# AutoCAD
## and its applications
## C O M P R E H E N S I V E

by

**Terence M. Shumaker**
Faculty Emeritus
Former Chairperson
Drafting Technology
Autodesk Premier Training Center
Clackamas Community College, Oregon City, Oregon

**David A. Madsen**
Faculty Emeritus
Former Chairperson
Drafting Technology
Autodesk Premier Training Center
Clackamas Community College, Oregon City, Oregon

Former Board of Director
American Design Drafting Association

Publisher
**THE GOODHEART-WILLCOX COMPANY, INC.**
Tinley Park, Illinois
www.g-w.com

Library of Congress Catalog Card Number 2003054950
International Standard Book Number 1-59070-293-X

1 2 3 4 5 6 7 8 9 – 04 – 08 07 06 05 04 03

**Library of Congress Cataloging-in-Publication Data**

Shumaker, Terence M.
  AutoCAD and applications : Comprehensive 2004/ by Terence M. Shumaker, David A. Madsen.
    p. cm.
  Includes index
  ISBN 1-59070-293-X
  1. Computer graphics. 2. AutoCAD I. Madsen, David A. II. Title
T385.S46163   2004
620.0042'0285'5369—dc21

2003054950

# AutoCAD
## and its applications
# B A S I C S

AutoCAD 2004

by

**Terence M. Shumaker**
Faculty Emeritus
Former Chairperson
Drafting Technology
Autodesk Premier Training Center
Clackamas Community College, Oregon City, Oregon

**David A. Madsen**
Faculty Emeritus
Former Chairperson
Drafting Technology
Autodesk Premier Training Center
Clackamas Community College, Oregon City, Oregon

Former Board of Director
American Design Drafting Association

Publisher
**THE GOODHEART-WILLCOX COMPANY, INC.**
Tinley Park, Illinois
www.g-w.com

**Goodheart-Willcox Publisher Brand Disclaimer:** Brand names, company names, and illustrations for products and services included in this text are provided for educational purposes only, and do not represent or imply endorsement or recommendation by the authors or the publisher.

**Library of Congress Cataloging-in-Publication Data**

Shumaker, Terence M.
    AutoCAD and applications : basics 2004/ by Terence M. Shumaker,
David A. Madsen.
        p. cm.
    Includes index
    ISBN 1-59070-289-1
    1. Computer graphics. 2. AutoCAD I. Madsen, David A. II. Title
T385.S46145   2004
620.0042'0285'5369—dc21

                    2003052841

# Introduction

*AutoCAD and its Applications—Basics* is a text providing complete instruction in mastering fundamental AutoCAD® 2004 commands and drawing techniques. Typical applications of AutoCAD are presented with basic drafting and design concepts. The topics are covered in an easy-to-understand sequence and progress in a way that allows you to become comfortable with the commands as your knowledge builds from one chapter to the next. In addition, *AutoCAD and its Applications—Basics* offers the following features:

- Step-by-step use of AutoCAD commands.
- In-depth explanations of how and why commands function as they do.
- Extensive use of font changes to specify certain meanings.
- Examples and discussions of industry practices and standards.
- Actual screen captures of AutoCAD and Windows features and functions.
- Professional tips explaining how to use AutoCAD effectively and efficiently.
- Over two hundred exercises to reinforce the chapter topics. These exercises also build on previously learned material.
- Chapter tests for review of commands and key AutoCAD concepts.
- A large selection of drafting problems supplementing each chapter. Problems are presented as 3D illustrations, actual plotted industrial drawings, and engineering sketches.

With *AutoCAD and its Applications—Basics,* you learn AutoCAD commands and become acquainted with information in other areas:

- Office practices for firms using AutoCAD systems.
- Preliminary planning and sketches.
- Linetypes and their uses.
- Drawing geometric shapes and constructions.
- Special editing operations that increase productivity.
- Making multiview drawings (orthographic projection).
- Dimensioning techniques and practices, based on accepted standards.
- Drawing section views and designing graphic patterns.
- Creating shapes and symbols for different uses.
- Creating and managing symbol libraries.
- Sketching with AutoCAD.
- Basic 3D drawing and display.
- Plotting and printing drawings.
- Using Windows Explorer for organizing and managing files and directories.

## Fonts Used in This Text

Different typefaces are used throughout this text to define terms and identify AutoCAD commands. Important terms always appear in ***bold-faced italic, serif*** type. AutoCAD menus, commands, variables, dialog box names, and toolbar buttons are printed in **bold-faced, sans serif** type. File names, directory folder names, paths, and keyboard entry items appear in the body of the text in Roman, sans serif type. Keyboard keys are shown inside of square brackets [ ] and appear in Roman, sans serif type. For example, [Enter] means to press the Enter key.

Prompt sequences are set apart from the body text with space above and below and appear in Roman, sans serif type. Keyboard entry items in prompts appear in **BOLD-FACED, SANS SERIF** type, capital letters. In prompts, the [Enter] key is represented by the ⏎ symbol. In addition, commands, menus, and dialog boxes related to Microsoft® Windows® appear in Roman, sans serif type.

## Other Text References

For additional information, standards from organizations, such as ANSI (American National Standards Institute) and ASME (American Society of Mechanical Engineers) are referenced throughout the text. These standards are used to help you create drawings that follow industry, national, and international practices. Appendix G lists many of these standards.

Also for your convenience, other Goodheart-Willcox textbooks are referenced. Referenced textbooks include *AutoCAD and its Applications—Advanced, AutoLISP Programming—Principles and Techniques, Geometric Dimensioning and Tolerancing,* and *Process Pipe Drafting.* All these textbooks can be ordered directly from Goodheart-Willcox.

*AutoCAD and its Applications—Basics* covers basic AutoCAD applications. For a text covering the advanced AutoCAD applications, please refer to *AutoCAD and its Applications—Advanced.* Copies of these texts can be ordered directly from Goodheart-Willcox.

## Introducing the AutoCAD Commands

There are several ways to select AutoCAD drawing and editing commands. Selecting commands from the toolbars, the pull-down menus, or the digitizer tablet template menu is slightly different from entering them from the keyboard. All AutoCAD commands and related options in this text are introduced by providing all the commonly active command entry methods.

In many examples, command entries are shown as if they were typed at the keyboard. This allows the text to present the keyboard shortcuts, full command name, and prompts that appear on screen. Commands, options, and values you must enter are given in bold text, as shown below. The available keyboard shortcuts are given first to reinforce the quickest way for you to enter commands at the keyboard. Pressing the [Enter] (return) key is indicated with the ⏎ symbol.

```
Command: L or LINE⏎
Specify first point: 2,2⏎
Specify next point or [Undo]: 4,2⏎
Specify next point or [Undo]: ⏎
```

General input, such as picking a point or selecting an object, is presented in *italic, serif* type, as shown below.

```
Command: L or LINE⏎
Specify first point: (pick a point)
Specify next point or [Undo]: (pick another point)
Specify next point or [Undo]: ⏎
```

The command line, pull-down menu, and toolbar button menu entry methods are presented throughout the text. When a command is introduced, these methods are illustrated in the margin next to the text reference. The toolbar in which the button is located is also identified. The example in the margin next to this paragraph illustrates the various methods of initiating the **LINE** command.

Some commands and functions are handled more efficiently by picking a toolbar button or a menu command. Many of these procedures are described in numbered, step-by-step instructions. Experiment with all command entry methods to find the most convenient way for *you* to enter commands.

## Features New for AutoCAD 2004

AutoCAD has introduced many new features in AutoCAD 2004. When a new or updated feature is presented in this text, the graphic in the margin next to this paragraph is shown. This serves as an aid to users upgrading to AutoCAD 2004 from an earlier release.

## Flexibility in Design

*Flexibility* is the key word when using *AutoCAD and its Applications—Basics*. This text is an excellent training aid for individual instruction, as well as classroom instruction. *AutoCAD and its Applications—Basics* teaches you how to apply AutoCAD to common drafting tasks. It is also an invaluable resource for any professional using AutoCAD. When working through the text, you will see a variety of notices. These notices include Professional Tips, Notes, and Cautions. They will help you develop your AutoCAD skills.

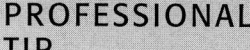

**PROFESSIONAL TIP** These ideas and suggestions are aimed at increasing your productivity and enhancing your use of AutoCAD commands and techniques.

**NOTE** A note explains important aspects of a command, menu, or activity. These aspects should be kept in mind while you are working through the text.

**CAUTION** A caution alerts you to potential problems if instructions or commands are used incorrectly or if an action can corrupt or alter files, folders, or disks. If you are in doubt after reading a caution, consult your instructor or supervisor.

*AutoCAD and its Applications—Basics* provides several ways for you to evaluate your performance. Included are the following:

- **Exercises.** Each chapter contains in-text exercises. These exercises instruct you to perform tasks that reinforce the material just presented. You can work through the exercises at your own pace.
- **Chapter Tests.** Each chapter includes a written test at the end of the chapter. Questions require you to give proper definitions, commands, options, and responses.
- **Drawing Problems.** There are a variety of drafting and design problems at the end of each chapter. These are presented as real-world CAD drawings, 3D illustrations, and engineering sketches. The problems are designed to make you think, solve problems, use design techniques, research and use proper drawing standards, and correct errors in the drawings or engineering sketches. Each drawing problem deals with one or more of seven technical

disciplines. Although doing all the problems will enhance your AutoCAD skills, you may be focusing on a particular discipline. The discipline related to a problem is indicated by a graphic in the margin next to the problem. These graphics and their descriptions are as follows:

 These problems address *mechanical* drafting and design applications, such as manufactured part designs.

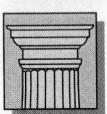 These problems address *architectural* and *structural* drafting and design applications, such as floor plans and presentation drawings.

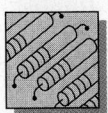 These problems address *electronics* drafting and design applications, such as electronic schematics, logic diagrams, and electrical part design.

 These problems address *civil* drafting and design applications, such as plot plans, plats, and landscape drawings.

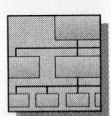 These problems address *graphic design* applications, such as text creation, logos, title blocks, and page layout.

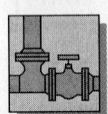 These problems address *piping* drafting and design applications, such as piping flow diagrams, pump design, and pipe layout.

 These problems address a variety of *general* drafting and design applications.

## About the Authors

Terence M. Shumaker is Faculty Emeritus, the former Chairperson of the Drafting Technology Department, and former Director of the Autodesk Premier Training Center at Clackamas Community College. Terence taught at the community college level for over 25 years. He has professional experience in surveying, civil drafting, industrial piping, and technical illustration. He is the author of Goodheart-Willcox's *Process Pipe Drafting* and coauthor of the *AutoCAD and its Applications* series (Releases 10, 11, 12, 13, and 14; AutoCAD 2000/2000i; and AutoCAD 2002 editions) and *AutoCAD Essentials.*

David A. Madsen is Faculty Emeritus, the former Chairperson of Drafting Technology and the Autodesk Premier Training Center at Clackamas Community College and former member of the American Design and Drafting Association Board of Directors. David was an instructor and a department chair at Clackamas Community College for nearly thirty years. In addition to community college experience, David was a Drafting Technology instructor at Centennial High School in Gresham, Oregon. David also has extensive experience in mechanical drafting, architectural design and drafting, and construction practices. He is the author of several Goodheart-Willcox drafting and design textbooks, including *Geometric Dimensioning and Tolerancing,* and coauthor of the *AutoCAD and its Applications* series (Releases 10, 11, 12, 13, and 14; AutoCAD 2000/2000i; and AutoCAD 2002 editions), *Architectural Drafting Using AutoCAD, Architectural AutoCAD,* and *AutoCAD Essentials.*

# Contents in Brief

## Acknowledgments

Special thanks from David Madsen to Ethan Collins, Eugene O'Day, and Ron Palma for their professional expertise in providing in-depth research and testing, technical assistance, reviews, and development of new materials for use throughout the text.

Special thanks from Terence Shumaker to Craig Black for his expert reviews, technical assistance, and contribution of new material for several chapters in this book. Craig is manager of the Autodesk Premier Training Center at Fox Valley Technical College in Appleton, Wisconsin.

### Technical Assistance and Contribution of Materials

Margo Bilson of Willamette Industries, Inc.
Fitzgerald, Hagan, & Hackathorn
Bruce L. Wilcox, Johnson and Wales University School of Technology

### Contribution of Photographs or Other Technical Information

Arthur Baker
Autodesk, Inc.
*CADalyst* magazine
*CADENCE* magazine
Chris Lindner
EPCM Services Ltd.
Harris Group, Inc.
International Source for Ergonomics
Jim Webster
Kunz Associates
Myonetics, Inc.
Norwest Engineering
Schuchart & Associates, Inc.
Willamette Industries, Inc.

## Trademarks

# Contents

## Drawing and Printing with AutoCAD

# Editing the Drawing

# AutoCAD Applications

## Dimensioning and Tolerancing

## Advanced Drawing Construction

## Basic 3D Drawing and Advanced Applications

# Appendices

## CHAPTER 1

# Introduction to AutoCAD Features

## Learning Objectives

After completing this chapter, you will be able to do the following:
- Describe the methods and procedures used in computer-aided drafting.
- Explain the value of planning your work and system management.
- Load AutoCAD from the Windows desktop.
- Describe the AutoCAD screen layout and user interface.
- Describe the function of dialog boxes.
- Identify the function of **DesignCenter** and the **Properties** window.
- Use the help system for online assistance.
- Use the features found in the **AutoCAD Help** window.
- Review the online product support.
- Define the use of function, control, and shortcut keys.

## The Tools of CAD

The computer and software are the principal components of the present-day design and drafting workstation. These tools make up a *system* referred to as *CAD*—computer-aided design or computer-aided drafting. Drafters, designers, and engineers use CAD to develop designs and drawings and to plot them on paper or film. Additionally, drawings and designs can be displayed as 3D models and animations or used in analysis and testing.

CAD has surpassed the use of manual drafting techniques because of its speed, power, accuracy, and flexibility, but it is not totally without its attendant problems and trade-offs. Although the uses of CAD designs are limited only by the imagination, it should be remembered that the computer hardware is sensitive to the slightest electrical impulses and the human body is sensitive to the repetitive motions required when using the tools.

## The AutoCAD Toolbox

Drawings and models are constructed in AutoCAD using XYZ coordinates. The *Cartesian (rectangular)* coordinate system is used most often and is discussed in Chapter 3. Angular layouts are created by measuring angles in a counterclockwise direction. Drawings can be annotated with text and described with a variety of dimensioning techniques. In addition, objects can be given colors, patterns, and textures. AutoCAD also provides you with the tools to create basic pictorial drawings, called *isometrics*, and powerful 3D solids and surface models.

## The Applications of AutoCAD

Using AutoCAD software and this text, you will learn how to construct, lay out, dimension, and annotate two-dimensional drawings. Should you wish to continue your study into 3D modeling, 3D rendering, and customization, *AutoCAD and its Applications—Advanced* can provide you with detailed instruction. Your studies will enable you to create a wide variety of drawings, designs, and 3D models in any of the drafting, design, and engineering disciplines.

AutoCAD drawings can have hundreds of colors and *layers*, which contain different kinds of information. Objects can also be shown as exploded assemblies or displayed in 3D. See **Figure 1-1**. In addition, objects in the drawing can be given "intelligence" in the form of *attributes*. These attributes are various kinds of data that turn a drawing into a graphical database. You can then ask questions of your drawing and receive a variety of information.

Using AutoCAD, you have the ability to construct 3D models that appear as wireframes or have surface colors and textures. The creation of solid models that have mass properties and can be analyzed is also possible with AutoCAD. The display in **Figure 1-2** is an example of a solid model created in AutoCAD. 3D drawings and models can be viewed in several ways. These models can also be colored and shaded, or *rendered*, to appear in a realistic format.

**Figure 1-1.**
A 3D model of a watch shown as an exploded assembly.

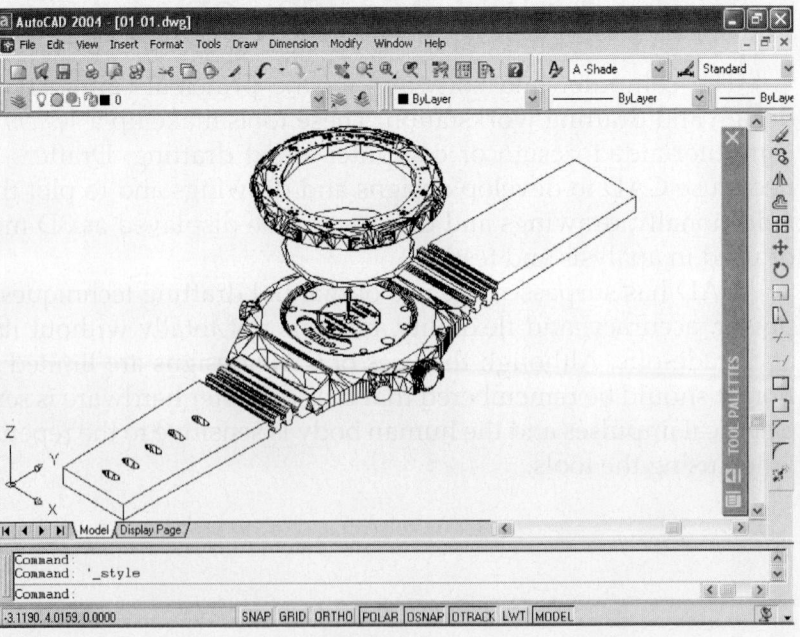

**Figure 1-2.**
A 3D model of a connecting rod. A—Model shown as a wireframe with edges marked by lines. B—Color and shading are added when the model is rendered. (Autodesk, Inc.)

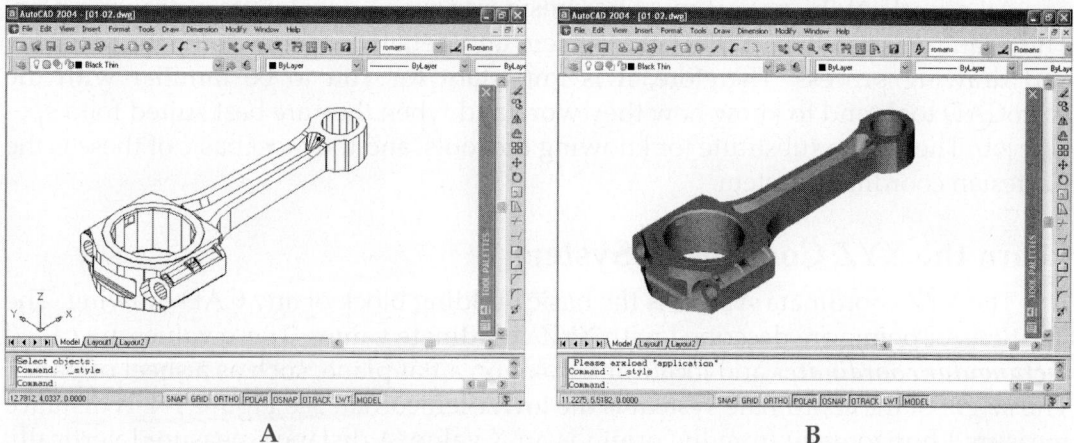

A                                                                          B

**Figure 1-3.**
This 3D piping model can be rotated and viewed from any location in 3D space. (Autodesk, Inc.)

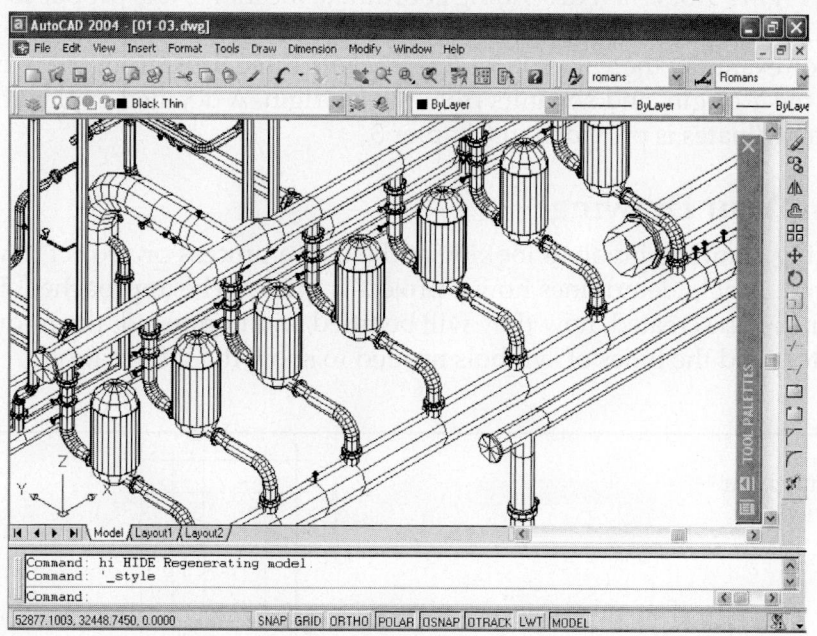

A powerful application of CAD software and 3D models is animation. The simplest form of animation is to dynamically rotate the model, in order to view it from any direction. See **Figure 1-3.** Drawings and models can also be animated so the model appears to move, rotate, and even explode into its individual components. An extremely useful form of animation is called a *walkthrough.* Using specialized software, you can plot a path through or around a model and replay it just like a movie. The logical next step in viewing the model is to actually be inside it and have the ability to manipulate and change the objects in it. This is called *virtual reality,* and it is achieved through the use of 3D models and highly specialized software and hardware.

All aspects of the project must be considered when developing a drawing plan. This requires careful use of the CAD system and detailed standards for the planning and drawing process. Therefore, it is important for you to be familiar with the AutoCAD tools and to know how they work and when they are best suited for a specific job. There is no substitute for knowing the tools, and the most basic of these is the Cartesian coordinate system.

## Learn the XYZ Coordinate System

The XYZ coordinate system is the basic building block of any CAD drawing. The locations of points are described with XYZ coordinate values. These values are called *rectangular coordinates* and locate any point on a flat plane, such as a sheet of paper. The *origin* of the coordinate system is the lower-left corner. See **Figure 1-4.** A distance measured horizontally from the origin is an X value. A distance measured vertically from the origin is a Y value.

Rectangular coordinates can also be measured in three-dimensional space. In this case, the third dimension rises up from the surface of the paper and is given a Z value. See **Figure 1-5.** When describing coordinate locations, it is proper to give the X value first, the Y value second, and the Z value third. Each number is separated by a comma. For example, the value of 3,1,6 represents three units from the X origin, one unit from the Y origin, and six units from the Z origin. A detailed explanation of rectangular coordinates is provided in Chapter 3.

## Planning Your Drawing

Drawing planning involves looking at the entire process or project in which you are involved. A plan determines how a project is going to be approached. It includes the drawings to be created, how they will be titled and numbered, the information to be presented, and the types of symbols needed to show the information.

**Figure 1-4.**
The 2D rectangular coordinate system.

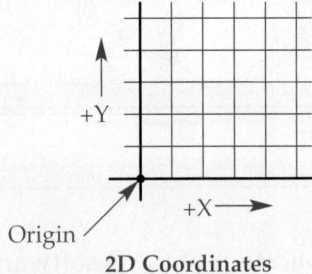

2D Coordinates

**Figure 1-5.**
The 3D rectangular coordinate system.

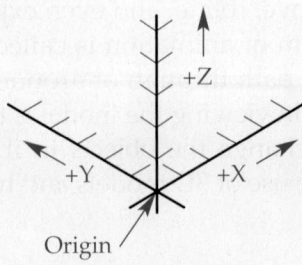

3D Coordinates

More specifically, drawing planning applies to how you create and manage a drawing or set of drawings. This includes which view or feature you draw first and the coordinates and AutoCAD commands you use to draw it. Drafters who begin constructing a drawing from the seat of their pants—creating symbols and naming objects, shapes, and views as they go—do not possess a good drawing plan. Those who plan, use consistent techniques, and adhere to school or company standards are developing good drawing habits.

Throughout this text you will find aids to help you develop good drawing habits. One of the first steps in developing your skills is to learn how to plan your work. The importance of planning cannot be emphasized enough. There is no substitute.

## Using Drawing Standards

*Standards* are guidelines for operating procedures, drawing techniques, and record keeping. Most schools and companies have established standards. It is important that standards exist and are used by all CAD personnel. Drawing standards may include the following items:

- Methods of file storage (location and name).
- File naming conventions.
- File backup methods and times.
- Drawing templates and title blocks.
- Drawing symbols.
- Dimensioning styles and techniques.
- Text styles.
- Layer settings.
- Plot styles.

Your standards may vary in content, but the most important aspect of standards is that they are used. When standards are used, your drawings are consistent, you become more productive, and the classroom or office functions more efficiently.

## Planning Your Work

Study the planning pyramids in **Figure 1-6.** The horizontal axes of the pyramids represent the amount of time spent on the project. The vertical axes represent the life of the project. The top level is the planning stage and the bottom level is the final execution of the project.

The pyramid on the right is pointed at the top and indicates a small amount of initial planning. As the project progresses, more and more time is devoted to planning, and less time is available for other tasks. This is *not* an ideal situation. The inverted pyramid on the left shows a lot of time devoted to initial planning. As the project advances, less planning time is needed, thus freeing more time for tasks related to the completion of the project.

**Figure 1-6.**
Planning pyramids illustrate time required for well planned and poorly planned projects.

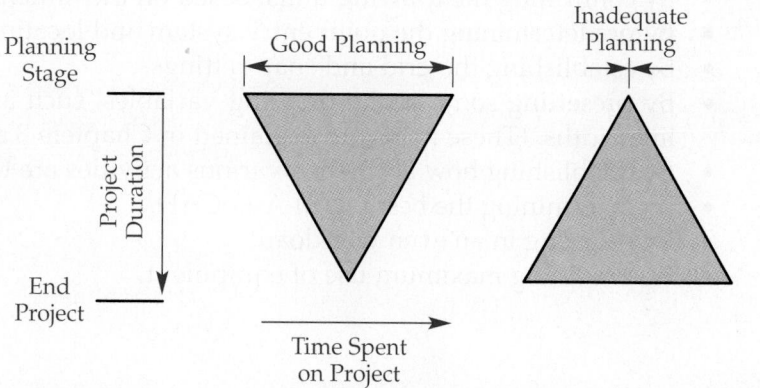

As you begin your CAD training, plan your drawing sessions thoroughly to organize your thoughts. Sketch the problem or design, noting the sizes and locations of features. List the drawing commands needed, in the order they are to be used. Schedule a regular time to use the computer and adhere to that time. Follow the standards your school or firm has set. These might include specific drawing names, project planning sheets, project logs, drawing layout procedures, special title blocks, and a location for drawing storage. Everyone using the computers in your school or company must follow the standards and procedures. Confusion may result if your drawings do not have the proper name, are stored in the wrong place, or have the wrong title block.

Develop the habit of saving your work regularly—at least every ten to fifteen minutes. The **SAVETIME** system variable can be set to automatically save your drawings at predetermined intervals. **SAVETIME** is covered in detail in Chapter 2. Drawings may be lost due to a software error, hardware malfunction, power failure, or your own mistakes. This is not common, but you should still be prepared for such an event.

You should develop methods of managing your work. This is critical to computer drafting and is discussed throughout the text. Keep the following points in mind as you begin your AutoCAD training:

✓ Plan your work and organize your thoughts.
✓ Learn and use your classroom or office standards.
✓ Save your work often.

If you remember to follow these three points, your grasp of the tools and methods of CAD will be easier. In addition, your experiences with the computer will be more enjoyable.

Remember the planning pyramids as you begin your study of AutoCAD. When you feel the need to dive blindly into a drawing or project, restrain yourself. Take the time needed for development of the project goals. Then proceed with the confidence of knowing where you are heading.

During your early stages of AutoCAD training, write down all the instructions needed to construct your drawing. Do this especially for your first few assignments. This means documenting every command and every coordinate point (dimension) needed. Develop a planning sheet for your drawings. Your time spent at the computer with AutoCAD will be more productive and enjoyable.

## Using Drawing Plan Sheets

A good work plan can save drawing time. Planning should include sketches. A rough preliminary sketch and a drawing plan can help in the following ways:

• By determining the drawing layout.
• By setting the overall size of the drawing by laying out the views and required free space.
• By confirming the drawing units, based on the dimensions provided.
• By predetermining the point entry system and locating the points.
• By establishing the grid and snap settings.
• By presetting some of the drawing variables, such as layers, linetypes, and linewidths. (These items are explained in Chapters 3 and 4.)
• By establishing how and when various activities are to be performed.
• By determining the best use of AutoCAD.
• By resulting in an even workload.
• By providing maximum use of equipment.

## Planning Checklist

In the early stages of your AutoCAD training, it is best to plan your drawing projects carefully. There is a tendency to want things to happen immediately—for things to be "automatic,"—but if you hurry and do little or no planning, you will become more frustrated. Therefore, as you begin each new project, step through the following planning checklist so the execution of your project goes smoothly:

✓ Analyze the problem.
✓ Study all engineering sketches.
✓ Locate all available resources and list for future use.
✓ Determine the applicable standards for the project.
✓ Sketch the problem.
✓ Decide on the number and kinds of views required.
✓ Determine the final plotted scale of the drawing and of all views.
✓ Determine the drawing sequence, such as lines, features, dimensions, and notes.
✓ List the AutoCAD commands to be used.
✓ Follow the standards and refer to resources as you work.

**PROFESSIONAL TIP**

AutoCAD is designed so you can construct drawings and models using the actual dimensions of the object. *Always draw in full scale.* The proper text and dimension size is set using scale factors. This is covered in detail in later chapters. The final scale of the drawing should be planned early, and it is shown on the plot.

## Working Procedures Checklist

As you begin learning AutoCAD, you will realize that several skills are required to become a proficient CAD user. The following list provides you with some hints to help you become comfortable with AutoCAD. These hints will also allow you to work quickly and efficiently. The following actions are discussed in detail in later chapters:

✓ Plan all work with pencil and paper before using the computer.
✓ Check the **Layers** and **Properties** toolbars at the top of the display screen and the status bar at the bottom to see which object property settings and drawing aids are in effect.
✓ Read the command line at the bottom of the display screen. Constantly check for the correct commands, instructions, or keyboard entry of data.
✓ Read the command line after keyboard entry of data before pressing the [Enter] key. Backspacing to erase incorrect typing is quicker than redoing the command.
✓ If using a multibutton puck, develop a good hand position that allows easy movement. Your button-pressing finger should move without readjusting your grip of the puck.
✓ Learn the meanings of all the buttons on your puck or mouse and use them regularly.
✓ Watch the disk drive lights to see when the disks are being accessed. Some disk access may take a few seconds. Knowing what is happening will lessen frustration and impatience.

✓ Think ahead. Know your next move.

✓ Learn new commands every day. Don't rely on just a few that seem to work. Find commands that can speed your work and do it more efficiently.

✓ Save your work every ten to fifteen minutes, in case a power failure or system crash deletes the drawing held in computer memory.

✓ If you are stumped, ask the computer for help. Use the online help to display valuable information about each command on the screen. Using AutoCAD's online help is discussed in detail later in this chapter.

## Exercise 1-1

○ Using a piece of paper and a pen or pencil, make a sketch similar to **Figure 1-4**. Label the origin, +X axis, and +Y axis. Sketch a dot located at the intersection of three units in the +X axis and three units in the +Y axis.

○ Provide a short discussion about why it is important to plan your work before you start a drawing in AutoCAD. Why should a sketch be part of your preliminary planning?

## Starting AutoCAD

AutoCAD 2004 is designed to operate with Windows XP Professional, Windows XP Home, Windows 2000 Professional, or Windows NT 4.0. These interfaces are nearly identical. If you see illustrations in this text that appear slightly different than your screen, do not be concerned, as the AutoCAD feature is the same.

When AutoCAD is first installed, Windows creates a ***program icon,*** which is displayed on the desktop. An ***icon*** is a small picture representing an application, accessory, file, or command. In addition to the icon, the program name is listed as an item in the Start menu, under the Autodesk item, which is found in the Programs menu.

**NOTE**

AutoCAD must first be installed properly on the computer before it can be used. Refer to the AutoCAD help system for detailed instructions on AutoCAD installation and configuration of peripheral devices, such as plotters, printers, and digitizers.

AutoCAD can be started using several different techniques. The quickest way to start AutoCAD is to double-click on the AutoCAD 2004 icon on the Windows desktop. See **Figure 1-7**.

**PROFESSIONAL TIP**

When AutoCAD is installed using unaltered settings, the label for the AutoCAD icon is AutoCAD 2004. The name can be quickly changed by picking the label, typing a new name, and pressing [Enter].

**Figure 1-7.**
Double-click the
AutoCAD 2004 icon
on the Windows
desktop to start
AutoCAD.

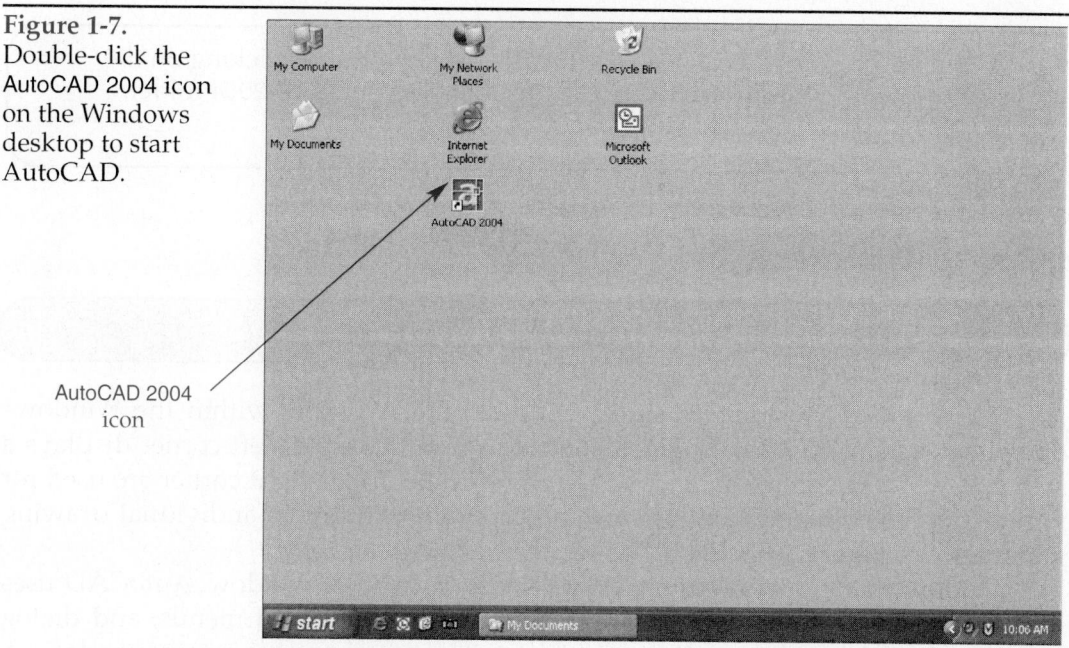

AutoCAD 2004
icon

**Figure 1-8.**
Pick AutoCAD 2004 in the Autodesk menu to load AutoCAD.

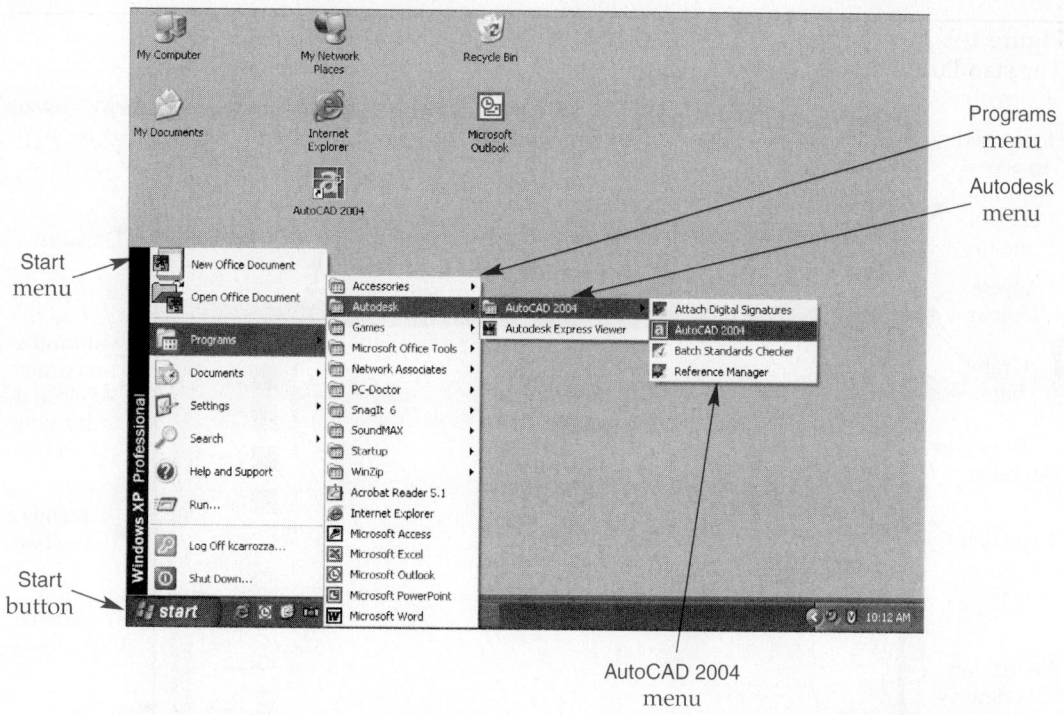

Programs
menu

Autodesk
menu

Start
menu

Start
button

AutoCAD 2004
menu

The second method for starting AutoCAD is to pick the Start button at the lower-left of the Windows desktop. This displays the Start menu. Next, move the pointer to Programs and either hold it there or pick to display the Programs menu. Move the pointer to Autodesk and click to show the Autodesk menu. Now move the pointer to the AutoCAD 2004 item and click. This displays all the items in the AutoCAD 2004 program group. Pick AutoCAD 2004 to load the software. See **Figure 1-8.**

**NOTE** You can also start AutoCAD by double-clicking on the acad.exe file in the Program Files/AutoCAD 2004 folder.

## The AutoCAD Window

The AutoCAD window is similar to any other window within the Windows operating system. Picking the small control icon in the upper-left corner displays a standard window control menu, and the icons in the upper-right corner are used for minimizing, maximizing, and closing the program window or individual drawing windows. See **Figure 1-9**.

Window sizing operations are done as with any other window. AutoCAD uses the familiar Windows style interface, with buttons, pull-down menus, and dialog boxes. Each of these items is discussed in detail in this chapter. Learning the layout, appearance, and proper use of these features will allow you to master AutoCAD quickly.

**Figure 1-9.**
The standard AutoCAD window.

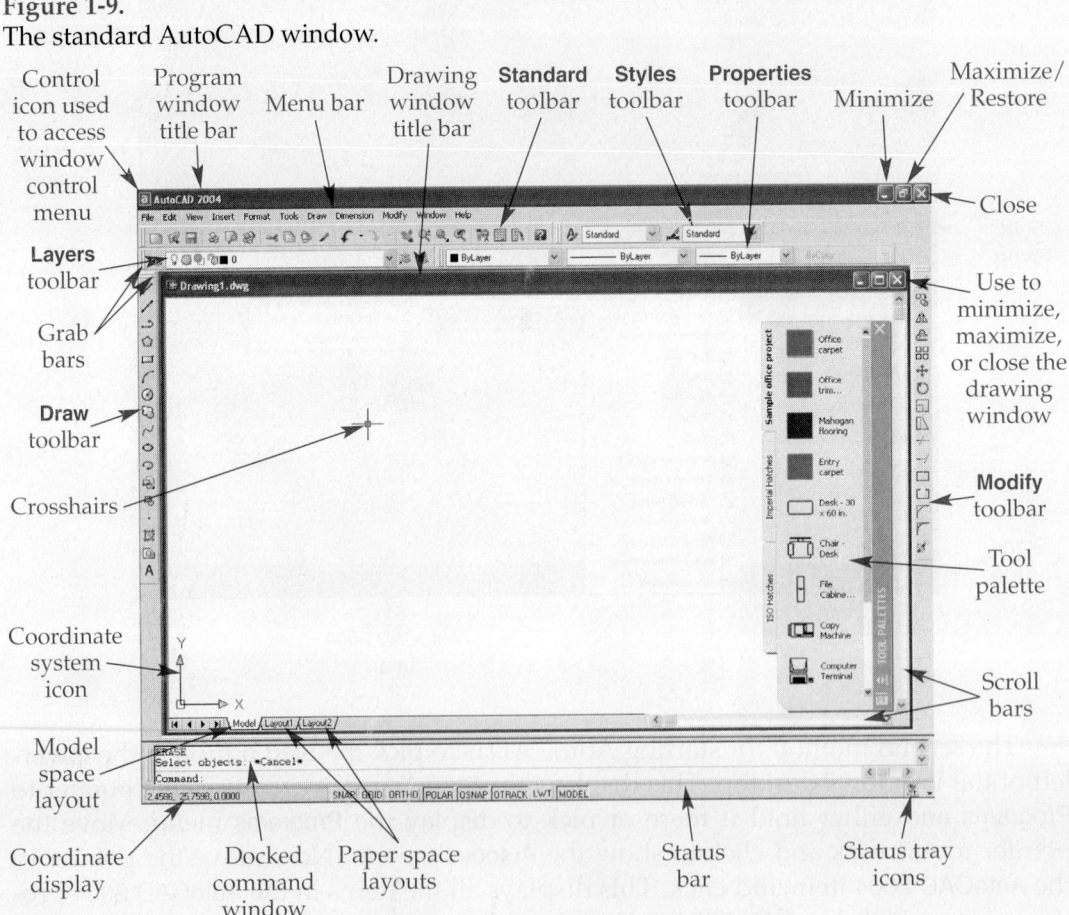

## Standard Screen Layout

The standard screen layout provides a large graphics, or drawing, area. The drawing area is bordered by *toolbars* at the left, right, and top and by the *command window* at the bottom. Look at your screen now and study the illustration in Figure 1-9. Note that the proportional size of the AutoCAD window features may vary depending on the display resolution of your computer system.

Many of the elements of the AutoCAD window are referred to as *floating*. This means the item can be freely resized or moved about the screen into new positions. Floating features are contained within a standard Windows border and display a title bar at the top. When you run AutoCAD for the first time, the AutoCAD window is displayed in a floating position on the desktop. A smaller window inside the AutoCAD window displays the drawing area for the currently open drawing file. Floating windows are moved and adjusted for size in the same manner as any other window; however, the drawing windows can only be adjusted and positioned within the AutoCAD window.

Some floating features, such as toolbars and the **Tool Palettes** window, can also be *docked* around the edges of the AutoCAD window. The toolbars displayed initially after installing AutoCAD are docked by default and do not display a title bar. To place a docked toolbar in a floating position, you can either double-click the grab bar or press and hold the pick button while pointing at the grab bar, and then move your mouse to drag the toolbar away from the edge of the window. The term *grab bar* refers to the two thin bars at the top or left edge of a docked toolbar. To dock a floating toolbar, double-click on the title bar or press and hold the pick button while pointing at the title bar and drag the toolbar to an edge of the AutoCAD window (top, bottom, left, or right). Then release the pick button. When the item is docked, it loses its border and title bar and becomes a part of the AutoCAD window. Floating features may be moved or docked at any time as needed.

Become familiar with these unique areas of the AutoCAD window and the information provided by each. The following list describes the function of each area. Each of these features will be discussed in detail later in this text:

- **Command window.** In its default position, this window is docked at the bottom of the AutoCAD window. It displays the Command: prompt and reflects any command entries you make. It also displays prompts that supply information to you or request input. This is where your primary communications with AutoCAD are displayed, so watch for any information shown on this line.
- **Menu bar.** The menu bar appears just below the title bar and displays a number of menu names. As with standard Windows menus, use the cursor to point at a menu name and press the pick button. This causes a *pull-down menu* to be displayed. Any time you pick an item followed by an *ellipsis* (…), a dialog box is displayed. A *dialog box* is a rectangular area that appears on the screen after you type or select certain commands. It contains a variety of options related to a specific command or function and provides a convenient means of supplying information to AutoCAD.
- **Scroll bars.** The scroll bars allow you to adjust your view of the drawing area by "sliding" the drawing from side to side or up and down.
- **Crosshairs.** This is your primary means of pointing to objects or locations within a drawing.
- **Coordinate system icon.** This indicates the current coordinate system and view orientation.
- **Toolbars.** Toolbars contain various buttons that activate AutoCAD commands. These toolbars can be moved, resized, modified, hidden, or docked as needed. Some toolbar buttons show a small black triangle in the lower-right corner. These buttons are called *flyouts*. Press and hold the pick button while pointing at a flyout to display a set of related buttons.

- **The Tool Palettes window.** The **Tool Palettes** window is similar to floating toolbars and contains frequently used block symbols and fill patterns that can be used in your drawings. Tool palettes are typically user customized with block symbols and hatch patterns to meet your specific needs. AutoCAD includes three sample palettes. Customizing tool palettes is covered later in this text.
- **Status bar.** This bar contains several buttons that display the current state of specific drawing control features and allow access for changing the settings of these features. To the right of the status bar is a tray with icons. These icons represent the presence of various drawing conditions. When a pull-down menu item is highlighted or you are pointing at a toolbar button, a brief explanation of the item is shown along the left side of the status bar.
- **Coordinate display.** This display field, found on the status bar, shows the XYZ crosshairs location, according to the current settings.
- **Standard toolbar.** In the default AutoCAD screen configuration, the **Standard** toolbar appears just above the **Layers** toolbar. When you move your pointing device to the toolbar, the crosshairs change to the familiar Windows arrow pointer. As you move your cursor across a toolbar button, a 3D border is displayed around the previously flat button. Holding the cursor motionless over a button for a moment displays a *tooltip*, which shows the name of the button in a small box at the cursor location. While the tooltip is visible, a brief explanation of what the button does is displayed along the status bar at the bottom left edge of the window.

The **Standard** toolbar contains a series of buttons that provide access to several of AutoCAD's drawing setup and control commands. Each of these features is identified and briefly described in **Figure 1-10**. These features are discussed in detail later in this text.

Figure 1-10.
The **Standard** toolbar and its components.

A—**Grab Bar.** A "grab" handle for relocating toolbars.
B—**New.** Begins a new drawing.
C—**Open.** Opens an existing drawing for editing and revision.
D—**Save.** Writes the drawing information currently in memory to a file.
E—**Plot.** Sends the drawing information to a hardcopy device, such as a printer or plotter.
F—**Plot Preview.** Displays a preview of the drawing layout prior to plotting.
G—**Publish.** Prints drawing sheets to an electronic file.
H—**Cut to Clipboard.** "Cuts" (removes) a specified portion of your drawing geometry, storing it in the Windows Clipboard.
I—**Copy to Clipboard.** Copies a specified portion of the drawing geometry, storing it in the Windows Clipboard.

J—**Paste from Clipboard.** "Pastes" (inserts) the contents of the Windows Clipboard to a specified location in your drawing.
K—**Match Properties.** Copies the properties from one object to one or more objects.
L—**Undo.** Cancels the effects of the last command or operation.
M—**Undo Drop-Down.** Provides a list of previous operations that can be undone.
N—**Redo.** Can be used to "redo" or restore operations previously canceled by the **Undo** command.
O—**Redo Drop-Down.** Provides a list of previously undone operations to restore in the current drawing.
P—**Pan Realtime.** Displays the hand cursor and moves the display in the graphics screen dynamically in "realtime."

Q—**Zoom Realtime.** Displays the Zoom cursor and increases or decreases the displayed size of objects in the drawing area.
R—**Zoom Flyout.** Displays a series of buttons that activate the **ZOOM** command options.
S—**Zoom Previous.** Restores the previous display to the drawing area.
T—**Properties.** Displays the **Properties** palette, where you can set properties for new objects or modify the properties of existing objects.
U—**DesignCenter.** Activates **DesignCenter**, allowing drawing information to be shared between multiple drawings.
V—**Tool Palettes.** Turns the **Tool Palettes** window on or off.
W—**Help.** Activates AutoCAD's online help facility.

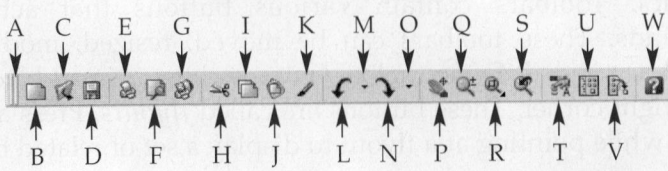

AutoCAD and its Applications—Basics

**Figure 1-11.**
The **Styles** toolbar and its components.

A—**Text Style Manager.** Displays the **Text Style** dialog box where text styles can be created and managed.

B—**Text Style Control.** Displays the current text style and provides a list of available text styles in the drawing.

C—**Dimension Style Manager.** Displays the **Dimension Style Manager** dialog box where dimension styles can be created and managed.

D—**Dim Style Control.** Displays the current dimension style and provides a list of available dimension styles in the current drawing.

- **Styles toolbar.** In the default AutoCAD screen configuration, the **Styles** toolbar appears to the right of the **Standard** toolbar. This toolbar contains buttons and display fields relative to text and dimension styles. These features are identified and briefly explained in **Figure 1-11.**

- **Layers and Properties toolbars.** In the default AutoCAD screen configuration, the **Layers** and **Properties** toolbars appear just above the drawing area, below the **Standard** and **Styles** toolbars. These toolbars contain buttons and display fields for setting and adjusting the properties of objects in a drawing. Each of these features is identified and briefly explained in **Figure 1-12.**

**Figure 1-12.**
The **Layers** and **Properties** toolbars and their components.

**Layers Toolbar:**

A—**Layer Properties Manager.** Displays the **Layer Properties Manager**, where drawing layers can be created and managed.

B—**Layer Control Drop-Down.** Displays the current drawing layer, provides a list of available drawing layers, and allows the control of different display properties of each.

C—**Make Object's Layer Current.** Allows the selection of a drawing object to change the current drawing layer to that of the selected object.

D—**Layer Previous.** Activates the previous layer control display.

**Properties Toolbar:**

E—**Color Control.** Displays the current object creation color, provides a list of colors, and allows the accessing of the **Select Color** dialog box.

F—**Linetype Control.** Displays the current object creation linetype, provides a list of loaded linetypes in the current drawing, and allows access to the **Linetype Manager** dialog box.

G—**Lineweight Control.** Displays the current object creation lineweight and provides a list of available lineweights.

H—**Plot Style Control.** Displays the current object creation plot style and provides a list of additional plot styles and the accessing of the **Current Plot Style** dialog box.

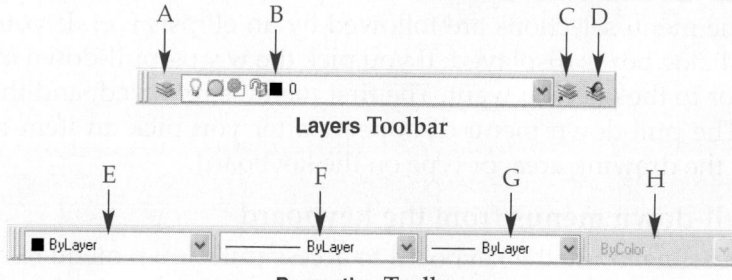

Layers Toolbar

Properties Toolbar

**Figure 1-13.**
The AutoCAD menu bar. Pull-down menus are accessed by picking the words in this bar.

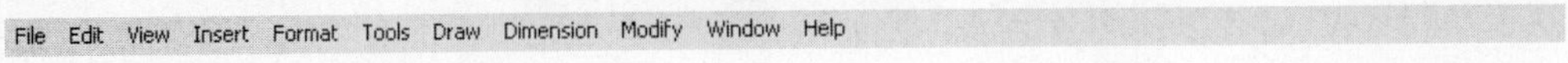

File   Edit   View   Insert   Format   Tools   Draw   Dimension   Modify   Window   Help

## Pull-Down Menus

The AutoCAD pull-down menus are located on the menu bar at the top of the screen. As with a toolbar, when you move your pointing device to the menu bar, the crosshairs change to the arrow pointer. From **Figure 1-13**, you can see that the default menu bar has eleven pull-down menu items: **File**, **Edit**, **View**, **Insert**, **Format**, **Tools**, **Draw**, **Dimension**, **Modify**, **Window**, and **Help**.

 **NOTE** During the AutoCAD installation process, an additional menu known as the **Express Tools** is available. Installing this menu provides you with an **Express** pull-down menu, which includes additional tools for improved functionality and productivity during your drawing processes. **Express Tool** functions are discussed where applicable throughout this text.

Most of the available menu selections can be found in both the toolbars and the pull-down menus system. Some menu selections, however, are found in only one of these two menu areas—so it is important to be familiar with the layout and use of both toolbars and pull-down menus. To see how a pull-down menu works, move your cursor to the **View** menu and press the pick button. A pull-down menu appears below **View**. See **Figure 1-14A.** Commands are easily selected by picking a menu item with your pointing device.

Notice that several of the commands in the **View** pull-down menu have a small arrow to the right. When one of these items is selected, a *cascading menu* appears. A cascading menu has additional options for the previous selection. See **Figure 1-14B.**

Some of the menu selections are followed by an ellipsis (...). If you pick one of these items, a dialog box is displayed. If you pick the wrong pull-down menu, simply move the cursor to the one you want. The first menu is removed, and the new menu is displayed. The pull-down menu disappears after you pick an item in the menu, pick a point in the drawing area, or type on the keyboard.

### Accessing pull-down menus from the keyboard

It is also possible to use the keyboard to access pull-down menu items by typing shortcuts. These shortcut keystrokes are called *menu accelerator keys*. They allow access to any pull-down menu selection using an [Alt]+[*key*] combination on the keyboard. For instance, the **File** menu can be accessed by first pressing the [Alt] key and then pressing the [F] key. Pressing [Alt] and then [D] accesses the **Draw** menu, and so on. For AutoCAD releases prior to 2004, the menu accelerator keys were automatically displayed. One character of each pull-down menu title or command was underlined on

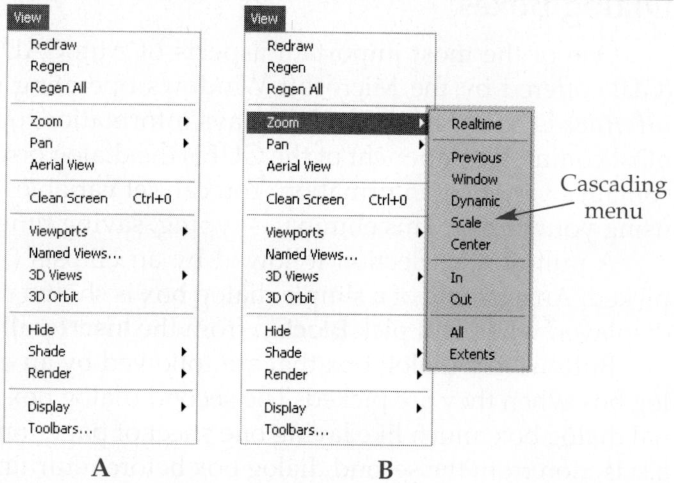

**Figure 1-14.**
Using the pull-down menus.
A—When you pick **View**, this pull-down menu is displayed.
B—A pull-down menu item followed by an arrow indicates a cascading menu. Selecting the item displays the cascading menu (shown here highlighted).

| View | | View | | |
|---|---|---|---|---|
| Redraw | | Redraw | | |
| Regen | | Regen | | |
| Regen All | | Regen All | | |
| Zoom ▶ | | **Zoom ▶** | | Realtime |
| Pan ▶ | | Pan ▶ | | Previous |
| Aerial View | | Aerial View | | Window |
| Clean Screen   Ctrl+0 | | Clean Screen   Ctrl+0 | | Dynamic |
| Viewports ▶ | | Viewports ▶ | | Scale |
| Named Views... | | Named Views... | | Center |
| 3D Views ▶ | | 3D Views ▶ | | In |
| 3D Orbit | | 3D Orbit | | Out |
| Hide | | Hide | | All |
| Shade ▶ | | Shade ▶ | | Extents |
| Render ▶ | | Render ▶ | | |
| Display ▶ | | Display ▶ | | |
| Toolbars... | | Toolbars... | | |

Cascading menu

**A**        **B**

screen. To display the accelerator keys with an underline in AutoCAD 2004, you need to press the [Alt] key.

Once a pull-down menu is displayed, a menu item can be selected using a single character key. For example, suppose you want to zoom in closer to your work. First press [Alt] and then [V] to access the **View** menu. Then, press [Z] to select the **Zoom** command. Finally, press [I] to select the **In** option.

---

**PROFESSIONAL TIP**

Once a pull-down menu is displayed, you can use the up, down, right, and left arrow keys to move to different items in the menu and to display cascading menus. When an item followed by an arrow is highlighted, press the right arrow key to display the cascading menu. Remove the menu by pressing the left arrow. Press [Enter] to select a highlighted item.

---

**NOTE**

There are many individual character key and key combination shortcuts available for Windows and Windows-based applications. Refer to your Microsoft Windows documentation for a complete list of keyboard shortcuts.

---

**Exercise 1-3**

○ Continue from Exercise 1-2 or start AutoCAD.
○ Open each pull-down menu and read the options found in each menu without picking any options.
○ Use each of the methods explained in the previous discussion to open pull-down menus.
○ Keep AutoCAD open for the next exercise. If you must quit, pick **Exit** in the **File** pull-down menu, and then pick **No** in the AutoCAD alert box.

---

# Dialog Boxes

One of the most important aspects of AutoCAD is the graphical user interface (GUI) offered by the Microsoft Windows operating environment. A *graphical user interface* is how the software displays information, options, and choices for you. The most common component of the GUI is the dialog box. A *dialog box* is a box that may contain a variety of information. You can set variables and select items in a dialog box using your cursor. This eliminates typing, saving time and increasing productivity.

A pull-down selection followed by an ellipsis (…) displays a dialog box when picked. An example of a simple dialog box is shown in **Figure 1-15.** This dialog box is displayed when you pick **Block…** from the **Insert** pull-down menu.

Buttons in a dialog box that are followed by an ellipsis (…) display another dialog box when they are picked. The second dialog box is displayed on top of the original dialog box, much like laying one sheet of paper on top of another. You must make a selection from the second dialog box before returning to the original dialog box.

There are standard parts to all dialog boxes. If you take a few minutes to review the following brief descriptions, you will find it much easier to work with the dialog boxes. Detailed discussions are provided in later chapters.

- **Command buttons.** When you pick a command button, something happens immediately. The most common buttons are **OK** and **Cancel**. Another common button is **Help**. See **Figure 1-15.** If a button has a dark border, it is the default. Pressing the [Enter] key accepts the default. If a button is "grayed-out," it cannot be selected. Buttons can also lead to other things. A button with an ellipsis (…) leads to another dialog box. A button with an arrow symbol (<) requires you to make a selection in the drawing area.
- **Radio buttons.** When you press a selector button on your car radio, the station changes. Only one station can play at a time. Likewise, only one item in a group of radio buttons can be highlighted or active at one time. See **Figure 1-16.**
- **Check box.** A check box, or toggle, displays a "✓" when it is on (active). If the box is empty, the option is off. See **Figure 1-16.**
- **List box.** A list box contains a list of items or options. You can scan through the list using the scroll bar (if present) or the keyboard arrow keys. Either highlight the desired item with the arrow keys and press [Enter] or simply select it using your pointing device. See **Figure 1-17.**

**Figure 1-15.**
A dialog box is displayed when you pick an item that is followed by an ellipsis. The dialog box shown here appears after you select **Block…** from the **Insert** pull-down menu.

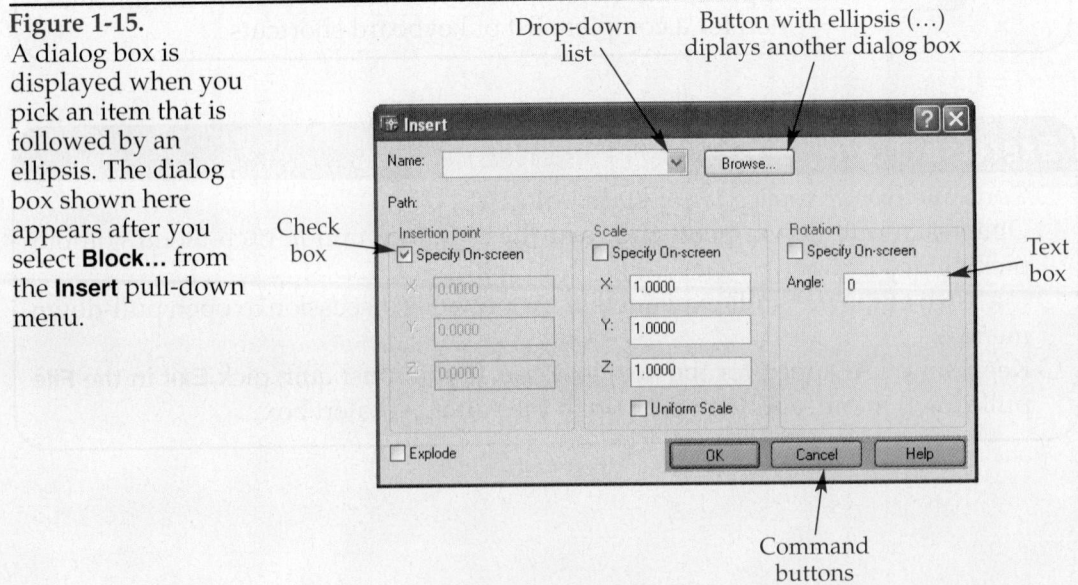

Drop-down list

Button with ellipsis (…) diplays another dialog box

Check box

Text box

Command buttons

AutoCAD and its Applications—Basics

**Figure 1-16.**
Only one radio button in a group can be highlighted at a time. A "✓" in a check box indicates the item is active (on). Any number of check boxes can be active in a given group.

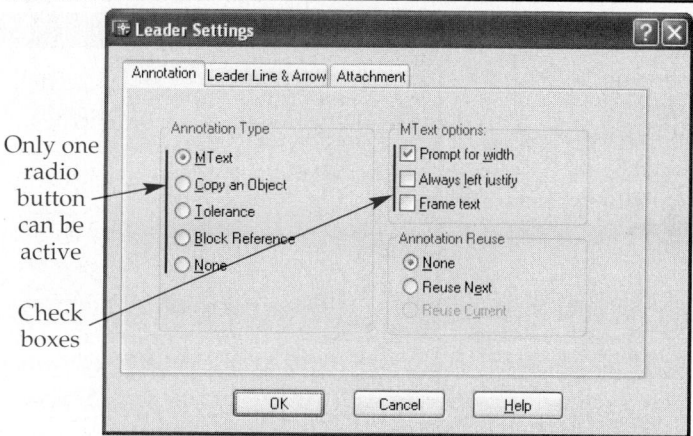

Only one radio button can be active

Check boxes

**Figure 1-17.**
A list box contains a list of items related to the dialog box. A drop-down list is displayed when you pick the drop-down arrow.

List box

Use scroll bar and arrows to move through list

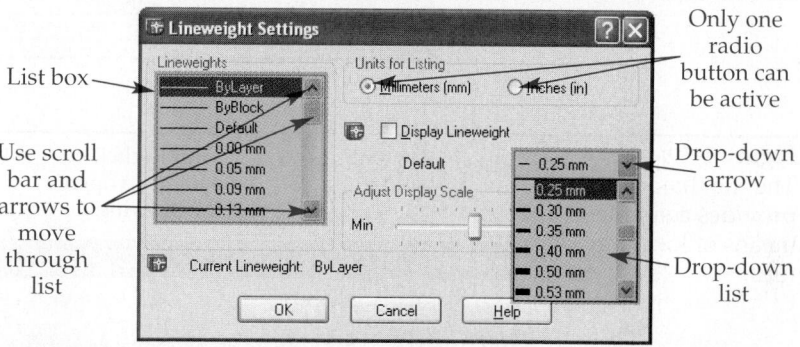

Only one radio button can be active

Drop-down arrow

Drop-down list

- **Drop-down list box.** The drop-down list box is similar to the standard list box, except only one item is initially shown. The remaining items are hidden until you pick the drop-down arrow. When you pick the drop-down arrow, the drop-down list is displayed below the initial item. You can then pick from the expanded list or use the scroll bar to find the item you need. See **Figure 1-17.**
- **Text box.** You can enter a name or single line of information using the text box. See **Figure 1-18.** When the currently selected text box is empty, the cursor appears as a flashing vertical bar, positioned at the far left side of the box. If there is existing text in the box, it appears highlighted. Any characters you then type will replace the highlighted text. Pressing either the [Backspace] key, space bar, or [Delete] key deletes all the highlighted text. You can edit existing text using the cursor keys [Home], [End], right arrow, and left arrow. The [Home] key moves the cursor to the beginning of the line of text, and the [End] key moves to the end of the line. The right and left arrow keys move the cursor one character to the right or left, respectively. By using the [Ctrl] key in conjunction with the right or left arrow key, you can move the cursor to the next word or the previous word, respectively.
- **File dialog box.** The file dialog box provides a simple means of locating and specifying file names using the familiar Windows style dialog box. The example in **Figure 1-19** shows a file dialog box for selecting one or more drawing file names to open for editing. By *double-clicking* a folder name in the list, you can "open" it. Its contents are then displayed in the list box where items can be selected. The **Look in:** drop-down list displays the directory tree and allows you to browse for a storage device or folder. The **Files of type:** drop-down list is used to specify the type of file for which you are searching. Once a file name is selected in the list box, it appears in the **File name:** text box, and its image appears in the **Preview** box. When selecting more than one file name, each file name appears in the **File name:** text box in quotation marks.

**Figure 1-18.**
You can enter a name, number, or single line of information in a text box. Several text boxes are shown here highlighted.

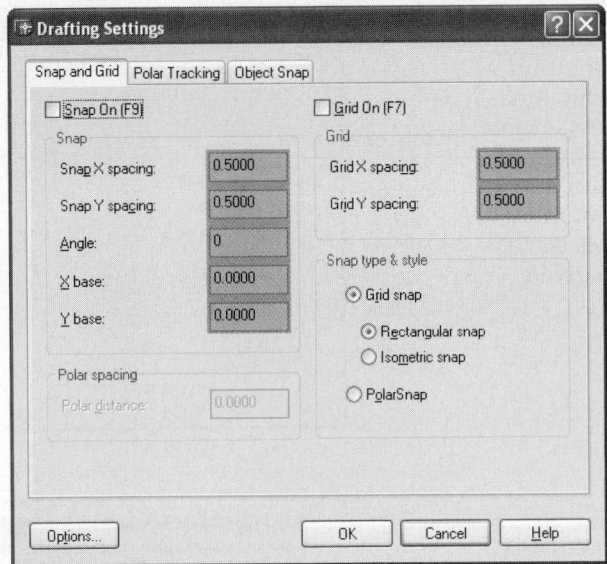

**Figure 1-19.**
The file dialog box provides a simple means of locating files.

Current folder

Double-click on a name to open the drawing

Image of selected drawing

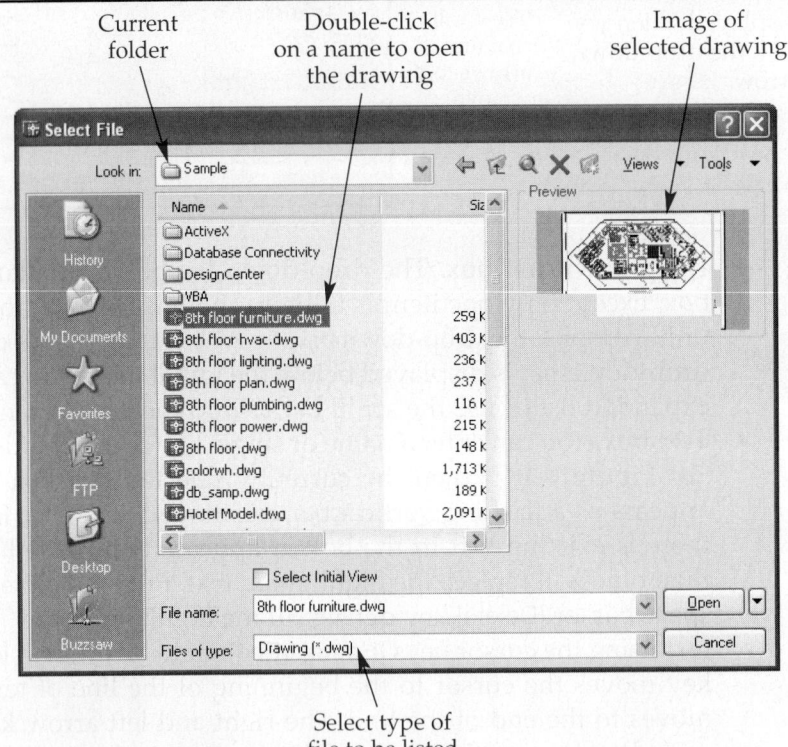

Select type of file to be listed

NOTE    The standard **Select File** dialog box is discussed in more detail in Chapter 2.

- **Scroll bars and buttons.** The scroll bar can be compared to an elevator sitting next to a list of items. The top arrow, or scroll button, points to the top floor, and the bottom arrow points to the basement. The box in the middle is the elevator. If you pick the elevator and hold down the pick button, you can move the box up or down. This displays additional items in the upper or lower floors of a list box. Pick the blank area above the elevator box to scroll up one page. Pick below the elevator box to scroll down one page. If you want to scroll up or down one file at a time, simply pick the up or down arrows. Horizontal scroll bars and buttons operate in the same manner. See **Figure 1-20.**
- **Preview box or image tile.** A preview box is an area of a dialog box that displays a "picture" of the item you select, such as a hatching style, linetype, or text font. See **Figure 1-21.** For many image tiles, picking anywhere on the image changes the associated setting and updates the image accordingly.
- **Tab.** A dialog box tab is much like an index tab used to separate sections of a notebook or the label tabs on the top of a manila file folder. Many dialog boxes in AutoCAD contain two or more "pages" or "panels," each with a tab at the top. Each tab displays a new set of related options. While the dialog box is displayed, you can pick any number of tabs in order to select options. The dialog box will only be dismissed when the **OK** button or the **Cancel** button is picked. See **Figure 1-22.**
- **Alerts.** Alerts can be displayed in two forms. A note may appear in the lower-left corner of the original dialog box, or a separate alert dialog box may appear. See **Figure 1-23.**

**Figure 1-20.**
Use scroll bars and buttons to scroll through a listing or to view sections of a drawing.

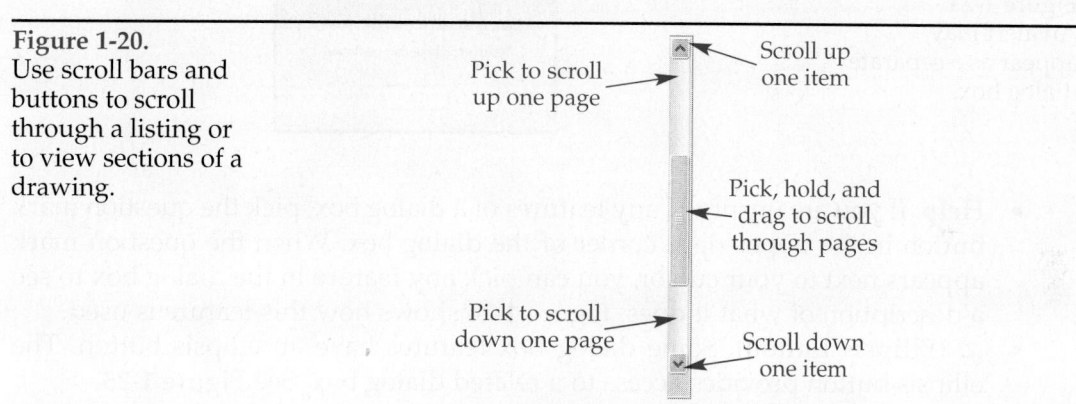

**Figure 1-21.**
An image tile displays the selected setting. Many image tiles, such as the ones shown here, can be picked to change the setting.

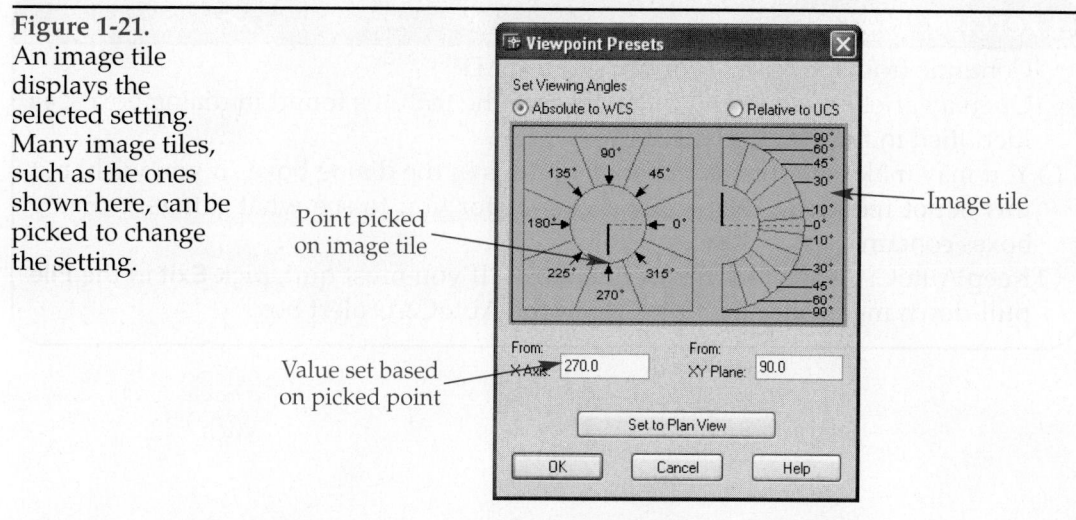

**Figure 1-22.**
A dialog box tab is much like an index tab used to separate sections of a notebook. Each tab displays a new set of related options.

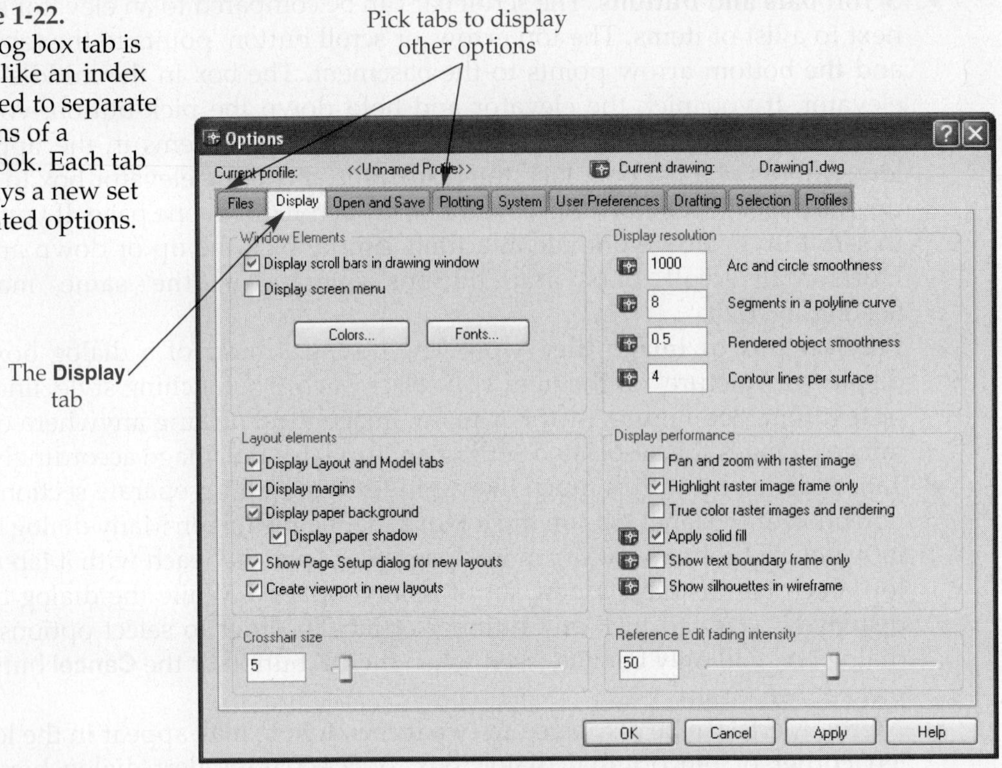

Pick tabs to display other options

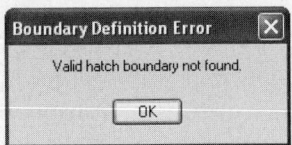

The **Display** tab

**Figure 1-23.**
An alert may appear as a separate dialog box.

**Boundary Definition Error**

Valid hatch boundary not found.

OK

- **Help.** If you are unsure of any features of a dialog box, pick the question mark button in the upper-right corner of the dialog box. When the question mark appears next to your cursor, you can pick any feature in the dialog box to see a description of what it does. **Figure 1-24** shows how this feature is used.
- **... (Ellipsis button).** Some dialog box features have an ellipsis button. The ellipsis button provides access to a related dialog box. See **Figure 1-25**.

---

## Exercise 1-4

○ Continue from Exercise 1-3 or start AutoCAD.
○ Open a variety of dialog boxes to observe the features found in dialog boxes, as identified in the previous discussion.
○ You may make selections or change options in the dialog boxes if you wish, but this is not required. This is just a chance for you to see what different dialog boxes contain.
○ Keep AutoCAD open for the next exercise. If you must quit, pick **Exit** in the **File** pull-down menu, and then pick **No** in the AutoCAD alert box.

**Figure 1-24.**
Using the question mark button. A—Pick the question mark button, and a question mark appears next to the cursor. B—Pick any feature in the dialog box, and a brief description is displayed.

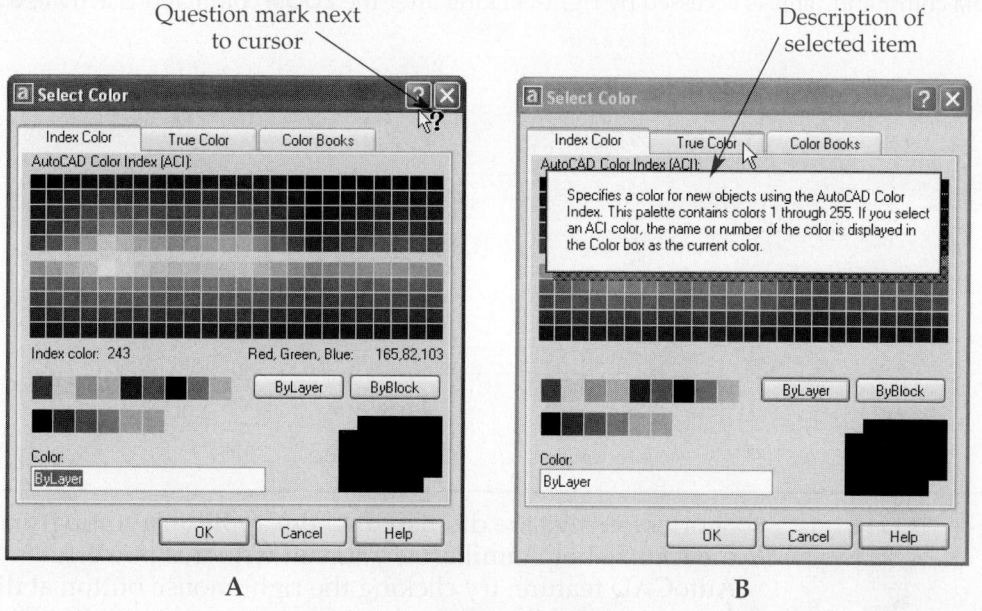

Question mark next
to cursor

Description of
selected item

A                                                                 B

**Figure 1-25.**
The ... (ellipsis) button displays a dialog box providing additional options related to the dialog feature it is next to. The ellipsis button shown here is picked to display a dialog box for defining and modifying text styles.

Ellipsis
button

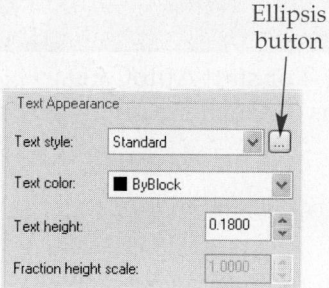

## Shortcut Menus

AutoCAD makes extensive use of shortcut menus to simplify and accelerate command entries. Sometimes referred to as *cursor menus* because they are displayed at the cursor location, these context sensitive menus are accessed by right-clicking. Because they are context sensitive, the shortcut menu content varies based on the location of the pointer when you right-click and the current conditions, such as whether a command is active or whether an object is selected.

When you right-click in the drawing area with no command active, the first item displayed on the shortcut menu is typically an option to repeat the previously used command or operation. See **Figure 1-26A.** If you right-click while a command is active, the shortcut menu contains options specific to the command. See **Figure 1-26B.**

**Figure 1-26.**
The context sensitive shortcut menus in AutoCAD provide instant access to commands and options related to what you are doing at the time. A—If a command is not currently active, the top menu pick repeats the previous command. B—This menu displays options for the **ZOOM** command. This is accessed by right-clicking after the **ZOOM** command is activated.

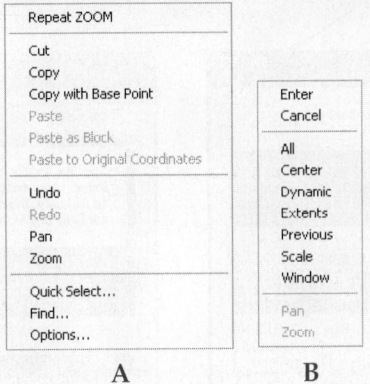

A                                      B

 **NOTE** Shortcut menus are discussed where applicable throughout the text. To help familiarize yourself with this powerful AutoCAD feature, try clicking the right mouse button at different times while you are learning to use new AutoCAD commands or when practicing various dialog box operations. You can significantly increase your productivity in AutoCAD by learning to use these features effectively.

## Exercise 1-5

○ Continue from Exercise 1-4 or start AutoCAD.
○ Access the shortcut menus to see their contents by right-clicking in the following locations:
  ○ Command window.
  ○ Drawing area.
  ○ Toolbar buttons.
  ○ Docking area beside a toolbar.
  ○ Layout tabs.
  ○ Tool palettes.
○ You can close a shortcut menu by pressing [Esc] or picking an area off the menu.
○ Keep AutoCAD open for the next exercise. If you must quit, pick **Exit** in the **File** pull-down menu, and then pick **No** in the AutoCAD alert box.

## Image Tile Menus

An image tile appears similar to a preview box and displays an image of the available object, pattern, or option. AutoCAD uses several menus composed of images. See **Figure 1-27**. To choose the object you want to use, simply pick the image tile or text label in the list box. Image tile menus allow for easy selection, since you can see the shape or item represented by the image. To select an image, move your pointing device to it and pick.

Figure 1-27.
Image tile menus
graphically display
options or
selections.

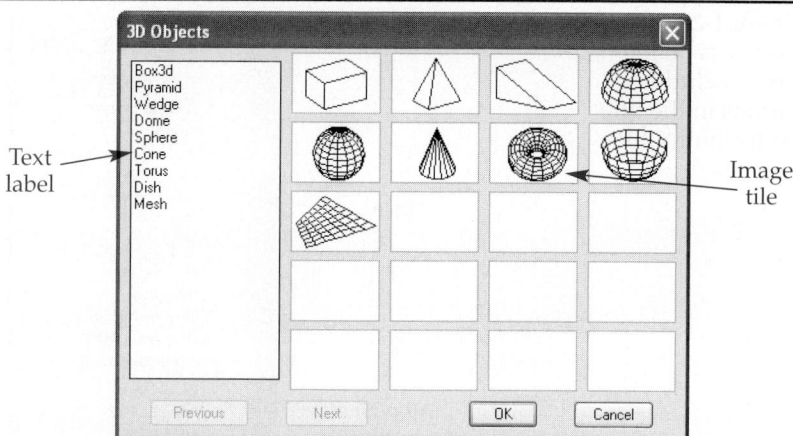

Text label

Image tile

## Modeless Dialog Boxes

Some AutoCAD features are presented in a special type of window that is sometimes referred to as a *modeless dialog box* or window. Features displayed in this manner include the **DesignCenter**, the **Properties** window, and the **Tool Palettes** window. Unlike standard dialog boxes, these windows can be docked or resized and do not need to be closed in order to enter commands and work within the drawing.

Similar to the way you move toolbars, press and hold the pick button over the title bar to reposition or dock these items. Each of the modeless dialog boxes includes a series of buttons that allow you to close, hide, or control the properties of the windows. See **Figure 1-28.** The **Auto-hide** button allows the window to minimize out of your way when the cursor is away from the window. To restore or maximize the window, simply move the cursor over the title bar. Each modeless dialog box also contains a **Properties** button, which allows you to control how the window operates and displays within AutoCAD.

### DesignCenter

**DesignCenter** is a powerful drawing information manager that provides a simple tool for effectively reusing and sharing drawing content. One of the primary productivity benefits of using CAD is that once something has been created, you can use it repeatedly in any number of drawings or drawing projects. Many types of drawing elements are similar or the same in numerous drawings, such as common drawing details, frequently used subassemblies or parts, and drawing layouts. **DesignCenter** lets you conveniently "drag and drop" drawing content to copy it from one drawing to another. *Drag and drop* is a feature that allows you to perform tasks by picking and holding the pick button while you drag the item and release the pick button to drop it in the desired location.

**Figure 1-28.**
Modeless dialog boxes include buttons in the title bar to control their behavior.

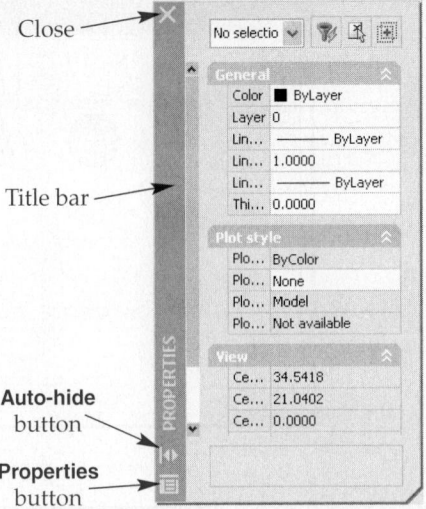

Close

Title bar

Auto-hide button

Properties button

**Figure 1-29.**
**DesignCenter**. A—When you first start **DesignCenter**, it is opened in the center of the AutoCAD window. B—**DesignCenter** in a docked state. The grab bar along the top can be used to "float" **DesignCenter**.

Grab bar

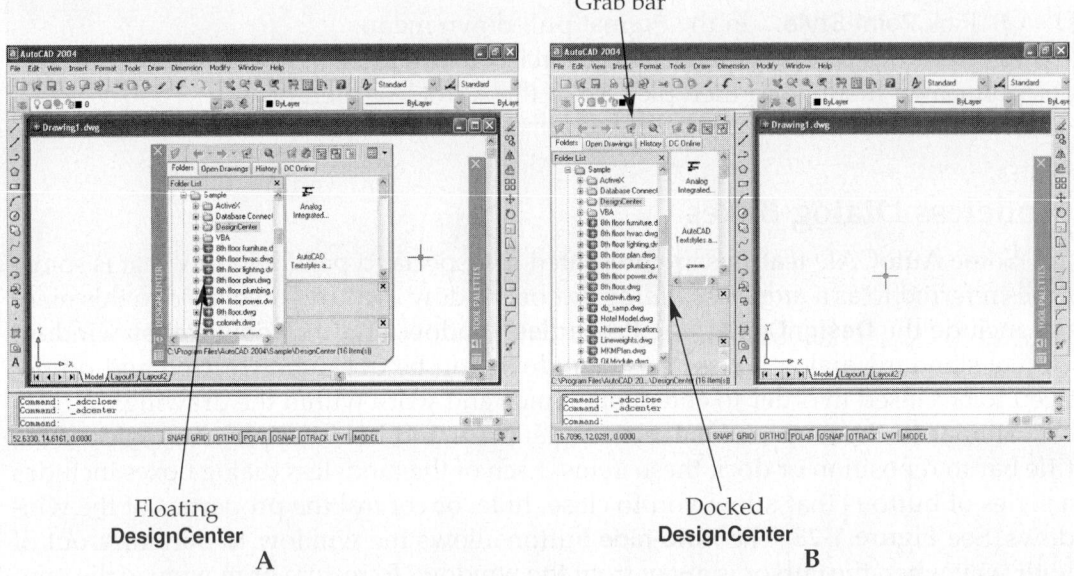

Floating
**DesignCenter**
A

Docked
**DesignCenter**
B

When you first start **DesignCenter**, it is opened in the center of the AutoCAD window. See **Figure 1-29A**. **Figure 1-29B** shows **DesignCenter** in a docked state. If the **DesignCenter** has been docked, double-click on the grab bar to change to the floating state. Double-click on the title bar to return to the docked position. The use of this powerful information management system is discussed throughout the text where it applies.

### Properties window

The **Properties** window lets you manage the properties of new and existing objects in a drawing. This window can be docked to the side of the AutoCAD window or left floating. When docked, the window's resizing bar allows you to adjust the size to suit your needs. The actual use of the **Properties** window is explained where it applies throughout this text.

## Tool Palettes window

The default **Tool Palettes** window includes three sample palettes. See **Figure 1-30.** These different tabs provide access to frequently used block symbols and hatch fill patterns. These palettes can be customized with your own symbols or hatch patterns, and new palettes can also be created. This process is explained later in this text. The **Properties** button on this modeless dialog box includes a **Transparency...** option, which allows the palette to display transparently so drawing geometry behind the palette can be viewed, as shown in **Figure 1-31.**

---

 **PROFESSIONAL TIP**

You can move the modeless dialog boxes to the side of the AutoCAD window without docking them by holding the [Ctrl] key while positioning the windows where desired.

---

**Figure 1-30.**
Three sample palettes are included with AutoCAD 2004.

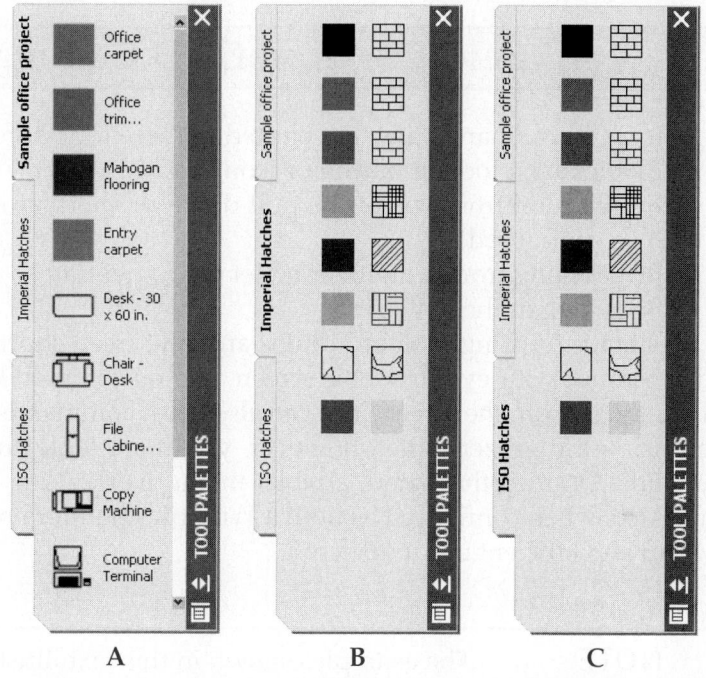

A    B    C

---

**Figure 1-31.**
Tool palettes can be set to be transparent by picking the **Properties** button in the title bar.

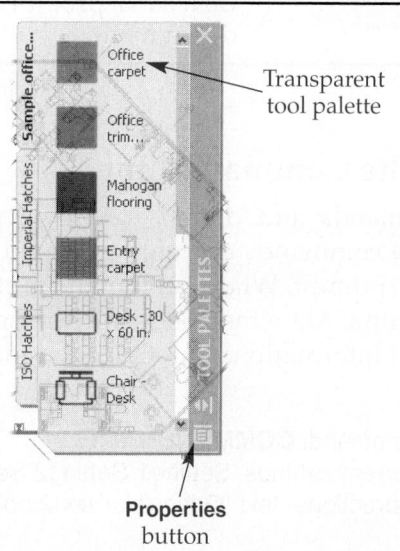

Transparent tool palette

**Properties** button

---

○ Continue from Exercise 1-6 or start AutoCAD.
○ Open the **Properties** window by pressing the [Ctrl]+[1] key combination.
○ Dock the **Properties** window to the right of the screen.
○ Open **DesignCenter** by pressing the [Ctrl]+[2] key combination.
○ Make the **Properties** window and **DesignCenter** floating. Move them around on the screen.
○ Use the [Ctrl] key to position the **Properties** window and **DesignCenter** to the left of the screen without docking them.
○ Close **DesignCenter.**
○ Set the **Properties** window to auto-hide.
○ Keep AutoCAD open for the next exercise. If you must quit, pick **Exit** in the **File** pull-down menu, and then pick **No** in the AutoCAD alert box.

## Selecting AutoCAD Commands

AutoCAD commands may be selected in these four different ways:
- By picking a toolbar button or icon.
- By selecting from one of the pull-down or shortcut menus (or screen menus, if so configured).
- By selecting from a digitizer tablet menu overlay.
- By typing at the keyboard.

The advantage of using toolbar buttons and on-screen shortcut menus is you do not need to remove your eyes from the screen. Typing commands may not require you to turn your eyes from the screen. You can also learn commands quickly by typing them. When using a digitizer tablet, however, you must look down to pick tablet menu commands. On the other hand, a tablet menu overlay can show almost every command. Also, when configured as both a Windows pointer and a digitizer, a tablet is a powerful and efficient input device.

 **NOTE** The examples shown in this text illustrate each of the AutoCAD commands as they appear when typed at the Command: prompt and when picked from toolbars and pull-down menus.

## Using the Command Line

Commands and options can be typed directly into the command window. AutoCAD commands can only be typed when the command window displays the Command: prompt. When a command is started, whether from a menu selection or by typing, AutoCAD either performs the specified operation or prompts you for any additional information. AutoCAD commands have a standard format, structured as follows:

Command: **COMMANDNAME**↵
Current settings: Setting1 Setting2 Setting3
Instructional text [Option1/oPtion2/opTion3/...] <default option or value>:

If the command has associated settings or options, these are displayed as shown. The instructional text indicates what you should do at this point, and all available options are shown within the square brackets. Each option has a unique combination of uppercase characters that can be entered at the prompt rather than typing the entire option name. If a default option is displayed in the angle brackets, you can press the [Enter] key to accept it rather than entering the value again.

AutoCAD provides you with the ability to select previously used commands by using the up and down arrow keys. For example, if you want to use the **CIRCLE** command that was used a few steps prior to your present position, press the up arrow key on the keyboard until the command you need is displayed at the Command: prompt. Then press [Enter] to activate it. This capability can be used to execute a typed command that is misspelled. For example, suppose you type LINE3 and press [Enter]. The following message appears:

Unknown command "LINE3". Press F1 for help.

Just press the up arrow key, then press [Backspace] to delete the number three (3) and press [Enter] to execute the **LINE** command. This is a timesaving feature if you like to type commands at the Command: prompt.

Right-clicking in the command window displays a shortcut menu with a cascading menu showing a list of commands you have used recently. See **Figure 1-32**. This list shows up to six recently used command names. Pick a command name from the list to use that command again.

**Figure 1-32.**
The shortcut menu displayed when you right-click in the command window offers a cascading menu listing commands you have used recently.

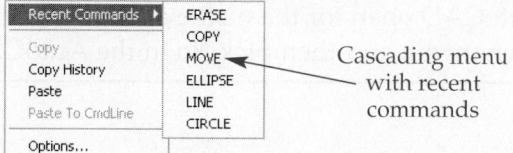

Cascading menu with recent commands

---

## Exercise 1-8

◯ Continue from Exercise 1-7 or start AutoCAD.

◯ Type the following command and follow the instructions:

Command: **LINE.**↵
Specify first point: *(pick a point in the drawing area)*
Specify next point or [Undo]: *(pick another point away from the first point)*
Specify next point or [Undo]: ↵
Command:

◯ Use the up and down arrows keys to access previously issued commands, and then return to the current Command: prompt.

◯ Right-click in the command window to see the shortcut menu.

◯ Keep AutoCAD open for the next exercise. If you must quit, pick **Exit** in the **File** pull-down menu, and then pick **No** in the AutoCAD alert box.

---

## AutoCAD Tablet Menu

A digitizer tablet can accept an overlay or menu containing a large selection of AutoCAD commands. Other specialized programs that operate with AutoCAD can have similar menus. This text presents commands as if they are typed at the keyboard or selected from menus, dialog boxes, or toolbars. If you want to use a digitizer tablet to pick commands, the tablet must first be configured (arranged) before the menu can be used.

When you use a digitizer with AutoCAD, the cursor can be moved within only the active drawing area on screen. Therefore, menu selections can be made only from the tablet menu overlay. Since all the AutoCAD commands do not fit on the tablet, you still need to select toolbar buttons or make selections from the pull-down menus. In addition, using the tablet requires you to take your eyes off the screen and look down at the overlay. After picking a tablet command, look at the command line to be sure you picked what you desired.

The AutoCAD tablet menu is shown in **Figure 1-33.** If you plan on using a digitizer with a tablet menu, take some time and study its arrangement. Become familiar with the command groups and try to remember where each command is located. The quicker you learn the layout of the menu, the more efficient your drawing sessions will be.

### Exercise 1-9

○ Skip this exercise if a tablet menu is not used.
○ Continue from Exercise 1-8 or start AutoCAD.
○ Use the AutoCAD tablet menu to access commands to see how the menu works, as compared to other options you have tried.
○ Keep AutoCAD open for the next exercise. If you must quit, pick **Exit** in the **File** pull-down menu, and then pick **No** in the AutoCAD alert box.

## Getting Help

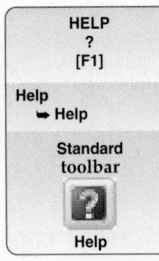

If you need help with a specific command, option, or program feature, AutoCAD provides a powerful and convenient online help system. There are several ways to access this feature. The fastest method is to press the [F1] function key. This displays the **AutoCAD 2004 Help** window. The first time you use the help system, the **Contents** tab lists the names of the available online reference guides for the AutoCAD help system. You can also display the **AutoCAD 2004 Help** window by selecting the **?** button at the right end of the **Standard** toolbar, by picking **Help** from the **Help** pull-down menu, or by typing ? or HELP at the Command: prompt.

**PROFESSIONAL TIP** If you are unfamiliar with how to use a Windows help system, it is suggested you spend time now exploring all the topics under **AutoCAD Help** in the **Contents** tab of the **AutoCAD 2004 Help** window.

**Figure 1-33.**
The AutoCAD tablet menu. (Autodesk, Inc.)

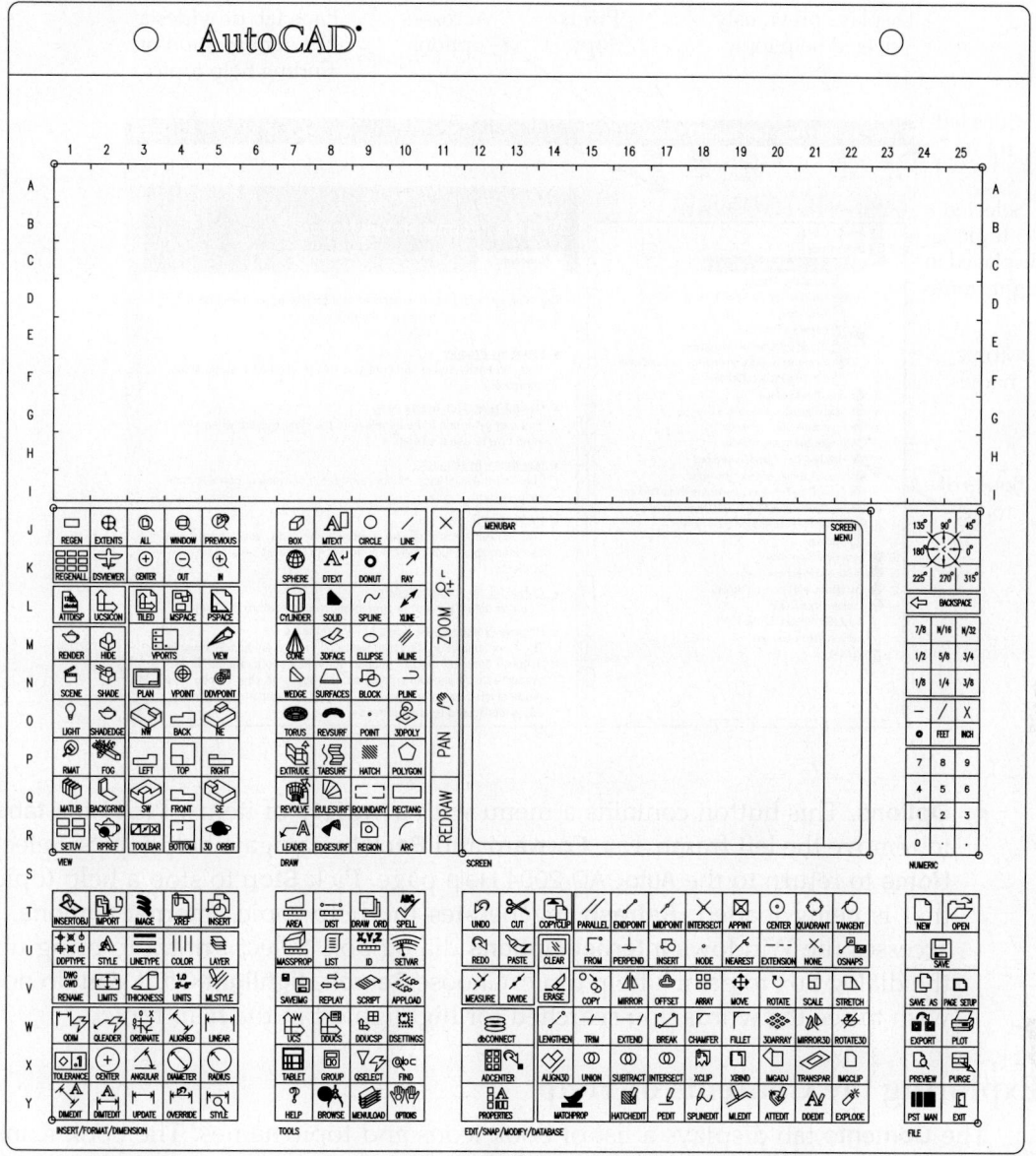

The **AutoCAD 2004 Help** window consists of two frames. See **Figure 1-34.** The left frame, which has five tabs, is used to locate help topics. The right frame displays the selected help topics. In addition to the two frames, the following buttons are located in the **AutoCAD 2004 Help** window:

- **Hide/Show.** This button controls the visibility of the left frame. When you pick **Hide**, the left frame disappears, the **Show** button replaces the **Hide** button, and the buttons appear above the right frame. Pick the **Show** button to view the left frame.
- **Back.** Pick this button to view the previously displayed help topic.
- **Forward.** Pick this button to go forward to help pages you viewed before pressing the **Back** button.
- **Home.** Picking this button takes you to the AutoCAD 2004 Help page.
- **Print.** If you want to print a help topic, pick this button. Then, you must specify if you want to print the selected help topic or the selected heading and all subtopics.

**Figure 1-34.**
The **AutoCAD 2004 Help** window.

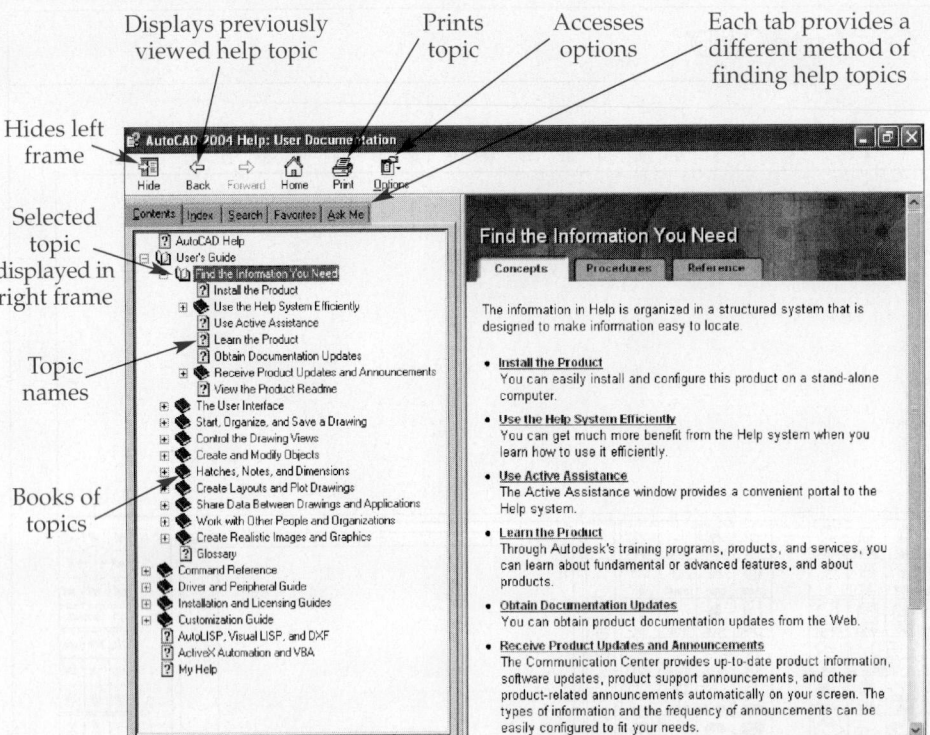

Hides left frame

Displays previously viewed help topic

Prints topic

Accesses options

Each tab provides a different method of finding help topics

Selected topic displayed in right frame

Topic names

Books of topics

- **Options.** This button contains a menu with a variety of items. Pick **Hide tabs** to remove the left frame. Use **Forward** and **Back** to navigate help topics. Select **Home** to return to the AutoCAD 2004 Help page. Pick **Stop** to stop a help topic that is being loaded. **Refresh** regenerates the help topic. **Internet Options...** accesses the Windows **Internet Options** dialog box. Select **Print...** to bring up the dialog box to print a help topic. Choose **Search Highlight Off** if you do not wish to see the words you searched for highlighted in the help topic.

## Exploring the Contents of Help

The **Contents** tab displays a list of book icons and topic names. The book icons represent the organizational structure of books of topics within the AutoCAD documentation. See **Figure 1-34**. Topics contain the actual help information; the icon used to represent a topic is a sheet of paper with a question mark. To open a book or a help topic, double-click on its name or icon. **Figure 1-34** shows the list of items displayed when one of the books is opened. Double-click on the Find the Information You Need topic to display a window with a discussion of this topic. Step-by-step instructions, as well as useful tips, are provided in this window.

The **Contents** tab lists each of the help documents within the AutoCAD help system. The following documents are available:

- **AutoCAD Help.** This document provides a general introduction to the help section.

- **User's Guide.** This is the most useful help area for most AutoCAD users. The User's Guide contains many "chapters" explaining how various tasks are accomplished using AutoCAD. New AutoCAD users should explore the User's Guide to become comfortable using the program.

- **Command Reference.** This reference contains an alphabetical listing of commands, system variables, and command aliases, along with information on utilities and standard libraries.
- **Driver and Peripheral Guide.** This guide describes techniques of installing and configuring pointing devices, printers, plotters, and external databases.
- **Installation and Licensing Guides.** This document includes topics for installing AutoCAD under a stand-alone or network license.
- **Customization Guide.** This guide provides direction in customizing the AutoCAD environment, aliases, and menus, along with an introduction to programming languages.
- **AutoLISP, Visual LISP, and DXF.** This help area provides access to four documents used for advanced customization and programming:
  - AutoLISP Reference
  - AutoLISP Developer's Guide
  - AutoLISP Tutorial
  - DXF Reference
- **ActiveX Automation and VBA.** This document provides access to three documents used for advanced customization and programming:
  - ActiveX and VBA Developer's Guide
  - ActiveX and VBA Reference
  - Connectivity Automation Reference
- **My Help.** This help area allows you to create your own groups of help topics.

When you first view the **Contents** tab, these nine help documents are listed. A small plus symbol (+) and a closed book symbol precede five of the document names. These symbols indicate that these documents are condensed. To expand these documents, pick the plus sign or double-click on the document name. This expands the documents and lists subtopics. If a subtopic has a plus symbol, it can also be expanded to reveal subtopics within the subtopic. When a topic is picked, the right frame shows the help topic.

---

**PROFESSIONAL TIP**  While a help window is displayed, pressing the right mouse button displays a shortcut menu containing many of the items found in the pull-down menus.

---

## Using the Index Tab

Although the **Contents** tab of the **AutoCAD Help** window is useful for displaying all the topics in an expanded table of contents manner, it is not very useful when searching for a specific item. In this case, most people refer to the index. This is the function of the **Index** tab. See **Figure 1-35.**

The index can be used in two ways. The first is to scroll through the alphabetical list of items in the list box. This takes time because the list is lengthy. The second way is to follow the instructions above the text box: Type in the keyword to find. As you type each new character, the lower list changes to match your entry as close as possible. Test this by slowly typing the letters lin and notice the entry that appears highlighted at the top of the list. See **Figure 1-35.** If you were searching for information on drawing lines, you could now double-click on the specific item in the list.

Some items refer to several topics. In this case, the **Topics Found** dialog box is displayed. See **Figure 1-36.** Click on the topic you wish to see and pick the **Display** button. When you display the topic, a help screen is presented that includes **Concepts**, **Procedures**, and **Reference** tabs.

---

**Figure 1-35.**
The **Index** tab displays an index listing.

Entered text     AutoCAD selects topic that most nearly matches entry

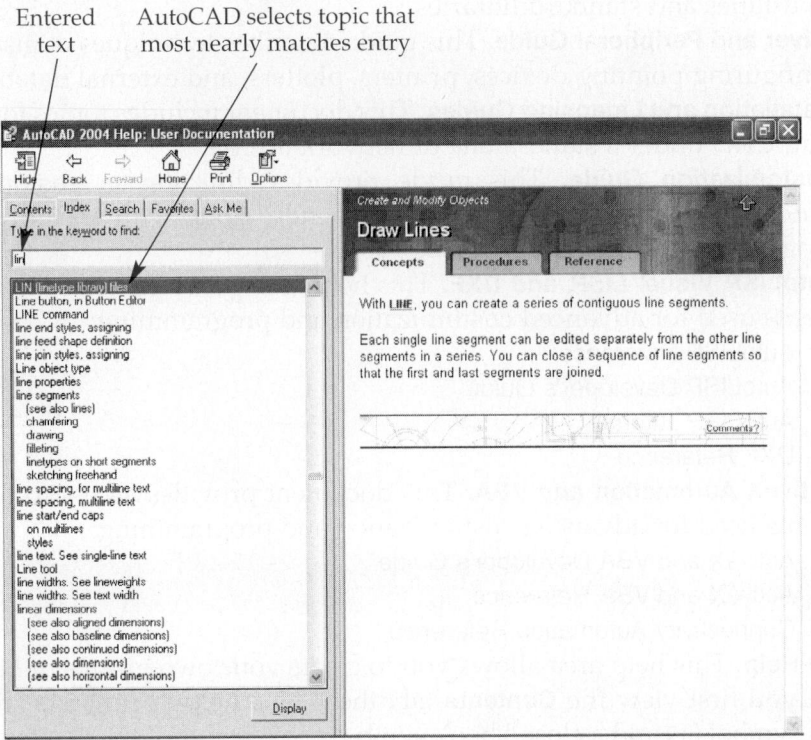

**Figure 1-36.**
The **Topics Found** dialog box.

Select from list of topics

Pick to display topic

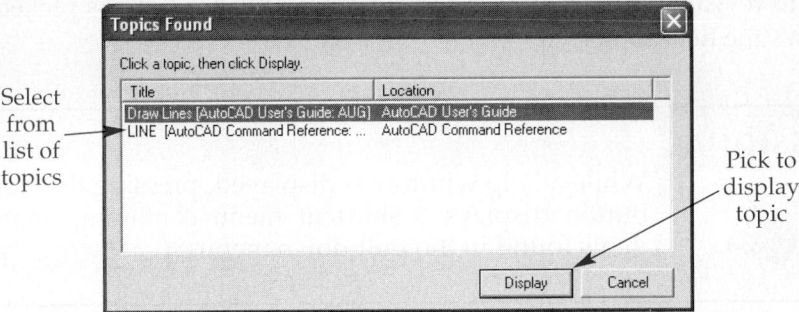

The **Concepts** tab provides a general description and explanation of the topic. See **Figure 1-37.** The text may include hyperlinks, which access additional help information when picked. The **Procedures** tab provides step-by-step instructions related to the topic. See **Figure 1-38.** The **Reference** tab lists hyperlinks to similar topics. See **Figure 1-39.**

At the upper-right corner of each page is an up arrow. Pick this arrow to move to the next higher level in the help system. All tabs include a **Comments** hyperlink at the bottom of the page. Select this link to send a message regarding the help topic to Autodesk Technical Publications.

## Using the Search Tab

The **Search** tab can be used to search for specific words or phrases. See **Figure 1-40.** Type the search entry into the **Type in the word(s) to search for:** text box. Pick the arrow button next to the text box to select the AND, OR, NEAR, and NOT search operators. After typing the search entry, pick the **List Topics** button to list all topics containing the search entry. Double-click on a listed help topic (or select the topic and pick the **Display** button) to have the topic displayed in the right frame.

**Figure 1-37.**
The **Concepts** tab provides a general explanation of the topic.

Pick to go to a higher
level in the help system

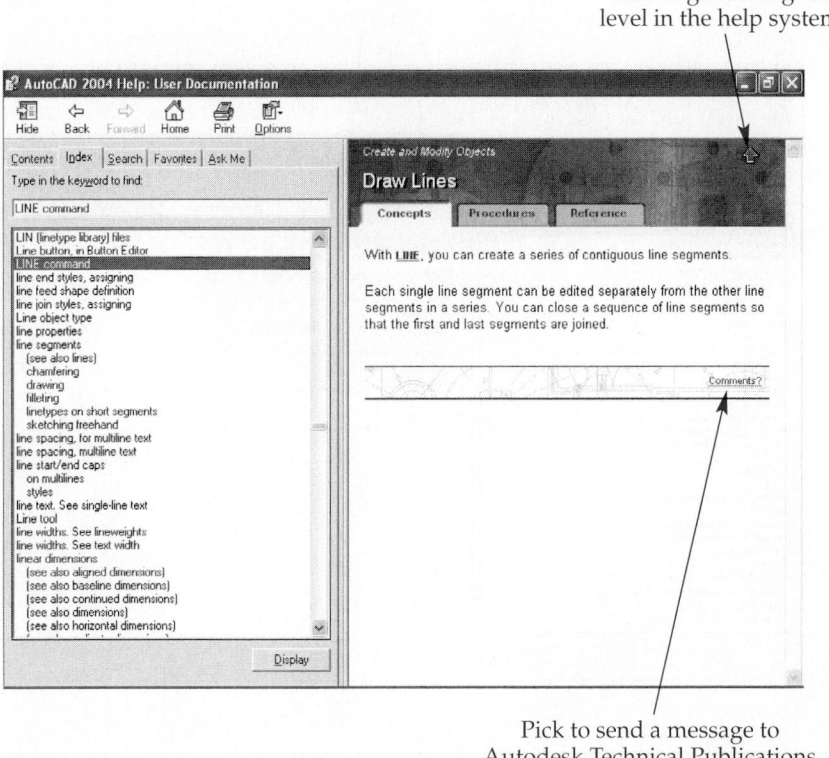

Pick to send a message to
Autodesk Technical Publications

**Figure 1-38.**
The **Procedures** tab lists step-by-step instructions related to the help topic.

Step-by-step procedure for
using the **LINE** command

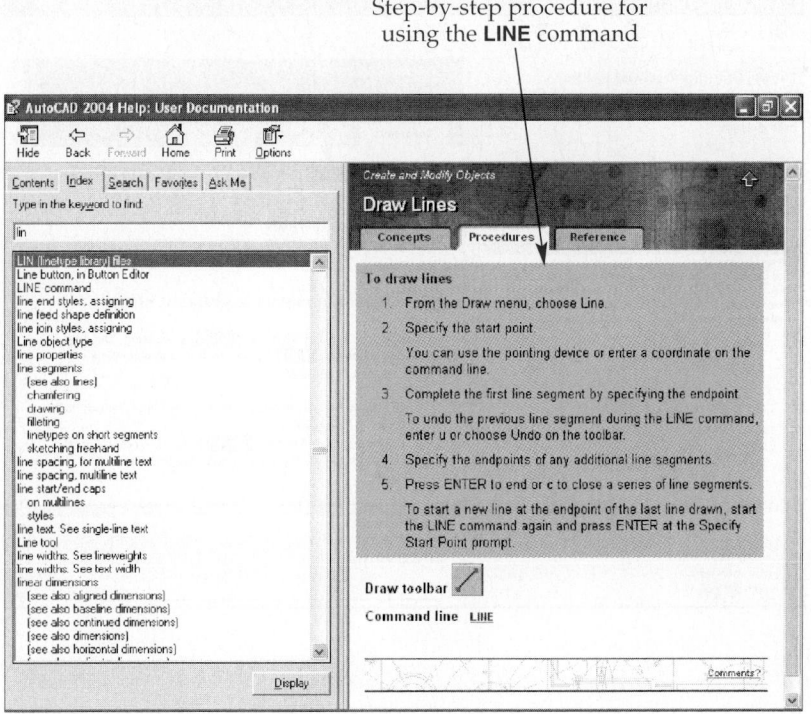

**Figure 1-39.**
The **Reference** tab lists related commands and system variables.

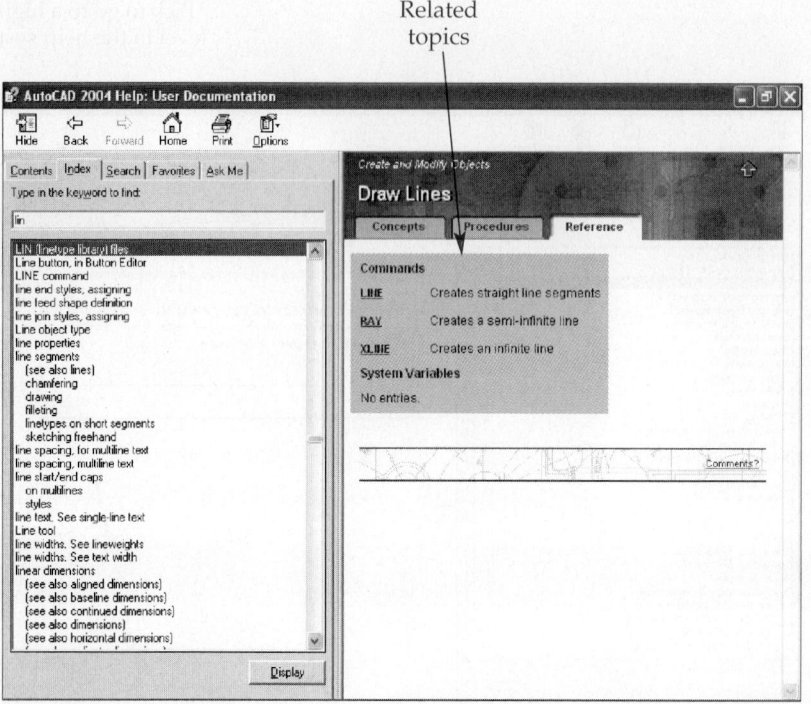

**Figure 1-40.**
The **Search** tab allows you to conduct a detailed search.

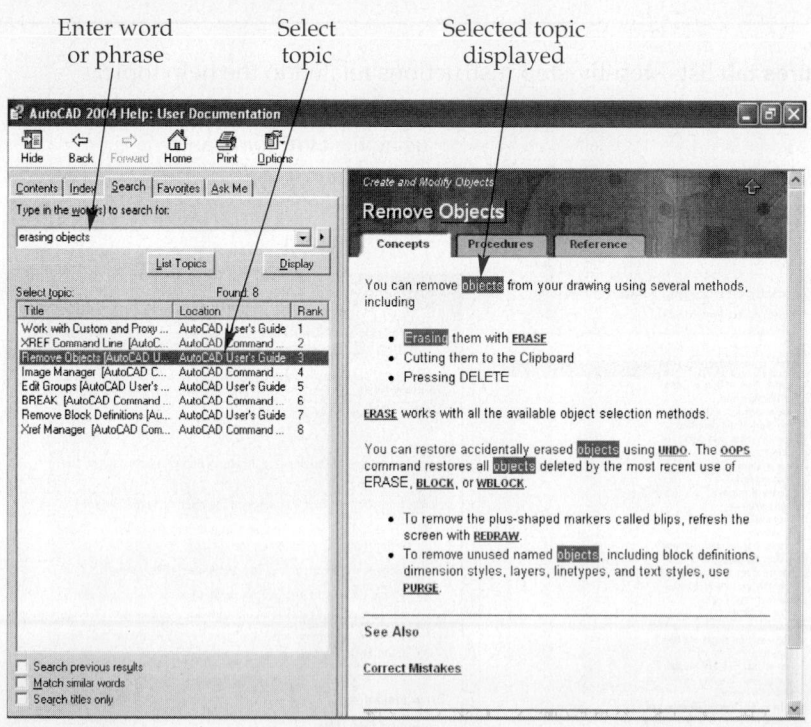

## Using the Favorites Tab

The **Favorites** tab can be used to list help topics for future reference. To save a help topic, display the topic in the right frame, access the **Favorites** tab, and then pick the **Add** button. See **Figure 1-41**. The topic is listed in the **Topics:** window. When you want to access this topic in the future, simply access the **Favorites** tab, select the topic from the list, and pick the **Display** button. This is much easier than navigating through the **Contents** tab to find a help topic. Use the **Remove** button to delete help topics from the **Favorites** tab.

## Using the Ask Me Tab

You can sort help topics by posing a question or typing a phrase in the **Ask Me** tab. First, use the **List of components to search:** drop-down list to select the help documents most likely to contain the desired help information. The User's Guide and Command Reference contain help topics on basic issues. Then, type the question you want answered in the **Type in a question and press Enter** text box. You can also enter phrases. Press [Enter], and hyperlinks to help topics are listed in the window. Pick a hyperlink to display the help topic in the right frame. See **Figure 1-42**.

---

**Figure 1-41.**
Save useful topics in the **Favorites** tab for easy reference in the future.

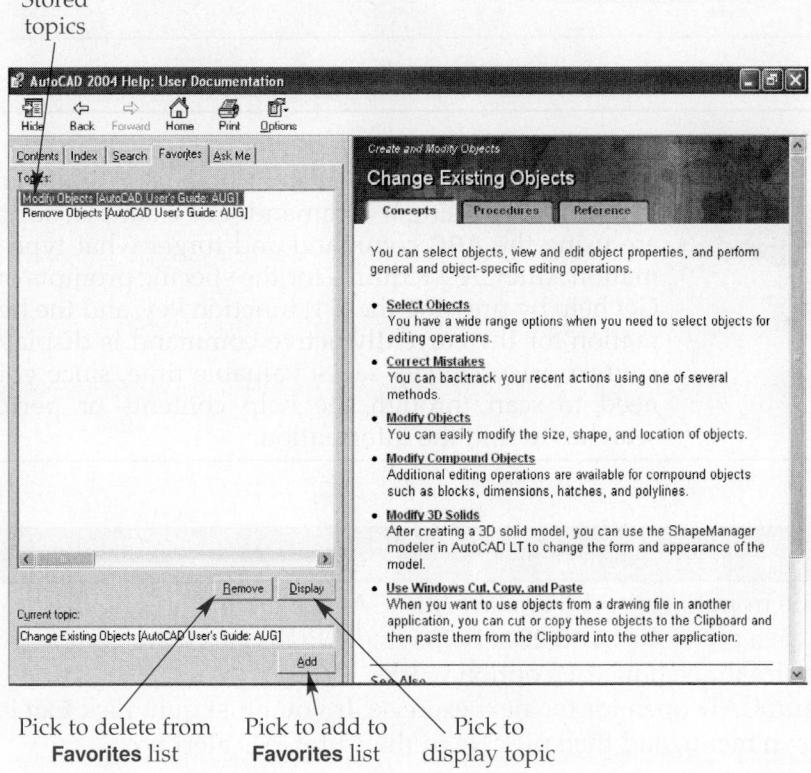

Stored topics

Pick to delete from **Favorites** list    Pick to add to **Favorites** list    Pick to display topic

**Figure 1-42.**
The **Ask Me** tab provides another method to locate help topics.

Enter a question       Select "books"       Topics
or phrase            to search           listed

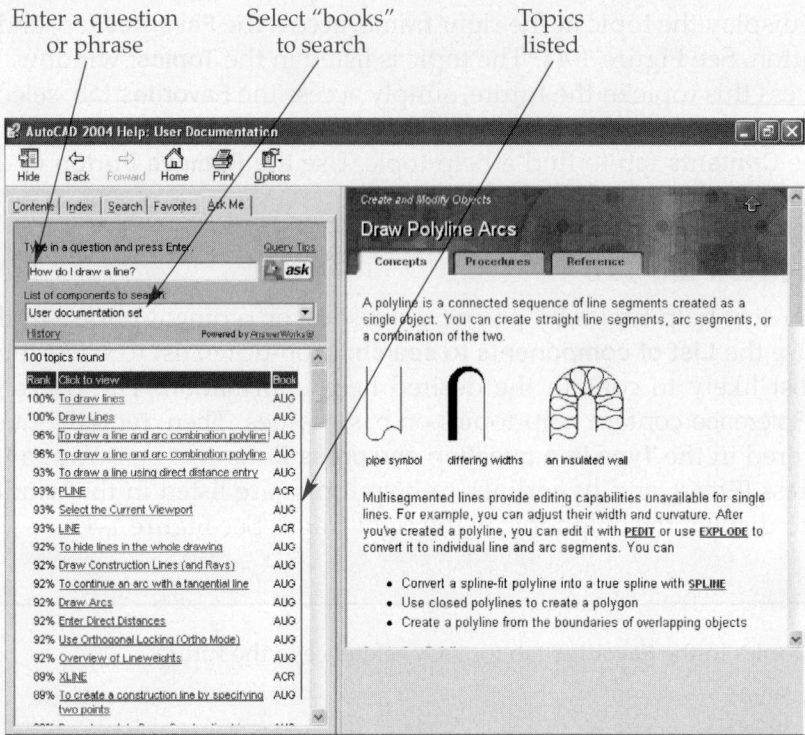

---

**PROFESSIONAL TIP**

AutoCAD's help function can also be used while you are in the process of using a command. For example, suppose you are using the **ARC** command and forget what type of information AutoCAD requires for the specific prompts on screen. Get help by pressing the [F1] function key, and the help information for the currently active command is displayed. This *context oriented help* saves valuable time, since you do not need to scan through the help contents or perform any searches to find the information.

---

## Exercise 1-10

○ Continue from Exercise 1-9 or start AutoCAD.
○ Access each of the **AutoCAD 2004 Help** window tabs and search out help topics of your choice to see how each option works.
○ Keep AutoCAD open for the next exercise. If you must quit, pick **Exit** in the **File** pull-down menu, and then pick **No** in the AutoCAD alert box.

---

## Active Assistance

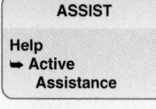

ASSIST

Help
➡ Active
   Assistance

**Active Assistance** is a help window that monitors your actions and displays information relative to the command currently being accessed. It can be activated by selecting **Active Assistance** from the **Help** pull-down menu or by typing ASSIST at the Command: prompt.

The **Active Assistance** window is shown in **Figure 1-43**. It provides brief help information for the active command or dialog box. When you enter a command, the **Active Assistance** window displays content related to the command. As its name suggests, the **Active Assistance** window remains active as you work in AutoCAD.

Right-click in the **Active Assistance** window to display the **Active Assistance** shortcut menu. This menu includes the following options:

- **Home.** This option displays the How to Use Active Assistance topic in the window. This topic provides brief descriptions of the **Active Assistance** window and its options.
- **Back.** This option displays the previous topic.
- **Forward.** This option returns to the topic displayed prior to using the **Back** option. This option is only enabled after the **Back** option is used.
- **Print.** This option prints the displayed topic.
- **Settings.** Pick **Settings...** to access the **Active Assistance Settings** dialog box. See **Figure 1-44**. The check box at the top of the dialog box allows you to specify whether or not the **Active Assistance** window is displayed when AutoCAD is launched.

    The four options in the **Activation** area control when the **Active Assistance** window is displayed. The **All commands** option has the **Active Assistance** window open at all times and displays help for all AutoCAD commands. The **New and enhanced commands** option displays the window for commands new to AutoCAD 2004. The **Dialogs only** option opens the window when a dialog box is accessed. When **On demand** is selected, you must use the **ASSIST** command to open the window.

Figure 1-43.
The **Active Assistance** window provides brief information on the active command or dialog box.

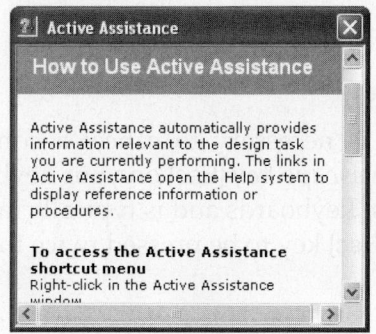

Figure 1-44.
Display of the **Active Assistance** window is controlled by the settings in the **Active Assistance Settings** dialog box.

Display when AutoCAD is launched

Select when **Active Assistance** window is displayed

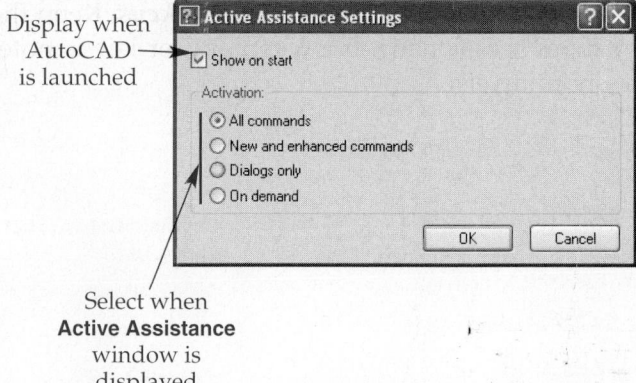

## Using the Online Product Support

Product support is a comprehensive support tool provided with AutoCAD 2004. It is accessed by picking the **Online Resources** cascading menu in the **Help** pull-down menu, and then selecting **Product Support**. This powerful support tool features a knowledge base of information designed to help you find fast answers to questions, solutions for problems, and guidance for finding additional support and technical assistance.

---

### Exercise 1-11

○ Continue from Exercise 1-10 or start AutoCAD.

○ If you have an Internet connection, pick **Product Support** from the **Online Resources** cascading menu in the **Help** pull-down menu and observe the contents.

○ Keep AutoCAD open for the next exercise. If you must quit, pick **Exit** in the **File** pull-down menu, and then pick **No** in the AutoCAD alert box.

---

## Keys and Buttons

AutoCAD provides several ways of performing a given task. Many keys on the keyboard allow you to quickly perform many functions. In addition, multibutton pointing devices also use buttons for AutoCAD commands. Become familiar with the meaning of these keys and buttons to help improve your performance with AutoCAD.

### The [Esc] Key

Any time it is necessary to cancel a command and return to the Command: prompt, press the *escape key* [Esc] on your keyboard. This key is found on the upper-left corner of most keyboards and is typically labeled Esc. Some command sequences may require the [Esc] key to be pressed twice to completely cancel the operation.

### Control Keys

Most computer programs use *control key* functions to perform common tasks. Control key functions are used by pressing and holding the [Ctrl] key while pressing a second key. These keys are also called *accelerator keys*. Keep the following list close at hand and try them occasionally. If a command or key is noted as a "toggle," it is either on or off—nothing else.

| Key Combination | Result |
| --- | --- |
| [Ctrl]+[A] | Select all |
| [Ctrl]+[B] | Snap mode (toggle) |
| [Ctrl]+[C] | **COPYCLIP** command |
| [Ctrl]+[D] | Coordinate display on status line (toggle) |
| [Ctrl]+[E] | Crosshairs in isoplane positions left/top/right (toggle) |
| [Ctrl]+[F] | Osnap mode (toggle) |
| [Ctrl]+[G] | Grid mode (toggle) |
| [Ctrl]+[K] | **HYPERLINK** command |
| [Ctrl]+[L] | Ortho mode (toggle) |
| [Ctrl]+[N] | **NEW** command |
| [Ctrl]+[O] | **OPEN** command |
| [Ctrl]+[P] | **PLOT** (print) command |
| [Ctrl]+[Q] | **QUIT** (exit) command |
| [Ctrl]+[R] | Toggle viewport |
| [Ctrl]+[S] | **SAVE** command |
| [Ctrl]+[T] | Tablet mode (toggle) |
| [Ctrl]+[U] | Polar mode (toggle) |
| [Ctrl]+[V] | **PASTECLIP** command |
| [Ctrl]+[W] | Object Snap Tracking (toggle) |
| [Ctrl]+[X] | **CUTCLIP** command |
| [Ctrl]+[Y] | **REDO** command |
| [Ctrl]+[Z] | **UNDO** command |
| [Ctrl]+[0] | Clean Screen mode (toggle) |
| [Ctrl]+[1] | **Properties** window (toggle) |
| [Ctrl]+[2] | **DesignCenter** (toggle) |
| [Ctrl]+[3] | **Tool Palettes** window (toggle) |
| [Ctrl]+[6] | **dbConnect Manager** (toggle) |

## Function Keys

Function keys provide instant access to commands. They can also be programmed to perform a series of commands. The function keys are located along the top of the keyboard. Depending on the brand of keyboard, there will be either ten or twelve function keys. These are numbered from [F1] to [F12]. AutoCAD uses eleven function keys. These are listed below. As you become proficient with AutoCAD, you might program the function keys to do specific tasks using other computer programs.

| Function Key | Result |
|---|---|
| [F1] | **HELP** command |
| [F2] | Flip screen between graphics and text windows (toggle) |
| [F3] | Object Snap mode (toggle) |
| [F4] | Tablet mode (toggle) |
| [F5] | Isoplane mode (toggle) |
| [F6] | Coordinate display (toggle) |
| [F7] | Grid mode (toggle) |
| [F8] | Ortho mode (toggle) |
| [F9] | Snap mode (toggle) |
| [F10] | Polar mode (toggle) |
| [F11] | Object Snap Tracking (toggle) |

## Button Functions

If you are using a multibutton pointing device, you can select control key functions by pressing a single button. The default settings of the pointing device buttons are as follows:

| Button | Result |
|---|---|
| 0 | Pick |
| 1 | Return |
| 2 | **Object Snap** shortcut menu |
| 3 | Cancel |
| 4 | Snap mode (toggle) |
| 5 | Ortho mode (toggle) |
| 6 | Grid mode (toggle) |
| 7 | Coordinate display (toggle) |
| 8 | Crosshairs isoplane positions top/left/right (toggle) |
| 9 | Tablet mode (toggle) |

○ Continue from Exercise 1-11 or start AutoCAD.
○ Use some of the control keys, alt keys, and function keys to become comfortable with how they work.
○ If you are using a digitizer tablet and puck, use the button functions to see how they work.
○ Exit AutoCAD by picking **Exit** in the **File** pull-down menu, and then pick the **No** button in the AutoCAD alert box.

## Understanding Terminology

The following terms are used throughout the text and will help you select AutoCAD functions. You should become familiar with them:

- **Default.** A value maintained by the computer until you change it.
- **Pick** or **click.** Use the pointing device to select an item on the screen or tablet.
- **Button.** One of the screen toolbar or pointing device (puck) buttons.
- **Key.** A key on the keyboard.
- **Function key.** One of the keys labeled [F1]–[F12] along the top or side of the keyboard.
- **[Enter] (↵).** The [Enter] or [Return] key on the keyboard.
- **Command.** An instruction issued to the computer.
- **Option.** An aspect of a command that can be selected.

## Avoiding "Disk Full" Problems

When you save a drawing, AutoCAD allows you to specify a name and a location for the drawing file. The drawing will be saved in the AutoCAD program folder unless you specify a new one. You can also select the disk drive in which to save the drawing. The hard disk that contains the AutoCAD program folder is the default. New users to AutoCAD often want to save their drawings on a 3.5″ disk instead of on the hard drive.

Saving a drawing to the 3.5″ disk during a working session is not the most efficient way to operate AutoCAD. These drives are slow to store and access data. In addition, limited space on the 3.5″ disk can soon lead to a Not enough space on disk error. If you save your drawing directly to these disks, AutoCAD also places a backup drawing file with the same name in the same location as the original file. Each time you save the original drawing, the backup file is updated. Therefore, you actually have two drawing files instead of one.

Always save your work to the hard disk on a regular basis—*every ten to fifteen minutes.* If you must save a drawing to a 3.5″ disk, make it the last thing you do before you exit AutoCAD. You can also use the Windows Explorer at any time to quickly see if drawings will fit on your disk, and then copy them to the disk. Refer to Chapter 13 for a discussion of using the Windows Explorer. Chapter 2 discusses the techniques of starting and saving drawings properly.

## Chapter Test

*Answer the following questions on a separate sheet of paper.*

1. What system is used to construct drawings and models in AutoCAD?
2. Basic pictorial drawings are called _____.
3. Using the system referred to in Question 1, what is the proper notation for the values Z=4, X=2, and Y=5?
4. What is *drawing planning?*
5. Why is drawing planning important?
6. What is the first thing you should do as part of your planning checklist?
7. Why should you save your work every ten to fifteen minutes?
8. What are *standards?*
9. What scale should you use to draw in AutoCAD?
10. Why should you read the command line at the bottom of the screen?
11. How is AutoCAD represented on the Windows desktop?
12. What is the quickest method for starting AutoCAD?
13. Which toolbars are displayed by default when AutoCAD is launched?
14. What is a *grab bar?*
15. Which area displays the communication between you and AutoCAD?
16. What is the difference between a docked toolbar and a floating toolbar?
17. What are *menu accelerator keys?* How are they used? Give an example.
18. What is an *option?*
19. List the AutoCAD pull-down menus.
20. What is a *flyout menu?*
21. What is the function of tabs in a dialog box?
22. What must you do to a tablet before it can be used?
23. What are the functions of the following control keys?
    A. [Ctrl]+[B]
    B. [Ctrl]+[C]
    C. [Ctrl]+[D]
    D. [Ctrl]+[G]
    E. [Ctrl]+[O]
    F. [Ctrl]+[S]
24. Name the function keys that execute the same tasks as the following control keys:
    A. [Ctrl]+[B]
    B. [Ctrl]+[D]
    C. [Ctrl]+[G]
    D. [Ctrl]+[L]
    E. [Ctrl]+[T]
25. What is the difference between a *button* and a *key?*
26. What do you call a value that is maintained by the computer until you change it?
27. What type of pull-down menu item has an arrow to the right?
28. What type of menu contains a group of symbols or patterns?

29. What is an *image tile*?
30. What is *context oriented help,* and how is it accessed?
31. How do you open a folder in a file dialog box in order to see its contents?
32. What is the area in a dialog box that displays a "picture" of the item you select?
33. What is the function of the **...** (ellipsis) button?
34. How do you access a shortcut menu?
35. What is the purpose of a shortcut menu?
36. Why are shortcut menus considered context sensitive?
37. Name a powerful drawing information manager that provides a simple tool for efficiently reusing and sharing drawing content.
38. Name the window that lets you manage the properties of new and existing objects in a drawing.
39. How do you access previously used commands?
40. Identify the quickest way to access the **AutoCAD 2004 Help** window.
41. What happens to the cursor when you pick the question mark in the upper-right corner of a dialog box?
42. What is the purpose of the cursor mentioned in Question 41?
43. Describe the purpose of the book icons in the **Contents** tab of the **AutoCAD 2004 Help** window.
44. How do you use the **Index** tab of the **AutoCAD 2004 Help** window to find information on a topic?
45. Identify the tab in the **AutoCAD 2004 Help** window that allows you to do a detailed search based on one or more words.
46. How do you access help regarding a currently active command?
47. What is the purpose of the **Active Assistance** window?
48. What is Online Product Support?
49. Why shouldn't you save your work to a 3.5" floppy disk?
50. What is the purpose of the **SAVETIME** variable?

## Problems

1. Interview your drafting instructor or supervisor and try to determine what type of drawing standards exist at your school or company. Write them down and keep them with you as you learn AutoCAD. Make notes as you progress through this text on how you use these standards. Also note how the standards could be changed to better match the capabilities of AutoCAD.

2. Research your drafting department standards. If you do not have a copy of the standards, acquire one. If AutoCAD standards have been created, make notes as to how you can use these in your projects. If no standards exist in your department or company, make notes as to how you can help develop standards. Write a report on why your school or company should create CAD standards and how they would be used. Discuss who should be responsible for specific tasks. Recommend procedures, techniques, and forms, if necessary. Develop this report as you progress through your AutoCAD instruction and as you read through this book.
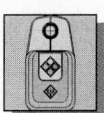

3. Develop a drawing planning sheet for use in your school or company. List items you think are important for planning a CAD drawing. Make changes to this sheet as you learn more about AutoCAD.

4. Load AutoCAD from the Windows desktop using one of the three methods discussed in this chapter. Perform the following tasks:
   A. Open the **AutoCAD 2004 Help** window.
   B. In the **Contents** tab, expand the User's Guide category.
   C. Pick the Find the Information You Need topic, then pick the Use the Help System Efficiently hyperlink in the right pane.
   D. If you have access to a printer, print the topic.
   E. Look up the Use Active Assistance topic.
   F. Close the **AutoCAD 2004 Help** window, and then close AutoCAD.

5. Load AutoCAD by selecting the proper items, using the Start button on the Windows task bar.
   A. Move the pointer over the buttons in the **Standard** toolbar and read the notes on the status bar at the bottom of the screen.
   B. Move the pointer to the second button in the **Standard** toolbar and read the note on the status bar.
   C. Slowly move the pointer over each of the buttons on the **Styles** and **Layers** toolbars and read the tooltips. Do the same on the **Draw** and **Modify** toolbars at the sides of the screen.
   D. Pick the **File** pull-down menu to display it. Using the right arrow key, move through all the pull-down menus. Use the left arrow key to return to the **Draw** pull-down menu. Use the down arrow key to move to the **Circle** command, then use the right arrow key to display the **Circle** options in the cascading menu.
   E. Press the [Esc] key to dismiss the menu.
   F. Close AutoCAD by picking **Exit** in the **File** pull-down menu.

6. Draw a freehand sketch of the screen display. Label each of the screen areas. To the side of the sketch, write a short description of each screen area's function.

## Learning Objectives

After completing this chapter, you will be able to do the following:
- Plan an AutoCAD drawing.
- Use the AutoCAD **Quick Setup** wizard.
- Use the AutoCAD **Advanced Setup** wizard.
- Use an AutoCAD template.
- Start a drawing from scratch.
- Manage drawings in the Multiple Design Environment (MDE).
- Save a drawing under a different name.
- Specify how often your work is automatically saved.
- Save AutoCAD drawings for older releases.
- Save and open AutoCAD drawings in a DXF format.
- Open a saved drawing.
- Search for AutoCAD files.
- Explain how to open an AutoCAD drawing using Windows Explorer.
- Use the **Partial Open** option and the **Partial Load** command.
- Use the **CLOSE** and **EXIT** commands.

## Planning Your AutoCAD Drawing

Effective planning can greatly reduce the amount of time it takes to set up and complete a drawing. Drawing setup involves many factors affecting the quality and accuracy of your final drawing. AutoCAD helps make this planning process easy by providing a variety of automated setup options that help you begin a drawing. Even with these options, you still need to know the basic elements that make up your drawing. Some basic planning decisions include the following:
- The sheet size on which the drawing will be plotted.
- The units of measure being used.
- The precision required for the drawing.
- The name of the drawing.

This chapter discusses all of these AutoCAD setup options. It also provides an opportunity to experiment with them.

## Starting a New File Using a Template

In AutoCAD, templates store standard drawing settings and may contain predefined drawing layouts, title blocks, and other common drawing components. When you begin a drawing using a template, all the settings and contents of the template file are added to the new drawing. Using a template means the drawing setup process is already complete and you are ready to begin drafting immediately. In addition to reducing drawing setup time, templates also help to maintain consistent standards in each of your drawings. AutoCAD also allows you to start a new drawing based on an existing drawing file. A drawing file used as a template is also referred to as a *prototype drawing.*

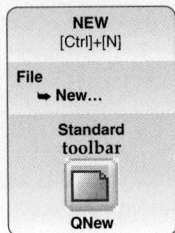

When you open the AutoCAD program, a new drawing is started automatically. This drawing is based on a template file containing default settings. If you use this drawing, you need to set the drawing specifications, such as units of measurement, text settings, and dimension settings. To start a drawing based on a template file, pick the **QNew** button from the **Standard** toolbar, select **New...** from the **File** pull-down menu, enter NEW at the Command: prompt, or use the [Ctrl]+[N] key combination. This displays the **Select template** dialog box, as seen in **Figure 2-1.**

The **Select template** dialog box lists the templates found in the default template folder. A variety of templates conforming to accepted industry standards are included with AutoCAD. You will notice all the files have a .dwt extension, which stands for *drawing template.* If you just want to open a blank file, use the acad.dwt template for English settings or the acadiso.dwt template for metric settings. To open a template file, select the file, and then pick the **Open** button or double-click on the file.

Placing the cursor on a template file in the **Select template** dialog box displays a preview in the **Preview** window. The template files provided with AutoCAD use a naming system indicating the drafting standard referenced, the size of the title block in the preset layout, and the plot style settings used. Plot styles are introduced in Chapter 10.

Figure 2-1.
The **Select template** dialog box allows you to select a pre-configured drawing file called a *template file.*

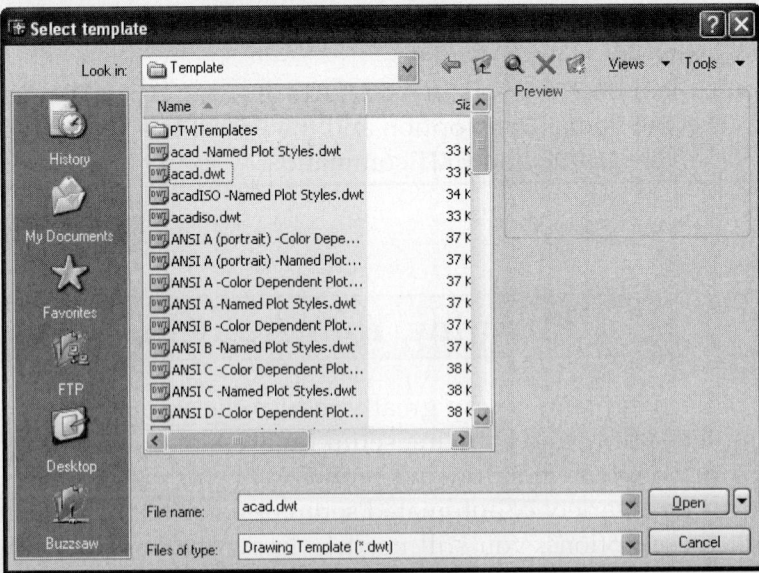

Drafters often think of the drawing size as sheet size. The *sheet size* is the size of the paper you will use to lay out and plot the final drawing. It takes into account the size of the drawing and additional space for dimensions, notes, and clear area between the drawing and borderlines. The sheet size also includes the title block, the revision block, zoning, and an area for general notes. In AutoCAD, the sheet size is specified in the **Page Setup** dialog box when defining your drawing layout. The **Page Setup** dialog box is discussed in Chapter 10.

ASME/ANSI standard sheet sizes and formats are specified in the documents ASME Y14.1, *Decimal Inch Drawing Sheet Size and Format,* and ASME Y14.1M, *Metric Drawing Sheet Size and Format.* The proper presentation of engineering changes is given in ASME Y14.35M, *Revision of Engineering Drawings and Associated Documents.* ASME Y14.1 lists sheet size specifications in inches, as follows:

| Size Designation | Size (in inches) |
|---|---|
| A | 8 1/2 × 11 (horizontal format) |
|  | 11 × 8 1/2 (vertical format) |
| B | 11 × 17 |
| C | 17 × 22 |
| D | 22 × 34 |
| E | 34 × 44 |
| F | 28 × 40 |
| Sizes G, H, J, and K are roll sizes. | |

ASME Y14.1M provides sheet size specifications in metric units. Standard metric drawing sheet sizes are designated as follows:

| Size Designation | Size (in millimeters) |
|---|---|
| A0 | 841 × 1189 |
| A1 | 594 × 841 |
| A2 | 420 × 594 |
| A3 | 297 × 420 |
| A4 | 210 × 297 |

Longer lengths are referred to as *elongated* and *extra-elongated* drawing sizes. These are available in multiples of the short side of the sheet size. **Figure 2-2** shows standard ANSI/ASME sheet sizes.

All the generic and ANSI templates provided with AutoCAD are based on decimal inches as the unit of measure. The architectural templates are set up for the feet and inches measurements typically used in architectural applications. DIN, ISO, and JIS A0 through JIS A4 template files are based on metric measurement settings.

**Figure 2-2.**
A—Standard drawing sheet sizes (ANSI Y14.1). B—Standard metric drawing sheet sizes (ASME Y14.1M).

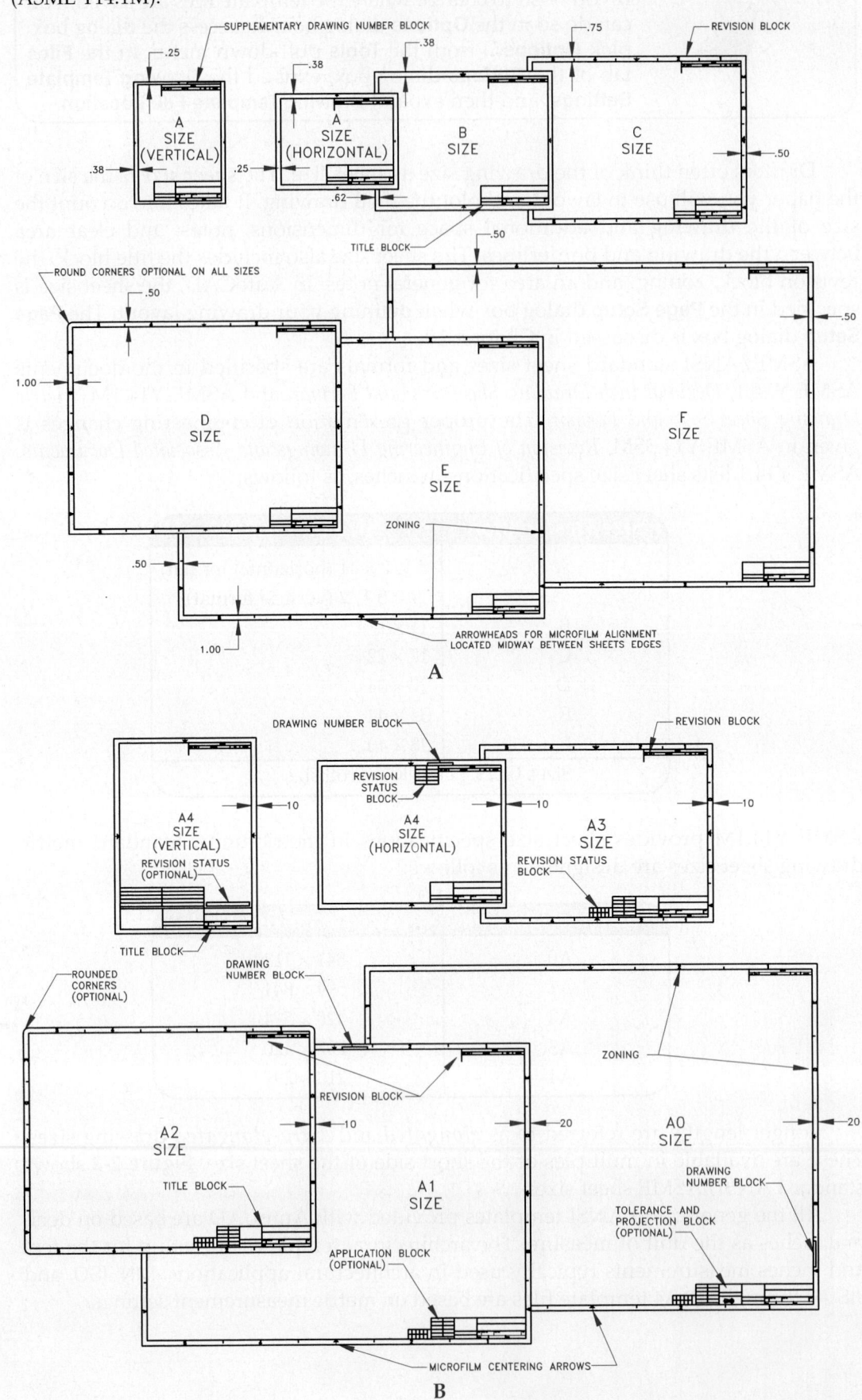

| NOTE  | *DIN* refers to the German standard *Deutsches Institut Für Normung,* which was established by the German Institute for Standardization. *ISO* is the International Organization for Standardization, and *JIS* is the Japanese Industry Standard. |
|---|---|

The ANSI, DIN, ISO, and JIS templates provide layouts with the title block located in the lower-right corner. The architectural templates provide a title block on the right side of the sheet, which is common in the architectural industry. The Template folder also contains the acad.dwt template, for starting a drawing using feet and inches, and the acadiso.dwt template, for using metric units. These options do not have layouts or title blocks already set up.

When using a setup wizard, you enter values defining the drawing settings. When using a template, these values are automatically set. Templates usually have values for the following drawing elements:

✓ Standard layouts with a border and title block.
✓ Grid and snap settings.
✓ Units and angle values.
✓ Text standards and general notes.
✓ Dimensioning settings.

A template option lets you start a drawing project with little or no drawing setup required. Sometimes, you may use a template with some or most of the required settings for the new drawing. After referencing the desired template, you can then adjust your drawing settings as needed for the type of drawing being created. When going through this text, you will discover many ways to adjust AutoCAD to match individual needs and professional applications. Each of these applications can be used to build customized templates.

## Exercise 2-1

○ Start AutoCAD if it is not already started.
○ Pick **New...** from the **File** pull-down menu.
○ Pick some of the template files to view their preview images.
○ Pick a template interesting you and start a new drawing. For example, pick an ANSI B template if you are interested in a B-size mechanical drawing, or choose one of the architectural templates if you are interested in architectural drawings.
○ The AutoCAD screen now displays the layout, border, and title block as defined in the selected template.
○ Pick the **Model** tab to make model space active.

## Starting a New Drawing

Besides using a template file, there are other ways to start a new drawing file. AutoCAD contains an option to have a different dialog box than **Select template** displayed when opening the program or using the **NEW** command. The dialog box allows you to open an existing file, use a Start from Scratch drawing, use a template file, or use a wizard to assist in setting up the drawing specifications. The **Show Startup dialog box** option from the **Startup:** drop-down list in the **System** tab of the **Options** dialog box displays the **Startup** dialog box when opening AutoCAD and the

NEW
[Ctrl]+[N]

File
➥ New...

**Figure 2-3.**
Setting the **Startup** option to **Show Startup dialog box** displays the **Create New Drawing** dialog box when using the **NEW** command.

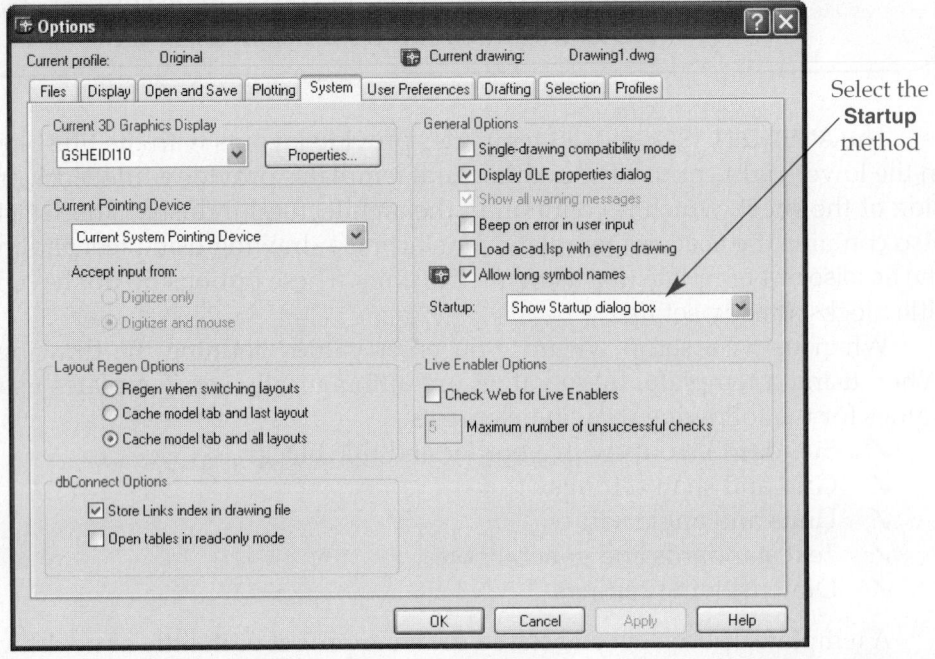

Select the **Startup** method

**Figure 2-4.**
The **Startup** dialog box opens when you begin AutoCAD. This dialog box can be turned off, and AutoCAD automatically starts with the drawing setup based on the template file acad.dwt.

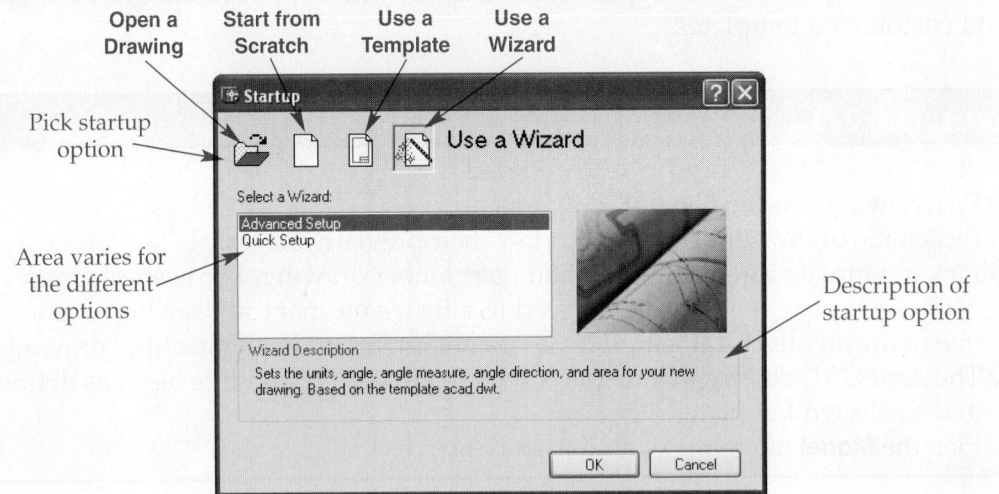

Open a Drawing

Start from Scratch

Use a Template

Use a Wizard

Pick startup option

Area varies for the different options

Description of startup option

**Create New Drawing** dialog box when using the **NEW** command. See **Figure 2-3.** Pick **Options...** from the **Tools** pull-down menu to access the **Options** dialog box.

With the **Show Startup dialog box** option on, when you open AutoCAD, the **Startup** dialog box is displayed. See **Figure 2-4.** If you already have AutoCAD open, you can start a new drawing using the **NEW** command. Access this command by picking **New...** from the **File** pull-down menu, pressing the [Ctrl] + [N] key combination, or typing NEW at the Command: prompt. This displays the **Create New Drawing** dialog box, which is almost identical to the **Startup** dialog box. The only difference is, in the **Create New Drawing** dialog box, the **Open a Drawing** option is grayed out. This is because, if you are already in an AutoCAD session, you would use the **OPEN** command to open an existing drawing instead of the **NEW** command.

A row of four buttons near the top of the dialog box presents each of the available startup options. Holding the cursor over a button displays a tooltip. The following options are available:

- **Open a Drawing.** Opens an existing drawing.
- **Start from Scratch.** Starts a new drawing based on the initial default settings contained in the acad.dwt (English) or acadiso.dwt (metric) templates. You can then set up all other drawing specifications.
- **Use a Template.** Starts a new drawing based on a template. A *template* is a file containing standard settings, which are applied to the new drawing. AutoCAD offers a selection of templates based on accepted industry standards, but you can also create your own templates or use any existing drawing file as a template.
- **Use a Wizard.** Provides a step-by-step method of defining the drawing settings.

These options define the drawing appearance by setting items, such as dimensioning features, pattern scales, and text size, to match the selected drawing units and drawing area. The option you select in the **Startup** dialog box is presented as the default option for the next use of the **NEW** command.

In **Figure 2-4**, the **Use a Wizard** option is selected. A *wizard* consists of AutoCAD setup options automatically controlling scale factors for dimension settings, text height, and other drawing settings, based on the information you provide. Two setup options are found in the list:

- **Quick Setup.** Allows a drawing to be quickly started by defining the drawing area and required units of measure.
- **Advanced Setup.** Provides the same options found in the **Quick Setup**, but with additional control and flexibility.

Picking an option displays a description of the wizard. Pick **Quick Setup** or **Advanced Setup** to access the appropriate wizard.

## Using the Quick Setup Wizard

The following discussion explains how to start a new drawing using the **Quick Setup** option. To access the **Quick Setup** wizard, pick the **Use a Wizard** button in the **Create New Drawing** dialog box, and then choose the **Quick Setup** option. The **QuickSetup** dialog box, shown in **Figure 2-5**, is displayed. The drawing units are set in the **Units** page of the **QuickSetup** dialog box, and the initial size of the drawing area is set in the **Area** page. Use the **Next** and **Back** buttons to display the needed page. A list along the left edge of the dialog box shows the names of the pages and displays a small arrow next to the name of the currently displayed page. When you have adjusted all desired settings, pick the **Finish** button from the last page of the wizard.

### Setting units of measure

There are several options for setting drawing units in the **Units** page of the **QuickSetup** dialog box. The initial default setting is **Decimal** units, using four decimal place precision. The default units, precision, and drawing area settings are based on the current settings found in the acad.dwt template. An example of the current units and precision settings is displayed in the preview image on the right. The units setting can be changed by picking the desired radio button. When a radio button is picked, the selected option becomes active. An example of the new active option is then displayed in the preview image. The units options are as follows:

- **Decimal.** These units are used to create drawings in decimal inches or millimeters. Decimal units are normally used on mechanical drawings for manufacturing. This option conforms to the ASME Y14.5M dimensioning and tolerancing standard. The initial default precision is four decimal places.

**Figure 2-5.**
The **QuickSetup** dialog box contains two pages. The **Units** page, displayed first, uses an initial default of **Decimal** units.

Marker indicates active page

Select type of units

Preview of selected units

Pick to access **Area** page

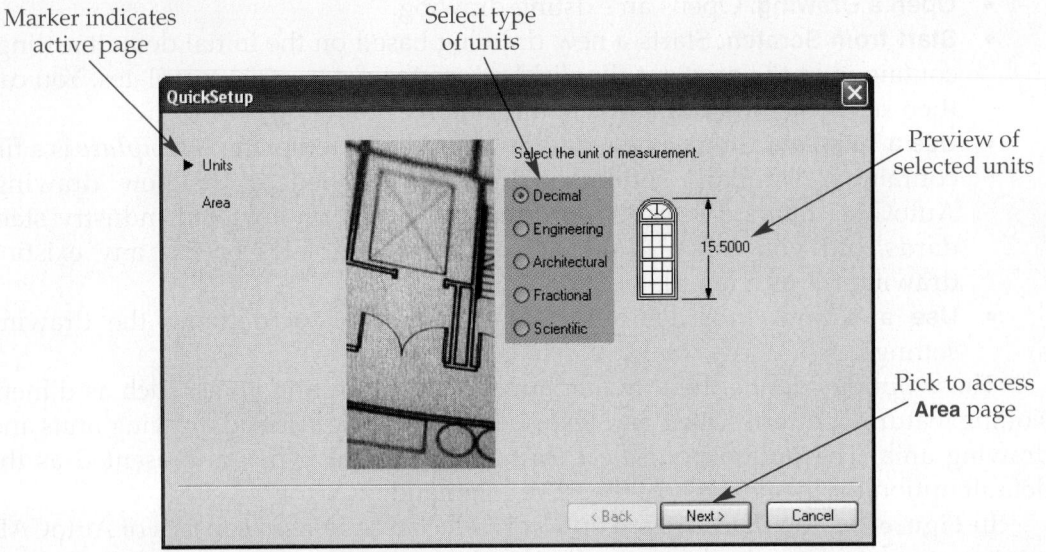

**Figure 2-6.**
In addition to decimal, other types of units are available. Select the units appropriate for your drawing.

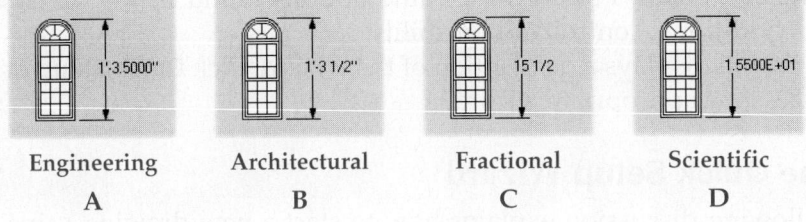

| Engineering | Architectural | Fractional | Scientific |
| A | B | C | D |

- **Engineering.** These units are often used in civil drafting projects, such as maps, plot plans, dam and bridge construction, and topography. The initial default precision is four decimal places. The example from the preview image is shown in **Figure 2-6A.**
- **Architectural.** Architectural, structural, and other drawings use these units when measurements are in feet, inches, and fractional inches. The initial default precision is 1/16". The example from the preview image is shown in **Figure 2-6B.**
- **Fractional.** This option is used for drawings having fractional parts of any common unit of measure. The initial default precision is 1/16. The example from the preview image is shown in **Figure 2-6C.**
- **Scientific.** These units are used when very large or small values are applied to a drawing. These applications take place in industries such as chemical engineering and astronomy. The initial default precision is four decimal places. The preview image in **Figure 2-6D** shows 1.5500E+01. The E+01 means the base number is multiplied by 10 to the first power.

After selecting the type of units applicable to the drawing, pick the **Next** button to access the **Area** page.

> **NOTE** You can pick the **Cancel** button in any of the startup dialog
> boxes to skip the setup process and go directly to the
> AutoCAD window. This starts the drawing session using
> the current **Start from Scratch** default settings. You can then
> adjust these settings as needed.

### Setting the drawing area

AutoCAD refers to the drawings you create as *models.* Models are drawn full-size in *model space.* Model space is active when the **Model** tab is selected. See **Figure 2-7.** When you finish drawing the model, you then switch to *layout space,* where the drawing layout is organized as necessary to be printed on paper. Model space and layout space are fully explained in Chapter 10 of this text. All text material prior to Chapter 10 is presented based on model space being active.

An AutoCAD drawing is created in actual size, using the desired units of measure. If you are drawing an object measured in feet and inches, you draw using feet and inches in AutoCAD. If you are creating a mechanical drawing for manufacturing, the drawing is full-size, using decimal inches or millimeters. You draw the objects full-size, regardless of the type of drawing, the units used, or the size of the final layout on paper. AutoCAD allows you to specify the size of the actual area required for your drawing and refers to this as the *model space drawing limits.* The model space drawing limits can be changed at any time during the drawing process.

Now you are ready to set the drawing area, or model space drawing limits. The **Area** page of the **QuickSetup** dialog box is accessed by picking the **Next** button on the **Units** page. See **Figure 2-8.** There are **Width:** and **Length:** text boxes with default sheet size settings of 12.0000 and 9.0000.

Change the width and length as desired by entering new values in the text boxes. The drawing area is set in full-scale units and should be large enough for the model being created. For example, if you are designing a 50′ × 30′ building, your drawing area will need to be larger than 50′ × 30′ to allow room for dimensions, notes, and other features. The preview image displays the orientation and dimensions of the specified drawing area. Pick the **Finish** button when you are done.

Figure 2-7.
Model space is
active when the
**Model** tab is
selected.

The **Model**
tab is selected

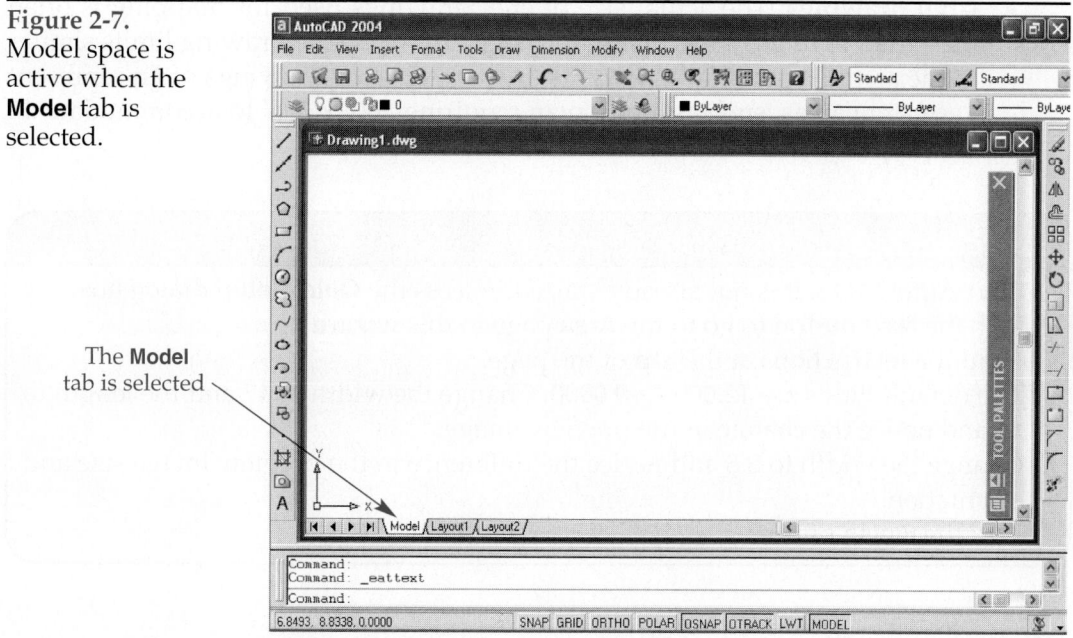

**Figure 2-8.**
The **Area** page of the **QuickSetup** dialog box. The model space drawing limits, or drawing area, default setting is 12 × 9 units.

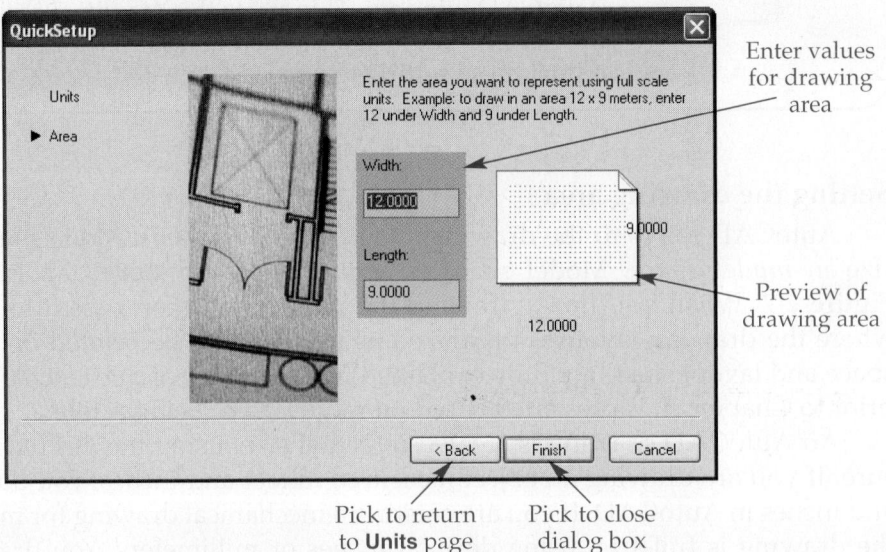

Keep in mind that the size of your drawing area does not need to conform to standard sheet sizes because the sheet size is specified when you define the drawing layout. Additionally, you can change the drawing limits at any time if more or less space is required to complete the drawing. This is accomplished with the **LIMITS** command. The following list provides some professional guidelines you can use to set the drawing area width and length based on different units:

- **Inch and metric drawings.** Calculate the total widths and lengths of the objects included in all views, adding extra space between views and room for dimensions and notes. Use these values for your drawing area settings.
- **Architectural drawings.** The actual size of architectural drawings is based on foot and inch measurements. If you are drawing a 48' × 24' floor plan, allow 10' on each side for dimensions and notes to make a total drawing area 68' × 44'. When you select architectural units, AutoCAD automatically sets up the drawing for you to draw in feet and inches.
- **Civil drawings.** The actual size of civil drawings used for mapping is often measured in units of feet. This allows you to set up the drawing limits similar to the architectural application just discussed. Civil drawings often represent very large areas, such as a plot plan requiring 200' × 100' to accommodate all the property lines, dimensions, and notes.

## Exercise 2-2

○ Start AutoCAD if it is not already started. Access the **QuickSetup** dialog box.
○ Pick the **Next** button to go to the **Area** page in this wizard.
○ Read the instructions at the top of the page.
○ The default limits are 12.0000 × 9.0000. Change the width to 17 and the length to 11 and notice the change in the preview image.
○ Change the width to 8.5 and notice the difference in the preview image size and orientation.
○ Pick the **Finish** button.

AutoCAD and its Applications—Basics

**Figure 2-9.**
The **Advanced Setup** dialog box has five pages. This **Units** page is the same as the **Units** page in the **QuickSetup** dialog box, with the addition of the **Precision:** drop-down list.

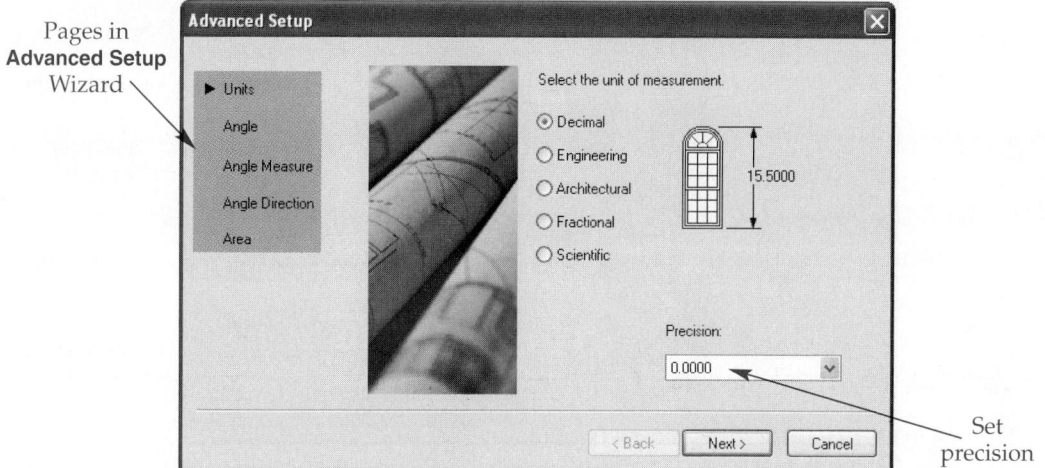

## Using the **Advanced Setup** Wizard

The **Advanced Setup** wizard provides more options and flexibility than the **Quick Setup** wizard does. To access the **Advanced Setup** wizard, pick the **Use a Wizard** button in the **Create New Drawing** dialog box. The **Advanced Setup** dialog box is shown in **Figure 2-9.** This dialog box has five pages. Use the pages in progressive order or as needed to set up your drawing.

The first page (**Units**) is similar to the **Units** page in the **Quick Setup** wizard discussed earlier. Unlike in the **Quick Setup** wizard, however, the unit precision can be set using the **Precision:** drop-down list. The last page (**Area**) is the same as the **Area** page in the **QuickSetup** dialog box. The other pages are described in the following sections.

### Setting angular units

Use the **Angle** page to select one of five angular unit options and the precision (display accuracy) of angles. **Figure 2-10** shows the **Angle** page. The angle measurement options are accessed by picking the desired radio button. The preview image shows a representation of units, and you can use the **Precision:** drop-down list to set the precision. These options are available:

- **Decimal Degrees.** This is the initial default setting. It is normally used in mechanical drafting, where degrees and decimal parts of a degree are commonly used.
- **Deg/Min/Sec.** This style is sometimes used in mechanical, architectural, structural, and civil drafting. The preview image in **Figure 2-11A** shows 90d, where the d is degrees. There are sixty minutes in one degree and sixty seconds in one minute.
- **Grads.** *Grad* is the abbreviation for *gradient.* The angular value is followed by a g, as shown in the preview image, **Figure 2-11B.** Gradients are units of angular measurement based on one-quarter of a circle having one hundred grads. A full circle has four hundred grads.
- **Radians.** A *radian* is an angular unit of measurement in which $2\pi$ radians = $360°$ and $\pi$ radians = $180°$. For example, a $90°$ angle has $\pi/2$ radians and an arc length of $\pi/2$. The preview image in **Figure 2-11C** gives the default value of a $90°$ angle as 2r (1.5708 displayed with zero decimal places). Changing the precision displays the radian value rounded to the specified decimal place.

**Figure 2-10.**
The **Angle** page is used to set the type of angular units. **Decimal Degrees** is the initial default.

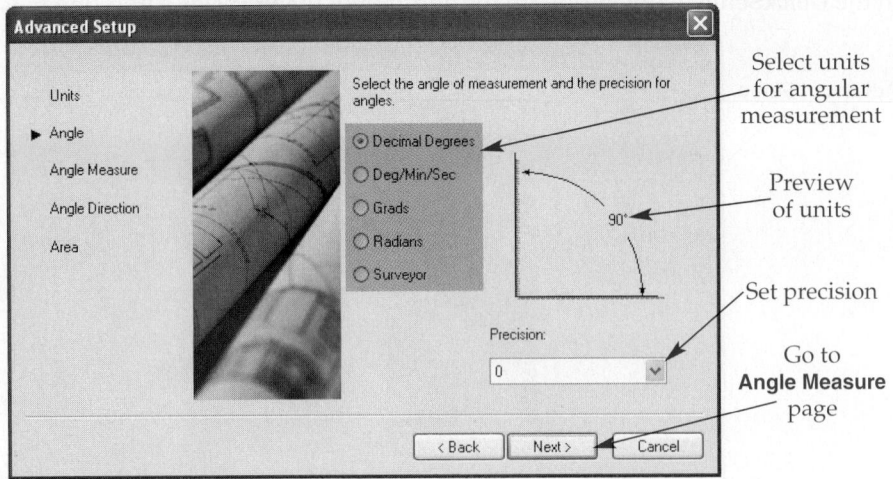

**Figure 2-11.**
In addition to decimal degrees, other types of angular units are available. Select the units appropriate for your drawing. All units are shown with the default precision.

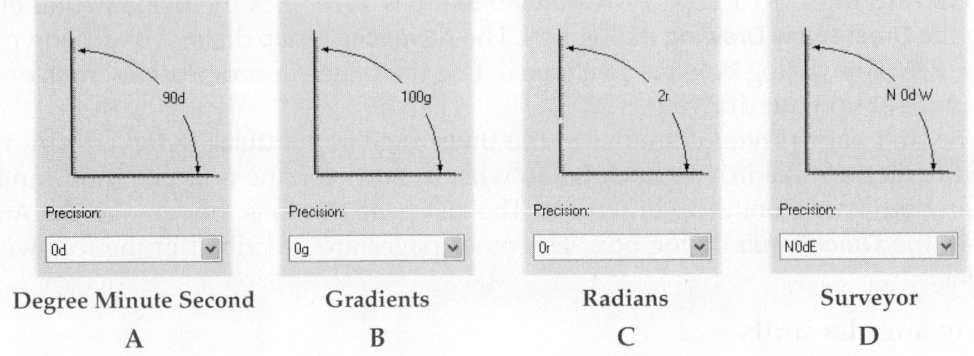

| Degree Minute Second | Gradients | Radians | Surveyor |
|:---:|:---:|:---:|:---:|
| A | B | C | D |

- **Surveyor.** Surveyor angles are measured using bearings. A *bearing* is the direction of a line with respect to one of the quadrants of a compass. Bearings are measured clockwise or counterclockwise (depending on the quadrant), beginning from either north or south. Bearings are measured in degrees, minutes, and seconds. An angle measuring 55°45′22″ from north toward west is expressed as N55°45′22″W. An angle measured 25°30′10″ from south toward east is expressed as S25°30′10″E. **Figure 2-11D** shows the preview as N0dE. Use the **Precision:** drop-down list to set measurement to degrees, degrees/minutes, or degree/minutes/seconds, or use it to set decimal display accuracy of the seconds part of the measurement.

Once you have selected the units and precision for angular measurement, pick the **Next** button to go to the **Angle Measure** page. See **Figure 2-12**. The orientation of the compass directions is the same as when you look at a map, with north at the top of the screen, east at the right, west at the left, and south at the bottom. Setting the angle measure establishes the direction for angle 0°. The AutoCAD default is **East**, or on the right side of the screen. The **North**, **West**, and **South** radio buttons are used to place 0° at those orientations. The **Other** option requires you to type a desired starting angle. After selecting the orientation for angular measurement, pick the **Next** button to go to the **Angle Direction** page.

     AutoCAD and its Applications—Basics

**Figure 2-12.**
In the **Angle Measure** page, the default angle zero direction is **East**.

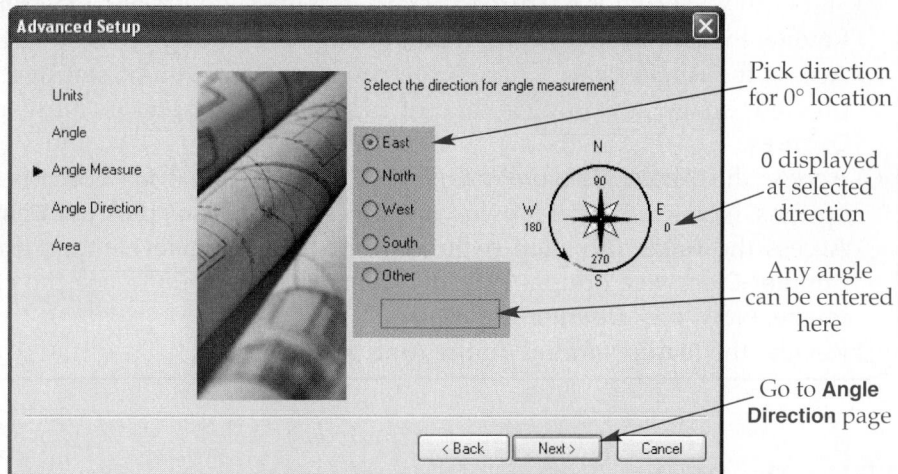

Pick direction for 0° location

0 displayed at selected direction

Any angle can be entered here

Go to **Angle Direction** page

**Figure 2-13.**
The **Angle Direction** page determines the positive direction of angle measurement from the direction specified in the **Angle Measure** page. The default angle direction is **Counter-Clockwise**.

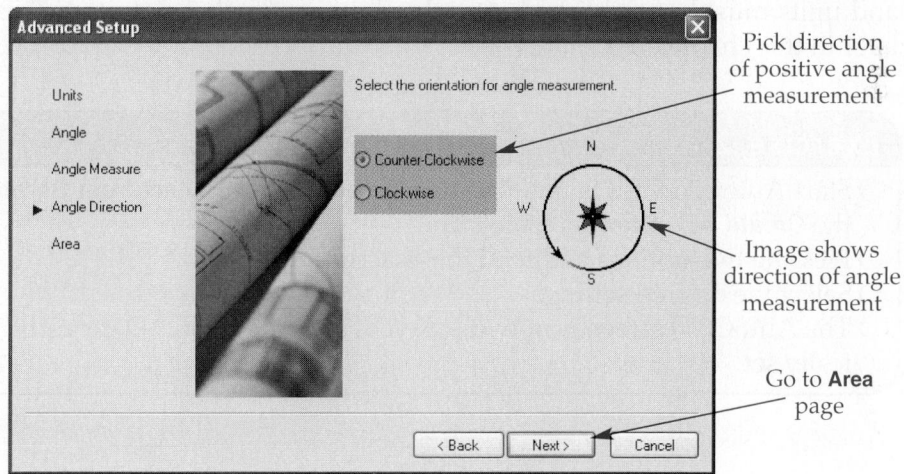

Pick direction of positive angle measurement

Image shows direction of angle measurement

Go to **Area** page

The **Angle Direction** page allows you to select **Counter-Clockwise** or **Clockwise** angle direction. The angle direction originates from the compass position set in the **Angle Measure** page. The default angle direction is **Counter-Clockwise**. **Figure 2-13** shows the default setting and related preview image.

---

**NOTE**

The values in the **Precision:** lists affect coordinate displays for units and angular measure, but have no effect on the accuracy of your drawing. The high accuracy of AutoCAD is maintained regardless of the display precision.

---

## Exercise 2-3

○ Start AutoCAD if it is not already started. Access the **Advanced Setup** dialog box.
○ Review the features found in the **Units** page previously covered in Exercise 2-2.
○ Access the **Angle** page. Change the precision to different settings. Look at the preview image as you pick each of the angle unit options. Now, pick **Decimal Degrees**.
○ Access the **Angle Measure** page. Pick each of the four compass orientation options. Notice how the preview image changes. Now, pick the **East** option.
○ Access the **Angle Direction** page and notice the preview image for the default **Counter-Clockwise** option. Pick the **Clockwise** option and see the change in the image. Now, pick **Counter-Clockwise.**
○ Review the features found on the **Area** page.

## Using the **Start from Scratch** Option

The **Start from Scratch** option in the **Create New Drawing** dialog box is used if you want to set up a drawing on your own. When it is picked, AutoCAD displays two options: **Imperial (feet and inches)** and **Metric**. Selecting an option displays a description in the **Tip** area. When a drawing is started from scratch, settings such as limits and units must be established after the drawing has been started. This is discussed later in this chapter.

## Exercise 2-4

○ Start AutoCAD if it is not already started. Pick the **Start from Scratch** button in the **Create New Drawing** dialog box.
○ Pick the two options and read the descriptions.
○ Select the desired setting.
○ The AutoCAD screen is now displayed, and all AutoCAD defaults are automatically set.

## Which Startup Option Should I Use?

Before starting an AutoCAD drawing, there should be some consideration of which startup option to use. Consider the following:

- **Use a Template.** Templates can be incredible productivity boosters. The provided template files may meet some personal needs, but creating new custom templates is where the greatest benefit is found. Custom templates allow you to use an existing drawing as a starting point for any new drawing. This option is extremely valuable for ensuring that everyone in a department, class, school, or company uses the same standards within their drawings.
- **Use a Wizard.** Wizards are often the best option when using AutoCAD as a design tool. In the design phase of a project, it may be too soon to be concerned about what the final drawing layout will look like. This option allows the size of the drawing area to be set up, including several of the drawing environment settings. It does not place a title block or border.
- **Start from Scratch.** Use this option to "play it by ear" when just sketching or when the start or end of a drawing project is unknown.

AutoCAD and its Applications—Basics

# Multiple Design Environment (MDE)

AutoCAD allows you to have multiple drawings open at the same time. This feature is referred to as the *Multiple Design Environment (MDE)* (sometimes called a *multiple document interface*, or *MDI)*. Most drafting projects are composed of a number of drawings, each presenting different aspects of a project. For example, in an architectural drafting project, required drawings might include a site plan, a floor plan, electrical and plumbing plans, and assorted detail drawings. Consider a mechanical assembly composed of several unique parts. The required drawings might include an overall assembly view, plus individual detail drawings of each component part. The drawings in such projects are closely related to one another. By opening two or more of these drawings at the same time, you can easily reference information contained in existing drawings, while working in a new drawing. AutoCAD even allows you to directly copy all or part of the contents from one drawing directly into another, using a simple drag-and-drop operation.

There are many ways to increase your drafting productivity through effective use of the MDE. These more advanced topics are covered throughout the text where they apply to the discussion material. The following information introduces the basic features and behaviors of the MDE.

## Controlling Drawing Windows

Each drawing you open or start in AutoCAD is placed in its own drawing window. Based on AutoCAD's initial default behavior, drawing windows are displayed in a floating state. This means the drawing area is displayed within a smaller window inside the main AutoCAD window. When multiple drawings are open at the same time, they are placed in a cascading arrangement by default. The name of each drawing is displayed on the left side of its title bar.

AutoCAD's drawing windows have the same control options as program windows on your desktop. They can be resized, moved, minimized, maximized, restored, and closed, using the same methods used for program windows on your desktop. **Figure 2-14** shows a summary of the standard window control functions available for drawing windows.

The drawing windows and the AutoCAD window have the same relationship as program windows have with the Windows desktop. When a drawing window is maximized, it fills the available area in the AutoCAD window. Minimizing a drawing window displays it as a reduced size title bar along the bottom of AutoCAD's drawing area. Drawing windows cannot be moved outside the AutoCAD window. **Figure 2-15** illustrates drawing windows in a floating state and minimized.

To work on any currently open drawing, just pick its title bar if it is visible. You can quickly cycle through all open drawings in sequence by pressing either the [Ctrl]+[F6] or [Ctrl]+[Tab] key combination. To go directly to a specific drawing when the title bars are not visible, access the **Window** pull-down menu in AutoCAD. The name of each open drawing file is displayed, and the active drawing shows a check mark next to it. See **Figure 2-16A.** Pick the name of the desired drawing to make it current. Up to nine drawing names are displayed on this menu. If more than nine drawings are open, a **More Windows...** selection is displayed. Picking this displays the **Select Window** dialog box, shown in **Figure 2-16B.**

The additional control options available in the **Window** pull-down menu include:

- **Close.** Closes the active window.
- **Close All.** Closes all open drawings.
- **Cascade.** Arranges the drawing windows that are not currently minimized in a cascade of floating windows, with the active drawing placed at the front.
- **Tile Horizontally.** Tiles the drawing windows that are not currently minimized in a horizontal arrangement, with the active drawing window placed in the top position.

Figure 2-14.
Drawing window control options.

| Window Control Buttons | | |
|---|---|---|
| **Button** | **Function** | **Description** |
| | Minimize | Displays window as a button along bottom of drawing window space in AutoCAD window. |
| | Restore | Returns window to floating state, at previous size and position, displays title bar. |
| | Maximize | Displays window at largest possible size, hides title bar. |
| | Close | Closes drawing, provides option to save drawing if any changes remain unsaved. |
| | Display window control menu | Displays pull-down menu with window control options. |

| Resizing Controls | | |
|---|---|---|
| **Cursor** | **Function** | **Usage** |
| ↕ | Size window vertically | Press and hold pick button while pointing at top or bottom border of window, then move mouse. |
| ↔ | Size window horizontally | Press and hold pick button while pointing at left or right border of window, then move mouse. |
| ↖ | Size window diagonally | Press and hold pick button while pointing at any corner on border of window, then move mouse. |
| ✛ | Move window | Press and hold pick button while pointing at title bar of window, then move mouse. |

Figure 2-15.
Drawing windows can be displayed in several ways. A—By default, drawings are displayed in floating windows. When multiple drawings are open, the windows are placed in a cascading arrangement. B—Minimized drawing windows are displayed as a reduced size title bar. Pick the title bar to display a window control menu.

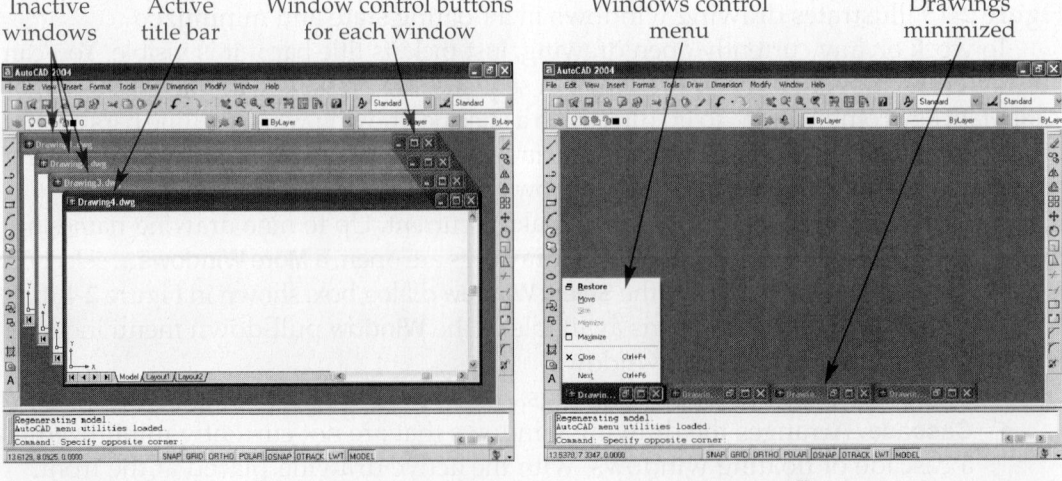

AutoCAD and its Applications—Basics

- **Tile Vertically.** Tiles the drawing windows that are not currently minimized in a vertical arrangement, with the active drawing window placed in the left position.
- **Arrange Icons.** Arranges minimized drawings neatly along the bottom of the AutoCAD drawing window area.

The effects of tiling the drawing windows vary, based on the number of windows being tiled and whether they are tiled horizontally or vertically. See **Figure 2-17.**

**Figure 2-16.**
Selecting the active drawing window. A—Pick the name of a drawing displayed on the **Window** pull-down menu to make it current. This menu also offers additional drawing window control options. B—When more than nine drawings are open, pick **More Windows...** from the **Window** pull-down menu to display the **Select Window** dialog box.

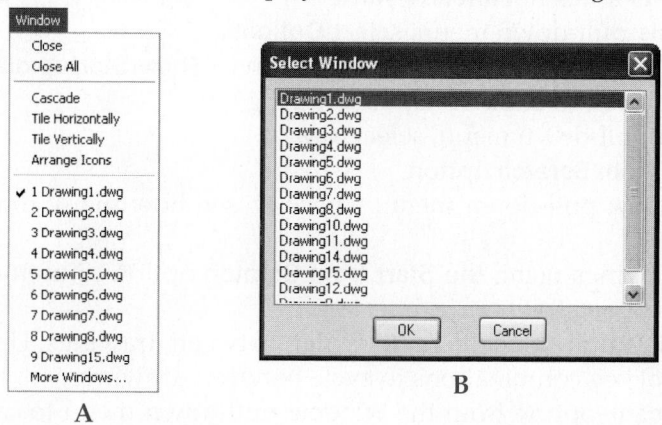

A
B

**Figure 2-17.**
Tiled drawing windows. A—Three drawing windows, tiled horizontally. B—Three drawing windows, tiled vertically. C—Four drawing windows, tiled either horizontally or vertically.

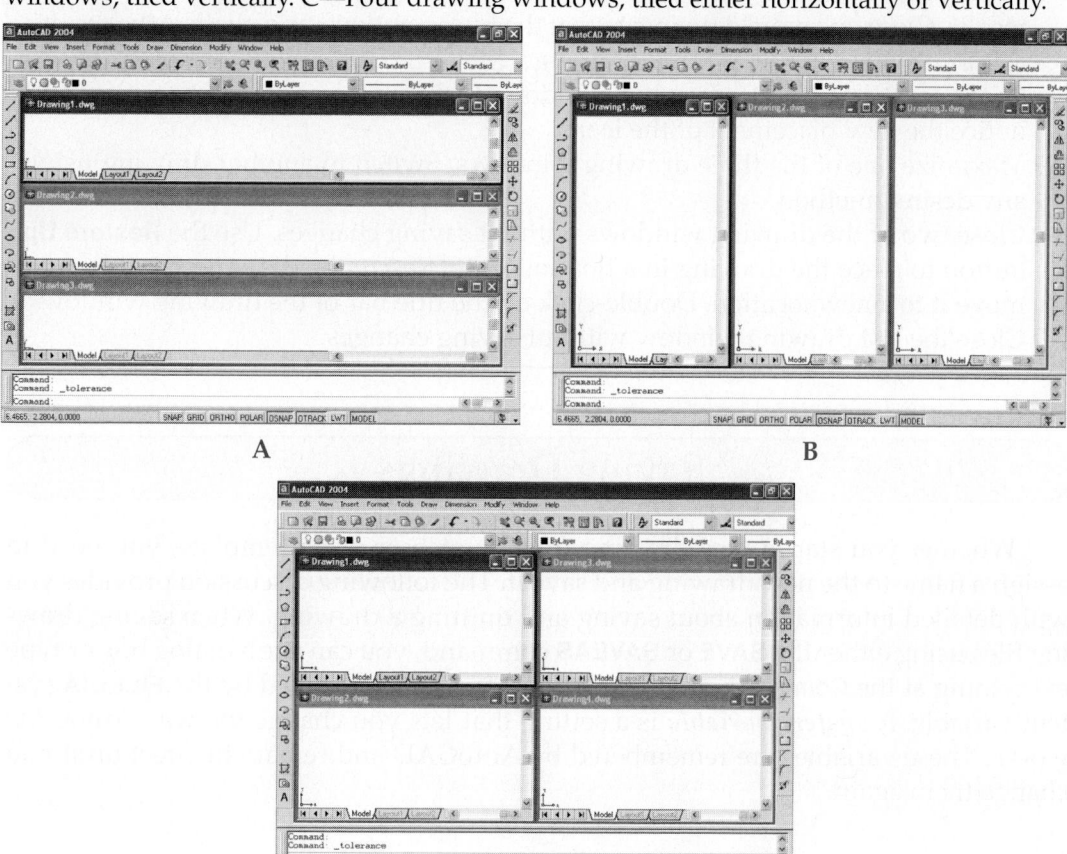

A
B

C

NOTE     Typically, you can change the active drawing as desired. There are some situations, however, when you cannot switch between drawings. For example, you cannot switch drawings during a dialog session. You must either complete or cancel the dialog box before switching is possible.

## Exercise 2-5

○ Start AutoCAD if it is not already started.
○ From the **Tools** pull-down menu, select **Options**.
○ Pick the **System** tab and set the **Startup** option to **Show Startup dialog box**.
○ Pick the **OK** button to close the **Options** dialog box.
○ From the **File** pull-down menu, select **New**.
○ Use the **Start from Scratch** option.
○ Pick the **Window** pull-down menu. Check to see how many drawing files are currently open.
○ Start new drawings using the **Start from Scratch** option until you have at least ten drawings open at the same time.
○ Use the **Window** pull-down menu to switch between drawings. Use the [Ctrl]+[F6] and [Ctrl]+[Tab] key combinations to cycle between drawings.
○ Pick the **Cascade** option from the **Window** pull-down menu to cascade the currently open drawing windows. Pick the **Tile Horizontally** and **Tile Vertically** options and observe the results of each action.
○ Use the **Close** button to close all except four drawing windows without saving any changes. Pick the **Tile Horizontally** and **Tile Vertically** options and observe the results. Close one more drawing, repeat the tile operations, and observe the results.
○ Minimize the remaining three drawings. Move the minimized drawings to different locations in the drawing window. Pick the **Arrange Icons** option and notice the new placement of the icons.
○ Maximize one of the three drawing windows. Switch to another drawing using any desired method.
○ Close two of the drawing windows without saving changes. Use the **Restore Up** button to place the drawing in a floating state. Resize the drawing window and move it to a new location. Double-click on the title bar of the drawing window.
○ Close the last drawing window without saving changes.

## Saving Drawings

Whether you start a new drawing from scratch or use a template, you need to assign a name to the new drawing and save it. The following discussion provides you with detailed information about saving and quitting a drawing. When saving drawing files using either the **SAVE** or **SAVEAS** command, you can use a dialog box or type everything at the Command: prompt. Dialog boxes are controlled by the **FILEDIA** system variable. A *system variable* is a setting that lets you change the way AutoCAD works. These variables are remembered by AutoCAD and remain in effect until you change them again.

There are two **FILEDIA** system variable settings. The default is 1, which displays dialog boxes at the appropriate times. When **FILEDIA** is set to 0, dialog boxes do not appear. You must then type the desired information at the prompt line. You can quickly change the **FILEDIA** system variable as follows:

Command: **FILEDIA**⏎
Enter new value for FILEDIA <1>: **0**⏎

In the following discussion, the **FILEDIA** variable is set to 1, unless otherwise specified.

## Naming Drawings

Drawing names may be chosen to identify a product by name and number—for example, VICE-101, FLOORPLAN, or 6DT1005. Your school or company probably has a drawing numbering system you can use. These drawing names should be recorded in a part numbering or drawing name log. Such a log serves as a valuable reference long after you forget what the drawings contain.

It is important to set up a system that allows you to determine the content of a drawing by the drawing name. Although it is possible to give a drawing file an extended name, such as Details for Top Half of Compressor Housing for ACME, Inc., Part Number 4011A, Revision Level C, this is normally not a practical way of sorting drawing information. Drawing titles should be standardized and may be most effective when making a clear and concise reference to the project, part number, process, sheet number, and revision level.

When a standardized naming system exists, a shorter name like ACME.4011A.C provides all the necessary information. If additional information is desirable for easier recognition, it can be added to the base name, for example: ACME 4011 A.C Compressor Housing.Top.Casting Details. Always record drawing names and provide information related to the drawings. The following rules and restrictions apply to naming all files, including AutoCAD drawings:

- A maximum of 256 characters can be used.
- Alphabetical and numeric characters and spaces, along with most punctuation symbols, can be used.
- The following characters cannot be used: quotation mark ("), asterisk (*), question mark (?), forward slash (/), and backward slash (\).

## Saving Your Work

You must save your drawing periodically to protect your work by writing the existing status of your drawing to disk. While working in AutoCAD, you should save your drawing every ten to fifteen minutes. This is very important! If there is a power failure, a severe editing error, or another problem, all the work saved prior to the problem will be usable. If you save only once an hour, a power failure could result in an hour of lost work. Saving your drawing every ten to fifteen minutes results in less lost work if a problem occurs.

There are three commands that allow you to directly save your work: **QSAVE**, **SAVEAS**, and **SAVE**. Also, any command or option ending the AutoCAD session provides a warning asking if you want to save changes to the drawing. This gives you a final option to either save or not save changes to the drawing.

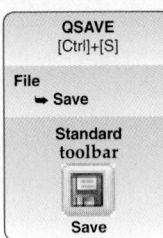

# Using the QSAVE Command

Of the three available saving commands, the most frequently used is the **QSAVE** command. **QSAVE** stands for *quick save*. The **QSAVE** command is accessed by picking the **Save** button from the **Standard** toolbar, picking the **Save** option from the **File** pull-down menu, typing QSAVE at the Command: prompt, or by pressing [Ctrl]+[S].

The **QSAVE** command response depends on whether or not the drawing already has a name. If the current drawing has a name, the **QSAVE** command updates the file based on the current state of the drawing. In this situation, **QSAVE** issues no prompts and displays no messages.

If the current drawing has not yet been named, the **QSAVE** command displays the **Save Drawing As** dialog box. See **Figure 2-18.** You must complete three steps in order to save your file:

1. Select the folder in which the file is to be saved.
2. Select the type of file to save, such as drawing (.dwg) or template (.dwt).
3. Enter a name for the file.

When selecting the folder in which the file will be stored, first select the disk drive from the **Save in:** drop-down list. Using this option, you can save to any available hard disk, floppy disk, or network drive. To move upward from the current folder, pick the **Up one level** button. To create a new folder in the current location, pick the **Create New Folder** button and type the name for the folder.

The **Files of type:** drop-down list offers options to save the drawing file in alternate formats. For most applications, this should be set to AutoCAD 2004 Drawing (*.dwg) when saving drawings. When saving a template file, this is set as AutoCAD Drawing Template (*.dwt).

If the drawing has not yet been named, the name Drawing1 appears in the **File name:** text box. Change this to the desired drawing name. You do not need to include the .dwg extension.

**Figure 2-18**
The **Save Drawing As** dialog box.

Select folder where
drawing will be saved

Move up one level
from current folder

Create a new
folder

Enter name

Select type of file
to save as

Once you have specified the correct location and file name, pick the **Save** button to save the drawing file. Keep in mind that you can either pick the **Save** button or just press the [Enter] key to activate the **Save** button and save the drawing.

> **NOTE** The **Save Drawing As** dialog box is a standard file selection dialog box. The features of this dialog box are discussed more thoroughly later in this chapter.

## Using the SAVEAS Command

The **SAVEAS** command is used in the following situations:
- When the current drawing already has a name and you need to save it under a different name.
- When you need to save the current drawing in an alternate format, such as a drawing file for AutoCAD/AutoCAD LT Release 2000, a DXF file, or a drawing template file.
- When you open one of your drawing template files and create a drawing. This leaves the drawing template unchanged and ready to use for other drawings.

The **SAVEAS** command is accessed by picking **Save As...** from the **File** pull-down menu or by typing SAVEAS at the Command: prompt. This command always displays the **Save Drawing As** dialog box. If the current drawing has already been saved, the current name and location are displayed. Confirm that the **Save in:** box displays the current drive and directory folder you want and that the **Files of type:** box displays the desired file type. Type the new drawing name in the **File name:** box and pick the **Save** button.

```
         SAVEAS
File
  ➥ Save As...
```

## Using the SAVE Command

The third command provided for directly saving a drawing is the **SAVE** command. The **SAVE** command is not commonly used and is only available at the command line by typing SAVE. The **SAVE** command displays the **Save Drawing As** dialog box, regardless of whether or not the drawing has been previously saved. Because of this, the **QSAVE** command is better for saving a drawing in progress, and the **SAVEAS** command is better for saving a drawing with a new name or location.

If you try to save the current drawing using the same name and location as another drawing file, AutoCAD issues a warning message in an alert box and allows you to cancel the operation or replace the current drawing with the one you are working on. If you actually need to replace the existing file, pick the **Yes** button to overwrite the file with the information in the current drawing. If you do not wish to overwrite the file, pick the **No** button to return to the **Save Drawing As** dialog box. To cancel the operation, pick the **Cancel** button. Be very careful—if you pick the **Yes** button, the current drawing replaces the other drawing.

> **NOTE** When saving a drawing to a different name, the **SAVE** command saves the drawing file with a different name, but leaves you in the current drawing. The **SAVEAS** command discards all changes to the original drawing file up to the last save. Before using the **SAVEAS** command, close the drawing file, and then reopen it to make sure all changes remain.

## Saving Your Work Automatically

AutoCAD can create an automatic backup copy of the active drawing. The backup file has a .bak extension and is created in the same folder where the drawing is located. When you save the drawing, the .dwg file is updated, and the .bak file is overwritten by the old .dwg file. Therefore, the backup file is always "one save behind" the drawing file.

This feature can be activated using the **Create backup copy with each save** check box in the **Open and Save** tab of the **Options** dialog box. See **Figure 2-19**. This dialog box can be accessed by selecting **Options...** from the **Tools** pull-down menu.

Before you can access a backup file, you must rename it. Use Windows Explorer to rename the file and change the file extension from .bak to .dwg. Once the file has been renamed, it can be opened in AutoCAD.

AutoCAD provides you with an automatic work-saving tool called *automatic save (autosave)*. All you need to do is enter the amount of time (in minutes) between saves in the **Open and Save** tab of the **Options** dialog box. The value is entered in the **Minutes between saves** text box in the **File Safety Precautions** area. See **Figure 2-19**, which shows a setting of fifteen minutes.

The autosave timer starts as soon as a change is made to the drawing. The timer is reset when the **SAVE**, **QSAVE**, or **SAVEAS** command is used. The drawing is saved when the first command is given after the autosave timer has been reached. For example, if you set the timer to fifteen minutes, work for fourteen minutes, and then let the computer remain idle for five minutes, an automatic save is not executed until the nineteen-minute interval, when you perform a command. Therefore, be sure to manually save your drawing if you plan to be away from your computer for an extended period of time.

The autosave feature is intended to be used in case AutoCAD shuts down unexpectedly. Therefore, when you close a drawing file, the autosave file associated with that drawing is automatically deleted from Windows. If AutoCAD does shut down unexpectedly, then the autosave file remains and can be used. The autosave drawing is always saved with the name of *DrawingName_n_n_nnnn*.sv$. If you need to use the

**Figure 2-19.**
Use the **Open and Save** tab in the **Options** dialog box to set the autosave timer value.

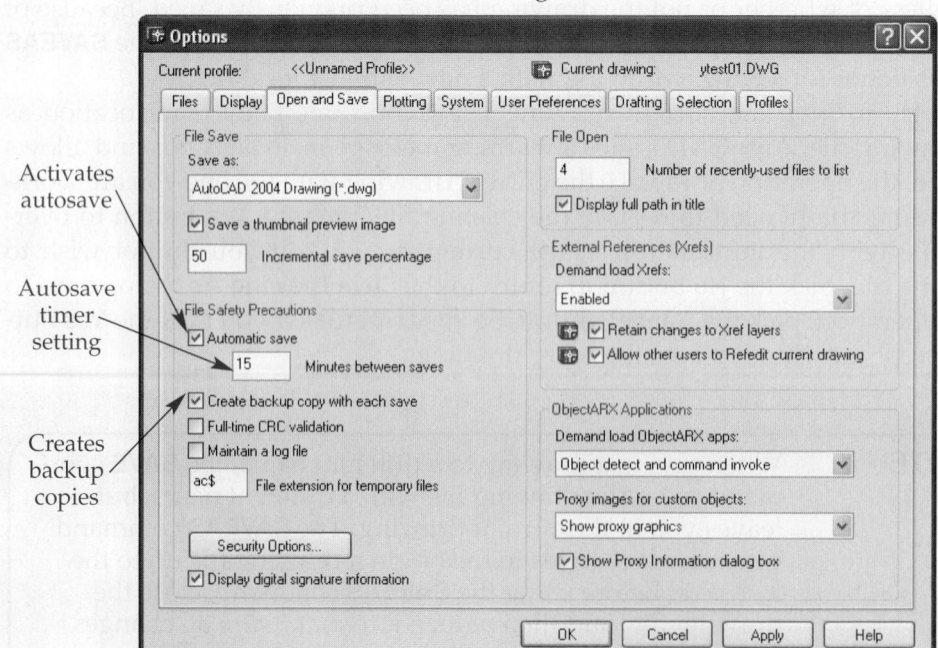

Activates autosave

Autosave timer setting

Creates backup copies

autosaved file, it can be renamed with a .dwg file extension, using Windows Explorer. Refer to Chapter 13 for more information on Windows Explorer.

> **NOTE** The **Automatic Save File Location** in the **Files** tab of the **Options** dialog box determines the folder where the autosaved files are saved. Pick **Options...** from the **Tools** pull-down menu to access this dialog box.

## Saving AutoCAD Drawings As Older Releases

The drawing file type saved by AutoCAD 2004 is a different file format than the file types saved by previous releases of AutoCAD. AutoCAD 2004 drawings can be saved in an AutoCAD 2000 format. This allows you to send AutoCAD 2004 drawings to businesses where older releases of AutoCAD are being used. This is also useful if you use AutoCAD 2004 at work or school and have an earlier release of AutoCAD at home.

To save as an older release, use the **SAVEAS** command. The **Save Drawing As** dialog box appears. Using the **Files of type:** drop-down list, select the **AutoCAD 2000/LT2000 Drawing** option to save the drawing as an AutoCAD 2000 format. AutoCAD 2002, AutoCAD 2000i, and AutoCAD 2000 all use AutoCAD 2000 format files. If you need to save the file in a format earlier than Release 2000, such as Release 14 or 13, you need to use the **AutoCAD R12/LT2 DXF** option, which is discussed in the following section.

After selecting the file format, specify the file name and location as previously discussed. When you save a version of a drawing in an earlier format, be sure to give it a different name than the AutoCAD 2004 version. This prevents you from accidentally overwriting your working drawing with the older format.

## Saving AutoCAD Drawings in a DXF format

Your AutoCAD drawings can be saved in Release 12, AutoCAD 2000, and AutoCAD 2004 DXF formats. The DXF (drawing exchange format, or drawing interchange file) format is used by AutoCAD users who may need to exchange files with other programs or import other software files into AutoCAD. The use of DXF files is explained fully in Chapter 13. This format allows you to send DXF drawings to businesses using older releases of AutoCAD or requiring DXF formatted files.

To save as a DXF format, use the **SAVEAS** command and select from the following file formats:

AutoCAD 2004 DXF (*.dxf)
AutoCAD 2000/LT2000 DXF (*.dxf)
AutoCAD R12/LT2 DXF (*.dxf)

## Opening Existing Drawings

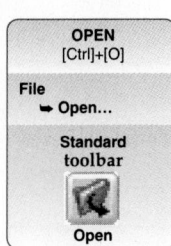

OPEN
[Ctrl]+[O]

File
↳ Open...

Standard
toolbar

Open

An existing drawing is one that has been previously saved. You can easily access any existing drawing with the **OPEN** command. To use the **OPEN** command, pick the **Open** button on the **Standard** toolbar, pick **Open...** from the **File** pull-down menu, press the [Ctrl]+[O] key combination, or type OPEN at the Command: prompt. The **Select File** dialog box appears. See **Figure 2-20.**

**Figure 2-20.**
The **Select File** dialog box is used to select a drawing to open. Notice the 8th floor drawing has been selected from the file list box and appears in the **File name:** text box.

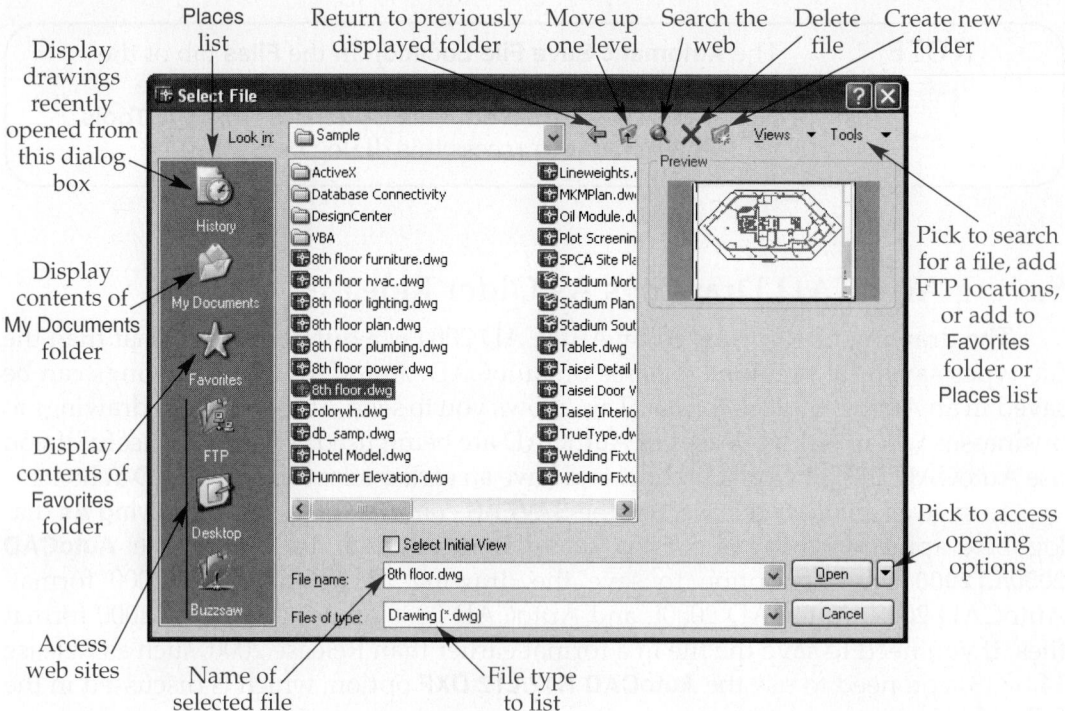

The **Select File** dialog box contains a list of folders and files. Double-click on a file folder to open it, and then double-click on the desired file to open it. The AutoCAD 2004\Sample folder is open, with the sample drawings displayed, in **Figure 2-20.**

When you pick an existing drawing, a picture of the drawing is displayed in the **Preview** image tile. This is an easy way for you to get a quick look at the drawing without loading the drawing into AutoCAD. You can view each drawing until you find the one you want.

After picking a drawing file name to highlight it, you can quickly highlight another drawing in the list by using the keyboard arrow keys. Use the up and down arrow keys to move vertically between files and use the left and right arrow keys to move horizontally. This enables you to scan through the drawing previews very quickly. An easy way to become familiar with the **Preview** image tile feature is to look at the sample drawings that come with AutoCAD. To do the following exercise, the sample drawings must have been loaded during the AutoCAD installation process.

## Exercise 2-6

○ Start AutoCAD and use the setup option of your choice.
○ Pick **Open...** from the **File** pull-down menu to access the **Select File** dialog box.
○ Display the contents of the AutoCAD 2004\Sample folder.
○ Pick any sample drawing and look at the **Preview** image tile. Pick as many drawings as you would like to preview. Use the cursor keys on your keyboard to scroll through the available files. Use the scroll bar to move the list from left to right as needed to display hidden files.
○ Pick the **Cancel** button.
○ If you want to exit AutoCAD, select **Exit** from the **File** pull-down menu.

AutoCAD and its Applications—Basics

# Accessing Files

The **Select File** dialog box includes the Places list along its left side. The Places list provides instant access to certain folders. The following buttons are available:

- **History.** Lists drawing files opened recently from the **Select File** dialog box.
- **My Documents/Personal.** Displays the files and folders contained in the My Documents or Personal folder for the current user. Whether you see My Documents or Personal depends on your operating system version.
- **Favorites.** Displays files and folders located in the Windows\Favorites folder.
- **FTP.** Displays available FTP (file transfer protocol) sites. To add or modify the listed FTP sites, select **Add/Modify FTP Locations** from the **Tools** menu in the **Select File** dialog box.
- **Desktop.** Lists the files, folders, and drives located on your desktop.
- **Buzzsaw.** Displays projects on the Buzzsaw Web site. Buzzsaw.com is designed for the building industry. After setting up a project hosting account, users can access project drawings from the Web site. This allows the various companies involved in the construction process to have instant access to the drawing files.

The **Select File** dialog box includes other features for selecting folders and files:

- **Back button.** Shows the previously displayed folder contents.
- **Up one level button.** Displays the contents of the folder containing the currently displayed file or folder.
- **Search the Web button.** Accesses the **Browse the Web** dialog box, from which you can open files from the Internet.
- **Delete button.** Deletes the selected file or folder.
- **Create New Folder button.** Creates a new folder within the folder being displayed.

# Finding Files

You can search for files from the **Select File** dialog box by picking **Find...** in the **Tools** menu. This accesses the **Find** dialog box, which is shown in **Figure 2-21**. If you know the file name for the drawing, enter it in the **Named:** text box. If you do not know the name, you can use wildcard characters (such as *) to narrow the search.

---

**Figure 2-21.**
Use the **Find** dialog box to locate drawing files.

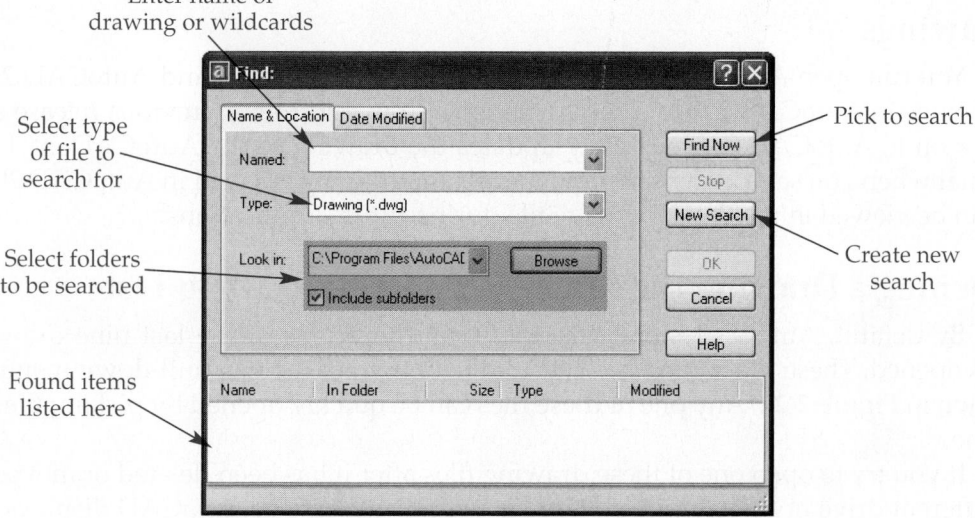

Enter name of drawing or wildcards

Select type of file to search for

Select folders to be searched

Found items listed here

Pick to search

Create new search

---

Choose the type of file from the **Type:** drop-down list. You can search for .dwg, .dws, .dxf, or .dwt files from the **Find** dialog box. If you are searching for another type of file, use the Windows Explorer search tool.

A search can be completed more quickly if you do not search the entire hard drive. If you know the folder in which the file is located, specify the folder in the **Look in:** text box. Pick the **Browse** button to select a folder from the **Browse for Folder** dialog box. Select the **Include subfolders** check box if you want the subfolders within the selected folder to be searched.

You can also search for files based on when they were last modified. The **Date Modified** tab provides options to search for files modified within a certain time period. This option is very useful if you wish to list all drawings modified within a specific week or month.

**PROFESSIONAL TIP**

While working in file dialog boxes, certain file management capabilities are available, similar to when you are using the Windows Explorer. To rename an existing file or folder, pick it once and pause for a moment, then pick the name again. This places the name in a text box for editing. Type the new name and press [Enter].

For a full listing of all the available options, point to a desired file folder, and then right-click. This displays a shortcut menu of available options for working with the file folder. Use one of the options or pick somewhere off the menu to close it.

**CAUTION**

Use extreme caution when deleting or renaming files and folders. Never delete or rename anything if you are not absolutely certain you should. If you are unsure, ask your instructor or system administrator for assistance.

## Opening Release 12, Release 13, Release 14, and AutoCAD 2000 Drawings

You can open AutoCAD Release 12, Release 13, Release 14, and AutoCAD 2000 drawings in AutoCAD 2004. When you open a drawing from a previous release and work on it, AutoCAD automatically updates the drawing to the AutoCAD 2004 file format when you save. After the previous release drawing is saved in AutoCAD 2004, it can be viewed in the **Preview** image tile during future applications.

### Opening a Drawing from the **File** Pull-Down Menu List

By default, AutoCAD stores the names and locations of the last nine drawing files opened. These file names are listed at the bottom of the **File** pull-down menu, as shown in **Figure 2-22.** Any one of these files can be quickly opened by picking the file name.

If you try to open one of these drawing files after it has been deleted or moved to a different drive or directory, AutoCAD is unable to locate it. AutoCAD displays the message Cannot find the specified drawing file. Please verify that the file exists. AutoCAD then opens the **Select File** dialog box.

Figure 2-22.
The **File** pull-down
menu contains a list
of the last nine
edited drawings.

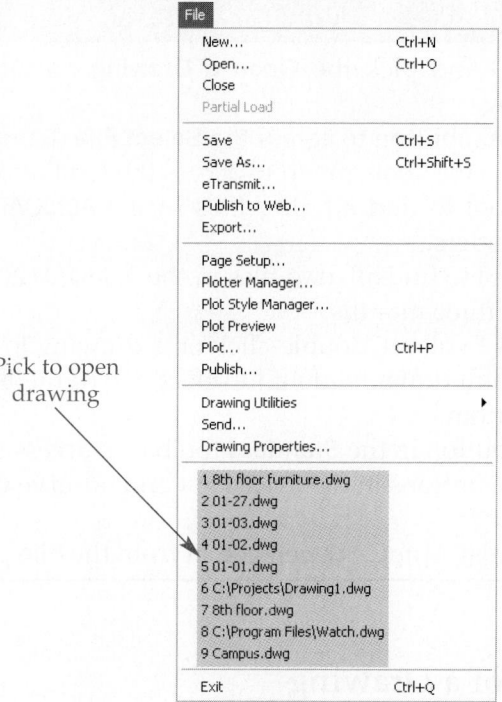

Pick to open
drawing

| File | |
|---|---|
| New... | Ctrl+N |
| Open... | Ctrl+O |
| Close | |
| Partial Load | |
| Save | Ctrl+S |
| Save As... | Ctrl+Shift+S |
| eTransmit... | |
| Publish to Web... | |
| Export... | |
| Page Setup... | |
| Plotter Manager... | |
| Plot Style Manager... | |
| Plot Preview | |
| Plot... | Ctrl+P |
| Publish... | |
| Drawing Utilities | ▶ |
| Send... | |
| Drawing Properties... | |
| 1 8th floor furniture.dwg | |
| 2 01-27.dwg | |
| 3 01-03.dwg | |
| 4 01-02.dwg | |
| 5 01-01.dwg | |
| 6 C:\Projects\Drawing1.dwg | |
| 7 8th floor.dwg | |
| 8 C:\Program Files\Watch.dwg | |
| 9 Campus.dwg | |
| Exit | Ctrl+Q |

**PROFESSIONAL TIP**

You can select the number of previous drawings displayed in the **File** pull-down menu in the **Number of recently-used files to list** text box in the **File Open** area of the **Open and Save** tab of the **Options** dialog box. Pick **Options...** from the **Tools** pull-down menu to access this dialog box.

## Using Windows Explorer to Open Drawings

You can open drawing files through the Windows Explorer program. This can be done in two ways. You can double-click on the file, and it will open in AutoCAD. If AutoCAD is not already loaded, AutoCAD will load, and the file will be opened. You can also drag-and-drop a file to the AutoCAD command line, and AutoCAD will open it. If AutoCAD is not open, you can drag-and-drop the file to the AutoCAD icon on your desktop. AutoCAD will then load and open the drawing file. For more information about the Windows Explorer, see Chapter 13.

## Opening DXF Files

You can open AutoCAD Release 12, Release 13, Release 14, AutoCAD 2000, and AutoCAD 2004 DXF files in AutoCAD 2004. When you open a DXF file and work on it, AutoCAD automatically updates the DXF file to the AutoCAD 2004 DXF file format when you save. After the previous release DXF is saved in AutoCAD 2004, it can be viewed in the **Preview** image tile during future applications. To open a DXF file, use the **OPEN** command and select DXF (*.dxf) in the **Files of type:** drop-down list. See Chapter 13 for more information on DXF files.

## Opening Part of a Drawing

When working with large drawings, you can use the **Partial Open** option to open only part of a drawing. You can select only certain views and, within those views, only specific layers. All views and layers not opened do not appear in the drawing area. For complex drawing, this can make editing much easier.

To partially open a drawing, select the drawing in the **Select File** dialog box, pick the drop-down arrow next to the **Open** button, and select **Partial Open**. This displays the **Partial Open** dialog box. See **Figure 2-23.** This dialog box displays the drawing views and layers in the selected drawing.

The drawing views are listed in the **View geometry to load** area. Views are discussed in Chapter 9. Select a view or select *Extents* or *Last*. The *Extents* option will load objects on the selected layers within the drawing extents. The *Last* option loads objects on the selected layers within the last saved view.

**Figure 2-23.**
The **Partial Open** dialog box.

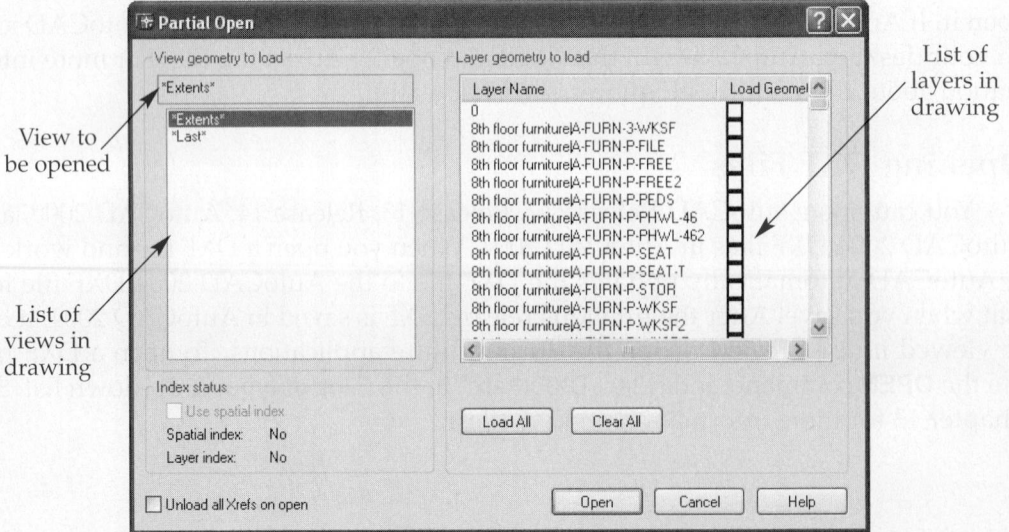

AutoCAD and its Applications—Basics

Select layers to be loaded in the **Layer geometry to load** area. Pick in the square next to the layer name to place a "✓" in the box. Only the checked layers can be loaded, and only the objects on those layers within the selected view will be loaded. Layers are discussed in Chapter 4.

> **NOTE**  Many of the topics identified in the previous and following discussions are explained in detail later in this text. Layers are discussed in Chapter 4. Creation and use of views are covered in Chapter 9.

## Using the **Partial Load** Command

After a drawing is partially open, you can load additional geometry from a view, a selected area, or layers into the drawing, using the **PARTIALOAD** command. You cannot unload any information currently loaded in the drawing. You can access the **PARTIALOAD** command by picking **Partial Load** from the **File** pull-down menu or by typing PARTIALOAD at the Command: prompt.

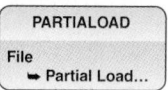

The **Partial Load** dialog box displays the views and layers available for specifying additional geometry to load into a partially open drawing. See **Figure 2-24.** This dialog box is nearly identical to the **Partial Open** dialog box. You can select additional views and layers to load into the drawing.

In addition to the features found in the **Partial Open** dialog box, the **Partial Load** dialog box also contains a **Pick a window** button. This button allows you to select a window to define the area from which objects should be loaded. All objects on the selected layers within the window are loaded.

Figure 2-24.
The **Partial Load** dialog box.

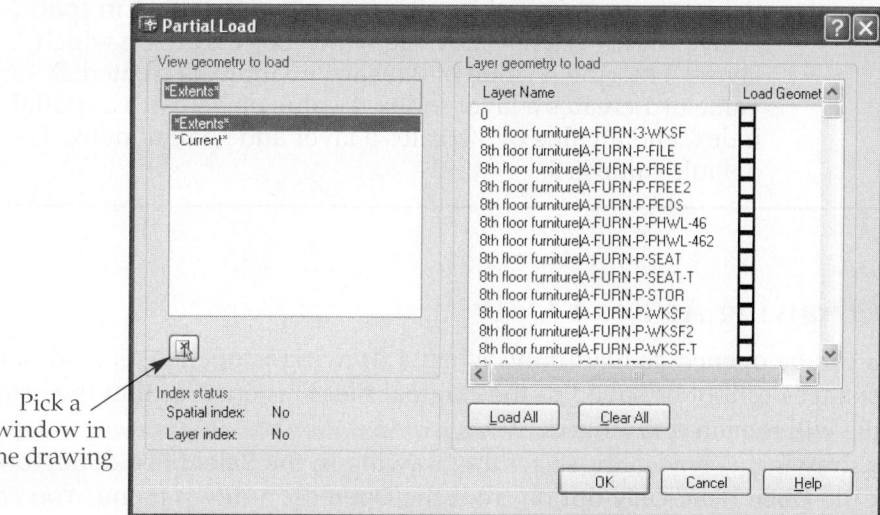

Pick a window in the drawing

**Figure 2-25.**
AutoCAD "remembers" if a file was previously partially opened. When you open the drawing again, one of these dialog boxes provides opening options. A—Using the **OPEN** command. B—Using the **Partial Open** option.

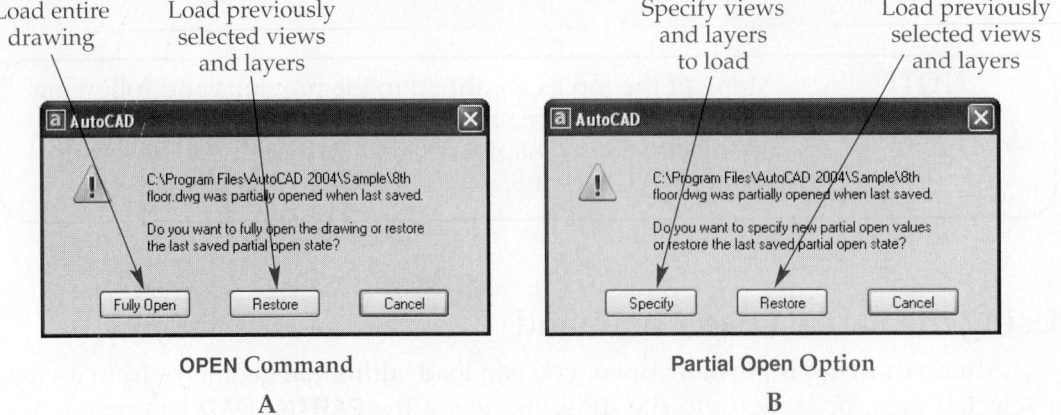

| Load entire drawing | Load previously selected views and layers | | Specify views and layers to load | Load previously selected views and layers |

OPEN Command
A

Partial Open Option
B

## Opening a Drawing That Has Been Partially Opened

When you partially open a drawing, make changes, and then save and close the drawing, AutoCAD "remembers" the file had been only partially opened. When you open the drawing again, one of the dialog boxes in **Figure 2-25** appears. The following options are available:

- **Fully Open.** Loads all views and layers in the drawing.
- **Restore.** Loads only the views and layers that had been previously loaded.
- **Cancel.** Cancels the command.
- **Specify.** Pick this button to specify views and layers to load.

---

**NOTE**   The **INDEXCTL** system variable controls whether or not layer and spatial indexes are saved with the drawing file. A spatial index organizes objects based on their location in space. A layer index is a list showing which objects are on which layers. Entering a value of 0 means no index is created. A value of 1 creates a layer index, a value of 2 creates a spatial index, and a value of 3 creates a layer and spatial index. The default value is 0.

---

## Opening a Drawing As Read-Only

Drawings can be opened as read-only. When a drawing is opened as read-only, the drawing changes cannot be saved to the original file. This ensures that the original drawing file will remain unchanged.

To open a drawing as read-only, select the drawing in the **Select File** dialog box, and then pick the **Open Read-Only** option from the **Open** drop-down menu. You can also select **Partial Open Read-Only** to use the **Partial Open** option with a read-only file. You can make changes to a drawing opened as read-only, but AutoCAD will not allow you to save the changes to the original file name. However, you can use the **SAVEAS** command to save the modified drawing file using a different name.

**Figure 2-26.**
This AutoCAD alert box is shown if you try to exit AutoCAD or close a drawing file without saving your work. This is an opportunity to decide what will be done with unsaved work.

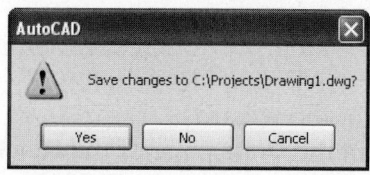

## Closing a Drawing

The **CLOSE** command is the primary way to exit out of a drawing file without ending the AutoCAD session. You can close the current drawing file by picking **Close** from the **File** pull-down menu or by typing CLOSE at the Command: prompt. If you enter the **CLOSE** command before saving your work, AutoCAD gives you a chance to decide what you want to do with unsaved work. The AutoCAD alert box shown in **Figure 2-26** appears. Press [Enter] to activate the highlighted **Yes** button. This saves the drawing. If the drawing is unnamed, the **Save Drawing As** dialog box appears. You can also pick the **No** button if you plan to discard any changes made to the drawing since the previous save. Pick the **Cancel** button if you decide not to close the drawing and want to return to the graphics window.

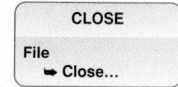

If you have multiple drawing windows open, you can close all of them simultaneously by selecting **Close All** from the **Window** pull-down menu. This command closes all open drawing files. Picking **Close** in the **Window** pull-down menu closes only the active drawing. This option is identical to the **CLOSE** command.

## Exiting AutoCAD

The **EXIT** command is the primary way to end an AutoCAD session. You can close the program by picking **Exit** from the **File** pull-down menu or by typing EXIT or QUIT at the Command: prompt. If you attempt to exit before saving your work, AutoCAD gives you a chance to decide what you want to do with unsaved work. The AutoCAD alert box shown in **Figure 2-26** appears.

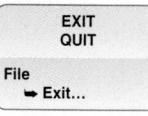

## Chapter Test

*Answer the following questions on a separate sheet of paper.*

1. Identify four basic planning decisions that need to be made before beginning a drawing.
2. By default, what is the name of the dialog box that opens when using the **NEW** command?
3. Which dialog box contains the setting that controls which dialog box displays when using the **NEW** command?
4. List the three options for starting a drawing available in the **Create New Drawing** dialog box.
5. What are AutoCAD wizards?
6. Name the setup option allowing you to quickly start a drawing by defining the drawing area and units.
7. Name the setup option providing units and angle control.

8. What is a template when used in AutoCAD?
9. Name the setup option allowing you to select from a list of files that store standard drawing settings and may contain predefined drawing layouts, title blocks, and other common drawing components.
10. Name the setup option asking you to select either English or metric units before opening the AutoCAD graphics window.
11. How do you open one of the wizards?
12. List the options found in the **Units** page of the **QuickSetup** dialog box.
13. This is an example of which type of unit: 15.500?
14. This is an example of which type of unit: 1'-3 1/2"?
15. This is an example of which type of unit: 15 1/2?
16. What is *sheet size?*
17. What are the dimensions of an ANSI/ASME B size sheet?
18. Is the size of an ANSI/ASME A2 sheet specified in inches or millimeters?
19. What is the purpose of layout space?
20. 90.00° is an example of which angle units option?
21. 90°30'15" is an example of which angle units option?
22. N45°30'15"W is an example of which angle units option?
23. What is the AutoCAD default direction and compass orientation for measuring angles?
24. What does the .dwt file extension stand for?
25. What is the purpose of the MDE?
26. How do you quickly cycle through all the currently open drawings in sequence?
27. How often should work be saved?
28. Name the command allowing you to quickly save your work without displaying the dialog box.
29. Name the system variable allowing you to control the dialog box display.
30. Name the pull-down menu where the **SAVE**, **SAVEAS**, and **OPEN** commands are located.
31. How do you exit AutoCAD without saving your work?
32. How do you set AutoCAD to automatically save your work at designated intervals?
33. What command do you use to save a drawing to a floppy disk?
34. Name the command accessed when you pick the **Save** button in the **Standard** toolbar.
35. Which option in the **Files of type:** list in the **Save Drawing As** dialog box should be used when saving a drawing file?
36. If a drawing has been previously saved, what is the difference between using the **QSAVE** and **SAVE** commands?
37. How do you search for a drawing file from the **Select File** dialog box?
38. What is displayed when you select the **Favorites** button in the **Select File** dialog box?
39. What is the purpose of the **Partial Open** option?
40. Which command is used to load additional objects into a partially opened drawing?
41. Identify the command you would use if you wanted to exit a drawing file, but remain in the AutoCAD session.
42. What happens if you use the **CLOSE** command before saving your work?
43. How can you simultaneously close all open drawing windows?
44. From which pull-down menu can you select the name of a recently opened drawing file and open it?
45. How can you set the number of files listed in the pull-down menu described in Question 44?

## Drawing Problems

1. Create a new drawing using the **Quick Setup** wizard. Use settings of your own choosing. Save the drawing as P2-1.dwg.

2. Create a new drawing using the **Advanced Setup** wizard and settings of your own choosing. Save the drawing as a drawing template file named P2-2.dwt.

3. Create a new drawing, based on one of the templates supplied by AutoCAD. Save the new drawing as an AutoCAD R2000 drawing file named P2-3.dwg.

*The following problems can be done if the AutoCAD 2004\Sample file folder is loaded. All drawings listed are found in that folder.*

4. Locate and preview or open the 8th Floor drawing. Describe the drawing in your own words.

5. Locate and preview or open the Oil Module drawing. Describe the drawing in your own words.

6. Locate and preview or open the Wilhome drawing. Describe the drawing in your own words.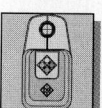

7. Locate and preview or open the Tablet drawing. Describe the drawing in your own words.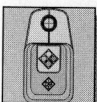

8. Locate and preview or open the SPCA Site Plan drawing. Describe the drawing in your own words.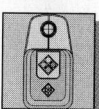

9. Locate and preview or open the Hotel Model drawing. Describe the drawing in your own words.

AutoCAD includes many standard templates. These templates include settings and title blocks for many standardized sheet sizes. Three such templates are shown here.

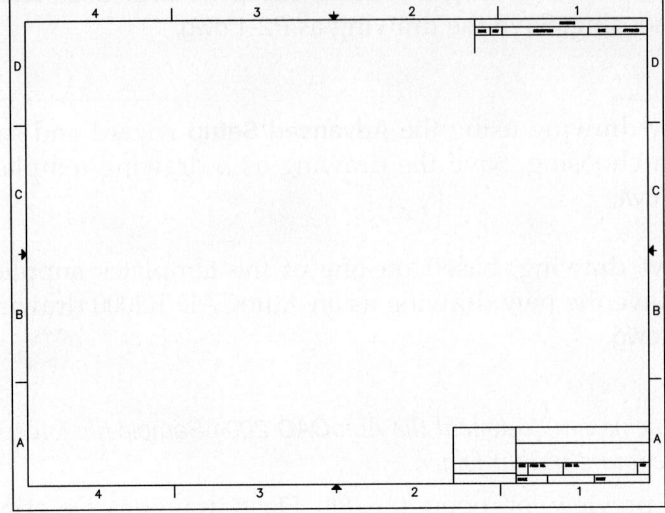

**ANSI C Title Block**

**Architectural Title Block**

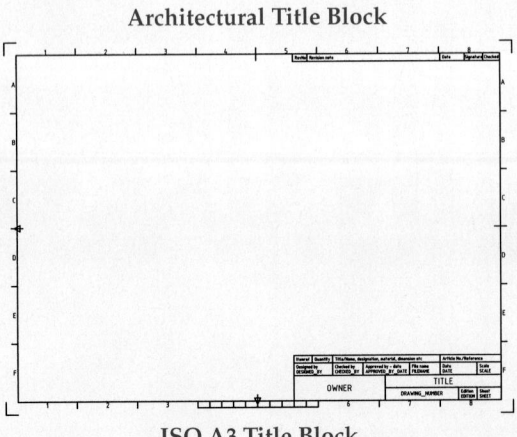

**ISO A3 Title Block**

# Introduction to Drawing and Editing

## Learning Objectives

After completing this chapter, you will be able to do the following:
- Display a grid of dots in the drawing area.
- Cancel a command.
- Adjust grid and snap settings.
- Create a template drawing.
- Use a variety of linetypes to construct an object.
- Select the **LINE** command to draw given objects.
- Use absolute, relative, and polar coordinate point entry systems.
- Use the screen cursor for point entry.
- Use the **MULTIPLE** command modifier.
- Use the Ortho mode and polar tracking.
- Use direct distance entry.
- Make revisions to objects using the **ERASE** command and its options.
- Make selection sets using the **Window**, **Crossing**, **WPolygon**, **CPolygon**, and **Fence** options.
- Remove and add objects to a selection set.
- Clean up the screen with the **REDRAW** command.
- Use the **OOPS** command to bring back an erased object.
- Use the **U** command to undo a command.
- Select stacked objects.

AutoCAD provides aids that help prepare the drawing layout, increase speed and efficiency, and ensure accuracy. These *drawing aids* include Grid mode and Snap mode. This chapter discusses each of these aids and how they are used to assist your drawing. AutoCAD automatically provides default drawing aids when you start a drawing, but you can change them to fit your own needs.

AutoCAD can be used to view and edit many formats of existing drawings, including drawing files found on the Internet. This chapter discusses how to create and use drawing templates and how to draw lines in AutoCAD. It also covers the different methods of editing the data you create with AutoCAD.

# Establishing a Grid on the Screen

AutoCAD provides a grid, or pattern of dots, on the screen to help you lay out a drawing. When the Grid mode is activated, this pattern of dots appears in the drawing area, as shown in **Figure 3-1**. The grid pattern shows only within the drawing limits to help clearly define the working area, and the spacing between dots can be adjusted.

**Figure 3-2** shows the **Snap and Grid** tab of the **Drafting Settings** dialog box. This dialog box can be used to turn the grid on and off and to set the grid spacing. To access the **Drafting Settings** dialog box, select **Drafting Settings...** from the **Tools** pull-down menu; right-click on the **GRID** or **SNAP** button in the status bar and select **Settings...** from the shortcut menu; or type DSETTINGS, DS, or SE at the Command: prompt. The grid can be turned on (displayed) or off (not displayed) by selecting the **Grid On** check box. Other methods for turning the grid on and off include using the **ON** and **OFF** options of the **GRID** command, picking the **GRID** button on the status bar, using the [Ctrl]+[G] key combination, pressing the [F7] function key, and using puck button 6.

The grid spacing can be set in the **Grid** area of the **Drafting Settings** dialog box. You can also set the grid spacing using the **GRID** command. Entering GRID at the Command: prompt provides the following prompt:

Command: **GRID**↵
Specify grid spacing(X) or [ON/OFF/Snap/Aspect] <*current*>: **.25**↵

You can press [Enter] to accept the default spacing value shown in brackets or enter a new value, as shown. If the grid spacing you enter is too close to display on the screen, you get the Grid too dense to display message. In this case, a larger grid spacing is required.

**Figure 3-1.**
Dots represent the grid spacing.

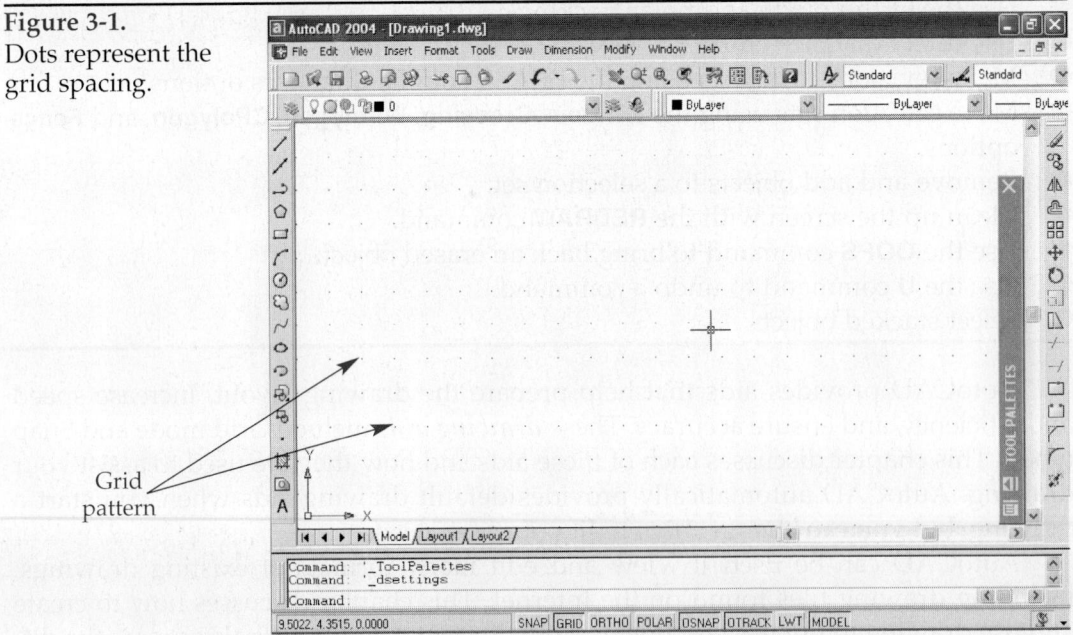

Grid
pattern

AutoCAD and its Applications—Basics

**Figure 3-2.**
Grid setting can be
made in the **Snap
and Grid** tab of the
**Drafting Settings**
dialog box.

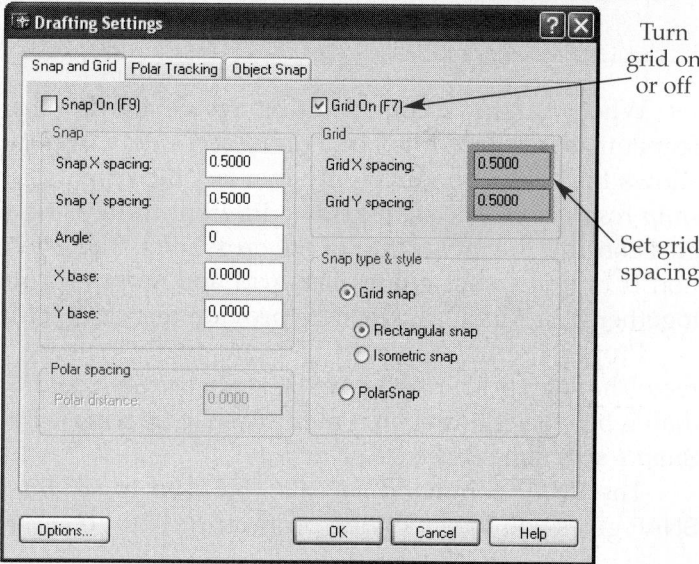

Turn
grid on
or off

Set grid
spacing

## Different Horizontal and Vertical Grid Units

To set different values for horizontal and vertical grid spacing, enter the appropriate values in the **Grid X spacing:** and **Grid Y spacing:** text boxes in the **Drafting Settings** dialog box. For example, **Figure 3-3** shows a horizontal spacing of 1 and a vertical spacing of .5. This can also be done using the **GRID** command. Type A (for the **Aspect** option) to set different values for the horizontal and vertical grid spacing.

**Figure 3-3.**
The X and Y grid
spacing units can be
set to different
values. Notice that,
here, the horizontal
spacing is greater
than the vertical
spacing.

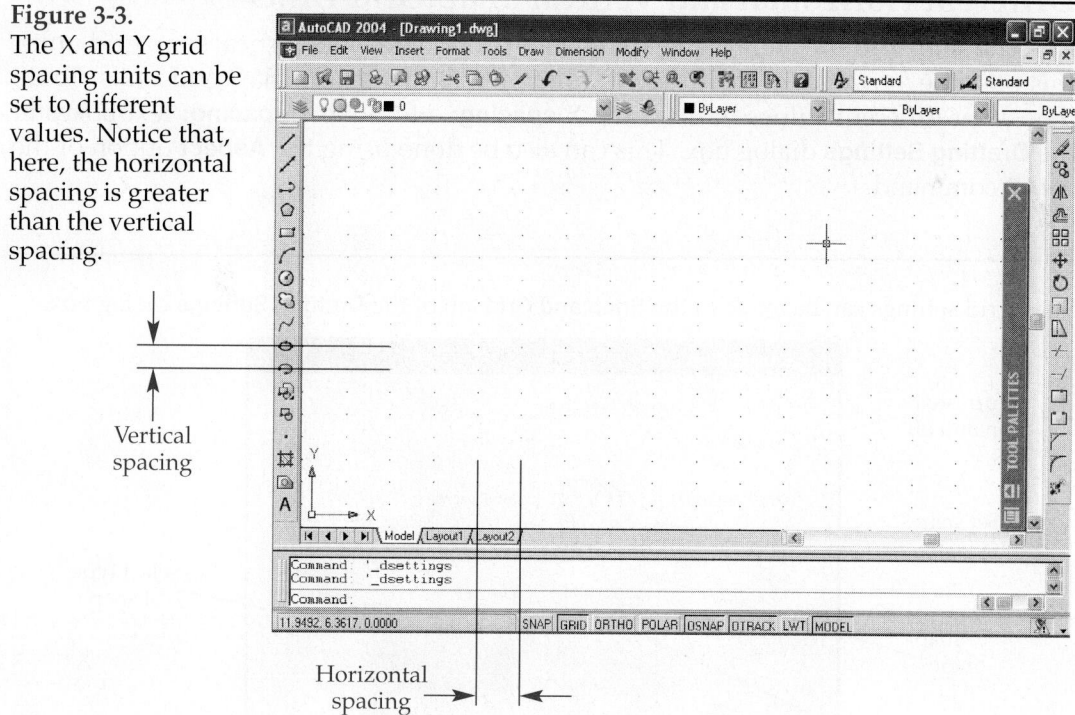

Vertical
spacing

Horizontal
spacing

When you move your pointing device, the crosshairs move freely on the screen. Sometimes it is hard to place a point accurately. You can set up an invisible grid that allows the cursor to move only in exact increments. This is called the *snap grid,* or *snap resolution.* The snap grid is different from using the **GRID** command. The snap grid controls the movement of the crosshairs. The grid discussed in the previous section is only a visual guide. The grid and snap grid settings can, however, be used together. The AutoCAD defaults provide the same settings for both.

Properly setting the snap grid can greatly increase your drawing speed and accuracy. The snap grid spacing can be set in the **Snap and Grid** tab of the **Drafting Settings** dialog box. See **Figure 3-4.** Enter the snap spacing values in the **Snap X spacing:** and **Snap Y spacing:** text boxes.

The **SNAP** command can also be used to set the invisible snap grid. Entering SNAP gives you the following prompt:

Command: **SNAP↵**
Specify snap spacing or [ON/OFF/Aspect/Rotate/Style/Type] <*current*>:

Pressing [Enter] accepts the value shown in brackets. The value you set remains the same until changed. The **OFF** option turns snap off, but the same snap spacing is again in effect when you turn snap on again. The snap spacing can be turned on or off at any time by clicking the **SNAP** button on the status bar, pressing [Ctrl]+[B], pressing the [F9] function key, selecting or deselecting the **Snap On** check box in the **Drafting Settings** dialog box, or pressing puck button 4.

## Different Horizontal and Vertical Snap Grid Units

The snap grid is usually set up with equal horizontal and vertical snap grid units. It is possible, however, to set different horizontal and vertical snap grid units. To do this, enter different values in the **Snap X spacing:** and **Snap Y spacing:** text boxes in the **Drafting Settings** dialog box. This can also be done using the **Aspect** option of the **SNAP** command.

**Figure 3-4.**
Snap grid settings can be made in the **Snap and Grid** tab of the **Drafting Settings** dialog box.

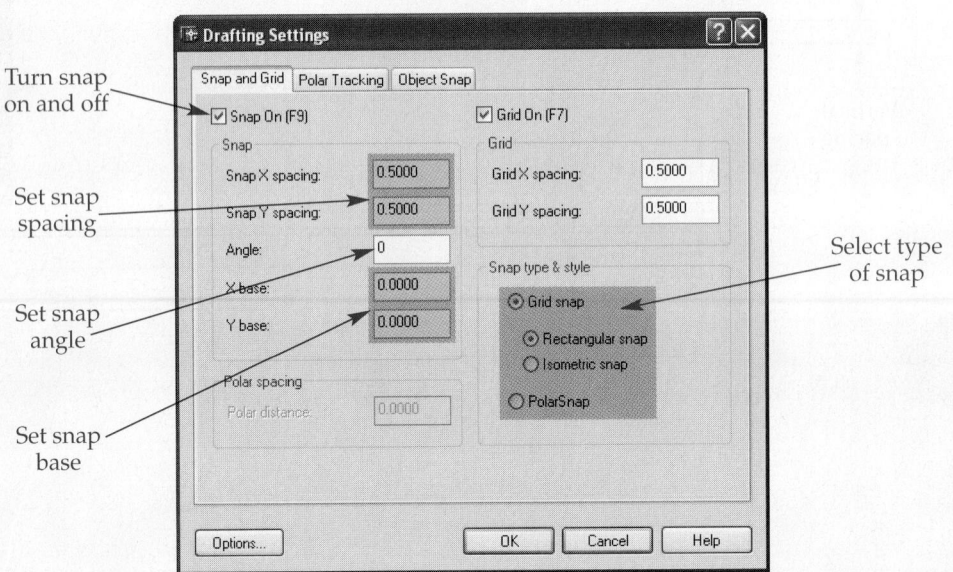

Turn snap on and off

Set snap spacing

Set snap angle

Set snap base

Select type of snap

The most effective use of the Snap mode quite often comes from setting an equal X and Y spacing to the lowest, or near lowest, increment of the majority of the feature dimensions. For example, this might be .0625 units in a mechanical drawing or 6″ in an architectural application. If many horizontal features conform to one increment and most vertical features correspond to another, then a snap grid can be set up using different X and Y values.

## Rotating the Snap Grid

The normal snap grid pattern consists of horizontal rows and vertical columns. Another option, however, is to rotate the snap grid. This technique is helpful when drawing an auxiliary view at an angle to other views of the drawing. When the snap grid is rotated, you are given the option of setting a new base point. The base point is the pivot around which the snap grid is rotated. The base point of a normal snap grid is the lower-left corner. It may be more convenient to set the base point at the location where you will begin the view.

Using the **Drafting Settings** dialog box, enter the snap angle in the **Angle:** text box and the new base point in the **X base:** and **Y base:** text boxes. These values can also be set using the **Rotate** option of the **SNAP** command. The grid automatically rotates counterclockwise about the base point when a positive rotation angle is given and clockwise when a negative rotation angle is given. **Figure 3-5** shows the relationship between the regular and rotated snap grids. Remember, the snap grid is invisible.

## Setting the Snap Type and Style

The **Snap type & style** area of the **Drafting Settings** dialog box allows you to select one of two types of snap grids: **Grid snap** or **PolarSnap**. **PolarSnap** allows you to snap to precise distances along alignment paths when using polar tracking. Polar tracking is discussed in Chapter 6. **Grid snap** has two styles: **Rectangular snap** and **Isometric**

**Figure 3-5.**
The snap grid is usually horizontal rows and vertical columns. It can be rotated, however, to help you draw. Notice the angle of the crosshairs. (The snap grid is invisible, but represented here by dots.)

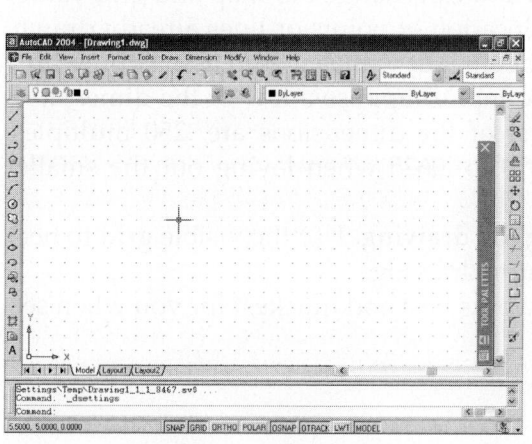

Default Snap Grid

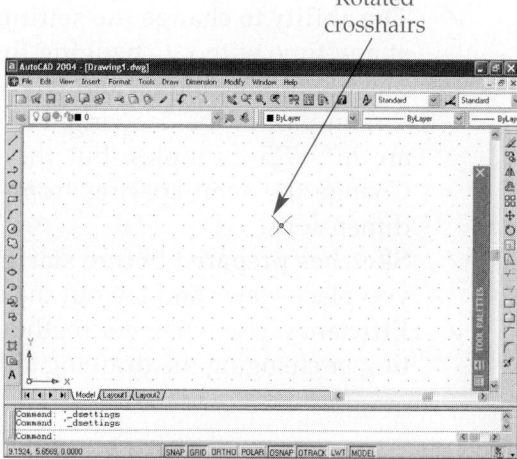

Rotated crosshairs

Rotated Snap Grid

**snap**. **Rectangular snap** is the standard style. **Isometric snap** is useful when creating isometric drawings (discussed in Chapter 25). Select the radio button(s) for the snap type and style you desire and pick the **OK** button. You can also use the **Type** and **Style** options of the **SNAP** command to change these settings. Use the **Type** option to select **Polar** or **Grid** and use the **Style** option to select **Standard** (Rectangular) or **Isometric**.

## Setting the Grid Spacing Relative to the Snap Spacing

The visible grid can be set to coincide with the invisible snap grid by choosing the **Snap** option after entering the **GRID** command. You can also set the dot spacing as a multiple of the snap units by entering the number of snap units between grid points. For example, 2X places grid points at every other snap unit. If the snap spacing is .25, and you specify 2X at the Specify grid spacing(X) or [ON/OFF/Snap/Aspect]: prompt, the grid spacing will be .5 units.

    Command: GRID↵
    Specify grid spacing(X) or [ON/OFF/Snap/Aspect] <0.5000>: 2X↵

**PROFESSIONAL TIP**

The Snap and Grid modes may be set at different values to complement each other. For example, the grid may be set at .5, and the snap may be set at .25. With this type of format, each mode plays a separate role in assisting drawing layout. This may also keep the grid from being too dense. You can quickly change these values at any time to have them best assist you.

## Factors to Consider When Setting Drawing Aids

The following factors will influence the drawing aid settings you choose to use:

✓ **The drawing units.** If the units are decimal inches, set the grid and snap values to standard decimal increments, such as .0625, .125, .25, .5, and 1 or .05, .1, .2, .5, and 1. For architectural units, use standard increments, such as 1, 6, and 12 (for inches) or 1, 2, 4, 5, and 10 (for feet).

✓ **The drawing size.** A very large drawing might have a grid spacing of 1.00, while a small drawing may use a spacing of .5 or less.

✓ **The value of the smallest dimension.** If the smallest dimension is .125, then an appropriate snap value would be .125, with a grid spacing of .25.

✓ **The ability to change the settings.** You can change the snap and grid values at any time without changing the location of points or lines already drawn. This should be done when larger or smaller values would assist you with a certain part of the drawing. For example, suppose a few of the dimensions are in .0625 multiples, but the rest of the dimensions are .250 multiples. Change the snap spacing from .250 to .0625 when laying out the smaller dimensions.

✓ **Sketches prepared before starting the drawing.** Use the visible grid to help you place views and lay out the entire drawing.

✓ **Efficiency.** Use whatever method works best and quickest for you when setting or changing the drawing aids.

# Changing Drawing Settings

After setting up AutoCAD, you are ready to begin drawing. The **Quick Setup** and **Advanced Setup** options provide convenient ways to initially set the drawing units and limits. These settings may need to be changed, however, while working on a drawing or when the drawing is finished. The drawing units may be changed at any time with the **UNITS** command, and the model space drawing limits can be changed with the **LIMITS** command.

## Changing Units

The **UNITS** command is the quickest way to set the units and angles. The **UNITS** command opens the **Drawing Units** dialog box for easy control of the settings. Picking **Units...** in the **Format** pull-down menu or typing UN or UNITS at the Command: prompt accesses this command. The **Drawing Units** dialog box is shown in **Figure 3-6**.

Linear units are specified in the **Length** area of the **Drawing Units** dialog box. The established units in the current drawing are presented as the default values. Select the desired linear units format from the **Type:** drop-down list and use the **Precision:** drop-down list to specify the linear units precision. Access the **Type:** and **Precision:** drop-down lists located in the **Angle** area of the **Drawing Units** dialog box to set the desired angular units format and precision. Selecting the **Clockwise** check box changes the direction for angular measurements to clockwise from the default of counterclockwise.

Pick the **Direction...** button to access the **Direction Control** dialog box. See **Figure 3-7**. The standard **East**, **North**, **West**, and **South** options are offered as radio buttons. Pick one of these buttons to set the compass orientation. The **Other** radio button activates the **Angle:** text box and the **Pick an angle** button. The **Angle:** text box allows an angle for zero direction to be entered. The **Pick an angle** button allows two points on the screen to be picked for establishing the angle zero direction.

UNITS
UN

Format
➥ Units...

## Changing Limits

The model space drawing limits can be changed using the **LIMITS** command. Entering LIMITS at the Command: prompt or picking **Drawing Limits** from the **Format** pull-down menu accesses the **LIMITS** command. The **LIMITS** command asks you to specify the coordinates for the lower-left corner and the upper-right corner of the drawing area. The lower-left corner is usually 0,0, but you can specify a different value. Press [Enter] to accept the 0,0 value for the lower-left corner default or type a

LIMITS

Format
➥ Drawing
Limits

Figure 3-6.
The **UNITS** command accesses the **Drawing Units** dialog box.

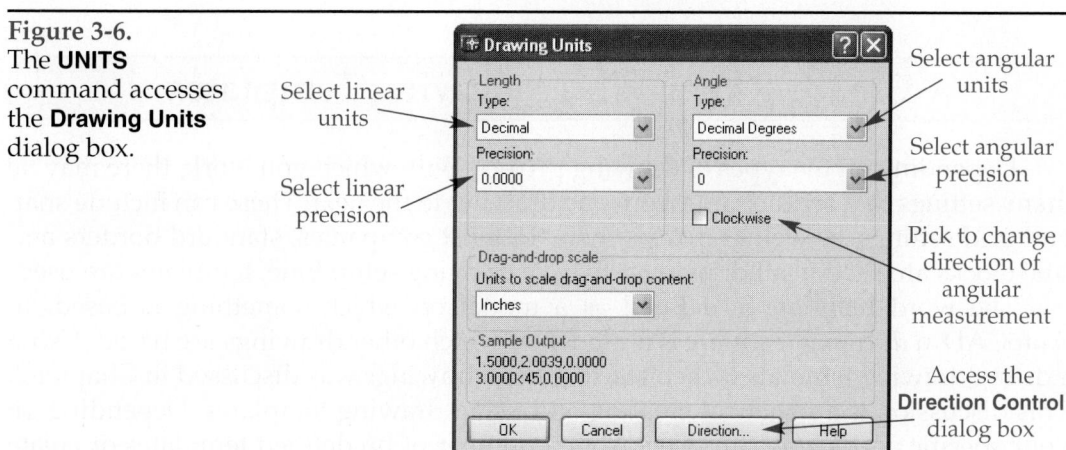

Select linear units
Select linear precision
Select angular units
Select angular precision
Pick to change direction of angular measurement
Access the **Direction Control** dialog box

Figure 3-7.
Picking the
**Direction...** button
in the **Drawing Units**
dialog box displays
the **Direction Control**
dialog box.

Select direction
of 0°

Specify another
angle

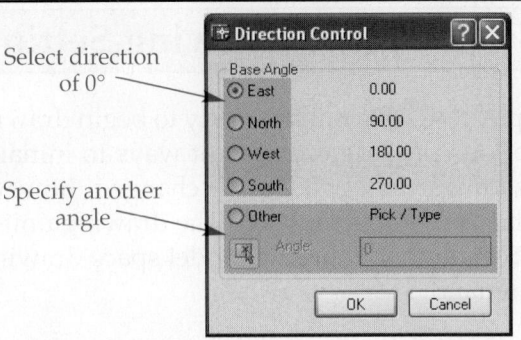

new value. The upper-right corner setting usually identifies the upper-right corner of the drawing area. If you want a 17″ × 11″ drawing area, then the upper-right corner setting should be 17,11. The first value is the horizontal measurement, and the second value is the vertical measurement of the limits. A comma separates the values. The command works like this:

    Command: **LIMITS.**↵
    Reset Model space limits:
    Specify lower left corner or [ON/OFF] <0.0000,0.0000>: ↵
    Specify upper right corner <12.0000,9.0000>: **17,11**↵
    Command:

The **LIMITS** command can also be used to turn the limits on or off by typing ON or OFF at the prompt. When the limits are turned on, AutoCAD restricts you from drawing outside of the rectangular area defined by the limits settings. Limits are typically turned off for most drafting applications.

### Exercise 3-1

○ Open AutoCAD if it is not already open. Use the startup option of your choice.
○ Access the AutoCAD window.
○ Open the **Drawing Units** dialog box and make the linear units Architectural, the angular measurements Decimal Degrees, the number of decimal places for angles = 3, and the direction for angle 0 = 3 o'clock, with angles measured counter-clockwise.
○ Pick **OK** to exit the **Drawing Units** dialog box.
○ Use the **LIMITS** command to turn the limits on and off.

## Creating and Using Drawing Templates

Depending on the types of drawing projects with which you work, there may be many settings that are the same from one drawing to the next. These can include snap and grid settings, as well as many others. In most companies, standard borders and title blocks are used in all drawings. To save drawing setup time, templates are used.

The word *template* is defined as a model on which something is based. In AutoCAD, a *drawing template* is a model on which other drawings are based. Using existing drawing templates when starting new drawings was discussed in Chapter 2. This discussion is a review of creating and using drawing templates. Depending on your specific needs, you can select from a number of predefined templates or create your own.

When you use a template, all the settings saved in the template are applied to your new drawing. The template file can supply any information normally saved in a drawing file, including settings and drawing objects. Many of the templates already have standard borders and title blocks, which are then created in your new drawing. The template drawing contains the setup options you choose, plus any snap and grid settings you use. As you continue through this text, you can add items to your templates, such as layer settings, company information, logos, text styles, plot styles, dimension styles, and bills of materials. All these settings are designed to your company or school specifications and based on your drawing applications.

## Creating Your Own Templates

If none of the predefined templates meet your needs, you can create and save your own custom templates. AutoCAD allows you to save *any* drawing as a template. A drawing template should be developed whenever several drawing applications require the same setup procedure. The template then allows the setup to be applied to any number of future drawings. Creating templates increases drafting productivity by decreasing setup requirements.

Some existing AutoCAD templates may be close to what you need and simply need fine-tuning. If the existing AutoCAD templates do not fit your needs, you may want to use a wizard to establish basic settings or even start from scratch. Some basic parameters that can be specified in a drawing template include units, limits, snap settings, and grid settings. You can also draw your own border and title block.

As you learn more about working with AutoCAD, you will find many other settings that can be included in your drawing templates. When you have everything needed in the template, the template is ready to save. Use the **SAVEAS** command to save a drawing template. Picking **Save As...** from the **File** pull-down menu or typing SAVEAS at the Command: prompt accesses the **SAVEAS** command. This command displays the **Save Drawing As** dialog box, as shown in **Figure 3-8.** To specify that the drawing is to be saved as a drawing template, pick AutoCAD Drawing Template (*.dwt) from the **Files of type:** drop-down list. The file list window then shows all the drawing templates currently found in the Template folder. You can store custom templates in another location, but it is recommended that they be stored in the Template folder.

**Figure 3-8.**
Saving a template.

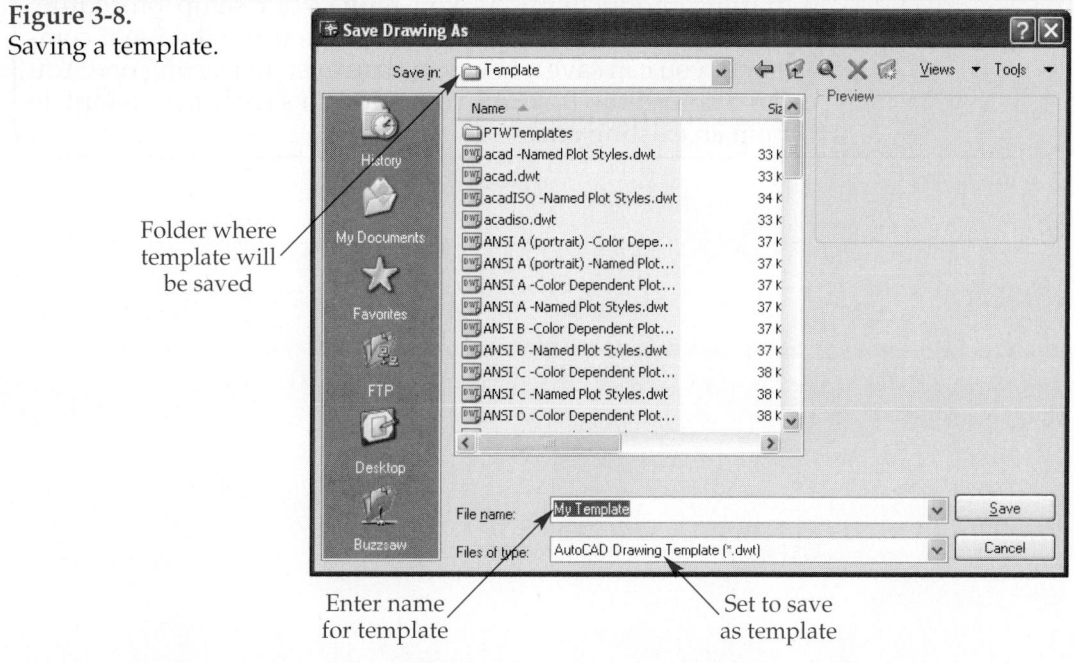

Folder where template will be saved

Enter name for template

Set to save as template

**Figure 3-9.**
Enter a description of the new template in the **Template Description** dialog box.

Enter description for template

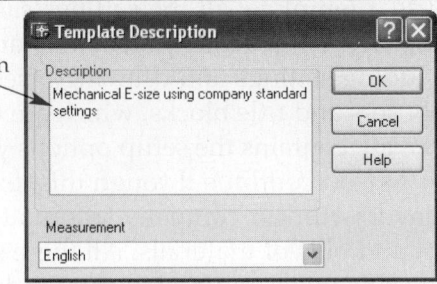

The contents of this folder are displayed by default when the **Select template** dialog box is displayed or the **Use a Template** option is selected in the **Startup** and **Create New Drawing** dialog boxes. After specifying the name and location for the new template file, pick the **Save** button in the **Save Drawing As** dialog box. The **Template Description** dialog box is now displayed, as shown in **Figure 3-9.** Use the **Description** area to enter a brief description of the template file you are saving. You can enter up to two hundred characters, but a brief description usually works best. Under the **Measurement** drop-down list, specify whether the units used in the template are English or metric, and then pick the **OK** button.

The template name should relate to the template, such as Mechanical A size, for a mechanical drawing on an A-size sheet. The template might be named for the drawing application, such as Architectural floor plans. The template name might be as simple as Template 1. The name should be written in a reference manual, along with documentation about what is included in the template. This provides future reference for you and other users. The template drawing you create is saved for you to open and use whenever it is needed. Now, you can exit AutoCAD, and when you start up again, the template you created is ready for you to use for preparing a new drawing.

**PROFESSIONAL TIP**

Generalized templates that set the units, limits, snap settings, and grid settings to specifications are useful, but keep in mind you can create any number of drawing templates. Templates containing more detailed settings can dramatically increase drafting productivity. As you refine your setup procedure, you can revise the template files. When using the **SAVE** command, you can save a new template over an existing one. You can also use the **SAVEAS** command to save a new template from an existing one.

○ Create one of the following templates based on the type of drawing you prefer. To create your template, begin a new drawing based on the existing template listed and set the specified grid and snap values.

  1. Name: MECHANICAL-IN-A
     Use: Mechanical drawings in inches on A-size sheet.
     Template: ANSI A -Color Dependent Plot Styles.dwt
     Grid = .25
     Snap = .125
  2. Name: MECHANICAL-IN-B
     Use: Mechanical drawings in inches on B-size sheet.
     Template: ANSI B -Color Dependent Plot Styles.dwt
     Grid = .5
     Snap = .25
  3. Name: MECHANICAL-MM-A3
     Use: Mechanical drawings in metric on A3-size sheet.
     Template: ISO A3 -Color Dependent Plot Styles.dwt
     Grid = 10
     Snap = 5
  4. Name: MECHANICAL-MM-A2
     Use: Mechanical drawings in metric on A2-size sheet.
     Template: ISO A2 -Color Dependent Plot Styles.dwt
     Grid = 20
     Snap = 10
  5. Name: ARCHITECTURAL-D
     Use: Architectural drawings on D-size sheet.
     Template: Architectural, English units -Color Dependent Plot Styles.dwt
     Grid = 24
     Snap = 6

○ Save the drawing template as explained in the previous discussion.
○ Record the information about your template in a notebook.
○ Create another new drawing template based on one of the previous options, but this time, design the template without a border or a title block by using a setup wizard.
○ Save the drawing template as explained in the previous discussion.
○ Record the information about your template in a notebook.

## Line Conventions

Drafting is a graphic language using lines, symbols, and words to describe products to be manufactured or constructed. Line conventions are standards based on line thickness and type. These standards are designed to enhance the readability of drawings. This section introduces line standards.

The American National Standards Institute (ANSI) recommends two line widths to establish contrasting lines in a drawing. Lines are described as thick or thin. For manual drafting, thick lines are twice as thick as thin lines, with recommended widths of 0.6 mm and 0.3 mm, respectively. A single line width for all types of lines is acceptable, however, on drawings prepared with a CAD system. **Figure 3-10** shows recommended line width and type as defined in ASME Y14.2M, *Line Conventions and Lettering*.

**Figure 3-10.**
Line conventions. (Adapted from ASME Y14.2M)

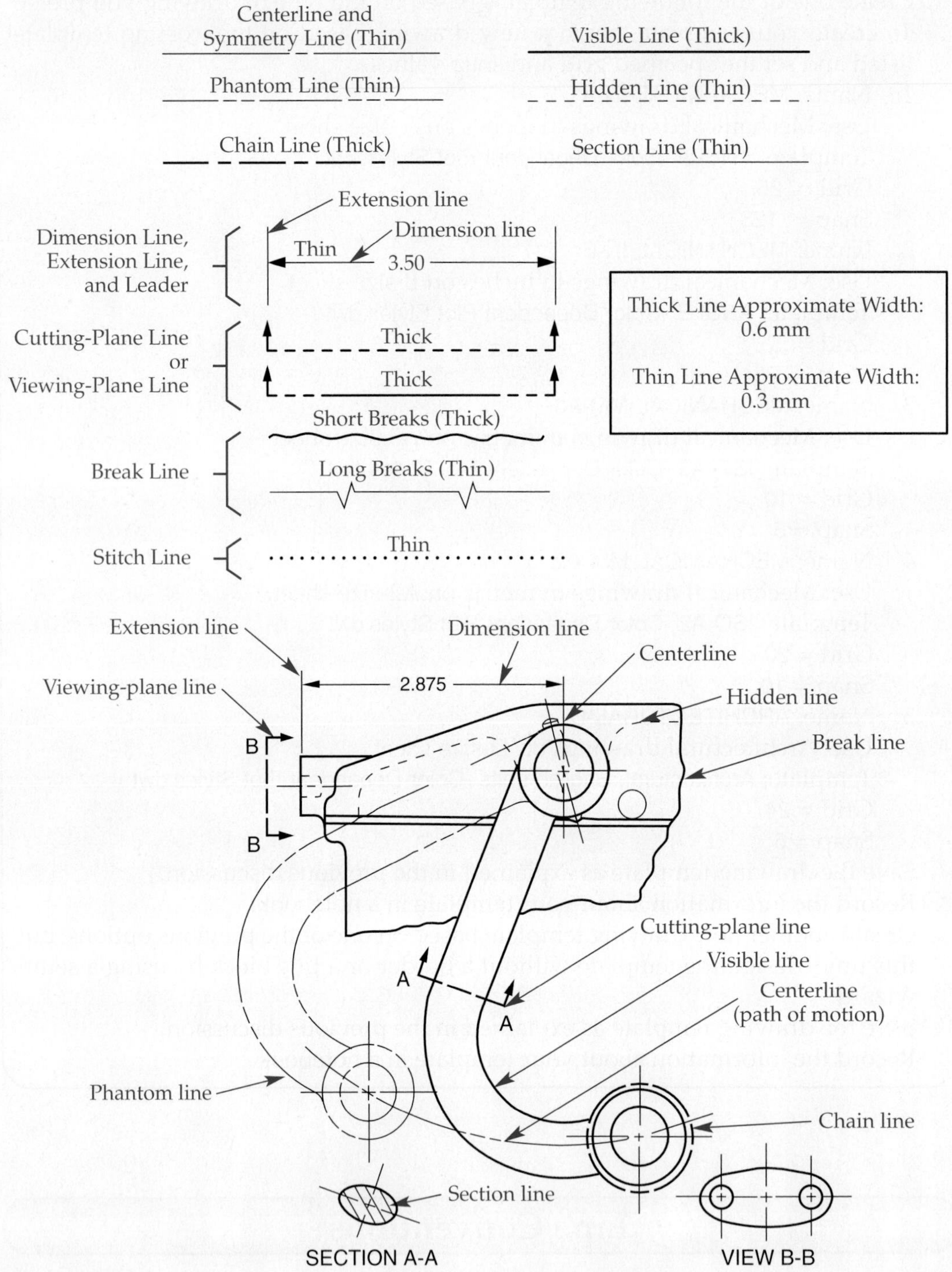

## Object Lines

*Object lines,* also called *visible lines,* are thick lines used to show the outline or contour of an object. See **Figure 3-11.** Object lines are the most common type of lines used in drawings. These lines should be twice as thick as thin lines.

## Hidden Lines

*Hidden lines,* often called *dashed lines,* are used to represent invisible features of an object, as shown in **Figure 3-11.** They are drawn thin so they clearly contrast with

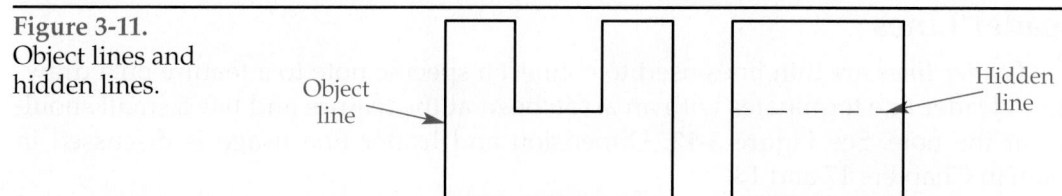

**Figure 3-11.**
Object lines and hidden lines.

Object line

Hidden line

object lines. When properly drawn at full size, the dashes are .125″ (3 mm) long and spaced .06″ (1.5 mm) apart. Be careful if the drawing is to be greatly reduced or scaled down during the plotting process. Reduced dashes may appear too small.

## Centerlines

*Centerlines* locate the centers of circles and arcs and show the axis of a cylindrical or symmetrical shape, as shown in **Figure 3-12.** They are thin lines consisting of alternating long and short dashes. The recommended dash lengths are .125″ (3 mm) for the short dashes and .75″ to 1.5″ (19 mm to 38 mm) for the long dashes. These lengths can be altered, depending on the size of the drawing. Spaces approximately .06″ (1.5 mm) long should separate the dashes. The small centerline dashes should cross only at the center of a circle.

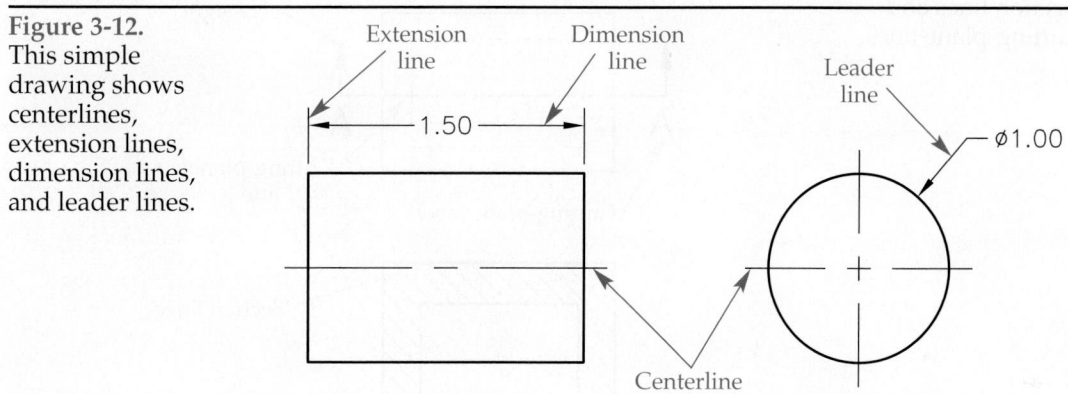

**Figure 3-12.**
This simple drawing shows centerlines, extension lines, dimension lines, and leader lines.

Extension line

Dimension line

Leader line

Ø1.00

1.50

Centerline

## Extension Lines

*Extension lines* are thin lines used to show the "extent" of a dimension, as shown in **Figure 3-12.** They begin a small distance from an object and extend .125″ (3 mm) beyond the last dimension line. Extension lines may cross object lines, hidden lines, and centerlines, but they may not cross dimension lines. Centerlines become extension lines when they are used to show the extent of a dimension. When this is done, there is no space where the centerline joins the extension line.

## Dimension Lines

*Dimension lines* are thin lines placed between extension lines to indicate a measurement. In mechanical drafting, the dimension line is normally broken near the center for placement of the dimension numeral, as shown in **Figure 3-12.** The dimension line normally remains unbroken in architectural and structural drawings. The dimension numeral is placed on top of an unbroken dimension line. Arrows terminate the ends of dimension lines, except in architectural drafting, where slashes or dots are often used.

## Leader Lines

*Leader lines* are thin lines used to connect a specific note to a feature on a drawing. A leader line terminates with an arrowhead at the feature and has a small shoulder at the note. See **Figure 3-12.** Dimension and leader line usage is discussed in detail in Chapters 17 and 18.

## Cutting-Plane and Viewing-Plane Lines

*Cutting-plane lines* are thick lines identifying the location of a section. *Viewing-plane lines* are drawn in the same style as cutting-plane lines, but identify the location of a view. Cutting-plane and viewing-plane lines may be drawn one of two ways, as shown in **Figure 3-10.** The use of viewing-plane and cutting-plane lines is discussed in detail in Chapters 6 and 21.

## Section Lines

*Section lines* are thin lines drawn in a section view to show where material has been cut away, as shown in **Figure 3-13.** Types of section lines and applications are discussed in Chapter 21.

**Figure 3-13.**
Section lines and cutting-plane lines.

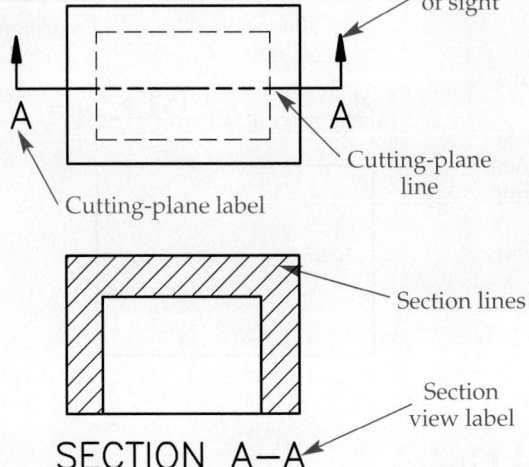

## Break Lines

*Break lines* show where a portion of an object has been removed for clarity or convenience. For example, the center portion of a very long part may be broken out so the two ends can be moved closer together for more convenient representation. There are several types of break lines shown in **Figure 3-14.**

## Phantom Lines

*Phantom lines* are thin lines with two short dashes alternating with long dashes. The short dashes are .125″ (3 mm) long, and the long dashes range from .75″ to 1.5″ (19 mm to 38 mm) in length, depending on the size of the drawing. Spaces between dashes are .06″ (1.5 mm). Phantom lines identify repetitive details, show alternate positions of moving parts, and locate adjacent positions of related parts. See **Figure 3-15.**

**Figure 3-14.**
Standard break lines.

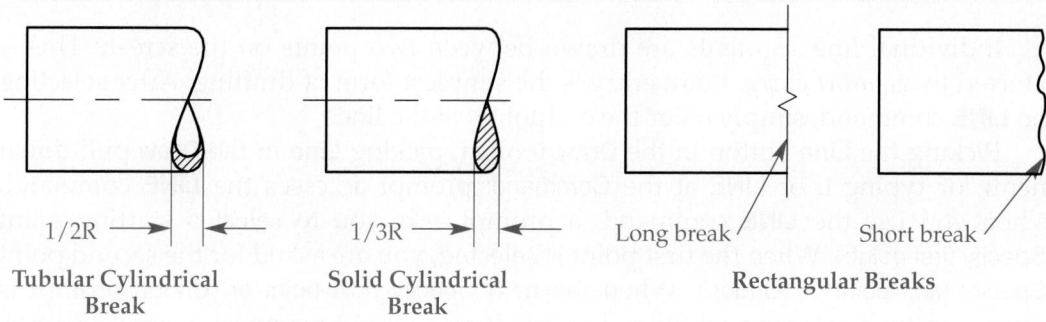

1/2R →| |←

**Tubular Cylindrical Break**

1/3R →| |←

**Solid Cylindrical Break**

Long break

Short break

**Rectangular Breaks**

**Figure 3-15.**
Phantom lines.

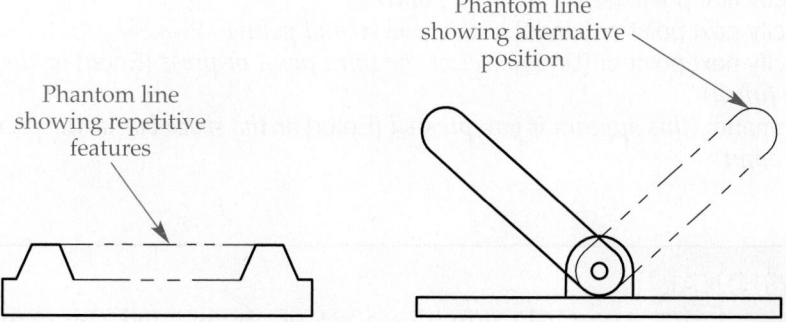

Phantom line showing repetitive features

Phantom line showing alternative position

# Chain Lines

*Chain lines* are thick lines of alternating long and short dashes. They show that the portion of the surface next to the chain line has special features or receives unique treatment. See **Figure 3-16.**

**Figure 3-16.**
Chain lines.

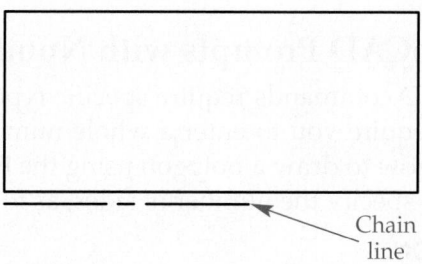

Chain line

# Drawing Lines with AutoCAD

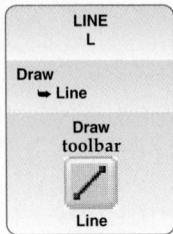

LINE
L

Draw
➥ Line

Draw
toolbar

Line

Individual line segments are drawn between two points on the screen. This is referred to as *point entry.* Point entry is the simplest form of drafting. After selecting the **LINE** command, simply enter the endpoints of the line.

Picking the **Line** button in the **Draw** toolbar, picking **Line** in the **Draw** pull-down menu, or typing L or LINE at the Command: prompt accesses the **LINE** command. When you use the **LINE** command, a prompt asks you to select a starting point (Specify first point:). When the first point is selected, you are asked for the second point (Specify next point or [Undo]:). When the next Specify next point or [Undo]: prompt is given, continue selecting additional points if you want to connect a series of lines. When you are finished, press the [Enter] key or the space bar to get back to the Command: prompt. The following command sequence is used for the **LINE** command:

Command: **L** *or* **LINE**↵
Specify first point: *(select the first point)*
Specify next point or [Undo]: *(select the second point)*
Specify next point or [Undo]: *(select the third point or press* [Enter] *or the space bar to finish)*
Command: *(this appears if you pressed* [Enter] *or the space bar at the previous prompt)*

**PROFESSIONAL TIP**

AutoCAD provides a set of abbreviated commands called *command aliases.* Command aliases are also called *keyboard shortcuts* because they reduce the amount of typing needed when entering a command at the keyboard. Using command aliases allows you to enter commands more quickly. For example, instead of typing LINE at the Command: prompt, you can type L, which is faster. Becoming familiar with the available command aliases can help you become more productive with AutoCAD.

## Responding to AutoCAD Prompts with Numbers

Many of the AutoCAD commands require specific types of numeric data. Some of AutoCAD's prompts require you to enter a whole number. For example, later in this book, you will learn how to draw a polygon using the **POLYGON** command. This command requires you to specify the number of sides, as follows:

Command: **POLYGON**↵
Enter number of sides <current>: **6**↵
Specify center of polygon or [Edge]: *(pick the center of the polygon)*
Enter an option [Inscribed in circle/Circumscribed about circle] <I>: ↵
Specify radius of circle: **2**↵
Command:

The Enter number of sides: prompt illustrates the simplest form of numeric entry in which any whole number may be used. Other entries require whole numbers that may be positive or negative. A number is understood to be positive without placing the plus (+) sign before the number. The minus (-) sign must, however, precede a negative number.

Much of your data entry may not be whole numbers. In these cases, any real number can be used and expressed as a decimal, as a fraction, or in scientific notation. These numbers may be positive or negative. Here are some examples of acceptable real numbers:

4.250
-6.375
1/2
1-3/4
2.5E+4 *(25,000)*
2.5E-4 *(0.00025)*

When entering fractions, the numerator and denominator must be whole numbers greater than zero. For example, 1/2, 3/4, and 2/3 are all acceptable fraction entries. Fractional numbers greater than one must have a dash between the whole number and the fraction. For example, 2-3/4 is entered for two and three quarters. The dash (-) separator is needed because a space acts just like pressing [Enter] and automatically ends the input. The numerator may be larger than the denominator, as in 3/2, *only* if a whole number is not used with the fraction. For example, 1-3/2 is not a valid input for a fraction. When you enter coordinates or measurements, the values used depend on the units of measurement.

- Values on inch drawings are understood to be in inches without placing the inch marks (") after the numeral. For example, 2.500 is automatically understood to be 2.500".
- When your drawing is set up for metric values, any entry is automatically expressed as millimeters.
- If you are working in an engineering or architectural environment, any value greater than 1' is expressed in inches, feet, or feet and inches. The values can be whole numbers, decimals, or fractions.
  - For measurements in feet, the foot symbol (') must follow the number, as in 24'.
  - If the value is in feet and inches, there is no space between the feet and inch value. For example, 24'6 is the proper input for the value 24'-6".
  - If the inch part of the value contains a fraction, the inch and fractional part of an inch are separated by a dash, such as 24'6-1/2.

Never mix feet with inch values greater than one foot. For example, 24'18" is an invalid entry. In this case, you should enter 25'6.

---

**PROFESSIONAL TIP**

Placing the inch mark (") after an inch value at the prompt line is acceptable, but not necessary. It takes more time and reduces productivity.

---

**NOTE**

AutoCAD accepts the inch (") and foot (') symbols in the command line only when the **UNITS** are set to either **Architectural** or **Engineering**. If the **UNITS** are not set to one of these, a message on the command line will read Requires numeric distance or second point.

---

# Point Entry Methods

There are several point entry techniques for drawing lines. Being familiar and skillful with these methods is very important. A combination of point entry techniques should be used to help reduce drawing time.

Each of the point entry methods uses the Cartesian, or rectangular, coordinate system. The *Cartesian coordinate system* is based on selecting distances from three intersecting axes. The point's distance from the intersection point, called the *origin*, in respect to each of these axes defines a *location*. In standard two-dimensional (2D) drafting applications, objects are drawn in the XY plane, and the Z axis is not referenced. Using the Z axis is discussed in Chapter 26 with three-dimensional (3D) drafting.

In 2D drafting, the origin divides the coordinate system into four quadrants within the XY plane. Points are located in relation to the origin, where X = 0 and Y = 0, or (0,0). **Figure 3-17** shows the X,Y values of points located in the Cartesian coordinate system.

When using AutoCAD, the origin (0,0) is usually at the lower-left corner of the drawing. This point also coincides with the lower-left corner of the drawing limits. This setup places all points in the upper-right quadrant, where both X and Y coordinate values are positive. See **Figure 3-18.** Methods of establishing points in the Cartesian coordinate system include using absolute coordinates, relative coordinates, and polar coordinates.

**Figure 3-17.**
The Cartesian coordinate system.

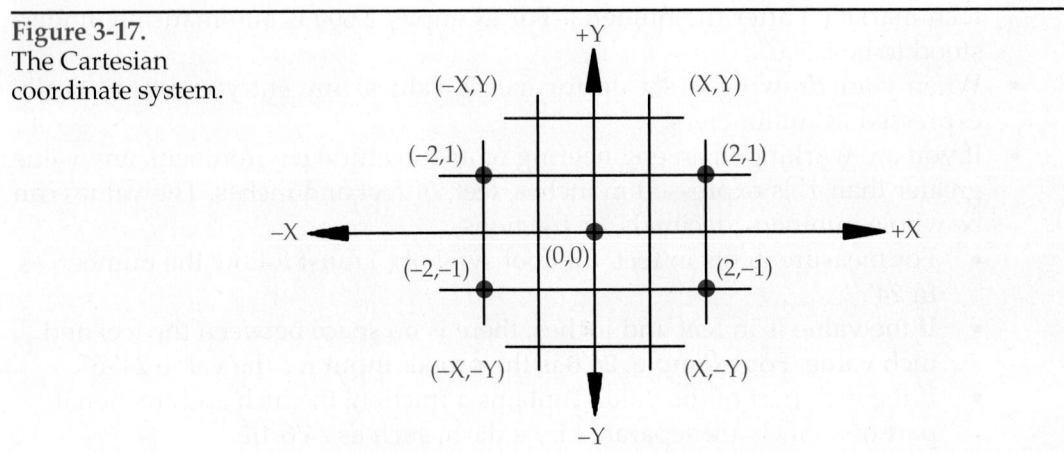

**Figure 3-18.**
The XY coordinate axes on the screen.

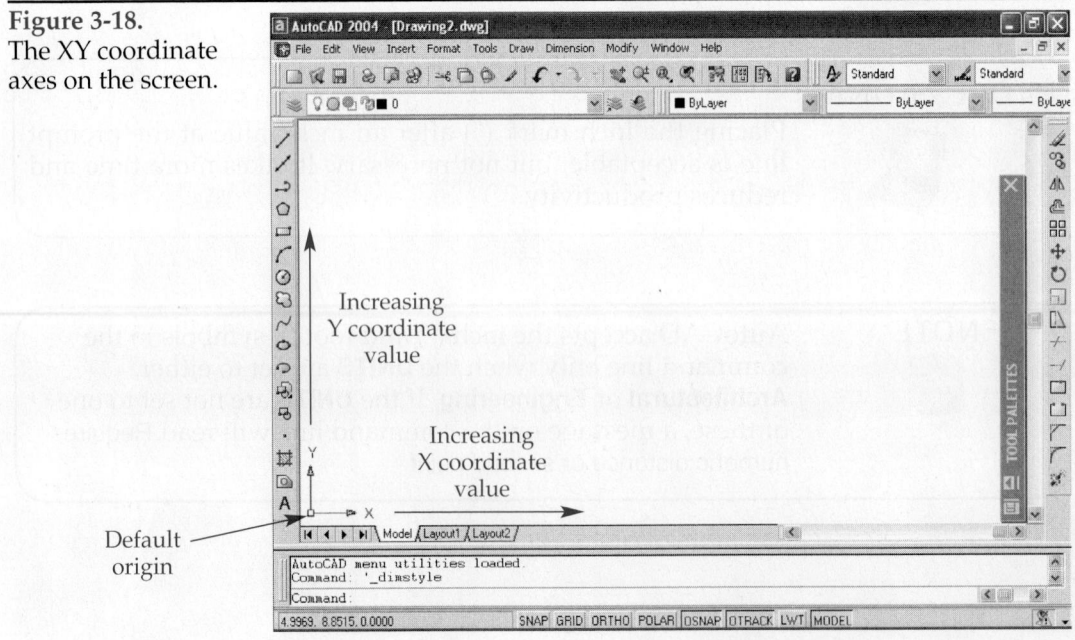

## Using absolute coordinates

Points located using the absolute coordinate system are measured from the origin (0,0). For example, a point where X = 4 and Y = 2 (4,2) is located four units horizontally and two units vertically from the origin, as shown in **Figure 3-19**. The coordinate display on the status bar registers the location of the selected point in XYZ coordinates.

The discussion and examples in this chapter reference only the XY coordinates for 2D drafting. Also note that the coordinate display reflects the current system of working units. Remember, when the absolute coordinate system is used, each point is located from 0,0. Follow these commands and point placements at your computer, as you refer to **Figure 3-20**:

> Command: **L** *or* **LINE**↵
> Specify first point: **4,2**↵
> Specify next point or [Undo]: **7,2**↵
> Specify next point or [Undo]: **7,6**↵
> Specify next point or [Close/Undo]: **4,6**↵
> Specify next point or [Close/Undo]: **4,2**↵
> Specify next point or [Close/Undo]: ↵
> Command:

**Figure 3-19.**
Locating points with absolute coordinates.

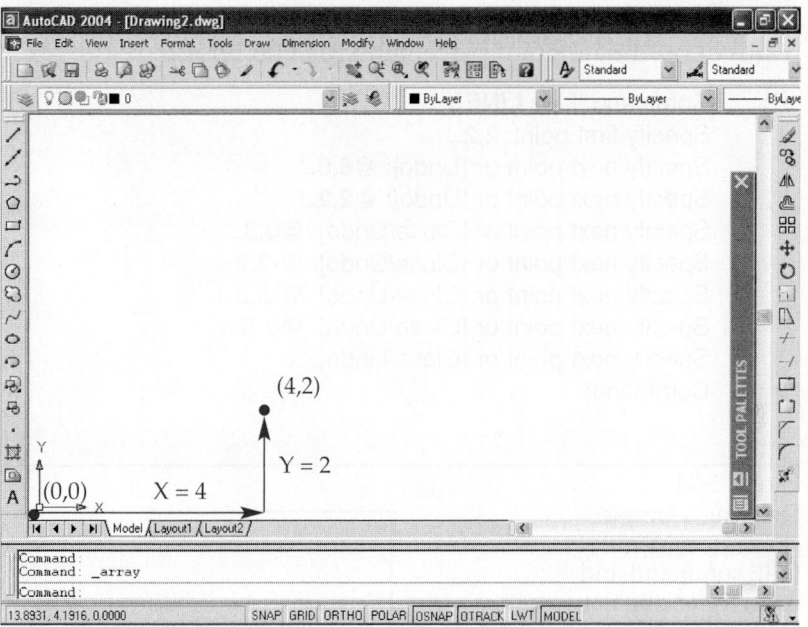

**Figure 3-20.**
Drawing simple shapes using the **LINE** command and absolute coordinates.

○ Start a new drawing or use one of your templates.
○ Given the absolute coordinates in the chart below, use the **LINE** command to draw the object.
○ Save the drawing as EX3-3.

| Point | Coordinates | Point | Coordinates |
|-------|-------------|-------|-------------|
| 1 | 0,0 | 5 | 0,2 |
| 2 | 9,0 | 6 | 0,1.5 |
| 3 | 9.5,.5 | 7 | .25,.5 |
| 4 | 9.5,2 | 8 | 0,0 |

## Using relative coordinates

*Relative coordinates* are located from the previous position, rather than from the origin. The relationship of points in the Cartesian coordinate system, shown in **Figure 3-17**, must be clearly understood before using this method. For relative coordinates, the @ symbol must precede your entry. Holding the [Shift] key and pressing the [2] key at the top of the keyboard selects this symbol. Follow these commands and relative coordinate point placements, as you refer to **Figure 3-21**:

Command: **L** *or* **LINE**↵
Specify first point: **2,2**↵
Specify next point or [Undo]: **@6,0**↵
Specify next point or [Undo]: **@2,2**↵
Specify next point or [Close/Undo]: **@0,3**↵
Specify next point or [Close/Undo]: **@-2,2**↵
Specify next point or [Close/Undo]: **@-6,0**↵
Specify next point or [Close/Undo]: **@0,-7**↵
Specify next point or [Close/Undo]: ↵
Command:

Figure 3-21.
Drawing a simple shape using the **LINE** command and relative coordinates. Notice that the coordinates are entered counterclockwise from the first point (2,2).

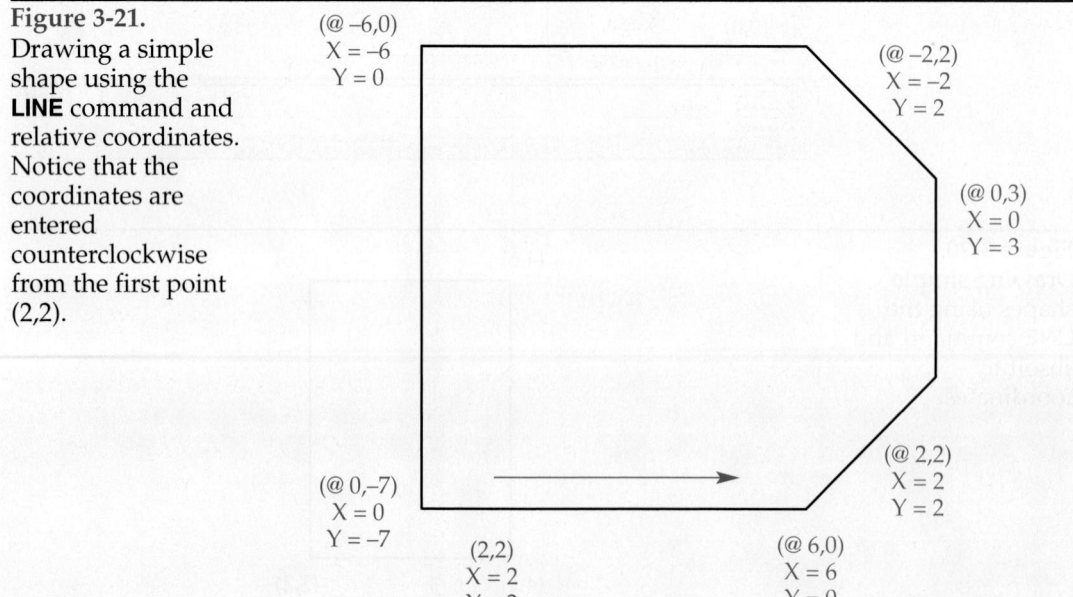

○ Start a new drawing or use one of your templates.
○ Use the **LINE** command to draw an object with the relative coordinates given in the chart below.
○ Save the drawing as EX3-4.

| Point | Coordinates | Point | Coordinates |
|-------|-------------|-------|-------------|
| 1 | 1,1 | 5 | @-9.5,0 |
| 2 | @9,0 | 6 | @0,-.5 |
| 3 | @.5,.5 | 7 | @.25,-1 |
| 4 | @0,1.5 | 8 | @-.25,-.5 |

## Using polar coordinates

A point located using *polar coordinates* is based on the distance from a fixed point at a given angle. First the distance is entered, then the angle. A < symbol separates the two values.

The angular values used for the polar coordinate format are shown in Figure 3-22. Consistent with standard AutoCAD convention, 0° is to the right, or east. Angles are then measured counterclockwise.

When preceded by the @ symbol, a polar coordinate point is measured from the previous point. If the @ symbol is not included, the coordinate is located relative to the origin. If you want to draw a line four units long from point 1,1, at a 45° angle, the following information must be typed:

        Command: **L** *or* **LINE**↵
        Specify first point: **1,1**↵
        Specify next point or [Undo]: **@4<45**↵
        Specify next point or [Undo]: ↵

Figure 3-22.
Angles used in the polar coordinate system.

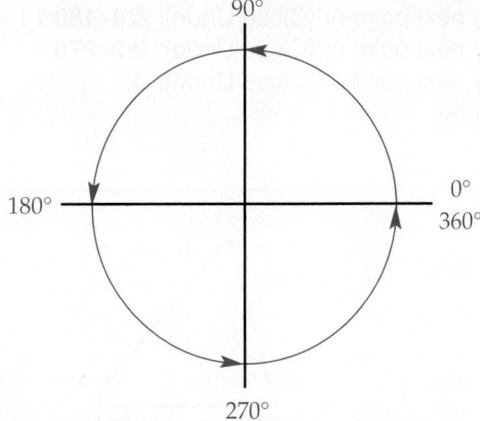

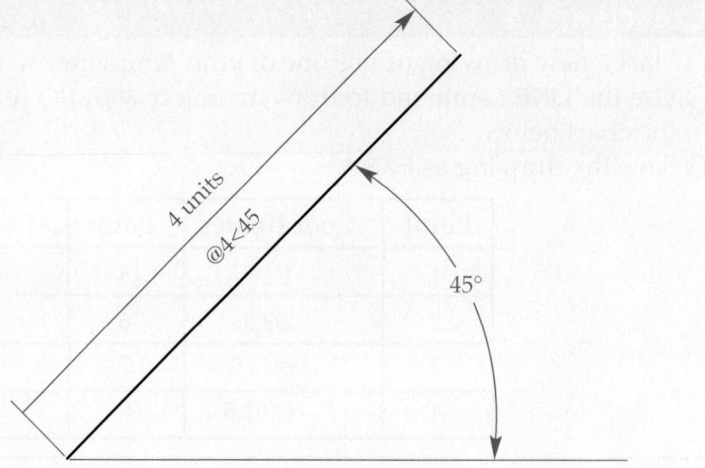

Figure 3-23.
Using polar
coordinates for the
**LINE** command.

4 units
@4<45
45°

Figure 3-23 shows the result of this command. The entry @4<45 means the following:

- **@.** Tells AutoCAD to measure from the previous point. This symbol must precede all relative coordinate inputs.
- **4.** Gives the distance, such as 4 units, from the previous point.
- **<.** Establishes that a polar or angular increment is to follow.
- **45.** Determines the angle, such as 45°, from 0°.

Now, follow these commands and polar coordinate points on your computer, as you refer to **Figure 3-24**:

Command: **L** *or* **LINE**↵
Specify first point: **2,6**↵
Specify next point or [Undo]: **@2.5<0**↵
Specify next point or [Undo]: **@3<135**↵
Specify next point or [Close/Undo]: **2,6**↵
Specify next point or [Close/Undo]: ↵
Command: ↵
LINE Specify first point: **6,6**↵
Specify next point or [Undo]: **@4<0**↵
Specify next point or [Undo]: **@2<90**↵
Specify next point or [Close/Undo]: **@4<180**↵
Specify next point or [Close/Undo]: **@2<270**↵
Specify next point or [Close/Undo]: ↵
Command:

Figure 3-24.
Using polar
coordinates to draw.

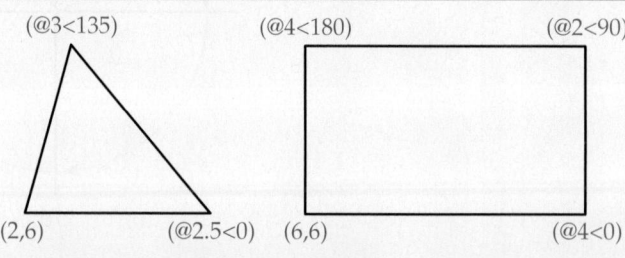

(@3<135)        (@4<180)                    (@2<90)

(2,6)        (@2.5<0)   (6,6)                (@4<0)

○ Start a new drawing or use one of your templates.
○ Use the **LINE** command to draw an object using the polar coordinates given in the chart below.
○ Save the drawing as EX3-5.

| Point | Coordinates | Point | Coordinates |
|:-----:|:-----------:|:-----:|:-----------:|
| 1 | 1,1 | 4 | @1.5<90 |
| 2 | @9<0 | 5 | @9.5<180 |
| 3 | @.7<45 | 6 | @2<270 |

### Picking points using the screen cursor

The pointing device can be used to move the crosshairs and pick points. The Grid and Snap modes normally should be turned on for precise point location. This assists in drafting presentation and maintains accuracy when using a pointing device. With Snap mode on, the crosshairs move in designated increments without any guesswork.

When you are using a pointing device, the command sequence is the same as when you are using coordinates. Points are picked when the crosshairs are at the desired location. After the first point is picked, the distance to the second point and the point's coordinates are displayed on the status line for reference. When picking points in this manner, there is a "rubberband" line connecting the "first point" and the crosshairs. The rubberband line moves as the crosshairs are moved, showing where the new line will be placed.

## Drawing Multiple Lines

The **MULTIPLE** command is used to automatically repeat commands issued at the keyboard. This technique can be used to draw repetitive lines, polylines, circles, arcs, ellipses, or polygons. For example, if you plan to draw several sets of line segments, type MULTIPLE at the Command: prompt, press the space bar to add a space, and then type L or LINE. AutoCAD automatically repeats the **LINE** command until you have finished drawing all the desired lines. You must cancel to get back to the Command: prompt. The **MULTIPLE** command is used as follows:

```
Command: MULTIPLE↵
Enter command name to repeat: L or LINE↵
Specify first point: (pick the first point)
Specify next point or [Undo]: (pick the second point)
Specify next point or [Undo]: (pick the third point or press [Enter])
Specify next point or [Close/Undo]: ↵
LINE Specify first point: (pick the first point)
Specify next point or [Undo]: (pick the second point)
Specify next point or [Undo]: (pick the third point or press [Enter])
Specify next point or [Close/Undo]: ↵
LINE Specify first point: (press [Esc] to cancel) *Cancel*
```

As you can see, AutoCAD automatically reissues the **LINE** command so you can draw another line (or lines). Press [Esc] to cancel the repeating command.

## The Coordinate Display

The area to the left side of the status bar shows the coordinate display window. The units setting determines the number of places displayed to the right of the decimal point. The coordinate display changes to represent the location of the cursor in relation to the origin. Each time a new point is picked or the pointing device is moved, the coordinates are updated.

Picking the coordinate display in the status bar or pressing the [Ctrl]+[D] key combination, the [F6] function key, or puck button 7 turns the coordinate display on and off. With coordinates on, the coordinates constantly change as the crosshairs move. With coordinates off, no coordinates are displayed.

There are three coordinate modes, and they are controlled by the **COORDS** system variable. Set this variable to 0 for a static display. This displays coordinates only when points are selected. Set the **COORDS** variable to 1 for a dynamic absolute display. Set the variable to 2 for a dynamic length/angle (polar) display. A typical absolute coordinate display gives X, Y, and Z coordinates, such as 6.2000,5.9000,0.0000. A polar coordinate display shows the distance and angle from the last point and the Z axis distance, such as 3.4000<180, 0.0000.

### Exercise 3-6

○ Start a new drawing, use one of your templates, or open a previous exercise.
○ Draw rectangles 3″ (76.2 mm) wide by 2″ (50.8 mm) high, using each point entry method from the following list. Experiment with the coordinate display options as you draw the rectangles.
  ○ Absolute coordinates.
  ○ Relative coordinates.
  ○ Polar coordinates.
  ○ The screen cursor.
○ Use the **MULTIPLE** and **LINE** commands to draw several different lines and shapes. Notice the advantage of remaining in the **LINE** command when several different line segments or shapes must be drawn.
○ Save the drawing as EX3-6.

## Drawing in Ortho Mode

The term *ortho* comes from *orthogonal*, which means "at right angles." The Ortho mode constrains points selected while drawing and editing to be only horizontal or vertical. The directions are in alignment with the current Snap grid.

The Ortho mode has a special advantage when drawing rectangular shapes because all corners are guaranteed to be square. See **Figure 3-25.** Picking the **ORTHO** button on the status bar; using the [F8] function key, puck button 5, or the [Ctrl]+[L] key combination; or typing ORTHO at the Command: prompt can activate and deactivate Ortho mode.

AutoCAD and its Applications—Basics

**Figure 3-25.**
Using Ortho mode.
A—Angled lines
cannot be drawn
with a pointing
device while Ortho
mode is turned on.
B—With Ortho mode
turned off, angled
lines can be drawn.

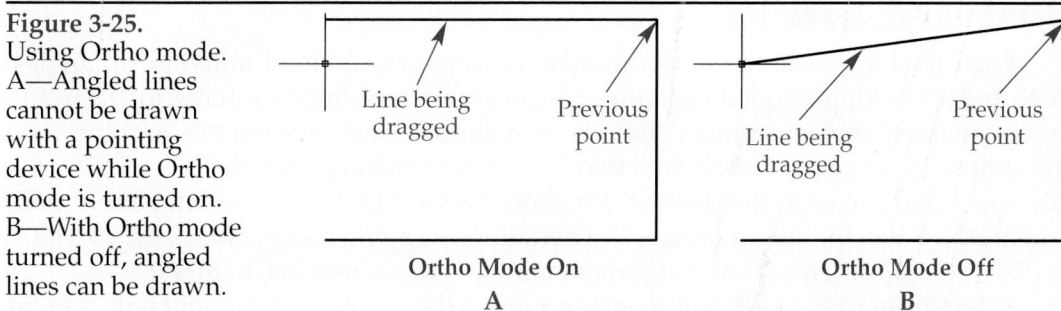

Ortho Mode On
A

Ortho Mode Off
B

## Using Direct Distance Entry

*Direct distance entry* is a method of entering points allowing you to use the cursor to specify the direction and use a keyboard entry to specify a distance. To draw a line using this point entry method, drag the cursor in any desired direction from the first point of the line. Then type a numerical value indicating the distance from that point.

The direct distance entry method works best in combination with the Ortho mode or polar tracking. **Figure 3-26** shows how to draw a rectangle using direct distance entry. Note that the Ortho mode is on for this example:

```
Command: L or LINE↵
Specify first point: 2,2↵
Specify next point or [Undo]: (drag the cursor to the right, type 3, and press [Enter])
Specify next point or [Undo]: (drag the cursor up, type 2, and press [Enter])
Specify next point or [Close/Undo]: (drag the cursor to the left, type 3, and press [Enter])
Specify next point or [Close/Undo]: (drag the cursor down, type 2, and press [Enter])
Specify next point or [Close/Undo]: ↵
Command:
```

**PROFESSIONAL TIP**

Direct distance entry is a convenient way to find points quickly and easily with a minimum amount of effort. Use direct distance entry with Ortho or Snap mode to draw objects with perpendicular lines. Direct distance entry can be used whenever AutoCAD expects a point coordinate value, including both drawing and editing commands.

**Figure 3-26.**
Using direct
distance entry to
draw lines a
designated distance
from a current
point. With Ortho
mode on, move the
cursor in the desired
direction and type
the distance.

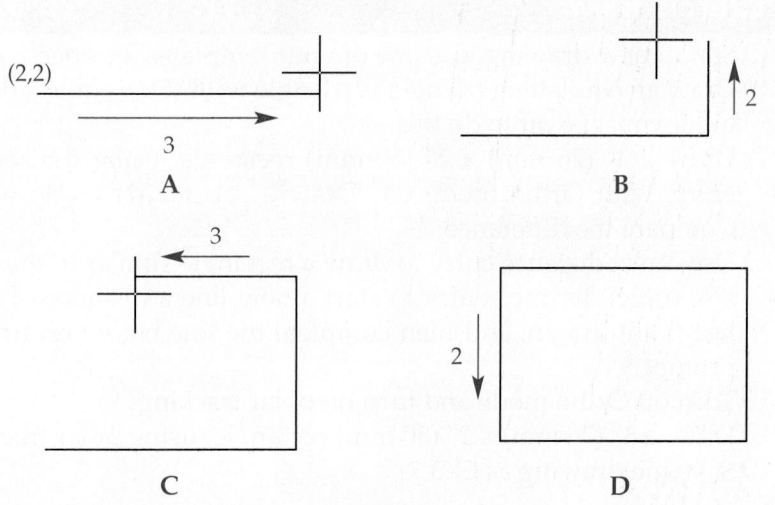

## Using Polar Tracking

Polar tracking is similar to Ortho mode, except you are not limited to 90° angles. With polar tracking toggled on, you can cause the drawing crosshairs to "snap" to any predefined angle increment. To turn on polar tracking, pick the **POLAR** button on the status bar or use the [F10] function key. Polar tracking provides visual aids. As you move the cursor in the desired direction, AutoCAD displays an alignment path and tooltip when the cursor crosses the default polar angle increments of 0°, 90°, 180°, or 270°. Setting different polar alignment angles is explained in Chapter 6.

After you start the **LINE** command and move the cursor in alignment with a polar tracking angle, all you have to do is type the desired distance value and press [Enter] to have the line drawn. Polar tracking is used, as follows, to draw the lines shown in **Figure 3-27**:

> Command: **L** or **LINE**.↵
> Specify first point: **2,2**.↵
> Specify next point or [Undo]: **2** (*drag the crosshairs while watching the tooltip; at 0°, press* [Enter])
> Specify next point or [Undo]: **3** (*drag the crosshairs while watching the tooltip; at 90°, press* [Enter])
> Specify next point or [Close/Undo]: ↵
> Command:

Polar tracking is discussed in detail in Chapter 6.

**Figure 3-27.**
Using polar tracking to draw lines at predefined angle increments.

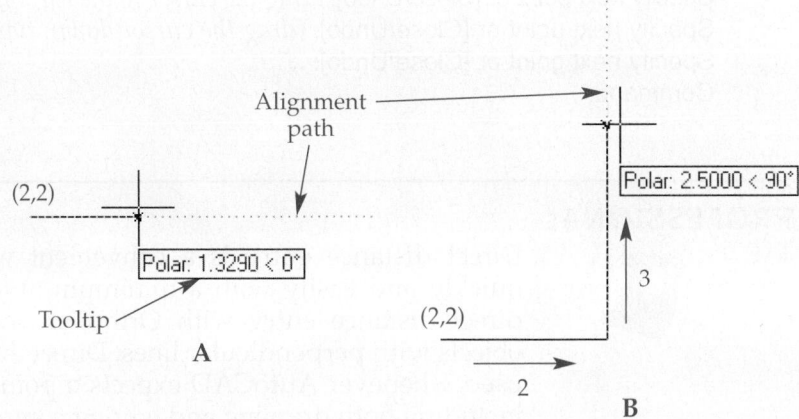

**Exercise 3-7**

○ Start a new drawing, use one of your templates, or open a previous exercise.
○ Draw an equilateral triangle (a triangle with three equal sides and angles). Ortho mode must be off to do this.
○ Draw a 3″ (76 mm) × 2″ (50 mm) rectangle, using the screen cursor for point entry, with Ortho mode off. Draw a second rectangle with Ortho mode on. Compare the difference.
○ Use direct distance entry to draw a rectangle similar to the one in **Figure 3-26**.
○ Use direct distance entry to start a new line a distance of your choice from the last point drawn, and then complete the line before returning to the Command: prompt.
○ Turn off Ortho mode and turn on polar tracking.
○ Draw a 3″ (76 mm) × 2″ (50 mm) rectangle, using polar tracking.
○ Save the drawing as EX3-7.

## Using the **Close** Line Option

A *polygon* is a closed plane figure with at least three sides. Triangles and rectangles are examples of polygons. Once you have drawn two or more line segments of a polygon, the endpoint of the last line segment can be connected automatically to the first line segment, using the **Close** option. To use this option, type C or CLOSE at the prompt line. In **Figure 3-28,** the last line is drawn using the **Close** option, as follows:

Command: **L** *or* **LINE.⏎**
Specify first point: *(pick Point 1)*
Specify next point or [Undo]: *(pick Point 2)*
Specify next point or [Undo]: *(pick Point 3)*
Specify next point or [Close/Undo]: *(pick Point 4)*
Specify next point or [Close/Undo]: **C.⏎**
Command:

**Figure 3-28.**
Using the **Close** option to complete a box.

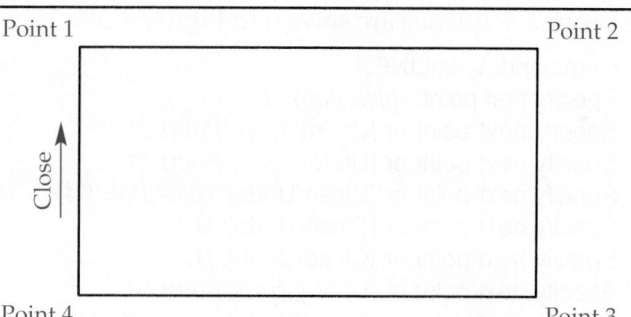

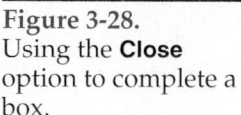

## Using the Line **Continue** Option

Suppose you draw a line, then exit the **LINE** command, but decide to go back and connect a new line to the end of the previous one. Type L to begin the **LINE** command. At the Specify first point: prompt, simply press the [Enter] key or the space bar. This action automatically connects the first endpoint of the new line segment to the endpoint of the previous one, as shown in **Figure 3-29.** The **Continue** option can also be used for drawing arcs, as discussed in Chapter 5. The following command sequence is used for continuing a line:

Command: **L** *or* **LINE.⏎**
Specify first point: *(press* [Enter] *or the space bar, and AutoCAD automatically picks the last endpoint of the previous line)*
Specify next point or [Undo]: *(pick the next point)*
Specify next point or [Undo]: *(press* [Enter] *to exit the command)*
Command:

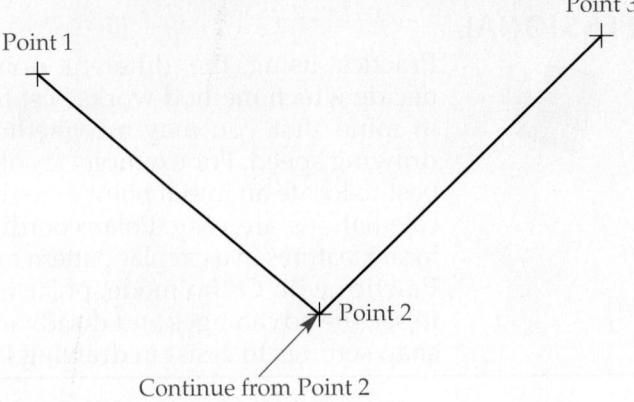

**Figure 3-29.**
Using the **Continue** option.

Point 1

Point 3

Point 2

Continue from Point 2

**PROFESSIONAL TIP**

Pressing the space bar or [Enter] repeats the previous command. If no other commands have been used since the line to be continued was drawn, pressing the space bar or [Enter] repeats the **LINE** command.

## Undoing the Previously Drawn Line

When drawing a series of lines, you may find you made an error. To delete the mistake while still in the **LINE** command, type U at the Specify next point or [Undo]: prompt and press [Enter]. Doing this removes the previously drawn line and allows you to continue from the previous endpoint. You can use the **Undo** option repeatedly to continue deleting line segments until the entire line is gone. The results of the following prompt sequence are shown in **Figure 3-30:**

> Command: **L** *or* **LINE**↵
> Specify first point: *(pick Point 1)*
> Specify next point or [Undo]: *(pick Point 2)*
> Specify next point or [Undo]: *(pick Point 3)*
> Specify next point or [Close/Undo]: *(pick Point 4)*
> Specify next point or [Close/Undo]: **U**↵
> Specify next point or [Close/Undo]: **U**↵
> Specify next point or [Undo]: *(pick Point 5)*
> Specify next point or [Close/Undo]: *(press* [Enter] *to exit the command)*
> Command:

**Figure 3-30.**
Using the **Undo** option while in the **LINE** command. Notice that the original Points 3 and 4 remain as blips until the screen is redrawn.

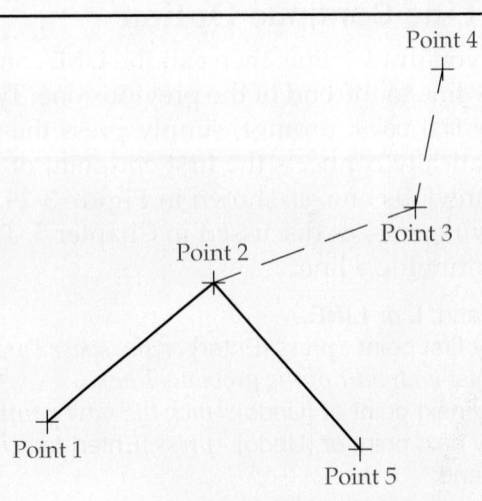

Point 4

Point 2

Point 3

Point 1

Point 5

# Canceling a Command

If you press the wrong key or misspell a word when entering a command or answering a prompt, use the [Backspace] key to correct the error. This works only if you notice your mistake *before* the [Enter] key is pressed. If you do enter an incorrect option or command, AutoCAD usually responds with an error message. You are then given another chance to enter the correct information or return to the Command: prompt. If you are not sure what has happened, reading the error message should tell you what you need to know.

Previous messages displayed in the command window are not always visible. Press the [F2] function key to display AutoCAD's text screen. This allows you to read the entire message. Also, you will be able to review the commands and options you entered. This may help you better understand what happened. You can press the [F2] key again to return to the graphics screen or use your cursor to pick any visible portion of the graphics screen to make it current again.

It is often necessary to stop the currently active command and return to AutoCAD's Command: prompt to either reenter a command or use another command. This can occur if an incorrect entry is made and you need to restart the command using the correct method or even if you simply decide to do something different. Pressing the [Enter] key or the space bar discontinues some commands, such as the **LINE** command. This exits the command and returns to the Command: prompt, where AutoCAD awaits a new command entry. There are many situations, however, where this does not work. One example of this is using the **Window** option of the **ZOOM** command. Pressing [Enter] does not discontinue the command. In this case, you must cancel the command. (The **ZOOM** command is discussed in detail in Chapter 9.)

You can cancel any active command or abort any data entry and return to the Command: prompt by pressing the [Esc] key. This key is usually located in the upper-left corner of your keyboard. It may be necessary to press the [Esc] key twice to completely cancel certain commands. Many multibutton digitizer pucks use button number 3 to cancel a command. Additionally, most of the toolbar buttons and pull-down menu options automatically cancel any currently active command before entering the new command. So, in a case where you wish to abort the current command and start a new one, simply pick the appropriate pull-down menu option or toolbar button.

*Editing* is the procedure used to correct mistakes or revise an existing drawing. There are many editing functions that help increase productivity. The basic editing operations **ERASE**, **OOPS**, and **U** are introduced in the next sections.

To edit a drawing, you must select items to modify. The Select objects: prompt appears whenever you need to select items in the command sequence. Whether you select only one object or hundreds of objects, you create a *selection set.* You can create a selection set using a variety of selection options, including the following:

- Window selection
- Crossing selection
- Window polygon selection
- Crossing polygon selection
- Selection fence

When you become familiar with the selection set options, you will find that they increase your flexibility and productivity.

In the following discussion and examples, several of the selection set methods are introduced using the **ERASE** command. Keep in mind, however, that these techniques can be used with most of the editing commands in AutoCAD whenever the Select objects: prompt appears. Any of the selection set methods can be enabled from the prompt line.

## Using the ERASE Command

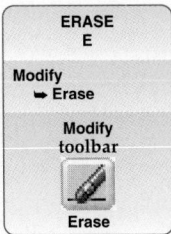

ERASE
E

Modify
↳ Erase

Modify
toolbar

Erase

The **ERASE** command is similar to using an eraser in manual drafting to remove unwanted information. With the **ERASE** command, however, you have a second chance. If you erase the wrong item, it can be brought back with the **OOPS** command. Picking the **Erase** button in the **Modify** toolbar, picking **Erase** in the **Modify** pull-down menu, or typing E or ERASE at the Command: prompt accesses the **ERASE** command.

When you enter the **ERASE** command, you are prompted to select an object to be erased, as follows:

Command: **E** *or* **ERASE**↵
Select objects: *(select the object(s) to be erased)*
Select objects: ↵
Command:

When the Select objects: prompt appears, a small box replaces the screen crosshairs. This box is referred to as the *pick box.* Move the pick box over the item to be erased and pick that item. The object is highlighted. Press the [Enter] key or the right mouse button, and the object is erased.

> **NOTE**
>
> The terms *entity* and *object* are interchangeable in AutoCAD. An entity or object is a predefined element you place in a drawing by means of a single command. For example, a line, a circle, an arc, or a single line of text is an entity or object.

After you pick the first object, the Select objects: prompt is redisplayed. You can then select another object to erase, as shown in **Figure 3-31.** If you are finished selecting objects, press the [Enter] key at the Select objects: prompt to "close" the selection set. The **ERASE** operation is completed, and you are returned to the Command: prompt.

**Figure 3-31.**
Using the **ERASE** command to erase a single object.

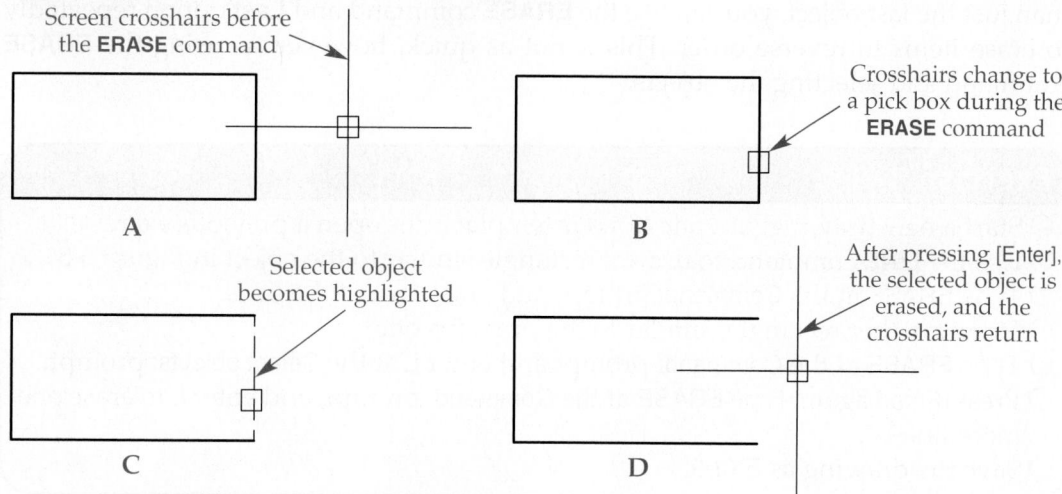

Screen crosshairs before
the **ERASE** command

Crosshairs change to
a pick box during the
**ERASE** command

A

B

Selected object
becomes highlighted

After pressing [Enter],
the selected object is
erased, and the
crosshairs return

C

D

## Making a single selection automatically

Normally, AutoCAD lets you pick as many items as you want for a selection set, and selected items are highlighted to let you know what has been picked. You also have the option of selecting a single item and having it automatically edited without first being highlighted. To do this, enter SI (for single) at the Select objects: prompt. To select several items with this method, use the **Window** or **Crossing** selection options (discussed later in this chapter). The command sequence is as follows:

Command: **E** *or* **ERASE**↵
Select objects: **SI**↵
Select objects: *(pick an individual item or use the* **Window** *or* **Crossing** *option to pick several items)*
Command:

Note that the Select objects: prompt did not return after the items were picked. The entire group is automatically edited (erased in this example) when you press [Enter] or pick the second corner of a window or crossing box.

**PROFESSIONAL TIP**

The **SI** (single) selection option is not commonly used as a command line option. This is because the option of picking an object and pressing [Enter] requires less keystrokes than the option of typing SI and pressing [Enter] does. The **SI** option is most commonly used when developing menu macros requiring single object selection.

## Using the Last selection option

The **ERASE** command's **Last** option saves time if you need to erase the last entity drawn. For example, suppose you draw a line and then want to erase it. The **Last** option will automatically select the line. Typing L at the Select objects: prompt selects the **Last** option:

Command: **E** *or* **ERASE**↵
Select objects: **L**↵
1 found
Select objects: ↵
Command:

Keep in mind that using the **Last** option only highlights the last visible item drawn. You must press [Enter] for the object to be erased. If you need to erase more than just the last object, you can use the **ERASE** command and **Last** option repeatedly to erase items in reverse order. This is not as quick, however, as using the **ERASE** command and selecting the objects.

---

### Exercise 3-9

○ Start a new drawing, use one of your templates, or open a previous exercise.
○ Use the **LINE** command to draw a rectangle similar to the object in **Figure 3-31**.
○ Type ERASE at the Command: prompt and erase two of the lines.
○ Draw another rectangle, similar to the previous one.
○ Type ERASE at the Command: prompt and enter L at the Select objects: prompt.
○ Press [Enter] again, type ERASE at the Command: prompt, and enter L to erase one more line.
○ Save the drawing as EX3-9.

---

### Using the Window selection option

The **W** or **Window** option can be used at any Select objects: prompt. This option allows you to draw a box, or "window," around an object or group of objects to select for editing. Everything entirely within the window can be selected at the same time. If portions of entities project outside the window, those entities are not selected. The command sequence looks like this:

> Command: **E** or **ERASE**↵
> Select objects: *(select a point below and to the left of the object(s) to be erased)*

When the Select objects: prompt is shown, select a point clearly below and to the left of the object to be erased. After you select the first point, the screen crosshairs change to a box-shaped cursor. It expands in size as you move the pointing device to the right. The box is a solid line. The next prompt is as follows:

> Specify opposite corner: *(pick the other corner above and to the right of the object(s) to be erased)*
> Select objects: ↵
> Command:

When the Specify opposite corner: prompt is shown, move the pointing device up and to the right so the box totally encloses the object(s) to be erased. Then pick to locate the second corner, as shown in **Figure 3-32.** All objects within the window become highlighted. When finished, press [Enter] or pick the right mouse button to complete the **ERASE** command.

You can also manually specify the **Window** selection option from the command line. You need to do this if the **PICKAUTO** variable (discussed later in this chapter) is set to 0. The command sequence is as follows:

> Command: **E** or **ERASE**↵
> Select objects: **W**↵
> Specify first corner: *(select a point outside of the object)*
> Specify opposite corner: *(pick the opposite corner of the window)*
> Select objects: ↵
> Command:

When you manually enter the **Window** option, you do not need to pick the first point to the left of the object(s) being erased. The "box" remains the **Window** box whether you move the cursor to the left or right.

AutoCAD and its Applications—Basics

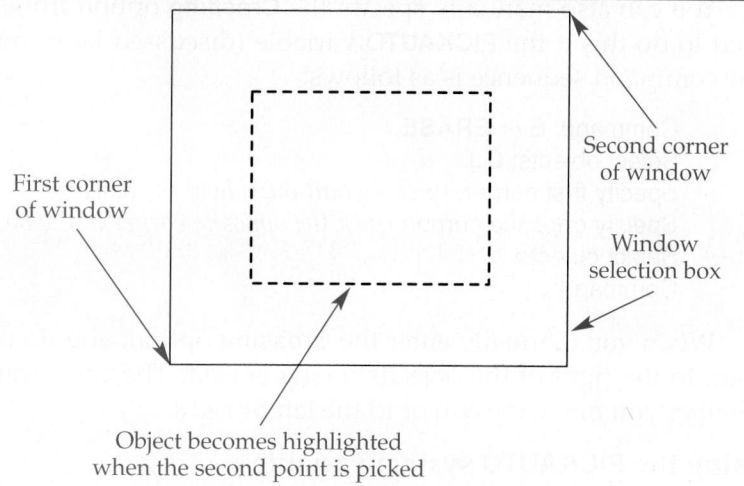

Figure 3-32.
Using the **Window**
selection option
with the **ERASE**
command.

First corner
of window

Second corner
of window

Window
selection box

Object becomes highlighted
when the second point is picked

## Using the Crossing selection option

The **Crossing** selection option is similar to the **Window** option. Entities within the box and those *crossing* the box, however, are selected. The **Crossing** box outline is dotted to distinguish it from the solid outline of the **Window** box. The command sequence for the **Crossing** option is as follows:

Command: **E** *or* **ERASE**↵
Select objects: *(pick a point to the right of the object(s) to be erased)*

When the Select objects: prompt is shown, select a point to the right of the object to be erased. After you select the first point, the screen crosshairs change to a box-shaped cursor. The cursor expands in size as you move the pointing device to the left. The next prompt is as follows:

Specify opposite corner: *(move the cursor to the left so the box encloses or crosses the object(s) to be erased and pick)*
Select objects: ↵
Command:

Remember, the crossing box does not need to enclose the entire object to erase it as the window box does. The crossing box needs only to "cross" part of the object. **Figure 3-33** shows how to erase three of the four lines of a rectangle using the **Crossing** option.

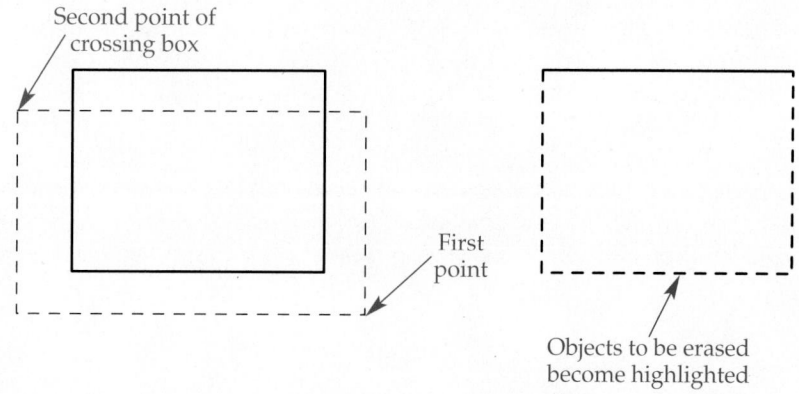

Figure 3-33.
Using the **Crossing**
box to erase objects.

Second point of
crossing box

First
point

Objects to be erased
become highlighted

You can also manually specify the **Crossing** option from the command line. You need to do this if the **PICKAUTO** variable (discussed later in this chapter) is set to 0. The command sequence is as follows:

Command: **E** *or* **ERASE**⏎
Select objects: **C**⏎
Specify first corner: *(pick a point outside of the object)*
Specify opposite corner: *(pick the opposite corner of the box)*
Select objects: ⏎
Command:

When you manually enter the **Crossing** option, you do not need to pick the first point to the right of the object(s) being erased. The "box" remains the **Crossing** box whether you move the cursor to the left or right.

### Using the PICKAUTO system variable

The **PICKAUTO** system variable controls automatic windowing when the Select objects: prompt appears. The **PICKAUTO** settings are ON = 1 (default) and OFF = 0. Change the **PICKAUTO** value by typing PICKAUTO at the Command: prompt and then entering the new value. By default, **PICKAUTO** is set to 1. At this setting, you can automatically use the **Window** or **Crossing** selection process.

With **PICKAUTO** set to 1, pick any left point outside the object, and then move the cursor to the right for a **Window** selection. The **Window** box outline is a solid line. Pick any right point outside the object and move the cursor to the left for a **Crossing** selection. The **Crossing** box is a dashed line.

You can use the automatic **Window** or **Crossing** option even if **PICKAUTO** is 0 (off). To do this, enter W (for window) or C (for crossing) at the Select objects: prompt, and then proceed as previously discussed.

### Using the Box selection option

Another way to begin the **Window** or **Crossing** selection option is to type BOX at the Select objects: prompt. You are then prompted to pick the first corner, which is the bottom left corner of a **Window** box or the right corner of a **Crossing** box. The command sequence is as follows:

Command: **E** *or* **ERASE**⏎
Select objects: **BOX**⏎
Specify first corner: *(pick the bottom left corner of a* **Window** *box or the right corner of a* **Crossing** *box)*
Specify opposite corner: *(pick the opposite corner of the box)*
Select objects: ⏎
Command:

○ Start a new drawing, use one of your templates, or open a previous exercise.
○ Set the **PICKAUTO** system variable to 0 (off).
○ Draw a square, using the **LINE** command with relative coordinates and the **Close** option.
○ Type ERASE at the Command: prompt and use the **Window** selection option. Place the window around the entire square to erase the square.
○ Draw a rectangle using the **LINE** command, Ortho mode, and direct distance entry.
○ Now, erase three of the four lines, using the **Crossing** selection.
○ Set the **PICKAUTO** system variable to 1 (on).
○ Draw a rectangle, using the **LINE** command and Snap mode.
○ Now, enter ERASE and automatically erase the square using a window.
○ Draw a rectangle, using the **LINE** command and absolute coordinates.
○ Enter ERASE and erase three sides of the square, using the automatic **Crossing** selection.
○ Save the drawing as EX3-10.

## Using the WPolygon selection option

The **Window** selection option requires you to place a rectangle completely around the entities to be erased. Sometimes it is awkward to place a rectangle around the items to erase. When this situation occurs, you can place a polygon (closed figure with three or more sides) of your own design around the objects with the **WPolygon** selection option.

To use the **WPolygon** option, type WP at the Select objects: prompt. Then, draw a polygon enclosing the objects. As you pick corners, the polygon drags into place. The command sequence for erasing the five middle squares in **Figure 3-34** is as follows:

```
Command: E or ERASE⏎
Select objects: WP⏎
First polygon point: (pick Point 1)
Specify endpoint of line or [Undo]: (pick Point 2)
Specify endpoint of line or [Undo]: (pick Point 3)
Specify endpoint of line or [Undo]: (pick Point 4)
Specify endpoint of line or [Undo]: ⏎
Select objects: ⏎
Command:
```

**Figure 3-34.**
Using the **WPolygon** selection option to erase objects.

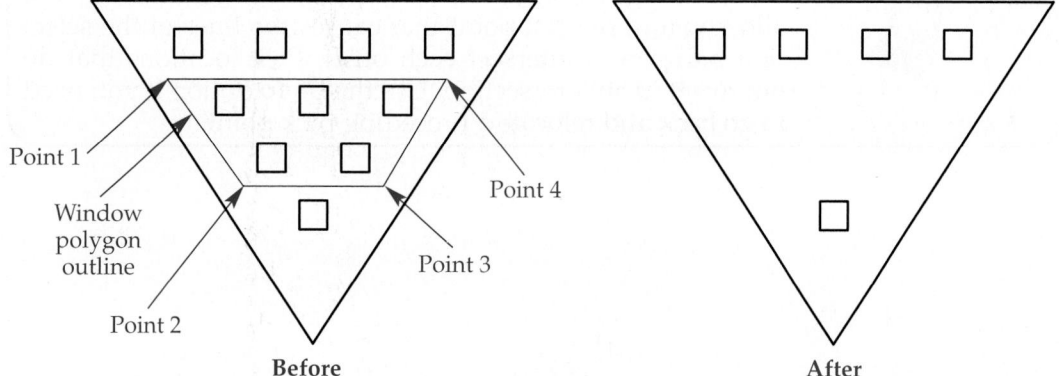

Point 1

Window polygon outline

Point 2

Point 3

Point 4

Before

After

---

If you do not like the last polygon point you picked, use the **Undo** option by entering U at the Specify endpoint of line or [Undo]: prompt.

### Using the **CPolygon** selection option

The **Crossing** selection option lets you place a rectangle around or through the objects to be erased. Sometimes it is difficult to place a rectangle around or through the items to be erased without coming into contact with other entities. When you want to use the features of the **Crossing** selection option, but prefer to use a polygon instead of a rectangle, enter CP at the Select objects: prompt. Then, proceed to draw a polygon enclosing or crossing the objects to erase. As you pick the points, the polygon drags into place. The **CPolygon** line is a dashed rubberband cursor. Suppose you want to erase everything inside the large triangle in **Figure 3-35**, except for the top and bottom horizontal lines. The command sequence to erase these lines is as follows:

Command: **E** *or* **ERASE**↵
Select objects: **CP**↵
First polygon point: *(pick Point 1)*
Specify endpoint of line or [Undo]: *(pick Point 2)*
Specify endpoint of line or [Undo]: *(pick Point 3)*
Specify endpoint of line or [Undo]: *(pick Point 4)*
Specify endpoint of line or [Undo]: ↵
Select objects: ↵
Command:

**Figure 3-35.**
Using the **CPolygon** selection option. Everything enclosed within and crossing the polygon is selected.

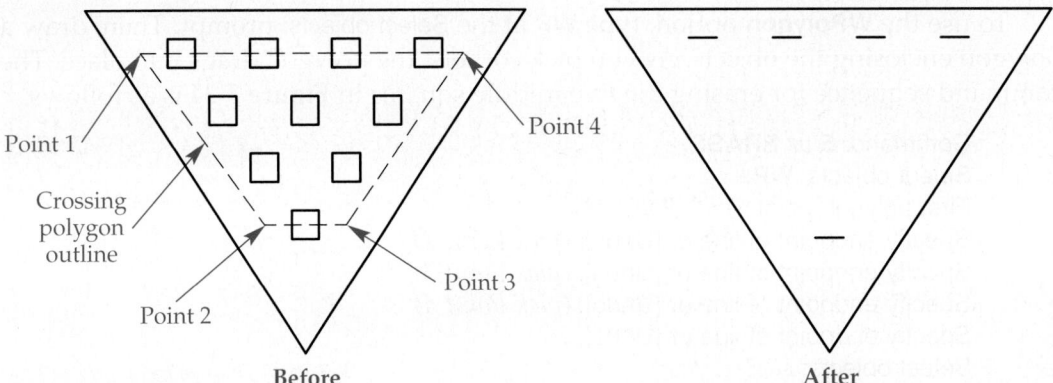

PROFESSIONAL TIP

When using **WPolygon** or **CPolygon**, AutoCAD does not allow you to select a point that causes the lines of the selection polygon to intersect each other. Pick locations that do not result in an intersection. Use the **Undo** option if you need to go back and relocate a preceding pick point.

AutoCAD and its Applications—Basics

## Using the Fence selection option

**Fence** is another selection option used to select several objects at the same time. When using the **Fence** option, you simply need to place a fence through the objects you want to select. Anything the fence passes through is included in the selection set. The fence can be straight or staggered, as shown in **Figure 3-36.** Type F at the Select objects: prompt and continue as follows:

Command: **E** *or* **ERASE**↵
Select objects: **F**↵
First fence point: *(pick Point 1)*
Specify endpoint of line or [Undo]: *(pick Point 2)*
Specify endpoint of line or [Undo]: *(pick Point 3)*
Specify endpoint of line or [Undo]: *(pick Point 4)*
Specify endpoint of line or [Undo]: *(pick Point 5)*
Specify endpoint of line or [Undo]: *(pick Point 6)*
Specify endpoint of line or [Undo]: ↵
Select objects: ↵
Command:

**Figure 3-36.**
Using the **Fence** selection option to erase entities. The fence can be either straight or staggered.

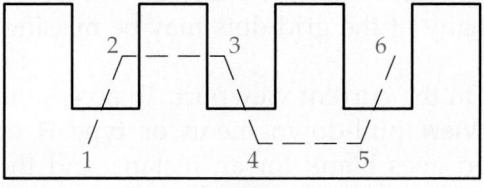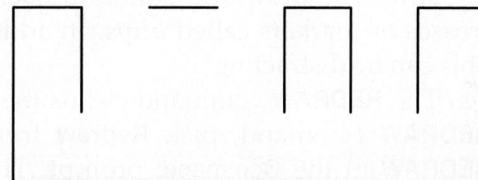

Before                              After

### Exercise 3-11

○ Start a new drawing, use one of your templates, or open a previous exercise.
○ Draw an object similar to the one shown in **Figure 3-34.**
○ Use the **WPolygon** selection option to erase the same items as shown in the figure.
○ Draw an object similar to the one shown in **Figure 3-35.**
○ Use the **CPolygon** selection option to erase the same items as shown in the figure.
○ Draw an object similar to the one shown in **Figure 3-36.**
○ Use the **Fence** selection option to erase the items shown in the figure.
○ Save the drawing as EX3-11.

## Removing from and adding to the selection set

When editing a drawing, a common mistake is to accidentally select an object you do not want to select. The simplest way to remove one or more objects from the current selection set is by holding down the [Shift] key and reselecting the objects. This is possible only for individual picks and implied windows. For an implied window, the [Shift] key must be held down while picking the first corner and then can be released for picking the second corner. If you accidentally remove the wrong object from the selection set, release the [Shift] key and pick it again.

To use other methods for removing objects from a selection set or for specialized selection needs, you can switch to the Remove objects mode by typing R at the Select objects: prompt. This changes the Select objects: prompt to Remove objects:. The command sequence is as follows:

Command: **E** *or* **ERASE**↵
Select objects: *(pick several objects, using any technique)*
Select objects: **R**↵
Remove objects: *(pick the objects you want removed from the selection set)*
Remove objects: ↵

Switch back to the selection mode by typing A (for Add) at the Remove objects: prompt. This restores the Select objects: prompt and allows you to select additional objects. This is how the **Add** feature works:

Remove objects: **A**↵
Select objects: *(continue selecting objects as needed)*
Select objects: ↵
Command:

## Cleaning up the Screen

After you draw and edit a number of objects, the screen is cluttered with small crosses or markers called *blips.* In addition, many of the grid dots may be missing. This can be distracting.

REDRAW
R

View
➥ Redraw

The **REDRAW** command cleans the screen in the current viewport. To access the **REDRAW** command, pick **Redraw** from the **View** pull-down menu or type R or REDRAW at the Command: prompt. The screen goes blank for an instant, and the cleaned drawing and screen return. The **REDRAW** and **REDRAWALL** commands are discussed in Chapter 9.

> **NOTE**
>
> Blips are used as visual aids. The **BLIPMODE** system variable controls whether or not blips are used. Blips are displayed when the **BLIPMODE** setting is 1 and are not displayed when the setting is 0 (default). Change the **BLIPMODE** value by typing BLIPMODE at the Command: prompt and then entering the new value.

## Using the OOPS Command

The **OOPS** command brings back the last object you erased. It is issued by typing OOPS at the Command: prompt. If you erased several objects in the same command sequence, all are brought back to the screen. Only the objects erased in the most recent erase procedure can be returned using **OOPS**.

## Using the U Command

While the **OOPS** command brings back the last object you erased, the **U** command undoes the last command. The **U** command is issued by typing U at the Command: prompt or by using the [Ctrl]+[Z] key combination. **OOPS** can be used only one time in sequence, while **U** can be issued until every command used since the editing session began has been undone. Even **OOPS** can be undone with the **U** command.

## Using the Previous Selection

The object selection options given up to this point in the chapter have used the example of the **ERASE** command. These selection options are also used when moving objects, rotating objects, and performing other editing functions. These basic editing commands are explained in Chapter 11.

Often, more than one sequential editing operation needs to be carried out on a specific group of objects. In this case, the **Previous** selection option allows you to select the same object(s) you just edited for further editing. You can select the **Previous** selection set by typing P at the Select objects: prompt. In the following example, a group of objects is erased, and the **OOPS** command is used to recover them. Then, the **ERASE** command is issued again, this time using the **Previous** selection option to access the previously selected objects:

Command: **E** *or* **ERASE**↵
Select objects: *(pick several items, using any selection technique)*
*n* found, *n* total
Select objects: ↵
Command: **OOPS**↵
Command: **E** *or* **ERASE**↵
Select objects: **P**↵
*n* found
Select objects: ↵
Command:

## Selecting All Objects in a Drawing

Sometimes, you may want to select every object in the drawing. To do this, type ALL at the Select objects: prompt, as follows:

Command: **E** *or* **ERASE**↵
Select objects: **ALL**↵
Select objects: ↵
Command:

This procedure erases everything in the drawing. You can use the **Remove** option at the second Select objects: prompt to remove certain objects from the set. You can also enter ALL after typing R to remove all objects from the set.

---

### Exercise 3-12

○ Start a new drawing, use one of your templates, or open a previous exercise.
○ Draw an object similar to the one shown in **Figure 3-36**.
○ Use the **SI** selection option to erase one line.
○ Use the **SI** selection option with a fence to erase any two lines.
○ Practice using the **Remove** and **Add** selection options by selecting six items to erase, removing two of the items from the selection set, and then adding three new entities.
○ Use the **REDRAW** command to clean up the screen.
○ Use the **ALL** selection option to erase everything from the drawing.
○ Use the **U** or **OOPS** command to get everything you erased back.
○ Save the drawing as EX3-12.

---

| NOTE  | When you are selecting objects to be erased, AutoCAD accepts only qualifying objects. *Qualifying object* refers to an object that is not on a locked layer and that passes through the pick box area at the point selected. Layers are discussed later in this book. |
|---|---|

## Cycling through Stacked Objects

One way to deal with stacked objects is to let AutoCAD cycle through the overlapping objects. *Cycling* is repeatedly selecting one item from a series of stacked objects until the desired object is highlighted. This works best when several objects cross at the same place or are very close together. To begin cycling through objects, hold down the [Ctrl] key while you make your first pick.

For the objects in **Figure 3-37**, pick the point where the four circles intersect. If there are two or more objects found crossing through the pick box area, the top object is highlighted. Now, you can release the [Ctrl] key. When you pick again, the top object returns, and the next one is highlighted. Every time you pick, another object becomes highlighted. In this way, you cycle through all the objects. When you have the desired object highlighted, press [Enter] to end the cycling process and return to the Select objects: prompt. Press [Enter] again to return to the Command: prompt. The following command sequence is used to erase one of the circles in **Figure 3-37**, but you can use this for any editing function:

Command: **E** *or* **ERASE**↵
Select objects: *(hold down the* [Ctrl] *key and pick)* <Cycle on> *(pick until you highlight the desired object and press* [Enter]*)*
<Cycle off>1 found
Select objects: *(select additional objects or press* [Enter]*)*
Command:

Figure 3-37.
Cycling through a series of stacked circles until the desired object is highlighted.

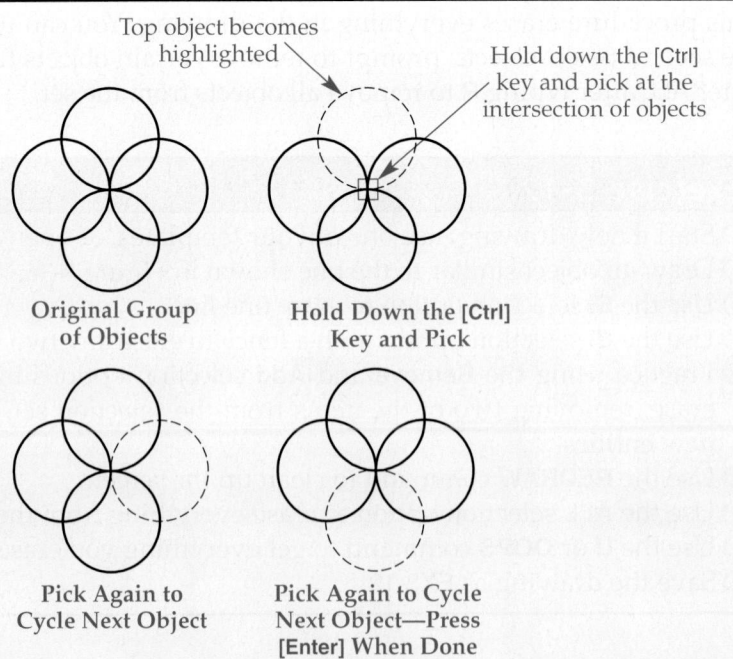

Top object becomes highlighted

Hold down the [Ctrl] key and pick at the intersection of objects

Original Group of Objects

Hold Down the [Ctrl] Key and Pick

Pick Again to Cycle Next Object

Pick Again to Cycle Next Object—Press [Enter] When Done

## Chapter Test

*Answer the following questions on a separate sheet of paper.*

1. How do you set grid spacing of .25?
2. How do you set snap spacing of .125?
3. Name the command used to place a pattern of dots on the screen.
4. Identify the pull-down menu selection that accesses a dialog box used to select drafting settings.
5. How do you activate the snap grid so the screen cursor will automatically move in precise increments?
6. How do you set different horizontal and vertical snap units?
7. Name three ways to access the **Drafting Settings** dialog box.
8. What command opens the **Drawing Units** dialog box?
9. Name three settings that can be specified in the **Drawing Units** dialog box.
10. What is the upper-right corner limit for an architectural drawing using a C-size (22″ × 17″) sheet and a scale of 4′ per inch when plotted, if the lower-left corner is 0,0?
11. Describe a template drawing.
12. Give the keyboard shortcuts for the **DSETTINGS** command.
13. How do you turn the grid on and off at the status bar?
14. What is the result of pressing the [Ctrl]+[B] key combination or the [F9] function key?
15. Give the commands and entries to draw a line from Point A to Point B to Point C and back to Point A. Then, return to the Command: prompt:
    - A. Command: _____
    - B. Specify first point: _____
    - C. Specify next point or [Undo]: _____
    - D. Specify next point or [Undo]: _____
    - E. Specify next point or [Close/Undo]: _____
16. Give the command sequence used to erase a group of objects using the **Windows** selection option and then bring them all back:
    - A. Command: _____
    - B. Select objects: _____
    - C. Specify first corner: _____
    - D. Specify opposite corner: _____
    - E. Select objects: _____
    - F. Command: _____
17. Give the command necessary to refresh the screen.
18. Identify the following linetypes:

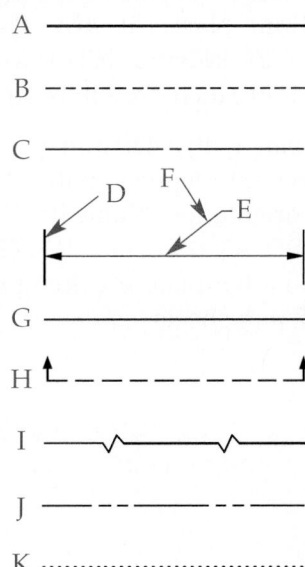

---

19. List two ways to discontinue drawing a line.
20. Name five point entry methods.
21. Identify three ways to turn on the coordinate display.
22. What does the coordinate display 2.750<90 mean?
23. What does the coordinate display 5.250,7.875 mean?
24. List four ways to turn on the Ortho mode.
25. Identify how you can continue drawing another line segment from a previously drawn line.
26. Define *stacked objects*.
27. How do the appearances of a window and a crossing box differ?
28. Name the command used to bring back the last object(s) erased before issuing another command.
29. List at least five ways to select an object to erase.
30. Explain, in general terms, how direct distance entry works.

## Drawing Problems

*The following problems can be saved as templates for future use. For Problems 1–3, use the Quick Setup wizard.*

1. Create a template with an 11″ × 8.5″ area and decimal units. Name it QK A SIZE (H) INCHES.dwt and include QUICK A SIZE (H) INCHES SETUP for its description. You now have a template for doing inch drawings on 11″ × 8.5″ (horizontal) sheets.

2. Create a template with an 8.5″ × 11″ area and decimal units. Name it QK A SIZE (V) INCHES.dwt and include QUICK A SIZE (V) INCHES SETUP for its description. You now have a template for doing inch drawings on 11″ × 8.5″ (vertical) sheets.

3. Create a template with a 594 mm × 420 mm area and decimal units. Name it QK A2 SIZE METRIC.dwt and include QUICK A2 SIZE METRIC SETUP for its description. You now have a template for doing metric (millimeters) drawings on 594 mm × 420 mm sheets.

*For Problems 4–5, use the Advanced Setup wizard.*

4. Create a template with a 17″ × 11″ area, decimal units with 0.000 precision, decimal degrees with 0.0 precision, and default angle measure and orientation. Name it ADV B SIZE INCHES.dwt and include ADVANCED B SIZE INCHES SETUP for its description. You now have a template for doing inch drawings on 17″ × 11″ sheets.

5. Create a template with a 420 mm × 297 mm area, decimal units with 0.0 precision, decimal degrees with 0.0 precision, and default angle measure and orientation. Name it ADV ISO A3 SIZE MM.dwt and include ADVANCED ISO A3 SIZE MILLIMETERS SETUP for its description. You now have a template for doing metric (millimeters) drawings on 420 mm × 297 mm sheets.

*For Problems 6–8, create new templates, using existing templates as models.*

6. Begin a new drawing and select the Ansi c -color dependent plot styles.dwt template. Use the **UNITS** command to set decimal units with 0.000 precision and decimal angles with 0.0 precision. The direction control should be set to the default values. Set the limits to 0,0 and 17,11. Name the drawing TEMP ANSI B.dwt and include ANSI B TEMPLATE SETUP for its description. You now have a template for doing inch drawings on 17″ × 11″ sheets with a border and a title block.

7. Begin a new drawing and select the Iso a3 -color dependent plot styles.dwt template. Use the **UNITS** command to set decimal units with 0.000 precision and decimal angles with 0.0 precision. The direction control should be set to the default values. Set the limits to 0,0 and 420,297. Name the drawing TEMP ISO A3.dwt and include ISO A3 TEMPLATE SETUP for its description. You now have a template for doing metric (millimeters) drawings on 420 mm × 297 mm sheets with a border and a title block.

8. Begin a new drawing and select the Architectural, english units -color dependent plot styles.dwt template. Use the **UNITS** command to set architectural units with 1/16″ precision and degrees/minutes/seconds angles with 0d00′00″ precision. The direction control should be set to the default values. Set the limits to 0,0 and 22,17. Name the drawing TEMP ARCH.dwt and include ARCHITECTURAL TEMPLATE SETUP for its description. You now have a template for doing architectural drawings on 22″ × 17″ sheets with a border and a title block.

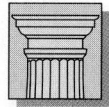

*For Problems 9 and 10, create templates from scratch.*

9. Begin a new drawing and select the **Start from Scratch** option. Select 0.00 as decimal units, 0.00 as decimal degrees, and 90° (North) for direction of the 0° angle. Make angles measure counterclockwise. Set the limits to 0,0 and 17,11. Save as a drawing template named SFS B SIZE INCHES and include START FROM SCRATCH B SIZE INCHES SETUP for its description. You now have a template for doing inch drawings on 17″ × 11″ sheets.

10. Begin a new drawing and select the **Start from Scratch** option. Select 0.00 as decimal units, 0.00 as decimal degrees, and 0° (East) for direction of the 0° angle. Make angles measure counterclockwise. Set the limits to 0,0 and 420,297. Save as a drawing template named SFS A3 SIZE METRIC and include START FROM SCRATCH A3 METRIC SETUP for its description. You now have a template for doing metric (millimeters) drawings on 420 mm × 297 mm sheets.

11. Open one of your templates from a previous problem or Exercise 3-2. Draw the specified objects as accurately as possible with grid and snap turned off. Use the **LINE** command and draw the following objects only on the left side of the screen:
    - Right triangle
    - Isosceles triangle
    - Rectangle
    - Square
    Save the drawing as P3-11.

12. Draw the same objects specified in Problem 11 on the right side of the screen. This time, make sure the snap grid is turned on. Observe the difference between having snap on in this problem and off in the previous problem. Save the drawing as P3-12.

13. Draw an object by connecting the following point coordinates. Save your drawing as P3-13. Make a print of your drawing if a printer is available.

| Point | Coordinates | Point | Coordinates |
|-------|-------------|-------|-------------|
| 1 | 2,2 | 8 | @-1.5,0 |
| 2 | @1.5,0 | 9 | @0,1.25 |
| 3 | @.75<90 | 10 | @-1.25,1.25 |
| 4 | @1.5<0 | 11 | @2<180 |
| 5 | @0,-.75 | 12 | @-1.25,-1.25 |
| 6 | @3,0 | 13 | @2.25<270 |
| 7 | @1<90 | | |

14. With the absolute, relative, and polar coordinate entry methods, draw the following shapes. Set the limits to 0,0 and 22,17; units to decimal; grid spacing to .5; and snap spacing to .0625. Draw Object A three times, using a different point entry system each time. Draw Object B once, using at least two methods of coordinate entry. Do not draw dimensions. Save your drawing as P3-14. Make a print of your drawing if a printer is available.

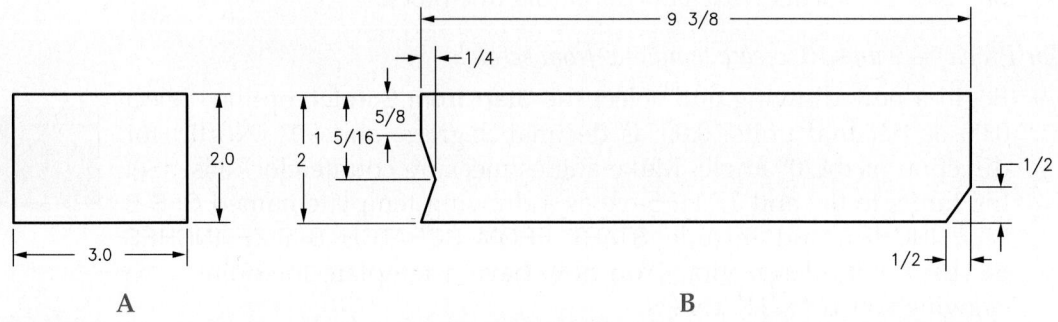

A

B

15. Draw the front elevation of this house. Create the dimensions proportional to the given drawings. Save the drawing as P3-15.

**CHAPTER 4**

# Using Layers, Modifying Object Properties, and Making Prints

## Learning Objectives

After completing this chapter, you will be able to do the following:
- Draw objects on separate layers.
- Create and manage drawing layers.
- Draw objects with different colors, linetypes, and lineweights.
- Filter the list of layers.
- Use the **Properties** window to change layers, colors, linetypes, and lineweights.
- Use **DesignCenter** to copy layers and linetypes between drawings.
- Learn the Express Tool commands to control layer behavior.
- Make prints of your drawings.

Chapter 3 introduced you to drawing and editing in AutoCAD. In addition to lines, many other types of objects are created in the course of producing most drawings. Many of these objects will be introduced in Chapter 5.

Regardless of the type of object drawn, all AutoCAD objects have properties. Some object properties—such as color and linetype—are common to many types of objects. Other properties—such as text height—are specific to a single object type. AutoCAD uses a layer system to simplify the process of assigning and modifying object properties. In addition, when using layer display options, you can create several different drawing sheets, views, and displays from a single drawing.

This chapter introduces the AutoCAD layer system and basic object properties. It also provides a brief introduction to printing and plotting. Printing and plotting will be covered in greater detail in Chapter 10.

## Introduction to Layers

In drafting, different elements or components of drawings might be separated by placing them on different sheets. When each sheet is perfectly aligned with the others, you have what is called an *overlay system.* In AutoCAD, the components of this overlay system are referred to as **layers.** All the layers can be reproduced together to reflect the entire design drawing. Individual layers might also be reproduced to show specific details or components of the design. Using layers increases productivity in several ways:

- ✓ Specific information can be grouped on separate layers. For example, the floor plan can be drawn on one layer, the electrical plan on another, and the plumbing plan on a third.
- ✓ Several plot sheets can be referenced from the same drawing file by modifying layer visibility.
- ✓ Drawings can be reproduced in individual layers, or the layers can be combined in any desired format. For example, the floor plan and electrical plan can be reproduced together and sent to an electrical contractor for a bid. The floor plan and plumbing plan can be reproduced together and sent to a plumbing contractor.
- ✓ Each layer can be assigned a different color, linetype, and lineweight to help improve clarity.
- ✓ Each layer can be plotted in a different color or pen width, or it can be not plotted at all.
- ✓ Selected layers can be turned off or frozen to decrease the amount of information displayed on the screen or to speed screen regeneration.
- ✓ Changes can be made to a layer promptly, often while the client watches.

## Layers Used in Different Drafting Fields

In mechanical drafting, views, hidden features, dimensions, sections, notes, and symbols might each be placed on separate layers. In architectural or civil drafting, there may be over one hundred layers. Layers can be created for floor plans, foundation plans, partition layouts, plumbing systems, electrical systems, structural systems, roof drainage systems, reflected ceiling systems, and HVAC systems. Interior designers may use floor plan, interior partition, and furniture layers. In electronics drafting, each level of a multilevel circuit board can be drawn on its own layer.

## Current Layer

As you have worked through the exercises in this book, you may have noticed that "0" appears in the **Layer Control** drop-down list on the **Layers** toolbar. See **Figure 4-1.** Layer 0 is the AutoCAD default current layer. Until another layer is defined and set current, all objects drawn are placed on and belong to Layer 0.

**PROFESSIONAL TIP**

Although Layer 0 is often the current layer when a new drawing is started, it is advisable to draw on layers you create other than Layer 0. Layer 0 is typically reserved for the creation of block symbols, which is discussed later in this text.

Figure 4-1.
0 appears in the **Layer Control** drop-down list on the **Layers** toolbar. Layer 0 is the AutoCAD default layer.

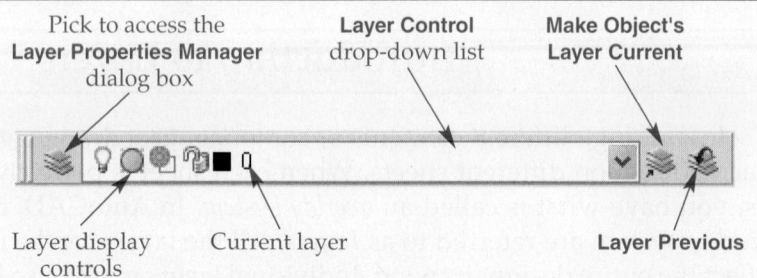

Pick to access the **Layer Properties Manager** dialog box

**Layer Control** drop-down list

**Make Object's Layer Current**

Layer display controls

Current layer

**Layer Previous**

## Naming Layers

Layers should be given names to reflect what is drawn on them. Layer names can have up to 255 characters and can include letters, numbers, and certain special characters, including spaces. Typical mechanical, architectural, and civil drafting layer names are as follows:

| Mechanical | Architectural | Civil |
|---|---|---|
| Object | Walls | Property Line |
| Hidden | Windows | Structures |
| Center | Doors | Roads |
| Dimension | Electrical | Water |
| Construction | Plumbing | Contours |
| Hatch | Furniture | Gas |
| Border | Lighting | Elevations |

For very simple drawings, layers can be named by linetype and color. For example, the layer name Continuous-White may have a continuous linetype drawn in white. The layer usage and color number, such as Object-7, can also be used to indicate an object line with color 7. Another option is to assign the linetype a numerical value. For example, object lines can be 1, hidden lines can be 2, and centerlines can be 3. If you use this method, keep a written record of your numbering system for reference.

Layers can also be given more complex names. The name might include the drawing number, color code, and layer content. The layer name Dwg100-2-Dimen, for example, could refer to drawing DWG100, color 2, and the fact that this layer is used for dimensions.

## The Layer Properties Manager

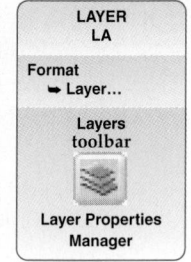

The **LAYER** command opens the **Layer Properties Manager** dialog box, shown in Figure 4-2. To display this dialog box, pick the **Layer Properties Manager** button from the **Layers** toolbar, select **Layer...** from the **Format** pull-down menu, or type LA or LAYER at the Command: prompt. Only one layer is required in an AutoCAD drawing. This layer is named 0 and cannot be renamed or purged from the drawing. As discussed earlier, however, it is often useful to have more than one layer in a drawing. The most important layer is the *current* layer because whatever you draw is placed on this layer. It is useful to think of the current layer as the *top* layer.

## Creating Layers

Layers should be added to a drawing to meet the needs of the current drawing project. To add a new layer, pick the **New** button from the **Layer Properties Manager** dialog box. A new layer listing appears, using a default name of Layer1. See Figure 4-3. The layer name is highlighted when the listing appears, allowing you to type in a new name.

**Figure 4-2.**
The **Layer Properties Manager** dialog box.

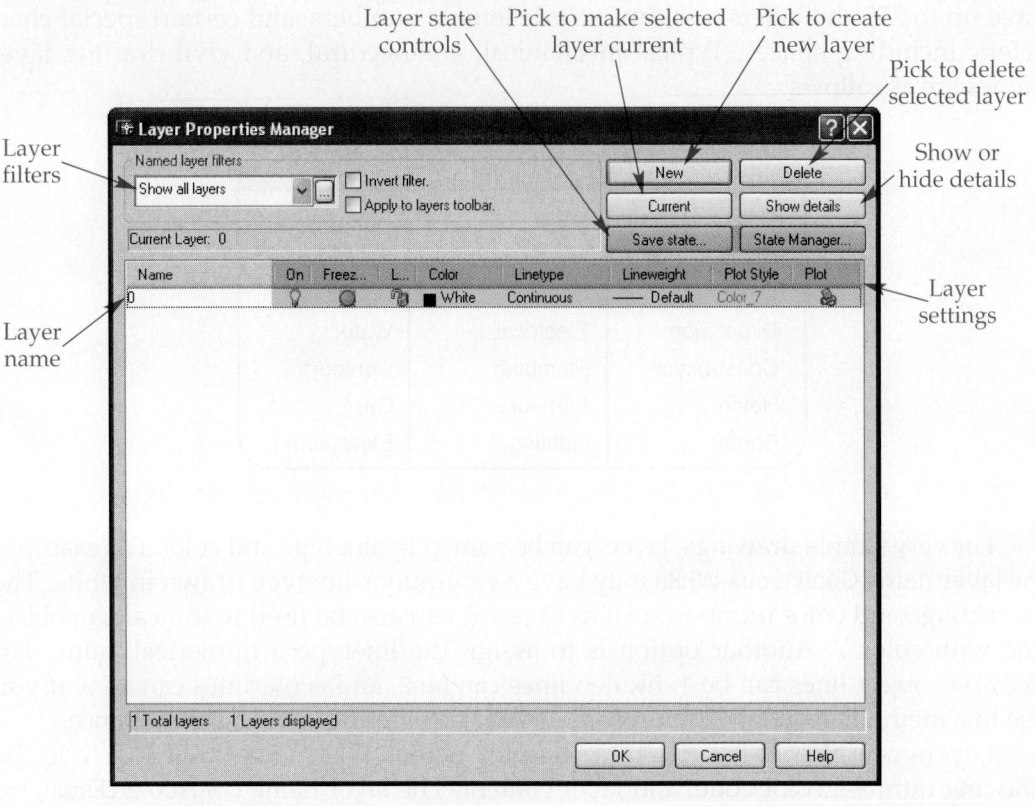

Layer state controls — Pick to make selected layer current — Pick to create new layer — Pick to delete selected layer — Layer filters — Show or hide details — Layer name — Layer settings

**Figure 4-3.**
A new layer is named Layer1 by default.

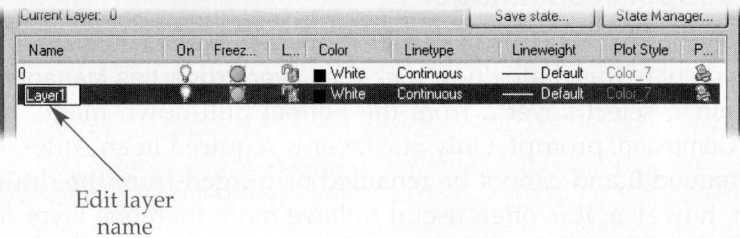

Edit layer name

You can also enter several new layer names at the same time. This is done by typing a layer name and then pressing the comma key. This drops the Layer1 listing below the previously entered name. Entering several layer names in this manner saves time because it keeps you from having to pick the **New** button each time. Pick the **OK** button when you are finished typing the new layer names. When you reopen the **Layer Properties Manager** dialog box, the new layer names are alphabetized, as shown in **Figure 4-4.**

> **NOTE**
> Sorting can be controlled by selecting the headings in the layer names window. Each time the **Layer Properties Manager** dialog box is reopened, however, the layers are sorted alphanumerically by default.

Figure 4-4.
Layer names are
automatically
placed in numerical
and alphabetical
order.

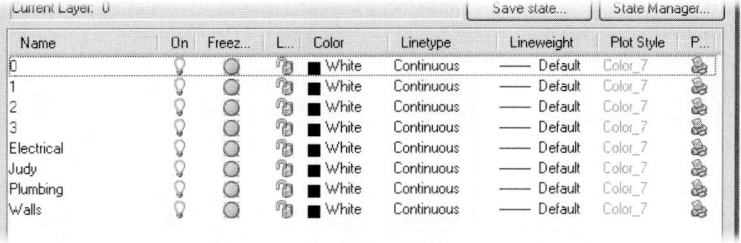

The **MAXSORT** system variable controls the sorting of layers. The default **MAXSORT** value is 1000. As long as the number of layers is less than the **MAXSORT** value, the layers are sorted numerically and alphabetically. If there are more layers than the **MAXSORT** value, the layers are sorted in the order in which they were created. The **MAXSORT** system variable also controls the sorting of symbol names and block names.

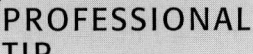

**PROFESSIONAL TIP**  If you need to exit the **Layer Properties Manager** dialog box after creating layers, pick the **OK** button to accept the creation of the new layers. Picking the **Close** button (**X**) causes the dialog box to be closed without saving the list of layers you created.

## Deleting Layers

Deleting a layer no longer in use is a simple process. First, select the layer, and then pick the **Delete** button. The layer is erased from the list box. If the selected layer is not deleted, an object in the drawing has been drawn on this layer.

## Setting the Current Layer

You can set a new current layer by double-clicking the layer name or highlighting the layer name in the layer list and then picking the **Current** button. To highlight the layer name, simply pick on top of the name. The current layer is specified in the status line above the layer list in the **Layer Properties Manager** dialog box and in the **Layer Control** drop-down list in the **Layers** toolbar.

### Exercise 4-1

◯ Start a new drawing or open one of your templates.
◯ Open the **Layer Properties Manager** dialog box.
◯ Start a list of layer names similar to those in **Figure 4-4**, but in a different order, or use other names of your own choosing. Enter a couple of the names by picking the **New** button after each entry.
◯ Continue the list of new layer names by pressing the comma key after each name to enter several names.
◯ Pick the **OK** button when you are done.
◯ Open the **Layer Properties Manager** dialog box again and see how AutoCAD automatically lists the layer names in alphanumeric order.
◯ Close the dialog box.
◯ Save as EX4-1.

**Figure 4-5.**
Layer settings can be changed by picking the icons in the **Layer Properties Manager** dialog box.

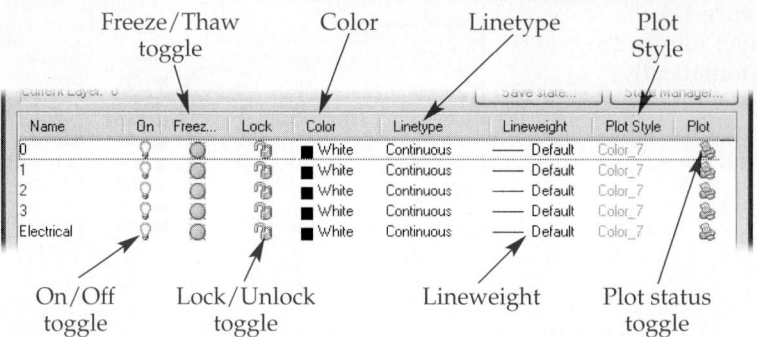

## Viewing the Status of Layers

The status of each layer is displayed in the **Layer Properties Manager** with icons to the right of the layer name. See **Figure 4-5.** If you position the pointer over an icon for a moment, a tooltip appears and tells what the icon refers to. Layer settings can be changed by picking the related icons.

- **Changing the layer name.** The layer name list box contains all the layers in the drawing. To change an existing name, pick the name once to highlight it, pause for a moment, and then pick it again. When you pick the second time, the layer name is highlighted with a text box around it and a cursor for text entry, allowing you to type a new layer name. Layer 0 cannot be renamed.

- **Turning layers on and off.** The lightbulb shows whether a layer is on or off. The yellow lightbulb means the layer is on; objects on that layer are displayed on-screen and can be plotted. If you pick on a yellow lightbulb, it turns gray, turning the layer off. If a layer is off, the objects on it are not displayed on-screen and are not plotted. Objects on a layer that has been turned off can still be edited when using advanced selection techniques and are regenerated when a drawing regeneration occurs.

On    Off

- **Thawing and freezing layers.** Layers are further classified as thawed or frozen. Similar to turned off layers, frozen layers are not displayed and do not plot. Objects on a frozen layer, however, cannot be edited and are not regenerated when the drawing regenerates. Freezing layers containing objects that do not need to be referenced for current drawing tasks can greatly speed up your system performance. The snowflake icon is displayed when a layer is frozen. Layers are normally thawed, which means objects on the layer are displayed on-screen. The sun icon is displayed for thawed layers. Picking the sun/snowflake icon toggles it to the other icon.

Thawed  Frozen

NOTE    It is important to note that objects on frozen layers cannot be modified, but objects residing on turned off layers can be modified. For example, if you turn off half your layers and use the **All** selection option with the **ERASE** command, even the objects on the turned off layers will be erased! The **ERASE** command does not, however, affect frozen layers.

Locked Unlocked

- **Unlocked and locked layers.** The unlocked and locked padlock symbols are for locking and unlocking layers. Layers are unlocked by default, but you can pick on the unlocked padlock to lock it. A locked layer remains visible, but objects on it cannot be edited. New objects can be added to a locked layer.

- **Layer color.** The color swatch shows the current default color for objects created on each layer. When you need to change the color for an existing layer, pick the swatch to display the **Select Color** dialog box. Working with colors is discussed later in this chapter.
- **Layer linetype.** The current linetype setting for each layer is shown in the **Linetype** list. Picking the linetype name opens the **Select Linetype** dialog box, where you can specify a new linetype. Working with linetypes is discussed later in this chapter.
- **Layer lineweight.** The current lineweight setting for each layer is shown in the **Lineweight** list. Picking the lineweight name opens the **Lineweight** dialog box, where you can specify a new lineweight. Working with lineweights is discussed later in this chapter.
- **Layer plot styles.** This setting changes the plot style associated with the selected layers. The plot style setting is disabled when you are working with color-dependent plot styles (the **PSTYLEPOLICY** system variable is set to 1). Otherwise, picking the plot style displays the **Select Plot Style** dialog box. Plot styles are discussed in Chapter 10.
- **Layer plot/no plot.** Select this toggle to turn off plotting for a particular layer. The "no plot" symbol is displayed over the printer image when the layer is not available to be plotted. The layer is still displayed, but not plotted.

Plot    No Plot

The following layer options appear only in paper space layout mode, which is discussed in Chapter 10:
- **Thawing and freezing layers in active and new viewports.** These settings, for floating model space views on layouts, are detailed in Chapter 23. The options are visible only when a layout tab is active.

## Exercise 4-2

○ Open EX4-1.
○ Open the **Layer Properties Manager** dialog box.
○ Use one of the layers you created in Exercise 4-1. Select the **?** button and pick each item in the dialog box. Read the help tip that appears.
○ Pick each icon to see it change settings or give you an AutoCAD message. Change each back to the original setting.
○ Pick the color swatch to open the **Select Color** dialog box. Look at the dialog box, and then pick **Cancel** to exit it.
○ Pick a linetype name to open the **Select Linetype** dialog box. Pick the **Cancel** button to exit the dialog box.
○ Pick a lineweight name to open the **Lineweight** dialog box. Pick the **Cancel** button to exit the dialog box.
○ Save your work. Exit AutoCAD or keep this drawing open for the next exercise.

## Working with Layers

Any setting you change affects all currently highlighted layer names. Highlighting layer names employs the same techniques used in file dialog boxes. You can highlight a single name by picking it. Picking another name deselects the previous name and highlights the new selection. You can use the [Shift] key to select two layers and all layer names between them on the listing. Holding the [Ctrl] key while picking layer names highlights or deselects each selected name without affecting any other selections.

**Figure 4-6.**
Right-clicking in the
list box of the **Layer
Properties Manager**
dialog box produces
this shortcut menu.
If a single layer is
selected, a **Make
Current** option is
also available.

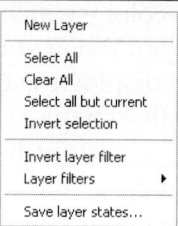

| New Layer |
| Select All |
| Clear All |
| Select all but current |
| Invert selection |
| Invert layer filter |
| Layer filters ▸ |
| Save layer states... |

A shortcut menu is also available while your cursor is in the layer list area of this dialog box. Press the right mouse button to display the shortcut menu shown in **Figure 4-6.** The options available on this menu are as follows:

- **New Layer.** Creates a new layer.
- **Select All.** Selects all layers.
- **Clear All.** Deselects all layers.
- **Select all but current.** Selects all layers, except the current layer.
- **Invert selection.** Deselects all selected layers and selects all deselected layers.
- **Invert layer filter.** Inverts the current filter setting. Filters are discussed later in this chapter.
- **Layer filters.** Displays a submenu with predefined filters. The choices are the following:
  - **Show all layers.**
  - **Show all used layers.**
  - **Show all Xref dependent layers.**
- **Save layer states**. Opens the **Save Layer States** dialog box, which is discussed later in this chapter.

### Exercise 4-3

○ Open EX4-1 if it is not already open.
○ Open the **Layer Properties Manager** dialog box.
○ Pick layer names to highlight each individually.
○ Use the [Shift] key to pick a group of consecutive layer names.
○ Use the [Ctrl] key to pick a group of nonsequential layer names.
○ Move the cursor inside the layer list area and pick the right mouse button. Try out the options in the shortcut menu.
○ Save your work. Exit AutoCAD or keep this drawing open for the next exercise.

## Setting the Layer Color

The number of layer colors available depends on your graphics card and monitor. Color systems usually support at least 256 colors, while many graphics cards support up to 16.7 million colors. Color settings can affect the appearance of plotted drawings. Lineweights can also be associated with drawing colors. This is discussed in Chapter 10. Colors should highlight the important features on the drawing and not cause eyestrain. AutoCAD allows you to assign colors to layers by selecting a color from the **Select Color** dialog box.

In order to assign a color to a layer, first highlight a layer name in the **Layer Properties Manager,** and then pick the color swatch associated with the layer name. AutoCAD then displays the **Select Color** dialog box. See **Figure 4-7.** This dialog box includes three different color tabs from which a color can be selected for use in your

Figure 4-7.
The **Select Color**
dialog box.

Index Color tab
255 colors

True Color tab
24 bit color

Color Books tab
Pantone colors

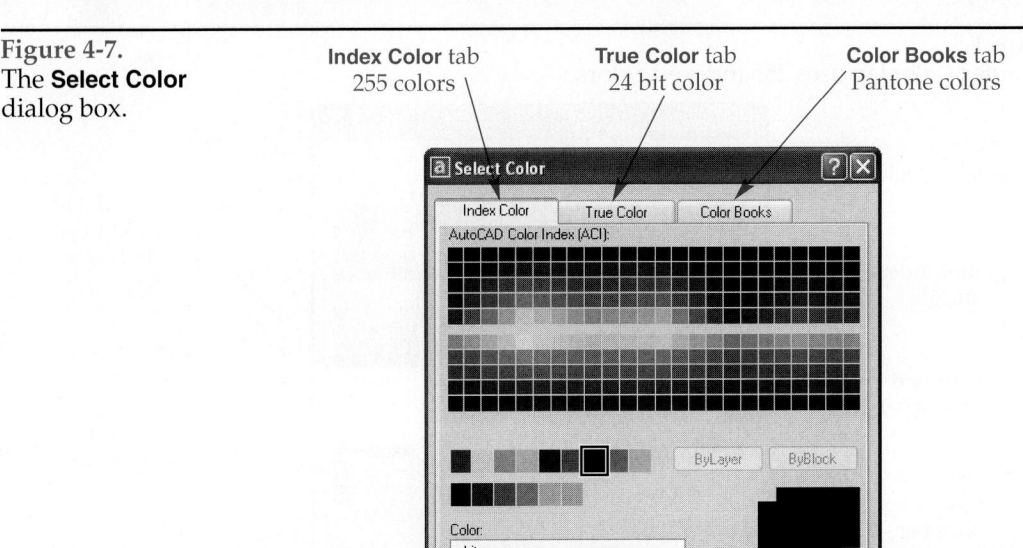

highlighted layer. These tabs are the **Index Color** tab, the **True Color** tab, and the **Color Books** tab. Each of these tabs includes different methods of obtaining colors for assignment to a layer. The tabs are described in the following sections.

### Index Color tab

This tab includes 255 color swatches from which you can choose a color. See **Figure 4-8**. This tab is commonly referred to as the **AutoCAD Color Index (ACI)**, as layer colors are coded by name and number. The first seven colors in the **ACI** include both a numerical index number and a name:

| Number | Color |
|--------|---------|
| 1 | Red |
| 2 | Yellow |
| 3 | Green |
| 4 | Cyan |
| 5 | Blue |
| 6 | Magenta |
| 7 | White |

To select a color, you can either pick the color swatch displaying the desired color or type the color name or number in the **Color:** text box. The first seven basic colors are listed in the table above. The color white (number 7) refers to white if the graphics screen background is black, and black if the background is white. All other colors can be accessed by their ACI numbers.

As you move the cursor around the color swatches, the **Index color:** note updates to show you the number of the color the cursor is hovering over. Beside the **Index color:** note is the **Red, Green, Blue:** (RGB) note. This indicates the RGB numbers used to mix the highlighted color. Once you pick a color, it is entered into the **Color:** text box. On the lower right of the dialog box is a preview of the newly selected color and a sample of the previously assigned color. Two additional buttons are also included: **ByLayer** and **ByBlock**. These are special colors assigned to geometry in the drawing, but they cannot be assigned to a layer name. These are discussed later in this text.

**Figure 4-8.**
The **Index Color** tab uses 255 indexed colors.

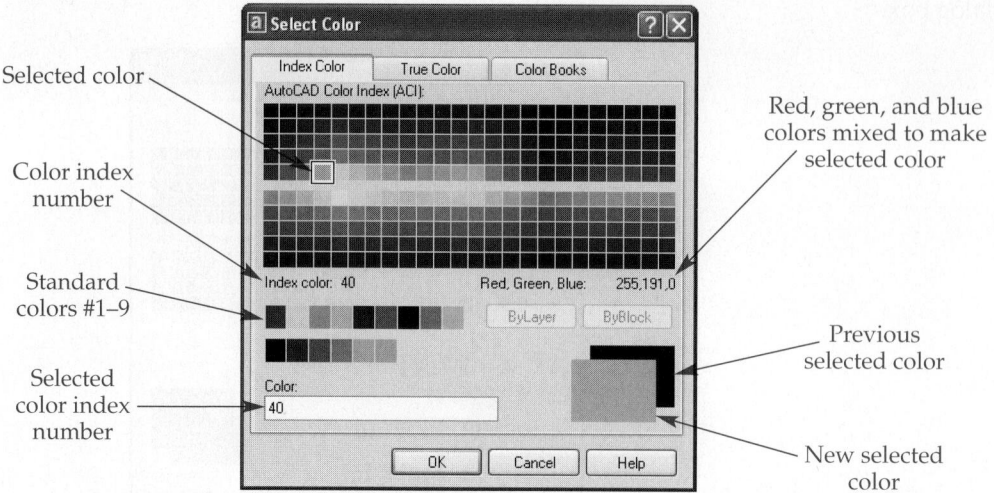

Selected color

Color index number

Standard colors #1–9

Selected color index number

Red, green, and blue colors mixed to make selected color

Previous selected color

New selected color

An easy way to investigate the ACI numbering system is to pick a color swatch and see what number appears in the **Color:** text box. After selecting a color, pick the **OK** button when you are ready. The color you picked is now displayed as the color swatch for the highlighted layer name in the **Layer Properties Manager** dialog box.

### True Color tab

The **True Color** tab allows you to specify a true color (24 bit color) using either Hue, Saturation, and Luminance (HSL) or Red, Green, and Blue (RGB) color models. **Figure 4-9A** shows the **True Color** tab with the HSL color model selected. The **True Color** tab is shown in **Figure 4-9B** with the RGB color model selected.

The HSL color model includes three text boxes allowing you to control the properties of the color. The hue represents a specific wavelength of light within the visible spectrum. Valid hue values range from 0–360 degrees. The saturation refers to the purity of the color. Valid saturation values range from 0–100 percent. Finally, the luminance specifies the brightness of the color. Valid luminance values range from 0–100 percent, where 0 percent represents black, 100 percent represents white, and 50 percent represents the optimal brightness of the color. Instead of adjusting the HSL colors through the text boxes, you can move the cursors in the spectrum preview screen and luminance slider bar and pick the approximate color you want. The true color specified is then translated to RGB values, which are displayed in the **Color:** text box.

The RGB color model includes three text boxes and three slider bars. Adjusting the values in the **Red:**, **Green:**, and **Blue:** text boxes causes the slider bars to be adjusted, with the mixed color displayed in the new color preview. The cursor can also be used to slide the marker along each bar to mix the colors.

### Color Books tab

The **Color Books** tab allows you to use third party color books, such as Pantone color books, to specify a color. See **Figure 4-10**. The **Color Book:** drop-down list includes several different color books, including several Pantone and RAL books. Once a book has been selected, the available colors within the book are displayed. (RAL colors, which were developed in Germany, are used internationally.) You can pick an area on the color slider or use the up and down keys to browse through the book. To select a color, use your pick button to pick on top of one of the color book swatches. As a color is selected, the equivalent RGB values are displayed on the right side of the dialog box, and the color is updated in the new color preview.

**Figure 4-9.**
The **True Color** tab uses 24 bit color. A—HSL color model. B—RGB color model.

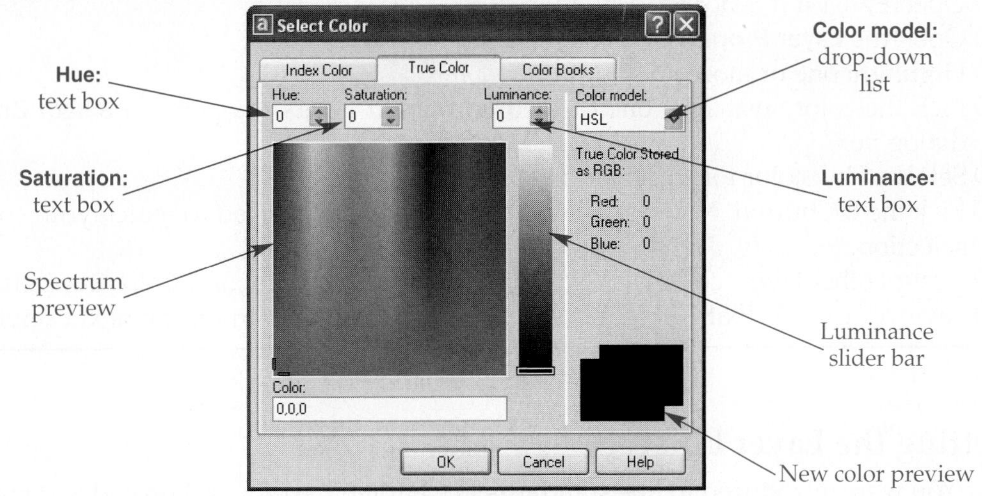

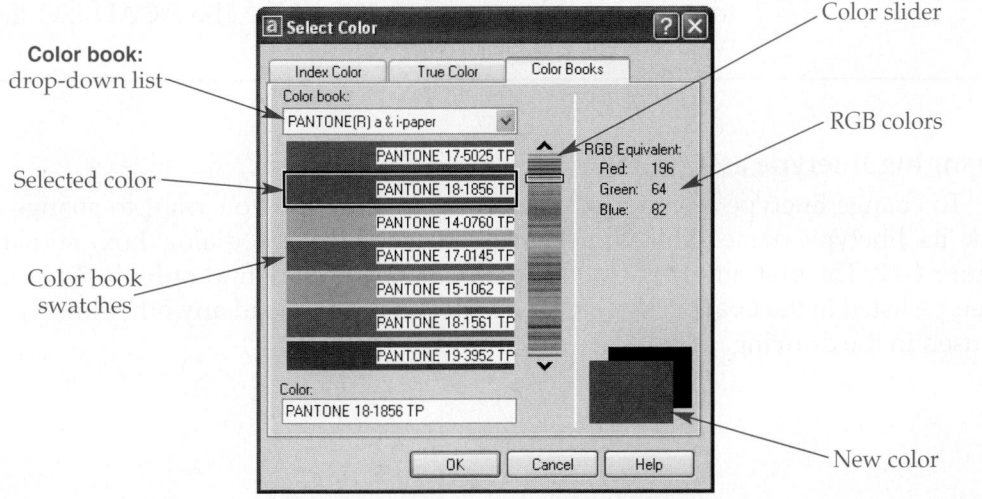

Hue:
text box

Saturation:
text box

Spectrum
preview

Color model:
drop-down
list

Luminance:
text box

Luminance
slider bar

New color preview

**HSL Color Model**
**A**

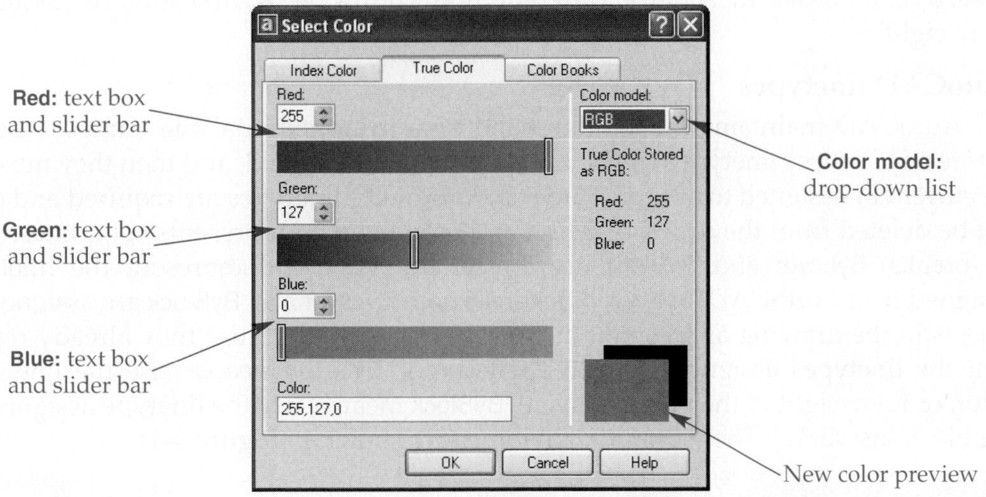

Red: text box
and slider bar

Green: text box
and slider bar

Blue: text box
and slider bar

Color model:
drop-down list

New color preview

**RGB Color Model**
**B**

**Figure 4-10.**
The **Color Books** tab uses Pantone and RAL colors.

Color book:
drop-down list

Selected color

Color book
swatches

Color slider

RGB colors

New color

## Setting the Layer Linetype

You were introduced to line standards in Chapter 3. AutoCAD provides standard linetypes that can be used at any time to match the ASME standards or the standards for other drafting applications you are using. You can also create your own custom linetypes. In order to achieve different line widths, it is necessary to assign a lineweight.

### AutoCAD linetypes

AutoCAD maintains its standard linetypes in an external file named acad.lin. Before any of these linetypes can be used, they must be loaded, and then they must be set current or assigned to a layer. Three of AutoCAD's linetypes are required and cannot be deleted from the drawing. The Continuous linetype represents solid lines with no breaks. ByLayer and ByBlock are logical linetypes and represent the linetype assigned to an AutoCAD layer or block insertion. ByLayer and ByBlock are assigned to objects in the drawing and cannot be assigned to layers because they already represent the linetypes assigned to individual layers. ByLayer means "use the linetype, color, or lineweight of the object's layer." ByBlock means "use the linetype assigned to the block insertion." The AutoCAD linetypes are shown in **Figure 4-11.**

**PROFESSIONAL TIP**

Two linetype definition files are available, acad.lin and acadiso.lin. The ACAD ISO linetypes found in both files are identical, but the non-ISO linetype definitions are scaled up 25.4 times in the acadiso.lin file. The scale factor of 25.4 is used to convert from inches to millimeters. The ACAD ISO linetypes are for metric drawings.

### Changing linetype assignments

To change linetype assignments, select the layer name you want to change and pick its linetype name. This displays the **Select Linetype** dialog box, shown in **Figure 4-12.** The first time you use this dialog box, you may find only the Continuous linetype listed in the **Loaded linetypes** list box. You need to load any other linetypes to be used in the drawing.

**Figure 4-11.**
The AutoCAD linetype library contains ACAD ISO, standard, and complex linetypes.

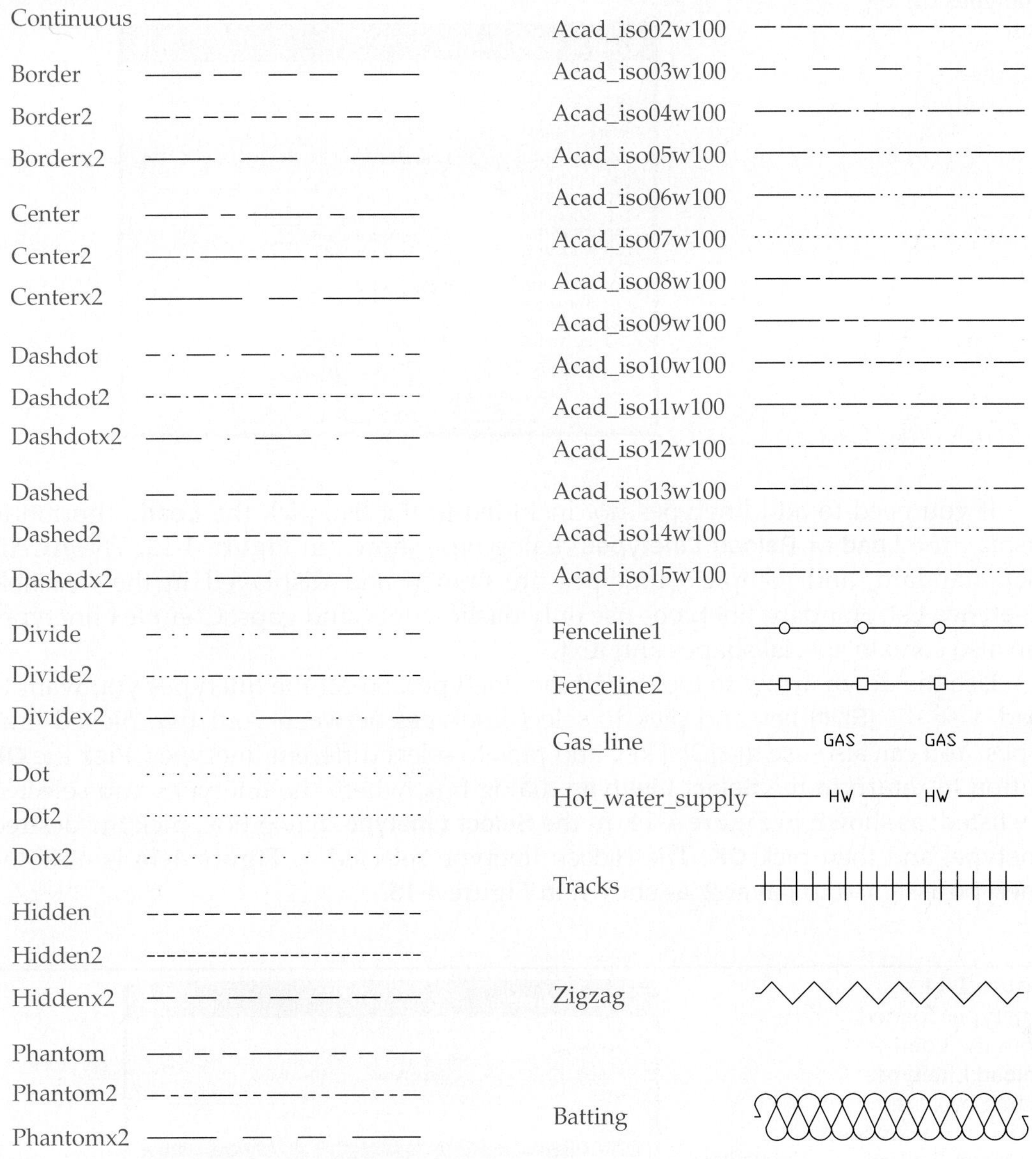

Continuous
Border
Border2
Borderx2
Center
Center2
Centerx2
Dashdot
Dashdot2
Dashdotx2
Dashed
Dashed2
Dashedx2
Divide
Divide2
Dividex2
Dot
Dot2
Dotx2
Hidden
Hidden2
Hiddenx2
Phantom
Phantom2
Phantomx2
Acad_iso02w100
Acad_iso03w100
Acad_iso04w100
Acad_iso05w100
Acad_iso06w100
Acad_iso07w100
Acad_iso08w100
Acad_iso09w100
Acad_iso10w100
Acad_iso11w100
Acad_iso12w100
Acad_iso13w100
Acad_iso14w100
Acad_iso15w100
Fenceline1
Fenceline2
Gas_line
GAS
GAS
Hot_water_supply
HW
HW
Tracks
Zigzag
Batting

**Figure 4-12.**
The **Select Linetype** dialog box.

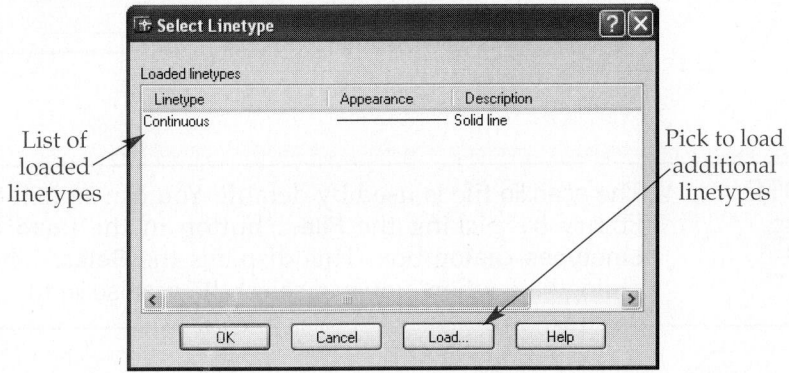

Select Linetype
Loaded linetypes
Linetype
Appearance
Description
Continuous
Solid line
OK
Cancel
Load...
Help
List of loaded linetypes
Pick to load additional linetypes

**Figure 4-13.**
The **Load or Reload Linetypes** dialog box.

Select file where linetype definitions are stored

Select linetypes to load into drawing

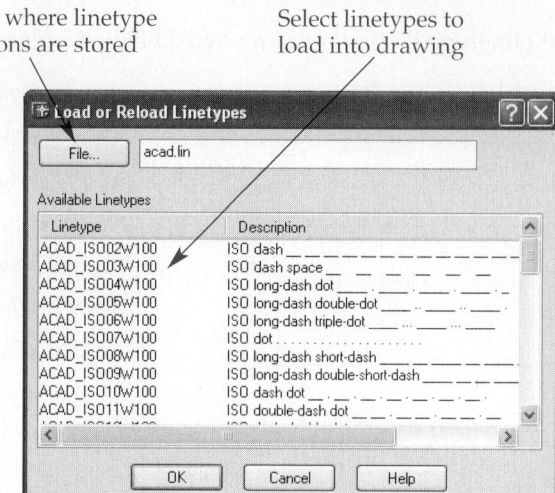

If you need to add linetypes not included in the list, pick the **Load...** button to display the **Load or Reload Linetypes** dialog box, shown in **Figure 4-13.** The ACAD ISO, standard, and complex linetypes are named and displayed in the **Available Linetypes** list. Standard linetypes use only dashes, dots, and gaps. Complex linetypes can also contain special shapes and text.

Use the down arrow to look at all the linetypes. Select the linetypes you want to load. Use the [Shift] key and pick to select linetypes between your two picked linetypes. You can also use the [Ctrl] key and pick to select different linetypes. Pick the **OK** button to return to the **Select Linetype** dialog box, where the linetypes you selected are listed, as shown in **Figure 4-14.** In the **Select Linetype** dialog box, pick the desired linetype, and then pick **OK**. The Hidden linetype selected in **Figure 4-14** is now the linetype assigned to Layer 2, as shown in **Figure 4-15.**

**Figure 4-14.**
Linetypes loaded from the **Load or Reload Linetypes** dialog box are added to the **Loaded linetypes** list box.

Loaded linetypes

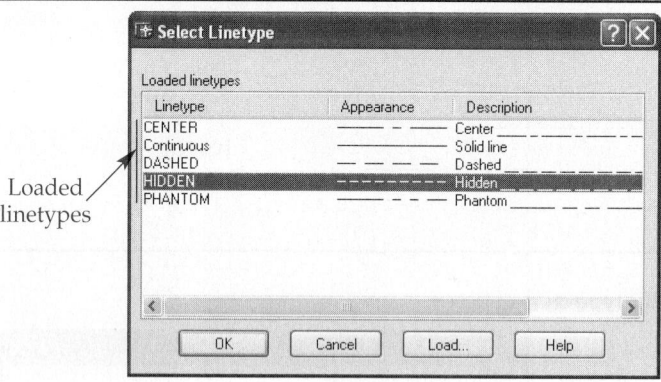

NOTE

The acad.lin file is used by default. You can switch to the ISO library by picking the **File...** button in the **Load or Reload Linetypes** dialog box. This displays the **Select Linetype File** dialog box, where you can select the acadiso.lin file.

AutoCAD and its Applications—Basics

**Figure 4-15.**
Objects drawn on layer 2 now have a Hidden linetype.

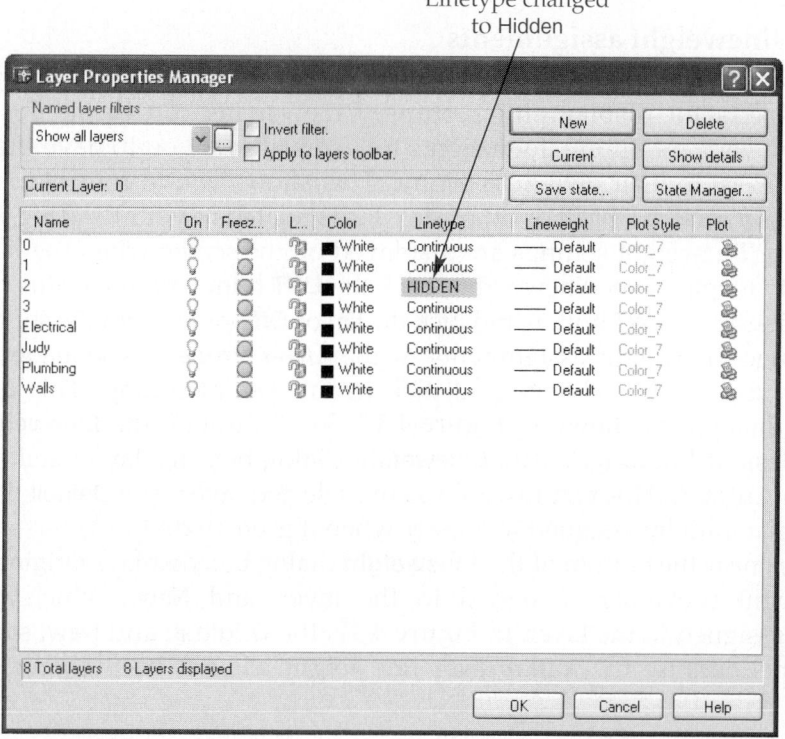

Linetype changed
to Hidden

## Managing linetypes

The **Linetype Manager** dialog box is a convenient place to load and access linetypes. This dialog box can be accessed by selecting **Linetype...** from the **Format** pull-down menu, selecting **Other...** in the **Linetype Control** drop-down list in the **Properties** toolbar, or typing LT or LINETYPE at the Command: prompt. See **Figure 4-16.**

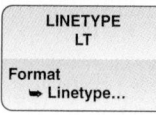

LINETYPE
LT

Format
➥ Linetype...

**Figure 4-16.**
The **Linetype Manager** dialog box.

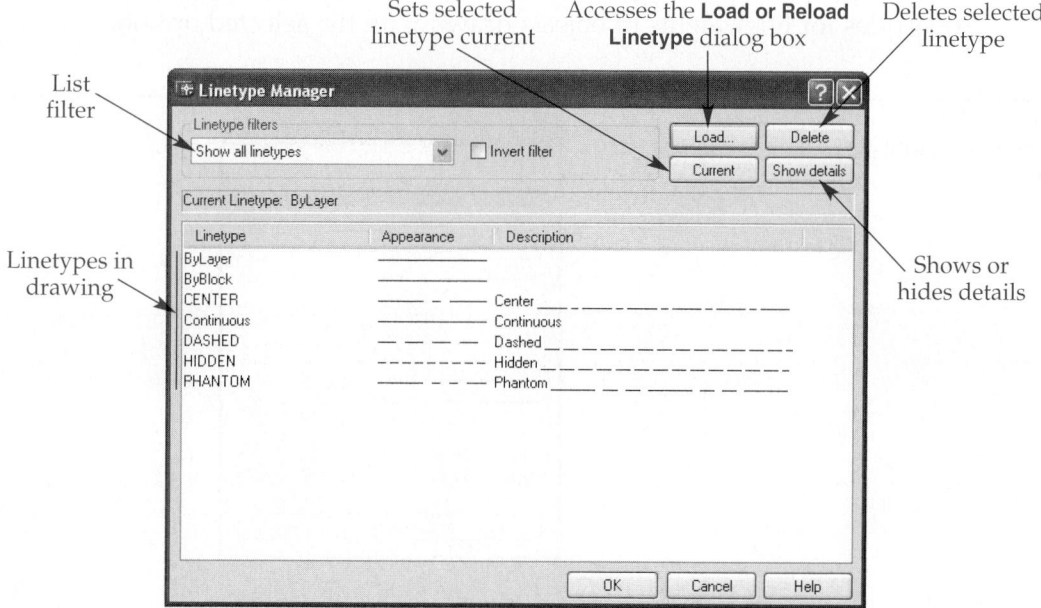

Sets selected
linetype current

Accesses the **Load or Reload
Linetype** dialog box

Deletes selected
linetype

List
filter

Linetypes in
drawing

Shows or
hides details

This dialog box is similar to the **Layer Properties Manager** dialog box. Picking the **Load...** button opens the **Load or Reload Linetypes** dialog box. Picking the **Delete** button deletes any selected non-used linetypes.

### Changing lineweight assignments

Like linetypes, lineweights can also be assigned to objects. *Lineweight* adds width to objects for display and plotting. Lineweights can be set for objects or assigned to layers. Assigning lineweights to layers allows you to have the objects on specific layers set to their own lineweights. This allows you to control the display of line thickness to match ASME or other standards related to your drafting application.

The layer lineweight settings are displayed on the screen when the lineweight is turned on. To toggle screen lineweights, click the **LWT** button on the status bar. You can also right-click on the **LWT** button and pick the **On** or **Off** option from the shortcut menu.

To change lineweight assignments in the **Layer Properties Manager**, select the layer name you want to change and pick its lineweight setting. This displays the **Lineweight** dialog box, shown in **Figure 4-17.** Scroll through the **Lineweights:** list to select the desired lineweight. The **Lineweight** dialog box displays fixed lineweights available in AutoCAD for you to apply to the selected layer. The Default lineweight is the lineweight initially assigned to a layer when it is created.

The area near the bottom of the **Lineweight** dialog box displays **Original:**, which is the lineweight previously assigned to the layer, and **New:**, which is the new lineweight assigned to the layer. In **Figure 4-17**, the **Original:** and **New:** specifications are the same, because the initial layer lineweight has not been changed from the default.

### Setting the current lineweight

Current lineweights are set in the **Lineweight Settings** dialog box, shown in **Figure 4-18.** The **Lineweight Settings** dialog box can be accessed by picking **Lineweight...** from the **Format** pull-down menu; typing LW, LWEIGHT, or LINEWEIGHT at the Command: prompt; or right-clicking on the **LWT** button on the status bar and then selecting **Settings...** from the shortcut menu. The following describes the features of the **Lineweight Settings** dialog box:

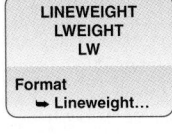

LINEWEIGHT
LWEIGHT
LW

Format
➥ Lineweight...

- **Lineweights.** Set the current lineweight by selecting the desired setting from the list. If lineweight is set to ByLayer, the object lineweight corresponds to the lineweight of its layer. The Default option lineweight width is controlled by the Default list options. Settings other than ByLayer, ByBlock, or Default are used as overrides for lineweights of objects drawn with the selected option.

Figure 4-17.
The **Lineweight** dialog box.

Select lineweight from list

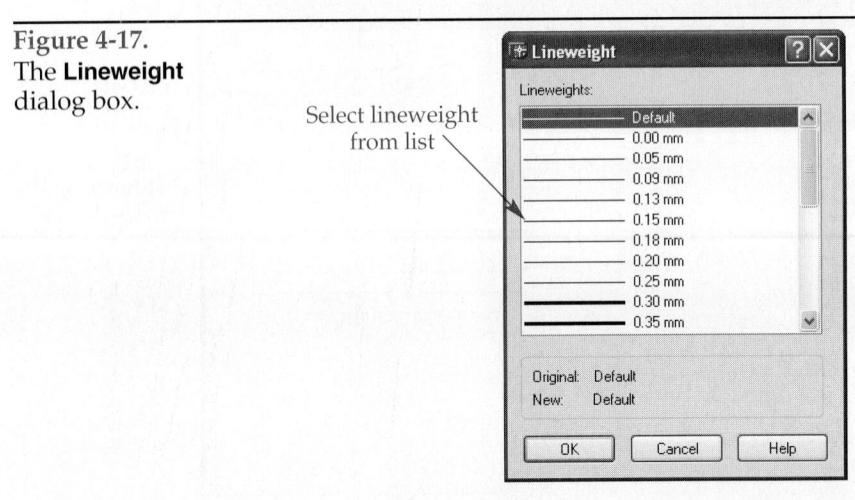

Figure 4-18.
The **Lineweight Settings** dialog box.

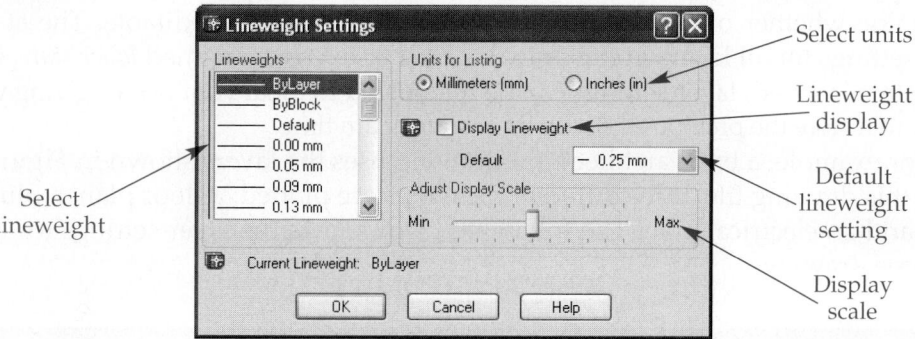

Select lineweight

Select units

Lineweight display

Default lineweight setting

Display scale

- **Units for Listing.** This area allows you to set the lineweight thickness to millimeters or inches.
- **Display Lineweight.** This is another way to turn lineweight thickness on or off. Check this box to turn lineweight on.
- **Default.** Select a lineweight default value from the drop-down list. This becomes the default lineweight for layers. The initial default setting is 0.010" or 0.25 mm. This is also controlled by the **LWDEFAULT** system variable.
- **Adjust Display Scale.** This scale allows you to adjust the lineweight display scale to improve the appearance of different lineweight widths. Adjustment of the lineweight display scale toward the **Max** value can reduce AutoCAD performance. A setting near the middle of the scale or toward **Min** may be preferred.
- **Current Lineweight.** This indicates the current lineweight setting.

---

NOTE

An object's individual properties, such as color, linetype, and lineweight, can be assigned "by layer" or "by object." It is important to note that assigning properties "by object" overrides any assignments made "by layer." For example, if a line's color property is ByLayer, the line obtains its color from the color of the layer on which it is drawn. If that same line's color is changed "by object" to a green color, however, the line is green regardless of the layer color. This is also true for linetype and lineweight.

---

## Exercise 4-5

○ Open EX4-1 if it is not already open.
○ Open the **Select Linetype** dialog box and notice the default linetype.
○ Pick the **Load...** button and load the ACAD_ISO02W100, Center, Dashed, Hidden, and Phantom linetypes.
○ Pick the **OK** button.
○ Apply the Hidden, Center, and Phantom linetypes to the layers of your choice.
○ Apply the lineweight of 0.60 mm to the Walls layer.
○ Open the **Lineweight Settings** dialog box and experiment with lineweight settings. Draw a few lines after each setting to see the results.
○ Save your work. Exit AutoCAD or keep this drawing open for the next exercise.

---

## Layer States

Layer settings, such as on/off, frozen/thawed, plot/no plot, and locked/unlocked, determine whether or not a layer is displayed, plotted, and editable. The status of layer settings for all layers in the drawing can be saved as a named *layer state*. Once a layer state is saved, layer settings can be readjusted to meet your needs, giving you the ability to restore the previously saved layer state at anytime.

For example, a basic architectural drawing uses the layers shown in **Figure 4-19**. From this drawing file, three different drawings are plotted: a floor plan, a plumbing plan, and an electrical plan. The following chart shows the layer settings for each of the three drawings:

| | Floor Plan | Plumbing Plan | Electrical Plan |
|---|---|---|---|
| **0** | Off | Off | Off |
| **Dimension-Electrical** | Frozen | Frozen | On/Thawed |
| **Dimension-Floor Plan** | On/Thawed | Frozen | Frozen |
| **Dimension-Plumbing** | Frozen | On/Thawed | Frozen |
| **Electrical** | Frozen | Frozen | On/Thawed |
| **Floor Plan Notes** | On/Thawed | Frozen | Frozen |
| **Plumbing** | Frozen | On/Thawed | Frozen |
| **Title Block** | On/Thawed | Locked | Locked |
| **Walls** | On/Thawed | Locked | Locked |
| **Windows and Doors** | On/Thawed | Frozen | Frozen |

**Figure 4-19.**
Layers for a basic architectural drawing.

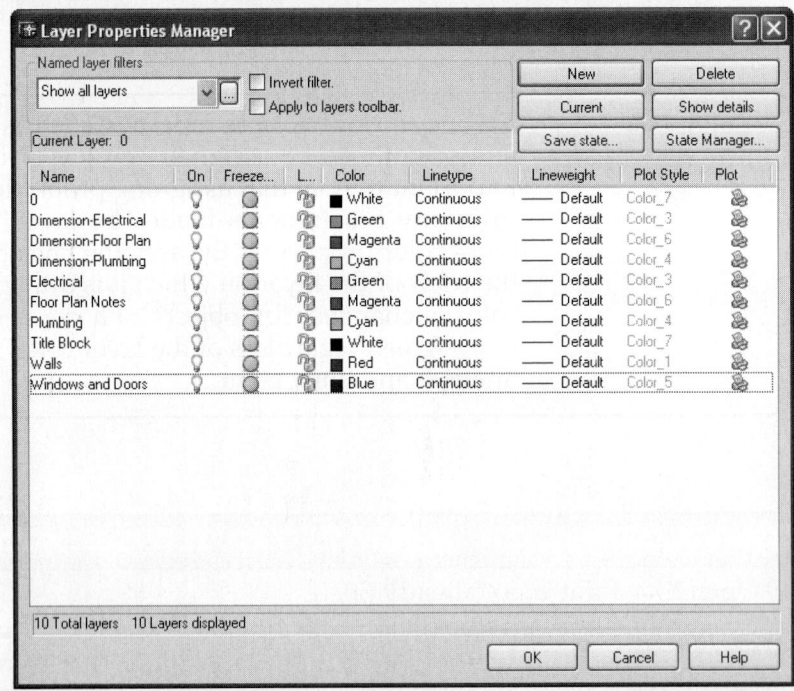

Each of the three groups of settings can be saved as an individual layer state. Once the layer state is created, the settings can be restored by simply restoring the layer state. This is easier than changing the settings for each layer individually.

To save a layer state, first adjust the layer settings you wish to save. Pick the **Save state...** button to access the **Save Layer States** dialog box. See **Figure 4-20**. Enter a

         AutoCAD and its Applications—Basics

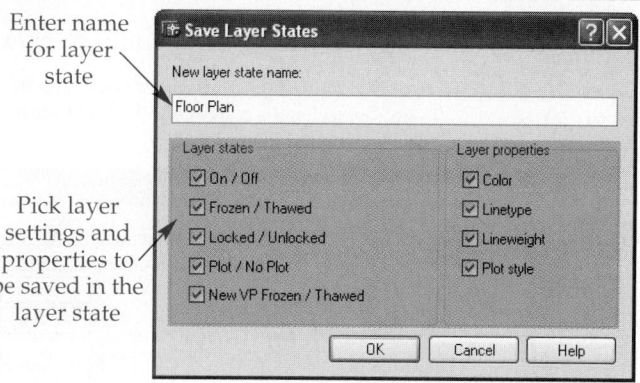

**Figure 4-20.**
Only selected settings and properties are saved in the layer state. Those settings not saved are not reset when the layer state is restored.

Enter name for layer state

Pick layer settings and properties to be saved in the layer state

name for the layer state and pick the settings and properties to be saved. Only saved settings and properties are reset when the layer state is restored. For this example, the three layer states (with settings) shown in **Figure 4-21** are created.

Once a layer state is saved, it can be restored at any time. By restoring a layer state, the layer settings are automatically changed to match the settings saved in the layer state. To restore a layer state, pick the **State Manager...** button in the **Layer Properties Manager** dialog box. This accesses the **Layer States Manager** dialog box. See **Figure 4-22.** Select a layer state from the **Layer states** list and pick one of the following buttons:

- **Restore.** Restores the settings saved in the selected layer state.
- **Edit.** Accesses the **Edit layer state** dialog box, where you can select which settings and properties are saved in the layer state. You cannot change the value of layer settings in this dialog box.
- **Rename.** Allows you to rename the layer state.
- **Delete.** Deletes the selected layer state.
- **Import.** Accesses the **Import layer state** dialog box, where you can select an LAS file containing an existing layer state. Imported layer states are listed in the **Layer states** list in the **Layer State Manager**. Select the imported layer state and pick the **Restore** button to have the settings restored.

**Figure 4-21.**
The layer states and saved layer settings.

| Name | On | Freeze... | L... | Color |
|------|----|-----------|------|-------|
| 0 | | | | White |
| Dimension-Electrical | | | | Green |
| Dimension-Floor Plan | | | | Magenta |
| Dimension-Plumbing | | | | Cyan |
| Electrical | | | | Green |
| Floor Plan Notes | | | | Magenta |
| Plumbing | | | | Cyan |
| Title Block | | | | White |
| Walls | | | | Red |
| Windows and Doors | | | | Blue |

Floor Plan

| Name | On | Freeze... | L... | Color |
|------|----|-----------|------|-------|
| 0 | | | | White |
| Dimension-Electrical | | | | Green |
| Dimension-Floor Plan | | | | Magenta |
| Dimension-Plumbing | | | | Cyan |
| Electrical | | | | Green |
| Floor Plan Notes | | | | Magenta |
| Plumbing | | | | Cyan |
| Title Block | | | | White |
| Walls | | | | Red |
| Windows and Doors | | | | Blue |

Plumbing Plan

| Name | On | Freeze... | L... | Color |
|------|----|-----------|------|-------|
| 0 | | | | White |
| Dimension-Electrical | | | | Green |
| Dimension-Floor Plan | | | | Magenta |
| Dimension-Plumbing | | | | Cyan |
| Electrical | | | | Green |
| Floor Plan Notes | | | | Magenta |
| Plumbing | | | | Cyan |
| Title Block | | | | White |
| Walls | | | | Red |
| Windows and Doors | | | | Blue |

Electrical Plan

**Figure 4-22.**
Use the **Layer States Manager** dialog box to restore, modify, import, or export existing layer states.

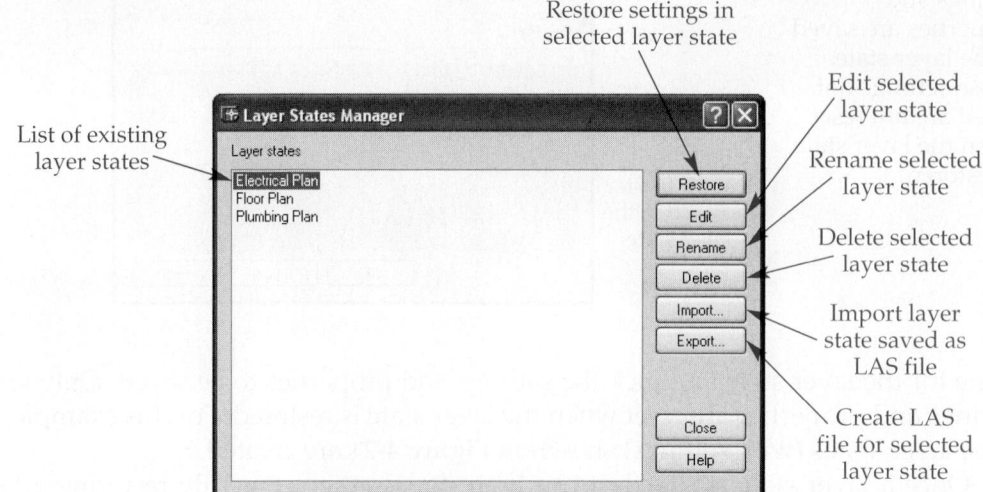

Restore settings in selected layer state

List of existing layer states

Edit selected layer state

Rename selected layer state

Delete selected layer state

Import layer state saved as LAS file

Create LAS file for selected layer state

- **Export.** Saves the layer state as a LAS file and imports it into other drawings. This allows you to share layer states between drawings containing identical layers. Pick this button to access the **Export layer state** dialog box, where you can specify a name and location for the LAS file.

**PROFESSIONAL TIP**
If you have a drawing that does not contain layer names, importing a layer state file (.las) causes the layers from the layer state to be added to your drawing.

**NOTE**
The **Express** pull-down menu includes a **Layer Manager...** tool found in the **Layers** cascading menu. This tool also creates layer states in a drawing, but allows you to save these as LAY files. This utility is very similar to the **Layer States Manager** dialog box discussed previously. This tool is primarily for pre-AutoCAD 2000 users who would have used this older routine to create layer states.

## Using Layer Details

The **Layer Properties Manager** dialog box contains a **Show details** button. When selected, a new area is displayed at the bottom of the existing dialog box, as shown in **Figure 4-23**, and the **Show details** button changes to a **Hide details** button. The features of the **Details** area are disabled unless one or more of the layers in the layer list are highlighted. The **Details** area provides an alternate way of entering the same information that can be entered in the upper area.

**Figure 4-23.**
The **Details** area of the expanded **Layer Properties Manager** dialog box.

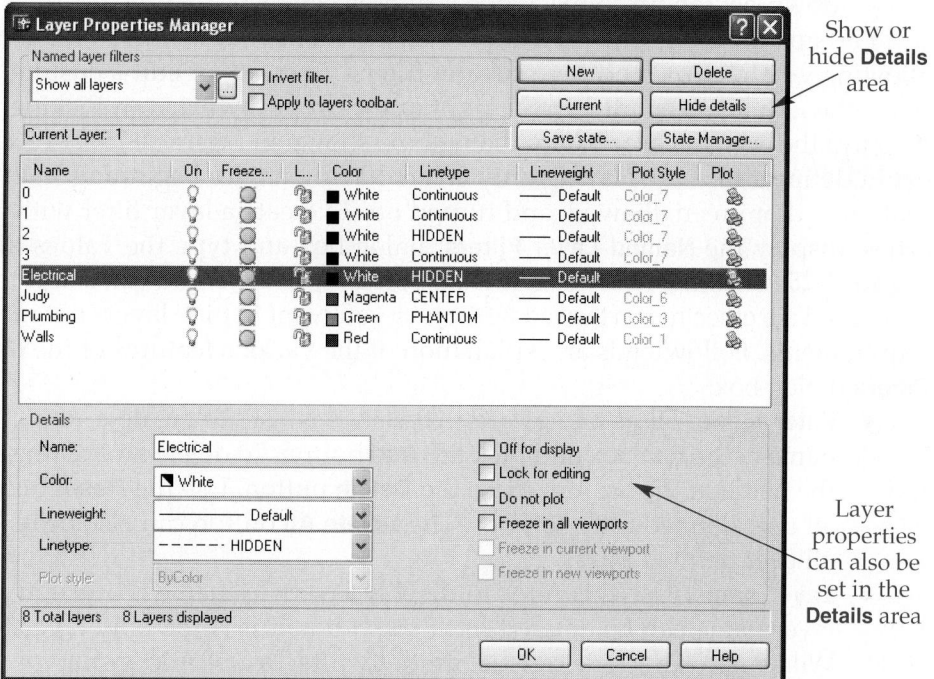

Show or hide **Details** area

Layer properties can also be set in the **Details** area

## Layer Filters

In some applications, large numbers of layer names may be used to assist in drawing information management. Having all layer names showing at the same time in the layer list can make it more difficult to work with your drawing layers. *Layer filters* are used to screen, or filter, out any layers you do not want displayed in the **Layer Properties Manager** dialog box. The **Named layer filters** area of the **Layer Properties Manager** provides options for filtering out unwanted layer names. See Figure 4-24. The default options are explained below:

- **Show all layers.** This is the default option, and it shows all defined layer names.
- **Show all used layers.** The current layer and any layers containing drawing objects are displayed.
- **Show all Xref dependent layers.** Xrefs are discussed in Chapter 23. This displays all layers brought in with externally referenced drawings.
- **Invert filter.** In addition to the default layer filter options, you can also invert, or reverse, the layer filter setting. For example, there is a choice to show all used layers, but what if you want to show all unused layers? In this case, you would check the **Invert filter** toggle to invert, or reverse, your choice.

**Figure 4-24.**
The **Named layer filters** area provides options for filtering layers.

Select filter

Pick to create or edit custom filters

Pick to reverse filter

Pick to filter list in toolbar

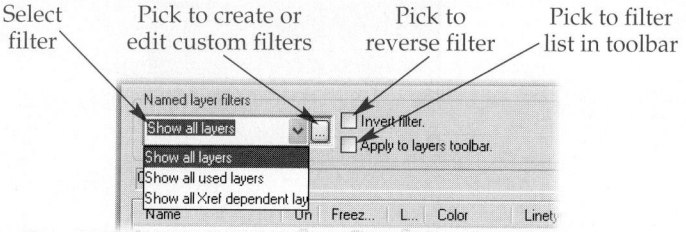

- **Apply to layers toolbar.** Check this toggle if you want only the layers matching the current filter displayed in the **Layers** toolbar. The **Layer Control** drop-down list tooltip shows when a filter is active.

Perhaps the most powerful aspect of the **Named layer filters** area is the feature allowing you to create and save custom filters. To create or edit a custom layer filter, select the **...** (ellipsis) button to the right of the drop-down arrow. Picking this button displays the **Named Layer Filters** dialog box, shown in **Figure 4-25**. For example, you could define a filter displaying only layers having names beginning with *a* or *b*, and that are red or green, thawed, and turned on. To create a layer filter with these properties, display the **Named Layer Filters** dialog box and type the values displayed in **Figure 4-25**. Click the **Add** button when you are finished. You can select the layer filter named a b green red on thawed whenever you want to hide layers not meeting these requirements. Following is an explanation of the various features of the **Named Layer Filters** dialog box:

- **Filter name.** Filter names are saved in this list. To create a new filter, type a name in the text box and pick the **Add** button. To delete an existing filter, select the name in the list and press the **Delete** button. Use the **Reset** button to clear all user defined filter settings. The **Delete All** button can also be used to delete all user defined filters.
- **Layer name.** Use this filter to display layers by name. For example, a single layer name can be entered in this text box if it is the only layer to be listed. Wildcard characters can be used to filter a specific group of layers. For example, the layer name W* would filter all layers beginning with *W*, such as Wall01, Wall02, and Wall03. An entry of Door,Window,W* would display the Door and Window layers, plus all layers beginning with *W*.
- **On/Off.** Use this filter to display only the names of layers that are either on or off. The default for this setting is to display both cases.
- **Freeze/Thaw.** Use this filter to display either only frozen or only thawed layer names.
- **Current viewport.** Use this filter to display layer names frozen or thawed in the current viewport. (Viewport concepts are discussed in Chapter 10.)
- **New viewport.** Use this filter to display layer names frozen or thawed in new viewports.

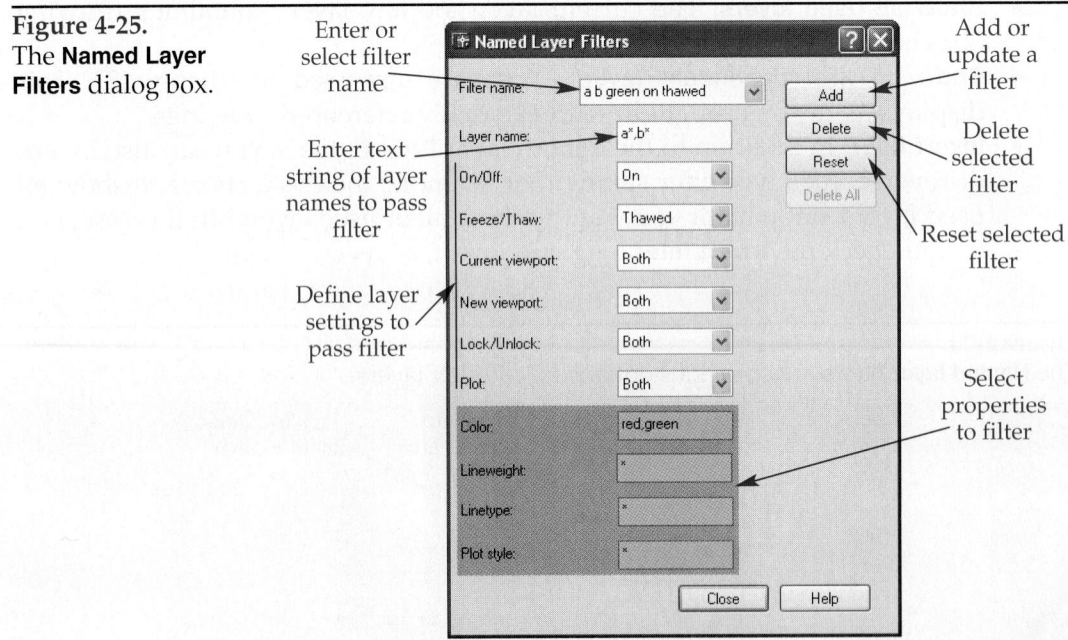

**Figure 4-25.**
The **Named Layer Filters** dialog box.

Enter or select filter name

Enter text string of layer names to pass filter

Define layer settings to pass filter

Add or update a filter

Delete selected filter

Reset selected filter

Select properties to filter

- **Lock/Unlock.** Use this filter to display either only locked or only unlocked layer names.
- **Plot.** Use this filter to display layer names that either plot or do not plot.
- **Color.** Use this filter to display layer names by color designation. Use color numbers or names. For example, you can use red or 1.
- **Lineweight.** Use this filter to display layer names by lineweight designation.
- **Linetype.** Use this filter to display layer names by linetype.
- **Plot style.** Use this filter to display layer names by plot style.

## Exercise 4-6

○ Open EX4-1 if it is not already open.
○ Add a layer named A with color green and a layer named B with color red.
○ Create a named layer filter with the following specifications:

| | |
|---|---|
| **Filter name:** | a b green red on thawed |
| **Layer name:** | a*,b* |
| **On/Off:** | On |
| **Freeze/Thaw:** | Thawed |
| **Current viewport:** | Both |
| **New viewport:** | Both |
| **Lock/Unlock:** | Both |
| **Plot:** | Both |
| **Color:** | red,green |
| **Lineweight:** | * |
| **Linetype:** | * |
| **Plot style:** | * |

○ Select the **Apply to layers toolbar** check box and see the results in the **Layers** toolbar layer list. Deselect the **Apply to layers toolbar** check box and look at the results in the **Layers** toolbar layer list.
○ Save the exercise as EX4-6.

## Quickly Setting a Layer Current

You can quickly make another layer current by using the **Layer Control** drop-down list located in the **Layers** toolbar. The name of the current layer is displayed in the box. Pick the drop-down arrow, and a layer list appears, as shown in **Figure 4-26.**

Pick a layer name from the list, and that layer is set current. When many layers are defined in the drawing, the vertical scroll bar can be used to move up and down through the list. Selecting a layer name to set as current automatically closes the list and returns you to the drawing editor. When a command is active, the drop-down

Figure 4-26.
The **Layer Control** drop-down list is located on the left side of the **Layers** toolbar. All layers are listed with icons representing their state and color. Pick on a layer name to make it current.

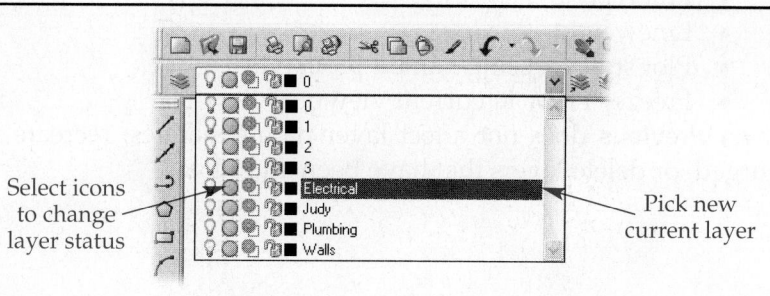

Select icons to change layer status

Pick new current layer

button is grayed out, and the list is not available. You can also use the **CLAYER** system variable to make a layer current. The **Layer Control** drop-down list has the same status icons as the **Layer Properties Manager** dialog box. By picking an icon, you can change the state of the layer.

**PROFESSIONAL TIP** Layers are meant to simplify the drafting process. They separate different details of the drawing and can reduce the complexity of what is displayed. If you set color and linetype by layer, do not reset and mix entity linetypes and color on the same layer. Doing so can mislead you and your colleagues when trying to find certain details. Always maintain accurate records of your template drawings.

## Making the Layer of an Existing Object Current

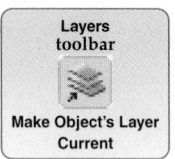

Layers toolbar

Make Object's Layer Current

Another quick way to set the current layer is to use the **Make Object's Layer Current** button in the **Layers** toolbar. When you pick this button, AutoCAD asks you to select an object on the layer you want to make current:

```
Command: (_ai_molc)
Select object whose layer will become current: (pick an object to make its layer current)
Plumbing is now the current layer.
Command:
```

## Restoring the Previous Layer Settings

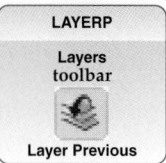

LAYERP

Layers toolbar

Layer Previous

After changing layer properties, you can restore the previous layer settings by picking the **Layer Previous** button in the **Layers** toolbar or typing LAYERP at the Command: prompt. Once the command has been executed, the Command: prompt displays a message stating if the command was successful or if it failed:

```
Command: LAYERP↵
Restored previous layer status.
```

The **Layer Previous** command only affects layer operations. Therefore, after using commands to draw, modify, and zoom, you can use the **Layer Previous** command to restore the last layer state without affecting any other functions. The following layer properties are restored by the **Layer Previous** command:

- On/Off
- Freeze/Thaw
- Lock/Unlock
- Color
- Linetype
- Lineweight
- Plot style (if using named plot styles)
- Freeze/Thaw in current viewport

**Layer Previous** does not affect layer name changes, recreate layers that have been purged, or delete layers that have been added.

# Changing Object Properties

PROPERTIES
PROPS
CH
MO

Modify
➡ Properties

Standard
toolbar

Properties

You should always draw objects on an appropriate layer, but layer settings are not permanent. You can change an object's layer if needed. You can also change other properties of the object, such as color and linetype. Using the **Properties** toolbar or the **Properties** window modifies these properties.

To modify properties using the **Properties** toolbar, select the object, and then use the drop-down lists in the appropriate control boxes to change the properties. After you have changed the properties, press [Esc] to deselect the object. To modify an object's properties using the **Properties** window, pick the **Properties** button in the **Standard** toolbar, select **Properties** from the **Modify** pull-down menu, or type PROPS, CH, MO, or PROPERTIES at the Command: prompt. If an object has been selected, you can right-click on it and pick **Properties** from the shortcut menu. When you use one of these options, AutoCAD displays the **Properties** window, shown in **Figure 4-27**. You can also double-click on many objects to automatically select the object and open the **Properties** window.

The properties of the selected object are listed in the **Properties** window. The specific properties listed vary, depending on the type of object selected. Properties such as layer, linetype, and color are listed in the **General** category.

To modify a particular object property, first, find the property in the **Properties** window, and then select its value. Depending on the type of value, a specific editing method is activated. Use this tool to change the value. For example, if you want to change an object's layer, pick Layer to highlight it, as in **Figure 4-27**. A drop-down arrow is displayed to the right of the layer name. Pick the arrow to access the Layer drop-down list. Pick the layer name you want to use for the selected object's layer. You can use this same process to change the color, linetype, or lineweight of a selected object.

You can work in AutoCAD with the **Properties** window open and available for use. You can move the **Properties** window by picking and holding on the title bar while you move the mouse. If you want to close the **Properties** window, select the **X** in the upper-left corner.

Figure 4-27.
The **Properties** window is used to modify the properties of the selected object.

Select property

Use drop-down arrow to access list of layers

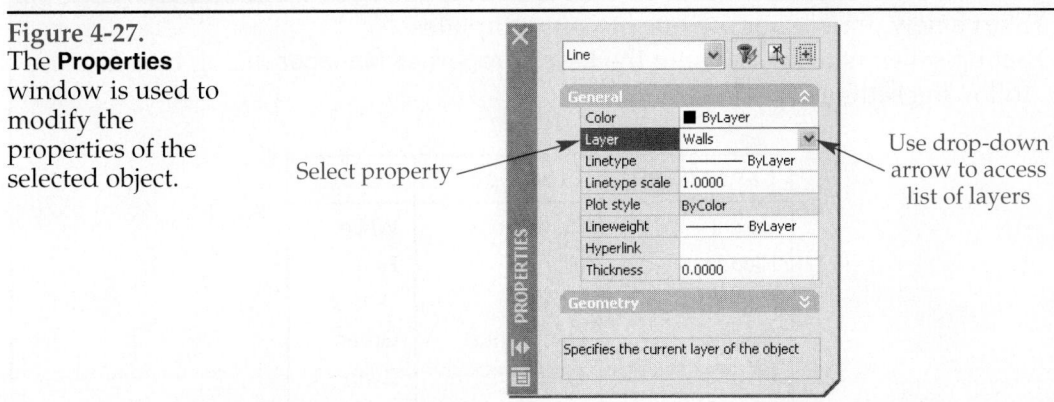

**NOTE**

Modifying object properties using the **Properties** window is covered in greater depth in Chapter 12.

---

## Exercise 4-7

○ Open EX4-6 if it is not already open.
○ Use the **Layer Control** drop-down list in the **Layers** toolbar to experiment with making different layers current. Draw an object each time you change to a new current layer. Draw objects based on what you have already learned, such as line segments.
○ Use the **Make Object's Layer Current** button to select an object in the drawing and make its layer current. Be sure the object you select is not on the current layer.
○ Select an object and change its layer. Do this again, but this time, select more than one object and change the layer in the **Properties** window.
○ Use the **Properties** window to make other changes to objects, such as color and linetype.
○ Save your work. Exit AutoCAD or keep this drawing open for the next exercise.

## Overriding Layer Settings

Color, linetype, and lineweight settings reference layer settings by default. This means when you create a layer, you also establish a color, linetype, and lineweight to go with the layer. This is what it means when the color, linetype, and lineweight are specified as ByLayer. This is the most common method for managing these settings. Sometimes, however, you may need objects to reference a specific layer, but have specific color, linetype, or lineweight properties different than the layer settings. In such a situation, the color, linetype, and lineweight can be set to an *absolute* value, and current layer settings are ignored. The term ***absolute***, as used here and in future content, refers to an object being assigned specific properties that are not reliant on a layer or block for their definitions.

## Exercise 4-8

○ Start a new drawing or use one of your templates.
○ Set up seven new layers using the **Layer Properties Manager** dialog box. Use the following settings:

| Layer name | Linetype | Color |
|------------|----------|--------|
| Object | Continuous | White |
| Hidden | Hidden | Red |
| Center | Center | Yellow |
| Electric | Continuous | Green |
| Phantom | Phantom | Cyan |
| Dot | Dot | Blue |
| Dim | Continuous | Magenta |

○ Establish a new template with the specified layers by saving with a name of your choice. Record the template name and the settings in a notebook for future reference.

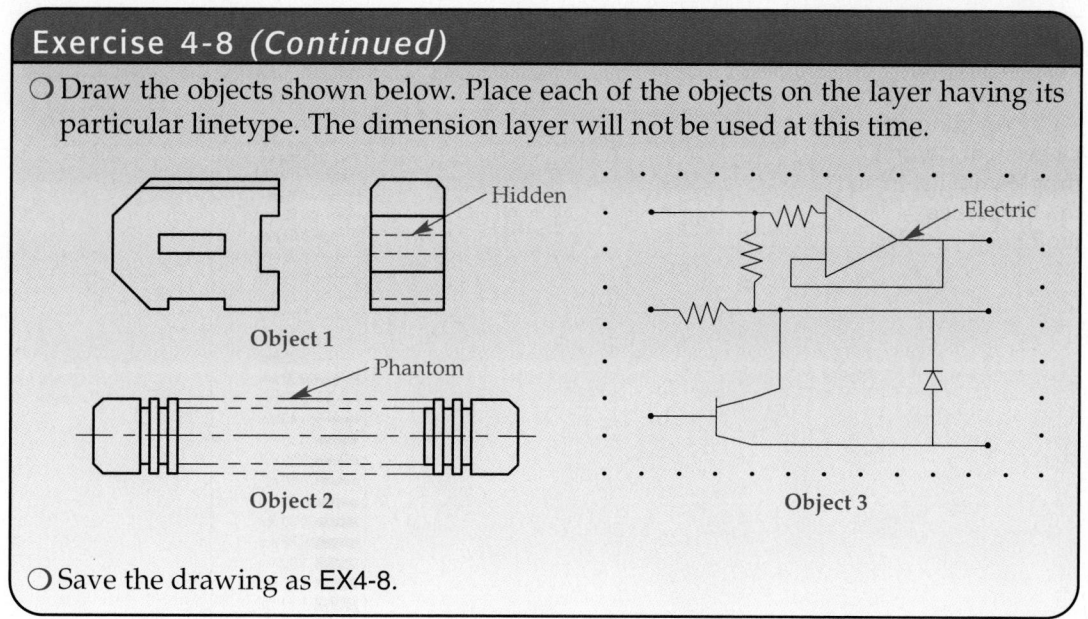
## Setting Color

The current object color can be easily set by selecting the **Color Control** drop-down list from the **Properties** toolbar. See **Figure 4-28**. The default setting is ByLayer. This is the recommended setting for most applications. To change this setting, pick another color from the list. If the color you want is not on the list, you can pick the item at the bottom of the list, labeled **Select Color**, to display the **Select Color** dialog box, or you can type COL or COLOR at the Command: prompt. Once an absolute color is specified, all new objects are drawn in the specified color, regardless of the current layer settings. Another way to set the current object color is by using the **CECOLOR** system variable. **CECOLOR** stands for *current entity color.* This variable is set as follows:

    Command: **CECOLOR**↵
    Enter new value for CECOLOR <BYLAYER>: *(enter new color value)*

**Figure 4-28.**
The current object color is easily set by opening the **Color Control** drop-down list in the **Properties** toolbar. This control box is also used to change the color of selected objects.

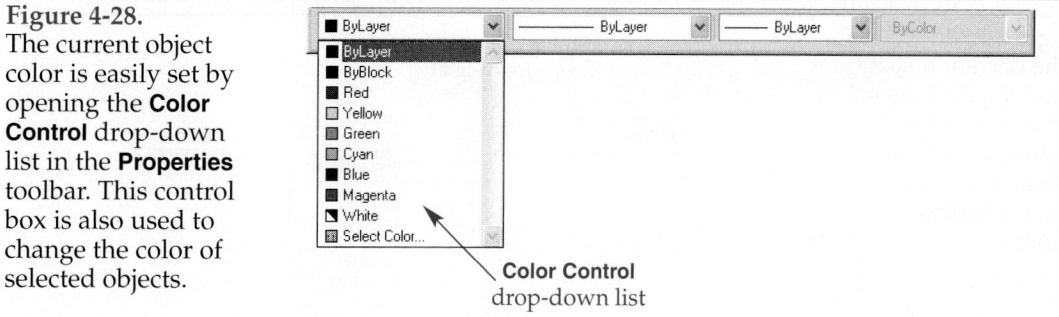

Color Control
drop-down list

## Setting Lineweight

Similar to the current object color, you can set the current object lineweight to differ from the layer settings. To set the current object lineweight, pick the **Lineweight Control** drop-down list from the **Properties** toolbar and select the desired linetype. See **Figure 4-29**. You can also directly adjust the system variable controlling the current object linetype. This variable is called **CELWEIGHT**. Set the **CELWEIGHT** system variable in a similar manner as you set the **CECOLOR** system variable. If ByLayer is desired, you must enter −1.

**Figure 4-29.**
The current object lineweight is easily set by opening the **Lineweight Control** drop-down list in the **Properties** toolbar.

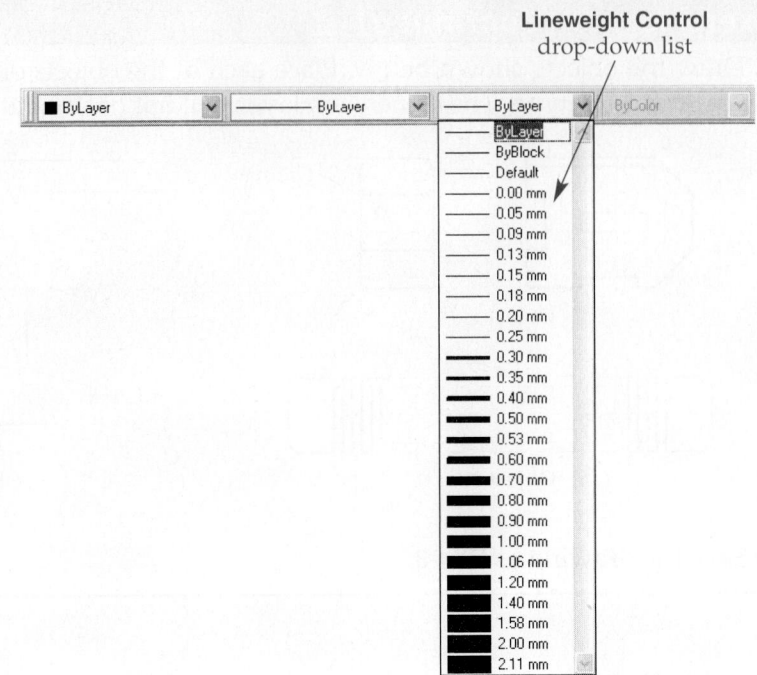

## Setting Linetype

Similar to the current object lineweight, you can set the current object linetype to be separate from any layer settings. To set the current object linetype, pick the **Linetype Control** drop-down list from the **Properties** toolbar and select the desired linetype. See **Figure 4-30**. If the linetype you want has not been loaded into the current drawing yet, it will not appear in the listing. You can select **Other...** from the list to load the **Linetype Manager** so new linetypes can be loaded.

You can also directly adjust the system variable controlling the current object linetype. This variable is called **CELTYPE**, for *current entity linetype*. Set the **CELTYPE** system variable in the same manner as you set the **CECOLOR** and **CELWEIGHT** system variables.

**Figure 4-30.**
The current object linetype is easily set by opening the **Linetype Control** drop-down list in the **Properties** toolbar.

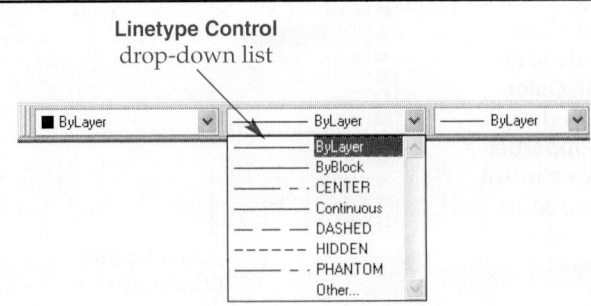

### Setting the linetype scale

The linetype scale sets the lengths of dashes and spaces in linetypes. When you start AutoCAD with a wizard or template, the global linetype scale is automatically set to match the units you select. The global linetype scale can, however, be overridden at the object level. A *global* change is a change affecting all linetypes in the current drawing.

The default object linetype scale factor is 1.0. As with layers, the linetype scale can be changed at the object level. One reason for changing the default linetype scale is to make your drawing more closely match standard drafting practices.

Earlier, you were introduced to the **Properties** window. When a line object is selected to modify, a Linetype scale property is listed. You can change the linetype scale of the object by entering a new value in this field. A value less than 1.0 makes the dashes and spaces smaller than those in the global setting, while a value greater than 1.0 makes the dashes and spaces larger than those in the global setting. Using this information, you can experiment with different linetype scales until you achieve your desired results. Be careful when changing linetype scales to avoid making your drawing look odd, with a variety of line formats. **Figure 4-31** shows a diagram comparing different linetype scale factors.

### Changing the global linetype scale

The **LTSCALE** variable can be used to make a global change to the linetype scale. The default global linetype scale factor is 1.0000. Any line with dashes initially assumes this factor.

---

**Figure 4-31.**
Drawing the same linetype at different linetype scales.

| Scale Factor | Line |
| --- | --- |
| 0.5 | 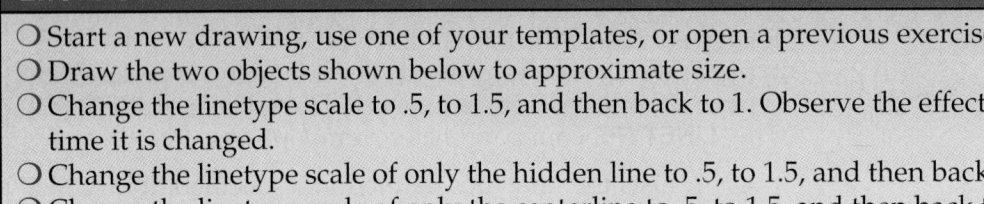 |
| 1.0 | |
| 1.5 | |

To change the linetype scale for the entire drawing, type **LTSCALE** at the Command: prompt. The current value is listed. Enter the new value and press [Enter]. A Regenerating model message appears, as the global linetype scale is changed for all lines on the drawing.

---

### Exercise 4-9

○ Start a new drawing, use one of your templates, or open a previous exercise.
○ Draw the two objects shown below to approximate size.
○ Change the linetype scale to .5, to 1.5, and then back to 1. Observe the effect each time it is changed.
○ Change the linetype scale of only the hidden line to .5, to 1.5, and then back to 1.
○ Change the linetype scale of only the centerline to .5, to 1.5, and then back to 1.

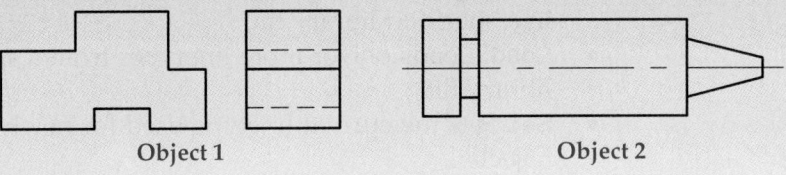

Object 1          Object 2

○ Experiment with other linetype scales if you wish, and then change the scale back to 1.
○ Save the drawing as EX4-9.

---

## Reusing Drawing Content

In nearly every drafting discipline, individual drawings created as part of a given project are likely to share a number of common elements. All the drawings within a specific drafting project generally have the same set of standards. Drawing features, such as the text size and font used for annotation, standardized dimensioning methods and appearances, layer names and properties, drafting symbols, drawing layouts, and even typical drawing details, are often duplicated in many different drawings. These and other components of CAD drawings are referred to as *drawing content.* One of the most fundamental advantages of CAD systems is the ease with which content can be shared between drawings. Once a commonly used drawing feature has been defined, it can be used again as needed, in any number of drawing applications.

The creation and use of drawing template files was covered in Chapters 2 and 3. Drawing templates represents one way to reuse drawing content that has already been defined. Creating your own customized drawing template files provides an effective way to start each new drawing using standard settings.

Drawing templates, however, provides only a starting point. During the course of a drawing project, you may need to add content to the current drawing that has been defined previously in another drawing. Some drawing projects may require you to revise an existing drawing rather than start a completely new drawing. For other projects, you may need to duplicate the standards used in a drawing a client has supplied.

AutoCAD provides a powerful drawing content manager called **DesignCenter**. **DesignCenter** allows you to reuse drawing content that has already been defined in previous drawings by using a drag-and-drop operation. **DesignCenter** was introduced in Chapter 1.

**DesignCenter** is used to manage several categories of drawing content, including blocks, dimension styles, layers, layouts, linetypes, text styles, and externally referenced drawings. Layers and linetypes are discussed in this chapter, but the other content types are introduced in the chapters where they apply. The following discussion details the features of **DesignCenter** and shows how layer and linetype content found in existing drawings can be reused in other drawing projects.

## Using DesignCenter to Copy Layers and Linetypes

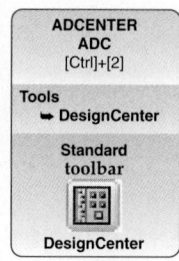

**DesignCenter** is activated by picking the **DesignCenter** button on the **Standard** toolbar, picking **DesignCenter** from the **Tools** pull-down menu, typing ADC or ADCENTER at the Command: prompt, or using the [Ctrl]+[2] key combination. This displays **DesignCenter**. See **Figure 4-32**.

It is not necessary to open a drawing in AutoCAD in order to view or access its content. **DesignCenter** allows you to directly load content from any accessible drawing. You can also use **DesignCenter** to browse through existing drawing files and view their contents, or you can use its advanced search tools to look for specific drawing content.

**DesignCenter** allows you to easily share content between drawings currently open in AutoCAD. To copy content, first select the drawing from which the content is to be copied. The drawing is selected from the tree view pane. If the tree view is not

---

**Figure 4-32.**
**DesignCenter** is used to copy content from one drawing to another.

Pick to select drawings from hard drives and network locations

Pick to select from open drawings

Pick to select recently opened drawings

**Tree View Toggle**

Select display mode for the preview palette

Tree view pane

Selected drawing

Preview palette

C:\Program Files\AutoCAD 2004\Sample\DesignCenter\Fasteners - US.dwg (7 Item(s))

---

already visible, toggle it on by picking the **Tree View Toggle** button in the **DesignCenter** toolbar. The first three tabs on the **DesignCenter** toolbar control the tree view display:

- **Folders.** Pick this tab to display the folders and files found on the hard drive and network.
- **Open Drawings.** Pick this tab to list only the currently opened drawings.
- **History.** Pick this tab to list recently opened drawings.

Pick the plus sign (+) next to a drawing icon to view the content categories for the drawing. Each category of drawing content is listed with a representative icon. Pick the Layers icon to load the palette with the layer content found in the selected drawing. The preview palette now displays all the available layer content. See **Figure 4-33.**

To select layers from the palette, use standard Windows selection methods. The [Shift] and [Ctrl] keys are used for selecting multiple items. In this example, the drawing is selected first, and the Layers content is picked. The preview palette displays the available content. Select the desired layers and use one of the following options to import them into the current drawing:

- **Drag and drop.** Move the cursor over the top of the desired icon in the preview palette. Press and hold down the pick button on your pointing device. Drag the cursor to the opened drawing. See **Figure 4-34.** Release the pick button, and the selected content is added to your current drawing file.
- **Add from shortcut menu.** Select the desired icon(s) in the preview palette and right-click to open the shortcut menu. Pick the **Add Layer(s)** option, and the selected content is added to your current drawing.
- **Copy from shortcut menu.** This option is identical to the **Add Layer(s)** option, except you select **Copy** from the shortcut menu instead of **Add Layer(s)**. Now, move the cursor to the drawing where you want the content added and right-click to open the shortcut menu. Select **Paste**, and the selected contents are added to the current drawing.

To select more than one icon at one time, hold down the [Shift] key and pick the first and last icon in a group. You can also hold down the [Ctrl] key to select multiple icons individually. The copied layers are now available in the active drawing. See **Figure 4-35.** If the name of a layer being loaded already exists in the destination drawing, that layer name and its settings are ignored. The existing settings for the layer are preserved, and a message is displayed at the command line indicating the duplicate settings were ignored.

Figure 4-33.
Displaying the layers found in a drawing using **DesignCenter**.

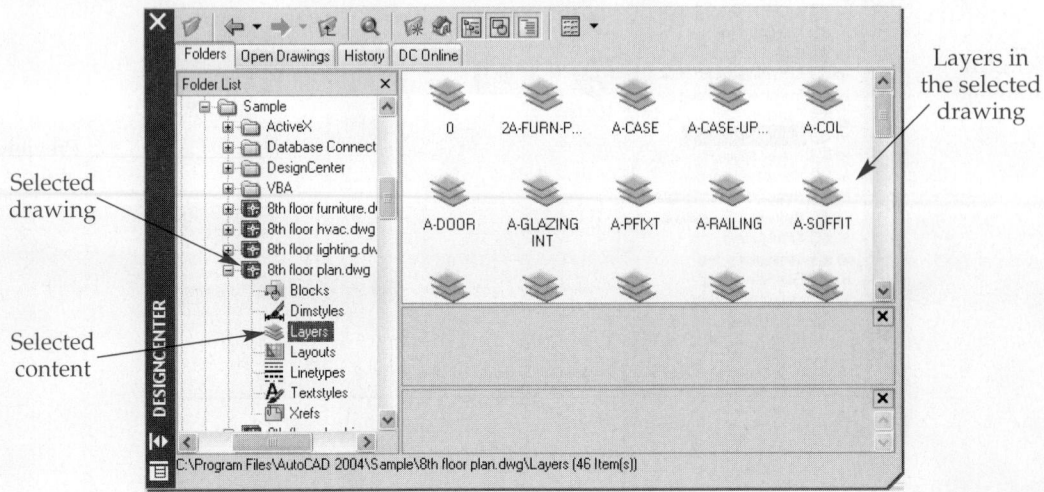

**Figure 4-34.**
To copy layers shown in **DesignCenter** into the current drawing, first select the layers to be copied, then drag and drop them into the drawing area of the current drawing.

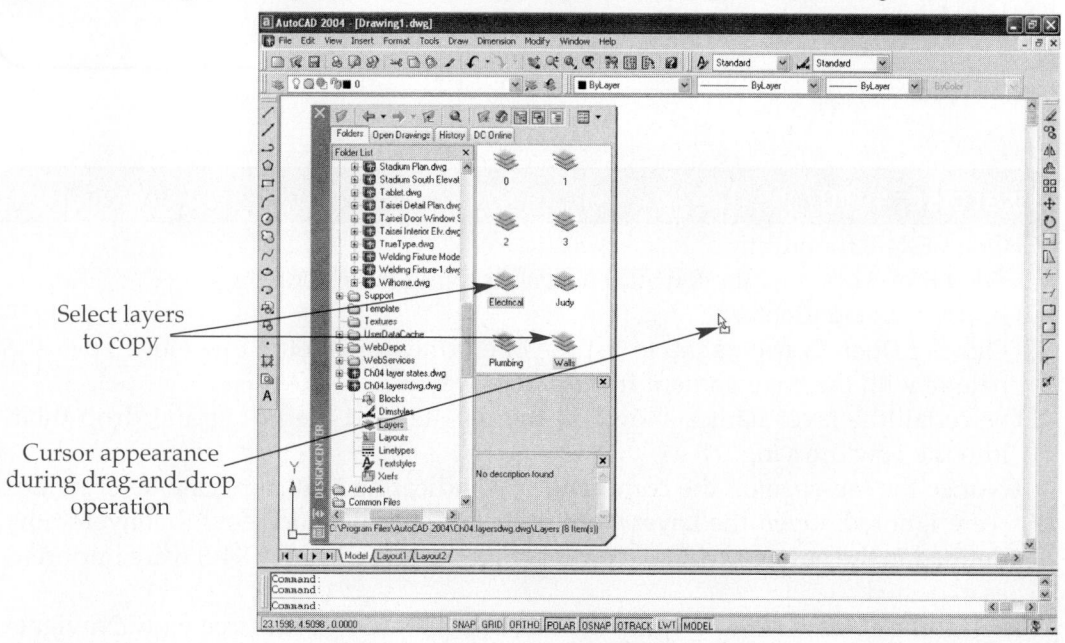

Select layers to copy

Cursor appearance during drag-and-drop operation

**Figure 4-35.**
The copied layers now appear in the **Layer Control** drop-down list of the current drawing.

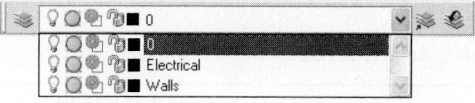

Linetypes can be copied using the same procedure. In the tree view, select the drawing containing the linetypes to be copied. Select Linetypes to display the line-types in the preview palette. See **Figure 4-36.** Select the linetypes to be copied, and then use drag and drop or the shortcut menu to add the linetypes to the current drawing.

**Figure 4-36.**
Linetypes can also be displayed in the preview palette.

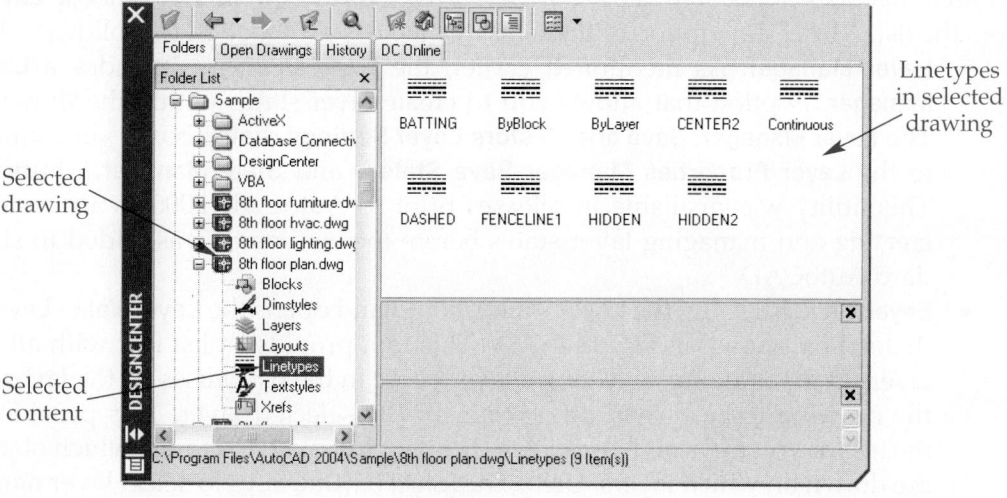

Selected drawing

Selected content

Linetypes in selected drawing

NOTE  **DesignCenter** is a very powerful tool. Specific applications of **DesignCenter** are provided throughout this text.

---

## Exercise 4-10

○ Open EX4-8 for editing.

○ Keep EX4-8 open while you start a new drawing from scratch.

○ Activate **DesignCenter**.

○ Pick the **Open Drawings** tab to list the open drawings in the tree view. Load the palette with the layer content from EX4-8.dwg.

○ Select all the layer names shown in the palette, and then drag and drop them into the new drawing.

○ Notice the message on the command line indicating that duplicate layer names were ignored. Open the **Layer Control** drop-down list and view the layers now defined in the new drawing to confirm that the layers from EX4-8 were imported as expected.

○ Select the **Folders** tab to display the desktop hierarchy in the tree view. Navigate to the AutoCAD 2004\Sample folder.

○ In the tree view window, select the Wilhome drawing file and load the linetype content into the palette.

○ Select the TINYDASH and THREEDOT linetypes and load them into the new drawing.

○ Save the new drawing as EX4-10.

---

## Additional Layering Tools

In addition to the standard layering tools discussed throughout this chapter, the **Express** pull-down menu includes a **Layers** cascading menu with several useful layering tools. An **ET: Layers** toolbar is also available by right-clicking in a docked toolbar area that does not contain a toolbar. Select the **Express** menu, then choose **Layers** from the list. A brief description of the tools available is provided in the following list:

- **Layer Manager.** As mentioned earlier, the **Express** menu includes a **Layer Manager...** option that allows you to create layer states within the drawing. The **Layer Manager: Save and Restore Layer Settings** dialog box is very similar to the **Layer Properties Manager Save State...** and **State Manager...** buttons. This utility was available in releases prior to AutoCAD 2000 as a means of creating and managing layer states before the command was added to standard AutoCAD.

- **Layer Walk.** Selecting the **Layer Walk...** command opens the **LayerWalk - Layers:** dialog box, shown in **Figure 4-37A.** This tool provides a list box with all the layers in the drawing. Selecting a layer name in the list causes all the layers in the drawing to be turned off, except for the selected layer. This provides a means for you to "walk" through a drawing full of layers to see which objects are drawn on which layers. Using the [Shift] or [Ctrl] keys to select layer names causes the objects on those layers to display.

**Figure 4-37.**
The **LayerWalk - Layers:** dialog box. A—Selected layers are displayed in the drawing area. B—Entering a filter in the filter drop-down lists only layers matching the filter criteria.

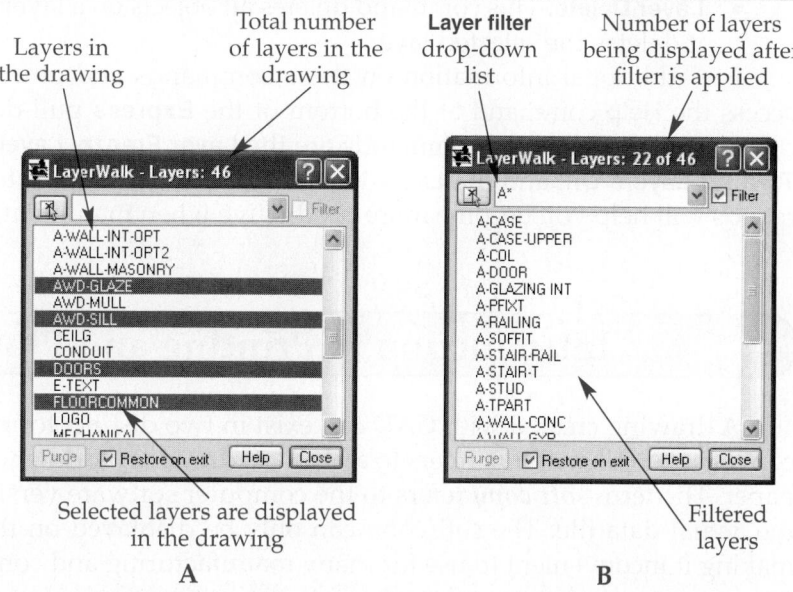

Layers in the drawing

Total number of layers in the drawing

**Layer filter** drop-down list

Number of layers being displayed after filter is applied

Selected layers are displayed in the drawing

A

Filtered layers

B

You can also enter a character in the filter list to have the **LayerWalk** routine filter for layers with specific characters. Layers meeting your filter criteria are then displayed in the list box. See **Figure 4-37B.**

- **Layer Match.** Using this command allows you to select objects that need their layer to match another object's layer. First, select the objects whose layers will be changed, and then select an object whose layer will be matched.
- **Change to Current Layer.** This command allows you to pick objects on a layer and have them moved to the current layer.
- **Copy Objects to New Layer.** Use this command to copy objects in the drawing to a new layer and move the copies to a new location. This command displays the **COPYTOLAYER** dialog box, where you can select the layer to which the objects will be moved. After selecting the layer, you have the option of choosing a base point to move the layers from and a displacement point or new location for the copied objects.
- **Layer Isolate.** This command turns off all the layers in the drawing, except for the layer of an object you choose.
- **Isolate Layer to Current Viewport.** This command is similar to **Layer Isolate**, except it freezes the selected layer in all paper space viewports other than the current viewport. Layer control for paper space viewports is discussed later in this text.
- **Layer Off.** You can use this command when you desire to turn off a layer. Select an object whose layer you wish to turn off, and the layer is turned off.
- **Turn All Layers On.** This command turns on all layers that have been turned off.
- **Layer Freeze.** Similar to the **Layer Off** command, this command freezes the layer of an object you select.
- **Thaw All Layers.** This command thaws all frozen layers in the drawing.
- **Layer Lock.** Use this command to lock the layer of an object you select.
- **Layer Unlock.** Use this command to unlock any locked layers in the drawing.
- **Layer Merge.** This command causes you to merge objects on two layers to a single layer. First select the objects that need to be moved to a different layer. Next, select an object on the layer where you want the first selected objects to be merged. Once you have done this, the layer of the first selected objects is deleted from the drawing.

- **Layer Delete.** This command deletes all objects on a layer you choose, and then it deletes the selected layer.

For additional information on these commands and other **Express** commands, access the **Help** command at the bottom of the **Express** pull-down menu. The most commonly used **Express** commands are the **Layer Freeze**, **Layer Off**, **Thaw All Layers**, **Turn All Layers On**, and the **Layer Isolate** commands. Getting to know these as commands will help you become more productive when manipulating layer displays.

## Introduction to Printing and Plotting

A drawing created with CAD can exist in two distinct forms: hard copy and soft copy. The term *hard copy* refers to a physical drawing a printer or plotter produces on paper. The term *soft copy* refers to the computer software version of the drawing, or the actual data file. The soft copy can only be displayed on the computer monitor, making it inconvenient to use for many manufacturing and construction purposes. If the power to the computer is turned off, the soft copy drawing is not available.

A hard copy drawing is extremely versatile. It can be rolled up or folded and taken down to the shop floor or out to a construction site. A hard copy drawing can be checked and redlined without a computer or CAD software. Although CAD is the standard throughout the world for generating drawings, the hard copy drawing is still a vital tool in industry.

AutoCAD supports two types of hard copy devices—printers and plotters. Printers and plotters take the soft copy images you draw in AutoCAD and transfer them onto paper. There are several types of *printers*, including dot matrix, ink-jet, laser, and thermal transfer. Dot matrix printers are normally used to make low-quality check prints, while the better quality ink-jet, laser, and thermal printers may be used for quick check prints of formal drawings. Print size for most of these printers is 8.5″ × 11″ or 8.5″ × 14″.

Large format hard copy devices are commonly referred to as *plotters*. These include ink-jet, thermal, electrostatic, pen, and pencil plotters. These plotters are capable of producing a hard copy with varying line widths and color output. Pen plotters have been the industry standard for preparing large format hard copies. They are called *pen plotters* because they use liquid ink, fiber tip pens, or pens with pencil lead. Multipen plotters can provide different line thicknesses and colors. Even though pen plotters can plot very quickly, it takes quite some time to plot a large, complex drawing. Since plotting with pen plotters can often be time-consuming, ink-jet, thermal transfer, and laser plotters are rapidly replacing pen plotters in industry.

Laser printers and plotters draw lines on a revolving plate charged with high voltage. The laser light causes the plate to discharge while an ink toner adheres to the laser-drawn image. Pressure or heat then bonds the ink to the paper. The quality of the laser printer or plotter depends on the number of dots per inch (dpi). Laser printers are commonly 600 and 1200 dpi.

Thermal printers use tiny heat elements to burn dots into treated paper. The electrostatic process uses a line of closely spaced, electrically charged, wire nibs to produce dots on coated paper. Ink-jet plotters spray droplets of ink onto the paper to produce dot matrix images.

The information found in this chapter is provided to give you only the basics, so you can make your first plot. Chapter 10 explores the detailed aspects of printing and plotting. Prints and plots are made using the **Plot** dialog box. Access this dialog box by selecting **Plot...** from the **File** pull-down menu, picking the **Plot** button in the **Standard** toolbar, pressing the [Ctrl]+[P] key combination, or typing PLOT at the Command: prompt. You can also right-click on a **Model** or **Layout** tab and select **Plot...** from the shortcut menu.

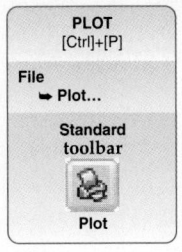

PLOT
[Ctrl]+[P]

File
➥ Plot...

Standard
toolbar

Plot

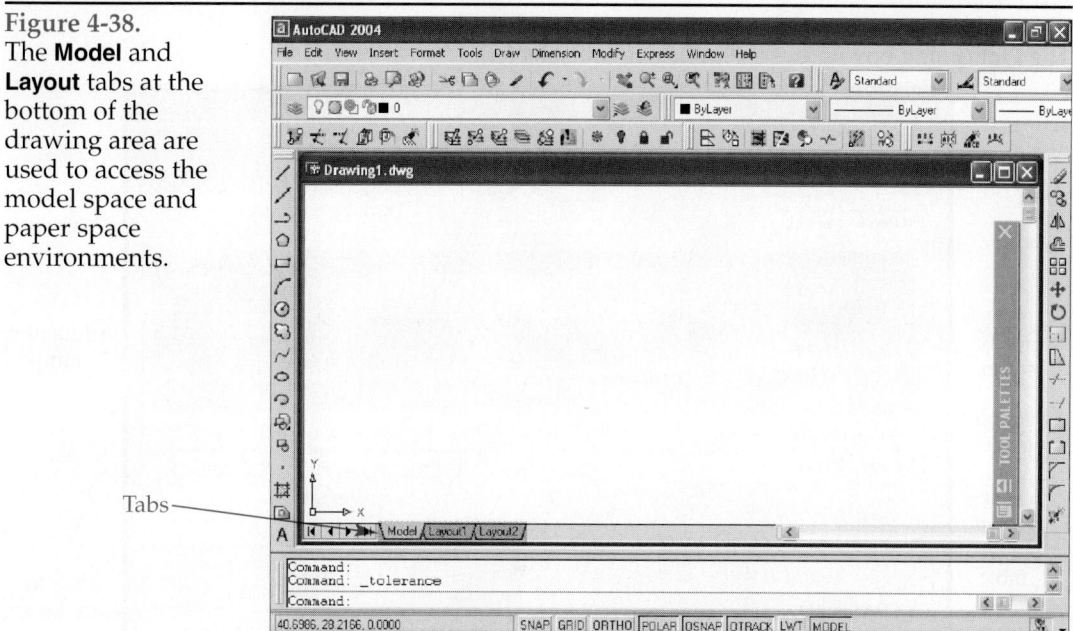

**Figure 4-38.**
The **Model** and **Layout** tabs at the bottom of the drawing area are used to access the model space and paper space environments.

Tabs

The first step in making an AutoCAD drawing is to create a model. The *model* is composed of various objects, such as lines, circles, and text. The model is created by drawing in the **Model** tab at the bottom of the drawing area. See **Figure 4-38.** The model is created in an environment called *model space.*

Once the model is completed, a layout can be created. A *layout* can contain various views of the model, a title block, and other annotations. In addition, the layout includes page setup information (such as paper size and margins) and plotter configuration data (information related to the specific model of printer or plotter being used). Layouts are created using the **Layout** tabs at the bottom of the drawing area. Layouts are created in an environment called *paper space,* and a single drawing can have multiple layouts.

Drawings can be plotted from the **Model** tab of the drawing area or from one of the **Layout** tabs. The following discussion will address plotting from the **Model** tab only. Creating and plotting layouts is addressed in Chapter 10.

## Plot Device Tab

The **Plot** dialog box is shown in **Figure 4-39** with the **Plot Device** tab displayed. The features of this tab will be discussed in detail in Chapter 10. The following is a brief introduction to some of the features:

- **Plotter configuration.** This area displays the name of the currently selected plotter and allows you to select a different plotter or printer. For now, it is assumed that your instructor or CAD system manager has taken care of the plotter configuration.
- **Plot style table (pen assignments).** All objects created in AutoCAD have a plot style property, just as all objects have a layer and color property. The plot style property determines how the object is plotted. The plot style table contains definitions for a collection of plot styles. This area displays the name of the currently selected plot style table and allows you to select a different table. This topic is described in detail in Chapter 10.
- **Plot stamp.** A plot stamp is text information included on a printed or plotted drawing. A plot stamp can include information such as the drawing name or the date and time the drawing was printed.

**Figure 4-39.**
The **Plot** dialog box with the **Plot Device** tab selected.

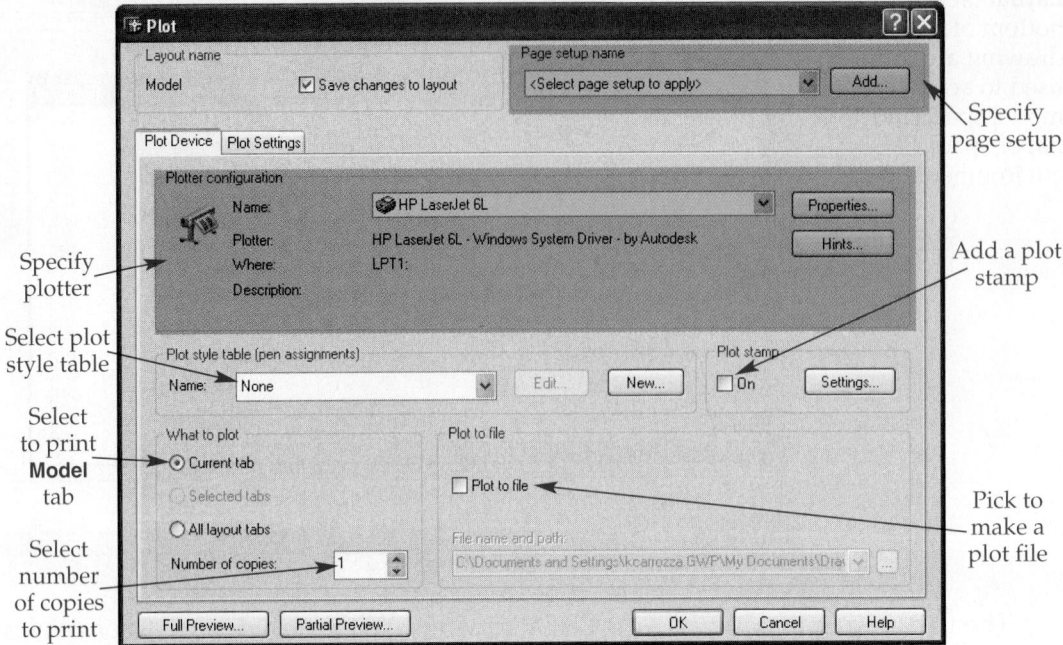

- **What to plot.** The **Current tab** option is used to plot from the **Model** tab. You can adjust the **Number of copies:** setting to make multiple plots.
- **Plot to file.** If you select the **Plot to file** check box, you can write your plot to a file, rather than to a printing device. This is useful because many graphics programs can import and convert drawing information in the form of plot files.

## Making a Plot

There are many plotting options available. In this section, one method of creating a plot from the **Model** tab is discussed. Refer to **Figure 4-40** as you read through the following plotting procedure:

1. Access the **Plot** dialog box and select the **Plot Settings** tab.
2. Check the plot device and paper size specifications in the **Paper size and paper units** area.
3. Select what is to be plotted in the **Plot area** section. The following options are available:
   - **Limits.** This option plots everything inside the defined drawing limits.
   - **Extents.** This option plots only the area of the drawing where objects are drawn.
   - **Display.** This option plots the current screen display.
   - **Window.** Pick the **Window** button to manually select a rectangular area of the drawing to plot. When you pick this button, the drawing window returns, and you can select the window. After you select the second corner of the window, the **Plot** dialog box returns.
4. Select an option in the **Drawing orientation** area. Choose **Portrait** or **Landscape** to orient your drawing vertically (portrait) or horizontally (landscape). The **Plot upside-down** option rotates the paper 180°.
5. Set the scale in the **Plot scale** area. Because you draw full-scale in AutoCAD, you typically need to scale drawings either up or down to fit the paper. Scale is measured as a ratio of either inches or millimeters to drawing units. Select a predefined scale from the **Plot Scale** drop-down list or enter your own values into the custom fields. Choose Scaled to Fit from the **Plot Scale** drop-down list to let AutoCAD automatically shrink or stretch the plot area to fill the paper.

**Figure 4-40.**
The **Plot** dialog box with the **Plot Settings** tab selected.

Pick whether to plot vertically or horizontally on the paper

Select area to plot

Preview plot

Set scale

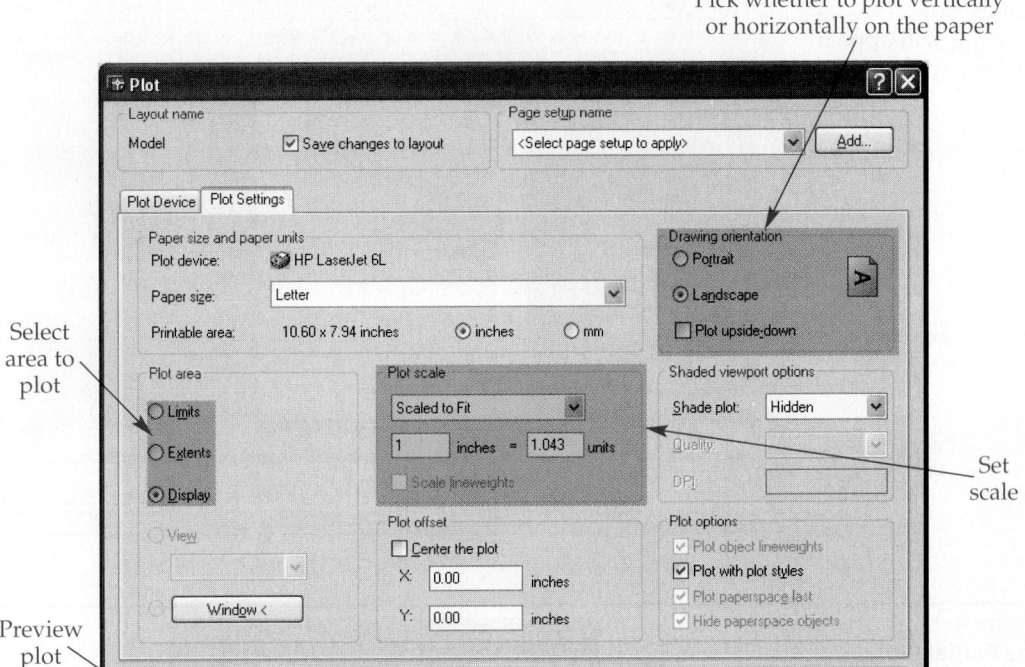

6. If desired, use the **Plot offset** area to set additional left and bottom margins around the plot or to center the plot.

7. Preview the plot. Pick the **Full Preview...** button to display the sheet as it will look when it is plotted. See **Figure 4-41.** The cursor appears as a magnifying glass with + and – symbols. The plot preview image zooms if you hold the left mouse button and move the cursor. Press [Esc] to exit the preview. The **Partial Preview...** button displays the **Partial Plot Preview** dialog box. See **Figure 4-42.** This shows the area of the paper and the area of the plotted drawing.

8. Pick the **OK** button in the **Plot** dialog box to send the data to the plotting device.

Before you pick the **OK** button to send your drawing to the plotter, there are several items you should check:

✓ The printer or plotter is plugged in.

✓ The cable from your computer to printer or plotter is secure.

✓ The printer has paper.

✓ Paper is properly loaded in the plotter and grips or clamps are in place.

✓ Ink cartridges or plotter pens are inserted correctly.

✓ The plotter area is clear for paper movement.

**PROFESSIONAL TIP**

You can stop a plot in progress at any time by using the [Esc] key. Keep in mind that it may take a while for some plotters or printers to terminate the plot, depending on the amount of the drawing file that has already been sent. Turning the plotter off purges all plot data from the plotter's internal buffer.

**Figure 4-41.**
A full preview of
the plot shows
exactly how the
drawing will appear
on the paper.

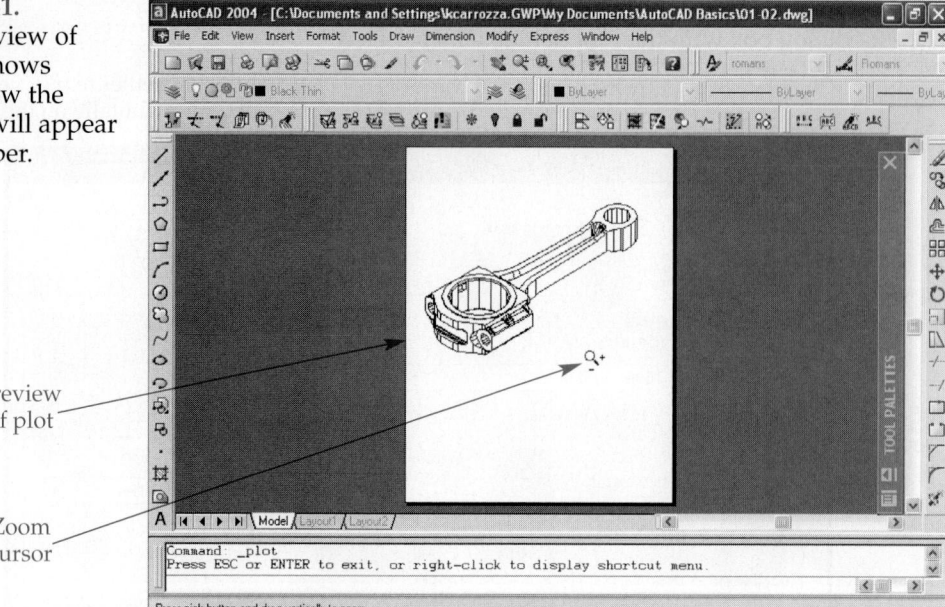

Preview
of plot

Zoom
cursor

**Figure 4-42.**
The **Partial Plot
Preview** dialog box
shows the location
of the paper
margins and the
area covered by the
drawing.

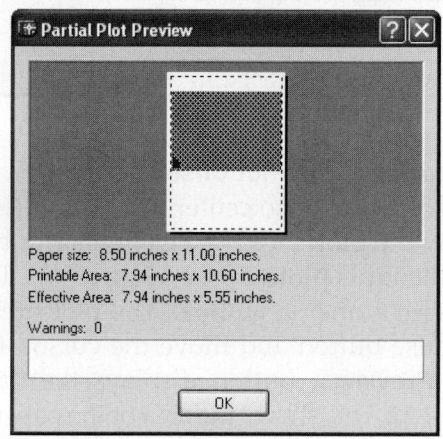

Exercise 4-11

○ Open any of your previous drawings.
○ Access the **Plot** dialog box.
○ Set the plot scale to Scaled to Fit, and set the plot area to **Display**.
○ Pick the **Partial Preview...** button and observe the display. Press the [Esc] key.
○ Pick the **Full Preview...** button and observe the results. A full representation of your drawing should be displayed as it will appear when printed on the paper. Press the [Esc] key.
○ Experiment by changing the drawing orientation, followed by viewing a full preview after each change.
○ Select the **Window** button and window a small portion of your drawing.
○ Do another full preview to see the results. End the preview.
○ Set the plot area to **Display** and preview the drawing. Make a print if a printer is available for your use.
○ Exit AutoCAD.

# Chapter Test

*Answer the following questions on a separate sheet of paper.*

1. What is the default linetype in AutoCAD?
2. Name at least ten of AutoCAD's standard linetypes.
3. List the seven standard color names and numbers.
4. How are new layer names entered when creating several layers at the same time without using the **New** button in the **Layer Properties Manager** dialog box?
5. Which pull-down menu contains the **Layer...** option?
6. Identify three ways to access the **Layer Properties Manager** dialog box.
7. What condition must exist before a linetype can be used in a layer?
8. How do you make another layer current in the **Layer Properties Manager** dialog box?
9. How do you change a layer's linetype in the **Layer Properties Manager** dialog box?
10. How is the **Select Color** dialog box displayed from the **Layer Properties Manager** dialog box?
11. How do you load several linetypes at the same time from the **Load or Reload Linetypes** dialog box?
12. What is the state of a layer *not* displayed on the screen and *not* calculated by the computer when the drawing is regenerated?
13. Describe the purpose of locking a layer.
14. Are locked layers visible?
15. How do you know if a layer is off, thawed, or unlocked in the **Layer Properties Manager** dialog box?
16. Describe the purpose of layer filters.
17. Identify two ways to directly access property options for changing the layer, linetype, or color of an existing object.
18. Identify the following layer status icons:

   A.

   B.

   C.

   D.

   E.

   F.

19. How do you make the layer of an existing object current?
20. How do you make another layer current by using the **Layers** toolbar?
21. Which button in the **Layer Properties Manager** allows you to save layer settings so they can be restored at a later time?
22. Why is ByLayer referred to as a logical color, linetype, and lineweight?
23. Define a *global change*.
24. In the tree view area of **DesignCenter**, how do you view the content categories of one of the listed open drawings?
25. Briefly explain how drag and drop works.
26. How do you display all the available layer contents from a drawing in the **DesignCenter** preview palette?
27. Define *hard copy* and *soft copy*.
28. Identify four ways to access the **Plot** dialog box.
29. Describe the difference between the **Display** and **Window** options in the **Plot area** section of the **Plot** dialog box.
30. What is a major advantage of doing a plot preview?

## Drawing Problems

*Before beginning these problems, set up template drawings with layer names, colors, linetypes, and lineweights for the type of drawing you are creating. Do not draw dimensions. Be sure to do preliminary planning for each drawing as discussed in this chapter.*

1. Draw the plot plan shown below. Use the linetypes shown, which include Continuous, Hidden, Phantom, Centerline, Fenceline2, and Gas_line. Make your drawing proportional to the example. Save the drawing as P4-1.

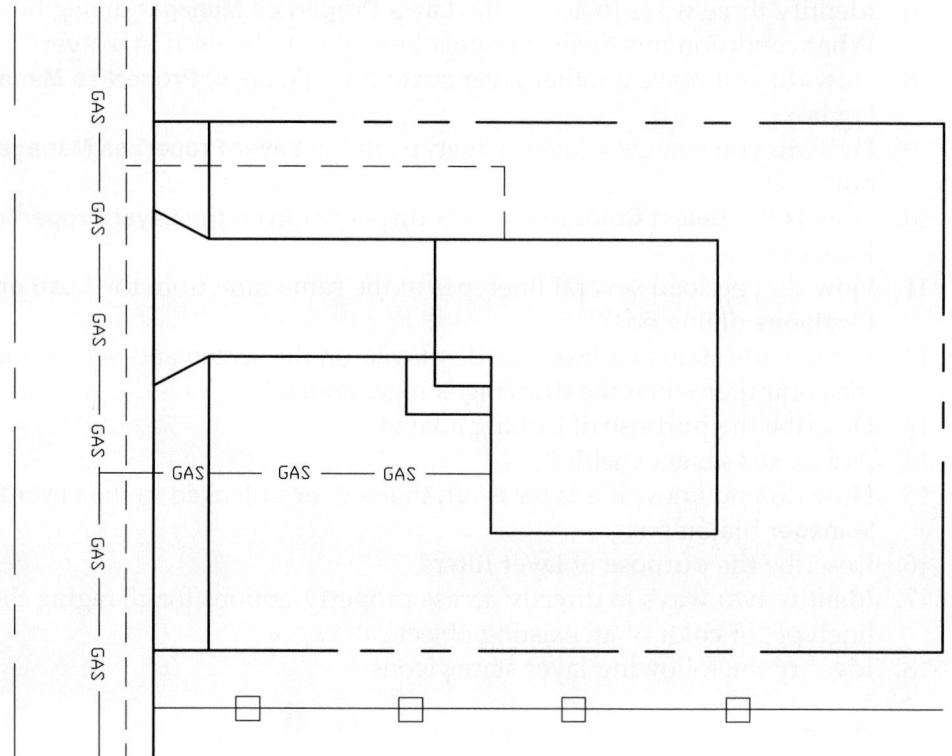

2. Draw the chart for the door schedule. Make the measurements for the rows and columns approximately the same as in the givin problem. Do not draw the text. It will be added in Chapter 8. Save the drawing as P4-2.

| | | DOOR SCHEDULE | | |
|---|---|---|---|---|
| SYM. | SIZE | TYPE | | QTY. |
| ① | 36 x 80 | S.C. RP. METAL INSULATED | | 1 |
| ② | 36 x 80 | S.C. FLUSH METAL INSULATED | | 2 |
| ③ | 32 x 80 | S.C. SELF CLOSING | | 2 |
| ④ | 32 x 80 | HOLLOW CORE | | 5 |
| ⑤ | 30 x 80 | HOLLOW CORE | | 5 |
| ⑥ | 30 x 80 | POCKET SLDG. | | 2 |

3. Draw the line chart shown below. Use the linetypes shown, which include **Continuous**, **Hidden**, **Phantom**, **Centerline**, **Fenceline1**, and **Fenceline2**. Make your drawing proportional to the given example. Save the drawing as P4-3.

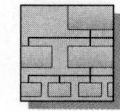

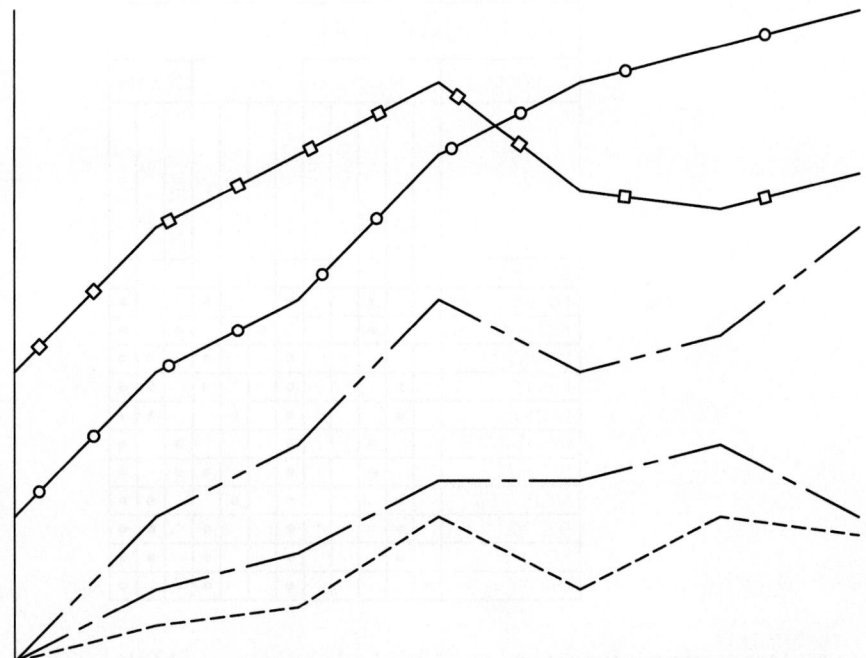

4. Draw the chart for the window schedule. Make the measurements for the rows and columns approximately the same as shown. Do not draw the hexagons or text. They will be added in Chapter 8. Save the drawing as P4-4.

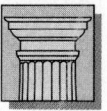

# WINDOW SCHEDULE

| SYM. | SIZE | MODEL | ROUGH OPEN | QTY. |
|---|---|---|---|---|
| A | 12 x 60 | JOB BUILT | VERIFY | 2 |
| B | 96 x 60 | W4N5 CSM. | 8'-0 3/4" x 5'-0 7/8" | 1 |
| C | 48 x 60 | W2N5 CSM. | 4'-0 3/4" x 5'-0 7/8" | 2 |
| D | 48 x 36 | W2N3 CSM. | 4'-0 3/4" x 3'-6 1/2" | 2 |
| E | 42 x 42 | 2N3 CSM. | 3'- 6 1/2" x 3'-6 1/2" | 2 |
| F | 72 x 48 | G64 SLDG. | 6'-0 1/2" x 4'-0 1/2" | 1 |
| G | 60 x 42 | G536 SLDG. | 5'-0 1/2" x 3'-6 1/2" | 4 |
| H | 48 x 42 | G436 SLDG. | 4'-0 1/2" x 3'-6 1/2" | 1 |
| J | 48 x 24 | A41 AWN. | 4'-0 1/2" x 2'-0 7/8" | 3 |

5. Draw the chart for the interior finish schedule. Make the measurements for the rows and columns approximately the same as in the given problem. Do not draw the solid circles or the text. They will be added in Chapter 8. Save the drawing as P4-5.

| INTERIOR FINISH SCHEDULE | | | | | | | | | | | | |
|---|---|---|---|---|---|---|---|---|---|---|---|---|
| ROOM | FLOOR | | | | | WALLS | | | | CEILING | | |
| | VINYL | CARPET | TILE | HARDWOOD | CONCRETE | PAINT | PAPER | TEXTURE | SPRAY | SMOOTH | BROCADE | PAINT |
| ENTRY | | | | | • | | | | | | | |
| FOYER | | | • | | | • | | • | | | | • |
| KITCHEN | | | • | | | | | • | | • | | • |
| DINING | | | | • | | • | | • | | • | • | • |
| FAMILY | | • | | | | • | | • | | • | • | • |
| LIVING | | • | | | | • | | | • | • | • | • |
| MSTR. BATH | | | • | | | • | | | | • | | • |
| BATH #2 | | | • | | | • | | • | | • | | • |
| MSTR. BED | | • | | | | • | | | • | • | • | • |
| BED #2 | | • | | | | • | | • | | • | | • |
| BED #3 | | • | | | | • | | • | | • | | • |
| UTILITY | • | | | | | • | | • | | • | • | • |

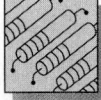

6. Draw the integrated circuit block diagram. Make your drawing proportional to the given problem. Do not draw the circle, line connections, or text. Save the drawing as P4-6.

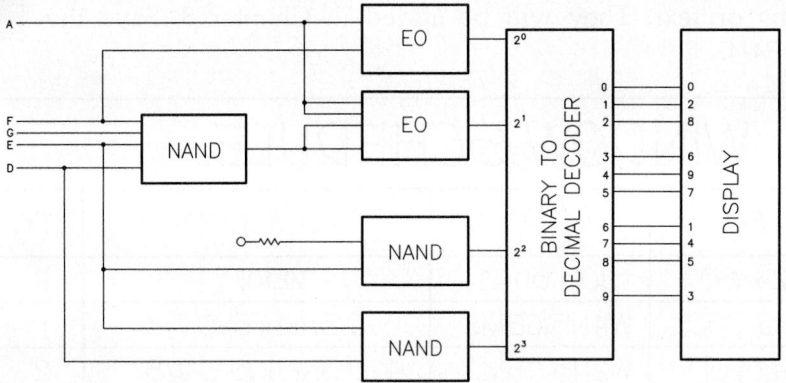

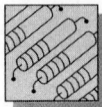

7. Draw the robotics system block diagram. Make your drawing proportional to the given problem. Do not draw the arrowheads or text. Save the drawing as P4-7.

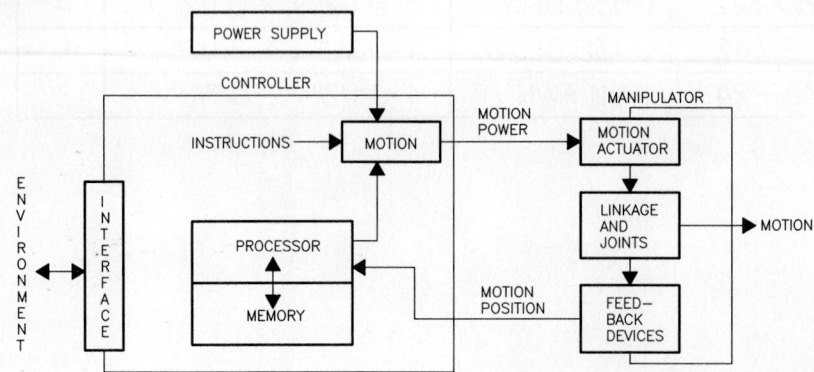

182    AutoCAD and its Applications—Basics

## CHAPTER 5

# Drawing Basic Shapes

## Learning Objectives

After completing this chapter, you will be able to do the following:
- Use **DRAGMODE** to observe an object being dragged into place.
- Draw circles using the **CIRCLE** command options.
- Identify and use the @ symbol function.
- Draw arcs using the **ARC** command options.
- Use the **ELLIPSE** command to draw ellipses and elliptical arcs.
- Draw polygons.
- Use the **RECTANG** command to draw rectangles, and explore other rectangle options.
- Draw donuts.
- Use the **Revision Cloud** tool to mark up drawings.

The decisions you make when drawing circles and arcs with AutoCAD are similar to those made when drawing the items manually. AutoCAD provides many ways to create circles and arcs using the **CIRCLE** and **ARC** commands. These include the center location and radius or diameter, or where the outline of the circle or arc should be located. AutoCAD also includes additional drawing tools such as the **ELLIPSE**, **POLYGON**, **RECTANG**, and **DONUT** commands to draw a wide variety of shapes. Other provided tools include the **Revision Cloud** tool, which is used to mark up drawings.

## Watching Objects Drag into Place

Chapter 3 showed how the **LINE** command displays an image that is "dragged" across the screen before the second endpoint is picked. This image is called a *rubberband*. The **CIRCLE**, **ARC**, **ELLIPSE**, **POLYGON**, and **RECTANG** commands also display a rubberband image to help you decide where to place the object.

For example, when you draw a circle using the **Center, Radius** option, a circle image appears on the screen after you pick the center point. This image gets larger or smaller as you move the pointer. When the desired circle size is picked, the dragged image is replaced by a solid-line circle. See **Figure 5-1.**

**Figure 5-1.**
Dragging a circle to
its desired size.

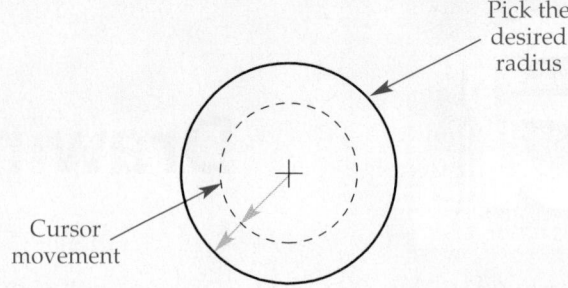

The **DRAGMODE** system variable affects the visibility of the rubberband. The **DRAGMODE** can be set to on, off, or automatic by typing DRAGMODE at the Command: prompt and pressing [Enter] as follows:

Command: **DRAGMODE**↵
Enter new value [ON/OFF/Auto] <Auto>: *(type* ON, OFF, *or* A *and press* [Enter]*)*

The current (default) mode is shown in brackets. Pressing the [Enter] key keeps the existing status.

When **DRAGMODE** is on, you must enter DRAG during a command sequence to see the objects drag into place. The following command sequence shows you how to activate the **DRAGMODE** while in the **CIRCLE** command.

Command: **CIRCLE**↵
Specify center point for circle or [3P/2P/Ttr (tan tan radius)]: *(pick a center point)*
Specify radius of circle or [Diameter]: **DRAG**↵ *(the circle drags into place as you move the cursor and pick the desired radius)*
Command:

Selecting **OFF** disables **DRAGMODE**. This means that you will not see the objects drag into place. Even if you enter DRAG, AutoCAD ignores the request. When you set **DRAGMODE** to **Auto**, you see objects automatically dragged into place for all commands that support dragging. This is the default setting. Many users prefer to have the **DRAGMODE** set to **Auto**.

## Drawing Circles

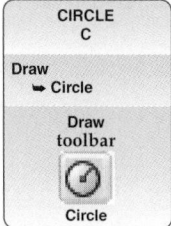

CIRCLE
C

Draw
↪ Circle

Draw
toolbar

Circle

The **CIRCLE** command is activated by picking the **Circle** button in the **Draw** toolbar, selecting **Circle** from the **Draw** pull-down menu, or entering C or CIRCLE at the Command: prompt. The options available in the **Circle** cascading menu are shown in **Figure 5-2.**

**Figure 5-2.**
The **Circle** cascading
menu in the **Draw**
pull-down menu.

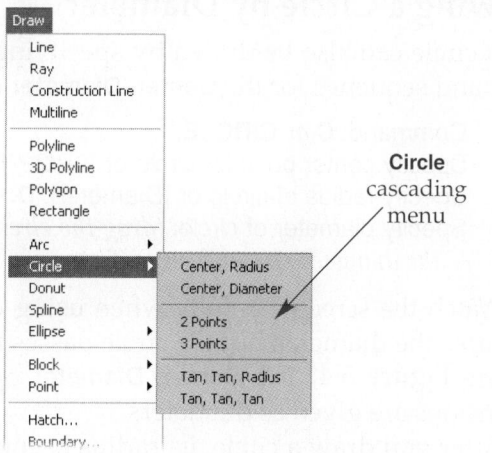

Circle
cascading
menu

## Drawing a Circle by Radius

A circle can be drawn by specifying the center point and the radius. The *radius* is
the distance from the center to the circumference of a circle or arc. The *circumference*
is the perimeter or distance around the circle.

After accessing the **Center, Radius** option, you are asked to pick the center point
followed by the radius. If the radius is picked on the screen, watch the coordinate display to help you locate the exact radius. The following command sequence is used to
draw the circle in **Figure 5-3:**

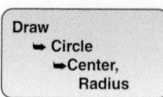

Draw
➥ Circle
➥Center,
Radius

> Command: **C** *or* **CIRCLE**.⏎
> Specify center point for circle or [3P/2P/Ttr (tan tan radius)]: *(select a center point)*
> Specify radius of circle or [Diameter]: *(drag the circle to the desired radius and pick,*
>    *or type the radius size and press* [Enter])

**Figure 5-3.**
Drawing a circle by
specifying the
center point and
radius.

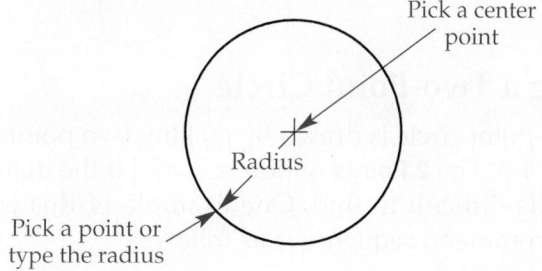

Pick a center
point

Radius

Pick a point or
type the radius

**NOTE**

The radius value you enter is stored as the **CIRCLERAD** system variable. This system variable is the default radius setting the next time you use the **CIRCLE** command. If
**CIRCLERAD** is set to zero, no default radius is provided the
next time you use the **CIRCLE** command.

## Drawing a Circle by Diameter

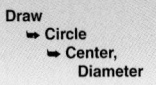
Draw
➥ Circle
➥ Center,
   Diameter

A circle can also be drawn by specifying the center point and the diameter. The command sequence for the **Center, Diameter** option is as follows:

Command: **C** *or* **CIRCLE**↵
Specify center point for circle or [3P/2P/Ttr (tan tan radius)]: *(select a center point)*
Specify radius of circle or [Diameter]: **D**↵
Specify diameter of circle: *(drag the circle to the desired diameter and pick, or type the diameter size and press* [Enter]*)*

Watch the screen carefully when using the **Center, Diameter** option. The pointer measures the diameter, but the circle passes midway between the center and the cursor. See **Figure** 5-4. The **Center, Diameter** option is convenient because most circle dimensions are given as diameters.

After you draw a circle, its radius becomes the default for the next circle. If you use the **Diameter** option, the previous default setting is converted to a diameter. If you use the **Radius** option to draw a circle after using the **Diameter** option, AutoCAD changes the default to a radius measurement based on the previous diameter. If you set **CIRCLERAD** to a value such as .50, then the default for a circle drawn with the **Diameter** option is automatically 1.00 (twice the default radius).

**Figure 5-4.**
Drawing a circle using the **Center, Diameter** option. Notice that AutoCAD calculates the circle's position as you move the cursor.

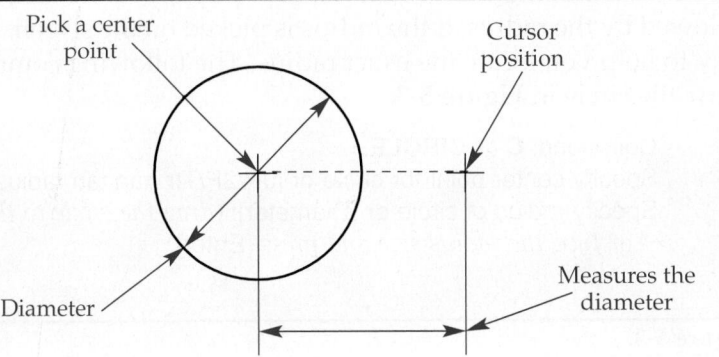

## Drawing a Two-Point Circle

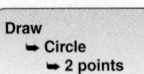
Draw
➥ Circle
➥ 2 points

A two-point circle is drawn by picking two points on opposite sides of the circle. See **Figure** 5-5. The **2 Points** option is useful if the diameter of the circle is known, but the center is difficult to find. One example of this is locating a circle between two lines. The command sequence is as follows:

Command: **C** *or* **CIRCLE**↵
Specify center point for circle or [3P/2P/Ttr (tan tan radius)]: **2P**↵
Specify first end point of circle's diameter: *(select a point)*
Specify second end point of circle's diameter: *(select a point)*

AutoCAD automatically calculates the radius of the circle. This is the default radius the next time the **CIRCLE** command is used.

**Figure 5-5.**
Drawing a circle by selecting two points.

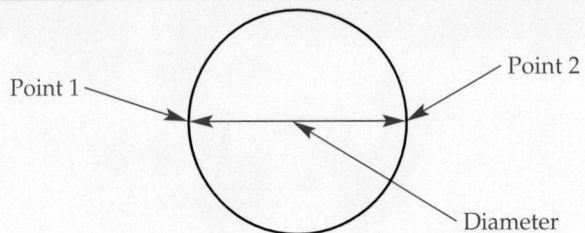

## Drawing a Three-Point Circle

If three points on the circumference of a circle are known, the **3 Points** option is the best method to use. The three points can be selected in any order. See **Figure 5-6**. The command sequence is as follows:

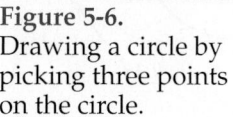

Command: **C** *or* **CIRCLE.⏎**
Specify center point for circle or [3P/2P/Ttr (tan tan radius)]: **3P.⏎**
Specify first point on circle: *(select a point)*
Specify second point on circle: *(select a point)*
Specify third point on circle: *(select a point)*

AutoCAD automatically calculates the radius of the circle. This becomes the default radius the next time the **CIRCLE** command is used.

**Figure 5-6.**
Drawing a circle by picking three points on the circle.

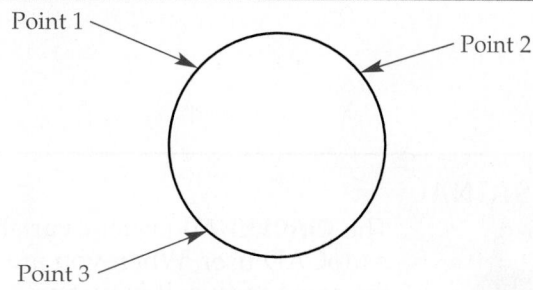

## Drawing a Circle Tangent to Two Objects

The term *tangent* refers to a line, circle, or arc that comes into contact with an arc or circle at only one point. That point is called the ***point of tangency***. A line drawn from the circle's center to the point of tangency is perpendicular to the tangent line. A line drawn between the centers of two tangent circles passes through the point of tangency. You can draw a circle tangent to given lines, circles, or arcs.

The **Tan, Tan, Radius** option creates a circle having a specific radius and tangent to two objects. Once the **Tan, Tan, Radius** option is selected, select the lines, arcs, or circles that the new circle will be tangent to. The radius of the circle is also required. To assist you in picking the objects, AutoCAD uses the **Deferred Tangent** object snap by default. (Object snap modes are covered in Chapter 6.) When you see the **Deferred Tangent** symbol, move it to the objects that you want to pick. The command sequence is as follows:

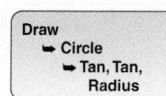

Command: **C** *or* **CIRCLE.⏎**
Specify center point for circle or [3P/2P/Ttr (tan tan radius)]: **T.⏎**
Specify point on object for first tangent of circle: *(pick the first line, circle, or arc)*
Specify point on object for second tangent of circle: *(pick the second line, circle, or arc)*
Specify radius of circle <current>: *(type a radius value and press* [Enter]*)*

If the radius entered is too small, AutoCAD gives you the message: Circle does not exist. AutoCAD automatically calculates the radius of the circle. This is the default radius the next time the **CIRCLE** command is used. Two examples of this option are shown in **Figure 5-7**.

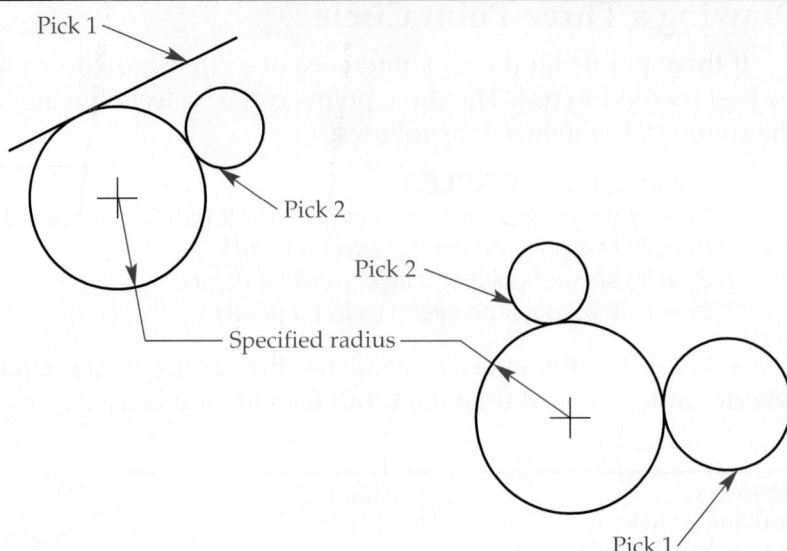

Figure 5-7.
Two examples of drawing circles tangent to two given objects using the **Tangent, Tangent, Radius** option.

Pick 1

Pick 2

Pick 2

Specified radius

Pick 1

---

PROFESSIONAL TIP

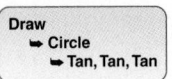

The **CIRCLERAD** system variable is normally not set by the AutoCAD user. When you are creating multiple circles with the same radius, it is normally quicker to just draw the first circle using the **CIRCLE** command and then draw the rest of the circles using the automatically set default radius of the first circle.

## Drawing a Circle Tangent to Three Objects

Draw
→ Circle
  → Tan, Tan, Tan

The **Tan, Tan, Tan** option allows you to draw a circle tangent to three existing objects. This option creates a three-point circle using the three points of tangency. See **Figure 5-8.** Selecting the pull-down option is the same as using the **3 Points** option at the Command: prompt with the **TAN** object snap:

> Command: **C** or **CIRCLE.⏎**
> Specify center point for circle or [3P/2P/Ttr (tan tan radius)]: **3P⏎**
> Specify first point on circle: **TAN.⏎**
> to (pick an object)
> Specify second point on circle: **TAN.⏎**
> to (pick an object)
> Specify third point on circle: **TAN.⏎**
> to (pick an object)
> Command:

---

NOTE

Unlike the **TTR** option, the **Tan, Tan, Tan** option does not automatically recover when a point prompt is answered with a pick where no tangent exists. In such a case, the **TAN** mode must be manually reactivated for subsequent attempts to make that pick. **TAN** (tangent) is one of the object snap modes discussed in Chapter 6 of this text. For now, if this happens, type TAN and press [Enter] at the point selection prompt. This returns the aperture box so you can pick again.

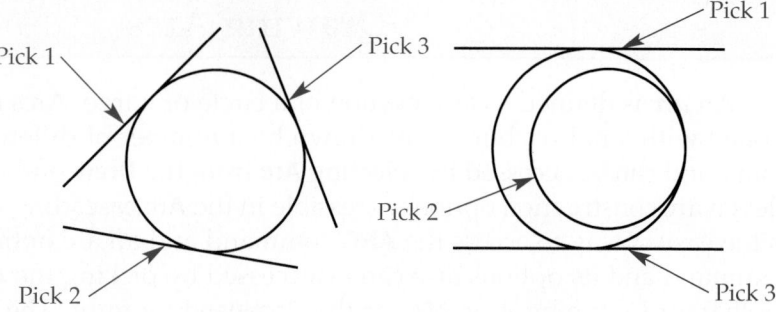

**Figure 5-8.**
Two examples of drawing circles tangent to three given objects.

Pick 1    Pick 3    Pick 1

Pick 2    Pick 2    Pick 3

## Using the @ Symbol to Specify the Last Coordinates

The @ symbol can be used to input the coordinates last entered. For example, suppose you want to draw a circle with a center at the end of the line just drawn. Enter the @ symbol when asked for a center point. The command sequence is as follows:

Command: **L** *or* **LINE**↵
Specify first point: **4,4**↵
Specify next point or [Undo]: **8,4**↵
Specify next point or [Undo]: ↵
Command: **C** *or* **CIRCLE**↵
Specify center point for circle or [3P/2P/Ttr (tan tan radius)]: **@**↵

The @ symbol automatically issues the coordinate 8,4 (end of the last line) as the center of the circle. The 8,4 value is saved in the **LASTPOINT** system variable. The @ symbol retrieves the **LASTPOINT** value.

Another application of the @ symbol is drawing concentric circles (circles with the same center). To do this, draw a circle using the **Center, Radius** or the **Center, Diameter** option. Then, enter the **CIRCLE** command again and type @ when asked for the center point. This automatically places the center of the new circle at the center of the previous circle.

### Exercise 5-1

○ Begin a new drawing or use one of your templates.
○ Set the **CIRCLERAD** system variable to 0.
○ Use the **Center, Radius** option of the **CIRCLE** command to draw a circle similar to the one shown in **Figure 5-3**.
○ Use the **Center, Diameter** option of the **CIRCLE** command to draw the circle shown in **Figure 5-4**.
○ Draw two vertical parallel lines two units apart. Then use the **2 Point** option of the **CIRCLE** command to draw a circle tangent to the two lines.
○ Use the **3 Point** option of the **CIRCLE** command to draw the circle shown in **Figure 5-6**.
○ Use the **Tangent, Tangent, Radius** option of the **CIRCLE** command to draw the circles shown in **Figure 5-7**.
○ Use the **Tan, Tan, Tan** option to draw circles tangent to the existing objects as in **Figure 5-8**.
○ Draw a line. Use the **Center, Radius** option of the **CIRCLE** command and the @ symbol to place the circle's center at the endpoint of the line.
○ Draw three concentric circles using @ and the **CIRCLE** command.
○ Set **CIRCLERAD** to .5 and draw circles using each **CIRCLE** command option. Compare the prompts to those from the first circles drawn in this exercise.
○ Save the drawing as EX5-1.

# Drawing Arcs

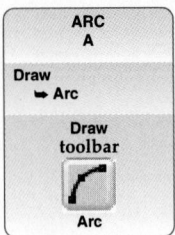

ARC
A

Draw
➡ Arc

Draw
toolbar

Arc

An *arc* is defined as any portion of a circle or curve. Arcs are commonly dimensioned with a radius, but can be drawn by a number of different methods. The **ARC** command can be accessed by selecting **Arc** from the **Draw** pull-down menu. There are eleven arc construction options accessible in the **Arc** cascading menu, **Figure 5-9**. This is the easiest way to access the **ARC** command and an arc option. However, the **ARC** command and its options also can be accessed by picking the **Arc** button in the **Draw** toolbar, or by typing A or ARC at the Command: prompt. The **3 Points** option is the default when using the toolbar button or the Command: prompt.

**Figure 5-9.**
The **Arc** cascading menu in the **Draw** pull-down menu.

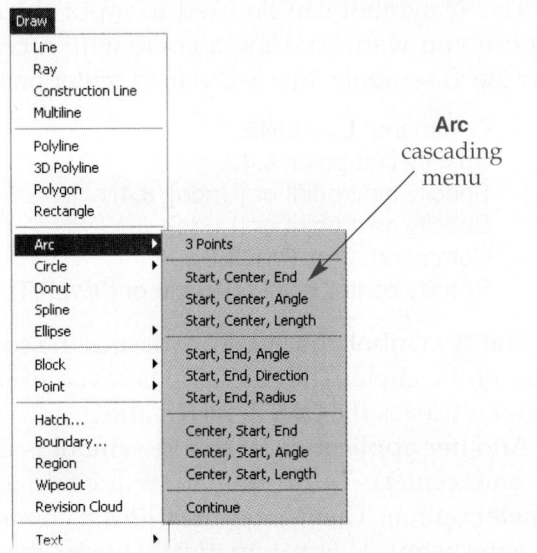

PROFESSIONAL
TIP

It is easiest to select the desired **ARC** option using the **Arc** cascading menu in the **Draw** pull-down menu. When an **ARC** option is selected, AutoCAD automatically prompts you for the next required input.

## Drawing a Three-Point Arc

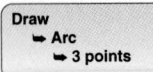

Draw
➡ Arc
➡ 3 points

The **3 Points** option asks for the start point, second point along the arc, and then the endpoint. See **Figure 5-10**. The arc can be drawn clockwise or counterclockwise and is dragged into position as the endpoint is located. The command sequence is as follows:

Command: **A** *or* **ARC**↵
Specify start point of arc or [Center]: *(select the first point on the arc)*
Specify second point of arc or [Center/End]: *(select the second point on the arc)*
Select end point of arc: *(select the arc's endpoint)*
Command:

Figure 5-10.
Drawing an arc by
picking three points.

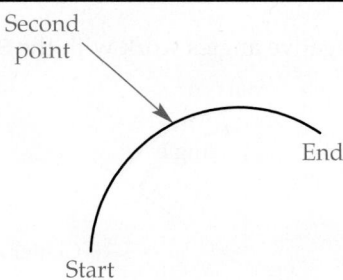

## Drawing Arcs Using the **Start, Center, End** Option

Use the **Start, Center, End** option when you know the start, center, and endpoint
locations for the arc. Picking the start and center points establishes the arc's radius.
The point selected for the endpoint determines the arc length. The selected endpoint
does not have to be on the radius of the arc. See **Figure 5-11.** The command sequence
is as follows:

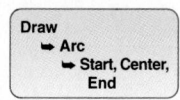

Draw
➥ Arc
 ➥ Start, Center,
  End

> Command: **A** or **ARC.**↲
> Specify start point of arc or [Center]: *(select the first point on the arc)*
> Specify second point of arc or [Center/End]: **C**↲
> Specify center point of arc: *(select the arc's center point)*
> Specify end point of arc or [Angle/chord Length]: *(select the arc endpoint)*
> Command:

Figure 5-11.
Using the **Start,
Center, End** option.
Notice the endpoint
does not have to be
on the arc.

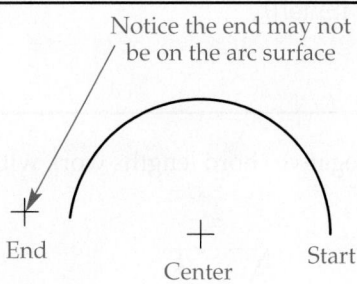

## Drawing Arcs Using the **Start, Center, Angle** Option

When the arc's included angle is known, the **Start, Center, Angle** option may be
the best choice. The *included angle* is an angle formed between the center, start point,
and endpoint of the arc. The arc is drawn counterclockwise, unless a negative angle is
specified. See **Figure 5-12.** The following shows the command sequence with a 45°
included angle:

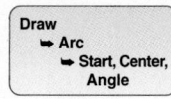

Draw
➥ Arc
 ➥ Start, Center,
  Angle

> Command: **A** or **ARC.**↲
> Specify start point of arc or [Center]: *(select the first point on the arc)*
> Specify second point of arc or [Center/End]: **C**↲
> Select center point of arc: *(select the arc center point)*
> Specify end point of arc or [Angle/chord Length]: **A**↲
> Specify included angle: **45**↲
> Command:

**Figure 5-12.**
How positive and negative angles work with the **Start, Center, Angle** option.

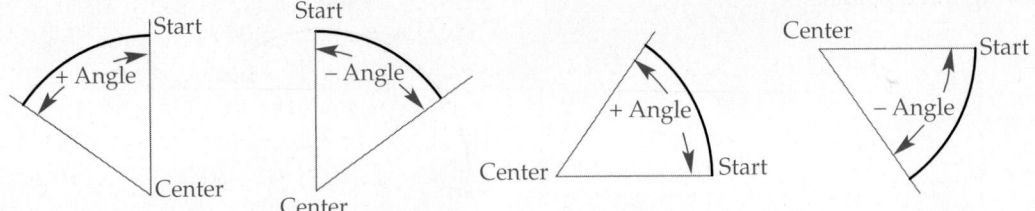

## Drawing Arcs Using the **Start, Center, Length** Option

Draw
➥ Arc
  ➥ Start, Center, Length

The chord length can be determined using a chord length table (see Appendix I). A one-unit radius arc with an included angle of 45° has a chord length of .765 units. Arcs are drawn counterclockwise. Therefore, a positive chord length gives the smallest possible arc with that length. A negative chord length results in the largest possible arc. See **Figure 5-13.** The following shows the command sequence with a chord length of .765:

> Command: **A** *or* **ARC**↵
> Specify start point of arc or [Center]: *(select the first point on the arc)*
> Specify second point of arc or [Center/End]: **C**↵
> Specify center point of arc: *(select the arc center point)*
> Specify end point of arc or [Angle/chord Length]: **L**↵
> Specify length of chord: *(type .765 for the smaller arc or –.765 for the larger arc, and press* [Enter]*)*
> Command:

**Figure 5-13.**
How positive and negative chord lengths work with the **Start, Center, Length** option.

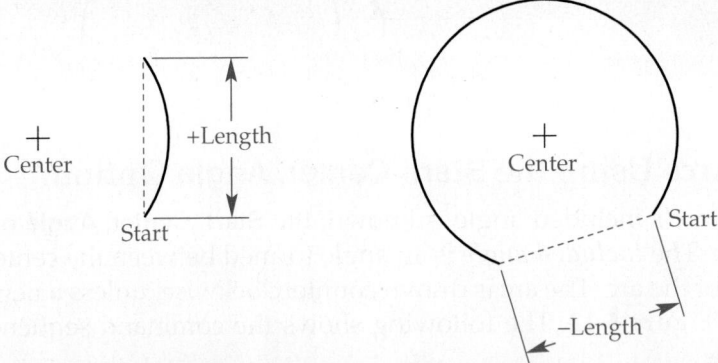

---

### Exercise 5-2

○ Begin a new drawing or use one of your templates.
○ Use the **3 Points** option of the **ARC** command to draw arcs similar to those shown in **Figure 5-10.**
○ Use the **Start, Center, End** option of the **ARC** command and draw the arc shown in **Figure 5-11.**
○ Use the **Start, Center, Angle** option of the **ARC** command and draw the arcs shown in **Figure 5-12.**
○ Use the **Start, Center, Length** option of the **ARC** command and draw the arcs shown in **Figure 5-13.**
○ Save the drawing as EX5-2.

# Drawing Arcs Using the Start, End, Angle Option

An arc can also be drawn by picking the start point, endpoint, and entering the included angle. A positive included angle draws the arc counterclockwise, while a negative angle produces a clockwise arc. See **Figure 5-14**. The command sequence is as follows:

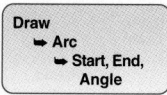

Command: **A** *or* **ARC↵**
Specify start point of arc or [Center]: *(select the first point on the arc)*
Specify second point of arc or [Center/End]: **E↵**
Specify end point of arc: *(select the arc endpoint)*
Specify center point of arc or [Angle/Direction/Radius]: **A↵**
Specify included angle: *(type a positive or negative angle and press* [Enter]*)*
Command:

**Figure 5-14.**
How positive and negative angles work with the **Start, End, Angle** option.

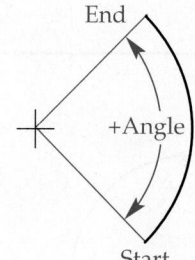
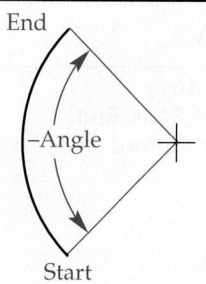

# Drawing Arcs Using the Start, End, Radius Option

A positive radius value for the **Start, End, Radius** option results in the smallest possible arc between the start point and endpoint. A negative radius gives the largest arc possible. See **Figure 5-15**. Arcs can only be drawn counterclockwise with this option. The command sequence is as follows:

Command: **A** *or* **ARC↵**
Specify start point of arc or [Center]: *(select the first point on the arc)*
Specify second point of arc or [Center/End]: **E↵**
Specify end point of arc: *(select the arc endpoint)*
Specify center point of arc or [Angle/Direction/Radius]: **R↵**
Specify radius of arc: *(pick or type a positive or negative radius and press* [Enter])
Command:

**Figure 5-15.**
Using the **Start, End, Radius** option with a positive and negative radius.

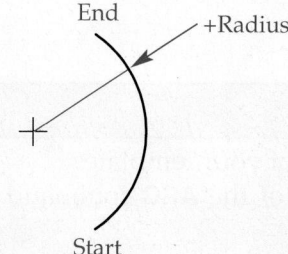
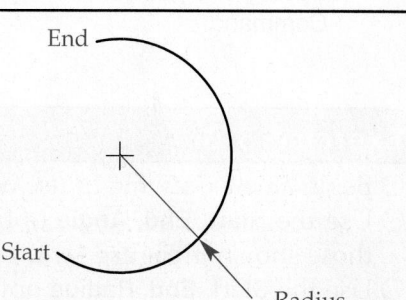

## Drawing Arcs Using the Start, End, Direction Option

Draw
➡ Arc
  ➡ Start, End,
     Direction

An arc can be drawn by picking the start point, endpoint, and entering the direction of rotation in degrees. The distance between the points and the number of degrees determines the arc's location and size. The arc is started tangent to the direction specified, with the direction being measured from the 0° mark as shown in **Figure 5-16**. The command sequence is as follows:

Command: **A** *or* **ARC**↵
Specify start point of arc or [Center]: *(select the first point on the arc)*
Specify second point of arc or [Center/End]: **E**↵
Specify end point of arc: *(select the arc endpoint)*
Specify center point of arc or [Angle/Direction/Radius]: **D**↵
Specify tangent direction for the start point of arc: *(pick the direction from the start point, or type the direction in degrees and press [Enter])*
Command:

**Figure 5-16.**
Using the **Start, End, Direction** option.

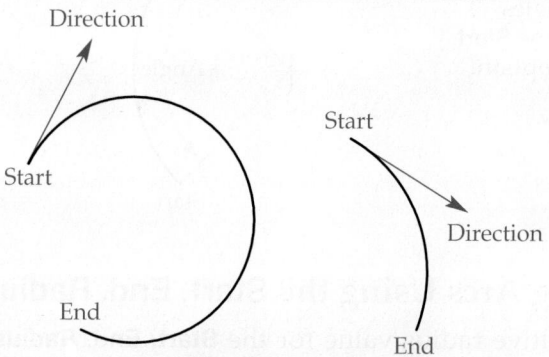

## Drawing Arcs Using the Center, Start, End Option

Draw
➡ Arc
  ➡ Center,
     Start, End

The **Center, Start, End** option is a variation of the **Start, Center, End** option. See **Figure 5-17**. Use the **Center, Start, End** option when it is easier to begin by locating the center. The command sequence is as follows:

Command: **A** *or* **ARC**↵
Specify start point of arc or [Center]: **C**↵
Specify center point of arc: *(pick the center point)*
Specify start point of arc: *(pick the start point)*
Specify end point of arc or [Angle/chord Length]: *(pick the arc's endpoint)*
Command:

### Exercise 5-3

○ Begin a new drawing or use one of your templates.
○ Use the **Start, End, Angle** option of the **ARC** command to draw arcs similar to those shown in **Figure 5-14**.
○ Use the **Start, End, Radius** option of the **ARC** command to draw the arcs shown in **Figure 5-15**.
○ Use the **Start, End, Direction** option of the **ARC** command to draw the arcs shown in **Figure 5-16**.
○ Use the **Center, Start, End** option of the **ARC** command to draw the arc shown in **Figure 5-17**.
○ Save the drawing as EX5-3.

**Figure 5-17.**
Using the **Center, Start, End** option. Note that the endpoint does not have to be on the arc.

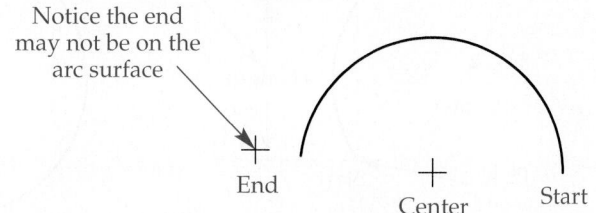

Notice the end
may not be on the
arc surface

End     Center     Start

## Drawing Arcs Using the **Center, Start, Angle** Option

The **Center, Start, Angle** option is a variation of the **Start, Center, Angle** option. Use the **Center, Start, Angle** option when it is easier to begin by locating the center. **Figure 5-18** shows how positive and negative angles work with this option. The command sequence is as follows:

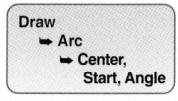

Draw
→ Arc
   → Center,
     Start, Angle

> Command: **A** *or* **ARC**↵
> Specify start point of arc or [Center]: **C**↵
> Specify center point of arc: *(pick the center point)*
> Specify start point of arc: *(pick the start point)*
> Specify end point of arc or [Angle/chord Length]: **A**↵
> Specify included angle: *(pick the included angle or type a positive angle or negative angle and press* [Enter])
> Command:

**Figure 5-18.**
How positive and negative angles work with the **Center, Start, Angle** option.

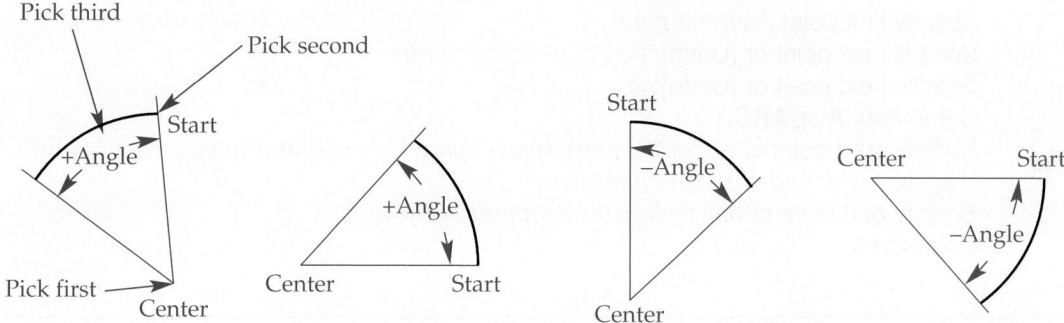

Pick third

Pick second

Start

+Angle

Pick first

Center

+Angle

Center    Start

Start

−Angle

Center

Center    Start

−Angle

## Drawing Arcs Using the **Center, Start, Length** Option

The **Center, Start, Length** option is a variation of the **Start, Center, Length** option. Use the **Center, Start, Length** option when it is easier to begin by locating the center. **Figure 5-19** shows how positive and negative chord lengths work with this option. The command sequence is as follows:

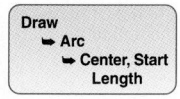

Draw
→ Arc
   → Center, Start
     Length

> Command: **A** *or* **ARC**↵
> Specify start point of arc or [Center]: **C**↵
> Specify center point of arc: *(pick the center point)*
> Specify start point of arc: *(pick the start point)*
> Specify end point of arc or [Angle/chord Length]: **L**↵
> Specify length of chord: *(pick, or type the chord length and press* [Enter])
> Command:

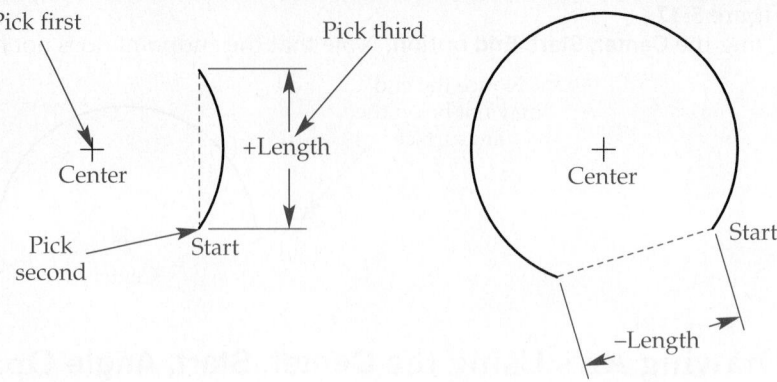

**Figure 5-19.**
How positive and negative chord lengths work with the **Center, Start, Length** option.

## Continuing Arcs from a Previously Drawn Arc or Line

Draw
→ Arc
→ Continue

An arc can be continued from the previous arc or line. To do so, pick **Continue** from the **Arc** cascading menu in the **Draw** pull-down menu. The **Continue** option can also be accessed by beginning the **ARC** command and then pressing the [Enter] key, pressing the space bar, or selecting **Enter** from the shortcut menu when prompted to:

Specify start point of arc or [Center]: *(press space bar or [Enter] to place start point of the arc at end of the previous line or arc)*

When a series of arcs are drawn in this manner, each consecutive arc is tangent to the object before it. The start point and direction are taken from the endpoint and direction of the previous arc. See **Figure 5-20.**

The **Continue** option can also be used to quickly draw an arc tangent to the endpoint of a previously drawn line. See **Figure 5-21.** The command sequence is as follows:

Command: **L** *or* **LINE.**↵
Specify first point: *(select a point)*
Specify next point or [Undo]: *(select a second point)*
Specify next point or [Undo]: ↵
Command: **A** *or* **ARC.**↵
Specify start point of arc or [Center]: *(press space bar or [Enter] to place start point of the arc at end of the previous line)*
Specify end point of arc: *(select the endpoint of the arc)*
Command:

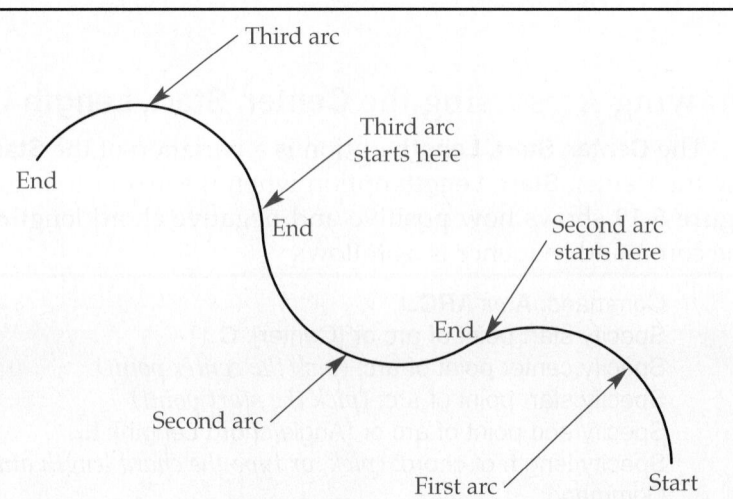

**Figure 5-20.**
Using the **Continue** option to draw three arcs.

**Figure 5-21.**
An arc continuing from the previous line. Point 2 is the start of the arc and Point 3 is the end of the arc.

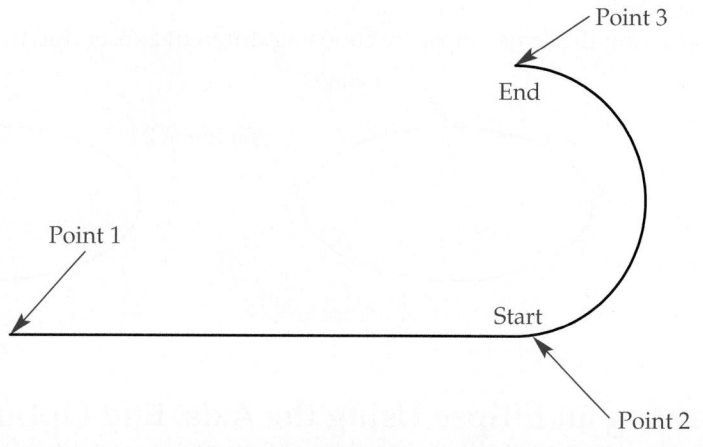

## Exercise 5-4

○ Begin a new drawing or use one of your templates.
○ Use the **Center, Start, Angle** option of the **ARC** command to draw arcs similar to those shown in **Figure 5-18**.
○ Use the **ARC** command and the **Continue** option to draw the arcs shown in **Figure 5-20**.
○ Use the **ARC** command and the **Continue** option as described in the text to draw an arc connected to a previously drawn line, as shown in **Figure 5-21**.
○ Save the drawing as EX5-4.

## Drawing Ellipses

When a circle is viewed at an angle, an elliptical shape is seen. For example, a 30° ellipse is created if a circle is rotated 60° from the line of sight. The parts of an ellipse are shown in **Figure 5-22**. The **ELLIPSE** command can be accessed by selecting **Ellipse** from the **Draw** pull-down menu, picking the **Ellipse** button in the **Draw** toolbar, or entering EL or ELLIPSE at the Command: prompt. An ellipse can be drawn using different options of the **ELLIPSE** command.

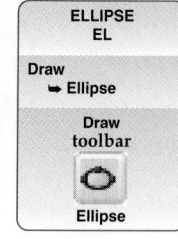

ELLIPSE
EL

Draw
➡ Ellipse

Draw
toolbar

Ellipse

**Figure 5-22.**
Parts of an ellipse.

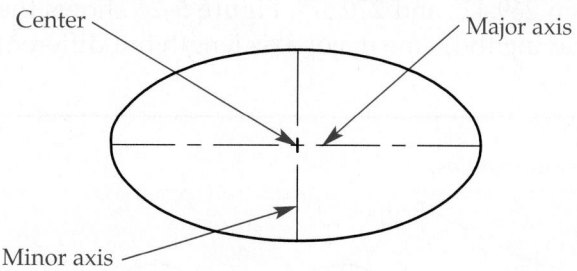

**Figure 5-23.**
Constructing the same ellipse by choosing different axis endpoints.

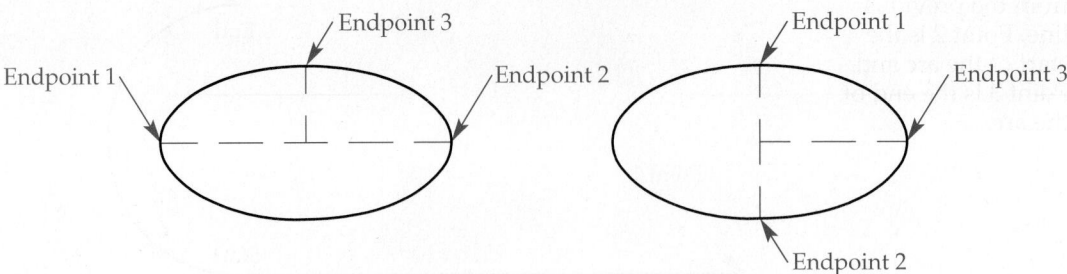

Endpoint 3

Endpoint 1

Endpoint 2

Endpoint 1

Endpoint 3

Endpoint 2

## Drawing an Ellipse Using the **Axis, End** Option

The **Axis, End** option establishes the first axis and one endpoint of the second axis. The first axis may be either the major or minor axis, depending on what is entered for the second axis. The longer of the two axes is always the major axis. After you pick the first axis, the ellipse is dragged by the cursor until the point is picked. The command sequence for the ellipses in **Figure 5-23** is as follows:

Command: **EL** *or* **ELLIPSE**↵
Specify axis endpoint of ellipse or [Arc/Center]: *(select an axis endpoint)*
Specify other endpoint of axis: *(select the other endpoint of the axis)*
Specify distance to other axis or [Rotation]: *(select a distance from the midpoint of the first axis to the end of the second axis and press* [Enter]*)*
Command:

If you respond to the Specify distance to other axis or [Rotation]: prompt with R for rotation, AutoCAD assumes you have selected the major axis with the first two points. The next prompt requests the angle that the corresponding circle is rotated from the line of sight to produce the ellipse. The command sequence is as follows:

Command: **EL** *or* **ELLIPSE**↵
Specify axis endpoint of ellipse or [Arc/Center]: *(select a major axis endpoint)*
Specify other endpoint of axis: *(select the other endpoint of the major axis)*
Specify distance to other axis or [Rotation]: **R**↵
Specify rotation around major axis: *(type a rotation angle, such as* 30, *and press* [Enter]*)*
Command:

The 30 response draws an ellipse that is created when a circle is rotated 30° from the line of sight. A 0 response draws an ellipse with the minor axis equal to the major axis—that is, a circle. AutoCAD rejects any rotation angle between 89.42° and 90.57° or between 269.42° and 270.57°. **Figure 5-24** shows the relationship between several ellipses having the same major axis length but different rotation angles.

**Figure 5-24.**
Ellipse rotation angles.

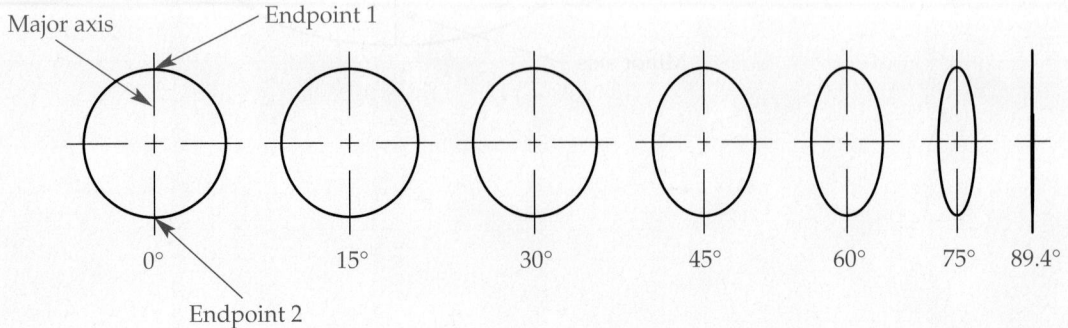

Major axis

Endpoint 1

0°      15°      30°      45°      60°      75°   89.4°

Endpoint 2

**Figure 5-25.**
Drawing an ellipse by picking the center and endpoints of two axes.

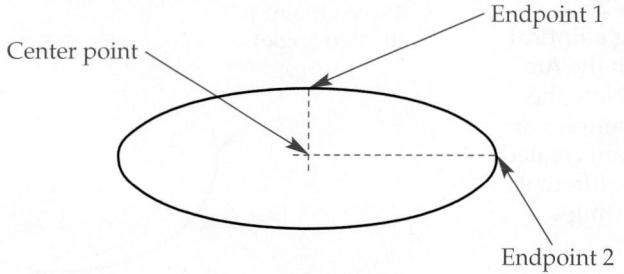

Center point

Endpoint 1

Endpoint 2

## Drawing an Ellipse Using the **Center** Option

An ellipse can also be constructed by specifying the center point and one endpoint for each of the two axes. See **Figure 5-25.** The command sequence for this option is as follows:

Draw
➥ Ellipse
➥ Center

> Specify axis endpoint of ellipse or [Arc/Center]: **C↵**
> Specify center of ellipse: *(select the ellipse center point)*
> Specify endpoint of axis: *(select the endpoint of one axis)*
> Specify distance to other axis or [Rotation]: *(select the endpoint of the other axis)*

The rotation option can be used instead of selecting the second axis endpoint.

---

### Exercise 5-5

○ Begin a new drawing or use one of your templates.
○ Use the **Axis, End** option of the **ELLIPSE** command to draw the ellipses shown in **Figure 5-23.**
○ Use the **Center** and **Rotation** options of the **ELLIPSE** command to draw some ellipses similar to **Figure 5-24.**
○ Use the **Center** option of the **ELLIPSE** command to draw the ellipse shown in **Figure 5-25.**
○ Save the drawing as EX5-5.

---

## Drawing Elliptical Arcs

The **Arc** option of the **ELLIPSE** command is used to draw elliptical arcs. The command sequence for the **Arc** option is as follows:

Draw
➥ Ellipse
➥ Arc

> Command: **EL** *or* **ELLIPSE↵**
> Specify axis endpoint of ellipse or [Arc/Center]: **A↵**
> Specify axis endpoint of elliptical arc or [Center]: *(pick the first axis endpoint)*
> Specify other endpoint of axis: *(pick the second axis endpoint)*
> Specify distance to other axis or [Rotation]: *(pick the distance for the second axis)*
> Specify start angle or [Parameter]: **0↵**
> Specify end angle or [Parameter/Included angle]: **90↵**
> Command:

Once the second endpoint of the first axis is picked, you can drag the shape of a full ellipse. This can help you visualize the other axis. The distance for the second axis is from the ellipse center to the point picked. Then, enter a start angle. The start and end angles are the angular relationships between the ellipse center and the arc endpoints. The angle of the elliptical arc is established from the angle of the first axis. A 0° start angle is the same as the first endpoint of the first axis. A 45° start angle is 45° counterclockwise from the first endpoint of the first axis. End angles are also established counterclockwise from the start point. **Figure 5-26** shows the elliptical arc

---

**Figure 5-26.**
Drawing elliptical arcs with the **Arc** option. Note the three examples at the bottom created by three different angle settings.

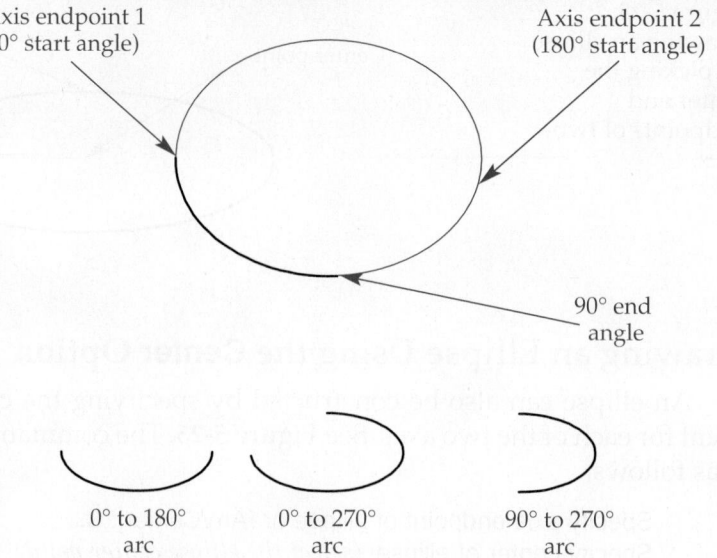

Axis endpoint 1
(0° start angle)

Axis endpoint 2
(180° start angle)

90° end
angle

0° to 180°
arc

0° to 270°
arc

90° to 270°
arc

drawn with the previous command sequence, and displays sample arcs with different start and end angles.

## Using the **Parameter** option

The **Parameter** option requires the same input as the other elliptical arcs until the Specify start angle or [Parameter]: prompt. The difference is that AutoCAD uses a different means of vector calculation to create the elliptical arc. The results are similar, but the command sequence is as follows:

    Specify start angle or [Parameter]: **P↵**
    Specify start parameter or [Angle]: (pick the start point)
    Specify end parameter or [Angle/Included angle]: (pick the end point)
    Command:

## Using the **Included** option

The **Included** option establishes an included angle beginning at the start angle. An included angle is an angle that is formed by two sides, or in this case, the angle formed by the endpoints and center of the arc. This option requires the same input as the other elliptical arcs until the Specify end angle or [Parameter/Included angle]: prompt. The command sequence is as follows:

    Specify end angle or [Parameter/Included angle]: **I↵**
    Specify included angle for arc <current>: **180↵**
    Command:

## Rotating an elliptical arc around its axis

The **Rotation** option for drawing an elliptical arc is similar to the **Rotation** option when drawing a full ellipse, which was discussed earlier. This option allows you to rotate the elliptical arc about the first axis by specifying a rotation angle. Refer back to **Figure 5-24** for examples of various rotation angles. This option requires the same input as the other elliptical arcs until the Specify distance to other axis or [Rotation]: prompt. The command sequence is as follows:

    Specify distance to other axis or [Rotation]: **R↵**
    Specify rotation around major axis: (enter rotation value)
    Specify start angle or [Parameter]: (enter start angle)
    Specify end angle or [Parameter/Included angle]: (enter end angle)
    Command:

### Drawing an elliptical arc using the Center option

The **Center** option for drawing an elliptical arc lets you establish the center of the ellipse. See **Figure 5-27.** This option requires the same input as the other elliptical arcs until the Specify axis endpoint of elliptical arc or [Center]: prompt. The command sequence is as follows:

> Specify axis endpoint of elliptical arc or [Center]: **C↵**
> Specify center of elliptical arc: *(select the ellipse center point)*
> Specify endpoint of axis: *(select endpoint of axis)*
> Specify distance to other axis or [Rotation]: *(select the endpoint of the other axis)*
> Specify start angle or [Parameter]: **0↵**
> Specify end angle or [Parameter/Included angle]: **180↵**
> Command:

---

**Figure 5-27.**
Drawing elliptical arcs with the **Center** option.

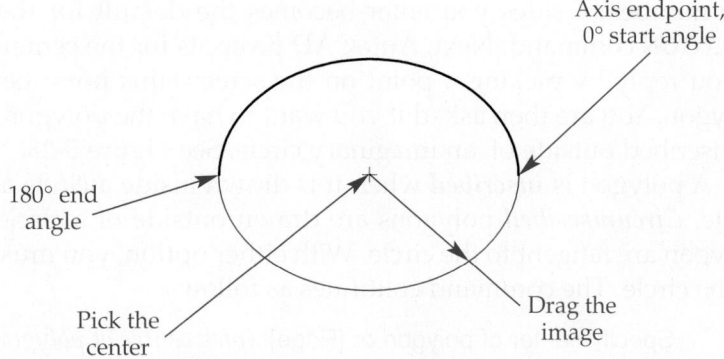

Axis endpoint,
0° start angle

180° end
angle

Pick the
center

Drag the
image

---

**NOTE**

The setting of the **PELLIPSE** system variable affects the way an ellipse can be edited. An ellipse drawn while **PELLIPSE** is set at 0 is a true elliptical object, while an ellipse drawn while **PELLIPSE** is set at 1 is a polyline ellipse. A true elliptical object maintains its elliptical shape during grip editing. (Grip editing is discussed in Chapter 12 of this text.) The vertices of a polyline ellipse can be moved out of the elliptical shape. The **Arc** option of the **ELLIPSE** command is not available when **PELLIPSE** is set to 1.

---

## Exercise 5-6

○ Begin a new drawing or use one of your templates.
○ Use the **Arc** option of the **ELLIPSE** command to draw the following elliptical arcs:
  ○ Use axis endpoints, axis distance, start angle = 0, and end angle = 90, similar to **Figure 5-26.**
  ○ Use the same options as in the previous instructions to draw a 0° to 180° arc, 0° to 270° arc, and a 90° to 270° arc, similar to the samples in **Figure 5-26.**
  ○ Use the **Parameter** option to draw an elliptical arc of your own design.
  ○ Use the **Rotation** option to rotate an elliptical arc 45° about its axis.
  ○ Use the **Included** option to draw an elliptical arc with a 180° included angle and another with a 90° included angle.
  ○ Use the **Center** option to draw an elliptical arc of your own design.
○ Save the drawing as EX5-6.

---

# Drawing Regular Polygons

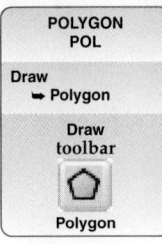

POLYGON
POL

Draw
➡ Polygon

Draw
toolbar

Polygon

A *regular polygon* is any closed-plane geometric figure with three or more equal sides and equal angles. For example, a hexagon is a six-sided regular polygon. The **POLYGON** command is used to draw any regular polygon with up to 1024 sides.

The **POLYGON** command can be accessed by selecting **Polygon** from the **Draw** pull-down menu, picking the **Polygon** button in the **Draw** toolbar, or entering POL or POLYGON at the Command: prompt. Regardless of the method used to select the command, you are first prompted for the number of sides. If you want an octagon (polygon with eight sides), enter 8 as follows:

> Command: **POL** *or* **POLYGON**↵
> Enter number of sides *<current>*: **8**↵

The number of sides you enter becomes the default for the next time you use the **POLYGON** command. Next, AutoCAD prompts for the center or edge of the polygon. If you reply by picking a point on the screen, this point becomes the center of the polygon. You are then asked if you want to have the polygon inscribed within, or circumscribed outside of, an imaginary circle. See **Figure 5-28.**

A polygon is *inscribed* when it is drawn inside a circle and its corners touch the circle. *Circumscribed* polygons are drawn outside of a circle where the sides of the polygon are tangent to the circle. With either option, you must then specify the radius of the circle. The command continues as follows:

> Specify center of polygon or [Edge]: (*pick center of polygon*)
> Enter an option [Inscribed in circle/Circumscribed about circle] *<current>*: (*respond with I or C and press* [Enter])
> Specify radius of circle: (*type the radius, such as 2, and press* [Enter], *or pick a point on the screen at the desired distance from the center*)

The **I** or **C** option you select becomes the default for the next polygon. The Specify center of polygon or [Edge]: prompt allows you to pick the center or specify the edge. Notice that picking the center is the default. If you want to draw the polygon by specifying the length of one of the edges, enter E for the **Edge** option and pick edge endpoints as follows:

> Specify center of polygon or [Edge]: **E**↵
> Specify first endpoint of edge: (*pick a point*)
> Specify second endpoint of edge: (*pick second point*)

**Figure 5-28.**
Drawing an inscribed and a circumscribed polygon.

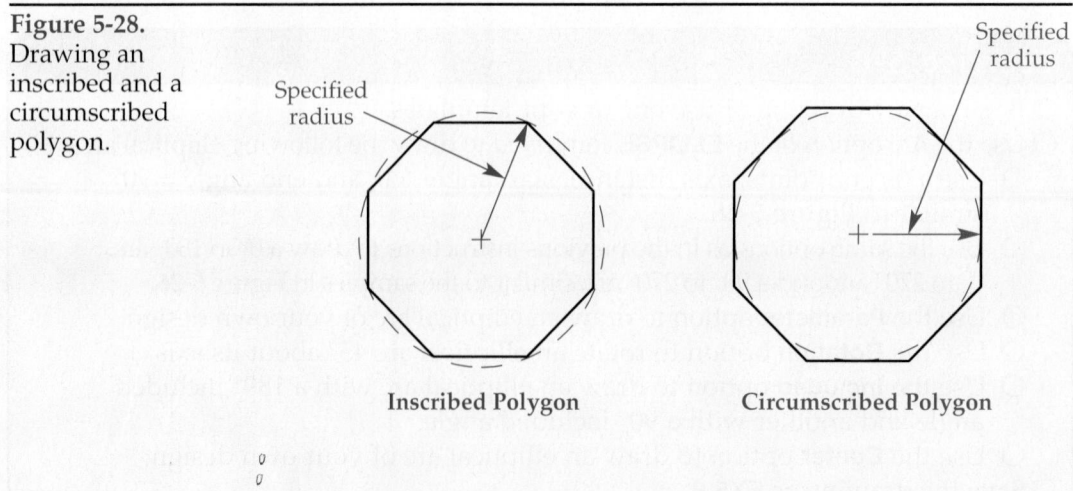

Specified radius

Specified radius

Inscribed Polygon

Circumscribed Polygon

After you pick the endpoints of one side, the rest of the polygon sides are drawn counterclockwise using the length specified by the two picked endpoints.

Polygons are polylines and can be easily edited using the **PEDIT** (polyline edit) command, which is discussed in Chapter 15 of this text. For example, a polygon can be given width using the **Width** option of the **PEDIT** command.

Hexagons (six-sided polygons) are commonly drawn as bolt heads and nuts on mechanical drawings. Keep in mind that these features are normally dimensioned across the flats. To draw a polygon to be dimensioned across the flats, circumscribe it. The radius you enter is equal to one-half the distance across the flats. The distance across the corners (inscribed polygon) is specified when the polygon must be confined within a circular area. One example is the boundary of a swimming pool deck in architectural drafting. Notice the distance across the flats and the distance across the corners in **Figure 5-29**.

**Figure 5-29.**
Specifying the distance across the flats and between the corners of a polygon.

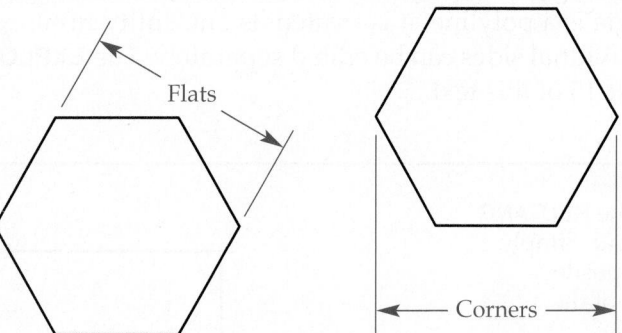

## Setting the Number of Polygon Sides

AutoCAD allows you to set the default number of polygon sides with the **POLYSIDES** system variable. This value can be set in your template for future use, but is automatically reset to 4 in a new drawing. Type POLYSIDES at the Command: prompt and enter the number of default sides for the **POLYGON** command. The value you specify for the default is used until you change the value again using the **POLYSIDES** system variable or the **POLYGON** command.

### Exercise 5-7

○ Begin a new drawing or use one of your templates.
○ Draw a hexagon with a distance of three units across the flats. Then draw another hexagon measuring three units across the corners.
○ Draw an octagon with a horizontal edge that is 1.75 units long.
○ Draw a pentagon circumscribed about a circle having a 2.25 diameter.
○ Save the drawing as EX5-7.

# Drawing Rectangles

AutoCAD's **RECTANG** command allows you to easily draw rectangles. When using this command, pick one corner and then the opposite diagonal corner to establish the rectangle. See **Figure 5-30**. The **RECTANG** command can be accessed by picking **Rectangle** in the **Draw** pull-down menu, by picking the **Rectangle** button in the **Draw** toolbar, or entering REC, RECTANG, or RECTANGLE at the Command: prompt:

> Command: **REC**, **RECTANG**, *or* **RECTANGLE**↵
> Specify first corner point or [Chamfer/Elevation/Fillet/Thickness/Width]: *(select the first corner of the rectangle)*
> Specify other corner point or [Dimensions]: *(select the second corner)*
> Command:

Rectangles are polylines and can be edited using the **PEDIT** command. Since a rectangle is a polyline, it is treated as one entity until exploded. After it is exploded, the individual sides can be edited separately. The **EXPLODE** command is discussed in Chapter 15 of this text.

**Figure 5-30.**
Using the **RECTANG** command. Simply pick opposite corners of the rectangle.

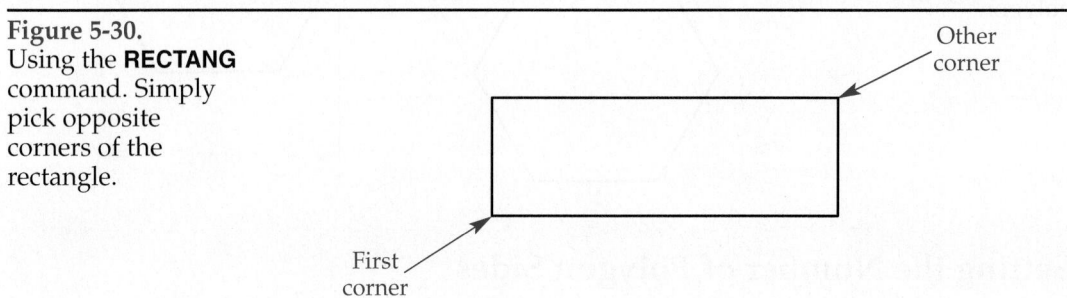

Other corner

First corner

## Drawing Rectangles with Line Width

The **Width** option of the **RECTANG** command is used to adjust the width of the rectangle in the XY plane. Setting line width for rectangles is similar to setting width for polylines, which is discussed in Chapters 14 and 15.

The following sequence is used to create a rectangle with .03 wide lines:

> Command: **REC**, **RECTANG**, *or* **RECTANGLE**↵
> Specify first corner point or [Chamfer/Elevation/Fillet/Thickness/Width]: **W**↵
> Specify line width for rectangles <*current*>: **.03**↵

You can press [Enter] at the Specify line width for rectangles: prompt to have the rectangle polylines drawn with the default polyline width. If you enter a value at this prompt, the polylines are drawn using the specified width.

After setting the rectangle width, you can either select another option or draw the rectangle. Continue selecting options until you have set the characteristics correctly, then draw the rectangle. If a width is set, any new rectangles drawn use the width you entered. To reset the width to the initial default, enter the Width option and then specify a width of 0. Now, new rectangles are drawn using a standard "0 width" line.

## Drawing Chamfered Rectangles

A *chamfer* is an angled corner on an object. Drawing chamfers is covered in detail in Chapter 11 of this text. This is a brief introduction to drawing chamfers on rectangles. To draw chamfers on rectangles, use the **Chamfer** option of the **RECTANG** command. The rectangle created will have chamfers drawn automatically.

After you select the **Chamfer** option, you must provide the chamfer distances, **Figure 5-31.** The command sequence is as follows:

> Command: **REC**, **RECTANG**, *or* **RECTANGLE**.↵
> Specify first corner point or [Chamfer/Elevation/Fillet/Thickness/Width]: **C**↵
> Specify first chamfer distance for rectangles <*current*>: *(enter the first chamfer distance)*
> Specify second chamfer distance for rectangles <*current*>: *(enter the second chamfer distance)*
> Specify first corner point or [Chamfer/Elevation/Fillet/Thickness/Width]:

**Figure 5-31.**
A chamfer is an angled corner. Two distances are used to calculate the chamfer.

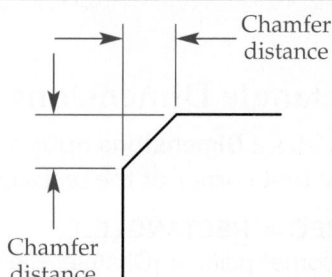

After setting the chamfer distances, you can either draw the rectangle or select another option. If you select the **Fillet** option, the chamfers will not be drawn.

The default chamfer distances are the chamfer distances or fillet radius used to draw the previous rectangle. If the default for the first chamfer distance is zero and you enter a different value, the new distance becomes the default for the second chamfer distance. However, if the default chamfer distances are nonzero values, a new value entered for the first distance does *not* become the default for the second distance.

As with the **Width** option, if you set the **Chamfer** option's distances to a value greater than 0, any new rectangles created are automatically chamfered. New rectangles will continue to be created with chamfers until you reset the chamfer distances to 0 or use the **Fillet** option to create rounded corners.

## Drawing Filleted Rectangles

A *fillet* is a rounded corner on an object, **Figure 5-32.** Drawing fillets is covered in detail in Chapter 11 of this text. This is a brief introduction to drawing fillets on rectangles.

Fillets are automatically drawn on rectangles using the **Fillet** option of the **RECTANG** command. After selecting the option, you must enter the fillet radius:

> Command: **REC**, **RECTANG**, *or* **RECTANGLE**.↵
> Specify first corner point or [Chamfer/Elevation/Fillet/Thickness/Width]: **F**↵
> Specify fillet radius for rectangles <*current*>: *(enter a fillet radius or press* [Enter] *to accept the default)*
> Specify first corner point or [Chamfer/Elevation/Fillet/Thickness/Width]:

The default fillet radius is the radius of the previously drawn rectangle. Once a fillet radius is specified, the **RECTANG** command will automatically draw fillets on rectangles. In order to draw rectangles without fillets, the fillet radius must be set to 0. **Figure 5-33** shows examples of rectangles drawn with chamfers and fillets.

Figure 5-32.
A fillet is a rounded
corner.

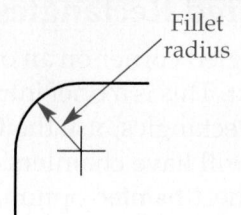

Fillet
radius

Figure 5-33.
Chamfered and
filleted rectangles.
A—A rectangle
drawn with
chamfers. B—A
rectangle drawn
with fillets.

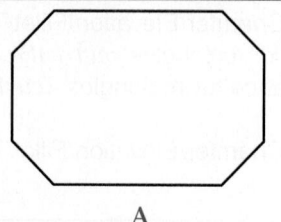

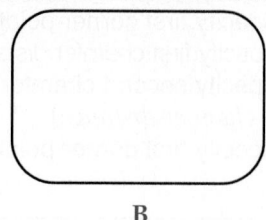

A

B

## Specifying Rectangle Dimensions

AutoCAD provides a **Dimensions** option for the **RECTANG** command. The option is available after the first corner of the rectangle is picked:

> Command: **REC** *or* **RECTANGLE.**↵
> Specify first corner point or [Chamfer/Elevation/Fillet/Thickness/Width]: *(pick first corner point)*
> Specify other corner point or [Dimensions]:

Enter D to access the **Dimensions** option. You are then prompted to enter the length and width of the rectangle. In the following example, a $5 \times 3$ rectangle is specified:

> Specify other corner point or [Dimensions]: **D**↵
> Specify length for rectangles <*current*>: **5.**↵
> Specify width for rectangles <*current*>: **3.**↵
> Specify other corner point or [Dimensions]: *(move crosshairs to desired quadrant and pick point)*.

After specifying the length and width, the Specify other corner point or [Dimensions]: prompt is displayed. If you wish to change the dimensions, select the **Dimensions** option again. If the dimensions are correct, you can specify the other corner point to complete the rectangle. When using the **Dimensions** option, the second corner point determines which of four possible rectangles is drawn. See **Figure 5-34.**

**Figure 5-34.**
When using the **Dimensions** option of the **RECTANGLE** command, the orientation of the rectangle relative to the first corner point is determined by the second corner point.

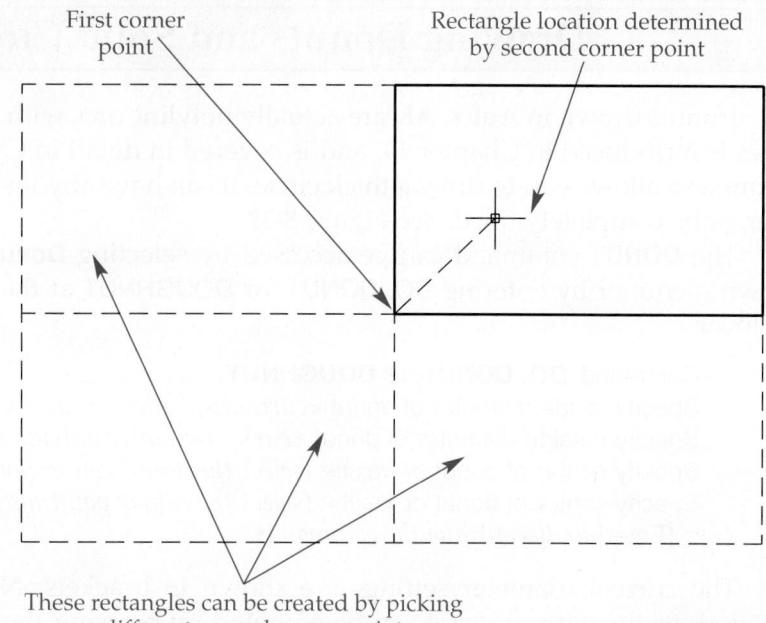

First corner point

Rectangle location determined by second corner point

These rectangles can be created by picking a different second corner point

## Additional RECTANG Options

There are two other options available when using the **RECTANG** command. These options remain effective for multiple uses of the command:

- **Elevation.** This option sets the elevation of the rectangle along the Z axis. The default value is 0.
- **Thickness.** This option gives the rectangle depth along the Z axis (into the screen). The default value is 0.

A combination of these options can be used to draw a single rectangle. For example, a rectangle can have fillets and a .03 line width.

---

### Exercise 5-8

○ Begin a new drawing or use one of your templates.
○ Use the **RECTANG** command to draw a rectangle.
○ Use the **RECTANG** command to draw a rectangle with .03 line width.
○ Use the **RECTANG** command to draw rectangles similar to **Figure 5-33.**
○ Use the **Dimensions** option of the **RECTANGLE** command to draw a rectangle that is 6 units wide and 4 units high. Make the first corner point the lower-left corner of the rectangle.
○ Create another rectangle using the lower-right corner of the previous rectangle as the first corner point. Use the **Dimensions** option to make the rectangle 3.5 units wide and 7 units high. Position the rectangle so the first corner is the upper-left corner.
○ Save the drawing as EX5-8.

---

# Drawing Donuts and Solid Circles

Donuts drawn in AutoCAD are actually polyline arcs with width. Drawing polylines is introduced in Chapter 14, and is covered in detail in Chapter 15. The **DONUT** command allows you to draw a thick circle. It can have any inside and outside diameter, or be completely filled. See **Figure 5-35.**

DONUT
DOUGHNUT
DO

Draw
➥ Donut

The **DONUT** command can be accessed by selecting **Donut** from the **Draw** pull-down menu, or by entering DO, DONUT, or DOUGHNUT at the Command: prompt as follows:

Command: **DO**, **DONUT**, *or* **DOUGHNUT.**↵
Specify inside diameter of donut *<current>*: *(enter inside diameter)*
Specify outside diameter of donut *<current>*: *(enter outside diameter)*
Specify center of donut or <exit>: *(select the donut center point)*
Specify center of donut or <exit>: *(select the center point for another donut, or press* [Enter] *to discontinue the command)*

The current diameter settings are shown in brackets. New diameters can be entered, or the current value can be accepted by pressing the [Enter] key. An inside diameter of 0 produces a solid circle.

After selecting the center point, the donut appears on the screen. You may pick another center point to draw the same size donut in a new location. The **DONUT** command remains active until you press [Enter] or cancel by pressing [Esc].

When the **FILL** mode is turned off, donuts appear as segmented circles or concentric circles. **FILL** can be used transparently by entering 'FILL while inside the **DONUT** command. Then, enter ON or OFF as needed. The fill display for previously drawn donuts is updated when the drawing is regenerated.

**Figure 5-35.**
Examples of donuts.

  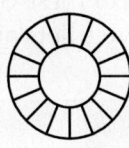 

Fill On          Fill On          Fill Off          Fill Off
                 ID = 0                              ID = 0

---

NOTE       The setting for the inside diameter and outside diameter of donuts are stored in the **DONUTID** and **DONUTOD** system variables, respectively. If the value of **DONUTID** is greater than the value of **DONUTOD**, the values are switched when the next donut is drawn.

○ Begin a new drawing or use one of your templates.
○ Draw a donut with a .5 inside diameter and a 1.5 outside diameter.
○ Draw a donut with a 0 inside diameter and a 1.5 outside diameter.
○ Turn the **FILL** mode off and enter REGEN to see what happens to the donuts.
○ Set **DONUTID** to .25 and **DONUTOD** to .75.
○ Enter DONUT at the Command: prompt and draw a donut using the defaults.
○ Use a transparent **FILL** command ('**FILL**) to turn **FILL** on while in the **DONUT** command. Now, draw two more donuts.
○ Select **Donut** from the **Draw** pull-down menu and draw three more donuts.
○ Save the drawing as EX5-9.

## Using the Revision Cloud

A revision cloud is a polyline of sequential arcs that forms a cloud-shaped object. See **Figure 5-36.** This type of object is typically used by people who review drawings and mark notes and changes. The revision cloud points the drafter to a specific portion of the drawing that may need to be edited.

To create a **Revision Cloud**, pick a starting location, move the cursor to shape the cloud, and then move the cursor toward the beginning of the cloud. AutoCAD automatically closes the cloud and ends the command. This command can be entered by selecting **Revision Cloud** from the **Draw** pull-down menu, picking the **Revcloud** button from the **Draw** toolbar, or by entering REVCLOUD at the Command: prompt. The following prompt is displayed after entering this command:

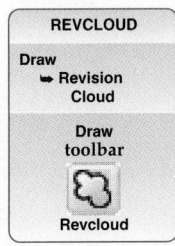

REVCLOUD

Draw
➥ Revision
Cloud

Draw
toolbar

Revcloud

Command: **REVCLOUD**↵
Minimum arc length: *current* Maximum arc length: *current*
Specify start point or [Arc length/Object] <*current option*>:

**Figure 5-36.**
The revision cloud can be used to identify areas of a drawing that have been modified.

Revision cloud and note
identify change to drawing

To begin drawing the revision cloud, pick a starting point in the drawing. After picking the starting point, the prompt tells you to: Guide crosshairs along cloud path.... Move the cursor around the objects to be enclosed until you come close to the starting point. AutoCAD then closes the cloud and prompts you with: Revision cloud finished.

The size of the arcs is determined by entering the **Arc length** option. This value measures the length of an arc from its starting point to its ending point. You can change this value to any desired value. Upon entering the **Arc length** option, you are prompted for the following:

> Specify start point or [Arc length/Object] <current option>: **A**↵
> Specify minimum length of arc <current size>: (enter a minimum arc length)
> Specify maximum length of arc <current size>: (enter the maximum arc length)
> Specify start point or [Object] <Object>: (pick a starting point for the cloud or select an object to turn into a revision cloud)

Varying the minimum and maximum values causes the revision cloud to have an uneven, hand-drawn look. The actual size of the arc is the length value multiplied by the dimension scale (**DIMSCALE** variable) so revision clouds appear the same size in drawings with different scales.

Circles, closed polylines, ellipses, polygons, and rectangles can be converted to revision clouds by selecting the **Object** option. The command sequence follows:

> Command: **REVCLOUD**↵
> Minimum arc length: current Maximum arc length: current
> Specify start point or [Arc length/Object] <current option>: **O**↵
> Select object: (pick the object to convert to a revision cloud)
> Reverse direction [Yes/No] <default>: (enter N, or Y to reverse the cloud arcs)
> Command:

The polyline and dimension scale topics related to this discussion are covered in detail later in this text.

---

### Exercise 5-10

○ Open one of your previously created drawings.
○ Create a layer named Revisions, set the color to red, and set the layer current.
○ Use the **REVCLOUD** command to create a revision cloud around a portion of your drawing.
○ Draw a circle around another portion of the drawing and then convert it to a revision cloud.
○ Save the drawing as EX5-10.

---

## Chapter Test

*Answer the following questions on a separate sheet of paper.*

1. Give the command, entries, and actions required to draw a circle with a 2.5 unit diameter:
   A.  Command: _____
   B.  Specify center point for circle or [3P/2P/Ttr (tan tan radius)]: _____
   C.  Specify radius of circle or [Diameter]: _____
   D.  Specify diameter of circle: _____

2. Give the command, entries, and actions required to draw a circle that has a 1.75 unit radius and is tangent to an existing line and circle:
   A. Command: _____
   B. Specify center point for circle or [3P/2P/Ttr (tan tan radius)]: _____
   C. Specify point on object for first tangent of circle: _____
   D. Specify point on object for second tangent of circle: _____
   E. Specify radius of circle: _____
3. Give the command, entries, and actions needed to draw a three-point arc:
   A. Command: _____
   B. Specify start point of arc or [Center]: _____
   C. Specify second point of arc or [Center/End]: _____
   D. Specify end point of arc: _____
4. Give the command, entries, and actions needed to draw an arc, beginning with the center point and having a 60° included angle:
   A. Command: _____
   B. Specify start point of arc or [Center]: _____
   C. Specify center point of arc: _____
   D. Specify start point of arc: _____
   E. Specify end point of arc or [Angle/chord Length]: _____
   F. Specify included angle: _____
5. Give the command, entries, and actions required to draw an arc tangent to the endpoint of a previously drawn line:
   A. Command: _____
   B. Specify start point of arc or [Center]: _____
   C. Specify end point of arc: _____
6. Give the command, entries, and actions needed to draw an ellipse with the **Axis, End** option:
   A. Command: _____
   B. Specify axis endpoint of ellipse or [Arc/Center]: _____
   C. Specify other endpoint of axis: _____
   D. Specify distance to other axis or [Rotation]: _____
7. Give the command, entries, and actions necessary to draw a hexagon measuring 4″ (102 mm) across the flats:
   A. Command: _____
   B. Enter number of sides: _____
   C. Specify center of polygon or [Edge]: _____
   D. Enter an option [Inscribed in circle/Circumscribed about circle]: _____
   E. Specify radius of circle: _____
8. Give the responses required to draw two donuts with a .25 inside diameter and a .75 outside diameter:
   A. Command: _____
   B. Specify inside diameter of donut: _____
   C. Specify outside diameter of donut: _____
   D. Specify center of donut or <exit>: _____
   E. Specify center of donut or <exit>: _____
   F. Specify center of donut or <exit>: _____
9. Describe why the @ symbol can be used by itself for point selection.
10. Define the term *included angle*.
11. List the three input options that can be used to draw an arc tangent to the endpoint of a previously drawn arc.
12. Given the distance across the flats of a hexagon, would you use the **Inscribed** or **Circumscribed** option to draw the hexagon?
13. Describe how a solid circle can be drawn.

14. Identify how to access the option that allows you to draw a circle tangent to three objects.
15. Identify two ways to access the **Arc** option for drawing elliptical arcs.
16. Name the AutoCAD system variable that lets you draw a true ellipse or a polyline ellipse with the **ELLIPSE** command.
17. Name the pull-down menu where the **RECTANG** command is found.
18. What is the default option if the **ARC** command is typed at the Command: prompt?
19. Give the easiest keyboard shortcut for the following commands:
    A. **CIRCLE**
    B. **ARC**
    C. **ELLIPSE**
    D. **POLYGON**
    E. **RECTANG**
    F. **DONUT**
20. Name the command option that is designed specifically for drawing rectangles with line width.
21. Name the command option that is used to draw rectangles with rounded corners.
22. Describe how you would draw a rectangle with different chamfer distances at each corner.
23. What is the **ELLIPSE** rotation angle that causes you to draw a circle?
24. Explain how to turn the **FILL** mode off while inside the **DONUT** command.
25. Name the system variable used to set the default radius when drawing circles.
26. How do you close the revision cloud?

## Drawing Problems

*Start AutoCAD and use one of the setup options or use a template. Do not draw dimensions or text. Use your own judgment and approximate dimensions if needed.*

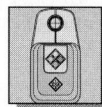

1. You have just been given the sketch of a new sports car design (shown below). You are asked to create a drawing from the sketch. Use the **LINE** command and selected shape commands to draw the car. Do not be concerned with size and scale. Consider the commands and techniques used to draw the car, and try to minimize the number of entities. Save your drawing as P5-1.

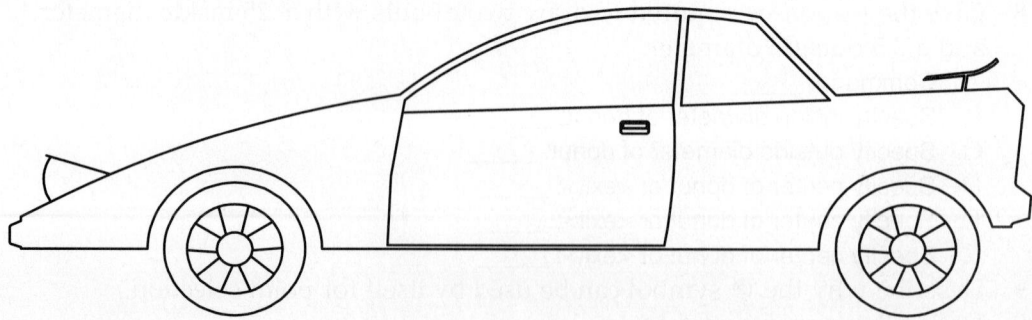

2. You have just been given the sketch of an innovative new truck design (shown below). You are asked to create a drawing from the sketch. Use the **LINE** command and selected shape commands to draw the truck resembling the sketch. Do not be concerned with size and scale. Save your drawing as P5-2.

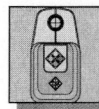

3. Use the **LINE** and **CIRCLE** command options to draw the objects below. Do not include dimensions. Save the drawing as P5-3.

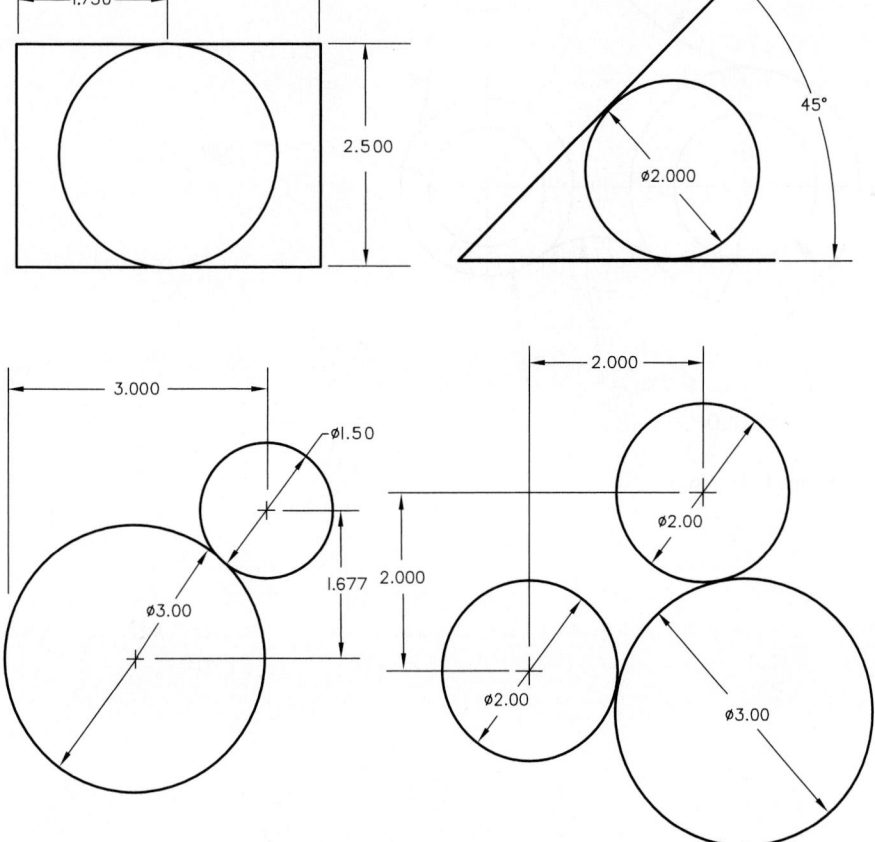

4. Use the **CIRCLE** and **ARC** command options to draw the object below. Do not include dimensions. Save the drawing as P5-4.

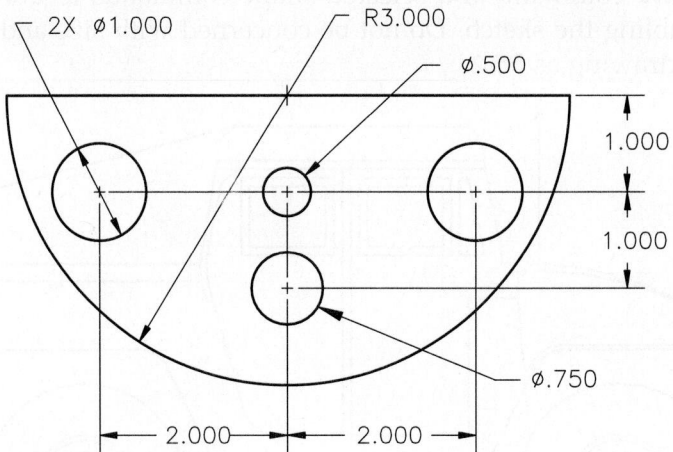

5. Draw the following object. Do not include dimensions.

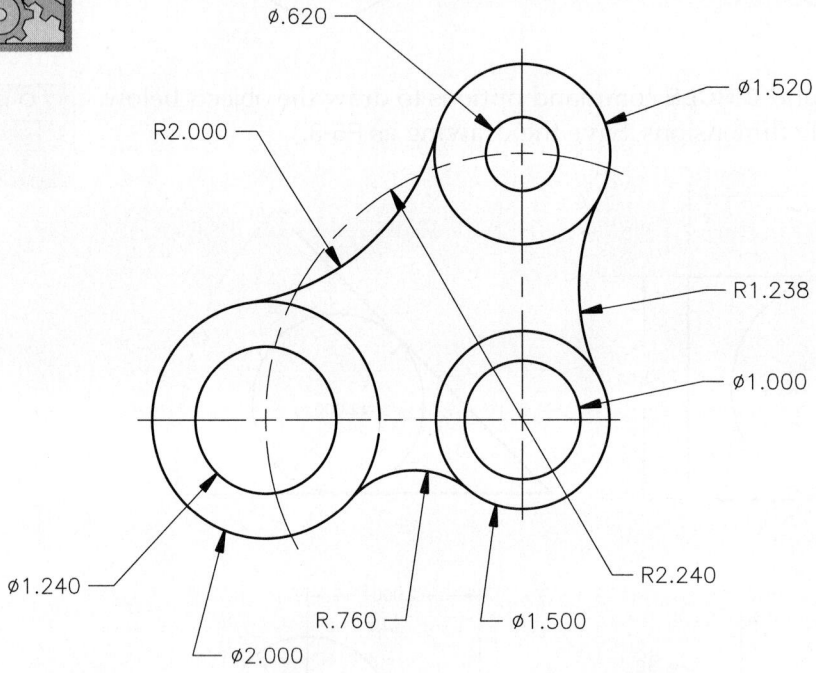

(Art courtesy of Bruce L. Wilcox)

6. Draw the pressure cylinder shown below. Use the **Arc** option of the **ELLIPSE** command to draw the cylinder ends. Do not draw the dimensions. Save the drawing as P5-6.

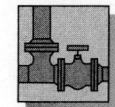

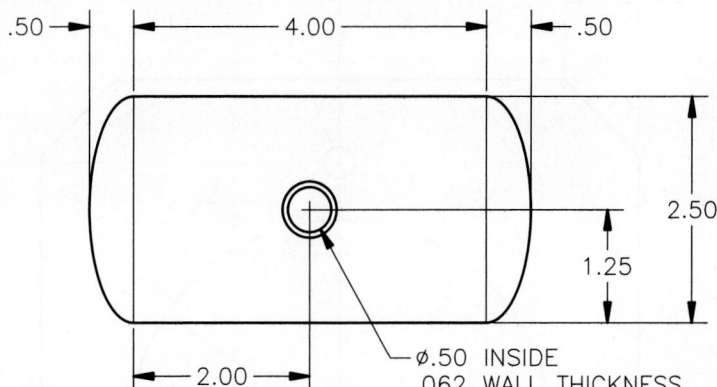

7. Draw the hex head bolt pattern shown below. Do not draw dimensions. Save the drawing as P5-7.

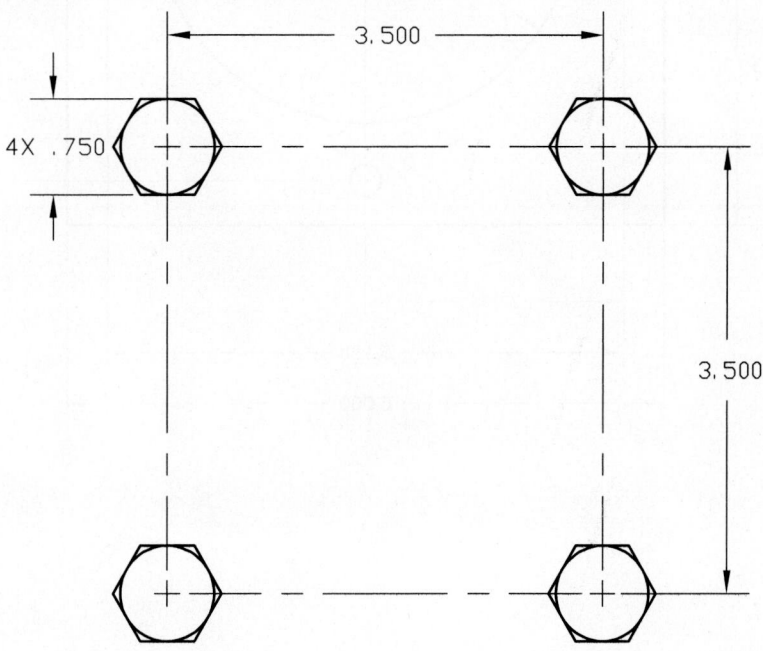

8. Draw the spacer below. Do not draw the dimensions.

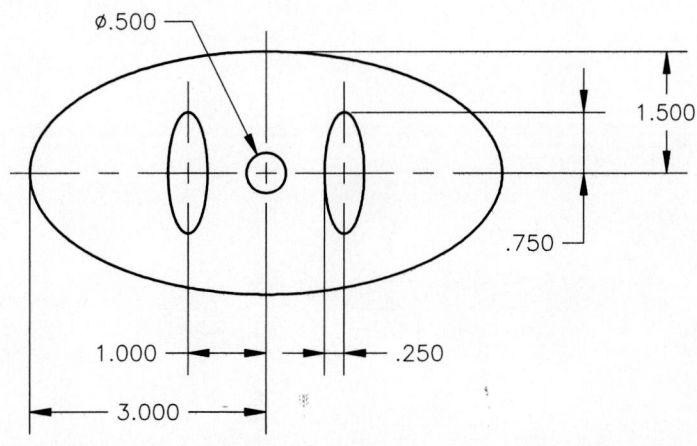

9. Draw the following object. Do not include dimensions.

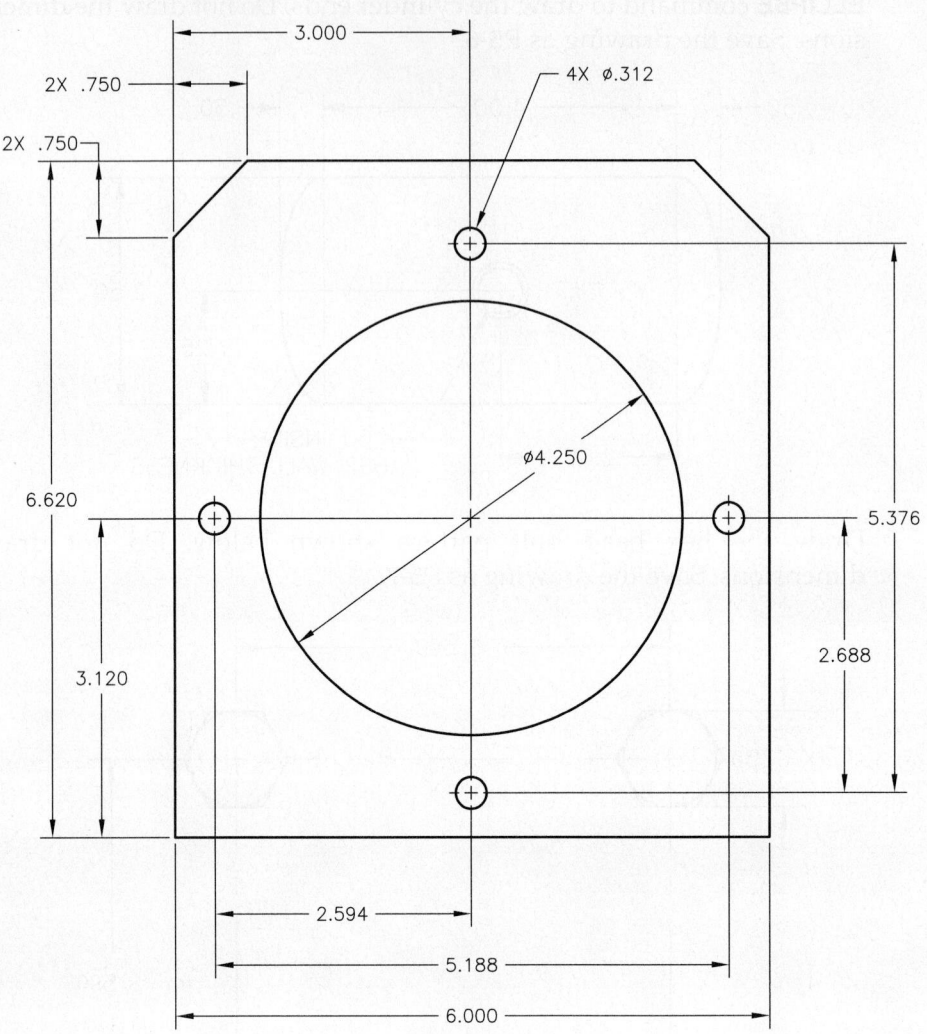

10. Draw the following object. Do not include dimensions.

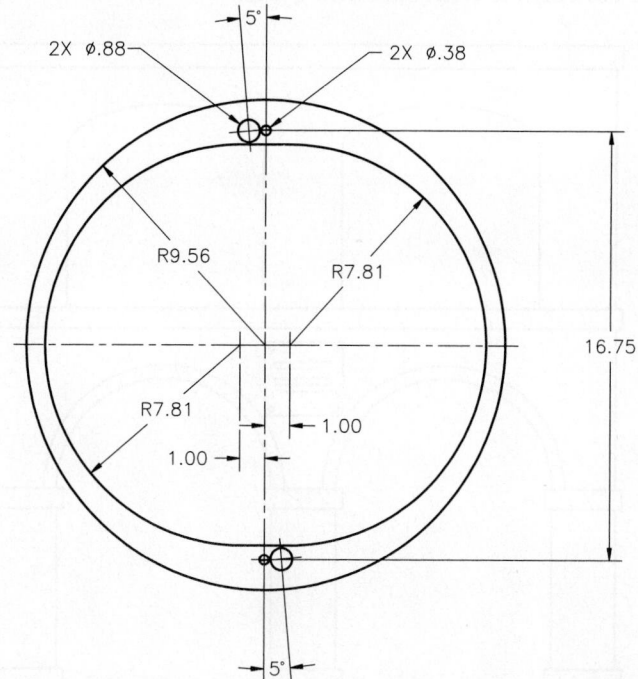

11. Create this controller integrated circuit diagram. Use a rule or scale to keep the proportion as close as possible. Do not include the text.

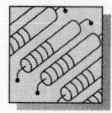

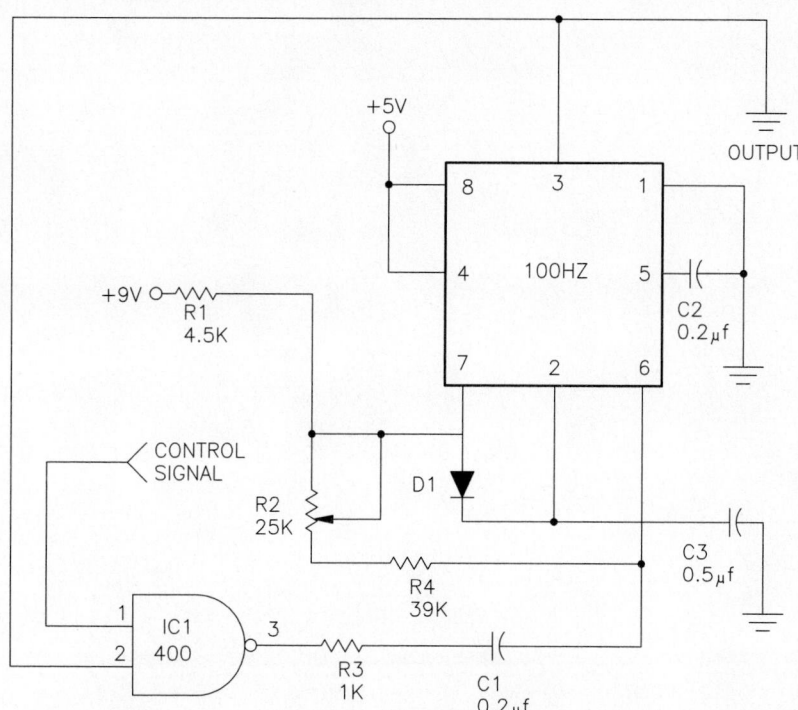

12. Draw this elevation using the **ARC**, **CIRCLE**, and **RECTANG** commands. Do not be concerned with size and scale.

# Object Snap, Geometric Constructions, and Multiview Drawings

## Learning Objectives

After completing this chapter, you will be able to do the following:
- Use object snap modes to create precision drawings.
- Use object snap overrides for single point selections.
- Set running object snap modes for continuous use.
- Use the AutoSnap features to speed up point specifications.
- Adjust marker size based on point selection needs.
- Use temporary tracking and AutoTrack modes to locate points relative to other points in a drawing.
- Use polar tracking and polar snap.
- Use the **OFFSET** command to draw parallel lines and curves.
- Divide existing objects into equal lengths using the **DIVIDE** command.
- Use the **MEASURE** command to set designated increments on an existing object.
- Create orthographic multiview drawings.
- Adjust snap grid and UCS settings to construct auxiliary views.
- Use construction lines to assist in drawing orthographic views and auxiliary views.

This chapter explains how the powerful **OSNAP** command features are used when creating and editing your drawing. **OSNAP** means *object snap*. Object snap allows you to instantly locate exact points relative to existing objects. A feature called *AutoSnap™* can be used to visually preview and confirm snap point options prior to point selection. Other point selection methods, such as object snap tracking, polar tracking, and X and Y coordinate filters, allow you to locate points relative to existing points. This chapter continues with an explanation of how to create parallel offset copies, divide objects, and place point objects. Creating multiview drawings using orthographic projection and construction lines is also covered.

## Snapping to Specific Features

Object snap is one of the most useful tools found in AutoCAD. It increases your drafting ability, performance, and productivity. The term *object snap* refers to the cursor's ability to "snap" exactly to a specific point or place on an object. The advantage of object snap is that you do not have to pick an exact point.

The AutoSnap feature is enabled by default. With AutoSnap active, visual cues are displayed while using object snap. This helps you in visualizing and confirming candidate points for object snap.

These visual cues appear as *markers* displayed at the current selection point. **Figure 6-1** shows two examples of visual cues provided by AutoSnap. The endpoint of a line object is being picked in **Figure 6-1A**. The visual cue for an **Endpoint** object snap is shown as a square when the cursor is placed close to the line object. After a brief pause, a tooltip is displayed, indicating the object snap mode. In **Figure 6-1B**, a point that is tangent to an existing circle is being selected. The AutoSnap symbol for a tangency point is shown as a circle with a tangent horizontal line.

Another visual clue that is displayed with some object snaps, and also with AutoTrack options, is an alignment path. An *alignment path* is a dashed line that shows the path upon which an object would be drawn if aligned as desired with another object. For example, you will see a parallel alignment path created when drawing parallel objects using the **Parallel** object snap. An *extension path* is a type of alignment path that is displayed when using the **Extension** object snap to find the imaginary extension of an existing object.

The default settings for AutoSnap are used for this discussion of the object snap features. Changing AutoSnap settings and features is discussed later in this chapter.

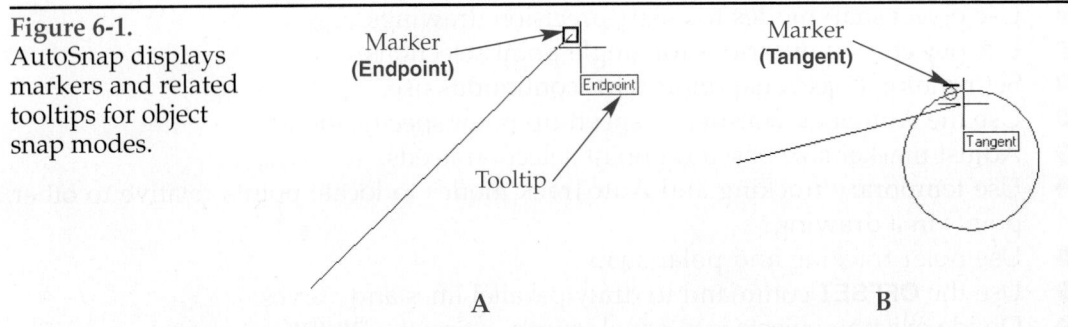

**Figure 6-1.**
AutoSnap displays markers and related tooltips for object snap modes.

# Object Snap Modes

Object snap modes determine the point to which the cursor snaps. These modes can be activated using one of several different methods. After entering a command, an object snap override can be typed at the prompt line or selected from the **Object Snap** shortcut menu shown in **Figure 6-2**. To activate this menu, hold down the [Shift] key and right-click your mouse or pick the [Enter] button on your puck. Object snap overrides are also available as buttons in the **Object Snap** toolbar, **Figure 6-3.**

To activate the **Object Snap** toolbar, select **Toolbars...** from the **View** pull-down menu. Then, select **Object Snap** in the **Toolbars** tab of the **Customize** dialog box. Pick the **Close** button to close the **Customize** dialog box. You can keep the **Object Snap** toolbar floating or you can dock it at the edge of the graphics window in a location that is convenient to access.

*Object snap override* refers to the entry of an object snap mode at a point specification prompt. A *point specification prompt* is any prompt that asks you to enter or pick a point coordinate. Object snap overrides are active for one point specification only, and they override any previously set object snap modes for that one entry.

A *running object snap mode* stays active for all point selections until it is changed. Running object snap modes are discussed later in this section.

**Figure 6-2.**
The **Object Snap**
shortcut menu
provides quick
access to object snap
overrides.

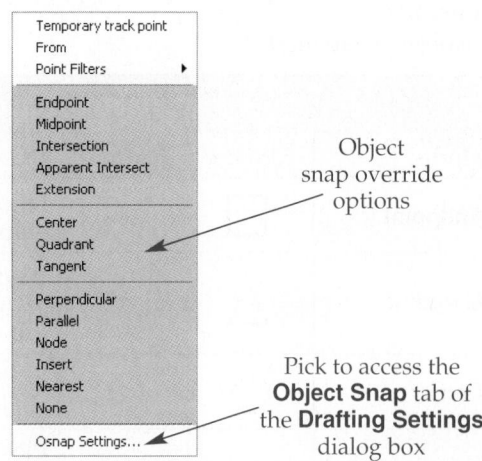

Object
snap override
options

Pick to access the
**Object Snap** tab of
the **Drafting Settings**
dialog box

**Figure 6-3.**
The **Object Snap**
toolbar.

NOTE

When AutoCAD is configured to display screen menus, the object snap modes screen menu can be accessed by picking **** near the top of the current screen menu.

The table in **Figure 6-4** summarizes the object snap modes. Included with each mode is the marker that appears on-screen and its button from the **Object Snap** toolbar. Each object snap mode selects a different portion of an object. When you activate an object snap override from the prompt line, you only need to enter the first three letters of the desired object snap mode.

**PROFESSIONAL TIP**

Remember that object snap overrides are not commands, but are used in conjunction with commands. If you type MID or PER at the Command: prompt, AutoCAD displays an "Unknown Command" error message.

Practice with the different object snap modes to find the ones that work best in various situations. Object snap can be used during many commands, such as **LINE**, **CIRCLE**, **ARC**, **MOVE**, **COPY**, and **INSERT**. The most common uses for object snap are discussed in the following sections.

Figure 6-4.
The object snap modes.

| Object Snap Modes | | | |
|---|---|---|---|
| **Mode** | **Marker** | **Button** | **Description** |
| **Endpoint** | □ | 🖉 | Finds the nearest endpoint of a line, arc, polyline, elliptical arc, spline, ellipse, ray, solid, or multiline. |
| **Midpoint** | △ | 🖉 | Finds the middle point of any object having two endpoints, such as a line, polyline, arc, elliptical arc, polyline arc, spline, ray, solid, xline, or multiline. |
| **Center** | ○ | ⊙ | Locates the center point of a radial object, including circles, arcs, ellipses, elliptical arcs, and radial solids. |
| **Quadrant** | ◇ | ◈ | Picks the closest of the four quadrant points that can be found on circles, arcs, elliptical arcs, ellipses, and radial solids. (Not all of these objects may have all four quadrants.) |
| **Intersection** | ✕ | ✕ | Picks the closest intersection of two objects. |
| **Apparent Intersection** | ⊠ | ✕ | Selects a visual intersection between two objects that appear to intersect on screen in the current view, but may not actually intersect each other in 3D space. |
| **Extension** | + | ---- | Finds a point along the imaginary extension of an existing line, polyline, arc, polyline arc, elliptical arc, spline, ray, xline, solid, or multiline. |
| **Insertion** | ⌐⌐ | 🔄 | Finds the insertion point of text objects and blocks. |
| **Perpendicular** | ⌐ | ⊥ | Finds a point that is perpendicular to an object from the previously picked point. |
| **Parallel** | ∥ | ∥ | Used to find any point along an imaginary line parallel to an existing line or polyline. |
| **Tangent** | ⊽ | ⊙ | Finds points of tangency between radial and linear objects. |
| **Nearest** | ⊠ | 🖉 | Locates the point on an object closest to the crosshairs. |
| **Node** | ⊗ | ○ | Picks a point object drawn with the **POINT**, **DIVIDE**, or **MEASURE** command. |
| **None** | | 🚫 | Turns running object snap off. |

## Endpoint Object Snap

In many cases, you need to connect a line, arc, or center point of a circle to the endpoint of an existing line or arc. Select the **Endpoint** object snap mode and move the cursor past the midpoint of the line or arc toward the end to be picked. A small square marks the endpoint that will be picked.

AutoCAD and its Applications—Basics

In **Figure 6-5**, the following command sequence is used to connect a line to the endpoint of an existing line:

Command: **L** *or* **LINE**.⏎
Specify first point: *(pick a point)*
Specify next point or [Undo]: *(pick the* **Endpoint** *button on the* **Object Snap** *toolbar, type END, or pick* **Endpoint** *from the* **Object Snap** *shortcut menu)*
of *(move the cursor near the end of the line and pick)*
Specify next point or [Undo]: ⏎
Command:

The **Endpoint** object snap can be used to quickly select the endpoints of all types of lines and arcs. It is often selected as a running object snap.

Figure 6-5.
Using **Endpoint**
object snap.

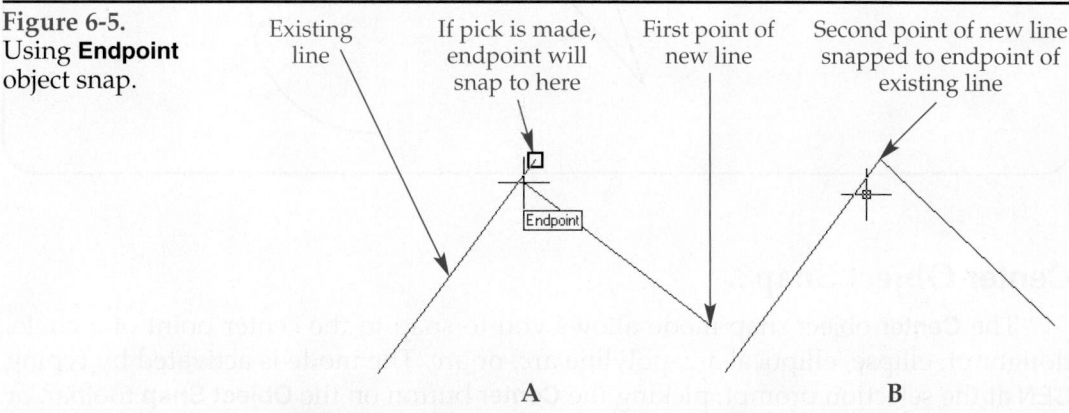

Existing line

If pick is made, endpoint will snap to here

First point of new line

Second point of new line snapped to endpoint of existing line

Endpoint

A

B

## Midpoint Object Snap

The **Midpoint** object snap mode finds and picks the midpoint of a line, polyline, or arc. During a command, type MID at the prompt, pick the **Midpoint** button on the **Object Snap** toolbar, or select **Midpoint** from the **Object Snap** shortcut menu to activate this object snap mode. Next, position the cursor near the midpoint of the object. A small triangle will mark the midpoint. See **Figure 6-6**.

Figure 6-6.
Using **Midpoint**
object snap.

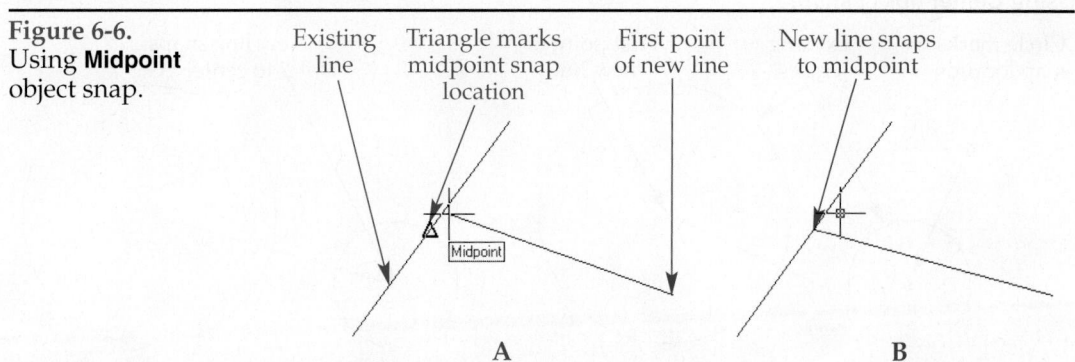

Existing line

Triangle marks midpoint snap location

First point of new line

New line snaps to midpoint

Midpoint

A

B

○ Start AutoCAD and use the setup option of your choice.
○ Use the **Endpoint** and **Midpoint** object snap modes to draw the object shown below. Draw Line 1, then Line 2 connecting to the endpoint of Line 1. Draw Line 3 from the endpoint of Line 2 to the midpoint of Line 1. Draw Arc A with one end connected to the endpoint of Line 1.
○ Save the drawing as EX6-1.

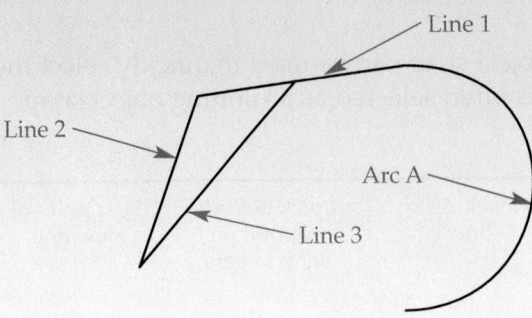

## Center Object Snap

The **Center** object snap mode allows you to snap to the center point of a circle, doughnut, ellipse, elliptical arc, polyline arc, or arc. The mode is activated by typing CEN at the selection prompt, picking the **Center** button on the **Object Snap** toolbar, or picking **Center** from the **Object Snap** shortcut menu. When you move the cursor onto the object whose center point is to be located, a small circle and plus sign will mark the center point.

Be sure to move the cursor near the perimeter, not the center point, of the object. For example, when locating the center of a large circle, the **Center** object snap mode will *not* locate the center if the cursor is not near the perimeter of the circle. In **Figure 6-7**, the **Center** object snap is used to draw a line to the center of a circle.

Figure 6-7.
Using **Center** object snap.

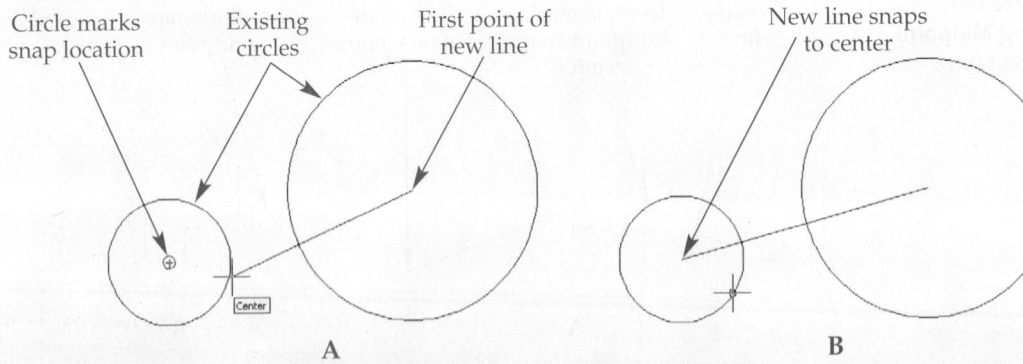
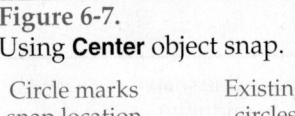

## Quadrant Object Snap

A *quadrant* is a quarter section of a circle, doughnut, ellipse, elliptical arc, polyline arc, or arc. The **Quadrant** object snap mode finds the 0°, 90°, 180°, and 270° positions on a circle, doughnut, or arc, **Figure 6-8.**

Figure 6-8.
The quadrants of a
circle.

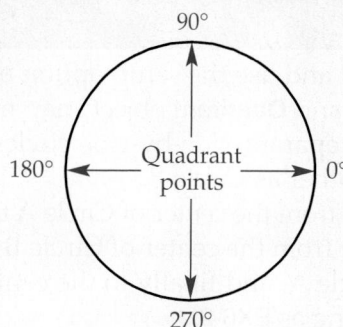

When picking quadrants, locate the crosshairs near the intended quadrant on the circle, doughnut, or arc. For example, **Figure 6-9** illustrates the use of the **Quadrant** object snap mode to locate the center point of a new circle at the quadrant of an existing circle. The command sequence is as follows:

Command: **C** *or* **CIRCLE.**↵
Specify center point for circle or [3P/2P/Ttr (tan tan radius)]: *(pick the **Quadrant** button in the **Object Snap** toolbar, type QUA, or pick **Quadrant** from the **Object Snap** shortcut menu)*
of *(move the cursor near the desired quadrant and pick)*
Specify radius of a circle or [Diameter]: *(pick a radius)*

Figure 6-9.
Using **Quadrant**
object snap.

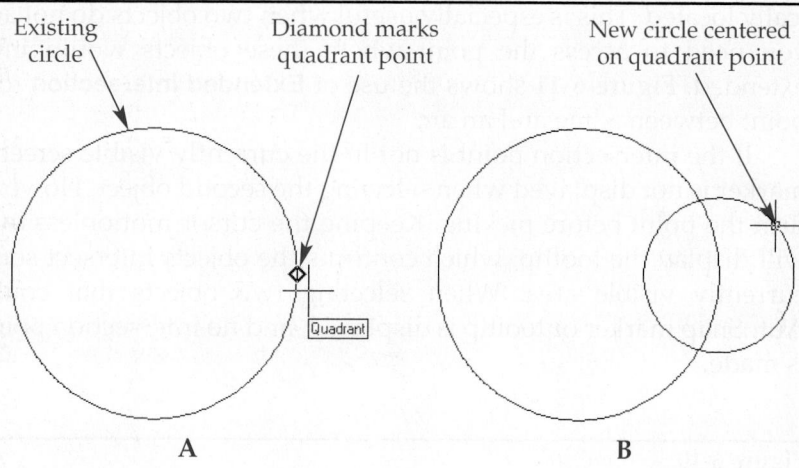

A                                           B

**NOTE**  Quadrant positions are unaffected by the current angle zero direction, but always coincide with the current WCS (world coordinate system). The WCS is discussed later in this chapter. The quadrant points of a circle, doughnut, or arc are at the top, bottom, left, and right, regardless of the rotation of the object. However, the quadrant points of ellipses and elliptical arcs rotate with the object.

## Intersection Object Snap

The **Intersection** object snap mode is used to snap to the intersection of two or more objects. This mode is activated by typing INT at the selection prompt, picking the **Intersect** button, or picking **Intersection** from the **Object Snap** shortcut menu. Then move the cursor near the intersection. A small "X" marks the intersection. See **Figure 6-10.**

When picking a point for an **Intersection** object snap, the "X" appears only when the cursor is close to the intersection point of two objects. If the cursor is near an object, but not close to an actual intersection, the tooltip reads Extended Intersection, and the AutoSnap marker is followed by an ellipsis ( … ). When using **Extended Intersection**, you select the objects one at a time and the intersection point is automatically located. This is especially useful when two objects do not actually intersect, and you need to access the point where these objects would intersect if they were extended. **Figure 6-11** shows the use of **Extended Intersection** to find an intersection point between a line and an arc.

If the intersection point is not in the currently visible screen area, the AutoSnap marker is not displayed when selecting the second object. However, you can still confirm the point before picking. Keeping the cursor motionless over the second object will display the tooltip, which confirms the objects intersect somewhere beyond the currently visible area. When selecting two objects that could not intersect, no AutoSnap marker or tooltip is displayed, and no intersection point is found if the pick is made.

Figure 6-10.
Using **Intersection**
object snap.

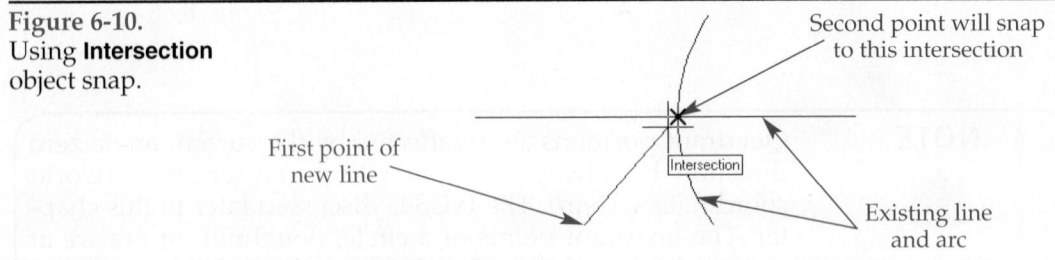

Second point will snap to this intersection

First point of new line

Intersection

Existing line and arc

**Figure 6-11.**
Finding the extended intersection of two objects. A—Select the first object. B—When the second object is selected, the extended intersection becomes the snap point. C—The completed line.

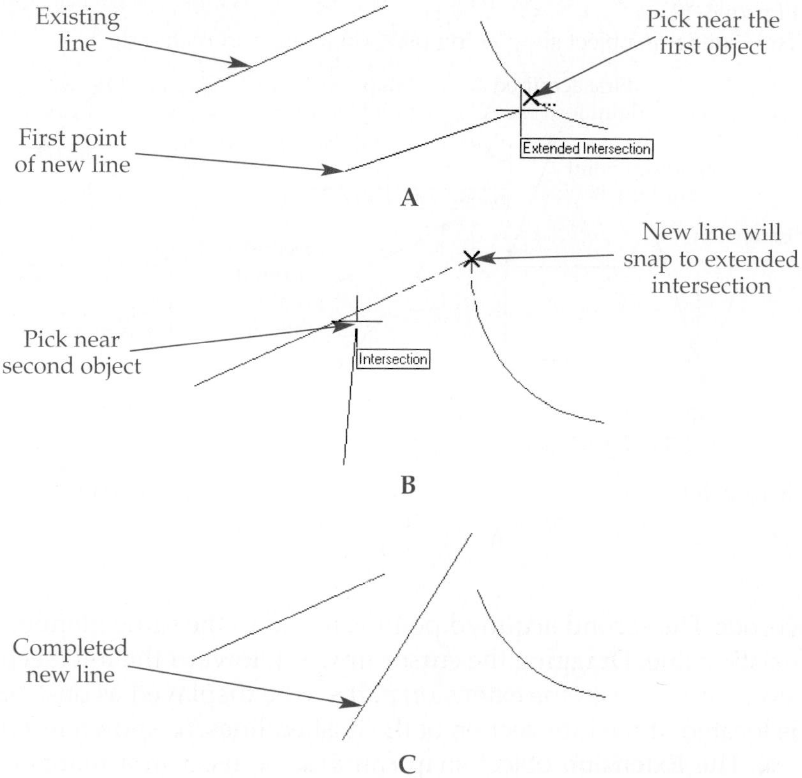

Existing line

Pick near the first object

First point of new line

Extended Intersection

**A**

New line will snap to extended intersection

Pick near second object

Intersection

**B**

Completed new line

**C**

## Apparent Intersection Object Snap

The *apparent intersection* is the point where two objects created in 3D space appear to intersect based on the current view. Three-dimensional objects that are far apart may appear to intersect when viewed from certain angles. Whether they intersect or not, this option returns the coordinate point where the objects appear to intersect. This is a valuable option when working with 3D drawings. Creating and editing 3D objects is discussed in Chapter 26 of this text, and in *AutoCAD and its Applications—Advanced.*

## Extension Object Snap

The **Extension** object snap mode is used to find any point along the imaginary extension of an existing line, polyline, or polyline arc. This mode is activated by typing EXT at the selection prompt, picking the **Extension** button on the **Object Snap** toolbar, or picking **Extension** from the **Object Snap** shortcut menu. The extension object snap differs from most other snaps because it requires more than one selection point. The initial point(s), called the *acquired point,* is not selected in the typical manner but is found by simply moving the cursor over the line, polyline, or polyline arc from which the new object is to be extended. When the object is found, a (+) symbol marks the location. If the new object is to be created at the intersection of extensions from two objects, the cursor must be placed over the second object to locate its extension path. The last point, which is the actual snap point, can be placed anywhere along the extension path, including the intersection of two extension paths. The *extension path,* represented by a dashed line or arc, extends from the acquired point to the current location of the mouse.

Line A in **Figure 6-12** is an example of the way the **Extension** object snap can create a new line at the intersection of extension paths from two existing objects. The first acquired point is found by moving the cursor directly over the corner of the rectangle. The tooltip for the extension is displayed, and the (+) marker becomes visible at the

**Figure 6-12.**
The **Extension** object snap being used on a line and rectangle.

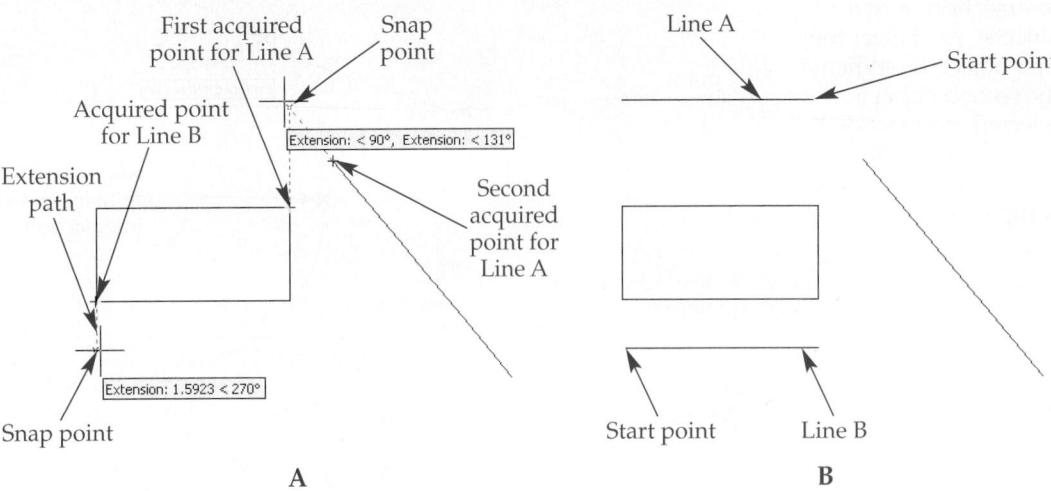

First acquired
point for Line A

Snap
point

Line A

Start point

Acquired point
for Line B

Extension: < 90°,  Extension: < 131°

Second
acquired
point for
Line A

Extension
path

Extension: 1.5923 < 270°

Snap point

Start point

Line B

A

B

corner. The second acquired point is found in the same manner at the endpoint of the existing line. Dragging the cursor upward, toward the intersection point of the extension paths, causes the extension paths to be displayed as dashed lines. The snap point is located at the intersection of the dashed lines, as shown in **Figure 6-12.**

The **Extension** object snap can also be used in a manner similar to temporary tracking and the **From** object snap, which are discussed later in this chapter. In **Figure 6-12,** the **Extension** snap and direct distance entry are used to start Line B 1.5 units away from the corner of the rectangle.

---

### Exercise 6-3

○ Start AutoCAD and use the setup option of your choice.
○ Draw a rectangle and an angled line to the right of the rectangle, as shown in **Figure 6-12A.**
○ Use the **Extension** object snap mode to draw Line A and Line B similar to those in **Figure 6-12B.**
○ Save the drawing as EX6-3.

---

## Perpendicular Object Snap

In geometric construction, it is common to draw one object perpendicular to another. This is done using the **Perpendicular** object snap mode. To activate this mode, type PER at the selection prompt, pick the **Perpendicular** button in the **Object Snap** toolbar, or pick **Perpendicular** from the **Object Snap** shortcut menu. A small right-angle symbol appears at the snap point. This mode can be used with arcs, elliptical arcs, ellipses, splines, xlines, multilines, polylines, solids, traces, or circles.

**Figure 6-13** shows an example of the **Perpendicular** object snap being used to locate the endpoint of a line. The endpoint is positioned so that the new line is perpendicular to the existing line. In **Figure 6-14,** the first point of the line is selected with the **Perpendicular** object snap. The tooltip reads Deferred Perpendicular. The term *deferred perpendicular* means that the calculation of the perpendicular point is delayed until another point is picked. The second endpoint determines the location of the first endpoint.

**Figure 6-13.**
Drawing a line from a point perpendicular to an existing line. The **Perpendicular** object snap mode is used to select the second endpoint.

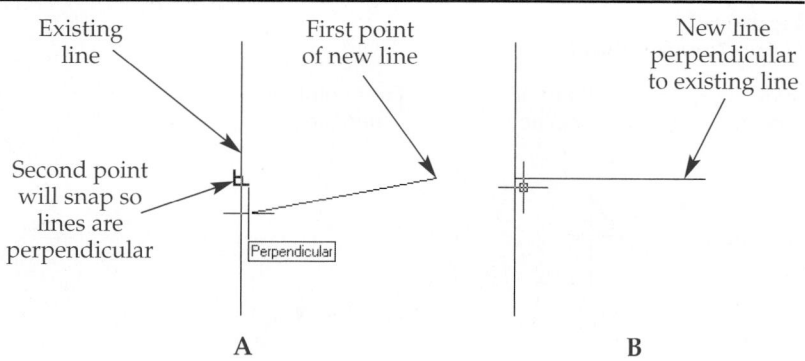

**Figure 6-14.**
Deferring the perpendicular location until the second point is selected. The **Perpendicular** object snap mode is used to select the first endpoint.

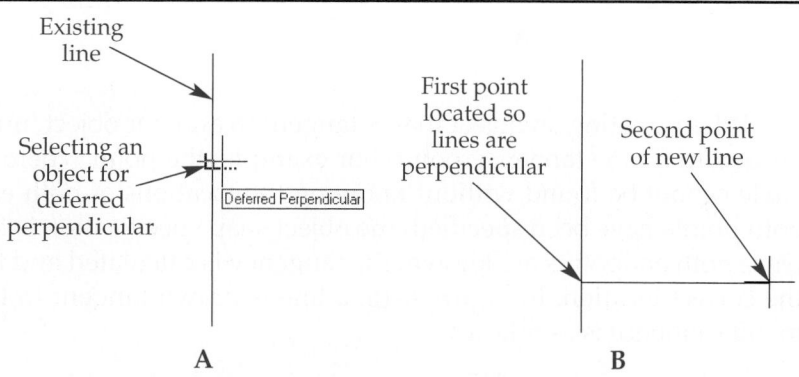

It is important to understand that perpendicularity is calculated from points picked, and not as a relationship between objects. Also, perpendicularity is measured at the point of intersection, so it is possible to draw a line that is perpendicular to a circle or an arc.

---

### Exercise 6-4

○ Start AutoCAD and use the setup option of your choice.
○ Draw a horizontal line, and a circle above the line. Add a new line from the circle's center, perpendicular to the first line.
○ Draw two intersecting lines and a separate circle. Add a line from the circle's center to the intersection of the lines.
○ Draw two nonintersecting, nonparallel lines. Draw a line from the endpoint of one line to the point where it would intersect the other line if it were extended.
○ Save the drawing as EX6-4.

---

## Tangent Object Snap

The **Tangent** object snap is similar to the **Perpendicular** object snap. However, instead of aligning the objects perpendicularly, it aligns objects tangentially. To activate this mode, type TAN at the selection prompt, pick the **Tangent** button on the **Object Snap** toolbar, or pick **Tangent** from the **Object Snap** shortcut menu. A small circle with a horizontal line appears at the snap point.

In **Figure 6-15**, the endpoint of a line is located using the **Tangent** object snap mode. The first point is selected normally. Then, the **Tangent** object snap mode is activated and the cursor is placed near the tangent point on the circle. AutoCAD determines the tangent point and places the snap point (and the endpoint) there.

**Figure 6-15.**
Using **Tangent** object snap.

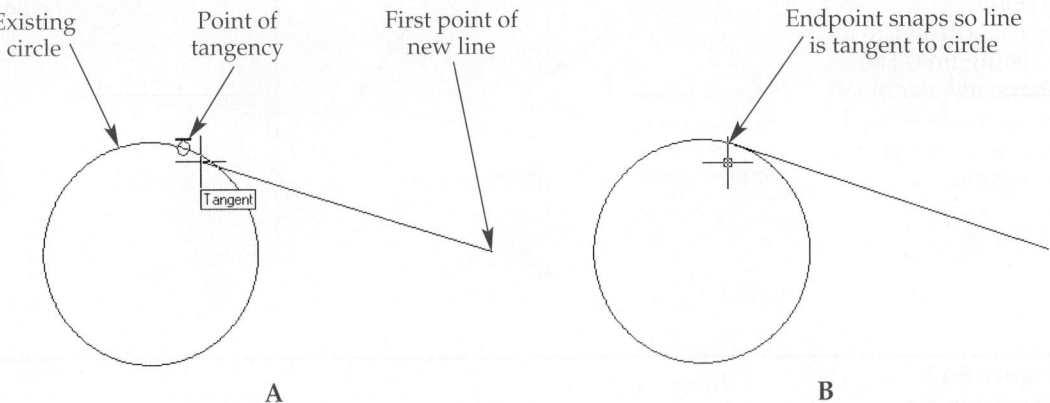

Existing circle

Point of tangency

First point of new line

Endpoint snaps so line is tangent to circle

Tangent

A

B

When creating an object that is tangent to another object, multiple points may be needed to fix the tangency point. For example, the point where a line is tangent to a circle cannot be found without knowing the locations of both ends of the line. Until both points have been specified, the object snap specification is for *deferred tangency*. Once both endpoints are known, the tangency is calculated and the object is drawn in the correct location. In **Figure 6-16**, a line is drawn tangent to two circles. The command sequence is as follows:

Command: **L** *or* **LINE**↵
Specify first point: *(pick the* **Tangent** *button on the* **Object Snap** *toolbar, type* TAN, *or pick* **Tangent** *from the* **Object Snap** *shortcut menu.)*
tan to *(pick the first circle)*
Specify next point or [Undo]: *(pick the* **Tangent** *button on the* **Object Snap** *toolbar, type* TAN, *or pick* **Tangent** *from the* **Object Snap** *shortcut menu.)*
tan to *(pick the second circle)*
Specify next point or [Undo]: ↵
Command:

---

### Exercise 6-5

○ Start AutoCAD and use the setup option of your choice.
○ Draw a line tangent to an existing circle.
○ Draw two circles and then draw a line tangent to both of the circles.
○ Use the **Tangent** object snap to draw two lines that are tangent to the circles but do not cross.
○ Save the drawing as EX6-5.

---

## Parallel Object Snap

The process of drawing, moving, or copying objects that are not horizontal or vertical is improved with the **Parallel** object snap mode. This option is used to find any point along an imaginary line that is parallel to an existing line or polyline. Polylines are discussed in Chapter 14. To activate the **Parallel** object snap mode, type PAR at the selection prompt, pick the **Parallel** button on the **Object Snap** toolbar, or pick **Parallel** from the **Object Snap** shortcut menu.

**Figure 6-16.**
Drawing a line
tangent to two circles.

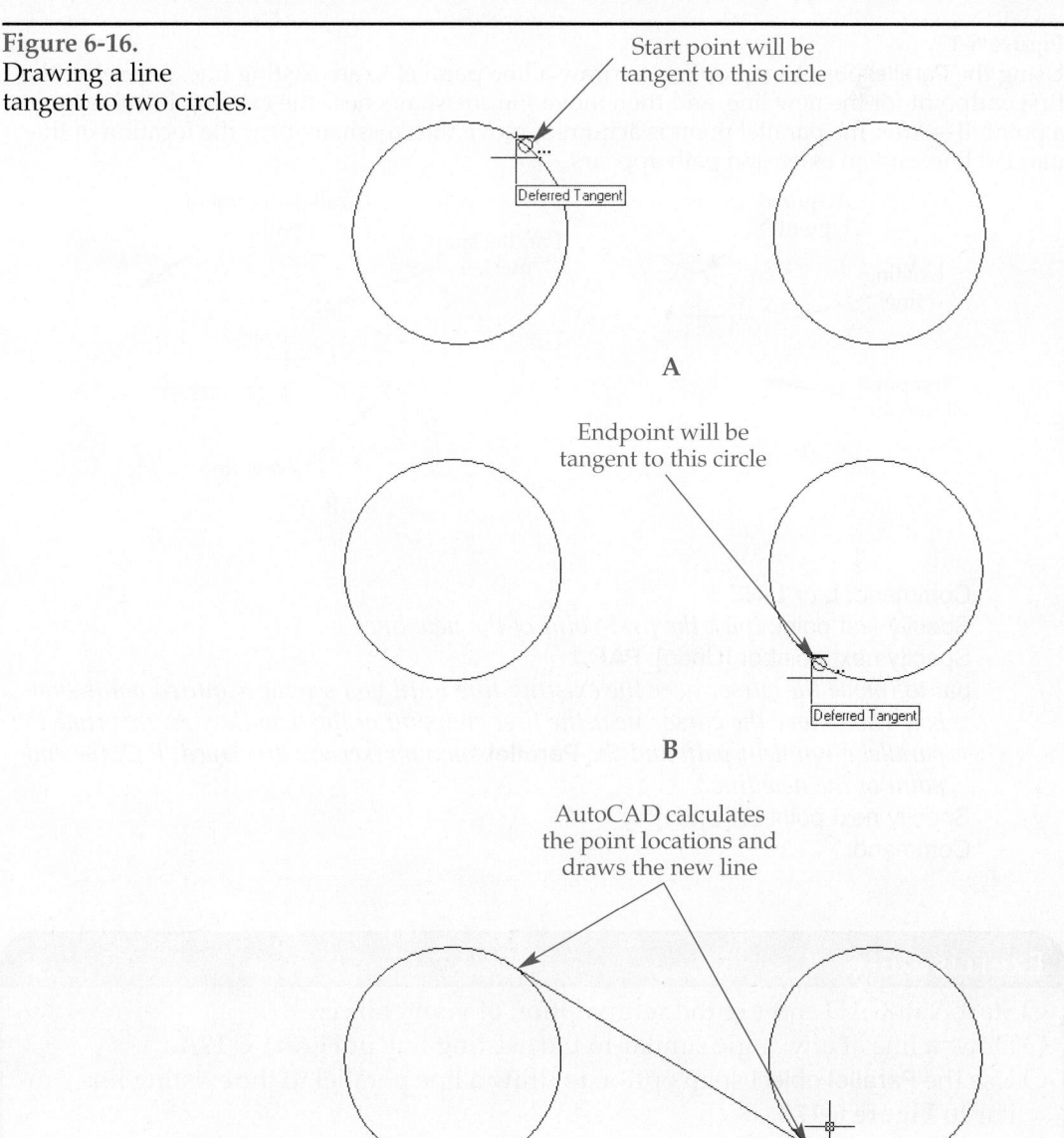

Start point will be
tangent to this circle

Deferred Tangent

**A**

Endpoint will be
tangent to this circle

Deferred Tangent

**B**

AutoCAD calculates
the point locations and
draws the new line

**C**

The **Parallel** object snap is similar to the **Extension** object snap because it requires more than one selection point. The first point, called the *acquired point,* is found by pausing the cursor over the line to which the new object is to be parallel. When the object is found and you move the cursor in a direction parallel to the existing line, a (//) symbol marks the existing line. A dashed line, parallel to the existing line, extends from the cursor's location into space. This line is known as the *parallel alignment path.* The last point, which is the actual snap point, can be placed anywhere along the parallel alignment path. When the alignment path is displayed, the **Parallel** snap marker appears on the line from which the parallel is used. Picking any location along the parallel alignment path creates the second point of the parallel line. **Figure 6-17** shows an example of the **Parallel** object snap being used to draw a line parallel to an existing line. The following command sequence is used:

**Figure 6-17.**
Using the **Parallel** object snap option to draw a line parallel to an existing line. A—Select the first endpoint for the new line, and then move the crosshairs near the existing line to acquire a point. B—After the parallel point is acquired, move the crosshairs near the location of the parallel line, and an extension path appears.

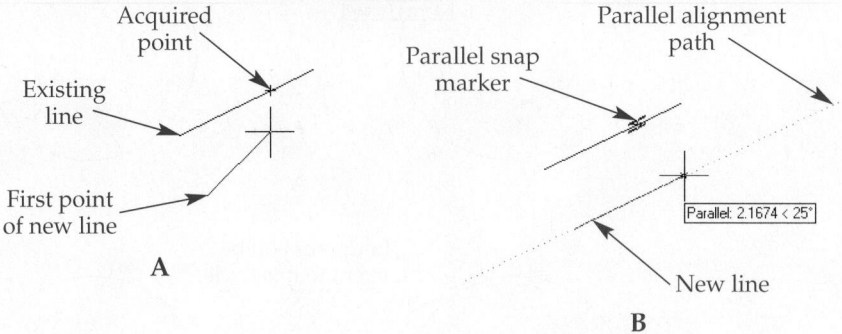

```
Command: L or LINE↵
Specify first point: (pick the first point of the new line)
Specify next point or [Undo]: PAR↵
par to (move the cursor over the existing line until you see the acquired point sym-
    bol. Then move the cursor near the first endpoint of the new line. At this time the
    parallel alignment path and the Parallel snap marker are displayed. Pick the end-
    point of the new line.)
Specify next point or [Undo]: ↵
Command:
```

### Exercise 6-6

○ Start AutoCAD and use the setup option of your choice.
○ Draw a line at any angle similar to the existing line in **Figure 6-17A.**
○ Use the **Parallel** object snap option to draw a line parallel to the existing line similar to **Figure 6-17B.**
○ Save the drawing as EX6-6.

## Node Object Snap

Point objects can be snapped to using the **Node** object snap mode. In order for object snap to find the point object, the point must be in a visible display mode. Controlling the point display mode is covered later in this chapter.

## Nearest Object Snap

When you need to specify a point that is on an object but cannot be located with any of the other object snap modes, the **Nearest** mode can be used. This object snap locates the point on the object closest to the crosshair location. It should be used when you want an object to touch an existing object, but the location of the intersection is not critical.

Consider drawing a line object that is to end on another line. Trying to pick the point with the crosshairs is inaccurate because you are relying only on your screen and mouse resolution. The line you draw may fall short or extend past the line. Using **Nearest** ensures that the point is precisely on the object.

AutoCAD and its Applications—Basics

When AutoCAD uses object snap modes, it searches the entire drawing database for the specified type of point nearest to the crosshairs. When working on complex drawing, you may want to use the **Quick** mode, which selects the first point satisfying the snap mode. The **Quick** mode must be activated at the Command: prompt, and is only effective for a single selection. It is activated by preceding the object snap mode with QUI and a comma. For example, the following command sequence would be used to activate the **Tangent** object snap mode in **Quick** mode:

Command: **L** *or* **LINE.**↵
Specify first point: **QUI,TAN.**↵

## Setting Running Object Snaps

The previous discussion explained how to use object snaps by activating the individual mode at the selection prompt. However, if you plan to use object snaps continuously, you can set *running object snaps*. You preset the running object snap modes, and AutoCAD automatically activates them at all point selection prompts.

You can set a running object snap mode using the **Object Snap** tab in the **Drafting Settings** dialog box. Pick **Drafting Settings…** from the **Tools** pull-down menu, pick the **Object Snap Settings** button from the **Object Snap** toolbar, right-click on the **OSNAP** or **OTRACK** button on the status bar and select **Settings…** from the shortcut menu, or type OS, OSNAP, or DDOSNAP at the Command: prompt. You can also type DSETTINGS at the Command: prompt to access the **Drafting Settings** dialog box.

The **Object Snap** tab of the **Drafting Settings** dialog box is shown in **Figure 6-18.** Notice that the **Endpoint**, **Intersection**, **Extension**, and **Parallel** modes are active. You can use this dialog box at any time to discontinue a running object snap or to set additional modes.

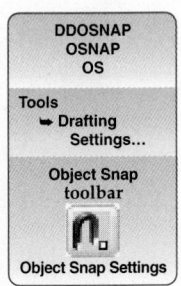

DDOSNAP
OSNAP
OS

Tools
➥ Drafting
   Settings…

Object Snap
toolbar

Object Snap Settings

**Figure 6-18.**
Running object snap modes can be set in the **Drafting Settings** dialog box.

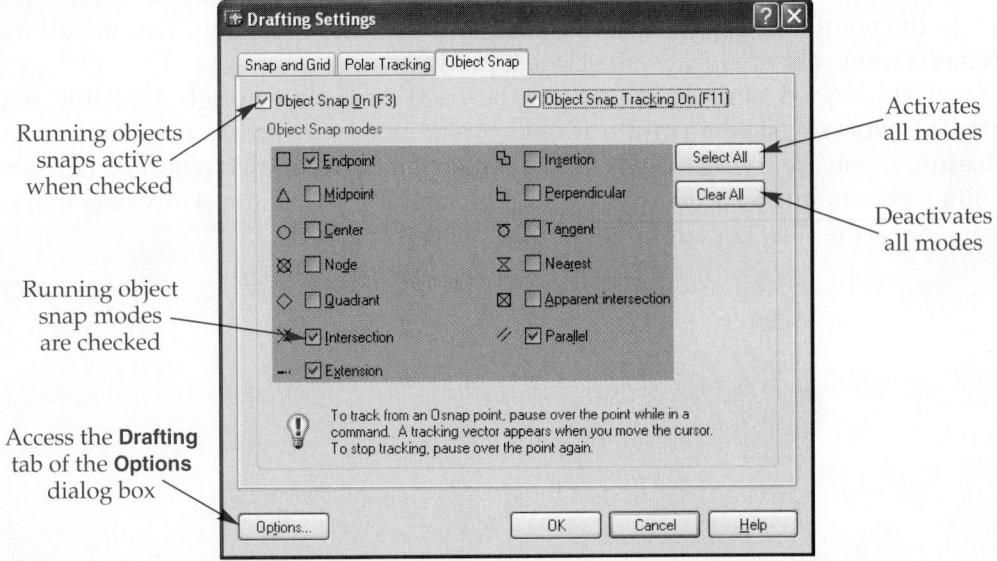

## Toggling, Disabling, and Overriding Running Object Snap

Running object snap is active at all point selection prompts, but is temporarily suspended when an object snap override is entered. The override is temporary, and is active for a single point selection only. Any currently running object snap mode is reactivated for the next pick.

To make a single point selection without the effects of any running object snap modes, enter the **None** object snap mode. To activate the **None** object snap mode, type NON at the selection prompt, select the **Snap to None** button on the **Object Snap** toolbar, or select **None** from the **Object Snap** shortcut menu.

When you need to make several point specifications without the aid of object snap, you can toggle it off by clicking the **OSNAP** button on the status bar at the bottom of the AutoCAD window. The advantages of this method are that you can make several picks, and then restore the same running object snap modes by clicking **OSNAP** again. You can also right-click on the **OSNAP** button and pick **Off** from the shortcut menu (pick **On** to restore the running object snaps), pick the **Object Snap On (F3)** check box in the **Drafting Settings** dialog box, or press the [F3] key on your keyboard. Any of these options can be used to reactivate running object snaps.

You can remove the active checks in the **Drafting Settings** dialog box as needed to disable running object snaps. You can also pick the **Clear All** button to disable all running modes. Select desired running object snaps by picking the associated box or pick the **Select All** button to activate all object snaps.

## Using Multiple Object Snap Modes

As shown with the examples of running object snap, more than one object snap mode can be made active at once. When multiple modes are running at the same time, each of the modes is checked for possible points, and the closest point is selected.

For example, assume the **Endpoint** and **Midpoint** object snap modes are active. The AutoSnap marker locates either an endpoint or the midpoint of a line, depending on which is closest to the location of the crosshairs. This can cause conflicts between some object snap modes. For example, no matter where you pick a circle, the closest quadrant point is always closer than the center of the circle. This means that when **Quadrant** and **Center** are both active, a quadrant point is always selected when moving the crosshairs over a circle. To make the **Center** snap marker appear, move the crosshairs over the circle and then over the circle's center.

The **Nearest** object snap mode causes conflicts with almost every other mode. The nearest mode does not move the selection point to a nearby feature of an object, but picks the point on the object closest to the current cursor location. This means that the **Nearest** mode always locates the closest point.

The [Tab] key on your keyboard can be used to cycle through available snap points. This works well when multiple object snap modes are active. For example, use this feature if you are trying to select the intersection between two objects where several other objects intersect nearby. To use this feature, when the AutoSnap marker appears, press the [Tab] key until the desired point is marked.

By default, a keyboard entry overrides any currently running object snap modes. This behavior is controlled by the **OSNAPCOORD** system variable. The value of **OSNAPCOORD** can be set as follows:

- **0.** Running object snap settings override absolute coordinate entry.
- **1.** Keyboard entry overrides object snap settings.
- **2.** Keyboard entry overrides object snap settings except in scripts.

This can also be changed by selecting **Options...** from the **Tools** pull-down menu, selecting the **User Preferences** tab in the **Options** dialog box, and selecting the appropriate radio button in the **Priority for Coordinate Date Entry** section.

## Exercise 6-7

○ Start AutoCAD and use the setup option of your choice.
○ Set the **Endpoint**, **Midpoint**, and **Perpendicular** running object snaps and practice using them in at least two situations. Drawings similar to **Figure 6-5**, **Figure 6-6**, and **Figure 6-13** can be used.
○ Change the running object snap to **Center** and **Tangent**, and use each twice in creating a simple drawing. Drawings similar to **Figure 6-7** and **Figure 6-16** can be used.
○ Discontinue the running object snaps.
○ Save the drawing as EX6-7.

Use the object snap modes not only when drawing, but also when editing. With practice, using object snaps will become second nature and greatly increase your productivity and accuracy.

## AutoSnap Settings

The AutoSnap feature makes object snap much easier to use. However, if you do not wish to have the additional visual cues while using object snap, you can turn the AutoSnap feature off. To customize the appearance and functionality of the AutoSnap feature, access the **Object Snap** tab of the **Drafting Settings** dialog box and pick the **Options...** button in the lower left-hand corner. This opens the **Drafting** tab of the **Options** dialog box, shown in **Figure 6-19**. To activate an AutoSnap option, check the corresponding checkbox:

- **Marker.** Toggles the AutoSnap marker display.
- **Magnet.** Toggles the AutoSnap magnet. When active, the magnet snaps the cursor to the object snap point.

**Figure 6-19.**
Setting AutoSnap features.

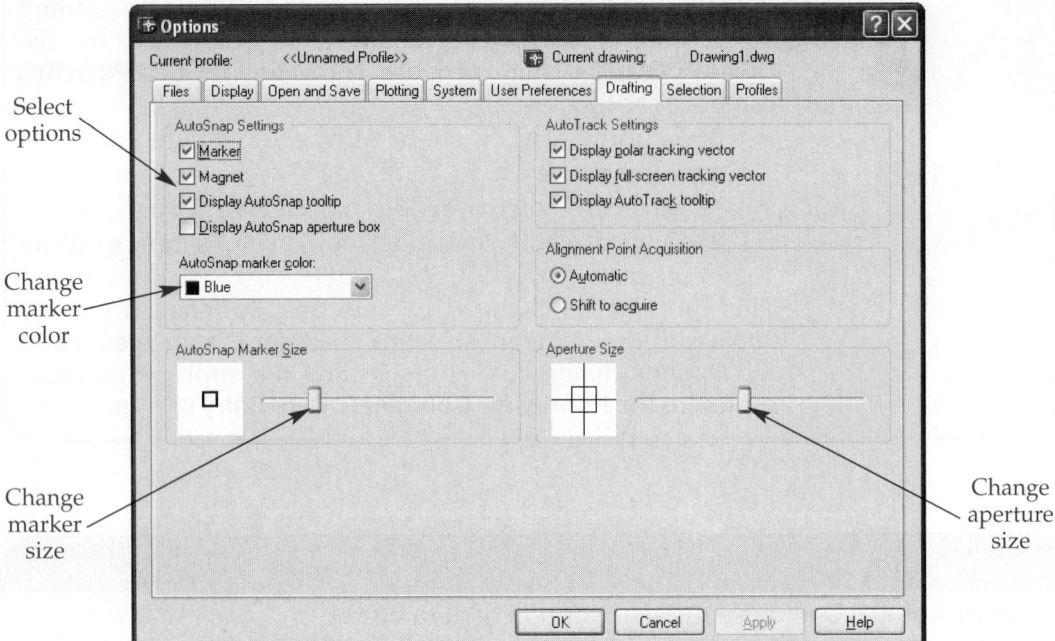

Select options

Change marker color

Change marker size

Change aperture size

- **Display AutoSnap tooltip.** Toggles the tooltip display.
- **Display AutoSnap aperture box.** Toggles the display of the aperture.

The marker size and color can also be adjusted to suit your needs. For example, the default marker color is yellow, but this is difficult to see if you have the graphics screen background set to white. Pick the down arrow to access the **AutoSnap marker color:** drop-down list, and select the desired color. At higher screen resolutions, a larger marker size improves visibility. Move the slider at the **AutoSnap Marker Size:** area to change the size.

The **AUTOSNAP** system variable controls the display of AutoSnap markers and tooltips and turns the AutoSnap magnet on or off. The **OSMODE** system variable uses bit codes to set object snap modes.

---

**Exercise 6-8**

○ Start AutoCAD and use the setup option of your choice.
○ Open the **Drafting Settings** dialog box and then the **Options** dialog box.
○ Move the **AutoSnap Marker Size** slider and watch the image change to represent the marker size.
○ Change the marker color to red.
○ Use the newly revised marker size and color to draw objects of your choice with the object snaps.
○ Save the drawing as EX6-8.

---

## Changing the Aperture Size

When selecting a point using object snaps, the cursor must be within a specific range of a candidate point before it is located. The object snap detection system finds everything within a square area centered at the cursor location. This square area is called the *aperture* and is invisible by default.

AutoCAD and its Applications—Basics

To display the aperture, open the **Drafting Settings** dialog box and pick the **Options...** button from the **Object Snap** tab. The **Drafting** tab of the **Options** dialog box appears. Activate the **Display AutoSnap aperture box** check box. Having the aperture visible may be helpful when you are first learning to work with object snap. The **APBOX** system variable turns the AutoSnap aperture box on or off.

To change the size of the aperture, move the slider in the **Aperture Size** area. Various aperture sizes are shown in **Figure 6-20.** The aperture size can also be set by typing APERTURE at the Command: prompt. The size of the aperture is measured in *pixels*. Pixels are the dots that make up a display screen.

Keep in mind that the *aperture* and the *pick box* are different. The aperture is displayed on the screen when object snap modes are active. The pick box appears on the screen for any command that activates the Select objects: prompt.

**Figure 6-20.**
Aperture box size is measured in pixels. The three examples here are not shown at actual size, but are provided to show the size relationship between different settings.

5 Pixels          10 Pixels          20 Pixels

### Exercise 6-9

○ Open EX6-7.
○ Display the aperture.
○ Change the aperture size to 5 pixels. Draw lines to existing objects using the object snap modes of your choice.
○ Change the aperture size to 20 pixels. Again, draw lines to the existing objects using the object snap modes of your choice.
○ Observe the difference in aperture size. Determine your personal preference between the 5 and 20 pixel sizes as compared to the AutoCAD default of 10 pixels.
○ Save the drawing as EX6-9.

## Using Temporary Tracking to Locate Points

*Tracking* is a system that allows you to visually locate points in a drawing relative to other points. Tracking creates a new point using the X coordinate of one tracking point and the Y coordinate of another. The tracking feature can be used at any point specification prompt, just like object snap. Tracking can also be used in combination with object snap.

To activate temporary tracking, pick the **Temporary Tracking Point** button from the **Object Snap** toolbar, type TT at the selection prompt, or pick **Temporary track point** from the **Object Snap** shortcut menu.

For example, tracking can be used to place a circle at the center of a rectangle. See **Figure 6-21.** The X coordinate of the rectangle's center corresponds to the midpoint of the horizontal lines. The Y coordinate of the rectangle's center corresponds to the midpoint of the vertical lines. Temporary tracking can be used to combine these two points to find the center of the rectangle using this sequence:

**Figure 6-21.**
Using temporary tracking to locate the center of a rectangle. A—The midpoint of the left line is acquired. B—The midpoint of the bottom line is acquired. C—The center point of the circle is located at the intersection of the alignment paths.

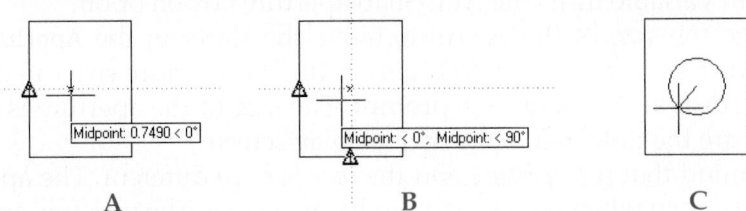

A        B        C

```
Command: C or CIRCLE.↵
Specify center point for circle or [3P/2P/Ttr (tan tan radius)]: TT↵
Specify temporary OTRACK point: MID↵
of (pick one of the vertical lines and move the cursor horizontally)
Specify center point for circle or [3P/2P/Ttr (tan tan radius)]: TT↵
Specify temporary OTRACK point: MID↵
of (pick one of the horizontal lines and move the cursor vertically)
Specify center point for circle or [3P/2P/Ttr (tan tan radius)]: (select the point where
      the two alignment paths cross intersect)
Specify radius of circle or [Diameter] <current>: ↵
Command:
```

The direction of the orthogonal line determines whether the X or Y component is used. In the previous example, after picking the first tracking point, the cursor is moved horizontally. This means the Y axis value of the previous point is being used and tracking is now ready for an X coordinate specification.

After moving the cursor horizontally, you may notice that movement is locked in a horizontal mode. If you need to move the cursor vertically, move the cursor back to the previously picked point and then drag vertically. Use this method anytime you need to switch between horizontal and vertical movement.

## Using the From Point Selection Option

The **From** point selection mode is another tracking tool that can be used to locate points based on existing geometry. The **From** point selection mode allows you to establish a relative coordinate, polar coordinate, or direct distance entry from a specified reference base point.

Access the **From** option by selecting the **Snap From** button in the **Object Snap** toolbar, selecting **From** in the **Object Snap** shortcut menu, or typing FRO at a point selection prompt. The example in **Figure 6-22** shows the center point for a circle being established as a polar distance from the midpoint of an existing line. The command sequence is shown here:

```
Command: C or CIRCLE.↵
Specify center point for circle or [3P/2P/Ttr (tan tan radius)]: FRO.↵
Base point: MID↵
of (pick line)
<Offset>: @2<45↵
Specify radius of circle or [Diameter] <current>: .75↵
Command:
```

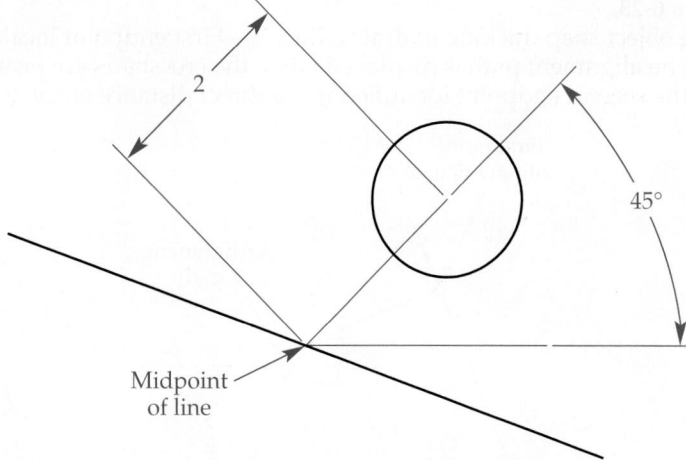

**Figure 6-22.**
Using the **From** point selection mode following the command sequence given in the text.

2

45°

Midpoint
of line

# Using AutoTracking to Locate Points

The temporary tracking mode, discussed earlier, allows the relative placement of a point for a single task. The AutoTrack™ mode enables this feature to be activated at all times, similar to running object snaps. The purpose of AutoTracking is to reduce the need for construction lines and keyboard entry.

There are two AutoTrack modes: object snap tracking and polar tracking. Both modes provide alignment paths to aid in precise point location relative to existing points. Any command requiring a point selection, such as the **COPY**, **MOVE**, and **LINE** commands, can make use of these modes.

## Object Snap Tracking

Object snap tracking is always used in conjunction with object snaps. When this mode is active, placing the crosshairs near an AutoSnap marker will acquire the point. Once a point is acquired, horizontal and vertical alignment paths are available for locating points.

Object snap tracking is toggled on and off with the [F11] function key or the **OTRACK** button on the status bar. This mode is only available for points selected by the currently active object snap modes. When running object snaps are active, all selected object snap modes are available for object snap tracking. However, these modes are not available for object snap tracking if running object snaps are deactivated.

In **Figure 6-23,** object snap tracking is used in conjunction with the **Perpendicular** and **Midpoint** running object snaps to draw a line that is 2 units long and perpendicular

**Figure 6-23.**
Using object snap tracking to draw a line. A—First endpoint located at midpoint of existing line. The alignment path is displayed when the crosshairs are near. B—The completed line, with the second endpoint identified using direct distance entry along the alignment path.

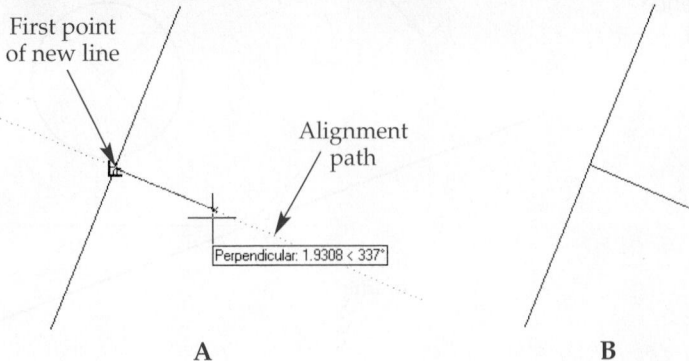

First point
of new line

Alignment
path

Perpendicular: 1.9308 < 337°

A

B

to the existing, slanted line. The running object snap modes are set before the following command sequence is initiated, and the **OSNAP** and **OTRACK** buttons on the status are active.

> Command: **L** *or* **LINE**.↵
> Specify first point: *(pick the midpoint of the existing line)*
> Specify next point or [Undo]: *(pause the crosshairs near the first point to acquire it, and then position the crosshairs as shown in* **Figure 6-23A** *to activate perpendicular alignment path)* **2**.↵
> Specify next point or [Undo]: ↵
> Command:

---

**PROFESSIONAL TIP**

AutoTracking is similar in performance to the **Extended** object snap. Experiment with a combination of just the **Endpoint** object snap mode and AutoTracking. Then try a combination of **Endpoint** and **Extended** object snap modes without AutoTracking to see the difference. Notice that without object snap tracking, you cannot drag in a direction perpendicular to an endpoint.

---

**Exercise 6-11**

○ Start AutoCAD and use the setup option of your choice.
○ Set the **Midpoint** and **Perpendicular** running object snaps.
○ Draw a line similar to the line in **Figure 6-23A**.
○ Use object snap tracking to draw a new line perpendicular to the midpoint of the first line and 5 units away, similar to **Figure 6-23B**.
○ Save the drawing as EX6-11.

---

AutoCAD and its Applications—Basics

# Polar Tracking

The Ortho mode, discussed in Chapter 3, forces the cursor movement to orthogonal (horizontal and vertical) orientations. When Ortho mode is turned on and the **LINE** command is in use, all new line segments are drawn at 0°, 90°, 180°, or 270°. Polar tracking works in much the same way, but allows for a greater range of angles.

Polar tracking can be turned on and off by selecting the **POLAR** button from the status bar or by using the [F10] function key. AutoCAD automatically turns Ortho off when polar tracking is on, and turns polar tracking off when Ortho is on. You cannot use polar tracking and Ortho at the same time.

When the polar tracking mode is turned on, the cursor snaps to preset incremental angles when a point is being located relative to another point. For example, when using the **LINE** command, polar tracking is not active for the first endpoint selection, but is available for the second and subsequent point selections. Polar alignment paths are displayed as dashed lines whenever the cursor comes into alignment with any of these preset angles.

To set incremental angles, use the **Polar Tracking** tab in the **Drafting Settings** dialog box. To access this dialog box, right-click on the **POLAR** button from the status bar and then select **Settings...**, pick **Drafting Settings...** from the **Tools** pull-down menu, or type DSETTINGS or DS at the Command: prompt. **Figure 6-24** shows the **Polar Tracking** tab of the **Drafting Settings** dialog box.

The following features are found in the **Polar Tracking** tab:

- **Polar Tracking On (F10).** Check this box, press the [F10] key, or pick the **POLAR** button on the status bar to turn polar tracking on.
- **Polar Angle Settings area.** This area of the dialog box allows you to set the desired polar angle increments. It contains the following items:
  - **Increment angle:.** This drop-down list is set at 90.0 by default. This setting provides angle increments every 90°. Open the drop-down list to select from a variety of preset angles. The setting in **Figure 6-24** (30) provides polar tracking in 30° increments. The increment angle can also be adjusted by changing the value of the **POLARANG** system variable.

**Figure 6-24.**
The **Polar Tracking** tab of the **Drafting Settings** dialog box.

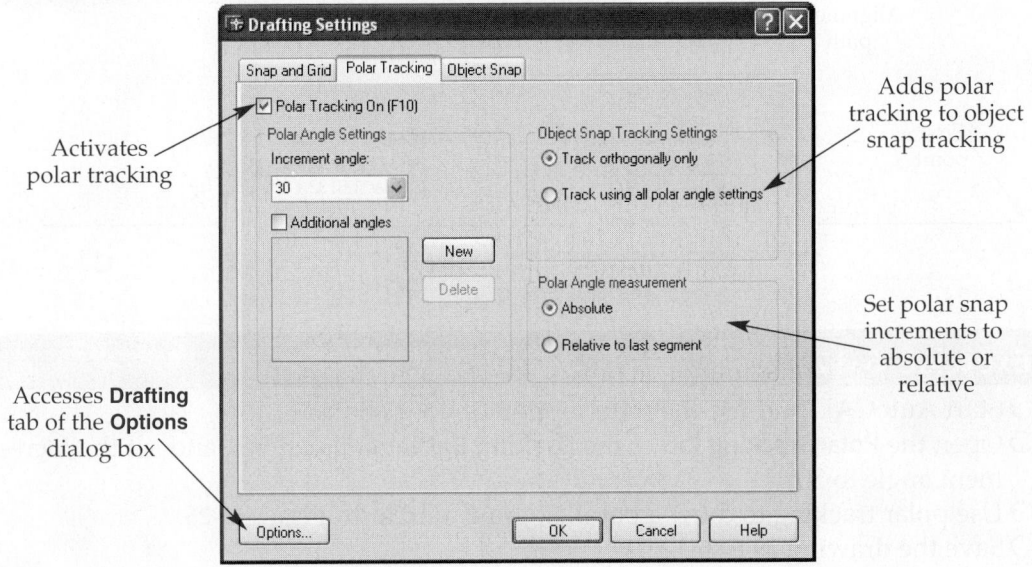

Activates polar tracking

Accesses **Drafting** tab of the **Options** dialog box

Adds polar tracking to object snap tracking

Set polar snap increments to absolute or relative

- **Additional angles.** This check box activates your own angle increments. To do this, pick the **New** button to open a text box in the window. Type the desired angle. Pick the **New** button each time you want to add another angle. The additional angles are used together with the incremental angle setting when you use polar tracking. Use the **Delete** button to remove angles from the list. You can make the additional angle(s) inactive by turning off the **Additional angles** check box. An additional angle can also be added or changed using the **POLARADDANG** system variable.
- **Object Snap Tracking Settings area.** This area is used to set the angles available with object snap tracing. If **Track orthogonally only** is selected, only horizontal and vertical alignment paths are active. If **Track using all polar angle settings** is selected, alignment paths for all polar snap angles are active.
- **Polar Angle measurement area.** This setting determines if the polar snap increments are constant or relative to the previous segment. If **Absolute** is selected, the polar snap angles are measured from the base angle of 0° set for the drawing. If **Relative to Last Segment** is checked, each increment angle is measured from a base angle established by the previously drawn segment.

**Figure 6-25** shows a parallelogram being drawn with polar tracking active and set for 30° angle increments and absolute polar angle measurements. The following command sequence creates the parallelogram:

Command: **L** *or* **LINE**↵
Specify first point: *(select the first point)*
Specify next point or [Undo]: *(drag the cursor to the right while the polar alignment path indicates <0°)* **3**↵
Specify next point or [Undo]: *(drag the cursor to the 60° polar alignment path)* **1.5**↵
Specify next point or [Close/Undo]: *(drag the cursor to the 180° polar alignment path)* **3**↵
Specify next point or [Close/Undo]: **C**↵
Command:

---

**Figure 6-25.**
Using polar tracking with 30° angle increments to draw a parallelogram. A—After the first side is drawn, the alignment path and direct distance entry are used to create the second side. B—Horizontal alignment path is used for the third side. C—Parallelogram completed with the **Close** option.

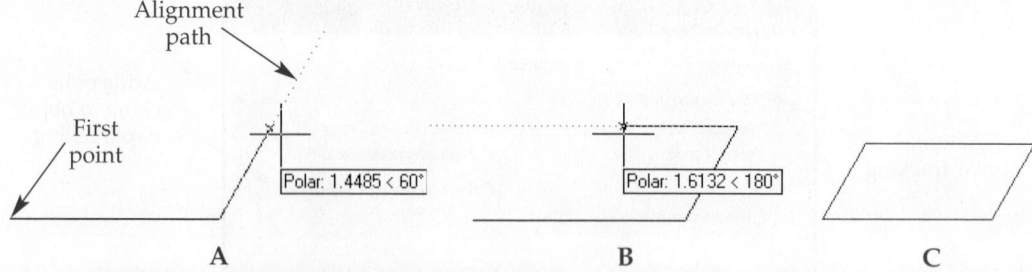

Alignment path

First point

Polar: 1.4485 < 60°

Polar: 1.6132 < 180°

A                    B                    C

---

## Exercise 6-12

○ Start AutoCAD and use the setup option of your choice.
○ Open the **Polar Tracking** tab of the **Drafting Settings** dialog box and set the increment angle to 30.
○ Use polar tracking to draw a parallelogram similar to **Figure 6-25**.
○ Save the drawing as EX6-12.

## Polar tracking with polar snaps

Polar tracking can also be used in conjunction with polar snaps. If polar snaps are used when drawing the parallelogram in **Figure 6-25**, there would be no need to type the length of the line, because you set both the angle increment and a length increment. The desired angle and length increment are established in the **Snap and Grid** tab of the **Drafting Settings** dialog box. You can open this dialog box as previously described, or you can right-click on the status bar **SNAP** button and pick **Settings...** from the shortcut menu. This opens the **Drafting Settings** dialog box as shown in **Figure 6-26**.

To activate polar snap, pick the **Polar snap** button in the **Snap type & style** area of the dialog box. Picking this button activates the **Polar spacing** area and deactivates the **Snap** area. The length of the polar snap increment is set in the **Polar distance:** box. If the **Polar distance:** setting is 0, the polar snap distance will be the orthogonal snap distance.

**Figure 6-27** shows a parallelogram being drawn with 30° angle increments and length increments of .75. The lengths of the parallelogram sides are 1.5 and .75.

**Figure 6-26.**
The **Snap and Grid** tab of the **Drafting Settings** dialog box is used to set the polar snap spacing.

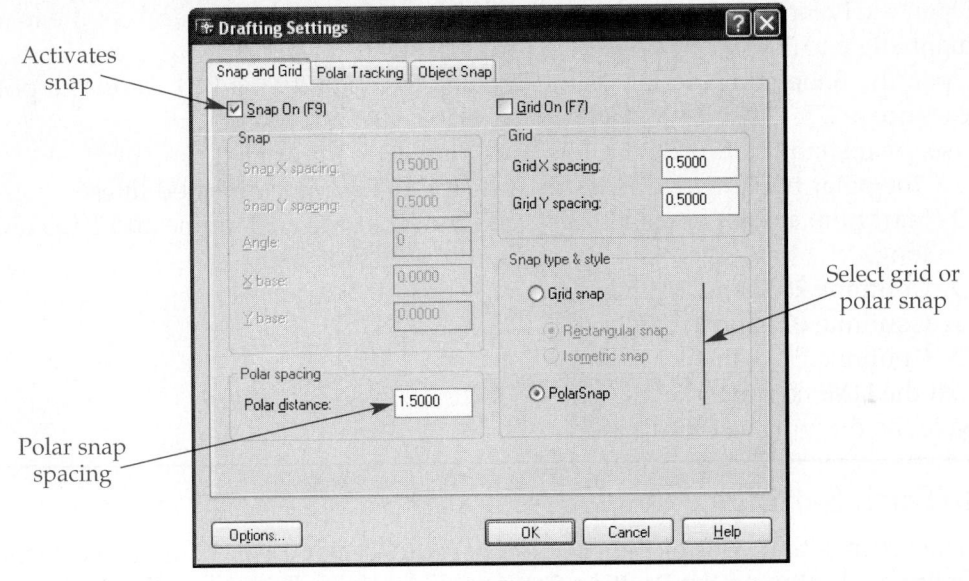

**Figure 6-27.**
Drawing a parallelogram with polar snap.

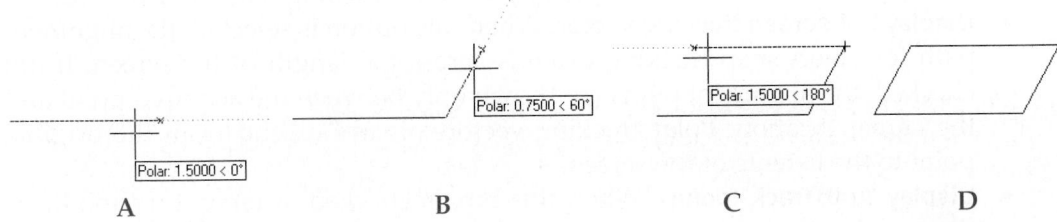

## Using polar tracking overrides

It takes some time to set up the polar tracking and the polar snap options, but it is worth the effort if you have several objects to draw that can take advantage of this feature. If you want to perform polar tracking for only one point, you can use the polar tracking override to do this easily. This works for the specified angle if polar tracking is on or off. To activate a polar tracking override, enter a left angle bracket (<) followed by the desired angle when AutoCAD asks you to specify a point. The following command sequence uses a 30° override to draw a line 1.5 units long:

Command: **L** *or* **LINE.**↵
Specify first point: *(pick a start point for the line)*
Specify next point or [Undo]: **<30.**↵
Angle override: 30
Specify next point or [Undo]: *(move the cursor in the desired 30° direction)* **1.5.**↵
Specify next point or [Undo]: ↵
Command:

---

### Exercise 6-13

○ Start AutoCAD and use the setup option of your choice.
○ Open the **Polar Tracking** tab of the **Drafting Settings** dialog box and set the increment angle to 30.
○ Open the **Snap and Grid** tab of the **Drafting Settings** dialog box to set the polar distance at .75.
○ Use polar snap to draw a parallelogram similar to **Figure 6-27.**
○ Use the polar tracking overrides to draw the following connected lines:
　○ Start from a point of your choice and draw a line at a 67° angle and 1.125 units long.
　○ Continue 293° and 1.125 long.
　○ Continue 67° and 1.125 long.
　○ Continue 293° and 1.125 long.
○ Exit the **LINE** command.
○ Save the drawing as EX6-13.

---

## AutoTrack Settings

The settings that control the function of AutoTracking can be accessed through the **Options...** button on the **Drafting Settings** dialog box. This opens the **Options** dialog box to the **Drafting** tab. This tab was illustrated in **Figure 6-19.**

The following options are available in the **AutoTrack Settings** area:

- **Display polar tracking vector.** When this feature is selected, the alignment path is displayed. When this option is off, no polar tracking path is displayed.
- **Display full-screen tracking vector.** When this option is selected, the alignment path for object snap tracking extends across the length of the screen. If not checked, the alignment paths are shown only between the acquired point and the cursor location. Polar tracking vectors always extend from the original point to the extents of the screen.
- **Display AutoTrack tooltip.** When this box is checked, a temporary tooltip is displayed with the AutoTrack alignment paths.

The options in the **Alignment Point Acquisition** area determine how the object snap tracking alignment paths are selected:

- **Automatic.** When this option is selected, points are acquired whenever the cursor is paused over an object snap point.

- **Shift to acquire.** When this option is selected, the [Shift] key must be pressed to acquire an object snap point and use object snap tracking. AutoSnap markers are still displayed and normal object snap can be used without pressing the [Shift] key. If many running object snaps are set, it may be useful to use this option to reduce the number of paths displayed across the screen.

The **TRACKPATH** system variable stores the alignment path display settings, and the **POLARMODE** system variable stores the alignment point acquisition method.

## Point Filters

Tracking allows you to combine the X coordinate of one point and the Y coordinate of another point to locate a new point. You can also directly access the X or Y coordinates of a point by using point filters. *Filters* allow you to select any aspect of an object while filtering out other objects, items, or features.

There are many uses for filters. Filters used for layer control were introduced in Chapter 4. Point filters and object selection filters are completely discussed in Chapter 7.

## Drawing Parallel Lines and Curves

OFFSET
O

Modify
➥ Offset

Modify
toolbar

Offset

The **OFFSET** command is used to draw concentric circles, arcs, curves, polylines, and parallel lines. This command is accessed by picking **Offset** in the **Modify** pull-down menu, picking the **Offset** button in the **Modify** toolbar, or typing O or OFFSET at the Command: prompt. When selected, the command produces the following prompt:

> Command: **O** *or* **OFFSET**↵
> Offset distance or [Through] <*current*>:

Type a distance or pick a point for the parallel object to be drawn through. The last offset distance used is shown in brackets. If you want to draw two parallel circles a distance of .1 unit apart, use the following command sequence. Refer to **Figure 6-28.**

> Command: **O** *or* **OFFSET**↵
> Specify offset distance or [Through] <*current*>: **.1**↵
> Select object to offset or <exit>: *(pick the object)*
> Specify point on side to offset: *(pick the side of the object for the offset to be drawn)*
> Select object to offset or <exit>: *(select another object or press* [Enter]*)*

When the Select object to offset prompt first appears, the screen cursor turns into a pick box. After the object is picked, the screen cursor turns back into crosshairs. No other selection option (such as window or crossing) works with the **OFFSET** command.

Figure 6-28.
Drawing an offset using a designated distance.

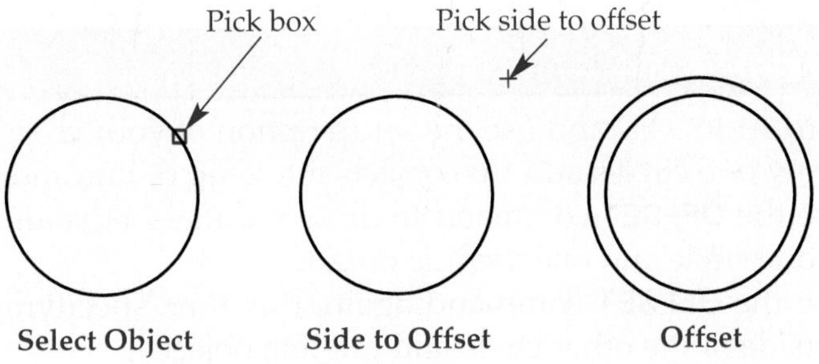

Pick box    Pick side to offset

Select Object    Side to Offset    Offset

**Figure 6-29.**
Drawing an offset through a given point.

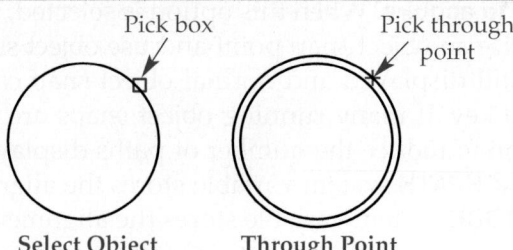

Pick box

Pick through point

Select Object          Through Point

The other option is to pick a point that the offset is drawn through. Type T as follows to produce the results shown in **Figure 16-29:**

    Command: **O** *or* **OFFSET.**⏎
    Specify offset distance or [Through] <*current*>: **T**⏎
    Select object to offset or <exit>: *(pick the object)*
    Specify through point: *(pick the point that the offset will be drawn through)*
    Select object to offset or <exit>: ⏎

Object snap modes can be used to assist in drawing an offset. For example, suppose you have a circle and a line and want to draw a concentric circle tangent to the line. Refer to **Figure 6-30** and the following command sequence:

    Command: **O** *or* **OFFSET.**⏎
    Specify offset distance or [Through] <*current*>: **QUA.**⏎
    of *(pick the existing circle)*
    Specify second point: **PER.**⏎
    to *(pick the existing line)*
    Select object to offset or <exit>: *(pick the existing circle)*
    Specify point on side to offset: *(pick between the circle and line)*
    Select object to offset or <exit>: ⏎
    Command:

**Figure 6-30.**
Using **OFFSET** to draw a concentric circle tangent to a line.

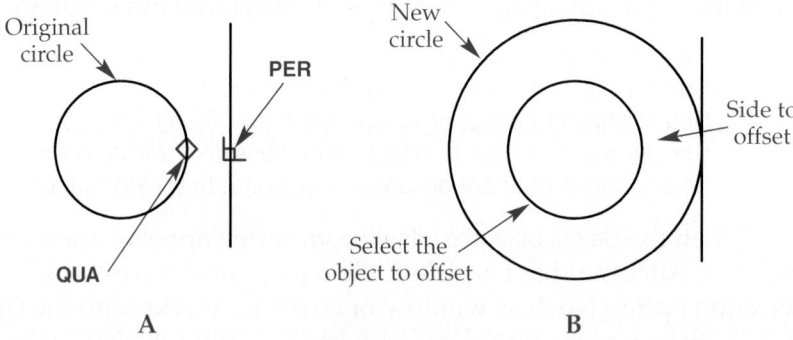

Original circle

New circle

PER

Side to offset

Select the object to offset

QUA

A                                        B

---

## Exercise 6-14

○ Start AutoCAD and use the setup option of your choice.
○ Draw two circles and two objects made up of line and arc segments.
○ Use the **OFFSET** command to draw parallels a distance of .2 units on the inside of one circle and one arc-line object.
○ Use the **OFFSET** command again, this time specifying a **Through** point on the outside of the other circle and arc-line object.
○ Save the drawing as EX6-14.

AutoCAD and its Applications—Basics

## Dividing an Object

DIVIDE
DIV

Draw
➥ Point
➥ Divide

A line, circle, arc, or polyline can be divided into an equal number of segments using the **DIVIDE** command. To start the **DIVIDE** command, select **Divide** from the **Point** cascading menu of the **Draw** pull-down menu, or type DIV or DIVIDE.

The **DIVIDE** command does not physically break an object into multiple parts. It places point objects or blocks at the locations where the breaks would occur if the object were actually divided into multiple segments.

Suppose you have drawn a line and want to divide it into seven equal parts. Enter the **DIVIDE** command and select the object to divide. Then, enter the number of segments. Refer to **Figure 6-31.** The procedure is as follows:

Command: **DIV** *or* **DIVIDE.**↵
Select object to divide: *(pick the object)*
Enter the number of segments or [Block]: **7.**↵
Command:

The **Block** option of the **DIVIDE** command allows you to place a block at each division point. To initiate the **Block** option, type B at the prompt. You are then asked if the block is to be aligned with the object. A *block* is a previously drawn symbol or shape. Blocks are discussed in detail in Chapter 22 of this text.

After the number of segments is given, the object is divided with points. However, by default, points are displayed as dots, which may not show very well. Notice that in **Figure 6-31** the appearance of the marks has been changed by changing the point style. To change the point style, select **Point Style...** from the **Format** pull-down menu and selecting a new point style from the **Point Style** dialog box. Drawing points and setting point style is discussed later in this chapter.

**Figure 6-31.**
Using the **DIVIDE** command. Note that the default marks (points) have been changed to Xs.

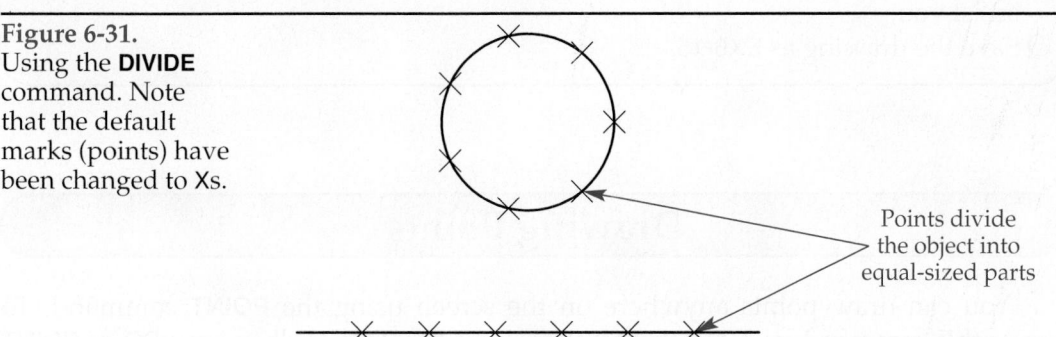

Points divide the object into equal-sized parts

## Dividing Objects at Specified Distances

MEASURE
ME

Draw
➥ Point
➥ Measure

Unlike the **DIVIDE** command, where an object is divided into a specified number of parts, the **MEASURE** command places marks a specified distance apart. To activate the **MEASURE** command, pick **Measure** from the **Point** cascading menu of the **Draw** pull-down menu, or by typing ME or MEASURE at the Command: prompt. The line shown in **Figure 6-32** is measured with .75 unit segments as follows:

Command: **ME** *or* **MEASURE.**↵
Select object to measure: *(pick an object)*
Specify length of segment or [Block]: **.75**↵

**Figure 6-32.**
Using the **MEASURE**
command. Notice
that the last segment
may be shorter than
the others, depending
on the total length
of the object.

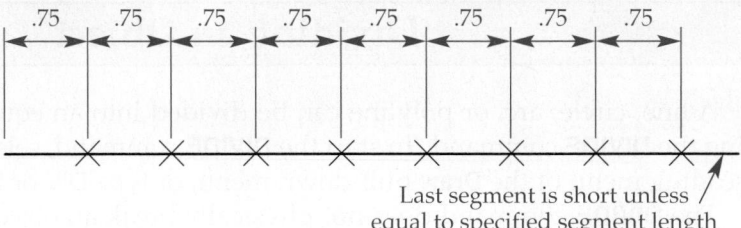

Last segment is short unless
equal to specified segment length

Measuring begins at the end closest to where the object is picked. All increments are equal to the entered segment length except the last segment, which may be shorter. The point style determines the type of marks placed on the object, just as it does with the **DIVIDE** command. Blocks can be inserted at the given distances using the **Block** option of the **MEASURE** command.

---

## Exercise 6-15

○ Start AutoCAD and use the setup option of your choice.
○ Select the X point style from the **Point Style** dialog box.
○ Draw two circles of any diameter and two lines of any length.
○ Use the **DIVIDE** command to divide one circle into 10 equal parts and one line into 5 equal parts.
○ Use the **MEASURE** command to divide the other circle into .5 unit parts and the other line into .75 unit parts.
○ Draw two parallel vertical lines. Make each line 3″ (75 mm) long and space them 4″ (100 mm) apart. Use the **DIVIDE** command to divide the line on the left into 10 equal increments. Draw horizontal parallel lines from each division on the left line over to the right line. Use the **Node** and **Perpendicular** object snap options to assist you.
○ Save the drawing as EX6-15.

---

## Drawing Points

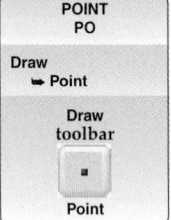

POINT
PO

Draw
➡ Point

Draw
toolbar

Point

You can draw points anywhere on the screen using the **POINT** command. To access this command, pick the **Point** button from the **Draw** toolbar, type PO or POINT at the Command: prompt, or select one of the options from the **Point** cascading menu in the **Draw** pull-down menu. The command sequence is as follows:

Command: **PO** *or* **POINT**⏎
Current point modes: PDMODE=0 PDSIZE=0.0000
Specify a point: *(type point coordinates or pick with pointing device)*
Command:

If you need to place only a single point object, use the keyboard command or select the **Single Point** option from the **Point** cascading menu. After drawing a single point, you are returned to the Command: prompt. If you need to draw multiple points, use the **Point** button on the **Draw** toolbar or the **Multiple Point** option from the **Point** cascading menu. Press [Esc] to exit the command.

When the **POINT** command is used, the current point modes are listed at the command line. The **PDMODE** system variable specifies the type of point marker, and the **PDSIZE** system variable specifies the size of the point marker. The appearance of the point is controlled by the point style, which is set in the **Point Style** dialog box.

AutoCAD and its Applications—Basics

**NOTE** If the point style is set as dots and blips are active, the blip covers the dot when the point is selected. Enter REDRAW at the Command: prompt and press [Enter] to erase the blip.

## Setting Point Style

The style and size of points are set using the **Point Style** dialog box, **Figure 6-33.** This dialog box is accessed by selecting **Point Style...** from the **Format** pull-down menu or by entering DDPTYPE at the Command: prompt.

The **Point Style** dialog box contains twenty different point styles. The current point style is highlighted. To change the style, simply pick the graphic image of the desired style.

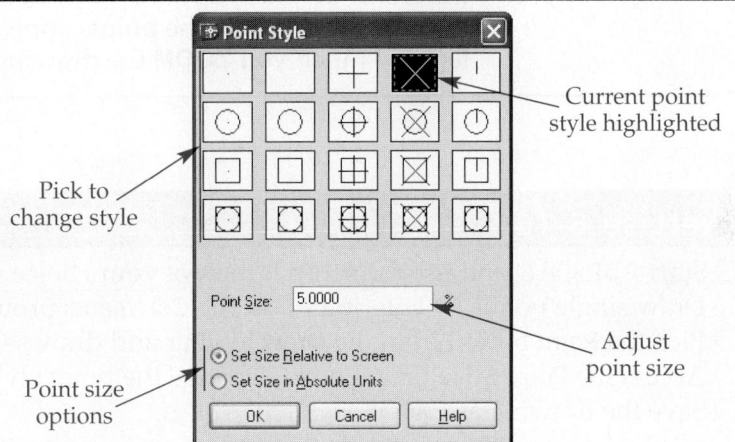

Figure 6-33.
The **Point Style** dialog box. This is a quick way to select the point style and to change the point size.

Current point style highlighted

Pick to change style

Adjust point size

Point size options

**NOTE** The point style is stored in the **PDMODE** system variable. This variable can be changed at the Command: prompt. The **PDMODE** values of the point styles shown in the top row of the **Point Style** dialog box are 0 through 4, from left to right. These are the basic point styles. Add a circle (second row in dialog box) by adding 32 to the basic **PDMODE** value. Add 64 to draw a square (third row), and add 96 to draw a circle and square (bottom row). For example, a point display of an X inside a circle has a **PDMODE** value of 35. That is the sum of the X value of 3 and the circle value of 32.

Set the point size by entering a value in the **Point Size:** text box of the **Point Style** dialog box. Pick the **Set Size Relative to Screen** option button if you want the point size to change in relation to different display options. Picking the **Set Size in Absolute Units** option button makes the points appear the same size no matter what display option is used. The effect of these options is shown in **Figure 6-34.**

---

Figure 6-34.
Points sized with
the **Relative to
Screen** setting
change size as the
drawing is zoomed.
Points sized with
the **Absolute Units**
setting remain a
constant size.

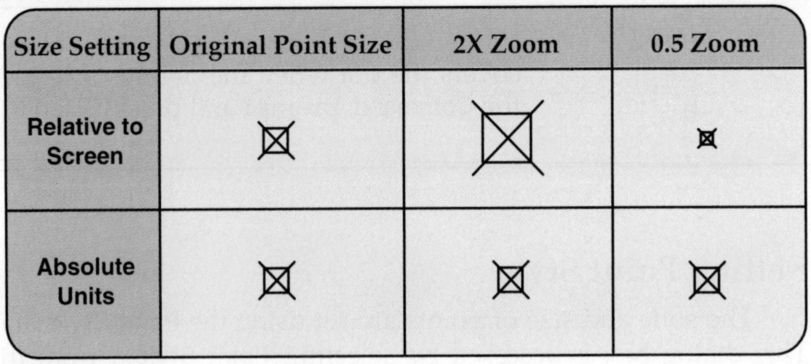

| Size Setting | Original Point Size | 2X Zoom | 0.5 Zoom |
|---|---|---|---|
| Relative to Screen | ⊠ | ⊠ | ⊠ |
| Absolute Units | ⊠ | ⊠ | ⊠ |

NOTE  The point size and relative/absolute settings can also be modified by changing the **PDSIZE** (point display size) system variable. Positive **PDSIZE** values change size in relation to different display options (relative to screen). Negative **PDSIZE** values make the points appear the same size no matter how much you **ZOOM** the drawing (absolute units).

## Exercise 6-16

○ Start AutoCAD and use the setup option of your choice.
○ Draw single points by entering PO at the Command: prompt.
○ Pick the **Point** button from the **Draw** toolbar and draw several points.
○ Access the **Point Style** dialog box to change the point style.
○ Save the drawing as EX6-16.

## Orthographic Multiview Drawings

Each field of drafting has its own method to present views of a product. Architectural drafting uses plan views, exterior elevations, and sections. In electronics drafting, symbols are placed in a schematic diagram to show the circuit layout. In civil drafting, contour lines are used to show the topography of the land. Mechanical drafting uses *multiview drawings*.

This section discusses multiview drawings. Multiview drawings are based on the standard ASME Y14.3M, *Multiview and Sectional View Drawings*. The use of construction lines for view alignment and for geometric construction is also explained.

The views of a multiview drawing are created through orthographic projection. *Orthographic projection* involves projecting object features onto an imaginary plane. This imaginary plane is called a *projection plane*. The imaginary projection plane is placed parallel to the object. Thus, the line of sight is perpendicular to the object. This results in views that appear two-dimensional, **Figure 6-35.**

Six two-dimensional views show all sides of an object. The six views are the front, right side, left side, top, bottom, and rear. The views are placed in a standard arrangement so others can read the drawing. The front view is the central, or most important, view. Other views are placed around the front view, **Figure 6-36.**

**Figure 6-35.**
Obtaining a front
view with
orthographic
projection.

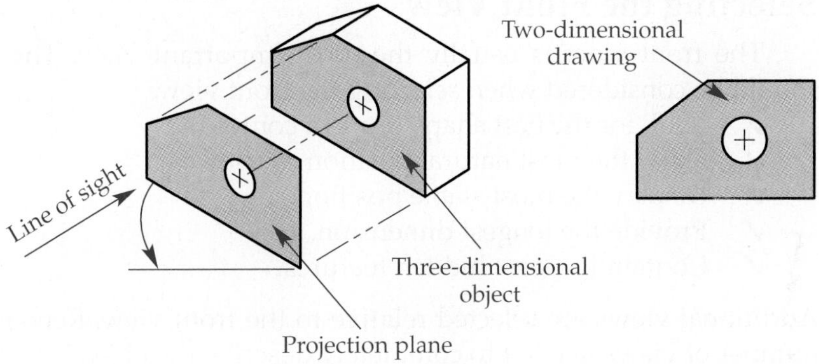

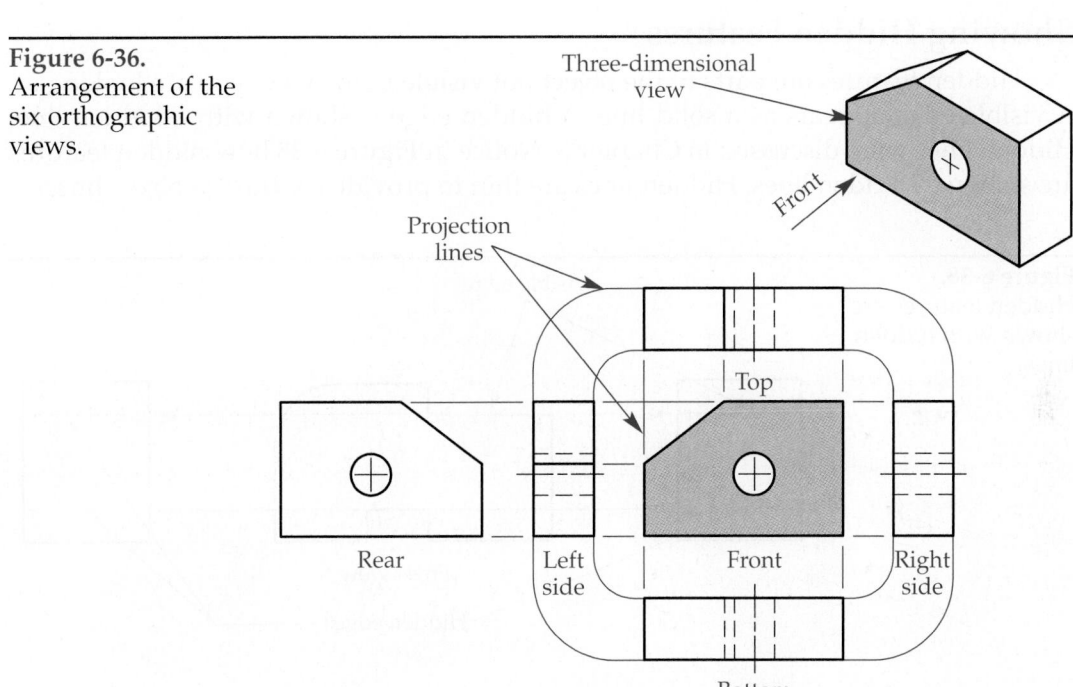

There are very few products that require all six views. The number of views needed depends on the complexity of the object. Use only enough views to completely describe the object. Drawing too many views is time-consuming and can clutter the drawing. In some cases, a single view may be enough to describe the object. The object shown in **Figure 6-37** needs only two views. These two views completely describe the width, height, depth, and features of the object.

**Figure 6-36.**
Arrangement of the
six orthographic
views.

**Figure 6-37.**
The views you
choose to describe
the object should
show all height,
width, and depth
dimensions.

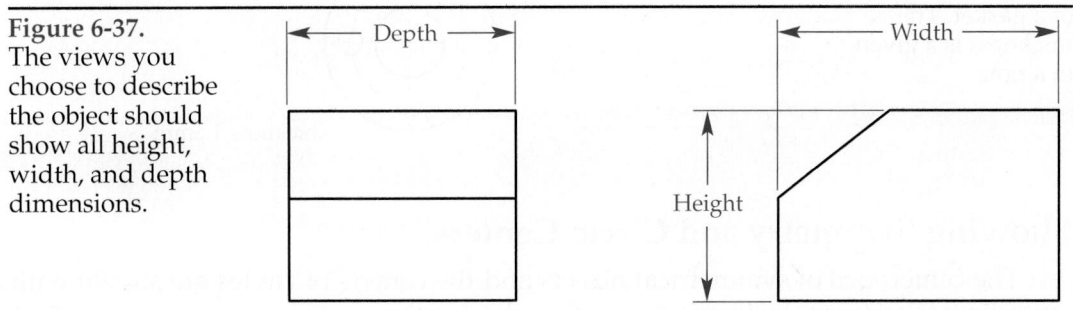

## Selecting the Front View

The front view is usually the most important view. The following guidelines should be considered when selecting the front view:

- ✓ Look for the best shape or most contours.
- ✓ Show the most natural position of use.
- ✓ Display the most stable position.
- ✓ Provide the longest dimension.
- ✓ Contain the least hidden features.

Additional views are selected relative to the front view. Remember, choose only the number of views needed to completely describe the object's features.

## Showing Hidden Features

Hidden features are parts of the object not visible in the view you are looking at. A visible edge appears as a solid line. A hidden edge is shown with a hidden line. Hidden lines were discussed in Chapter 3. Notice in **Figure 6-38** how hidden features are shown as hidden lines. Hidden lines are thin to provide contrast to object lines.

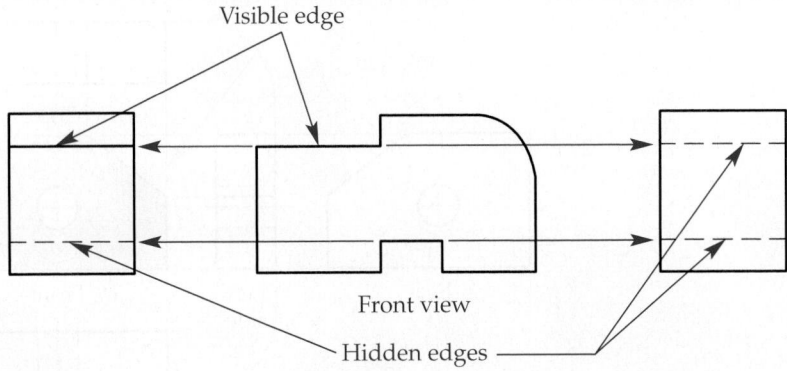

**Figure 6-38.**
Hidden features are shown with hidden lines.

## One-View Drawings

In some instances, an object can be fully described using one view. A thin part, such as a gasket, can be drawn with one view. See **Figure 6-39.** The thickness is given as a note in the drawing or in the title block. A cylindrical object can also be drawn with one view. The diameter dimension is given to identify the object as round.

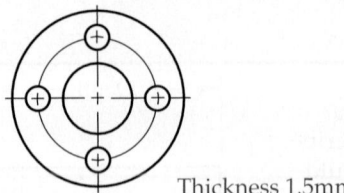

**Figure 6-39.**
A one-view drawing of a gasket. The thickness is a given in a note.

Thickness 1.5mm

## Showing Symmetry and Circle Centers

The centerlines of symmetrical objects and the centers of circles are shown with centerlines. For example, in one view of a cylinder, the axis is drawn as a centerline. In the other view, centerlines cross to show the center in the circular view. See **Figure 6-40.** The only place that the small centerline dashes should cross is at the center of a circle.

**Figure 6-40.** Drawing centerlines. A—For a cylinder. B—For a round hole.

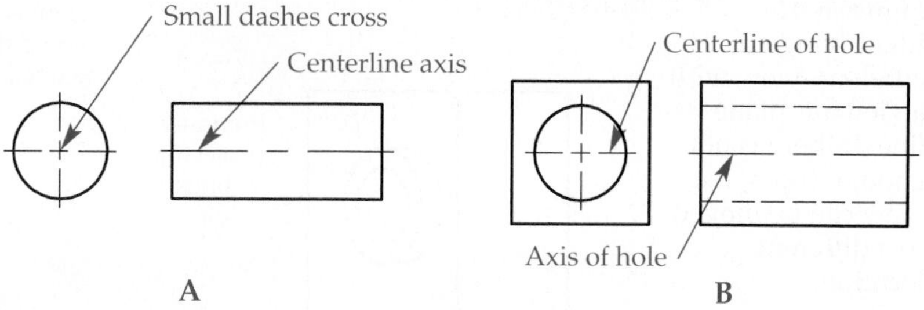

Small dashes cross

Centerline axis

Centerline of hole

Axis of hole

A

B

## Drawing Auxiliary Views

In most cases, an object is completely described using a combination of one or more of the six standard views. However, sometimes the multiview layout is not enough to properly identify some object surfaces. It may then be necessary to draw auxiliary views.

*Auxiliary views* are typically needed when a surface on the object is at an angle to the line of sight. These slanted surfaces are *foreshortened*, meaning they are shorter than the true size and shape of the surface. To show this surface in true size, an auxiliary view is needed. Foreshortened dimensions are not recommended.

Auxiliary views are drawn by projecting lines perpendicular (90°) to a slanted surface. Usually, one projection line remains on the drawing. It connects the auxiliary view to the view where the slanted surface appears as a line. The resulting auxiliary view shows the surface in true size and shape. For most applications, the auxiliary view need only show the slanted surface, not the entire object. This is called a *partial auxiliary view* and is shown in **Figure 6-41.**

In many situations, there may not be enough room on the drawing to project directly from the slanted surface. The auxiliary view is then placed elsewhere, **Figure 6-42.** A viewing-plane line is drawn next to the view where the slanted surface appears as a line. The *viewing-plane line* is drawn with a thick dashed or phantom line in accordance with ASME Y14.2M. It is terminated with bold arrowheads that point toward the slanted surface.

**Figure 6-41.** Auxiliary views show the true size and shape of an inclined surface.

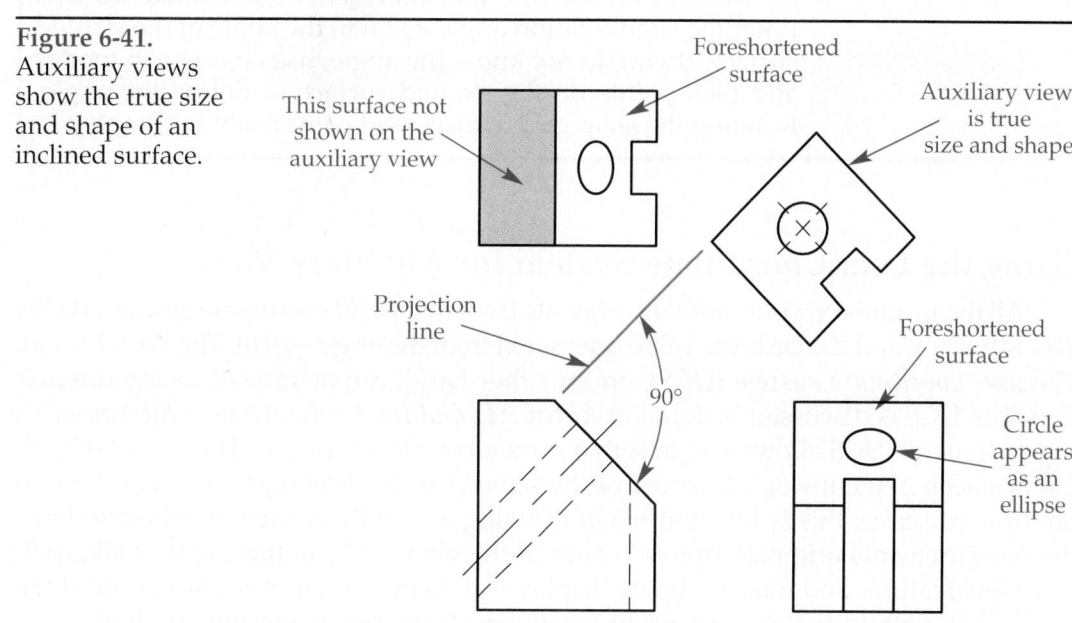

Foreshortened surface

This surface not shown on the auxiliary view

Auxiliary view is true size and shape

Projection line

90°

Foreshortened surface

Circle appears as an ellipse

**Figure 6-42.**
Identifying an
auxiliary view with
a viewing-plane
line. If there is not
enough room, the
view can be moved
to a different
location.

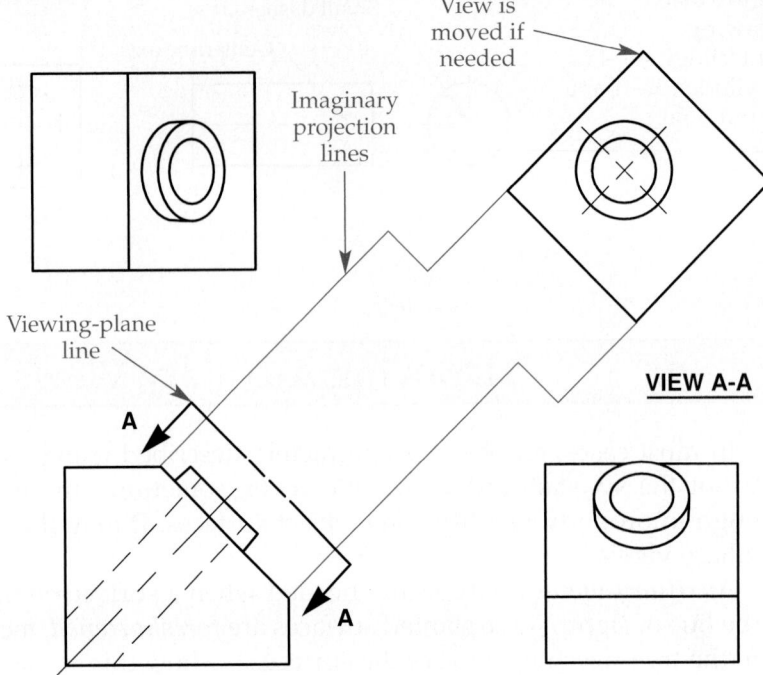

Each end of the viewing-plane line is labeled with a letter. The letters relate the viewing-plane line with the proper auxiliary view. A title such as VIEW A-A is placed under the auxiliary view. When more than one auxiliary view is drawn, labels continue with B-B through Z-Z (if necessary). The letters *I*, *O*, and *Q* are not used because they may be confused with numbers. An auxiliary view drawn away from the standard view retains the same angle as if it is projected directly.

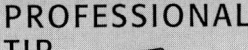

PROFESSIONAL
TIP

Changing the rotation angle of the snap grid is especially useful for drawing auxiliary views. After the views have been drawn, access the **SNAP** command. Then, pick the base point for rotation on the line that represents the slanted surface. Enter the snap rotation angle equal to the angle of the slanted surface. If you do not know the angle, use object snap modes and pick points on the slanted surface to define the angle. Rotating the snap grid is discussed completely in Chapter 3.

## Using the User Coordinate System for Auxiliary Views

All the features on your drawing originate from the *world coordinate system (WCS)*. This is the X, Y, and Z coordinate values measured from the origin (0,0,0). The WCS is fixed. The *user coordinate system (UCS)*, on the other hand, can be moved to any orientation. The UCS is discussed in detail in *AutoCAD and its Applications—Advanced*.

In general, UCS allows you to set your own coordinate origin. The UCS 0,0,0 origin has been in the lower-left corner of the screen for the drawings you have done so far. In many cases this is fine, but when drawing an auxiliary view it is best to have the measurements originate from a corner of the view. This, in turn, makes all auxiliary view features and the coordinate display true as measured from the corner of the view. This method makes it easier to locate and later dimension the auxiliary view features.

254  AutoCAD and its Applications—Basics

**Figure 6-43.**
Relocating the origin and rotating the Z axis of the UCS system. A—Rotating the UCS to align with the auxiliary view angle. B—The UCS icon displayed at the current UCS origin at the corner of the auxiliary view.

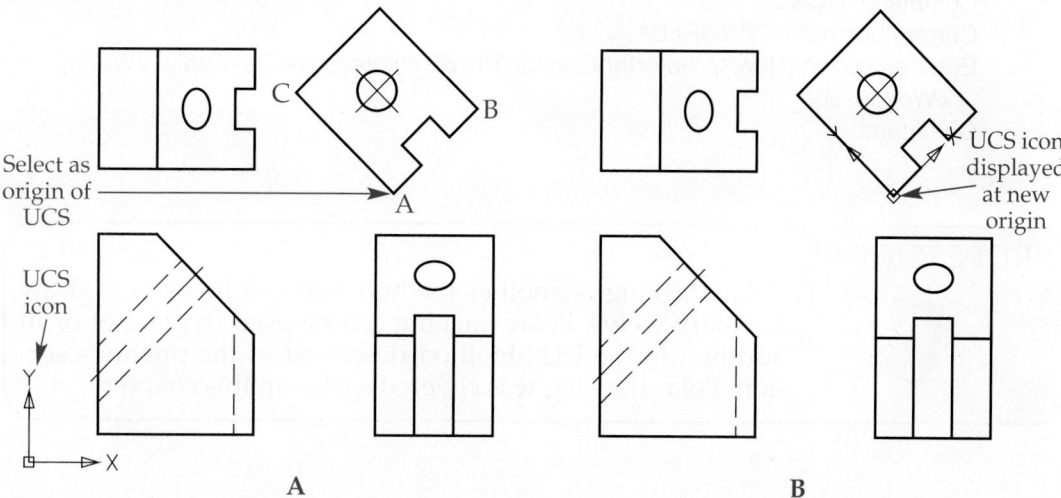

A                                                    B

Figure 6-43 shows an example of aligning the UCS to the auxiliary view. First, draw the principal views, such as the front, top, and right side. Then, move the UCS origin to a location that coincides with a corner of the auxiliary view.

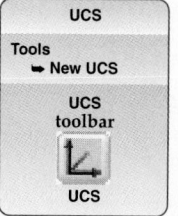

To move the UCS origin, type UCS at the Command: prompt, select the **UCS** button on the **UCS** toolbar, or select **3 Point** option in the **New UCS** cascading menu of the **Tools** pull-down menu. The command sequence is as follows:

Command: **UCS.**
Current ucs name: *WORLD*
Enter an option [New/Move/orthoGraphic/Prev/Restore/Save/Del/Apply/?/World]
    <World>: **N.**
Specify origin of new UCS or [ZAxis/3point/OBject/Face/View/X/Y/Z] <0,0,0>: **3.**
Specify new origin point <0,0,0>: *(select Point A as shown in Figure 6-43)*
Specify point on positive portion of X-axis <current>: *(select Point B)*
Specify point on positive-Y portion of the UCS X-Y plane <current>: *(select Point C)*
Command:

The icon is rotated and moved as shown in **Figure 6-43B.** If you want the UCS displayed in the lower-left corner of the drawing area, select **Named UCS...** from the **Tools** pull-down menu. This displays the **UCS** dialog box. In the **Settings** tab, uncheck the **Display at UCS origin point** checkbox.

Before you begin drawing the auxiliary view, use the **Save** option of the **UCS** command to name and save the new UCS:

Command: **UCS.**
Current ucs name: *NO NAME*
Enter an option [New/Move/orthoGraphic/Prev/Restore/Save/Del/Apply/?/World]
    <World>: **S.**
Enter name to save current UCS or [?]: **AUX.**
Command:

Now, proceed by drawing the auxiliary view. When you have finished, select the **World UCS** button from the **UCS** toolbar or enter the UCS command and use the default **World** option to reset the UCS back to the WCS origin:

Command: **UCS.**↵
Current ucs name: *WORLD*
Enter an option [New/Move/orthoGraphic/Prev/Restore/Save/Del/Apply/?/World]
   <World>: ↵
Command:

---

**PROFESSIONAL TIP**

Polar tracking is another method that can be used to draw auxiliary views. Polar tracking can be used in place of or in addition to the UCS method described in the previous section. Polar tracking was covered earlier in this chapter.

---

## Drawing Construction Lines

In drafting terminology, *construction lines* are lines used for layout purposes. They are not part of the drawing. In manual drafting, they are either drawn very lightly or removed so they do not reproduce.

AutoCAD has construction lines and rays that can be used for such purposes. For example, you can use construction lines and rays to project features between views for accurate placement, for geometric constructions, or to coordinate geometric locations for object snap selections. The AutoCAD command that lets you draw construction lines is **XLINE**, while rays are drawn with the **RAY** command. Both commands can be used for similar purposes, however, the **XLINE** command has more options and flexibility than the **RAY** command.

### Using the XLINE Command

The **XLINE** command creates xline objects. An *xline object* is an infinite length line designed for use as a construction line. Although these lines are infinite, they do not change the drawing extents. This means that they have no effect on zooming operations.

The xlines can be modified by moving, copying, trimming, and other editing operations. Editing commands such as **TRIM** or **FILLET** change the object type. For example, if one end of an xline is trimmed off, it becomes a ray object. A *ray* is considered semi-infinite because it is infinite in one direction only. If the infinite end of a ray is trimmed off, it becomes a line object.

Construction lines and rays are drawn on the current layer and plot the same as other objects. This may cause conflict with the other lines on that layer. A good way to handle this problem is to set up a special layer just for construction lines.

The **XLINE** command can be accessed by picking the **Construction Line** button in the **Draw** toolbar, by picking **Construction Line** in the **Draw** pull-down menu, or by typing XL or XLINE at the Command: prompt. The **XLINE** command sequence appears as follows:

Command: **XL** *or* **XLINE.**↵
Specify a point or [Hor/Ver/Ang/Bisect/Offset]:

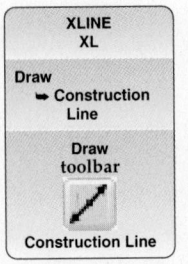

XLINE
XL

Draw
➥ Construction
Line

Draw
toolbar

Construction Line

The following **XLINE** options are available:

- **From point.** This **XLINE** default allows you to specify two points that the construction line passes through. The first point of an xline is called the *root point.* After you pick the first point, the Through point: prompt allows you to select as many points as you like. Xlines are created between every point and the root point. Use the object snap modes to accurately pick points:

  Command: **XL** *or* **XLINE**↵
  Specify a point or [Hor/Ver/Ang/Bisect/Offset]: *(pick a point)*
  Specify through point: *(pick a second point)*
  Specify through point: *(pick another second point)*
  Specify through point: *(draw more construction lines or press* [Enter]*)*
  Command:

  **Figure 6-44** shows how construction lines can be used to help project features between views.

- **Hor (H).** This option draws a horizontal construction line through a single specified point. It serves the same purpose as the default option, but the line is automatically drawn horizontally and you only have to pick one point.

- **Ver (V).** This option draws a vertical construction line through the specified point.

**Figure 6-44.**
Using the **XLINE** command default option. You can also use the **XLINE Hor** option.

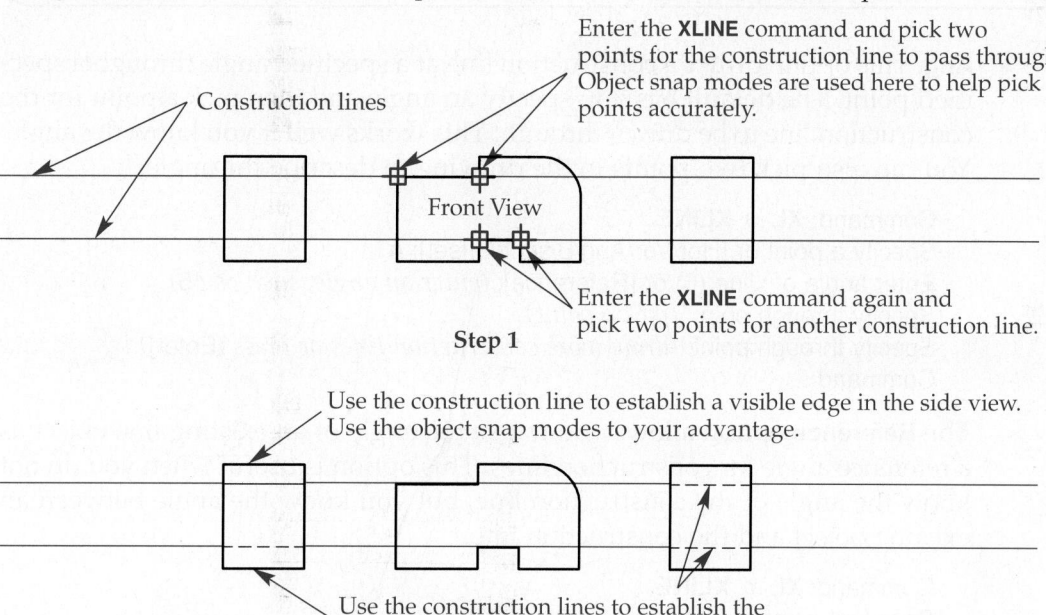

○ Start AutoCAD and use the setup option of your choice. One of your templates may already have proper layers and linetypes.

○ Set up layers and linetypes as needed. Review Chapter 4 if necessary.

○ Draw the four views of the object shown below. Use construction lines to locate the hidden lines in the top and side views. Do not draw dimensions.

○ Save the drawing as EX6-17.

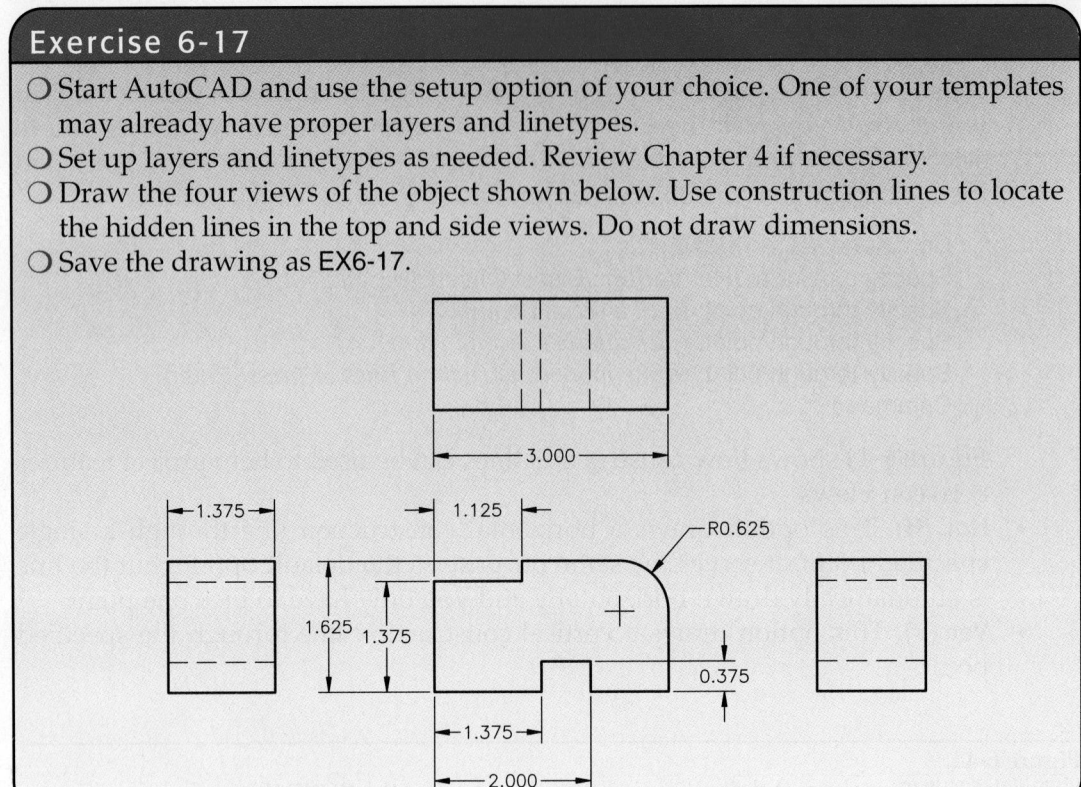

- **Ang.** This option draws a construction line at a specified angle through a specified point. The default lets you specify an angle and then pick a point for the construction line to be drawn through. This works well if you know the angle. You can also pick two points in the drawing to describe the angle:

  Command: **XL** *or* **XLINE**↵
  Specify a point or [Hor/Ver/Ang/Bisect/Offset]: **A**↵
  Enter angle of xline (0) or [Reference]: *(enter an angle, such as* 45*)*
  Specify through point: *(pick a point)*
  Specify through point: *(draw more construction lines or press* [Enter]*)*
  Command:

  The **Reference** option allows you to use the angle of an existing line object as a reference angle for construction lines. This option is useful when you do not know the angle of the construction line, but you know the angle between an existing object and the construction line:

  Command: **XL** *or* **XLINE**↵
  Specify a point or [Hor/Ver/Ang/Bisect/Offset]: **A**↵
  Enter angle of xline (0) or [Reference]: **R**↵
  Select a line object: *(pick a line)*
  Enter angle of xline <*current*>: **90**↵
  Specify through point: *(pick a point)*
  Specify through point: *(draw more construction lines or press* [Enter]*)*
  Command:

  **Figure 16-45** shows the **Ang** option used to draw construction lines establishing the location of an auxiliary view.

**Figure 6-45.**
Using the **XLINE** command **Ang** option.

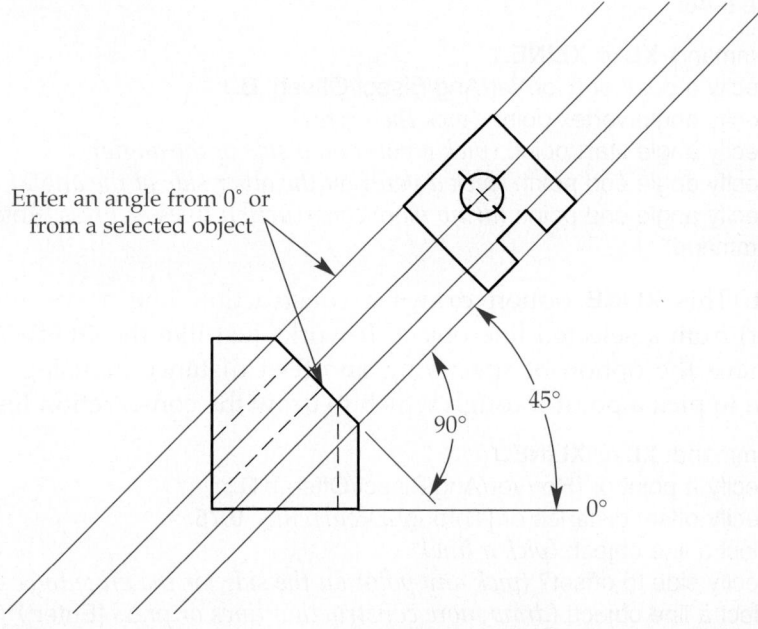

Enter an angle from 0° or
from a selected object

90°

45°

0°

## Exercise 6-18

○ Start AutoCAD and use the setup option of your choice.
○ Draw the front, top, and auxiliary views of the object shown below. Do not draw dimensions.
○ Save the drawing as EX6-18.

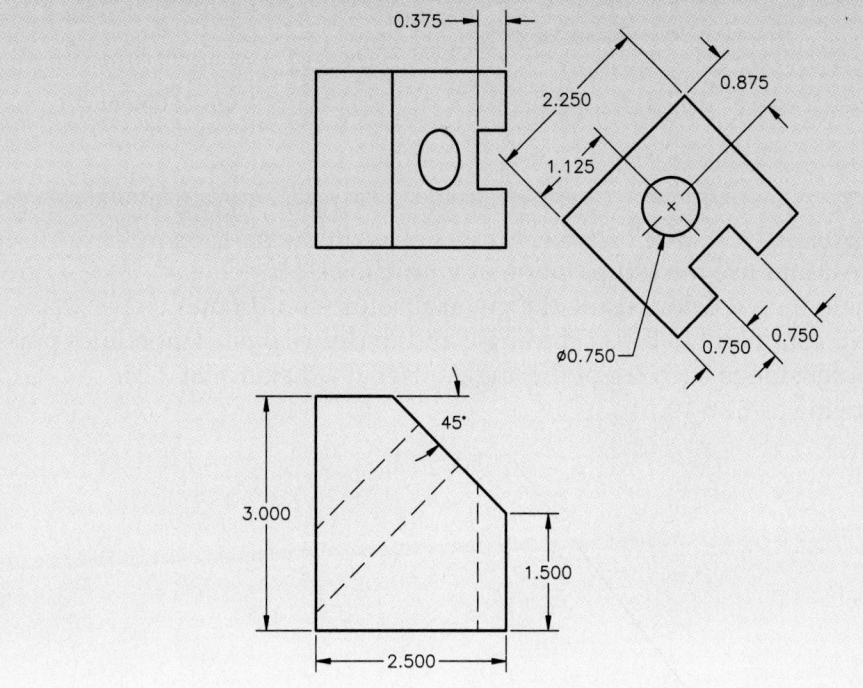

- **Bisect.** This option draws a construction line that bisects a specified angle. This is a convenient tool for use in some geometric constructions, as shown in Figure 6-46:

> Command: **XL** *or* **XLINE**⏎
> Specify a point or [Hor/Ver/Ang/Bisect/Offset]: **B**⏎
> Specify angle vertex point: *(pick the vertex)*
> Specify angle start point: *(pick a point on a side of the angle)*
> Specify angle end point: *(pick a point on the other side of the angle)*
> Specify angle end point: *(draw more construction lines or press* [Enter]*)*
> Command:

- **Offset.** This **XLINE** option draws a construction line a specified distance (offset) from a selected line object. It works just like the **OFFSET** command. You have the option of specifying an offset distance or using the **Through** option to pick a point through which to draw the construction line:

> Command: **XL** *or* **XLINE**⏎
> Specify a point or [Hor/Ver/Ang/Bisect/Offset]: **O**⏎
> Specify offset distance or [Through] *<current>*: **0.75**⏎
> Select a line object: *(pick a line)*
> Specify side to offset? *(pick any point on the side for the xline to be drawn)*
> Select a line object: *(draw more construction lines or press* [Enter]*)*
> Command:

**Figure 6-46.**
Using the **XLINE** command **Bisect** option.

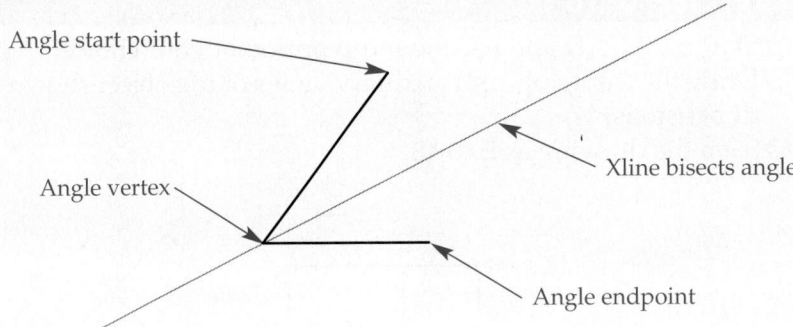

Angle start point

Angle vertex

Xline bisects angle

Angle endpoint

---

## Exercise 6-19

- ○ Start AutoCAD and use the setup option of your choice.
- ○ Draw the angle shown below using the given absolute coordinates.
- ○ Use the **XLINE** command to bisect the angle and to draw construction lines parallel to the outer side of each leg of the angle offset at a distance of .525.
- ○ Save the drawing as EX6-19.

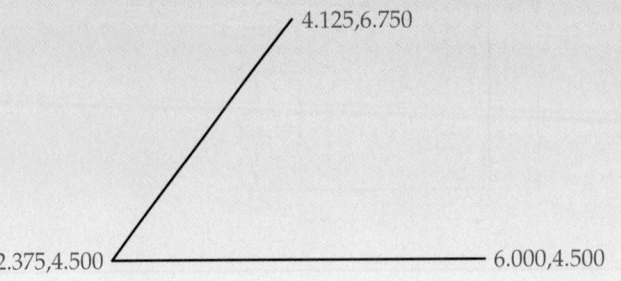

4.125,6.750

2.375,4.500          6.000,4.500

## Using the RAY Command

The **RAY** command is limited compared to the **XLINE** command. The **RAY** command allows you to specify the point of origin and a point the ray passes through. In this manner, the **RAY** command works much like the default option of the **XLINE** command. However, the ray extends beyond only the second pick point. The **XLINE** command results in a construction line that extends both ways from the pick points.

The **RAY** command can be accessed by picking **Ray** in the **Draw** pull-down menu or by typing RAY at the Command: prompt. The **RAY** command sequence is as follows:

RAY

Draw
 ➡ Ray

```
Command: RAY↵
Specify start point: (pick a point)
Specify through point: (pick a second point)
Specify through point: (draw more construction lines or press [Enter])
Command:
```

Both the **RAY** command and the **XLINE** command allow the creation of multiple objects. You must press [Enter] to end the command.

## Editing Construction Lines and Rays

The construction lines that you create using the **XLINE** and **RAY** commands can be edited and modified using standard editing commands. These commands are introduced in Chapter 11 and Chapter 12.

The construction lines will change into a new object type when infinite ends are trimmed off. A trimmed xline becomes a ray. A ray that has its infinite end trimmed becomes a normal line object. Therefore, in many cases, your construction lines can be modified to become part of the actual drawing. This approach can save a significant amount of time in many drawings.

## Chapter Test

*Answer the following questions on a separate sheet of paper.*

1. Give the command and entries needed to draw a line to the midpoint of an existing line:
   A. Command: _____
   B. Specify first point: _____
   C. Specify next point or [Undo]: _____
   D. of _____
2. Give the command and entries needed to draw a line tangent to an existing circle and perpendicular to an existing line:
   A. Command: _____
   B. Specify first point: _____
   C. to _____
   D. Specify next point or [Undo]: _____
   E. to _____
3. Give the command sequence required to draw a concentric circle inside an existing circle at a distance of .25:
   A. Command: _____
   B. Specify offset distance or [Through] <*current*>: _____
   C. Select object to offset or <exit>: _____
   D. Specify point on side to offset: _____
   E. Select object to offset or <exit>: _____

4. Give the command and entries needed to divide a line into 24 equal parts:
   A. Command: _____
   B. Select the object to divide: _____
   C. Enter the number of segments or [Block]: _____
5. Define *object snap*.
6. Define *quadrant*.
7. Define *running object snap*.
8. How do you set running object snaps?
9. How do you access the **Drafting Settings** dialog box to change object snap settings?
10. Describe the object snap override.
11. How do you change the aperture size?
12. What value would you specify to make the aperture half the default value?
13. How is the running object snap discontinued?
14. List two ways to establish an offset distance using the **OFFSET** command.
15. What is the difference between the **DIVIDE** and **MEASURE** commands?
16. If you use the **DIVIDE** command and nothing appears to happen, what should you do?
17. How do you access the **Point Style** dialog box?
18. How do you change the point size in the **Point Style** dialog box?
19. How do you activate the **Object Snap** shortcut menu?
20. Define *AutoSnap*.
21. What is an AutoSnap tooltip?
22. Name the following AutoSnap markers:

   A.         B.         C.

   D.         E.         F.

   G.         H.         I.

   J.         K.         L.

23. What does it mean when the tooltip reads Deferred Perpendicular?
24. What is the situation when the tooltip reads Extended Intersection?
25. What conditions must exist for the tooltip to read Tangent?
26. What is a deferred tangency?
27. Which object snaps depend on "acquired points" to function?
28. If you are using running object snaps and you want to make a single point selection without the effects of the running object snaps, what do you do?
29. If you are using running object snaps and you want to make several point specifications without the aid of object snap, but you want to continue the same running object snaps after making the desired point selections, what is the easiest way to temporarily turn the running object snaps off?
30. What do you do if there are multiple AutoSnap selection possibilities within range of the cursor and you want to select a specific one of the possibilities?
31. Define *AutoTracking*.
32. Which feature should be used in conjunction with AutoTracking?
33. How do you turn AutoSnap off?
34. How do you change the color of the AutoSnap marker?

35. How do you draw a single point and how do you draw multiple points?
36. Provide at least four guidelines for selecting the front view of an orthographic multiview drawing.
37. When can a part be shown with only one view?
38. When is an auxiliary view needed and what does an auxiliary view show?
39. What is the angle of projection from the slanted surface into the auxiliary view?
40. Name the AutoCAD command that allows you to draw construction lines.
41. What is the difference between the construction lines drawn with the command identified in Question 40 and rays drawn with the **RAY** command?
42. Why is it a good idea to put construction lines on their own layer?
43. Name the option that can be used to bisect an angle with a construction line.

## Drawing Problems

*Load AutoCAD for each of the following problems and use one of your templates or start a new drawing using your own variables.*

1. Draw the object below using the object snap modes. Save the drawing as P6-1 (omit dimensions).

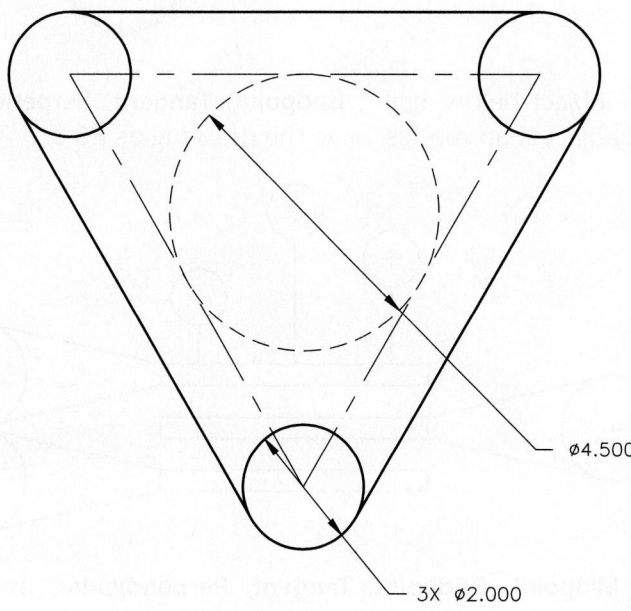

ø4.500

3X ø2.000

2. Draw the highlighted objects below, then use the object snap modes indicated to draw the remaining objects. Save the drawing as P6-2.

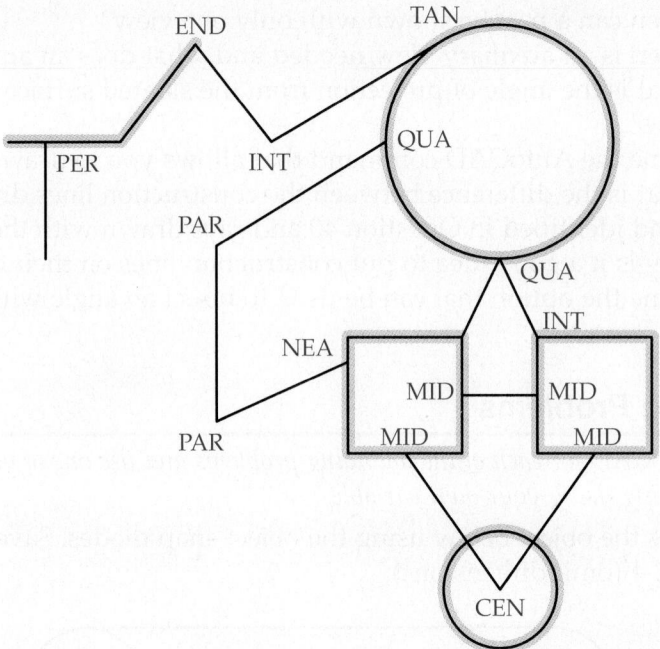

3. Draw the object below using **Endpoint**, **Tangent**, **Perpendicular**, and **Quadrant** object snap modes. Save the drawing as P6-3.

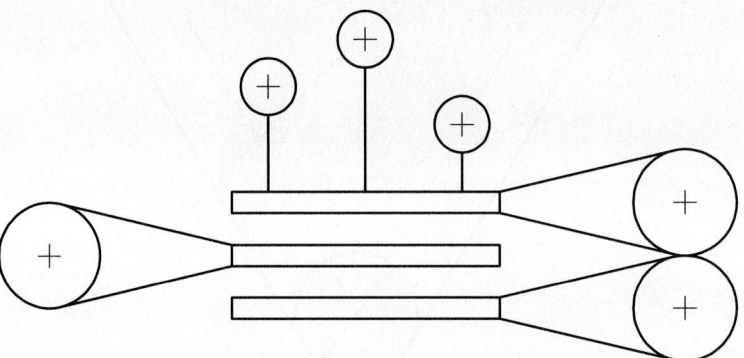

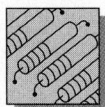

4. Use the **Midpoint**, **Endpoint**, **Tangent**, **Perpendicular,** and **Quadrant** object snap modes to draw these electrical switch schematics. Do not draw text or arrowheads. Save the drawing as P6-4.

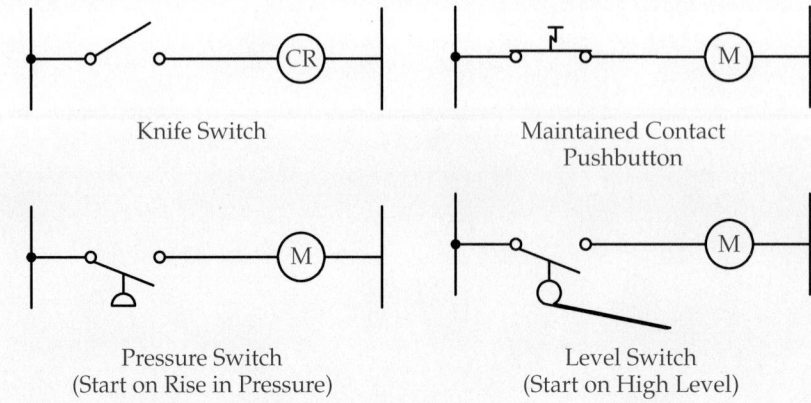

Knife Switch

Maintained Contact Pushbutton

Pressure Switch
(Start on Rise in Pressure)

Level Switch
(Start on High Level)

5. Draw the front and side views of this offset support. Use construction lines. Do not draw the dimensions. Save your drawing as P6-5.

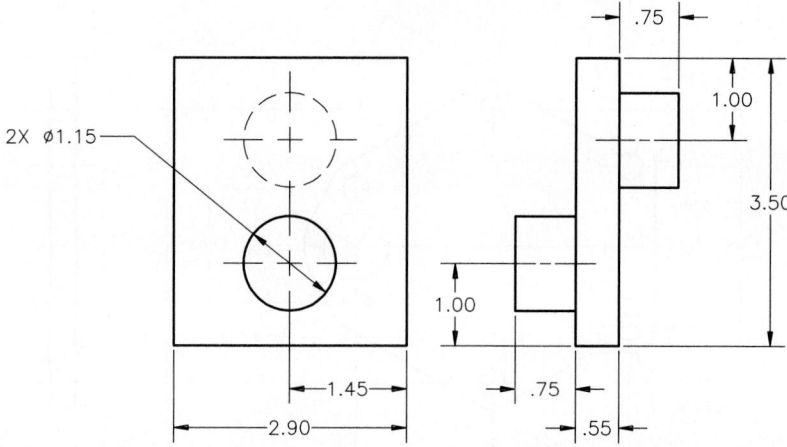

6. Draw the top and front views of this hitch bracket. Use construction lines. Do not draw the dimensions. Save your drawing as P6-6.

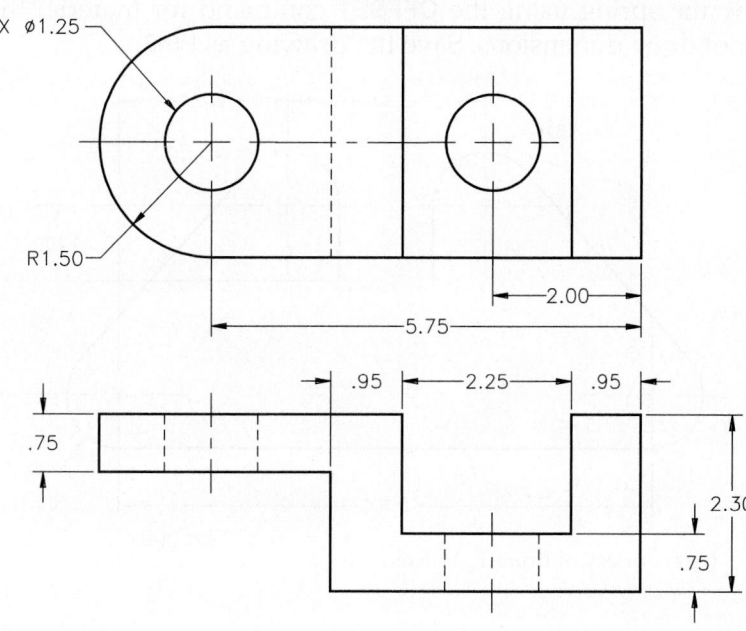

7. Draw this aluminum spacer. Use object snap modes and construction lines. Do not draw dimensions. Save the drawing as P6-7.

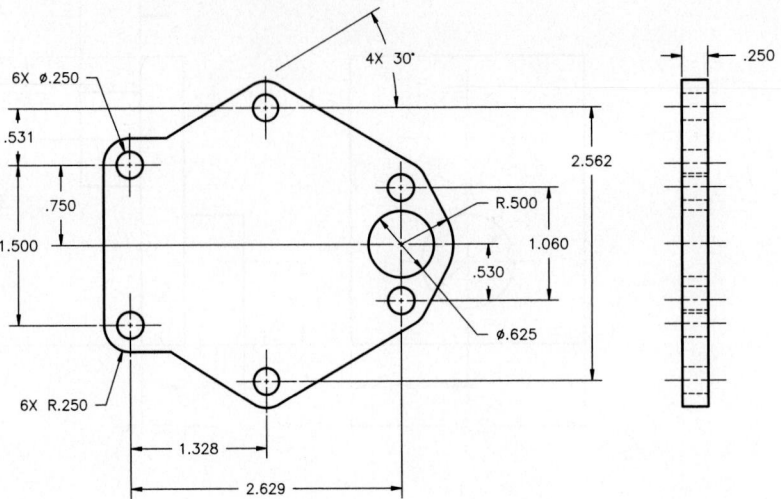

8. Draw the spring using the **OFFSET** command for material thickness. Do not draw dimensions. Save the drawing as P6-8.

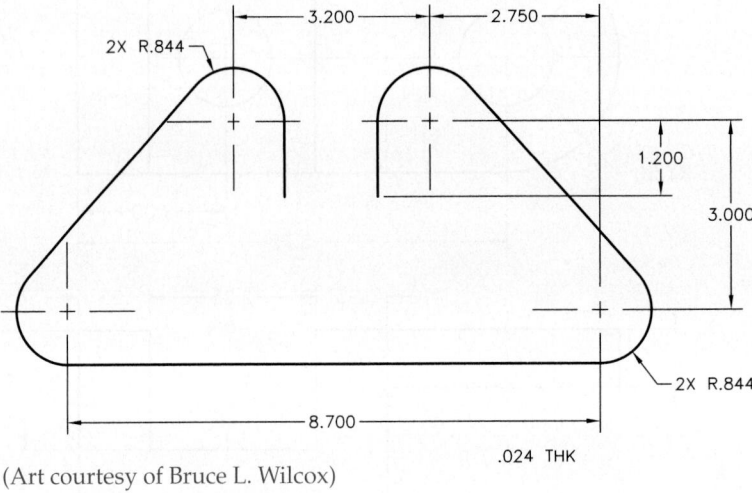

(Art courtesy of Bruce L. Wilcox)

9. Draw the gasket without dimensions. Save the drawing as P6-9.

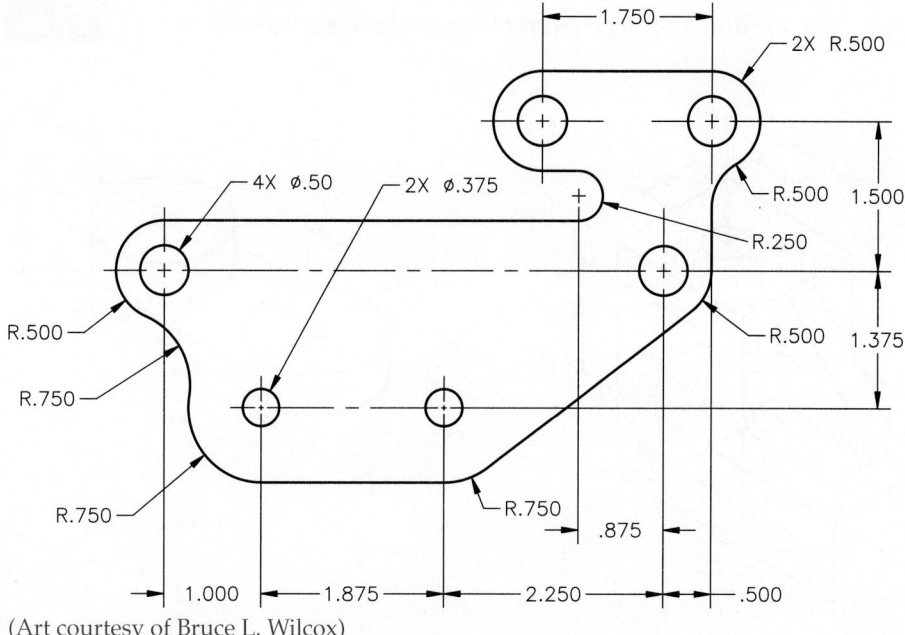

(Art courtesy of Bruce L. Wilcox)

10. Draw the sheet metal chassis without dimensions. Use object snap tracking and polar tracking to your advantage. Save the drawing as P6-10.

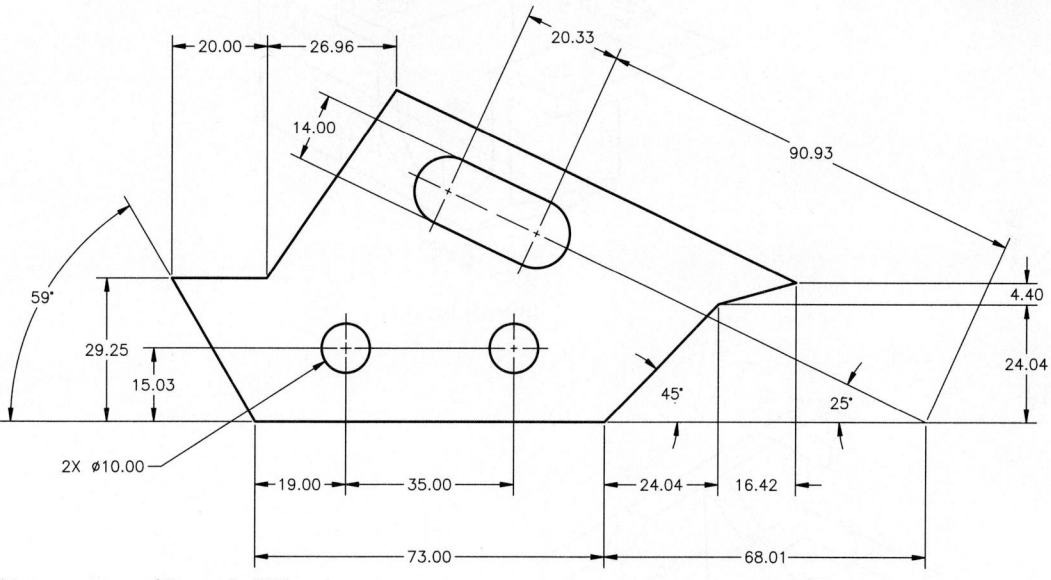

(Art courtesy of Bruce L. Wilcox)

*In Problems 11 through 15, draw the views needed to completely describe the objects. Use object snap modes, AutoTrack modes, and construction lines as needed. Do not dimension. Save the drawings as P6-(problem number), such as P6-11, P6-12, etc.*

11.

Brace

12.

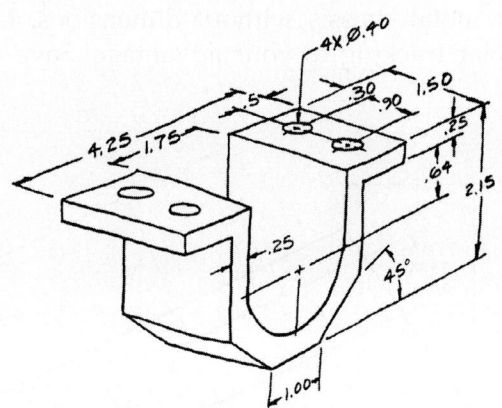

Connector

13.

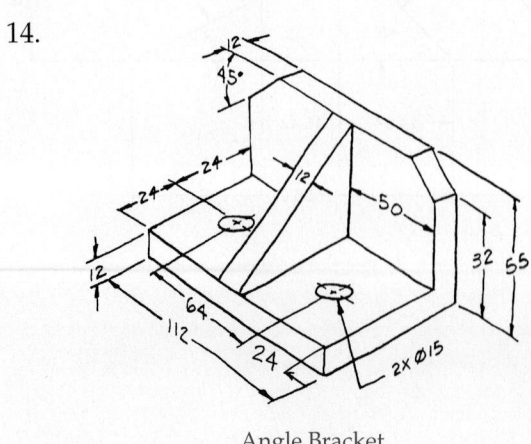

Journal Bracket

14.

Angle Bracket
(Metric)

15.

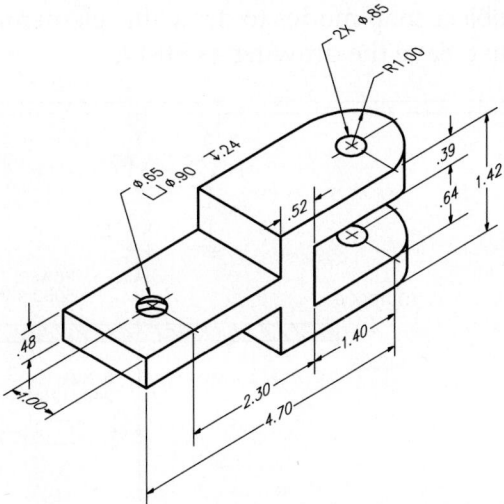

Hitch Bracket

16. Draw the views of this pillow block, including the auxiliary view. Use construction lines. Do not draw the dimensions. Save your drawing as P6-16.

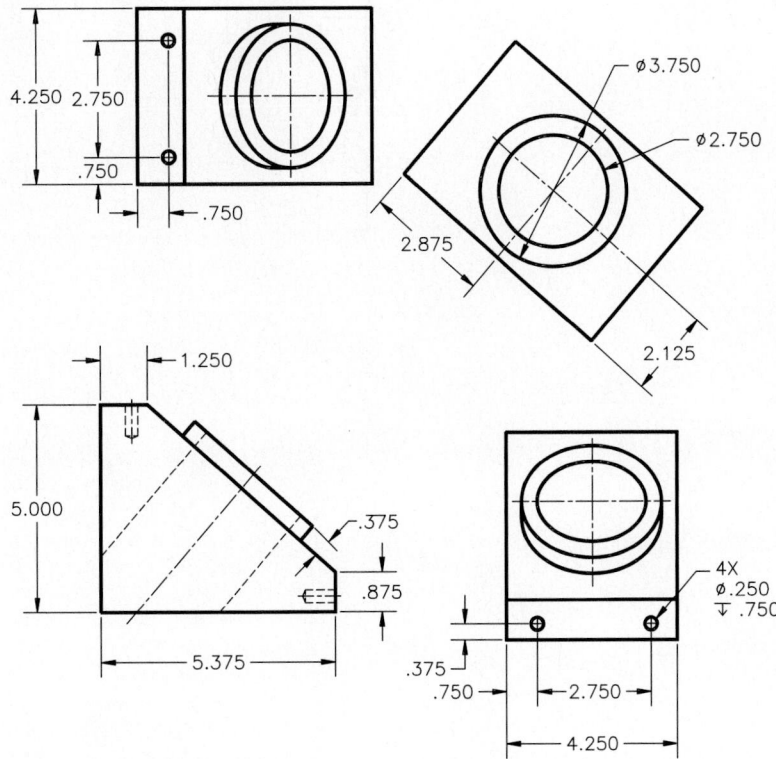

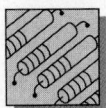

17. Use object snap modes to draw this elementary diagram. Do not draw the text. Save the drawing as P6-17.

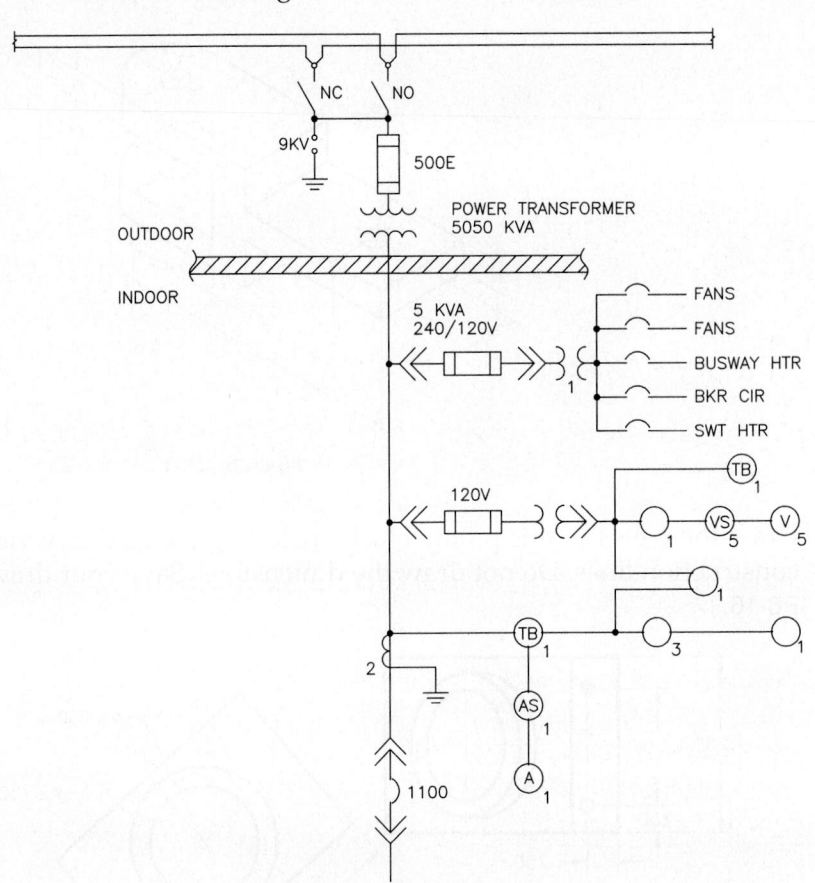

# Using the Geometry Calculator and Filters

## Learning Objectives

After completing this chapter, you will be able to do the following:
- Use the geometry calculator to make mathematical calculations.
- Make calculations and use information based on existing drawing geometry.
- Add objects to drawings using the geometry calculator and object snaps.
- Make point selections using point filters.
- Use selection set filters to create custom selection sets according to object types and object properties.

AutoCAD commands require precise input. Often, the input is variable and based on objects or locations within a drawing. AutoCAD provides a feature known as the *geometry calculator* to help find and use this type of information.

The geometry calculator and its use are explained in this chapter. Fundamental math calculations and drafting applications are presented. Complex mathematical calculations are also possible. Also covered in this chapter is the **FILTER** command, which allows you to customize a selection set by filtering objects based on object type and object properties.

## Using the Geometry Calculator

AutoCAD's geometry calculator allows you to extract and use existing information in your drawing. The geometry calculator also allows you to perform basic mathematical calculations at the command line or supply an expression as input to a prompt.

The geometry calculator is accessed by typing CAL at the Command: prompt. You are then prompted for an expression. After you type the mathematical expression and press [Enter], AutoCAD automatically simplifies, or "solves," the expression and returns the result. For example:

> Command: **CAL**↵
> \>\> Expression: **2+2**↵
> 4
> Command:

CAL

## Basics of the Geometry Calculator

The geometry calculator is more powerful than most hand-held calculators because it can directly access drawing information and can supply input to an AutoCAD prompt. The types of expressions that can be entered include numeric expressions and vector expressions. A *numeric expression* refers to a mathematical process using numbers, such as the expressions solved using normal calculators. A *vector expression* is an expression involving a point coordinate location.

To use the geometry calculator, you must understand the sequence and format of an expression. The geometry calculator evaluates expressions according to the standard mathematical rules of precedence. This means that expressions within parentheses are simplified first, starting with the innermost set and proceeding outward. Mathematical operators are evaluated in the standard order: exponents first, multiplication and division next, addition and subtraction last. Operators of equal precedence are evaluated from left to right.

## Making Numeric Entries

The same methods of entering numbers at AutoCAD prompts are also acceptable for calculator expressions. When entering feet and inches, either of the accepted formats can be used. This means that 5'-6" can also be entered as 5'6". The 5'-6" value can also be entered as 66 inches. When a number expressed in feet and inches is entered, AutoCAD automatically converts to inches:

```
Command: CAL↵
>> Expression: 24'6"↵
294.0
```

> **NOTE**
> An entry at the Expression: prompt must be completed by pressing [Enter]. Pressing the space bar adds a space to your entry; it does not act as a return at this prompt.

## Using Basic Math Functions

The basic mathematical functions used in numeric expressions include addition, subtraction, multiplication, division, and exponential notation. Parentheses are used to group symbols and values into sets. The symbols used for the basic mathematical operators are shown in the following table.

| Symbol | Function | Example |
|--------|----------|---------|
| + | Addition | 3+26 |
| - | Subtraction | 270–15.3 |
| * | Multiplication | 4*156 |
| / | Division | 256/16 |
| ^ | Exponent | 22.6^3 |
| ( ) | Grouped expressions | 2*(16+2^3) |

The following examples use the **CAL** command to solve each type of mathematical functions.

> Command: **CAL**⏎
> \>\> Expression: **17.375+5.0625**⏎
> 22.4375

> Command: **CAL**⏎
> \>\> Expression: **17.375–5.0625**⏎
> 12.3125

> Command: **CAL**⏎
> \>\> Expression: **12*18.25**⏎
> 219.0

> Command: **CAL**⏎
> \>\> Expression: **27'8"/4**⏎
> 83.0

> Command: **CAL**⏎
> \>\> Expression: **9^2**⏎
> 81.0

> Command: **CAL**⏎
> \>\> Expression: **(17.375+5.0625)+(4.25*3.75)–(18.5/2)**⏎
> 29.125

An *integer* is a whole number; it has no decimal or fractional part. The geometry calculator has limits when working with integer values. Integers greater than 32,767 or less than –32,768 must be presented as real numbers. When working with values outside this range, type a decimal point and a zero (.0) after the value.

## Exercise 7-1

○ Start a new drawing. Use the **CAL** command to calculate:
  ○ 28.125+37.625
  ○ 16.875–7.375
  ○ 6.25+3.5
  ○ (25.75÷4)+(5.625×3)
  ○ $3.625^2$
  ○ (12.125×3)+(24÷3+5.25)–(3.75÷1.5)

## Making Unit Conversions

The calculator has a function called **CVUNIT** that lets you convert one type of unit into another. For example, inches can be converted to millimeters or liters can be converted to gallons. The order of elements in the **CVUNIT** function is:

**CVUNIT**(*value,from units,to units*)

For example, to convert 4.7 kilometers to the equivalent number of feet:

> Command: **CAL**⏎
> \>\> Expression: **CVUNIT(4.7,kilometers,feet)**⏎
> 15419.9

If the units of measure you specify are either incompatible or are not defined in the acad.unt file, the message

> \>\> Error: CVUNIT failed to convert units

is displayed and the prompt is reissued.

The **CVUNIT** function can work with units of distance, angles, volume, mass, time, and frequency. The units available for conversion are specified in the file acad.unt found in the AutoCAD \Support folder. This file can be edited to include additional units of measure if needed.

**Exercise 7-2**

○ Start a new drawing. Use the **CAL** command to convert:
  - ○ 8.625 inches to millimeters
  - ○ 34.5 millimeters to inches
  - ○ 5.5 kilometers to miles
  - ○ 12 gallons to liters
  - ○ 47 hours to minutes

## Point Entry

While the numeric functions of the calculator provide many useful capabilities, the most powerful use of the geometry calculator is its ability to find and use geometric information. Information such as point coordinates can be entered as input to the geometry calculator.

A point coordinate is entered as one, two, or three numbers separated by commas and enclosed in square brackets. The numbers represent the XYZ coordinates. For example [4,7,2], [2.1,3.79], or [2,7.4,0]. Any value that is zero can be omitted, as well as commas immediately in front of the right bracket. For example:

| | |
|---|---|
| [2,2] | is the same as [2,2,0] |
| [,,6] | is the same as [0,0,6] |
| [5] | is the same as [5,0,0] |
| [] | is the same as [0,0,0] |

Direction can be entered using any accepted AutoCAD format, including polar and relative coordinates, as shown in the following table.

| Coordinate entry | Entry format |
|---|---|
| Polar | [*dist<angle*] |
| Relative | [@*x, y, z*] |

These options provide the ability to determine locations, distances, and directions within a drawing. For example, to determine a point coordinate value for a location that is 6 units at an angle within the XY plane of 45° from the point 2,2,0, use the sequence:

Command: **CAL**↵
>> Expression: **[2,2,0]+[6<45]**↵
(6.24264 6.24264 0.0)

In an application of this type, the point answer is returned in parentheses with spaces to separate the numbers instead of commas. Calculations can also be performed within the point coordinate specification. For example:

>> Expression: **[2+3,2+3,0]+[1,2,0]**↵
(6.0 7.0 0.0)

A point location can be specified using the @ symbol. Entering this symbol supplies the current value of the **LASTPOINT** system variable:

> Command: **CAL**↵
> \>> Expression: **@**↵
> (*point coordinates*)

The reference to (*point coordinates*) in this command sequence represents the point coordinate values returned by AutoCAD. The actual coordinate values will vary based on user input.

Besides entering coordinates at the prompt, you can also specify point coordinates by picking with the cursor. The **CUR** function is used to specify a point picked with the cursor:

> Command: **CAL**↵
> \>> Expression: **CUR**↵
> \>> Enter a point: (*pick a point*)
> (*point coordinates*)

This method can also be used as part of a calculation:

> \>> Expression: **CUR+[1,2]**↵
> \>> Enter a point: (*pick a point*)
> (*point coordinates*)

---

### Exercise 7-3

○ Start a new drawing. Use the **CAL** command to find the following point coordinates using the shortest entry format.
  ○ [2,2,0]+[6<30]
  ○ [4,3,0]+[2,2,0]
○ Use the cursor to select a point within the **CAL** command.
○ Use the cursor to pick a point and add 3,2,0.

---

## Using the CAL Command Transparently

The **CAL** command can also be used transparently (within another command). To use the geometry calculator transparently, enter the command as **'CAL** (an apostrophe followed by CAL). When the **CAL** command is used transparently, the result is supplied as input to the current prompt.

The following example uses direct distance entry combined with the geometry calculator to provide the correct length of a line. The line being drawn is 8.0 inches times 1.006.

> Command: **L** *or* **LINE**↵
> Specify first point: (*pick first point*)
> Specify next point or [Undo]: **'CAL**↵ (*drag cursor in appropriate direction to set the angle of the line*)
> \>> Expression: **8*1.006**↵
> 8.048
> Specify next point or [Undo]: ↵

The calculator evaluates the expression and automatically supplies the result of 8.048 at the Specify next point or [Undo]: prompt. When AutoCAD receives a single numeric value at a point prompt, it is automatically understood as a direct distance entry value. An application of this type of calculation might be including a shrinkage allowance for a casting or forging pattern.

---

○ Start a new drawing.
○ Use the **CAL** command transparently to draw a line using direct distance entry from a point located at 2,4 to 6×1.0625.
○ Save the drawing as EX7-4.

## Using the Object Snap Modes

Object snap points can also be specified as point coordinates to the geometry calculator. The object snaps provide the accuracy that is often needed when finding points on an object. The following example shows the **Endpoint** object snap used to identify a specific point on an object. Note that you *must* use the letter abbreviation. Typing the full snap name will result in an error.

> Command: **CAL**↵
> >> Expression: **END**↵
> >> Select entity for END snap: *(pick an object)*
> *(point coordinates)*

The next example uses the **Endpoint** object snap to find the end of a line and add the point coordinate of 2 at 45°.

> Command: **CAL**↵
> >> Expression: **END+[2<45]**↵
> >> Select entity for END snap: *(pick an object)*
> *(point coordinates)*

You can use the geometry calculator to provide information based on selected points. For example, the following sequence can be used to find the point midway between two points selected with the cursor.

> Command: **CAL**↵
> >> Expression: **(CUR+CUR)/2**↵
> >> Enter a point: *(pick a point)*
> >> Enter a point: *(pick a point)*
> *(point coordinates)*

This same technique can be used with any desired object snap mode. For example, to divide the distance between the center of a circle and the endpoint of a line by two:

> Command: **CAL**↵
> >> Expression: **(CEN+END)/2**↵
> >> Select entity for CEN snap: *(pick the circle)*
> >> Select entity for END snap: *(pick the line)*
> *(point coordinates)*

The previous sequence can be used within the **LINE** command to draw a line that starts halfway between the center of an existing circle and the endpoint of an existing line, as shown in **Figure 7-1.**

> Command: **L** *or* **LINE**↵
> Specify first point: **'CAL**↵
> >> Expression: **(CEN+END)/2**↵
> >> Select entity for CEN snap: *(pick the circle)*
> >> Select entity for END snap: *(pick the line)*
> *(point coordinates)*
> Specify next point or [Undo]:

**Figure 7-1.**
Finding a point
halfway between
the center of a circle
and the endpoint of
a line.

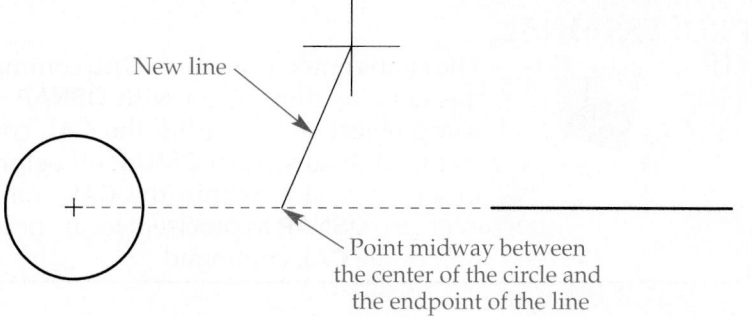

New line

Point midway between
the center of the circle and
the endpoint of the line

**Figure 7-2.**
Locating the center
of a circle two units
to the right of the
midpoint of a line.

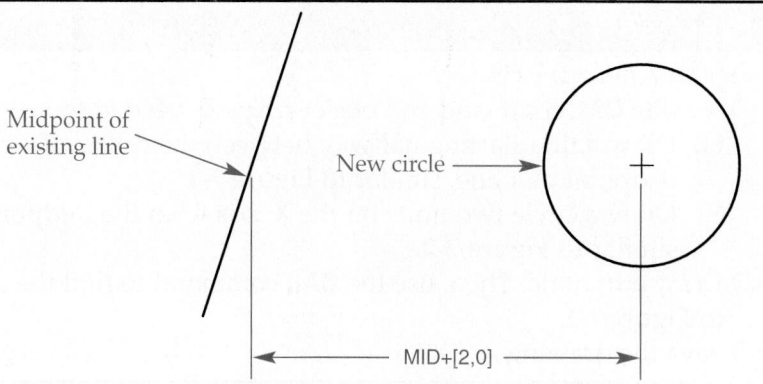

Midpoint of
existing line

New circle

MID+[2,0]

The following sequence is used to create a circle with its center located two units along the X axis from the midpoint of an existing line, as shown in **Figure 7-2.**

> Command: **C** *or* **CIRCLE**↵
> Specify center point for circle or [3P/2P/Ttr (tan tan radius)]: **'CAL**↵
> \>> Expression: **MID+[2,0]**↵
> \>> Select entity for MID snap: *(pick the line object)*
> *(point coordinates)*
> Specify radius of circle or [Diameter] *<current>*:

The next sequence determines the centroid (center of mass) of a triangle defined by picking three endpoints, as shown in **Figure 7-3.**

> Command: **CAL**↵
> \>> Expression: **(END+END+END)/3**↵
> \>> Select entity for END snap: *(pick first corner of the triangle)*
> \>> Select entity for END snap: *(pick second corner of the triangle)*
> \>> Select entity for END snap: *(pick third corner of the triangle)*
> *(point coordinates)*

**Figure 7-3.**
Locating the center
of mass of a
triangle.

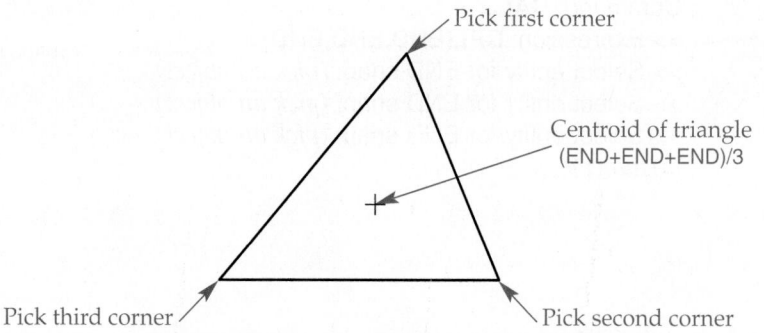

Pick first corner

Centroid of triangle
(END+END+END)/3

Pick third corner

Pick second corner

### Exercise 7-5

○ Start a new drawing.
○ Use the **CAL** command and object snaps as needed to:
  ○ Draw a line starting halfway between the center of a circle and the endpoint of a line, similar to **Figure 7-1**.
  ○ Draw a circle two units on the X axis from the midpoint of a line, similar to **Figure 7-2**.
○ Draw a triangle. Then, use the **CAL** command to find the center of mass, similar to **Figure 7-3**.
○ Save the drawing as EX7-5.

## Calculating Distances

There are three basic calculator functions used to calculate distances in a drawing. These are the **DIST**, **DPL**, and **DPP** functions.

The **DIST** function performs a simple distance calculation between the two specified points. It is entered as **DIST(***P1***,***P2***)** where $P1$ = Point 1 and $P2$ = Point 2. Similar to all calculator functions, the points can be entered manually or picked. The **DIST** function is used in the following sequence to find a distance between two endpoints of a line:

> Command: **CAL**↵
> \>> Expression: **DIST(END,END)**↵
> \>> Select entity for END snap: *(pick an object)*
> \>> Select entity for END snap: *(pick an object)*
> *(distance)*

The **DPL** function calculates the perpendicular distance between a point ($P$) and a line passing through two other points ($P1$ and $P2$). It is written as **DPL(***P***,***P1***,***P2***)**. See **Figure 7-4**. The following is an example using **DPL** with the endpoint object snap. The order of selection is P, P1, and then P2:

> Command: **CAL**↵
> \>> Expression: **DPL(END,END,END)**↵
> \>> Select entity for END snap: *(pick an object)*
> \>> Select entity for END snap: *(pick an object)*
> \>> Select entity for END snap: *(pick an object)*
> *(distance)*

Figure 7-4.
Finding the shortest
distance between a
point and a line.

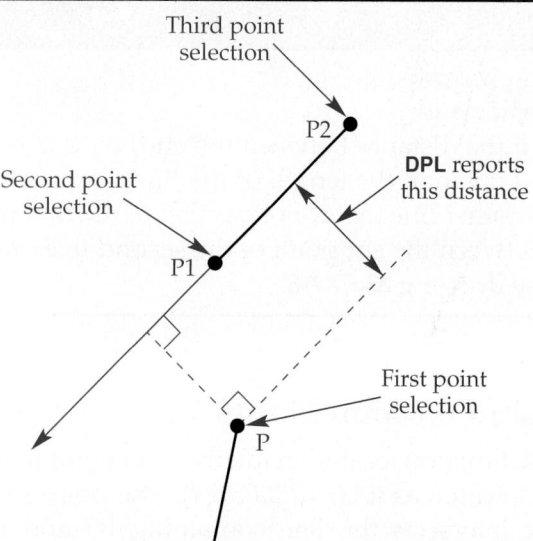

DPP function is much like the **DPL** function except it finds the shortest distance between a point (*P*) and a plane defined by three other points (*P1*, *P2*, and *P3*). See **Figure 7-5**. The **DPP** function is written as **DPP(*P*,*P1*,*P2*,*P3*)**. The points for **DPP** can be entered manually or picked. The following example calculates the distance between the point 2,2,6 and three random points on the XY plane:

```
Command: CAL↵
>> Expression: DPP([2,2,6],CUR,CUR,CUR)↵
>> Enter a point: (pick a point)
>> Enter a point: (pick a point)
>> Enter a point: (pick a point)
6.0
```

If Point P is on the same plane as the three points picked to define the plane, the returned value is 0. Notice in the command sequence that Point P is defined with the coordinates 2,2,6, which means it is located six units above the XY plane.

**Figure 7-5.**
Finding the shortest
distance between a
point and a plane.

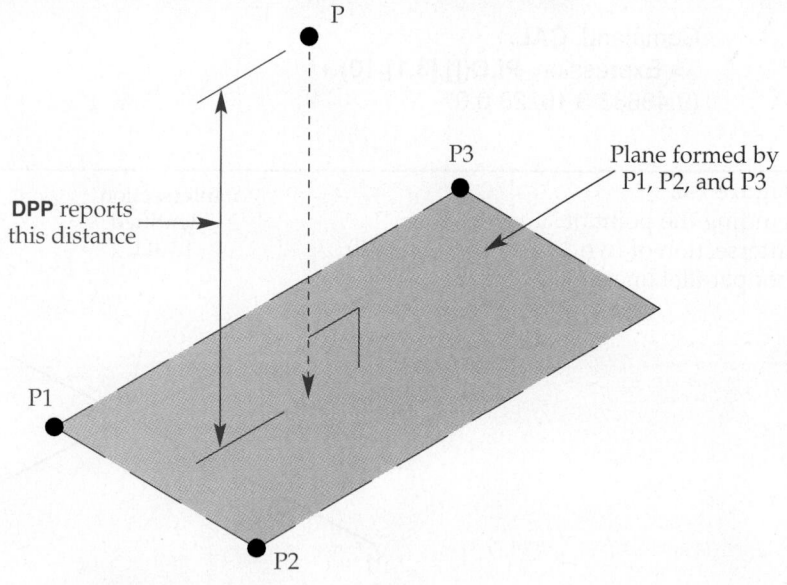

○ Start a new drawing.
○ Draw a line and:
  ○ Find the distance between the endpoints.
  ○ Find one-half the length of the line.
○ Draw another line that is not parallel to the first line. Find the perpendicular distance between the endpoint of the second line and the first line.
○ Save the drawing as EX7-6.

## Finding Intersection Points

The **ILL** function locates an intersection point between two nonparallel lines. This function is written as **ILL(***P1,P2,P3,P4***)**. The point location where the line containing P1 and P2 intersects the line containing P3 and P4 is identified. An actual line between P1 and P2 (or P3 and P4) is not necessary. This function finds a hypothetical intersection as though the lines are infinite in length. The following sequence shows the use of the **ILL** function to find the intersection of the lines shown in **Figure 7-6:**

```
Command: CAL↵
>> Expression: ILL([2,5,0],[4,6,0],[4,5,0],[2,6,0])↵
(3.0 5.5 0.0)
```

If the two lines, or hypothetical extensions of the two lines, do not intersect, the message:

```
>> Error: The two lines in function ILL do not intersect or are collinear.
```

is displayed and the >>Expression: prompt is returned.

## Finding a Point on a Line

The **PLD** function finds a point that is a specified distance from the start point of a line passing through two points (*P1* and *P2*) and on the line. It is written as **PLD(***P1,P2,Dist***)**. It is not necessary for an actual line to exist. The following sequence finds a point along a line passing through 0,0 and 3,1 that is 10 units from the start point, as shown in **Figure 7-7**.

```
Command: CAL↵
>> Expression: PLD([],[3,1],10)↵
(9.48683 3.16228 0.0)
```

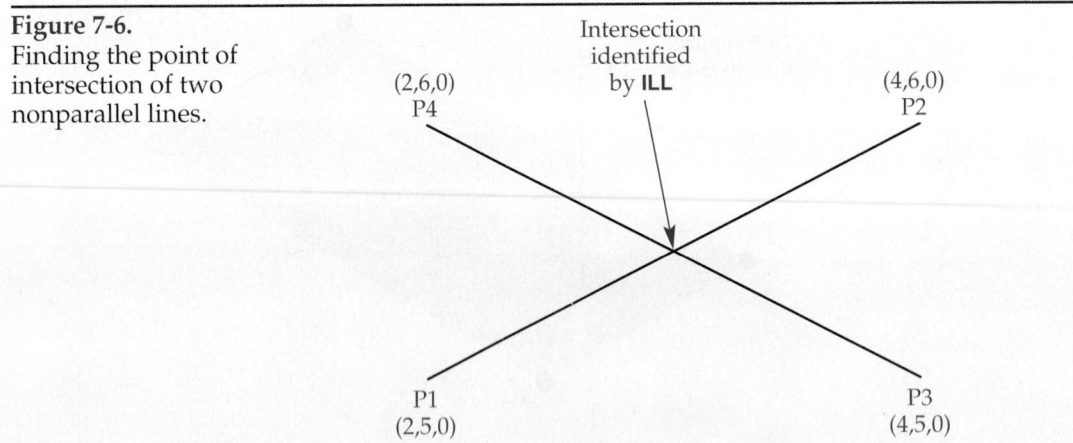

**Figure 7-6.**
Finding the point of intersection of two nonparallel lines.

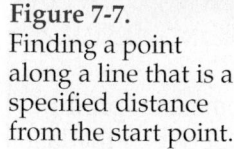

**Figure 7-7.**
Finding a point
along a line that is a
specified distance
from the start point.

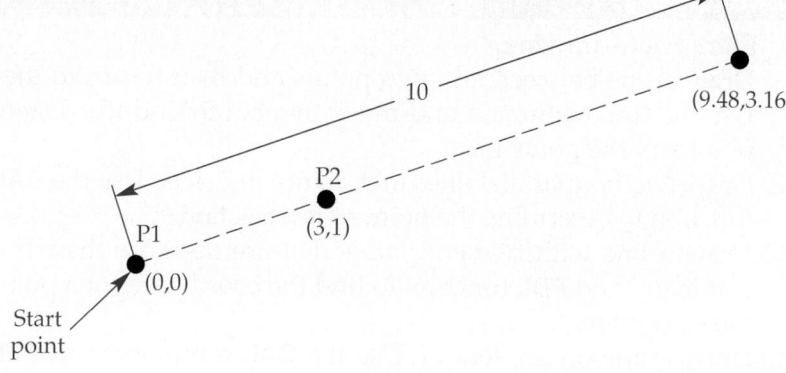

The **PLT** function provides another means of finding a point along a line. It finds a point that is along a line passing through two points (*P1* and *P2*) and located from the start point based on a specified scale (*T* parameter). The *T* parameter is simply a scale factor relative to the distance between P1 and P2. The function is written as **PLT**(*P1,P2,T*). The following sequence locates a point that is three-quarters of the way along the length of the specified line:

```
Command: CAL↵
>> Expression: PLT([],[2,2],.75)↵
(1.5 1.5 0.0)
```

If *T*=0, then the point location is the same as *P1*. If *T*=1, then the point location is the same as *P2*. A *T* value of .5 identifies the midpoint between *P1* and *P2*. A *T* value of 2 locates a point along the line that is a distance from the start point equal to twice the length of the line. **Figure 7-8** shows several examples.

**Figure 7-8.**
Finding a point
along a line based
on the scale of the
line length.

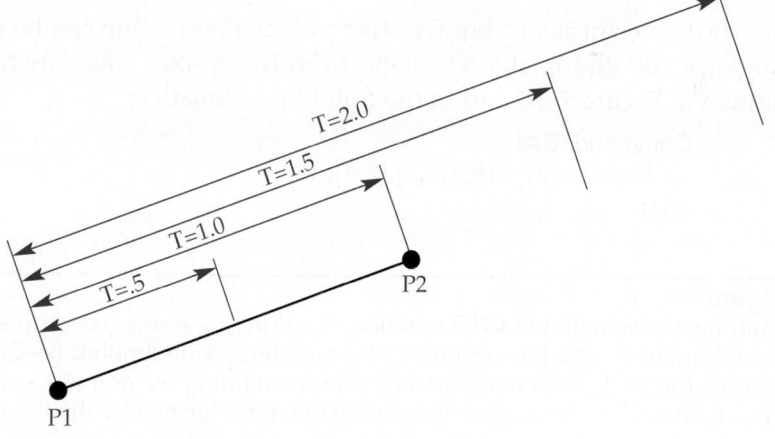

○ Start a new drawing.

○ Draw a line between any two points and then return to the Command: prompt. Use the **CAL** command and the @ symbol to find the distance between the last point and the point 4,4,0.

○ Draw two nonparallel lines that do not intersect. Use the **CAL** command and **ILL** function to determine the point of intersection.

○ Draw a line with two endpoints that are no more than 1″ apart. Use the **CAL** command and **PDL** function to find the coordinates of a point that is 3.375″ from the start point.

○ Draw a line of any length. Use the **CAL** command and **PLT** function to find a point that is on the line and a distance from the start point equal to one-quarter of the line length.

○ Save the drawing as EX7-7.

## Finding an Angle

The **ANG** function finds the angle between two lines. As with other calculator functions, the lines need not physically exist in the drawing. This function can be entered several different ways, depending on the nature of the angle you are trying to calculate.

To find the angle of a vector from the X axis in the XY plane, enter **ANG**(*coordinates*). The coordinate values are entered within parentheses. The coordinates can be manually entered or a point can be selected using object snap options. The following sequence shows this method being used to enter the coordinates of a point along the line shown in **Figure 7-9A**.

```
Command: CAL↵
>> Expression: ANG([1,1,0])↵
45.0
```

If the vector is not known, two points along a line can be used to determine the angle of the line in the XY plane from the X axis. The function is **ANG**(*P1, P2*), as shown in **Figure 7-9B** and in the following sequence:

```
Command: CAL↵
>> Expression: ANG([2,2],[4,4])↵
45.0
```

**Figure 7-9.**
Finding angles with the **ANG** function. A—Entering a single coordinate returns the angle from horizontal of a line containing 0,0 and the specified point. B—Entering two coordinates returns the angle from horizontal of a line containing the points. C—Entering three coordinates finds the angle between the two lines formed by the three points.

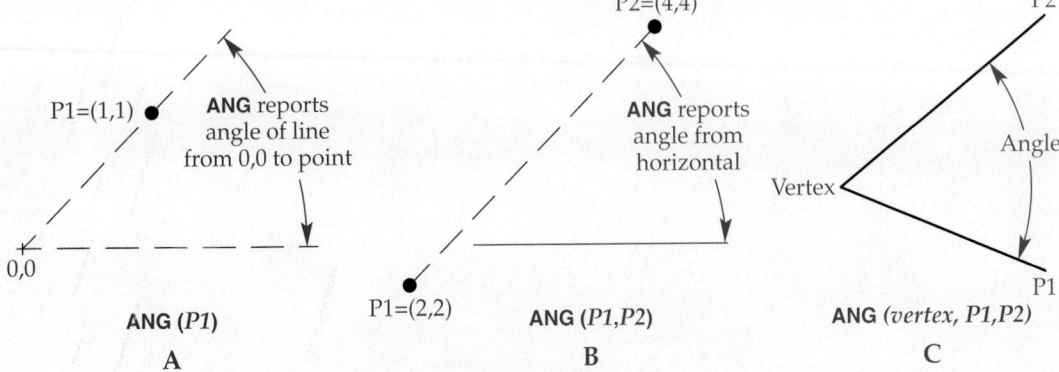

You can also calculate an included angle by specifying a vertex and a point on each side, or leg, of the angle. A *vertex* is the intersection of two lines. An ***included angle*** is the angle formed between the vertex and the sides of the angle. The formula is entered as **ANG(***vertex*,*P1*,*P2***)**, **Figure 7-9C**. The following example determines the angle between two lines. The **Endpoint** object snap is used to precisely pick points.

>    Command: **CAL**↵
>    \>> Expression: **ANG(END,END,END).**↵
>    \>> Select entity for END snap: *(pick vertex)*
>    \>> Select entity for END snap: *(pick end of first line)*
>    \>> Select entity for END snap: *(pick end of second line)*
>    *(angle)*

## Finding a Radius

You can use the **RAD** function to find the radius of an arc, circle, or 2D polyline arc. The command sequence is:

>    Command: **CAL**↵
>    \>> Expression: **RAD**↵
>    \>> Select circle, arc or polyline segment for RAD function: *(select a circle)*
>    *(radius)*

You can easily draw objects to match the radius of an existing object using the **RAD** function. The following example uses **RAD** to supply the radius value for a circle to match that of the existing circle, as shown in **Figure 7-10**.

>    Command: **C** *or* **CIRCLE**↵
>    Specify center point for circle or [3P/2P/Ttr (tan tan radius)]: *(pick the center point of the new circle)*
>    Specify radius of circle or [Diameter] <*current*>: '**CAL**↵
>    \>> Expression: **RAD**↵
>    \>> Select circle, arc or polyline segment for RAD function: *(select the existing circle)*
>    *(radius of existing circle)*
>    Command:

**Figure 7-10.**
Using the **RAD** function to create a circle equal in diameter to an existing circle.

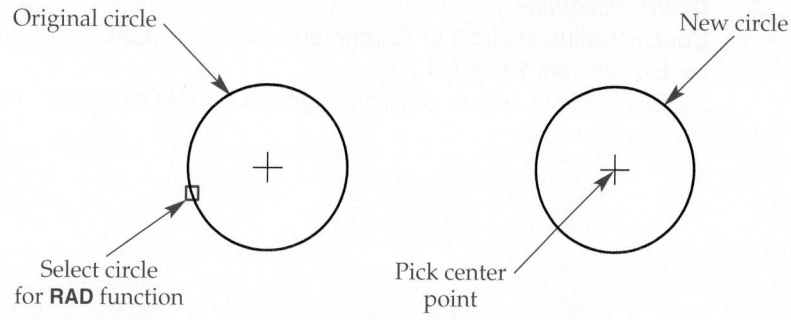

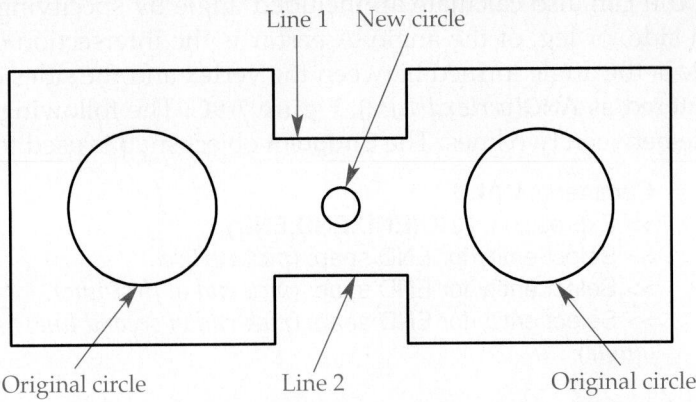

Figure 7-11.
Combining
calculator functions
to revise a circle and
place it in a new
position.

Line 1    New circle

Original circle          Line 2          Original circle

## Combining Calculator Functions

Calculator functions can be combined. For example, suppose you want to draw a new circle that is 25% the size of the original circle and placed in a new position that also needs to be calculated. Look at Figure 7-11 as you use the following command sequence:

Command: **C** *or* **CIRCLE**↵
Specify center point for circle or [3P/2P/Ttr (tan tan radius)]: **'CAL**↵
>> Expression: **(MID+MID)/2**↵
>> Select entity for MID snap: *(pick Line 1)*
>> Select entity for MID snap: *(pick Line 2)*
*(point coordinates)*

This locates the center point of the new circle vertically halfway between the midpoints of Line 1 and Line 2. Now, instruct AutoCAD to calculate a new radius that is 25% of the size of the original circle:

Specify radius of circle or [Diameter] <*current*>: **'CAL**↵
>> Expression: **.25*RAD**↵
>> Select circle, arc, or polyline segment for RAD function: *(pick one of the original circles)*
Command:

A new circle that is 25% of the size of the original circle is drawn at the calculated location.

Another application of the **CAL** command is shown in Figure 7-12 where a new circle is placed 3″ along a centerline from an existing circle. The new circle is 1.5 times larger than the original circle. The command sequence is:

Command: **C** *or* **CIRCLE**↵
Specify center point for circle or [3P/2P/Ttr (tan tan radius)]: **'CAL**↵
>> Expression: **PLD(CEN,END,3)**↵
>> Select entity for CEN snap: *(pick the original circle)*
>> Select entity for END snap: *(pick near the right end of the centerline)*
*(point coordinates)*
Specify radius of circle or [Diameter] <*current*>: **'CAL**↵
>> Expression: **1.5*RAD**↵
>> Select circle, arc, or polyline segment for RAD function: *(pick the original circle)*

Figure 7-12.
Copying a circle
along a centerline
and resizing it.

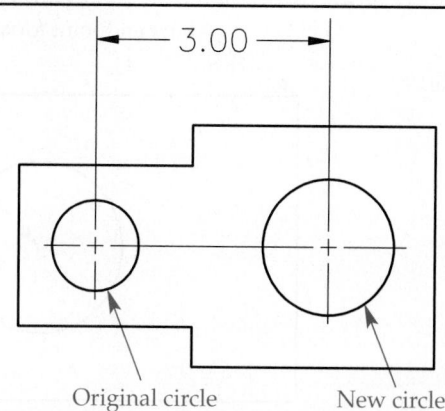

Original circle          New circle

## Exercise 7-9

○ Start a new drawing.
○ Draw a circle of any size.
○ Using the **RAD** function of the **CAL** command, draw another circle of equal diameter at any location.
○ Use the **CAL** command to assist you in making a drawing similar to **Figure 7-11**.
○ Save the drawing as EX7-9.

## Geometry Calculator Shortcut Functions

To make using the geometry calculator as efficient as possible, some of the most commonly used calculator tasks have shortcuts. The basic abbreviations are shown in the following table.

| Function | Replaces | Description |
|---|---|---|
| DEE | DIST(END,END) | Distance between two selected endpoints |
| ILLE | ILL(END,END,END,END) | Intersection of two lines defined by four selected endpoints |
| MEE | (END+END)/2 | Point midway between two selected endpoints |

These functions work exactly the same way as the longer format that you have already learned. Look at each of the shortcut options as you review earlier discussions covering the actual functions used by the shortcuts. For example, you can use the **DEE** shortcut to determine the length of a line:

> Command: **CAL**↵
> >> Expression: **DEE**↵
> >> Select one endpoint for DEE: *(pick one end of the line)*
> >> Select another endpoint for DEE: *(pick the other end)*
> *(distance)*

The command sequence to draw a circle at the center of a rectangle using the **MEE** function, as shown in **Figure 7-13**, is:

> Command: **C** *or* **CIRCLE**↵
> Specify center point for circle or [3P/2P/Ttr (tan tan radius)]: **'CAL**↵
> >> Expression: **MEE**↵
> >> Select one endpoint for MEE: *(pick one corner of the rectangle)*
> >> Select another endpoint for MEE: *(pick the opposite corner of the rectangle)*
> *(coordinates)*
> Specify radius of circle or [Diameter] <*current*>: *(type a radius and press* [Enter] *or pick a radius)*

Figure 7-13.
Centering a circle
within a rectangle
using the **CAL**
command.

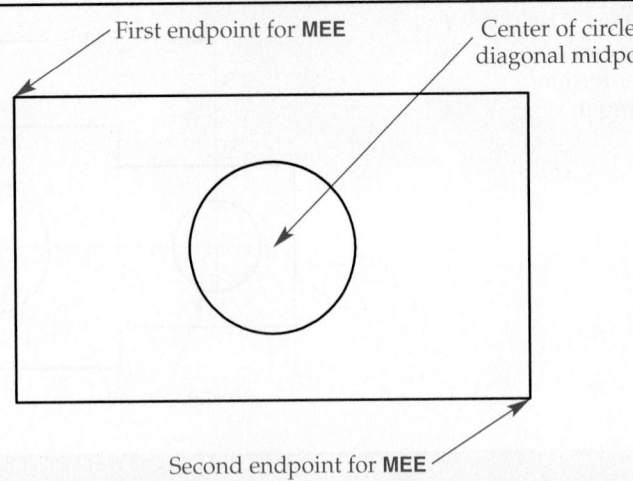

First endpoint for **MEE**

Center of circle at
diagonal midpoint

Second endpoint for **MEE**

**Exercise 7-10**

○ Start a new drawing.
○ Draw a line and then use **DEE** to determine the length.
○ Draw two intersecting lines and then use the **ILLE** function to find the intersection point.
○ Use the **MEE** function to help you create a drawing similar to **Figure 7-13**.
○ Save the drawing as EX7-10.

## Using Advanced Math Functions

A number of advanced mathematical functions are also supported by the geometry calculator. These include logarithmic and exponential functions, as well as some data modification and conversion functions. For example, you can calculate the square root of 25:

```
Command: CAL↵
>> Expression: SQRT(25)↵
5.0
```

The following table shows each of the advanced math operators supported by the geometry calculator.

| Function | Description |
|----------|-------------|
| **LN**(x) | Returns the natural log of a number. |
| **LOG**(x) | Returns the base-10 log of a number. |
| **EXP**(x) | Returns the natural exponent (or antilog) of a number. |
| **EXP10**(x) | Returns the base-10 exponent of a number. |
| **SQR**(x) | Returns a number squared. |
| **SQRT**(x) | Returns the square root of a number. |
| **ABS**(x) | Returns the absolute value (magnitude) of a number. |
| **ROUND**(x) | Rounds a number to the nearest integer value. |
| **TRUNC**(x) | Removes the decimal value of a number, returning the integer value. |

# Using Trigonometric Functions

When creating drawings, you often need to work with distances and angles. The geometry calculator supports several trigonometric functions for the calculations of distances and angles in a drawing. **Figure 7-14** shows the basic trigonometric operators and formulas.

The geometry calculator assumes the input for angular values is in degrees unless otherwise specified. This is regardless of the current angular units setting in AutoCAD. To enter angular data as degrees (d), minutes (') and seconds ("), use the format 30d45'15". If the minute or second value is zero, it can be omitted from the entry. For example, 42d0'30" can be written as 42d30". However, the degree value must be given, even if it is zero.

To enter a value in radians, use an *r* as a suffix for the number, such as 1.2r. A suffix of *g* indicates that the value is in grads, such as 50.00g. The geometry calculator output is always decimal degrees, regardless of the angular units style used for the input, except for the **D2R**(*angle*) function. The available trigonometric operators are shown in the following table.

| Function | Description |
|----------|-------------|
| **SIN**(*angle*) | Returns the sine of the angle. |
| **COS**(*angle*) | Returns the cosine of the angle. |
| **TANG**(*angle*) | Returns the tangent of the angle. |
| **ASIN**(*angle*) | Returns the arcsine of the angle. |
| **ACOS**(*angle*) | Returns the arccosine of the angle. |
| **ATAN**(*angle*) | Returns the arctangent of the angle. |
| D2R(*angle*) | Converts from degrees to radians. |
| R2D(*angle*) | Converts from radians to degrees. (Note: Do not use *r* suffix for this function.) |
| PI | The constant pi ($\pi$, 3.14159…) |

To provide an example of using trigonometric functions in the geometry calculator, the following sequence solves for angle *A* in **Figure 7-14.** The length of side *a* is 4.182 and side *c* is 5.136. Since the length of side *a* divided by the length of side *c* is equal to the sine of angle *A*, the arcsine of *a* ÷ *c* is equal to angle *A*:

```
Command: CAL↵
>> Expression: ASIN(4.182/5.136)↵
54.5135
```

**Figure 7-14.**
The elements of a right triangle and related trigonometric functions.

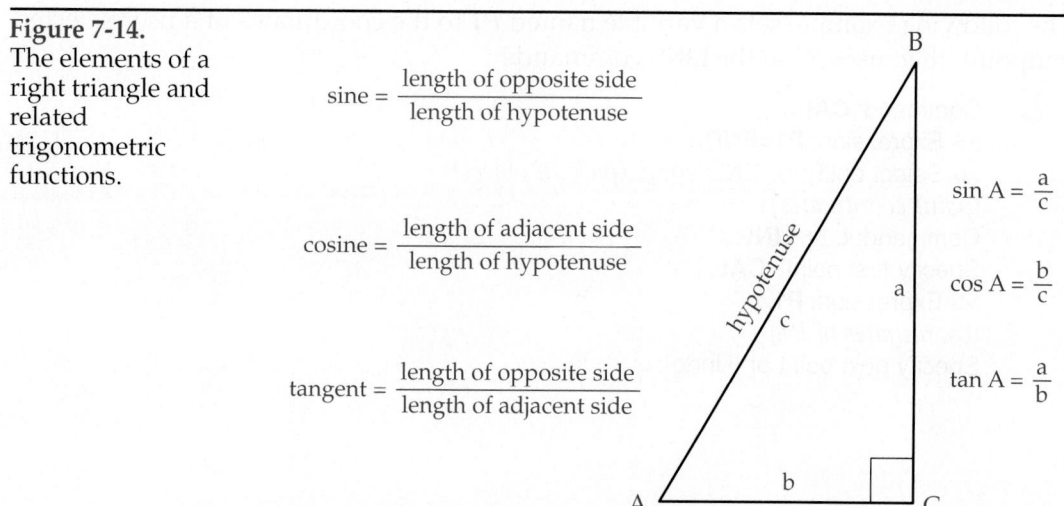

$$\text{sine} = \frac{\text{length of opposite side}}{\text{length of hypotenuse}}$$

$$\text{cosine} = \frac{\text{length of adjacent side}}{\text{length of hypotenuse}}$$

$$\text{tangent} = \frac{\text{length of opposite side}}{\text{length of adjacent side}}$$

$$\sin A = \frac{a}{c}$$

$$\cos A = \frac{b}{c}$$

$$\tan A = \frac{a}{b}$$

The returned value of 54.5135 indicates that angle $A$ is 54.5135°. Using the information in **Figure 7-14** and the geometry calculator, you can quickly solve for missing information needed to complete a drawing.

The constant *pi* ($\pi$) is presented in the trigonometry functions table. This constant is also used in circular formulas, such as $\pi R^2$ (circular area) or $2\pi R$ (circumference).

---

### Exercise 7-11

○ Start a new drawing.
○ Solve the following math problems with the geometry calculator.
  ○ Square root of 79.
  ○ 23 squared.
  ○ Sine of 30 degrees.
  ○ Cosine of 30 degrees.
  ○ Calculate the hypotenuse of a right triangle with side $a = 6$ and side $b = 2.5$. Refer to **Figure 7-14.**
  ○ Calculate angle $A$ of a right triangle with side $a = 6$ and side $b = 2.5$. Refer to **Figure 7-14.**
○ Save the drawing as EX7-11.

---

## Setting and Using Variables with the Geometry Calculator

The geometry calculator has the ability to save values by assigning them to a user-defined variable. A *variable* is a text item that represents a value stored for later use. Calculator variables can store only numeric, point, or vector data. The following example sets a variable named $X$ to a value of 1.2.

```
Command: CAL↵
>> Expression: X=1.25↵
1.25
```

The variable can be entered at a prompt by using the transparent **CAL** command:

```
Command: C or CIRCLE↵
Specify center point for circle or [3P/2P/Ttr (tan tan radius)]: (pick a center point)
Specify radius of circle or [Diameter] <current>: 'CAL↵
>> Expression: X
1.25
```

This extracts the value of the variable $X$ (1.25) and uses this as the radius of the circle. The following example sets a variable named *P1* to the coordinates of a user-selected endpoint, then uses *P1* in the **LINE** command:

```
Command: CAL↵
>> Expression: P1=END↵
>> Select entity for END snap: (pick an object)
(point coordinates)
Command: L or LINE↵
Specify first point: 'CAL↵
>> Expression: P1↵
(coordinates of P1)
Specify next point or [Undo]: ↵
```

## Using AutoCAD System Variables in the Geometry Calculator

In AutoCAD, many values are given a special name and stored for access whenever needed. These are called *system variables,* and their values depend on the current drawing or environment. The geometry calculator has a specialized function named **GETVAR** that allows you to use values stored in AutoCAD system variables. To retrieve a system variable, type **GETVAR(***variable name***)** at the Expression: prompt. The following example shows the drawing area being increased by multiplying the upper-right limits by 4:

> Command: **LIMITS**↵
> Reset Model space limits:
> Specify lower left corner or [ON/OFF] <0.0000,0.0000>: ↵
> Specify upper right corner <12.0000,9.0000>: **'CAL**↵ *(notice the current maximum limits are 12,9)*
> >> Expression: **4*GETVAR(LIMMAX)**↵
> (48.0 36.0 0.0)
> Command:

If you use the **LIMITS** command again, you will see the upper-right value has increased to 48,36.

A complete listing of system variables is available by typing **SETVAR** at the Command: prompt, followed by typing ?. This gives you the Enter variable(s) to list <*>: prompt. The default * lists all of the variables:

> Command: **SETVAR**↵
> Enter variable name or [?]: **?**↵
> Enter variable(s) to list <*>: ↵

This opens the **AutoCAD Text Window**, where all the system variables and their settings are listed. Continue pressing [Enter] to see the complete list. Press the [F2] key to return to the graphics window.

## Introduction to Filters

*Filters* allow you to select any aspect of an object on the screen while "filtering out" other objects, items, or features. A variety of applications for filters are covered in the rest of this chapter and throughout this text where specific applications are discussed. Filters used for layer control were introduced in Chapter 4.

## Drawing with X and Y Filters

X and Y filters control X and Y coordinates. There is also a Z filter for the Z coordinate, which is used in 3D applications. When working in 2D, the Z value is 0. The discussion in this section involves using the **LINE** command with X and Y filters.

.X
.Y

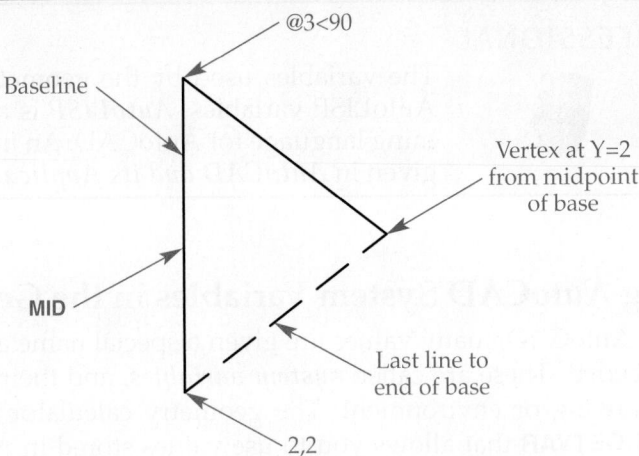

Figure 7-15.
Constructing an
isosceles triangle
using a Y filter.

Baseline

@3<90

Vertex at Y=2
from midpoint
of base

MID

Last line to
end of base

2,2

Suppose you want to construct an isosceles triangle with a height of 2″ from the baseline that you draw first. Refer to **Figure 7-15.** First, use this command sequence to establish the base of the triangle:

Command: **L** *or* **LINE**↵
Specify first point: **2,2**↵
Specify next point or [Undo]: **@3<90**↵

Now, place the vertex 2″ from the midpoint of the baseline:

Specify next point or [Undo]: **.Y**↵
of **MID**↵
of *(pick the baseline)*
of (need XZ): **@2,0**↵

When not specified, as in @2,0, the Z value is assumed to be 0. Finally, complete the triangle with the **Close** option:

Specify next point or [Undo]: **C**↵
Command:

Earlier in this chapter you learned to construct a circle at the center of a rectangle using the geometry calculator expression **(END+END)/2** (or **MEE** shortcut function). The same operation can be performed using X and Y filters. As an example, suppose you want to place the center of a circle at the center of a rectangle, as shown in **Figure 7-16.** The command sequence is:

Command: **C** *or* **CIRCLE**↵
Specify center point for circle or [3P/2P/Ttr (tan tan radius)]: **.X**↵
of **MID**↵
of *(pick a horizontal line)*
of (need YZ): **MID**↵
of *(pick a vertical line)*
Specify radius of circle or [Diameter] <current>: *(specify the radius)*
Command:

In this example, the X value is filtered before the YZ value. However, the same operation can be performed by filtering the Y value first, and then the XZ value.

AutoCAD and its Applications—Basics

Pick near midpoint
Pick near
the midpoint
Pick or type
a radius value


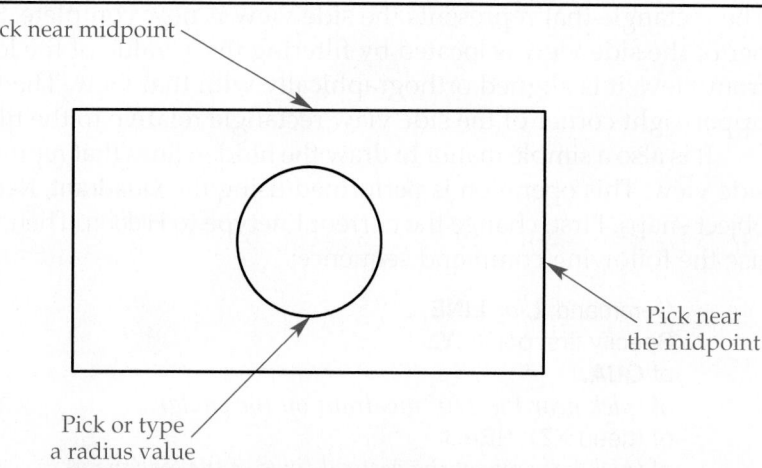

**Figure 7-16.** Centering a circle inside a rectangle using X and Y filters.

**Exercise 7-12**

- ❍ Start AutoCAD and use the setup option of your choice.
- ❍ Use the X and Y filters as previously discussed to assist you in making a drawing similar to Figures 7-15 and 7-16.
- ❍ Save the drawing as EX7-12.

## Using X and Y Filters to Project Views

If you draw the object shown in **Figure 7-17** on a drafting board, you would probably draw the front view first. Then, using drafting instruments, you might project construction lines and points from the front view to complete the right side view. Filters can be used to perform similar projection operations.

The front view of a rectangular object can be drawn very efficiently using the **RECTANG** command. The circle can then be constructed using X and Y filters, as previously described. Then, the command sequence to draw the side view is:

Command: **REC** *or* **RECTANG**↵
Specify first corner point or [Chamfer/Elevation/Fillet/Thickness/Width]: **.Y**↵
of **END**↵
of *(pick near the endpoint of the bottom horizontal line)*
of (need XZ): *(pick a point to set distance between the views)*
Specify other corner point or [Dimensions]: **@2.5,5**↵
Command:

8.50
4.25
2.50
5.00
2.50
ø2.50


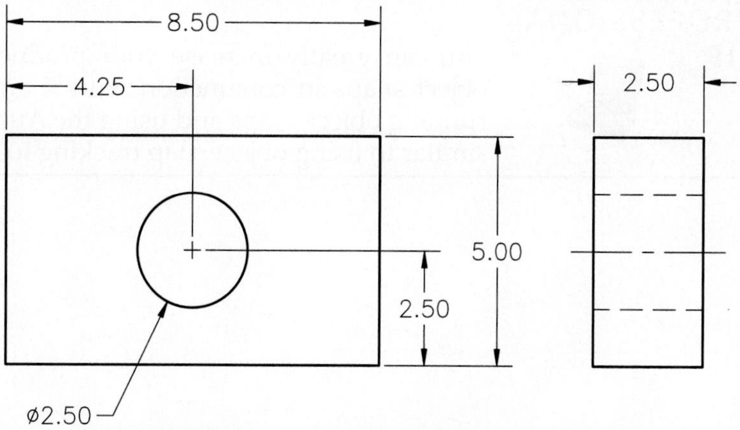

**Figure 7-17.** A simple orthographic drawing.

The rectangle that represents the side view is now complete. Since the lower-left corner of the side view is located by filtering the Y value of the lower-right corner of the front view, it is aligned orthographically with that view. The @2.5,5 entry locates the upper-right corner of the side view rectangle relative to the filtered point.

It is also a simple matter to draw the hidden lines that represent the circle seen in the side view. This operation is performed using the **Quadrant**, **Nearest**, and **Perpendicular** object snaps. First, change the current linetype to Hidden. Then, refer to **Figure 7-18** and use the following command sequence:

> Command: **L** *or* **LINE**↵
> Specify first point: **.Y**↵
> of **QUA**↵
> of *(pick near the 270° quadrant on the circle)*
> of (need XZ): **NEA**↵
> of *(pick near one of the vertical lines of the side view)*
> Specify next point or [Undo]: **PER**↵
> of *(pick on the opposite vertical line in the side view)*
> Specify next point or [Undo]: ↵
> Command:

**Figure 7-18.**
"Projecting" lines using X and Y filters.

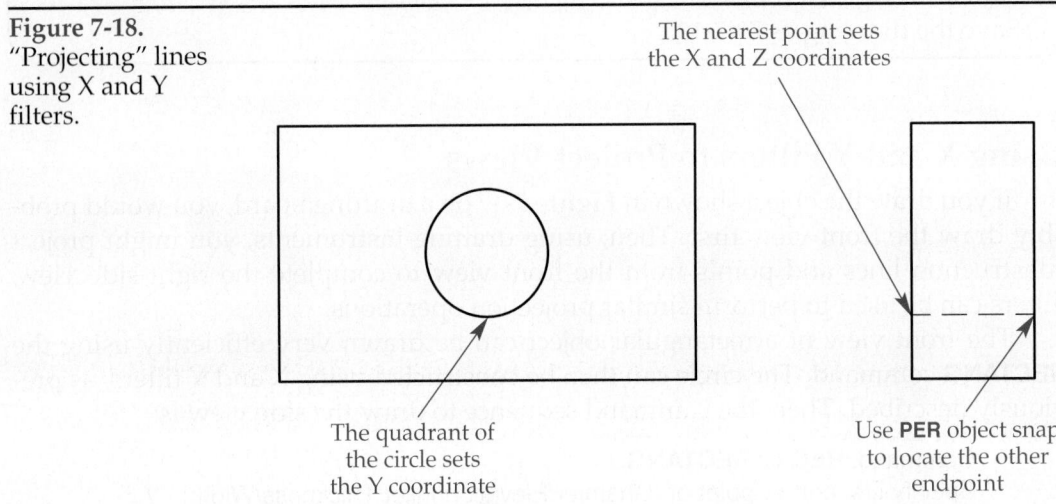

The nearest point sets the X and Z coordinates

The quadrant of the circle sets the Y coordinate

Use **PER** object snap to locate the other endpoint

Now that one of the hidden lines is drawn, you can repeat the procedure to draw the second hidden line. However, an easier way is to use the **OFFSET** command to offset the first hidden line at the required distance.

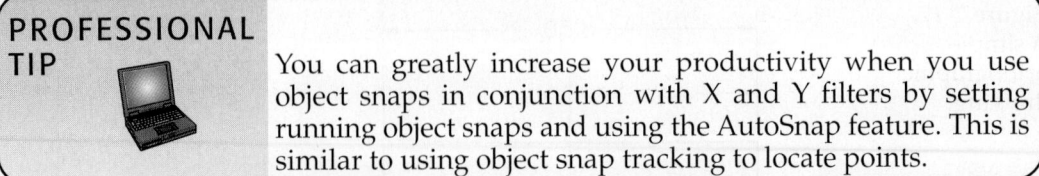

**PROFESSIONAL TIP**

You can greatly increase your productivity when you use object snaps in conjunction with X and Y filters by setting running object snaps and using the AutoSnap feature. This is similar to using object snap tracking to locate points.

## Creating Selection Sets

When creating complex drawings, you often need to perform the same editing operation to many objects. For example, assume you have designed a complex metal part with over 40 holes for 1/8″ bolts. A design change occurs, and you are notified that 3/16″ bolts will be used instead of 1/8″ bolts. Therefore, the hole size will also change. You could select and modify each circle individually, but it would be more efficient to create a selection set of all the circles and then modify them simultaneously.

AutoCAD provides two methods of creating selection sets: the **QSELECT** (quick select) command and the **FILTER** command. The **QSELECT** command is used to create simple selection sets by specifying object types and property values for selection. The **FILTER** command provides additional selection criteria and allows you to save selection sets.

### Using Quick Select to Create Selection Sets

One way to filter for different objects in a drawing is by using the **QSELECT** command. With **QSELECT**, you can quickly create a selection set based on the filtering criteria you specify. To access the command, pick **Quick Select...** in the **Tools** pull-down menu, type QSELECT at the Command: prompt, or right-click in the drawing area and choose **Quick Select...** from the shortcut menu. This displays the **Quick Select** dialog box. See **Figure 7-19.** You can also open the **Quick Select** dialog box by picking the **Quick Select** button in the **Properties** window.

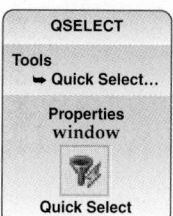

QSELECT

Tools
➥ Quick Select...

Properties
window

Quick Select

A selection set can be defined in several ways using the **Quick Select** dialog box:

- Pick the **Select objects** button and select the objects on screen.
- Specify an object type (such as text, line, or circle) to be selected throughout the drawing.
- Specify a property (such as a color or layer) that objects must possess in order to be selected.

Once the selection criteria are defined, you can use the radio buttons in the **How to apply:** area to include or exclude the defined objects.

Look at **Figure 7-20** as you follow this example that uses the **Quick Select** command:

1. Select **Quick Select...** from the **Tools** pull-down menu to open the **Quick Select** dialog box.
2. In the **Apply to:** drop-down list, select **Entire drawing**. If you access the **Quick Select** dialog box after a selection set is defined there is also a **Current selection** option that allows you to create a subset of the existing set.
3. In the **Object type:** drop-down list, select **Multiple**. This will allow you to select any object type. The drop-down list contains all the object types in the drawing.

Figure 7-19
Selection sets can be defined in the **Quick Select** dialog box.

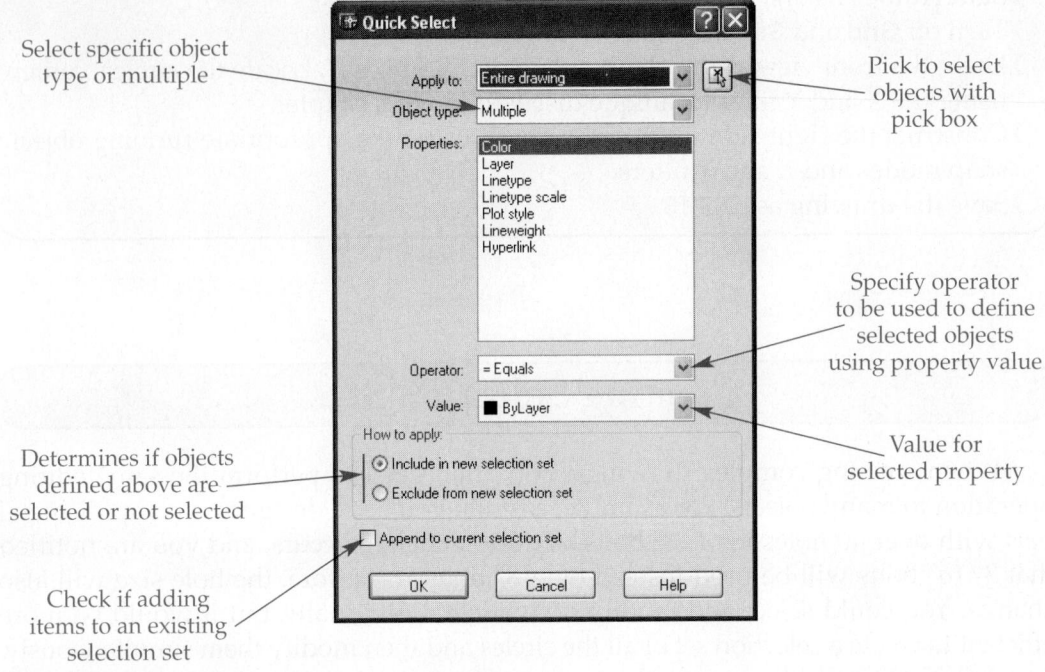

Select specific object type or multiple

Pick to select objects with pick box

Specify operator to be used to define selected objects using property value

Value for selected property

Determines if objects defined above are selected or not selected

Check if adding items to an existing selection set

Figure 7-20.
Creating selection sets with the **Quick Select** dialog box. A—Objects in drawing.
B—Selection set containing objects with the display color specified. C—Circle object added to initial selection set.

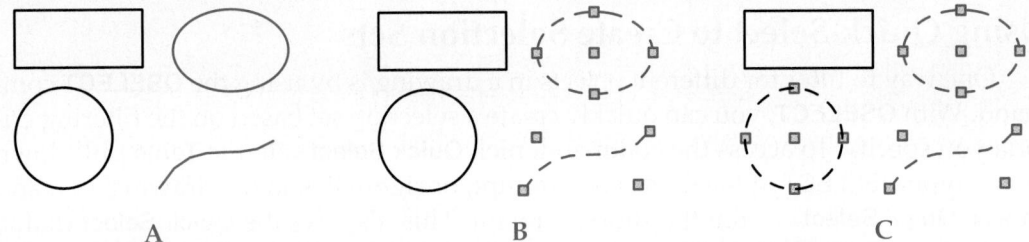

A         B         C

4. In the **Properties:** list, select **Color**. The items in the **Properties:** list vary depending on what is specified in the **Object type:** drop-down list.
5. In the **Operator:** drop-down list, select **= Equals**.
6. The **Value:** drop-down list contains values corresponding to the entry in the **Properties:** drop-down list. In this case, color values are listed. Select the color of the right-hand objects in **Figure 7-20A**.
7. Under the **How to apply:** area, pick the **Include in new selection set** radio button.
8. Pick the **OK** button.

AutoCAD selects all objects with the color specified in the **Value:** drop-down list, as shown in **Figure 7-20B**.

Once a set of objects has been selected, the **Quick Select** dialog box can be used to refine the selection set. Use the **Exclude from new selection set** option to exclude objects or use the **Append to current selection set** option to add objects. The following procedure refines the selection set created above to include any circles in the drawing that have a black color.

1. While the initial set of objects is selected, right-click in the drawing area and select **Quick Select...** from the shortcut menu to open the **Quick Select** dialog box.

2. Check the **Append to current selection set** check box at the bottom of the dialog box. AutoCAD automatically selects the **Entire drawing** option in the **Apply to:** drop-down list.
3. Select **Circle** in the **Object type:** drop-down list, **Color** in the **Properties:** drop-down list, **= Equals** in the **Operator:** drop-down list, and **Black** (or **ByLayer**, as appropriate) in the **Value:** drop-down list.
4. In the **How to apply:** area, pick the **Include in new selection set** radio button.
5. Pick the **OK** button. The selection now appears as shown in **Figure 7-20C**.

## Using Filters to Create a Selection Set

The **FILTER** command is used to create a list of property criteria that must be met in order for a specific object to be selected. Filter lists can be created for use at any time. These filter lists are accessed at any Select object: prompt.

The **FILTER** command is accessed by typing FI or FILTER. This opens the **Object Selection Filters** dialog box, **Figure 7-21**. The **FILTER** command can also be used transparently by typing 'FILTER at the Select object: prompt.

The three major areas of the **Object Selection Filters** dialog box are the list box, the **Select Filter** area, and the **Named Filters** area. The list box is where the current filter list data is displayed, the **Select Filter** area is used to specify filter criteria, and the **Named Filters** area is used to save filters for future use.

FILTER
FI

### Entering filter data

The **Select Filter** area of the **Object Selection Filters** dialog box is where filter data are entered. The drop-down list and edit boxes can be used to enter the values for the filters. Objects in a drawing can even be selected to develop a filter.

The three edit boxes correspond to X, Y, and Z point coordinates. They are enabled as needed for entering different types of filter information. When the filter drop-down list reads **Arc**, it refers to an object type. Since no further information is required about the object type, the edit boxes are all disabled. Setting the filter to **Arc Center** enables all three edit boxes, which are used to define the center point. When **Arc Radius** is selected, only the top edit box is enabled because only a single value is required. An example of each of these situations is shown in **Figure 7-22**.

For many filter specifications, such as layer, linetype, and color, the **Select...** button is enabled. When picked, this button displays the appropriate dialog box for showing the available options. For example, if **Color** is the specified filter, the **Select...** button displays the standard **Select Color** dialog box.

**Figure 7-21.**
The **Object Selection Filters** dialog box.

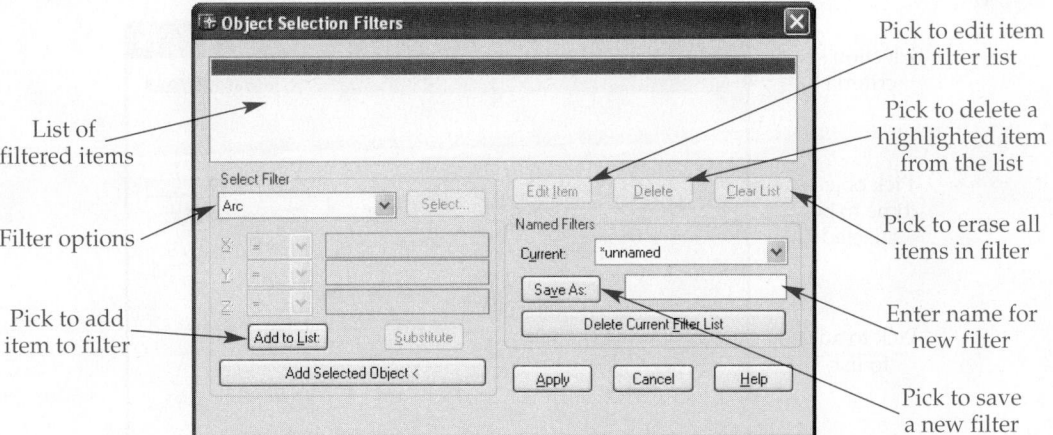

Chapter 7 Using the Geometry Calculator and Filters

**Figure 7-22.**
This shows examples of filter items with the **X:**, **Y:**, and **Z:** edit boxes enabled as needed.

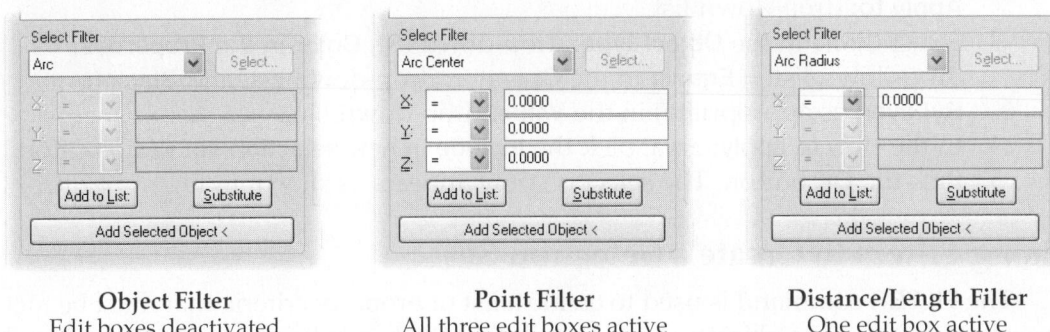

| **Object Filter** | **Point Filter** | **Distance/Length Filter** |
|---|---|---|
| Edit boxes deactivated | All three edit boxes active | One edit box active |

Once the desired filter and value(s) are specified, you must add these data to the list. Pick the **Add to List** button to add the new item to the existing filter list. The list at the top of the dialog box is updated.

To use an existing object as a basis for a filter list, pick the **Add Selected Object** button. This temporarily closes the **Object Selection Filters** dialog box and gives you a Select object: prompt. Once an object is selected, you are returned to the dialog box. The information from the selected object is placed in the filter list. Since you may not need all of the filter list specifications that result from picking an object, the filter list can now be edited as needed.

To remove an item from the filter list, highlight it and pick the **Delete** button. To clear the entire list and start over, pick the **Clear List** button. To edit an item in the list, highlight the item and pick the **Edit Item** button. Editing the filter list is discussed in more detail later in this chapter.

To introduce applications of selection filters, the following example creates a simple filter list that selects only circle objects:

Command: **FI** *or* **FILTER.**⏎

This displays the **Object Selection Filters** dialog box. In the **Select Filter** area, pick the drop-down list to see the selection filter options. From this list, select **Circle**. To add this specification to the filter list, pick the **Add to List** button. The list box now displays this selection criteria as **Object = Circle**. This shows that only circle objects will be selected. See **Figure 7-23.** To use the selection filter, pick the **Apply** button. The dialog box is closed, and the following prompt is issued:

**Figure 7-23.**
Setting the filter so that only circles are selected.

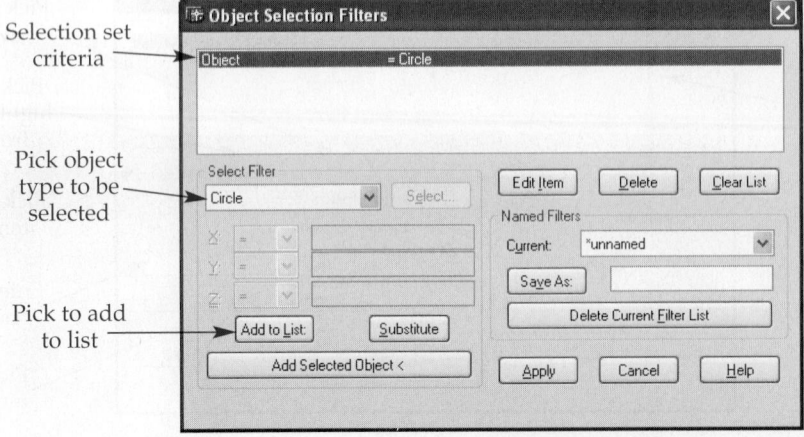

AutoCAD and its Applications—Basics

**Figure 7-24.**
All objects are
filtered out except
for the circles.

Selection
window

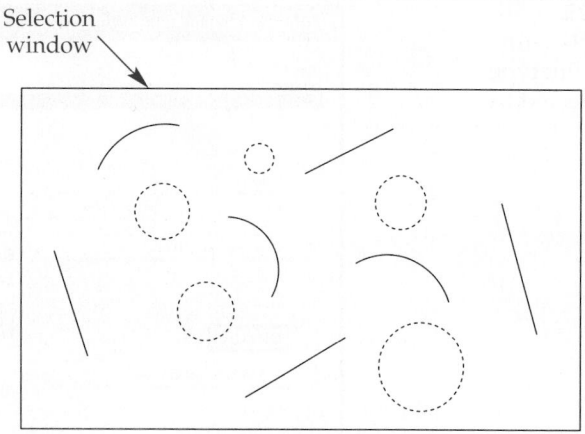

Applying filter to selection.
Select objects: *(use window, crossing, fence, or* **ALL** *to select objects)*

The prompt tells you that the filter is active. In **Figure 7-24,** a selection window is created around a group of lines, arcs, and circles. Because the filter is set to allow only circle objects, all other object types are filtered out of the selection. AutoCAD reports the number of objects found and the number filtered out (not selected):

13 found 8 were filtered out.
Select objects:

To exit the filtered selection, press [Enter] at the Select objects: prompt. The message Exiting filtered selection appears on the command line and the selected objects are displayed with grips. If the **FILTER** command was entered transparently, pressing [Enter] displays the message Resuming *(command)* command. That command's normal Select objects: prompt is displayed.

Filter lists can be expanded to select only objects with specific properties. The next example creates a filter list that selects only line objects that have a CENTER linetype. The steps are:

1. Enter the **FILTER** command and clear the list box by picking the **Clear List** button. This starts a new filter list.
2. From the drop-down list in the **Select Filter** area, select **Line**, then pick the **Add to List** button. This adds the filter **Object = Line** to the list box.
3. Select **Linetype** in the drop-down list and then pick the **Select...** button to display the **Select Linetype(s)** dialog box. Select the CENTER linetype and pick the **OK** button.
4. Pick the **Add to List** button. The **Object Selection Filters** dialog box should appear as shown in **Figure 7-25.**

By adding additional filters to the filter list, a filter can be extremely specific when needed. Filters for a specific location or a specific text string can be useful when selecting items in very large, complex drawings.

---

### Exercise 7-14

○ Start AutoCAD and use the setup option of your choice.
○ Draw a group of lines, arcs, and circles similar to **Figure 7-24.**
○ Use the **FILTER** command to create a filter that selects only circles.
○ Use a selection window around all objects and observe which are selected.
○ Save the drawing as EX7-14.

---

**Figure 7-25.**
Line objects with
**CENTER** linetype
will be selected by
this filter.

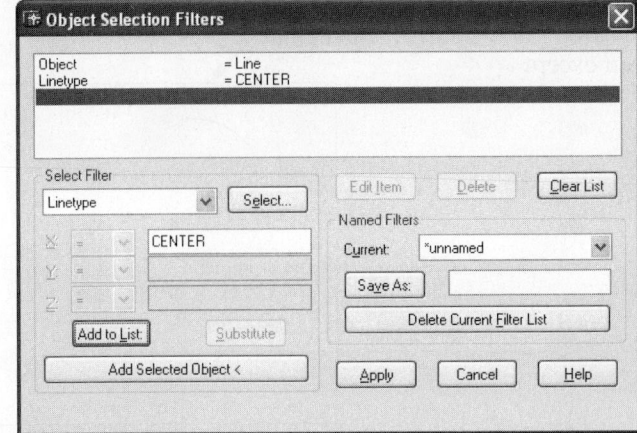

## Working with relative operators

The term *relative operator* refers to functions that determine the relationship between data items. These relationships include equality, inequality, greater than, less than, and combinations such as greater than or equal to and less than or equal to. Each of the three edit boxes in the **Select Filter** area are preceded by a relative operator drop-down list. By default, the operator is as "equal to" when the list is enabled. An appropriate relative operator can be selected for each data field.

For example, a relative operator can be used to select all arcs that have a radius of 2.5 or greater. To do this, the filter specification is **Arc Radius** with 2.5 entered in the enabled edit box. Then, select the greater than or equal to symbol (**>=**) in the relative operator drop-down list. See **Figure 7-26.** The following chart shows the relative operator functions:

| Symbol | Meaning |
|--------|---------|
| = | Equal to |
| != | Not equal to |
| < | Less than |
| <= | Less than or equal to |
| > | Greater than |
| >= | Greater than or equal to |
| × | Equal to any value |

**Figure 7-26.**
The greater than or
equal to filtering
option.

Relative operator
drop-down list

Enter setting
value

Pick to select
an object with
properties
to be filtered

Pick after editing
an item from the
filter list

## Editing the filter list

Editing capabilities are provided that allow you to modify and delete filter list items. If you accidentally enter an incorrect filter specification, you can easily correct it using these steps.

1. Highlight the item in the filter list that you need to edit and pick the **Edit Item** button. The values for the selected specification are then entered in the **Select Filter** area and can be freely edited.
2. Change the values as necessary.
3. Pick the **Substitute** button when finished. The edited filter specification is substituted for the highlighted item. Be sure to pick **Substitute** and not **Add to List**; otherwise, you end up with two different values for the same filter specification in the filter list.

To remove an item from the filter list, highlight it and select the **Delete** button. Only one filter specification can be deleted at a time using this method. If you need to remove all of the current specifications and start over, pick the **Clear List** button.

## Creating named filters

The most powerful feature of CAD is being able to benefit from work you have already done. By reusing previous work instead of repeating the work to produce duplicate results, you increase your efficiency and overall productivity levels.

Complex filter lists can be time-consuming to develop. However, AutoCAD allows you to name and save filter lists. Then, you can recall the lists for future use. The **Named Filters** area of the **Object Selection Filters** dialog box is used to create and manage these lists.

When you have created a filter list that you plan to use again, it should be named and saved. When the filter list is completed and tested, follow these steps to name and save the list.

1. Pick in the edit box to the right of the **Save As:** button.
2. Type a short, descriptive name in the edit box. The name for a filter list can be up to 18 characters in length. These named filter lists are stored in a file named filter.nfl and are available until deleted.
3. Pick the **Save As:** button to save the named filter.

To delete a saved filter list, make it current by picking the filter name in the **Current:** drop-down list. Then, pick the **Delete Current Filter List** button.

---

### Exercise 7-15

○ Start AutoCAD and use the setup option of your choice.
○ Establish the filter list that was used in Exercise 7-14. Name and save it as CIRCLE.
○ Save the drawing as EX7-15.

---

## Using filters on a drawing

Filters can increase productivity, but you must learn to recognize situations when they can be used. Imagine that you have just created the flowchart in Figure 7-27. You are then asked to change all of the text inside the flowchart to a new layer and color for plotting considerations. You could use the **Properties** window and individually select each word on the chart, but you decide to use the **FILTER** command to make the job easier. Access the command to open the **Object Selection Filters** dialog box, and follow these steps.

1. Pick the **Add Selected Object** button. The drawing returns with a Select object: prompt. Pick a text element within any one of the boxes.

---

**Figure 7-27.**
Original flowchart requiring modification.

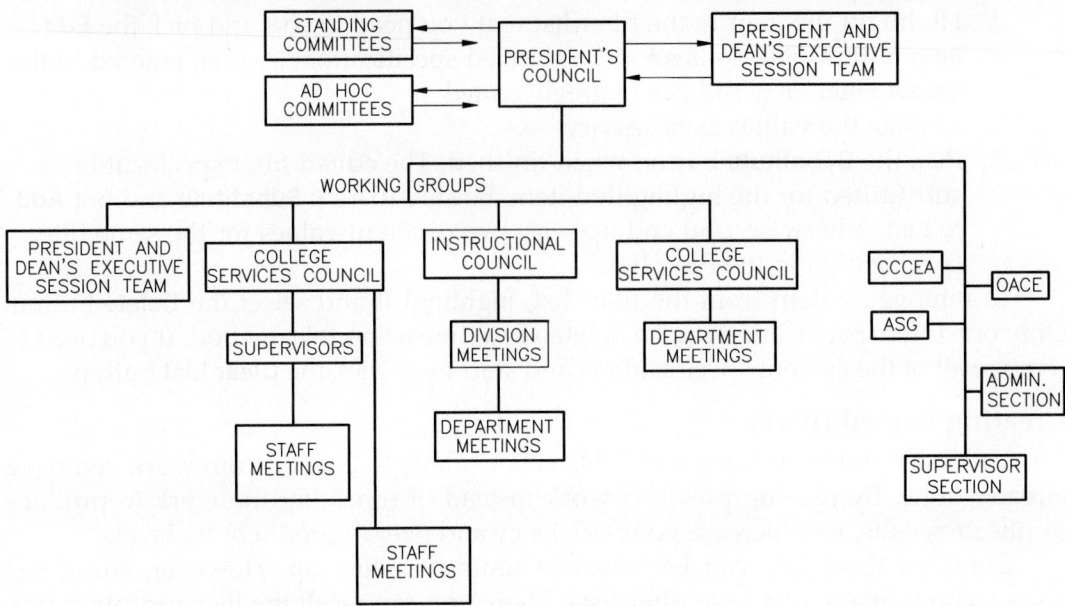

## GROUP DECISION MAKING PROCESS

2. The dialog box returns and displays the characteristics of the text you picked. Highlight items such as Text Position and Text Value and pick the **Delete** button for each. See **Figure 7-28.** These filters are not needed because they limit the filter list to specific aspects of the text.

3. Enter a filter name, such as TEXT, in the **Save As:** text box and then pick the **Save As:** button. TEXT becomes the current filter name.

4. Pick the **Apply** button. The drawing returns and you are prompted:

> Select object:
> Applying filter to selection.
> Select objects: **ALL**↵
> Select objects: Specify opposite corner: 144 found
> 106 were filtered out.
> *(the text within the flowchart is now highlighted)*
> Select objects: ↵
> Exiting filter selection.
> Command:

5. All text is selected and displayed with grips.

6. Use the **Properties** window or other editing method to modify the selected text. The revised flowchart is shown in **Figure 7-29.**

---

**Figure 7-28.**
Deleting selection filters that are too specific.

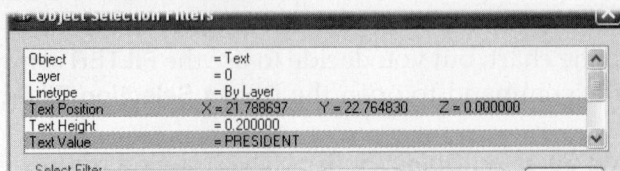

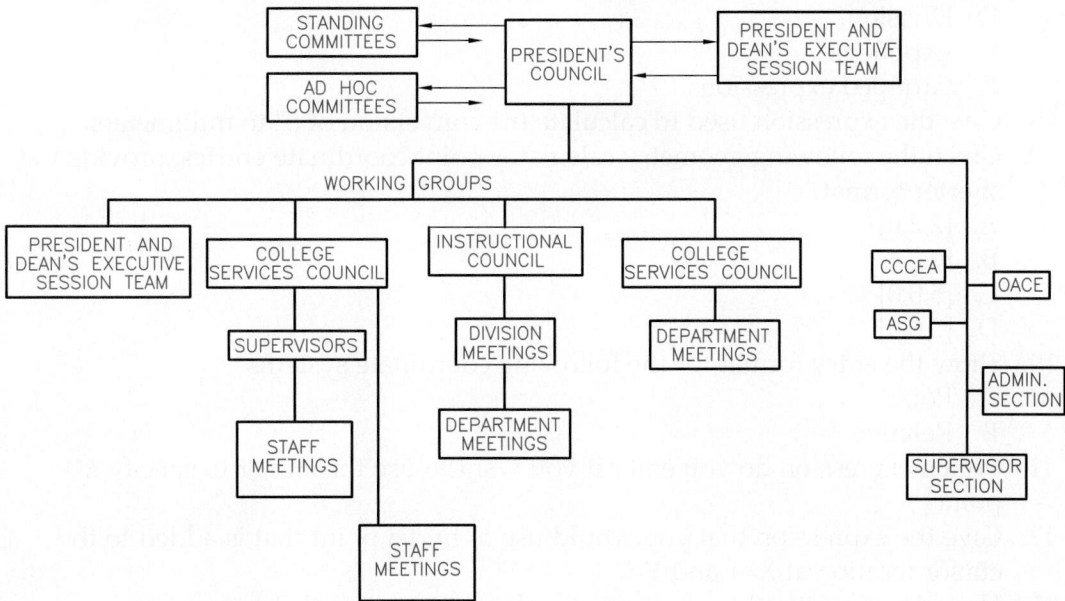

GROUP DECISION MAKING PROCESS

## Express Selection

You can greatly increase your productivity when using the **Get Selection Set** express tool for selecting objects on the same layer(s). The **Get Selection Set** express tool is used as follows:

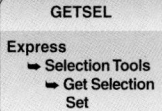

1. Pick **Get Selection Set** in the **Selection Tools** cascading menu in the **Express** pull-down or type GETSEL at the Command: prompt.
2. Select an object on the source layer you want to edit.
3. Select an object of the type you want and a selection set, or press [Enter] for all objects.
4. Start the editing command of your choice.
5. At the Select objects: prompt type P for the previous selection set.

Note that after using the **Get Selection Set** express tool that no objects are selected with grips. You must use the **Previous** option at a Select objects: prompt to select the objects.

## Chapter Test

*Answer the following questions on a separate sheet of paper.*

1. Identify the command that starts the geometry calculator.
2. Define *expression*.
3. What is the order of operations within an expression?
4. Give an example of an integer.
5. Give an example of a real number.
6. Show three examples of how the measurement *five feet six inches* can be entered when using the **CAL** command.

7. Give the proper symbol to use for the following math functions.
   A. Addition.
   B. Subtraction.
   C. Multiplication.
   D. Division.
   E. Exponent.
   F. Grouped expressions.
8. Give the expression used to calculate the conversion of 8″ to millimeters.
9. Given the following geometry calculator point coordinate entries, provide the shorter format.
   A. [2,2,0]
   B. [0,0,6]
   C. [5,0,0]
   D. [0,0,0]
10. Show the entry format for the following coordinate systems.
    A. Polar.
    B. Relative.
11. Which expression do you enter if you want to use the cursor to specify a point?
12. Give the expression that you would use to find a point that is added to the cursor location at X=1 and Y=2.
13. How do you enter the geometry calculator transparently?
14. Why are object snaps often used when finding points for the geometry calculator?
15. How do you enter an object snap within the geometry calculator?
16. Give the expression used to find the distance halfway between the endpoints of two lines.
17. Give the expression used to calculate the distance between the center of two circles.
18. Give the expression used to find the shortest distance from the end of a line to another line with two available endpoints.
19. Give the expression needed to find the distance between the last point used in AutoCAD and the point located at coordinates 4,4,0.
20. Identify the function that is used to find the intersection point between two nonparallel lines.
21. Name the function that is used to find an angle.
22. Give the expression used to identify the included angle when the vertex and sides are available.
23. Provide the function that is used to find the radius of a circle, arc, or 2D polyline.
24. Give the shortcut functions for the following applications.
    A. Distance between two selected endpoints.
    B. Intersection of two lines defined by four selected endpoints.
    C. Point midway between two selected endpoints.
25. Give the function for the following math operations.
    A. Returns a number squared.
    B. Returns the square root of a number.
26. Give an example of the full format for entering degrees, minutes, and seconds in the geometry calculator.
27. Give the trigonometric functions for the following operations.
    A. Returns the sine of angle.
    B. Returns the cosine of angle.
    C. Returns the tangent of angle.
28. Give the function for calculating the constant pi.

29. A _____ is a text item that represents another value that can be accessed later as needed.
30. What is the purpose of X, Y, and Z filters?
31. Name the command that allows you to quickly create a selection set based on the filtering criteria that you specify.
32. Identify four ways to open the **Quick Select** dialog box.
33. Define *filters.*
34. How do you enter the **FILTER** command transparently?
35. What happens when you enter the **FILTER** command?
36. What is the purpose of the list box in the **Object Selection Filters** dialog box?
37. What is the purpose of the **Select Filter** area in the **Object Selection Filters** dialog box?
38. What is the purpose of the **Named Filters** area in the **Object Selection Filters** dialog box?
39. How do you remove an item from the filter list?
40. How do you clear the entire filter list and start over again?
41. Which relative operator is used to select all arcs that have a radius of 4.3 or less?
42. If you want to use filters to make changes to the text on your drawing and you pick one of the text objects, the dialog box displays the characteristics of the text you picked. Why is it best to delete items such as Text Position and Text Value?
43. If you add circles to the filter list, what happens when a selection window is placed around a group of lines, arcs, and circles?
44. Identify two ways to specify a linetype in a filter list.
45. Provide the following relative operator symbols.
    A. Not equal to.
    B. Less than.
    C. Less than or equal to.
    D. Greater than.
    E. Greater than or equal to.
    F. Equal to any value.

## Drawing Problems

*Use the **CAL** command to calculate the result of the following equations.*

1. $27.375 + 15.875$
2. $16.0625 - 7.1250$
3. $5 \times 17'\text{-}8''$
4. $48'\text{-}0'' \div 16$
5. $(12.625 + 3.063) + (18.250 - 4.375) - (2.625 - 1.188)$
6. $7.25^2$

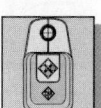

7. Show the calculation and answer that would be used with the **LINE** command to make an 8″ line 1.006 in./in. longer in a pattern to allow for shrinkage in the final casting. Show only the expression and answer.
8. Solve for the deflection of a structural member. The formula is written as $PL^3/48EI$, where P = pounds of force, L = length of beam, E = Modulus of Elasticity, and I = moment of inertia. The values to be used are P = 4000 lbs, L = 240″, and E = 1,000,000 lbs/in². The value for I is the result of the beam (Width × Height³)/12, where Width = 6.75″ and Height = 13.5″.

9. Convert 4.625″ to millimeters.
10. Convert 26 mm to inches.
11. Convert 65 miles to kilometers.
12. Convert 5 gallons to liters.
13. Calculate the coordinate located at 4,4,0 + 3<30.
14. Calculate the coordinate located at (3 + 5,1 + 1.25,0) + (2.375,1.625,0).
15. Find the square root of 360.
16. Calculate 3.25 squared.

*Given the following right triangle, make the required trigonometry calculations.*

17. Length of side *c* (hypotenuse).
18. Sine of angle *A*.
19. Sine of angle *B*.
20. Cosine of angle *A*.
21. Tangent of angle *A*.
22. Tangent of angle *B*.

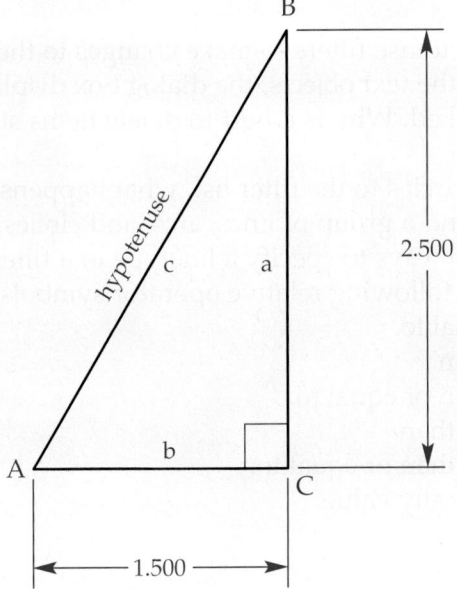

23. Create the following drawing. Use the **CAL** command and object snaps as needed to help you. Do not draw dimensions. Save the drawing as P7-23.

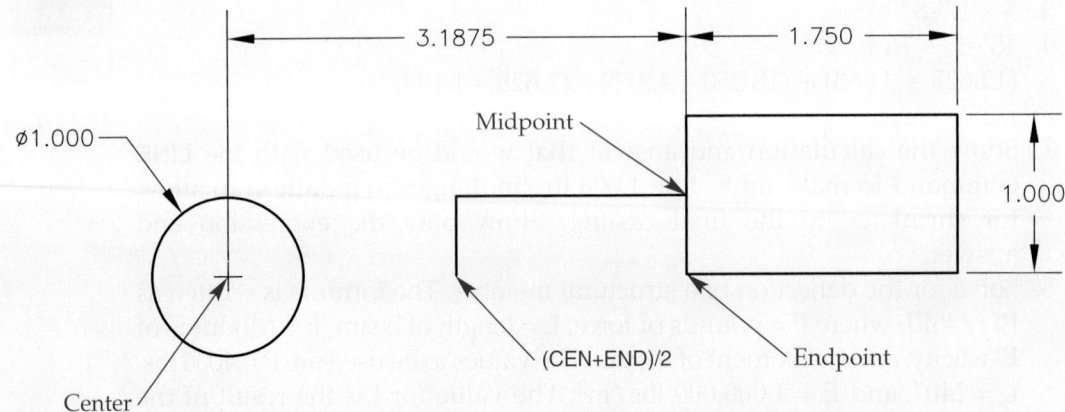

24. Open P7-23 and add the circle as shown below. Save the drawing as P7-24.

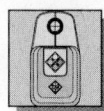

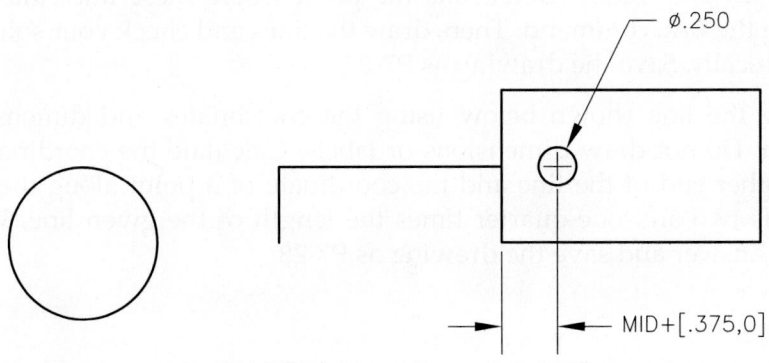

Ø.250

MID+[.375,0]

25. Create the following drawing. Use the **CAL** command and object snaps as needed to help you. Place the circle with its center at the centroid (center of mass) of the triangle. Do not draw dimensions. Save the drawing as P7-25.

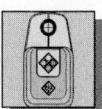

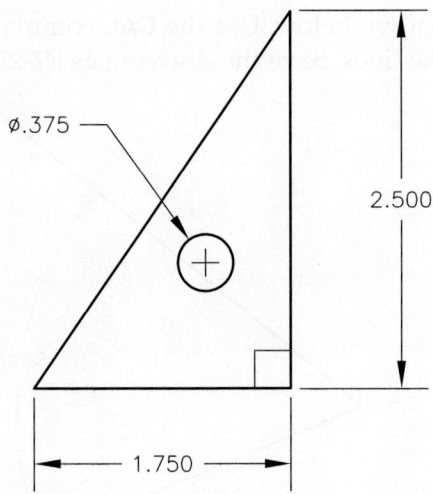

Ø.375

2.500

1.750

26. Draw the lines shown below using the dimensions given. Do not draw dimensions or labels. Save the drawing as P7-26. Then, calculate:
    A. Length of Line A.
    B. Length of Line B.
    C. Shortest distance between Point P and Line B.

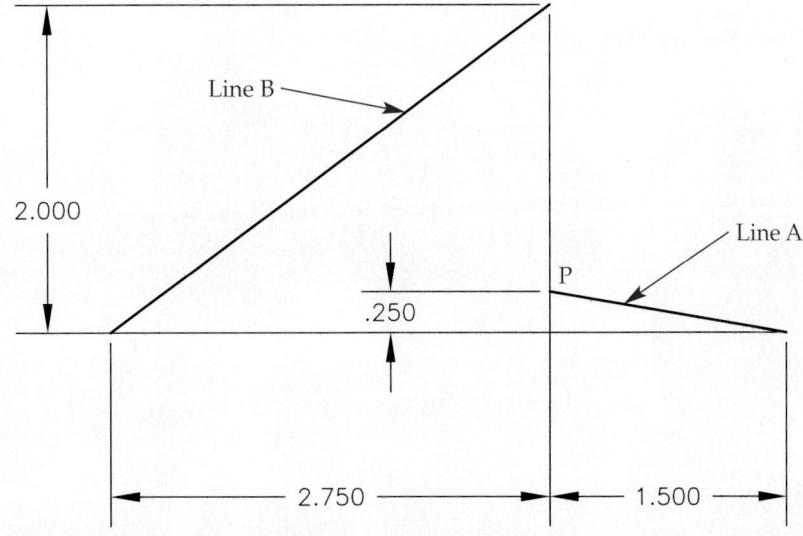

Line B

Line A

P

2.000

.250

2.750

1.500

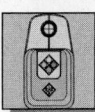

27. Line A has endpoints at 2.88,8.88 and 6.50,6.75. Line B has endpoints at 1.75,7.25 and 6.5,8.5. Determine the point where these lines intersect using the **CAL** command. Then, draw the lines and check your solution graphically. Save the drawing as P7-27.

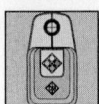

28. Draw the line shown below using the coordinates and dimensions given. Do not draw dimensions or labels. Calculate the coordinate at the other end of the line and the coordinate of a point along the line that is two and one-quarter times the length of the given line. Write your answer and save the drawing as P7-28.

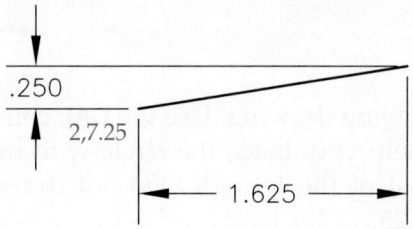

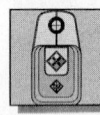

29. Draw the lines shown below. Use the **CAL** command to determine the angle between the lines. Save the drawing as P7-29.

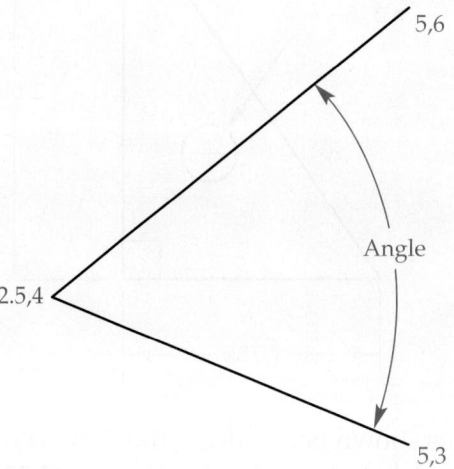

30. Draw a rectangle measuring 3.125 × 5.625. Use the **CAL** command to center a .75 diameter circle in the rectangle. Save the drawing as P7-30.

31. Draw the following object. Do not include dimensions. Then, use the **CAL** command to add another circle with a diameter that is 30% of the size of the existing circle. Center the new circle between the midpoints of Line 1 and Line 2. Save the drawing as P7-31.

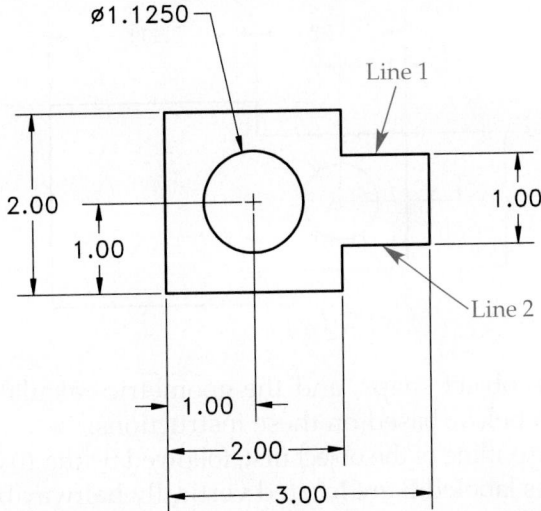

32. Draw the following object. Do not include dimensions. Then, use the **CAL** command to create another circle with the same diameter as the existing circle. Place the center of the new circle .5" above a point that is midway between the center of the existing circle and the midpoint of the right-hand line of the object. Save the drawing as P7-32.

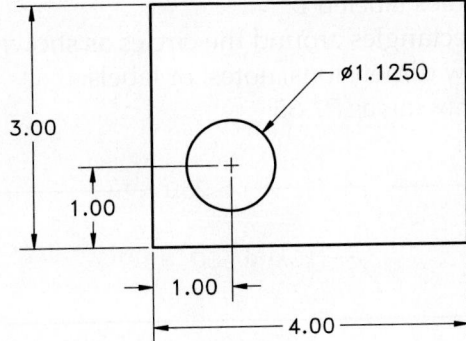

33. Use the X and Y filters to draw an isosceles triangle with a vertical base-line measuring 4.5" long and 5.75" high. Save the drawing as P7-33.

34. Draw the object shown below. Do not dimension the drawing. Then, use the **CAL** command to create another circle with a diameter that is 150 percent (1.5X) of the existing circle. Vertically center the new circle 3″ to the right of the existing circle. Save the drawing as P7-34.

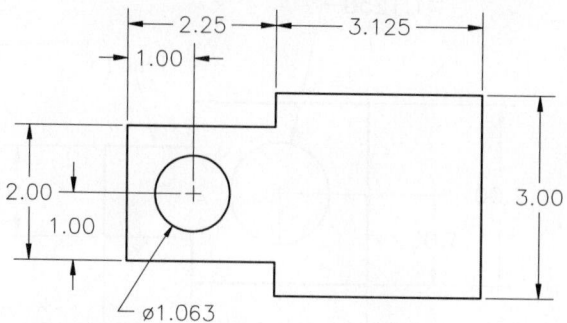

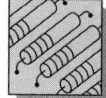

35. Use tracking, object snaps, and the geometric calculator to draw the object shown below based on these instructions:
    A.  Draw the outline of the object first, followed by the 10 ⌀.500 holes (A).
    B.  The holes labeled B are located vertically halfway between the centers of the holes labeled A. They have a diameter one-quarter the size of the holes labeled A.
    C.  The holes labeled C are located vertically halfway between the holes labeled A and B. Their diameter is three-quarters of the diameter of the holes labeled B.
    D.  The holes labeled D are located horizontally halfway between the centers of the holes labeled A. These holes have the same diameter as the holes labeled B.
    E.  Draw the rectangles around the circles as shown.
    F.  Do not draw dimensions, notes, or labels.
    G.  Save the drawing as P7-35.

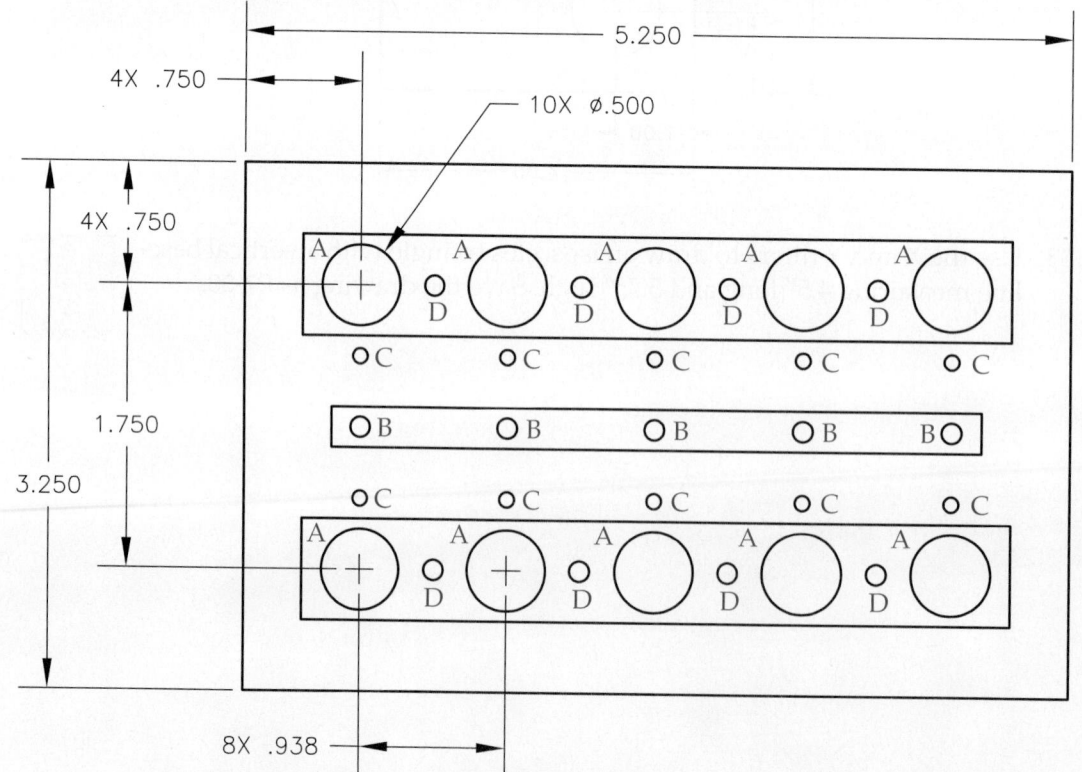

36. Open **P7-35**. Use a selection filter to erase all circles less than ⌀.500. Name and save the filter set. Save the drawing as **P7-36**.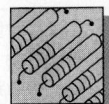

37. Draw the following roof plan. Do not dimension. Use the **CAL MEE** function to mirror the roof. Then, use the **FILTER** command to change the color of the roof and the linetype to CENTER. Finally, use the **FILTER** command to change the building outline to a continuous linetype. Save the drawing as **P7-37**.

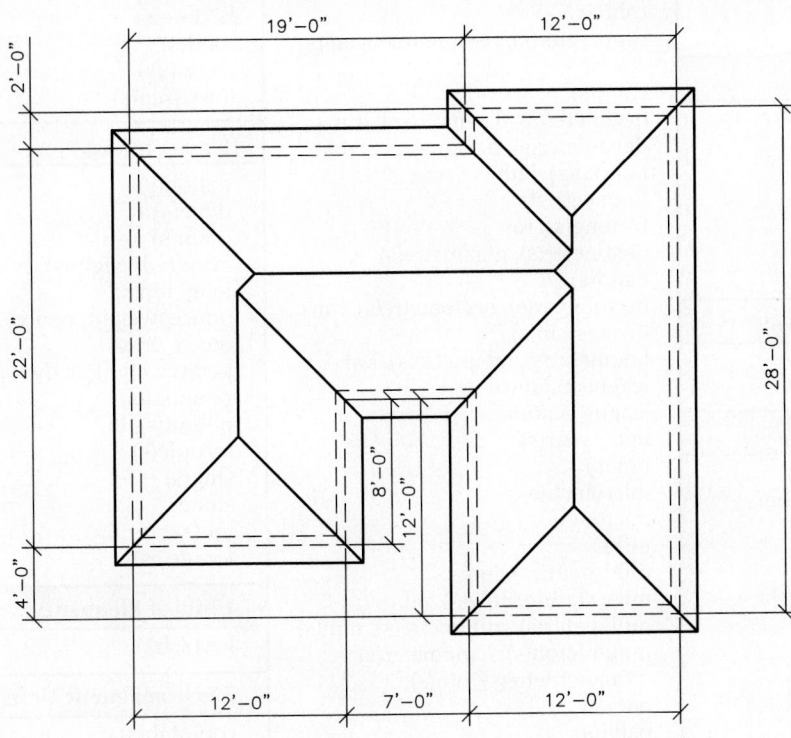

This chart lists the units of measure (and acceptable abbreviations) that can be converted using the **CVUNIT** function. These units are defined in the acad.unt file. You can customize this file to have additional units of measure available for conversion.

## Units Defined for Conversion with CVUNIT function

### Basic SI Units

meter(s), metre(s), m
kilogram(s), kg
second(s), sec
ampere(s), amp(s)
kelvin, k
candela, cd

### Derived SI Units

celsius, centigrade, c
rankine
fahrenheit
gram(s), gm, g
newton(s), n
pascal, pa
joule(s)

### Exponent Synonyms

square, sq
cubic, cu

### Units of Volume

barrel(s), bbl
board_f(oot.eet), fbm
bushel(s), bu
centiliter(s), cl
cord(s)
cc
decistere(s)
dekaliter(s), dal
dekastere(s)
dram(s)
dry_pint(s)
dry_quart(s)
firkin(s)
gallon(s), gal
gill(s)
hectoliter(s)
hogshead(s), hhd
kilderkin(s)
kiloliter(s)
liter(s)
milliliter(s), ml
minim(s)
fluid_ounce(s)
peck(s)
pint(s), fluid_pint(s)
pottle(s)
puncheon(s)
quart(s), qt, fluid_quart(s)
register_ton(s)
seam(s)
stere(s)
tun(s)

### Circular Measure

circle(s)
radian(s)
degree(s)
grad(s)
quadrant(s)

### Units of Length

Angstrom(s)
astronomical_unit(s), au
bolt(s)
cable(s)
caliber
centimeter(s), centimetre(s), cm(s)
chain(s)
cubit(s)
decimeter(s), decimetre(s), dm
dekameter(s), dekametre(s), dam
fathom(s), fath
f(oot.eet), ft, '
furlong(s), fur
gigameter(s), gigametre(s)
hand(s)
hectometer(s), hectometre(s), hm
inch(es), in(s), "
kilometer(s), kilometre(s), km
league_nautical
league_statute
light_year(s)
link(s)
microinch(es)
micron(s)
mil(s)
mile_nautical, inm
mile_statute, mile(s), mi
millimeter(s), millimetre(s), mm(s)
millimicron(s), nanometer(s),
    nanometre(s), nm(s)
pace(s)
palm(s)
parsec(s)
perch(es)
pica(s)
point(s)
rod(s), pole(s)
rope(s)
skein(s)
span(s)
survey_f(oot.eet)
yard(s), yd

### Units of Time

centur(y.ies)
day(s)
decade(s)
fortnight(s)
hour(s), hr
milleni(um.a)
minute(s), min
sidereal_year(s)
tropical_year(s)
week(s), wk
year(s), yr

### Solid Measure

sphere(s)
hemisphere(s)
steradian(s)

### Units of Area

acre(s)
are(s)
barn(s)
centare(s)
hectare(s)
rood(s)
section(s)
township(s)

### Units of Mass

dalton(s)
dyne(s)
grain(s)
hundredweight(s), cwt
long_ton(s)
ounce_weight, ounce(s), oz
ounce_troy
pennyweight(s), dwt, pwt
poundal(s)
pound(s), lb
scruple(s)
slug(s)
stone
ton(s)
tonn(e.es)

### Units of Frequency

hertz, hz

### Electromagnetic Units

coulomb(s)
farad(s)
henr(y.ies)
ohm(s)
siemens
tesla(s)
volt(s), v
watt(s), w
weber(s)

### Dimensionless Prefixes

deca
hecto
kilo
mega
giga
tera
peta
exa

### Fractions

deci
centi
milli
micro
nano
pico
femto
atto

## CHAPTER 8

# Placing Text on Drawings

## Learning Objectives

After completing this chapter, you will be able to do the following:

- Use and discuss proper text standards.
- Use the **TEXT** command to create single-line text.
- Make multiple lines of text with the **MTEXT** command.
- Create text styles.
- Use **DesignCenter** to manage text styles.
- Draw special symbols using control characters.
- Underscore and overscore text.
- Explain the purpose of the Quick Text mode and use the **QTEXT** command.
- Edit existing text.
- Check your spelling.
- Search for and replace material automatically.
- Design title blocks for your drawing template.
- Use the text tools in the **Express** pull-down menu.

Words and notes on drawings have traditionally been added by hand lettering. This is a slow, time-consuming task. Computer-aided drafting programs have reduced the tedious nature of adding notes to a drawing. In computer-aided drafting, lettering is referred to as *text*.

There are advantages of computer-generated text over hand-lettering techniques. When performed by computer, lettering is fast, easier to read, and more consistent. This chapter shows how text can be added to drawings. Also explained is the proper text presentation based on ASME Y14.2M, *Line Conventions and Lettering*.

## Text Standards

Company standards often dictate how text appears on a drawing. The minimum recommended text height on engineering drawings is .125″ (3 mm). All dimension numbers, notes, and other text information should be the same height. Titles, subtitles, captions, revision information, and drawing numbers can be .188″ to .25″ (5 mm to 6.5 mm) high. Many companies specify a .188″, or 5/32″ (5 mm), lettering height for standard text. This text size is easy to read even after the drawing is reduced.

Figure 8-1.
Vertical and inclined
text.

ABC.. abc.. 123..
*ABC.. abc.. 123..*

Vertical or inclined text may be used on a drawing, depending on company preference. See **Figure 8-1.** One or the other is recommended, but do not use both. The recommended slant for inclined text is 68° from horizontal. Computer-generated text offers a variety of styles for specific purposes, such as titles or captions. Text on a drawing is normally uppercase, but lowercase letters are used in some instances.

Numbers in dimensions and notes are the same height as standard text. When fractions are used in dimensions, the fraction bar should be placed horizontally between the numerator and denominator using full-size numbers. Fractions can be stacked when using the **MTEXT** command. However, many notes placed on drawings have fractions displayed with a diagonal (/) fraction bar. A dash or space is usually placed between the whole number and the fraction. See **Figure 8-2.**

## Scale Factors for Text Height

Scale factors and text heights should be determined before beginning a drawing. They are best incorporated as values within your template drawing files. Scale factors are important because this value is used to make sure the text is plotted at the proper height. The scale factor is multiplied by the desired plotted text height to get the AutoCAD text height.

The scale factor is always a reciprocal of the drawing scale. For example, if you wish to plot a drawing at a scale of 1/2″ = 1″, calculate the scale factor as follows:

    1/2″ = 1″
    .5″ = 1″
    1/.5 = 2 The scale factor is 2.

An architectural drawing that is to be plotted at a scale of 1/4″ = 1′-0″ has a scale factor calculated as follows:

    1/4″ = 1′-0″
    .25″ = 12″
    12/.25 = 48 The scale factor is 48.

The scale factor of a civil engineering drawing that has a scale of 1″ = 60′ is calculated as follows:

    1″ = 60′
    1″ = (60 × 12)″
    720/1 = 720 The scale factor is 720.

**Figure 8-2.**
Examples of numbers for different units of measure.

| Decimal Inch | | Fractional Inch | | | Millimeter | | |
|---|---|---|---|---|---|---|---|
| 2.750 | .25 | $2\frac{3}{4}$ | 2−3/4 | 2 3/4 | 2.5 | 3 | 0.7 |

If your drawing is in millimeters with a scale of 1:1, the drawing can be converted to inches with the formula 1″ = 25.4 mm. Therefore, the scale factor is 25.4. When the metric drawing scale is 1:2, then the scale factor for converting to inches is 1″ = 25.4 × 2, or 1″ = 50.8. The scale factor is 50.8.

After the scale factor has been determined, you should then calculate the height of the AutoCAD text. In a 1″ = 1″ scaled drawing, the scale factor equals 1. Therefore, the text height in the drawing will be 1/8″ high, because the text height multiplied by a scale factor of 1 equals 1/8″ high text. However, if you are working on a civil engineering drawing with a scale of 1″ = 60′, text drawn at 1/8″ high appears as a dot. Remember that the drawing you are working on is 720 times larger than it is when plotted at the proper scale. Therefore, you must multiply the text height by the 720 scale factor to have text in correct proportion on the screen:

text height × scale factor = model space scaled text height
.125″ × 720 = 90″ The proper text height in model space is 90″.

An architectural drawing with a scale of 1/4″ = 1′-0″ has a scale factor of 48. Text that is to be 1/8″ high when printed should be drawn 6″ high (1/8″ × 48 = 6″).

## Text Composition

*Composition* refers to the spacing, layout, and appearance of the text. With manual lettering, it is necessary to space letters freehand. Spacing is performed automatically with computer-generated text.

Notes should be placed horizontally on the drawing. AutoCAD automatically sets lines of text apart at an equal distance. This helps maintain the identity of individual notes.

The term *justify* means to align the text to fit a given location. For example, left-justified text is aligned along an imaginary left border. Most lines of text are left-justified.

## Using AutoCAD to Draw Text

AutoCAD provides you with two basic systems for creating text. There is line text for creating single-line text objects, and multiline text for preparing paragraphs of text. The **TEXT** command is used to create single-line text. This text is entered at the command line. The **MTEXT** command is used to create paragraph text. This text is entered in the *multiline text editor*. Each command is used differently, but the options are similar. Text styles allow you to make the text look the way you want.

### Single-Line Text

The **TEXT** command allows you to see the text on the screen as you type. The **TEXT** command creates single-line text. This means that each line of text is a single text object. **TEXT** is most useful for text items that require only one line of text. Whenever the text has more than one line or requires mixed fonts, sizes, or colors, multiline text should be used.

The **TEXT** command can be issued by picking **Single Line Text** from the **Text** cascading menu in the **Draw** pull-down menu, picking the **Single Line Text** button in the **Text** toolbar, or entering TEXT at the Command: prompt as follows:

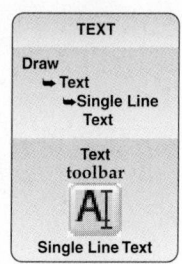

TEXT

Draw
➥ Text
  ➥Single Line Text

Text toolbar

Single Line Text

Command: **TEXT**↵
Current text style: "Standard" Text height: *current*
Specify start point of text or [Justify/Style]: *(pick a starting point)*
Specify height <*current*>: *(enter the scaled text height value or press [Enter])*
Specify rotation angle of text <0>: *(enter a value or press [Enter])*
Enter text: *(type text and press [Enter])*
Enter text: *(type the next line of text or press [Enter] to complete)*
Command:

When the Enter text: prompt appears, a text cursor equal in size to the text height appears on the screen at the text start point. **TEXT** can be used to enter multiple lines of text simply by pressing [Enter] at the end of each line. The Enter text: prompt is repeated for the next line of text. The text cursor automatically moves to the start point one line below the preceding line. Each line of text is a single object. Press [Enter] twice to exit the command and keep what you have typed. You can cancel the command at any time by pressing the [Esc] key. This action erases any incomplete lines of text.

While in the **TEXT** command, the screen crosshairs can be moved independently of the text cursor box. Selecting a new start point completes the line of text being entered and begins a new line at the selected point. Thus, multiple lines of text may be entered anywhere in the drawing without exiting the command. This saves a lot of drafting time. The following are a few aspects of the **TEXT** command to be aware of:

- ✓ When you end the **TEXT** command, the entered text is erased from the screen, and then regenerated.
- ✓ Regardless of the type of justification selected, the cursor box appears as if the text is left-justified. However, when you end the **TEXT** command, the text disappears and is then regenerated with the alignment you requested.
- ✓ When you use a control code sequence for a symbol, the control code, not the symbol, is displayed. When you complete the command, the text disappears and is then regenerated showing the proper symbol. Control codes are discussed later in this chapter.
- ✓ If you cancel the **TEXT** command, an incomplete line will be deleted.

## TEXT and command line editing

When using the **TEXT** command, you can perform editing at the command line. The following keys are used to edit the entered material:

- [↑]. The up arrow key moves backward through previously entered commands, allowing them to become a text entry. You might think of it as moving *up* the list of previous commands.
- [↓]. After moving backward through any number of previous lines, the down arrow key moves forward again. You might think of this as moving back *down* the list of previously entered commands.
- [←]. The left arrow key moves the cursor left through the text currently on the command line. Doing this allows you to reposition the cursor to insert text or words that were skipped when entering the text.
- [→]. After using the left arrow key, the right arrow key moves the typing cursor back to the right.
- **[Home].** Moves the cursor to the home position, which is in front of the first character typed at the command line.
- **[End].** Moves the cursor back to the far right, at the very end of the text typed at the command line.
- **[Insert].** Toggles the command line between Insert mode and Overwrite mode. When in Insert mode, any new text is inserted at the cursor position, and any text existing to the right of the cursor is moved to the right. When in Overwrite mode, new text entered replaces the character at the cursor position.
- **[Delete].** Deletes the character to the right of the text cursor.
- **[Backspace].** Deletes the character to the left of the text cursor.

In previous releases of AutoCAD, the **DTEXT** command was used to create single-line text. This command has been replaced by the **TEXT** command. If you enter DTEXT or its alias, DT, at the Command: prompt, the **TEXT** command is activated.

### The **Start point** option

After entering the **TEXT** command, you are given the Specify start point of text or [Justify/Style]: prompt. The default option allows you to select a point on the screen where you want the text to begin. This point becomes the lower-left corner of the text. After you pick the start point, the prompt reads:

    Specify Height <*current*>:

This prompt allows you to enter the text height. The default value is 0.2000. This is where the scaled text height needs to be entered. The previously selected letter height can be displayed as the current value. If you want letters that are .5 units high, then enter .5. The next prompt is:

    Specify rotation angle of text <0>:

The default value for the rotation angle is 0, which places the text horizontally. The values rotate text in a counterclockwise direction. The text pivots about the starting point as shown in **Figure 8-3**.
The last prompt is:

    Enter text:

Type the desired text and press [Enter]. If no other justification is selected, the text is left-justified, as shown in **Figure 8-4**.

**Figure 8-3.**
Different rotation angles for text. The starting point is indicated here with a plus sign.

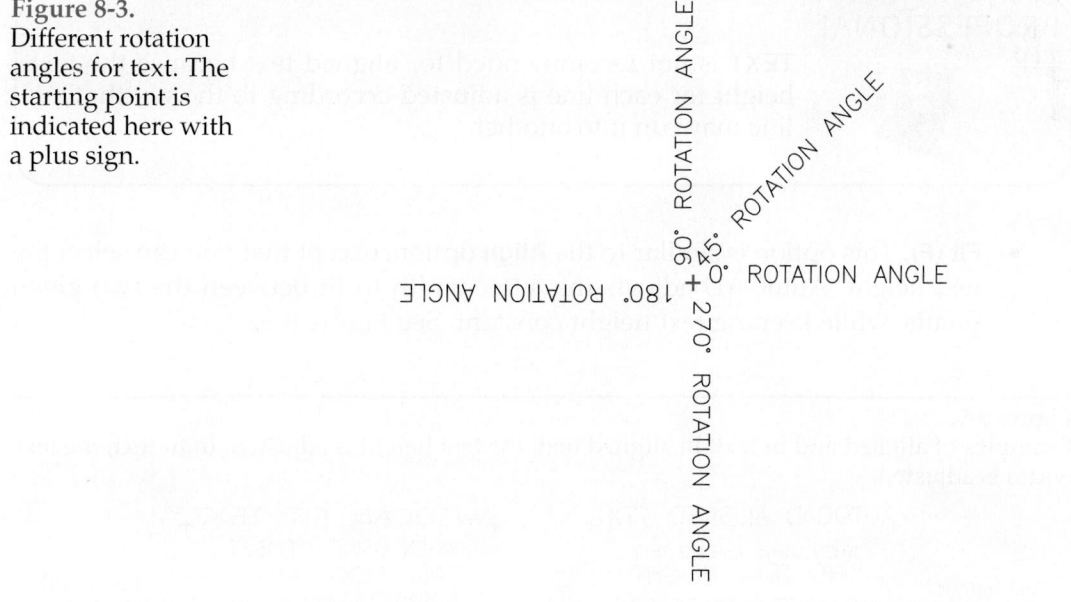

**Figure 8-4.**
Left-justified text with the start point shown.

AUTOCAD LEFT-JUSTIFIED TEXT

**NOTE**

If the default angle orientation or direction (**ANGBASE** and **ANGDIR** system variables) is changed, the text rotation is affected.

## The Justify option

The **TEXT** command offers a variety of justification options. Left-justification is the default. If you want another option, enter J at the Specify start point of text [Justify/Style]: prompt. When you select the **Justify** option, you can use one of several text alignment options. These options can be seen in the command sequence below, and are explained in the next sections.

```
Command: TEXT↵
Current text style: "Standard" Text height: 0.2000
Specify start point of text or [Justify/Style]: J↵
Enter an option [Align/Fit/Center/Middle/Right/TL/TC/TR/ML/MC/MR/BL/BC/BR]:
```

- **Align (A).** When this option is selected, you are prompted for two points between which the text string is confined. The beginning and endpoints can be placed horizontally or at an angle. AutoCAD automatically adjusts the text width to fit between the selected points. The text height is also changed with this option. The height varies according to the distance between the points and the number of characters. See **Figure 8-5.**

**PROFESSIONAL TIP**

**TEXT** is not recommended for aligned text because the text height for each line is adjusted according to the width. One line may run into another.

- **Fit (F).** This option is similar to the **Align** option, except that you can select the text height. AutoCAD adjusts the letter width to fit between the two given points, while keeping text height constant. See **Figure 8-5.**

**Figure 8-5.**
Examples of aligned and fit text. In aligned text, the text height is adjusted. In fit text, the text width is adjusted.

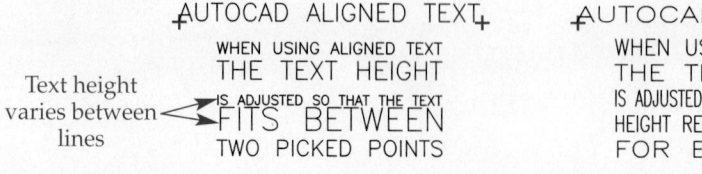

- **Center (C).** This option allows you to select the center point for the baseline of the text. Enter the letter height and rotation angle after picking the center point.
- **Middle (M).** This option allows you to center text both horizontally and vertically at a given point. The letter height and rotation can also be changed.
- **Right (R).** This option justifies text at the lower-right corner. The point is entered at the Specify right endpoint of text baseline: prompt. The letter height and rotation can also be entered. The command sequence is similar to the sequence for the **Start point** option. **Figure 8-6** compares the **Center**, **Middle**, and **Right** options.

## Other text alignment options

There are a number of text alignment options that allow you to place text on a drawing in relation to the top, bottom, middle, left side, or right side of the text. These alignment options are shown in **Figure 8-7.** These options are shown as abbreviations that correlate to the **TEXT** prompt line. To use one of these options, type the two letters for the desired option and press [Enter].

**Figure 8-6.**
Three justification options with start point shown.
A—Using the **Center** text option.
B—Using the **Middle** text option.
C—Using the **Right** text option.

**Figure 8-7.**
Using the **TL, TC, TR, ML, MC, MR, BL, BC,** and **BR** text alignment options. Notice what the abbreviations stand for.

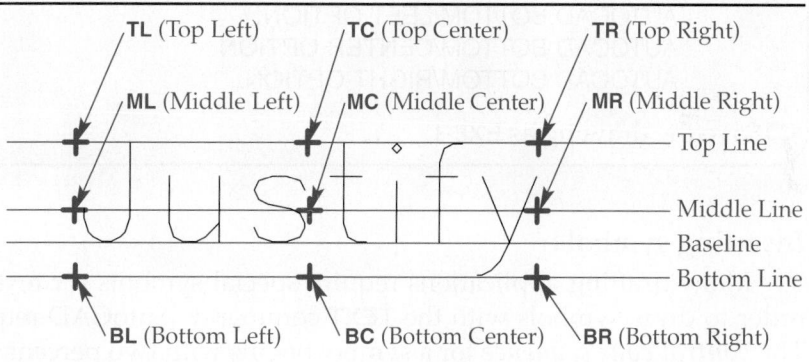

PROFESSIONAL TIP

If you already know which text alignment option you want to use in your drawing, you can enter it at the Specify start point of text or [Justify/Style]: prompt without entering J. Just type the letter or letters of the desired option and press [Enter].

○ Start AutoCAD and use the setup option of your choice.

○ Use the **TEXT** command to type the following lines of text exactly as shown using the **Start point** option. Use .25″ (6 mm) letter height and 0° rotation angle.

> LETTERING HAS TYPICALLY BEEN A SLOW, TIME-CONSUMING TASK. COMPUTER-AIDED DRAFTING HAS REDUCED THE TEDIOUS NATURE OF PREPARING LETTERING ON A DRAWING. IN CAD, LETTERING IS REFERRED TO AS TEXT. COMPUTER-GENERATED TEXT IS FAST, CONSISTENT, AND EASIER TO READ.

○ Use the **TEXT** command to type the following information. For each line, change the text justification option to obtain the format given. Use .5″ (12 mm) letter height and 0° rotation angle.

> AUTOCAD TEXT LEFT-JUSTIFIED USING THE START POINT OPTION.
> AUTOCAD TEXT RIGHT-JUSTIFIED USING THE RIGHT OPTION.
> AUTOCAD TEXT ALIGNED USING THE ALIGN OPTION.
> AUTOCAD TEXT CENTERED USING THE CENTER OPTION.
> AUTOCAD FIT TEXT USING THE FIT OPTION.
> AUTOCAD TEXT USING THE MIDDLE OPTION.

○ Use the **TEXT** command to type the following information. For each line, change the text justification option to obtain the format given in each statement. Use .5″ (12 mm) letter height and 0° rotation angle.

> AUTOCAD TOP/LEFT OPTION.
> AUTOCAD TOP/CENTER OPTION.
> AUTOCAD TOP/RIGHT OPTION.
> AUTOCAD MIDDLE/LEFT OPTION.
> AUTOCAD MIDDLE/CENTER OPTION.
> AUTOCAD MIDDLE/RIGHT OPTION.
> AUTOCAD BOTTOM/LEFT OPTION.
> AUTOCAD BOTTOM/CENTER OPTION.
> AUTOCAD BOTTOM/RIGHT OPTION.

○ Save the drawing as EX8-1.

### Inserting symbols

Many drafting applications require special symbols for text and dimensions. In order to draw symbols with the **TEXT** command, AutoCAD requires a control code. The *control code sequence* for a symbol begins with two percent signs (%%). The next character you enter represents the symbol. These control codes are used for single-line text objects that are generated with the **TEXT** command. The following list gives the most popular control code sequences:

| Control Code | Description | Symbol |
|---|---|---|
| %%D | Degrees symbol | ° |
| %%P | Plus/minus sign | ± |
| %%C | Diameter symbol | Ø |

**Figure 8-8.**
A— The control sequence %%C creates the Ø (diameter) symbol.
B—The control sequence %%U underscores text.

Ø2.75
A

## UNDERSCORING TEXT

B

For example, in order to add the note Ø2.75, the control sequence %%C2.75 is entered at the Enter text: prompt. See **Figure 8-8A.**

A single percent sign can be added normally. However, when a percent sign must precede another control sequence, %%% can be used to force a single percent sign. For example, suppose you want to type the note 25%±2%. You must enter 25%%%%P2%.

### Drawing underscored or overscored text

Text can be underscored (underlined) or overscored by typing a control sequence in front of the line of text. The control sequences are:

%%O = overscore
%%U = underscore

For example, the note <u>UNDERSCORING TEXT</u> must be entered at the Enter text: prompt as %%UUNDERSCORING TEXT. The resulting text is shown in **Figure 8-8B.** A line of text may require both underscoring and overscoring. For example, the control sequence %%O%%ULINE OF TEXT produces the note with both underscore and overscore.

The %%O and %%U control codes are toggles that turn overscoring and underscoring on and off. Type %%U preceding a word or phrase to turn underscoring on. Type %%U after the desired word or phrase to turn underscoring off. Any text following the second %%U then appears without underscoring. For example, <u>DETAIL A</u> HUB ASSEMBLY would be entered as %%UDETAIL A%%U HUB ASSEMBLY.

---

**PROFESSIONAL TIP**

Many drafters prefer to underline labels such as <u>SECTION A-A</u> or <u>DETAIL B</u>. Rather than draw line or polyline objects under the text, use **Middle** or **Center** justification modes and underscoring. The view labels are automatically underlined and centered under the views or details they identify.

---

### Exercise 8-2

○ Start AutoCAD and use the setup option of your choice.
○ Use the **TEXT** command and control codes to type the following:

45°
1.375±.005
Ø3.875
79%
<u>UNDERSCORING TEXT</u>

○ Save the drawing as EX8-2.

---

# Multiline Text

The **MTEXT** command is used to create multiline text objects. Instead of each line being an individual object, all the lines are part of the same object. The **MTEXT** command is accessed by picking the **Multiline Text** button in the **Draw** or **Text** toolbar, picking **Multiline Text...** in the **Text** cascading menu of the **Draw** pull-down, or entering T, MT, or MTEXT at the Command: prompt.

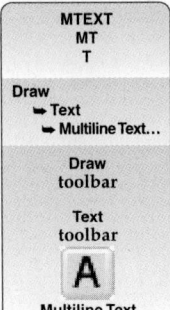
After entering the **MTEXT** command, AutoCAD asks you to specify the first and opposite corners of the text boundary. The *text boundary* is a box within which your text will be placed. When you pick the first corner of the text boundary, the cursor changes to a box with grayed out letters that represent the current text height. Move the box until you have the desired size for your paragraph and pick the opposite corner. See **Figure 8-9.**

When drawing the text boundary, an arrow in the boundary shows the direction of text flow. While the width of the boundary provides a limit to the width of the text paragraphs, it does not affect the possible height. The boundary height is automatically resized to fit the actual text entered. The direction of the flow indicates where the boundary is expanded, if necessary. This is the command sequence:

```
Command: T, MT, or MTEXT↵
Current text style: "Standard" Text height: 0.2000
Specify first corner: (pick the first corner)
Specify opposite corner or [Height/Justify/Line spacing/Rotation/Style/Width]: (pick
    the opposite corner)
```

After picking the text boundary, the multiline text editor appears. See **Figure 8-10.** The multiline text editor is divided into the **Text Formatting** toolbar and the *text editor*. The **Text Formatting** toolbar controls the properties of text entered into the text editor. The text editor includes a paragraph ruler where indent stops and an indent marker are located. A cursor is located within the text editor. This cursor is the height set in the **Text Formatting** toolbar. This is where text is entered to create a paragraph.

As mentioned earlier, notes in drawings are often presented using uppercase text. Right-clicking inside the text editor displays a shortcut menu. The **AutoCAPS** option is found in this menu. Selecting this option turns on the caps lock on the keyboard each time the multiline text editor is accessed. The caps lock is turned off when you exit the multiline text editor so text in other programs is not all uppercase. Additional options are available in the text editor shortcut menu. These are discussed later.

**Figure 8-9.**
The text boundary is a box within which your text will be placed. The arrow indicates the direction of text flow.

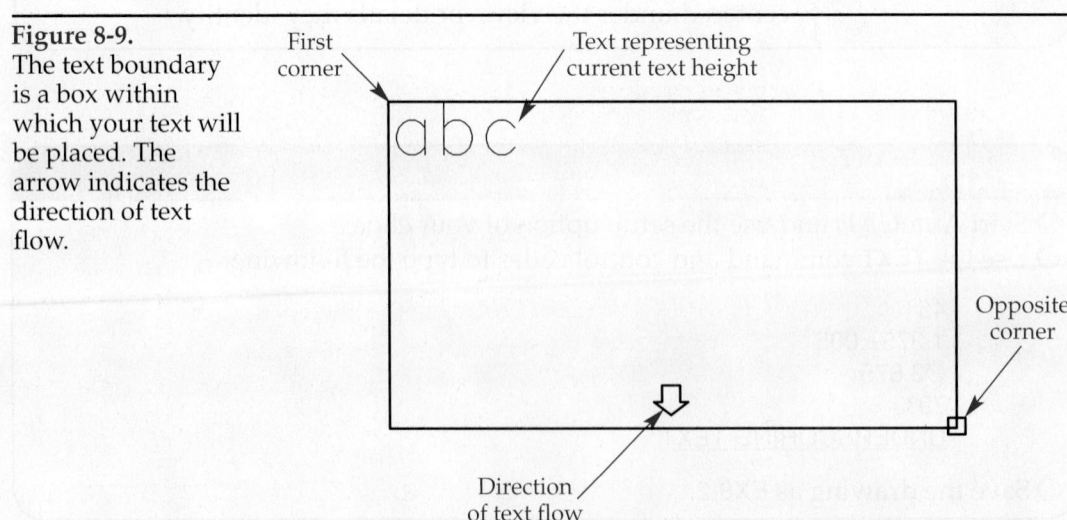

**Figure 8-10.**
The multiline text editor with the **AutoCAPS** shortcut menu deactivated.

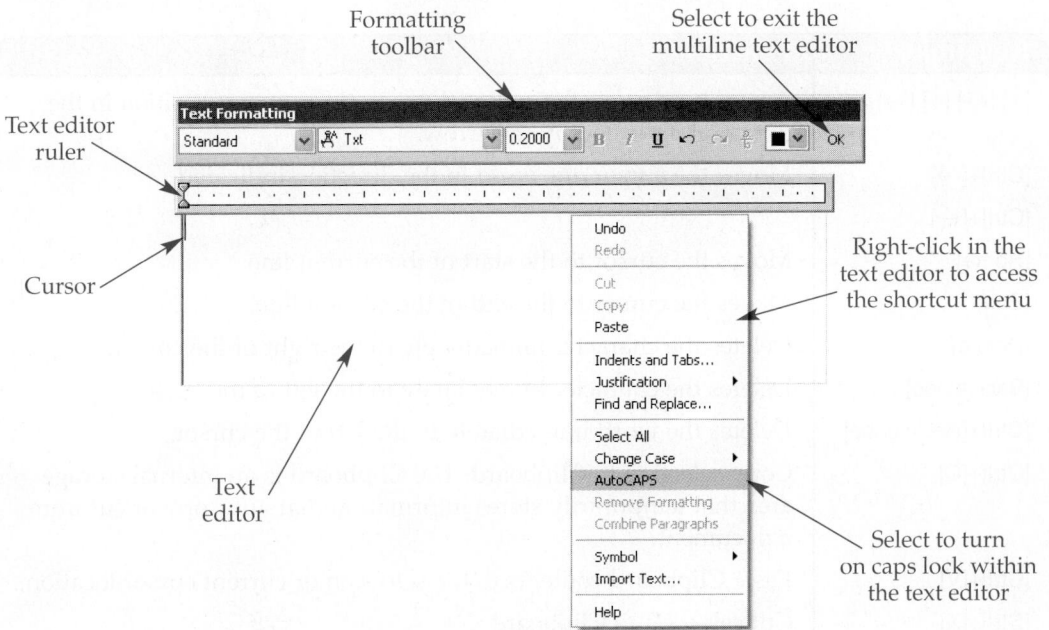

When the text editor is filled with text and a new line is added, previous lines begin to be hidden and a scroll bar is displayed at the right. Use the scroll bar to move up and down to access lines in the text editor. Pressing the [Enter] key causes a new line to be entered. Pressing [Enter] twice creates a blank line between lines of text. Tabs can also be used to line up columns of text. When finished entering text in the editor, pick the **OK** button in the **Text Formatting** toolbar to exit the text editor.

---

### Exercise 8-3

○ Start AutoCAD and use the setup option of your choice.
○ Access the **MTEXT** command and create a text boundary that is 4″ (100 mm) wide and 2″ (50 mm) high. Hint: use relative coordinates.
○ Type anything you want.
○ Type enough text or press the [Enter] key enough times so the scroll bar is displayed on the right.
○ Pick the **OK** button when done to see the text displayed on the screen.
○ Save the drawing as EX8-3.

---

## Modifying character properties with the multiline text editor

The multiline text editor is displayed after you define the text boundary. The **Text Formatting** toolbar controls the properties of the text entered in the text editor. Additional text controls can also be accessed by right-clicking within the text editor. This section describes all features within the toolbar, text editor, and shortcut menu.

---

While entering text in the multiline text editor, there are a number of keystroke combinations that are available. These combinations are as follows:

| Keystroke | Function |
|---|---|
| [↑] [←] [↓] [→] | Arrow keys move the cursor through the text one position in the direction indicated by the arrow. |
| [Ctrl]+[→]<br>[Ctrl]+[←] | Moves the cursor one word in the direction indicated. |
| [Home] | Moves the cursor to the start of the current line. |
| [End] | Moves the cursor to the end of the current line. |
| [Delete] | Deletes the character immediately to the right of the cursor. |
| [Backspace] | Deletes the character immediately to the left of the cursor. |
| [Ctrl]+[Backspace] | Deletes the word immediately to the left of the cursor. |
| [Ctrl]+[C] | Copy selection to Clipboard. The Clipboard is an internal storage area that temporarily stores information that you copy or cut from a document. |
| [Ctrl]+[V] | Paste Clipboard contents to the selection or current cursor location. |
| [Ctrl]+[X] | Cut selection to Clipboard. |
| [Ctrl]+[Z] | Undo. |
| [Enter] | Ends the current paragraph, starting a new one on the next line. |
| [Page Up]<br>[Page Down] | These keys move the cursor up to 28 rows in the indicated direction. |
| [Ctrl]+[Page Up]<br>[Ctrl]+[Page Down] | These keys move the cursor to the top or bottom of the currently visible page of text. |
| [Ctrl]+[Home] | Moves the cursor to Line 1, Column 1. |
| [Ctrl]+[End] | Moves the cursor to the last character position. |
| [Ctrl]+[A] | Selects all text in the current multiline text object. |
| [Shift]+[→]<br>[Shift]+[←] | Selects or deselects text. Increases or decreases the selection by one character at a time, depending on the direction indicated. |
| [Shift]+[↑]<br>[Shift]+[↓] | Selects or deselects text. Increases or decreases the selection by one line at a time, depending on the direction indicated. |
| [Ctrl]+[Shift]+[→]<br>[Ctrl]+[Shift]+[←] | Selects or deselects text. Increases or decreases the selection by one word at a time, depending on the direction indicated. |
| [Esc] | Closes the multiline text editor and loses any changes made. |

**PROFESSIONAL TIP**

Text can be pasted from any text-based application into the multiline text editor. For example, you can copy text from an application such as Microsoft® Word, and then paste it into the multiline text editor. The pasted text retains its properties. Likewise, text copied or cut from the multiline text editor can be pasted into another text-based application.

As you move the cursor into the editing window, it changes shape. If you have used other Windows text editors, this is a familiar text cursor shape. Pointing to a character position within the text and pressing the pick button causes the cursor to be placed at the selected location. You can then begin typing or editing as needed. If you begin typing where the text cursor is initially placed, your text begins in the upper-left corner of the text boundary.

Text is selected as it is with most standard Windows text editors. Place the cursor at one end of the desired selection, press and hold the pick button. Drag the cursor until the desired text is highlighted, then release the pick button. Now, any editing operations you perform affect the highlighted text. For example, a copy or cut operation places the highlighted text on the Clipboard. One other way to highlight text is to move your mouse to the word you would like to highlight and double-click it with the pick button. To entirely replace the highlighted text with new text, either paste the new text from the Clipboard or begin typing. The selection is erased and the new text appears in its place.

**Figure 8-11** illustrates the features found in the **Text Formatting** toolbar. Keep in mind that *selected text* refers to text that you have highlighted in the text window:

- **Style.** This drop-down list includes a list of the different text styles in the drawing. A text style is a type of font usage definition. A *font* is a family of text characters. It controls features such as the font used, if it appears to be vertical or inclined, and if it is created backwards. Text styles are covered in detail later in this chapter. Selecting a style from this list sets the **Font** drop-down with the font assigned to the style.
- **Font.** Pick the down arrow to open the drop-down list of available text fonts. Picking one of the options allows the selected text to have its font changed or newly entered text to use this font type. This overrides the font used in the current style. Txt is the default text font.
- **Text height.** This option allows selected text or new text to have its height changed. This overrides the current setting of the **TEXTSIZE** system variable and the text height set within the text style.
- **Bold.** Pick this button to have the selected text become bold. This only works with some TrueType fonts. The SHX fonts do not have this capability.

**Figure 8-11.**
The **Text Formatting** toolbar.

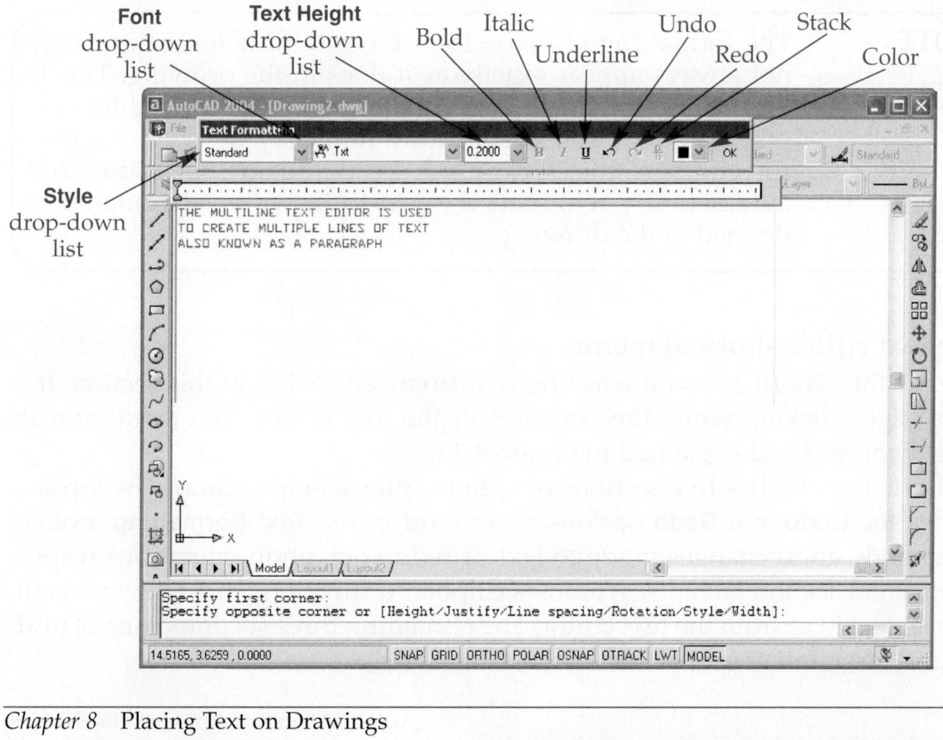

- **Italic.** Pick this button to have the selected text become italic. This only works with some TrueType fonts. The SHX style fonts do not have this capability.
- **Underline.** Picking this button underlines selected text.

**NOTE** If you select text that is already bold, picking the **Bold** button returns the text to its normal appearance. This is also true for italic and underline.

- **Undo.** Pick this button to undo the previous activity.
- **Redo.** Redoes undone operations.
- **Stack.** This button allows selected text to be stacked vertically or diagonally. To use this feature for drawing a vertically stacked fraction, place a forward slash between the top and bottom items. Then select the text with your pointing device and pick the button. This button is also used for unstacking text that has been previously stacked. You can also use the caret (^) character between text if you want to stack the items without a fraction bar. This is called a *tolerance stack*. Typing a number sign (#) between selected numbers results in a diagonal fraction bar. See **Figure 8-12.**
- **Color.** The color is set ByLayer as default, but you can change the text color by picking one of the colors found in the **Color** drop-down list.

**Figure 8-12.**
Different types of stack characters.

| | Selected Text | Stacked Text |
|---|---|---|
| **Vertical Fraction** | $1/2$ | $\frac{1}{2}$ |
| **Tolerance Stack** | $1\,{}^{\wedge}2$ | $\frac{1}{2}$ |
| **Diagonal Fraction** | $1\#2$ | $\frac{1}{2}$ |

**NOTE** The formatting of text within the multiline text editor may not always appear exactly as it does in the drawing. This is most commonly true when a substitute font is used for display in the editor. A substitute font may be wider or narrower than the font used in the drawing. AutoCAD automatically reformats the text to fit within the boundary defined in the drawing.

### Using the text editor shortcut menu

The text editor shortcut menu was briefly introduced earlier in this section. It is accessed by right-clicking while the cursor is in the text editor. The menu and its options are displayed and explained in **Figure 8-13.**

This shortcut menu has five sections of options, plus a help section. The top section includes the **Undo** and **Redo** options also found in the **Text Formatting** toolbar. These commands undo changes made to text or redo your undo operations respectively. The second section includes Windows Clipboard functions that allow you cut, copy, or paste text to or from the text editor. The remaining three sections control multiline text and text content properties.

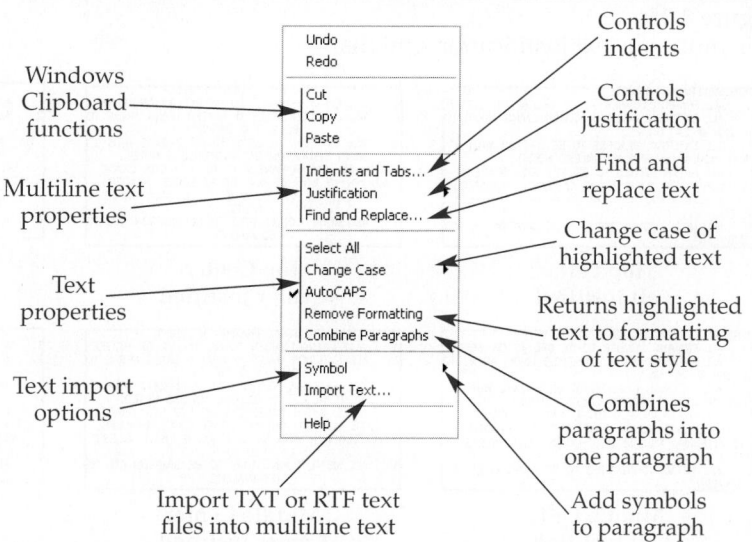

**Figure 8-13.**
The text editor shortcut menu is accessed by right-clicking while the cursor is in the text editor.

Windows Clipboard functions

Multiline text properties

Text properties

Text import options

Controls indents

Controls justification

Find and replace text

Change case of highlighted text

Returns highlighted text to formatting of text style

Combines paragraphs into one paragraph

Add symbols to paragraph

Import TXT or RTF text files into multiline text

## Multiline text properties

The third section in the shortcut menu controls indentations and the justification of the multiline text object. Also included in this section is a find and replace tool to locate text in the paragraph and replace it with a different piece of text. Each of these commands is described as follows:

- **Indents and Tabs.** Selecting this option will open the **Indents and Tabs** dialog box, **Figure 8-14.** This dialog box allows you to set up the indentation for the first line of a paragraph of text as well as the remaining portion of a paragraph. Each time a new paragraph is started, the **First line** indent is used. As text is entered in the editor and is wrapped to the next line, the **Paragraph** indent is used. The **Tab stop position** allows you to set up a cursor stop position when the [Tab] key is pressed. Entering a new value and picking the **Set** button allows you to set up several additional tab locations in the paragraph. Picking the **Clear** button removes the highlighted tab location.
- **Justification.** Selecting this option produces a cascading menu of justification options. These options are similar to the text justification described earlier, except they apply to the entire paragraph of text. **Figure 8-15** displays the different justification options and how they relate to multiline text object.
- **Find and Replace.** When this command is picked, the **Replace** dialog box is displayed. See **Figure 8-16.** Enter the text you are searching for in the **Find what:** text box. Then pick the **Find Next** button to highlight it. Next, enter the text that will be substituted in the **Replace with:** text box. You can then pick the **Replace** or the **Replace All** button to replace the highlighted text or all words that match your search criteria.

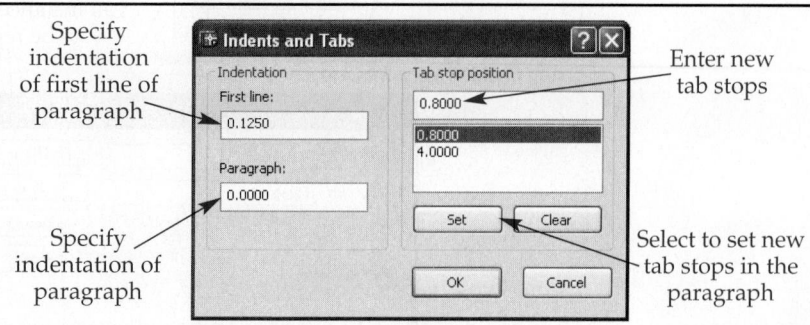

**Figure 8-14.**
The **Indents and Tabs** dialog box is used to set up indentations within the multiline text object.

Specify indentation of first line of paragraph

Specify indentation of paragraph

Enter new tab stops

Select to set new tab stops in the paragraph

**Figure 8-15.**
The multiline text justification options.

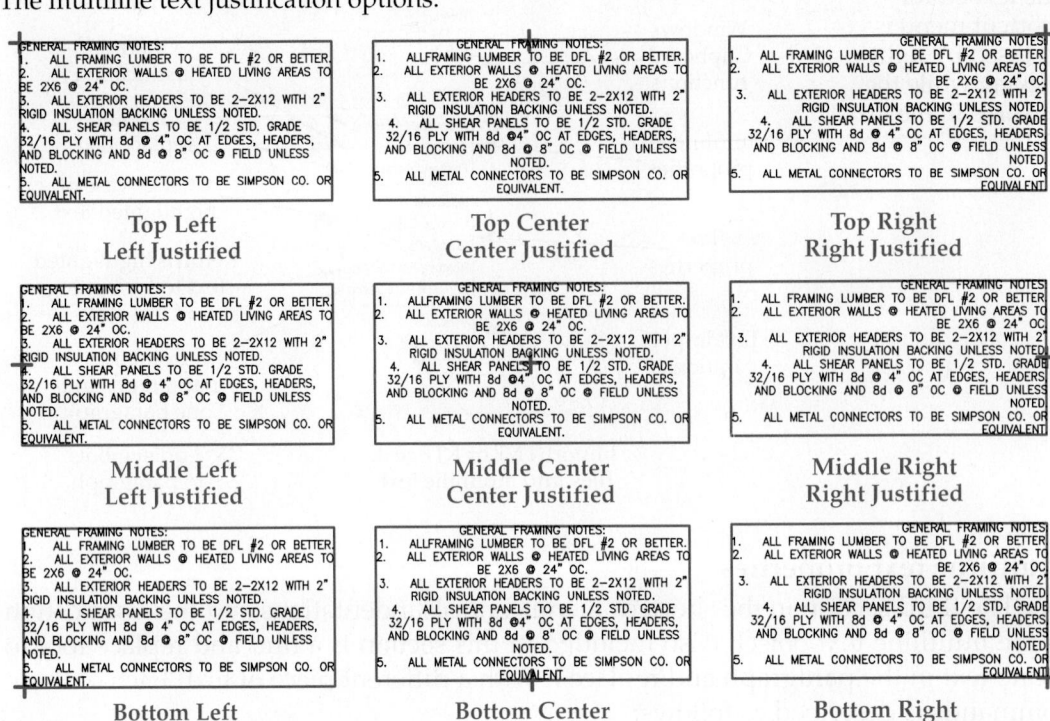

Top Left
Left Justified

Top Center
Center Justified

Top Right
Right Justified

Middle Left
Left Justified

Middle Center
Center Justified

Middle Right
Right Justified

Bottom Left
Left Justified

Bottom Center
Center Justified

Bottom Right
Right Justified

+ This symbol represents the insertion point

**Figure 8-16.**
Using the **Find and Replace** option. A—Searching for a word. B—Replacing the text.

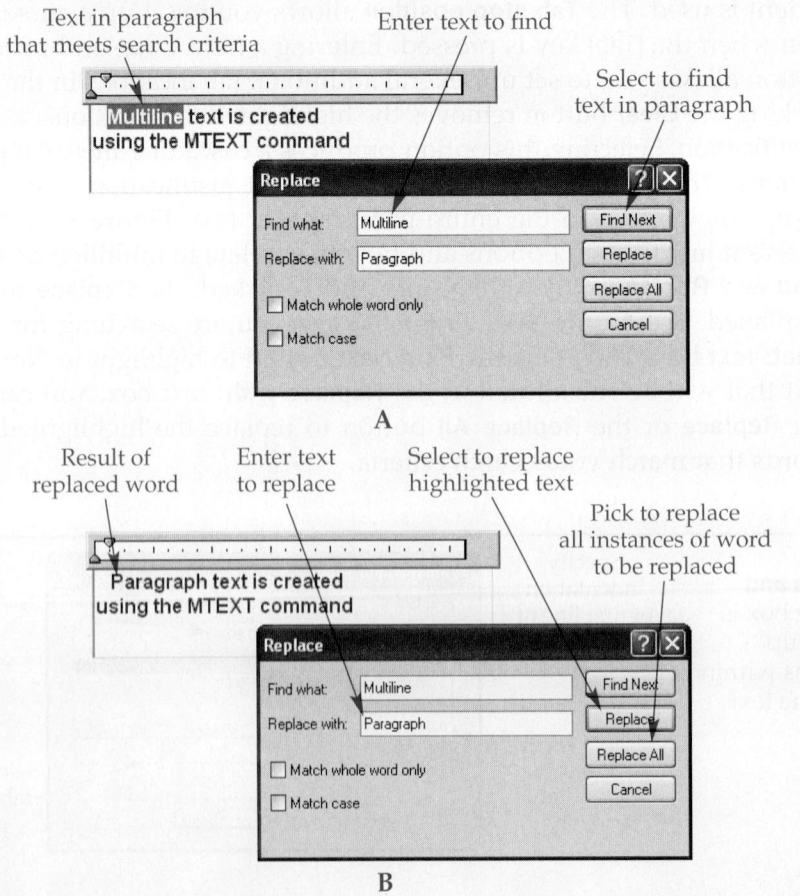

The **Match whole word only** check box is used to specify a search for a whole word, and not part of another word. For example, if **Match whole word only** is not checked, a search for the word *the* would find those letters wherever they occur—including as part of other words, such as o<u>the</u>r or we<u>athe</u>r. You can also select the **Match case** check box if you are searching for words that are case specific.

## Controlling text properties

The fourth section within the shortcut menu controls how text is created, formatted, and selected. The following options are available:

- **Select All.** This option selects all lines of text within the multiline text object being created or modified.
- **Change Case.** This cascading menu includes the **UPPERCASE** and **lowercase** options. First highlight text in the text editor to be modified, and then access either the **UPPERCASE** or the **lowercase** options. The **UPPERCASE** option changes all highlighted text to uppercase, and the **lowercase** option will change the highlighted text to lowercase.
- **AutoCAPS.** This option was described earlier. When selected, this option causes the [Caps Lock] button on the keyboard to be turned on so that text will be entered in uppercase.
- **Remove Formatting.** This option removes formatting such as bold, italic, or underline from any highlighted text in the text editor.
- **Combine Paragraphs.** This option causes any lines of highlighted text that form multiple paragraphs to be combined into a single paragraph.

## Importing text and symbols

The fifth section on the shortcut menu includes two options for importing text and adding symbols to the multiline text object. These are described as follows:

- **Symbol.** Picking this option displays the cascading menu shown in **Figure 8-17**. This option allows the insertion of symbols at the text cursor location. The first three options include the **Degrees**, **Plus/Minus**, and **Diameter** symbols. The **Non-breaking Space** option keeps two separate words together. The **Other...** option opens the **Character Map** dialog box, **Figure 8-18**. To use this dialog box, pick the desired TrueType symbols from the **Font:** drop-down list. The following are the steps for using a symbol or symbols:
  1. Pick the desired symbol and then pick the **Select** button. The selected symbol is displayed in the **Characters to copy:** box.
  2. Pick the **Copy** button to have the selected symbol or symbols copied to the Clipboard.
  3. Pick the **Close** button to close the dialog box.
  4. Back in the multiline text editor, place the text cursor where you want the symbols displayed.
  5. Move the screen cursor to anywhere inside the text editor and right-click to display the shortcut menu. Pick the **Paste** option to paste the symbol at the cursor location.

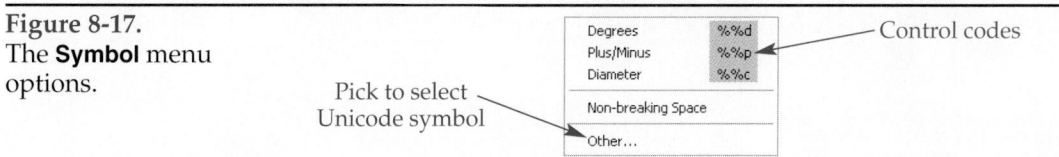

**Figure 8-17.**
The **Symbol** menu options.

Figure 8-18.
The **Character Map**
dialog box.

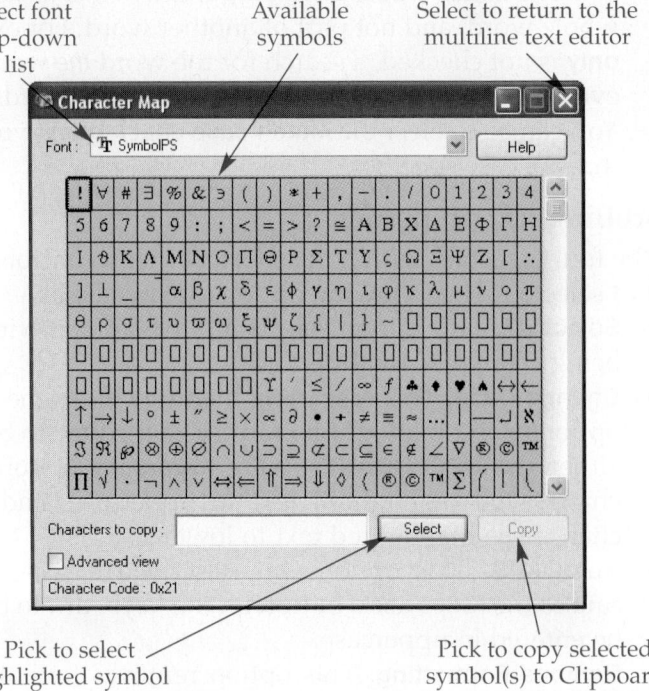

Select font
drop-down
list

Available
symbols

Select to return to the
multiline text editor

Pick to select
highlighted symbol

Pick to copy selected
symbol(s) to Clipboard

- **Import Text.** This allows you to import text from an existing text file directly into the multiline text editor. The text file can be either a standard ASCII text file (TXT) or an RTF (rich text format) file. The imported text becomes a part of the current multiline text object.

  When this option is selected, the **Select File** dialog box is displayed. Select the text file to be imported and pick the **Open** button. If you import text while a portion of text is highlighted in the text editor, the **Inserting Text** dialog box shown in **Figure 8-19** appears. This dialog allows you to replace the highlighted text with the imported text, have the inserted text be placed after the highlighted text, or replace all of the text in the text editor with the text being inserted.

Figure 8-19.
When importing
text into the
multiline text editor
while text is
highlighted, the
**Inserting Text** dialog
box provides
insertion options.

Imported text
replaces selection

Imported text
follows selection

Imported text
replaces all text in
multiline text editor

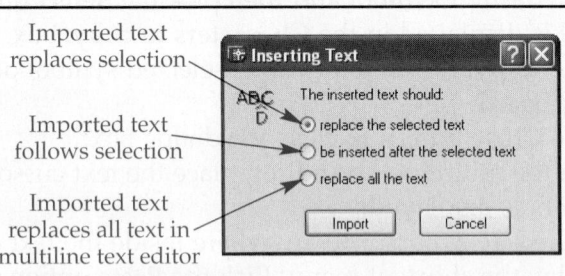

○ Start AutoCAD and use the setup option of your choice.

○ Use the **MTEXT** command to create a text boundary that is 4″ (100 mm) wide by 2″ (50 mm) high.

○ Type the following text paragraph:

> Entering a paragraph of text is quick and easy with the MTEXT command. The MTEXT command opens the multiline text editor, where text is typed and edited as needed. The MTEXT command is accessed by picking Multiline Text in the Text cascading menu of the Draw pull-down menu, by picking the Multiline Text button in the Draw toolbar, or by entering MTEXT at the Command: prompt.

○ Use the shortcut menu to select the entire paragraph and then change the height to .125″ (3 mm) and change the font from txt to Romans.

○ Select the entire paragraph again and this time change the font to Arial. Now notice that the **Bold** and **Italic** buttons are active. This is because the Arial font is a TrueType font.

○ Make the word MTEXT bold.

○ Make the words multiline text editor italic.

○ Add the following statement to your paragraph:

> The multiline text editor also makes it easy to enter the symbols for degrees (°), plus/minus (±), diameter (∅), greater than (>), and Omega (Ω).

○ Pick the **OK** button.

○ Save the drawing as EX8-4.

## Additional formatting

In addition to the shortcut menu items described above, the multiline text editor includes a couple of other right-click shortcut items. When right-clicking over the text editor ruler, a shortcut menu appears with two options. See **Figure 8-20.** The **Indents and Tabs...** option accesses the **Indents and Tabs** dialog box described earlier. Picking the **Set Mtext Width...** option displays the **Set Mtext Width** dialog box where a new width for the paragraph can be specified. The width is set initially when you pick the two corners of the text boundary.

The width of the multiline text object can also be modified by moving the cursor to the right side of the ruler. The cursor changes to a double arrow cursor. Press and hold the pick button to stretch the text editor wider or narrower.

Earlier in this section, the **Stack** button on the **Text Formatting** toolbar was discussed. When you enter a fraction in the text editor for the first time, the **AutoStack Properties** dialog box is displayed. See **Figure 8-21.** This dialog box allows you to enable AutoStacking, which causes the entered fraction to stack with a horizontal or diagonal fraction bar. You can also choose to remove the leading space between a whole number and the fraction. This dialog box is displayed each time a fraction is entered. If you decide that you do not want this dialog box to pop up each time you

**Figure 8-20.**
Right-clicking on the text editor ruler yields a shortcut menu that controls the indents and width of the multiline text object.

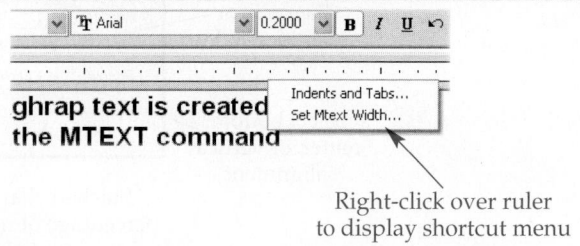

Right-click over ruler to display shortcut menu

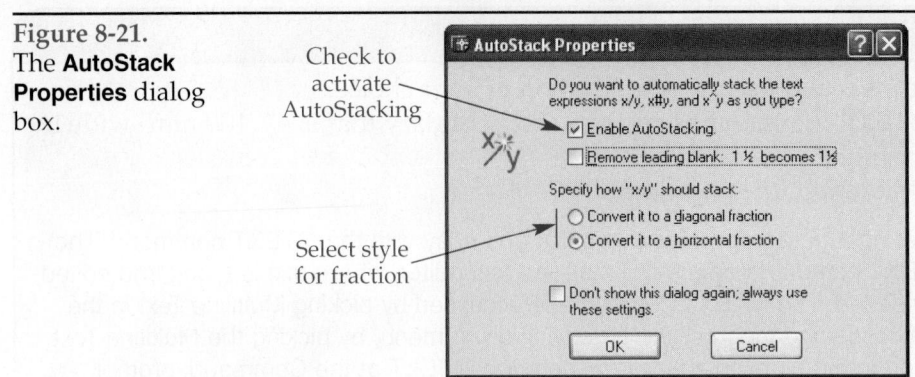

Figure 8-21.
The **AutoStack Properties** dialog box.

Check to activate AutoStacking

Select style for fraction

create a fraction, you can pick the **Don't show this dialog again; always use these settings** check box. Selecting this option causes new fractions to be created with the last settings you specified.

If you highlight a fraction and right-click, the shortcut menu appears with two additional options. The first option is **Unstack**, which causes the fraction to unstack. The upper and lower values are placed on a single line with the appropriate character (^, #, or /) displayed between the numbers. The second option is **Properties**, which displays the **Stack Properties** dialog box. The features of this dialog box are described in Figure 8-22.

## Exercise 8-5

○ Start AutoCAD and use the setup option of your choice.
○ Use the **MTEXT** command to create a text boundary that is 4″ (100 mm) wide by 2″ (50 mm) high.
○ Type the following text paragraph:

> Multiline text is created using the MTEXT command. This provides you with the opportunity to place several lines of text on a drawing and have all of the lines act as one text object. It also gives you the convenience of entering and editing the text in the multiline text editor.

○ Change the width to 2″ (50 mm) and observe the effect.
○ Change the width back to 4″ (100 mm).
○ Change the justification to a few different options to see the results. Change the justification back to top left.
○ Pick the **OK** button.
○ Save the drawing as EX8-5.

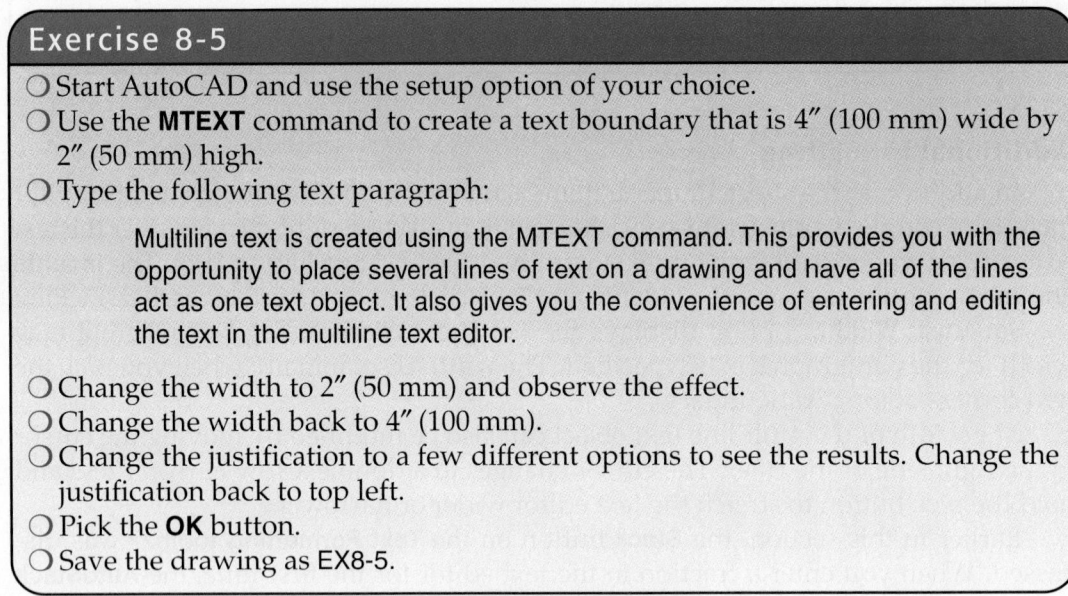

Figure 8-22.
The **Stack Properties** dialog box.

Top and bottom numbers in stack

Set horizontal, diagonal, or tolerance style

Select bottom, center, or vertical alignment

Stacked character size as percentage of normal text size

Return to default settings

Access the **AutoStack Properties** dialog box

## Setting multiline text options at the command line

When creating multiline text, you can preset some of the settings so that they do not have to be done within the text editor. These options are available from the command line when you begin creating the text boundary. Two of these options are not available anywhere else except from the command line.

After picking the first boundary corner for the text, the Specify opposite corner or [Height/Justify/Line spacing/Rotation/Style/Width]: prompt is displayed. You can select any of the options by entering the appropriate letter at the prompt. The following command sequence shows an example:

        Command: **T**, **MT**, *or* **MTEXT**↵
        Current text style: Standard. Text height: 0.2000
        Specify first corner: *(pick the first boundary corner)*
        Specify opposite corner or [Height/Justify/Line spacing/Rotation/Style/Width]: **H**↵
        Specify height <0.2000>: **.125**↵
        Specify opposite corner or [Height/Justify/Line spacing/Rotation/Style/Width]: **J**↵
        Enter justification [TL/TC/TR/ML/MC/MR/BL/BC/BR] <TL>: **MC**↵
        Specify opposite corner or [Height/Justify/Line spacing/Rotation/Style/Width]: **L**↵
        Enter line spacing type [At least/Exactly] <At least>: **E**↵
        Enter line spacing factor or distance <1x>: **2X**↵
        Specify opposite corner or [Height/Justify/Line spacing/Rotation/Style/Width]: **R**↵
        Specify rotation angle <0>: **30**↵
        Specify opposite corner or [Height/Justify/Line spacing/Rotation/Style/Width]: **S**↵
        Enter style name or [?] <Standard>: ↵
        Specify opposite corner or [Height/Justify/Line spacing/Rotation/Style/Width]: **W**↵
        Specify width: **4**↵

A value specified in the **Width** option automatically sets the text boundary width and opens the multiline text editor.

The two options available at the Command: prompt are **Line spacing** and **Rotation**. The **Line spacing** option is used to control line spacing for newly created text. When the option is first entered, the Enter line spacing type [At least/Exactly] <At least>: prompt is displayed. Entering the **At least** option automatically adds spaces between lines based on the height of the character in the line. The **Exactly** option forces the line spacing to be the same for all lines of the multiline text object. After selecting one of these options, the Enter line spacing factor or distance <1x>: prompt is displayed. A number followed by an X specifies the spacing increment. This spacing increment is the vertical distance from the bottom of one line to the bottom of the next line of multiline text. For example, single-spaced lines are a value of 1X, and double spaced lines are a value of 2X.

The **Rotation** option allows you to specify a rotation angle for the text. After entering the rotation option the Specify rotation angle <0>: prompt is displayed. Enter a rotation value in degrees. After the text has been entered in the text editor and the **OK** button has been selected, the multiline text object is rotated at the desired angle.

---

NOTE

The **–MTEXT** command can be used to enter a multiline text object without using the multiline text editor. The options at the Command: prompt are identical to the options for the **MTEXT** command. Lines of text are entered at the Mtext: prompt, similar to the entry of single-line text.

---

# AutoCAD Text Fonts

A *font* is a particular letter face design. The standard AutoCAD text fonts are shown in **Figure 8-23.** These fonts have .shx file extensions.

The txt font is the AutoCAD default. The txt font is rather rough in appearance and may not be the best choice for your application, even though the txt font requires less time to regenerate than other fonts. The Romans (roman simplex) font is smoother than txt. It closely duplicates the single-stroke lettering that has long been the standard for most drafting. The complex and triplex fonts are multistroke fonts for drawing titles and subtitles. The gothic and italic fonts are ornamental styles. In addition, AutoCAD provides several standard symbol fonts.

Several additional AutoCAD fonts provide special alphabets or symbols that are accessed by typing specific keys. This is called *character mapping*. Character mapping for non-Roman and symbol fonts is displayed in **Figure 8-24.**

*TrueType* fonts are scaleable and have an outline. *Scaleable* means the font can be displayed on the screen or printed at any size and still maintain proportion. TrueType fonts have an outline, but they appear filled in the AutoCAD window. When you plot or print, the fonts can be filled or shown as an outline. The **TEXTFILL** system variable controls this appearance. The **TEXTFILL** default is 1, which draws filled fonts. A setting of 0 draws the font outlines.

**Figure 8-23.**
Standard AutoCAD text and symbol fonts.

AutoCAD and its Applications—Basics

**Figure 8-24.**
Character mapping for non-Roman and symbol fonts.

| | A | B | C | D | E | F | G | H | I | J | K | L | M | N | O | P | Q | R | S | T | U | V | W | X | Y | Z |
|---|---|---|---|---|---|---|---|---|---|---|---|---|---|---|---|---|---|---|---|---|---|---|---|---|---|---|
| Greekc | Α | Β | Χ | Δ | Ε | Φ | Γ | Η | Ι | ϑ | Κ | Λ | Μ | Ν | Ο | Π | Θ | Ρ | Σ | Τ | Υ | ∇ | Ω | Ξ | Ψ | Ζ |
| Greeks | Α | Β | Χ | Δ | Ε | Φ | Γ | Η | Ι | ϑ | Κ | Λ | Μ | Ν | Ο | Π | Θ | Ρ | Σ | Τ | Υ | ∇ | Ω | Ξ | Ψ | Ζ |
| Syastro | ☉ | ☿ | ♀ | ⊕ | ♂ | ♃ | ♄ | ♅ | ♆ | ♇ | ☽ | ♋ | ✳ | ♌ | ♋ | ♈ | ♉ | ♊ | ♋ | ♌ | ♍ | ♎ | ♏ | ♐ | ♑ | ♒ |
| Symap | ○ | □ | △ | ◇ | ☆ | + | × | ∗ | ● | ■ | ▲ | ◀ | ▼ | ▶ | ★ | ↑ | ± | ↑ | ↗ | ⍟ | ♠ | ♣ | ♦ | ⊕ | © | ♻ | △ |
| Symath | ℵ | ′ | \| | ‖ | ± | ∓ | × | · | ÷ | = | ≠ | ≡ | < | > | ≤ | ≥ | ∝ | ~ | √ | ⊂ | ∪ | ⊃ | ∩ | ∈ | → | ↑ |
| Symeteo | · | · | ∗ | ▲ | ▄ | ↘ | ∧ | ∩ | ∩ | ∪ | ∪ | ’ | ‘ | ʃ | ∽ | ∞ | ℝ | ϛ | — | ╱ | \| | ╲ | ￣ | ╱ | ╱ |
| Symusic | · | ♩ | ♪ | ◡ | ○ | ● | ♯ | ♮ | ♭ | — | – | × | ↱ | 𝄞 | ℗: | 𝄡 | • | > | --- | ⌐ | ∧ | ＝ | ▽ |

Samples of several TrueType fonts are shown in **Figure 8-25**. The architect's hand-lettered font Stylus BT is an excellent choice for the artistic appearance desired on architectural drawings. Try them and use the one you like the best.

**Figure 8-25.**
Some of the many TrueType fonts available.

**Swiss 721**

| | |
|---|---|
| swiss (regular) | abcdABCD12345 |
| swissi (italic) | *abcdABCD12345* |
| swissb (bold) | **abcdABCD1234** |
| swissbi (bold italic) | ***abcdABCD12345*** |

**Monospace 821**

| | |
|---|---|
| monos (monospaced) | abcdABCD12345 |
| monosi (italic) | *abcdABCD12345* |

**Dutch 801 (serif)**

| | |
|---|---|
| dutch (regular) | abcdABCD12345 |
| dutchi (italic) | *abcdABCD12345* |
| dutchb (bold) | **abcdABCD12345** |
| dutchbi (bold italic) | ***abcdABCD12345*** |

**Architect's Hand Lettered**

| | |
|---|---|
| stylus BT | abcdABCD 12345 |

**Bank Gothic (all caps)**

| | |
|---|---|
| bgothl (light) | ABCDABCD 1 2345 |
| bgothm (medium) | ABCDABCD 1 2345 |

**Commercial Script**

| | |
|---|---|
| comsc (regular) | *abcdABCD12345* |

**Vineta (shadow)**

| | |
|---|---|
| vinet (regular) | **abcdABCD12345** |

**Commercial Pi**

| | |
|---|---|
| compi (regular) | ©®©® ± °′″ ●●-■ |

**Universal Math**

| | |
|---|---|
| umath (regular) | αβψδABΨΔ + − × ÷ = |

**PROFESSIONAL TIP**

TrueType fonts and other complex text fonts can be very taxing on system resources. This can slow down display changes and increase drawing regeneration time significantly. Use these fonts only when necessary. When you must use complex fonts, set your system variables to speed-optimized settings.

# AutoCAD Text Styles

Text styles are variations of fonts. A *text style* gives height, width, obliquing angle (slant), and other characteristics to a text font. You may have several text styles that use the same font, but with different characteristics. By default, the Standard text style uses the txt font, 0 degrees rotation angle, width of 1, and 0 degrees obliquing angle.

## Selecting and Modifying Text Styles

STYLE
ST

Format
➥ Text Style...

Styles
toolbar

Text Style Manager

Text styles are created, modified, and deleted using the **Text Style** dialog box, shown in **Figure 8-26**. Access this dialog box by picking **Text Style...** from the **Format** pull-down menu, selecting the **Text Style Manager** button in the **Styles** toolbar, or by entering ST or STYLE at the Command: prompt. The following describes the features found in this dialog box:

- **Style Name area.** Set a new current text style by making a selection from the drop-down list. Use the **New...** button to create a new text style and the **Rename...** button to rename a selected style. If you need to delete a style, use the **Delete** button.
- **Font area.** This area of the **Text Style** dialog box is where you select an available font, style of the selected font, and text height.
  - **Font Name.** This drop-down list is used to access the available fonts. The default font is txt.shx. All SHX fonts are identified with an AutoCAD compass symbol, while the TrueType fonts have the TrueType symbol.
  - **Font Style.** This drop-down list is inactive unless the selected font has options available, such as bold or italic. None of the SHX fonts have additional options, but some of the TrueType fonts may. For example, the SansSerif font has Regular, Bold, BoldOblique, and Oblique options. Each option provides the font with a different appearance.

**Figure 8-26.**
The **Text Style** dialog box is used to set the characteristics of a text style.

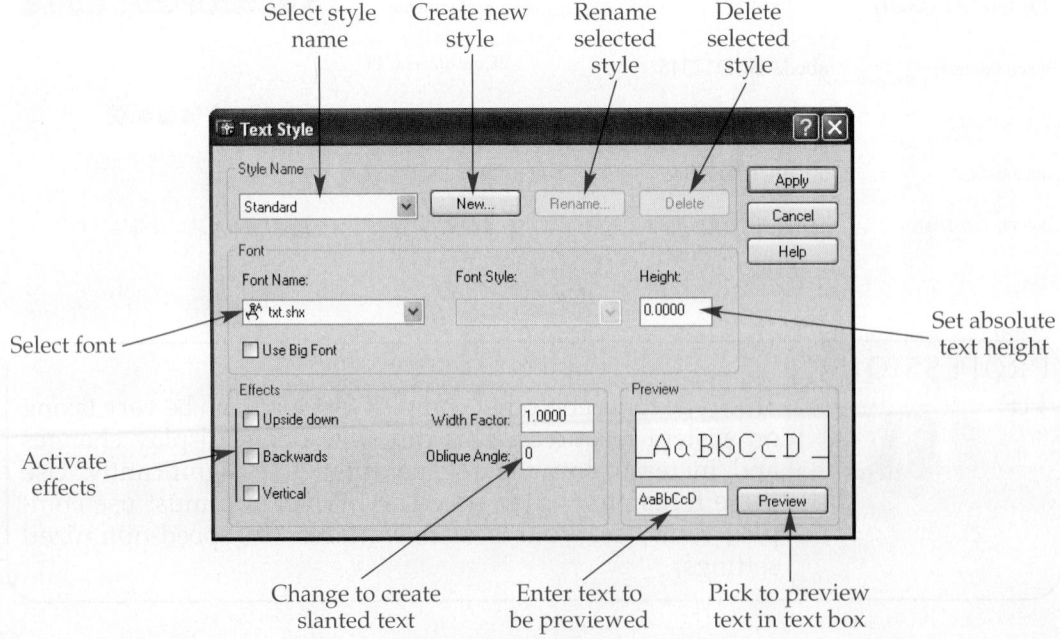

- **Height.** This text box is used to set the text height. The default is 0.0000. This allows you to set the text height in the **TEXT** command. If you set a value such as .125, the text height becomes fixed for this text style and you are not prompted for the text height. Setting a text height value other than zero saves time during the command process, but also eliminates your flexibility. ASME recommended text heights were discussed earlier in this chapter.

---

**NOTE**  The default text height is stored in the **TEXTSIZE** system variable. When a text style has a height other than 0, the style height overrides any default value stored in this variable.

---

**PROFESSIONAL TIP**  It is recommended that a text height value of 0 be used for text styles used in dimensions. Dimension styles allow you to specify a text height value for the annotation text. By specifying a text height in the text style, the dimension text height is overridden. Dimension styles are discussed later in this text.

---

- **Use Big Font.** Asian and other large format fonts (called *Big Fonts*) are activated with this check box. The Big Font is used as a supplement to define many symbols not available in normal font files.
- **Effects area.** This area of the **Text Style** dialog box is used to set the text format. It contains the following options, which are shown in **Figure 8-27**:
  - **Upside down.** This check box is off by default. When it is checked, the text you draw is placed upside down.
  - **Backwards.** When the box is checked, text that you draw is placed backwards.
  - **Vertical.** This check box is inactive for all TrueType fonts. A check in this box makes SHX font text vertical. Text on drawings is normally placed horizontally, but vertical text can be used for special effects and graphic designs. Vertical text works best when the rotation angle is 270°.

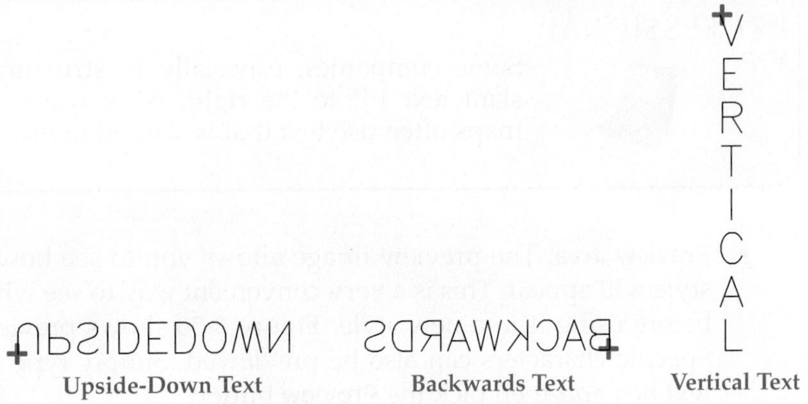

---

Figure 8-27.
Special effects for
text styles can be set
in the **Text Style**
dialog box.

UPSIDEDOWN
Upside-Down Text

BACKWARDS
Backwards Text

V
E
R
T
I
C
A
L
Vertical Text

The multiline text editor only displays the text horizontally, right-side up, and forward. Any special effects such as vertical, backwards, or upside down take effect when you pick **OK** to exit the editor.

- **Width Factor.** This text box provides a value that defines the text character width relative to the height. A width factor of 1 is the default. A width factor greater than 1 expands the characters, and a factor less than 1 compresses the characters. See **Figure 8-28.**
- **Oblique Angle.** This text box allows you to set an angle at which text is slanted. The zero default draws characters vertically. A value greater than 0 slants the characters to the right, while a negative value slants characters to the left. See **Figure 8-29.** Some fonts, such as *italic,* are already slanted.

**Figure 8-28.**
Text width factors are set in the **Text Style** dialog box.

| Width Factor | Text |
|---|---|
| 1 | ABCDEFGHIJKLM |
| .5 | ABCDEFGHIJKLMNOPQRSTUVWXY |
| 1.5 | ABCDEFGHI |
| 2 | ABCDEFG |

**Figure 8-29.**
Text obliquing angles are set in the **Text Style** dialog box.

| Obliquing Angle | Text |
|---|---|
| 0 | ABCDEFGHIJKLM |
| 15 | *ABCDEFGHIJKLM* |
| –15 | ABCDEFGHIJKLM |

 Some companies, especially in structural drafting, like to slant text 15° to the right. Also, water features named on maps often use text that is slanted to the right.

- **Preview area.** The preview image allows you to see how the selected font or style will appear. This is a very convenient way to see what the font looks like before using it in a new style. **Figure 8-30** shows previews of various fonts. Specific characters can also be previewed. Simply type the characters in the text box and then pick the **Preview** button.

**Figure 8-30.**
The **Preview** image shows a sample of the font. A—The Scripts font. B—The Gothice font. C—The Italic font.

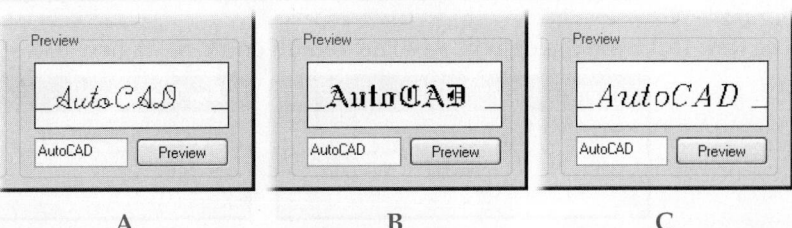

A                  B                  C

## Exercise 8-6

○ Start AutoCAD with the setup option of your choice.
○ Open the **Text Style** dialog box.
○ Access the **Style Name** drop-down list and look through the available options. Select a few of the options that you want to see displayed in the preview image.
○ Go to the **Font Name** drop-down list and select a few different fonts to see their image in the preview tile. Pick the SansSerif font and then open the **Font Style** drop-down list. Pick each of the options as you watch the preview image change to represent your selection.
○ Turn the **Upside down** and **Backwards** check boxes on and then off while you watch the preview image.
○ Change the width factor to 2, .5, and back to 1 while you watch the **Preview** image.
○ Change the obliquing angle to 15, 30, –15, –30, and then back to 0 while you watch the **Preview** image.
○ Type your own desired characters in the box to the left of the **Preview** button and then pick the button.
○ Pick the **Close** button.
○ Exit AutoCAD or leave this drawing open for the next exercise.

## Creating a New Text Style

If you start a new drawing with the AutoCAD default template, the only text style available is the Standard style. The Standard text style is based on the txt font, which is not very attractive. This may not suit your needs.

What if you want to create a text style for mechanical drawings that uses the Romans font and characters .125″ high? You want to have this available as the most commonly used text on your drawings. You decide to name the style ROMANS-125. This is a name that you can remember, because it uses Romans font characters that are .125″ high. It is still a good idea to record the name and details about the text styles you create and keep this information in a log for future reference.

Text style names can have up to 255 characters, including letters, numbers, dashes (–), underlines (_), and dollar signs ($). You can enter uppercase or lowercase letters. The following explains the steps to use to create this text style:

1. Open the **Text Style** dialog box. Standard is the current style with txt.shx as the font, and a zero text height.
2. Pick the **New...** button. This opens the **New Text Style** dialog box, **Figure 8-31A**. Notice style1 is in the **Style Name** text box. You can keep a text style name like style1 or style2, but this is not descriptive. Type ROMANS-125 in the box and then pick the **OK** button. See **Figure 8-31B**. ROMANS-125 is now displayed in the **Style Name** text box of the **Text Style** dialog box.
3. Go to the **Font Name** drop-down list, find romans.shx, and pick it. The font is now romans.shx.

Figure 8-31.
The **New Text Style** dialog box. A—The default entry. B—A new text style entered.

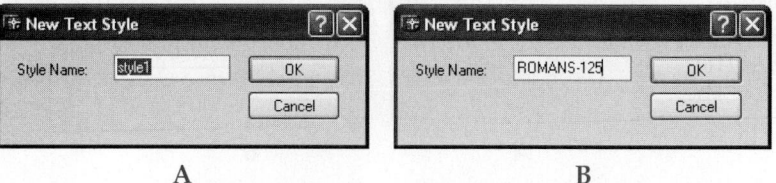

A                                    B

Figure 8-32.
The **Text Style** dialog box showing the changes in the style, font, and height.

New style name

Font for new style

Height for new style

4. Change the value in the **Height** text box to .125. **Figure 8-32** shows the work done in Steps 2, 3, and 4.
5. Pick the **Apply** button and then the **Close** button. The new ROMANS-125 text style is now part of your drawing.

Now, ROMANS-125 is the default style when you use the **TEXT** or **MTEXT** commands. If you want to create a similar text style for your architectural drawings, you might consider a style name called ARCHITECTURAL-125. For this style, set the font name to Stylus BT and the height to .125.

**PROFESSIONAL TIP**

You can make the text style name the same as the font name if you wish. In some cases, this is a clear and concise way of naming the style.

## Exercise 8-7

○ Start AutoCAD with the setup option of your choice.
○ Open the **Text Style** dialog box.
○ Create a text style named ROMANS-125 if you commonly do mechanical drawings, or ARCHITECTURAL-125 if you commonly do architectural drawings.
   ○ For ROMANS-125, set the font name to romans.shx and the height to .125.
   ○ For ARCHITECTURAL-125, set the font name to Stylus BT and the height to .125.
○ Pick the **Apply** button and then close the **Text Style** dialog box.
○ Try out your new text style with the **TEXT** and **MTEXT** commands.
○ Create a text style named ROMANS if you commonly do mechanical drawings, or ARCHITECTURAL if you commonly do architectural drawings.
   ○ For ROMANS, set the font name to romans.shx and the height to 0.
   ○ For ARCHITECTURAL, set the font name to Stylus BT and the height to 0.
○ Pick the **Apply** button and then close the **Text Style** dialog box.
○ Try out your new text style with the **TEXT** and **MTEXT** commands.
○ Save the drawing as EX8-7.

---

**PROFESSIONAL TIP**  To save valuable drafting time, add text styles to your template drawings. If only a single text height is needed in the template, set the text height for the style. Do not forget to consider the scale factor when entering the text height. Enter the scaled text height for the style.

## Changing, Renaming, and Deleting Text Styles

You can change the current text style without affecting existing text objects. The changes are applied only to text added using that style.

Existing text styles are easily renamed in the **Text Style** dialog box. Select the desired style name in the **Style Name** text box and pick the **Rename...** button. This opens the **Rename Text Style** dialog box, which is similar to the **New Text Style** dialog box. Change the text style name in the **Style Name** text box and pick the **OK** button.

---

**NOTE**  Styles can also be renamed using the **Text styles** option of the **Rename** dialog box. This dialog box is accessed by selecting **Rename...** from the **Format** pull-down menu or by entering RENAME at the Command: prompt.

---

You can also delete an existing text style in the **Text Style** dialog box by picking the desired style name in the **Style Name** drop-down list followed by picking the **Delete** button. If you try to delete a text style that has been used to create text objects in the drawing, AutoCAD gives you the following message:

   Style is in use, can't be deleted.

This means that there are text objects in the drawing that reference this style. If you want to delete the style, change the text objects in the drawing to a different style. You cannot delete or rename the Standard style.

---

**NOTE**

If you change the font and orientation of an existing text style, all text items with that style are redrawn with the new values.

## Importing Text Styles from Existing Drawings

**DesignCenter** can be used to import text styles from existing drawing files. **DesignCenter** allows you to browse through drawing files to find desired text styles, and then add the needed style into your current drawing file. For a complete introduction to the **DesignCenter**, see Chapter 1.

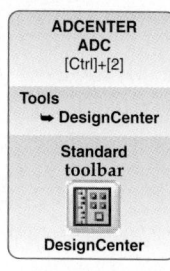
The **DesignCenter** can be accessed by picking the **DesignCenter** button on the **Standard** toolbar, selecting **DesignCenter** from the **Tools** pull-down menu, entering ADC or ADCENTER at the Command: prompt, or using the [Ctrl]+[2] key combination. See **Figure 8-33**.

The following procedure is used to import a text style into the current drawing:

1. In the tree view area, locate the existing drawing containing the text style to be copied.
2. Double-click on the file name or pick the plus (+) sign next to it to list the various types of content within the drawing.
3. Pick the Textstyles content in the tree view. This displays the text styles.
4. Select the text style or text styles to be copied into the drawing. You can then copy the text style in any of the following ways:

   - **Drag and drop.** Move the cursor over the top of the desired text style(s), press and hold the pick button on your pointing device, and drag the cursor to the drawing area of the opened drawing. Let go of the pick button and the text style(s) is added to your current drawing file.
   - **Shortcut menu.** Position the cursor over the desired text style and right-click to open the shortcut menu. See **Figure 8-33**. Pick the **Add Text Style(s)** option, and the text style is added to your current drawing.
   - **Copy and paste.** Use the shortcut menu as described in the previous method, but select the **Copy** option. Move the cursor to the drawing where you want the text style added, then right-click your mouse button and select the **Paste** option from the shortcut menu. The copied text style is added to the current drawing.

**Figure 8-33.**
**DesignCenter** allows you to copy a text style from an existing drawing into the current drawing.

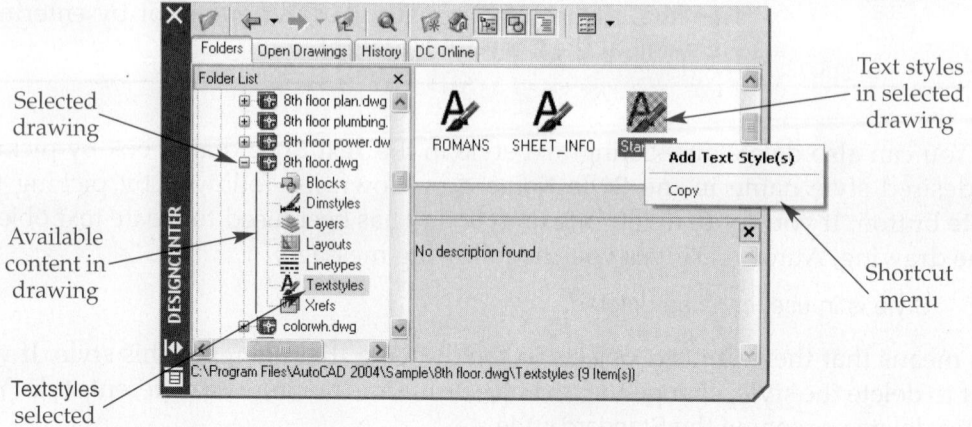

**PROFESSIONAL TIP** To select more than one text style at one time to import into your current drawing file, hold down the [Shift] key and pick the first and last text styles in a group of text styles, or hold down the [Ctrl] key to select multiple text styles individually.

**NOTE** New text styles can be created at the Command: prompt with the **-STYLE** command. After entering the command, you are prompted to enter the new style name and properties (such as font, height, and obliquing angle).

## Exercise 8-8

○ Start a new drawing and create four text styles. Save this drawing as EX8-8a and close the drawing.

○ Open a drawing you created in an earlier chapter that contains only the Standard text style.

○ Use **DesignCenter** to insert text styles into the current drawing from EX8-8a by following these instructions:

   ○ Insert one text style at a time, using each of the three methods to insert each text style.

   ○ Insert two text styles at the same time. If a duplicate insertion of text styles is inserted, AutoCAD ignores this duplication by giving you this message: Textstyle(s) added. Duplicate definitions will be ignored.

   ○ Insert all four text styles at the same time.

○ Save the exercise as EX8-8.

## Redrawing Text Quickly

Text often requires a great deal of time to regenerate, redraw, and plot because each character is drawn with many individual vectors (line segments). The Quick Text mode makes text appear as rectangles equal to the height and length of each text string. This speeds regeneration and plotting time. The Quick Text mode is turned on and off with the **QTEXT** (quick text) command. **Figure 8-34** shows a comparison between displays when the Quick Text mode is on and off.

The **QTEXT** command is entered at the Command: prompt. If the last setting was off, the command line appears as follows:

QTEXT

    Command: **QTEXT**↵
    Enter mode [ON/OFF] <Off>:

Enter ON to activate Quick Text mode and quicken the redraw time. This mode can also be activated by selecting the **Show text boundary frame only** option in the **Display performance** area of the **Display** tab of the **Options** dialog box. This dialog box can be accessed by selecting **Options...** from the **Tools** pull-down menu.

---

**Figure 8-34.**
Comparison of
Quick Text mode
turned on and off.

Quick Text Mode On

THE QUICK TEXT MODE IS USED TO
SPEED REGENERATION TIME IN
COMPLEX DRAWINGS.

Quick Text Mode Off

> **NOTE**
>
> If you print with Quick Text mode on, the text prints as box outlines, not as actual text. If you want the actual text to print, turn Quick Text mode off before printing.

## Revising Text with DDEDIT

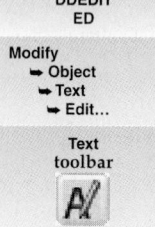

DDEDIT
ED

Modify
→ Object
→ Text
→ Edit...

Text
toolbar

Edit Text

Text editing is accomplished using the **DDEDIT** command. **DDEDIT** is accessed by picking **Text** and then **Edit...** from the **Object** cascading menu in the **Modify** pull-down menu, entering ED or DDEDIT at the Command: prompt, or selecting the **Edit Text** button on the **Text** toolbar. The **DDEDIT** command can also be accessed by selecting the text object, right-clicking, and selecting **Mtext Edit...** or **Text Edit...** from the shortcut menu.

If you pick single-line text, you get the **Edit Text** dialog box, **Figure 8-35.** Enter the new text string in the **Text:** text box. If you pick text that was drawn with the **MTEXT** command, you get the multiline text editor. Multiline text is also drawn with the **LEADER** command, which is explained in Chapter 17.

**Figure 8-35.**
The **DDEDIT**
command activates
the **Edit Text** dialog
box if the selected
text object was
created with the
**TEXT** command.

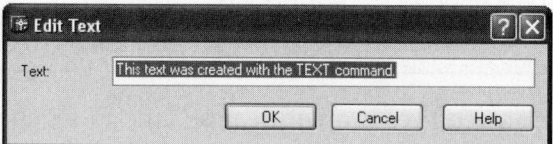

> **PROFESSIONAL TIP**
>
>
>
> You can double-click on a text object to edit it. Double-clicking on a single-line text object (**TEXT**) opens the **Edit Text** dialog box. Double-clicking on a multiline text object (**MTEXT**) opens the multiline text editor.

AutoCAD and its Applications—Basics

## Exercise 8-9

○ Start AutoCAD and use the setup option of your choice.
○ Use the **TEXT** command to place the following text:

   3068 SOLID CORE PANELED ENTRY DOOR SC306 ACME DOOR CO.

○ Use the **DDEDIT** command to change the text to read:

   3'-0" × 6'-8" STEEL FRAME PANELED ENTRY DOOR ER44 CECO ENTRY SYSTEMS.

○ Turn the Quick Text mode on, then off. Observe the results. Do not forget to use **REGEN** to change the display.
○ Save the drawing as EX8-9.

## Changing Text with the Properties Window

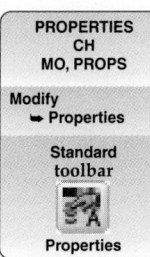

PROPERTIES
CH
MO, PROPS

Modify
➥ Properties

Standard
toolbar

Properties

The **Properties** window can be used to change text. The **Properties** window can be opened by picking the **Properties** button on the **Standard** toolbar, selecting **Properties** from the **Modify** pull-down menu, or entering CH, MO, PROPS, or PROPERTIES at the Command: prompt. You can also open the **Properties** window by selecting the desired text and then right-clicking and selecting **Properties** from the shortcut menu.

You have two options for selecting text to change. You can select the desired text and then display the **Properties** window, or you can display the **Properties** window and then select the desired text. If you display the **Properties** window first, you may need to move the window before you can select the text (if the window covers the text you want to pick). Either way, the **Properties** window is opened, as shown in **Figure 8-36.**

Notice the top of the window displays Text in the box. This informs you that a text object has been selected. If multiple objects are selected, the drop-down list is used to select which object has its properties displayed.

The properties of the text object are displayed in different categories within the window. Picking on top of a property allows you to modify its value. The text properties are divided into the following categories:

- **General.** These general properties are found in nearly all AutoCAD object types. The general properties include color, layer, linetype, linetype scale, plot style, lineweight, hyperlink, and thickness.
- **Text.** Text properties are common to text and multiline text objects. These properties were explained earlier in this chapter and include items such as justification, rotation, and style.
- **Geometry.** The geometry properties are the X, Y, and Z coordinate locations of the text insertion point.
- **Misc.** The miscellaneous settings are the Upside down and Backward properties. These properties are not listed for multiline text objects.

To change a property, pick the property or property setting with the cursor. The property setting can then be edited. For some properties, a pull-down can be used to select other settings. See **Figure 8-37.**

After you make the desired changes to your text, press [Enter] to apply the changes or pick the "X" in the **Properties** window title bar to close the **Properties** window. Then press the [Esc] key to deselect the text.

**Figure 8-36.**
The **Properties** window shows the properties of the selected text. Note the properties of text created with the **TEXT** command are slightly different from the properties of text created with the **MTEXT** command.

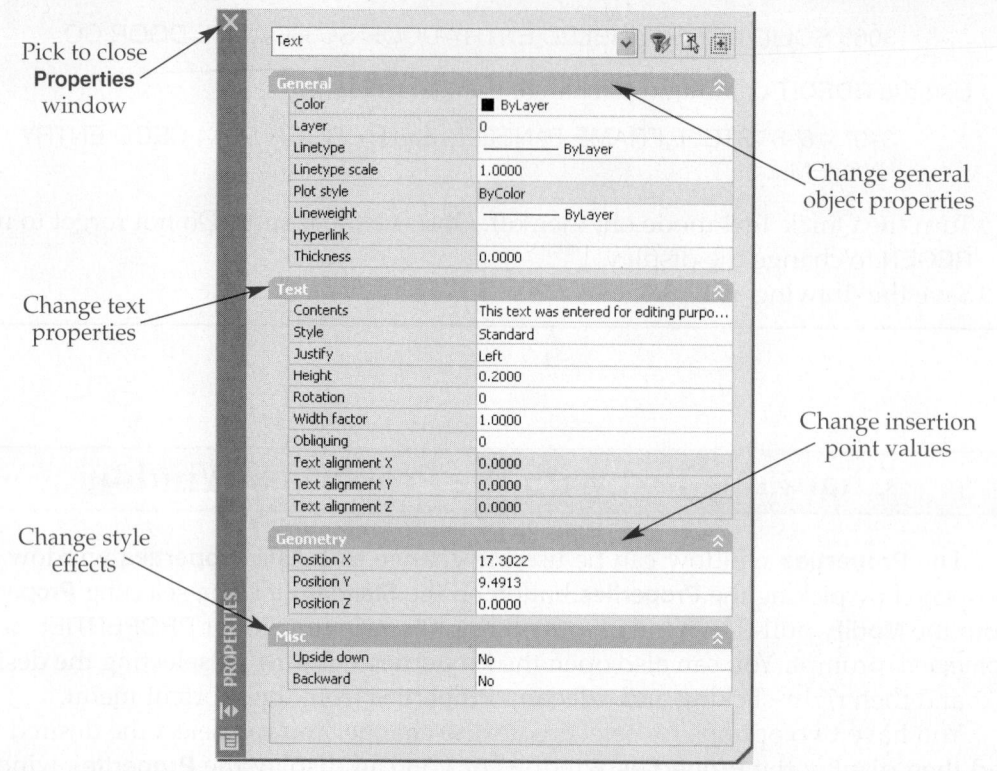

Pick to close **Properties** window

Change text properties

Change style effects

Change general object properties

Change insertion point values

**Figure 8-37.**
Modifying a property using the **Properties** window. When the **Justify** property is picked, the drop-down arrow appears next to the Left setting. Picking the arrow exposes the drop-down menu shown.

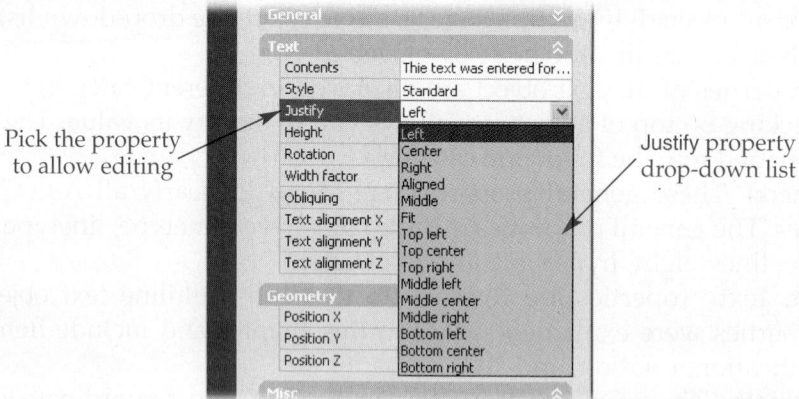

Pick the property to allow editing

Justify property drop-down list

The **Properties** window can also be used to change multiline text. When you select the multiline text to change, the **Properties** window appears with MText identified as the selected object, as shown in **Figure 8-38**. The properties listed are similar to those listed for a text object. The properties that differ for the two objects are described below:

- **Contents.** Allows you to edit the text by picking the button at the right to open the multiline text editor.
- **Direction.** Allows you to specify the horizontal or vertical direction of the multiline text object.
- **Width.** Allows you to specify the width of the multiline text object.

**Figure 8-38.**
The **Properties** window with a multiline text object selected. Note the list of properties is slightly different than the list for a text object.

Selected object type

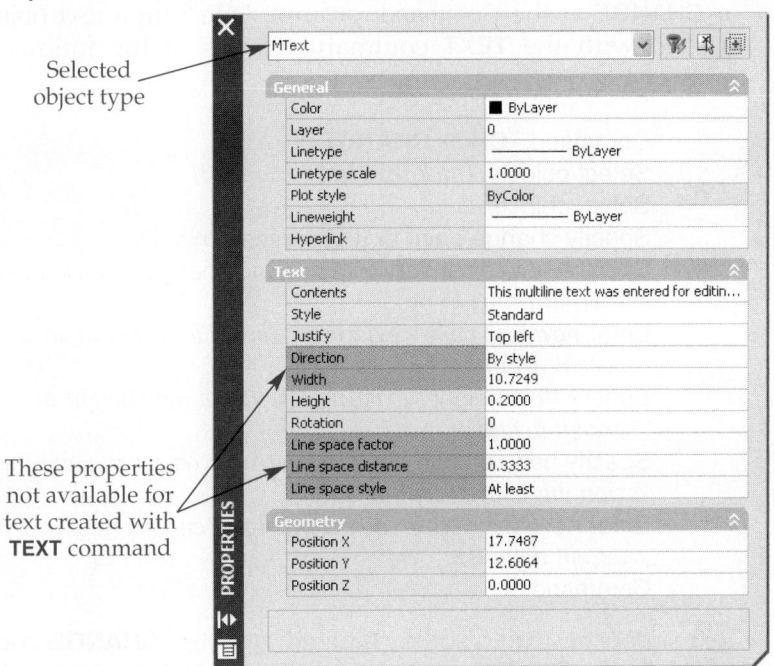

These properties not available for text created with **TEXT** command

- **Line Space Factor.** Allows you to specify the line spacing factor of the multi-line text object.
- **Line Space Distance.** Allows you to specify the line spacing to an absolute value measured in drawing units.
- **Line Space Style.** Allows you to specify the line spacing style of the multiline text object.

## Exercise 8-10

○ Start AutoCAD and use the setup option of your choice.
○ Use the **MTEXT** command to place the following text on your drawing (incorrectly as shown) using ROMANS style and .125 text height. Insert the first boundary corner at 1,4 and the opposite corner at 9.5,2.5.

1. INTERPRET DEMINSIONIN AND TOLERENCING
   PER ANSI Y14.5M–1982.
2. MOVE ALL BURRS AND EDGES.
3. ALL FILLETS AND ROUNDS ARE .125 R.
4. FINISH ALL OVER.

○ Use the **Properties** window to modify the above text as follows:
  ○ Change the text to read:

1. INTERPRET DIMENSIONING AND TOLERANCING PER ASME
   Y14.5M–1994.
2. REMOVE ALL BURRS AND SHARP EDGES.
3. ALL FILLETS AND ROUNDS R.125.
4. FINISH ALL OVER 62 MICROINCHES.

  ○ Change the color to Blue.
  ○ Change the justification to Bottom right.
  ○ Change the insertion point to 8,2.
○ Save the drawing as EX8-10.

NOTE

The **CHANGE** command can also be used to modify single-line text objects. This command is accessed by entering -CH or CHANGE at the Command: prompt. Selecting a text object created with the **TEXT** command results in the following prompts:

> Command: **-CH** *or* **CHANGE**↵
> Select objects: *(pick text to be changed)*
> Select objects: ↵
> Specify change point or [Properties]: ↵
> Specify new text insertion point <no change>: *(pick a new text location)*
> Enter new text style *<existing>*: *(enter a new style or accept default)*
> Specify new height *<existing>*: *(enter a new height or accept default)*
> Specify new rotation angle *<existing>*: *(enter a new rotation angle or accept default)*
> Enter new text *<selected text string>*: *(enter a new text or accept default)*
> Command:

Text properties can also be changed with the **CHANGE** command. At the Specify change point or [Properties]: prompt, enter P for properties. You will receive the following prompt:

> Enter property to change [Color/Elev/LAyer/LType/ltScale/LWeight/Thickness]:

Enter the property you wish to change.

The **CHANGE** command cannot be used to specify a new insertion point for text created with the **MTEXT** command. Also, the thickness and elevation of **MTEXT** objects cannot be changed with this command.

## Scaling Text

Changing the height of text objects can be accomplished using the **SCALETEXT** command. The **SCALETEXT** command allows you to scale text objects in relation to their individual insertion points or in relation to a single base point. **SCALETEXT** is accessed by picking **Scale** from the **Text** cascading menu of the **Object** cascading menu in the **Modify** pull-down menu, entering SCALETEXT at the Command: prompt, or selecting the **Scale Text** button on the **Text** toolbar.

**SCALETEXT** works with single-line and multiline text objects. You can select both types of text objects simultaneously when using the **SCALETEXT** command. The prompts for the **SCALETEXT** command are as follows:

> Command: **SCALETEXT**↵
> Select objects: *(select the text object(s) to be scaled)*
> Enter a base point option for scaling
> [Existing/Left/Center/Middle/Right/TL/TC/TR/ML/MC/MR/BL/BC/BR] <Existing>: *(specify justification for base point)*
> Specify new height or [Match object/Scale factor] *<default>*: *(specify scaling option)*
> Command:

SCALETEXT

Modify
➥ Object
➥ Text
➥ Scale

Text
toolbar

Scale Text

All the justification options except **Existing** and **Left** are shown in **Figures 8-6** and **8-7**. Using the **Existing** option scales the text objects using their existing justification setting as the base point. Using the **Left** option scales the text objects using their lower-left point as the base point. **Figure 8-39** shows text with different justification points being scaled using the **Existing** option. Notice how the text is scaled in relation to its own justification setting.

After specifying the justification to be used as the base point, AutoCAD prompts for the scaling type. The **Specify new height** option (default) allows you to type a new value for the text height. All the selected text objects change to the new text height. The **Match object** option allows you to pick an existing text object. The selected text object's height adopts the text height from the picked text object. Use the **Scale factor** option to scale text objects that have different heights in relation to their current heights. Using a scale factor of 2 scales all the selected text objects to twice their current size.

---

**Figure 8-39.**
Using the **Existing** option of the **SCALETEXT** command, text objects are scaled using their individual justification settings.

BL Justification
MC Justification
TR Justification

Original Text

BL Justification
MC Justification
TR Justification

Text Scaled Using
Existing Base Point Option

---

## Changing Text Justification

If you use the **Properties** window to change the justification setting of a text object, the text object(s) move to adjust to the new justification point. The justification point does not move. To change the justification point without moving the text, use the **JUSTIFYTEXT** command. **JUSTIFYTEXT** is accessed by picking **Justify** from the **Text** cascading menu of the **Object** cascading menu from the **Modify** pull-down menu, entering JUSTIFYTEXT at the Command: prompt, or by selecting the **Justify Text** button on the **Text** toolbar.

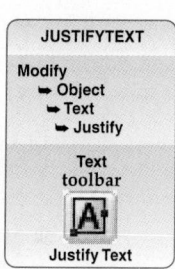

JUSTIFYTEXT

Modify
➡ Object
➡ Text
➡ Justify

Text
toolbar

Justify Text

---

### Exercise 8-11

○ Start AutoCAD and use the setup option of your choice.
○ Using the **TEXT** command, place three lines of text in the drawing. Give each line a different height and justification.
○ Use the **SCALETEXT** command to scale the text height up two times their current values.
○ Use the **JUSTIFYTEXT** command to change all the text objects to have the same justification setting.

---

# Checking Your Spelling

You have been introduced to editing text on the drawing using the **DDEDIT** command and the **Properties** window. You can use these methods to change lines of text and even correct spelling errors. However, AutoCAD has a powerful and convenient tool for checking the spelling on your drawing.

SPELL
SP

Tools
➥ Spelling...

To check spelling, enter SP or SPELL at the Command: prompt or pick **Spelling** from the **Tools** pull-down menu. After entering the command, you are asked to select the text to be checked. You need to pick each line of single-line text or make one pick on multiline text to select the entire paragraph. You can enter the **All** selection method to select all text in the drawing.

The **Check Spelling** dialog box is displayed. See **Figure 8-40.** The following describes the features found in the **Check Spelling** dialog box:

- **Current dictionary: American English.** The dictionary being used is identified at the top of the dialog box. You can change to a different dictionary by picking the **Change Dictionaries...** button.
- **Current word.** Displays a word that may be spelled incorrectly.
- **Suggestions.** Gives you a list of possible correct spellings for the current word. The highlighted word in the first box is AutoCAD's best guess. Following the highlighted word is a list of other choices. If there are many choices, a scroll bar is available for you to use. If you do not like the word that AutoCAD has highlighted, move the cursor arrow to another word and pick it. The word you pick then becomes highlighted in the list and is shown in the **Suggestions** text box. If none of the words in the **Suggestion** text box or list are correct and the current word is not correct either, you can enter the correct word in the **Suggestions** text box.
- **Ignore.** Pick this button to skip the current word. In **Figure 8-40,** ASME is not a misspelled word, it just is not recognized by the dictionary. You would select the **Ignore** button and the spell check goes on to the next word.
- **Ignore All.** Pick this button if you want AutoCAD to ignore all words that match the currently found misspelled word.
- **Change.** Pick this button to replace the current word with the word in the **Suggestions** text box.
- **Change All.** Pick this button if you want to replace the **Current word** with the word in the **Suggestions** text box throughout the entire selection set.

Figure 8-40.
The **Check Spelling** dialog box.

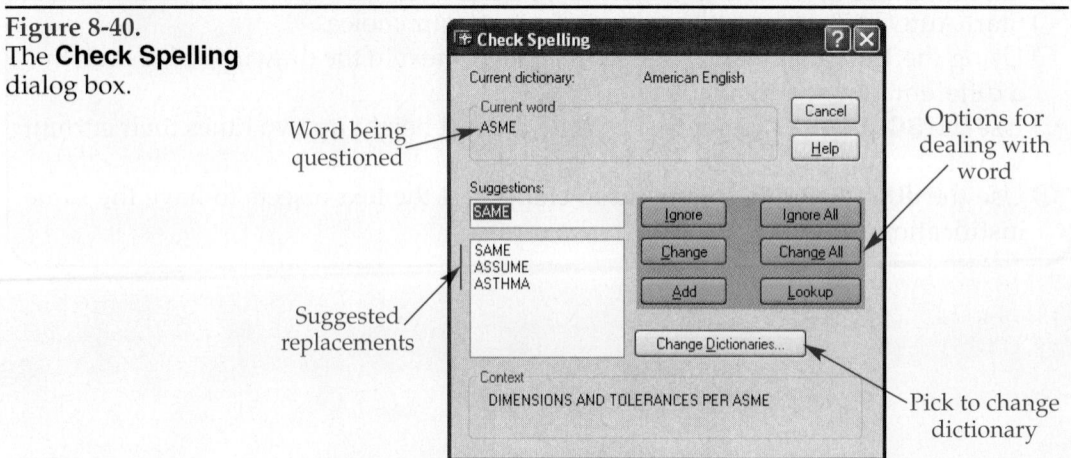

- **Add.** Pick this button to add the current word to the custom dictionary. You can add words with up to 63 characters.
- **Lookup.** This button asks AutoCAD to check the spelling of the word you enter in the **Suggestions** text box.
- **Context.** At the bottom of the dialog box, AutoCAD displays the line of text where the current word was found.

## Changing Dictionaries

AutoCAD provides you with several dictionaries: one American English, two British English, and two French. There are also dictionaries available for 24 different languages. Pick the **Change Dictionaries...** button to access the **Change Dictionary** dialog box. See **Figure 8-41.**

The areas of the **Change Dictionary** dialog box are as follows:
- **Main dictionary area.** This is where you can select one of the many language dictionaries to use as the current dictionary. To change the main dictionary, pick the down arrow to access the drop-down list. Next, pick the desired language dictionary from the list. The main dictionary is protected and cannot be added to.
- **Custom dictionary area.** This displays the name of the current custom dictionary, sample.cus by default. You can create your own custom dictionary by entering a new file name with a .cus extension. Words can be added or deleted and dictionaries can be combined using any standard text editor. If you use a word processor such as Microsoft Word or WordPerfect, be sure to save the file as *text only*, with no special text formatting or printer codes.

**Figure 8-41.**
The **Change Dictionaries** dialog box.

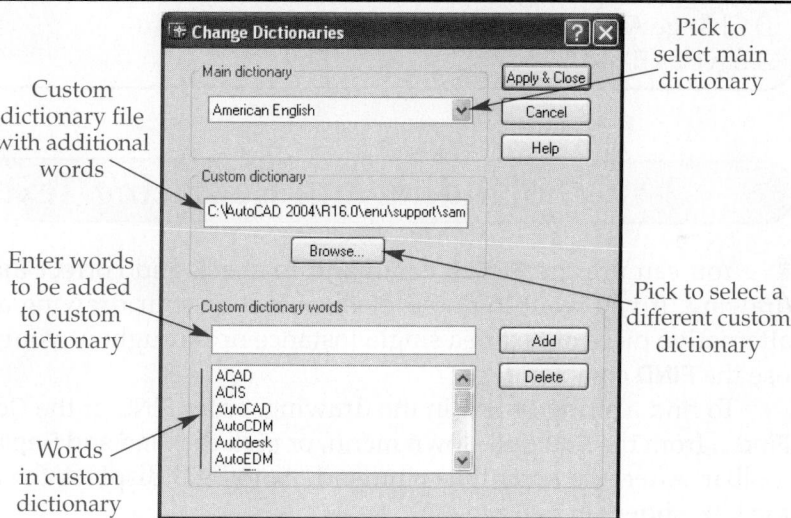

Custom dictionary file with additional words

Enter words to be added to custom dictionary

Words in custom dictionary

Pick to select main dictionary

Pick to select a different custom dictionary

**PROFESSIONAL TIP**
You can create custom dictionaries for various disciplines. For example, when in a mechanical drawing, common abbreviations and brand names might be added to a mech.cus file. A separate file named arch.cus might contain common architectural abbreviations and frequently used brand names.

- **Browse....** Pick this button to access the **Select Custom Dictionary** dialog box.
- **Custom dictionary words area.** Type a word in the text box that you either want to add or delete from the custom dictionary. For example, ASME Y14.5M is custom text used in engineering drafting. Pick the **Add** button to accept the custom word in the text box, or pick the **Delete** button to remove the word from the custom dictionary. Custom dictionary entries may be up to 32 characters in length.

---

**NOTE**  The current main and custom dictionaries are stored in the **DCTMAIN** and **DCTCUST** system variables, respectively.

---

### Exercise 8-12

○ Start AutoCAD and use the setup option of your choice.
○ Use the **MTEXT** command to type the following paragraph exactly as shown:

    1. ENTERPRETT DEMINSIONIN AND TOLERENCING
       PER ANSI Y14.5M–1982.
    2. REMOV ALL BURRS AND EDJES.
    3. ALL PHILLETS AND ROUNDS ARE .125 R.
    4. FINIS ALL OVER.

○ Check the spelling and correct the misspelled words.
○ Change ANSI Y14.5M-1982 to ASME Y14.5M-1994.
○ Save as EX8-12.

---

## Finding and Replacing Text

You can use the **SPELL** command to check and correct the spelling of text in a drawing. If you want to find a piece of text in your drawing and replace it with an alternative piece of text in a single instance or throughout your drawing, you should use the **FIND** command.

FIND

Edit
→ Find...

Text
toolbar

Find and Replace

To find a string of text in the drawing, enter FIND at the Command: prompt, pick **Find...** from the **Edit** pull-down menu, or pick the **Find and Replace** button on the **Text** toolbar. After you enter the command, AutoCAD displays the **Find and Replace** dialog box, shown in **Figure 8-42.**

The **Find and Replace** dialog box contains the following elements:
- **Find text string.** Specify the text string that you want to find in this text box. Enter a string, or choose one of the six most recently used strings from the drop-down list.
- **Replace with.** Specify the text string you want to replace in this text box. Enter a string, or choose one of the most recently used strings from the drop-down list.
- **Search in.** Specify whether to search the entire drawing or only the current selection. If there is a current selection set, **Current selection** is the default value. If there is no current selection set, **Entire drawing** is the default value. Picking the **Select Objects** button closes the dialog box temporarily for you to select objects in your drawing. Press [Enter] to return to the dialog box.

**Figure 8-42.**
The **Find and Replace** dialog box.

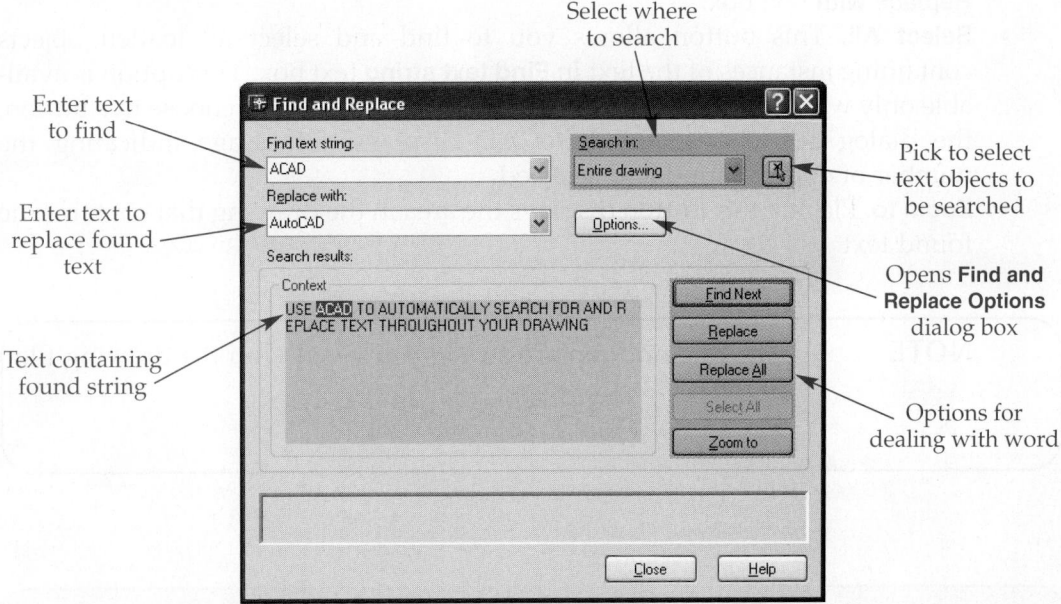

Enter text to find

Enter text to replace found text

Text containing found string

Select where to search

Pick to select text objects to be searched

Opens **Find and Replace Options** dialog box

Options for dealing with word

- **Options….** This button displays the **Find and Replace Options** dialog box, in which you can define the type of objects and words that you want to find. See **Figure 8-43.** The following options are available:
  - **Include area.** This area allows you to specify the type of objects you want to include in the search. By default, all options are selected.
  - **Match Case.** This check box allows you to include the case of the text in **Find text string** as part of the search criteria.
  - **Find Whole Words Only.** This check box allows you to find only whole words that match the text in **Find text string**.
- **Context.** This area displays and highlights the currently found text string in its surrounding context. If you choose **Find Next**, AutoCAD refreshes the **Context** area and displays the next found text string in its surrounding context.
- **Find/Find Next.** This button allows you to find the text in **Find text string** text box. Once you find the first instance of the text, the **Find** button becomes **Find Next** button, which you can use to find the next instance.
- **Replace.** This button allows you to replace found text with the text entered in the **Replace with** text box.

**Figure 8-43.**
The **Find and Replace Options** dialog box.

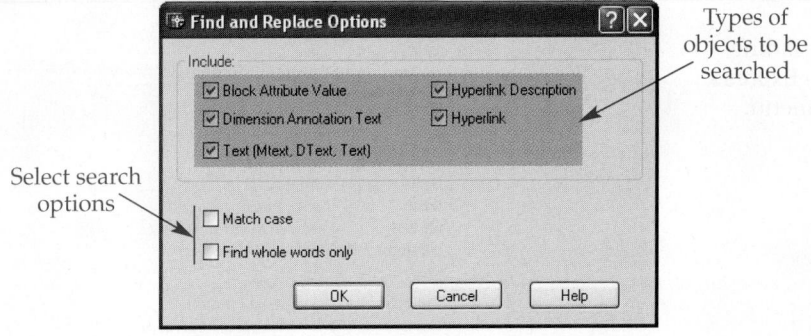

Types of objects to be searched

Select search options

- **Replace All**. This button allows you to find all instances of the text entered in the **Find text string** text box and replace all occurrences with the text in the **Replace with** text box.
- **Select All**. This button allows you to find and select all loaded objects containing instances of the text in **Find text string** text box. This option is available only when searching the **Current selection**. When you choose this button, the dialog box closes and AutoCAD displays a message indicating the number of objects found and selected.
- **Zoom to**. Picking this button displays the area in the drawing that contains the found text.

> **NOTE**
>
> The find and replace strings are saved with the drawing file and may be reused.

## Using Text Express Tools

Where applicable, Express Tools have been mentioned in this text. The **Express** pull-down menu includes a **Text** cascading menu with several commands. See **Figure 8-44**.

### Using Remote Text

*Remote text (RTEXT)* is text created from an ASCII text file or DIESEL expression. *ASCII* (American Standard Code for Information Interchange) is a form of code that allows you to type values and codes similar to a word processing program. ASCII text editors like Windows Notepad can be used to write text and save the file as a TXT file. A *DIESEL expression* is a type of programming code that looks at AutoCAD variables to determine a function.

To use the **Remote Text** command, select **Remote Text** from the **Text** cascading menu in the **Express** pull-down menu, or enter RTEXT at the Command: prompt. The following sequence is used to bring an ASCII text file into an AutoCAD drawing as a piece of remote text.

```
RTEXT

Express
  ⇒ Text
    ⇒ Remote Text
```

    Command: **RTEXT**↵
    Current settings: Style=Romand Height=3/16" Rotation=0
    Enter an option [Style/Height/Rotation/File/Diesel] <File>: **F**↵

**Figure 8-44.**
The **Text** cascading menu in the **Express** pull-down menu.

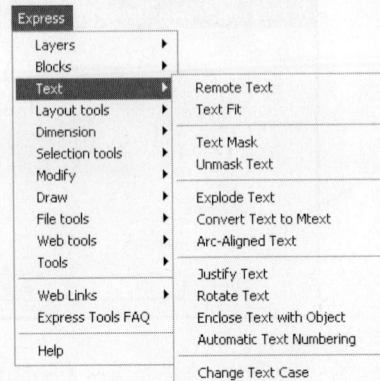

AutoCAD and its Applications—Basics

This accesses the **Select text file** dialog box. Browse for a file with a TXT extension, highlight it, and select the **Open** button. You then receive the following prompts:

> Specify start point of RText: *(pick a start point for the text)*
> Current values: Style=Romand Height=3/16" Rotation=0
> Enter an option [Style/Height/Rotation/Edit]: ⏎
> Command:

This process adds a piece of remote text into the drawing. The remote text maintains a link back to the file that was used for the remote text object.

### Editing remote text

The **RTEDIT** command is used to edit remote text. **RTEDIT** is accessed by entering RTEDIT at the Command: prompt. Once a remote text object is selected, you are given the following **RTEDIT** options:

- **Style.** Enter a new style for the remote text.
- **Height.** Change the height of the remote text object.
- **Rotation.** Allows you to rotate the text.
- **Edit.** Choose this option to open the ASCII file for editing.

### Using a DIESEL expression

A DIESEL expression is more powerful than bringing in a TXT file, because it is an interactive code that is updated each time the drawing file is opened. An example of this is code that displays the drawing name of the drawing file or displays the current date. The following sequence is used to place a DIESEL expression into remote text:

> Command: **RTEXT**⏎
> Current settings: Style=Romand Height=3/16" Rotation=0
> Enter an option [Style/Height/Rotation/File/Diesel] <File>: **D**⏎

This accesses the **Edit Rtext** dialog box. Entering the code Drawing file: $(getvar, "dwgname") in this dialog box displays the name of the drawing in the drawing file. Enter Drawing file: $(getvar, "dwgname") and select the **OK** button. See **Figure 8-45.**

> Specify start point of RText: *(pick a start point for the text)*
> Current values: Style=Romand Height=3/16" Rotation=0
> Enter an option [Style/Height/Rotation/Edit]: *(enter an option or press [Enter] to end the command)*
> Command:

**Figure 8-45.**
The **Edit RTEXT** dialog box allows you to type in a DIESEL expression.

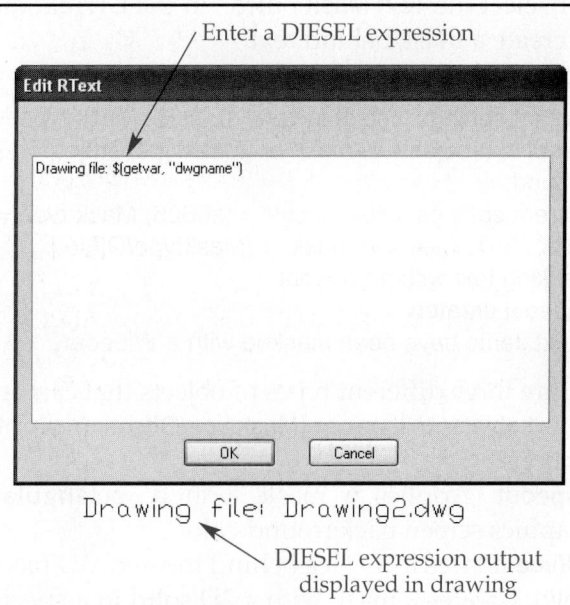

Enter a DIESEL expression

Drawing file: $(getvar, "dwgname")

Drawing file: Drawing2.dwg

DIESEL expression output displayed in drawing

Other examples of DIESEL expressions are shown below. To include the directory path and the drawing file name, use the following DIESEL expression:

Drawing name: $(getvar, "dwgprefix")$(getvar, "dwgname")

The output looks like this:

Drawing file: D:\Drawings\2002102\A-FP1.dwg

To show the date and the time that the drawing was opened, use the following DIESEL expression:

$(edtime, 0, MON DD"," YYYY - H:MMam/pm)

The output looks like this:

Jan 09, 2004 - 11:12pm

Additional DIESEL expressions can be found in the Express Tools help section. See *AutoCAD and its Applications—Advanced* for more information on DIESEL expressions.

## Using the TEXTFIT Command

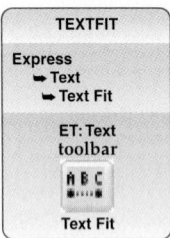

TEXTFIT

Express
➥ Text
➥ Text Fit

ET: Text toolbar

Text Fit

The **TEXTFIT** command stretches or shrinks text objects by specifying a new start and endpoint for the text. To access the command, select **Text Fit** in the **Text** cascading menu in the **Express** tools pull-down menu, enter TEXTFIT at the Command: prompt, or select the **Text Fit** button in the **ET:Text** toolbar. The following sequence displays how the **TEXTFIT** command works:

Command: **TEXTFIT**⏎
Select Text to stretch or shrink: *(select a piece of text)*
Specify end point or [Start point]: *(enter S to select a new start point)*
Specify new starting point: *(select a new start point)*
ending point: *(select a new end point)*
Command:

## Creating a Text Mask

TEXTMASK

Express
➥ Text
➥ Text Mask

ET: Text toolbar

Text Mask

The **TEXTMASK** command creates a masking object behind selected single-line or multiline text objects so that any objects behind the text do not display through the text. See **Figure 8-46**. To access the **TEXTMASK** command, select **Text Mask** from the **Text** cascading menu in the **Express** pull-down menu, enter TEXTMASK at the Command: prompt, or select the **Text Mask** button in the **ET:Text** toolbar. The following sequence is used to create a mask behind text:

Command: **TEXTMASK**⏎
Current settings: Offset factor = 0.0625, Mask type = Wipeout
Select text objects to mask or [Masktype/Offset]: *(select text objects)*
1 found
Current settings: Offset factor = 0.0625, Mask type = Wipeout
Select text objects to mask or [Masktype/Offset]: ⏎
Masking text with a Wipeout
Wipeout created.
1 text items have been masked with a Wipeout.

There are three different types of objects that can be used as a mask. Enter an M at the Select text objects to mask or [Masktype/Offset]: prompt to choose from one of the following options:

- **Wipeout.** Applies a mask with a rectangular frame displayed with the graphics screen background color.
- **3dface.** Places a 3D face behind the text. 3D faces are covered later in this text.
- **Solid.** Creates a mask with a 2D solid in a specified color.

**Figure 8-46.**
A—Text with no mask. B—Text with a text mask.

When creating a mask, AutoCAD offsets the mask a specified distance from the edges of the text. To change the offset distance, enter O at the Select text objects to mask or [Masktype/Offset]: prompt. AutoCAD then prompts you to Enter offset factor relative to text height. Enter the distance from the edge of the text that you want the mask to cover.

### Using the UNTEXTMASK command

The **UNTEXTMASK** command removes a mask from text that has been masked with the **Text Mask** command. To access the **UNTEXTMASK** command, select **Unmask Text** from the **Text** cascading menu in the **Express** pull-down menu, or enter UNTEXTMASK at the Command: prompt.

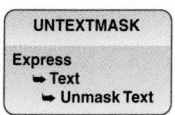

## Exploding Text

The **TXTEXP** command allows you to explode single-line or multiline text objects into individual lines, polylines, and arcs. To access the **TXTEXP** command, select **Explode Text** from the **Text** cascading menu in the **Express** pull-down menu, pick the **Explode Text** button in the **ET:Text** toolbar, or enter TXTEXP at the Command: prompt.

## Converting Single-Line Text to Multiline Text Objects

The **TXT2MTXT** command allows you to convert single-line text into a multiline text object. This command is accessed by selecting **Convert Text to Mtext** in the **Text** cascading menu in the **Express** pull-down menu, or by entering TXT2MTXT at the Command: prompt. Single-line text can be converted to a single line of multiline text or multiple single lines can be converted and combined into one multiline text object.

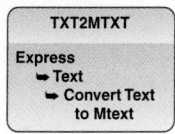

## Aligning Text with an Arc

The **ARCTEXT** command creates text that is curved or arced. In order to create arced text, an arc must exist in the drawing. To access this command, select **Arc-Aligned Text** in the **Text** cascading menu in the **Express** pull-down menu, select the **Arc-Aligned Text** button in the **ET:Text** toolbar, or enter ARCTEXT at the Command: prompt. Once the command is accessed, you are prompted to select an arc. Select the arc you want to use for the arced text. After the arc is selected, the **ArcAlignedText Workshop - Create** dialog box is displayed. See **Figure 8-47.**

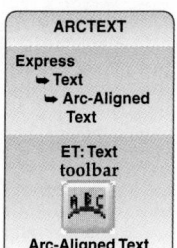

The **ArcAlignedText Workshop - Create** dialog box includes several options for controlling the output of the arced text. The areas within the dialog box are:

- **Buttons.** The pick buttons across the top of the dialog box control text location relative to the arc and its length. Backwards and concave text are available as well as several alignment tools.
- **Color.** This drop-down list allows you to specify the color of the text.
- **Font.** The first drop-down list specifies a text style to use and the second allows you to specify a font.
- **Text.** The **Text:** text box is where you can enter the desired text.
- **Properties.** This section includes additional properties that can be applied to the text.

Pick the **OK** button when finished configuring the arced text. If the text needs to be modified, access the **Arc-Aligned Text** command again and select the arced text.

**Figure 8-47.**
The **ArcAlignedText Workshop - Create** dialog box.

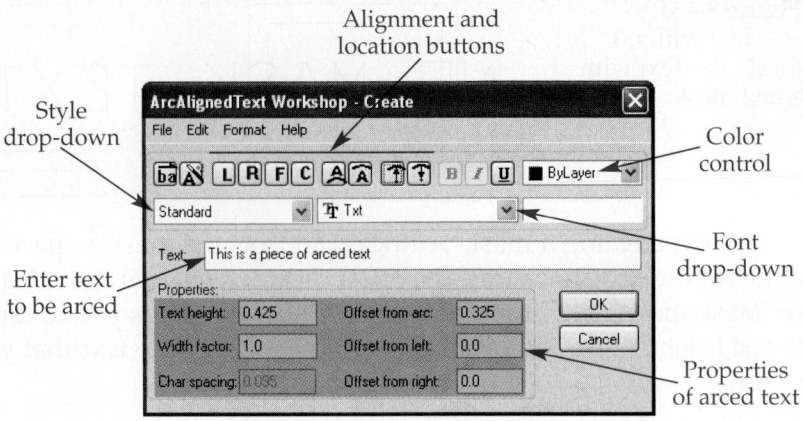

Style drop-down

Alignment and location buttons

Color control

Font drop-down

Enter text to be arced

Properties of arced text

After you are finished with the text, the arc used to designate the arc text can be erased if desired.

## Justifying Text

The **Justify Text** command is similar to the **JUSTIFYTEXT** command explained earlier. It performs virtually the same way as the **JUSTIFYTEXT** command.

## Rotating Text

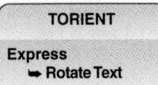

TORIENT

Express
➡ Rotate Text

The **TORIENT** command allows you to rotate text, multiline text, or attributes around their insertion points, at a specified rotation angle. You can access this command by selecting **Rotate Text** from the **Text** cascading menu in the **Express** pull-down menu, or by entering TORIENT at the Command: prompt. The following prompt sequence rotates five pieces of text 30°:

Command: **TORIENT**↵
Select TEXT, MTEXT, ATTDEF, or BLOCK inserts w/ attributes…
Select objects: *(pick the text objects to be rotated)*
5 found
Select objects: *(continue to select objects to be rotated or press* [Enter]*)*
New absolute rotation <Most Readable>: **30**↵
5 objects modified.
Command:

The **Most Readable** option orients the text to the most readable right-side up, right-read orientation.

## Placing an Object around Text

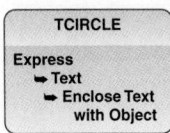

TCIRCLE

Express
➡ Text
　➡ Enclose Text
　　with Object

The **TCIRCLE** command allows you to place a circle, slot, or rectangle around one or more pieces of text, multiline text, or attributes. Access this command by picking **Enclose Text with Object** from the **Text** cascading menu in the **Express** pull-down menu, or enter TCIRCLE at the Command: prompt.

# Automatically Numbering Text Strings

You can add sequential numbers to individual lines of text or to each line within a multiline text object. Use the **Automatic Text Numbering** command found in the **Text** cascading menu under the **Express** pull-down menu, or enter TCOUNT at the Command: prompt. When the command has been accessed, you are prompted to select objects, then pick a sorting method:

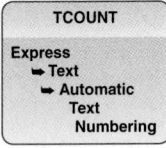

> Command: **TCOUNT**↵
> Select objects: *(pick the text objects numbered)*
> 5 found
> Select objects: *(continue selecting objects or press* [Enter]*)*
> Sort selected objects by [X/Y/Select-order] *<current value>*:

The following sorting options are available:
- **X.** Places numbers by increasing the X coordinate value of the selected text.
- **Y.** Places numbers by decreasing the Y coordinate value of the selected text.
- **Select-order.** Places numbers according to the order in which the text was selected.

After specifying the sorting method the following prompt is displayed:

> Specify starting number and increment (Start, increment) <1,1> *(enter the starting number followed by a comma, then the incremental number)*

The next prompt allows you to specify the placement of the numbers:

> Placement of numbers in text [Overwrite/Prefix/Suffix/Find&Replace..] *<current value> (pick an option or pick* [Enter] *for the default)*

The following placement options are available:
- **Overwrite.** Replaces the selected text with a number.
- **Prefix.** Adds a number to the beginning of the line.
- **Suffix.** Adds the number to the end of the line.
- **Find&Replace.** Replaces a specified text string with a number.

When finished, numbers are added to the selected strings of text.

## Changing Case

The **TCASE** command is similar to the **Change Case** option in the multiline text editor. However, this command can be used to change the case of text, multiline text, attributes, and dimension text. Access this command by selecting **Change Text Case** from the **Text** cascading menu in the **Express** pull-down menu, or enter TCASE at the Command: prompt. After selecting text to change its case, the **TCASE – change text case** dialog box is displayed as shown in **Figure 8-48**. This dialog box provides you with five case options to apply to your text. Select an option then press the **OK** button to apply the changes.

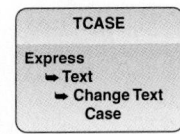

Figure 8-48.
The **TCASE – change text case** dialog box allows you to change the case of selected text.

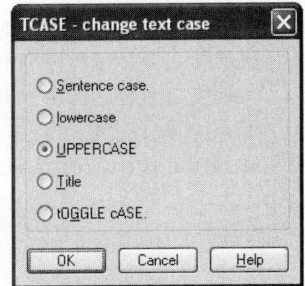

Text presentation is important on any drawing. It is a good idea to plan your drawing using rough sketches to allow room for text and notes. Some things to consider when designing the drawing layout include:

✓ Arrange text to avoid crowding.

✓ Place related notes in groups to make the drawing easy to read.

✓ Place all general notes in a common location. Locate notes in the lower-left corner or above the title block when using ASME standards. Place notes in the upper-left corner when using military standards.

✓ Always use the spell checker.

## Chapter Test

*Answer the following questions on a separate sheet of paper.*

1. Give the command and inputs required to use the **TEXT** command to display the following text string: IT IS FAST AND EASY TO DRAW TEXT USING AUTOCAD. The text must be .375 units high, have the default txt font, and fit between two points:
   A. Command: _____
   B. Specify start point of text or [Justify/Style]: _____
   C. Enter an option [Align/Fit/Center/Middle/Right/TL/TC/TR/ML/MC/MR/BL/BC/BR]: _____
   D. Specify first endpoint of text baseline: _____
   E. Specify second endpoint of text baseline: _____
   F. Specify height: _____
   G. Enter text: _____

2. How do you turn on the Quick Text mode if it is currently off using the Command: prompt?

3. List three ways to access the **TEXT** command.

4. Give the letter you must enter for the following justification options when using the **TEXT** command:
   A. Left-justified text.
   B. Right-justified text.
   C. Text between two points without regard for text height.
   D. Center the text horizontally and vertically.
   E. Text between two points with a fixed height.
   F. Center text along a baseline.
   G. Top and left horizontal.
   H. Middle and right horizontal.
   I. Bottom and center horizontal.

5. List the **TEXT** command **Justify** options.

6. How would you specify a text style with a double width factor?

7. How would you specify a text style with a 15° angle?

8. How would you specify vertical text?

9. Give the control sequence required to draw the following symbols when using the **TEXT** command:
   A. 30°
   B. 1.375 ±.005
   C. Ø24
   D. <u>NOT FOR CONSTRUCTION</u>

10. Why use the Quick Text mode rather than have the actual text displayed on the screen?
11. When setting text height in the **Text Style** dialog box, what value do you enter so text height can be altered each time the **TEXT** command is used?
12. List a command that lets you alter the location, style, height, and wording of existing single-line text.
13. Identify the command used to revise existing single-line text on the drawing by using the **Edit Text** dialog box.
14. When editing single-line text, how do you remove the character located in front of the text cursor?
15. When using the **Edit Text** dialog box, how do you move the text cursor to the left without removing text characters?
16. When using the **Edit Text** dialog box, how do you remove all of the text to the right of the text cursor?
17. When editing text in the **Text:** text box, the flashing vertical bar is called the

    _____.

18. Determine the AutoCAD text height for text to be plotted .188″ high using a half (1″ = 2″) scale. (Show your calculations.)
19. Determine the AutoCAD text height for text to be plotted .188″ high using a scale of 1/4″ = 1′-0″. (Show your calculations.)
20. What would you do if you just completed editing a line of text and discovered you made a mistake? Assume you are still in the **Edit Text** dialog box.
21. Identify two ways to move around inside the **Text:** box of the **Edit Text** dialog box.
22. What happens when you press the space bar or the [Backspace] key when the text inside the **Text:** text box is highlighted?
23. What happens when you press [Ctrl]+[X] when the text within the **Text:** text box is highlighted?
24. Name the command that lets you make multiline text objects.
25. How does the width of the multiline text boundary affect what you type?
26. What happens if the multiline text that you are entering exceeds or is not as long as the boundary length that you initially establish?
27. What happens when you pick the first corner followed by the other corner of the multiline text boundary?
28. Name the command that you enter if you want to enter multiline text at the Command: prompt rather than in a text editor.
29. Name two commands that allow you to edit multiline text.
30. How are fractions drawn when using the **TEXT** command?
31. How do you draw stacked fractions when using the **MTEXT** command?
32. What is the keyboard shortcut for the **TEXT** command?
33. What does a width factor of .5 do to the text when compared with the default width factor of 1?
34. What do you get when using the **DDEDIT** command on multiline text?
35. What is the keyboard shortcut for the **MTEXT** command?
36. How do you move the text cursor down one line at a time in the multiline text editor?
37. What happens when you pick the **Other...** option in the **Symbol** command of the text editor shortcut menu?
38. Name the internal storage area that temporarily stores information you copy or cut from a document.
39. When you are in the multiline text editor, how do you open the text editor shortcut menu?
40. What is the purpose of the **Set Mtext Width** option found in the shortcut menu when you right-click over the multiline text editor ruler?

41. Describe how to find a word or words in a text object and have the word or words replaced with another word or words.
42. Describe how you would create a text style that has the name ROMANS-125_15, uses the romans.shx font, has a fixed height of .125, a text width of 1.25, and an obliquing angle of 15.
43. Name the feature that allows you to move the cursor over the top of the desired text style in **DesignCenter**, hold down the pick button, and drag the cursor to the opened drawing.
44. Identify and briefly describe two methods that can be used to import an existing text style from **DesignCenter** to another drawing when you right-click over the desired text style.
45. Describe the two methods that can be used to select more than one text style at a time to import into your drawing from **DesignCenter**.
46. When using the **SCALETEXT** command, which base point option would you select to keep the text object(s) current justification point?
47. What is the difference between using the **JUSTIFYTEXT** command and using the **Properties** window to change the justification point of a text object?
48. Identify three ways to access the AutoCAD spell checker.
49. What is the purpose of the word found in the **Current word** box of the **Check Spelling** dialog box?
50. How do you change the **Current word** if you do not think the word that is displayed in the **Suggestions:** text box of the **Check Spelling** dialog box is the correct word, but one of the words in the list of suggestions is the correct word?
51. What is the purpose of the **Add** button in the **Check Spelling** dialog box?
52. How do you change the main dictionary for use in the **Check Spelling** dialog box?
53. Outline at least five steps that are used to create a new text style with the **Text Style** dialog box.
54. Identify at least four different ways to open the **Properties** window, including all keyboard shortcuts.
55. Describe two ways to select text objects to change when using the **Properties** window.
56. How do you change the text layer in the **Properties** window?
57. Explain how to edit text in the **Properties** window.
58. Name the command that allows you to find a piece of text and replace it with an alternative piece of text in a single instance or for every instance in your drawing.

AutoCAD and its Applications—Basics

## Drawing Problems

1. Start AutoCAD, use the setup option of your choice, and create text styles as needed. Use the **TEXT** command to type the following information. Change the text style to represent each of the four fonts named. Use a .25 unit text height and 0° rotation angle. Save the drawing as P8-1.

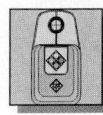

> TXT–AUTOCAD'S DEFAULT TEXT FONT WHICH IS AVAILABLE FOR USE WHEN YOU BEGIN A DRAWING.
> ROMANS–SMOOTHER THAN TXT FONT AND CLOSELY DUPLICATES THE SINGLE-STROKE LETTERING THAT HAS BEEN THE STANDARD FOR DRAFTING.
> ROMANC–A MULTISTROKE DECORATIVE FONT THAT IS GOOD FOR USE IN DRAWING TITLES
> ITALICC–AN ORNAMENTAL FONT SLANTED TO THE RIGHT AND HAVING THE SAME LETTER DESIGN AS THE COMPLEX FONT.

2. Start AutoCAD and use the setup option of your choice and create text styles as needed. Change the options as noted in each line of text. Then use the **TEXT** command to type the text, changing the text style to represent each of the four fonts named. Use a .25 unit text height. Save the drawing as P8-2.

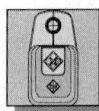

> TXT–EXPAND THE WIDTH BY THREE.
> MONOTXT–SLANT TO THE LEFT –30°.
> ROMANS–SLANT TO THE RIGHT 30°.
> ROMAND–BACKWARDS.
> ROMANC–VERTICAL.
> ITALICC–UNDERSCORED AND OVERSCORED.
> ROMANS–USE 16d NAILS @ 10″ OC.
> ROMANT–⌀32 (812.8).

3. Start AutoCAD and use the setup option of your choice. Create text styles with a .375 height with the following font: Arial, BankGothic LtBT, CityBlueprint, Stylus BT, Swis 721 BdOul BT, Vineta BT, and Wingdings. Use the **TEXT** command to type the complete alphabet and numbers 1–10 for the text fonts, all symbols available on the keyboard, and the diameter, degree, and plus/minus symbol. Save the drawing as P8-3.

4. Use the **MTEXT** command to type the following text using a text style with Romans font and .125 text height. The heading text height is .25. Check your spelling. Save the drawing as P8-4.

## NOTES:

1. INTERPRET DIMENSIONS AND TOLERANCES PER ASME Y14.5M–1994.
2. REMOVE ALL BURRS AND SHARP EDGES.

CASTING NOTES UNLESS OTHERWISE SPECIFIED:

1. .31 WALL THICKNESS.
2. R.12 FILLETS.
3. R.06 ROUNDS.
4. 1.5°–3.0° DRAFT.
5. TOLERANCES:
   ±1° ANGULAR
   ±.03 TWO PLACE DIMENSIONS.
6. PROVIDE .12 THK MACHINING STOCK ON ALL MACHINE SURFACES.

5.  Use the **MTEXT** command to type the following text using a text style with Stylus BT font and .125 text height. The heading text height is .188. After typing the text exactly as shown, edit the text with the following changes:
    A.  Change the \ in item 7 to 1/2.
    B.  Change the [ in item 8 to 1.
    C.  Change the 1/2 in item 8 to 3/4.
    D.  Change the ^ in item 10 to a degree symbol.
    E.  Check your spelling after making the changes.
    F.  Save as drawing P8-5.

## COMMON FRAMING NOTES:

1.  ALL FRAMING LUMBER TO BE DFL #2 OR BETTER.
2.  ALL HEATED WALLS @ HEATED LIVING AREAS TO BE 2 X 6 @ 24" OC.
3.  ALL EXTERIOR HEADERS TO BE 2-2 X 12 UNLESS NOTED, W/ 2" RIGID INSULATION BACKING UNLESS NOTED.
4.  ALL SHEAR PANELS TO BE 1/2" CDX PLY W/8d @ 4" OC @ EDGE, HDRS, & BLOCKING AND 8d @ 8" OC @ FIELD UNLESS NOTED.
5.  ALL METAL CONNECTORS TO BE SIMPSON CO. OR EQUAL.
6.  ALL TRUSSES TO BE 24" OC. SUBMIT TRUSS CALCS TO BUILDING DEPT. PRIOR TO ERECTION.
7.  PLYWOOD ROOF SHEATHING TO BE \ STD GRADE 32/16 PLY LAID PERP TO RAFTERS. NAIL W/8d @ 6" OC @ EDGES AND 12" OC @ FIELD.
8.  PROVIDE [ 1/2" STD GRADE T&G PLY FLOOR SHEATHING LAID PERP TO FLOOR JOISTS. NAIL W/10d @ 6" OC @ EDGES AND BLOCKING AND 12" OC @ FIELD.
9.  BLOCK ALL WALLS OVER 10'-0" HIGH AT MID.
10. LET-IN BRACES TO BE 1 X 4 DIAG BRACES @ 45^ FOR ALL INTERIOR LOAD BEARING WALLS.

6.  Open P4-4 and complete the window schedule by entering a text style with the Stylus BT font. Create a layer for the text. Draw the hexagonal symbols in the SYM column. Save the drawing as P8-6.

7.  Open P4-2 and complete the door schedule by entering a text style with the Stylus BT font. Create a layer for the text. Draw the circle symbols in the SYM column. Save the drawing as P8-7.

8.  Open P4-5 and complete the finish schedule by entering a text style with the Stylus BT font. Save the drawing as P8-8.

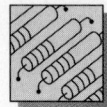

9.  Open P4-6 and complete the block diagram by entering the text using a text style with the Romans font. Create a layer for the text. Save the drawing as P8-9.

10. Open P4-7 and complete the block diagram by entering a text style with the Romans font. Create a layer for the text. Save the drawing as P8-10.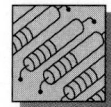

11. Open P5-11 and add text to the circuit diagram. Use a text style with the Romans font. Create a layer for the text. Save the drawing as P8-11.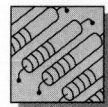

12. Add title blocks, borders, and text styles to the template drawings you created in earlier chapters. Create a Border layer for the borderlines and thick title block lines. Create a Title block layer for thin title block lines and text. Make three template drawings with borders and title blocks for your future drawings. Use the following guidelines:
    A. Prototype 1 for A-size, 8 1/2 × 11 drawings, named TITLEA–MECH.
    B. Prototype 2 for B-size, 11 × 17 drawings, named TITLEB–MECH.
    C. Prototype 3 for C-size, 17 × 22 drawings, named TITLEC–MECH.
    D. Set the following values for the drawing aids:
       Units = three-place decimal
       Grid = .500
       Snap = .250
    E. Draw a border 1/2″ from the drawing limits.
    F. Design a title block using created text styles. Place it in the lower-right corner of each drawing. The title block should contain the following information: company or school name, address, date, drawn by, approved by, scale, title, drawing number, material, revision number. See the example below.
    G. Record the information about each template in a log.

| R - | | CHANGE | | DATE | ECN |
|---|---|---|---|---|---|
| SPECIFICATIONS | | HYSTER COMPANY | | | |
| | | THIS PRINT CONTAINS CONFIDENTIAL INFORMATION WHICH IS THE PROPERTY OF HYSTER COMPANY. BY ACCEPTING THIS INFORMATION THE BORROWER AGREES THAT IT WILL NOT BE USED FOR ANY PURPOSE OTHER THAN THAT FOR WHICH IT IS LOANED. | | | |
| UNLESS OTHERWISE SPECIFIED DIMENSIONS ARE IN INCHES MILLIMETERS AND TOLERANCES FOR: | | DR. | SCALE | | DATE |
| ___ PLACE DIMS± _____ : ___ PLACE DIMS± _____ ANGLES ± _____ : WHOLE DIMS± _____ | | CK. MAT'L. | CK. DESIGN | | REL. ON ECN |
| | | NAME | | | |
| MODEL | DWG. FIRST USED | SIMILAR TO | | | |
| DEPT. | PROJECT | LIST DIVISION | H | PART NO. | R |

13. Draw a small parts list (similar to the one shown below) connected to your C-size prototype title block.
   A. Enter PARTS LIST with a style containing a complex font.
   B. Enter the other information using text and the **TEXT** command. Do not exit the **TEXT** command to start a new line of text.
   C. Save the drawing as TITLEC-PARTS.
   D. Record the information about the template in a log.

| 3 | HOLDING PINS | 12 |
|---|---|---|
| 2 | SIDE COVERS | 3 |
| 1 | MAIN HOUSING | 1 |
| KEY | DESCRIPTION | QTY |

PARTS LIST

UNLESS OTHERWISE SPECIFIED
ALL DIMENSIONS IN

INCHES

AND TOLERANCES FOR:

1 PLACE DIMS: ±.1
2 PLACE DIMS: ±.01
3 PLACE DIMS: ±.005
ANGULAR: ±30'
FRACTIONAL: ±.1/32
FINISH: 125? in.

JANE'S
DESIGN

| DR: JANE | SCALE: FULL | DATE: XX–XX–XX | APPD: |
|---|---|---|---|

MATERIAL: MILD STEEL

NAME: XXX–XXXX

| FIRST USED ON: | SIMILAR TO: | B | PART NO: 123–321 | REV: 0 |
|---|---|---|---|---|

14. Draw an architectural template for a 17″ × 22″ or 22″ × 34″ sheet size with a title block along the right side similar to the one shown below. Use the same layout and layer instructions given for Problem 12. Save the drawing as ARCH. Record the information about the template in a log.

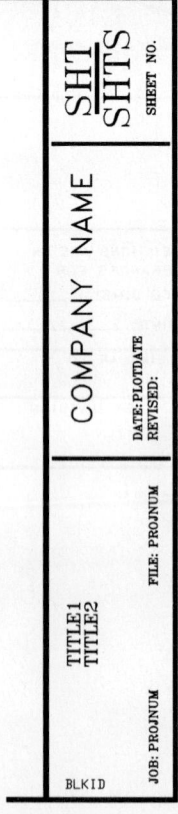

15. Draw title blocks with borders for your electrical, piping, and general drawings. Use the same instructions provided in Problem 12. The title block can be similar to the one displayed with Problem 12, but the area for mechanical drafting tolerances is not required. Research sample title blocks to come up with your design. Save the templates as ELEC A, ELEC B, PIPE A, PIPE B, or another name related to the drawing type and sheet size.

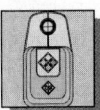

16. Draw the AND/OR schematic shown below. Save your drawing as P8-16.

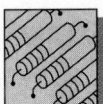

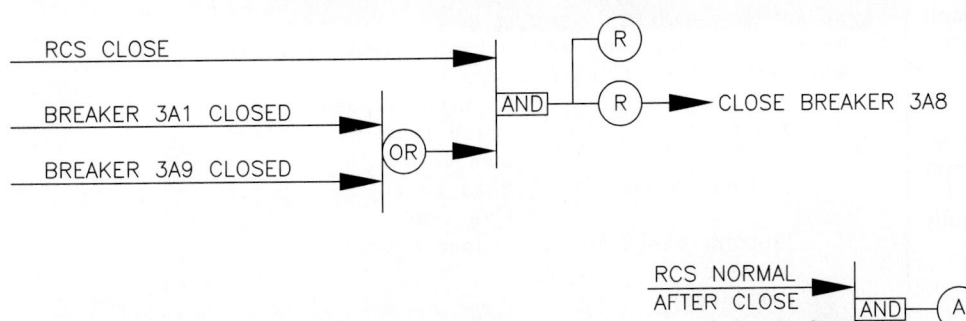

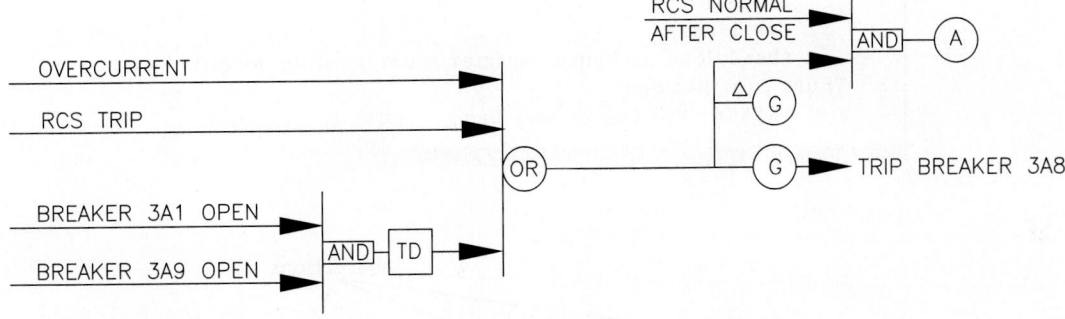

17. Draw the controller schematic shown below. Save your drawing as P8-17.

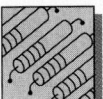

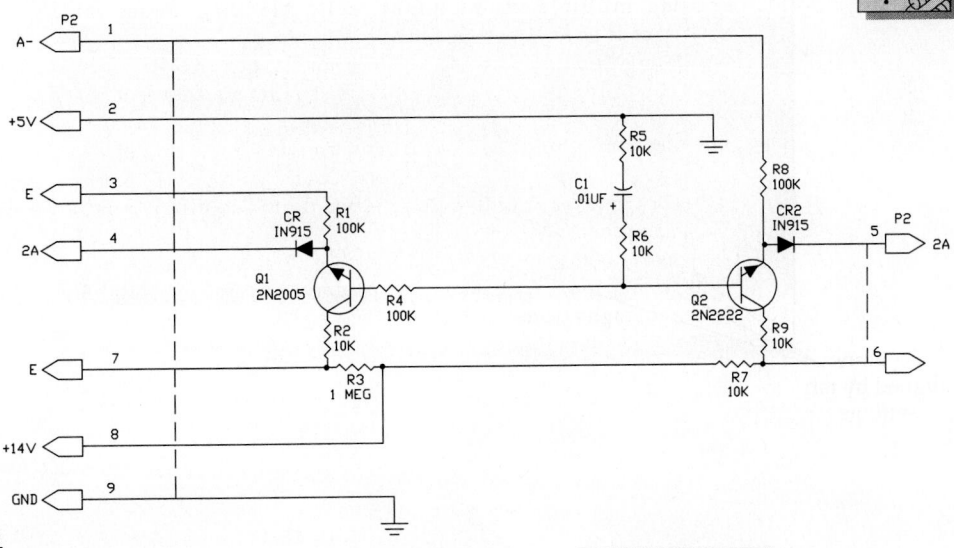

The text editor ruler illustrates the tab and indent settings for the paragraph in which the cursor is located. These examples show how different settings can be used within the same set of notes. The additional tabs set for Note 12 below align the columns automatically. Tabs and indents can be set in the **Indents and Tabs** dialog box or can be set by picking and dragging in the text editor ruler.

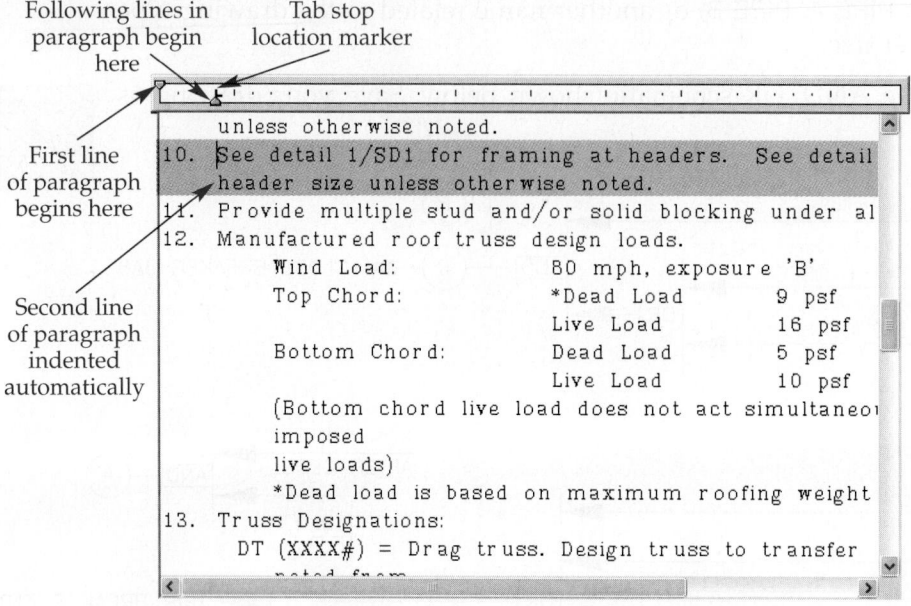

Following lines in paragraph begin here

Tab stop location marker

First line of paragraph begins here

Second line of paragraph indented automatically

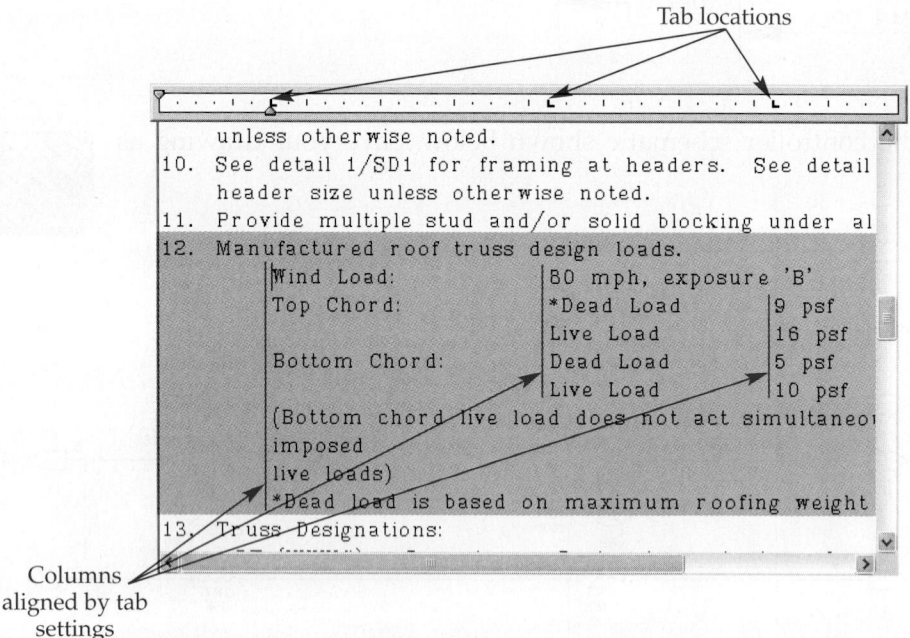

Tab locations

Columns aligned by tab settings

## CHAPTER 9

# Drawing Display Options

## Learning Objectives

After completing this chapter, you will be able to do the following:

- Explain the differences between the **REDRAW** command and the **REGEN** command.
- Magnify a small part of the drawing to work on details.
- Move the display window to reveal portions of the drawing outside the boundaries of the monitor.
- Create named views that can be recalled instantly.
- Use the **Aerial View** window.
- Define the terms model space and paper space.
- Create multiple viewports in the graphics window.
- Create 3D viewpoints with the **3DORBIT** command and preset viewpoints.
- Control display order.

You can view a specific portion of a drawing using the AutoCAD display commands. The **ZOOM** command allows you to enlarge or reduce the amount of the drawing displayed. The portion displayed can also be moved using the **PAN** command. Panning is like looking through a camera and moving the camera across the drawing. Using the **Aerial View** window, you can locate a particular area of the drawing to view. The **VIEW** command allows you to create and name specific views of the drawing. When further drawing or editing operations are required, the view can be quickly and easily recalled.

Display functions allow you to work in model space or paper space. *Model space* is used for drawing and designing, while *paper space* is used for plotting. Detailed information on the use of model space and paper space to prepare multiview drawings is provided in Chapter 10.

This chapter also discusses the differences between the **REDRAW** and **REGEN** commands. Additionally, using the **REGENAUTO** and **VIEWRES** commands to achieve optimum display speeds and quality is discussed.

# Redrawing and Regenerating the Screen

REDRAW
R

View
➥ Redraw

A *blip* is a small cross that is displayed when a point is picked on the screen. See **Figure 9-1.** These blips are not part of your drawing; they simply stay on the screen until it is redrawn. The **REDRAW** command is used to clean the blips from the screen and refresh objects after editing operations.

Redraw the screen by selecting **Redraw** from the **View** pull-down menu or by entering R or REDRAW at the Command: prompt.

**Figure 9-1.**
Tiny crosshairs, or blips, appear on the screen when a point is selected.

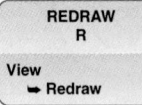

Blips

**PROFESSIONAL TIP**

Using **REDRAW** every time blips appear slows your drawing sessions. Redraw the screen only when the blips interfere with the drawing process.

The **REDRAW** command simply refreshes the current screen. To regenerate the screen, the **REGEN** command is used. This command recalculates all drawing object coordinates and regenerates the display based on the current zoom magnification. For example, if you have zoomed in on objects in your drawing and curved edges appear to be straight segments, using **REGEN** will smooth the curves.

REGEN
RE

View
➥ Regen

To access the **REGEN** command, pick **Regen** from the **View** pull-down menu or enter RE or REGEN at the Command: prompt. The screen is immediately regenerated.

Blips are often turned off to eliminate the need for redraws. Blips can be turned on or off by entering the **BLIPMODE** command at the Command: prompt and then entering either ON or OFF as desired.

Turning **BLIPMODE** off affects the current drawing only. If you want blips to be off in new drawings, turn **BLIPMODE** off in the template drawing.

## Getting Close to Your Work

The ability to *zoom in* (magnify) a drawing allows designers to create extremely small items, such as the electronic circuits found in a computer. The **ZOOM** command is a helpful tool that you will use often. The different options of the **ZOOM** command are discussed in the next sections.

### The ZOOM Options

Each of the **ZOOM** options can be accessed by its corresponding button in the **Standard** toolbar, or by selecting the option in the **Zoom** cascading menu from the **View** pull-down menu. All the buttons in the **Zoom** flyout are also found in the **Zoom** toolbar. See **Figure 9-2.** All **ZOOM** options except **In** and **Out** are available at the Command: prompt:

ZOOM
Z

View
↳ Zoom

    Command: **Z** *or* **ZOOM**↵
    Specify corner of window, enter a scale factor (nX or nXP), or
    [All/Center/Dynamic/Extents/Previous/Scale/Window] <real time>:

The **ZOOM** options are as follows:
- **real time.** The default option allows you to perform realtime zooming. This interactive zooming is discussed later in this chapter.
- **All.** Zooms to the edge of the drawing limits. If objects are drawn beyond the limits, the **All** option zooms to the edges of your geometry. Always use this option after you change the drawing limits.
- **Center.** Zoom the center of the display screen to a picked point. If you want to zoom to the center of an area of the drawing and want to magnify the view as well, then pick the center and height of the area in the drawing. Rather than a height, a magnification factor can be entered by typing a number followed by an X, such as 4X. The current value represents the height of the screen in drawing units. Entering a smaller number enlarges the image size, while a larger number reduces it. The command sequence is as follows:

    [All/Center/Dynamic/Extents/Previous/Scale/Window] <real time>: **C**↵
    Specify center point: *(pick a center point)*
    Enter magnification or height <*current*>: **4X**↵
    Command:

- **Dynamic.** Allows for a graphic pan and zoom with the use of a view box that represents the screen. This option is discussed in detail later in the chapter.
- **Extents.** Zooms to the extents (or edges) of the geometry in a drawing. This is the portion of the drawing area that contains drawing objects.
- **Window.** Pick opposite corners of a box. Objects in the box enlarge to fill the display. The **Window** option is the default if you pick a point on the screen upon entering the **ZOOM** command.
- **Scale.** The following prompt appears when you select the **Scale** option:

    Enter a scale factor (nX or nXP):

**Figure 9-2.**
**ZOOM** command options. A—The **Zoom** flyout button on the **Standard** toolbar. B—The **Zoom** cascading menu. C—The **Zoom** toolbar contains the same buttons as the **Zoom** flyout.

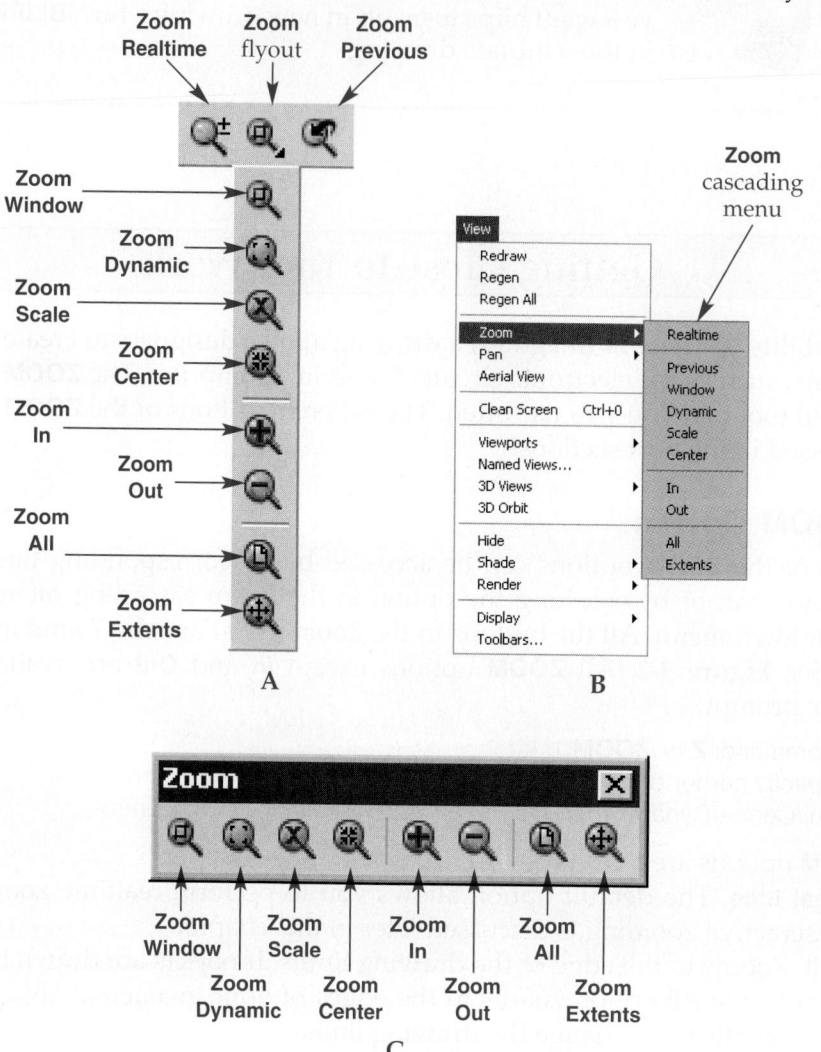

There are two options, **nX** or **nXP**. The **nX** option scales the display relative to the current display. To use this option, type a positive number, then X, and then press [Enter]. For example, enter 2X to magnify the current display "two times." To reduce the display, enter a number less than 1. For example, if you enter .5X, objects appear half as large as they did in the previous display.

The **nXP** option is used in conjunction with model space and paper space. It scales a drawing in model space relative to paper space and is used primarily in the layout of scaled multiview drawings. A detailed discussion of this option is given in Chapter 10.

Both of the **Scale** options can be entered at the initial **ZOOM** command prompt. For example, enter the following to enlarge the current display by a factor of three:

Command: **Z** or **ZOOM**↵
[All/Center/Dynamic/Extents/Previous/Scale/Window] <real time>: **3X**↵
Command:

- **Previous.** Returns to the previous display. You can go back ten displays, one at a time.
- **In.** This option is available only on the toolbar and the pull-down menu. It automatically executes a 2X zoom scale factor.
- **Out.** This option is available only on the toolbar and the pull-down menu. It automatically executes a .5X zoom scale factor.

## Performing Realtime Zoom

When using the command line, the default option of the **ZOOM** command is **real time**. A *realtime zoom* can be viewed as it is performed. It is activated by pressing [Enter] at the **ZOOM** command prompt, by picking the **Zoom Realtime** button in the **Standard** toolbar, by picking **Realtime** in the **Zoom** cascading menu in the **View** pull-down menu, or by right-clicking in the drawing area and selecting **Zoom** in the short-cut menu.

Realtime zooming allows you to see the model move on the screen as you zoom. It is the quickest and easiest method for adjusting the magnification of drawings on the screen.

The Zoom cursor (a magnifying glass icon with a plus and minus) is displayed when realtime zoom is executed. Press and hold the left mouse button (pick button) and move the pointer up to zoom in (enlarge) and down to zoom out (reduce). When you have achieved the display you want, release the button. If the display needs further adjustment after the initial zoom, press and hold the left mouse button again and move the pointer to get the desired display. To exit once you are done, press the [Esc] key, the [Enter] key, or right-click to get the shortcut menu and pick **Exit**.

If you right-click while the Zoom cursor is active, a shortcut menu is displayed. See **Figure 9-3.** This menu appears at the Zoom cursor location and contains six viewing options.

- **Pan.** Activates the **PAN Realtime** option. This allows you to adjust the placement of the drawing on the screen. If additional zooming is required, right-click again to display the shortcut menu and pick **Zoom**. In this manner you can toggle back and forth between **PAN** and **ZOOM Realtime** to accurately adjust the view. A detailed explanation of the **PAN** command is given later in the chapter.
- **Zoom.** Activates the **ZOOM Realtime** option. A check appears to the left of this option if it is active.
- **3D Orbit.** When this is selected, AutoCAD allows you to change your point of view around your drawing. Similar to **ZOOM**, this option is used to move around a 3D object. A detailed explanation of **3D Orbit** is provided later in this chapter.
- **Zoom Window.** Activates the **ZOOM Window** option and changes the cursor display. See **Figure 9-4.** You can pick opposite corners of a window but you must press and hold the pick button and drag the window box to the opposite corner, then release the pick button.

---

**Figure 9-3.**
The shortcut menu appears at the Zoom cursor location and contains six viewing options.

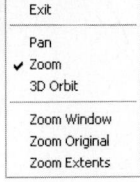

**Figure 9-4.**
The cursor changes when **Zoom Window** is selected from the shortcut menu.

- **Zoom Previous.** Restores the previous display before any realtime zooming or panning had occurred. This is a handy function if the current display is not to your liking, and it would be easier to start over rather than to make further adjustments.
- **Zoom Extents.** Zooms to the extents of the drawing geometry.

## Enlarging with a Window

The **ZOOM Window** option requires that you pick opposite corners of a rectangular window enclosing the area to be zoomed. The first point you pick is automatically accepted as the first corner of the zoom window. After this corner is picked, move the mouse, and a box appears showing the area that will be displayed or zoomed into once the second corner is picked. The box grows and shrinks as you move the pointing device. When the second corner is picked, the center of the window becomes the center of the new screen display. **Figure 9-5** shows **ZOOM Window** used on a drawing.

## Accurate Displays with a Dynamic Zoom

The **ZOOM Dynamic** option allows you to accurately specify the portion of the drawing you want displayed. This is done by constructing a *view box*. This view box is proportional to the size of the display area of your screen. If you are looking at a zoomed-in view when **ZOOM Dynamic** is selected, the entire drawing is displayed on the screen. To practice with this command, load any drawing into AutoCAD. Then, select the **ZOOM Dynamic** option.

The screen is now occupied by three boxes. See **Figure 9-6**. A fourth box is displayed later. Each box has a specific function:

- **Drawing extents.** (blue dotted line) This box shows the area of the drawing that is occupied by drawing objects. It is the same area that is displayed with **ZOOM Extents**.

**Figure 9-5.**
Using the **ZOOM Window** option. A—Select the corners of a window (shown here highlighted). B—The selected window fills the drawing screen. To return to the original view, use the **ZOOM Previous** option.

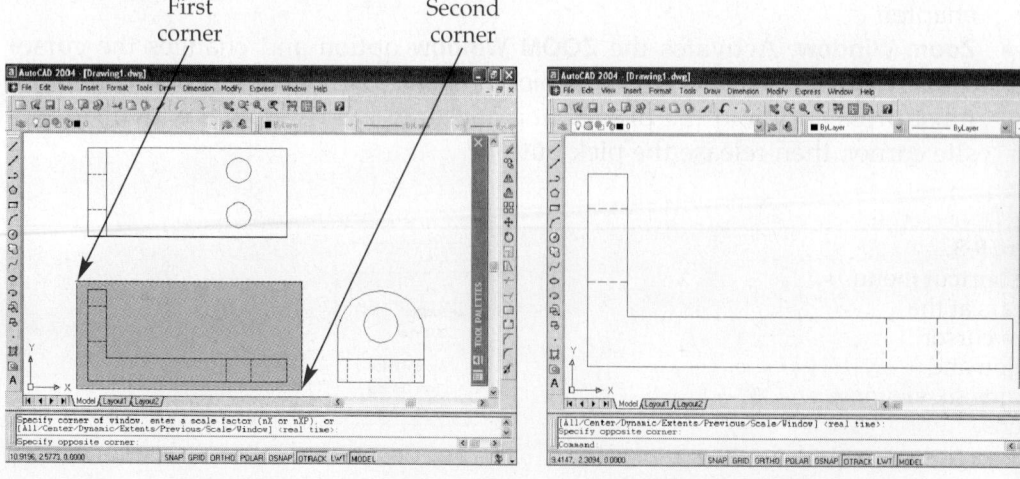

First corner     Second corner

A                                                    B

AutoCAD and its Applications—Basics

**Figure 9-6.**
Features of the
**ZOOM Dynamic**
option.

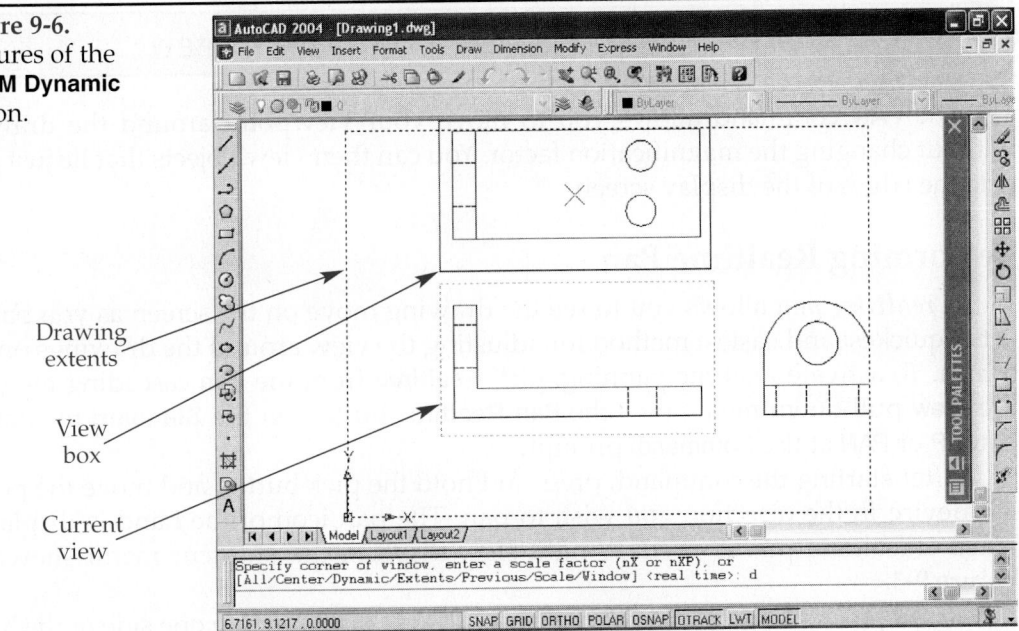

Drawing
extents

View
box

Current
view

- **Current view.** (green dotted line) This is the view that was displayed before you selected **ZOOM Dynamic**.
- **Panning view box.** (X in the center) Move the pointing device to find the center point of the desired zoomed display. When you press the pick button, the zooming view box appears.
- **Zooming view box.** (arrow on right side) This box allows you to decrease or increase the area that you wish to zoom. Move the pointer to the right and the box increases in size. Move the pointer to the left and the box shrinks. You can also pan up or down with the zooming view box. The only restriction is that you cannot move the box to the left.

The **ZOOM Dynamic** command is not complete until you press [Enter]. If you press the pick button to select the zooming view box, you can resize the viewing area. Press the pick button again and the panning view box reappears. The panning view box can then be repositioned over the area desired. In this manner, you can fine-tune the exact display needed. This is also helpful in defining permanent views, which is discussed later in this chapter.

---

### Exercise 9-1

○ Start AutoCAD and load a drawing from a previous exercise or drawing problem.
  ○ Enlarge and reduce the drawing using **Zoom Realtime**.
  ○ Move around the drawing using **Pan Realtime**.
  ○ Select **ZOOM Window** and enlarge a portion of the drawing.
  ○ Select **ZOOM Window** again, to move in closer to a detail.
  ○ Use **ZOOM Previous** to return to the last display.
  ○ Select **ZOOM Extents** to show only the drawing entities.
  ○ Select **ZOOM All** to display the entire drawing limits.
  ○ Select **ZOOM Dynamic**. Maneuver the view box to select a portion of the drawing.
  ○ Use **ZOOM Dynamic** to enlarge the display.
  ○ Save the drawing as EX9-1, then quit the drawing session.

---

The **PAN** command allows you to move your viewpoint around the drawing without changing the magnification factor. You can then view objects that lie just outside the edges of the display screen.

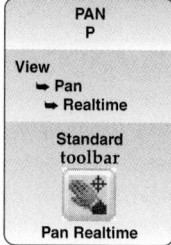

PAN
P

View
➥ Pan
➥ Realtime

Standard
toolbar

Pan Realtime

## Performing Realtime Pan

A *realtime pan* allows you to see the drawing move on the screen as you pan. It is the quickest and easiest method for adjusting the view around the drawings on the screen. To activate realtime panning, pick **Realtime** from the **Pan** cascading menu in the **View** pull-down menu, pick the **Pan Realtime** button on the **Standard** toolbar, or enter P or PAN at the Command: prompt.

After starting the command, press and hold the pick button and move the pointing device in the direction you wish to pan. The pan icon of the hand is displayed when a realtime pan is used. A right-click displays the shortcut menu shown in **Figure 9-3**.

If you pan to the edge of your drawing, a bar is displayed on one side of the hand cursor. The bar correlates to the side of the drawing. For example, if you reach the left side of the drawing, a bar and arrow appear on the left side of the hand. These icons are shown in **Figure 9-7**.

**Figure 9-7.**
A bar and arrow appear by the hand cursor when you pan to the edge of the drawing.

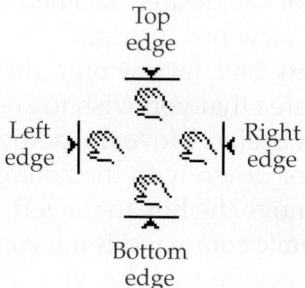

Top edge

Left edge

Right edge

Bottom edge

## Picking the Pan Displacement

The *pan displacement* is the distance the drawing is moved on the screen. You can pick the displacement by selecting **Point** from the **Pan** cascading menu in the **View** pull-down menu or by entering -P or -PAN at the Command: prompt. The following prompt appears:

Command: **-P** *or* **-PAN**↵
Specify base point or displacement:

You can specify a base point by picking a point or entering absolute coordinates. You are then prompted to select a second point. The display window is moved the distance between the points.

You can also enter the displacement, or the distance the display window is to be moved, by giving coordinates. The coordinates can be either relative or absolute.

## Using Pan Presets

The **Pan** cascading menu in the **View** pull-down menu includes four preset directional options: **Left**, **Right**, **Up**, and **Down**. See **Figure 9-8**. Select one of the options to move the display in the indicated direction.

**Figure 9-8.**
The **Pan** options can be found in the **Pan** cascading menu of the **View** pull-down menu.

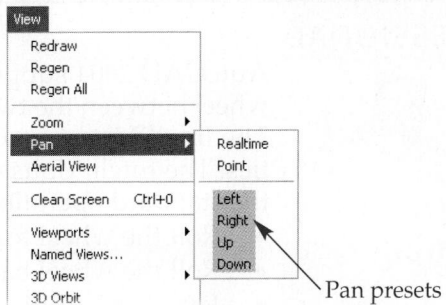

Pan presets

## Using Scroll Bars to Pan

The scroll bars found at the bottom and to the right of the drawing area can also be used to pan the display. See **Figure 9-9**. Pick the arrows at the end of the scroll bar to pan in small increments. Select the scroll bar itself to pan in larger increments. Position the cursor over the box in the scroll bar, pick the left-click and hold it, and then move the mouse to see realtime panning in the horizontal or vertical direction.

**Figure 9-9.**
The drawing area scroll bars can be used for panning operations.

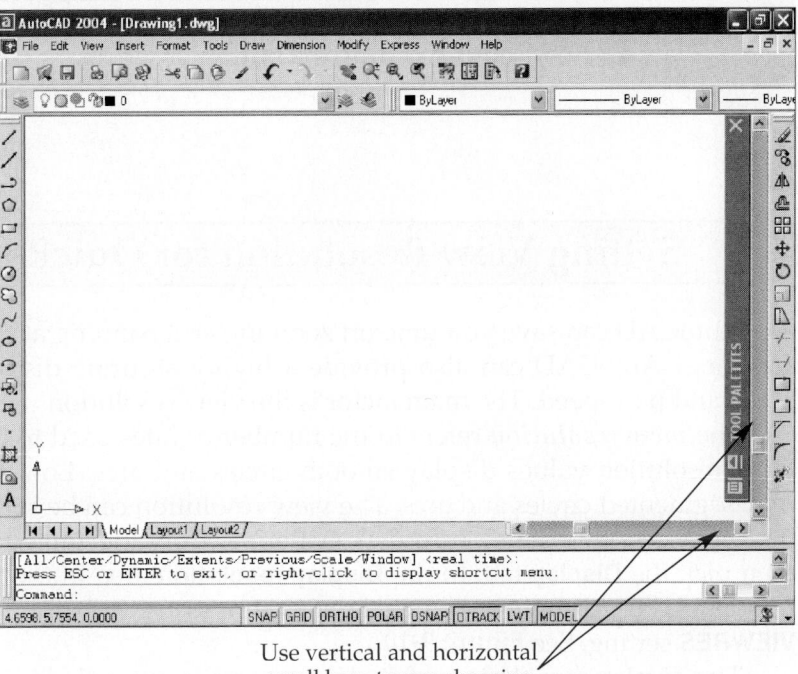

Use vertical and horizontal scroll bars to pan drawing

**NOTE** The drawing area scroll bars can be activated and deactivated by selecting the **Display scroll bars in drawing window** option in the **Window Elements** area of the **Display** tab of the **Options** dialog box. To access this dialog box, select **Options...** from the **Tools** pull-down menu or right-click in the drawing area and select **Options...** from the shortcut menu.

AutoCAD 2004 supports the IntelliMouse. This mouse has a wheel between the two normally functioning mouse buttons. The IntelliMouse provides you with zoom and pan capabilities. The IntelliMouse has these basic functions in addition to the standard operation of the two buttons:

- Roll the wheel forward or away from you to zoom in.
- Roll the wheel backward or toward you to zoom out.
- Press and hold the wheel button down and move the mouse to pan.
- Double-click on the wheel to zoom to the drawing extents.

The **ZOOMFACTOR** system variable controls the incremental movement of the wheel. By default, the zoom factor is set to 10 percent. Thus, each increment in the wheel rotation changes the zoom level by 10 percent.

The **MBUTTONPAN** system variable controls the behavior of the third button or wheel to support the **PAN** command or the **Object Snap** shortcut menu. A 0 supports the action defined in the menu (MNU) file and 1 supports panning when you hold and drag the button or wheel.

## Setting View Resolution for Quick Displays

AutoCAD can save you time on zooming and panning at the expense of display accuracy. AutoCAD can also provide a highly accurate display at the expense of zoom and pan speed. The main factor is the view resolution.

The *view resolution* refers to the number of lines used to draw circles and arcs. High resolution values display smooth circles and arcs. Low resolution values display segmented circles and arcs. The view resolution can be set in the **Options** dialog box. To access this dialog box, pick **Options...** from the **Tools** pull-down menu, and then pick the **Display** tab. In the **Display resolution** area in the upper-right corner of the dialog box is the **Arc and circle smoothness** text box. This contains the current **VIEWRES** setting. See **Figure 9-10.**

The display smoothness of circles and arcs is controlled by the **VIEWRES** setting. It can vary between 1 and 20000. The default setting is 1000, which produces a relatively smooth circle. A number smaller than 1000 causes circles and arcs to be drawn with fewer vectors (straight lines). See **Figure 9-11.** A number larger than 1000 causes more vectors to be included in the circles.

It is important to remember that the **VIEWRES** setting is a display function only and has no effect on the plotted drawing. A drawing is plotted using an optimum number of vectors for the size of circles and arcs. In other words, if a circle you draw looks like a polygon in the drawing area before **REGEN** is used, it will look like a circle when the drawing is plotted.

**Figure 9-10.**
The view resolution (**VIEWRES**) variable can be set in the **Options** dialog box.

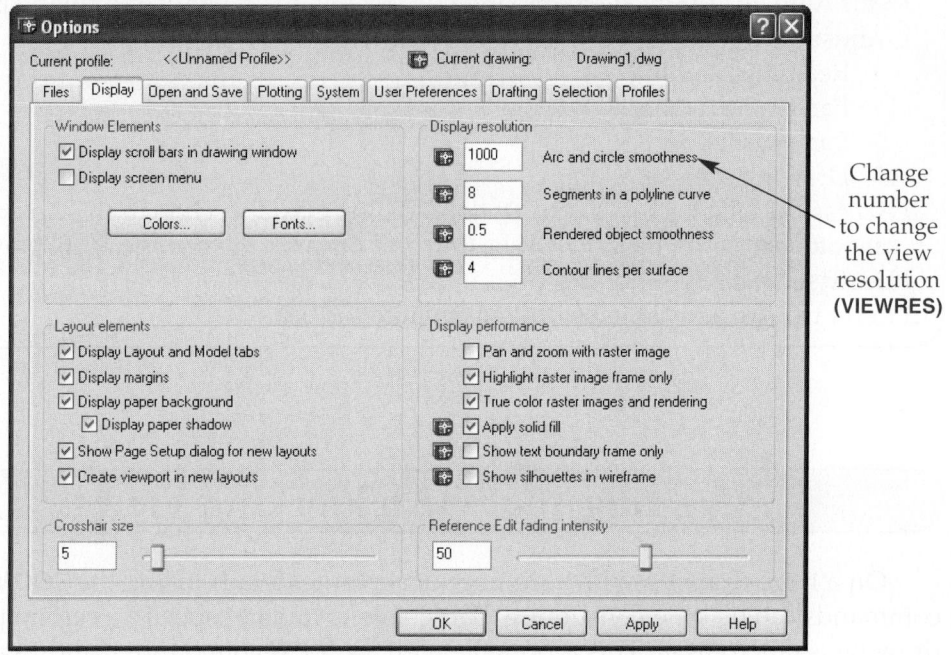

Change number to change the view resolution (**VIEWRES**)

**Figure 9-11.**
The higher the **VIEWRES** value, the smoother a circle will appear.

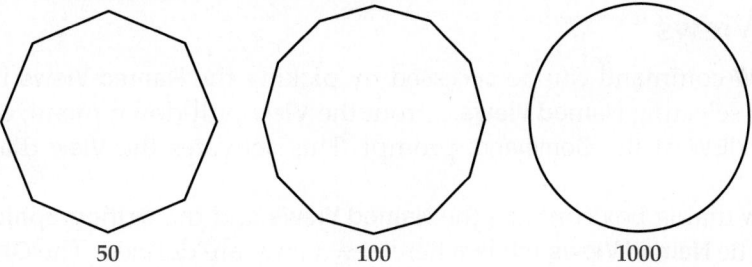

50          100          1000

NOTE

You can change the **VIEWRES** setting by entering VIEWRES at the Command: prompt. A Do you want fast zooms? prompt appears. This prompt is no longer useful, but remains in AutoCAD so programs written for earlier versions will still function properly.

○ Start AutoCAD and load a drawing from a previous exercise or drawing problem.
○ Adjust the display using each of the following options:
   ○ Realtime panning.
   ○ Pan displacement.
   ○ Pan presets.
   ○ Drawing area scroll bars.
○ Access the **Display** tab of the **Options** dialog box and change the **Arc and circle smoothness** to 10. Pick the **OK** button and observe the change in display.
○ Draw some circles and arcs.
○ Reset the **Arc and circle smoothness** value to 1000.

# Creating Your Own Working Views

On a large drawing with a number of separate details, using the **ZOOM** and **PAN** commands can be time-consuming. Being able to quickly specify a certain part of the drawing is much easier. This is possible with the **VIEW** command. It allows you to create named views of any area of the drawing. A view can be a portion of the drawing, such as the upper-left quadrant, or it can represent an enlarged portion. After the view is created, you can instruct AutoCAD to display it at any time.

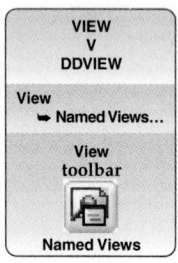

VIEW
V
DDVIEW

View
➥ Named Views...

View
toolbar

Named Views

## Creating Views

The **VIEW** command can be accessed by picking the **Named Views** button in the **View** toolbar, selecting **Named Views...** from the **View** pull-down menu, or entering V, VIEW, or DDVIEW at the Command: prompt. This activates the **View** dialog box. See **Figure 9-12.**

The **View** dialog box contains the **Named Views** and the **Orthographic & Isometric Views** tabs. The **Named Views** tab is where new views are defined. The **Orthographic & Isometric Views** tab provides preset views around the drawing in AutoCAD.

**Figure 9-12.**
Select a different view in the **View** dialog box. Create a new view by selecting the **New...** button.

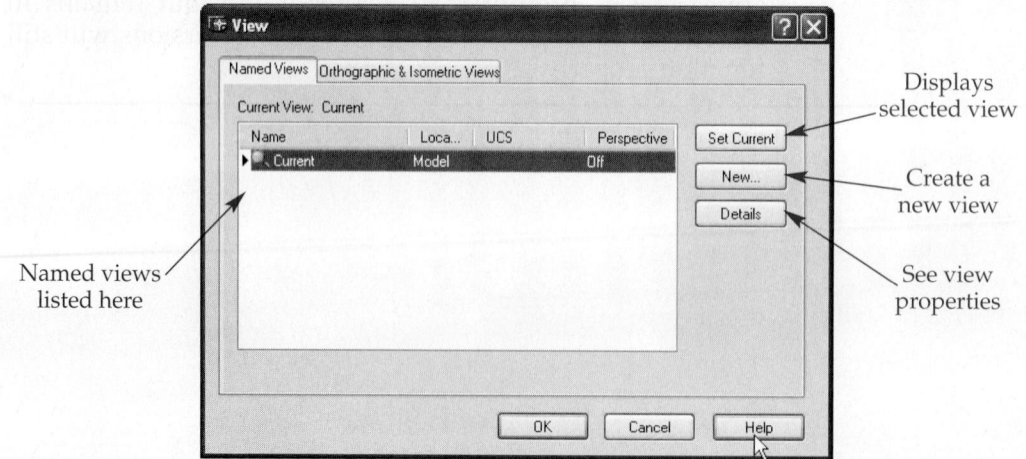

Displays
selected view

Create a
new view

See view
properties

Named views
listed here

A list of currently defined views is shown in the **Named Views** tab. If you want to save the current display as a view, pick the **New...** button to access the **New View** dialog box, **Figure 9-13.** Now, type the desired view name in the **View name:** edit box. The **Current Display** option button is the default. Click **OK** and the view name is added to the list. AutoCAD creates a view from what is currently being displayed in the graphics window.

If you want to use a window to define the view, pick the **Define Window** radio button in the **New View** dialog box, and then pick the **Define View Window** button. You are prompted to Specify first corner. Pick two points to define a window. After the second corner is selected, the **New View** dialog box reappears. Pick the **OK** button and the **View** dialog box is updated to reflect the new view.

**Figure 9-13.**
In the **New View** dialog box, name the new view and define the window.

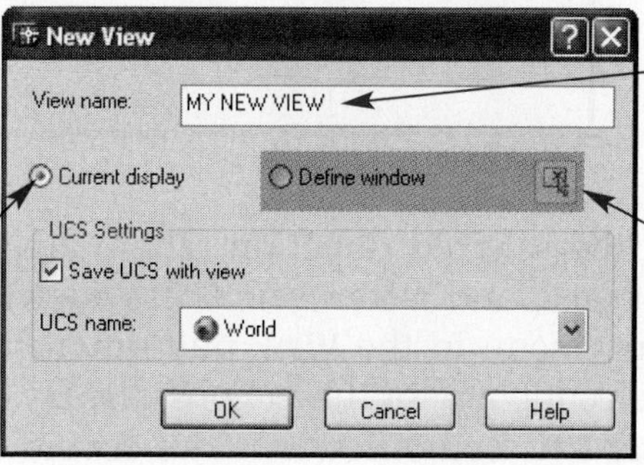

Enter name for new view

Define new view as current display

Define view with window

To display one of the listed views, pick its name from the list in the **Named Views** tab and pick the **Set Current** button. The name of the current view appears in the **Current View:** label below the **Named Views** tab. Now, pick the **OK** button and the screen displays the selected view.

To delete a view displayed in the **View** dialog box, first pick the view name in the list in the **Named Views** tab to highlight it, then right-click the mouse. A shortcut menu appears. Select the **Delete** option in the shortcut menu. The view name is immediately removed from the list. Notice that when a view is highlighted, you can right-click the mouse for other shortcut menu options. You can set a view current with the **Set Current** option, use the **Rename** option to rename a view, delete a view with the **Delete** option, or get a detailed description of the selected view by picking the **Details...** option. Selecting **Details...** opens the **View Details** dialog box, which provides a variety of information about the view. This dialog box can also be accessed by selecting the **Details** button in the **View** dialog box. A discussion of these values related to 3D drawings is given in *AutoCAD and its Applications—Advanced.*

The **Orthographic & Isometric Views** tab in the **View** dialog box allows you to quickly choose a preset view around the drawing. See **Figure 9-14.** Notice that the icons display the side of the drawing that will be viewed. There are orthogonal views such as Top, Bottom, Front, Back, Left, and Right. Picking any of these icons, then pressing the **Set Current** button changes the view in AutoCAD so you are looking at your

**Figure 9-14.**
The **Orthographic & Isometric Views** tab contains six orthographic views and four isometric views.

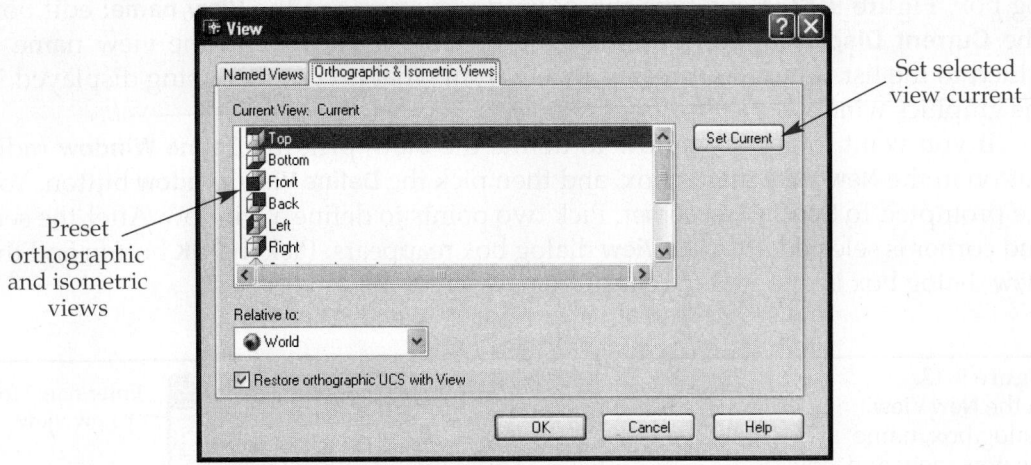

Preset orthographic and isometric views

Set selected view current

drawing from the selected direction. There are isometric views such as Southwest, Southeast, Northeast, and Northwest. These views can also be selected from the **3D Views** cascading menu in the **View** pull-down menu or from the **View** toolbar. See **Figure 9-15.** Selecting any of these icons displays a 3D view (isometric) of the drawing. Orthogonal and isometric views are covered in greater depth in *AutoCAD and its Applications—Advanced*.

**Figure 9-15.**
Preset orthographic and isometric views can also be selected in the **3D Views** cascading menu in the **View** pull-down menu or from the **View** toolbar.

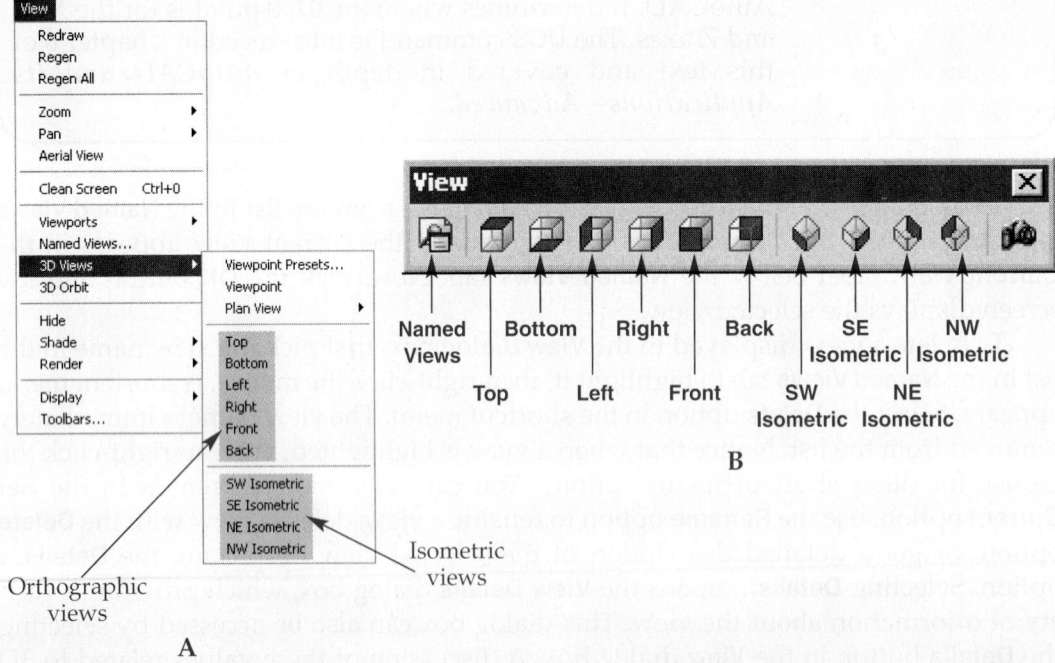

Orthographic views

Isometric views

Named Views

Bottom · Right · Back · SE Isometric · NW Isometric

Top · Left · Front · SW Isometric · NE Isometric

A

B

## Working with Views at the **Command:** Prompt

The **-VIEW** command allows you to create and set views at the Command: prompt. When -V or -VIEW is entered at the Command: prompt, you are presented with the following options:

-VIEW<br>-V

Enter an option [?/Orthographic/Delete/Restore/Save/Ucs/Window]:

- **?.** This option lists currently defined view names. You are prompted for which views to list. Responding with [Enter] accepts the default and displays all currently defined view names.
- **Orthographic.** This option changes the view to one of the orthographic views that you choose. You are prompted for which orthographic view to display.
- **Delete.** This option removes unneeded views. After selecting this option, you are prompted to enter the name of the view to be deleted. Type the name and press [Enter].
- **Restore.** A saved view can be displayed on the screen using this option. Simply enter the name of the view you want to display at the Enter view name to restore: prompt. The view is then immediately displayed.
- **Save.** This option creates a new view. Enter the new view name at the Enter view name to save: prompt. The current display becomes the new view.
- **UCS.** This option allows you to save the current UCS with any new views you create. You are prompted with Save current UCS with named views? [Yes/No].
- **Window (W).** This option also creates a new view and prompts for a window selection.

## Using Transparent Display Commands

To begin a new command, you usually need to complete or cancel the current command. Most menu picks automatically cancel the command in progress before initiating the new one. However, some commands function without canceling an active command.

A *transparent command* temporarily interrupts the active command. After the transparent command is completed, the command that was interrupted is resumed. Therefore, it is not necessary to cancel the initial command. Many display commands can be used transparently, including **REDRAW**, **PAN**, **AV**, and **ZOOM** options.

Suppose that while drawing a line, you need to place a point somewhere off the screen. One option is to cancel the **LINE** command. Then zoom out to see more of the drawing and select **LINE** again. A more efficient method is to use **PAN** or **ZOOM** while still in the **LINE** command. An example of drawing a line to a point off the screen is as follows:

Command: **L** *or* **LINE**↵
Specify first point: *(pick a point)*
Specify next point or [Undo]: *(pick the* **Pan** *button or enter* 'PAN*)*
>>Press Esc or Enter to exit, or right-click to display shortcut menu. *(pan to the location desired then press* [Enter]*)*
Resuming LINE command.
Specify next point or [Undo]: *(pick a point)*
Specify next point or [Undo]: ↵
Command:

The double prompt (>>) indicates that a command has been put "on hold" while you use a transparent command. The transparent command must be completed before the original command is returned. At that time, the double prompt disappears.

The above procedure is similar when using the **ZOOM** command. When typed at the keyboard, an apostrophe (') is used before the command. To connect a line to a small feature, enter 'Z or 'ZOOM.

---

PROFESSIONAL
TIP

The **Pan**, **Zoom**, and **View** buttons activate commands transparently.

---

PROFESSIONAL
TIP

A transparent redraw is executed when **Redraw** is picked from the **View** pull-down menu. Commands such as **GRID**, **SNAP**, and **ORTHO** can be used transparently, but it is quicker to activate these modes with the appropriate function keys or from the status bar.

## Exercise 9-3

○ Begin a new drawing or use one of your templates.
○ Set the drawing limits at 12,9, grid spacing at .5, and snap spacing at .25.
○ Construct the two arcs shown below.
○ Window a view of the left arc and name it 1. Restore view 1.
○ Pick the **Pan Realtime** button and pan to display the arc on the right.
○ Select the **LINE** command and snap to the top of the arc.
○ Pick the upper endpoint of the right arc as the second endpoint of the line.
○ Restore view 1.
○ Begin a second line, selecting the lower arc endpoint as the first endpoint.
○ Use the **ZOOM Dynamic** command transparently to display the bottom half of the right arc.
○ Pick the lower endpoint of the right arc as the second endpoint of the line.
○ Use **ZOOM Realtime** or **ZOOM Dynamic** to show the completed object.
○ Save the drawing as EX9-3.

VIEW 1

2X R1.0

# Using the Aerial View

When working on a large drawing, you can spend a lot of time zooming and panning the graphics window trying to locate a particular detail or feature. One of the most powerful display features in AutoCAD is the **Aerial View** window. **Aerial View** is a navigation tool that lets you see the entire drawing in a separate window, locate the detail or feature you want, and move to it quickly. You can zoom in on an area, change the magnification, and match the view in the graphics window to the one in the **Aerial View** window (or vice versa).

To open the **Aerial View** window, pick **Aerial View** from the **View** pull-down menu or enter AV or DSVIEWER at the Command: prompt. The entire drawing is then displayed in the **Aerial View** window. See **Figure 9-16.**

The **Aerial View** window initially appears at the lower right of the drawing area, but can be moved to any convenient location on the screen. To do so, pick the title bar of the **Aerial View** window, hold down the left mouse button, and drag the window to a new location.

The menu bar in the **Aerial View** window contains three pull-down menus and three buttons. See **Figure 9-17.** The buttons provide the same options found in the **View** pull-down menu:

- **Zoom In.** Increases the magnification of the image in the **Aerial View** window.
- **Zoom Out.** Decreases the magnification of the image in the **Aerial View** window.
- **Global.** Displays the entire generated drawing area (the extents of the drawing) in the **Aerial View** window.

AV
DSVIEWER

View
↦ Aerial View

Figure 9-16.

The **Aerial View** window (shown here highlighted) is initially in the lower-right corner of the screen.

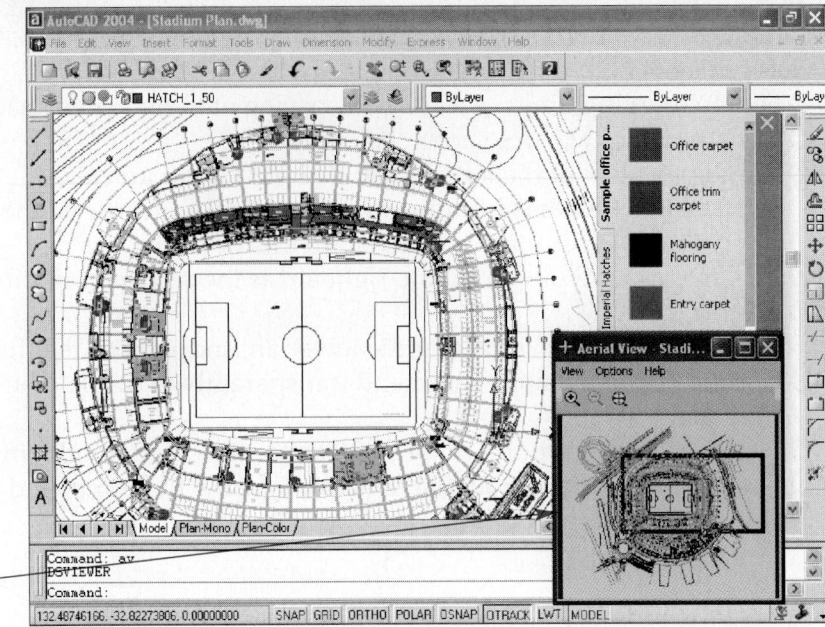

Aerial View window

Figure 9-17.
The **Aerial View** window has pull-down menus and a toolbar. These contain options for working with the window.

Pull-down menus

Zoom In

Zoom Out

Global

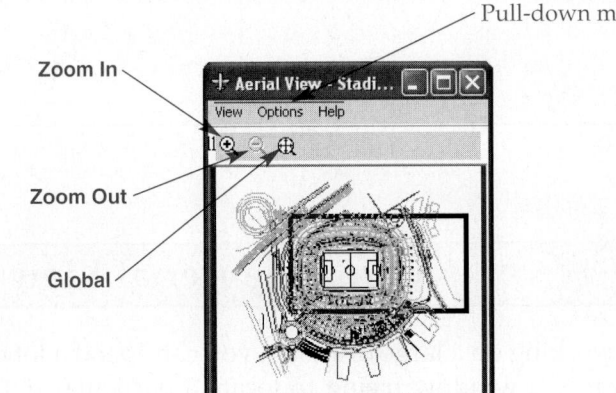

The **Options** pull-down menu contains the following **Aerial View** window options:

- **Auto Viewport.** When on, switching to a different tiled viewport automatically causes the new viewport to be displayed in the aerial view window. When off, AutoCAD will not update the **Aerial View** window to match the active viewport.
- **Dynamic Update.** This causes the **Aerial View** window to update its display after each change in the drawing. Enable this only if your display system is very fast.
- **Realtime Zoom.** Activating this will update the drawing view area as you zoom and pan in the **Aerial View** window.
- **Aerial View Help.** Opens the AutoCAD help to the **Aerial View** section.

The **Aerial View** window is similar to the **Zoom Dynamic** command. When using the **Aerial View**, the overall drawing can be viewed. There is a current view box that can be resized by pressing the pick button. Moving the pointing device right or left shrinks or enlarges the current view. Press the pick button again and by moving the pointing device around you can pan around in the window. When the desired view has been obtained, right-click and AutoCAD will set that as the current view.

You can also right-click inside the **Aerial View** window to get a shortcut menu that accesses the functions described earlier. Best of all, you can use the **Aerial View** zoom and pan functions transparently while a drawing or editing command is in progress.

## Exercise 9-4

○ Start AutoCAD and open the 8th floor lighting.dwg drawing in the AutoCAD 2004\Sample folder.

○ Activate the **Aerial View** and zoom toward the bottom-left corner of the drawing to include the LUMINAIRE SCHEDULE. Click the left mouse button to resize the window. Click the pick button again to exit the resizing window when the desired window size has been selected.

○ Move the current view box around until it is toward the top of the drawing.

○ Zoom out to view the entire map using the **Global** button in the **Aerial View** window.

○ Resize your **Aerial View** window so it occupies at least one-quarter of your display screen.

○ Pick the **Zoom In** button in the **Aerial View** window to zoom the **Aerial View** window.

○ Pick inside the **Aerial View** window to pan around the drawing.

○ When you are finished experimenting with the **Aerial View**, quit the session without saving.

## Model Space and Paper Space

*Model space* can be thought of as the *space* where you draw and design in AutoCAD. The term *model* has more meaning when working in 3D, but you can consider any drawing or design as a model, even if it is two-dimensional. An introduction of User Coordinate Systems and the UCS icon is given in Chapter 6 of this text, and a detailed discussion is in *AutoCAD and its Applications—Advanced*.

*Paper space* is a *space* you use to lay out a drawing or model to be plotted. Basically, it is as if you place a sheet of paper on the screen, then insert, or *reference*, one or more drawings to the paper. In order to enter paper space, you can pick one of the layout tabs at the bottom of the screen. See **Figure 9-18.** You can also use the **MODEL** or **PAPER** button on the status bar to switch between model space and paper space. The button displays the current environment, and picking it switches to the other environment.

Remember that you should create all your drawings and designs in the **Model** tab, not in the **Layout** tab. Only paper layouts for plotting purposes should be created in the **Layout** tab. To return to model space, pick the **Model** tab.

**Figure 9-18.**
The layout tabs are located at the bottom of the drawing area window. The **PAPER** button indicates the paper space environment is active. The button reads **MODEL** when you are working in model space.

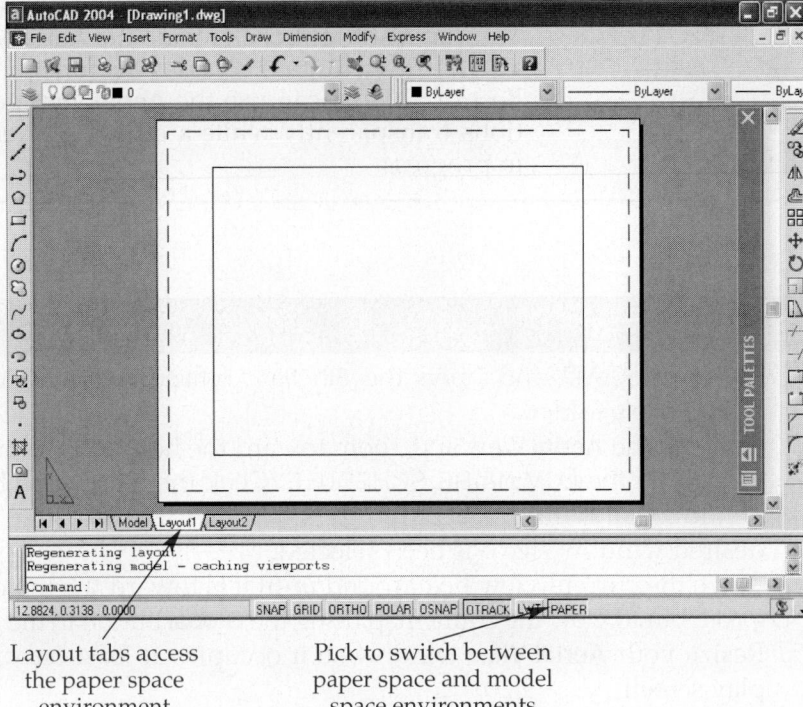

Layout tabs access the paper space environment

Pick to switch between paper space and model space environments

Do not be confused by model space and paper space. The discussion in Chapter 10 provides you with additional understanding. Right now, think of these terms in the following manner:

| Tab | Environment | Status Bar Button | Activity |
|-----|-------------|-------------------|----------|
| **Model** | Model space | **MODEL** | Drawing and design |
| **Layout** | Paper space | **PAPER** | Plotting and printing |

## Tiled Viewports

The **Model** tab drawing area can be divided into various viewports. These viewports are called *tiled viewports.* Another type of viewports, *floating viewports,* can be created in the **Layout** tab. Tiled viewports are created in model space, floating viewports are created in paper space.

By default, there is only one viewport in the drawing area. Additional viewports can be added. The edges of tiled viewports butt against one another like floor tile. The tiled viewports cannot overlap.

Viewports are different "tiles," or views, in the same drawing. Only one viewport can be active at any given time. The active viewport has a bold outline around its edges. See **Figure 9-19.**

AutoCAD and its Applications—Basics

**Figure 9-19.**
An example of three tiled viewports in model space. All viewports contain the same objects, but the display in each viewport can be unique.

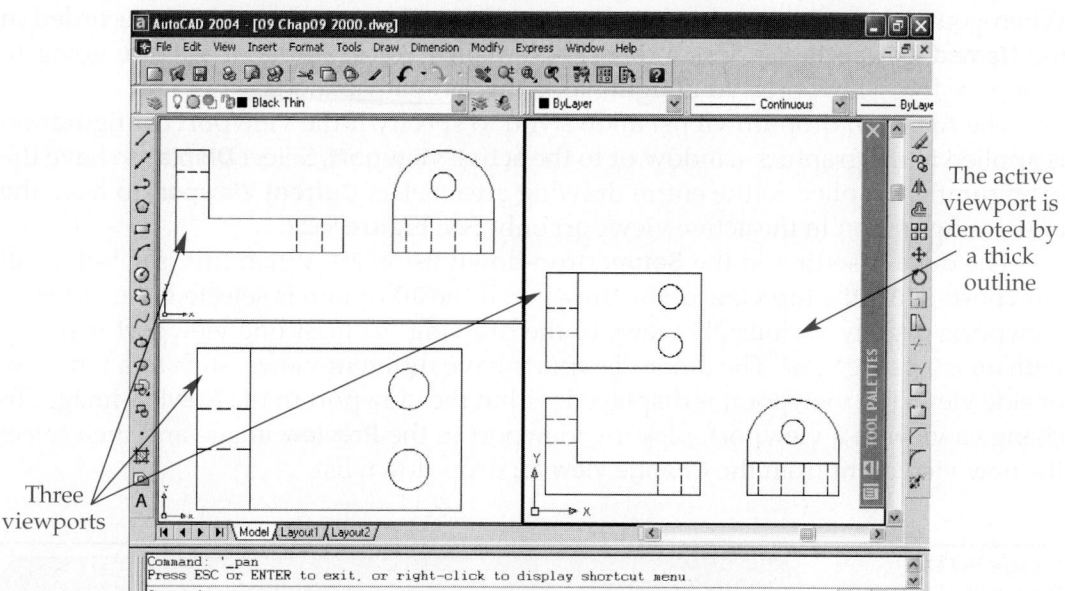

Three viewports

The active viewport is denoted by a thick outline

## Creating Tiled Viewports

Viewports can be created using the **Viewports** dialog box, **Figure 9-20.** Picking the **Display Viewports Dialog** button from either the **Layouts** or **Viewports** toolbar can access this dialog box. You can also enter VPORTS at the Command: prompt, or select **New Viewports...** from the **Viewports** cascading menu in the **View** pull-down menu.

The **New Viewports** tab is shown in **Figure 9-20.** The **Standard viewports:** list contains many preset viewport configurations. The configuration name identifies the number of viewports and the arrangement or location of the largest viewport. These

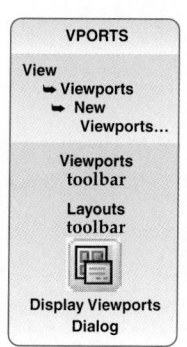

VPORTS

View
→ Viewports
→ New
Viewports...

Viewports toolbar

Layouts toolbar

Display Viewports Dialog

**Figure 9-20.**
Specify the number and arrangement of tiled viewports in the **New Viewports** tab of the **Viewports** dialog box.

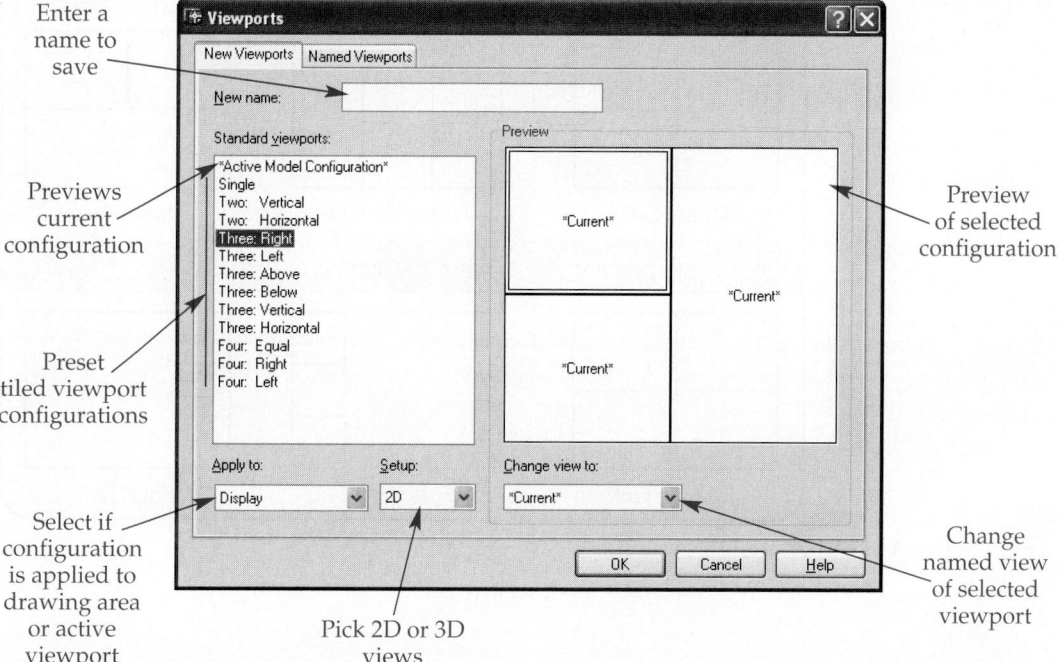

Enter a name to save

Previews current configuration

Preset tiled viewport configurations

Select if configuration is applied to drawing area or active viewport

Pick 2D or 3D views

Preview of selected configuration

Change named view of selected viewport

configurations are shown in **Figure 9-21.** Select one, and a preview appears in the **Preview** area. Select \*Active Model Configuration\* to preview the current configuration.

You can name and save a configuration. Enter a name in the **New name:** text box. When you pick the **OK** button, the new named viewport configuration is recorded in the **Named Viewports** tab. Use a descriptive name. For example, if you are going to configure four viewports, you might name this as Four Viewports.

The **Apply to:** drop-down list allows you to specify if the viewport configuration is applied to the graphics window or to the active viewport. Select **Display** to have the configuration applied to the entire drawing area. Select **Current Viewport** to have the new configuration in the active viewport only. See **Figure 9-22.**

The default setting in the **Setup:** drop-down list is **2D**. When this is selected, all viewports show the top view of the drawing. If the **3D** option is selected, the different viewports display various 3D views of the drawing. At least one viewport is set up with an isometric view. The other viewports have different views, such as a top view or side view. The viewpoint is displayed within the viewport in the **Preview** image. To change a view in a viewport, pick the viewport in the **Preview** image and then select the new viewpoint from the **Change view to:** drop-down list.

**Figure 9-21.**
Preset tiled viewport configurations are available in the **New Viewports** tab of the **Viewports** dialog box.

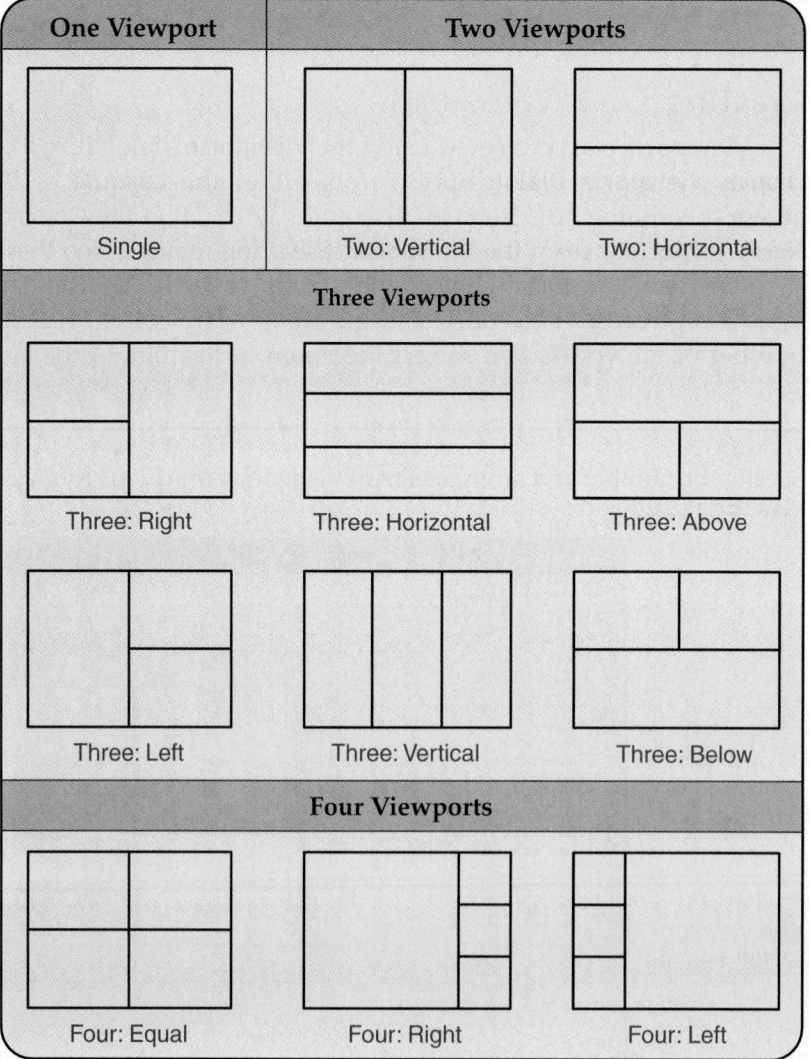

**Figure 9-22.**
Viewport configurations can be applied to the drawing area or the active viewport.
A—Original configuration (Three: Right). B—Use the **Current Viewport** option to create additional
viewports within the active viewport. Here, the Two: Vertical configuration is specified for the
active viewport.

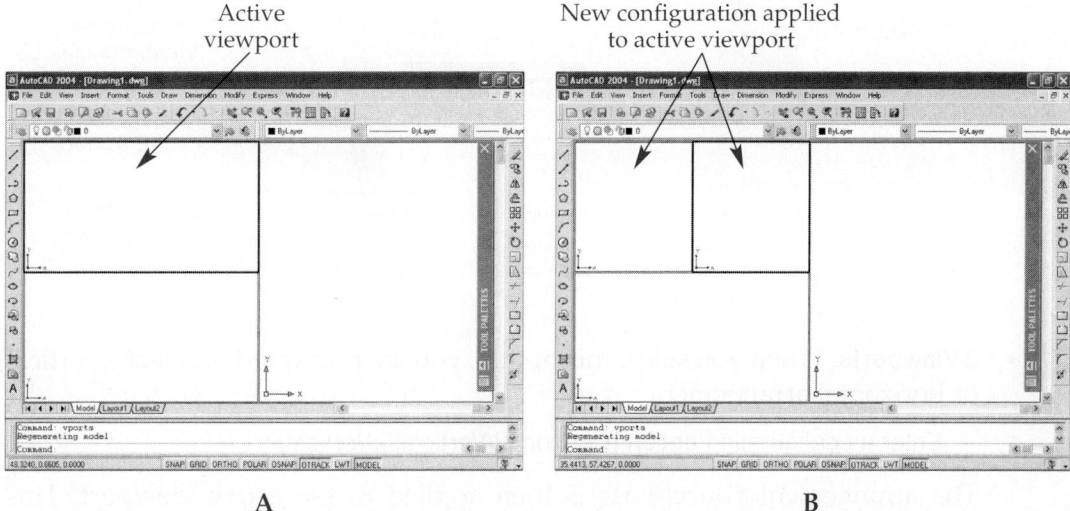

Active viewport

New configuration applied to active viewport

A                                B

The **Named Viewports** tab displays the names of saved viewport configurations
and gives you a preview of each. See **Figure 9-23.** Select the named viewport configuration and pick **OK** to apply it to the drawing area. Named viewport configurations
cannot be applied to the active viewport.

You can also select a viewport configuration from the **Viewports** cascading menu
in the **View** pull-down menu, shown in **Figure 9-24.** The following configuration
options are available:

- **1 Viewport.** This option replaces the current viewport configuration with a
  single viewport.

**Figure 9-23.**
The **Named Viewports** tab.

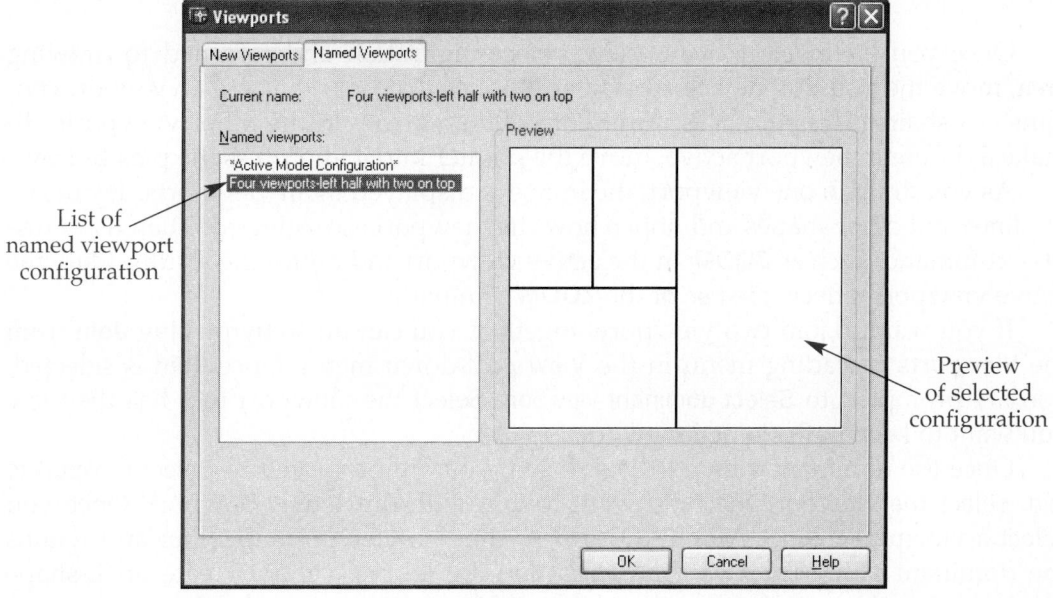

List of named viewport configuration

Preview of selected configuration

**Figure 9-24.**
The **Viewports** cascading menu in the **View** pull-down menu.

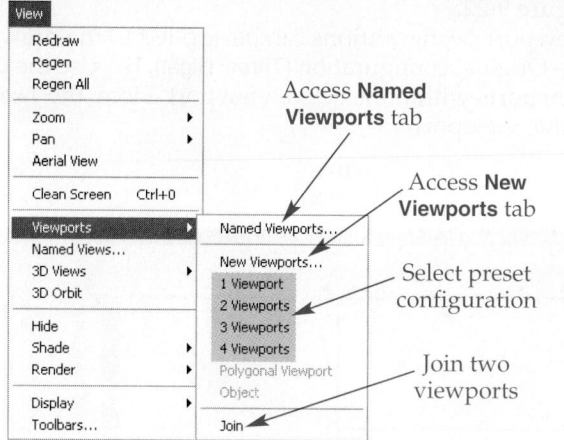

Access **Named Viewports** tab

Access **New Viewports** tab

Select preset configuration

Join two viewports

- **2 Viewports.** When you select this option, you are prompted to select a vertical or horizontal arrangement:

    Enter a configuration option [Horizontal/Vertical] <Vertical>:

  The arrangement you choose is then applied to the active viewport. This configuration does not replace the current viewport configuration.
- **3 Viewports.** The following prompt appears when you select this option:

    Enter a configuration option [Horizontal/Vertical/Above/Below/Left/Right] <Right>:

  The arrangement you choose is then applied to the active viewport. This configuration does not replace the current viewport configuration.
- **4 Viewports.** This option creates four equal viewports within the active viewport.

**NOTE** The AutoCAD graphics window can be divided into *tiled viewports*, of which only 64 can be available at one time. You can check this number using the **MAXACTVP** (maximum active viewports) system variable at the Command: prompt.

Once you have selected the viewport configuration and returned to drawing area, move the pointing device around and notice that only the active viewport contains crosshairs. The pointer is represented by an arrow in the other viewports. To make a different viewport active, move the pointer into it and press the pick button.

As you draw in one viewport, the image is displayed in all viewports. Try drawing lines and other shapes and notice how the viewports are affected. Then use a display command, such as **ZOOM**, in the active viewport and notice the results. Only the active viewport reflects the use of the **ZOOM** command.

If you want to join two viewports together, you can do so by picking **Join** from the **Viewports** cascading menu in the **View** pull-down menu. Once **Join** is selected, you are prompted to Select dominant viewport. Select the viewport that has the view you want to keep in the joined viewport.

Once the dominant viewport is selected, you are prompted to Select viewport to join. Select the viewport that you want to join with the active viewport. Once you select a viewport to join, AutoCAD "glues" the two viewports together and retains the dominant view. The two viewports you are joining cannot create an L-shape viewport. In other words, the two edges of the viewports must be the same size in order to join them.

The **-VPORTS** command can be used to create viewports at the Command: prompt. Enter -VPORTS and the following prompt appears:

Command: **-VPORTS**↵
Enter an option
[Save/Restore/Delete/Join/SIngle/?/2/<3>/4] <3>:

The options are similar to those already discussed.

## Uses of Tiled Viewports

Viewports in model space can be used for both 2D and 3D drawings. They are limited only by your imagination and need. See *AutoCAD and its Applications—Advanced* for examples of the tiled viewports in 3D. The nature of 2D drawings, whether mechanical multiview, architectural construction details, or unscaled schematic drawings, lend themselves well to viewports.

Several sample drawings are included with the AutoCAD software. If AutoCAD was installed using default settings, the sample drawings should be located in the AutoCAD 2004\Sample folder. Check with your instructor or supervisor to locate these drawings, or browse through the folders to determine their locations. The sample drawings include a variety of drawing and design disciplines and are excellent for testing and practice. You should use these drawings, especially when learning the display commands.

### Exercise 9-5

○ Start AutoCAD and open the wilhome.dwg drawing from the AutoCAD 2002\Sample folder.
○ When the drawing is displayed on the screen, you should see a house floor plan and several elevations. Press the **Model** tab to make model space active. Zoom into various locations to get familiar with the drawing.
○ Use the **Viewports** dialog box to create three viewports. The large viewport should be on the right.
○ Use realtime panning to center the drawing in the large viewport. Use realtime zooming to enlarge the drawing to fill the viewport.
○ In the upper-left viewport, use **ZOOM Window** to find the AQUARIUM elevation in the upper-left corner of the drawing.
○ Pick the lower-left viewport and zoom in on the Grand Room at the upper-right of the house. Use realtime pan and zoom to locate the entertainment center.
○ Quit without saving the drawing.

# Floating Viewports

The layout tabs are used to set up a page to be printed or plotted. The paper space environment is activated when you switch from the **Model** tab to a layout tab. Viewports created in paper space are called floating viewports. These *floating viewports* are actually holes cut into the paper in the layout tab so that the model space drawing can be seen. These viewports are separate objects and can overlap, thus the term "floating viewports," as they can be moved around.

After floating viewports are created, display commands are used to modify the model space "showing through" the viewport. Editing commands such as **MOVE**, **ERASE**, and **COPY** can be used in paper space to modify the viewports.

As you work through the following sections describing floating viewports, be sure a layout tab is selected on your AutoCAD screen.

> **NOTE**  The first time you select a layout tab, the **Page Setup** dialog box appears. This dialog box will be discussed in Chapter 10. For the time being, simply pick the **OK** button to access the layout tab.

## Creating Floating Viewports

The process of creating floating viewports in paper space is nearly identical to the process of creating tiled viewports in model space. A viewport configuration can be selected from the **Viewports** dialog box, which was discussed earlier in this chapter. Also, the **MVIEW** command options can be used to create single or multiple viewports.

As discussed earlier, when model space is active, the **Viewports** dialog box creates tiled viewports. When paper space is active, it creates floating viewports. This dialog box differs slightly depending on the current environment—model space or paper space. The **Apply to:** drop-down list found in model space becomes the **Viewport spacing:** text box in paper space. Use this setting to specify the space around the edges of the floating viewports. See **Figure 9-25**.

Floating viewports can also be created using the **MVIEW** command.

MVIEW
MV

```
Command: MV or MVIEW↵
Specify corner of viewport or
    [ON/OFF/Fit/Hideplot/Lock/Object/Polygonal/Restore/2/3/4] <Fit>:
```

The default option is to define a rectangular floating viewport by selecting opposite corners. See **Figure 9-26**.

The **2**, **3**, and **4** options provide preset viewport configurations similar to the **Viewports** dialog box. These options can also be selected from the **Viewports** cascading menu in the **View** pull-down menu, as was discussed for tiled viewports.

The remaining options are described as follows:

- **ON and OFF.** These options activate and deactivate the model space display within a viewport. When you enter the **OFF** option, you are prompted to select the viewports to be affected. Use the **ON** option to reactivate the viewport.
- **Fit.** This default option creates a single rectangular floating viewport that fills the entire printable area on the sheet.
- **Hideplot.** This option prevents hidden lines in a 3D model from being plotted. This option is covered in greater detail in *AutoCAD and its Applications— Advanced.*

**Figure 9-25.**
When paper space is active, the **New Viewports** tab in the **Viewports** dialog box contains the **Viewport Spacing:** setting.

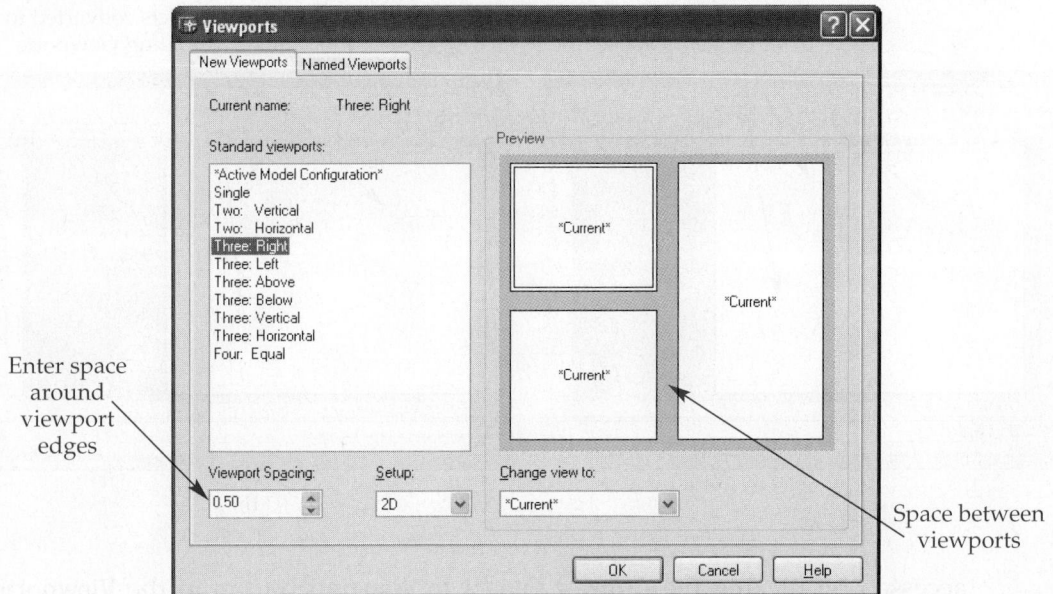

Enter space around viewport edges

Space between viewports

**Figure 9-26.**
Creating a rectangular floating viewport using the **MVIEW** command.

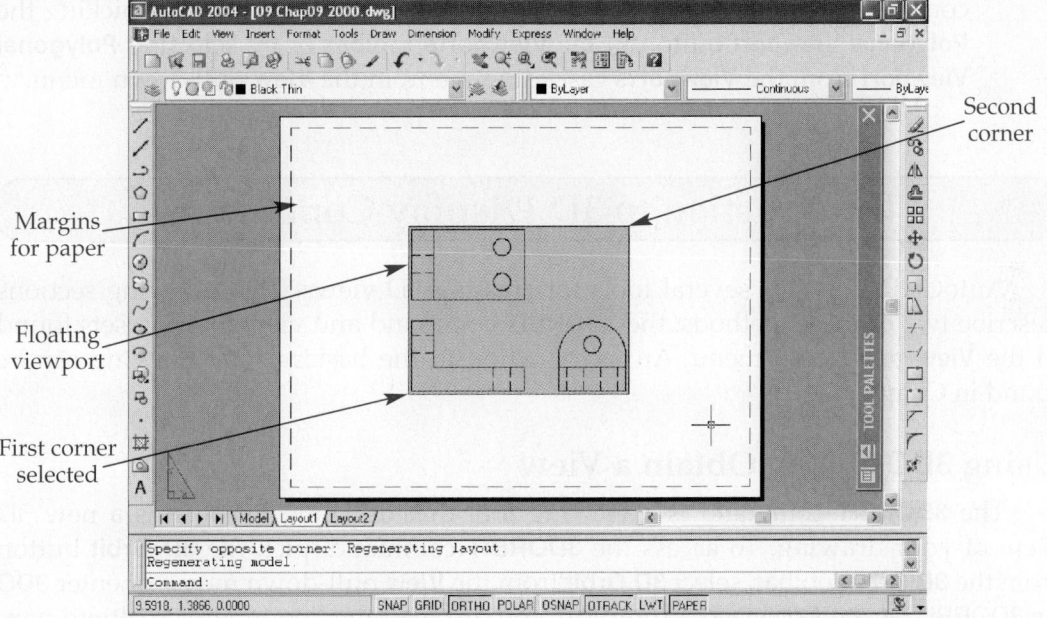

Second corner

Margins for paper

Floating viewport

First corner selected

- **Lock.** This option allows you to lock the view in one or more viewports. When a viewport is locked, objects within the viewport can be still edited and new objects can be added, but you are unable to use display commands such as **ZOOM** and **PAN**. This option is also used to unlock a locked viewport.
- **Restore.** Converts saved viewport configurations into individual floating viewports.
- **Object.** Use this option to change a closed object drawn in paper space into a floating viewport. Circles, ellipses, polygons, and other closed shapes can be used as floating viewport outlines. See **Figure 9-27.** This option can also be

**Figure 9-27.**
Viewports can be created from closed objects. A—Draw the objects in paper space.
B—Objects converted to viewports.

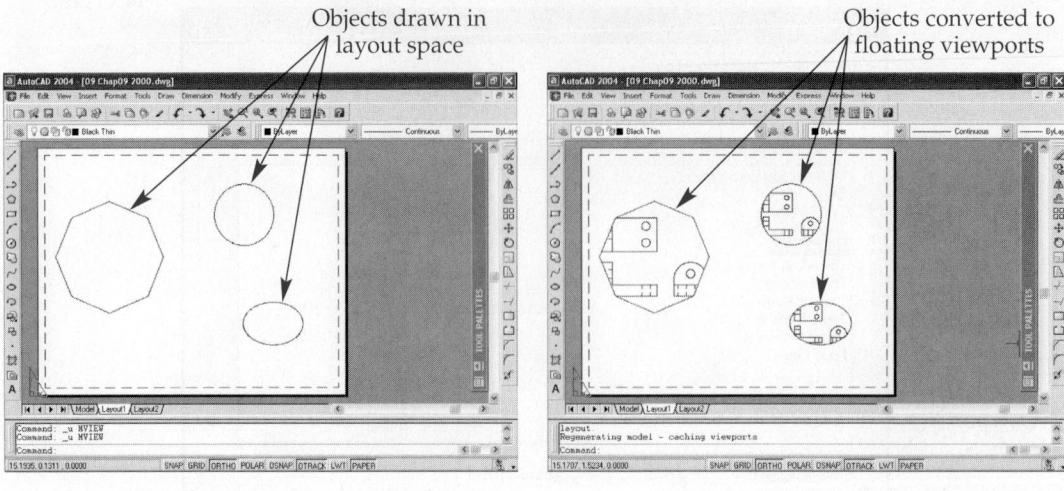

Objects drawn in
layout space

Objects converted to
floating viewports

A

B

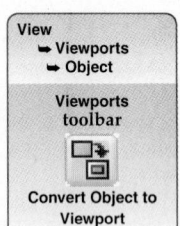

View
➡ Viewports
➡ Object

Viewports
toolbar

Convert Object to
Viewport

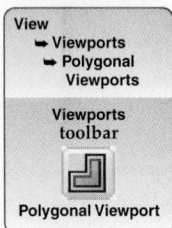

View
➡ Viewports
➡ Polygonal
Viewports

Viewports
toolbar

Polygonal Viewport

accessed by picking the **Convert Object to Viewport** button in the **Viewports** toolbar or by selecting **Object** from the **Viewports** cascading menu in the **View** pull-down menu.

- **Polygonal.** Use this option to draw a floating viewport outline using a polyline. Polylines are discussed in Chapter 14. The viewport shape can be any closed shape composed of lines and arcs. This option can also be accessed by picking the **Polygonal Viewport** button in the **Viewports** toolbar or by selecting **Polygonal Viewport** from the **Viewports** cascading menu in the **View** pull-down menu.

## Introduction to 3D Display Commands

AutoCAD provides several tools for creating 3D views. The following sections describe two of these methods: the **3DORBIT** command and viewpoint presets found in the **View** pull-down menu. An introduction to the basics of 3D drawing can be found in Chapter 26.

### Using 3DORBIT to Obtain a View

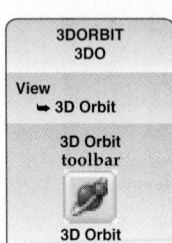

3DORBIT
3DO

View
➡ 3D Orbit

3D Orbit
toolbar

3D Orbit

The **3DORBIT** command is a viewing tool that dynamically obtains a new 3D view of your drawing. To access the **3DORBIT** command, pick the **3D Orbit** button from the **3D Orbit** toolbar, select **3D Orbit** from the **View** pull-down menu, or enter 3DO or 3DORBIT at the Command: prompt. If you are realtime zooming or realtime panning, you can right-click and select **3D Orbit** from the shortcut menu.

Once the **3DORBIT** command is accessed, a 3D view appears in the active viewport. The UCS (User Coordinate System) is changed to a shaded 3D icon, and an arcball, which is a circle divided into four quadrants by smaller circles, appears in the middle of the viewport. See **Figure 9-28.**

The drawing crosshairs also change to a sphere encircled with two lines. By holding down the pick button and moving your pointing device, a 3D view can be obtained. By dragging the pointing device you can see your new viewpoint adjust. It is like walking around your drawing and moving your eye position up, down, and around.

**Figure 9-28.**
When you activate the **3DORBIT** command, the arcball, shaded UCS icon, and 3D Orbit cursor appear. You can then rotate the objects in 3D space.

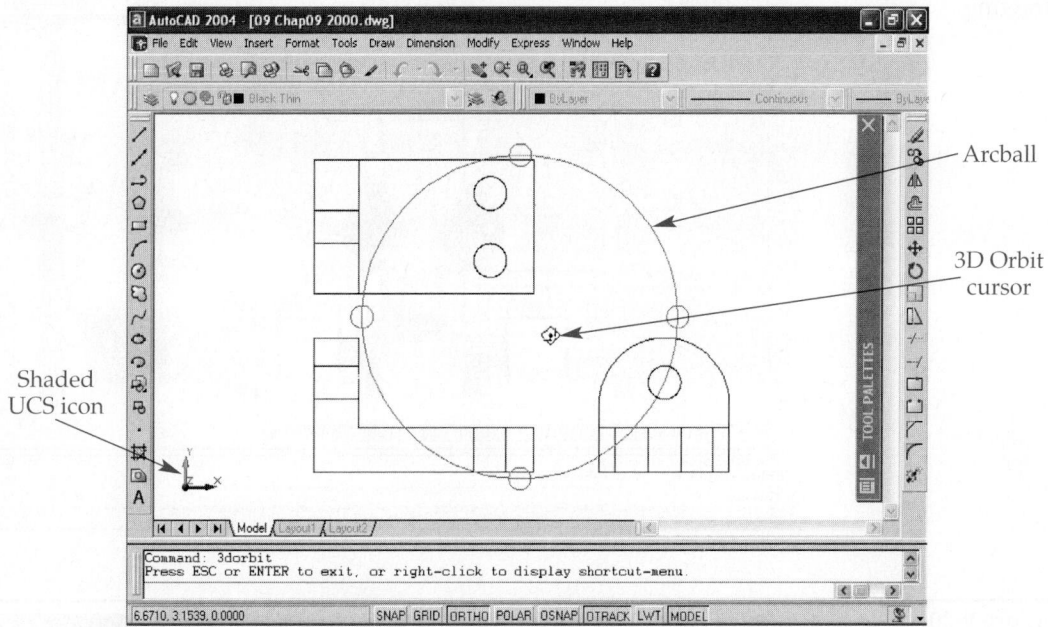

If the cursor is moved over the top of one of the quadrant circles on the arcball, it changes shape, showing you the direction the view can be rotated. If the right mouse button is pressed, a shortcut menu appears so you can use realtime zoom or realtime pan. There are several other options and possibilities with the **3DORBIT** command. The **3DORBIT** command is covered in greater detail in *AutoCAD and its Applications—Advanced*.

## Using Preset Isometric and Orthographic Views

When creating 3D drawings, viewports can be used to display different 3D views of the object or structure. The **3DORBIT** command can be used to specify the viewpoint in each viewport. Another method of specifying viewpoints is using the preset isometric and orthographic viewpoints available in the **View** pull-down menu.

The following example provides an introduction to using the preset 3D viewpoints using the Oil Module.dwg drawing in the AutoCAD 2004\Sample folder. First, open the Oil Module.dwg drawing. The drawing that appears is a 3D model of oil piping. It is displayed in a model tab from a northwest isometric view.

Select **Top** from the **3D Views** cascading menu in the **View** pull-down menu. This sets the viewpoint for an orthographic top view, which is the same as a plan view. Your display should look like **Figure 9-29**.

Access the **Viewports** dialog box and select the Three: Right configuration. Next, make the large viewport active by picking anywhere inside it. Then, select **2D Wireframe** from the **Shade** cascading menu in the **View** pull-down menu. This allows viewing of the model in a wireframe view.

Select the **NE Isometric** option from the **3D Views** cascading menu in the **View** pull-down menu. The model is now displayed as if you were viewing it from an elevated location from the northeast. Use the **ZOOM** command to display the "nearest" corner of the model, as shown in **Figure 9-30**.

Pick a point within the upper-left viewport to make it active. Select the **Right** option from the **3D Views** cascading menu in the **View** pull-down menu to create a right elevation view. Use the **ZOOM** command to display the corner shown in the large viewport. Repeat the process in the lower-left viewport using the **Back** option

**Figure 9-29.**
Plan (top) view of
the Oil Module
drawing.

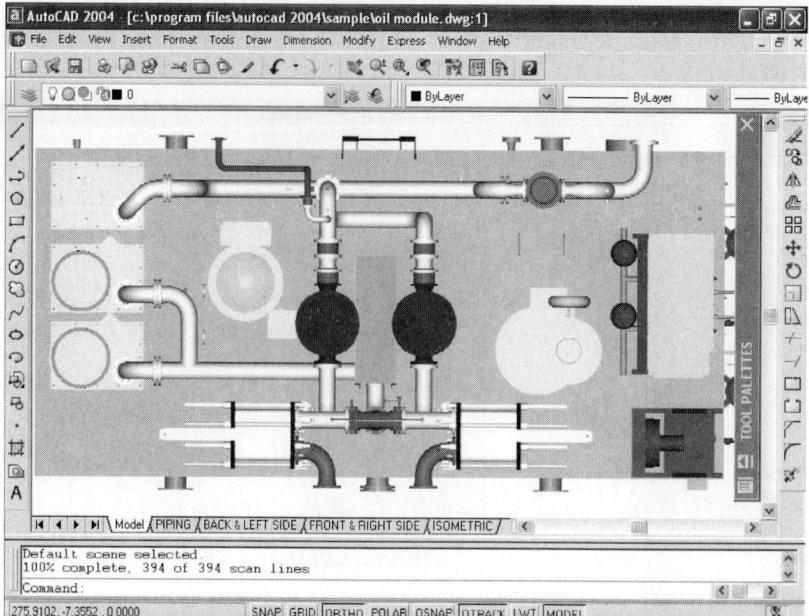

**Figure 9-30.**
The large viewport
set to the NE
isometric viewpoint
and shaded.

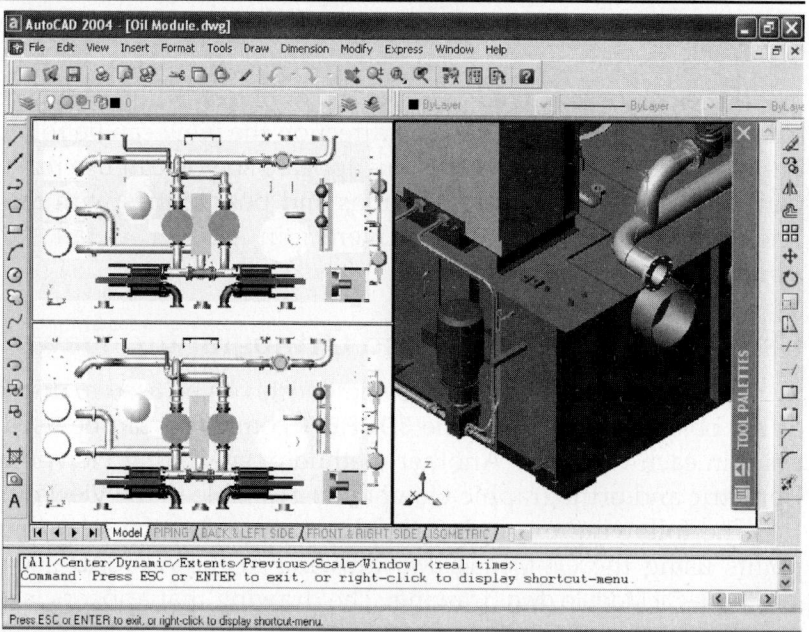

instead of the **Right** option. Finally, activate each viewport and enter HIDE at the Command: prompt to remove hidden lines. The **HIDE** command affects only the active viewport, so you will need to enter the command three times. The finished drawing is shown in **Figure 9-31.**

AutoCAD and its Applications—Basics

Figure 9-31.
Three different 3D
views of the Oil
Module drawing.

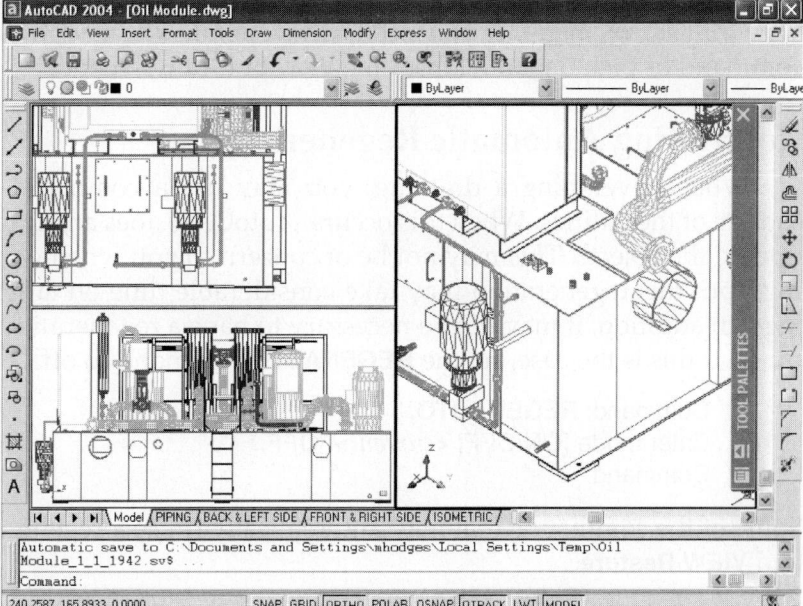

 **NOTE**

In addition to the **3DORBIT** command and the preset 3D viewpoints, there are several other tools available in AutoCAD to establish 3D views. The **DVIEW** command defines a viewing "camera" and "target" for precise control of the view. The **VPOINT** or **DDVPOINT** command allows you to define a viewing direction by entering coordinates at the Command: prompt or by dynamically positioning a compass and tripod. The tool you choose to use to establish a 3D view depends on the subject and requirements of the view. All of the 3D viewing tools are discussed thoroughly in *AutoCAD and its Applications—Advanced*.

## Exercise 9-6

○ Open the Oil Module.dwg drawing, select the **Model** tab, and pick the **Top** viewpoint.
○ Create three viewports in a configuration of your choosing.
○ Select an object within the drawing and create a different 3D view of the model in each viewport.
○ Use the **HIDE** command in each viewport to remove hidden lines.
○ Close the drawing without saving.

## Redrawing and Regenerating Viewports

Since each viewport is a separate screen, you can redraw or regenerate a single viewport at a time without affecting the others. The **REGEN** (regenerate) command instructs AutoCAD to recalculate all objects in the drawing. This takes considerably longer than a **REDRAW**, especially if the drawing is large. However, **REGEN** can clarify a drawing by smoothing out circles, arcs, ellipses, and splines.

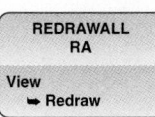

REDRAWALL
RA

View
➥ Redraw

REGENALL
REA

View
➡ Regen All

To redraw all viewports, use the **REDRAWALL** command or pick **Redraw** from the **View** pull-down menu. If you need to regenerate all viewports, use the **REGENALL** command or pick **Regen All** from the **View** pull-down menu.

### Controlling Automatic Regeneration

When developing a drawing, you may use a command that changes certain aspects of the entities. When this occurs, AutoCAD does an automatic regeneration to update the objects. This may not be of concern to you when working on small drawings, but this regeneration may take considerable time on large and complex drawings. In addition, it may not be necessary to have a regeneration of the drawing at all times. If this is the case, set the **REGENAUTO** command to off.

Command: **REGENAUTO.**↵
Enter mode [ON/OFF] <*current*>: **OFF**↵
Command:

Some of the commands that may automatically cause a regeneration are **PLAN**, **HIDE**, and **VIEW Restore**.

## Controlling the Order of Display

DRAWORDER
DR

Tools
➡ Display Order
  ➡ Bring Above
    Objectt

Draw Order
toolbar

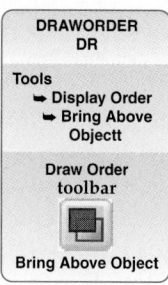

Bring Above Object

AutoCAD has the ability to display both raster and vector images in the graphics window. A *raster image* is composed of dots, or *pixels*, and is also referred to as a *bit map*. Raster images contain no XYZ coordinate values. Objects in a *vector image* (drawing), such as those created in AutoCAD, are given XYZ coordinate values. All these objects are composed of points, or *vectors*, connected by straight lines.

Drawings containing both raster and vector images can have objects that overlap each other. For example, in **Figure 9-32A** the raster image of the **Zoom Previous** button is imported into AutoCAD and overlays the vector image of the text label. In this case the text label should be displayed on top of the raster image. To do this, use the **DRAWORDER** command by picking **Bring Above Object** in the **Display Order** cascading menu of the **Tools** pull-down menu, pick the **Bring Above Object** button in the **Draw Order** toolbar, or enter DR or DRAWORDER at the Command: prompt. The drawing is then displayed and plotted as shown in **Figure 9-32B**.

The drawing order is the order in which objects are displayed and/or plotted. If an object is moved to the top of the drawing order, it is displayed and plotted first. If one object is moved above another object, it is displayed on top—the text in **Figure 9-32B**. These order and arrangement functions are handled by the following **DRAWORDER** options:

- **Above object.** The selected object is moved above the reference object.
- **Under object.** The selected object is moved below the reference object.
- **Front.** The selected object is placed to the front of the drawing.
- **Back.** The selected object is placed to the back of the drawing.

Figure 9-32.
A—An imported raster image obscures part of a vector drawing.
B—The **DRAWORDER** command is used to bring the vector drawing above the raster image.

A

B

## Clearing the Screen

The AutoCAD window can become crowded in the course of a drawing session. Each toolbar and modeless dialog box displayed on-screen reduces the size of the drawing area. As the drawing area gets smaller, less of the drawing is visible. This can make drafting difficult. You can quickly maximize the size of the drawing area using the **Clean Screen** tool.

The **Clean Screen** tool removes all toolbars, modeless dialog boxes, and title bars from the AutoCAD window. See **Figure 9-33.** The **Clean Screen** tool is accessed by picking **Clean Screen** form the **View** pull-down menu or using the [Ctrl]+[0] (zero) key combination. To return to the normal display, use the [Ctrl]+[0] (zero) key combination.

[Ctrl]+[0]

View
➥ Clean Screen

PROFESSIONAL
TIP

The **Clean Screen** tool can be helpful when you have multiple drawings displayed. Only the active drawing is displayed when the **Clean Screen** tool is used. This allows you to work more efficiently within one of the drawings. You can use the **Window** pull-down menu options to switch between drawings.

**Figure 9-33.**
Using the **Clean Screen** tool. A—Initial display with default toolbars displayed. B—Display after using the **Clean Screen** tool.

Original
Display

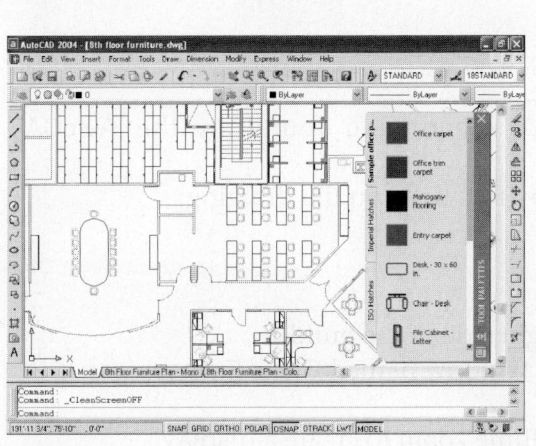

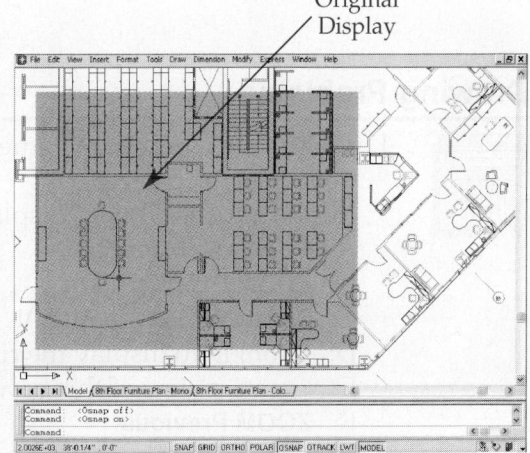

A

B

## Chapter Test

*Answer the following questions on a separate sheet of paper.*

1. What is the difference between the **REDRAW** and **'REDRAW** commands?
2. What are *blips* and how does **REDRAW** affect them?
3. Which command allows you to change the display of blips?
4. Give the proper command option and value to automatically zoom to a 2X scale factor.
5. What is the difference between **ZOOM Extents** and **ZOOM All**?
6. During the drawing process, when should you use **ZOOM**?
7. How many different boxes are displayed during the **ZOOM Dynamic** command?
8. What is a *pan displacement*?
9. When using the **ZOOM Dynamic** option, what represents the current view?
10. What is the purpose of the **PAN** command?
11. Explain how scroll bars can be used to pan the drawing display.
12. How do you access the **PAN** command presets?
13. What is *view resolution*?
14. In which dialog box is circle and arc smoothness set?
15. How do you create a named view of the current screen display?
16. How do you display an existing view?
17. How would you obtain a listing of existing views?
18. How is a transparent display command entered at the keyboard?
19. What is the effect of picking **Global** from the **View** pull-down menu in the **Aerial View** window?
20. What is the function of the **Auto Viewport** option of the **Aerial View** window?
21. Cite several advantages of **Aerial View** over other display commands.
22. Explain the difference between model space and paper space.
23. What type of viewports is created in model space?
24. What type of viewports is created in paper space?
25. What is the purpose of the **Preview** area of the **Viewports** dialog box?
26. Explain the procedures and conditions that need to exist when joining viewports.
27. What commands allow you to create 3D views in a drawing or viewport?
28. Which pull-down menu contains preset 3D viewpoint options?
29. Which command regenerates all of the viewports?
30. What is the function of **REGENAUTO**?

## Drawing Problems

1. Open the drawing named wilhome.dwg found in the AutoCAD 2004\Sample folder.
   Perform the following display functions on the drawing:
   A. Select the **Model** tab.
   B. **ZOOM Extents**.
   C. Create a view named All.
   D. Zoom in to display the right side of the building.
   E. Create a view of this new window named Grand Entrance.
   F. **ZOOM Previous**.
   G. Use realtime pan and realtime zoom to create a display of the lower-left staircase.
   H. Create a view of this display named Kitchen Elevations.
   I. Display the view named All.
   J. Save the drawing as P9-1.

2. Load one of your own mechanical template drawings that contains a border and title block. Do the following:
    A. Zoom into the title block area. Create and save a view named Title.
    B. Zoom to the extents of the drawing and create and save a view named All.
    C. Determine the area of the drawing that will contain notes, parts list, or revisions. Zoom into these areas and create views with appropriate names such as Notes, Partlist, and Revisions.
    D. Divide the drawing area into commonly used multiview sections. Save the views with descriptive names such as Top, Front, Rightside, and Leftside.
    E. Restore the view named All.
    F. Save the drawing as P9-2, or as a template.
3. Load one of your own template drawings used for architectural layout that contains a border and title block. Do the following:
    A. Zoom into the title block area. Create and save a view named Title.
    B. Zoom to the extents of the drawing and create and save a view named All.
    C. Determine the area of the drawing that will contain notes, schedules, or revisions. Zoom into these areas and create views with appropriate names such as Notes, Schedules, and Revisions.
    D. Restore the view named All.
    E. Save the drawing as P9-3, or as a template.
4. Open the drawing named Oil Module.dwg drawing. This drawing should be in the AutoCAD 2004\Sample folder. Then perform the following:
    A. Make sure the **Model** tab is active. Set the named view FRONT as the current view.
    B. Pick **4 Viewports** from the **Viewports** cascading menu in the **View** pull-down menu. In each viewport, zoom to a different quadrant of the drawing. Pick **2D Wireframe** from the **Shade** cascading menu in the **View** pull-down menu in each viewport.
    C. Create named views of different parts of the module, such as LowerRight, LowerLeft, UpperRight, and UpperLeft.
    D. In the upper-right viewport, **ZOOM All** and create a view named All.
    E. Use **3DORBIT** to obtain a 3D view in the upper-right viewport and use the **HIDE** command to remove the hidden lines.
    F. Make the upper-left viewport active and split it into four equal viewports.
    G. In each of the new viewports, restore your named views from step C.
    H. Pick **Join** from the **Viewports** cascading menu in the **View** pull-down menu to join the two far-right viewports together. Make the 3D view the dominant view.
    I. In the lower-left viewport, restore the **All** view.
    J. Save the drawing as P9-4 only if required by your instructor.

Elevation section. (Steve D. Bloedel)

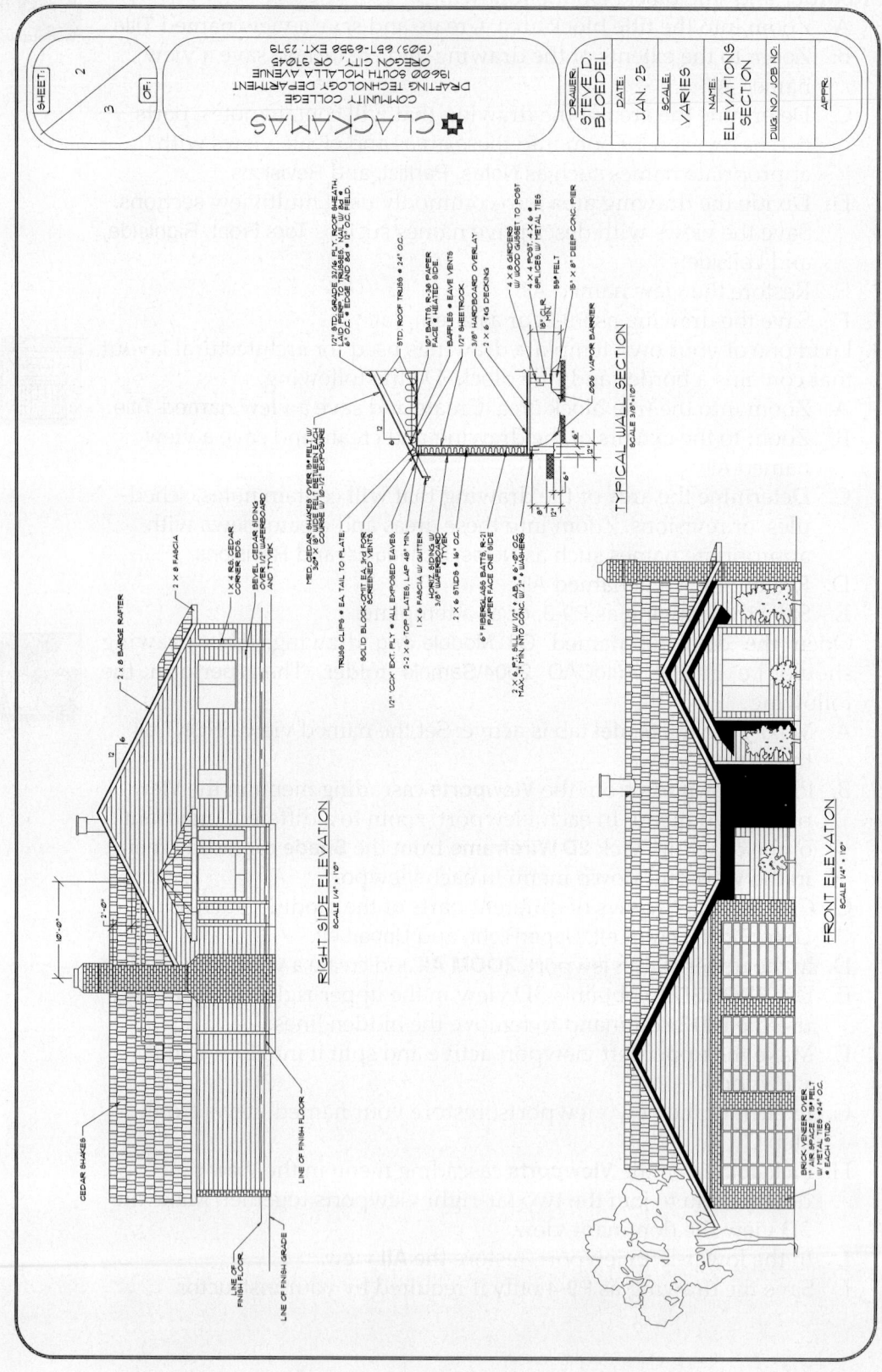

## CHAPTER 10

# Layouts, Plotting, and Printing

## Learning Objectives

After completing this chapter, you will be able to do the following:
- Print and plot a drawing.
- Set up layouts using title blocks and viewports.
- Create new layouts.
- Manage layouts.
- Select a plotting device and modify a plotting device configuration.
- Explain plot styles, plot style tables, and plot style modes.
- Create and modify plot styles and plot style tables.
- Attach plot style tables to drawings and layouts.
- Assign plot styles to drawings, layers, and objects.
- Select plot settings.
- Calculate scale factors based on drawing scale.
- Create a plot file.
- Plot a group of drawings using the Batch Plot utility.
- Explain keys to efficient plotting.

Often, the end result of your AutoCAD work will be a plotted drawing. It is far easier for a construction crew in the field to use a printed copy of the drawing rather than using a computer to view the DWG file. Therefore, it is important that you understand the various plotting options available in AutoCAD.

Paper space, model space, the **Model** tab, and layout tabs were discussed in Chapter 9. Each layout tab can be set to plot different views of the objects using different plotting settings. This allows you to create several different plots using a single drawing.

## Plotting Procedure

You can create plots from the **Model** tab (model space) and from the layout tabs (paper space). The general procedures for both cases are similar. The following steps are explained later in this chapter:
1. Create the drawing objects in the **Model** tab (model space). If you are creating a layout, create the floating viewports, title block, and other desired items in a layout tab (paper space).

2. Configure the plotting device if it is not already configured.
3. Access the **Page Setup** or **Plot** dialog box and specify values for the plotting settings. Each tab (**Model** and layout) can have its own settings, so each layout can produce a different plot.
4. Plot the drawing.

## Layout and Plotting Terms

It is important to understand the terminology used when discussing model space, paper space, layouts, and plotting. Therefore, this section provides you with a quick overview of the commands and functions that enable you to lay out and plot a drawing. These terms are described in greater detail later in this chapter.

- **Model space.** This is the drawing environment in which the drawing objects are constructed. Model space is active when the **Model** tab is selected. Model space is also activated when you double-click inside a floating viewport in a layout tab.
- **Paper space.** This is the drawing environment used to create plotting layouts, which are arrangements of various objects (such as floating viewports, title blocks, and annotations) on the page to be plotted. Paper space is active by default when a layout tab is selected. If you double-click inside a floating viewport in a layout tab, the viewport becomes active and model space is entered. To switch back to paper space, double-click in an area outside the floating viewport.
- **Layouts.** A layout is the manner in which a drawing is arranged in paper space. A layout may contain a title block, one or more viewports, and annotations. Each drawing can have multiple layouts, and each layout is shown as a tab along the bottom of the drawing area. Each layout can have different page setup and plotting settings.
- **Page setups.** A page setup is the manner in which the drawing is displayed on a sheet of paper in order to create a layout. Most of the aspects of how the drawing is plotted can be established in a page setup, from the plot device to pen settings to scales. These settings can even be saved in the drawing file as a named page setup, which can be recalled each time the drawing is plotted.
- **Layout settings.** These settings are created in the **Page Setup** dialog box and include paper size and drawing units, paper orientation, plot area, plot scale, plot offset, and plot options.
- **Plotters window.** The **Plotters** window allows you to add, delete, configure, and reconfigure plotters. It can be accessed by selecting **Plotter Manager...** from the **File** pull-down menu. When a device is configured, the settings are saved in a PC3 file.
- **Plot styles.** Plot styles contain settings that are applied to objects when they are plotted. A *color-dependent plot style* is applied to all objects with a specific color. A *named plot style* can be assigned to an object or layer.
- **Plot style tables.** A plot style table is a collection of plot styles. There are two types of plot style tables: color-dependent and named. A plot style table can only contain plot styles of a single *plot style mode* (either color-dependent or named). The **Model** tab and each layout tab can have a unique plot style table attached. Only plot styles in the attached plot style table can be used within a tab.
- **Plot Styles window.** The **Plot Styles** window allows you to manage all your plot style table files. From here you can open and edit the plot styles within a plot style table. You can also create new plot style tables.

- **Plot settings.** These settings are created in the **Plot** dialog box and include the same items found in the **Page Setup** dialog box. They control how the drawing is printed on paper. Although this may seem like the last step in the process, plot settings can be created at the beginning of a project and then saved to be used again.
- **Batch Plotting.** Once drawing files have been assigned layouts, page setups, and plot parameters, they can be grouped in *batch list* files using the Batch Plot utility. These files can then be configured to plot off-line or in the background as a group, or "batch," while the user continues with other tasks. Batch plot files are saved with a .bp3 extension and can be created without opening a full session of AutoCAD.

## Layout Settings

A *layout* shows the arrangement of objects on a sheet of paper for plotting purposes. A layout may include a title block, floating viewports showing your model space drawing, and annotation.

A single drawing can have multiple layouts. Named layouts are displayed as tabs along the bottom of the drawing area. Each layout tab represents a different paper space configuration.

When you start AutoCAD, a new drawing is started automatically. This drawing is based on a template file containing default settings and has two layouts by default. These layouts are identified by the **Layout1** and **Layout2** tabs below the drawing area. When you pick a layout tab for the first time, the **Page Setup** dialog box for the layout appears. This dialog box allows you to complete a variety of settings for the plotting device and the layout of the drawing on a sheet of paper. This dialog box is discussed later in this chapter. For the time being, select the **OK** button in this dialog box to enter the **Layout1** tab.

When a layout tab is selected, an image showing a preview of the final printed drawing is shown. See **Figure 10-1**. The dashed line around the edge of the paper represents the page margins. The solid lines show the outline of a floating viewport. By default, a single viewport is created.

Figure 10-1.
A layout is displayed when a layout tab is selected. The layout provides a preview of how the plotted drawing will appear.

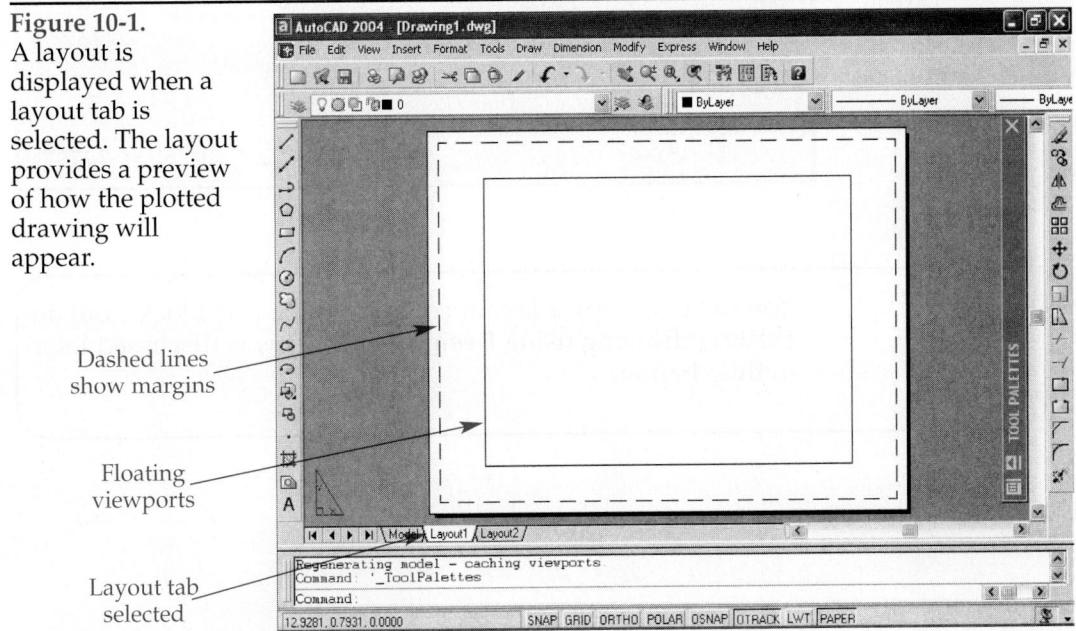

Dashed lines show margins

Floating viewports

Layout tab selected

## Working in Layout Tabs

A layout can contain many types of objects, including floating viewports, a title block, and notes. Assembling these items in a layout allows you to see exactly what the final plot will look like.

Several settings that affect the display of layouts are contained in the **Layout elements** area of the **Display** tab in the **Options** dialog box. See **Figure 10-2**. Access this dialog box by selecting **Options...** from the **Tools** pull-down menu. Use the default settings until you are comfortable working with layouts.

### Inserting a title block

Most layouts contain a title block. Title blocks are generally saved in a template file and then inserted as a block when needed. A block is a single object comprising multiple individual objects. See Chapter 22 for a complete discussion on blocks.

It is best to insert a title block into the layout and then save it as a template file. You can then start a new drawing based on the template, and the layout with the title block will already be created.

To insert a title block, select **Block...** from the **Insert** pull-down menu to access the **Insert** dialog box. Pick the **Browse...** button and select the title block drawing to be inserted. **Figure 10-3** shows the ANSI A title block inserted into a layout.

Figure 10-2.
Layout display
options are found in
the **Options** dialog
box.

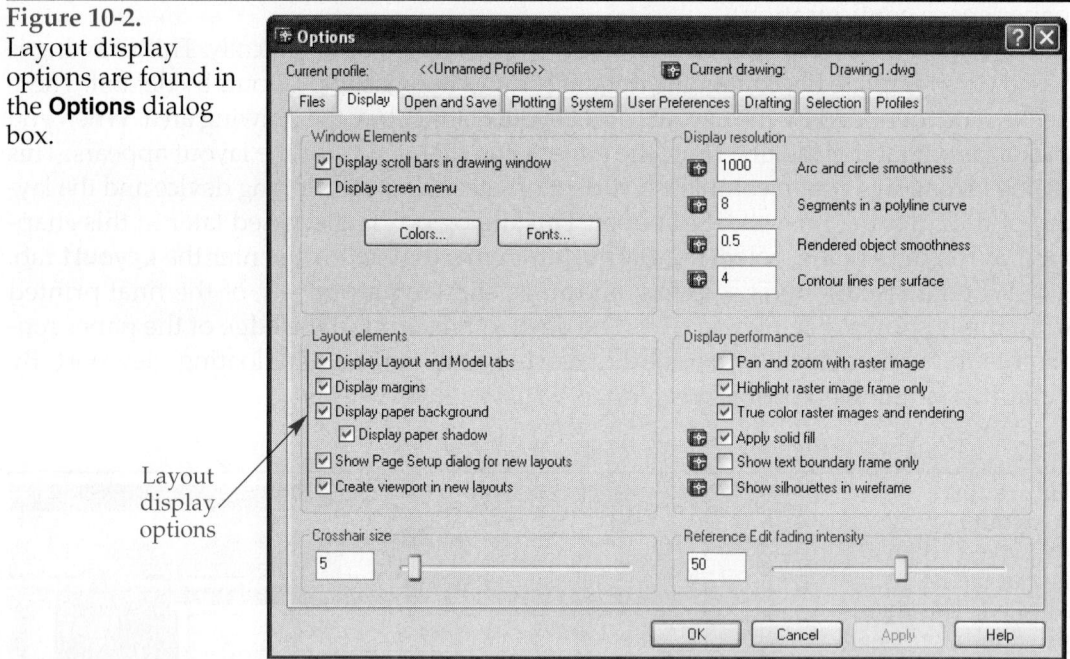

Layout
display
options

**NOTE**

You can also copy a layout containing the title block from an existing drawing using **DesignCenter**. This is discussed later in this chapter.

**Figure 10-3.**
The ANSI A title block inserted into the layout. Note the viewport created by default has been deleted.

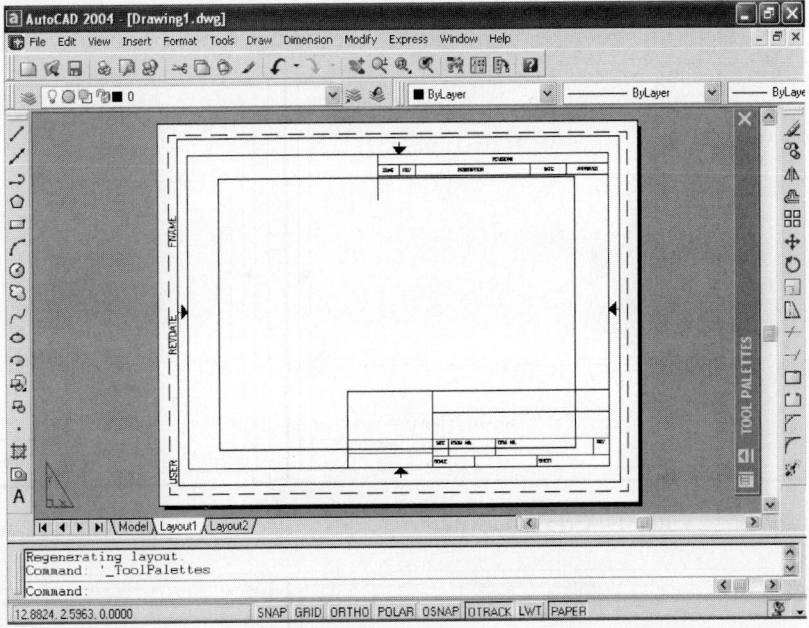

## Working with floating viewports

Chapter 9 explained how to create floating viewports in a layout. Once the viewports are created, the display within the viewport must be set to show the correct part of the model space drawing.

Create the floating viewports after the title block has been inserted. This will allow you to position the viewports so they do not interfere with the title block. Floating viewports are created using the **Viewports** dialog box or the **MVIEW** command. This is discussed in Chapter 9.

**Figure 10-4** illustrates the following procedure for establishing the display in two floating viewports:

1. Create the first viewport using the **Viewports** dialog box. The model space drawing is visible in the viewport.
2. Create a second viewport.
3. Double-click in the new viewport to enter model space.
4. Use the **XP** option of the **ZOOM** command or the scale drop-down list on the **Viewports** toolbar to scale the drawing. Use realtime panning to display the part of interest in the drawing.
5. Double-click outside of the viewports to activate paper space. Use grips or the **STRETCH** command to resize the viewport.

Using multiple viewports in a layout allows you to illustrate different aspects of the drawing. Using multiple layouts, various types of drawings can be created from a single drawing model. This is a very simple example of the use of floating viewports within a layout. **Figure 10-5** shows the viewports created by the **Std. 3D Engineering Views** option available in the **Create Layout** wizard. The viewports show the three primary orthographic views and an isometric view. The **Create Layout** wizard is discussed later in this chapter.

CAUTION

If you use zoom to adjust the drawing inside the viewport, the drawing may no longer be to scale. Always use the **ZOOM XP** option or the scale drop-down list on the **Viewports** toolbar as the final step prior to plotting to be certain the drawing is scaled inside the viewport.

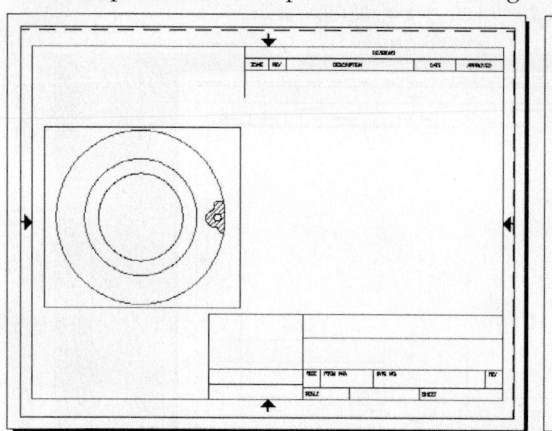

Step 1—Create viewport.

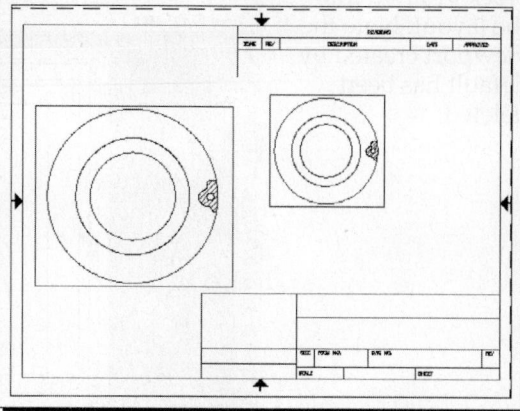

Step 2—Create second viewport.

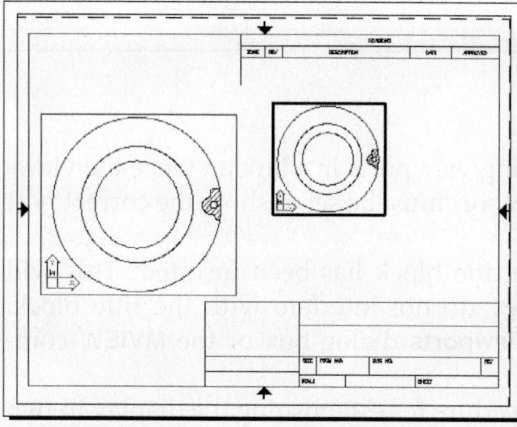

Step 3—Make second viewport active.

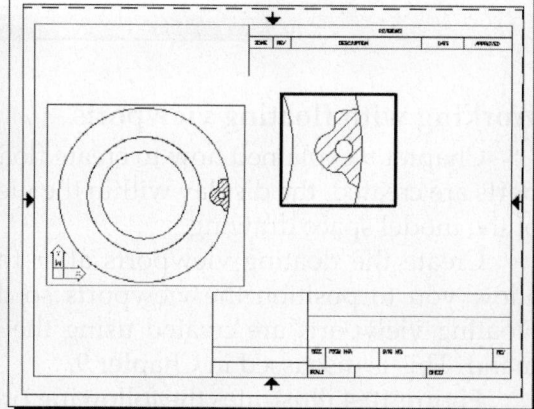

Step 4—Zoom and pan display in second viewport.

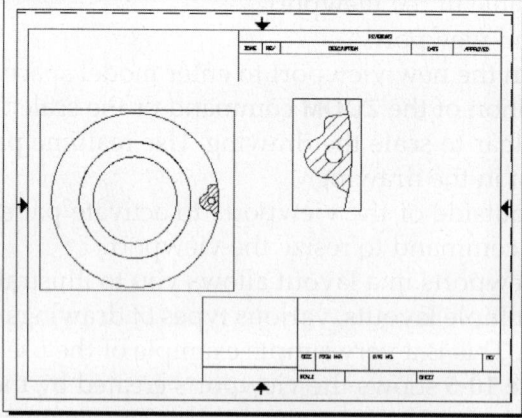

Step 5—Resize viewport.

**Figure 10-5.**
This example shows the ANSI D title block and the **Std. 3D Engineering Views** viewport configuration. This configuration is available in the **Create Layout** wizard.

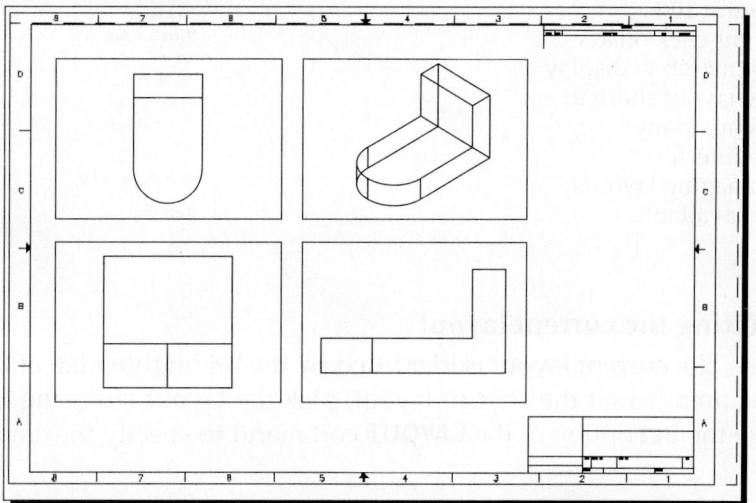

○ Start a new drawing from scratch.
○ Create the following layers with the specified properties:

| Layer | Color | Linetype |
|-------|-------|----------|
| Circle | Blue | Continuous |
| Line | Red | Hidden |
| Ellipse | Green | Phantom |
| Rectangle | Magenta | Dashed |

○ Draw a circle, line, ellipse, and rectangle, each on the appropriate layer.
○ Perform a **ZOOM Extents**.
○ Access the **Layout1** tab, cancel the **Page Setup** dialog box, and delete the default viewport.
○ Create an arrangement of viewports using the Three: Left preset configuration.
○ Modify the display within the viewports so that all objects are shown in the larger, left viewport, the circle is shown in the top-right viewport, and the ellipse is shown in the lower-right viewport. Double-click in a viewport to make it active.
○ Save this drawing as EX10-1. It will be used for other exercises in this chapter.

## Managing Layouts

The **LAYOUT** command allows you to manage layouts. To access this command, type LO or LAYOUT at the Command: prompt:

Command: **LO** *or* **LAYOUT**↵
Enter layout option [Copy/Delete/New/Template/Rename/SAveas/Set/?] <set>:

You are prompted to select a **LAYOUT** command option. Some of these options are also available in the **Layouts** toolbars or the **Layout** cascading menu of the **Insert** pull-down menu. You can also position the cursor over a layout tab and right-click to display the layout shortcut menu, **Figure 10-6**. This shortcut menu also contains many **LAYOUT** command options.

**Figure 10-6.**
Right-click on a
layout tab to display
the layout shortcut
menu. Many
options for
managing layouts
are available.

| New layout |
| From template... |
| Delete |
| Rename |
| Move or Copy... |
| Select All Layouts |
| Activate Previous Layout |
| Activate Model Tab |
| Page Setup... |
| Plot... |

## Setting the current layout

The current layout is identified by the highlighted tab at the bottom of the drawing area. To set the current layout, pick the layout tab using the cursor. You can also use the **Set** option of the **LAYOUT** command to specify the current layout.

**PROFESSIONAL TIP**

If you are selecting options from the layout shortcut menu, you must have the appropriate layout set as current before selecting the command. For example, if you select **Delete** from the layout shortcut menu, the current layout is deleted. If you work at the Command: prompt, the current layout is the default but you can specify a different layout.

## Listing layouts

If a drawing has several layouts or layouts with fairly long names, all layout tabs may not be visible. When this is the case, you can use the four buttons to the left of the tab list to view the tabs. See **Figure 10-7.** The two outer arrows display the left and right ends of the tab list. The inner arrows move the list one tab in the indicated direction. Changing the display of the tab list does not affect the current tab. You still must pick a tab to set it as current.

The **?** option of the **LAYOUT** command can be used to list all layouts within the drawing. After selecting this option, you must switch to the **AutoCAD Text Window** to view the list. To do this, select **Text Window** from the **Display** cascading menu in the **View** pull-down menu or use the [F2] function key.

**Figure 10-7.**
Use the arrows to select which layout tabs are displayed.

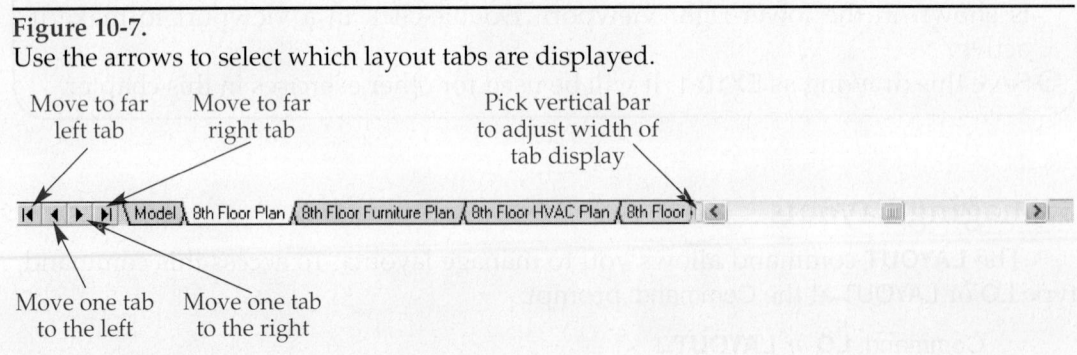

Move to far left tab

Move to far right tab

Pick vertical bar to adjust width of tab display

Move one tab to the left

Move one tab to the right

Model / 8th Floor Plan / 8th Floor Furniture Plan / 8th Floor HVAC Plan / 8th Floor

### Creating a new layout

There are several methods of creating new layouts. A new layout can be created from scratch or they can be copied from existing drawing and template files. Finally, a layout within the drawing can be copied to create a new layout. These methods are described as follows:

- **New layout from scratch.** Use the **New** option of the **LAYOUT** command to create a new layout. You can also create a new layout by selecting **New Layout** from the **Layout** cascading menu in the **Insert** pull-down menu, picking the **New Layout** button in the **Layouts** toolbar, or by right-clicking on a layout tab and selecting **New layout** from the layout shortcut menu. If you select the option from the command line, toolbar, or pull-down menu, the following prompt appears:

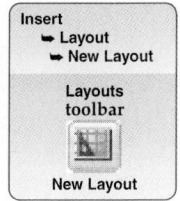

Insert
→ Layout
→ New Layout

Layouts toolbar

New Layout

> Enter new Layout name <Layout3>: *(type a name or accept default name)*

The layout name appears on the layout tab. If you use the **New layout** option in the layout shortcut menu, the new layout is created with the default name. You can then use the **Rename** option to change the name.

- **New layout from template.** This option creates a new layout based on a layout stored in an existing drawing or template file. Select this option by using the **Template** option of the **LAYOUT** command, selecting **Layout from Template...** from the **Layout** cascading menu in the **Insert** pull-down menu, or picking the **Layout from Template** button in the **Layouts** toolbar. You can also right-click on a layout tab and select **From template...** in the layout shortcut menu.

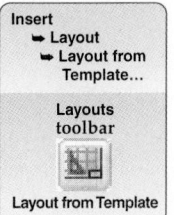

Insert
→ Layout
→ Layout from Template...

Layouts toolbar

Layout from Template

When you select this option, the **Select Template From File** dialog box is displayed, **Figure 10-8A.** The Template folder in the path set by the AutoCAD 2004 Drawing Template File Location is selected by default. To verify the location of AutoCAD 2004 template files, access the **Files** tab in the **Options** dialog box and check the path listed under the Drawing Template File Location.

Select the drawing file or template file containing the layout to be copied and pick the **Open** button. If you selected the command option from the short-cut menu, toolbar, or pull-down menu, the **Insert Layout(s)** dialog box appears. See **Figure 10-8B.** This dialog box lists all layouts in the selected file. Highlight the layout(s) you want to copy and pick the **OK** button.

If you select this option from the command line, the **Insert Layout(s)** dialog box does not appear. Instead, you are prompted to enter the name of the layout to copy.

---

**PROFESSIONAL TIP**

It is much easier to select layouts to copy using the **Insert Layout(s)** dialog box than it is to enter the name at the Command: prompt. Therefore, use the shortcut menu, toolbar, or pull-down menu to select this **LAYOUT** command option.

---

**Figure 10-8.**
Creating a new layout from another drawing or template. A—Select the drawing or template containing the layout. B—Highlight the layout(s) to be added to the current drawing.

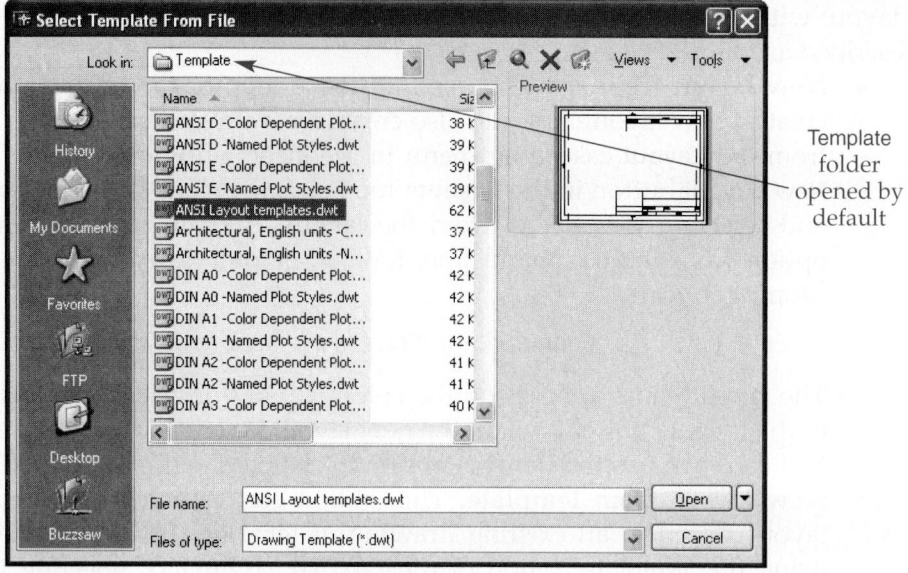

A

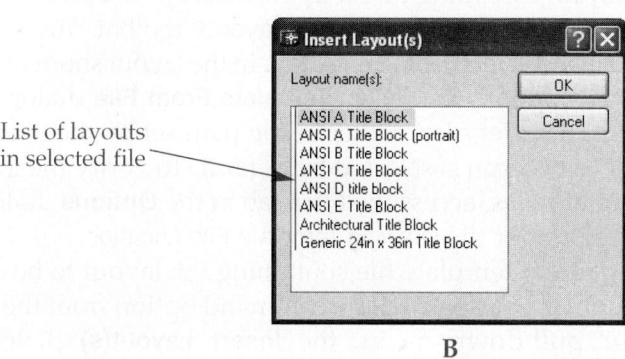

B

- **Copy layout in drawing.** You can create a new layout by copying an existing layout. If you use the **Copy** option of the **LAYOUT** command, enter the name of the layout to copy, and then enter the name for the new copy. The current layout is the default layout to copy. If a name for the copy is not entered, AutoCAD uses the current layout name plus a number in parentheses. For example, if the current layout is named **Layout3**, the following prompts appear:

  Command: **LO** *or* **LAYOUT**⏎
  Enter layout option [Copy/Delete/New/Template/Rename/SAveas/Set/?] <set>: **C**⏎
  Enter name of layout to copy <Layout3>: ⏎
  Enter layout name for copy <Layout3 (2)>: ⏎
  Layout "Layout3" copied to "Layout3 (2)".

  You can also copy an existing layout by selecting **Move or Copy...** from the layout shortcut menu. This option provides no opportunity to change the layout to be copied; the current layout tab is copied. When you select this option, the **Move or Copy** dialog box appears, **Figure 10-9.** Activate the **Create a copy** check box, and then select which layout the new layout tab should be to the left of. The default name is automatically assigned to the new layout. Use the **Rename** option to change it.

Figure 10-9.
The **Move or Copy** dialog box is used to reorganize the layout tabs and to copy layout tabs within a drawing. It is accessed through the layout shortcut menu.

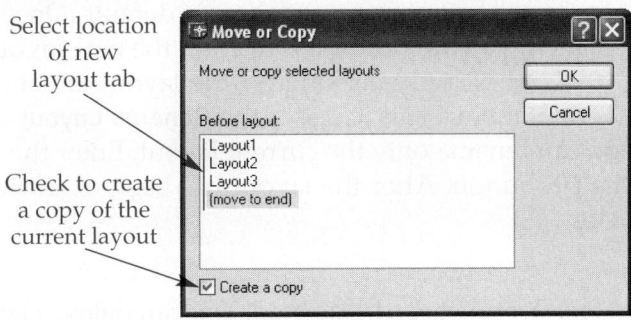

Select location of new layout tab

Check to create a copy of the current layout

- **Using the Create Layout wizard.** You can create a new layout using the **Create Layout** wizard. To access this wizard, select **Layout Wizard** from the **Layout** cascading menu in the **Insert** pull-down menu or select **Create Layout...** from the **Wizards** cascading menu in the **Tools** pull-down menu. The pages of the wizard allow you to specify a title block, viewports, and many page setup values. These page setup values are discussed later in this chapter.

## Copying layouts with DesignCenter

Layouts are included as a type of content that can be viewed using **DesignCenter**. To access **DesignCenter**, select **DesignCenter** from the **Tools** pull-down menu, pick the **DesignCenter** button in the **Standard** toolbar, enter ADC or ADCENTER at the Command: prompt, or use the [Ctrl]+[2] key combination.

To copy a layout from an existing drawing or template, first locate the drawing in the **DesignCenter** tree view. Then select Layouts to display the layouts within the drawing. See **Figure 10-10**. Select the layout(s) to be copied and then use the **Add Layout(s)** or copy and paste options from shortcut menus or drag-and-drop to insert the layouts in the current drawing.

## Renaming a layout

The name of the layout appears on its tab. Layouts created by default are named **Layout$n$**, where $n$ is a number. A layout created by copying another layout has the same name as the initial layout, followed by a number in parentheses. For example, the first copy of **Layout2** is named **Layout2 (1)**.

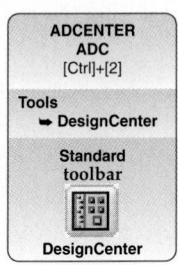

ADCENTER
ADC
[Ctrl]+[2]

Tools
→ DesignCenter

Standard
toolbar

DesignCenter

Figure 10-10.
Layouts can be shared between drawings using **DesignCenter**.

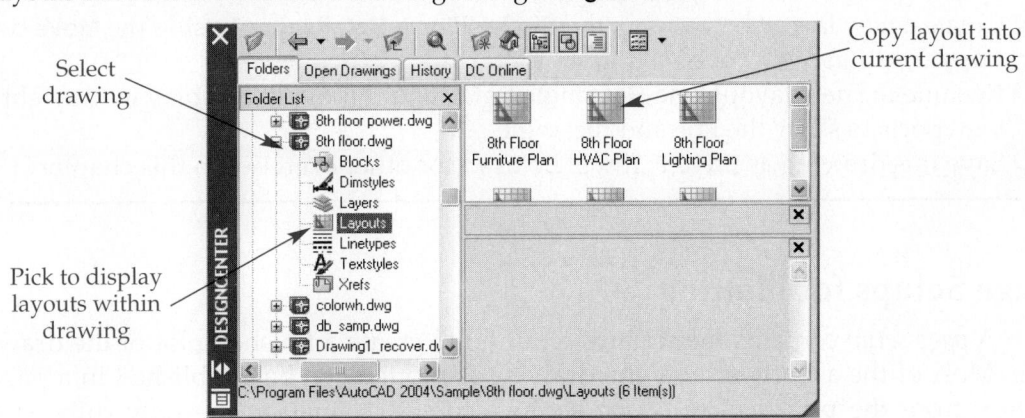

Select drawing

Pick to display layouts within drawing

Copy layout into current drawing

Layouts are easier to work with when they have a descriptive name. Layouts can be renamed using the **Rename** option of the **LAYOUT** command. When you select the **Rename** option of the **LAYOUT** command, you are prompted to enter the name of the layout to be renamed. The current layout is provided as a default. Once you have entered the layout to be renamed, you are prompted to enter the new layout name.

You can also rename a layout by right-clicking on the layout tab and selecting **Rename** from the layout shortcut menu. This accesses the **Rename Layout** dialog box. If you select this option, you can rename only the current layout. Enter the new name in the text box and pick the **OK** button. After the layout has been renamed, the new name is displayed on the tab.

### Deleting a layout

When a layout is no longer useful, it can be deleted. You can delete a layout using the **Delete** option of the **LAYOUT** command. You can also delete the active layout by right-clicking on the layout tab and selecting **Delete** from the layout shortcut menu.

When you use the **Delete** option of the **LAYOUT** command, you are prompted to enter the name of the layout to be deleted. The current layout is provided as the default.

If you select **Delete** from the layout shortcut menu, an alert box warns you that the layout will be permanently deleted. Pick the **OK** button to delete the layout.

### Saving a layout

The **Saveas** option of the **LAYOUT** command is used to save a single layout as a drawing template or drawing file. The following is the command sequence:

Command: **LO** or **LAYOUT**↵
Enter layout option [Copy/Delete/New/Template/Rename/SAveas/Set/?] <set>: **SA**↵
Enter layout to save to template <*current layout*>: *(enter name of layout or accept default)*

After you specify the layout to save, the **Create Drawing File** dialog box appears. You can save the layout in a DWT, DWG, or DXF file. Enter the file name and pick the **SAVE** button. The layout is now saved in the new file.

---

### Exercise 10-2

○ Open EX10-1 if it is not already open.
○ Rename **Layout1** as **Circle-Ellipse Detail**.
○ Save and close EX10-1.
○ Begin a new drawing from scratch.
○ Delete the **Layout2** layout by right-clicking on the tab and then selecting **Delete** from the layout shortcut menu.
○ Open **DesignCenter** and copy the **Circle-Ellipse Detail** layout from the EX10-1.dwg drawing file. Close **DesignCenter**.
○ Create a new layout by copying the **Circle-Ellipse Detail** layout using the **Move or Copy...** option in the layout shortcut menu.
○ Rename the new layout **Line-Rectangle Detail** and modify the display in the right viewports to show the line and rectangle.
○ Save this drawing as EX10-2. It will be used for other exercises in this chapter.

---

## Page Setups for Plotting

A *page setup* contains the settings required to create a finished plot of the drawing. Most of the aspects of how the drawing is plotted can be established in a page setup, from the plot device to pen settings to scales. In fact, the only difference between the **Page Setup** and **Plot** dialog boxes is that the **Page Setup** dialog box does not provide plot preview buttons.

Each layout can have a unique page setup. Therefore, the **Page Setup** dialog box is always tied to the active **Model** tab or layout tab. These settings can even be saved in the drawing file as a named page setup, which can be recalled each time the drawing is plotted. Therefore, the setup becomes a productivity tool since it decreases the amount of time preparing a drawing for plotting.

The settings that compose the page setup are set in the **Page Setup** dialog box. This dialog box is accessed by selecting **Page Setup...** from the **File** pull-down menu, picking the **Page Setup** button in the **Layouts** toolbar, typing PAGESETUP at the Command: prompt, or right-clicking on a layout tab and selecting **Page Setup...** from the layout shortcut menu. The **Page Setup** dialog box is shown in **Figure 10-11.**

The **Page Setup** dialog box contains two tabs: one for selecting the plot device, and the other for selecting the layout settings. In addition, areas at the top of the dialog box display the current layout name and the current page setup name. The **Layout name** text box is for display only, and shows the name of the current layout. The **Page setup name** text box displays the name of the current page setup.

The page setup settings fall into several categories. These areas are discussed in the following sections of the text:

- **Plot device settings.** These settings deal with selecting and configuring the printer or plotter on which the drawing is to be output.
- **Plot style table.** This table contains plot styles. These plot styles determine how an object appears in the plotted drawing. Color, linetype, and lineweight can be determined by an object's plot style, along with line end treatment and fill style.
- **Plot settings.** These settings, which include the paper size and orientation, control what part of the drawing is plotted, as well as the drawing scale and other plotting parameters.

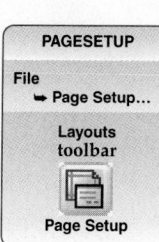

PAGESETUP

File
↳ Page Setup...

Layouts
toolbar

Page Setup

---

**PROFESSIONAL TIP**

In the planning stages of your work, create one or more page setups for the drawing and save them in a template drawing.

---

**Figure 10-11.**
The **Page Setup** dialog box.

Name of layout

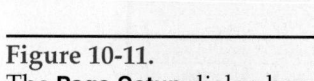
Available tabs

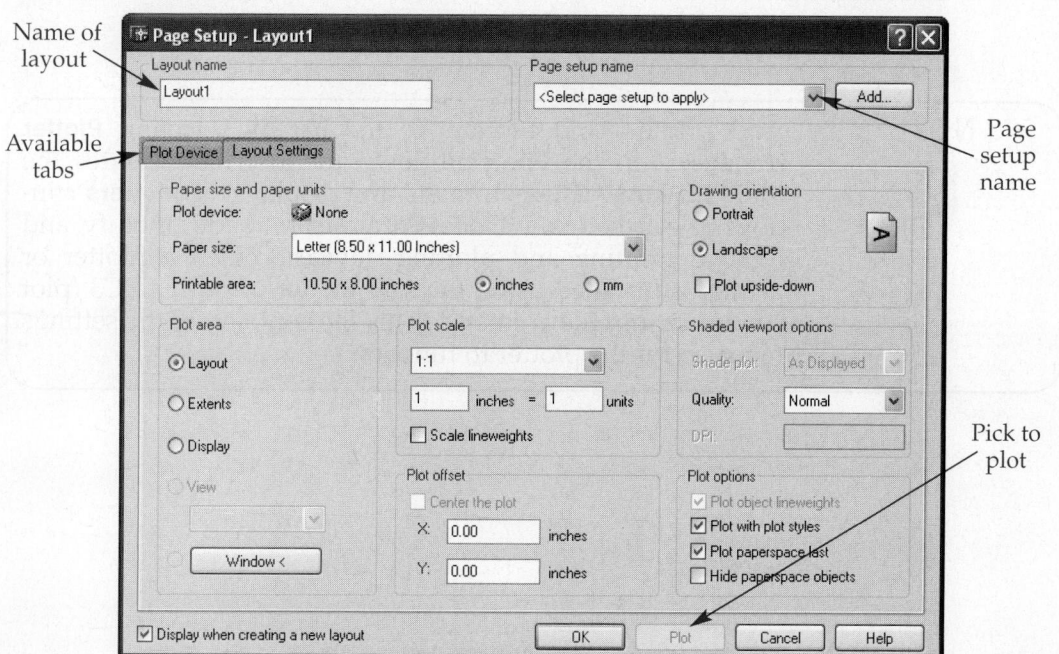

Page setup name

Pick to plot

Before printing or plotting, make sure that your output device is configured properly. AutoCAD displays information about the currently configured printer or plotter in the **Plot Device** tab of the **Page Setup** dialog box. See **Figure 10-12.**

You can use this tab to change many of the printer or plotter specifications. The current device is displayed in the **Plotter configuration** area. When additional devices are configured, you can make a different one current by picking it from the **Name:** drop-down list.

**Figure 10-12.**
The **Plot Device** tab of the **Page Setup** dialog box.

Select device from list of configured devices

Information about selected device

Edit plot device configuration

Select plot style table

---

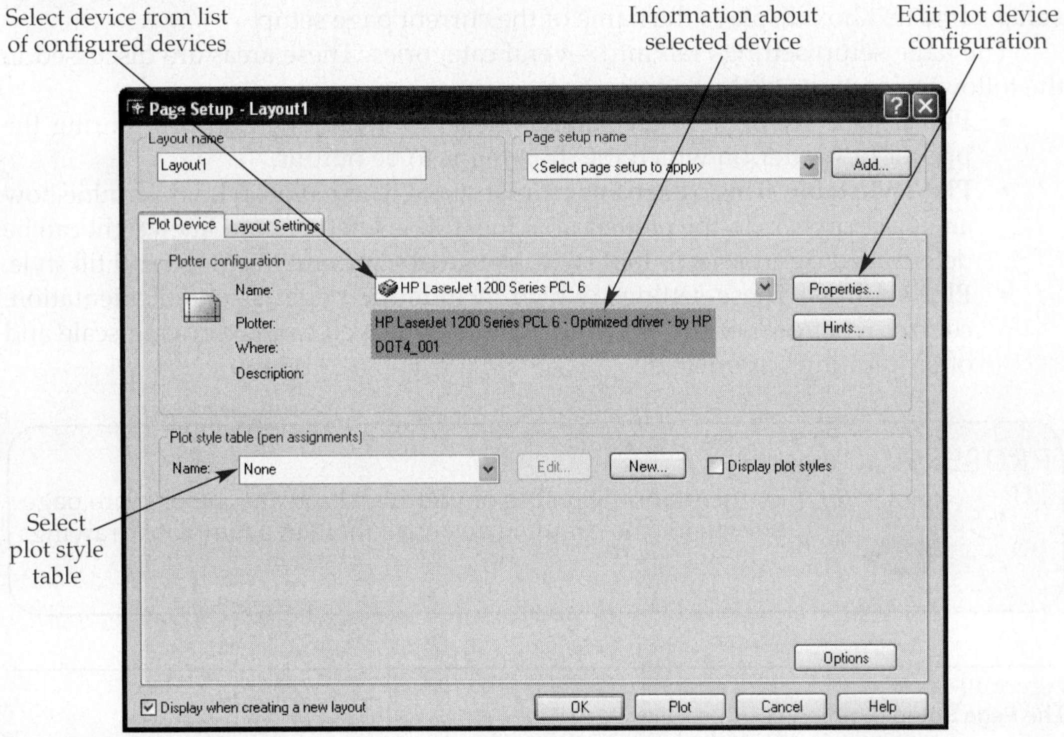

**NOTE**

Add printers and plotters to the list by selecting **Plotter Manager...** in the **File** pull-down menu. This executes the **PLOTTERMANAGER** command and displays the **Plotters** window. Select the Add-A-Plotter Wizard icon to add, modify, and remove printing and plotting devices. When a plotter or printer is installed using the **Add Plotter** wizard, a PC3 (plot configuration) file is created. This file contains all the settings required for the plotter to function.

# Modifying the Plotter Configuration

To change the properties of the current plot device, pick the **Properties...** button in the **Plotter configuration** area. This opens the **Plotter Configuration Editor** dialog box. See **Figure 10-13.** Three tabs provide access to the plotting device property settings:

- **General tab.** General information about the current plotter is displayed in this tab. The only item you can change is the description.
- **Ports tab.** Use this tab to pick a port to send the plot to, plot to a file, or select **AutoSpool**. Using **AutoSpool**, plot files can be sent to a *plot spooler* file, which automatically plots the drawing in the background while you continue to work.
- **Device and Document Settings tab.** This tab displays a tree list of all the settings applicable to the current plotting device. Clicking on the desired icon enables you to modify specific settings. Items in this list displayed in brackets (< >) can be changed. The **Custom Properties** item is highlighted by default because it contains the properties most often changed. Pick the **Custom Properties...** button to display the properties dialog box specific to your plotter. Pick the **Save As...** button to save your changes to a PC3 file.

---

**Figure 10-13.**
The **Plotter Configuration Editor** dialog box. The **Device and Document Settings** tab is shown here.

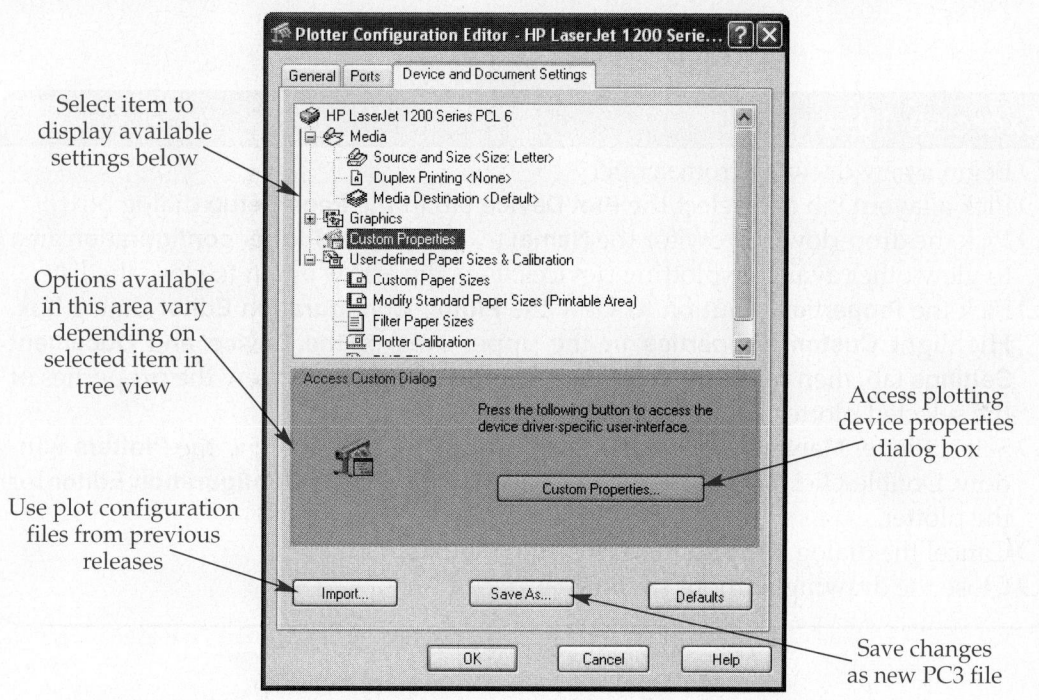

Select item to display available settings below

Options available in this area vary depending on selected item in tree view

Use plot configuration files from previous releases

Access plotting device properties dialog box

Save changes as new PC3 file

It is good practice to create a new PC3 file and preserve the original. If you have old plot configuration files from AutoCAD Release 13 (PCP) or AutoCAD Release 14 (PC2), they can be imported into the current settings by picking the **Import...** button. Settings contained in these two files that can be used by AutoCAD 2004 are plotter name, port information, pen optimization level, paper size, and resolution.

**CAUTION** Avoid editing and saving modified PC3 files unless you have been instructed to do so. These files are critical to the proper functioning of your plotter.

## Specifying a Plot Style Table

The **Plot style table** area is located in the middle of the **Plot Device** tab of the **Page Setup** dialog box. This area allows you to list and select customized pen assignment files for specialized plotting purposes. Use the default of **None** until you possess a good understanding of plot style tables. Plot style tables are discussed in the following section.

**NOTE** If you want to plot a drawing without using a plot style, pick **None** in the **Plot style table** area of the **Page Setup** dialog box.

---

### Exercise 10-3

○ Begin a new drawing from scratch.
○ Pick a layout tab and select the **Plot Device** tab in the **Page Setup** dialog box.
○ Pick the drop-down arrow for the **Name:** text box in the **Plotter configuration** area to view other available plotting devices. Pick the arrow again to close the list.
○ Pick the **Properties...** button to view the **Plotter Configuration Editor** dialog box. Highlight **Custom Properties** in the upper area of the **Device and Document Settings** tab, then select the **Custom Properties...** button to view the properties of the selected plotter. Cancel all dialog boxes.
○ Select **Plotter Manager...** from the **File** pull-down menu to view the **Plotters** window. Double-click on a plotter icon to display the **Plotter Configuration Editor** for the plotter.
○ Cancel the dialog box and then close the **Plotters** window.
○ Close the drawing without saving.

---

## Plot Styles

The properties of objects in an AutoCAD drawing, such as color, layer, linetype, and lineweight, are used as defaults for plotting. This means that all colors, linetypes, and lineweights will be plotted exactly as they appear in the drawing. You also have the ability to create multiple plots of the same drawing using different plot style tables. A *plot style table* is a named file that provides complete control over pen settings for plotted drawings.

*Plot styles* are basically a variety of pen settings that control, among other things, the color, thickness, linetype, line end treatment, and fill style of drawing objects. Plot styles can be assigned to any object or layer.

In AutoCAD Release 14, a variety of pen parameters were controlled by the **Pen Assignments** dialog box. Most of these features are now managed with the **Plot Style Table Editor** dialog box, which is discussed in detail later in this chapter. Other aspects of plotter functions, such as pen speed, default line width, and optimization, are now stored in the PC3 plotter configuration file.

## Plot Style Attributes

By default, objects are drawn without a plot style. When no plot style is applied, objects are plotted according to their assigned properties, such as color, linetype, and lineweight. The finished plot appears identical to the on-screen display.

A plot style is a collection of several properties. When a plot style is assigned to an object, the plot style properties replace the object's properties *for plotting purposes only*. For example, assume a drawing has a layer named Blue, which has blue selected as its color. A line drawn on this layer appears blue on screen. If no plot style is assigned to the line, it will plot as blue also. Now assume a plot style is created with the color red set as one of its properties. This plot style is assigned to the line. The line will now be plotted as red. However, the line still appears blue on screen, because the plot style only takes effect when the object is plotted.

The following properties can be set in a plot style.

- **Color.** A color specified in a plot style will override the object color in the drawing. Use object color is the default setting. This setting plots the object with the same color shown on screen. The following options related to color can also be specified.
  - **Dithering.** *Dithering* is the intermingling of dots of various colors to produce what appears to be a new color. Dithering is either enabled or disabled. It is ignored if the plotter does not support it. Dithering may create incorrect linetypes when plotting pale colors or thin lines. It is best to test dithering to see if it produces the best results. Dithering can be used regardless of the object color selected.
  - **Convert to Grayscale.** If this option is selected, the object's colors are converted to grayscale if the plotter supports it. If this is not selected, the object colors are used. This option is illustrated in **Figure 10-14**.
  - **Use Assigned Pen Number.** This setting only applies to pen plotters. Available pens range from 1 to 32. The assigned pen number cannot be changed if the plot style color is set to Use object color, or if you are editing a plot style in a color-dependent plot style table. In this case, the value is set to Automatic. If you enter 0 for pen number, the field reads Automatic. AutoCAD selects a pen based on the plotter configuration.
  - **Virtual Pen Number.** Pen numbers between 1 and 255 allow non-pen plotters to simulate pen plotters using virtual pens. A 0 or Automatic setting instructs AutoCAD to assign a virtual pen from the AutoCAD Color Index (ACI).
  - **Screening.** This affects the amount of ink placed on the paper while plotting. A value of 0 produces the color white, and 100 plots the color's full intensity. The effects of screening are shown in **Figure 10-15.**
  - **Linetype.** If you select a plot style linetype, it overrides the object's linetype when plotted. The default value (Use object linetype) plots the object using the linetype displayed on screen. An adaptive adjustment setting adjusts the linetype scale to keep the linetype pattern complete. This is activated by default.

**Figure 10-14.**
The effects of the Convert to grayscale plot style setting.

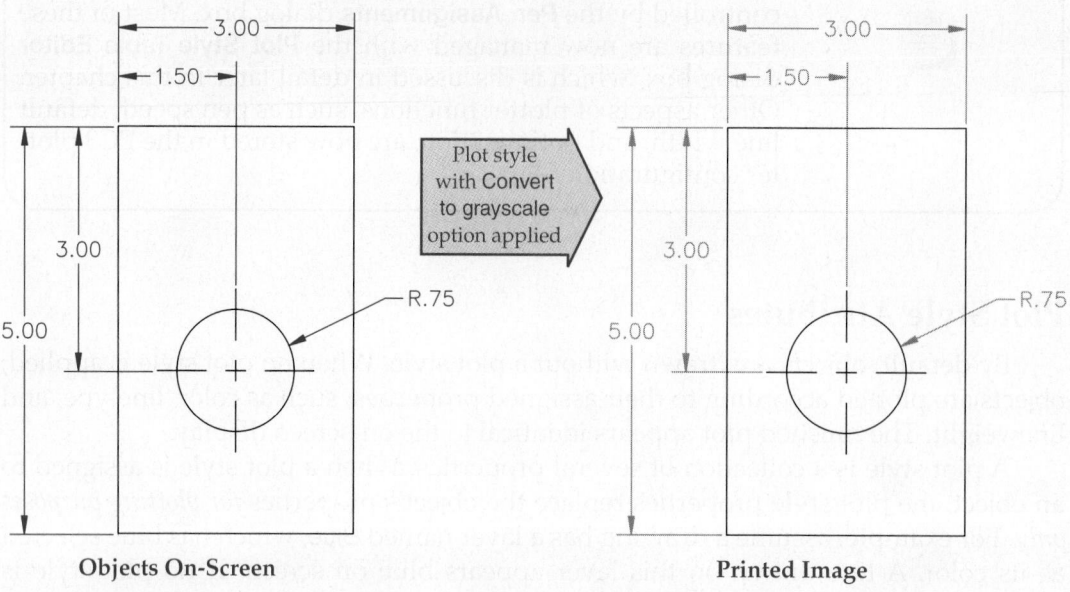

Objects On-Screen          Printed Image

**Figure 10-15.**
Using the screening plot style settings.

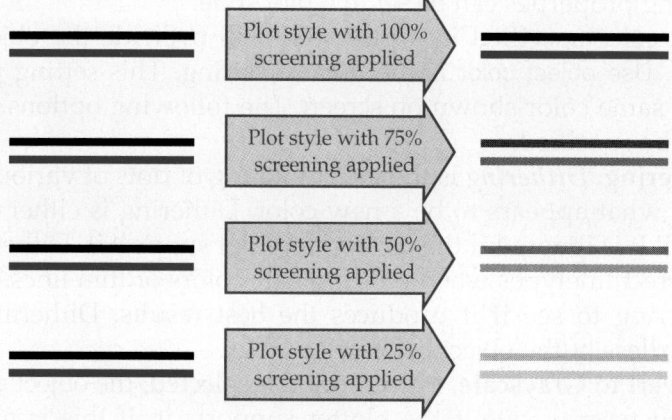

- **Lineweight.** Select a lineweight from this list if you want the plotted lineweight to override the object property in the AutoCAD drawing. The default value is Use object lineweight.
- **Line End Style.** If you select a line end style from this list, the line end style is added to the endpoints when plotted. **Figure 10-16** illustrates the end style options. Note that the lines must be relatively thick for the end styles to be noticeable. The default setting is Use object end style.
- **Line Join Style.** If you select a line join style from this list, it overrides the object's line join style when the drawing is plotted. The default setting is Use object join style, but you can select one of the following line end styles: Miter, Bevel, Round, and Diamond.
- **Fill Style.** If you select a fill style from this list, it overrides the object's fill style when the drawing is plotted. The default setting is Use object fill style, but you can select one of the fill styles shown in **Figure 10-17**.

**Figure 10-16.**
End line style options can be specified within a plot style.

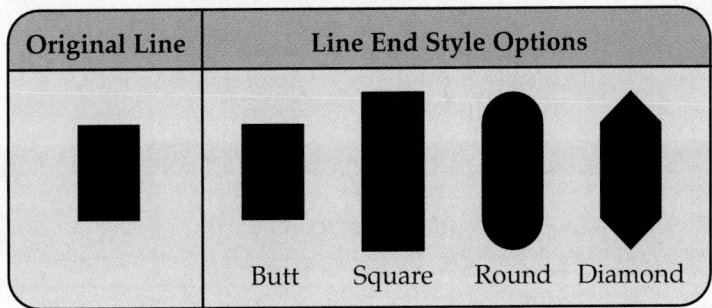

| Original Line | Line End Style Options | | | |
|---|---|---|---|---|
| | Butt | Square | Round | Diamond |

**Figure 10-17.**
These fill styles can be set for a plot style.

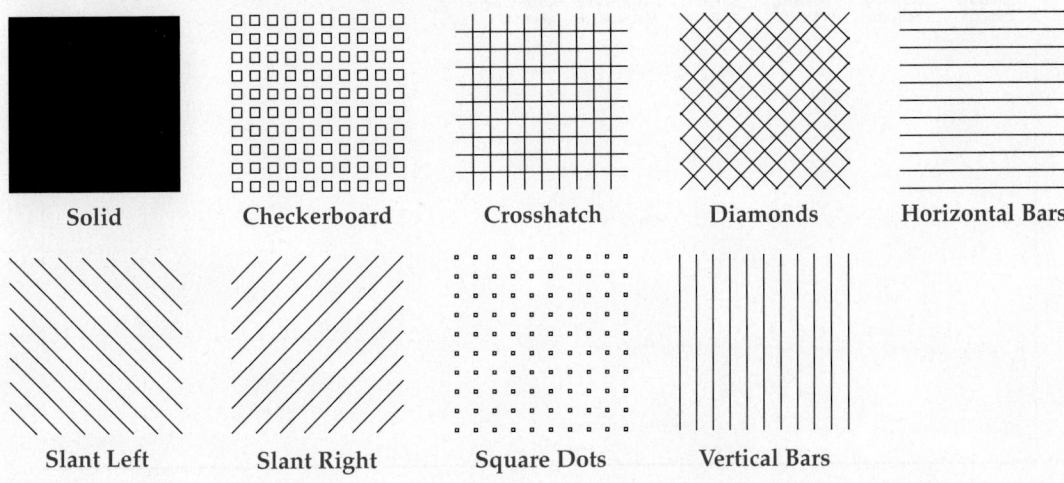

Solid　　Checkerboard　　Crosshatch　　Diamonds　　Horizontal Bars

Slant Left　　Slant Right　　Square Dots　　Vertical Bars

## Plot Style Modes

There are two plot style modes: color-dependent and named. You can create a *color-dependent plot style* in which each color can be assigned values for the various plotting properties. These settings are saved in a *color-dependent plot style table* file with a CTB extension.

A *named plot style* is assigned to objects. The settings in the named plot style override the object properties when the object is plotted. *Named plot style tables* are saved in a file with an STB extension. These tables allow you to use color properties in the drawing without having the object's color tied to its plotting characteristics. These tables are useful if, for example, you are working on a multiphase project in which different components of the drawing must be highlighted, subdued, or plotted in a specific lineweight or linetype.

## Plot Style Tables

AutoCAD is supplied with several plot style tables. You can also create and save your own customized tables. Plot style tables are given file names with CTB or STB extensions. These files are saved in the path set by the AutoCAD 2004 Plot Style Table Search Path. To verify the location of AutoCAD 2004 plot style table, access the **Files** tab in the **Options** dialog box and check the path listed under the Plot Style Table Search Path.

To view the available plot style tables, select **Plot Style Manager...** from the **File** pull-down menu or enter STYLESMANAGER at the Command: prompt. The **Plot Styles** window is displayed. See **Figure 10-18.**

**Figure 10-18.**
Double-click on an icon to edit the plot style table. Select the Add-A-Plot Style Table Wizard icon to create a new table.

Double-click to create
a new plot style table

Named plot style
table icon

Color-dependent
plot style table icon

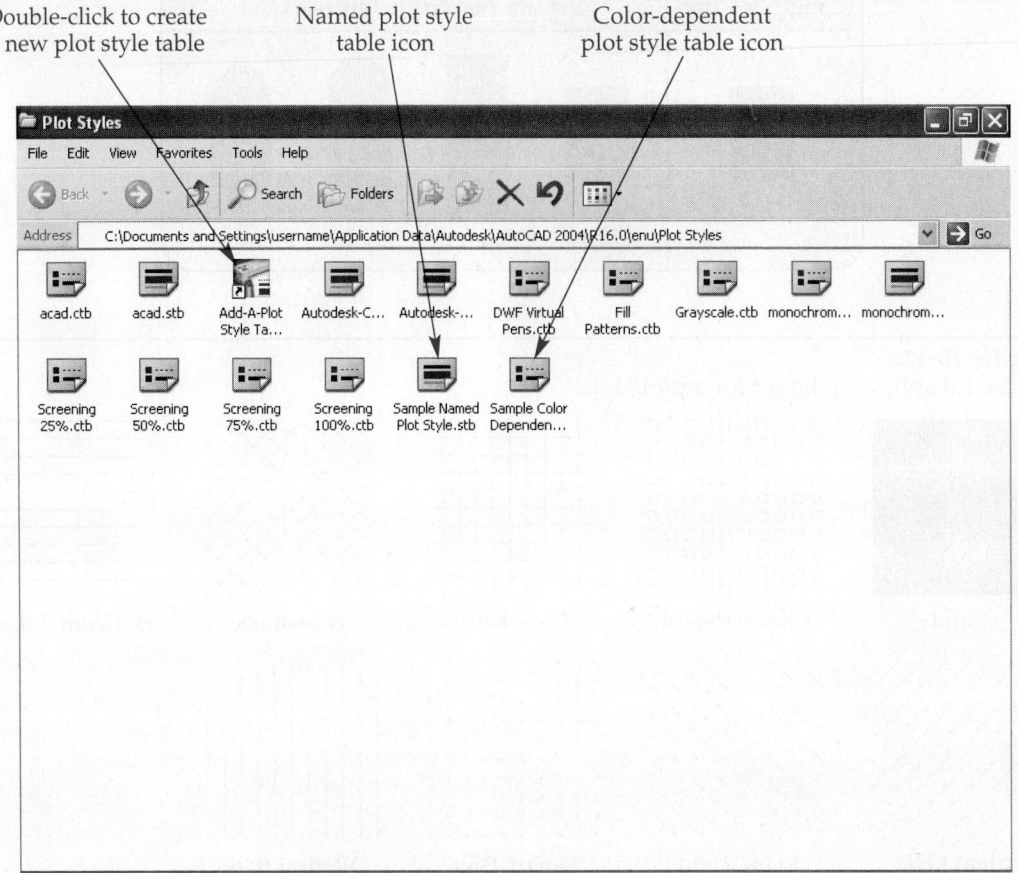

The **Plot Styles** window displays icons for each of the saved plot style tables. There is also an icon to access the **Add Plot Style Table** wizard. You can double-click on an icon to access the **Plot Style Table Editor** dialog box. This dialog box, which is discussed later in the chapter, is used to edit the plot style table.

### Creating a plot style table

Create a named plot style table if you know that components of the drawing or project, such as layouts, layers, and objects, will be plotted at different times using different colors, linetypes, lineweights, or area fills.

Plot style tables are created using the **Add Plot Style Table** wizard. To access this wizard, select **Add Plot Style Table...** from the **Wizards** cascading menu of the **Tools** pull-down menu. You can also select the Add-A-Plot Style Table Wizard icon in the **Plot Styles** window, which is discussed later in the chapter. The **Add Plot Style Table** wizard is displayed. Read the introductory page and pick **Next** to access the **Begin** page. See **Figure 10-19.** Four options are available:

- **Start from scratch.** Constructs a new plot style table. The **Browse File** page is skipped with this option because the new plot style table is not based on any existing settings.
- **Use an existing plot style table.** Copies an existing plot style table to be used as a template for a new one. The **Table Type** page is skipped when this option is selected because the plot style mode is determined by the file selected as the template.

AutoCAD and its Applications—Basics

**Figure 10-19.**
Select the basis for the plot style table in the **Begin** page of the **Add Plot Style Table** wizard.

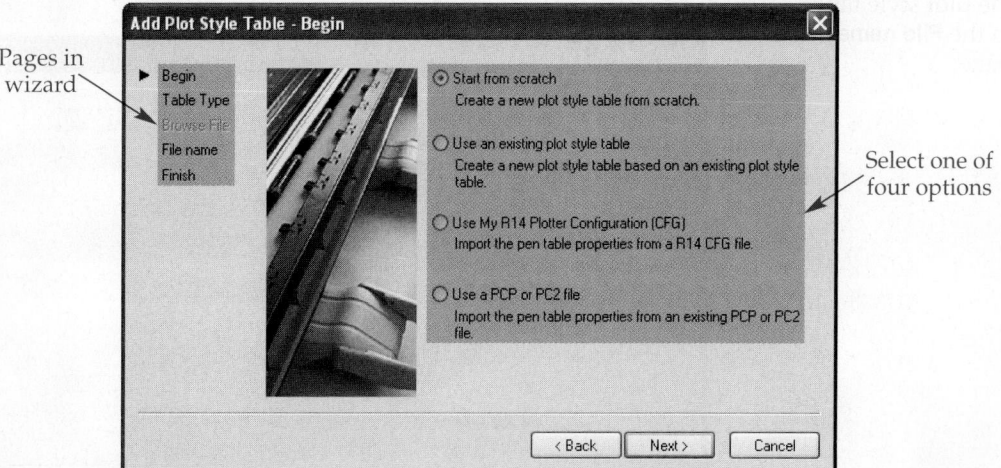

Pages in wizard

Select one of four options

- **Use My R14 Plotter Configuration (CFG).** Copies the pen assignments from the acad14.cfg file to be used as a template for a new one. This option should be used if you did not save either a PCP or PC2 file in Release 14.
- **Use a PCP or PC2 file.** Pen assignments saved previously in a Release 14 PCP or PC2 file are used to make a new plot style table.

After you have selected the beginning plot style table option, press **Next** to go to the **Table Type** page. See **Figure 10-20.** This page is not displayed if the **Use an existing plot style table** option was selected. Select the **Named Plot Style Table** option to use the named plot style mode, and then pick **Next**.

Select the file on which the plot style table is to be based in the **Browse File** page. Enter the file name in the text box or pick the **Browse...** button to display a **Select File** dialog box. The type of file you select depends on the selected beginning plot style table option. If you are using a CFG file, you must also select the plotter or printer to use.

**Figure 10-20.**
Select the plot style mode in the **Table Type** page. This page does not appear if the new table is based on an existing plot style table.

Select plot style mode

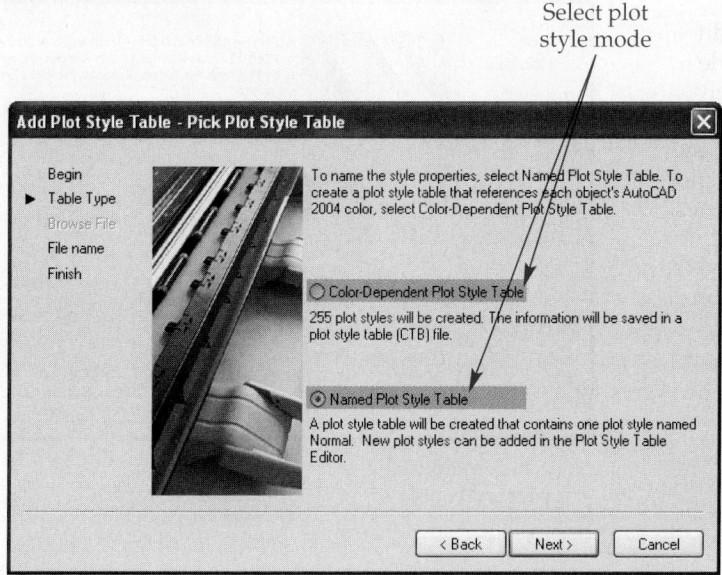

Enter name for
plot style table

**Figure 10-21.**
Enter the name for
the plot style table
in the **File name**
page.

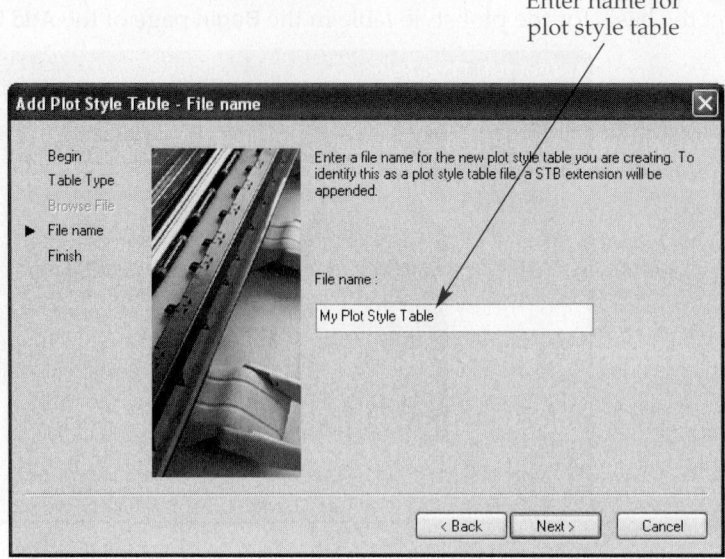

Enter name for
plot style table

After selecting the appropriate file, pick the **Next** button to access the **File name** page. See **Figure 10-21.** Enter a name for the new plot style table. A CTB extension is added to color-dependent plot style tables, and an STB extension is added to named plot style tables.

Once you have entered the plot style table name, pick **Next** to display the **Finish** page. See **Figure 10-22.** Pick the check box at the bottom of the page to attach this plot style table to all new drawings by default. That is, the plot style table will be listed in the **Plot style table area** of the **Page Setup** dialog box. This check box is only available if you are creating a plot style using the mode (color-dependent or named) specified in the **Default plot style behavior for new drawings** area of the **Plotting** tab in the **Options** dialog box. This tab is discussed later in the chapter.

You can edit the new plot style table by selecting the **Plot Style Table Editor...** button, which accesses the **Plot Style Table Editor** dialog box. This is discussed later in the chapter.

**Figure 10-22.**
The **Finish** page
allows you to edit
the new plot style
table immediately
and to attach the
new table to all new
drawings (if the plot
style mode matches
the setting in the
**Options** dialog box).

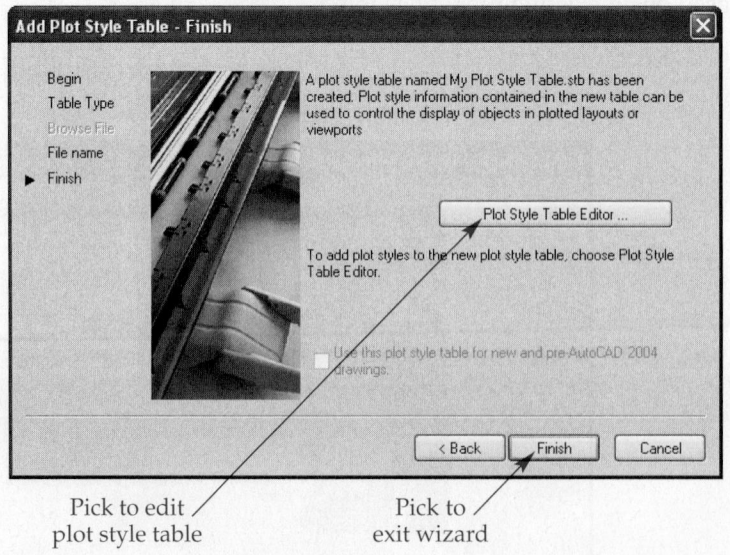

Pick to edit
plot style table

Pick to
exit wizard

Pick **Finish** and the new plot style table is created. The new file is saved in the folder path set by the Plot Style Table Search Path. To verify the location of this file and other AutoCAD 2004 support files, access the **Files** tab in the **Options** dialog box and check the path listed under the Plot Style Table Search Path. A corresponding icon is added to the **Plot Styles** window.

> NOTE
>
> The **Wizards** cascading menu also contains an **Add Named Plot Style Table...** or **Add Color-Dependent Plot Style Table...** option. The plot style mode set for the drawing determines which option is available. The pages in these wizards are identical to the **Add Plot Style Table** wizard with the following exceptions:
> - On the **Begin** page, the **Use an existing plot style table** option is not available.
> - There is no **Table Type** page.
> - The **Finish** page includes an option to attach the new plot style table to the current drawing.

## Exercise 10-4

○ Start a new drawing from scratch.
○ Use the **Add Plot Style Table** wizard to create a new color-dependent plot style table called My Color-Dependent Table. Create the table from scratch.
○ Create a second color-dependent plot style table named My Second C-D Table.
○ Use the **Add Plot Style Table** wizard to create a new named plot style table called My Named Table. Create the table from scratch.
○ Access the **Plot Styles** window to see the icons for the new tables.
○ Close all drawings and leave AutoCAD open for the next exercise.

### Editing a plot style table

Plot style properties are set in the **Plot Style Table Editor** dialog box. To access this dialog box, double-click on the icon for the desired plot style table in the **Plot Styles** window. You can also select the **Edit...** button in the **Plot style table** area of the **Plot Device** tab in the **Page Setup** dialog box.

The **Plot Style Table Editor** dialog box is used to edit both color-dependent and named plot style tables. Color-dependent plot style tables contain 255 preset plot styles—one for each ACI color. A new named plot style table contains one preset plot style, Normal.

The **Plot Style Table Editor** contains three tabs. The **General** tab contains information about the plot style table. See **Figure 10-23.** Enter a description in the text box. The **Apply global scale factor to non-ISO linetypes and fill patterns** option scales all non-ISO linetypes and fill patterns by the value entered in the **Scale factor** text box.

The **Table View** and **Form View** tabs are used to set the plot style attributes and, for named plot style tables, to create and delete plot styles. These tabs are shown in **Figure 10-24.**

When editing a named plot style table, the Normal plot style is created automatically. This plot style cannot be modified, and is assigned to all layers by default. To create a new plot style, pick the **Add Style** button. In the **Table View** tab, this inserts a new table with the name Style *n* highlighted at the top. Enter a new name. In the **Form View** tab, the **Add Plot Style** dialog box appears. Enter a new name and pick the **OK** button.

**Figure 10-23.**
Information about a
plot style table is
contained in the
**General** tab of the
**Plot Style Table
Editor** dialog box.

Plot style table
being edited

Enter a description for
the plot style table

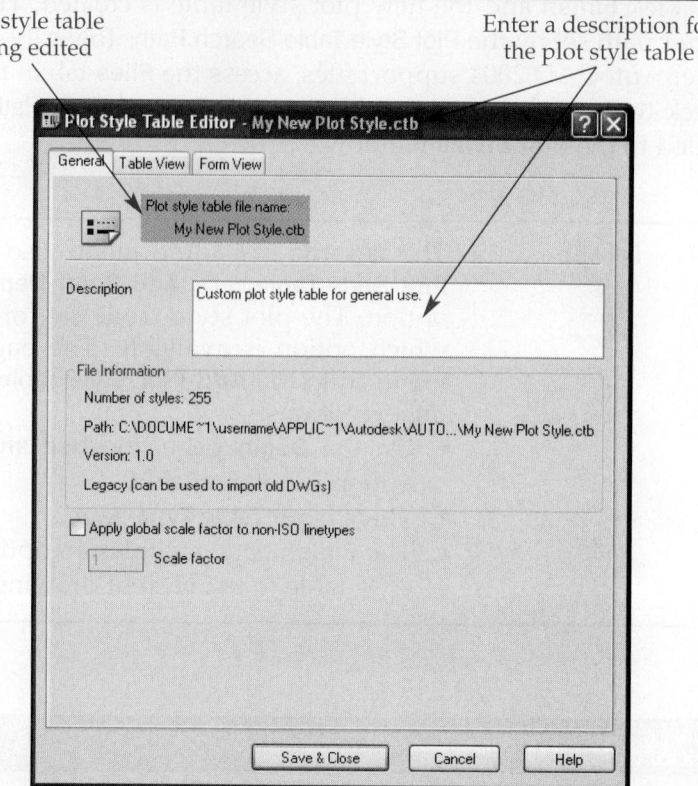

If you wish to delete a named plot style, pick the **Delete Style** button in either tab. If the **Form View** tab is displayed, the current style is deleted. If the **Table View** tab is displayed, first pick in the gray bar above the name of the plot style to be deleted, then pick the **Delete Style** button.

To modify plot style attributes in the **Table View** tab, first use the scroll bar to display the plot style to be edited. Pick the value to be changed and you can modify it with a text box or drop-down list. This editing procedure is similar to changing object properties in the **Properties** window.

The **Form View** tab lists all the attributes in a different format. To view all of the settings for a specific plot style, simply pick the plot style in the **Plot styles:** list box. The properties of the selected plot style are listed in the **Properties** area. Modify the properties using the drop-down lists provided.

Pick the **Save As...** button to change the table name, or pick the **Save & Close** button to save the current file and exit.

---

NOTE  Once a plot style table is created, it can be used on new drawings and drawings created in previous releases of AutoCAD.

---

**Figure 10-24.**
Plot style table settings are modified in the **Plot Style Table Editor** dialog box. A—The **Table View** tab for a named plot style table. B—The **Form View** tab for a color-dependent plot style table.

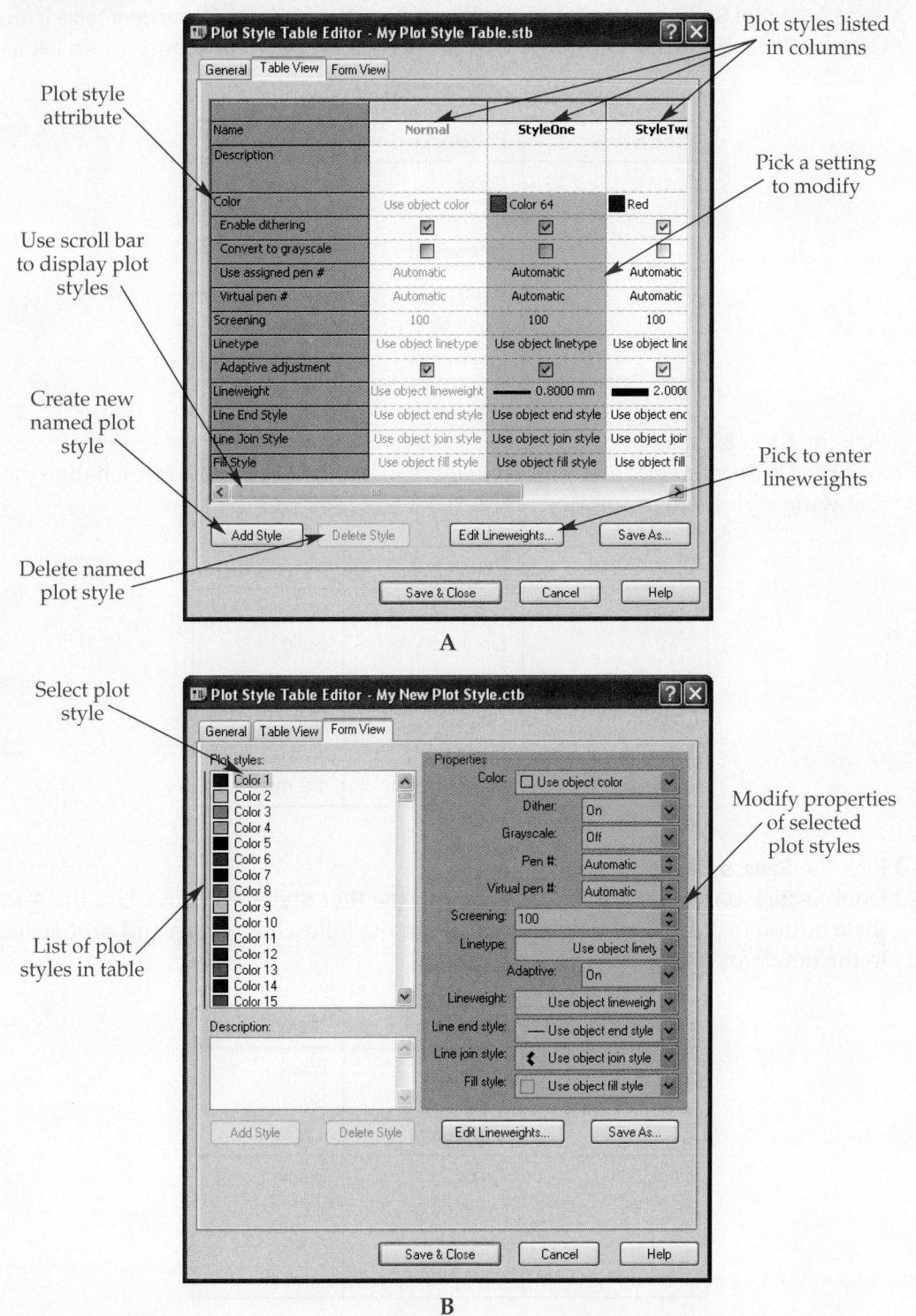

A

B

## Exercise 10-5

○ Start a new drawing from scratch.
○ Access the **Plot Styles** window and double-click on the My Color-Dependent Table icon.
○ Use the **Table View** tab to modify the properties of the following plot styles as specified:

| Plot Style | Property | New Value |
|---|---|---|
| Color 5 | Color | Black |
| | Linetype | Solid |
| | Lineweight | 1.2 mm |
| Color 3 | Color | Black |
| | Linetype | Solid |
| | Lineweight | 1.2 mm |

○ Pick the **Save & Close** button.
○ Edit the My Second C-D Table plot style table using the **Form View** tab. Change the following styles and properties:

| Plot Style | Property | New Value |
|---|---|---|
| Color 1 | Color | Black |
| | Linetype | Solid |
| | Lineweight | 1.2 mm |
| Color 6 | Color | Black |
| | Linetype | Solid |
| | Lineweight | 1.2 mm |

○ Pick the **Save & Close** button.
○ Double-click on the My Named Table icon in the **Plot Styles** window. Use the **Add Style** button to create two new styles. Assign the following names and properties to the new plot styles:

| Plot Style | Property | New Value |
|---|---|---|
| Black 100% | Color | Black |
| | Linetype | Solid |
| | Lineweight | 1.2 mm |
| Black 50% | Color | Black |
| | Screening | 50 |
| | Linetype | Solid |
| | Lineweight | 1.2 mm |

○ Pick the **Save & Close** button.
○ Close the drawing.

# Applying Plot Styles

In order to assign plot styles, plot style tables must be specified in the drawing. The **Model** tab and each individual layout tab can be assigned one plot style table each. Only the styles within the attached plot style table can be applied within the layout.

The plot style mode (color-dependent or named) for a drawing is determined when the drawing is first created. The setting is found in the **Plotting** tab of the **Options** dialog box. To access the **Options** dialog box, select **Options...** from the **Tools** pull-down menu or enter OP or OPTIONS at the Command: prompt. You can also right-click in the drawing area and select **Options...** from the shortcut menu. If the **Page Setup** or **Plot** dialog box is open, you can also select the **Options** button in the **Plot Device** tab.

The **Plotting** tab of the **Options** dialog box is shown in **Figure 10-25**. The plot style mode for new drawings is determined by the setting in the **Default plot style behavior for new drawings** area. By default, the **Use color dependent plot styles** option is selected. When this option is selected, new drawings are set to use only color-dependent plot styles. The default plot style behavior setting can also be set using the **PSTYLEPOLICY** system variable (0 for named plot style mode and 1 for color-dependent mode).

The **Default plot style table** drop-down list can be used to set a default plot style table. When None is selected, objects in the new drawing are plotted based on their on-screen properties. The default plot style table is applied to the **Model** tab and layout tabs in new drawings. However, the plot style table can be changed at any time in the **Page Setup** dialog box.

If you select the **Use named plot styles** option, the drop-down lists below the default plot style table are activated. You can select the default plot styles for layer 0 and for objects. You can select any plot styles from the default plot style table.

The **Add or Edit Plot Style Tables...** button accesses the **Plot Styles** window. This window allows you to edit existing plot style tables and create new plot style tables.

---

**Figure 10-25.**
Use the **Plotting** tab of the **Options** dialog box to set default plot style modes and tables for new drawings.

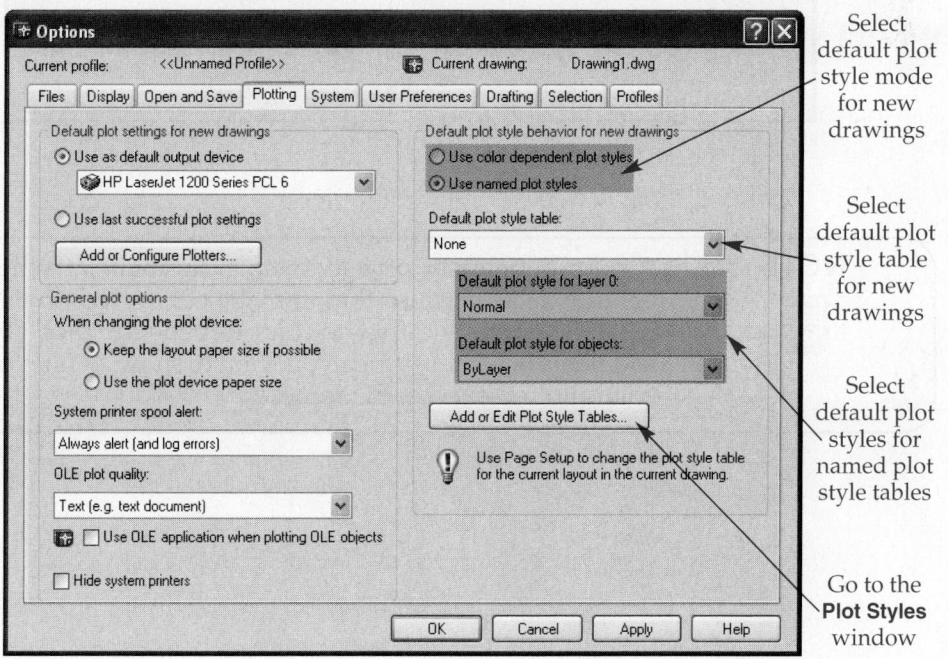

### Applying color-dependent plot styles

Color-dependent plot style tables contain 255 plot styles—one for each color available for display in AutoCAD. You cannot add or delete plot styles in a color-dependent table. When you assign a color-dependent plot style table to a layout, the property values set for the plot styles override the on-screen display values during plotting.

Color-dependent plot styles can only be applied to drawings created while the **Use color dependent plot styles** option was selected as the default plot style behavior in the **Options** dialog box. Each of the **Model** and layout tabs can have a different plot style table assigned.

To assign a color-dependent plot style table, access the **Page Setup** dialog box. Select the **Plot Device** tab, and then pick the plot style table from the **Plot style table** drop-down list. See **Figure 10-26.** The selected plot style table is applied to the active **Model** or layout tab.

**Figure 10-26.**
Selecting a plot style table for a layout.

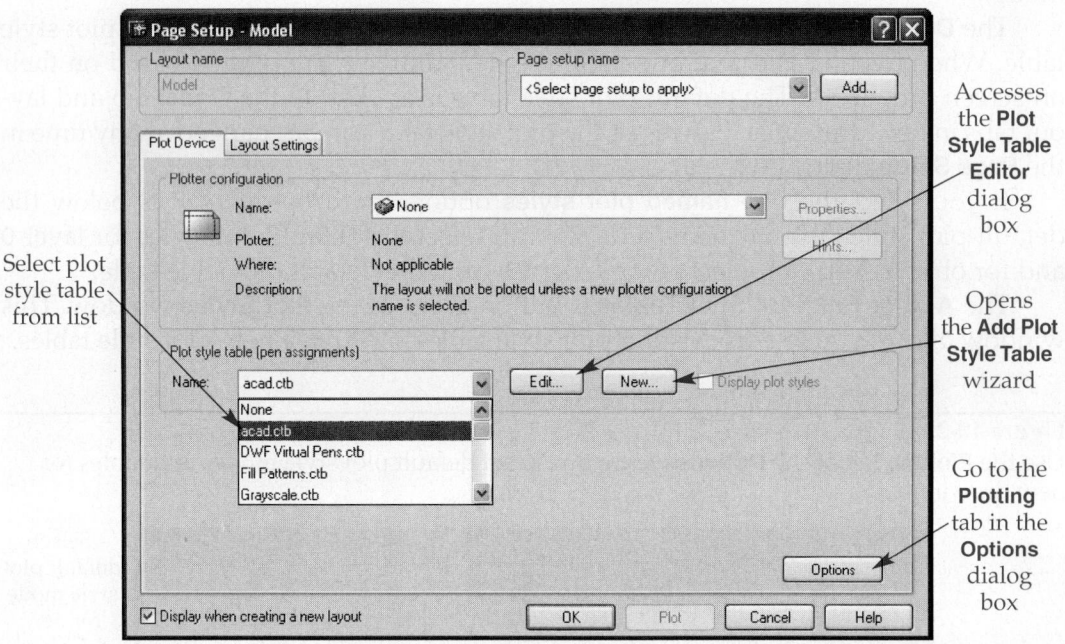

Select plot style table from list

Accesses the **Plot Style Table Editor** dialog box

Opens the **Add Plot Style Table** wizard

Go to the **Plotting** tab in the **Options** dialog box

---

**NOTE**

A color-dependent plot style table cannot be attached to layers or objects because they may be composed of a variety of colors. Remember that a color-dependent plot style table should be used only when you want to show all lines of a single color plotted exactly the same.

---

### Applying named plot styles

In order for named plot styles to be used in a drawing, the drawing must have been created with the **Use named plot styles** option selected as the default plot style behavior in the **Options** dialog box. The drawing could also be based on a template with named plot styles.

The **Model** tab and each layout tab can have a named plot style table attached. When you select a plot style table for the **Model** tab, you are also presented the option of selecting the plot style table for all layout tabs. However, each layout tab can have a different plot style table.

Once the named plot style tables have been assigned to the **Model** tab and layout tabs, plot styles can be assigned to objects and layers. A plot style assigned to an object will override a plot style assigned to a layer, just as a color or linetype assigned to an object will override the layer setting.

Plot styles can be assigned to layers in the **Layer Properties Manager** dialog box, **Figure 10-27.** To access this dialog box, pick the **Layer Properties Manager** button from the **Layers** toolbar, select **Layer...** from the **Format** pull-down menu, or type LA or LAYER at the Command: prompt.

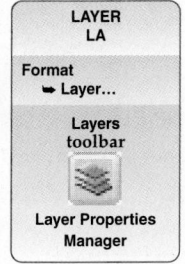

LAYER
LA

Format
↳ Layer...

Layers
toolbar

Layer Properties
Manager

**Figure 10-27.**
Named plot styles can be assigned to layers using the **Layer Properties Manager** dialog box.

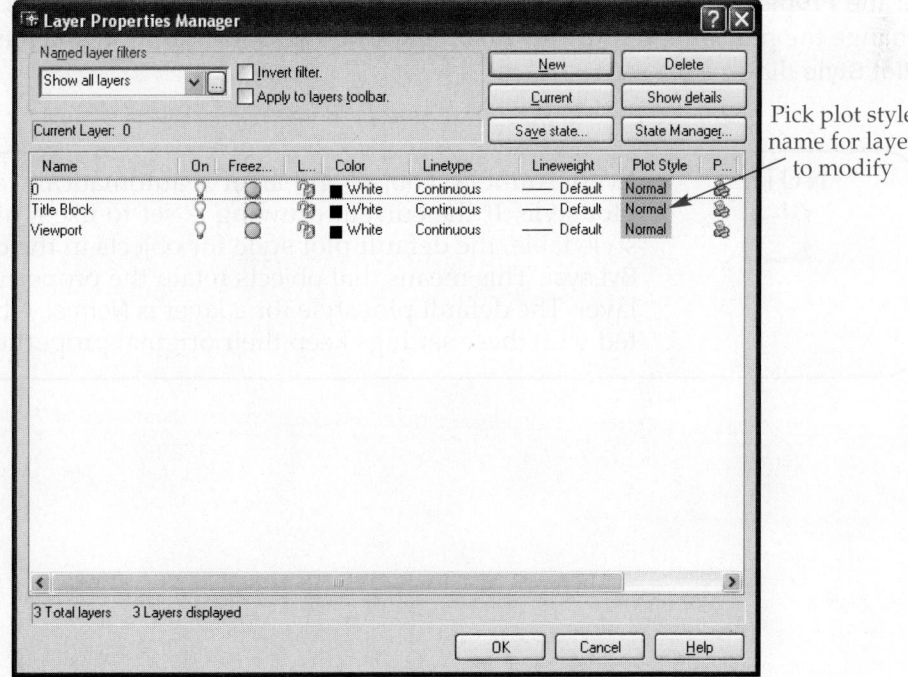

Pick plot style
name for layer
to modify

Figure 10-28.
Use the **Select Plot Style** dialog box to select a plot style for a layer.

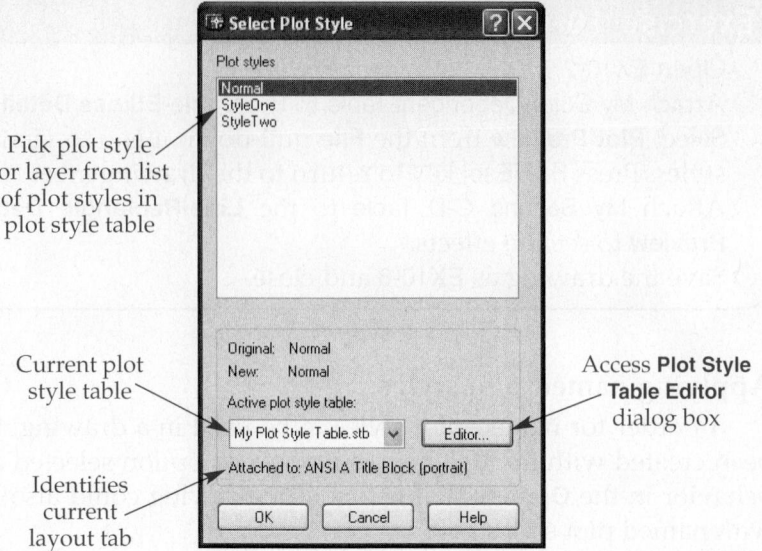

Pick plot style for layer from list of plot styles in plot style table

Current plot style table

Identifies current layout tab

Access **Plot Style Table Editor** dialog box

To modify the plot style, pick the current plot style listed for the layer. The **Select Plot Style** dialog box is displayed, **Figure 10-28.** This dialog box lists the plot styles available in the plot style table attached to the current tab. You can select a different plot style table from the **Active plot style table:** drop-down list. If you select another plot style table, the change is reflected in the **Plot style table** area of the **Page Setup** dialog box. Pick the **Editor...** button to access the **Plot Style Table Editor** dialog box.

Named plot styles can also be applied to objects. When a plot style is applied to an object, the plot style remains attached to the object in all layout tabs. If the plot style attached to the object is contained in the plot style table attached to the layout tab, the object will be plotted with the plot style settings. However, if the plot style assigned to the object is not found within the plot style table attached to the layout tab, the object is plotted according to its on-screen display settings.

Modifying an object's plot style is similar to modifying an object's layer, color, or linetype. You can select the new plot style from the **Plot Style Control** drop-down list in the **Properties** toolbar (**Figure 10-29A**), or you can use the **Properties** window to change the plot style (**Figure 10-29B**). Selecting the Other... option accesses the **Select Plot Style** dialog box.

---

NOTE

Every AutoCAD object and layer is automatically assigned a plot style. If the current drawing is set to use a named plot style table, the default plot style for objects in the drawing is ByLayer. This means that objects retain the properties of their layer. The default plot style for a layer is Normal. Objects plotted with these settings keep their original properties.

---

Figure 10-29.
Assigning a new plot style to an object. A—Using the **Plot Style Control** drop-down list in the
**Properties** toolbar. B—Using the **Properties** window.

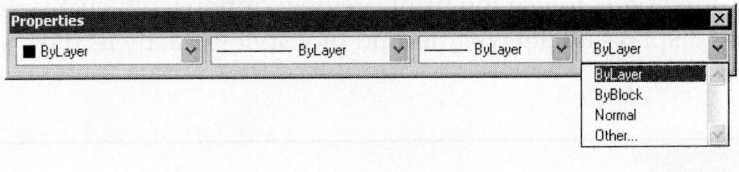

A

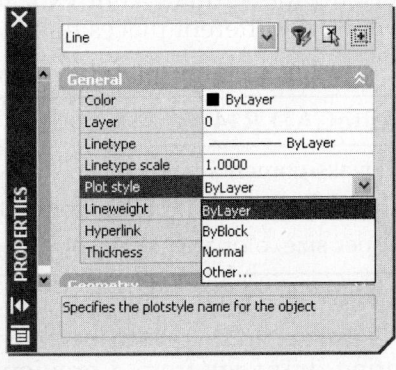

B

## Exercise 10-7

○ Open EX10-2.
○ Select all four objects. Right-click and select **Copy** from the shortcut menu. Press [Esc] twice to deselect the objects.
○ Access the **Plotting** tab of the **Options** dialog box. In the **Default plot style behavior for new drawings** area, select the **Use named plot styles** option.
○ Close the drawing without saving.
○ Create a new drawing from scratch.
○ Right-click in the drawing area and select **Paste** from the shortcut menu. Pick an insertion point.
○ Perform a **ZOOM Extents**.
○ Use **DesignCenter** to copy the **Circle-Ellipse Detail** layout and **Line-Rectangle Detail** layout from EX10-2.dwg. Close **DesignCenter**.
○ Delete the **Layout1** and **Layout2** tabs.
○ Attach My Named Table plot style table to the **Circle-Ellipse Detail** layout.
○ Pick the **Model** tab and select None as the plot style table.
○ Change the plot style property of the circle to Black 100%. Change the plot style property of the ellipse to Black 50%.
○ Perform a plot preview of the **Model** tab and **Circle-Ellipse Detail** layout and compare the differences.
○ Save the drawing as EX10-7.

## Viewing Plot Style Effects Before You Plot

The display of lineweights in an AutoCAD drawing is controlled by the **LWDISPLAY** system variable. If **LWDISPLAY** is on, lineweights are displayed on screen. Similarly, it is possible to display plot style effects on screen to see how they will appear. To do so, pick the **Display plot styles** check box in the **Plot style table** area of the **Plot Device** tab in the **Page Setup** dialog box. Keep in mind that these two display features can increase the time required to regenerate drawings, and may decrease the performance of AutoCAD.

A quicker method is to use the print preview options, which are discussed later in the text. This displays all lineweights and plot styles exactly as they will appear on the plotted drawing.

**PROFESSIONAL TIP**

Imported plot settings from PCP and PC2 files are distributed in three different places in AutoCAD 2004.

| AutoCAD R14 | AutoCAD 2004 |
|---|---|
| Pen assignments | Plot style table |
| Optimization level/plotter connection | PC3 file |
| Paper size, plot area, scale, origin, offset | Page setup |

This is important if you are involved in a project that requires updating drawings from a previous release of AutoCAD to AutoCAD 2004 format and you wish to retain all of your plot settings.

## Plotting Settings

A majority of the values that must be set prior to plotting can be established and saved in layouts, viewports, layers, plot style tables, and template drawings. If you plan your work well, there should be very little, if anything, you will have to set prior to plotting. Take a look at some of the items required for plotting, and where they can be saved.

| Item | Location |
|---|---|
| Border and title block | Layout |
| View scales | Viewport (**Zoom XP**) |
| Text height | Drawing |
| Object color, lineweight, and end style | Layers and plot style tables |
| Plot device | Page setup |
| Plot style table | Page setup |
| Paper size and drawing orientation | Page setup |
| Plot scale, area, offset, and options | Page setup |

If you prepare for plotting as soon as you begin a new drawing, the act of plotting may mean just a few clicks of your pointing device.

Selecting the desired output device and plot style table was discussed earlier in this chapter. Once these settings are complete, you can specify the plot settings in the **Plot Settings** tab of the **Plot** dialog box or in the **Layout Settings** tab of the **Page Setup** dialog box. See **Figure 10-30**.

**Figure 10-30.**
A—The **Plot Settings** tab of the **Plot** dialog box. B—The **Layout Settings** tab of the **Page Setup** dialog box.

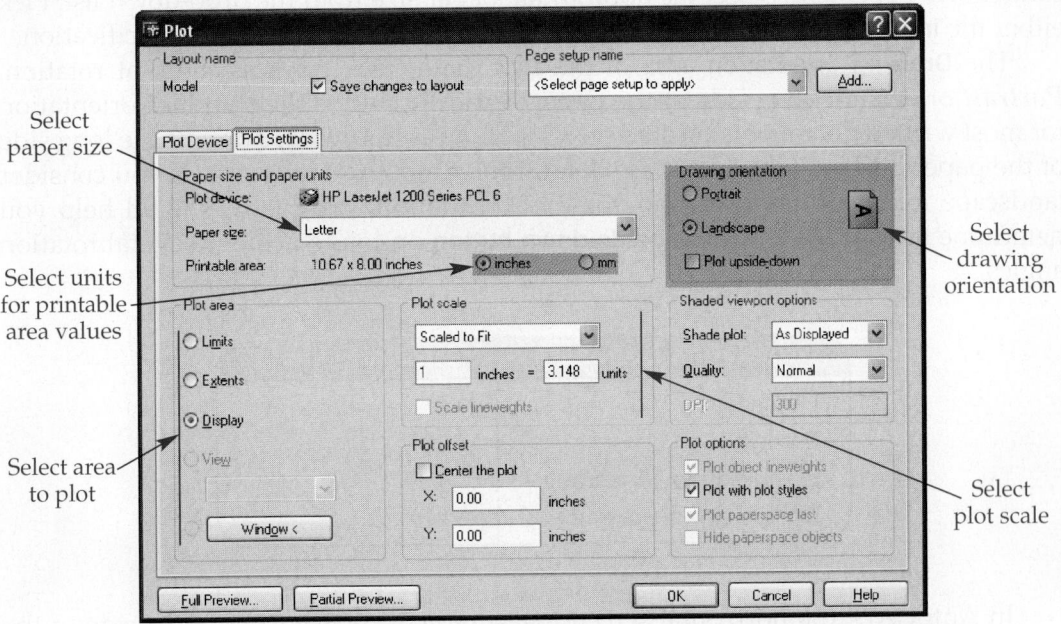

Select paper size

Select units for printable area values

Select area to plot

Select drawing orientation

Select plot scale

A

B

**NOTE**  The settings discussed in the next sections can be set in either the **Plot** or **Page Setup** dialog boxes. You are not asked for a layout name in the **Page Setup** dialog box since it is tied to a named layout.

## Paper Size, Units, and Drawing Orientation

The **Paper size and paper units** area of the **Plot Settings** tab in the **Plot** dialog box controls the paper size. Select the appropriate paper size from the drop-down list. Pick either the **inches** or **mm** radio button to set the units for the paper size specification.

The **Drawing orientation** area of the **Plot** dialog box controls the plot rotation. *Portrait* orients the long side of the paper vertically, and is the standard orientation for most written documents printed on 8.5 × 11 paper. *Landscape* orients the long side of the paper horizontally, and is the default for AutoCAD drawings. If you consider landscape format to be a rotation angle of 0°, the following table should help you determine how to use the **Plot upside-down button** option to achieve several rotation angles.

| Orientation Buttons | Rotation Angle |
|---|---|
| Landscape | 0° |
| Portrait | 90° |
| Upside-down landscape | 180° |
| Upside-down portrait | 270° |

In AutoCAD, the horizontal screen measurement relates to the long side of the paper, the landscape format. However, you might create a drawing, form, or chart in portrait format. This format orients the long side of the plot vertically. AutoCAD rotates plots in 90° increments, as shown in the previous table. **Figure 10-31** illustrates the result of a 90° portrait rotation.

**Figure 10-31.**
The long side of the plot is oriented vertically in a 90° portrait rotation.

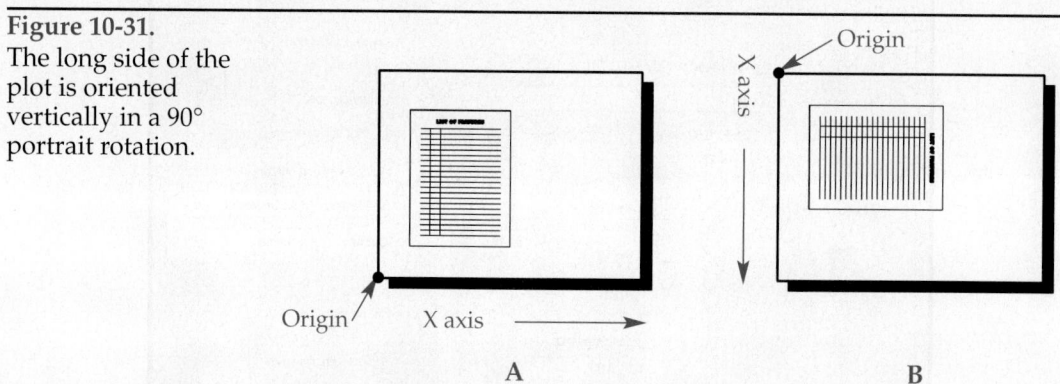

## Plotting Area

The **Plot area** area of the **Plot Settings** tab allows you to choose the portion of the drawing to be plotted, and how it is to be plotted. The five radio button options are described as follows:

- **Layout/Limits.** The **Layout** option is displayed when plotting a layout. Everything inside the margins of the layout is plotted. The **Limits** option is displayed when plotting the **Model** tab. This option plots everything inside the defined drawing limits.
- **Extents.** The **Extents** option plots only the area of the drawing in which objects are drawn. Before using this option, zoom the extents to include all drawn objects to verify exactly what will be plotted. Be aware that border lines around your drawing (like the title block) may be clipped off if they are at the extreme edge of the screen. This often happens because you are requesting the plotter to plot at the extreme edge of its active area.

- **Display.** This option plots the current screen display.
- **View.** Use this option to plot named views, which were discussed in Chapter 9. This option is disabled if no views have been saved in the drawing. Select the name of the view from the drop-down list. This option is available only when the **Model** tab is current.
- **Window.** This option appears grayed-out until you pick the **Window...** button. You must define two opposite corners of a window around the portion of the drawing to be plotted.

> **NOTE**
> If the window you define is too close to an object, some portion of that object may be clipped off in your plot. If this happens, simply adjust the window size the next time you plot. You can prevent these errors by using the plot preview options.

## Shaded Viewport Options

AutoCAD 2004 allows viewports to be plotted in shaded modes. If a viewport has been designated to be plotted in **Wireframe** or **Hidden** mode, no options from this area of the **Plot** dialog box are editable. If a viewport is designated to be plotted in **As Displayed** or **Rendered** mode, you have the option of setting the quality of the shading for the viewports. Each predefined quality setting has a certain dots per inch (dpi) setting associated with it. If you choose **Custom** in the **Quality:** drop-down list, enter a value in the **DPI:** text box.

## Plot Offset

The **Plot offset** area controls how far the drawing is offset from the lower-left corner of the paper. See **Figure 10-32.**

The origin of a plotter is the lower-left corner of the plot media. To begin plotting a drawing at that point, leave the values shown in the **X:** and **Y:** text boxes at 0.00. If you want to move the drawing away from the default origin, change the required values in the text boxes. For example, to move the drawing four units to the right and three units above the plotter origin, enter 4 in the **X:** text box, and 3 in the **Y:** text box.

**Figure 10-32.**
The **Plot offset** area controls how far the drawing is offset from the lower-left corner of the paper.

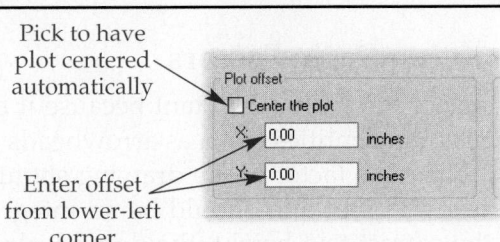

Pick to have plot centered automatically

Enter offset from lower-left corner

## Other Plotting Options

The **Plot options** area of the **Plot** dialog box contains a list of four items that can affect the time and resources required to plot a drawing. Apply these options only when required for the plot by picking the appropriate check box. The following options are available:

- **Plot object lineweights.** Lines having a lineweight other than 0 are plotted using the appropriate thickness. This box is checked by default.
- **Plot with plot styles.** All plot styles attached to the drawing and its components are plotted.
- **Plot paperspace last.** Paper space objects are plotted first by default. If this box is checked, paper space objects are plotted last. Since there are no paper space objects present in the **Model** tab, this option is available only when plotting from a layout tab.
- **Hide paperspace objects.** This option removes hidden lines from 3D objects that have been created in paper space. This option is only available when you are plotting from a layout tab. This option affects only objects drawn in paper space. It does not affect any 3D objects within a viewport. To plot objects within viewports with hidden lines removed, you must change the Shade plot property of the viewport. To do this, select the layout tab, pick the viewport, and open the **Properties** window. Pick the Shade plot property and change the setting to Hidden. See **Figure 10-33**.

**Figure 10-33.**
In order to plot objects in a floating viewport with hidden lines removed, the Shade plot setting for the viewport must be Hidden.

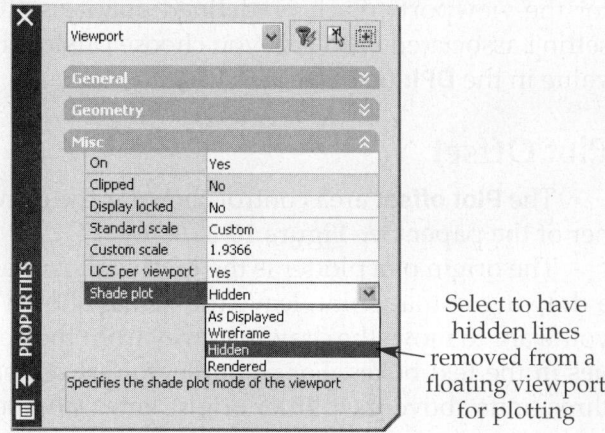

Select to have hidden lines removed from a floating viewport for plotting

## Determining Drawing Scale Factors

The proper scale factor is vitally important because it ensures that text, dimension values, and dimensioning entities (such as arrowheads and tick marks) are plotted at the proper size. The scale factor of the drawing should already be established by the time you are ready to plot and should be an integral part of your template drawings. To obtain the correct text height, the desired plotted text height is multiplied by the scale factor. The scale factor is also used in scaling dimensions.

**NOTE**

Determine the plot scale and scale factor when you begin the drawing. If you find the drawing scale factor does not correspond to the plotting scale, you will need to update dimensions and text.

AutoCAD and its Applications—Basics

The scale factor is always the reciprocal of the drawing scale. For example, if you wish to plot a mechanical drawing at a scale of 1/2″ = 1″, calculate the scale factor as follows:

> 1/2″ = 1″
> .5″ = 1″
> 1 ÷ .5 = 2 *(The scale factor is 2)*

An architectural drawing to be plotted at a scale of 1/4″ = 1′-0″ has a scale factor calculated as follows:

> 1/4″ = 1′-0″
> .25″ = 12″
> 12 ÷ .25 = 48 *(The scale factor is 48)*

The scale factor of a civil engineering drawing that has a scale of 1″ = 60′ is calculated as follows:

> 1″ = 60′
> 1″ = 60 × 12 = 720″ *(The scale factor is 720)*

Once the scale factor of the drawing has been determined, calculate the height of the text in AutoCAD. If text height is to be plotted at 1/8″, it should not be drawn at that height. Remember, all geometry created in AutoCAD should be drawn at full scale.

For example, if you are working on a civil engineering drawing with a scale of 1″ = 60′, the scale factor equals 720. Text drawn 1/8″ high appears as a dot. The full-size civil engineering drawing in AutoCAD is 720 times larger than it will be when plotted at the proper scale. Therefore, you must multiply the text height by 720 in order to get text that appears in correct proportion on the screen. For 1/8″ high text to appear correctly on screen, calculate the AutoCAD text height as follows:

> 1/8″ × 720
> .125 × 720 = 90 *(The proper height of the text is 90)*

Remember, scale factors and text heights should be determined before beginning a drawing. The best method is to incorporate these as values within your template drawing files.

### Scaling the plot

AutoCAD drawing geometry is created at full scale, and the drawing is scaled at the plotter to fit on the sheet size. The **Plot scale** area of the **Plot** dialog box is used to specify the plot scale. The **Scale:** drop-down list contains a selection of 34 different decimal and architectural scales, including Custom and Scaled to Fit. See **Figure 10-34.** The **Custom:** text boxes allow you to specify the plot scale as a ratio of plotted units to drawing units. An architectural drawing to be plotted at 1/4″ = 1′-0″ can be entered in the text boxes as:

> 1/4″ = 1′ *or* .25 = 12 *or* 1 = 48

A mechanical drawing to be plotted at a scale of 1/2″ = 1″ can be entered in the text boxes as:

> 1/2″ = 1″ *or* .5 = 1 *or* 1 = 2

Pick Scaled to Fit in the **Scale:** drop-down list if you want AutoCAD to automatically adjust your drawing to fit on the paper. This is useful if you have a C-size pen plotter but need to plot a D-size or E-size drawing. However, keep in mind that you may have considerable blank space left on the paper, depending on the size and proportions of your drawing.

Figure 10-34.
The **Scale:** drop-
down list contains a
selection of 34
different decimal
and architectural
scales, including
Custom and Scaled to
Fit.

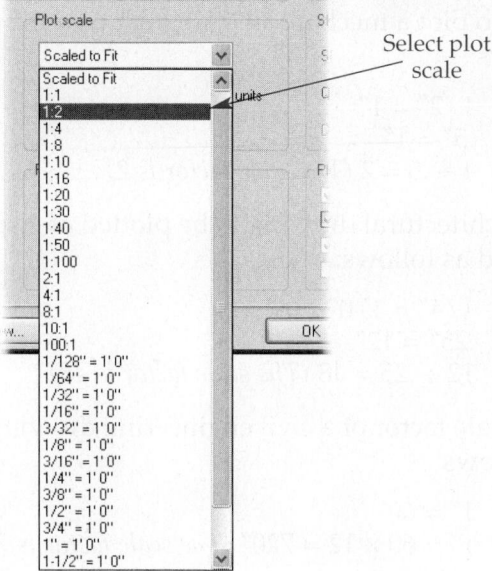

The Scaled to Fit option is also useful if you are printing a large drawing on a dot matrix or laser printer that can only use A-size sheets. The drawing is automatically scaled down to fit the size of the printer paper.

## Calculating the drawing area and limits

To calculate the available area on a sheet of paper at a specific scale, use this formula:

Scale factor × Media size = Limits

For example, the limits of a B-size (17″ × 11″) sheet of paper at 1/2″ = 1″ scale (scale factor = 2) can be calculated as follows:

2 × 17 = 34 (X distance)
2 × 11 = 22 (Y distance)

Thus, the limits of a B-size sheet at the scale of 1/2″ = 1″ are 34,22. The same formula applies to architectural scales. The limits of a C-size architectural sheet (24″ × 18″) at a scale of 1/4″ = 1′-0″ (scale factor = 48) can be determined as follows:

48 × 24 = 1152″          = 96′ (X distance)

Use the same formula to calculate the Y distance for the 18″ side of the paper. Refer to the charts in Appendix E to find the limits for common scales on various paper sizes for each drafting field.

**CAUTION**

Before you plot a drawing, always check the **PSLTSCALE** system variable. This variable controls paper space linetype scaling, and is set to 1 by default. This means that all linetype dash lengths and spaces will be scaled to the paper space scale. For most plotting purposes, **PSLTSCALE** should be set to zero.

If **PSLTSCALE** is set to 1, your viewports can be zoomed to different magnifications and the linetype scale will be the same in all viewports. If **PSLTSCALE** is set to 0, viewports zoomed to varying magnifications will also appear to have differing linetype scales.

## Previewing the Plot

Depending on their size and complexity, drawings can require long plotting times. By previewing a plot before it is sent to the output device, you can catch errors, saving material and valuable plot time. This feature is controlled by the **Full Preview...** and **Partial Preview...** buttons at the lower-left corner of the **Plot** dialog box.

If **Partial Preview...** is selected, AutoCAD displays the **Partial Plot Preview** dialog box, shown in **Figure 10-35.** The outline is the paper size, and the dashed line represents the printable area. The paper dimensions are given for reference. The area the image occupies is called the *effective area.* The effective area dimensions are noted and the outline of this area is filled with a blue hatch pattern. While this preview shows you how the drawing compares to the paper size, the final plot depends on how the printer or plotter is set up.

If there is something wrong with the relationship of the display and the paper, AutoCAD gives you messages in the **Warnings:** text box. These warnings give you an opportunity to make corrections and then preview the plot again. You may encounter the following warnings:

- Effective area too small to display.
- Origin forced effective area off paper.
- Plotting area exceeds paper maximum.

Notice the small symbol in the upper-left corner of the effective area in **Figure 10-35.** This is the *orientation icon.* When the orientation icon appears in the upper-left corner, it indicates the landscape orientation. The icon is in the lower-left corner for a portrait orientation, the lower-right corner for an upside-down landscape orientation, and the upper-right corner for an upside-down portrait orientation.

**Figure 10-35.**
If **Partial Preview...** is selected, AutoCAD displays the **Partial Plot Preview** dialog box.

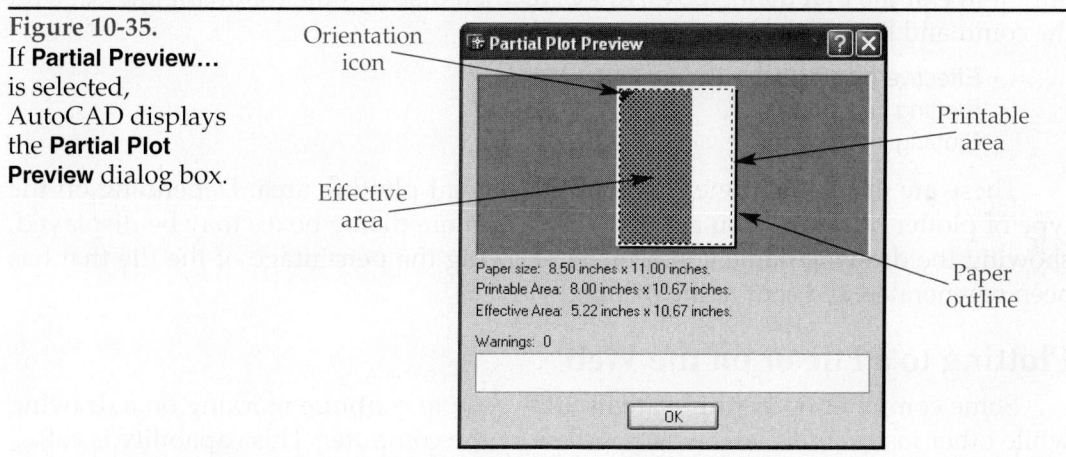

Orientation icon

Printable area

Effective area

Paper outline

**PROFESSIONAL TIP**

Rather than using the orientation icon in the **Partial Plot Preview** dialog box to determine the drawing orientation, use the graphic image in the **Drawing orientation** area of the **Plot** dialog box.

Pick the **Full Preview...** button to display the drawing as it will actually appear on the plotted hard copy. The display reflects any plot style tables that have been attached to the drawing. Displaying the full preview takes the same amount of time as a drawing regeneration. Therefore, the drawing size determines how quickly the image is produced.

Figure 10-36.
Right-click to
display the shortcut
menu when a plot
preview is
displayed.

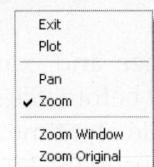

Exit
Plot

Pan
✓ Zoom

Zoom Window
Zoom Original

The drawing is displayed inside a paper outline. The cursor assumes the shape of the zoom icon. Press and hold the pick button as you move the cursor up to enlarge, and down to reduce. Right-click to display the shortcut menu shown in **Figure 10-36.** It provides several display options, a **Plot** option, and an **Exit** option. The shortcut menu is handy because it allows you to closely examine the drawing before you commit to plotting. You can also press [Esc] or [Enter] to return to the **Plot** dialog box.

A full preview is also displayed by picking **Plot Preview** in the **File** pull-down menu. This selection bypasses the **Plot** dialog box.

Before you pick **OK** in the **Plot** dialog box, there are several items you should check:
- ✓ The printer or plotter is plugged in and turned on.
- ✓ The parallel or serial cable to the computer is secure.
- ✓ The pen carousel is loaded and secure, or the pen is in the plotter arm.
- ✓ Pens of proper color and thickness are in correct locations in the pen carousel or rack.
- ✓ The plot media is properly loaded in the plotter and paper grips or clamps are in place.
- ✓ The printer or plotter area is clear for unblocked paper movement.

Once you are satisfied with all plotter parameters and are ready to plot, pick the **OK** button to exit the **Plot** dialog box. AutoCAD then displays the following message on the command line:

Effective plotting area: (xx) wide by (yy) high
Plotting viewport n
Plotting viewport n

These are the actual dimensions of the current plotting area. Depending on the type of plotter or printer you are using, one or more dialog boxes may be displayed, showing the drawing name and a meter showing the percentage of the file that has been regenerated and sent to the printer.

## Plotting to a File or on the Web

Some computer operating systems allow you to continue working on a drawing while other instructions are being handled by the computer. This capability is called *multitasking* and is a standard feature of the Windows and Unix operating systems. For those operating systems capable of true multitasking, it can be extremely handy to redirect plot output to an external file. This plot file can then be sent directly to a configured plotter while you continue working on a drawing.

Redirecting plot output to a PLT file is good practice if you have only one office or class computer connected to a printer or plotter. This is also the case if your office or school uses a plot spooler. A plot spooler is connected to a plotter and is basically a "smart" disk drive with memory. It reads the PLT file from disk and sends the drawing data to the plotter. A plot spooler removes the need of having a computer connected to the plotter.

Additionally, plot files can be stored in a plot queue on the file server in a networked computer environment. A *plot queue* is a lineup, or list of files, waiting to be plotted. The PLT files can be loaded in the queue and started while users on the network continue doing other work. The Batch Plot utility can also be used to plot a group of PLT files.

AutoCAD and its Applications—Basics

If you want to redirect plot output to a file, pick the **Plot to file** check box in the **Plot Device** tab of the **Plot** dialog box. See **Figure 10-37A.** After picking this check box, the note (this file only) is displayed after **Plot to file**. This activates the **File name and path:** text box, which is normally disabled. The location displayed is the path of the current drawing. You can select a previous file location from the drop-down list, or use the browse button (...) to open the **Browse for Plot File** dialog box to navigate to a new location. See **Figure 10-37B.** From here you can save the plot file to a location on the World Wide Web. You must have an Internet browser, such as Netscape or Microsoft Internet Explorer, in order to use this feature. In addition, you must have access to a web site using File Transfer Protocol (FTP). With these capabilities, you can copy, move, rename, and delete files and folders found on the Web.

**Figure 10-37.**
A—Use the settings in the **Plot to file** area to create a plot file. B—Use the **Browse for Plot File** dialog box to select plot file or new location.

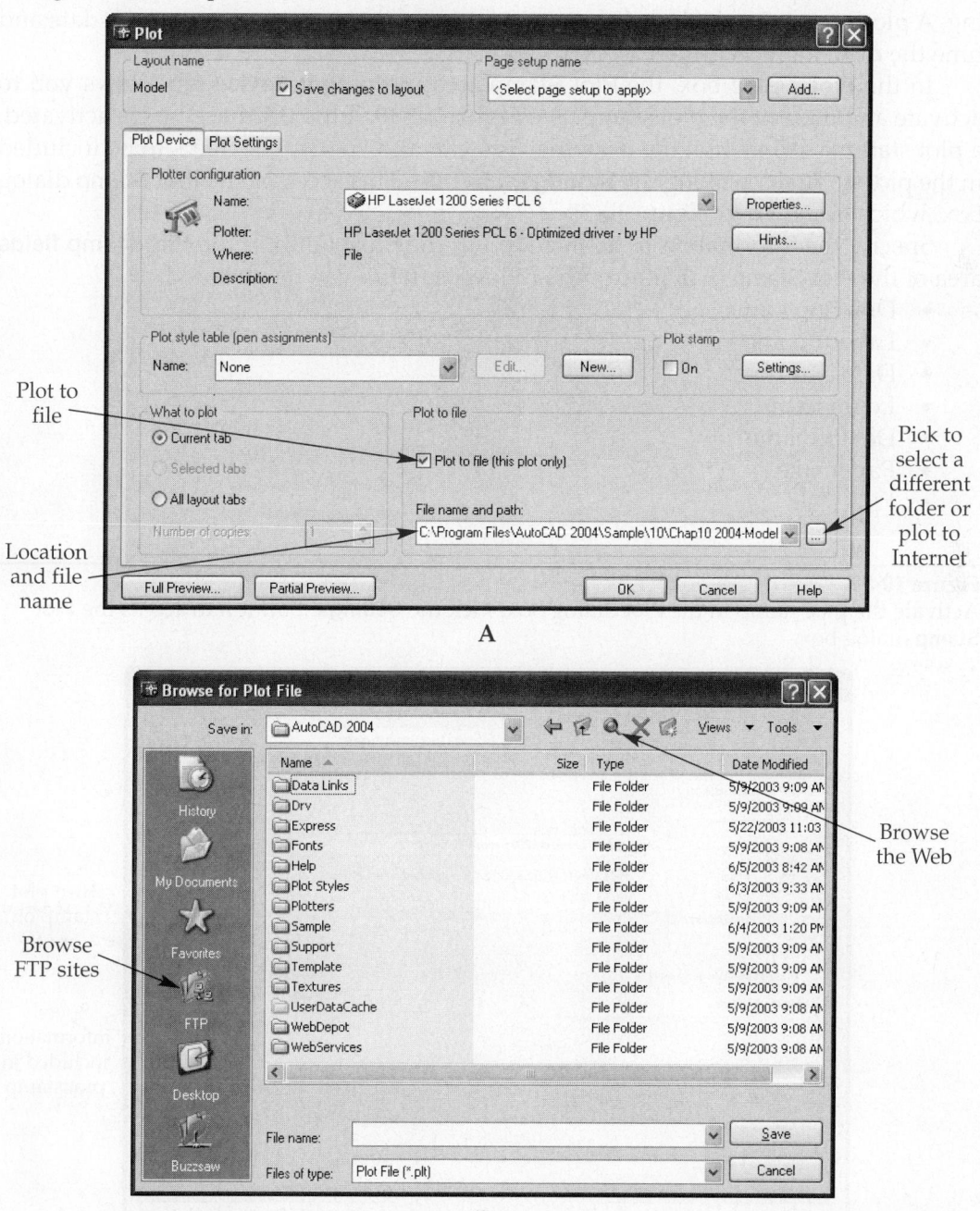

A

B

Observe that saved plot files are automatically given the extension PLT. The plot file name defaults to the current drawing name, with the addition of either "-model" or "-layout," depending on whether the **Model** tab or a layout tab is current. To provide a different name for the plot file, enter the name in the **File name:** text box and pick **OK**. Pick **OK** to close the dialog box and create the plot file.

> **NOTE**
> AutoCAD's Internet features are discussed in detail in *AutoCAD and its Applications—Advanced.*

## Adding a Plot Stamp

A plot stamp is specific text information included on a printed or plotted drawing. A plot stamp may include information such as the drawing name or the date and time the drawing was printed.

In the **Plot** dialog box, the **Plot Stamp** area in the **Plot Device** tab allows you to activate and modify the plot stamp. See **Figure 10-38.** If the **On** check box is activated, a plot stamp is printed on the drawing. You can also specify the items to be included in the plot stamp by picking the **Settings...** button. This accesses the **Plot Stamp** dialog box, which is shown in **Figure 10-39.**

Specify the information to be included in the plot stamp in the **Plot stamp fields** area of the **Plot Stamp** dialog box. The following items can be included:

- Drawing name
- Layout name
- Date and time
- Login name
- Device name
- Paper size
- Plot scale

Figure 10-38.
Activate the plot stamp in the **Plot** dialog box. Pick the **Settings...** button to access the **Plot Stamp** dialog box.

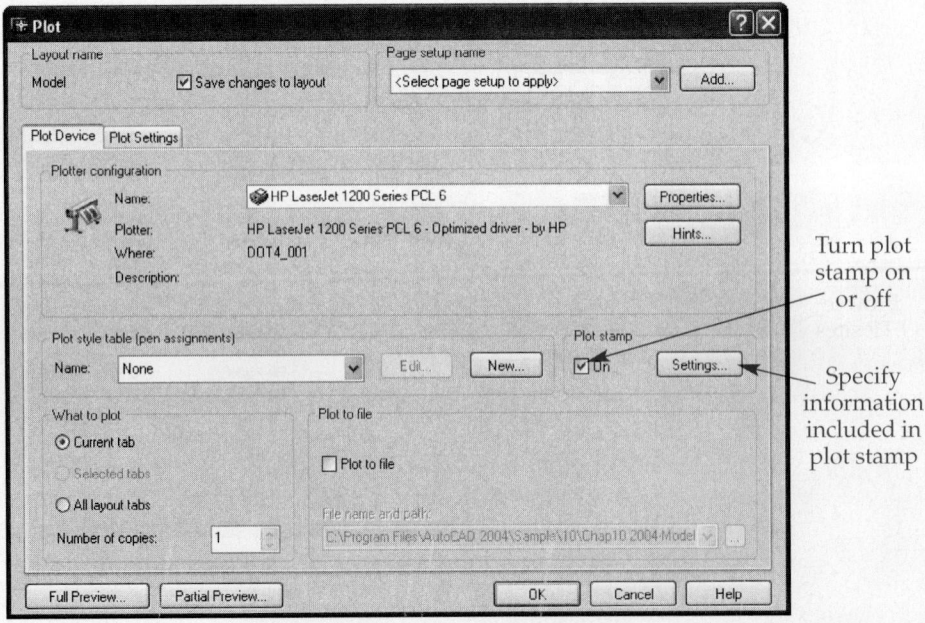

**Figure 10-39.**
Use the **Plot Stamp** dialog box to specify the information included in the plot stamp. You can save plot stamp settings as PSS files.

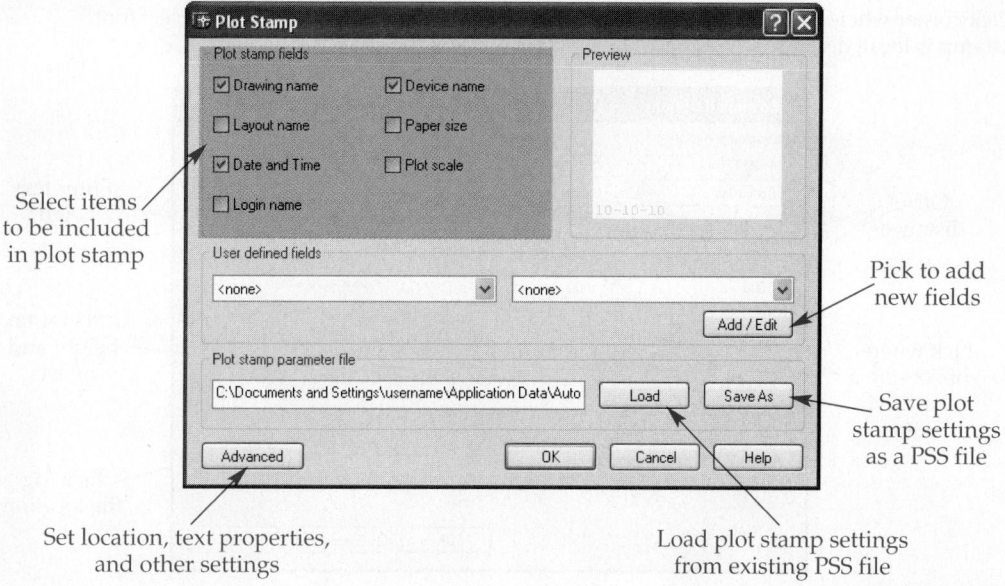

Select items to be included in plot stamp

Pick to add new fields

Save plot stamp settings as a PSS file

Set location, text properties, and other settings

Load plot stamp settings from existing PSS file

You can create additional plot stamp items in the **User defined fields** area. For example, you could add a field for the client name, the project name, or the contractor who will be using the drawing.

The **Preview** area provides a preview of the location and orientation of the plot stamp. The preview does not show the actual plot stamp text.

Plot stamp settings can be saved in a PSS (plot stamp parameter) file. If you load an existing PSS file, the settings saved in the file are automatically set in the **Plot Stamp** dialog box.

Additional plot stamp options are set in the **Advanced Options** dialog box. To access this dialog box, pick the **Advanced...** button in the **Plot Stamp** dialog box. The **Advanced Options** dialog box is shown in Figure 10-40. The following options are available:

- **Location and offset.** Pick the corner where the plot stamp begins from the drop-down list. If you want the plot stamp to print upside-down, pick the **Stamp upside-down** check box. The orientation is set by picking Horizontal or Vertical from the **Orientation** drop-down list. The X offset and Y offset distance is entered in the text boxes. The offset distances are measured relative to the printable area or paper border.
- **Text properties.** Specify the text font and height. Pick the **Single line plot stamp** check box if you want the plot stamp constrained to a single line. If this check box is not checked, the plot stamp will be printed in two lines.
- **Plot stamp units.** Select the plot stamp units. The plot stamp units can be different from the drawing units.
- **Log file location.** Pick the **Create a log file** check box to create a log file of plotted items. Specify the name of the log file in the text box. Pick **Browse...** to specify the location of the log file.

---

**NOTE**

The log file settings are independent of the plot stamp settings. Thus, you can produce a log file without creating a plot stamp or have a plot stamp without producing a log file.

---

**Figure 10-40.**
Specify the plot stamp location, orientation, text font and size, and units in the **Advanced Options** dialog box.

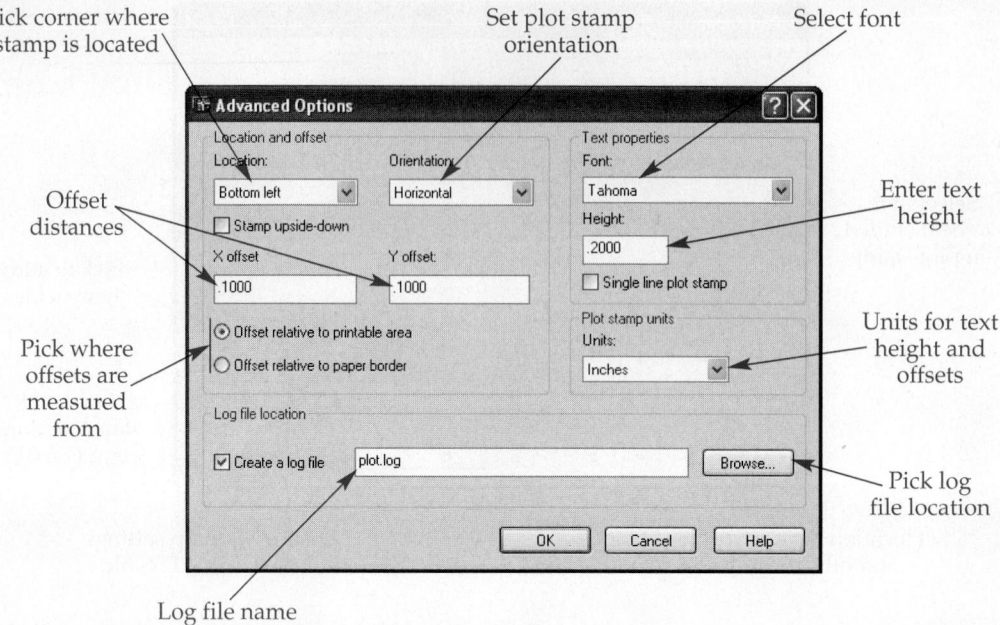

Pick corner where stamp is located

Set plot stamp orientation

Select font

Offset distances

Pick where offsets are measured from

Enter text height

Units for text height and offsets

Pick log file location

Log file name

## Additional Plotting Options

The **Plotting** tab of the **Options** dialog box contains general plotting settings, some of which will seldom have to be changed. See **Figure 10-41**. To access this dialog box, select **Options...** from the **Tools** pull-down menu. This tab provides several general plotting options. The **Default plot style behavior for new drawings** options have been discussed previously. The other areas are discussed briefly here.

**Figure 10-41.**
General plotting settings are found in the **Plotting** tab of the **Options** dialog box.

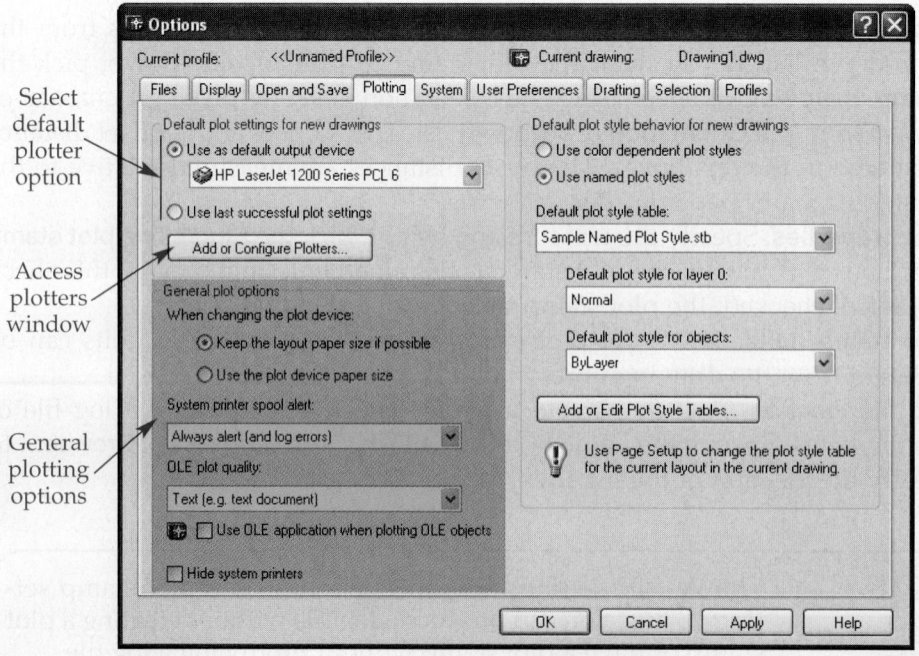

Select default plotter option

Access plotters window

General plotting options

- **Default plot settings for new drawings.** The default setting is **Use as default output device**. The device can be selected from the drop-down list. The **Use last successful plot settings** option retains the previous plot settings. Picking the **Add or Configure Plotters** button displays the **Plotters** window.
- **General plot options.** This area allows you to use either the **Keep the layout paper size if possible** option, regardless of the plotter selected, or the **Use the plot device paper size** option. If you choose to keep the layout size, AutoCAD will use the paper size specified in the **Layout Settings** tab of the **Page Setup** dialog box. If this size cannot be plotted, AutoCAD defaults to the size listed in the plotter's PC3 file. These radio buttons reflect the setting of the **PAPERUPDATE** system variable.
  - **System printer spool alert.** If a port conflict occurs during plotting and a drawing is spooled to a system printer, AutoCAD can display an alert and log the error. This drop-down list gives four options for alerting and logging errors.
  - **OLE plot quality.** *OLE* is an acronym for *object linking and embedding* and refers to any text or graphic object that is imported from another software application. This drop-down list allows you to select the type of OLE objects that will be plotted. The **OLEQUALITY** system variable also controls this option.
  - **Use OLE application when plotting OLE objects.** If this check box is activated, applications used to create OLE objects are launched. This may be desirable if you wish to use the OLE software to adjust the quality of the object. This option is also controlled by the **OLESTARTUP** system variable.

## Using the Batch Plot Utility

The Batch Plot utility adds a powerful dimension to printing and plotting. Using this utility, you can create a list of drawings to be printed and then instruct AutoCAD to begin plotting while you return to work on other projects. The Batch Plot utility opens a temporary session of AutoCAD for its purposes, but does not allow you to edit drawings or adjust plot parameters in any way. To use this feature, locate the Batch Plot utility program file, batchplt.exe, located in the AutoCAD 2004 program folder. See **Figure 10-42.**

CAUTION

Use the Batch Plot utility only if you have previously created all required drawings, layouts, page setups, and PC3 files. Always preview your plots to check for accuracy before saving any of the files. Valuable time may be wasted if you do not plan your plots accurately.

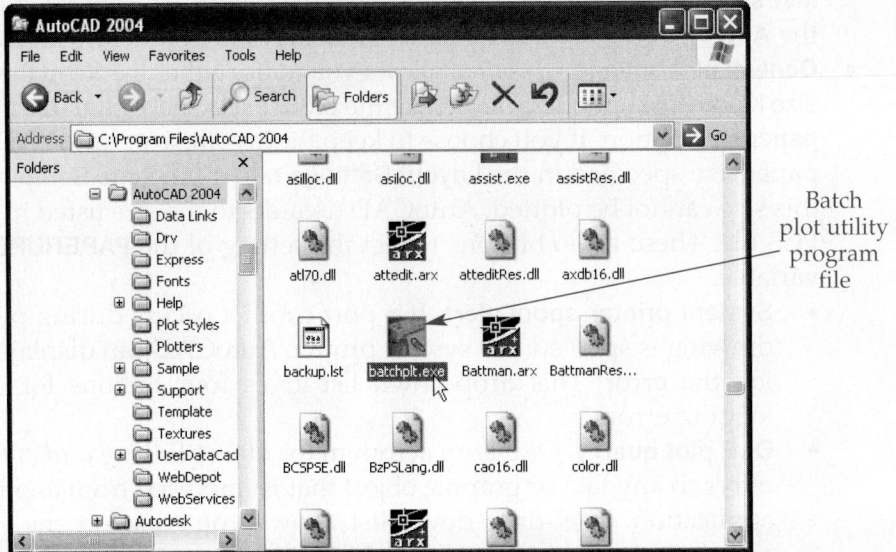

Batch plot utility program file

## Batch Plot Checklist

Before you use the Batch Plot utility, be sure you have completed the following tasks. Following these guidelines is important if the utility is to run successfully.

✓ Check each drawing to be plotted for accuracy and completeness. If you are plotting a view, display the named view to be plotted before saving the drawing. The default view is plotted by the Batch Plot utility.

✓ Conduct a full preview of the drawing to check for the accuracy of all plot parameters.

✓ Verify the PC3 file if a single plotter is to be used, and carefully check the layout and page setup parameters before creating the batch list.

✓ If more than one drawing is to be plotted using the same plotter, but the drawings have different plot parameters, verify the layouts and page setups to be used for each drawing. If different configurations of the same plot device are to be used, create individual PC3 files before creating the batch list.

✓ If batch drawings will use different devices, carefully check the configurations of each device and save them as PC3 files.

## Creating a New Batch Plot List

As previously stated, the Batch Plot utility program is a stand-alone program accessed using the batchplt.exe program file found in the AutoCAD 2004 program folder. The **AutoCAD Batch Plot Utility** dialog box is displayed after double-clicking on this file name. See **Figure 10-43.**

---

NOTE

In the following discussion, Batch Plot utility commands are selected from the pull-down menus. Most commands can also be selected using the appropriate toolbar buttons. You can also right-click on a selected drawing to display a shortcut menu.

---

Figure 10-43.
The **AutoCAD Batch Plot Utility** dialog box.

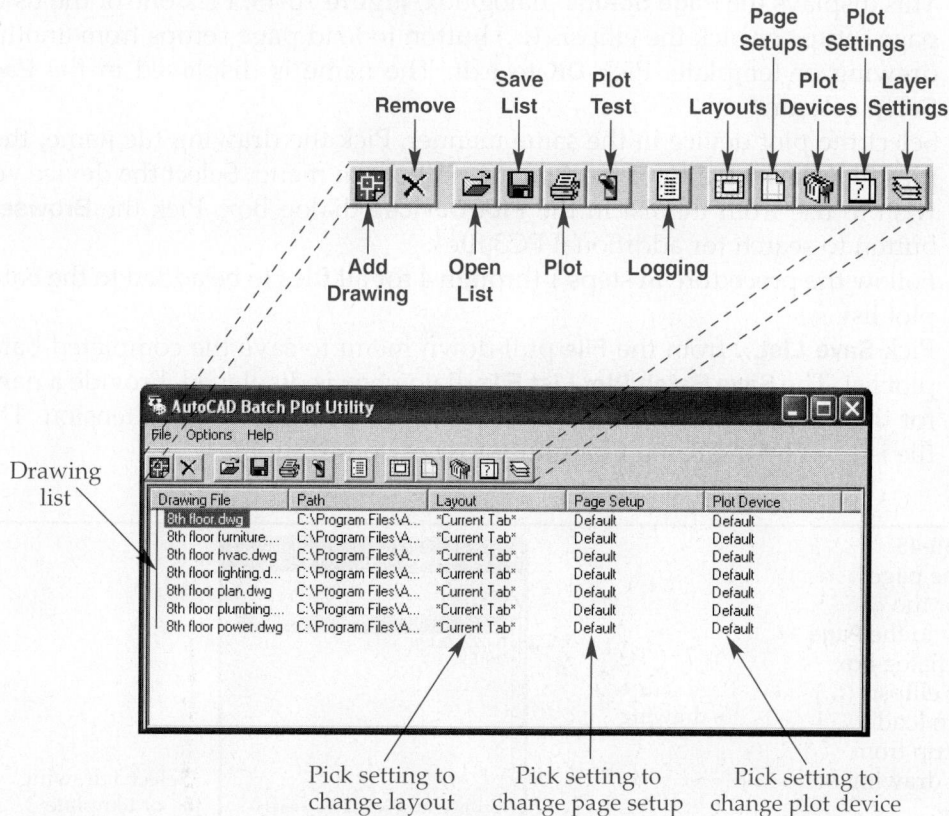

The first step in using the Batch Plot utility is to make a list of the drawings to be plotted using the following steps:

1. Pick **Add Drawing...** from the **File** pull-down menu to add a drawing to the **Drawing File** list. This displays the **Add Drawing File** dialog box, which is a standard file dialog box. Select the desired drawing and pick **OK**.
2. To assign a layout to plot, first pick the drawing name in the **Drawing File** list to highlight it. Next, select **Layouts...** from the **Options** pull-down menu. This displays the **Layouts** dialog box, **Figure 10-44**. Pick the **Show all layouts** button for a complete list of layouts in the selected drawing. Pick the desired layout(s) and then pick **OK**. The selection is displayed in the **Layout** column.

Figure 10-44.
Select the layout(s) to be plotted from the **Layouts** dialog box.

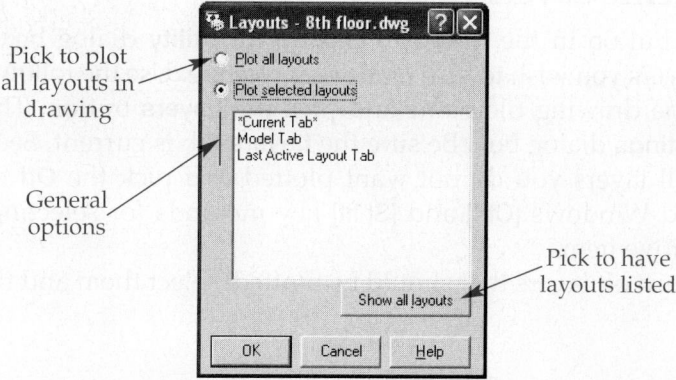

3. To assign a page setup, first pick the drawing name in the **Drawing File** list to highlight it. Next, select **Page Setups...** from the **Options** pull-down menu. This displays the **Page Setups** dialog box, **Figure 10-45.** Pick one of the listed page setups or pick the ellipsis (**...**) button to load page setups from another drawing or template. Pick **OK** to exit. The name is displayed in the **Page Setup** column.
4. Select the plot device in the same manner. Pick the drawing file name, then pick **Plot Devices...** from the **Options** pull-down menu. Select the device you wish to use from the list in the **Plot Devices** dialog box. Pick the **Browse...** button to search for additional PC3 files.
5. Follow the procedure in steps 1 through 4 for all files to be added to the batch plot list.
6. Pick **Save List...** from the **File** pull-down menu to save the completed batch plot list. The **Save Batch Plot List File** dialog box is displayed. Provide a name for the file and pick **Save**. This saves the file with a BP3 file extension. This file is used by the Batch Plot utility to plot your drawings.

**Figure 10-45.**
Select the page setup for the drawing in the **Page Setups** dialog box. Pick the ellipsis (**...**) button to load a page setup from another drawing or template.

Page setups in drawing

Select a drawing or template

**PROFESSIONAL TIP**

Even though a specific page setup and plot device is associated with a drawing, you can still override them in the Batch Plot utility and select page setups from other drawings, or any other PC3 file you have created.

## Plotting Specific Layers

The **Layers** button in the **AutoCAD Batch Plot Utility** dialog box allows you to specify which layers you wish to turn off during plotting. Use the following procedure:
1. Select the drawing file name and pick the **Layers** button. This displays the **Plot Settings** dialog box. Be sure the **Layers** tab is current. See **Figure 10-46.**
2. Select all layers you do not want plotted and pick the **Off** button. Use the standard Windows [Ctrl] and [Shift] key methods for selecting alternate and consecutive items.
3. If you turn off layers that should be plotted, select them and then pick the **On** button.

Figure 10-46.
Select the layers you do not want plotted and pick the **Off** button.

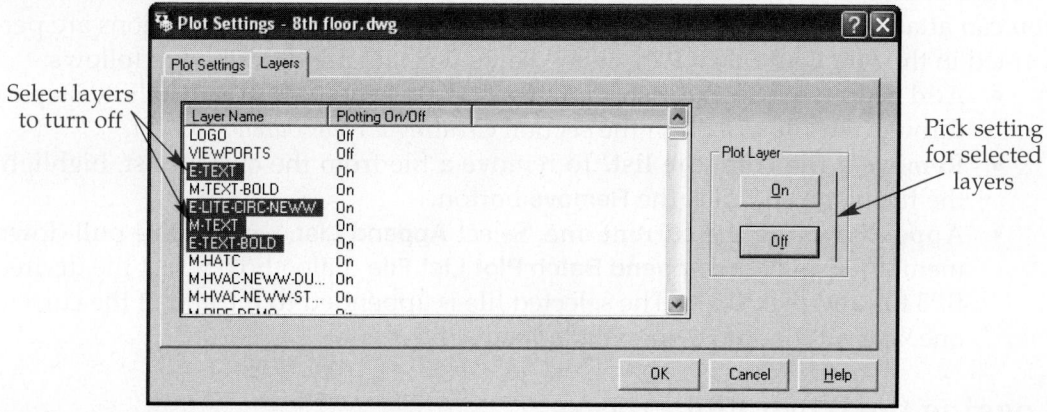

## Selecting the Area to Plot

The **Plot Settings** button in the **AutoCAD Batch Plot Utility** dialog box enables you to control the area of the drawing you wish to plot, and the scale with which to plot it. Selecting this button displays the **Plot Settings** tab of the **Plot Settings** dialog box. Three areas in this tab allow you to control what is plotted. See **Figure 10-47.**

- **Plot Area.** This area provides the same options available in the standard **Page Setup** or **Plot** dialog box, except the **Window** option is not available. When active, the **View** drop-down list shows all named views in the drawing file.
- **Plot Scale.** Change the plot scale in this area if necessary. If a page setup has not been associated with the selected drawing file, then the plot scale area will reflect the most recent setting in the **Plot** dialog box. If a page setup has been associated with the selected drawing file, then the **Plot Scale** area displays that value. Make it a habit to check this area carefully to ensure that the drawing is plotted at the proper scale.
- **Plot to file.** Enter a file name and location if you wish to have the batch list create a plot file.

Figure 10-47.
The **Plot Settings** dialog box enables you to control the area of the drawing you wish to plot, and the scale with which to plot it.

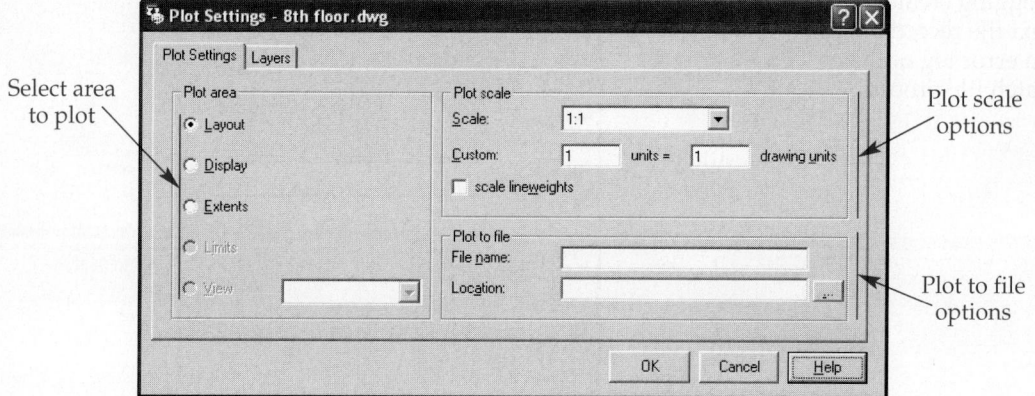

## Editing a Batch Plot List File

You can open an existing batch plot list file and add or delete files. In addition, you can attach (append) another BP3 file to the current one. These functions are performed in the **AutoCAD Batch Plot Utility** dialog box and are described as follows:

- **Add a drawing to the list.** Pick the **Add Drawing** button and follow steps 1 through 4 as described in the section *Creating a New Batch Plot List*.
- **Remove a file from the list.** To remove a file from the current list, highlight the file name and pick the **Remove** button.
- **Append a list to the current one.** Select **Append List...** in the **File** pull-down menu to display the **Append Batch Plot List File** dialog box. Select the desired BP3 file and pick **Open**. The selected file is appended to the end of the current one, and all files are displayed in the list box.

## Logging the Batch Plot Process

*Logging* creates a text file record and an error log of the batch file process. Pick the **Logging** button in the **AutoCAD Batch Plot Utility** dialog box, or pick **Logging...** in the **File** pull-down menu to display the logging options. See **Figure 10-48.** Plot journal logging and error logging are enabled by default, but can be disabled by picking the **Enable journal logging** or **Enable error logging** check boxes. The default bpjournl.log file and bperror.log files are saved in the Documents and Settings\\*username*\\My Documents folder. You can change the names and location of the log files by entering names in the **File name** text box, or by picking the **Browse...** button to display the **Journal Filename** or **Error Log Filename** dialog boxes.

A record of each batch plot overwrites the previous log file by default. If keeping a record of batch plotting is important, be sure the **Append** radio button is selected. Pick the **Overwrite** radio button if you want only the last batch plotted file to be kept on record.

Two options allow you to add lines of text to the log files.

- **Header.** Use this option to add a single line of text to the current log file. The text is the first line printed in the current log file.
- **Comment.** Use this option to add a line of text for each drawing in the file. The text is the first line printed in the log for a specific drawing. A different line of text can be entered for each drawing.

**Figure 10-48.**
Logging creates a text file record and an error log of the batch file process.

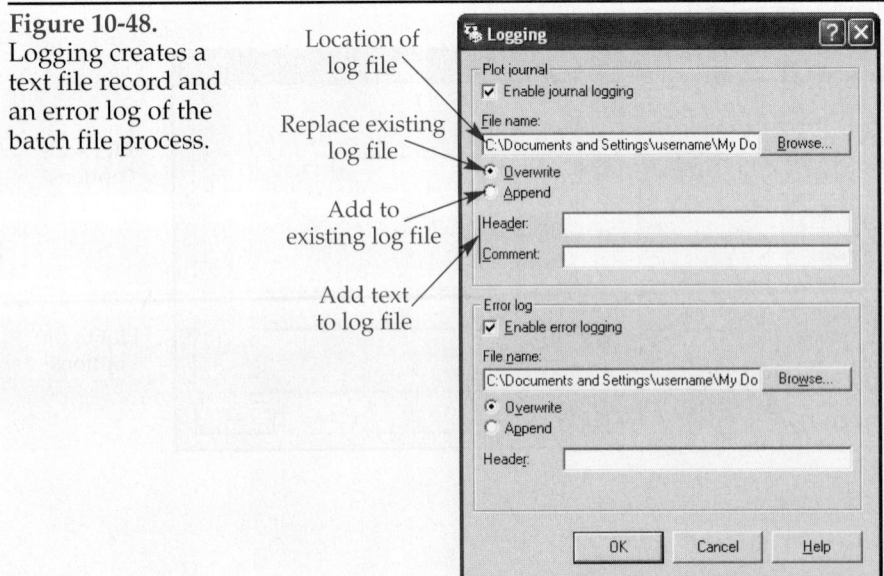

Location of log file

Replace existing log file

Add to existing log file

Add text to log file

## Testing the Batch Plot

The **Plot Test** button in the **AutoCAD Batch Plot Utility** dialog box provides a quick test for your batch plot file without actually plotting the drawings. The results of the test, including any problems that are found, are displayed in the **Plot Test Results** dialog box. A variety of problems can occur, especially if the drawing is being plotted on a different computer than the one it was drawn on. This is common with drawings that contain xref files (see Chapter 23), special fonts, and symbols. Always try to remedy these problems before performing a batch plot.

## Plotting a Batch Plot List

After the batch list is complete, you can choose to close the current session without plotting by picking **Exit** from the **File** pull-down menu. Be sure to save the current list first.

Pick the **Plot** button to begin plotting the list. When the plotting begins, you can open AutoCAD and continue working on other projects, or open any other application while the Batch Plot utility works in the background. A check mark appears next to the drawing name as it is successfully printed. An "X" appears next to drawings that do not plot. Minimize the **AutoCAD Batch Plot Utility** dialog box to remove it from the screen.

# Plotting Hints

Plotting can slow down productivity in an office or a classroom if not done efficiently. Establish and follow a procedure for using the plotter, and instruct all drafters, engineers, and other plotter users of the proper operating procedures. Post these in strategic locations.

## Planning Your Plots

*Planning* is again the key word when dealing with plots. In the same way you planned the drawing, you must plan the plot. The following items need to be considered when planning:

  ✓ Size and type of plotting media, such as bond paper, vellum, or polyester film.
  ✓ Type of title block.
  ✓ Location and scale of multiple views.
  ✓ Origin location, and scale of the drawing.
  ✓ Color, thickness, and types of pens to be used.
  ✓ Speed of pens.
  ✓ Orientation of 3D views.
  ✓ Portion to be plotted: layout, view, window, display, limits, or extents.

This is only a sample of decisions that should be made before you begin plotting. Remember, the plotter is the funnel that all drawings must go through before they are evaluated, approved, and sent to production or the client. When a bottleneck develops at the plotter, the time savings of a CAD system can be drastically reduced.

Use preprinted borders and title blocks whenever possible to decrease plotting time. Use block attributes for the title block information that will change with each drawing. A title block with defined attributes can be inserted into any drawing or plotted separately before or after the drawing. This eliminates drawing borders and title blocks every time you create a drawing. Refer to Chapter 24 for a discussion of title block attributes.

## Eliminate Unnecessary Plots

The easiest way to eliminate the problems associated with plotting is to eliminate plotting. Make plots *only* when absolutely necessary. This results in time and money savings. A few additional suggestions include the following:

✓ Obtain approvals of designs while the drawings are on screen.
✓ Transfer files or disks for the checker's comments.
✓ Create a special layer with a unique color for markups. Freeze or erase this layer when finally making a plot.
✓ Use a "redlining" software package that enables the checker to review the drawing and apply markups to it without using AutoCAD.
✓ Check drawings on disk. Use a special layer for comments.
✓ Use a printer when check prints are sufficient.
✓ Avoid making plots for backups. Rather, save your drawing files to three different locations, such as the hard disk, a diskette at your workstation, and a diskette at another location. These may also be supplemented with a backup on tape cartridges, optical disks, or other external storage devices.

## If You Must Plot...

Industry still exists on a paper-based system. Therefore, it is important that plotters are used efficiently. This means using the plotter only for what is required. Here are a few hints for doing just that.

✓ Ask yourself, "Do I *really* need a plot?" If the answer is an unqualified *yes*, then proceed.
✓ Plan your plot!
✓ Pick the least busy time to make the plot.
✓ If more than one plotter is available, use the smallest, least complex model.
✓ Select the smallest piece of paper possible.
✓ Use the lowest quality paper possible.
✓ Decide on only one pen color and thickness to make the plot.
✓ Use the most inexpensive pen possible.
✓ Use the fastest pen speed to achieve quality without pen skipping.
✓ Use a continuous linetype when possible. Hidden and center linetypes increase plot time significantly and cause pen wear. This is not as much of a factor with penless plotters, such as laser and inkjet devices.
✓ Create batch plot files and use batch plotting at times when plotter and printer use is light.

## Producing Quality Plots

When you must plot the highest quality drawing for reproduction, evaluation, or presentation, use your plotter in a manner that does the job right the first time. Keep in mind these points before making that final plot.

✓ Choose the device that will produce the quality of print needed. Select the right tool for the job.

✓ Choose the paper type and size appropriate for the project.

✓ Set pen speeds slow enough to produce good lines without skipping.

✓ If using wet ink pens, select the proper ink for your climate.

✓ Apply the appropriate plot style table for color plotting.

## Chapter Test

*Answer the following questions on a separate sheet of paper.*

1. What is paper space?
2. Which drawing environment (space) is active when the **Model** tab is selected?
3. What is a layout?
4. How do you create floating viewports in a layout?
5. When working in a layout tab, how do you activate a viewport in order to zoom or pan the viewport display?
6. List three methods used to create a new layout tab.
7. When creating a new layout by copying an existing layout, why is it better to select the command option from the shortcut menu rather than using the toolbar button?
8. How can you rename a layout?
9. If all layout tabs are not visible on screen, how do you select a tab that is not currently visible?
10. List the types of files a layout can be saved as.
11. How do you access the **Plotter Configuration Editor** from the **Page Setup** dialog box?
12. List five properties that can be set within a plot style.
13. Name the two plot style modes and the file extensions for their plot style tables.
14. What is a plot style table?
15. How do you access the **Plot Styles** window?
16. How do you create a new plot style table?
17. When you create a new color-dependent plot style table, how many plot styles does it contain?
18. When you create a new named plot style table, how many plot styles does it contain?
19. List two ways to access the **Plot Style Table Editor**.
20. What determines the plot style mode for a drawing?
21. Explain how you can specify a plot style table to be attached to all new drawings by default.
22. How does a color-dependent plot style table attached to a layout affect the plotting of the layout?
23. Plot styles of which plot style mode can be attached to layers and objects?
24. Explain how to assign a plot style to a layer.
25. Name two methods of assigning a plot style to an object.
26. What setting is used to have the effect of plot styles displayed in a layout?

27. Calculate the scale factors for drawings with the following scales:
    A. 1/4″ = 1″
    B. 1/8″ = 1′-0″
    C. 1″ = 30′
28. Calculate the drawing limits for the following scales and sheet sizes:
    A. 2″ = 1″ scale, 17 × 11 sheet size
    B. 1/2″ = 1′-0″ scale, 48 × 36 sheet size
    C. 1″= 10′ scale, 36 × 24 sheet size
29. Define *plot file* and explain how it is used.
30. Define *plot queue*.
31. What do you enter in the **Plot** dialog box to make the plotted drawing twice the size of the soft copy drawing?
32. What do you enter to specify a plot scale of 1/4″ = 1′-0″?
33. What system variable controls paper space linetype scaling?
34. Name the pull-down menu where the **Plot...** command is found.
35. How do you add a printer or plotter to the **Plot Device** tab of the **Plot** dialog box?
36. What is the difference between a PC2 file and a PC3 file?
37. How do you save a plot file named PLOT1 to a 3.5″ disk?
38. Identify the two types of paper orientation.
39. List an advantage of the partial preview format.
40. Cite two advantages of the full preview format.
41. Identify at least one disadvantage of the full preview format.
42. What is the purpose of batch plotting?
43. How do you access the **AutoCAD Batch Plot Utility** dialog box?
44. Explain why you should plan your plots.
45. Provide the best method to speed up the plotting process in a classroom or company.
46. Check prints are best generated on a(n) _____.
47. What type of paper and pens should be used for a check plot?
48. What type of paper and pens should be used for a final plot?

*For Questions 49–53, specify if the statement is true or false.*

49. Plot styles can be added to and deleted from color-dependent plot style tables.
50. Plot styles can be added to and deleted from named plot style tables.
51. The plot style mode of a drawing cannot be changed.
52. A plot style assigned to a layer will override a plot style assigned to an object on the layer when the drawing is plotted.
53. If a drawing has multiple layouts, all layouts must use the same plot style table.

## Drawing Problems

1. Create a new B-size decimal template drawing for use with mechanical (machine) parts. Use the following guidelines:
   A. Create a layout with the border and title block.
   B. Establish the appropriate settings to make this a half-scale (1″= 2″) drawing.
   C. Create three different text styles: one to plot at 1/8″ high, another at 3/16″ high, and a third at 1/4″ high. Set the text heights and linetype scale according to the values given in the chart in Appendix H.
   D. Save the drawing template as MECH-B-HALF.DWT.

2. Create a new C-size architectural template drawing. Use the following guidelines:
   A. Create a layout with the border and title block. Set units to architectural and set the area to 160' × 120'. Select to work on the drawing without the layout visible.
   B. Establish the appropriate settings to make this a 1/8"= 1'-0" scale drawing.
   C. Create three different text styles: one to plot at 1/8" high, another at 3/16" high, and a third at 1/4" high. Set the text heights and linetype scale according to the values given in the chart in Appendix H.
   D. Save the drawing as ARCH-C-EIGHTH.DWT.

3. Create a new C-size civil engineering template drawing. Use the following guidelines:
   A. Create a layout with the border and title block. Set units to engineering, angle to surveyor, angle measure to east, angle direction to counterclockwise, and set the area to 1000' × 750'. Select to work on the drawing while viewing the layout.
   B. Establish the appropriate settings to make this a 1" = 50' scale drawing.
   C. Create three different text styles: one to plot at 1/8" high, another at 3/16" high, and a third at 1/4" high. Set the text heights and linetype scale according to the values given in the chart in Appendix H.
   D. Save the drawing as CIVIL-C-1=50.DWT.

4. Open one of your drawings from Chapter 8. Plot the drawing on B-size paper using the **Limits** option. Use different color pens for each color in the drawing.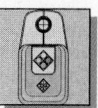

5. Zoom in on a portion of the drawing used for Problem 4 and select the **Display** plotting option. Rotate the plot 90° and fit it on the paper.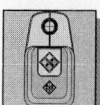

6. Using the same drawing used in Problem 4, use the **Window** option. Window a detailed area of the drawing. Plot the drawing to fit the paper size chosen.

7. Draw the views needed to describe the object completely. Set up appropriate layers, colors, and linetypes. Do not dimension the drawing. Plot from a layout tab using a scale of 1:1. Save the problem as P10-7.

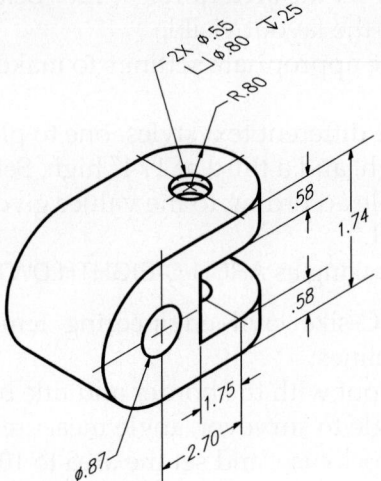

8. Draw the stainless steel stud shown on a B-size sheet at a scale of 2:1 (2 times actual size). Use a template drawing with a single floating model space viewport. Do not dimension the drawing. Be sure that paper space is active before using the **PLOT** command. Save the drawing as P10-8. Set the plot scale at 1:1.

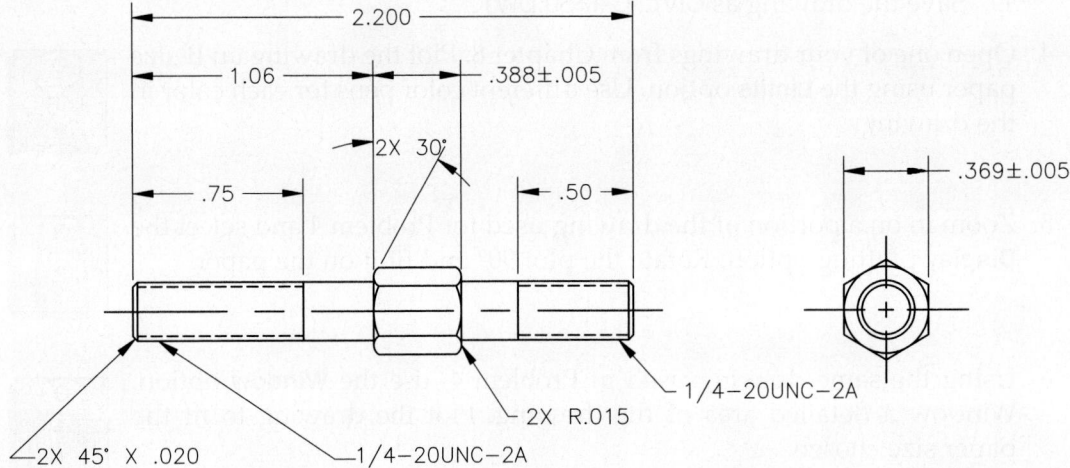

9. Draw the schematic shown on an A-size sheet at full scale. The size of the components is not important, but keep the same proportions as shown. Using color-dependent plot styles, have the equipment (shown in color in the diagram) plot with a lineweight of 0.8 mm and 80% screening. Plotted text height should be 1/8". Save the drawing as P10-9. Plot in paper space at 1:1.

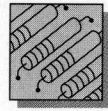

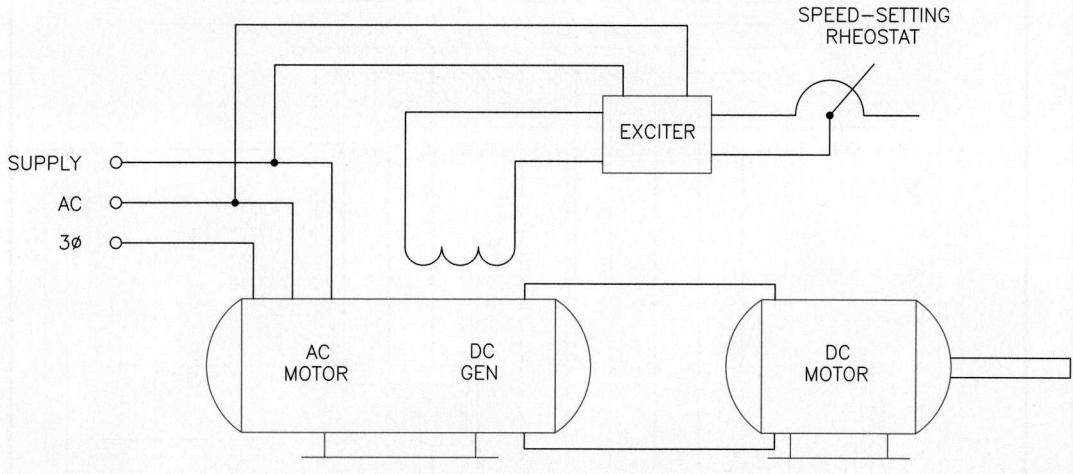

10. Draw the schematic shown on a B-size sheet at full scale. The size of the components is not important, but keep the same proportions as shown. Plotted text height should be 1/8". Create four layouts with the names and displays as follows:
    A. The **Entire Schematic** layout plots the entire schematic.
    B. The **3 Wire Control** layout plots only the 3 Wire Control diagram.
    C. The **Motor** layout plots the motor symbol and connections in the lower-center of the schematic.
    D. The **Schematic** layout plots schematic without the 3 Wire Control and motor components.
    Save the drawing as P10-10. Plot in paper space at 1:1.

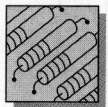

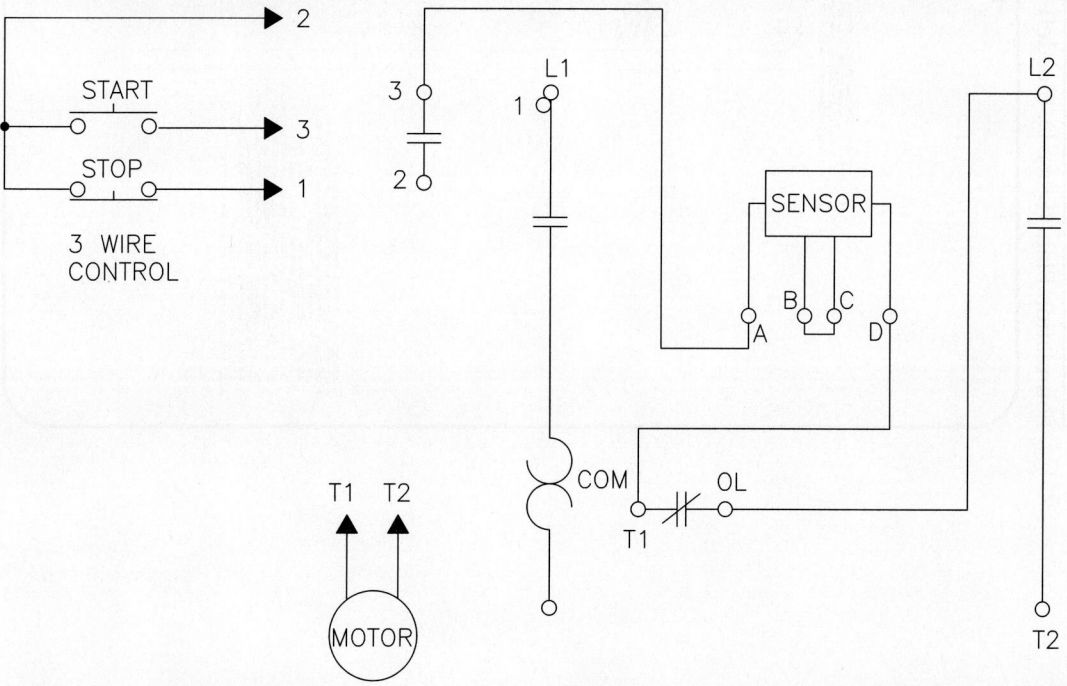

Foundation Plan. (Steve D. Bloedel)

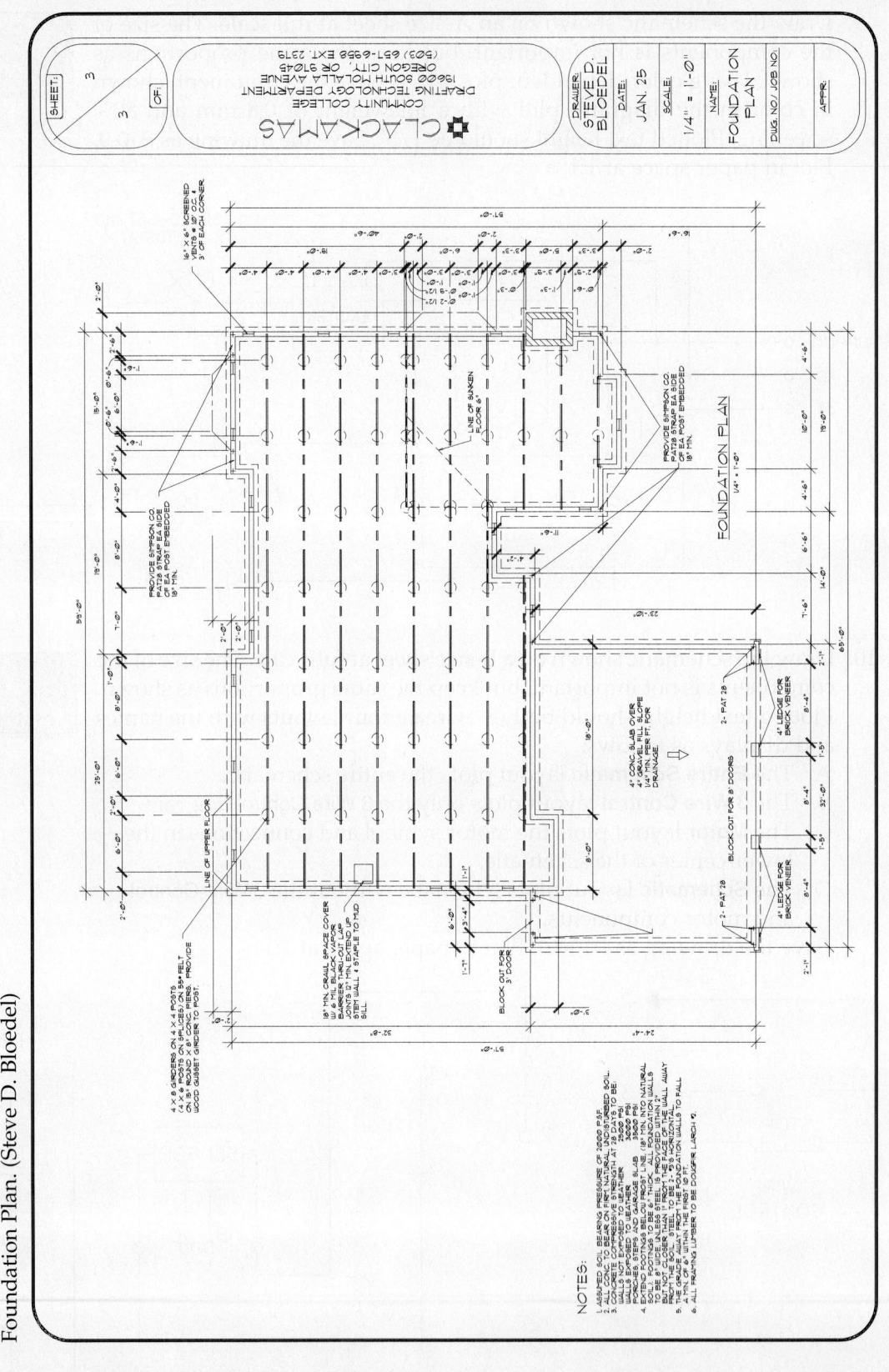

# CHAPTER 11

# Basic Editing Commands

## Learning Objectives

After completing this chapter, you will be able to do the following:

- Draw chamfers and angled corners with the **CHAMFER** command.
- Use the **FILLET** command to draw fillets, rounds, and other rounded corners.
- Remove portions of lines, circles, and arcs using the **BREAK** command.
- Use the **TRIM** and **EXTEND** commands to edit objects.
- Relocate objects using the **MOVE** command.
- Make single and multiple copies of existing objects using the **COPY** command.
- Draw mirror images of objects using the **MIRROR** command.
- Change the angular position of objects using the **ROTATE** command.
- Create arrangements of objects using the **ARRAY** command.
- Use the **ALIGN** command to simultaneously move and rotate objects.
- Change the size of objects using the **SCALE** command.
- Modify the lengths and heights of objects using the **STRETCH** and **LENGTHEN** commands.
- Create selection sets and object groups using the **GROUP** command.

This chapter explains commands and methods for changing a drawing. With manual drafting techniques, editing and modifying a drawing can take hours or even days. AutoCAD, however, makes the same editing tasks simpler and quicker. In Chapter 3, you learned how to draw and erase lines. The **ERASE** command is one of the most commonly used editing commands. You also learned how to select objects by picking with the cursor or using a window box, crossing box, window polygon, crossing polygon, or fence. The items selected are referred to as a *selection set.*

Many of the same selection methods and techniques can be used for the editing commands discussed in this chapter. You will learn how to draw angled and rounded corners. You will also learn how to move, copy, rotate, scale, and create mirror images of existing objects. These features are found in the **Modify** toolbar and the **Modify** pull-down menu. The editing commands discussed in this chapter are basically divided into two general groups—editing individual features of a drawing and editing major portions of a drawing. Commands typically used to edit individual features of a drawing include the following:

- **CHAMFER**
- **FILLET**
- **BREAK**

- **TRIM**
- **EXTEND**
- **LENGTHEN**

The following commands are used to edit entire drawings or major portions of a drawing, though they can also be used to edit individual features:

- **MOVE**
- **COPY**
- **ROTATE**
- **ARRAY**
- **MIRROR**
- **SCALE**
- **STRETCH**
- **CHANGE**
- **GROUP**

# Drawing Chamfers

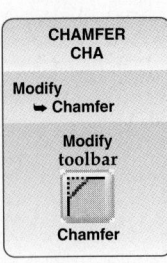

CHAMFER
CHA

Modify
↳ Chamfer

Modify
toolbar

Chamfer

A *chamfer* in mechanical drafting is a small angled surface used to relieve a sharp corner. AutoCAD defines a *chamfer* as "any angled corner on the drawing." A chamfer's distance from the corner determines the chamfer's size. A 45° chamfer is the same distance from the corner in each direction. See **Figure 11-1.** Chamfers were introduced in Chapter 5.

Chamfers are drawn between two lines that may or may not intersect. They can also connect polylines, xlines, and rays. Selecting the **Chamfer** button in the **Modify** toolbar, picking **Chamfer** from the **Modify** pull-down menu, or typing CHA or CHAMFER at the Command: prompt accesses the **CHAMFER** command. The following shows the default values and available options when you enter the **CHAMFER** command:

Command: **CHA** *or* **CHAMFER**↵
(TRIM mode) Current chamfer Dist1 = <*current*>, Dist2 = <*current*>
Select first line or [Polyline/Distance/Angle/Trim/Method/mUltiple]:

The current settings are displayed for your reference. Chamfers are established with two distances or one distance and an angle. The default value is 0.5 for both distances. This produces a 45° × 0.5 chamfered corner. The following is a brief description of each **CHAMFER** option:

- **Polyline.** Use this option if you want to chamfer all the eligible corners on a polyline. The term *eligible* means the chamfer distance is small enough to work on the corner.
- **Distance.** This option lets you set the chamfer distance for each line from the corner.

**Figure 11-1.**
Examples of different chamfers.

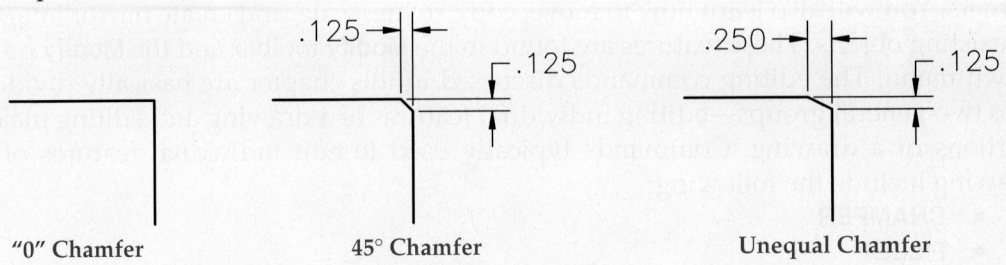

AutoCAD and its Applications—Basics

- **Angle.** This option uses a chamfer distance on the first selected line and applies a chamfer angle to determine the second line chamfer.
- **Trim.** Enter this to set the Trim mode. If **Trim** is on, the selected lines are trimmed or extended as required from the corner before creating the chamfer line. If **No trim** is active, the Trim mode is off. In this case, the selected lines are not trimmed or extended, and only the chamfer line is added.
- **Method.** This is a toggle that sets the chamfer method to either **Distance** or **Angle**. **Distance** and **Angle** values can be set without affecting each other.
- **Multiple.** Using this option repeats the chamfer command until you press the [Enter] key. After successfully chamfering two objects, you are prompted to Select first line or [Polyline/Distance/Angle/Trim/Method/mUltiple]: again, which is basically restarting the command, using the last settings.

## Setting the Chamfer Distance

The chamfer distance must be set before you can draw chamfers. The distances you set remain in effect until changed. Most drafters set the chamfer distance as exact values, but you can pick two points to set the distance. The following procedure is used to set the chamfer distance:

Command: **CHA** or **CHAMFER.⏎**
(TRIM mode) Current chamfer Dist1 = *<current>*, Dist2 = *<current>*
Select first line or [Polyline/Distance/Angle/Trim/Method/mUltiple]: **D.⏎**
Specify first chamfer distance *<current>*: *(specify a distance, such as .25)*
Specify second chamfer distance *<current>*: *(press* [Enter] *for the current distance or type a new value)*
Select first line or [Polyline/Distance/Angle/Trim/Method/mUltiple]:

Now you are ready to draw chamfers. Select the first and second lines:

Select first line or [Polyline/Distance/Angle/Trim/Method/mUltiple]: *(pick the first line)*
Select second line: *(pick the second line)*

After the lines are picked, AutoCAD automatically chamfers the corner. Objects can be chamfered even when the corners do not meet. AutoCAD extends the lines as required to generate the specified chamfer and complete the corner if Trim mode is on. If Trim mode is off, AutoCAD does not extend the lines to complete the corner. This is discussed later.

If the specified chamfer distance is so large that the chamfered objects disappear, AutoCAD does not perform the chamfer. Instead, a message, such as Distance is too large, is given. If you want to chamfer additional corners, press [Enter] to repeat the **CHAMFER** command. The results of several chamfering operations are shown in Figure 11-2.

> **NOTE**
> For the distance method, the first and second chamfer distance values are stored in system variables. The first distance is stored in the **CHAMFERA** system variable, and the second distance is stored in the **CHAMFERB** system variable.

Figure 11-2.
Using the **CHAMFER**
command.

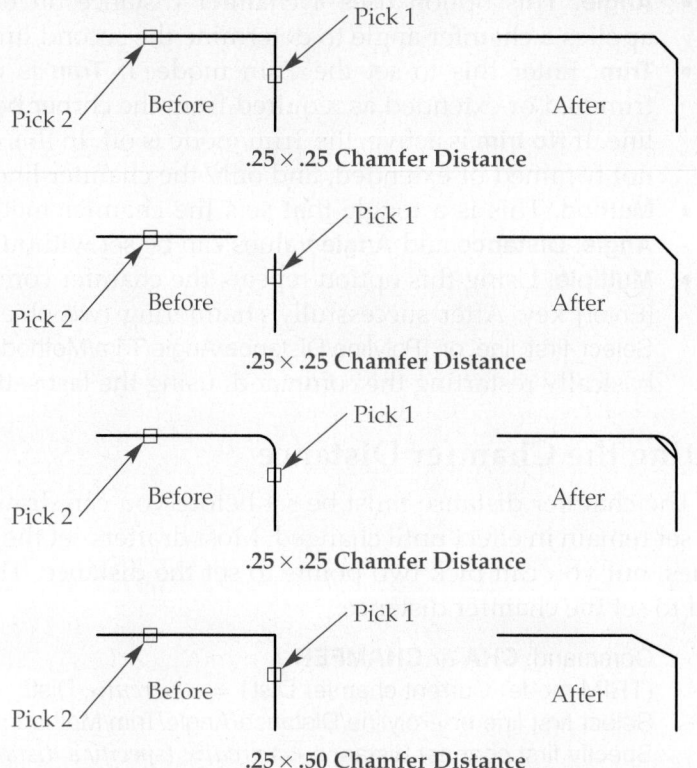

Pick 1

Before

After

.25 × .25 Chamfer Distance

Pick 2

Pick 1

Before

After

.25 × .25 Chamfer Distance

Pick 2

Pick 1

Before

After

.25 × .25 Chamfer Distance

Pick 2

Pick 1

Before

After

.25 × .50 Chamfer Distance

Pick 2

## Chamfering the Corners of a Polyline

Polylines are objects that can be made up of many different widths and shapes. Drawing and editing polylines is discussed further in Chapter 14 and Chapter 15. All corners of a closed polyline can be chamfered at one time. Enter the **CHAMFER** command, select the **Polyline** option, and then select the polyline. The corners of the polyline are chamfered to the distance values set. If the polyline was drawn without using the **Close** option, the beginning corner is not chamfered, as shown in **Figure 11-3**.

## Setting the Chamfer Angle

Instead of setting two chamfer distances, you can set the chamfer distance for one line and set an angle to determine the chamfer to the second line. To do this, use the **Angle** option. See **Figure 11-4**:

Command: **CHA** *or* **CHAMFER**.↵
(TRIM mode) Current chamfer Dist1 = *<current>*, Dist2 = *<current>*
Select first line or [Polyline/Distance/Angle/Trim/Method/mUltiple]: **A**↵
Specify chamfer length on the first line *<current>*: *(enter a chamfer distance—.5, for example)*

Figure 11-3.
Using the **Polyline** option of the **CHAMFER** command.

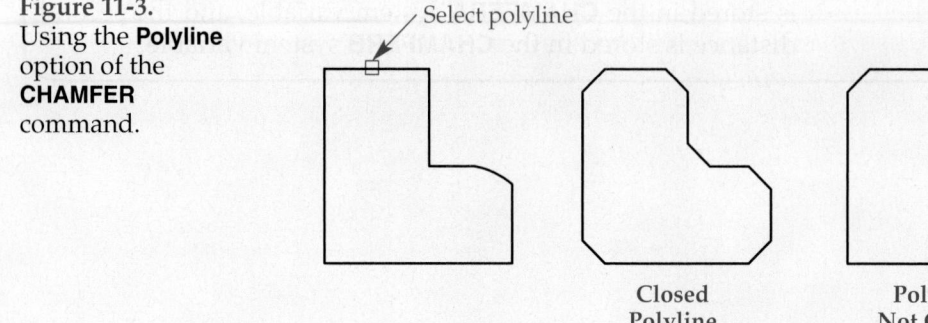

Select polyline

Closed
Polyline

Polyline
Not Closed

Figure 11-4.
Using the **Angle** option of the **CHAMFER** command with the chamfer length set at .5 and the angle set at 45°.

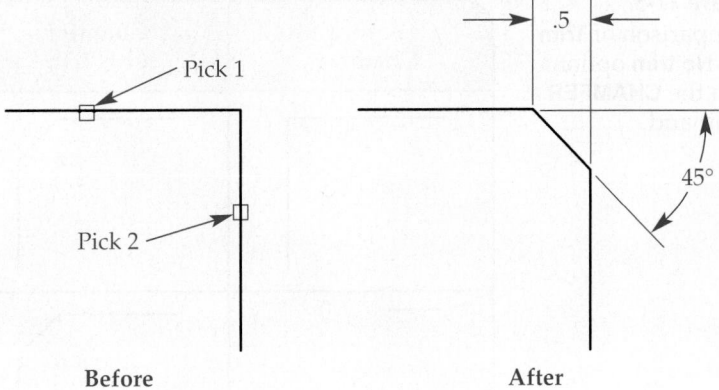

Before          After

Specify chamfer angle from the first line <current>: *(enter an angle—45, for example)*
Select first line or [Polyline/Distance/Angle/Trim/Method/mUltiple]: *(pick the first line)*
Select second line: *(pick the second line)*
Command:

---

NOTE

For the angle method, the chamfer distance and angle values are stored in system variables. The chamfer distance is stored in the **CHAMFERC** system variable, and the chamfer angle is stored in the **CHAMFERD** system variable.

---

## Exercise 11-1

○ Begin a new drawing or use one of your templates.
○ Use the **Distance** option of the **CHAMFER** command to draw the objects shown in **Figure 11-1**.
○ Draw the "Before" objects shown in **Figure 11-2**. Use the **Distance** option to change them to the "After" objects.
○ Draw the "Before" object shown in **Figure 11-4**, and then use the **Angle** option of the **CHAMFER** command to create the "After" object.
○ Save the drawing as EX11-1.

## Setting the Chamfer Method

When you set chamfer distances or a distance and an angle, AutoCAD maintains the setting until you change it. You can set the values for each method without affecting the other. Use the **Method** option if you want to toggle between drawing chamfers by **Distance** and by **Angle**. The default option contains the values you previously set:

Command: **CHA** *or* **CHAMFER**⏎
(TRIM mode) Current chamfer Length = <current>, Angle = <current>
Select first line or [Polyline/Distance/Angle/Trim/Method/mUltiple]: **M**⏎
Enter trim method [Distance/Angle] <Angle>: **D**⏎
Select first line or [Polyline/Distance/Angle/Trim/Method/mUltiple]: *(pick the first line)*
Select second line: *(pick the second line)*
Command:

---

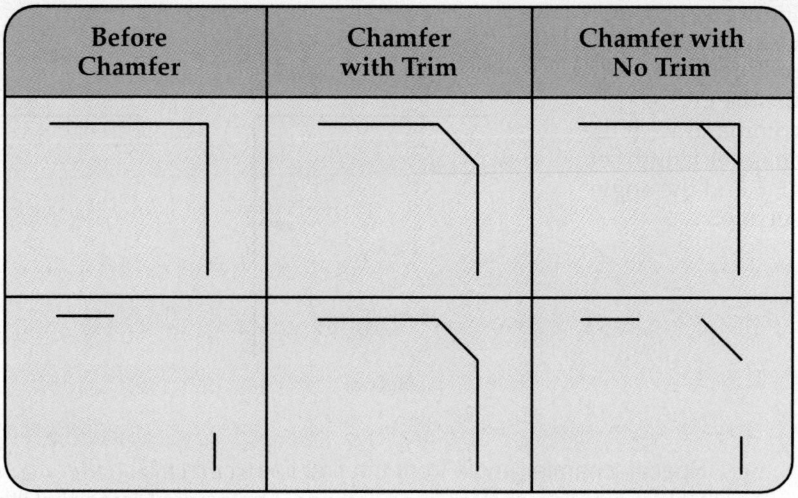

**Figure 11-5.**
Comparison of **Trim** and **No trim** options with the **CHAMFER** command.

| Before Chamfer | Chamfer with Trim | Chamfer with No Trim |
|---|---|---|
| | | |
| | | |

## Setting the Chamfer Trim Mode

You can have the selected lines automatically trimmed with the chamfer, or you can have the selected lines remain in the drawing after the chamfer, as shown in **Figure 11-5.** To set this, enter the **Trim** option, and then select either T for **Trim** or N for **No trim**:

> Command: **CHA** *or* **CHAMFER.**↵
> (TRIM mode) Current chamfer Dist1 = *<current>*, Dist2 = *<current>*
> Select first line or [Polyline/Distance/Angle/Trim/Method/mUltiple]: **T.**↵
> Enter Trim mode option [Trim/No trim] <Trim>: **N.**↵
> Select first line or [Polyline/Distance/Angle/Trim/Method/mUltiple]: *(pick the first line)*
> Select second line: *(pick the second line)*
> Command:

You can also use the **TRIMMODE** system variable to set **Trim** or **No trim** by typing TRIMMODE at the Command: prompt. A 1 setting trims the lines before chamfering, while a 0 setting does not trim the lines.

## Making Multiple Chamfers

To make several chamfers on the same object, select the **Multiple** option of the **CHAMFER** command by typing U at the Select first line or [Polyline/Distance/Angle/Trim/Method/mUltiple]: prompt. The prompt for a first line repeats. When you have made all the chamfers needed, press [Enter].

---

NOTE

The **TRIMMODE** system variable affects both the **FILLET** and **CHAMFER** commands. If the **Polyline** option is used with the **No trim** option active, any chamfer lines created are not part of the polyline.

---

AutoCAD and its Applications—Basics

When the **CHAMFER** or **FILLET** command is set to **Trim**, lines not connecting at a corner are automatically extended, and the chamfer or fillet is applied. When the **No trim** option is used, however, these lines are not extended, but the chamfer or fillet is drawn anyway. If you have lines drawn short of a corner and you want them to connect to the chamfer or fillet, you need to extend them when you draw with the **No trim** option active.

---

## Exercise 11-2

○ Begin a new drawing or use one of your templates.
○ Draw the "Before" objects shown in **Figure 11-5**, and then use the Trim mode as needed to create the "After" objects.
○ Save the drawing as EX11-2.

---

## Drawing Rounded Corners

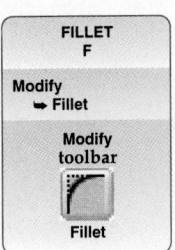

FILLET
F

Modify
➡ Fillet

Modify
toolbar

Fillet

In mechanical drafting, an inside rounded corner is called a *fillet.* An outside rounded corner is called a *round.* AutoCAD refers to all rounded corners as *fillets.*

Fillets were introduced in Chapter 5 when drawing filleted corners on rectangles with the **RECTANG** command. The **FILLET** command draws a rounded corner between intersecting and nonintersecting lines, circles, and arcs. To access the **FILLET** command, pick the **Fillet** button on the **Modify** toolbar, select **Fillet** from the **Modify** pull-down menu, or type F or FILLET at the Command: prompt.

Fillets are sized by radius. The default radius is 0.5. A new radius is specified first by typing R on the prompt line for the **Radius** option, as follows. See **Figure 11-6**.

Command: **F** *or* **FILLET**↵
Current settings: Mode = TRIM, Radius = *<current>*
Select first object or [Polyline/Radius/Trim/mUltiple]: **R**↵
Specify fillet radius *<current>*: *(type the fillet radius—.25, for example—and press* [Enter]; *you can also press* [Enter] *to accept the current value)*
Select first object or [Polyline/Radius/Trim/mUltiple]: *(pick the first object to be filleted)*
Select second object: *(pick the other object to be filleted)*
Command:

---

Figure 11-6.
Using the **FILLET** command.

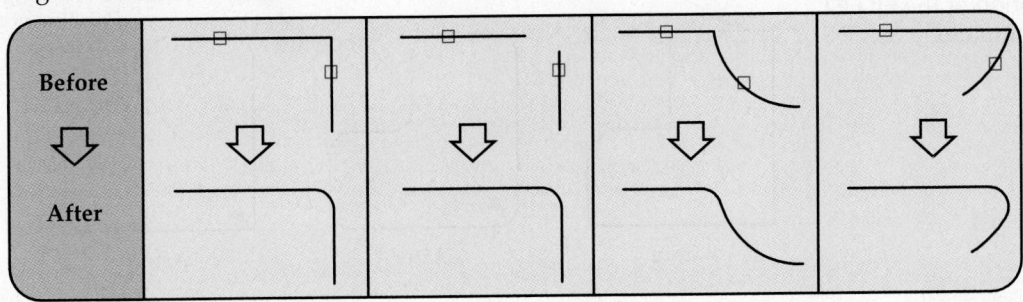

The value of the radius for fillets is stored in the **FILLETRAD** system variable. This variable is changed when you enter a new value using the **Radius** option of the **FILLET** command. You can also change **FILLETRAD** at the Command: prompt.

## Exercise 11-3

○ Begin a new drawing or use one of your templates.
○ Draw the "Before" objects shown in **Figure 11-6.** Use the **FILLET** command as needed to create the "After" objects.
○ Save the drawing as EX11-3.

## Rounding the Corners of a Polyline

Fillets can be drawn at all corners of a closed polyline by selecting the **Polyline** option. The current fillet radius is used with this option. Polylines are fully explained in Chapter 14 and Chapter 15. The command sequence used to draw the objects in **Figure 11-7** is as follows:

```
Command: F or FILLET.↓
Current settings: Mode = TRIM, Radius = 0.2500
Select first object or [Polyline/Radius/Trim/mUltiple]: P.↓
Select 2D polyline: (pick the polyline)
n lines were filleted
Command:
```

AutoCAD tells you how many lines were filleted. The Command: prompt returns. If the polyline was drawn without using the **Close** option, the beginning corner is not filleted.

## Setting the Fillet Trim Mode

The **TRIMMODE** system variable and the **Trim** option control whether or not the **FILLET** command trims object segments extending beyond the fillet radius point. When the Trim mode is active, objects are trimmed. When the Trim mode is inactive, the filleted objects are not changed after the fillet is inserted, as shown in **Figure 11-8.** Use the **Trim** option like this:

```
Command: F or FILLET.↓
Current settings: Mode = TRIM, Radius = 0.2500
Select first object or [Polyline/Radius/Trim/mUltiple]: T.↓
Enter Trim mode option [Trim/No trim] <Trim>: N.↓
```

**Figure 11-7.**
Using the **Polyline** option of the **FILLET** command.

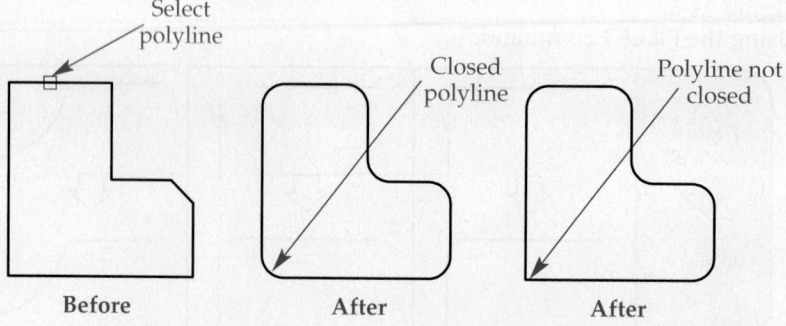

**Figure 11-8.**
Using the **Trim** option of the **FILLET** command.

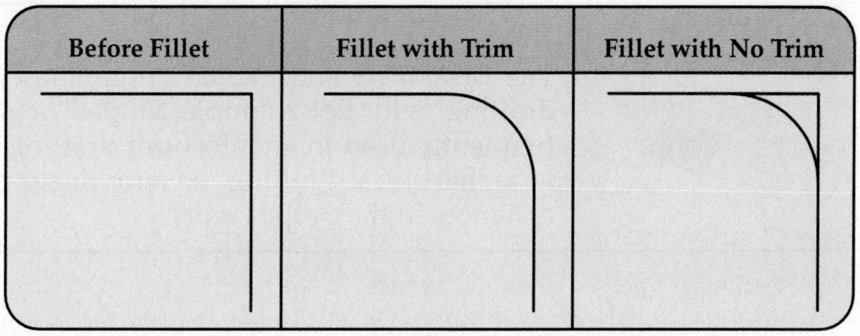

| Before Fillet | Fillet with Trim | Fillet with No Trim |
|---|---|---|

Select first object or [Polyline/Radius/Trim/mUltiple]: *(pick the first object)*
Select second object: *(pick the second object)*
Command:

If the lines to be filleted do not connect at the corner, they are automatically extended when the Trim mode is on. They are not extended, however, when using the **No trim** option. If you do not want a separation between the line and the filleted corner, extend the lines to the corner before filleting.

## Filleting Parallel Lines

You can also draw a fillet between parallel lines. When parallel lines are selected, a radius is placed between the two lines. In Trim mode, a longer line is trimmed to match the length of a shorter line. The radius of a fillet between parallel lines is always half of the distance between the two lines, regardless of the radius setting for the **FILLET** command.

## Making Multiple Fillets

To make several fillets on the same object, select the **Multiple** option of the **FILLET** command by typing U at the Select first object or [Polyline/Radius/Trim/mUltiple]: prompt. The prompt for a first object repeats. When you have made all the fillets needed, press [Enter].

---

**PROFESSIONAL TIP**  Using the **FILLET** or **CHAMFER** command with a 0 fillet radius or 0 chamfer distances is a quick and convenient way to create square corners.

---

### Exercise 11-4

○ Begin a new drawing or use one of your templates.
○ Draw a corner similar to the one on the left in **Figure 11-8.** Make two copies of the object.
○ Use the **Trim** and **No trim** options to create the objects shown on the right in **Figure 11-8.**
○ Draw two parallel lines with different lengths. Fillet one end of the lines using the **Trim** option. Use the **No trim** option on the other end.
○ Save the drawing as EX11-4.

---

## Removing a Section from an Object

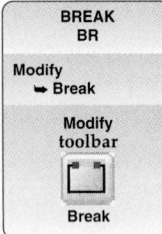

BREAK
BR

Modify
↦ Break

Modify
toolbar

Break

The **BREAK** command is used to remove a portion of a line, circle, arc, trace, or polyline. This command can also be used to divide a single object into two objects. Picking the **Break** button in the **Modify** toolbar, picking **Break** in the **Modify** pull-down menu, or typing BR or BREAK at the Command: prompt accesses the **BREAK** command. When using the **BREAK** command, the following prompts appear:

> Command: **BR** *or* **BREAK**↵
> Select object: *(pick the object)*
> Specify second break point or [First point]: *(pick second break point or type F to select first break point)*

The **BREAK** command requires you to select the object to be broken, the first break point, and the second break point. When you select the object, the point you pick is also used as the first break point by default. If you wish to select a different first break point, type F at the Specify second break point or [First point]: prompt to select the **First point** option. After both break points are specified, the part of the object between the two points is deleted. See **Figure 11-9**.

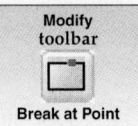

Modify
toolbar

Break at Point

The **BREAK** command can also be used to split an object in two without removing a portion. Selecting the same point for both the first and second break points does this. This can be accomplished by entering @ at the Specify second break point or [First point]: prompt. The @ symbol repeats the coordinates of the previously selected point. Using the **BREAK** command without removing a portion of the object is shown in **Figure 11-10**.

When breaking arcs or circles, always work in a counterclockwise direction. Otherwise, you may break the portion of the arc or circle you want to keep. If you want to break off the end of a line or arc, pick the first point on the object. Pick the second point slightly beyond the end to be cut off. See **Figure 11-11**. When you pick a second point not on the object, AutoCAD selects the point on the object nearest the point you picked.

---

**Figure 11-9.**
Using the **BREAK** command to break an object. The first pick can be used to select both the object and the first break point.

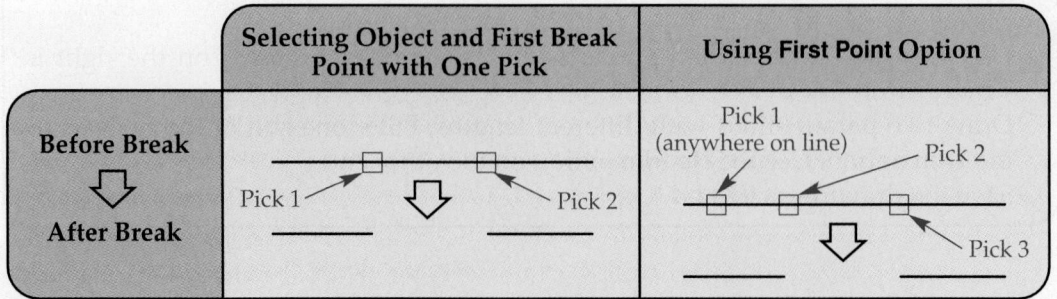

**Figure 11-10.**
Using the **BREAK** command to break an object at a single point, without removing any of the object. Select the same point as the first and second break points.

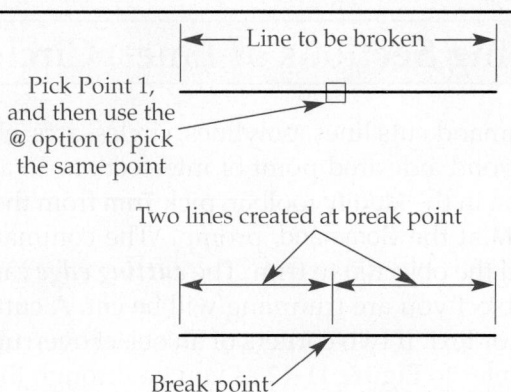

Line to be broken

Pick Point 1, and then use the @ option to pick the same point

Two lines created at break point

Break point

**Figure 11-11.**
Using the **BREAK** command on circles and arcs.

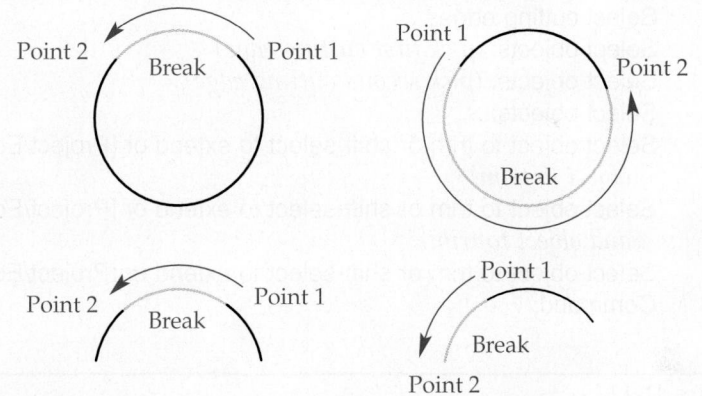

Point 2   Break   Point 1

Point 1   Point 2   Break

Point 2   Break   Point 1

Point 1   Break   Point 2

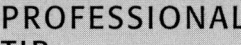

**PROFESSIONAL TIP**

You may want to turn running object snaps off if they conflict with the points you are trying to pick when using the **BREAK** command. Picking the **OSNAP** button on the status bar is an easy way to temporarily override the running object snaps.

**Exercise 11-5**

○ Begin a new drawing or use one of your templates.
○ Draw two horizontal lines and use the **BREAK** command to break each line at two points, similar to **Figure 11-9.**
○ Draw two horizontal lines and use the **BREAK** command to break each line at one point, similar to **Figure 11-10.**
○ Draw two circles and two arcs and break each similar to **Figure 11-11.**
○ Save the drawing as EX11-5.

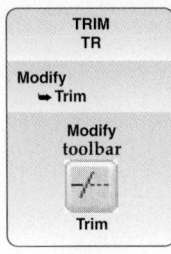

TRIM
TR

Modify
➥ Trim

Modify
toolbar

Trim

The **TRIM** command cuts lines, polylines, circles, arcs, ellipses, splines, xlines, and rays extending beyond a desired point of intersection. To access the **TRIM** command, pick the **Trim** button in the **Modify** toolbar, pick **Trim** from the **Modify** pull-down menu, or type TR or TRIM at the Command: prompt. The command requires you to pick a "cutting edge" and the object(s) to trim. The *cutting edge* can be an object defining the point where the object you are trimming will be cut. A cutting edge can be an object such as a line, arc, or text. If two corners of an object overrun, select two cutting edges and two objects. Refer to **Figure 11-12** as you go through the following sequence:

```
Command: TR or TRIM↵
Current settings: Projection=UCS, Edge=None
Select cutting edges …
Select objects: (pick first cutting edge)
Select objects: (pick second cutting edge)
Select objects: ↵
Select object to trim or shift-select to extend or [Project/Edge/Undo]: (pick the first
    object to trim)
Select object to trim or shift-select to extend or [Project/Edge/Undo]: (pick the sec-
    ond object to trim)
Select object to trim or shift-select to extend or [Project/Edge/Undo]: ↵
Command:
```

**Figure 11-12.**
Using the **TRIM** command. Note the cutting edges.

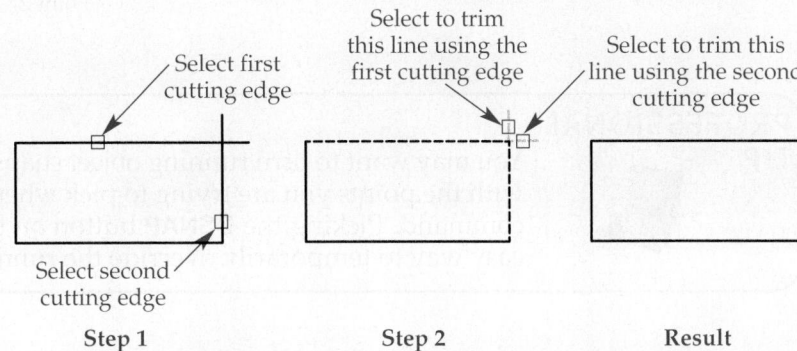

NOTE

You can access the **EXTEND** command while using the **TRIM** command. After selecting the cutting edge, hold the [Shift] key while selecting an object to extend the object to the cutting edge. The **EXTEND** command is discussed in the following section.

## Trimming without Selecting a Cutting Edge

You can quickly trim objects back to the nearest intersection by hitting the [Enter] key at the first Select objects: prompt, instead of picking a cutting edge. Picking an object that intersects with another object trims the selected object to the first object. If there are multiple objects interseting the object to be trimmed, it is trimmed back to the first intersection. After trimming an object, you can select other objects to be trimmed without having to restart the command. When you are done trimming, press the [Enter] key to exit the command. The command sequence for this **TRIM** method is as follows:

> Command: **TR** *or* **TRIM**↵
> Current settings: Projection=UCS, Edge=None
> Select cutting edges ...
> Select objects: ↵
> Select object to trim or shift-select to extend or [Project/Edge/Undo]: *(pick the object to trim)*
> Select object to trim or shift-select to extend or [Project/Edge/Undo]: *(pick the object to trim)*
> Select object to trim or shift-select to extend or [Project/Edge/Undo]: ↵
> Command:

## Trimming to an Implied Intersection

An *implied intersection* is the point where two or more objects would meet if they were extended. Trimming to an implied intersection is possible using the **Edge** option of the **TRIM** command. When you enter the **Edge** option, the choices are **Extend** and **No extend**. When **Extend** is active, AutoCAD checks to see if the cutting edge object will extend to intersect the object to be trimmed. If so, the implied intersection point can be used to trim the object. This does not change the cutting edge object at all. The command sequence for the **TRIM** operation shown in **Figure 11-13** is as follows:

> Command: **TR** *or* **TRIM**↵
> Current settings: Projection=UCS, Edge=None
> Select cutting edges ...
> Select objects: *(pick the cutting edge)*
> Select objects: ↵
> Select object to trim or shift-select to extend or [Project/Edge/Undo]: **E**↵
> Enter an implied edge extension mode [Extend/No extend] <No extend>: **E**↵
> Select object to trim or shift-select to extend or [Project/Edge/Undo]: *(pick the object to trim)*
> Select object to trim or shift-select to extend or [Project/Edge/Undo]: ↵
> Command:

The **Edge** option can also be set using the **EDGEMODE** system variable. **Extend** is active when the **EDGEMODE** is 1. With this setting, the cutting edge object is checked to see if it will extend to intersect the object to be trimmed. The **No extend** option is set when **EDGEMODE** is set to 0. Set the **EDGEMODE** system variable by typing EDGEMODE at the Command: prompt and entering the new value.

---

**Figure 11-13.**
Trimming to an implied intersection.

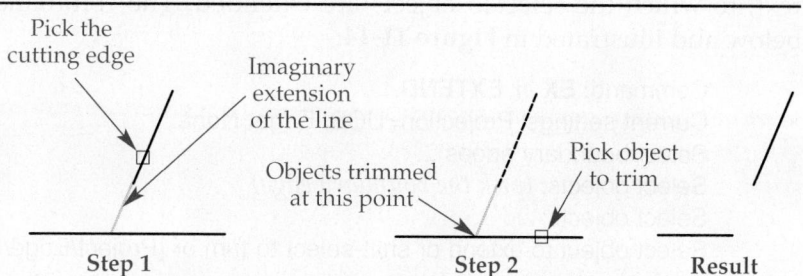

Pick the cutting edge

Imaginary extension of the line

Objects trimmed at this point

Pick object to trim

Step 1    Step 2    Result

## Using the Undo Option

The **TRIM** command has an **Undo** option that allows you to cancel the previous trimming without leaving the command. This is useful when the result of a trim is not what you expected. To undo the previous trim, simply type U immediately after performing an unwanted trim. The trimmed portion returns, and you can continue trimming other objects:

Command: **TR** or **TRIM**↵
Current settings: Projection=UCS, Edge=Extend
Select boundary edges ...
Select objects: *(pick the first cutting edge)*
Select objects: ↵
Select object to trim or shift-select to extend or [Project/Edge/Undo]: *(pick the object to trim)*
Select object to trim or shift-select to extend or [Project/Edge/Undo]: **U**↵
Command has been completely undone.
Select object to trim or shift-select to extend or [Project/Edge/Undo]: *(pick the object to trim)*
Select object to trim or shift-select to extend or [Project/Edge/Undo]: ↵
Command:

## Introduction to the Project Mode

In a 3D drawing environment, some lines may appear to intersect, but not actually intersect. In such a case, using the **Project** option of the **TRIM** command can allow trimming operations. The **PROJMODE** system variable also controls this option. Using AutoCAD for 3D drawing is explained in *AutoCAD and its Applications—Advanced*.

## Extending Lines

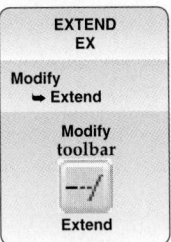

EXTEND
EX

Modify
↳ Extend

Modify
toolbar

Extend

The **EXTEND** command is the opposite of the **TRIM** command. It is used to lengthen lines, elliptical arcs, rays, open polylines, and arcs to meet other objects. **EXTEND** does not work on closed polylines because an unconnected endpoint does not exist.

To use the **EXTEND** command, pick the **Extend** button in the **Modify** toolbar, select **Extend** from the **Modify** pull-down menu, or type EX or EXTEND at the Command: prompt. The command format is similar to **TRIM**. You are asked to select boundary edges, as opposed to cutting edges. *Boundary edges* are objects, such as lines, arcs, or text, to which the selected objects are extended. The command sequence is shown below and illustrated in **Figure 11-14**:

Command: **EX** or **EXTEND**↵
Current settings: Projection=UCS, Edge=None
Select boundary edges ...
Select objects: *(pick the boundary edge)*
Select objects: ↵
Select object to extend or shift-select to trim or [Project/Edge/Undo]: *(pick the object to extend)*
Select object to extend or shift-select to trim or [Project/Edge/Undo]: ↵
Command:

If there is nothing for the selected line to meet, AutoCAD gives the message Object does not intersect an edge.

Figure 11-14.
Using the **EXTEND**
command. Note the
boundary edges.

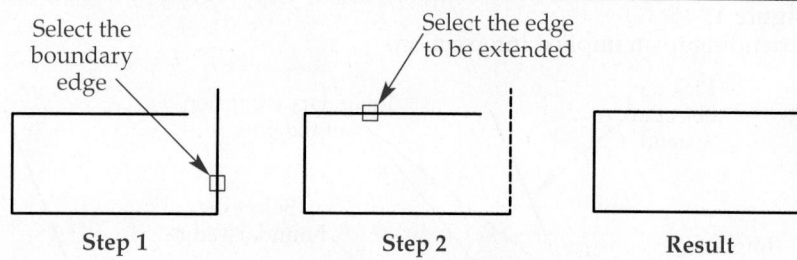

Select the
boundary
edge

Select the edge
to be extended

Step 1                    Step 2                    Result

NOTE    You can access the **TRIM** command while using the **EXTEND**
command. After selecting the boundary edge, hold the [Shift]
key while selecting an object to trim the object at the boundary edge.

## Extending without Selecting a Boundary Edge

You can quickly extend objects to the nearest object by hitting the [Enter] key at
the first Select objects: prompt, instead of picking a boundary edge. Using this
method, the selected object automatically extends it to the nearest object in its path. If
there is no object to extend to, a message on the command line reads Object does not
intersect an edge. After extending an object, you can select other objects to be extended
or press the [Enter] key to exit the command. The command sequence for this **EXTEND**
method is as follows:

Command: **EX** *or* **EXTEND**↵
Current settings: Projection=UCS, Edge=None
Select boundary edges ...
Select objects: ↵
Select object to extend or shift-select to trim or [Project/Edge/Undo]: *(pick the object
    to extend)*
Select object to extend or shift-select to trim or [Project/Edge/Undo]: ↵
Command:

## Extending to an Implied Intersection

You can extend an object to an implied intersection using the **Edge** option in the
**EXTEND** command. When you enter the **Edge** option, the choices are **Extend** and **No
extend**, similar to the choices for the **TRIM** command. When **Extend** is active, the
boundary edge object is checked to see if it intersects an object when it is extended. If
so, the implied intersection point can be used as the boundary for the object to be
extended, as shown in **Figure 11-15.** This does not change the boundary edge object at all.

Command: **EX** *or* **EXTEND**↵
Current settings: Projection=UCS, Edge=None
Select boundary edges ...
Select objects: *(pick the boundary edge)*
Select objects: ↵
Select object to extend or shift-select to trim or [Project/Edge/Undo]: **E**↵
Enter an implied edge extension mode [Extend/No extend] <No extend>: **E**↵
Select object to extend or shift-select to trim or [Project/Edge/Undo]: *(pick the object
    to extend)*
Select object to extend or shift-select to trim or [Project/Edge/Undo]: ↵
Command:

**Figure 11-15.**
Extending to an implied intersection.

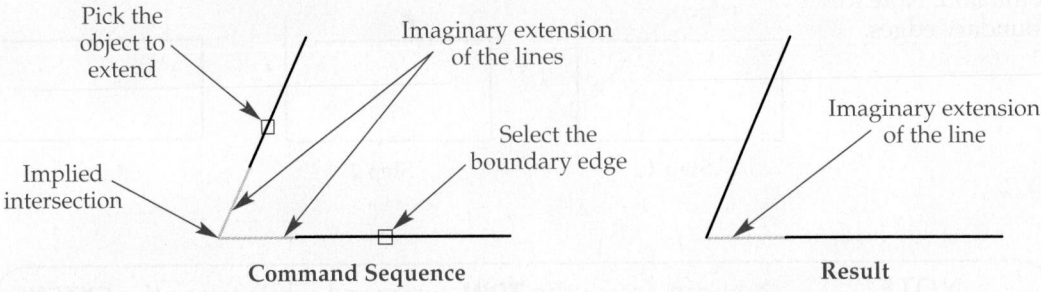

The **Edge** option can also be set using the **EDGEMODE** system variable, as previously discussed with the **TRIM** command.

## Using the Undo Option

The **Undo** option in the **EXTEND** command can be used to reverse the previous operation without leaving the **EXTEND** command. The command sequence is the same as discussed for the **TRIM** command.

## The Project Mode of the EXTEND Command

In a 3D drawing, some lines may appear to intersect in a given view, but not actually intersect. In such a case, you can use the **Project** option or the **PROJMODE** system variable as explained for the **TRIM** command.

## Changing Lines and Circles

The endpoint location of a line or the radius of a circle can be altered using the **CHANGE** command. To access the **CHANGE** command, type -CH or CHANGE at the Command: prompt. The keyboard shortcut is a hyphen (-) typed before CH. You are then prompted to select the objects to change. After the objects are selected, AutoCAD prompts for the change point. The *change point* is the new endpoint or radius location. The **CHANGE** command also has a **Properties** option. This option can be used to change several properties of the selected object.

**PROFESSIONAL TIP**

The **CHANGE** command is normally an inefficient command to use. It is easier to relocate line endpoints using grip editing (discussed in Chapter 12). You can modify object properties more easily using the **Properties** window or the **Properties** toolbar.

Remove to A, B

Trim to corner

Remove to angle

A    B

Remove to C, D

C

Break

D

E    F

Extend to implied corner

Remove to E, F

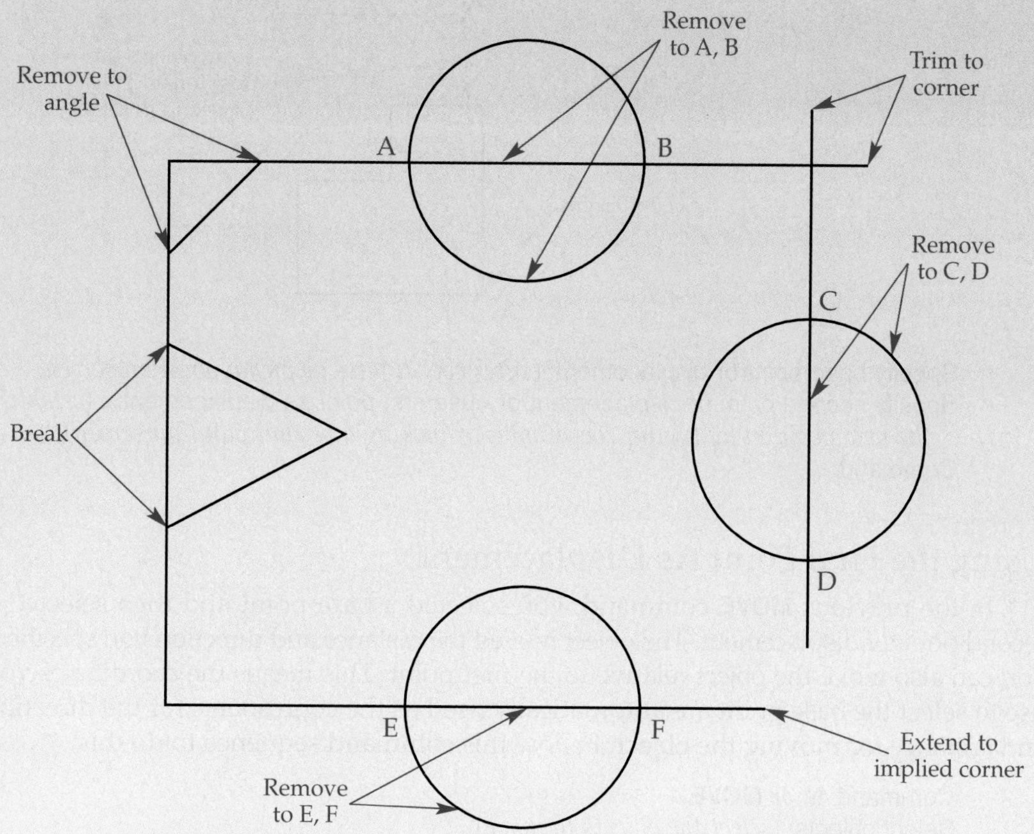

# Moving an Object

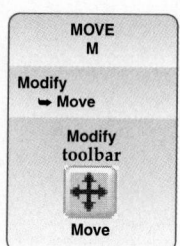

MOVE
M

Modify
➥ Move

Modify
toolbar

Move

In many situations, you may find that the location of a view or feature is not where you want it. This problem is easy to fix using the **MOVE** command. Picking the **Move** button in the **Modify** toolbar, picking **Move** from the **Modify** pull-down menu, or typing M or MOVE at the Command: prompt accesses the **MOVE** command.

After the **MOVE** command is accessed, AutoCAD asks you to select the objects to be moved. Use any of the selection set options to select the objects. Once the items are selected, the next prompt requests the base point or displacement. The *base point* provides a reference point. Most drafters select a point on an object, the corner of a view, or the center of a circle. The next prompt asks for the second point of displacement. This is the new position. All selected entities are moved the distance from the base point to the displacement point.

The following **MOVE** operation relates to the object shown in **Figure 11-16**. As the base point is picked, the object is automatically dragged into position. This is the command sequence:

```
Command: M or MOVE↵
Select objects: (select the object or objects to be moved)
Select objects: ↵
```

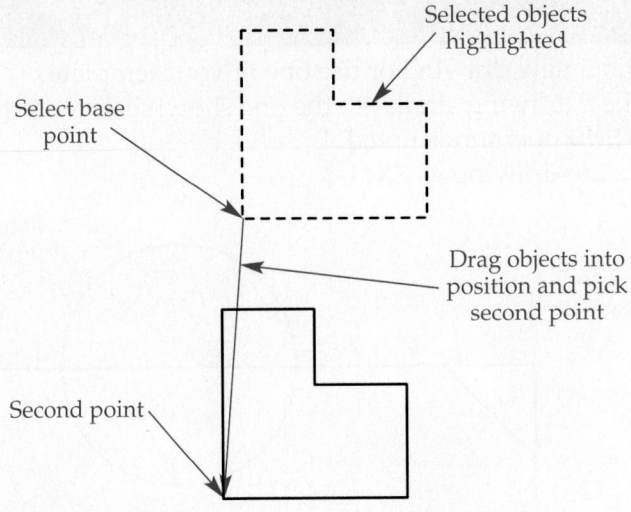

**Figure 11-16.**
Using the **MOVE** command. When you select the object to be moved, it becomes highlighted.

Selected objects highlighted

Select base point

Drag objects into position and pick second point

Second point

Specify base point or displacement: *(enter coordinates or pick a point on screen)*
Specify second point of displacement or <use first point as displacement>: *(establish the new position by typing coordinates or picking a second point on screen)*
Command:

## Using the First Point As Displacement

In the previous **MOVE** command, you selected a base point and then selected a second point of displacement. The object moved the distance and direction you specified. You can also move the object relative to the first point. This means the coordinates you use to select the base point are automatically used as the coordinates for the direction and distance for moving the object. Follow this command sequence to do this:

Command: **M** *or* **MOVE**↵
Select objects: *(select the objects to move)*
Select objects: ↵
Specify base point or displacement: **2,4**↵
Specify second point of displacement or <use first point as displacement>: ↵ *(the object moves a distance and direction equal to the coordinates specified for the base point, which is 2 units in the X direction and 4 units in the Y direction, for this example)*
Command:

**PROFESSIONAL TIP**

Always use object snap modes to your best advantage with editing commands. For example, suppose you want to move an object to the center point of a circle. Use the **Center** object snap mode to select the center of the circle as the base point.

AutoCAD and its Applications—Basics

# Copying Objects

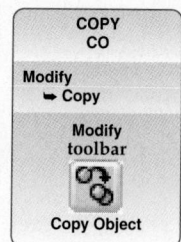

COPY
CO

Modify
➡ Copy

Modify
toolbar

Copy Object

The **COPY** command is used to make a copy of an existing object or objects. To access the **COPY** command, pick the **Copy** button in the **Modify** toolbar, select **Copy** from the **Modify** pull-down menu, or type CO or COPY at the Command: prompt. The command prompts are the same as the **MOVE** command. When a second point of displacement is picked, however, the original object remains, and a copy is drawn. The following command sequence is illustrated in **Figure 11-17:**

> Command: **CO** or **COPY**↵
> Select objects: (select the objects to be copied)
> Select objects: ↵
> Specify base point or displacement, or [Multiple]: (select base point or enter displacement)
> Specify second point of displacement or <use first point as displacement>: (pick second point or press [Enter] if displacement was specified)
> Command:

The **COPY** command is similar to the **MOVE** command. You can either specify a base point and a second point of displacement or simply specify a displacement. If you specify a displacement, a copy of the object is made at the specified location.

## Making Multiple Copies

To make several copies of the same object, select the **Multiple** option of the **COPY** command by typing M at the Specify base point or displacement, or [Multiple]: prompt. The prompt for a second point of displacement repeats. When you have made all the copies needed, press [Enter]. The results are shown in **Figure 11-18.**

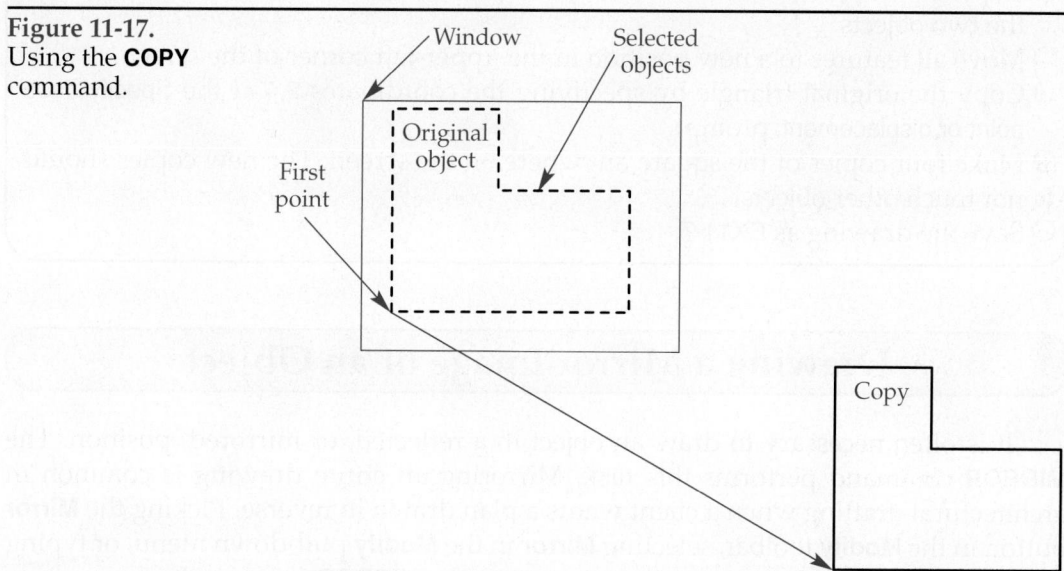

Figure 11-17.
Using the **COPY**
command.

Window

Selected
objects

Original
object

First
point

Copy

**Figure 11-18.**
Using the **Multiple**
option of the **COPY**
command.

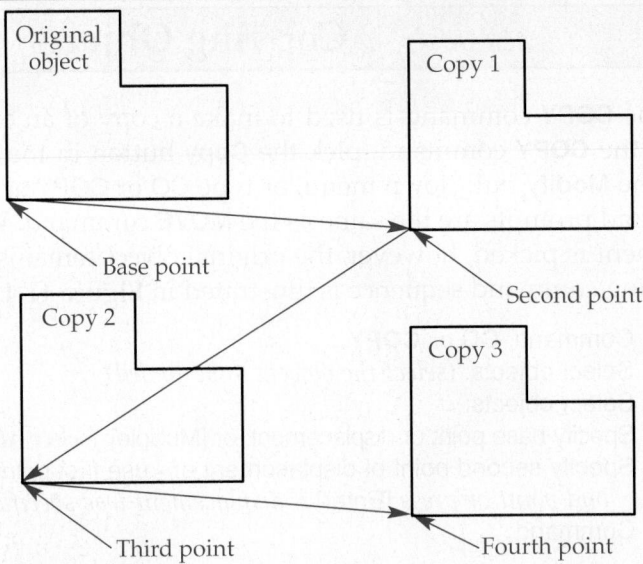

## Drawing a Mirror Image of an Object

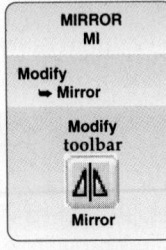

MIRROR
MI

Modify
➥ Mirror

Modify
toolbar

Mirror

It is often necessary to draw an object in a reflected, or mirrored, position. The **MIRROR** command performs this task. Mirroring an entire drawing is common in architectural drafting when a client wants a plan drawn in reverse. Picking the **Mirror** button in the **Modify** toolbar, selecting **Mirror** in the **Modify** pull-down menu, or typing MI or MIRROR at the Command: prompt accesses the **MIRROR** command.

### Selecting the Mirror Line

When you enter the **MIRROR** command, you select the objects to mirror and then select a mirror line. The *mirror line* is the hinge about which objects are reflected. The objects and any space between the objects and the mirror line are reflected. See **Figure 11-19.**

**Figure 11-19.**
When an object is reflected about a mirror line, the space between the object and the mirror line is also mirrored.

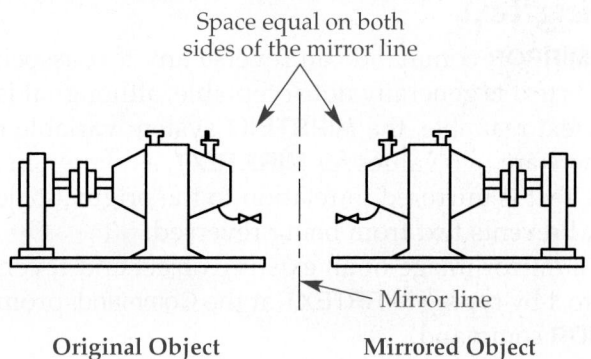

Space equal on both sides of the mirror line

Mirror line

Original Object          Mirrored Object

The mirror line can be placed at any angle. Once you pick the first endpoint, a mirrored image appears and moves with the cursor. Once you select the second mirror line endpoint, you have the option to delete the original objects. Refer to **Figure 11-20** and the following command sequence:

Command: **MI** *or* **MIRROR**↵
Select objects: *(select objects to be mirrored)*
Select objects: ↵
Specify first point of mirror line: *(pick the first point on the mirror line)*
Specify second point of mirror line: *(pick the second point on the mirror line)*
Delete source objects? [Yes/No] <N>: *(type Y and press [Enter] to delete the original objects; you can also press [Enter] to accept the default and keep the original objects)*
Command:

**Figure 11-20.**
Using the **MIRROR** command. You have the option to delete the old objects.

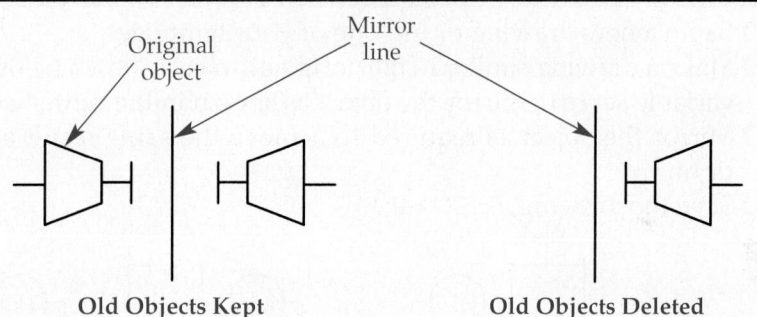

Original object          Mirror line

Old Objects Kept          Old Objects Deleted

## Exercise 11-8

○ Begin a new drawing or use one of your templates.
○ Draw the half object shown below. Complete the entire object using the **MIRROR** command. Do not dimension.
○ Save the drawing as EX11-8.

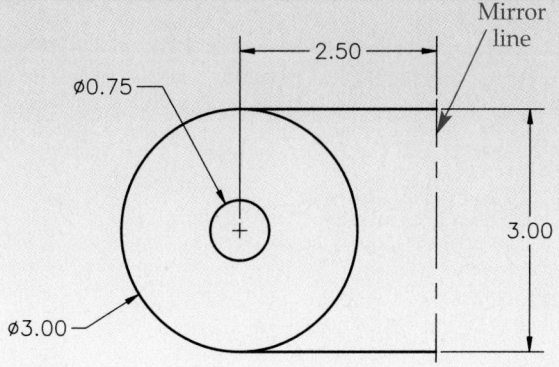

Mirror line

2.50

⌀0.75

3.00

⌀3.00

## Mirroring Text

The **MIRROR** command can reverse any text associated with the selected object. Backwards text is generally not acceptable, although it is used for reverse imaging. To keep the text readable, the **MIRRTEXT** system variable must be 0. This is the default value. There are two values for **MIRRTEXT**, as shown in **Figure 11-21:**

- **1.** Text is mirrored in relation to the original object. This is the default value.
- **0.** Prevents text from being reversed.

To draw a mirror image of an existing object and reverse the text, set the **MIRRTEXT** variable to 1 by typing MIRRTEXT at the Command: prompt and entering 1. Proceed to the **MIRROR** command.

**Figure 11-21.**
The **MIRRTEXT** system variable options.

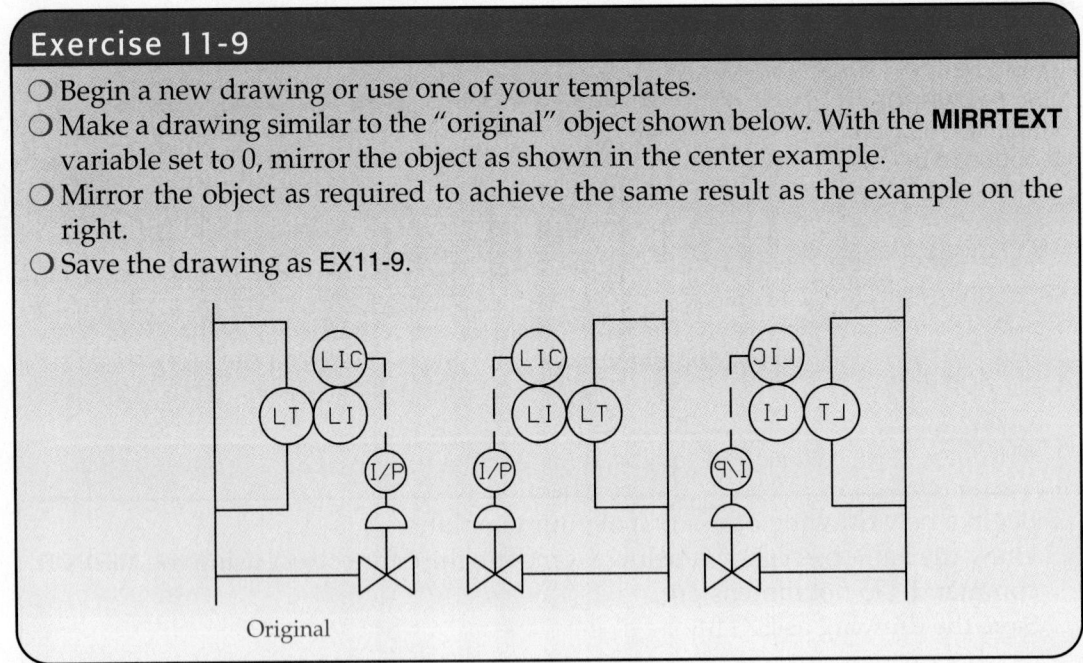

Mirror line

MIRRTEXT(1)     (1)TXƎTᴚᴚIM

MIRRTEXT(0)     MIRRTEXT(0)

### Exercise 11-9

○ Begin a new drawing or use one of your templates.
○ Make a drawing similar to the "original" object shown below. With the **MIRRTEXT** variable set to 0, mirror the object as shown in the center example.
○ Mirror the object as required to achieve the same result as the example on the right.
○ Save the drawing as **EX11-9.**

Original

# Rotating Existing Objects

Design changes often require an object, feature, or view to be rotated. For example, the office furniture layout may have to be moved, copied, or rotated for an interior design. AutoCAD allows you to easily revise the layout to obtain the final design.

To rotate selected objects, pick the **Rotate** button on the **Modify** toolbar, pick **Rotate** from the **Modify** pull-down menu, or type RO or ROTATE at the Command: prompt. Objects can be selected using any of the selection set options. Once the objects are selected, pick a base point and enter a rotation angle. A negative rotation angle revolves the object clockwise. A positive rotation angle revolves the object counterclockwise. See **Figure 11-22**. The **ROTATE** command sequence appears as follows:

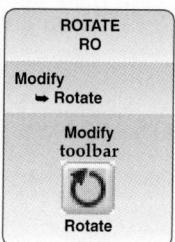

> Command: **RO** *or* **ROTATE**↵
> Current positive angle in UCS: ANGDIR=counterclockwise  ANGBASE=0
> Select objects: *(select the objects)*
> Select objects: ↵
> Specify base point: *(pick the base point or enter coordinates; press [Enter])*
> Specify rotation angle or [Reference]: *(type a positive or negative rotation angle and press [Enter]; you can also pick a point on screen)*
> Command:

If an object is already rotated and you want a different angle, you can change the angle in two ways. Both ways involve using the **Reference** option after selecting the object for rotation. The first way is to specify the existing angle and then the new angle. See **Figure 11-23A**:

> Specify rotation angle or [Reference]: **R**↵
> Specify the reference angle <0>: **135**↵
> Specify the new angle: **180**↵

The other method is to pick a reference line on the object and rotate the object in relationship to the reference line. See **Figure 11-23B**:

> Specify rotation angle or [Reference]: **R**↵
> Specify the reference angle <0>: *(pick an endpoint of a reference line that forms the existing angle)*
> Specify second point: *(pick the other point of the reference line that forms the existing angle)*
> Specify the new angle: *(specify a new angle, such as 180, and press [Enter])*

---

**Figure 11-22.**
Rotation angles.

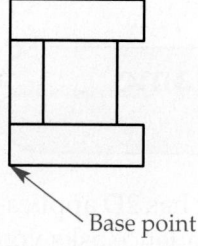

Base point

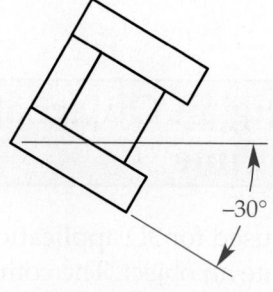

−30°

**−30° Rotation**

30°

**30° Rotation**

---

Figure 11-23.
Using the **Reference**
option of the
**ROTATE** command.
A—Entering
reference angles.
B—Selecting points
on a reference line.

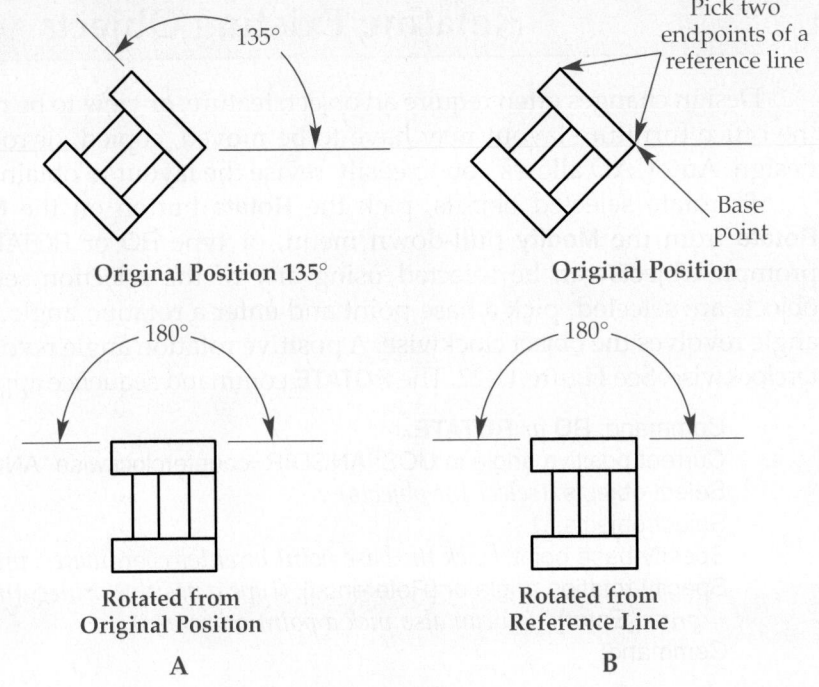

Original Position 135°

Pick two
endpoints of a
reference line

Original Position

Base
point

180°

180°

Rotated from
Original Position

**A**

Rotated from
Reference Line

**B**

**PROFESSIONAL TIP**

Always use the object snap mode to your best advantage
when editing. For example, suppose you want to rotate an
object. It may be difficult to find an exact corner without
using object snap mode. To select the base point, use the
**Endpoint** or **Intersection** object snap mode.

## Exercise 11-10

○ Begin a new drawing or use one of your templates.
○ Draw a 2.25 unit square.
○ Rotate the square to 75°. Using the **Reference** option, rotate the square another
45°. Finally, rotate the square back to 0°.
○ Save the drawing as EX11-10.

## Moving and Rotating an Object at the Same Time

The **ALIGN** command is primarily used for 3D applications, but it has 2D applications when you want to move and rotate an object. The command sequence asks you
to select objects and then asks for three source points and three destination points. For
2D applications, you only need two source points and two destination points. Press
[Enter] when the prompt requests the third source and destination points. The *source
points* define a line related to the object's original position. The *destination points*
define the location of this line relative to the object's new location.

**Figure 11-24.**
Using the **ALIGN** command to move and rotate a kitchen cabinet layout against a wall.

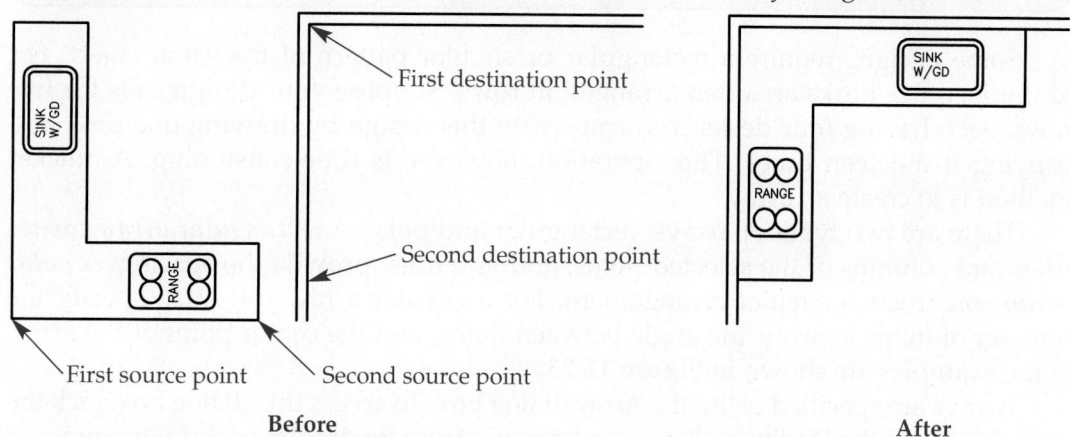

First destination point

Second destination point

First source point    Second source point

**Before**    **After**

To access the **ALIGN** command, pick **Align** in the **3D Operation** cascading menu of the **Modify** pull-down menu or type AL or ALIGN at the Command: prompt. The command sequence is as follows. Refer to **Figure 11-24:**

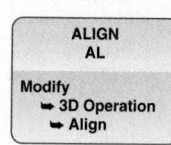

ALIGN
AL

Modify
➥ 3D Operation
➥ Align

> Command: **AL** *or* **ALIGN.**↵
> Select objects: *(select the objects)*
> Select objects: ↵
> Specify first source point: *(pick the first source point)*
> Specify first destination point: *(pick the first destination point)*
> Specify second source point: *(pick the second source point)*
> Specify second destination point: *(pick the second destination point)*
> Specify third source point or <continue>: ↵
> Scale objects based on alignment points? [Yes/No] <N>: *(enter Y to scale the object if the distance between the source points is different than the distance between the destination points)*
> Command:

---

## Exercise 11-11

○ Begin a new drawing or use one of your templates.
○ Make a drawing similar to the one shown below. Do not add text or leaders.
○ Use the **ALIGN** command to move and rotate Part A into position with Part B. S1 is the first source point, and S2 is the second source point. D1 is the first destination point, and D2 is the second destination point.
○ Save the drawing as EX11-11.

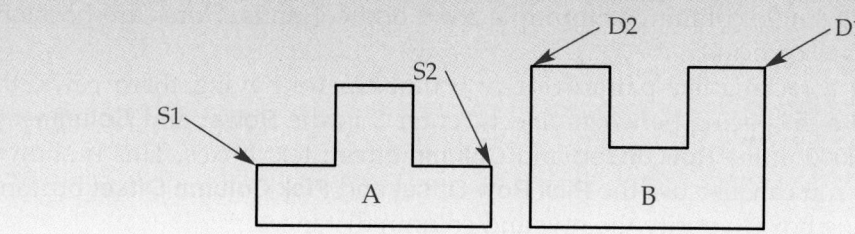

---

# Creating Multiple Objects with ARRAY

Some designs require a rectangular or circular pattern of the same object. For example, office desks are often arranged in rows. Suppose your design calls for five rows, each having four desks. You can create this design by drawing one desk and copying it nineteen times. This operation, however, is time-consuming. A quicker method is to create an array.

There are two types of arrays: rectangular and polar. A *rectangular array* creates rows and columns of the selected items, and you must provide the spacing. A *polar array* constructs a circular arrangement. For a circular array, you must specify the number of items to array, the angle between items, and the center point of the array. Some examples are shown in **Figure 11-25.**

Arrays are specified using the **Array** dialog box. To access this dialog box, pick the **Array** button in the **Modify** toolbar, select **Array...** from the **Modify** pull-down menu, or enter AR or ARRAY at the Command: prompt. All input needed to create the array is specified in the **Array** dialog box. See **Figure 11-26.** Use the **Rectangular Array** and **Polar Array** radio buttons to specify the type of array. Pick the **Select objects** button to return to the AutoCAD window and pick the objects to be included in the array.

Figure 11-25.
Examples of arrays
created with the
**ARRAY** command.

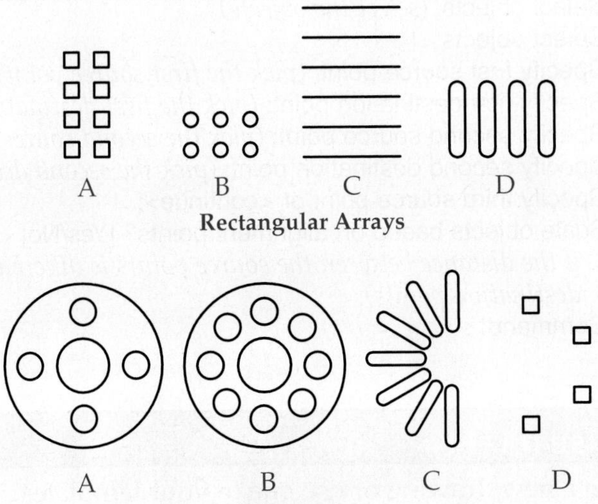

Rectangular Arrays

Polar Arrays

## Arranging Objects in a Rectangular Pattern

A rectangular array places objects in line along the X and Y axes. You can specify a single row, a single column, or multiple rows and columns. *Rows* are horizontal, and *columns* are vertical.

To create a rectangular pattern for a .5 unit square having three rows, three columns, and a .5 spacing between objects, enter 3 in the **Rows:** and **Columns:** text boxes and 1.0000 in the **Row offset:** and **Column offset:** text boxes. This is shown in **Figure 11-26.** You can also use the **Pick Row Offset** and **Pick Column Offset** buttons in the **Array** dialog box to specify the row and column distances.

The original object and resulting array are shown in **Figure 11-27.** When giving the distance between rows and columns, be sure to include the width and height of the object. **Figure 11-27** shows how to calculate the distance between objects in a rectangular array.

AutoCAD and its Applications—Basics

**Figure 11-26.**
The **Array** dialog box options for a rectangular array.

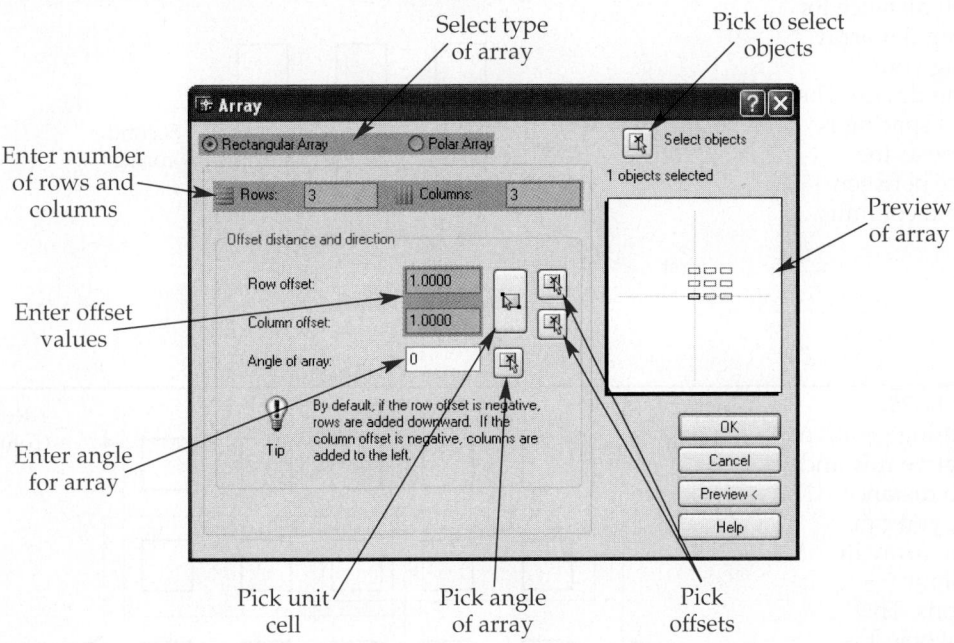

**Figure 11-27.**
The original object (in dashed lines) and the created rectangular array. Note how the distance between rows and columns is determined.

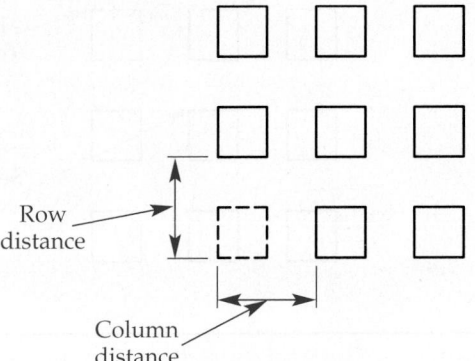

Row distance

Column distance

 AutoCAD allows you to specify the distance separating objects with your pointing device. This distance is called the *unit cell.* The unit cell distance is the same as the distance between rows and columns. It is entered with the pointing device, however, just like selecting a window. See **Figure 11-28.** The second point's distance and direction from the first point determines the X and Y spacing for the array. To specify a unit cell, pick the **Pick Both Offsets** button in the **Array** dialog box.

 **Figure 11-29** shows how you can place arrays in four directions by entering either positive or negative row and column distance values. The dashed box is the original object. The row and column distance is 1 unit, and the box is .5 units square. Specifying the unit cell distance can create a quick row and column arrangement in any direction. For example, in **Figure 11-30,** the second unit cell corner is picked below and to the left of the first corner.

 You can also create an angled rectangular array. Enter the angle in the **Angle of array:** text box or pick the **Pick Angle of Array** button to specify the angle with the crosshairs. The column and row alignments are rotated, not the objects. See **Figure 11-31.**

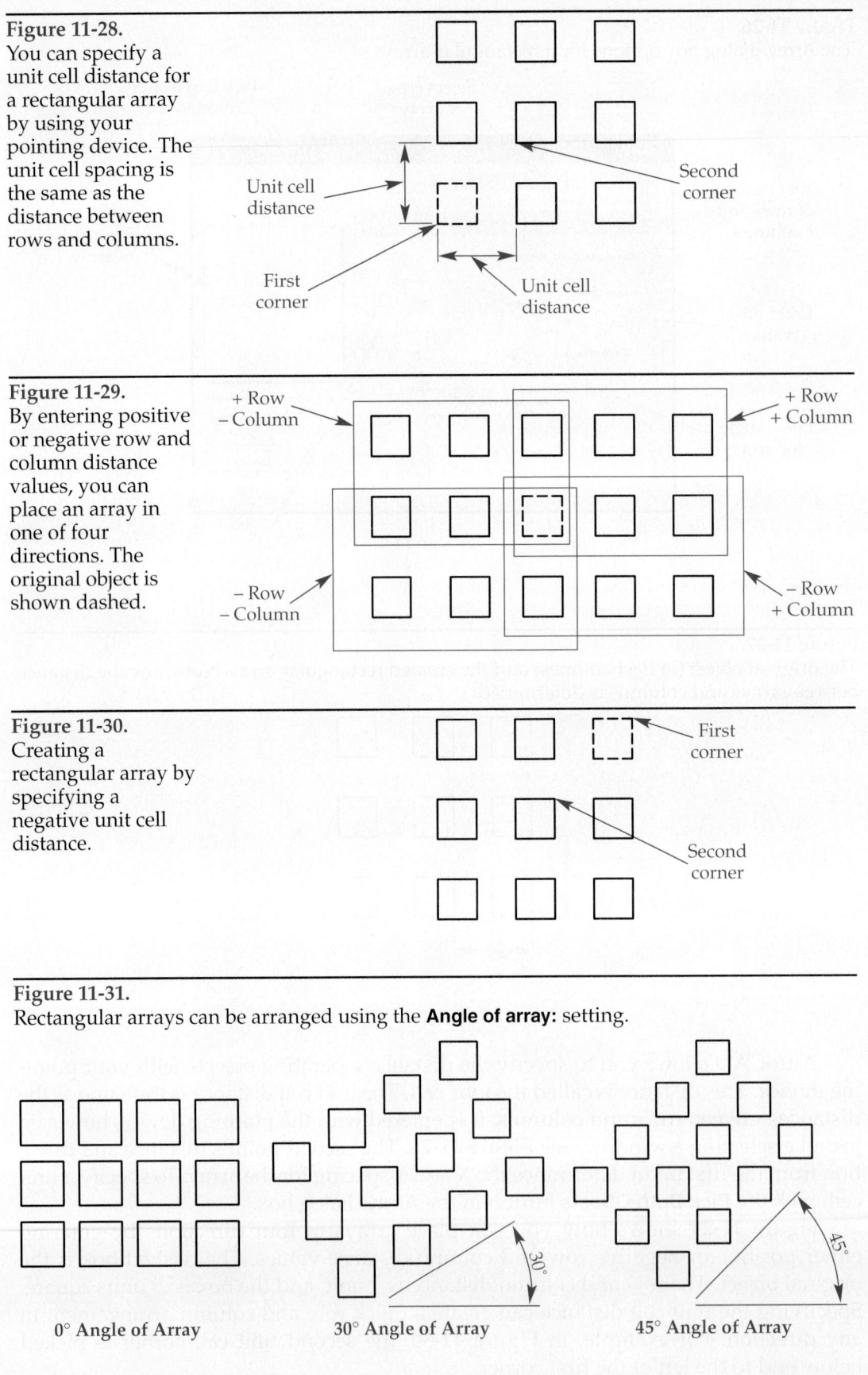

**Figure 11-28.**
You can specify a unit cell distance for a rectangular array by using your pointing device. The unit cell spacing is the same as the distance between rows and columns.

Unit cell distance

Second corner

First corner

Unit cell distance

**Figure 11-29.**
By entering positive or negative row and column distance values, you can place an array in one of four directions. The original object is shown dashed.

+ Row
– Column

+ Row
+ Column

– Row
– Column

– Row
+ Column

**Figure 11-30.**
Creating a rectangular array by specifying a negative unit cell distance.

First corner

Second corner

**Figure 11-31.**
Rectangular arrays can be arranged using the **Angle of array:** setting.

0° Angle of Array

30° Angle of Array

45° Angle of Array

30°

45°

# Arranging Objects around a Center Point

A polar array creates a circular pattern with the selected object. To create a polar array, pick the **Polar Array** radio button in the **Array** dialog box. See **Figure 11-32.** Pick the **Select objects** button to return to the drawing area and select the object to be arrayed. Once you have selected the object, the **Array** dialog box returns.

The next step in creating a polar array is to specify the center point. This is the point about which the objects in the array will be rotated. Enter the coordinates for the center point in the **X:** and **Y:** text boxes or pick the **Pick Center Point** button to select the center point in the drawing area.

After selecting the center point, you must specify the type of polar array to be created using the **Method:** drop-down list. The selected method determines which settings in the dialog box are available. Three methods are available:

- **Total number of items & Angle to fill.**
- **Total number of items & Angle between items.**
- **Angle to fill & Angle between items.**

The **Total number of items:** setting is the total number of objects to be in the array, including the originally selected object. If you do not know how many items will be in the array, use the **Angle to fill & Angle between items** method. The **Angle to fill:** setting can be positive or negative. To array the object in a counterclockwise direction, enter a positive angle. To array the object in a clockwise direction, enter a negative angle. Enter 360 to create a complete circular array. The **Angle between items:** setting specifies the angular distance between adjacent objects in the array. For example, if you were creating a circular pattern of five items spaced 18° apart, you would enter 5 in the **Total number of items:** text box and 18 in the **Angle between items:** text box.

You can have the objects rotated as they are copied around the center point by checking the **Rotate items as copied** check box. This keeps the same face of the object always pointing toward the center point. If objects are not rotated as they are copied, they remain in the same orientation as the original object. See **Figure 11-33.**

When AutoCAD creates a polar array, the base point of the object is rotated and remains at a constant distance from the center point. The default base point varies for different types of objects, as shown in the following table:

**Figure 11-32.**
The **Array** dialog box options for a polar array.

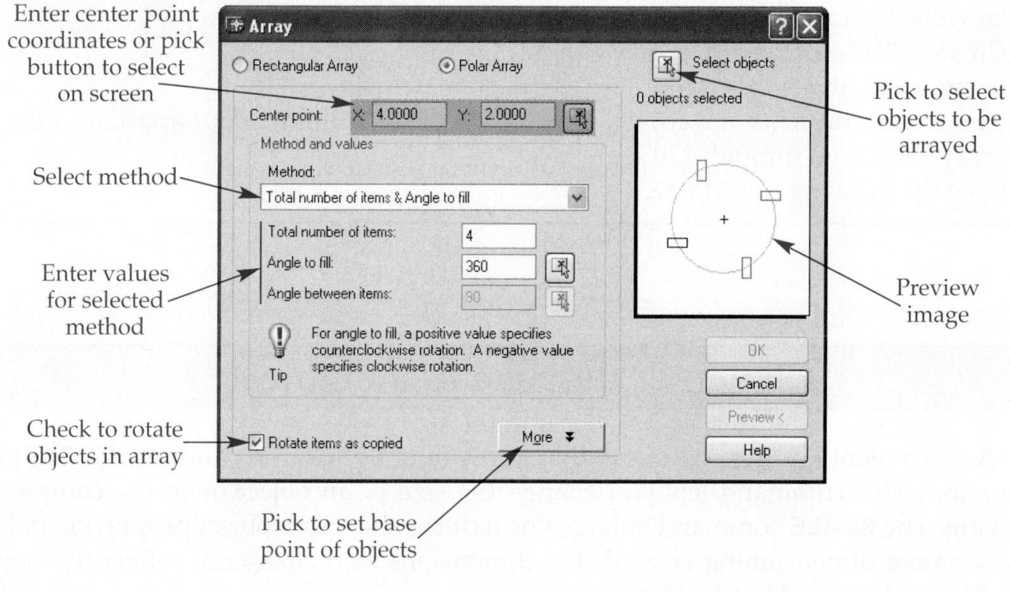

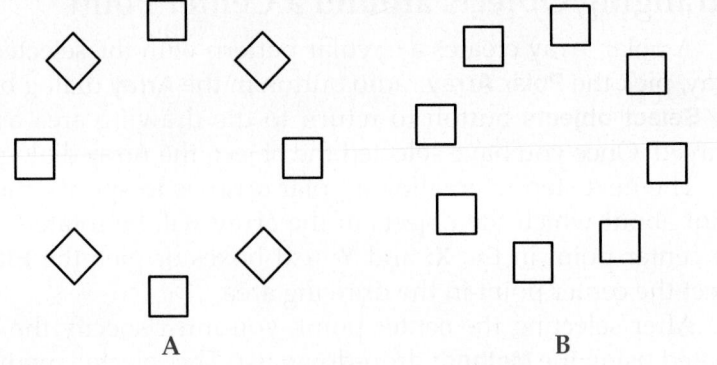

Figure 11-33.
Rotating objects in a
polar array. A—The
square is rotated as
it is arrayed. B—The
square is not rotated
as it is arrayed.

A                                                                B

| Object Type | Default Base Point |
| --- | --- |
| Arc, circle, ellipse | Center |
| Rectangle, polygon | First corner |
| Line, polyline, donut | Starting point |
| Block, text | Insertion point |

If the default base point does not produce the desired array, you can select a different
base point for the selected object. Pick the **More** button in the **Array** dialog box to display the **Object base point** area. Deactivate the **Set to object's default** check box. Enter
a new base point in the text boxes or pick the button to select a base point on screen.

### Exercise 11-12

○ Start a new drawing or use one of your templates.
○ Draw a ⌀1″ circle.
○ Create a rectangular array of five columns and three rows, with 2″ spacing
between the centers of the circles in both directions. Make the original circle the
lower-left object in the array.
○ Create a second rectangular array using the original circle as the upper-right
object in the array. Create three columns and five rows, with .5″ clear spacing
between the circles.
○ Create a 360° polar array of five circles.
○ Copy one of the circles to the side of the polar array.
○ Create an array with the copied circle. Each circle should be 30° apart, and the
array should go through 270°.
○ Save the drawing as EX11-12.

## Changing the Size of an Object

A convenient editing command that saves hours of drafting time is the **SCALE**
command. This command lets you change the size of an object or of the complete
drawing. The **SCALE** command enlarges or reduces the entire object proportionately.
If associative dimensioning is used, the dimensions also change to reflect the new
size. This is discussed in Chapter 18.

To scale objects, pick the **Scale** button in the **Modify** toolbar, pick **Scale** from the **Modify** pull-down menu, or type SC or SCALE at the Command: prompt. The command sequence is as follows:

Command: **SC** *or* **SCALE**↵
Select objects: *(select objects to be scaled)*
Select objects: ↵
Specify base point: *(select the base point)*
Specify scale factor or [Reference]:

Specifying the scale factor is the default option. Enter a number to indicate the amount of enlargement or reduction. For example, if you want to double the scale, type 2 at the Specify scale factor or [Reference]: prompt, as shown in **Figure 11-34**. The chart in **Figure 11-35** shows sample scale factors.

**Figure 11-34.**
Using the **SCALE** command. The base point does not move, but every other point in the object does.

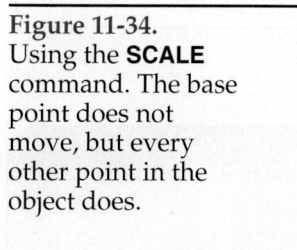
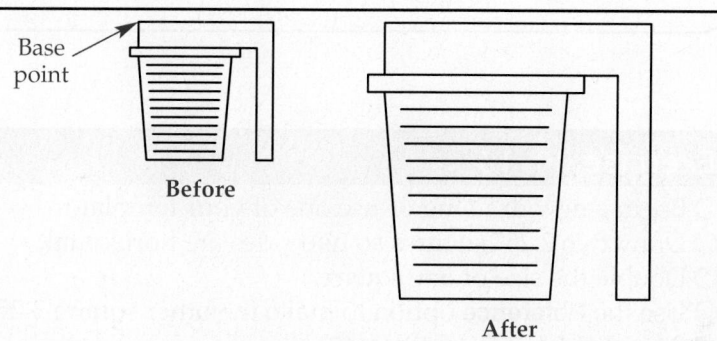

Base point

Before

After

**Figure 11-35.**
Different scale factors and the resulting sizes.

| Scale Factor | Resulting Size |
|---|---|
| 10 | 10 × bigger |
| 5 | 5 × bigger |
| 2 | 2 × bigger |
| 1 | Equal to existing size |
| .75 | 3/4 of original size |
| .50 | 1/2 of original size |
| .25 | 1/4 of original size |

## Using the **Reference** Option

An object can also be scaled by specifying a new size in relation to an existing dimension. For example, suppose you have a shaft that is 2.50″ long and you want to make it 3.00″ long. To do so, use the **Reference** option as follows, as shown in **Figure 11-36**:

Specify scale factor or [Reference]: **R**↵
Specify reference length <1>: **2.5**↵
Specify new length: **3**↵
Command:

Figure 11-36.
Using the **Reference**
option of the **SCALE**
command.

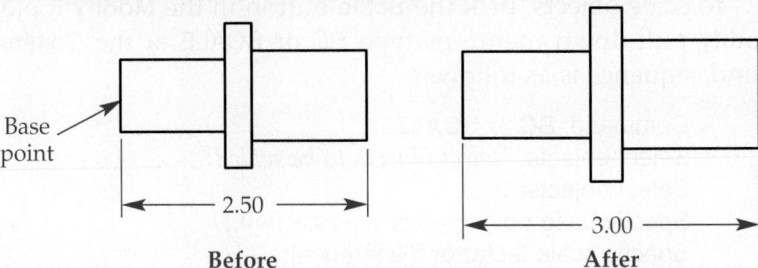

Base
point

2.50

Before

3.00

After

NOTE    The **SCALE** command changes all dimensions of an object
proportionately. If you want to change only the width or
length of an object, use the **STRETCH** or **LENGTHEN** command.

## Exercise 11-13

○ Begin a new drawing or use one of your templates.
○ Draw two 2.25″ squares so two sides are horizontal.
○ Double the size of one square.
○ Use the **Reference** option to make the other square 3.25″ long on one side.
○ Save the drawing as EX11-13.

## Stretching an Object

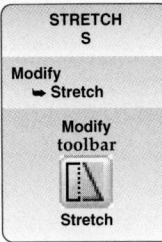

STRETCH
S

Modify
➥ Stretch

Modify
toolbar

Stretch

The **SCALE** command changes the length and width of an object proportionately.
The **STRETCH** command changes only one dimension of an object. In manual drafting, it is common to increase the length of a part, while leaving the diameter or width
the same. In architectural design, room sizes may be stretched to increase the square
footage.

When using the **STRETCH** command, you can select objects with a crossing window or crossing polygon. To use a crossing window, type C at the Select objects:
prompt or drag your selection window from right to left. To access the **STRETCH**
command, pick the **Stretch** button in the **Modify** toolbar, pick **Stretch** from the **Modify**
pull-down menu, or type S or STRETCH at the Command: prompt. The command
sequence is as follows:

Command: **S** *or* **STRETCH**↵
Select objects to stretch by crossing-window or crossing-polygon…
Select objects: *(select the first corner of a crossing window)*
Specify opposite corner: *(pick the second corner)*
Select objects: *(pick additional objects or press* [Enter]*)*

Select only the portion of the object to be stretched, as shown in **Figure 11-37.** If you
select the entire object, the **STRETCH** command works like the **MOVE** command. Next, you
are asked to pick the base point. This is the point from which the object will be stretched.
Pick a new position for the base point. As you move the screen cursor, the object is

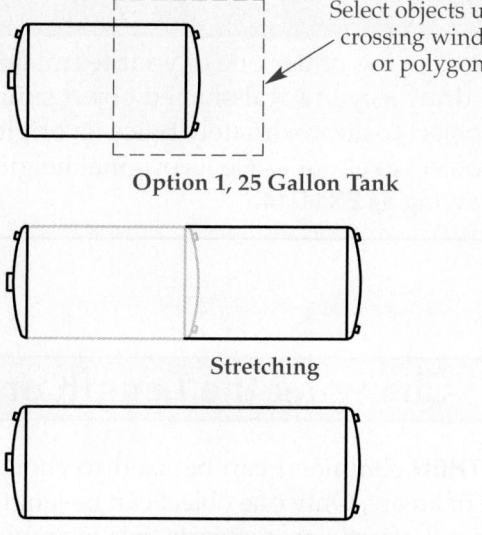

Figure 11-37.
Using the **STRETCH** command.

Select objects using crossing window or polygon

Option 1, 25 Gallon Tank

Stretching

Option 2, 50 Gallon Tank

stretched or compressed. When the displayed object is stretched to the desired position, pick the new point. The command sequence after selecting objects is as follows:

Specify base point or displacement: *(pick the base point for the stretch to begin)*
Specify second point of displacement or <use first point as displacement>: *(pick the final location of the base point)*
Command:

The example in **Figure 11-37** shows the object being stretched. This is a common use of the **STRETCH** command. You can also use the **STRETCH** command to reduce the size of an object.

## Using the Displacement Option

The displacement option works the same with the **STRETCH** command as with the **MOVE** and **COPY** commands. After selecting the objects to be stretched, enter a displacement, as shown in the following:

Specify base point or displacement: *(enter an X and Y displacement, such as* 2,3*)*
Specify second point of displacement or <use first point as displacement>: ↵
Command:

When you press [Enter] at the Specify second point of displacement: prompt, the object is automatically stretched as you specified with the X and Y coordinates. In this case, the object is stretched two units in the X direction and three units in the Y direction.

**PROFESSIONAL TIP**

It may not be common to have objects lined up in a convenient manner for using the crossing box selection method with the **STRETCH** command. You should consider using the crossing polygon selection method to make selecting the objects easier. Also, make sure the **DRAGMODE** variable is turned on so you can watch the object stretch to its new size. If the stretched object is not what you expected, cancel the command with the [Esc] key. The **STRETCH** command and other editing commands discussed in this chapter work well with the Ortho mode on. This restricts the object movement to only horizontal and vertical directions.

## Changing the Length of an Object

The **LENGTHEN** command can be used to change the length of objects and the included angle of an arc. Only one object can be lengthened at a time. The **LENGTHEN** command does not affect closed objects. For example, you can lengthen a line, polyline, arc, elliptical arc, or spline, but you cannot lengthen a closed polygon or circle.

To access the **LENGTHEN** command, pick **Lengthen** from the **Modify** pull-down menu or type LEN or LENGTHEN at the Command: prompt. When you select an object, AutoCAD gives you the current length, if the object is linear, or the included angle, if the object is an arc:

LENGTHEN
LEN

Modify
➥ Lengthen

Command: **LEN** *or* **LENGTHEN**↵
Select an object or [DElta/Percent/Total/DYnamic]: *(pick an object)*
Current length: *current*
Select an object or [DElta/Percent/Total/DYnamic]:

Each option is described below:

- **Delta.** The **Delta** option allows you to specify a positive or negative change in length, measured from the endpoint of the selected object. The lengthening or shortening happens closest to the selection point and changes the length by the amount entered. See **Figure 11-38**.

    Command: **LEN** *or* **LENGTHEN**↵
    Select an object or [DElta/Percent/Total/DYnamic]: **DE**↵
    Enter delta length or [Angle] <0.000> *(enter the desired length—.75, for example)*
    Select an object to change or [Undo]: *(pick the object)*
    Select an object to change or [Undo]: *(select another object to lengthen or press*
        [Enter] *to exit the command)*
    Command:

Figure 11-38.
Using the **Delta**
option of the
**LENGTHEN**
command.

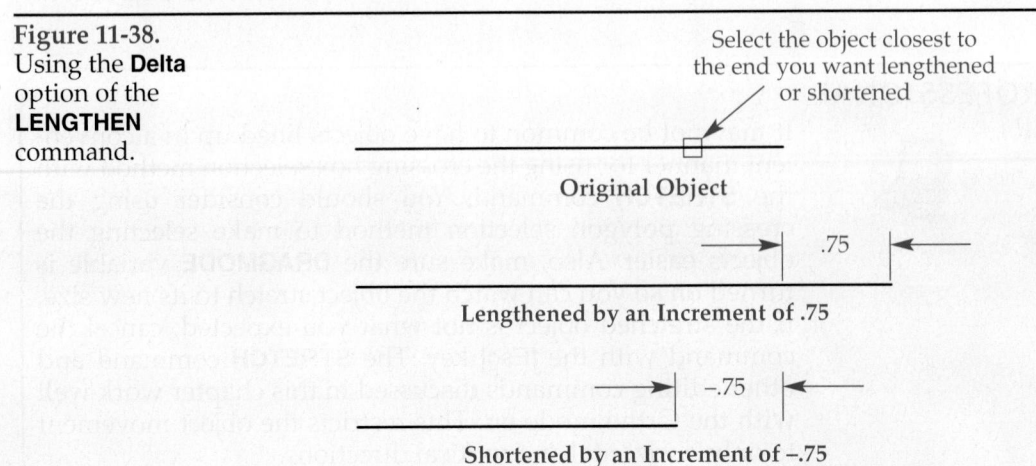

Select the object closest to
the end you want lengthened
or shortened

Original Object

.75

Lengthened by an Increment of .75

–.75

Shortened by an Increment of –.75

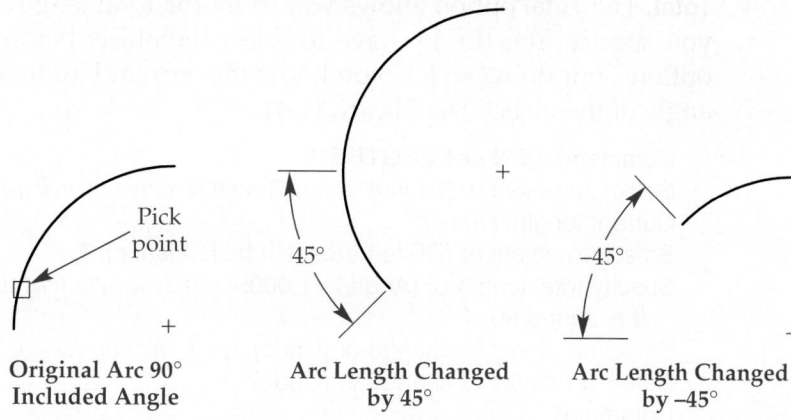

**Figure 11-39.**
Using the **Angle** suboption of the **LENGTHEN** command's **Delta** option.

Pick point

Original Arc 90°
Included Angle

45°

Arc Length Changed by 45°

−45°

Arc Length Changed by −45°

The **Delta** option has an **Angle** suboption that lets you change the included angle of an arc by a specified angle. The command sequence is as follows, as shown in **Figure 11-39:**

Command: **LEN** *or* **LENGTHEN**↵
Select an object or [DElta/Percent/Total/DYnamic]: **DE**↵
Enter delta length or [Angle] <*current*>: **A**↵
Enter delta angle <0>: *(enter an angle, such as 45)*
Select an object to change or [Undo]: *(pick the arc)*
Select an object to change or [Undo]: ↵
Command:

- **Percent.** The **Percent** option allows you to change the length of an object or the angle of an arc by a specified percentage. If you consider the original length to be 100 percent, you can make the object shorter by specifying less than 100 percent or longer by specifying more than 100 percent. Look at **Figure 11-40** and follow this command sequence:

Command: **LEN** *or* **LENGTHEN**↵
Select an object or [DElta/Percent/Total/DYnamic]: **P**↵
Enter percentage length <100.0000>: **125**↵
Select an object to change or [Undo]: *(pick the object)*
Select an object to change or [Undo]: ↵
Command:

**Figure 11-40.**
Using the **Percent** option of the **LENGTHEN** command.

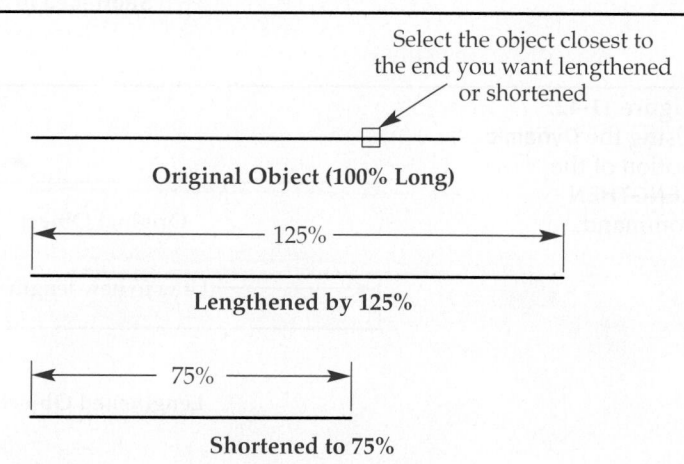

Select the object closest to the end you want lengthened or shortened

Original Object (100% Long)

125%

Lengthened by 125%

75%

Shortened to 75%

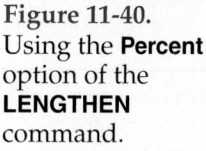

- **Total.** The **Total** option allows you to set the total length or angle to the value you specify. You do not have to select the object before entering one of the options, but doing so lets you know the current length and, if it is an arc, the angle of the object. See **Figure 11-41**.

  Command: **LEN** *or* **LENGTHEN**↵
  Select an object or [DElta/Percent/Total/DYnamic]: *(pick an object)*
  Current length: *current*
  Select an object or [DElta/Percent/Total/DYnamic]: **T**↵
  Specify total length or [Angle] <1.000>: *(enter a new length, such as* 3.75, *or* A, *if it is an angle)*
  Select an object to change or [Undo]: *(pick the object)*
  Select an object to change or [Undo]: ↵
  Command:

- **Dynamic.** This option lets you drag the endpoint of the object to the desired length or angle with the screen cursor. See **Figure 11-42**. It is helpful to have the grid and snap set to usable increments when using this option. This is the command sequence:

  Command: **LEN** *or* **LENGTHEN**↵
  Select an object or [DElta/Percent/Total/DYnamic]: **DY**↵
  Select an object to change or [Undo]: *(pick the object)*
  Specify new end point *(move the cursor to the desired length and pick)*
  Select an object to change or [Undo]: ↵
  Command:

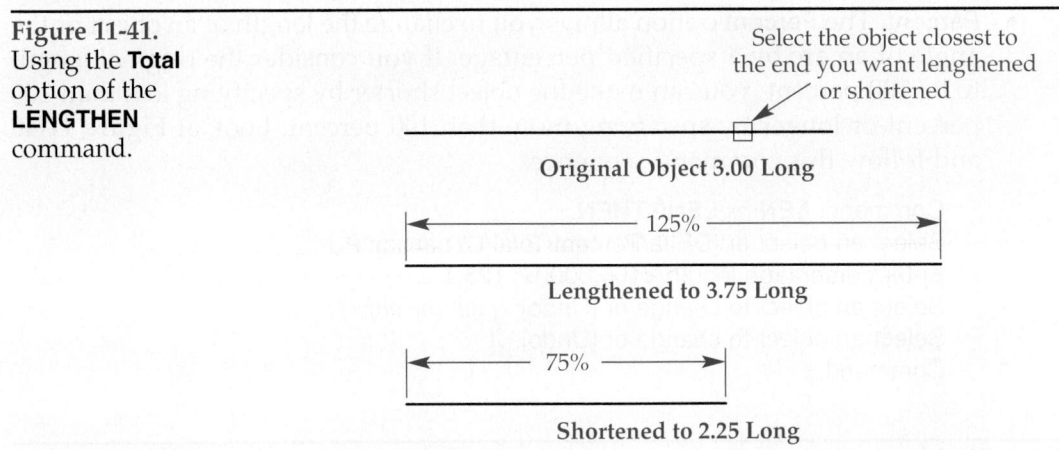

Figure 11-41.
Using the **Total** option of the **LENGTHEN** command.

Select the object closest to the end you want lengthened or shortened

Original Object 3.00 Long

— 125% —

Lengthened to 3.75 Long

— 75% —

Shortened to 2.25 Long

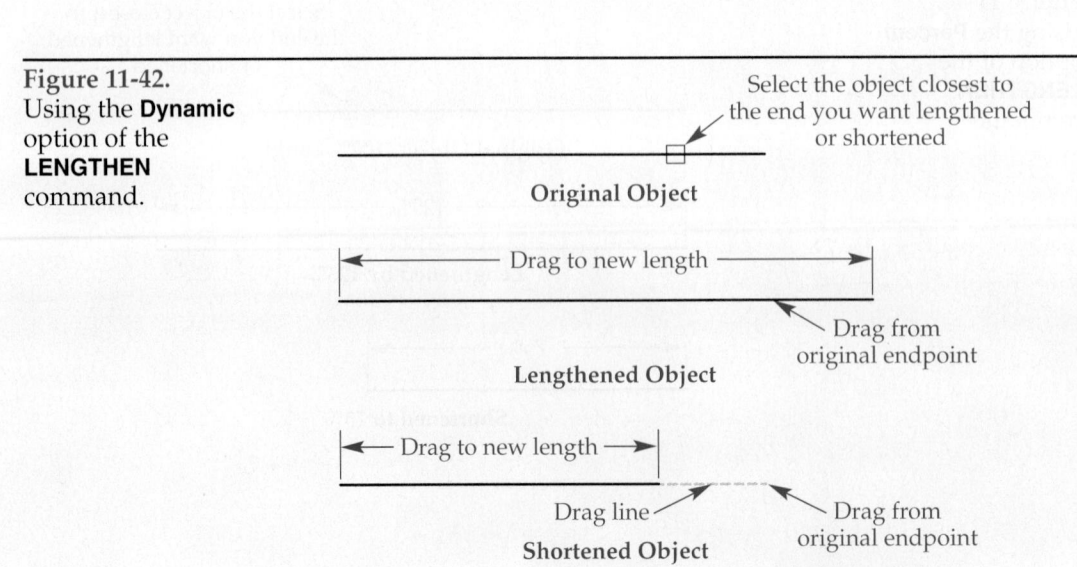

Figure 11-42.
Using the **Dynamic** option of the **LENGTHEN** command.

Select the object closest to the end you want lengthened or shortened

Original Object

Drag to new length

Lengthened Object

Drag from original endpoint

Drag to new length

Drag line

Drag from original endpoint

Shortened Object

AutoCAD and its Applications—Basics

○ Begin a new drawing or use one of your templates.
○ Use the **LENGTHEN** command and the following options to draw objects similar to the ones specified in the given figure numbers. (Note: Use the **COPY** command to make two copies of each original object, one for lengthening and one for shortening.)
  ○ **Delta.** Figure 11-38 and Figure 11-39.
  ○ **Percent.** Figure 11-40.
  ○ **Total.** Figure 11-41.
  ○ **Dynamic.** Figure 11-42.
○ Save the drawing as EX11-15.

**NOTE** Only lines and arcs can be lengthened dynamically. A spline's length can only be decreased. Splines are discussed in Chapter 15.

## Selecting Objects for Future Editing

Throughout this chapter, you have worked with the basic editing commands by entering the command and then selecting the object to be edited. You can also set up AutoCAD to let you select the object first and then enter the desired editing command. The settings controlling object selection are found in the **Selection** tab of the **Options** dialog box. These settings are discussed in Chapter 12.

The **SELECT** command is used to preselect an object or group of objects for future editing. It is designed to increase your productivity. Often, you are working with the same set of objects—moving, copying, or scaling them. Set these aside as a selection set with the **SELECT** command. Continue to perform another drawing task. To return to those objects set aside, enter P for **Previous** at the Select objects: prompt. Only the last selection set you make can be modified. The command sequences for creating a selection set and then moving it are as follows:

> Command: **SELECT**↵
> Select objects: *(use any method to select an individual object or group of objects)*
> Select objects: *(select additional objects or press* [Enter])
> Command:

This creates a selection set. Later, when you want to move these objects, use the **Previous** option as follows:

> Command: **M** *or* **MOVE**↵
> Select objects: **P**↵ *(this selects the object or group of objects previously selected using the* **SELECT** *command)*
> Select objects: ↵
> Specify base point or displacement: *(pick the base point)*
> Specify second point of displacement or <use first point as displacement>: *(pick the new location of the base point)*
> Command:

## Exercise 11-16

○ Begin a new drawing or use one of your templates.
○ Draw two circles with 1.5″ (40 mm) radii spaced .25″ (6 mm) apart.
○ Use the **SELECT** command to select both circles for future editing.
○ Draw at least three other small objects.
○ Use the **COPY** command and the **Previous** option to copy the original two circles to a new location.
○ Save the drawing as EX11-16.

## Creating Object Groups

A *group* is a named selection set. These selection sets are saved with the drawing and, therefore, exist between multiple drawing sessions. Objects can be members of more than one group, and groups can be nested. *Nesting* means placing one group inside of another group.

An object existing in multiple groups creates an interesting situation. For example, if a line and an arc are grouped and then the arc is grouped with a circle, moving the first group moves the line and arc, and moving the second group moves the arc and circle. Nesting can be used to place smaller groups into larger groups for easier editing.

By default, selecting one object within a group causes the entire group to be selected. This setting can be changed in the **Selection** tab of the **Options** dialog box, with the **Object grouping** check box in the **Selection Modes** area. Typing G or GROUP at the Command: prompt accesses the **GROUP** command. Either of these entry methods displays the **Object Grouping** dialog box, shown in **Figure 11-43**.

There are many elements found in the **Object Grouping** dialog box. The text box displays the **Group Name** and lists whether or not the group is selectable. If a group is selectable, picking any object in it selects the entire group. Making a group nonselectable allows individual objects within the group to be edited.

The **Group Identification** area has several components:
- **Find Name.** This button displays a dialog list of all groups with which an object is associated. When you pick this button, a Pick a member of a group prompt appears. Once you pick an object, the **Group Member List** dialog box lists any groups with which the object is associated.
- **Highlight.** This button allows a group name to be specified and then highlights all its members in the drawing editor. This allows you to see the parts of the drawing identified as the members of that group. Pick the **Continue** button or press [Enter] to return to the **Object Grouping** dialog box.

GROUP
G

**Figure 11-43.**
The **Object Grouping** dialog box. The different elements are shown here highlighted.

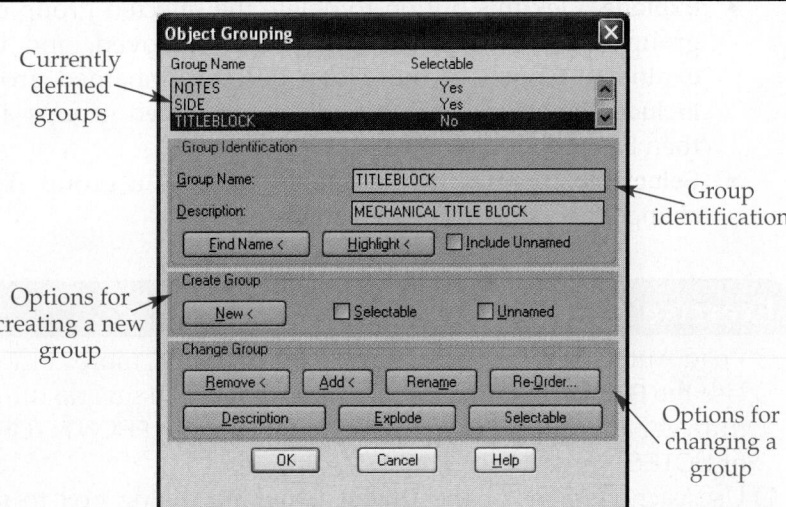

Currently defined groups

Group identification

Options for creating a new group

Options for changing a group

- **Include Unnamed.** This check box causes unnamed groups to be listed with named groups. Unnamed groups are given a default name by AutoCAD in the format of *A$x$, where $x$ is an integer value that increases with each new group, such as *A6. Unnamed groups can be named later using the **Rename** option.

The **Create Group** area contains the options for creating a new group:

- **New.** This button creates a new group from the selected objects using the name entered in the **Group Name:** text box. AutoCAD issues a Select objects for grouping: prompt after you enter a new name in the **Group Name:** text box.
- **Selectable.** A check in this box sets the initial status of the **Selectable** value as Yes for the new group. This is indicated in the **Selectable** list described earlier. No check here specifies No in the **Selectable** list. This can be changed later.
- **Unnamed.** This indicates whether or not the new group will be named. If this box is checked, AutoCAD assigns its own default name as detailed previously.

The **Change Group** area of the **Object Grouping** dialog box shows the options for changing a group:

- **Remove.** Pick this button to remove objects from a group definition.
- **Add.** This button allows objects to be added to a group definition.
- **Rename.** Pick this button to change the name of an existing group. Unnamed groups can be renamed.
- **Re-Order.** Objects are numbered in the order they are selected when defining the group. The first object is numbered 0, not 1. This button allows objects to be reordered within the group. For example, if a group contains a set of instructions, you can reorder the instructions to suit the typical steps used. The **Order Group** dialog box is displayed when you pick this button. The elements of this dialog box are briefly described as follows:
  - **Group Name.** Displays the name of the selected group.
  - **Description.** Displays the description for the selected group.
  - **Remove from position (0-$n$).** Position number of the object to reorder, where $n$ is the total number of objects found in the group. You place the desired order in the text box to the right of this and the next two features.
  - **Replace at position (0-$n$).** Position to which the number is being moved.
  - **Number of objects (1-$n$).** Displays the number of objects or the range to reorder.
  - **Reverse Order.** Pick this button to have the order of all members in the group reversed.
- **Description.** Updates the group with the new description entered in the **Description:** text box.

- **Explode.** Pick this button to delete the selected group definition, but not the group's objects. The group name is removed, and the original group is exploded. Copies of the group become unnamed groups. By selecting the **Include Unnamed** check box, these unnamed groups are displayed and can then be exploded, if needed.
- **Selectable.** Toggles the selectable value of a group. This is where you can change the value in the **Selectable** list.

---

**Exercise 11-17**

○ Load AutoCAD and open one of your previous, more complex drawings.
○ Use the **GROUP** command to name and describe several different elements of the drawing as groups. For example, for views, use FRONT, TOP, SIDE, TITLEBLOCK, or NOTES.
○ Use each element of the **Object Grouping** dialog box to see the effect on the groups you have named.
○ Save the drawing as EX11-17.

---

## Chapter Test

*Answer the following questions on a separate sheet of paper.*

1. Give the command and entries used to draw a .125 × .125 chamfer:
   A. Command: _____
   B. Select first line or [Polyline/Distance/Angle/Trim/Method/mUltiple]: _____
   C. Specify first chamfer distance <*current*>: _____
   D. Specify second chamfer distance <*current*>: _____
   E. Select first line or [Polyline/Distance/Angle/Trim/Method/mUltiple]: _____
   F. Select second line: _____

2. Give the command and entries required to produce .50 radius fillets on all corners of a closed polyline:
   A. Command: _____
   B. Select first object or [Polyline/Radius/Trim/mUltiple]: _____
   C. Specify fillet radius <*current*>: _____
   D. Select first object or [Polyline/Radius/Trim/mUltiple]: _____
   E. Select second object: _____

3. Give the command, entries, and actions required to move an object from Position A to Position B:
   A. Command: _____
   B. Select objects: _____
   C. Select objects: _____
   D. Specify base point or displacement: _____
   E. Specify second point of displacement or <use first point as displacement>: _____

4. Give the command and entries needed to make two copies of the same object:
   A. Command: _____
   B. Select objects: _____
   C. Select objects: _____
   D. Specify base point or displacement, or [Multiple]: _____
   E. Specify base point: _____
   F. Specify second point of displacement or <use first point as displacement>: _____
   G. Specify second point of displacement or <use first point as displacement>: _____

5. Give the command and entries necessary to draw a reverse image of an existing object and remove the existing object:
   A. Command: _____
   B. Select objects: _____
   C. Select objects: _____
   D. Specify first point of mirror line: _____
   E. Specify second point of mirror line: _____
   F. Delete source objects? [Yes/No] <N>: _____
6. Give the command and entries needed to rotate an object 45° clockwise:
   A. Command: _____
   B. Select objects: _____
   C. Select objects: _____
   D. Specify base point: _____
   E. Specify rotation angle or [Reference]: _____
7. Give the command and entries required to reduce the size of an entire drawing by one-half:
   A. Command: _____
   B. Select objects: _____
   C. Select objects: _____
   D. Specify base point: _____
   E. Specify scale factor or [Reference]: _____
8. Define the term *displacement*, as it relates to the **MOVE** and **COPY** commands.
9. Explain the difference between the **MOVE** and **COPY** commands.
10. List two locations drafters normally choose as the base point when using the **MOVE** or **COPY** commands.
11. Describe the purpose of the **SELECT** command.
12. What is a *selection set?*
13. How do you select objects for editing that have previously been picked using the **SELECT** command?
14. How is the size of a fillet specified?
15. Identify the selection method or methods issued by AutoCAD when using the **STRETCH** command.
16. How do you cancel the **STRETCH** command?
17. The **EXTEND** command is the opposite of the _____ command.
18. Name the system variable used to preset the fillet radius.
19. In what direction should you pick points to break a portion out of a circle or arc?
20. Name the command that trims an object to a cutting edge.
21. Name the command associated with boundary edges.
22. The **MOVE**, **COPY**, **TRIM**, **EXTEND**, and **STRETCH** commands are located in the _____ pull-down menu.
23. What is the difference between polar and rectangular arrays?
24. What four values should you know before you create a rectangular array?
25. Define the term *unit cell.*
26. Name the command that can be used to move and rotate an object simultaneously.
27. Describe the difference between the **Trim** and **No trim** options when using the **CHAMFER** and **FILLET** commands.
28. What is the purpose of the **Method** option in the **CHAMFER** command?
29. How can you split an object in two without removing a portion?
30. Name the option in the **TRIM** and **EXTEND** commands allowing you to trim or extend to an implied intersection.
31. How do you use the Smart mode with the **TRIM** and **EXTEND** commands?

32. Identify the **LENGTHEN** command option corresponding to each of the following descriptions:
   A. Changes a length or arc angle by a percentage of the total.
   B. Drags the endpoint of the object to the desired length or angle.
   C. Allows a positive or negative change in length from the endpoint.
   D. Sets the total length or angle to the value specified.
33. Define a *group*.
34. How do you access the **Object Grouping** dialog box?
35. Describe how you create a new group.
36. Suppose an object is 1.5″ (38 mm) wide and you want to create a rectangular array with .75″ (19 mm) spacing between objects. What should you specify for the distance between columns?
37. How do you create a rotated rectangular array?
38. What values should you know before you create a polar array?
39. How do you specify a clockwise polar array rotation?
40. Give the keyboard shortcuts for the following commands:
   A. **CHAMFER**
   B. **FILLET**
   C. **BREAK**
   D. **TRIM**
   E. **EXTEND**
   F. **CHANGE**
   G. **MOVE**
   H. **COPY**
   I. **MIRROR**
   J. **ROTATE**
   K. **ALIGN**
   L. **SCALE**
   M. **LENGTHEN**
   N. **ARRAY**

## Drawing Problems

*Use your templates as appropriate for each of the following problems. Start a new drawing for each problem, unless indicated otherwise.*

1. Draw Object A using the **LINE** and **ARC** commands. Make sure the corners overrun and the arc is centered, but does not touch the lines. Use the **TRIM**, **EXTEND**, and **MOVE** commands to make Object B. Save the drawing as P11-1.

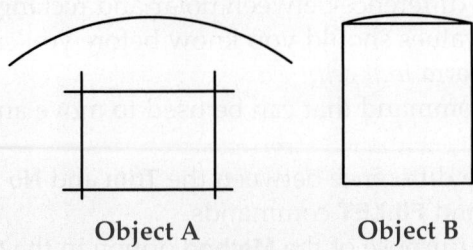

Object A          Object B

2. Open drawing P11-1 for further editing (Object A). Using the **STRETCH** command, change the shape to Object B. Make a copy of the new revision. Change the copy to represent Object C. Save the drawing as P11-2.

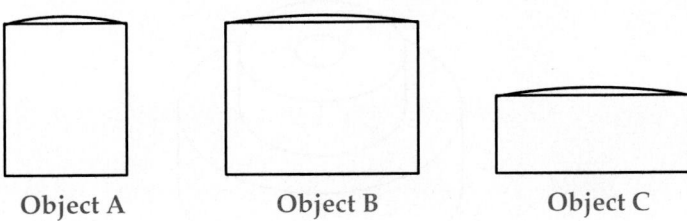

       Object A             Object B             Object C

3. Refer to **Figure 11-37** in this chapter. Draw and make three copies of the object shown in Option 1. Stretch the first copy to twice its length, as shown in Option 2. Stretch the second copy to twice its height. Double the size of the third copy using the **SCALE** command. Save the drawing as P11-3.

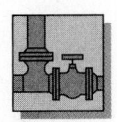

4. Draw Objects A, B, and C shown below, without dimensions. Move Objects A, B, and C to new positions. Select a corner of Object A and the centers of Objects B and C as the base points. Save the drawing as P11-4.

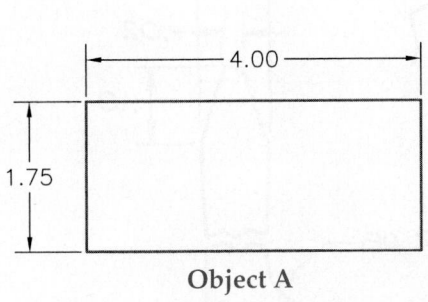
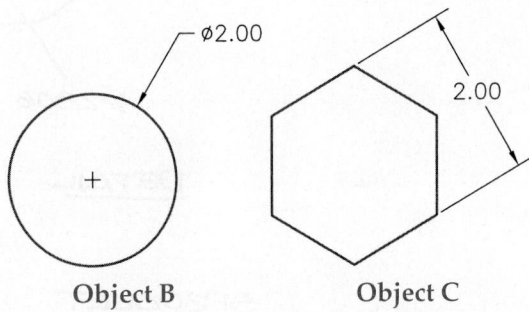

       Object A             Object B             Object C

5. Draw Objects A, B, and C shown in Problem 11-4 on the left side of the screen. Make a copy of Object A two units to the right. Make four copies of Object B three units, center-to-center, to the right using the **Multiple** option. Make three copies of Object C three units, center-to-center, to the right. Save the drawing as P11-5.

6. Draw the object shown using the **ELLIPSE**, **COPY**, and **LINE** commands. The rotation angle of the ellipse is 60°. Use the **BREAK** or **TRIM** command when drawing and editing the lower ellipse. Save the drawing as P11-6.

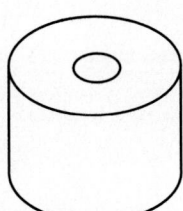

7. Open drawing P11-6 for further editing. Shorten the height of the object using the **STRETCH** command as shown below. Next, add to the object as indicated. Save the drawing as P11-7.

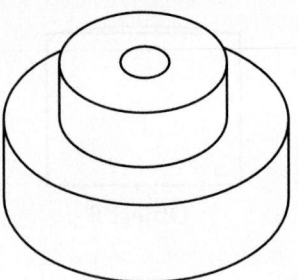

8. You have been given an engineer's sketches and notes to construct a drawing of a sprocket. Create a front and side view of the sprocket using the **ARRAY** command. Place the drawing on one of your templates. Do not add dimensions. Save the drawing as P11-8.

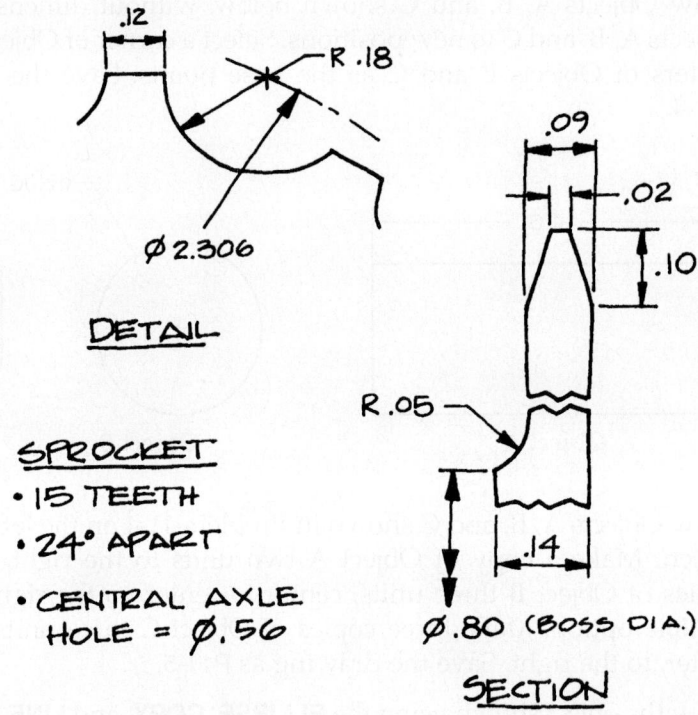

.12

R .18

Ø 2.306

DETAIL

SPROCKET
• 15 TEETH
• 24° APART
• CENTRAL AXLE
HOLE = Ø.56

.09

.02

.10

R .05

.14

Ø.80 (BOSS DIA.)

SECTION

9. Draw Object A without dimensions. Use the **CHAMFER** and **FILLET** commands to your best advantage. Draw a mirror image as Object B. Now, remove the original view and move the new view so Point 2 is at the original Point 1 location. Save the drawing as P11-9.

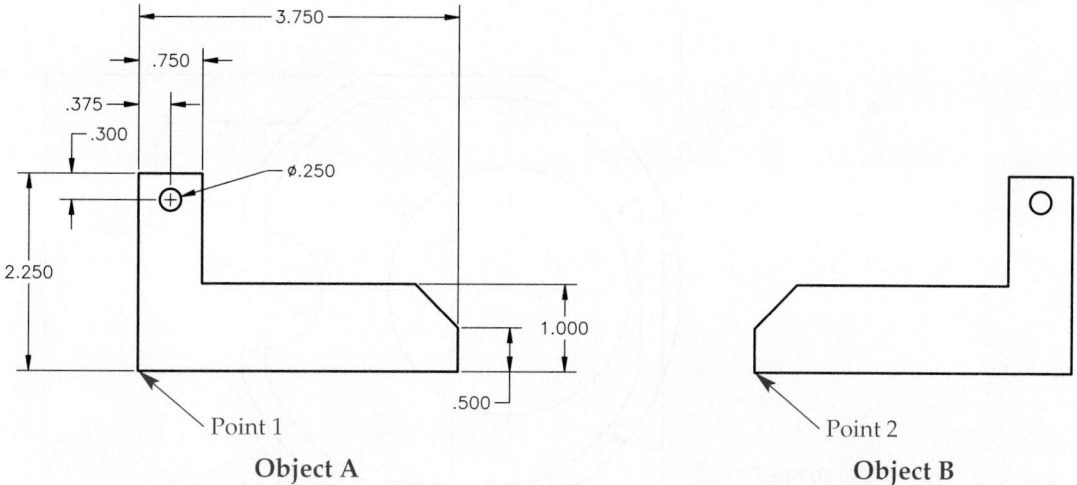

Object A                                    Object B

10. Draw the object shown below without dimensions. The object is symmetrical; therefore, draw only one half. Mirror the other half into place. Use the **CHAMFER** and **FILLET** commands to your best advantage. All fillets and rounds are .125. Save the drawing as P11-10.

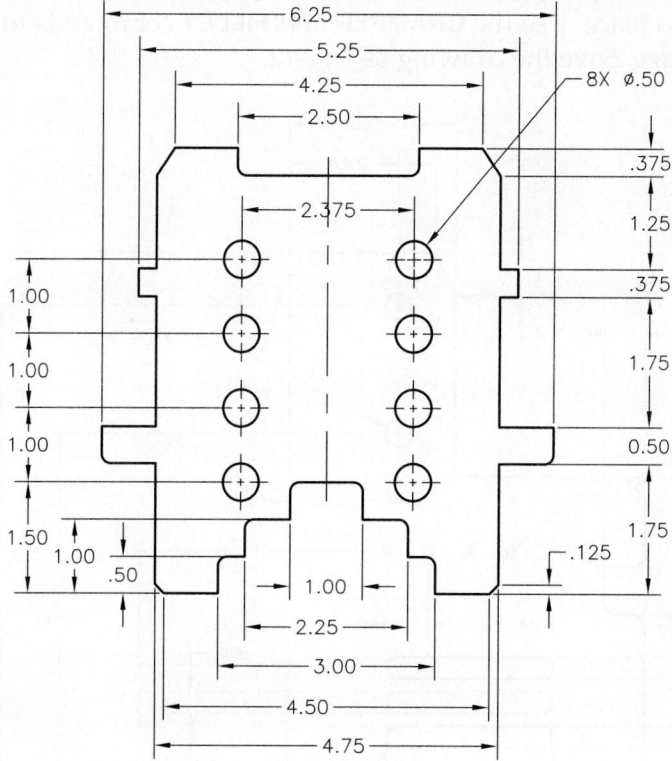

---

11. Use the **TRIM**, **OSNAP**, and **OFFSET** commands to assist you in drawing this object. Do not draw centerlines or dimensions. Save the completed drawing as P11-11.

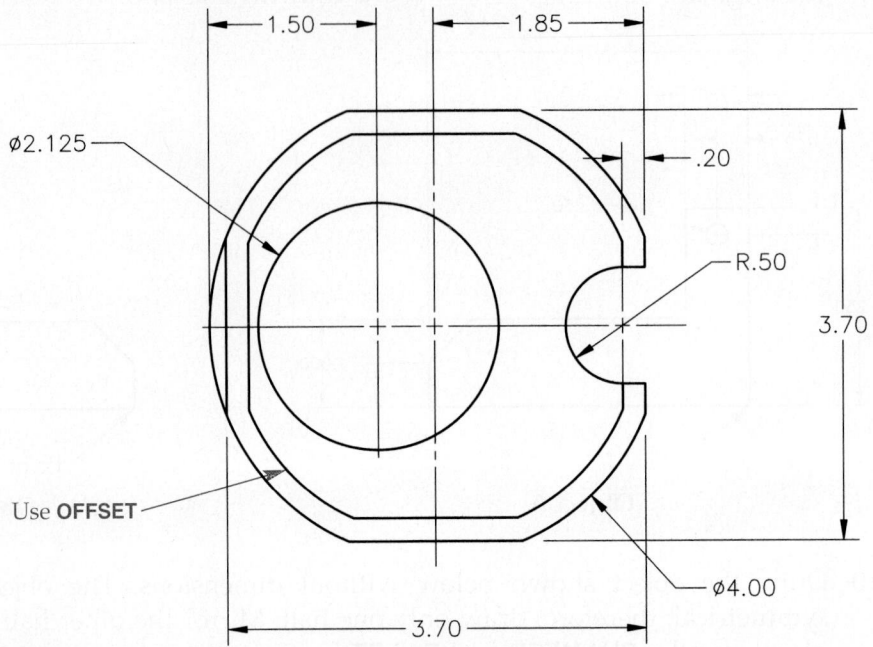

12. Draw the object shown below without dimensions. Mirror the right half into place. Use the **CHAMFER** and **FILLET** commands to your best advantage. Save the drawing as P11-12.

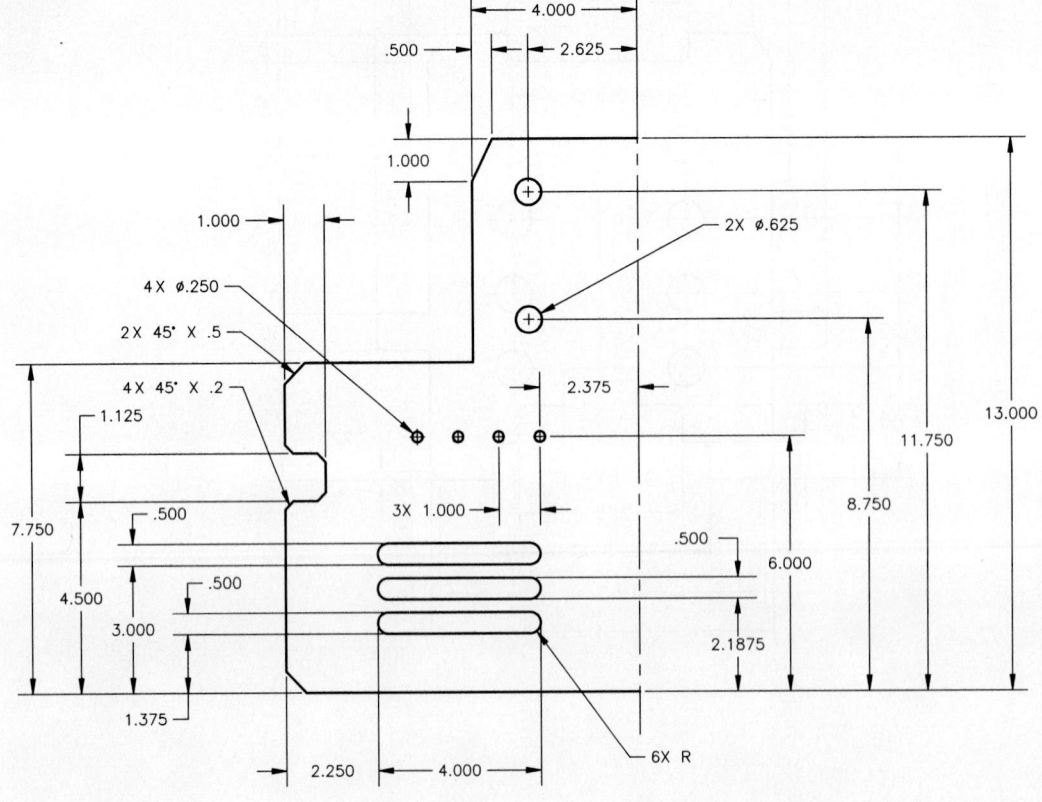

13. Redraw the objects shown below. Mirror the drawing, but have the text remain readable. Delete the original image during the mirroring process. Save the drawing as P11-13.

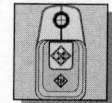

2b1

TRANSFER

5a2 4a1 8a1

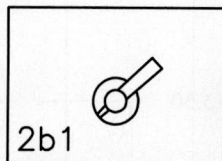

LTS.HTRS.FANS

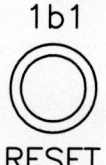

2b1

1b1

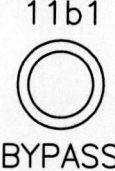

RESET

11b1

BYPASS

14. Draw the following object views using the dimensions given. Use **ARRAY** to construct the hole and tooth arrangements. Use one of your templates for the drawing. Do not add dimensions. Save the drawing as P11-14.

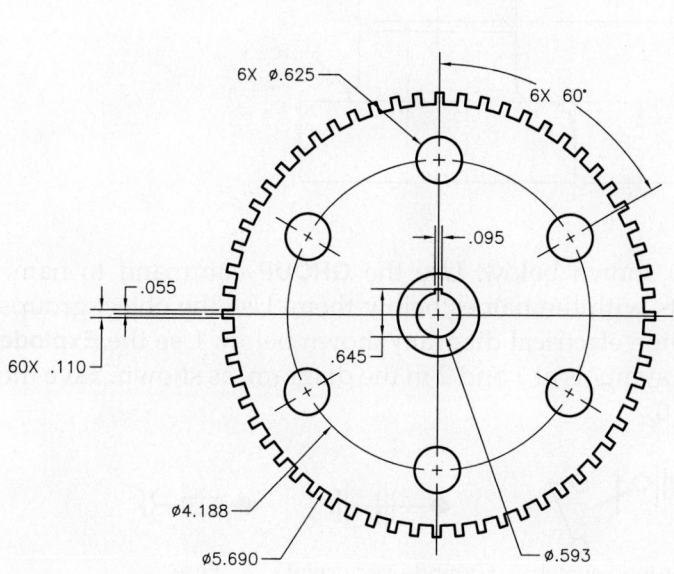

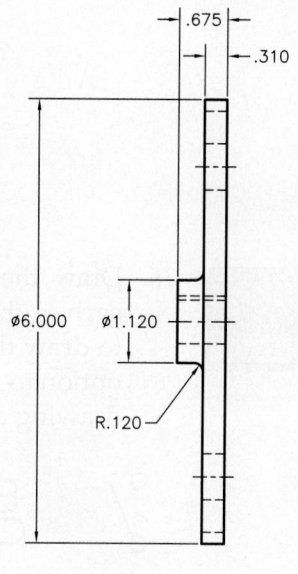

15. Draw the following object without dimensions. Use the **TRIMMODE** setting to your advantage. Save the drawing as P11-15.

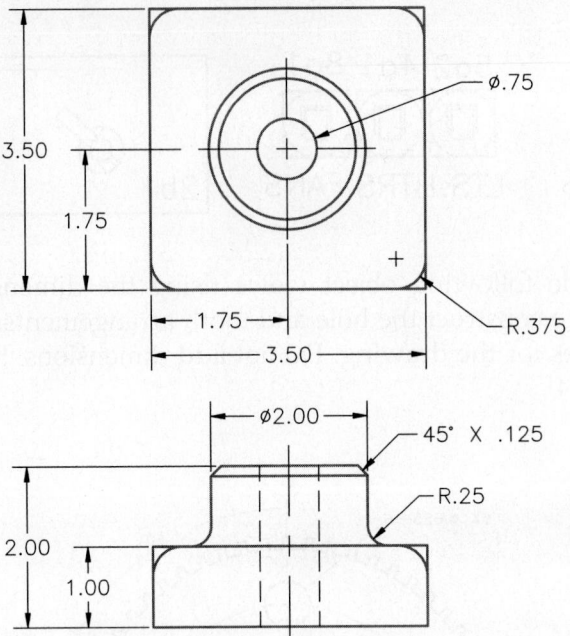

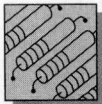

16. Draw the objects shown below. Use the **GROUP** command to name each of the objects with the names below them. Use the object groups to draw the one-line electrical diagram shown below. Use the **Explode** option to edit the symbols at 1 and 2 in the diagram, as shown. Save the drawing as P11-16.

Switch   Regulator   Ground-switch   Ground-overcurrent   Fuse

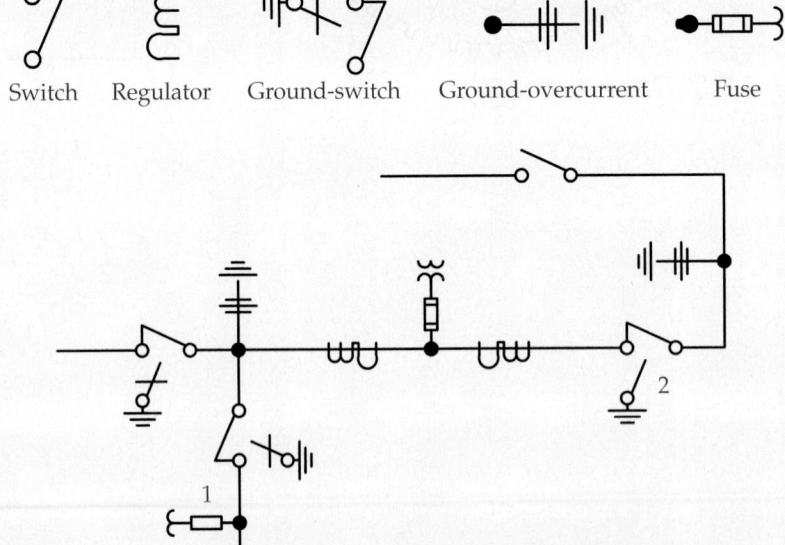

17. Draw the following bracket. Do not include dimensions in your drawing. Use the **FILLET** command where appropriate. Save the drawing as P11-17.

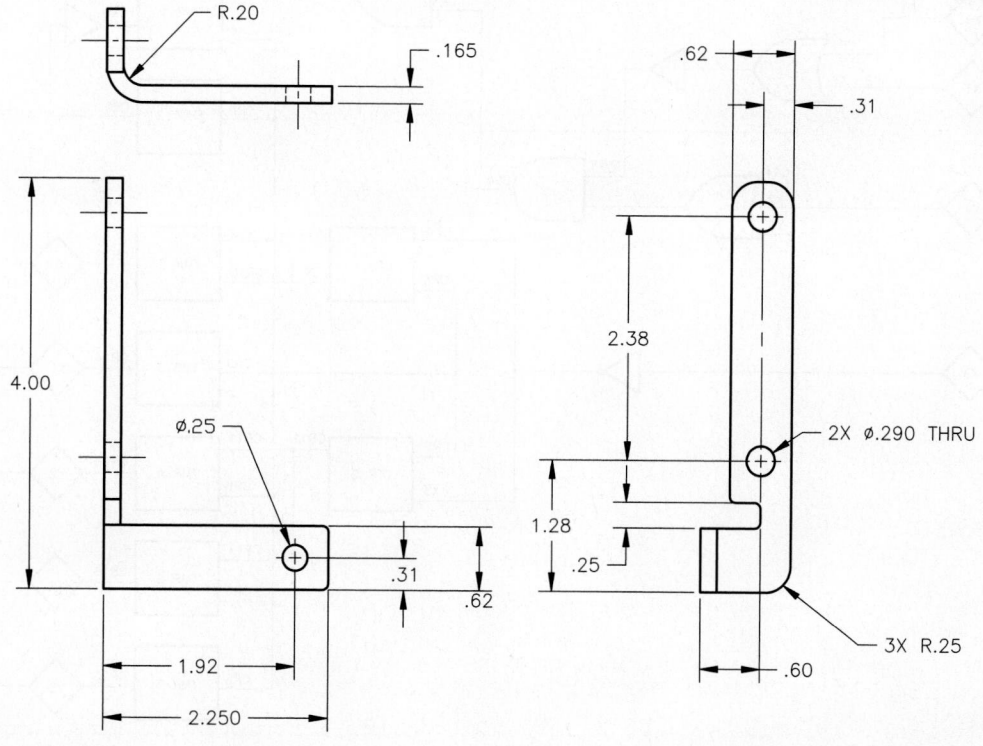

ALL FILLETS AND ROUNDS R.06

18. Draw this refrigeration system schematic. Save the drawing as P11-18.

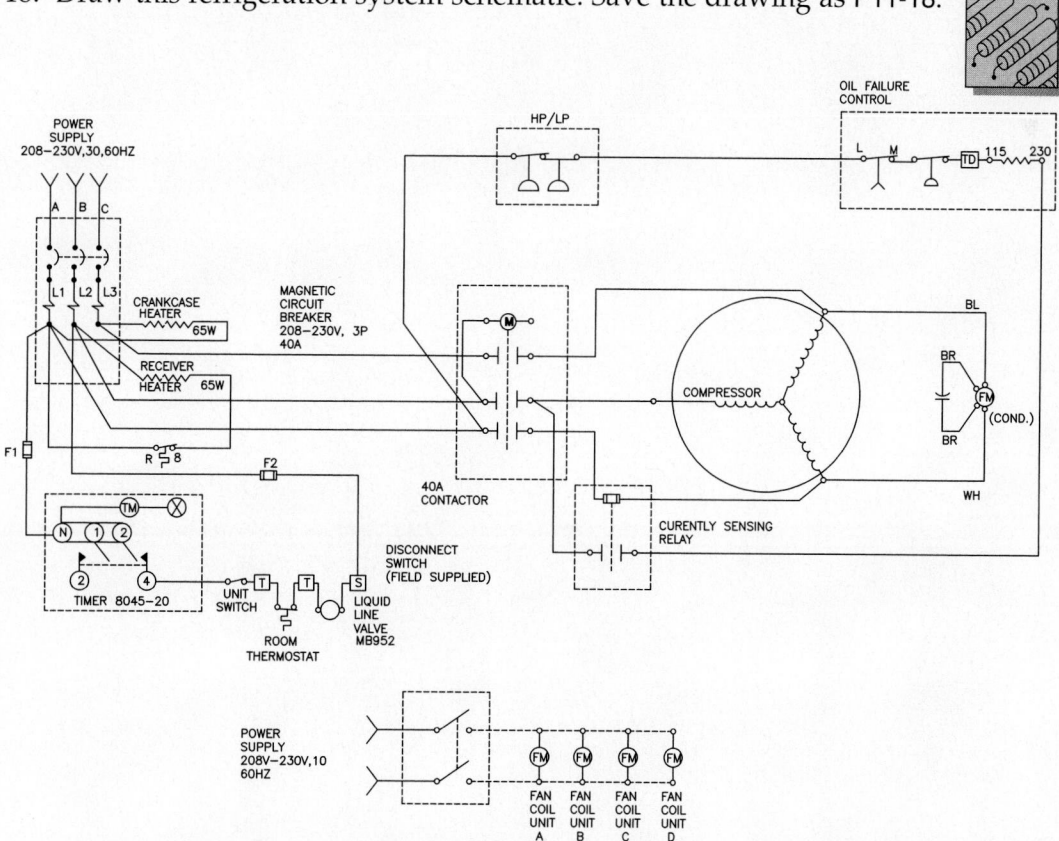

19. Draw this timer schematic. Save the drawing as **P11-19**.

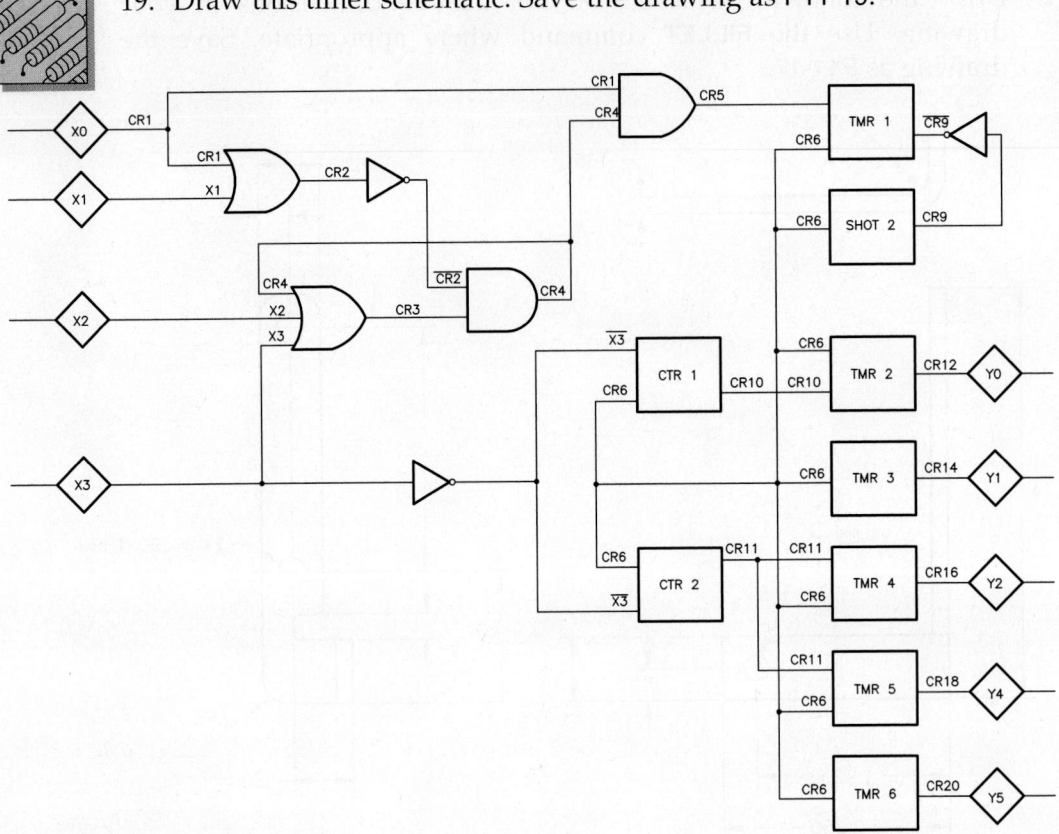

20. The following engineering sketch shows a steel column arrangement on a concrete floor slab for a new building. The I-shaped symbols represent the steel columns. The columns are arranged in "bay lines" and "column lines." The column lines are numbered 1, 2, and 3. The bay lines are labeled A through G. The width of a bay is 24'-0". Line balloons, or tags, identify the bay and column lines. Draw the arrangement, using **ARRAY** for the steel column symbols and the tags. Do not dimension the drawing. The following guidelines will help you.

A. Begin a new drawing, named P11-20, or use an architectural template.
B. Select architectural units and specify a 36 × 24 sheet size. Determine the scale required for the floor plan to fit on this sheet size and specify your limits accordingly.
C. Draw the steel column symbol to the dimensions given.
D. Set the grid spacing at 2'-0" (24").
E. Set the snap spacing at 12".
F. Draw all other objects.
G. Place text inside the balloon tags. Set the running object snap mode to **Center** and **Justify** the text to **Middle**. Make the text height 6".
H. Place a title block on the drawing.
I. Save the drawing as P11-20.

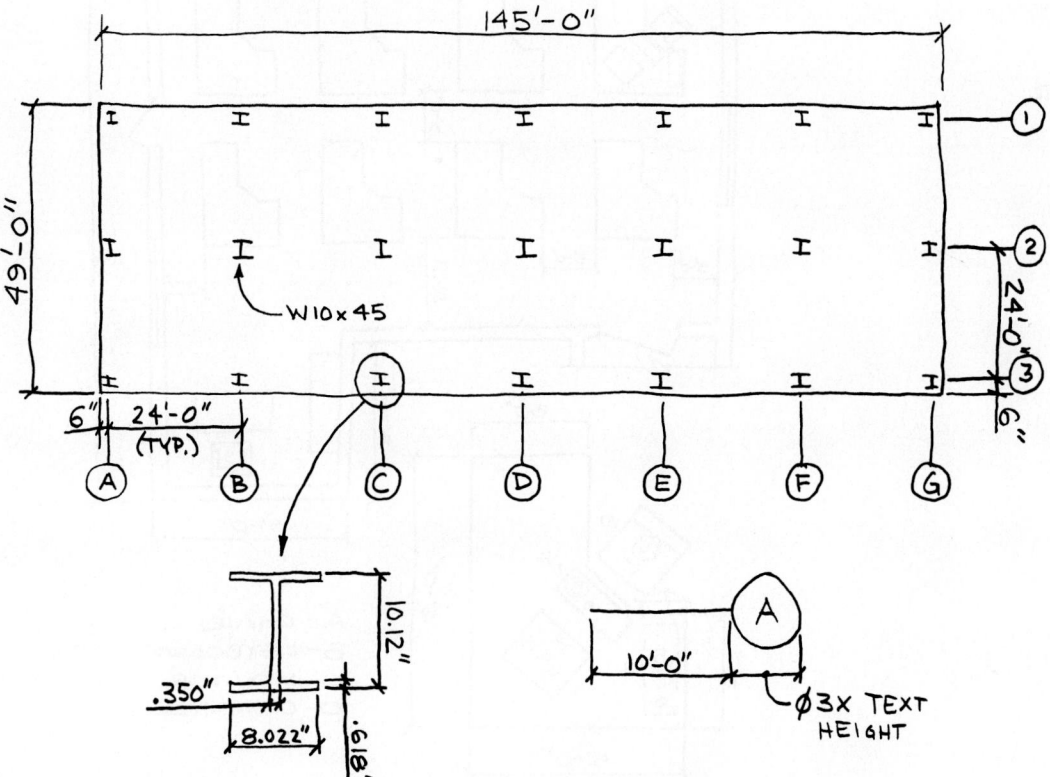

21. The engineering sketch given is a proposed office layout of desks and chairs. One desk is shown with the layout of a chair, keyboard, monitor, and tower-mounted computer (drawn with dotted lines). All the desk workstations should have the same configuration. The exact sizes and locations of the doors and windows are not important for this problem. Use the following guidelines to complete this problem.
   A. Begin a new drawing, called P11-21.
   B. Choose architectural units.
   C. Select a C-size template drawing and be sure to create the drawing in model space. Use the **ZOOM nXP** option to display the drawing at a scale fitting the C-size layout.
   D. Use the appropriate drawing and editing commands to complete this problem quickly and efficiently.
   E. Draw the desk and computer hardware to the dimensions given.
   F. Do not dimension the drawing. Plot a paper space layout tab at a one-to-one scale.
   G. Save the drawing as P11-21.

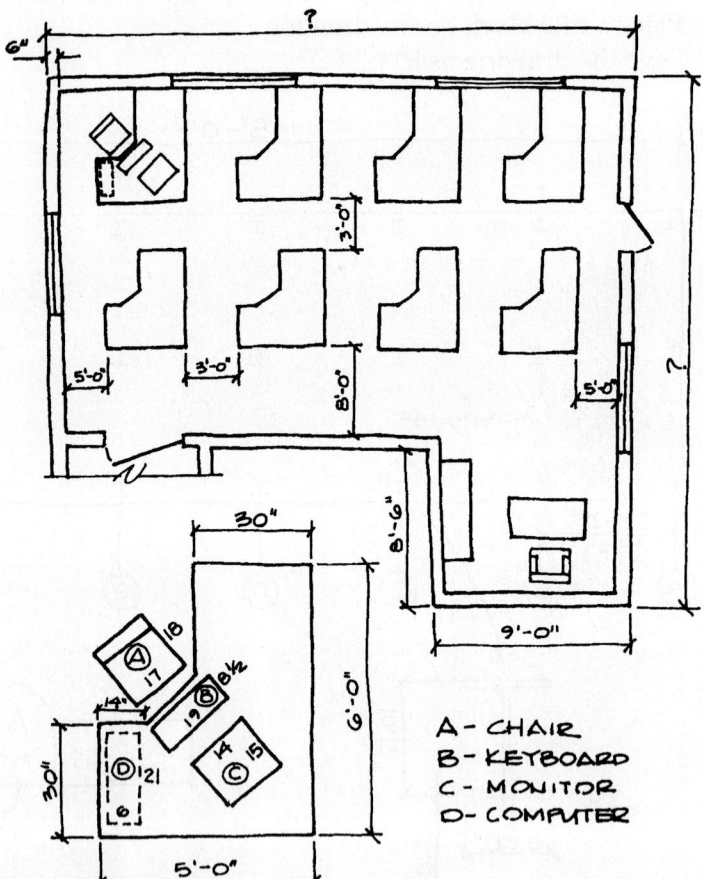

A - CHAIR
B - KEYBOARD
C - MONITOR
D - COMPUTER

## CHAPTER 12

# Automatic Editing

## Learning Objectives

After completing this chapter, you will be able to do the following:

- Use grips to do automatic editing with the **STRETCH**, **COPY**, **MOVE**, **ROTATE**, **SCALE**, and **MIRROR** commands.
- Identify the system variables used for automatic editing.
- Perform automatic editing with the **Properties** window.
- Use the **MATCHPROP** command to match object properties.

In Chapter 11, you learned how to use commands that let you do a variety of drawing and editing activities with AutoCAD. These editing commands give you maximum flexibility and increase productivity. This chapter takes editing a step further, however, by allowing you to first select an object and then automatically perform editing operations.

## Automatic Editing with Grips

*Hold, grab,* and *grasp* are all words synonymous with *grip.* In AutoCAD, **grips** are features on an object that are highlighted with small boxes. For example, the grips on a straight line are the endpoints and midpoint. When grips are used for editing, you can select an object to automatically activate the grips. Pick any of the small boxes to perform **STRETCH**, **COPY**, **MOVE**, **ROTATE**, **SCALE**, or **MIRROR** operations.

When grips are enabled and there is no command active, a pick box is located at the intersection of the screen crosshairs. You can pick any object to activate the grips. **Figure 12-1** shows what grips look like on several different objects. For text, the grip box is located at the insertion point.

You can control grip settings in the **Selection** tab of the **Options** dialog box. The **Options** dialog box is opened by picking **Options...** in the **Tools** pull-down menu or by right-clicking and selecting **Options...** from the shortcut menu. You can access the **Selection** tab of the **Options** dialog box directly by typing GR or DDGRIPS at the Command: prompt. The **Selection** tab in the **Options** dialog box is shown in **Figure 12-2.**

```
DDGRIPS
GR

Tools
➥ Options...
```

**Figure 12-1.**
Grips are placed at strategic locations on objects.

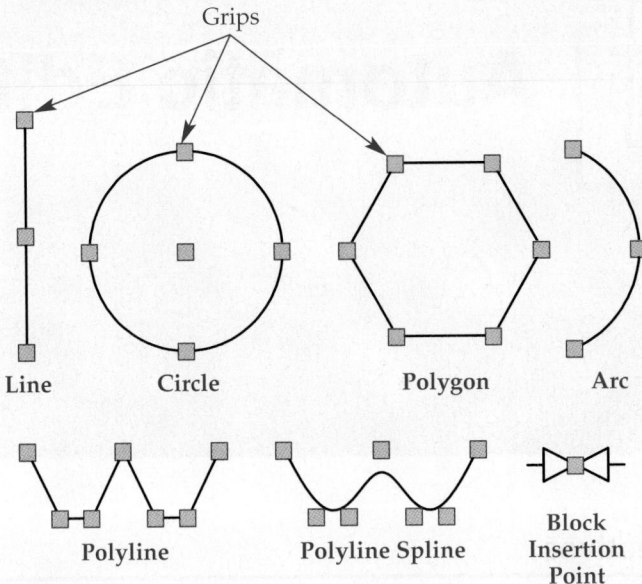

Grips

Line    Circle          Polygon      Arc

Polyline    Polyline Spline    Block
Insertion
Point

**Figure 12-2.**
The **Selection** tab of the **Options** dialog box contains grip control settings.

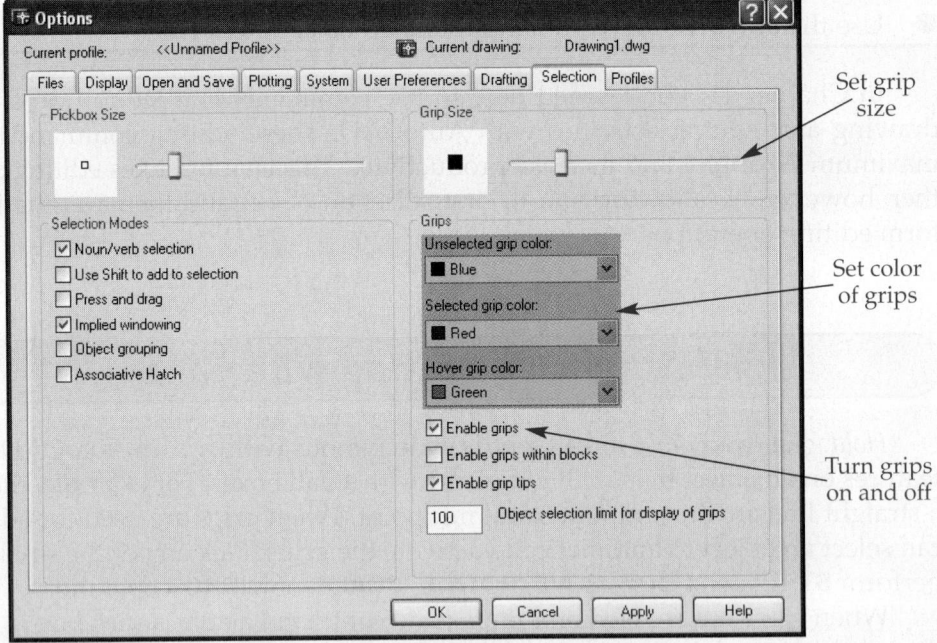

Set grip size

Set color of grips

Turn grips on and off

The **Pickbox Size** scroll bar lets you adjust the size of the pick box. The sample in the image tile gets smaller or larger as you move the scroll bar. Stop when you have the desired size. The pick box size is also controlled by the **PICKBOX** system variable, where the desired size is set in pixels.

The **Grip Size** scroll bar in the **Selection** tab of the **Options** dialog box lets you graphically change the size of the grip box. The sample in the image tile gets smaller or larger as you move the scroll bar. Change the grip size to whatever works best for your drawing. Very small grip boxes may be difficult to pick. The grips may overlap, however, if they are too large.

The grip size can be given a numerical value at the Command: prompt using the **GRIPSIZE** system variable. To change the default setting of 5, enter GRIPSIZE at the Command: prompt, and then type a desired size in pixels.

The three color drop-down lists allow you to change the color of grips. The grips displayed when you first pick an object are referred to as *unselected grips* because you have not yet picked a grip to perform an operation. An unselected grip is a filled-in square using the color of the **Unselected grip color:** setting. Unselected grips are blue by default and are called *warm.*

After you pick a grip, it is called a *selected grip.* A selected grip appears as a filled-in square using the **Selected grip color:** setting. Selected grips are red by default and are called *hot.* If more than one object is selected and has warm grips, what you do with the hot grips affects all the selected objects. Objects having warm and hot grips are highlighted and are part of the selection set.

You can remove highlighted objects from a selection set by holding down the [Shift] key and picking the objects to be removed. The [Shift] key can also be used to add or remove hot grips. If you want to make more than one grip hot, hold the [Shift] key down, and then select the grip. To add more grips to the hot grip selection set, continue to hold the [Shift] key down and select the other grips. With the [Shift] key held down, selecting a hot grip (red) returns it to the warm (blue) stage. **Figure 12-3** shows two different circles being modified by using hot grips. Moving the crosshairs over a warm grip and pausing changes the color of the grip to the **Hover grip color:** setting found in the **Selection** tab of the **Options** dialog box. By default, this color is set to green. This is useful when multiple grips are close together. Pausing over the warm grip and letting it change color ensures that you select the correct grip.

You can also control grip color with the **GRIPCOLOR**, **GRIPHOT**, and **GRIPHOVER** system variables. **GRIPCOLOR** controls the color of warm grips, and **GRIPHOT** regulates the color of hot grips. The hover grip color can be changed by using the **GRIPHOVER** system variable. When you enter one of these variables, simply set the color number as desired.

Notice the three check boxes in the **Grips** area. Pick the **Enable grips** check box to turn grips on or off. This setting can also be set using the **GRIPS** system variable.

**Figure 12-3.**
You can modify multiple objects by using the [Shift] key to select grips to make them hot.

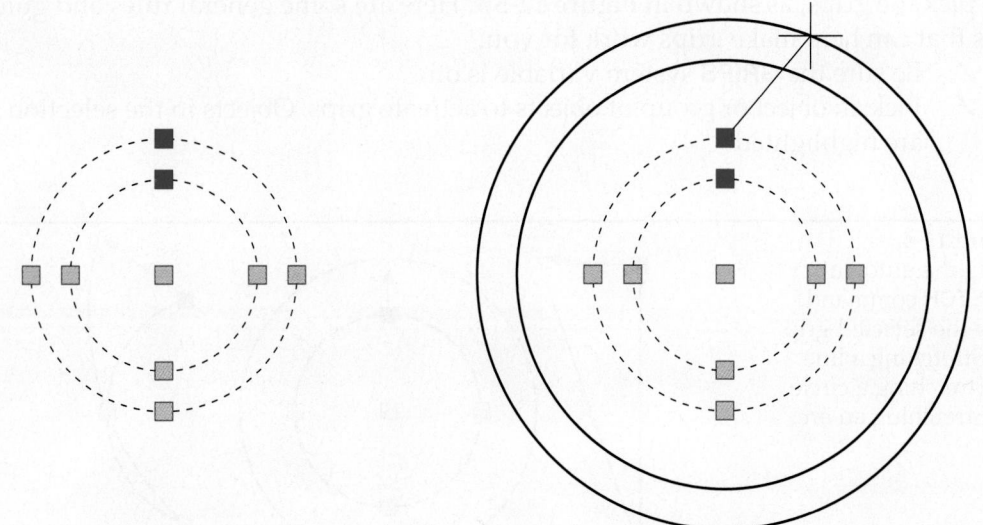

Pick the **Enable grips within blocks** check box to have grips displayed on every subobject of a block. A *block* is a special symbol designed for multiple uses. Blocks are discussed in detail in Chapter 22. When this check box is off, the grip location for a block is at the insertion point, as shown in **Figure 12-1.** Grips in blocks can also be controlled with the **GRIPBLOCK** system variable.

When the **Enable grip tips** box is checked, a tip displays relating to the selected object. This option only works on custom objects supporting grip tips. Standard AutoCAD objects do not have grip tips. The **GRIPTIPS** system variable also controls this option.

## Using Grips

To activate grips, move the pick box to the desired object and pick. The object is highlighted, and the warm grips are displayed. To select a grip, move the pick box to the desired grip and pick it. Notice the crosshairs snap to a grip. When you pick a grip, the command line shows the following prompt:

```
** STRETCH **
Specify stretch point or [Base point/Copy/Undo/eXit]:
```

This activates the **STRETCH** command. All you have to do is move the cursor to make the selected object stretch, as shown in **Figure 12-4.** If you pick the middle grip of a line or arc or the center grip of a circle, the object moves. These are the other options:

- **Base point.** Type B and press [Enter] to select a new base point.
- **Copy.** Type C and press [Enter] if you want to make one or more copies of the selected object.
- **Undo.** Type U and press [Enter] to undo the previous operation.
- **Exit.** Type X and press [Enter] to exit the command. The hot grip is gone, but the warm grips remain. You can also use the [Esc] key to cancel the command. Canceling twice removes the selected and unselected grips and returns to the Command: prompt.

You can pick objects individually or use a window or crossing box. **Figure 12-5** shows how you can stretch features of an object after selecting all the objects. Step 1 in **Figure 12-5A** stretches the first corner, and Step 2 stretches the second corner. You can also make more than one grip hot at the same time by holding down the [Shift] key as you pick the grips, as shown in **Figure 12-5B.** Here are some general rules and guidelines that can help make grips work for you:

- ✓ Be sure the **GRIPS** system variable is on.
- ✓ Pick an object or group of objects to activate grips. Objects in the selection set are highlighted.

Figure 12-4.
Using the automatic **STRETCH** command. Note the selected grip.
A—Stretching a line.
B—Stretching a circle.
C—Stretching an arc.

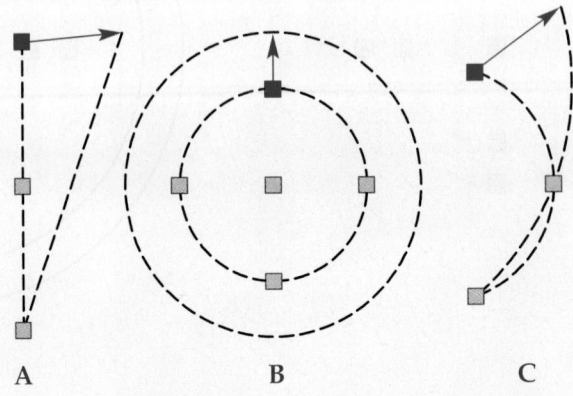

A                    B                    C

**Figure 12-5.**
Stretching an object. A—Select corners to stretch individually. B—Select several hot grips by holding down the [Shift] key.

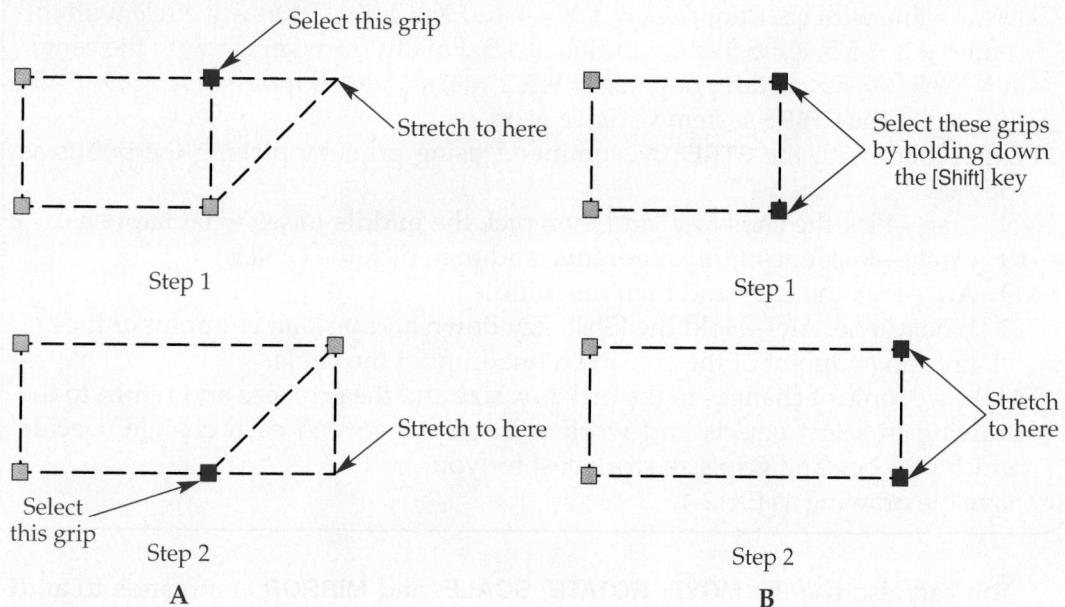

- ✓ Pick a warm grip to make it hot.
- ✓ Make multiple grips hot by holding the [Shift] key while picking warm grips.
- ✓ If more than one object has hot grips, they are all affected by the editing commands.
- ✓ Remove objects from the selection set by holding down the [Shift] key and picking them, thus making the grips warm.
- ✓ Return objects to the selection set by picking them again.
- ✓ Remove hot grips from the selection set by pressing the [Esc] key to cancel. Cancel again to remove all grips from the selection set. You can also right-click and select **Deselect All** from the shortcut menu to remove all grips.

**PROFESSIONAL TIP**

When editing with grips, you can enter coordinates to help improve your accuracy. Remember that any of the coordinate entry methods work.

○ Start a new drawing or use one of your templates.

○ Draw a line with coordinates X = 2, Y = 4 and X = 2, Y = 7. Draw a circle with the center at X = 5.5, Y = 5.5 and a radius of 1.5. Finally, draw an arc with the center at X = 8.5, Y = 5.5; a start point of X = 9.5, Y = 4; and an endpoint of X = 9.5, Y = 7.

○ Make sure the **GRIPS** system variable is on.

○ Experiment with the **STRETCH** command using grips by picking the points as follows:

   ○ Line—Pick the ends first, and then pick the middle to see what happens.

   ○ Circle—Pick one of the quadrants, and then pick the center.

   ○ Arc—Pick the ends and then the middle.

   ○ Line, Circle, Arc—Hold the [Shift] key down and pick an endpoint of the line, an endpoint of the arc, and a quadrant of the circle.

○ Make a couple of changes to the pick box size and the grip size and return to the drawing to select objects and work with grips between each change. Decide which pick box and grip size work best for you.

○ Save the drawing as EX12-1.

You can also use the **MOVE**, **ROTATE**, **SCALE**, and **MIRROR** commands to automatically edit objects. All you have to do is pick the object, and then select one of the grips. When you see the \*\* STRETCH \*\* command, press [Enter] to cycle through the command options:

```
** STRETCH **
Specify stretch point or [Base point/Copy/Undo/eXit]: ↵
** MOVE **
Specify move point or [Base point/Copy/Undo/eXit]: ↵
** ROTATE **
Specify rotation angle or [Base point/Copy/Undo/Reference/eXit]: ↵
** SCALE **
Specify scale factor or [Base point/Copy/Undo/Reference/eXit]: ↵
** MIRROR **
Specify second point or [Base point/Copy/Undo/eXit]: ↵
```

As an alternative to pressing [Enter], you can enter the first two characters of the desired command from the keyboard. Type MO for **MOVE**, MI for **MIRROR**, RO for **ROTATE**, SC for **SCALE**, and ST for **STRETCH**.

AutoCAD also allows you to right-click and access a grips shortcut menu, as shown in **Figure 12-6.** This menu is only available after a grip has been turned into a hot grip. The shortcut menu allows you to access the five grip editing options without using the keyboard. All you have to do is pick **Move, Mirror, Rotate, Scale,** or **Stretch** as needed. Another option in the shortcut menu is **Base Point**. This option allows you to select a base point other than the hot grip. The shortcut menu also provides direct access to the **Copy** option, which is explained later in this chapter. The **Undo** option closes the shortcut menu and returns to the current grip activity.

An added bonus in the grips shortcut menu is the **Properties** option. Selecting this opens the **Properties** window, where you can change properties of the objects being edited. Selecting the **Exit** option closes the grips shortcut menu and removes the hot grip.

Figure 12-6.
The grips shortcut
menu appears when
a grip is selected
and you right-click.

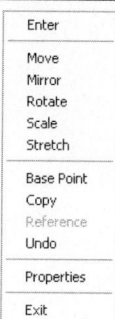

| |
|---|
| Enter |
| Move |
| Mirror |
| Rotate |
| Scale |
| Stretch |
| Base Point |
| Copy |
| Reference |
| Undo |
| Properties |
| Exit |

**NOTE**

When AutoCAD is configured to display a screen menu, the **Move**, **Mirror**, **Rotate**, **Scale**, and **Stretch** automatic editing commands appear in a separate screen menu whenever a grip is selected.

**PROFESSIONAL TIP**

Many of the conventional AutoCAD editing operations can be performed when warm grips are displayed on screen and the **PICKFIRST** variable is set to 1 (its default value). The editing commands can be selected from the pull-down menus, selected from the toolbars, or entered at the Command: prompt. For example, the **ERASE** command can be used to clear the screen of all objects displayed with warm grips by first picking the objects and then selecting the **ERASE** command.

## Moving an Object Automatically

If you want to move an object with grips, select the object, pick a grip to use as the base point, and then press [Enter] to cycle through the commands until you get to this prompt:

```
** MOVE **
Specify move point or [Base point/Copy/Undo/eXit]:
```

The selected grip becomes the base point. Move the object to a new point by picking the new location. You may want to use object snap mode or coordinates to place it in a new location. The **MOVE** operation is complete, as shown in **Figure 12-7.** If you accidentally pick the wrong grip or want to have a base point other than the selected grip, type B and press [Enter] for the **Base point** option. Pick a new base point.

### Exercise 12-2

○ Start a new drawing or use one of your templates.
○ Draw a 1.5″ (38 mm) diameter circle with the center at X = 2, Y = 3.
○ Use grips to move the circle 2″ (50 mm) to the right.
○ Save the drawing as EX12-2.

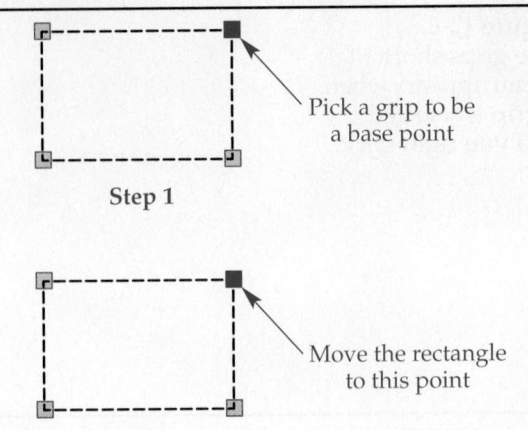

**Figure 12-7.**
The automatic
**MOVE** command.
The selected grip
becomes the base
point for the move.

Pick a grip to be
a base point

Step 1

Move the rectangle
to this point

Step 2

## Copying an Object Automatically

The **Copy** option is found in each of the editing commands. When using the **STRETCH** command, the **Copy** option allows you to make multiple copies of the object you are stretching. Holding down the [Shift] key while performing the first **STRETCH** operation accesses the **Multiple** option. The prompt looks like this:

```
** STRETCH (multiple) **
Specify stretch point or [Base point/Copy/Undo/eXit]:↵
```

The **Copy** option in the **MOVE** command is the true form of the **COPY** command. You can activate the **Copy** option by typing C, as follows:

```
** MOVE **
Specify move point or [Base point/Copy/Undo/eXit]: C↵
** MOVE (multiple) **
Specify move point or [Base point/Copy/Undo/eXit]: (make as many copies as desired
   and enter X, press [Esc], or select Exit from the grips shortcut menu to exit)
```

Holding down the [Shift] key while performing the first **MOVE** operation also accesses the **Copy** option. The **Copy** option works similarly in each of the editing commands. Try it with each to see what happens. When you are in the **STRETCH** or **MOVE** command, you can also access the **Copy** option directly by picking the right mouse button to open the grips shortcut menu.

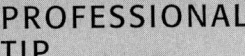

**PROFESSIONAL
TIP**

When in the **Copy** option of the **MOVE** command, if you make the first copy and then hold the [Shift] key, the distance of the first copy automatically becomes the snap spacing for additional copies.

## Exercise 12-3

○ Start a new drawing or use one of your templates.
○ Use the **RECTANG** command to draw the objects shown in A, B, C, and D below. Do not draw dimensions.
○ Use the **Copy** option of the **STRETCH** command to make Object A look similar to the example on the right.
○ Use the **Copy** option of the **STRETCH** command to make Object B look similar to the example on the right. Make two grips hot for this to work.
○ Use the **Copy** option of the **MOVE** command to make multiple copies to the right of Object C.
○ Use the **MOVE** command to make multiple copies to the right of Object D, while holding down the [Shift] key.
○ Save the drawing as EX12-3.

## Rotating an Object Automatically

To automatically rotate an object, select the object, pick a grip to use as the base point, and press [Enter] until you see this prompt:

```
** ROTATE **
Specify rotation angle or [Base point/Copy/Undo/Reference/eXit]:
```

Now, move your pointing device to rotate the object. Pick the desired rotation point or enter a rotation angle at the Command: prompt.

Type R and press [Enter] if you want to use the **Reference** option. The **Reference** option may be used when the object is already rotated at a known angle and you want to rotate it to a new angle. The reference angle is the current angle, and the new angle is the desired angle. **Figure 12-8** shows the **ROTATE** options.

Figure 12-8.
The rotation angle
and **Reference**
option of the
**ROTATE** command.

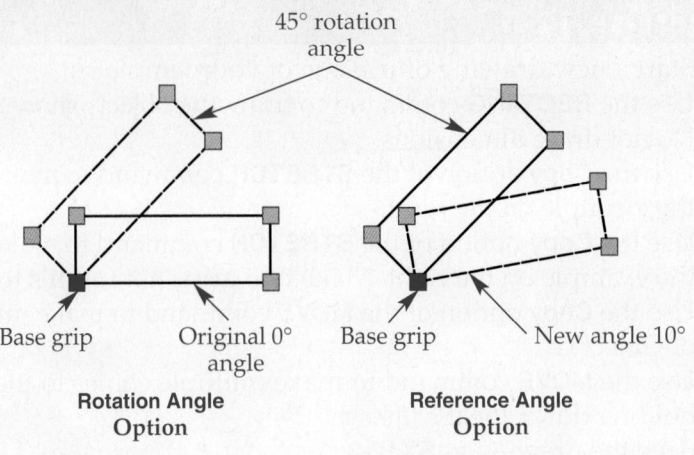

45° rotation
angle

Base grip    Original 0°    Base grip    New angle 10°
angle

**Rotation Angle**
**Option**

**Reference Angle**
**Option**

## Exercise 12-4

○ Start a new drawing or use one of your templates.
○ Use the **RECTANG** command to draw a rectangle similar to the one shown on the left in **Figure 12-8.** Orient the long sides so they are at 0°.
○ Use grips to rotate the object 45°.
○ Rotate the object again, to 20°, using the **Reference** option.
○ Save the drawing as EX12-4.

## Scaling an Object Automatically

If you want to scale an object with grips, cycle through the editing options until you get this prompt:

    ** SCALE **
    Specify scale factor or [Base point/Copy/Undo/Reference/eXit]:

Move the screen cursor and pick when the object is dragged to the desired size. You can also enter a scale factor to automatically increase or decrease the scale of the original object. You can use the **Reference** option if you know a current length and a desired length. The selected base point remains in the same place when the object is scaled. **Figure 12-9** shows the two **SCALE** options.

Figure 12-9.
The options for the
automatic **SCALE**
command include
the **scale factor**
option and the
**Reference** option.

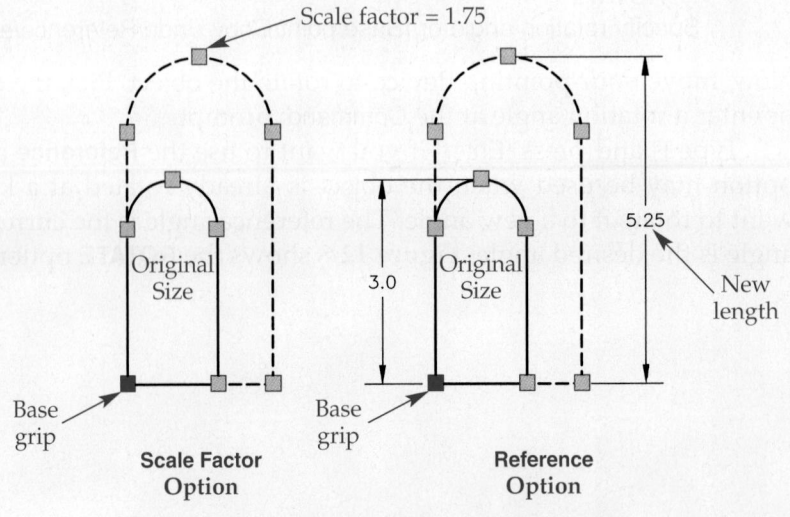

Scale factor = 1.75

Original
Size

Original
Size

3.0

5.25

New
length

Base
grip

Base
grip

**Scale Factor**
**Option**

**Reference**
**Option**

## Mirroring an Object Automatically

If you want to mirror an object using grips, the selected grip becomes the first point of the mirror line. Press [Enter] to cycle through the editing commands until you get this prompt:

```
** MIRROR **
Specify second point or [Base point/Copy/Undo/eXit]:
```

Use the **Base point** option to reselect the first point of the mirror line. Pick another grip or any point on the screen as the second point of the mirror line. See **Figure 12-10**. Unlike the standard **MIRROR** command, the automatic **MIRROR** command does not give you the option to delete the old objects. The old objects are deleted automatically. If you want to keep the original object while mirroring, use the **Copy** option in the **MIRROR** command.

**Figure 12-10.**
When using the automatic **MIRROR** command, the selected grip becomes the first point of the mirror line, and the original object is automatically deleted.

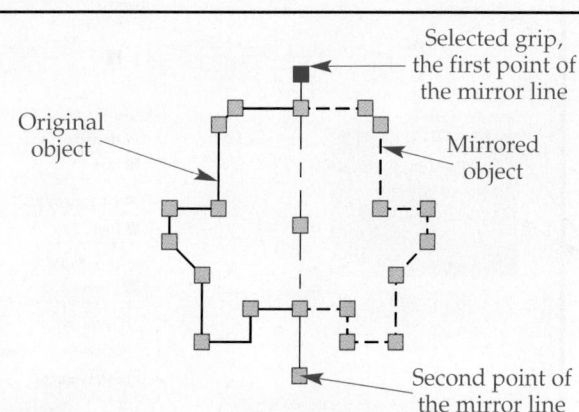

# Basic Editing Versus Automatic Editing

In Chapter 11, you were introduced to basic editing. Basic editing allows you to first enter a command and then select the desired object to be edited. You can also set system variables so you first select the desired objects and then enter the desired command. The automatic editing features discussed in this chapter use grips and related editing commands to edit an object automatically, after first selecting the object.

The **Selection Modes** area of the **Selection** tab in the **Options** dialog box allows you to control the way you use editing commands. See **Figure 12-11.** Select or deselect the following options, based on your own preferences:

- **Noun/verb selection.** When you first select objects and then enter a command, it is referred to as the *noun/verb* format. The pick box is displayed at the screen crosshairs. A "✓" in this check box means the noun/verb method is active. The **PICKFIRST** system variable can also be used to set the **Noun/verb selection**. When using the *verb/noun* format, you enter the command before selecting the object. Remove the "✓" from the **Noun/verb selection** check box to enter the command before making a selection.

**Figure 12-11.**
The **Selection Modes** area of the **Selection** tab in the **Options** dialog box.

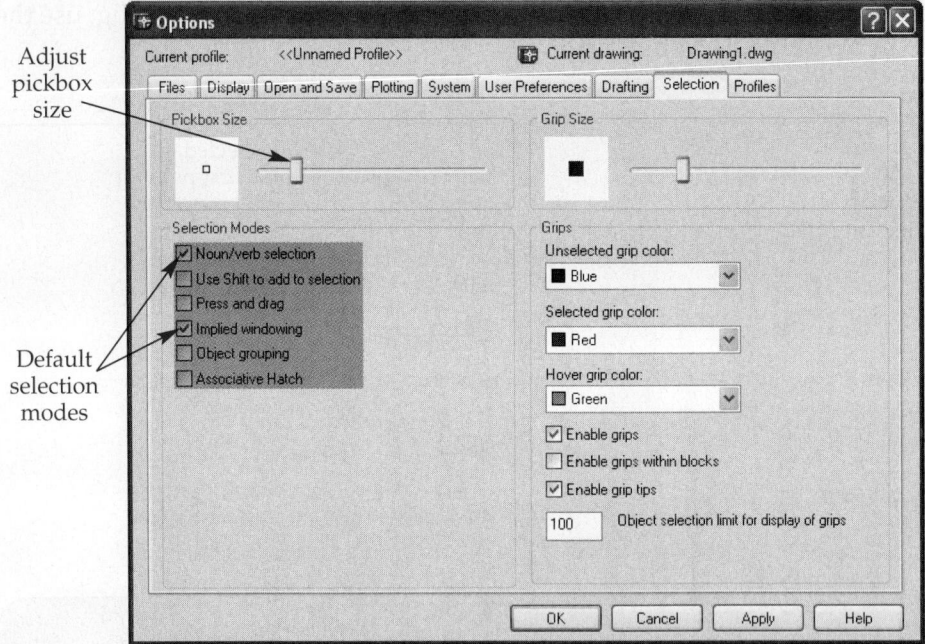

Adjust pickbox size

Default selection modes

NOTE

Some editing commands, such as **FILLET, CHAMFER, DIVIDE, MEASURE, OFFSET, EXTEND, TRIM,** and **BREAK,** require you to enter the command before you select the object.

AutoCAD and its Applications—Basics

- **Use Shift to add to selection.** When this check box is off, every object or group of objects you select is highlighted and added to the selection set. If you pick this check box, it changes the way AutoCAD accepts objects you pick. For example, if you pick an object, it is highlighted and added to the selection set. If you pick another object, however, it is highlighted, and the first one is removed from the selection set. This means you can only select one object by picking or one group of objects with a selection window. If you want to add more items to the selection set, you must hold down the [Shift] key as you pick them. Turning off the **PICKADD** system variable does the same thing as turning on this feature.
- **Press and drag.** This is the same as turning on the **PICKDRAG** system variable. With **Press and drag** on, you create a selection window by picking the first corner and moving the cursor while holding down the pick button. Release the pick button when you have the desired selection window. By default, this option is off. This means you need to pick both the first and second corners of the desired selection window.
- **Implied windowing.** By default, this option is on. This means you can automatically create a window by picking the first point and moving the cursor to the right to pick the second point, or you can make a crossing box by picking the first point and moving the cursor to the left to pick the second point. This is the same as turning on the **PICKAUTO** system variable. This does not work if **PICKDRAG** is on.
- **Object grouping.** This option controls whether or not AutoCAD recognizes grouped objects as singular objects. When it is off, the individual elements of a group can be selected for separate editing without having to first explode the group.
- **Associative Hatch.** The default is off, which means, if an associative hatch is moved, the hatch boundary does not move with it. Select this toggle if you want the boundary of an associative hatch to move when you move the hatch pattern. It is a good idea to have this on for most applications. Hatches and hatch boundaries are fully explained in Chapter 21.

## Setting Object Sorting Methods

The **Object Sorting Methods** area, shown in **Figure 12-12,** appears when you pick the **User Preferences** tab in the **Options** dialog box. The check boxes in the **Object Sorting Methods** area allow you to control the order in which objects are displayed or plotted. The check boxes are explained as follows:
- **Object selection.** Objects selected using a windowing method are placed in the selection set in the order they occur in the drawing database.
- **Object snap.** Object snap modes find objects in the order they occur in the drawing database.
- **Regens.** Objects are displayed by a drawing regeneration in the order they occur in the drawing database.
- **Plotting.** Objects are plotted in the order they occur in the drawing database.

NOTE  The **SORTENTS** system variable also controls object sorting using bit values.

**Figure 12-12.**
The **User Preferences** tab of the **Options** dialog box.

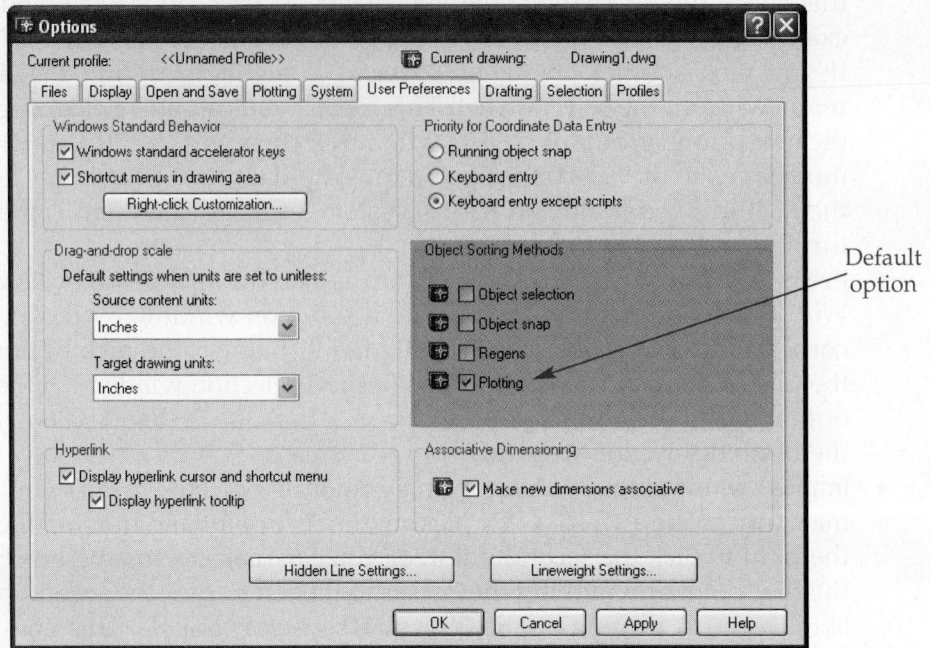

Default
option

Notice, in **Figure 12-12**, that only one of the check boxes is checked. Object sorting takes time and should only be used if the drawing or application software you are using requires object sorting. Turn the **Object selection** sorting on if you want AutoCAD to find the last object drawn when selecting overlapping objects.

### Exercise 12-7

○ Start a new drawing, use one of your templates, or open a previous exercise.
○ Open the **Selection** tab in the **Options** dialog box.
○ Pick the **User Preferences** tab to see the **Object Sorting Methods** area.
○ Cancel the dialog box.
○ Quit the drawing session without saving or keep it open for the next exercise.

## Using the Properties Window

PROPERTIES
PROPS
CH, MO
[Ctrl]+[1]

Modify
➡ Properties

Standard
toolbar

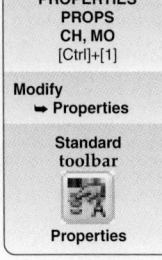

Properties

An object can be edited automatically using the **Properties** window. To edit an object using the **Properties** window, pick the **Properties** button from the **Standard** toolbar; pick **Properties** from the **Modify** pull-down menu; or type MO, CH, PROPS, or PROPERTIES at the Command: prompt. You can also toggle the **Properties** window on and off using the [Ctrl]+[1] key combination. If an object has already been selected, you can also access the **Properties** window by right-clicking and selecting **Properties** from the shortcut menu.

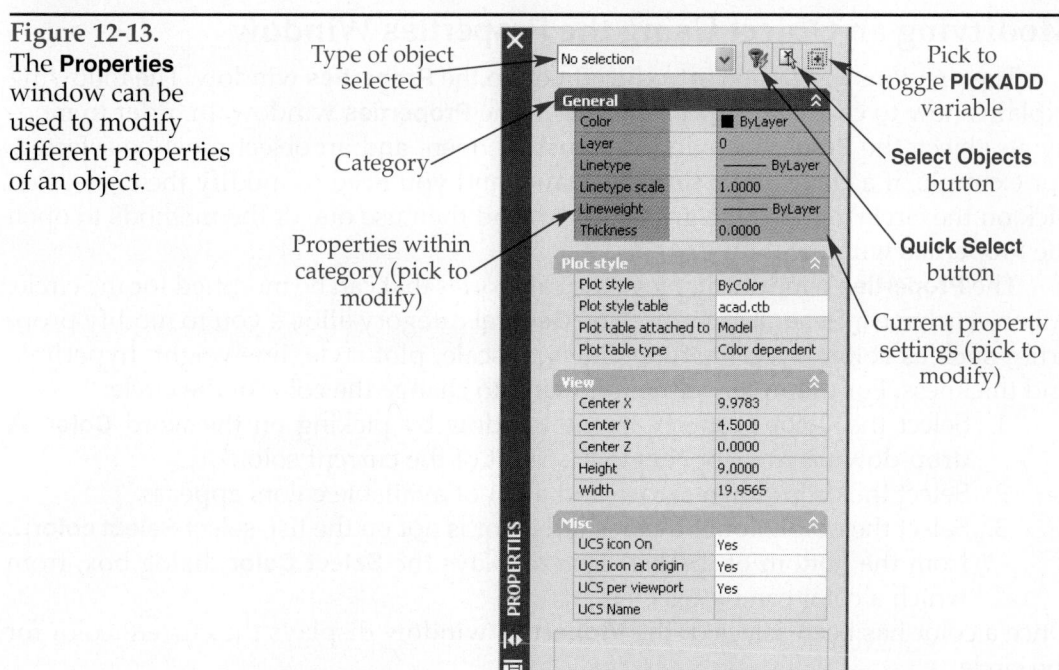

**Figure 12-13.**
The **Properties** window can be used to modify different properties of an object.

Type of object selected

Category

Properties within category (pick to modify)

Pick to toggle **PICKADD** variable

**Select Objects** button

**Quick Select** button

Current property settings (pick to modify)

The **Properties** window appears, as shown in **Figure 12-13**. The **Properties** window can be docked in the drawing area similar to a toolbar. This was discussed in Chapter 1.

While the **Properties** window is displayed, you can enter commands and continue to work in AutoCAD. You can close the box by picking the **X** in the top left corner, picking the **Properties** button on the **Modify** toolbar, or using the [Ctrl] + [1] key combination.

When you access the **Properties** window without first selecting an object, No selection can be seen in the top drop-down list. This means AutoCAD does not have any objects selected to modify. The four categories—**General**, **Plot style**, **View**, and **Misc**—list the current settings for the drawing.

Underneath each category is a list of object properties. For example, in **Figure 12-13**, the current color is ByLayer. To change a property, pick the property or its current value. Once the property is highlighted, one of the following methods is used to set the new value:

- A drop-down arrow with a list of values.
- A pick point button, which allows you to pick a new coordinate location.
- A text box, which is opened when you select certain properties, such as the radius of an arc. Entering a new value in this box allows you to change the radius.

Once a property to be modified has been selected, a description of what that property does is shown at the bottom of the dialog box.

In the upper-right portion of the **Properties** window are three buttons. Pick the **Quick Select** button to access the **Quick Select** dialog box, where you can create object selection sets. This dialog box is discussed in Chapter 7. Picking the **Select Objects** button deselects the currently selected objects and changes the crosshairs to a pick box. The third button toggles the value of the **PICKADD** system variable, which determines whether or not you need to hold the [Shift] key when adding objects to a selection set.

## Modifying an Object Using the Properties Window

The previous discussion introduced you to the **Properties** window. The following explains how to change object properties in the **Properties** window. In order to modify an object, the **Properties** window must be open, and an object must be selected. For example, if a circle and a line are drawn and you need to modify the circle, first pick on the circle to make the grips appear, and then use one of the methods to open the **Properties** window.

The **Properties** window displays the categories that can be modified for the circle. All objects have a **General** category. The **General** category allows you to modify properties such as color, layer, linetype, linetype scale, plot style, lineweight, hyperlink, and thickness. For example, do the following to change the color of the circle:

1. Select the **Color** property in the window by picking on the word **Color**. A drop-down arrow appears to the right of the current color.
2. Select the drop-down arrow, and a list of available colors appears.
3. Select the new color. If the desired color is not on the list, select **Select color...** from the bottom of the list. This displays the **Select Color** dialog box, from which a color can be selected.

Once a color has been selected, the **Properties** window displays the current color for the circle.

A description of each of the properties in the **General** category follows:

- **Color.** Pick this property to display a drop-down arrow from which a color can be selected. At the bottom of the drop-down list is the **Select Color...** option, which displays the **Select Color** dialog box showing all the colors available.
- **Layer.** Select the desired layer for the object here. Layers are discussed in Chapter 4.
- **Linetype.** Select the desired linetype for the object.
- **Linetype scale.** To change the individual object's linetype, highlight the value and type a new scale value. The linetype scale for an individual object is a multiplier of the **LTSCALE** system variable. This was discussed in Chapter 4.
- **Plot style.** Picking on this property displays a drop-down arrow with various plot styles. Initially, only one style is available: ByColor. In order to create a list of plot styles, you must create a plot style table. Plotting and plot styles are discussed in Chapter 10.
- **Lineweight.** Select the desired lineweight for the object. Lineweights are discussed in Chapter 4.
- **Hyperlink.** Picking on this property displays a ... (ellipsis) button. By selecting this button, you can access the **Insert Hyperlink** dialog box. Use this dialog box to add a hyperlink to a graphical object, a description, or a URL address to an object.
- **Thickness.** This property allows you to change the thickness of a 3D object in a text box. Thickness is discussed in Chapter 26.

As stated earlier, all objects have a **General** category. Depending on the type of object that has been selected to modify, other categories are also displayed. See **Figure 12-14.** One of the most common categories is **Geometry**. Although most objects have a **Geometry** category, the properties within the categories vary, depending on the type of object. Typically, there are three properties that allow you to change the absolute coordinates for the object by specifying the X, Y, and Z coordinates. Pick one of these properties, and a pick button is displayed. The button allows you to pick a point in your drawing for the new location. In addition to the pick button, the value for the coordinate can also be changed in a text box.

When multiple objects are selected, you can use the **Properties** window to modify all the objects, or you can pick only one of the selected objects to be modified. The drop-down list displays the types of objects selected. See **Figure 12-15.** Select All to

**Figure 12-14.**
The **Properties** window with a line object selected. Notice there are only two categories that can be modified for the line object.

Type of object selected

General properties

These values cannot be directly modified, but change if endpoints are modified

Start point and endpoint coordinates

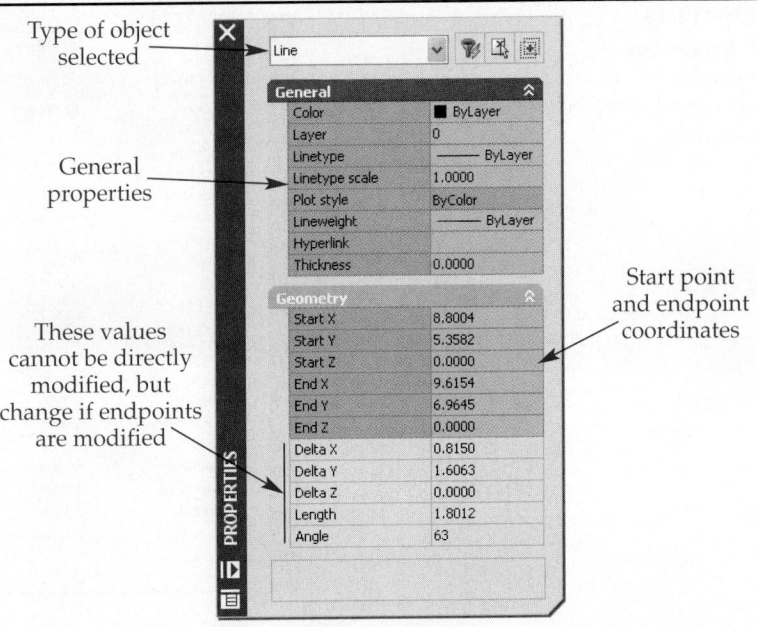

**Figure 12-15.**
The **Properties** window with three objects selected. You can edit the objects individually or all together by selecting All (3).

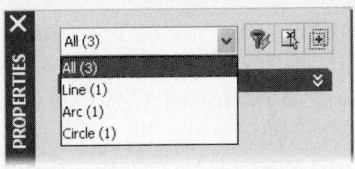

change the properties of all selected objects. Only properties shared by all selected objects are displayed when All is selected. To modify only one object, select the appropriate object type.

When all the changes to the object have been made, press the [Esc] button on the keyboard to clear the grips and remove the object from the **Properties** window. The object is now displayed in the drawing window with the desired changes. For example, if you select a circle, two categories appear in the **Properties** window—**General** and **Geometry**. See **Figure 12-16.** The **Geometry** category displays the current location of the center of the circle by showing three properties: **Center X**, **Center Y**, and **Center Z**. To choose a new center location for the circle, select the appropriate property. Pick a new point or type the coordinate values. There are also other properties that can be modified for the circle, such as the **Radius**, **Diameter**, **Circumference**, and **Area**. By changing any of these values, you are modifying the size of the circle.

---

NOTE

The **Properties** window is discussed where appropriate throughout this text.

---

**Figure 12-16.**
The **Properties** window with a Circle object selected for editing.

Type of object selected

Pick to modify location

Pick button

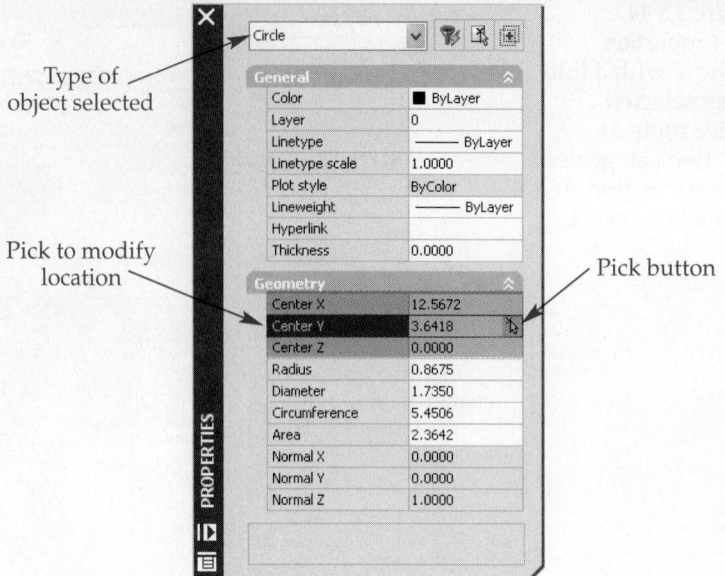

---

## Exercise 12-8

○ Start a new drawing, use one of your templates, or open a previous exercise.
○ Draw a line with endpoint coordinates X = 2, Y = 3, and X = 2, Y = 6.
○ Draw a circle with a radius of 1.250 and a center location of X = 6, Y = 4.5.
○ Use the **TEXT** command with .25 text height to position the word LINE below the line and the word CIRCLE below the circle.
○ Use the **Properties** window to edit the line as follows:
  ○ Change the start point to X = 6.750, Y = 3.770.
  ○ Change the endpoint to X = 6.750, Y = 6.750.
○ Use the **Properties** window to edit the circle as follows:
  ○ Change the center location to X = 7.125, Y = 5.25.
  ○ Change the radius to .375.
○ Change the LINE label to a text height of .125" and place it above the line.
○ Change the CIRCLE label to read Circle and justify the middle of it with the center of the circle. Modify the text height to be .375".
○ Save the drawing as EX12-8.

---

**PROFESSIONAL TIP**

If you are trying to pick an object that is on top of another, AutoCAD may not pick the one you want. AutoCAD picks the last thing you drew, however, if **Object selection** is on in the **Object Sorting Methods** area in the **User Preferences** tab of the **Options** dialog box.

# Changing the Properties of an Object at the Command: Prompt

Object properties can be changed at the Command: prompt using the **CHANGE** and **CHPROP** commands. Select the **Properties** option of the **CHANGE** command, as follows:

> Command: **-CH** *or* **CHANGE**↵
> Select objects: *(pick the object)*
> Select objects: ↵
> Specify change point or [Properties]: **P**↵
> Enter property to change [Color/Elev/LAyer/LType/ltScale/LWeight/Thickness
> /Plotstyle]:

The following properties can be changed with the **CHANGE** command:
- **Color.** Changes the color of the selected object.
- **Elevation.** Changes the elevation in 3D drawings.
- **Layer.** Changes the layer designation.
- **Linetype.** Changes the current linetype of a selected object to a linetype that has been loaded using the **LINETYPE** command.
- **Linetype scale.** Changes the individual object linetype scale.
- **Lineweight.** Changes the individual object's lineweight.
- **Thickness.** Changes the thickness in 3D drawings.
- **Plot style.** Changes the named plot style for the object. This option is not available in drawings using color-dependent plot styles.

The **CHPROP** (change property) command lets you change only properties of an object. It does not allow for a point change, as does the **CHANGE** command. This is the command sequence for **CHPROP**:

> Command: **CHPROP**↵
> Select objects: *(pick the object)*
> Select objects: ↵
> Enter property to change [Color/LAyer/LType/ltScale/LWeight/Thickness/Plotstyle]:

Except for **Elevation**, the **CHPROP** options are the same as those discussed for the **CHANGE** command.

## Exercise 12-9

- ◯ Start a new drawing or use one of your templates.
- ◯ Draw a vertical line on the left side of the screen, a circle in the middle, and a hexagon on the right side.
- ◯ Load the Center, Hidden, and Phantom linetypes.
- ◯ Use the **CHANGE** command to change the line's linetype to CENTER and the hexagon's linetype to PHANTOM.
- ◯ Use the **CHPROP** command to change the circle's linetype to HIDDEN and the color to RED.
- ◯ Use the **CHPROP** command to change the hexagon's color to YELLOW.
- ◯ Save the drawing as EX12-9.

One of the advantages of AutoCAD is the capability of editing in more than one drawing at a time. This allows you to copy objects from one drawing to another drawing. You can also refer to another drawing to obtain information (such as a distance) while working in a different drawing.

To take a look at how this works, use the **OPEN** command to first open EX12-8. Use the **OPEN** command again to open EX12-9. Two drawings have now been opened in AutoCAD. In the **Window** pull-down menu, pick **Tile Horizontally**. This "tiles" the two open drawings. See **Figure 12-17**.

**Figure 12-17.**
Multiple drawings can be tiled to make editing easier.

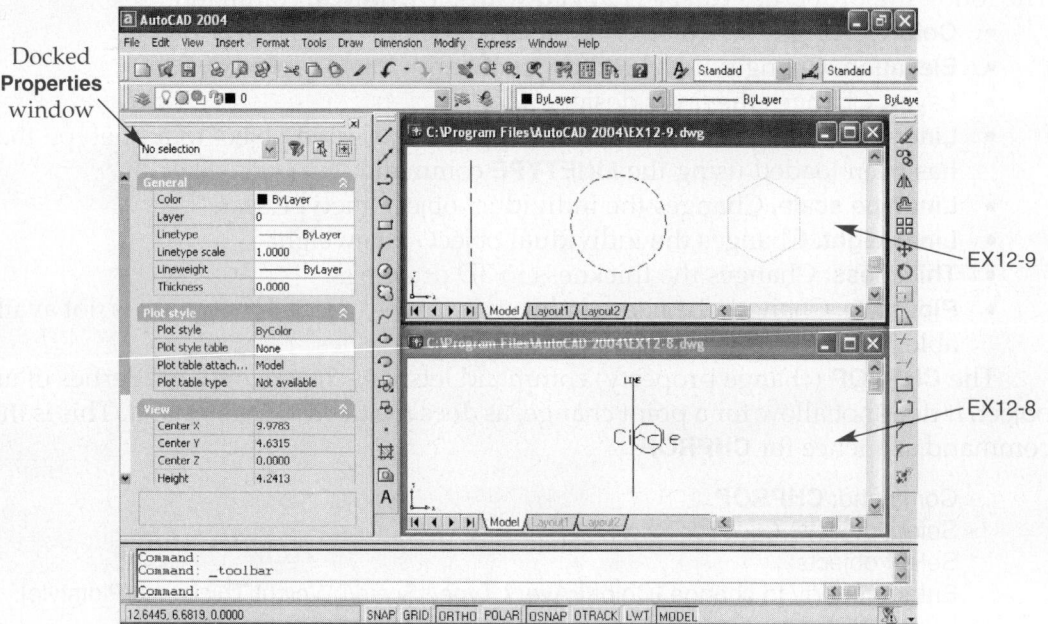

**NOTE**  The Multiple Design Environment (MDE) is discussed in more detail in Chapter 2.

## Copying Objects between Drawings

The Windows function *copy and paste* is used to copy an object from one drawing to another. To use this feature in AutoCAD, the object you intend to copy must be selected with grips. For example, if you want to copy the circle from drawing EX12-9 to drawing EX12-8, you would first select the circle. Once the circle is selected, right-click to get the shortcut menu shown in **Figure 12-18**. The shortcut menu has two options allowing you to copy to the Windows Clipboard:

- **Copy.** This option takes selected objects from AutoCAD and places them on the Windows Clipboard to be used in another application or another AutoCAD drawing.

Figure 12-18.
Right-click to access
this shortcut menu
to select one of the
copy options.

```
Repeat HELP

Cut
Copy
Copy with Base Point
Paste
Paste as Block
Paste to Original Coordinates

Erase
Move
Copy Selection
Scale
Rotate

Deselect All

Quick Select...
Find...
Properties
```

- **Copy with Base Point.** This option also copies the selected objects to the Clipboard, but allows you to specify a base point to position the copied object when it is pasted. When using this option, AutoCAD prompts you to select a base point. Select a logical base point, such as a corner or center point of the object.

Once you have selected one of the two copy options, make the second drawing active by picking inside of it. Right-click, and a shortcut menu is displayed, as shown in **Figure 12-19**. Notice the copy options remain available, but three paste options are now available below the copy options. The paste options are only available if there is something on the Clipboard. The three options are described below:

- **Paste.** This option pastes any information from the Clipboard into the current drawing. If the **Copy with Base Point** option was used to place objects in the Clipboard, the objects being pasted are attached to the crosshairs at the specified base point.
- **Paste as Block.** This option "joins" all objects in the Clipboard when they are pasted into the drawing. The pasted objects act like a block in that they are single objects joined together to form one object. Blocks are covered in Chapter 22. Use the **EXPLODE** command to get the objects to act individually again.
- **Paste to Original Coordinates.** This option pastes the objects from the Clipboard to the same coordinates at which they were located in the original drawing.

You can also copy objects between drawings using a drag-and-drop operation. To do so, first open both drawings and arrange their windows so they are both visible in the drawing area. Select the object to be copied, and then press and hold the pick button. Move the cursor into the other drawing and release the pick button. The object is automatically copied into the second drawing.

Figure 12-19.
Right-click to access
this shortcut menu
and select one of the
paste options to
paste an object from
the Clipboard to a
drawing.

```
Repeat PAN

Cut
Copy
Copy with Base Point
Paste
Paste as Block
Paste to Original Coordinates

Undo
Redo
Pan
Zoom

Quick Select...
Find...
Options...
```

# Matching Properties

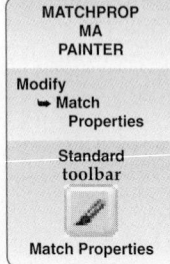

MATCHPROP
MA
PAINTER

Modify
➥ Match
   Properties

Standard
toolbar

Match Properties

The **MATCHPROP** command allows you to copy properties from one object to one or more objects. This can be done in the same drawing or between drawings. To access the **MATCHPROP** command, select the **Match Properties** button from the **Standard** toolbar; select **Match Properties** from the **Modify** pull-down menu; or enter MA, MATCHPROP, or PAINTER at the Command: prompt. The following is the prompt sequence:

Command: **MA**, **MATCHPROP**, *or* **PAINTER**↵
Select source object: *(pick the object with the properties you want to paint)*

When you first access the **MATCHPROP** command, AutoCAD prompts you for the source object. The source object is the object with all the properties you would like to copy to another object or series of objects. Once the source object has been selected, AutoCAD displays the properties it will paint to the destination object. The next prompt reads:

Select destination object(s) or [Settings]:

This allows you to pick the objects you want to receive the properties of the source object. If you want the properties painted to all objects in the drawing, type ALL at this prompt.

To change the properties to be painted, access the **Settings** option by typing S and pressing [Enter], as follows:

Select destination object(s) or [Settings]: **S**↵

The **Property Settings** dialog box now appears, showing the types of properties that can be painted. See **Figure 12-20**. The following describes the major areas of the **Property Settings** dialog box:

- **Basic Properties.** This area lists the general properties of the selected object. If you do not want the property to be copied, deselect the appropriate check box. All active properties will be transferred to the destination objects.
- **Special Properties.** In addition to general properties, you can also paint over dimension styles, text styles, and hatch patterns. These properties are replaced in the destination object if these check boxes are active.

Figure 12-20.
**Figure 12-20.**
The **Property Settings** dialog box for the **MATCHPROP** command. Select the properties to
paint onto a new object.

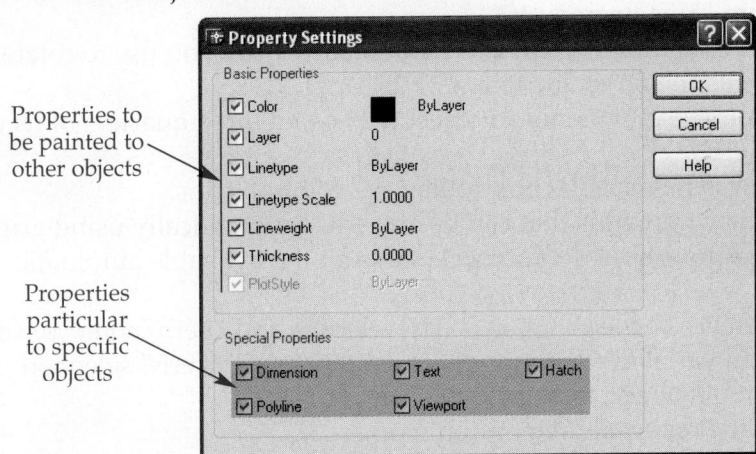

Properties to
be painted to
other objects

Properties
particular
to specific
objects

For example, if you want to paint only the color property and text style of one text
object to another text object, uncheck all boxes except the **Color** and **Text** property
check boxes.

**NOTE**

To use the **MATCHPROP** command between drawings, select
the source object from one drawing and the destination
object from another.

**PROFESSIONAL
TIP**

Use the **Partial Open** option in the **Open** command to partially open existing drawings to be used as source objects for
copying or property matching. **Partial Open** is discussed in
Chapter 2.

## Exercise 12-11

○ Open drawings EX12-9 and EX12-10, and then tile the drawings horizontally.
○ Make the EX12-9 drawing active.
○ Use the **MATCHPROP** command to paint the color and linetype of the hexagon to
the circle you pasted in drawing EX12-10.
○ Open one of your previous drawings containing text, such as a Chapter 8 exer-
cise or problem.
○ Create a new text style different from the text style on the existing drawing. Use
the Romand.shx font in the text style, for example. Use the **MATCHPROP** com-
mand to change all text to the new text style.
○ Save the drawing as EX12-11.

## Chapter Test

*Answer the following questions on a separate sheet of paper.*

1. How do you turn grips on and off?
2. Which option of the automatic **ROTATE** command would you use to rotate an object from an existing 60° angle to a new 25° angle?
3. What scale factor is used to scale an object to become three-quarters of its original size?
4. Name the two system variables controlling the color of grips.
5. Name the editing commands that can be accessed automatically using grips.
6. When grips are active, how do you cycle through the available automatic commands?
7. Explain the difference between "noun/verb" selection and "verb/noun" selection.
8. Name the system variable allowing you to set the "noun/verb" selection.
9. What does **Use Shift to add to selection** mean?
10. Describe how the **Press and drag** option works.
11. Name the system variable used to turn on the **Press and drag** option.
12. Name the system variable that turns on the **Implied windowing** option.
13. Identify two ways to access the **Options** dialog box.
14. Explain two ways to change the pick box size.
15. Explain how you would change the radius of a circle from 1.375 to 1.875 using the **Properties** window.
16. Identify the pull-down menu and the item you pick from this menu to access the **Properties** window.
17. How would you change the linetype of an object using the **Properties** window?
18. Name the command allowing you to change the location of an object or object properties at the Command: prompt.
19. Name the command used at the Command: prompt to change only the properties of an object.
20. How do you change the color of an object using the **Properties** window?
21. How do you access the grips shortcut menu?
22. What is the purpose of the **Base Point** option in the grips shortcut menu?
23. Explain the function of the **Undo** option in the grips shortcut menu.
24. Describe the purpose of the **Properties** option in the grips shortcut menu.
25. What happens when you choose the **Exit** option from the grips shortcut menu?
26. What command is used to quickly change the properties of objects to match the properties of a different object?
27. What is the purpose of the **Selection** tab found in the **Options** dialog box?
28. How do you change an existing text reading AutoCAD to read AutoCAD 2004 by using the **Properties** window?
29. Name the option used to have a group of objects joined as a block when they are pasted.
30. When you use the option described in Question 29, how do you separate the objects back into individual objects?

# Drawing Problems

*Use templates as appropriate for each of the following problems. Use grips and the associated editing commands or other editing techniques discussed in this chapter.*

1. Draw the objects labeled A, below, and then use the **STRETCH** command to make them look like the objects labeled B. Do not include dimensions. Save the drawing as P12-1.

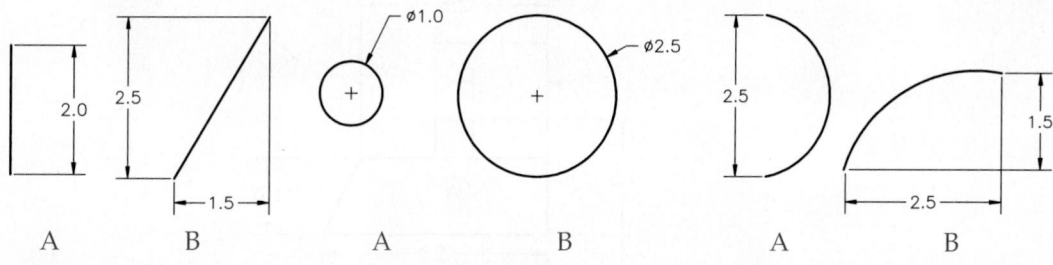

|       |       |       |       |       |       |
|-------|-------|-------|-------|-------|-------|
| A     | B     | A     | B     | A     | B     |

2. Draw the object labeled A, below. Using the **Copy** option of the **MOVE** command, copy the object to the position labeled B. Edit Object A so it resembles Object C. Edit Object B so it looks like Object D. Do not include dimensions. Save the drawing as P12-2.

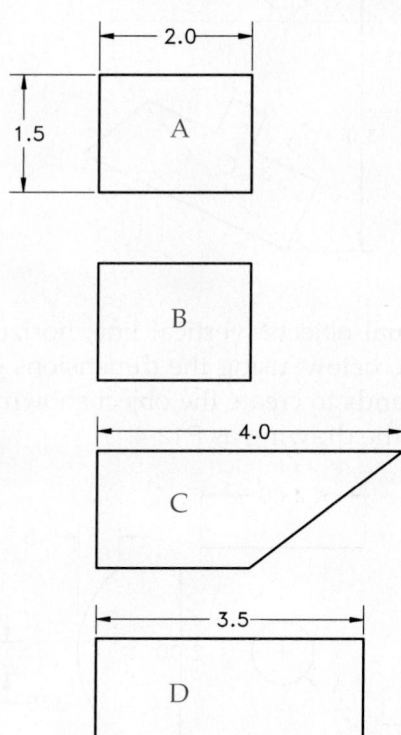

3. Draw the object labeled A, below. Copy the object, without rotating it, to a position below, as indicated by the dashed lines. Rotate the object 45°. Copy the rotated object labeled B to a position below, as indicated by the dashed lines. Use the **Reference** option to rotate the object labeled C to 25°, as shown. Do not include dimensions. Save the drawing as P12-3.

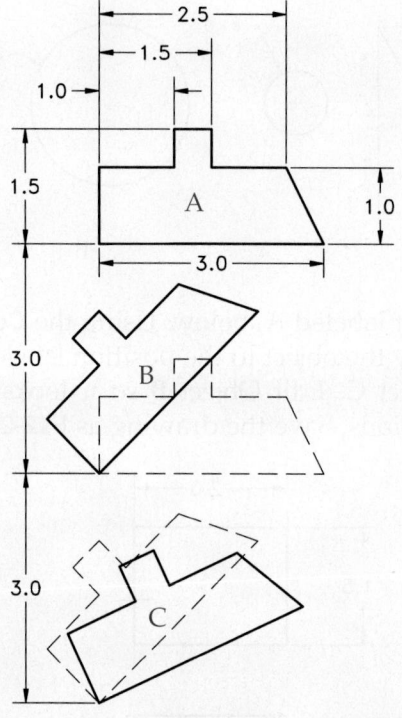

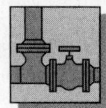

4. Draw the individual objects (vertical line, horizontal line, circle, arc, and C shape) in A, below, using the dimensions given. Use grips and the editing commands to create the object shown in B. Do not include dimensions. Save the drawing as P12-4.

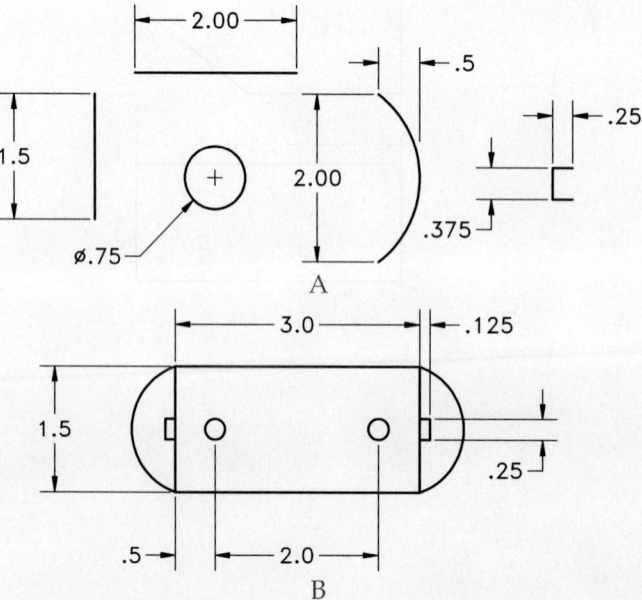

5. Use the completed drawing from Problem 12-4. Erase everything except the completed object and move it to a position similar to A, below. Copy the object two times to positions B and C. Use the automatic **SCALE** command to scale the object in position B to 50 percent of its original size. Use the **Reference** option of the **SCALE** command to enlarge the object in position C from the existing 3.0 length to a 4.5 length, as shown in C. Do not include dimensions. Save as P12-5.

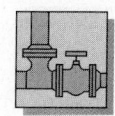

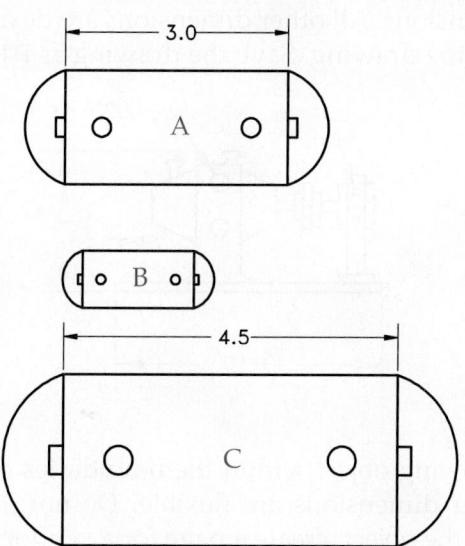

6. Draw the dimensioned partial object shown in A. Do not include dimensions. Mirror the drawing to complete the four quadrants, as shown in B. Change the color of the horizontal and vertical parting lines to red and the linetype to Center. Save the drawing as P12-6.

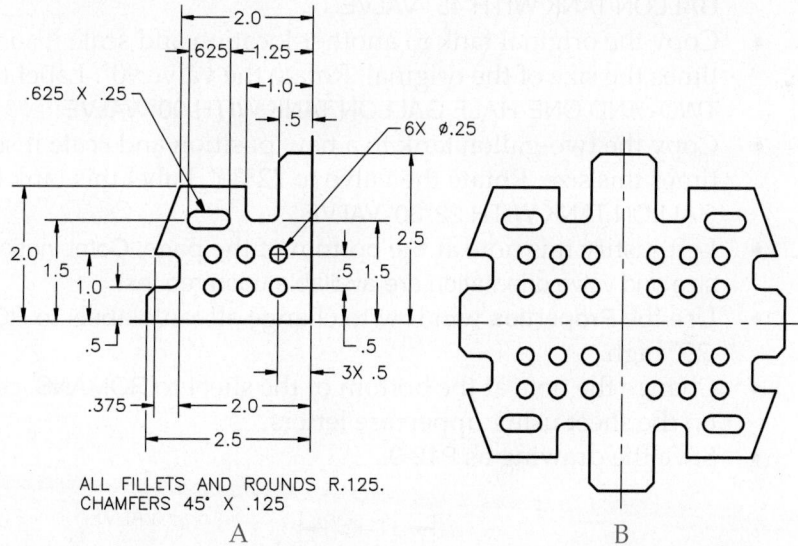

ALL FILLETS AND ROUNDS R.125.
CHAMFERS 45° X .125

7. Load the final drawing you created in Problem 12-6. Use the **Properties** window to change the diameters of the circles from .25 to .125. Change the linetype of the slots to Phantom. Be sure the linetype scale allows the linetypes to be displayed. Save the drawing as P12-7.

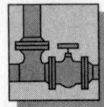

8. Use the editing commands discussed in this chapter to assist you in drawing the following object. Draw the object within the boundaries of the given dimensions. All other dimensions are flexible. Do not include dimensions in the drawing. Save the drawing as P12-8.

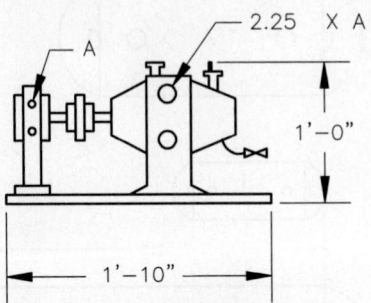

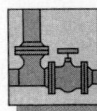

9. Draw the following object within the boundaries of the given dimensions. All other dimensions are flexible. Do not include dimensions. After drawing the object, create a page for a vendor catalog, as follows:
   - All labels should be ROMAND text, centered directly below the view. Use a text height of .125.
   - Label the drawing ONE-GALLON TANK WITH HORIZONTAL VALVE.
   - Keep the valve the same scale as the original drawing in each copy.
   - Copy the original tank to a new location and scale it so it is two times its original size. Rotate the valve 45°. Label this tank TWO-GALLON TANK WITH 45° VALVE.
   - Copy the original tank to another location and scale it so it is 2.5 times the size of the original. Rotate the valve 90°. Label this tank TWO- AND ONE-HALF GALLON TANK WITH 90° VALVE.
   - Copy the two-gallon tank to a new position and scale it so it is two times this size. Rotate the valve to 22°30'. Label this tank FOUR-GALLON TANK WITH 22°30' VALVE.
   - Left-justify this note at the bottom of the page: Combinations of tank size and valve orientation are available upon request.
   - Use the **Properties** window to change all tank labels to ROMANC, .25" high.
   - Change the note at the bottom of the sheet to ROMANS, centered on the sheet using uppercase letters.
   - Save the drawing as P12-9.

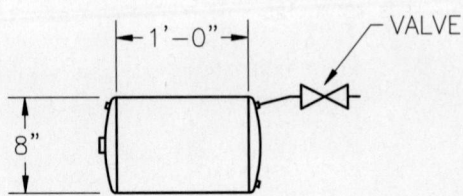

## Learning Objectives

After completing this chapter, you will be able to do the following:
- Explain the meaning and use of Windows file extensions.
- Select, display, and arrange folders and files in Windows Explorer.
- Manage files and folders using Windows Explorer.
- Search for files and folders using Windows Explorer.
- Copy, move, delete, and rename files using Windows Explorer.
- Format and copy diskettes using Windows Explorer.
- Perform drag-and-drop operations using Windows Explorer.
- Manage critical files using the **Options** dialog box.
- Import and export a variety of file types in AutoCAD.

AutoCAD works with several types of computer files. The files are identified by a three-letter file extension at the end of the file name. Windows® Explorer provides a variety of tools to help you manage these files and the folders where they are stored. This chapter covers many of those functions.

AutoCAD can write drawing files in a variety of formats, many of which are compatible with other popular software applications. You can export the industry standard DXF file for use with other CAD packages or specific applications. Files can also be exported for use in the design and animation software programs Autodesk VIZ® and 3ds max®, or for use in the stereolithography process. In addition, you can import several different file types into AutoCAD.

## Types of File Names

Drawing file names can be up to 255 characters long. They can contain letters, numbers, spaces, dollar signs ($), hyphens (-), and underscores (_). When you begin a new drawing, AutoCAD adds a file extension to the end of the file name. This extension is .dwg. If you name a drawing Building 340, AutoCAD adds the extension to create the file name of Building 340.dwg. When you open the drawing to edit, you only have to type Building 340. AutoCAD knows to look for that file, plus the .dwg extension. File names are not case-sensitive. This means that you can name a drawing PROBLEM 20-12, but Windows interprets Problem 20-12 as the same file name. See **Figure 13-1.**

**Figure 13-1.**
File names are not case sensitive. This alert box appears when you attempt to save as an already existing file.

Existing file name

New file name

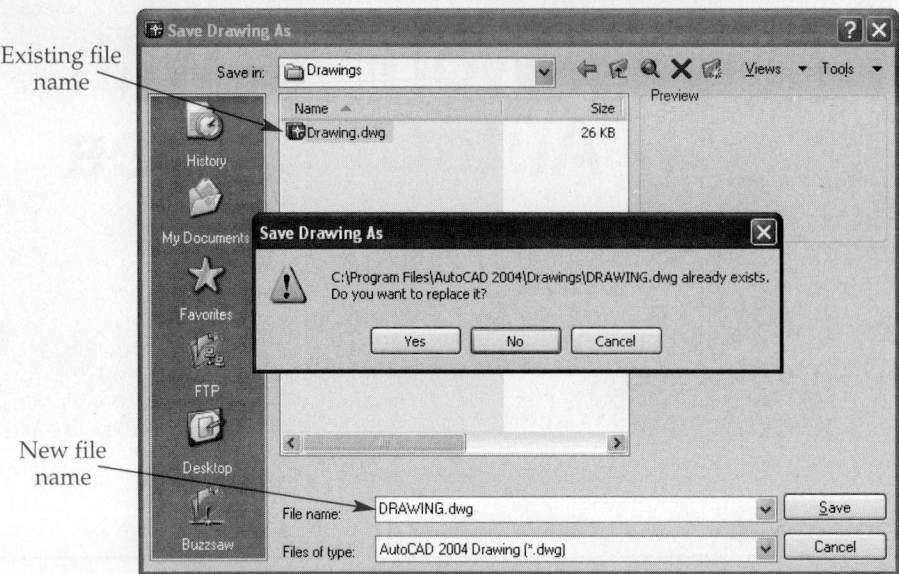

After you edit the Building 340.dwg file and save it again, the original is converted to a backup file. Its file extension is automatically changed to .bak (backup). AutoCAD maintains a current DWG file and one BAK file. If you revise and save the Building 340 drawing again, the BAK file is erased and the previous DWG file becomes the backup. Only a newly revised drawing is given the .dwg file extension.

Some common file extensions used by AutoCAD and Windows include the following:

| AutoCAD | |
|---------|---|
| BAK | Backup copy of a drawing file |
| DCL | Dialog control language description file |
| DWG | Drawing file |
| DWT | Drawing template file |
| LIN | File containing the linetypes used by AutoCAD |
| MNU | Menu source file |
| PAT | Hatch patterns file |
| PLT | Plot file |
| DWF | Design web format |
| **Windows** | |
| BMP | Bitmap file |
| CLP | Windows Clipboard file |
| COM | Command file |
| DLL | Dynamic-link library file |
| EXE | Executable file |
| INI | Initialization file |
| WMF | Windows metafile |

**PROFESSIONAL TIP**

Saving backup files is the default behavior of AutoCAD. This feature is controlled by the **Create backup copy with each save** option in the **File Safety Precautions** area of the **Open and Save** tab of the **Options** dialog box. The creation of backup files can be disabled to reduce the amount of time required to save, but this is not advised for most applications. If a drawing file becomes corrupt, a backup file may be the only way to recover data that would otherwise be lost. Recovering lost or damaged drawing data is discussed later in this chapter.

**NOTE**

Refer to Appendix B for important information on hard disk structure and management. This information is applicable to any classroom or business application.

# Introduction to Windows Explorer

Windows Explorer is a program that allows you to manage and display folders and files. To activate Windows Explorer, right-click the Start menu button and select Explore from the shortcut menu.

**NOTE**

The functions of the Windows Explorer are very similar in Windows NT, Windows 2000, and Windows XP. However, there are some minor differences. This chapter is based on the Windows Explorer provided with Windows XP. The material in the chapter is still applicable if you are using a different operating system, but the window may appear slightly different.

## Elements of Windows Explorer

When you use Windows Explorer, you will see the contents of the current drive displayed as a directory tree. The *directory tree* is a graphic representation of the directory structure and the folders and files it contains. When you start Windows Explorer, the window displays the contents of the current drive. See **Figure 13-2**. The window is divided in half with a vertical *split bar*. The left half of the window, referred to as the folders pane, displays the directory tree. The right half of the window, the contents pane, lists the contents of the current folder. You can drag the split bar to the left or to the right to display more or less of the contents in each side of the window.

At the right of the window is a list of the folders and files contained in the selected folder. A folder icon appears next to each folder in this list. A *file icon* indicating the file type appears next to each file name. Program files (EXE and BAT files), document files (TXT and DOC files), and other types of files are each represented with a specific icon.

**Figure 13-2.**
The folders pane of Windows Explorer displays the directory tree, while the contents pane displays the files and subfolders within the selected folder.

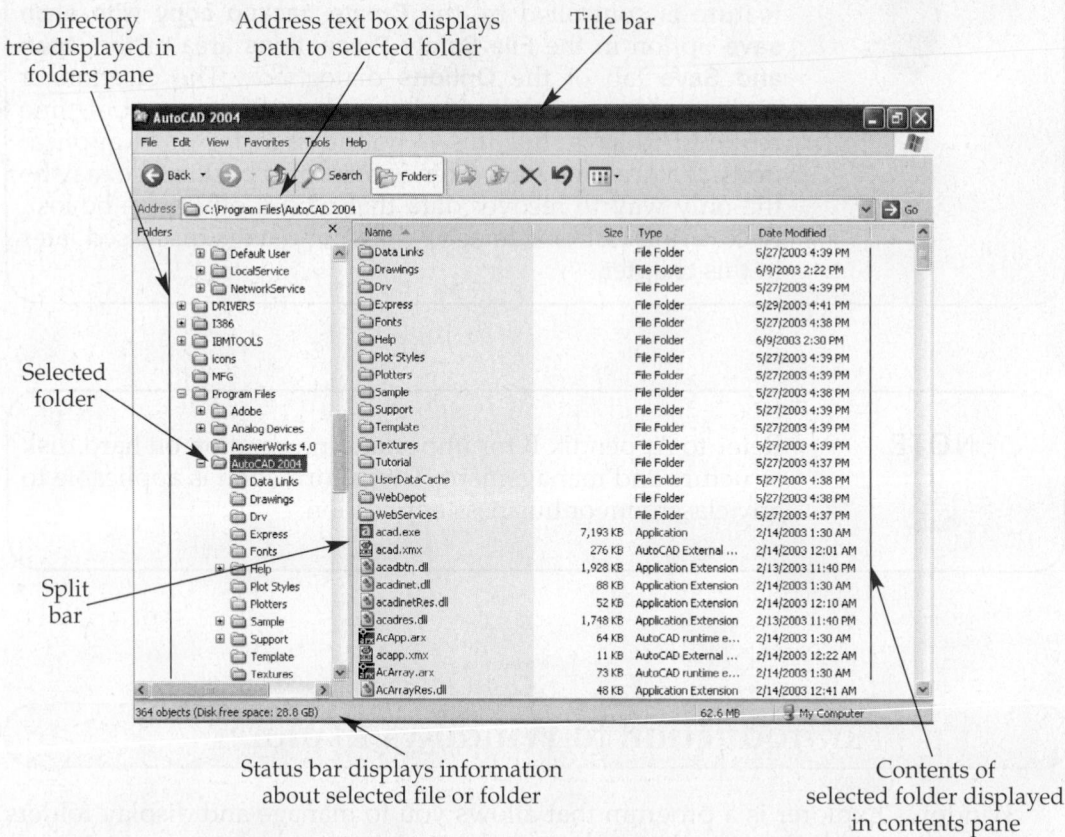

Directory tree displayed in folders pane

Address text box displays path to selected folder

Title bar

Selected folder

Split bar

Status bar displays information about selected file or folder

Contents of selected folder displayed in contents pane

You must first select a file or folder in Windows Explorer before you can work with it. When you want to select a file or folder, place the cursor over the desired file or folder icon and pick. You can select more than one file or folder by pressing and holding the [Ctrl] key as you pick with your pointing device. The items you select are highlighted. Any operations you perform are applied to the selected files and folders. More information about file and folder selection appears later in this chapter.

*Drive icons* represent each of the drives on your computer. These are listed below the My Computer icon near the top of the list in the folders pane. See **Figure 13-3.** The text to the right of each icon lists the label and the drive letter for each drive. Each type of drive is represented by a different icon. You can see that the diskette drive (A:) is represented with a different icon than those used for the hard disks (C: and T:). To work with the contents of one of the available drives, pick the desired drive icon. This displays the drive's contents in the pane on the right.

Just below the Windows Explorer title bar are pull-down menus. The menus displayed depend on your operating system. Many of the commands located in these menus are explored later in this chapter.

Finally, as with all Microsoft Windows applications, Windows Explorer can be moved, resized, closed, and minimized to the taskbar at any time. Standard methods are used to perform these activities.

AutoCAD and its Applications—Basics

**Figure 13-3.**
Drive icons are listed under the My Computer icon.

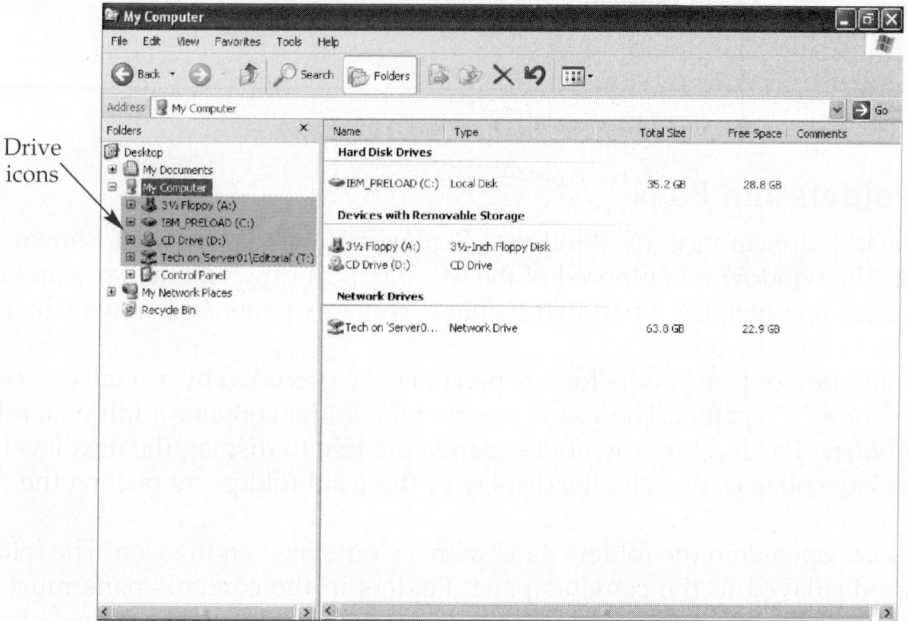

Drive icons

## Accessing Windows Explorer Commands

Most commands used in Windows Explorer can be accessed in several ways. Commands can be activated from a toolbar button, pull-down menu, or shortcut menu. Some commands can also be accessed through keyboard shortcuts.

Toolbar buttons enable you to perform a variety of functions quickly. The toolbar display is toggled on and off by selecting an option from the Toolbars cascading menu of the View pull-down menu. A check mark next to a toolbar name indicates that it is active.

**Figure 13-4** provides quick identification of the default toolbar available in Windows Explorer. The functions of these buttons are described later in this chapter when applicable. Additional functions can be added to the toolbar by selecting Customize... from the Toolbars cascading menu in the View pull-down menu.

**Figure 13-4.**
Many file management options are available in the Windows Explorer toolbar.

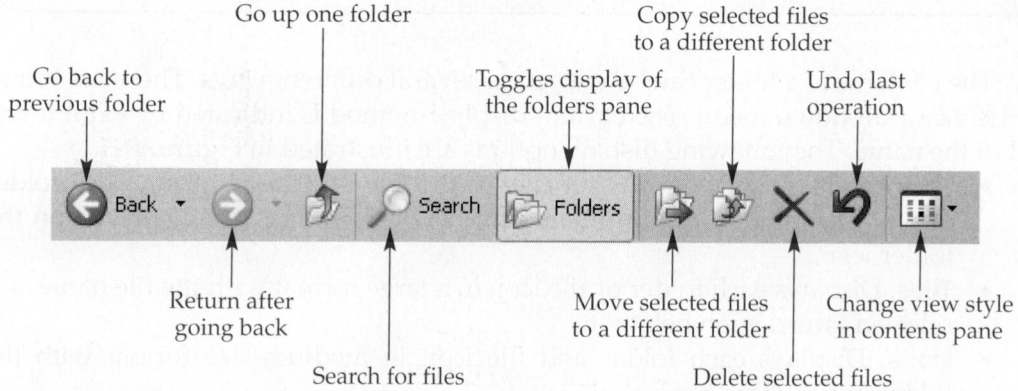

Go up one folder

Copy selected files to a different folder

Go back to previous folder

Toggles display of the folders pane

Undo last operation

Return after going back

Move selected files to a different folder

Change view style in contents pane

Search for files

Delete selected files

## Listing Folders and Files

The default appearance of Windows Explorer is similar to that shown in **Figure 13-2.** The window is composed of the title bar, pull-down menu bar, standard toolbar, Address text box, Links bar, folders pane, contents pane, and status bar. The Links bar is not active by default.

Folder and device icons in the folders pane may be preceded by a small box containing a "+" or a "−" symbol. The + indicates that the folder contains additional folders, or *subfolders*. Picking the + symbol expands the tree to display the next level of folders. You can collapse, or hide, the display of these subfolders by picking the "−" symbol.

Folders are opened in the folders pane with a single pick on the icon. The folder contents are displayed in the contents pane. Folders in the contents pane must be double-clicked to open. An open folder is automatically closed when a new one is selected and opened.

The contents of a folder can be viewed in several different ways. These are found in the View pull-down menu. The current display method is indicated by a dot to the left of the name. The following display options are illustrated in **Figure 13-5.**

- **Thumbnails.** Displays icons for files and folders in large format. If a folder contains graphics files, thumbnail images of those files are displayed on the folder icon.
- **Tiles.** Displays each folder or file icon in a large format with the file name and selected information below it.
- **Icons.** Displays each folder and file icon in medium-size format with the folder or file name beneath it.
- **List.** Represents files and folders with small icons with file names to the right. The list fills the height of the contents pane. Files that do not fit in the first column are listed in additional columns to the right. Use the horizontal scroll bar to display them.

**Figure 13-5.**
There are several ways to have files listed in the contents pane.

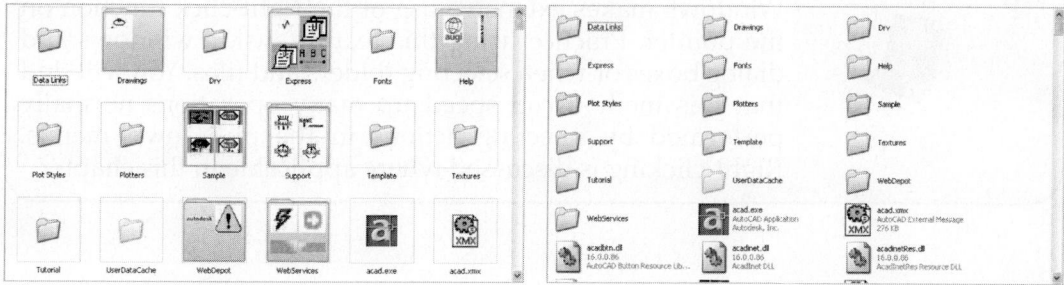

Thumbnails

Tiles

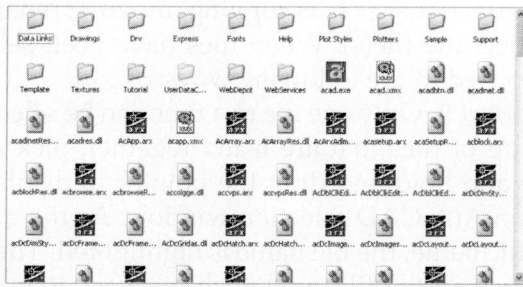

Icons

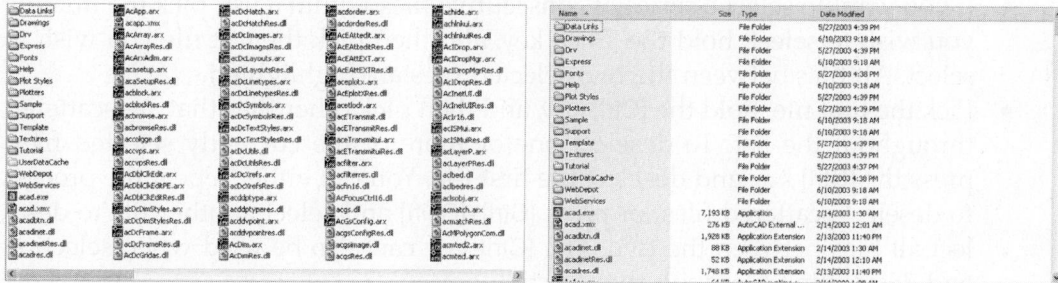

List

Details

- **Details.** Displays folders and files as a single column of small icons. The file name, size, type, and the date and time the file was last modified are listed to the right of each icon. Additional details can be added using the Choose Details... option in the View pull-down menu.

These view options can also be selected using the Views button at the right side of the toolbar. Selecting the Views button accesses a drop-down list of the options. Viewing and arranging options can also be selected by right-clicking on any open area of the contents pane, selecting an option from the shortcut menu.

## Basic Windows Explorer Functions

Before using the Windows Explorer to manage your folders and files, it is best to have a good understanding of how these items are selected and what kinds of actions Windows Explorer is capable of performing.

## Selecting Files

When performing functions such as copying, moving, renaming, and deleting, it is first necessary to select the file(s). When files have been selected, they are highlighted. Files can be selected in the following ways:

- Pick the file to select it. Only one file at a time can be selected with this method.
- To select a group of files that are listed together, pick a point that does not highlight a file and hold and drag the pointer to display a dashed selection box similar to an AutoCAD selection window. As the dashed box touches or surrounds the file name, the file name is highlighted. The selection box should surround or touch all the files you wish to select. Release the pick button to complete the selection. See **Figure 13-6.**
- If you want to select a series of consecutive files within a list, pick the first file you wish to select, hold the [Shift] key, and then pick the last file you wish to select. All files between the two selected files are highlighted.
- Pick the first file, hold the [Ctrl] key, and then pick other files that are scattered throughout the list. To deselect one or more of the currently selected files, press the [Ctrl] key and deselect the first file. You can either repeat the process to deselect scattered files, or press [Ctrl]+[Shift] and select another file to deselect all files between the two. The [Ctrl] key can also be used when selecting and deselecting files with the selection box.

**Figure 13-6.**
A group of files that are listed together can be selected by picking and dragging the dashed box so that all files are highlighted.

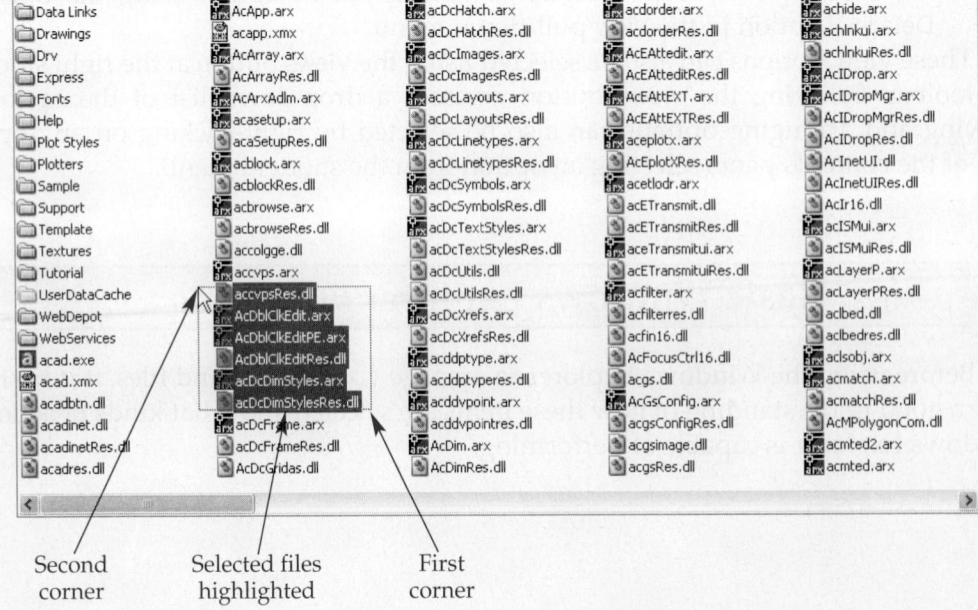

Second corner    Selected files highlighted    First corner

- Press the [Tab] key to activate the contents pane, and then use the arrow keys to locate and highlight a single file. This selection method also supports [Ctrl] and [Shift] key combinations.

Once you have selected files by one or more of the methods listed here, you can perform the required function.

---

## Exercise 13-1

○ Activate Windows Explorer and insert a diskette that contains drawing files.
○ Use the Windows Explorer to do the following:
  ○ Adjust the visibility of the Windows Explorer toolbars to match your preferences.
  ○ List all files in the AutoCAD 2004\Sample folder.
  ○ List all files on your diskette.
  ○ View the file list using large icons.
  ○ View the file list details.
  ○ Select a group of files from your diskette using the selection box method.
○ Close Windows Explorer.

---

## Selecting Multiple Folders and Files

You can select a consecutive group of items by picking the first item, and then pressing and holding the [Shift] key while picking the last item in the group. Two or more groups of consecutive files can be selected as follows:

1. Pick the first item in a group. Hold the [Shift] key and pick the last item in the group.
2. Press the [Ctrl] key and select the first item in the second group.
3. Press the [Ctrl]+[Shift] keys and pick the last item in the group. This selects the second group.
4. Press the [Ctrl] key and select the first item in the third group.
5. Press the [Ctrl]+[Shift] keys and pick the last item in the group. This selects the third group.
6. Continue in this manner until all groups are selected.

If the files or folders you need to select far outnumber those that will remain unselected, use the following technique:

1. Pick Select All from the Edit pull-down menu or press the [Ctrl]+[A] key combination. This selects all folders and files in the current drive or folder.
2. Deselect the items that you do not want to be part of the selected group by holding down the [Ctrl] key and picking the item(s) you wish to remove.

The following is a good method to use if only a few files or folders are to remain unselected:

1. Select only the files that are not to be acted on.
2. Pick Invert Selection from the Edit pull-down menu. This automatically deselects the items you picked and selects all remaining items.

The status bar at the bottom of Windows Explorer displays the number of objects selected and the total number of bytes in the selected items. Check the status bar when selecting files to be copied to storage media. You can quickly see if the total file sizes exceed the storage capacity of the media.

You may wish to hide the status bar to make more room to display folders and files. To toggle the status bar on and off, pick Status Bar from the View pull-down menu.

---

## Arranging Folder and File Icons

Once you have selected the display that suits your needs, you can quickly arrange the icons by one of four methods. These are selected by picking Arrange Icons from the View pull-down menu.

- **by Name.** Displays icons alphabetically. Folders are always listed first, then files. If the view is set to Thumbnail, Tile, or Icon, the icons are arranged alphabetically in rows beginning at the upper-left and progressing to the right on each row. If the view is set to List or Details, the files are arranged alphabetically in columns.
- **by Type.** Displays icons by file type. Folders are always displayed first, and then files are listed alphabetically according to the three-letter file extension.
- **by Size.** Files are listed from smallest number of bytes to largest.
- **by Date.** Displays files by the date they were last modified. If the view is set to Thumbnail, Tile, or Icon, the icons are arranged in rows, with most recent on the left. If the view is set to List or Details, the icons are arranged in columns.

When icons are displayed in the Thumbnail, Tile, or Icon formats, you can choose to move them around and arrange them to suit your needs or let Windows Explorer arrange them for you. The Auto Arrange option is the default and automatically arranges icons in rows and columns. To activate the Auto Arrange option, open the View pull-down menu and select Auto Arrange from the Arrange Icons by cascading menu. A check mark means the option is active. To turn this option off, select it to remove the check mark. Now you can freely pick and drag icons to new locations.

If your arrangement gets too messy, you can align the icons into the nearest rows and columns by picking Align to Grid in the Arrange Icons by cascading menu. This option does not produce the compact arrangement that Auto Arrange provides, but merely moves icons to the nearest row and column. Gaps in the arrangement remain.

The Show in Groups option in the Arrange Icons by cascading menu arranges the icons in labeled groups. These groups are labeled according to the criteria used to sort the files. For example, if you selected the Size viewing option, the groups might be labeled Tiny, Small, Medium, and Large. If you selected the Modified viewing option, the groups might be labeled Today, Yesterday, Earlier this year, Two years ago, and A long time ago.

---

**NOTE**  When the Details option is active, you can automatically reverse the order of listing by picking any one of the column headings in the contents pane. For example, picking Size displays files first from largest to smallest, then folders. Pick Size again to return to the default display of folders first, then files from smallest to largest. Test this feature by picking each of the column headings.

---

## Launching Applications with Windows Explorer

Many of the files that appear in Windows Explorer are associated with application programs. By double-clicking on the file icon or file name, you can load the file and simultaneously start the application with which it is associated. Double-clicking on a drawing file loads AutoCAD and opens the drawing.

## Searching for Files

Before you can manage your files and folders, you must locate them. Windows provides a variety of options within Windows Explorer to help you find the items you need. To begin a search, pick the Search button of the Windows Explorer toolbar. The folders pane is replaced with the Search Companion pane. See **Figure 13-7.**

---

AutoCAD and its Applications—Basics

**Figure 13-7.**
The Search Companion is used to search for files.

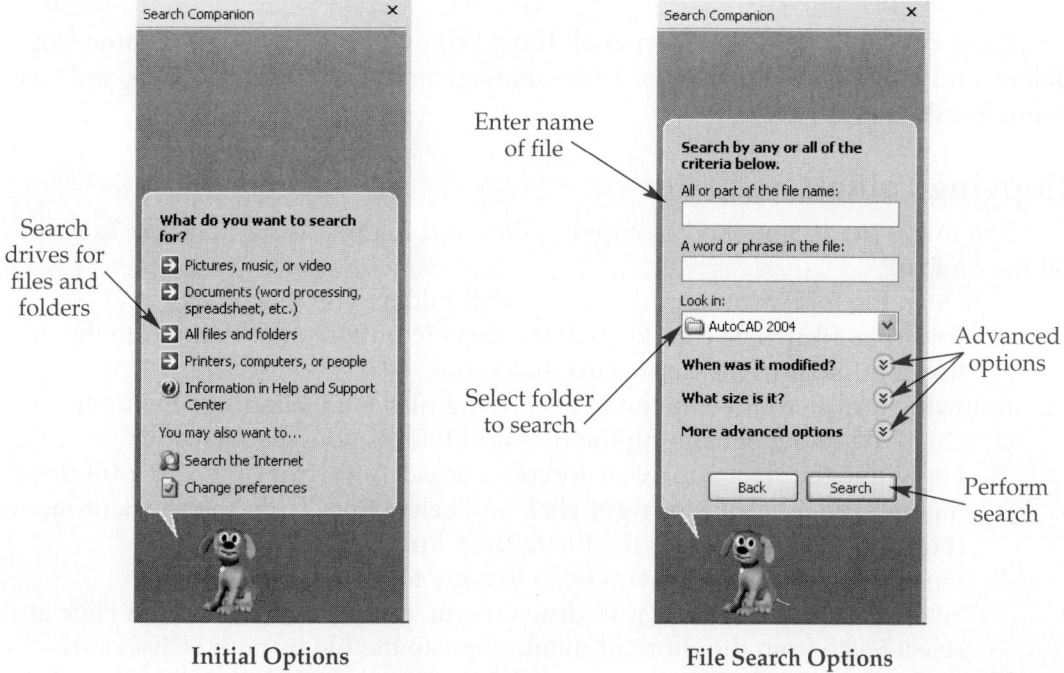

Initial Options            File Search Options

## Conducting a basic search

Begin by accessing the Search Companion. Use the following procedure to search for a file:

1. At the What do you want to search for? prompt, select the All files and folders button.
2. Enter the name of the file you want to search for in the All or part of the name: text box.
3. In the Look in: drop-down list, select the drive and folder in which you wish to begin the search.
4. Pick the Search button to begin the search. If the item you need is found, it is displayed in the contents pane. You may stop the search at any time by pressing the Stop button.
5. Pick the Start a new Search button to begin a new search.

## Additional search options

You can refine and narrow your searches by entering modification dates, words and phrases that appear within the file, file sizes, and miscellaneous criteria. Review the Help and Support Center for more information on using these advanced search options.

### Exercise 13-2

○ Insert one of your diskettes in the A: drive and select 3.5" Floppy (A:) from the folders pane.

○ Experiment with listing the files by date, size, name, and type.

○ Select the first three files on the disk using [Shift] key method.

○ Add the last three files to your selection using the [Ctrl] and [Shift] key combinations.

○ Search the local hard drive to find a file named osk.exe.

○ Double-click on the osk.exe file to launch the application.

○ Close the application and pick the Folders button in the Windows Explorer toolbar to exit the Search Companion.

Keep Windows Explorer open at all times. You will often need to rename, copy, delete, and move files and folders. These management functions are quick and easy using Windows Explorer.

## Copying Folders and Files

The following is a method of copying files and folders using the Copy To button on the toolbar:

1. Open the folder containing the files and folders you wish to copy.
2. Select the files to be copied, pick the Copy To button, and then locate the destination folder in the Copy Items dialog box.

The following are alternative methods of copying files with Windows Explorer:

1. Open the folder containing the files and folders you wish to copy.
2. Highlight the files you wish to copy. Select Copy from the Edit pull-down menu, press [Ctrl]+[C], or right-click and select Copy from the shortcut menu (**Figure 13-8**). This copies the file to the Clipboard.
3. Open the folder or drive you wish to copy to.
4. Select Paste from the Edit pull-down menu, press [Ctrl]+[V], or right-click and select Paste from the shortcut menu to paste the file from the Clipboard.

The same steps can be used to copy a folder or a group of files. Use one of the selection methods previously mentioned to highlight the group.

Figure 13-8.
If you right-click a selected file, this shortcut menu allows you to access Windows Explorer commands quickly.

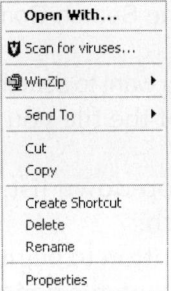

## Moving Folders and Files

The following is the procedure for moving files and folders using the Move To button on the toolbar:

1. Open the folder containing the files and folders you wish to move.
2. Select the files and folders to be moved, pick the Move To button on the toolbar, and select the destination folder in the Move Items dialog box.

The following are alternative methods of moving files with Windows Explorer:

1. Open the folder containing the files and folders you wish to move.
2. Highlight the file or files to be moved. Select Cut from the Edit pull-down menu, press [Ctrl]+[X], or right-click and select Cut from the shortcut menu. This deletes the file and places it in the Clipboard.
3. Open the folder or drive you wish to move the item to.
4. Select Paste from the Edit pull-down menu, press [Ctrl]+[V], or right-click and select Paste from the shortcut menu to paste the file from the Clipboard.

Drag-and-drop operations provide faster and easier ways to copy or move files and folders. These options are discussed later in this chapter.

## Renaming Folders and Files

Before a folder or file can be renamed, it must be selected. After selecting the file, proceed in the following manner:

1. Pick Rename from the File pull-down menu or right-click the file name and select Rename from the shortcut menu.
2. Type the new name. Be sure to include the three-letter file extension if it is displayed.
3. Press [Enter] or pick anywhere on the screen.

You can also use the following procedure to quickly rename a folder or file without using the Rename command:

1. Pick the file or folder to select it.
2. Pick it again and a blinking cursor appears at the end of the name.
3. Type the new name and press [Enter] or pick anywhere on the screen.

---

**PROFESSIONAL TIP**

If the files in the contents pane are displayed with the three-letter file extension, you must include the extension when renaming a file. If you omit the extension, a Windows alert informs you that the file may be unusable if the extension is changed. You can avoid this problem by doing the following:

1. Pick Folder Options... in the Tools pull-down menu.
2. Pick the View tab in the Folder Options dialog box.
3. Put a check in the Hide file extensions for known file types check box.
4. Pick OK to exit.

By performing this operation, files in the contents pane are displayed without the three-letter extensions. Therefore, when you rename a file, Windows automatically retains the file extension. This provides you with a fail-safe method for renaming files.

---

## Deleting Folders and Files

Windows stores the items you delete from the hard drive in the Recycle Bin. Items that are deleted from network and floppy drives are permanently deleted and *are not* sent to the Recycle Bin. Delete folders and files as follows:

1. Select the folders and files to be deleted.
2. Pick the Delete button on the toolbar, select Delete from the File pull-down menu, press the [Delete] key, or right-click on the file name and select Delete from the shortcut menu.
3. If the file will be sent to the Recycle Bin, the Confirm File Delete dialog box asks if you are sure you want to send the file to the Recycle Bin. Pick Yes to send the file to the Recycle Bin. If the file is being deleted from a network or floppy drive, the Confirm File Delete dialog box will ask you if you are sure you want to delete the file. Pick Yes to permanently delete the file.

The Recycle Bin is a repository for deleted files. If for any reason you feel that a file has been deleted by mistake, open the Recycle Bin and restore the file as follows:

1. Display the Windows desktop.
2. Double-click on the Recycle Bin icon to open the Recycle Bin.
3. Select the files you wish to restore.
4. Pick Restore from the File pull-down menu. The files are removed from the Recycle Bin and returned to the location they were at prior to deletion.

## Viewing the Properties of a File

You can quickly display detailed information about any folder or file as follows:

1. Select the file.
2. Pick Properties from the File pull-down menu or right-click on the file name and select Properties from the shortcut menu. The Properties dialog box is displayed. See **Figure 13-9**.

**Figure 13-9.**
The Properties dialog box displays details about the file.

File name

File information

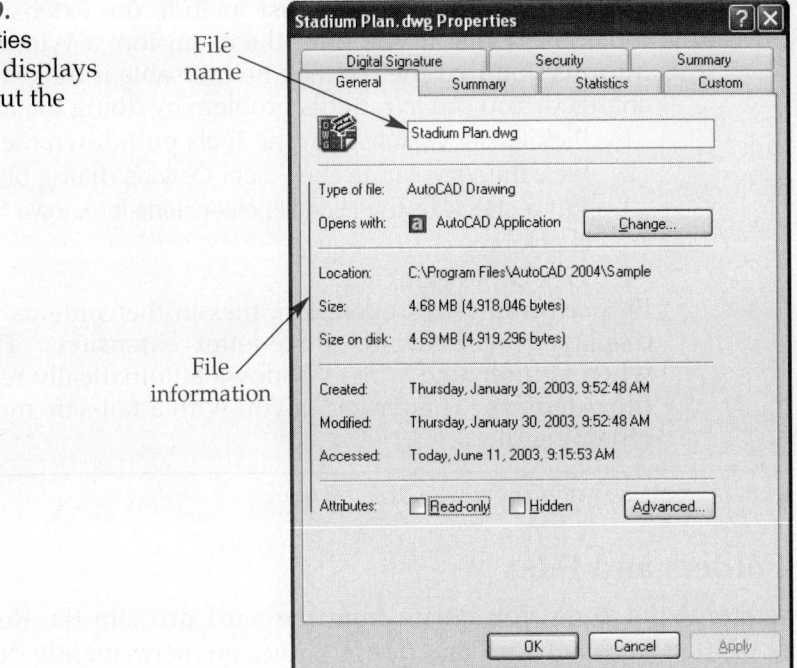

## Creating a New Folder

Organizing the files on your hard disk is a very important component of computer system maintenance. It is often desirable to keep block symbols, hatch patterns, and script files in separate subfolders. Once you have created a new folder, you can move and copy files and subfolders to it from other locations on your hard disk.

1. Pick the drive or folder icon where you want the new folder to appear.
2. Pick Folder from the New cascading menu in the File pull-down menu. Alternatively, you can right-click in the contents pane, and then pick New and Folder from the shortcut menu. A New Folder icon and label appear in the contents pane.
3. Type a new name and press [Enter]. The folder is ready to be used.

Avoid saving your files in the AutoCAD program directories or folders. It is best to create new folders for your work. Always check with your instructor or supervisor before creating new folders or performing any disk management function. The same naming conventions used for file names apply to folder names.

## Disk Operations Using Windows Explorer

A variety of disk operations can also be performed with the Windows Explorer. These operations include formatting, labeling, and copying diskettes. Each of these functions is located in the shortcut menu that appears after right-clicking on the disk drive icon, **Figure 13-10**.

**Figure 13-10.**
This shortcut menu appears after right-clicking on the disk drive icon.

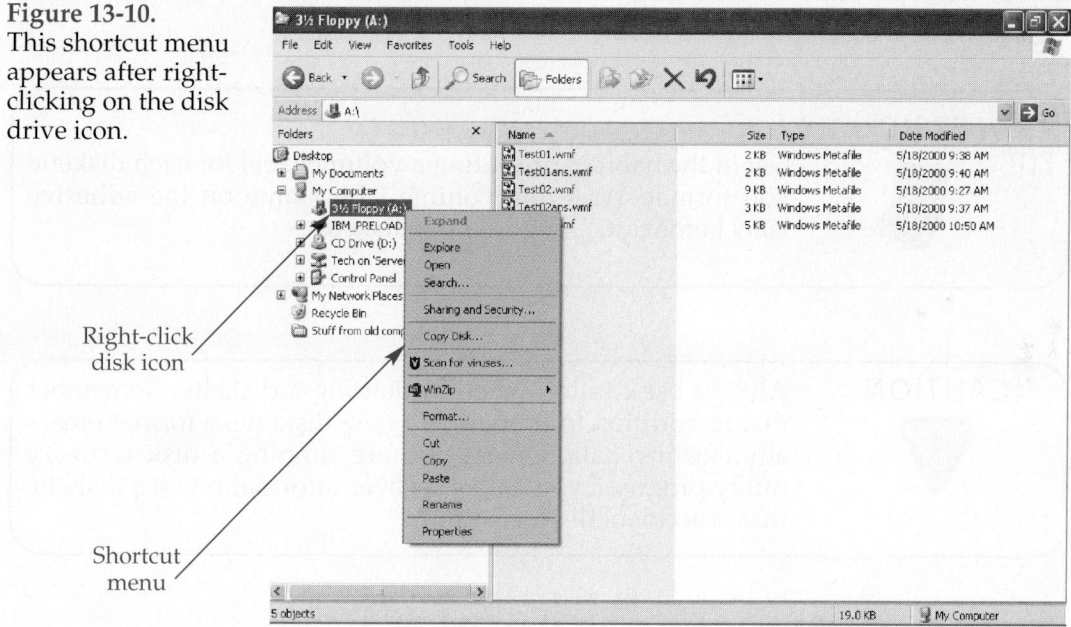

Right-click disk icon

Shortcut menu

### Formatting a Diskette

New diskettes must be formatted before they can be used. Although preformatted diskettes can be purchased, formatting is a process that is useful for thoroughly cleaning a diskette. The formatting process prepares a diskette so information can be copied to it. If the diskette you intend to format has previously been used, Windows Explorer detects this and informs you accordingly before it removes any existing data from the diskette. To format a diskette, do the following:

1. Insert a diskette into the appropriate disk drive.
2. Right-click on the diskette name or icon. Select Format... from the shortcut menu.

---

*Chapter 13  Working with AutoCAD Files*                                                    555

Figure 13-11.
The Format dialog
box.

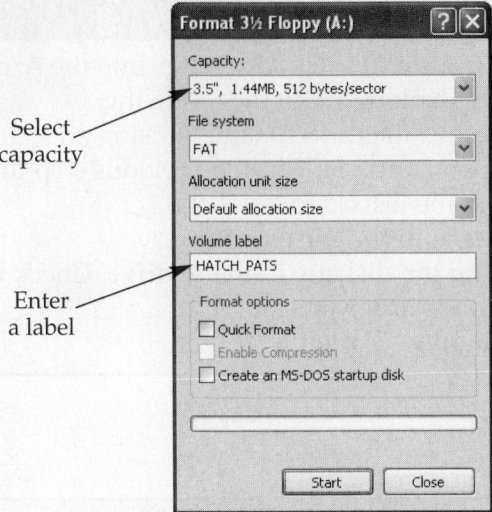

Select capacity

Enter a label

3. The Format dialog box then appears, **Figure 13-11.**
4. Select the capacity of the diskette to be formatted from the drop-down list in the Capacity: list box.
5. If you want to provide a label for the diskette, enter the desired name in the Label: text box. A label is an identifying name for the diskette. The name is shown in the title bar of the directory window.
6. Pick the Start button to begin formatting the diskette.
7. When the formatting is complete, pick OK.

**PROFESSIONAL TIP** Get in the habit of providing a volume label for each diskette you format. Write the volume label name on the adhesive label before attaching it to the diskette.

**CAUTION** Always use caution when formatting a diskette. Remember that in addition to preparing a new diskette, a format erases any existing data. Unless you are running a disk recovery utility program, you *cannot* recover information on a diskette that is accidentally formatted.

## Copying a Diskette

Throughout this text you have been advised to always make a backup copy of your AutoCAD drawings on portable storage media such as 3.5" diskettes or Zip disks. It is also a good idea to have a second backup of your original backup. You can easily copy the contents of one diskette to another using Windows Explorer. To copy a diskette, do the following:
1. Insert the source diskette in the drive you want to copy from. If your computer has two drives, you can insert the destination diskette in the second drive. The destination diskette is called the *copy to* diskette.
2. Right-click the drive icon for the source diskette in the folders pane.
3. Select Copy Disk... from the shortcut menu. The Copy Disk dialog box appears, **Figure 13-12.**

AutoCAD and its Applications—Basics

**Figure 13-12.**
The Copy Disk dialog box.

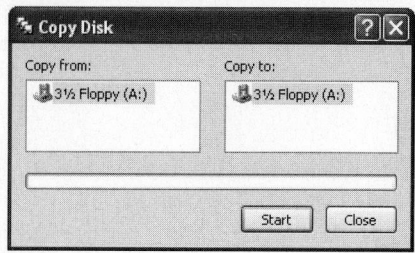

4. Labels and icons representing the available drives are shown in the Copy Disk dialog box. Select the appropriate icons for the Copy from: and the Copy to: disks.
5. Pick the Start button. A Copy Disk alert asks you to insert the diskette you want to copy from. Insert the proper diskette and pick OK. If you have selected to use two different disk drives, you will be asked to insert both the source and destination diskettes. If using a single disk drive computer, you will have to switch diskettes when prompted.
6. At the next Copy Disk alert, insert the diskette you want to copy to and pick OK.
7. The contents of the source diskette are then copied to the destination diskette.

 **CAUTION** The Copy Disk command not only copies, it formats! Therefore, there is no need to spend time formatting a diskette before making a copy. Be certain your destination diskette is blank or only has unneeded files on it.

 **PROFESSIONAL TIP** Single-density (360 KB) and double-density (720 KB) diskettes can be read in Windows XP, but *cannot* be formatted or copied. If you receive an error while trying to copy a diskette that you know to be good, make sure it is a high-density diskette (1.44 MB).

## Protecting Your Diskettes

Dust, heat, cold, magnets, cigarette smoke, and coffee do great damage to your diskettes. Placing your diskette on or near any other electrical or magnetic device can quickly ruin your files. This includes your digitizer tablet! A ringing telephone can even be a dangerous enemy of the diskette because of its magnetic field. Beyond physical damage, you or someone else could write over the files on a diskette, or put files on the wrong diskette, making them difficult or impossible to find.

The easiest way to protect the data on your diskette from accidental erasure is to use the write-protect tab. The write-protect tab is a small, sliding tab located on the bottom side of the diskette. Notice that the write-protect tab is in effect when it is moved toward the edge of the diskette. Use the point of a pen or your fingernail to slide the tab. See **Figure 13-13.**

When the tab is in the write-protect position, you cannot format, save, or copy files to that diskette. However, the files can be read from the diskette. Windows Explorer displays a dialog box with a write-protect error message if you attempt to format or save to a write-protected diskette. If you must use the diskette for writing or formatting purposes, simply move the write-protect tab to the appropriate position.

**Figure 13-13.**
To prevent your files from being erased, move the write-protect tab to the "read only" position.

Write-protect tab

---

**Exercise 13-4**

○ Insert one of your blank diskettes into the A: drive.

○ Use the Format command to format the diskette and label it PROBLEMS.

○ Copy a drawing file from the AutoCAD 2004\Sample folder from the hard disk to the diskette.

○ Use the Copy Disk command to make a backup copy of the PROBLEMS diskette.

## Additional Disk Management Functions

The shortcut menu that is displayed by right-clicking on the diskette drive icon **(Figure 13-10)** provides several other functions for managing the contents of diskettes. The following list briefly describes these options:

- **Expand.** Expands one branch of the directory tree for the selected drive.
- **Explore.** Displays the contents of the diskette in the contents pane.
- **Open.** Opens a separate window that displays all folders and files on the diskette.
- **Search.** Opens a new Windows Explorer window with the Search Companion active.
- **Sharing and Security.** Allows you to configure shares for the selected drive.
- **Properties.** Opens the Properties dialog box for the diskette. The General tab displays general information about the diskette and provides a text box for naming the diskette. The Tools tab provides three tools that allow you to check the diskette for errors, defragment data stored on the diskette, and back up the diskette to a tape drive. The Hardware tab provides information about the various drives installed on the computer. The Sharing tab allows you to configure shares for the drive. Check the Windows online help for additional information on these tools.

---

**NOTE**    Many software applications place new options on the short-cut menu, so your menu may show additional options that are not listed here.

---

# Drag-and-Drop Operations with Windows Explorer

The drag-and-drop functionality in Windows makes many common Windows Explorer operations faster and easier. Drag-and-drop options are provided for copying, moving, and deleting files and folders. When you drag any file or folder to a new location on the same disk drive, the items are moved to the new location. Dragging an item to a different disk drive creates a copy on the second disk drive. If the default operation is not what you need, you can drag the files or folders using the second mouse button (the right-click button). When you drop the items, a shortcut menu appears listing the available options. For example, the shortcut menu shown in **Figure 13-14** is displayed when dragging an item to an alternate location on the same disk drive. Because moving the file is the default operation, the **Move Here** option is shown in bold text. You can select from the other options or pick Cancel. To delete files or folders, you can drag them to the Recycle Bin icon on either the desktop or in the folders pane.

The Windows Explorer can also be used to dynamically drag and drop file icons into the AutoCAD drawing area. This powerful capability allows you to open drawings, insert drawing files as blocks, insert text files as multiline text, and import PostScript and raster files. Drag-and-drop operations can also be used to load menu, linetype, shape, script, and slide files, as well as AutoLISP and ARX applications.

The following table lists the different kinds of drag-and-drop operations that can be used in AutoCAD. Also listed are the required file name extensions, the related AutoCAD commands, and the chapters in this text where additional command information can be found.

**Figure 13-14.**
The drag-and-drop
shortcut menu
provides additional
flexibility for drag-
and-drop operations.

Copy Here
**Move Here**
Create Shortcuts Here

Cancel

| Operation | File Extension | Related Command | Related Chapter |
|-----------|----------------|-----------------|-----------------|
| Load a linetype file | LIN | **LINETYPE** | Chapter 4 |
| Insert a text file | TXT | **MTEXT** | Chapter 8 |
| Load a shape font | SHP | **COMPILE** | Chapter 8 |
| Insert a drawing file | DWG | **INSERT** | Chapter 23 |
| Open a drawing file | DWG | **OPEN** | Chapter 2 |
| Print a drawing | DWG | **PLOT** | Chapter 10 |
| Load a slide file | SLD | **VSLIDE** | Chapter 27 |
| Run a script file | SCR | **SCRIPT** | Chapter 27 |
| Insert a DXF file | DXF | **INSERT** | Chapter 13 |
| Open a DXF file | DXF | **OPEN** | Chapter 13 |
| Load a DXB file | DXB | **DXBIN** | Chapter 13 |

Additional files that can be used with drag-and-drop procedures are discussed in *AutoCAD and its Applications—Advanced.* The following table lists those files:

| Operation | File Extension | Related Command |
|-----------|----------------|-----------------|
| Load ADS and ARX applications | EXE, ARX | **XLOAD** |
| Import a PostScript image | EPS, PS | **PSIN** |
| Load a menu file | MNU | **MENU** |
| Insert an AutoLISP routine | LSP | **LOAD** |

## Dragging and Dropping a Text File

You will learn in Chapter 22 that AutoCAD objects, such as text, can be saved to disk and inserted into other drawing files. A text file created with a text editor outside of AutoCAD can also be inserted into a drawing using drag-and-drop if it is saved as a TXT file. To drag a text file into AutoCAD, do the following:

1. Start both AutoCAD and Windows Explorer. Arrange the display windows so that both are visible.
2. In Windows Explorer, open the folder that contains the text file you want to insert.
3. Select the text file icon, drag it into the AutoCAD drawing area, and then release the mouse button. The text is inserted in the current text style and on the current layer.

The text file is inserted as a multiline text object, and appears with grips. The location of the text can be quickly changed with the grips.

External text files can be created with Notepad, WordPad, or your own ASCII text editor. Remember that the text file must have a TXT extension. Without this extension, a text file is not associated with an application and cannot be inserted.

**PROFESSIONAL TIP**

If you use the right mouse button when dragging a text file into AutoCAD, a shortcut menu offers additional options. The **Insert here** option produces the same result as a regular drag-and-drop operation. Optionally, you can attach a hyperlink to an existing drawing object or cancel the operation. Using hyperlinks in AutoCAD is discussed in *AutoCAD and its Applications—Advanced*.

## Using Drag and Drop to Print a Drawing

You can plot a drawing by dragging the drawing file icon directly to the appropriate printer icon. The drawing file icon you select is opened in the drawing editor using the **FILEOPEN** command. This command allows you to open a file without using a dialog box, regardless of the setting of the **FILEDIA** system variable. To use the **FILEOPEN** command, AutoCAD must first set Single Document Interface mode active by setting the **SDI** system variable to 1. Once the drawing appears in the drawing area, the **Plot** dialog box is displayed. You can then modify the printing parameters as required and print the drawing. After exiting the **Plot** dialog box, **SDI** is reset to its previous value.

To print a drawing on the system printer using drag and drop, do the following:

1. Launch AutoCAD and then launch Windows Explorer.
2. Locate and select the folder containing the drawing that you wish to print. Right-click the folder icon and select Explore from the shortcut menu. Arrange and resize the windows as necessary so that the contents pane of each window is visible.

**Figure 13-15.**
Use two Windows Explorer windows to print a drawing with the drag-and-drop method.

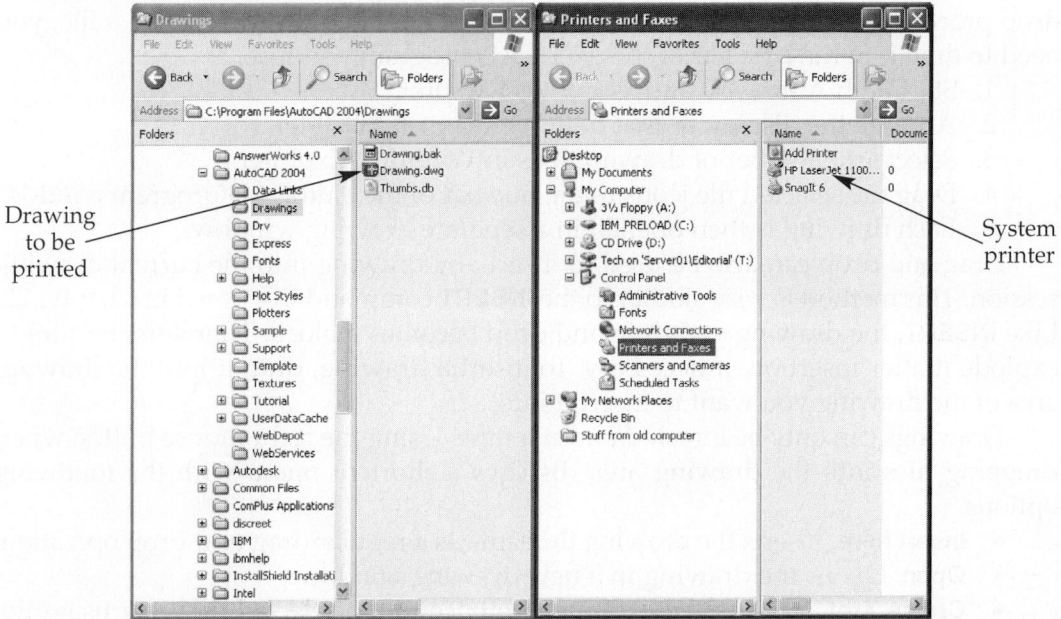

Drawing to be printed

System printer

3. In the original window, select and expand the Control Panel branch, and select Printers and Faxes. See **Figure 13-15.**
4. Select the file you wish to print in the second Windows Explorer window and drag it to the desired printer icon in the original Windows Explorer window. Release the mouse button.
5. The AutoCAD program window is moved to the front, the file is opened, and the **Plot** dialog box is displayed.
6. Make any necessary adjustments to the plotting parameters. Pick **OK** to print the drawing.

The following is an alternative method of plotting a drawing file from Windows Explorer:
1. Launch AutoCAD and then launch Windows Explorer.
2. Locate the drawing you wish to print and right-click on it. Select Print from the shortcut menu.

**PROFESSIONAL TIP**

You can place a printer icon on the Windows desktop and avoid having to open the My Computer and Printers windows. Simply create a Windows shortcut by pressing the [Ctrl] key, then picking and dragging the printer icon to a location on the desktop. The label below this icon will change to "Shortcut to...". To change the label, pick the name to highlight it and then pick it again to edit. Type a new name, then press [Enter]. Now when you need to print a document, just drag the file name from Windows Explorer and drop it on the new printer icon.

# Dragging and Dropping Drawing Files into AutoCAD

One or more drawing files can be easily opened in AutoCAD using a drag-and-drop procedure. It is important to remember that when you want to open a file, you need to drag it to the *title bar* of the AutoCAD program window.

1. Start both AutoCAD and Windows Explorer.
2. Arrange the display so that both windows are visible.
3. Select any number of drawing files in Windows Explorer.
4. Drag the selected file icons to the title bar of the AutoCAD program window.
5. Each drawing is then opened in a separate drawing window.

Drag and drop can also be used to insert any drawing into the current drawing session. This method is very similar to the **INSERT** command discussed in Chapter 22. Like **INSERT**, the drawing you drag and drop becomes a block. Therefore, be sure to explode it after insertion, if necessary. To insert a drawing, drag it into the drawing area of the drawing you want to insert it into.

Drawings can only be inserted one at a time. Using the right mouse button when dragging files into the drawing area displays a shortcut menu with the following options:

- **Insert here.** Inserts the drawing the same as a regular drag-and-drop operation.
- **Open.** Opens the drawing in a new drawing window.
- **Create Xref.** Attaches an external reference to the selected drawing using the drop point as the insertion location and default scale and rotation.
- **Create Hyperlink here.** Creates a hyperlink to the drawing attached to a selected object.
- **Cancel.** Stops the drag-and-drop operation.

## Exercise 13-5

○ Launch both Windows Explorer and AutoCAD. Arrange the display windows so that both are visible.
○ Open a directory containing one or more DWG files.
○ Using the methods described previously, drag one or more drawing file icons on to the AutoCAD program window title bar.
○ Drag a drawing file icon into a drawing window. Answer the prompts for insertion point, scale, and rotation angle, and then explode the inserted drawing.
○ Use Notepad to create a simple text file. Make the notes specific to your particular application. Save the file as a TXT file.
○ Drag the text file into the AutoCAD drawing window.

**NOTE** This chapter has introduced you to only some of the features within Windows Explorer. Become familiar with *all* the functions offered by this useful tool. By making Windows Explorer an integral part of your daily work, you can greatly increase your productivity.

# Recovering a Damaged Drawing

A damaged drawing file is one that has been corrupted and cannot be loaded into the AutoCAD drawing editor with the **OPEN** command. Drawings can be corrupted in the following ways:

- A bad or corrupted diskette.
- Running out of disk space during a drawing session.
- Power failures.
- Hardware or software problems.

A valuable resource for recovering lost or damaged drawing data is the backup file. By default, AutoCAD creates a BAK file when you save a drawing—so a BAK file stores the drawing prior to your most recent save operation. A BAK file is also a drawing file, but it uses a different file extension.

AutoCAD does not allow you to open BAK files directly. To open a BAK file, it must be renamed to end in a .dwg file extension. Note that Windows Explorer must be configured to display file extensions to be able to change them.

When a BAK file does not provide the best solution, AutoCAD provides a method for recovering most damaged files. You can type RECOVER at the Command: prompt, or select **Recover...** from the **Drawing Utilities** cascading menu in the **File** pull-down menu. This displays the **Select File** dialog box. Select the proper folder and file and AutoCAD attempts to recover the damaged drawing. If it is successful, the file is loaded into the drawing editor, and it can be worked on normally. If you do not save the file before exiting AutoCAD, the recovered drawing is lost.

There is also an automatic saving feature in AutoCAD that creates a temporary backup file during a drawing session. This file can be a valuable backup if you find your drawing is corrupted as a result of an improper termination or system crash. By default, AutoCAD names the automatically saved file *DrawingName_n_n_nnnn*.sv$ and saves it in the C:\Documents and Settings\\*User*\Local Settings\Temp folder. If you need to use this file, you must rename it as a DWG file in Windows Explorer.

| RECOVER |
| --- |
| File |
| ➥ Drawing |
| Utilities |
| ➥ Recover... |

# Using the AUDIT Command

| AUDIT |
| --- |
| File |
| ➥ Drawing |
| Utilities |
| ➥ Audit |

You can perform a diagnostic check on your drawing files with the **AUDIT** command. This checks for and corrects errors. You have the option of fixing errors or leaving them.

```
Command: AUDIT↵
Fix any errors detected? [Yes/No] <N> ↵
  1         Blocks audited
 55         Blocks audited
Pass    1    539      objects audited
Pass    2    539      objects audited
Pass    3    5500     objects audited
Total errors found 0 fixed 0
Command:
```

If you answer no, as in the above example, all errors are listed for your reference, but they are not fixed. To fix errors in the transferred drawing, type Y at the Fix any errors detected? prompt.

AutoCAD displays the errors and notifies you that they are fixed like this:

```
3          Blocks audited
Pass    1    29      objects audited
Pass    2    14      objects audited
Total errors found 2 fixed 2
```

If the system variable **AUDITCTL** is set to 1 (on), AutoCAD automatically creates an audit report that lists the corrections made. This report is given the same name as the drawing, but has an ADT file extension. The file is placed in the same directory as the drawing. This is an ASCII text file (American Standard Code for Information Interchange). You can open this file and read the information using any ASCII text editor, such as Windows Notepad or WordPad.

## Listing the Audit Report

It is not necessary to leave AutoCAD to display the audit report. Simply pick Programs, Accessories, and then Notepad from the Start menu.

To list the audit report, first select Open... from the File menu. Then, select the audit file. Pick OK and the contents of the file are displayed on the screen. After reviewing the file, you can exit Notepad.

## Understanding AutoCAD's Temporary Files

AutoCAD maintains several temporary files while you are working on a drawing. You might consider these as "worksheets" that AutoCAD opens, much like the notes, references, sketches, and calculations you may have scattered around your desk. These files are created automatically to store portions of the AutoCAD program not currently in use and information related to the current drawing file. These files are critical to AutoCAD's operation, and must be maintained and safeguarded properly.

## Program Swap Files

AutoCAD uses a virtual memory system. *Virtual memory* is a combination of memory and hard disk space. The main program file for AutoCAD is named acad.exe. It is a large file—over 6.6 MB. If there is not enough room in your computer's physical memory (RAM) to store the program, AutoCAD creates *pages* of the program in free space on your hard disk drive.

A virtual memory system keeps only the part of the program that is currently being used in physical memory. If additional portions of the program are needed, AutoCAD creates a page on the hard disk and writes the least-used portion of the program to that page. The new portion of the program that is requested is written to physical memory. Thus, AutoCAD creates a *paging* system using virtual memory. The least-used pages are written to a page called a *swap file*, and are held there until needed again.

When required, AutoCAD's paging system automatically creates and maintains a swap file. These files are critical to AutoCAD, and must never be deleted while you are in a drawing session. Should you experience an improper termination of AutoCAD, and the drawing file is not saved properly, these swap files may be left open. In that case, the files are no longer of use and can be deleted, but only *after* you have exited AutoCAD.

## Temporary Files

The second piece of AutoCAD's virtual memory system is called the *pager*. The pager is similar to the swap file system, but creates temporary storage space for drawing file information. The entire contents of a small drawing may fit into your computer's physical memory, but as the drawing grows larger, portions of it must be temporarily removed. AutoCAD creates a *page file* for the least-used portion of your drawing, and opens the physical memory for new drawing data. When the drawing data contained in the page file is needed, it is *paged* back into memory. These temporary files are given the file extension of AC$. These are vital files and must never be deleted while working in AutoCAD.

If AutoCAD should terminate improperly, these page files are left open in the temporary files directory—usually C:\Documents and Settings\\*User*\Local Settings\Temp. If AutoCAD is no longer running, the AC$ files left behind are no longer of any use, and can be deleted. Always delete these files with Windows Explorer, and never while you are working in AutoCAD.

## Creating a Workspace for Temporary Files

The default workspace for AutoCAD's temporary files is C:\Documents and Settings\\*User*\Local Settings\Temp. You can create a folder on your hard drive and tell AutoCAD to always use that folder for storage of temporary files. Use the following procedure to allocate space for these files:

1. Pick **Options...** in the **Tools** pull-down menu or right-click and select **Options...** from the shortcut menu. This displays the **Options** dialog box.
2. Pick the **Files** tab.
3. Pick the + symbol to the left of Temporary Drawing File Location. The current location is displayed. See **Figure 13-16.**
4. Pick the current directory (folders) path to select it.
5. Pick the **Browse...** button to display the **Browse for Folder** dialog box.
6. Find the folder you want to use for temporary files and select it. Pick **OK** to exit.

**Figure 13-16.**
The location of temporary drawing files can be specified in the **Options** dialog box.

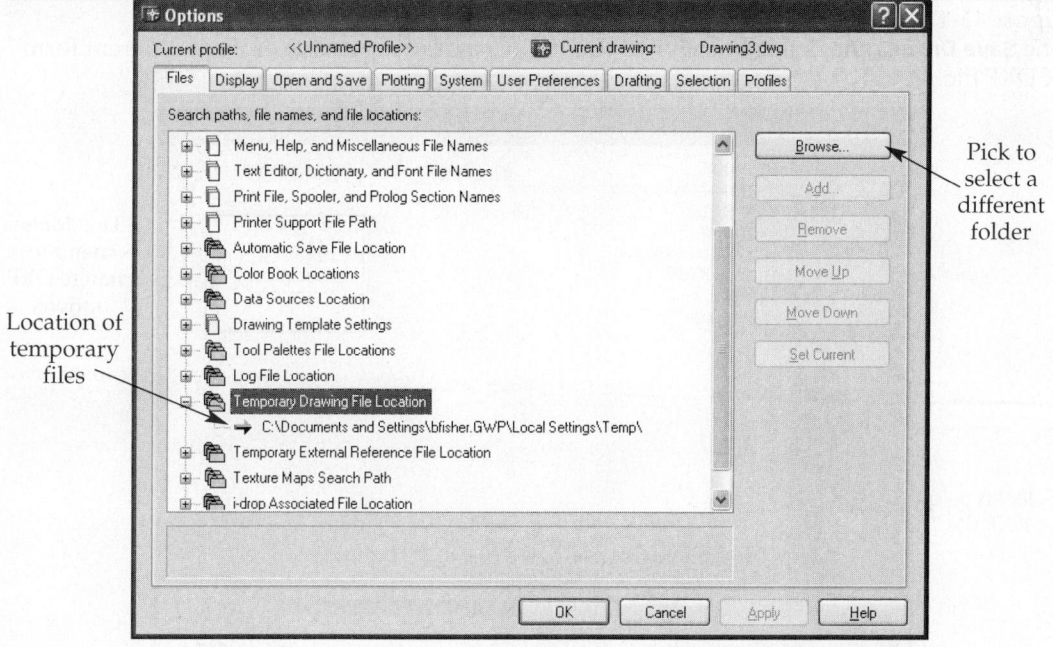

> **NOTE**
>
> After you complete step 3 on the previous page, you can type in a new location if you know the exact path. Be sure to specify the drive letter and complete path. For example, if you created a folder on the C: drive in the \AutoCAD 2004 folder named Tempfile, the proper path to type is C:\AutoCAD 2004\Tempfile.

# Importing and Exporting Files

AutoCAD provides you with the ability to work with files other than DWG files. You can import external data into a drawing, or export the current drawing to files that can be used in other programs for rendering, animation, desktop publishing, presentations, stereolithography, and solid modeling. This section provides a brief overview of AutoCAD's capabilities in importing and exporting a variety of different files.

## DXF Files

The DXF file format is commonly used for sharing drawing files with CAD applications other than AutoCAD. *DXF* is an acronym for *drawing interchange format*. A DXF file is simply an ASCII text file that defines the objects and settings within a drawing. You can save an entire drawing or just selected objects as a DXF file using either the **SAVEAS** or **WBLOCK** command.

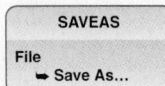

When using **SAVEAS**, select the desired DXF version from the **Files of type:** list. You can save the DXF file to be compatible with AutoCAD 2004, AutoCAD 2000/LT 2000, or AutoCAD R12/LT2. See **Figure 13-17.** From the **Save Drawing As** dialog box, pick **Options...** from the **Tools** menu to access the **DXF Options** tab of the **Saveas Options** dialog box. The available options are as follows:

- **ASCII.** Writes the DXF file in a standard ASCII text format.
- **BINARY.** Writes the DXF file using a binary file format. This option can reduce the size of the translated file by 25% or more.

---

**Figure 13-17.**
The **Save Drawing As** dialog box allows you to save a drawing as one of three different forms of DXF file.

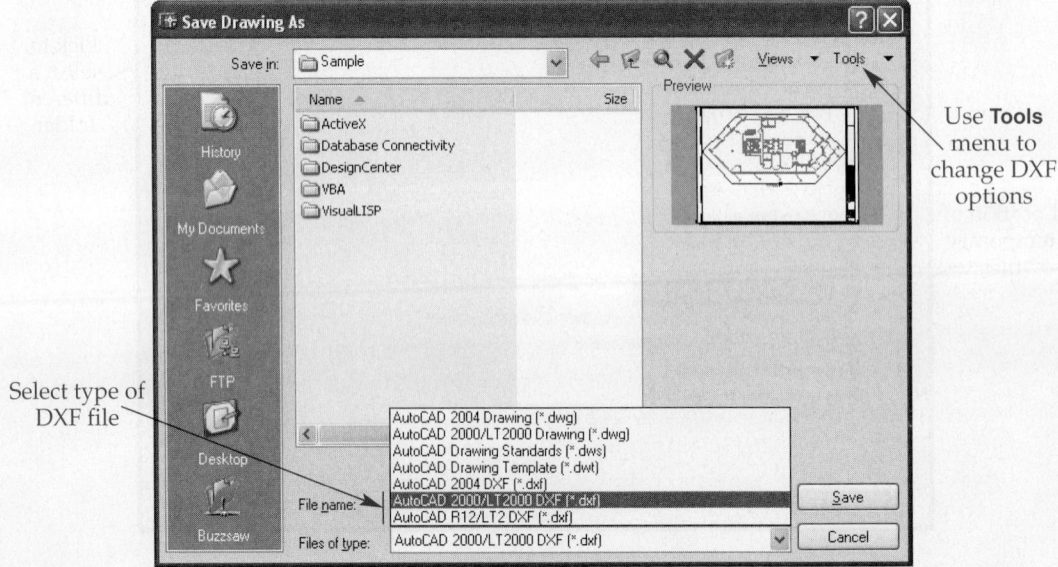

AutoCAD and its Applications—Basics

- **Select objects.** Allows selection of specific drawing objects to be saved to the DXF file.
- **Save thumbnail preview image.** Saves a preview image with the file.
- **Decimal places of accuracy (0 to 16).** Specifies the decimal places of precision for ASCII format DXF files.

To write a DXF file using the **WBLOCK** command, specify a file name with a .dxf extension in the **File Name:** text box in the **Write Block** dialog box. The **WBLOCK** command automatically creates an AutoCAD 2004 format DXF file.

WBLOCK

Existing DXF files can be opened directly with the **OPEN** command, or their contents can be inserted into the current drawing using the **INSERT** command. To access DXF files in the file selection dialog boxes displayed by these commands, specify DXF (*.dxf) in the **Files of type:** list.

### DXF applications

There are several applications for which you will want to convert an AutoCAD file to DXF format. The most common application is sharing drawings with CAM systems or other CAD systems. Numerical control (NC) programs also use DXF files. The file is used to translate the shape and features of a machine part to code that can be used for lathes, milling machines, and drill presses. In addition, desktop publishing programs use DXF files to translate drawings into images that can be inserted into a page layout. Also, programs that perform stress analysis and calculations often rely on DXF drawings.

## Importing a Scanned File

*Scanning* is the process of creating an electronic file from a hard copy. Scanners reflect light off the hard copy and translate this data into an electronic file. Many scanning programs create a DXB (drawing interchange binary) file after scanning an existing paper drawing with a camera or plotter-mounted scanner. The file created is in binary code. The **DXBIN** command converts this code into drawing data. This drawing data becomes an AutoCAD drawing file with a .dwg extension.

To import a DXB file, pick **Drawing Exchange Binary...** from the **Insert** pull-down menu, or type DXBIN at the Command: prompt. The **Select DXB File** dialog box appears. Select the scanned file and pick the **Open** button. You can then edit the drawing using typical AutoCAD commands. After editing the drawing, it can be saved as a drawing file.

DXBIN

Insert
➡ Drawing
Exchange
Binary...

## Autodesk VIZ and 3D Studio Files

Autodesk VIZ and 3ds max® are programs that allow you to design, render, and animate 3D models. Both of these applications can use the 3D Studio (3DS) file format. You can export or import 3D Studio files with AutoCAD.

To export a 3D Studio file, type 3DSOUT at the Command: prompt. Next, you are prompted to select objects. Select all the objects you wish to export and press [Enter]. The **3D Studio Output File** dialog box is displayed. Enter the file name in the **File name:** text box. Press [Enter] or pick **Save** when you are finished. Exporting a 3D Studio file can also be executed using the **EXPORT** command or selecting **Export...** from the **File** pull-down menu and then picking the **3D Studio (*.3ds)** file type in the **Export Data** dialog box.

3DSOUT

File
➡ Export...

You can import an existing 3D Studio file into AutoCAD by selecting **3D Studio...** from the **Insert** pull-down menu. The **3D Studio File Import** dialog box is displayed. Select the appropriate 3DS file from the list and press [Enter]. You can also import a 3D Studio file by typing 3DSIN at the Command: prompt.

3DSIN

Insert
➡ 3D Studio...

## Solid Model Files

A *solid* is a 3D object composed of a specific material and possessing unique characteristics related to its shape and composition. These characteristics are called *mass properties*. Solids are created in AutoCAD with one of several commands found in the **Solids** cascading menu of the **Draw** pull-down menu.

The term *solid modeling* refers to the process of constructing a model from one or more 3D solid shapes called *primitives* and performing any necessary editing functions to create the final product. This procedure is discussed in detail in *AutoCAD and its Applications—Advanced*.

**ACISOUT**

File
  ➥ Export...

A solid model is frequently used with analyzing and testing software and in part manufacturing. The **ACISOUT** command converts AutoCAD drawings into a file format that is useful for these purposes. To activate the **ACISOUT** command, choose **Export...** from the **File** pull-down menu. Pick **ACIS (*.sat)** in the **Files of type:** drop-down list of the **Export Data** dialog box. When you pick **OK**, you are prompted to select objects. Use any of the standard selection methods to choose the solid objects, then press [Enter]. If ACISOUT is typed at the Command: prompt, the **Create ACIS File** dialog box is displayed instead of the **Export Data** dialog box. Notice that SAT file is the default setting. Do not change this. Type the file name in the **File name:** text box and press [Enter] or pick **Save**. The SAT file is stored in ASCII format.

**ACISIN**

Insert
  ➥ ACIS File...

Solid model data stored in the SAT file can be read back into AutoCAD using the **ACISIN** command. When you enter this command, the **Select ACIS File** dialog box is displayed. Pick the file from the list, then pick **Open** or press [Enter]. You can also activate the **ACISIN** command by picking **ACIS File...** in the **Insert** pull-down menu.

> **PROFESSIONAL TIP**
>
> The ASCII file created by the **ACISOUT** command may be from three to four times smaller than the DWG file. For this reason, it may be more efficient to store 3D solid models as SAT files rather than DWG files. When you need to work with the model in AutoCAD for any purpose, simply use the **ACISIN** command. This command creates solid objects from the model data stored in the SAT file.

## Stereolithography Files

*Stereolithography* is a technology that can create a three-dimensional plastic prototype model using a computer-generated solid model, a laser, and a vat of liquid polymer. This technology is also referred to as *rapid prototyping* because a prototype 3D model can be designed and formed in a short amount of time, without using standard manufacturing processes. Most software used to create a stereolithograph can read an STL file. AutoCAD can export a drawing file to the STL format, but *cannot* import an STL file.

**STLOUT**

File
  ➥ Export...

To activate the **STLOUT** command, type STLOUT at the Command: prompt. You are then prompted to select a single object. Select one object and press [Enter]. You are then asked if you want to create a binary STL file. If you answer no to this prompt, an ASCII file is created. Keep in mind that a binary STL file may be much smaller than the ASCII STL file. After you choose the type of file to create, the **Create STL File** dialog box is displayed. Type the file name in the **File name:** text box and pick **Save** or press [Enter]. You can also create an STL file by selecting **Export...** from the **File** menu and then selecting **Lithography (*.stl)** in the **Export Data** dialog box.

## Postscript Files

PostScript is a copyrighted page description language developed by Adobe Systems. This language is widely used in the desktop publishing industry. AutoCAD drawing files can be exported to the EPS PostScript file format by typing PSOUT at the Command: prompt. The **Create PostScript File** dialog box is displayed. You can also pick **Export...** from the **File** pull-down menu to display the **Export Data** dialog box. Then, pick **Encapsulated PS (*.eps)** in the file type drop-down list. Type the file name in the **File name:** text box and pick **Save** or press [Enter].

There are additional options for exporting PostScript files. To set these options, select **Options...** from the **Tools** menu in the **Create PostScript File** dialog box or **Export Data** dialog box. This accesses the **PostScript Out Options** dialog box, which allows you to fine-tune the content and appearance of the exported EPS file. The use of PostScript files is discussed in detail in *AutoCAD and its Applications—Advanced*.

PSOUT

File
➥ Export...

## Additional Files

Three additional files are listed in the **Export Data** dialog box and are defined here:
- **Metafile (.wmf).** A Windows file that contains vector information. It can be scaled and retain its resolution. See *AutoCAD and its Applications—Advanced* for a detailed discussion of metafiles.
- **DXX Extract (.dxx).** An extract file of attribute information contained in a block. This file is created using the **ATTEXT** command, which is discussed in Chapter 24.
- **Bitmap (.bmp).** A *bitmap* is a digital image composed of bits, or screen pixels. A bitmap is also referred to as a *raster image*. Unlike the metafile format, a bitmap contains no vector information. Bitmaps are discussed in *AutoCAD and its Applications—Advanced*.

## Chapter Test

*Answer the following questions on a separate sheet of paper.*

1. What is a file type extension?
2. What types of files are identified by the following extensions?
   A. BAK
   B. LIN
   C. MNU
   D. PLT
   E. BMP
   F. EXE
3. How do you launch Windows Explorer?
4. How do you list all files on the diskette in the A: drive?
5. In the Windows Explorer, how do you open a folder in the folders pane to view its files in the contents pane?
6. Using Windows Explorer, how do you select several files that are scattered randomly throughout the file list?
7. What is the procedure for changing a file name?
8. How can a file be moved to a new location?
9. How are files initially deleted?
10. How are files removed from the Recycle Bin to prevent being permanently deleted?
11. What are the two panes in Windows Explorer?

12. Write the correct path name for a drawing file named houseplan located in the Architectural subfolder, which is a branch of the Projects folder on the C: hard disk drive.
13. How can you select a consecutive group of items?
14. Which AutoCAD command is activated by dragging and dropping a drawing file into AutoCAD?
15. What three-letter file extension is valid when using drag-and-drop to place text in an AutoCAD drawing?
16. What is the purpose of Windows Explorer's *split bar*?
17. Describe the right-clicking process for creating a new folder.
18. How can 3.5″ diskettes be protected to prevent data from being written to them accidentally?
19. How can a damaged file be recovered?
20. What command allows you to run a diagnostic check of a drawing file?
21. What type of memory system does AutoCAD use to create pages of the program on the hard disk?
22. What is the name of the backup drawing file that AutoCAD creates when you save a drawing?
23. Define the following abbreviations.
    A. DXF.
    B. DXB.
24. What commands can be used to create a DXF file?
25. What commands can be used to access the contents of an existing DXF file?
26. List some of the programs that can use DXF files.
27. When would you use the **DXBIN** command?
28. Name five types of files that can be imported into AutoCAD.
29. Why might it be more efficient to store solid models in the form of SAT files rather than as drawing files?
30. What is an STL file and what is it used for?

## Problems

*Obtain the permission of your instructor or system administrator before creating or deleting folders, formatting or labeling diskettes, deleting files, or using any Windows Explorer command that can alter the structure of the hard disk files and directories.*

1. Make backup copies of all your diskettes. Use the Copy command in Windows Explorer. Copy the files in two different ways.
    A. Copy all DWG files to the new diskette. Then copy all BAK files to the new diskette.
    B. Copy a second diskette, or recopy the first diskette.
    C. List the files on your backup diskette. Be sure that files with both .dwg and .bak extensions have been copied. Then rename all files with the .bak extension to have an .old extension.

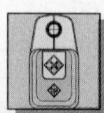

2. Get a printed listing of the files contained on one diskette. Ask your instructor or supervisor for assistance if you are not familiar with the printer.

3. Load one of your simple drawings into the AutoCAD graphics window. Create a DXF file of the drawing. Generate a printed copy of the contents of the DXF file.

4. This problem involves making new subfolders and copying drawing files to them.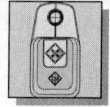
   A. Make your own subfolder under the AutoCAD 2004 folder. Name it using your initials.
   B. Make the new subfolder current.
   C. Copy all your drawing files from one 3.5″ diskette to the sub-folder.
   D. Make a subfolder within your new directory and name it Bak.
   E. Make the Bak subfolder current.
   F. Copy all of your BAK files into the Bak subfolder.
   G. Open a separate window for each of your subfolders.

5. Make a new subfolder of the folder you created in Problem 4. Name the new subfolder Test.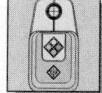
   A. Copy the contents of the Bak subfolder into Test.
   B. Display the contents of the Test subfolder in the contents pane.
   C. Rename one of the files in the Test subfolder to hey.you.
   D. Use the Search command and list all files with a .you file extension.
   E. Copy the hey.you file to the Bak subfolder and rename it who.me.
   F. Use the Search command and list all files with a .me file extension.
   G. Copy who.me to one of your 3.5″ diskettes and name it yes.you.
   H. Delete the three files you just created.
   I. Activate the Bak subfolder and delete it and all the files it contains.

6. Format four diskettes in a row without exiting the Format dialog box. Provide volume labels for the diskettes as they are formatted. When all formatting is complete, change the names of each diskette label without formatting the diskettes again.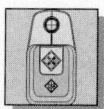

7. Use the copy disk option of Windows to make backup copies of all your 3.5″ diskettes that are used for drawing and data file storage. Label the diskettes that are copied with the same labels as the originals, but add a designation that indicates either "backup" or "copy."

8. Create a diskette that you use only for storage of DXF files. Open your drawing files and save them as DXF files to the diskette. Keep this diskette for backup purposes.

9. If you have access to a scanner, create a DXB file from an old, hand-drawn print. Import the DXB file using the **DXBIN** command. Compare the new AutoCAD drawing with the original.

In addition to Windows Explorer, several other programs are included with the Windows operating system. The particular programs available depend on your Windows installation. Some typical programs are shown here.

Calculator

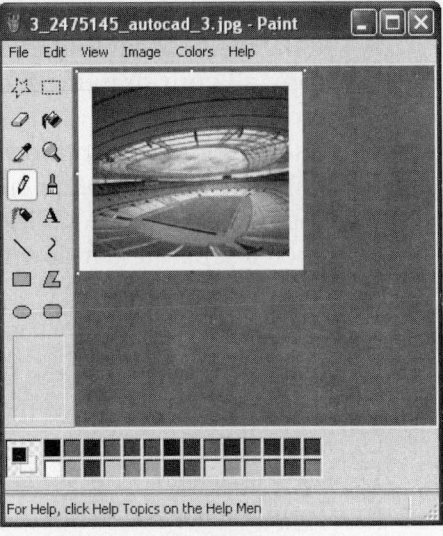

Paint

Windows Media Player

AutoCAD and its Applications—Basics

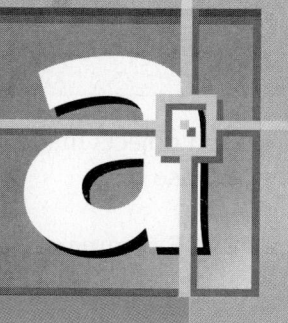

## CHAPTER 14

# Introduction to Polylines and Multilines

## Learning Objectives

After completing this chapter, you will be able to do the following:

- Use the **PLINE** command to draw polyline objects.
- Draw objects with the **TRACE** command.
- Explain the functions of the **UNDO** and **REDO** commands.
- Compare the results of using the **FILL** mode on and off.
- Use the **MLINE** command to draw multilines.
- Create your own multiline styles with the **MLSTYLE** command.
- Edit multiline intersections, corners, and vertices.
- Perform drawing tasks with the **SKETCH** command.

Polylines and multilines are two AutoCAD features that provide you with endless possibilities for design and drafting applications. This chapter introduces you to the use of polylines and fully explains how to create drawing features with multilines. You will also see how to sketch freehand with AutoCAD. A complete discussion of drawing polyline arcs and editing polylines is provided in Chapter 15.

The term *polyline* is composed of the words "poly" and "line." *Poly* means *many*. A *polyline* is a single object that can be made up of one or more line segments. Each line segment can vary in width. Polylines are drawn with the **PLINE** command and its various options. The **TRACE** command is similar to the **PLINE** command and also introduced in this chapter.

*Multilines* are combinations of parallel lines consisting of individual lines called *elements.* Multilines can have up to 16 individual line elements. You can offset the elements as needed to create a desired pattern for any field of drafting (for example, architectural, schematic, or mechanical drafting). Multilines are drawn using the **MLINE** command and its options.

The **PLINE** command is used to draw polylines and any related objects made up of line segments. Polylines have advantages over normal lines because they:

- Can be drawn as thick or tapered lines.
- Have much more flexibility than lines drawn with the **TRACE** command.
- Can be used with any linetype.
- Can be edited using advanced editing features.
- Can be drawn as closed polygons.
- Have an area and perimeter that can be determined easily.
- Can be used to draw a single object comprised of arcs and straight lines of varying thickness.

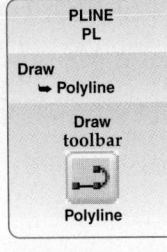

```
PLINE
PL

Draw
  ➥ Polyline

Draw
toolbar

Polyline
```

The function of the **PLINE** command is similar to the function of the **LINE** command. However, there are additional command options. Also, all segments of a polyline are treated as a single object. To draw a polyline, you can pick the **Polyline** button on the **Draw** toolbar, pick **Polyline** from the **Draw** pull-down menu, or type PL or PLINE at the Command: prompt:

```
Command: PL or PLINE↵
Specify start point: (select a point)
Current line-width is 0.0000
Specify next point or [Arc/Halfwidth/Length/Undo/Width]: (select the next point)
```

A line width of 0.0000 produces a line of minimum width. If this is acceptable, select the endpoint of the line segment. If additional line segments are drawn, the endpoint of the first line segment automatically becomes the starting point of the next line segment. When done drawing line segments, press [Enter] or [Esc] to end the **PLINE** command and return to the Command: prompt.

## Setting the Polyline Width

If it is necessary to change the width of a line segment, enter the **PLINE** command and select the first point. Then, use the **Width** option:

```
Command: PL or PLINE↵
Specify start point: (select a point)
Current line-width is 0.0000
Specify next point or [Arc/Halfwidth/Length/Undo/Width]: W↵
```

When the **Width** option is selected, you are asked to specify the starting and ending widths of the line. The starting width value becomes the default setting for the ending width. Therefore, to draw a line segment with one width, press [Enter] at the second prompt. If a tapered line segment is desired, enter different values for the starting and ending widths. After the widths are specified, the rubberband line from the first point reflects the width settings.

The following command sequence draws the line segment shown in **Figure 14-1.** Notice that the starting and ending points of the line are located at the center of the line segment's width.

```
Command: PL or PLINE↵
Specify start point: 4,4↵
Current line-width is 0.0000
Specify next point or [Arc/Halfwidth/Length/Undo/Width]: W↵
Specify starting width <0.0000>: .25↵
Specify ending width <0.2500>: ↵
Specify next point or [Arc/Halfwidth/Length/Undo/Width]: 8,4↵
Specify next point or [Arc/Close/Halfwidth/Length/Undo/Width]: ↵
Command:
```

**Figure 14-1.**
A thick polyline drawn using the **Width** option of the **PLINE** command.

Start point (4,4)    Endpoint (8,4)

## Drawing a Tapered Polyline

By entering different starting and ending width values, a tapered polyline is drawn, **Figure 14-2**. In the following example, the starting width is .25 units, and the ending width is .5 units:

```
Command: PL or PLINE↵
Specify start point: 4,4↵
Current line-width is 0.0000
Specify next point or [Arc/Halfwidth/Length/Undo/Width]: W↵
Specify starting width <0.0000>: .25↵
Specify ending width <0.2500>: .5↵
Specify next point or [Arc/Halfwidth/Length/Undo/Width]: 8,4↵
Specify next point or [Arc/Close/Halfwidth/Length/Undo/Width]: ↵
Command:
```

The **Width** option of the **PLINE** command can be used to draw an arrowhead. To do so, specify 0 as the starting width and then use any desired ending width.

**Figure 14-2.**
The **PLINE Width** option can be used to draw a wide, tapered polyline.

Start point (4,4)    Endpoint (8,4)

.25 units wide    .5 units wide

## Using the Halfwidth Option

The **Halfwidth** option of the **PLINE** command allows you to specify the width of the polyline from the center to one side. After picking the first point of the polyline, enter the **Halfwidth** option. Then, specify starting and ending values. Notice that the polyline in **Figure 14-3** is twice as wide as the polyline in **Figure 14-2** even though the same width values are entered.

```
Specify next point or [Arc/Halfwidth/Length/Undo/Width]: H↵
Specify starting half-width <0.0000>: .25↵
Specify ending half-width <0.2500>: .5↵
```

**Figure 14-3.**
Specifying the width of a polyline with the **Halfwidth** option of the **PLINE** command. Notice that a starting value of .25 produces a polyline width of .5 units and an ending value of .5 produces a polyline width of 1 unit.

Start point (4,4)    Endpoint (8,4)

.5 units wide    1 unit wide

## Using the Length Option

The **Length** option of the **PLINE** command allows you to draw a polyline parallel to the previous polyline. After drawing a polyline, reissue the **PLINE** command and pick a starting point. Then, enter the **Length** option and give the desired length:

```
Command: PL or PLINE↵
Specify start point: (pick the starting point for the first polyline)
Current line-width is 0.0000
Specify next point or [Arc/Halfwidth/Length/Undo/Width]: (pick the endpoint for the
    first polyline)
Specify next point or [Arc/Close/Halfwidth/Length/Undo/Width]: ↵
Command: ↵
PLINE
Specify start point: (pick a starting point for the second polyline)
Current line-width is 0.0000
Specify next point or [Arc/Halfwidth/Length/Undo/Width]: L↵
Specify length of line: (enter or pick any desired length for the second polyline)
Specify next point or [Arc/Close/Halfwidth/Length/Undo/Width]: ↵
Command:
```

The second polyline is drawn parallel to the previous polyline with the length you specified.

## Undoing Previously Drawn Polylines

While inside the **PLINE** command, you can use the **Undo** option of the command to erase the last line segment. To do so, type U on the prompt line and press [Enter]. Each time you use the **Undo** option, another line segment is erased. The segments are removed in reverse order (from the order in which they were drawn). This is a quick way to go back and correct the polyline while remaining in the **PLINE** command.

```
Specify next point or [Arc/Close/Halfwidth/Length/Undo/Width]: U↵
Specify next point or [Arc/Close/Halfwidth/Length/Undo/Width]:
```

After you press [Enter], the last polyline segment drawn is automatically removed. The rubberband is attached to the end of the line segment that was drawn before the undone segment. You can now continue to draw additional line segments or undo another segment. You can use the **Undo** option to remove all of the polyline segments up to the first point of the polyline. You cannot, however, specify a new first point for the polyline.

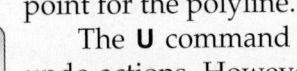

The **U** command (*not* the **Undo** option of the **PLINE** command) is also used to undo actions. However, the **U** command is used to undo the actions of the previous command. After a command has been completed, pick the **Undo** button on the **Standard** toolbar, pick **Undo** from the **Edit** pull-down menu, press the [Ctrl]+[Z] key combination, or type U at the Command: prompt and press [Enter]. The **U** command can also be activated by right-clicking in the drawing area and selecting **Undo** from the shortcut menu. AutoCAD indicates which command was undone on the prompt line:

```
Command: U↵
PLINE
Command:
```

In this example, the **PLINE** command was the last command. Therefore, it was the command whose actions were undone. You can reissue the **U** command to continue undoing commands. However, you can only undo one command at a time and they must be undone in the order in which they were used. The **UNDO** command has a number of options not available with the **U** command, including the ability to undo more than one command. The **UNDO** command is discussed later in this chapter.

AutoCAD and its Applications—Basics

## Exercise 14-1

○ Start a new drawing or use one of your templates.
○ Use the **PLINE** command to draw several objects of your own design. Vary the line width for each object.
○ Draw three different types of arrowheads by specifying different starting and ending widths for the line segments.
○ Set the polyline width to .125. Draw a single polyline. Using the **Length** option, draw two more polylines with the same width and a length of 4 units.
○ Save the drawing as EX14-1.

## Drawing Thick Lines Using the TRACE Command

When it is necessary to draw wide lines, the **TRACE** command can be used instead of the **PLINE** command. To use the **TRACE** command, type TRACE at the Command: prompt. Then, specify the trace width and select points as you would with the **LINE** command. The current trace width is stored in the **TRACEWID** system variable.

```
Command: TRACE↵
Specify trace width <current>: (enter width)
Specify start point: (select start point)
Specify next point: (select second point)
Specify next point: (select additional points or press [Enter] to complete)
Command:
```

When you use the **TRACE** command, objects are made up of *trace segments.* Trace segment ends are mitered to fit the next segment. Therefore, the previous trace segment is not drawn on screen until the next endpoint is specified. There is no close option with the **TRACE** command. Also, all segments drawn with the command must be the same width. However, you can reissue the command and draw new trace segments with a different width. Also, you can edit with grips to create a single segment of varying width.

## Exercise 14-2

○ Start a new drawing or use one of your templates.
○ Use the **TRACE** command to draw several objects of your own design. Vary the trace width for each object.
○ Save the drawing as EX14-2.

## Using the UNDO Command

As mentioned earlier in this chapter, the **UNDO** command is different from the **U** command. The **UNDO** command offers several options that allow you to undo a single command or a number of commands at once. The command sequence is:

```
Command: UNDO↵
Enter the number of operations to undo or [Auto/Control/BEgin/End/Mark/Back] <1>:
```

The default option allows you to designate the number of previous command sequences you wish to remove. For example, if you enter 1, the previous command sequence is undone. If you enter 2, the previous two command sequences are undone. AutoCAD tells you which commands were undone with a message on the prompt line:

```
Command: UNDO↵
Enter the number of operations to undo or [Auto/Control/BEgin/End/Mark/Back]: 2↵
PLINE LINE
Command:
```

## UNDO Options

There are several other options for the **UNDO** command. When the **Auto** option is on, any commands that are part of a group and used to perform a single operation are removed together. For example, when a command contains other commands, all of the commands in that group are removed as one single command. The **Auto** option is active by default. If it is turned off, each command in a group of commands is treated individually.

The **Control** option allows you to specify how many of the **UNDO** command options you want active. You can even disable the **UNDO** command altogether. To use the **Control** option, type C after issuing the **UNDO** command:

```
Enter the number of operations to undo or [Auto/Control/BEgin/End/Mark/Back]: C↵
Enter an UNDO control option [All/None/One] <All>: (enter a control option and
    press [Enter])
```

Selecting the **All** suboption keeps the full range of **UNDO** command options active. This is the default setting. The **None** suboption disables the **U** and **UNDO** commands. When the **U** command is entered, the following prompt appears:

```
Command: U↵
U command disabled. Use UNDO command to turn it on
```

This prompt indicates how to reactivate the **U** and **UNDO** commands. If you type UNDO at the Command: prompt, the following appears:

```
Command: UNDO↵
Enter an UNDO control option [All/None/One] <All>:
```

To reactivate all of the **UNDO** options, press [Enter] to accept the default **All**.

The **One** suboption limits **UNDO** to one operation only. When this suboption is active and you issue the **UNDO** command, the following prompt appears:

```
Command: UNDO↵
Control/<1>: ↵
LINE
Everything has been undone
Command:
```

If you attempt to enter a number higher than one, you get an error message. You can type C at the Control/<1>: prompt to display the **Control** suboptions.

When you use the **UNDO** command, AutoCAD maintains an "undo" file. This file saves previously used **UNDO** commands. All **UNDO** entries saved before disabling **UNDO** with the **Control None** suboption are discarded. This frees up some disk space and may be valuable information for you to keep in mind if you ever get close to having a full disk. If you want to continue using the **U** and **UNDO** commands to some extent, then you might consider using the **UNDO Control One** suboption. This allows you to keep using the **U** and **UNDO** commands to a limited extent while freeing up disk space holding current information about **UNDO**.

The **BEgin** and **End** options of the **UNDO** command are used together to perform several undo operations at once. They allow you to group a series of commands and treat them as a single command. Once the group is defined, the **U** command is then used to remove the commands that follow the **BEgin** option, but precede the **End** option. These options are useful if you can anticipate the possible removal of several commands that are entered consecutively. For example, if you think you may want to undo the next three commands altogether, do the following:

Command: **UNDO**↵
Enter the number of operations to undo or [Auto/Control/BEgin/End/Mark/Back]: **BE**↵
Command: **L** or **LINE**↵ *(this is the first command in the group)*
Specify first point: *(pick a point)*
Specify next point or [Undo]: *(pick an endpoint)*
Specify next point or [Undo]: ↵
Command: **PL** or **PLINE**↵
Specify start point: *(pick a point)*
Current line-width is 0.0000
Specify next point or [Arc/Halfwidth/Length/Undo/Width]: *(pick an endpoint)*
Specify next point or [Arc/Halfwidth/Length/Undo/Width]: ↵
Command: **L** or **LINE**↵
Specify first point: *(pick a point)*
Specify next point or [Undo]: *(pick an endpoint)*
Specify next point or [Undo]: ↵ *(this completes the last command in the group)*
Command: **UNDO**↵
Enter the number of operations to undo or [Auto/Control/BEgin/End/Mark/Back]: **E**↵
Command: **U**↵
GROUP
Command:

Since the three commands that were executed between the **BEgin** and **End** options, the **U** command treats them as one command and undoes all three. Note that the **BEgin** option must precede the command sequence and the **End** option must immediately follow the last command in the group to be undone.

The **UNDO Mark** option allows you to insert a marker in the undo file. Then, the **UNDO Back** option undoes all commands issued after the marker was inserted. For example, if you do not want certain work to be undone by the **Back** option, enter the **Mark** option after completing the work:

Command: **UNDO**↵
Enter the number of operations to undo or [Auto/Control/BEgin/End/Mark/Back]: **M**↵
Command:

Now, continue working. To undo all work since the marker was inserted, reissue the **UNDO** command and enter the **Back** option.

> Command: **UNDO**↵
> Enter the number of operations to undo or [Auto/Control/BEgin/End/Mark/Back]: **B**↵

If no marker has been inserted, everything in the entire drawing is undone. AutoCAD questions your choice:

> This will undo everything. OK? <Y>:

If you want everything that you have drawn and edited to be undone, press [Enter]. If not, type N or NO and press [Enter], or press the [Esc] key.

---

**PROFESSIONAL TIP**

The **UNDO Mark** option can be used to assist in the design process. For example, if you are working on a project and have completed a portion of the design, you can mark the spot with the **Mark** option and then begin work on the next design phase. If anything goes wrong with this part of the design, you can simply use the **UNDO Back** option to remove everything back to the mark.

---

**CAUTION**

Be very careful when using the **UNDO Back** option. Entering this option can undo everything in the entire drawing. You can bring back what you have undone if you use the **REDO** command immediately after using the **UNDO Back** option. If you use any other command, even **REDRAW**, after using **UNDO Back**, the drawing is lost forever. The **REDO** command is explained later in this chapter.

---

AutoCAD 2004
NEW FEATURE

## Using the UNDO List

The **UNDO** list allows you to graphically select a number of commands to undo. Using this feature performs the same function as using the **UNDO** command and entering a number. Access the **UNDO** list by picking the down arrow to the right of the **Undo** button on the **Standard** toolbar. A small window containing a sequential list of commands is displayed below the button, **Figure 14-4.** The first (top) command in the list is the most recent command. Commands must be undone in reverse order. To select a number of commands, move the cursor down. The commands that will be undone are highlighted. To execute the undo operation, pick the last command to undo. All commands executed after the one selected will be undone along with the selected command. Using this list is an easy way to undo back to an exact command without having to figure out how many commands have been issued since.

**Figure 14-4.**
The **UNDO** list accessed from the **Standard** toolbar.

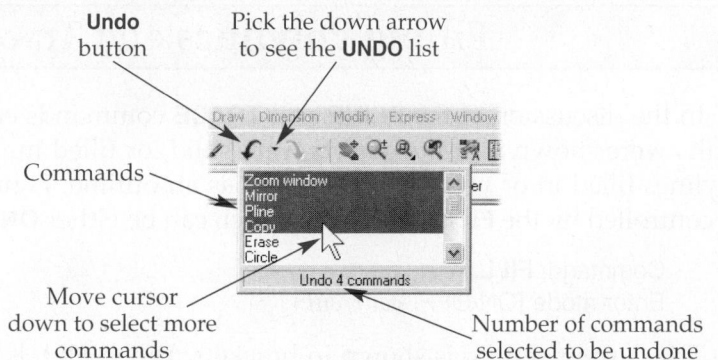

Undo button

Pick the down arrow to see the **UNDO** list

Commands

Move cursor down to select more commands

Number of commands selected to be undone

## Redoing the Undone

The **REDO** command is used to reverse the action of the **UNDO** and **U** commands. Type REDO at the Command: prompt, pick **Redo** from the **Edit** pull-down menu, press the [Ctrl]+[Y] key combination, or pick the **Redo** button from the **Standard** toolbar to activate the command.

The **REDO** command works only *immediately* after undoing something. **REDO** does *not* bring back polyline segments that were removed using the **Undo** option of the **PLINE** command.

If multiple undos are performed, any or all of the commands that were undone can be redone using the **REDO** list. Pick the down arrow next to the **Redo** button on the **Standard** toolbar. The list window is displayed, which shows the commands that were undone and can be redone. This list functions in the same way as the **UNDO** list discussed earlier.

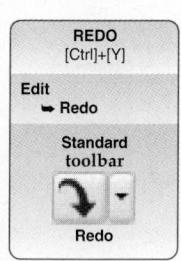

REDO
[Ctrl]+[Y]

Edit
↳ Redo

Standard toolbar

Redo

AutoCAD 2004
NEW FEATURE

---

### Exercise 14-3

○ Start a new drawing or use one of your templates.
○ Use the **PLINE** command to draw:
  ○ A rectangle measuring 2 units by 4 units with a line width of 0.
  ○ A rectangle measuring 2 units by 4 units with a line width of .125.
  ○ A polyline 6 units long with a .125 starting width and a .250 ending width.
  ○ A polyline 6 units long. Using the **Halfwidth** option, draw the polyline with a starting half-width of .125 and an ending half-width of .250.
○ Use the **U** command to remove the last three polylines.
○ Use the **REDO** list to bring back the last two removed polylines.
○ Save the drawing as EX14-3.

---

# Filling Polylines and Traces

FILL

In the discussion of the **PLINE** and **TRACE** commands earlier in this chapter, the results were shown as if the objects were solid, or filled in. You can have traces and polylines filled in or you can show them as an outline, **Figure 14-5**. These functions are controlled by the **FILL** command, which can be either **ON** or **OFF**.

Command: **FILL**↵
Enter mode [ON/OFF] <*current*>:

The current setting is shown in brackets. When **FILL** is on, traces and polylines appear filled after they are drawn. When **FILL** is off, traces and polylines appear as outlines and the corners are mitered. The **REGEN** command is used to display traces and polylines with the new setting.

OPTIONS
OP

Tools
➥ Options...

The **FILL** mode can also be set with the **Apply solid fill** check box in the **Options** dialog box. The check box is located in the **Display performance** area of the **Display** tab. When checked, **FILL** is on.

**Figure 14-5.**
Examples of **FILL** mode on and off.

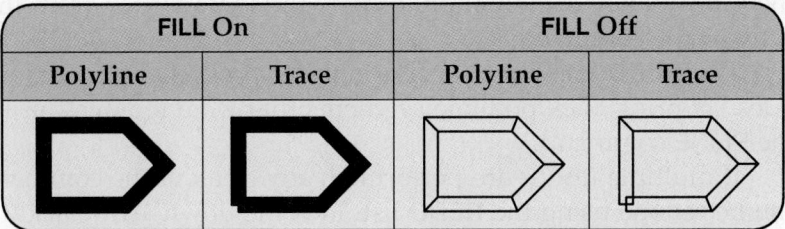

| FILL On | | FILL Off | |
|---------|---------|----------|---------|
| Polyline | Trace | Polyline | Trace |

---

**PROFESSIONAL TIP**

When there are many wide polylines or traces in a drawing, it is best to have **FILL** turned off. This saves time when redrawing, regenerating, or plotting a check copy of the drawing. Turn **FILL** on for the final plotting.

---

## Exercise 14-4

○ Start a new drawing or use one of your templates.
○ Use the **TRACE** command to draw a 2 unit by 4 unit rectangle with a .125 line width. Draw another rectangle with a .25 line width.
○ Use the **PLINE** command to draw a 2 unit by 4 unit rectangle with a .125 line width. Draw another rectangle with a .25 line width.
○ Turn **FILL** off and on and observe the difference.
○ Use the **REGEN** command with **FILL** on and off, and notice the regeneration speed in each situation. There may not be much difference with a fast computer unless the file starts to become large.
○ Save the drawing as EX14-4.

# Drawing Multilines

*Multilines* are objects that can consist of up to 16 parallel lines. The lines in a multiline are called *elements.* The **MLINE** command is used to draw multilines. A multiline configuration, or style, can be set using the **MLSTYLE** command. The default AutoCAD multiline style has two elements and is called STANDARD.

The **MLINE** command is accessed by picking **Multiline** from the **Draw** pull-down menu or by typing ML or MLINE at the Command: prompt:

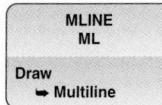

> Command: **ML** *or* **MLINE**↵
> Current settings: Justification = Top, Scale = 1.00, Style = STANDARD
> Specify start point or [Justification/Scale/STyle]: **2,2**↵
> Specify next point: **6,2**↵
> Specify next point or [Undo]: **6,6**↵
> Specify next point or [Close/Undo]: **2,6**↵
> Specify next point or [Close/Undo]: **C**↵
> Command:

The prompts and options for the **MLINE** command are similar to those for the **LINE** command. As shown in the previous command sequence, you can use the **Close** option at the last prompt to close a polygon. Enter U during the command sequence to undo the previously drawn multiline segment. The object created in the previous command sequence is shown in **Figure 14-6.** You can see AutoCAD's STANDARD multiline style consists of two parallel lines. If you pick on the line to display grips, you can see that the entered coordinates correspond to the inner square.

**Figure 14-6.**
A multiline object created with AutoCAD's STANDARD multiline style.

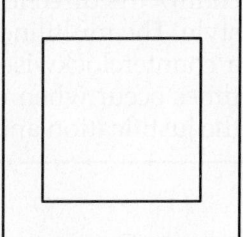

## Multiline Justification

Multiline justification determines how the resulting lines are offset from the definition points provided. *Definition points* are the points you pick or coordinates you enter when drawing multilines. The justification is based on counterclockwise movement and can be specified only once during a single **MLINE** command sequence. The justification options are **Top** (default), **Zero**, and **Bottom**.

To change the justification, type J at the first prompt displayed after entering the **MLINE** command. Then, enter the first letter of the desired justification format (T, Z, or B). The results of the three different justification options using identical point entries are shown in **Figure 14-7.** Observe each orientation as you go through the following command sequence:

> Command: **ML** *or* **MLINE**↵
> Current settings: Justification = Top, Scale = 1.00, Style = STANDARD
> Specify start point or [Justification/Scale/STyle]: **J**↵
> Enter justification type [Top/Zero/Bottom] <*current*>: (*type* T, Z, *or* B, *and press* [Enter])
> Current settings: Justification = *specified value*, Scale = 1.00, Style = STANDARD
> Specify start point or [Justification/Scale/STyle]: **2,2**↵

**Figure 14-7.**
Multilines drawn using each of the three justification options. The definition points (represented by plus symbols) are picked in a counterclockwise rotation.

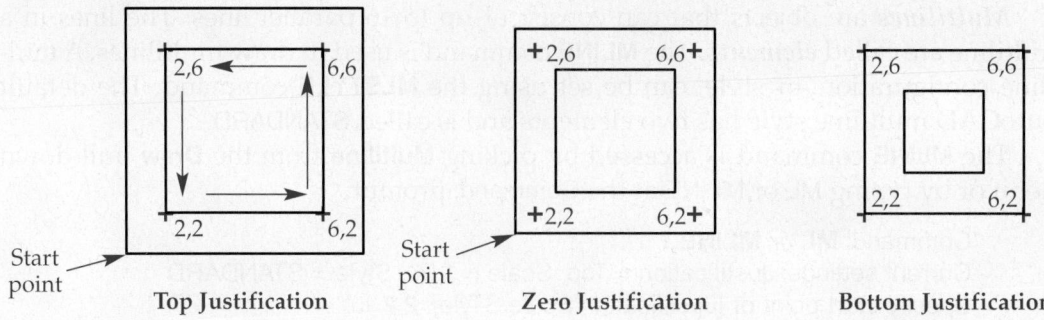

Specify next point: **6,2**↵
Specify next point or [Undo]: **6,6**↵
Specify next point or [Close/Undo]: **2,6**↵
Specify next point or [Close/Undo]: **C**↵
Command:

The current multiline justification setting is stored in the **CMLJUST** system variable. You can change the setting by entering 0 for the **Top** option, 1 for the **Zero** option, or 2 for the **Bottom** option.

---

**PROFESSIONAL TIP**

As shown in **Figure 14-7**, the multiline justification options control the direction of the offsets for elements of the current style. The multiline segments in these examples are drawn in a counterclockwise direction. Unexpected results can sometimes occur when using the **MLINE** command, depending on the justification and drawing direction.

---

**Exercise 14-5**

○ Start a new drawing or use one of your templates.
○ Use the **MLINE** command and its justification options to draw three objects similar to the ones shown in **Figure 14-7**.
○ Observe the difference between the justification options.
○ Save the drawing as EX14-5.

---

## Adjusting the Multiline Scale

The **MLINE** Scale option is a multiplier applied to the offset distance specified in the multiline style. The multiline style is defined with the **MLSTYLE** command. The multiplier is stored in the **CMLSCALE** system variable. The example in the previous section used a scale setting of 1 (default). With this setting, the distance between multiline elements is equal to 1 times the offset distance. For example, if the offset distance is 0.5, the distance between multiline elements is 0.5 when the multiline scale is 1. However, if the multiline scale is specified as 2, the distance between multiline elements is 1 (0.5 × 2).

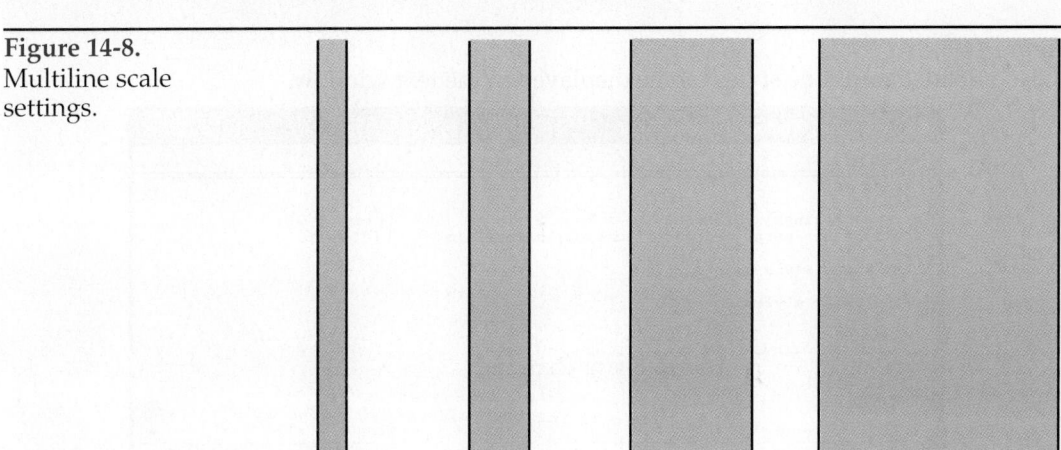

**Figure 14-8.**
Multiline scale settings.

Scale = .25        Scale = .5        Scale = 1        Scale = 2

The multiline scale is set to 2 in the next example. Multilines drawn with different scale settings are shown in **Figure 14-8.**

> Command: **ML** *or* **MLINE**↵
> Current settings: Justification = Top, Scale = 1.00, Style = STANDARD
> Specify start point or [Justification/Scale/STyle]: **S**↵
> Enter mline scale <1.00>: **2**↵
> Current settings: Justification = Top, Scale = 2.00, Style = STANDARD
> Specify start point or [Justification/Scale/STyle]:

---

### Exercise 14-6

○ Start a new drawing or use one of your templates.
○ Use the **MLINE** command and the **Scale** option to draw three objects similar to the ones shown in **Figure 14-8.**
○ Observe the difference between the multiline scales.
○ Save the drawing as EX14-6.

---

## Changing the Multiline Style

You can specify the current multiline style by using the **STyle** option of the **MLINE** command. However, before a new multiline style can be accessed, it must be created and saved using the **MLSTYLE** command. To use a saved multiline style, enter ST to access the **STyle** option and then enter the style name:

> Command: **ML** *or* **MLINE**↵
> Current settings: Justification = Top, Scale = 1.00, Style = STANDARD
> Specify start point or [Justification/Scale/STyle]: **ST**↵
> Enter mline style name or [?] : **ROAD1**↵
> Justification = Top, Scale = 1.00, Style = ROAD1
> Specify start point or [Justification/Scale/STyle]:

If you forget the name of the desired multiline style, you can enter ? at the Enter mline style name or [?]: prompt. The text window is opened and the currently loaded multiline styles are listed, **Figure 14-9.** Then, type the name of the style you want to use.

If you try to specify a multiline style that is not loaded, the **Load multiline style from file** dialog box is displayed. You can look for the desired multiline style in the acad.mln file library. Or, pick the **Tools** button and then **Find...** to open the **Find:** dialog

**Figure 14-9.**
A list of loaded multiline styles can be displayed in the text window.

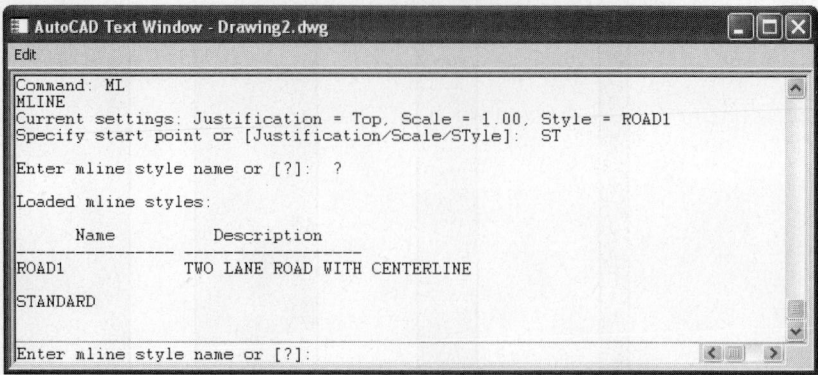

box. This dialog box allows you to search other files for the multiline style. The **Find** dialog box is discussed in Chapter 2. If the desired multiline style does not exist in the file you select, AutoCAD displays the message:

> Multiline style *style name* not found in *path and file selected*.
> You can use the "MLSTYLE" command to load it from another file.

## Creating Multiline Styles

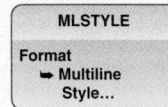

Multiline styles are defined using the **MLSTYLE** command. The current style is stored in the **CMLSTYLE** system variable. The **MLSTYLE** command can be accessed by picking **Multiline Style...** from the **Format** pull-down menu. You can also type MLSTYLE at the Command: prompt.

The **MLSTYLE** command displays the **Multiline Styles** dialog box, **Figure 14-10**. This is where multiline styles can be defined, edited, and saved. Styles can be saved to an external file so they can be used in other drawings. The image tile in the center of the **Multiline Styles** dialog box displays a representation of the current multiline style. The options provided in the **Multiline Style** area of the **Multiline Styles** dialog box are described as follows:

- **Current: drop-down list.** The **Current:** drop-down list allows you to set a different style as the current style. Pick the arrow and select the style from the list. Specifying a different style changes the setting of the **CMLSTYLE** system variable. Until you create or load a multiline style, the only style available is STANDARD.

---

**Figure 14-10.**
The **Multiline Styles** dialog box is used to define, edit, and save multiline styles.

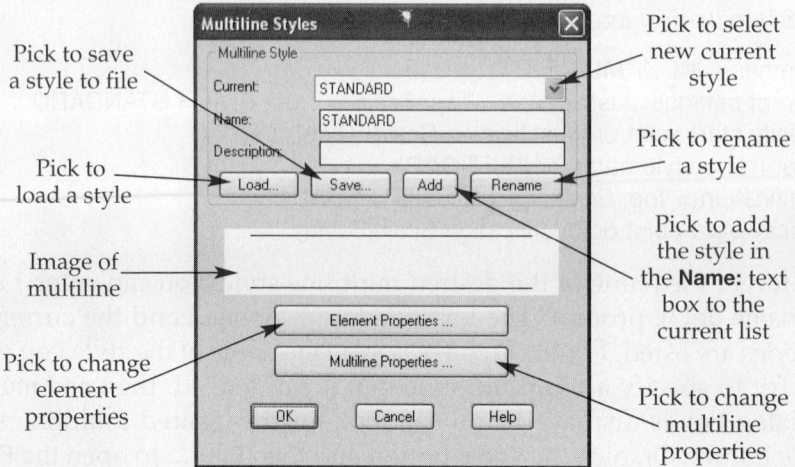

Pick to save a style to file

Pick to select new current style

Pick to load a style

Pick to rename a style

Image of multiline

Pick to add the style in the **Name:** text box to the current list

Pick to change element properties

Pick to change multiline properties

MLSTYLE

Format
➥ Multiline
    Style...

*AutoCAD and its Applications—Basics*

- **Name: text box.** This text box is used to enter the name for a new style. It is also for renaming an existing style.
- **Description: text box.** An optional description of your multiline style may be entered in this text box. This is discussed later in this chapter.
- **Load... button.** This button allows you to load a multiline style from an external multiline definition file.
- **Save... button.** This button is used to save a style to a file. To add the style to an existing definition file, specify the existing file name in the **Save Multiline Style** dialog box that appears.
- **Add button.** This button saves the style under the name specified in the **Name:** text box and adds the multiline style name to the list of defined styles.
- **Rename button.** Pick this button to rename the multiline style under the name specified in the **Name:** text box.

## Using the Element Properties Dialog Box

Picking the **Element Properties...** button in the **Multiline Styles** dialog box displays the **Element Properties** dialog box, **Figure 14-11**. This dialog box is where you define the elements of the current multiline style. It is also where you define the elements for a new multiline style.

- **Elements: area.** This area displays the current offset, color, and linetype settings for each multiline element. Picking one of the elements in this area allows it to be modified.
- **Add button.** A multiline style definition can have from one to 16 different elements. Pick this button to add a new element to the multiline style definition. The new element has the settings **Offset** = 0.0, **Color** = BYLAYER, and **Ltype** = ByLayer. See **Figure 14-12**. Once a new element is added, its properties can be changed.
- **Delete button.** Pick this button to delete the element highlighted in the **Elements:** area.
- **Offset text box.** The value in this text box is the offset from 0 justification. This value can be positive, negative, or zero. This offset value is the value on which the **MLINE Scale** option operates.
- **Color... button.** Used to change the display color of the element highlighted in the **Elements:** area. Pick the button or the color swatch to open the **Select Color** dialog box. Then, pick the color you wish to assign to the element. Pick the **OK** button to close the **Select Color** dialog box. The new color is displayed in the color swatch and its name appears in the text box to the right of the color swatch. You can also change the color by typing the name of a color in the text box.

Figure 14-11.
The **Element Properties** dialog box is used to add elements to a multiline style.

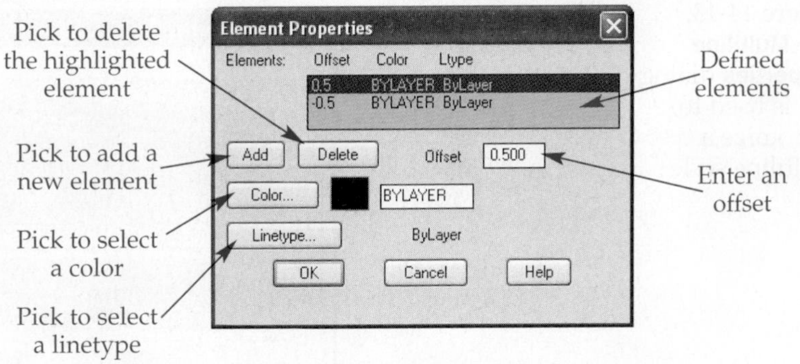

Pick to delete the highlighted element

Pick to add a new element

Pick to select a color

Pick to select a linetype

Defined elements

Enter an offset

Figure 14-12.
The new element is
added to the
multiline style.

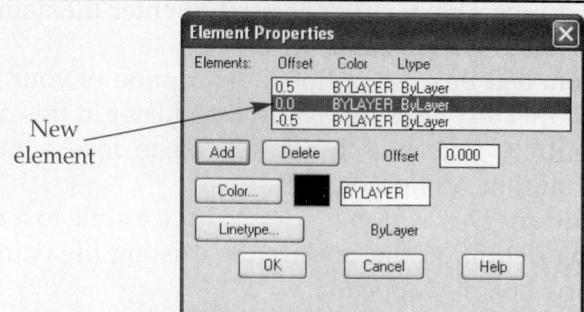

New element

- **Linetype... button.** Used to change the linetype of the element highlighted in the **Elements:** area. Picking the button displays the **Select Linetype** dialog box. Then, pick the desired linetype from the list. Linetypes must be loaded before they can be used (see Chapter 4). Pick **OK** to close the **Select Linetype** dialog box. The new linetype is assigned to the highlighted element.

Once the elements have been modified, pick **OK** to exit the **Element Properties** dialog box. The changes to the multiline style definition are displayed in the image tile in the **Multiline Styles** dialog box.

## Using the Multiline Properties Dialog Box

Picking the **Multiline Properties...** button in the **Multiline Styles** dialog box opens the **Multiline Properties** dialog box. See **Figure 14-13.** This dialog box offers additional options for customizing multiline styles. You can add caps and segment joints to multiline elements. You can also add a background color, or fill, to the multiline. When done making changes, pick **OK** to return to the **Multiline Styles** dialog box.

- **Display joints check box.** When checked, joints are displayed on the multiline. *Joints* are lines that connect the vertices of adjacent multiline elements. Joints are also referred to as *miters.* Multilines drawn with and without joints are shown in **Figure 14-14.**
- **Caps area.** The settings in this area control the placement of caps on multilines. *Caps* are lines connecting the corresponding vertices of the beginning or ending points of the multiline elements. Using the check boxes, caps can be set at the start points, endpoints, or both. Several examples of different cap options are shown in **Figure 14-15.**

  The caps can be drawn as arcs. Arcs can be set to connect the ends of the outermost elements only, pairs of inner elements, or both the outer and inner elements. There must be at least two multiline elements for outer arcs to be drawn. Arcs are drawn tangent to the elements they connect.

Figure 14-13.
The **Multiline Properties** dialog box is used to customize a multiline style.

Activate to display joints

Settings for caps

Check to enable **Fill** settings

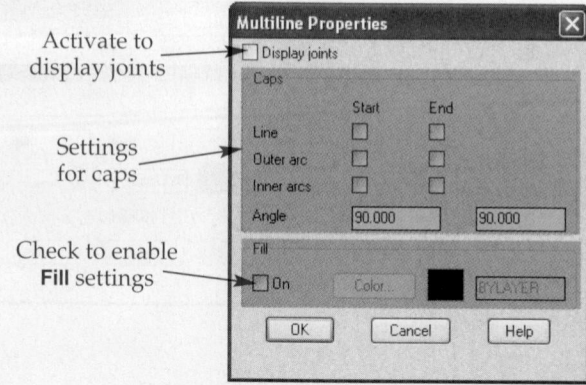

**Figure 14-14.**
Multilines can be drawn with or without displayed joints.

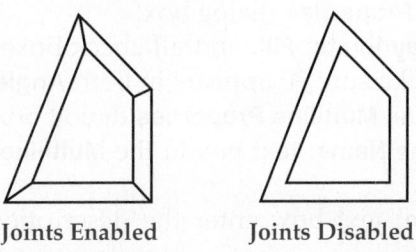

Joints Enabled     Joints Disabled

**Figure 14-15.**
Various cap options used with multilines.

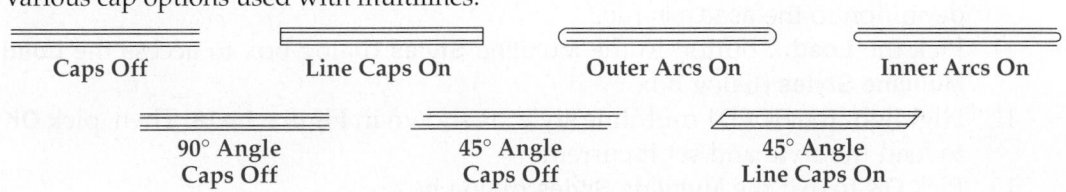

Caps Off     Line Caps On     Outer Arcs On     Inner Arcs On

90° Angle
Caps Off     45° Angle
Caps Off     45° Angle
Line Caps On

You can change the angle of the caps relative to the direction of the multiline elements. To do so, enter values in the **Angle** text boxes. There is a text box for the start points and one for the endpoints.

- **Fill area.** If the **On** check box labeled is checked, the multiline is filled with a solid pattern. The color of the pattern is shown in the color swatch. To change the color, pick the **Color...** button or the color swatch. Then, choose a new color in the **Select Color** dialog box. You can also change the color by typing the color name in the text box to the right of the color swatch. Multilines drawn with the **Fill** setting on and off are shown in **Figure 14-16.**

**Figure 14-16.**
The multiline **Fill** setting allows you to draw multilines with a solid fill pattern.

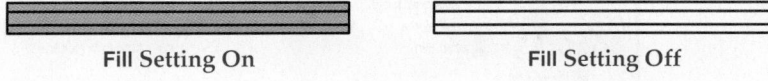

Fill Setting On     Fill Setting Off

## Creating and Using a Multiline Style

Now that you have seen how the **MLINE** and **MLSTYLE** commands work, you can create your own multiline style and draw multilines with it. Suppose you need to draw a multiline for a two-lane road to be used in a mapping project. The following procedure is used to create the style and draw the multiline.

1. Open the **Multiline Styles** dialog box. Pick the **Element Properties...** button to open the **Element Properties** dialog box.
2. Add one new element. Then, set the following elements properties.

| Offset | Color | Ltype |
|--------|--------|--------|
| 0.25 | BYLAYER | ByLayer |
| 0.0 | YELLOW | CENTER2 |
| −0.25 | BYLAYER | ByLayer |

3. Pick **OK** to close the **Element Properties** dialog box.
4. Pick the **Multiline Properties…** button in the **Multiline Styles** dialog box to display the **Multiline Properties** dialog box.
5. Be sure the **Display joints**, **Fill**, and all check boxes in the **Caps** area are not checked. Also, make sure 90 appears in both **Angle** text boxes.
6. Pick **OK** to close the **Multiline Properties** dialog box.
7. Type ROAD1 in the **Name:** text box in the **Multiline Style** area of the **Multiline Styles** dialog box.
8. In the **Description:** text box, enter the description TWO LANE ROAD WITH CENTERLINE.
9. Pick the **Save…** button to display the **Save Multiline Style** dialog box.
10. Select the file acad.mln so its name appears in the **File name:** text box, as shown in **Figure 14-17**. Then, pick the **Save** button to add the multiline style definition to the acad.mln file.
11. Pick the **Load…** button in the **Multiline Styles** dialog box to access the **Load Multiline Styles** dialog box.
12. Highlight the ROAD1 multiline style, as shown in **Figure 14-18**. Then, pick **OK** to load the style and set it current.
13. Pick **OK** to exit the **Multiline Styles** dialog box.
14. Using the **MLINE** command, draw the multiline shown in **Figure 14-19**:

> Command: **ML** *or* **MLINE.**⏎
> Current settings: Justification = Top, Scale = 1.00, Style = ROAD1
> Specify start point or [Justification/Scale/STyle]: *(enter start point)*
> Specify next point: *(enter endpoint)*
> Specify next point or [Undo]: ⏎
> Command:

**Figure 14-17.**
Use the **Save Multiline Style** dialog box to save the ROAD1 style to the acad.mln file.

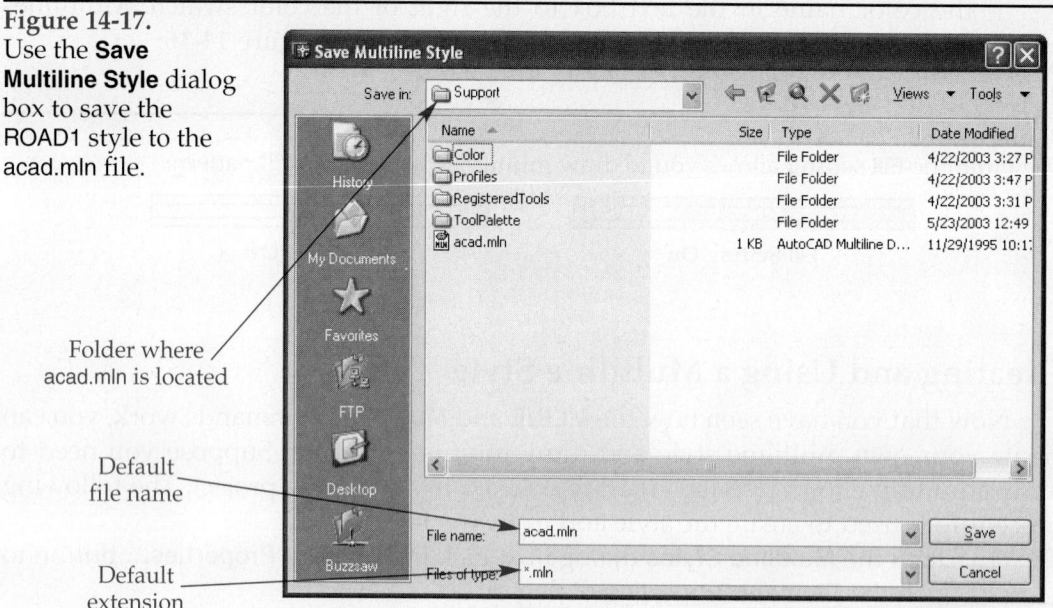

Folder where acad.mln is located

Default file name

Default extension

Figure 14-18.
The **Load Multiline Styles** dialog box.

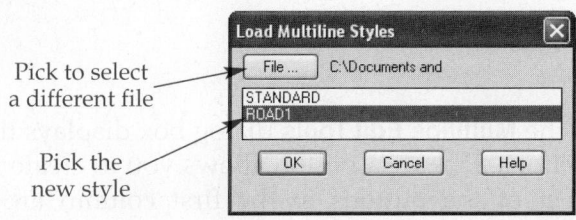

Pick to select
a different file

Pick the
new style

Figure 14-19.
A multiline drawn with the ROAD1 style.

---

## Exercise 14-7

○ Start a new drawing or use one of your templates.
○ Use the **MLSTYLE** and **MLINE** commands to create:
  ○ A multiline with joints similar to the one shown in **Figure 14-14**.
  ○ Multilines with several types of caps similar to those shown in **Figure 14-15**.
  ○ A multiline with the **Fill** setting on and a color of your choice.
  ○ A multiline defined with a style similar to that shown in **Figure 14-19**, but with a different linetype.
○ Save the drawing as EX14-7.

---

## Editing Multilines

The **MLEDIT** command permits limited editing operations for multiline objects. Access this command by picking **Multiline...** from the **Object** cascading menu in the **Modify** pull-down menu or by typing MLEDIT at the Command: prompt. This displays the **Multiline Edit Tools** dialog box, **Figure 14-20**. This dialog box contains four columns of image buttons. Each column contains three image buttons of related command options. The image on each button gives you an example of what to expect when using the editing option. The name of the **MLEDIT** option is displayed in the lower-left corner of the dialog box when you pick an image button.

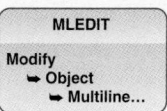

Figure 14-20.
The **Multiline Edit Tools** dialog box has 12 different options. Refer to the text for an explanation of each option.

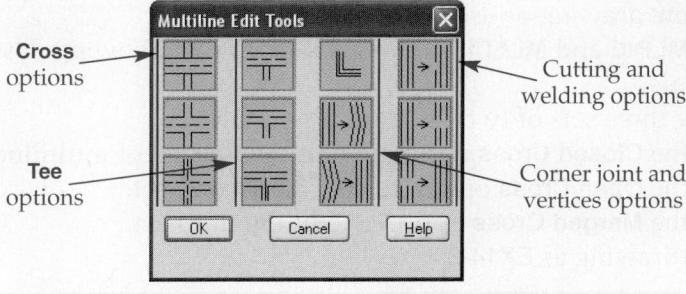

**Cross** options

**Tee** options

Cutting and welding options

Corner joint and vertices options

---

Once you pick the **OK** button, the dialog box is closed. You are prompted on the Command: line to continue with the command. The command options are described in the following sections.

## Editing Intersections

The first (left) column in the **Multiline Edit Tools** dialog box displays three different types of multiline intersections. Picking a button allows you to create the type of intersection shown. The effect of the buttons in the first column are shown in **Figure 14-21** and described below.

- **Closed Cross.** When using this option, the first multiline selected is called the background and the second multiline is called the foreground. A *closed cross* is created by trimming the background while the foreground remains unchanged. The trimming is apparent, not actual. This means the line visibility of the background multiline is changed, but it is still a single multiline. The command sequence is:

  Command: **MLEDIT↵**
  *(In the* **Multiline Edit Tools** *dialog box, pick the* **Closed Cross** *image button and then* **OK***)*
  Select first mline: *(pick the background multiline)*
  Select second mline: *(pick the foreground multiline and the intersection is created)*
  Select first mline or [Undo]: *(select the background multiline of another intersection, type* U *to undo the intersection, or press* [Enter] *to end the command)*

- **Open Cross.** Select the **Open Cross** image button to trim all of the elements of the first multiline and only the outer elements of the second multiline, as shown in **Figure 14-21**. The command sequence is the same as that used for the **Closed Cross** option.

- **Merged Cross.** The **Merged Cross** image button allows you to trim the outer elements of both multilines. The inner elements are not changed. See **Figure 14-21**.

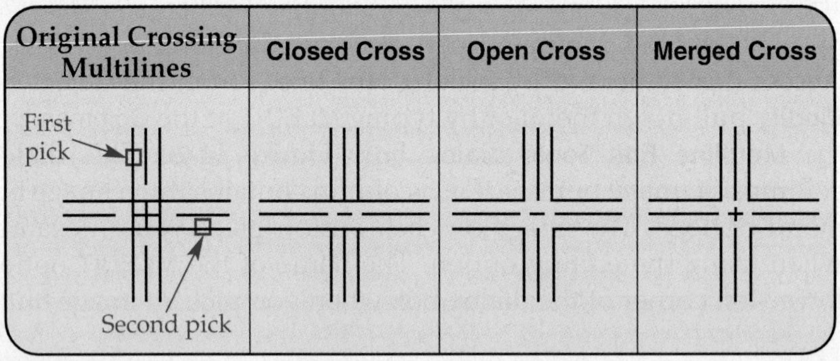

Figure 14-21.
Creating a **Closed Cross, Open Cross,** and **Merged Cross** intersection with the **MLEDIT** command.

| Original Crossing Multilines | Closed Cross | Open Cross | Merged Cross |
|---|---|---|---|

---

### Exercise 14-8

○ Start a new drawing or use one of your templates.
○ Use the **MLINE** and **MLEDIT** commands to do the following. Use **Figure 14-21** as an example.
  ○ Draw three sets of two intersecting multilines.
  ○ Use the **Closed Cross** option to edit the first set of multilines.
  ○ Use the **Open Cross** option to edit the second set.
  ○ Use the **Merged Cross** option to edit the third set.
○ Save the drawing as EX14-8.

Figure 14-22.
Using the **MLEDIT**
**Tee** options to edit
multiline tees.

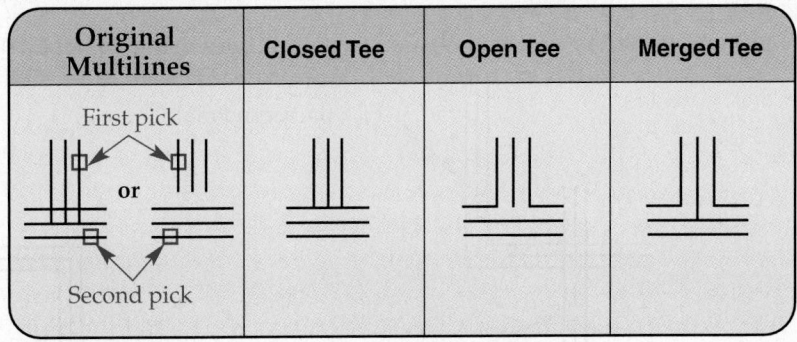

| Original Multilines | Closed Tee | Open Tee | Merged Tee |
|---|---|---|---|

## Editing Tees

The image buttons in the second column of the **Multiline Edit Tools** dialog box are used for editing multiline tees. The results of using the tee options are illustrated in **Figure 14-22.** The three options are:

- **Closed Tee.** Pick the **Closed Tee** option to have AutoCAD trim or extend the first selected multiline to its intersection with the second multiline.
- **Open Tee.** The **Open Tee** option is similar to the **Closed Tee** option. It allows you to trim the elements where a trimmed or extended multiline intersects with another multiline. The first pick specifies the multiline to trim or extend and the second pick specifies the intersecting multiline. The intersecting multiline is trimmed and left open where the two multilines join.
- **Merged Tee.** The **Merged Tee** option is similar to the **Open Tee** option. It trims the intersecting multiline after the first multiline is trimmed or extended. However, the inner elements are joined. This creates an open appearance with the outer elements while merging the inner elements.

### Exercise 14-9

○ Start a new drawing or use one of your templates.
○ Use the **MLINE** and **MLEDIT** commands to do the following. Use **Figure 14-22** as an example.
  ○ Draw three sets of two multilines that meet, or nearly meet, at a tee.
  ○ Use the **Closed Tee** option to edit the first set of multilines.
  ○ Use the **Open Tee** option to edit the second set.
  ○ Use the **Merged Tee** option to edit the third set.
○ Save the drawing as EX14-9.

## Editing Corner Joints and Multiline Vertices

The image buttons in the third column of the **Multiline Edit Tools** dialog box provide options for creating corner joints and editing multiline vertices. The three options are:

- **Corner Joint.** This option allows you to create a corner joint between two multilines. The first multiline is trimmed or extended to its intersection with the second multiline, as shown in **Figure 14-23.**

**Figure 14-23.**
A corner joint can be created between two multilines using the **MLEDIT Corner Joint** option.

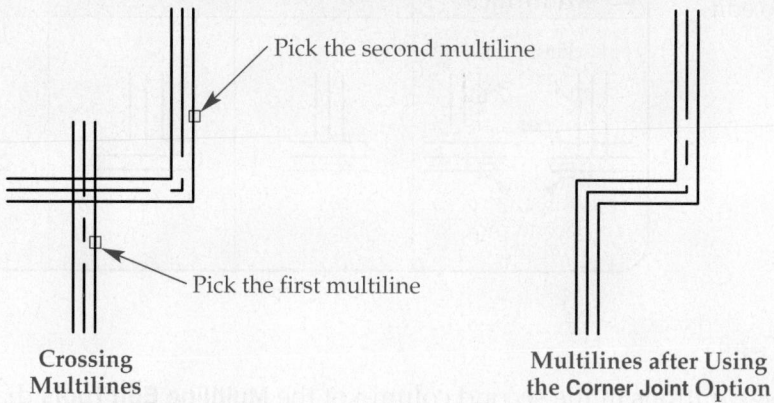

Pick the second multiline

Pick the first multiline

Crossing
Multilines

Multilines after Using
the **Corner Joint** Option

- **Add Vertex.** This option adds a vertex to an existing multiline at the location you pick, **Figure 14-24**. The command sequence differs slightly from the sequences used with the other **MLEDIT** options. After you select the **Add Vertex** option and pick **OK**, you are prompted with:

  Select mline: *(pick a location on the multiline for the new vertex)*
  Select mline or [Undo]: ↵
  Command:

- **Delete Vertex.** This option allows you to remove a vertex from an existing multiline. The vertex closest to the location you pick is deleted, **Figure 14-24**. The command sequence is the same as for the **Add Vertex** option.

**Figure 14-24.**
The **MLEDIT Add Vertex** and **Delete Vertex** options are used to edit multiline vertices.

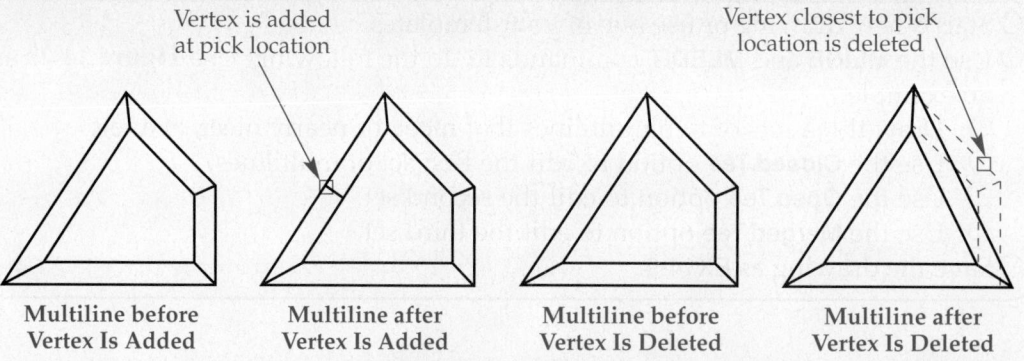

Vertex is added
at pick location

Vertex closest to pick
location is deleted

Multiline before
Vertex Is Added

Multiline after
Vertex Is Added

Multiline before
Vertex Is Deleted

Multiline after
Vertex Is Deleted

## Exercise 14-10

○ Start a new drawing or use one of your templates.
○ Use the **MLINE** and **MLEDIT** commands to do the following:
  ○ Draw multilines similar to the unedited objects shown in **Figure 14-23**. Then, use the **Corner Joint** option to create an object similar to the edited example.
  ○ Draw multilines similar to the unedited objects shown in **Figure 14-24**. Then, use the **Add Vertex** and **Delete Vertex** options to create objects similar to the edited examples.
○ Save the drawing as EX14-10.

AutoCAD and its Applications—Basics

# Cutting and Welding Multilines

The fourth column of image buttons in the **Multiline Edit Tools** dialog box is used for *cutting* a portion out of a single multiline element or the entire multiline. The spaces between multiline elements can also be connected. AutoCAD refers to the connecting operation as *welding*. The **MLEDIT** cutting and welding options are:

- **Cut Single.** This option allows you to cut a single multiline element between two specified points, as shown in **Figure 14-25**. Cutting only affects the visibility of elements and does not separate a multiline object. The multiline is still a single object. After selecting the **Cut Single** option and picking **OK**, you are prompted with:

  > Select mline: *(pick a location for the first cutting point on the multiline)*
  > Select second point: *(pick a location for the second cutting point)*
  > Select mline or [Undo]: ↵
  > Command:

- **Cut All.** This option cuts all elements of a multiline between specified points. See **Figure 14-25**. The multiline is still a single object even though it appears to be separated.
- **Weld All.** This option allows you to repair all cuts in a multiline. Select the **Weld All** image button. Then, pick **OK** and select a point on each side of the cut multiline. The multiline is restored to its precut condition.

**Figure 14-25.**
The **MLEDIT** cutting options allow you to cut single multiline elements or entire multilines between two specified points.

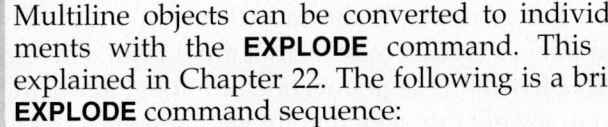

| Original Multiline | Cut Single | Cut All |
|---|---|---|
| | Pick points | |

---

**PROFESSIONAL TIP**

Multiline objects can be converted to individual line segments with the **EXPLODE** command. This command is explained in Chapter 22. The following is a brief look at the **EXPLODE** command sequence:

> Command: **X** *or* **EXPLODE.**↵
> Select objects: *(pick the object to explode)*
> x found
> Select objects: ↵
> Command:

○ Start a new drawing or use one of your templates.
○ Use the **MLINE** and **MLEDIT** commands to do the following:
  ○ Draw multilines similar to those illustrated on the left in
    **Figure 14-25**.
  ○ Use the **Cut Single** and **Cut All** options to create objects similar to the
    edited multilines shown.
  ○ Use the **Weld All** option to restore the multilines to their original conditions.
○ Save the drawing as EX14-11.

# Sketching with AutoCAD

*Sketching* is a feature of AutoCAD that allows you to draw objects as if you were sketching with pencil and paper. Sketching is done with the **SKETCH** command. While this command is not commonly used, it does have value for certain applications. It is sometimes used when it is necessary to draw a contour that is not defined by geometric shapes or lines. Other examples of applications for freehand sketching in AutoCAD include:

- Contour lines on topographic maps.
- Maps of countries and states.
- Architectural landscape symbols such as trees, bushes, and plants.
- Graphs and charts.
- Graphic designs, such as those found on a greeting card.
- Short breaks, such as those used in mechanical drafting.

Before using the **SKETCH** command, it is best to turn the **Snap** and **Ortho** modes off because they limit the cursor's movement. Normally, you want total control over the cursor when sketching. Then use the **SKETCH** command:

    Command: SKETCH↵
    Record increment <0.1000>:

The *record increment* is the length of each sketch line element generated as you move the cursor. For example, if the record increment is set to 0.1000 (the default value), sketched images consist of lines that are 0.1 units in length. An increment setting of 1 creates sketched line segments one unit long. Reducing the increment setting increases the accuracy of your sketched image. However, record increments less than 0.1 greatly increase the drawing file size. To view the chosen record increment, turn **ORTHO** on and draw a set of stair steps. The smallest horizontal and vertical elements represent the length of the record increment. If **SNAP** is turned on, the record increment then becomes equal to the snap spacing. A comparison of record increments is shown in **Figure 14-26**. After the record increment is entered, the command continues:

    Pen eXit Quit Record Erase Connect .

This prompt displays the **SKETCH** subcommands. Once you see this prompt, a subcommand can be accessed by entering its corresponding capitalized letter. Pressing the left mouse button activates the **Pen** subcommand.

The buttons on a multibutton puck can also be used to activate the **SKETCH** subcommands. The normal puck buttons for the **Snap** (4) and **Ortho** (5) modes remain disabled as long as the **SKETCH** command is active. The following table lists the keyboard entries and puck buttons used to access each subcommand.

Figure 14-26.
Record increments used with the **SKETCH** command.

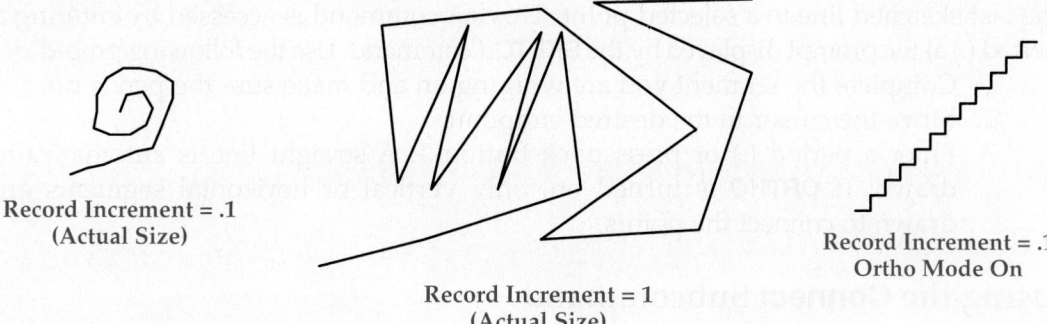

Record Increment = .1
(Actual Size)

Record Increment = 1
(Actual Size)

Record Increment = .1
Ortho Mode On

| Subcommand | Keyboard Entry | Puck Button | Subcommand Function |
|------------|----------------|-------------|---------------------|
| Pen | P | 0 | Toggles pen up and down. |
| Period | . | 1 | Draws a line from the end-point of a sketched line. |
| Record | R | 2 | Records sketched lines as permanent. |
| eXit | X, spacebar, or [Enter] | 3 | Records sketched lines and exits the **SKETCH** command. |
| Quit | Q or [Esc] | 4 | Removes all unrecorded objects. |
| Erase | E | 5 | Erases all unrecorded objects. |
| Connect | C | 6 | Allows connection to the endpoint of a sketched line when pen is up. |

Sketch segments are by default line objects. You can use the **SKPOLY** system variable to create sketched lines that are defined as polyline objects. A **SKPOLY** system variable setting of 0 is for line objects and 1 for polyline objects.

## Drawing Sketched Lines

After entering the **SKETCH** command, actual sketching is done with the **Pen** subcommand. Using this subcommand is similar to sketching with paper and pencil. When the pencil is "down," you are ready to draw. When the pencil is "up," you are thinking about what to draw next or moving to the next location. After issuing the **SKETCH** command, enter P to toggle the pen down and begin sketching. You can also press your left mouse button to move the pen up and down. Move the cursor around to create a line. Enter P again or press your left mouse button to toggle the pen up and stop sketching.

**PROFESSIONAL TIP**

If you do not consider yourself an artist, trace an existing design. Tape the design to a digitizer and move the cursor along the outline of the shape with the pen down. Move the pen up when you want to specify a new sketching location.

## Using the Period (.) Subcommand

The **Period** subcommand allows you to draw a straight line from the endpoint of the last sketched line to a selected point. This subcommand is accessed by entering a period (.) at the prompt displayed by the **SKETCH** command. Use the following procedure.

1. Complete the segment you are working on and make sure the pen is up.
2. Move the cursor to the desired endpoint.
3. Enter a period (.) or press puck button 1. A straight line is automatically drawn. If **ORTHO** is turned on, only vertical or horizontal segments are drawn to connect the points.

## Using the **Connect** Subcommand

It is common to toggle the pen up to pause from sketching or to make a menu selection. When the pen is up, you can return to the last sketched point and resume sketching by using the **Connect** subcommand. To do so, enter C or press puck button 6. AutoCAD responds with this message:

Connect: Move to endpoint of line.

Move the cursor to the end of the previously sketched line. As soon as the crosshairs touch the previously drawn line, the pen automatically moves down and you can resume sketching.

## Using the **Erase** Subcommand

You can erase line segments while sketching. If you make a mistake, enter E for the **Erase** subcommand or press puck button 5. The pen may be up or down. If the pen is down, it is automatically raised. AutoCAD responds with the message:

Erase: Select end of delete. <Pen up>

Move the cursor to erase any portion of the sketch. Every part of the sketch from the last point to the portion you select will be erased. When finished, enter P or press puck button 0. If you decide not to erase anything, enter E or press puck button 5. AutoCAD returns to the **SKETCH** command prompt after issuing the message Erase aborted.

## Recording Sketched Lines

Sketched lines are displayed in color when you first begin to sketch. These lines are referred to as *temporary lines*. Temporary lines become *permanent lines* and are displayed in their final color after they are *recorded.* You can record lines and remain in the **SKETCH** command by entering R or pressing puck button 2. You can also record lines and exit the **SKETCH** command by entering X or pressing the spacebar, [Enter], or puck button 3. AutoCAD responds with a message indicating the number of lines recorded. For example, if you created 32 lines, the message reads 32 lines recorded.

## Quitting the **SKETCH** Command

To quit the **SKETCH** command without recording any lines, enter Q or press the [Esc] key or puck button 4. This removes all temporary lines and returns you to the Command: prompt.

## Managing Storage Space with the **SKETCH** Command

Sketching rapidly consumes computer storage space. For example, the sketch of a rose shown in **Figure 14-27** may be less than 50KB as a JPEG file. However, created using the **SKETCH** command and saved as an AutoCAD drawing file, this drawing is

**Figure 14-27.**
A rose drawn using the **SKETCH** command. (Courtesy of Susan Waterman)

nearly 1.5MB. Therefore, the **SKETCH** command should be used only when necessary. The record increment should be set as large as possible, but low enough that the results are pleasing.

## Exercise 14-12

○ Start a new drawing or use one of your templates.
○ Use the **SKETCH** command to sketch a bush, tree, or houseplant in plan (top) view.
○ Save the drawing as EX14-12.

## Chapter Test

*Answer the following questions on a separate sheet of paper.*

1. Give the command and entries required to draw a polyline from Point A to Point B with a beginning width of .500 and an ending width of 0.
   A. Command: _____
   B. Specify start point: _____
      Current line-width is 0.0000
   C. Specify next point or [Arc/Halfwidth/Length/Undo/Width]: _____
   D. Specify starting width <0.0000>: _____
   E. Specify ending width <.500>: _____
   F. Specify next point or [Arc/Halfwidth/Length/Undo/Width]: _____
   G. Specify next point or [Arc/Close/Halfwidth/Length/Undo/Width]: _____

2. Give the command and entries needed to draw a multiline with zero justification and the saved style ROAD1.
   A. Command: _____
   B. Current settings: Justification = Top, Scale = 1.00, Style = STANDARD
   C. Specify start point or [Justification/Scale/STyle]: _____
   D. Enter mline style name or [?]: _____
      Current settings: Justification = Top, Scale = 1.00, Style = ROAD1
   E. Specify start point or [Justification/Scale/STyle]: _____
   F. Enter justification type [Top/Zero/Bottom] <top>: _____
      Current settings: Justification = Zero, Scale = 1.00, Style = ROAD1
   G. Specify start point or [Justification/Scale/STyle]: _____
   H. Specify next point: _____
   I. Specify next point or [Undo]: _____
3. How do you draw a filled arrow using the **PLINE** command?
4. Name two commands that can be used to draw wide lines.
5. Which **PLINE** command option allows you to specify the width from the center to one side?
6. What is an advantage of leaving the **FILL** mode turned off?
7. What is the difference between picking **Undo** from the **Edit** pull-down menu and entering the **UNDO** command?
8. Name the command that is used to bring back an object that was previously removed using **UNDO**.
9. Name the **MLINE** command option that establishes how the resulting lines are offset based on the definition points provided.
10. Name the option that controls the multiplier value for the offset distances specified with the **MLINE** command.
11. How do you access the **Multiline Styles** dialog box?
12. Describe the function of the **Add** button in the **Element Properties** dialog box.
13. Describe the function of the **Linetype...** button in the **Element Properties** dialog box.
14. Define *caps*.
15. List the settings in the **Multiline Properties** dialog box that control the options for placing end caps on multilines.
16. Define *joints*.
17. What is displayed when you enter the **MLEDIT** command?
18. How do you access one of the **MLEDIT** options?
19. List the three options that are used for editing multiline intersections with the **MLEDIT** command.
20. Name the **MLEDIT** option in which the intersecting multiline is trimmed and left open after the first multiline is trimmed or extended to its intersection with the intersecting multiline.
21. Name the **MLEDIT** option that allows you to remove a vertex from an existing multiline.
22. Name the **MLEDIT** option that lets you remove a portion from an individual multiline element.
23. Name the **MLEDIT** option that removes all of the elements of a multiline between two specified points.
24. Name the **MLEDIT** option that repairs all cuts in a multiline between two selected points.
25. Explain why the **Snap** and **Ortho** modes should be turned off for most sketching applications.

## Drawing Problems

1. Use the **PLINE** command to draw the following object with a .032 line width. Do not draw dimensions. Save the drawing as P14-1.

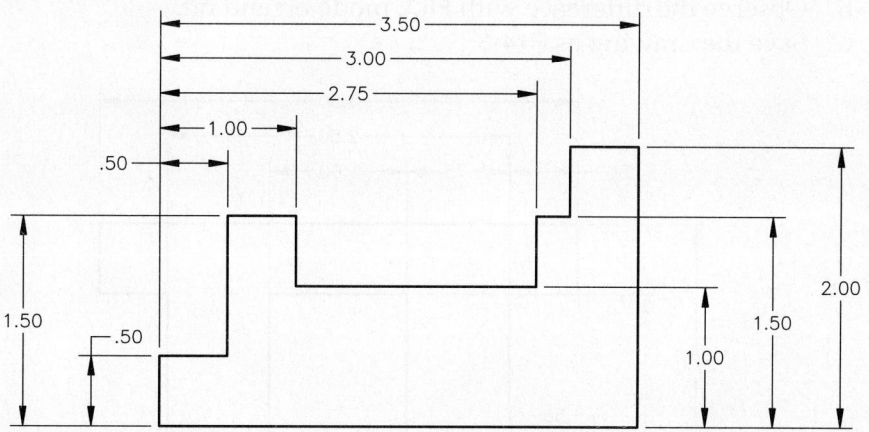

2. Use the **PLINE** command to draw the following object with a .032 line width. Do not draw dimensions. Save the drawing as P14-2.

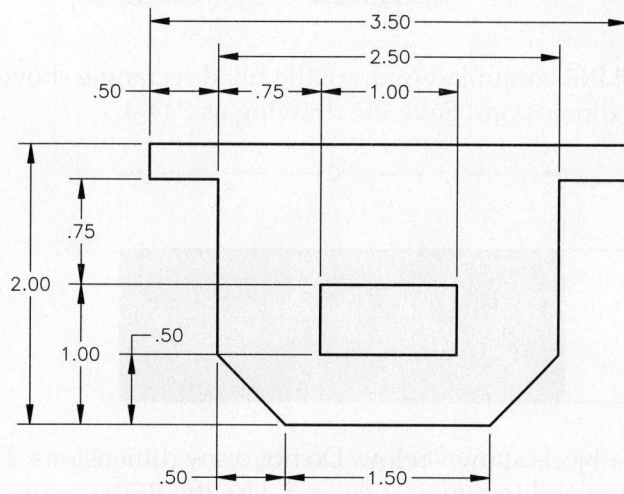

3. Use the **TRACE** command to draw the following object with a .032 line width. Do not draw dimensions.
   A. Turn off the **FILL** mode and use the **REGEN** command. Then, turn on **FILL** and reissue the **REGEN** command.
   B. Observe the difference with **FILL** mode on and off.
   C. Save the drawing as P14-3.

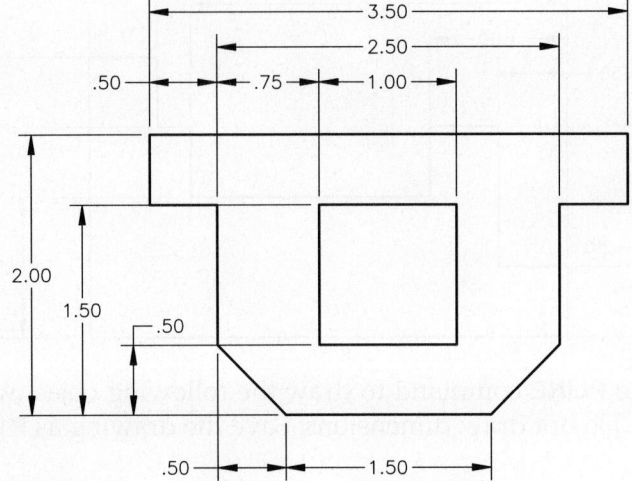

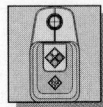

4. Use the **PLINE** command to draw the filled rectangle shown below. Do not draw dimensions. Save the drawing as P14-4.

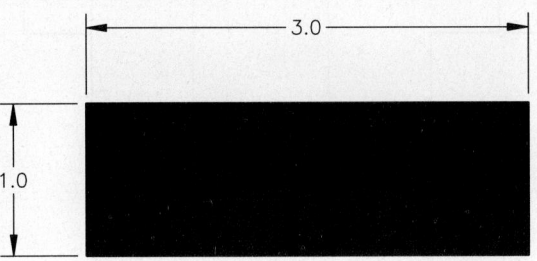

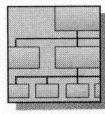

5. Draw the objects shown below. Do not draw dimensions. Then, use the **UNDO** command to remove Object B. Use the **REDO** command to bring Object B back. Save the drawing as P14-5.

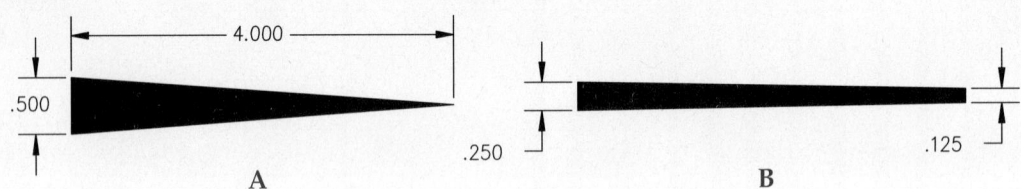

6. Draw the object shown below. Do not draw dimensions. Set decimal units, .25 grid spacing, and .0625 snap spacing. Set the limits to 11,8.5. Save the drawing as P14-6.

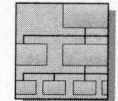

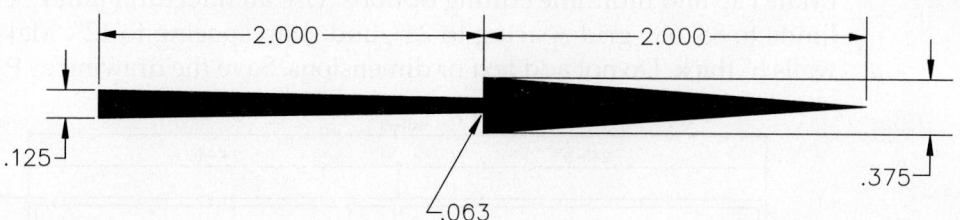

7. Open P4-7 and add the arrowheads. Draw one arrowhead using the **PLINE** command and then use the necessary editing commands to place the rest. Refer to the original problem. Save the drawing as P14-7.

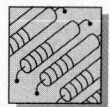

8. Draw the objects shown using the **MLINE** command. Use the justification options indicated with each illustration. Set the limits to 11,8.5, grid spacing to .50, and snap spacing to .25. Set the offset for the multiline elements to .125. Do not add text or dimensions. Save the drawing as P14-8.

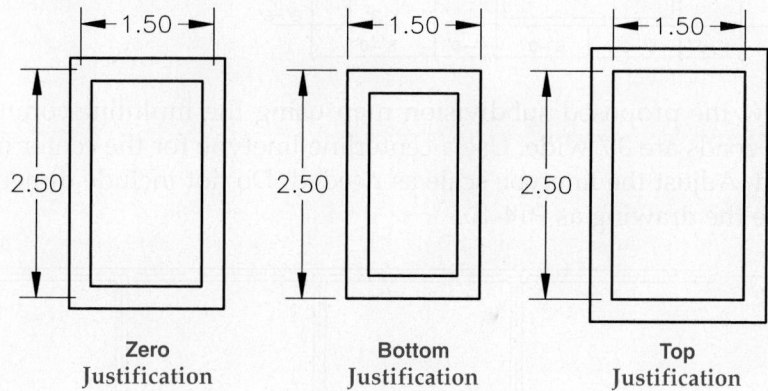

Zero Justification          Bottom Justification          Top Justification

9. Draw the partial floor plan shown using the multiline commands. Carefully observe how the dimensions correlate with the multiline elements to determine your justification settings. Also, use the appropriate cap and multiline editing options. Use architectural units. Set the limits to 88',68', grid spacing to 24", and snap spacing to 12". Make all walls 6" thick. Do not add text or dimensions. Save the drawing as P14-9.

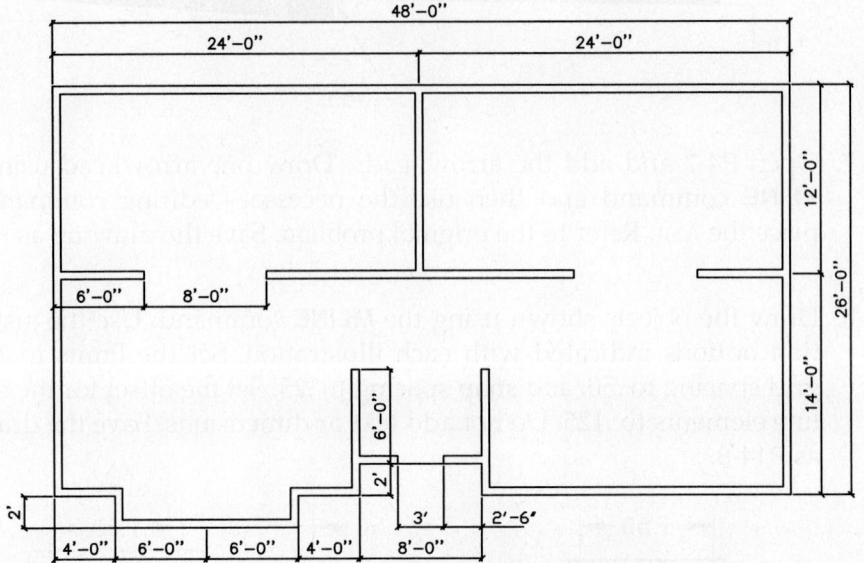

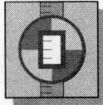

10. Draw the proposed subdivision map using the multiline commands. The roads are 30' wide. Use a centerline linetype for the center of each road. Adjust the linetype scale as needed. Do not include dimensions. Save the drawing as P14-10.

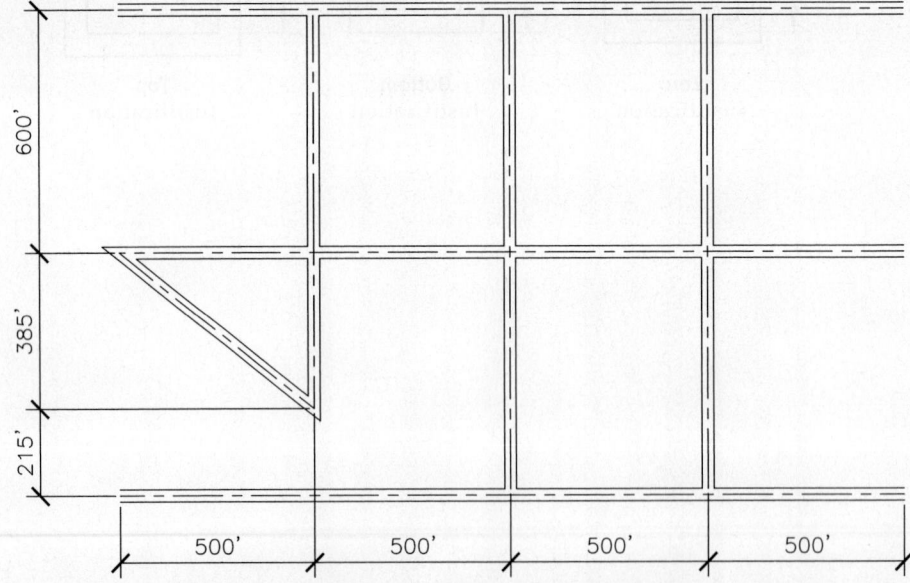

AutoCAD and its Applications—Basics

11. Draw the partial floor plan shown below using multilines for the walls.
    Do not dimension the floor plan. Save the drawing as P14-11.

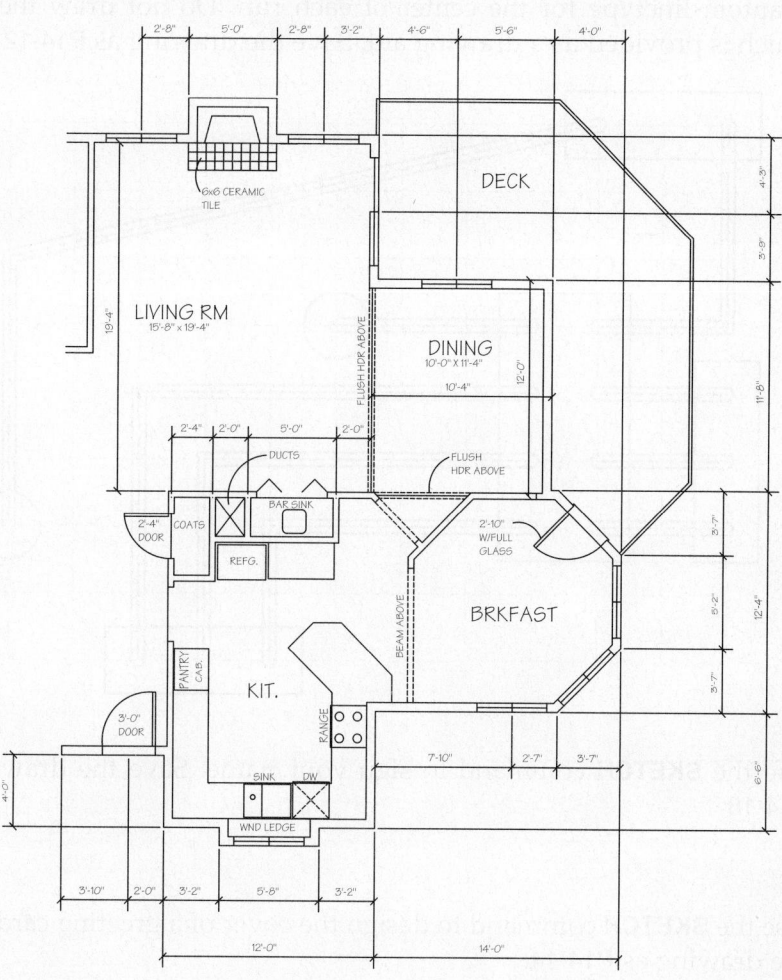

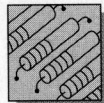

12. Draw the proposed electrical circuit using the multiline commands. Establish a line offset that is proportional to the given layout. Use a phantom linetype for the center of each run. Do not draw the grid, which is provided as a drawing aid. Save the drawing as P14-12.

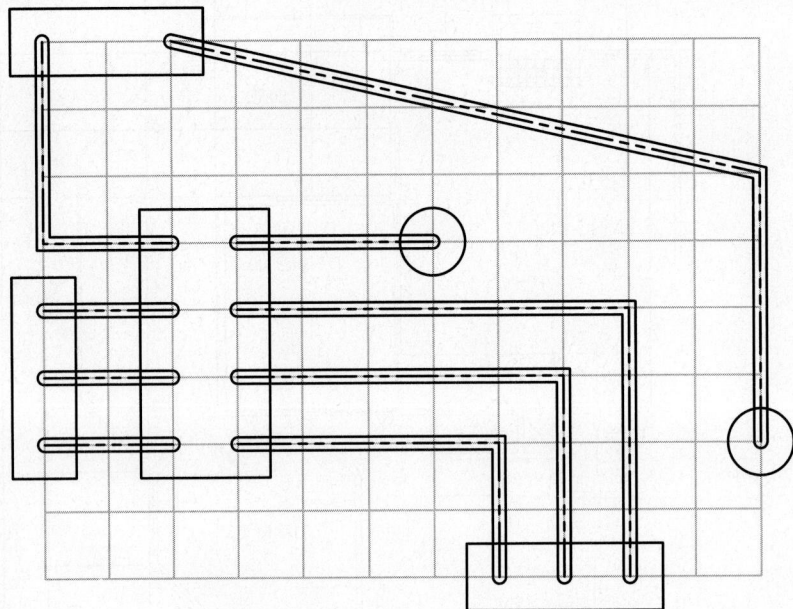

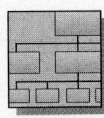

13. Use the **SKETCH** command to sign your name. Save the drawing as P14-13.

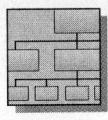

14. Use the **SKETCH** command to design the cover of a greeting card. Save the drawing as P14-14.

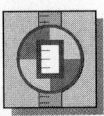

15. Locate a map of your state and make a photocopy. Tape the copy to your digitizer. Using the **SKETCH** command:
    A. Trace the outline of the map.
    B. Include all major rivers and lakes.
    C. Save the drawing as P14-15.

## CHAPTER 15

# Drawing and Editing Polylines and Splines

## Learning Objectives

After completing this chapter, you will be able to do the following:
- Use the **PLINE** command to draw straight and curved polylines.
- Edit existing polylines with the **PEDIT** command.
- Describe the function of each **PEDIT** command option.
- Use the **EXPLODE** command to change polylines into individual line and arc segments.
- Draw and edit spline curves.
- Create a polyline boundary.

The **PLINE** command was introduced in Chapter 14 as a way to draw thick and tapered lines. The discussion focused on line-related options, such as **Width**, **Halfwidth**, and **Length**. The editing functions were limited to the **ERASE** and **UNDO** commands. As you will find in this chapter, the **PLINE** command can also be used to draw a variety of special shapes, limited only by your imagination. This chapter explains how to use the **PLINE** command to create polyline arcs and introduces advanced editing commands for polylines. This chapter also discusses how to convert polylines into smooth curves and how to create and edit true spline curves.

The **PLINE** command can be accessed by picking the **Polyline** button in the **Draw** toolbar or selecting **Polyline** from the **Draw** pull-down menu. You can also type PL or PLINE at the Command: prompt.

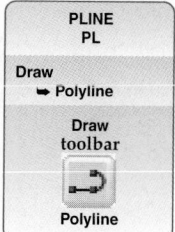

PLINE
PL

Draw
➡ Polyline

Draw
toolbar

Polyline

## Drawing Polyline Arcs

The **Arc** option of the **PLINE** command is similar to the **ARC** command except that the **PLINE Width** and **Halfwidth** options can be used to set an arc width. The arc width can range from 0 up to the radius of the arc. A polyline arc can also be drawn with different starting and ending widths using the **Width** option. The arc shown in **Figure 15-1** was drawn with the following command sequence.

    Command: **PL** or **PLINE**↵
    Specify start point: (pick the first point)
    Current line-width is 0.0000
    Specify next point or [Arc/Halfwidth/Length/Undo/Width]: **W**↵

Figure 15-1.
A polyline arc with
different starting
and ending widths.

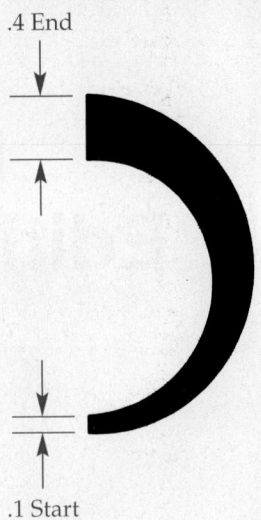

.4 End

.1 Start

Specify starting width <*current*>: **.1**↵
Specify ending width <*current*>: **.4**↵
Specify next point or [Arc/Halfwidth/Length/Undo/Width]: **A**↵
Specify endpoint of arc or
[Angle/CEnter/Direction/Halfwidth/Line/Radius/ Second pt/Undo/Width]: (*pick the arc endpoint*)
Specify endpoint of arc or
[Angle/CEnter/CLose/Direction/Halfwidth/Line/Radius/ Second pt/Undo/Width]: ↵
Command:

## Drawing a Continuous Polyline Arc

A polyline arc continued from a previous line or polyline is tangent to the last object drawn. The arc's center is determined automatically, but you can pick a new center. If a straight polyline is continued from a polyline arc, the arc's tangent direction remains the same as that of the previous line, arc, or polyline. This may not be what you want. In this case, it may be necessary to specify a setting with one of the **PLINE Arc** options. These options are **Angle**, **CEnter**, **CLose**, **Direction**, **Radius**, and **Second pt** (second point). The options are very similar to the **ARC** command options and are explained in the following sections.

## Specifying the Included Angle

The following is an example of using the **Angle** option inside the **PLINE Arc** command sequence to specify an angle for a polyline arc. The angle value is based on the number of degrees in a circle. Therefore, a value of 180 draws a half circle, 270 draws 3/4 of a circle, and so on. The values 0 and 360 cannot be entered. A negative value draws the arc in a clockwise direction. The object drawn in the following sequence is illustrated in **Figure 15-2**.

Command: **PL** *or* **PLINE**↵
Specify start point: (*pick the first point*)
Current line-width is 0.4000
Specify next point or [Arc/Halfwidth/Length/Undo/Width]: **A**↵
Specify endpoint of arc or
[Angle/CEnter/Direction/Halfwidth/Line/Radius/ Second pt/Undo/Width]: **A**↵
Specify included angle: (*specify the included angle,* 60 *in this case, and press* [Enter])
Specify endpoint of arc or [CEnter/Radius]: (*pick the arc endpoint*)
Specify endpoint of arc or
[Angle/CEnter/CLose/Direction/Halfwidth/Line/Radius/ Second pt/Undo/Width]: ↵
Command:

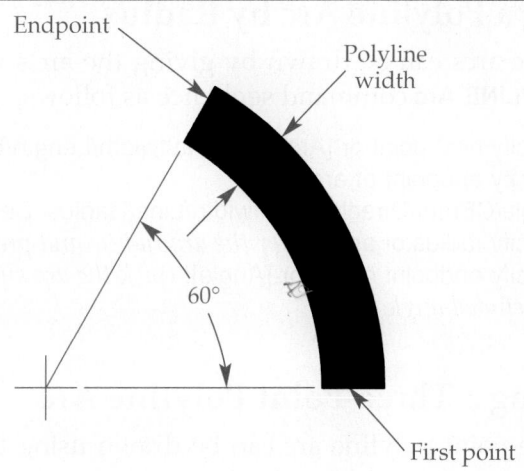

**Figure 15-2.**
Drawing a polyline arc with a specified angle.

Endpoint

Polyline width

60°

First point

## Using the CEnter Option

When a polyline arc is drawn as a continuation of a polyline segment, the center point of the arc is automatically calculated. You may want to pick a new center point if the polyline arc does not continue from another object or if the center point calculated is not suitable. The **CEnter** option allows you to specify a new center point for the arc. It is used as follows:

Command: **PL** *or* **PLINE**↵
Specify start point: *(pick the first point)*
Current line-width is 0.4000
Specify next point or [Arc/Halfwidth/Length/Undo/Width]: *(pick the endpoint of the first segment)*
Specify next point or [Arc/Close/Halfwidth/Length/Undo/Width]: **A**↵
Specify endpoint of arc or
[Angle/CEnter/CLose/Direction/Halfwidth/Line/Radius/ Second pt/Undo/Width]: **CE**↵
   *(notice that two letters, CE, are required for this option)*
Specify center point of arc: *(pick the desired arc center point)*
Specify endpoint of arc or [Angle/Length]: *(select the arc endpoint, or type A or L, and press [Enter])*

If the endpoint is picked, the polyline arc is drawn. If A is entered, the next prompt is:

Specify included angle: *(enter an included angle and press [Enter])*

If L is entered at the Specify endpoint of arc or [Angle/Length]: prompt, the next prompt is:

Specify length of chord: *(enter a chord length and press [Enter])*

## Using the Direction Option

The **Direction** option alters the bearing of the arc. The default option places a polyline arc tangent to the last polyline, arc, or line. This option is used to change this and can also be entered when you are drawing an unconnected polyline arc. The **Direction** option functions much like the **Direction** option of the **ARC** command. The following is an example of using the **Direction** option inside the **PLINE Arc** command sequence.

Specify next point or [Arc/Close/Halfwidth/Length/Undo/Width]: **A**↵
Specify endpoint of arc or
[Angle/CEnter/CLose/Direction/Halfwidth/Line/Radius/ Second pt/Undo/Width]: **D**↵
Specify the tangent direction for the start point of arc: *(enter a direction in positive or negative degrees, or pick a point on either side of the start point)*
Specify endpoint of the arc: *(select an endpoint)*

## Drawing a Polyline Arc by Radius

Polyline arcs can be drawn by giving the arc's radius. Enter the **Radius** option inside the **PLINE Arc** command sequence as follows:

Specify next point or [Arc/Close/Halfwidth/Length/Undo/Width]: **A⏎**
Specify endpoint of arc or
[Angle/CEnter/Direction/Halfwidth/Line/Radius/ Second pt/Undo/Width]: **R⏎**
Specify radius of arc: *(enter the arc radius and press [Enter])*
Specify endpoint of arc or [Angle]: *(pick the arc endpoint or enter* A *to specify an
    included angle)*

## Specifying a Three-Point Polyline Arc

A three-point polyline arc can be drawn using the **Second pt** option. The command sequence after entering the **Arc** option is:

Specify endpoint of arc or
[Angle/CEnter/Direction/Halfwidth/Line/Radius/ Second pt/Undo/Width]: **S⏎**
Specify second point on arc: *(pick the second point on the arc)*
Specify end point of arc: *(pick the endpoint to complete the arc)*

## Using the CLose Option

The **CLose** option saves drafting time by automatically adding the last segment to close a polygonal shape. Using this option inside the **PLINE Arc** command sequence closes the shape with a polyline arc segment, rather than a straight polyline. See **Figure 15-3**. Notice that CL is entered at the prompt line to distinguish this option from the **CEnter** option:

Specify endpoint of arc or
[Angle/CEnter/CLose/Direction/Halfwidth/Line/Radius/ Second pt/Undo/Width]: **CL⏎**

**Figure 15-3.**
Using the **CLose** option inside the **PLINE Arc** command sequence to close a polygonal shape.

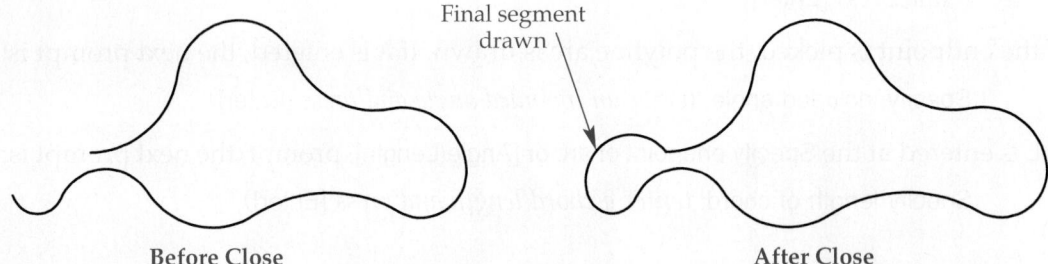

Final segment
drawn

**Before Close**                    **After Close**

○ Start a new drawing or use one of your templates.
○ Draw several continuous polyline arcs. Draw at least four segments and use the **CLose** option to close the polyline.
○ Draw a polyline arc by picking endpoints and specifying a 90° included angle. Then continue from the first arc with another 90° polyline arc.
○ Draw a polyline arc using two endpoints and a center point.
○ Specify two endpoints, a center point, and an included angle to draw a polyline arc.
○ Specify endpoints and a positive direction to draw a polyline arc. Then, see how using a negative direction affects the arc.
○ Specify the endpoints for a 1.5 unit radius polyline arc.
○ Draw a polyline arc by picking three points.
○ Save the drawing as EX15-1.

## Presetting Polyline Widths

You can preset a constant width for polylines with the **PLINEWID** system variable. This can save you valuable drafting time if you are drawing many wide lines of the same thickness. To specify a setting, type PLINEWID at the Command: prompt. Then, enter a new value. When you are done drawing wide polylines, be sure to set the value of **PLINEWID** to 0.

Objects drawn with the **POLYGON** command are constructed with polylines. However, the width of these objects is not affected by the **PLINEWID** system variable.

## Revising Polylines Using the PEDIT Command

Polylines are drawn as multiple segments. A single polyline may be drawn as a straight segment joined to an arc segment and completed with another straight segment. Even though you have drawn separate segments, AutoCAD puts them all together. The result is one polyline treated as a single object. When editing a polyline, you must edit it as one object or divide it into its individual segments. These changes are made with the **PEDIT** and **EXPLODE** commands. The **EXPLODE** command is discussed later in this chapter.

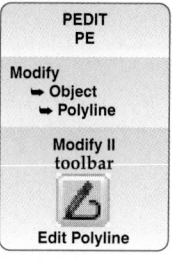

PEDIT
PE

Modify
➥ Object
➥ Polyline

Modify II
toolbar

Edit Polyline

The **PEDIT** command is accessed by picking the **Edit Polyline** button on the **Modify II** toolbar, typing PE or PEDIT at the Command: prompt, or selecting **Polyline** from the **Object** cascading menu in the **Modify** pull-down menu. You can also select a polyline, right-click in the drawing area, and choose **Polyline Edit** from the shortcut menu. The **PEDIT** command is initiated as follows:

Command: **PE** or **PEDIT**↵
Select polyline or [Multiple]: *(select the polyline)*

When selecting a wide polyline, you must pick on the edge of a polyline segment rather than in the center. If you want to edit more than one polyline, type M to select the **Multiple** option. If the polyline you want to change was the last object drawn, simply type L for **Last** at the Select polyline: prompt. If the object you select is a line or arc object, the following message is displayed.

Object selected is not a polyline
Do you want to turn it into one? <Y>

---

Entering Y or pressing [Enter] turns the selected object into a polyline. Type N and press [Enter] to leave the object as is. The command then continues. The command options are explained later in this chapter.

You can have AutoCAD automatically turn lines and arcs into polylines without displaying the previous prompt. The value of the **PEDITACCEPT** system variable controls this feature. When set to 0, you are prompted when a line or arc is selected. When the system variable is set to 1, AutoCAD automatically turns selected lines and arcs into polylines. The command then continues normally.

Circles drawn with the **CIRCLE** command cannot be changed to polylines for editing purposes. Polyline circles can be created by using the **PLINE Arc** option and drawing two 180° arcs, or by using the **DONUT** command.

---

**PROFESSIONAL TIP**  A group of connected lines and arcs can be turned into a continuous polyline by using the **PEDIT Join** option. This option is discussed later in this chapter.

---

## Revising a Polyline As One Unit

A polyline can be edited as a single object or it can be divided into individual segments. The segments can then be revised individually. This section discusses the options for changing the entire polyline. The command sequence is:

Command: **PE** *or* **PEDIT**↵
Select polyline or [Multiple]: *(pick a polyline)*
Enter an option [Close/Join/Width/Edit vertex/Fit/Spline/Decurve/Ltype gen/Undo]:

There is no default option for the **PEDIT** command; you must select one of the options. Pressing [Enter] returns you to the Command: prompt.

### Opening and Closing a Polyline

You may decide that you need to close an open polyline or open a closed polyline. These functions are performed with the **Open** and **Close** options of the **PEDIT** command. Open and closed polylines are shown in **Figure 15-4**.

If you select a closed polyline, AutoCAD displays the **Open** option along with the other **PEDIT** command options. Enter this option to open the polyline by removing the last segment.

The **Open** option is only available if the polygon was closed using the **Close** option of the **PLINE** command. It is not displayed if the polyline was closed by manually drawing the final segment. Instead, the **Close** option is displayed.

---

Figure 15-4.
Open and closed polylines.

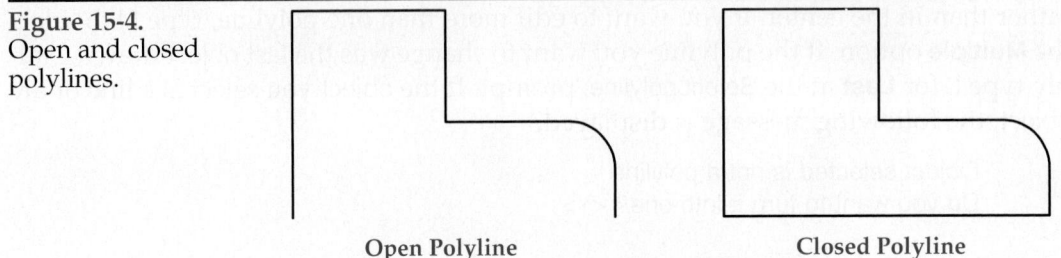

Open Polyline | Closed Polyline

---

AutoCAD and its Applications—Basics

If you select an open polyline, the **Close** option is displayed instead of the **Open** option. Enter this option to close the polyline.

## Joining Polylines to Other Polylines, Lines, and Arcs

Polylines, lines, and arcs that are connected can be joined to create a single polyline. This is done with the **Join** option of the **PEDIT** command. This option works only if the polyline and other existing objects meet *exactly*. They cannot cross, nor can there be any spaces or breaks between the objects. See **Figure 15-5**. The command sequence to join objects to a polyline is:

Command: **PE** *or* **PEDIT**↵
Select polyline or [Multiple]: *(select the original polyline)*
Enter an option [Close/Join/Width/Edit vertex/Fit/Spline/Decurve/Ltype gen/Undo]: **J**↵
Select objects: *(select all of the objects to be joined)*
Select objects: ↵
*n* segments added to polyline
Enter an option [Close/Join/Width/Edit vertex/Fit/Spline/Decurve/Ltype gen/Undo]: ↵
Command:

Select each object to be joined or group the objects with one of the selection set options. The original polyline can be included in the selection set, but it does not need to be. See **Figure 15-6**. If you select lines and arcs to join, AutoCAD automatically converts these objects to polylines, regardless of the **PEDITACCEPT** setting.

**Figure 15-5.**
Features that can and cannot be joined using the **PEDIT Join** option.

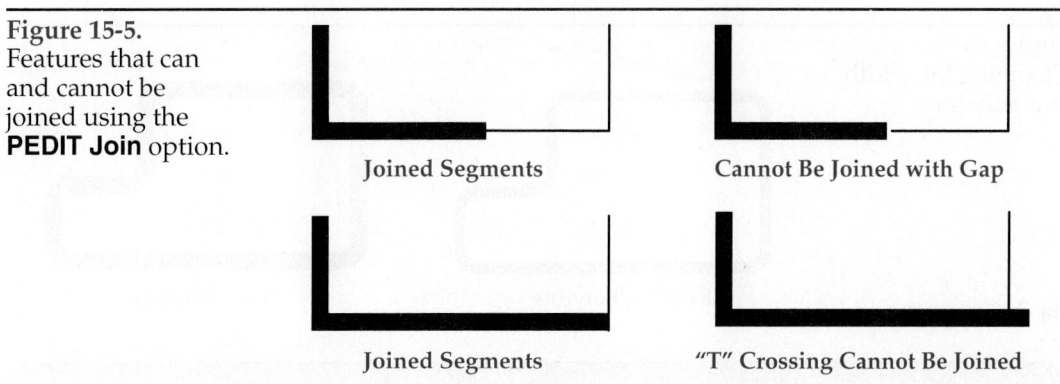

Joined Segments

Cannot Be Joined with Gap

Joined Segments

"T" Crossing Cannot Be Joined

**Figure 15-6.**
Joining a polyline to other connected lines and arcs.

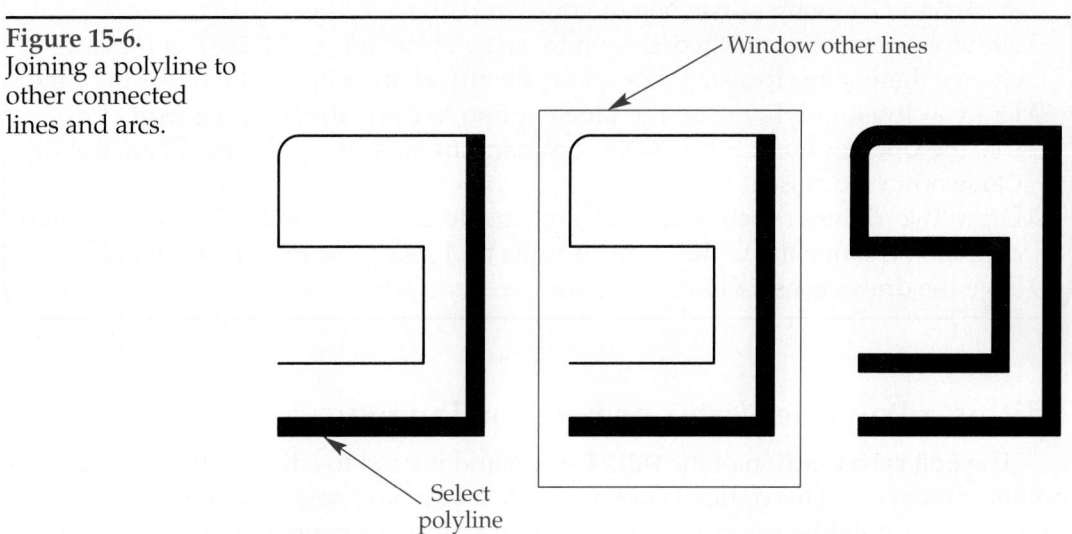

Window other lines

Select polyline

## Changing the Width of a Polyline

The **Width** option of the **PEDIT** command allows you to change a polyline width to a new width. The width of the original polyline can be constant or it can vary. However, *all* segments will be changed to the constant width you specify. To change a polyline from a .06 width to a .1 width, follow these steps:

Command: **PE** *or* **PEDIT**↵
Select polyline or [Multiple]: *(pick the polyline)*
Enter an option [Close/Join/Width/Edit vertex/Fit/Spline/Decurve/Ltype gen/Undo]: **W**↵
Specify new width for all segments: **.1**↵
Enter an option [Close/Join/Width/Edit vertex/Fit/Spline/Decurve/Ltype gen/Undo]: ↵
Command:

An unedited polyline and a new polyline after using the **PEDIT Width** option are shown in **Figure 15-7**. The width of donuts can be changed using this procedure as well.

Figure 15-7.
Changing the width
of a polyline.

— Pick

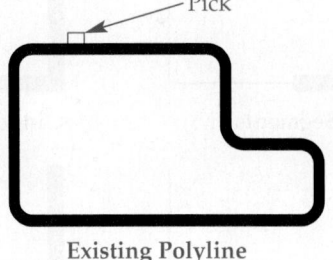

Existing Polyline

New Polyline

---

**Exercise 15-2**

○ Start a new drawing or use one of your templates.
○ Draw a series of connected lines and arcs. Then, use the **PEDIT** command to change these items to a single polyline. Finally, change the width of the polyline.
○ Draw a closed polyline. Use the **Close** option to draw the final segment.
○ Use the **Open** option of the **PEDIT** command to open the polyline. Then, use the **Close** option to close it again.
○ Draw two donuts, each with a .5 unit inside diameter and a 1.0 unit outside diameter. Change the width of the donuts to .1 using the **PEDIT** command.
○ Save the drawing as EX15-2.

---

## Editing a Polyline Vertex or Point of Tangency

The **Edit vertex** option of the **PEDIT** command is used to edit polyline vertices and points of tangency. This option is not available if you have selected multiple polylines for editing. A polyline *vertex* is where straight polyline segments meet and a *point of tangency* is where straight polyline segments or polyline arcs join other polyline arcs. When you enter the **Edit vertex** option, an "X" marker appears on screen at the first polyline vertex or point of tangency. The **Edit vertex** option has 10 suboptions, as shown in the following command sequence and explained below.

Command: **PE** *or* **PEDIT**↵
Select polyline or [Multiple]: *(pick the polyline)*
Enter an option [Close/Join/Width/Edit vertex/Fit/Spline/Decurve/Ltype gen/Undo]: **E**↵
Enter a vertex editing option [Next/Previous/Break/Insert/Move/Regen/Straighten/ Tangent/Width/eXit] <N>:

- **Next.** Moves the "X" marker on screen to the next vertex or point of tangency on the polyline.
- **Previous.** Moves the "X" marker to the previous vertex or point of tangency on the polyline.
- **Break.** Breaks the polyline between two vertices or points of tangency.
- **Insert.** Adds a new polyline vertex at a selected point.
- **Move.** Moves a polyline vertex to a new location.
- **Regen.** Generates the revised version of the polyline.
- **Straighten.** Straightens polyline arc segments or multiple segments between two points.
- **Tangent.** Specifies a tangent direction for curve fitting when using the **PEDIT Fit** option.
- **Width.** Changes the width of a polyline segment.
- **eXit.** Returns the **PEDIT** command prompt.

Only the current point identified by the "X" marker is affected by editing functions. In **Figure 15-8**, the marker is moved clockwise through the points using the **Next** option and counterclockwise using the **Previous** option. If you edit the vertices of a polyline and nothing appears to happen, use the **Regen** suboption to regenerate the polyline.

## Making Breaks in a Polyline

You can break a polyline into two separate polylines with the **Break** suboption of the **Edit vertex** option of the **PEDIT** command. Once the **Edit vertex** option is entered, use the **Next** or **Previous** suboption to move the "X" marker to the first vertex where the polyline is to be broken. Then, enter the **Break** suboption:

Enter an option [Close/Join/Width/Edit vertex/Fit/Spline/Decurve/Ltype gen/Undo]: **E**↵
Enter a vertex editing option [Next/Previous/Break/Insert/Move/Regen/Straighten/ Tangent/Width/eXit] <N>: *(use **Next** and **Previous** to move the "X" marker to the position where you want the break to begin)*
Enter a vertex editing option [Next/Previous/Break/Insert/Move/Regen/Straighten/ Tangent/Width/eXit] <N>: **B**↵

---

Figure 15-8.
Using the **Next** and **Previous** vertex editing suboptions to specify polyline vertices. Note the different positions of the "X" marker.

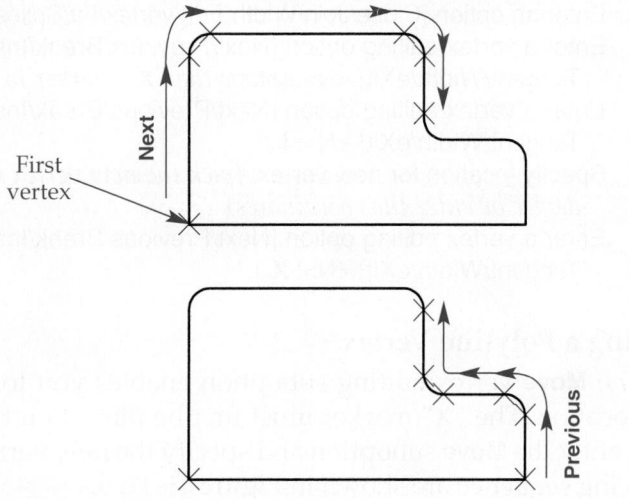

AutoCAD uses vertex at the marker as the first break point. The command sequence continues:

> Enter an option [Next/Previous/Go/eXit] <N>: *(move the "X" marker to the second vertex of the break)*
> Enter an option [Next/Previous/Go/eXit] <N>: **G**↵

The **Go** suboption instructs AutoCAD to remove the portion of the polyline between the two points. You can also break the polyline without removing a segment by specifying **Go** without moving to a second vertex. The results of the following command sequence are illustrated in **Figure 15-9.** The polyline was drawn clockwise.

> Enter a vertex editing option
> [Next/Previous/Break/Insert/Move/Regen/Straighten/Tangent/Width/eXit] <N>: *(move to Point 1)*
> Enter a vertex editing option
> [Next/Previous/Break/Insert/Move/Regen/Straighten/Tangent/Width/eXit] <N>: **B**↵ *(specifies Point 1)*
> Enter an option [Next/Previous/Go/eXit] <N>: **P**↵ *(specifies Point 2)*
> Enter an option [Next/Previous/Go/eXit] <P>: ↵ *(specifies Point 3)*
> Enter an option [Next/Previous/Go/eXit] <P>: ↵ *(specifies Point 4)*
> Enter an option [Next/Previous/Go/eXit] <P>: **G**↵ *(breaks the polyline between Points 1 and 4)*

**Figure 15-9.**
Using the **Break** vertex editing suboption to break a polyline and remove a portion.

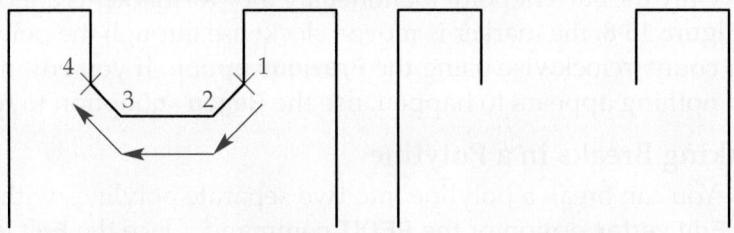

Break Points Specified    New Polylines

## Inserting a New Vertex in a Polyline

A new vertex can be added to a polyline using the **Insert** vertex editing suboption. The inserted vertex can be inserted on an existing polyline segment, but does not need to be. First, use the **Next** or **Previous** suboption to locate the vertex next to where you want the new vertex. Refer to **Figure 15-10** as you go through the following command sequence.

> Enter an option [Close/Join/Width/Edit vertex/Fit/Spline/Decurve/Ltype gen/Undo]: **E**↵
> Enter a vertex editing option [Next/Previous/Break/Insert/Move/Regen/Straighten/Tangent/Width/eXit] <N>: *(move the "X" marker to the desired location)*
> Enter a vertex editing option [Next/Previous/Break/Insert/Move/Regen/Straighten/Tangent/Width/eXit] <N>: **I**↵
> Specify location for new vertex: *(pick the new vertex location using your pointing device or enter the coordinates)*
> Enter a vertex editing option [Next/Previous/Break/Insert/Move/Regen/Straighten/Tangent/Width/eXit] <N>: **X**↵

## Moving a Polyline Vertex

The **Move** vertex editing suboption enables you to move a polyline vertex to a new location. The "X" marker must first be placed on the vertex you want to move. Then, enter the **Move** suboption and specify the new vertex location. The results of the following sequence are shown in **Figure 15-11.**

**Figure 15-10.**
Using the **Insert** vertex editing suboption to add a new vertex to a polyline.

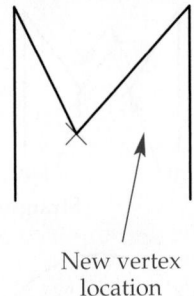
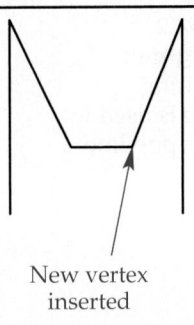

New vertex location

New vertex inserted

**Figure 15-11.**
Using the **Move** vertex editing suboption to place a polyline vertex at a new location.

Existing vertex

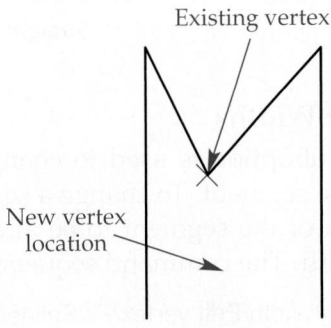
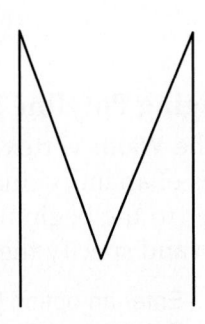

New vertex location

**Vertex Moved**

Enter an option [Close/Join/Width/Edit vertex/Fit/Spline/Decurve/Ltype gen/Undo]: **E**↵
Enter a vertex editing option [Next/Previous/Break/Insert/Move/Regen/Straighten/ Tangent/Width/eXit] <N>: *(move the "X" marker to the vertex to be moved)*
Enter a vertex editing option [Next/Previous/Break/Insert/Move/Regen/Straighten/ Tangent/Width/eXit] <N>: **M**↵
Specify new location for marked vertex: *(pick the desired location with your pointing device or enter the coordinates)*
Enter a vertex editing option [Next/Previous/Break/Insert/Move/Regen/Straighten/ Tangent/Width/eXit] <N>: **X**↵

## Straightening Polyline Segments or Arcs

The **Straighten** vertex editing suboption allows you to straighten polyline segments or arcs between two points. The command sequence is:

Enter an option [Close/Join/Width/Edit vertex/Fit/Spline/Decurve/Ltype gen/Undo]: **E**↵
Enter a vertex editing option [Next/Previous/Break/Insert/Move/Regen/Straighten/ Tangent/Width/eXit] <N>: *(move the "X" marker to the first point of the segments to be straightened)*
Enter a vertex editing option [Next/Previous/Break/Insert/Move/Regen/Straighten/ Tangent/Width/eXit] <N>: **S**↵
Enter an option [Next/Previous/Go/eXit] <N>: *(move the "X" marker to the last point of the segments to be straightened)*
Enter an option [Next/Previous/Go/eXit] <N>: **G**↵

If the "X" marker is not moved before G is entered, AutoCAD straightens the segment from the first marked point to the next vertex. This provides a quick way to straighten an arc. See **Figure 15-12.**

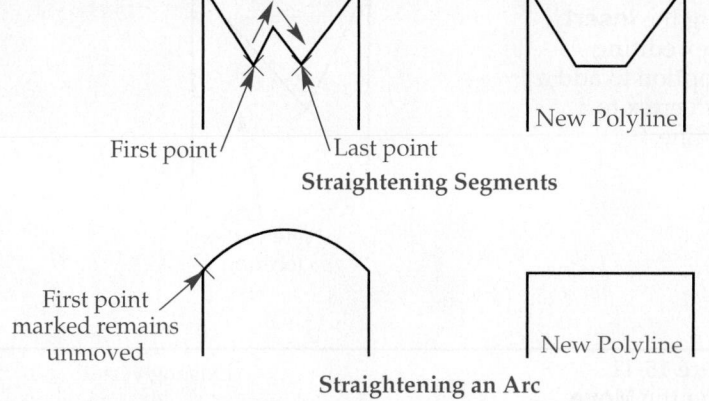

**Figure 15-12.**
The **Straighten** vertex editing suboption is used to straighten polyline segments.

First point    Last point

**Straightening Segments**

New Polyline

First point marked remains unmoved

**Straightening an Arc**

New Polyline

## Changing Polyline Segment Widths

The **Width** vertex editing suboption is used to change the starting and ending widths of an individual polyline segment. To change a segment width, move the "X" marker to the beginning vertex of the segment to be altered. Then, enter the **Width** option and specify the new width. The command sequence is:

Enter an option [Close/Join/Width/Edit vertex/Fit/Spline/Decurve/Ltype gen/Undo]: **E**↵
Enter a vertex editing option [Next/Previous/Break/Insert/Move/Regen/Straighten/Tangent/Width/eXit] <N>: *(move the "X" marker to the beginning vertex of the segment to be changed)*
Enter a vertex editing option [Next/Previous/Break/Insert/Move/Regen/Straighten/Tangent/Width/eXit] <N>: **W**↵
Specify starting width for next segment <*current width of segment*>: *(enter the revised starting width and press* [Enter]*)*
Specify ending width for next segment <*revised starting width*>: *(enter the revised ending width and press* [Enter]*, or press* [Enter] *to keep the width the same as the starting width)*
Enter a vertex editing option [Next/Previous/Break/Insert/Move/Regen/Straighten/Tangent/Width/eXit] <N>: **R**↵

Notice the default starting width value is the current width of the segment to be changed. The default ending width value is the same as the revised starting width. If nothing appears to happen to the segment when you specify the ending width and press [Enter], enter the **Regen** option to have AutoCAD draw the revised polyline. See **Figure 15-13.**

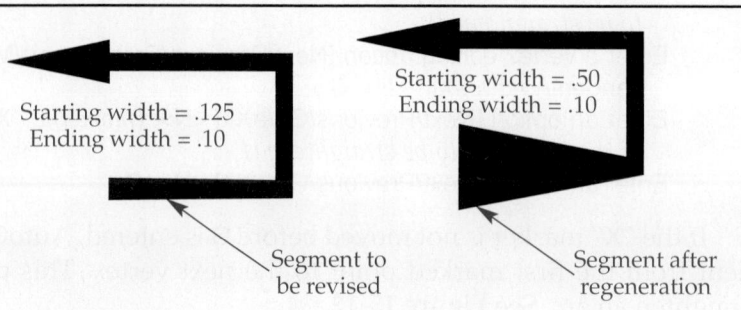

**Figure 15-13.**
Changing the width of a polyline segment with the **Width** vertex editing suboption. Use the **Regen** suboption to display the change.

Starting width = .125
Ending width = .10

Starting width = .50
Ending width = .10

Segment to be revised

Segment after regeneration

## Making Smooth Curves out of Polylines

In some situations, you may need to convert a polyline into a series of smooth curves. One example of this is a graph. A graph may show a series of plotted points as a smooth curve rather than straight segments. This process is called *curve fitting* and is accomplished using the **Fit** option and the **Tangent** vertex editing suboption of the **PEDIT** command.

The **Fit** option allows you to construct pairs of arcs passing through control points. You can specify the control points or you can simply use the vertices of the polyline. The more closely spaced the control points, the smoother the curve.

Prior to curve fitting, each vertex can be given a tangent direction. AutoCAD then fits the curve based on the tangent directions that you set. However, you do not need to enter tangent directions. Specifying tangent directions is a way to edit vertices when the **PEDIT Fit** option does not produce the best results.

The **Tangent** vertex editing suboption is used to edit tangent directions. After entering the **PEDIT** command and the **Edit vertex** option, move the "X" marker to each vertex to be changed. Enter the **Tangent** suboption for each specified vertex and enter a tangent direction in degrees or pick a point in the expected direction. The direction you choose is then indicated by an arrow placed at the vertex. The command sequence is:

> Enter an option [Close/Join/Width/Edit vertex/Fit/Spline/Decurve/Ltype gen/Undo]: E↵
> Enter a vertex editing option [Next/Previous/Break/Insert/Move/Regen/Straighten/ Tangent/Width/eXit] <N>: *(move the "X" marker to the desired vertex)*
> Enter a vertex editing option [Next/Previous/Break/Insert/Move/Regen/Straighten/ Tangent/Width/eXit] <N>: T↵
> Specify direction of vertex tangent: *(specify a direction in positive or negative degrees and press [Enter] or pick a point in the desired direction)*

Continue by moving the marker to each vertex that you want to change, entering the **Tangent** suboption for each vertex, and selecting a tangent direction. Once the tangent directions are given for all vertices to be changed, enter the **PEDIT Fit** option.

You can also enter the **PEDIT** command, select a polyline, and then enter the **Fit** option without adjusting tangencies if desired. The polyline shown in **Figure 15-14** was made into a smooth curve using the following steps.

> Command: **PE** *or* **PEDIT**↵
> Select polyline or [Multiple]: *(pick the polyline to be edited)*
> Enter an option [Close/Join/Width/Edit vertex/Fit/Spline/Decurve/Ltype gen/Undo]: F↵

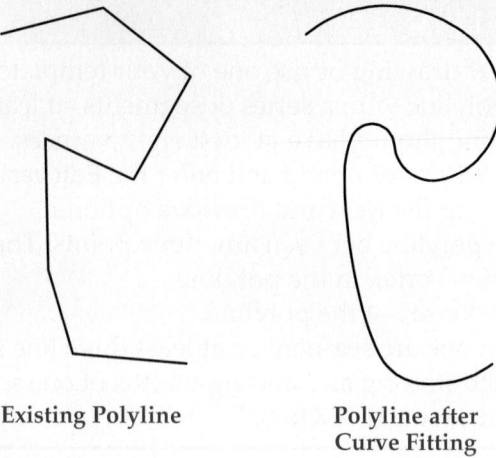

**Figure 15-14.**
Using the **PEDIT Fit** option to turn a polyline into a smooth curve.

Existing Polyline                   Polyline after Curve Fitting

If the resulting curve does not look like what you had anticipated, enter the **Edit vertex** option. Then, make changes using the various vertex editing suboptions as necessary.

## Using the PEDIT Spline Option

When a polyline is edited with the **PEDIT Fit** option, the resulting curve passes through each of the polyline's vertices. The **PEDIT Spline** option also smoothes the corners of a straight-segment polyline. However, this option produces different results. The resulting curve passes through the first and last control points or vertices only. The curve *pulls* toward the other vertices, but does not pass through them. The **Spline** option is used as follows:

    Command: **PE** *or* **PEDIT**↵
    Select polyline or [Multiple]: *(pick the polyline to be edited)*
    Enter an option [Close/Join/Width/Edit vertex/Fit/Spline/Decurve/Ltype gen/Undo]: **S**↵

The results of using the **Fit** and **Spline** options on a polyline are illustrated in **Figure 15-15.**

**Figure 15-15.**
A comparison of polylines edited with the **PEDIT Fit** and **Spline** options.

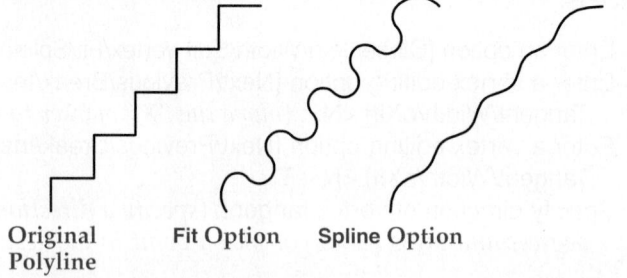

Original Polyline        Fit Option        Spline Option

## Straightening All Segments of a Polyline

The **PEDIT Decurve** option returns a polyline edited with the **Fit** or **Spline** options to its original form. However, the information entered for tangent directions is kept for future reference. You can also use the **Decurve** option to straighten the curved segments of a polyline. See **Figure 15-16.**

    Command: **PE** *or* **PEDIT**↵
    Select polyline: *(pick the polyline to be edited)*
    Enter an option [Close/Join/Width/Edit vertex/Fit/Spline/Decurve/Ltype gen/Undo]: **D**↵

**Figure 15-16.**
The **PEDIT Decurve**
option is used to
straighten the
curved segments of
a polyline.

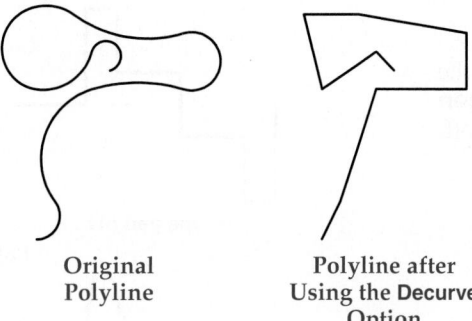

Original          Polyline after
Polyline        Using the **Decurve**
                       Option

**PROFESSIONAL
TIP**

If you make a mistake while editing a polyline, remember
that the **Undo** option is available inside the **PEDIT** command.
Using the **Undo** option more than once allows you to step
backward through each operation. The **UNDO** command can
also be used at the Command: prompt to undo all of the effects
of the last **PEDIT** command.

### Exercise 15-4

○ Start a new drawing or use one of your templates.
○ Draw a polyline with at least five vertices. Make the polyline smooth using the
**Fit** option of the **PEDIT** command.
○ Return the polyline to its original form using the **PEDIT Decurve** option.
○ Practice with the **Undo** option by first drawing a series of polyline segments.
After using the **PEDIT** command to make several changes, use the **Undo** option to
return to the original polyline.
○ Save the drawing as EX15-4.

## Changing the Appearance of Polyline Linetypes

The **PEDIT Ltype gen** (linetype generation) option determines how linetypes
other than Continuous appear in relation to the vertices of a polyline. For example,
when a Center linetype is used and the **Ltype gen** option is disabled, the polyline has
a long dash at each vertex. When the **Ltype gen** option is activated, the polyline is
generated with a constant pattern in relation to the polyline as a whole. The difference between using the **Ltype gen** option off and on is illustrated in **Figure 15-17.** Also
shown are the effects these settings have on spline curves. To turn the **Ltype gen**
option on:

    Command: **PE** *or* **PEDIT**↵
    Select polyline or [Multiple]: *(pick the polyline)*
    Enter an option [Close/Join/Width/Edit vertex/Fit/Spline/Decurve/Ltype gen/Undo]: **L**↵
    Enter polyline linetype generation option [ON/OFF] <Off>: **ON**↵

You can also change the **Ltype gen** option setting for new polylines with the
**PLINEGEN** system variable. This variable must be set before the polyline is drawn.
Changing the setting does not affect existing polylines. The settings for the **PLINEGEN**
system variable are 0 (off) and 1 (on).

Figure 15-17.
A comparison of
polylines with the
**PEDIT Ltype gen**
option on and off.

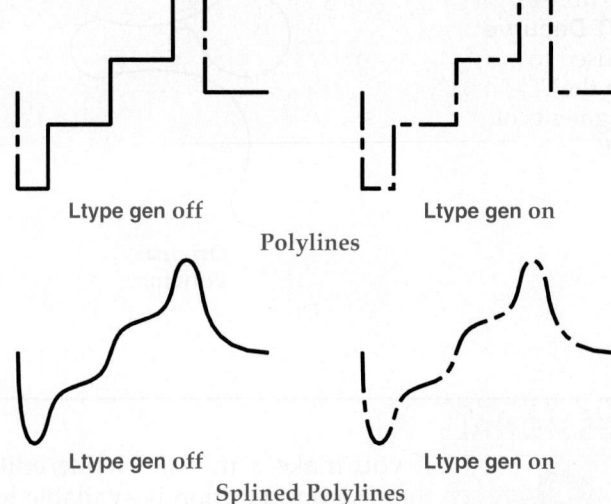

Ltype gen off      Ltype gen on

Polylines

Ltype gen off      Ltype gen on

Splined Polylines

## Converting a Polyline into Individual Line and Arc Segments

A polyline is a single object composed of line and arc segments. The **EXPLODE** command allows you to change a polyline into a series of individual lines and arcs. You can then edit each segment individually. The resulting segments are not, however, polylines. When a wide polyline is exploded, the resulting line or arc is redrawn along the centerline of the original polyline. See **Figure 15-18.**

To explode an object, pick the **Explode** button on the **Modify** toolbar, select **Explode** from the **Modify** pull-down menu, or type X or EXPLODE at the Command: prompt. You are then asked to select objects:

EXPLODE
X

Modify
➥ Explode

Modify
toolbar

Explode

Command: **X** *or* **EXPLODE.**↵
Select objects: *(pick the polyline to be exploded)*
Select objects: ↵

The **EXPLODE** command removes all width characteristics and tangency information. AutoCAD reminds you of this fact if you explode a wide polyline with the message:

Exploding this polyline has lost width information.
The UNDO command will restore it.

Figure 15-18.
Exploding a wide
polyline.

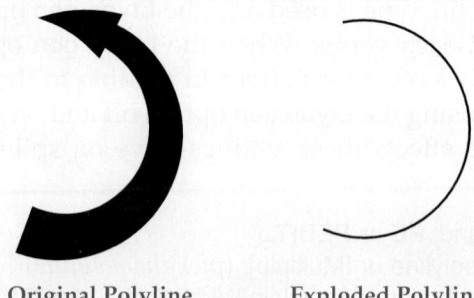

Original Polyline      Exploded Polyline

## Additional Methods for Smoothing Polylines

The methods for smoothing polylines that were introduced earlier in this chapter focused on using the **Fit** and **Spline** options of the **PEDIT** command. With the **Fit** option, the resulting *fit curve* passes through the polyline vertices. The **Spline** option creates a *spline curve* that passes through the first and last control points or vertices. The resulting curve *pulls* toward the other vertices but does not pass through them.

The **Spline** option creates a curve that approximates a true B-spline. AutoCAD's **SPLINE** command creates a true B-spline curve. You can choose between one of two types of calculations used by the **Spline** option to create the curve—cubic and quadratic. A *cubic curve* is extremely smooth. A *quadratic curve* is not as smooth as a cubic curve, but it is smoother than a curve produced with the **Fit** option. Like a cubic curve, a quadratic curve passes through the first and last control points. The remainder of the curve is tangent to the polyline segments between the intermediate control points, as shown in **Figure 15-19.**

The **SPLINETYPE** system variable determines whether AutoCAD draws cubic or quadratic curves. The default setting is 6. At this setting, a cubic curve is drawn when using the **Spline** option of the **PEDIT** command. If the **SPLINETYPE** system variable is set to 5, a quadratic curve is generated. The only valid values for **SPLINETYPE** are 5 and 6.

**Figure 15-19.**
A comparison of curves drawn with the **PEDIT Fit** and **Spline** options. The **SPLINETYPE** system variable controls whether a quadratic or cubic curve is drawn with the **Spline** option.

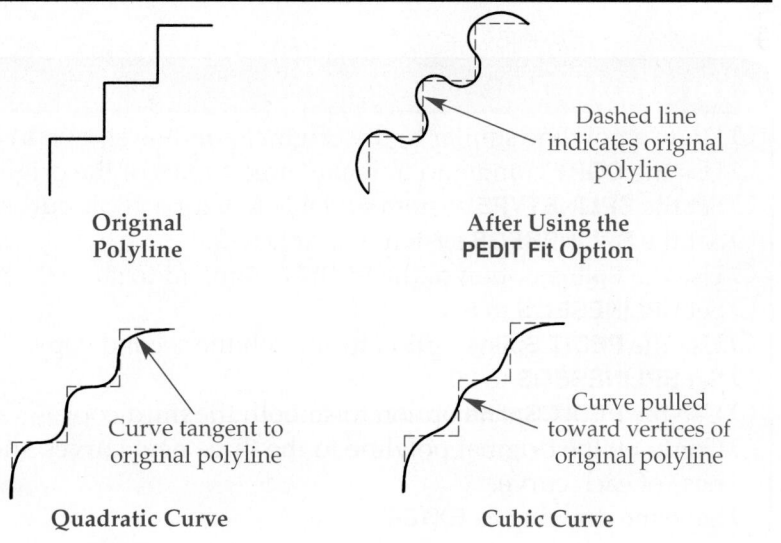

Original Polyline

After Using the PEDIT Fit Option

Dashed line indicates original polyline

Curve tangent to original polyline

Quadratic Curve

Curve pulled toward vertices of original polyline

Cubic Curve

The **SPLINESEGS** system variable controls the number of line segments used to construct spline curves. It can be set at the Command: prompt or in the **Segments in a polyline curve** text box in the **Display** resolution area of the **Display** tab of the **Options** dialog box. The **SPLINESEGS** default value is 8, which creates a fairly smooth spline curve with moderate regeneration time. If you decrease the value, the resulting spline curve is less smooth. If you increase the value, the resulting spline curve is smoother but the regeneration time and drawing file size is increased. The relationship between **SPLINESEGS** values and spline curves is shown in **Figure 15-20.**

**Figure 15-20.**
A comparison of curves drawn with different settings for the **SPLINESEGS** system variable.

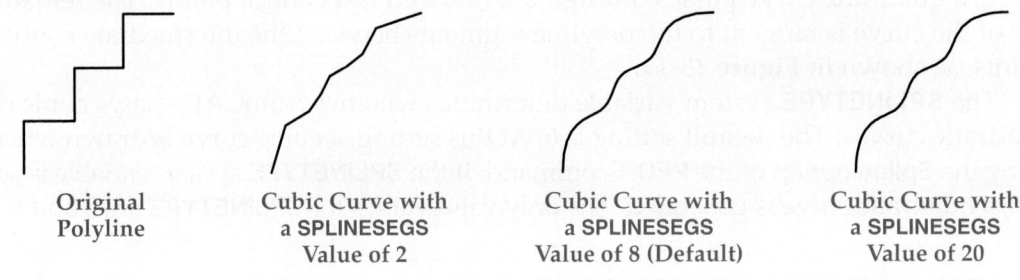

| Original Polyline | Cubic Curve with a SPLINESEGS Value of 2 | Cubic Curve with a SPLINESEGS Value of 8 (Default) | Cubic Curve with a SPLINESEGS Value of 20 |

## Drawing Curves Using the SPLINE Command

The **SPLINE** command is used to create a special type of curve called a nonuniform rational B-spline (NURBS). A NURBS curve is considered to be a true spline. A spline created by fitting a spline curve to a polyline is merely a linear approximation of a true spline and is not as accurate. An additional advantage of spline objects over smoothed polylines is that splines use less disk space.

To access the **SPLINE** command, pick the **Spline** button on the **Draw** toolbar, pick **Spline** from the **Draw** pull-down menu, or type SPL or SPLINE at the Command: prompt. A spline is created by specifying the control points along the curve using any standard coordinate entry method.

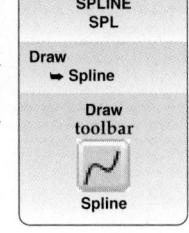

Command: **SPL** *or* **SPLINE**↵
Specify first point or [Object]: **2,2**↵
Specify next point: **4,4**↵
Specify next point or [Close/Fit tolerance] <start tangent>: **6,2**↵
Specify next point or [Close/Fit tolerance] <start tangent>: ↵
Specify start tangent: ↵
Specify end tangent: ↵
Command:

When you have given all of the necessary points along the spline, pressing [Enter] ends the point specification process and allows the start tangency and end tangency to be entered. Specifying the tangents changes the direction in which the spline curve begins and ends. Pressing [Enter] at these prompts accepts the default direction, as calculated by AutoCAD, for the specified curve. The results of the previous command sequence are shown in **Figure 15-21**.

**Figure 15-21.**
A spline drawn with the **SPLINE** command using the AutoCAD defaults for the start and end tangents.

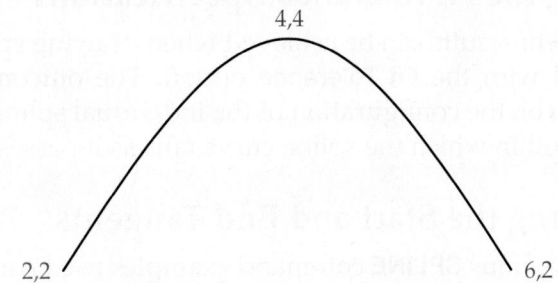

---

**NOTE**  If only two points are specified along the spline curve, an object that looks like a line is created, but the object is a spline.

---

Figure 15-22.
Using the **Close**
option of the
**SPLINE** command
with AutoCAD
default tangents to
draw a closed
spline. Compare
this spline to the
object shown in
Figure 15-21.

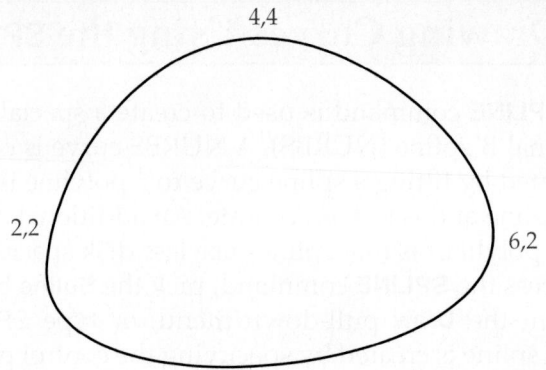

## Drawing Closed Splines

The **Close** option of the **SPLINE** command enables you to draw closed splines, Figure 15-22. The command sequence is:

> Command: **SPL** *or* **SPLINE**↵
> Specify first point or [Object]: **2,2**↵
> Specify next point: **4,4**↵
> Specify next point or [Close/Fit tolerance] <start tangent>: **6,2**↵
> Specify next point or [Close/Fit tolerance] <start tangent>: **C**↵
> Specify tangent: ↵
> Command:

After closing a spline, you are prompted to specify a tangent direction for the start/end point of the spline. Pressing [Enter] accepts the default calculated by AutoCAD.

## Altering the Fit Tolerance Specifications

Different results can be achieved when drawing splines by altering the specifications used with the **Fit Tolerance** option. The outcomes of different settings vary, depending on the configuration of the individual spline object. The setting specifies a *tolerance* within which the spline curve falls as it passes through the control points.

## Specifying the Start and End Tangents

The previous **SPLINE** command examples used AutoCAD's default start and end tangents. You can set start and end tangent directions by entering values at the prompts that appear after you pick the points of the spline. The tangency is based on the tangent direction of the selected point. The results of using the horizontal and vertical tangent directions using **Ortho** mode are shown in **Figure 15-23**. The command sequence is:

> Command: **SPL** *or* **SPLINE**↵
> Specify first point or [Object]: **2,2**↵
> Specify next point: **4,4**↵
> Specify next point or [Close/Fit tolerance] <start tangent>: **6,2**↵
> Specify next point or [Close/Fit tolerance] <start tangent>: ↵
> Specify start tangent: *(move cursor in tangent direction and press* [Enter]*)*
> Specify end tangent: *(move cursor in tangent direction and press* [Enter]*)*
> Command:

Figure 15-23.
These splines were
drawn through the
same points but
have different start
and end tangent
directions. The
tangent directions
are indicated by the
arrows.

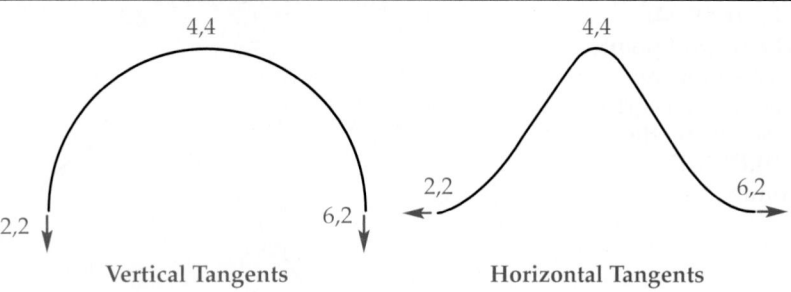

Vertical Tangents        Horizontal Tangents

## Converting a Spline-Fitted Polyline to a Spline

A spline-fitted polyline object can be converted to a spline object using the **Object** option of the **SPLINE** command. This option works for either 2D or 3D objects. The command sequence is as follows:

Command: **SPL** *or* **SPLINE**↵
Specify first point or [Object]: **O**↵
Select objects to convert to splines…
Select objects: *(pick the spline-fitted polyline)*
Select objects: ↵
Command:

---

### Exercise 15-8

○ Start a new drawing or use one of your templates.
○ Draw the spline shown in **Figure 15-21.** Use the AutoCAD default tangents.
○ Draw a similar spline to the right of the first one using the **Close** option and default tangents.
○ Draw two splines similar to the objects shown in **Figure 15-23.** Use **Ortho** mode for the start and end tangents.
○ Save the drawing as EX15-8.

---

## Editing Splines

The **SPLINEDIT** command allows you to edit spline objects. Several editing options are available. Control points can be added, moved, or deleted to alter the shape of an existing curve. A spline can also be opened or closed. In addition, you can change the start and end tangents.

To access the **SPLINEDIT** command, pick the **Edit Spline** button on the **Modify II** toolbar, pick **Spline** from the **Object** cascading menu in the **Modify** pull-down menu, or enter SPE or SPLINEDIT at the Command: prompt. The command sequence is:

Command: **SPE** *or* **SPLINEDIT**↵
Select spline: *(pick a spline)*

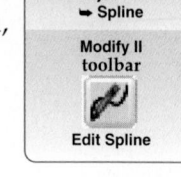

SPE
SPLINEDIT

Modify
➥ Object
➥ Spline

Modify II
toolbar

Edit Spline

When you pick a spline, the control points are identified by grips, as shown in **Figure 15-24.** The command sequence continues:

Enter an option [Fit data/Close/Move vertex/Refine/rEverse/Undo]:

The **SPLINEDIT** command options are described in the following sections.

**Figure 15-24.**
The control points
on a spline are
displayed as grips
when using the
**SPLINEDIT**
command.

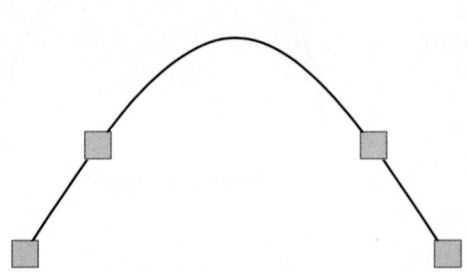

## Editing Fit Data

The **Fit data** option of the **SPLINEDIT** command allows spline control points to be edited. Spline control points are called *fit points*. The **Fit data** option has several suboptions:

```
Command: SPE or SPLINEDIT↵
Select spline: (pick a spline)
Enter an option [Fit data/Close/Move vertex/Refine/rEverse/Undo]: F↵
Enter a fit data option
[Add/Close/Delete/Move/Purge/Tangents/toLerance/eXit] <eXit>:
```

Each of the **Fit data** suboptions is explained next. See **Figure 15-25** for examples of using these options.

- **Add.** This suboption allows you to add new fit points to a spline definition. When adding, a fit point can be located by picking a point or entering coordinates. Fit points appear as unselected grips. When one is selected, it becomes highlighted along with the next fit point on the spline. You can then add a fit point between the two highlighted points. If the endpoint of the spline is selected, only the endpoint becomes highlighted. If the start point of the spline is selected, the following prompt is issued:

  ```
  Specify new point or [After/Before]: <exit>:
  ```

  This prompt asks whether to insert the new fit point before or after the existing one. Respond by entering A or B accordingly. When a fit point is added, the spline curve is refit through the added point. See **Figure 15-25**.

  The **Add** option functions in a running mode. This means that you can continue to add points as needed. By pressing [Enter] at a Specify new point <exit>: prompt, you can select other existing fit points. Therefore, points can be added anywhere on the spline.

- **Close/Open.** If the selected spline is open, the **Close** suboption is displayed. If the spline is closed, the **Open** suboption is displayed. These options allow you to open a closed spline or close an open spline.

- **Delete.** The **Delete** suboption allows you to delete fit points as needed. However, at least two fit points must remain. Even when only two points remain, the object is still defined as a spline although it looks like a line. Like the **Add** option, the **Delete** option operates in a running mode, allowing as many deletions as needed. The spline is recurved through the remaining fit points.

- **Move.** This suboption allows fit points to be moved as necessary. When the **Move** option is entered, the start point of the spline is highlighted. You can specify a different location simply by picking a new point with your left mouse button. You can also specify other fit points to move. The options are explained as follows:

**Figure 15-25.**
Examples of using the **SPLINEDIT Fit Data** suboptions to edit a spline. Compare the original spline to each of the edited objects.

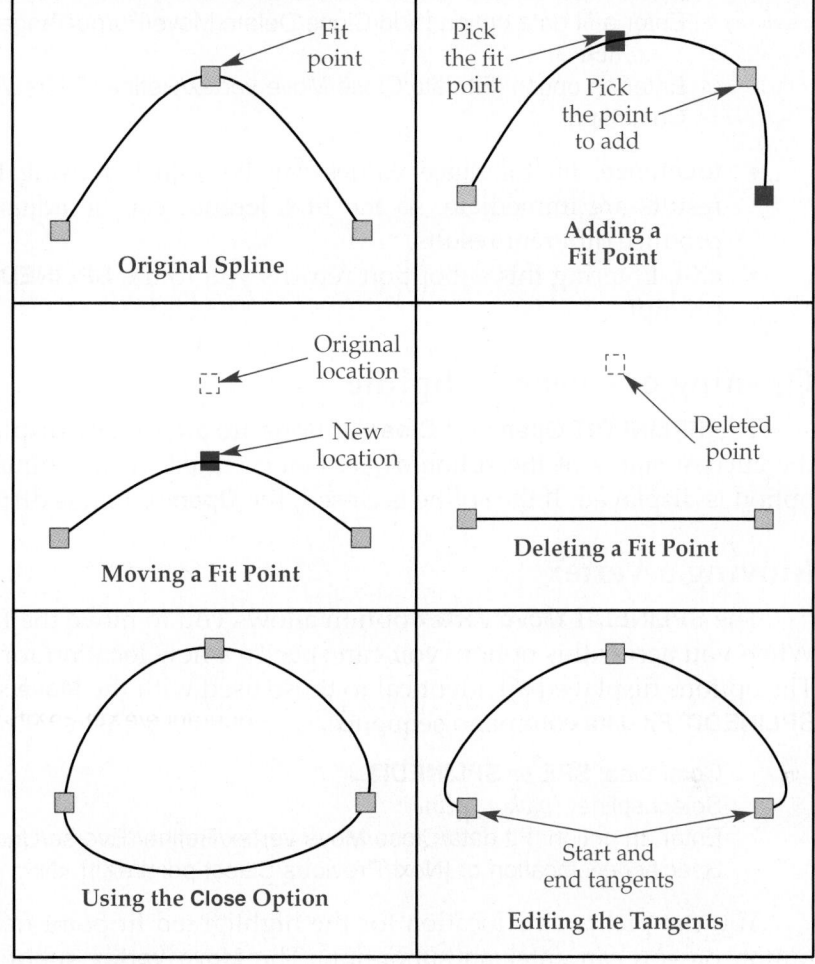

- **Specify new location.** This suboption allows you to move the currently highlighted point to a specified location.
- **Next.** This suboption highlights the next fit point. It is activated by pressing [Enter].
- **Previous.** Entering this suboption highlights the previous fit point.
- **Select point.** This suboption allows you to pick a different fit point to move rather than using the **Next** or **Previous** options.
- **eXit.** This suboption returns you to the **Fit Data** suboption prompt.
- **Purge.** This suboption lets you remove fit point data from a spline. After using this option, the resulting spline is not as easy to edit. In very large drawings where many complex splines are created, such as Geographical Information Systems (GIS) drawings, purging fit point data reduces the file size by simplifying the definition. Once a spline is purged, the **Fit Data** option is no longer displayed by the **SPLINEDIT** command for the purged spline.
- **Tangents.** This suboption allows editing of the start and end tangents for an open spline and editing of the start tangent for a closed spline. The tangency is based on the direction of the selected point. You can also use the **System default** option to set the tangency values to the AutoCAD defaults:

```
Command: SPE or SPLINEDIT↵
Select spline: (pick a spline)
Enter an option [Fit data/Close/Move vertex/Refine/rEverse/Undo]: F↵
Enter a fit data option [Add/Close/Delete/Move/Purge/Tangents/toLerance/eXit]
    <eXit>: T↵
Specify start tangent or [System default]: S↵
```

Specify end tangent or [System default]: **S**↵
Enter a fit data option [Add/Close/Delete/Move/Purge/Tangents/toLerance/eXit]
    <eXit>: ↵
Enter an option [Fit data/Close/Move vertex/Refine/rEverse/Undo]: ↵
Command:

- **toLerance.** Fit tolerance values can be adjusted using this suboption. The results are immediate, so the fit tolerance can be adjusted as necessary to produce different results.
- **eXit.** Entering this suboption returns you to the **SPLINEDIT** command option prompt.

## Opening or Closing a Spline

The **SPLINEDIT Open** and **Close** options are alternately displayed, depending on the current status of the spline object being edited. If the spline is open, the **Close** option is displayed. If the spline is closed, the **Open** option is displayed.

## Moving a Vertex

The **SPLINEDIT Move vertex** option allows you to move the fit points of a spline. When you access this option, you can specify a new location for a selected fit point. The options displayed are identical to those used with the **Move** suboption inside the **SPLINEDIT Fit data** command sequence.

Command: **SPE** *or* **SPLINEDIT**↵
Select spline: *(pick a spline)*
Enter an option [Fit data/Close/Move vertex/Refine/rEverse/Undo]: **M**↵
Specify new location or [Next/Previous/Select point/eXit] <N>:

You can pick a new location for the highlighted fit point using your left mouse button or you can enter an suboption. The **Move vertex** suboptions are explained below:

- **Specify new location.** Allows you to move the currently highlighted point to a specified location.
- **Next.** Highlights the next fit point.
- **Previous.** Highlights the previous fit point.
- **Select point.** Allows you to pick a different fit point to move, rather than cycling through points with the **Next** or **Previous** suboptions.
- **eXit.** Returns you to the **SPLINEDIT** command prompt.

---

### Exercise 15-9

○ Start a new drawing or use one of your templates.
○ Draw a spline similar to the original spline in **Figure 15-25**. Use the AutoCAD default tangents.
○ Copy the original spline to five locations, similar to the layout in **Figure 15-25**.
○ Use the **SPLINEDIT** command to add a control point to the upper-right spline.
○ Close the middle-left spline.
○ Delete the top control point of the middle-right spline.
○ Move the top control point of the lower-left spline.
○ Change the start and end tangents of the lower-right spline.
○ Save the drawing as EX15-9.

---

          *AutoCAD and its Applications—Basics*

# Smoothing or Reshaping a Section of the Spline

The **SPLINEDIT Refine** option allows fine tuning of the spline curve. Fit points can be added to help smooth or reshape a section of the spline. When you use this option, the fit point data is removed from the spline. The command sequence is:

Command: **SPE** *or* **SPLINEDIT**.↲
Select spline: *(pick a spline)*
Enter an option [Fit data/Close/Move vertex/Refine/rEverse/Undo]: **R**↲
Enter a refine option [Add control point/Elevate order/Weight/eXit] <eXit>:

- **Add control point.** This option allows you to specify new fit points on a spline as needed.
- **Elevate order.** The *order* of a spline is the degree of the spline polynomial +1. In simple terms, it is the degree of refinement of the spline. For example, a cubic spline has an order of 4. Elevating the order of a spline causes more control points to appear on the curve for greater control. In **Figure 15-26**, the order of the spline is elevated from 4 to 6. The order setting can be from 4 to 26, but it cannot be adjusted downward. For example, if the order is set to 24, the only remaining settings are 25 and 26.
- **Weight.** This option allows you to change the *weight*, or "pull," of individual control points. The default setting of 1.0000 can be adjusted to a higher or lower value. When all control points have the same weight, they exert the same amount of pull on the spline. When a weight value is lessened for a control point, the spline is not pulled as close to the point as before. Likewise, when a weight value is increased, the control point exerts more pull on the spline. See **Figure 15-26**. The weight setting must be positive. The control point selection suboptions of the **Weight** option are the same as those used with the **SPLINEDIT Move vertex** option. You can specify a new weight for the highlighted control point by using the **Enter new weight** option:

Enter a refine option [Add control point/Elevate order/Weight/eXit] <eXit>: **W**↲
Enter new weight (current = 1.0000) or [Next/Previous/Select point/eXit] <N>:
   *(enter a positive number)*

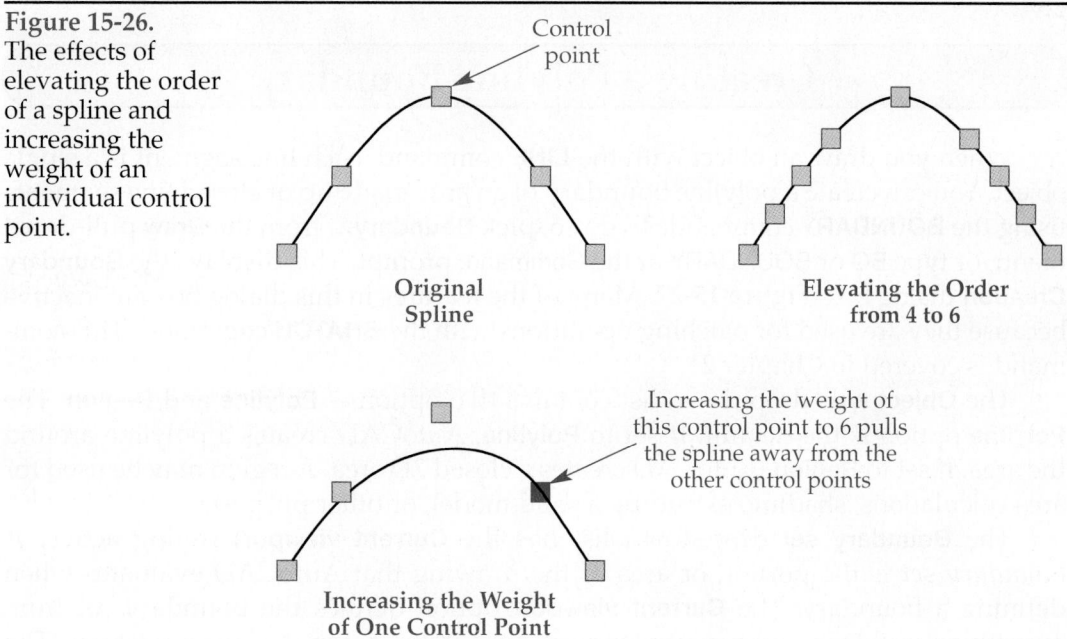

**Figure 15-26.**
The effects of elevating the order of a spline and increasing the weight of an individual control point.

Control point

Original Spline

Elevating the Order from 4 to 6

Increasing the weight of this control point to 6 pulls the spline away from the other control points

Increasing the Weight of One Control Point

## Reversing the Order of Spline Control Points

The **rEverse** option of the **SPLINEDIT** command allows you to reverse the listed order of the spline control points. This makes the previous start point the new endpoint and the previous endpoint the new start point. Using this option affects the various control point selection options as a result.

## Undoing SPLINEDIT Changes

The **SPLINEDIT Undo** option undoes the previous change made to the spline. You can also use this option to undo changes back to the beginning of the current **SPLINEDIT** command sequence.

## Exiting the SPLINEDIT Command

To exit the **SPLINEDIT** command, press [Enter] or type X and press [Enter] at the following prompt after making changes:

> Enter an option [Close/Move vertex/Refine/rEverse/Undo/eXit] <eXit>: ↵
> Command:

---

### Exercise 15-10

○ Start a new drawing or use one of your templates.
○ Draw a spline similar to the original spline shown in **Figure 15-26**. Use the AutoCAD default tangents.
○ Copy the original spline to two locations, similar to the layout in **Figure 15-26**.
○ Use the **SPLINEDIT** command on one of the new splines to elevate the order of control points.
○ Use the **SPLINEDIT** command to increase the weight of one of the control points on the other spline.
○ Save the drawing as EX15-10.

---

## Creating a Polyline Boundary

BOUNDARY
BO

Draw
↳ Boundary...

When you draw an object with the **LINE** command, each line segment is a single object. You can create a polyline boundary of an area made up of closed line segments using the **BOUNDARY** command. To do so, pick **Boundary...** from the **Draw** pull-down menu, or type BO or BOUNDARY at the Command: prompt. This displays the **Boundary Creation** dialog box, **Figure 15-27**. Many of the features in this dialog box are inactive because they are used for hatching operations with the **BHATCH** command. This command is covered in Chapter 21.

The **Object type** drop-down list contains two options—**Polyline** and **Region**. The **Polyline** option is the default. If set to **Polyline**, AutoCAD creates a polyline around the area. If set to **Region**, AutoCAD creates a closed 2D area. A region may be used for area calculations, shading, extruding a solid model, or other purposes.

The **Boundary set** drop-down list has the **Current viewport** setting active. A *boundary set* is the portion or area of the drawing that AutoCAD evaluates when defining a boundary. The **Current viewport** option defines the boundary set from everything visible in the current viewport, even if it is not in the current display. The **New** button, located to the right of the drop-down list, allows you to define a boundary set. When you pick this button, the **Boundary Creation** dialog box closes and the

AutoCAD and its Applications—Basics

**Figure 15-27.**
The **Boundary Creation** dialog box.

Select the type of boundary object

Select the boundary set

Pick to include or exclude objects inside the boundary

Pick to create a polyline or region boundary

Pick to define a new boundary set

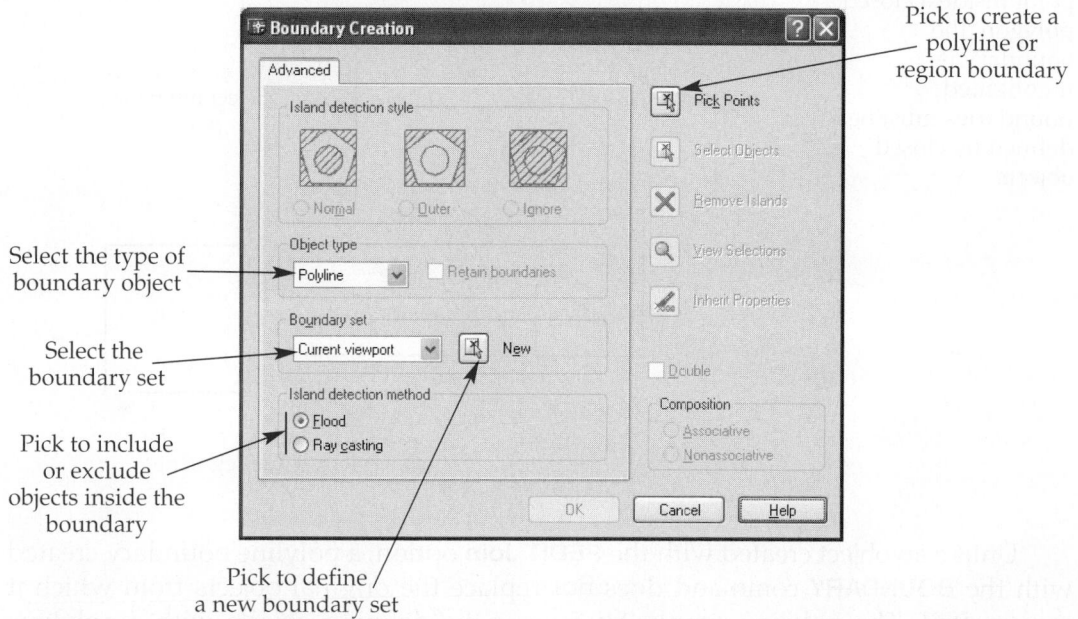

Select objects: prompt appears. You can then select the objects you want to use to create a boundary set. After you are done, press [Enter]. The **Boundary Creation** dialog box returns with **Existing set** active in the **Boundary set** drop-down list. This means that the boundary set is defined from the objects that you selected.

The **Island detection method** area is used to specify whether objects within the boundary are used as boundary objects. Objects inside a boundary are called *islands*, **Figure 15-28.** There are two options in the **Island detection method** area. Activate the **Flood** radio button if you want islands to be included as boundary objects. Activate the **Ray casting** radio button if you do not want to include islands as boundary objects.

The only other active feature in the **Boundary Creation** dialog box is the **Pick Points** button, which is located in the upper-right corner. When you pick this button, the **Boundary Creation** dialog box closes and the Select internal point: prompt appears. If the point you pick is inside a closed polygon, the boundary is highlighted, as shown in **Figure 15-29.** If the point you pick is not within a closed polygon, the **Boundary Definition Error** alert box appears. Pick **OK**, close the area in which you want to pick, and try again.

**Figure 15-28.**
Objects within a boundary, called islands, can be included or excluded when defining a boundary set.

Boundary

Area within boundary

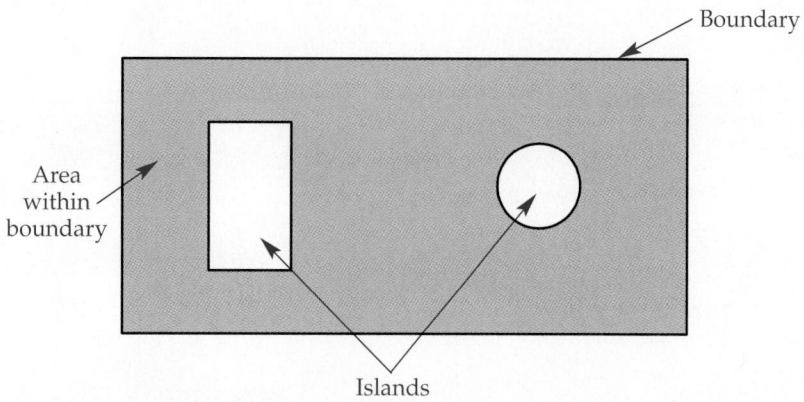

Islands

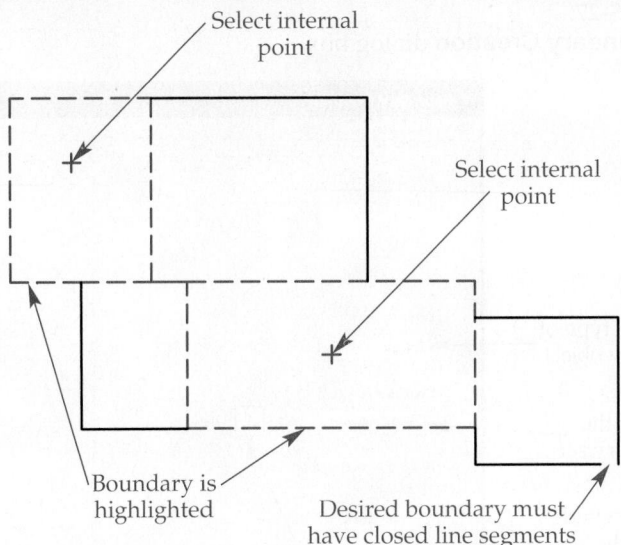

**Figure 15-29.**
When you select a point inside a closed polygon, the boundary is highlighted. Boundaries must be defined by closed objects.

Select internal point

Select internal point

Boundary is highlighted

Desired boundary must have closed line segments

Unlike an object created with the **PEDIT Join** option, a polyline boundary created with the **BOUNDARY** command does not replace the original objects from which it was created. The polyline simply *traces* over the defining objects with a polyline. Thus, the separate objects still exist and are *underneath* the newly created boundary. To avoid duplicate geometry, move the boundary to another location on screen, erase the original defining objects, and then move the boundary back to its original position.

**PROFESSIONAL TIP**

Area calculations can be simplified by first using the **BOUNDARY** command, or by joining objects with the **PEDIT Join** option, before issuing the **AREA** command. Then, use the **AREA Object** option to perform the area calculation. The **AREA** command is covered in Chapter 16. If you want to retain the original separate objects and the **PEDIT Join** option was used, explode the joined polyline after the area calculation. If the **BOUNDARY** command was used, simply erase the polyline boundary after the calculation.

# Chapter Test

*Answer the following questions on a separate sheet of paper.*

1. Give the command and entries required to create a polyline arc with a starting width of 0 and an ending width of .25. Draw the arc from a known center to an endpoint.
   - A. Command: _____
   - B. Specify start point: _____
   - C. Specify next point or [Arc/Close/Halfwidth/Length/Undo/Width]: _____
   - D. Specify starting width: _____
   - E. Specify ending width: _____
   - F. Specify next point or [Arc/Close/Halfwidth/Length/Undo/Width]: _____
   - G. Specify endpoint of arc or [Angle/CEnter/CLose/Direction/Halfwidth/Line/Radius/ Second pt/Undo/Width]: _____
   - H. Specify center point of arc: _____
   - I. Specify endpoint of arc or [Angle/Length]: _____
   - J. Specify endpoint of arc or [Angle/CEnter/CLose/Direction/Halfwidth/Line/Radius/ Second pt/Undo/Width]: _____

2. Give the command and entries required to turn three connected lines into a single polyline.
   - A. Command: _____
   - B. Select polyline or [Multiple]: _____
   - C. Object selected is not a polyline.
     Do you want to turn it into one? <Y>: _____
   - D. Enter an option [Close/Join/Width/Edit vertex/Fit/Spline/Decurve/Ltype gen/Undo]: _____
   - E. Select objects: _____
   - F. Select objects: _____
   - G. Select objects: _____
   - H. Enter an option [Close/Join/Width/Edit vertex/Fit/Spline/ Decurve/Ltype gen/Undo]: _____

3. Which system variable controls the display of the prompt in 2C?

4. Give the command and entries needed to change the width of a polyline from .1 to .25.
   - A. Command: _____
   - B. Select polyline or [Multiple]: _____
   - C. Enter an option [Close/Join/Width/Edit vertex/Fit/Spline/Decurve/Ltype gen/Undo]: _____
   - D. Specify new width for all segments: _____
   - E. Enter an option [Close/Join/Width/Edit vertex/Fit/Spline/Decurve/Ltype gen/Undo]: _____

*For Questions 5 through 11, give the **PEDIT Edit vertex** option that relates to the definition given.*

5. Moves the "X" marker to the next position.
6. Moves a polyline vertex to a new location.
7. Breaks a polyline at a point or between two points.
8. Generates the revised version of a polyline.
9. Specifies a tangent direction.
10. Adds a new polyline vertex.
11. Returns you to the **PEDIT** command prompt.
12. Which **PEDIT** command option and suboption allow you to change the starting and ending widths of a polyline?
13. Why may it appear that nothing happens after you change the starting and ending widths of a polyline?

---

14. Name the **PEDIT** command option and the **Edit vertex** suboption used for curve fitting.
15. Which command will remove all width characteristics and tangency information from a polyline?
16. Which two **PEDIT** command options allow you to open a closed polyline and close an open polyline?
17. When you enter the **Edit vertex** option of the **PEDIT** command, where is the "X" marker placed by AutoCAD?
18. How do you move the "X" marker to edit a different polyline vertex?
19. Can you use the **Fit** option of the **PEDIT** command without using the **Tangent** vertex editing suboption first?
20. Explain the difference between a fit curve and a spline curve.
21. Compare a quadratic curve, cubic curve, and fit curve.
22. Discuss the appearance of a quadratic curve.
23. Which **SPLINETYPE** system variable setting allows you to draw a quadratic curve?
24. Which **SPLINETYPE** setting allows you to draw a cubic curve?
25. Name the system variable that can be set to adjust the smoothness of a spline curve.
26. Name the pull-down menu and menu selections used to access the polyline editing options.
27. Explain how you can adjust the way polyline linetypes are generated using the **PEDIT** command.
28. Name the system variable that allows you to alter the way polyline linetypes are generated.
29. Name the command used to create a polyline boundary.
30. Name the command that can be used to create a true spline.
31. How do you accept the AutoCAD defaults for the start and end tangents of a spline?
32. Name the **SPLINE** command option that allows you to turn a spline-fitted polyline into a true spline.
33. Name the command that allows you to edit splines.
34. What is the purpose of the **Add** suboption of the **SPLINEDIT Fit data** option?
35. What is the minimum number of fit points for spline?
36. Name the **SPLINEDIT** option that allows you to move the fit points in a spline.
37. What is the purpose of the **SPLINEDIT Refine** option?
38. Identify the **SPLINEDIT Refine** suboption that lets you increase, but not decrease, the number of control points appearing on a spline curve.
39. Name the **SPLINEDIT** refine option that controls the pull exerted by a control point on a spline.
40. How many operations can you undo inside the **SPLINEDIT** command with the **Undo** option?

## Drawing Problems

*Start a new drawing for each of the following problems. Specify your own units, limits, and other settings to suit each problem.*

1. Draw the single polyline shown below. Use the **PLINE Arc**, **Width**, and **Close** options to complete the shape. Set the polyline width to 0, except at the points indicated. Save the drawing as P15-1.

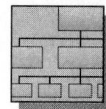

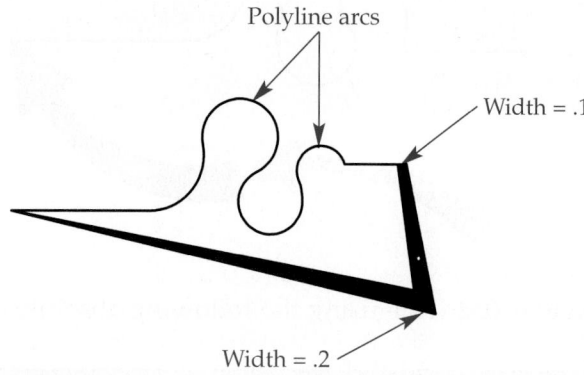

2. Draw the two curved arrows shown below using the **PLINE Arc** and **Width** options. The arrowheads should have a starting width of 1.4 and an ending width of 0. The body of each arrow should have a beginning width of .8 and an ending width of .4. Save the drawing as P15-2.

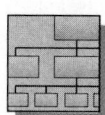

3. Open drawing P15-1 and make a copy of the original object to edit. Use the **PEDIT** command to change the object drawn into a rectangle. Use the **PEDIT Decurve** and **Width** options and the **Straighten**, **Insert**, and **Move** vertex editing suboptions. Save the completed drawing as P15-3.

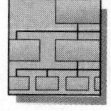

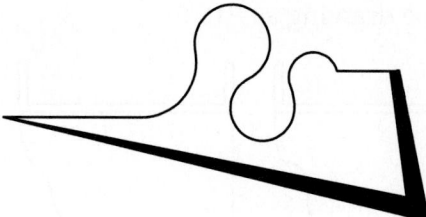

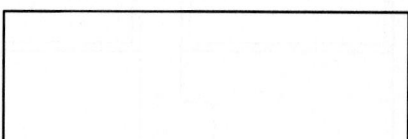

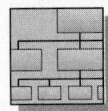

4. Open drawing P15-2 and make the following changes. Then, save the drawing as P15-4.
   A. Combine the two polylines using the **PEDIT Join** option.
   B. Change the beginning width of the left arrow to 1.0 and the ending width to .2.
   C. Draw a polyline .062 wide similar to Line A as shown.

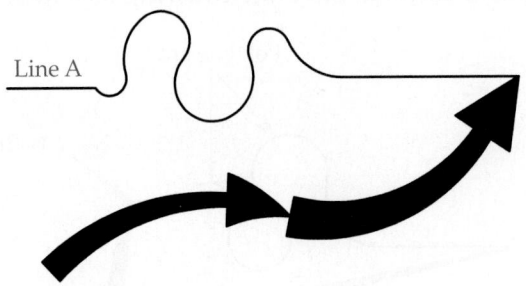

Line A

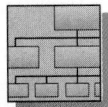

5. Draw a polyline .032 wide using the following absolute coordinates.

| Point | Coordinates | Point | Coordinates | Point | Coordinates |
|-------|-------------|-------|-------------|-------|-------------|
| 1 | 1,1 | 5 | 3,3 | 9 | 5,5 |
| 2 | 2,1 | 6 | 4,3 | 10 | 6,5 |
| 3 | 2,2 | 7 | 4,4 | 11 | 6,6 |
| 4 | 3,2 | 8 | 5,4 | 12 | 7,6 |

Copy the polyline three times so there are four polylines. Use the **PEDIT Fit** option to smooth the first copy. Use the **PEDIT Spline** option to turn the second copy into a quadratic curve. Make the third copy into a cubic curve. Use the **PEDIT Decurve** option to return one of the three copies to its original form. Save the drawing as P15-5.

6. Use the **PLINE** command to draw a patio plan similar to the one shown in Example A below. Draw the house walls 6" wide. Copy the drawing three times and use the **PEDIT** command to create the remaining designs shown. Use the **Fit** option for Example B, a quadratic spline for Example C, and a cubic spline for Example D. Change the **SPLINETYPE** system variable as required. Save the drawing as P15-6.

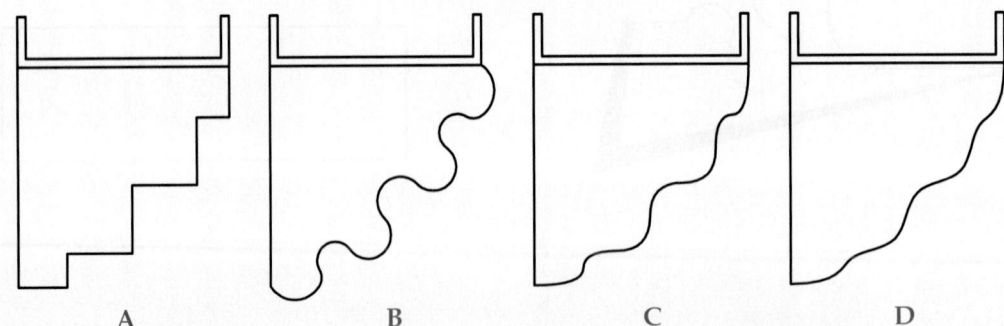

A           B           C           D

7. Open drawing P15-6 and create four new patio designs. This time, use grips to edit the polylines and create designs similar to Examples A, B, C, and D below. Save the drawing as P15-7.

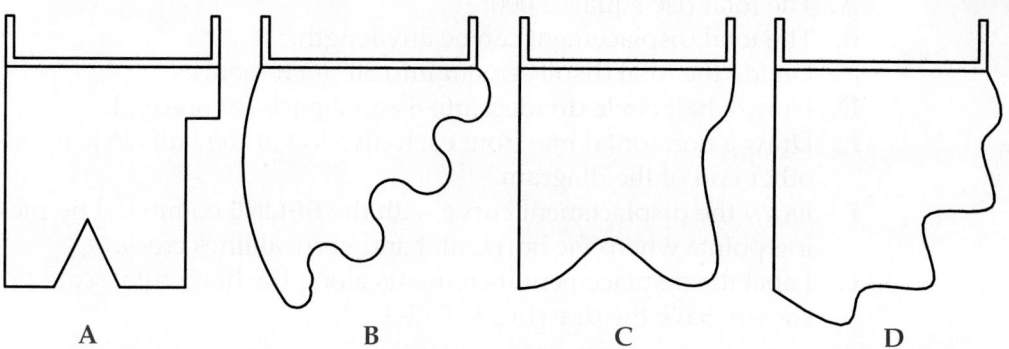

A            B            C            D

8. Use **SPLINE** and other commands, such as **ELLIPSE**, **MIRROR**, **OFFSET**, and **PLINE**, to design an architectural door knocker similar to the one shown. Use an appropriate text command and font to place your initials in the center. Save the drawing as P15-8.

9. Use the **SPLINE** command to draw the curve for the cam displacement diagram below. Use the following guidelines and the given drawing to complete this problem.
   A. The total rise equals 2.000.
   B. The total displacement can be any length.
   C. Divide the total displacement into 30° increments.
   D. Draw a half circle divided into 6 equal parts on one end.
   E. Draw a horizontal line from each division of the half circle to the other end of the diagram.
   F. Draw the displacement curve with the **SPLINE** command by picking points where the horizontal and vertical lines cross.
   G. Label the displacement increments along the horizontal scale as shown. Save the drawing as P15-9.

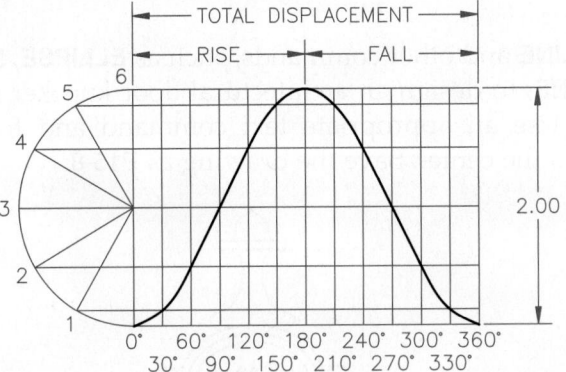

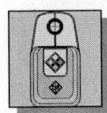

10. Draw a spline similar to the original spline shown below. Copy the spline seven times to create a layout similar to the one given. Perform the **SPLINEDIT** operations identified under each of the seven copies. Save the drawing as P15-10.

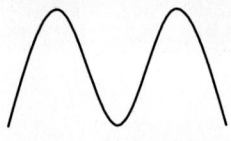

Original Spline

Close

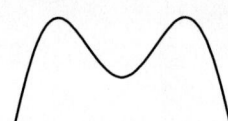

Move a Control Point

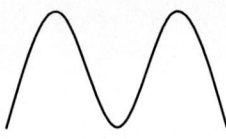

Elevate the Order to 10

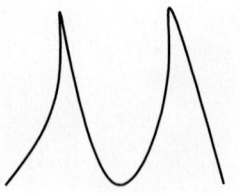

Add Two Control Points

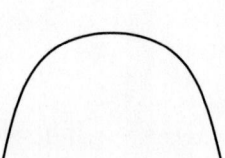

Delete a Control Point

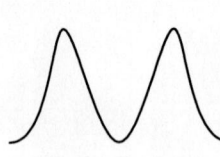

Edit the Tangents

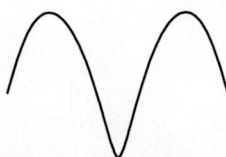

Increase the Weight of a Control Point to 4

## CHAPTER 16

# Obtaining Information about the Drawing

## Learning Objectives

After completing this chapter, you will be able to do the following:

- Use the **AREA** command to calculate the area of an object by adding and subtracting objects.
- List data related to a single point, object, group of objects, or an entire drawing.
- Find the distance between two points.
- Identify a point location.
- Determine the amount of time spent in a drawing session.
- Determine the status of drawing parameters.

When working on a drawing, you may need to ask AutoCAD for information about the drawing, such as object distances and areas. You can also ask AutoCAD to tell you how much time you have spent on a drawing. The commands that allow you to do this include **AREA**, **DBLIST** (database list), **DIST** (distance), **ID** (identification), **LIST**, **STATUS**, and **TIME**.

These commands are accessed from the **Inquiry** cascading menu in the **Tools** pull-down menu. You can also access these commands from the **Inquiry** toolbar. See **Figure 16-1**. To display this toolbar, pick **Toolbars...** from the **View** pull-down menu. Then, check the check box next to **Inquiry** in the **Toolbars** tab and pick **Close**. You can also display the toolbar by right-clicking on any visible toolbar and selecting **Inquiry** from the shortcut menu.

> **NOTE**
>
>
>
> The **Region/Mass Properties** button or pull-down menu entry provides data related to the properties of a 2D region or 3D solid. This topic is discussed in *AutoCAD and its Applications—Advanced.*

**Figure 16-1.**
The inquiry commands are grouped in the **Inquiry** cascading menu in the **Tools** pull-down menu and on the **Inquiry** toolbar.

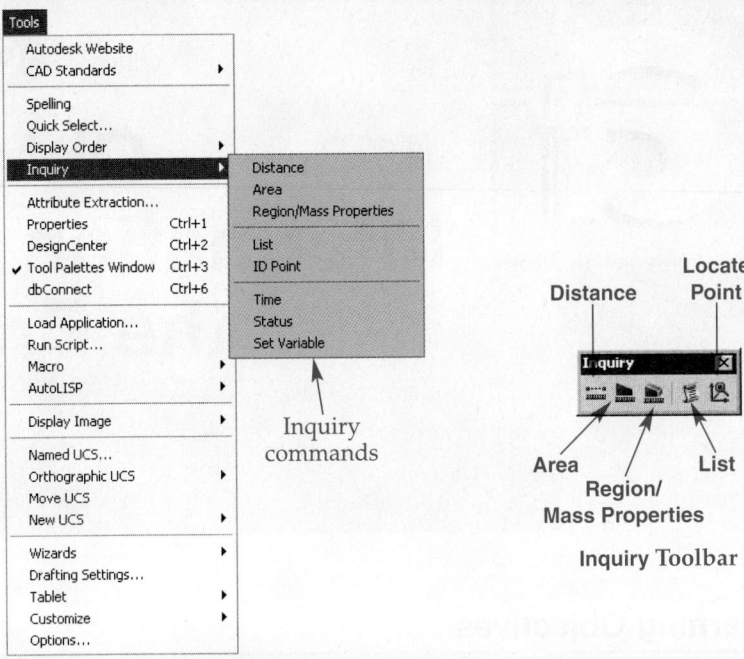

Inquiry commands

Inquiry Cascading Menu

Inquiry Toolbar

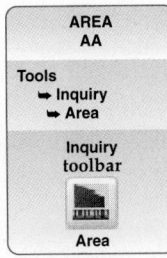

AREA
AA

Tools
➡ Inquiry
➡ Area

Inquiry toolbar

Area

## Finding the Area of Shapes and Objects

The most basic function of the **AREA** command is to find the area of any object, circle, polygon, polyline, or spline. The command sequence is:

Command: **AA** *or* **AREA**↵
Specify first corner point or [Object/Add/Subtract]: **O**↵
Select objects: *(pick the object)*
Area = *n.nn*, Circumference = *n.nn*
Command:

The two numeric values represented by *n.nn* indicate the area and circumference of the object. The second value returned by the **AREA** command varies depending on the type of object selected, as shown in the following table:

| Object | Value returned |
|---|---|
| Line | Does not have an area (no value given) |
| Polyline | Length or perimeter |
| Circle | Circumference |
| Spline | Length or perimeter |
| Rectangle | Perimeter |

**PROFESSIONAL TIP**

AutoCAD gives you the area between three or more points picked on the screen, even if the three points are not connected by lines. The perimeter of the selected points is also given.

---

Shapes drawn with polylines do not need to be closed for AutoCAD to calculate their area. AutoCAD calculates the area as if a line segment connects the first and last points.

To find the area of a shape created with the **LINE** command, pick all the vertices of that shape. This is the default mode of the **AREA** command. Setting a running object snap mode such as **Endpoint** or **Intersection** will help you pick the vertices. See **Figure 16-2.**

> Command: **AREA**↵
> Specify first corner point or [Object/Add/Subtract]: *(pick point 1)*
> Specify next corner point or press ENTER for total: *(pick point 2)*
> Specify next corner point or press ENTER for total: *(continue picking points until all corners of the object have been selected; then press* [Enter]*)*
> Area = *n.nn*, Perimeter = *n.nn*
> Command:

**Figure 16-2.**
Pick all vertices to find the area of an object drawn with the **LINE** command.

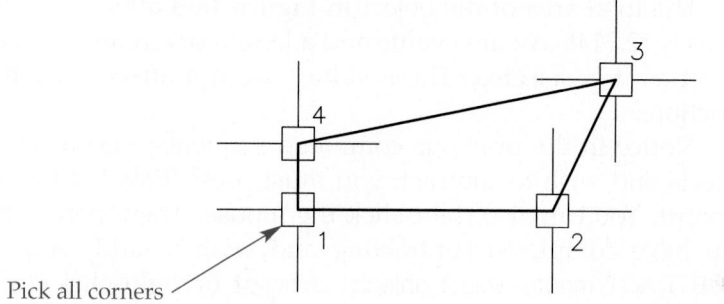

Pick all corners

## Adding and Subtracting Areas

If you use the **Add** option of the **AREA** command, you can pick multiple objects or areas. As you add objects or areas, a running total of the area is automatically calculated. The **Subtract** option allows you to remove objects or areas from the selection set. Once either of these options is entered, the **AREA** command remains in effect until canceled.

The next example shows how to use these two options in the same operation. Polyline-based objects are selected in the operation. Refer to **Figure 16-3** as you go through the following command sequence:

> Command: **AREA**↵
> Specify first corner point or [Object/Add/Subtract]: **A**↵
> Specify first corner point or [Object/Subtract]: **O**↵
> (ADD mode) Select objects: *(pick the polyline)*
> Area = 13.7854, Length = 20.1416
> Total area = 13.7854
> (ADD mode) Select objects: ↵
> Specify first corner point or [Object/Subtract]: **S**↵
> Specify first corner point or [Object/Add]: **O**↵
> (SUBTRACT mode) Select objects: *(pick the first circle)*
> Area = 0.7854, Circumference = 3.1416
> Total area = 13.0000
> (SUBTRACT mode) Select objects: *(pick the second circle)*
> Area = 0.7854, Circumference = 3.1416
> Total area = 12.2146
> (SUBTRACT mode) Select objects: ↵
> Specify first corner point or [Object/Add]: ↵
> Command:

**Figure 16-3.**
To calculate the area of an object drawn with the **PLINE** command, first select the outer boundary of the object using the **AREA** command **Add** option. Then, select the inner boundaries (the circles) using the **AREA** command **Subtract** option. This will calculate the area of the object.

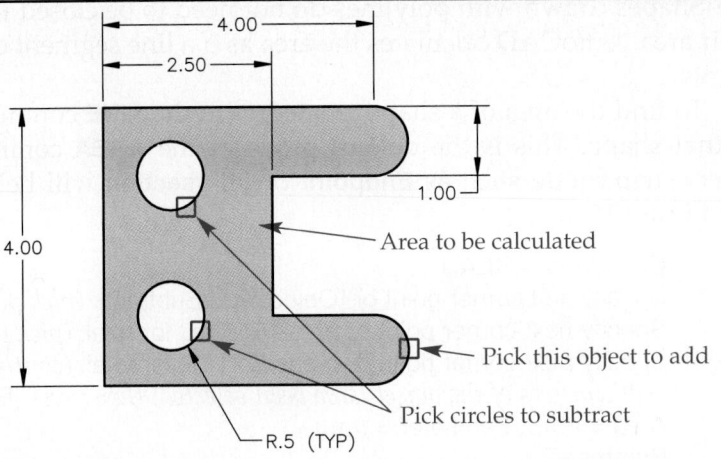

4.00

2.50

1.00

4.00

Area to be calculated

Pick this object to add

Pick circles to subtract

R.5 (TYP)

The total area of the object in **Figure 16-3** after subtracting the areas of the two holes is 12.2146. An area value and a length or circumference value are given for each object as it is selected. These values are not affected by the adding or subtracting functions.

Notice in the previous command sequence that when you are finished adding objects and wish to subtract, you must press [Enter] at the (ADD mode) Select objects: prompt. You can also right-click the mouse. Then, type S to enter subtract mode. If you have completed subtracting and wish to add, you must press [Enter] at the (SUBTRACT mode) Select objects: prompt or right-click the mouse. Then, type A to enter Add mode.

**PROFESSIONAL TIP**

Calculating area, circumference, and perimeter values of shapes drawn with the **LINE** command can be time-consuming. You must pick each vertex on the object. If you need to calculate areas, it is best to create lines and arcs with the **PLINE** or **SPLINE** command. Then use the **AREA** command **Object** option when adding or subtracting objects.

## Exercise 16-1

○ Start a new drawing or use one of your templates.
○ Draw the objects shown below. Use the dimensions given. The exact locations of the cutout and holes are not important.
○ Use the **AREA** command to determine the:
   1. Area of large rectangle.
   2. Perimeter of large rectangle.
   3. Perimeter of small rectangle.
   4. Circumference of one circle.
   5. Area of large rectangle minus the areas of the three shapes.
○ Save the drawing as EX16-1. This drawing is used for the next exercise.

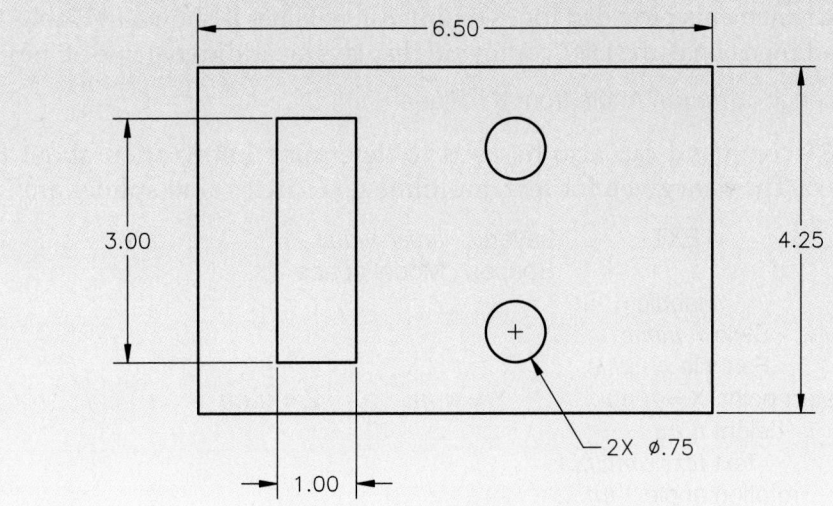

## Listing Drawing Data

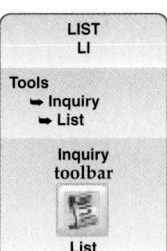

LIST
LI
Tools
➥ Inquiry
  ➥ List
Inquiry
toolbar
List

The **LIST** command enables you to display data about any AutoCAD object. Line lengths, circle or arc locations and radii, polyline widths, and object layers are just a few of the items you can identify with the **LIST** command. You can select several objects to list. The command sequence is:

Command: **LI** *or* **LIST**↵
Select objects: *(pick one or more objects using any selection method)*
Select objects: ↵

When you press [Enter], the data for each of the objects picked are displayed in the text window. The following data are given for a line:

LINE          Layer:        *layer name*
                    Space:        Model space
              Handle = *nn*
from point,    X = *nn.nn*        Y = *nn.nn*        Z = *nn.nn*
  to point,    X = *nn.nn*        Y = *nn.nn*        Z = *nn.nn*
Length = *nn.nn*,        Angle in XY Plane = *nn.nn*
      Delta X = *nn.nn*,        Delta Y = *nn.nn*,        Delta Z = *nn.nn*

The delta X and delta Y values indicate the horizontal and vertical distances between the *from point* and *to point* of the line. These two values, along with the length and angle, provide you with four measurements for a single line. An example of the

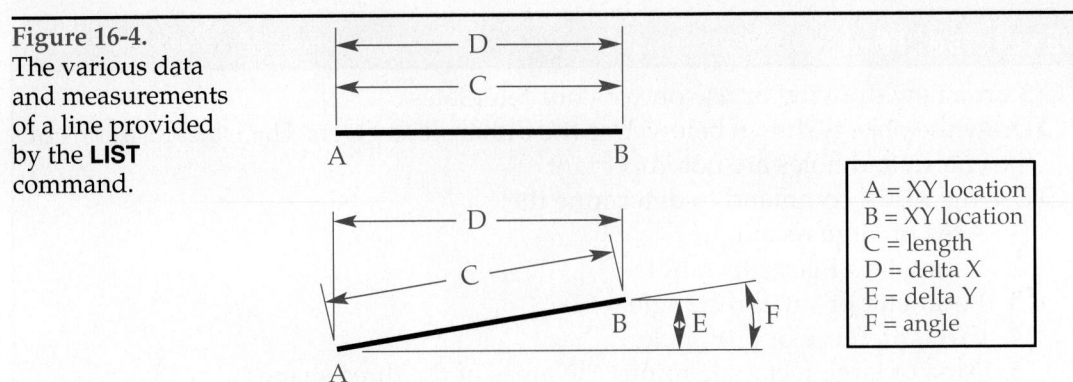

**Figure 16-4.**
The various data and measurements of a line provided by the **LIST** command.

A = XY location
B = XY location
C = length
D = delta X
E = delta Y
F = angle

data and measurements provided for two-dimensional lines is shown in **Figure 16-4.** If a line is three-dimensional, the **LIST** command displays an additional line of information:

3D Length = *nn.nn*, Angle from XY Plane = *nn.nn*

The **LIST** command can also be used to determine information about text and multiline text. The data given for text, multiline text, circles, and splines are:

```
TEXT              Layer:    layer name
                  Space:    Model space
        Handle = nn
     Style = name
     Font file = name
start point, X = n.nn      Y = n.nn        Z = n.nn
     height n.nn
        text text contents
     rotation angle   nn
     width scale factor      n.nn
     obliquing angle         nn
generation normal
```

```
MTEXT             Layer:    layer name
                  Space:    Model space
        Handle = nn
Location:         X = n.nn      Y = n.nn        Z = n.nn
Width:            n.nn
Normal:           X = n.nn      Y = n.nn        Z = n.nn
Rotation:         nn
Text style:       style name
Text height:      n.nn
Line spacing:     Multiple n.nn = n.nn
Attachment:       corner of multiline text insertion point
Flow direction:   direction text is read based on language
Contents:         multiline text contents
```

```
CIRCLE       Layer:     layer name
             Space:     Model space
Handle = nn
           center point,    X = n.nn        Y = n.nn        Z = n.nn
           radius           n.nn
       circumference        n.nn
             area           n.nn


SPLINE       Layer:     layer name
             Space:     Model space
Handle = nn
              Length:    n.nn
               Order:    n.nn
          Properties:    Planar, Non-Rational, Non-Periodic
   Parametric Range:     Start n.nn
                         End n.nn
Number of control points:    n
      Control Points:    X = n.nn,        Y = n.nn,        Z = n.nn
                         (the XYZ of all control points are listed)
Number of fit points:    n
           User Data:    Fit Points
                         X = n.nn,        Y = n.nn,        Z = n.nn
                         (the XYZ of all fit points are listed)
    Fit point tolerance: n.nn
```

**PROFESSIONAL TIP**

The **LIST** command is the most powerful inquiry command in AutoCAD. It provides all the information you need to know about an object. Also, when selecting an object from the polyline family, the **LIST** command reports the area and perimeter of the object so you do not need to use the **AREA** command. The **LIST** command also reports an object's color and linetype, unless both are "by layer."

## Listing Drawing Data for All Objects

The **DBLIST** (database list) command lists all data for every object in the current drawing. This command is initiated by typing DBLIST at the Command: prompt. The information is provided in the same format used by the **LIST** command. As soon as you enter the **DBLIST** command, the data begin to quickly scroll up the screen in the text window. The scrolling stops when a complete page (or screen) is filled with database information. Press [Enter] to scroll to the end of the next page. Use the scroll buttons to move forward and backward through the listing.

If you find the data you need, press the [Esc] key to exit the **DBLIST** command. You can exit the text window by pressing the [F2] function key.

The **DIST** (distance) command is used to find the distance between two points. As with the **AREA** command, use object snap modes to accurately pick locations. The **DIST** command provides the distance between the points and the angle of the line from the positive X axis. It also gives delta X, Y, and Z dimensions.

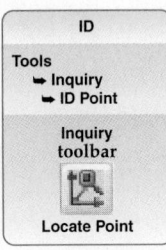

DIST
DI

Tools
➥ Inquiry
➥ Distance

Inquiry
toolbar

Distance

To access the **DIST** command, pick the **Distance** button in the **Inquiry** toolbar, select **Distance** from the **Inquiry** cascading menu in the **Tools** pull-down menu, or type DI or DIST at the Command: prompt. The button and pull-down selections issue the command transparently and can be used within other commands.

Command: **DI** or **DIST**↵
Specify first point: (select point)
Specify second point: (select point)
Distance = n.nn, Angle in XY Plane = n, Angle from XY Plane = n
Delta X = n.nn, Delta Y = n.nn, Delta Z = n.nn
Command:

# Identifying Point Locations

ID

Tools
➥ Inquiry
➥ ID Point

Inquiry
toolbar

Locate Point

The **ID** command gives the coordinate location of a single point on screen. This command can be used to find the coordinates of a line endpoint or the center of a circle. Simply pick the point to be identified when the Specify point: prompt appears. Use the object snap modes for accuracy.

Command: **ID**↵
Specify point: (select the point)
X = nn.nn          Y = nn.nn          Z = nn.nn
Command:

In conjunction with "blip" mode, the **ID** command can help you identify where a coordinate is on screen. Suppose you want to see where the point (X = 8.75, Y = 6.44) is located. Enter these numbers at the Specify point: prompt. AutoCAD responds by placing a blip (marker) at that exact location. In order to use this feature, the **BLIPMODE** system variable must be on.

Command: **BLIPMODE**↵
Enter mode [ON/OFF] <ON>: **ON**↵
Command: **ID**↵
Specify point: **8.75,6.44**↵
X = 8.75 Y = 6.44 Z = 0.00
Command:

○ Open EX16-1 if it is not currently on screen.

○ Use the **LIST** command to display information about one circle and one line on the drawing.

○ Enter the **DBLIST** command to display information about your drawing.

○ Press the [Enter] key to display the end of the list and then press the [Esc] key to exit the command.

○ Use the proper command and object snap modes to find:

○ Distance between the center points of the two circles.

○ Distance between the center point of the lower circle and the lower-left corner of the large rectangle.

○ Distance between the lower-left and upper-right corners of the large rectangle.

○ Coordinates of the center point of the upper circle.

○ Coordinates of the lower-left corner of the small rectangle.

○ Coordinates of the midpoint of the large rectangle's right side.

○ Location of point (6,4) on your screen.

○ Save the drawing as EX16-2 and quit.

## Checking the Time

TIME

Tools
➥ Inquiry
➥ Time

The **TIME** command allows you to display the current time, time related to your drawing, and time related to the current drawing session. The following information is displayed in the text window when the **TIME** command is entered:

```
Command: TIME↵
Current time:                 Wednesday, February 14, 2004 at 13:39:22:210 PM
Times for this drawing:
  Created:                    Monday, February 12, 2004 at 10:24:48:130 AM
  Last updated:               Monday, February 12, 2004 at 14:36:23:46 PM
  Total editing time:         0 days 01:23:57:930
  Elapsed timer (on):         0 days 00:35:28:650
  Next automatic save in:     0 days 01:35:26:680
Enter option [Display/ON/OFF/Reset]:
```

There are a few things to keep in mind when checking the text window display after issuing the **TIME** command. First, the drawing creation time starts when you begin a new drawing, not when a new drawing is first saved. Second, the **SAVE** command affects the Last updated: time. However, if you exit AutoCAD and do not save the drawing, all time in that session is discarded. Finally, you can time a specific drawing task by using the **TIME** command **Reset** option to reset the elapsed timer.

When the **TIME** command is issued, the times shown in the text window are static. This means that none of the times are being updated. You can request an update by using the **Display** option:

```
Enter option [Display/ON/OFF/Reset]: D↵
```

When you enter the drawing area, the timer is on by default. If you want to stop the timer, simply enter OFF at the Enter option [Display/ON/OFF/Reset]: prompt. If the timer is off, enter ON to start it again.

---

**NOTE** The Windows operating system maintains the date and time settings for the computer. You can change these settings in the Windows Control Panel. To access the Control Panel, pick Settings and then Control Panel from the Start menu.

### Exercise 16-3

❍ Open any of your saved drawings.
❍ Enter the **TIME** command and study the information that is displayed.
❍ If the current date and time are incorrect, inform your instructor or supervisor. Then, set the correct date and time.
❍ Update the **TIME** command display.
❍ Reset the elapsed timer.
❍ Exit AutoCAD without saving your drawing.

## Determining the Drawing Status

**STATUS**
Tools
➥ Inquiry
➥ Status

While working on a drawing, you may forget some of the drawing parameters, such as the limits, grid spacing, or snap values. All the information about a drawing can be displayed using the **STATUS** command. Access this command by typing STATUS at the Command: prompt or selecting **Status** from the **Inquiry** cascading menu in the **Tools** pull-down menu. The drawing information is displayed in the text window. See **Figure 16-5.**

The number of objects in a drawing refers to the total number of objects—both erased and existing. Drawing aid settings are shown along with the current settings for layer, linetype, and color. These topics are discussed in later chapters of this text. Free drawing (dwg) disk space represents the space left on the drive containing your drawing file.

**Figure 16-5.**
The drawing information listed by the **STATUS** command is shown in the text window.

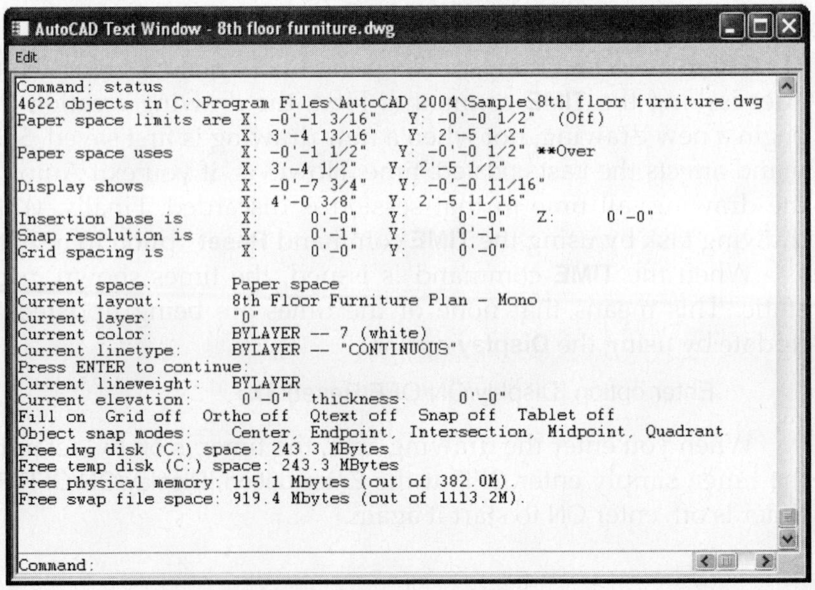

```
AutoCAD Text Window - 8th floor furniture.dwg
Edit
Command: status
4622 objects in C:\Program Files\AutoCAD 2004\Sample\8th floor furniture.dwg
Paper space limits are X: -0'-1 3/16"   Y: -0'-0 1/2"  (Off)
                       X: 3'-4 13/16"   Y: 2'-5 1/2"
Paper space uses       X: -0'-1 1/2"   Y: -0'-0 1/2" **Over
                       X: 3'-4 1/2"   Y: 2'-5 1/2"
Display shows          X: -0'-7 3/4"   Y: -0'-0 11/16"
                       X: 4'-0 3/8"   Y: 2'-5 11/16"
Insertion base is      X:    0'-0"   Y:    0'-0"   Z:    0'-0"
Snap resolution is     X:    0'-1"   Y:    0'-1"
Grid spacing is        X:    0'-0"   Y:    0'-0"

Current space:        Paper space
Current layout:       8th Floor Furniture Plan - Mono
Current layer:        "0"
Current color:        BYLAYER -- 7 (white)
Current linetype:     BYLAYER -- "CONTINUOUS"
Press ENTER to continue:
Current lineweight:   BYLAYER
Current elevation:     0'-0"  thickness:      0'-0"
Fill on  Grid off  Ortho off  Qtext off  Snap off  Tablet off
Object snap modes:    Center, Endpoint, Intersection, Midpoint, Quadrant
Free dwg disk (C:) space: 243.3 MBytes
Free temp disk (C:) space: 243.3 MBytes
Free physical memory: 115.1 Mbytes (out of 382.0M).
Free swap file space: 919.4 Mbytes (out of 1113.2M).

Command:
```

When you have completed reviewing the information, press [F2] to close the text window. You can also switch to the graphics window without closing the text window by picking anywhere inside the graphics window or using the Windows [Alt]+[Tab] feature.

**NOTE** Another way to move between the graphics window and the text window is provided with the AutoCAD commands **GRAPHSCR** and **TEXTSCR**. Typing TEXTSCR at the Command: prompt displays the text window. Typing GRAPHSCR closes the text window. You can also open to the text window by selecting **Text Window** from the **Display** cascading menu in the **View** pull-down menu.

## Chapter Test

*Answer the following questions on a separate sheet of paper.*

1. To add the areas of several objects when using the **AREA** command, when do you select the **Add** option?
2. When using the **AREA** command, explain how picking a polyline is different from picking an object drawn with the **LINE** command.
3. What information is provided by the **AREA** command?
4. What is the **LIST** command used for?
5. Describe the meaning of delta X and delta Y.
6. What is the function of the **DBLIST** command?
7. How do you cancel the **DBLIST** command?
8. What are the two purposes of the **ID** command?
9. What information is provided by the **TIME** command?
10. When does the drawing creation time start?

## Drawing Problems

1. Draw the object shown below using the dimensions given. Check the time when you start the drawing. Draw all of the features using the **PLINE** and **CIRCLE** commands. Use the **Object**, **Add**, and **Subtract** options of the **AREA** command to calculate the following measurements:
   A. Area and perimeter of Object A.
   B. Area and perimeter of Object B.
   C. Area and circumference of one of the circles.
   D. Area of Object A minus the area of Object B.
   E. Area of Object A minus the areas of the other three features.
   F. Enter the **TIME** command and note the editing time spent on your drawing. Save the drawing as P16-1.

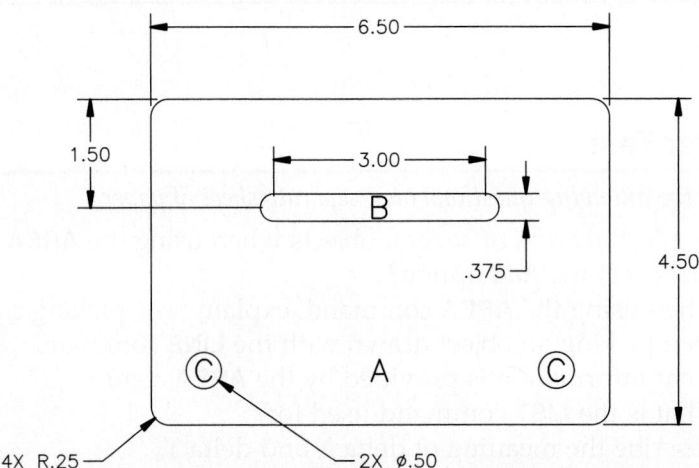

2. Draw the deck shown below using the **PLINE** command. Draw the hexagon using the **POLYGON** command. Use the following guidelines to complete this problem:
   A. Specify architectural units for your drawing. Use 1/2" fractions and decimal degrees. Leave the remaining settings for the drawing units at the default values.
   B. Set the limits to 100',80' and perform a **ZOOM All**.
   C. Set the grid spacing to 2' and the snap spacing to 1'.
   D. Calculate the measurements listed below.
      a. Area and perimeter of Object A.
      b. Area and perimeter of Object B.
      c. Area of Object A minus the area of Object B.
      d. Distance between Point C and Point D.
      e. Distance between Point E and Point C.
      f. Coordinates of Points C, D, and F.
   E. Enter the **DBLIST** command and check the information listed for your drawing.
   F. Enter the **TIME** command and note the total editing time spent on your drawing.
   G. Save the drawing as P16-2.

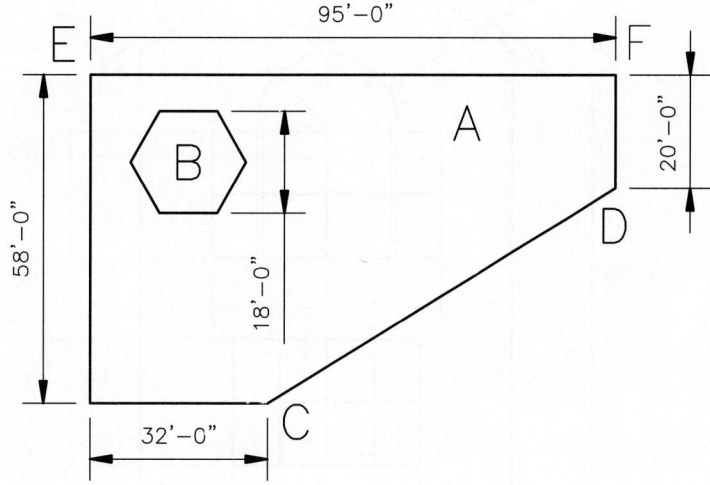

3. The drawing below is a view of the gable end of a house. Draw the house using the dimensions given. Draw the windows as single lines only (the location of the windows is not important). The spacing between the second-floor windows is 3″. The width of this end of the house is 16′-6″. The length of the roof is 40′. You may want to use the **PLINE** command to assist in creating specific shapes in this drawing, except as noted above. Save the drawing as P16-3. Then, calculate the following:

A. Total area of the roof.
B. Diagonal distance from one corner of the roof to the other.
C. Area of the first-floor window.
D. Total area of all second-floor windows, including the 3″ space between them.
E. Siding will cover the house. What is the total area of siding for this end?

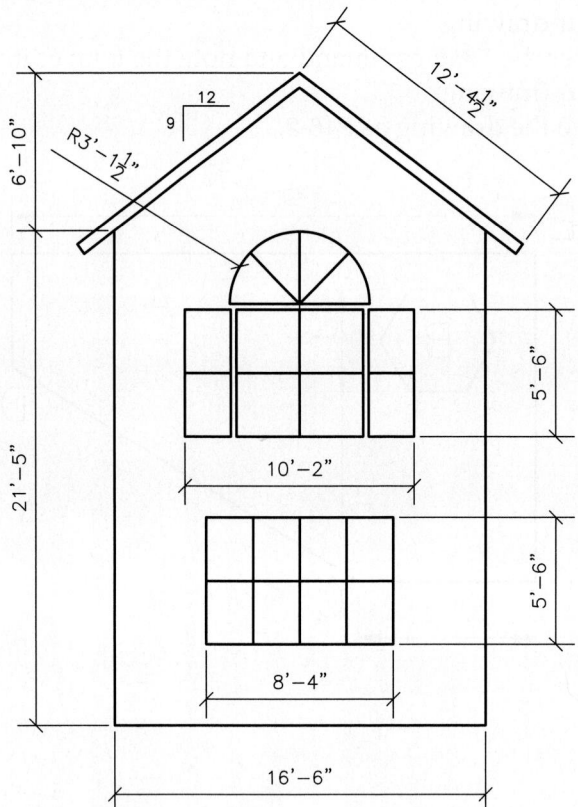

4. The drawing shown below is a side view of a pyramid. The pyramid has four sides. Create an auxiliary view showing the true size of a pyramid face. Save the drawing as **P16-4**. Using inquiry techniques, calculate:
    A. Area of one side.
    B. Perimeter of one side.
    C. Area of all four sides.
    D. Area of the base.
    E. True length (distance) from the midpoint of the base on one side to the apex.

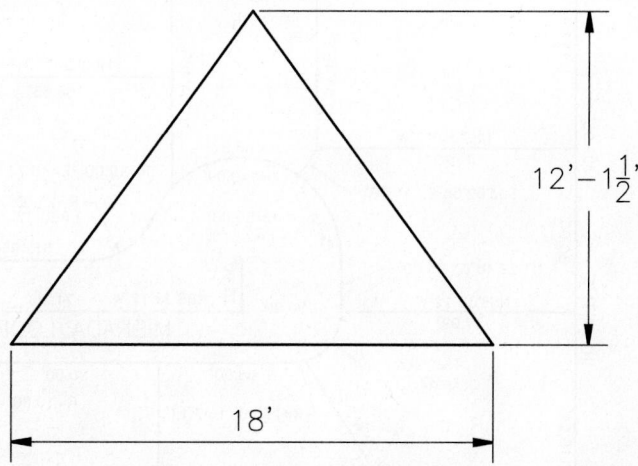

5. Draw the property plat shown below. Label property line bearings and distances only if required by your instructor. Calculate the area of the property plat in square feet and convert to acres. Save the drawing as **P16-5**.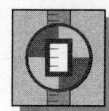

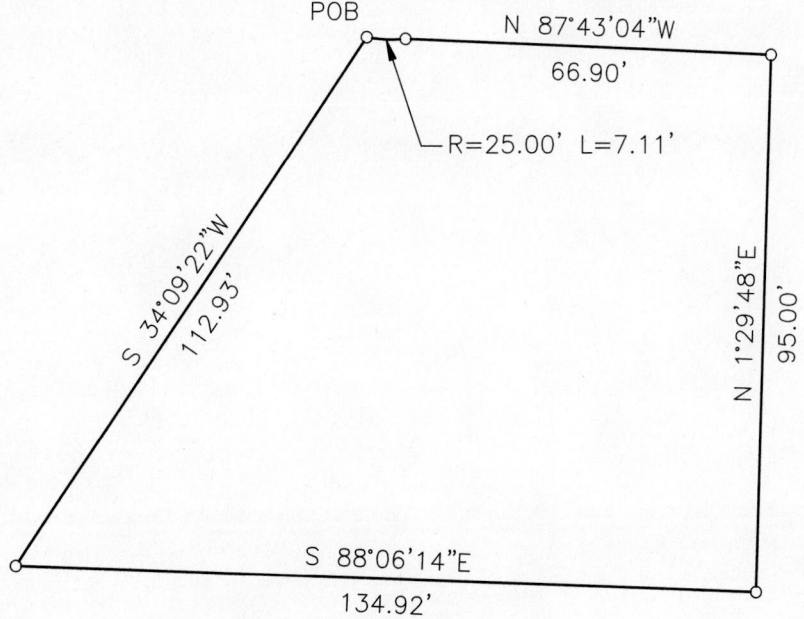

6. Draw the subdivision plat shown below. Label the drawing as shown. Calculate the acreage of each lot and record each value as a label inside the corresponding lot (for example, .249 AC). Save the drawing as P16-6.

# Basic Dimensioning Practices

## Learning Objectives

After completing this chapter, you will be able to do the following:

- Use the dimensioning commands to dimension given objects to ASME and other drafting standards.
- Control the appearance of dimensions.
- Add linear, angular, diameter, and radius dimensions to a drawing.
- Set the appropriate units and decimal places for dimension numbers.
- Use text size and style consistent with ASME and other professional standards.
- Use the proper character codes to display symbols within dimension text.
- Add dimensions to a separate layer.
- Place general notes on drawings.
- Draw datum and chain dimensions.
- Add dimensions for multiple items using the **QDIM** command.
- Dimension curves.
- Draw oblique dimensions.
- Use the **QLEADER** command to draw specific notes with linked leader lines.
- Dimension objects with arrowless tabular dimensions.
- Prepare thread symbols and notes.
- Create and use dimension styles.
- Create dimension style overrides.

*Dimensions* are given to describe the size, shape, and location of features on an object or structure. The dimension may consist of numerical values, lines, symbols, and notes. Typical AutoCAD dimensioning features and characteristics are shown in **Figure 17-1.**

Each drafting field (such as mechanical, architectural, civil, and electronics) uses a different type of dimensioning technique. It is important for a drafter to place dimensions in accordance with company and industry standards. The standard emphasized in this text is ASME Y14.5M-1994, *Dimensioning and Tolerancing*. The *M* in Y14.5M means the standard is written with metric numeric values. ASME Y14.5M-1994 is published by The American Society of Mechanical Engineers (ASME). The standard can be ordered directly from ASME, 345 E. 47th Street, New York, NY 10017. It can also be obtained from the American National Standards Institute (ANSI), 1430 Broadway, New York, NY 10018. This text discusses the correct application of both inch and metric dimensioning.

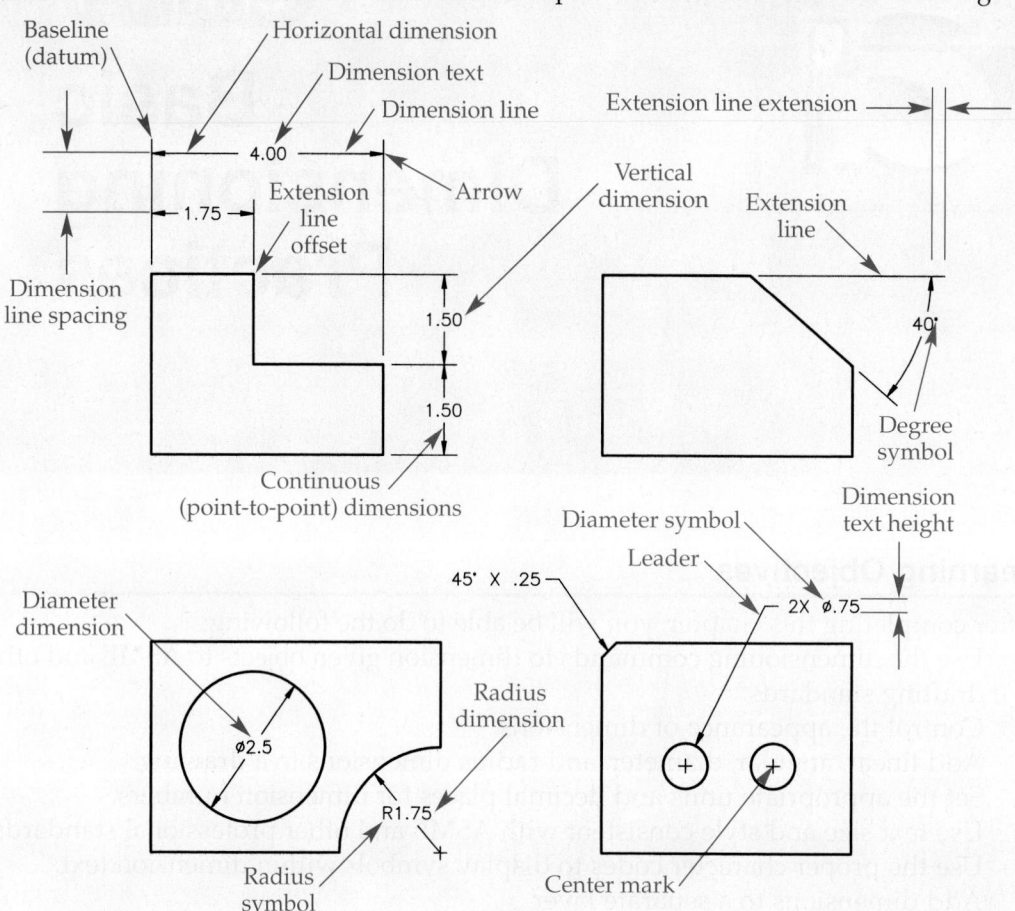

AutoCAD's dimensioning functions provide you with unlimited flexibility. Commands allow you to dimension linear distances, circles, and arcs. You can also place a note with an arrow and leader line pointing to the feature. In addition to these commands, dimension styles allow you to control the height, width, style, and spacing of individual components of a dimension.

This text covers the comprehensive elements of AutoCAD dimensioning in four chapters. This chapter covers fundamental standards and practices for dimensioning. Chapter 18 covers editing procedures for dimensions. Chapter 19 covers dimensioning applications with tolerances. Chapter 20 covers geometric dimensioning and tolerancing practices. If you use AutoCAD for mechanical drafting in the manufacturing industry, you may want to study all four dimensioning chapters. If your business is in another field, such as architectural design, you may want to learn the basics covered in Chapters 17 and 18 and skip Chapters 19 and 20.

This chapter will get you started dimensioning immediately with AutoCAD. As you progress, you will learn about dimension settings that can be used to control the way dimensions are presented. You can control things such as the space between dimension lines; arrowhead size and type; and text style, height, and position. You will also learn how to create dimension styles that have settings used on the types of drawings done at your company or school.

When you dimension objects with AutoCAD, the objects are automatically measured exactly as you have them drawn. This makes it important for you to draw accurate original objects and features. Use the object snaps to your best advantage when dimensioning.

# Dimension Arrangement

Dimensions are meant to communicate information about the drawing. Different industries and companies apply similar techniques for presenting dimensions. The two most accepted arrangements of text are unidirectional and aligned.

## Unidirectional Dimensioning

Unidirectional dimensioning is typically used in the mechanical drafting field. The term *unidirectional* means *one direction*. This system has all dimension numbers and notes placed horizontally on the drawing. They are read from the bottom of the sheet.

Unidirectional dimensions normally have arrowheads on the ends of dimension lines. The dimension number is usually centered in a break near the center of the dimension line. See **Figure 17-2**.

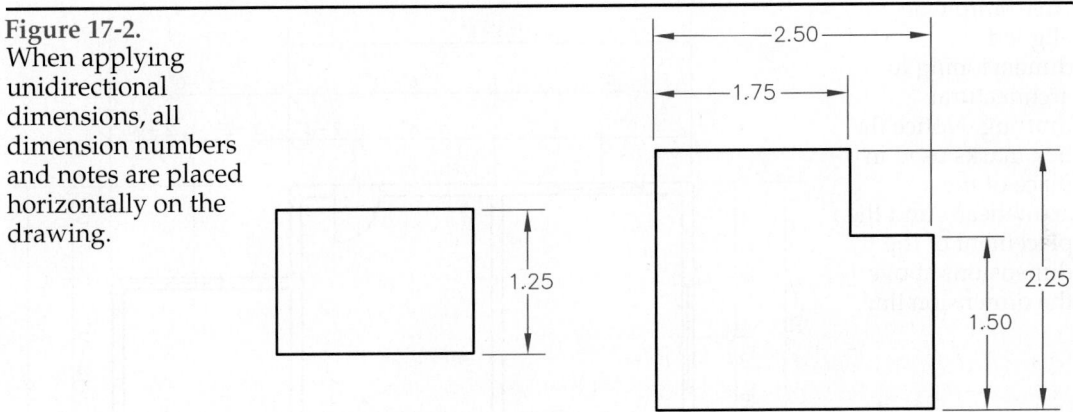

**Figure 17-2.** When applying unidirectional dimensions, all dimension numbers and notes are placed horizontally on the drawing.

## Aligned Dimensioning

Aligned dimensions are typically placed on architectural or structural drawings. The term *aligned* means the dimension numbers are lined up with the dimension lines. The dimension numbers for horizontal dimensions read horizontally. Dimension numbers for vertical dimensions are placed so they are read from the right side of the sheet. See **Figure 17-3**. Numbers for dimensions placed at an angle read at the same angle as the dimension line. Notes are usually placed so they read horizontally.

When using the aligned system, terminate dimension lines with tick marks, dots, or arrowheads. In architectural drafting, the dimension number is generally placed above the dimension line and tick marks are used as terminators. See **Figure 17-4.**

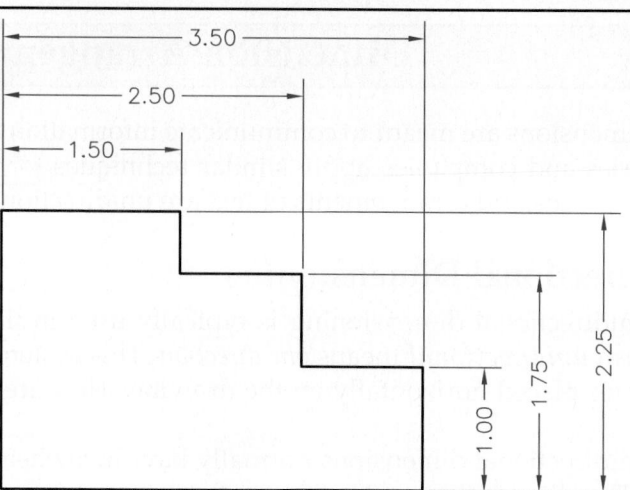

**Figure 17-3.**
In the aligned dimensioning system, dimension numbers for horizontal dimensions read horizontally. Dimension numbers for vertical dimensions are placed so they read from the right side of the sheet.

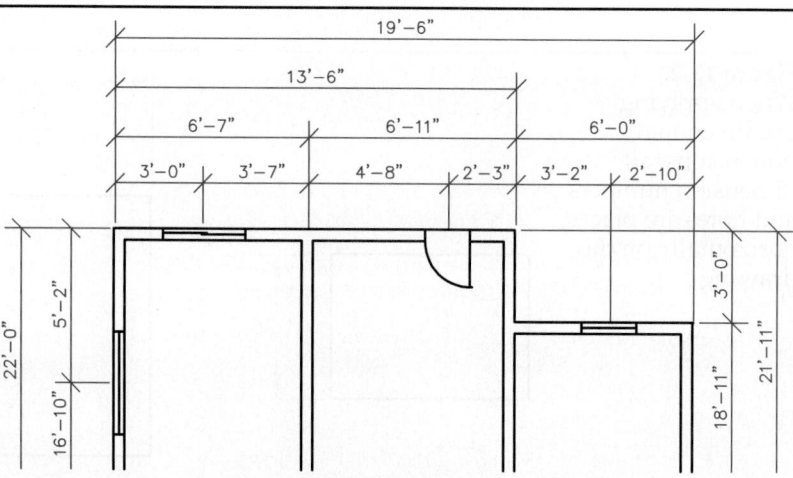

**Figure 17-4.**
An example of aligned dimensioning in architectural drafting. Notice the tick marks used in place of the arrowheads and the placement of the dimensions above the dimension line.

## Drawing Dimensions with AutoCAD

AutoCAD has a variety of dimensioning applications that fall into five fundamental categories: linear, angular, diameter, radius, and ordinate. These applications allow you to perform nearly every type of dimensioning practice needed for your discipline.

## Drawing Linear Dimensions

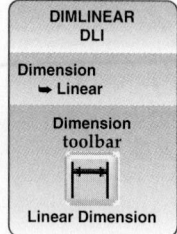

DIMLINEAR
DLI

Dimension
➥ Linear

Dimension
toolbar

Linear Dimension

*Linear* means straight. In most cases, dimensions measure straight distances, such as horizontal, vertical, or slanted surfaces. The **DIMLINEAR** command allows you to measure the length of an object and place extension lines, dimension lines, dimension text, and arrowheads automatically. To do this, pick the **Linear Dimension** button in the **Dimension** toolbar, select **Linear** from the **Dimension** pull-down menu, or type DLI or DIMLINEAR at the Command: prompt. The command sequence is:

> Command: **DLI** *or* **DIMLINEAR**↵
> Specify first extension line origin or <select object>: *(pick the origin of the first extension line)*
> Specify second extension line origin: *(pick the origin of the second extension line)*

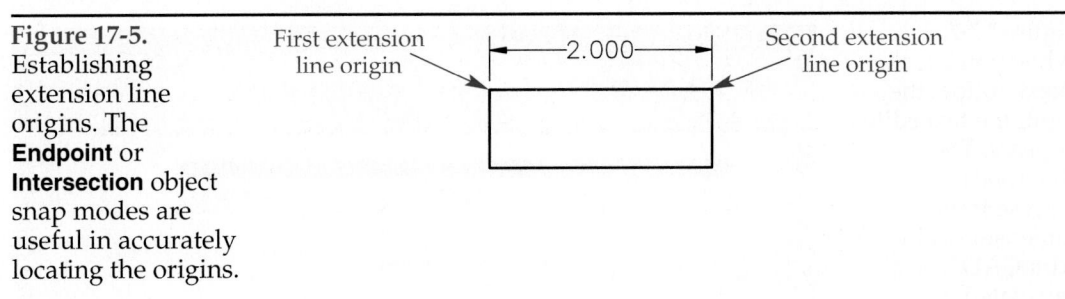

**Figure 17-5.** Establishing extension line origins. The **Endpoint** or **Intersection** object snap modes are useful in accurately locating the origins.

First extension line origin

2.000

Second extension line origin

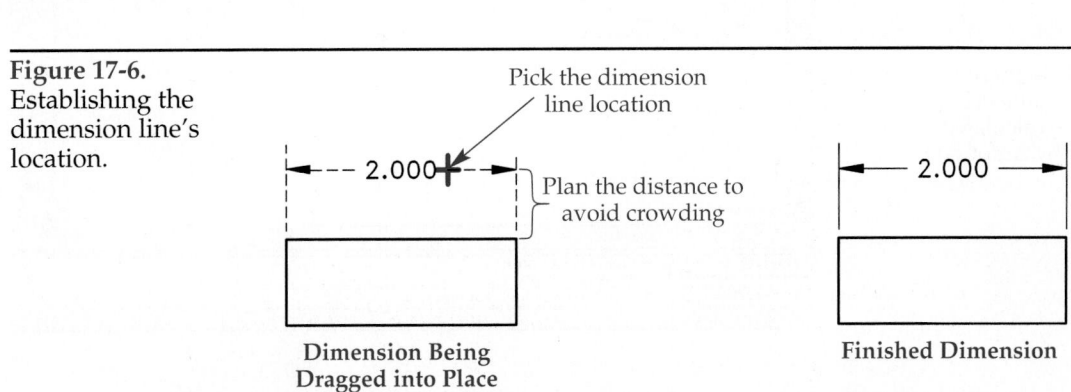

**Figure 17-6.** Establishing the dimension line's location.

Pick the dimension line location

2.000

Plan the distance to avoid crowding

**Dimension Being Dragged into Place**

2.000

**Finished Dimension**

The points you pick are the extension line origins. See **Figure 17-5.** Place the crosshairs directly on the corners of the object where the extension lines begin. Use object snap modes for accuracy.

The **DIMLINEAR** command allows you to generate horizontal, vertical, or rotated dimensions. After selecting the object or points of origin for dimensioning, the command continues:

Specify dimension line location or [Mtext/Text/Angle/Horizontal/Vertical/Rotated]:

- **Specify dimension line location.** This is the default. Simply drag the dimension line to a desired location and pick. See **Figure 17-6.** This is where preliminary plan sheets and sketches help you determine proper distances to avoid crowding. The extension lines, dimension line, dimension text, and arrowheads are automatically drawn after the location is picked.

- **Mtext.** Accesses the multiline text editor and the **Text Formatting** toolbar, **Figure 17-7.** Here you can provide a specific measurement or text format for the dimension. See Chapter 8 for a complete description of the multiline text editor and the **Text Formatting** toolbar. The chevrons (< >) represent the current dimension value. Edit the dimension text and pick **OK.** For example, the ASME standard recommends that a reference dimension be displayed enclosed in parenthesis. Type an open and closed parenthesis around the chevrons to create a reference dimension. If you want the current dimension value changed, delete the chevrons and type the new value. If you want the chevrons to be part of the dimension text, type the new value inside or next to the chevrons. While this is not an ASME standard, it may be needed for some applications.

- **Text.** Uses the command line to change dimension text. This is convenient if you prefer to type the desired text rather than using the multiline text editor. The **Text** and **Mtext** options both create multiline text objects. The **Text** option displays the current dimension value in brackets and allows you to accept this value by pressing [Enter] or type a new value. The command sequence is:

Specify dimension line location or [Mtext/Text/Angle/Horizontal/Vertical/Rotated]: T↵
Enter dimension text <2.875>:

Figure 17-7.
When you use the
**Mtext** option, the
multiline text editor
appears. The
chevrons (< >)
represent the
dimension value
AutoCAD has
calculated.

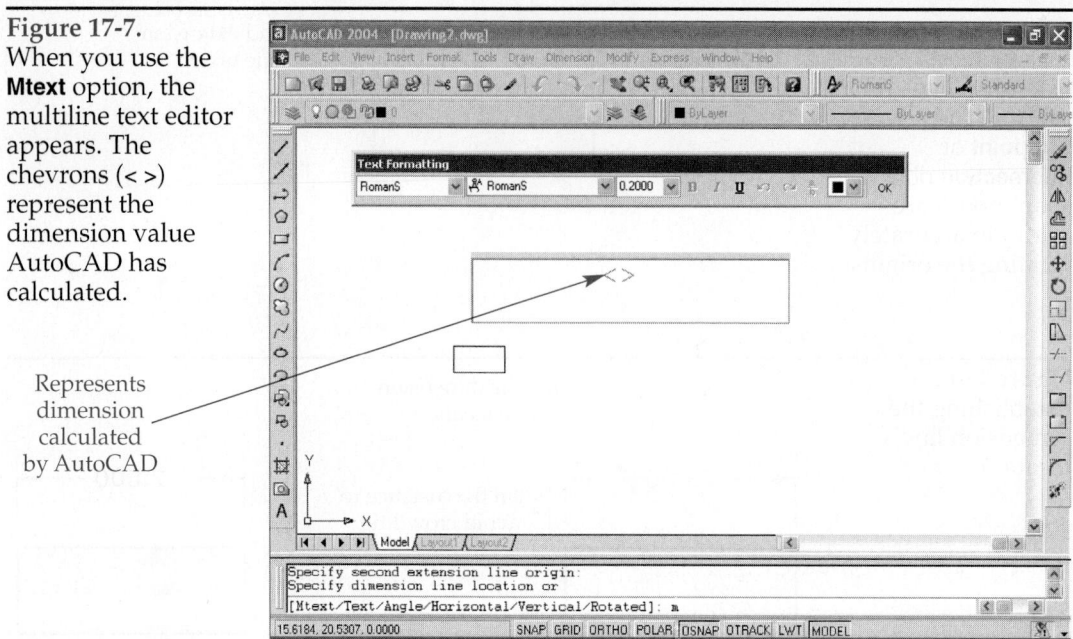

Represents
dimension
calculated
by AutoCAD

Pressing [Enter] accepts the current value. Type a new value, such as placing the chevrons inside parentheses to create a reference dimension:

Enter dimension text <2.875>: **(<>)**↵

- **Angle.** Allows you to change the dimension text angle. This option can be used when creating rotated dimensions or for adjusting the dimension text to a desired angle. The sequence is:

   Specify dimension line location or [Mtext/Text/Angle/Horizontal/Vertical/Rotated]: **A**↵
   Specify angle of dimension text: *(enter desired angle)*

- **Horizontal.** Sets the dimension to a horizontal distance only. This may be helpful when dimensioning the horizontal distance of a slanted surface. The **Mtext**, **Text**, and **Angle** options are available again in case you want to change the dimension text value or angle.

- **Vertical.** Sets the dimension being created to a vertical distance only. This option may be helpful when dimensioning the vertical distance of a slanted surface. Like the **Horizontal** option, the **Mtext**, **Text**, and **Angle** options are available.

- **Rotated.** Allows an angle to be specified for the dimension line. A practical application is dimensioning to angled surfaces and auxiliary views. This technique is different from other dimensioning commands because you are asked to provide a dimension line angle. See **Figure 17-8.** The command sequence is:

   Specify dimension line location or [Mtext/Text/Angle/Horizontal/Vertical/Rotated]: **R**↵
   Specify angle of dimension line <0>: *(enter a value, such as* 45, *or pick two points on the line to be dimensioned)*

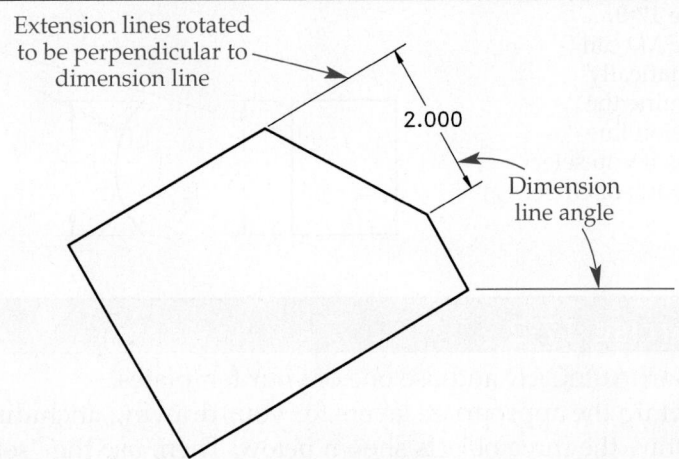

**Figure 17-8.**
Rotating a dimension for an angled view.

Extension lines rotated to be perpendicular to dimension line

2.000

Dimension line angle

## Selecting an Object to Dimension

In the previous discussion, the extension line origins were picked in order to establish the extents of the dimension. Another powerful AutoCAD dimensioning option allows you to pick a single line, circle, or arc to dimension. This works when you are using the **DIMLINEAR**, **DIMALIGNED**, and **QDIM** commands; the latter two are discussed later. You can use this option anytime you see the Specify first extension line origin or <select object>: prompt. Press [Enter] and then pick the object being dimensioned. When you select a line or arc, AutoCAD automatically begins the extension lines from the endpoints. If you pick a circle, the extension lines are drawn from the closest quadrant and its opposite quadrant. See **Figure 17-9**.

**Figure 17-9.**
AutoCAD can automatically determine the extension line origins if you select a line, arc, or circle.

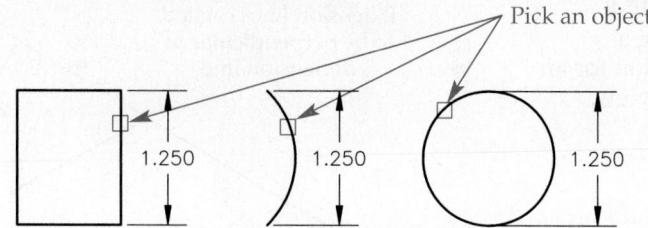

Pick an object

1.250    1.250    1.250

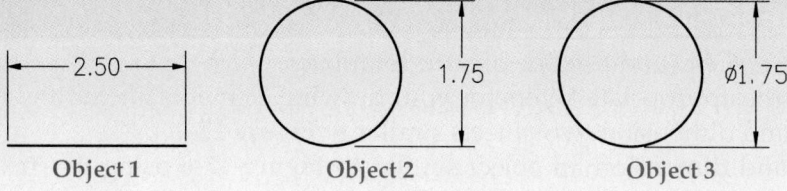
**PROFESSIONAL TIP**

Dimensioning in AutoCAD should be performed as accurately and neatly as possible. You can achieve consistently professional results by using the following guidelines.

- Always construct drawing geometry accurately. Never truncate, or round-off, decimal values when entering locations, distances, or angles. For example, enter .4375 for 7/16 rather than .44.

- Set the desired precision level before beginning your dimensioning. Most drawings have varying levels of precision for specific drawing features, so select the most common precision level to start with and adjust the precision as needed for each dimension. Setting the dimension precision is explained later in this chapter.

- Always use the precision drawing aids to ensure the accuracy of dimensions. If the point being dimensioned does not coincide with a snap point or a known coordinate, use an appropriate object snap override.

- *Never* type a different dimension value than what appears in the brackets. If a dimension needs to change, revise the drawing or dimensioning variables accordingly. The ability to change the dimension in the brackets is provided by AutoCAD so that a different text format can be specified for the dimension. Prefixes and suffixes can also be added to the dimension in the brackets. A typical example of a prefix might be to specify the number of times a dimension occurs, such as **4X 1.750**. Other examples of this capability appear later in this chapter.

# Dimensioning Angled Surfaces and Auxiliary Views

When dimensioning a surface drawn at an angle it may be necessary to align the dimension line with the surface. For example, auxiliary views are normally placed at an angle. In order to properly dimension these features, the **DIMALIGNED** command or the **Rotated** option of the **DIMLINEAR** command can be used.

## Using the **DIMALIGNED** Command

DIMALIGNED
DAL

Dimension
➡ Aligned

Dimension
toolbar

Aligned Dimension

The **DIMALIGNED** command can be accessed by picking the **Aligned Dimension** button on the **Dimension** toolbar, picking **Aligned** in the **Dimension** pull-down menu, or typing DAL or DIMALIGNED at the Command: prompt. The results of the **DIMALIGNED** command are displayed in Figure 17-10. The command sequence is:

Command: **DAL** *or* **DIMALIGNED**↵
Specify first extension line origin or <select object>: *(pick first extension line origin)*
Specify second extension line origin: *(pick second extension line origin)*
Specify dimension line location or
[Mtext/Text/Angle]: *(pick the dimension line location)*
Dimension text = 2.250
Command:

**Figure 17-10.**
The **DIMALIGNED** dimensioning command allows you to place dimension lines parallel to angled features.

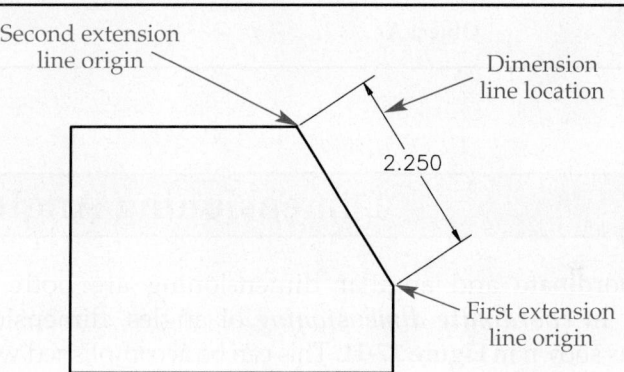

Second extension
line origin

Dimension
line location

2.250

First extension
line origin

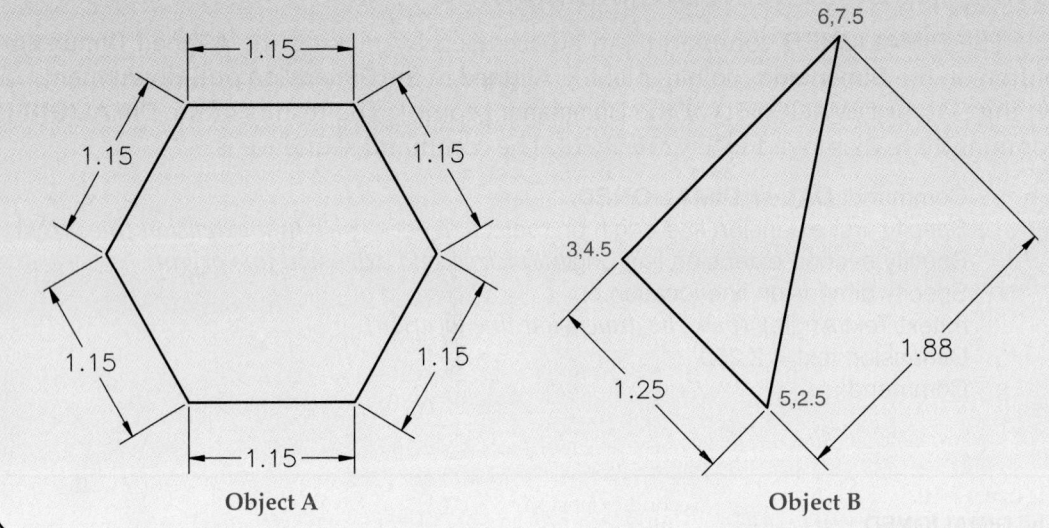
## Dimensioning Angles

Coordinate and angular dimensioning are both accepted for dimensioning angles. In *coordinate dimensioning* of angles, dimensions locate the corner of the angle, as shown in **Figure 17-11.** This can be accomplished with the **DIMLINEAR** command.

*Angular dimensioning* locates one corner with a dimension and provides the value of the angle in degrees. See **Figure 17-12.** You can dimension the angle between any two nonparallel lines. The intersection of the lines is the angle's vertex. AutoCAD automatically draws extension lines if they are needed. The angular unit of measure is set in the dimension style, which is discussed later in this chapter.

The **DIMANGULAR** command is used for the angular method. It is accessed by picking the **Angular Dimension** button on the **Dimension** toolbar, picking **Angular** in the **Dimension** pull-down menu, or by entering DAN or DIMANGULAR at the Command: prompt. The dimension in **Figure 17-12A** was drawn with the following sequence.

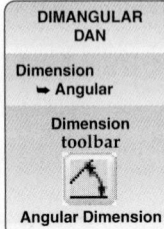

DIMANGULAR
DAN

Dimension
➡ Angular

Dimension
toolbar

Angular Dimension

Command: **DAN** or **DIMANGULAR**↵
Select arc, circle, line, or <specify vertex>: (*pick the first leg of the angle to be dimensioned*)
Select second line: (*pick the second leg of the angle to be dimensioned*)
Specify dimension arc line location or [Mtext/Text/Angle]: (*pick the desired location of the dimension line arc*)
Dimension text = 30
Command:

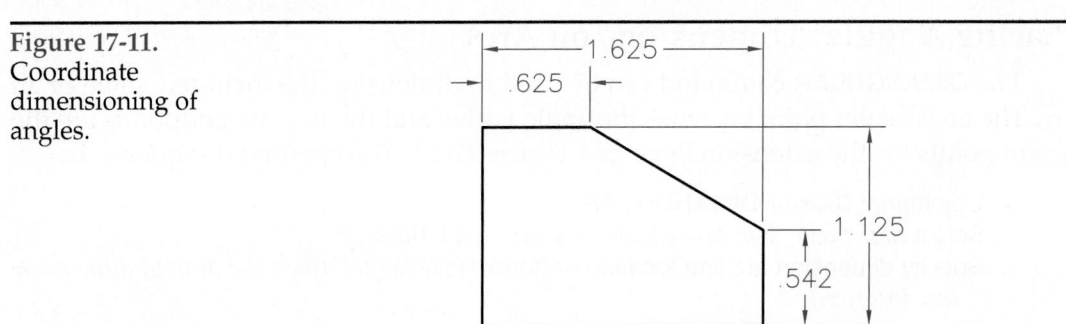

**Figure 17-11.**
Coordinate
dimensioning of
angles.

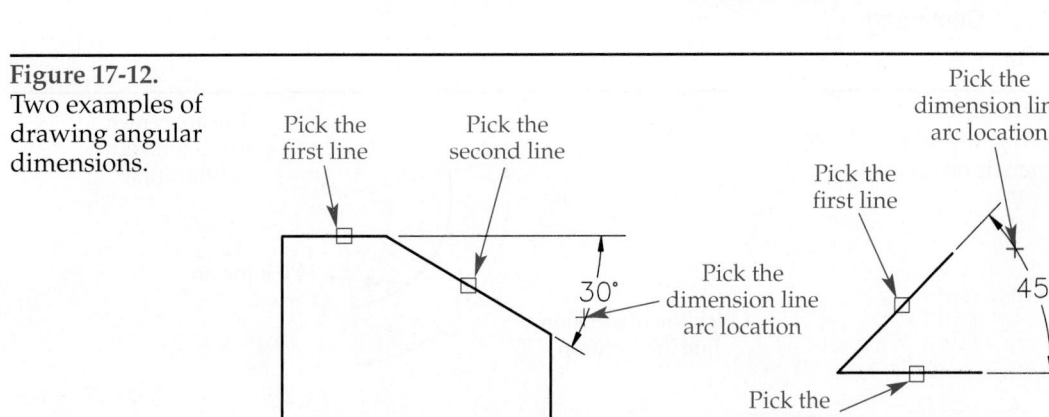

**Figure 17-12.**
Two examples of
drawing angular
dimensions.

Pick the
first line

Pick the
second line

Pick the
dimension line
arc location

30°

A

Pick the
dimension line
arc location

Pick the
first line

45°

Pick the
second line

B

The last prompt asks you to pick the dimension line arc location. If there is enough space, AutoCAD places the dimension text, dimension line arc, and arrowheads inside the extension lines. If there is not enough room between extension lines for the arrowheads and numbers, AutoCAD automatically places the arrowheads outside and the number inside the extension lines. If space is very tight, AutoCAD may place the dimension line arc and arrowheads inside and the text outside, or place everything outside of the extension lines. See **Figure 17-13.**

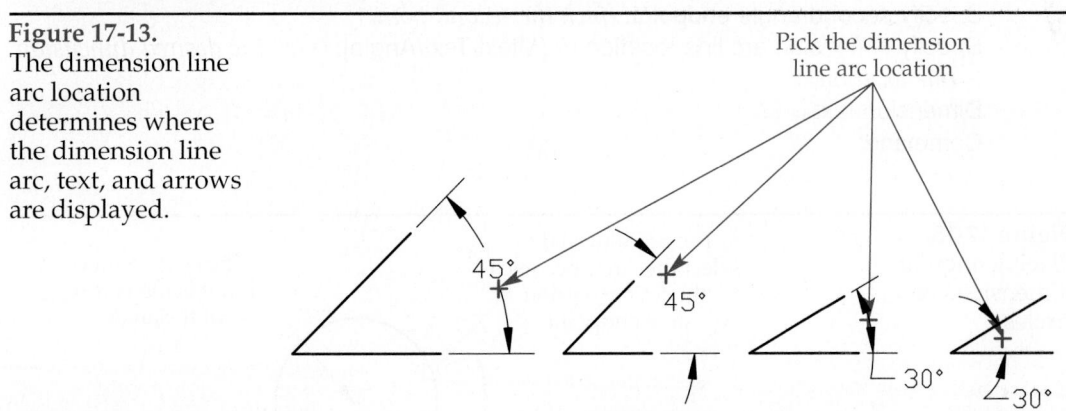

**Figure 17-13.**
The dimension line
arc location
determines where
the dimension line
arc, text, and arrows
are displayed.

Pick the dimension
line arc location

45°

45°

30°

30°

## Placing Angular Dimensions on Arcs

The **DIMANGULAR** command can be used to dimension the included angle of an arc. The arc's center point becomes the angle vertex and the two arc endpoints are the origin points for the extension lines. See **Figure 17-14**. The command sequence is:

Command: **DAN** *or* **DIMANGULAR**↵
Select arc, circle, line, or <specify vertex>: *(pick the arc)*
Specify dimension arc line location or [Mtext/Text/Angle]: *(pick the desired dimension line location)*
Dimension text = 128
Command:

Figure 17-14.
Placing angular
dimensions on arcs.

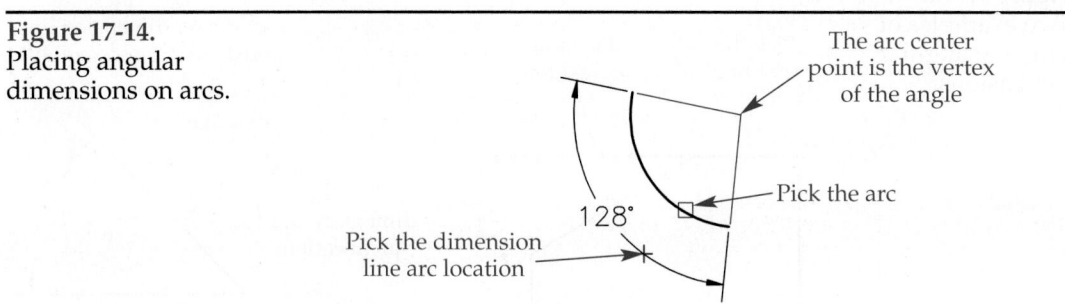

## Placing Angular Dimensions on Circles

The **DIMANGULAR** command can also be used to dimension a portion of a circle. The circle's center point becomes the angle vertex and two picked points are the origin points for the extension lines. See **Figure 17-15**. The command sequence is:

Command: **DAN** *or* **DIMANGULAR**↵
Select arc, circle, line, or <specify vertex>: *(pick the circle)*

The point you pick on the circle is the endpoint of the first extension line. You are then asked for the second angle endpoint, which is the endpoint of the second extension line:

Specify second angle endpoint: *(pick the second point)*
Specify dimension arc line location or [Mtext/Text/Angle]: *(pick the desired dimension line location)*
Dimension text = 85
Command:

Figure 17-15.
Placing angular
dimensions on
circles.

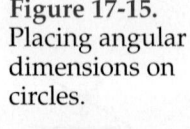
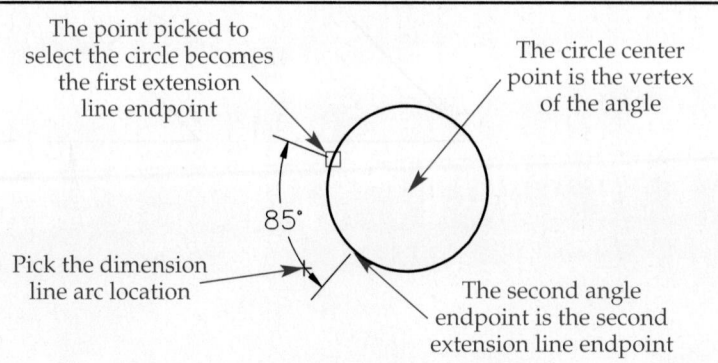

Using angular dimensioning for circles increases the number of possible solutions for a given dimensioning requirement, but the actual uses are limited. One professional application is dimensioning an angle from a quadrant point to a particular feature without having to first draw a line to dimension. Another benefit of this option is the ability to specify angles that exceed 180°.

## Angular Dimensioning through Three Points

You can also establish an angular dimension through three points. The points are the angle vertex and two angle line endpoints. See **Figure 17-16.** To do this, press [Enter] after the first prompt:

> Command: **DAN** or **DIMANGULAR.**⏎
> Select arc, circle, line, or <specify vertex>: ⏎
> Specify angle vertex: *(pick a vertex point; a rubberband connects the vertex and the cursor to help locate the endpoints)*
> Specify first angle endpoint: *(pick the first endpoint)*
> Specify second angle endpoint: *(pick the second endpoint)*
> Non-associative dimension created.
> Specify dimension arc line location or [Mtext/Text/Angle]: *(pick the desired dimension line location)*
> Dimension text = 60

This method also dimensions angles over 180°.

**Figure 17-16.**
Angular dimensions using three points.

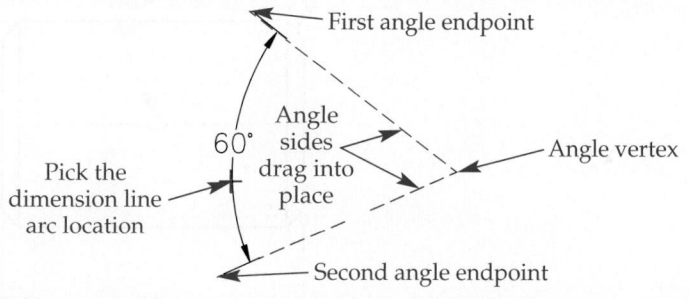

## Exercise 17-4

- Start AutoCAD and use one of your templates.
- Set up the appropriate layers for your drawing elements, including a layer for dimensions.
- Draw the object shown below.
- Use the **LINEAR** and **ANGULAR** dimensioning commands to dimension the object exactly as shown.
- Save the drawing as EX17-4.

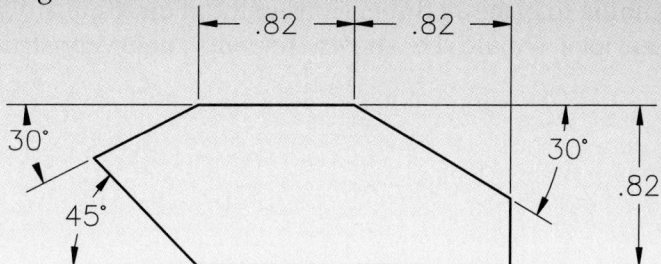

Dimensioning practices often depend on product requirements, manufacturing accuracy, standards, and tradition. Dimensional information includes size dimensions, location dimensions, and notes. Two techniques that identify size and location are chain and datum dimensioning. Which method is used depends on the accuracy of the product and the drafting field. Both methods are covered later in this chapter.

## Size Dimensions and Notes

*Size dimensions* provide the size of physical features. They include lines, notes, or dimension lines and numbers. Size dimensioning practices depend on the techniques used to dimension different geometric features. See **Figure 17-17.** A *feature* is considered any physical portion of a part or object, such as a surface, hole, window, or door. Dimensioning standards are used so an object designed in one place can be manufactured or built somewhere else.

Specific notes and general notes are the two types of notes on a drawing. *Specific notes* relate to individual or specific features on the drawing. They are attached to the feature being dimensioned using a leader line. *General notes* apply to the entire drawing and are placed in the lower-left corner, upper-left corner, or above or next to the title block. Where they are placed depends on company or school practice.

**Figure 17-17.**
Size dimensions and
specific notes.

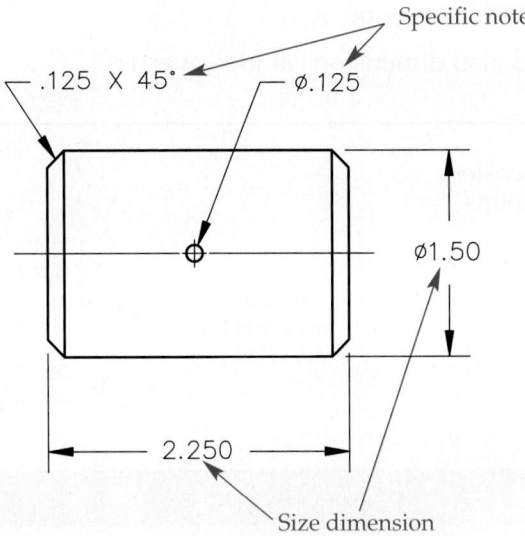

## Dimensioning Flat Surfaces and Architectural Features

In mechanical drafting, flat surfaces are dimensioned by giving measurements for each feature. If there is an overall dimension provided, you can omit one of the dimensions. The overall dimension controls the omitted dimension. In architectural drafting, it is common to place all dimensions without omitting any of them. The idea is that all dimensions should be shown to help make construction easier. See **Figure 17-18.**

Figure 17-18.
Dimensioning flat
surfaces and
architectural
features.

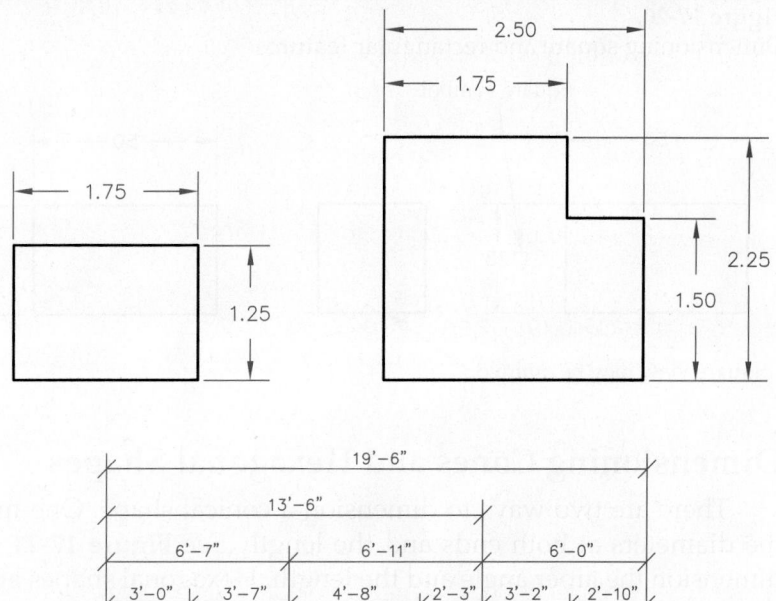

## Dimensioning Cylindrical Shapes

Both the diameter and length of a cylindrical shape can be dimensioned in the view in which the cylinder appears rectangular. See Figure 17-19. This allows the view in which the cylinder appears as a circle to be omitted.

Figure 17-19.
Dimensioning
cylindrical shapes.

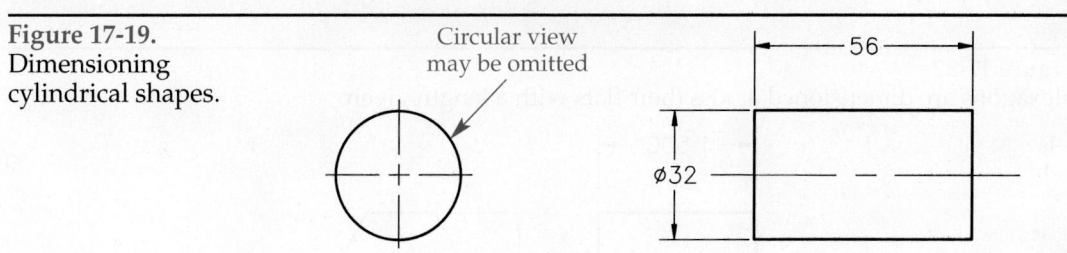

Circular view
may be omitted

## Dimensioning Square and Rectangular Features

Square and rectangular features are usually dimensioned in the views in which the length and height are shown. The square symbol can be used preceding the dimension for the square feature. See Figure 17-20. The square symbol must be created as a block and inserted. Blocks are discussed in Chapter 22 of this text.

**Figure 17-20.**
Dimensioning square and rectangular features.

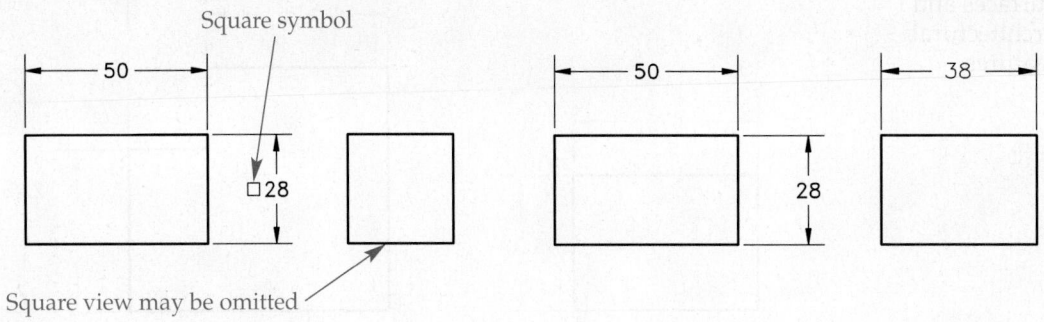

**Dimensioning Cones and Hexagonal Shapes**

There are two ways to dimension a conical shape. One method is to dimension the diameters at both ends and the length. See **Figure 17-21.** Another method is to dimension the taper angle and the length. Hexagonal shapes are dimensioned by giving the distance across the flats and the length. See **Figure 17-22.**

**Figure 17-21.**
Dimensioning conical shapes. These shapes can also be dimensioned with an angle and length.

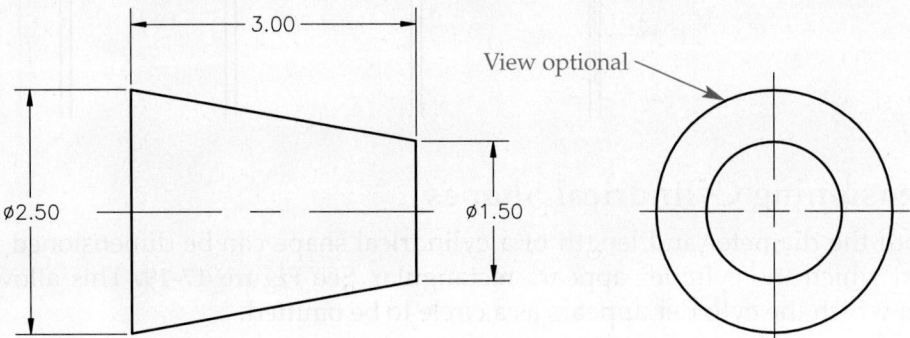

**Figure 17-22.**
Hexagons are dimensioned across their flats with a length given.

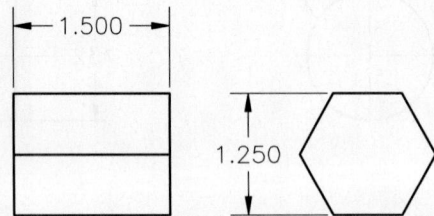

○ Start AutoCAD and use one of your templates.

○ Set up the appropriate layers for your drawing elements, including a layer for dimensions.

○ Draw the objects shown below. Hint: To orient the hexagon as shown, use a six-sided circumscribed polygon. When prompted to enter the radius value, type @.625<0. Use object snap modes, along with X and Y filters, object snap tracking, or construction lines to assist you in drawing the side view of the hexagon.

○ Dimension the objects exactly as shown using the proper dimensioning commands and techniques.

○ Save the drawing as EX17-5.

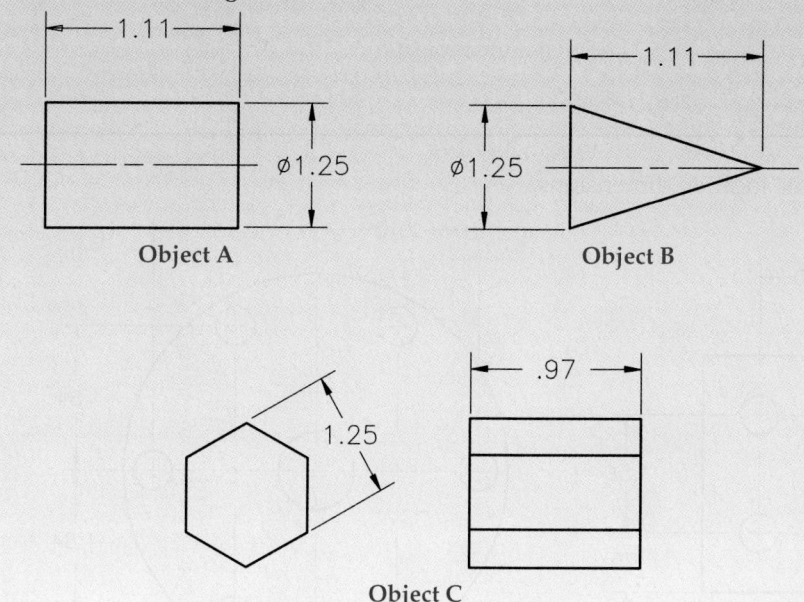

# Location Dimensions

*Location dimensions* are used to locate features on an object. They do not provide the size. Holes and arcs are dimensioned to their centers in the view in which they appear circular. Rectangular features are dimensioned to their edges. See **Figure 17-23.** In architectural drafting, windows and doors are dimensioned to their centers on the floor plan.

Rectangular coordinates and polar coordinates are the two basic location dimensioning systems. *Rectangular coordinates* are linear dimensions used to locate features from surfaces, centerlines, or center planes. AutoCAD performs this type of dimensioning using a variety of dimensioning commands. The most frequently used dimensioning command is **DIMLINEAR** and its options. See **Figure 17-24.**

The *polar coordinate system* uses angular dimensions to locate features from surfaces, centerlines, or center planes. The angular dimensions in the polar coordinate system are drawn using AutoCAD's **DIMANGULAR** command. See **Figure 17-25.**

**Figure 17-23.**
Locating circular and rectangular features.

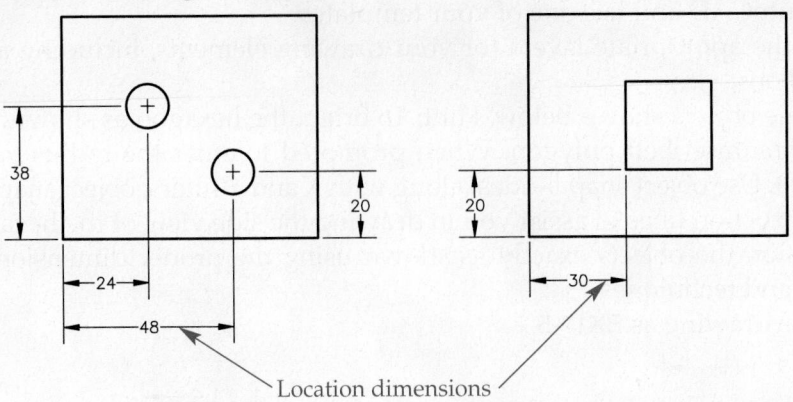

Location dimensions

**Figure 17-24.**
Rectangular coordinate location dimensions.

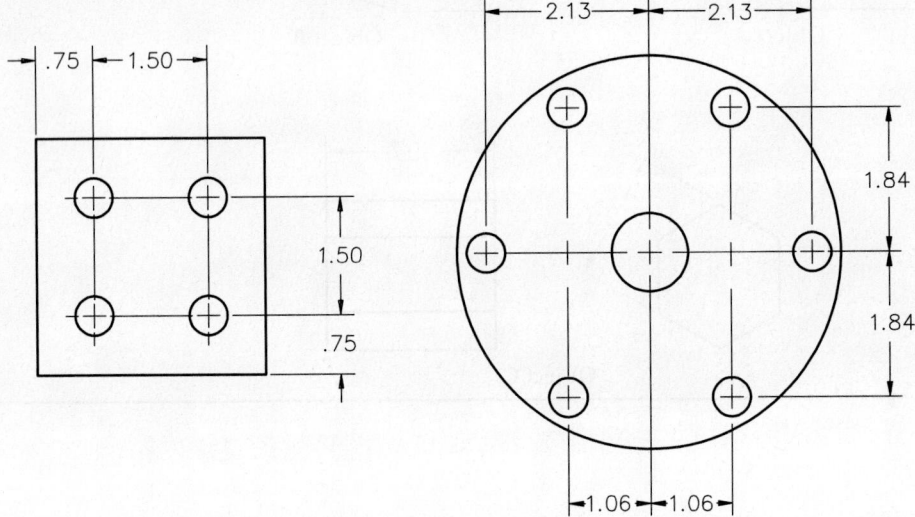

**Figure 17-25.**
Polar coordinate location dimensions.

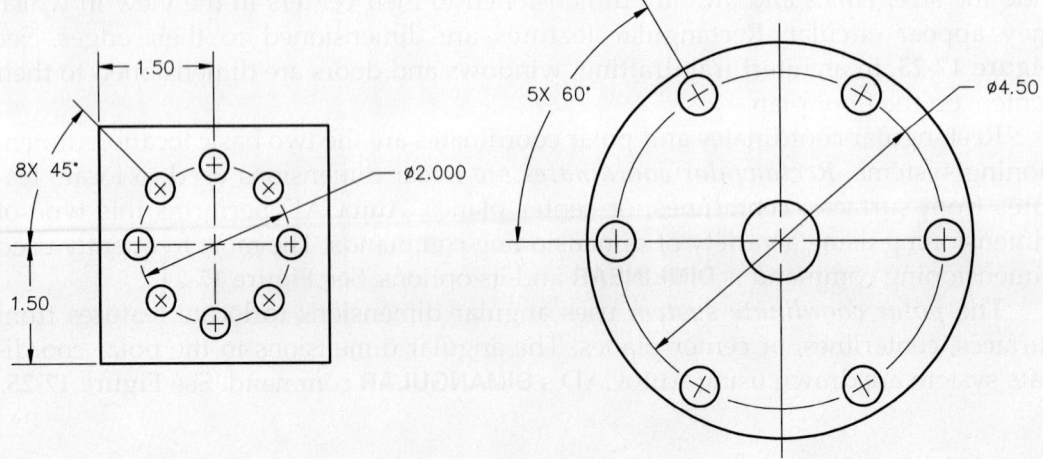

AutoCAD and its Applications—Basics

# Datum and Chain Dimensioning

With *datum dimensioning,* or *baseline dimensioning,* dimensions on an object originate from common surfaces, centerlines, or center planes. Datum dimensioning is commonly used in mechanical drafting because each dimension is independent of the others. This achieves more accuracy in manufacturing. **Figure 17-26** shows an object dimensioned with surface datums.

*Chain dimensioning,* also called *point-to-point dimensioning,* places dimensions in a line from one feature to the next. Chain dimensioning is sometimes used in mechanical drafting. However, there is less accuracy than with datum dimensioning since each dimension is dependent on other dimensions in the chain. Architectural drafting uses chain dimensioning in most applications. **Figure 17-27** shows two examples of chain dimensioning. In mechanical drafting, it is common to leave one dimension blank and provide an overall dimension. Architectural drafting practices usually show dimensions all the way across plus an overall dimension.

**Figure 17-26.**
Datum dimensioning.

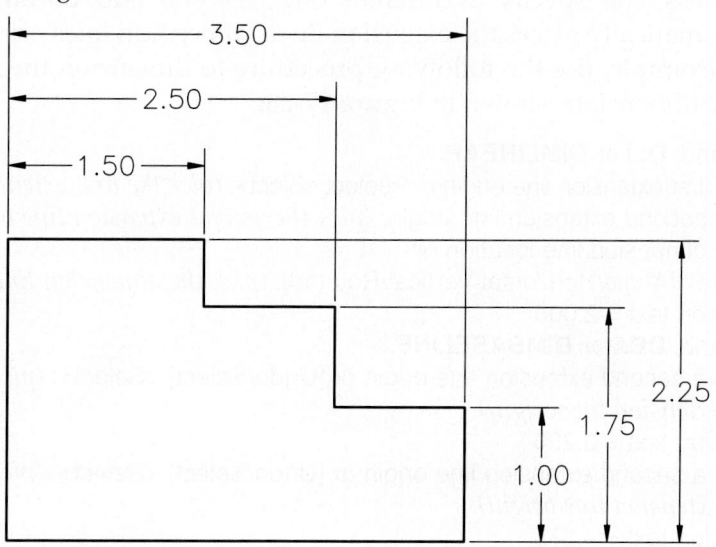

**Figure 17-27.**
Chain dimensioning.

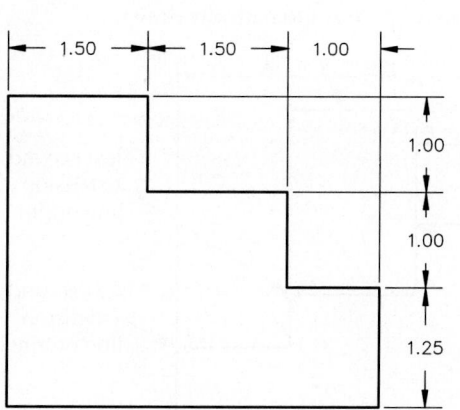
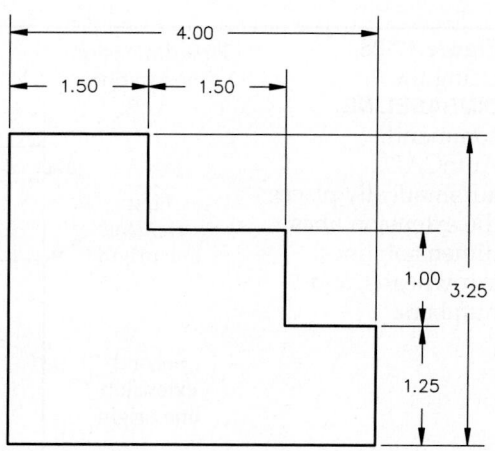

## Making Datum and Chain Dimensioning Easy

AutoCAD refers to datum dimensioning as *baseline* and chain dimensioning as *continue.* Datum dimensioning is controlled by the **DIMBASELINE** command. Chain dimensioning is controlled by the **DIMCONTINUE** command. The **DIMBASELINE** and **DIMCONTINUE** commands are used in the same manner. The prompts and options are the same. Use the **Undo** option in the **DIMBASELINE** or **DIMCONTINUE** commands to undo previously drawn dimensions.

## Datum Dimensions

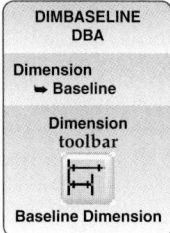

DIMBASELINE
DBA

Dimension
➥ Baseline

Dimension
toolbar

Baseline Dimension

Datum dimensions are created by picking the **Baseline Dimension** button in the **Dimension** toolbar, picking **Baseline** in the **Dimension** pull-down menu, or by entering either DBA or DIMBASELINE at the Command: prompt. Baseline dimensions can be created with linear, ordinate, and angular dimensions. Ordinate dimensions are discussed later in this chapter.

When you enter the **DIMBASELINE** command, AutoCAD asks you to Specify a second extension line origin. This is because a baseline dimension is a continuation of an existing dimension. Therefore, a dimension must exist before using the command. AutoCAD automatically selects the most recently drawn dimension as the base dimension unless you specify a different one. As you add datum dimensions, AutoCAD automatically places the extension lines, dimension lines, arrowheads, and numbers. For example, use the following procedure to dimension the series of horizontal baseline dimensions shown in **Figure 17-28**.

Command: **DLI** *or* **DIMLINEAR**↵
Specify first extension line origin or <select object>: *(pick the first extension line origin)*
Specify second extension line origin: *(pick the second extension line origin)*
Specify dimension line location or
[Mtext/Text/Angle/Horizontal/Vertical/Rotated]: *(pick the dimension line location)*
Dimension text = 2.000
Command: **DBA** *or* **DIMBASELINE**↵
Specify a second extension line origin or [Undo/Select] <Select>: *(pick the next second extension line origin)*
Dimension text = 3.250
Specify a second extension line origin or [Undo/Select] <Select>: *(pick the next second extension line origin)*
Dimension text = 4.375
Specify a second extension line origin or [Undo/Select] <Select>: ↵
Select base dimension: ↵
Command:

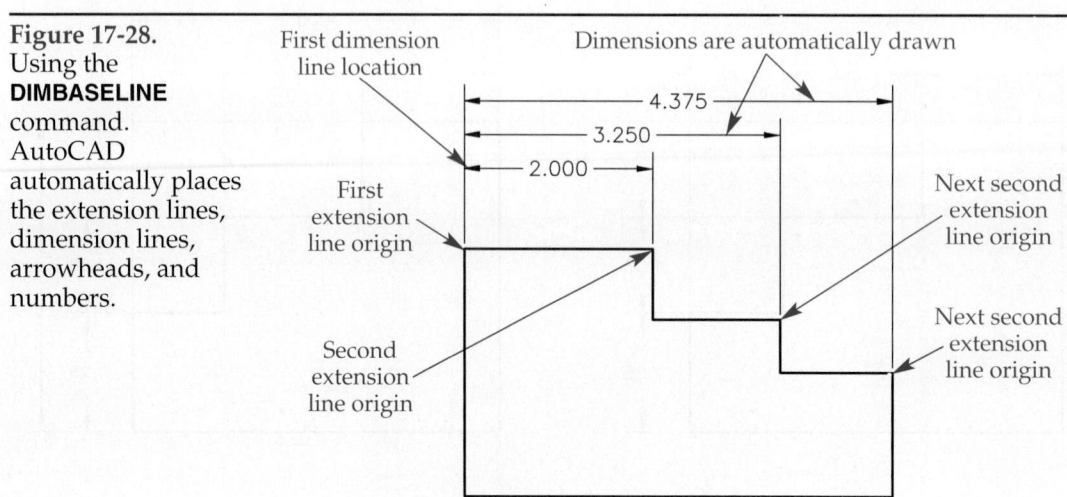

Figure 17-28. Using the **DIMBASELINE** command. AutoCAD automatically places the extension lines, dimension lines, arrowheads, and numbers.

First dimension line location

Dimensions are automatically drawn

4.375
3.250
2.000

First extension line origin

Second extension line origin

Next second extension line origin

Next second extension line origin

You can continue to add baseline dimensions until you press [Enter] twice to return to the Command: prompt. Notice as you pick additional dimension extension line origins that AutoCAD automatically places the dimension text; you do not specify a location.

If you want to add datum dimensions to an existing dimension other than the most recently drawn one, use the **Select** option by pressing [Enter] at the first prompt. At the Select base dimension: prompt, pick the dimension to serve as the base. When picking a dimension to use as the baseline, the extension line nearest the point where you select the dimension is used as the baseline point. Then, select the new second extension line origins as described earlier.

You can also draw baseline dimensions to angular features. First, draw an angular dimension. Then, enter the **DIMBASELINE** command. You can also pick an existing angular dimension other than the one most recently drawn. **Figure 17-29** shows angular baseline dimensions.

**Figure 17-29.**
Using the
**DIMBASELINE**
command to datum
dimension angular
features.

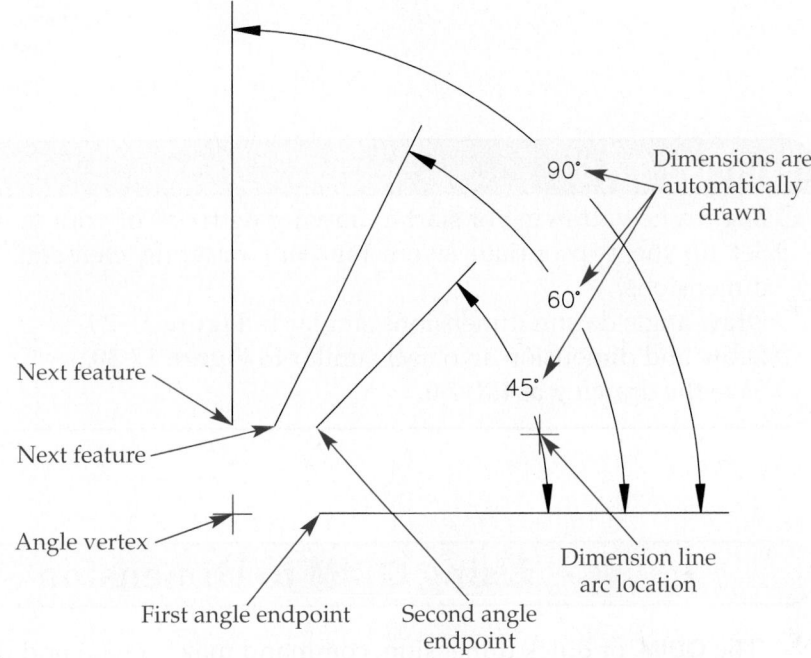

## Chain Dimensions

As previously mentioned, when creating chain dimensions you will receive the same prompts and options received while creating datum dimensions. Chain dimensioning is shown in **Figure 17-30.** Chain dimensions (continue dimensions) are created by picking the **Continue Dimension** button on the **Dimension** toolbar, picking **Continue** in the **Dimension** pull-down menu, or by entering DCO or DIMCONTINUE at the Command: prompt. Continue dimensions can be created with linear, ordinate, and angular dimensions. Ordinate dimensions are discussed later in this chapter.

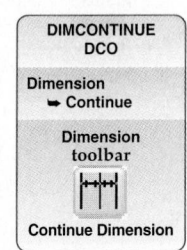

DIMCONTINUE
DCO

Dimension
➥ Continue

Dimension
toolbar

Continue Dimension

**PROFESSIONAL TIP**
You do not have to use **DIMBASELINE** or **DIMCONTINUE** immediately after a dimension that is to be used as a base or chain. You can come back later and use the **Select** option as previously discussed. Then, select the dimension you want to use and draw the datum or chain dimensions that you need.

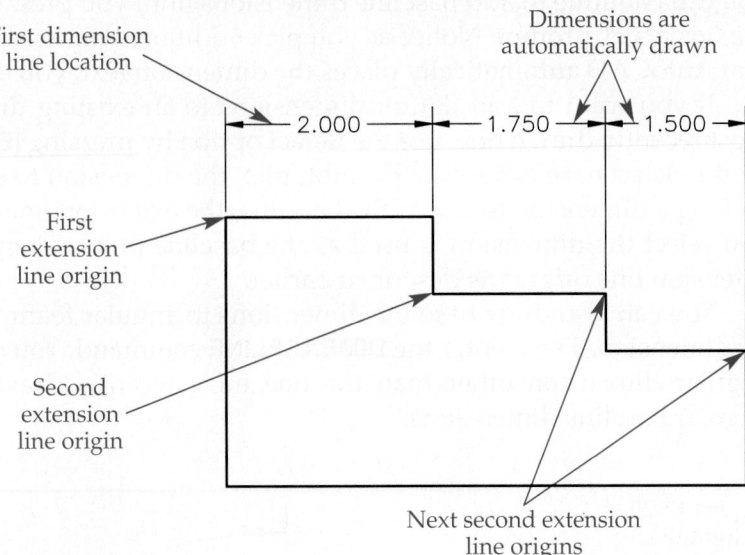

**Figure 17-30.**
Using the
**DIMCONTINUE**
command to create
chain dimensions.

First dimension
line location

Dimensions are
automatically drawn

2.000   1.750   1.500

First
extension
line origin

Second
extension
line origin

Next second extension
line origins

---

---

# Using QDIM to Dimension

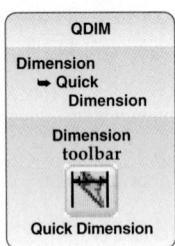

QDIM

Dimension
➥ Quick
   Dimension

Dimension
toolbar

Quick Dimension

    The **QDIM**, or quick dimension, command makes chain and datum dimensioning easy by eliminating the need to define the exact points being dimensioned. Often, the points that need to be selected for dimensioning are the endpoint of a line or the center of an arc. AutoCAD automates the process of point selection in the **QDIM** command by finding those points for you. The **QDIM** command can be accessed by selecting **Quick Dimension** from the **Dimension** pull-down menu, picking the **Quick Dimension** button on the **Dimension** toolbar, or entering QDIM at the Command: prompt.

    The type of geometry selected affects the **QDIM** output. If a single polyline is selected, **QDIM** attempts to draw linear dimensions to every vertex of the polyline. If a single arc or circle is selected, then **QDIM** draws a radius or diameter dimension. If multiple objects are selected, linear dimensions are drawn to the vertex of every line or polyline and to the center of every arc or circle. In each case, AutoCAD finds the points automatically. The command line sequence is:

Command: **QDIM**↵
Associative dimension priority = Endpoint
Select geometry to dimension: *(pick several lines, polylines, arcs and/or circles)*
Select geometry to dimension: ↵
Specify dimension line position, or
[Continuous/Staggered/Baseline/Ordinate/Radius/Diameter/datumPoint/Edit/seTtings]
    <current>: *(pick a position for the dimension lines)*
Command:

---

                                              AutoCAD and its Applications—Basics

Figure 17-31.
The **QDIM** command can dimension multiple features or objects at the same time.

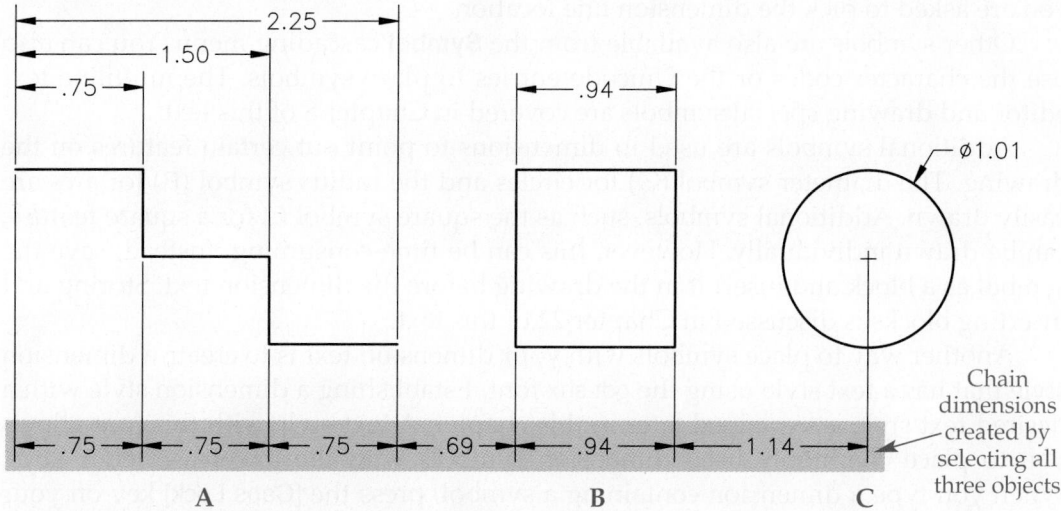

The dimensions at the bottom showing labels: 2.25, 1.50, .75, .94, ∅1.01, .75, .75, .75, .69, .94, 1.14, A, B, C, Chain dimensions created by selecting all three objects

**Figure 17-31** shows examples of different types of objects being dimensioned with the **QDIM** command. The upper dimensions are created by selecting each object separately. The lower dimensions are created by selecting all objects at once.

The **Continuous**, **Staggered**, **Baseline**, **Ordinate**, **Radius**, and **Diameter** options relate to the different modes of dimensioning discussed earlier in this chapter. In **Figure 17-31**, Object A was dimensioned with the **Baseline** option of the **QDIM** command. The command sequence is:

Command: **QDIM**↵
Select geometry to dimension: *(pick polyline shown in Figure 17-31A)*
Specify dimension line position, or
[Continuous/Staggered/Baseline/Ordinate/Radius/Diameter/datumPoint/Edit/seTtings]
<Continuous>: **B**↵
Specify dimension line position, or
[Continuous/Staggered/Baseline/Ordinate/Radius/Diameter/datumPoint/Edit/seTtings]
<Baseline>: *(pick a vertical or horizontal position for the dimension line)*
Command:

The dimensions at the bottom of **Figure 17-31** are created using the **Continuous** option of the **QDIM** command and selecting all three objects.

The **QDIM** command can also be used as a way to edit any existing associative dimension. Editing dimensions and a description of the **datum Point, Edit,** and **Setting** options of the **QDIM** command are discussed in Chapter 18.

## Including Symbols with Dimension Text

After you select a feature to dimension, AutoCAD responds with the measurement (dimension number). In some cases, such as dimensioning radii and diameters, AutoCAD automatically places the radius (R) or diameter (∅) symbol before the dimension number. However, in other cases related to linear dimensioning, this is not automatic. The recommended ASME standard for a diameter dimension is to place the diameter symbol (∅) before the number. This can be done using the **Mtext** option of the dimensioning commands. When the multiline text editor appears, place the cursor in the location where you want the symbol, such as in front of the chevrons.

Then, right-click to display the shortcut menu and select **Diameter** from the **Symbol** cascading menu. After you pick **OK** in the text editor, the command continues and you are asked to pick the dimension line location.

Other symbols are also available from the **Symbol** cascading menu. You can also use the character codes or the Unicode entries to place symbols. The multiline text editor and drawing special symbols are covered in Chapter 8 of this text.

Additional symbols are used in dimensions to point out certain features on the drawing. The diameter symbol (⌀) for circles and the radius symbol (R) for arcs are easily drawn. Additional symbols, such as the square symbol ( ) for a square feature, can be drawn individually. However, this can be time-consuming. Instead, save the symbol as a block and insert it in the drawing before the dimension text. Storing and inserting blocks is discussed in Chapter 22 of this text.

Another way to place symbols with your dimension text is to create a dimension style that has a text style using the gdt.shx font. Establishing a dimension style with a desired text style is explained later in this chapter. A text style with this font allows you to place commonly used dimension symbols with the lowercase letter keys. When you type a dimension containing a symbol, press the [Caps Lock] key on your keyboard to activate caps lock. By doing this, text is uppercase. When a symbol needs to be inserted, you can press the [Shift] key and the letter that corresponds to the desired symbol.

Often-used ASME symbols are shown in **Figure 17-32**. The letter in parentheses is the lowercase letter that you press at the keyboard to make the symbol. Additional geometric dimensioning and tolerancing (GD&T) symbols are available by pressing other keyboard keys. GD&T is covered in Chapter 20.

**Figure 17-32.**
Common dimensioning symbols and how to draw them. The lowercase letter displayed in parentheses with some symbol names is the keystroke for placing the symbol with the gdt.shx font.

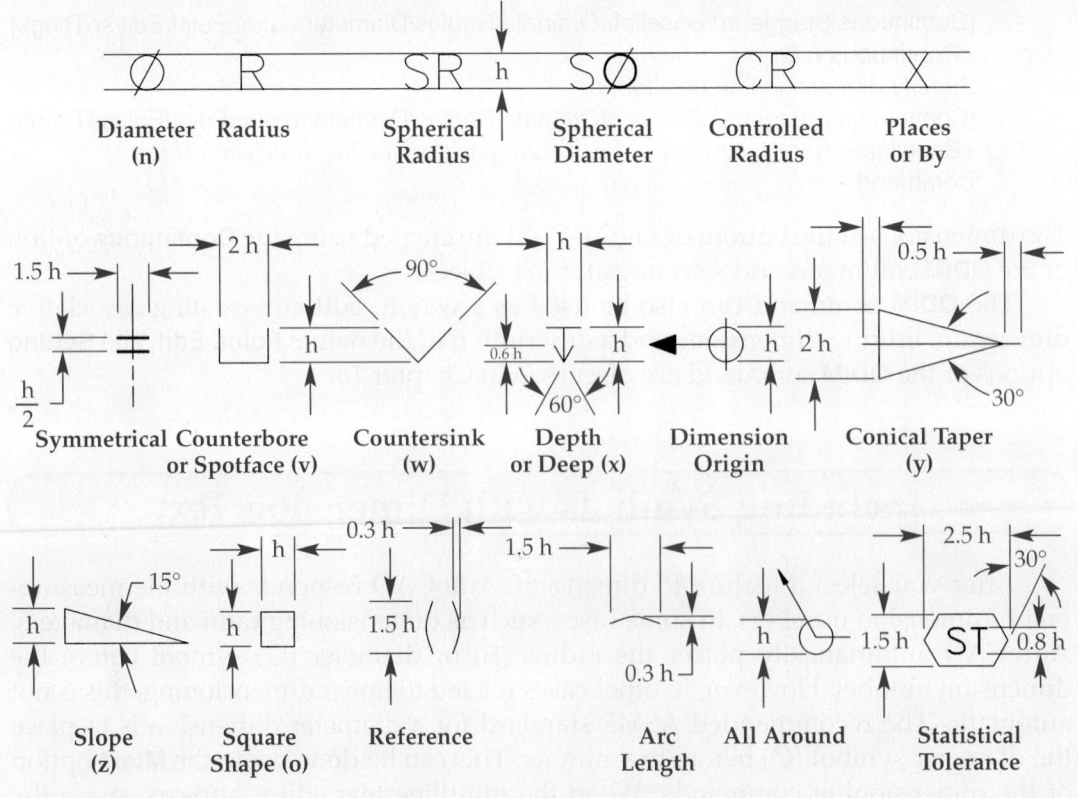

AutoCAD and its Applications—Basics

## Drawing Center Dashes or Centerlines in a Circle or Arc

When small circles or arcs are dimensioned, the **DIMDIAMETER** and **DIMRADIUS** commands leave center dashes. If the dimension of a large circle crosses through the center, the dashes are left out. However, you can manually add center dashes and centerlines with the **DIMCENTER** command. The command is accessed by picking the **Center Mark** button on the **Dimension** toolbar, picking **Center Mark** in the **Dimension** pull-down menu, or entering DCE or DIMCENTER at the Command: prompt. The command sequence is:

> Command: **DCE** *or* **DIMCENTER**↵
> Select arc or circle: (*pick the arc or circle*)
> Command:

When the circle or arc is picked, center marks are automatically drawn. The size of the center marks or the amount that the centerlines extend outside the circle or arc is controlled by the **Center Mark for Circles** area in the **Lines and Arrows** tab of the **Modify Dimension Style** dialog box. Later in this chapter you will see how to control all settings for the display of dimensions using dimension styles. **Figure 17-33** shows the difference between drawing center marks and centerlines in arcs and circles.

**Figure 17-33.**
Arcs and circles displayed with center marks and centerlines.

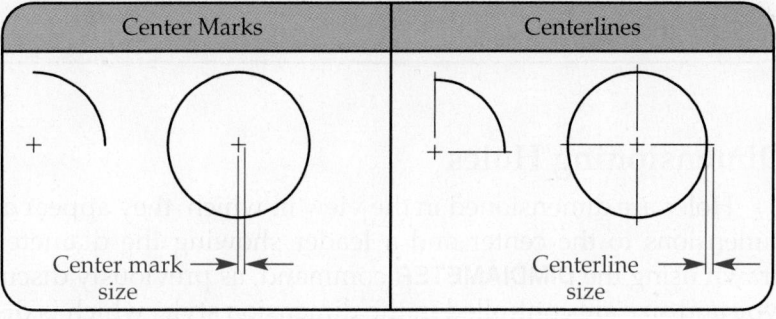

## Dimensioning Circles

Circles are normally dimensioned by giving the diameter. The ASME standard for dimensioning arcs is to give the radius. However, AutoCAD allows you to dimension either a circle or an arc with a diameter dimension. Diameter dimensions are produced by picking the **Diameter Dimension** button on the **Dimension** toolbar, picking **Diameter** in the **Dimension** pull-down menu, or entering DDI or DIMDIAMETER at the Command: prompt. You are then asked to select the arc or circle.

When using the **DIMDIAMETER** command, a leader line and diameter dimension value are attached to the cursor when you pick the desired circle or arc. You can drag the leader to any desired location and length before picking where you want it. The resulting leader points to the center of the circle or arc just as recommended by the ASME standard. See **Figure 17-34.** The command sequence is:

> Command: **DDI** *or* **DIMDIAMETER**↵
> Select arc or circle: (*pick the circle*)
> Dimension text = 1.250
> Specify dimension line location or [Mtext/Text/Angle]: (*pick the dimension line location*)
> Command:

In the right margin near the top:

**DIMCENTER**
**DCE**

Dimension
➡ Center Mark

Dimension
toolbar

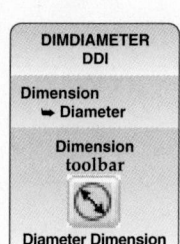

Center Mark

In the right margin near the bottom:

**DIMDIAMETER**
**DDI**

Dimension
➡ Diameter

Dimension
toolbar

Diameter Dimension

**Figure 17-34.** Using the **DIMDIAMETER** command with the AutoCAD dimensioning variable defaults.

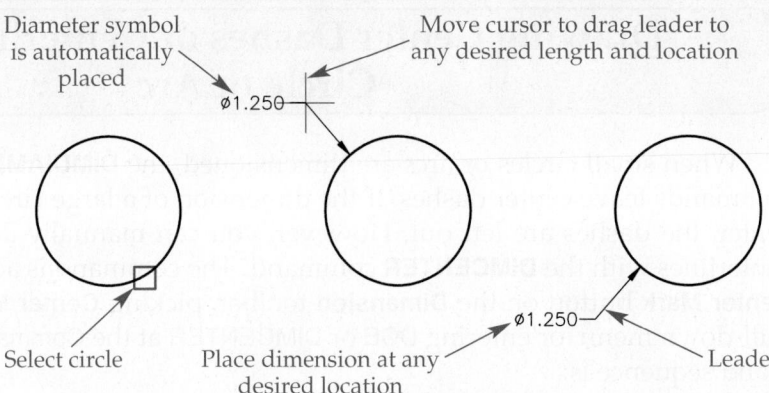

Diameter symbol is automatically placed

Move cursor to drag leader to any desired length and location

ø1.250

Select circle

Place dimension at any desired location

ø1.250

Leader

You also have the **Mtext**, **Text**, and **Angle** options that were introduced earlier. Use the **Mtext** or **Text** option if you want to change the text value or the **Angle** option if you want to change the angle of the text.

---

### Exercise 17-7

○ Start AutoCAD and use one of your templates.
○ Set up the appropriate layers for your drawing elements, including one for dimensions.
○ Draw and dimension an object similar to **Figure 17-34**.
○ Save the drawing as EX17-7.

---

## Dimensioning Holes

Holes are dimensioned in the view in which they appear as circles. Give location dimensions to the center and a leader showing the diameter. Leader lines can be drawn using the **DIMDIAMETER** command, as previously discussed. The center mark type and size are controlled in the dimension style, which is discussed later. Multiple holes of the same size can be noted with one hole dimension, such as 2X Ø.50. See **Figure 17-35**. Use the **Mtext** or **Text** option to create this dimension. The **Angle** option can be used to change the angle of the text numbers, but it is not commonly done.

---

**PROFESSIONAL TIP**

The ASME standard recommends a small space between the object and the extension line. This happens when the **Offset from Origin** setting within the dimension style is set to its default or some other desired positive value. This is very useful *except* when providing dimensions to centerlines for the location of holes. When the endpoint of the centerline is picked, a positive value leaves a space between the centerline and the beginning of the extension line. This is not a preferred practice. Change the **Offset from Origin** setting to 0 to remove the gap. Be sure to change back to its positive setting when dimensioning other objects.

Use of the **Dimension Style Manager** dialog box to set this and other dimensioning settings is fully explained later in this chapter.

---

AutoCAD and its Applications—Basics

Figure 17-35.
Dimensioning holes.

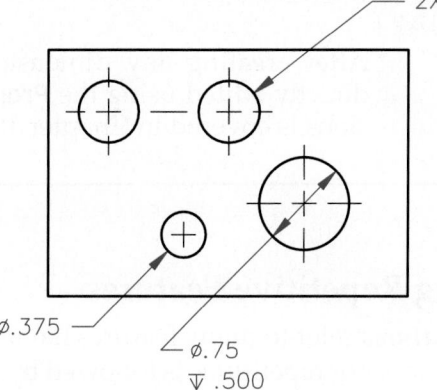

## Dimensioning for Manufacturing Processes

A *counterbore* is a larger-diameter hole machined at one end of a smaller hole. It provides a place for the head of a bolt. A *spotface* is similar to a counterbore except that it is not as deep. The spotface provides a smooth, recessed surface for a washer. A *countersink* is a cone-shaped recess at one end of a hole. It provides a mating surface for a screw head of the same shape. A note for these features is provided using symbols. First, locate the centers in the circular view. Then, place a leader providing machining information in a note. See **Figure 17-36.**

Symbols for this type of application can be customized, as discussed in Chapter 22. These symbols can also be drawn by creating a dimension style with a text style using the gdt.shx font, as explained earlier in this chapter. The symbols and related gdt.shx keyboard letter used to make the symbol are displayed in **Figure 17-32.**

The **DIMDIAMETER** command gives you multiline text to use during the creation of the dimension. Additional text can be added by editing the dimension text, since it is actually an mtext object.

Figure 17-36.
Dimension notes for machining processes. The symbols can be inserted as blocks or as lowercase letters when the gdt.shx font is used.

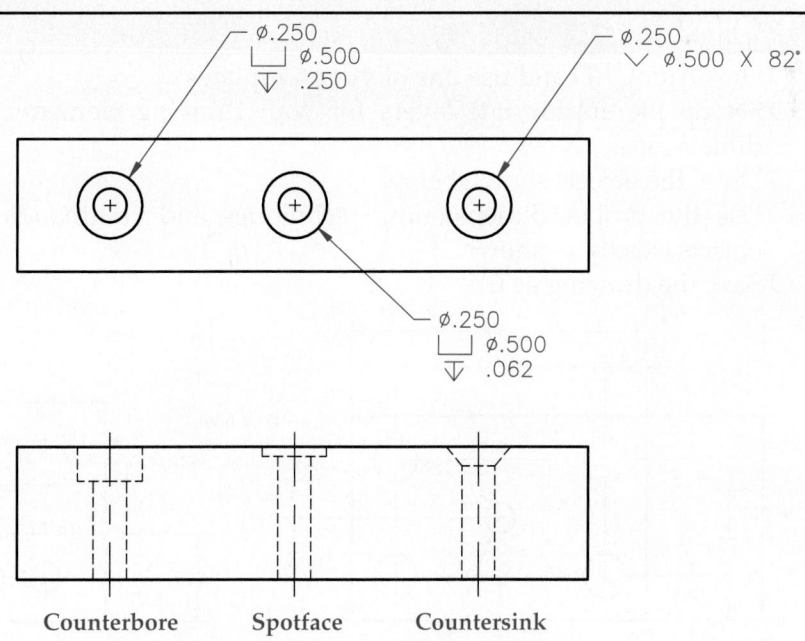

After creating any dimension, the dimension text can be directly edited using the **Properties** window. Editing dimensions is covered in Chapter 18 of this text.

## Dimensioning Repetitive Features

*Repetitive features* refer to many features having the same shape and size. When this occurs, the number of repetitions is followed by an X, a space, and the size dimension. The dimension is then connected to the feature with a leader. See **Figure 17-37**.

**Figure 17-37.**
Dimensioning repetitive features (shown in color).

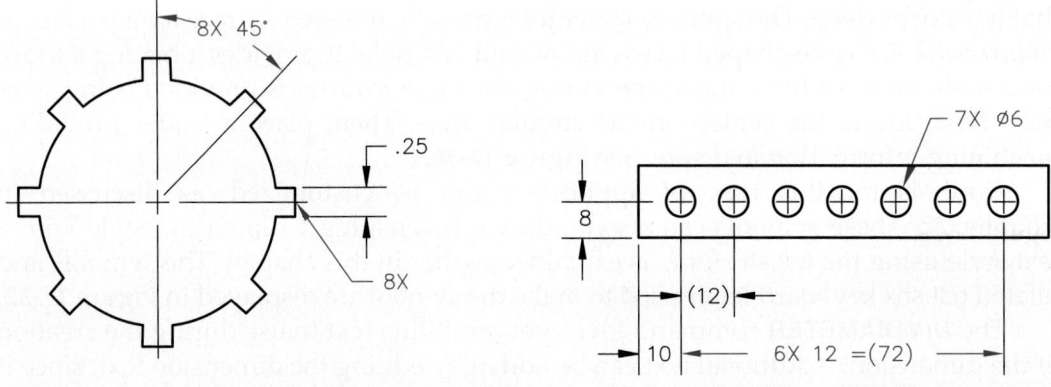

### Exercise 17-8

○ Start AutoCAD and use one of your templates.
○ Set up the appropriate layers for your drawing elements, including one for dimensions.
○ Draw the objects shown below.
○ Use the proper dimensioning techniques and commands to dimension the objects exactly as shown.
○ Save the drawing as EX17-8.

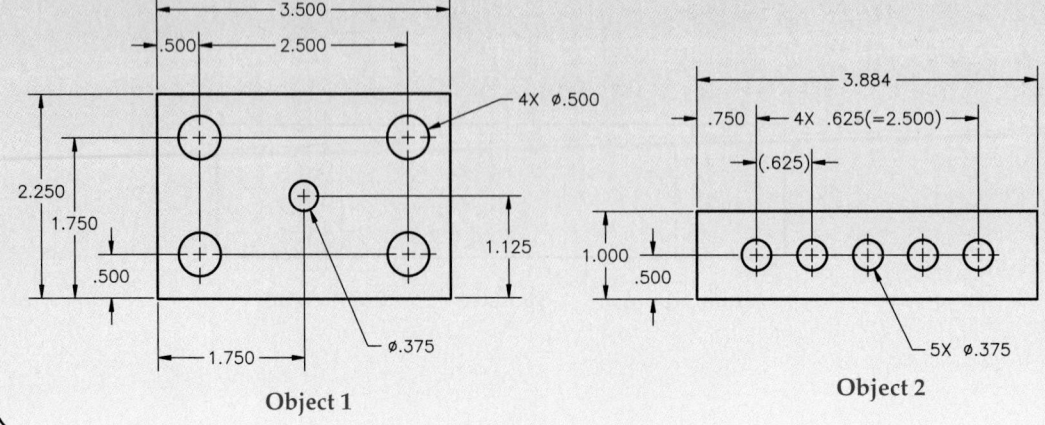

Object 1                                      Object 2

DIMRADIUS
DRA

Dimension
➡ Radius

Dimension
toolbar

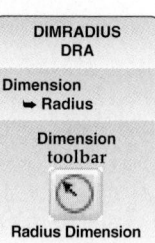

Radius Dimension

# Dimensioning Arcs

The standard for dimensioning arcs is a radius dimension. A radius dimension is placed with the **DIMRADIUS** command. Access this command by picking the **Radius Dimension** button on the **Dimension** toolbar, picking **Radius** in the **Dimension** pull-down menu, or entering either DRA or DIMRADIUS at the Command: prompt.

When you pick the desired arc or circle to dimension, a leader line and radius dimension value are attached to the cursor. You can drag the leader to any desired location and length before picking where you want it. The resulting leader points to the center of the arc or circle as recommended by the ASME standard. See **Figure 17-38.** The command sequence is:

> Command: **DRA** *or* **DIMRADIUS.**↵
> Select arc or circle: *(pick an arc)*
> Dimension text = 0.750
> Specify dimension line location or [Mtext/Text/Angle]: *(drag the leader to a desired location and pick)*
> Command:

As with the previous dimensioning commands, you can use the **Mtext** or **Text** option to change the dimension text. You can also use the **Angle** option to change the angle of the text value.

**Figure 17-38.**
Using the **DIMRADIUS** command to dimension arcs with AutoCAD dimensioning defaults.

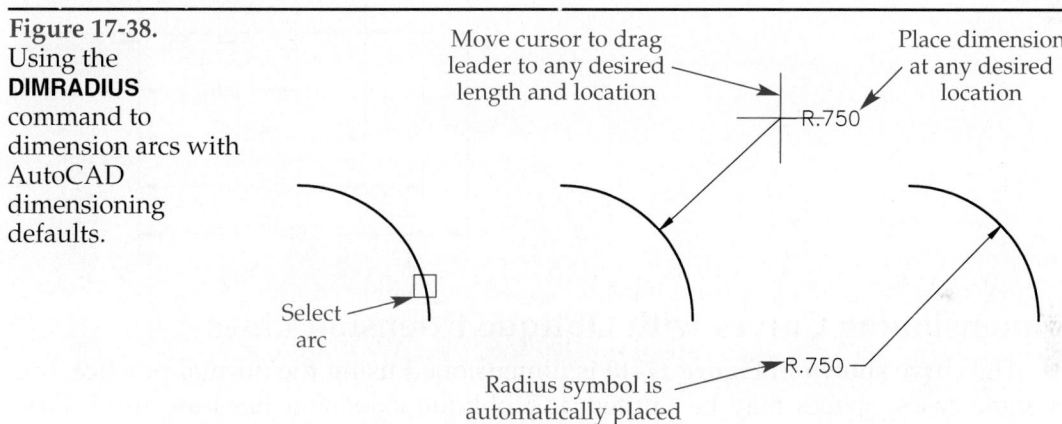

## Dimensioning Fillets and Rounds

Small inside arcs are called *fillets.* Small arcs on outside corners are called *rounds.* Fillets are designed to strengthen inside corners. Rounds are used to relieve sharp corners. Fillets and rounds can be dimensioned individually as arcs or in a general note. The general note such as ALL FILLETS AND ROUNDS R.125 UNLESS OTHERWISE SPECIFIED is usually placed near the title block. See **Figure 17-39.**

**Figure 17-39.**
Dimensioning fillets and rounds.

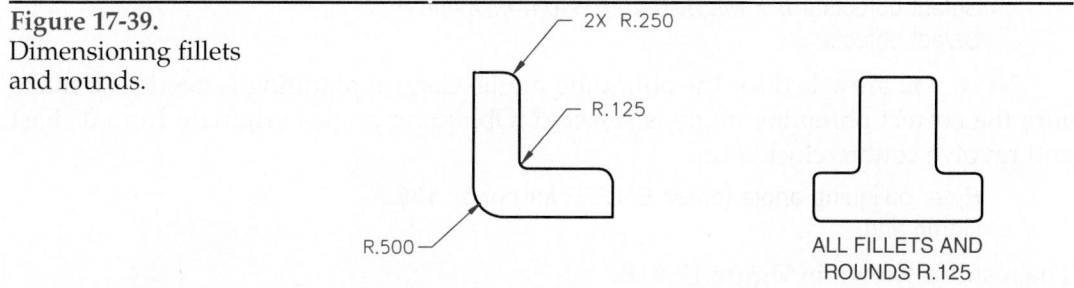

---

○ Start AutoCAD and use one of your templates.
○ Set up the appropriate layers for your drawing elements, including one for dimensions.
○ Draw and dimension an object similar to **Figure 17-38**.
○ Draw and dimension objects similar to **Figure 17-39**.
○ Save the drawing as EX17-9.

## Dimensioning Curves

When possible, curves are dimensioned as arcs. When they are not in the shape of a constant-radius arc, they should be dimensioned to points along the curve using the **DIMLINEAR** command. See **Figure 17-40**.

Figure 17-40.
Dimensioning
curves that do not
have a constant
radius.

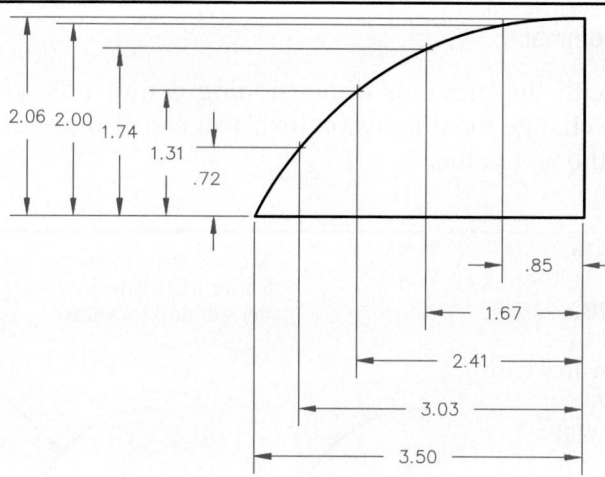

## Dimensioning Curves with Oblique Extension Lines

The curve shown in **Figure 17-40** is dimensioned using the normal practice, but, in some cases, spaces may be limited and oblique extension lines are used. First, dimension the object using the **DIMLINEAR** command as appropriate, even if dimensions are crowded or overlap. See **Figure 17-41A**.

The .150 and .340 dimensions are to be placed at an oblique angle above the view. The **Oblique** option of the **DIMEDIT** command is used to draw oblique dimensions. The **DIMEDIT** command is explained in detail in Chapter 18. The command option is accessed by picking **Oblique** in the **Dimension** pull-down menu. After selecting the command, you are asked to select the objects. Pick the dimensions to be redrawn at an oblique angle. In this case, the .150 and .340 dimensions are selected.

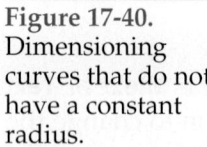

DIMEDIT

Dimension
→ Oblique

Command: **DIMEDIT**↵
Enter type of dimension editing [Home/New/Rotate/Oblique] <Home>: **O**↵
Select objects: *(pick the .150 and .340 dimensions)*
Select objects: ↵

Next, you are asked for the obliquing angle. Careful planning is needed to make sure the correct obliquing angle is selected. Obliquing angles originate from 0° East and revolve counterclockwise.

Enter obliquing angle (press ENTER for none): **135**↵
Command:

The result is shown in **Figure 17-41B**.

Figure 17-41.
Drawing
dimensions with
oblique extension
lines.

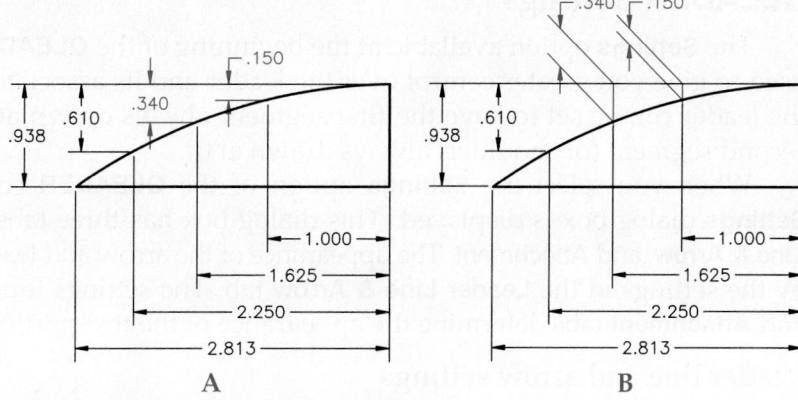

A                                    B

## Drawing Leader Lines

The **DIMDIAMETER** and **DIMRADIUS** commands automatically place leaders on the drawing. The **QLEADER** command allows you to begin and end a leader line where you desire. You can also place single or multiple lines of text with the leader. This command is ideal for:

- Adding specific notes to the drawing.
- Staggering a leader line to go around other drawing features. Keep in mind that staggering leader lines is not a recommended ASME standard.
- Drawing a double leader. Drawing two leaders from one note is not a recommended ASME standard.
- Making custom leader lines.
- Drawing curved leaders for architectural applications.

The **QLEADER** command creates leader lines and related notes that are considered complex objects. This command provides you with the flexibility to place tolerances and multiple lines of text with the leader. Some of the leader line characteristics, such as arrowhead size, are controlled by the dimension style settings. Other features, such as the leader format and annotation style, are controlled by the **Settings** option within the **QLEADER** command. An *annotation* is text such as notes and dimensions on a drawing.

The **QLEADER** command is accessed by picking the **Quick Leader** button in the **Dimension** toolbar, selecting **Leader** in the **Dimension** pull-down menu, or typing LE or QLEADER at the Command: prompt. The first two prompts look like the **LINE** command, with the Specify from point: and Specify to point: prompts. This allows you to pick where the leader begins and ends.

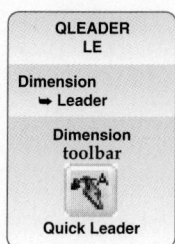

QLEADER
LE

Dimension
➥ Leader

Dimension
toolbar

Quick Leader

> Command: **LE** *or* **QLEADER**.⏎
> Specify first leader point, or [Settings] <Settings>: *(pick the leader start point)*
> Specify next point: *(pick the second leader point, which is the start of the leader shoulder)*
> Specify next point: *(press* [Enter] *and the shoulder is drawn automatically)*
> Specify text width <0.0000>: ⏎
> Enter first line of annotation text <Mtext>: *(enter text)*
> Enter next line of annotation text: ⏎

In this example, AutoCAD automatically draws a leader shoulder in front of the text.

In mechanical drafting, properly drawn leaders have one straight segment extending from the feature to a horizontal shoulder that is 1/4" (6 mm) long. While most other fields also use straight leaders, AutoCAD provides the option of drawing curved leaders, which are commonly used in architectural drafting. This is done with the **Settings** option of the command.

## QLEADER Settings

The **Settings** option available at the beginning of the **QLEADER** command can be used to give you greater control over the leader and its associated text. For example, the leader can be set to have the first segment always drawn at a 45° angle and the second segment (or shoulder) always drawn at 0°.

When you select the **Settings** option of the **QLEADER** command, the **Leader Settings** dialog box is displayed. This dialog box has three tabs: **Annotation**, **Leader Line & Arrow**, and **Attachment**. The appearance of the arrow and leader line is determined by the settings in the **Leader Line & Arrow** tab. The settings found in the **Annotation** and **Attachment** tabs determine the appearance of the text portion of the leader.

### Leader line and arrow settings

The **Leader Line & Arrow** tab of the **Leader Settings** dialog box is shown in **Figure 17-42.** The settings in this tab determine the type of arrowhead, type of leader line, angles for leader line and shoulder, and number of requested points.

The **Leader Line** area is used to specify the shape of the leader line. A leader with straight-line segments is drawn by picking the **Straight** radio button. A curved leader is drawn by picking the **Spline** radio button. The spline leader is commonly used in architectural drafting. **Figure 17-43** shows examples of the spline and straight leader lines.

**Figure 17-42.**
The **Leader Line & Arrow** tab of the **Leader Settings** dialog box.

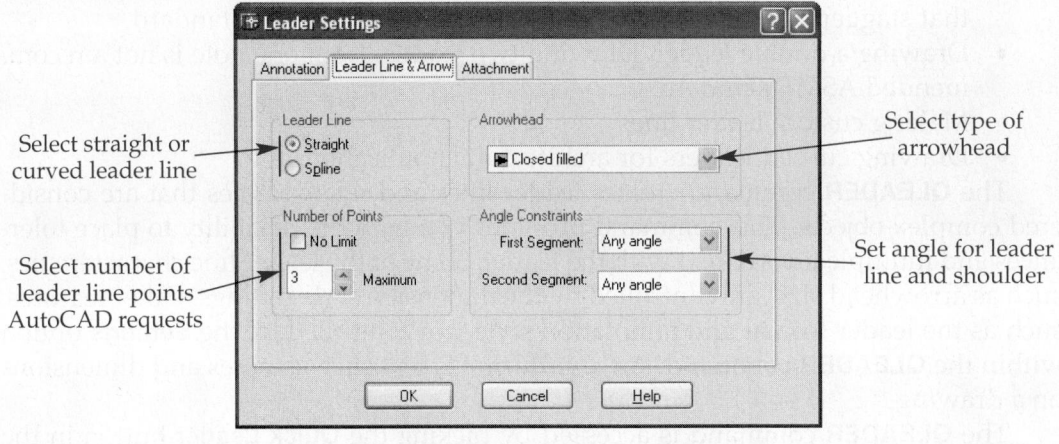

**Figure 17-43.**
The type of leader line (straight or spline) is set in the **Leader Line & Arrow** tab of the **Leader Settings** dialog box.

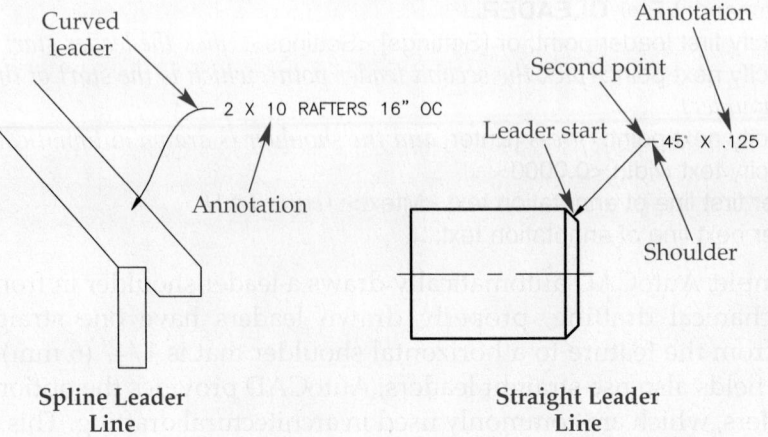

You can also set the maximum number of vertices on the leader line. This is set in the **Number of Points** area. Set a maximum number of vertices in the **Maximum** text box or select the **No Limit** check box to have an unlimited number. After the maximum number is reached, the **QLEADER** command automatically stops drawing the leader and asks for text information. To use less than the maximum number of points, press the [Enter] key at the Specify next point prompt. If the leader is a line object, a value of three for the maximum number of points defines a maximum total of two line segments.

The **Arrowhead** area uses the default value assigned to leaders within the current dimension style. To change the appearance of the arrowhead, pick the drop-down list and select a terminator from the full range of choices. Changing the **Arrowhead** setting creates a dimension style override, which is discussed later in this chapter.

The first two segments of the leader line can be restricted to certain angles. These angles are set in the **Angle Constraints** area. The options for each segment are **Any angle**, **Horizontal**, **90**, **45**, **30**, or **15**. The **Ortho** mode setting overrides the angle constraints so it is advisable to turn **Ortho** mode off while using this command.

**PROFESSIONAL TIP**

The ASME standard for leaders does not recommend a leader line that is less than 15° or greater than 75° from horizontal. Use the **Angle Constraints** settings in the **Leader Settings** dialog box to help maintain these standards.

### Leader text settings

The **Annotation** and **Attachment** tabs of the **Leader Settings** dialog box control the way text is used with the leader line. The **Annotation** tab contains settings that specify the type of object used for annotation, additional options for mtext objects, and tools that automatically repeat annotations. The **Attachment** tab has options for specifying the point where the leader line shoulder meets an mtext annotation object.

The **Annotation** tab is shown in **Figure 17-44**. The **Annotation Type** area determines which type of entity is inserted and attached to the end of the leader line. The following options are available.

- **MText.** This is the default setting, causing a multiline text object to be inserted after the leader lines are drawn. See **Figure 17-45A.**
- **Copy an Object.** This option allows an mtext, text, block, or tolerance object to be copied from the current drawing and inserted at the end of the current leader line. This is useful when the same note or symbol is required in many places throughout a drawing. After drawing the leader line, the Select an object to copy: prompt appears. The selected object is placed at the end of the shoulder. See **Figure 17-45B.**
- **Tolerance.** This displays the **Geometric Tolerance** dialog box for creation of a feature control frame after the leader line is drawn. See **Figure 17-45C.** Geometric tolerancing is explained in detail in Chapter 20 of this text.
- **Block Reference.** This option inserts a specified block at the end of the leader. A *block* is a symbol that was previously created and saved. Blocks can be inserted into other drawings. These multiple-use symbols are explained in detail in Chapter 22 of this text. Blocks can be scaled during the insertion process. A special symbol block named Target is inserted in **Figure 17-45D.**
- **None.** This option ends the leader with no annotation of any kind. See **Figure 17-45E.** The **None** option can be used as a way to create multiple leaders for a single leader annotation, as shown in **Figure 17-46.** Multiple leaders are not a recommended ASME standard, but they are used for some

**Figure 17-44.**
The **Annotation** tab of the **Leader Settings** dialog box.

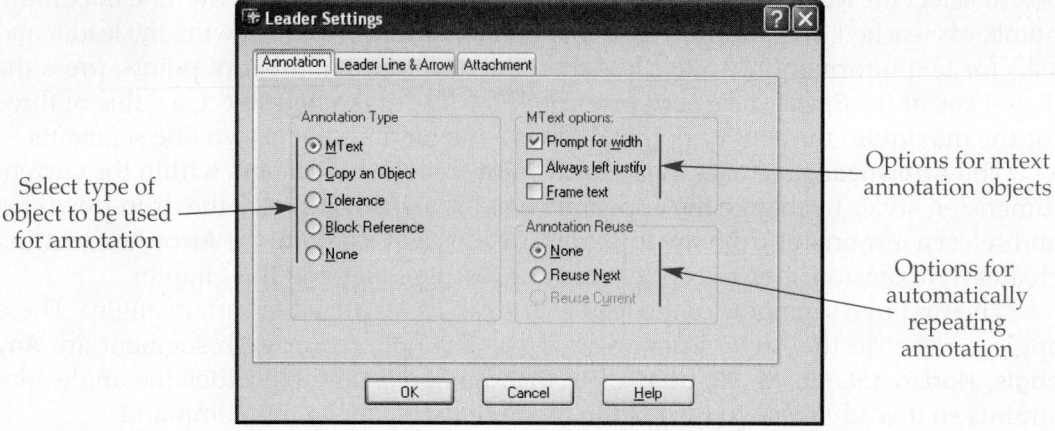

Select type of
object to be used
for annotation

Options for mtext
annotation objects

Options for
automatically
repeating
annotation

**Figure 17-45.**
The annotation type is selected in the **Annotation** tab of the **Leader Settings** dialog box.

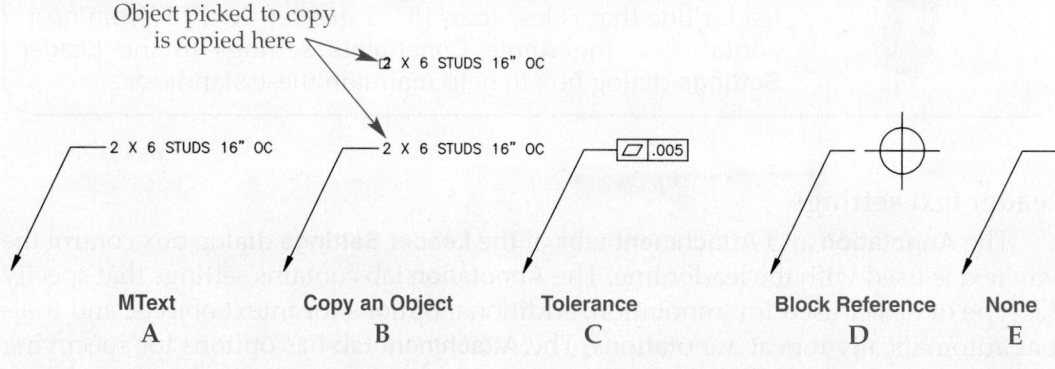

Object picked to copy
is copied here

2 X 6 STUDS 16" OC

2 X 6 STUDS 16" OC        2 X 6 STUDS 16" OC        .005

| MText | Copy an Object | Tolerance | Block Reference | None |
|-------|----------------|-----------|-----------------|------|
| A | B | C | D | E |

**Figure 17-46.**
Use the **None** annotation option when drawing multiple leaders.

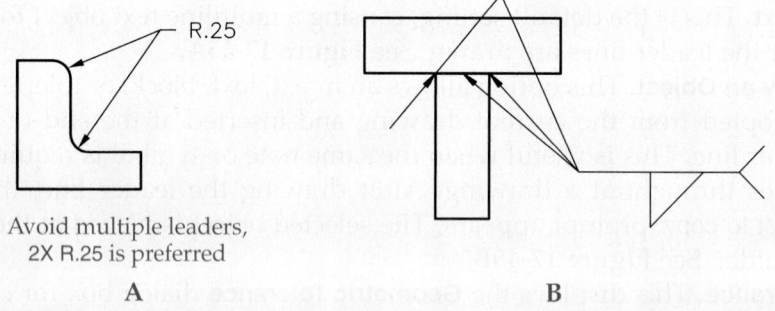

R.25

Avoid multiple leaders,
2X R.25 is preferred

A                                            B

applications, such as the leader for welding symbols. The welding symbol shown in **Figure 17-46B** was created as a block and then inserted using the **Block Reference** annotation option.

You can automatically repeat the previous leader annotation using the options in the **Annotation Reuse** area. The default option is **None**. This allows you to specify the annotation when creating a leader. If you wish to use an annotation repeatedly, select the **Reuse Next** option and then create the first leader and annotation. When you create another leader, the setting automatically changes to **Reuse Current** and the annotation is inserted. The annotation is repeated for all new leaders until the **Annotation Reuse** setting is changed back to **None**.

The **MText options** area of the **Annotation** tab is only available if **MText** is selected as the annotation type. These settings can be overridden by selecting the **MText** option during the **QLEADER** command. The following options are available.

- **Prompt for width.** If checked, you are prompted to define the size of the mtext box. If this option is not checked, a value of 0 (no text wrapping) is assigned to the mtext box.
- **Always left justify.** Forces the mtext to be left justified, regardless of the direction of the leader line.
- **Frame text.** Creates a box around the mtext text box. The default properties of the frame are controlled by the dimension line settings of the current dimension style.

The **Attachment** tab is only available when the **MText** option is selected in the **Annotation Type** area of the **Annotation** tab. This tab contains options that determine how the mtext object is positioned relative to the endpoint of the leader line shoulder. See **Figure 17-47.** Different options can be specified for mtext to the right of the leader line and mtext to the left of the leader line. These options are shown in **Figure 17-48.**

The **Underline bottom line** option causes a line to be drawn along the bottom of the mtext box. When this check box is selected, the choices for text on left and right side become grayed-out.

**Figure 17-47.**
The **Attachment** tab of the **Leader Settings** dialog box determines the location of the mtext annotation relative to the leader line shoulder.

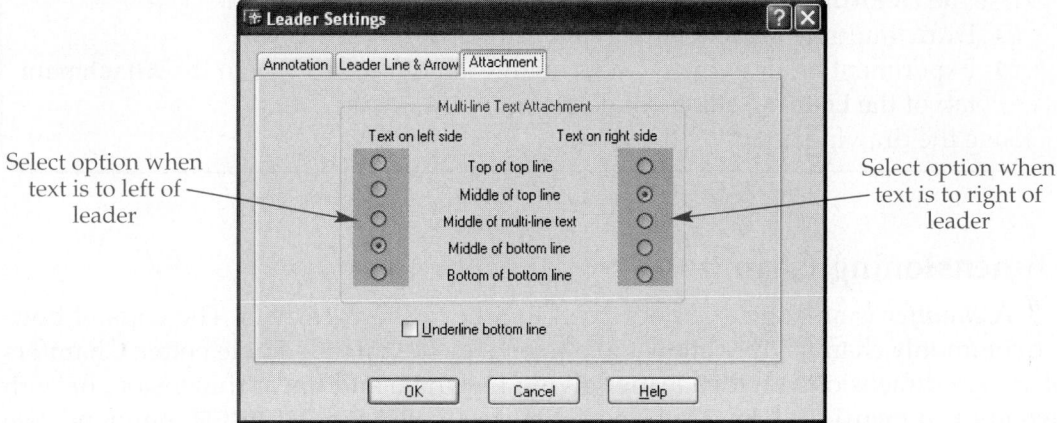

**PROFESSIONAL TIP**

Common drafting practice is to use the **Middle of bottom line** option for left-sided text and the **Middle of top line** option for right-sided text. These are the default settings.

**NOTE**

The **LEADER** command can also be used to draw leaders. This command does not provide the convenience, flexibility, and ability to easily comply with drafting standards as does the **QLEADER** command.

**Figure 17-48.**
Placement of mtext is controlled by the options in the **Attachment** tab of the **Leader Settings** dialog box. Shaded examples are the recommended ASME standard.

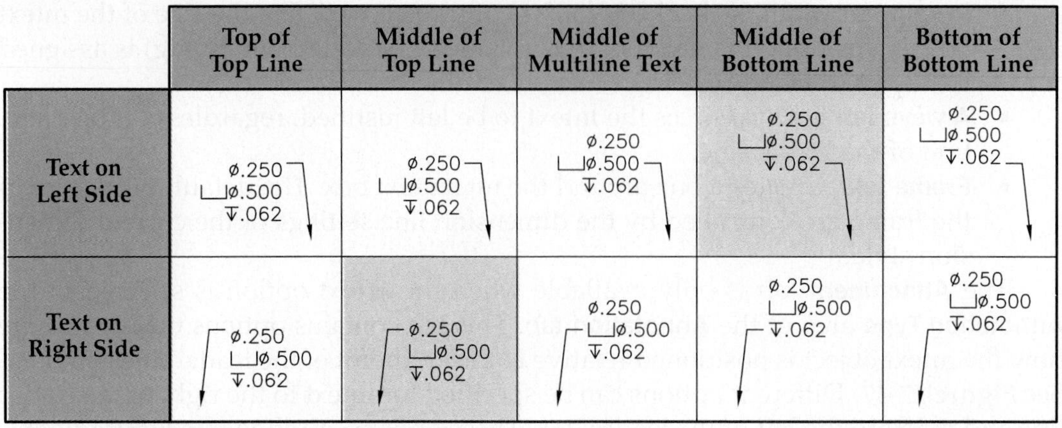

| | Top of Top Line | Middle of Top Line | Middle of Multiline Text | Middle of Bottom Line | Bottom of Bottom Line |
|---|---|---|---|---|---|
| **Text on Left Side** | ⌀.250 ⌴⌀.500 ∇.062 | ⌀.250 ⌴⌀.500 ∇.062 | ⌀.250 ⌴⌀.500 ∇.062 | ⌀.250 ⌴⌀.500 ∇.062 | ⌀.250 ⌴⌀.500 ∇.062 |
| **Text on Right Side** | ⌀.250 ⌴⌀.500 ∇.062 | ⌀.250 ⌴⌀.500 ∇.062 | ⌀.250 ⌴⌀.500 ∇.062 | ⌀.250 ⌴⌀.500 ∇.062 | ⌀.250 ⌴⌀.500 ∇.062 |

## Exercise 17-10

○ Start AutoCAD and use one of your templates.
○ Set up the appropriate layers for your drawing elements, including one for dimensions.
○ Draw and dimension objects similar to **Figure 17-43**.
○ Use the **QLEADER** command to:
    ○ Draw multiple leaders with a note similar to **Figure 17-46**.
    ○ Experiment by drawing a leader with each of the settings in the **Attachment** tab of the **Leader Settings** dialog box.
○ Save the drawing as EX17-10.

## Dimensioning Chamfers

A *chamfer* is an angled surface used to relieve sharp corners. The ends of bolts are commonly chamfered to allow them to engage the threaded hole better. Chamfers of 45° are dimensioned with a leader giving the angle and linear dimension, or with two linear dimensions. This can be accomplished using the **QLEADER** command. See **Figure 17-49**.

Chamfers other than 45° must have either the angle and a linear dimension or two linear dimensions placed on the view. See **Figure 17-50**. The **DIMLINEAR** and **DIMANGULAR** commands are used for this purpose.

## Exercise 17-11

○ Start AutoCAD and use one of your templates.
○ Set up the appropriate layers for your drawing elements, including one for dimensions.
○ Draw and dimension objects similar to **Figure 17-49**.
○ Draw and dimension objects similar to **Figure 17-50**.
○ Save the drawing as EX17-11.

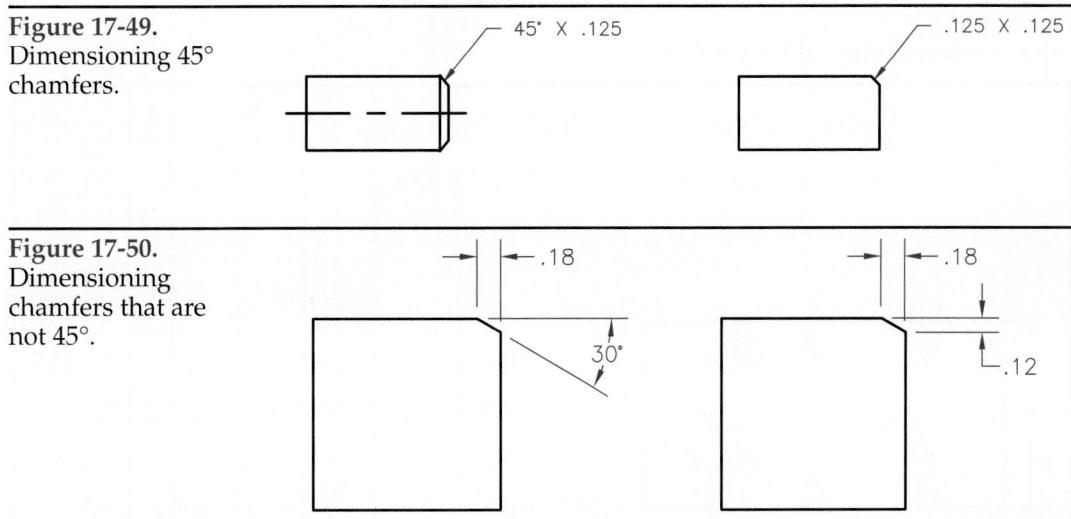

**Figure 17-49.**
Dimensioning 45°
chamfers.

45° X .125

.125 X .125

**Figure 17-50.**
Dimensioning
chamfers that are
not 45°.

.18

30°

.18

.12

## Alternate Dimensioning Practices

It is becoming common to omit dimension lines in industries where computer-controlled machining processes are used. Arrowless, tabular, and chart dimensioning are three types of dimensioning that omit dimension lines. These three types are discussed in the next sections.

### Arrowless Dimensioning

*Arrowless dimensioning* is becoming popular in mechanical drafting. It is also used in electronics drafting, especially for chassis layout. This type of dimensioning has only extension lines and numbers. Dimension lines and arrowheads are omitted. Dimension numbers are aligned with the extension lines. Each dimension number represents a dimension originating from a common point. This starting, or 0, dimension is typically known as a *datum,* or *baseline.* Holes or other features are labeled with identification letters. Sizes for these features are given in a table placed on the drawing. See **Figure 17-51.**

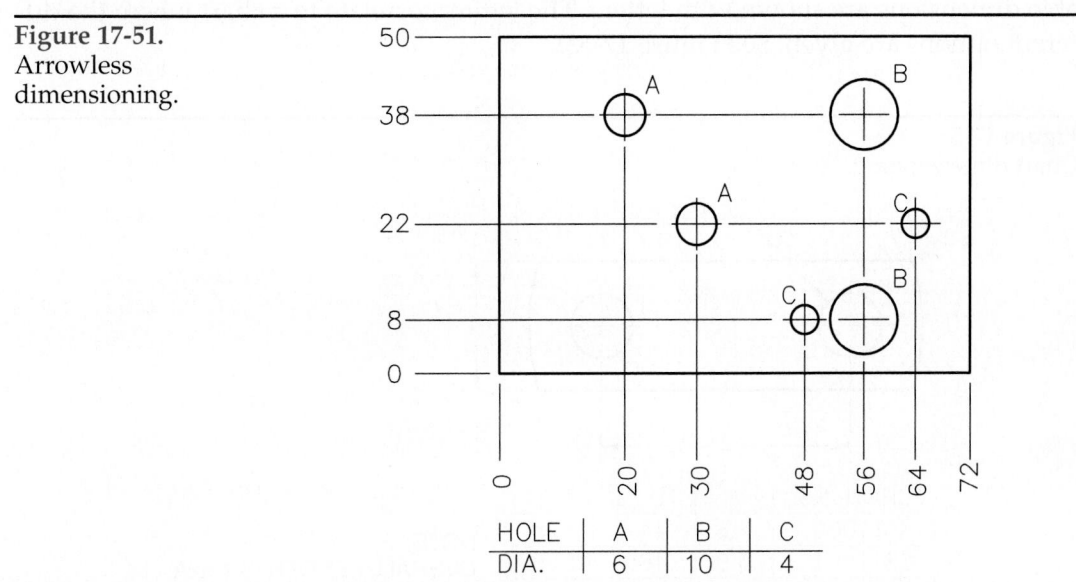

**Figure 17-51.**
Arrowless
dimensioning.

| HOLE | A | B | C |
|------|---|---|---|
| DIA. | 6 | 10 | 4 |

Figure 17-52.
Tabular dimensioning. (Doug Major)

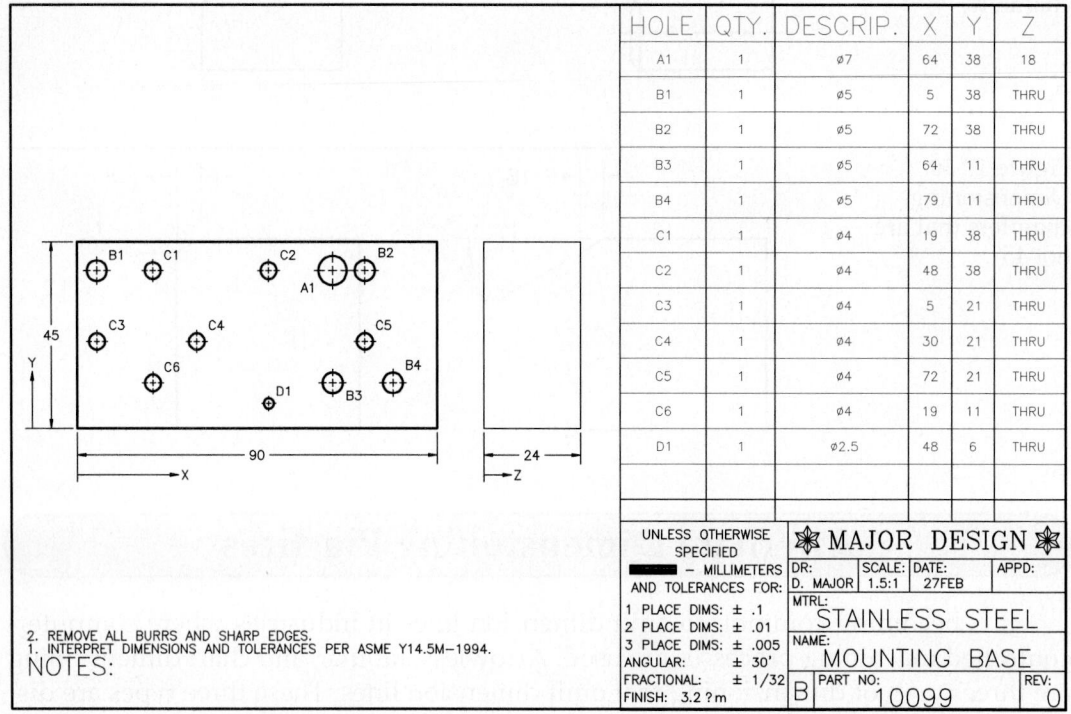

| HOLE | QTY. | DESCRIP. | X | Y | Z |
|------|------|----------|----|----|------|
| A1 | 1 | ⌀7 | 64 | 38 | 18 |
| B1 | 1 | ⌀5 | 5 | 38 | THRU |
| B2 | 1 | ⌀5 | 72 | 38 | THRU |
| B3 | 1 | ⌀5 | 64 | 11 | THRU |
| B4 | 1 | ⌀5 | 79 | 11 | THRU |
| C1 | 1 | ⌀4 | 19 | 38 | THRU |
| C2 | 1 | ⌀4 | 48 | 38 | THRU |
| C3 | 1 | ⌀4 | 5 | 21 | THRU |
| C4 | 1 | ⌀4 | 30 | 21 | THRU |
| C5 | 1 | ⌀4 | 72 | 21 | THRU |
| C6 | 1 | ⌀4 | 19 | 11 | THRU |
| D1 | 1 | ⌀2.5 | 48 | 6 | THRU |

NOTES:
1. INTERPRET DIMENSIONS AND TOLERANCES PER ASME Y14.5M−1994.
2. REMOVE ALL BURRS AND SHARP EDGES.

| UNLESS OTHERWISE SPECIFIED | ✳ MAJOR DESIGN ✳ | | | |
|---|---|---|---|---|
| ▬▬ − MILLIMETERS AND TOLERANCES FOR: | DR: D. MAJOR | SCALE: 1.5:1 | DATE: 27FEB | APPD: |
| 1 PLACE DIMS: ± .1 2 PLACE DIMS: ± .01 3 PLACE DIMS: ± .005 | MTRL: STAINLESS STEEL | | | |
| ANGULAR: ± 30' | NAME: MOUNTING BASE | | | |
| FRACTIONAL: ± 1/32 FINISH: 3.2 ?m | B | PART NO: 10099 | | REV: 0 |

## Tabular Dimensioning

*Tabular dimensioning* is a form of arrowless dimensioning where dimensions to features are shown in a table. Each feature is labeled with a letter or number that correlates to the table. The table gives the location of features from the X and Y axes. It also provides the depth of features from a Z axis, when appropriate. See **Figure 17-52.**

## Chart Dimensioning

*Chart dimensioning* may take the form of unidirectional, aligned, arrowless, or tabular dimensioning. It provides flexibility in situations where dimensions change as requirements of the product change. The views of the product are drawn and variable dimensions are shown with letters. The letters correlate to a chart where the different options are given. See **Figure 17-53.**

Figure 17-53.
Chart dimensioning.

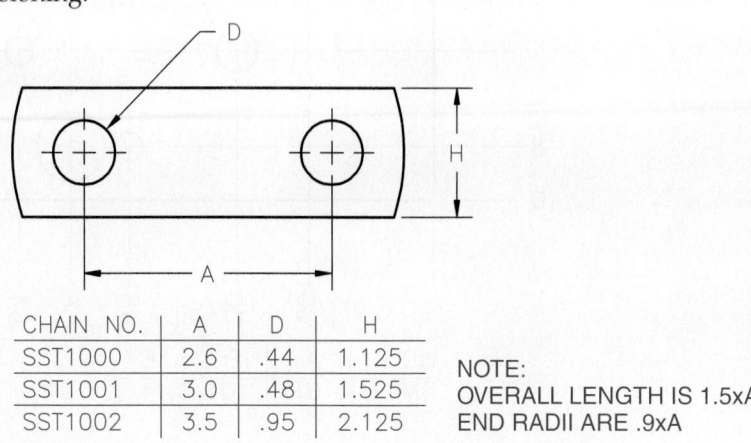

| CHAIN NO. | A | D | H |
|-----------|-----|-----|-------|
| SST1000 | 2.6 | .44 | 1.125 |
| SST1001 | 3.0 | .48 | 1.525 |
| SST1002 | 3.5 | .95 | 2.125 |

NOTE:
OVERALL LENGTH IS 1.5xA
END RADII ARE .9xA

## WCS and UCS

The world coordinate system (WCS) origin, the 0,0,0 coordinate, has been in the lower-left corner of the screen for the drawings you have already completed. In most cases, this is fine. However, when doing arrowless dimensioning, it is best to have the dimensions originate from a primary datum, which is often a corner of the object. Depending on how the object is drawn, this point may or may not align with the WCS origin.

The WCS is fixed; the user coordinate system (UCS), on the other hand, can be moved to any orientation desired. The UCS is discussed in detail in *AutoCAD and its Applications—Advanced*. In general, the UCS allows you to set your own coordinate system.

All arrowless dimensions drawn in AutoCAD originate from the current UCS origin. Move the UCS origin to the corner of the object or the appropriate datum feature by selecting **Move UCS** from the **Tools** pull-down menu. You are then prompted to specify a new origin point. Use an object snap mode to select the corner of the object or appropriate datum feature. In **Figure 17-54A**, the UCS is moved to an appropriate location.

When done drawing arrowless dimensions from a datum, you can leave the UCS origin at the datum or move it back to the WCS origin. To return to the WCS, select **World** from the **New UCS** cascading menu in the **Tools** pull-down menu.

## Drawing Arrowless Dimensions

AutoCAD refers to arrowless dimensioning as *ordinate dimensioning.* These dimensions are drawn using the **DIMORDINATE** command, which is accessed by picking the **Ordinate Dimension** button on the **Dimension** toolbar, picking **Ordinate** in the **Dimension** pull-down menu, or entering DOR or DIMORDINATE at the Command: prompt. When using this command, AutoCAD automatically places an extension line and number along X and Y coordinates.

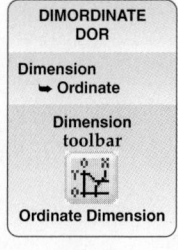

Since you are working in the XY plane, it is often best to have **Ortho** mode on. Also, if there are circles on your drawing, use the **DIMCENTER** command to place center marks in the circles, as shown in **Figure 17-54B**. This makes your drawing conform to ASME standards and provides something to pick when dimensioning the circle locations.

Now, you are ready to start placing the ordinate dimensions. Enter the **DIMORDINATE** command:

> Command: **DOR** *or* **DIMORDINATE.**↵
> Specify feature location: (*pick the feature to be dimensioned*)

When the Specify feature location: prompt appears, move the screen cursor to the point or feature to be dimensioned. If the feature is the corner of the object, pick the corner. If the feature is a circle, pick the end of the center mark. This leaves the required space

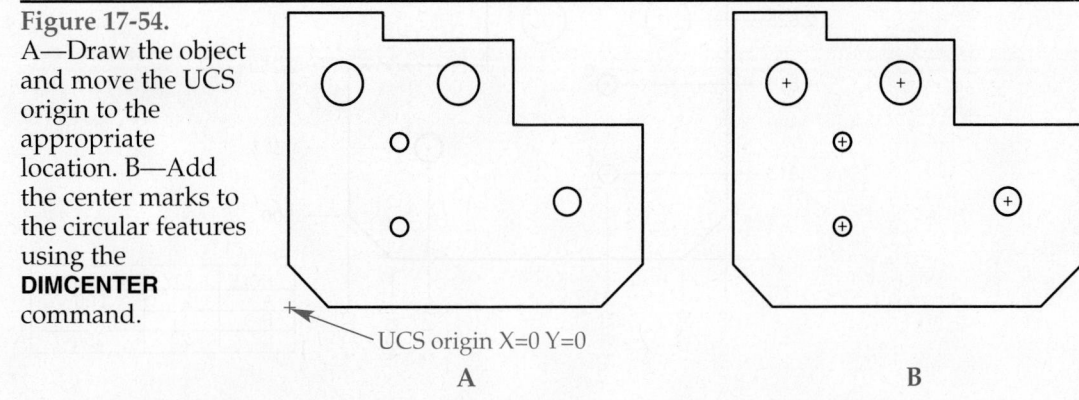

**Figure 17-54.**
A—Draw the object and move the UCS origin to the appropriate location. B—Add the center marks to the circular features using the **DIMCENTER** command.

UCS origin X=0 Y=0

A

B

between the center mark and the extension line. Zoom in if needed and use the object snap modes. The next prompt asks for the leader endpoint, which actually refers to the extension line endpoint.

> Specify leader endpoint or [Xdatum/Ydatum/Mtext/Text/Angle]: *(pick the endpoint of the extension line)*
> Dimension text = 0.500

If the X axis or Y axis distance between the feature and the extension line endpoint is large, the default axis may not be the desired axis for the dimension. When this happens, use the **Xdatum** or **Ydatum** option to tell AutoCAD from which axis the dimension originates. The **Mtext**, **Text**, and **Angle** options are identical to the options available with other dimensioning commands. Pick the leader endpoint to complete the command.

**Figure 17-55** shows the ordinate dimensions placed on the object. Notice the dimension text is aligned with the extension lines. Aligned dimensioning is standard with ordinate dimensioning. Finally, complete the drawing by adding any missing lines, such as centerlines or fold lines. Identify the holes with letters and correlate a dimensioning table. See **Figure 17-56**.

**Figure 17-55.**
Placing ordinate dimensions.

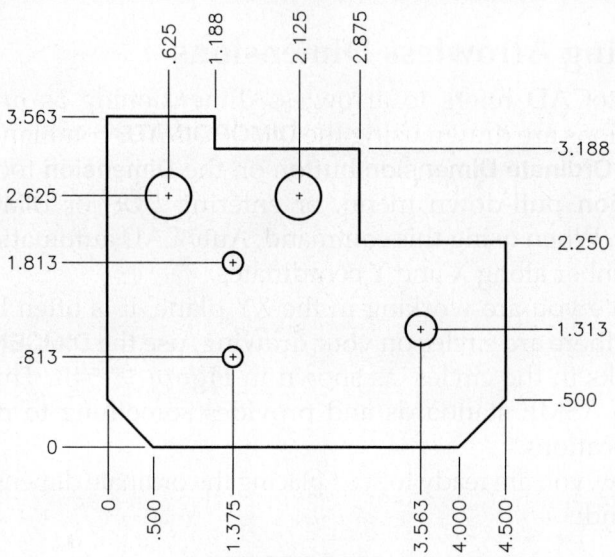

**Figure 17-56.**
Completing the drawing.

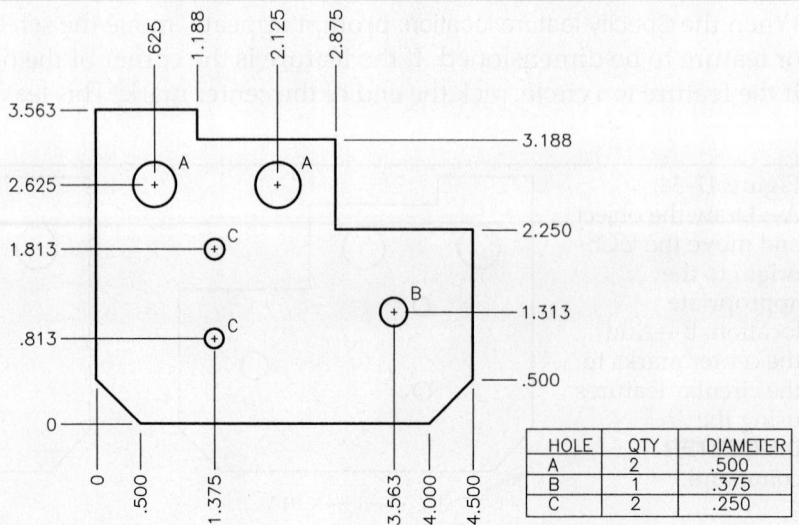

| HOLE | QTY | DIAMETER |
|------|-----|----------|
| A | 2 | .500 |
| B | 1 | .375 |
| C | 2 | .250 |

Most ordinate dimensioning tasks work best with **Ortho** mode on. However, when the extension line is too close to an adjacent dimension number, it is best to stagger the extension line as shown in the following illustration. With **Ortho** mode off, the extension line is automatically staggered when you pick the offset second extension line point as demonstrated.

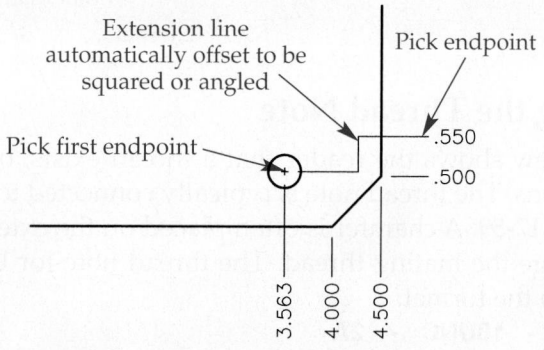

Extension line
automatically offset to be
squared or angled

Pick endpoint

Pick first endpoint

.550

.500

3.563  4.000  4.500

## Exercise 17-12

○ Start AutoCAD and use one of your templates.
○ Set up the appropriate layers for your drawing elements, including one for dimensions.
○ Draw the object shown in **Figure 17-51**. Use ordinate dimensioning to dimension the drawing.
○ Save the drawing as EX17-12.

# Thread Drawings and Notes

There are many different thread forms. The most common forms are the Unified and metric screw threads. The parts of a screw thread are shown in **Figure 17-57**.

Threads are commonly shown on a drawing with a simplified representation. Thread depth is shown with a hidden line. This method is used for both external and internal threads. See **Figure 17-58**.

**Figure 17-57.**
Parts of a screw thread.

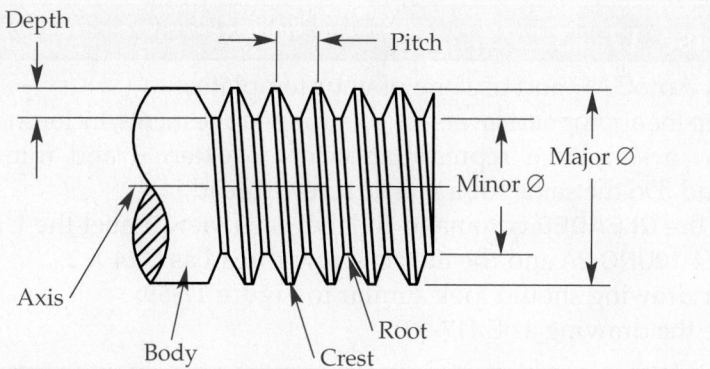

Depth

Pitch

Major ∅

Minor ∅

Axis

Body

Crest

Root

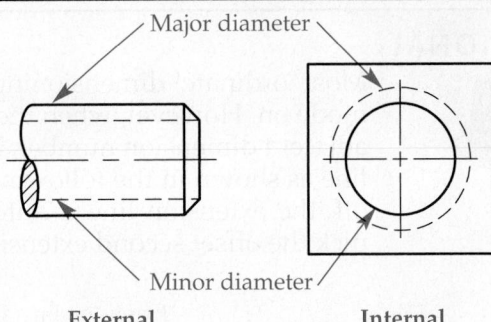

**Figure 17-58.**
Simplified thread representations.

Major diameter

Minor diameter

External          Internal

## Showing the Thread Note

The view shows the reader that a thread exists, but the thread note gives exact specifications. The thread note is typically connected to the thread view with a leader. See **Figure 17-59.** A chamfer is often placed on the external thread. This makes it easier to engage the mating thread. The thread note for Unified screw threads must be specified in the format:

    **3/4    - 10UNC - 2A**
    (1)       (2) (3)    (4) (5)
    (1)  Major diameter of thread, given as fraction or number.
    (2)  Number of threads per inch.
    (3)  Thread series. UNC = Unified National Coarse. UNF = Unified National Fine.
    (4)  Class of fit. 1 = large tolerance. 2 = general purpose tolerance. 3 = tight tolerance.
    (5)  A = external thread. B = internal thread.

The thread note for metric threads is specified in the format:

    **M  14 X 2**
    (1) (2)  (3)
    (1) M = metric thread.
    (2) Major diameter in millimeters.
    (3) Pitch in millimeters.

There are too many Unified and metric screw threads to discuss here. Refer to the *Machinery's Handbook,* available from Goodheart-Willcox Publisher, or a comprehensive drafting text for more information.

**Figure 17-59.**
Displaying the thread note with a leader.

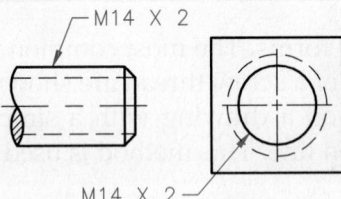

M14 X 2

M14 X 2

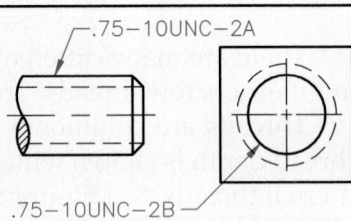

.75–10UNC–2A

.75–10UNC–2B

---

### Exercise 17-13

○ Start AutoCAD and use one of your templates.
○ Set up the appropriate layers for your drawing elements, including one for dimensions.
○ Draw a simplified representation of an external and internal Unified screw thread. Do the same for a metric screw thread.
○ Use the **QLEADER** command to label each view. Label the Unified screw thread as 3/4-10UNC-2A and the metric screw thread as M14 X 2.
○ Your drawing should look similar to **Figure 17-59.**
○ Save the drawing as EX17-13.

## Dimension Styles

The appearance of dimensions, from the size and the style of the text to the color of the dimension line, is controlled by over 70 different settings. *Dimension styles* are saved configurations of these settings. So far in this chapter, you have used only a few of these settings. The dimension settings that you used were introduced to help you perform specific tasks.

A dimension style is created by changing the dimension settings as needed to achieve the desired dimension appearance for your drafting application. For example, the dimension style for mechanical drafting probably has Romans text font placed in a break in the dimension line and the dimension lines are terminated with arrowheads. See **Figure 17-3**. The dimension style for architectural drafting may use CityBlueprint or Stylus BT text font placed above the dimension line and dimension lines are terminated with slashes. See **Figure 17-4.**

The dimension style can have dimensions based on national or international standards, or may be set up to match company or school applications and standards. The dimensioning that you have been doing in this chapter is based on the AutoCAD Standard dimension style. This dimension style uses the AutoCAD default settings and variables.

## Creating Dimension Styles

You might think of dimension styles as the dimensioning standards you use. Dimension styles are usually established for a specific type of drafting field or application. You can customize dimension styles to correspond to drafting standards such as ASME/ANSI, International Organization for Standardization (ISO), military (MIL), architectural, structural, civil, or your own school or company standards.

Dimension styles are created using the **Dimension Style Manager** dialog box. See **Figure 17-60.** This dialog box is accessed by picking the **Dimension Styles** button on the **Dimension** toolbar, **Dimension Style...** in the **Format** pull-down menu, or **Style...** in the **Dimension** pull-down menu. You can also type D, DST, DDIM, DIMSTY, or DIMSTYLE at the Command: prompt.

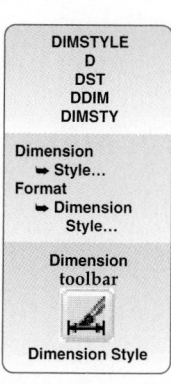

DIMSTYLE
D
DST
DDIM
DIMSTY

Dimension
➥ Style...
Format
➥ Dimension
Style...

Dimension
toolbar

Dimension Style

**Figure 17-60.**
The **Dimension Style Manager** dialog box. The Standard dimension style is the AutoCAD default.

Current dimension style

List of dimension styles

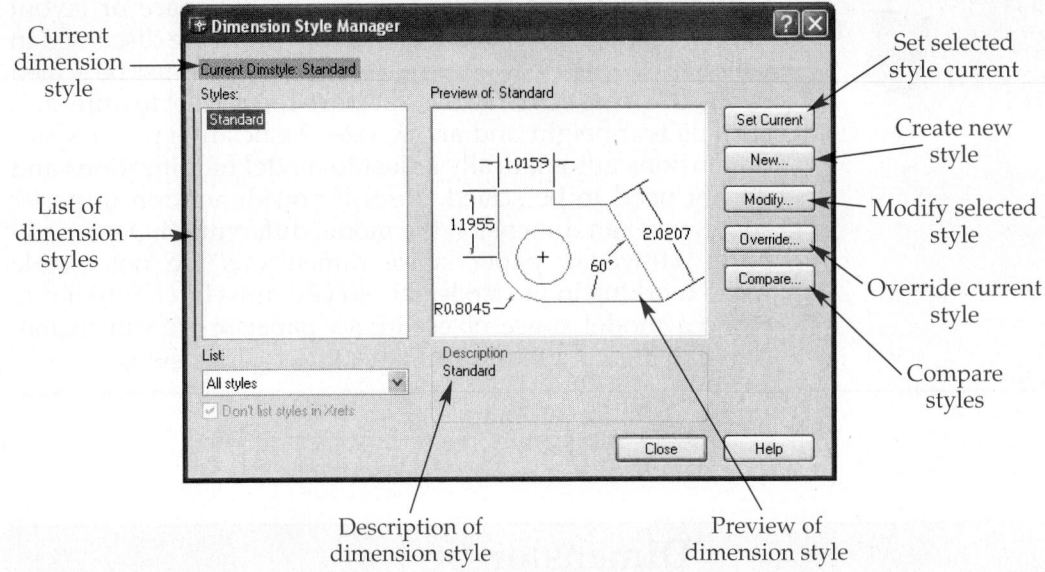

Set selected style current

Create new style

Modify selected style

Override current style

Compare styles

Description of dimension style

Preview of dimension style

The current dimension style, which is initially Standard, is noted at the top of the **Dimension Style Manager** dialog box. The **Styles:** box displays the dimension styles found within the current drawing. The selection in the **List:** drop-down list controls whether all styles or only the styles in use are displayed in the **Styles:** box.

If there are external reference drawings (xrefs) within the current drawing, the **Don't list styles in Xrefs** box can be checked to eliminate xref-dependent dimension styles from the **Styles:** box. This is often valuable because xref dimension styles cannot be used to create new dimensions. External references are discussed in Chapter 23.

The **Description** area and **Preview of:** image provide information about the selected dimension style. The Standard dimension style is the AutoCAD default. If you change any of the AutoCAD default dimension settings without first creating a new dimension style, the changes are automatically stored in a dimension style override.

There are additional options found in the **Dimension Style Manager** dialog box. These include:

- **Set Current.** This button makes the dimension style selected in the **Styles:** box current. When a dimension style is current, all new dimensions are created in that style. Existing dimensions are not affected by a change to the current style. Xref-dependent dimension styles cannot be set current.
- **New.** Use this button to create a new dimension style. When you pick this button, the **Create New Dimension Style** dialog box is displayed. See **Figure 17-61.** The following options are available in this dialog box:
  - **New Style Name.** Give your new dimension style a descriptive name, such as Architectural or Mechanical.
  - **Start With.** This option helps you save time by basing the settings for a new style on an existing dimension style. Xref dimension styles can be selected from this dialog box only if they were displayed in the **Dimension Style Manager** dialog box.
  - **Use for.** The choices in this drop-down list are **All dimensions**, **Linear dimensions**, **Angular dimensions**, **Radius dimensions**, **Diameter dimensions**, **Ordinance dimensions**, and **Leaders and Tolerances**. Use the **All dimensions** option to create a new dimension style. If you select one of the other options, you create a "substyle" of the dimension style specified in the **Start With:** text box. The settings in the new style are applied to the dimension type selected in this drop-down list.

**Figure 17-61.**
The **Create New Dimension Style** dialog box.

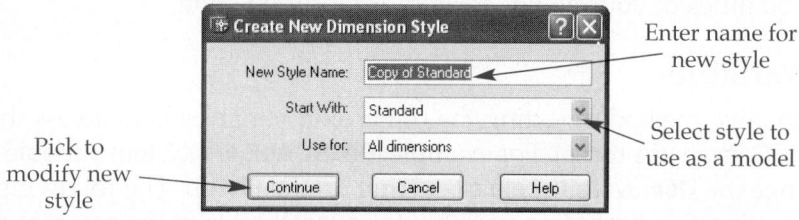

Pick to modify new style

Enter name for new style

Select style to use as a model

- Pick the **Continue** button to access the **New Dimension Style** dialog box.
- **Modify.** Selecting this button opens the **Modify Dimension Style** dialog box, which allows you to make changes to the style highlighted in the **Styles** list. Xref styles cannot be modified.
- **Override.** An *override* is a temporary change to the current style settings. Including a text prefix for just a few of the dimensions on a drawing is an example of an override. Picking this button opens the **Override Current Style** dialog box. This button is only available for the current style. Once an override is created it is made current and is displayed as a branch, called the *child*, of the style from which it is created. The dimension style from which the child is created is called the *parent.* The override settings are lost when any other style, including the parent, is set current.
- **Compare.** Sometimes it is useful to view the details of two styles to determine the differences. When the **Compare...** button is selected, the **Compare Dimension Styles** dialog box is opened. You can compare two styles by entering the name of one style in the **Compare:** drop-down list and the name of the other in the **With:** drop-down list. The differences between the selected styles are displayed in the dialog box.

The **New Dimension Style**, **Modify Dimension Style**, and **Override Current Style** dialog boxes have the same tabs. See **Figure 17-62.** The **Lines and Arrows**, **Text**, **Fit**, **Primary Units**, **Alternate Units**, and **Tolerances** tabs access the settings used for changing the way dimensions are displayed. These are discussed in the next sections.

**Figure 17-62.**
The **Lines and Arrows** tab of the **Modify Dimension Style** dialog box.

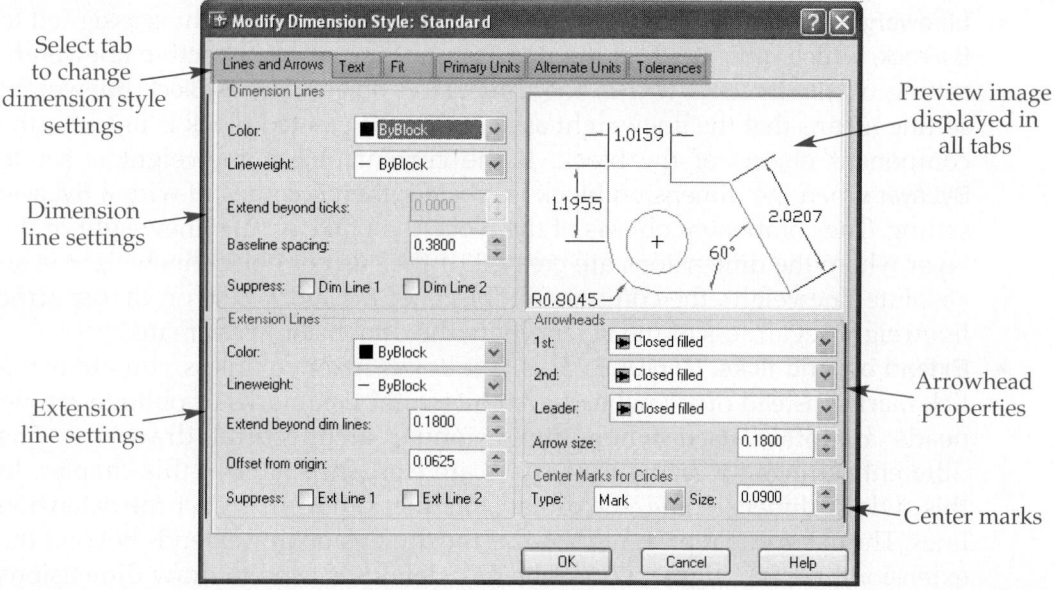

Select tab to change dimension style settings

Dimension line settings

Extension line settings

Preview image displayed in all tabs

Arrowhead properties

Center marks

After completing the information on all tabs, pick the **OK** button to return to the **Dimension Style Manager** dialog box. Select **Set Current** to have all new dimensions take on the qualities of your newly created or modified style.

## System Variables

An alternative method of setting the dimension variables is to access the variables directly at the Command: prompt. For example, **DIMSCALE** is a system variable that can be used to change the **Use overall scale of:** setting on the **Fit** tab. The following shows an example of setting the dimension variable for overall scale at the command line.

> Command: **DIMSCALE**↵
> Enter new value for DIMSCALE <*current*>: *(enter a new value)*

In this book, the system variables are noted in parenthesis where applicable.

## Using the **Lines and Arrows** Tab

When the **New** (or **Modify**) button is selected from the **Dimension Style Manager** dialog box, the **New** (or **Modify**) **Dimension Style** dialog box is displayed with six tabs: **Lines and Arrows**, **Text**, **Fit**, **Primary Units**, **Alternate Units**, and **Tolerances**. As adjustments are made to the current dimension style, an image on each tab updates to graphically reflect those changes. The **Lines and Arrows** tab controls all settings for the display of the lines, arrowheads, leaders, and center marks of dimension strings. See **Figure 17-62**.

The **Dimension Lines** area is used to change the format of the dimension line with the following settings.

- **Color.** (**DIMCLRD**) By default, the dimension line color is assigned ByBlock, which indicates that the line assumes the currently active color setting of all elements within the dimension object. The ByBlock color setting means that the color assigned to the created block is used for the component objects of the block. All associative dimensions are created as block objects. Blocks are symbols designed for multiple use and are explained in Chapter 22. Associative dimensions are discussed in this chapter and in Chapter 18. If the current entity color is set to ByLayer when the dimension block is created, then it comes in with a ByLayer setting. The component objects of the block then take on the color of the layer where the dimensions are created. If the current object color is an absolute color, then the component objects of the block take on that specific color regardless of the layer where the dimension was created.

- **Lineweight.** (**DIMLWD**) By default, the dimension line lineweight is assigned to ByBlock, which indicates that the line assumes the currently active lineweight setting of all elements within the dimension object. The ByBlock lineweight setting means that the lineweight assigned to the created block is used for the component objects of the block. If the current object lineweight is set to ByLayer when the dimension block is created, then it comes in with a ByLayer setting. The component objects of the block then take on the lineweight of the layer where the dimensions are created. If the current object lineweight is an absolute lineweight, the component objects of the block take on that specific lineweight regardless of the layer where the dimension was created.

- **Extend beyond ticks.** (**DIMDLE**) This text box is inactive unless you are using tick marks instead of arrowheads. Architectural tick marks or oblique arrowheads are often used when dimensioning architectural drawings. The different settings for arrowhead styles are explained later in this chapter. In this style of dimensioning, the dimension lines often cross over the extension lines. The extension represents how far the dimension line extends beyond the extension line. See **Figure 17-63**. The 0.00 default is used to draw dimensions that are not extended past the extension lines.

**Figure 17-63.**
Using the **Extend beyond ticks** settings to allow the dimension line to extend past the extension line. With the default value of 0, the dimension line does not extend.

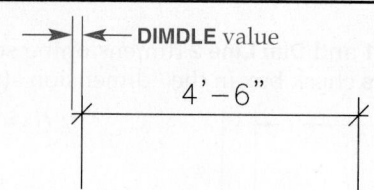

- **Baseline spacing.** (**DIMDLI**) This text box allows you to change the spacing between the dimension lines of baseline dimensions created with the **DIMBASELINE** command. The default spacing is .38 units, which is generally too close for most drawings. Try other values to help make the drawing easy to read. **Figure 17-64** shows the dimension line spacing.
- **Suppress.** (**DIMSD1** and **DIMSD2**) This option has two toggles that prevent the display of the first, second, or both dimensions lines and their arrowheads. The **Dim Line 1** and **Dim Line 2** check boxes refer to the first and second points picked when the dimension is created. Both dimension lines are displayed by default. The results of using these options are shown in **Figure 17-65**.

The **Extension Lines** area of the **Lines and Arrows** tab is used to change the format of the extension lines with the following dimension settings.

- **Color.** (**DIMCLRE**) The color choice made here controls the extension line color. The default value is ByBlock.
- **Lineweight.** (**DIMLWE**) The lineweight setting controls the lineweight of the extension lines.
- **Extend beyond dim lines.** (**DIMEXE**) This text box is used to set the extension line extension, which is the distance the extension line runs past the last dimension line. See **Figure 17-66.** The default value is 0.18; an extension line extension of .125 is common on most drawings.
- **Offset from origin.** (**DIMEXO**) This text box is used to change the distance between the object and the beginning of the extension line. See **Figure 17-66.** Most applications require this small offset. The default is .0625. When an extension line meets a centerline, use a setting of 0.0 to prevent a gap.

**Figure 17-64.**
The **Baseline spacing** setting controls the spacing between dimension lines.

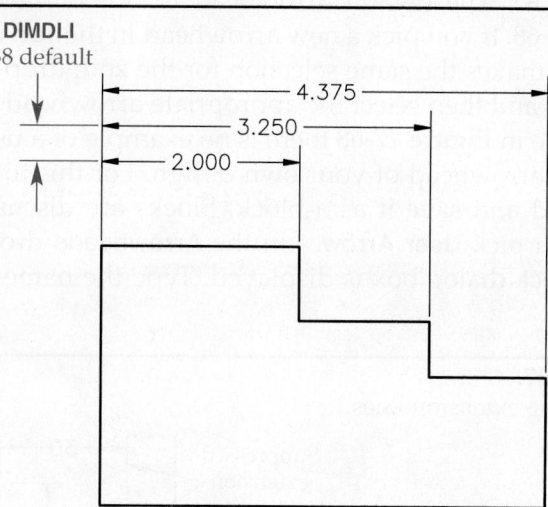

**Figure 17-65.**
Using the **Dim Line 1** and **Dim Line 2** dimensioning settings. "Off" is equivalent to an unchecked **Suppress** check box in the "dimension style" dialog box.

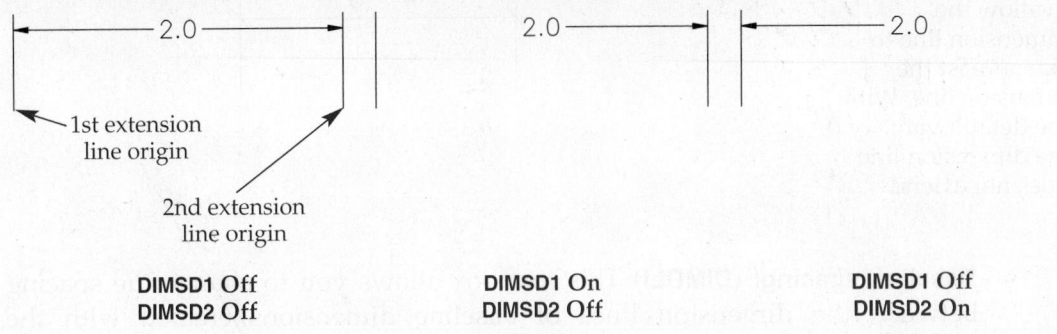

DIMSD1 Off
DIMSD2 Off

DIMSD1 On
DIMSD2 Off

DIMSD1 Off
DIMSD2 On

**Figure 17-66.**
The extension line extension (**Extend beyond dim lines**) and the extension line offset (**Offset from origin**).

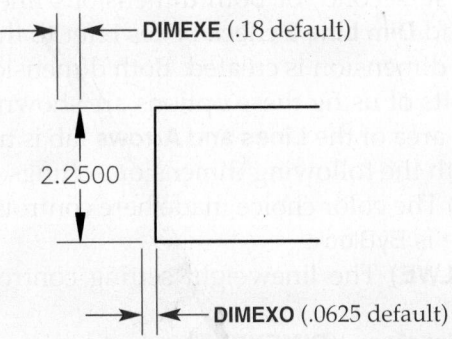

DIMEXE (.18 default)

2.2500

DIMEXO (.0625 default)

- **Suppress. (DIMSE1** and **DIMSE2)** This option is used to suppress the first, second, or both extension lines using the **Ext Line 1** and **Ext Line 2** check boxes. Extension lines are displayed by default. An extension line might be suppressed, for example, if it coincides with an object line. See **Figure 17-67.**

The **Arrowheads** area provides several different arrowhead options and controls the arrowhead size. Use the appropriate drop-down list to select the arrowhead used for the **1st** arrowhead (**DIMBLK1**), **2nd** arrowhead (**DIMBLK2**), and **Leader** arrowhead (**DIMDRBLK**). The default arrowhead is closed filled; other options are shown in **Figure 17-68.** If you pick a new arrowhead in the **1st:** drop-down list, AutoCAD automatically makes the same selection for the **2nd:** drop-down list. Check your drafting standards and then select the appropriate arrowhead.

Notice in **Figure 17-68** there is no example of a user arrow. This option is used to access an arrowhead of your own design. For this to work, you must first design an arrowhead and save it as a block. Blocks are discussed in Chapter 22 of this text. When you pick **User Arrow...** in the **Arrowheads** drop-down list, the **Select Custom Arrow Block** dialog box is displayed. Type the name of your custom arrow block in

**Figure 17-67.**
Suppressing extension lines.

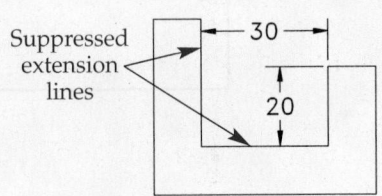

Suppressed extension lines

30

20

**Figure 17-68.**
Examples of dimensions drawn using the options found in the **Arrowhead** drop-down list.

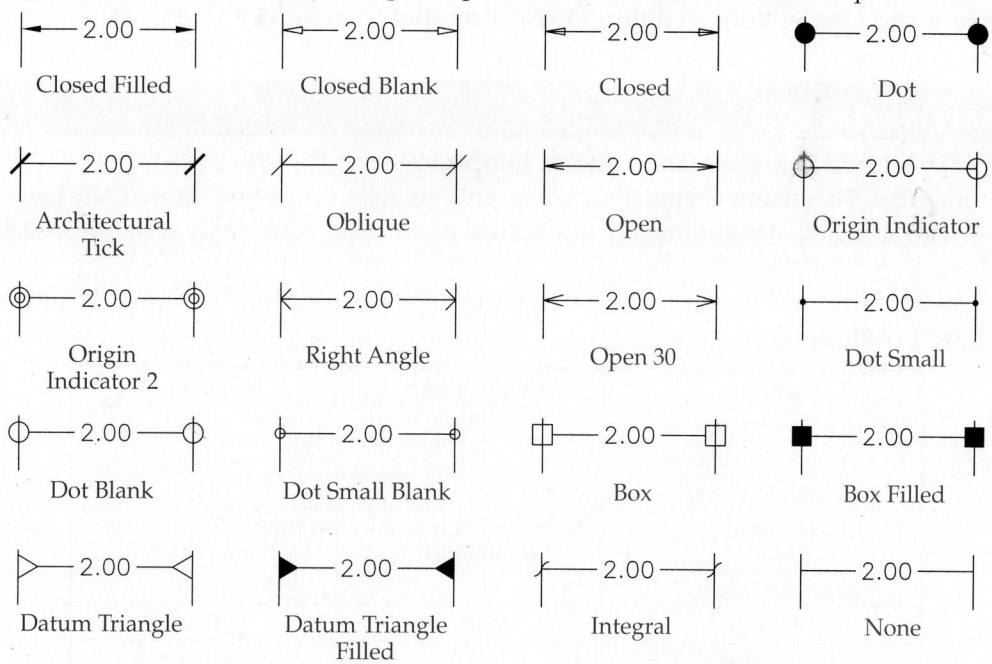

the **Select from Drawing Blocks:** text box and then pick **OK** to have the arrow used for the style. The name of the block is then displayed in the **Arrowheads** drop-down list.

When you select the oblique or architectural tick arrowhead, the **Extend beyond ticks:** text box in the **Dimension Lines** area is activated. This allows you to enter a value for a dimension line projection beyond the extension line. The default value is zero, but some architectural companies like to project the dimension line past the extension line. Refer to **Figure 17-63.**

The **Arrow Size:** text box (**DIMASZ**) allows you to change the size of arrowheads. The default value is .18. An arrowhead size of .125″ is common on mechanical drawings. **Figure 17-69** shows the arrowhead size value.

The **Center Marks for Circles** area (**DIMCEN**) of the **Lines and Arrows** tab allows you to select the way center marks are placed in circles and arcs. The **Type:** drop-down list contains the following options.

- **None.** Provides for no center marks to be placed in circles and arcs.
- **Mark.** Used to place only center marks without centerlines.
- **Line.** Places center marks and centerlines.

After selecting either the **Mark** or **Line** option, you can place center marks on circles and arcs by using the **DIMCENTER** command. The results of drawing center marks and centerlines are shown in **Figure 17-33.**

---

**Figure 17-69.**
The default arrow size is .18.

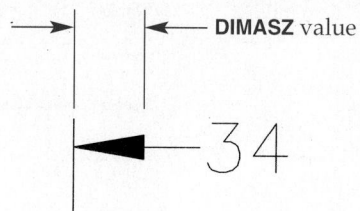

---

The **Size:** text box in the **Center Marks for Circles** area is used to change the size of the center mark and centerline. The default size is .09. The size specification controls the **Mark** and **Line** options in different ways, as shown in **Figure 17-33.**

## Using the Text Tab

Changes can be made to dimension text by picking the **Text** tab in the **New** (or **Modify**) **Dimension Style** dialog box. See **Figure 17-70.**

The **Text Appearance** area is used to set the dimension text style, color, height, and frame. The options in this area are:

**Figure 17-70.**
The **Text** tab of the **Modify Dimension Style** dialog box.

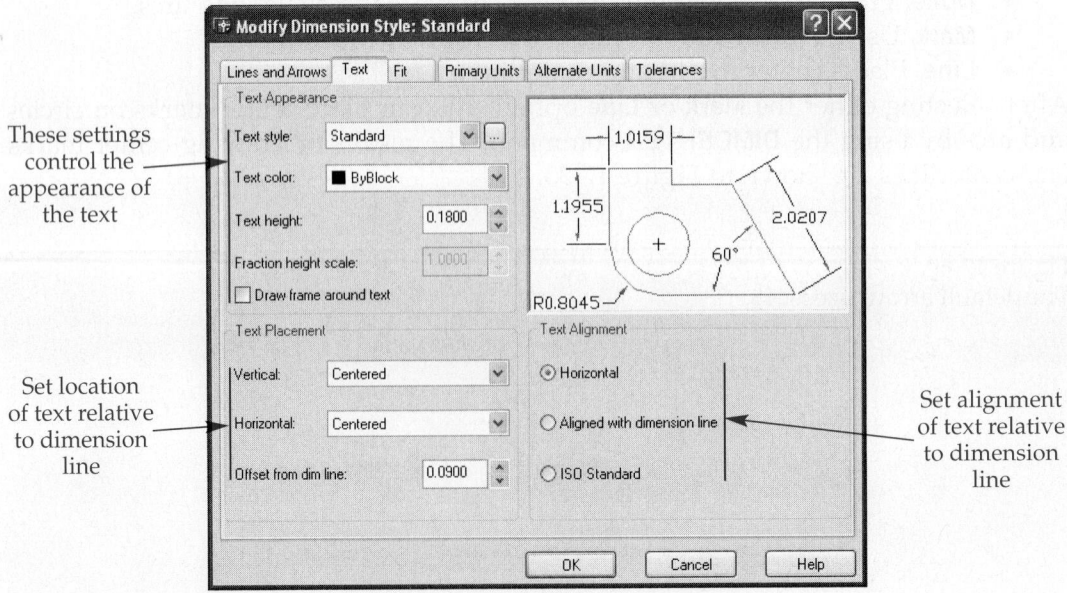

These settings control the appearance of the text

Set location of text relative to dimension line

Set alignment of text relative to dimension line

- **Text style. (DIMTXSTY)** The dimension text style uses the Standard text style by default. Text styles must be loaded in the current drawing before they are available for use in dimension text. Pick the desired text style from the drop-down list.
- **Text color. (DIMCLRT)** The dimension color default is ByBlock. Use the drop-down list to select a color for the text. If the color is not in the drop-down list, pick **Select Color...** to select a color from the **Select Color** dialog box.
- **Text height. (DIMTXT)** The dimension text height is set by entering the desired value in this text box. Dimension text height is commonly the same as the text height found on the rest of the drawing except for titles, which are larger. The default dimension text height is .18, which is an acceptable standard. Many companies use a text height of .125. The ASME standard recommends text height between .125 and .188. The text height for titles and labels is usually between .18 and .25.
- **Fraction height scale. (DIMTFAC)** This setting controls the height of fractions for architectural or fractional unit dimensions. The value in this box is multiplied by the text height value to determine the height of the fraction. A value of 1.0 creates fractions that are the same text height as regular (nonfractional) text, which is the normally accepted standard. A value less than 1.0 makes the fraction smaller than the regular text height.
- **Draw frame around text. (DIMGAP)** If checked, AutoCAD draws a rectangle around the text. The distance between the text and the frame is determined by the setting for the **Offset from dim line** value, which is explained later in this chapter.

The **Text Placement** area of the **Text** tab is used to place the text relative to the dimension line. See **Figure 17-71.** The preview image changes to represent the selections you make. The **Vertical: (DIMTAD)** drop-down list has the following options for the vertical justification.

- **Centered.** This option is the default. It places dimension text centered in a gap provided in the dimension line. This is the dimensioning practice commonly used in mechanical drafting and many other fields.
- **Above.** This option is generally used for architectural drafting and building construction. The dimension text is placed horizontally and above horizontal dimension lines. For vertical and angled dimension lines, the text is placed in a gap provided in dimension line. Architectural drafting commonly uses *aligned dimensioning* in which the dimension text is aligned with the dimension lines and all text reads from either the bottom or right side of the sheet. An additional setting to provide this is discussed later.

**Figure 17-71.**
Dimension text justification options. A—Vertical justification options, with the horizontal Centered justification. B—Horizontal justification options, with the vertical Centered justification.

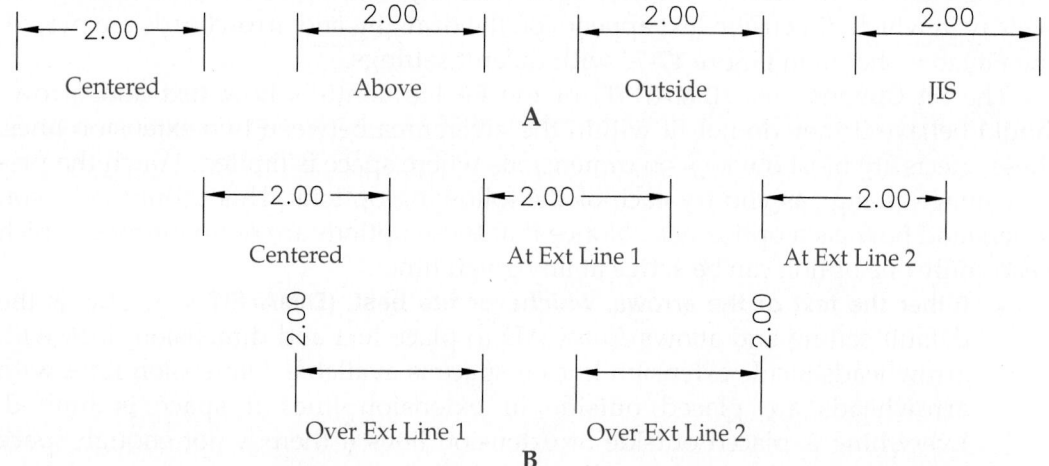

A

B

- **Outside.** This option places the dimension text outside the dimension line and either above or below a horizontal dimension line or to the right or left of a vertical dimension line. The direction you move the cursor determines the above/below and left/right placement.
- **JIS.** This is the option to use when dimensioning for the Japanese Industrial Standards.

In addition to the vertical placement of the dimension text, you can control the horizontal placement. The **Horizontal: (DIMJUST)** drop-down list has the following options for the horizontal justification.

- **Centered.** This option is the AutoCAD default. It places dimension text centered between the extension lines.
- **At Ext Line 1.** This option locates the text next to the extension line placed first.
- **At Ext Line 2.** This option locates the text next to the extension line placed second.
- **Over Ext Line 1.** This option places the text aligned with and over the first extension line. This practice is not commonly used.
- **Over Ext Line 2.** This option places the text aligned with and over the second extension line. This practice is also not commonly used.

The **Offset from dim line: (DIMGAP)** text box is used to set the gap between the dimension line and the dimension text. This setting also controls the distance between the leader shoulder and the text, and the space between the basic dimension box and the text. Basic dimensions are used in geometric tolerancing and explained in Chapter 19. The default gap is .09. The gap should be set to half the text height. **Figure 17-72** shows the gap in linear and leader dimensions.

The **Text Alignment** area (**DIMTOH** and **DIMTIH**) of the **Text** tab allows you to control the alignment of dimension text. This area is used when you want to draw unidirectional dimensions or aligned dimensions, which were discussed earlier in this chapter. The **Horizontal** option draws unidirectional dimensions commonly used for mechanical manufacturing drafting applications. The **Aligned with dimension line** option creates aligned dimensions, which are typically used for architectural dimensioning. The **ISO Standard** option creates aligned dimensions when the text falls between the extension lines and horizontal dimensions when the text falls outside the extension lines.

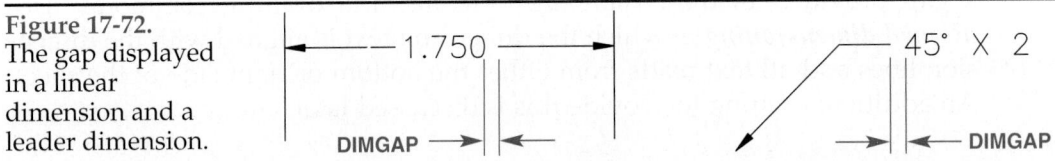

Figure 17-72.
The gap displayed in a linear dimension and a leader dimension.

## Using the Fit Tab

The **Fit** tab in the **New** (or **Modify**) **Dimension Style** dialog box is used to establish the way in which dimension text appears on the drawing and arrowheads are placed. The **Fit** tab is shown in **Figure 17-73** with default settings.

The **Fit Options** area (**DIMATFIT**) of the **Fit** tab controls how text and arrows should behave if they do not fit within the given area between two extension lines. These effects are most obvious on dimensions where space is limited. Watch the preview image change as you try each of the following options. This should help you understand how each option acts. Notice that these options are radio buttons, which means only one option can be active at any given time.

- **Either the text or the arrows, whichever fits best. (DIMATFIT = 3)** This is the default setting and allows AutoCAD to place text and dimension lines with arrowheads inside extension lines if space is available. Dimension lines with arrowheads are placed outside of extension lines if space is limited. Everything is placed outside of extension lines if there is not enough space between extension lines.

**Figure 17-73.**
The **Fit** tab of the **Modify Dimension Style** dialog box.

Description of selected option

Text and arrows fit options

Placement of grip-edited dimension text

Set scale for dimension features

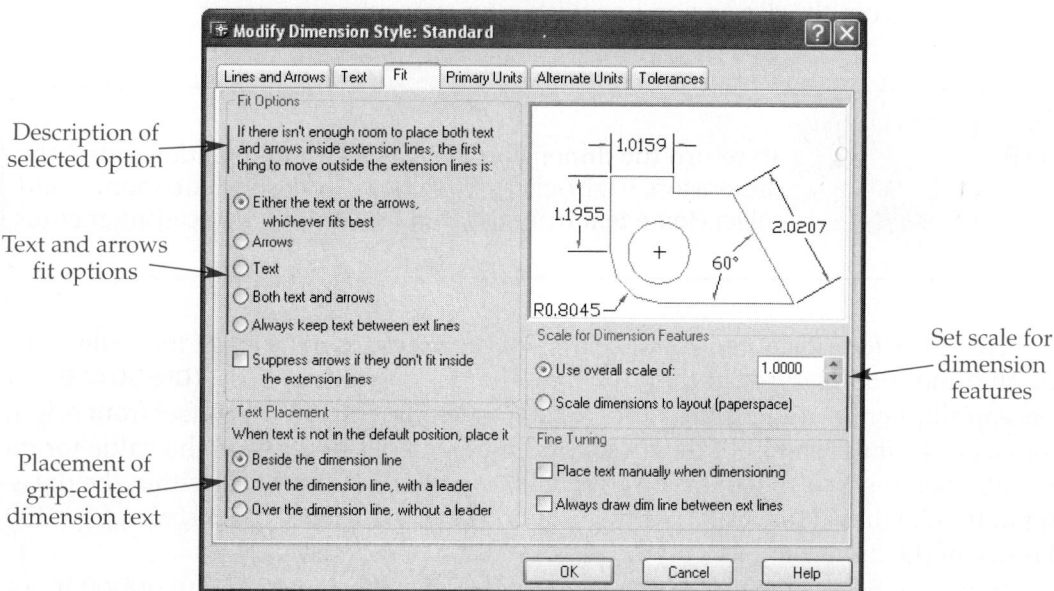

- **Arrows. (DIMATFIT** = 1) The text, dimension line, and arrowheads are placed inside the extension lines if there is enough space. The text is placed outside if there is enough space for only the arrowheads and dimension line inside the extension lines. Everything is outside if there is not enough room for anything inside.
- **Text. (DIMATFIT** = 2) The text, dimension line, and arrowheads are placed inside the extension lines if there is enough space for everything. If there is enough space for only the text inside the extension lines, then the dimension lines and arrowheads are placed outside. Everything is outside if there is not enough room for the text inside.
- **Both text and arrows. (DIMATFIT** = 0) When this option is used, AutoCAD places the text, dimension line, and arrowheads inside the extension lines if there is enough space, or everything is placed outside the extensions if there is not enough space.
- **Always keep text between ext lines. (DIMTIX)** This option always places the dimension text between the extension lines. This may cause problems when there is limited space between extension lines.
- **Suppress arrows if they don't fit inside the extension lines. (DIMSOXD)** This option removes the arrowheads if they do not fit inside the extension lines. Use this with caution because it can create dimensions that violate standards.

Sometimes it becomes necessary to move the dimension text from its default position. The text can be moved by grip editing the text portion of the dimension. The options in the **Text Placement** area (**DIMTMOVE**) of the **Fit** tab instruct AutoCAD how to handle these grip editing situations. The following options are available.

- **Beside the dimension line. (DIMTMOVE** = 0) When the dimension text is grip edited and moved, the text is constrained to move with the dimension line and can only be placed within the same plane as the dimension line.
- **Over the dimension line, with a leader. (DIMTMOVE** = 1) When the dimension text is grip edited and moved, the text can be moved in any direction away from the dimension line. A leader line is created that connects the text to the dimension line.

- **Over the dimension line, without a leader. (DIMTMOVE** = 2) When the dimension text is grip edited and moved, the text can be moved in any direction away from the dimension line without a connecting leader.

PROFESSIONAL TIP

To return the dimension text to its default position, select the dimension, right-click to display the shortcut menu, and select **Home text** from the **Dim Text position** cascading menu.

The **Scale for Dimension Features** area of the **Fit** tab is used to set the scale factor for all dimension features in the drawing. The **Use overall scale of: (DIMSCALE** > 0) sets a multiplier for dimension settings, such as text height and the offset from origin. For example, if the height of the dimensioning text is set to .125 and the value for the overall scale is set to 100, then the dimension text can be measured within the drawing to be 12.5 units (100 × .125). If the drawing is plotted with a plot scale of 1 = 100, the size of the dimension text on the paper measures .125 units.

Select the **Scale dimensions to layout (paperspace)** (**DIMSCALE** = 0) option if you are dimensioning in a floating viewport in a layout (paper space) tab. It allows the overall scale to adjust according to the active floating viewport by setting the overall scale equal to the viewport scale factor.

The **Fine Tuning** area of the **Fit** tab provides you with maximum flexibility in controlling where you want to place dimension text. The **Place text manually when dimensioning** (**DIMUPT**) option gives you control over text placement and dimension line length outside extension lines. The text can be placed where you want it, such as moved to the side within the extension lines, or placed outside of the extension lines.

The **Always draw dim line between ext lines** (**DIMTOFL**) option forces AutoCAD to place the dimension line inside the extension lines, even when the text and arrowheads are outside. The default application is with the dimension line and arrowheads outside the extension lines. **Figure 17-74** shows the difference between checked (**DIMTOFL** on) and unchecked (**DIMTOFL** off). Forcing the dimension line inside the extension lines is not an ASME standard, but it may be preferred by some companies.

**Figure 17-74.**
The effects of the **Always draw dim line between ext lines** option of the **Fine Tuning** area of the **Fit** tab.

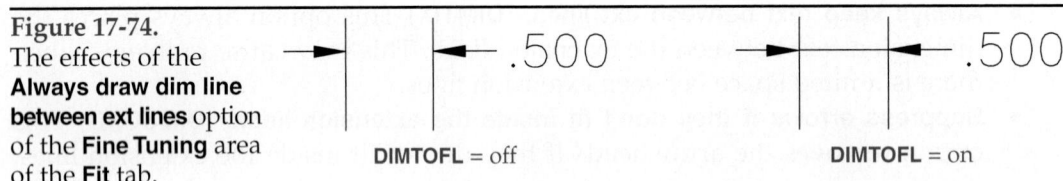

DIMTOFL = off

DIMTOFL = on

PROFESSIONAL TIP

When dimensioning mechanical drawings it is common to have **Place text manually when dimensioning** on, centered horizontal and vertical justification, and horizontal text alignment.

For architectural drafting it is typical to have **Place text manually when dimensioning** on, **Always draw dimension line** on, centered horizontal justification, above vertical justification, and text aligned with dimension lines.

## Using the Primary Units Tab

The **Linear Dimensions** area of the **Primary Units** tab of the **New** (or **Modify**) **Dimension Style** dialog box is used to set units for linear dimensions. See **Figure 17-75.** This area has the following setting options.

- **Unit format. (DIMLUNIT/DIMALTU)** Select the type of units for dimension text from this drop-down list. The default selection is **Decimal** units. A definition and examples of the different units are provided in Chapter 2 of this text.
- **Precision. (DIMDEC/DIMALTD)** This drop-down list allows you to decide how many zeros follow the decimal place when decimal-related units are selected. The default is 0.0000; 0.00 and 0.000 settings are also common in mechanical drafting. When fractional units are selected, the precision values are related to the smallest desired fractional denominator. The default is 1/16″ but you can choose other options ranging from 1/256″ to 1/2″; 0″ displays no fractional values. A variety of dimension precision may be found on the same drawing.
- **Fraction format. (DIMFRAC)** The options for controlling the display of fractions are **Diagonal**, **Horizontal**, and **Not Stacked**. The **Fraction format** option is only available if the **Architectural** or **Fractional** style is selected for the unit format.

**Figure 17-75.**
The **Primary Units** tab of the **Modify Dimension Style** dialog box.

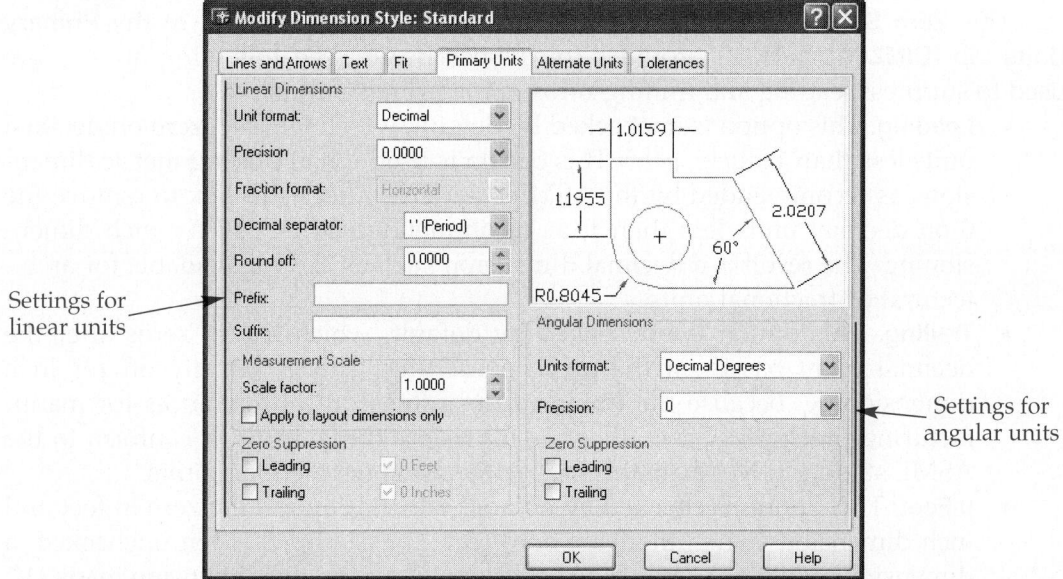

Settings for linear units

Settings for angular units

- **Decimal separator. (DIMDSEP)** Decimal numbers may use commas, periods, or spaces as separators. The '.' **(Period)** option is the default. The **Decimal separator** option is not available if the **Architectural** or **Fraction** style is selected for the unit format.
- **Round off. (DIMRND/DIMALTRND).** This text box specifies the accuracy of rounding for dimension numbers. The default is zero, which means that no rounding takes place and all dimensions are placed exactly as measured. If you enter a value of .1, all dimensions are rounded to the closest .1 unit. For example, an actual measurement of 1.188 is rounded to 1.2.
- **Prefix. (DIMPOST/DIMAPOST)** *Prefixes* are special notes or applications placed in front of the dimension text. A typical prefix might be SR3.5 where SR means spherical radius. When a prefix is used on a diameter or radius dimension, the prefix replaces the ∅ or R symbol.
- **Suffix. (DIMPOST/DIMAPOST)** *Suffixes* are special notes or applications placed after the dimension text. A typical suffix might be 3.5 MAX, where MAX is the abbreviation for maximum. The abbreviation IN can also be used when one or more inch dimensions are placed on a metric dimensioned drawing or a suffix of MM on one or more millimeter dimensions are placed on an inch drawing.

**PROFESSIONAL TIP**

Usually, a prefix or suffix is not used on every dimension in the drawing. A prefix or suffix is normally a special specification and might be used in only a few cases. Because of this, you might set up a special dimension style for these applications or enter them when needed by using the **MText** or **Text** option of the related dimensioning command.

The **Measurement Scale** area within the **Linear Dimensions** area of the **Primary Units** tab is used to set the scale factor of linear dimensions. Set the value in the **Scale factor:** text box (**DIMLFAC**). If a value of 1 is set, dimension values are displayed the same as they are measured. If the setting is 2, dimension values are twice as much as the measured amount. For example, an actual measurement of 2 inches is displayed as 2 with a scale factor of 1, but the same measurement is displayed as 4 when the scale factor is 2. Placing a check in the **Apply to layout dimensions only (DIMLFAC** < 0) check box makes the linear scale factor active only when dimensioning in a layout tab.

This **Zero Suppression** area within the **Linear Dimensions** area of the **Primary Units** tab (**DIMZIN/DIMALTZ**) provides four check boxes. The following options are used to suppress leading and trailing zeros in the primary units.
- **Leading.** This option is unchecked by default, which leaves a zero on decimal units less than 1, such as 0.5. This option is used when placing metric dimensions as recommended by the ASME standard. Check this box to remove the 0 on decimal units less than 1, as recommended by ASME for inch dimensioning. The result is a decimal dimension such as .5. Not available for architectural or fractional units.
- **Trailing.** This option is unchecked by default, which leaves zeros after the decimal point based on the precision setting. This is usually off for inch dimensioning, because the trailing zeros often control tolerances for manufacturing processes. Check this box for metric dimensions to conform to the ASME standard. Not available for architectural or fractional units.
- **0 Feet.** This option is checked by default, which removes the zero in feet and inch dimensions when there are zero feet. For example, when unchecked, a dimension may read 0'-11". When checked, however, the dimension reads 11". Only available for architectural or fractional units.

*AutoCAD and its Applications—Basics*

- **0 Inches.** This option is checked by default, which removes the zero when the inch part of feet and inch dimensions is less than one inch, such as 12'-7/8". If checked, the same dimension reads 12'-0 7/8". Also, it removes the zero from a dimension with no inch value; 12' rather than 12'-0". Only available for architectural or fractional units.

The **Angular Dimensions** area of the **Primary Units** tab is used to set the desired type of angular units for dimensioning. Angular units are discussed in the section in Chapter 2 on AutoCAD setup and with the **UNITS** command. The setup options and **UNITS** command do not control the type of units used for dimensioning. The following settings are found in this area.

- **Units format.** (**DIMAUNIT**) The default setting is **Decimal Degrees**. The other options are **Degrees Minutes Seconds**, **Gradians**, and **Radians**. Select the desired option from the drop-down list.
- **Precision.** (**DIMADEC**) Sets the desired precision of the angular dimension number. Select an option from the drop-down list.
- **Zero Suppression.** (**DIMAZIN**) This area of the **Angular Dimensions** area is used to keep or remove leading or trailing zeros on the angular dimension.

## Using the Alternate Units Tab

The **Alternate Units** tab of the **Dimension Style** dialog box is used to set alternate units. See **Figure 17-76**. *Alternate units*, or *dual dimensioning,* have inch measurements followed by millimeters in brackets, or millimeters followed by inches in brackets. Dual dimensioning practices are no longer a recommended ASME standard. ASME recommends that drawings be dimensioned using inch or metric units only. However, the use of alternate units can be used in many other applications.

The **Display alternate units** (**DIMALT**) check box must be checked in order to activate the settings. The tab has many of the same settings found in the **Primary Units** tab. The **Multiplier for alt units** (**DIMALTF**) setting is multiplied by the primary unit to establish the value for the alternate unit. 25.4 is the default because an inch value is multiplied by 25.4 to convert it to millimeters. The **Placement** area controls the location of the alternate-unit dimension. The two options are **After primary value** and **Below primary value**.

**Figure 17-76.**
The **Alternate Units** tab of the **Modify Dimension Style** dialog box.

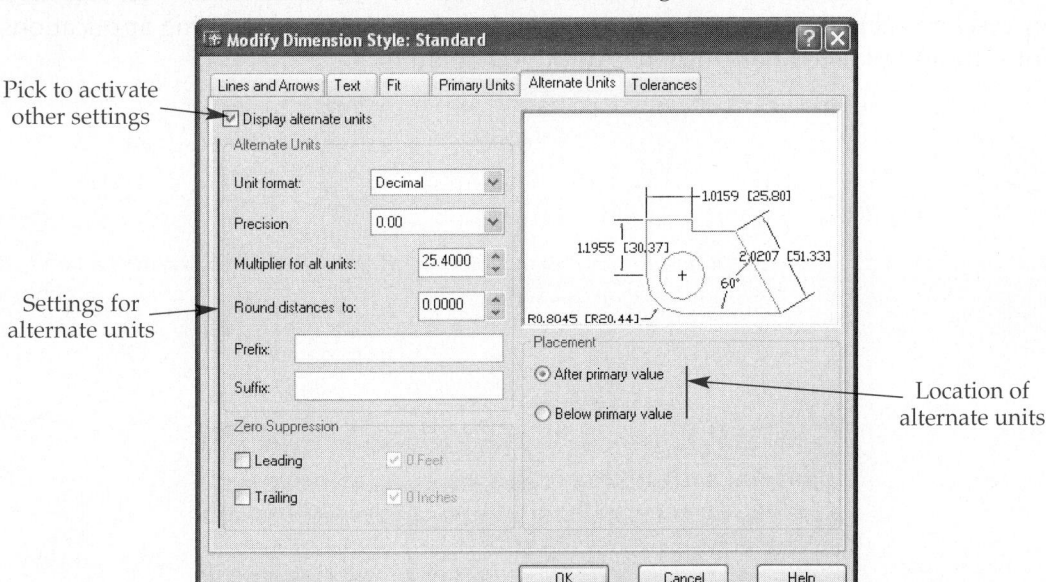

NOTE  The final tab in the **Modify Dimension Style** dialog box, **Tolerances**, is discussed in Chapter 19.

## Exercise 17-16

○ Start AutoCAD and use one of your templates.
○ Create text styles using the ROMANS and Stylus BT text fonts.
○ Open the **Dimension Style Manager** dialog box. With the Standard style selected, pick the **Modify** button.
○ Pick the **Primary Units** tab. Set the primary units to three-place decimal.
○ Access the **Text** tab. Make note of the options in the **Style:** drop-down list.
○ Set text height at .125 and the **Offset from dim line** to .05.
○ Draw a dimension 5.625 in length using ROMANS font with the dimension text centered in a gap provided in the dimension line.
○ Draw another dimension 5.625 using Stylus BT font with the dimension text above the dimension line.
○ Save the drawing as EX17-16.

## Making Your Own Dimension Styles

Creating and recording dimension styles is part of your AutoCAD management responsibility. You should carefully evaluate the items contained in the dimensions for the type of drawings you do. During this process, be sure to carefully check company or national standards to verify the accuracy of your plan. Then, make a list of features and values for the dimensioning settings you use based on what you have learned in this chapter. When you are ready, use the **Dimension Style Manager** dialog box options to establish dimension styles named to suit your drafting practices.

The following chart provides possible settings for two dimension style. One list is for mechanical manufacturing and the other is for architectural drafting applications. For settings not listed here, use the AutoCAD defaults.

| Setting | Mechanical (Inch) | Architectural |
|---|---|---|
| Dimension line spacing | .50 | .75 |
| Extension line extension | .125 | .18 |
| Extension line offset | .0625 | .08 |
| Arrowhead options | Closed filled, closed, or open | Architectural tick, dot, closed filled, oblique, or right angle |
| Arrowhead size | .125 | .18 |
| Center | Line | Mark |
| Center size | .25 | .25 |
| Text placement | Manually | Manually |
| Vertical justification | Centered | Above |
| Text alignment | Horizontal | Aligned with dimension line |
| Primary units | Decimal (default) | Architectural |
| Dimension precision | 0.000 | 1/16" |
| Zero suppression (metric) | Leading off Trailing on | Leading off Trailing on |
| Zero suppression (inch) | Leading on Trailing off | Leading on Trailing off |
| Angles | Decimal degrees (default) | Deg/min/sec |
| Tolerances | By application | None |
| Text style | gdt | Stylus BT |
| Text height | .125 | .125 |
| Text gap | .05 | .1 |

## Exercise 17-17

○ Create your own list of dimension style settings for the type of drafting you perform.
○ Open the **Dimension Style Manager** dialog box and change the settings as needed to match the list you created.
○ Save the dimension style with a name that describes the list you made.
○ Save as EX17-17.

## Overriding Existing Dimensioning Variables

Generally, it is appropriate to have one or more dimension styles set to perform specific tasks that relate to your dimensioning practices. However, there are situations where a few dimensions require settings that are not covered by your basic styles. These situations may be too few and far between to warrant creating a new style. For example, assume you have the value for **Offset from origin** set at .0625, which conforms to ASME standards. However, in your final drawing there are three dimensions that require a 0 **Offset from origin** setting. For these dimensions, you can perform a *dimension style override* and temporarily alter the settings for the dimension style without actually modifying the style.

# Dimension Style Override for Existing Dimensions

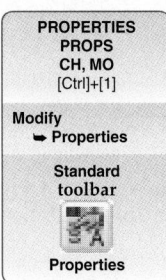
To override the dimension style of an existing dimension, first select the dimension. Then, open the **Properties** window by picking the **Properties** button on the **Standard** toolbar, selecting **Properties** from the **Modify** pull-down menu, or typing PROPERTIES at the Command: prompt. You can also right-click in the viewport and select **Properties** from the shortcut menu or double-click on the selected dimension.

The dimension properties listed in the **Properties** window are broken down into eight categories. See **Figure 17-77.** To change an existing property or value, access the proper category and pick the property to highlight it. You can then change the corresponding value. Refer to Chapter 12 for a discussion on how to make changes in the **Properties** window.

The changes made in the **Properties** window are overrides to the dimension style for the selected dimension. The changes do not alter the original dimension style. Also, the changes are not applied to new dimensions.

**Figure 17-77.**
The **Properties** window can be used to edit dimension properties and create a dimension style override.

| Text | |
|---|---|
| Fractional type | Horizontal |
| Text color | ByBlock |
| Text height | 0.1800 |
| Text offset | 0.0900 |
| Text outside... | Off |
| Text pos hor | Centered |
| Text pos vert | Centered |
| Text style | Standard |
| Text inside a... | Off |
| Text position X | 37.2090 |
| Text position Y | 14.1319 |
| Text rotation | 0 |
| Measurement | 4.0000 |
| Text override | |

| Lines & Arrows | |
|---|---|
| Arrow 1 | Closed filled |
| Arrow 2 | Closed filled |
| Arrow size | 0.1800 |
| Dim line LW | ByBlock |
| Ext line LW | ByBlock |
| Dim line 1 | On |
| Dim line 2 | On |
| Dim line color | ByBlock |
| Dim line ext | 0.0000 |
| Ext line 1 | On |
| Ext line 2 | On |
| Ext line color | ByBlock |
| Ext line ext | 0.1800 |
| Ext line offset | 0.0625 |

| Rotated Dimension | |
|---|---|
| **General** | |
| Color | ByLayer |
| Layer | 0 |
| Linetype | ByLayer |
| Linetype scale | 1.0000 |
| Plot style | ByColor |
| Lineweight | ByLayer |
| Hyperlink | |
| Associative | Yes |
| **Misc** | |
| Dim style | Standard |
| Lines & Arrows | |
| Text | |
| Fit | |
| Primary Units | |
| Alternate Units | |
| Tolerances | |

| Primary Units | |
|---|---|
| Decimal sepa... | . |
| Dim prefix | |
| Dim suffix | |
| Dim roundoff | 0.0000 |
| Dim scale linear | 1.0000 |
| Dim units | Decimal |
| Suppress lea... | No |
| Suppress tra... | No |
| Suppress zer... | Yes |
| Suppress zer... | Yes |
| Precision | 0.0000 |

| Fit | |
|---|---|
| Dim line forced | Off |
| Dim line inside | On |
| Dim scale ov... | 1.0000 |
| Fit | Best fit |
| Text inside | Off |
| Text movem... | Keep dim line with text |

| Tolerances | |
|---|---|
| Tolerance di... | None |
| Tolerance lim... | 0.0000 |
| Tolerance lim... | 0.0000 |
| Tolerance po... | Middle |
| Tolerance pr... | 0.0000 |
| Tolerance su... | No |
| Tolerance su... | No |
| Tolerance su... | Yes |
| Tolerance su... | Yes |
| Tolerance te... | 1.0000 |
| Alt Toleranc... | 0.00 |
| Alt tolerance... | No |
| Alt tolerance... | No |
| Alt tolerance... | Yes |
| Alt tolerance... | Yes |

| Alternate Units | |
|---|---|
| Alt enabled | Off |
| Alt format | Decimal |
| Alt precision | 0.00 |
| Alt round | 0.0000 |
| Alt scale factor | 25.4000 |
| Alt suppress ... | No |
| Alt suppress ... | No |
| Alt suppress ... | Yes |
| Alt suppress ... | Yes |
| Alt prefix | |
| Alt suffix | |

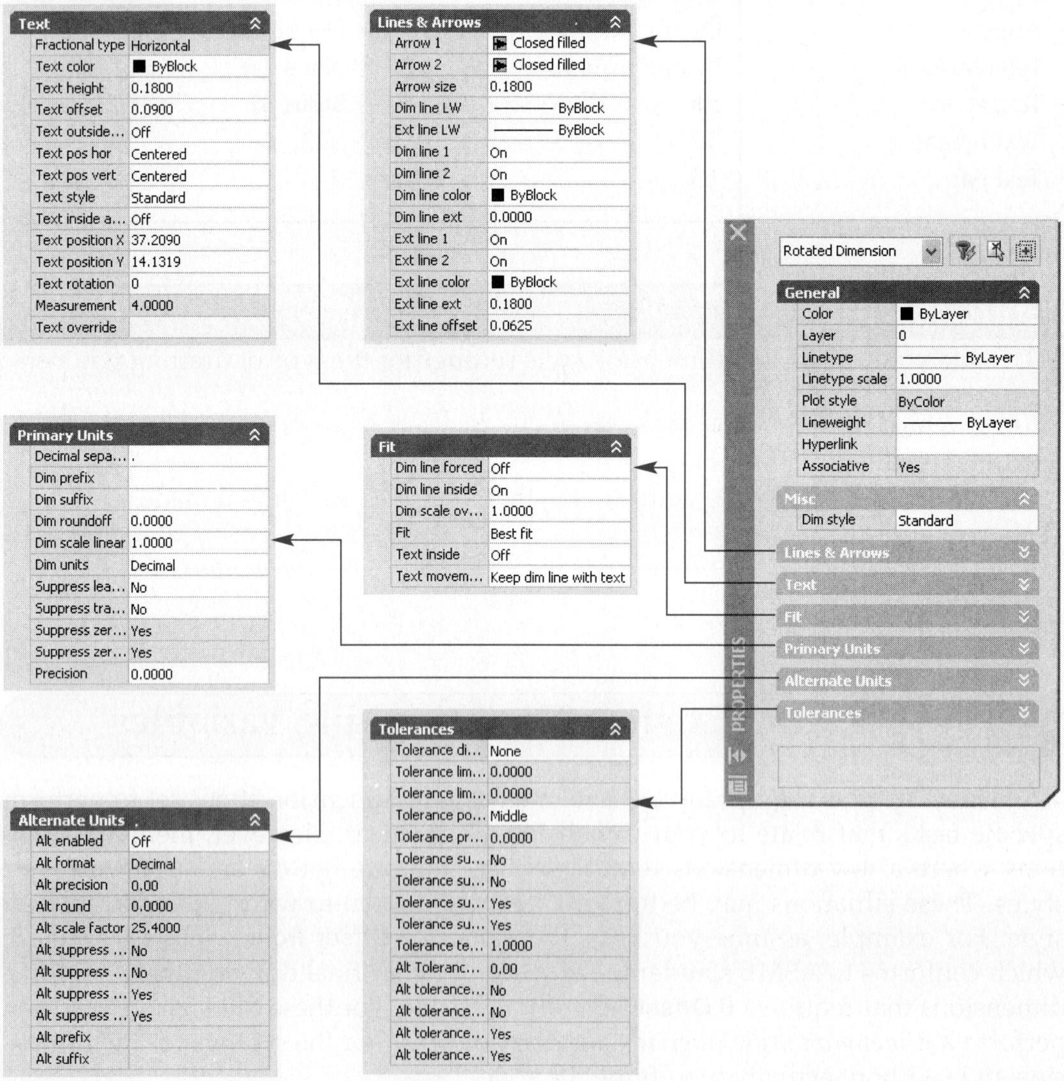

## Dimension Style Override for New Dimensions

To override the dimension style for dimensions you are about to draw, open the **Dimensions Style Manager**. Then, select the dimension style that you are going to override from the **Styles** list. Finally, pick the **Override...** button to display the **Override Current Style** dialog box. This dialog box has the same features as the **New** (or **Modify**) **Dimensioning Style** dialog box. Make any changes to the style and pick the **OK** button. The style you overrode now has a branch under it labeled **<style overrides>**, which is set as the current style. Close the **Dimension Style Manager** and draw the needed dimensions.

To clear the overrides, return to the **Dimension Style Manager** and set any other style current. However, this will discard the overrides. If you want to incorporate the overrides into the style that was overridden, right-click on the **<style overrides>** name and select **Save to current style** from the shortcut menu. To save the changes to a new style, pick the **New...** button. Then, select **<style overrides>** in the **Start With** drop-down list in the **Create New Dimension Style** dialog box. Finally, in the **New Dimension Style** dialog box, simply pick **OK** to save the overrides as a new style.

## Dimension Style Override on the Command Line

A dimension style is really a set of dimensioning variable values. Individual dimensioning variables can be overridden using the command line and the **DIMOVERRIDE** command. This has a similar effect to overriding a style for existing dimensions using the **Properties** window. However, you must be very familiar with the dimensioning variable names and which aspect of the dimension style they control. Also, the command can only change existing dimensions. For example, to change the **Offset from origin** setting, which is controlled by the **DIMEXO** system variable, use the **DIMOVERRIDE** command:

DIMOVERRIDE
DOV

Command: **DOV** *or* **DIMOVERRIDE**↵
Enter dimension variable name to override or [Clear overrides]: **DIMEXO**↵
Enter new value for dimension variable <0.0625>: **0**↵
Enter dimension variable name to override: *(type another variable name to override or press* [Enter]*)*
Select objects: *(select the dimension or dimensions to override)*
Select objects: ↵
Command:

The **DIMEXO** variable automatically changes from .0625 to 0 on the selected dimensions. To clear any overrides, use the **Clear** option. Exiting the command discards all overrides.

---

**PROFESSIONAL TIP**

Carefully evaluate the dimensioning requirements in a drawing before performing a style override. It may, in fact, be better to create a new style. For example, if a number of the dimensions in the current drawing all require the same overrides, then generating a new dimension style is a good idea. If only one or two dimensions need the same overrides, performing an override may be more productive.

---

○ Start AutoCAD and use one of your templates.
○ Create a new dimensioning style with the following settings:
  Arrowhead size = .1
  Text offset from dimension line = .05
  Dimension line extend beyond ticks = .12
  Dimension line baseline spacing = .5
  Extension line offset from origin = .06
○ Make a drawing similar to **Figure 17-40.**
○ Use the **QDIM** command with the baseline option to dimension the object.
○ After dimensioning the drawing, override the **Extension Line offset from origin:** setting and change it to a value of 0 on all dimensions except the overall dimensions.
○ Save the drawing as EX17-18.

---

**NOTE**

Dimensions can also be created in dimensioning mode. To access dimensioning mode, type DIM at the Command: prompt. The Command: prompt becomes the Dim: prompt and you can enter dimensioning commands. To exit dimensioning mode, press the [Esc] key and the Command: prompt is displayed.

This method was common in earlier releases of AutoCAD, but has become a relatively inefficient method of command entry. Newer dimensioning commands, such as **QLEADER** and **QDIM**, cannot be accessed from the Dim: prompt.

---

## Chapter Test

*Answer the following questions on a separate sheet of paper.*

1. What are the recommended standard units of measure for mechanical drawings?
2. Name the units of measure commonly used in architectural and structural drafting. Show an example.
3. What is the recommended height for dimension numbers and notes on drawings?
4. Name the pull-down menu where the **Linear**, **Aligned**, and **Radius** dimensioning commands are found.
5. Name the two dimensioning commands that provide linear dimensions for angled surfaces.
6. Name the **DIMLINEAR** option that opens the multiline text editor for changing the dimension text.
7. Name the **DIMLINEAR** option that allows you to change dimension text at the prompt line.
8. What is the keyboard shortcut (command alias) for the **DIMBASELINE** command?
9. Which command other than **DIMBASELINE** can be used to create baseline dimensions?
10. Name at least three modes of dimensioning available through the **QDIM** command.
11. Name the command used to dimension angles in degrees.
12. AutoCAD refers to chain dimensioning as _____.
13. AutoCAD refers to datum dimensioning as _____.

---

14. The command used to provide diameter dimensions for circles is _____.
15. The command used to provide radius dimensions for arcs is _____.
16. What does the *M* mean in the title of the standard ASME Y14.5M-1994?
17. Does a text style have to be loaded before it can be accessed for use in dimension text?
18. How do you access the **DIMRADIUS** and **DIMDIAMETER** commands from a pull-down menu?
19. How do you place a datum dimension from the origin of the previously drawn dimension?
20. How do you place a datum dimension from the origin of a dimension that was drawn during a previous drawing session?
21. Which type of dimensions are created when you select multiple objects in the **QDIM** command?
22. Oblique extension lines are drawn using the _____ command and by accessing the _____ option.
23. Define *annotation.*
24. Identify how to access the **QLEADER** command using:
    A. Toolbar.
    B. Pull-down menu.
    C. Command: prompt.
25. Text placed using the **QLEADER** command is a _____ text object.
26. Describe the purpose of the **Copy an object** option in the **Leader Settings** dialog box.
27. Define *arrowless dimensioning.*
28. AutoCAD refers to arrowless dimensioning as _____ dimensioning.
29. Name the pull-down menu selection that allows you to draw arrowless dimensions.
30. What is the importance of the user coordinate system (UCS) when drawing arrowless dimensions?
31. Identify the elements of this Unified screw thread note: 1/2-13 UNC-2B.
    A. 1/2.
    B. 13.
    C. UNC.
    D. 2.
    E. B.
32. Identify the elements of this metric screw thread note: M 14 X 2.
    A. M.
    B. 14.
    C. 2.
33. How does the arrowhead specified for the dimension style affect the arrowhead used with the **QLEADER** command?
34. Name the dialog box that is used to create dimension styles.
35. Identify at least three ways to access the dialog box identified in Question 34.
36. Define an AutoCAD *dimension style.*
37. Name the dialog box tab used to control the appearance of dimension lines, extension lines, arrowheads, and center marks.
38. Name the dialog box tab used to control dimensioning settings that adjust the location of dimension lines, dimension text, arrowheads, and leader lines.
39. Name the dialog box tab used to control the dimensioning settings that display the dimension text.
40. Name at least four arrowhead types that are available in the **Lines and Arrows** tab for common use on architectural drawings.
41. Identify the dialog box tab used to control the dimension text location as you place the dimension.

42. Name the area in the **Modify Dimension Style** dialog box in which vertical justification of text can be set.

43. Which option for the vertical justification mentioned in Question 42 is commonly used in mechanical drafting?

44. Define *primary units*.

45. Given the following dimension text examples, identify if the application is for inch decimal drawings, metric decimal drawings, or architectural drawings.
    A. 12'-6"
    B. 0.5
    C. .500

## Drawing Problems

*Use the startup option of your choice or use one of your templates. Set limits, units, dimension styles, and other parameters as needed. Use the following general guidelines.*

A. Use dimension styles and text fonts that match the type of drawing as discussed in this chapter.

B. Use grids and object snap modes to your best advantage.

C. Apply dimensions accurately using ASME or other related industry/architectural standards. Dimensions are in inches, or feet and inches, unless otherwise specified.

D. Set separate layers for dimensions and other features.

E. Plot drawings with proper line weights.

F. For mechanical drawings, place general notes 1/2" from lower-left corner:

    3. UNLESS OTHERWISE SPECIFIED, ALL DIMENSIONS ARE IN INCHES *(or MILLIMETERS as applicable)*.

    2. REMOVE ALL BURRS AND SHARP EDGES.

    1. INTERPRET DIMENSIONS AND TOLERANCES PER ASME Y14.5M-1994.

    NOTES:

G. Save each drawing as P17-*(problem number)*.

    1.

Title: Shaft
Material: SAE 1030

2.

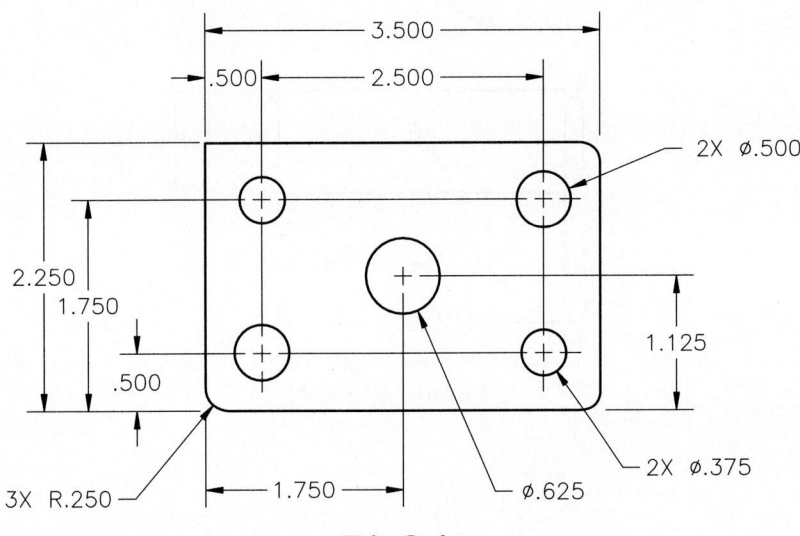

Title: Gasket

3.

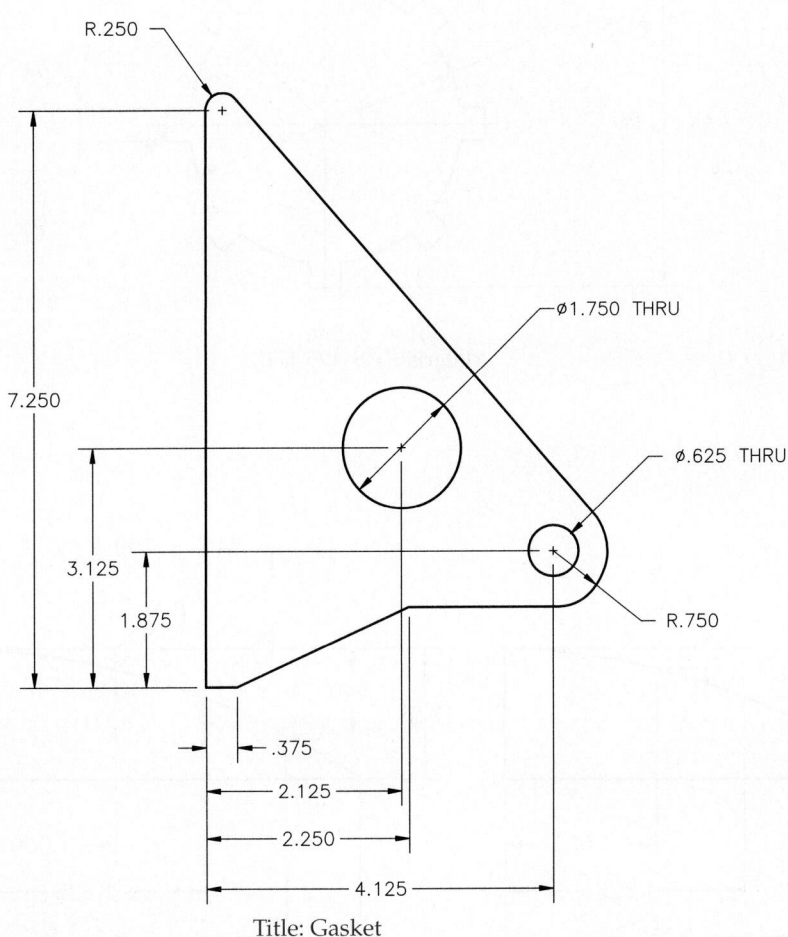

Title: Gasket

4.

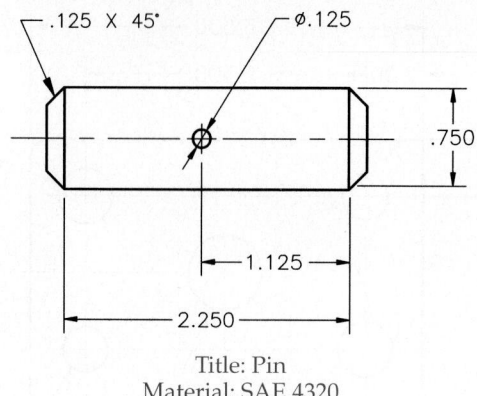

.125 X 45°    ∅.125

.750

1.125

2.250

Title: Pin
Material: SAE 4320

5.

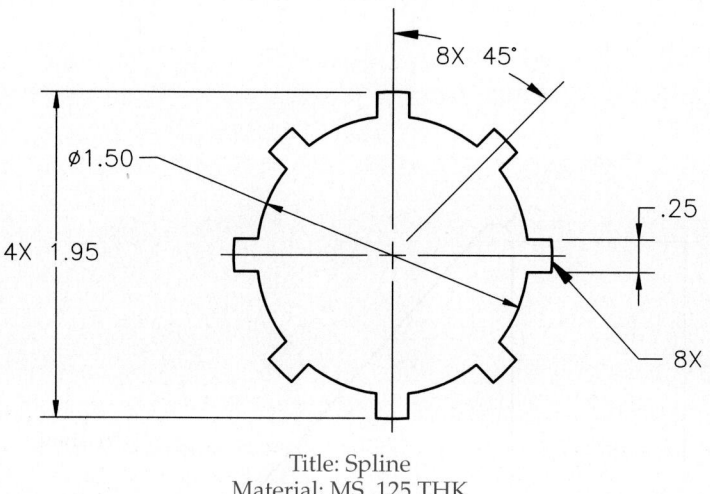

8X 45°

∅1.50

4X 1.95

.25

8X

Title: Spline
Material: MS .125 THK

6.

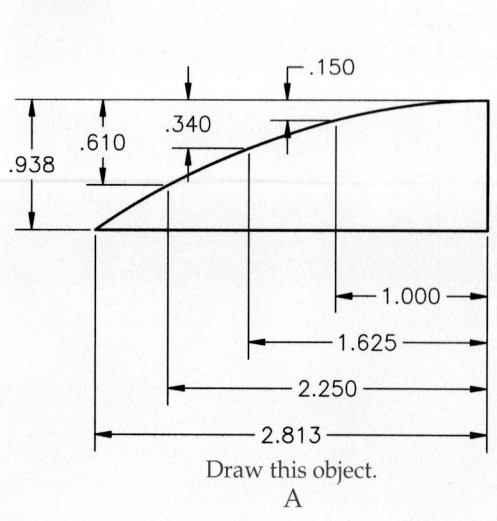

.150

.340

.610

.938

1.000

1.625

2.250

2.813

Draw this object.
A

.340 .150

.610

.938

1.000

1.625

2.250

2.813

Modify the dimensions as shown here.
B

Title: Shim

7.

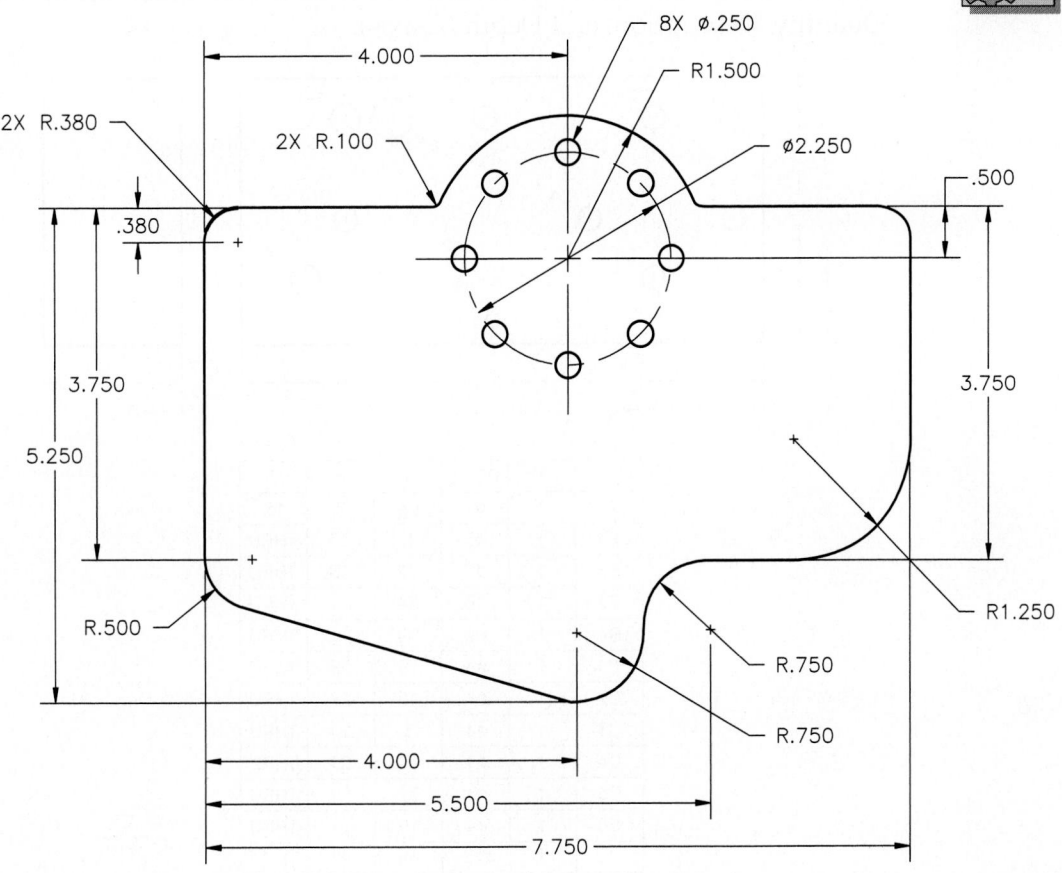

8.

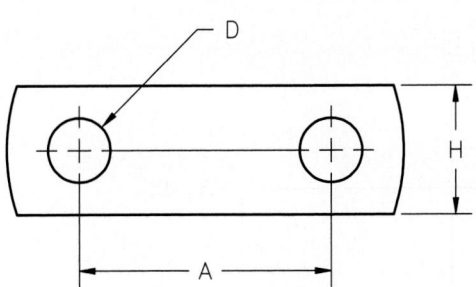

D

H

A

| CHAIN NO. | A | D | H |
|-----------|-----|-----|-------|
| SST1000 | 2.6 | .44 | 1.125 |
| SST1001 | 3.0 | .48 | 1.525 |
| SST1002 | 3.5 | .95 | 2.125 |

Note:
Overall Length is 1.5xA
end radii are .9xA

Title: Chain Link
Material: Steel

9. Convert the given drawing to a drawing with the holes located using arrowless dimensioning based on the X and Y coordinates given in the table. Place a table above your title block with Hole (identification), Quantity, Description, and Depth (Z-axis).

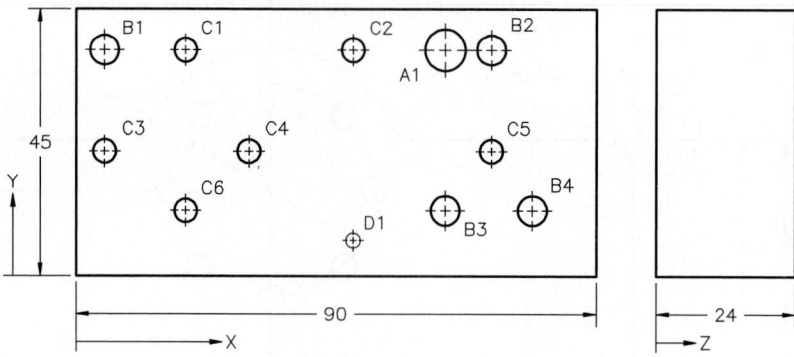

| HOLE | QTY | DESC | X | Y | Z |
|------|-----|------|----|----|------|
| A1 | 1 | ø7 | 64 | 38 | 18 |
| B1 | 1 | ø5 | 5 | 38 | THRU |
| B2 | 1 | ø5 | 72 | 38 | THRU |
| B3 | 1 | ø5 | 64 | 11 | THRU |
| B4 | 1 | ø5 | 79 | 11 | THRU |
| C1 | 1 | ø4 | 19 | 38 | THRU |
| C2 | 1 | ø4 | 48 | 38 | THRU |
| C3 | 1 | ø4 | 5 | 21 | THRU |
| C4 | 1 | ø4 | 30 | 21 | THRU |
| C5 | 1 | ø4 | 72 | 21 | THRU |
| C6 | 1 | ø4 | 19 | 11 | THRU |
| D1 | 1 | ø2.5 | 48 | 6 | THRU |

Title: Base
Material: Bronze

10.

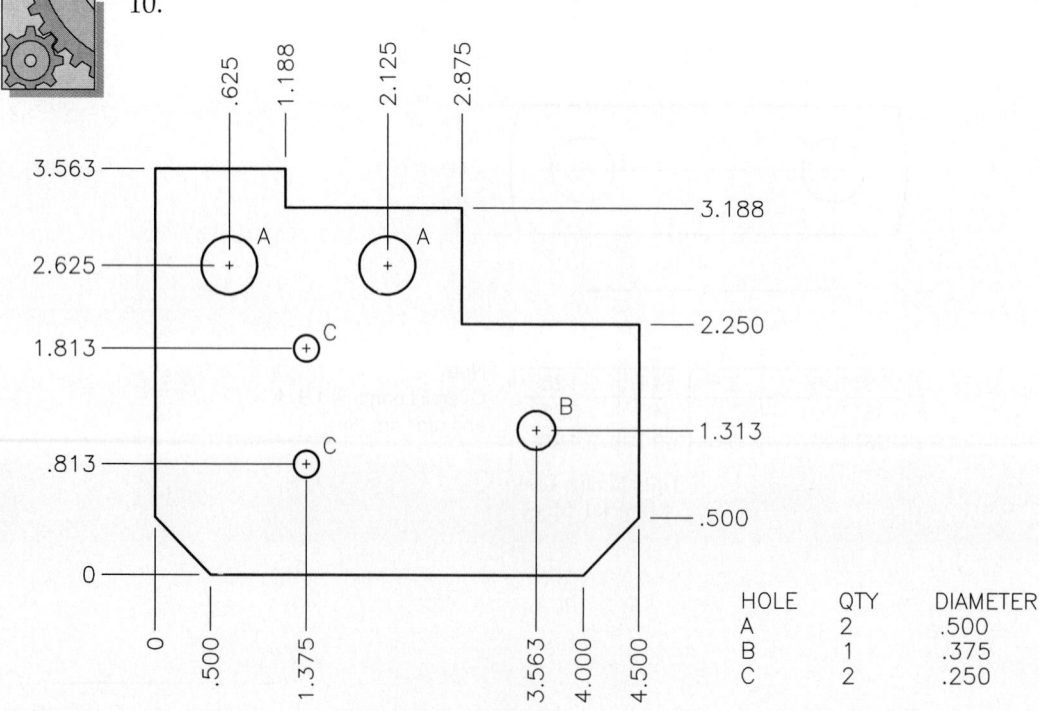

| HOLE | QTY | DIAMETER |
|------|-----|----------|
| A | 2 | .500 |
| B | 1 | .375 |
| C | 2 | .250 |

Title: Chassis
Material: Aluminum .100 THK

11.

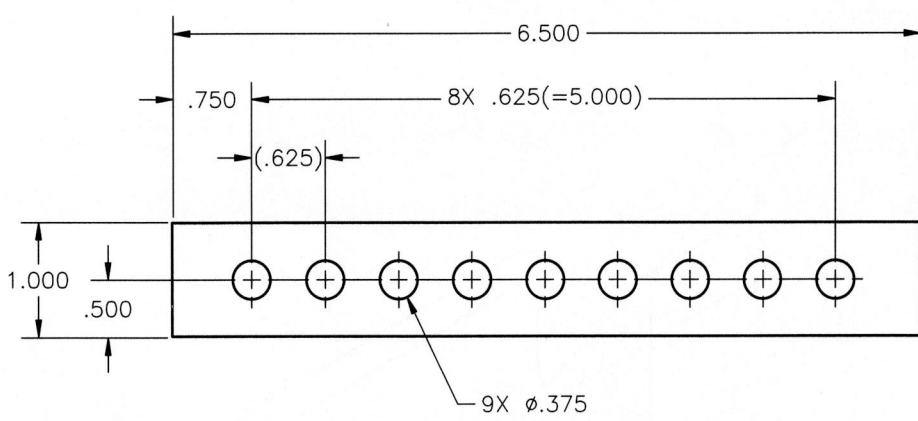

12.

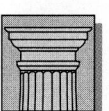

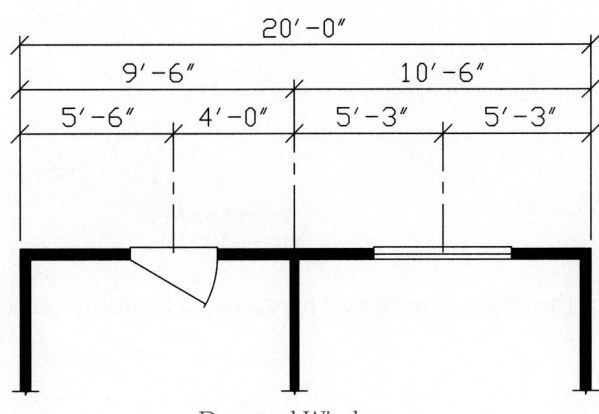

Door and Window

13.

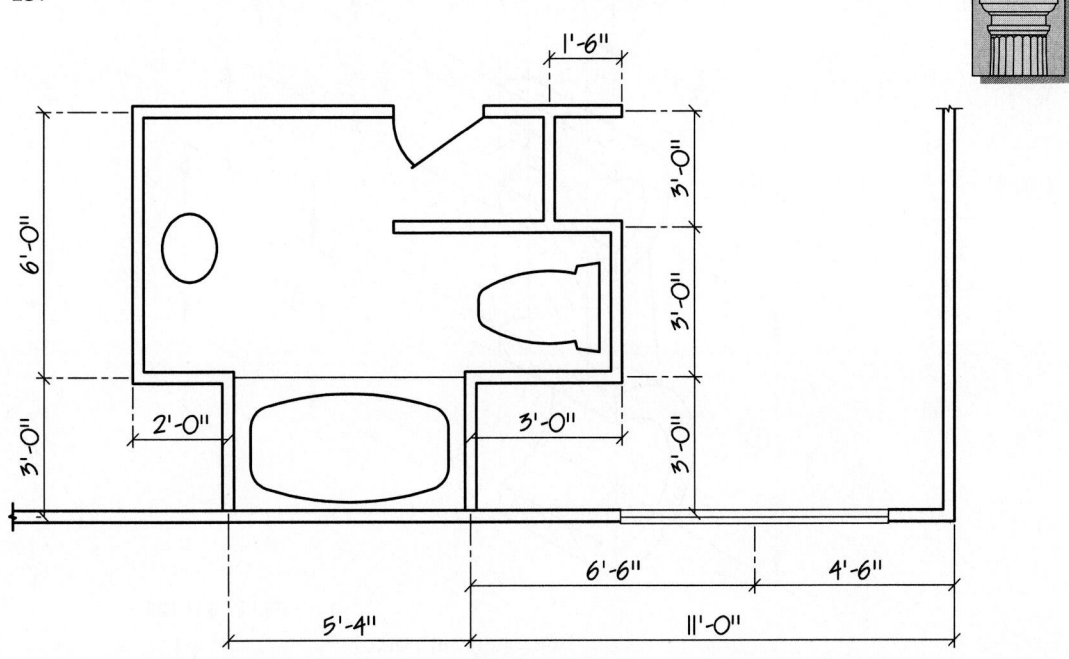

Title: Bathroom Area

*For Problems 14–16, use the isometric drawing provided to create a multiview drawing for the part. Include only the views necessary to fully describe the object. Dimension according to the ASME standards discussed in this chapter using a dimension style appropriate for mechanical drafting.*

14.

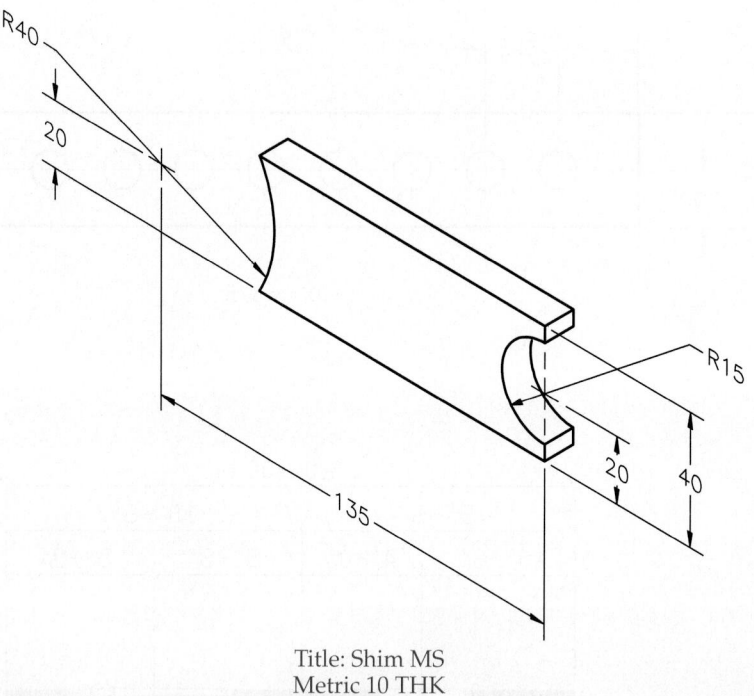

Title: Shim MS
Metric 10 THK

15.  Half of the object is removed for clarity. The entire object should be drawn.

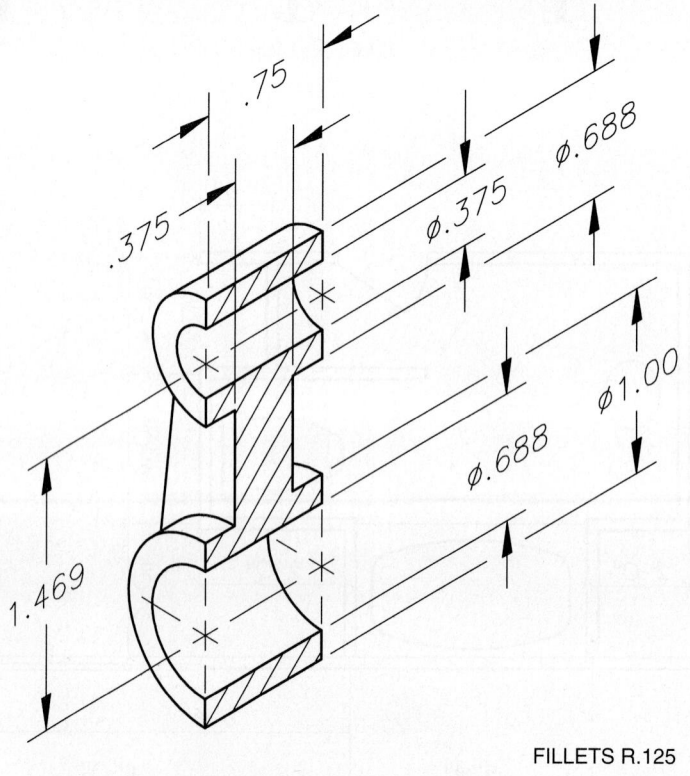

FILLETS R.125

Title: Shaft Support
Material: Cast Iron (CI)

16. Half of the object is removed for clarity. The entire object should be drawn.

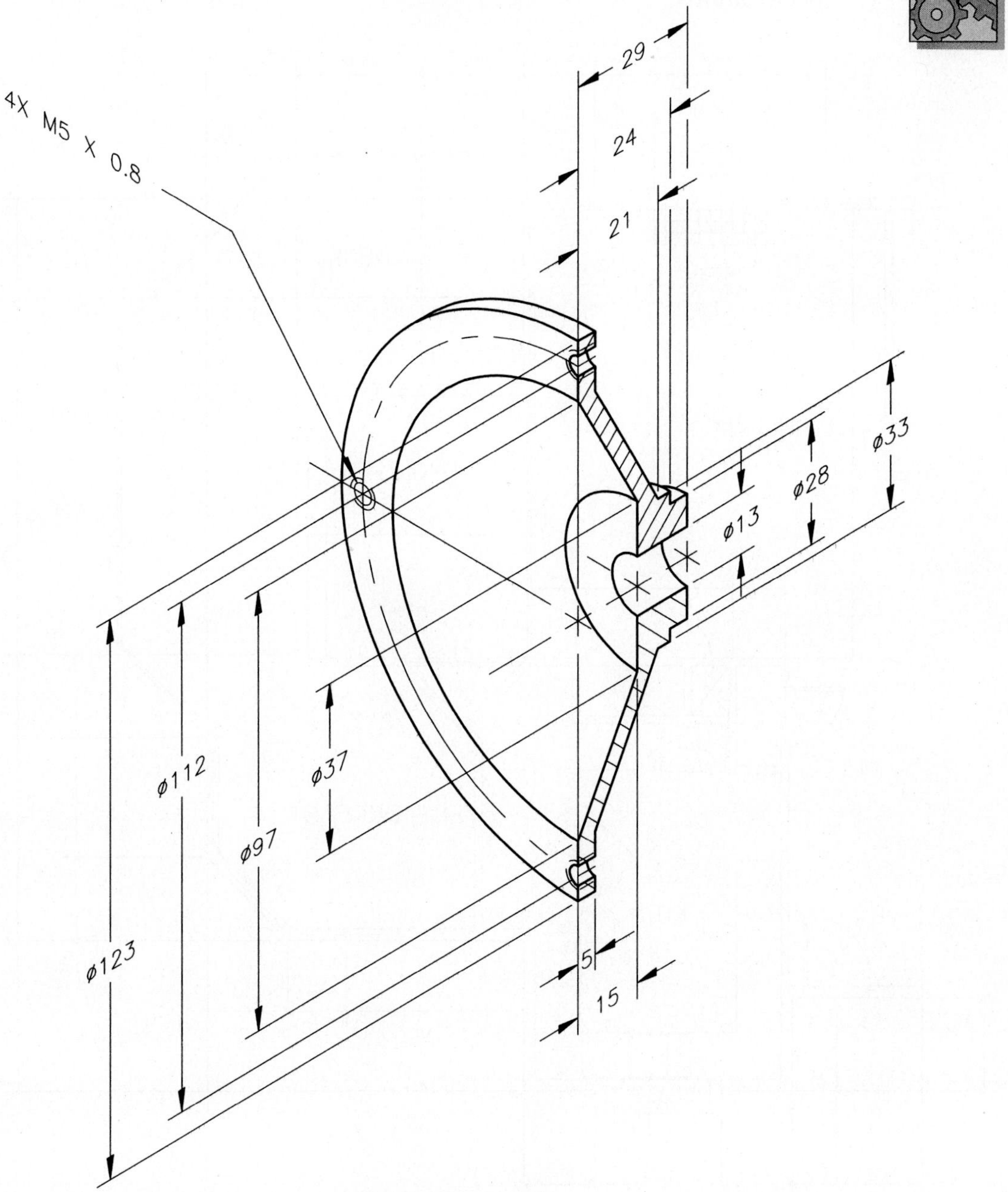

4X M5 X 0.8

29

24

21

ø33

ø28

ø13

ø112

ø37

ø97

ø123

5

15

Title: Transmission Cover
Material: Cast Iron (CI)
Metric

17. Draw this floor plan. Size the windows and the doors to your own specifications.

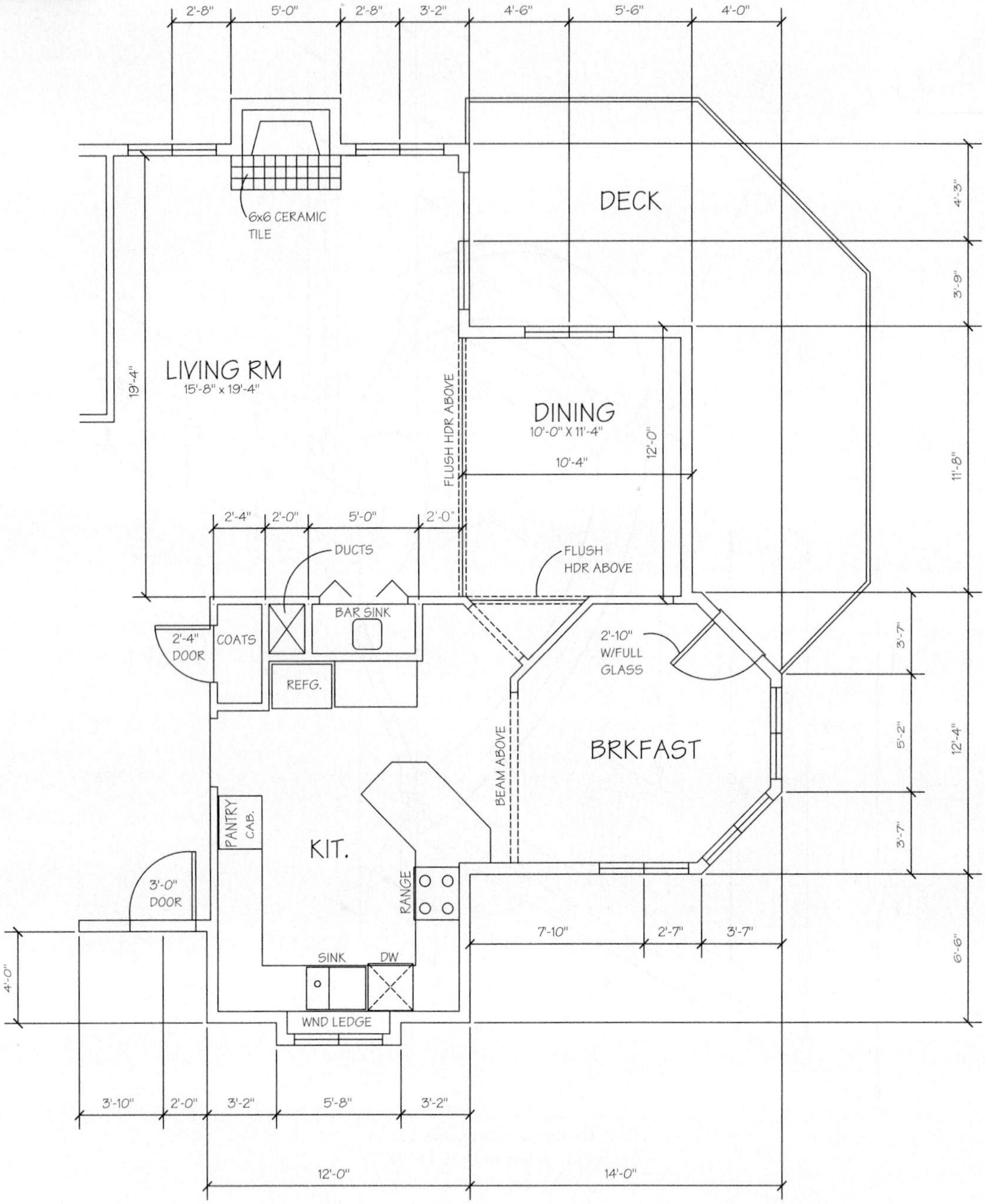

2'-8" 5'-0" 2'-8" 3'-2" 4'-6" 5'-6" 4'-0"

DECK

4'-3"

3'-9"

6x6 CERAMIC
TILE

LIVING RM
15'-8" x 19'-4"

19'-4"

DINING
10'-0" X 11'-4"

FLUSH HDR ABOVE

12'-0"

11'-8"

10'-4"

2'-4" 2'-0" 5'-0" 2'-0"

DUCTS

FLUSH
HDR ABOVE

BAR SINK

2'-4"
DOOR

COATS

2'-10"
W/FULL
GLASS

3'-7"

REFG.

BRKFAST

5'-2"

12'-4"

PANTRY
CAB.

KIT.

BEAM ABOVE

3'-7"

RANGE

3'-0"
DOOR

6'-6"

SINK

DW

4'-0"

7'-10" 2'-7" 3'-7"

WND LEDGE

3'-10" 2'-0" 3'-2" 5'-8" 3'-2"

12'-0" 14'-0"

18.

| HOLE LAYOUT | | | |
|---|---|---|---|
| KEY | SIZE | DEPTH | NO. REQD |
| A | ⌀.250 | THRU | 6 |
| B | ⌀.125 | THRU | 4 |
| C | ⌀.375 | THRU | 4 |
| D | R.125 | THRU | 2 |

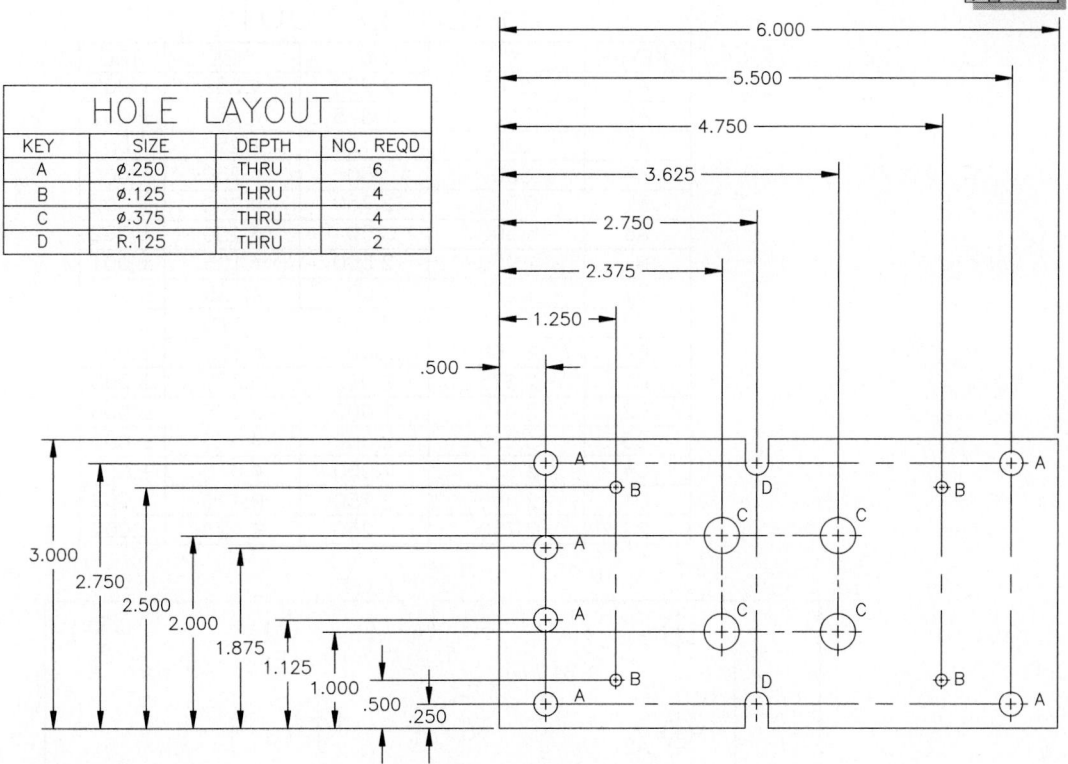

Title: Chassis Base (datum dimensioning)
Material: 12 gage Aluminum

19.

| HOLE LAYOUT | | | |
|---|---|---|---|
| KEY | SIZE | DEPTH | NO. REQD |
| A | ⌀.250 | THRU | 6 |
| B | ⌀.125 | THRU | 4 |
| C | ⌀.375 | THRU | 4 |
| D | R.125 | THRU | 2 |

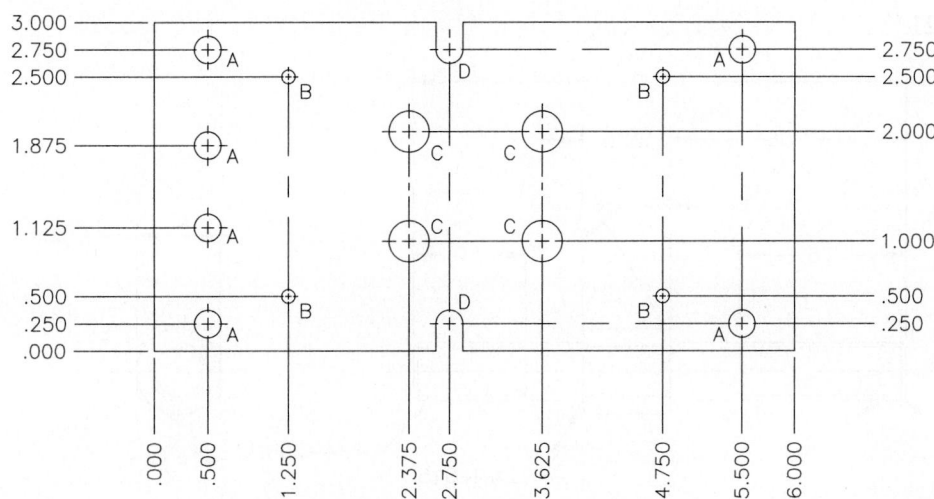

Title: Chassis Base (arrowless dimensioning)
Material: 12 gage Aluminum

20.

## HOLE LAYOUT

| KEY | X | Y | SIZE | TOL |
|-----|-----|-----|------|-----|
| A1 | .500 | 2.750 | ⌀.250 | ±.002 |
| A2 | .500 | 1.875 | ⌀.250 | ±.002 |
| A3 | .500 | 1.125 | ⌀.250 | ±.002 |
| A4 | .500 | .250 | ⌀.250 | ±.002 |
| A5 | 5.500 | 2.750 | ⌀.250 | ±.002 |
| A6 | 5.500 | .250 | ⌀.250 | ±.002 |
| B1 | 1.250 | 2.500 | ⌀.125 | ±.001 |
| B2 | 1.250 | .500 | ⌀.125 | ±.001 |
| B3 | 4.750 | 2.500 | ⌀.125 | ±.001 |
| B4 | 4.750 | .500 | ⌀.125 | ±.001 |
| C1 | 2.375 | 2.000 | ⌀.375 | ±.005 |
| C2 | 2.375 | 1.000 | ⌀.375 | ±.005 |
| C3 | 3.625 | 2.000 | ⌀.375 | ±.005 |
| C4 | 3.625 | 1.000 | ⌀.375 | ±.005 |
| D1 | 2.750 | 2.750 | R.125 | ±.002 |
| D2 | 2.750 | .250 | R.125 | ±.002 |

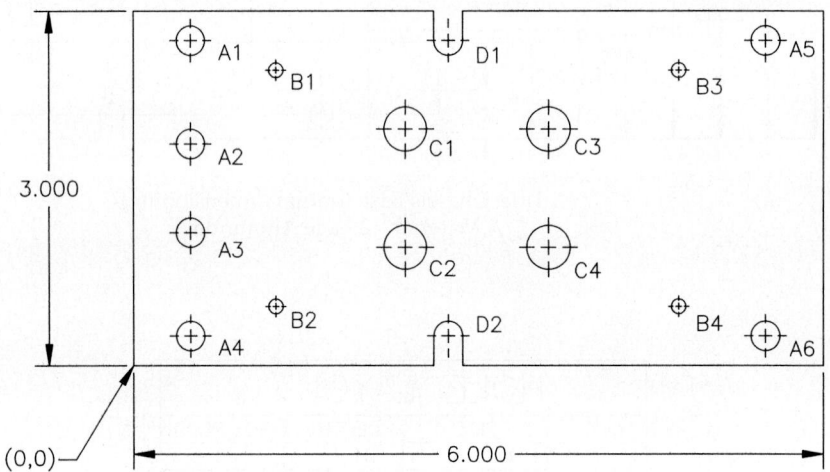

Title: Chassis Base (arrowless tabular dimensioning)
Material: 12 gage Aluminum

21.

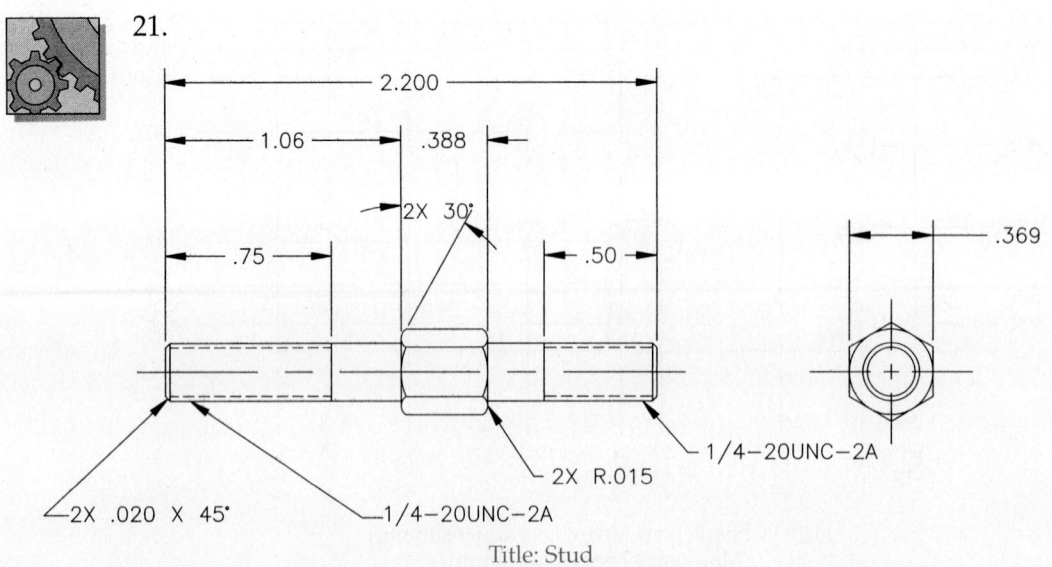

Title: Stud
Material: Stainless Steel

AutoCAD and its Applications—Basics

22.

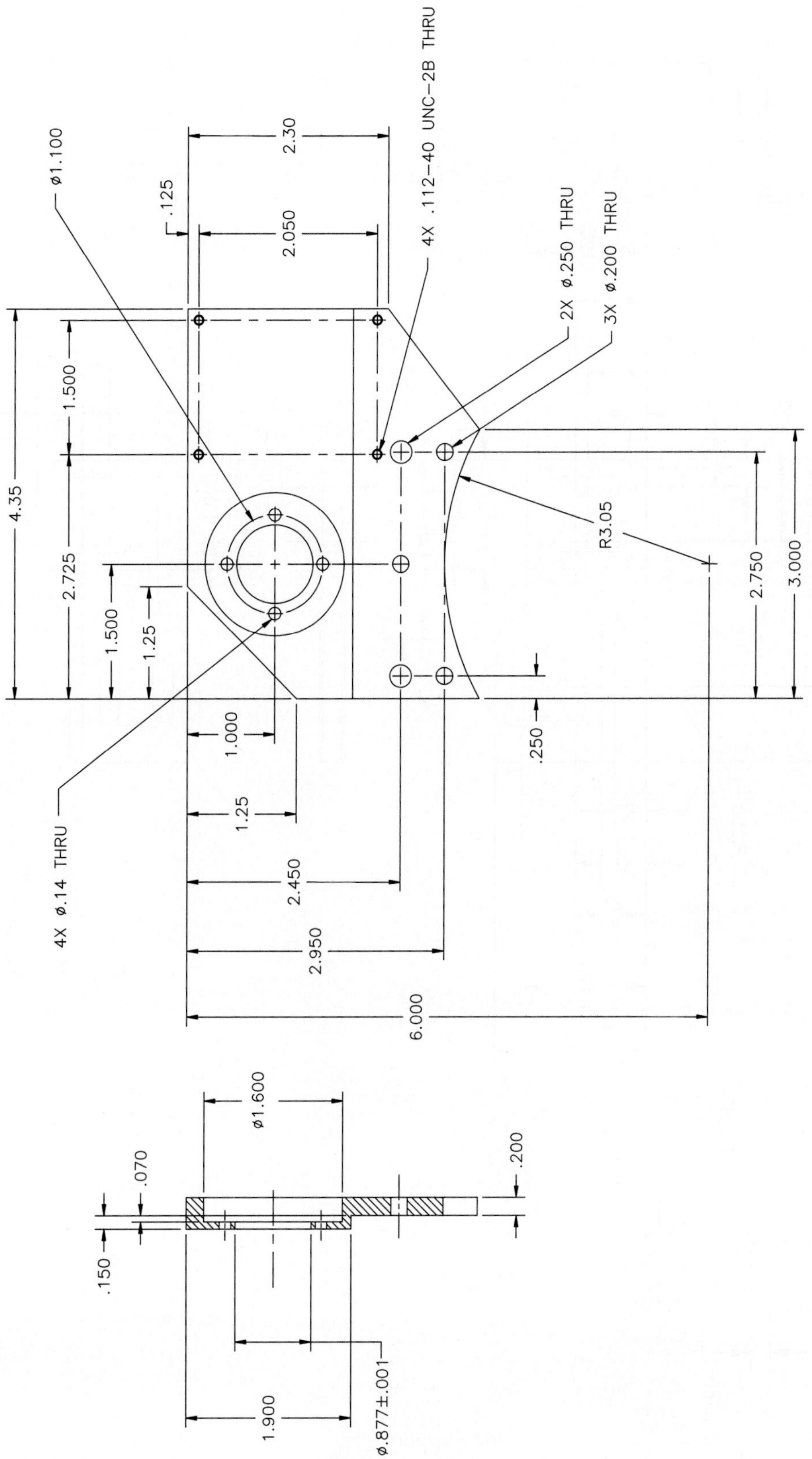

Ø1.100

2.30

.125

2.050

4X .112-40 UNC-2B THRU

2X Ø.250 THRU

3X Ø.200 THRU

4.35

1.500

2.725

1.500

1.25

R3.05

2.750

3.000

1.000

.250

1.25

4X Ø.14 THRU

2.450

2.950

6.000

Ø1.600

.070

.200

.150

1.900

Ø.877±.001

Title: Bracket
Material: SAE 1040

23.

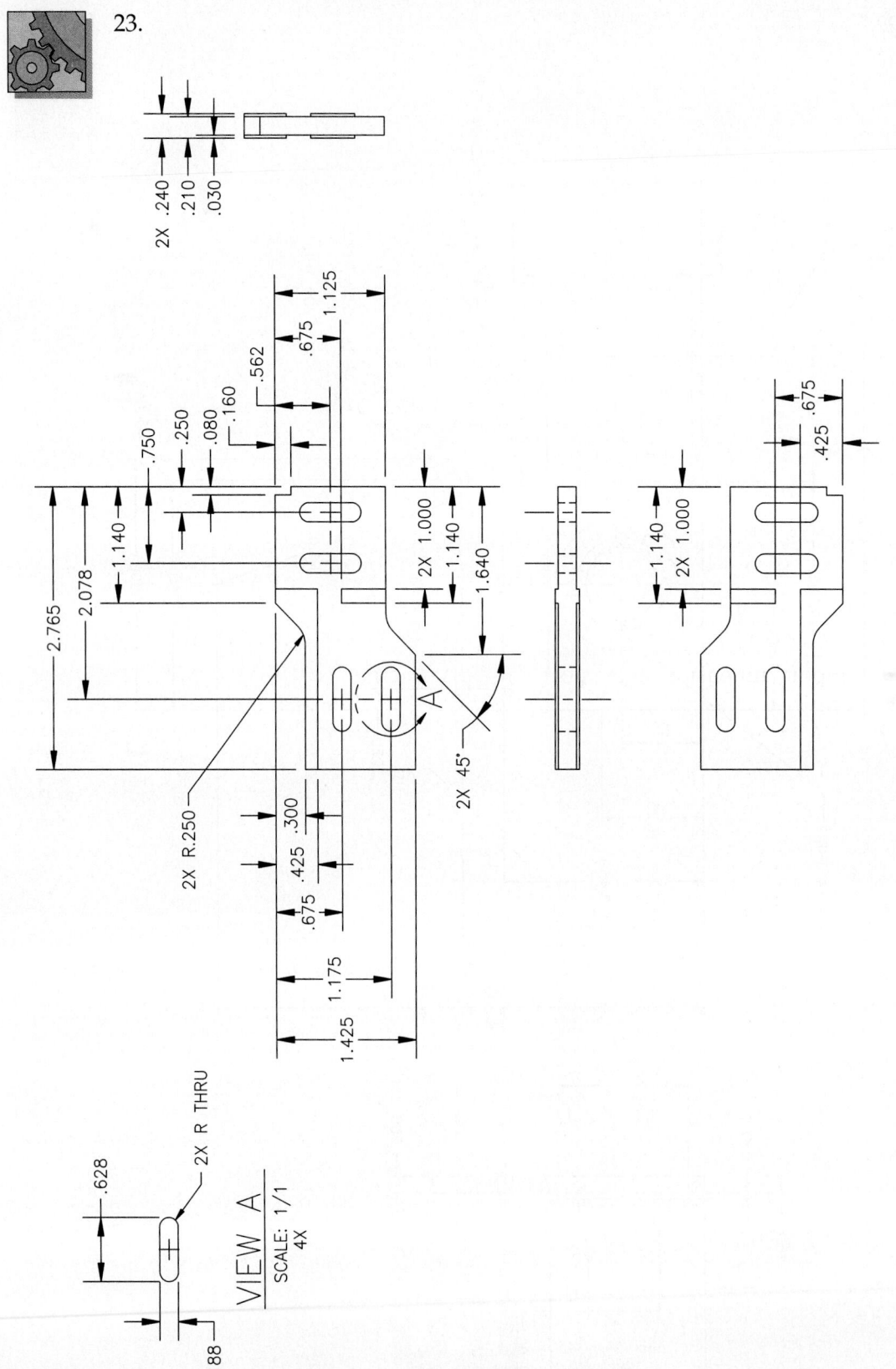

Title: Support
Material: Aluminum

## CHAPTER 18

# Editing Dimensions

## Learning Objectives

After completing this chapter, you will be able to do the following:
- Make changes to existing dimensions.
- Update a dimension to reflect the current dimension style.
- Import dimension styles from another drawing.
- Use the **Properties** window to edit individual dimension properties.
- Edit individual elements of associative dimensions.

The tools used to edit dimensions vary from simple erasing techniques to object editing commands. Often, the dimensioned object is edited and the dimensions are automatically updated to reflect the changes. This chapter provides you with a variety of useful techniques for editing dimensions.

## Erasing Dimensions

In Chapter 3, you were introduced to the **ERASE** command. Among the many selection options used with this command are **Last**, **Previous**, **Window**, **Crossing**, **WPolygon**, **CPolygon**, and **Fence**.

Erasing existing features such as large groups of dimensions often becomes difficult. For example, the objects may be very close to other parts of the drawing. When there are many objects, it is usually time-consuming to erase each one individually. When this situation occurs, the **Crossing**, **CPolygon**, and **Fence** selection options of the **ERASE** command are useful. A comparison of using the **Window** and **Crossing** selection options with the **ERASE** command on a group of dimensions is shown in Figure 18-1. For a review of these techniques, refer to Chapter 3.

**PROFESSIONAL TIP**

Dimensions are block objects inside of AutoCAD. After erasing dimensions, use the **PURGE** command to purge the erased dimension blocks. The **PURGE** command is discussed in Chapter 22.

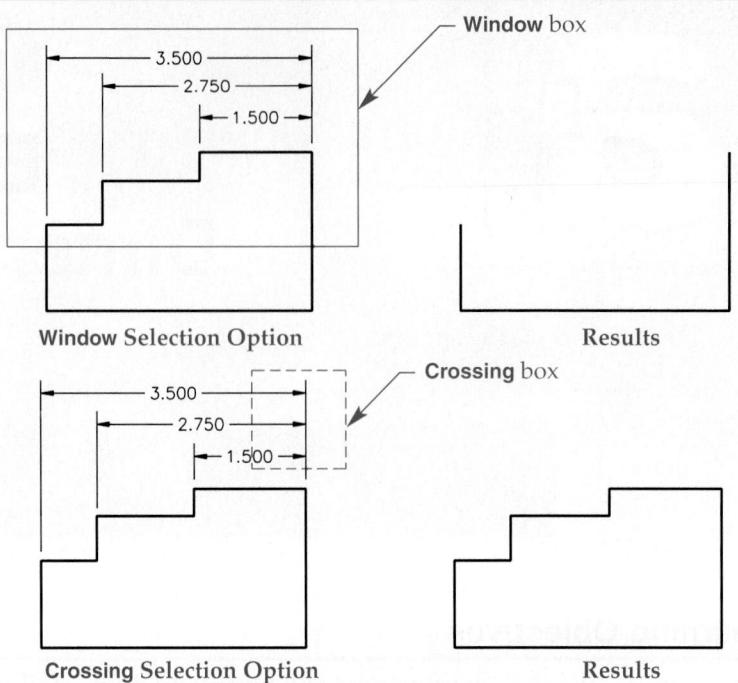

Figure 18-1.
Using the **Window** and **Crossing** selection options of the **ERASE** command to erase dimensions.

Window Selection Option

Window box

Results

Crossing box

Crossing Selection Option

Results

## Editing Dimension Text Values

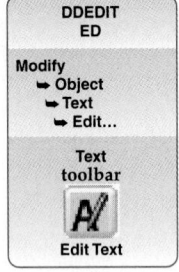

DDEDIT
ED

Modify
➡ Object
↳ Text
↳ Edit...

Text
toolbar

Edit Text

The **DDEDIT** command can be used to edit existing dimension text. You can add a prefix or suffix to the text, or edit the dimension text format. This is useful when you wish to alter dimension text without creating a new dimension. For example, a linear dimension does not automatically place a diameter symbol with the text value. Using the **DDEDIT** command is one way to place this symbol on the dimension once it has already been placed in the drawing.

You can access the **DDEDIT** command by picking **Text** and then **Edit...** from the **Object** cascading menu in the **Modify** pull-down menu. You can also type ED or DDEDIT at the Command: prompt. When you enter this command, the following prompt is displayed:

Select an annotation object or [Undo]:

After you select a dimension to edit, the multiline text editor and **Text Formatting** toolbar are displayed. See **Figure 18-2**. The two chevrons (< >) represent the existing dimension text. To add a diameter symbol to the text, place the cursor at the position that you want to add the symbol and right-click. Then, select **Diameter** from the **Symbol** cascading menu. This adds the %%c control code, which displays the diameter symbol in the text object. Pick the **OK** button on the **Text Formatting** toolbar to close the multiline text editor. The result of changing an existing dimension in this manner is shown in **Figure 18-3**.

PROFESSIONAL
TIP

You can replace the brackets representing the dimension value with numeric values. However, if the dimension is subsequently stretched, trimmed, or extended, the dimension text value will not change. Therefore, try to leave the default value.

**Figure 18-2.**
The multiline text editor can be used to edit existing dimension text.

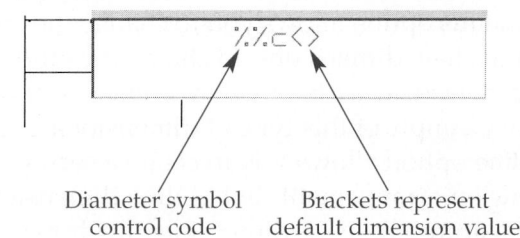

Diameter symbol control code

Brackets represent default dimension value

**Figure 18-3.**
Using the **DDEDIT** command to add a diameter symbol to an existing dimension.
A—Original dimension.
B—Diameter symbol added.

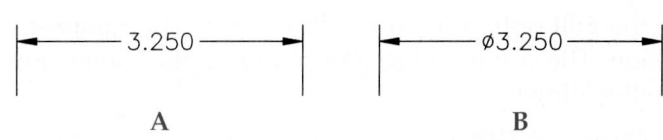

3.250

A

ø3.250

B

## Exercise 18-1

○ Start a new drawing or use one of your templates.
○ Draw and dimension an object similar to the one shown in the upper-left corner of **Figure 18-1.**
○ Make a copy of the object and position it directly below the original object.
○ Use the **Window** selection option of the **ERASE** command to remove the dimensions of the first object, as shown in the top example of **Figure 18-1.**
○ Use the **Crossing** selection option of the **ERASE** command to remove the dimensions of the second object, as shown in the bottom example of **Figure 18-1.**
○ Draw an original object and add a dimension similar to the one shown in **Figure 18-3A.**
○ Use the **DDEDIT** command to add a diameter symbol to the dimension.
○ Save the drawing as EX18-1.

## Editing Dimensions with the QDIM Command

The **QDIM** command can be used to place a new dimension in a drawing. This was discussed in Chapter 17. The **QDIM** command can also be used to perform several dimension editing operations. You can change the arrangement of an existing dimension, add an additional dimension, or remove an existing dimension. The **QDIM** command can be accessed by picking the **Quick Dimension** button on the **Dimension** toolbar, picking **Quick Dimension** from the **Dimension** pull-down menu, or typing QDIM at the Command: prompt. The **QDIM** command sequence is:

Command: **QDIM**↵
Associative dimension priority = Endpoint
Select geometry to dimension: *(pick the dimension to edit)*

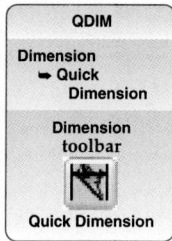

QDIM

Dimension
➡ Quick
      Dimension

Dimension
toolbar

Quick Dimension

Select geometry to dimension: ↵
Specify dimension line position, or
[Continuous/Staggered/Baseline/Ordinate/Radius/Diameter/datumPoint/Edit/seTtings]
    <Continuous>:

The **Continuous** option allows you to change the arrangement of a selected group of dimensions to chain dimensions. In chain, or continuous, dimensioning the dimensions are placed next to each other in a line, or end to end. This is discussed in Chapter 17. An example of this type of dimensioning is shown in **Figure 18-4A.**

The **Baseline** option allows you to create a series of baseline dimensions from an existing dimension arrangement. In baseline dimensioning, all dimensions originate from common features. Baseline dimensions are drawn in **Figure 18-4B.** In the example shown, the **Baseline** option has been used to change the dimensioning arrangement from continuous in **Figure 18-4A** to baseline.

The **Edit** option allows you to add dimensions to, or remove dimensions from, a selected group and then automatically reorder the group. You can use the **Add** suboption of the **Edit** option to add a dimension. The **Remove** option is used to remove a dimension. The command sequence to add the dimension shown in **Figure 18-4C** to the baseline dimensions is:

Command: **QDIM**↵
Associative dimensions priority = Endpoint
Select geometry to dimension: *(select all dimensions in the group to change)*
Select geometry to dimension: ↵
Specify dimension line position, or
[Continuous/Staggered/Baseline/Ordinate/Radius/Diameter/datumPoint/Edit/seTtings]
    <Baseline>: **E**↵
Indicate dimension point to remove, or [Add/eXit] <eXit>: **A**↵
Indicate dimension point to add, or [Remove/eXit] <eXit>: *(pick the location or feature for which the dimension is to be added)*
One dimension point added.
Indicate dimension point to add, or [Remove/eXit] <eXit>: ↵
Specify dimension line position, or
[Continuous/Staggered/Baseline/Ordinate/Radius/Diameter/datumPoint/Edit/seTtings]
    <Baseline>: *(pick a location for the baseline dimension arrangement)*

The dimensions are then automatically realigned after you pick a location for the arrangement. You do not have to pick all of the dimensions in the group. However, if you do not pick the entire group you must select the location carefully. The spacing for the edited dimension and the dimensions in the group that were not selected may not be consistent.

---

**Figure 18-4.**
The **QDIM** command can be used to change existing dimension arrangements and add or remove dimensions.

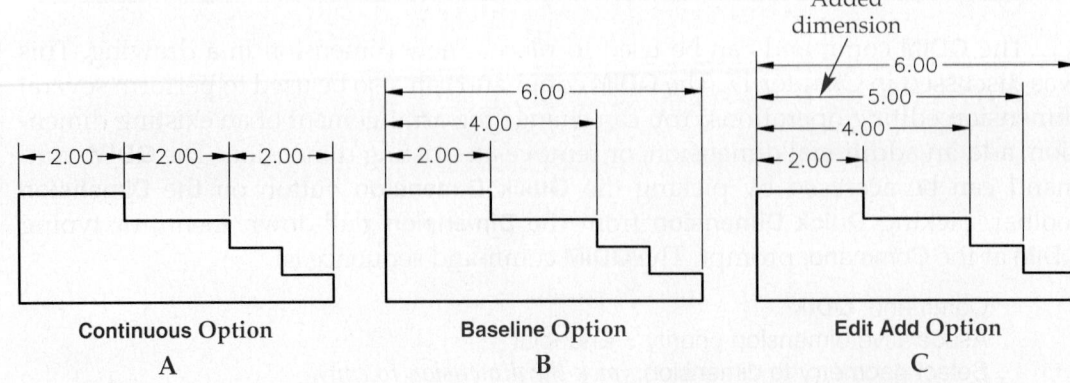

Continuous Option
A

Baseline Option
B

Edit Add Option
C

AutoCAD and its Applications—Basics

## Editing Dimension Text Placement

Good dimensioning practice requires that adjacent dimension text be *staggered*, rather than stacked. As an example, in **Figure 18-5,** one of the dimensions has been moved to a new location to separate the text elements. The **DIMTEDIT** command allows you to change the placement and orientation of an existing associative dimension text value. An *associative dimension* is one in which all elements of the dimension (including the dimension line, extension lines, arrowheads, and text) act as a single object. Thus, when an associative dimension is selected for editing, the entire dimension is highlighted. Associative dimensioning is controlled by the **DIMASSOC** system variable and is active by default.

To access the **DIMTEDIT** command, pick the **Dimension Text Edit** button on the **Dimension** toolbar, pick one of the options from the **Align Text** cascading menu in the **Dimension** pull-down menu, or enter DIMTEDIT at the Command: prompt. After entering the command, select the dimension to be altered.

If the **DIMASSOC** system variable was on when the dimension was created, the text of the selected dimension automatically drags with the screen cursor. This allows you to relocate the text with your pointing device. If you pick a point, AutoCAD automatically moves the text and reestablishes the break in the dimension line. You can also select from the options that are displayed on the command line during this sequence:

Specify new location for dimension text or [Left/Right/Center/Home/Angle]:

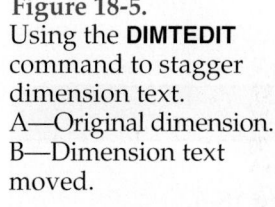

DIMTEDIT

Dimension
➡ Align Text

Dimension
toolbar

Dimension Text Edit

Figure 18-5.
Using the **DIMTEDIT** command to stagger dimension text.
A—Original dimension.
B—Dimension text moved.

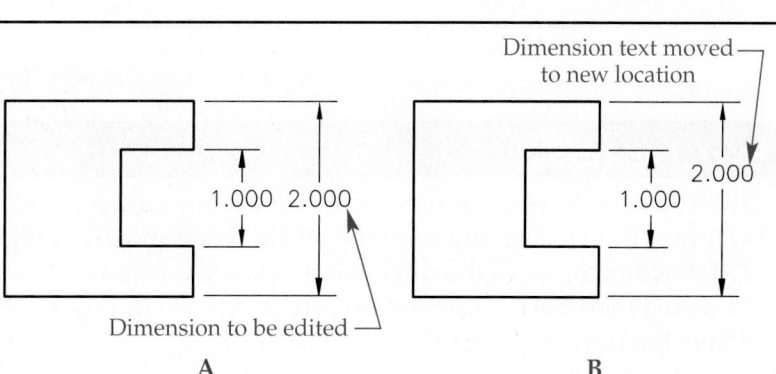

Dimension text moved to new location

2.000

1.000

1.000  2.000

Dimension to be edited

A                    B

- **Left.** Moves horizontal text to the left and vertical text down.
- **Right.** Moves horizontal text to the right and vertical text up.
- **Center.** Centers the dimension text on the dimension line.
- **Home.** Moves relocated text back to its original position.
- **Angle.** Allows you to place dimension text at an angle. When the **Angle** option is entered, you are asked to specify a rotation angle. The text is then rotated about its middle point.

The result after using each of the **DIMTEDIT** command options is shown in Figure 18-6.

Figure 18-6.
A comparison of the options used with the **DIMTEDIT** command.

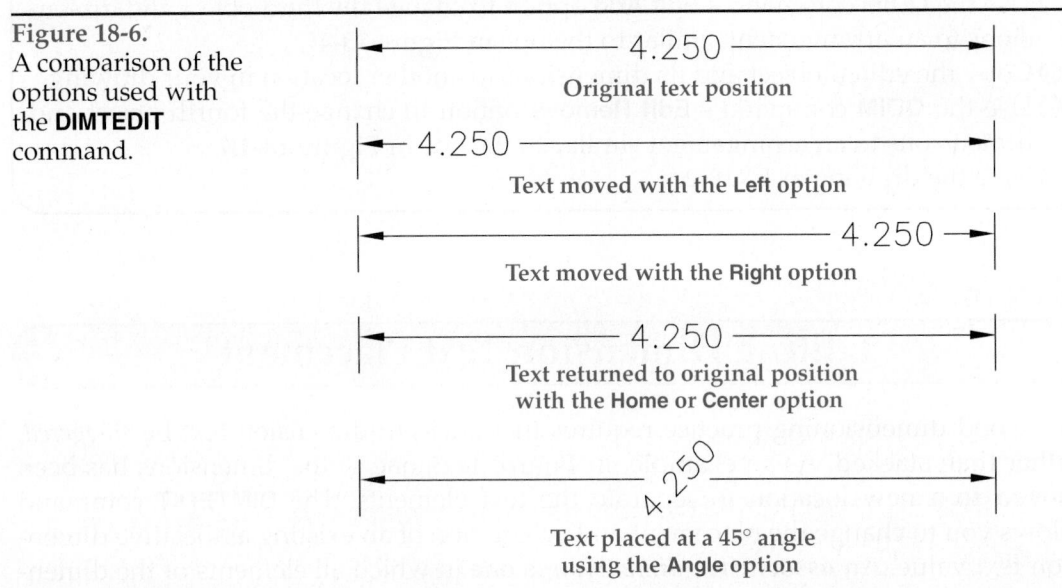

4.250
Original text position

4.250
Text moved with the **Left** option

4.250
Text moved with the **Right** option

4.250
Text returned to original position with the **Home** or **Center** option

4.250
Text placed at a 45° angle using the **Angle** option

NOTE You can locate dimension text as desired without using automatic horizontal justification by activating the **Place text manually when dimensioning** check box, which is located in the **Fit** tab of the **New** (or **Modify**) **Dimension Style** dialog box.

PROFESSIONAL TIP If you wish to relocate existing dimension text, using grips is the quickest way to adjust the text position. This method requires only picks and no command entry. Simply pick the dimension, pick the dimension text grip, and then drag the text to the new location.

Exercise 18-3

○ Start a new drawing or use one of your templates.
○ Draw a dimension similar to the original one shown in **Figure 18-6.**
○ Make four copies of the dimension below the original.
○ Use the **DIMTEDIT** command options as shown in **Figure 18-6.**
○ Save the drawing as EX18-3.

## Using the DIMEDIT Command

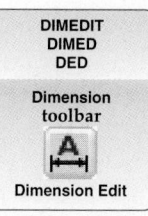

The **DIMEDIT** command can be used to change the text value, text placement, or extension lines of an existing dimension. You can access the **DIMEDIT** command by picking the **Dimension Edit** button on the **Dimension** toolbar or by entering DED, DIMED, or DIMEDIT at the Command: prompt. This command has four options that can be used to edit individual or multiple dimensions.

Command: **DED, DIMED,** *or* **DIMEDIT**↵
Enter type of dimension editing [Home/New/Rotate/Oblique] <Home>:

- **Home.** The default option; identical to the **Home** option of the **DIMTEDIT** command.
- **New.** Allows you to specify new dimension text and is similar to the **DDEDIT** command. After entering this option, the multiline text editor is displayed. Enter a prefix or suffix for the text and pick **OK**. The Select objects: prompt then appears. Any dimensions that are selected assume the new text.
- **Rotate.** Used to rotate dimension text; similar to the **Angle** option of the **DIMTEDIT** command.
- **Oblique.** Allows you to change the angle of the extension lines. The **Oblique** option can also be accessed directly by picking **Oblique** from the **Dimension** pull-down menu.

## Shortcut Menu Options

If you select a dimension and right-click, a shortcut menu is displayed. See **Figure 18-7.** The shortcut menu contains the following dimension-specific options:

- **Dim Text position.** The options in this cascading menu automatically move the dimension text.
- **Precision.** The options in this cascading menu allow you to easily adjust the number of decimal places displayed in a dimension text value.
- **Dim Style.** This cascading menu allows you to create a new dimension style based on the properties of the selected dimension. You can also change the dimension style of the dimension. In addition to the **Dim Style** option in the shortcut menu, there are other methods of changing the dimension style of an existing dimension. These are discussed in the next sections.

Figure 18-7.
Select a dimension
and then right-click
to access this
shortcut menu.

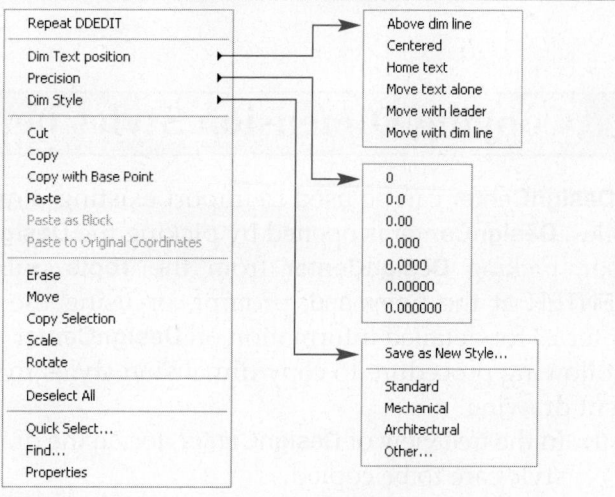

## Changing the Dimension Style

So far you have learned how to edit dimension text, text placement, dimension group arrangements, and other elements of existing dimensions. In addition to these operations, you will often find it necessary to change the dimension style of a dimension. You can also import dimension styles from a separate drawing for use in the current drawing. These methods are discussed in the following sections.

As discussed in Chapter 17, you can create dimension styles by specifying settings for text styles, positioning elements, and other properties in the **Dimension Style Manager** dialog box. When there are a number of dimension styles used in your drawing, you may need to change the style of an existing dimension to a different style. A dimension's style can be changed using any of the following methods:

- **Dim Style cascading menu in the shortcut menu.** Select the dimension and right-click to display the shortcut menu. Select a new dimension style from the cascading menu.
- **Dim Style Control drop-down list in the Dimension toolbar.** Select the dimension and then select the new dimension style from this drop-down list. See **Figure 18-8**.
- **Dim Style Control drop-down list in the Styles toolbar.** Select the dimension and then select the new dimension style from this drop-down list.
- **Properties window.** Select a new dimension style in the **Misc** category. Refer to Chapter 12 for a discussion on how to change settings in the **Properties** window.
- **Update option.** The **Update** dimension command changes the style of the selected dimension to the current dimension style. This command can be accessed by picking the **Dimension Update** button on the **Dimension** toolbar or by selecting **Update** from the **Dimension** pull-down menu.

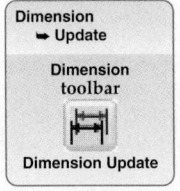

Dimension
➡ Update

Dimension
toolbar

Dimension Update

**Figure 18-8.**
The **Dim Style Control** drop-down list on the **Dimension** toolbar can be used to change the style of an existing dimension.

Dim Style Control
drop-down list

## Copying Dimension Styles between Drawings

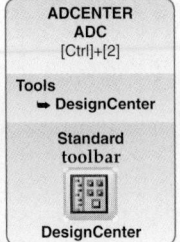

ADCENTER
ADC
[Ctrl]+[2]

Tools
➡ DesignCenter

Standard
toolbar

DesignCenter

**DesignCenter** can be used to import existing dimension styles from other drawing files. **DesignCenter** is opened by picking the **DesignCenter** button on the **Standard** toolbar, picking **DesignCenter** from the **Tools** pull-down menu, typing ADC or ADCENTER at the Command: prompt, or using the [Ctrl]+[2] key combination. See Chapter 23 for detailed information on **DesignCenter**. Once **DesignCenter** is open, use the following procedure to copy dimension styles from an existing drawing into the current drawing.

1. In the tree view of **DesignCenter**, locate the drawing from which the dimension styles are to be copied.
2. Expand the drawing tree and highlight Dimstyles.

Figure 18-9.
Copying dimension styles using **DesignCenter**.

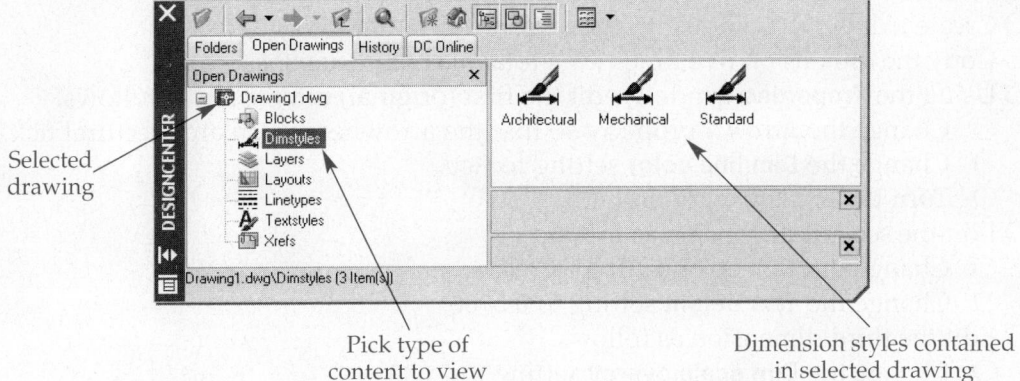

Selected drawing

Pick type of content to view

Dimension styles contained in selected drawing

3. The dimension styles in the drawing are shown in the preview palette. See **Figure 18-9**.
4. Select the dimension style(s) to be copied. Use the [Ctrl] and [Shift] keys to select multiple items. Then, right-click and select **Add Dimstyle(s)** from the shortcut menu to copy the styles to the current drawing. You can also use the **Cut** and **Paste** options from the shortcut menus or simply drag the dimension style icon and drop it into the drawing area.

---

**Exercise 18-4**

○ Begin a new drawing.
○ Open **DesignCenter**.
○ Use the tree viewing area to select a drawing from Chapter 17 containing dimension styles that you created.
○ Expand the drawing tree and highlight Dimstyles.
○ Import the dimension styles from the Chapter 17 drawing into the current drawing.
○ Close **DesignCenter**.
○ Open the **Dimension Style Manager** dialog box to verify that the styles have been copied.
○ Save the drawing as EX18-4.

---

## Using the **Properties** Window to Edit Dimensions

The **Properties** window can be used to change the various text, justification, and formatting properties of selected dimensions. However, as discussed in Chapter 17, doing so creates a dimension style override for the edited dimensions. Also, as discussed earlier in this chapter, you can assign a different style to the selected dimension using the **Properties** window.

## Exercise 18-5

○ Start a new drawing or use one of your templates.
○ Create a dimension similar to the one shown in **Figure 18-3B**.
○ Copy the dimension five times for a total of six dimensions.
○ Using the **Properties** window, edit the first (original) dimension as follows.
  ○ Change the **Arrow 1** property so that the arrowhead is an architectural tick.
  ○ Change the **Dim line color** setting to Red.
  ○ Turn the **Ext line 1** option off.
○ Edit the second dimension as follows.
  ○ Change the **Text color** setting to Yellow.
  ○ Change the **Text height** setting to 0.5000.
○ Edit the third dimension as follows.
  ○ Change the **Dim scale overall** setting to 2.000.
○ Edit the fourth dimension as follows.
  ○ Change the **Dim units** setting to Fractional.
  ○ Change the **Precision** setting to 0 1/256.
○ Edit the fifth dimension as follows.
  ○ Turn the **Alt enabled** option on.
  ○ Change the **Alt precision** setting to 0.0000.
○ Edit the sixth dimension as follows.
  ○ Change the **Tolerance display** setting to Limits.
  ○ Change the **Tolerance limit lower** setting to 0.0001.
  ○ Change the **Tolerance limit upper** setting to 0.0002.
○ Save the drawing as EX18-5.

## Using the MATCHPROP Command

The dimension editing methods presented in this chapter have focused on updating individual dimension properties and changing dimensions to a different dimension style. You can also edit dimensions by matching the properties of one dimension to another. The **MATCHPROP** command allows you to select the properties of one dimension and apply those properties to one or more existing dimensions.

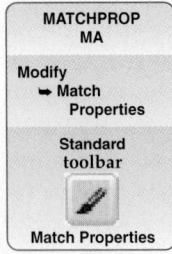

MATCHPROP
MA

Modify
➥ Match
  Properties

Standard
toolbar

Match Properties

The **MATCHPROP** command can be accessed by picking the **Match Properties** button on the **Standard** toolbar, selecting **Match Properties** from the **Modify** pull-down menu, or entering MA or MATCHPROP at the Command: prompt. This command is covered more completely in Chapter 12. The command sequence is:

Command: **MA** *or* **MATCHPROP**.↵
Select source object: (*pick the dimension from which to copy the style*)
Current active settings: Color Layer Ltype Ltscale Lineweight Thickness PlotStyle
  Text Dim Hatch
Select destination object(s) or [Settings]: (*pick one or more dimensions to which the
  style is to be applied*)
Select destination object(s) or [Settings]: ↵
Command:

After you select the dimensions to change, press [Enter] and all of the destination dimensions are updated to reflect the properties of the source dimension.

For the **MATCHPROP** command to work with dimensions, the **Dimension** setting must be active. You can check this after you have selected the source object. When the Current active settings: prompt line appears, Dim should appear with the other settings. (Notice that the **Dimension** setting is active in the previous command sequence.) If this setting does not appear when you are prompted to select a destination object, enter S for the **Settings** option. This displays the **Property Settings** dialog box. Activate the **Dimension** check box in the **Special Properties** area and pick **OK**. Then, select the destination dimensions.

---

**PROFESSIONAL TIP**

The style of the source dimension is applied to the destination dimensions. If the dimension style of the source dimension has been overridden, the "base" style is applied along with the dimension style override. Reapplying the "base" style will remove the overrides.

---

### Exercise 18-6

◯ Open drawing EX18-5.
◯ Use the **MATCHPROP** command to match the properties of the first dimension to the remaining dimensions.
◯ Save the drawing as EX18-6.

---

## Editing Associative Dimensions

As discussed earlier in this chapter, an associative dimension is made up of a group of individual elements and treated as a single object. When an associative dimension is selected for editing, the entire group of elements is highlighted. If you use the **ERASE** command, for example, you can pick the dimension as a single object and erase all the elements at once.

One benefit of associative dimensioning is that it permits existing dimensions to be updated as an object is edited. This means that when a dimensioned object is edited the dimension value automatically changes to match the edit. The automatic update is only applied if you accepted the default text value during the original dimension placement, or if you kept the value represented by chevrons (< >) in the multiline text editor. This provides you with an important advantage when editing an associative-dimensioned drawing. Any changes to objects are automatically transferred to the dimensions.

Associative dimensioning is controlled by the **DIMASSOC** dimension variable. **DIMASSOC** is set by entering DIMASSOC at the Command: prompt. You can also open the **Options** dialog box and select the **User Preferences** tab. Then, check or uncheck the **Make new dimensions associative** option in the **Associative Dimensioning** area.

There are three settings for the **DIMASSOC** dimension variable: 0, 1, and 2. A setting of 0 turns off associative dimensioning. In this case, elements of the dimension are created separately, as if the dimension is exploded. The dimension is not updated when the object is edited. With a setting of 1, the components that make up a dimension are grouped together, but the dimension is not associated with an object. If you edit the object, you also have to edit the dimension.

---

**Figure 18-10.**
The original drawing was created with associative dimensions. The drawing was revised using grips to change the rectangle dimensions, the **Properties** window to modify the circle diameter, and the **MOVE** command to relocate the circle. The dimensions automatically updated to the new object geometry.

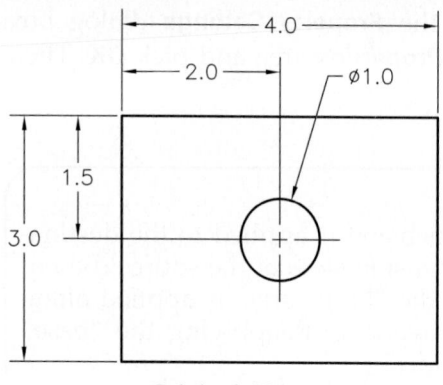

Original Object

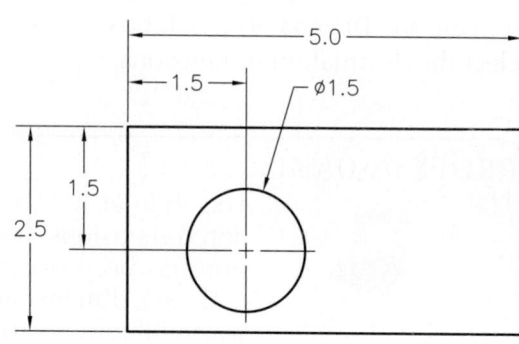

Revised Drawing

If **DIMASSOC** is set to 2, the components that make up a dimension are grouped and the dimension is associated with the object. If the object is stretched, trimmed, or extended, the dimension updates automatically. See **Figure 18-10.** An associative dimension also updates when using grips or the **MOVE, MIRROR, ROTATE,** or **SCALE** commands.

In the **Options** dialog box, checking the **Make new dimensions associative** check box sets **DIMASSOC** to 2. If you uncheck the check box, the **DIMASSOC** value is to its previous value other than 2 (either 1 or 0).

NOTE

Associative dimensions in paper space attached to model space objects also automatically update when the object is edited.

DIMREASSOCIATE
DRE

Dimension
➡ Reassociate
  Dimensions

Nonassociative dimensions can be converted to associative dimensions using the **DIMREASSOCIATE** command. To access this command, select **Reassociate Dimensions** from the **Dimension** pull-down menu or type DRE or DIMREASSOCIATE at the Command: prompt. You are prompted to select the dimensions to be associated. After selecting the dimensions, an X marker appears at the first extension line endpoint. Select the point on an object with which to associate this extension line. Then, select the associated point for the second extension line.

Use the **Next** option to advance to the next definition point. You can also use the **Select object** option to select an object with which to associate the dimension. The extension line endpoints are then automatically associated with the object endpoints.

DISASSOCIATE
DDA

To disassociate a dimension from an object, type DDA or DISASSOCIATE at the Command: prompt and then select the dimension. The dimension objects will still be grouped together, but the dimension will not be associated with an object.

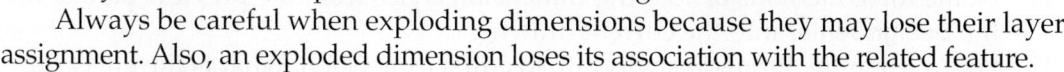

## Exercise 18-7

○ Draw and dimension an object similar to the original drawing in **Figure 18-10**. Be sure to use associative dimensions.

○ Modify the objects using a variety of editing methods and observe the dimensions automatically update.

○ Save the drawing as EX 18-7.

## Exploding an Associative Dimension

EXPLODE
X

Modify
➡ Explode

Modify
toolbar

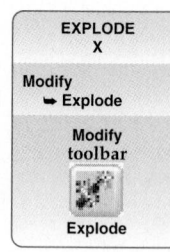

Explode

As previously discussed, the component parts of an associative dimension cannot be edited separately. An associative dimension is treated as one object even though it consists of extension lines, a dimension line, arrowheads, and text. At times, you may find it necessary to edit the individual parts. For example, you may want to erase the text without erasing the dimension line, arrowheads, or extension lines. To do this, you must first explode the dimension using the **EXPLODE** command.

Always be careful when exploding dimensions because they may lose their layer assignment. Also, an exploded dimension loses its association with the related feature.

**PROFESSIONAL TIP**    One way to edit individual dimension properties without removing the associative dimensioning feature is to use the **Properties** window to create a dimension style override.

## Dimension Definition Points

When you draw an associative dimension, the points used to specify the dimension location and the center point of the dimension text are called the *definition points,* or *defpoints.* When a dimension location is redefined, the revised position is based on the definition points. The definition points are located on the Defpoints layer. This layer is automatically created by AutoCAD. The definition points are displayed with the dimension.

Normally, the Defpoints layer does not plot. The definition points are plotted only if the Defpoints layer is renamed and the layer is set to plot. The definition points are displayed when the dimensioning layer is on, even if the Defpoints layer is turned off.

If you select an object for editing and wish to include the dimensions in the edit, then you must include the definition points of the dimension in the selection set. If you need to snap to a definition point only, use the **Node** object snap.

# Chapter Test

*Answer the following questions on a separate sheet of paper.*

1. Name at least three selection options that can be used to easily erase a group of dimensions surrounding an object without erasing any part of the object.
2. Explain how you would add a diameter symbol to a dimension text value using the **DDEDIT** command.
3. Which command and option can you use to add a new baseline dimension to an existing set of baseline dimensions?
4. Define *associative dimension.*
5. Name the command that allows you to control the placement and orientation of an existing associative dimension text value.
6. What happens when you use the **New** option of the **DIMEDIT** command?
7. Name the **DIMEDIT** option that is used to change extension lines to an angle of your choice.
8. Which three command options related to dimension editing are available in the shortcut menu accessed when a dimension is selected?
9. Name three methods of changing the dimension style of a dimension.
10. How does the **Dimension Update** command affect selected dimensions?
11. Name three methods of copying dimension styles from the preview palette of the **DesignCenter** into the current drawing.
12. When using the **Properties** window to edit a dimension, what is the effect on the dimension style?
13. How do you access the **Property Settings** dialog box?
14. Why is it important to have associative dimensions for editing objects?
15. Describe the differences between the dimensions created using the three **DIMASSOC** settings.
16. Which **Options** dialog box setting controls associative dimensioning?
17. Which command is used to convert nonassociative dimensions to associative dimensions?
18. Which command is used to convert associative dimensions to nonassociative dimensions?
19. What are definition points?
20. On which layer are definition points automatically located by AutoCAD?

## Drawing Problems

1. Open P17-1 and edit as follows.
   A. Erase the left side view.
   B. Stretch the vertical dimensions to provide more space between dimension lines. Be sure the space you create is the same between all vertical dimensions.
   C. Stagger the existing vertical dimension numbers if they are not staggered as shown in the original problem.
   D. Erase the 1.750 horizontal dimension and then stretch the 5.255 and 4.250 dimensions to make room for a new datum dimension from the baseline to where the 1.750 dimension was located. This should result in a new baseline dimension that equals 2.750. Be sure all horizontal dimension lines are equally spaced.
   E. Save the drawing as P18-1.

2. Open P17-2 and edit as follows.
   A. Stretch the total length from 3.500 to 4.000, leaving the holes the same distance from the edges.
   B. Fillet the upper-left corner. Modify the 3X R.250 dimension accordingly.
   C. Save the drawing as P18-2.

3. Open P17-4 and edit as follows.
   A. Use the existing drawing as the model and make four copies.
   B. Leave the original drawing as it is and edit the other four pins in the following manner, keeping the ∅.125 hole exactly in the center of each pin.
   C. Make one pin have a total length of 1.500.
   D. Create the next pin with a total length of 2.000.
   E. Edit the third pin to a length of 2.500.
   F. Change the last pin to a length of 3.000.
   G. Organize the pins on your drawing in a vertical row ranging in length from the smallest to the largest. You may need to change the drawing limits.
   H. Save the drawing as P18-3.

4. Open P17-5 and edit as follows.
   A. Modify the spline to have 12 projections, rather than eight.
   B. Change the angular dimension, linear dimension, and 8X dimension to reflect the modification.
   C. Save the drawing as P18-4.

5. Open P17-11 and edit as follows.
   A. Stretch the total length from 6.500 to 7.750.
   B. Add two more holes that continue the equally spaced pattern of .625 apart.
   C. Change the 8X .625(=5.00) dimension to read 10X .625(=6.250).
   D. Save the drawing as P18-5.

6. Open P17-13 and edit as follows.
   A. Make the bathroom 8'-0" wide by stretching the walls and vanity that are currently 6'-0" wide to 8'-0". Do this without increasing the size of the water closet compartment. Provide two equally spaced oval sinks where there is currently one.
   B. Save the drawing as P18-6.

7. Open P17-18 and edit as follows.
   A. Lengthen the part .250 on each side for a new overall dimension of 6.500.
   B. Change the width of the part from 3.000 to 3.500 by widening an equal amount on each side.
   C. Save the drawing as P18-7.

8. Open P17-21 and edit as follows.
   A. Shorten the .75 thread on the left side to .50.
   B. Shorten the .388 hexagon length to .300.
   C. Save the drawing as P18-8.

## CHAPTER 19

# Dimensioning with Tolerances

## Learning Objectives

After completing this chapter, you will be able to do the following:
- Define and use dimensioning and tolerancing terminology.
- Identify different types of tolerance dimensions.
- Create dimension styles with specified tolerance settings.
- Prepare drawings with dimensions and tolerances from engineering designs, sketches, and layouts.

This chapter discusses the basics of tolerancing and explains how to prepare dimensions with tolerances for mechanical manufacturing drawings. Chapter 17 introduced you to the creation of dimension styles and explained how to set the specifications for dimension geometry, fit format, primary units, alternate units, and text. Dimensioning for mechanical drafting usually uses the following AutoCAD settings, depending on company practices.

## Lines and Arrows

- The dimension line spacing for baseline dimensioning is usually more than the .38 default.
- The extension line extension is .125 and the extension line offset is .0625.
- Arrowheads are closed filled, closed blank, closed, or open.
- A small dot is used on a leader pointing to a surface.
- The centerline option is used for center marks for circles and located arcs. Fillets and rounds generally have no center marks.

## Fit Format

- The manually defined format is convenient for flexible text placement.
- The best fit option for text and arrows is common, but other format options work better for some applications.
- Horizontal and vertical justification is usually in centered format.
- Text placement is normally inside and outside horizontal for unidirectional dimensioning.

## Primary Units, Text, and Tolerances

- Objects are dimensioned in inches or millimeters.
- The primary units are typically decimal with the number of decimal places controlled by the feature tolerance.
- Using alternate units for dual dimensioning is not a recommended ASME practice.
- The text is usually placed using the Romans font, a height of .125, and a gap of .0625.
- The tolerance method depends on the application.

## Tolerancing Fundamentals

A *tolerance* is the total amount that a specific dimension is permitted to vary. A tolerance is not given to values identified as reference, maximum, minimum, or stock sizes. The tolerance may be applied directly to the dimension, indicated by a general note, or identified in the drawing title block. See **Figure 19-1.**

The *limits* of a dimension are the largest and smallest numerical values that the feature can be. In **Figure 19-2A**, the dimension is stated as 12.50±0.25. This is referred to as *plus-minus dimensioning.* The tolerance of this dimension is the difference between the maximum and minimum limits. The upper limit is 12.75 (12.50 + 0.25), and the lower limit is 12.25 (12.50 – 0.25). If you take the upper limit and subtract the lower limit, the tolerance is .50.

The specified dimension is the part of the dimension from where the limits are calculated. The specified dimension of the feature shown in **Figure 19-2** is 12.50. A tolerance on a drawing may be displayed with plus-minus dimensioning, or the limits may be calculated and shown as in **Figure 19-2B**. Many schools and companies prefer the second method, which is called *limits dimensioning.* This is because the limits are given and calculations are not required.

**Figure 19-1.**
Tolerances can be specified on the dimension, in a general note, or in the drawing title block.

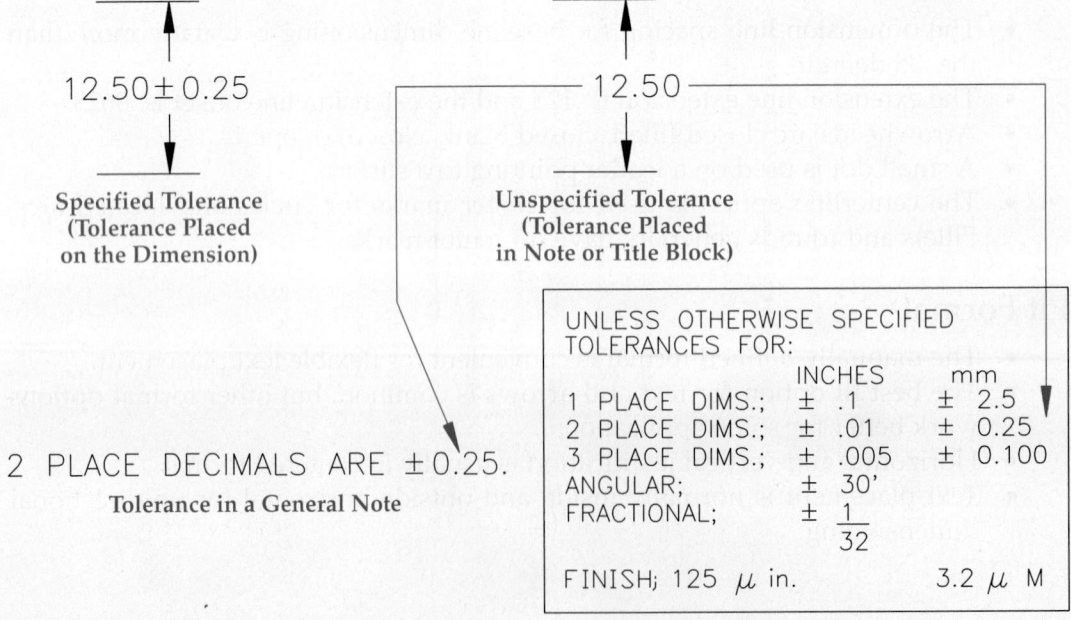

Tolerances in a General Note

Figure 19-2.

Examples of plus-minus dimensioning and limits dimensioning.

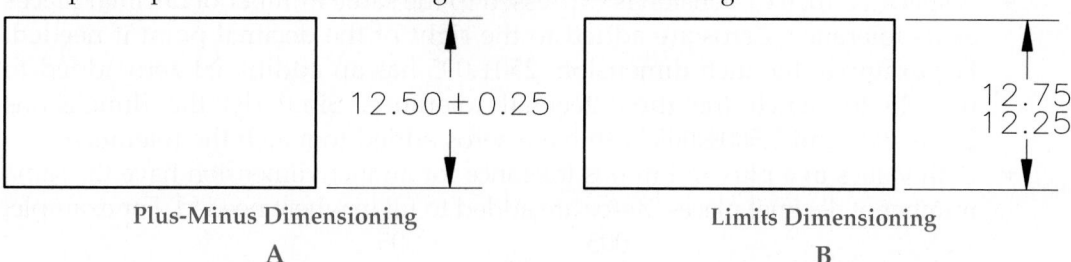

Plus-Minus Dimensioning

A

Limits Dimensioning

B

A *bilateral tolerance* permits variance in both the positive and negative directions from the specified dimension. An *equal bilateral tolerance* has the same variance in both directions. In an *unequal bilateral tolerance,* the variance from the specified dimension is not the same in both directions. See **Figure 19-3.**

A *unilateral tolerance* is permitted to increase or decrease in only one direction from the specified dimension. See **Figure 19-4.**

Figure 19-3.
Examples of bilateral tolerances.

$$24^{+0.08}_{-0.20}$$

Metric

$$.750^{+.002}_{-.003}$$

Inch

**Unequal Bilateral Tolerance**

$$24\pm0.1$$

Metric

$$.750\pm.005$$

Inch

**Equal Bilateral Tolerance**

Figure 19-4.
The variance of a unilateral tolerance is in only one direction from the specified dimension.

$$24^{0}_{-0.2}$$

$$.625^{+.000}_{-.004}$$

$$24^{+0.2}_{0}$$

$$.625^{+.004}_{-.000}$$

Metric

Inch

## Assigning Decimal Places to Dimensions and Tolerances

The standard ASME Y14.5M, *Dimensioning and Tolerancing,* has separate recommendations for the way the number of decimal places is displayed for inch and metric dimensions. Examples of decimal dimension values in inches and metric units are shown in **Figure 19-3** and **Figure 19-4.** The following are some general rules.

## Inch Dimensioning

- A specified inch dimension is expressed to the same number of decimal places as its tolerance. Zeros are added to the right of the decimal point if needed. For example, the inch dimension .250±.005 has an additional zero added to the .25 to match the three-decimal tolerance. Similarly, the dimensions 2.000±.005 and 2.500±.005 both have zeros added to match the tolerance.
- Both values in a plus and minus tolerance for an inch dimension have the same number of decimal places. Zeros are added to fill in where needed. For example:

$$\begin{matrix} +.005 \\ -.010 \end{matrix} \quad not \quad \begin{matrix} +.005 \\ -.01 \end{matrix}$$

## Metric Dimensioning

- The decimal point and zeros are omitted from the dimension when the metric dimension is a whole number. For example, the metric dimension 12 has no decimal point followed by a zero. This rule is true unless tolerance values are displayed.
- When a metric dimension includes a decimal portion, the last digit to the right of the decimal point is not followed by a zero. For example, the metric dimension 12.5 has no zero to the right of the 5. This rule is true unless tolerance values are displayed.
- Both values in a plus and minus tolerance for a metric dimension have the same number of decimal places. Zeros are added to fill in where needed.
- Zeros are not added after the specified dimension to match the tolerance. For example, both 24±0.25 and 24.5±0.25 are correct. However, some companies prefer to add zeros after the specified dimension to match the tolerance, in which case 24.00±0.25 and 24.50±0.25 are both correct.

## Setting Primary Units

DDIM
D

Format
➥ Dimensioin
Style

Dimension
toolbar

Dimension Style

As discussed in Chapter 17, a dimension style can be created with specific formatting, justification, and text settings. The **Dimension Style Manager** dialog box is used to create dimension styles. See **Figure 19-5.** This dialog box is accessed by picking the **Dimension Style** button on the **Dimension** toolbar, picking **Dimension Style...** from the **Format** pull-down menu, or entering D or DDIM at the Command: prompt.

Figure 19-5.
The **Dimension Style Manager** dialog box.

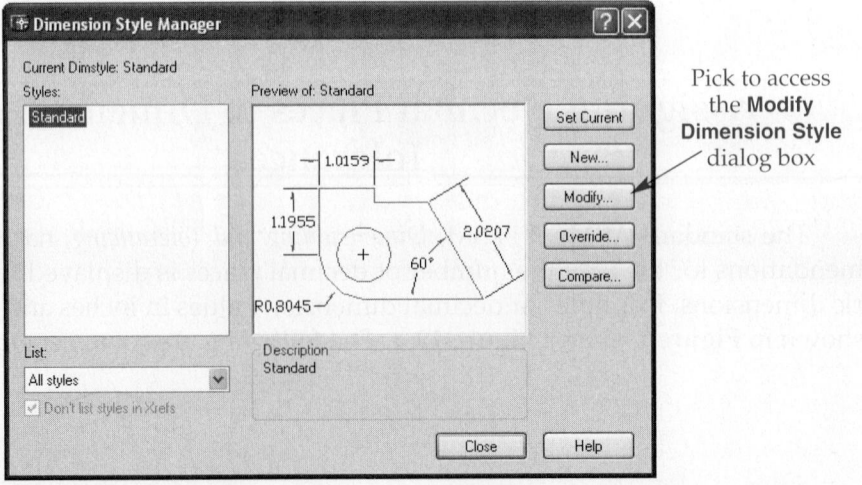

Pick to access the **Modify Dimension Style** dialog box

**Figure 19-6.**
Settings for the unit format and precision of linear dimensions are located in the **Primary Units** tab.

Set the precision for specified dimensions

Settings should match the **Zero Suppression** tolerance format settings in the **Tolerances** tab

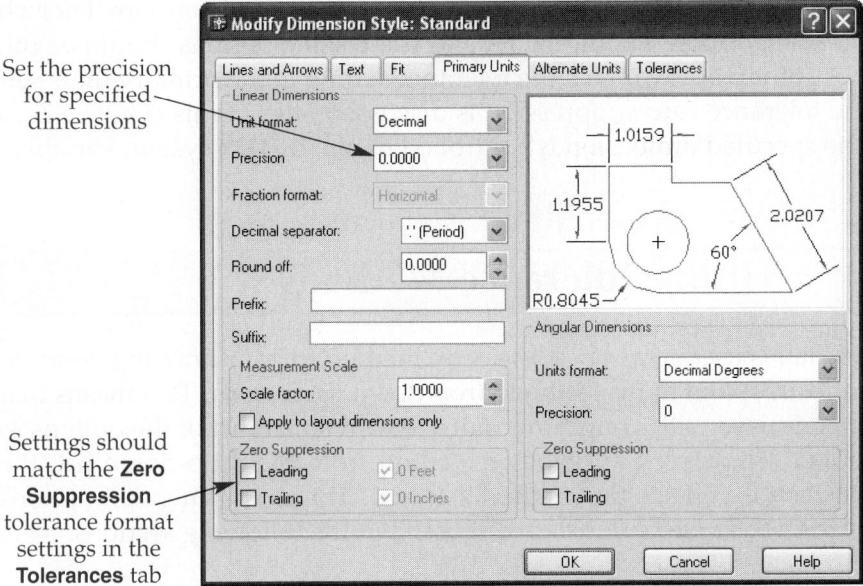

In the **Dimension Style Manager** dialog box, highlight the style you want to modify and pick the **Modify...** button to access the **Modify Dimension Style** dialog box. The **Primary Units** tab is used to set the type of units and precision of the dimension. See **Figure 19-6.** The **Tolerances** tab allows you to set the tolerance format values. See **Figure 19-7.**

In the **Linear Dimensions** area of the **Primary Units** tab, the **Precision** drop-down list allows you to specify the number of zeros displayed after the decimal point of the specified dimension. The ASME standard recommends that the precision for the dimension and the tolerance be the same for inch dimensions, but it may be different for metric values, as previously discussed. After setting the primary unit precision, AutoCAD will automatically make the default for the tolerance precision in the **Tolerances** tab the same.

**Figure 19-7.**
The **Tolerances** tab contains formatting settings for tolerance dimensions.

Select a tolerance method

Set the precision for tolerance dimensions

Settings should match the **Zero Suppression** linear dimension settings in the **Primary Units** tab

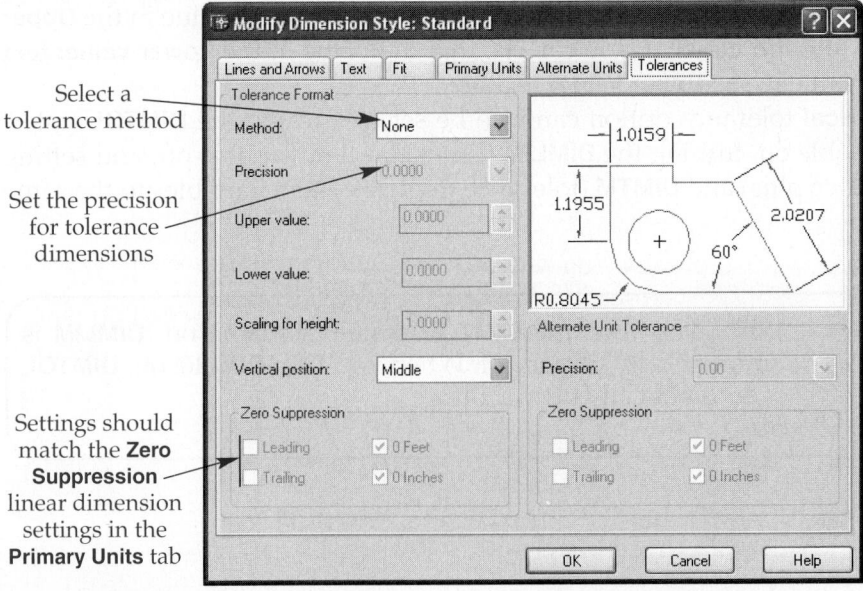

The **Zero Suppression** settings were explained in Chapter 17. The suppression settings for linear dimensions in the **Primary Units** tab should be the same as the **Zero Suppression** tolerance format settings in the **Tolerances** tab. For example, the **Leading** options should be off and the **Trailing** options should be on for metric dimensions. For inch dimensions, the **Leading** options should be on and the **Trailing** options should be off. AutoCAD does not automatically match the tolerance setting to the primary units setting. Changing the tolerance zero suppression is discussed later in this chapter. Zero suppression for the specified dimension is controlled by the **DIMZIN** system variable.

## Setting Tolerance Methods

The **Tolerances** tab is used to apply a tolerance method to your drawing. Refer to **Figure 19-7.** The default option in the **Method:** drop-down list is **None**. This means that no tolerance method is used with your dimensions. As a result, most of the options in this area are disabled. If you pick a tolerance method from the drop-down list, the resulting image in the tab reflects the method selected. The drop-down list options are shown in **Figure 19-8.** These options are discussed in the following sections.

**Figure 19-8.**
A tolerance dimensioning method can be selected from the options in the **Method:** drop-down list, located in the **Tolerance Format** area of the **Tolerances** tab.

Select a tolerance method

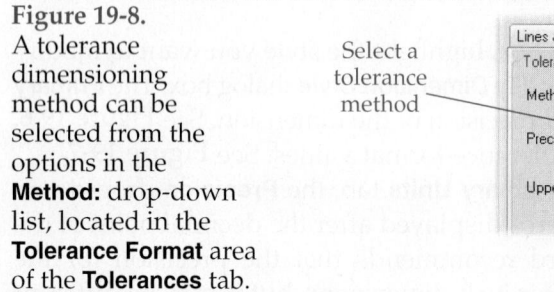

### Symmetrical Tolerance Method

The **Symmetrical** tolerance dimensioning option is used to draw dimension text that displays an equal bilateral tolerance in the plus/minus format. When the **Symmetrical** option is selected, the **Upper value:** text box, **Scaling for height:** text box, and **Vertical position:** drop-down list are activated. The preview image displays an equal bilateral tolerance. See **Figure 19-9.** You can enter a tolerance value in the **Upper value:** text box. Although inactive, you can see that the value in the **Lower value:** text box matches the value in the **Upper value:** text box.

The **Symmetrical** tolerance option can also be set by turning the **DIMTOL** (tolerance) system variable on, turning the **DIMLIM** (limits) system variable off, and setting the **DIMTP** (tolerance plus) and **DIMTM** (tolerance minus) system variables to the same numerical value.

| NOTE  | When you turn the **DIMTOL** system variable on, **DIMLIM** is automatically turned off. When you turn **DIMLIM** on, **DIMTOL** is automatically turned off. |
| --- | --- |

Figure 19-9.
Setting the **Symmetrical** tolerance method option current with an equal bilateral tolerance value of 0.005.

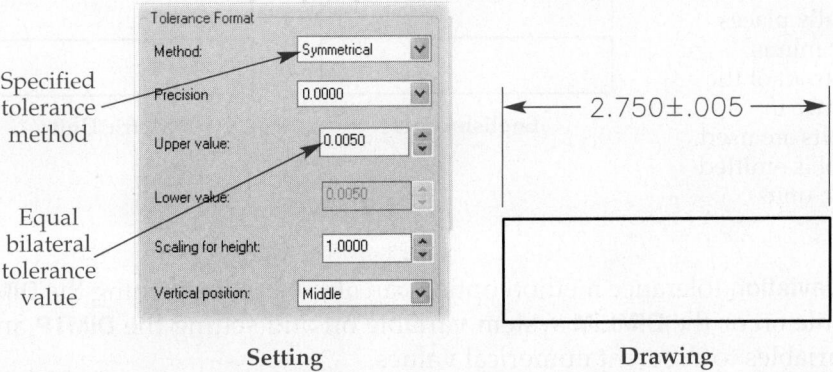

Specified tolerance method

Equal bilateral tolerance value

Setting                    Drawing

### Exercise 19-1

○ Start a new drawing or use one of your templates.
○ Set the required units, precision, zero suppression, and tolerance method to draw an object with equal bilateral tolerance dimensioning. Draw and dimension an object similar to the one shown in **Figure 19-9**.
○ Save the drawing as EX19-1.

## Deviation Tolerance Method

AutoCAD refers to an unequal bilateral tolerance as a *deviation.* This means that the tolerance deviates (departs) from the specified dimension with two different values. The deviation tolerance method can be set by selecting **Deviation** in **Method:** drop-down list of the **Tolerances** tab. After selecting this option, the **Upper value:** and **Lower value:** text boxes are activated so that you can enter the desired upper and lower tolerance values. See **Figure 19-10**. The preview image in the tab changes to match a representation of an unequal bilateral tolerance.

The **Deviation** option can also be used to draw a unilateral tolerance by entering zero for either the **Upper value:** or **Lower value:** setting. If you are using inch units, AutoCAD includes the plus or minus sign before the zero tolerance. When metric units are used, the sign is omitted for the zero tolerance. See **Figure 19-11**.

Figure 19-10.
Setting the **Deviation** tolerance method option current with unequal bilateral tolerance values.

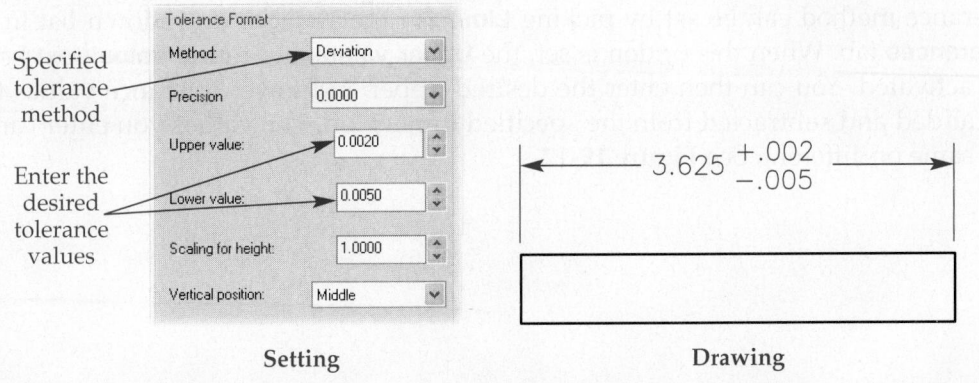

Specified tolerance method

Enter the desired tolerance values

Setting                    Drawing

**Figure 19-11.**
When a unilateral tolerance is specified, AutoCAD automatically places the plus or minus symbol in front of the zero tolerance if English units are used. The symbol is omitted with metric units.

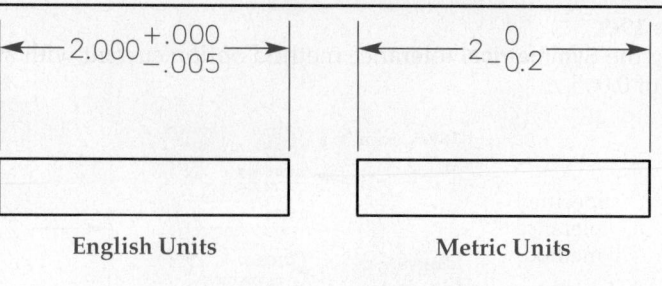

English Units          Metric Units

The **Deviation** tolerance method option can also be set by turning the **DIMTOL** system variable on or the **DIMLIM** system variable off and setting the **DIMTP** and **DIMTM** system variables to different numerical values.

NOTE

The **MEASUREMENT** system variable is used to change between English (inch) units and metric units. If the variable is set to 0, English units are active. A setting of 1 corresponds to metric units.

## Exercise 19-2

○ Start a new drawing or use one of your templates.
○ Set the required units, precision, zero suppression, and tolerance method to draw and dimension the following.
   ○ An object with an unequal bilateral tolerance dimension, similar to the one shown in **Figure 19-10.**
   ○ An object with a unilateral tolerance dimension, similar to the example shown with English units in **Figure 19-11.**
   ○ Change the **MEASUREMENT** system variable to 1. Draw another object and apply the same unilateral dimension used with the previous object. Note the differences.
○ Save the drawing as EX19-2.

## Limits Tolerance Method

In limits dimensioning, the tolerance limits are given and no calculations from the specified dimension are required (unlike plus-minus dimensioning). The limits tolerance method can be set by picking **Limits** in the **Method:** drop-down list in the **Tolerances** tab. When this option is set, the **Upper value:** and **Lower value:** text boxes are activated. You can then enter the desired upper and lower tolerance values that are added and subtracted from the specified dimension. The values you enter can be the same or different. See **Figure 19-12.**

Figure 19-12.
Selecting the **Limits** tolerance method and setting limit values.

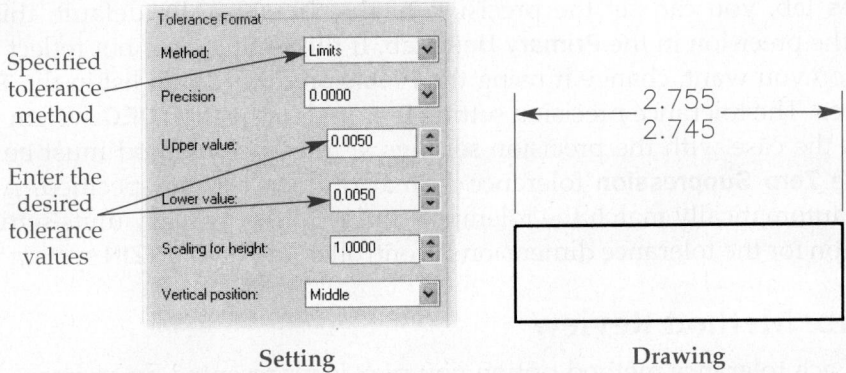

Specified tolerance method

Enter the desired tolerance values

Setting

Drawing

## Basic Tolerance Method

The basic tolerance method is used to draw basic dimensions. A *basic dimension* is considered to be a theoretically perfect dimension and is used in geometric dimensioning and tolerancing, which is covered in Chapter 20. The basic tolerance method can be set by picking **Basic** in the **Method:** drop-down list in the **Tolerances** tab. With this setting, the **Upper value:** and **Lower value:** options in the **Tolerance Format** area are disabled because a basic dimension has no tolerance. A basic dimension is distinguished from other dimensions by a rectangle placed around the dimension number, as shown in **Figure 19-13**.

Figure 19-13.
The **Basic** tolerance method is used for basic dimensioning. The dimension text for a basic dimension is placed inside a rectangle.

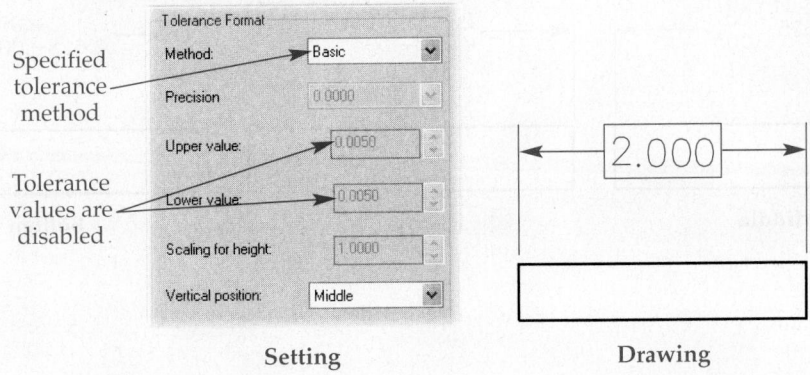

Specified tolerance method

Tolerance values are disabled

Setting

Drawing

## Tolerance Precision and Zero Suppression

After a tolerance method is specified in the **Method:** drop-down list of the **Tolerances** tab, you can set the precision of the tolerance. By default, this setting matches the precision in the **Primary Units** tab. If the setting does not reflect the level of precision you want, change it using the **Precision** drop-down list in the **Tolerance Format** area. The tolerance precision setting is stored in the **DIMTDEC** system variable.

As is the case with the precision settings, a tolerance method must be selected before the **Zero Suppression** tolerance format options can be specified. AutoCAD does not automatically match the tolerance setting to the primary units setting. Zero suppression for the tolerance dimension is controlled by the **DIMTZIN** system variable.

## Tolerance Method Review

✓ Each tolerance method option you pick is represented by an image preview in the **Modify Dimension Style** dialog box.

✓ When drawing inch tolerance dimensions, you should activate the **Leading Zero Suppression** tolerance format option in the **Tolerances** tab. The same option should be activated for linear dimensions in the **Primary Units** tab. You can then properly draw inch tolerance dimensions without placing the zero before the decimal point, as recommended by ASME standards. These settings would allow you to draw a tolerance dimension such as .625±.005.

✓ When drawing metric tolerance dimensions, deactivate the **Leading Zero Suppression** tolerance format option in the **Tolerances** tab. Deactivate the same option for linear dimensions in the **Primary Units** tab. This allows you to place a metric tolerance dimension with the zero before the decimal point, as recommended by ASME standards (for example, a dimension such as 12±0.2).

## Tolerance Justification

You can control the alignment, or justification, of deviation tolerance dimensions using the options in the **Vertical position:** drop-down list in the **Tolerance Format** area of the **Tolerances** tab. The **Middle** option centers the tolerance with the specified dimension and is the default. This is also the recommended ASME practice. The other justification options are **Top** and **Bottom**. Deviation tolerance dimensions displaying each of the justification options are shown in **Figure 19-14.** The justification for deviation tolerance dimensions is controlled by the **DIMTOLJ** system variable.

**Figure 19-14.**
Examples of the tolerance justification options for deviation tolerance dimensions.

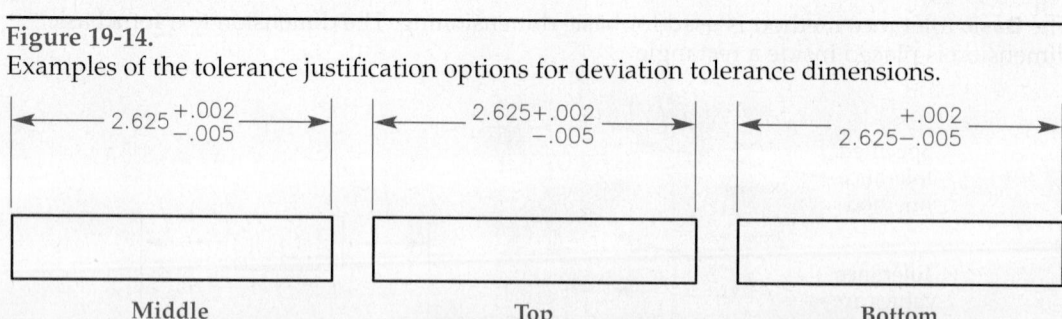

Middle          Top          Bottom

## Tolerance Height

You can set the text height of the tolerance dimension in relation to the text height of the specified dimension. This is done using the **Scaling for height:** text box in the **Tolerance Format** area of the **Tolerances** tab. The default of 1.0000 makes the tolerance dimension text the same height as the specified dimension text. This is the recommended ASME standard. If you want the tolerance dimension height to be three-quarters as high as the specified dimension height, enter .75 in the **Scaling for height:** text box. Some companies prefer this practice to keep the tolerance part of the dimension from taking up additional space. Examples of tolerance dimensions with different text heights are shown in **Figure 19-15.** The tolerance text height is controlled by the **DIMTFAC** system variable.

**Figure 19-15.**
Using different scale settings for the text height of tolerance dimensions.

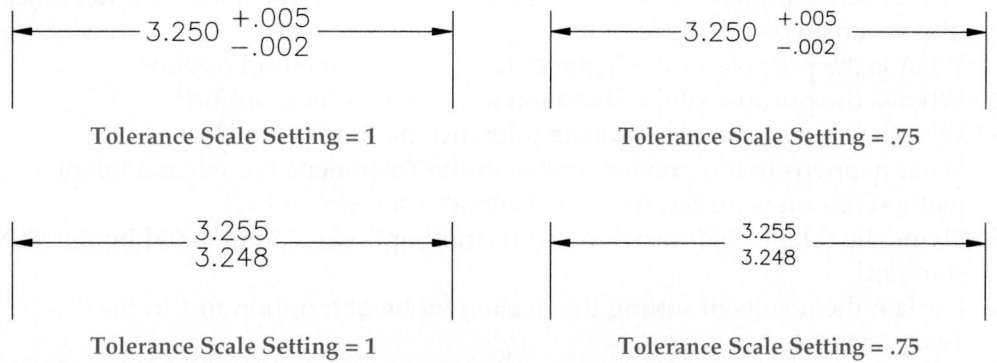

Exercise 19-4

○ Start a new drawing or use one of your templates.
○ Set the required units, precision, zero suppression, tolerance method, justification, and height to draw:
  ○ Three dimensioned objects similar to the examples shown in **Figure 19-14.**
  ○ Four dimensions similar to the examples shown in **Figure 19-15.**
○ Save the drawing as **EX19-4.**

## Chapter Test

*Answer the following questions on a separate sheet of paper.*

1. Define the term *tolerance.*
2. Give an example of an equal bilateral tolerance in inches and in metric units.
3. Give an example of an unequal bilateral tolerance in inches and in metric units.
4. What are the limits of the tolerance dimension 3.625±.005?
5. Give an example of a unilateral tolerance in inches and in metric units.
6. Which dialog box is used to create dimension styles? How is it accessed?
7. How do you open the **Tolerances** tab?
8. How do you set the number of zeros displayed after the decimal point for a tolerance dimension?
9. Which zero suppression settings should be specified for linear and tolerance dimensions when using metric units?
10. Which zero suppression settings should be specified for linear and tolerance dimensions when using inch units?
11. What is the purpose of the **Symmetrical** tolerance method option?
12. What is the purpose of the **Deviation** tolerance method option?
13. What is the purpose of the **Limits** tolerance method option?
14. What happens to the preview image in the **Tolerances** tab when a tolerance method option is picked from the **Method:** drop-down list?
15. Name the tolerance dimension justification option recommended by the ASME standard.
16. Explain the results of setting the **Scaling for height:** option to 1 in the **Tolerances** tab.
17. What setting would you use for the **Scaling for height:** option if you wanted the tolerance dimension height to be three-quarters of the specified dimension height?

# Drawing Problems

*Set the limits, units, dimension style options, and other parameters as needed for the following problems. Use the guidelines given below.*

A.  Draw and dimension the necessary views for the following drawings to exact size. These problems are presented in 3D; draw the proper 2D views for each.

B.  Apply dimensions accurately using ASME standards. Create dimension styles that suit the specific needs of each drawing. For example, save different dimension styles for metric and inch dimensions.

C.  Create separate layers for the views and dimensions.

D.  Plot the drawings with 0.6 mm object lines and 0.3 mm thin lines.

E.  Place the following general notes in the lower-left corner of each drawing.

   3. UNLESS OTHERWISE SPECIFIED, ALL DIMENSIONS ARE IN MILLIMETERS. *(or* INCHES *as applicable)*
   2. REMOVE ALL BURRS AND SHARP EDGES.
   1. INTERPRET PER ASME Y14.5M-1994.
   NOTES:

F.  Save the drawings as P19-1, P19-2, and so on.

1.

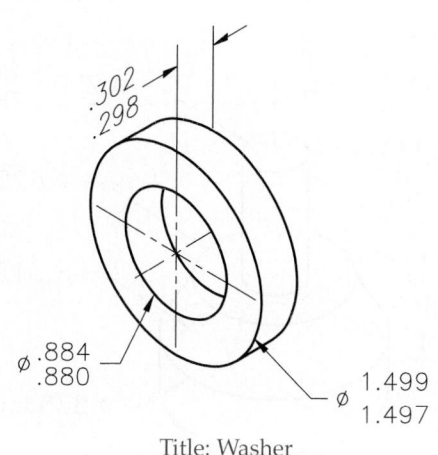

Title: Washer
Material: SAE 1020
Inch

2.

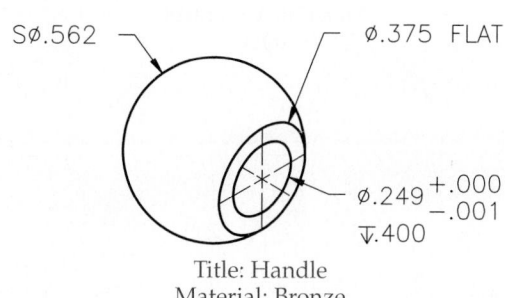

Title: Handle
Material: Bronze
Inch

3.

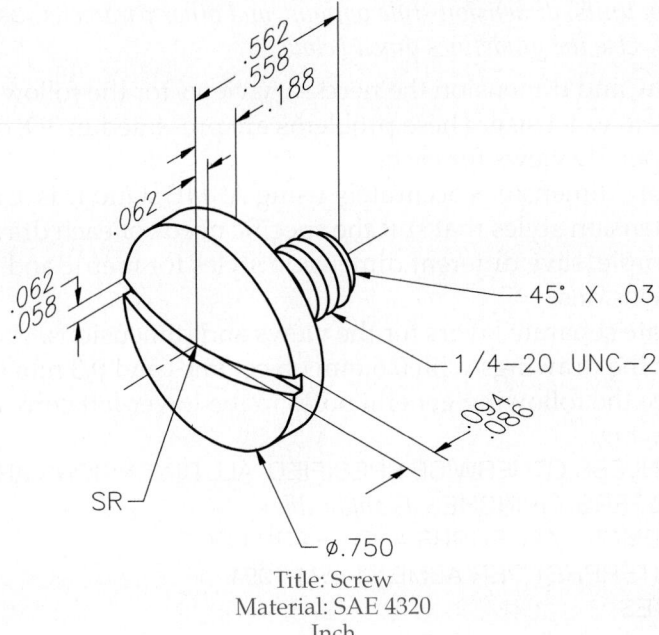

45° X .03

1/4—20 UNC—2

SR

⌀.750

Title: Screw
Material: SAE 4320
Inch

4.

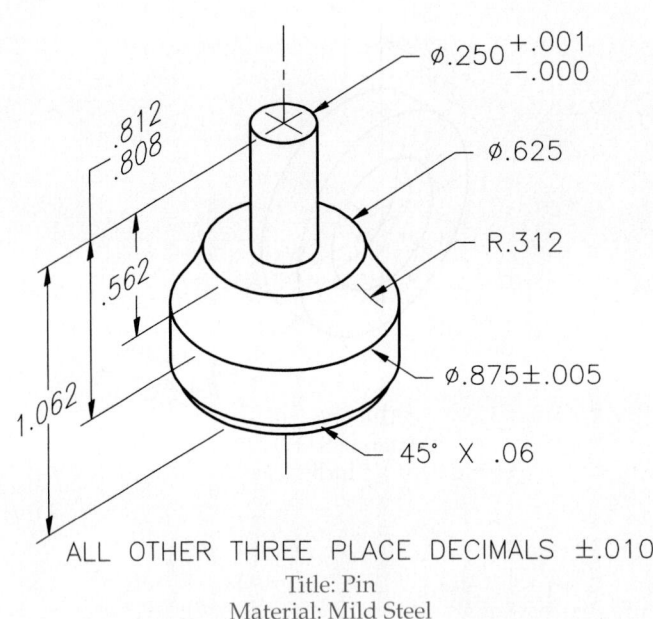

⌀.250 +.001 −.000

⌀.625

R.312

⌀.875±.005

45° X .06

ALL OTHER THREE PLACE DECIMALS ±.010

Title: Pin
Material: Mild Steel
Inch

5. This object is shown as a section for clarity. Do not draw a section.

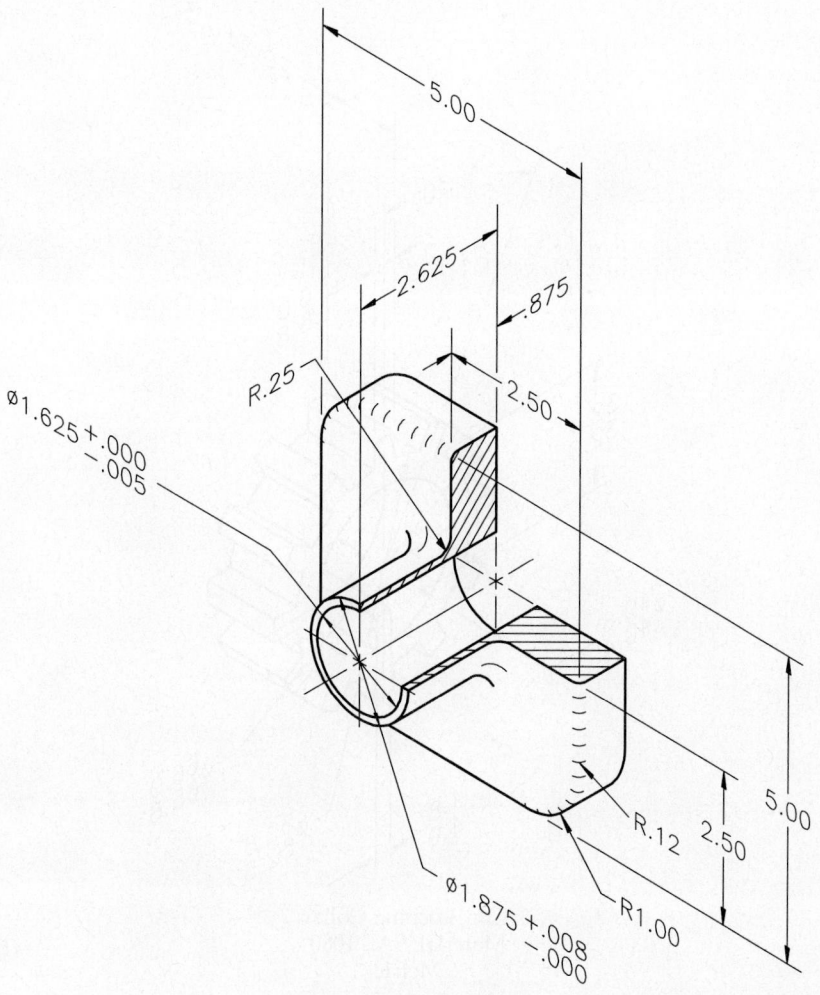

Title: Thrust Washer
Material: SAE 5150
Inch

6.

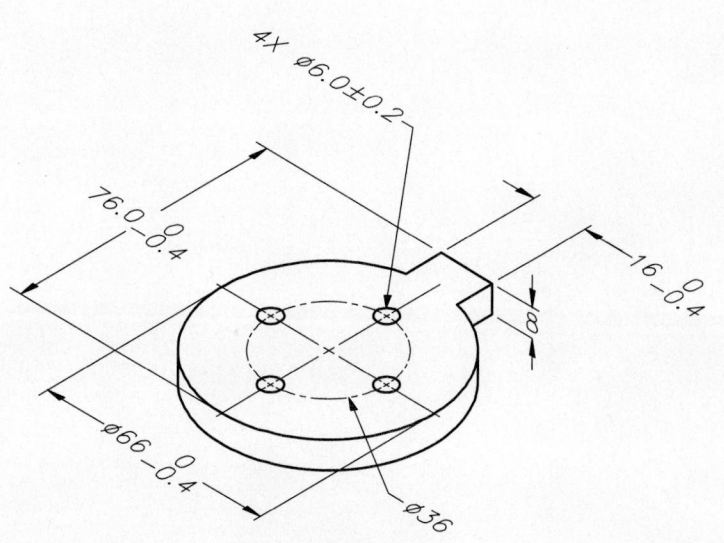

Title: Spacer
Material: Cold Rolled Steel
Metric

7.

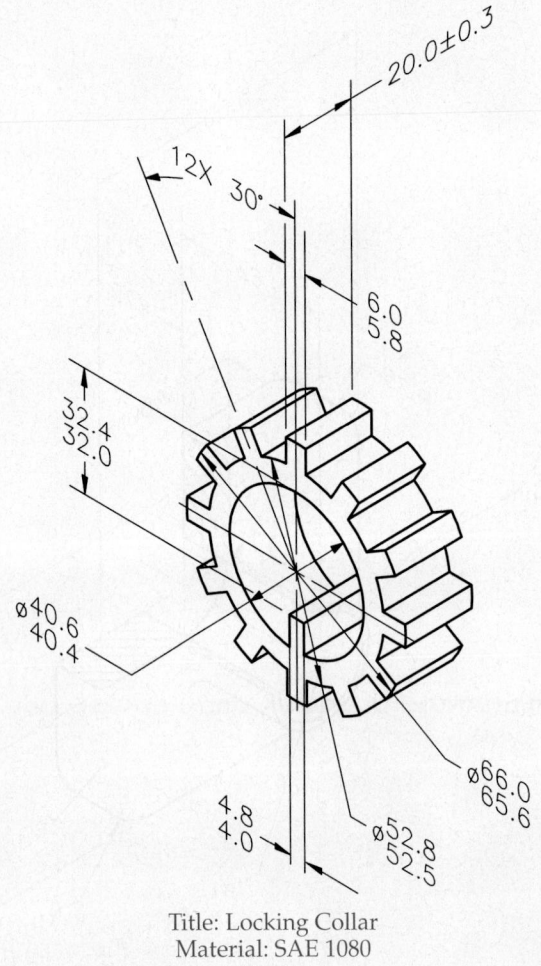

20.0±0.3

12X 30°

6.0
5.8

32.4
32.0

ø40.6
40.4

ø66.0
65.6

4.8
4.0

ø52.8
52.5

Title: Locking Collar
Material: SAE 1080
Metric

## CHAPTER 20

# Geometric Dimensioning and Tolerancing

## Learning Objectives

After completing this chapter, you will be able to do the following:
- Identify symbols used in geometric dimensioning and tolerancing.
- Use the **TOLERANCE**, **QLEADER**, and **LEADER** commands to create geometric tolerancing symbols.
- Draw and edit feature control frames.
- Draw datum feature symbols.
- Place basic dimensions on a drawing.

This chapter is an introduction to geometric dimensioning and tolerancing (GD&T) principles as adopted by the American National Standards Institute (ANSI) and published by the American Society of Mechanical Engineers (ASME) for engineering and related document practices. The standard is ASME Y14.5M-1994, *Dimensioning and Tolerancing*. **Geometric tolerancing** is a general term that refers to tolerances used to control the form, profile, orientation, runout, and location of features on an object.

The drafting applications covered in this chapter use the AutoCAD geometric tolerancing capabilities and additional recommendations to comply with the ASME Y14.5M-1994 standard. This chapter is only an introduction to geometric dimensioning and tolerancing. For complete coverage of GD&T, refer to *Geometric Dimensioning and Tolerancing* published by The Goodheart-Willcox Company, Inc. Before beginning this chapter, it is recommended that you have a solid understanding of dimensioning and tolerancing standards and AutoCAD applications. This introductory material is presented in Chapters 17 through 19 of this text.

The discussion in this chapter divides the dimensioning and geometric tolerancing symbols into five basic types:
- Dimensioning symbols.
- Geometric characteristic symbols.
- Material condition symbols.
- Feature control frames.
- Datum feature symbols.

When you draw GD&T symbols, it is recommended that you place them on a dimensioning layer so the symbols and text can be plotted as lines that have the same thickness as extension and dimension lines (.01" or .3 mm). The suggested text font is Romans. These practices correspond with the standard ASME Y14.2M-1992, *Line Conventions and Lettering*.

# Dimensioning Symbols

*Symbols* represent specific information that would be difficult and time-consuming to duplicate in note form. Symbols must be clearly drawn to the required size and shape so they communicate the desired information uniformly. Symbols are recommended by ASME Y14.5M because they are an international language; they are read the same way in any country. In an international economy, it is important to have effective communication on engineering drawings. Symbols make this communication process uniform. ASME Y14.5M also states that the adoption of dimensioning symbols does not prevent the use of equivalent terms or abbreviations in situations where symbols are considered inappropriate.

Symbols aid in clarity, presentation of the drawing, and reduction of drawing time. Creating and using AutoCAD symbols is covered later in this chapter and in Chapter 22. A sample group of recommended dimensioning symbols is shown in **Figure 20-1**.

**Figure 20-1.**
Dimensioning symbols recommended by ASME Y14.5M-1994.

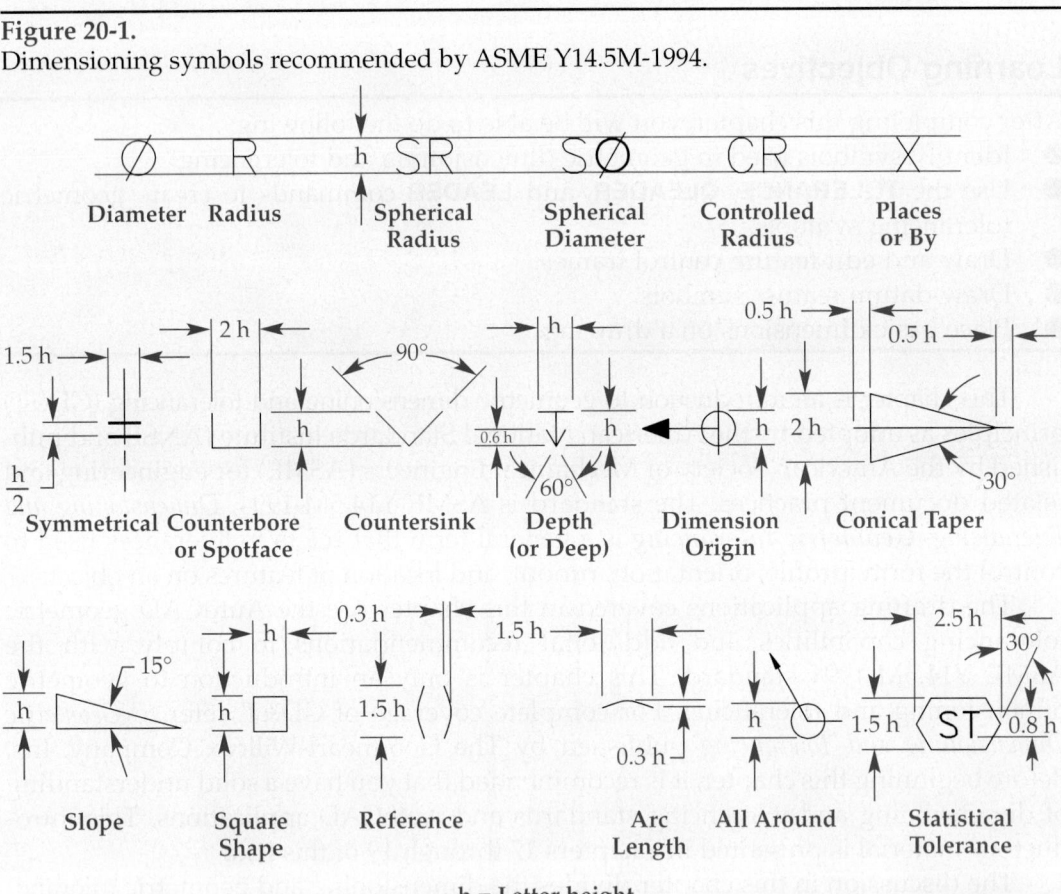

h = Letter height

# Geometric Characteristic Symbols

In GD&T, symbols are used to provide specific controls related to the form of an object, orientation of features, outlines of features, relationship of features to an axis, or location of features. These symbols are known as *geometric characteristic* symbols. Geometric characteristic symbols are separated into five types: form, profile, location, orientation, and runout, as shown in **Figure 20-2**.

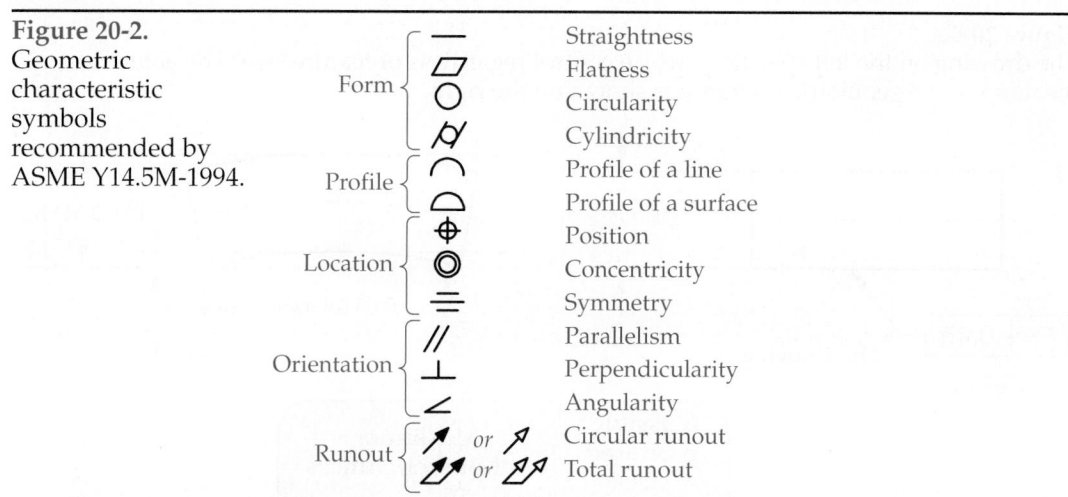

Figure 20-2. Geometric characteristic symbols recommended by ASME Y14.5M-1994.

| | Straightness |
| Form | Flatness |
| | Circularity |
| | Cylindricity |
| Profile | Profile of a line |
| | Profile of a surface |
| Location | Position |
| | Concentricity |
| | Symmetry |
| Orientation | Parallelism |
| | Perpendicularity |
| | Angularity |
| Runout | Circular runout |
| | Total runout |

## Material Condition Symbols

*Material condition symbols* are often referred to as *modifying symbols* because they modify the geometric tolerance in relation to the produced size or location of the feature. Material condition symbols are only used in geometric dimensioning applications. The symbols used in a feature control frame to indicate maximum material condition (MMC) or least material condition (LMC) are shown in **Figure 20-3**. Regardless of feature size (RFS) is also a material condition. However, there is no symbol for RFS because it is assumed for all geometric tolerances and datum references unless MMC or LMC is specified.

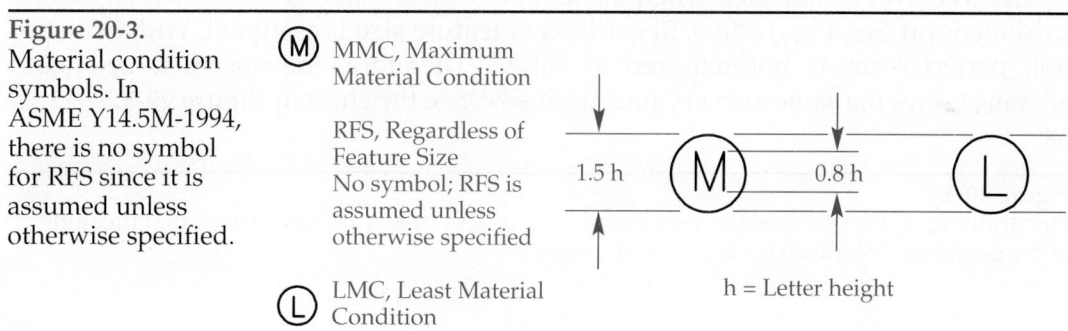

Figure 20-3. Material condition symbols. In ASME Y14.5M-1994, there is no symbol for RFS since it is assumed unless otherwise specified.

Ⓜ MMC, Maximum Material Condition

RFS, Regardless of Feature Size No symbol; RFS is assumed unless otherwise specified

Ⓛ LMC, Least Material Condition

1.5 h  Ⓜ  0.8 h  Ⓛ

h = Letter height

## Surface Control, Regardless of Feature Size

Regardless of feature size is assumed as the material condition when there is no material condition symbol following the geometric tolerance in a feature control frame. *Regardless of feature size (RFS)* means the geometric tolerances remain the same regardless of the actual produced size. The term *produced size,* when used here, means the actual size of the feature when measured after manufacture.

When a feature control frame is connected to a feature surface with a leader or an extension line, it is referred to as *surface control.* See **Figure 20-4**. The geometric characteristic symbol shown is straightness, but the application is the same for any characteristic.

Look at the chart in **Figure 20-4** and notice how the possible sizes range from 6.20 (MMC) to 5.80 (LMC). With surface control, perfect form is required at MMC. *Perfect form* means the object cannot exceed a true geometric form boundary established at

**Figure 20-4.**
The drawing on the left specifies surface control regardless of feature size. The actual meaning of the geometric tolerance is shown on the right.

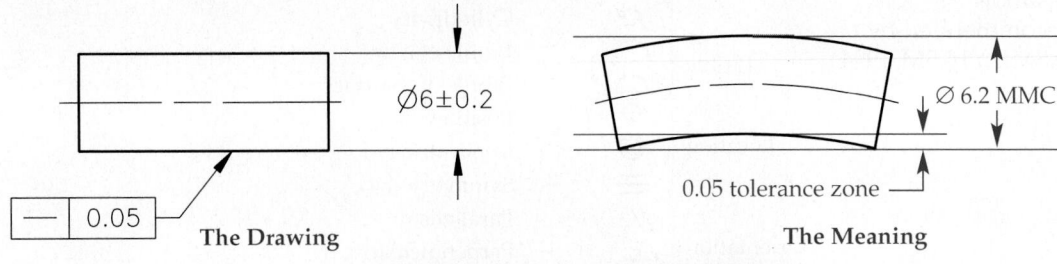

|  | Possible produced sizes | Maximum out-of-straightness |
|---|---|---|
| MMC | 6.20 | * 0 |
|  | 6.10 | 0.05 |
|  | 6.00 | 0.05 |
|  | 5.90 | 0.05 |
| LMC | 5.80 | 0.05 |

* Perfect form required

maximum material condition. The geometric tolerance at MMC is zero, as shown in the chart. As the produced size varies from MMC in the chart, the geometric tolerance increases until it equals the amount specified in the feature control frame.

## Axis Control, Regardless of Feature Size

*Axis control* is indicated when the feature control frame is shown with a diameter dimension. See **Figure 20-5.** Regardless of feature size is assumed. With axis control, perfect form is not required at MMC. Therefore, the specified geometric tolerance stays the same at every produced size. See the chart in **Figure 20-5.**

**Figure 20-5.**
The drawing on the left specifies axis control regardless of feature size. The actual meaning of the geometric tolerance is shown on the right.

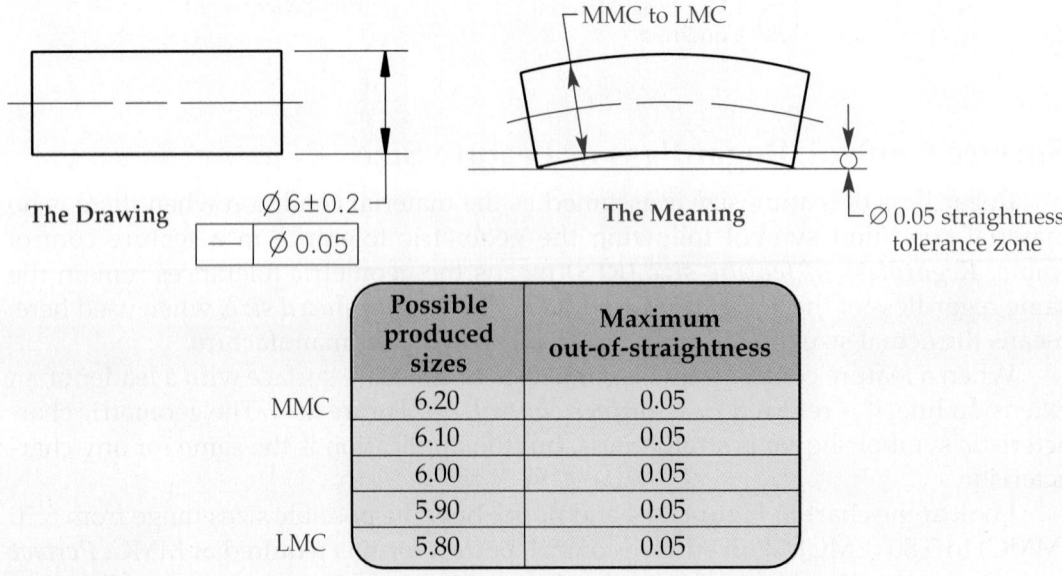

|  | Possible produced sizes | Maximum out-of-straightness |
|---|---|---|
| MMC | 6.20 | 0.05 |
|  | 6.10 | 0.05 |
|  | 6.00 | 0.05 |
|  | 5.90 | 0.05 |
| LMC | 5.80 | 0.05 |

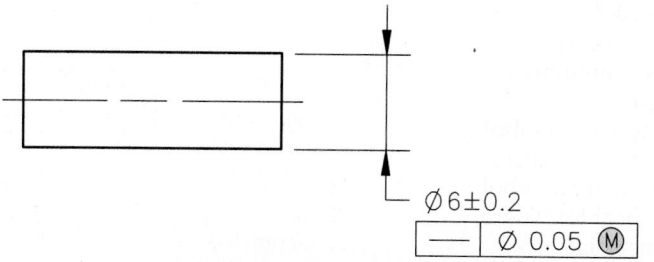

**Figure 20-6.**
The drawing specifies maximum material condition applied to a feature. The symbol for MMC is shown highlighted.

Ø6±0.2

⌀ 0.05 Ⓜ

| | Possible produced sizes | Maximum out-of-straightness |
|---|---|---|
| MMC | 6.20 | 0.05 |
| | 6.10 | 0.15 |
| | 6.00 | 0.25 |
| | 5.90 | 0.35 |
| LMC | 5.80 | 0.45 |

## Maximum Material Condition Control

If the material condition control is *maximum material condition (MMC)*, the symbol for MMC must be placed in the feature control frame. See **Figure 20-6**. When this application is used, the specified geometric tolerance is held at the maximum material condition produced size. See the chart in **Figure 20-6**. Then, as the produced size varies from MMC, the geometric tolerance increases equal to the change. The maximum geometric tolerance is at the LMC produced size.

## Least Material Condition Control

If the material condition control is *least material condition (LMC)*, the symbol for LMC must be placed in the feature control frame. When this application is used, the specified geometric tolerance is held at the least material condition produced size. Then, as the produced size varies from LMC, the geometric tolerance increases equal to the change. The maximum geometric tolerance is at the MMC produced size.

## Feature Control Frame

The geometric characteristic, geometric tolerance, material condition, and datum reference (if any) for an individual feature are specified by means of a feature control frame. The *feature control frame* is divided into compartments containing the geometric characteristic symbol in the first compartment, followed by the geometric tolerance. Where applicable, the geometric tolerance is preceded by the diameter symbol, which describes the shape of the tolerance zone, and is followed by a material condition symbol (if other than RFS). See **Figure 20-7**.

When a geometric tolerance is related to one or more datums, the datum reference letters are placed in compartments following the geometric tolerance. *Datums* are considered theoretically perfect surfaces, planes, points, or axes. When there is a multiple datum reference, both datum reference letters are separated by a dash and placed in a single compartment after the geometric tolerance. A *multiple datum reference* is established by two datum features, such as an axis established by two datum diameters. Several feature control frames with datum references are shown in **Figure 20-8**.

**Figure 20-7.**
Feature control frames containing the geometric characteristic symbol, geometric tolerance, and diameter symbol (as applicable). There is no material condition symbol for RFS since it is assumed. Note that the geometric tolerance is expressed as a total, not a plus-minus value.

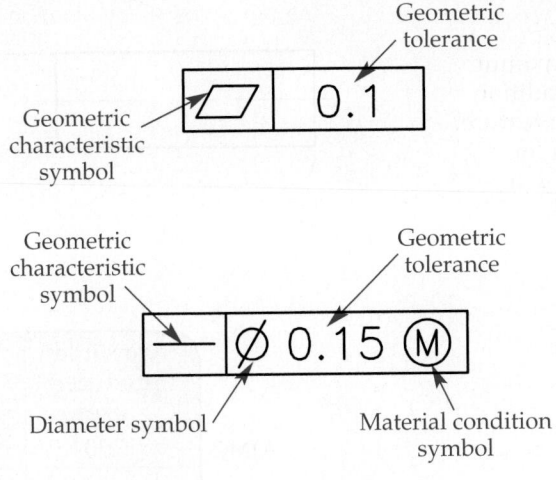

**Figure 20-8.**
Examples of datum references indicated in feature control frames.

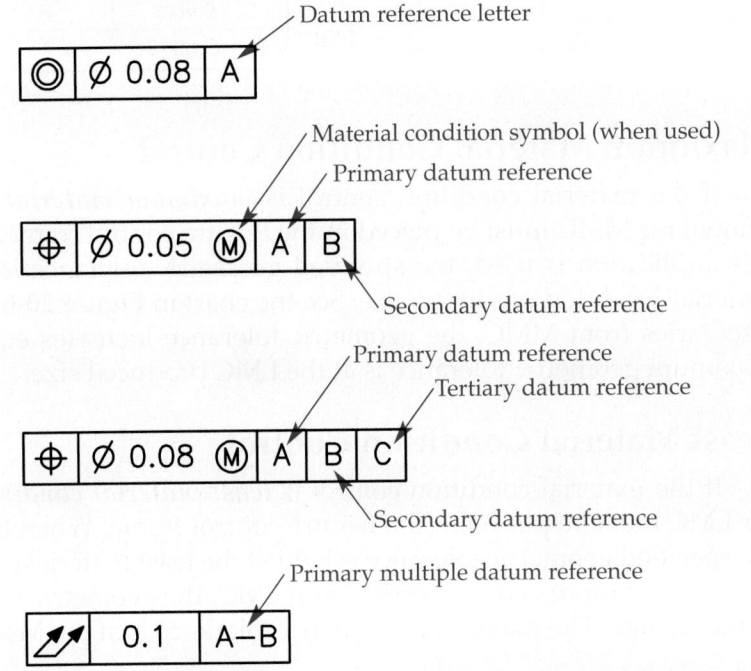

There is a specific order used to display elements in a feature control frame. See **Figure 20-9.** Notice the datum reference letters can be followed by a material condition symbol where applicable.

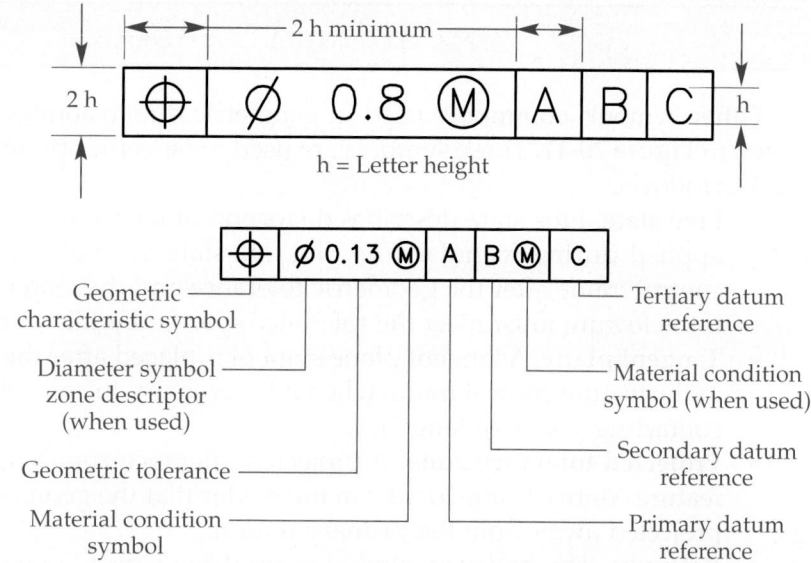

**Figure 20-9.**
The order of elements in a feature control frame.

Geometric characteristic symbol

Diameter symbol zone descriptor (when used)

Geometric tolerance

Material condition symbol

Tertiary datum reference

Material condition symbol (when used)

Secondary datum reference

Primary datum reference

## Basic Dimensions

A *basic dimension* is considered a theoretically perfect dimension. Basic dimensions are used to describe the theoretically exact size, profile, orientation, and location of a feature. These dimensions provide the basis from which permissible variations are established by tolerances on other dimensions, in notes, or in feature control frames. In simple terms, a basic dimension tells you where the geometric tolerance zone or datum target is located.

Basic dimensions are shown on a drawing with a rectangle placed around the dimension text, as shown in **Figure 20-10.** A general note can also be used to identify basic dimensions in some applications. For example, the note UNTOLERANCED DIMENSIONS LOCATING TRUE POSITION ARE BASIC indicates the dimensions that are basic. The basic dimension rectangle is a signal to the reader to look for a geometric tolerance in a feature control frame related to the features being dimensioned.

**Figure 20-10.**
Basic dimensions are identified with a rectangle drawn around the text.

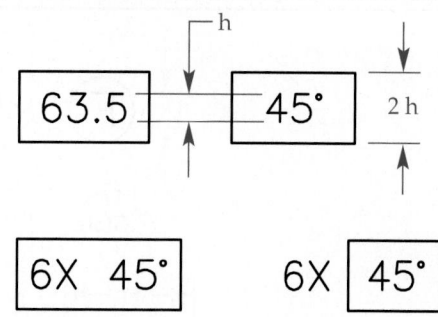

The number of times or places may be applied to a basic dimension by placement inside or outside of the basic dimension symbol.

h = Letter height

# Additional Symbols

Other symbols commonly used in geometric dimensioning and tolerancing are shown in **Figure 20-11.** These symbols are used for specific applications, and are identified as follows.

- **Free state.** Free state describes distortion of a part after the removal of forces applied during manufacture. The free state symbol is placed in the feature control frame after the geometric tolerance and the material condition (if any) if the feature must meet the tolerance specified while in free state.
- **Tangent plane.** A tangent plane symbol is placed after the geometric tolerance in the feature control frame when it is necessary to control a feature surface by contacting points of tangency.
- **Projected tolerance zone.** A projected tolerance zone symbol is placed in the feature control frame to inform the reader that the geometric tolerance zone is projected away from the primary datum.
- **Between.** The between symbol is used with profile geometric tolerances to identify where the profile tolerance is applied.
- **Statistical tolerance.** The statistical tolerance symbol is used to indicate that a tolerance is based on statistical tolerancing. *Statistical tolerancing* is the assigning of tolerances to related dimensions based on the requirements of statistical process control. *Statistical process control (SPC)* is a method of monitoring and adjusting a manufacturing process based on statistical signals. The statistical tolerancing symbol is placed after the dimension or geometric tolerance that requires SPC. See **Figure 20-12.** When the feature can be manufactured by either SPC or conventional means, both the statistical tolerance with the statistical tolerance symbol and the conventional tolerance must be shown. An appropriate general note should accompany the drawing. Either of the two following notes is acceptable:
- FEATURES IDENTIFIED AS STATISTICAL TOLERANCED SHALL BE PRODUCED WITH STATISTICAL PROCESS CONTROL.
- FEATURES IDENTIFIED AS STATISTICAL TOLERANCED SHALL BE PRODUCED WITH STATISTICAL PROCESS CONTROL, OR THE MORE RESTRICTIVE ARITHMETIC LIMITS.

**Figure 20-11.**
Additional recommended dimensioning symbols.

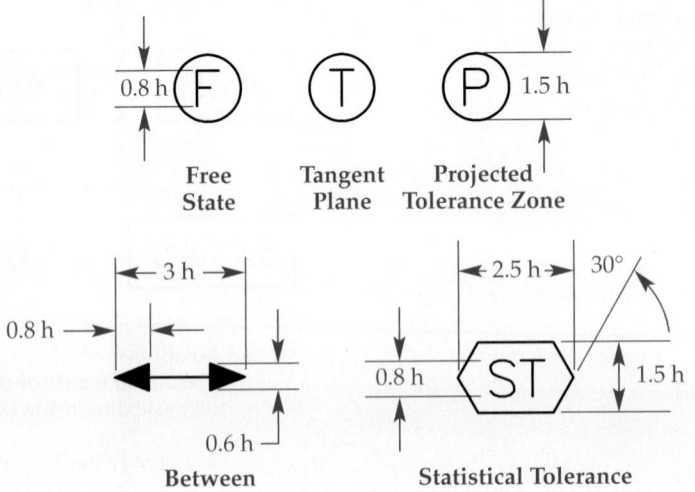

**Figure 20-12.**
Different ways to apply a statistical tolerance. The statistical tolerance symbol is shown here highlighted.

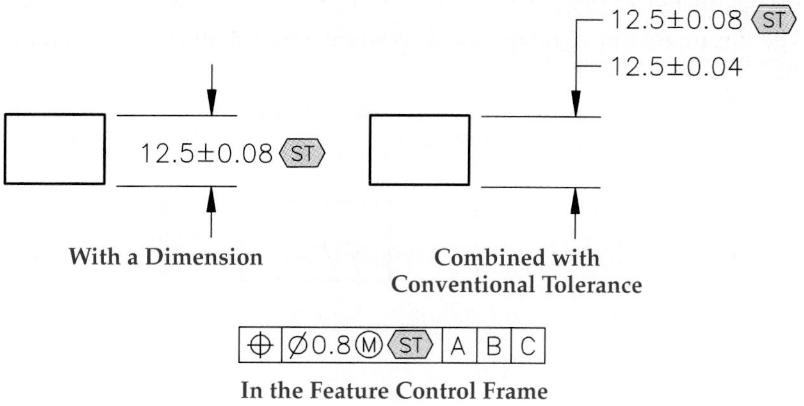

12.5±0.08 〈ST〉

**With a Dimension**

12.5±0.08 〈ST〉
12.5±0.04

**Combined with Conventional Tolerance**

⊕ Ø0.8 Ⓜ 〈ST〉 A B C

**In the Feature Control Frame**

## Datum Feature Symbols

As discussed previously, datums refer to theoretically perfect surfaces, planes, points, or axes. In this introduction to datum-related symbols, the datum is assumed. In geometric dimensioning and tolerancing, the datums are identified with a *datum feature symbol.*

Each datum feature requiring identification must have its own identification letter. Any letter of the alphabet can be used to identify a datum except *I, O,* or *Q.* These letters can be confused with the numbers 1 or 0. On drawings where the number of datums exceeds 23, double letters are used, starting with *AA* through *AZ,* and then *BA* through *BZ.* Datum feature symbols can be repeated only as necessary for clarity.

In **Figure 20-13,** the datum feature symbol recommended by ASME Y14.5M-1994 is shown. The datum feature symbol used in drawings prior to the release of ASME Y14.5M-1994 is distinctively different. The previously used datum feature symbol is shown in **Figure 20-14.**

**Figure 20-13.**
The datum feature symbol based on ASME Y14.5M-1994.

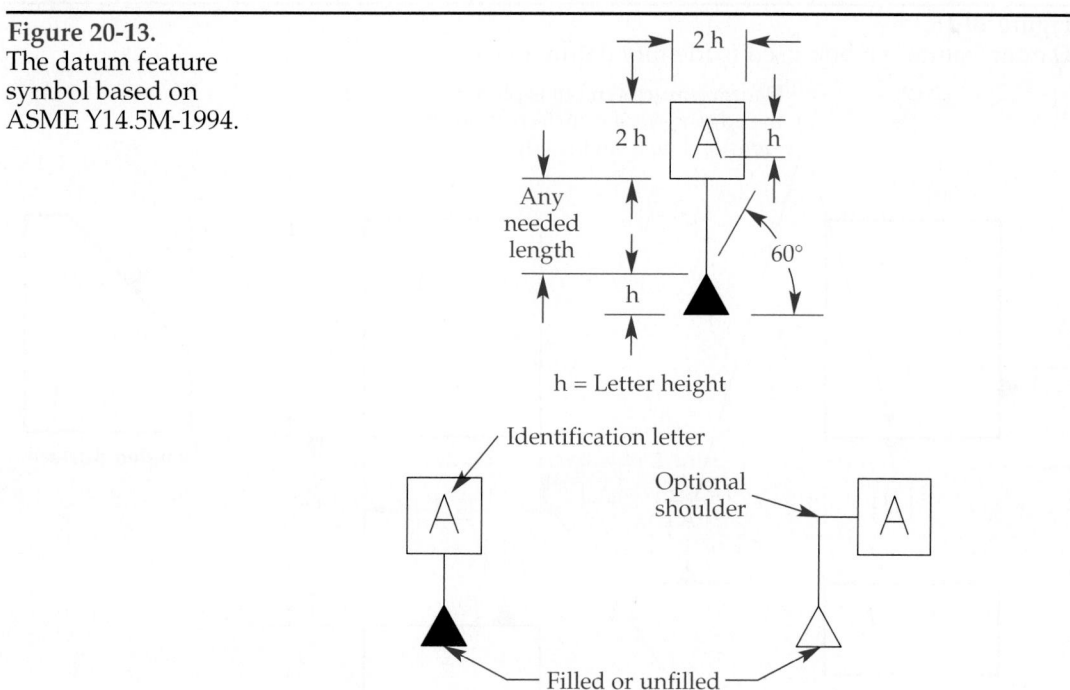

h = Letter height

Identification letter

Optional shoulder

Filled or unfilled

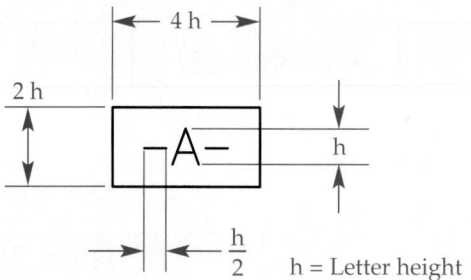

## Applications of the Datum Feature Symbol

When a surface is used to establish a datum plane on a part, the datum feature symbol is placed on the edge view of the surface or on an extension line in the view where the surface appears as a line. See **Figure 20-15.** A leader line can also be used to connect the datum feature symbol to the view.

When the datum is an axis, the datum feature symbol can be placed on the drawing using one of the following methods. See **Figure 20-16.**

- The symbol can be placed on the outside surface of a cylindrical feature.
- The symbol can be centered on the opposite side of the dimension line arrowhead.
- The symbol can replace the dimension line and arrowhead when the dimension line is placed outside the extension lines.
- The symbol can be placed on a leader line shoulder.
- The symbol can be placed below, and attached to, the center of a feature control frame.

Elements on a rectangular symmetrical part or feature can be located and dimensioned in relationship to a datum center plane. Datum center plane symbols are shown in **Figure 20-17.**

**Figure 20-15.**
Datum feature symbols used to identify datum planes.

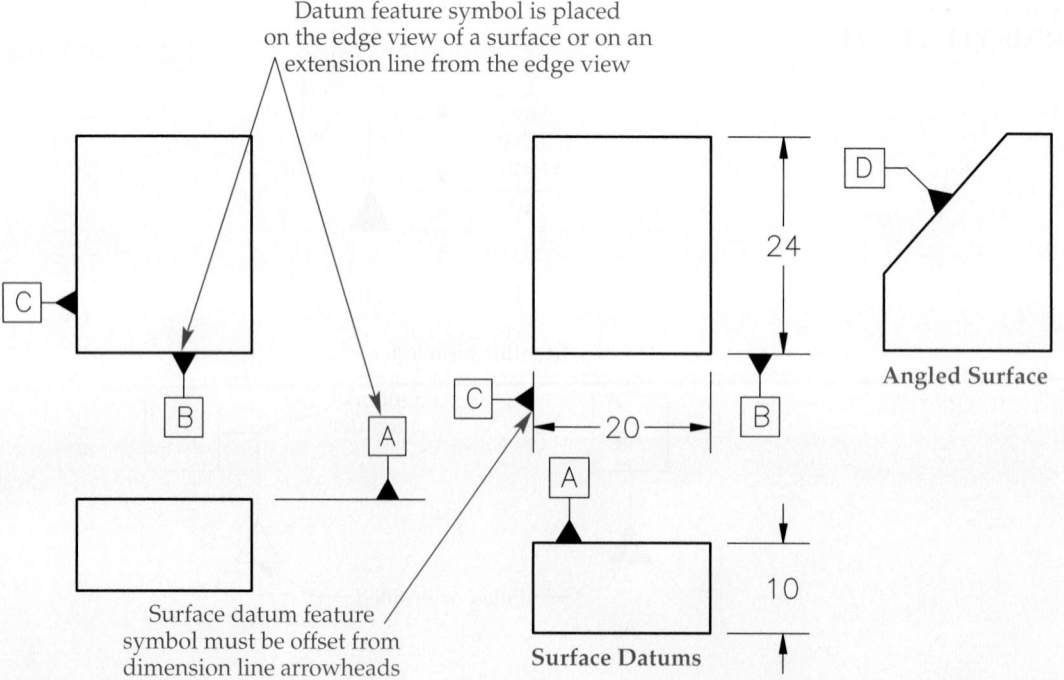

**Figure 20-16.**
Different methods
of using the datum
feature symbol to
represent a datum
axis.

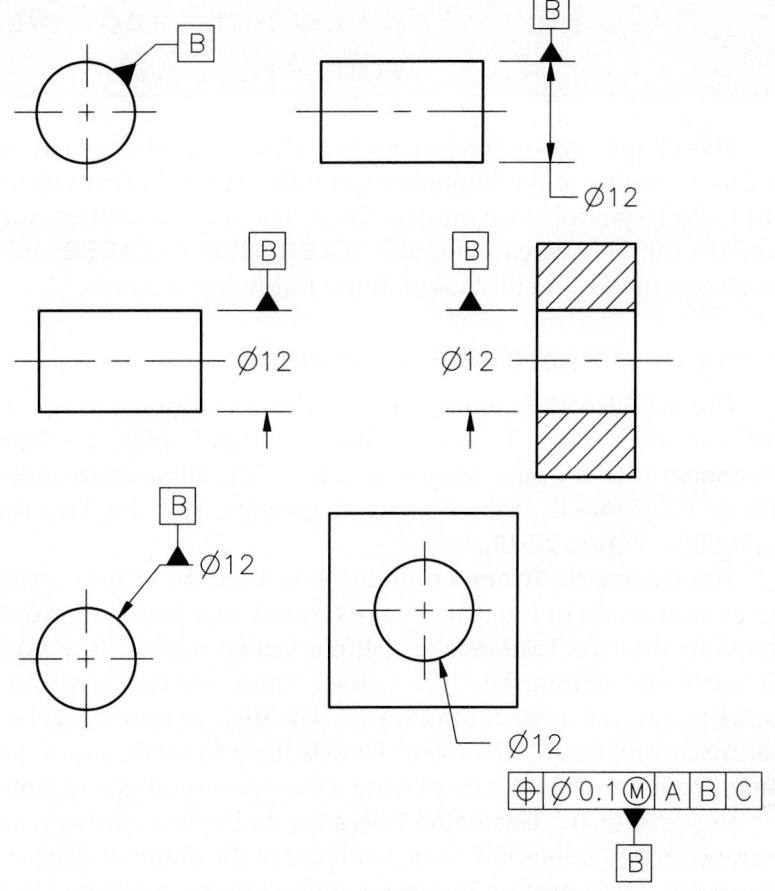

**Figure 20-17.**
Placing datum
center plane
symbols. Axis and
center plane datum
feature symbols
must align with, or
replace, the
dimension line
arrowhead. Or, the
datum feature
symbol must be
placed on the
feature, leader
shoulder, or feature
control frame.

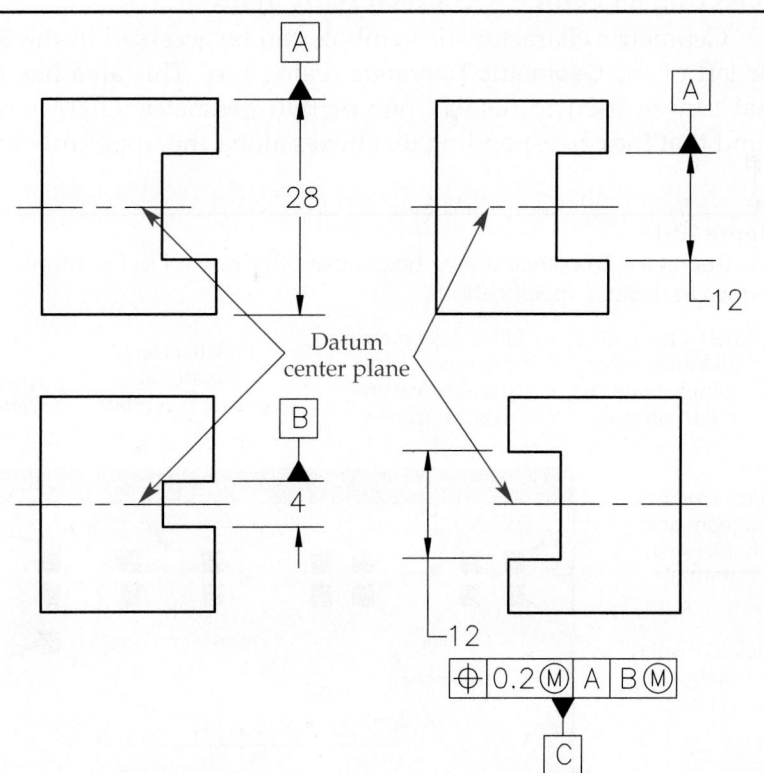

# Geometric Dimensioning and Tolerancing with AutoCAD

This chapter has given you an introduction to the appearance and use of geometric dimensioning and tolerancing symbols. AutoCAD provides you with the ability to add GD&T symbols to your drawings. The feature control frame and related GD&T symbols can be created using the **TOLERANCE**, **QLEADER**, and **LEADER** commands. These commands are discussed in the following sections.

## Using the TOLERANCE Command

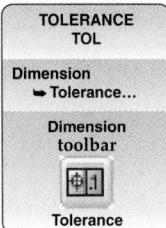

TOLERANCE
TOL

Dimension
➥ Tolerance...

Dimension
toolbar

Tolerance

The **TOLERANCE** command provides tools for creating GD&T symbols and feature control frames. To access this command, pick the **Tolerance** button on the **Dimension** toolbar, pick **Tolerance...** from the **Dimension** pull-down menu, or enter TOL or TOLERANCE at the Command: prompt. This displays the **Geometric Tolerance** dialog box, **Figure 20-18**.

The **Geometric Tolerance** dialog box is divided into areas containing compartments that relate to the components found in a feature control frame. The compartments in the two **Tolerance** and three **Datum** areas allow you to specify geometric tolerance and datum reference values. There are two levels in each area that can be used to create a feature control frame. The first, or upper, level is used to make a single feature control frame. The lower level is used to create a double feature control frame. There are also options for displaying a diameter symbol and a modifying symbol.

In addition, the **Geometric Tolerance** dialog box allows you to display a projected tolerance zone symbol and value, and part of the datum feature symbol. The options and features in the **Geometric Tolerance** dialog box are explained in the following sections.

### Selecting a geometric characteristic symbol

Geometric characteristic symbols can be accessed in the **Sym** area located at the far left of the **Geometric Tolerance** dialog box. This area has two image tile buttons that can be used to display one or two geometric characteristic symbols. Keep in mind that the corresponding text boxes along the upper row in each area are used for

---

**Figure 20-18.**
The **Geometric Tolerance** dialog box is used to draw GD&T symbols and feature control frames to desired specifications.

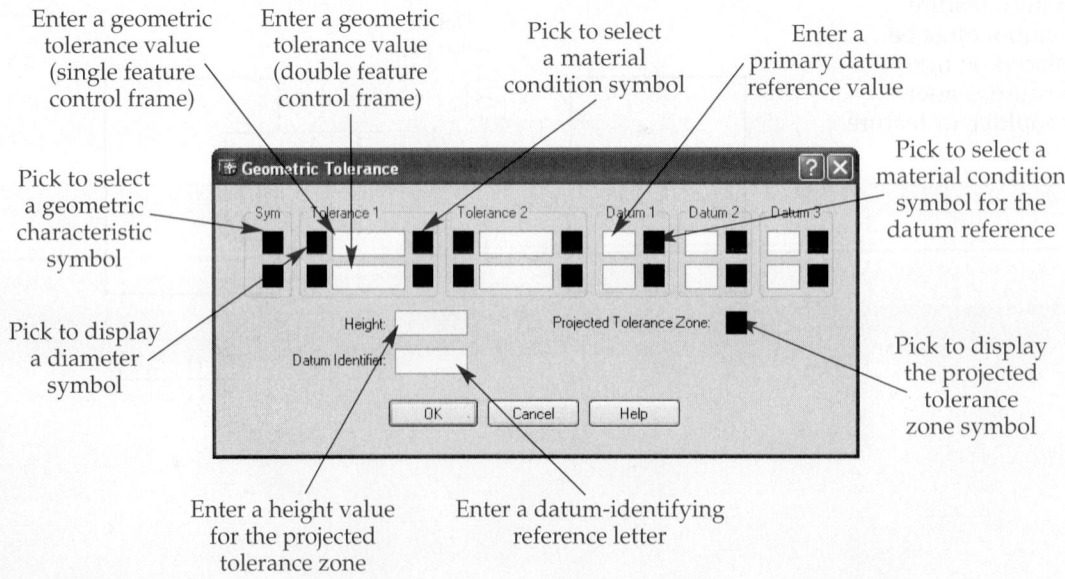

Enter a geometric tolerance value (single feature control frame)

Enter a geometric tolerance value (double feature control frame)

Pick to select a material condition symbol

Enter a primary datum reference value

Pick to select a geometric characteristic symbol

Pick to select a material condition symbol for the datum reference

Pick to display a diameter symbol

Pick to display the projected tolerance zone symbol

Enter a height value for the projected tolerance zone

Enter a datum-identifying reference letter

a single feature control frame. The text boxes in the lower row are used to create a double feature control frame.

Picking one of the image tile buttons in the **Sym** area opens the **Symbol** dialog box, **Figure 20-19**. Pick a symbol to have it displayed in the **Sym** image tile that you selected. After making a selection, the **Geometric Tolerance** dialog box returns. You can pick the same image tile again to select a different symbol, if you wish. To remove a previously selected symbol, pick the blank image tile in the lower-right corner of the **Symbol** dialog box.

### Tolerance 1 area

The **Tolerance 1** area of the **Geometric Tolerance** dialog box allows you to enter the first geometric tolerance value used in the feature control frame. If you are drawing a single feature control frame, enter the desired value in the upper text box. If you are drawing a double feature control frame, also enter a value in the lower text box. Double feature control frames, discussed later in this chapter, are used for applications such as unit straightness, unit flatness, composite profile tolerance, composite positional tolerance, and coaxial positional tolerance. You can add a diameter symbol by picking the image tile to the left of the text box. Pick the diameter image tile again to remove the diameter symbol.

The image tile to the right of the text box is used to place a material condition symbol. When you pick this image tile, the **Material Condition** dialog box appears, **Figure 20-20**. Pick the desired symbol to have it displayed in the image tile you selected. In the example given, an MMC symbol is selected. To remove a material condition symbol, pick the blank tile in the **Material Condition** image tile menu. The RFS symbol in **Figure 20-20** was used in ANSI Y14.5M-1982. The symbol is not used in ASME Y14.5M-1994 because RFS is assumed unless otherwise specified.

In **Figure 20-21**, a position symbol is shown in the **Sym** image tile and 0.5 is entered as the tolerance value in the upper text box in the **Tolerance 1** area. The tolerance value is preceded by a diameter symbol and followed by an MMC symbol. Remember that a zero precedes metric decimals but not inch decimals.

---

**Figure 20-19.**
The **Symbol** dialog box is used to select a geometric characteristic symbol for use in a feature control frame.

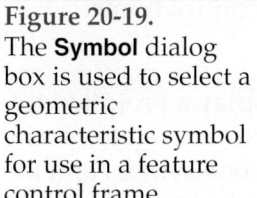 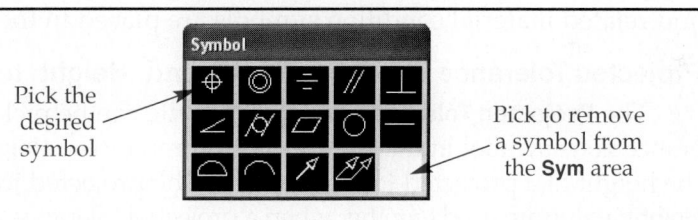

Pick the desired symbol

Pick to remove a symbol from the **Sym** area

---

**Figure 20-20.**
The **Material Condition** dialog box. Pick the desired material condition symbol for the geometric tolerance and datum reference as needed. Notice the symbol for RFS is available. This symbol is not used in ASME Y14.5M-1994, but it may be needed when editing older drawings.

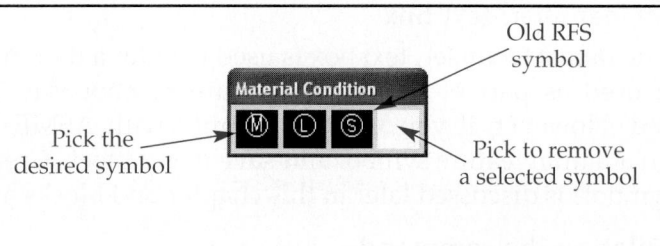

Old RFS symbol

Pick the desired symbol

Pick to remove a selected symbol

---

**Figure 20-21.**
The **Geometric Tolerance** dialog box with a diameter symbol, geometric tolerance value, and MMC material condition symbol added to the **Tolerance 1** area.

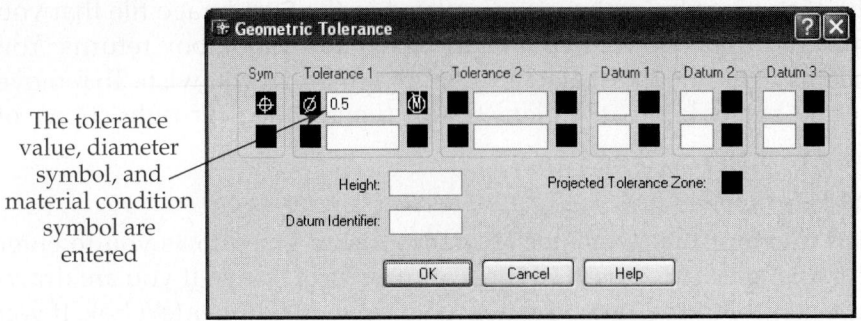

The tolerance value, diameter symbol, and material condition symbol are entered

### Tolerance 2 area

The **Tolerance 2** area of the **Geometric Tolerance** dialog box is used for the addition of a second geometric tolerance to the feature control frame. This is not a common application, but it may be used in some cases where there are restrictions placed on the geometric tolerance specified in the first compartment. For example, the second geometric tolerance value of 0.8 MAX means that the specification given in the first compartment is maintained but cannot exceed 0.8 maximum.

### Datum areas

The **Datum 1** area of the **Geometric Tolerance** dialog box is used to establish the information needed for the primary datum reference compartment. Like the **Tolerance** areas, this area offers two levels of text boxes to create single or double feature control frames. You can also specify a material condition symbol for the datum reference by picking the image tile next to the corresponding text box to open the **Material Condition** dialog box.

The **Datum 2** and **Datum 3** areas are used to specify the secondary and tertiary datum reference information. Refer to **Figure 20-9** to see how the datum reference and related material condition symbols are placed in the feature control frame.

### Projected Tolerance Zone: image tile and Height: text box

The **Projected Tolerance Zone:** image tile can be picked to display a projected tolerance zone symbol in the feature control frame. The **Height:** text box is used to specify the height of a projected tolerance zone. The projected tolerance zone symbol and the **Height:** value are used together when a projected tolerance zone is applied to the drawing. The use of a projected tolerance zone in a drawing is discussed later in this chapter.

### Datum Identifier: text box

The **Datum Identifier:** text box is used to enter a datum-identifying reference letter to be used as part of the datum feature symbol. An uppercase letter should be entered. However, if you want to comply with ASME Y14.5M-1994, you need to design a datum feature symbol and save it as a block. Creating your own dimensioning symbols is discussed later in this chapter and blocks are discussed in Chapter 22.

### Completing the command

After you have entered all the desired information in the **Geometric Tolerance** dialog box, pick **OK**. See **Figure 20-22A**. The following prompt is then displayed on the command line.

> Enter tolerance location: *(pick the location for the feature control frame to be drawn)*
> Command:

The feature control frame for the given example is shown in **Figure 20-22B**.

Figure 20-22.
A—When the desired values have been specified in the **Geometric Tolerance** dialog box, pick **OK**. In this example, primary, secondary, and tertiary datum reference values have been added and are shown highlighted along with the geometric tolerance value. B—The feature control frame created by the values specified in the dialog box.

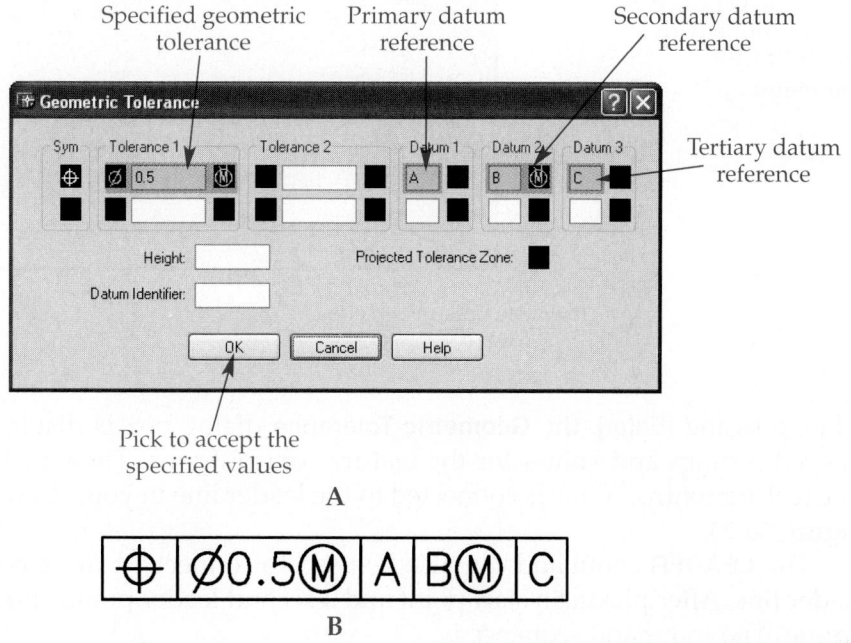

Specified geometric tolerance

Primary datum reference

Secondary datum reference

Tertiary datum reference

Pick to accept the specified values

A

B

---

## Exercise 20-1

○ Start a new drawing or use one of your templates.
○ Draw feature control frames as shown in **Figure 20-7** and **Figure 20-8**.
○ Save the drawing as EX20-1.

---

## Using the **QLEADER** and **LEADER** Commands to Place GD&T Symbols

In many cases, leader lines are connected to feature control frames or other GD&T symbols in order to identify toleranced features. The **QLEADER** and **LEADER** commands enable you to draw leader lines and access the dialog boxes used to create feature control frames in one operation. Refer to Chapter 17 for a complete discussion of the **QLEADER** command.

The **QLEADER** command can be accessed by picking the **Quick Leader** button on the **Dimension** toolbar, picking **Leader** from the **Dimension** pull-down menu, or by entering LE or QLEADER at the Command: prompt. When you enter this command, use the **Settings** option to open the **Leader Settings** dialog box, **Figure 20-23**. Then, pick the **Tolerance** radio button in the **Annotation** tab to connect a feature control frame or datum feature symbol to a leader line. The command sequence is:

> Command: **LE** or **QLEADER**
> Specify first leader point, or [Settings] <Settings>: *(when the **Leader Settings** dialog box is displayed, pick the **Tolerance** radio button and then **OK**)*
> Specify first leader point, or [Settings] <Settings>: *(pick the leader start point)*
> Specify next point: *(pick the next leader point)*
> Specify next point: ↵

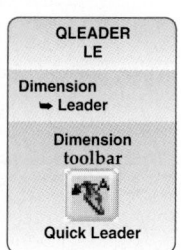

QLEADER
LE

Dimension
➡ Leader

Dimension
toolbar

Quick Leader

---

Figure 20-23.
The **Leader Settings**
dialog box. Activate
the **Tolerance** radio
button when
placing a feature
control frame with
the **QLEADER**
command.

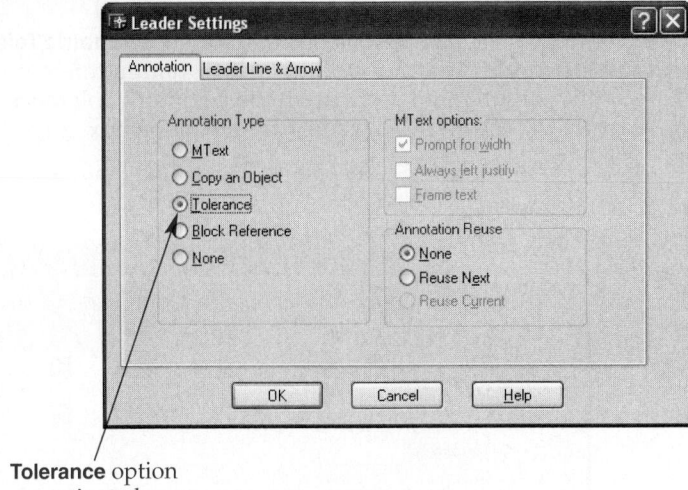

Tolerance option
activated

After pressing [Enter], the **Geometric Tolerance** dialog box is displayed. Specify the
desired settings and values for the feature control frame. Then, pick the **OK** button.
The feature control frame is connected to the leader line in your drawing, as shown in
**Figure 20-24.**

The **LEADER** command can also be used to connect a feature control frame to a
leader line. After picking a start point and a second leader point, enter the **Annotation**
option. The command sequence is:

LEADER
LEAD

Command: **LEAD** *or* **LEADER**
Specify leader start point: (*pick the leader start point*)
Specify next point: (*pick the next point of the leader*)
Specify next point or [Annotation/Format/Undo] <Annotation>: ↵
Enter first line of annotation text or <options>: ↵
Enter an annotation option [Tolerance/Copy/Block/None/Mtext] <Mtext>: **T**

Entering the **Tolerance** annotation option displays the **Geometric Tolerance** dialog
box. You can then establish the feature control frame information. When you pick **OK**,
the feature control frame is connected to the leader shoulder.

Figure 20-24.
After completing
the **QLEADER**
command, the
feature control
frame is connected
to the leader line.

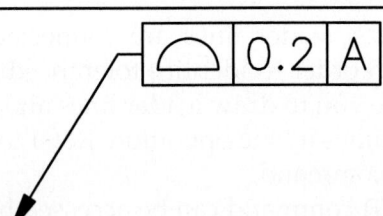

### Exercise 20-2

○ Open drawing EX20-1.
○ Using the **QLEADER** or **LEADER** command, draw the feature control frame
  shown in **Figure 20-24.**
○ Save the drawing as EX20-2.

# Introduction to Projected Tolerance Zones

In some situations where positional tolerance is used entirely in out-of-squareness, it may be necessary to control perpendicularity and position next to the part. The use of a ***projected tolerance zone*** is recommended when variations in perpendicularity of threaded or press-fit holes may cause the fastener to interfere with the mating part. A projected tolerance zone is usually specified for a fixed fastener, such as the threaded hole for a bolt or the press-fit hole for a pin. The length of a projected tolerance zone can be specified as the distance the fastener extends into the mating part, the thickness of the part, or the height of a press-fit stud. The normal positional tolerance extends through the thickness of the part.

However, this application can cause an interference between the location of a thread or press-fit object and its mating part. This is because the attitude of a fixed fastener is controlled by the actual angle of the threaded hole. There is no clearance available to provide flexibility. For this reason, the projected tolerance zone is established at true position and extends away from the primary datum at the threaded feature. The projected tolerance zone provides a larger tolerance because it is projected away from the primary datum, rather than within the thread. A projected tolerance is also easier to inspect than the tolerance applied to the pitch diameter of the thread. This is because a thread gauge with a post projecting above the threaded hole can be used to easily verify the projected tolerance zone with a coordinate measuring machine (CMM).

## Representing a Projected Tolerance Zone

One method for displaying the projected tolerance zone is to place the projected tolerance zone symbol and height in the feature control frame after the geometric tolerance and related material condition symbol. The related thread specification is then connected to the section view of the thread symbol. With this method, the projected tolerance zone is assumed to extend away from the threaded hole at the primary datum. See **Figure 20-25**.

**Figure 20-25.**
A projected tolerance zone representation with the length of the projected tolerance zone given in the feature control frame. The projected tolerance zone symbol is shown highlighted.

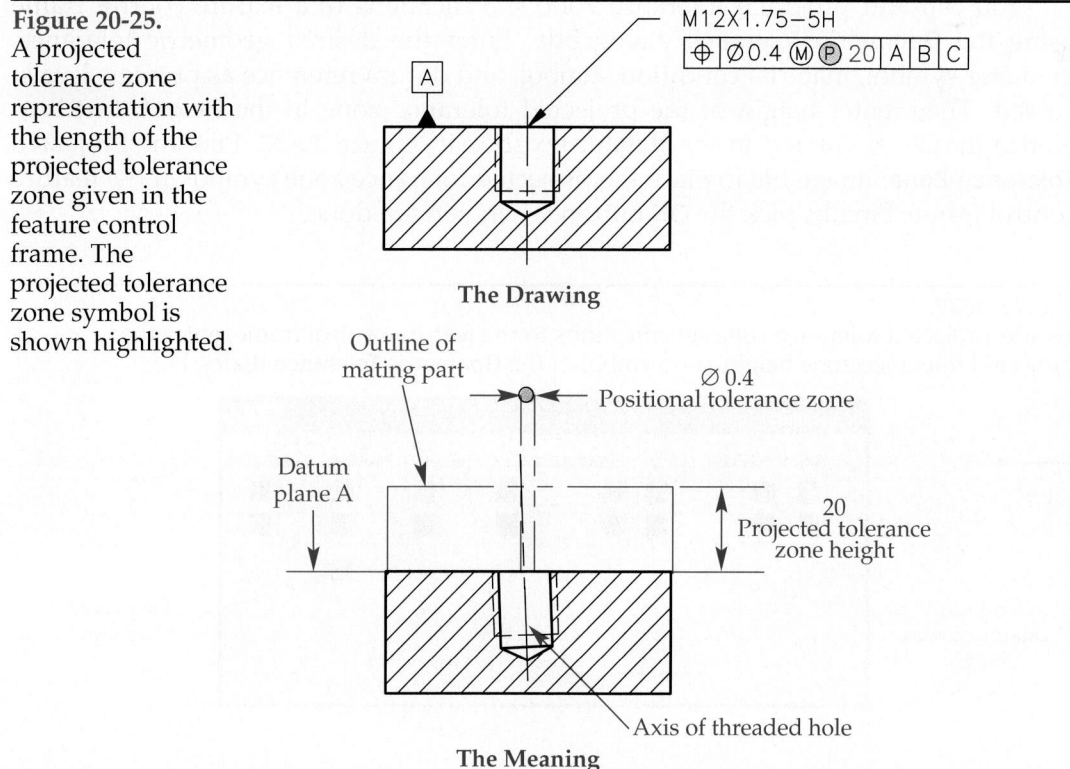

**Figure 20-26.**
A projected tolerance zone representation with the length of the projected tolerance zone shown with a chain line and a minimum dimension in the adjacent view.

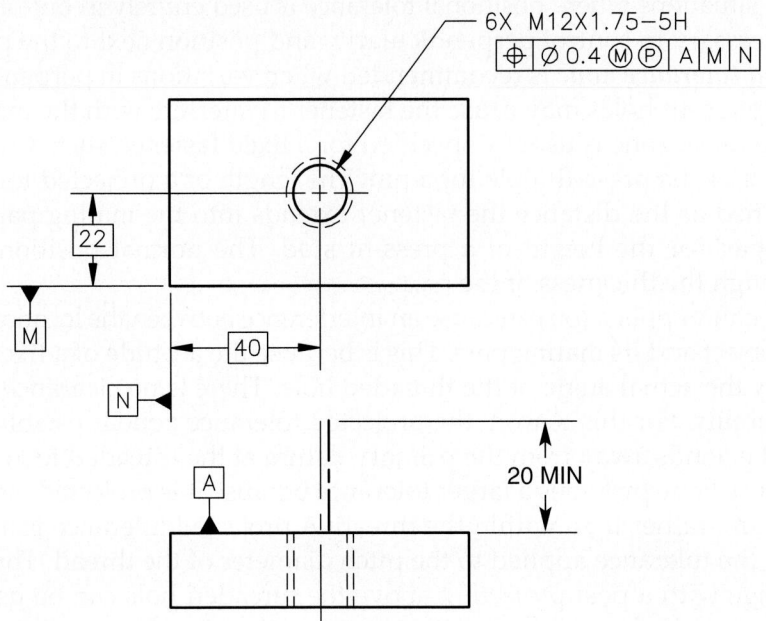

To provide additional clarification, the projected tolerance zone can be shown using a chain line in the view where the related datum appears as an edge and the minimum height of the projection is dimensioned. See **Figure 20-26.** The projected tolerance zone symbol is shown alone in the feature control frame after the geometric tolerance and material condition symbol (if any). The meaning is the same as previously discussed.

## Drawing the Projected Tolerance Zone

You can add projected tolerance zone specifications to a feature control frame using the **Geometric Tolerance** dialog box. Enter the desired geometric tolerance, diameter symbol, material condition symbol, and datum reference as previously discussed. Then, enter height of the projected tolerance zone in the **Height:** text box. Notice that 24 is entered in the **Height:** text box in **Figure 20-27.** Pick the **Projected Tolerance Zone:** image tile to place the projected tolerance zone symbol in the feature control frame. Finally, pick the **OK** button when you are done.

**Figure 20-27.**
To add projected tolerance zone specifications to the feature control frame, enter the projected tolerance zone height and symbol in the **Geometric Tolerance** dialog box.

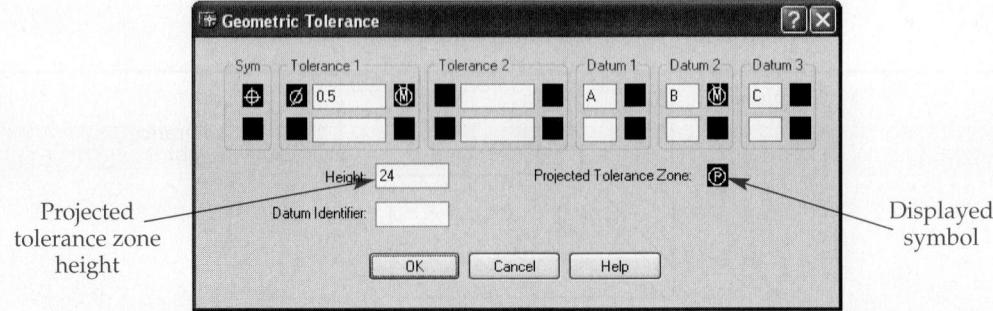

AutoCAD and its Applications—Basics

**Figure 20-28.**
The feature control frame created by the values specified in **Figure 20-27**. The AutoCAD projected tolerance zone compartment conforms to ANSI Y14.5M-1982 standards. See **Figure 20-25** and **Figure 20-26** for applications of the projected tolerance zone as recommended by ASME Y14.5M-1994.

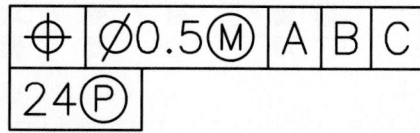

Now, place the feature control frame in the desired location in the drawing. Notice in **Figure 20-28** that AutoCAD displays the projected tolerance zone height in a separate compartment below the feature control frame. This representation is in accordance with ANSI Y14.5M-1982. The ASME Y14.5M-1994 convention has no lower compartment, as shown in **Figure 20-25**.

If you want to dimension the projected tolerance zone height with a chain line, then omit the value in the **Height:** text box in the **Geometric Tolerance** dialog box and only pick the **Projected Tolerance Zone:** image tile. This adds a compartment below the feature control frame with only the projected tolerance zone symbol. This representation is in accordance with ANSI Y14.5M-1982, but it does not match the ASME Y14.5M-1994 convention illustrated in **Figure 20-26**.

## Exercise 20-3

○ Open drawing EX20-1.
○ Draw the feature control frame and projected tolerance zone compartment shown in **Figure 20-28**.
○ Save the drawing as EX20-3.

## Drawing a Double Feature Control Frame

Several GD&T applications require that the feature control frame be doubled in height, with two sets of geometric tolerancing values provided. These applications include unit straightness and flatness, composite positional tolerance, and coaxial positional tolerance.

To draw a double feature control frame, first use the **TOLERANCE** command and create the desired first level of the feature control frame in the **Geometric Tolerance** dialog box as previously discussed. You can also use the **QLEADER** or **LEADER** command if you are connecting the feature control frame to a leader line. Next, pick the lower image tile in the **Sym** area. When the **Symbol** dialog box is displayed again, pick another geometric characteristic symbol. This results in two symbols displayed in the **Sym** area. Continue specifying the needed information in the lower-level **Tolerance** and **Datum** compartments. Sample entries for a double feature control frame are shown in **Figure 20-29**.

If the two symbols in the **Sym** image tiles are the same, then the double feature control frame is drawn with one geometric characteristic symbol displayed in a single compartment. See **Figure 20-30A**. This is acceptable if only one geometric characteristic symbol is required for the feature-relating control, but it is inappropriate if you need to display the same geometric characteristic symbol twice. If you are drawing a double feature control frame with different geometric characteristic symbols for a combination control, then the feature control frame must have two separate compartments. See **Figure 20-30B**.

**Figure 20-29.**
Specifying information for a double feature control frame in the **Geometric Tolerance** dialog box.

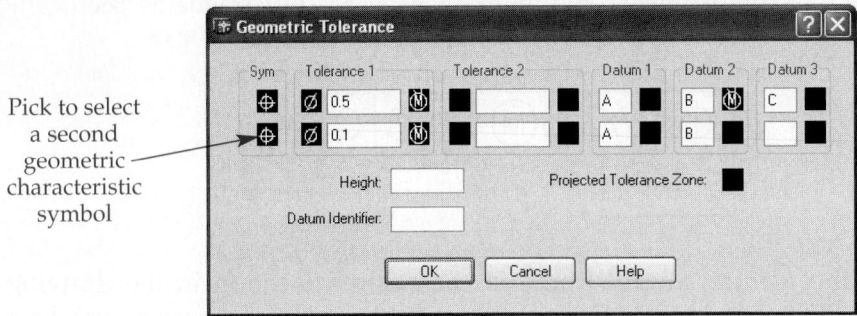

Pick to select a second geometric characteristic symbol

**Figure 20-30.**
A—If only one geometric characteristic symbol entered in the **Geometric Tolerance** dialog box is required for display, it is shown once in the first compartment of the double feature control frame. B—If two different symbols are used, they are displayed in separate compartments.

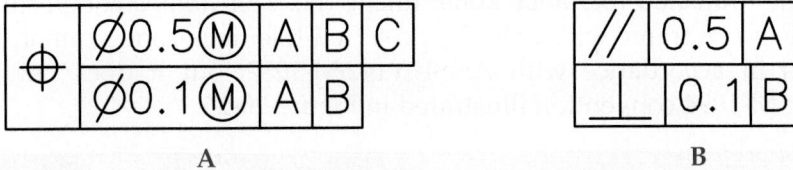

A

B

---

**Exercise 20-4**

○ Open drawing EX20-1.
○ Draw the double feature control frames shown in **Figure 20-30**.
○ Save the drawing as EX20-4.

---

## Drawing Datum Feature Symbols

As discussed earlier in this chapter, datums in a drawing are identified by datum feature symbols. You can draw datum feature symbols using the **TOLERANCE**, **QLEADER**, or **LEADER** commands. When you access the **Geometric Tolerance** dialog box, enter the desired datum reference letter in the **Datum Identifier:** text box. See **Figure 20-31**.

After picking **OK**, place the datum feature symbol at the desired location in your drawing. You can also draw a datum feature symbol connected to a feature control frame by selecting the desired geometric characteristic symbol and entering the necessary information in the **Geometric Tolerance** dialog box. In **Figure 20-32**, datum feature symbols are shown with and without a feature control frame. Notice the symbols are placed inside squares. This complies with the ANSI Y14.5M-1982 standard, rather than ASME Y14.5M-1994. In order to match the ASME Y14.5M-1994 standard, the symbols need to be drawn as shown in **Figure 20-13**. One way to do this is to create your own symbols that you can insert as needed. Creating and saving your own symbols are discussed in Chapter 22.

Before you learn how to create your own symbols, you can modify the symbols shown in **Figure 20-32** by establishing a dimension style with leader line terminators set to **Datum triangle** or **Datum triangle filled**. These leader options are available in the

**Figure 20-31.**
Using the **Geometric Tolerance** dialog box to enter a datum-identifying reference letter. This letter is used to create the datum feature symbol.

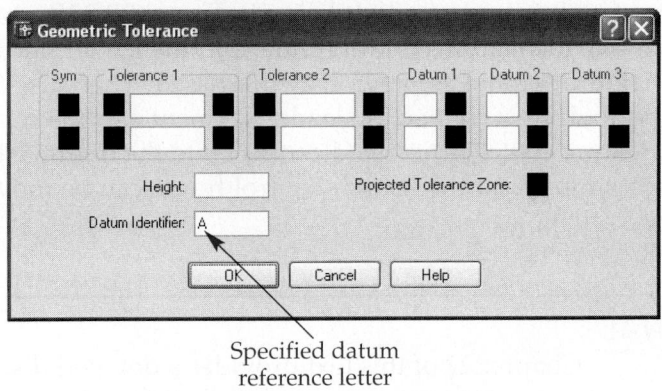

Specified datum
reference letter

**Figure 20-32.**
A—A datum feature symbol drawn without a feature control frame. B—A datum feature symbol drawn with a feature control frame. Note the symbols in A and B do not comply with the ASME Y14.5M-1994 standard.

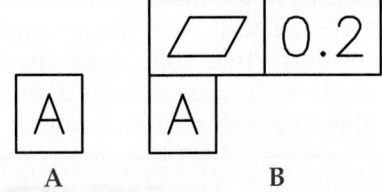

**Leader:** drop-down list in the **Arrowheads** area of the **Lines and Arrows** tab in the **Modify Dimension Style** dialog box. Creating dimension styles with the **Dimension Style Manager** and the **Modify Dimension Style** dialog boxes are discussed in Chapter 17.

After creating a dimension style that uses datum triangles for leader arrowheads, enter the **QLEADER** or **LEADER** command to draw a leader segment that connects to the datum feature symbol as shown in **Figure 20-33A**. This modifies the symbol in **Figure 20-32A**. Use the object snap modes to help you properly position the leader with the symbol. If you use the **QLEADER** command, make sure the annotation setting is set to **Mtext**. Then, pick the leader start point and endpoint, and then press

**Figure 20-33.**
A—To draw a datum feature symbol in accordance with ASME Y14.5M-1994, create a dimension style that uses the **Datum triangle** or **Datum triangle filled** leader arrowhead option. Then, use the **QLEADER** or **LEADER** command to connect a leader arrow to the existing symbol. B—If a feature control frame is to be used, the datum feature symbol, leader line, and feature control frame must be drawn separately.

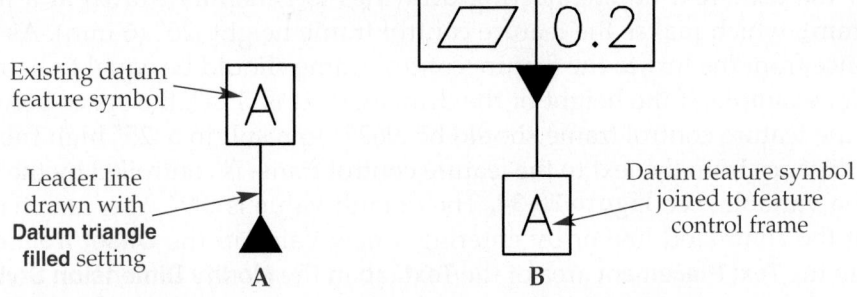

Existing datum
feature symbol

Leader line
drawn with
**Datum triangle
filled** setting

Datum feature symbol
joined to feature
control frame

[Enter]. When prompted for the text width, press the [Esc] key. If you use the **LEADER** command, pick the leader line points, and then use the **None** suboption of the **Annotation** option to specify no annotation text.

To modify the datum feature symbol shown in **Figure 20-32B,** you must draw the datum feature symbol, the feature control frame, and the leader line separately. First, draw the datum feature symbol as previously discussed. Then, use the **QLEADER** or **LEADER** command to draw a connecting leader segment as shown in **Figure 20-33B.** Finally, draw the feature control frame and connect it to the datum triangle as shown. The datum feature symbol and the feature control frame can be moved as needed to allow for proper positioning.

---

**PROFESSIONAL TIP**

Chapter 22 of this text provides a detailed discussion on how to create your own symbol libraries. A *symbol library* is a related group of symbols. It is recommended that you design dimensioning symbols that are not available in AutoCAD, such as the datum feature symbol that is recognized by ASME Y14.5M-1994. This symbol is shown in **Figure 20-13.**

Your symbol library might include the counterbore, countersink, depth, and other dimensioning symbols illustrated in **Figure 20-1.** These symbols are easily drawn if you establish a dimension style that uses the gdt.shx font. Chapter 17 explains how to create such a dimension style to help you draw these symbols when needed.

---

**Exercise 20-5**

○ Start a new drawing or use one of your templates.
○ Draw the datum feature symbol shown in **Figure 20-32A.**
○ Modify the symbol to look like the one shown in **Figure 20-33A.**
○ Draw the datum feature symbol and feature control frame shown in **Figure 20-33B.**
○ Save the drawing as EX20-5.

---

## Controlling the Height of the Feature Control Frame

Referring to **Figure 20-9,** the height of the feature control frame is twice the height of the text. Text on engineering drawings is generally drawn at a height of .125″ (3 mm), which makes the feature control frame height .25″ (6 mm). As a result, the distance from the text to the feature control frame should be equal to half the text height. For example, if the height of the drawing text is .125″, the space between the text and the feature control frame should be .0625″ to result in a .25″ high frame.

The distance from the text to the feature control frame is controlled by the **DIMGAP** dimension variable. See **Figure 20-34.** The default value is .09″. You can change this setting at the command line or by entering a new value in the **Offset from dim line:** text box in the **Text Placement** area of the **Text** tab in the **Modify Dimension Style** dialog

**Figure 20-34.**
The **DIMGAP** dimension variable setting controls the distance from the text to the feature control frame.

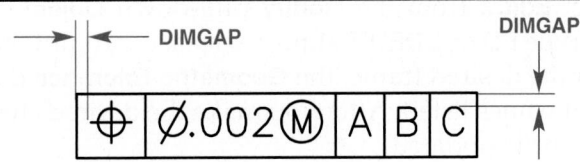

box. The setting also controls the gap between the dimension line and the dimension text for linear dimensions and the space between the dimension text and the rectangle for basic dimensions. Basic dimensions are discussed in the next section.

## Drawing Basic Dimensions

A basic dimension is shown in **Figure 20-35.** Basic dimensions can be automatically drawn by setting a basic tolerance in the **Tolerance** tab of the **Modify Dimension Style** dialog box, as discussed in Chapter 19. It is recommended that you establish a separate dimension style for basic dimensions because not all of your dimensions on a drawing will be basic. The **Offset from dim line:** setting (**DIMGAP**) in the **Text** tab of the **Modify Dimension Style** dialog box controls the space between the basic dimension text and the rectangle around the dimension.

**Figure 20-35.**
An AutoCAD basic dimension.

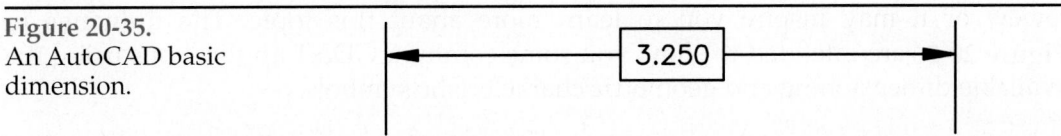

### Exercise 20-6

○ Start a new drawing or use one of your templates.
○ Create a new dimension style named GDT. With the dimension text height set to .125", change the space between the text and the feature control frame to .0625" (half the text height).
○ Use the new dimension style to draw the feature control frame shown in **Figure 20-34.**
○ Draw the basic dimension shown in **Figure 20-35.**
○ Save the drawing as EX20-6.

## Editing Feature Control Frames

A feature control frame acts as one object. When you pick any location on the frame, the entire object is selected. You can edit feature control frames using AutoCAD editing commands such as **ERASE, COPY, MOVE, ROTATE,** and **SCALE.** The **STRETCH** command only allows you to move a feature control frame. This effect is similar to the results of using the **STRETCH** command with text objects.

You can edit the values inside a feature control frame by using the **DDEDIT** command. To access the command, double-click on the feature control frame you wish to

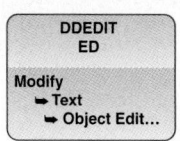

edit, select **Edit...** from the **Modify** pull-down **Object** cascading and **Text** cascading menu, or type ED or DDEDIT at the Command: prompt. When you enter this command and select the desired frame, the **Geometric Tolerance** dialog box is displayed with all the current values listed. After you make the desired changes and pick **OK**, the feature control frame is updated.

You can also use the **DDEDIT** command to edit basic dimensions. When you select a basic dimension for editing, the multiline text editor is displayed. You can then edit the basic dimension as you would any other dimension.

> **NOTE**
>
> If you double-click on a dimension, AutoCAD opens the **Properties** dialog box instead of the multiline text editor.

## Sample GD&T Applications

This chapter is intended to give you a general overview of GD&T applications and basic instructions on how to draw GD&T symbols using AutoCAD. If you are in the manufacturing industry, you may have considerable use for geometric dimensioning and tolerancing. The support information presented in this chapter may be a review or it may inspire you to learn more about this topic. The drawings in **Figure 20-36** are intended to show you some common GD&T applications using the available dimensioning and geometric characteristic symbols.

**Figure 20-36.**
Examples of typical geometric dimensioning and tolerancing applications using various dimensioning and geometric characteristic symbols.

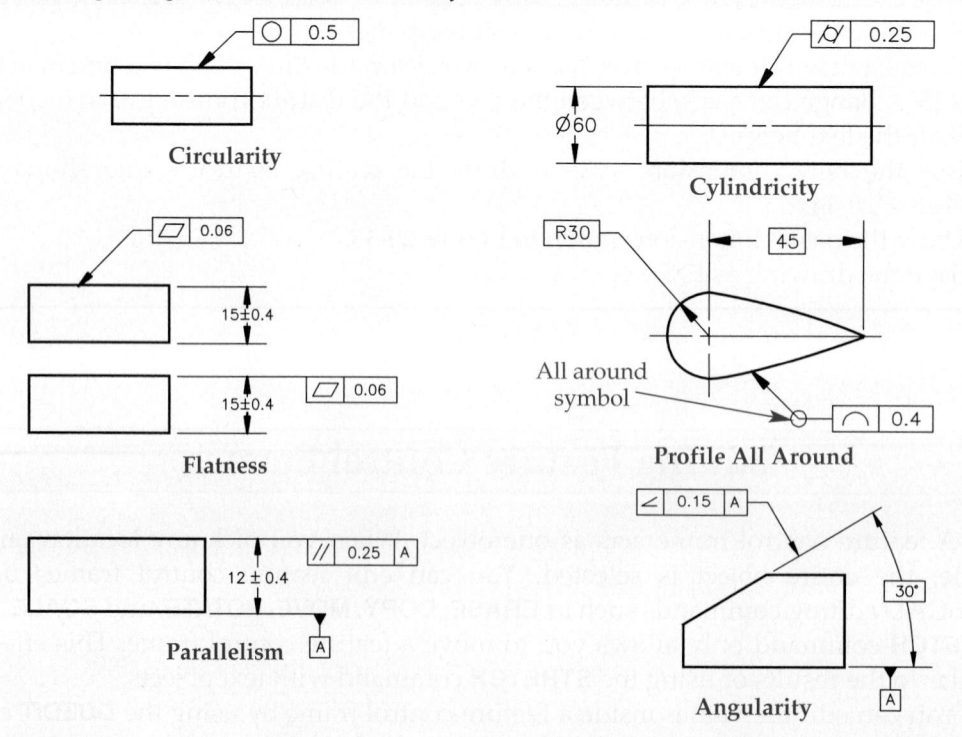

*(Continued)*

**Figure 20-36.**
*(Continued)*

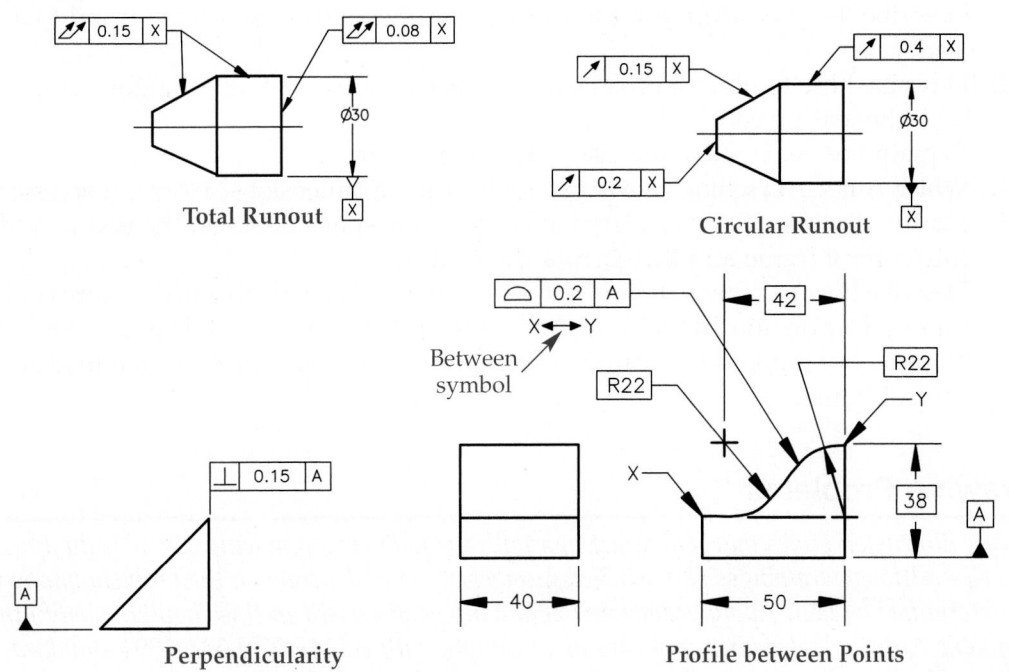

Total Runout

Circular Runout

Perpendicularity

Profile between Points

## Chapter Test

*Answer the following questions on a separate sheet of paper.*

1. Identify each of the following geometric characteristic symbols.

    A. ⎯  H. ◎

    B. ⟋⟍  I. ⎓

    C. ○  J. //

    D. ⌀  K. ⊥

    E. ⌒  L. ∠

    F. ⌓  M. ↗

    G. ⊕  N. ↗↗

2. Identify the parts of the feature control frame shown below.

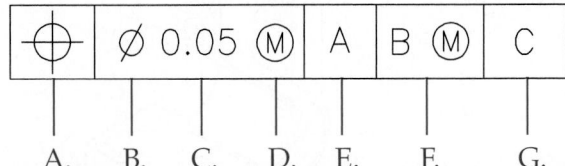

   A.   B.   C.   D.   E.   F.   G.

3. Name the current standard for dimensioning and tolerancing that is adopted by the American National Standards Institute and published by the American Society of Mechanical Engineers.
4. Name three commands that can be used to draw a feature control frame.
5. Identify the dialog box that contains settings used to create a feature control frame.
6. How do you access the **Symbol** dialog box in which a geometric characteristic symbol can be selected?

7. How do you remove a geometric characteristic symbol from one of the image tiles in the **Sym** area of the **Geometric Tolerance** dialog box?
8. Describe the procedure used to draw a feature control frame connected to a leader line.
9. Describe how to place a projected tolerance zone symbol and height value with the feature control frame.
10. Explain how to create a double feature control frame.
11. Which AutoCAD setting allows you to draw basic dimensions? How is it accessed?
12. Identify the AutoCAD setting that controls the space between the text in a feature control frame and the surrounding frame.
13. Describe how to draw a datum feature symbol without an attached feature control frame. How do you add a leader line with a filled datum triangle to the symbol?
14. Name the command that can be used to edit the existing values in a feature control frame.

## Drawing Problems

*Create dimension styles that will assist you with the following problems. Draw fully dimensioned multiview drawings. The required number of views depends on the problem and is to be determined by you. Apply geometric tolerancing as discussed in this chapter. Modify the available AutoCAD drawing applications to comply with ASME Y14.5M-1994 standards. The problems are presented in accordance with ASME Y14.5M-1994.*

1. Open drawing P19-5. Edit the drawing by adding the geometric tolerancing applications shown below. Untoleranced dimensions are ±.02 for two-place decimal precision and ±.005 for three-place decimal precision. If you did not draw P19-5, then start a new drawing and draw the problem now. The problem is shown as a cutaway for clarity. You do not need to draw a section. Save the drawing as P20-1.

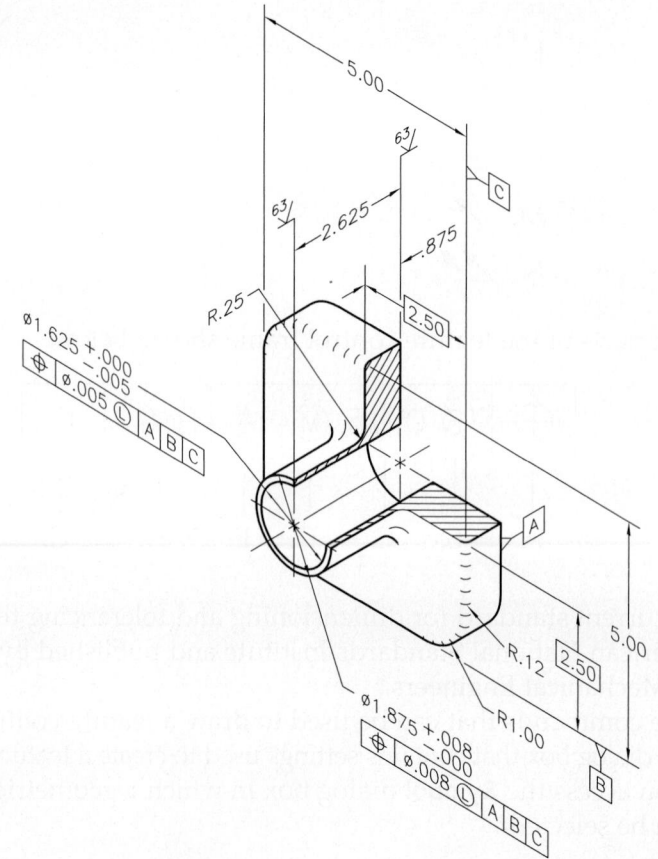

2. Open drawing P19-6. Edit the drawing by adding the geometric tolerancing applications shown below. Untoleranced dimensions are ±0.5. If
you did not draw P19-6, then start a new drawing and draw the
problem now. Save the drawing as P20-2.

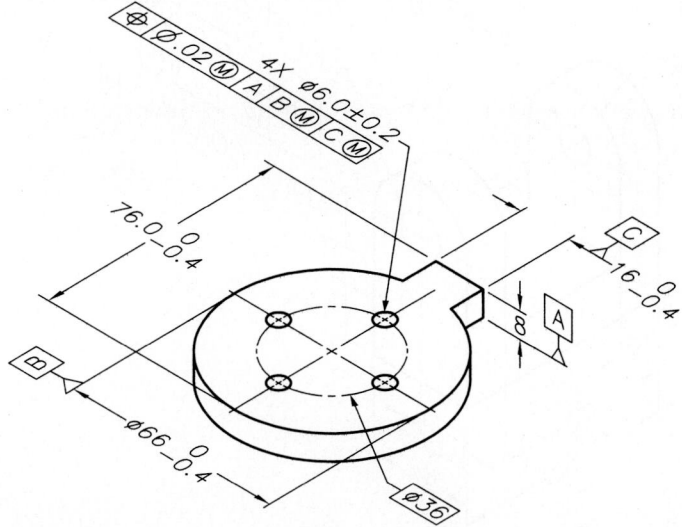

3. Open drawing P19-7. Edit the drawing by adding the geometric tolerancing applications shown below. If you did not draw P19-7, start a
new drawing and draw the problem now. Save the drawing as P20-3.

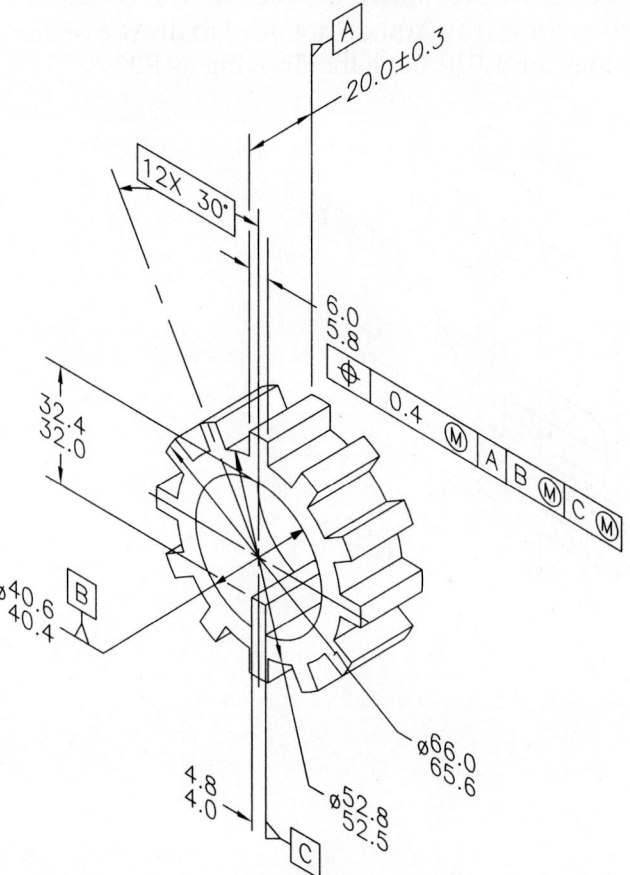

---

4. Draw the following object as previously instructed. Untoleranced dimensions are ±0.3. Save the drawing as P20-4.

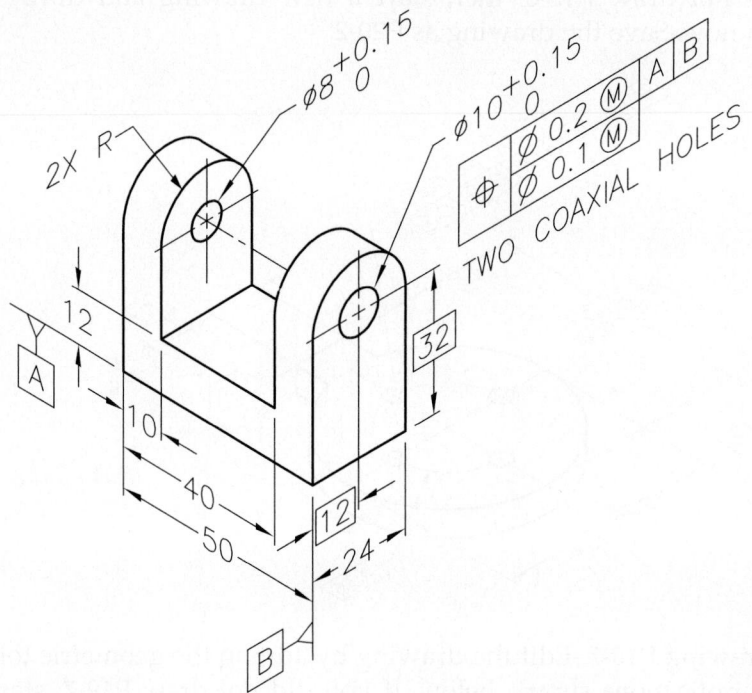

5. Draw the following object as previously instructed. The problem is shown with a full section for clarity. You do not need to draw a section. Untoleranced dimensions are ±.010. Save the drawing as P20-5.

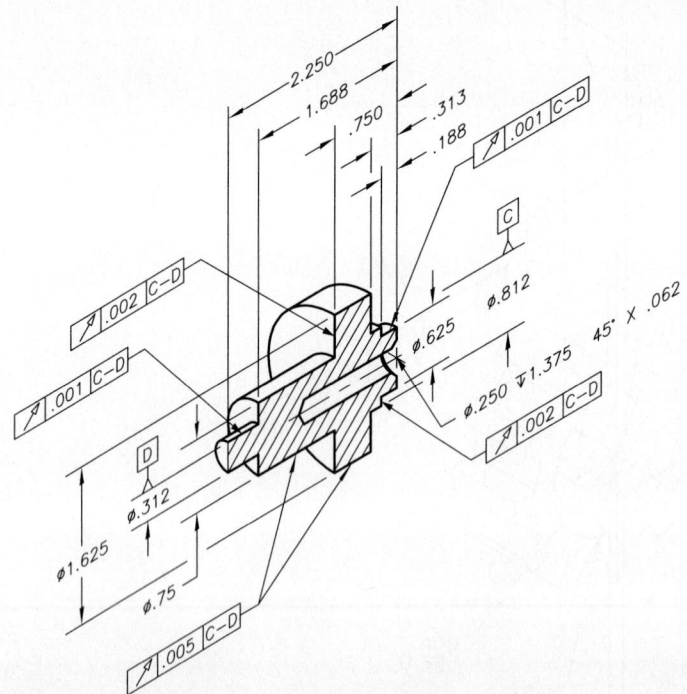

6. Open drawing P17-22. Edit the drawing by adding the geometric tolerancing applications shown below. If you did not draw P17-22, start a new drawing and draw the problem now. Save the drawing as P20-6.

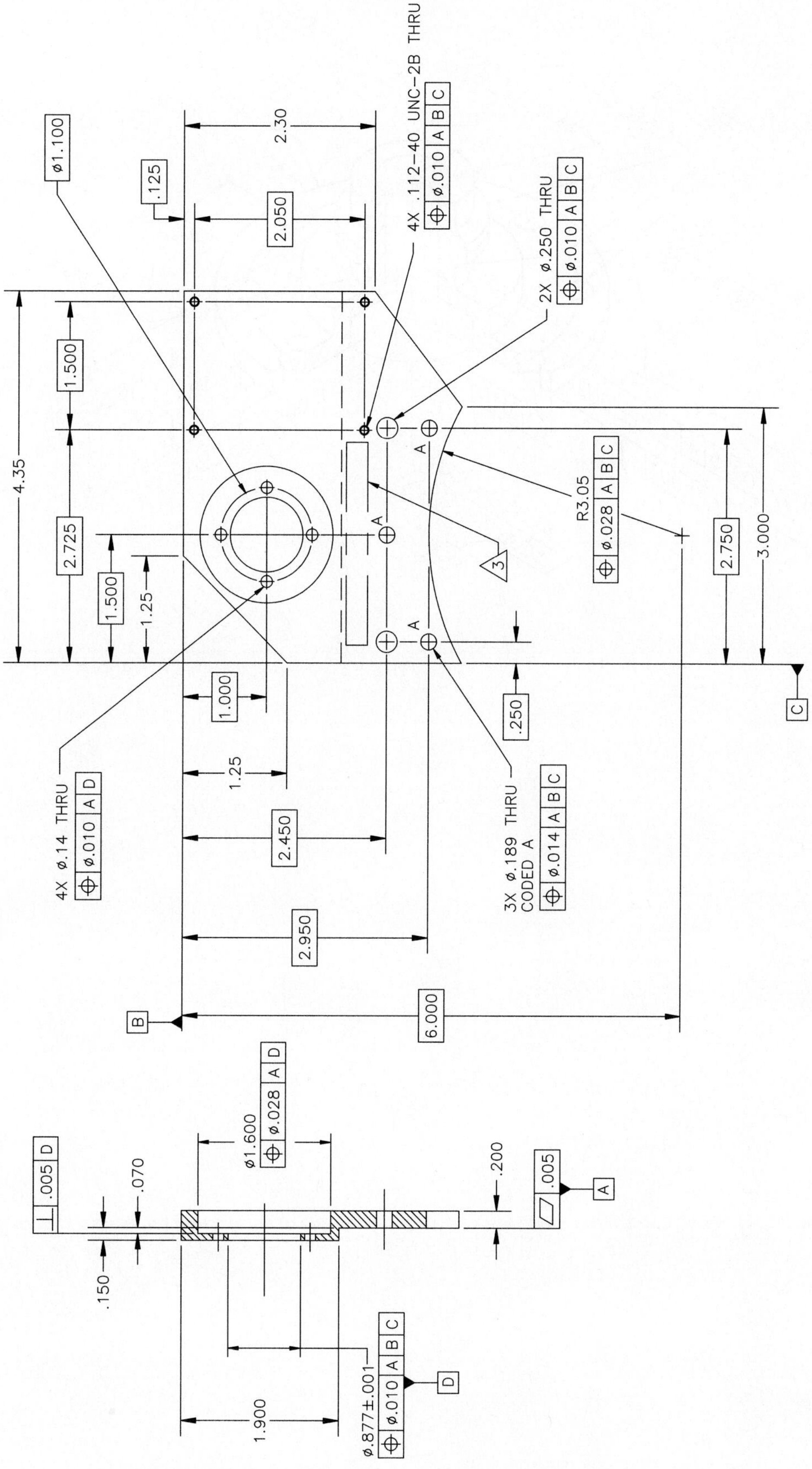

7. Draw the following object as previously instructed. The problem is shown with a half section for clarity. You do not need to draw a section. Untoleranced dimensions are ±.010. Save the drawing as P20-7.

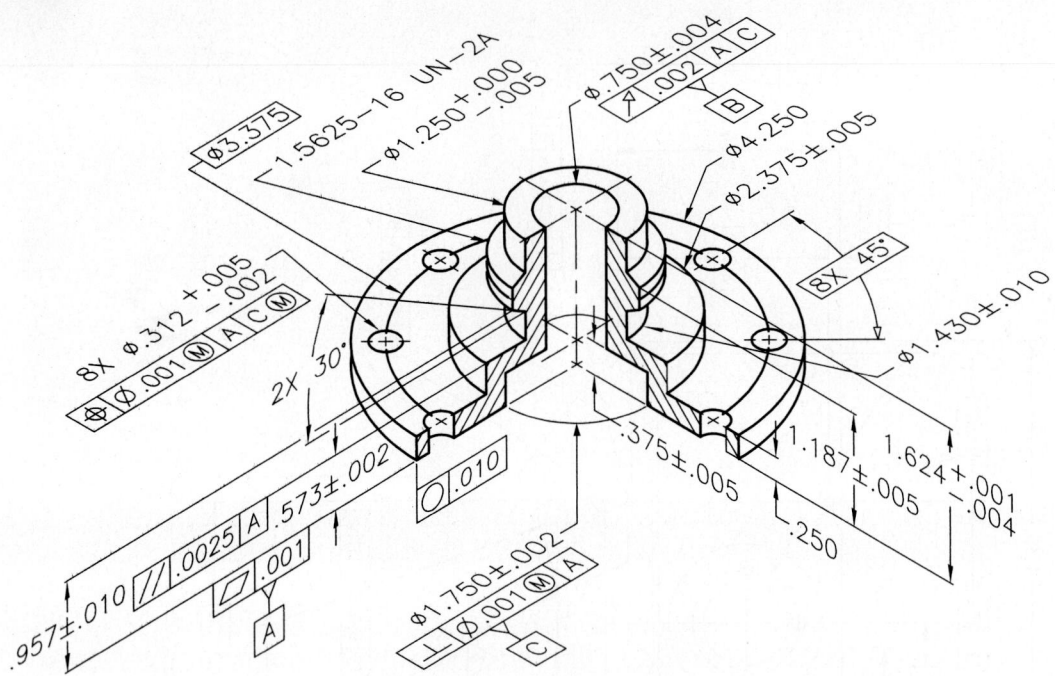

## Learning Objectives

After completing this chapter, you will be able to do the following:
- Identify sectioning techniques.
- Use sections and dimensioning practices to draw objects given in engineering sketches.
- Draw section material using the **BHATCH** and **SOLID** commands.
- Insert hatch patterns into drawings using **DesignCenter** and the **Tool Palettes**.
- Edit existing hatch patterns with the **HATCHEDIT** command.

In mechanical drafting, internal features in drawings appear as hidden lines. It is poor practice to dimension to hidden lines, but these features must be dimensioned. Therefore, section views are used to clarify the hidden features.

Section views show internal features as if a portion of the object is cut away. They are used in conjunction with multiview drawings to completely describe the exterior and interior features of an object.

When sections are drawn, a *cutting-plane line* is placed in one of the views to show where the cut was made. The cutting-plane line is the *saw* that cuts through the object to expose internal features. It is drawn with a thick dashed or phantom line in accordance with ASME Y14.2M, *Line Conventions and Lettering*. The arrows on the cutting-plane line indicate the line of sight when looking at the section view.

The cutting-plane lines are often labeled with letters that relate to the proper section view. A title, such as SECTION A-A, is placed under the view. When more than one section view is drawn, labels continue with B-B through Z-Z. The letters *I*, *O*, and *Q* are not used because they may be confused with numbers.

Labeling multiple section views is necessary for drawings with multiple sections. When only one section view is present and its location is obvious, a label is not needed. Section lines are used in the section view to show where the material has been cut away. See **Figure 21-1**.

Sectioning is also used in other drafting fields, such as architectural and structural drafting. Cross sections through buildings show the construction methods and materials. See **Figure 21-2**. The cutting-plane lines used in these fields are often composed of letter and number symbols. This helps coordinate the large number of sections found in a set of architectural drawings.

**Figure 21-1.**
A three-view
multiview drawing
with a full section
view.

Direction
of sight

Cutting-plane label

Cutting-
plane line

A ⌐                    ⌐ A

Regular
Multiviews

Section
lines

SECTION A—A

Section-view label

**Section View**

**Figure 21-2.**
An architectural
sectional view.
(Alan Mascord,
Design Associates)

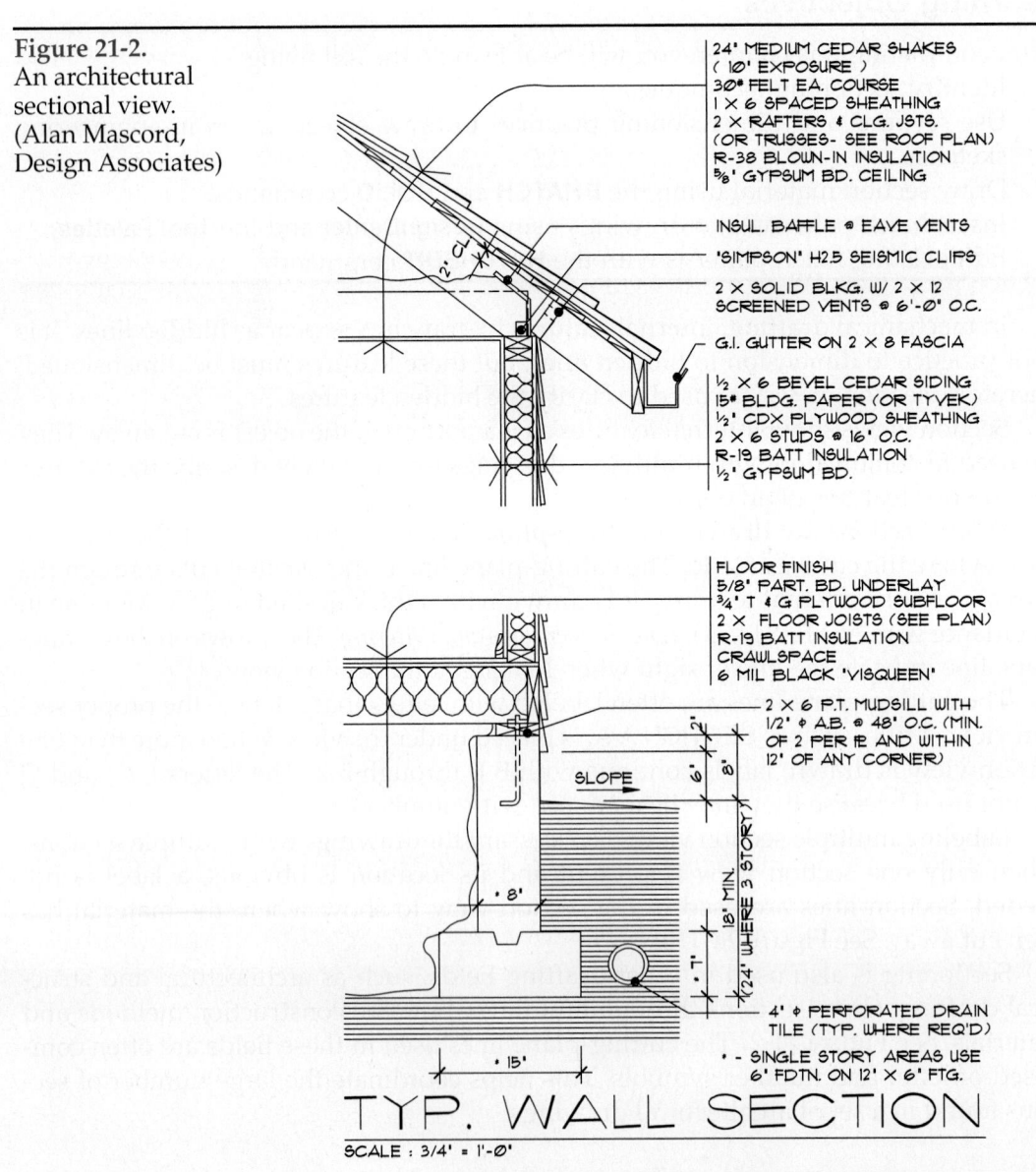

24' MEDIUM CEDAR SHAKES
( 10' EXPOSURE )
30# FELT EA. COURSE
1 × 6 SPACED SHEATHING
2 × RAFTERS & CLG. JSTS.
(OR TRUSSES- SEE ROOF PLAN)
R-38 BLOWN-IN INSULATION
5/8' GYPSUM BD. CEILING

INSUL. BAFFLE @ EAVE VENTS

'SIMPSON' H2.5 SEISMIC CLIPS

2 × SOLID BLKG. W/ 2 × 12
SCREENED VENTS @ 6'-0" O.C.

G.I. GUTTER ON 2 × 8 FASCIA

1/2 × 6 BEVEL CEDAR SIDING
15# BLDG. PAPER (OR TYVEK)
1/2' CDX PLYWOOD SHEATHING
2 × 6 STUDS @ 16' O.C.
R-19 BATT INSULATION
1/2' GYPSUM BD.

FLOOR FINISH
5/8' PART. BD. UNDERLAY
3/4' T & G PLYWOOD SUBFLOOR
2 × FLOOR JOISTS (SEE PLAN)
R-19 BATT INSULATION
CRAWLSPACE
6 MIL BLACK 'VISQUEEN'

2 × 6 P.T. MUDSILL WITH
1/2' ø A.B. @ 48' O.C. (MIN.
OF 2 PER ft. AND WITHIN
12' OF ANY CORNER)

SLOPE

4' ø PERFORATED DRAIN
TILE (TYP. WHERE REQ'D)

* - SINGLE STORY AREAS USE
6' FDTN. ON 12' × 6' FTG.

TYP. WALL SECTION

SCALE : 3/4' = 1'-0'

There are many types of sections available for the drafter to use. The section used depends on the detail to be sectioned. For example, one object may require the section be taken completely through the object. Another may only need to remove a small portion to expose the interior features.

*Full sections* remove half the object. See **Figure 21-1.** In this type of section, the cutting-plane line passes completely through the object along a center plane.

*Offset sections* are the same as full sections, except the cutting-plane line is staggered. This allows you to cut through features that are not in a straight line. See **Figure 21-3.**

*Half sections* show one-quarter of the object removed. The term *half* is used because half of the view appears in section and the other half is shown as an exterior view. Half sections are commonly used on symmetrical objects. A centerline is used to separate the sectioned part of the view from the unsectioned portion. Hidden lines are normally omitted from the unsectioned side. See **Figure 21-4.**

*Aligned sections* are used when a feature is out of alignment with the center plane. In this case, an offset section will distort the image. The cutting-plane line cuts through the feature to be sectioned. It is then rotated to align with the center plane before projecting into the section view. See **Figure 21-5.**

*Revolved sections* clarify the contour of objects that have the same shape throughout their length. The section is revolved in place within the object, or part of the view may be broken away. See **Figure 21-6.** This section makes dimensioning easier.

*Removed sections* serve much the same function as revolved sections. The section view is removed from the regular view. A cutting-plane line shows where the section was taken. When multiple removed sections are taken, the cutting planes and related views are labeled. Drawing only the ends of the cutting-plane lines simplifies the views. See **Figure 21-7.**

*Broken-out sections* show only a small portion of the object removed. This section is used to clarify a hidden feature. See **Figure 21-8.**

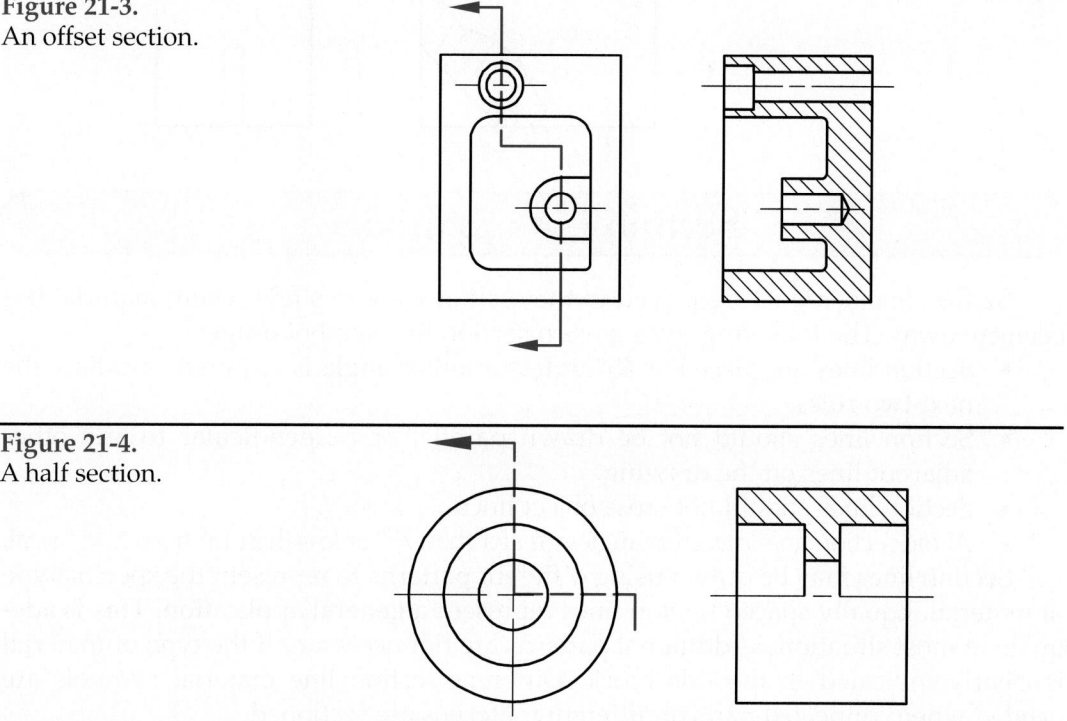

**Figure 21-3.**
An offset section.

**Figure 21-4.**
A half section.

**Figure 21-5.**
An aligned section.

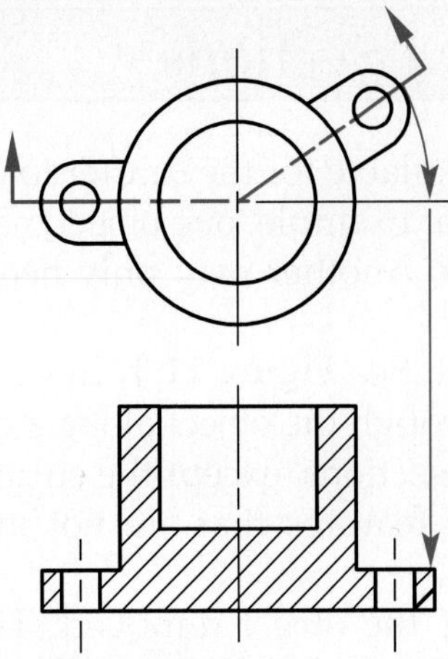

Rotate to
center plane

Project to
section view

**Figure 21-6.**
A revolved section.

**Figure 21-7.**
Removed sections.

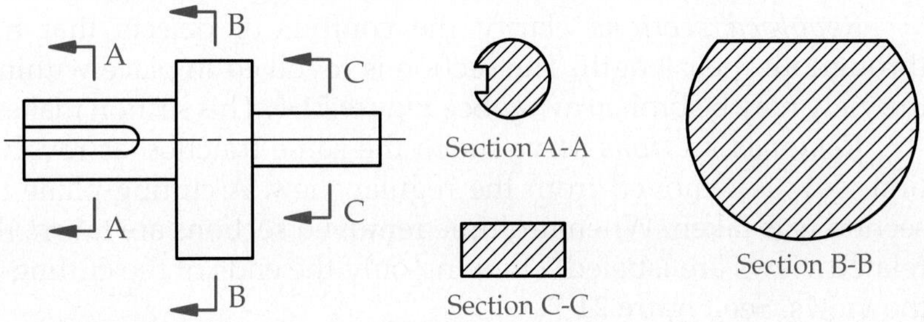

B

A

C

Section A-A

A

C

Section B-B

B

Section C-C

**Figure 21-8.**
A broken-out
section.

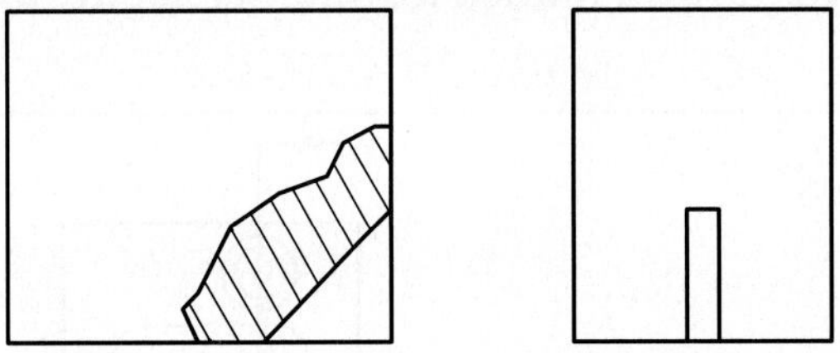

## Section Line Symbols

Section line symbols are placed in the section view to show where material has been cut away. The following rules govern section line symbol usage:
- Section lines are placed at 45° unless another angle is required to satisfy the next two rules.
- Section lines should not be drawn parallel or perpendicular to any other adjacent lines on the drawing.
- Section lines should not cross object lines.
- Avoid section lines placed at angles greater than 75° or less than 15° from horizontal.

Section lines may be drawn using different patterns to represent the specific type of material. Equally spaced section lines represent a general application. This is adequate in most situations. Additional patterns are not necessary if the type of material is clearly indicated in the title block. Different section line material symbols are needed when connected parts of different materials are sectioned.

AutoCAD has standard section line symbols available. These are referred to as *hatch patterns*. These symbols are located in the acad.pat file. The AutoCAD pattern labeled ANSI31 is the general section line symbol and is the default pattern in a new drawing. It is also used when representing cast iron in a section. When you change to a different hatch pattern, the new pattern becomes the default in the current drawing until it is changed.

The ANSI32 symbol is used for sectioning steel. Other standard AutoCAD hatch patterns are shown in **Figure 21-9**.

**Figure 21-9.**
Standard AutoCAD hatch patterns. (Autodesk, Inc.)

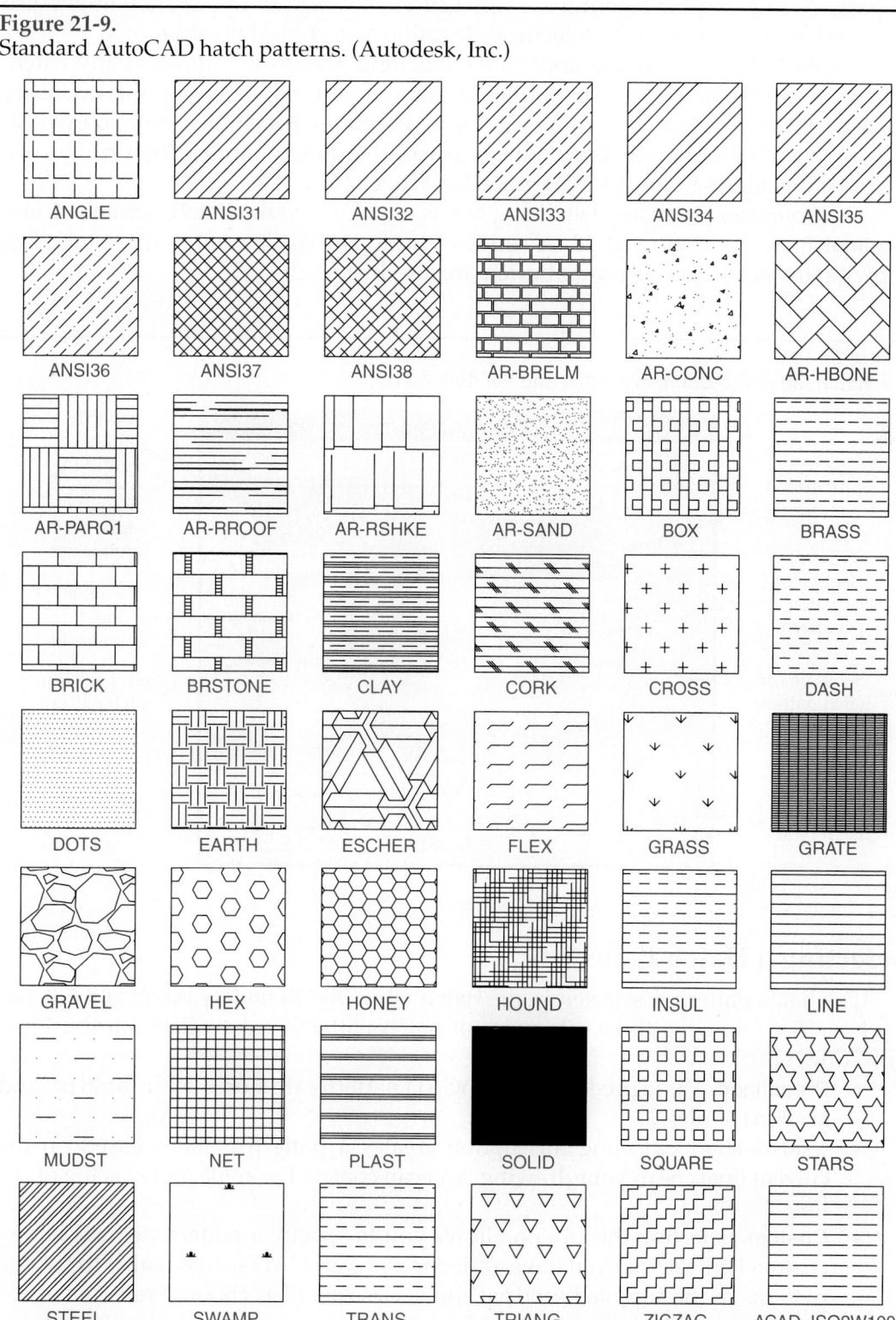

When very thin objects are sectioned, the material may be completely blackened or filled in. AutoCAD refers to this as *solid*. The ASME Y14.2M standard recommends that very thin sections be drawn without section lines or solid fill.

## Drawing Section Lines and Hatch Patterns

AutoCAD hatch patterns are not limited to sectioning. They can be used as artistic patterns in a graphic layout for an advertisement or promotion. They might also be added as shading on an architectural elevation or technical illustration.

The **BHATCH** command simplifies the hatching process by automatically hatching any enclosed area. Hatch patterns are selected and applied using the **Boundary Hatch and Fill** dialog box. Access this dialog box with the **BHATCH** command by picking the **Hatch** button on the **Draw** toolbar, by picking **Hatch...** in the **Draw** pull-down menu, or by entering H or BHATCH at the Command: prompt.

The **Boundary Hatch and Fill** dialog box is divided into the **Hatch**, **Advanced**, and **Gradient** tabs. See **Figure 21-10.** A series of buttons that determine the method of applying the hatch and a **Preview** button are also included.

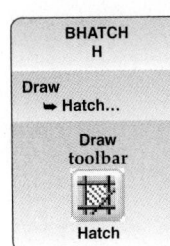

BHATCH
H

Draw
→ Hatch...

Draw
toolbar

Hatch

---

**Figure 21-10.**
The **Hatch** tab of the **Boundary Hatch and Fill** dialog box.

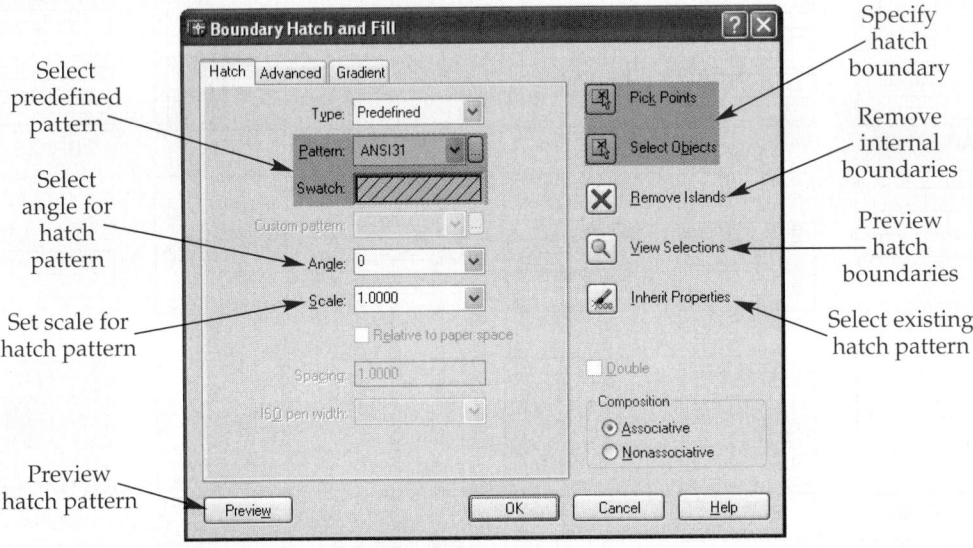

### Selecting a Hatch Pattern

The hatch pattern is selected in the **Hatch** tab of the **Boundary Hatch and Fill** dialog box. The following three categories of hatch patterns are available in the **Type:** drop-down list:

- **Predefined.** These predefined AutoCAD patterns are stored in the acad.pat and acadiso.pat files.
- **User defined.** Selecting this option creates a pattern of lines based on the current linetype in your drawing. You can control the angle and spacing of the lines.
- **Custom.** Selecting this option allows you to specify a pattern defined in any custom PAT file that you have added to the AutoCAD search path. (To use the patterns in the supplied acad.pat and acadiso.pat files, choose Predefined.)

## Predefined hatch patterns

AutoCAD has many predefined hatch patterns. These patterns are contained in the acad.pat and acadiso.pat files. To select a predefined hatch pattern, select Predefined in the **Type:** drop-down list and then select the predefined pattern. You can select the pattern from the **Pattern:** drop-down list, or you can pick the ellipsis (**...**) button next to the **Pattern:** drop-down arrow to display the **Hatch Pattern Palette** dialog box. See **Figure 21-11.**

The **Hatch Pattern Palette** dialog box provides sample images of the predefined hatch patterns. The hatch patterns are divided among the four tabs: **ANSI**, **ISO**, **Other Predefined**, and **Custom**. Select the desired pattern from the appropriate tab, and pick the **OK** button to return to the **Boundary Hatch and Fill** dialog box. The selected pattern is displayed in the **Swatch:** tile and listed in the **Pattern:** text box. You can also access the **Hatch Pattern Palette** dialog box by picking the image displayed in the **Swatch:** tile.

You can control the angle and scale of any predefined pattern using the **Angle:** and **Scale:** drop-down lists. For predefined ISO patterns, you can also control the ISO pen width using the **ISO pen width:** drop-down list.

An object can be hatched solid by selecting the Solid predefined pattern or selecting an option from the **Gradient** tab. This is discussed later in this chapter.

## User defined hatch patterns

A user defined hatch pattern is a pattern of lines drawn using the current linetype. The angle for the pattern relative to the X axis is set in the **Angle:** text box, and the spacing between the lines is set in the **Spacing:** text box.

You can also specify double hatch lines by selecting the **Double** check box on the right side of the **Boundary Hatch and Fill** dialog box. This check box is only available when User defined is selected in the **Type:** drop-down list. **Figure 21-12** shows examples of user defined hatch patterns.

AutoCAD stores the selected angle in the **HPANG** system variable and the spacing in the **HPSPACE** system variable. AutoCAD stores the setting of the **Double** check box in the **HPDOUBLE** system variable.

**Figure 21-11.**
The **Hatch Pattern Palette** dialog box can be used to select a predefined or custom hatch pattern.

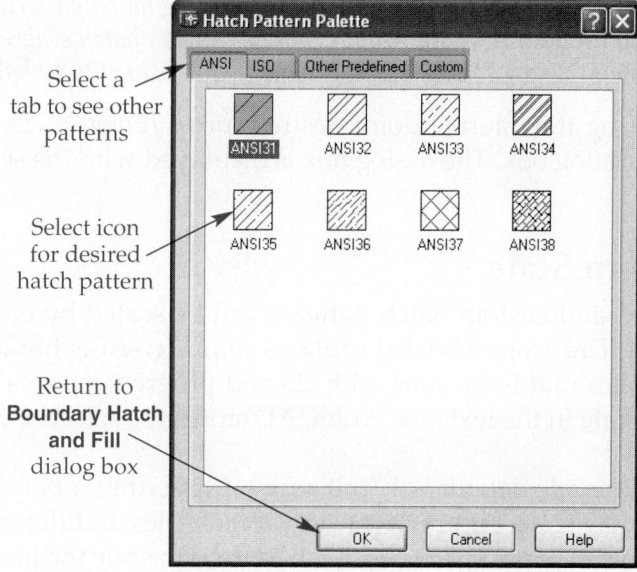

Select a tab to see other patterns

Select icon for desired hatch pattern

Return to **Boundary Hatch and Fill** dialog box

Figure 21-12.
Examples of different hatch angles and spacing.

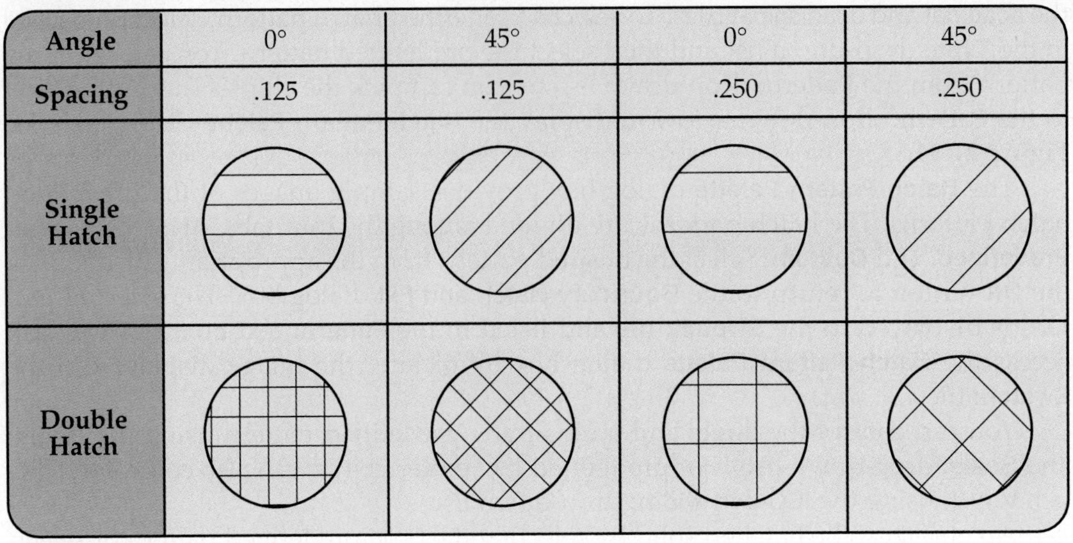

| Angle | 0° | 45° | 0° | 45° |
|---|---|---|---|---|
| Spacing | .125 | .125 | .250 | .250 |
| Single Hatch | | | | |
| Double Hatch | | | | |

## Custom hatch patterns

You can create custom hatch patterns and save them in PAT files. When you select **Custom** in the **Type:** drop-down list, the **Custom pattern:** drop-down list is enabled. You can select a custom pattern from this drop-down list, or pick the ellipsis (**...**) button to select the pattern from the **Custom** tab of the **Hatch Pattern Palette** dialog box. You can set the angle and scale of custom hatch patterns, just as you can with predefined hatch patterns.

### Selecting an existing pattern

You can specify the hatch pattern by selecting an identical hatch pattern from the drawing. Picking the **Inherit Properties** button allows you to select a previously drawn hatch pattern and use it for the current hatch pattern settings. The prompts look like this:

> Select associative hatch object: *(pick the desired hatch pattern)*
> Inherited Properties: Name *<hatch name>*, Scale *<hatch scale>*, Angle *<hatch angle>*
> Select internal point: *(pick a point inside the new area to be hatched)*

After picking the internal point desired, press [Enter] to return to the **Boundary Hatch and Fill** dialog box. The dialog box is displayed with the settings of the selected pattern.

## Hatch Pattern Scale

Predefined and custom hatch patterns can be scaled by entering a value in the **Scale:** text box. The drop-down list contains common scales broken down in .25 increments. The scales in this list start with .25 and progress to a scale of 2, although you can type any scale in the text box. AutoCAD stores the selected scale in the **HPSCALE** system variable.

The pattern scale default is 1 (full scale). If the drawn pattern is too tight or too wide, enter a new scale. **Figure 21-13** shows examples of different scales.

The **Relative to paper space** check box is used to scale the hatch pattern relative to paper space units. Use this option to easily display hatch patterns at a scale appropriate for your layout.

Figure 21-13.
Hatch pattern scale
factors.

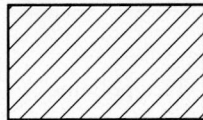
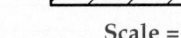
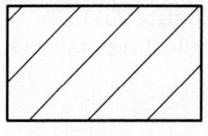

Scale = 1          Scale = 2          Scale = 3

**PROFESSIONAL TIP**

When you start AutoCAD with a wizard, the hatch pattern scale factor is automatically set based on the information you provide. The adjusted settings are related to the full scale of the objects you draw. You can leave the settings as established by AutoCAD or you can change them. If you are using a template or starting AutoCAD from scratch, you can set the hatch pattern scale factor to match the drawing size.

Enter a larger scale factor when hatching large areas. This makes your section lines look neater and saves regeneration and plot time. For metric drawings, set the hatch scale to 25.4, because 1″ = 25.4 mm.

## Selecting Areas to Be Hatched

Areas to be hatched can be selected by one of two methods: picking points or selecting objects. Both of these selection methods are accessed by picking a button in the **Boundary Hatch and Fill** dialog box.

Using the **Pick Points** button is the easiest method of defining an area to be hatched. When you pick the button, the drawing returns. Pick a point within the region to be hatched, and AutoCAD automatically defines the boundary around the selected point.

More than one internal point can be selected. When you are finished selecting points, press [Enter] and the **Boundary Hatch and Fill** dialog box returns. Then pick the **OK** button, and the feature is automatically hatched. See **Figure 21-14**.

Figure 21-14.
Defining the hatch
boundary by
picking a point.

Move the screen cursor
and pick a point inside the
area to be hatched

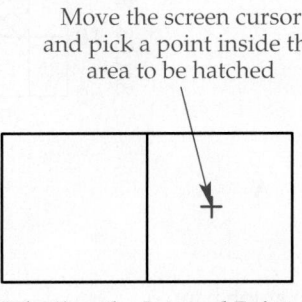
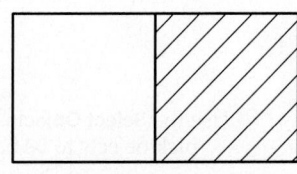

Selecting the Internal Point                    The Results

**NOTE**

When you are at the Select internal point: prompt, you can enter U or UNDO to undo the last selection, in case you picked the wrong area. You can also undo the hatch pattern by entering U at the Command: prompt after the pattern is drawn. However, you can preview the hatch before applying it to save time.

Figure 21-15.
Selecting objects to be hatched.

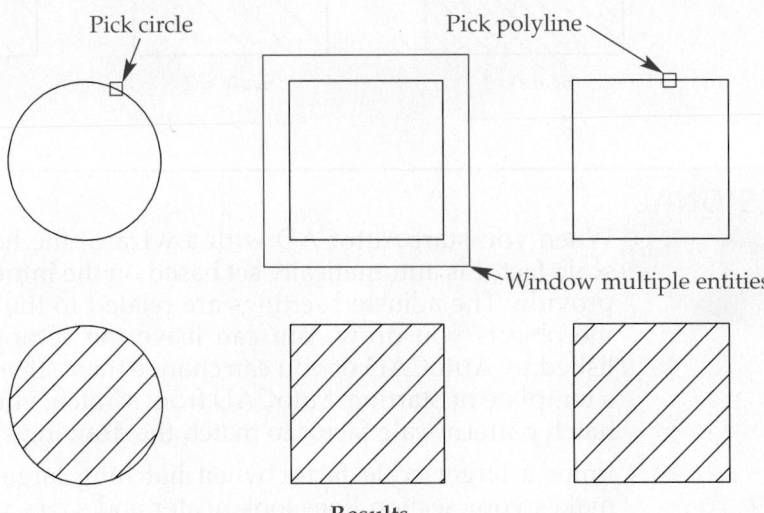

The **Select Objects** button is used to define the hatch boundary if you have items that you want to hatch by picking the object, rather than picking inside the object. See **Figure 21-15**. These items can be circles, polygons, or closed polylines. This method works especially well if the object to be hatched is crossed by other objects, such as the graph lines that cross the bars in **Figure 21-16**. Picking a point inside the bar results in the hatch displayed in **Figure 21-16A**. You can pick inside each individual

Figure 21-16.
A—Applying a hatch pattern to objects that cross each other using the **Pick Points** button.
B—Applying a hatch pattern to a closed polygon using the **Select Objects** button.

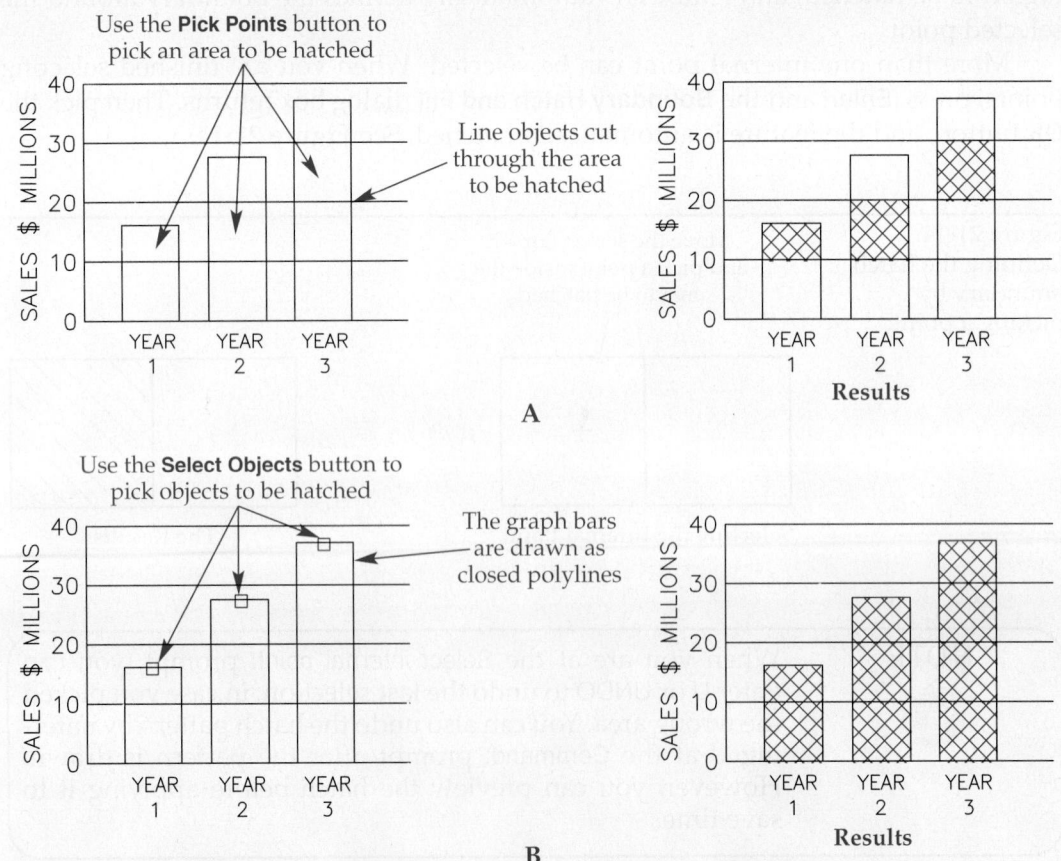

area of each bar, but this can be time-consuming. If the bars were drawn using a closed polyline, all you have to do is use the **Select Objects** button to pick each bar. See **Figure 21-16B**.

The **Select Objects** button can also be used to pick an object inside an area to be hatched to exclude it from the hatch pattern. An example of this is the text shown inside the hatch area of **Figure 21-17**.

**Figure 21-17.**
Using the **Select Objects** button to exclude an object from the hatch pattern.

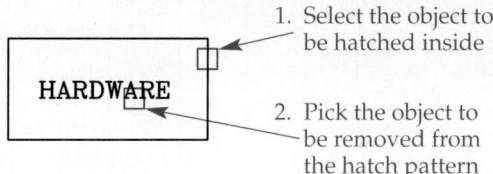

1. Select the object to be hatched inside

2. Pick the object to be removed from the hatch pattern

Results

## Islands

Boundaries inside another boundary are known as *islands*. AutoCAD can then either ignore these internal boundary objects and hatch through them or consider them as islands and hatch around them. See **Figure 21-18**.

When you use the **Pick Points** button to hatch an internal area, islands are left unhatched by default, as shown in **Figure 21-18B**. However, if you want islands to be hatched, pick the **Remove Islands** button in the **Boundary Hatch and Fill** dialog box after selecting the internal point. The drawing window returns with the following prompts:

> Select island to remove: (*pick the islands to remove*)
> <Select island to remove>/Undo: ↵

Select the islands to remove and press [Enter] to return to the dialog box. The island objects are now hatched. See **Figure 21-18C**.

The **Advanced** tab of the **Boundary Hatch and Fill** dialog box allows you to set the island detection style and the island detection method. See **Figure 21-19**.

The **Island detection style** area is used to specify the method for hatching islands. If no islands exist, specifying an island detection style has no effect. There are three options that allow you to choose the features to be hatched. These options are illustrated by the image tiles in the dialog box. The three style options are:

- **Normal.** This option hatches inward from the outer boundary. If AutoCAD encounters an island, it turns off hatching until it encounters another island.

**Figure 21-18.**
A—Original objects.
B—Using the **Pick Points** button to hatch an internal area leaves islands unhatched.
C—After picking an internal point, use the **Remove Islands** button and pick the islands. This allows the islands to be hatched.

Pick an internal point

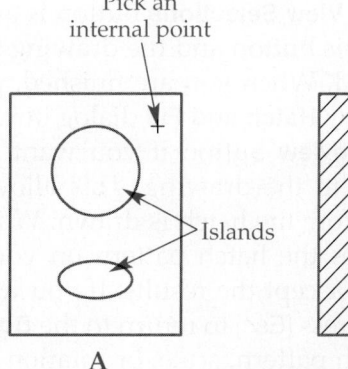

Islands

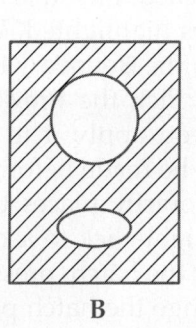

A                B                C

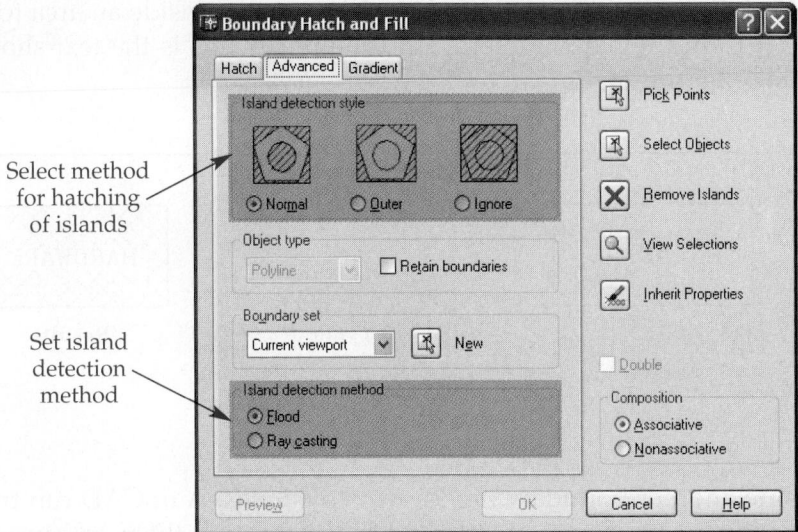

Select method
for hatching
of islands

Set island
detection
method

Then the hatching is reactivated. Every other closed boundary is hatched with this option.

- **Outer.** This option hatches inward from the outer boundary. AutoCAD turns hatching off when it encounters an island and does not turn it back on. AutoCAD hatches only the outermost level of the structure and leaves the internal structure blank.
- **Ignore.** This option ignores all islands and hatches everything within the selected boundary.

The **Island detection method** area has two options: **Flood** and **Ray casting**. These options determine whether internal boundaries are defined as islands when hatching. The **Flood** option is selected by default. This setting allows you to leave internal objects unhatched. Pick the **Ray casting** option if you want to ignore island boundaries and hatch through the islands.

## Previewing the Hatch

Before applying a hatch pattern to the selected area, you can use preview tools to be sure the hatch pattern and hatch boundary settings are correct. The following buttons, which are found in the **Boundary Hatch and Fill** dialog box, can be used to preview the boundary and hatch pattern:

- **View Selections button.** You can instruct AutoCAD to let you see the boundaries of selected objects. The **View Selections** button is available after picking objects to be hatched. Pick this button and the drawing is displayed with the hatch boundaries highlighted. When you are finished, press [Enter] or right-click to return to the **Boundary Hatch and Fill** dialog box.
- **Preview button.** Pick the **Preview** button if you want to look at the hatch pattern before you apply it to the drawing. This allows you to see if any changes need to be made before the hatch is drawn. When using this option, AutoCAD temporarily places the hatch pattern on your drawing. You can press [Enter] or right-click to accept the results. If you want to make changes after previewing the hatch, press [Esc] to return to the **Boundary Hatch and Fill** dialog box. Change the hatch pattern, scale, or rotation angle as needed and preview the hatch again. When you are satisfied with the preview of the hatch, pick the **OK** button in the **Boundary Hatch and Fill** dialog box to have it applied to the drawing.

# Hatch Pattern Composition

The **BHATCH** command creates associative hatch patterns by default, but can be set to create nonassociative patterns. *Associative hatch patterns* update automatically when the boundary is edited. If the boundary is stretched, scaled, or otherwise edited, the hatch pattern automatically fills the new area with the original hatch pattern. Associative hatch patterns can be edited using the **HATCHEDIT** command, which is discussed later in this chapter.

The **Composition** area of the **Boundary Hatch and Fill** dialog box has **Associative** and **Nonassociative** options. The **Associative** option is on by default. When selected, the **Nonassociative** option creates a nonassociative hatch that is independent of its boundaries. This means that if you pick only the hatch boundary to edit, the hatch pattern does not change with it. For example, if you pick a hatch boundary to scale, only the boundary is scaled while the pattern remains the same. You need to select both the boundary and the pattern before editing if you want to modify both.

## Exercise 21-1

○ Start AutoCAD and use one of your templates with a Hatch layer.

○ Open the **Boundary Hatch and Fill** dialog box. Pick the ellipsis (**...**) button next to **Pattern:** to view the pattern lists and images. Select several different images to see what happens.

○ Use the **LINE** command to draw an object similar to the one shown here. The exact dimensions are up to you. Be sure each area of the object is closed.

○ Use the **BHATCH** command to make a full section of the object, as shown in the right object. Use the ANSI31 hatch pattern.

○ Draw the bar graph shown in **Figure 21-16** without text. Use a closed polyline to draw the graph bars. Use the **Select Objects** option to select the bars for hatching.

○ Draw the HARDWARE box shown in **Figure 21-17**. Hatch the area inside the box without hatching the text.

○ Use closed polylines to draw the object in **Figure 21-18A**. Copy the object to a position directly below the original. Use the **Pick Points** option to hatch the object as shown in **Figure 21-18B**. Use the **Pick Points** button and the **Remove Islands** button to hatch the object as shown in **Figure 21-18C**.

○ Preview each hatch pattern before you apply it to be sure the results are what you expect.

○ Initiate the **BHATCH** command and pick the **Inherit Properties** button. Pick a hatch pattern on your drawing that is different from the current hatch pattern settings. Notice that the name and settings of the selected pattern become current.

○ Save the drawing as EX21-1.

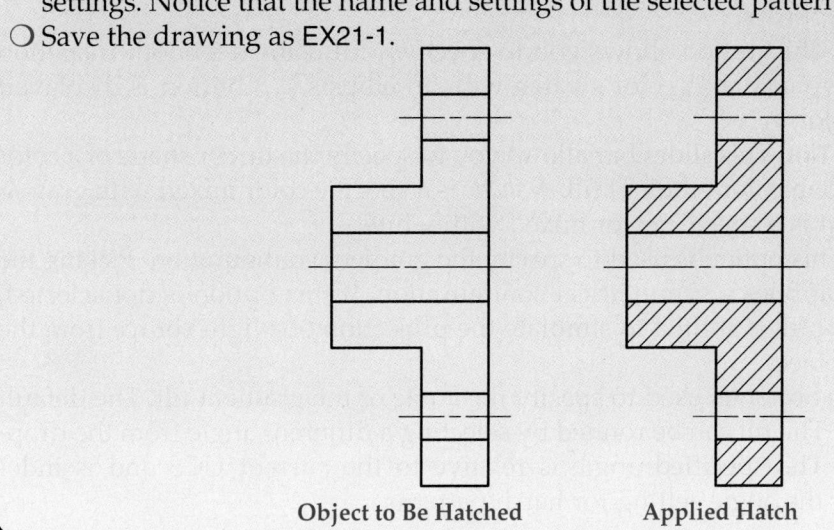

Object to Be Hatched          Applied Hatch

Figure 21-20.
Using the Solid
hatch pattern to
make a basic solid
hatch object.

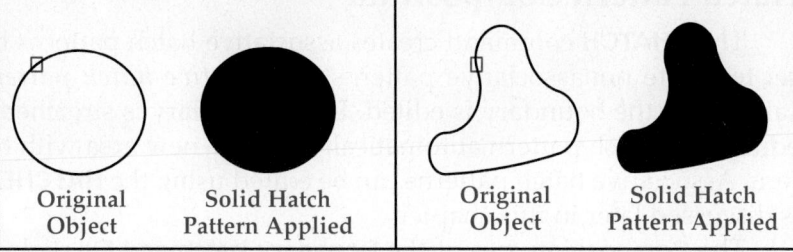

Original | Solid Hatch | Original | Solid Hatch
Object | Pattern Applied | Object | Pattern Applied

## Creating Solid Hatch Patterns

As discussed earlier in this chapter, solid hatches can be created with the **Solid** predefined hatch pattern. See **Figure 21-20.** This pattern can be accessed from the **Pattern:** drop-down list in the **Boundary Hatch and Fill** dialog box or the **Other Predefined** tab in the **Hatch Pattern Palette** dialog box. The pattern can be assigned a color. However, the hatching options used with other predefined hatches are not available. This is a quick way to fill a closed object solid. Filled objects can also be created with the **SOLID** command. This command is discussed later in this chapter.

More advanced types of fills can be applied to closed objects by using the gradient fill hatching options available with the **BHATCH** command. A *gradient fill* is a shading transition between the tones of one color or two separate colors. Gradient fills can be used to simulate color-shaded objects. There are nine different gradient fill patterns available. They are accessed in the **Gradient** tab of the **Boundary Hatch and Fill** dialog box. See **Figure 21-21.**

The fills are based on linear sweep, spherical, radial, and curved shading. They create the appearance of a lit surface with a gradual transition from an area of highlight to a filled area. When two colors are used, a transition from light to dark between the colors is simulated.

As with other types of hatch patterns, gradient fills are associative when applied by default. They can also be edited in the same way as other hatch patterns with the **HATCHEDIT** command.

The options in the **Gradient** tab of the **Boundary Hatch and Fill** dialog box include settings for one or two fill colors, gradient configuration, and fill angle. The options are as follows:

- **One Color.** This is the default option. It specifies a fill that has a smooth transition between the darker shades and lighter tints of one color. To select a color, pick the ellipsis (**...**) button next to the color swatch to access the **Select Color** dialog box. When the **One color** option is active, the **Shade** and **Tint** slider bar appears.
- **Two Color.** This option allows you to specify a fill using a smooth transition between two colors. A color swatch with an ellipsis (**...**) button is displayed for each color.
- **Shade and Tint.** This slider bar allows you to specify the tint or shade of a color used for a one-color gradient fill. A *shade* is a specific color mixed with gray or black. A *tint* is a specific color mixed with white.
- **Centered.** This option is used to specify the gradient configuration. Picking the check box applies a symmetrical configuration. If this option is not selected, the gradient fill is shifted to simulate the projection of a light source from the left of the object.
- **Angle.** This option is used to specify the angle of the gradient fill. The default angle is 0°. The fill can be rotated by selecting a different angle from the drop-down list. The specified angle is relative to the current UCS and is independent of the angle setting for hatch patterns.

**Figure 21-21.**
The **Gradient** tab of the **Boundary Hatch and Fill** dialog box contains options for creating gradient fill hatch patterns. There are nine types of gradient patterns available.

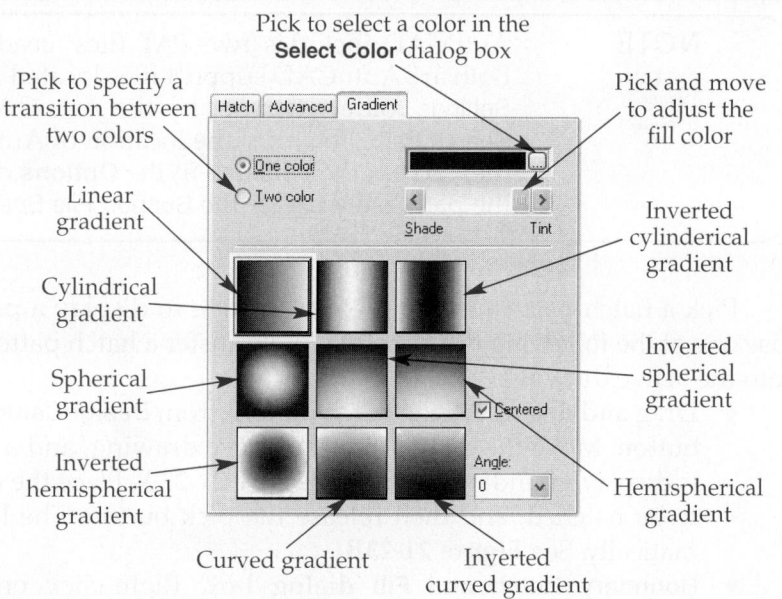

Pick to select a color in the **Select Color** dialog box

Pick to specify a transition between two colors

Pick and move to adjust the fill color

Linear gradient

Cylindrical gradient

Inverted cylinderical gradient

Spherical gradient

Inverted spherical gradient

Inverted hemispherical gradient

Hemispherical gradient

Curved gradient

Inverted curved gradient

## Using DesignCenter to Insert Hatch Patterns

Hatch patterns can be readily located and previewed before they are inserted using **DesignCenter**. To insert a hatch pattern into the current drawing, you can use a drag-and-drop operation. To access **DesignCenter**, pick the **DesignCenter** button on the **Standard** toolbar, select **DesignCenter** from the **Tools** pull-down menu, type ADC or ADCENTER at the Command: prompt, or use the [Ctrl]+[2] key combination. To drag and drop a hatch pattern from **DesignCenter**, you need to select a PAT file. Once the PAT file is selected, the hatch patterns it contains are displayed in the preview palette. See **Figure 21-22.**

**Figure 21-22.**
Pick a PAT file in **DesignCenter** to display the available hatch patterns in the preview palette.

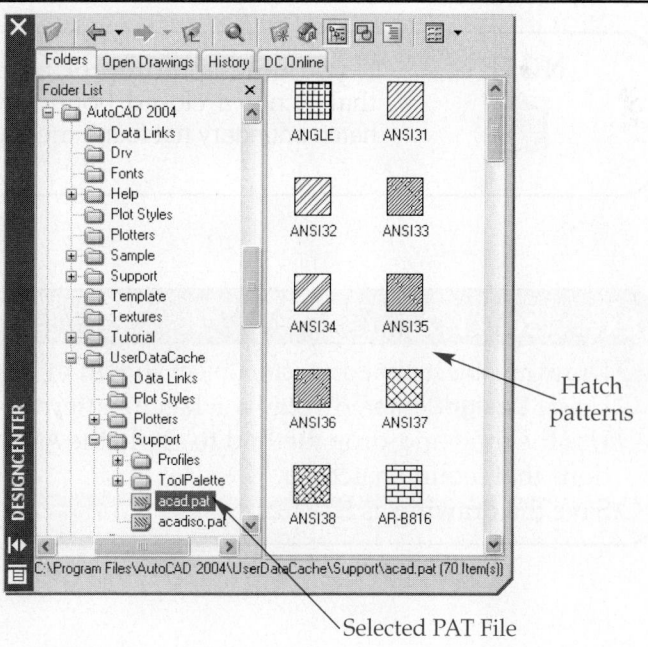

Hatch patterns

Selected PAT File

AutoCAD includes two PAT files: acad.pat and acadiso.pat. Both are AutoCAD support files located in the Documents and Settings folder path set by the AutoCAD 2004 Support File Search Path. To verify the location of AutoCAD 2004 support files, access the **Files** tab in the **Options** dialog box and check the path listed under the Support File Search Path.

Pick a hatch pattern in the preview palette to display a preview of the pattern. Use one of the following three methods to transfer a hatch pattern from **DesignCenter** into the active drawing:

- **Drag and drop.** Pick the hatch pattern from **DesignCenter** and hold the mouse button. Move the cursor into the active drawing, and a hatch pattern symbol is displayed under the cursor, **Figure 21-23A**. Place the cursor within the area to be hatched, and then release the pick button. The hatch is applied automatically. See **Figure 21-23B**.
- **Boundary Hatch and Fill dialog box.** Right-click on a hatch pattern in **DesignCenter** and select **BHATCH...** from the shortcut menu to access the **Boundary Hatch and Fill** dialog box. The selected hatch pattern is displayed automatically.
- **Copy and paste.** Hatch patterns can also be inserted using a copy and paste operation. Right-click on the hatch pattern in **DesignCenter** and pick **Copy** from the shortcut menu. Move the cursor into the active drawing, right-click, and select **Paste** from the shortcut menu. The hatch pattern symbol is displayed beneath the cursor. Pick within the area to be hatched, and the hatch pattern is automatically applied.

When hatch patterns are inserted from **DesignCenter**, the angle, scale, and island detection settings match the settings of the previous hatch pattern. If you wish to change these settings after inserting the hatch pattern, use the **HATCHEDIT** command.

NOTE

If you drag-and-drop or paste a hatch pattern into an area that is not a closed boundary, AutoCAD displays the Valid hatch boundary not found message at the Command: prompt.

## Exercise 21-2

○ Draw an object similar to the object shown in **Figure 21-23A**.
○ Using **DesignCenter**, display the hatch patterns available in the acad.pat file.
○ Use the drag-and-drop method to apply the ANSI31 hatch pattern to the four sections that require hatching.
○ Save the drawing as EX21-2.

**Figure 21-23.**
When a hatch pattern is selected in the preview palette, a preview image appears.
A—The hatch pattern symbol appears under the cursor during the drag-and-drop and
paste operations. B—The hatch pattern added to the drawing.

Selected
hatch
pattern

Preview
of hatch
pattern

Hatch
pattern
symbol
under
cursor

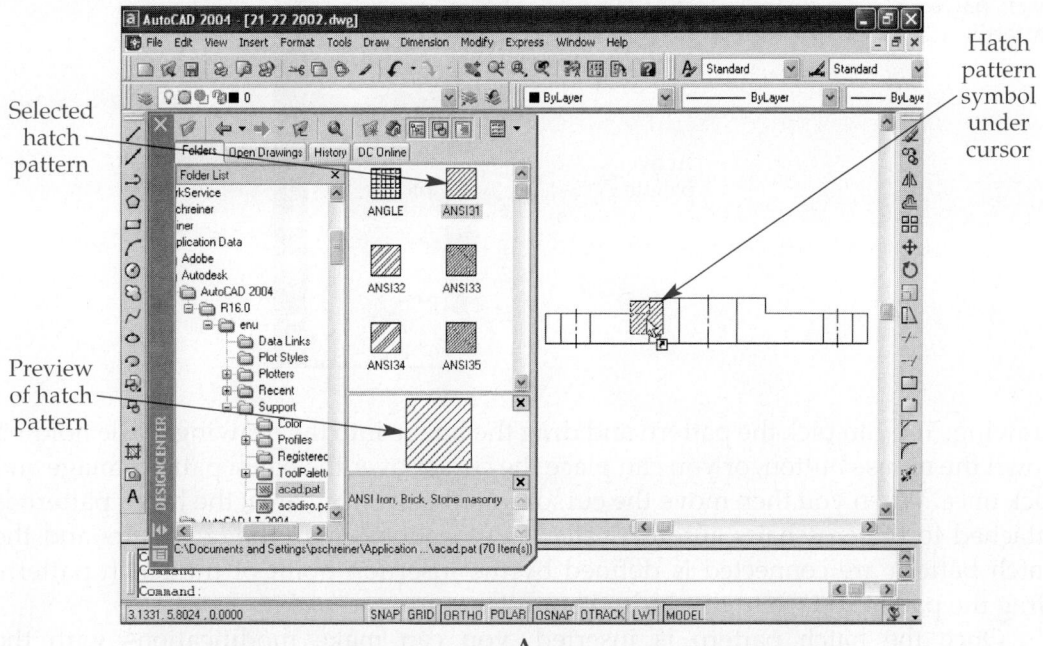

**A**

Inserted
hatch
pattern

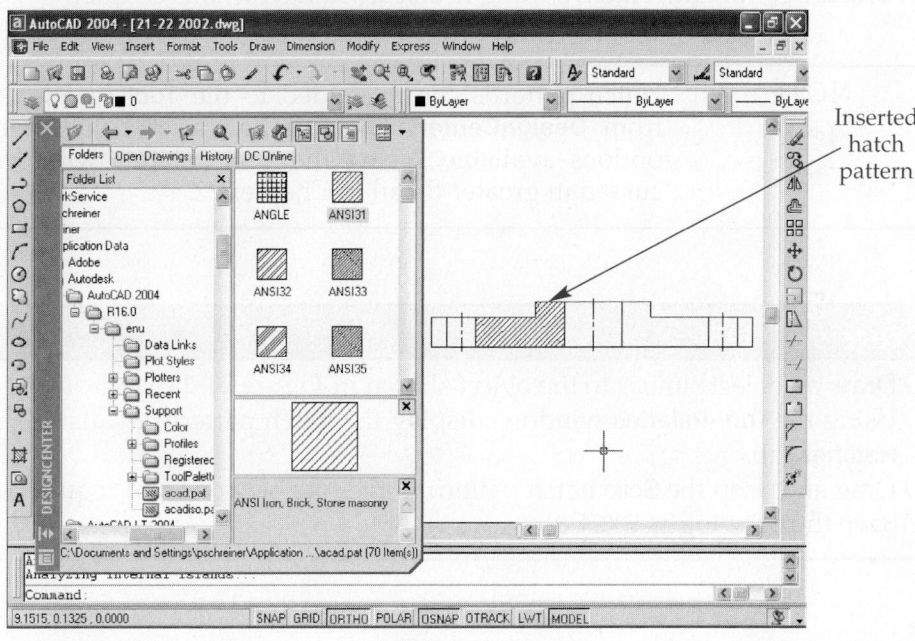

**B**

## Using Tool Palettes to Insert Hatch Patterns

Inserting hatch patterns with the **Tool Palettes** window is similar to inserting
them with **DesignCenter**. As with **DesignCenter**, a pattern can be previewed in a window before it is applied. To open the **Tool Palettes** window, pick the **Tool Palettes** button on the **Standard** toolbar, select **Tool Palettes Window** from the **Tools** pull-down
menu, enter TP or TOOLPALETTES at the Command: prompt, or use the [Ctrl]+[3] key
combination. The **Tool Palettes** window is shown in **Figure 21-24.**

To drag and drop a hatch pattern from the **Tool Palettes**, select the tab in which
the pattern resides. There are two ways to drag the pattern for insertion into the

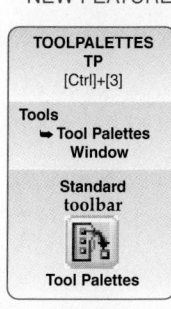

TOOLPALETTES
TP
[Ctrl]+[3]

Tools
➡ Tool Palettes
Window

Standard
toolbar

Tool Palettes

Figure 21-24.
The **Tool Palettes**
window can be
used to access and
insert hatch
patterns.

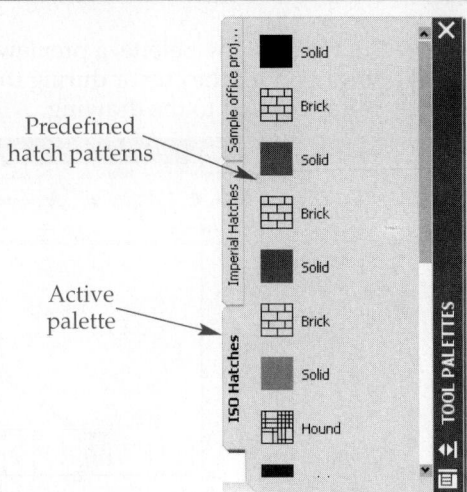

Predefined
hatch patterns

Active
palette

drawing. You can pick the pattern and drag the image into the drawing while holding down the mouse button, or you can place the cursor over the hatch pattern image and pick once. When you then move the cursor into the drawing area, the hatch pattern is attached to the crosshairs automatically. The location where the crosshairs and the hatch pattern are connected is defined by the insertion point of the hatch pattern. Drag the pattern image to the desired boundary area and pick.

Once the hatch pattern is inserted, you can make modifications with the **HATCHEDIT** command. Hatch editing is discussed later in this chapter.

NOTE

Hatch patterns can be added to the **Tool Palettes** window from **DesignCenter**. There are a variety of customization options available. Using the **Tool Palettes** window is discussed in greater detail in Chapter 22.

## Exercise 21-3

○ Draw an object similar to the object shown in **Figure 21-23A.**
○ Using the **Tool Palettes** window, display the hatch patterns available in the **ISO Hatches** tab.
○ Drag and drop the Solid hatch pattern to the four sections that require hatching.
○ Save the drawing as EX21-3.

PROFESSIONAL
TIP

Another way to insert hatch patterns is to use the **SUPERHATCH** command available with the AutoCAD Express Tools. If the Express Tools are installed, this command can be accessed from the **Draw** cascading menu in the **Express** pull-down menu or the **Express Standard** toolbar. You can also enter SUPERHATCH at the Command: prompt. Using the **SUPERHATCH** command is similar to normal hatching. However, instead of using predefined patterns, it allows you to use an image, block, external reference, or wipeout as a hatch pattern. Access the **AutoCAD Express Tools Help** window for more information about the **SUPERHATCH** command.

## Correcting Errors in the Boundary

The **BHATCH** command works well unless you have an error in the hatch boundary. The most common error is a gap in the boundary. This can be very small and difficult to detect, and happens when you do not close the geometry. However, AutoCAD is quick to let you know by displaying the **Boundary Definition Error** alert box. See **Figure 21-25**. Pick the **OK** button and then return to the drawing to find and correct the problem. **Figure 21-26** shows an object where the corner does not close. The error is too small to see on the screen, but using the **ZOOM** command reveals the problem. Fix the error and use the **BHATCH** command again.

Another error message occurs when you pick a point outside the boundary area. When this happens, you also get the **Boundary Definition Error** alert. All you have to do is pick **OK** and then select a point inside the boundary you want hatched.

---

**Figure 21-25.**
A **Boundary Definition Error** alert box is displayed if problems occur in your hatching operation.

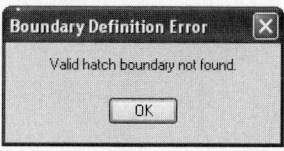

---

**Figure 21-26.**
Using the **ZOOM** command to find the source of the hatching error.

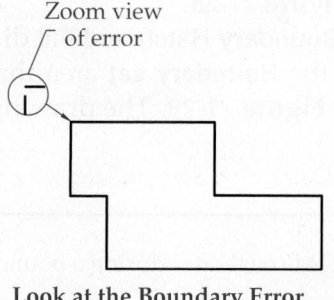

Zoom view of error

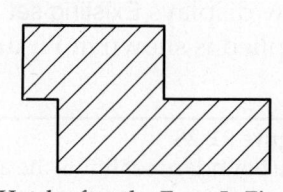

Look at the Boundary Error

Hatch after the Error Is Fixed

---

**PROFESSIONAL TIP**

When creating an associative hatch, it is best to specify only one internal point per hatch block placement. If you specify more than one internal point in the same operation, AutoCAD creates one hatch object from all points picked. This can cause unexpected results when trying to edit what appears to be a separate hatch object.

## Improving Boundary Hatching Speed

In most situations, boundary hatching works with satisfactory speed. Normally, the **BHATCH** command evaluates the entire drawing visible on screen to establish the boundary. This process can take some time on a large drawing.

You can improve the hatching speed and resolve other problems using options found in the **Advanced** tab in the **Boundary Hatch and Fill** dialog box. See **Figure 21-27**.

The drop-down list in the **Boundary set** area specifies what is evaluated when hatching. The default setting is Current viewport. If you want to limit what AutoCAD evaluates when hatching, you can define the boundary area so the **BHATCH** command

---

Figure 21-27.
The **Advanced** tab of the **Boundary Hatch and Fill** dialog box provides options to improve hatching efficiency.

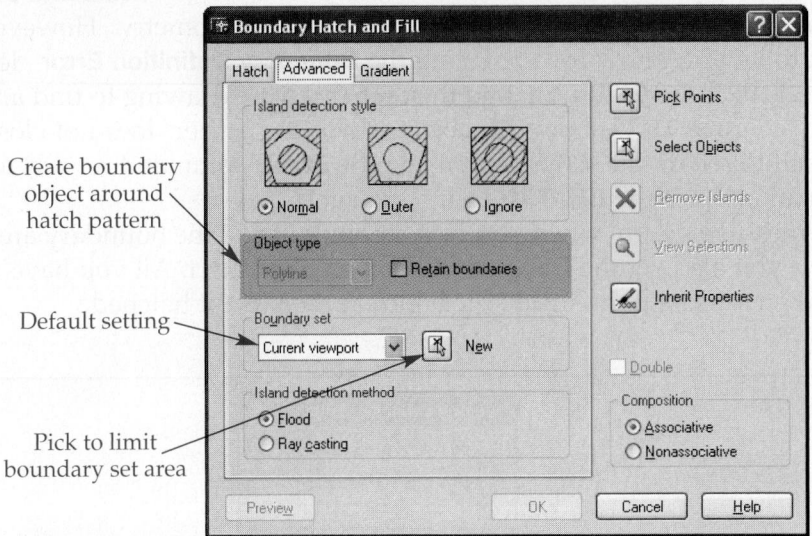

Create boundary object around hatch pattern

Default setting

Pick to limit boundary set area

only considers a specified portion of the drawing. To do this, pick the **New** button. Then at the Select objects: prompt, use a window to select the features of the object to be hatched. This is demonstrated in **Figure 21-28.**

After selecting the object(s), the **Boundary Hatch and Fill** dialog box returns, displaying the **Advanced** tab. Notice in the **Boundary set** area that the drop-down list now displays Existing set as shown in **Figure 21-29.** The drawing with hatch patterns applied is shown in **Figure 21-30.**

**Figure 21-28.**
The boundary set limits the area that AutoCAD evaluates during a boundary hatching operation.

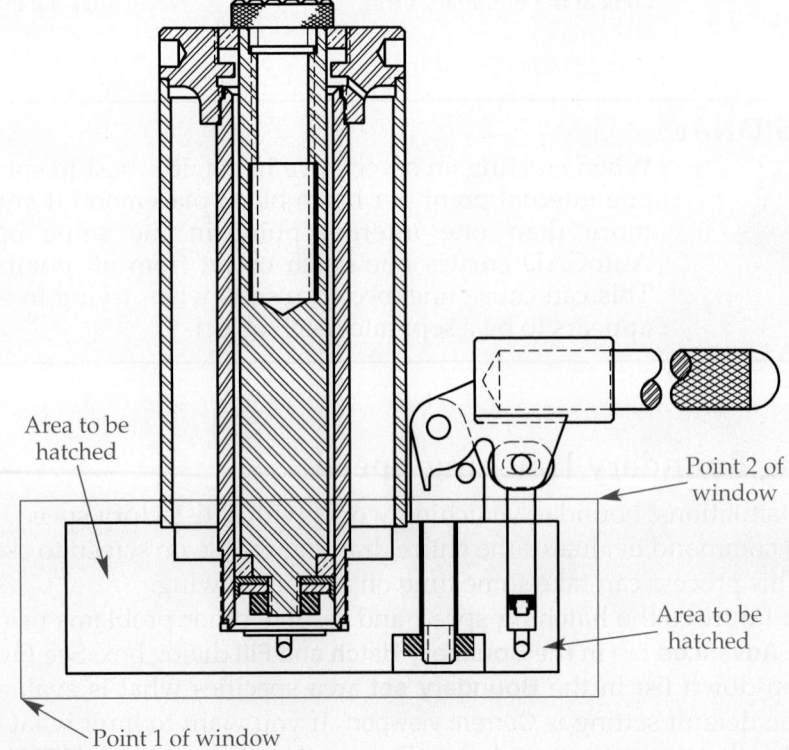

Area to be hatched

Point 2 of window

Area to be hatched

Point 1 of window

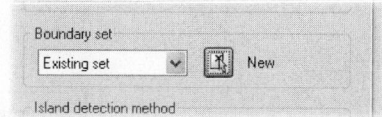

Boundary set

Existing set    New

Island detection method

**Figure 21-30.**
Results of hatching the drawing in **Figure 21-28** after selecting a boundary set.

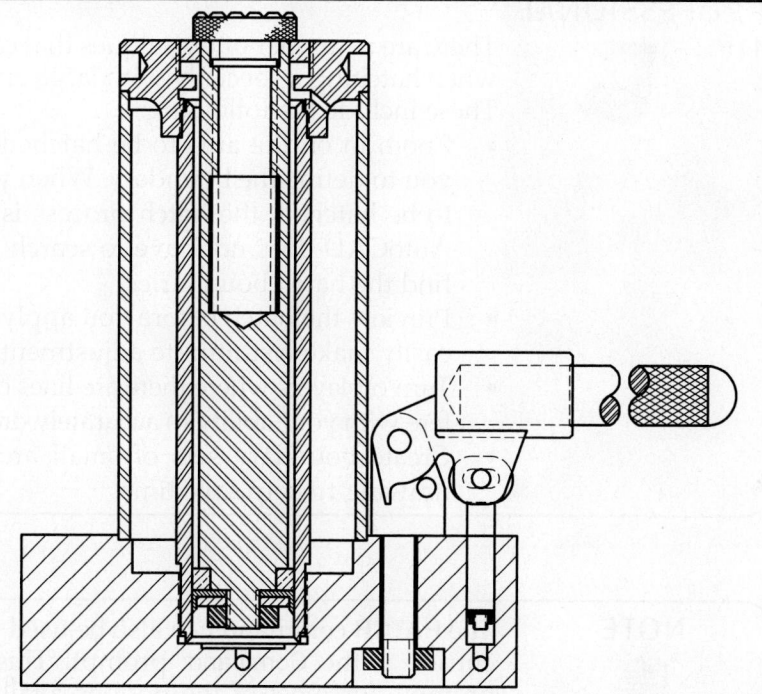

You can make as many boundary sets as you wish. However, the last one made remains current until another is created. The **Retain boundaries** check box in the **Object type** area can be selected as soon as a boundary set is made. Checking this box allows you to keep the boundary of a hatched area as a polyline, and new boundaries will continue to be saved as polylines whenever you create a boundary area. The default is no check in this box, so the hatched boundaries are not saved as polylines.

When you use the **BHATCH** command and pick an internal area to be hatched, AutoCAD automatically creates a temporary boundary around the area. If the **Retain boundaries** check box is unchecked, the temporary boundaries are automatically removed when the hatch is complete. However, if you check the **Retain boundaries** check box, the hatch boundaries are kept when the hatch is completed.

When the **Retain boundaries** check box is checked, the **Object type** drop-down list is activated. See **Figure 21-31.** Notice that the drop-down list has two options: Polyline (the default) and Region. If Polyline is selected, the boundary is a polyline object around the hatch area. If Region is selected, then the hatch boundary is the hatched region. A *region* is a closed two-dimensional area.

Figure 21-31.
There are two object
type options for
saving a boundary.
These options are
only available if the
**Retain boundaries**
option is checked.

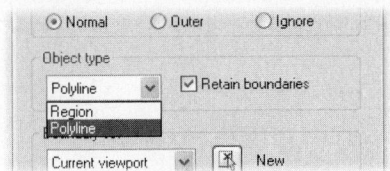

PROFESSIONAL
TIP

There are a number of techniques that can help you save time when hatching, especially with large and complex drawings. These include the following:

- Zoom in on the area to be hatched to make it easier for you to define the boundary. When you zoom into an area to be hatched, the hatch process is much faster because AutoCAD does not have to search the entire drawing to find the hatch boundaries.
- Preview the hatch before you apply it. This allows you to easily make last-minute adjustments.
- Turn off layers where there are lines or text that might interfere with your ability to accurately define hatch boundaries.
- Create boundary sets of small areas within a complex drawing to help save time.

NOTE

The **HATCH** command can also be used to hatch objects using entries at the Command: prompt. This command provides prompts for most of the options available in the **Boundary Hatch and Fill** dialog box. The **HATCH** command creates nonassociative hatch patterns, so it is recommended that you use the **Boundary Hatch and Fill** dialog box to hatch objects. For more information on the **HATCH** command, refer to the AutoCAD help system.

## Editing Hatch Patterns

You can edit hatch boundaries and hatch patterns with grips and editing commands such as **ERASE**, **COPY**, **MOVE**, **ROTATE**, and **SCALE**. If a hatch pattern is associative, whatever you do to the hatch boundary is automatically done to the associated hatch pattern. As explained earlier, a hatch pattern is associative if the **Associative** option in the **Boundary Hatch and Fill** dialog box is active.

A convenient way to edit a hatch pattern is by using the **HATCHEDIT** command. You can access this command by picking **Hatch...** from the **Object** cascading menu in the **Modify** pull-down menu, picking the **Edit Hatch** button on the **Modify II** toolbar, or entering HE or HATCHEDIT at the Command: prompt. You can also double-click on the hatch pattern you wish to edit. The command sequence is as follows:

Command: **HE** *or* **HATCHEDIT**↵
Select associative hatch object: *(pick the hatch pattern to edit)*

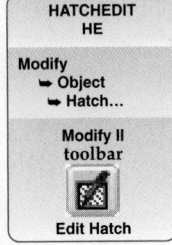

HATCHEDIT
HE

Modify
↳ Object
↳ Hatch...

Modify II
toolbar

Edit Hatch

When you select a hatch pattern or patterns to edit, the **Hatch Edit** dialog box is displayed. See **Figure 21-32**. The **Hatch Edit** dialog box has the same features as the **Boundary Hatch and Fill** dialog box, except that only the items that control hatch pattern characteristics are available.

The available features work just like they do in the **Boundary Hatch and Fill** dialog box. You can change the pattern type, scale, or angle; remove the associative qualities; set the inherit properties of an existing hatch pattern; or use the **Advanced** or **Gradient** tab options to edit the hatch pattern. You can also preview the edited hatch before applying it to your drawing.

**Figure 21-32.**
The **Hatch Edit** dialog box is used to edit hatch patterns. Notice that only the options related to hatch characteristics are available.

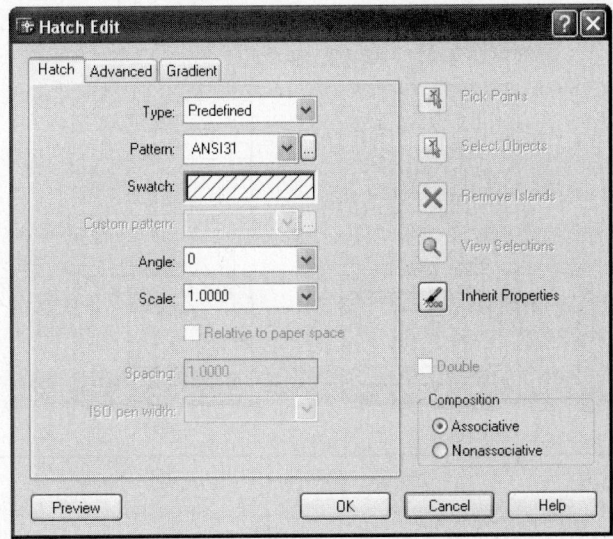

**PROFESSIONAL TIP**

The **MATCHPROP** command can also be used to inherit the properties of an existing hatch pattern and apply it to the hatch pattern you wish to edit. This command can be used to apply existing hatch patterns to objects in the current drawing file or to objects in other drawing files that are open in AutoCAD.

**Exercise 21-4**

○ Start AutoCAD and use one of your templates that has a Hatch layer.
○ Draw each of the objects displayed at each of the A positions shown on the next page.
○ Be sure the hatch pattern is associative.
○ Copy the objects at the A positions to B and C positions.
○ Use the **HATCHEDIT** command to change the hatch patterns of the copied objects to the representations found at the B and C positions.
○ Adjust the hatch pattern, scale, angle, and style to obtain the figures shown.

*(Continued)*

○ Save as EX21-4.

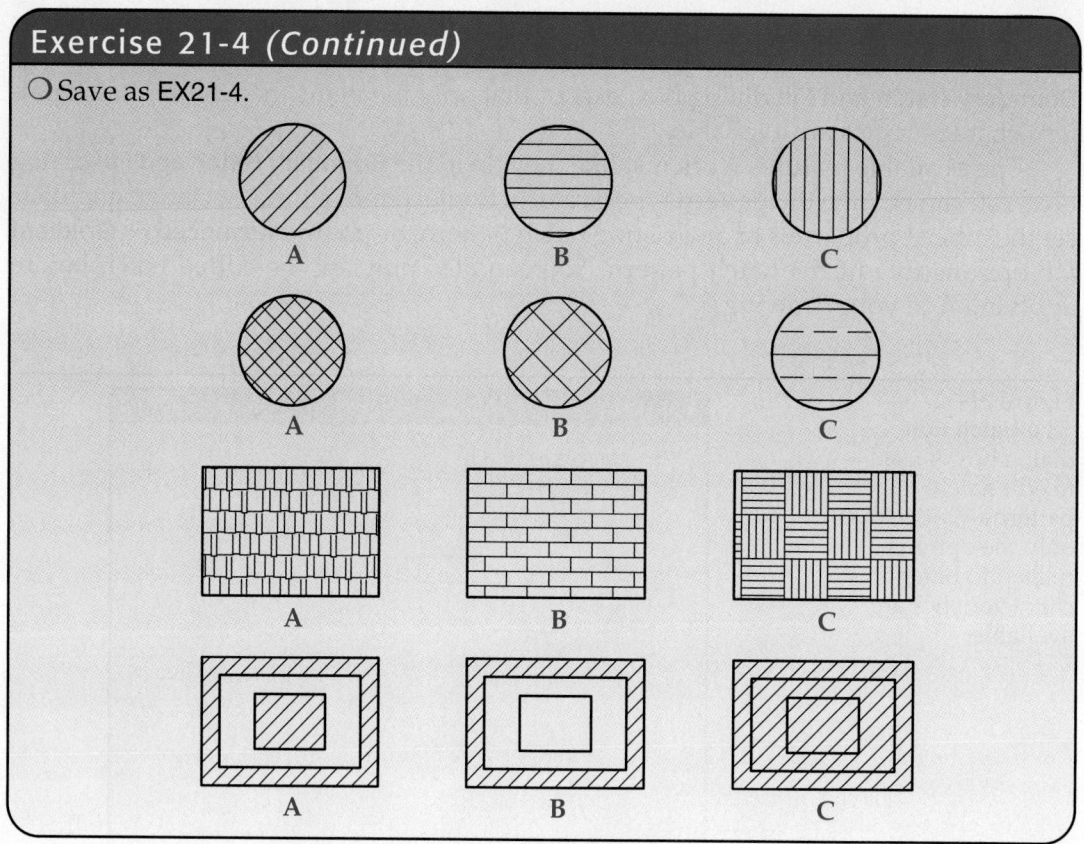

## Editing Associative Hatch Patterns

When you edit an object with an associative hatch pattern, the hatch pattern changes to match the edit. For example, the object in **Figure 21-33A** is stretched and the hatch pattern matches the new object. When the island in **Figure 21-33B** is erased, the hatch pattern is automatically revised to fill the area where the island was located. As long as the original boundary is being edited, the associative hatch will update. After you erase the island in **Figure 21-33B,** a new island cannot be added, because it was not originally calculated to be a part of the hatch boundary.

**Figure 21-33.**
Editing objects with associative hatch patterns. The hatch pattern changes to match the edit.

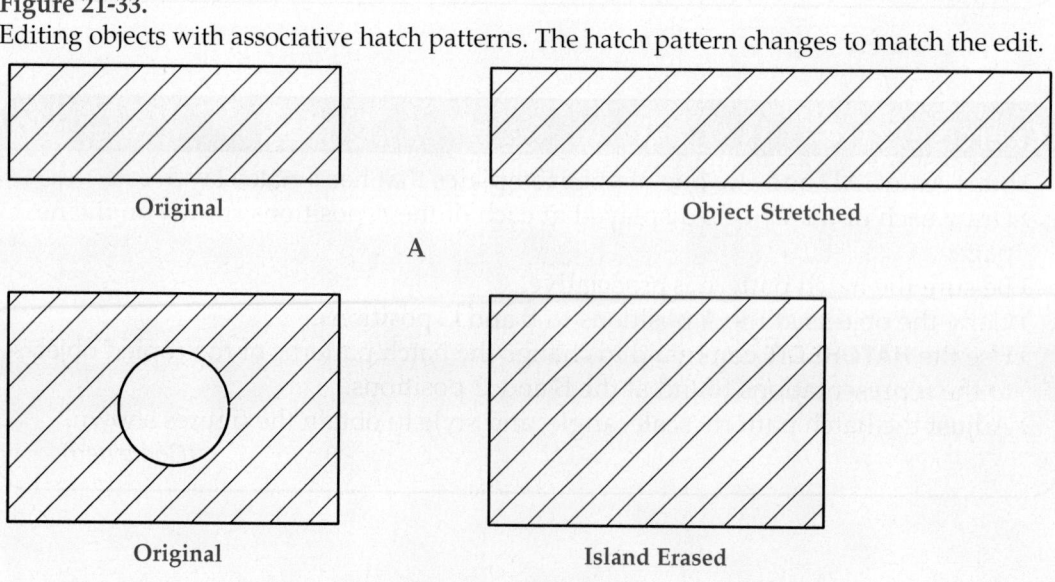

## Drawing Objects with Solid Fills

In previous chapters, you have learned that polylines, polyarcs, trace segments, and doughnuts may be filled in solid when **FILL** mode is on. When **FILL** is off, these objects are drawn as outlines only. The **SOLID** command works in much the same manner except that it fills objects or shapes that are already drawn and fills areas that are simply defined by picking points.

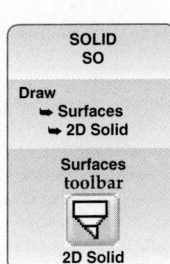

```
SOLID
SO

Draw
  ➥ Surfaces
  ➥ 2D Solid

Surfaces
toolbar

2D Solid
```

The **SOLID** command is accessed by picking the **2D Solid** button from the **Surfaces** toolbar, picking **2D Solid** from the **Surfaces** cascading menu in the **Draw** pull-down menu, or entering SO or SOLID at the Command: prompt. You are then prompted to select points. If the object to fill solid is rectangular, pick the corners in the numbered sequence shown in **Figure 21-34**.

Notice that AutoCAD prompts you for another third point after the first four. This prompt allows you to fill in additional parts of the same object, if needed. AutoCAD assumes that the third and fourth points of the previous solid are now points one and two for the next solid. The subsequent points you select fill in the object in a triangular fashion. Continue picking points, or press [Enter] to stop. The following sequence draws the object shown in **Figure 21-35**:

```
Command: SO or SOLID
Specify first point: (pick point 1)
Specify second point: (pick point 2)
Specify third point: (pick point 3)
Specify fourth point or <exit>: (pick point 4 and the rectangular portion is drawn)
Specify third point: (pick point 5)
Specify fourth point or <exit>: ↵
Specify third point: ↵
```

**Figure 21-34.**
Using the **SOLID** command. Select the points in the order shown.

**Figure 21-35.**
The **SOLID** command allows you to enter a second "third point" (point 5 here) after entering the fourth point.

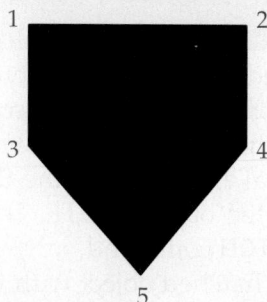

Different types of solid arrangements can be drawn by altering the numbering sequence. See **Figure 21-36.** Also, the **SOLID** command can be used to draw filled shapes without prior use of the **LINE**, **PLINE**, or **RECTANG** commands; simply pick the points. Consider using various object snap modes when picking the points of existing geometry.

**Figure 21-36.**
Using a different numbering sequence for the **SOLID** command will give you different results.

## PROFESSIONAL TIP

Keep in mind that many solids and dense hatches require extensive regeneration. On a complex drawing, create filled solids and hatching on a separate layer and keep the layer frozen until you are ready to plot the drawing. Many solids and dense hatch patterns also adversely affect plot time. Save plotting time by making check plots with **FILL** mode off.

## Exercise 21-6

○ Start AutoCAD and use one of your templates.
○ Create a new layer named Solid-Magenta and draw all solids on this layer.
○ Practice using the **SOLID** command by drawing the objects shown in Figures **21-34, 21-35,** and **21-36.**
○ Save the drawing as EX21-6.

# Chapter Test

*Answer the following questions on a separate sheet of paper.*

*For Questions 1–6, name the type of section identified in each of the following statements:*

1. Half of the object is removed, the cutting-plane line generally cuts completely through along the center plane.
2. Used primarily on symmetrical objects, the cutting-plane line cuts through one-quarter of the object.
3. The cutting-plane line is staggered through features that do not lie in a straight line.
4. The section is turned in place to clarify the contour of the object.
5. The section is rotated and located from the object. The location of the section is normally identified with a cutting-plane line.
6. A small portion of the view is removed to clarify an internal feature.
7. AutoCAD's standard section line symbols are called _____.
8. In which pull-down menu can you select **Hatch...** to display the **Boundary Hatch and Fill** dialog box?
9. Name the two files that contain hatch patterns that can be copied from **DesignCenter**.
10. Explain the purpose and function of the ellipsis (**...**) buttons in the **Boundary Hatch and Fill** dialog box.
11. Identify two ways to select a predefined hatch pattern in the **Boundary Hatch and Fill** dialog box.
12. Explain how you set a hatch scale in the **Boundary Hatch and Fill** dialog box.
13. Explain how to use an existing hatch pattern on a drawing as the current pattern for your next hatch.
14. Describe the purpose of the **Preview** button found in the **Boundary Hatch and Fill** dialog box.
15. What happens if you try to hatch an area where there is a gap in the boundary?
16. How do you limit AutoCAD hatch evaluation to a specific area of the drawing?
17. Define *associative hatch pattern*.
18. How do you change the hatch angle in the **Boundary Hatch and Fill** dialog box?
19. Describe the fundamental difference between using the **Pick Points** and the **Select Objects** buttons in the **Boundary Hatch and Fill** dialog box.
20. If you use the **Pick Points** button inside the **Boundary Hatch and Fill** dialog box to hatch an area, how do you hatch around an island inside the area to be hatched?
21. How do you use the **BHATCH** command to hatch an object with text inside without hatching the text?
22. Name the command that may be used to edit existing associative hatch patterns.
23. How does the **Hatch Edit** dialog box compare to the **Boundary Hatch and Fill** dialog box?
24. Explain the three island detection style options.
25. What happens if you erase an island inside an associative hatch pattern?
26. What is the result of stretching an object that is hatched with an associative hatch pattern?
27. In addition to the **BHATCH** command, what command can be used to fill an object solid?
28. What are gradient fill hatch patterns? How are they created with the **BHATCH** command?
29. Explain how to use drag-and-drop to insert a hatch pattern from **DesignCenter** into an active drawing.
30. Explain two ways to use drag-and-drop for inserting a hatch pattern from the **Tool Palettes** window into the drawing.

## Drawing Problems

*For Problems 1–4, use the following guidelines:*

A. Use an appropriate template with a mechanical drawing title block.
B. Create separate layers for views, dimensions, and section lines.
C. Place the following general notes 1/2″ from the lower-left corner.

    2.  REMOVE ALL BURRS AND SHARP EDGES
    1.  INTERPRET PER ASME Y14.5M-1994
    NOTES:

1. Draw the full section shown on the right. Save the drawing as P21-1.

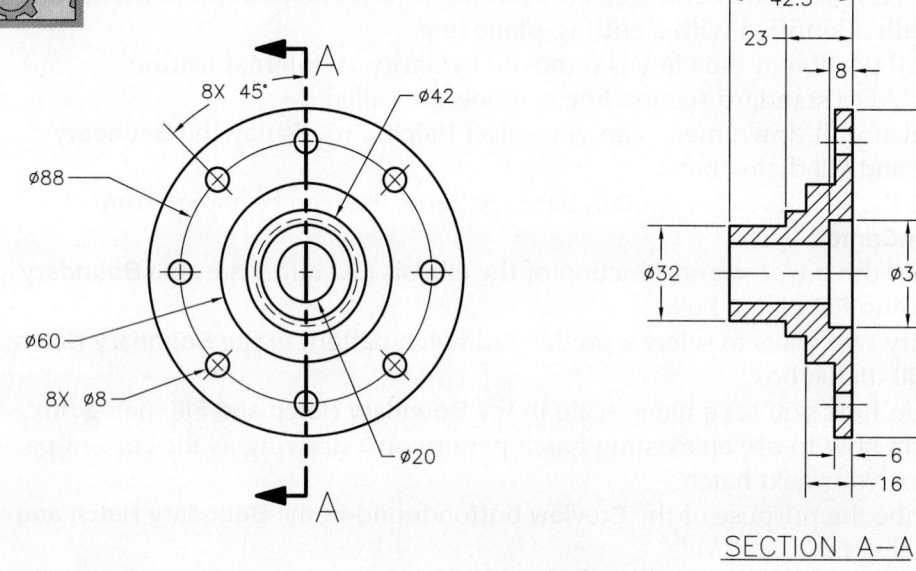

SECTION A–A

Name: Hub
Material: Cast Iron

2. Draw the half section shown in the center. Add the additional notes: OIL QUENCH 40-45C, CASE HARDEN .020 DEEP, and 59-60 ROCKWELL C SCALE. Save the drawing as P21-2.

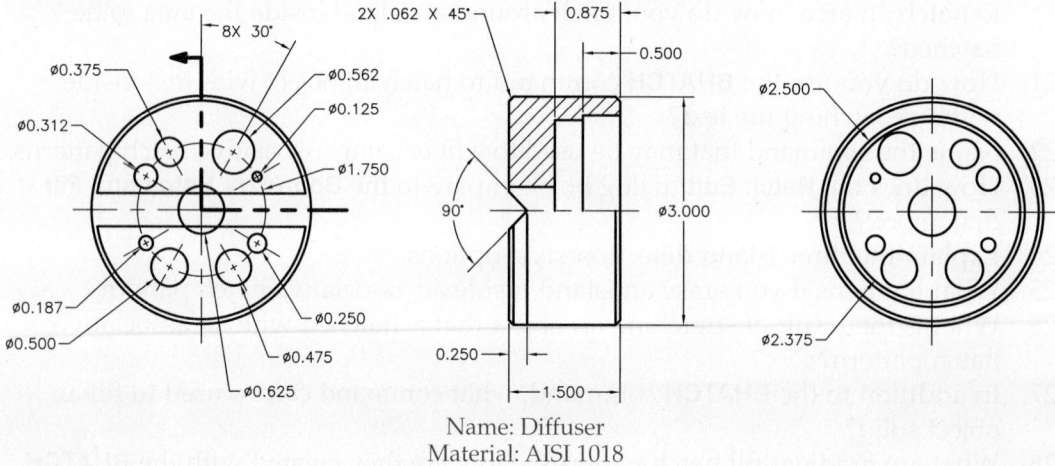

Name: Diffuser
Material: AISI 1018

3. Draw the aligned section shown on the right. Add the additional notes: FINISH ALL OVER 1.63mm UNLESS OTHERWISE SPECIFIED and ALL DIMENSIONS ARE IN MILLIMETERS. Save the drawing as P21-3.

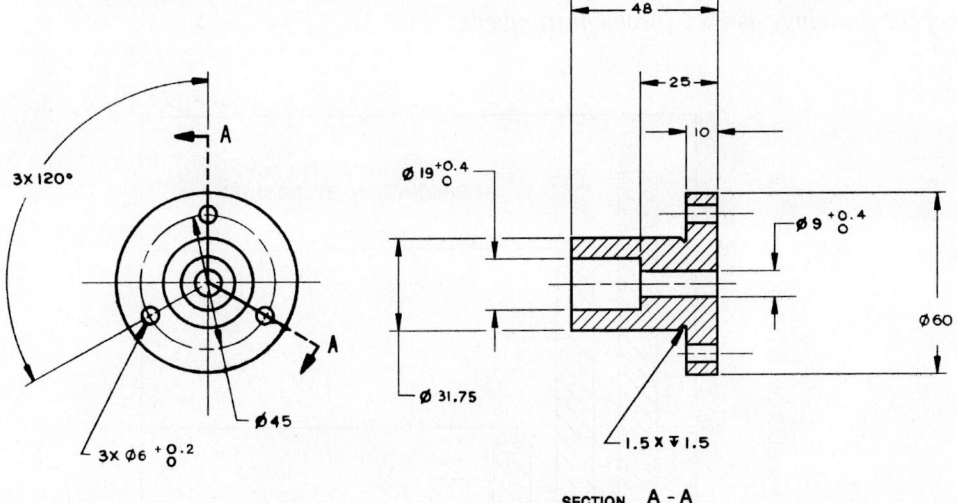

SECTION A-A

Name: Bushing
Material: SAE 1030

4. Draw the aligned section shown on the right. Add the additional notes: FINISH ALL OVER 1.63mm UNLESS OTHERWISE SPECIFIED and ALL DIMENSIONS ARE IN MILLIMETERS. Save the drawing as P21-4.

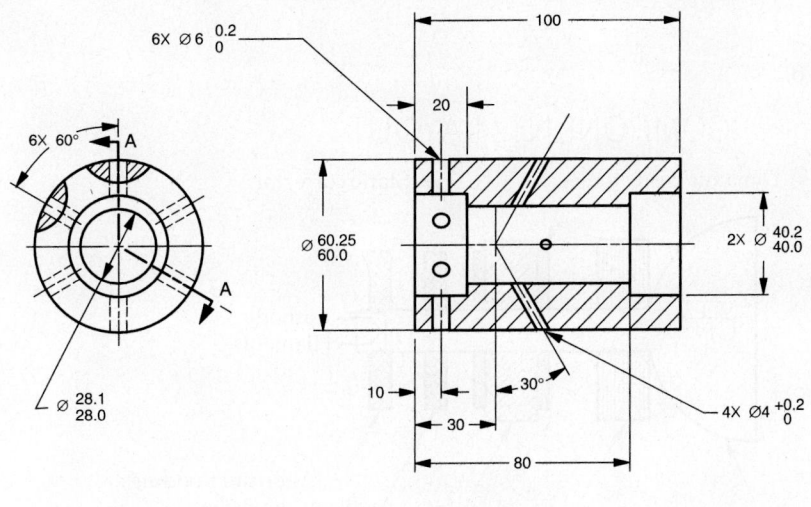

SECTION A-A

Name: Nozzle
Material: Phosphor Bronze

*For Problems 5–14, draw the following problems using commands discussed in this chapter and in previous chapters. Use templates that are appropriate for the specific problems. Use text styles that correlate with the problem content. Place dimensions and notes when needed. Make your drawings proportional to the given problems when dimensions are not given. Save each of the drawings as* **P21**-*(problem number).*

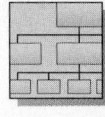

5.

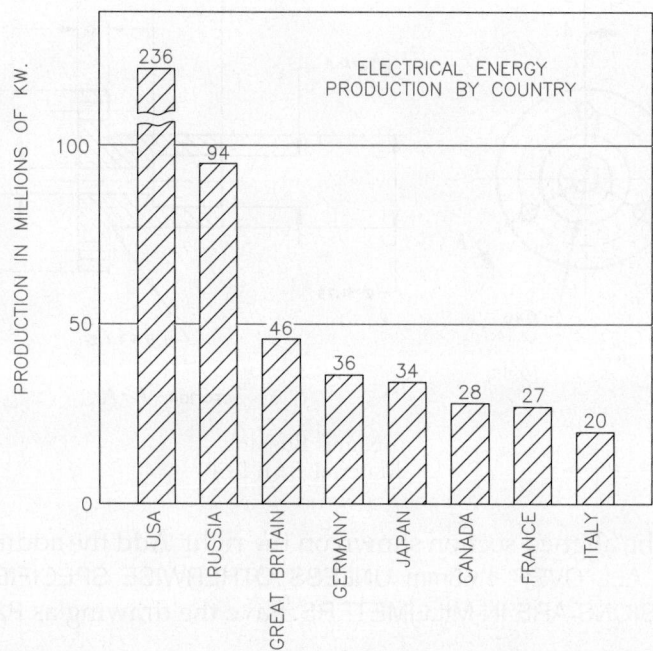

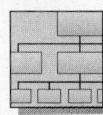

6.

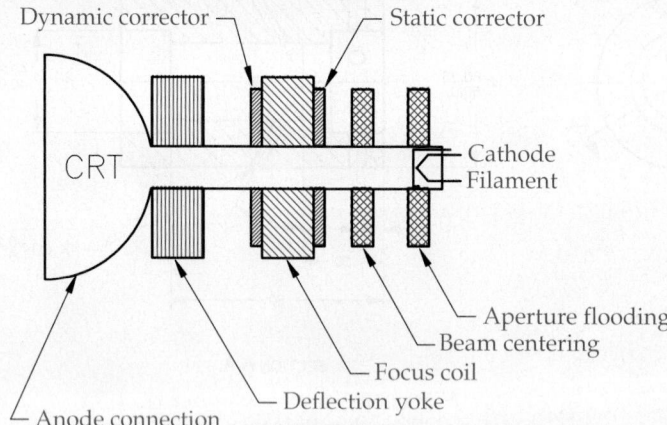

7.

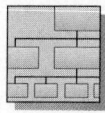

## SOLOMAN SHOE COMPANY

PERCENT OF TOTAL SALES EACH DIVISION

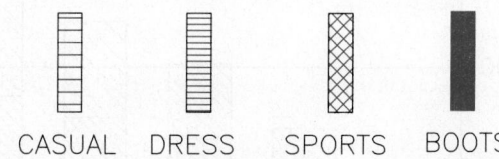

CASUAL   DRESS   SPORTS   BOOTS

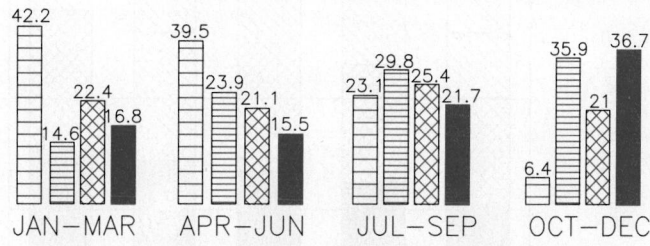

42.2
14.6  22.4  16.8
JAN—MAR

39.5
23.9  21.1  15.5
APR—JUN

23.1  29.8  25.4  21.7
JUL—SEP

35.9  36.7
6.4  21
OCT—DEC

8.

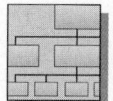

## DIAL TECHNOLOGIES
### EXPENSE BUDGET
**FISCAL YEAR**

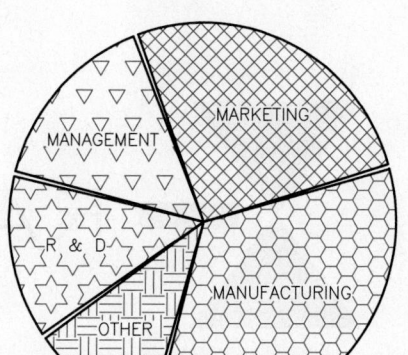

MANAGEMENT   MARKETING

R & D

OTHER   MANUFACTURING

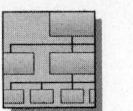

9.

## SALES HISTORY

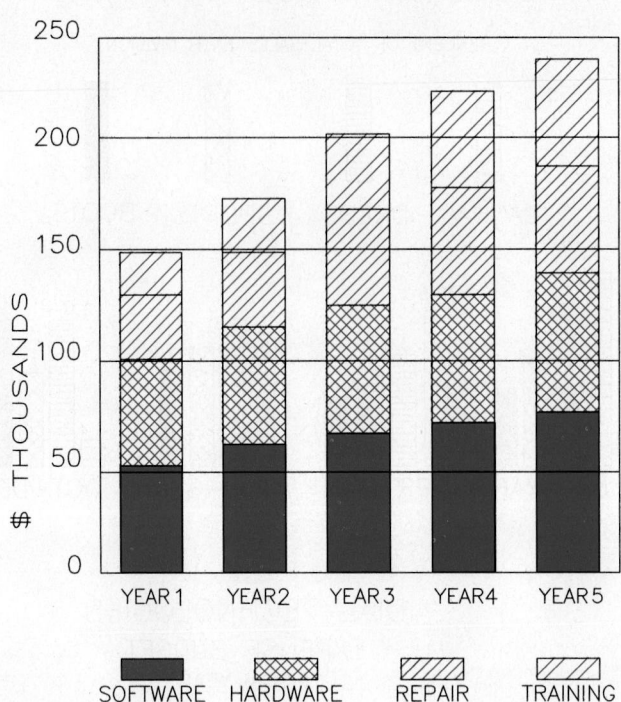

10.

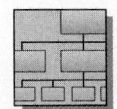

11.

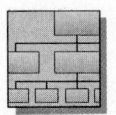

12.

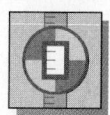

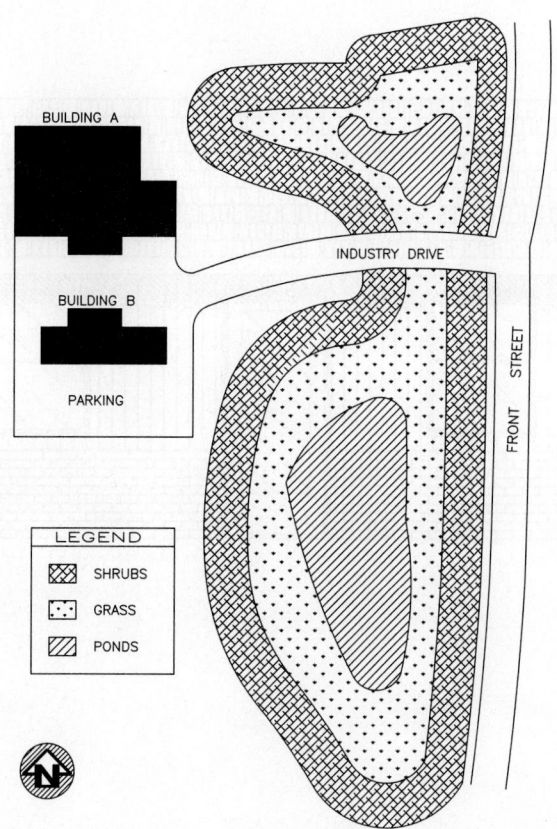

BUILDING A

BUILDING B

PARKING

INDUSTRY DRIVE

FRONT STREET

LEGEND
SHRUBS
GRASS
PONDS

13.

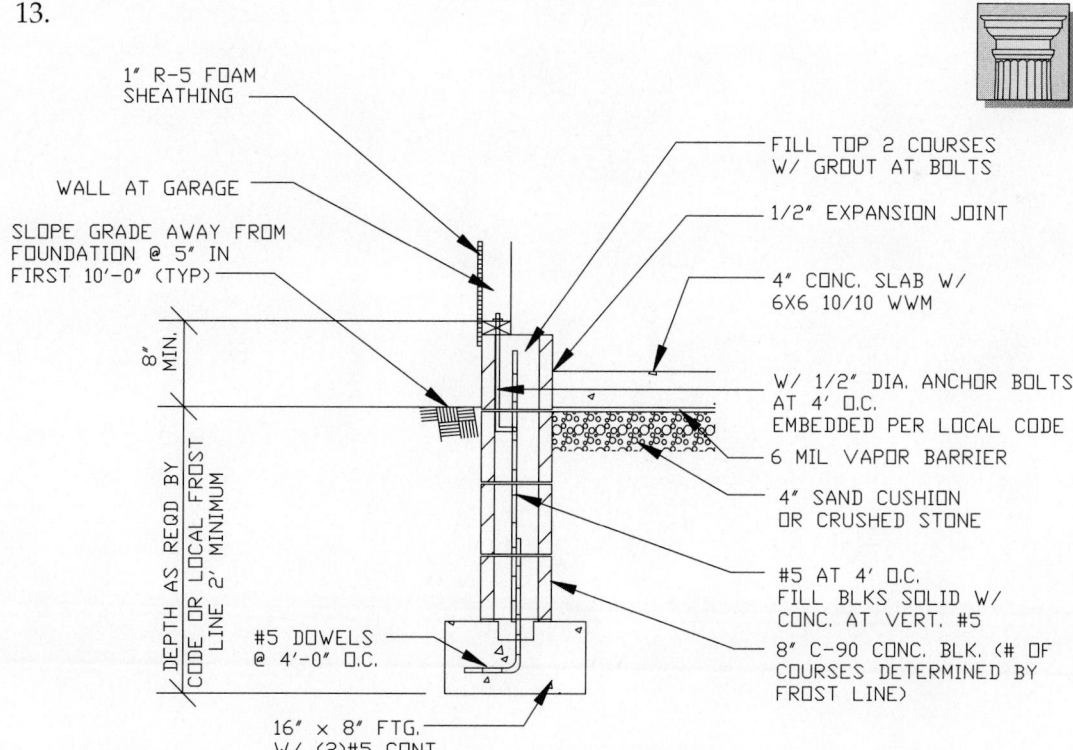

1" R-5 FOAM
SHEATHING

WALL AT GARAGE

SLOPE GRADE AWAY FROM
FOUNDATION @ 5" IN
FIRST 10'-0" (TYP)

8" MIN.

DEPTH AS REQD BY
CODE OR LOCAL FROST
LINE 2' MINIMUM

#5 DOWELS
@ 4'-0" O.C.

16" x 8" FTG.
W/ (2)#5 CONT.

FILL TOP 2 COURSES
W/ GROUT AT BOLTS

1/2" EXPANSION JOINT

4" CONC. SLAB W/
6X6 10/10 WWM

W/ 1/2" DIA. ANCHOR BOLTS
AT 4' O.C.
EMBEDDED PER LOCAL CODE

6 MIL VAPOR BARRIER

4" SAND CUSHION
OR CRUSHED STONE

#5 AT 4' O.C.
FILL BLKS SOLID W/
CONC. AT VERT. #5

8" C-90 CONC. BLK. (# OF
COURSES DETERMINED BY
FROST LINE)

14.

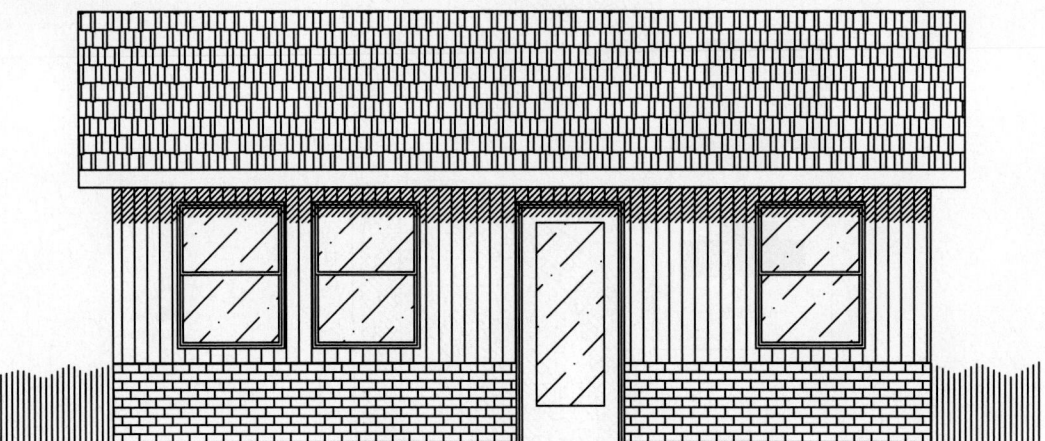

# Creating Symbols for Multiple Use

## Learning Objectives

After completing this chapter, you will be able to do the following:

- Create and save blocks.
- Insert blocks into a drawing.
- Edit a block and update it in a drawing.
- Insert drawings and blocks into drawings using **DesignCenter**.
- Insert blocks into drawings using the **Tool Palettes** window.
- Create blocks that are saved independent of the drawing.
- Construct and use a symbol library of blocks.
- Customize tool palettes.

One of the greatest benefits of AutoCAD is its ability to store symbols for future use. These symbols, or *blocks*, can be inserted into a drawing and scaled and rotated in one operation. If a block is edited, drawings containing the block can be updated to include the new version. There are two types of blocks used in AutoCAD. A *block* created with the **BLOCK** command is stored within a drawing. A *wblock* created with the **WBLOCK** command is saved as a separate drawing file. Both types of blocks can be shared between drawings. Blocks can be copied between drawings using **DesignCenter** or the **Tool Palettes** window, and wblocks can be inserted into drawings using **DesignCenter**, the **Tool Palettes** window, and the **INSERT** command. Both types of blocks can be used to create a *symbol library*, which is a related group of symbols.

When a drawing is inserted or referenced, it becomes part of the drawing on screen, but its content is not added to the current drawing file. Any named objects, such as blocks and layers, are referred to as *dependent symbols*. When a dependent symbol is revised, a drawing that references it is automatically updated by AutoCAD the next time it is opened.

## Creating Symbols As Blocks

The ability to draw and store symbols is one of the greatest time-saving features of AutoCAD. The **BLOCK** command is used to create a symbol within a specific drawing file. The block can then be inserted as many times as needed into the drawing in which it was defined with the **INSERT** command. It can also be copied into other drawings using **DesignCenter** or tool palettes. A pre-drawn block created with the **WBLOCK** command can be inserted as many times as needed into *any* drawing with the **INSERT** command. Upon insertion, both types of blocks can be scaled and rotated to meet the drawing requirements.

There are advantages to creating and storing symbols as blocks rather than as individual drawing files. However, the best method for block usage depends on the needs of the user and the project. This chapter discusses the construction and management of blocks, wblocks, and symbol libraries. Blocks are discussed in the following sections.

## Constructing Blocks

A block can be any shape, symbol, view, or drawing that you use more than once. Before constructing a block, review the drawing you are working on. This is where a sketch of your drawing can be useful. Look for any shapes, components, notes, and assemblies that are used more than once. These can be drawn once and then saved as blocks.

---

**PROFESSIONAL TIP**

Blocks that vary in size from one drawing to the next should be drawn to fit inside a one-unit square. It does not matter if the object is measured in feet, inches, or millimeters. This makes it easy to scale the symbol later when you insert it into a drawing.

---

## Drawing the Block Components

Draw a block as you would any other drawing geometry. If you want the block to have the color and linetype of the layer it will be inserted on, be sure to set layer 0 current before you begin drawing the block. If you forget to do this and draw the objects on another layer, simply use the **Properties** window or **Properties** toolbar to place all the objects on layer 0 before using the **BLOCK** command.

When you finish drawing the object, determine the best location on the symbol to use as an insertion point. When you insert the block into a drawing, the symbol is placed with its insertion point on the screen cursor. Several examples of commonly used blocks with their insertion points highlighted are shown in **Figure 22-1**.

---

**Figure 22-1.**
Common drafting symbols and their insertion points for placement on drawings. The insertion points are shown as colored dots.

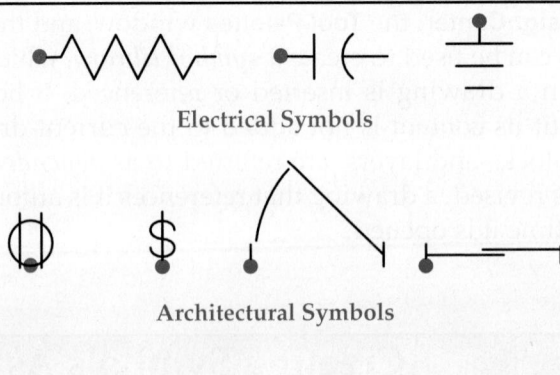

Electrical Symbols

Architectural Symbols

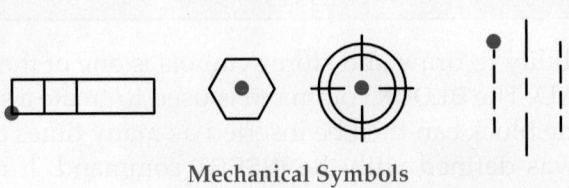

Mechanical Symbols

---

If it is important that the block maintains a specific color and linetype regardless of the layer it is to be used on, be sure to set the color and linetype before drawing the objects. On the other hand, if the block can assume the current color and linetype when the block is inserted into a drawing, set the current object color and linetype to ByBlock.

To set the color to ByBlock, pick ByBlock in the **Color Control** drop-down list of the **Properties** toolbar. You can also pick **Color…** from the **Format** pull-down menu to access the **Select Color** dialog box. Pick the **ByBlock** button as shown in **Figure 22-2.**

To set the linetype to ByBlock, pick ByBlock in the **Linetype Control** drop-down list of the **Properties** toolbar. Or, pick **Linetype…** from the **Format** pull-down menu to display the **Linetype Manager** dialog box. Pick ByBlock in the **Linetype** list and then pick the **Current** button. See **Figure 22-3.**

Once the current color and linetype are both set to ByBlock, you can create blocks. A block created with these settings assumes the current color and linetype when it is inserted into a drawing, regardless of the current layer setting.

---

**Figure 22-2.**
After picking **Color…** from the **Format** pull-down menu to display the **Select Color** dialog box, pick the **ByBlock** button to have the block assume the current color when it is inserted into a drawing.

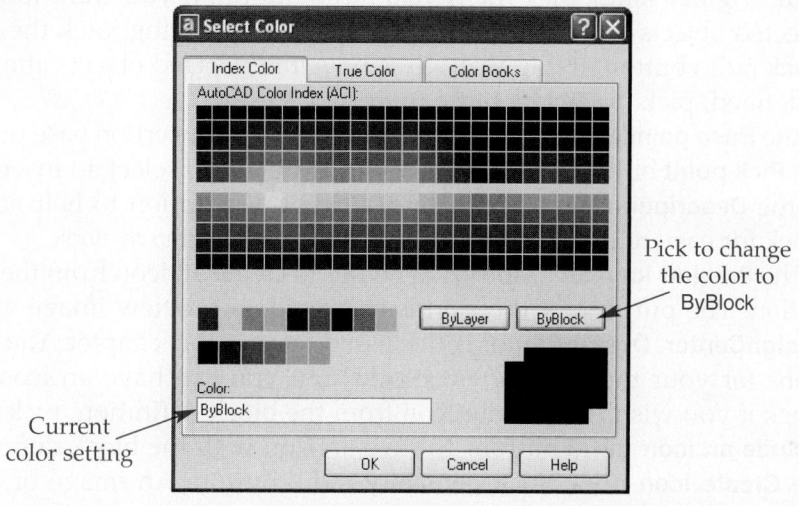

---

**Figure 22-3.**
To set the ByBlock linetype current, pick ByBlock in the **Linetype** list of the **Linetype Manager** dialog box and then pick the **Current** button.

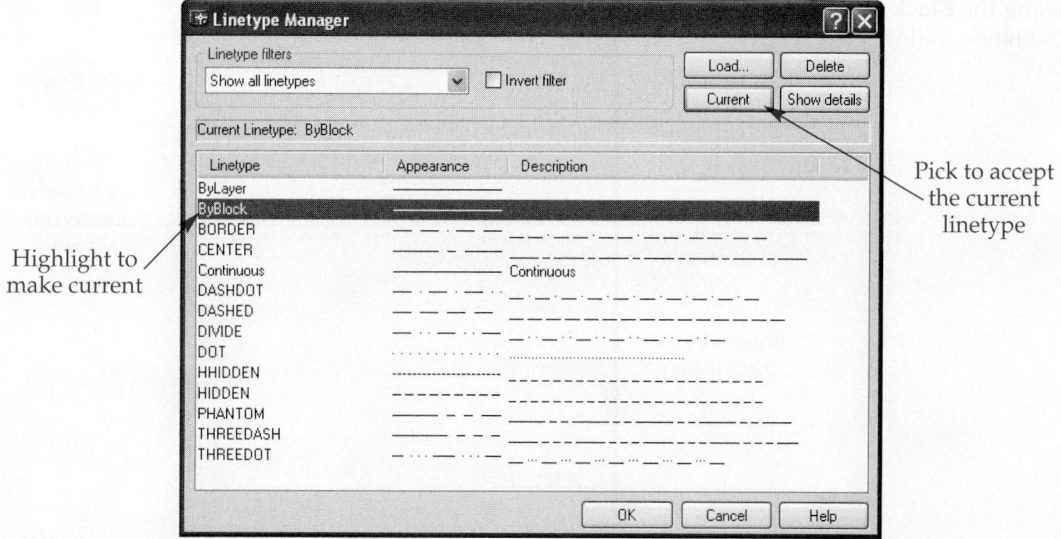

---

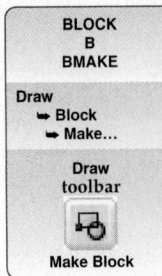

BLOCK
B
BMAKE

Draw
➥ Block
➥ Make...

Draw
toolbar

Make Block

# Creating Blocks

When you draw a shape or symbol, you have not yet created a block. To save your object as a block, pick the **Make Block** button on the **Draw** toolbar, pick **Make...** from the **Block** cascading menu in the **Draw** pull-down menu, or enter B, BLOCK, or BMAKE at the Command: prompt. Any one of these methods displays the **Block Definition** dialog box, **Figure 22-4.** The process for creating a block is as follows:

1. In the **Name:** text box, enter a name for the block, such as PUMP. The name cannot exceed 255 characters. It can include numbers, letters, and spaces, as well as the dollar sign ($), hyphen (-), and underscore (_).

2. In the **Objects** area, pick the **Select objects** button to use your pointing device to select objects for the block definition. The drawing area returns and you are prompted to select objects. Select all the objects that will make up the block. Press [Enter] when you are done. The **Block Definition** dialog box reopens, and the number of objects selected is shown in the **Objects** area. If you want to create a selection set, use the **Quick Select** button to define a filter for your selection set.

3. In the **Objects** area, specify whether to retain, convert, or delete the selected objects. If you want to keep the selected objects in the current drawing (in their original state), pick the **Retain** radio button. If you want to replace the selected objects with one of the blocks you are creating, pick the **Convert to block** radio button. If you want to remove the selected objects after the block is defined, pick the **Delete** radio button.

4. In the **Base point** area, enter the coordinates for the insertion base point or pick the **Pick point** button to use your pointing device to select an insertion point.

5. In the **Description:** text box, enter a textual description to help identify the block for easy reference, such as This is a vacuum pump symbol.

6. In the **Preview icon** area, specify whether to create an icon from the block definition. The purpose of the icon is to provide a preview image when using **DesignCenter**. **DesignCenter** is discussed later in this chapter. You may want icons for your most important blocks, but you can have an icon for every block if you wish. To omit an icon from the block definition, pick the **Do not include an icon** radio button. To save an icon with the block definition, pick the **Create icon from block geometry** radio button. An image of the icon is then displayed to the right.

**Figure 22-4.**
Blocks are created using the **Block Definition** dialog box.

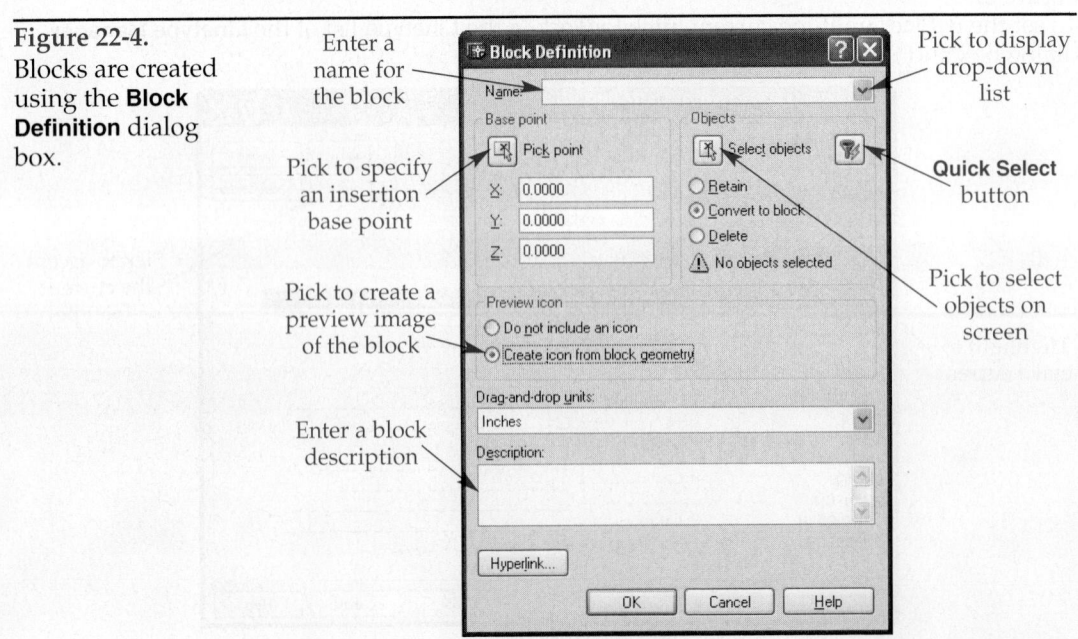

Enter a name for the block

Pick to display drop-down list

Pick to specify an insertion base point

**Quick Select** button

Pick to create a preview image of the block

Pick to select objects on screen

Enter a block description

7. Use the **Drag-and-drop units:** drop-down list to specify the type of units **DesignCenter** will use when inserting the block.

8. After you have finished defining the block, pick **OK**.

The **Convert to block** radio button is active by default. If you select the **Delete** option and then decide that you want to keep the original geometry in the drawing after you have defined the block, you can enter the **OOPS** command. This returns the original objects to the screen, whereas entering U at the Command: prompt or picking the **Undo** button from the **Standard** toolbar removes the block from the drawing.

---

**NOTE**  The **Block Definition** dialog box contains a **Hyperlink...** button. Pick this button to access the **Insert Hyperlink** dialog box to insert a hyperlink in the block. Hyperlinks and other Internet features for AutoCAD are discussed in *AutoCAD and its Applications—Advanced.*

---

To verify that the block was saved properly, access the **Block Definition** dialog box. Pick the **Name:** drop-down list button to display a list of all blocks in the current drawing. The block names are organized in numerical and alphabetical order. If there are more than six blocks in your drawing, a scroll bar appears to the right of the list so that you can access the remaining blocks.

The **-BLOCK** command can also be used to create new blocks and list existing blocks. Access this command by entering **-B** or **-BLOCK** at the Command: prompt. When the **-BLOCK** command is entered, the options in the **Block Definition** dialog box are presented as prompts on the command line. To display a list of block names, use the **?** option as follows:

```
-BLOCK
-B
```

> Command: **-B** *or* **-BLOCK**↵
> Enter block name or [?]: **?**↵
> Enter block(s) to list <*>

Press [Enter] to list all of the blocks in the current drawing. The following information is then displayed in the **AutoCAD Text Window**:

> Defined blocks.
>     "PUMP"
> 
> | User Blocks | External References | Dependent Blocks | Unnamed Blocks |
> |---|---|---|---|
> | 1 | 0 | 0 | 0 |

This listing reports each block name, as well as the different types of blocks and the number of each type in the drawing. When you create a block, you have actually created a *block definition*. Therefore, the first entry in the block listing is that of *defined* blocks. *User blocks* are those created by you. *External references* are drawings referenced with the **XREF** command. (External references are discussed in Chapter 23.) Blocks that reside in a referenced drawing are called *dependent blocks*. *Unnamed blocks* are objects such as associative and nonassociative dimensions.

Try stepping through the process of creating a block again. Draw a one-unit square and name it PLATE. See **Figure 22-5**. After creating the block, be sure to confirm that the PLATE block was saved by using the **-BLOCK** command.

---

**Figure 22-5.**
The procedure for drawing a one-unit square and defining it as a block.
A—Draw the block.
B—Pick the insertion base point. C—Select the square using the **Window** selection option or any other suitable option.

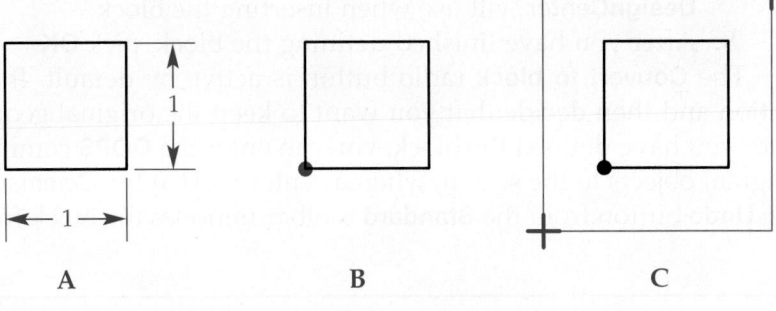

A                    B                    C

**PROFESSIONAL TIP**

Blocks can be used when creating other blocks. Suppose you design a complex part or view that will be used repeatedly. You can insert existing blocks into the view and then save the entire object as a block. This is called *nesting*, where larger blocks contain smaller blocks. The larger block must be given a different name. Proper planning and knowledge of all existing blocks can speed up the drawing process and the creation of complex parts.

---

**Exercise 22-1**

○ Start a new drawing or use one of your templates. Specify decimal units.
○ Set layer 0 current. Draw a circle with a one-unit diameter and add centerlines as shown below.
○ Create a block of the circle and centerlines and name it CIRCLE.
○ Pick the center of the circle as the insertion base point.
○ Save the drawing as EX22-1.

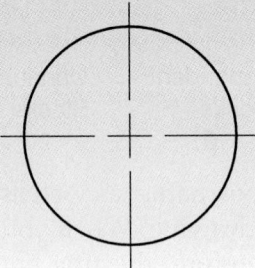

---

## Using Blocks in a Drawing

Once a block has been created, it is easy to insert it into a drawing. First, determine a proper size and rotation angle for the block. Blocks are normally inserted on specific layers, so set the proper layer *before* inserting the block. Once a block has been inserted into a drawing, it is referred to as a *block reference*.

# Inserting Blocks

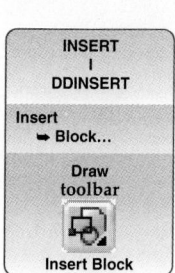
Blocks are placed on your drawing with the **INSERT** command. Enter I, INSERT, or DDINSERT at the Command: prompt, pick the **Insert Block** button from the **Draw** toolbar, or pick **Block...** from the **Insert** pull-down menu. This accesses the **Insert** dialog box, **Figure 22-6.**

Pick the **Name:** drop-down list button to access the defined blocks in the current drawing. Highlight the name of the block you wish to insert. If the list of block names is long, use the scroll bar to display additional blocks. You may also enter the name of the block in the **Name:** text box. Once the desired block has been chosen, you must specify the insertion location, scale, and rotation angle. You can also specify whether to explode the block upon inserting it. The option buttons and other features in the **Insert** dialog box are described as follows:

- **Browse... button.** Pick this button to display the **Select Drawing File** dialog box and select a drawing file for insertion into the current drawing.
- **Insertion point area.** If the **Specify On-screen** check box is activated, you can pick an insertion point on screen and insert the block dynamically. If you wish to insert the block using absolute coordinates, disable the check box and enter the coordinates in the **X:**, **Y:**, and **Z:** text boxes. Entering coordinates in this manner is referred to as using *preset values*. If preset values are used, the block is immediately inserted at the specified coordinates when you pick **OK**.
- **Scale area.** The **Scale** area allows you to specify scale values for the block in relation to the X, Y, and Z axes. By default, the **Specify On-screen** check box is inactive. This causes the block to be inserted at a one-to-one scale once the insertion point has been selected. If you want to be prompted for the scale at the command line when inserting the block, activate the **Specify On-screen** check box. If the check box is inactive, you can enter scale values in the **X:**, **Y:**, and **Z:** text boxes. If you activate the **Uniform Scale** check box, you can simply specify a scale value for the X axis. The same value is then used for the Y and Z axes when the block is inserted.
- **Rotation area.** The **Rotation** area allows you to insert the block at a specified angle. By default, the **Specify On-screen** check box is inactive and the block is inserted at an angle of zero. If you want to use a different angle, enter a value in the **Angle:** text box. If you want to be prompted for the rotation angle at the command line when inserting the block, activate the **Specify On-screen** check box.

**Figure 22-6.**
The **Insert** dialog box allows you to select and prepare a block for insertion. Select the block you wish to insert from the drop-down list or enter the block name in the **Name:** text box.

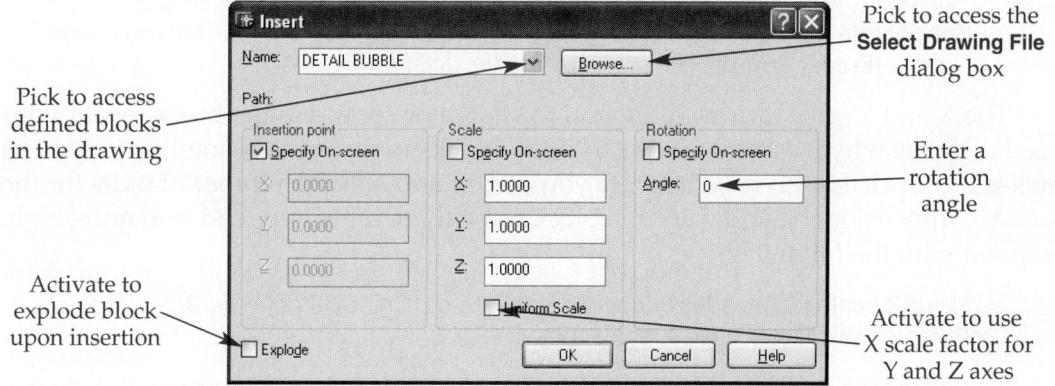

- **Explode check box.** When a block is created, it is saved as a single object. Therefore, it is defined as a single object when inserted in the drawing, no matter how many objects were used to create the block. Activate the **Explode** check box if you wish to explode the block into its original objects for editing purposes. If you explode the block upon insertion, it will assume its original properties, such as its original layer, color, and linetype.

When you pick the **OK** button, prompts appear for any values defined as **Specify On-screen** in the **Insert** dialog box. If you are specifying the insertion point on screen, the following prompt appears:

> Specify insertion point or [Scale/X/Y/Z/Rotate/PScale/PX/PY/PZ/PRotate]: *(pick the point to insert the block)*

If you select one of the options, the new value will override any setting in the **Insert** dialog box. The following options are available:

- **Scale.** This option affects the overall scale of the X, Y, and Z axes.
- **X.** Entering this option affects only the X scale factor.
- **Y.** Entering this option affects only the Y scale factor.
- **Z.** Entering this option affects only the Z scale factor.
- **Rotate.** This option sets the rotation angle.
- **PScale.** This option allows you to preview the scale of the X, Y, and Z axes. You are then prompted to enter the actual scale factors.
- **PX.** This option allows you to preview the scale of the X axis. You are then prompted to enter the actual scale factor.
- **PY.** This option allows you to preview the scale of the Y axis. You are then prompted to enter the actual scale factor.
- **PZ.** This option allows you to preview the scale of the Z axis. You are then prompted to enter the scale factor.
- **PRotate.** This option is used to preview the rotation angle. You are then prompted to enter the actual rotation angle.

If you are specifying the scale factor on screen, the following prompt appears:

> Enter X scale factor, specify opposite corner, or [Corner/XYZ] <1>: *(pick a point, or enter a value for the scale)*

Moving the cursor scales the block dynamically as it is dragged. If you want to scale the block visually, pick a point when the object appears correct. If you enter an X scale factor or press [Enter] to accept the default scale value, you are then prompted with the following:

> Enter Y scale factor <use X scale factor>: *(enter a value or press [Enter] to accept the same scale specified for the X axis)*

If you are specifying the rotation angle on screen, the following prompt appears:

> Specify rotation angle <0>: *(pick a point, enter a value for the rotation angle and press [Enter], or press [Enter] to accept the default angle)*

The X and Y scale factors allow you to stretch or compress the block to suit your needs. This is why it is a good idea to draw blocks to fit inside a one-unit square. It makes the block easy to scale because you can enter the exact number of units for the X and Y dimensions. If you want the block to be three units long and two units high, respond with the following:

> Enter X scale factor, specify opposite corner, or [Corner/XYZ] <1>: **3**↵
> Enter Y scale factor <use X scale factor>: **2**↵

Notice that the prompt for the Y scale factor allows you to accept the X scale factor for Y by simply pressing [Enter]. The object shown in **Figure 22-7** was given several different X and Y scale factors using the **INSERT** command.

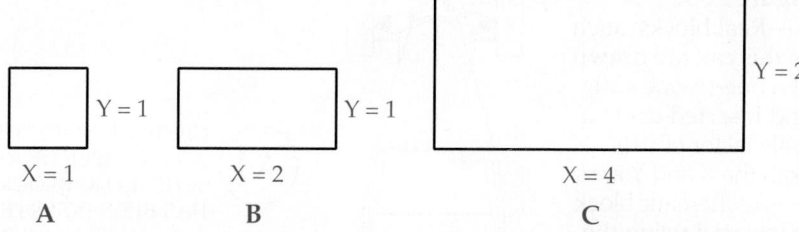

Figure 22-7.
A comparison of
different X and
Y scale factors used
for inserting the
PLATE block.

Y = 1    X = 1    **A**

Y = 1    X = 2    **B**

Y = 2    X = 4    **C**

## Block Insertion Options

It is possible to create a mirror image of a block by simply entering a negative value for the scale factor. For example, entering -1 for both the X scale factor and the Y scale factor mirrors the block to the opposite quadrant of the original orientation specified and retains the original size. Different mirroring techniques are shown in **Figure 22-8**. The insertion point is indicated by a dot.

An approximate dynamic scaling technique is made possible by using the **Corner** option inside the **INSERT** command sequence. You can size the block dynamically as you move the cursor if the **DRAGMODE** system variable is set to **Auto**. Use the **Corner** option as follows:

Enter X scale factor, specify opposite corner, or [Corner/XYZ] <1>: **C.**↲
Specify opposite corner: (*move the cursor to change the size of the block and pick a point or enter absolute coordinates*)

If you pick a point on screen, be sure to pick a point above and to the right of the insertion point to insert the block as drawn. Picking a corner point below or to the left of the insertion point generates a mirror image such as those shown in **Figure 22-8**.

In addition to the scaling options previously discussed, a block that is scaled during insertion can be classified as a *real block*, a *schematic block*, or a *unit block*. A ***real block*** is one that is drawn at a one-to-one scale. It is then inserted into the drawing using 1 for both the X and Y scale factors. Examples of real blocks could include a car design, a bolt, or a pipe fitting. See **Figure 22-9A**.

Figure 22-8.
Negative and
positive scale
factors have
different effects
when used to insert
a block.

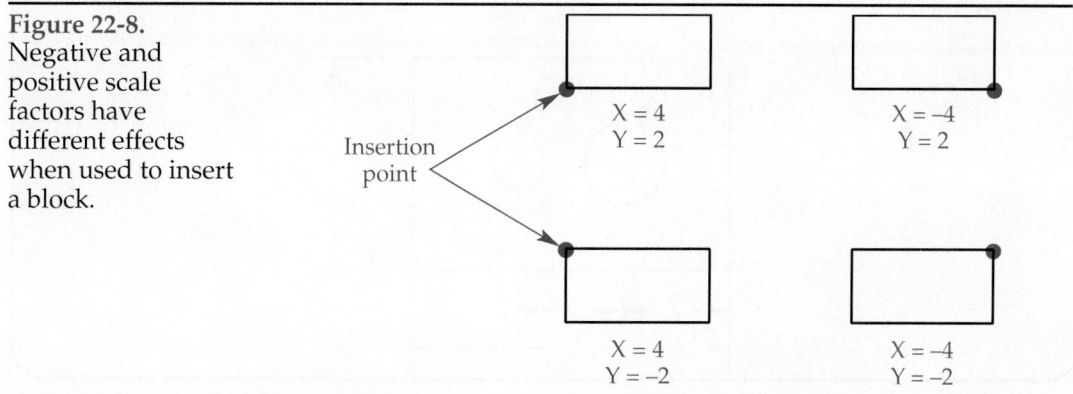

Insertion point

X = 4    Y = 2

X = −4    Y = 2

X = 4    Y = −2

X = −4    Y = −2

**Figure 22-9.**
A—Real blocks, such as this car, are drawn at a one-to-one scale and inserted using a scale factor of 1 for both the X and Y axes. B—A schematic block is inserted using the scale factor of the drawing for the X and Y axes. C—A 2D unit block can be inserted at different scales for the X and Y axes.

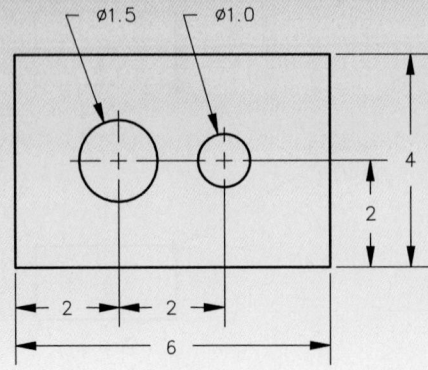

GENERAL NOTE: THIS IS AN EXAMPLE OF A SCHEMATIC BLOCK THAT HAS BEEN INSERTED BY THE SCALE FACTOR.

Scale
X = 48
Y = 48

X = 1
Y = 1

Scale
X = 4
Y = 12

A                          B                          C

A *schematic block* is a block that is originally drawn at a one-to-one scale. It is then inserted into the drawing using the scale factor of the drawing for both the X and Y scale values. Examples of schematic blocks could include notes, detail bubbles, or section symbols. See **Figure 22-9B.**

*Unit blocks* are also originally drawn at a one-to-one scale. There are three different types of unit blocks. One example of a *1D unit block* is a 1″ line object that is turned into a block. A *2D unit block* is any object that can fit inside a 1″ × 1″ square. A *3D unit block* is any object that can fit inside a 1″ cube. To use a unit block, insert the block and determine the individual scale factors for each axis. For example, a 1D unit block could be inserted at a scale of 4, which would turn the line into a 4″ line. A 2D unit block could be assigned different scale factors for the X and Y axes, such as 48 for the X axis and 72 for the Y axis. See **Figure 22-9C.** A 3D unit block could be inserted at different scales for the X, Y, and Z axes.

## Exercise 22-2

○ Open EX22-1 if it is not currently on your screen.
○ Draw a 1 × 1 square on layer 0 and define it as a block named PLATE.
○ Insert the PLATE block into the drawing. Enter an X scale factor of 6 and a Y scale factor of 4.
○ Insert the CIRCLE block twice into the drawing as shown. The small circle is one unit in diameter and the large circle is 1.5 units in diameter.
○ Make a block of the entire drawing and name it PLATE-1. Pick the lower-left corner as the insertion point.
○ Insert the PLATE-1 block into your drawing and enter a scale of –1, –1. Also during insertion, rotate the object 45°.
○ Save the drawing as EX22-2.

Ø1.5        Ø1.0

2        2

6

4

2

## The Effects of Layers on Blocks

Blocks retain the property characteristics of the layer(s) on which they were drawn. In Chapter 4, you learned that all objects in AutoCAD are created in ByLayer mode by default. This means the object color and linetype properties are dictated by the layer on which objects are created. For example, suppose the CIRCLE block was drawn on layer 1 with the color red and a dashed linetype. When inserted, the block appears red and dashed, no matter what layer it is inserted on. If different colors, linetypes, or even layers are used in a block, they also remain the same when the block is inserted on a different layer. Therefore, a block defined in ByLayer mode retains its properties when inserted into a drawing (or another drawing, if the block was saved as a drawing file). If the layers included in the inserted block do not exist in the drawing, AutoCAD automatically creates them.

For a block to assume the property characteristics of the layer it is inserted on, it must be created on layer 0. Suppose you create the CIRCLE block on layer 0 and insert it on layer 1. The block becomes part of layer 1 and thus assumes the color and linetype of that layer. Exploding the CIRCLE block returns the objects back to layer 0 and to the original color and linetype assigned to layer 0.

An exception occurs if objects within the block are drawn using an explicit color or linetype; in other words, the objects are not drawn using the default ByLayer mode. In this case, the exploded CIRCLE block objects would retain their original properties.

## Changing the Layer, Color, and Linetype of a Block

If you insert a block on the wrong layer, or if you wish to change the color or linetype properties of the block, you can use the **Properties** window to modify it. Select the block to modify, and its properties are listed. See **Figure 22-10.** Notice that Block Reference is specified in the drop-down list. You can now modify the selected block.

To modify the layer of the selected block, pick **Layer** in the **General** category. A drop-down arrow appears, allowing you to access the layer you want to use for the block. Once the new layer has been selected, pick the X at the upper-right corner of the **Properties** window to close the window. The block is now changed to the proper layer.

You may also want to change the color or linetype of a block. If the block was originally created on layer 0, it will assume the color and linetype of the current layer when it is inserted. If it was created on another layer, it will retain its original color and linetype.

**Figure 22-10.**
The **Properties** window allows you to change the layer, color, linetype, and other properties of a block.

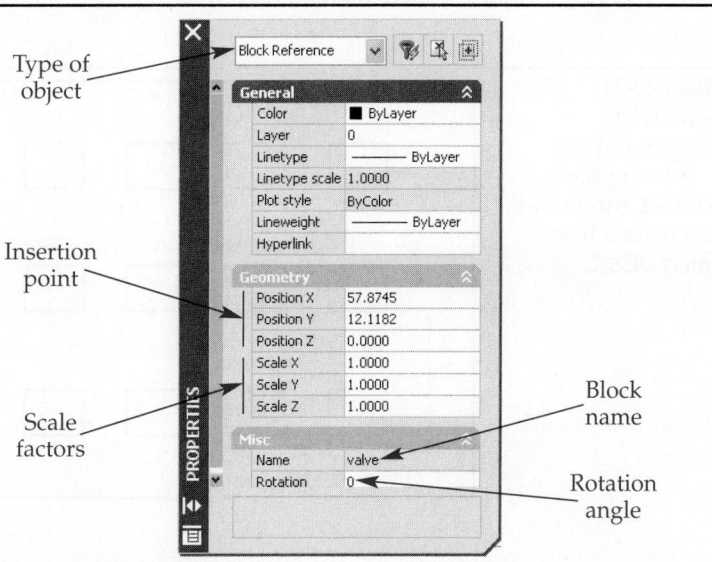

Type of object
Insertion point
Scale factors
Block name
Rotation angle

If you wish to change the color or linetype of an inserted block, you can access the **Properties** window and select the corresponding property in the **General** section after selecting the block. Select the desired color or linetype from the corresponding drop-down list.

## Inserting Multiple Copies of a Block

The features of the **INSERT** and **ARRAY** commands are combined using the **MINSERT** (multiple insert) command. This method of inserting and arraying blocks saves time and disk space. To access the **MINSERT** command, type MINSERT at the Command: prompt.

An example of an application using the **MINSERT** command is the arrangement of desks on a drawing. Suppose you want to draw the layout shown in **Figure 22-11**. First, specify architectural units and set the limits to 30',22'. Draw a 4' × 3' rectangle and save it as a block named DESK. The arrangement is to be three rows and four columns. Make the horizontal spacing between desks 2', and the vertical spacing 4'. Use the following command sequence:

```
Command: MINSERT↵
Enter block name or [?]: <current>: DESK↵
Specify insertion point or [Scale/X/Y/Z/Rotate/PScale/PX/PY/PZ/PRotate]: (pick a point)
Enter X scale factor, specify opposite corner, or [Corner/XYZ] <1>: ↵
Enter Y scale factor <use X scale factor>: ↵
Specify rotation angle <0>: ↵
Enter number of rows (---) <1>: 3↵
Enter number of columns (|||) <1>: 4↵
Enter distance between rows or specify unit cell (---): 7'↵
Specify distance between columns (|||): 6'↵
```

**Figure 22-11.**
To create an arrangement of desks using the **MINSERT** command, first create a block named DESK.

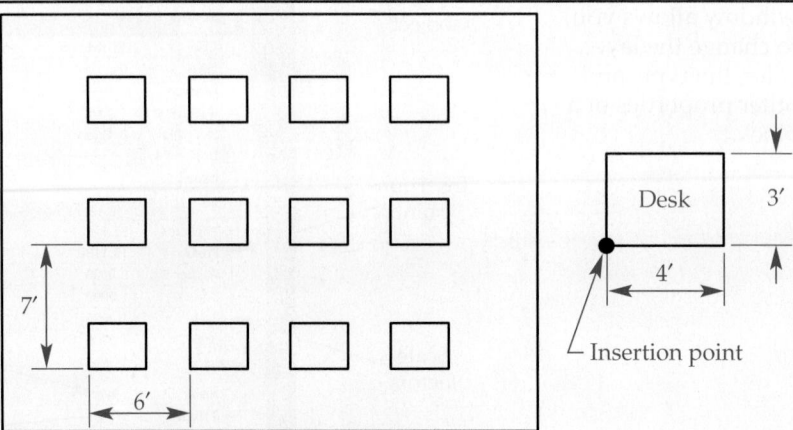

The resulting arrangement is shown in **Figure 22-11.** The complete pattern takes on the characteristics of a block, except that an array created with the **MINSERT** command cannot be exploded. Since the array cannot be exploded, you can use the **Properties** window to modify the number of rows and columns, change the spacing between objects, or change the layer, color, or linetype properties. If the initial block is rotated, all arrayed objects are also rotated about their insertion points. If the arrayed objects are rotated about the insertion point while using the **MINSERT** command, all objects are aligned on that point.

**PROFESSIONAL TIP**

As an alternative to the previous example, if you were working with different desk sizes, a 2D unit block may serve your purposes better than an exact size block. To create a 5′ × 3′-6″ (60″ × 42″) desk, for example, insert a one-unit square block using either the **INSERT** or **MINSERT** command, and enter the following for the X and Y scale factors:

Enter X scale factor, specify opposite corner, or
    [Corner/XYZ] <1>: **60**↵
Enter Y scale factor <use X scale factor>: **42**↵

A 2D unit block can be used in this manner for a variety of objects.

---

## Exercise 22-3

○ Start a new drawing or use one of your templates. Specify architectural units and set the limits to 80′,60′. Then, perform a **ZOOM All**.
○ Draw the chair shown below and save it as a block named CHAIR.
○ Use the **MINSERT** command twice to create the theater arrangement. The sides of the chairs should touch. Each row on either side of the aisle should have 10 chairs. The spacing between rows is 4′. The width of the center aisle is 5′.
○ Consider where you should insert the first chair to obtain the pattern.
○ Save the drawing as EX22-3.

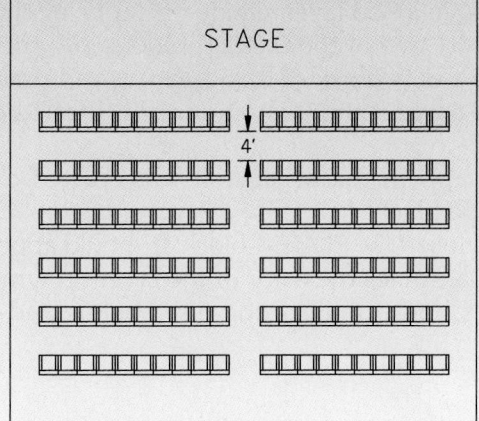

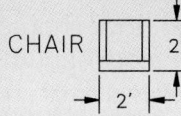

---

## Inserting Entire Drawings

The **INSERT** command can be used to insert an entire drawing file into the current drawing. To do so, enter the **INSERT** command and pick the **Browse...** button in the **Insert** dialog box to access the **Select Drawing File** dialog box. You can then select a drawing file to insert, as discussed earlier in this chapter.

When one drawing is inserted into another, the inserted drawing becomes a block reference. As a block, it may be moved to a new location with a single pick. The drawing is inserted on the current layer, but it does not inherit the color, linetype, or thickness properties of that layer. You can explode the inserted drawing back to its original objects if desired. Once exploded, the drawing objects revert to their original layers. A drawing that is inserted brings any existing block definitions, layers, linetypes, text styles, and dimension styles into the current drawing.

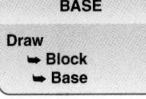

By default, every drawing has an insertion point of 0,0,0. (This is the insertion point used for a drawing file when you insert it into the current drawing.) If you want to change the insertion point of the drawing you need to insert, you can use the **BASE** command. Pick **Base** from the **Block** cascading menu in the **Draw** pull-down menu, or enter BASE at the Command: prompt as follows:

Command: **BASE**↵
Enter base point <0.0000, 0.0000, 0.0000>: *(pick a point or enter new coordinates)*

The new base point now becomes the insertion point for the drawing.

---

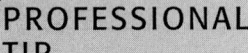

**PROFESSIONAL TIP**

When working on a drawing, it is common practice in industry to refer to other drawings to check features or dimensions. In many instances, the prints are not available and must be produced. You can avoid such delays by using the **INSERT** command. When you need to reference another drawing, simply insert it into your current drawing. When you are done checking the features or dimensions you need, simply use the **UNDO** command to undo the **INSERT** operation or erase the inserted drawing.

---

### Exercise 22-4

○ Open EX22-2.
○ If your drawing does not have a Red layer, create one and set it current.
○ Draw a 6 × 4 rectangle. Insert two of the CIRCLE blocks into the rectangle, both one unit in diameter. Make a new block of this drawing and name it PLATE-2.
○ Erase all objects on screen and set the 0 layer current. Insert both the PLATE-1 and PLATE-2 blocks.
○ The PLATE-2 block should appear red because it was created on the Red layer. The PLATE-1 block should be black.
○ Set the Red layer current and insert the PLATE-1 block. It should appear red because it was created on layer 0 and assumes the color of the layer on which it is inserted.
○ Enter the **BASE** command. Choose an insertion point below and to the left of the objects on screen.
○ Save the drawing as EX22-4.
○ Start a new drawing.
○ Insert drawing EX22-4 into your new drawing. The insertion point used is the one you established using the **BASE** command.
○ Enter any editing command and select a line on one of the PLATE blocks. The entire drawing should be highlighted, since the drawing is actually one large block.
○ Do not save the drawing.

---

# Using DesignCenter to Insert Blocks

Blocks or drawing files can be readily located and previewed before they are inserted using **DesignCenter**. You can insert blocks or entire drawings into your current drawing using the drag-and-drop capability of **DesignCenter**. You can also browse through existing drawings for blocks, show images of blocks and drawings, and display other information about saved blocks or files.

To access **DesignCenter**, pick the **DesignCenter** button on the **Standard** toolbar, select **DesignCenter** from the **Tools** pull-down menu, enter ADC or ADCENTER at the Command: prompt, or use the [Ctrl]+[2] key combination. When **DesignCenter** opens, it displays the content that was last selected in it. **DesignCenter** is able to do this because it keeps a history of the drawing files and the content that had been previously accessed. The **Tree View** area, located on the left side of the **DesignCenter** window, is used to navigate to drawing files. The right side of **DesignCenter** is called the **Content** area. This area displays the available content from what is selected in the **Tree View** area. See **Figure 22-12**. If a folder is selected on the **Tree View** side, the **Content** area displays all the drawing files within that folder. If a named object category is selected within a drawing file, such as Blocks, then the **Content** area displays all the blocks that are in that drawing file.

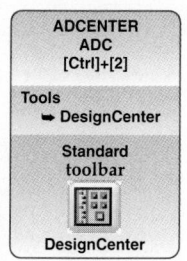

The **DesignCenter** toolbar buttons and tabs contain features for navigating to drawing file content and viewing options. **Figure 22-13** shows the button options available on the **DesignCenter** toolbar. The following features are used for navigation:

- **Load**. Displays the **Load** dialog box. Selecting a file and picking **Open** makes the drawing file active in **DesignCenter**.
- **Back**. Shows the last drawing file content that was selected. Picking the **Back** pull-down arrow shows a list of the previous drawing file content.
- **Forward**. If the **Back** button has been used, the **Forward** button is available. Picking it shows the last drawing file content that was selected. Picking the **Forward** pull-down arrow shows a list of the previous drawing file content.
- **Up**. Moves up one folder from the current one in the folder hierarchy.
- **Search**. Opens the **Search** dialog box, which allows you to search for drawings by specifying various criteria.

---

**Figure 22-12.**
The **DesignCenter** is used to search for existing blocks and drawing files for insertion into the current drawing.

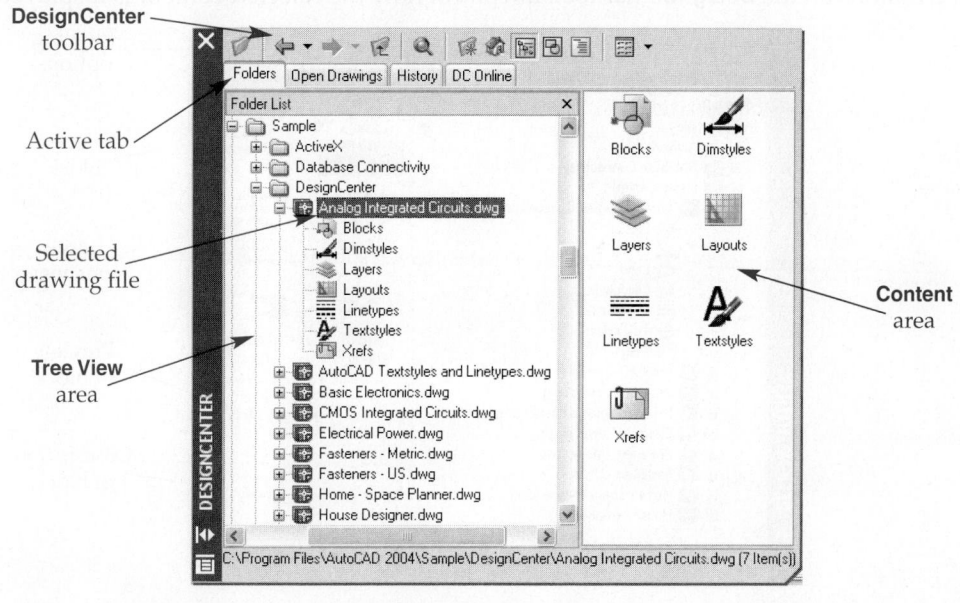

---

Figure 22-13.
The **DesignCenter** toolbar.

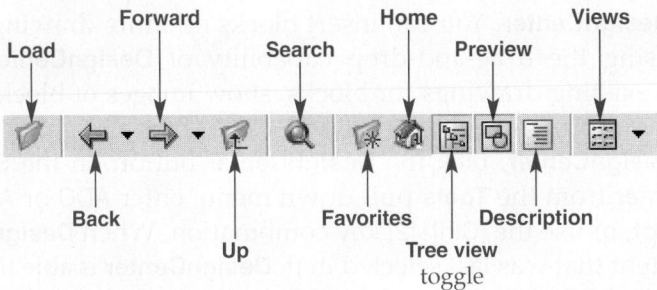

Load     Forward     Search     Home     Preview     Views

Back     Up     Favorites     Tree view toggle     Description

- **Favorites.** Displays the content of the **Favorites** folder. Content can be added to the **Favorites** folder by right-clicking over an item in the **Tree View** area or the **Content** area and selecting **Add to Favorites** from the right-click menu. This could be a drive letter, a folder, a drawing file, or any named objects within a drawing file, such as Blocks or Layers.
- **Home.** Selecting the **Home** button moves to the *home* content in **DesignCenter**. By default, *home* is the DesignCenter folder located in the AutoCAD 2004\Sample folder. To change this, right-click over an item in the **Tree View** area and select **Set as Home** from the right-click menu. This could be a drive letter, folder, or drawing file. The home location should be your most commonly accessed item in **DesignCenter**.

The last four buttons on the **DesignCenter** toolbar control viewing options within the **DesignCenter** window. The areas controlled by these options are shown in Figure 22-14. The following features are available:

- **Tree View toggle.** This button controls whether the **Tree View** area is hidden. The toggle only works when the **Folders** or **Open Drawings** tab is current.
- **Preview.** This is a toggle that displays or hides the **Preview** area. If no preview was saved for the selected content, the area is empty.
- **Description.** This is a toggle that displays or hides the **Description** area. If a description was given when a block was created, the related text is displayed in this area. If no description was given, the area displays *No description found*.

Figure 22-14.
Viewing options on the **DesignCenter** toolbar control how the selected content is displayed.

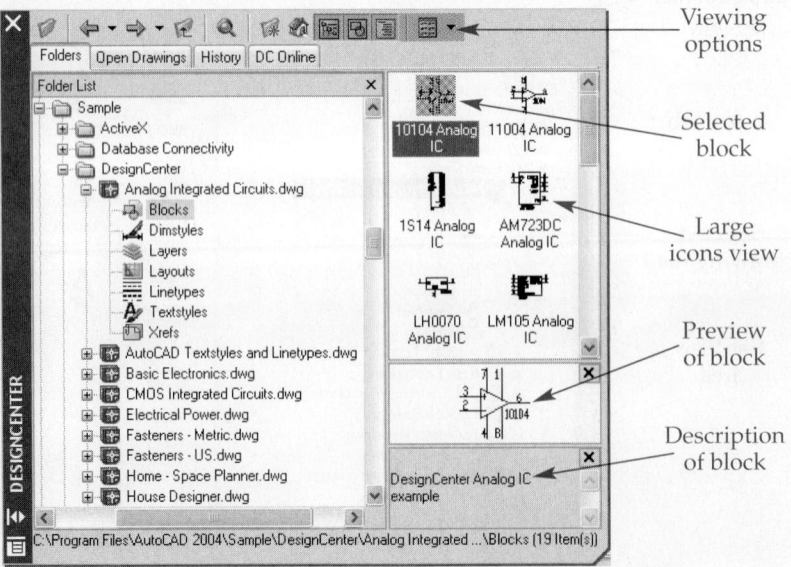

Viewing options

Selected block

Large icons view

Preview of block

Description of block

- **Views.** This button is used to control how the display appears in the **Content** area. Content can be displayed using large icons, small icons, a list view, or a detailed view.

When **DesignCenter** is opened, the active tab is set to **Folders**. This shows the hierarchy of files and folders on your computer, including network drives. Navigating in the **Folder List** view is similar to using Windows Explorer. The **Open Drawings** tab displays all the open drawing files in the current AutoCAD session. The **History** tab displays the most recently accessed files in **DesignCenter**. The **DC Online** tab gives you access to drawing content that can be downloaded from the Internet on the DesignCenter Online Web page.

To view the blocks that belong to a drawing, click on the Blocks icon in the **Tree View** area or double-click on the Blocks icon in the **Content** area. Once the desired block has been found, you can use a drag-and-drop operation or the **Insert** dialog box to insert it into the current drawing.

To use drag and drop, move the cursor over the top of the block in the **Content** area, press and hold down the pick button on your pointing device, and drag the cursor to the opened drawing. Release the pick button and the block is inserted into the drawing. The block is inserted based on the type of drag-and-drop units specified when creating the block. For example, if the original block was a 1″ × 1″ square, and the drag-and-drop units specified were feet when the block was created, then the block will be a 12″ × 12″ square when it is inserted from **DesignCenter**.

You can access the **Insert** dialog box while inserting a block from **DesignCenter** by right-clicking on the block icon in the **Content** area. When the shortcut menu appears, select **Insert Block...** to activate the **INSERT** command. This allows you to scale, rotate, or explode the block during insertion.

To insert an entire drawing using **DesignCenter**, select the folder in which the drawing resides in the **Tree View** area. Any drawings in the selected folder appear in the **Content** area. Use drag-and-drop to insert them into the current drawing. You can also right-click on a drawing icon and select **Insert as Block...** from the shortcut menu. In addition to blocks and drawings, **DesignCenter** can be used to insert dimension styles, layers, layouts, linetypes, text styles, and xrefs.

## Using the Tool Palettes to Insert Blocks

Tool palettes provide another way to access blocks for insertion into a drawing. This feature is similar to **DesignCenter** in the way that blocks can be previewed before inserting them. To open the **Tool Palettes** window, pick the **Tool Palettes** button on the **Standard** toolbar, select **Tool Palettes Window** from the **Tools** pull-down menu, enter TP or TOOLPALETTES at the Command: prompt, or use the [Ctrl]+[3] key combination. The **Tool Palettes** window is shown in **Figure 22-15.** The window is divided into tool palettes, each with a tab. The tool palettes are used to store blocks and hatch patterns.

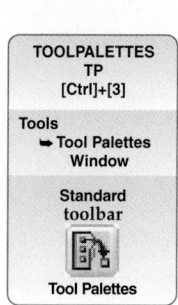

To insert a block from the **Tool Palettes** window, select the tool palette tab in which the block resides and locate the block. Use the scroll bar on the side of the window to move up or down in the tool palette. When the block is located, place the cursor over the block icon. You can use the drag-and-drop method, or you can pick once on the block icon. Then, move the cursor into the drawing area and pick again to place the block. When a block is selected in the tool palette with a single pick, the block is attached to the crosshairs once the cursor is moved into the drawing area. The location where the crosshairs and the block are connected is defined by the insertion point of the block.

When inserting a block in this manner, you can access scaling and rotation options for the block at the command line before picking an insertion point. Enter S to scale the block along the XYZ axes or R to specify a rotation angle for the block. Blocks inserted from tool palettes are automatically scaled based on a ratio of the current drawing scale to the scale used in the original block definition.

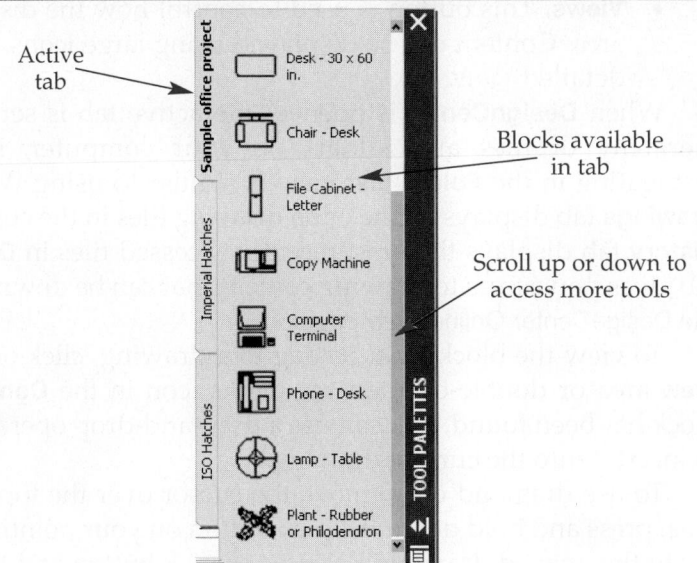

**Figure 22-15.**
The **Tool Palettes** window. Blocks may be inserted into the current drawing from a selected tab.

Active tab

Blocks available in tab

Scroll up or down to access more tools

Blocks can be added to tool palettes from **DesignCenter**. The **Tool Palettes** window is discussed in greater detail later in this chapter.

---

## Exercise 22-5

○ Start a new drawing or use one of your templates.
○ Open **DesignCenter**.
○ In the **Tree View** area, navigate to the AutoCAD 2004/Sample/DesignCenter folder.
○ Insert two blocks from the Fasteners-US.dwg file.
○ Insert two blocks from the Basic Electronics.dwg file.
○ Save the file as EX22-5.
○ Start a new drawing or use one of your templates.
○ Open the **Tool Palettes** window.
○ Insert two blocks from the **Sample office project** tab. Adjust the scale of each block when inserting.
○ Do not save the drawing.

---

# Editing Blocks

AutoCAD gives you the ability to edit blocks in the current drawing. This is referred to as *in-place reference editing*. This allows you to make minor changes to blocks, wblocks, or drawings that have been inserted in the current drawing. This type of editing can be used to modify the selected block reference as well as the original block definition. When editing blocks within a drawing, changes made to one block reference can be automatically applied to all instances of the same block in the drawing. When editing wblocks and inserted drawings, changes can be made without the need to open the original file. In-place editing cannot be used on blocks that have been inserted into a drawing with the **MINSERT** command.

If you do not use in-place reference editing, blocks must first be broken into their original components before they can be edited. Two methods can be used to break blocks apart. One involves the **INSERT** command and the **Explode** option in the **Insert**

AutoCAD and its Applications—Basics

dialog box. This method is used at the time of insertion. The other method involves the **EXPLODE** command and can be done at any time. These methods are discussed later in this chapter.

## Editing Blocks in Place

You can edit a block in-place by using the **REFEDIT** command. This command is accessed by typing REFEDIT at the Command: prompt, using the **Refedit** toolbar, or by picking **Edit Reference In-Place** from the **Xref and Block Editing** cascading menu in the **Modify** pull-down menu.

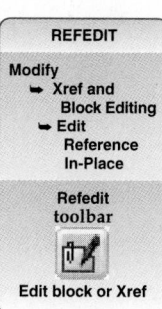

To display the **Refedit** toolbar, right-click on any displayed toolbar button and pick **Refedit**. See **Figure 22-16**. The button on the left of the toolbar is **Edit Block or Xref**. You can use this button to access the **REFEDIT** command. When you enter the **REFEDIT** command, you get this prompt:

Command: **REFEDIT**↵
Select reference: *(select the block to edit)*

Now the **Reference Edit** dialog box is displayed. See **Figure 22-17**. The features and options in the **Identify Reference** tab are explained as follows:

- **Reference name: area.** This area displays the name of the selected block and any references nested within the selected block. **Figure 22-18** shows a block nested within the selected block.
- **Preview area.** An image of the selected block is displayed here. You can cycle through nested blocks by picking the reference name. The preview image changes to display the currently selected block.
- **Automatically select all nested objects**. This option in the **Path:** area makes all of the block objects available for editing, including nested blocks.

---

Figure 22-16.
The **Refedit** toolbar.

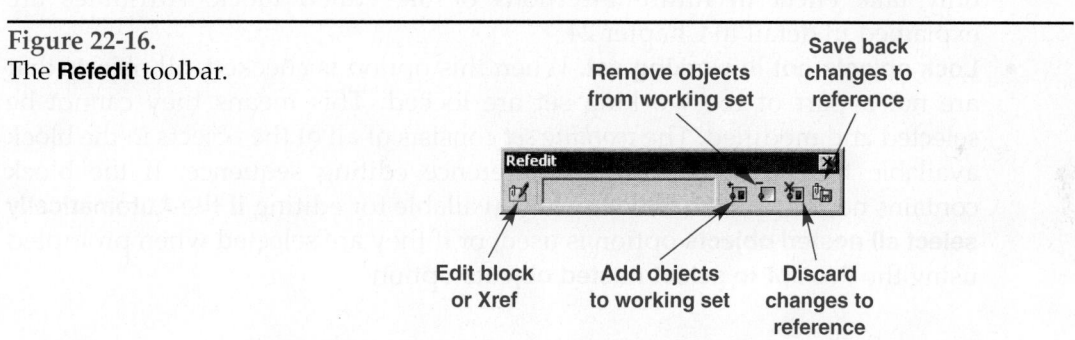

---

Figure 22-17.
The **Reference Edit** dialog box.

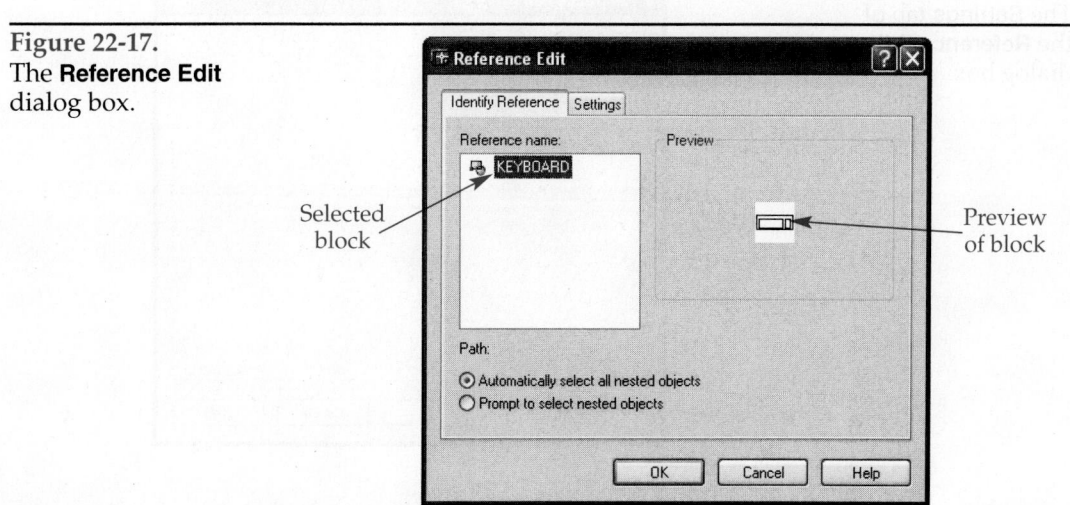

---

Figure 22-18.
Nested blocks are
shown in the tree
view of the
**Reference Edit**
dialog box.

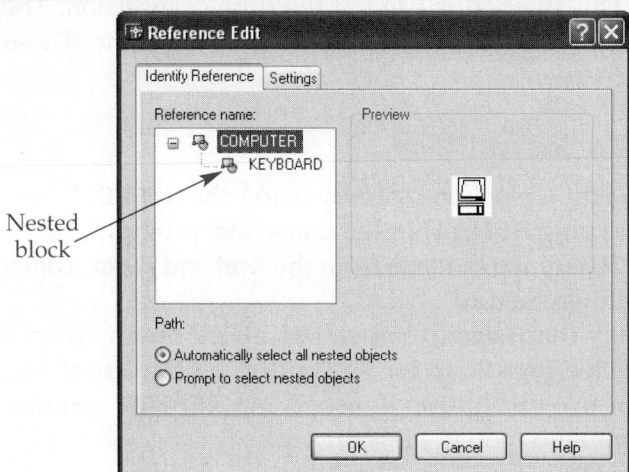

Nested
block

- **Prompt to select nested objects.** If this option is used, AutoCAD prompts you to select nested objects. Individual objects can then be selected for editing.

The **Reference Edit** dialog box also contains the **Settings** tab. See **Figure 22-19.** The options in this tab are explained as follows:

- **Create unique layer, style, and block names.** This option controls the naming of layers and other named objects extracted from the reference. If this option is active, named objects are given a prefix such as $#$.
- **Display attribute definitions for editing.** If this option is checked, the block attributes and attribute definitions in the reference are available for editing. The attributes of the original block reference are unchanged when your changes are saved to the block being edited. The edited attribute definitions only take effect in future insertions of the edited block. Attributes are explained in detail in Chapter 24.
- **Lock objects not in working set.** When this option is checked, all objects that are not a part of the working set are locked. This means they cannot be selected and modified. The *working set* consists of all of the objects in the block available for editing during the reference editing sequence. If the block contains nested objects, they are only available for editing if the **Automatically select all nested objects** option is used, or if they are selected when prompted using the **Prompt to select nested objects** option.

Figure 22-19.
The **Settings** tab of
the **Reference Edit**
dialog box.

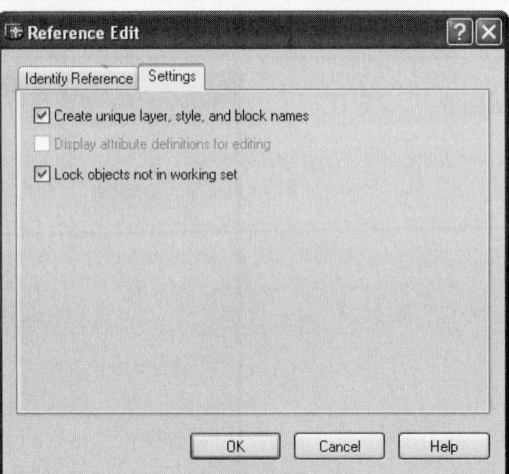

Once all settings are made in the **Reference Edit** dialog box, pick the **OK** button to begin editing the block. If the **Prompt to select nested objects** option is used, you get the following prompts:

Select nested objects: *(select the objects in the block to edit)*

Pick all objects in the block to be edited, then press [Enter].

Select nested objects: ↵
*n* items selected
Use REFCLOSE or the Refedit toolbar to end reference editing session.
Command:

If multiple insertions of the same block are displayed, be sure to pick the one you originally selected.

When the Command: prompt is available, all the objects in the drawing are grayed out, except the objects you selected. Now use any drawing or editing commands to alter the object as desired. Pick the **Save back changes to reference** button on the **Refedit** toolbar. Pick **OK** at the AutoCAD alert shown in **Figure 22-20** if you want to continue with the save. Changes to the edited block are displayed immediately. The changes also affect other insertions of the same block and future insertions of the block.

Objects that are selected for the working set appear brighter than other objects. Objects that are not a part of the working set are faded. The percent of fading is controlled in the **Display** tab of the **Options** dialog box. A maximum of 90% fading is allowed, and the default is 50%.

Objects that are added to the drawing during the edit can be removed from the working set. The additional buttons on the **Refedit** toolbar are described below.

- **Add objects to working set.** Any object that is drawn during the in-place edit is automatically added to the working set. Additional existing objects can be added with this feature. If an object is added to the working set, it is removed from the host drawing. The **REFSET** command allows you to add to or remove objects from the working set.
- **Remove objects from working set.** Use this feature to remove objects from the working set. When an object is removed from the set, it appears faded. If an object is removed from the working set, it is added to the host drawing.
- **Discard changes to reference.** Pick this button if you want to exit the reference edit function without saving changes to the object. The **REFCLOSE** command allows you to save or discard changes to the working set, and closes reference editing.

The **REFEDIT** command can also be used on the command line by entering -REFEDIT at the Command: prompt. This is the command sequence:

Command: **-REFEDIT**↵
Select reference: *(select the block to change)*

---

**Figure 22-20.**
This dialog box appears after editing the selected objects within the block and picking the **Save back changes to reference** button.

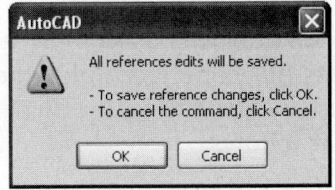

At the next prompt, type O and press [Enter] to accept the currently highlighted reference, or press [Enter] to use the **Next** option:

> Select nesting level [Ok/Next] <Next>: ↵
> Select nesting level [Ok/Next] <Next>: **O**↵
> Enter object selection method [All/Nested] <All>: (*Press* [Enter] *for all or type* N *to select*): **N**↵
> Select nested objects: (*select objects within the block to edit and press* [Enter])
> Display attribute definitions [Yes/No] <No>: (*type* Y *or* [Enter] *for No*)
> Use REFCLOSE or the Refedit toolbar to end reference editing session.
> Command: (*use drawing and editing commands as needed to edit the block*)

Use the **Save back changes to reference** button on the **Refedit** toolbar as previously discussed, or enter the **REFCLOSE** command and use one of its options. The **Save** option is used as follows:

> Command: **REFCLOSE**↵
> Enter option [Save/Discard reference changes] <Save>: ↵

The AutoCAD alert box is displayed. Pick **OK** to accept the changes.

---

## Exercise 22-6

○ Open EX22-2.
○ Use the **REFEDIT** command to change the original PLATE-1 block by changing the ∅1.0 and the ∅1.5 circles to ∅1.25 each.
○ Save the changes.
○ Save the drawing as EX22-6.

---

## Exploding a Block during Insertion

If you wish to edit the individual objects of a block at the time of insertion, you can insert a block and explode it in a single operation. This is done by picking the **Explode** check box in the **Insert** dialog box, as discussed earlier in this chapter. If you are using the **-INSERT** command, enter an asterisk (*) before the block name as follows:

> Command: **-INSERT**↵
> Enter block name or [?] <current>: **\*PLATE-1**↵
> Specify insertion point for block: (*pick a point*)
> Specify scale factor for XYZ axes: (*specify the scale and press* [Enter])
> Specify rotation angle <0>: ↵

The inserted geometry is not part of a block. It consists of individual objects that have their original properties and can be edited.

## Using the EXPLODE Command

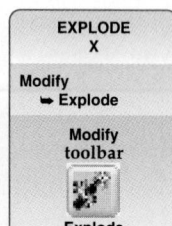

EXPLODE
X

Modify
↪ Explode

Modify
toolbar

Explode

The **EXPLODE** command is used to break apart any existing block, polyline, or dimension. To access this command, pick the **Explode** button on the **Modify** toolbar, select **Explode** from the **Modify** pull-down menu, or enter X or EXPLODE at the Command: prompt as follows:

> Command: **X** *or* **EXPLODE**↵
> Select objects: (*pick the block*)
> Select objects: ↵

---

When the block is exploded, the component objects are quickly redrawn. The individual objects can now be changed individually. To see if the **EXPLODE** command worked properly, select any object that was formerly part of the block. Only that object should be highlighted. If so, the block was exploded properly.

## Redefining Existing Blocks

Earlier in this chapter, you learned how to use the **REFEDIT** command to edit a block. Once the block is modified and the changes are saved, all instances of that block in the drawing are also updated. This can also be accomplished by what is referred to as redefining a block by using the **EXPLODE** and **BLOCK** commands together. To redefine an existing block, follow this procedure:

1. Insert the block to be redefined anywhere in your drawing.
2. Make sure you know where the insertion point of the block is located.
3. Explode the inserted block using the **EXPLODE** command.
4. Edit the block as needed.
5. Recreate the block definition using the **BLOCK** command.
6. Give the block the same name and the same insertion point it originally had.
7. Select the objects to be included in the block.
8. Pick **OK**. When a message from AutoCAD appears and asks if you want to redefine the block, pick **Yes**.
9. When the **BLOCK** command is complete, all insertions of the block are updated.

A common mistake is to forget to use the **EXPLODE** command before redefining the block. When you try to create the block again with the same name, an alert box indicating the block references itself is displayed. This means you are trying to create a block that already exists. Once you press the **OK** button, the alert box disappears and the **Block Definition** dialog box is redisplayed. Press the **Cancel** button, explode the block to be redefined, and try again.

NOTE

You can also redefine existing blocks using the **-BLOCK** command instead of the **Block Definition** dialog box. This command was covered earlier in this chapter. After the block has been inserted and exploded, and the necessary changes have been made, issue the **-BLOCK** command. Enter the same block name, enter Y or YES to redefine the block, pick the same insertion point, and select the revised objects. Finally, press [Enter] to redefine the block.

## Understanding the Circular Reference Error

As described in the previous example, when you try to redefine a block that already exists (using the same name), AutoCAD informs you that the block references itself. The concept of a block *referencing itself* may be a little difficult to grasp at first without fully understanding how AutoCAD works with blocks. A block can be composed of any objects, including other blocks. When using the **BLOCK** command to incorporate an existing block into a new block, AutoCAD must make a list of all the objects that compose the new block. This means AutoCAD must refer to any existing block definitions that are selected to be part of the new block. If you select an instance, or reference, of the block being redefined as a component object for the new definition, a problem occurs. You are trying to redefine a block name using a previous version of the block with the same name. In other words, the new block refers to a block of the same name, or *references itself*.

For example, assume you create a block named BOX that is composed of four line objects in the shape of a square, and insert it. You then decide the block needs to be changed so that it contains a small circle in the lower-left corner. If the original BOX block is exploded, all that is left are the four line objects. After drawing the required circle, you can enter the **BLOCK** command and recreate a block named BOX by selecting the four lines and the circle as the component objects. Redefining a block destroys the old definition and creates a new one. Any blocks with the same name are redefined with the updated changes. Make sure you want to redefine the block before agreeing to do so. Otherwise, give the block a new name. The correct way to redefine a block is shown in **Figure 22-21.**

Alternately, assume you do not explode the block, but still draw the circle and try to redefine the block. By selecting the BOX block *and* the circle, a new block named BOX would now be a block reference of the BOX block with a circle. The old block definition of BOX has not been destroyed, but a new definition has been attempted. Thus, AutoCAD is trying to define a new block named BOX by using an instance of the BOX block. This is referred to as a *circular reference*, and is what is meant by a block referencing itself. See **Figure 22-21.**

**Figure 22-21.**
A—The correct procedure for redefining a block. B—Redefining a block that has not first been exploded creates an invalid circular reference.

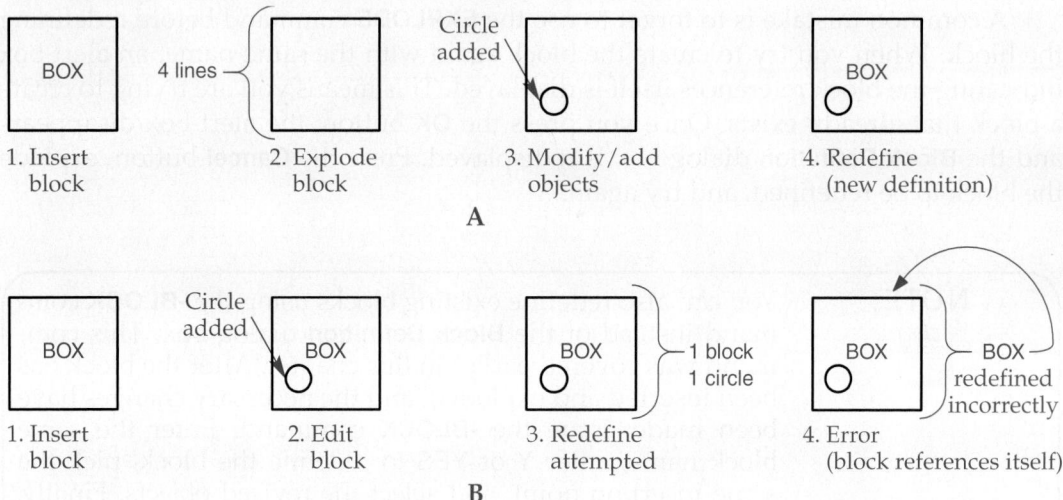

# Creating a Block from a Drawing File

You can create a block from any existing drawing. This allows you to avoid redrawing the object as a block, thus saving time. Remember, if something has already been drawn, try to use it as a block rather than redrawing it. Use the **-INSERT** command in the following manner to define a block named BOLT from an existing drawing file named fastener.dwg:

Command: **-INSERT**↵
Enter block name or [?]: <current>: **BOLT=FASTENER**↵
Specify insertion point or [Scale/X/Y/Z/Rotate/PScale/PX/PY/PZ/PRotate]: *(press the [Esc] key)*

The drawing is not inserted on screen because the command is canceled. However, a block named BOLT is saved and added to the drawing file, and it can be used in the same manner as any other block.

AutoCAD and its Applications—Basics

The same procedure is possible using the **Insert** dialog box. Using the **Browse...** button, select the fastener file. The selected file is then displayed in the **Name:** text box. Use this text box to change the name from fastener to BOLT and pick **OK**. The file can be inserted into the drawing, or you can press the [Esc] key to exit the command. A block named BOLT has now been created from the file and can be used as desired.

---

### Exercise 22-7

○ Open EX22-3.
○ Insert the CHAIR block anywhere on the drawing.
○ Explode the chair you just inserted.
○ Add a feature to the chair, such as a headrest (keep it simple).
○ Create a block named CHAIR from the revised chair.
○ Confirm that you want to redefine the block, and pick the same insertion point used by the original CHAIR block.
○ When the **BLOCK** command is completed, all chairs should be updated to reflect the changes.
○ Save the drawing as EX22-7.

---

## Creating Blocks As Drawing Files

Blocks created with the **BLOCK** command are stored in the drawing in which they are made. The **WBLOCK** (write block) command allows you to create a drawing (DWG) file out of a block. You can also use the **WBLOCK** command to create a global block from any object (it does not have to be first saved as a block). The resulting drawing file can then be inserted as a block into any drawing.

There are several ways to use the **WBLOCK** command. To see how the first method works, open drawing EX22-1. Convert the CIRCLE block to a permanent block by making it a separate drawing file. Use the following procedure:

> Command: **W** *or* **WBLOCK.**⏎

The **Write Block** dialog box appears, **Figure 22-22.** This dialog box is similar to the **Block Definition** dialog box. Pick the **Block:** radio button, and then select the CIRCLE block from the drop-down list in the **Source** area. Specify where you want to save the wblock by typing in a path or picking the ellipsis (...) button next to the **File name and path:** drop-down list (if the path shown is not the desired location). By default, the new drawing file has the same name as the block. This is shown with the folder path in the **File name and path:** entry in **Figure 22-22.** Picking the ellipsis (...) button displays the **Browse for Drawing File** dialog box. Navigate to the folder where you want to save the file, confirm the name of the file in the **File name:** field, and then pick the **Save** button. This returns you to the **Write Block** dialog box. Select the type of units that **DesignCenter** will use to insert the block in the **Insert units:** drop-down list. When you are finished, pick **OK**.

The above sequence wrote a new block, with the name HOLE, to a drawing file on disk. You can now use the **INSERT** command to insert the wblock into the current drawing or any other drawing.

---

Pick to create
a wblock from a
saved block

Selected block

File location

Pick to access
the **Browse for Folder**
dialog box

Pick to specify
insertion units used
by **DesignCenter**

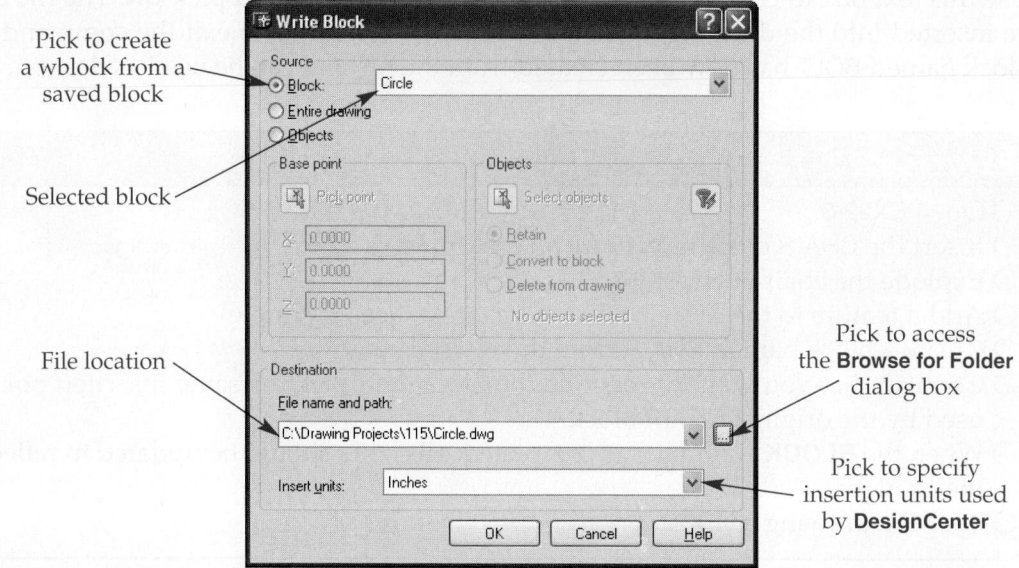

**NOTE**  When another drawing is inserted into the current drawing, the referenced drawing acts as a block. It is a single object and its individual components cannot be edited unless the **REFEDIT** command is used or the block is exploded.

## Creating a New Wblock

Suppose you want to create a wblock from a shape you have just drawn, but you have not yet made a block. The following sequence is used to save a selected object as a drawing file. First, enter the **WBLOCK** command and select the **Objects** radio button in the **Write Block** dialog box (it is active by default). Pick the **Select objects** button to select the objects for the drawing file. Next, pick the **Pick point** button to select the insertion point. You can also enter coordinates in the **X:**, **Y:**, and **Z:** text boxes. If the path shown in the **File name and path:** text box is not where you want to save the file, access the **Browse for Drawing File** dialog box by picking the ellipsis (**...**) button. Navigate to the folder where you want to save the file. Specify the name of the file in the **File name:** field and then pick the **Save** button. In the **Write Block** dialog box, select the type of units that **DesignCenter** will use to insert the block in the **Insert units:** drop-down list. When you are through, pick **OK**. See **Figure 22-23**.

This sequence is the same as that used with the **BLOCK** command. However, the wblock is saved to disk as a drawing file, *not* as a block in the current drawing. Be sure to specify the correct file path in the **File name and path:** text box when using the **Write Block** dialog box. A drawing file named desk that is to be saved in the blocks folder on the C: hard drive, for example, would be saved as c:\blocks\desk.

**Figure 22-23.**
Using the **Write Block** dialog box to create a wblock from selected objects without first defining a block.

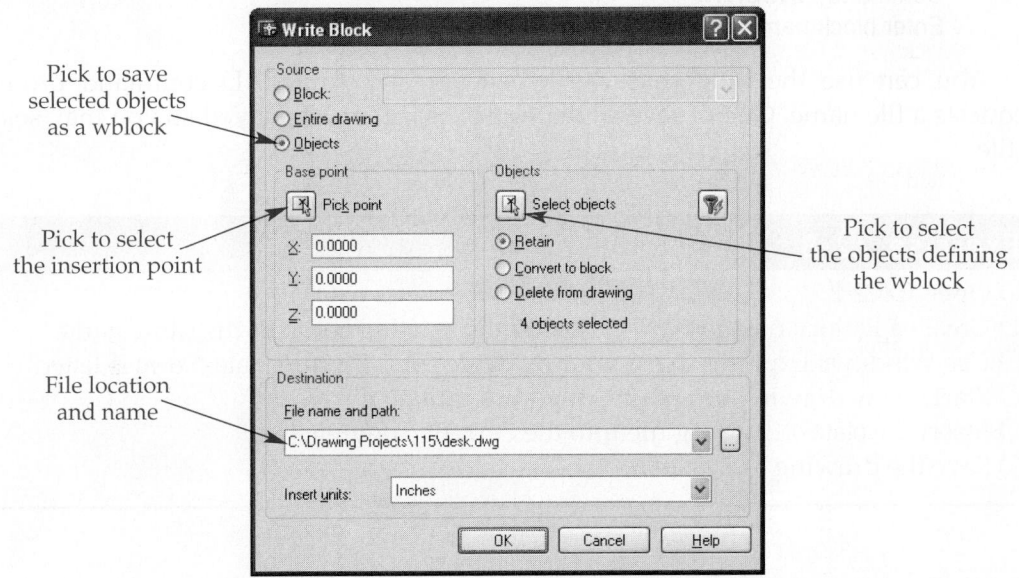

Pick to save selected objects as a wblock

Pick to select the insertion point

Pick to select the objects defining the wblock

File location and name

## Storing a Drawing As a Wblock

An entire drawing can also be stored as a wblock. To do this, pick the **Entire drawing** radio button in the **Write Block** dialog box. Specify the location to save the wblock and give it a name using the **File name and path:** text box. Select the type of units **DesignCenter** will use to insert the block in the **Insert units:** drop-down list, and pick **OK** when you are through.

In this case, the whole drawing is saved to disk as if you had used the **SAVE** command. The difference is that all unused blocks are deleted from the drawing. If the drawing contains any unused blocks, this method reduces the size of a drawing considerably.

PROFESSIONAL TIP

Using the **Entire drawing** wblock option is a good way to remove named objects that are unused in your drawing to reduce the file size. Use this routine when you have completed a drawing and decide the unused blocks, layers, styles, and other unused objects are no longer needed. The **PURGE** command can also be used to remove any unused layers, linetypes, text styles, dimension styles, multiline styles, blocks, and shapes. But the process is slower than using the **Entire drawing** wblock option. The **PURGE** command is discussed later in this chapter.

## Inserting a Drawing File with the Select Drawing File Dialog Box

When you use the **INSERT** command, you have the option to insert a block *or* a wblock. Picking the **Browse...** button in the **Insert** dialog box activates the **Select Drawing File** dialog box. You can then scroll through the files in any folder on the current drive, or on another drive, and pick the file name you need. This was discussed earlier in this chapter.

If you enter the **-INSERT** command, you can access the **Select Drawing File** dialog box by entering a tilde (~) when prompted for the block name as follows:

Command: **-INSERT**↵
Enter block name or [?]: <*current*>: **~**↵

You can use the tilde character whenever any AutoCAD command prompt requests a file name. One of several dialog boxes is then displayed so you may select a file.

---

### Exercise 22-8

○ Open EX22-2.
○ Create a wblock named PLATE-1 using the existing block of the same name.
○ Use Windows Explorer to list your drawing files. Be sure plate-1.dwg is listed.
○ Start a new drawing or use one of your templates.
○ Insert the plate-1 drawing file into the current drawing.
○ Save the drawing as EX22-8.

---

## Revising an Inserted Drawing

You may find that you need to revise a drawing file that has been used in other drawings. If this happens, you can quickly update any drawing in which the revised drawing is used. For example, if a drawing file named pump was modified after being used several times in a drawing, simply enter the **-INSERT** command, and type an equal sign (=) after the block name to update all the references to the pump drawing:

Command: **-INSERT**↵
Enter block name or [?]: <*current*>: **PUMP=**↵
Block "pump" already exists. Redefine it? [Yes/No] <N>: **Y**↵
Block "pump" redefined
Regenerating model.
Specify insertion point or [Scale/X/Y/Z/Rotate/PScale/PX/PY/PZ/PRotate]: (*press the* [Esc] *key*)

All of the pump references are automatically updated, and by pressing the [Esc] key to cancel the command, no new insertions of the pump drawing are made.

Suppose you had inserted a drawing file named fastener into your current drawing, but then saved it as a block and named it screw. Now you have decided to revise the fastener drawing. The screw block can be updated using the **-INSERT** command as follows:

Command: **-INSERT**↵
Enter block name or [?]: <*current*>: **SCREW=FASTENER**↵
Block "screw" already exists. Redefine it? [Yes/No] <N>: **Y**↵
Block "screw" redefined
Regenerating model.
Specify insertion point or [Scale/X/Y/Z/Rotate/PScale/PX/PY/PZ/PRotate]: (*press the* [Esc] *key*)

## Symbol Libraries

As you become proficient with AutoCAD, you will want to start constructing symbol libraries. A *symbol library* is a collection of related shapes, views, symbols, and other content used repeatedly in drawings. Some drafters incorporate symbols into screen and tablet menus. These customization methods are discussed in detail in *AutoCAD and its Applications—Advanced.* Arranging a storage system for frequently used symbols increases productivity and saves time. First, you need to establish how the symbols are stored (as blocks or drawing files) and then determine where they will be stored for insertion into different drawings.

### Blocks Versus Separate Drawing Files

As discussed earlier, the main difference between the **BLOCK** and **WBLOCK** commands is that a block is saved with the drawing in which it is created and the **WBLOCK** command saves the block as a separate drawing file. A complete drawing file occupies more disk space than a block. Also, a drawing file can contain many blocks; once the drawing file is inserted into the current drawing, all the blocks in the drawing file are also inserted into the drawing.

If you decide to use blocks, each person in the office or class must have access to the drawing that contains the blocks. This is often done by creating the blocks in a template file or a separate drawing file. If individual drawing files are used rather than blocks, each student or employee must have access to the files.

### Creating a Symbol Library

Once a set of related block definitions is created, you can arrange the blocks in a symbol library. This can consist of a single drawing file or several files. Each block should be identified with a name and insertion point location. Whether the symbols are being stored in a single drawing file or as individual files, several guidelines can be used to create the symbol library:

- Assign one person to initially create the symbols for each specialty.
- Follow class or company symbol standards.
- When using blocks, save one group of symbols per drawing file. When using individual drawing files, name the files accordingly so they can be assigned to separate folders on the hard drive. For example, you may want to create several different symbol libraries based on the following types of symbols:
  - ✓ Electronic
  - ✓ Electrical
  - ✓ Piping
  - ✓ Mechanical

- ✓ Structural
- ✓ Architectural
- ✓ Landscaping
- ✓ Mapping

- Print a hard copy of the symbol library. Include a representation of the symbol, its insertion point, any other necessary information, and where it is located. A sample is shown in **Figure 22-24.** Provide all users of the symbols with a copy of the listing.
- If a network drive is not in use, copy the symbol library file(s) to each work-station in the class or office.
- Keep backup copies of all files in a secure place.
- When symbols are revised, update all files containing the edited symbols.
- Inform all users of any changes to saved symbols.

**Figure 22-24.**
A printed copy of piping flow diagram blocks stored in a symbol library. Each colored dot indicates the insertion point, and is not part of the block.

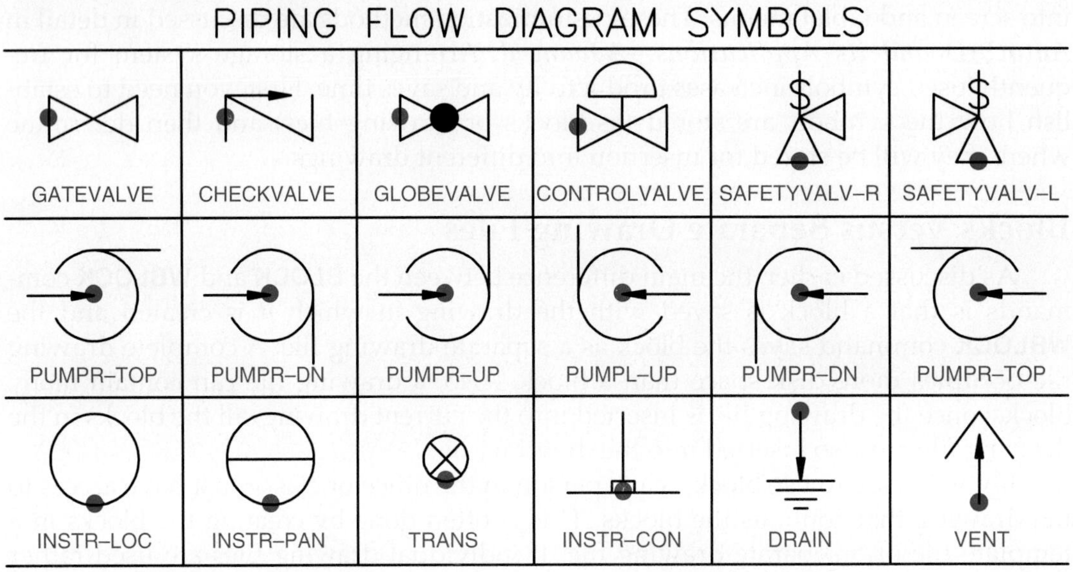

## PIPING FLOW DIAGRAM SYMBOLS

| GATEVALVE | CHECKVALVE | GLOBEVALVE | CONTROLVALVE | SAFETYVALV–R | SAFETYVALV–L |
| PUMPR–TOP | PUMPR–DN | PUMPR–UP | PUMPL–UP | PUMPR–DN | PUMPR–TOP |
| INSTR–LOC | INSTR–PAN | TRANS | INSTR–CON | DRAIN | VENT |

## Storing Symbol Drawings

The local or network hard disk drive is one of the best places to store a symbol library. It is easily accessed, quick, and more convenient to use than portable media. Writable CDs or other media can be used for backup purposes if a network drive with an automatic backup function is not available. In the absence of a network or modem, portable media can be used to transport files from one workstation to another.

There are several methods of storing symbols on the hard drive. Symbols can be saved as wblocks and organized within folders. It is recommended to store symbols outside of the AutoCAD 2004 folder. This will keep the system folder uncluttered and allow you to differentiate which folders and files were originally installed with AutoCAD. A good idea is to create a Blocks folder for storing your blocks, as shown in **Figure 22-25.**

Symbols can also be saved as blocks within a drawing. The symbols are then inserted using **DesignCenter** or the **Tool Palettes** window. When using this system, symbols can be grouped within several drawing files. For example, electrical symbols can be saved in an electrical.dwg drawing, and piping symbols can be saved in a

Figure 22-25.
An efficient way to store blocks saved as drawing files is to set up a Blocks folder containing folders for each type of symbol on the hard drive.

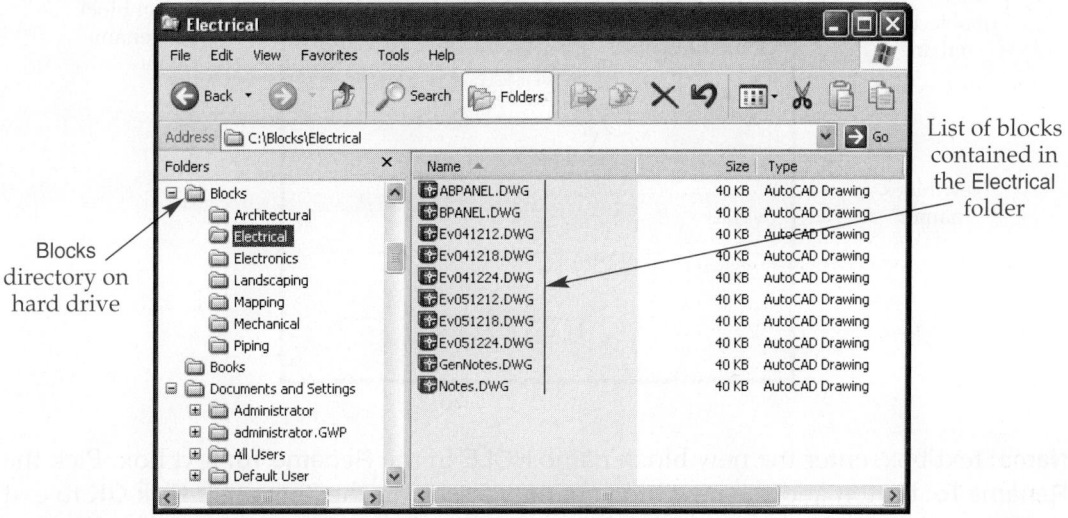

Blocks directory on hard drive

List of blocks contained in the Electrical folder

piping.dwg drawing. Limit the number of symbols within a drawing to a reasonable amount so the symbols can be found relatively easily in **DesignCenter**. If there are too many blocks within a drawing, it may be difficult to locate the desired symbol.

Drawing files saved on the hard drive should be arranged in a logical manner. The following guidelines also apply:

- All workstations in the class or office should have folders with the same names.
- One person should be assigned to update and copy symbol libraries to all workstation hard drives.
- Drawing files should be copied onto each workstation's hard drive from a master CD or network server.
- The master and backup versions of the symbol libraries should be kept in separate locations.

NOTE

A number of symbol libraries can be found on the DesignCenter Online Web page. The symbols are downloadable and include material from manufacturers and online catalogs. Links to Web sites are also provided. The DesignCenter Online Web page can be accessed in the **DC Online** tab in **DesignCenter**.

## Renaming Blocks

Blocks can be renamed using the **RENAME** command. Access this command by selecting **Rename...** from the **Format** pull-down menu or entering REN or RENAME at the Command: prompt. This displays the **Rename** dialog box, **Figure 22-26.**

To change the name of the CIRCLE block to HOLE, select Blocks from the **Named Objects** list. A list of block names defined in the current drawing then appears in the **Items** list. Pick CIRCLE to highlight it in the list. When this name appears in the **Old**

RENAME
REN

Format
➥ Rename...

**Figure 22-26.**
The **Rename** dialog box allows you to change the name of a block and other named objects.

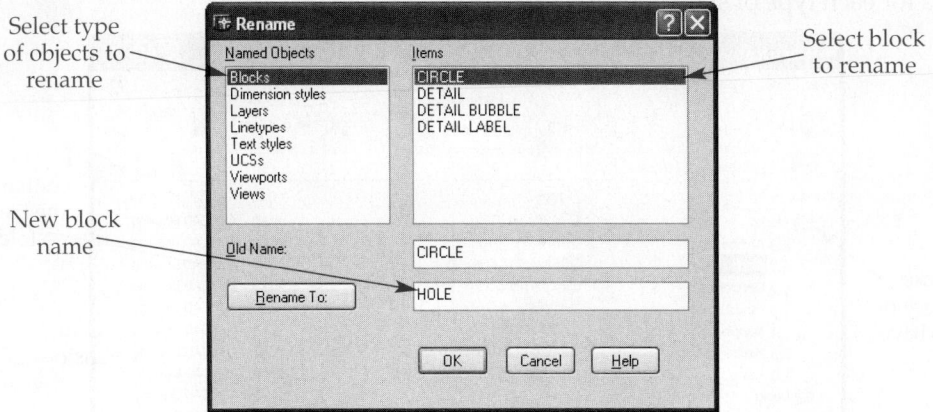

Select type of objects to rename

Select block to rename

New block name

**Name:** text box, enter the new block name HOLE in the **Rename To:** text box. Pick the **Rename To:** button and the new block name appears in the **Items** list. Pick **OK** to exit the **Rename** dialog box.

>
> **NOTE**
>
> Since AutoCAD does not permit the renaming of layer 0 or the Continuous linetype, these two named objects do not appear in the **Items** list in the **Rename** dialog box.

## Deleting Named Objects

As discussed in the previous section, a block is a named object. In many drawing sessions, not all of the named objects in a drawing are used. For example, your drawing may contain several layers, text styles, and blocks that are not used. Since these objects occupy disk space, it is good practice to delete or *purge* the unused objects with the **PURGE** command.

PURGE
PU

File
➡ Drawing
   Utilities
➡ Purge...

The **PURGE** command accesses the **Purge** dialog box, Figure 22-27. To access this dialog box, select **Purge...** from the **Drawing Utilities** cascading menu in the **File** pull-down menu or type PU or PURGE at the Command: prompt.

Select the appropriate radio button at the top of the dialog box to view content that can be purged or to view content that cannot be purged.

Before purging, select the **Confirm each item to be purged** check box to have an opportunity to review each item before it is deleted. If you wish to purge nested items, check the **Purge nested items** check box.

If you want to purge only some items, use the tree view to locate and highlight the items, and then pick the **Purge** button. If you want to purge all unused items, pick the **Purge All** button.

Figure 22-27.
The **Purge** dialog box.

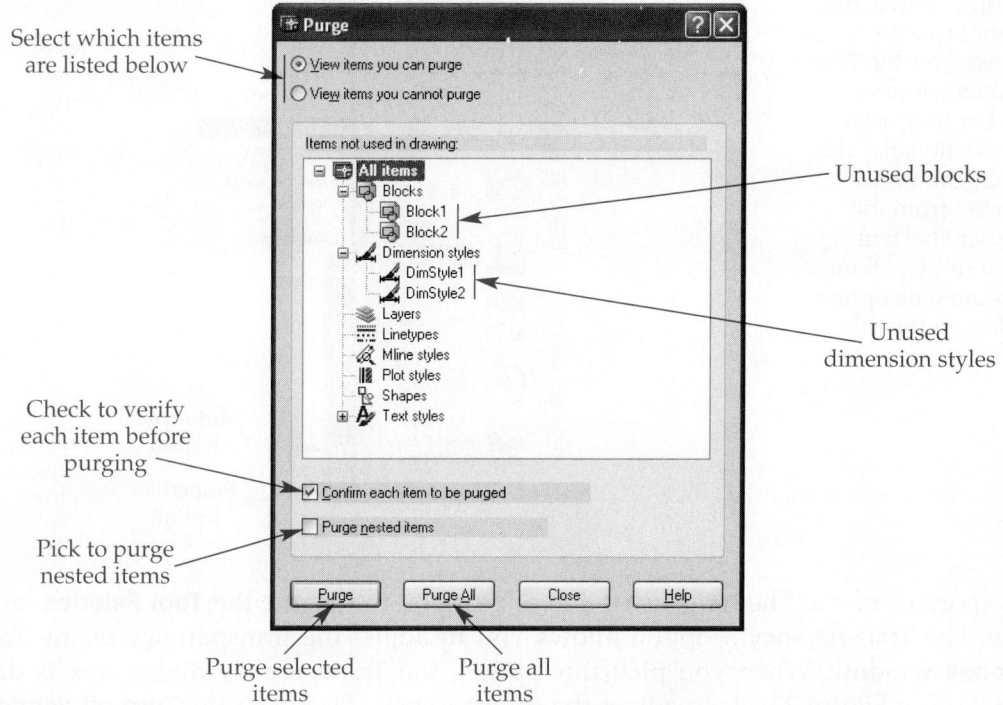

Select which items
are listed below

Unused blocks

Unused
dimension styles

Check to verify
each item before
purging

Pick to purge
nested items

Purge selected
items

Purge all
items

## Using and Customizing the Tool Palettes

Earlier in this chapter, you used the **Tool Palettes** window to insert blocks into a drawing. The **Tool Palettes** window provides a number of ways to manage frequently used blocks, drawing files, and hatch patterns. This section discusses the various features in the **Tool Palettes** window and the different methods available to customize tool palettes. As previously discussed, content is arranged in different palette tabs and can be added from **DesignCenter**. To open the **Tool Palettes** window, pick the **Tool Palettes** button on the **Standard** toolbar, select **Tool Palettes Window** from the **Tools** pull-down menu, enter TP or TOOLPALETTES at the Command: prompt, or use the [Ctrl]+[3] key combination.

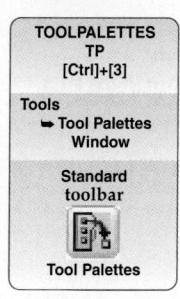

TOOLPALETTES
TP
[Ctrl]+[3]

Tools
➡ Tool Palettes
Window

Standard
toolbar

Tool Palettes

### Modifying the Appearance of the **Tool Palettes** Window

By default, only the vertical title bar of the **Tool Palettes** window is visible when it is opened. When the cursor is moved over the title bar, the tool palettes are displayed. Once the cursor is outside the window, the tool palettes disappear. This is controlled by the **Auto-hide** setting. This setting can be toggled on and off by picking the **Auto-hide** button on the title bar or by right-clicking on the **Tool Palettes** window title bar and picking **Auto-hide** from the shortcut menu. You can also access the shortcut menu by picking the **Properties** button on the title bar. See **Figure 22-28**.

The title bar shortcut menu contains several other options that affect the appearance of the **Tool Palettes** window. The **Allow Docking** option controls whether the window can be docked. When this option is checked, the window is dockable. The **Tool Palettes** window is docked and resized in the same manner as any AutoCAD toolbar. You can also move, resize, or close the window by using the related option in the title

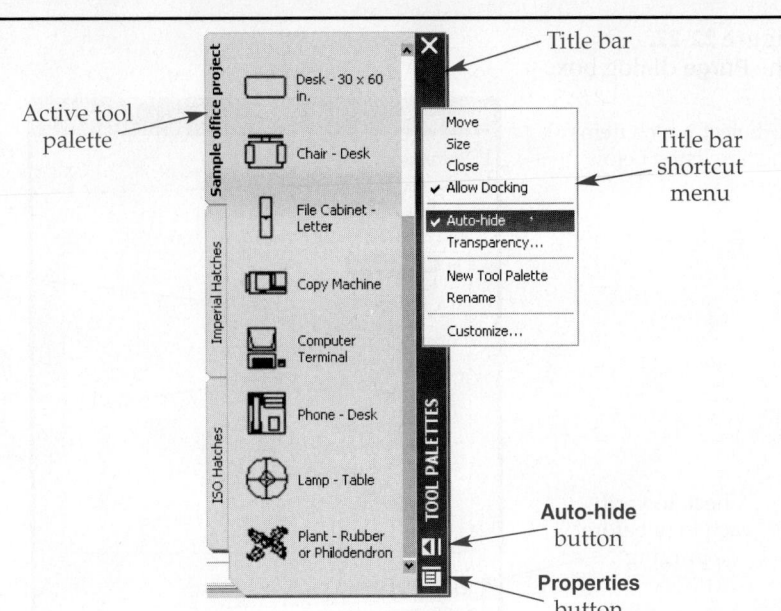

**Figure 22-28.**
When the **Auto-hide** option is active, the cursor must be moved over the **Tool Palettes** window title bar to display the palette tabs. This option can be selected from the title bar shortcut menu or by picking the **Auto-hide** option button on the title bar.

Active tool palette

Title bar

Title bar shortcut menu

Auto-hide button

Properties button

bar shortcut menu. The **Rename** option allows you to rename the **Tool Palettes** window. The **Transparency...** option allows you to adjust the transparency of the **Tool Palettes** window. When you pick this option, the **Transparency** dialog box is displayed. See **Figure 22-29.** To adjust the transparency, deactivate the **Turn off window transparency** setting and move the **Transparency Level** slider. The lowest transparency setting is active by default. Moving the slider to the right makes the window more transparent.

The **New Tool Palette** and **Customize...** options in the title bar shortcut menu allow you to create new palettes, import or export palettes, and arrange the order of palettes in the **Tool Palettes** window. These options are discussed in the *Creating and Arranging Palettes* section.

## Locating and Viewing Content

As previously discussed, each tool palette in the **Tool Palettes** window has its own tab. There are a number of ways to navigate through the tools, or content, in each palette. In addition, viewing options are available to display the content in different ways.

To view the content in a tool palette, click on the related tab to open it. If the **Tool Palettes** window contains more palettes than what is displayed on screen, pick on the edge of the lowest tab to display a selection menu listing the palette tabs. Locate the name of the tab to access the related tool palette.

The tool area in each palette can be navigated by using one of two scroll methods. If all of the content of a selected palette does not fit in the window, the remainder can be viewed by using the scroll bar or the scroll hand. The scroll hand appears when the cursor is placed in an empty area in the tool area. Picking and dragging scrolls the tool area up and down.

**Figure 22-29.**
The transparency level of the **Tool Palettes** window is set in the **Transparency** dialog box.

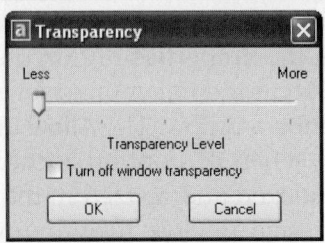

Figure 22-30.
Viewing options for
each tool palette can
be accessed by
right-clicking in the
tool area and
displaying the tool
area shortcut menu.

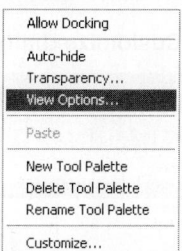

Allow Docking

Auto-hide
Transparency...
View Options...

Paste

New Tool Palette
Delete Tool Palette
Rename Tool Palette

Customize...

By default, the tools in each palette are represented by icons. The appearance of the tools can be adjusted to suit user preference. To access the viewing options in a palette, right-click in the tool area to display the shortcut menu. See **Figure 22-30.** This shortcut menu contains some of the same options listed in the title bar shortcut menu. The **View Options...** listing is used to set viewing options. The options in the lower areas of the menu are used to create, delete, rename, and rearrange tool palettes. These options and the **Paste** option are discussed in the sections that follow.

Picking **View Options...** displays the **View Options** dialog box, **Figure 22-31.** The size of the preview image for a tool can be adjusted by moving the **Image size:** slider. The **View style:** radio button options control how the content is displayed. The three options are described as follows:

- **Icon only.** This setting displays just the icon (a preview image).
- **Icon with text.** This setting displays the icon and the name of the tool.
- **List view.** This setting displays the icon and the name of each tool in the palette in a single-column format.

In the **Apply to:** drop-down list, you can specify how the view settings are assigned. The settings can be applied to the current palette only or to all palettes.

Figure 22-31.
Settings in the **View Options** dialog box control how the content is displayed in each tool palette.

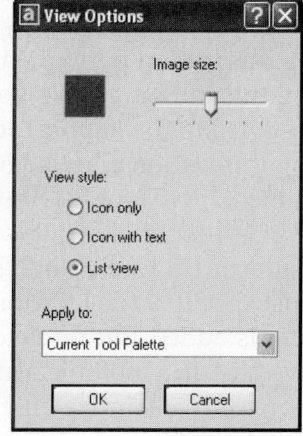

## Creating and Arranging Palettes

There are three sample palettes provided by AutoCAD in the **Tool Palettes** window. Using a simple procedure, you can quickly create new palettes and assign blocks and hatch patterns to them from **DesignCenter**. To create a new palette, right-click on the **Tool Palettes** title bar or in a tool area. Select **New Tool Palette** from the shortcut menu. You are then prompted to enter a name for the tool palette tab. Choose a name that identifies the content the palette will store. Adding blocks to a tool palette is discussed in the next section.

You can rename or delete existing palettes and change the order in which they appear. You can also import a palette saved as a file and place it in the **Tool Palettes**

**Figure 22-32.**
The **Tool Palettes** tab of the **Customize** dialog box.

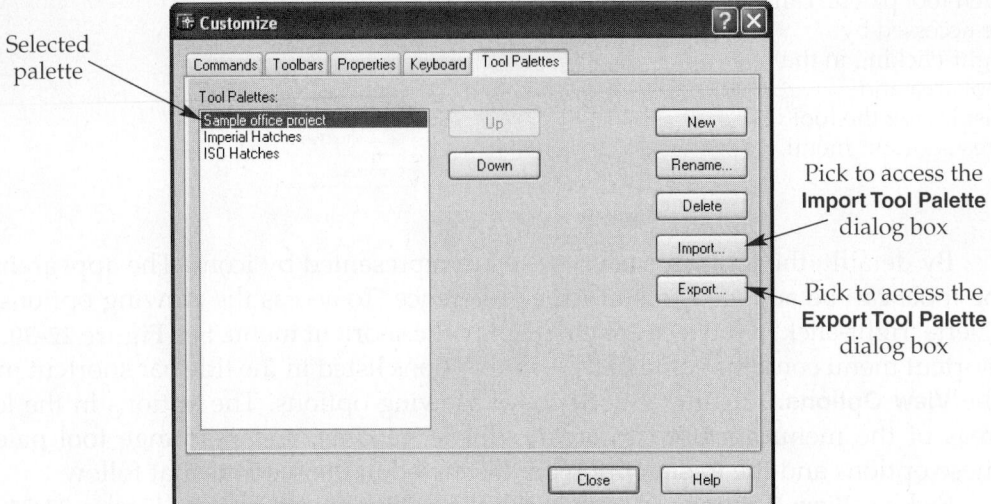

Selected palette

Pick to access the **Import Tool Palette** dialog box

Pick to access the **Export Tool Palette** dialog box

window. To access the palette tab options, right-click in a tool area and select the **Customize...** option. This opens the **Customize** dialog box with the **Tool Palettes** tab current. See **Figure 22-32.** The palette tabs are listed in the **Tool Palettes:** list. To modify a tab, highlight its name in the list. The options available in the **Customize** dialog box are described as follows:

- **Up**. Picking this button moves the selected palette up in the **Tool Palettes:** list. This rearranges the order of the palette tabs.
- **Down**. Picking this button moves the selected palette down in the **Tool Palettes:** list.
- **New**. Picking this button creates a new tool palette.
- **Rename**. Picking this button allows you to rename the selected palette.
- **Delete**. Picking this button permanently deletes the selected palette.
- **Import**. Picking this button allows you to import a tool palette that has been saved (exported) using the **Import Tool Palette** dialog box.
- **Export**. Picking this button allows you to export, or save, the selected palette as a file using the **Export Tool Palette** dialog box.

When you create a new tool palette, it is good practice to export it as a file to create a backup copy. Exporting a tool palette saves it to a file with an XTP extension. When saving, you must specify a file location.

When new content is added to or deleted from a tool palette, you can export it again to update the saved file. In a multiple AutoCAD user environment, tool palettes can be imported and exported to maximize efficiency. For example, on one workstation, tool palettes can be created and then exported to a network drive. The tool palettes can then be imported to other workstations.

> **NOTE**
>
> The path for AutoCAD's default tool palette files is specified in the Tool Palettes File Locations listing. To verify the location of this path, access the **Files** tab in the **Options** dialog box and check the path listed under Tool Palettes File Locations.

**Figure 22-33.**
Right-clicking on a drawing name in **DesignCenter** and selecting **Create Tool Palette** will create a new palette in the **Tool Palettes** window with the name of the drawing file. All the blocks defined in the drawing become tools in the palette.

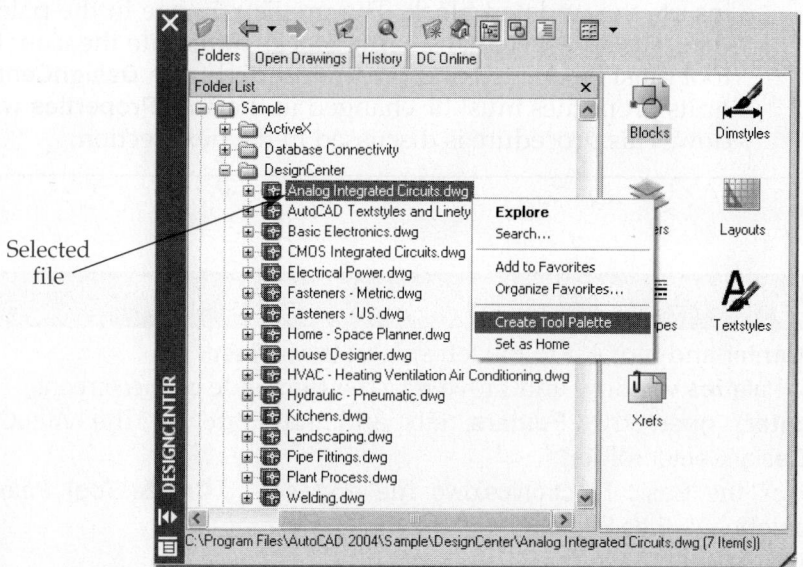

Selected file

## Adding Blocks to a Tool Palette

**DesignCenter** is used to add blocks and hatch patterns to tool palettes. You can use **DesignCenter** to create individual tools as well as a new palette. For example, a palette can be created with all the blocks in a single drawing file by right-clicking on the drawing file name in **DesignCenter** and selecting **Create Tool Palette** from the shortcut menu. See **Figure 22-33.** In the example shown, a new palette is created from the Analog Integrated Circuits file. The resulting palette consists of all the blocks in the file and has the same name as the file. A palette can also be created in this manner by expanding the contents of a drawing file in the **Tree View** area and right-clicking over the Blocks listing in either the **Tree View** area or the **Content** area. When the shortcut menu appears, select **Create Tool Palette.**

Individual blocks can be added to a tool palette from **DesignCenter** by using a drag-and-drop operation. First, display the blocks to be added in the **Content** area of **DesignCenter**. Then, open the **Tool Palettes** window and display the tool palette that will store the blocks. Finally, drag each block from **DesignCenter** and drop it into the tool palette. If the palette is not already created, you can right-click on the block icon and select **Create Tool Palette** from the shortcut menu. This creates a new palette containing the selected block in a single operation. You are then prompted for a new name for the palette.

An entire drawing file can be added to a tool palette from **DesignCenter** by picking the folder where the file resides in the **Tree View** area and then dragging the file from the **Content** area into a tool palette. When the file is inserted into a drawing from the **Tool Palettes** window, it becomes a block in the drawing.

If you have multiple drawing files in a folder and want to create a tool palette that consists of all of the blocks combined from all of the drawing files, navigate to the folder in the **Tree View** area of **DesignCenter.** Next, right-click over the folder and select **Create Tool Palette of Blocks.** A new palette is created in the **Tool Palettes** window with the name of the folder.

A block that has been added to a tool palette is directly linked to the drawing file in which it resides. If the block has been modified in the source file, inserting it from a tool palette inserts the updated block. The preview image in the palette does not reflect changes to the block. To update the icon, the tool must be deleted and then reinserted from **DesignCenter**, or its properties must be changed in the **Tool Properties** window. This procedure is discussed in the next section.

### Exercise 22-9

○ Open **DesignCenter** and move it to the left side of the screen.

○ Open the **Tool Palettes** window and move it to the right side of the screen.

○ In **DesignCenter**, open the **Folders** tab and navigate to the AutoCAD 2004\Sample\DesignCenter folder.

○ Right-click over the Basic Electronics.dwg file and select **Create Tool Palette**. Rename the palette tab Elec Symbols.

○ In **DesignCenter**, select the Electrical Power.dwg file.

○ In the **Content** area, double-click on Blocks to display the blocks in the Electrical Power.dwg file.

○ Drag as many blocks as you wish from **DesignCenter** into the Elec Symbols palette.

## Modifying Tools and Tool Properties

When working with several different palettes in the **Tool Palettes** window, it may be useful to copy or move the content of one palette to another. In addition, you may want to change the properties of blocks in certain palettes so that they vary from those in the source file or other palettes. Blocks residing in tool palettes can be modified to have different properties when inserted, such as different scales and rotation angles. Hatch patterns can be modified in the same manner. For example, you may want to specify a different angle for an inserted pattern. The properties override the defined object properties when the object is inserted.

A tool within a palette can be copied, moved, deleted, or renamed by right-clicking on the tool icon. This displays a tool shortcut menu, **Figure 22-34.** Property changes can be made by first displaying the same menu. The **Cut** option is used to remove a tool from one palette and move it to another. After picking **Cut**, select another palette tab, right-click in the tool area, and select **Paste** from the shortcut menu to move the tool to the new palette. The **Copy** option is used in the same way as the **Cut** option, except a copy is placed in the new palette and the tool remains in the original palette.

To delete a tool, right-click on its icon and select **Delete Tool** from the shortcut menu. When this option is selected, an alert dialog box appears. Selecting **OK** permanently deletes the tool.

To rename a tool, right-click on its icon and select **Rename** from the shortcut menu. Depending on the viewing option set in the **View Options** dialog box, the name of the tool may be displayed with the tool in the **Tool Palettes** window. If the name is not displayed, picking **Rename** temporarily displays the tool name so it can be renamed.

Figure 22-34.
A tool shortcut menu with modification options is displayed by right-clicking on a tool in a palette. Selecting **Properties...** opens the **Tool Properties** window.

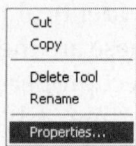

Cut
Copy

Delete Tool
Rename

Properties...

The properties of a tool can be viewed and modified by right-clicking on its icon and selecting **Properties...** from the shortcut menu. This opens the **Tool Properties** window. See **Figure 22-35**. The properties displayed depend on whether a block or hatch pattern is selected. In either case, a preview of the tool appears in the **Image:** area, and the name appears in the **Name:** text box. A description may be entered for the object in the **Description:** text box if desired.

In the **Tool Properties** window for a block, the first category is labeled **Insert**. See **Figure 22-35A**. The properties that appear are described as follows:

- **Name**. This is the name of the block in the source drawing file that will be inserted. It has to be the exact name of a block that has been defined in the source file.
- **Source file**. This is the location and name of the drawing file in which the block resides. To modify this setting, select the **Source file** setting. Then pick the ellipsis (...) button. This opens the **Select Linked Drawing** dialog box, which allows you to change the source drawing file.
- **Scale**. This value specifies the scale of the block in relation to the size at which the block was created.
- **Rotation**. This value specifies the rotation angle used when the block is inserted.
- **Explode**. This setting determines whether the block is exploded when inserted. The default setting is **No**.

Figure 22-35.
A—The **Tool Properties** window for a block tool. B—The **Tool Properties** window for a hatch pattern tool.

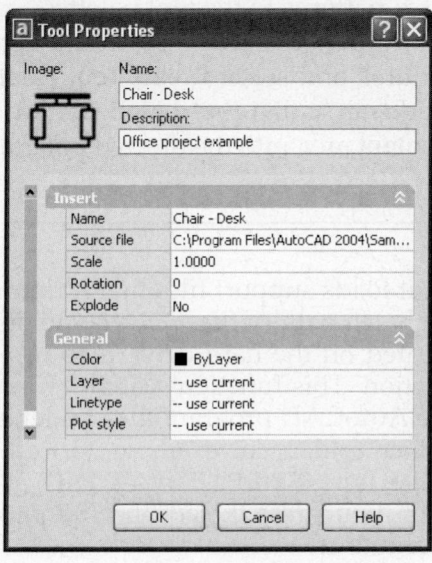

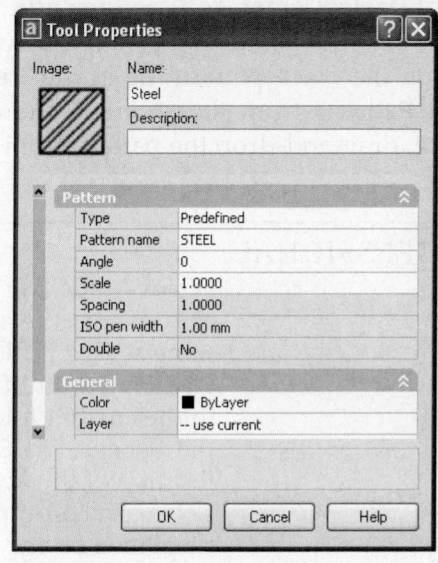

A                                        B

In the **Tool Properties** window for a hatch pattern, the first category is labeled **Pattern**. The settings correspond to the options specified in the **Boundary Hatch** dialog box. Hatch patterns are discussed in Chapter 21.

The **Tool Properties** window has identical property settings in the **General** category for blocks and hatch patterns. These are the **Color**, **Layer**, **Linetype**, **Plot style**, and **Lineweight** settings. As with other object properties, these settings may be modified to produce different results when inserting a block or hatch pattern from the **Tool Palettes**.

---

### Exercise 22-10

○ Open the **Tool Palettes** window.
○ Right-click over the title bar and select **New Tool Palette**.
○ Name the new palette My Blocks.
○ Open the **Sample Office Project** palette.
○ Right-click over the Phone-Desk tool and pick **Copy** from the shortcut menu.
○ Open the My Blocks palette.
○ Right-click in the tool area and select **Paste** from the shortcut menu.
○ Right-click over the Phone-Desk tool in the My Blocks palette and select **Delete Tool**.
○ Right-click in the tool area of the My Blocks palette and select **Delete Tool Palette**.

---

## Adding Hatch Patterns to a Palette

Hatch patterns can be added to tool palettes from **DesignCenter** using the same procedures involved with blocks. The pattern must first be defined in an AutoCAD hatch pattern file. As discussed in Chapter 21, hatch pattern files have a PAT extension. The hatch patterns provided with AutoCAD are stored in the acad.pat and acadiso.pat files. These files must be first located in **DesignCenter** to access AutoCAD's predefined hatch patterns. By default, these files are AutoCAD support files stored in the Support File Search Path folder. This path location can be determined by accessing the **Files** tab in the **Options** dialog box and identifying the path listed under Support File Search Path.

Once a hatch pattern file is located, its contents can be displayed in the **Content** area of **DesignCenter**. You can then add the hatch patterns to the tool palettes.

To create a palette that contains all of the hatch patterns in a single PAT file, right-click on the hatch pattern file in the **Tree View** area and select **Create Tool Palette of Hatch Patterns** from the shortcut menu. To add an individual hatch pattern to a palette, drag-and-drop the pattern from the **Content** area into the desired palette.

---

**PROFESSIONAL TIP**

When AutoCAD opens, it loads support files that it needs to run, such as the acad.pat hatch pattern file. One way to determine where a file is located on the hard drive is to use the **FINDFILE** AutoLISP function. This function searches for files in the current folder, the AutoCAD program files folder, and the Support File Search Path folder. For example, to find the location of the acad.pat file, type (FINDFILE "ACAD.PAT") at the Command: prompt. When you press [Enter], the file path is displayed on the command line.

---

# Chapter Test

*Answer the following questions on a separate sheet of paper.*

1. Define *symbol library*.
2. Which color and linetype settings should be used if you want a block to assume the current color and linetype when it is inserted into a drawing?
3. When should a block be drawn to fit inside a one-unit square, and what type of block is this called when it is inserted?
4. A block name can be _____ characters long.
5. What are two ways to access a listing of all blocks in the current drawing?
6. Describe the term *nesting* in relation to blocks.
7. How do you preset block insertion variables using a dialog box?
8. Describe the effect of entering negative scale factors when inserting a block.
9. Why would the **Corner** option be used when scaling a block during insertion?
10. What properties do blocks drawn on a layer other than layer 0 assume when inserted?
11. Why would you draw blocks on layer 0?
12. What is a limitation of an array pattern created with the **MINSERT** command?
13. What is the purpose of the **BASE** command?
14. Explain the difference between the **Scale** and **PScale** preset options used with the **INSERT** command.
15. Identify the two methods that allow you to break an inserted block into its individual objects for editing purposes.
16. Suppose you have found that a block was incorrectly drawn. Unfortunately, you have already inserted the block 30 times. How can you edit all of the blocks quickly?
17. What is the primary difference between blocks created with the **BLOCK** and **WBLOCK** commands?
18. After entering the **-INSERT** command, what would you enter when prompted for a block name to define a block named RESISTOR from an existing drawing file named electrical.dwg?
19. Explain two ways to remove all unused blocks from a drawing.
20. Suppose you revise a drawing named desk. However, this drawing had been inserted several times into another drawing and saved as a block named DESK2. How would you update the DESK2 insertions?
21. What advantage is offered by having a symbol library of blocks in a single drawing, rather than using wblocks?
22. What is the purpose of the **PURGE** command?
23. Name the capability of **DesignCenter** that allows you to easily insert a block into a drawing.
24. Which tab in **DesignCenter** displays the hierarchy of files and folders on your computer and network drives?
25. Which tab in **DesignCenter** displays all currently open drawings?
26. Give the dimensions of a block when it is inserted from **DesignCenter** if the original block was a 1″ × 1″ square and the inserted units were specified in feet.
27. How are blocks and hatch patterns added to the **Tool Palettes** window?
28. What is the purpose of the **Export** button in the **Customize** dialog box?
29. What is the best way to create a tool palette that consists of all the blocks in a drawing file?
30. What feature is used to specify the properties of a block, such as the insertion scale, when it is inserted from tool palettes?

## Drawing Problems

1. Create a symbol library for one of the drafting disciplines listed below, and then save it as a template or drawing file. Then, after checking with your instructor, draw a problem using the library. If you save the symbol library as a template, start the problem with the template. If you save it as a drawing file, start a new drawing and insert the symbol library into it.

   Specialty areas you might create symbols for include:
   - Mechanical (machine features, fasteners, tolerance symbols).
   - Architectural (doors, windows, fixtures).
   - Structural (steel shapes, bolts, standard footings).
   - Industrial piping (fittings, valves).
   - Piping flow diagrams (tanks, valves, pumps).
   - Electrical schematics (resistors, capacitors, switches).
   - Electrical one-line (transformers, switches).
   - Electronics (IC chips, test points, components).
   - Logic diagrams (AND gates, NAND gates, buffers).
   - Mapping, civil (survey markers, piping).
   - Geometric tolerancing (feature control frames).

   Save the drawing as P22-1 or choose an appropriate file name, such as ARCH-PRO or ELEC-PRO.

2. Display the symbol library created in Problem 1 on screen and print a hard copy. Put the printed copy in your notebook as a reference.

3. Open P11-20 from Chapter 11. The sketch for this drawing is shown  below. Erase all copies of the symbols that were made, leaving the original objects intact. These include the steel column symbols and the bay and column line tags. Then do the following:

    A. Make blocks of the steel column symbol and the tag symbols.

    B. Use the **MINSERT** command or the **ARRAY** command to place the symbols in the drawing.

    C. Dimension the drawing as shown in the sketch.

    D. Save the drawing as P22-3.

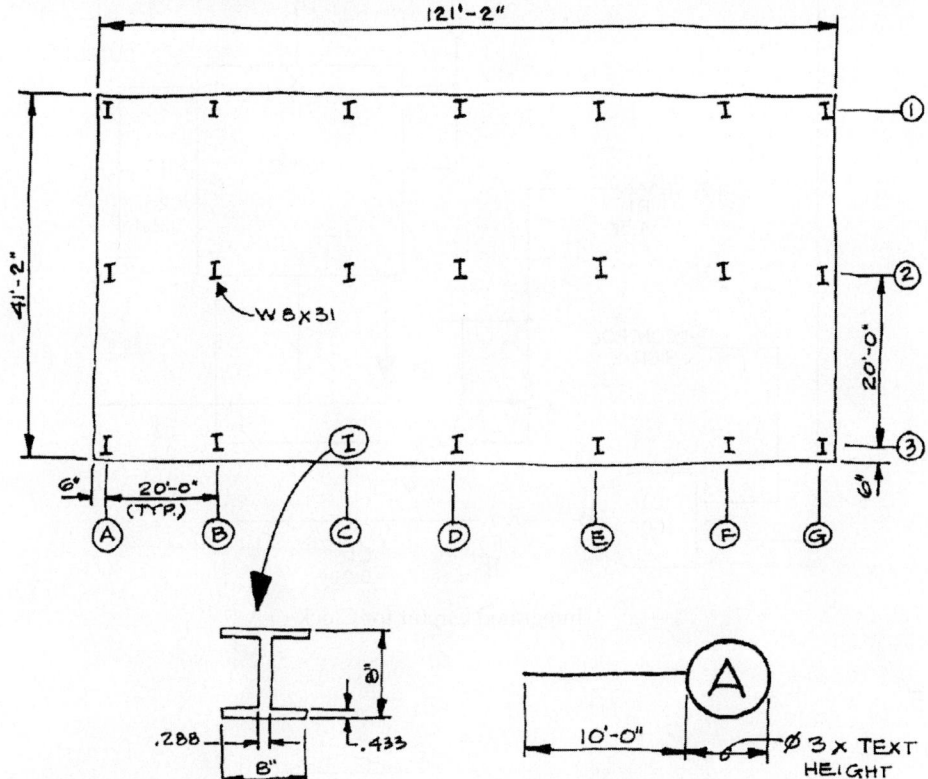

*Problems 4–6 represent a variety of electrical schematics, piping flow diagrams, and logic diagrams created using symbols as blocks. Create each drawing as shown (the drawings are not drawn to scale). The symbols should first be created as blocks or wblocks and then saved in a symbol library using one of the methods discussed in this chapter. Place a border and title block on each drawing. Save the drawings as P22-4, P22-5, and so on.*

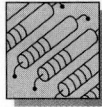

4.

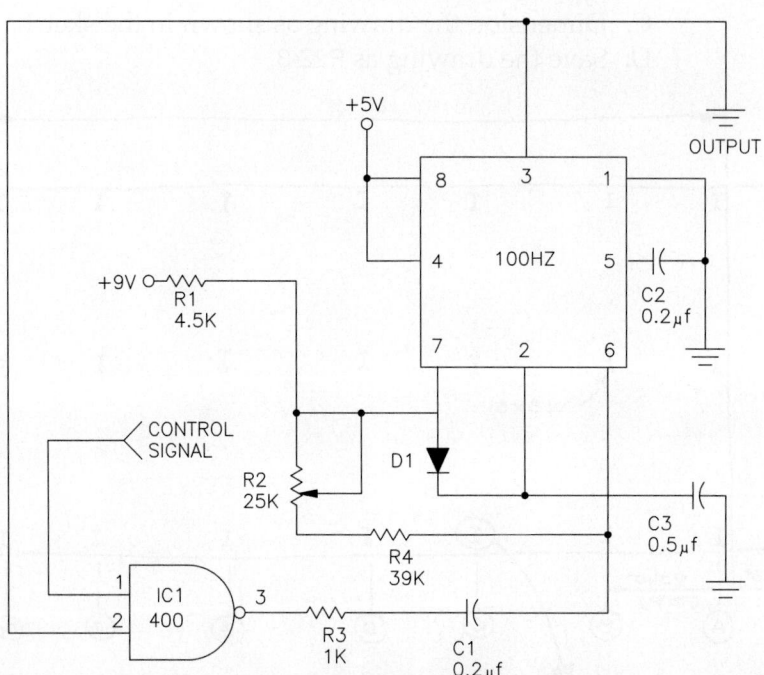

Integrated Circuit for Clock

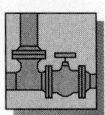

5.

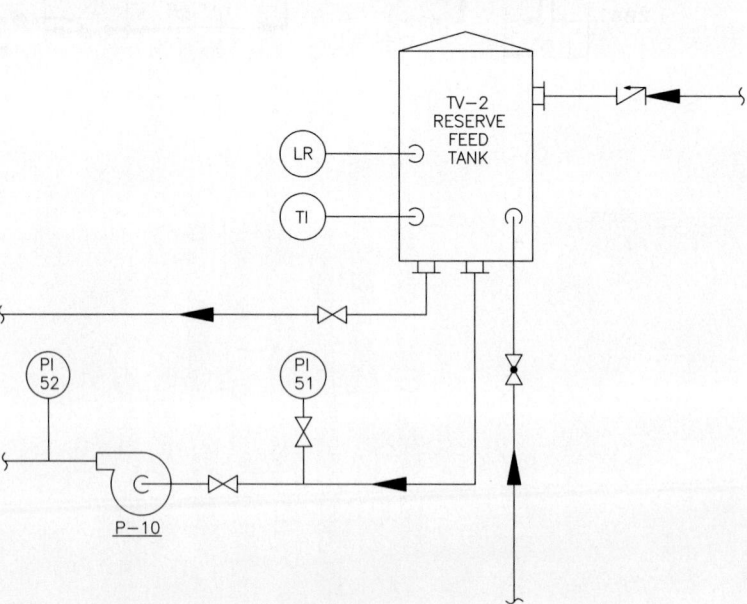

Piping Flow Diagram

AutoCAD and its Applications—Basics

6.

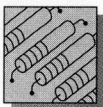

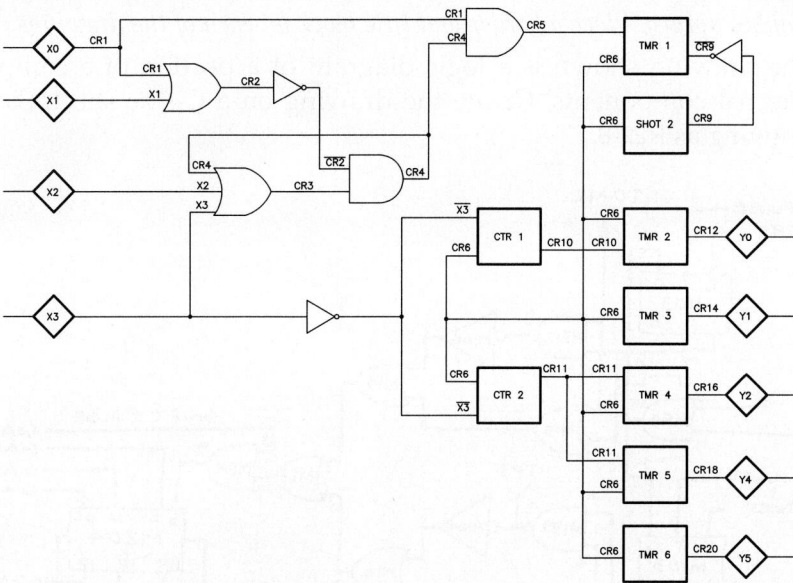

Logic Diagram of Marking System

7. Open **P11-21** from Chapter 11. The sketch for this drawing is shown below. Erase all of the desk workstations except one. Then do the following:

   A. Create a block of the workstation.
   B. Insert the block into the drawing using the **MINSERT** command.
   C. Dimension one of the workstations as shown in the sketch.
   D. Save the drawing as P22-7.

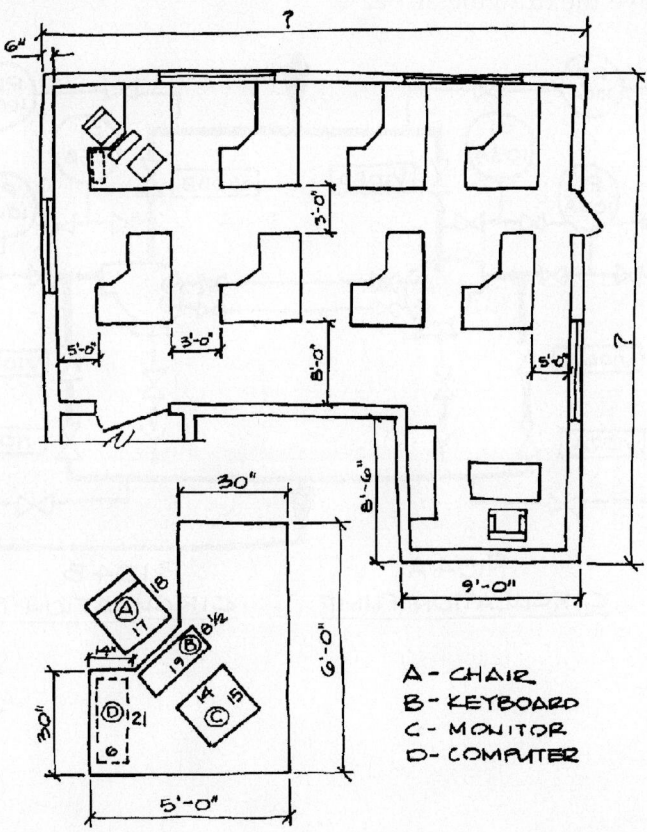

A - CHAIR
B - KEYBOARD
C - MONITOR
D - COMPUTER

*Problems 8–12 are presented as engineering sketches. They are schematic drawings created using symbols and are not drawn to scale. The symbols should first be drawn as blocks and then saved in a symbol library. Place a border and title block on each of the drawings.*

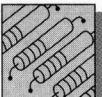

8. The drawing shown is a logic diagram of a portion of a computer's internal components. Create the drawing on a C-size sheet. Save the drawing as P22-8.

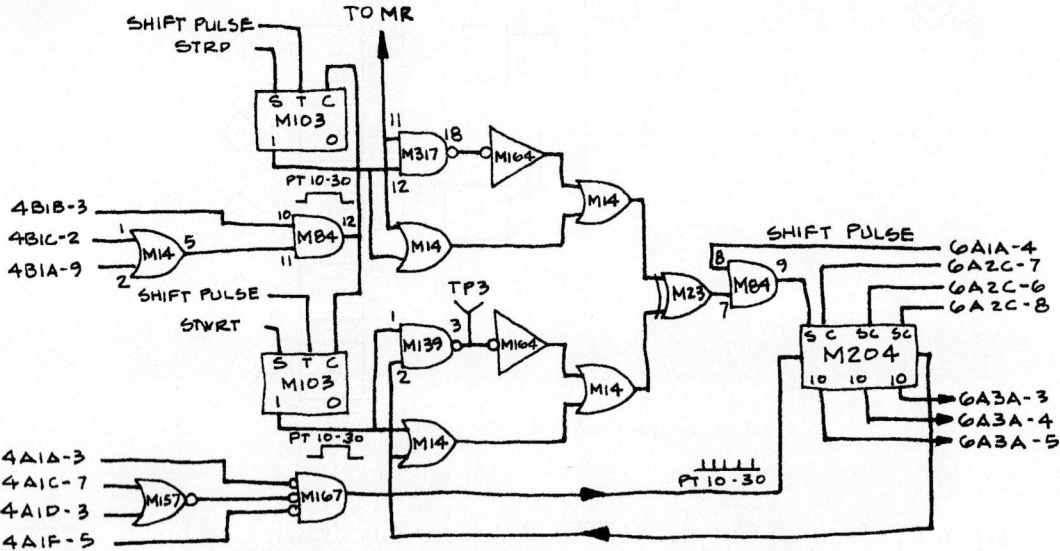

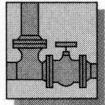

9. The drawing shown is a piping flow diagram of a cooling water system. Create the drawing on a B-size sheet. Look closely at this drawing. Using blocks and the correct editing commands, it may be easier to complete than you think. Draw the thick flow lines with polylines. Save the drawing as P22-9.

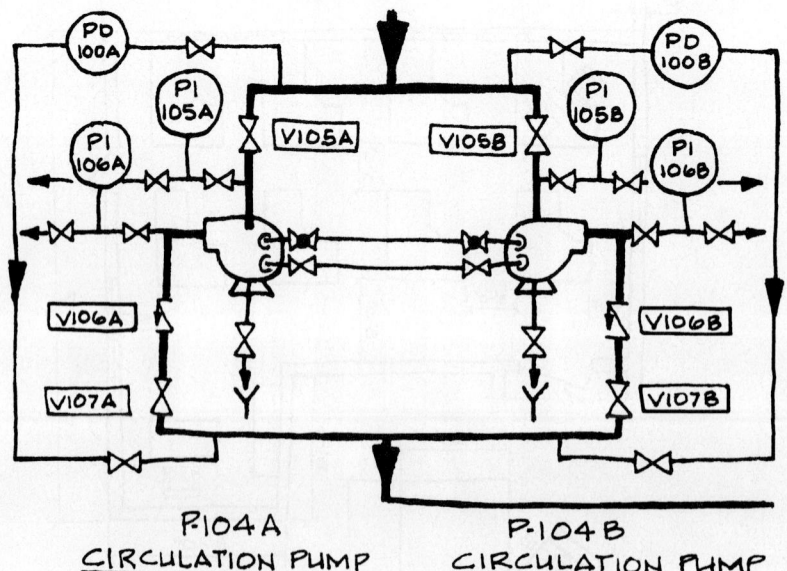

10. The drawing shown is the general arrangement of a basement floor plan for a new building. The engineer has shown one example of each type of equipment. Use the following instructions to complete the drawing: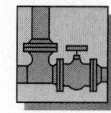

A. Create the drawing on a C-size sheet.

B. All text should be 1/8" high, except the text for the bay and column line tags, which should be 3/16" high. The line balloons for the bay and column lines should be twice the diameter of the text height.

C. The column and bay line steel symbols represent wide-flange structural shapes, and should be 8" wide × 12" high.

D. The PUMP and CHILLER installations (except PUMP #4 and PUMP #5) should be drawn per the dimensions given for PUMP #1 and CHILLER #1. Use the dimensions shown for the other PUMP units.

E. TANK #2 and PUMP #5 (P-5) should be drawn per the dimensions given for TANK #1 and PUMP #4.

F. Tanks T-3, T-4, T-5, and T-6 are all the same size, and are aligned 12' from column line A.

G. Plan this drawing carefully and create as many blocks as possible to increase your productivity. Dimension the drawing as shown, and provide location dimensions for all equipment not shown in the engineer's sketch.

H. Save the drawing as P22-10.

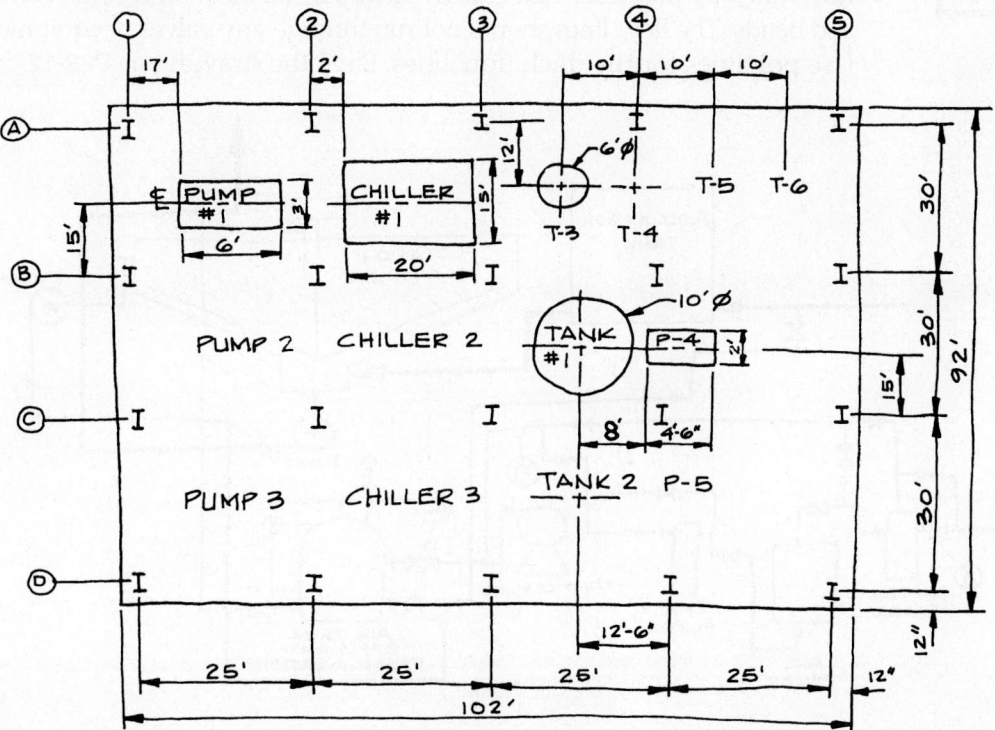

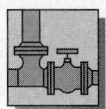

11. The drawing saved as P22-10 must be revised. The engineer has provided you with a sketch of the necessary revisions. It is up to you to alter the drawing as quickly and efficiently as possible. The dimensions shown on the sketch below *do not* need to be added to the drawing; they are provided for construction purposes only. Revise P22-10 so that all chillers and the four tanks reflect the changes. Save the drawing as P22-11.

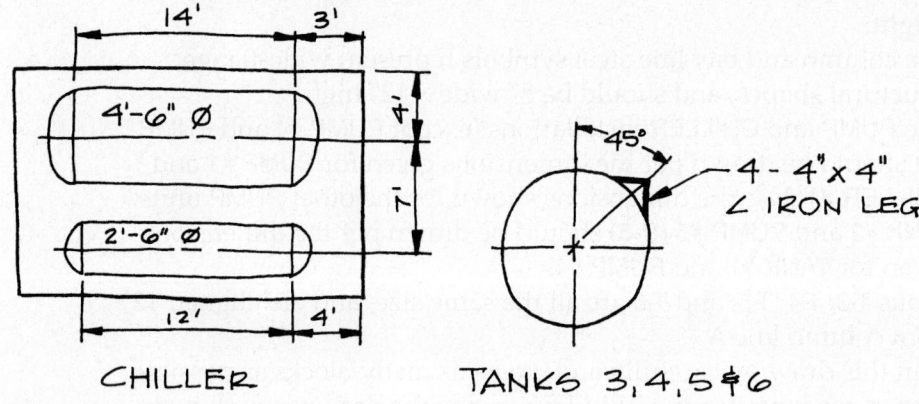

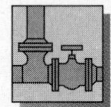

12. The piping flow diagram shown is part of an industrial effluent treatment system. Draw it on a C-size sheet. Eliminate as many bends in the flow lines as possible. Place arrowheads at all flow line intersections and bends. The flow lines should not run through any valves or equipment. Use polylines for the thick flow lines. Save the drawing as P22-12.

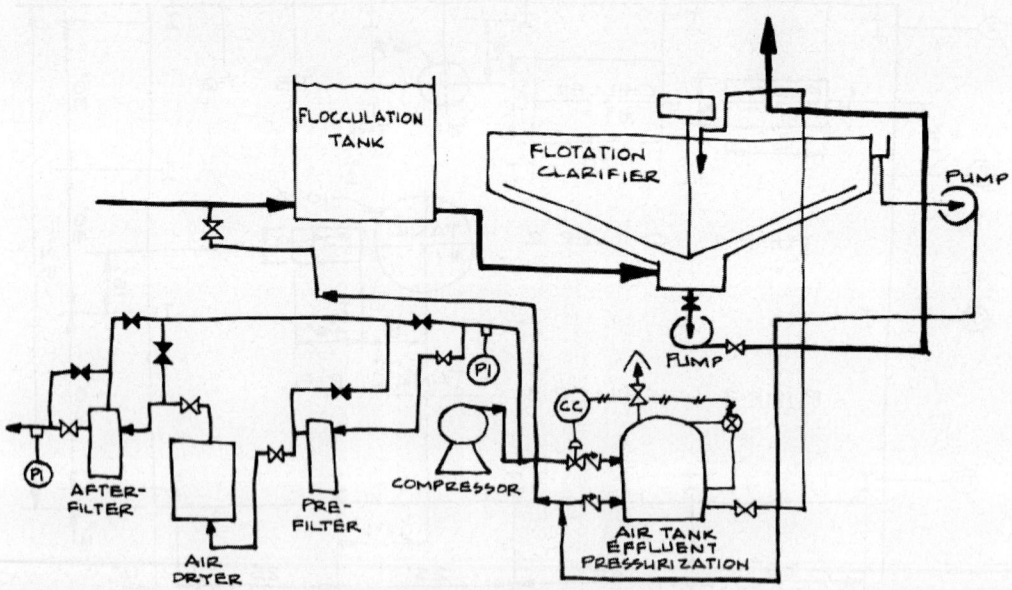

## CHAPTER 23

# External References

## Learning Objectives

After completing this chapter, you will be able to do the following:
- Define the function of external references.
- Reference an existing drawing into the current drawing using the **XREF** command.
- Bind external references and selected dependent objects to a drawing.
- Use **DesignCenter** to attach external references.
- Edit external references in the current drawing.
- Use external references to create a multiview layout.
- Control the display of layers in viewports using the **Layer Properties Manager** dialog box.

When you create multiple objects in a drawing by copying them, the drawing file grows in size. This is because AutoCAD must maintain a complete description of the geometry of each copied object. On the other hand, when you use a block to represent multiple objects, AutoCAD maintains only one description of the block's geometry. All other instances of the block are recorded as X, Y, and Z coordinates, and AutoCAD refers to the original block definition to obtain the block's data. The size of a drawing is decreased considerably if blocks are used rather than copied objects. Blocks are discussed in Chapter 22.

AutoCAD enables you to go even further in your efforts to control the size of drawing files and maximize efficiency with the **XREF** command. This command allows you to incorporate, or *reference*, one or more existing drawings into the current drawing without adding them to the contents of the current file. This procedure is excellent for applications in which existing base drawings or complex symbols and details must be shared by several users, or are used often. This chapter discusses the **XREF** command and illustrates how it can be used to reference drawings and create a multiview layout with views displayed at a variety of scale values.

Any machine or electrical appliance contains a variety of subassemblies and components. These components are assembled to create the final product. The final product occupies a greater amount of space and weighs more than any of the individual parts. In the same way, a drawing composed of a variety of blocks and inserted drawings grows much larger and occupies more disk space than the individual symbols and components.

AutoCAD allows you to *reference* existing drawings to the master drawing you are currently working on. When you externally reference (xref) a drawing, the drawing's geometry is not added to the current drawing (unlike the geometry of inserted drawing files), but it is displayed on screen. This makes for much smaller files. It also allows several people in a class or office to reference the same drawing file, with the assurance that any revisions to the reference drawing will be displayed in any drawing where it is used.

The **XREF** command is used to reference other drawing files into the master drawing. To access this command, pick the **External Reference** button from either the **Reference** or **Insert** toolbar, pick **Xref Manager...** from the **Insert** pull-down menu, or enter XREF or XR at the Command: prompt. This displays the **Xref Manager** dialog box, **Figure 23-1.** This dialog box is a complete management tool for your external references.

Reference drawings can be used in two basic ways:

- To construct a drawing using predrawn symbols or details, a method similar to the use of blocks.
- Before plotting, to lay out a drawing composed of multiple views or details, using different existing drawings. This technique is discussed later in the chapter.

XREF
XR

Insert
➥ Xref Manager...

Reference or Insert
toolbar

External Reference

Figure 23-1.
The **Xref Manager** dialog box provides access to all options for externally referenced files.

Pick to attach an external reference to current drawing

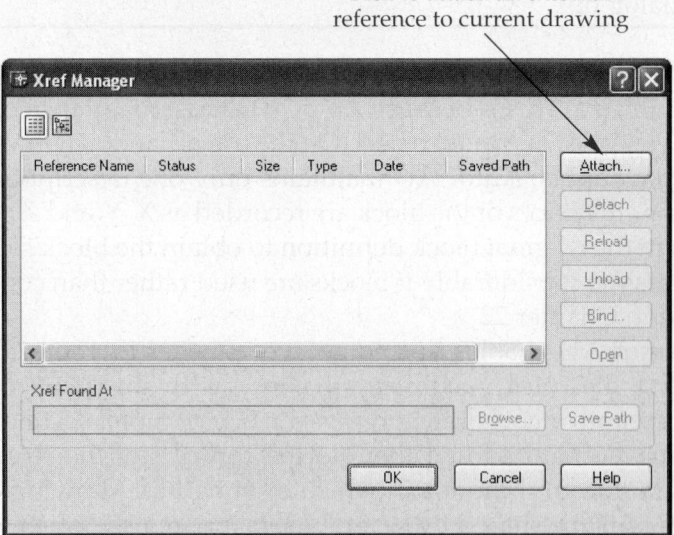

## Benefits of External References

One of the most important benefits of using xrefs is that whenever the master drawing is opened, the latest versions of the xrefs are displayed. If the original externally referenced drawings are modified between the time you revise the master and the time you open and plot it, all revisions are automatically reflected. This is because AutoCAD reloads each xref whenever the master drawing is loaded.

There are other significant advantages to using xrefs. They can be nested, and you can use as many xrefs as needed for any drawing. This means that a detail referenced to the master drawing can be composed of smaller details that are themselves xrefs. You can also attach other xrefs to the referenced drawing and have such updates automatically added to the master drawing when it is opened.

## Attaching an External Reference to the Current Drawing

Using the **XREF** command is similar to using the **INSERT** command. A referenced drawing that is inserted into the current drawing is said to be *attached*. To attach the reference to the current drawing, enter the **XREF** command and pick the **Attach...** button in the **Xref Manager** dialog box. This displays the **Select Reference File** dialog box. This is a standard file dialog box. Use this dialog box to access the appropriate folder and select the desired drawing file to attach. Pick **Open** when you are finished.

Once a file to attach has been specified, the **External Reference** dialog box is displayed, **Figure 23-2.** This dialog box is used to indicate how and where the reference is to be placed in the current drawing. The name and the path of the currently selected xref are shown in the upper-left corner of the dialog box. To change the drawing to be attached, pick the **Browse...** button and select the new file in the **Select Reference File** dialog box. When attaching an xref, pick the **Attachment** option in the **Reference Type** area. This option is active by default. Working with the **Overlay** option is discussed later in this chapter.

If there is more than one external reference already in the current drawing, you can attach another copy of an xref by picking the **Name:** drop-down list arrow. You can also attach an existing xref by highlighting the desired reference name in the **Xref Manager** dialog box and picking the **Attach...** button.

The lower portion of the **External Reference** dialog box contains the options for the xref insertion location, scaling, and rotation angle. The text boxes in the **Insertion point** area allow you to enter 2D or 3D coordinates for insertion of the xref if the **Specify On-screen** check box is inactive. Activate this check box if you wish to specify the insertion location on screen. Scale factors for the xref can be set in the **Scale** area. By default, the X, Y, and Z scale factors are set to 1. You can enter new values in the corresponding text boxes, or activate the **Specify On-screen** check box to display scaling

---

**Figure 23-2.**
The **External Reference** dialog box is used to specify how an external reference is placed in the current drawing.

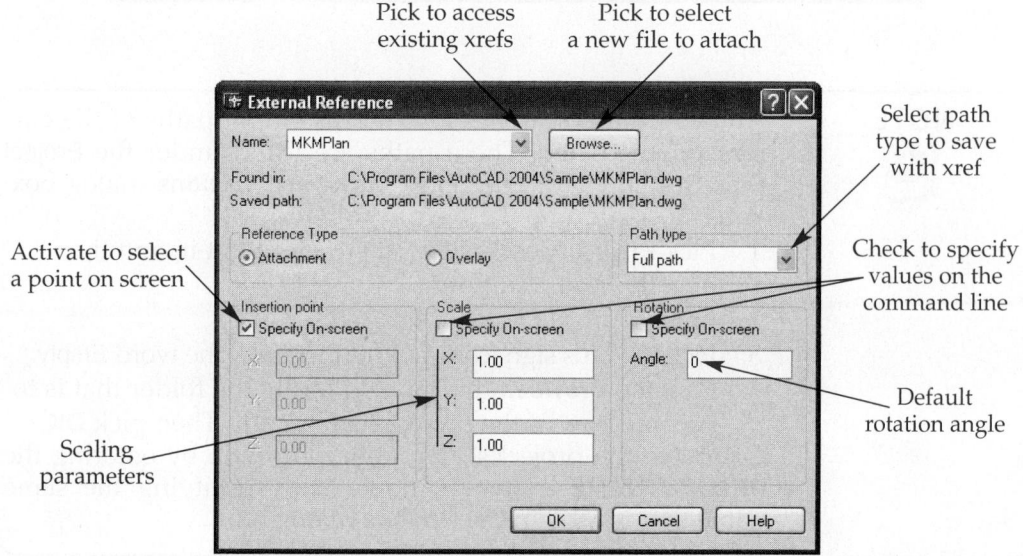

prompts on the command line. The rotation angle for the inserted xref is 0 by default. You can specify a different rotation angle in the **Angle:** text box, or activate the **Specify On-screen** check box if you wish to be prompted at the command line.

The **Path type** drop-down list is used to set how the path to the xref file will be stored by AutoCAD. This path is then used to find the xref file when the master file is opened. The resulting path is displayed in the **Xref Manager** dialog box, **Figure 23-3.** It also appears under the xref name in the **Saved path:** listing in the **External Reference** dialog box. There are three path options. They are described as follows:

- **Full path**. This option saves the full path to the xref drawing file. It is active by default. It specifies an *absolute path.*
- **Relative path**. This option saves the path relative to the file it is being referenced into (the current file). This option cannot be used if the xref file is on a local or network drive other than the drive that stores the master file.
- **No path**. This option does not save the path to the xref file. When this option is used, the xref file can only be found and loaded if the path to the file is included in one of the Support File Search Path locations or if the xref file is in the same folder as the master file. The Support File Search Path locations are specified in the **Files** tab of the **Options** dialog box.

**Figure 23-3.**
An xref file attached to the current drawing can be referenced with a full path, a relative path, or no path. The type of path used is displayed in the **Saved Path** column in the **Xref Manager** dialog box.

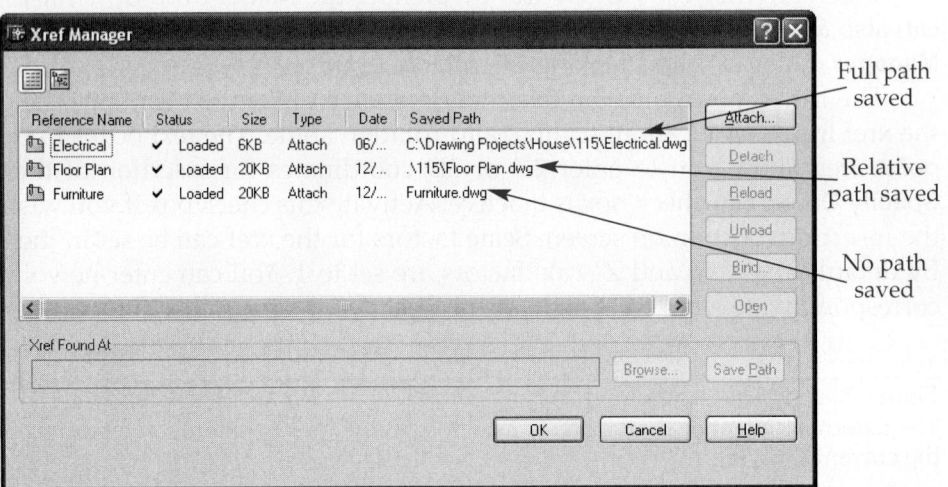

Full path saved

Relative path saved

No path saved

AutoCAD also searches for xref files in all paths of the current project name. These paths are listed under the Project Files Search Path in the **Files** tab of the **Options** dialog box. You can create a new project as follows:

1. Pick Project Files Search Path to highlight it, and then pick the **Add...** button.
2. Enter a project name if desired.
3. Pick the plus sign icon (+), and then pick the word Empty.
4. Pick the **Browse...** button and locate the folder that is to become part of the project search path. Then pick **OK**.

Complete the project search path definition by entering the **PROJECTNAME** system variable and specifying the same name that is used in the **Options** dialog box.

With the **Full path** option, xref drawing location is defined by its location on the computer system. That is, the xref drawings must be located in the same drive location and folder location specified in the saved path. The master drawing can be moved to any location, but the xref drawings must remain in the saved path location. This option is acceptable if it is unlikely that the master and xref drawings will be copied to another computer or drive or moved to another folder. If you will be sharing your drawings with a client or eventually archiving the drawings, the **Relative path** option is more appropriate.

The **Relative path** option defines the saved path relative to the location of the master drawing. If the master drawing and xref files are contained within a single folder and subfolders, this folder can be copied to any location without losing the connection between files. For example, the folder can be copied from the C: drive of one computer to the D: drive of another computer, to a folder on a CD, or to an archive server. If these types of transfers were performed with the **Full path** option, you would need to open the master drawing after copying and redefine the saved paths for all xref files.

In the **Saved Path** list in the **Xref Manager** dialog box, AutoCAD uses prefixes to define the relative paths to xref files. Referring to **Figure 23-3**, the path to the Floor Plan reference file is preceded by the characters .\. The period (.) represents the folder containing the master drawing. From that folder, AutoCAD "looks in" the 115 folder, where the Floor Plan drawing is found. A similar specification is used for the Elevation reference file in **Figure 23-4.** In this instance, the Elevation file is found in the same folder as the master drawing. The specification for the Wall reference file is preceded by the characters ..\. The double period (..) instructs AutoCAD to move up one folder

**Figure 23-4.**
This figure shows the relation between symbols in the **Saved Path** list and file locations within the folder structure.

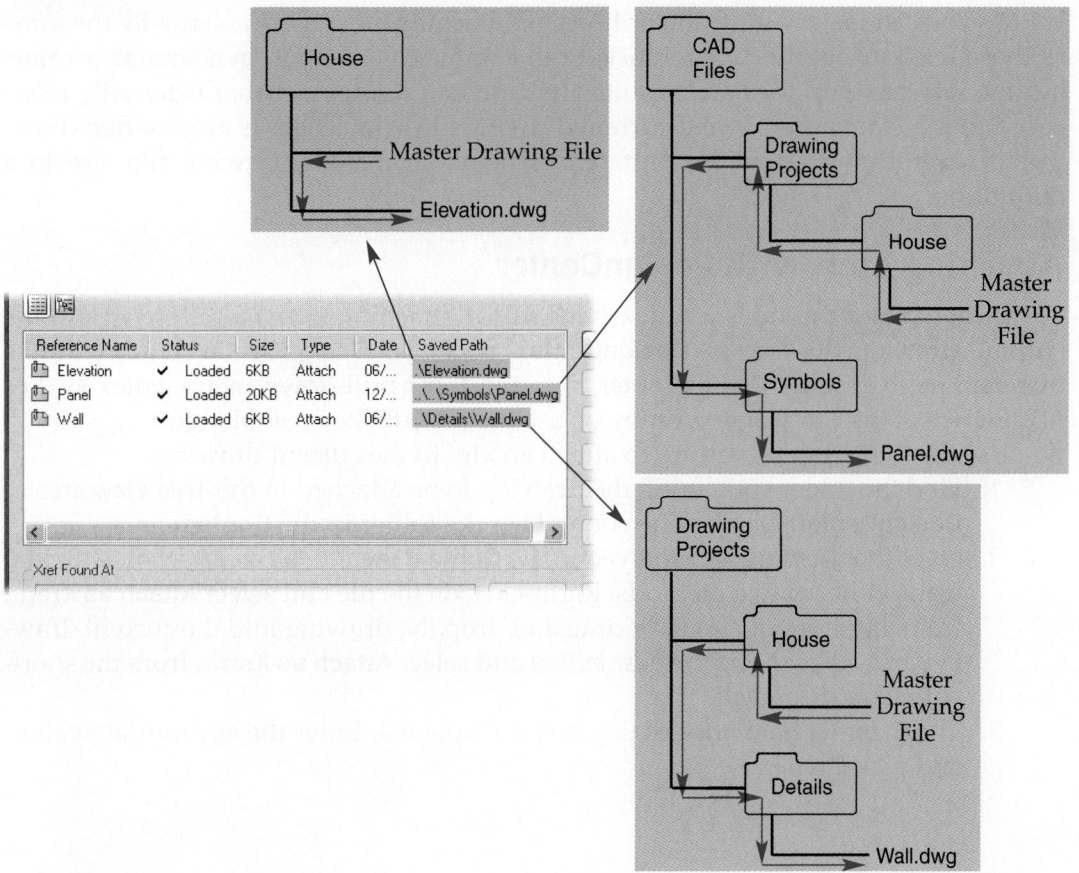

level from the current location. The double period can be repeated to move up multiple folder levels. For example, the Panel reference file in **Figure 23-4** is found by moving up two folder levels from the folder of the master drawing and then opening the Symbols folder.

> **NOTE**  The path saved to the xref is one of several locations searched by AutoCAD when a master drawing is opened and an xref must be loaded. When a file containing xrefs is opened, AutoCAD will try several ways to load each xref. The order in which AutoCAD searches path locations for loading xref files is as follows:
> 1. The path associated with the xref (the full path or a relative path).
> 2. The current folder of the master drawing.
> 3. The project paths specified in the Project Files Search Path.
> 4. The support paths specified in the Support File Search Path.
> 5. The Start in: folder path specified for the AutoCAD application shortcut (accessed with the **Properties** option in the desktop icon right-click menu).

After specifying a path type and reference type for an xref in the **External Reference** dialog box, the xref may be inserted into the current drawing. In the example given in **Figure 23-2,** the file C:\Program Files\AutoCAD 2004\Sample\MKMPlan.dwg is selected for attachment. Because the **Specify On-screen** check box in the **Insertion point** area is activated, the dialog box disappears when you pick **OK**. The xref is attached to your cursor and you are prompted for the insertion point. You can use any valid point specification option, including object snap modes.

As you can see, the insertion options for attaching an xref are essentially the same as those used when inserting a block. Both commands function in a similar manner, but the internal workings and results are different. Remember that externally referenced files are not added to the current drawing file's database, as are inserted drawings. Therefore, using external references helps keep your drawing file size to a minimum.

## Attaching Xrefs with DesignCenter

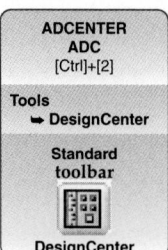

**DesignCenter** provides a quick method for attaching external references to the current drawing. To access **DesignCenter**, pick the **DesignCenter** button in the **Standard** toolbar, select **DesignCenter** from the **Tools** pull-down menu, enter ADC or ADCENTER at the Command: prompt, or use the [Ctrl]+[2] key combination.

Use the following procedure to attach an xref to the current drawing:
1. Find the folder containing the drawing to be attached in the **Tree View** area of **DesignCenter**. Display the contents of the folder in the **Content** area.
2. Once the drawing is displayed in the **Content** area, you can attach it as an xref using either of two methods. Right-click on the file and select **Attach as Xref...** from the shortcut menu, or drag and drop the drawing into the current drawing area *using the right mouse button* and select **Attach as Xref...** from the shortcut menu displayed.
3. The **External Reference** dialog box is displayed. Enter the appropriate values and pick **OK**.

## Overlaying the Current Drawing with an External Reference

There are many situations in which you may want to see what your drawing looks like with another drawing overlaid on it. Overlaying the current drawing with an external reference file allows you to temporarily view the xref without attaching it. This is accomplished by activating the **Overlay** option button in the **External Reference** dialog box after selecting an xref.

The difference between an overlaid xref and an attached xref is related to the way in which nested xrefs are handled. *Nesting* occurs when an externally referenced file is referenced by an xref file that has been attached to the current drawing. The xref file that is attached is known as the *parent xref*. When an xref is overlaid, any nested xrefs that it contains are displayed if those xrefs were *attached*, but not if they were *overlaid*. In other words, any nested overlays are not carried into the master drawing with the parent xref.

## Detaching, Reloading, and Unloading

As discussed earlier, each time you open a master drawing containing an attached xref, the xref is also loaded and appears on screen. This attachment remains permanent until you remove or *detach* it. This is done by highlighting the reference name in the **Xref Manager** dialog box and picking the **Detach** button. When you detach an externally referenced file, all instances of the xref are erased, and all referenced data is removed from the current drawing. All xrefs nested within the detached file are also removed. The actual detachment does not occur until you press **OK** and close the dialog box. This is helpful if you accidentally detach an xref, because you can simply press **Cancel** to prevent the detachment and return to the drawing.

There may be situations where you need to update or *reload* an xref file in the master drawing. For example, if an externally referenced file is edited by another user while the master drawing is open, the version on disk may be different than the version currently displayed. To update the xref, highlight the reference name in the **Xref Manager** dialog box and pick the **Reload** button. This forces AutoCAD to read and display the most recently saved version of the drawing.

When you need to temporarily remove an xref file without actually detaching it, you can *unload* the xref. To do so, highlight the reference name in the **Xref Manager** dialog box and pick the **Unload** button. When an xref is unloaded, it is not displayed or regenerated, and AutoCAD's performance is increased. To display the xref again, access the **Xref Manager** dialog box and pick the **Reload** button.

## Using the Xref Manager Dialog Box

In addition to attaching xref files, you can use the **Xref Manager** dialog box to access current information about any referenced file in the master drawing. Each of the labeled columns in this dialog box lists information, **Figure 23-5.** The file names in the **Reference Name** column can be displayed in either list view or tree view. The list view display mode is active by default. It can be activated by picking the **List View** button, located at the upper-left corner of the dialog box, or by pressing the [F3] key. The labeled columns displayed in list view are described as follows:

- **Reference Name.** This column lists the names of all existing external references.
- **Status.** This column describes the current status of each xref. The xref status can be classified as one of the following:
  - **Loaded.** The xref is attached to the drawing.
  - **Unloaded.** The xref is not displayed or regenerated.
  - **Unreferenced.** The xref has nested xrefs that are not found or are unresolved. An unreferenced xref is not displayed.
  - **Not Found.** The xref file was not found in valid search paths.
  - **Unresolved.** The xref file is missing or cannot be found.

**Figure 23-5.**
Additional information on referenced files is displayed in the **Xref Manager** dialog box.

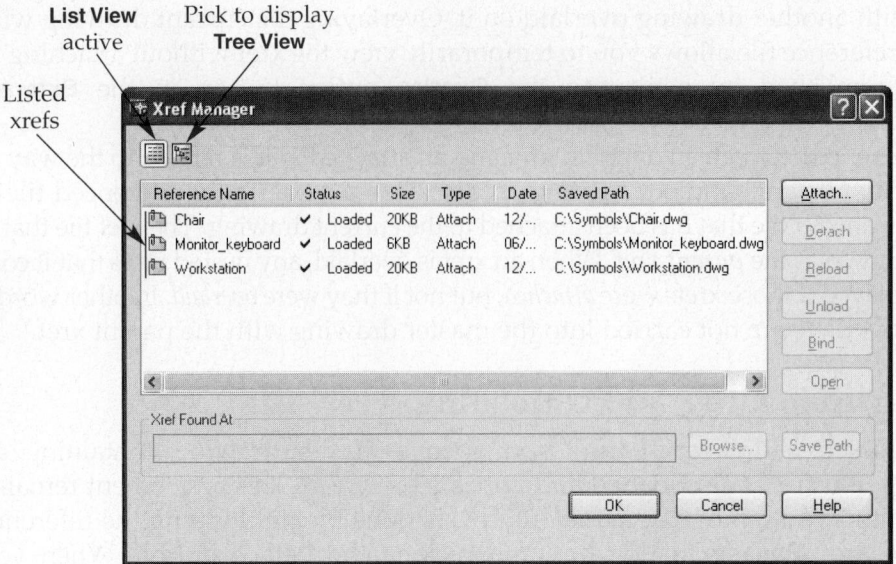

- **Orphaned.** The parent of the nested xref cannot be found.
- **Reload.** The xref is marked to be reloaded. Loading and unloading both occur after the dialog box is closed.
- **Unload.** The xref is marked to be unloaded.
- **Size.** The file size for each xref is listed in this column.
- **Type.** This column indicates whether the xref was attached or referenced as an overlay.
- **Date.** The last modification date for the file being referenced is indicated in this column.
- **Saved Path.** This column lists the path name saved with the xref. If only a file name appears here, the path has not been saved.

**PROFESSIONAL TIP**

In the list view display mode, the column widths can be adjusted as necessary to view incomplete information. To adjust the width of a column, move your cursor to the edge of the button at the top of the column until the cursor changes to a horizontal resizing cursor. Press and hold your left mouse button and drag the column to the desired width. The column width adjustments you make are used for subsequent displays of the dialog box. If the columns extend beyond the width of the dialog box window, a horizontal scroll bar appears at the bottom of the list.

To quickly see a listing of your externally referenced files that shows nesting levels, pick the **Tree View** button or press the [F4] key. See **Figure 23-6.** In the tree view display mode, the drawing is indicated with the standard AutoCAD drawing file icon, and xrefs appear as a sheet of paper with a paper clip. Nesting levels are shown in a format that is similar to the arrangement of folders. The xref icon can take on different appearances, depending on the current status of the xref. An xref whose status is unloaded or not found will have an icon that is grayed out. An upward arrow shown with the icon means the xref has just been reloaded, and a downward arrow means the xref has just been unloaded.

Figure 23-6.
The tree view display mode shows nested xref levels and the status of each xref.

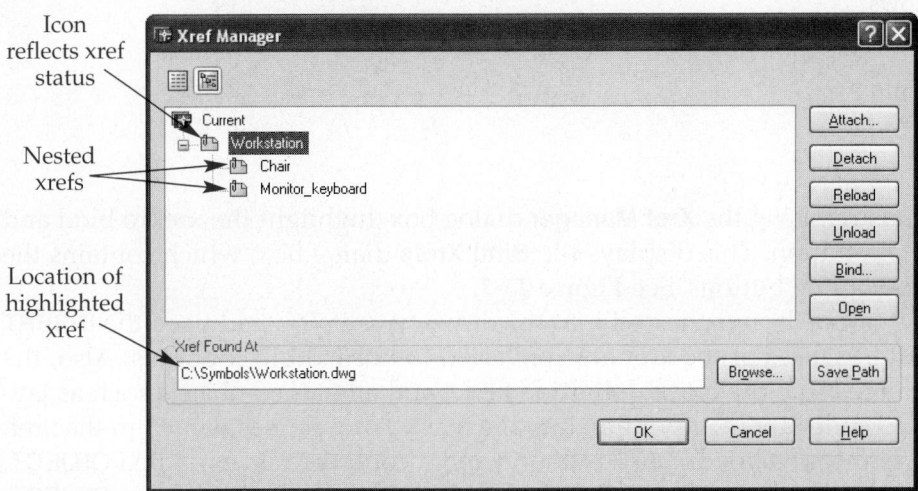

Icon reflects xref status

Nested xrefs

Location of highlighted xref

## Updating the Xref Path

As previously discussed, a file path saved with an externally referenced file is displayed in the **Saved Path** column of the **Xref Manager** dialog box. If an xref file is not found in the **Saved Path** location when the master drawing is opened, AutoCAD searches along the *library* path, which includes the current drawing folder and the Support File Search Path locations set in the **Files** tab of the **Options** dialog box. If a file with a matching name is found, it is resolved. In such a case, the **Saved Path** location differs from where the file was actually found. You can check this in the **Xref Manager** dialog box by highlighting an xref name and then comparing the path listed in the **Saved Path** column with the listing in the **Xref Found At** area. To update the **Saved Path** location, pick the **Save Path** button.

When a referenced drawing has been moved and the new location is not on the library path, its status is indicated as Not Found. You can update the path to refer to the new location by selecting the **Browse...** button in the **Xref Found At** area. Using the **Select new path** dialog box, go to the new folder and select the desired file. Then, press **Open** to update the path. When you pick **OK**, the xref is automatically reloaded into the drawing.

## Binding an External Reference

An externally referenced file can be made a permanent part of the master drawing as if it had been inserted with the **INSERT** command. This is called *binding* an xref. Binding is useful when you need to send the full drawing file to a plotting service, or to a client.

Before an xref is bound, all dependent objects in the externally referenced file, such as blocks, dimension styles, layers, linetypes, and text styles, are named differently by AutoCAD. When an xref is attached to the master drawing, dependent objects are renamed so the xref name precedes the actual object name. The names are separated by a vertical bar symbol ( | ). For example, prior to binding, a layer named Notes within an externally referenced drawing file named Title comes into the master drawing as Title|Notes. This is done to distinguish the xref-dependent layer name from the same layer name in the master drawing. When an xref file is bound to the master drawing, the dependent objects are renamed again to reflect that they have become a permanent part of the drawing. There are different renaming methods, depending on the type of binding that is performed.

Figure 23-7.
The **Bind Xrefs**
dialog box allows
you to specify how
the xref is
incorporated into
the master drawing.

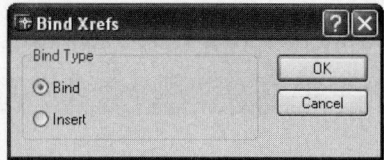

To bind an xref using the **Xref Manager** dialog box, highlight the xref to bind and select the **Bind...** button. This displays the **Bind Xrefs** dialog box, which contains the **Bind** and **Insert** option buttons. See **Figure 23-7**.

The **Insert** option brings the xref into the drawing as if you had used the **INSERT** command. All instances of the xref are converted to normal block objects. Also, the drawing is entered into the block definition table, and all named objects such as layers, blocks, and styles are incorporated into the master drawing as named in the xref. For example, if an xref named PLATE is bound and it contains a layer named OBJECT, the xref-dependent layer PLATE|OBJECT becomes the locally defined layer OBJECT. All other xref-dependent objects are stripped of the xref name, and they assume the properties of the locally defined objects with the same name. The **Insert** binding option provides the best results for most purposes.

The **Bind** option also brings the xref in as a native part of the master drawing and converts all instances of the xref to blocks. However, the xref name is kept with the names of all dependent objects, and the vertical line in each of the names is replaced with two dollar signs with a number in between. For example, a layer named Title|Notes is renamed Title$0$Notes when the xref is bound using the **Bind** option. The number inside the dollar signs is automatically incremented if a local object definition with the same name exists. For example, if Title$0$Notes already exists in the drawing, the layer is renamed to Title$1$Notes. In this manner, unique names are created for all xref-dependent object definitions that are bound. Any of the named objects can be renamed as desired using the **RENAME** command.

In some cases, you may only need to incorporate one or more specific named objects from an xref into the master drawing, rather than the entire xref. If you only need selected items, it can be counterproductive to bind an entire drawing. In this case, you can bind only the named objects you select. This technique is covered later in this chapter.

## Clipping an External Reference

A frequent need with externally referenced files is to display only a specific portion of a drawing. AutoCAD allows you to create a boundary that displays a subregion of an external reference. All geometry occurring outside the border is invisible. Objects that are partially within the subregion appear to be trimmed at the boundary. Although these objects appear trimmed, the referenced file is not changed in any way. Clipping is applied to a selected instance of an xref, and not to the actual xref definition.

The **XCLIP** command is used to create and modify clipping boundaries. To access the **XCLIP** command, pick the **External Reference Clip** button from the **Reference** toolbar, pick **Xref** from the **Clip** cascading menu in the **Modify** pull-down menu, or enter XC or XCLIP at the Command: prompt. The prompt sequence for creating a rectangular boundary for an xref is as follows:

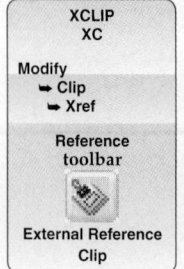

XCLIP
XC

Modify
➥ Clip
➥ Xref

Reference
toolbar

External Reference
Clip

    Command: **XC** or **XCLIP**↵
    Select objects: (select any number of xref objects)
    Select objects: ↵
    Enter clipping option
    [ON/OFF/Clipdepth/Delete/generate Polyline/New boundary] <New>: ↵

The Select objects: prompt allows you to select any number of xrefs to be clipped. Then press [Enter] to accept the default **New boundary** option. This option allows you to select the clipping boundary. The other options of the **XCLIP** command include the following:

- **ON and OFF.** The clipping feature can be turned on or off as needed by using these options.
- **Clipdepth.** This option allows a front and back clipping plane to be defined. The front and back clipping planes define what portion of a 3D drawing is displayed. An introduction to 3D drawing techniques is given in Chapter 26 of this text. Clipping of 3D models is discussed in *AutoCAD and its Applications—Advanced.*
- **Delete.** To remove a clipping boundary completely, use this option.
- **generate Polyline.** This option allows you to create a polyline object to represent the clipping border of the selected xref.

After the **New boundary** option is selected, the **XCLIP** command sequence continues as follows:

Specify clipping boundary:
[Select polyline/Polygonal/Rectangular] <Rectangular>: *(press* [Enter] *to create a rectangular boundary)*
Specify first corner: *(pick the first corner)*
Specify opposite corner: *(pick the other corner)*

An example of using the **XCLIP** command is illustrated in **Figure 23-8.** Note the geometry outside of the clipping boundary is no longer displayed after the command is completed. A clipped xref can be edited just like an unclipped xref. The clipping boundary moves with the xref. Note also that nested xrefs are clipped according to the clipping boundary for the parent xref.

If you do not wish to create a rectangular clipping boundary after selecting an xref, there are two other options for defining a boundary. These options are described as follows:

- **Select polyline.** This option allows you to select an existing polyline object as a boundary definition. The border can be composed only of straight line segments, so any arc segments in the selected polyline are treated as straight line segments. If the polyline is not closed, the start and end points of the boundary are connected.

**Figure 23-8.**
A clipping boundary is used to clip selected areas of an xref. A—Using the **Rectangular** boundary selection option. B—The clipped xref.

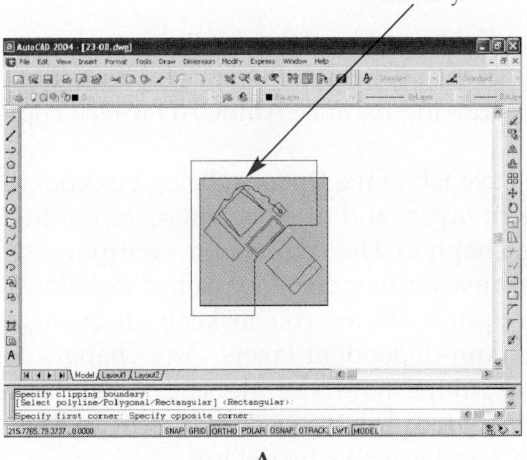
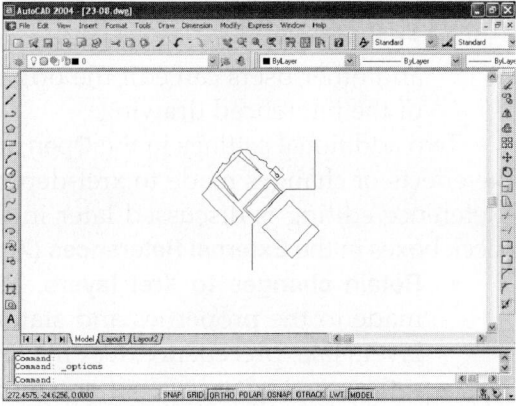

A                                                        B

- **Polygonal.** This option allows an irregular polygon to be drawn as a boundary. This option is similar to the **WPolygon** selection option, and allows a fairly flexible boundary definition.

The clipping boundary is invisible by default. The boundary can be displayed by setting the **XCLIPFRAME** system variable to 1.

---

**PROFESSIONAL TIP**

If a drawing will be used as an external reference, it is good practice to save the file with spatial and layer indexes. *Spatial* and *layer indexes* are lists that organize objects by their location in 3D space and their layer name. These lists help improve the performance of AutoCAD when referencing drawings with frozen layers and clipping boundaries. Layers that are frozen are not loaded when demand loading is enabled, and any areas outside clipping boundaries are also not loaded. (Demand loading is discussed in the next section.)

You can create spatial and layer indexes using the **Save Drawing As** dialog box. The procedure is as follows:
1. Pick **Options** from the **Tools** menu and make sure the **DWG Options** tab is active in the **Saveas Options** dialog box.
2. In the **Index type:** drop-down list, pick the type of index required. The default option is **None**.
3. Pick **OK**, and then save the drawing.

---

## Using Demand Loading

*Demand loading* controls how much of an external reference file is loaded when it is attached to the master drawing. When demand loading is enabled, the only portion of the xref file loaded is the part necessary to regenerate the master drawing. This improves performance and saves disk space because the entire xref file is not loaded. For example, any data on frozen layers, as well as any data outside of clipping regions, is not loaded.

Demand loading is enabled by default. To check or change the setting, open the **Open and Save** tab of the **Options** dialog box. The three demand loading options are found in the **Demand load Xrefs:** drop-down list in the **External References (Xrefs)** area. The options are described as follows:
- **Enabled.** When this option is active, demand loading is turned on. While the drawing is being referenced, the xref file is kept open and other users cannot edit the file.
- **Disabled.** Enabling this option turns off demand loading.
- **Enabled with copy.** When this option is active, demand loading is turned on, and other users can edit the original drawing because AutoCAD uses a copy of the referenced drawing.

Two additional settings in the **Open and Save** tab of the **Options** dialog box control the effects of changes made to xref-dependent layers and in-place reference editing. (Reference editing is discussed later in this chapter.) The settings are controlled by check boxes in the **External References (Xrefs)** area. Each option is explained as follows:
- **Retain changes to Xref layers.** This option allows you to keep all changes made to the properties and states of xref-dependent layers. Any changes to layers take precedence over the layer settings in the xref file. The edited properties are retained even if an xref is reloaded. The **VISRETAIN** system variable also controls this function. It is set to 1 and is active by default.

AutoCAD and its Applications—Basics

- **Allow other users to Refedit current drawing.** This option controls whether the current drawing can be edited in place by others while it is open and when it is referenced by another file. This option is active by default and is controlled by the **XEDIT** system variable.

## Binding Dependent Objects to a Drawing

As discussed earlier, binding allows you to make all dependent objects in an xref file a permanent part of the master drawing. Dependent objects include named items such as blocks, dimension styles, layers, linetypes, and text styles. Before binding, you cannot directly use any dependent objects from a referenced drawing in the master drawing. For example, a layer that exists only in a referenced drawing cannot be made current in the master drawing. The same applies for text styles.

When a drawing is referenced to the master drawing, all dependent named objects are renamed. All xref-dependent layer names are given the name of the referenced drawing, followed by the vertical bar symbol ( | ), and then the name of the layer. This naming convention enables you to quickly identify which layers belong to a specific referenced drawing. In **Figure 23-9**, the **Layer Properties Manager** dialog box shows how layer names in the master drawing are distinguished from those belonging to different xref files.

There may be cases where you wish to individually bind an xref-dependent named object, such as a layer or block, rather than the entire xref file. This can be done using the **XBIND** command.

To access the **XBIND** command, pick the **External Reference Bind** button from the **Reference** toolbar, pick **Object** from the **Modify** pull-down menu and then pick **Bind...** from the **External Reference** cascading menu, or enter XB or XBIND at the Command: prompt. This displays the **Xbind** dialog box, **Figure 23-10**. This dialog box allows you to select individual xref-dependent objects for binding.

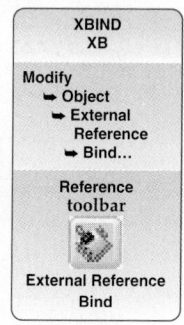

**Figure 23-9.**
Xref-dependent layer names in the master drawing are preceded by the xref drawing name and the vertical bar symbol ( | ).

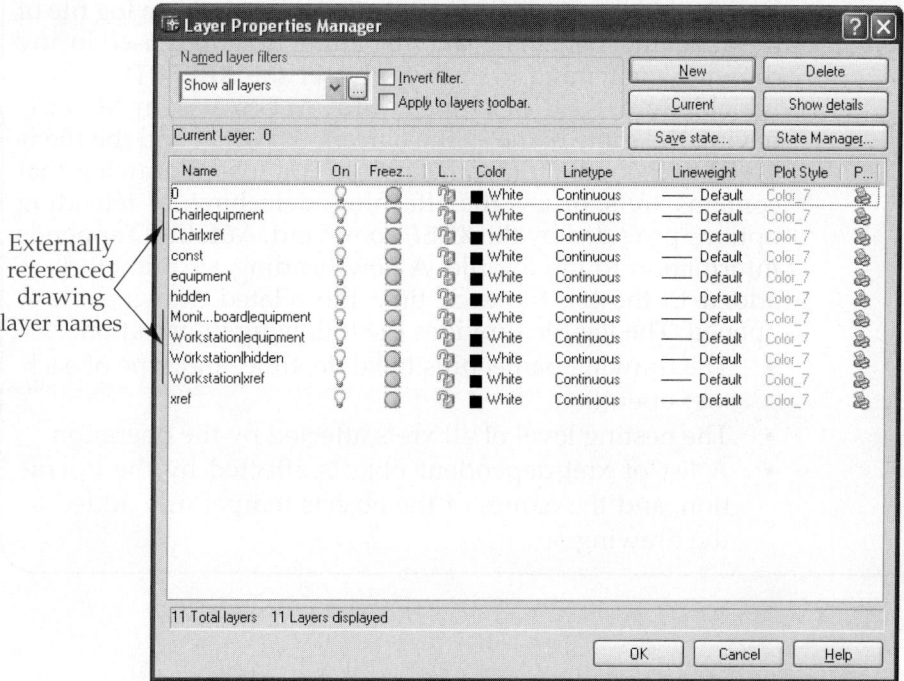

**Figure 23-10.**
The **Xbind** dialog box is used to individually bind xref-dependent objects to the master drawing.

Referenced drawing

Object groups within xref

Dependent object

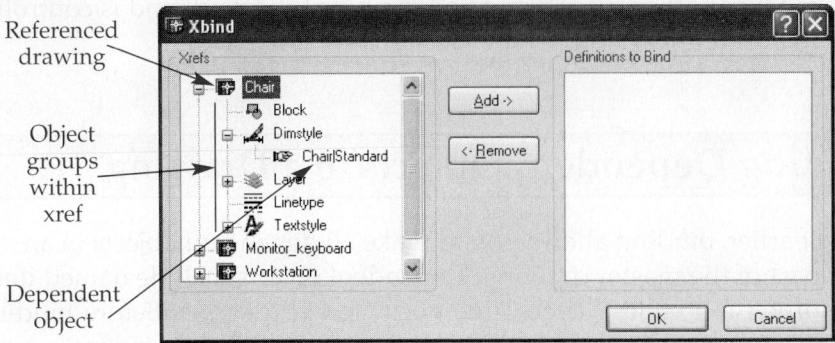

The three xrefs shown are indicated by the AutoCAD drawing file icons. Click the plus sign to expand the listing and display the contents of the xref file.

To select an individually named object from a group, you must first expand the group listing by clicking on the plus sign next to the corresponding icon. To select an object for binding, highlight it and pick the **Add** button. The names of all objects selected and added are displayed in the **Definitions to Bind** list. When all desired objects have been selected, pick the **OK** button. A message displayed on the command line indicates how many objects of each type were bound.

Individual objects that are bound using the **XBIND** command are renamed in the same manner as objects that are bound using the **Bind** option in the **Bind Xrefs** dialog box. In addition to being renamed, a bound layer can also be assigned a linetype that was not previously defined in the master drawing. An automatic bind is performed so the required linetype definition can be referenced by the new layer. A new linetype name, such as xref1$0$hidden, is created for the linetype. In similar fashion, a previously undefined block may be automatically bound to the master drawing as a result of binding nested blocks.

As discussed earlier, bound objects can be renamed as desired. This is done using the **RENAME** command.

---

**NOTE**

You can instruct AutoCAD to create and maintain a log file of the attaching, detaching, and reloading functions used in any drawing containing xrefs. Simply set the **XREFCTL** system variable to 1. At this setting, AutoCAD creates an XLG file having the same name as the current drawing, and the file is saved in the same folder. Each time you load a drawing that contains xrefs, or use the attaching, detaching, or reloading options provided by the **XREF** command, AutoCAD appends information to the log file. A new heading, or title block, is added to the log file each time the related drawing file is opened. The log file provides the following information:

- The drawing name, plus the date, time, and type of each xref operation.
- The nesting level of all xrefs affected by the operation.
- A list of xref-dependent objects affected by the operation, and the names of the objects temporarily added to the drawing.

---

# Editing Reference Drawings

Reference drawings can be edited *in place,* or within the master drawing. This function, called *reference editing,* allows you to edit reference drawings without opening the original xref file. Any changes can then be saved to the original drawing while remaining inside the master drawing.

> **NOTE**
> In-place reference editing is best suited for minor revisions. Larger revisions should be done inside the original drawing. Making major changes with in-place editing can decrease the performance of AutoCAD because additional disk space is used.

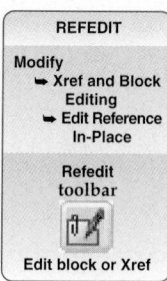

The **REFEDIT** command is used to edit externally referenced drawings in place. To issue this command, pick the **Edit block or Xref** button from the **Refedit** toolbar, pick **Edit Reference In-Place** from the **Xref and Block Editing** cascading menu in the **Modify** pull-down menu, or enter REFEDIT at the Command: prompt.

    Command: **REFEDIT**↵
    Select reference:

This prompt asks you to select a reference to edit. After you make a selection, the **Reference Edit** dialog box is displayed with the **Identify Reference** tab active, **Figure 23-11.** A preview of the selected xref is shown in the **Preview** panel, and the name of the file is highlighted. In the example shown, the Workstation reference drawing has been selected.

In the **Path:** area, the radio button labeled **Automatically select all nested objects** is active by default. Using this option makes all the xref objects available for editing. If you wish to only edit certain xref objects, then the **Prompt to select nested objects** option can be used. When this option is selected, the Select nested objects: prompt is displayed after picking **OK**. This prompt asks you to pick objects that belong to the previously selected xref. Pick all lines and any other geometry of the object to be edited, and then press [Enter]. The nested objects that you select make up the *working set.* If multiple instances of the same xref are displayed, be sure to pick objects from the one you originally selected.

---

**Figure 23-11.**
The **Reference Edit** dialog box lists the name of the selected reference drawing and displays an image preview.

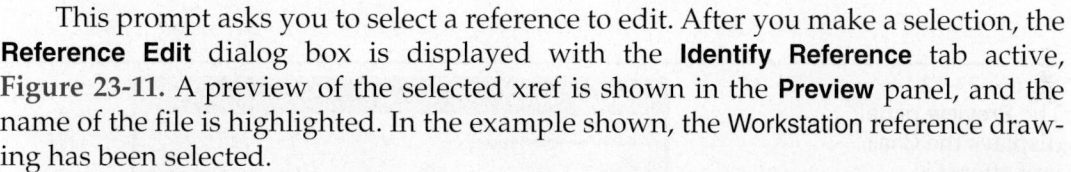

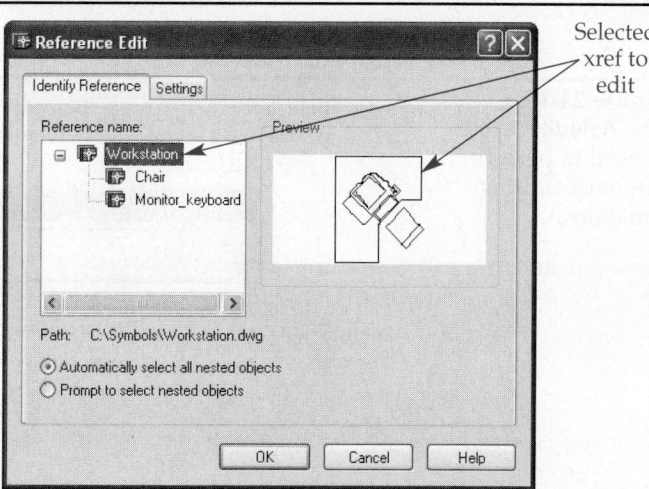

Selected xref to edit

---

Additional options for reference editing are available in the **Settings** tab of the **Reference Edit** dialog box. The **Create unique layer, style, and block names** option controls the naming of selected layers and objects that are *extracted*, or temporarily removed from the drawing, for editing purposes. If this check box is selected, layer and object names are given the prefix $n$, with *n* representing an incremented number. This is similar to the renaming method used when an xref is bound.

The **Display attribute definitions for editing** option is only available if a block object is selected in the **Identify Reference** tab of the **Reference Edit** dialog box. Checking this option allows you to edit any attribute definitions included in the reference. Attributes are covered in detail in Chapter 24.

To prevent accidental changes to objects that do not belong to the working set, you can check the **Lock objects not in working set** option. This makes all objects outside of the working set unavailable for selection when in reference editing mode.

If the selected xref file contains other references, the **Reference name:** area lists all nested xrefs and blocks in tree view. In the example given, Chair is a nested xref in the Workstation xref. If you pick the drawing file icon next to Chair in the tree view, an image preview is displayed. See **Figure 23-12.**

When you are through making settings, pick **OK** to begin editing the xref file. The **Refedit** toolbar is displayed in the drawing area, **Figure 23-13.** This toolbar displays the name of the selected reference drawing and is left on screen for the remainder of the reference editing session. You can use the toolbar to add objects to the working set, remove objects from the working set, and save or discard changes to the original xref file.

**Figure 23-12.**
The **Preview** panel displays the Chair xref after it is selected in tree view.

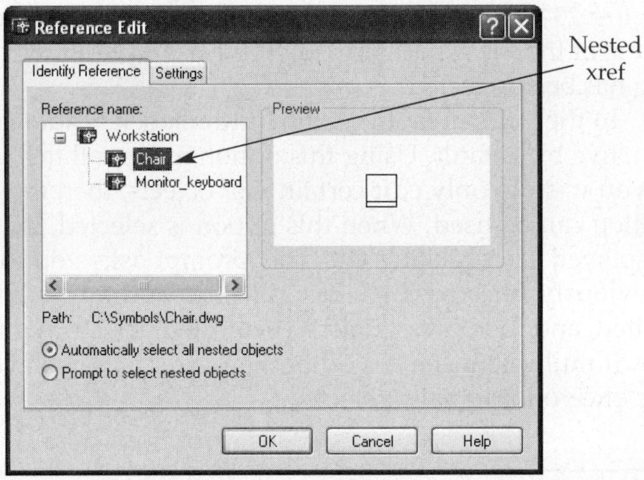

**Figure 23-13.**
The **Refedit** toolbar is used to perform reference editing functions.

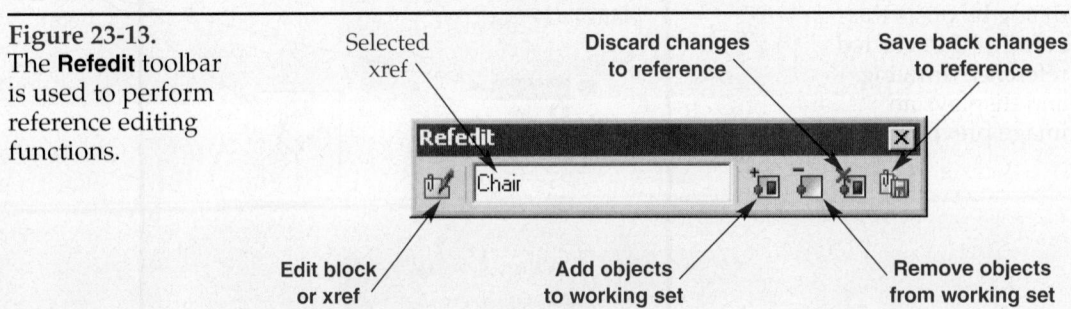

Any object that is drawn during the in-place edit is automatically added to the working set. Additional existing objects can also be added to the working set by using the **Add objects to working set** button. If an object is added to the working set, it is extracted, or removed, from the host drawing. The **REFSET** command allows you to add objects to the working set, or remove objects, during the in-place edit. The **Remove objects from working set** button allows you to remove selected objects from the working set. When a previously extracted object is removed, it is added back to the host drawing.

After you define the working set, it appears differently from the rest of the drawing. All nonselected objects are faded, or grayed out, **Figure 23-14A.** The objects in the working set appear in the normal display mode. The nonselected objects are displayed at a percentage of the normal display. The percentage of fading is 50% by default and can be changed by accessing the **Display** tab in the **Options** dialog box. Enter a value in the **Reference Edit fading intensity** text box in the lower-right corner, or move the slider. A maximum fading value of 90% is allowed.

Once the working set has been defined, you can use any drawing or editing commands to alter the object. In the example given in **Figure 23-14A,** the chair has been selected from the workstation so that arms can be added.

Once the necessary changes have been made, pick the **Save back changes to reference** button from the **Refedit** toolbar. If you wish to exit the reference editing session without saving changes, pick the **Discard changes to reference** button. If you save changes, pick **OK** when AutoCAD asks if you wish to continue with the save and redefine the xref. All instances of the xref are then immediately updated. See **Figure 23-14B.**

**Figure 23-14.**
Reference editing.
A—Objects in the drawing that are not a part of the working set are grayed out during the reference editing session. B—All instances of the xref are immediately updated after reference editing.

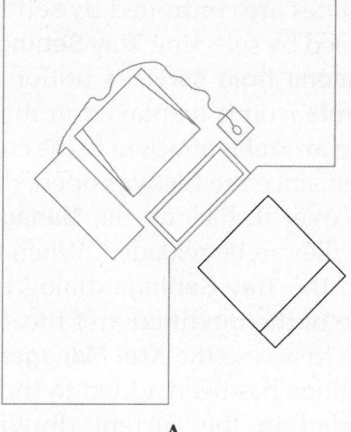
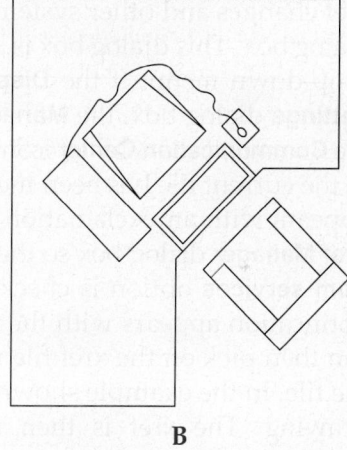

A                                    B

**CAUTION**
All reference edits made in this manner are saved back to the original drawing file, and affect any master drawing that references the file when the master is opened. For this reason, it is critically important that external references be edited only with the permission of your instructor or supervisor.

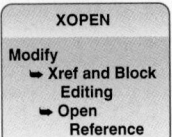

## Opening an External Reference File

Using the **REFEDIT** command allows you to edit xref objects within the current drawing. An xref file can also be opened from within its parent drawing into a new AutoCAD drawing window. This is essentially the same procedure as using the **OPEN** command, but much quicker. To use the **XOPEN** command, pick **Open Reference** from the **Xref and Block Editing** cascading menu in the **Modify** pull-down menu or enter XOPEN at the Command: prompt.

Command: **XOPEN**↵
Select Xref:

Selecting any object that is a part of an xref opens the xref drawing file into a new AutoCAD drawing window. Picking the **Window** pull-down menu shows all the drawing files that are open in the AutoCAD session.

Once changes are made to the xref file and saved, the xref file needs to be reloaded in the master drawing file. Use the **Xref Manager** dialog box to reload the modified xref file. This ensures that the master file you are working in is up-to-date.

Xref files can also be opened by selecting an object that is part of the xref file in the drawing area and selecting **Open Xref** from the right-click menu. You can also select an xref in the **Xref Manager** dialog box and pick the **Open** button.

## The Manage Xrefs Icon

When changes are made to parent drawings for xrefs used in a master drawing, a notification appears in the AutoCAD status bar tray. This tray is located in the lower-right corner of the drawing window. Changes are indicated by the appearance of the **Manage Xrefs** icon, a balloon message, or both. Notifications in the status bar tray for xref changes and other system updates are controlled by settings in the **Tray Settings** dialog box. This dialog box is accessed by selecting **Tray Settings...** from the status bar drop-down menu. If the **Display icons from services** option is checked in the **Tray Settings** dialog box, the **Manage Xrefs** icon is displayed in the status bar tray next to the **Communication Center** icon when an xref is attached to the current drawing. If an xref in the current file has been modified since the file was opened, the **Manage Xrefs** icon appears with an exclamation sign over it. Picking the **Manage Xrefs** icon opens the **Xref Manager** dialog box so the xref file can be reloaded. When the **Display notifications from services** option is checked in the **Tray Settings** dialog box, a balloon message notification appears with the name of the modified xref file. See **Figure 23-15A.** You can then pick on the xref file name to access the **Xref Manager** dialog box and reload the file. In the example shown, a phone has been added to the Workstation parent xref drawing. The xref is then reloaded in the current drawing named Office. See **Figure 23-15B.**

**Figure 23-15.**
The **Manage Xrefs** icon in the AutoCAD status bar tray provides a notification when an xref file has been modified and saved. A—A balloon message is displayed with an exclamation point over the icon. B—Reloading the xref file updates the current drawing and changes the appearance of the icon.

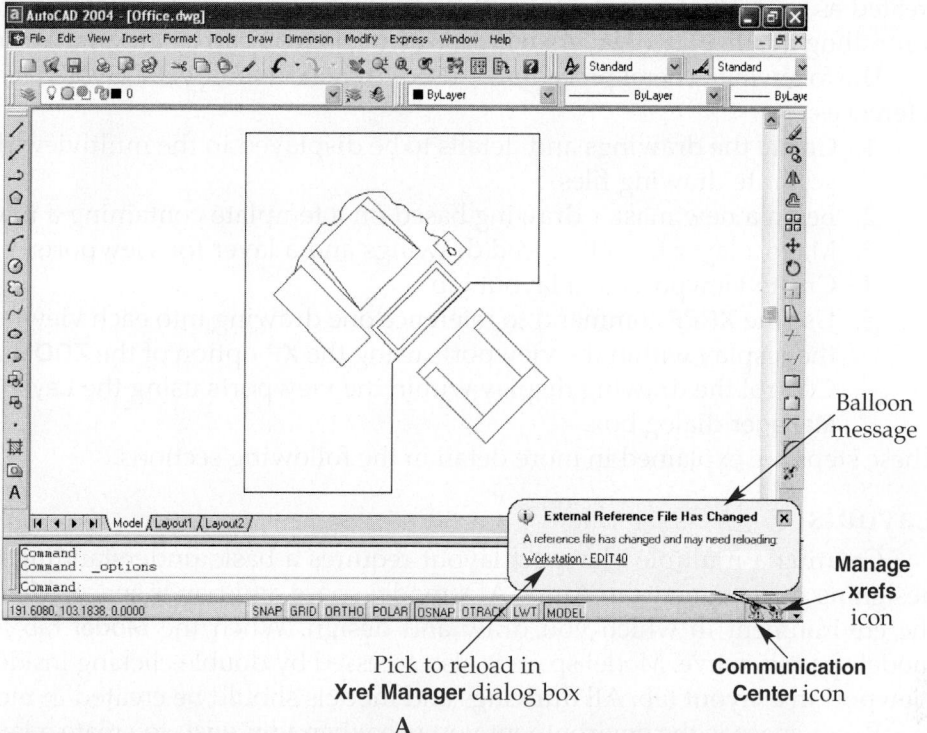

Balloon message

Manage xrefs icon

Pick to reload in **Xref Manager** dialog box

**Communication Center** icon

A

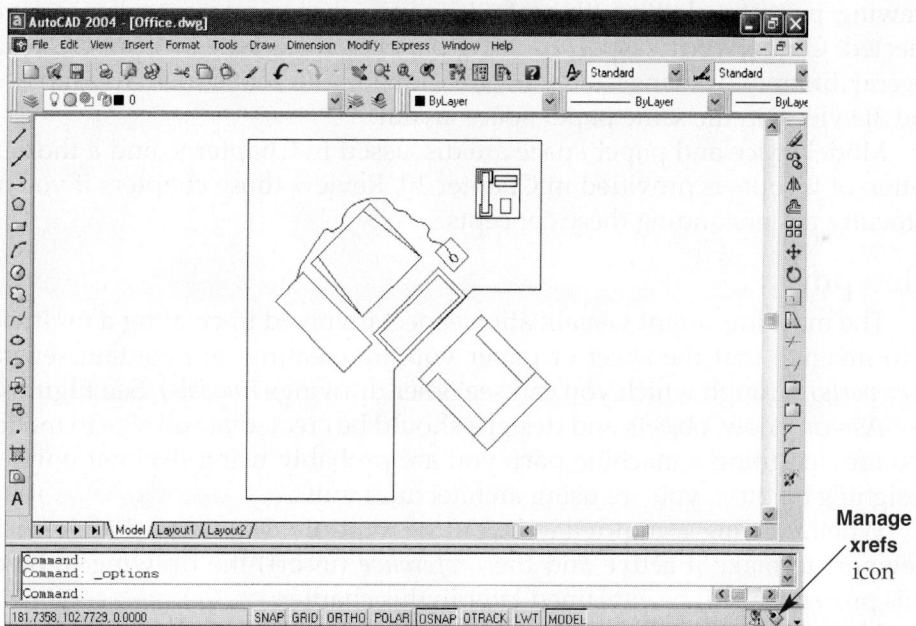

Manage xrefs icon

B

## Using Xrefs in Multiview Layouts

Multiview mechanical drawings and architectural construction drawings often contain sections and details drawn at different scales. These sections and details can be created as separate drawing files and then attached as xrefs to a master drawing. By controlling the display of layers within viewports, you can create a multiview layout.

The following general procedure is used to create a multiview layout using external references:

1. Create the drawings and details to be displayed in the multiview drawing as separate drawing files.
2. Begin a new master drawing based on a template containing a title block.
3. Make a layer for referenced drawings and a layer for viewports.
4. Create viewports in a layout tab.
5. Use the **XREF** command to reference one drawing into each viewport. Adjust the display within the viewports using the **XP** option of the **ZOOM** command. Control the drawing display within the viewports using the **Layer Properties Manager** dialog box.

These steps are explained in more detail in the following sections.

### Layouts

Creating a multiple viewport layout requires a basic understanding of the two designing environments in AutoCAD: model space and paper space. *Model space* is the environment in which you draw and design. When the **Model** tab is selected, model space is active. Model space is also accessed by double-clicking inside a floating viewport in a layout tab. All drawings and models should be created in model space.

Paper space is the environment you use when you wish to create a layout of the drawing prior to plotting. By default, paper space is active when a layout tab is selected. One powerful aspect of using paper space is that you can create a layout of several different drawings and views, each with different scales. You can even mix 2D and 3D views in the same paper space layout.

Model space and paper space are discussed in Chapter 9, and a thorough explanation of layouts is provided in Chapter 10. Review those chapters if you are having difficulty understanding these concepts.

### Viewports

The most important visualization aspect involved in creating a multiview layout is to imagine that the sheet of paper you are creating will contain several cutouts *(viewports)* through which you can see other drawings *(models)*. See **Figure 23-16.**

As you know, objects and designs should be created at full size in model space. If you are designing a machine part, you are probably using decimal units. If you are designing a house, you are using architectural units.

When creating a multiview layout of multiple drawings, double-click inside a viewport to make it active and then *reference* (insert) the drawing to be displayed. This procedure will be explained later in this chapter.

Now, imagine the C-size paper is hanging up in front of you, and the first viewport is cut 12″ wide and 12″ high. You want to display the floor plan of a house inside the opening. If you then place the full-size model of the floor plan directly behind the C-size paper, the house will extend many feet beyond the edges of the paper. How can you place the drawing within the viewport? You know the floor plan should be displayed inside the viewport at a scale of 1/4″ = 1′-0″. The scale factor of 1/4″ = 1′-0″ is 48. Therefore, you need to move the floor plan model away from the C-size paper until it is 1/48 (the reciprocal of 48) the size it is now. When you do that, the entire floor plan fits inside the viewport you cut. This is accomplished with the **XP** (times paper space) option of the **ZOOM** command, which is discussed later in this chapter. See **Figure 23-17.**

AutoCAD and its Applications—Basics

Figure 23-16.
Views of other drawings can be seen through viewports cut into paper space.

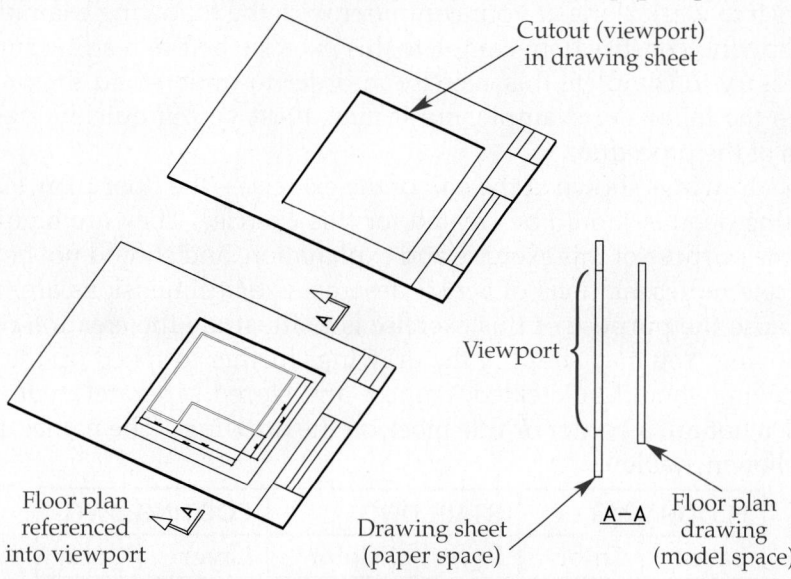

## Constructing a Multiview Drawing

Now that you have a good idea of the multiview layout process, the following example leads you through the details of the procedure. This example uses a house floor plan, a stair detail, and a footing detail. This drawing is *not* among the sample drawings furnished with AutoCAD. Instead, the drawing is based on Exercise 23-1. Complete Exercise 23-1 before working through the example.

**Figure 23-17.**
A floor plan placed inside a viewport.

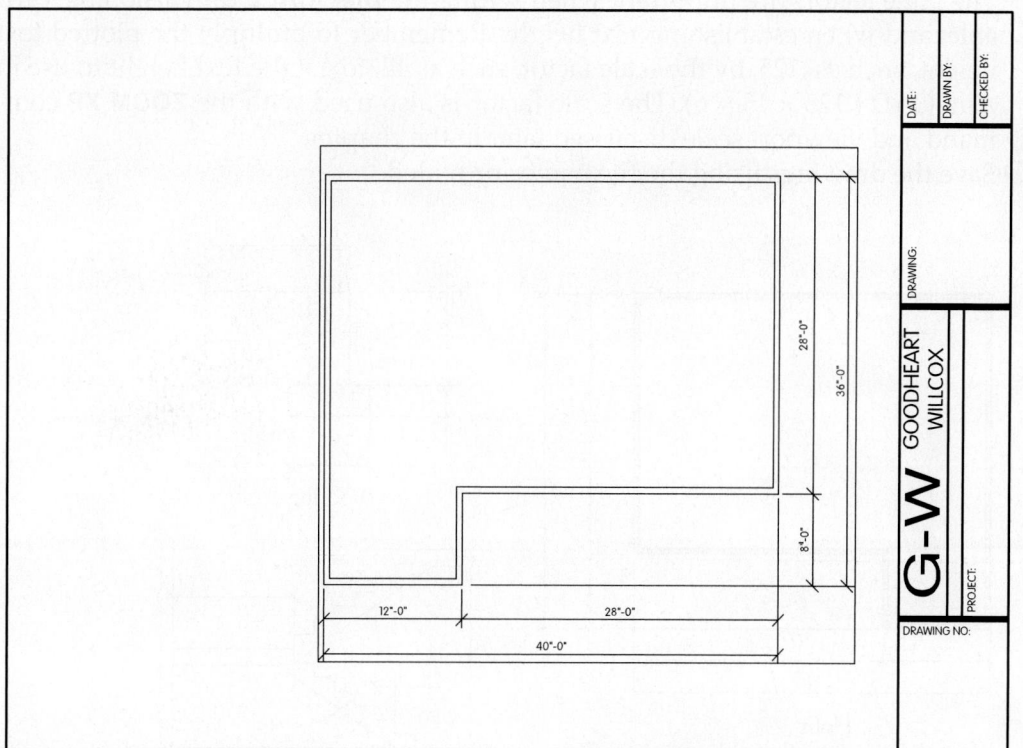

## Exercise 23-1

○ If you wish to work along at your computer with the following example of multiview drawing construction, complete this exercise before reading further. It is not necessary to complete this exercise in order to understand the process discussed in the following example, but it may assist you in quickly grasping the concepts of the procedure.

○ The three drawings shown at the end of the exercise—the floor plan, stair detail, and footing detail—should be created for this exercise. They are highly simplified for the purpose of this exercise and explanation, and should not be regarded as complete representations of actual designs. Exact dimensions are not necessary because the purpose of this exercise is to illustrate the creation of a multiview drawing. You may simplify the drawings further to speed up the exercise.

○ Each drawing should be created, named, and stored separately with different names. Do not put a border or title block on the drawings. The names are shown in the following table:

| FLOOR.DWG | | STAIR.DWG | | FOOTING.DWG | |
|---|---|---|---|---|---|
| **Layer** | **Color** | **Layer** | **Color** | **Layer** | **Color** |
| Wall | White | Wall | Yellow | Floor | Green |
| Dimen | Cyan | Floor | White | Foot | White |
| Notes | Red | Stair | Green | Dimen | Cyan |
| | | Foot | White | Notes | Red |
| | | Dimen | Cyan | Earth | Yellow |
| | | Notes | Red | | |

○ Use the following scales and scale factors when constructing each of the drawings.

FLOOR.DWG: 1/4″ = 1′-0″ (Scale factor = 48)
STAIR.DWG: 3/8″ = 1′-0″ (Scale factor = 32)
FOOTING.DWG: 3/4″ = 1′-0″ (Scale factor = 16)

The scale factors are important when setting the **DIMSCALE** dimensioning variable, and when establishing text height. Remember to multiply the plotted text height, such as .125, by the scale factor, such as 48, to get the text height to use in AutoCAD (.125 × 48 = 6). The scale factor is also used with the **ZOOM XP** command and viewport scale discussed later in the chapter.

○ Save the drawings using the file names provided.

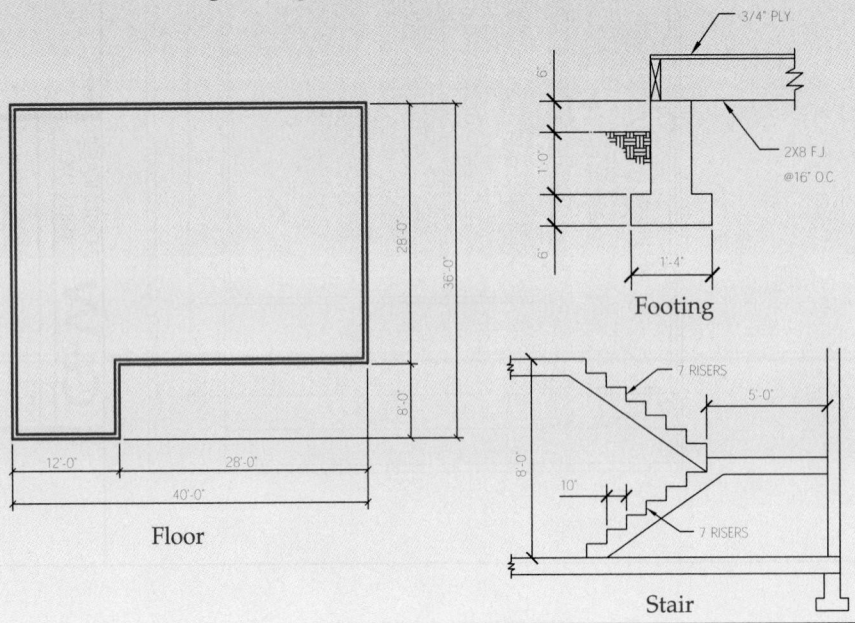

Floor

Footing

Stair

# Initial Drawing Setup

The first aspect of drawing setup is to place a border and title block on the screen. These items are created in the layout tab. They should be the proper size for the plot you wish to make. This can be accomplished in one of the following ways, depending on the depth of your preparation:

- Draw a border on a separate layer, then draw a title block.
- Draw a border and insert a predrawn title block.
- Open or insert a predrawn standard border and title block template containing all constant text and attributes for variable information. The Architectural, English units template drawing is a D-size sheet, but is appropriate for this example. It contains one viewport, which shows as a thin line just inside the left border line. Erase this viewport before creating a new one.

The method you use is not of primary importance for this example, but it is always best to use existing borders and title blocks to maximize efficiency and consistency.

**PROFESSIONAL TIP**

This initial setup phase is unnecessary if your school or company uses preprinted border and title block sheets. You might use a *phantom* border and title block sheet on the screen for layout purposes, and to add additional information to the title block. This phantom information can be frozen before plotting.

When setting up a drawing, first display a paper space layout, then set the units to match the type of drawing you are creating. Be sure the extents of your border and title block match the maximum active plotting area, or *clip limits*, of your plotter. This example uses a standard architectural C-size sheet (18″ × 24″), and assumes that the plotter's active area is .75″ less along the top and bottom and 1.25″ less on the sides, for a total plotting area of 16.5″ × 21.5″.

**NOTE**

Use the page setup options to accurately create an appropriate layout based on a specific plotter or printer and its available paper sizes. Settings selected in the **Page Setup** dialog box are immediately reflected in the selected layout. See Chapter 10 for information on the **Page Setup** dialog box.

Set the units for the new layout as follows (if you do not use a template):
1. Pick a layout tab.
2. Set the following in the **Drawing Units** dialog box:
   - Architectural units.
   - Units precision = 1/2″.
   - System of angle measure = Decimal degrees.
   - Angle precision = 0.
   - Direction for angle 0 = East.
   - Angles measured counterclockwise.
3. Perform a **Zoom all**.

## Creating New Layers

The border and title block should be on a separate layer, so you may want to create a new layer called Border or Title and assign it a separate color. Be sure to make this new layer current before you draw the border. If you wish to use an existing border and title block, insert it now.

One of the principal functions of this example is to use existing drawings in a layout. The house floor plan, stairs, and footing drawings will not become a part of the new drawing, but they will be *referenced* to the current drawing in order to save drawing file space. Therefore, you should also create a new layer for these drawings and name it Xref. Assign the Xref layer the color of 7.

The referenced drawings will fit inside viewports. These viewports can be any shape and are given the object name of viewport. Therefore, they can be edited like any other AutoCAD object. Create a layer called Viewports for these entities and assign it a color.

The layers of any existing drawings that you reference (xref) into your new drawing remain intact. Therefore, you do not have to create additional layers unless you want to add information to your drawing.

If you do not have an existing C-size architectural border and title block, you can draw a border at this time. Make the Border layer current and draw a polyline border using the **RECTANG** command at the dimensions of 16.5″ × 21.5″. Draw a title block if you wish. Your screen should look similar to **Figure 23-18**.

**Figure 23-18.**
The border and title block in paper space.

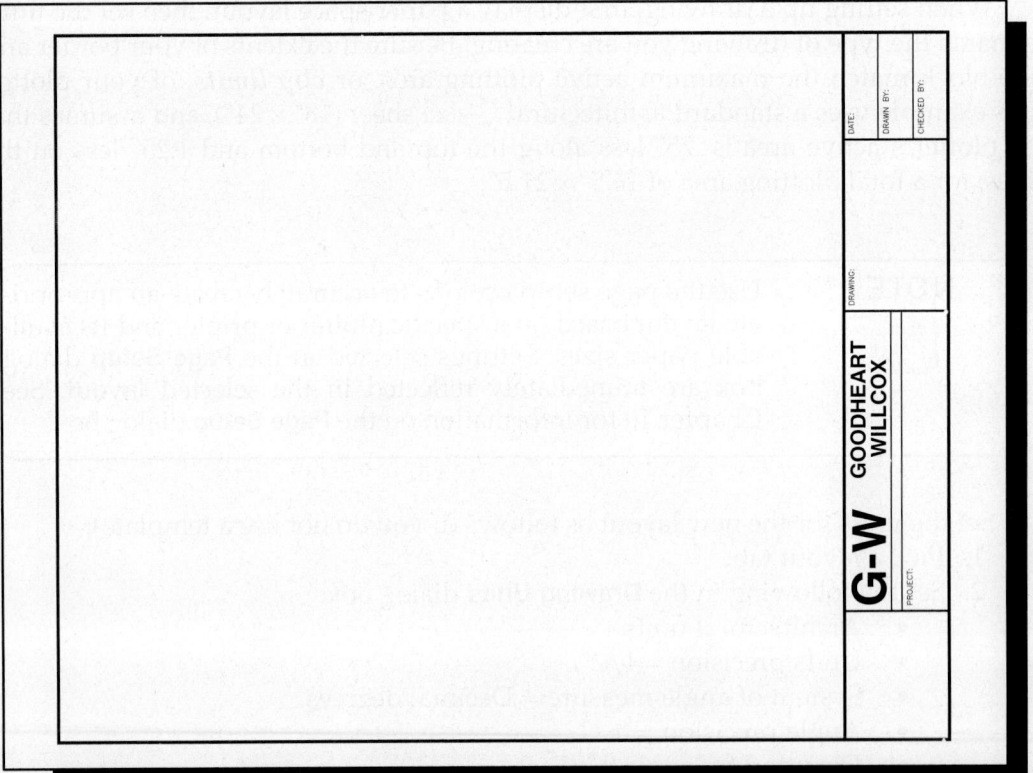

## Creating Viewports

The process of creating viewports is completed in a paper space layout because viewports are *cut* out of the paper. When creating a drawing in a layout, your screen represents a sheet of paper. You will now create an opening through which you can view a referenced drawing.

Methods of creating viewports are explained in Chapter 9. For this example, you can select the **Single Viewport** button in the **Viewports** toolbar to create each viewport. Be sure to set the Viewports layer current before creating the viewport. This allows the viewports to be turned off for plotting. Select two points to create a 12″ × 12″ viewport positioned as shown in **Figure 23-19**.

At this point, you can continue creating as many viewports as required. However, this example continues the process and references a drawing into the new viewport.

**Figure 23-19.**
A viewport added to the drawing in paper space.

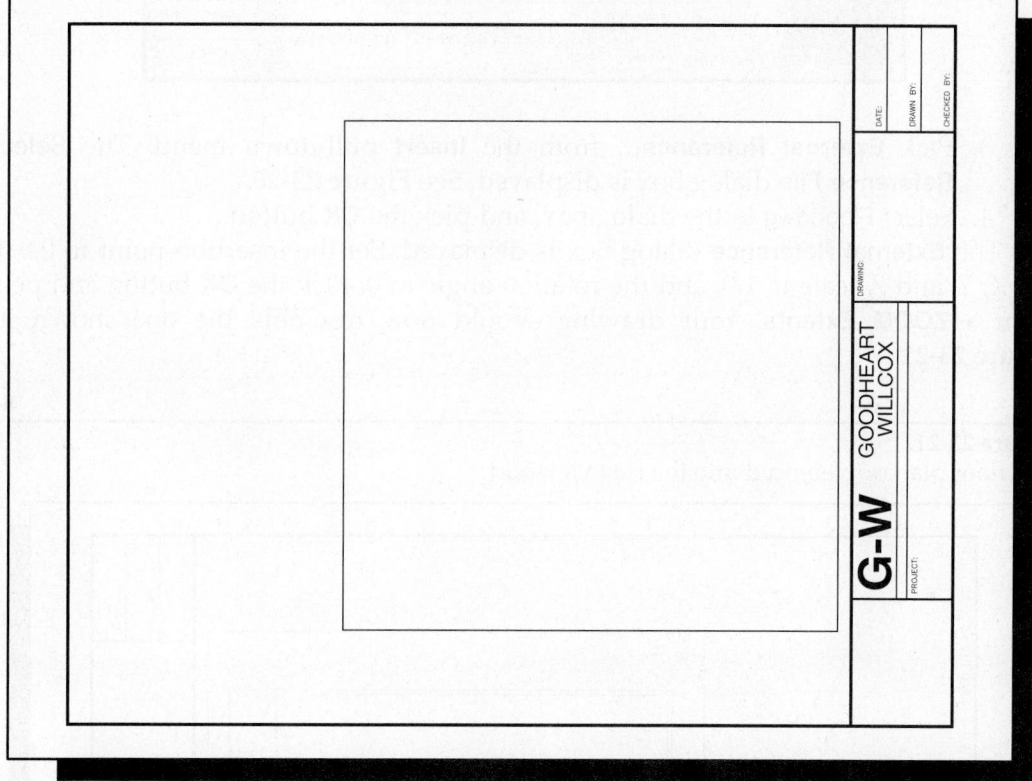

## Placing Views in the Drawing

You will use the new viewport to insert the drawing of the floor plan named Floor. Instead of using the **INSERT** command, which combines an existing drawing with the new one, use the **XREF** command so that AutoCAD creates a *reference* to the Floor drawing. This allows the size of the new drawing to remain small because the Floor drawing has not been combined with it.

The following procedure allows you to enter model space, reference an existing drawing to the new one, and zoom the view to see the referenced drawing.

1. If the layout tab is active, double-click inside the viewport to activate model space within the viewport.
2. Set the Xref layer current.

**Figure 23-20.**
The Floor.dwg drawing is selected in the **Select Reference File** dialog box.

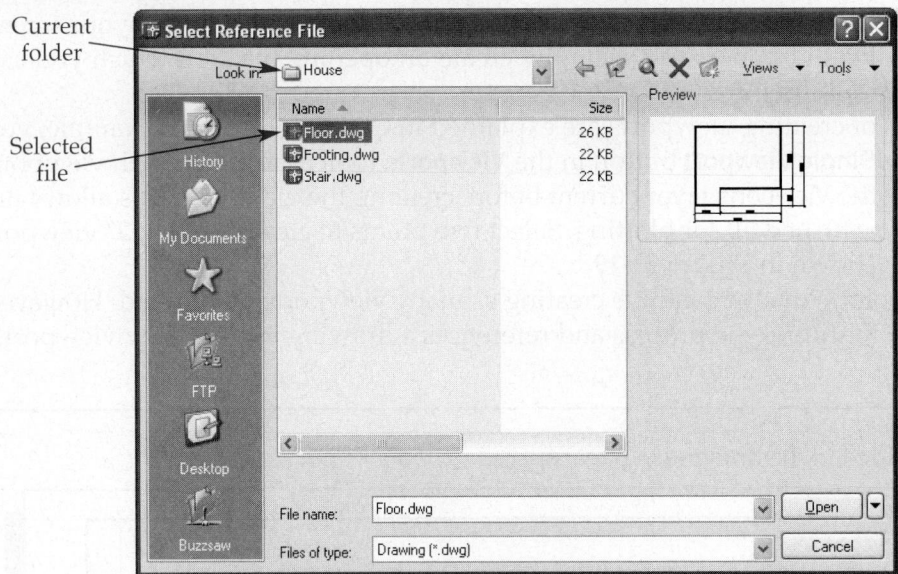

Current folder

Selected file

3.  Pick **External Reference...** from the **Insert** pull-down menu. The **Select Reference File** dialog box is displayed. See **Figure 23-20**.
4.  Select Floor.dwg in the dialog box, and pick the **OK** button.

The **External Reference** dialog box is displayed. Set the insertion point to 0,0,0, the X, Y, and Z scale to 1.0, and the rotation angle to 0. Pick the **OK** button and perform a **ZOOM Extents**. Your drawing should now resemble the one shown in **Figure 23-21**.

**Figure 23-21.**
The floor plan is referenced into the first viewport.

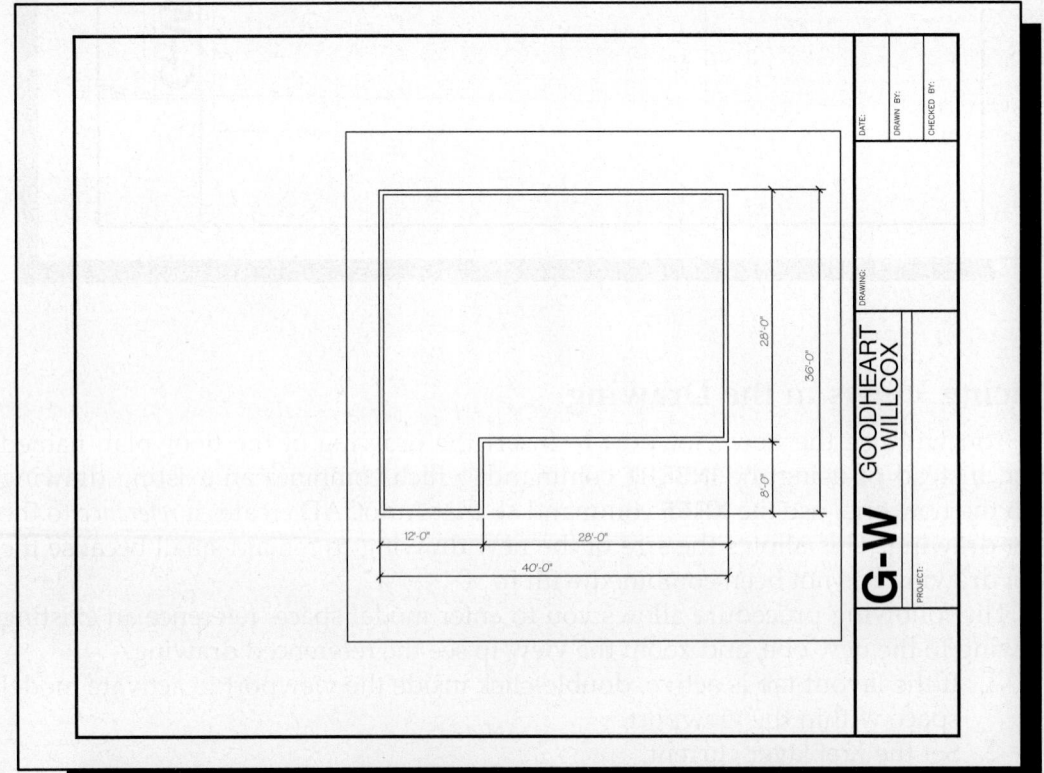

All layers on the referenced drawing are added to the new drawing. These layers can be distinguished from existing layers because the drawing name is automatically placed in front of the layer name and separated by a vertical bar symbol (|). This naming convention is shown in the **Layer Control** drop-down list in the **Object Properties** toolbar and in the **Layer Properties Manager** dialog box.

## Scaling a Drawing in a Viewport

When a drawing has been referenced and placed in a viewport, it is ready to be scaled. After using the **Extents** option of the **ZOOM** command, the referenced drawing fills the viewport. However, this does not imply that the drawing is displayed at the correct scale.

The scale factor of each view of the multiview drawing is important to remember; it is the scale used to size your drawing in the viewport. The scale factor is used in conjunction with the **XP** option of the **ZOOM** command, or it can be selected from the **Viewports** toolbar. Since the intended final scale of the floor plan on the plotted drawing is to be 1/4″ = 1′-0″, the scale factor is 48, or 1/48 of full size. A detailed discussion of determining scale factors is given in Chapter 10.

Be sure you are still in the model space environment within the viewport. Enter the following:

```
Command: Z or ZOOM↵
Specify corner of window, enter a scale factor (nX or nXP), or
[All/Center/Dynamic/Extents/Previous/Scale/Window] <real time>: 1/48XP↵
```

The scale can also be set by picking 1/4″ = 1′ from the scale drop-down list in the **Viewports** toolbar. See **Figure 23-22.** The drawing may not change much in size, depending on the size of the viewport. Also, keep in mind the viewport itself is an object that can be moved or stretched if needed. Remember to change to paper space when editing the size of the viewport. If part of your drawing extends beyond the edge of the viewport after applying the scale, simply use grips or the **STRETCH** command to change the size of the viewport.

**Figure 23-22.**
The scale can be set by picking 1/4″ = 1′ from the drop-down list in the **Viewports** toolbar.

Pick to display the scale drop-down list

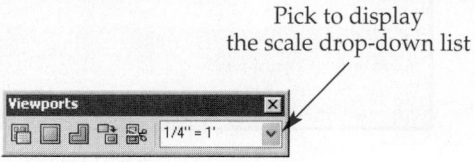

**PROFESSIONAL TIP**
You can use any display command inside a viewport. If a drawing is not centered after scaling, simply use **PAN** to move it around. If lines of a drawing touch a viewport edge, those lines will not be visible if the viewport layer is frozen or turned off.

## Controlling Viewport Layer Visibility

If you create another viewport, the floor plan will immediately fill it. This is because a viewport is just a window through which you can view a drawing or 3D model that has been referenced to the current drawing. One way to control what is visible in subsequent viewports is to freeze all layers of the Floor drawing in any new viewports that are created. Access the **Layer Properties Manager** dialog box and set all layers from the Floor xref to be frozen in new viewports by picking the icons in the **New VP Freeze** column. See **Figure 23-23.** When the snowflake icon appears in this column, the layer is not displayed in any new viewports.

The frozen or thawed status in the current viewport is controlled by the icons in the **Current VP Freeze** column.

**Figure 23-23.**
The snowflake icons in the **New VP Freeze** column indicate that the layers will be frozen in new viewports.

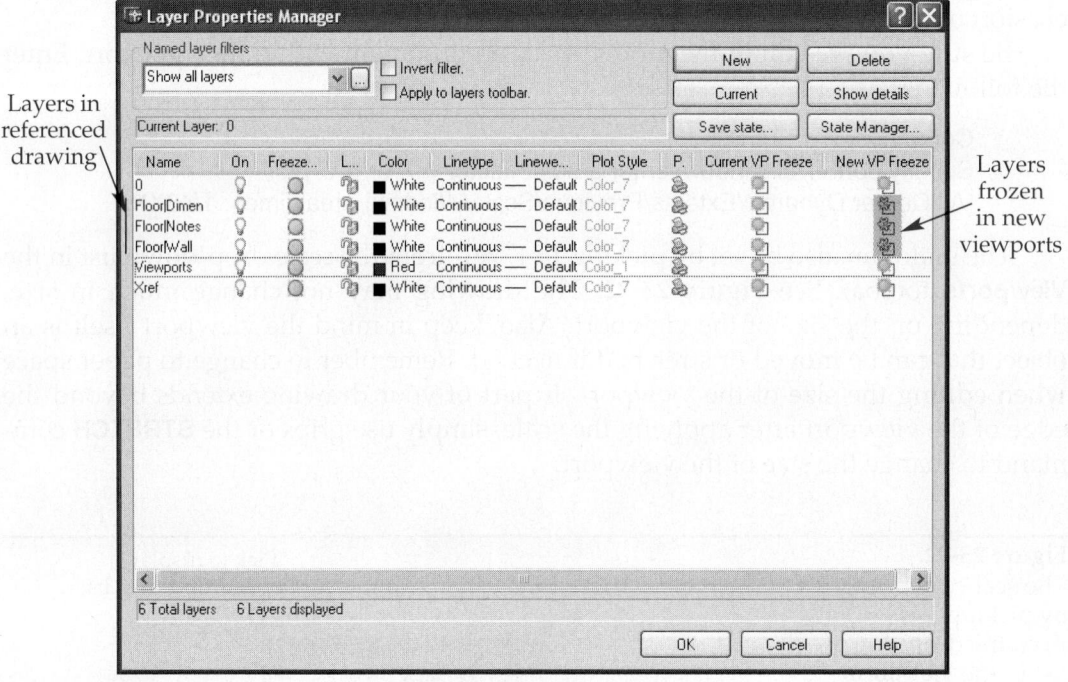

Layers in referenced drawing

Layers frozen in new viewports

**NOTE**

The **New VP Freeze** and **Current VP Freeze** settings in the **Layer Properties Manager** dialog box can also be set using the **VPLAYER** command at the Command: prompt.

## Creating Additional Viewports

The previous example of creating a viewport and referencing a drawing to it is the same process that is used to create the additional two viewports for the Stair and Footing drawings. In this case, two viewports are created before using the **XREF** command. If you know the number, size, and location of all viewports needed on a multi-view drawing, it may save time to create them all at once.

> **PROFESSIONAL TIP**
>
> Viewports can always be added, deleted, or resized on a drawing. So, if your class or company uses standard sheet layouts containing several views, create and save templates that contain viewports.

Now that the floor plan layers will be frozen in new viewports, the other two viewports can be created. Use the following procedure:

1. Double-click outside the viewport to activate paper space.
2. Set the Viewports layer current.
3. Draw a viewport to the dimensions shown in **Figure 23-24** using the **Polygonal Viewport** button in the **Viewports** toolbar.
4. Draw a third viewport 6″ wide and 5″ high.

The final arrangement of the three viewports is shown in **Figure 23-25**.

Now that the viewports are complete, you can begin referencing the remaining two drawings. The following procedure uses **DesignCenter** to reference the Stair drawing:

1. Set the current layer to Xref, and double-click in the lower-left viewport to make model space active.
2. Activate **DesignCenter**. Locate the folder that contains the Stair.dwg file and pick it. Files contained in the selected folder are displayed in the **Content** area.
3. Right-click on the Stair.dwg file and select **Attach as Xref...** from the shortcut menu. The **External Reference** dialog box is displayed. Use 0,0,0 for the insertion point, 1.0 for the scale, and 0 for the rotation angle.
4. Press [Ctrl]+[2] to temporarily dismiss **DesignCenter**.

**Figure 23-24.**
Draw this polygonal viewport.

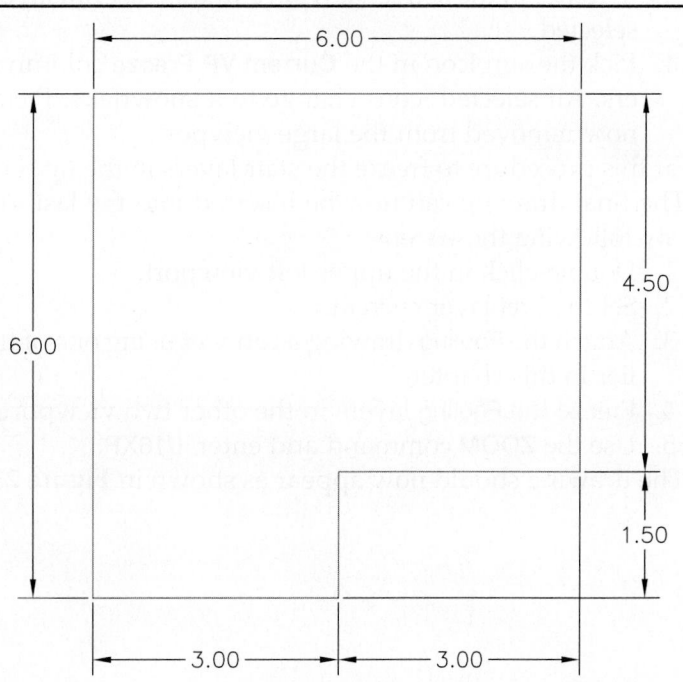

**Figure 23-25.**
Two additional viewports are placed and sized in the drawing.

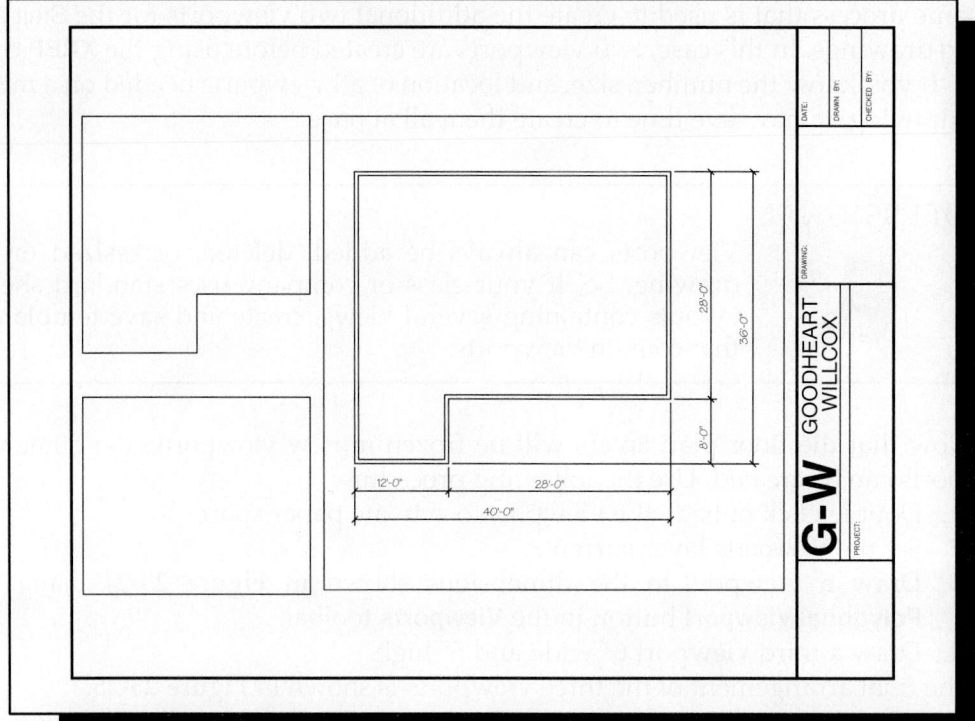

5. The scale factor for the Stair drawing is 32. Use the **ZOOM** command and enter 1/32XP to scale the drawing correctly.

The drawing now appears as shown in **Figure 23-26.** Notice the Stair drawing is shown in all three viewports. Use the **Layer Properties Manager** dialog box to freeze the stair layers in selected viewports using the following procedure:

1. Pick in the large viewport to make it active.
2. Open the **Layer Properties Manager** dialog box.
3. Select all layers that begin with the name of the referenced drawing you wish to freeze in the active viewport. In this case, all layers that begin with Stair are selected.
4. Pick the sun icon in the **Current VP Freeze** column of one of the selected layers. All selected icons change to a snowflake. Pick **OK**. The Stair drawing is now removed from the large viewport.

Repeat this procedure to freeze the stair layers in the upper-left viewport.

The final drawing can now be inserted into the last viewport. Prepare the third view by following these steps:

1. Double-click in the upper-left viewport.
2. Set the Xref layer current.
3. Attach the Footing drawing as an xref using one of the methods explained earlier in this chapter.
4. Freeze the Footing layers in the other two viewports.
5. Use the **ZOOM** command and enter 1/16XP.

The drawing should now appear as shown in **Figure 23-27.**

AutoCAD and its Applications—Basics

**Figure 23-26.**
The reference drawing Stair is displayed in all viewports. Use the **Layer Properties Manager** dialog box to restrict its visibility.

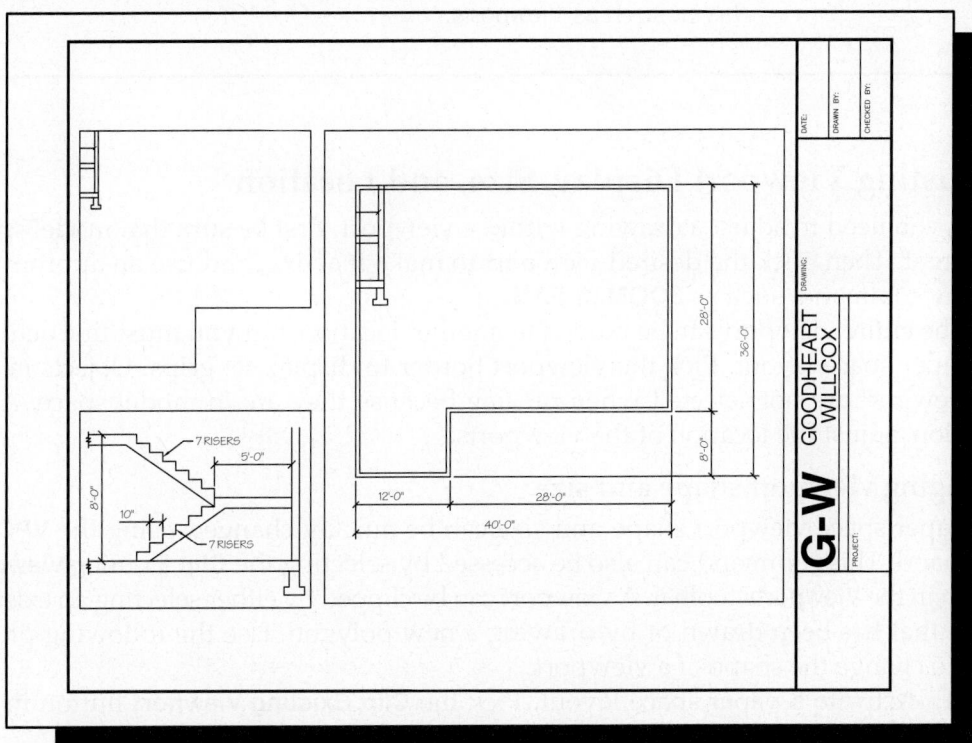

**Figure 23-27.**
The drawing is completed by referencing the Footing drawing.

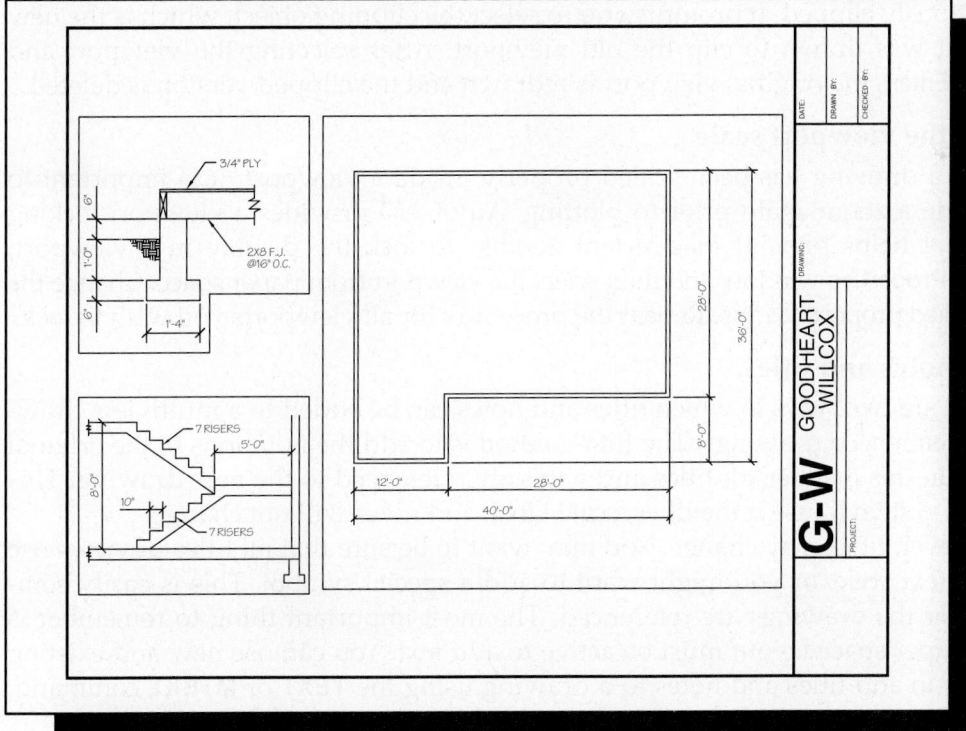

## Adjusting Viewport Display, Size, and Location

If you need to adjust a drawing within a viewport, first be sure that model space is current. Then, pick the desired viewport to make it active, and use an appropriate display command, such as **ZOOM** or **PAN**.

The entire viewport can be moved to another location, but you must first activate the paper space layout. Pick the viewport border to display its grips. Objects inside the viewport are not selected when picking because they are in model space. After selection, adjust the location of the viewports.

### Changing viewport shape and size

Paper space viewport shape and size can be quickly changed using the **VPCLIP** command. This command can also be accessed by selecting the **Clip Existing Viewport** button in the **Viewports** toolbar. A viewport can be clipped by either selecting an existing shape that has been drawn or by drawing a new polygon. Use the following procedure to change the shape of a viewport.

1. Activate a paper space layout. Pick the **Clip Existing Viewport** button in the **Viewports** toolbar.
2. Select the outline of the viewport to be resized.
3. Select the new clipping object, such as a circle that has been previously drawn over the current viewport. The old viewport is deleted.

The **Delete** option of the **VPCLIP** command enables you to delete a viewport that was previously clipped. It prompts you to select the clipping object, which is the new shape that was drawn to clip the old viewport. After selecting the viewport and pressing [Enter], the original viewport is redrawn and the clipped version is deleted.

### Locking the viewport scale

Once a drawing has been scaled properly inside a viewport, it is important to avoid using a zoom again prior to plotting. AutoCAD provides a viewport locking feature that helps prevent inadvertent zooms. To lock the display in a viewport, access the **Properties** window and then select the viewport from paper space. Change the Display locked property to Yes. Repeat the procedure for all viewports you wish to lock.

### Adding notes and titles

There are two ways in which titles and notes can be added to a multiview drawing with referenced drawings. The first method is to add the notations to the original drawing. In this manner, all titles and notes are referenced to the new drawing. This is the best system to use if the titles, scale label, and notes will not change.

However, titles may change. You may want to be sure that all titles of views use the same text style, or you might want to add a special symbol. This is easily completed after the drawings are referenced. The most important thing to remember is that the paper space layout must be active to add text. You can use new and existing text styles to add titles and notes to a drawing using the **TEXT** or **MTEXT** command. See **Figure 23-28.**

**Figure 23-28.**
The completed drawing with titles added and viewport outlines turned off.

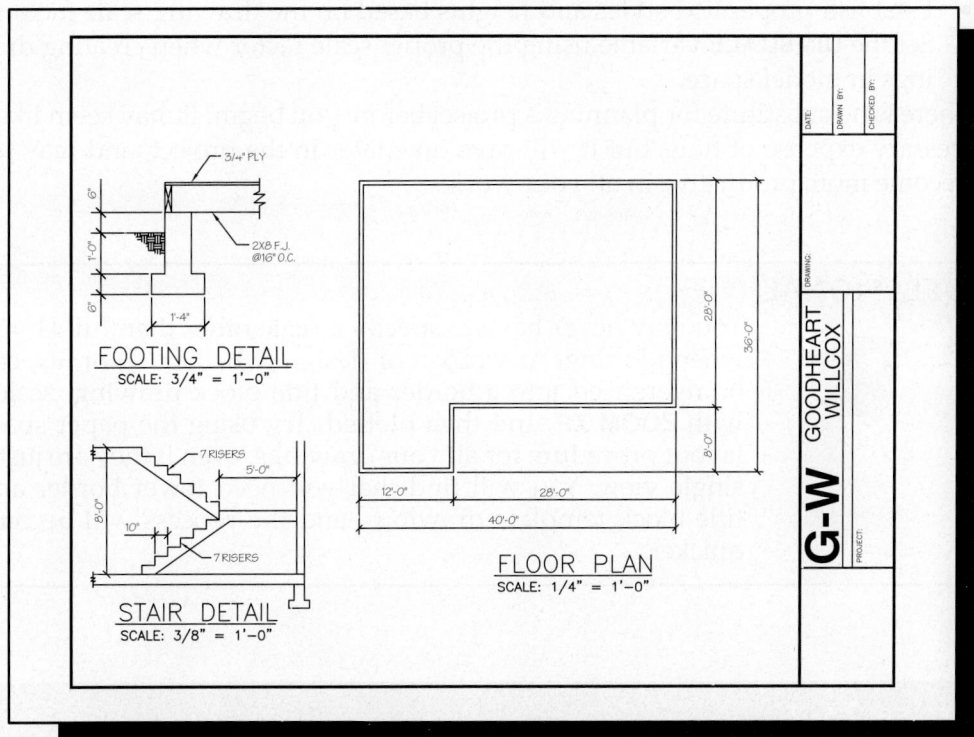

## Removing viewport outlines

The viewport outlines can be turned off for plotting purposes, as shown in **Figure 23-28.** Open the **Layer Properties Manager** dialog box and click on the plot icon for the appropriate layer. A diagonal slash is placed over the symbol, indicating that the layer will not plot.

---

NOTE  If you freeze the Viewports layer and a box still surrounds one of the views, you are probably still in model space. Remember that a box outlines the current viewport in model space. Enter PS at the Command: prompt or pick the **Model** button on the status bar to enter paper space and the outline disappears.

---

## Plotting a Multiview Drawing

You have already taken care of scaling the views because you used the **XP** option of the **ZOOM** command when you referenced them. The drawing that now appears on your screen in paper space can be plotted at full scale, 1 = 1, with the **PLOT** command.

Using the **PLOT** command in this manner is a simple procedure, but only if you planned your drawing at the start of the project. The process of creating a properly scaled multiview layout will go smoothly if you have planned the project. Review the following items, and keep them in mind when starting any drawing or design project—especially one that involves the creation of a multiview paper space layout.

- Determine the size of paper to be used.
- Determine the type of title block, notes, revision blocks, parts lists, etc., that will appear on the drawing.

---

- Prepare a quick sketch of the view layouts and their plotted scales.
- Determine the scales to be used for each viewport.
- Establish proper text styles and heights based on the drawing scale factors.
- Set the **DIMSCALE** variable using the proper scale factor when creating drawings in model space.

There is no substitute for planning a project before you begin. It may seem like an unnecessary expense of time, but it will save time later in the project, and may help you become more productive in all your work.

---

**PROFESSIONAL TIP**

You may never have to specify a scale other than full (1 = 1) when plotting. Any object or design, whether 2D or 3D, can be referenced into a border and title block drawing, scaled with **ZOOM XP**, and then plotted. Try using the paper space layout procedure for all your drawings, even if they are just a single view. You will find that you need fewer border and title block template drawings, and the process will become quicker.

---

## Exercise 23-2

○ Begin a new drawing using a C-size template with a title block.
○ Create a layer for referenced drawings (Xref) and a layer for viewports (Viewport).
○ Select a paper space layout tab.
○ Create an arrangement of three viewports on the Viewport layer. Leave space in the upper-right corner for an additional viewport.
○ **ZOOM** to display the open area in the upper-right corner of the drawing.
○ Create a single viewport in the current screen display.
○ Reference the Floor drawing used in Exercise 23-1 into one of the viewports in the group of three viewports. Be sure the Xref layer is current.
○ Save the drawing as EX23-2.

## Chapter Test

*Answer the following questions on a separate sheet of paper.*

1. When inserting an xref, how does the **Overlay** option differ from the **Attach** option?
2. What effect does the use of referenced drawings have on drawing file size?
3. When are xrefs updated in the master drawing?
4. Why would you want to bind a dependent object to a master drawing?
5. What does the layer name WALL$0$NOTES mean?
6. Name the system variable that controls the creation of the xref log file.
7. What are spatial and layer indexes and what function do they perform?
8. What are the three types of paths that can be used for storing an xref?
9. What command is used to edit external references in place?
10. What command allows you to open a parent xref drawing into a new AutoCAD drawing window by selecting the xref in the master drawing?
11. What is the function of the **VPCLIP** command?

12. What is the purpose of locking a viewport?
13. Indicate the command and value you would use to specify a 1/2″ = 1′-0″ scale inside a viewport.
14. How do you freeze all layers of a referenced drawing inside any new viewports?
15. Do you need to be in paper space or model space in order to resize a viewport?
16. Explain why you should plan your plots.

## Drawing Problems

1. Open one of your dimensioned drawings from Chapter 18. Construct a multiview layout and generate a plot on C-size paper.
   A. Create four viewports of equal size, separated by 1″ of empty space.
   B. Select each viewport and display a different view of the drawing.
   C. Plot the drawing and be sure to use the scale of 1:1.
   D. Save the drawing as P23-1.

2. Open one of your dimensioned drawings from Chapter 18. Construct a multiview layout and generate a plot on C-size or B-size paper. Plot at the scale of 1:1.

3. Open one of your dimensioned drawings from Chapter 19. Construct a multiview layout and generate a plot on C-size or B-size paper. Plot at the scale of 1:1.

4. Open one of your dimensioned drawings from Chapter 20. Construct a multiview layout and generate a plot on C-size or B-size paper. Plot at the scale of 1:1.

5. Open one of your drawings from Chapter 21. Construct a multiview layout and generate a plot on C-size or B-size paper. Plot at the scale of 1:1.

AutoCAD can create an e-mail transmittal containing a master drawing and any reference drawings. All of the files listed in this dialog box would be packaged for electronic transmittal. This feature is discussed in *AutoCAD and its Applications— Advanced.*

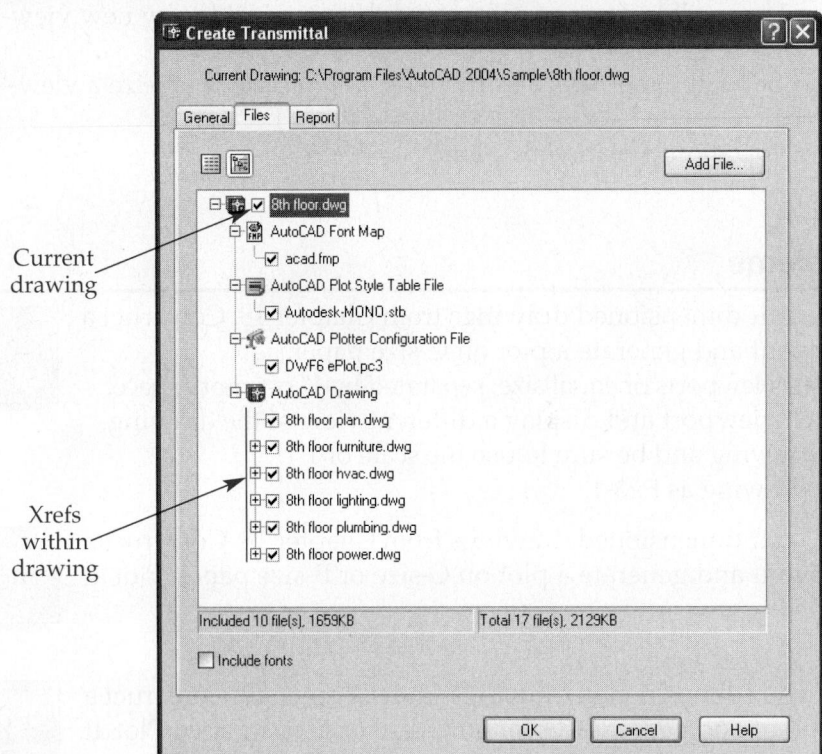

Current drawing

Xrefs within drawing

## CHAPTER 24

# Assigning Attributes and Generating a Bill of Materials

## Learning Objectives

After completing this chapter, you will be able to do the following:
- Assign attributes to blocks.
- Edit attributes defined for existing blocks.
- Create a template file for the storage of block attribute data.
- Extract attribute values to create a bill of materials.

Blocks become more useful when written information is provided with them. It is even more helpful to assign information that is either visible (displayed) or hidden. From this data, a list very similar to a bill of materials can be requested and printed.

Written or numerical values assigned to blocks are called *attributes* by AutoCAD. Attribute information can be *extracted* from the drawing, in addition to being used as text. Several blocks with attributes are shown in **Figure 24-1**.

**Figure 24-1.**
Examples of blocks with defined attributes.

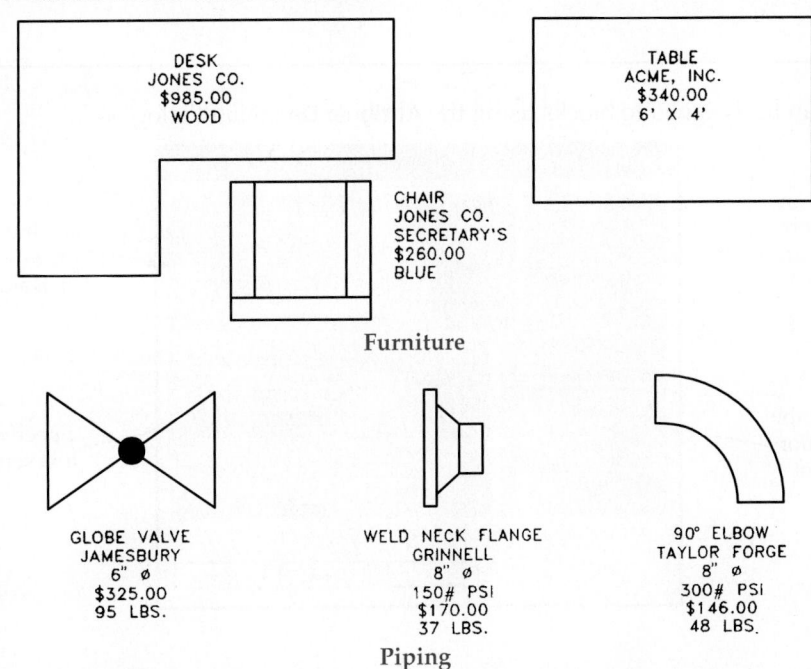

Attributes are created using the **Attribute Definition** dialog box. Inserted attribute values can be modified using the **Enhanced Attribute Editor**. Attribute definitions are modified using the **Block Attribute Manager**. Finally, block and attribute text data can be exported into other applications using the **Attribute Extraction** wizard.

## Assigning Attributes to Blocks

The first step in defining attributes for a block is to decide what information about the block is needed. In most cases, the name of the object should be your first attribute. This could be followed by other attribute items, such as the manufacturer, type, size, price, and weight. After you determine which attributes to assign, decide how you should be prompted to enter a value for each attribute. A typical prompt, for example, might be What is the size?

Suppose you are drawing a valve symbol for a piping flow diagram. You might want to list all the product-related data along with the symbol. The number of attributes needed is limited only by the project requirements.

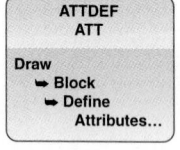

Once the symbol is drawn, you can use the **ATTDEF** (attribute define) command to assign attributes. To access this command, pick **Define Attributes...** from the **Block** cascading menu in the **Draw** pull-down menu, or enter ATT or ATTDEF at the Command: prompt. This displays the **Attribute Definition** dialog box, **Figure 24-2**.

This dialog box is divided into four areas. Each area allows you to set the specific aspects of an attribute. The four areas, their components, and other features in the **Attribute Definition** dialog box are described as follows:

- **Mode area.** Use this area to specify any of the attribute modes you wish to set. The following is a description of each mode option:
  - **Invisible.** If you want the attribute to be shown with the inserted block, leave the **Invisible** check box inactive. If you activate this check box, the attribute will not be displayed when the block is inserted.
  - **Constant.** If the value of the attribute should always be the same, activate the **Constant** check box. All future uses of the block will display the same attribute value, and you will not be prompted for a new value. If you wish to use different attribute values for inserted blocks, leave this check box inactive.

**Figure 24-2.**
Attributes can be assigned to blocks using the **Attribute Definition** dialog box.

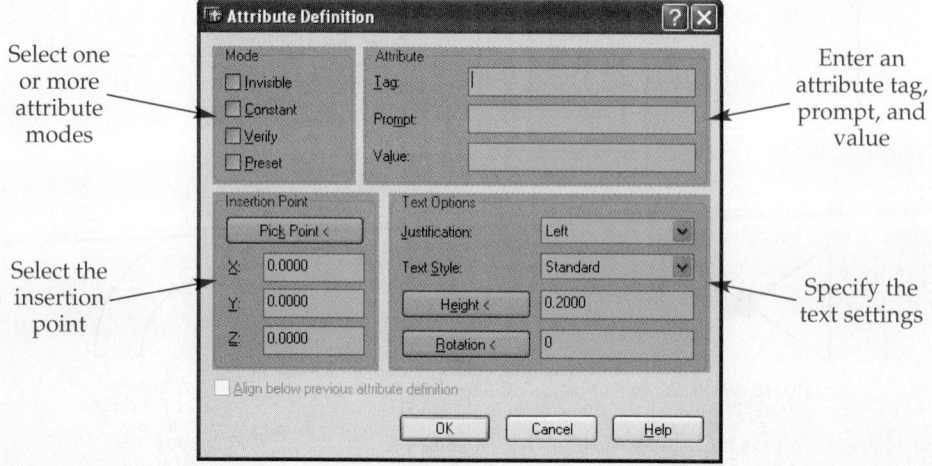

- **Verify.** Activate the **Verify** check box if you want a verification prompt to ask you whether the specified attribute value is correct when you insert the block.
- **Preset.** If you want the attribute to assume preset values during insertion, activate the **Preset** check box. This option disables the attribute prompt. Leave this check box inactive if you wish to display the normal prompt.

If you do not activate any of the attribute modes, you will be prompted to enter values for all attributes, and they will be visible when inserted with a block.

- **Attribute area.** This area lets you assign a tag, prompt, and value to the attribute in the corresponding text boxes. The entries in these text boxes can contain up to 256 characters. If the first character in an entry is a space, start the string with a backslash (\). If the first character is a backslash, begin the entry with two backslashes (\\). Each feature is described as follows:
  - **Tag: text box.** Use this text box to enter the name, or tag, of the attribute. You must enter a name or number. Any characters can be used except spaces. All text is displayed in uppercase.
  - **Prompt: text box.** Use this text box to enter a statement for AutoCAD to prompt with when the block is inserted. For example, if Size is specified as the attribute tag, you might enter What is the valve size? or Enter valve size: as the prompt. If the **Constant** attribute mode is set, this option is inactive.
  - **Value: text box.** The entry in this text box is used as a *default* attribute value when the block is inserted. You do not have to enter anything in this text box. You might decide to enter a message regarding the type of information needed, such as 10 SPACES MAX or NUMBERS ONLY. The default value is displayed in chevrons (< >) when you are prompted for the attribute value.
- **Text Options area.** This area allows you to specify the justification, style, height, and rotation angle for attribute text. The options in this area are described as follows:
  - **Justification.** You can use the **Justification:** drop-down list to select a justification option for the attribute text. The default option is Left.
  - **Text Style.** Access the **Text Style:** drop-down list to select one of the text styles in the current drawing. The default style is Standard.
  - **Height.** Use the text box to the right of the **Height** button to specify the height of the attribute text. Selecting the **Height** button temporarily returns you to the drawing area and allows you to indicate the text height by picking points on screen. Once the points are picked, the dialog box returns and the corresponding height is shown in the text box.
  - **Rotation.** To specify a rotation angle for the attribute text, enter an angular value in the text box next to the **Rotation** button. This button and the text box work in the same manner as the **Height** button and text box.
- **Insertion Point area.** This area is used to select the location for the attribute. Selecting the **Pick Point** button temporarily returns you to the drawing area and allows you to pick a point on screen. You can also enter coordinates in the text boxes.
- **Align below previous attribute definition check box.** When you first access the **Attribute Definition** dialog box, this check box is grayed out. After you create a block attribute, you can press [Enter] to reissue the **ATTDEF** command and create another attribute. If you want the next attribute to be placed below the first with the same justification, pick this check box. When you do this, the **Text Options** and **Insertion Point** areas become inactive.

When you are finished defining the attribute, pick **OK**. The attribute tag is then placed on screen. If you set the attribute mode to **Invisible**, do not be dismayed; this is the only time the tag appears. When the block is inserted, you are prompted for information based on the attribute definition.

Once you have created attributes for an object, you can use the **BLOCK** or **WBLOCK** command to define the object as a block. Blocks are discussed in Chapter 22. When creating the block, be sure to select all of the objects and attributes that go with the block. Select the attribute definitions in the order that you would like to be prompted or have them appear in the **Enter Attributes** dialog box. If you select the attribute definitions using either the **Window** or **Crossing** selection method, you will be prompted for the attribute values in the *reverse* order of creation of the attribute definitions. When creating the block, activate the **Delete** option button in the **Block Definition** dialog box. When the block is created, the selected objects should disappear, as well as the attributes. If any attributes remain on screen, undo the command and try again, making sure that all of the attributes are selected.

---

**NOTE**  Attributes can be defined at the Command: prompt using the **-ATTDEF** command. To access this command, enter -ATT or -ATTDEF at the Command: prompt. The command sequence then provides all the options found in the **Attribute Definition** dialog box.

---

**PROFESSIONAL TIP**  If you create attributes in the order in which you want to be prompted for their values, and the **Window** or **Crossing** selection method is used to select them for inclusion in the block, the attribute prompting will be in the *reverse* order of the desired prompting. This can be rectified by inserting the block, exploding it, and redefining the block. When specifying the new definition, pick the attributes by using the **Window** or **Crossing** selection method. This will reverse the order of the attribute prompting once again, thereby placing the prompts in the initially desired order.

---

## Editing Attribute Definitions

DDEDIT
ED

Modify
➥ Object
 ➥ Text
  ➥ Edit...

Text
toolbar

Edit Text

Occasionally, you may need to change certain aspects of text attributes *before* they are included in a block or definition. If you only want to change the tag, prompt, or default value assigned to a text attribute, you may do so quickly using the **DDEDIT** command. To access the **DDEDIT** command, pick the **Edit Text** button on the **Text** toolbar, select **Text** and then **Edit...** from the **Object** cascading menu in the **Modify** pull-down menu, or enter ED or DDEDIT at the Command: prompt. When you select the attribute, the **Edit Attribute Definition** dialog box is displayed, **Figure 24-3**. Revise the **Tag:**, **Prompt:**, or **Default:** values.

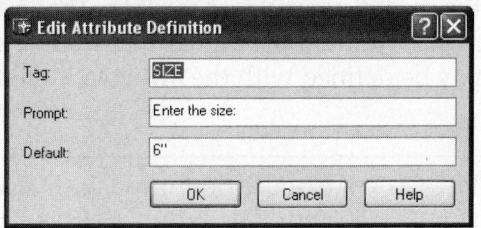

## Using the Properties Window

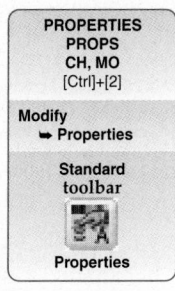

PROPERTIES
PROPS
CH, MO
[Ctrl]+[2]

Modify
➥ Properties

Standard
toolbar

Properties

The **Properties** window provides expanded editing capabilities for attributes. To activate the **Properties** window, pick the **Properties** button on the **Standard** toolbar, pick **Properties** from the **Modify** pull-down menu, enter CH, MO, PROPS, or PROPERTIES at the Command: prompt, or use the [Ctrl]+[2] key combination. You can also select the attribute to be edited, while no command is active, and then right-click and select **Properties** from the shortcut menu to display the **Properties** window.

**Figure 24-4** shows the **Properties** window with an attribute selected. You can change the color, linetype, layer, or thickness of the selected attribute in the **General** section. The attribute tag, prompt, and default value entries are listed in the **Text** section. You can select **Tag**, **Prompt**, or **Value** to change the corresponding values. There are also options to change the text style, justification, height, rotation angle, width factor, and obliquing angle in the **Text** section. You can change the insertion point of the text attribute in the **Geometry** section by using the **Position** options to enter new coordinates. Additional text options are available in the **Misc** section.

Figure 24-4.
The **Properties** window can be used to modify attributes.

Selected object to edit

Pick to change the attribute tag

Pick to change an attribute mode setting

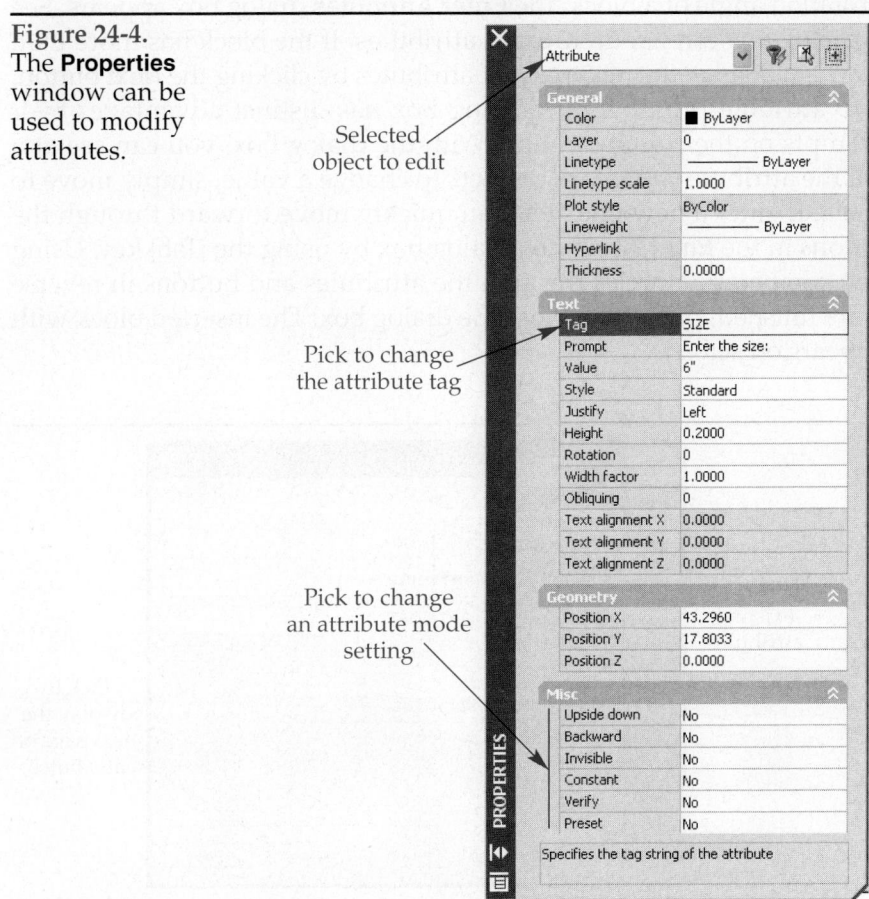

Perhaps the most powerful feature of the **Properties** window for editing attributes is the ability to change the attribute modes that were originally defined. As discussed earlier, an attribute may be defined with the **Invisible**, **Constant**, **Verify**, or **Preset** modes active.

NOTE

Attribute definitions can also be modified using the **CHANGE** command. Enter -CH or CHANGE at the Command: prompt and select the attribute. You are then prompted to modify the insertion point, text style, height, rotation angle, tag, prompt, and default value.

## Inserting Blocks with Attributes

When you use the **INSERT** command to place a saved block with attributes in your drawing, you are prompted for additional information after the insertion point, scale factors, and rotation angle are specified. The prompt statement that you entered with the **ATTDEF** command appears, and the default attribute value appears in brackets. Accept the default by pressing [Enter], or provide a new value. The attribute is then displayed with the block.

Attribute prompts may be answered using a dialog box if the **ATTDIA** system variable is set to 1 (on). After issuing the **INSERT** command and entering the insertion point, scale, and rotation angle of a block, the **Enter Attributes** dialog box appears. See **Figure 24-5**. This dialog box can list up to eight attributes. If the block has more than eight attributes, you can display the next page of attributes by clicking the **Next** button.

Responding to attribute prompts in a dialog box has distinct advantages over answering the prompts on the command line. With the dialog box, you can see at a glance whether all the attribute values are correct. To change a value, simply move to the incorrect value and enter a new one. You can quickly move forward through the attributes and buttons in the **Enter Attributes** dialog box by using the [Tab] key. Using the [Shift]+[Tab] key combination cycles through the attributes and buttons in reverse order. When you are finished, pick **OK** to close the dialog box. The inserted block with attributes then appears on screen.

Figure 24-5.
The **Enter Attributes** dialog box allows you to enter or change attribute definitions when a block is inserted.

Accept or change the existing attributes

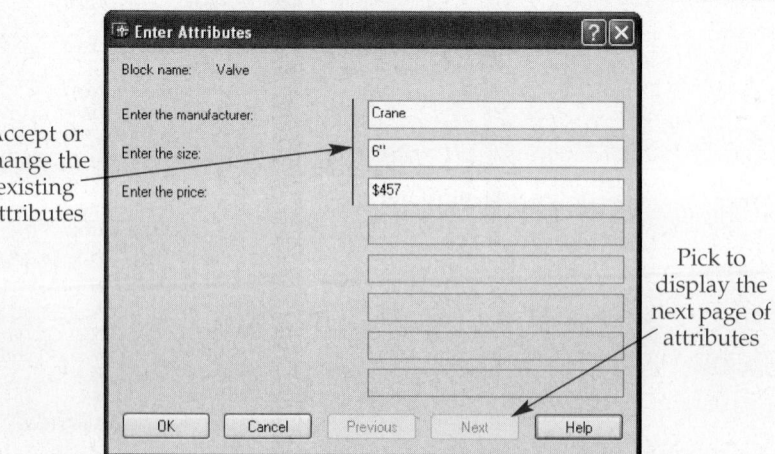

Pick to display the next page of attributes

Set the **ATTDIA** system variable to 1 in your template drawings to automatically activate the **Enter Attributes** dialog box whenever you insert a block with attributes.

## Exercise 24-1

○ Start a new drawing using your A-size or B-size architectural template.
○ Draw the valve symbol shown.

GATE
CRANE
6"
$457

○ Assign the attributes listed in the table below using the **ATTDEF** command.

| Tag | Prompt | Value | Mode |
|-----|--------|-------|------|
| Type | *(None)* | GATE | Constant |
| Mfr. | Enter the valve manufacturer: | CRANE | Invisible |
| Size | Enter the size: | 6" | Normal and preset |
| Price | Enter the price: | $457 | Invisible and Verify |

○ Create the block. Include the valve symbol and the attributes in the block definition and name it VALVE.
○ Use the **INSERT** command to insert the VALVE block into your drawing. Enter new values for the attributes if you wish. You should be prompted twice for the price if the **Verify** mode was set properly (if you are not using the **Enter Attributes** dialog box).
○ Save the drawing as EX24-1.

## Attribute Prompt Suppression

Some drawings may use blocks with attributes that always retain their default values. In this case, there is no need to be prompted for the attribute values when inserting a block. You can turn off the attribute prompts by setting the **ATTREQ** system variable to 0.

After making this setting, try inserting the VALVE block. Notice that none of the attribute prompts appear. The **ATTREQ** system variable setting is saved with the drawing. To display attribute prompts again, change the setting back to 1.

Part of your project and drawing planning should involve the setting of system variables such as **ATTREQ**. Setting **ATTREQ** to 0 before using blocks can save time in the drawing process. Always remember to set **ATTREQ** back to 1 when you want to use the prompts instead of accepting defaults. When anticipated attribute prompts are not issued, you should check the current **ATTREQ** setting and adjust it if necessary.

## Controlling the Display of Attributes

Attributes are intended to contain valuable information about the blocks in your drawings. This information is normally not displayed on screen or during plotting. The principal function of attributes is to generate materials lists and to speed accounting. In most cases, you can use the **TEXT** and **MTEXT** commands to create specific labels or other types of text. To control the display of attributes on screen, use the **ATTDISP** (attribute display) command. This command can be accessed by picking **Attribute Display** from the **Display** cascading menu in the **View** pull-down menu, or by entering ATTDISP at the Command: prompt. There are three options:

- **Normal.** This option displays attributes exactly as you created them. This is the default setting.
- **ON.** This option displays *all* attributes, including those defined with the **Invisible** mode.
- **OFF.** This option suppresses the display of all attributes.

PROFESSIONAL TIP

After attributes have been drawn, defined with blocks, and checked for correctness, hide them by entering the **Off** option of the **ATTDISP** command. If attributes are left on, they clutter the screen and lengthen regeneration time. In a drawing where attributes should be visible but are not, check the current setting of **ATTDISP** and adjust it if necessary.

## Changing Attribute Values

As discussed earlier, you can edit attributes before they are included in a block using the **DDEDIT** command or the **Properties** window. However, once a block with attributes is inserted in a drawing, different commands are used to edit the inserted attributes. Inserted attribute values can be modified using the **Enhanced Attribute Editor**.

The **Enhanced Attribute Editor** is used to modify attributes within a single block. To access this dialog box, pick the **Edit Attribute** button on the **Modify II** toolbar, select **Attribute** and then **Single...** from the **Object** cascading menu in the **Modify** pull-down menu, or enter EATTEDIT at the Command: prompt. You are then prompted to select a block. Pick the block containing the attributes you wish to modify, and the **Enhanced Attribute Editor** is displayed. See **Figure 24-6.**

The **Enhanced Attribute Editor** contains three tabs. The **Attribute** tab is displayed when the dialog box is initially accessed, with the attributes within the selected block listed in the window. If you want to select a different block to modify, pick the **Select block** button. Pick the attribute to be modified. Enter a new value for the attribute in the **Value:** text box.

Other properties of the selected attribute can be modified using the two other tabs. The **Text Options** tab allows you to modify the text properties of the attribute. See **Figure 24-7.** The **Properties** tab, **Figure 24-8,** contains settings for the object properties of the attribute.

After editing the attribute values and properties, pick the **Apply** button to have the changes reflected on screen. Pick the **Select block** button to modify another block, or pick the **OK** button to close the dialog box.

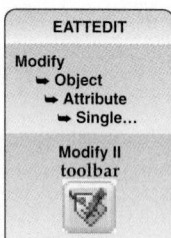

EATTEDIT

Modify
→ Object
→ Attribute
→ Single...

Modify II toolbar

Edit Attribute

**Figure 24-6.**
Select the attribute to be modified and change its value in the **Attribute** tab of the **Enhanced Attribute Editor**.

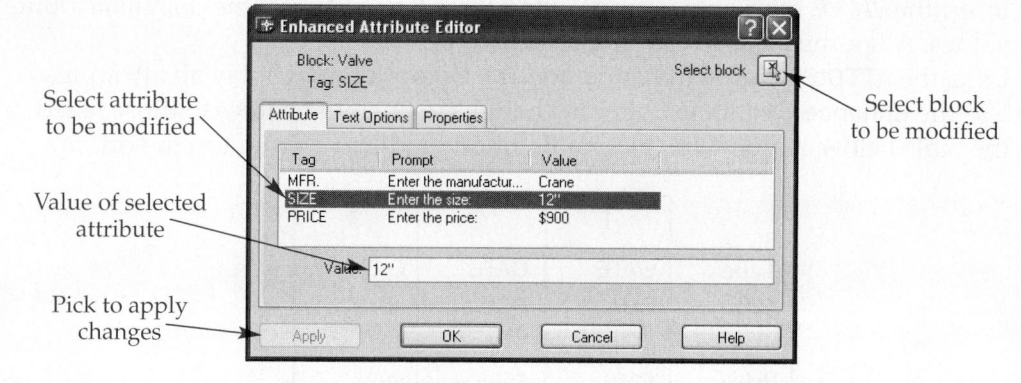

**Figure 24-7.**
The **Text Options** tab provides options in addition to those set in the **Attribute Definition** dialog box.

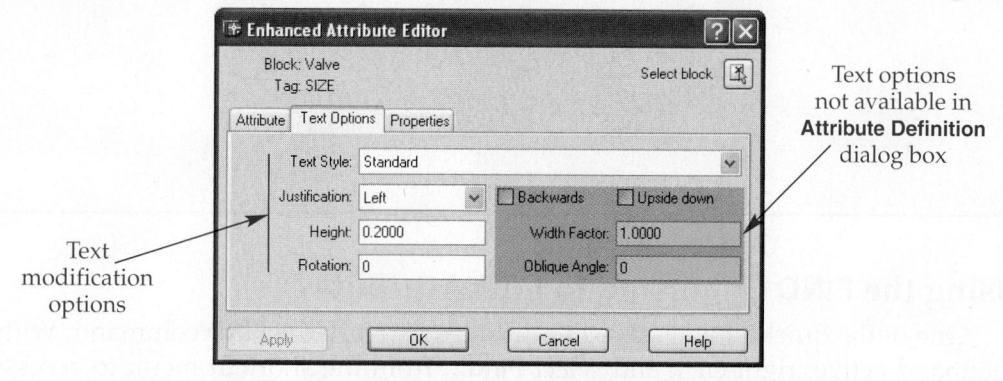

**Figure 24-8.**
The **Properties** tab can be used to modify an attribute's object properties.

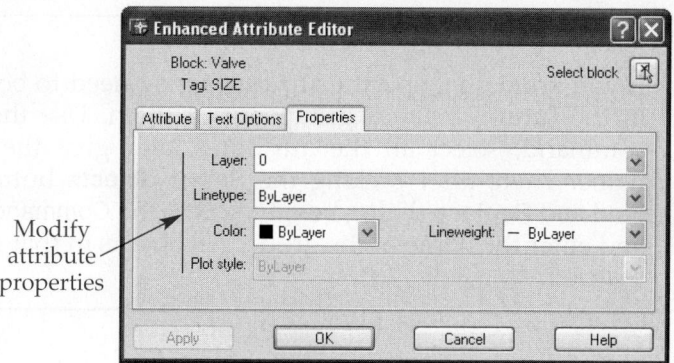

> **NOTE**
>
>
>
> You can also change the values of inserted attributes using the **ATTEDIT** command. This command accesses the **Edit Attributes** dialog box, which is identical to the **Enter Attributes** dialog box shown in **Figure 24-5**. However, this dialog box has fewer options than the **Enhanced Attribute Editor**, and the command is more difficult to access. Therefore, it is recommended that you use the **Enhanced Attribute Editor** for all attribute value modifications.

○ Open EX24-1.
○ Insert the VALVE block into your drawing three times. Accept the default attribute values. Align the blocks vertically as shown below.
○ Issue the **ATTDISP** command and enter the **On** option to display all attributes.
○ Use the **Enhanced Attribute Editor** to change the attribute values to those listed in the table below. Assume the blocks are numbered 1 to 3, from top to bottom.

|  | 1 | 2 | 3 |
|---|---|---|---|
| Type | GATE | GATE | GATE |
| Mfr. | CRANE | POWELL | JENKINS |
| Size | 4" | 8" | 10" |
| Price | $376 | $563 | $837 |

○ Save the drawing as EX24-2.

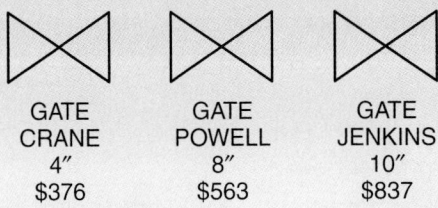

| GATE | GATE | GATE |
|---|---|---|
| CRANE | POWELL | JENKINS |
| 4" | 8" | 10" |
| $376 | $563 | $837 |

## Using the FIND Command to Edit Attributes

One of the quickest ways to edit attributes is to use the **FIND** command. With no command active, right-click and select **Find...** from the shortcut menu to access the **Find and Replace** dialog box. You can then search the entire drawing for an attribute, or you can search a selected group of objects. The **Find and Replace** dialog box is discussed in detail in Chapter 8.

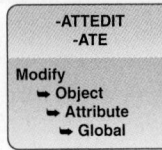

PROFESSIONAL TIP

If you know that specific attributes may need to be changed in the future, make a group out of them. Use the **GROUP** command, select all the attributes, and give the group a name. Then, after picking the **Select objects** button in the **Find and Replace** dialog box, type G at the Command: prompt and enter the name of the group. All objects in that group are selected.

## Editing Attribute Values and Properties at the Command Line

The **Enhanced Attribute Editor** allows you to edit attribute values by selecting blocks one at a time. You can also edit several block attributes at once, edit attributes individually, or change attribute properties by answering prompts on the command line. This type of attribute editing is done using the **-ATTEDIT** command. To access this command, select **Attribute** and then **Global** from the **Object** cascading menu in the **Modify** pull-down menu, or enter -ATE or -ATTEDIT at the Command: prompt:

-ATTEDIT
-ATE

Modify
↪ Object
  ↪ Attribute
    ↪ Global

    Command: **-ATE** *or* **-ATTEDIT**↵
    Edit attributes one at a time? [Yes/No] <Y>:

AutoCAD and its Applications—Basics

This prompt asks if you want to edit attributes individually. Pressing [Enter] at this prompt allows you to select any number of different block attributes for individual editing. AutoCAD lets you edit them all, one at a time, without leaving the command. It is also possible to change the same attribute on several insertions of the same block. If you enter the **-ATTEDIT** command and respond with No, you may change specific letters, words, and values of a single attribute. This lets you change all other insertions, or instances, of the same block, and is known as *global editing*. For example, suppose a block named with the attribute RESISTOR was inserted on a drawing in 12 locations. However, you misspelled the attribute as RESISTER. If you enter the **-ATTEDIT** command and specify No when asked whether to edit attributes individually, you can edit the attribute *globally*.

Each **-ATTEDIT** editing technique allows you to determine the exact block and attribute specifications to edit. The following prompts appear after you specify individual or global editing:

> Enter block name specification <*>:
> Enter attribute tag specification <*>:
> Enter attribute value specification <*>:

To selectively edit attribute values, respond to each prompt with the correct name or value. You are then prompted to select one or more attributes. Suppose you receive the following message after entering an attribute value and selecting an attribute:

> 0 found

You have picked an attribute that was not specified correctly. It is often quicker to press [Enter] at each of the three specification prompts and then *pick* the attribute you need to edit.

## Editing Several Insertions of the Same Attribute

A situation may occur where a block having a wrong or misspelled attribute value is inserted several times. For example, in **Figure 24-9**, the VALVE block was inserted three times with the manufacturer's name specified as CRANE. Unfortunately, the name was supposed to be POWELL. To change the attribute for each insertion, enter the **-ATTEDIT** command and specify global editing. Respond to the prompts in the following manner:

> Command: **-ATE** *or* **-ATTEDIT**↵
> Edit attributes one at a time? [Yes/No] <Y>: **N**↵
> Performing global editing of attribute values.
> Edit only attributes visible on screen? [Yes/No] <Y>: ↵
> Enter block name specification <*>: ↵
> Enter attribute tag specification <*>: ↵
> Enter attribute value specification <*>: ↵
> Select Attributes: *(pick* CRANE *on each of the* VALVE *blocks and press* [Enter] *when completed)*
> 3 attributes selected.
> Enter string to change: **CRANE**↵
> Enter new string: **POWELL**↵

After pressing [Enter], each of the CRANE attributes on the blocks selected is changed to the new value POWELL.

Figure 24-9.
Using the global editing technique with the **-ATTEDIT** command allows you to change the same attribute on several block insertions.

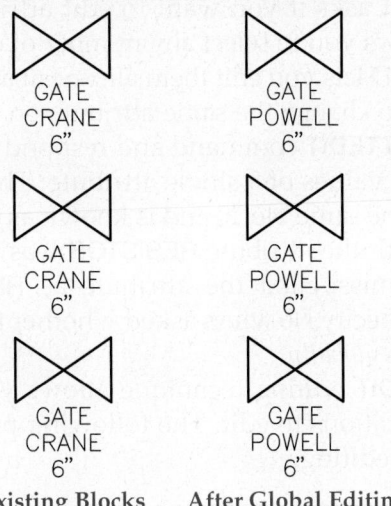

GATE
CRANE
6"

GATE
POWELL
6"

GATE
CRANE
6"

GATE
POWELL
6"

GATE
CRANE
6"

GATE
POWELL
6"

**Existing Blocks**     **After Global Editing**

## PROFESSIONAL TIP

Use care when assigning the **Constant** mode to attribute definitions. The **-ATTEDIT** command displays 0 found if you attempt to edit an inserted block attribute with a **Constant** mode setting. The inserted block must then be exploded and redefined. Assign the **Constant** mode only to attributes you know will not change.

## Exercise 24-3

○ Open EX24-1.
○ Insert the VALVE block into your drawing in three locations.
○ Issue the **ATTDISP** command and set the attribute display to **On**.
○ Enter the **-ATTEDIT** command and specify global editing. Change the name of the manufacturer from CRANE to POWELL on each of the blocks. Then, reenter the command and change the price from $457 to $487.
○ Save the drawing as EX24-3.

## NOTE

The **-ATTEDIT** command can also be used to edit individual attribute values and properties. However, it is more efficient to use the **Enhanced Attribute Editor** for changing individual attributes.

# Changing Attribute Definitions

Before saving an attribute within a block, you can modify the tag, prompt, and default value using the **DDEDIT** command. Once an attribute is saved in a block definition, you must use the **Block Attribute Manager** to change the attribute definition.

The **Block Attribute Manager** is accessed by picking the **Block Attribute Manager** button from the **Modify II** toolbar, selecting **Attribute** and then **Block Attribute Manager...** from the **Object** cascading menu in the **Modify** pull-down menu, or by entering BATTMAN at the Command: prompt. The **Block Attribute Manager** is shown in **Figure 24-10**.

The **Block Attribute Manager** lists the attributes for the selected block. To select a block, select it from the **Block:** drop-down list or pick the **Select block** button to return to the drawing area and pick the block. By default, the tag, prompt, default value, and modes for each attribute are listed.

The attribute list reflects the order in which prompts appear when a block is inserted. To change the order, use the **Move Up** and **Move Down** buttons to change the location of the selected attribute within the list. To delete an attribute, pick the **Remove** button.

You can select the attribute properties to be listed in the **Block Attribute Manager** by picking the **Settings...** button. This accesses the **Settings** dialog box, **Figure 24-11**. Select the properties to list in the **Display in list** area. When the **Emphasize duplicate tags** setting is active, attributes with identical tags are highlighted in red. Select the **Apply changes to existing references** option if you want the changes applied to existing blocks.

To modify an attribute definition, select the attribute in the **Block Attribute Manager** and then pick the **Edit...** button. This displays the **Edit Attribute** dialog box, **Figure 24-12**. The **Attribute** tab allows you to modify the modes, tag, prompt, and default value. Use the check boxes in the **Mode** area to select the desired modes. Enter new text strings in the **Tag:**, **Prompt:**, and **Default:** text boxes. The **Text Options** and **Properties** tabs are identical to the same tabs found in the **Enhanced Attribute Editor** with the exception of the **Auto preview changes** check box. These tabs allow you to modify the object properties of the attributes. If the **Auto preview changes** check box is checked, changes to attributes are displayed in the drawing area immediately. After modifying the attribute definition in the **Edit Attribute** dialog box, pick the **OK** button to return to the **Block Attribute Manager**.

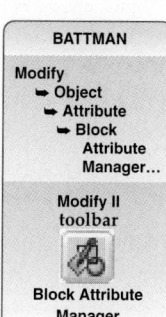

BATTMAN

Modify
➥ Object
➥ Attribute
➥ Block
  Attribute
  Manager...

Modify II
toolbar

Block Attribute
Manager

**Figure 24-10.**
Use the **Block Attribute Manager** to change attribute definitions, delete attributes, and change the order of attribute prompts.

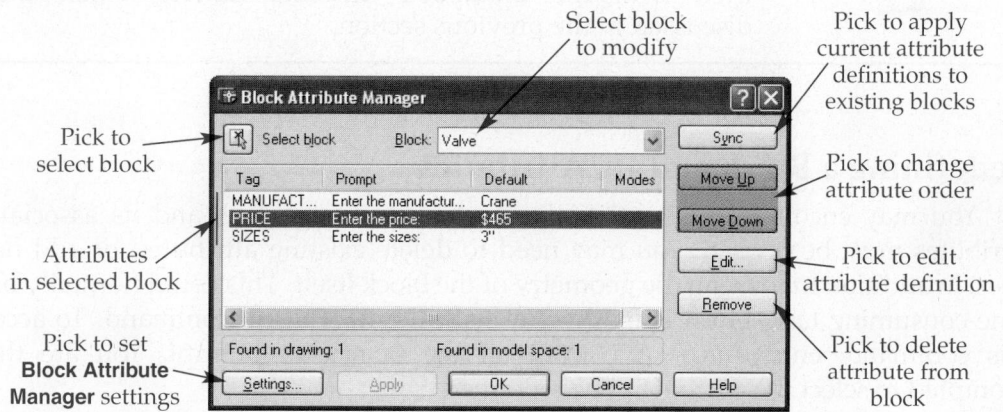

**Figure 24-11.**
The **Settings** dialog box controls the display of the attribute list in the **Block Attribute Manager**.

Select attribute properties to list in **Block Attribute Manager**

Identifies duplicate tags

Updates existing blocks

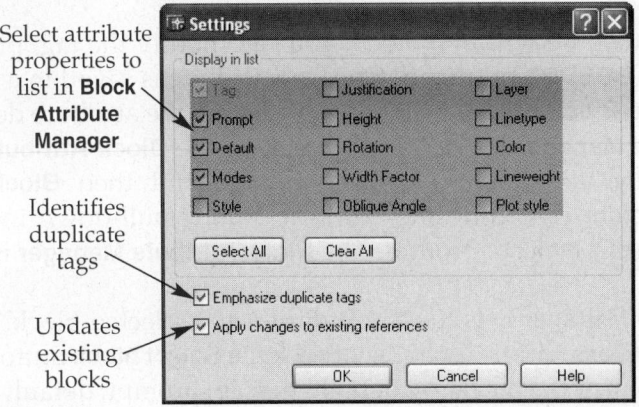

**Figure 24-12.**
Use the **Edit Attribute** dialog box to modify attribute definitions and properties.

Use these tabs to modify attribute properties

Select modes

Modify attribute definition

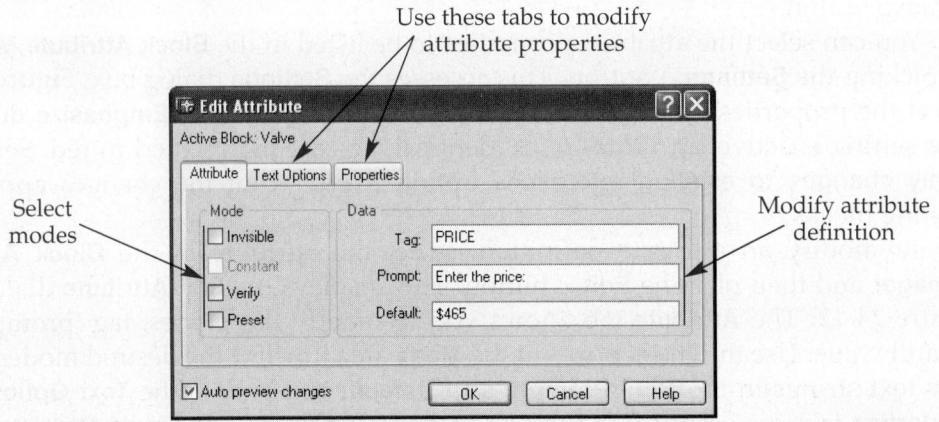

After modifying attributes within a block, all future insertions of the block will reflect the changes. Existing blocks are updated if the **Apply changes to existing references** option is selected in the **Settings** dialog box. If this option is not selected, the existing blocks retain the original attribute definitions.

NOTE

The **Block Attribute Manager** modifies attribute definitions—it does not modify attribute values. Attribute values are modified with the **Enhanced Attribute Editor**, which was discussed in the previous section.

## Redefining a Block and Its Attributes

You may encounter a situation in which an existing block and its associated attributes must be revised. You may need to delete existing attributes, or add new ones, in addition to revising the geometry of the block itself. This could normally be a time-consuming task, but it is made easy with the **ATTREDEF** command. To access this command, enter AT or ATTREDEF at the Command: prompt. You are then prompted to select the attribute to be redefined.

When redefining a block and its attributes, a copy of the existing block must be exploded prior to using the **ATTREDEF** command, or completely new geometry must be used. If this is not done, the following error message will be displayed:

New block has no attributes.

Once you explode the existing block, or draw new geometry, you can use the **ATTREDEF** command. The sequence is as follows:

Command: **AT** *or* **ATTREDEF**↵
Enter name of the block you wish to redefine: *(enter the block name and press* [Enter]*)*
Select objects for new Block...
Select objects: *(select the block geometry and all new and existing attributes and press* [Enter]*)*
Specify insertion base point of new Block: *(pick the insertion base point)*

After you pick the insertion point, all existing instances of the redefined block and attributes will be immediately updated. If any of the old attributes were omitted from the redefined block, they will not be included in the new version.

---

**NOTE**  All objects within a block, including attributes, can be edited using the **REFEDIT** command. This command is discussed in Chapter 22. When using **REFEDIT** to modify attributes, be sure to select the **Display attribute definitions for editing** option in the **Reference Edit** dialog box. Attribute definitions can then be modified using the **DDEDIT** command. You cannot change attribute values with this method.

---

## Using Attributes to Automate Drafting Documentation

So far you have seen that attributes are extremely powerful tools for assigning textual information to drawing symbols. However, attributes may also be used to automate any detailing or documentation task that requires a great deal of text. Such tasks include the creation of title block information and revision block data, as well as the generation of a parts list or list of materials.

### Attributes and Title Blocks

After a drawing is completely drawn and dimensioned, it is then necessary to fill out the information used in the drawing title block. This is usually one of the more time-consuming tasks associated with drafting documentation, and it can be efficiently automated by assigning attributes. The following guidelines are suggested:

1. The title block format is first drawn in accordance with industry or company standards. Use the correct layer(s), and be sure to include your company or school logo in the title block. If you work in an industry that produces items for the federal government, also include the applicable FSCM code in the title block. A typical A-size title block drawn in accordance with the ASME Y14.1, *Decimal Inch Drawing Sheet Size and Format* standard is illustrated in **Figure 24-13.**

---

Figure 24-13.
A title block sheet must adhere to applicable standards. This title block is for an A-size sheet and adheres to the ASME Y14.1, *Decimal Inch Drawing Sheet Size and Format* standard.

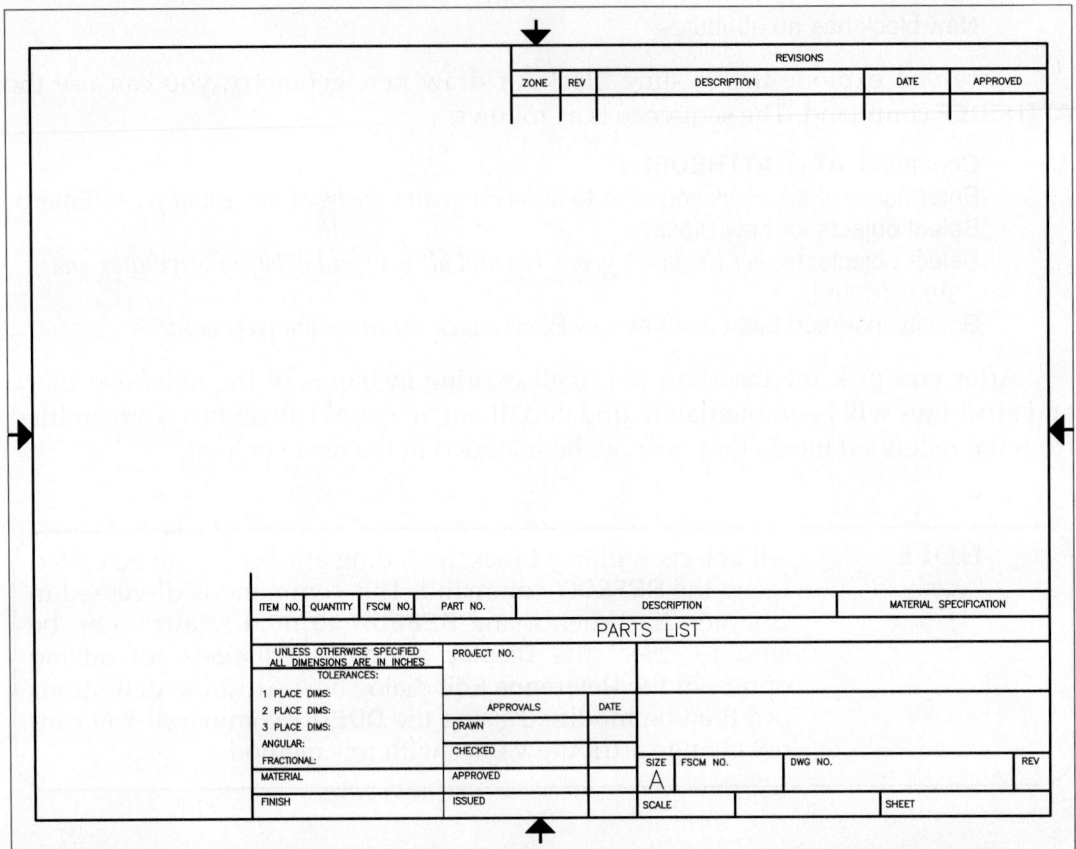

| | | REVISIONS | | | |
|---|---|---|---|---|---|
| ZONE | REV | DESCRIPTION | | DATE | APPROVED |

| ITEM NO. | QUANTITY | FSCM NO. | PART NO. | DESCRIPTION | MATERIAL SPECIFICATION |
|---|---|---|---|---|---|

PARTS LIST

**NOTE** The FSCM (Federal Supply Code for Manufacturers) is a five-digit numerical code identifier applicable to any organization that produces items used by the federal government. It also applies to government activities that are responsible for the development of certain specifications, drawings, or standards that control the design of items.

2. After drawing the title block, create a separate layer for the title block attributes. By placing the attributes on a separate layer, you can easily suppress the title block information by freezing the layer that contains the attributes. This can greatly reduce redraw and regeneration times. When you are ready to plot the finished drawing, simply thaw the frozen layer.

3. Define attributes for each area of the title block. As you create the attributes, determine the appropriate text height and justification for each definition. Attributes should be defined for the drawing title, drawing number, drafter, checker, dates, drawing scale, sheet size, material, finish, revision letter, and tolerance information. See **Figure 24-14.** Include any other information that may be specific to your organization or application.

4. Assign default values to the attributes wherever possible. As an example, if your organization consistently specifies the same overall tolerances on drawing dimensions, the tolerance attributes can be assigned default values.

| ITEM NO. | QUANTITY | FSCM NO. | PART NO. | | DESCRIPTION | | MATERIAL SPECIFICATION | | |
|---|---|---|---|---|---|---|---|---|---|

PARTS LIST

| UNLESS OTHERWISE SPECIFIED ALL DIMENSIONS ARE IN INCHES TOLERANCES: | | PROJECT NO. PROJECT | | | | | | |
|---|---|---|---|---|---|---|---|---|
| 1 PLACE DIMS: | TOL1 | | | | | | | |
| 2 PLACE DIMS: | TOL2 | APPROVALS | DATE | | TITLE | | | |
| 3 PLACE DIMS: | TOL3 | DRAWN DRAWN | DATE | | | | | |
| ANGULAR: | ANGL | CHECKED CHECKED | DATE | SIZE | FSCM NO. | DWG NO. | | REV |
| FRACTIONAL: | FRAC | | | A | | NUMBER | | REV |
| MATERIAL MATERIAL | | APPROVED APPROVED | DATE | | | | | |
| FINISH FINISH | | ISSUED ISSUED | DATE | SCALE SCALE | | SHEET SHEET | | |

Insertion point

**PROFESSIONAL TIP**

The size of each title block area imposes limits on the number of characters you can have in a line of text. You can provide a handy cue to yourself by including a reminder in the attribute. When defining an attribute in which you wish to place a reminder, include the information in the attribute prompt. For example, the prompt could read Enter drawing name (15 characters max):. Each time a block or drawing containing the attribute is used, the prompt will display the reminder.

Once you have defined each attribute in the title block, the **WBLOCK** command can be used to save the drawing as a file to disk so that it can be inserted into a new drawing. You can also use the **BLOCK** command to create a block of the defined attributes within the current file, which can then be saved as a template or wblock file. Both methods are acceptable and are explained as follows:

- **WBLOCK method.** The **WBLOCK** command saves a drawing file to disk so that it can be inserted into any drawing that is currently open. Be sure to use 0,0 as the insertion point for the title block. Drawings used in this manner should be given descriptive names. An A-size title block, for example, could be named TITLEA or FORMATA. To utilize the wblock file, begin a new drawing and insert the template drawing. After locating and scaling the drawing, the attribute prompts are displayed. If the **ATTDIA** system variable is set to 1, all of the attributes can be accepted or edited in the **Enter Attributes** dialog box. When you pick **OK** to close the dialog box, the attributes are placed in the title block. This method requires that you begin with a new drawing, and that you know the information requested by the attribute prompts.
- **BLOCK method.** If you use the **BLOCK** command, you can use the **Block Definition** dialog box to create a block of the defined attributes in the title block. When you select the objects for the block, be sure to select *only* the defined attributes you have created. Do not select the headings of the title block areas, or any of the geometry in the title block. When you pick the insertion base point, select a corner of the title block that will be convenient to use each time this block is inserted into a drawing. The point indicated in **Figure 24-14** shows an appropriate location for the insertion base point. Finally, activate the **Delete** option button in the **Block Definition** dialog box so the attribute definitions will be removed from the title block (when you insert the block later, the attribute values will be inserted where the attribute definitions

were located). You can also place the attribute definitions on a separate layer and freeze it so that the original attributes will not be displayed. The current drawing now contains a block of defined attributes for use in the title block.

If you save the drawing as a template file and begin a new drawing using the template, the title block data can be entered at any time during the creation of the new drawing. To do so, issue the **INSERT** command, enter the name of the block in the **Insert** dialog box, and pick the proper insertion base point. The attribute prompts are then either displayed on the command line or in a dialog box, depending on the value of the **ATTDIA** system variable.

Regardless of the method used, title block data can be entered quickly and accurately without the use of text commands. If the attributes are entered using the **Enter Attributes** dialog box, all the information can be seen at once, and mistakes can be corrected quickly. Attributes can be easily edited at a later date if necessary. The completed title block after insertion of the attribute block created in **Figure 24-14** is shown in **Figure 24-15**.

**Figure 24-15.**
The title block after insertion of the attributes. When the drawing is complete, dates and approvals can be added.

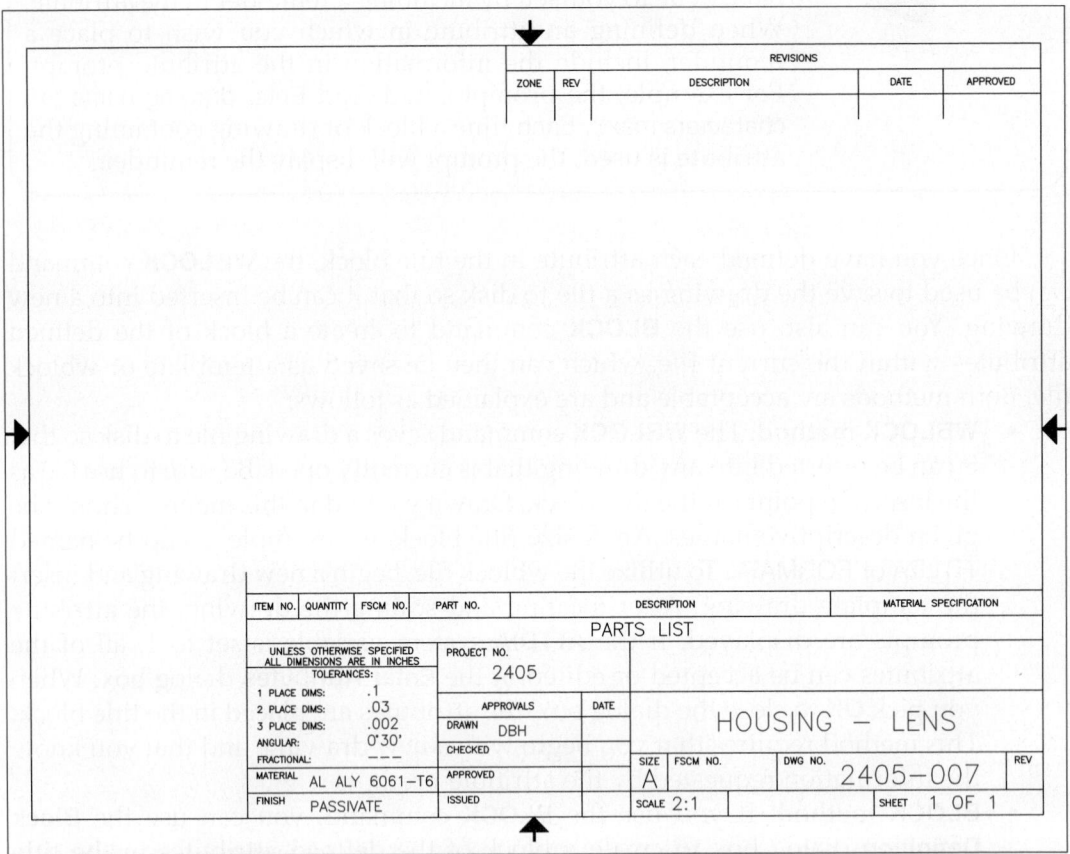

## Attributes and Revision Blocks

It is almost certain that a detail drawing will require revision at some time in the use of a product. Typical changes that occur include design improvements and the correction of drafting errors. The first time that a drawing is revised, it is usually assigned the revision letter *A*. If necessary, revision letters continue with *B* through *Z*, but the letters *I*, *O*, and *Q* are not used, because they might be confused with numbers.

Title block formats include an area specifically designated to record all drawing changes. This area is normally located at the upper-right of the title block sheet, and is commonly called the *revision block*. The revision block provides space for the revision letter, a description of the change, the date, and approvals. These items are entered in columns. A column for the zone is optional, and need only be added if applicable. *Zones* appear in the margins of a title block sheet and are indicated by alphabetical and numeric entries. They are used for reference purposes the same way reference letters and numbers are used to identify a street or feature on a road map. Although A-size and B-size title blocks may include zones, they are rarely needed.

Block attributes provide a handy means of completing the necessary information in a revision block. Refer to **Figure 24-16** as you follow these steps:

1. First, create the drawing geometry for the revision block using the appropriate layer(s).
2. Define attributes that describe the zone (optional), revision letter, description of change, date, and change approval on a separate layer.
3. Use left-justified text for the change description attribute, and middle-justified text for the remainder of the attributes.
4. Use the **WBLOCK** command to save the revision block and attributes as a drawing file. Use a descriptive name such as REVBLK or REV. Keep in mind that each line of the revision block has its own border lines. Therefore, the borders must be saved with the attributes. Use the upper-left endpoint of the revision block as the insertion point.

Now, after a drawing has been revised, simply insert the revision block at the correct location. If the **ATTDIA** system variable is set to 1, you can answer the attribute prompts in the **Enter Attributes** dialog box. After providing the change information, pick the **OK** button and the completed revision block is automatically added to the title block sheet. See **Figure 24-17.**

---

**Figure 24-16.**
The revision block consists of lines and defined attributes. The border lines must be drawn as part of the block, and the upper-left corner is used as the insertion point.

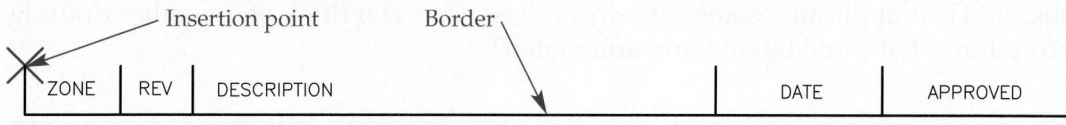

---

**Figure 24-17.**
The completed revision block after it is inserted into the drawing.

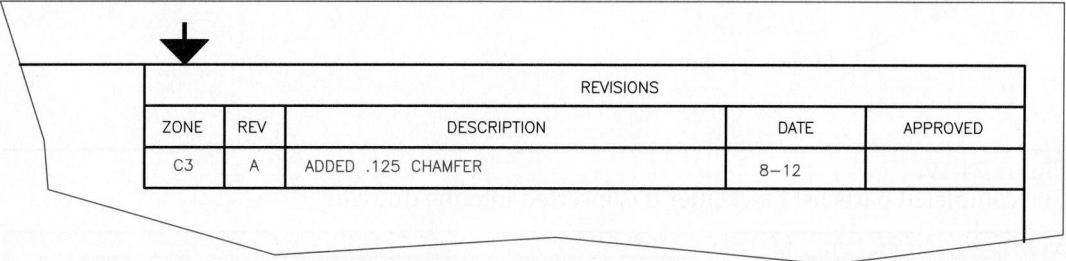

---

## Attributes and Parts Lists

Assembly drawings require a parts list, or list of materials, that provides information about each component of the assembly or subassembly. This information includes the quantity, FSCM code (when necessary), part number, description, and item number for each component. In some organizations, the parts list is generated as a separate document, usually in an 8 1/2″ × 11″ format. In other companies, it is common practice to include the parts list on the face of the assembly drawing. Whether they are created as a separate document or as part of the assembly drawing itself, parts lists provide another example of how attributes may be used to automate the documentation process.

Refer once again to the title block in **Figure 24-13**. Observe the section specifically designated for a parts list, located just above the title block area. Now, consider the example illustrated in **Figure 24-18** as you follow these guidelines:

1. First, create a parts list block using the appropriate drawing layer(s).
2. On a separate layer, define attributes that describe the quantity, FSCM code (when necessary), part number, item description, material specification, and item number for the components of an assembly drawing.
3. Use left-justified text for the item description attribute and middle-justified text for the other attributes.
4. Use the **WBLOCK** command to save the parts list block to disk with a descriptive name, such as PL for parts list or BOM for bill of materials. You can also use the **BLOCK** command to create a block of the parts list in the current drawing. Use the lower-left endpoint of the parts list block as the insertion point, as shown in **Figure 24-18**.

Now, after an assembly drawing has been completed, simply insert the parts list block into the drawing at the correct location. If the **ATTDIA** system variable is set to 1, you can answer the attribute prompts in the **Enter Attributes** dialog box. After providing the necessary information, click **OK** and the completed parts list block is automatically added to the title block sheet. See **Figure 24-19**. Repeat the procedure as many times as required for each component of the assembly drawing.

From the preceding examples, you can see that block attributes are powerful objects. Their applications are virtually endless. Can you think of any other drafting procedures that could be similarly automated?

**Figure 24-18.**
The parts list block is drawn with defined attributes and the insertion point located at the lower-left endpoint.

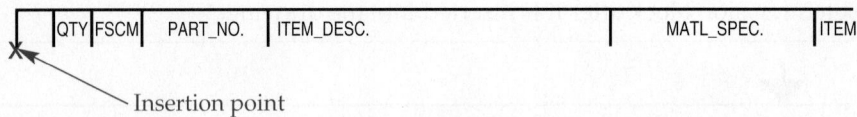

**Figure 24-19.**
The completed parts list block after it is inserted into the drawing.

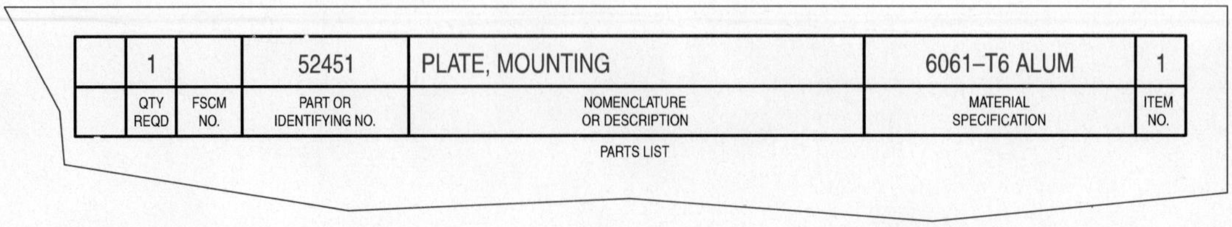

| | 1 | | 52451 | PLATE, MOUNTING | 6061–T6 ALUM | 1 |
|---|---|---|---|---|---|---|
| | QTY REQD | FSCM NO. | PART OR IDENTIFYING NO. | NOMENCLATURE OR DESCRIPTION | MATERIAL SPECIFICATION | ITEM NO. |
| | | | | PARTS LIST | | |

# Collecting Attribute Information

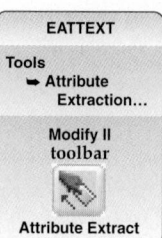
EATTEXT

Tools
➥ Attribute
    Extraction...

Modify II
toolbar

Attribute Extract

Attribute values and definitions can be extracted from a drawing and organized in a text file. This process, called *attribute extraction*, is useful for creating bills of materials, schedules, and parts lists. AutoCAD creates a text file containing the attribute information in a tabular format. You can select the specific blocks, attributes, and values to be extracted.

Attributes are extracted using the **Attribute Extraction** wizard. To access this wizard, pick the **Attribute Extract** button from the **Modify II** toolbar, select **Attribute Extraction...** from the **Tools** pull-down menu, or enter EATTEXT at the Command: prompt.

The first step in extracting attributes is to select the objects or drawings from which the information is to be gathered. The **Select Drawing** page of the **Attribute Extraction** wizard, shown in **Figure 24-20**, provides three options:

- **Select Objects.** Use this option if you want to include only some of the blocks in the current drawing. After selecting the radio button, the **Select Objects** button is activated. Pick this button to return to the drawing area and select the blocks to be included. You can select blocks from the current drawing only.
- **Current Drawing.** Pick this option to include all blocks in the current drawing.
- **Select Drawings.** Use this option to gather information from blocks from multiple drawings. After picking the radio button, the ellipsis (**...**) button is activated. Pick the ellipsis (**...**) button to access the **Select Files** dialog box. Selected drawings are listed in the **Drawing Files** list.

After selecting the blocks to be included, pick the **Next** button to advance to the **Settings** page. The options on this page allow you to include blocks from external reference files and blocks nested within other blocks. These boxes are checked by default. Uncheck the **Include xrefs** and **Include nested blocks** check boxes if you wish to exclude either type of object.

The **Use Template** page allows you to select a template file to automatically select the attributes to be extracted. See **Figure 24-21.** If this is the first use of the **Attribute Extraction** wizard, there will not be a template file saved and available for use. However, if attribute and block information have been extracted, a saved template file could be used. To select a template, pick the **Use template** radio button, which activates the **Use Template...** button. Pick this button to access the **Open** dialog box and select the BLK file.

---

**Figure 24-20.**
Select the blocks from which to extract information using the **Select Drawing** page.

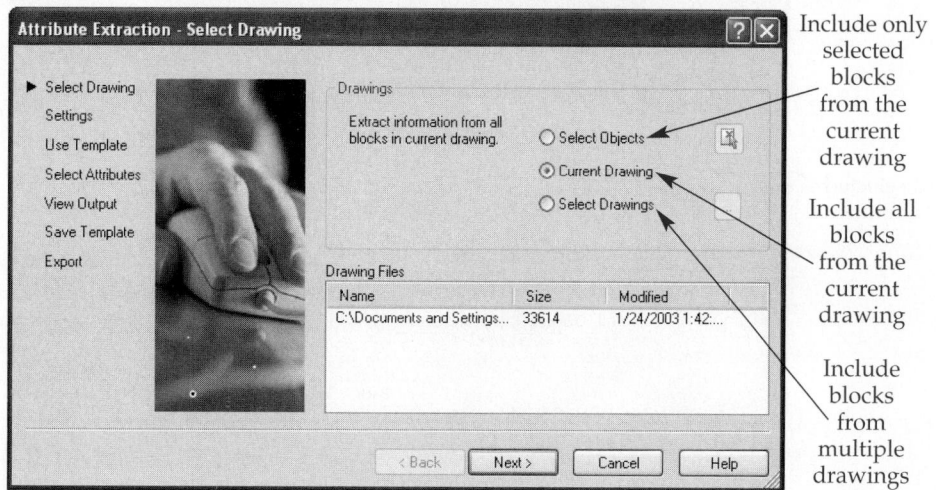

**Figure 24-21.**
Select a template of preset block and attribute values to be extracted using the **Use Template** page.

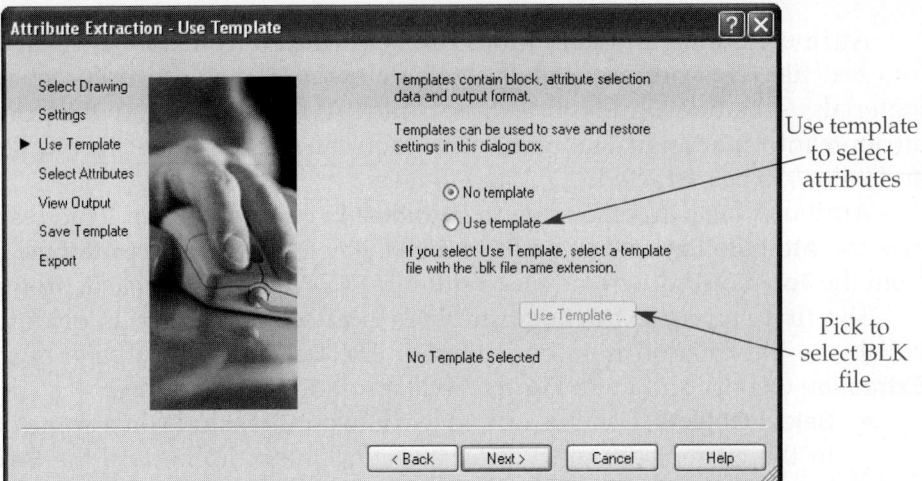

The **Select Attributes** page, **Figure 24-22,** lists the selected blocks and the attributes contained in those blocks. This page is divided into two tables. On the left is a list of all selected blocks. This list shows the block name and the number of times the block appears in the drawing. You can enter an alias for the block in the Block Alias Name column. On the right is a list of the attributes for the selected block. By default, all attributes are selected. Uncheck all attributes by selecting the **Uncheck All** button and then check only those attributes to be extracted to the output file. If a template file was selected in the previous step, the blocks and attributes are automatically selected to match the template.

You often need to be selective when listing blocks and attributes. In most cases, only certain types of attribute data need to be extracted from a drawing. This requires guidelines for AutoCAD to use when sorting through a drawing for attribute information. The guidelines for picking out specific attributes from blocks are specified using the **Select Attributes** page. This information is then used by AutoCAD to list the attributes when you create an extract file.

**Figure 24-22.**
Use the **Select Attributes** page to check the items to be extracted.

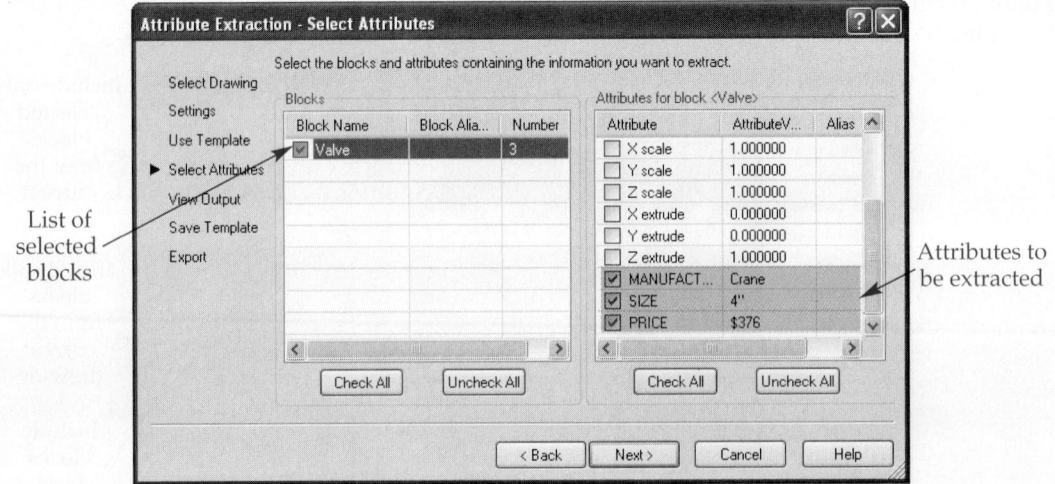

AutoCAD and its Applications—Basics

In addition to extracting attributes, AutoCAD can extract information about certain block characteristics. These include the following:

- **Name.** The block name.
- **Number.** The number of block insertions made.
- **X insertion point.** The X coordinate of the block insertion point.
- **Y insertion point.** The Y coordinate of the block insertion point.
- **Z insertion point.** The Z coordinate of the block insertion point.
- **Layer.** The name of the layer the block is inserted on.
- **Orient.** The rotation angle of the block.
- **X scale.** The insertion scale factor for the X axis.
- **Y scale.** The insertion scale factor for the Y axis.
- **Z scale.** The insertion scale factor for the Z axis.
- **X extrude.** The X value of the block extrusion direction.
- **Y extrude.** The Y value of the block extrusion direction.
- **Z extrude.** The Z value of the block extrusion direction.

After selecting the attributes to be extracted, pick the **Next** button to access the **View Output** page, **Figure 24-23.** A table displaying the results of the query is presented on this page. Two views of the information are available. Switch between the two views by selecting the **Alternate View** button. The view you select determines the format of the information when it is extracted. The information can also be copied to

**Figure 24-23.**
Use the **View Output** page to select the format of the information being extracted.

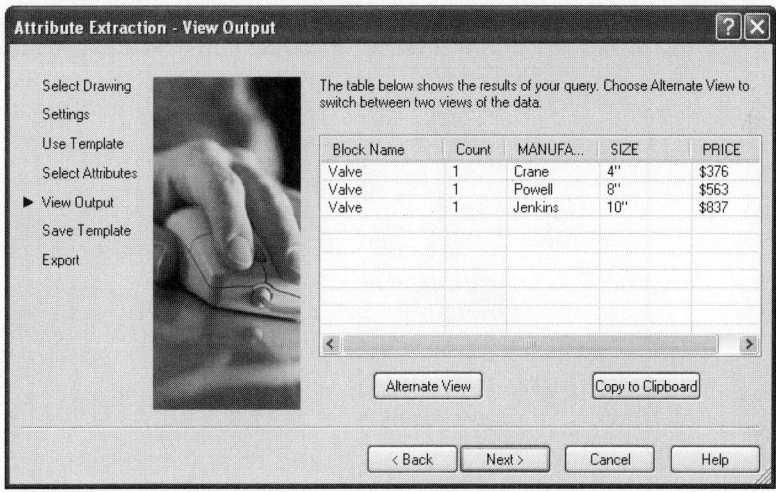

Initial View

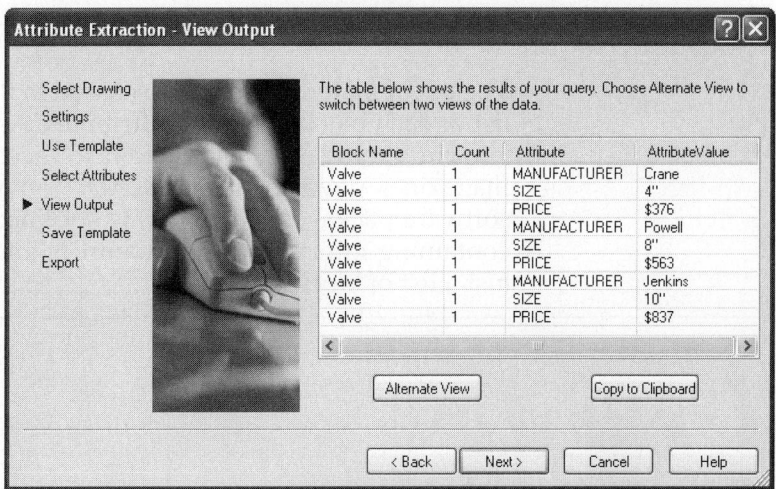

Alternate View

the Clipboard. To do this, select the **Copy to Clipboard** button. The information is copied to the Clipboard in the same format as that displayed in the table.

After viewing the output, the **Save Template** page provides an opportunity to save a template file. The template file stores the block and attribute selections made in the **Select Attributes** page as a BLK file. This template could then be used to automatically make the attribute selection for similar extractions in the future.

The last page in the wizard is the **Export** page, **Figure 24-24.** A file name and a file type are required on this page. The file name is entered in the **File Name** text box. Pick the ellipsis (**...**) button to select a folder location.

The type of file to be saved is selected in the **File Type** drop-down list. If Microsoft Excel and Microsoft Access are installed, the XLS and MDB formats are available. The default formats that are always available are comma-separated (CSV) and tab-separated (TXT). Pick the **Finish** button to export the file and return to the current drawing.

The extract file can be displayed on screen by opening the file in Windows Notepad. An example of the extract file in comma-separated and tab-separated formats is shown in **Figure 24-25.** Decide which format is most suitable for your application. Regardless of the extract file format chosen, you may print the file from Windows Notepad by selecting Print from the File pull-down menu.

**Figure 24-24.**
Enter the file name and select the file type using the **Export** page.

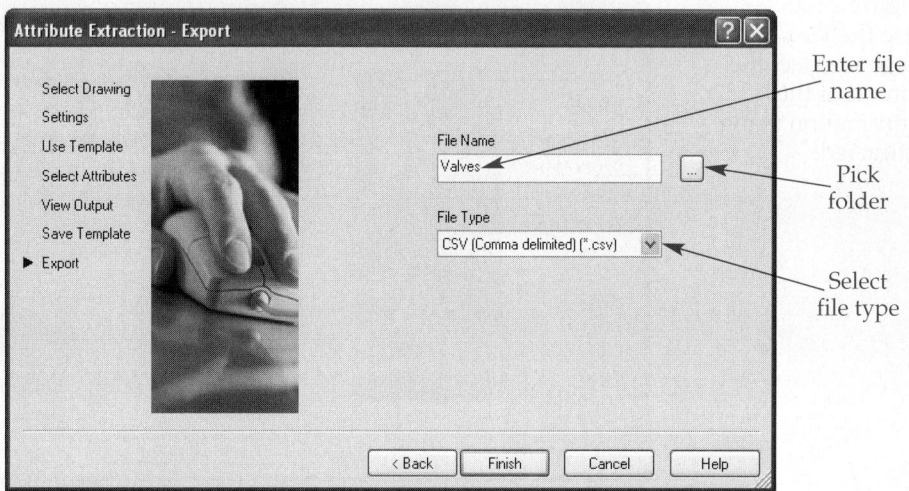

PROFESSIONAL
TIP

The bill of materials listing discussed in this chapter is a basic list of each block's selected attributes. As you become familiar with AutoCAD, customize it to meet your needs. Study magazines devoted to AutoCAD. You will find numerous software packages that generate specialized bills of material containing information on quantities and totals, rather than just a list of blocks.

**Figure 24-25.**
Extract files opened in Windows Notepad.

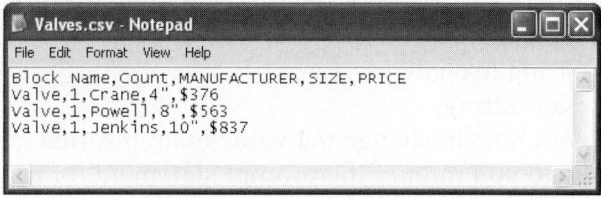

Comma-Separated File (CSV)

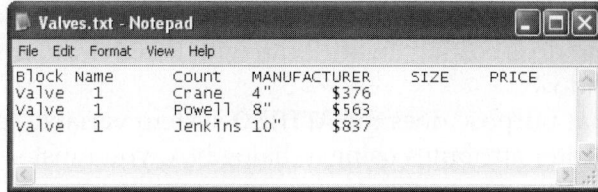

Tab-Separated File (TXT)

**NOTE**

The **ATTEXT** and **-ATTEXT** commands can also be used to extract block and attribute information. These commands are more cumbersome than the **Attribute Extraction** wizard. For additional information on these commands, refer to the Command Reference in the AutoCAD help system.

---

### Exercise 24-4

○ Open EX24-2.
○ Use the **Attribute Extraction** wizard to extract the attribute information from the inserted blocks.
○ Save the extracted information as a comma-separated file.
○ Enter Windows Notepad and open the extract file to display the bill of materials on screen.

---

## Chapter Test

*Answer the following questions on a separate sheet of paper.*

1. What is an *attribute*?
2. Explain the purpose of the **ATTDEF** command.
3. Define the function of the following four attribute modes:
   A. Invisible
   B. Constant
   C. Verify
   D. Preset
4. What attribute information does the **ATTDEF** command request?
5. Identify two ways to edit attributes before they are included within a block.
6. How can you change an existing attribute from **Visible** to **Invisible**?
7. List the three options for the **ATTDISP** command.
8. What is meant by *global* attribute editing?
9. How does individual attribute editing differ from global editing?

---

10. Identify the purpose of the following two prompts in the global attribute editing routine.
    A. String to change:
    B. New string:
11. Explain how to change the value of an inserted attribute.
12. How do you modify the prompt statement for an attribute that is saved within a block?
13. After a block with attributes has been saved, what method can you use to change the order of prompts when the block is inserted?
14. How does editing an attribute with **DDEDIT** differ from using the **Properties** window?
15. What purpose does the **ATTREQ** system variable serve?
16. To enter attributes using a dialog box, you must set the **ATTDIA** system variable to _____.
17. List three uses for extracted block and attribute data.
18. Explain the function served by a template file when using the **Attribute Extraction** wizard.
19. Describe the three selection options available in the **Select Drawing** page of the **Attribute Extraction** wizard.
20. How does the setting in the **View Output** page of the **Attribute Extraction** wizard affect the final extracted file?

## Drawing Problems

1. Start AutoCAD and start a new drawing. Draw the structural steel wide flange shape using the dimensions given. Do not dimension the drawing. Create attributes for the drawing using the information given. Make a block of the drawing and name it W12X40. Insert the block once to test the attributes. Save the drawing as P24-1.

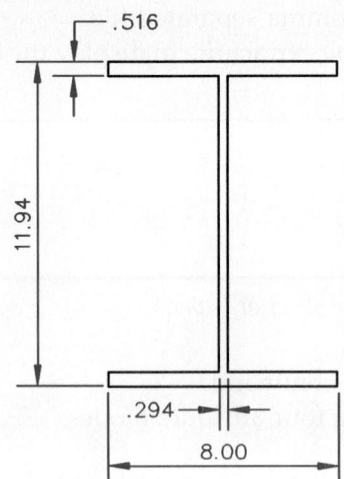

| Attributes | | | |
|---|---|---|---|
| | Steel | W12 × 40 | Visible |
| | Mfgr | Ryerson | Invisible |
| | Price | $.30/lb | Invisible |
| | Weight | 40 lbs/ft | Invisible |
| | Length | 10′ | Invisible |
| | Code | 03116WF | Invisible |

2. Open the drawing in Problem 1 (P24-1) and construct the floor plan shown using the dimensions given. Dimension the drawing. Insert the block W12X40 six times as shown. Required attribute data is given in the chart below the drawing. Enter the appropriate information for the attributes as you are prompted. Note the steel columns labeled 3 and 6 require slightly different attribute data. You can speed the drawing process by using **ARRAY** or **COPY**. Save the drawing as P24-2.

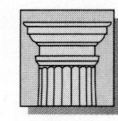

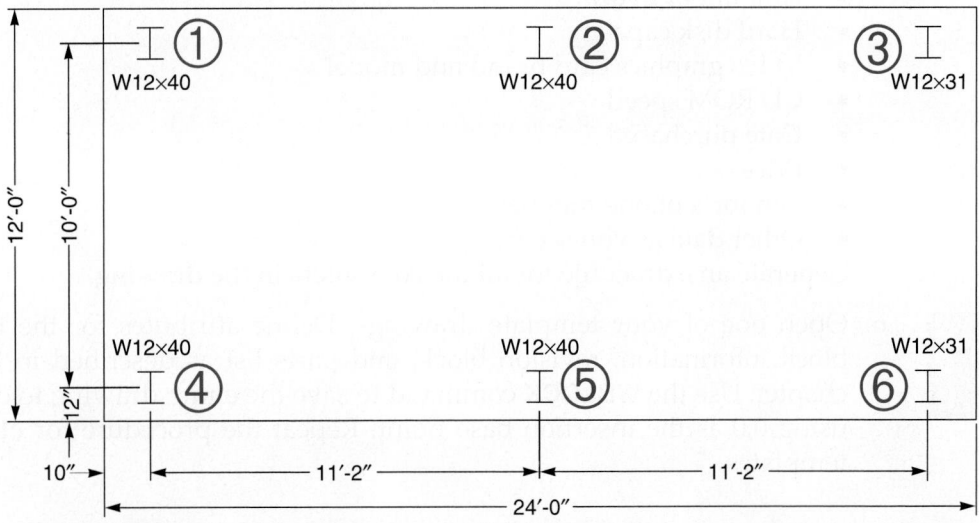

| | Steel | Mfgr | Price | Weight | Length | Code |
|---|---|---|---|---|---|---|
| Blocks ①, ②, ④, & ⑤ | W12 × 40 | Ryerson | $.30/lb | 40 lbs/ft | 10′ | 03116WF |
| Blocks ③ & ⑥ | W12 × 31 | Ryerson | $.30/lb | 31 lbs/ft | 8.5′ | 03125WF |

3. Open Problem 2 (P24-2). Create a tab-separated extraction file for the blocks in the drawing. Extract the following information for each block:
   - Block name
   - Steel
   - Manufacturer
   - Price
   - Weight
   - Length
   - Code

   Save the file as P24-3.txt.

4. Select a drawing from Chapter 22 and create a bill of materials for it using the **Attribute Extraction** wizard. Use the comma-separated format to display the file. Display the file in Windows Notepad.

5. Create a drawing of the computer workstation layout in the classroom or office in which you are working. Provide attribute definitions for all the items listed here.

- Workstation ID number
- Computer brand name
- Model number
- Processor chip
- Amount of RAM
- Hard disk capacity
- Video graphics card brand and model
- CD ROM speed
- Date purchased
- Price
- Vendor's phone number
- Other data as you see fit

Generate an extract file for all the computers in the drawing.

6. Open one of your template drawings. Define attributes for the title block information, revision block, and parts list as described in this chapter. Use the **WBLOCK** command to save the entire drawing to disk using 0,0 as the insertion base point. Repeat the procedure for other templates.

# Isometric Drawing

## Learning Objectives

After completing this chapter, you will be able to do the following:
- Describe the nature of isometric and oblique views.
- Set an isometric grid.
- Construct isometric objects.
- Create isometric text styles.
- Demonstrate isometric and oblique dimensioning techniques.

Being able to visualize and draw three-dimensional shapes is a skill that every drafter, designer, and engineer should possess. This is especially important in 3D modeling. However, there is a distinct difference between drawing a view that *looks* three-dimensional and creating a *true* 3D model.

A 3D model can be rotated on the display screen and viewed from any angle. The computer calculates the points, lines, and surfaces of the objects in space. Three-dimensional models are introduced in Chapter 26. This chapter focuses on creating views that *look* three-dimensional using some special AutoCAD functions and two-dimensional coordinates and objects.

## Pictorial Drawing Overview

The word *pictorial* means "like a picture." It refers to any realistic form of drawing. Pictorial drawings show height, width, and depth. Several forms of pictorial drawings are used in industry today. The least realistic is oblique. However, this is the simplest type. The most realistic, but also the most complex, is perspective. Isometric drawing falls midway between the two as far as realism and complexity are concerned.

### Oblique Drawings

An *oblique drawing* shows objects with one or more parallel faces having true shape and size. A scale is selected for the orthographic, or front faces. Then, an angle for the depth (receding axis) is chosen. The three types of oblique drawings are *cavalier*, *cabinet*, and *general*. See **Figure 25-1**. These vary in the scale of the receding axis. The receding axis is drawn at half scale for a cabinet view and at full scale for a cavalier. The general oblique is normally drawn with a 3/4 scale for the receding axis.

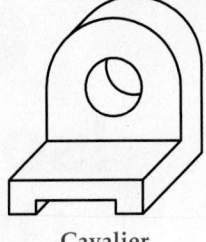
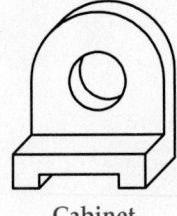

**Figure 25-1.**
The three types of oblique drawings differ in the scale of the receding axis.

| Cavalier | Cabinet | General |

## Isometric Drawings

*Isometric drawings* are more realistic than oblique drawings. The entire object appears as if it is tilted toward the viewer. The word *isometric* means "equal measure." This equal measure refers to the angle between the three axes (120°) after the object has been tilted. The tilt angle is 35°16′. This is shown in **Figure 25-2.** The 120° angle corresponds to an angle of 30° from horizontal. When constructing isometric drawings, lines that are parallel in the orthogonal views must be parallel in the isometric view.

The most appealing aspect of isometric drawing is that all three axis lines can be measured using the same scale. This saves time, while still producing a pleasing pictorial of the object. This type of drawing is produced when you use Isometric Snap mode, discussed later.

Closely related to isometric drawing are *dimetric* and *trimetric.* These forms of pictorial drawing differ from isometric in the scales used to measure the three axes. Dimetric drawing uses two different scales and trimetric uses three scales. Using different scales is an attempt to create *foreshortening.* This means the lengths of the sides appear to recede. The relationship between isometric, dimetric, and trimetric drawings is illustrated in **Figure 25-3.**

**Figure 25-2.**
An object is tilted 35°16′ to achieve an isometric view having 120° between the three axes. Notice how the highlighted face corresponds to each view.

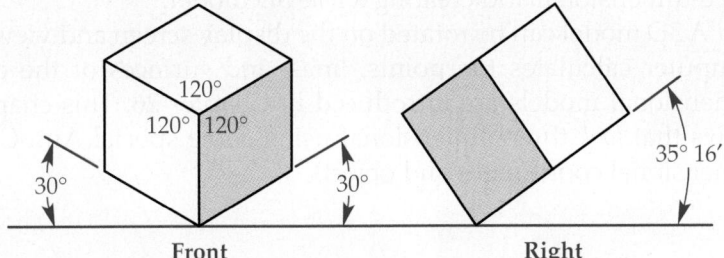

**Figure 25-3.**
Isometric, dimetric, and trimetric differ in the scales used to draw the three axes. The isometric shown here has the scales represented as one. You can see how the dimetric and trimetric scales vary.

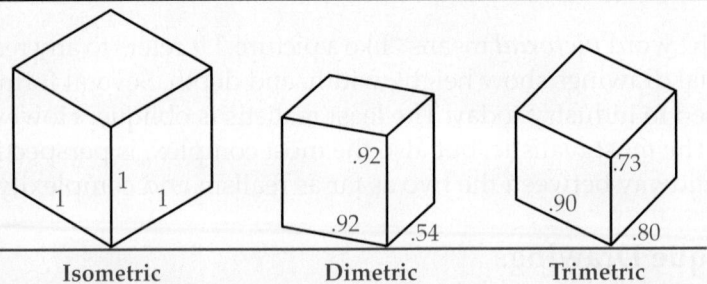

## Perspective Drawing

The most realistic form of pictorial drawing is a *perspective drawing.* The eye naturally sees objects in perspective. Look down a long hall and notice that the wall and floor lines seem to converge in the distance at an imaginary point. That point is called the *vanishing point.* The most common types of perspective drawing are *one-point* and *two-point.* These forms of pictorial drawing are often used in architecture. They are also used in the automotive and aircraft industries. Examples of one-point and two-point perspectives are shown in **Figure 25-4.** A perspective of a true 3D model can be produced in AutoCAD using the **DVIEW** and **3DORBIT** commands. See *AutoCAD and its Applications—Advanced* for complete coverage of **DVIEW** and **3DORBIT**.

**Figure 25-4.**
An example of one-point perspective and two-point perspective.

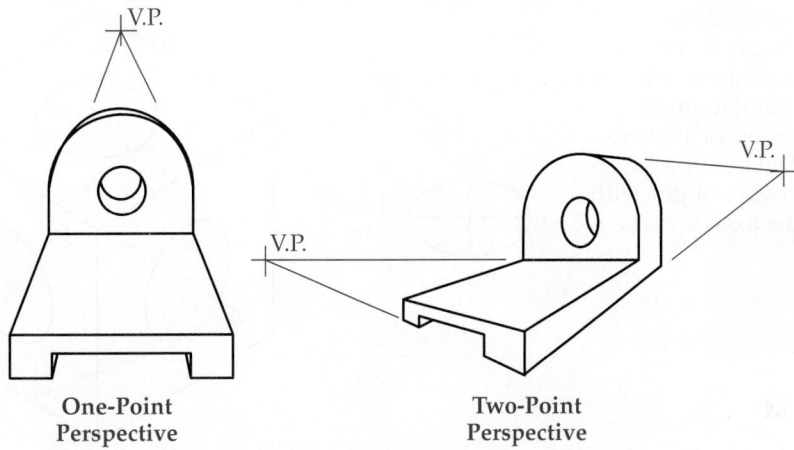

One-Point
Perspective

Two-Point
Perspective

## Isometric Drawing

The most common method of pictorial drawing used in industry is isometric. These drawings provide a single view showing three sides that can be measured using the same scale. An isometric view has no perspective and may appear somewhat distorted. Two of the isometric axes are drawn at 30° to horizontal; the third at 90°. See **Figure 25-5.**

The three axes shown in **Figure 25-5** represent the width, height, and depth of the object. Lines that appear horizontal in an orthographic view are placed at a 30° angle. Lines that are vertical in an orthographic view are placed vertically. These lines are parallel to the axes. Any line parallel to an axis can be measured and is called an *isometric line.* Lines that are not parallel to the axes are called *nonisometric lines* and cannot be measured. Note the two nonisometric lines in **Figure 25-5.**

Circular features shown on isometric objects must be oriented properly or they appear distorted. The correct orientation of isometric circles on the three principle planes is shown in **Figure 25-6.** Circles appear as ellipses on an isometric. The small diameter (minor axis) of the ellipse must always align on the axis of the circular feature. Notice that the centerline axes of the holes in **Figure 25-6** are parallel to one of the isometric planes.

A basic rule to remember about isometric drawing is that lines parallel in an orthogonal view must be parallel in the isometric view. AutoCAD's **ISOPLANE** feature makes that task, and the positioning of ellipses, easy.

**Figure 25-5.**
Layout of the
isometric axes.
Lines that are not
parallel to any of
the three axes are
called nonisometric
lines.

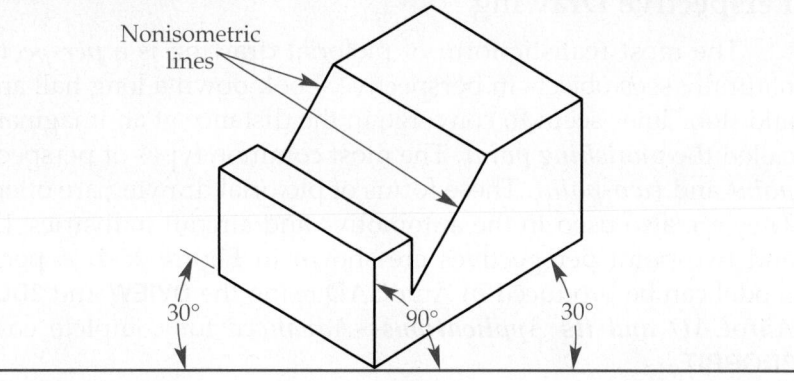

Nonisometric
lines

30°          90°          30°

**Figure 25-6.**
Proper isometric
circle (ellipse)
orientation on
isometric planes.
The minor axis
always aligns with
the axis centerline.

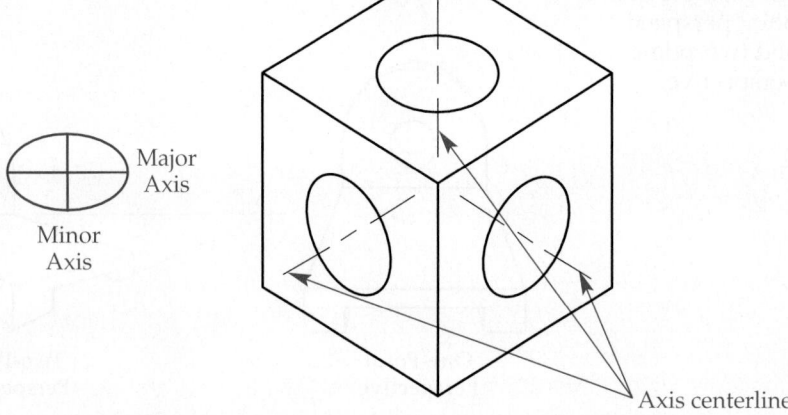

Major
Axis

Minor
Axis

Axis centerline

**PROFESSIONAL TIP**

If you are ever in doubt about the proper orientation of an ellipse in an isometric drawing, remember that the minor axis of the ellipse must always be aligned on the centerline axis of the circular feature. This is shown clearly in **Figure 25-6.**

## Settings for Isometric Drawing

DSETTINGS
DS
SE
DDRMODES

Tools
➡ Drafting
Settings...

You can quickly set your isometric variables in **Snap and Grid** tab of the **Drafting Settings** dialog box. See **Figure 25-7.** To access this dialog box, enter DS, SE, DSETTINGS, or DDRMODES at the Command: prompt, or select **Drafting Settings...** from the **Tools** pull-down menu. This dialog box can also be accessed by right-clicking on the **SNAP** or **GRID** status bar button and then selecting **Settings...** from the shortcut menu.

To activate the isometric snap grid, pick the **Isometric snap** radio button in the **Snap type & style** area. Notice that the **Snap X spacing** and **Grid X spacing** text boxes are now grayed-out. Since X spacing relates to horizontal measurements, it is not used in the isometric mode. You can only set the Y spacing for grid and snap in isometric. Be sure to check the **Snap On (F9)** and **Grid On (F7)** check boxes if you want **Snap** and **Grid** modes to be activated. Pick the **OK** button and the grid dots on the screen are displayed in an isometric orientation, as shown in **Figure 25-8.** If the grid dots are not visible, turn the grid on. You may also need to zoom in or out to display the grid.

**Figure 25-7.**
The **Drafting Settings** dialog box allows you to make settings needed for isometric drawing.

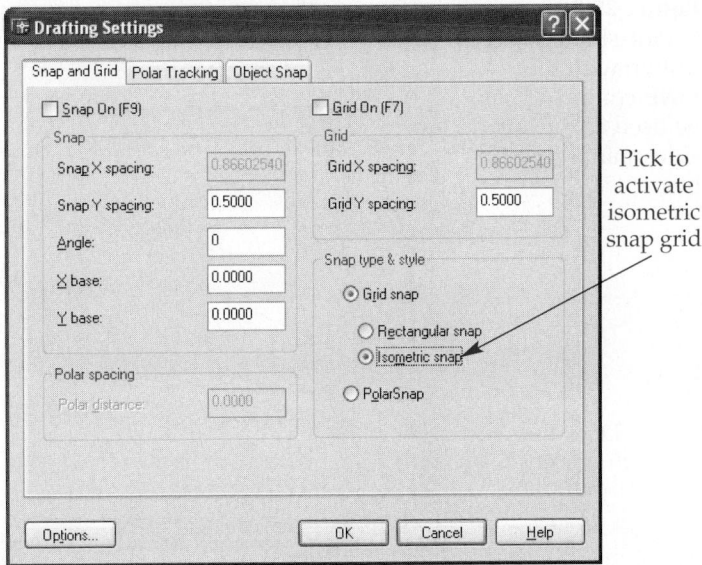

Pick to activate isometric snap grid

**Figure 25-8.**
An example of an isometric grid setup in AutoCAD.

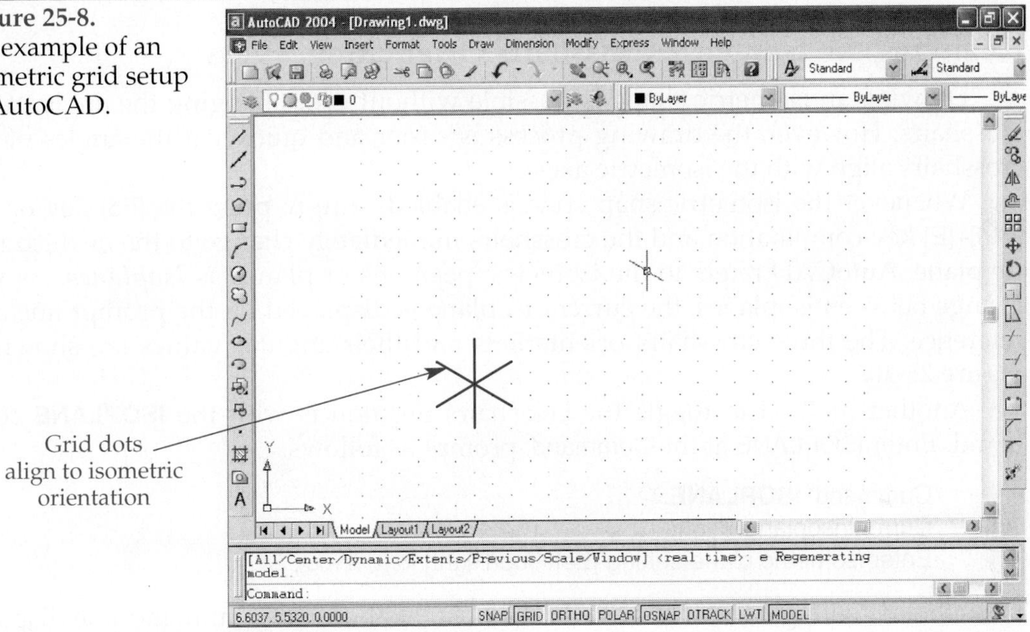

Grid dots align to isometric orientation

Notice the crosshairs appear angled. This aids you in drawing lines at the proper isometric angles. Try drawing a four-sided surface using the **LINE** command. Draw it so that it appears to be the left side of a box in an isometric layout. See **Figure 25-9.** To draw nonparallel surfaces, you can change the angle of the crosshairs to make your task easier, as discussed in the next section.

To turn off the Isometric Snap mode, pick the **Rectangular snap** radio button in the **Snap type & style** area. The Isometric Snap mode is turned off and you are returned to the drawing area when you pick the **OK** button.

> **NOTE**
>
> You can also set the Isometric Snap mode at the Command: prompt with the **SNAP** command. Type SNAP or SN, select the **Style** option, and then type I to select **Isometric**.

Figure 25-9.
A four-sided object drawn with the **LINE** command can be used as the left side of an isometric box.

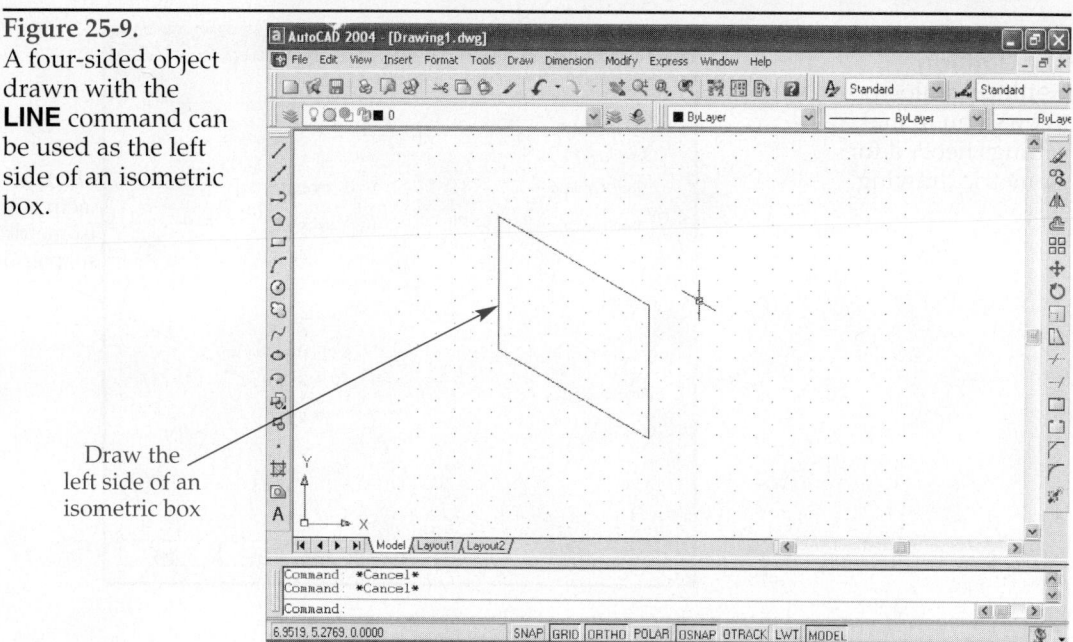

Draw the left side of an isometric box

## Changing the Isometric Crosshairs Orientation

Drawing an isometric shape is possible without ever changing the angle of the crosshairs. However, the drawing process is easier and quicker if the angles of the crosshairs align with the isometric axes.

Whenever the isometric snap style is enabled, simply press the [F5] key or the [Ctrl]+[E] key combination and the crosshairs immediately change to the next isometric plane. AutoCAD refers to the isometric positions or planes as *isoplanes.* As you change between isoplanes, the current isoplane is displayed on the prompt line as a reference. The three crosshairs orientations and their angular values are shown in **Figure 25-10.**

Another method to toggle the crosshairs position is with the **ISOPLANE** command. Enter ISOPLANE at the Command: prompt as follows.

> Command: **ISOPLANE**↵
> Current isoplane: Right
> Enter isometric plane setting [Left/Top/Right] <*current*>: ↵

Press [Enter] to toggle the crosshairs to the next position. The command line displays the new isoplane setting. You can toggle immediately to the next position by pressing [Enter] at the Command: prompt to repeat the **ISOPLANE** command and pressing [Enter] again. To specify the plane of orientation, type the first letter of that position. The **ISOPLANE** command can also be used transparently.

Figure 25-10.
The three isometric crosshairs positions can be changed using the [F5] function key, the [Ctrl]+[E] key combination, or using the **ISOPLANE** command.

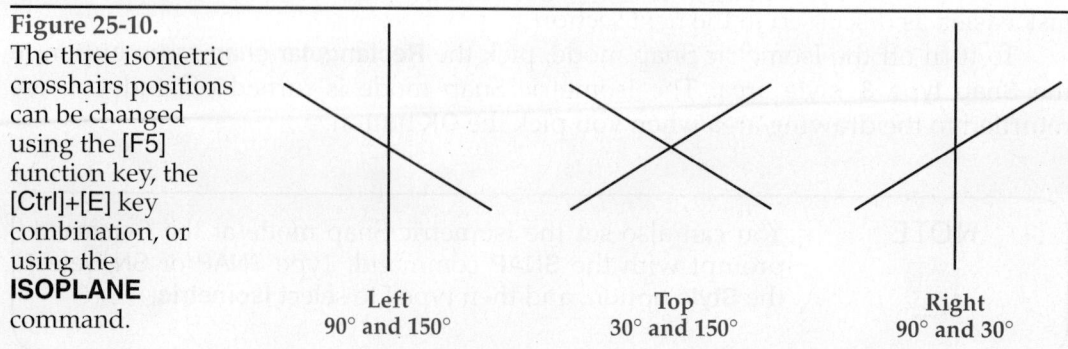

Left
90° and 150°

Top
30° and 150°

Right
90° and 30°

The crosshairs are always in one of the isoplane positions when Isometric Snap mode is in effect. An exception occurs during a display or editing command when a multiple selection set method (such as a window) is used. In these cases, the crosshairs change to the normal vertical and horizontal positions. At the completion of the display or editing command, the crosshairs automatically revert to their former isoplane orientation.

**PROFESSIONAL TIP**

The quickest way to change the isoplane is to press the [F5] function key or press the [Ctrl]+[E] key combination.

---

### Exercise 25-1

○ Use one of your templates to begin a new drawing.
○ Set the grid spacing at .5.
○ Use the **Drafting Settings** dialog box to activate Isometric Snap mode. Specify .25 vertical spacing.
○ Use the **LINE** command to draw the objects shown below. Do not dimension the objects.
○ Change the isoplane orientation as needed.
○ Save the drawing as EX25-1.

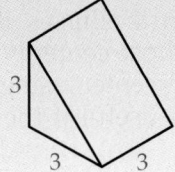
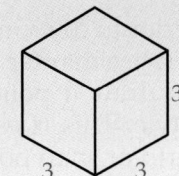

---

## Isometric Ellipses

Placing an isometric ellipse on an object is easy with AutoCAD because of the **Isocircle** option of the **ELLIPSE** command. An ellipse is positioned automatically on the current isoplane. To use the **ELLIPSE** command, first make sure you are in Isometric Snap mode. Then, pick the **Ellipse** button on the **Draw** toolbar, select **Axis, End** from the **Ellipse** cascading menu in the **Draw** pull-down menu, or enter EL or ELLIPSE at the Command: prompt. Once the **ELLIPSE** command is initiated, the following prompts appear.

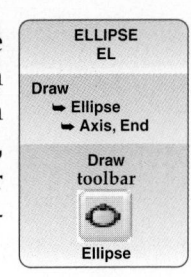

ELLIPSE
EL

Draw
➥ Ellipse
➥ Axis, End

Draw
toolbar

Ellipse

    Specify axis endpoint of ellipse or [Arc/Center/Isocircle]: I↵
    Specify center of isocircle: *(pick a point)*
    Specify radius of isocircle or [Diameter]:

Once you select the **Isocircle** option, pick the center point and then set the radius or diameter. The **Center** option does not allow you to create isocircles. Also, the **Isocircle** option only appears when you are in Isometric Snap mode.

Always check the isoplane position before placing an ellipse (isocircle) on your drawing. You can dynamically view the three positions that an ellipse can take. Initiate the **ELLIPSE** command, enter the **Isocircle** option, pick a center point, and press [F5] to toggle the crosshairs orientation. See **Figure 25-11.** The ellipse rotates each time you toggle the crosshairs.

---

**Figure 25-11.**
The orientation of
an isometric ellipse
is determined by the
crosshairs
orientation.

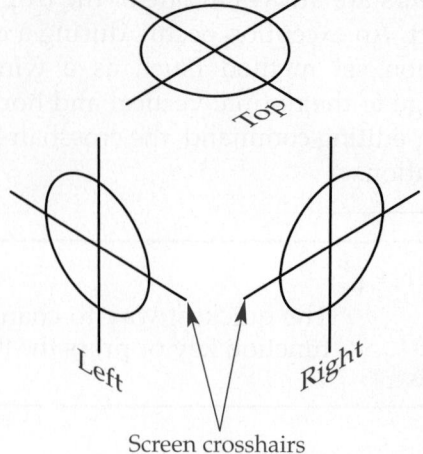

Top

Left

Right

Screen crosshairs

The isometric ellipse (isocircle) is a true ellipse. If selected, grips are displayed at the center and four quadrant points. See **Figure 25-12.** However, do not use grips to resize or otherwise adjust an isometric ellipse. As soon as you resize an isometric ellipse in this manner, its angular value is changed and it is no longer isometric. You can use the center grip to move the ellipse. Also, if you rotate an isometric ellipse while Ortho mode is on, it will not appear in a proper isometric plane. You *can* rotate an isometric ellipse from one isometric plane to another, but you must enter a value of 120°.

**PROFESSIONAL TIP**

Prior to drawing isometric ellipses, it is good practice to first place a marker at the ellipse center point. A good technique is to draw a point at the center using an easily visible point style. This is especially useful if the ellipse does not fall on grid or snap points.

**Figure 25-12.**
An isometric ellipse
has grips at its four
quadrant points and
center.

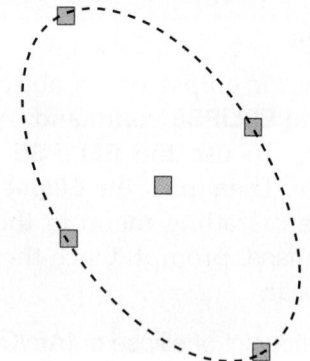

○ Open EX25-1 if this drawing is not already on your screen.
○ Select the **ELLIPSE** command to place an ellipse on the three sides of the object, as shown below.
○ Draw the numbered ellipses in the following manner.
　○ Pick a radius of .5 using the cursor to draw Ellipse 1.
　○ Enter a radius of .75 at the keyboard to draw Ellipse 2.
　○ Enter D and then a diameter of .6 at the keyboard to draw Ellipse 3.
○ Save the drawing as EX25-2.

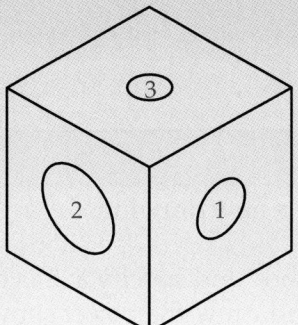

## Constructing Isometric Arcs

The **ELLIPSE** command can also be used to draw an isometric arc of any included angle. To construct an isometric arc, use the **Arc** option of the **ELLIPSE** command while in **Isometric mode**. To access the **Arc** option, pick the **Ellipse** button on the **Draw** toolbar, enter EL or ELLIPSE at the Command: prompt, or select **Arc** from the **Ellipse** cascading menu in the **Draw** pull-down menu. If you use the toolbar button or command line, you must then type A at the Command: prompt to enter the **Arc** option. Once the **Arc** option is initiated, the following prompts appear.

> Specify axis endpoint of elliptical arc or [Center/Isocircle]: I↵
> Specify center of isocircle: *(pick the center of the arc)*
> Specify radius of isocircle or [Diameter]: *(pick the radius or type a value and press* [Enter]*)*
> Specify start angle or [Parameter]: *(pick a start angle or type a value and press* [Enter]*)*
> Specify end angle or [Parameter/Included angle]: *(pick an end angle or type an included angle value and press* [Enter]*)*
> Command:

A common application of isometric arcs is drawing fillets and rounds. Once a round is created in isometric, the edge (corner) of the object sits back from its original, unfilleted position. See **Figure 25-13A.** You can draw the complete object first, then trim away the excess after locating the fillets. You can also draw the isometric arcs and then the connecting lines. Either way, the center point of the ellipse is a critical feature, and should be located first. The left-hand arc in **Figure 25-13A** was drawn first and copied to the back position. Use Ortho mode to help quickly draw 90° arcs.

The next step is to move the original edge to its new position, which is tangent to the isometric arcs. You can do this by snapping the endpoint of the line to the quadrant point of the arc. See **Figure 25-13B.** Notice the grips on the line and on the arc. The endpoint of the line is snapped to the quadrant grip on the arc. The final step is to trim away the excess lines and arc segment. The completed feature is shown in **Figure 25-13C.**

Rounded edges, when viewed straight on, cannot be shown as complete-edge lines that extend to the ends of the object. Instead, a good technique to use is a broken line in the original location of the edge. This is clearly shown in the figure in Exercise 25-3.

**Figure 25-13.**
Fillets and rounds can be drawn with the **Arc** option of the **ELLIPSE** command.

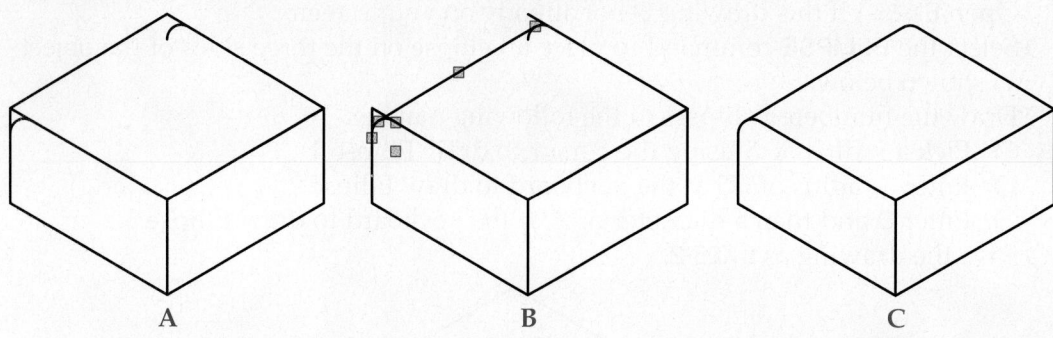

A          B          C

---

## Exercise 25-3

○ Start AutoCAD and begin a new drawing.
○ Set the grid spacing to .5.
○ Turn on Isometric Snap mode and specify a .25 vertical spacing for the snap.
○ Use the **LINE** command and draw the object shown below. Change the isoplane as needed. Do not dimension the object.
○ Use the **ELLIPSE** command and **Arc** option to complete the object. All fillets and rounds have a radius of .25.
○ Save the drawing as EX25-3.

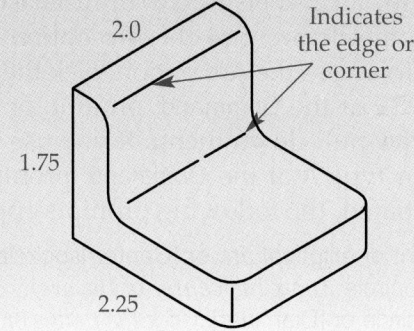

2.0

Indicates
the edge or
corner

1.75

2.25

---

## Creating Isometric Text Styles

Text placed in an isometric drawing should appear to be parallel to one of the isometric planes. Text should align with the plane to which it applies. Text may be located on the object or positioned away from it as a note. Drafters and artists occasionally neglect this aspect of pictorial drawing and it shows on the final product.

Properly placing text on an isometric drawing involves creating new text styles. **Figure 25-14** illustrates possible orientations of text on an isometric drawing. These examples were created using only two text styles. The text styles have an obliquing angle of either 30° or –30°. The labels in **Figure 25-14** refer to the chart below. The angle in the figure indicates the rotation angle entered when using one of the **TEXT** commands. For example, ISO-2 90 means that the ISO-2 style was used and the text was rotated 90°. This technique can be applied to any font.

| Name  | Font   | Obliquing Angle |
|-------|--------|-----------------|
| ISO-1 | Romans | 30°             |
| ISO-2 | Romans | –30°            |

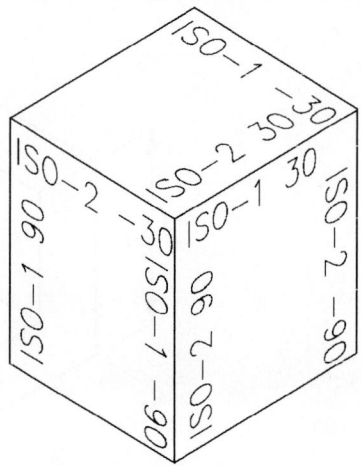

**Figure 25-14.**
Isometric text applications. The text shown here indicates which ISO style and angle were used.

---

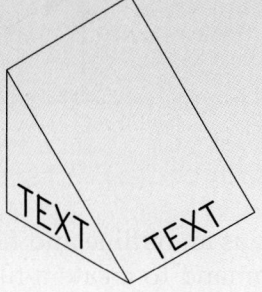
## Isometric Dimensioning

An important aspect of dimensioning in isometric is to place dimension lines, text, and arrowheads on the proper plane. Remember these guidelines:

✓  Extension lines should always extend the plane being dimensioned.
✓  The heel of the arrowhead should always be parallel to the extension line.
✓  Strokes of the text that would normally be vertical should always be parallel with the extension lines or dimension lines.

These techniques are shown on the dimensioned isometric part in **Figure 25-15.** AutoCAD does not automatically dimension isometric objects. You must first create isometric arrowheads and text styles. Then, manually draw the dimension lines and text as they should appear in each of the three isometric planes. This is time-consuming when compared to dimensioning normal 2D drawings.

You have already learned how to create isometric text styles. These can be set up in an isometric template drawing if you draw isometrics often. Examples of arrows for the three isometric planes are shown in **Figure 25-16.**

---

**Figure 25-15.**
A dimensioned isometric part. Note the text and arrowhead orientation in relation to the extension lines.

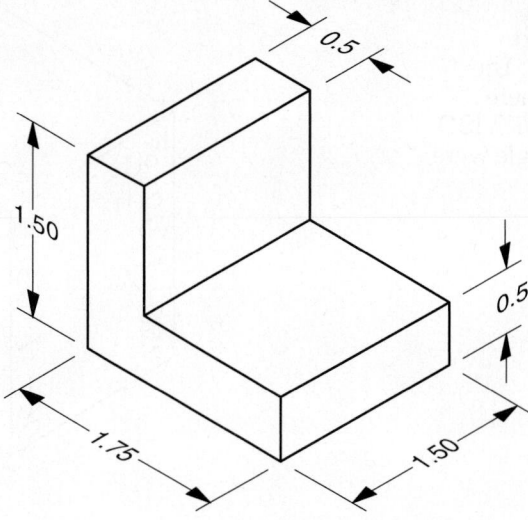

**Figure 25-16.**
Examples of arrowheads in each of the three isometric planes.

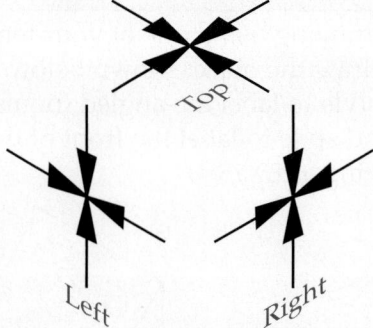

## Isometric Arrowheads

Arrowheads can be drawn as an outline and filled-in with a solid hatch pattern, or you can use the **SOLID** command to create a filled arrowhead. A variable-width polyline cannot be used because the heal of the arrowhead will not be parallel to the extension lines.

Every arrowhead does not need to be drawn individually. First, draw two isometric axes, as shown in **Figure 25-17A.** Then, draw one arrowhead like the one shown in **Figure 25-17B.** Use the **MIRROR** command to create additional arrows. As you create new arrows, move them to their proper plane.

Save each arrowhead as a block in your isometric template or prototype. Use block names that are easy to remember.

**Figure 25-17.**
Creating isometric arrowheads.
A—Draw the two isometric axes for arrowhead placement.
B—Draw the first arrowhead on one of the axis lines. Then, mirror the arrowhead to create others.

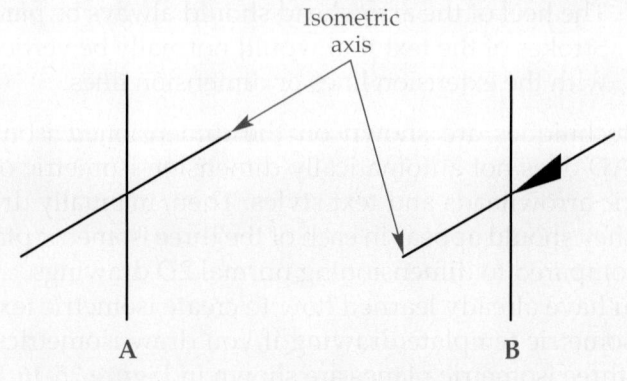

## Oblique Dimensioning

AutoCAD has a way to semiautomatically dimension isometric and oblique lines. First, the dimensions must be drawn using any of the linear dimensioning commands. **Figure 25-18A** illustrates an object dimensioned using the **DIMALIGNED** and **DIMLINEAR** commands. Then, use the **Oblique** option of the **DIMEDIT** command to rotate the extension lines. See **Figure 25-18B**.

To access the **Oblique** option, enter DED or DIMEDIT at the Command: prompt and then enter O for **Oblique**. You can also select **Oblique** from the **Dimension** pull-down menu. When prompted, select the dimension and enter the obliquing angle.

This technique creates suitable dimensions for an isometric drawing and is quicker than the previous method discussed. However, this method does not rotate the arrows so the arrowhead heels are aligned with the extension lines. It also does not draw the dimension text aligned in the plane of the dimension.

**Figure 25-18.**
Using the **Oblique** option of the **DIMEDIT** command, you can create semiautomatic isometric dimensions by editing existing dimensions.

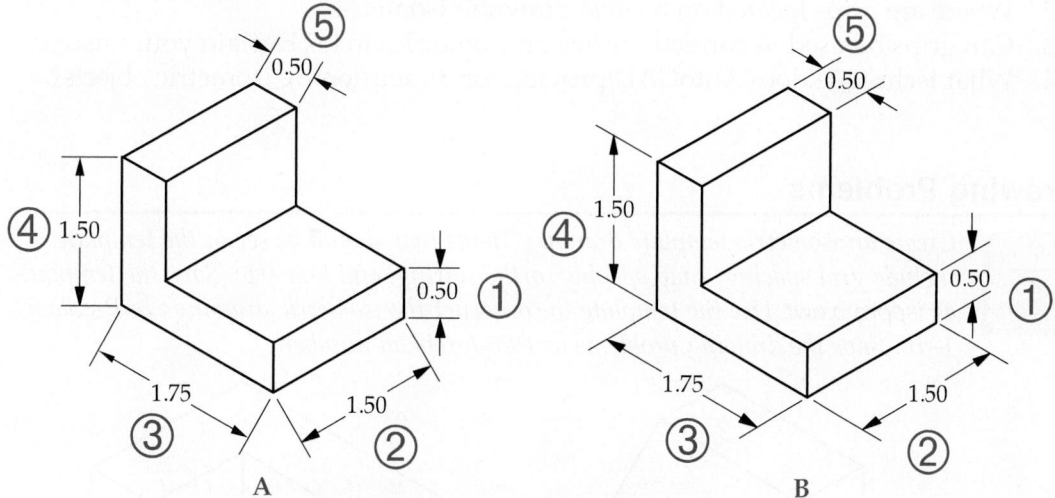

| Dimension | Obliquing Angle |
|-----------|-----------------|
| 1 | 30° |
| 2 | -30° |
| 3 | 30° |
| 4 | -30° |
| 5 | 30° |

## Chapter Test

*Answer the following questions on a separate sheet of paper.*

1. The simplest form of pictorial drawing is _____.
2. How does isometric drawing differ from oblique drawing?
3. How do dimetric and trimetric drawings differ from isometric drawings?
4. The most realistic form of pictorial drawing is _____.
5. What must be set in the **Drafting Settings** dialog box to turn on Isometric Snap mode and set a snap spacing of 0.2?
6. What function does the **ISOPLANE** command perform?
7. Which pull-down menu contains the command to access the **Drafting Settings** dialog box?
8. What factor determines the orientation of an isometric ellipse?
9. Name the command and option used to draw a circle in isometric.
10. Which text style setting allows you to create text that can be used on an isometric drawing?
11. Which command and two options must you select in order to draw isometric arcs?
12. Where are grips located on a circle drawn in isometric?
13. Can grips be used to correctly resize an isometric circle? Explain your answer.
14. What technique does AutoCAD provide for dimensioning isometric objects?

## Drawing Problems

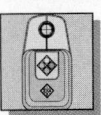

*Create an isometric template drawing. Items that should be set in the template include grid spacing, snap spacing, ortho setting, and text size. Save the template as* **isoproto.dwt.** *Use the template to construct the isometric drawings in Problems 1–10. Save the drawing problems as* **P25-***(problem number).*

1.

2.

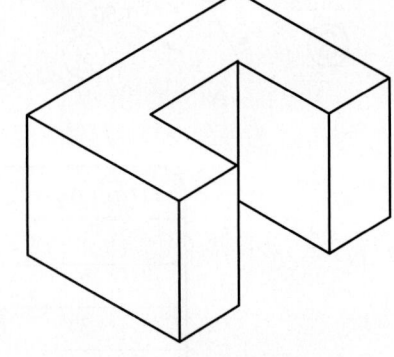

3.

4.

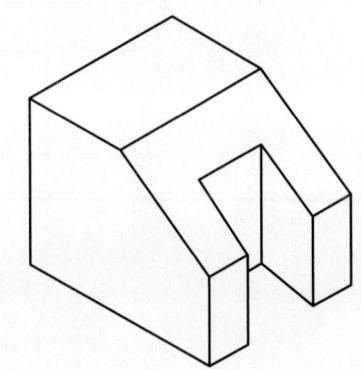

5.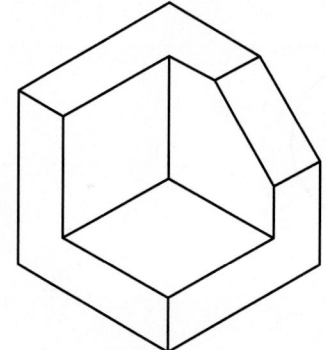

6.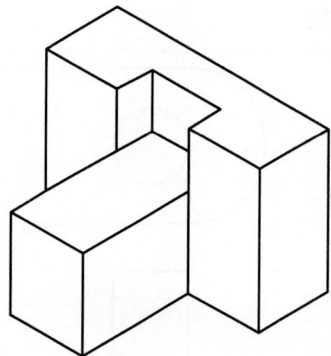

7.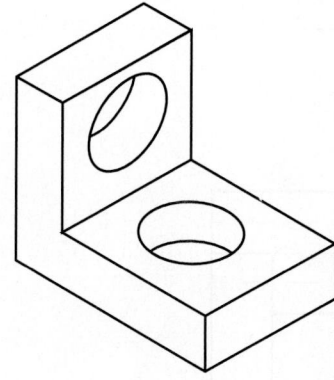

8.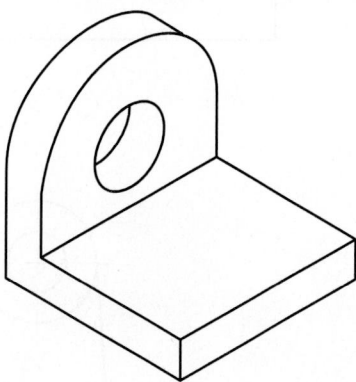

9.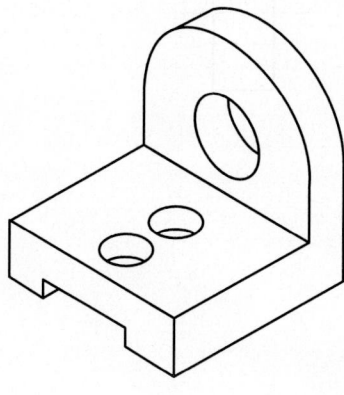

10.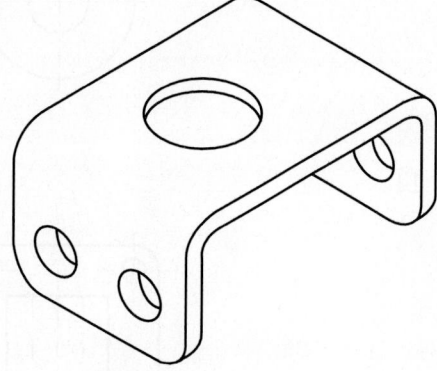

*For Problems 11–14, create isometric drawings using the views shown.*

11.

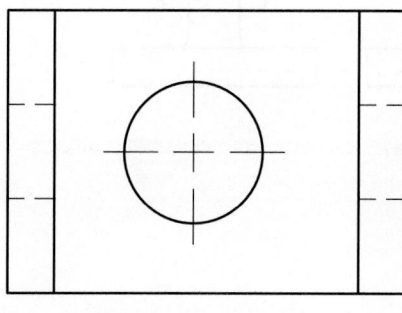
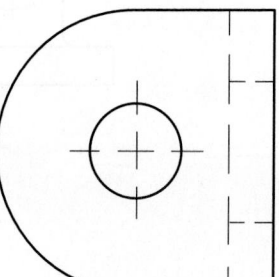

12.

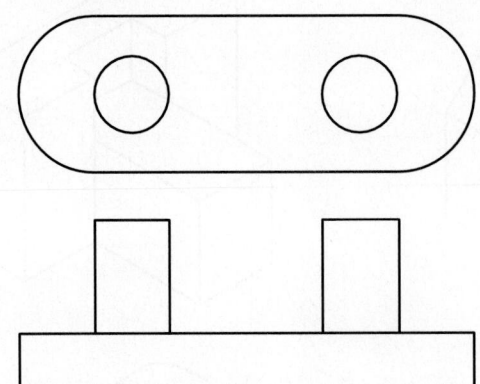

13.

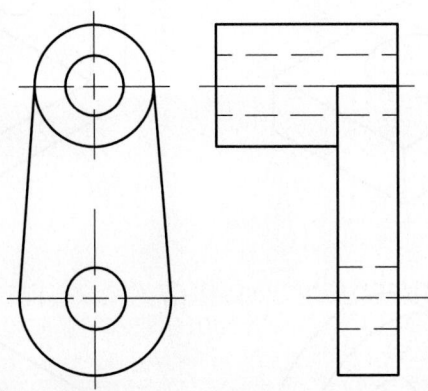

14.

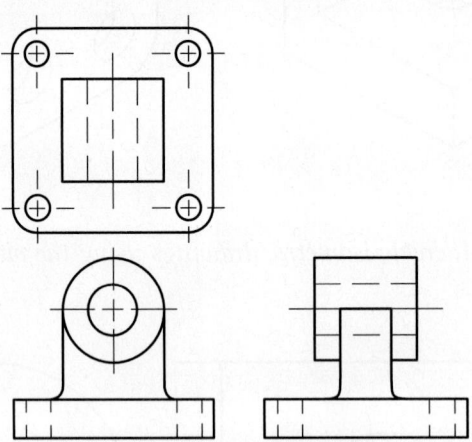

15. Construct a set of isometric arrowheads to use when dimensioning isometric drawings. Load your isometric template drawing. Create arrowheads for each of the three isometric planes. Save each arrowhead as a block. Name them with the first letter indicating the plane: T for top, L for left, and R for right. Also, number them clockwise from the top. See the example below for the right isometric plane. Do not include the labels in the blocks. Save the template again when finished.

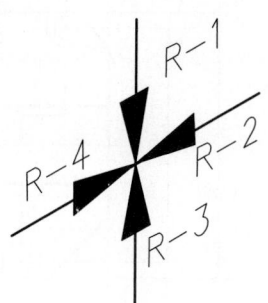

16. Create a set of isometric text styles like those shown in **Figure 25-14**. Load your template drawing and make a complete set in one font. Make additional sets in other fonts if you wish. Enter a text height of 0 so that you can specify the height when placing the text. Save the template when finished.

17. Begin a new drawing using your isometric template. Select one of the following problems from this chapter and dimension it: Problem 5, 7, 8, or 9. When adding dimensions, be sure to use the proper arrowhead and text style for the plane on which you are working. Save the drawing as P25-17.

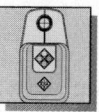

18. Create an isometric drawing of the switch plate shown below. Select a view that best displays the features of the object. Do not include dimensions. Save the drawing as P25-18.

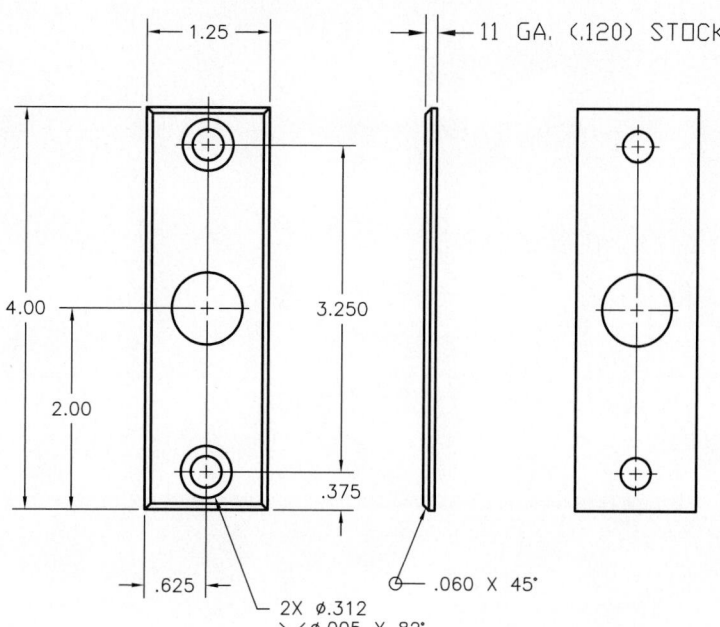

19. Create an isometric drawing of the retainer shown below. Select a view that best displays the features of the object. Do not include dimensions. Save the drawing as P25-19.

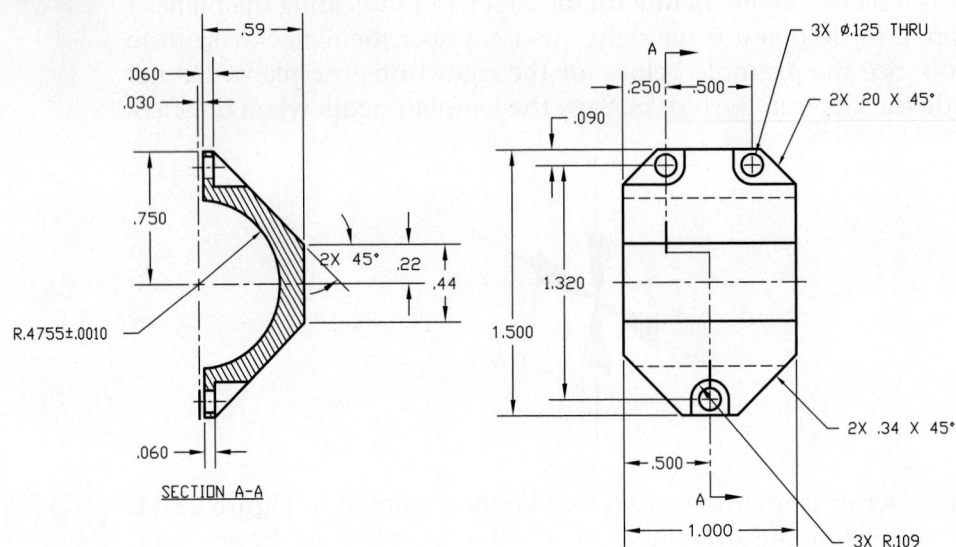

SECTION A-A

# Introduction to Three-Dimensional Drawing

## 26

## Learning Objectives

After completing this chapter, you will be able to do the following:
- Describe how to locate points in 3D space.
- Use the right-hand rule of 3D visualization.
- Display 3D objects from preset isometric viewpoints.
- Display 3D objects from any desired viewpoint.
- Construct wireframe objects.
- Construct solid primitives.
- Construct surface primitives.
- Create hidden displays.
- Create shaded displays.

Drafters and designers must have good three-dimensional (3D) visualization skills, such as the ability to see an object in three dimensions and to visualize it rotating in space. These skills are acquired by using 3D techniques to construct objects and by trying to picture two-dimensional sketches and drawings as 3D models.

Chapter 25 explained a method of representing a 3D object in two-dimensional space. This chapter provides an introduction to several aspects of true 3D drawing and visualization. A thorough discussion of 3D drawing, modeling, visualization, and display techniques is provided in *AutoCAD and its Applications—Advanced*.

## 3D Coordinates

To this point, you have been drawing in two dimensions (2D) in relation to X and Y coordinates. When drawing in 3D, however, a third coordinate measured along the Z axis is required. For 2D drawings, the Z coordinate is 0. Using X, Y, and Z coordinates you can locate any point in 3D space.

Look at **Figure 26-1.** Note that the positive Z values come up from the XY plane. Consider the surface of your computer screen as the XY plane. Anything behind the screen is negative Z and anything in front of the screen is positive Z.

**Figure 26-2A** shows a 2D drawing of the top of an object. The XY coordinate values of each point are shown. However, this is actually a 3D object. When displayed in a pictorial view, the Z coordinates can be seen. Notice in **Figure 26-2B** that the first two values of each coordinate match the X and Y values of the 2D view. Three-dimensional coordinates are always expressed as (X,Y,Z).

**Figure 26-1.**
A comparison of
2D and
3D coordinate
systems.

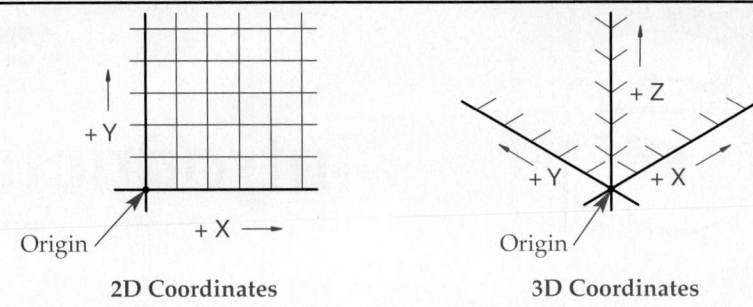

2D Coordinates                    3D Coordinates

**Figure 26-2.**
Each vertex of a
3D object must have
an X, Y, and Z value.

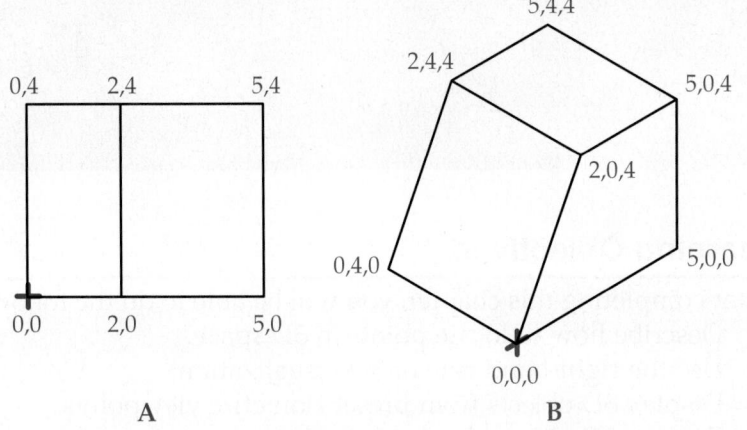

A                                  B

Study the nature of the 3D coordinate system. Be sure you understand Z values before you begin constructing 3D objects. It is important that you visualize and plan your design when working with 3D constructions.

**PROFESSIONAL TIP**

All points in three-dimensional space can be drawn using one of three coordinate entry methods—rectangular, spherical, or cylindrical. This chapter uses the rectangular coordinate entry method. For complete discussions on the spherical and cylindrical coordinate entry methods, please refer to *AutoCAD and its Applications—Advanced*.

## Exercise 26-1

- Study the multiview sketch below.
- Each tick mark is one unit. Use the correct dimensions as given in the multiview drawing.
- Given the 3D coordinate axes, freehand sketch a pictorial of the object.

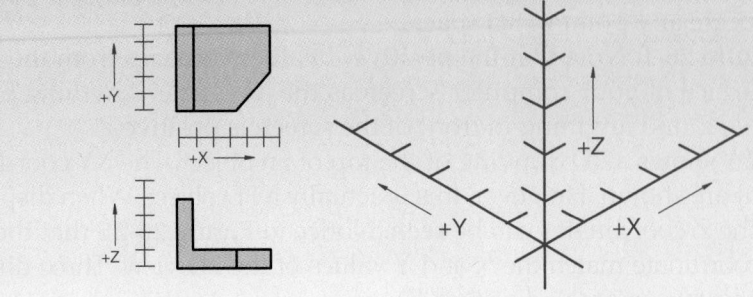

# The Right-Hand Rule

The *right-hand rule* is a representation of positive coordinate values in the three axis directions of a coordinate system. This rule requires that you hold the thumb, index finger, and middle finger of your right hand in front of you as shown in **Figure 26-3**. Although this may seem a bit unusual to do especially if you are sitting in the middle of a school library or computer lab, it can help you understand the nature of the three axes. If you discover that your 3D visualization skills are weak or that you are having trouble working with different UCSs, do not be afraid to use the right-hand rule. It is a useful technique for improving your 3D visualization skills.

Imagine that your thumb represents the X axis, your index finger the Y axis, and your middle finger the Z axis. Holding your hand in front of you, rotate your wrist so your middle finger is pointing directly at you. Now you see the plan view of the XY plane. The positive X axis is pointing to the right, the positive Y axis is pointing up, and the positive Z axis comes toward you. The origin (0,0,0) of this system is the palm of your hand.

The concept behind the right-hand rule can be visualized even better if you are sitting at a computer and the AutoCAD drawing area is displayed. If the UCS icon is not displayed in the lower-left corner of the screen, turn it on:

> Command: **UCSICON**↵
> Enter an option [ON/OFF/All/Noorigin/ORigin/Properties] <*current*>: **ON**↵

Now, orient your right hand as shown in **Figure 26-3** and position it next to the UCS (or WCS) icon. Your thumb and index finger should point in the same directions as the X and Y axes, respectively, on the UCS icon. Your middle finger will be pointing out of the screen. See **Figure 26-4**.

The right-hand rule can also be used to eliminate confusion when rotating the UCS. The UCS can rotate about any one of the three coordinate axes, just as a wheel rotates on an axle. Therefore, if you want to rotate about the X axis, keep your thumb stationary and turn your hand either toward or away from you. If you wish to rotate about the Y axis, keep your index finger stationary and turn your hand to the left or right. When rotating about the Z axis, keep your middle finger stationary and rotate your entire arm.

---

**Figure 26-3.**
Try positioning your hand as shown to understand the relationship of the X, Y, and Z axes.

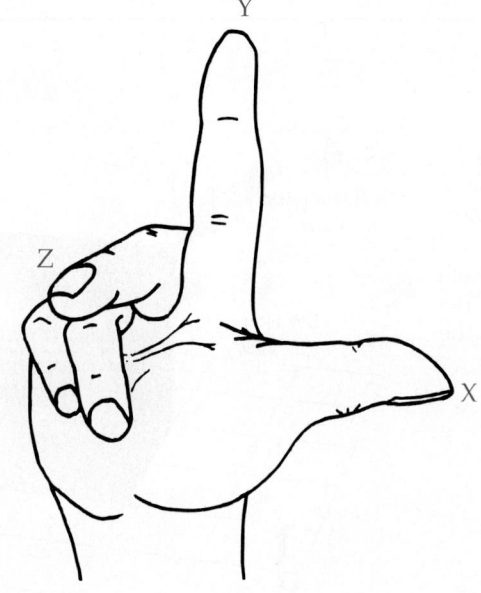

**Figure 26-4.**
Using the right-hand rule to view the WCS.

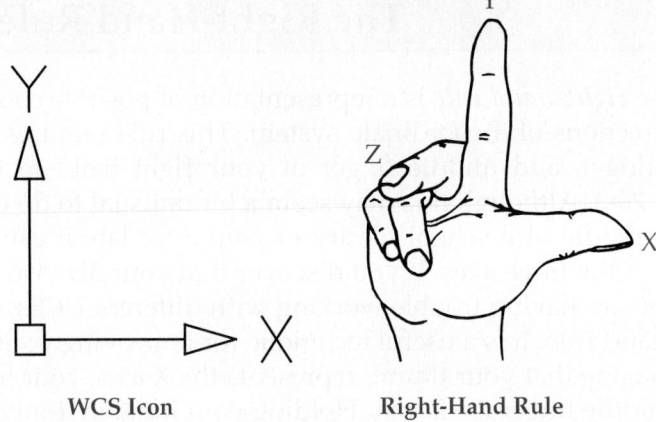

WCS Icon          Right-Hand Rule

Working with UCSs is introduced in Chapter 6 of this text. A complete discussion of working with and managing UCSs is provided in *AutoCAD and its Applications—Advanced.*

## Displaying 3D Views

It does not do much good to understand how to draw in 3D space if you cannot see what you draw in three dimensions. To this point, you have been looking at a plan, or top, view of the XY plane. AutoCAD provides several methods of changing your viewpoint to produce a 3D, or pictorial, view. The *viewpoint* is the location in space from which the object is viewed. Two methods of changing your viewpoint are discussed here.

### Isometric and Orthographic Viewpoint Presets

As you learned in Chapter 25, a 2D isometric drawing is based on angles of 120° between the three axes. AutoCAD provides preset viewpoints that allow you to view a 3D object from one of four locations. See **Figure 26-5.** Each of these viewpoints produces an isometric view of the object. In addition, AutoCAD has presets for the six standard orthographic views of an object. The isometric and orthographic viewpoint presets are based on the WCS.

**Figure 26-5.**
There are four preset isometric viewpoints in AutoCAD. This illustration shows the direction from which the cube will be viewed for each of the presets. The grid represents the XY plane of the WCS.

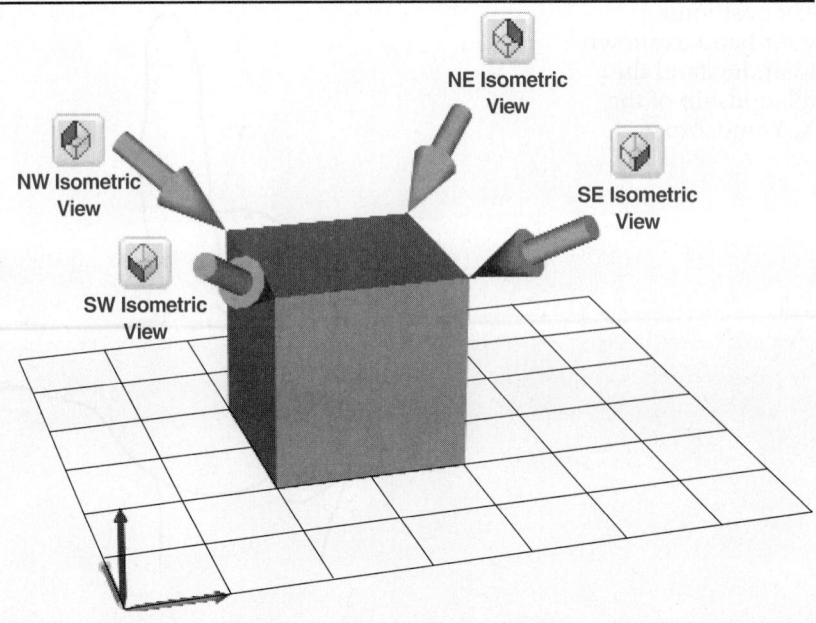

NE Isometric View

NW Isometric View

SE Isometric View

SW Isometric View

The four preset isometric views are southwest, southeast, northeast, and northwest. To switch your viewpoint to one of these presets, select **3D Views** from the **View** pull-down menu. Then, select **SW Isometric**, **SE Isometric**, **NE Isometric**, or **NW Isometric** from the cascading menu. You can also select the **SW Isometric**, **SE Isometric**, **NE Isometric**, or **NW Isometric** button on the **View** toolbar. This toolbar is not displayed by default.

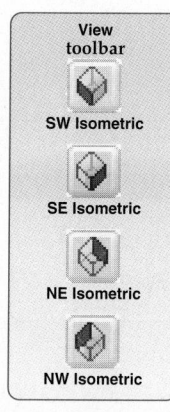

Once you select the command, the viewpoint in the current viewport is automatically changed to display an appropriate isometric view. Since these presets are based on the WCS, selecting a preset produces the same isometric view of the object regardless of the current UCS.

A view that looks straight down on the current drawing plane is called a *plan view*. For example, the default view when you start AutoCAD is a plan view of the WCS. When an isometric or other 3D view is displayed, you can easily switch to a plan view of the current UCS using the **PLAN** command. Type PLAN at the Command: prompt:

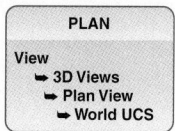

Command: **PLAN**↵
Enter an option [Current ucs/Ucs/World] <Current>: **W**↵ *(if you press [Enter], a plan view of the current UCS is displayed; the current UCS may or may not be the WCS)*
Regenerating model.
Command:

You can also create a plan view of the WCS by selecting **3D Views** in the **View** pull-down menu. Then, select **Plan View** in the cascading menu and **World UCS** in the next cascading menu.

The six orthographic presets are top, bottom, left, right, front, and back. To switch your viewpoint to one of these presets, select **3D Views** from the **View** pull-down menu. Then, select **Top**, **Bottom**, **Left**, **Right**, **Front**, or **Back** from the cascading menu. You can also select the **Top View**, **Bottom View**, **Left View**, **Right View**, **Front View**, or **Back View** button on the **View** toolbar. Once you select a preset, the view is changed to the corresponding orthographic view. Like the isometric presets, the orthographic presets are based on the WCS so the same view is displayed regardless of the current UCS.

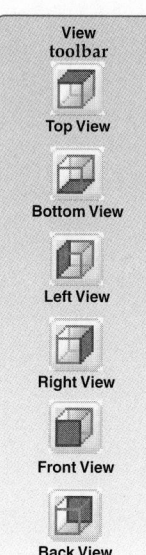

An important aspect of the orthographic presets is that selecting one not only changes the viewpoint, it changes the UCS to be plan to the orthographic view. All new objects are created on that UCS instead of the WCS (or previous UCS). Working with UCSs is explained in detail in *AutoCAD and its Applications—Advanced*. For the activities in this text, do not use the orthographic presets. However, the command sequence to change the UCS to the WCS is:

Command: **UCS**↵
Current ucs name: *LEFT* *(this name will match the name of the orthographic preset used to display the view)*
Enter an option [New/Move/orthoGraphic/Prev/Restore/Save/Del/Apply/?/World] <World>: **W**↵
Command:

---

**Exercise 26-2**

○ Open the drawing Oil Module.dwg from the AutoCAD Sample folder.
○ Use each one of the four isometric presets to display different views of the model. Note: This is a large model and it may take a few seconds for the command to work.
○ Close the drawing without saving the changes.

---

## Unlimited Viewpoints

You are not limited to the preset isometric viewpoints. In fact, you can view a 3D object from an unlimited number of viewpoints. The **3DORBIT** command allows you to dynamically rotate the view of the objects to create a new viewpoint.

3DORBIT
3DO

View
➥ 3D Orbit

To start the **3DORBIT** command, pick **3D Orbit** from the **View** pull-down menu or type 3DORBIT or 3DO at the Command: prompt. A green circle appears in the middle of the current viewport. See **Figure 26-6.** This is called the trackball, or arcball. Also, notice that the cursor changes. If you move it inside the trackball, it appears as two intersecting circles, as shown in **Figure 26-6.** If you move it outside of the trackball, the cursor appears as a single circle.

To change the view, pick anywhere inside the trackball and drag the cursor. The view is dynamically changed as you move the cursor. However, you are not rotating the *objects*, just the view. When you get the view you want, release the mouse button. The command remains active and you can further adjust the view. When done, right-click to display the shortcut menu. Then, select **Exit** from the menu. You can also press [Esc] to end the command. The **UNDO** command reverses the effects of the **3DORBIT** command.

Picking outside the trackball and dragging rotates the view about an axis extending out of the screen. Also, notice the circle "handles" at the four quadrants of the trackball. Picking in the right or left handle and dragging rotates the view about the vertical axis in the viewport. Picking in the top or bottom handle and dragging rotates the view about the horizontal axis in the viewport.

The **3DORBIT** command has many options. This discussion is merely an introduction to the command. The command options are covered in detail in *AutoCAD and its Applications—Advanced.*

---

**PROFESSIONAL TIP**

AutoCAD has other commands for changing the viewpoint whose functionality has largely been replaced by the more useful **3DORBIT** command. These commands include **VPOINT**, **DDVPOINT**, and **DVIEW**.

---

**Figure 26-6.**
Using the **3DORBIT** command to change the viewpoint.

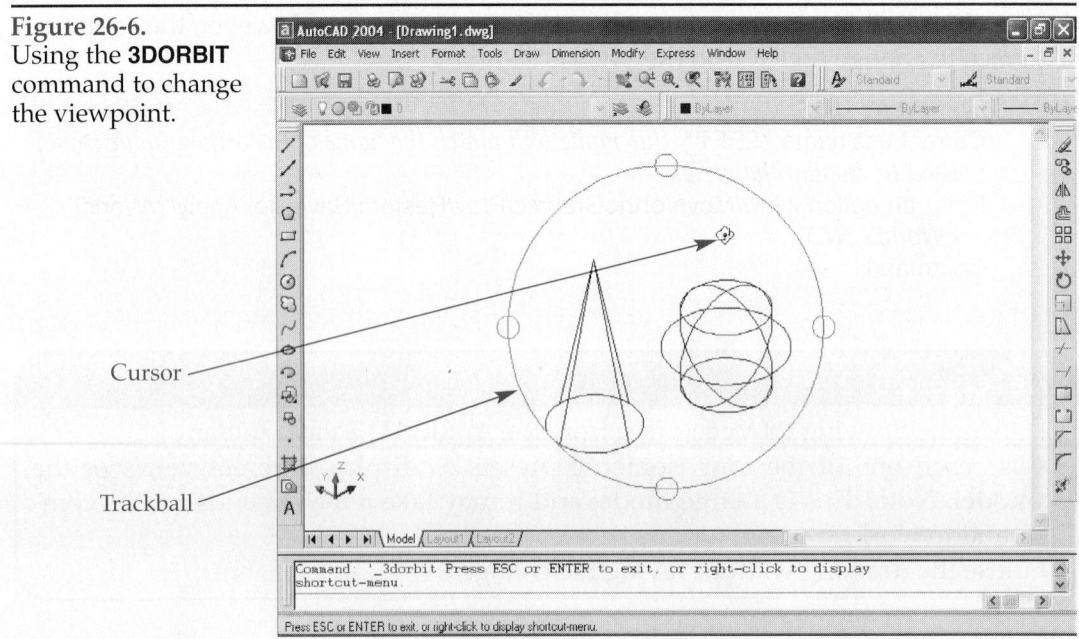

Cursor

Trackball

---

## Hiding Lines

When you display a 3D object in a pictorial view, such as from one of the isometric presets, AutoCAD displays all lines on the object. This includes the lines that represent the back of the object. See **Figure 26-7A.** This type of display is called a *wireframe display.* Often, it can be confusing looking at all of the lines. The **HIDE** command can be used to create a *hidden display* in which hidden lines are removed. See **Figure 26-7B.** The command is covered later in this chapter. However, to create a hidden display, simply type HIDE and the Command: prompt. Then, to return to a wireframe display, type REGEN at the Command: prompt.

**Figure 26-7.**
A—In a wireframe display, all lines are shown. B—In a hidden display, the lines that would be hidden from view are not shown. (Model courtesy of Autodesk, Inc.)

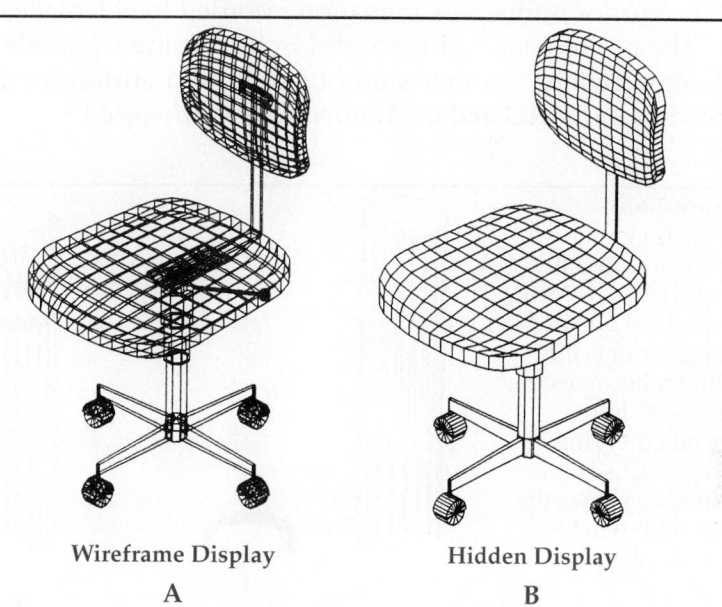

Wireframe Display
A

Hidden Display
B

## 3D Construction Techniques

Before constructing a 3D model, you should determine the purpose of your design. What will the model be used for—presentation, analysis, or manufacturing? This helps you determine which tools you should use to construct the model. Three-dimensional objects can be drawn in three basic forms—wireframe objects, solid models, and surface models.

A *wireframe object,* or model, is an object that is constructed of lines in 3D space. Wireframe models are hard to visualize because it is difficult to determine the angle of view and the nature of the surfaces. The **HIDE** command has no effect when used on a wireframe model because there is nothing to hide. All lines are always visible because there are no surfaces. There are not many practical applications for wireframe models. However, one application is to draw a wireframe and then place a skin, or surface, over the wireframe.

*Surface modeling* represents solid objects by creating a skin in the shape of the object. However, there is nothing inside the object. Think of a surface model as a hollow object. A surface model looks more like the real object than a wireframe and can be used for rendering. However, while more useful than wireframes, surface models have limited applications.

Like surface modeling, *solid modeling* represents the shape of objects, but also provides data related to the physical properties of the objects because it is composed of solid material. Solid models can be analyzed to determine mass, volume, moments of inertia, and centroid location. Some third-party programs allow you to perform finite element analysis on the model. In addition, solid models can be rendered. Most 3D objects are created as solid models.

In AutoCAD, both solid and surface models can be created from primitives. *Primitives* are basic shapes used as the foundation to create complex shapes. These basic shapes in AutoCAD include boxes, cylinders, spheres, and cones. Primitives can be modified to create a finished product. See **Figure 26-8**.

Surface and solid models can be exported from AutoCAD for use in animation and rendering software, such as 3ds max® or Autodesk VIZ®. Rendered models can be used in any number of presentation formats, including slide shows, black and white or color prints, and animation recorded to videotape, CD-ROM, or DVD.

The discussions and examples in this chapter provide an introductory view of 3D constructions. Further study of solid and surface modeling techniques is presented in *AutoCAD and its Applications—Advanced*.

**Figure 26-8.**
A—This cylinder and torus are solid primitives. B—With a couple of quick modifications, the cylinder becomes a stem with two machined O-ring grooves. C—This rendering shows the stem with two O-rings in place.

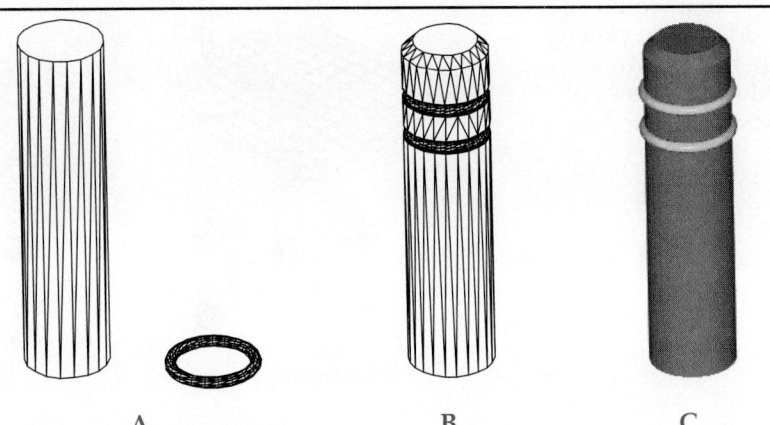

A                    B                    C

## Constructing Wireframe Objects

Wireframe objects, or wireframes, can be created with any combination of AutoCAD line objects, such as lines, polylines, circles, polygons, and so on. While the applications for wireframes are limited, drawing wireframes is a fundamental 3D skill that should be learned. Learning to draw wireframes provides valuable practice working in 3D space. In addition, the fundamentals of drawing wireframes can be applied to other 3D modeling techniques, such as creating a profile and axis for a revolved solid.

In this section, you will draw the object shown in **Figure 26-9** as a 3D wireframe. First, start a new drawing in AutoCAD and draw the top view using the dimensions shown. Use lines, polylines, circles, arcs, and rectangles as needed. Do not draw centerlines or dimensions. Next, display the drawing using the southwest isometric preset.

Figure 26-9.
You will use this
orthographic
drawing to create a
wireframe object.

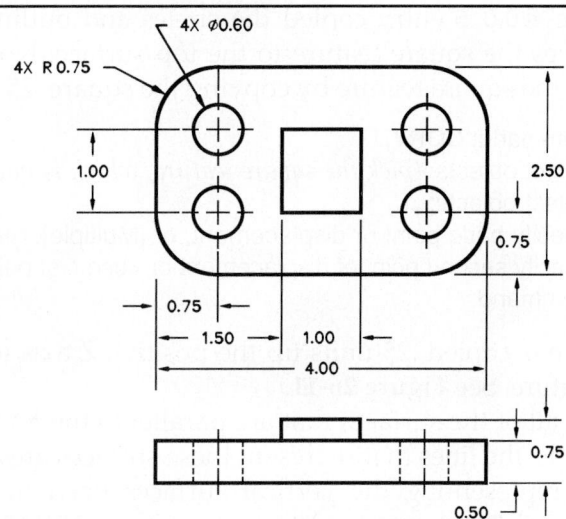

The "surfaces" of the part are imaginary planes between the lines that make up the wireframe. What you drew as the top view is actually the bottom surface of the part. You now need to add a thickness to the part. The base of the part is 0.50 thick, as shown in **Figure 26-9.** The four ∅0.60 circles are actually holes through the base. Therefore, the top and bottom surfaces of the base are represented by the outline and the four circles. Use the **COPY** command and relative displacement to create the top surface:

> Command: **COPY**↵
> Select objects: *(select the four circles and all lines that make up the outline of the part)*
> Select objects: ↵
> Specify base point or displacement, or [Multiple]: *(pick a point anywhere on screen)*
> Specify second point of displacement or <use first point as displacement>: **@0,0,.5**↵
> Command:

By specifying @0,0,.5 you tell AutoCAD that the second displacement point is 0 units on the X axis, 0 units on the Y axis, and .5 units on the Z axis from the first point. In other words, you have just copied the objects .5 units straight up the positive Z axis. See **Figure 26-10.**

Notice in **Figure 26-9** that the square feature is not a hole, but rather is extended from the top surface of the base. However, the square is currently on the bottom surface of the object. Therefore, you need to move the square to the top surface:

> Command: **MOVE**↵
> Select objects: *(select the square feature)*
> Select objects: ↵
> Specify base point or displacement: *(pick a point anywhere on screen)*
> Specify second point of displacement or <use first point as displacement>: **@0,0,.5**↵
> Command:

**Figure 26-10.**
The lines
representing the
bottom and top
surfaces of the base
are created.

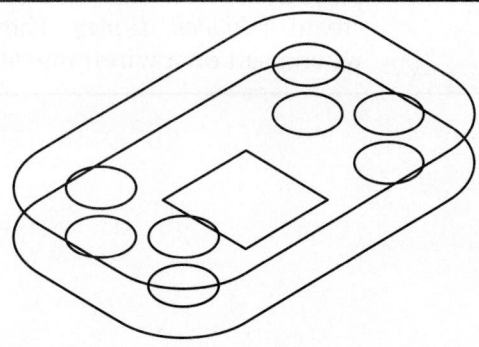

Just as the @0,0,.5 entry copied the circles and outline up the positive Z axis, this entry moves the square feature to the top surface. Now, you need to create the top surface of the square feature by copying the square .25 units up the positive Z axis:

Command: **COPY**↵
Select objects: *(pick the square feature, which is now on the top surface of the base)*
Select objects: ↵
Specify base point or displacement, or [Multiple]: *(pick any point on screen)*
Specify second point of displacement or <use first point as displacement>: **@0,0,.25**↵
Command:

The square is copied .25 units up the positive Z axis to create the top surface of the square feature. See **Figure 26-11.**

Now, all of the surfaces that are parallel to the XY plane have been "created." In other words, the lines that represent these surfaces are all correctly located. However, the lines representing the vertical surfaces need to be added. Set the **Endpoint**, **Midpoint**, and **Quadrant** object snaps and turn **OSNAP** on. Then, use the **LINE** command to connect endpoints and quadrants, as shown in **Figure 26-12A.**

The final wireframe is shown in **Figure 26-12B** after the viewpoint is changed using the **3DORBIT** command. Using the **HIDE** command has no effect on the display. This is because there are no actual surfaces in the model. The lines you see represent the edges of surfaces. Obviously, this type of 3D model has many drawbacks. However, you can now use this wireframe to create a surface or solid model. This approach to 3D modeling is covered in *AutoCAD and its Applications—Advanced.*

**Figure 26-11.**
The lines representing the bottom and top surfaces of the square feature are created.

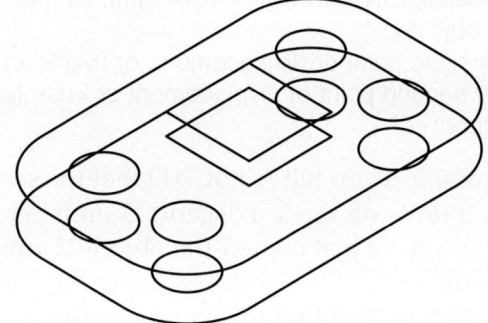

**PROFESSIONAL TIP**

Do not confuse a wireframe *object* with a wireframe *display*, which is a 3D surface or solid object with all lines displayed. Often, a drafter may say a 3D object is "displayed in wireframe." This means that the view of the object shows all lines, visible and hidden, not that the object is drawn as a wireframe object. If the **HIDE** command is used on a 3D object displayed in wireframe, the hidden lines will be removed to create a *hidden display.* The **HIDE** command has no effect when used on a wireframe *object.*

Figure 26-12.
A—Vertical lines, shown here in color, are added to complete the wireframe object. B—The viewpoint is changed and the **HIDE** command is used. Notice how the **HIDE** command does not suppress the display of any lines.

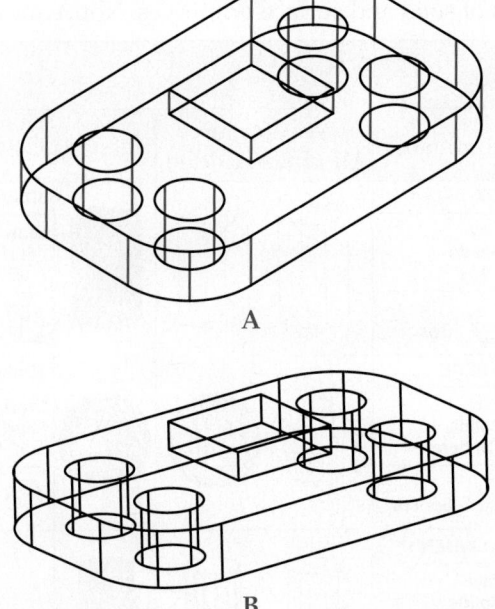

A

B

## Constructing Solid Primitives

As mentioned earlier, most 3D models are constructed as solids. This section provides an introduction to creating solid primitives. However, there are many more solid modeling techniques and methods available in AutoCAD. Extensive coverage of solid modeling is well beyond the scope of this text. Refer to *AutoCAD and its Applications—Advanced* for complete coverage of solid modeling.

The solid primitives that can be constructed in AutoCAD include a box, sphere, cylinder, cone, wedge, and torus. The commands to draw these primitives can be entered by selecting **Solids** in the **Draw** pull-down menu and then selecting the command in the cascading menu. You can also pick the appropriate button on the **Solids** toolbar or type the name of the solid, such as BOX, at the Command: prompt. See **Figure 26-13.** The **Solids** toolbar is not displayed by default.

> Draw
> ➥ Solids
>
> Solids
> toolbar

The information required to draw a primitive depends on the type of primitive being drawn. See **Figure 26-14.** For example, to draw a solid cylinder you must provide a center point for the base, a radius or diameter of the base, and the height of the cylinder:

```
Command: CYLINDER↵
Current wire frame density: ISOLINES = 4
Specify center point for base of cylinder or [Elliptical] <0,0,0>: 0,0,1↵
Specify radius for base of cylinder or [Diameter]: 2↵
Specify height of cylinder or [Center of other end]: 4↵
Command:
```

The cylinder is drawn with, normally, its base on the XY plane of the current USC. However, notice that the center of the base was specified as 0,0,1. This locates the center one unit up the positive Z axis from the XY plane of the current UCS. Also, notice that there are other options, such as creating a cylinder that is elliptical instead of round, specifying a diameter instead of a radius, and locating the center of the opposite end rather than providing a height. The command sequence for the other solid primitives is similar to that for a cylinder.

**Figure 26-13.**
A comparison of solid and surface primitives. Notice the differences in wireframe displays.

| Basic Primitive Shape | Solid | | | Surfaces | | |
|---|---|---|---|---|---|---|
| | Command | Wireframe All Lines/Hidden | Shaded | Command | Wireframe All Lines/Hidden | Shaded |
| Box | BOX / Draw Solids Box / Box |  | | 3D>Box / Draw Surfaces 3D Surfaces... / Box |  | |
| Sphere | SPHERE / Draw Solids Sphere / Sphere | 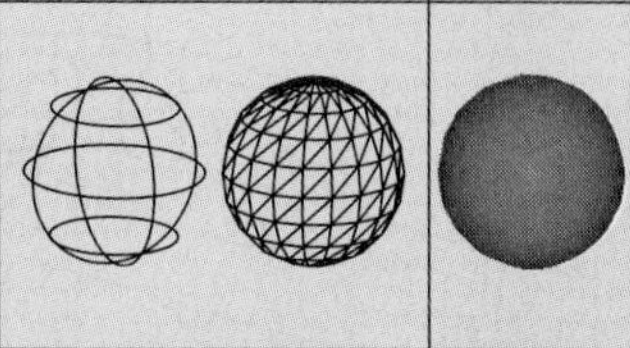 | | 3D>Sphere / Draw Surfaces 3D Surfaces... / Sphere |  | |
| Cylinder | CYLINDER / Draw Solids Cylinder / Cylinder | 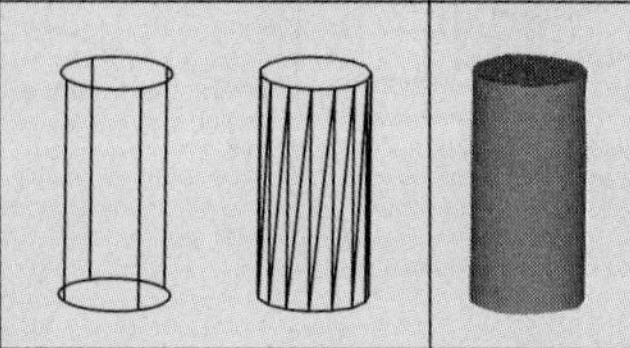 | | — | — | — |
| Cone | CONE / Draw Solids Cone / Cone | 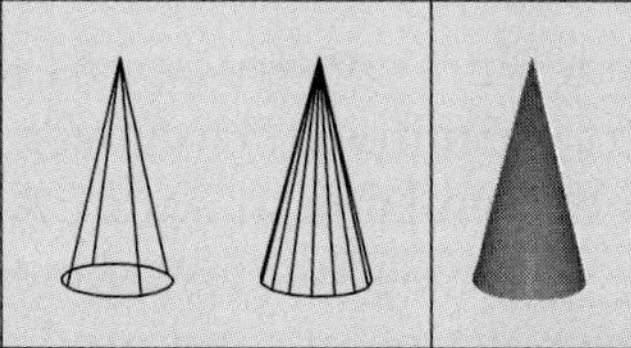 | | 3D>Cone / Draw Surfaces 3D Surfaces... / Cone |  | |
| Wedge | WEDGE / Draw Solids Wedge / Wedge |  | | 3D>Wedge / Draw Surfaces 3D Surfaces... / Wedge |  | |
| Torus | TORUS / Draw Solids Torus / Torus | 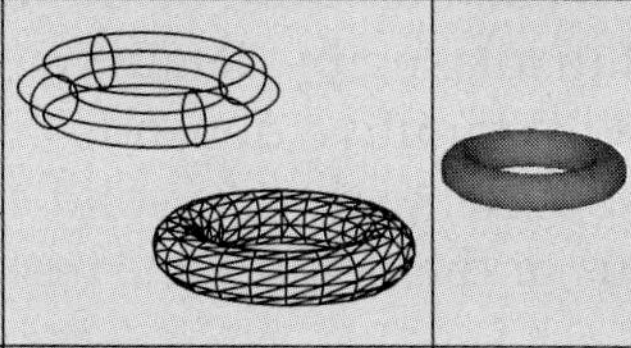 | | 3D>Torus / Draw Surfaces 3D Surfaces... / Torus | 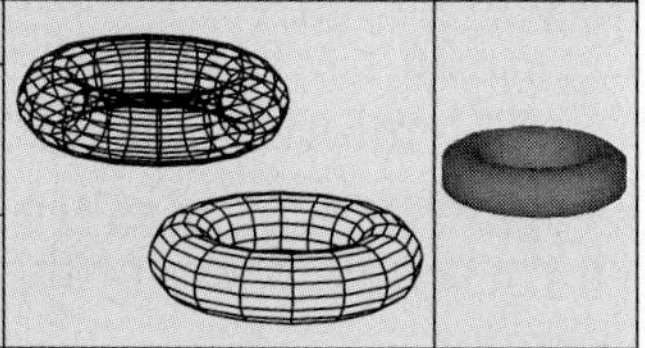 | |
| Pyramid | — | — | — | 3D>Pyramid / Draw Surfaces 3D Surfaces... / Pyramid | 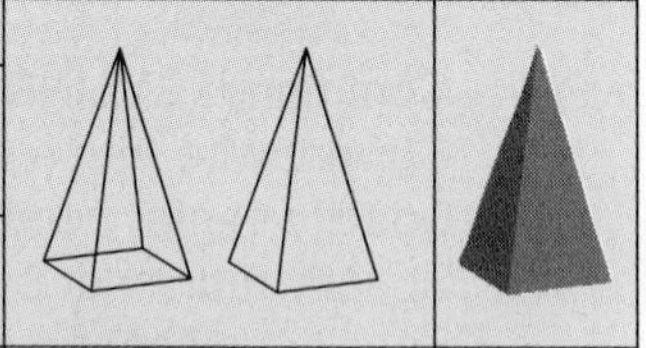 | |
| Dome | — | — | — | 3D>DOme / Draw Surfaces 3D Surfaces... / Dome | 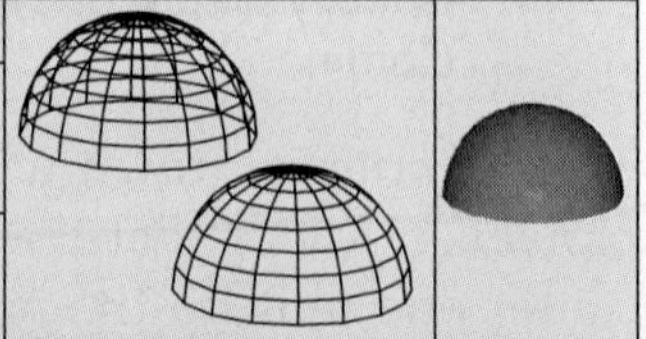 | |
| Dish | — | — | — | 3D>DIsh / Draw Surfaces 3D Surfaces... / Dish | 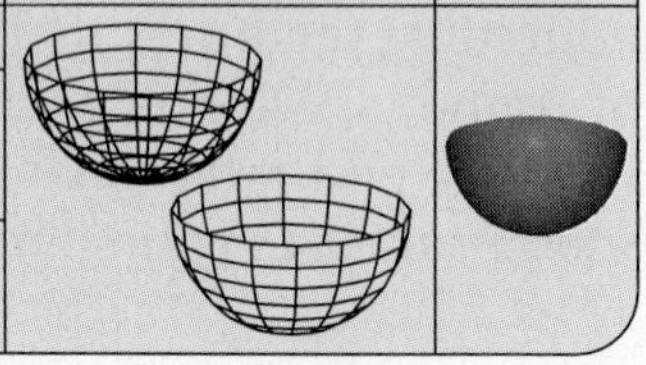 | |

Figure 26-14.
The basic information required to draw solid primitives.

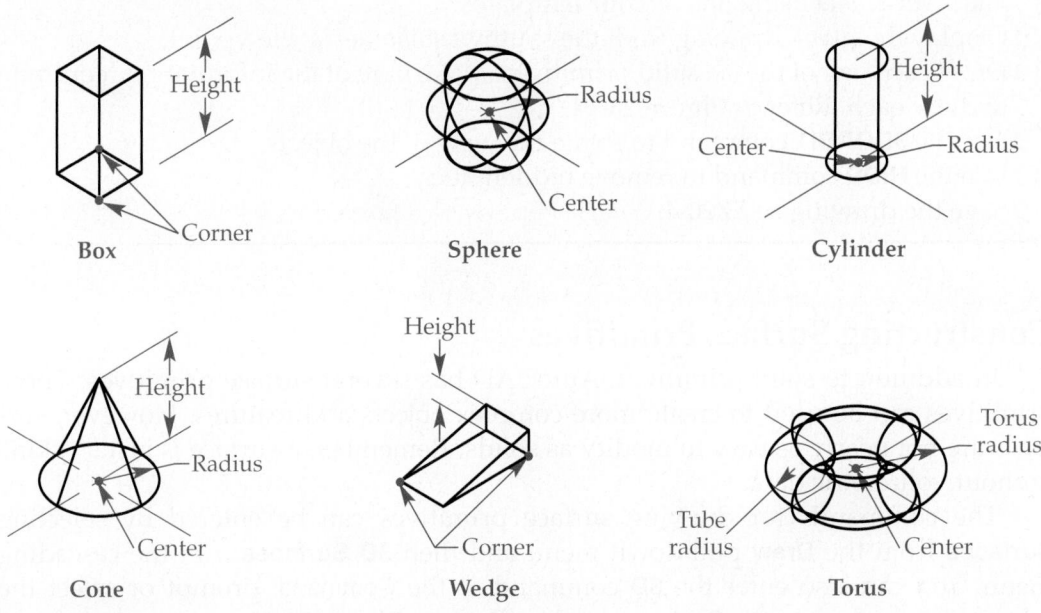

Certain familiar editing commands can be used on solid primitives. For example, you can fillet or chamfer the edges of a solid primitive. In addition, there are other editing commands that are specifically for use on solids. These are covered in detail in *AutoCAD and its Applications—Advanced*. The following is an example of placing a .125 chamfer on a cylinder:

```
Command: CHAMFER↵
(TRIM mode) Current chamfer Dist1 = 0.0000 Dist2 = 0.0000
Select first line or [Polyline/Distance/Angle/Trim/Method/mUltiple]: (pick the edge of
   the cylinder)
Base surface selection...
Enter surface selection option [Next/OK/ (current)] <OK>: ↵
Specify base surface chamfer distance: ↵
Specify other surface chamfer distance <0.1250>: ↵
Select an edge or [Loop]: (pick the edge again)
Select an edge or [Loop]: ↵
Command:
```

PROFESSIONAL
TIP  To see the object in 3D, use one of the isometric presets or the **3DORBIT** command. If you need to display a plan view of the current UCS, use the **PLAN** command.

## Constructing Surface Primitives

In addition to solid primitives, AutoCAD has several surface primitives. These primitives can be used to create more complex objects and features. However, surfaces are not nearly as easy to modify as solids. Remember, a surface is just a "skin" without volumetric data.

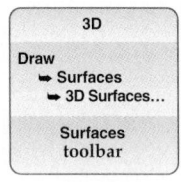

The commands for drawing surface primitives can be entered by selecting **Surfaces** from the **Draw** pull-down menu and then **3D Surfaces...** in the cascading menu. You can also enter the **3D** command at the Command: prompt or select the appropriate button on the **Surfaces** toolbar. Refer to **Figure 26-13.**

Using the pull-down menu displays the **3D Objects** dialog box, **Figure 26-15.** Notice the list box on the left of the dialog box and the image tiles on the right. The names correspond to the primitives shown on the image tiles. A primitive can be selected by picking either the name or the image. When selected, the image and the name are highlighted.

Once you select a surface primitive to draw, whether in the dialog box, on the command line, or from the toolbar, you are asked for certain information. The information required will depend on which primitive is being drawn. See **Figure 26-16.** For example, to draw a dome, you must provide a center, radius, and the number of segments for the dome:

> Command: **3D**↵ *(do not type the name of the surface primitive at the* Command: *prompt; you will draw a solid if you do)*
> Enter an option
> [Box/Cone/DIsh/DOme/Mesh/Pyramid/Sphere/Torus/Wedge]: **DO**↵
> Specify center point of dome: *(pick a point)*
> Specify radius of dome or [Diameter]: *(enter a radius or pick on the screen)*
> Enter number of longitudinal segments for surface of dome <16>: ↵
> Enter number of latitudinal segments for surface of dome <8>: ↵
> Command:

**Figure 26-15.**
Surface primitives can be drawn using the **3D Objects** dialog box.

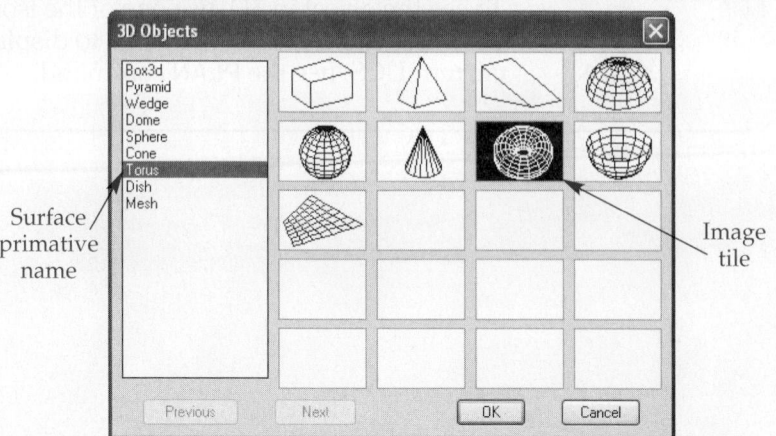

Surface primitive name

Image tile

**Figure 26-16.**
The basic information required to draw surface primitives.

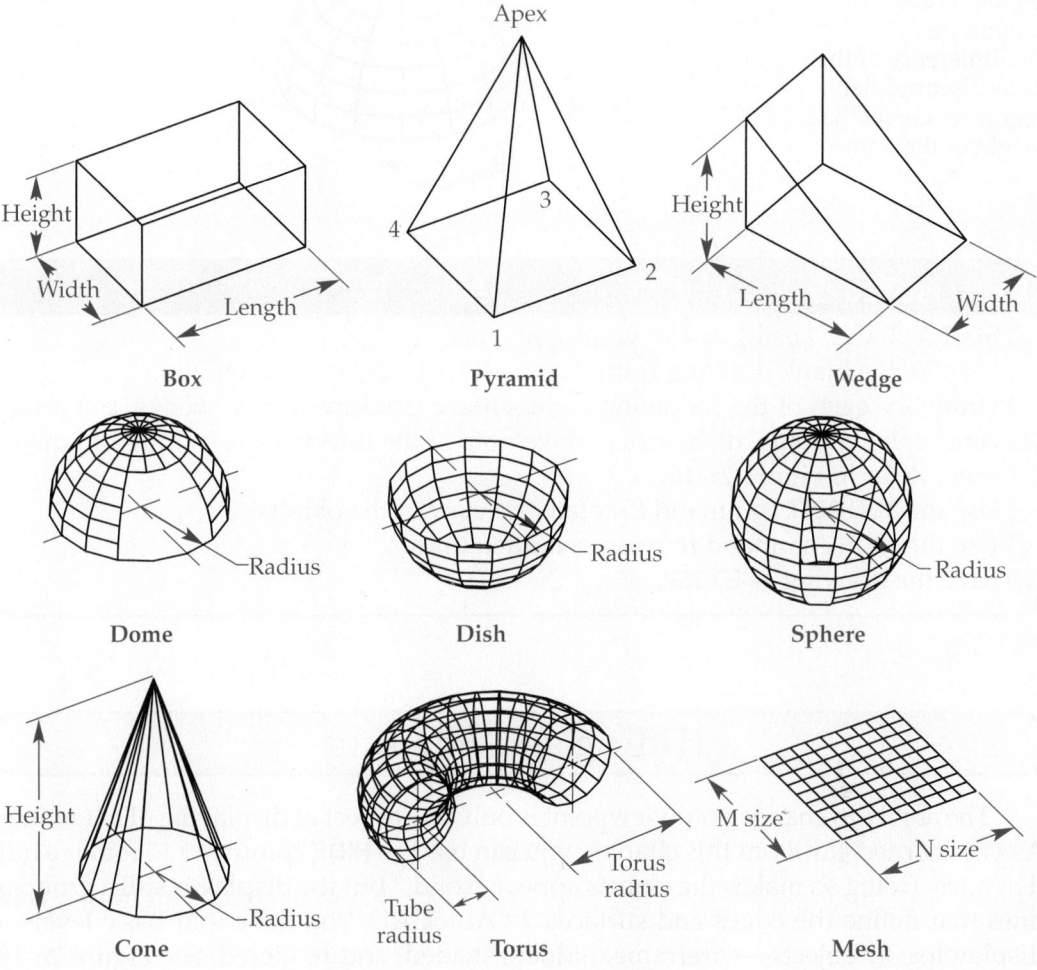

The dome is drawn with its base on the XY plane of the current UCS. To see a 3D view of the object, use the **3DORBIT** command or an isometric viewpoint.

Notice in the previous command sequence that you are asked for longitudinal and latitudinal segments. Longitudinal segments are around the circumference of the dome. Latitudinal segments are the north-south segments on the height of the dome. See **Figure 26-17.** For the surface primitives that contain curved surfaces—sphere, cone, dome, dish, torus—you must provide the number of segments for the object. The more segments used to define a curved surface, the smoother the surface appears. However, more segments also increases screen regeneration times.

---

**PROFESSIONAL TIP**   The number of segments for solids is controlled by the **FACETRES** system variable. Refer to *AutoCAD and its Applications—Advanced.*

---

Figure 26-17.
Longitudinal
segments are
around the
circumference of the
dome. Latitudinal
segments are on the
height of the dome.

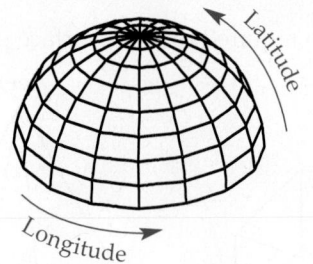

### Exercise 26-5

○ Start AutoCAD using one of your templates.
○ Display the blank drawing from the southwest isometric viewpoint.
○ Draw one each of the following eight surface primitives: box, wedge, pyramid, cone, sphere, dome, dish, torus. Make note of the information required to draw each. Refer to **Figure 26-16.**
○ Use the **3DORBIT** command to rotate the view of the objects.
○ Use the **HIDE** command to remove hidden lines.
○ Save the drawing as EX26-5.

## Hiding and Shading

The ability to change your viewpoint is only one aspect of displaying 3D drawings. As you learned earlier in this chapter, you can use the **HIDE** command to remove hidden lines. Doing so makes the objects appear "solid," but the display is still a group of lines that define the edges and surfaces. In AutoCAD, you have four basic levels of display for 3D objects—wireframe, hidden, shaded, and rendered. See **Figure 26-18.** Creating hidden and shaded displays are discussed in this section. For complete coverage of rendering with AutoCAD, refer to *AutoCAD and its Applications—Advanced.*

Figure 26-18.
The four basic levels of display available for a 3D model—wireframe, hidden, shaded, and rendered. (Model courtesy of Autodesk, Inc.)

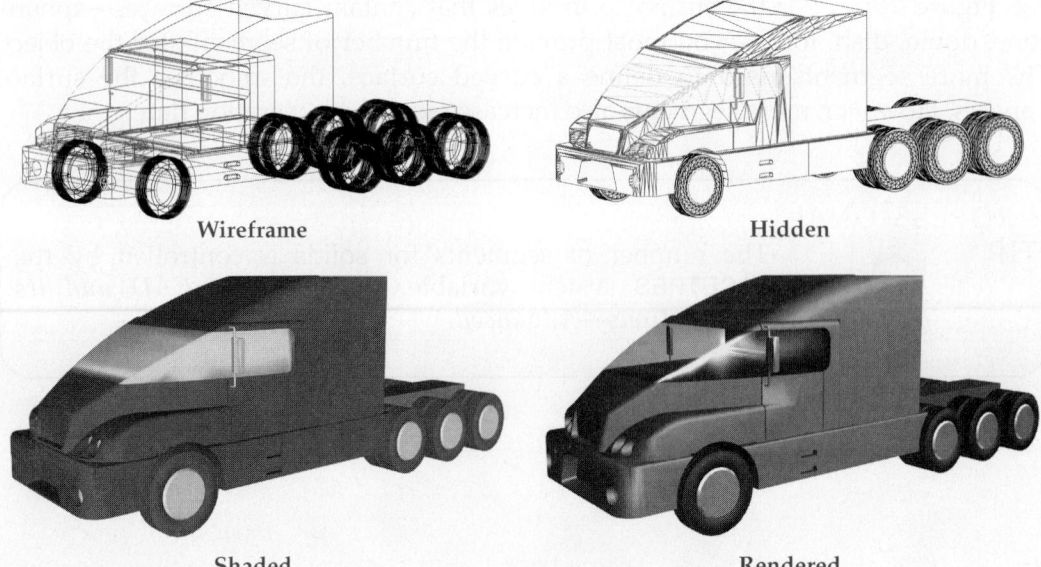

Wireframe

Hidden

Shaded

Rendered

# HIDE Command

The **HIDE** command was introduced earlier in this chapter. It is used to display a 3D object with hidden lines removed. Hidden lines are those lines on an object that would not be visible if the object were truly solid. For example, the features on the opposite side, or back, of the object would not be visible. Some internal features may also be hidden by the object. In a traditional 2D isometric drawing, these lines are drawn in a hidden linetype. In a wireframe display, all of the lines representing hidden features are visible. The **HIDE** command suppresses the display of these lines. However, the lines are not actually removed from the object.

To access the **HIDE** command, pick the **Hide** button in the **Render** toolbar, select **Hide** from the **View** pull-down menu, or enter HI or HIDE at the Command: prompt:

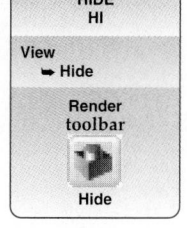

> Command: **HI** *or* **HIDE.**↵
> Regenerating model.
> Command:

The size and complexity of the drawing and the speed of your computer determines how long you must wait for the lines to be hidden. To redisplay the 3D object in a wireframe display, use the **REGEN** command. In addition, any command that performs a regeneration, such as **ZOOM Extents**, redisplays the hidden lines.

---

## Exercise 26-6

○ Start AutoCAD using one of your templates.
○ As solid primitives, draw a sphere, box, and cylinder using your own dimensions.
○ Display the objects in a 3D view using one of the preset isometric views or the **3DORBIT** command. If necessary, move the objects so that at least one is in front of another.
○ Use the **HIDE** command to create a hidden display.
○ Use the **REGEN** command to create a wireframe display.
○ Save the drawing as EX26-6.

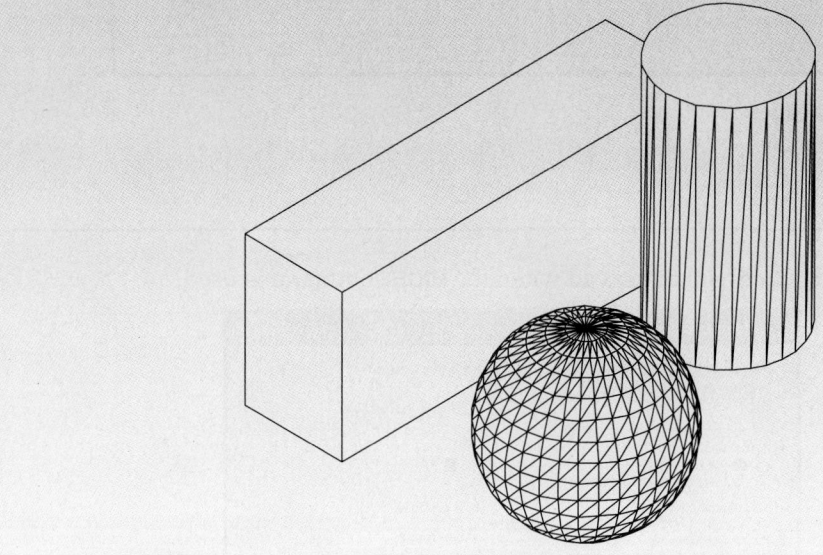

---

# Hidden Line Settings

By default, the **HIDE** command removes hidden lines from the display. However, you can have hidden lines displayed in a different linetype and color instead of removed. To set this, open the **Options** dialog box by right-clicking in the viewport and selecting **Options...** from the shortcut menu. You can also select **Options...** from the **Tools** pull-down menu or type OP or OPTIONS at the Command: prompt.

Once the **Options** dialog box is open, pick the **User Preferences** tab. See **Figure 26-19.** Then, pick the **Hidden Line Settings...** button at the bottom of the tab. The **Hidden Line Settings** dialog box is displayed, **Figure 26-20.** In the **Obscured Lines** area of the dialog box are drop-down lists from which you can select a linetype and color.

**Figure 26-19.**
The **Hidden Line Settings...** button is located in the **User Preferences** tab of the **Options** dialog box.

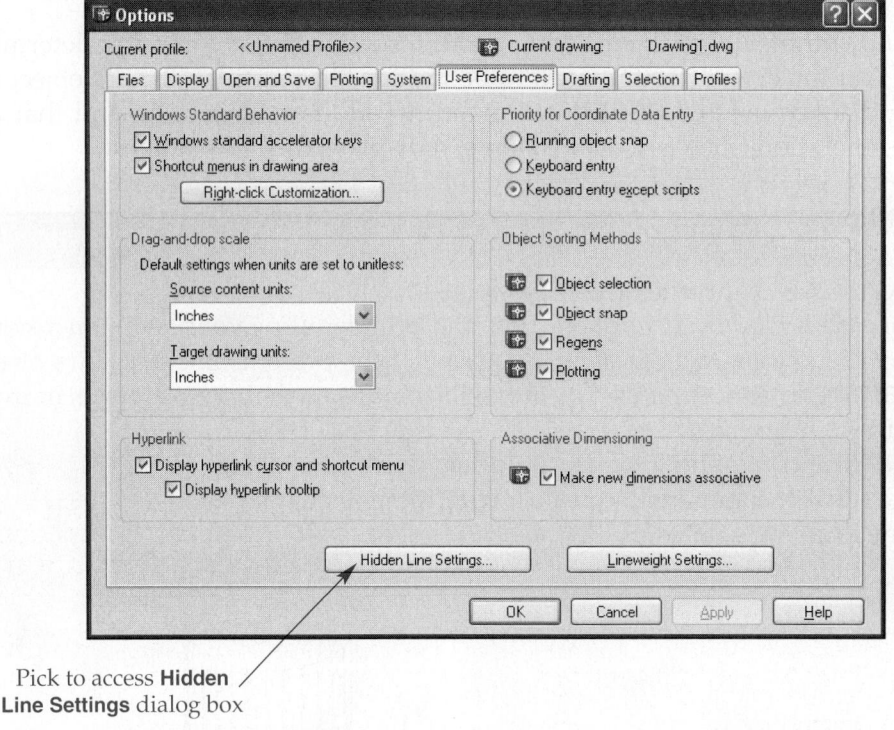

Pick to access **Hidden Line Settings** dialog box

**Figure 26-20.**
Changing how hidden lines are displayed when the **HIDE** command is used.

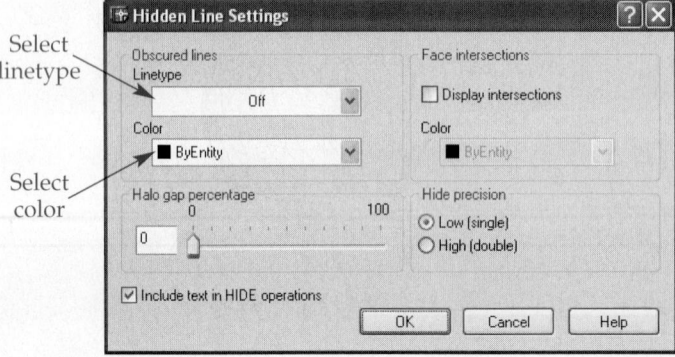

Select linetype

Select color

AutoCAD and its Applications—Basics

When the **Linetype** drop-down list is set to **Off**, the display of hidden lines is suppressed by the **HIDE** command. When a linetype is selected from the drop-down list, hidden lines are displayed in that linetype after the **HIDE** command is used. The linetypes available in the drop-down list are not the same as the linetypes loaded into your drawing.

When a linetype is selected, you can also change the display color of the hidden lines. Simply pick a color in the **Color** drop-down list. To have the hidden lines displayed in the same color as the object, select **ByEntity**, which is the default. The color setting has no effect when the **Linetype** drop-down list is set to **Off**.

When done making settings, pick the **OK** button to close the **Hidden Line Settings** dialog box. Then, pick the **OK** button to close the **Options** dialog box.

## SHADEMODE Command

The **SHADEMODE** command is used to create both hidden and shaded displays. In a shaded display, hidden lines are removed as with the **HIDE** command. In addition, the surfaces of the object are shaded in the same color as the object's display color. Refer to **Figure 26-18.** The **SHADE** command can also be used to shade an object. However, its functionality has been replaced by the **SHADEMODE** command, which offers much more flexibility.

To access the **SHADEMODE** command, select **Shade** from the **View** pull-down menu. Then, select a level of shading in the cascading menu. You can also type SHADEMODE at the Command: prompt and select an option. The **SHADEMODE** command options, or levels of shading, are:

- **2D Wireframe.** Creates a wireframe display in which all lines are displayed in their correct linetype and line weight.
- **3D Wireframe.** Creates a wireframe display in which all lines are displayed in a thin, continuous linetype regardless of their setting.
- **Hidden.** Creates a hidden display in which all lines are displayed in a thin, continuous linetype.
- **Flat Shaded.** Creates a shaded display. Smoothing groups are not applied to the objects. Therefore, all objects with curved surfaces appear faceted, or made up of flat faces.
- **Gouraud Shaded.** Creates a shaded display. Smoothing groups are applied to the objects. Therefore, curved surfaces appear smooth, not faceted. This is considered the highest shading level.
- **Flat Shaded, Edges On.** Creates a shaded display similar to the **Flat Shaded** option, but the edges are displayed. This would be like a flat-shaded **Hidden** option.
- **Gouraud Shaded, Edges On.** Creates a shaded display similar to the **Gouraud Shaded** option, but the edges are displayed. This would be like a gouraud-shaded **Hidden** option.

These options are also available within the **3DORBIT** command. With the **3DORBIT** command active, right-click to display the shortcut menu. Then, select **Shading Modes** to display the cascading menu. The **SHADEMODE** options are in this cascading menu.

The **REGEN** command does not redisplay a wireframe display after a hidden or shaded display is created with the **SHADEMODE** command. In order to redisplay a wireframe, you must use the **SHADEMODE** command and select either the **2D Wireframe** or **3D Wireframe** option. The **2D Wireframe** option is the type of wireframe display you have been working with to this point.

PROFESSIONAL
TIP

If you do a lot of drawing in 3D, you will probably find yourself using the **SHADEMODE** command very frequently. **SHADEMODE** is a good command for an alias. Using a command alias such as SM makes it much easier to enter the command. Creating command aliases is covered in Chapter 27.

## Exercise 26-7

○ Start AutoCAD and open the drawing Oil Module.dwg located in the AutoCAD Samples folder. Save it as EX26-7.
○ Type SHADEMODE at the Command: prompt (do not use the pull-down menu). Notice the default is **Gouraud**, which is the current shading level.
○ Select the **3D Wireframe** option. Notice how the display changes. This is a large model and may take some time to complete the operation.
○ Using the pull-down menu, change the level of shading from **3D Wireframe** to **Hidden; Flat; Flat Shaded, Edges On; Gouraud Shaded**; and then **Gouraud Shaded, Edges On**. Notice how the display changes for each option.
○ Use the **REGEN** command. Notice that the display remains shaded.
○ Use the **SHADEMODE** command and create a 2D wireframe display.
○ Save the drawing.

## Chapter Test

*Answer the following questions on a separate sheet of paper.*

1. What are the three coordinates needed to locate any point in 3D space?
2. In a 2D drawing, what is the value for the Z coordinate?
3. What purpose does the right-hand rule serve?
4. Which three fingers are used in the right-hand rule?
5. Which command controls the display of the UCS icon?
6. What is the definition of a *viewpoint?*
7. How many preset isometric viewpoints does AutoCAD have? List them.
8. How does changing the UCS impact using one of the preset isometric viewpoints?
9. List the six preset orthographic viewpoints.
10. When using a preset orthographic viewpoint, what happens to the UCS?
11. Which command allows you to dynamically change your viewpoint using an on-screen trackball?
12. Define *wireframe display.*
13. Define *hidden display.*
14. Define *wireframe object.*
15. Define *surface model.*
16. Define *solid model.*
17. Define *primitive.*
18. List the six solid primitives available in AutoCAD.
19. List the four surface primitives for which you must set the number of segments.
20. What are the four basic levels of display for 3D objects in AutoCAD?
21. Briefly describe how to have hidden lines displayed in red when the **HIDE** command is used.

22. List the seven options available with the **SHADEMODE** command.
23. What is the difference between a 2D wireframe and a 3D wireframe display created with the **SHADEMODE** command.
24. After the **SHADEMODE** command is used to create a shaded display, how do you redisplay a wireframe display?
25. Which shading level is considered the highest?

## Drawing Problems

1. Choose Problem 4, 5, or 6 from Chapter 25 and draw it using solid primitives. You will need to use the primitives as "building blocks" to create the object. Use object snaps and the **COPY**, **MOVE**, and **ROTATE** commands as needed. Change viewpoints to help in construction. Save the drawing as P26-1.

*For Problems 2–5, draw the objects in 3D form. Use solid primitives and object snaps with the **COPY**, **MOVE**, and **ROTATE** commands as needed. You will need to use the primitives as "building blocks" to create the object. Display the drawings from three different viewpoints. Use the **HIDE** and **SHADEMODE** commands as you draw to help in visualization. Save the drawings as P26-2, P26-3, P26-4, and P26-5.*

2.

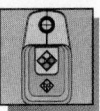

3.

4.

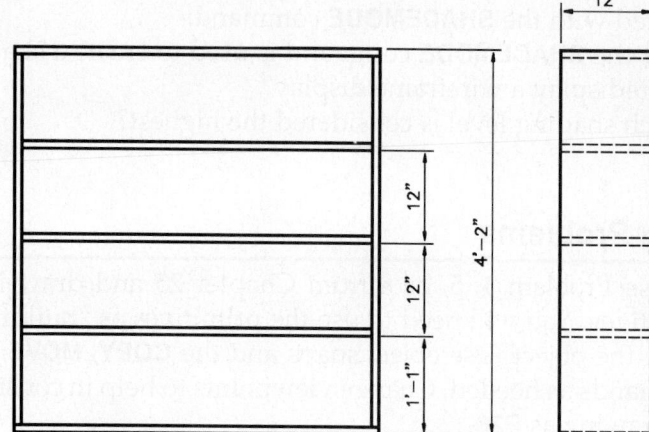

5.

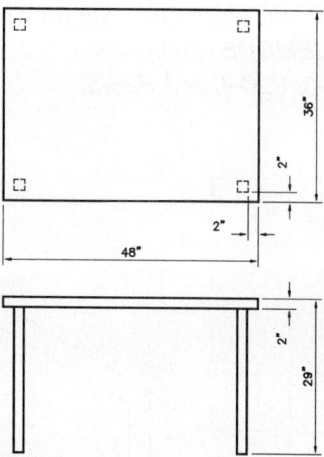

6. Construct a 3D model of the table shown.
   A. Use solid and/or surface primitives.
   B. Use the dimensions given.
   C. Use the **HIDE** and **SHADEMODE** commands as you go to help with visualization.
   D. Plot the table in wireframe display and hidden display.
   E. Alter the design of the table to include rounded tabletop corners or rounded feet. Try replacing the rectangular feet with spherical feet.

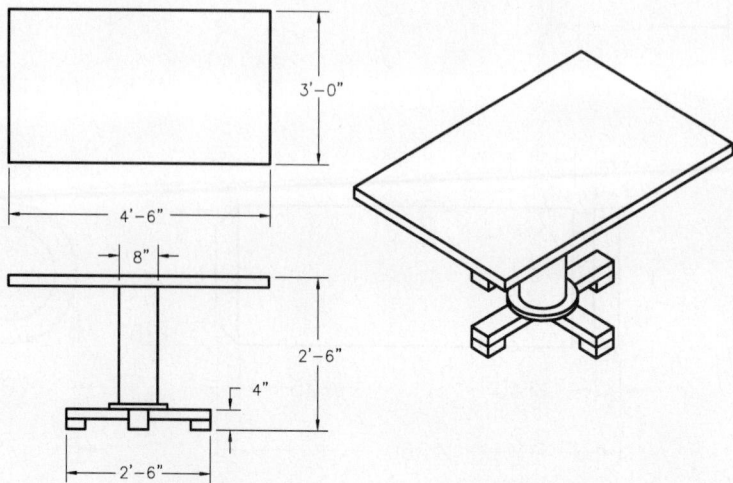

## CHAPTER 27

# External Commands, Script Files, and Slide Shows

## Learning Objectives

After completing this chapter, you will be able to do the following:
- Edit the acad.pgp file.
- Use a text editor to create script files.
- Create a continuous slide show of existing drawings.
- Use the **SLIDELIB** command to create a slide library.

This chapter introduces you to the use of scripts. A *script* is a series of commands and variables listed in a text file. When the script file is activated by AutoCAD, the entire list of commands is performed without additional input from the user. One useful script is a continuous slide show. It is excellent for client presentations, demonstrations, and grading drawings.

Scripts can be written with word processing and text editor programs. The Windows operating system includes three tools for writing ASCII (American Standard Code for Information Interchange) text files: MS-DOS EDIT, Notepad, and WordPad.

## Using Text Editors

As you become more experienced with AutoCAD, you will want to alter the program to suit your specific needs. Most of these alterations are done with a text editor program. Although Notepad lacks many formatting functions found in word processing programs, it can perform the text editing tasks required to customize AutoCAD.

### Word Processors

Many AutoCAD users rely on full-fledged word processing programs to create their text files. There are dozens of word processing programs commercially available. WordPad is a word processor included with Microsoft Windows. Like Notepad, WordPad can be accessed by picking Accessories in the Programs group of the Start menu. See **Figure 27-1**.

Figure 27-1.
Both the Windows
Notepad text editor
and the Windows
WordPad word
processor can be
accessed from the
Accessories menu.

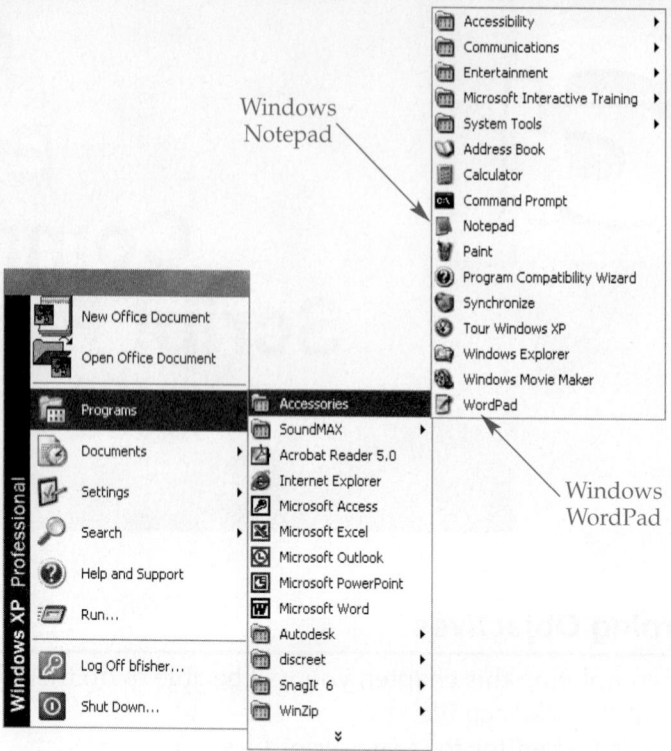

Other familiar Windows-compatible word processors include WordPerfect and Microsoft Word. These are excellent writing tools, but are far more sophisticated than is necessary to create text files for AutoCAD. If you create your AutoCAD text files with a word processor, save the document as a text-only (ASCII) file. This prevents the inclusion of special formatting codes, which makes the file unreadable by AutoCAD.

## Programmer's Text Editors

The best type of text editor, however, is a programmer's text editor. There are a wide variety of inexpensive yet powerful text editors available. These programs are designed for creating the type of files needed to customize AutoCAD. Programmer's editors are recommended over word processors because of their design, size, function, ease of use, and price. Norton Editor and Text Pad are excellent examples of programmer's editors available.

The Visual LISP Editor is a very good editor and is included with AutoCAD. It can be accessed by selecting **Visual LISP Editor** from the **AutoLISP** cascading menu in the **Tools** pull-down menu.

## The **ACAD.PGP** File

The acad.pgp (program parameters) file controls such features of AutoCAD as command aliases and external commands. The acad.pgp file is simply a text file, which can be edited with a word processor text editor. During the AutoCAD installation procedure, this file is placed in the Documents and Settings\\*User*\\Application Data\\Autodesk\\AutoCAD 2004\\R16.0\\enu\\Support folder. A portion of the acad.pgp file is shown in Notepad in **Figure 27-2**.

Modifying the acad.pgp file can be accomplished through the **Tools** pull-down menu. Go to **Tools,** then **Customize,** then **Edit Custom Files**, and then select **Program Parameters** (acad.pgp). This procedure opens Notepad and displays the acad.pgp file.

**Figure 27-2.**
The acad.pgp file opened in Notepad.

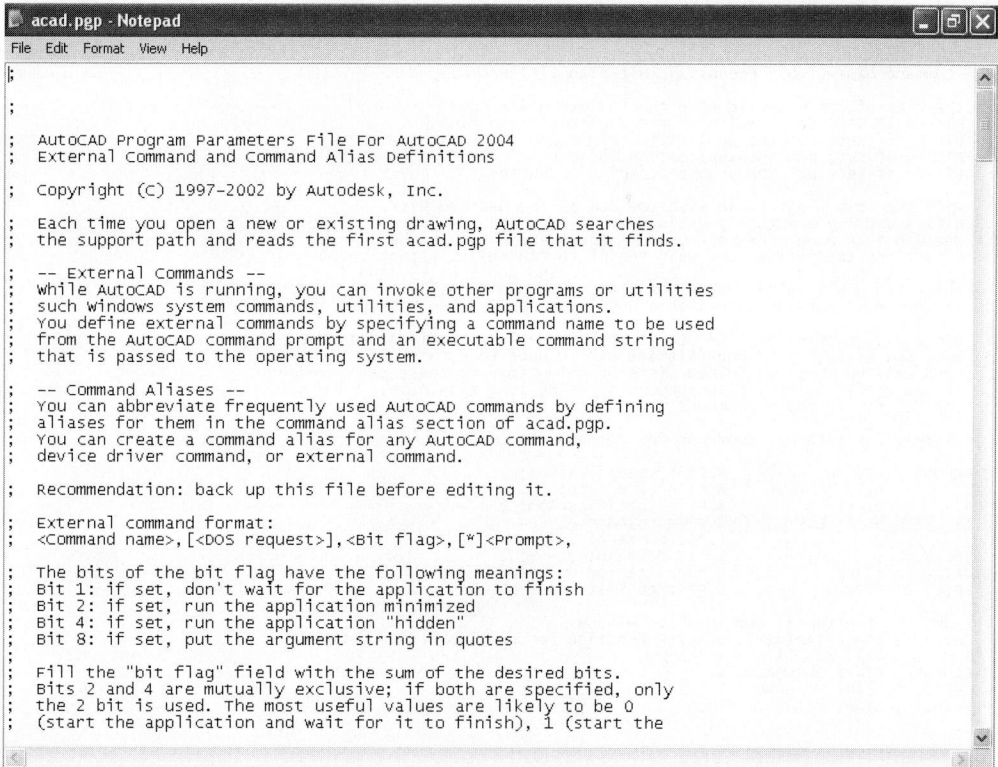

## External Commands

External commands carry out functions that are not part of AutoCAD. Each of these external commands is defined in the acad.pgp file. AutoCAD contains eleven external commands in the acad.pgp file, beginning with **CATALOG**. The first word on each line is the text that is typed at the Command: prompt in order to execute the external command. The second word represents the DOS command or program to be executed.

You can see in **Figure 27-3** that typing EDIT at the Command: prompt runs MS-DOS EDIT, a text editor. A comma separates each field in the EDIT entry. The fields are defined as follows:

- **EDIT.** The command typed at the AutoCAD Command: prompt.
- **START EDIT.** The command or program name executed after the external command name is typed. This is the text that would normally be entered at the DOS prompt (Windows command prompt) to run the text editor. Later in this chapter, instructions are provided for editing the acad.pgp file so you can run your favorite text editor.
- **9.** This bit flag value specifies certain program parameters. The meanings of the bit values are explained in the acad.pgp file.
- **File to edit:.** This is the prompt that appears after the command is typed.

**Figure 27-3.**
External commands are defined in the acad.pgp file.

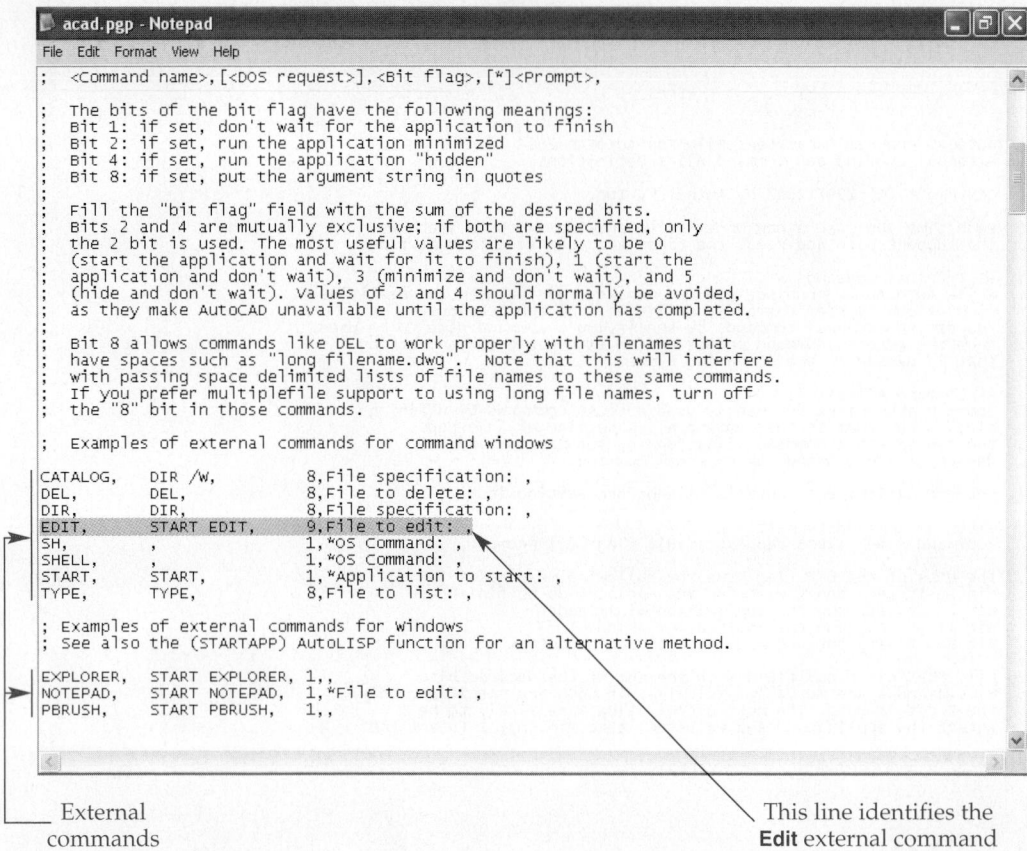

```
; <Command name>,[<DOS request>],<Bit flag>,["]<Prompt>,

;  The bits of the bit flag have the following meanings:
;  Bit 1: if set, don't wait for the application to finish
;  Bit 2: if set, run the application minimized
;  Bit 4: if set, run the application "hidden"
;  Bit 8: if set, put the argument string in quotes

;  Fill the "bit flag" field with the sum of the desired bits.
;  Bits 2 and 4 are mutually exclusive; if both are specified, only
;  the 2 bit is used. The most useful values are likely to be 0
;  (start the application and wait for it to finish), 1 (start the
;  application and don't wait), 3 (minimize and don't wait), and 5
;  (hide and don't wait). Values of 2 and 4 should normally be avoided,
;  as they make AutoCAD unavailable until the application has completed.

;  Bit 8 allows commands like DEL to work properly with filenames that
;  have spaces such as "long filename.dwg".  Note that this will interfere
;  with passing space delimited lists of file names to these same commands.
;  If you prefer multiplefile support to using long file names, turn off
;  the "8" bit in those commands.

;  Examples of external commands for command windows

CATALOG,    DIR /w,         8,File specification: ,
DEL,        DEL,            8,File to delete: ,
DIR,        DIR,            8,File specification: ,
EDIT,       START EDIT,     9,File to edit: ,
SH,         ,               1,*OS Command: ,
SHELL,      ,               1,*OS Command: ,
START,      START,          1,*Application to start: ,
TYPE,       TYPE,           8,File to list: ,

;  Examples of external commands for windows
;  See also the (STARTAPP) AutoLISP function for an alternative method.

EXPLORER,   START EXPLORER, 1,,
NOTEPAD,    START NOTEPAD,  1,*File to edit: ,
PBRUSH,     START PBRUSH,   1,,
```

External commands

This line identifies the **Edit** external command

## Command Aliases

AutoCAD allows you to abbreviate command names. This feature is called *command aliasing*. A list of predefined aliases furnished with AutoCAD can be displayed by viewing the contents of the acad.pgp file. You can do this by loading the file into Notepad or another text editor. Scroll down past the list of external commands and you will see the list of command aliases. This is an extensive list containing over 200 aliases. An example of some command aliases is provided here. See Appendix F for the complete listing.

```
A,      *ARC
C,      *CIRCLE
CO,     *COPY
E,      *ERASE
L,      *LINE
LA,     *LAYER
LT,     *LINETYPE
M,      *MOVE
P,      *PAN
PL,     *PLINE
R,      *REDRAW
T,      *MTEXT
Z,      *ZOOM
```

You can easily create your own aliases by editing this file. For example, if you want to add an alias **PP** for the **PLOT** command, enter the following below the **POLYGON** command in the acad.pgp file:

```
PP,     *PLOT
```

AutoCAD and its Applications—Basics

Figure 27-4.
The **Re-initialization**
dialog box.

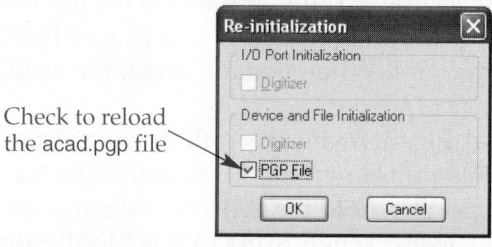

Check to reload
the acad.pgp file

Be sure to include the asterisk since it indicates to AutoCAD that this is an alias. Save the Notepad file. The revised acad.pgp file will not work until you restart AutoCAD or reload the acad.pgp file by entering the **REINIT** command. This displays the **Re-initialization** dialog box, shown in **Figure 27-4.** Pick the **PGP File** check box in this dialog box and then pick **OK** to reinitialize the acad.pgp file. After you reinitialize the acad.pgp file, your new command alias will work.

---

**NOTE**

The **Re-initialization** dialog box can also be used if you have one of your serial ports, such as COM1, configured for both a plotter and a digitizer. If you change the cable from plotter to digitizer, pick the **Digitizer** check boxes in both areas of the dialog box to reinitiate the digitizer.

---

## Editing the **ACAD.PGP** File

There are several tools available to edit the acad.pgp file. Notepad, MS-DOS EDIT, WordPad, or another text editor may be used. The easiest method of editing is to open the file with Notepad using the **Program Parameters** (acad.pgp) selection from the **Edit Custom Files** cascading menu from the **Customize** menu selection from the **Tools** pull-down menu.

---

**PROFESSIONAL TIP**

Always make backup copies of AutoCAD text files before editing them. If you "corrupt" one of these files through incorrect editing techniques, simply delete that file and restore the original.

---

The acad.pgp file can be easily altered to specify your personal text editor instead of the default MS-DOS Edit. For this example, we will set up an external command to access an imaginary editor called TextEditor. If you are currently running AutoCAD, use the method described above to open the acad.pgp file in Notepad.

Once the acad.pgp file is displayed in Notepad, you can move the flashing text cursor around the screen with the left, right, up, and down arrows, as well as the [Home], [Page Up], [Page Down], [Insert], [Delete], and [End] keys. You can also move the text cursor with your pointing device. Use the down arrow key or your pointing device to move the text cursor to the end of the line labeled:

    EDIT,    START EDIT,    9,File to edit: ,

Hit the [Enter] key to start a new line in the file. Type in the following new line of text:

    TE,      START TEXTEDIT,      9,File to edit: ,

---

Use the space bar to line up the new text with the text on the previous line to make it easier to read. These changes allow you to run TextEditor by typing TE at the AutoCAD Command: prompt. When you are done, the acad.pgp file should appear as shown in **Figure 27-5**.

To save the edited file, activate the pull-down menus at the top of the screen. Select **Save** from the **File** pull-down menu. To return to AutoCAD, press [Alt]+[Tab] to display the Task List, and then hold the [Alt] key while repeatedly pressing the [Tab] key. This cycles through the icons. When AutoCAD is highlighted, release the [Alt] key.

If you try using the new **TE** command in AutoCAD now, it will not work because AutoCAD is still using the original version of the acad.pgp file. Before the **TE** command can function, you must reinitialize the acad.pgp file by restarting AutoCAD or executing the **REINIT** command.

**Figure 27-5.**
**TE** has been added as a new command that will execute the TextEdit program.

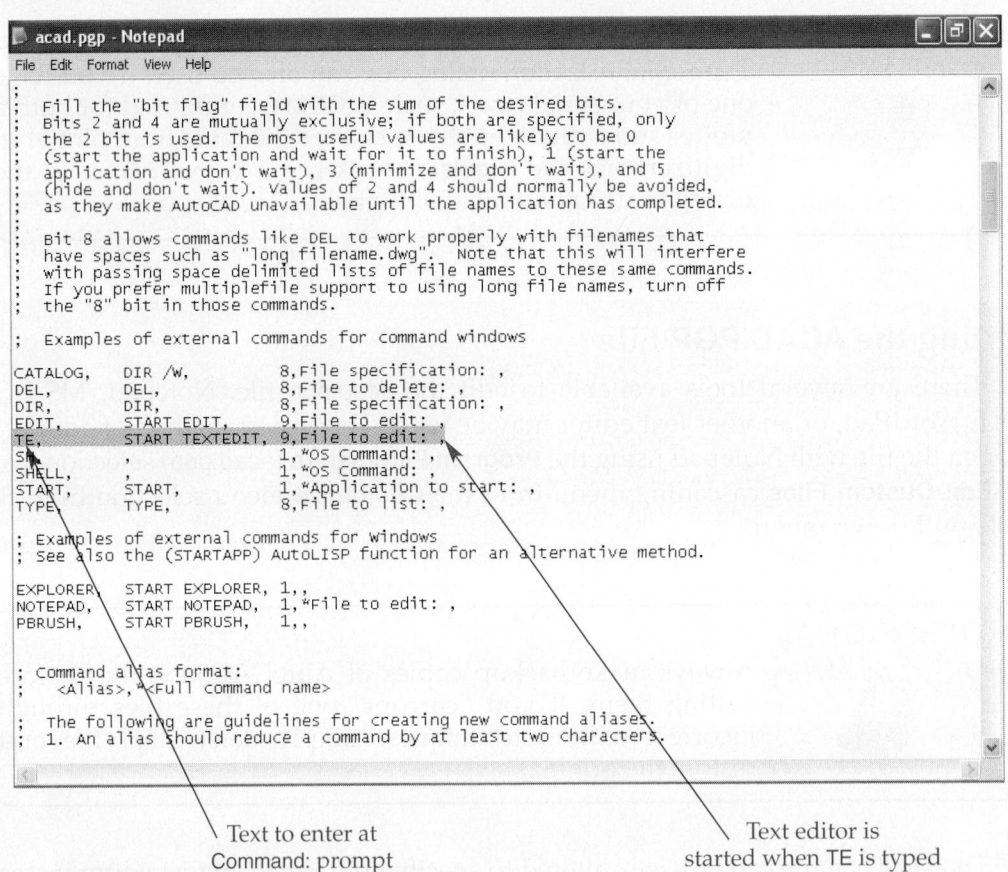

Text to enter at
Command: prompt

Text editor is
started when TE is typed

NOTE:  If you add an external command that references a new program, such as the text editor example above, you must make sure that the path to the program is listed in the **Support File Search Path** area in **Files** tab of **Options** dialog box. If the path to the program is not listed, it must be added before the command will work.

○ Open Windows Explorer and create a new folder named TextEdit in a location of your choice.

○ In Windows Explorer, locate and select the write.exe file in the Windows/System32 folder.

○ Holding the right-button on your pointing device, drag the file to the TextEdit folder. Select Copy Here from the shortcut menu.

○ Locate the file write.exe in the TextEdit folder and rename it to TextEdit.exe.

○ Load AutoCAD and open Notepad.

○ Use Notepad to add the **TE** external command to the acad.pgp file as described in the previous text. Make sure that you have a backup copy of acad.pgp before making your changes. Save the file and exit Notepad.

○ Open the **Options** dialog box and select the **Files** tab. Expand the **Support Files Search Path** tree and pick the **Add...** button. Enter C:\TextEdit in the text box.

○ Use the **REINIT** command.

○ Type TE at the Command: prompt.

## Creating Script Files to Automate AutoCAD

A *script file* is a list of commands that AutoCAD executes in sequence without input from the user. Scripts enable nonprogrammers to automate AutoCAD functions. Scripts can be used for specific functions, such as plotting a drawing with the correct **PLOT** command values and settings, or creating a slide show. A good working knowledge of AutoCAD commands is needed before you can confidently create a script file.

When writing a script file, use one command or option per line in the text file. This makes the file easier to fix if the script does not work properly. A return is specified by pressing [Enter] after typing a command. If the next option of a command is a default value to be accepted, press [Enter] again. This leaves a blank line in the script file, which represents pressing [Enter].

### Creating a Script

The following example shows how a script file can be used to save a drawing in AutoCAD 2000 DWG format. Write the script with Notepad or another text editor. Save the file as convert.scr in the Documents and Settings\\*User*\\Application Data\\Autodesk\\AutoCAD 2004\\R16.0\\enu\\Support folder.

**CAUTION**

A single incorrect entry in a script file can cause it to malfunction. Test the keystrokes at the keyboard as you write the script file and record them for future reference.

Many text editors and word processors save documents with .txt or .doc file extensions by default. Since scripts must end with the .scr file extension, you may have to use the Save As option in the text editor or word processor. Then, select All Files from the Save as type: menu in the Save As dialog box and save the file.

A comment can be inserted in a script file to provide information to the reader. Simply place a semicolon as the first character on the line and AutoCAD will not process that line. For example, the first line in the following script is a comment for information only:

; Saves the current drawing in AutoCAD 2000 DWG format. *(comment only)*
FILEDIA          *(sets the system variable that controls file dialog boxes)*
0 *(disables file dialog boxes)*
SAVEAS          *(command that saves the drawing in a format of your choice)*
2000    *(specifies the drawing is to be saved in the AutoCAD 2000 DWG format)*
    *(Enter accepts default file name and location)*
Y *(replaces the original file with the converted file)*
FILEDIA          *(sets the system variable that controls file dialog boxes)*
1 *(enables file dialog boxes)*

Figure 27-6 shows how the script file appears in the Windows Notepad.

Figure 27-6.
The conversion script file as it appears in Windows Notepad.

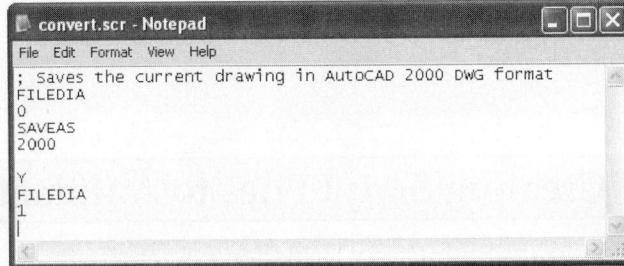

## Running a Script

SCRIPT
SCR

Tools
➥ Run Script...

To run the script, select **Run Script...** from the **Tools** pull-down menu or enter SCR or SCRIPT at the Command: prompt. Next, select the file name convert.scr from the **Select Script File** dialog box. See **Figure 27-7.** Then sit back and watch the script run.

All the commands, options, and text screens associated with the commands in the script are displayed in rapid succession on the screen. If the script stops before completion, a problem has occurred. Flip the screen to the **AutoCAD Text Window** ([F2]) to determine the last command executed. Return to your text editor and correct the problem. Most often, there are too many or too few returns. Another problem is spaces at the end of a line. If you suspect these errors, retype the line.

**Figure 27-7.**
The **Select Script File** dialog box.

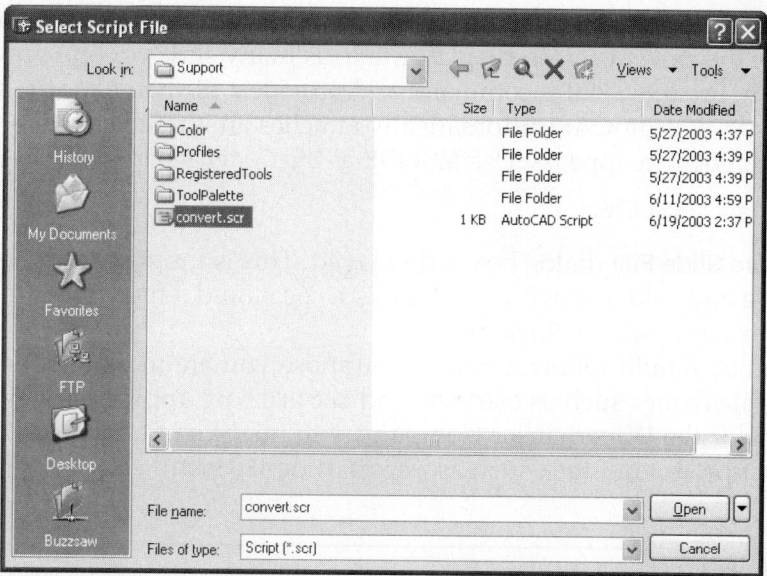

## Slides and Slide Shows

A *slide* in AutoCAD, similar to a slide in photography, is a snapshot of the drawing area display. Because of its nature, it cannot be edited or plotted. Slides can be viewed one at a time or as a continuous show. This is why slides are excellent for demonstrations, presentations, displays, and evaluation procedures.

You can create an impressive portfolio using a slide show. A *slide show* is a group of slides that are displayed at preset intervals. The slide show is controlled by a script file, which, as you learned from the previous examples, is a list of commands. Each slide is displayed for a specific length of time. The show can be continuous or can display each slide only once.

## Making and Viewing Slides

Creating slides is easy. First display the drawing for which you need a slide. You might display the entire drawing or zoom to a specific area or feature. AutoCAD creates a slide of the current screen display. Make as many slides of one drawing as you want. For each, use the **MSLIDE** command and provide a file name for the slide. Do not enter a file type, as AutoCAD automatically attaches an .sld file extension. If **FILEDIA** is set to 1, a dialog box appears. Use **MSLIDE** at the Command: prompt as follows:

MSLIDE

> Command: **MSLIDE**↵

The **Create Slide File** dialog box is displayed. This is the standard file dialog box. Pick the drive and folder in which the file is to be stored, enter the name in the **File name:** text box, and pick the **Save** button.

Slide names should follow a pattern. Suppose you are making slides for a class called cad1. File names such as cad1sld1 and cad1sld2 are appropriate. If working on project #4305 for the Weyerhauser Company, you might name the slide to reflect the client name or project number, such as weyersld1 or 4305sld1.

**PROFESSIONAL TIP**

To create a slide file at the highest resolution, set **VIEWRES** to its maximum value of 20000 before using the **MSLIDE** command. After making the slide, restore **VIEWRES** to its previous value.

VSLIDE

Viewing a slide is as simple as making one. Enter VSLIDE at the Command: prompt to initiate the **VSLIDE** command.

> Command: **VSLIDE**↵

The **Select Slide File** dialog box appears. Pick the slide you want to display and pick **OK**. The slide is displayed in the graphics window.

**PROFESSIONAL TIP**

Keep the AutoCAD 2004 folder free of drawings, slides, and AutoLISP files. This speeds the computer's access to AutoCAD files. Create a separate folder for slides or save slides on a diskette. If using diskettes, be sure to give the appropriate file name when creating slides.

### Exercise 27-3

- ○ Load any one of your drawings into the drawing editor.
- ○ Create a slide of the entire drawing, using an appropriate file name.
- ○ Make slides of two more drawings. Use similar naming techniques.
- ○ View each of the slides as they are created.
- ○ These slides are required to complete the next exercise.

AutoCAD and its Applications—Basics

# Writing a Slide Show Script File

A slide show script file contains only two or three commands. This depends on whether it is a single pass or continuous show. A slide show script file typically contains the following commands:

- **VSLIDE.** This command is used to display a slide. The name of the slide follows the command. If the slide name is preceded by an asterisk (*), the slide is preloaded and displayed at the following **VSLIDE** command. This second command is not followed by a slide name, since the slide is already preloaded.
- **DELAY.** Any slide file can be displayed for up to approximately 33 seconds using this command. Delays are given in milliseconds. A delay of four seconds is written as DELAY 4000.
- **RSCRIPT.** This command is used at the end of a continuous script file. It causes the script to repeat.

To create a slide show, begin by writing a script file with a text editor. The script in **Figure 27-8** creates a slide show with four slides. Each slide appears for three seconds, and the script repeats. Notice that the next slide is preloaded while the previous one is viewed.

In order to display the slides, AutoCAD must first locate them. If the slide files are located in one of the folders listed in the **Support Files Search Path** area of the **Files** tab of the **Options** dialog box, AutoCAD can locate them automatically. If the slide files are not in one of the folders listed, you must either add the folder to the list or supply the full paths (drive letter:\folder\file name) of the slide files in the **VSLIDE** commands in the script.

Figure 27-8.
The show.scr script file as it appears in the Windows Notepad.

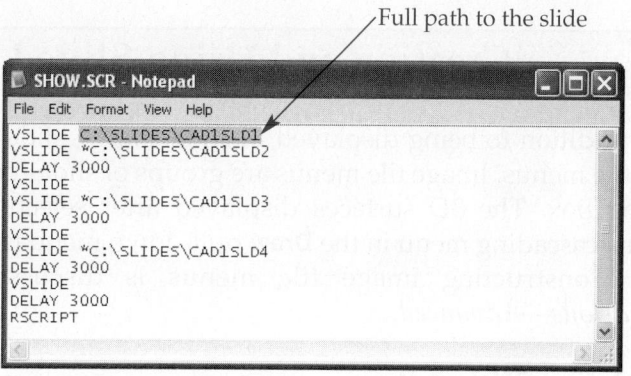

Full path to the slide

# Viewing the Slide Show

The slide show is started by entering SCR or SCRIPT at the Command: prompt or by picking **Run Script...** from the **Tools** pull-down menu. Select the script file name show.scr from the **Select Script File** dialog box.

The show begins and the commands in the script file are displayed at the Command: prompt as the slides appear. To stop the show, press the [Backspace] key. You can then work on a drawing, use DOS commands, or work with a text editor on another script file. When finished, resume the slide show where it left off by entering RESUME. Any script file can be interrupted and restarted in this manner.

If your slide show encounters an error and fails to finish the first time through, do not panic. Take the following steps to "debug," or correct, problems in your script file.

1. Run the script to see where it crashes (quits working).
2. Check the command line for the last command that was executed.

3. Look for error messages, such as:
   - **Can't open slide file** *xxxxx*. This indicates an incorrect slide file name.
   - *xxxxx* **Unknown command.** A command may be spelled incorrectly or a space may be left at the end of the line.
   - **Requires an integer value.** The delay value contains characters other than numerals or ends with a space.
4. Correct the problem in the script file and save the file.
5. Test the script.

The most common errors are misspelled commands and spaces at the end of lines. If you suspect there is a space at the end of a line, it is best to delete the line and retype it. If you use Notepad, it is easy to see if a space exists. The flashing cursor, when placed at the end of a line, does not rest on the last character.

---

### Exercise 27-4

- ○ Create a script file named EX27-4. Use Notepad or your own text editor. It is not necessary to be in the AutoCAD drawing editor to create the script file.
- ○ Include the three slides created in Exercise 27-3. If these slides have not been created, make slides of any three of your drawings.
- ○ Delay each slide for two seconds.
- ○ Make the show run continuously.
- ○ Run the slide show. Correct any errors and run it again until it recycles without failing.

---

## Creating and Using Slide Libraries

In addition to being displayed in slide shows, slide files are also used to create image tile menus. Image tile menus are groups of slides or vector images displayed in a dialog box. The 3D surfaces displayed after selecting **3D Surfaces...** from the **Surfaces** cascading menu in the **Draw** pull-down menu is an example of an image tile menu. Constructing image tile menus is discussed in *AutoCAD and its Applications—Advanced*.

### Creating a Slide Library

To create a slide library, you must use a utility program called slidelib.exe, which operates from the DOS prompt. By default, the slidelib.exe utility program is installed in the Program Files\AutoCAD 2004 folder.

After entering the **SLIDELIB** command, list the paths and filenames of the slides that are to be included in the slide library. For example, suppose you have four slides of pipe fittings in the \pipe subdirectory of the AutoCAD 2004 folder. Compile these files in a slide library called PIPE in the following manner:

SLIDELIB

```
Command: SH↵
OS Command: SLIDELIB PIPE↵
SLIDELIB 1.2 (3/8/89)
(C) Copyright 1987-1989, 1994, 1995 Autodesk, Inc.
   All Rights Reserved
\Program Files\AutoCAD 2004\PIPE\90elbow↵
\Program Files\AutoCAD 2004\PIPE\45elbow↵
\Program Files\AutoCAD 2004\PIPE\tee↵
\Program Files\AutoCAD 2004\PIPE\cap↵
↵
↵
Exit
Command:
```

After entering the last slide, press [Enter] three times to end the **SLIDELIB** command. The new slide library file is saved as pipe.slb.

## Viewing Slide Library Slides

**VSLIDE**

The **VSLIDE** command is also used to view slides contained in a slide library. First change **FILEDIA** to 0. Then, enter the **VSLIDE** command and provide the library name plus the slide name in parentheses as follows:

> Command: **FILEDIA**
> New value for FILEDIA <1>: **0**
>
> Command: **VSLIDE**↵
> Enter name of slide file to view: *<current directory>* **PIPE(90ELBOW)**

Use the **REDRAW** command to remove the slide from the screen to display the previous drawing.

---

**NOTE:** The path for the slide libraries must be listed in the **Support Files Search Path** area of the **Files** tab of the **Options** dialog box.

---

## Using the Slide Library in a Slide Show

The advantage of using a slide library for a slide show is that you do not need to preload slides. The script for a slide show of the four slides in the pipe.slb file would appear as follows:

```
VSLIDE PIPE(90ELBOW)
DELAY 1000
VSLIDE PIPE(45ELBOW)
DELAY 1000
VSLIDE PIPE(TEE)
DELAY 1000
VSLIDE PIPE(CAP)
DELAY 1000
REDRAW
```

The **REDRAW** command at the end of the slide show clears the screen and replaces the previous display. An **RSCRIPT** command instead of **REDRAW** repeats the show continuously.

---

## Chapter Test

*Answer the following questions on a separate sheet of paper.*

1. What precautions should you take when using a word processor to create text files for AutoCAD?
2. How do you activate Windows Notepad from the AutoCAD Command: prompt, and what is the name of the file that allows you to do it?
3. If you edit the acad.pgp file from within AutoCAD, what must you do for the new file definitions to take effect?
4. Describe external commands.
5. Commands located in the acad.pgp file are executed by _____.
6. Name the parts of a command listing found in the acad.pgp file.
7. What is a command alias, and how would you write one for the **POLYGON** command?
8. Define *script file.*
9. Why is it a good idea to put one command on each line of a script file?
10. List two common reasons why a script file might not work.
11. What two commands allow you to make and view slides?
12. What file extension is assigned to slide files?
13. Explain why it is a good idea to keep slide files in a separate folder rather than in the AutoCAD 2004 folder.
14. List the three commands used when writing a slide show.
15. To stop a slide show, press the _____ key.
16. How do you begin a slide show that has been stopped?
17. Briefly explain the method used to create a slide library.
18. Suppose you want to view a slide named VIEW1, which is in a slide library file called VIEWS. How must you enter its name at the Enter name of slide file to view: prompt?
19. What is the principal difference between a slide show script file written for a slide library and one written for a group of slides?

## Problems

1. If you use a text editor or word processor other than MS-DOS EDIT or Notepad, create a new command in the acad.pgp file that loads the text editor.

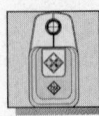

2. Create a new command for the acad.pgp file that activates the Windows Calculator.

3. Write a script file called notes.scr that does the following:
   A. Executes the **TEXT** command.
   B. Selects the **Style** option.
   C. Enters a style name.
   D. Selects the last point using the "@" symbol.
   E. Enters a text height of .25.
   F. Enters a rotation angle of 0.
   G. Inserts the text: NOTES:.
   H. Selects the **TEXT** command again.
   I. Enters location coordinates for first note.
   J. Enters a text height of .125.
   K. Enters a rotation angle of 0.
   L. Inserts the text: 1. INTERPRET DIMENSIONS AND TOLERANCES PER ASME Y14.5.
   M. Enters an [Enter] keystroke.
   N. Inserts the text: 2. REMOVE ALL BURRS AND SHARP EDGES.
   O. Enters the [Enter] twice at the Command: prompt to exit the command.

   Immediately before this script file is used, select the **ID** command and pick the point where you want the notes to begin. That point will be the "last point" used in the script file for the location of the word NOTES:. The script file, when executed, should draw the following:

   > NOTES:
   > 1. INTERPRET DIMENSIONS AND TOLERANCES PER ASME Y14.5.
   > 2. REMOVE ALL BURRS AND SHARP EDGES.

4. Create a slide show of your best AutoCAD drawings. This slide show should be considered as part of your portfolio for potential employers. Place all of the slides and the script file on a floppy disk. Make two copies of the portfolio disk on separate diskettes. Keep the following guidelines in mind:
   A. Do not delay slides longer than 5 seconds. You can always press the [Backspace] key to view a slide longer.
   B. One view of a drawing is sufficient unless the drawing is complex. If so, make additional slides of the drawing's details.
   C. Create a cover slide or title page slide that displays your name.
   D. Create an ending slide that says THE END.

5. Create a slide show that illustrates specific types of drawings. For example, you might make a slide show for dimensioned mechanical drawings or for electrical drawings. Having these specialized slide shows in your portfolio is useful if you apply for a job in a specific discipline. Store all slide shows on the same disk. Identify slide shows by their content as follows: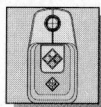

   > mech.scr—Mechanical
   > arch.scr—Architectural
   > pipe.scr—Piping
   > struct.scr—Structural
   > elect.scr—Electrical or Electronics
   > map.scr—Mapping
   > civil.scr—Civil

# APPENDIX A

# Glossary of Computer Terms

This appendix lists and defines some of the most commonly used terms in computer applications. It is intended as a reference for AutoCAD users who wish to review related hardware and software terminology.

## A

**Accelerator board:** A *graphics card* designed to increase the speed and power of the graphics processing duties of a computer. An accelerator board has its own microprocessor (CPU) and relieves the computer's CPU of some of the processing work. Accelerator boards may allow resolution of up to 1600 × 1200 and up to 16.7 million colors. Many industrial applications need high-end graphics accelerator boards because of the complexity of the models, renderings, and animations.

## B

**Bitmap:** A representative image consisting of rows and columns of dots, also known as a *raster image*. The number of dots in a bitmap defines the resolution of the image. A bitmap has no dimensional values. Many paint and draw programs create bitmap images and files. In AutoCAD, *vector images* are produced. Vector images are based on XYZ coordinate locations.

## C

**Card:** A thin plate, commonly known as a *board*, on which a variety of electronic chips are mounted. Also known as a *printed circuit board*, a card can be inserted into a computer to perform a variety of functions, from increasing the power of the computer's graphics to running other peripheral devices.

**CD-ROM:** A thin, plastic, optical disk that stores data and is read with a CD-ROM player using a laser. The average CD holds about 700 megabytes of information.

**CD-ROM drive:** A device used to play or read CD-ROMs.

**Chip:** A very small piece of silicon on which entire integrated electronic circuits are embedded. There are many different types of chips used in computer applications. *Microprocessor chips* run the computer, while *memory chips* temporarily store working information before it is saved to a storage device.

**CPU:** The abbreviation for *central processing unit*. The CPU is the heart of the computer. In personal computers, it is a microprocessor chip that handles all of the system's calculations.

## D

**Digitizer tablet:** The drawing board of the CAD workstation. A plastic or paper menu overlay containing AutoCAD commands and drawing symbols is commonly placed over the tablet. Items can be selected directly from the menu using a puck or stylus without looking at the screen. Movement of the pointing device is recorded and displayed on screen as the cursor position.

**Display device:** See *monitor*.

# F

**Floppy disk:** A form of storage media commonly known as a *diskette*. A 3.5″ disk can be formatted for either IBM/DOS compatible systems, or for Macintosh systems. The 3.5″ disk drive is the standard for new computers. Diskettes hold up to 1.44MB of information and are enclosed in a hard plastic shell that protects them from damage.

**Function keys:** The individual keys on a keyboard labeled [F1] through [F10] (or [F12]). In AutoCAD, the function keys are used to immediately perform commands and specific operations that would otherwise have to be entered or selected using a pointing device. Each of the function keys is discussed in Chapter 1 of this text.

# G

**Graphics card:** A *board* that controls graphics processing and the resolution of the computer monitor. Accelerator cards, or boards, can be inserted to allow the computer to process graphics faster and with higher resolution.

# H

**Hard disk drive:** A sealed unit that contains one or more metal disks, or platters, used to read and write computer data. Hard disks have a much greater storage capacity than floppy disks, and are measured in megabytes and gigabytes. Common hard disk sizes are 10 gigabyte (10 GB) to more than 40 gigabytes (40 GB). A small light on the front of the computer indicates when the hard disk drive is being accessed. Before AutoCAD can be used, it must be installed onto the hard disk drive from a CD-ROM.

**Hardware:** The physical pieces of equipment, such as the CPU, monitor, keyboard, printer or plotter, and diskettes used in computer-aided drafting and design.

# K

**Keyboard:** An input device that resembles a standard typewriter keyboard with additional keys located to the left, right, and top. The exact location and number of function keys (numbered [F1] through [F10] or [F12]) varies from one model to another. The keyboard can be used to enter AutoCAD commands or precise coordinate values.

# M

**Monitor:** A computer display output device that resembles a small television. Common monitor sizes are 15″, 17″, 19″, and 21″ (measured diagonally).

**Mouse:** A computer input device used to select items, perform cursor movement, and specify point locations on screen. A *mechanical mouse* has a roller ball on the bottom. The movement of the roller on any flat surface is sent to the computer and displayed as the movement of the screen cursor. Unlike a stylus or puck, a mouse can be lifted and moved to another position without affecting the location of the screen cursor.

An *optical mouse* uses a special reflective pad with grid lines. As the mouse is moved across the grid, a laser detects the movement and indicates the cursor location on screen. The optical mouse must remain on the pad in order to work.

# N

**Network:** A group of several connected computers that communicate with each other. Complex networks may have hundreds of computers or terminals working from a central computer called a *server*. Each workstation on the network still requires a CPU, an input device, and a display device.

---

# O

**Optical drive:** A disk drive that reads information from optical disks. The most popular optical drives use disks that are about the same size as standard magnetic 3.5" floppy disks, but thicker. While optical disks typically store up to 256 MB per disk (512 MB compressed), there are optical drives that store more than 4 GB (gigabyte) of data. Optical drives provide the reliability of optical media without the cost or vulnerability of magnetic media. Some types of optical disks can be rewritten with new data as required, just like magnetic floppies. They are also faster and more reliable for backups than magnetic tape drives.

# P

**Page:** A portion of the program or current drawing file that is kept in random access memory (RAM), or paged out to the hard disk for temporary storage.

**Peripheral:** A hardware device connected to the computer, such as a keyboard, monitor, printer, plotter, digitizer, modem, or scanner.

**Pixel:** A value used to measure screen resolution. Pixel means *picture element*. A pixel appears as a dot on screen, but it is actually a tiny rectangle. The display of a monitor is composed of horizontal rows and vertical columns of pixels. See *resolution*.

**Plotter:** A device used to output paper and film drawings. A plotter uses felt tip, ballpoint, or wet ink pens, inkjets, or pencils to place lines on paper. A *raster plotter*, such as an inkjet plotter, prints an entire row of the image at a time as the paper advances. A *pen plotter* constantly moves around the paper, drawing each vector separately. Plotting is covered in Chapters 4 and 10 of this text.

**Pointing device:** An input device that is used to move the screen cursor, specify point locations, and select commands. Items can be selected from the screen or a digitizer tablet menu. Commonly used pointing devices include the mouse, trackball, multibutton puck, and pen-shaped stylus. The puck and stylus are used in conjunction with a digitizer.

**Printer:** An output device that receives images and text from a computer for placement on paper. Some laser printers can output images with resolution up to 2400 dpi (dots per inch), but most are in the 600 dpi to 1200 dpi range. Some inkjet printers can output images with resolution up to 720 dpi. Many printers and plotters use the same technology, such as inkjet printing. Often, the only difference is in the size of the device.

**Puck:** A multibutton input device used with a digitizer tablet. A puck may have as many as 16 buttons. A set of small crosshairs in the puck serves as the pick point for this device. As the bottom surface of the puck slides on the digitizer surface, the movement controls the position of the screen cursor. One of the puck buttons, the pick button, is used to enter points and select menu commands. All the other buttons can be programmed to suit the user.

# R

**RAM:** The abbreviation for *random access memory*. RAM is made up of a group of data-holding blank chips and refers to the ability of the computer to randomly store and search for data in this area of memory. The chips are similar to empty storage boxes. When AutoCAD is loaded, the program files are placed into the computer's RAM. If your computer has a large amount of RAM, most of AutoCAD's files can be placed in the computer's memory. Some (or all) data in a drawing may also be initially placed in the computer's memory.

**Resolution:** The display quality of images on screen. The amount of resolution in an image determines how smooth or jagged the text and objects appear. Resolution is measured in *pixels*. A typical display resolution is 1280 × 1024, meaning the image can display 1280 pixels, or dots, horizontally, and 1024 dots vertically.

## S

**Serial port:** A socket or connector where a peripheral device, such as a modem or mouse, is plugged into the computer.

**Server:** A central computer that serves a network of computers or terminals. The hard disk drives in the server are normally large-capacity drives. Servers need to store a variety of software, and still have plenty of space for the numerous files created by computer users attached to the network. The network server can also store drawing files that may be needed by users in order to complete new drawings.

**Storage device:** Any drive or peripheral device that is used to save computer files. Common storage devices include floppy disk drives, hard disk drives, and CD-ROM drives.

**Storage media:** Any device used to store computer data, such as a floppy disk, hard disk, or CD-ROM.

**Stylus:** A pen-shaped pointing device used in conjunction with a digitizer tablet. A stylus is connected to the digitizer by a cable. When the point of the stylus is pressed down on the digitizer surface, a slight click can be felt and heard. This indicates that a point or menu item at the cursor's position on screen has been selected.

**Swap file:** A file containing the least-used portions, or pages, of a program on the hard disk. Swap files are used to store data that is not being currently used in physical memory. Pages stored in a swap file are held there until needed again.

## T

**Trackball:** A pointing device that enables you to move the screen cursor by rolling a ball. A trackball requires only the amount of table space needed for it to sit on (the only part that is rotated is the ball). A variety of trackballs are available, but most have two or three buttons, much like a mouse.

## V

**Virtual memory:** A memory system that uses a combination of RAM and hard disk space. A virtual memory system keeps only the part of the program that is being currently used in physical memory. If additional portions of the program are needed, AutoCAD creates a *page* on the hard disk and writes the least-used portion of the program to that page. See *swap file*.

# Managing the AutoCAD System

Any business—be it a bakery or engineering firm—relies on structure, organization, and standard procedures. A business lacking in one of these areas does not operate efficiently.

Computer systems can be used within the company structure for organization and procedure, or computers can contain the structural and organizational procedures themselves. In either case, the method in which computer systems are managed greatly affects the operation of the entire company.

Effective management of an AutoCAD system in a school or business means paying careful attention to the following items:

- ✓ The structure and makeup of the hard disk and mass storage devices.
- ✓ The location of all files and drawings.
- ✓ Storage procedures for student or employee drawing files.
- ✓ Drawing file backup procedures.
- ✓ The types of template drawings used for specific projects.
- ✓ The use and location of symbol libraries and reference drawings.
- ✓ The use and location of special screen and digitizer tablet menus.
- ✓ Drawing file creation procedures and naming conventions.
- ✓ Creation and distribution methods for new symbols and menus.
- ✓ Updating methods for software and hardware.
- ✓ Hardware maintenance.

Effective procedures and management techniques must be practiced by all students or employees. In addition, any personnel should look for ways that standards can be improved and revised for greater efficiency. In this text, read the section in Chapter 1 on using drawing standards and the section in Chapter 22 on creating and using symbol libraries.

## Management Procedures

One of your goals as an AutoCAD user should be to keep the computer system as efficient as possible. This means being organized and knowledgeable of school or company standards. You should also be aware of who has the authority to manage the system, and follow the system manager's guidelines.

If you are the system manager, develop standards and procedures, relay them to system users, and distribute up-to-date documentation, symbol libraries, menus, and standards. Revise standards as needed and distribute them to all users. In addition, incorporate software updates in a consistent and timely manner. Make the maintenance of hardware a priority.

# The System Manager

One or two people, depending on the size of the department or company, should be assigned as system manager. The manager has control over all functions of the computer system, and is in charge of preventing inconsistencies in procedure, drawing format, and file storage. The manager is responsible for the following:

- The scheduled use of computers.
- The structure of hard disk directories.
- Administration of the network server and user access to its files.
- The appearance and function of start-up menus and network log-in procedures.
- Implementation of file naming techniques.
- File storage and backup procedures.
- Drawing file access.
- The creation of symbol libraries.
- The development and distribution of written standards.
- Software and hardware upgrading.
- Hardware hygiene and maintenance.

When tasks are delegated, such as the creation of symbol libraries, be sure to include accurate sketches or drawings. Check and approve final drawings before distributing them to users.

# Developing Operating Standards and Procedures

The basis of system management is that everyone performs his or her job using the same procedures, symbols, and drawing techniques. A department that operates smoothly is probably using standards such as the following:

- File naming conventions.
- Methods of file storage that identify the location and name.
- File backup methods.
- Standard drawing sheet sizes and title blocks.
- Template drawings.
- The creation of blocks and symbols.
- Standard dimensioning techniques.
- Standard usage of layers, colors, linetypes, and text styles.
- Color schemes for plotting, and plot styles.
- The creation of screen and tablet menus.
- Organized storage of printed or plotted drawings.

Take the time initially to study the needs of your school or company. Meet with other department managers and users to determine the nature of their drawings. Always gain input from people who use the system and avoid making blanket decisions on your own.

Once needs have been established, develop a plan for implementing the required standards and procedures. Assign specific tasks to students or employees. Assemble the materials as they are completed and distribute the documentation and procedures to all users.

When developing procedures, begin with start-up procedures and work through the drawing process. Develop template drawings for specific types of projects first. The final aspects of system development should be the creation of screen and tablet menus and custom programs.

The hard disk drive is the heart of the AutoCAD computer system. It is the storage center for AutoCAD and other programs you use. In addition, it may hold hundreds of additional files, including drawings, templates, custom programs, slides, menu files, script files, and text files. The manner in which you work with the hard disk and arrange its contents can affect your productivity and drawing efficiency. Take time to assess the needs of your school or company and then organize your hard disk drives accordingly.

## File Maintenance

The integrity of saved files must be protected by everyone who works with the system. Procedures for file maintenance must be documented. Files of every type, including DWG, DWT, SLD, BAT, LSP, MNU, and BAK files, must have a secure storage area. Any hard disk directories, diskettes, optical discs, and magnetic tape storage areas must be kept clean of nonessential files. File maintenance procedures should include the following documentation:

- Location of essential AutoCAD files.
- Location of backup AutoCAD files.
- Printed contents of all hard disk directories for each workstation.
- Location and contents of all template drawings, supplemented with printed listings.
- Location and contents of all custom programs and associated menus.
- Location of all user files, including templates, drawings, slides, and text files.

Regardless of what you store on the hard disk, have a plan for it. Drawings should not be saved in the AutoCAD 2004 folder. Users should not be allowed to save files in the root directory. Decide on the nature of the hard disk structure and then stick to it. Make sure that all users are informed by documenting and distributing the standard procedures accordingly. Place copies of the procedures at each workstation.

Files to be used in conjunction with AutoCAD should be located in subfolders of the AutoCAD 2004 folder. Possible uses for subfolders include drawings, AutoLISP files, drivers, slides, and user folders. The individual files should reside within the subfolders. The subfolders of AutoCAD 2004 in **Figure B-1** are those that are automatically created when AutoCAD is installed. If you plan to store files within the AutoCAD folder tree, plan on creating new subfolders with names such as Drawings, Lisp, and Scripts. When specific types of files are kept in their own subfolders, file maintenance is easier.

Your hard disk planning should take into account future software. New programs should be installed in their own folders on the hard disk, and the files should be managed in the same fashion as the AutoCAD files. An example of a well-planned and closely managed hard disk structure is shown in **Figure B-2.**

## Maintaining Symbol Libraries and Menus

The development of symbol libraries and customized menus is one of the primary concerns of managing an AutoCAD system. In AutoCAD, symbols are created as *blocks*. See Chapter 22 of this text for a full discussion on drawing and saving block symbols.

Symbols must be consistent and up-to-date. User menus must also be consistent throughout the department or company. A vital aspect of maintaining standards and consistency is establishing a method for updating symbol libraries and menus. This task should be given to certain students or employees, with the results distributed to all users. The following guidelines should be used for developing and maintaining symbol libraries and selection menus:

- Establish drawing standards for the creation of symbols.
- Develop a symbol naming convention and storage system.

**Figure B-1.**
Specific subfolders in the AutoCAD 2004 folder are for files that are used with AutoCAD. These subfolders are automatically created when AutoCAD is installed.

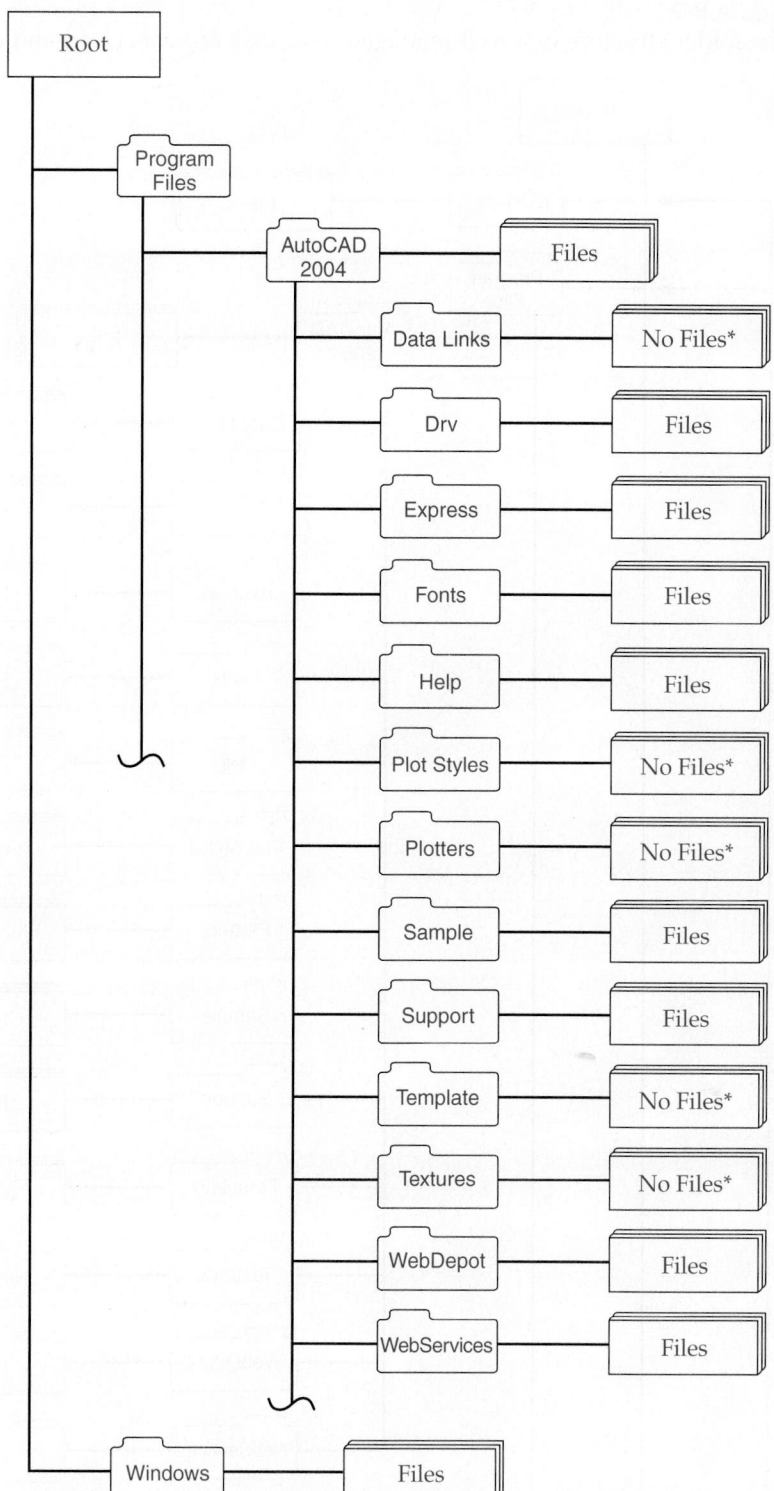

\* To verify the location of these files for AutoCAD 2004, while in AutoCAD access the **Files** tab in the **Options** dialog box. Check the specific file type, and the path is listed.

The folder structure of a well-managed hard disk appears clean and organized.

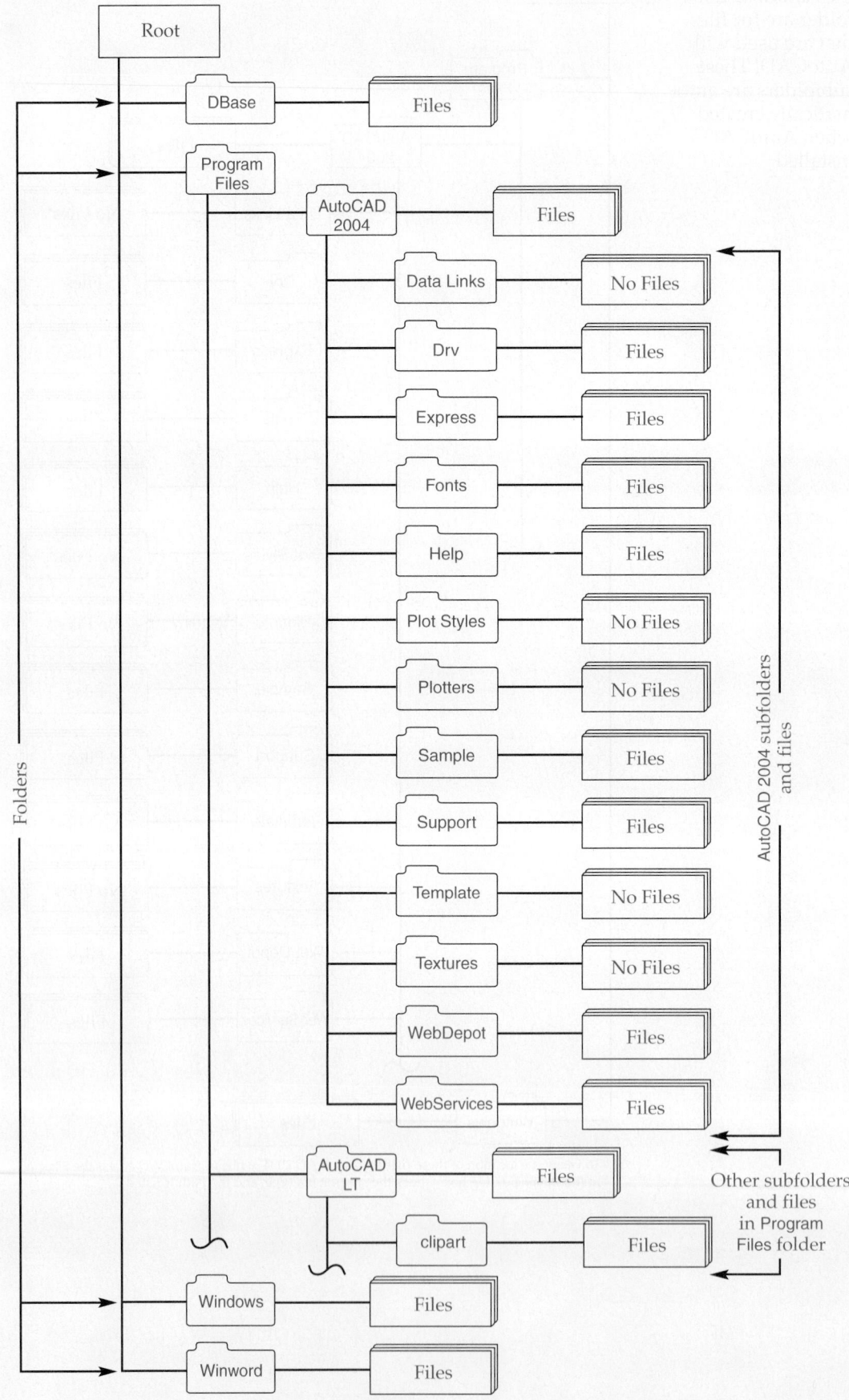

- Post a printed copy of all symbol libraries with their names and locations listed.
- Practice standards for the creation and maintenance of custom menus and toolbars.
- Assign the use of custom menus to specific departments.
- Make revisions to custom menus when necessary.
- Revise upgraded menus on all hard disks.

## Network Systems

There is an increasing need for drawing symbol consistency, accurate project time accounting, instant communication between coworkers, and data security. This has led to the popularity of *network systems*. A **network** is nothing more than several connected computers that communicate with each other. Complex networks have hundreds of computers or terminals working from a central computer called a **server**. Each workstation on the network still requires a CPU, an input device, and a display device. A diagram of a typical network system is shown in **Figure B-3**.

The hard disk drives in the server are normally large-capacity drives. They need to store a variety of software, and still have plenty of space for numerous files created by the computer users attached to the network. The network server can also store drawing files that may be needed by users in order to complete new drawings. For example, a base drawing of the walls of a structure can be stored on the server. When a student or employee needs to work on a new drawing of the plumbing or electrical layout of the structure, he or she can simply load the base drawing from the server into a networked computer and begin working. In most cases, the base drawing is preserved in its original form and a different name is given to the new drawing. AutoCAD provides a function that automatically locks a drawing when someone *checks it out* of the network. This means that only one person can work on a drawing at any given time, thus preventing several people from making different changes to the drawing.

**Figure B-3.**
A layout of a typical computer network system.

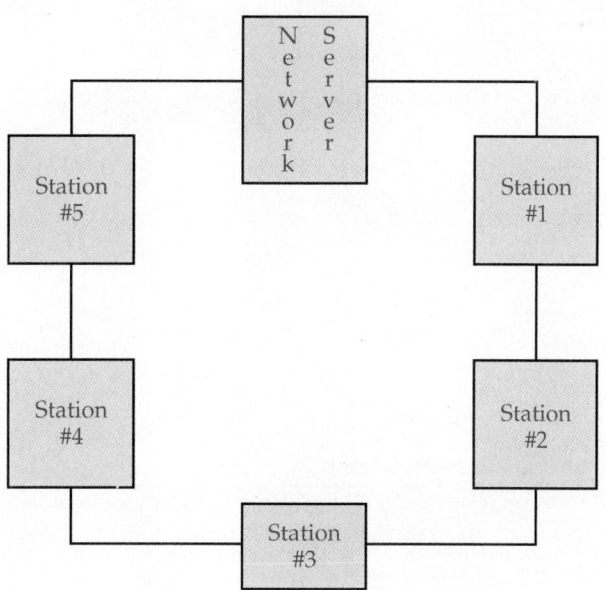

## Maintaining the Software

Software upgrades and releases are issued regularly. If you purchase upgrades, converting to new versions should be smooth and have little, if any, effect on production. Establish a procedure for upgrading all computers in the classroom or office. Inform all users of changes by providing a printed listing of new features. If you work for a company, schedule professional upgrade training for managers and employees at an authorized Autodesk Training Center (ATC) or an authorized Autodesk dealer. You can also get valuable training information on the World Wide Web at http://www.autodesk.com.

## Maintaining the Management System

All systems require continuous maintenance to function efficiently. Always enable users to contribute to the function of the system. Foster creativity by inviting suggestions. Meet with users and managers on a regular basis to learn what is functioning well and what is not. Remember, the system will function efficiently if a majority of those using it enjoy working with the system, and are encouraged to contribute to its growth and development.

# The Ergonomic Workstation

Ergonomics is the science of adapting the work environment to suit the needs of the worker. Since the advent of computers in the workplace in the early 1980s, an increasing number of work-related injuries and afflictions have been reported. By far, the most common of these are repetitive motion disorders (also called repetitive stress or strain). Carpal tunnel syndrome is probably the most well-known of these. Most injuries and disorders related to computer work are the result of the sedentary nature of the work, and the fast, repetitive motions of the hands and fingers on the keyboard and pointing devices.

Most disorders of this nature can be prevented to some extent by proper workstation configuration, good posture, and frequent exercises. **Figure C-1** shows a piece of ergonomic equipment for the computer workstation. Review the following checklist, and try to adhere to as many of the suggestions as possible. As is often the case, a small adjustment of equipment, or the investment of a few extra dollars, can prevent unnecessary future injuries and lost productivity.

- ✓ Obtain a good chair with proper back support, height, and tilt adjustment.
- ✓ Use adaptive devices such as forearm supports, wrist and palm rests, and keyboard drawers to help maintain a level wrist position in relation to the keyboard and pointing device.
- ✓ Avoid resting your wrists on a table while typing, and use a light stroke on the keys.
- ✓ Investigate the variety of ergonomic keyboards on the market and test for comfort and efficiency. (See website addresses at the end of this appendix.)
- ✓ Position the equipment and supplies of your workstation for ease of use and access. Use a document holder to keep documents at eye level.
- ✓ The screen should be placed 18" to 30" away from the eyes, and the top of the display screen should be at eye level.
- ✓ Lighting should not produce a glare on the screen.
- ✓ Provide under-desk space so feet can be placed on a tilted footrest, or at minimum, flat on the floor.
- ✓ Take short breaks throughout the day.
- ✓ Practice refocusing your eyes, and engaging in stretching exercises for hands, arms, shoulders, and neck on a regular basis.
- ✓ Be aware of how your body feels, especially any changes you feel in your shoulders, arms, wrists, and hands.
- ✓ Consult your doctor if you notice any numbness, aching, or tingling in your hands, wrists, or arms.

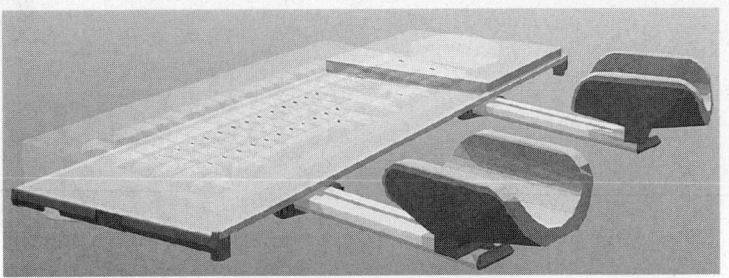

**Figure C-1.**
The forearm supports provide relief from muscle tension for computer operators and assist in the prevention of repetitive motion disorders. This design was created with AutoCAD. (Myonetics Inc.)

## Comfort in Your Workspace

Sitting in the same position for a long time causes fatigue. Properly arranging your workspace and improving your posture are two highly effective ways to reduce the strain and potential injuries associated with frequent computer use.

### Workspace Arrangement

An ergonomically correct workstation will add comfort to the job and help avoid serious injuries. A good chair is essential. The backrest and seat should provide firm support and adjust independently. The front of the seat should be curved to relieve pressure on the thighs. Keep thighs parallel to the floor. Rest your feet flat on the floor or on a footrest.

Use a light touch on the keyboard, keeping your hands and fingers relaxed. Your forearms should be parallel to the floor and your wrists in a neutral, comfortable position. Maintain about a 90° angle in the bend of your elbows.

The monitor should be adjusted so the top of the screen is at eye level, or slightly below. Place the monitor 20" to 24" (50 cm to 60 cm) in front of you, about an arm's length from the screen. Position the monitor to minimize glare from overhead lights, windows, or other light sources. If necessary, turn off lights or use less intense light-bulbs. Close curtains or blinds to block sunlight through windows. Change the brightness and contrast controls on the monitor as needed throughout the day. An antiglare filter placed over the screen is also an alternative.

### Posture and Exercise

No matter how comfortable or ergonomically correct your workstation is, you are still at risk for repetitive stress injuries. That is why you need to develop ergonomically sound work habits that include posture awareness and simple exercises. Repetitive stress injuries often develop slowly, over months or even years. You may not even be aware that an injury is developing until the pain becomes intense. These simple practices can help you avoid various types of injuries and disorders associated with using computers every day.

- **Maintain good posture.** The single best thing you can do is work on your posture. Computer users tend to tilt their shoulders and chin toward the screen. Don't allow your head to project forward. This places too much strain on the neck and shoulders. Also, avoid leaning on the armrests of the chair. Instead, type with the entire arm.

  Awareness is the key to maintaining good posture. Sit up straight! It is old-fashioned advice, but it applies more than ever in today's computerized workplace.

- **Get up from your desk.** Sitting for hours at a computer workstation without breaks puts tremendous stress on several areas of your body, including your neck, back, arms, wrists, and legs. Make a habit of getting out of your seat at least once every hour, even if it is only for a few minutes. If you can, walk outside during your break and get some fresh air. You'll return to your workstation feeling refreshed.

- **Practice periodic stretching and exercises.** When most of what you are doing all day is sitting still, moving only your fingers and eyes, the muscles in the rest of your body can become stiff and sore from lack of use. Taking a few moments to stretch periodically throughout the day can relax stiff joints and muscles, helping to avoid problems associated with prolonged muscular stress. Many simple stretching activities can be done right at your workstation without even leaving your seat.

- **Give your eyes a break.** You can greatly reduce eye strain with this simple practice: Every 15 minutes or so, look away from the computer screen and focus on something 20' or more away from you.

Several Internet sites provide useful information about preventing repetitive stress injures. Go to www.tifaq.com for answers to the most frequently asked questions about ergonomics and computer use injuries. It also has links to other useful websites, such as 3M Company's self-help site showing exercises that can be done without leaving your workstation. A good resource for college students by college students is www.eecs.harvard.edu/rsi. To learn about cutting-edge accessories including ergonomically designed keyboards, go to ergo.human.cornell.edu.

# AutoCAD System Variables

The following listing shows the AutoCAD system variables that can be stored within a drawing or template file. The value of each of these variables is written into the file when the drawing is saved, so the next time the drawing is opened, the values remain the same. Setting the values for most of these variables can be done by entering the variable name or by using the **SETVAR** command. Some variable values are derived by AutoCAD from the current condition of the drawing or the drawing environment, and cannot be directly set. These are referred to as *read-only* variables.

Each of the listings in this appendix provides a brief description of the system variable and the default setting when no specific drawing is referenced. The symbol (&c) indicates the variable is read-only.

## Variables Saved in Drawing

| Variable Name | Default Value | Description |
|---|---|---|
| AANGBASE | 0.0000 | Sets base angle to 0 relative to current UCS. |
| ANGDIR | 0 | Specifies counterclockwise or clockwise angle measurement. |
| ATTMODE | 1 | Display mode for block attributes. |
| AUNITS | 0 | Format for angular units. |
| AUPREC | 0 | Precision of angular units. |
| BACKZ | &c | Controls back clipping plane offset from the target plane. |
| CECOLOR | "BYLAYER" | Color of newly created objects. |
| CELTSCALE | 1.0000 | Individual object linetype scaling for new objects. |
| CELTYPE | "BYLAYER" | Linetype for newly created objects. |
| CELWEIGHT | -1 | Lineweight setting for new objects. |
| CHAMFERA | 0.0000 | First chamfer distance. |
| CHAMFERB | 0.0000 | Second chamfer distance. |
| CHAMFERC | 0.0000 | Chamfer length. |
| CHAMFERD | 0.0000 | Chamfer angle. |
| CLAYER | "0" | Currently active layer. |
| CMLJUST | 0 | Current multiline justification. |
| CMLSCALE | 1.0000 (imperial) or 20.000 (metric) | Scale factor for multiline features. |
| CMLSTYLE | "STANDARD" | Current multiline style name. |
| CPLOTSTYLE | "BYLAYER" | Current plot style setting for new objects. |
| CTAB | &c | Identifies the **Model** tab or a specific layout tab as current. |
| CVPORT | 2 | Identification number of current viewport. |
| DBCSTATE | 0 | Stores the state of the dbConnect Manager. |
| DIMADEC | 0 | Decimal places for angular dimensions. |
| DIMALT | off | Enables or disables alternate units dimensioning. |
| DIMALTD | 2 | Decimal places for alternate units dimensions. |

| Variable Name | Default Value | Description |
| --- | --- | --- |
| **DIMALTF** | 25.4000 | Alternate units dimension scale factor. |
| **DIMALTRND** | 0.00 | Rounding value for alternate dimension units. |
| **DIMALTTD** | 2 | Decimal places for alternate units tolerance values. |
| **DIMALTTZ** | 0 | Zero suppression for alternate units tolerance values. |
| **DIMALTU** | 2 | Units format for alternate units dimensions. |
| **DIMALTZ** | 0 | Zero suppression for alternate units dimension values. |
| **DIMAPOST** | "" | Prefix/suffix for alternate units dimensions. |
| **DIMASO** | on | Controls the associativity of dimension objects. |
| **DIMASSOC** | 2 | Controls associative dimensioning. |
| **DIMASZ** | 0.1800 | Dimension line and arrowhead size. |
| **DIMATFIT** | 3 | Controls placement of text and arrowheads when there is insufficient space between the extension lines. |
| **DIMAUNIT** | 0 | Unit format for angular dimension values. |
| **DIMAZIN** | 0 | Controls zero suppression for angular dimensions. |
| **DIMBLK** | "" | Block type to use for both arrowheads. |
| **DIMBLK1** | "" | Block type to use for first arrowhead. |
| **DIMBLK2** | "" | Block type to use for second arrowhead. |
| **DIMCEN** | 0.0900 | Controls placement of center marks or centerlines. |
| **DIMCLRD** | 0 | Dimension line, arrowhead, and leader line color. |
| **DIMCLRE** | 0 | Dimension extension line color. |
| **DIMCLRT** | 0 | Dimension text color. |
| **DIMDEC** | 4 | Decimal places for dimension values. |
| **DIMDLE** | 0.0000 | Dimension line extension beyond extension lines. |
| **DIMDLI** | 0.3800 | Incremental spacing between baseline dimensions. |
| **DIMDSEP** | "." | Specifies a single character to use as a decimal separator for decimal unit dimensions. |
| **DIMEXE** | 0.1800 | Extension line distance beyond dimension line. |
| **DIMEXO** | 0.0625 | Distance from origin points to extension lines. |
| **DIMFIT** | 3 | Obsolete. No effect except to preserve integrity of scripts. |
| **DIMFRAC** | 0 | Controls the fraction format used for architectural and fractional dimensions. |
| **DIMGAP** | 0.0900 | Gap size between dimension line and dimension text. |
| **DIMJUST** | 0 | Horizontal justification of dimension text. |
| **DIMLDRBLK** | 0 | Controls the type of arrowhead used for leaders. |
| **DIMLFAC** | 1.0000 | Scale factor for linear dimension values. |
| **DIMLIM** | off | Toggles creation of limits-style dimension text. |
| **DIMLUNIT** | 2 | Specifies units for all non-angular dimensions. |
| **DIMLWD** | -2 (BYBLOCK) | Lineweight value for dimension lines. |
| **DIMLWE** | -2 (BYBLOCK) | Lineweight value for extension lines. |
| **DIMPOST** | "" | Prefix/suffix for primary units dimension values. |
| **DIMRND** | 0.0000 | Rounding value for dimensions. |
| **DIMSAH** | off | Toggles appearance of arrowhead blocks. |
| **DIMSCALE** | 1.0000 | Global dimension feature scale factor. |
| **DIMSD1** | off | Toggles suppression of first dimension line. |
| **DIMSD2** | off | Toggles suppression of second dimension line. |
| **DIMSE1** | off | Toggles suppression of first extension line. |
| **DIMSE2** | off | Toggles suppression of second extension line. |
| **DIMSHO** | on | Obsolete. No effect except to preserve integrity of scripts. |
| **DIMSOXD** | off | Suppresses dimension lines outside extension lines. |

| Variable Name | Default Value | Description |
| --- | --- | --- |
| DIMSTYLE | ∿ | Name of current dimension style. |
| DIMTAD | 0 | Sets text placement relative to dimension line. |
| DIMTDEC | 4 | Decimal places for primary units tolerance values. |
| DIMTFAC | 1.0000 | Scale factor for fractional or tolerance text size. |
| DIMTIH | on | Orientation of text inside extension lines. |
| DIMTIX | off | Toggles forced placement of text between extension lines. |
| DIMTM | 0.0000 | Lower tolerance value for tolerance dimensions. |
| DIMTMOVE | 0 | Controls the format of dimension text when it is moved. |
| DIMTOFL | off | Toggles forced dimension line creation. |
| DIMTOH | on | Orientation of text outside extension lines. |
| DIMTOL | off | Toggles creation of appended tolerance dimensions. |
| DIMTOLJ | 1 | Vertical justification for dimension tolerance text. |
| DIMTP | 0.0000 | Upper tolerance value for tolerance dimensions. |
| DIMTSZ | 0.0000 | Controls size of dimension line tick marks drawn instead of arrowheads. |
| DIMTVP | 0.0000 | Vertical position of text above or below dimension line. |
| DIMTXSTY | "STANDARD" | Text style used for dimension text. |
| DIMTXT | 0.1800 | Size of dimension text. |
| DIMTZIN | 0 | Zero suppression for primary units tolerance values. |
| DIMUNIT | 2 | Obsolete. No effect except to preserve integrity of scripts. |
| DIMUPT | off | Controls user placement of dimension line and text. |
| DIMZIN | 0 | Zero suppression for primary units dimensions. |
| DISPSILH | 0 | Toggles display of wireframe silhouette curves. |
| DWGCODEPAGE | ∿ | **SYSCODEPAGE** value when drawing was created. |
| ELEVATION | 0.0000 | Current 3D elevation relative to current UCS. |
| EXTMAX | ∿ | Upper-right extents of drawing. |
| EXTMIN | ∿ | Lower-left extents of drawing. |
| EXTNAMES | 1 | Specifies the naming parameters for named objects. |
| FACETRES | 0.5000 | Smoothness of shaded objects and objects with hidden lines removed. |
| FILLETRAD | 0.0000 | Current fillet radius setting. |
| FILLMODE | 1 | Toggles fill for solid objects. |
| FRONTZ | ∿ | Front clipping plane offset from the target plane. |
| GRIDMODE | 0 | Toggles display of grid. |
| GRIDUNIT | 0.5000, 0.5000 | Current grid spacing in drawing units. |
| HALOGAP | 0 | Distance to shorten a haloed line |
| HANDLES | ∿ | Provides support for applications requiring handle access. |
| HIDETEXT | 1 | Determines if text objects are processed during the **HIDE** command. |
| HYPERLINKBASE | "" | File path specified for all relative hyperlinks in the drawing. |
| INDEXCTL | 0 | Controls creation and saving of layer and spatial indexes. |
| INSBASE | 0.0000, 0.0000, 0.0000 | Insertion point set by **BASE** command. |
| INSUNITS | 0 | Drawing units specified when inserting an object from **DesignCenter**. |
| INTERSECTIONCOLOR | 257 | Specifies color of intersection polylines. |
| INTERSECTIONDISPLAY | off | Specifies the display of intersection polylines. |
| ISOLINES | 4 | Number of isolines per surface on 3D objects. |
| LENSLENGTH | ∿ | Length of lens in millimeters for perspective view. |
| LIMCHECK | 0 | Toggles active limit checking for object creation. |

| Variable Name | Default Value | Description |
|---|---|---|
| LIMMAX | 12.0000, 9.0000 | Upper-right drawing limits. |
| LIMMIN | 0.0000, 0.0000 | Lower-left drawing limits. |
| LOGFILENAME | ∿ | Specifies path and name for the log file. |
| LTSCALE | 1.0000 | Current global linetype scale factor. |
| LUNITS | 2 | Current display format for linear units. |
| LUPREC | 4 | Current linear units precision value. |
| LWDISPLAY | 0 | Controls the display of lineweights within the **Model** tab and each individual layout tab. |
| MAXACTVP | 64 | Maximum number of active model space viewports. |
| MEASUREMENT | 0 | Sets drawing units as English or metric. |
| MIRRTEXT | 0 | Toggles mirroring technique for text objects. |
| OBSCUREDCOLOR | 257 | Specifies color for obscured lines |
| OBSCUREDLTYPE | 0 | Specifies linetype for obscured lines. |
| OLESTARTUP | 0 | Controls loading of the source application of an embedded OLE object when plotting. |
| ORTHOMODE | 0 | Toggles orthogonal drawing control. |
| PDMODE | 0 | Current point object display mode. |
| PDSIZE | 0.0000 | Current point object display size. |
| PELLIPSE | 0 | Controls the object type created with **ELLIPSE**. |
| PLINEGEN | 0 | Toggles linetype generation along a polyline. |
| PLINEWID | 0.0000 | Current polyline width value. |
| PROJECTNAME | "" | Assigns a project name to the current drawing. |
| PROXYGRAPHICS | 1 | Specifies whether images of proxy objects are saved in the drawing. |
| PSLTSCALE | 1 | Paper space linetype scale factor. |
| PSTYLEMODE | ∿ | Specifies the current plot style mode. |
| PUCSBASE | "" | The base UCS defining the origin and orientation of orthographic UCS settings in paper space only. |
| QTEXTMODE | "" | Toggles **Quick Text** display mode. |
| REGENMODE | 1 | Toggles automatic drawing regeneration. |
| SHADEDGE | 3 | Controls edge shading during rendering. |
| SHADEDIF | 70 | Sets ratio of diffuse reflective light to ambient light. |
| SKETCHINC | 0.1000 | Current **SKETCH** record increment value. |
| SKPOLY | 0 | Toggles creation of polyline objects by **SKETCH**. |
| SNAPANG | 0 | Snap/grid rotation angle in current viewport. |
| SNAPBASE | 0.0000, 0.0000 | Snap/grid origin point in current viewport. |
| SNAPISOPAIR | 0 | Isometric plane for current viewport. |
| SNAPMODE | 0 | Toggles snap mode. |
| SNAPSTYL | 0 | Current snap style. |
| SNAPUNIT | 0.5000, 0.5000 | Snap spacing for current viewport. |
| SORTENTS | 127 | Controls object sort order operations. |
| SPLFRAME | 0 | Toggles display of frames for spline-fit polylines. |
| SPLINESEGS | 8 | Current number of segments generated for each spline. |
| SPLINETYPE | 6 | Current type of spline generation by **PEDIT**. |
| SURFTAB1 | 6 | Tabulations generated for **RULESURF** and **TABSURF**, and mesh density in the M direction for **REVSURF** and **EDGESURF**. |
| SURFTAB2 | 6 | Mesh density in the N direction for **REVSURF** and **EDGESURF**. |
| SURFTYPE | 6 | Surface fitting type performed by **PEDIT Smooth**. |
| SURFU | 6 | Surface density for **PEDIT Smooth** in the M direction. |

| Variable Name | Default Value | Description |
| --- | --- | --- |
| **SURFV** | 6 | Surface density for **PEDIT Smooth** in the N direction. |
| **TARGET** | ~ | Location of target point in current viewport. |
| **TDCREATE** | ~ | Local time and date the current drawing was created. |
| **TDINDWG** | ~ | Total editing time for the current drawing. |
| **TDUCREATE** | ~ | Universal time and date the current drawing was created. |
| **TDUPDATE** | ~ | Local time and date of the last update and save. |
| **TDUSRTIMER** | ~ | User time elapsed. |
| **TDUUPDATE** | ~ | Universal time and date of the last update and save. |
| **TEXTSIZE** | 0.2000 | Default height of text drawn in current style. |
| **TEXTSTYLE** | "STANDARD" | Current text style name. |
| **THICKNESS** | 0.0000 | Current 3D solid thickness. |
| **TILEMODE** | 1 | Sets the **Model** tab or last layout tab current. |
| **TRACEWID** | 0.0500 | Current width for **TRACE** objects. |
| **TREEDEPTH** | 3020 | Maximum number of branches for tree-structured spatial index. |
| **TSTACKALIGN** | 1 | Sets the vertical justification of stacked text. |
| **TSTACKSIZE** | 70 | The stacked text character height, expressed as a percentage of the text's current height. |
| **UCSBASE** | "World" | The UCS defining the origin and orientation of orthographic UCS settings. |
| **UCSFOLLOW** | 0 | Toggles automatic change to plan view of current UCS. |
| **UCSICON** | 3 | Controls the display of the UCS icon. |
| **UCSNAME** | ~ | Name of the current UCS for the current space. |
| **UCSORG** | ~ | Origin point for the current UCS for the current space. |
| **UCSVP** | 1 | Controls the independence of UCS settings in active viewports in relation to the UCS of the current viewport. |
| **UCSXDIR** | ~ | X direction for the current UCS for the current space. |
| **UCSYDIR** | ~ | Y direction for the current UCS for the current space. |
| **UNITMODE** | 0 | Current units display format. |
| **USERI1-5** | 0 | USERI1, USERI2, USERI3, USERI4, and USERI5 are used for storage and retrieval of integer values. |
| **USERR1-5** | 0.0000 | USERR1, USERR2, USERR3, USERR4, and USERR5 are used for storage and retrieval of real numbers. |
| **USERS1-5** | "" | USERS1, USERS2, USERS3, USERS4, and USERS5 are used for storage and retrieval of text string data. |
| **VIEWCTR** | ~ | Center point location for current view in current viewport. |
| **VIEWDIR** | ~ | Viewing direction of the current view in current viewport. |
| **VIEWMODE** | ~ | Current viewing mode for the current viewport. |
| **VIEWSIZE** | ~ | Height of the current view in the current viewport. |
| **VIEWTWIST** | ~ | View twist angle for current viewport. |
| **VISRETAIN** | 1 | Controls visibility of layers in xref files. |
| **VSMAX** | ~ | Upper-right corner of the current viewport virtual screen. |
| **VSMIN** | ~ | Lower-left corner of the current viewport virtual screen. |
| **WORLDVIEW** | 1 | Controls automatic change of UCS for **DVIEW** and **VPOINT**. |
| **XCLIPFRAME** | 0 | Controls visibility of xref clipping boundaries. |
| **XEDIT** | 1 | Controls the reference editing capability of the current drawing when it is referenced by another drawing. |

The following listing shows the AutoCAD system variables that are saved with the AutoCAD configuration. These variables are not associated with, or saved in, the drawing file. The values will be the same in the next drawing session as they are when you leave the current drawing. The default values shown here represent the values existing prior to AutoCAD's initial configuration. The symbol (✍) indicates that the variable is read-only.

## Variables Saved in Registry

| Variable Name | Default Value | Description |
| --- | --- | --- |
| ACADLSPASDOC | 0 | Controls whether the acad.lsp file is loaded into every drawing, or just the first one opened in a single session. |
| APBOX | 0 | Turns the AutoSnap aperture box on or off. |
| APERTURE | 10 | Object snap target aperture height. |
| ATTDIA | 0 | Controls use of Command: prompt or dialog box. |
| ATTREQ | 1 | Use attribute defaults or request values from user. |
| AUDITCTL | 0 | Toggles the creation of an audit report (ADT) file. |
| AUTOSNAP | 63 | Controls display of the AutoSnap marker, tooltip, and magnet. |
| BLIPMODE | 0 | Controls display of marker blips. |
| CMDDIA | 1 | Enables or disables dialog boxes for a variety of commands. |
| COORDS | 1 | Controls dynamic coordinate updating. |
| CPROFILE | ✍ | Name of current profile. |
| CURSORSIZE | 5 | Controls the size of the screen cursor crosshairs as a percentage of the full screen size. |
| DCTCUST | "" | Current custom dictionary file name and path. |
| DCTMAIN | (varies by country) | Main dictionary file name. |
| DEFLPLSTYLE | "" | Default plot style for new layers. |
| DEFPLSTYLE | "" | Default plot style for new objects. |
| DELOBJ | 1 | Controls deletion of objects used to create other objects. |
| DEMANDLOAD | 3 | Specifies if and when AutoCAD demand loads a third-party application (if the drawing contains custom objects created in that application). |
| DRAGMODE | 2 | Controls display of object dragging. |
| DRAGP1 | 10 | Sets regen-drag input sampling rate. |
| DRAGP2 | 25 | Sets fast-drag input sampling rate. |
| DWGCHECK | 0 | Indicates whether a drawing was last edited using an application other than AutoCAD. |
| FILEDIA | 1 | Enables or disables file dialog boxes. |
| FONTALT | "simplex.shx" | Font file to be used when specified file is not found. |
| FONTMAP | "acad.fmp" | Font mapping file to be used. |
| GRIPBLOCK | 0 | Controls the assignment of grips within block objects. |
| GRIPCOLOR | 169 | Color of nonselected grips. |
| GRIPHOT | 1 | Color of selected grips. |
| GRIPHOVER | 3 | Controls the fill color of a grip when the cursor pauses over the grip. |
| GRIPOBJLIMIT | 100 | Suppresses the display of grips when the initial selection set includes more than the specified number of objects. |
| GRIPS | 1 | Toggles availability of grip editing modes. |

| Variable Name | Default Value | Description |
| --- | --- | --- |
| GRIPSIZE | 3 | Size of grip box in pixels. |
| GRIPTIPS | 1 | Controls the display of grip tips. |
| HPASSOC | 1 | Controls whether hatch patterns and gradient fills are associative. |
| IMAGEHLT | 0 | Controls the highlighting level for raster images. |
| INETLOCATION | "www.autodesk.com" | Internet location used by BROWSER. |
| INSUNITSDEFSOURCE | 1 | Drawing units specified for source content that is inserted into the current drawing. |
| INSUNITSDEFTARGET | 1 | Drawing units to be used in the current drawing when inserting content. |
| ISAVEBAK | 1 | Controls creation of a BAK file when saving. |
| ISAVEPERCENT | 50 | Determines amount of wasted space allowed in a drawing. |
| LAYOUTREGENCTL | 2 | Specifies how the display list is updated for model and layout tabs |
| LISPINIT | 1 | Controls preservation of AutoLISP functions from one drawing to another. |
| LOCALROOTPATH | ∾ | Stores the full path to the root folder where local customizable files were installed. |
| LOGFILEMODE | 0 | Specifies whether text window contents are written to a log file. |
| LOGFILEPATH | *varies* | Path used for the log files created for all drawings in a single session. |
| LWDEFAULT | 25 | Default lineweight value assigned to objects. |
| LWUNITS | 1 | Drawing units used for displayed lineweights. |
| MAXSORT | 1000 | Maximum number of symbol or block names sorted by listing commands. |
| MBUTTONPAN | 1 | Support level for the third button or wheel on a pointing device. |
| MEASUREINIT | *varies by country* | Sets initial drawing units as English or metric |
| MENUCTL | 1 | Toggles screen menu switching in response to commands. |
| MTEXTED | "INTERNAL" | Name of text editor for editing **MTEXT** objects. |
| MTEXTFIXED | 0 | Controls the appearance of the multiline text editor. |
| MTJIGSTRING | "abc" | Sets the content of the sample text displayed at the cursor location when the **MTEXT** command is started. |
| MYDOCUMENTSPREFIX | ∾ | Stores the full path to the My Documents folder for the user currently logged-on. |
| OFFSETGAPTYPE | 0 | Specifies how polylines are offset when a gap is created by the offset value. |
| OLEHIDE | 0 | Controls the display of OLE objects in AutoCAD. |
| OLEQUALITY | 1 | Default quality level for embedded OLE objects. |
| OSMODE | 4133 | Current object snap mode bit value. |
| OSNAPCOORD | 2 | Controls whether typed coordinates override object snap settings. |
| PALETTEOPAQUE | 0 | Controls whether windows can be made transparent. When transparency is unavailable or turned off, all palettes are opaque. |
| PAPERUPDATE | 0 | Controls display of a warning during plotting when the specified paper size differs from the default used by the plotter. |
| PEDITACCEPT | 0 | Suppresses display of the Object Selected Is Not a Polyline prompt in **PEDIT**. |
| PICKADD | 1 | Toggles additive selection of objects. |
| PICKAUTO | 1 | Toggles automatic windowing during selection process. |
| PICKBOX | 3 | Object selection pick box height in pixels. |
| PICKDRAG | 0 | Controls the selection window drawing method. |

| Variable Name | Default Value | Description |
|---|---|---|
| PICKFIRST | 1 | Controls the object selection and command entry sequence. |
| PICKSTYLE | 1 | Controls group and associative hatch selection. |
| PLINETYPE | 2 | Specifies whether AutoCAD uses optimized polylines. |
| PLOTROTMODE | 2 | Controls the orientation of plots. |
| PLQUIET | 0 | Controls display of plot-related dialog boxes and nonfatal errors resulting from batch plotting and scripts. |
| POLARADDANG | "" | Stores user-defined polar angles for AutoTracking. |
| POLARANG | 90 | Specifies the polar tracking angle increment value. |
| POLARDIST | 0.0000 | Snap increment used with polar snap. |
| POLARMODE | 0 | Specifies control settings for polar and object snap tracking. |
| PROJMODE | 1 | Controls the projection mode for **TRIM** and **EXTEND**. |
| PROXYNOTICE | 1 | Controls display of a notice when a proxy object is created. |
| PROXYSHOW | 1 | Controls display of proxy objects. |
| PROXYWEBSEARCH | 1 | Specifies how AutoCAD checks for object enablers. |
| PSPROLOG | "" | Name for prolog section read from acad.psf for **PSOUT**. |
| PSQUALITY | 75 | Controls rendering quality and fill on PostScript images. |
| PSTYLEPOLICY | 1 | Controls the association between the color property of an object and its plot style. |
| RASTERPREVIEW | 1 | Toggles saving of drawing preview image. |
| REMEMBERFOLDERS | 1 | Sets default path for **Look in** list in standard file selection dialog box. |
| REPORTERROR | 1 | Controls whether an error report can be sent to Autodesk if AutoCAD closes unexpectedly. |
| ROAMABLEROOTPREFIX | ↝ | Stores the full path to the root folder where roamable customizable files were installed. |
| RTDISPLAY | 1 | Controls the display of raster objects during realtime zooming or panning. |
| SAVEFILE | ↝ | Current automatic save file name. |
| SAVEFILEPATH | "C:\TEMP\" | Folder path used for all automatic save files in the current drawing session. |
| SAVETIME | 10 | Automatic save interval in minutes. |
| SDI | 0 | Enables or disables the Multiple Design Environment (MDE). |
| SHORTCUTMENU | 11 | Controls the availability of shortcut menus in the **Default**, **Edit**, and **Command** modes. |
| SIGWARN | 1 | Controls whether a warning is presented when a file with an attached digital signature is opened. |
| SNAPTYPE | 0 | Snap style defined for the current viewport. |
| STANDARDSVIOLATION | 2 | Specifies whether a user is notified of standards violations that exist in the current drawing when a nonstandard object is created or modified. |
| STARTUP | 0 | Controls whether the **Create New Drawing** dialog box is displayed when starting a new drawing with the **NEW** and **QNEW** commands. Also controls whether the Startup dialog box is displayed when the application is started. |
| TEXTFILL | 1 | Controls fill for TrueType fonts. |
| TOOLTIPS | 1 | Toggles display of toolbar tooltips. |
| TRACKPATH | 0 | Controls the display of AutoTracking alignment paths. |
| TRAYICONS | 1 | Controls whether a tray is displayed on the status bar. |
| TRAYNOTIFY | 1 | Controls whether service notifications are displayed in the status bar tray. |
| TRAYTIMEOUT | 5 | Controls the length of time (in seconds) that service notifications are displayed. |
| TREEMAX | 10000000 | Limits maximum number of nodes in spatial index tree. |

| Variable Name | Default Value | Description |
|---|---|---|
| TRIMMODE | 1 | Controls object trimming for **FILLET** and **CHAMFER**. |
| UCSAXISANG | 90 | The default angle used when a UCS is rotated around one of its axes. |
| UCSORTHO | 1 | Specifies whether the related orthographic UCS setting is restored when restoring an orthographic view. |
| UCSVIEW | 1 | Specifies whether the current UCS is saved when a named view is created. |
| WHIPARC | 0 | Controls the smoothness of circles and arcs. |
| WHIPTHREAD | 3 | Determines which operations use multithread processing. |
| XFADECTL | 50 | Controls the fading level for nonselected objects during reference editing. |
| XLOADCTL | 2 | Controls xref demand loading. |
| XLOADPATH | "" | Path for storage of temporary copies of demand-loaded xref files. |
| XREFCTL | 0 | Controls creation of external reference log (XLG) files. |
| XREFNOTIFY | 2 | Controls the notification for updated or missing xrefs. |
| ZOOMFACTOR | 10 | Controls the incremental change that occurs when zooming backward or forward with the IntelliMouse wheel. |

The following listing shows the AutoCAD system variables that are not saved when different values are assigned. These variables revert to default values when you open an existing drawing or start a new one. Many of these variables are read-only and reference information specific to the drawing or operating system. Other variables that are not saved are used to change standard features of AutoCAD, and are restored to default values in subsequent editing sessions to avoid unexpected results in common drafting procedures. Many of the variables listed here are commonly referenced or set when customizing. The symbol ( ✐ ) indicates the variable is read-only.

## Variables Not Saved

| Variable Name | Default Value | Description |
|---|---|---|
| ACADPREFIX | ✐ | Current support directory search path. |
| ACADVER | ✐ | Current AutoCAD version number, including patch level. |
| ACISOUTVER | 70 | Controls version of files created using the **ACISOUT** command. |
| ADCSTATE | ✐ | Determines whether **DesignCenter** is active or not. |
| AFLAGS | 0 | Current attribute flags settings. |
| AREA | ✐ | The last area calculated by **AREA**, **LIST**, or **DBLIST**. |
| BINDTYPE | 0 | Controls naming of xrefs when they are bound or edited in place. |
| CDATE | ✐ | Current date and time, presented as a real number. |
| CHAMMODE | 0 | Current chamfer method. |
| CIRCLERAD | 0.0000 | Default circle radius value. |
| CMDACTIVE | ✐ | Indicates what type of command is active. |
| CMDECHO | 1 | Controls echo of prompts and commands during the AutoLISP (command) function. |
| CMDNAMES | ✐ | Name of the currently active command(s). |
| COMPASS | 0 | Controls visibility of 3D compass in current viewport. |
| DATE | ✐ | Current Julian date, with the time represented as a fraction in a real number. |

| Variable | Default | Description |
|---|---|---|
| **DBMOD** | ∿ | Drawing modification status. |
| **DIASTAT** | ∿ | Exit method of the last dialog box session. |
| **DISTANCE** | ∿ | Last distance calculated by **DIST**. |
| **DONUTID** | 0.5000 | Default inside diameter for donuts. |
| **DONUTOD** | 1.0000 | Default outside diameter for donuts. |
| **DWGNAME** | ∿ | Name of current drawing. |
| **DWGPREFIX** | ∿ | Directory path for current drawing. |
| **DWGTITLED** | ∿ | Indicates if current drawing has been named. |
| **EDGEMODE** | 0 | Cutting and boundary edge determination method for **TRIM** and **EXTEND**. |
| **ERRNO** | 0 | Displays number of the appropriate error code when an AutoLISP function call causes an error AutoCAD detects. |
| **EXPERT** | 0 | Suppression level of warnings and double-check prompts. |
| **EXPLMODE** | 1 | **EXPLODE** support for nonuniformly scaled blocks. |
| **FACETRATIO** | 0 | Specifies the faceting aspect ratio for cylindrical and conic ACIS solids. |
| **FULLOPEN** | ∿ | Specifies if the current drawing is partially open. |
| **GFANG** | 0 | Specifies the angle of a gradient fill. Valid values are 0° through 360°. |
| **GFCLR1** | "RGB 000, 000, 255" | Specifies the color for a one-color gradient fill or the first color for a two-color gradient fill. |
| **GFCLR2** | "RGB 255, 255, 153" | Specifies the second color for a two-color gradient fill. |
| **GFCLRLUM** | 1.0000 | Makes the color a tint (mixed with white) or a shade (mixed with black) in a one-color gradient fill. |
| **GFCLRSTATE** | 1 | Specifies whether a gradient fill uses one color or two colors. |
| **GFNAME** | 1 | Specifies the pattern of a gradient fill. |
| **GFSHIFT** | 0 | Specifies whether the pattern in a gradient fill is centered or is shifted up and to the left. |
| **HIDEPRECISION** | 0 | Controls the precision of hiding and shading operations. |
| **HIGHLIGHT** | 1 | Toggles highlighting of selected objects. |
| **HPANG** | 0 | Current default hatch pattern angle. |
| **HPBOUND** | 1 | Object type created by **BHATCH** and **BOUNDARY**. |
| **HPDOUBLE** | 0 | Toggles double hatching for user-defined patterns. |
| **HPNAME** | "ANSI31" | Current default hatch pattern name. |
| **HPSCALE** | 1.0000 | Current default hatch pattern scale. |
| **HPSPACE** | 1.0000 | Current hatch pattern line spacing for user-defined patterns. |
| **INSNAME** | "" | Default block name for **INSERT**. |
| **LASTANGLE** | ∿ | Last arc angle entered or drawn. |
| **LASTPOINT** | 0.0000, 0.0000, 0.0000 | Last entered UCS coordinates for current space. |
| **LASTPROMPT** | ∿ | The last text displayed at the command line, including user input. |
| **LOCALE** | ∿ | ISO language code for the current running version of AutoCAD. |
| **LOGINNAME** | ∿ | Currently configured user name. |
| **MENUECHO** | 0 | Controls level of menu echo. |
| **MENUNAME** | ∿ | Currently loaded menu file name and path. |
| **MODEMACRO** | "" | Displays a text string or text written in DIESEL on the status line. |
| **NOMUTT** | 0 | Controls the suppression of messages that are normally displayed. |
| **OFFSETDIST** | 1.0000 | Default offset distance value. |
| **PERIMETER** | ∿ | Last perimeter value calculated by **AREA**, **LIST**, or **DBLIST**. |
| **PFACEVMAX** | ∿ | Maximum number of vertices per face. |

| PLATFORM | ∿ | Current operating system. |
|---|---|---|
| POLYSIDES | 4 | Default number of sides for **POLYGON**. |
| POPUPS | ∿ | Support level of display driver for pull-down menus. |
| PRODUCT | "AutoCAD" | Returns name of product. |
| PROGRAM | "acad" | Returns name of program. |
| PSVPSCALE | 0 | View scale factor used for new viewports. |
| REFEDITNAME | ∿ | Indicates whether reference editing is active and specifies the reference file name. |
| RE-INIT | 0 | Reinitializes the digitizer, digitizer port, and acad.pgp file. |
| SAVENAME | ∿ | Default drawing file save name. |
| SCREENBOXES | ∿ | Number of available boxes in the screen menu area. |
| SCREENMODE | ∿ | Current graphics/text state of the AutoCAD display. |
| SCREENSIZE | ∿ | Current viewport size in pixels. |
| SHPNAME | "" | Default shape file name. |
| SOLIDCHECK | 1 | Enables or disables solid validation for the current drawing session. |
| SYSCODEPAGE | ∿ | System code page specified in acad.xmf. |
| TABMODE | 0 | Enables or disables tablet mode. |
| TEMPPREFIX | ∿ | Directory name for placement of temporary files. |
| TEXTEVAL | 0 | Controls evaluation method for text strings. |
| TEXTQLTY | 50 | Resolution of text outlines for TrueType fonts. |
| TPSTATE | ∿ | Determines whether the **Tool Palettes** window is active or not. |
| TSPACEFAC | 1 | Controls the line spacing distance for multiline text as a factor of the text height. |
| TSPACETYPE | 1 | Specifies the line spacing used for multiline text. |
| UNDOCTL | ∿ | Current status of the **UNDO** command. |
| UNDOMARKS | ∿ | The number of **UNDO** marks that have been placed. |
| WMFBKGND | off | Controls the transparency of the background display of AutoCAD objects when they are output to a Windows metafile, copied to the Clipboard, or dragged and dropped into other applications. |
| WMFFOREGND | off | May modify the color of objects exported as Windows metafiles or copied to the Clipboard. |
| WORLDUCS | ∿ | Specifies whether the current UCS is the same as the WCS. |
| WRITESTAT | ∿ | Controls the read-only or write status of a drawing. |

# Drawing Sheet Sizes, Settings, and Scale Parameters

| Prototype Drawing Sheet Parameters | | | |
|---|---|---|---|
| Drawing Scale | D-size (34″ × 22″) Drawing Limits | C-size (22″ × 17″) Drawing Limits | B-size (17″ × 11″) Drawing Limits |
| 1″ = 1″ | 34,22 | 22,17 | 17,11 |
| 1/2″ = 1″ | 68,44 | 44,34 | 34,22 |
| 1/4″ = 1″ | 136,88 | 88,68 | 68,44 |
| 1/8″ = 1″ | 272,176 | 176,136 | 136,88 |
| 1″ = 1′-0″ | 408,264 | 264,204 | 204,132 |
| 3/4″ = 1′-0″ | 544,352 | 352,272 | 272,176 |
| 1/2″ = 1′-0″ | 816,528 | 528,408 | 408,264 |
| 3/8″ = 1′-0″ | 1088,704 | 704,544 | 544,352 |
| 1/4″ = 1′-0″ | 1632,1056 | 1056,816 | 816,528 |
| 3/16″ = 1′-0″ | 2176,1408 | 1408,1088 | 1088,704 |
| 1/8″ = 1′-0″ | 3264,2112 | 2112,1632 | 1632,1056 |
| 3/32″ = 1′-0″ | 4352,2816 | 2816,2176 | 2176,1408 |
| 1/16″ = 1′-0″ | 6528,4224 | 4224,3264 | 3264,2112 |

| Prototype Drawing Scale Parameters | | | |
|---|---|---|---|
| Drawing Scale | Dimension Scale (DIMSCALE) | Linetype Scale (LTSCALE) | Inversion Scale of Border & Parts List Blocks |
| 1″ = 1″ | 1 | .5 | 1 = 1 |
| 1/2″ = 1″ | 2 | 1 | 1 = 2 |
| 1/4″ = 1″ | 4 | 2 | 1 = 4 |
| 1/8″ = 1″ | 8 | 4 | 1 = 8 |
| 1″ = 1′-0″ | 12 | 6 | 1 = 12 |
| 3/4″ = 1′-0″ | 16 | 8 | 1 = 16 |
| 1/2″ = 1′-0″ | 24 | 12 | 1 = 24 |
| 3/8″ = 1′-0″ | 32 | 16 | 1 = 32 |
| 1/4″ = 1′-0″ | 48 | 24 | 1 = 48 |
| 3/16″ = 1′-0″ | 64 | 32 | 1 = 64 |
| 1/8″ = 1′-0″ | 96 | 48 | 1 = 96 |
| 3/32″ = 1′-0″ | 128 | 64 | 1 = 128 |
| 1/16″ = 1′-0″ | 192 | 96 | 1 = 192 |

## Architectural Sheet Size and Settings

| Paper size (in) | Approx. drawing area | Scale | Actual sheet limits | Approx. drawing limits | Text height 1/8" | Text height 1/4" | Scale factor | Ltscale |
|---|---|---|---|---|---|---|---|---|
| A<br>12 × 9 | 10 × 7.5 | 1″ = 1′–0″<br>1/2″ = 1′–0″<br>1/4″ = 1′–0″<br>1/8″ = 1′–0″ | 12′ × 9′<br>24′ × 18′<br>48′ × 36′<br>96′ × 72′ | 10′ × 7.5′<br>20′ × 15′<br>40′ × 30′<br>80′ × 60′ | 1.5<br>3.0<br>6.0<br>12.0 | 3.0<br>6.0<br>12.0<br>24.0 | 12<br>24<br>48<br>96 | 6<br>12<br>24<br>48 |
| B<br>18 × 12 | 16 × 11 | 1″ = 1′–0″<br>1/2″ = 1′–0″<br>1/4″ = 1′–0″<br>1/8″ = 1′–0″ | 18′ × 12′<br>36′ × 24′<br>72′ × 48′<br>144′ × 96′ | 16′ × 11′<br>32′ × 20′<br>64′ × 40′<br>128′ × 80′ | | | | |
| C<br>24 × 18 | 22 × 16 | 1″ = 1′–0″<br>1/2″ = 1′–0″<br>1/4″ = 1′–0″<br>1/8″ = 1′–0″ | 24′ × 18′<br>48′ × 36′<br>96′ × 72′<br>192′ × 144′ | 22′ × 16′<br>44′ × 32′<br>88′ × 64′<br>176′ × 28′ | | | | |
| D<br>36 × 24 | 34 × 22 | 1″ = 1′–0″<br>1/2″ = 1′–0″<br>1/4″ = 1′–0″<br>1/8″ = 1′–0″ | 36′ × 24′<br>72′ × 48′<br>144′ × 96′<br>288′ × 192′ | 34′ × 22′<br>68′ × 44′<br>136′ × 88′<br>272′ × 176′ | | | | |
| E<br>48 × 36 | 46 × 34 | 1″ = 1′–0″<br>1/2″ = 1′–0″<br>1/4″ = 1′–0″<br>1/8″ = 1′–0″ | 48′ × 36′<br>96′ × 72′<br>192′ × 144′<br>384′ × 288′ | 46′ × 34′<br>92′ × 68′<br>184′ × 136′<br>368′ × 272′ | | | | |

## Mechanical Sheet Size and Settings

| Paper size (in) | Approx. drawing area | Scale | Actual sheet limits | Approx. drawing limits | Text height 1/8" | Text height 1/4" | Scale factor | Ltscale |
|---|---|---|---|---|---|---|---|---|
| A<br>11 × 8.5 | 9 × 7 | 2″ = 1″<br>3/4″ = 1″<br>1/2″ = 1″<br>1/4″ = 1″ | 5.5 × 4.25<br>14.67 × 11.33<br>22 × 17<br>44 × 34 | 4.5″ × 3.5″<br>12″ × 9.33″<br>18″ × 14″<br>36″ × 28″ | .0625<br>.167<br>.25<br>.5 | .125<br>.33<br>.5<br>1.0 | .5<br>1.33<br>2<br>4 | .25<br>.67<br>1<br>2 |
| B<br>17 × 11 | 15 × 10 | 2″ = 1″<br>3/4″ = 1″<br>1/2″ = 1″<br>1/4″ = 1″ | 8.5 × 5.5<br>22.67 × 14.67<br>34 × 22<br>68 × 44 | 7.5″ × 5″<br>20″ × 13.33″<br>30″ × 20″<br>60″ × 40″ | | | | |
| C<br>22 × 17 | 20 × 15 | 2″ = 1″<br>3/4″ = 1″<br>1/2″ = 1″<br>1/4″ = 1″ | 11 × 8.5<br>29.33 × 14.67<br>44 × 34<br>88 × 68 | 10″ × 7.5″<br>26.67″ × 20″<br>40″ × 30″<br>80″ × 60″ | | | | |
| D<br>34 × 22 | 32 × 20 | 2″ = 1″<br>3/4″ = 1″<br>1/2″ = 1″<br>1/4″ = 1″ | 17 × 11<br>45.33 × 29.33<br>68 × 44<br>136 × 88 | 16″ × 10″<br>42.67″ × 26.67″<br>64″ × 40″<br>128″ × 80″ | | | | |
| E<br>44 × 34 | 42 × 32 | 2″ = 1″<br>3/4″ = 1″<br>1/2″ = 1″<br>1/4″ = 1″ | 22 × 17<br>58.67 × 45.33<br>88 × 68<br>176 × 136 | 21″ × 16″<br>56″ × 42.67″<br>84″ × 64″<br>168″ × 128″ | | | | |

| Paper size (in) | Approx. drawing area | Scale | Actual sheet limits | Approx. drawing limits | Text height 1/8 " | Text height 1/4 " | Scale factor | Ltscale |
|---|---|---|---|---|---|---|---|---|
| A 11 × 8.5 | 9 × 7 | 1″ = 10′<br>1″ = 20′<br>1″ = 30′<br>1″ = 50′ | 110′ × 85′<br>220′ × 170′<br>330′ × 255′<br>550′ × 425′ | 90′ × 70′<br>180′ × 140′<br>270′ × 210′<br>450′ × 350′ | 15<br>30<br>45<br>75 | 30<br>60<br>90<br>150 | 120<br>240<br>360<br>600 | 60<br>120<br>180<br>300 |
| B 17 × 11 | 15 × 10 | 1″ = 10′<br>1″ = 20′<br>1″ = 30′<br>1″ = 50′ | 170′ × 110′<br>340′ × 220′<br>510′ × 330′<br>850′ × 550′ | 150′ × 100′<br>300′ × 200′<br>450′ × 300′<br>750′ × 500′ | | | | |
| C 22 × 17 | 20 × 15 | 1″ = 10′<br>1″ = 20′<br>1″ = 30′<br>1″ = 50′ | 220′ × 170′<br>440′ × 340′<br>660′ × 510′<br>1100′ × 850′ | 200′ × 150′<br>400′ × 300′<br>600′ × 450′<br>1000′ × 750′ | | | | |
| D 34 × 22 | 32 × 20 | 1″ = 10′<br>1″ = 20′<br>1″ = 30′<br>1″ = 50′ | 340′ × 220′<br>680′ × 440′<br>1020′ × 660′<br>1700′ × 1100′ | 320′ × 200′<br>640′ × 400′<br>960′ × 600′<br>1600′ × 1000′ | | | | |
| E 44 × 34 | 42 × 32 | 1″ = 10′<br>1″ = 20′<br>1″ = 30′<br>1″ = 50′ | 440′ × 340′<br>880′ × 680′<br>1320′ × 1020′<br>2200′ × 1700′ | 420′ × 320′<br>840′ × 640′<br>1260′ × 960′<br>2100′ × 1600′ | | | | |

Civil Sheet Size and Settings

| Paper size (mm) | Approx. drawing area | Scale | Actual paper limits (mm) | Approx. drawing limits (mm) | Text height | | Scale factor | Ltscale |
|---|---|---|---|---|---|---|---|---|
| | | | | | 1/8 " | 1/4 " | | |
| A4 297 × 210 | 277 × 190 | 1 = 2 | 594 × 420 | 554 × 380 | .25 | .5 | 50.8 | 1 |
| | | 1 = 5 | 1485 × 1050 | 1385 × 950 | .625 | 1.25 | 127 | 2 |
| | | 1 = 10 | 2970 × 2100 | 2770 × 1900 | 1.25 | 2.5 | 254 | 5 |
| | | 1 = 20 | 5940 × 4200 | 5540 × 3800 | 2.5 | 5 | 508 | 10 |
| | | 1 = 50 | 14850 × 10500 | 13850 × 9500 | 6.25 | 12.5 | 1270 | 25 |
| | | 1 = 100 | 29700 × 21000 | 27700 × 19000 | 12.5 | 25 | 2540 | 50 |
| A3 420 × 297 | 400 × 277 | 1 = 2 | 820 × 594 | 780 × 554 | | | | |
| | | 1 = 5 | 2100 × 1485 | 2000 × 1385 | | | | |
| | | 1 = 10 | 4200 × 2970 | 4000 × 2770 | | | | |
| | | 1 = 20 | 8400 × 5940 | 8000 × 5540 | | | | |
| | | 1 = 50 | 21000 × 14850 | 20000 × 13850 | | | | |
| | | 1 = 100 | 42000 × 29700 | 40000 × 27700 | | | | |
| A2 594 × 420 | 577 × 400 | 1 = 2 | 1188 × 840 | 1148 × 800 | | | | |
| | | 1 = 5 | 2970 × 2100 | 2870 × 2000 | | | | |
| | | 1 = 10 | 5940 × 4200 | 5740 × 4000 | | | | |
| | | 1 = 20 | 11880 × 8400 | 11480 × 8000 | | | | |
| | | 1 = 50 | 29700 × 21000 | 28700 × 20000 | | | | |
| | | 1 = 100 | 59400 × 42000 | 57400 × 40000 | | | | |
| A1 841 × 594 | 801 × 554 | 1 = 2 | 1682 × 1188 | 1642 × 1148 | | | | |
| | | 1 = 5 | 4205 × 2970 | 4105 × 2870 | | | | |
| | | 1 = 10 | 8410 × 5940 | 8210 × 5740 | | | | |
| | | 1 = 20 | 16820 × 11880 | 16420 × 11480 | | | | |
| | | 1 = 50 | 42050 × 29700 | 41050 × 28700 | | | | |
| | | 1 = 100 | 84100 × 59400 | 82100 × 57400 | | | | |
| A0 1189 × 841 | 1149 × 801 | 1 = 2 | 2378 × 1682 | 2338 × 1642 | | | | |
| | | 1 = 5 | 5945 × 4205 | 5845 × 4105 | | | | |
| | | 1 = 10 | 11890 × 8410 | 11690 × 8210 | | | | |
| | | 1 = 20 | 23780 × 16820 | 23380 × 16420 | | | | |
| | | 1 = 50 | 59450 × 42050 | 58450 × 41050 | | | | |
| | | 1 = 100 | 118900 × 84100 | 116900 × 82100 | | | | |

**Metric Sheet Size and Settings**

# Command Aliases

| Command | Alias |
|---|---|
| 3DARRAY | 3A |
| 3DFACE | 3F |
| 3DORBIT | 3DO, ORBIT |
| 3DPOLY | 3P |
| ADCENTER | ADC |
| ALIGN | AL |
| APPLOAD | AP |
| ARC | A |
| AREA | AA |
| ARRAY | AR |
| -ARRAY | -AR |
| ATTDEF | ATT |
| -ATTDEF | -ATT |
| ATTEDIT | ATE |
| -ATTEDIT | -ATE, ATTE |
| BHATCH | BH, H |
| BLOCK | B |
| -BLOCK | -B |
| BOUNDARY | BO |
| -BOUNDARY | -BO |
| BREAK | BR |
| CHAMFER | CHA |
| CHANGE | -CH |
| CHECKSTANDARDS | CHK |
| CIRCLE | C |
| COLOR | COL, COLOUR |
| COPY | CO |
| DBCONNECT | DBC |
| DDEDIT | ED |
| DDGRIPS | GR |
| DDVPOINT | VP |
| DIMALIGNED | DAL |
| DIMANGULAR | DAN |
| DIMBASELINE | DBA |
| DIMCENTER | DCE |
| DIMCONTINUE | DCO |
| DIMDIAMETER | DDI |
| DIMDISASSOCIATE | DDA |
| DIMEDIT | DED |
| DIMLINEAR | DLI |
| DIMORDINATE | DOR |
| DIMOVERRIDE | DOV |
| DIMRADIUS | DRA |

| Command | Alias |
|---|---|
| DIMREASSOCIATE | DRE |
| DIMSTYLE | D, DST |
| DIST | DI |
| DIVIDE | DIV |
| DONUT | DO |
| DRAWORDER | DR |
| DSETTINGS | DS, SE |
| DTEXT | DT |
| DVIEW | DV |
| ELLIPSE | EL |
| ERASE | E |
| EXPLODE | X |
| EXPORT | EXP |
| EXTEND | EX |
| EXTRUDE | EXT |
| FILLET | F |
| FILTER | FI |
| GROUP | G |
| -GROUP | -G |
| HATCH | -H |
| HATCHEDIT | HE |
| HIDE | HI |
| IMAGE | IM |
| -IMAGE | -IM |
| IMAGEADJUST | IAD |
| IMAGEATTACH | IAT |
| IMAGECLIP | ICL |
| IMPORT | IMP |
| INSERT | I |
| -INSERT | -I |
| INSERTOBJ | IO |
| INTERFERE | INF |
| INTERSECT | IN |
| LAYER | LA |
| -LAYER | -LA |
| -LAYOUT | LO |
| LENGTHEN | LEN |
| LINE | L |
| LINETYPE | LT, LTYPE |
| -LINETYPE | -LT, -LTYPE |
| LIST | LI, LS |
| LTSCALE | LTS |
| LWEIGHT | LINEWEIGHT, LW |
| MATCHPROP | MA |
| MEASURE | ME |

| Command | Alias | Command | Alias |
|---------|-------|---------|-------|
| MIRROR | MI | SCALE | SC |
| MLINE | ML | SCRIPT | SCR |
| MOVE | M | SECTION | SEC |
| MSPACE | MS | SETVAR | SET |
| MTEXT | MT, T | SHADEMODE | SHA |
| -MTEXT | -T | SLICE | SL |
| MVIEW | MV | SNAP | SN |
| OFFSET | O | SOLID | SO |
| OPTIONS | OP, PR | SPELL | SP |
| OSNAP | OS | SPLINE | SPL |
| -OSNAP | -OS | SPLINEDIT | SPE |
| PAN | P | STANDARDS | STA |
| -PAN | -P | STRETCH | S |
| -PARTIALOPEN | PARTIALOPEN | STYLE | ST |
| PASTESPEC | PA | SUBTRACT | SU |
| PEDIT | PE | TABLET | TA |
| PLINE | PL | THICKNESS | TH |
| PLOT | PRINT | TILEMODE | TI |
| POINT | PO | TOLERANCE | TOL |
| POLYGON | POL | TOOLBAR | TO |
| PREVIEW | PRE | TOOLPALETTES | TP |
| PROPERTIES | CH, MO, PR, PROPS | TORUS | TOR |
| PROPERTIESCLOSE | PRCLOSE | TRIM | TR |
| PSPACE | PS | UCSMAN | UC |
| PUBLISHTOWEB | PTW | UNION | UNI |
| PURGE | PU | UNITS | UN |
| -PURGE | -PU | -UNITS | -UN |
| QLEADER | LE | VIEW | V |
| QUIT | EXIT | -VIEW | -V |
| RECTANGLE | REC | -VPOINT | -VP |
| REDRAW | R | WBLOCK | W |
| REDRAWALL | RA | -WBLOCK | -W |
| REGEN | RE | WEDGE | WE |
| REGENALL | REA | XATTACH | XA |
| REGION | REG | XBIND | XB |
| RENAME | REN | -XBIND | -XB |
| -RENAME | -REN | XCLIP | XC |
| RENDER | RR | XLINE | XL |
| REVOLVE | REV | XREF | XR |
| ROTATE | RO | -XREF | -XR |
| RPREF | RPR | ZOOM | Z |

# Drafting Standards and Related Documents

The following is a list of ANSI/ASME drafting standards or related documents. They are ANSI/ASME adopted, unless another standard developing organization, such as ANSI/NFPA, is indicated. For more information or to order standards, go to the ASME web site at www.asme.org.

## Abbreviations

Y14.38-1999, *Abbreviations and Acronyms*

## Dimensions

B4.1-1967 (R1999), *Preferred Limits and Fits for Cylindrical Parts*
B4.2-1978 (R1999), *Preferred Metric Limits and Fits*
B4.3-1978 (R1999), *General Tolerances for Metric Dimensioned Products*
B32.3-1984 (R1994), *Preferred Metric Sizes for Flat Metal Products*
B32.4M-1980 (R1994), *Preferred Metric Sizes for Round, Square, Rectangle, and Hexagon Metal Products*
B36.10M-2001, *Welded and Seamless Wrought Steel Pipe*
B36.19M-1985 (R1994), *Stainless Steel Pipe*

## Drafting Standards

Y14.1-1995, *Decimal Inch Drawing Sheet Size and Format*
Y14.1M-1995 (R2002), *Metric Drawing Sheet Size and Format*
Y14.2M-1992 (R2003), *Line Conventions and Lettering*
Y14.3M-1994 (R1999), *Multiview and Sectional View Drawings*
Y14.4M-1989 (R1999), *Pictorial Drawings*
Y14.5M-1994 (R1999), *Dimensioning and Tolerancing*
Y14.5.1-1994 (R1999), *Mathematical Definition of Y14.5*
Y14.5.2-2000, *Certification of GD&T Professionals*
Y14.6-2001, *Screw Thread Representation*
Y14.7.1-1971 (R2003), *Gear Drawing Standards-Part: For Spur, Helical, Double Helical, and Rack*
Y14.7.2-1978 (R1999), *Gear and Spline Drawing Standards-Part 2-Bevel and Hypoid Gears*
Y14.8M-1996 (R2002), *Castings and Forgings*
Y14.13M-1981 (R2003), *Mechanical Spring Representation*
Y14.18M-1986 (R2003), *Optical Parts*
Y14.24M-1999, *Types and Applications of Engineering Drawings*
Y14.32.1M-1994 (R1999), *Chassis Frames—Passenger Car and Light Truck—Ground Vehicle Practices*
Y14.34M-1996 (R2002), *Associated Lists*
Y14.35M-1997 (R2003), *Engineering Drawings and Associated Documents*
Y14.36M-1996 (R2002), *Surface Texture Symbols*
Y14.100M-2000, *Engineering Drawing Practices*

## Graphic Symbols

Y32.4-1977 (R1999), *Plumbing Fixture Diagrams Used in Architectural and Building Construction*

Y32.7-1972 (R1994), *Railroad Maps and Profiles*

Y32.18-1972 (R1998), *Mechanical and Acoustical Elements as Used in Schematic Diagrams*

ANSI/AWS A2.4-98, *Symbols for Welding, Brazing, and Nondestructive Examination*

ANSI/IEEE 315-1975, *Graphic Symbols for Electrical and Electronics Diagrams (Including Reference Designation Letters)*

ANSI/ISA S5.1-1984 (R1992), *Instrumentation Symbols and Identification*

ANSI/NFPA 170-1999, *Fire Safety Symbols*

## Metric System

SI-1, *Orientation and Guide for use of SI (Metric) Units*

Some of these standards are, and may in the future be, under review. Information in this appendix is subject to change. Some standards may be out of print.

# Drafting Symbols

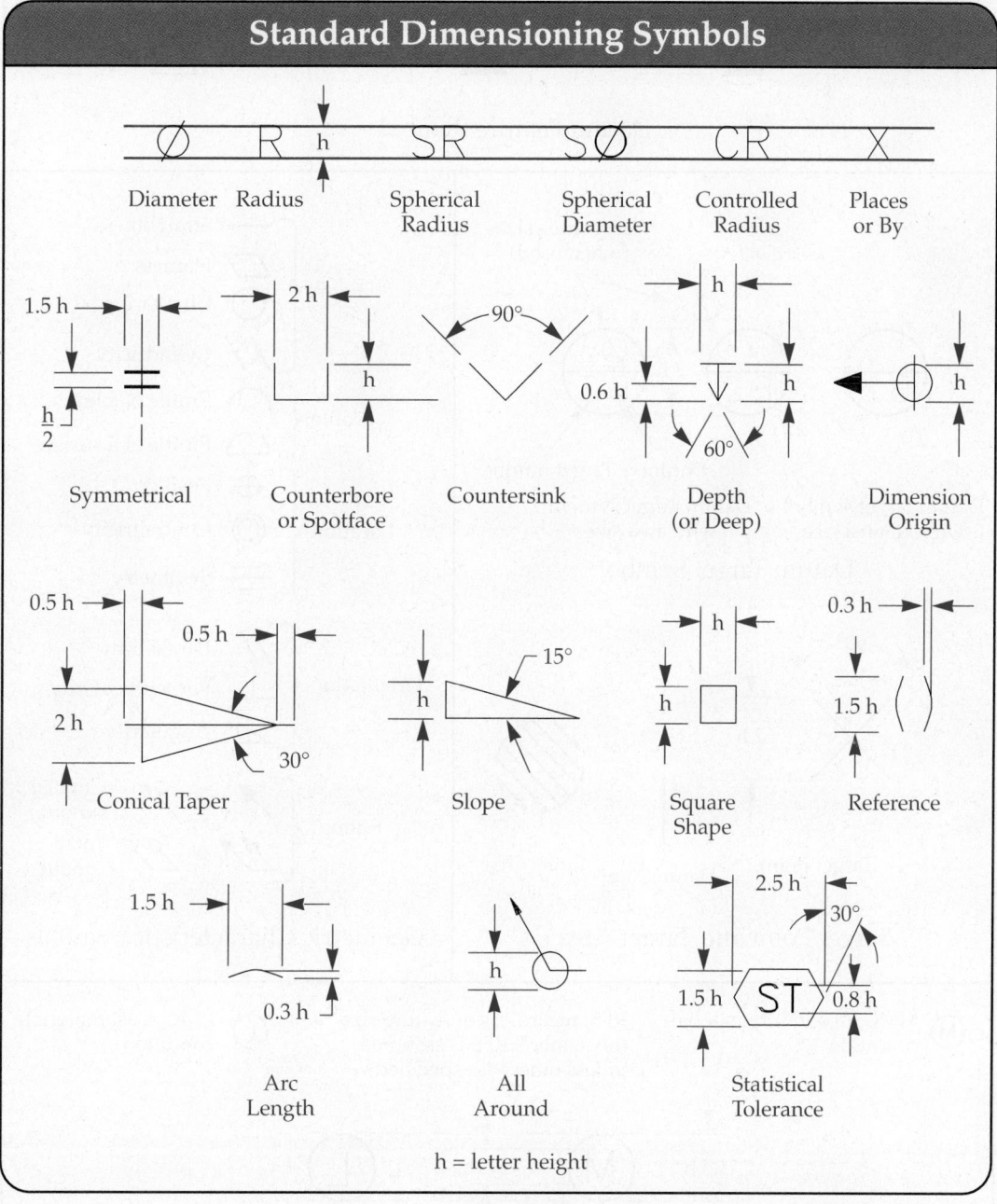

## Standard Dimensioning Symbols

Ø — Diameter
R — Radius
SR — Spherical Radius
SØ — Spherical Diameter
CR — Controlled Radius
X — Places or By

Symmetrical (1.5 h, h/2)
Counterbore or Spotface (2 h, h)
Countersink (90°)
Depth (or Deep) (h, 0.6 h, h, 60°)
Dimension Origin (h)

Conical Taper (0.5 h, 0.5 h, 2 h, 30°)
Slope (h, 15°)
Square Shape (h, h)
Reference (0.3 h, 1.5 h)

Arc Length (1.5 h, 0.3 h)
All Around (h)
Statistical Tolerance (2.5 h, 30°, 1.5 h, ST, 0.8 h)

h = letter height

# Geometric Dimensioning and Tolerancing Symbols

Datum Feature Symbol

Datum Target Symbol

Target Point and Target Area

Geometric Characteristic Symbols

Form — Straightness, Flatness, Circularity, Cylindricity

Profile — Profile of a line, Profile of a surface

Location — Position, Concentricity, Symmetry

Orientation — Parallelism, Perpendicularity, Angularity

Runout — Circular runout, Total runout

(M) MMC, maximum material condition

RFS, regardless of feature size (no symbol, RFS is assumed unless otherwise specified)

(L) LMC, least material condition

Material Condition Symbols

# Geometric Dimensioning and Tolerancing Symbols

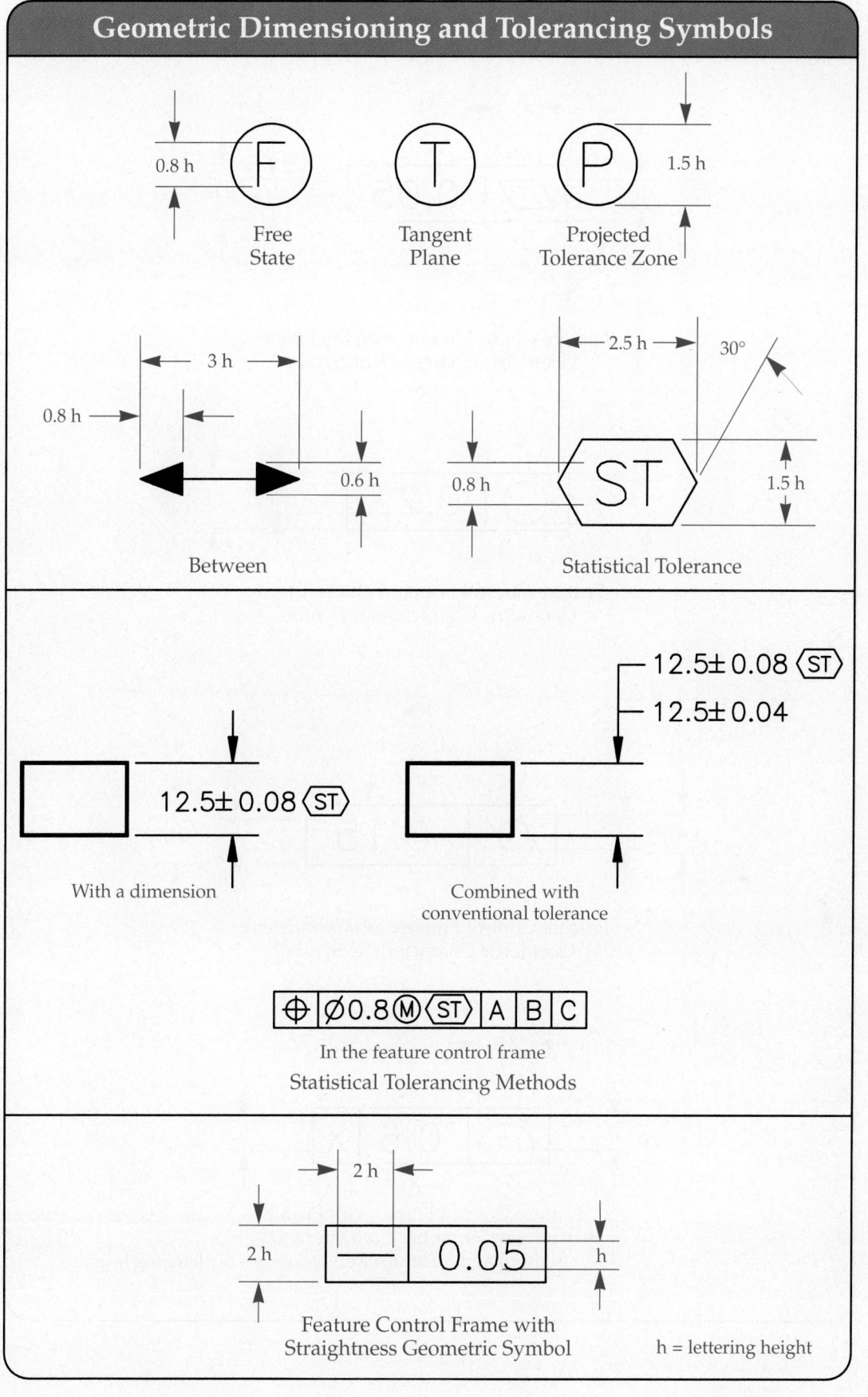

0.8 h

F

Free
State

T

Tangent
Plane

P

1.5 h

Projected
Tolerance Zone

3 h

0.8 h

0.6 h

Between

2.5 h

30°

0.8 h

ST

1.5 h

Statistical Tolerance

12.5± 0.08 ⟨ST⟩

With a dimension

12.5± 0.08 ⟨ST⟩
12.5± 0.04

Combined with
conventional tolerance

⊕ | Ø0.8Ⓜ⟨ST⟩ | A | B | C

In the feature control frame
Statistical Tolerancing Methods

2 h

2 h

— | 0.05

h

Feature Control Frame with
Straightness Geometric Symbol

h = lettering height

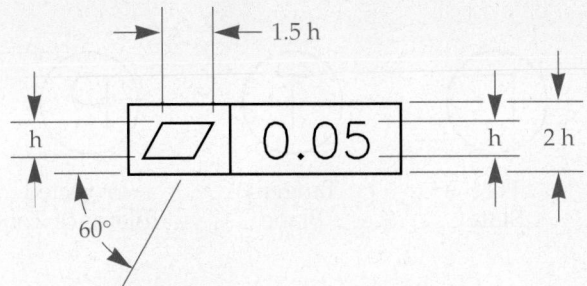

Feature Control Frame with the Flatness
Geometric Characteristic Symbol

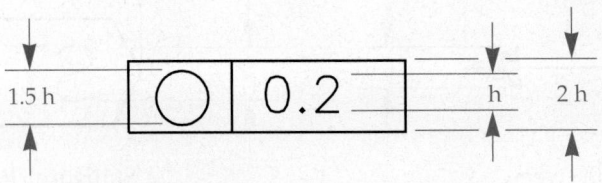

Feature Control Frame with Circularity
Geometric Characteristic Symbol

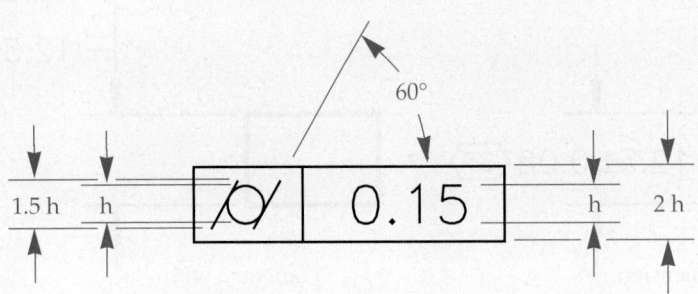

Feature Control Frame with Cylindricity
Geometric Characteristic Symbol

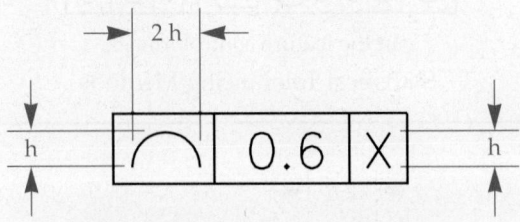

Feature Control Frame with Profile
of a Line Geometric Characteristic
Symbol and a Datum Reference          h = lettering height

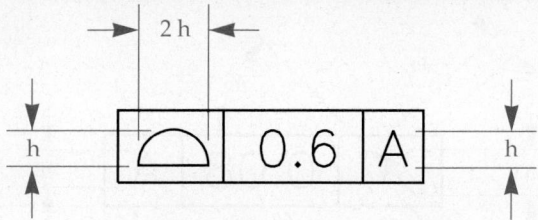

Feature Control Frame with Profile
of a Surface Geometric Characteristic
Symbol and a Datum Reference

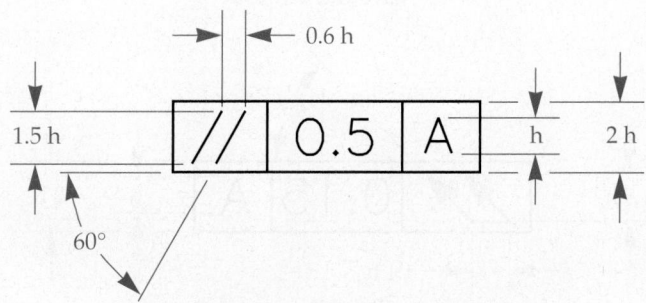

Feature Control Frame with
Parallelism Geometric Characteristic
Symbol and a Datum Reference

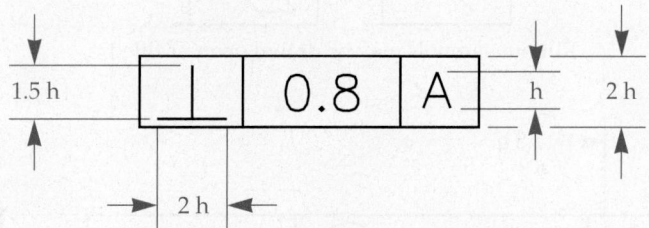

Feature Control Frame with
Perpendicularity Geometric Characteristic
Symbol and a Datum Reference

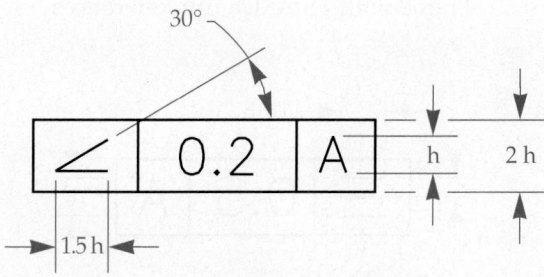

Feature Control Frame with
Angularity Geometric Characteristic
Symbol and a Datum Reference

h = lettering height

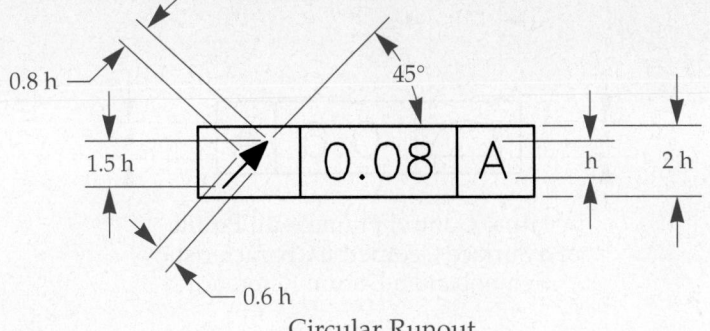

Circular Runout

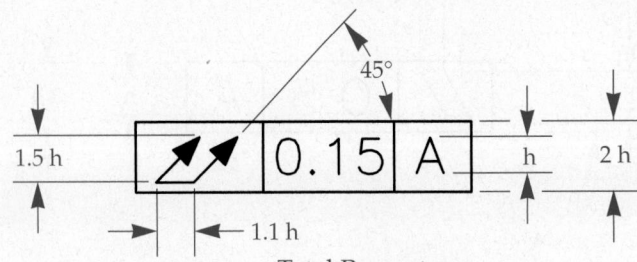

Total Runout

Runout symbols may be drawn open or filled

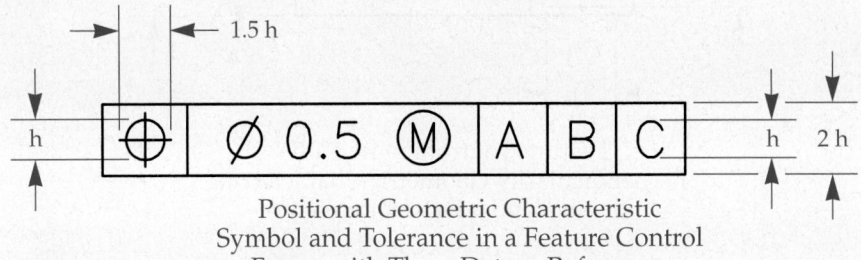

Positional Geometric Characteristic
Symbol and Tolerance in a Feature Control
Frame with Three Datum References

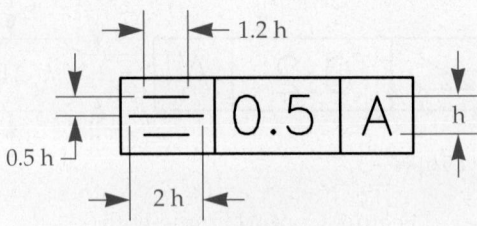

Feature Control Frame with Symmetry
Geometric Characteristic
Symbol and a Datum Reference

h = lettering height

# Single Line Piping Symbols

| Name | Screwed | | | Buttwelded | | |
|------|---------|---|---|------------|---|---|
| | Left Side | Front | Right Side | Left Side | Front | Right Side |
| 90° Elbow | | | | | | |
| 45° Elbow | | | | | | |
| Tee | | | | | | |
| 45° Lateral | | | | | | |
| Cross | | | | | | |
| Cap | | | | | | |
| Concentric Reducer | | | | | | |
| Eccentric Reducer | | | | | | |
| Union | | | | | | |
| Coupling | | | | | | |

# Common Symbols for Electrical Diagrams

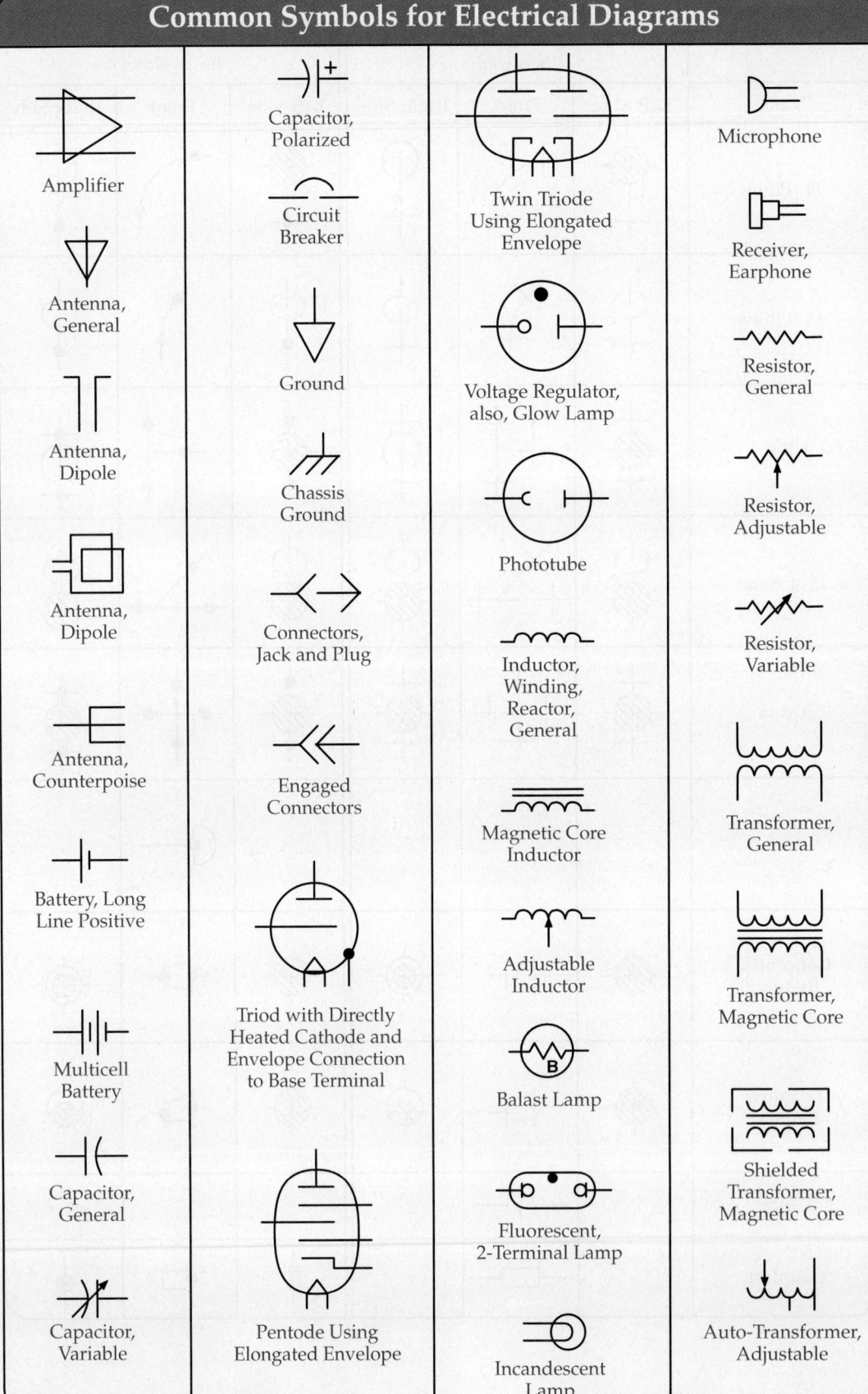

Amplifier

Antenna, General

Antenna, Dipole

Antenna, Dipole

Antenna, Counterpoise

Battery, Long Line Positive

Multicell Battery

Capacitor, General

Capacitor, Variable

Capacitor, Polarized

Circuit Breaker

Ground

Chassis Ground

Connectors, Jack and Plug

Engaged Connectors

Triod with Directly Heated Cathode and Envelope Connection to Base Terminal

Pentode Using Elongated Envelope

Twin Triode Using Elongated Envelope

Voltage Regulator, also, Glow Lamp

Phototube

Inductor, Winding, Reactor, General

Magnetic Core Inductor

Adjustable Inductor

Balast Lamp

Fluorescent, 2-Terminal Lamp

Incandescent Lamp

Microphone

Receiver, Earphone

Resistor, General

Resistor, Adjustable

Resistor, Variable

Transformer, General

Transformer, Magnetic Core

Shielded Transformer, Magnetic Core

Auto-Transformer, Adjustable

# Common Architectural Symbols

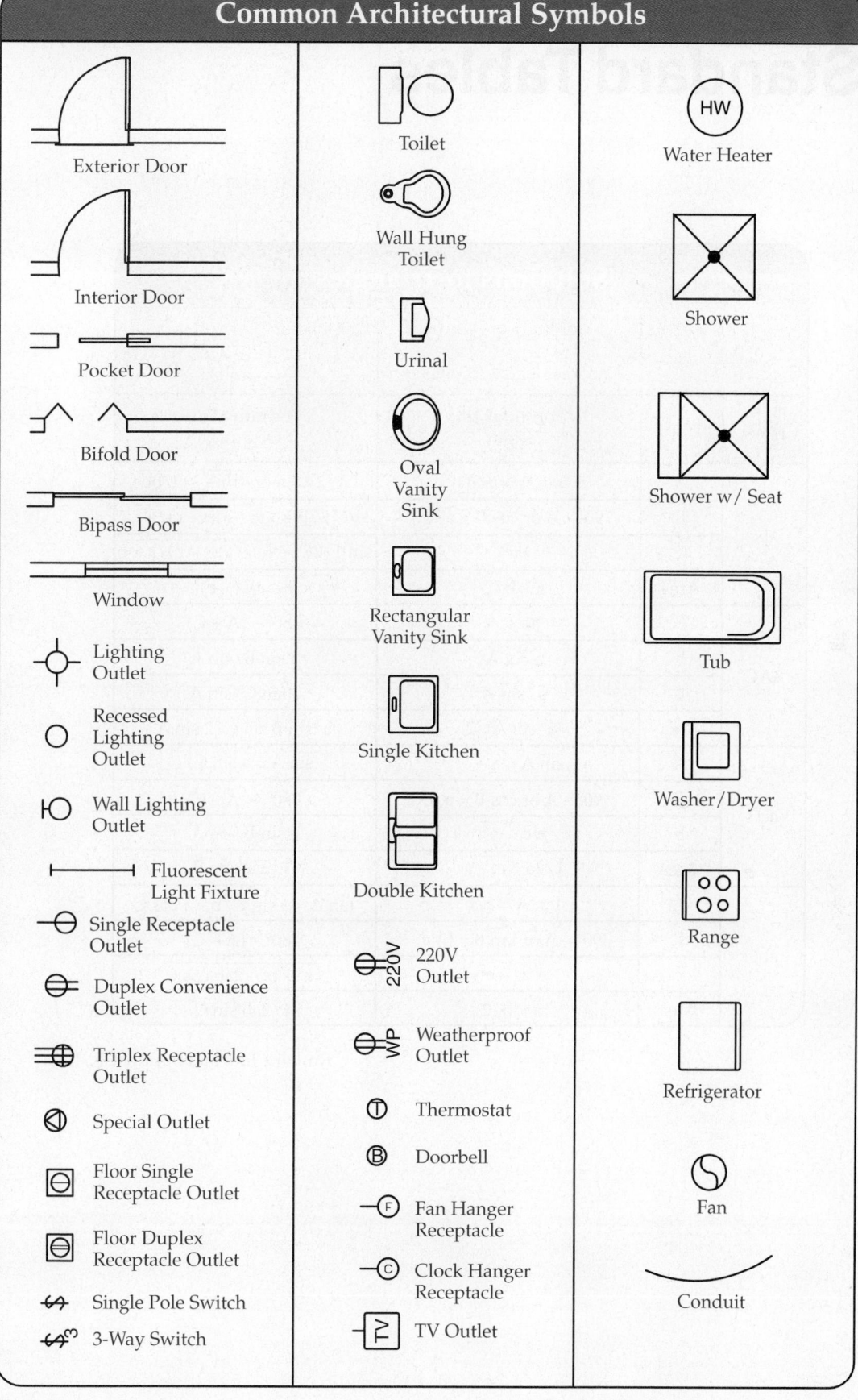

Exterior Door

Interior Door

Pocket Door

Bifold Door

Bipass Door

Window

Lighting Outlet

Recessed Lighting Outlet

Wall Lighting Outlet

Fluorescent Light Fixture

Single Receptacle Outlet

Duplex Convenience Outlet

Triplex Receptacle Outlet

Special Outlet

Floor Single Receptacle Outlet

Floor Duplex Receptacle Outlet

Single Pole Switch

3-Way Switch

Toilet

Wall Hung Toilet

Urinal

Oval Vanity Sink

Rectangular Vanity Sink

Single Kitchen

Double Kitchen

220V Outlet

Weatherproof Outlet

Thermostat

Doorbell

Fan Hanger Receptacle

Clock Hanger Receptacle

TV Outlet

Water Heater

Shower

Shower w/ Seat

Tub

Washer/Dryer

Range

Refrigerator

Fan

Conduit

# Standard Tables

| Solutions to Triangles | | | |
|---|---|---|---|
| $A + B + C = 180°$<br>$S = \dfrac{a+b+c}{2}$ | | Right | Oblique |
| **Have** | **Want** | **Formulas for Right** | **Formulas for Oblique** |
| abc | A | $\tan A = a/b$ | $1/2A = \sqrt{(s-b)(s-c)/bc}$ |
| | B | $90° - A$ or $\cos B = a/c$ | $\sin 1/2B = \sqrt{(s-a)(s-c)/a \times c}$ |
| | C | $90°$ | $\sin 1/2C = \sqrt{(s-a)(s-b)/a \times b}$ |
| | Area | $a \times b/2$ | $\sqrt{s \times (s-a)(s-b)(s-c)}$ |
| aAC | B | $90° - A$ | $180° - (A+C)$ |
| | b | $a \cot A$ | $a \sin B/\sin A$ |
| | c | $a/\sin A$ | $a \sin C/\sin A$ |
| | Area | $(a^2 \cot A)/2$ | $a^2 \sin B \sin C/2 \sin A$ |
| acC | A | $\sin A = a - c$ | $\sin A = a \sin C/c$ |
| | B | $90° - A$ or $\cos B = a/c$ | $180° - (A+C)$ |
| | b | $\sqrt{c^2 - a^2}$ | $c \sin B/\sin C$ |
| | Area | $1/2a \sqrt{c^2 - a^2}$ | $1/2\, ac \sin B$ |
| abC | A | $\tan A = a/b$ | $\tan A = a \sin C/b - a \cos C$ |
| | B | $90° - A$ or $\tan B = b/a$ | $180° - (A+C)$ |
| | c | $\sqrt{a^2 - b^2}$ | $\sqrt{a^2 + b^2 - 2ab \cos C}$ |
| | Area | $a \times b/2$ | $1/2ab \sin C$ |

Rutland Tool and Supply Co., Inc.

# Fraction, Decimal, and Metric Equivalents

| INCHES | | MILLI- METERS | INCHES | | MILLI- METERS |
|---|---|---|---|---|---|
| FRACTIONS | DECIMALS | | FRACTIONS | DECIMALS | |
| | .00394 | .1 | 15/32 | .46875 | 11.9063 |
| | .00787 | .2 | | .47244 | 12.00 |
| | .01181 | .3 | 31/64 | .484375 | 12.3031 |
| 1/64 | .015625 | .3969 | 1/2 | .5000 | 12.70 |
| | .01575 | .4 | | .51181 | 13.00 |
| | .01969 | .5 | 33/64 | .515625 | 13.0969 |
| | .02362 | .6 | 17/32 | .53125 | 13.4938 |
| | .02756 | .7 | 35/64 | .546875 | 13.8907 |
| 1/32 | .03125 | .7938 | | .55118 | 14.00 |
| | .0315 | .8 | 9/16 | .5625 | 14.2875 |
| | .03543 | .9 | 37/64 | .578125 | 14.6844 |
| | .03937 | 1.00 | | .59055 | 15.00 |
| 3/64 | .046875 | 1.1906 | 19/32 | .59375 | 15.0813 |
| 1/16 | .0625 | 1.5875 | 39/64 | .609375 | 15.4782 |
| 5/64 | .078125 | 1.9844 | 5/8 | .625 | 15.875 |
| | .07874 | 2.00 | | .62992 | 16.00 |
| 3/32 | .09375 | 2.3813 | 41/64 | .640625 | 16.2719 |
| 7/64 | .109375 | 2.7781 | 21/32 | .65625 | 16.6688 |
| | .11811 | 3.00 | | .66929 | 17.00 |
| 1/8 | .125 | 3.175 | 43/64 | .671875 | 17.0657 |
| 9/64 | .140625 | 3.5719 | 11/16 | .6875 | 17.4625 |
| 5/32 | .15625 | 3.9688 | 45/64 | .703125 | 17.8594 |
| | .15748 | 4.00 | | .70866 | 18.00 |
| 11/64 | .171875 | 4.3656 | 23/32 | .71875 | 18.2563 |
| 3/16 | .1875 | 4.7625 | 47/64 | .734375 | 18.6532 |
| | .19685 | 5.00 | | .74803 | 19.00 |
| 13/64 | .203125 | 5.1594 | 3/4 | .7500 | 19.05 |
| 7/32 | .21875 | 5.5563 | 49/64 | .765625 | 19.4469 |
| 15/64 | .234375 | 5.9531 | 25/32 | .78125 | 19.8438 |
| | .23622 | 6.00 | | .7874 | 20.00 |
| 1/4 | .2500 | 6.35 | 51/64 | .796875 | 20.2407 |
| 17/64 | .265625 | 6.7469 | 13/16 | .8125 | 20.6375 |
| | .27559 | 7.00 | | .82677 | 21.00 |
| 9/32 | .28125 | 7.1438 | 53/64 | .828125 | 21.0344 |
| 19/64 | .296875 | 7.5406 | 27/32 | .84375 | 21.4313 |
| 5/16 | .3125 | 7.9375 | 55/64 | .859375 | 21.8282 |
| | .31496 | 8.00 | | .86614 | 22.00 |
| 21/64 | .328125 | 8.3344 | 7/8 | .875 | 22.225 |
| 11/32 | .34375 | 8.7313 | 57/64 | .890625 | 22.6219 |
| | .35433 | 9.00 | | .90551 | 23.00 |
| 23/64 | .359375 | 9.1281 | 29/32 | .90625 | 23.0188 |
| 3/8 | .375 | 9.525 | 59/64 | .921875 | 23.4157 |
| 25/64 | .390625 | 9.9219 | 15/16 | .9375 | 23.8125 |
| | .3937 | 10.00 | | .94488 | 24.00 |
| 13/32 | .40625 | 10.3188 | 61/64 | .953125 | 24.2094 |
| 27/64 | .421875 | 10.7156 | 31/32 | .96875 | 24.6063 |
| | .43307 | 11.00 | | .98425 | 25.00 |
| 7/16 | .4375 | 11.1125 | 63/64 | .984375 | 25.0032 |
| 29/64 | .453125 | 11.5094 | 1 | 1.0000 | 25.4001 |

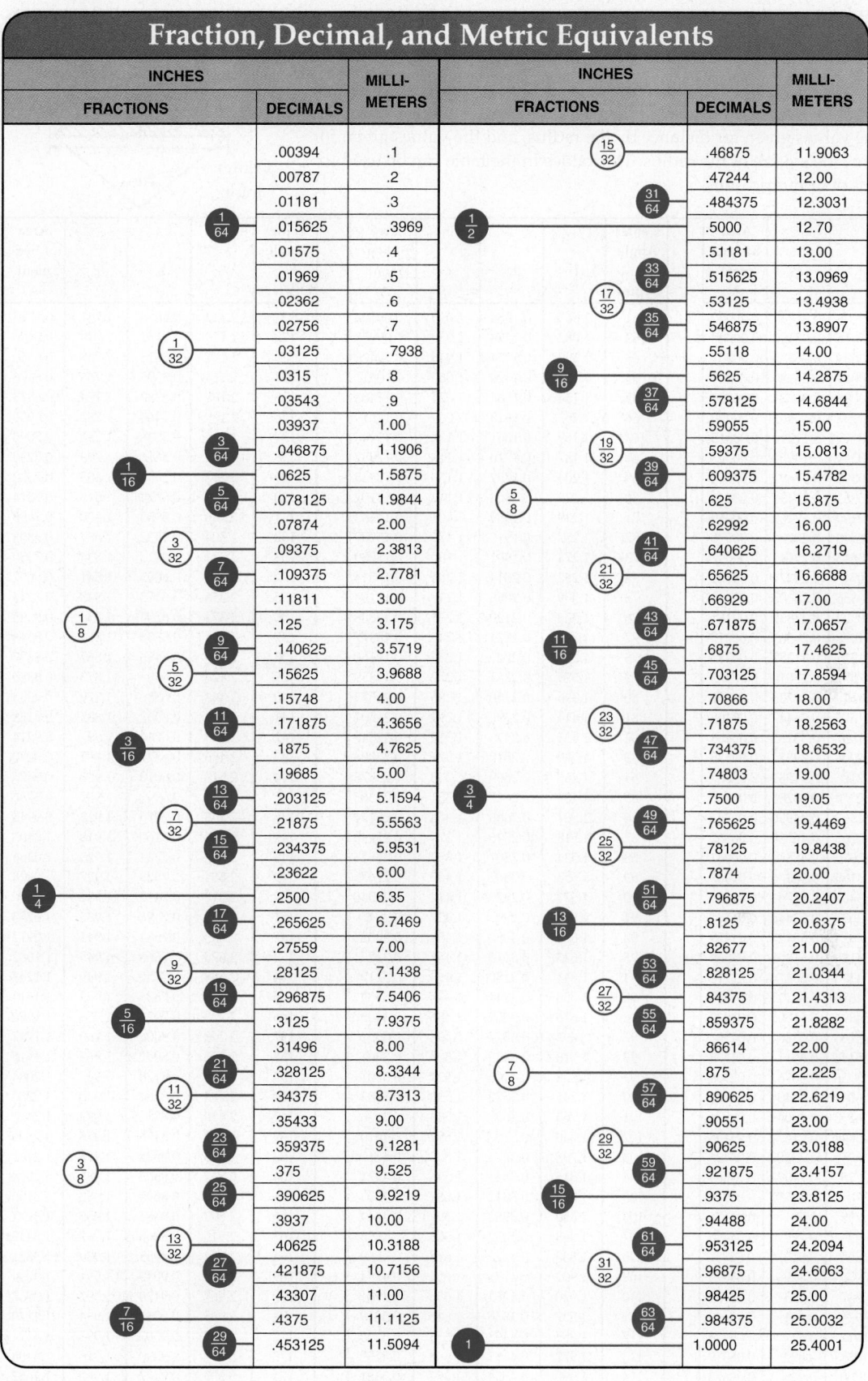

# Chord Length—Segments of Circles

Length of arc (*l*=radians), height of segment (*h*), length of chord (*c*), and area of segment (*A*) for angles from 1 to 180 degrees and radius = 1. For other radii, multiply the values given for distance by the radius, and the values given for the area by r², the square of the radius. The values in the table can be used for U.S. customary or metric units.

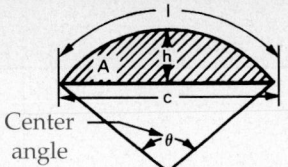

Center angle — θ

| Center Angle θ, Degrees | l | h | c | Area of Segment A | Center Angle θ, Degrees | l | h | c | Area of Segment A | Center Angle θ, Degrees | l | h | c | Area of Segment A |
|---|---|---|---|---|---|---|---|---|---|---|---|---|---|---|
| 1 | 0.01745 | 0.00004 | 0.01745 | 0.00000 | 61 | 1.065 | 0.1384 | 1.015 | 0.09502 | 121 | 2.112 | 0.5076 | 1.741 | 0.6273 |
| 2 | 0.03491 | 0.00015 | 0.03490 | 0.00000 | 62 | 1.082 | 0.1428 | 1.030 | 0.09958 | 122 | 2.129 | 0.5152 | 1.749 | 0.6406 |
| 3 | 0.05236 | 0.00034 | 0.05235 | 0.00001 | 63 | 1.100 | 0.1474 | 1.045 | 0.10428 | 123 | 2.147 | 0.5228 | 1.758 | 0.6540 |
| 4 | 0.06981 | 0.00061 | 0.06980 | 0.00003 | 64 | 1.117 | 0.1520 | 1.060 | 0.10911 | 124 | 2.164 | 0.5305 | 1.766 | 0.6676 |
| 5 | 0.08727 | 0.00095 | 0.08724 | 0.00006 | 65 | 1.134 | 0.1566 | 1.075 | 0.11408 | 125 | 2.182 | 0.5383 | 1.774 | 0.6813 |
| 6 | 0.10472 | 0.00137 | 0.10467 | 0.00010 | 66 | 1.152 | 0.1613 | 1.089 | 0.11919 | 126 | 2.199 | 0.5460 | 1.782 | 0.6950 |
| 7 | 0.12217 | 0.00187 | 0.12210 | 0.00015 | 67 | 1.169 | 0.1661 | 1.104 | 0.12443 | 127 | 2.217 | 0.5538 | 1.790 | 0.7090 |
| 8 | 0.13963 | 0.00244 | 0.13951 | 0.00023 | 68 | 1.187 | 0.1710 | 1.118 | 0.12982 | 128 | 2.234 | 0.5616 | 1.798 | 0.7230 |
| 9 | 0.15708 | 0.00308 | 0.15692 | 0.00032 | 69 | 1.204 | 0.1759 | 1.133 | 0.13535 | 129 | 2.251 | 0.5695 | 1.805 | 0.7372 |
| 10 | 0.17453 | 0.00381 | 0.17431 | 0.00044 | 70 | 1.222 | 0.1808 | 1.147 | 0.14102 | 130 | 2.269 | 0.5774 | 1.813 | 0.7514 |
| 11 | 0.19199 | 0.00460 | 0.19169 | 0.00059 | 71 | 1.239 | 0.1859 | 1.161 | 0.14683 | 131 | 2.286 | 0.5853 | 1.820 | 0.7658 |
| 12 | 0.20944 | 0.00548 | 0.20906 | 0.00076 | 72 | 1.257 | 0.1910 | 1.176 | 0.15279 | 132 | 2.304 | 0.5933 | 1.827 | 0.7803 |
| 13 | 0.22689 | 0.00643 | 0.22641 | 0.00097 | 73 | 1.274 | 0.1961 | 1.190 | 0.15889 | 133 | 2.321 | 0.6013 | 1.834 | 0.7950 |
| 14 | 0.24435 | 0.00745 | 0.24374 | 0.00121 | 74 | 1.292 | 0.2014 | 1.204 | 0.16514 | 134 | 2.339 | 0.6093 | 1.841 | 0.8097 |
| 15 | 0.26180 | 0.00856 | 0.26105 | 0.00149 | 75 | 1.309 | 0.2066 | 1.218 | 0.17154 | 135 | 2.356 | 0.6173 | 1.848 | 0.8245 |
| 16 | 0.27925 | 0.00973 | 0.27835 | 0.00181 | 76 | 1.326 | 0.2120 | 1.231 | 0.17808 | 136 | 2.374 | 0.6254 | 1.854 | 0.8395 |
| 17 | 0.29671 | 0.01098 | 0.29562 | 0.00217 | 77 | 1.344 | 0.2174 | 1.245 | 0.18477 | 137 | 2.391 | 0.6335 | 1.861 | 0.8546 |
| 18 | 0.31416 | 0.01231 | 0.31287 | 0.00257 | 78 | 1.361 | 0.2229 | 1.259 | 0.19160 | 138 | 2.409 | 0.6416 | 1.867 | 0.8697 |
| 19 | 0.33161 | 0.01371 | 0.33010 | 0.00302 | 79 | 1.379 | 0.2284 | 1.272 | 0.19859 | 139 | 2.426 | 0.6498 | 1.873 | 0.8850 |
| 20 | 0.34907 | 0.01519 | 0.34730 | 0.00352 | 80 | 1.396 | 0.2340 | 1.286 | 0.20573 | 140 | 2.443 | 0.6580 | 1.879 | 0.9003 |
| 21 | 0.36652 | 0.01675 | 0.36447 | 0.00408 | 81 | 1.414 | 0.2396 | 1.299 | 0.21301 | 141 | 2.461 | 0.6662 | 1.885 | 0.9158 |
| 22 | 0.38397 | 0.01837 | 0.38162 | 0.00468 | 82 | 1.431 | 0.2453 | 1.312 | 0.22045 | 142 | 2.478 | 0.6744 | 1.891 | 0.9314 |
| 23 | 0.40143 | 0.02008 | 0.39874 | 0.00535 | 83 | 1.449 | 0.2510 | 1.325 | 0.22804 | 143 | 2.496 | 0.6827 | 1.897 | 0.9470 |
| 24 | 0.41888 | 0.02185 | 0.41582 | 0.00607 | 84 | 1.466 | 0.2569 | 1.338 | 0.23578 | 144 | 2.513 | 0.6910 | 1.902 | 0.9627 |
| 25 | 0.43633 | 0.02370 | 0.43288 | 0.00686 | 85 | 1.484 | 0.2627 | 1.351 | 0.24367 | 145 | 2.531 | 0.6993 | 1.907 | 0.9786 |
| 26 | 0.45379 | 0.02563 | 0.44990 | 0.00771 | 86 | 1.501 | 0.2686 | 1.364 | 0.25171 | 146 | 2.548 | 0.7076 | 1.913 | 0.9945 |
| 27 | 0.47124 | 0.02763 | 0.46689 | 0.00862 | 87 | 1.518 | 0.2746 | 1.377 | 0.25990 | 147 | 2.566 | 0.7160 | 1.918 | 1.0105 |
| 28 | 0.48869 | 0.02970 | 0.48384 | 0.00961 | 88 | 1.536 | 0.2807 | 1.389 | 0.26825 | 148 | 2.583 | 0.7244 | 1.923 | 1.0266 |
| 29 | 0.50615 | 0.03185 | 0.50076 | 0.01067 | 89 | 1.553 | 0.2867 | 1.402 | 0.27675 | 149 | 2.601 | 0.7328 | 1.927 | 1.0428 |
| 30 | 0.52360 | 0.03407 | 0.51764 | 0.01180 | 90 | 1.571 | 0.2929 | 1.414 | 0.28540 | 150 | 2.618 | 0.7412 | 1.932 | 1.0590 |
| 31 | 0.54105 | 0.03637 | 0.53448 | 0.01301 | 91 | 1.588 | 0.2991 | 1.427 | 0.2942 | 151 | 2.635 | 0.7496 | 1.936 | 1.0753 |
| 32 | 0.55851 | 0.03874 | 0.55127 | 0.01429 | 92 | 1.606 | 0.3053 | 1.439 | 0.3032 | 152 | 2.653 | 0.7581 | 1.941 | 1.0917 |
| 33 | 0.57596 | 0.04118 | 0.56803 | 0.01566 | 93 | 1.623 | 0.3116 | 1.451 | 0.3123 | 153 | 2.670 | 0.7666 | 1.945 | 1.1082 |
| 34 | 0.59341 | 0.04370 | 0.58474 | 0.01711 | 94 | 1.641 | 0.3180 | 1.463 | 0.3215 | 154 | 2.688 | 0.7750 | 1.949 | 1.1247 |
| 35 | 0.61087 | 0.04628 | 0.60141 | 0.01864 | 95 | 1.658 | 0.3244 | 1.475 | 0.3309 | 155 | 2.705 | 0.7836 | 1.953 | 1.1413 |
| 36 | 0.62832 | 0.04894 | 0.61803 | 0.02027 | 96 | 1.676 | 0.3309 | 1.486 | 0.3405 | 156 | 2.723 | 0.7921 | 1.956 | 1.1580 |
| 37 | 0.64577 | 0.05168 | 0.63461 | 0.02198 | 97 | 1.693 | 0.3374 | 1.498 | 0.3502 | 157 | 2.740 | 0.8006 | 1.960 | 1.1747 |
| 38 | 0.66323 | 0.05448 | 0.65114 | 0.02378 | 98 | 1.710 | 0.3439 | 1.509 | 0.3601 | 158 | 2.758 | 0.8092 | 1.963 | 1.1915 |
| 39 | 0.68068 | 0.05736 | 0.66761 | 0.02568 | 99 | 1.728 | 0.3506 | 1.521 | 0.3701 | 159 | 2.775 | 0.8178 | 1.967 | 1.2084 |
| 40 | 0.69813 | 0.06031 | 0.68404 | 0.02767 | 100 | 1.745 | 0.3572 | 1.532 | 0.3803 | 160 | 2.793 | 0.8264 | 1.970 | 1.2253 |
| 41 | 0.71558 | 0.06333 | 0.70041 | 0.02976 | 101 | 1.763 | 0.3639 | 1.543 | 0.3906 | 161 | 2.810 | 0.8350 | 1.973 | 1.2422 |
| 42 | 0.73304 | 0.06642 | 0.71674 | 0.03195 | 102 | 1.780 | 0.3707 | 1.554 | 0.4010 | 162 | 2.827 | 0.8436 | 1.975 | 1.2592 |
| 43 | 0.75049 | 0.06958 | 0.73300 | 0.03425 | 103 | 1.798 | 0.3775 | 1.565 | 0.4117 | 163 | 2.845 | 0.8522 | 1.978 | 1.2763 |
| 44 | 0.76794 | 0.07282 | 0.74921 | 0.03664 | 104 | 1.815 | 0.3843 | 1.576 | 0.4224 | 164 | 2.862 | 0.8608 | 1.981 | 1.2934 |
| 45 | 0.78540 | 0.07612 | 0.76537 | 0.03915 | 105 | 1.833 | 0.3912 | 1.587 | 0.4333 | 165 | 2.880 | 0.8695 | 1.983 | 1.3105 |
| 46 | 0.803 | 0.0795 | 0.781 | 0.04176 | 106 | 1.850 | 0.3982 | 1.597 | 0.4444 | 166 | 2.897 | 0.8781 | 1.985 | 1.3277 |
| 47 | 0.820 | 0.0829 | 0.797 | 0.04448 | 107 | 1.868 | 0.4052 | 1.608 | 0.4556 | 167 | 2.915 | 0.8868 | 1.987 | 1.3449 |
| 48 | 0.838 | 0.0865 | 0.813 | 0.04731 | 108 | 1.885 | 0.4122 | 1.618 | 0.4669 | 168 | 2.932 | 0.8955 | 1.989 | 1.3621 |
| 49 | 0.855 | 0.0900 | 0.829 | 0.05025 | 109 | 1.902 | 0.4193 | 1.628 | 0.4784 | 169 | 2.950 | 0.9042 | 1.991 | 1.3794 |
| 50 | 0.873 | 0.0937 | 0.845 | 0.05331 | 110 | 1.920 | 0.4264 | 1.638 | 0.4901 | 170 | 2.967 | 0.9128 | 1.992 | 1.3967 |
| 51 | 0.890 | 0.0974 | 0.861 | 0.05649 | 111 | 1.937 | 0.4336 | 1.648 | 0.5019 | 171 | 2.985 | 0.9215 | 1.994 | 1.4140 |
| 52 | 0.908 | 0.1012 | 0.877 | 0.05978 | 112 | 1.955 | 0.4408 | 1.658 | 0.5138 | 172 | 3.002 | 0.9302 | 1.995 | 1.4314 |
| 53 | 0.925 | 0.1051 | 0.892 | 0.06319 | 113 | 1.972 | 0.4481 | 1.668 | 0.5259 | 173 | 3.019 | 0.9390 | 1.996 | 1.4488 |
| 54 | 0.942 | 0.1090 | 0.908 | 0.06673 | 114 | 1.990 | 0.4554 | 1.677 | 0.5381 | 174 | 3.037 | 0.9477 | 1.997 | 1.4662 |
| 55 | 0.960 | 0.1130 | 0.923 | 0.07039 | 115 | 2.007 | 0.4627 | 1.687 | 0.5504 | 175 | 3.054 | 0.9564 | 1.998 | 1.4836 |
| 56 | 0.977 | 0.1171 | 0.939 | 0.07417 | 116 | 2.025 | 0.4701 | 1.696 | 0.5629 | 176 | 3.072 | 0.9651 | 1.999 | 1.5010 |
| 57 | 0.995 | 0.1212 | 0.954 | 0.07808 | 117 | 2.042 | 0.4775 | 1.705 | 0.5755 | 177 | 3.089 | 0.9738 | 1.999 | 1.5184 |
| 58 | 1.012 | 0.1254 | 0.970 | 0.08212 | 118 | 2.059 | 0.4850 | 1.714 | 0.5883 | 178 | 3.107 | 0.9825 | 2.000 | 1.5359 |
| 59 | 1.030 | 0.1296 | 0.985 | 0.08629 | 119 | 2.077 | 0.4925 | 1.723 | 0.6012 | 179 | 3.124 | 0.9913 | 2.000 | 1.5533 |
| 60 | 1.047 | 0.1340 | 1.000 | 0.09059 | 120 | 2.094 | 0.5000 | 1.732 | 0.6142 | 180 | 3.142 | 1.0000 | 2.000 | 1.5708 |

## Area Equivalents

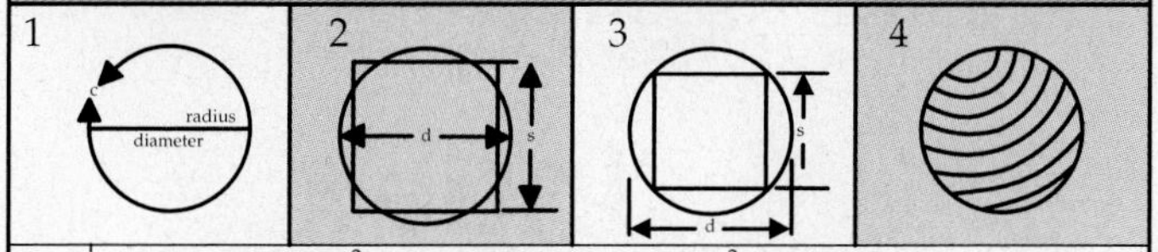

| | | | | |
|---|---|---|---|---|
| 1 | 2 | 3 | 4 | |

| | |
|---|---|
| 1 | area = radius$^2$ × 3.1416 or diameter$^2$ × .7854 |
| 1 | circumference = diameter × 3.1416 or diameter ÷ .3183 |
| 2 | when the area of a circle & square are equal, D = S × 1.128 |
| 2 | when the area of a circle & square are equal, S = D × .8862 |
| 3 | side of inscribed square – diameter × .7071 |
| 3 | diameter of circumscribing circle = S × 1.1412 |
| 4 | surface area of a sphere = diameter × circumference |
| 4 | volume of a sphere = diameter$^3$ × .5236 |

## Equivalents

### Fahrenheit and Celsius

$$°F = (1.8 × °C) + 32$$
$$°C = (°F − 32) ÷ 1.8$$

### Weight

1 gram = .03527 oz (av.)
1 oz = 28.35 grams
1 kilogram = 2.2046 pounds
1 pound = .04536 kilograms
1 metric ton = 2,204.6 pounds
1 ton (2000 lbs in U.S.) = 907.2 kg.

### Volume

1 U.S. quart = 0.946 liters
1 U.S. gallon = 3.785 liters
1 liter = 1.0567 U.S. quarts
1 liter = .264 U.S. gallons

## Length Conversions

| multiply | by | to obtain |
|---|---|---|
| Inches | 25.4 | Millimeters |
| Feet | 304.8 | Millimeters |
| Inches | 2.54 | Centimeters |
| Feet | 30.48 | Centimeters |
| Millimeters | .03937008 | Inches |
| Centimeters | .3937008 | Inches |
| Meters | 39.37008 | Inches |
| Millimeters | .003280840 | Feet |
| Centimeters | .03280840 | Feet |
| Inches | .0254 | Meters |

## Square Area Conversions

| multiply | by | to obtain |
|---|---|---|
| Millimeters | .00001076391 | Feet |
| Millimeters | .00155003 | Inches |
| Centimeters | .1550003 | Inches |
| Centimeters | .001076391 | Feet |
| Inches | 645.16 | Millimeters |
| Inches | 6.4516 | Centimeters |
| Inches | .00064516 | Meters |
| Feet | .09290304 | Meters |
| Feet | 929.0304 | Centimeters |
| Feet | 92,903.04 | Millimeters |

Rutland Tool and Supply Co., Inc.

# Index

# F

## S

# T

AutoCAD 2004

# AutoCAD
## and its applications
# A D V A N C E D

by

**Terence M. Shumaker**
Faculty Emeritus
Former Chairperson
Drafting Technology
Autodesk Premier Training Center
Clackamas Community College, Oregon City, Oregon

**David A. Madsen**
Faculty Emeritus
Former Chairperson
Drafting Technology
Autodesk Premier Training Center
Clackamas Community College, Oregon City, Oregon

Former Board of Director
American Design Drafting Association

## THE GOODHEART-WILLCOX COMPANY, INC.

Tinley Park, Illinois

www.g-w.com

Library of Congress Catalog Card Number 2003054952
International Standard Book Number 1-59070-291-3

1 2 3 4 5 6 7 8 9 – 04 – 08 07 06 05 04 03

**The Goodheart-Willcox Company, Inc., Brand Disclaimer:** Brand names, company names, and illustrations for products and services included in this text are provided for educational purposes only, and do not represent or imply endorsement or recommendation by the authors or the publisher.

**The Goodheart-Willcox Company, Inc., Safety Notice:** The reader is expressly advised to carefully read, understand, and apply all safety precautions and warnings described in this book or that might also be indicated in undertaking the activities and exercises described herein to minimize risk of personal injury or injury to others. Common sense and good judgment should also be exercised and applied to help avoid all potential hazards. The reader should always refer to the appropriate manufacturer's technical information, directions, and recommendations; then proceed with care to follow specific equipment operating instructions. The reader should understand these notices and cautions are not exhaustive.

The publisher makes no warranty or representation whatsoever, either expressed or implied, including but not limited to equipment, procedures, and applications described or referred to herein, their quality, performance, merchantability, or fitness for a particular purpose. The publisher assumes no responsibility for any changes, errors, or omissions in this book. The publisher specifically disclaims any liability whatsoever, including any direct, indirect, incidental, consequential, special, or exemplary damages resulting, in whole or in part, from the reader's use or reliance upon the information, instructions, procedures, warnings, cautions, applications or other matter contained in this book. The publisher assumes no responsibility for the activities of the reader.

The content of the AutoCAD software is subject to change between maintenance releases. The material in this book is based on the most recent maintenance release of AutoCAD available at the time of publication.

Library of Congress Cataloging-in-Publication Data

Shumaker, Terence M.
    AutoCAD and applications. Advanced 2004/ by Terence M. Shumaker, David A. Madsen.
        p. cm.
    ISBN 1-59070-291-3
    1. Computer graphics. 2. AutoCAD I. Madsen, David A. II. Title
T385.S4612    2003
620.0042'0285'5369—dc21
                                                        2003054952

# Introduction

*AutoCAD and its Applications—Advanced* provides complete instruction in mastering the AutoCAD 2004 3D modeling commands, Internet access using AutoCAD, and various customizing techniques. These topics are covered in an easy-to-understand sequence, and progress in a way that allows you to become comfortable with the commands as your knowledge builds from one chapter to the next. In addition, *AutoCAD and its Applications—Advanced* offers:

- Step-by-step use of AutoCAD commands.
- In-depth explanations of how and why commands function as they do.
- Extensive use of font changes to specify certain meanings. This is fully explained in the next section, *Fonts Used in This Text*.
- Examples and discussions of industrial practices and standards.
- Actual screen captures of AutoCAD and Windows features and functions.
- Professional tips explaining how to use AutoCAD effectively and efficiently.
- Exercises to reinforce the chapter topics. These exercises also build on previously learned material.
- Chapter tests for review of commands and key AutoCAD concepts.
- A large selection of modeling and customizing problems supplement each chapter. Problems are presented as 3D illustrations, actual plotted drawings, and engineering sketches.

With *AutoCAD and its Applications—Advanced* you not only learn AutoCAD commands, but you also become acquainted with:

- 3D object construction and layout techniques.
- Constructing models using different 3D coordinate systems.
- User coordinate systems.
- Model space viewports.
- 3D editing and display techniques.
- 3D text and dimensioning.
- Solid model construction, editing, and display.
- Surface modeling.
- Rendering.
- AutoCAD's database connectivity functions.
- Internet access from within AutoCAD.
- Customizing the AutoCAD environment.
- Customizing toolbars, pull-down menus, and image tiles.
- Customizing screen, button, and tablet menus.
- The basics of AutoLISP and dialog box (DCL) programming.
- Advanced AutoCAD features such as OLE.

## Fonts Used in This Text

Different typefaces are used throughout each chapter to define terms and identify AutoCAD commands. Important terms appear in *bold-italic face, serif* type. AutoCAD menus, commands, variables, dialog box names, and toolbar button names are printed in **bold-face, sans serif** type. File names, folder names, paths, and keyboard-entry items appear in the body of the text in Roman, sans serif type. Keyboard keys are shown inside of square brackets [ ] and appear in Roman, sans serif type. For example, [Enter] means to press the enter (return) key. In addition, commands, menus, and dialog boxes related to Microsoft Windows appear in Roman, sans serif type.

Prompt sequences are set apart from the body text with space above and below, and appear in Roman, sans serif type. Keyboard entry items in prompts appear in **bold-face, sans serif** type. In prompts, the [Enter] key is represented by the ⏎ symbol.

## Other Text References

This text focuses on advanced AutoCAD applications. Basic AutoCAD applications are covered in *AutoCAD and its Applications—Basics*, which is also available from Goodheart-Willcox Publisher. *AutoCAD and its Applications* texts are also available for AutoCAD Releases 10 through 2002.

For your convenience, other Goodheart-Willcox Publisher textbooks are referenced, including *AutoLISP Programming—Principles and Techniques*. These textbooks can be ordered directly from Goodheart-Willcox Publisher.

## Introducing the AutoCAD Commands

There are several ways to select AutoCAD drawing and editing commands. Selecting commands on a toolbar or from a pull-down menu is slightly different than entering them from the keyboard. All AutoCAD commands and related options are presented in this text using a variety of command entry methods.

In many examples, command entries are shown as if typed at the keyboard, allowing the text to present the full command name and the prompts that appear on screen. Commands, options, and values you must enter are given in **bold-face, sans serif** text, as shown in the following example. Pressing the [Enter] (return) key is indicated with the ⏎ symbol.

Command: **3DFACE**⏎
First point: **2,2**⏎
Second point: **4,2**⏎
Third point: **4,6**⏎
Fourth point: **2,6**⏎

General input, such as picking a point or selecting an object, is presented in *italic, serif font*, as shown below.

Command: **3DFACE**⏎
First point: *(pick a point)*
Second point: *(pick another point)*
Third point: *(pick a third point)*
Fourth point: *(pick the last point)*

The command line, toolbar button, and pull-down menu entry methods are presented throughout the text. When a command is introduced, these methods are illustrated in the margin next to the text reference. The toolbar on which the button is located is also identified. The example in the margin next to this paragraph illustrates the various methods of initiating the **HIDE** command.

HIDE
HI

View
➡ Hide

Render
toolbar

Hide

Some commands and functions are handled more efficiently by picking a toolbar button or a menu command. Many of these procedures are described in numbered, step-by-step instructions.

## Flexibility in Design

Flexibility is the key word when using *AutoCAD and its Applications—Advanced.* This text is an excellent training aid for both individual and classroom instruction. *AutoCAD and its Applications—Advanced* teaches you how to apply AutoCAD to common modeling and customizing tasks. It is also an invaluable resource for any professional using AutoCAD.

When working through the text, you will see a variety of notices. These include Professional Tips, Notes, and Cautions that help you develop your AutoCAD skills.

**PROFESSIONAL TIP**

These ideas and suggestions are aimed at increasing your productivity and enhancing your use of AutoCAD commands and techniques.

**NOTE**

A note alerts you to important aspects of a command function, menu, or activity that is being discussed. These aspects should be kept in mind while you are working through the text.

**CAUTION**

A caution alerts you to potential problems if instructions or commands are used incorrectly, or if an action can corrupt or alter files, folders, or disks. If you are in doubt after reading a caution, always consult your instructor or supervisor.

*AutoCAD and its Applications—Advanced* provides several ways for you to evaluate your performance. Included are:
- **Exercises.** Each chapter contains in-text exercises. These exercises allow you to perform tasks that reinforce the material just presented. You can work through the exercises at your own pace.
- **Chapter Tests.** Each chapter includes a written test at the end of the chapter. Questions require you to give the proper definition, command, option, or response to perform a certain task.

- **Drawing Problems.** There are a variety of drawing, design, and customizing problems at the end of each chapter. These are presented as real-world CAD drawings, 3D illustrations, and engineering sketches. The problems are designed to make you think, solve problems, use design techniques, research and use proper drawing standards, and correct errors in the drawings or engineering sketches.

Each drawing problem deals with one of six technical disciplines. Although doing all of the problems will enhance your AutoCAD skills, you may be focusing on a particular discipline. The discipline that a problem addresses is indicated by a graphic in the margin next to the problem number. The following graphics represent the disciplines.

 These problems address mechanical drafting and design applications, such as manufactured part designs.

 These problems address architectural and structural drafting and design applications, such as floor plans, furniture, and presentation drawings.

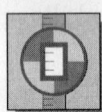 These problems address civil drafting and design applications, such as plot plans, plats, and landscape drawings.

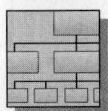 These problems address graphic design applications, such as text creation, title blocks, and page layout.

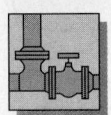 These problems address piping drafting and design applications, such as piping flow diagrams, tank drawings, and pipe layout.

 These problems address a variety of general drafting, design, and customization applications. These problems should be attempted by everyone learning advanced AutoCAD techniques for the first time.

---

NOTE

Some problems presented in this text are given as engineering sketches. These sketches are intended to represent the kind of material a drafter is expected to work from in a real-world situation. As such, engineering sketches often contain errors or slight inaccuracies and are most often not drawn according to proper drafting conventions and applicable standards. Errors in these problems are *intentional* to encourage the user to apply appropriate techniques and standards in order to solve the problem. As in real-world applications, sketches should be considered preliminary layouts. Always question inaccuracies in sketches and designs and consult the applicable standards or other resources.

---

## About the Authors

Terence M. Shumaker is Faculty Emeritus, the former Chairperson of the Drafting Technology Department, and former Director of the Autodesk Premier Training Center at Clackamas Community College. Terence taught at the community college level for over 25 years. He has professional experience in surveying, civil drafting, industrial piping, and technical illustration. He is the author of Goodheart-Willcox's *Process Pipe Drafting* and coauthor of the *AutoCAD and its Applications* series (Releases 10 through 2002 editions) and *AutoCAD Essentials.*

David A. Madsen is Faculty Emeritus, the former Chairperson of Drafting Technology and the Autodesk Premier Training Center at Clackamas Community College and former member of the American Design and Drafting Association Board of Directors. David was an instructor and a department chair at Clackamas Community College for nearly thirty years. In addition to community college experience, David was a Drafting Technology instructor at Centennial High School in Gresham, Oregon. David also has extensive experience in mechanical drafting, architectural design and drafting, and construction practices. He is the author of several Goodheart-Willcox drafting and design textbooks, including *Geometric Dimensioning and Tolerancing,* and coauthor of the *AutoCAD and its Applications* series (Releases 10 through 2002 editions), *Architectural Drafting Using AutoCAD, Architectural AutoCAD,* and *AutoCAD Essentials.*

## Acknowledgments

The authors and publisher would like to thank the following individuals and companies for their assistance and contributions.

### Contributing Authors

The authors wish to acknowledge a number of contributors for their professional expertise in providing in-depth research and testing, technical assistance, reviews, and development of new materials.

Craig Black contributed in many areas for this edition, including Chapter 23, Chapter 24, and Chapter 26. Craig is the manager of the AutoCAD Training Center and an instructor at Fox Valley Technical College in Appleton, WI. He has been working with FVTC as an ATC instructor since 1990 and has been using AutoCAD since 1985. Craig is an Autodesk Certified Instructor in AutoCAD, Mechanical Desktop, and Architectural Desktop and has conducted AutoCAD training at Autodesk University in Dallas, Los Angeles, San Francisco, and Philadelphia. He has twice been elected to the Autodesk Training Center Executive Committee, which is an advisory committee to Autodesk, Inc., concerning educational issues, and chaired the committee in 2001. Craig has industry and educational experience in AutoCAD menu customization, AutoLISP and DCL programming, and system management.

Rod Rawls for Chapter 19 through Chapter 25. Rod is an AutoCAD consultant and former instructor at the AutoCAD Premier Training Center, Clackamas Community College. He is also the coauthor of *AutoLISP Programming: Principles and Techniques* published by Goodheart-Willcox.

Ron Palma for part of Chapter 7, and Chapter 14 through 17. Ron is the owner and operator of 3D-DZYN in Canby, Oregon. Ron provides training, consulting, and technical support for Autodesk software products.

Ethan Collins for Chapter 18, Chapter 26, and Chapter 28. Ethan is a software specialist for Imaginit Technologies, and provides technical support for Autodesk software products.

## Contribution of Materials

Autodesk, Inc.
Bill Fane
*CADENCE* magazine
EPCM Services Ltd.
Fitzgerald, Hagan, & Hackathorn
Kunz Associates

## Trademarks

Autodesk, the Autodesk logo, 3D Studio MAX, 3ds max, 3D Studio VIZ, Autodesk VIZ, Advanced Modeling Extension, AME, AutoCAD, Heidi, Inventor, Mechanical Desktop, and *WHIP!* are registered trademarks, and AutoCAD DesignCenter, AutoCAD Learning Assistance, AutoSnap, AutoTrack, Volo View, and i-drop are trademarks of Autodesk, Inc., in the USA and/or other countries.

Microsoft, Windows, Windows NT, Windows 95, Windows 98, Windows 2000, Windows XP, Visual Basic, and Microsoft Word are trademarks of Microsoft Corporation.

dBase is a registered trademark of Ashton Tate.

IBM is a registered trademark of International Business Machines.

Other copyrights are owned by their respective owners.

# Brief Contents

# Expanded Contents

## Surface Model Construction and Editing

## Rendering, Materials, and Presentation Graphics

# Advanced AutoCAD Applications

# Introduction to Three-Dimensional Drawing

## Learning Objectives

After completing this chapter, you will be able to:
- Describe how to locate points in 3D space.
- Describe the right-hand rule of 3D visualization.
- Display 3D objects from preset isometric viewpoints.
- Display 3D objects from any desired viewpoint.
- Construct solid primitives.

The use of three-dimensional (3D) drawing and design as a tool is becoming more prevalent throughout industry. Companies are discovering the benefits of 3D modeling in design, visualization, testing, analysis, manufacturing, assembly, and marketing. Three-dimensional models also form the basis of computer animations and virtual worlds used with virtual reality systems. Drafters who can design objects, buildings, and "worlds" in 3D are in demand for a wide variety of positions, both inside and outside the traditional drafting and design disciplines.

The first thirteen chapters of this book present a variety of techniques for drawing and designing in 3D. The skills you learn will provide you with the ability to construct any object in 3D, and prepare you for entry into an exciting aspect of graphic communication.

To be effective in creating and using 3D objects, you must first have good 3D visualization skills, including the ability to see an object in three dimensions and to visualize it rotating in space. These skills can be obtained by using 3D techniques to construct objects and by trying to see two-dimensional sketches and drawings as 3D models. This chapter provides an introduction to several aspects of 3D drawing and visualization. Subsequent chapters expand on these aspects and provide a detailed examination of 3D drawing, editing, visualization, and display techniques.

## Using Rectangular 3D Coordinates

In two-dimensional drawing, you see one plane defined by two dimensions. These dimensions are usually located on the X and Y axes and what you see is the XY plane. However, in 3D drawing, another coordinate axis—the Z axis—is added. This results in two additional planes—the XZ plane and the YZ plane. If you are looking at a standard AutoCAD screen, the positive Z axis comes directly out of the screen toward you. AutoCAD can only draw lines in 3D if it knows the X, Y, and Z coordinate values of each point on the object. For 2D drawing, only two of the three coordinates (X and Y) are needed.

Compare the 2D and 3D coordinate systems shown in **Figure 1-1.** Notice that the positive values of Z in the 3D coordinate system come up from the XY plane. Consider the surface of your computer screen as the XY plane. Anything behind the screen is negative Z and anything in front of the screen is positive Z.

The object in **Figure 1-2A** is a 2D drawing showing the top view of an object. The XY coordinate values of the origin and each point are shown. Think of the object as being drawn directly on the surface of your screen. However, this is actually a 3D object. When displayed in a pictorial view, the Z coordinates can be seen. Notice in **Figure 1-2B** that the first two values of each coordinate match the X and Y values of the 2D view. Three-dimensional coordinates are always expressed as (X,Y,Z). The 3D object was drawn using positive Z coordinates. Therefore, the object comes out of your screen. The object can also be drawn using negative Z coordinates. In this case, the object would extend behind, or into, the screen.

Study the nature of the rectangular 3D coordinate system. Be sure you understand Z values before you begin constructing 3D objects. It is especially important that you carefully visualize and plan your design when working with 3D constructions.

**Figure 1-1.**
A comparison of 2D and 3D coordinate systems.

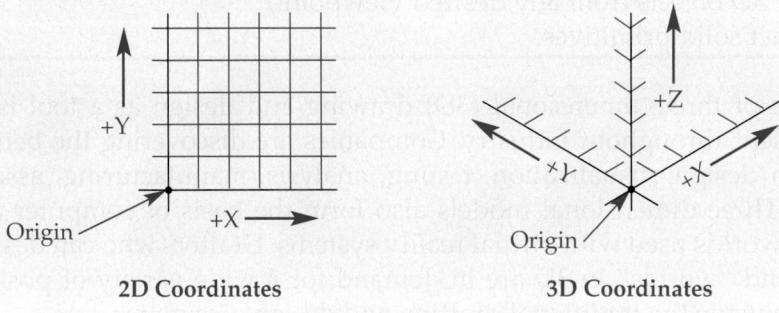

**2D Coordinates**          **3D Coordinates**

**Figure 1-2.**
A—The points making up a 2D object require only two coordinates. B—Each point of a 3D object must have an X, Y, and Z value. Notice that the first two coordinates (X and Y) are the same for each endpoint of a vertical line.

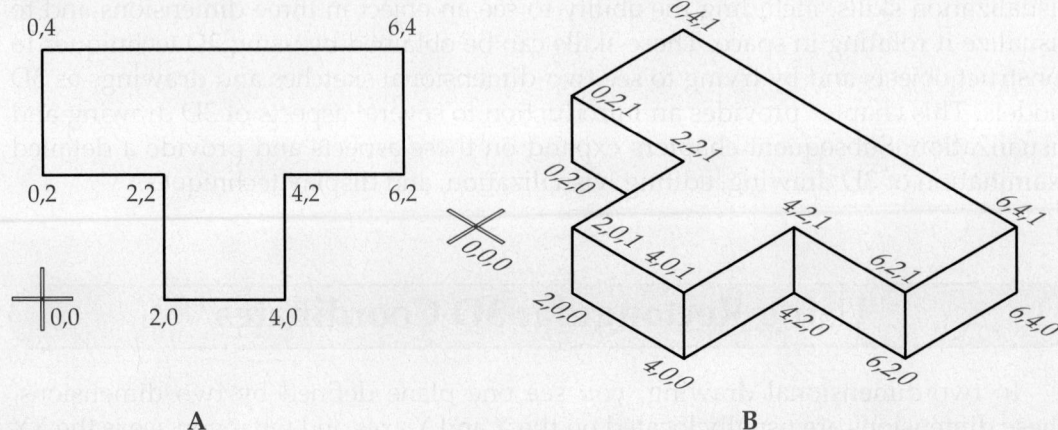

A          B

**PROFESSIONAL TIP**

All points in three-dimensional space can be drawn using one of three coordinate entry methods—rectangular, spherical, or cylindrical. This chapter uses the rectangular coordinate entry method. Complete discussions on the spherical and cylindrical coordinate entry methods are provided in Chapter 2.

---

### Exercise 1-1

○ Study the multiview sketch below.
○ Each tick mark represents one unit. Use the correct dimensions as given in the multiview sketch.
○ Freehand sketch the object pictorially using the axes of a 3D coordinate system.

---

## The Right-Hand Rule of 3D Drawing

In order to effectively draw in 3D, you must be able to visualize objects in 3D space. The *right-hand rule* is a simple method for visualizing the 3D coordinate system. It is a representation of the positive coordinate values in the three axis directions. AutoCAD's *user coordinate system (UCS)* and *world coordinate system (WCS)* are based on this concept of visualization.

To use the right-hand rule, position the thumb, index finger, and middle finger of your right hand as shown in **Figure 1-3**. Although this may seem a bit unusual, it can do wonders for your understanding of the three axes. Imagine that your thumb is the X axis, your index finger is the Y axis, and your middle finger is the Z axis. Hold your hand directly in front of you so that your middle finger is pointing directly at you, as shown in **Figure 1-3**. This is the plan view of the XY plane. The positive X axis is pointing to the right and the positive Y axis is pointing up. The positive Z axis comes toward you and the origin of this system is the palm of your hand.

The concept behind the right-hand rule can be visualized even better if you are sitting at a computer and the AutoCAD graphics window is displayed. If the UCS icon is not displayed in the lower-left corner of the screen, turn it on by selecting **Display** from the **View** pull-down menu, and then **UCS Icon** and **On**. Now, orient your right hand as shown in **Figure 1-3** and position it next to the UCS (or WCS) icon. Your index finger and thumb should point in the same directions as the Y and X axes, respectively, on the UCS icon. Your middle finger will be pointing out of the screen

---

*Chapter 1  Introduction to Three-Dimensional Drawing*      **19**

**Figure 1-3.**
Positioning your hand to use the right-hand rule to understand the relationship of the X, Y, and Z axes.

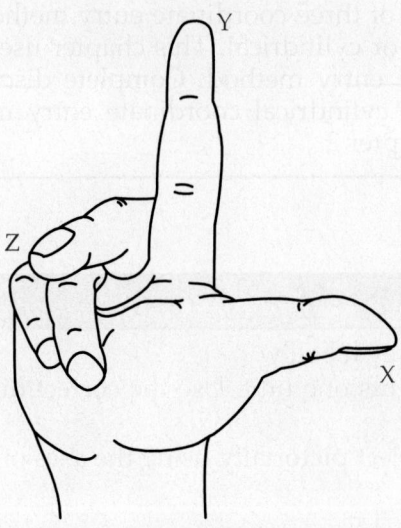

**Figure 1-4.**
A comparison of the UCS icon and the right-hand rule.

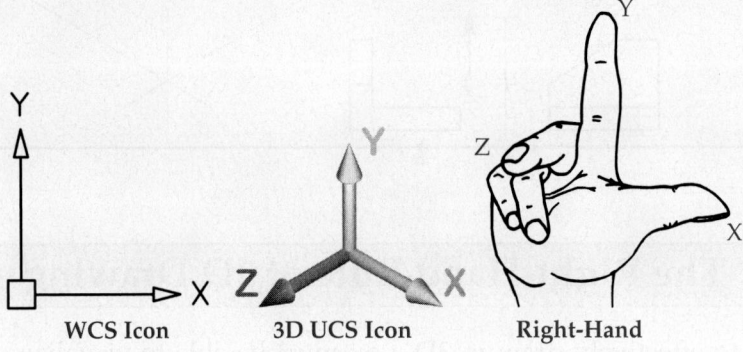

WCS Icon          3D UCS Icon          Right-Hand

directly at you, which is the Z axis. See **Figure 1-4.** Notice the middle illustration in the figure. This is the UCS icon shown when a 3D view is displayed using the **3DORBIT** command, which is discussed in the next section.

The right-hand rule can be used to eliminate confusion when rotating the UCS. The UCS can rotate on any of the three axes, just like a wheel rotates on an axle. Therefore, if you want to visualize how to rotate about the X axis, keep your thumb stationary and turn your hand either toward or away from you. If you wish to rotate about the Y axis, keep your index finger stationary and turn your hand to the left or right. When rotating about the Z axis, you must keep your middle finger stationary and rotate your entire arm.

If your 3D visualization skills are weak or you are having trouble visualizing different orientations of the UCS, use the right-hand rule. It is a useful technique for improving your 3D visualization skills. Rotating the UCS around one or more of the axes can become confusing if proper techniques are not used to visualize the rotation angles. Working with UCSs is introduced in Chapter 2; a complete discussion is provided in Chapter 3.

It does not do much good to understand how to draw in 3D space if you cannot see what you draw in three dimensions. To this point, you have been looking at a plan, or top, view of the XY plane. AutoCAD provides several methods of changing your viewpoint to produce a 3D, or pictorial, view. The *viewpoint* is the location in space from which the object is viewed. AutoCAD has several ways to display a 3D view of your drawing. These include preset isometric and orthographic viewpoints and the **3DORBIT** command.

## Isometric and Orthographic Viewpoint Presets

A 2D isometric drawing is based on angles of 120° between the three axes. AutoCAD provides preset viewpoints that allow you to view a 3D object from one of four isometric locations. See **Figure 1-5.** Each of these viewpoints produces an isometric view of the object. In addition, AutoCAD has presets for the six standard orthographic views of an object. The isometric and orthographic viewpoint presets are based on the WCS.

**Figure 1-5.**
There are four preset isometric viewpoints in AutoCAD. This illustration shows the direction from which the cube will be viewed for each of the presets. The grid represents the XY plane of the WCS.

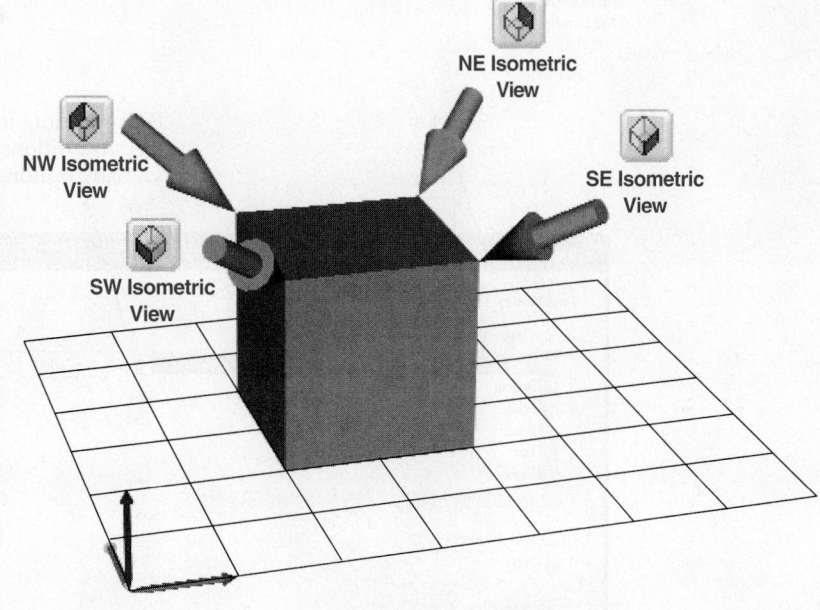

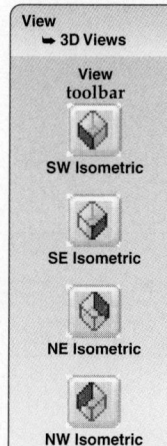

The four preset isometric views are southwest, southeast, northeast, and northwest. To switch your viewpoint to one of these presets, select **3D Views** from the **View** pull-down menu. Then, select **SW Isometric**, **SE Isometric**, **NE Isometric**, or **NW Isometric** from the cascading menu. You can also select the **SW Isometric**, **SE Isometric**, **NE Isometric**, or **NW Isometric** button on the **View** toolbar. This toolbar is not displayed by default. Picking the **Named Views** button on the **View** toolbar opens the **View** dialog box. In the **Orthographic & Isometric Views** tab of this dialog box, you can select one of the preset views. See **Figure 1-6.**

Once you select the command, the viewpoint in the current viewport is automatically changed to display an appropriate isometric view. Since these presets are based on the WCS, selecting a preset produces the same isometric view of the object regardless of the current UCS.

**Figure 1-6.**
A—The **3D Views** cascading menu provides various display options for the current drawing. B—Display options can also be selected from the **View** toolbar. C—The **Orthographic & Isometric Views** tab of the **View** dialog box contains the same orthographic and isometric viewing options provided by the **View** toolbar.

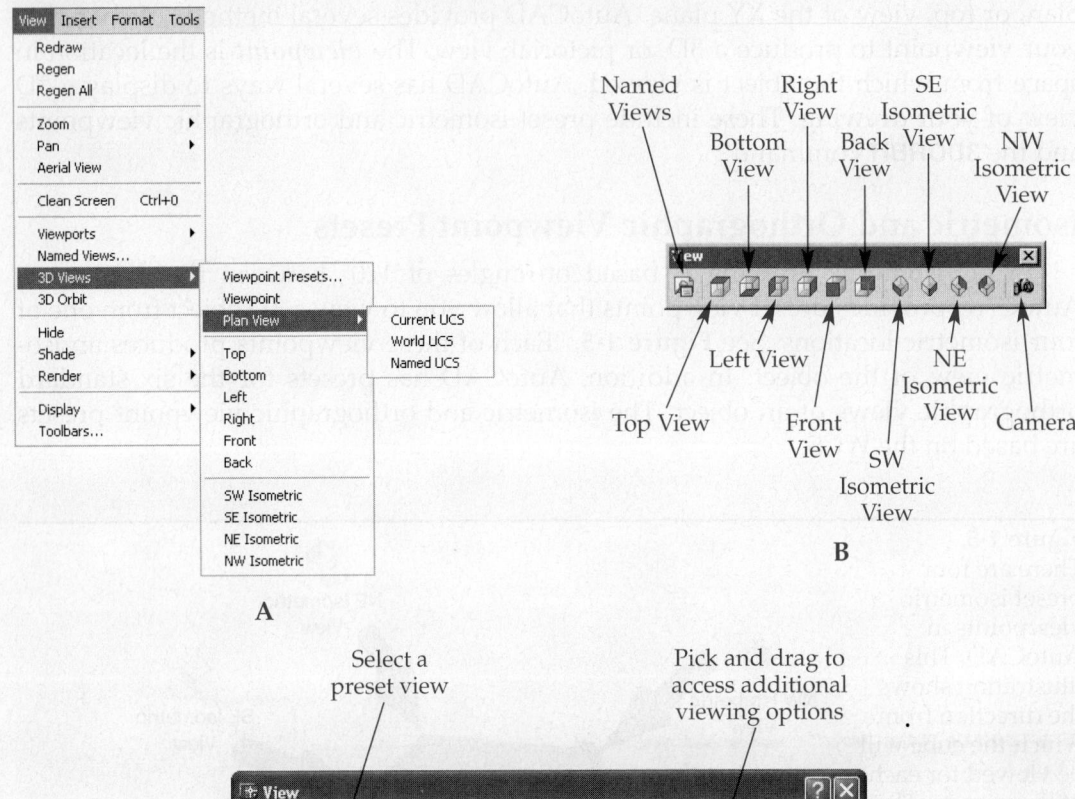

A view that looks straight down on the current drawing plane is called a *plan view.* For example, the default view when you start AutoCAD is a plan view of the WCS. When an isometric or other 3D view is displayed, you can easily switch to a plan view of the current UCS using the **PLAN** command. Type PLAN at the Command: prompt:

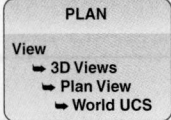

Command: **PLAN**↵
Enter an option [Current ucs/Ucs/World] <Current>: **W**↵ *(if you press [Enter], a plan view of the current UCS is displayed; the current UCS may or may not be the WCS)*
Regenerating model.
Command:

You can also create a plan view of the WCS by selecting **3D Views** in the **View** pull-down menu. Then, select **Plan View** in the cascading menu and **World UCS** in the next cascading menu. There are also **Current UCS** and **Named UCS** options in the cascading menu. The **PLAN** command is discussed in more detail in Chapter 5.

The six orthographic presets are top, bottom, left, right, front, and back. To switch your viewpoint to one of these presets, select **3D Views** from the **View** pull-down menu. Then, select **Top**, **Bottom**, **Left**, **Right**, **Front**, or **Back** from the cascading menu. You can also select the **Top View**, **Bottom View**, **Left View**, **Right View**, **Front View**, or **Back View** button on the **View** toolbar or use the **View** dialog box to select an orthographic preset. Once you select a preset, the view is changed to the corresponding orthographic view. Like the isometric presets, the orthographic presets are based on the WCS so the same view is displayed regardless of the current UCS.

An important aspect of the orthographic presets is that selecting one not only changes the viewpoint, it changes the UCS plan to the orthographic view. All new objects are created on that UCS instead of the WCS (or previous UCS). Working with UCSs is explained in detail in Chapter 3. However, the command sequence to change the UCS to the WCS is:

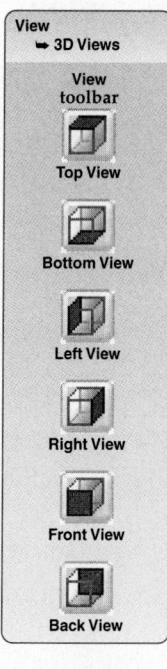

Command: **UCS**↵
Current ucs name: *LEFT* *(this name will match the name of the orthographic preset used to display the view)*
Enter an option [New/Move/orthoGraphic/Prev/Restore/Save/Del/Apply/?/World] <World>: **W**↵
Command:

---

## Exercise 1-2

○ Open the drawing Oil Module.dwg from the AutoCAD Sample folder.
○ Use each one of the four isometric presets to display different views of the model. Note: This is a large model and it may take a few seconds for the command to work.
○ Close the drawing without saving the changes.

---

## Unlimited Viewpoints

You are not limited to the preset isometric viewpoints. In fact, you can view a 3D object from an unlimited number of viewpoints. The **3DORBIT** command allows you to dynamically rotate the view of the objects to create a new viewpoint.

To start the **3DORBIT** command, pick **3D Orbit** from the **View** pull-down menu or type 3DORBIT or 3DO at the Command: prompt. A green circle appears in the middle of the current viewport. See **Figure 1-7.** This is called the trackball, or arcball. Also, notice that the cursor changes. If you move it inside the trackball, it appears as two intersecting circles, as shown in **Figure 1-7.** If you move it outside of the trackball, the cursor appears as a single circle.

To change the view, pick anywhere inside the trackball and drag the cursor. The view is dynamically changed as you move the cursor. However, you are not rotating the *objects,* just the view. When you get the view you want, release the mouse button. The command remains active and you can further adjust the view. When done, right-click to display the shortcut menu. Then, select **Exit** from the menu. You can also press [Esc] to end the command. The **UNDO** command reverses the effects of the **3DORBIT** command.

Picking outside the trackball and dragging rotates the view about an axis extending out of the screen. Also, notice the circle "handles" at the four quadrants of the trackball. Picking in the right or left handle and dragging rotates the view about the

**Figure 1-7.**
Using the **3DORBIT** command to change the viewpoint.

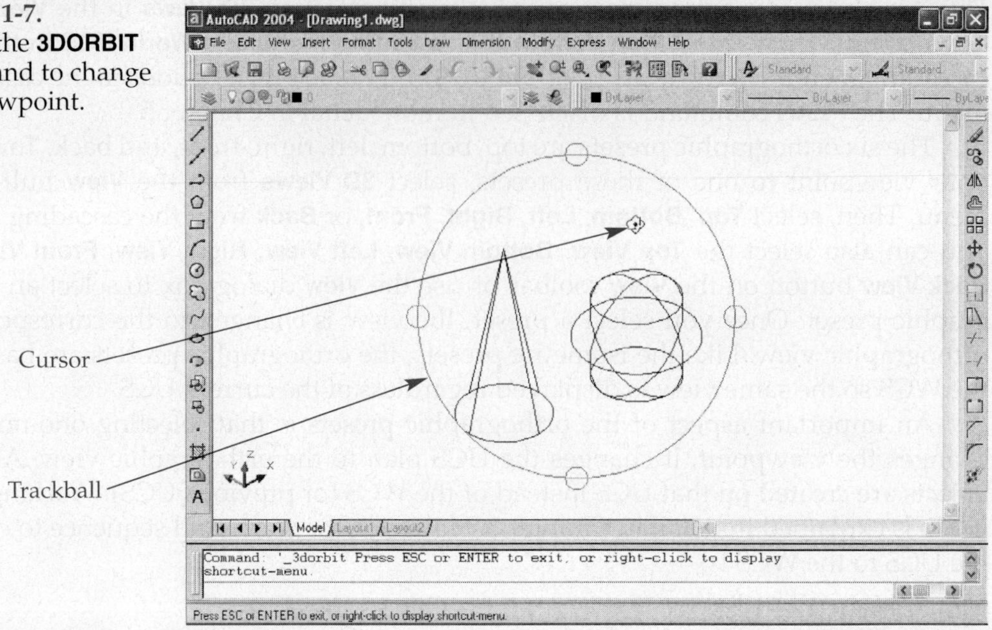

Cursor

Trackball

```
a AutoCAD 2004 - [Drawing1.dwg]
File  Edit  View  Insert  Format  Tools  Draw  Dimension  Modify  Express  Window  Help
```

```
Command: '_3dorbit Press ESC or ENTER to exit, or right-click to display
shortcut-menu.
```
```
Press ESC or ENTER to exit, or right-click to display shortcut-menu.
```

vertical axis in the viewport. Picking in the top or bottom handle and dragging rotates the view about the horizontal axis in the viewport.

The **3DORBIT** command has many options. This discussion is merely an introduction to the command. The command options are covered in detail in Chapter 5.

---

**PROFESSIONAL TIP**

AutoCAD has other commands for changing the viewpoint whose functionalities have largely been replaced by the more useful **3DORBIT** command. These commands include **VPOINT**, **DDVPOINT**, and **DVIEW**.

---

**Exercise 1-3**

○ Open the drawing Oil Module.dwg from the AutoCAD Sample folder.
○ Using the **3DORBIT** command, rotate the view. Display the model in a view that is not isometric. Note: This is a large model and it may take a few seconds for the command to work.
○ Exit the command.
○ Close the drawing without saving the changes.

---

## Hiding Lines

When you display a 3D object in a pictorial view, such as from one of the isometric presets, AutoCAD displays all lines on the object. This includes the lines that represent the back of the object or internal features. See **Figure 1-8A.** This type of display is called a *wireframe display.* Often, it can be confusing looking at all of the lines. The **HIDE** command can be used to create a *hidden display* in which hidden lines are removed. See **Figure 1-8B.** Hidden lines are those lines on an object that would not be visible if the object were truly solid. In a traditional 2D isometric drawing, these lines are drawn in a hidden linetype. In a wireframe display, all of the lines representing

**Figure 1-8.**
A—In a wireframe display, all lines are shown. B—In a hidden display, the lines that would be hidden from view are not shown. (Autodesk, Inc.)

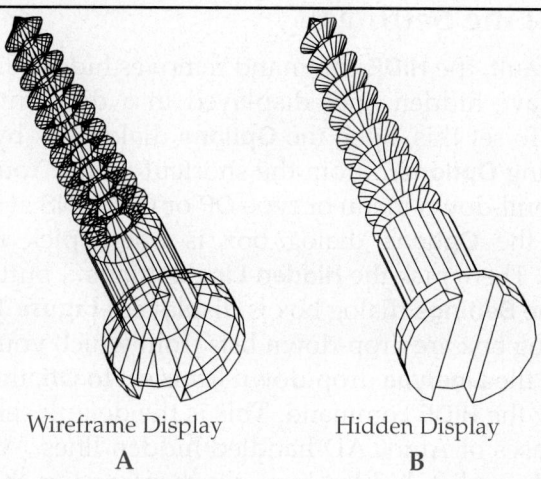

Wireframe Display
A

Hidden Display
B

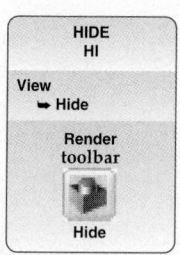

hidden features are visible. The **HIDE** command suppresses the display of these lines. However, the lines are not actually removed from the object.

To access the **HIDE** command, pick the **Hide** button on the **Render** toolbar, select **Hide** from the **View** pull-down menu, or enter HI or HIDE at the Command: prompt:

Command: **HI** *or* **HIDE.**↵
Regenerating model.
Command:

The size and complexity of the drawing and the speed of your computer determine how long you must wait for the lines to be hidden. To redisplay the 3D object in a wireframe display, use the **REGEN** command. In addition, any command that performs a regeneration, such as **ZOOM Extents**, redisplays the hidden lines.

The **HIDE** command not only affects the on-screen display—it also affects plots. To plot objects with hidden lines removed, use the following guidelines.

- **Plotting from the Model tab.**
  - Method 1. Open the **Plot** dialog box. Then, select **Hidden** from the **Shade Plot** drop-down list in the **Shaded Viewport options** area of the **Plot Settings** tab. Finally, plot the drawing.
  - Method 2. Issue the **HIDE** command. Then open the **Plot** dialog box. Select **As Displayed** from the **Shade Plot** drop-down list in the **Shaded Viewport options** area of the **Plot Settings** tab. Finally, plot the drawing.
- **Plotting from a layout tab.** When plotting from a layout tab the shade plot properties of the viewport(s) govern how the viewport is plotted. The viewport(s) can be set to plot hidden two different ways.
  - Method 1. Use the **Shademode** option of the **MVIEW** command.

    Command: **MV** *or* **MVIEW.**↵
    Specify corner of viewport or [ON/OFF/Fit/Shadeplot/Lock/Object/Polygonal/
      Restore/2/3/4] <Fit>: **S.**↵
    Shade plot? [As displayed/Wireframe/Hidden/Rendered] <As displayed>: **H.**↵
    Select objects: *(pick the viewport in which to hide lines when plotting)*
    Select objects: ↵
    Command:

    When you pick the viewport, pick the border of the viewport. Do not pick the objects in the viewport.
  - Method 2. Use the **Properties** window to set the **Shade plot** property of the viewport. To do this, select the layout tab, pick the viewport, and open the **Properties** window. Pick the **Shade plot** property and change the setting to **Hidden**.

# Hidden Line Settings

By default, the **HIDE** command removes hidden lines from the display. However, you can have hidden lines displayed in a different linetype and color instead of removed. To set this, open the **Options** dialog box by right-clicking in the viewport and selecting **Options...** from the shortcut menu. You can also select **Options...** from the **Tools** pull-down menu or type OP or OPTIONS at the Command: prompt.

Once the **Options** dialog box is open, pick the **User Preferences** tab. See **Figure 1-9.** Then, pick the **Hidden Line Settings...** button at the bottom of the tab. The **Hidden Line Settings** dialog box is displayed, **Figure 1-10.** In the **Obscured Lines** area of the dialog box are drop-down lists from which you can select a linetype and color.

When the **Linetype** drop-down list is set to **Off**, the display of hidden lines is suppressed by the **HIDE** command. This is the default setting and the way in which previous releases of AutoCAD handled hidden lines. When a linetype is selected from the drop-down list, hidden lines are displayed in that linetype after the **HIDE** command is used. The linetypes available in the drop-down list are not the same as the linetypes loaded into your drawing.

**Figure 1-9.**
The **Hidden Line Settings...** button is located in the **User Preferences** tab of the **Options** dialog box.

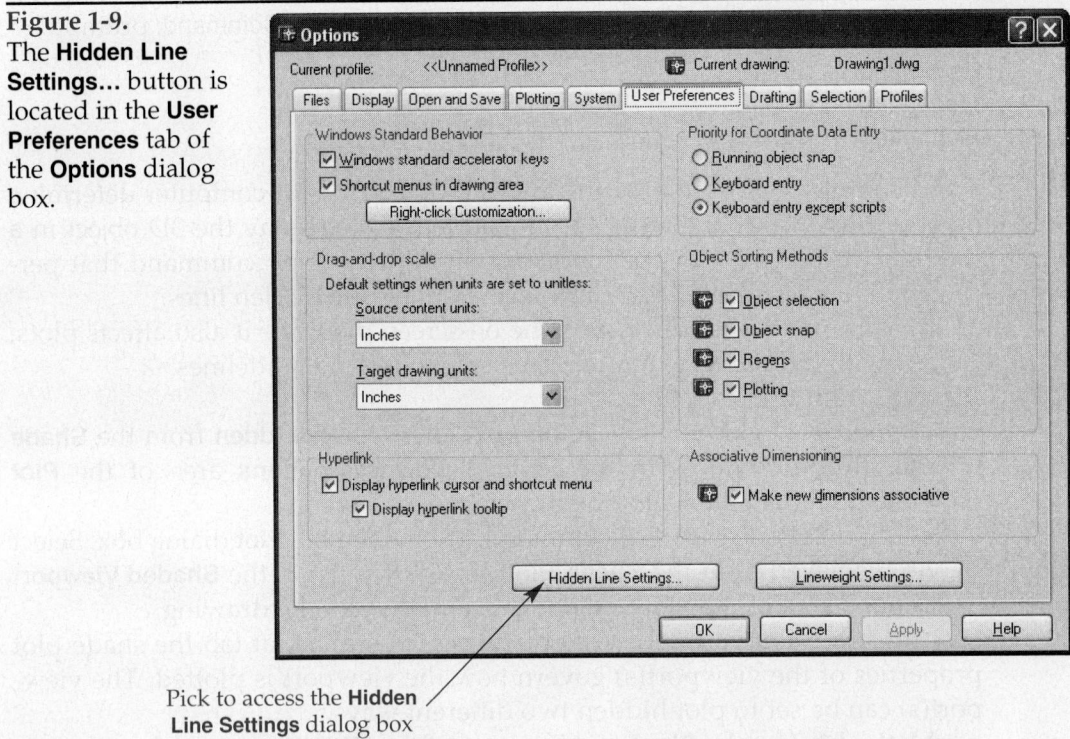

Pick to access the **Hidden Line Settings** dialog box

**Figure 1-10.**
Changing how hidden lines are displayed when the **HIDE** command is used.

Select a linetype

Select a color

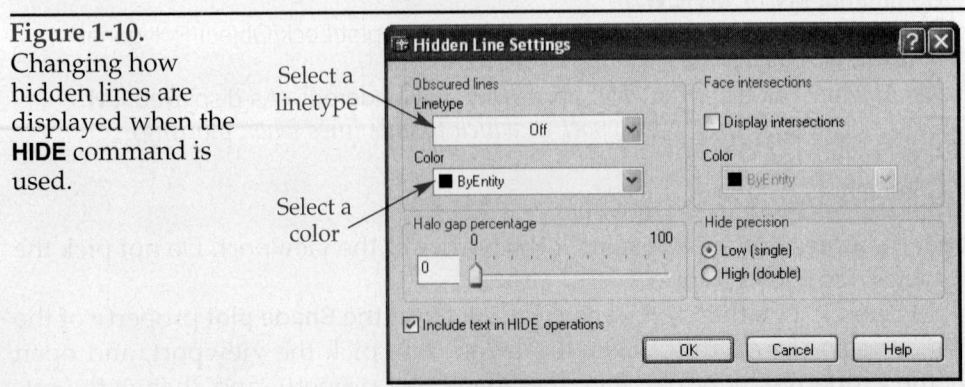

When a linetype is selected, you can also change the display color of the hidden lines. Simply pick a color in the **Color** drop-down list. To have the hidden lines displayed in the same color as the object, select **ByEntity**, which is the default. The color setting has no effect when the **Linetype** drop-down list is set to **Off**.

There are other settings in this dialog box related to hidden line display. These are:

- **Halo gap percentage.** Use this area to adjust the gap between the foreground edge and where the background edge starts to show. The distance is specified as a percentage of one unit. The gap is not affected by the zoom level.
- **Face Intersections.** This section is used to toggle the display of intersection polylines at the intersection of 3D surfaces and set the color of them.
- **Hide Precision.** The accuracy of hides and shades can be set in this section. **Low (single)** uses less memory while **High (double)** is more accurate but uses more memory, thereby possibly degrading performance.

When done making settings, pick the **OK** button to close the **Hidden Line Settings** dialog box. Then, pick the **OK** button to close the **Options** dialog box.

## 3D Construction Techniques

Before constructing a 3D model, you should determine the purpose of your design. What will the model be used for—presentation, analysis, or manufacturing? This helps you determine which tools you should use to construct the model. Three-dimensional objects can be drawn in three basic forms—wireframe objects, solid models, and surface models.

A *wireframe object,* or model, is an object that is constructed of lines in 3D space. Wireframe models are hard to visualize because it is difficult to determine the angle of view and the nature of the surfaces represented by the lines. The **HIDE** command has no effect when used on a wireframe model because there is nothing to hide. All lines are always visible because there are no surfaces. There are not many practical applications for wireframe models. However, one application is to draw a wireframe and then place a skin, or surface, over the wireframe. Another specialized application of 3D wireframe modeling is creating single-line piping diagrams for the process piping industry. An example of drawing a wireframe model is given in the next section.

*Surface modeling* represents solid objects by creating a skin in the shape of the object. However, there is nothing inside the object. Think of a surface model as a balloon filled with air. A surface model looks more like the real object than a wireframe and can be used for rendering. However, while more useful than wireframes, surface models have limited applications. Surface modeling is covered in Chapter 11 through Chapter 13.

Like surface modeling, *solid modeling* represents the shape of objects, but also provides data related to the physical properties of the objects. Solid models can be analyzed to determine mass, volume, moments of inertia, and centroid. A solid model is not just a skin, it represents a solid object. Some third-party programs allow you to perform finite element analysis on the model. In addition, solid models can be rendered. Most 3D objects are created as solid models. Solid modeling is covered in Chapter 6 through Chapter 10.

In AutoCAD, both solid and surface models can be created from primitives. *Primitives* are basic shapes used as the foundation to create complex shapes. These basic shapes in AutoCAD include boxes, cylinders, spheres, and cones. Primitives can be modified to create a finished product. See **Figure 1-11.**

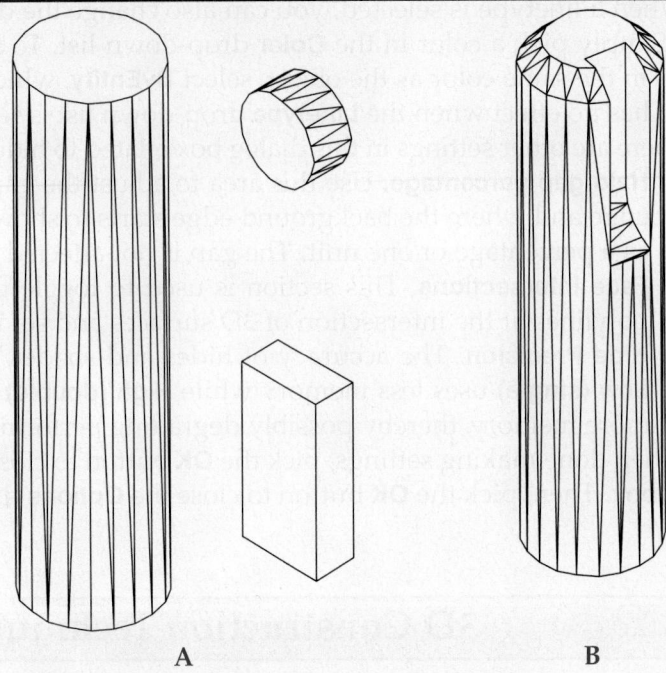

**Figure 1-11.**
A—These two cylinders and the box are solid primitives. B—With a couple of quick modifications, the large cylinder becomes a shaft with a machined keyway.

A                                                                 B

Surface and solid models can be exported from AutoCAD for use in animation and rendering software, such as 3ds max® or Autodesk VIZ®. Rendered models can be used in any number of presentation formats, including slide shows, black and white or color prints, and animation recorded to videotape, CD-ROM, or DVD. Surface and solid models can also be used to create virtual worlds for virtual reality applications.

## Constructing a Wireframe Object

To draw a wireframe object, you must know the XYZ coordinate values of each corner on the object. You can then use "line" commands, such as **LINE**, **CIRCLE**, **REC-TANGLE**, etc., to draw the object. Often, the lines representing the bottom (or most complex) horizontal surface are drawn first on the XY plane of the WCS. Then, this "surface" is copied along the Z axis and modified as needed. Finally, the lines representing the vertical surfaces are drawn to complete the object.

For example, first draw the 2D object shown in **Figure 1-12** using the **LINE** command. Next, copy the shape 1.5 units up the Z axis.

Command: **CO** or **COPY**↵
Select objects: *(select all lines in the shape)*
Select objects: ↵
Specify base point or displacement, or [Multiple]: *(pick anywhere in the drawing area)*
Specify second point of displacement or <use first point as displacement>: **@0,0,1.5**↵
Command:

By specifying @0,0,1.5 you tell AutoCAD that the second displacement point is 0 units on the X axis, 0 units on the Y axis, and 1.5 units on the Z axis from the first point. In other words, you have just copied the objects 1.5 units straight up the positive Z axis. This can be seen by displaying a pictorial view of the object using one of the preset isometric views. See **Figure 1-13**. To complete the wireframe object, use the **LINE** command and the **Endpoint** object snap to connect the corners of the object. See **Figure 1-14**.

**Figure 1-12.**
To draw a
wireframe, start by
drawing the top
view.

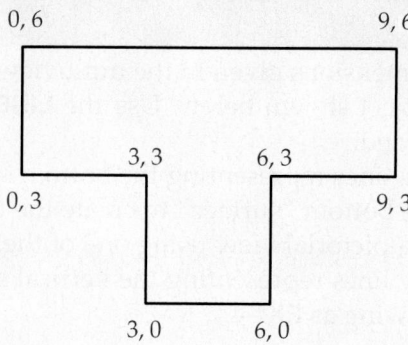

**Figure 1-13.**
The bottom
"surface" of the
wireframe is copied
along the Z axis to
create the top
"surface."

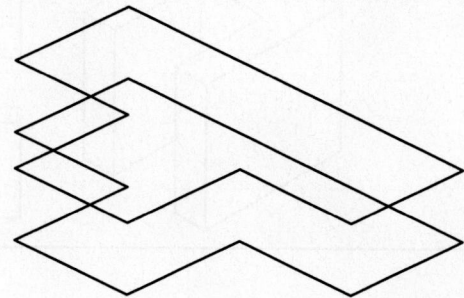

**Figure 1-14.**
To complete the
wireframe object,
connect the top and
bottom using the
**LINE** command and
the **Endpoint** object
snap.

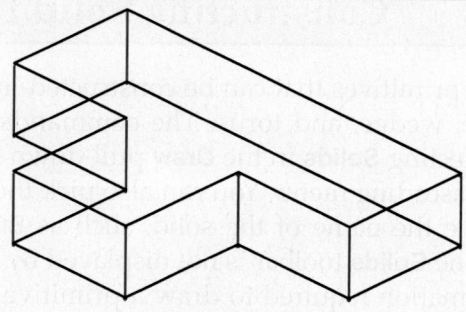

**PROFESSIONAL TIP**

Do not confuse a wireframe *object* with a wireframe *display*, which is a 3D surface or solid object with all lines displayed. Often, a drafter may say a 3D object is "displayed in wireframe." This means that the view of the object shows all lines, visible and hidden, not that the object is drawn as a wireframe object. If the **HIDE** command is used on a 3D object displayed in wireframe, the hidden lines will be removed to create a *hidden display*. The **HIDE** command has no effect when used on a wireframe *object*.

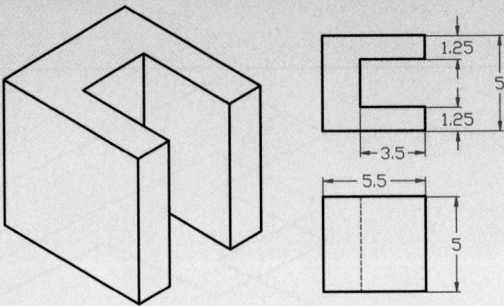
# Constructing Solid Primitives

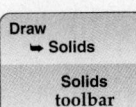

Draw
↳ Solids

Solids
toolbar

The solid primitives that can be constructed in AutoCAD include a box, sphere, cylinder, cone, wedge, and torus. The commands to draw these primitives can be entered by selecting **Solids** in the **Draw** pull-down menu and then selecting the command in the cascading menu. You can also pick the appropriate button on the **Solids** toolbar or type the name of the solid, such as BOX, at the Command: prompt. See **Figure 1-15.** The **Solids** toolbar is not displayed by default.

The information required to draw a primitive depends on the type of primitive being drawn. See **Figure 1-16.** For example, to draw a solid cylinder you must provide a center point for the base, a radius or diameter of the base, and the height of the cylinder:

```
Command: CYLINDER↵
Current wire frame density: ISOLINES = 4
Specify center point for base of cylinder or [Elliptical] <0,0,0>: 0,0,1↵
Specify radius for base of cylinder or [Diameter]: 2↵
Specify height of cylinder or [Center of other end]: 4↵
Command:
```

The cylinder is drawn with, normally, its base on the XY plane of the current UCS. However, notice that the center of the base was specified as 0,0,1. This locates the center one unit up the positive Z axis from the XY plane of the current UCS. Also, notice that there are other options, such as creating a cylinder that is elliptical instead of round, specifying a diameter instead of a radius, and locating the center of the opposite end rather than providing a height. The command sequence for the other solid primitives is similar to that for a cylinder.

Certain familiar editing commands can be used on solid primitives. For example, you can fillet or chamfer the edges of a solid primitive. In addition, there are other editing commands that are specifically for use on solids. You can also perform Boolean operations on solids. These operations allow you to add one solid to another, subtract one solid from another, or create a new solid based on how two solids overlap. Solid modeling construction and editing are discussed in detail in Chapter 6 through Chapter 10.

**Figure 1-15.**
A comparison of solid and surface primitives. Notice the differences between solids and surfaces in wireframe and hidden displays.

| Basic Primitive Shape | Solid | | | Surfaces | | |
|---|---|---|---|---|---|---|
| | Command | Wireframe All Lines/Hidden | Shaded | Command | Wireframe All Lines/Hidden | Shaded |
| Box | BOX / Draw Solids Box / Box |  |  | 3D>Box / Draw Surfaces 3D Surfaces… / Box |  | 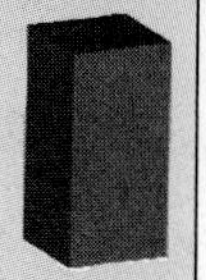 |
| Sphere | SPHERE / Draw Solids Sphere / Sphere | 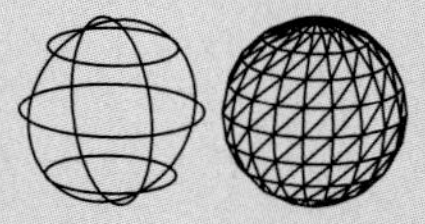 | 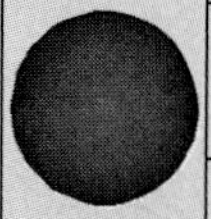 | 3D>Sphere / Draw Surfaces 3D Surfaces… / Sphere | 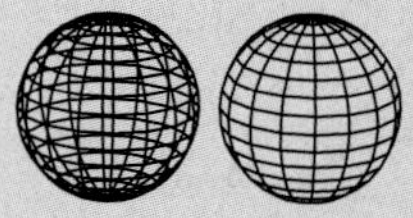 | 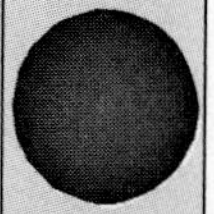 |
| Cylinder | CYLINDER / Draw Solids Cylinder / Cylinder | 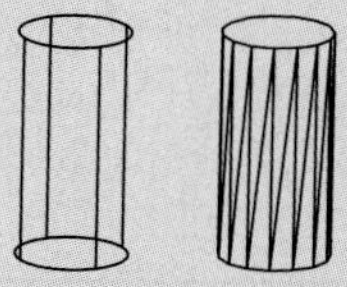 | 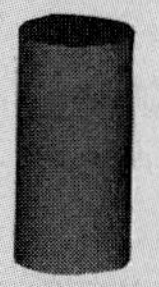 | — | — | — |
| Cone | CONE / Draw Solids Cone / Cone | 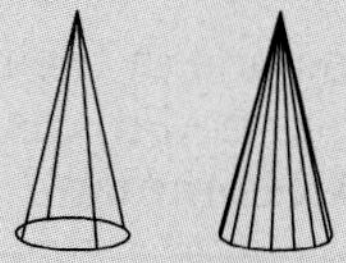 |  | 3D>Cone / Draw Surfaces 3D Surfaces… / Cone |  |  |
| Wedge | WEDGE / Draw Solids Wedge / Wedge |  |  | 3D>Wedge / Draw Surfaces 3D Surfaces… / Wedge |  |  |
| Torus | TORUS / Draw Solids Torus / Torus | 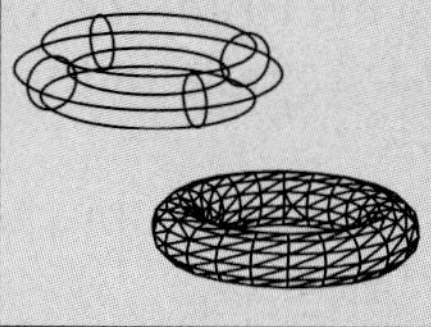 |  | 3D>Torus / Draw Surfaces 3D Surfaces… / Torus | 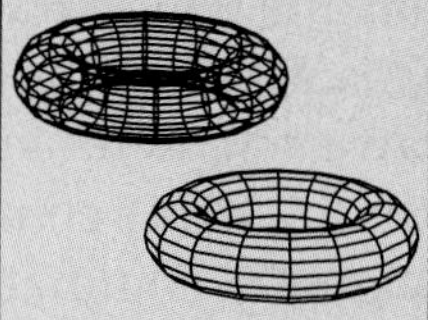 |  |
| Pyramid | — | — | — | 3D>Pyramid / Draw Surfaces 3D Surfaces… / Pyramid |  |  |
| Dome | — | — | — | 3D>DOme / Draw Surfaces 3D Surfaces… / Dome |  | |
| Dish | — | — | — | 3D>DIsh / Draw Surfaces 3D Surfaces… / Dish | 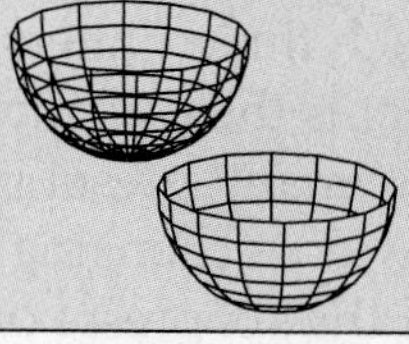 |  |

**Figure 1-16.**
The basic information required to draw solid primitives.

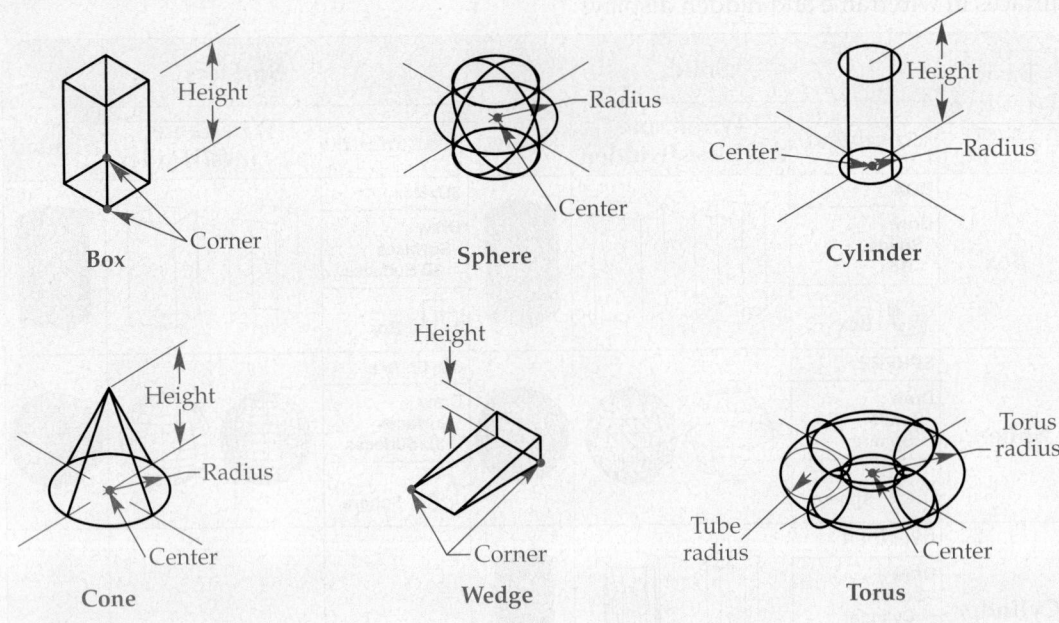

PROFESSIONAL TIP

To see the object in 3D, use one of the isometric presets or the **3DORBIT** command. If you need to display a plan view of the current UCS, use the **PLAN** command.

## Exercise 1-5

○ Start AutoCAD using one of your templates.
○ Display the blank drawing from the southwest isometric viewpoint.
○ Draw each one of the six solid primitives. Make note of the information required to draw each. Refer to **Figure 1-16.**
○ Use the **3DORBIT** command to rotate the view of the objects.
○ Use the **HIDE** command to remove hidden lines.
○ Save the drawing as EX1-5.

## Chapter Test

*Answer the following questions on a separate sheet of paper.*

1. What are the three coordinates needed to locate any point in 3D space?
2. In a 2D drawing, what is the value for the Z coordinate?
3. What purpose does the right-hand rule serve?
4. Which three fingers are used in the right-hand rule?
5. What is the definition of a *viewpoint?*
6. How many preset isometric viewpoints does AutoCAD have? List them.
7. How does changing the UCS impact using one of the preset isometric viewpoints?
8. List the six preset orthographic viewpoints.
9. When using a preset orthographic viewpoint, what happens to the UCS?

10. Which command allows you to dynamically change your viewpoint using an on-screen trackball?
11. Define *wireframe display*.
12. Define *hidden display*.
13. Define *wireframe object*.
14. Define *surface model*.
15. Define *solid model*.
16. Define *primitive*.
17. List the six solid primitives available in AutoCAD.
18. Briefly describe how to have hidden lines displayed in red when the **HIDE** command is used.

## Drawing Problems

*For Problems 1–4, draw the objects shown as wireframe objects. Use AutoCAD line commands, such as **LINE** and **CIRCLE**, to complete each object. Do not draw dimensions. Use your own dimensions for objects shown without dimensions. Save the drawings as* P1-*(problem number).*

1.

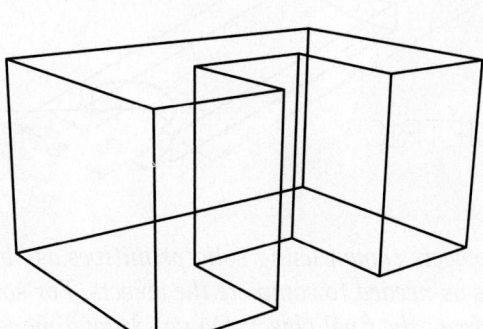 

2.

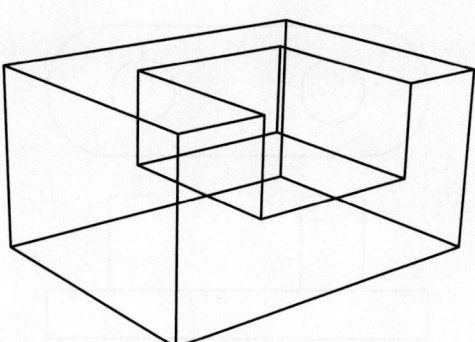 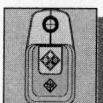

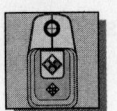

3.

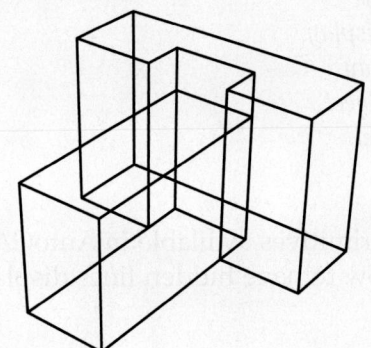

4.

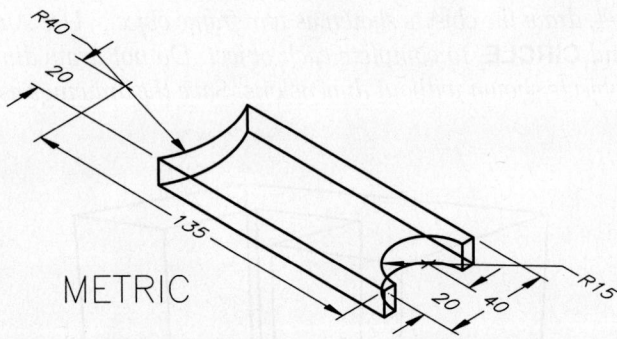

METRIC

*For Problems 5–10, draw the objects shown using solid primitives as "building blocks." Move and rotate the primitives as needed to complete the objects. For some objects, you may need to overlap primitives to create the final object. Do not draw dimensions. Use your own dimensions for objects shown without dimensions. Use the* **HIDE** *command to create a hidden display. Save the drawings as* **P1**-*(problem number).*

5.

6.

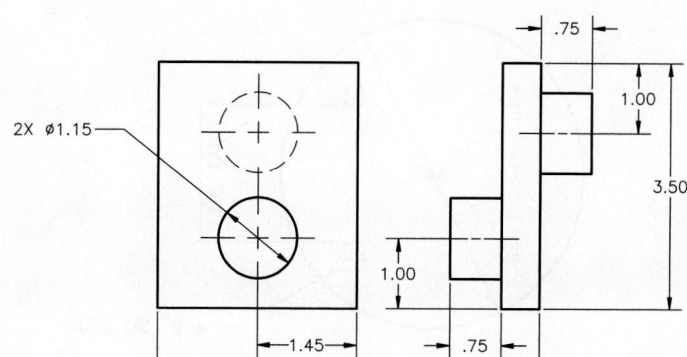

2X ⌀1.15

.75
1.00
3.50
1.00
1.45
2.90
.75
.55

7.

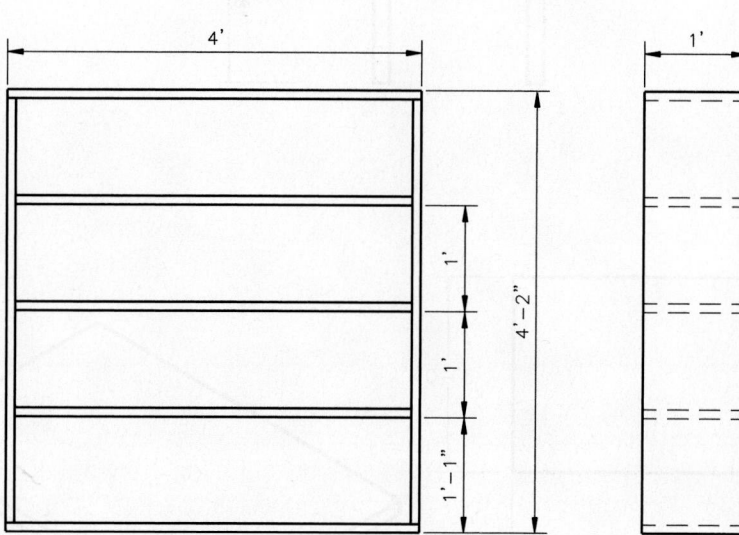

4'
1'
1'
1'
1'
1'–1"
4'–2"

8.

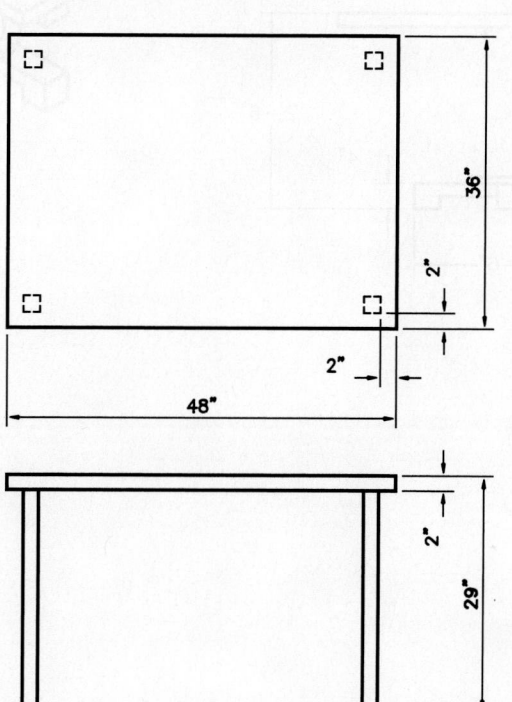

36"
2"
2"
48"
2"
2"
29"

# TABLE

9.

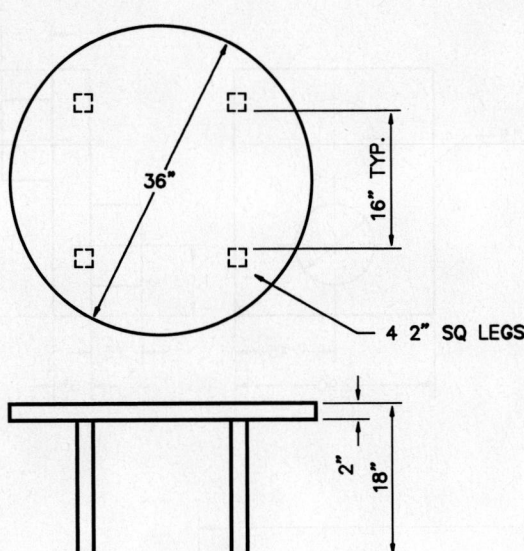

36"

16" TYP.

4 2" SQ LEGS

2"

18"

10.

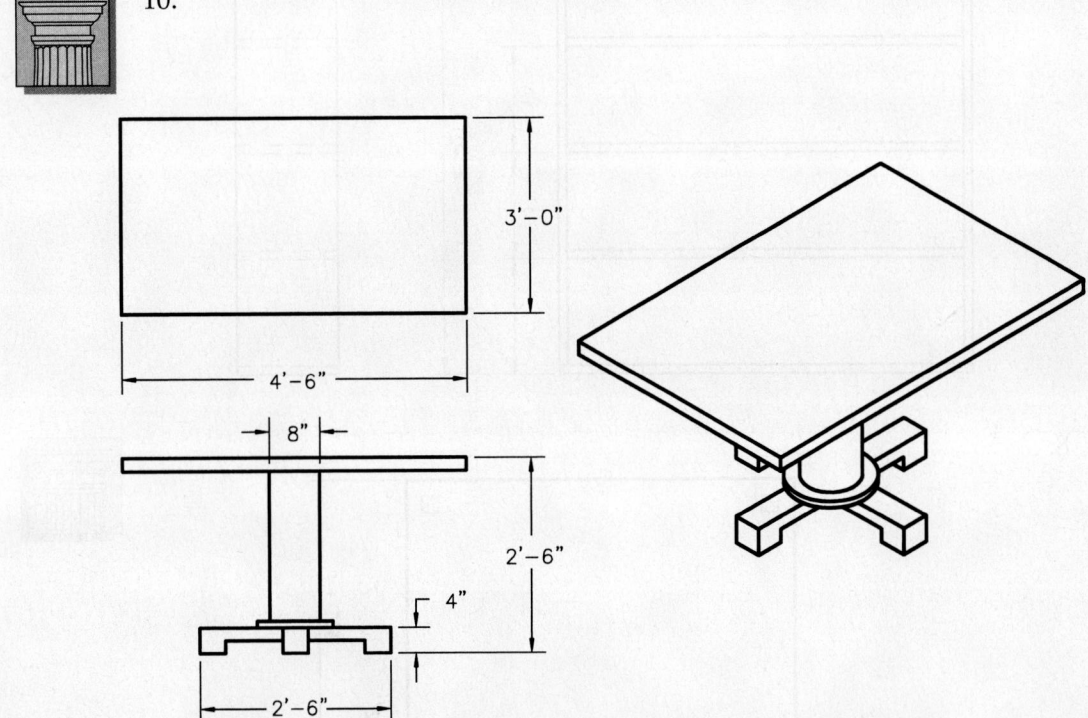

3'-0"

4'-6"

8"

2'-6"

4"

2'-6"

CHAPTER 2

# Three-Dimensional Coordinates and Constructions

## Learning Objectives

After completing this chapter, you will be able to:
- Describe the rectangular, spherical, and cylindrical methods of coordinate entry.
- Draw 3D polylines.
- Move and rotate the UCS.
- Create an accurate intersection between curved and flat surfaces.

As you learned in Chapter 1, any point in space can be located using X, Y, and Z coordinates. This type of coordinate entry is called rectangular coordinates. Rectangular coordinates are most commonly used for coordinate entry. However, there are actually three ways in which to locate a point in space. The other two methods of coordinate entry are spherical coordinates and cylindrical coordinates. These two coordinate entry methods are discussed in the following sections. In addition, this chapter introduces working with user coordinate systems (UCSs) and how to create accurate intersections in 3D space.

## Introduction to Spherical Coordinates

Locating a point in 3D space with *spherical coordinates* is similar to locating a point on Earth using longitudinal and latitudinal values, with the center of Earth representing the origin. Lines of longitude connect the North and South Poles and provide an east-west measurement on Earth's surface. Lines of latitude extend horizontally around Earth and provide a north-south measurement. The origin (Earth's center) can be that of the default world coordinate system (WCS) or the current user coordinate system (UCS). See **Figure 2-1A.**

When entering spherical coordinates, the longitude measurement is expressed as the angle *in* the XY plane and the latitude measurement is expressed as the angle *from* the XY plane. See **Figure 2-1B.** A distance from the origin is also provided. The coordinates represent a measurement from the equator toward either the north or south pole on Earth's surface. The following spherical coordinate entry is shown in **Figure 2-1B.**

**7.5<35<55**

**Figure 2-1.**
A—Lines of longitude, representing the highlighted latitudinal segments in the illustration below, run from north to south. Lines of latitude, representing the highlighted longitudinal segments below, run from east to west. B—Spherical coordinates require a distance, an angle *in* the XY plane, and an angle *from* the XY plane.

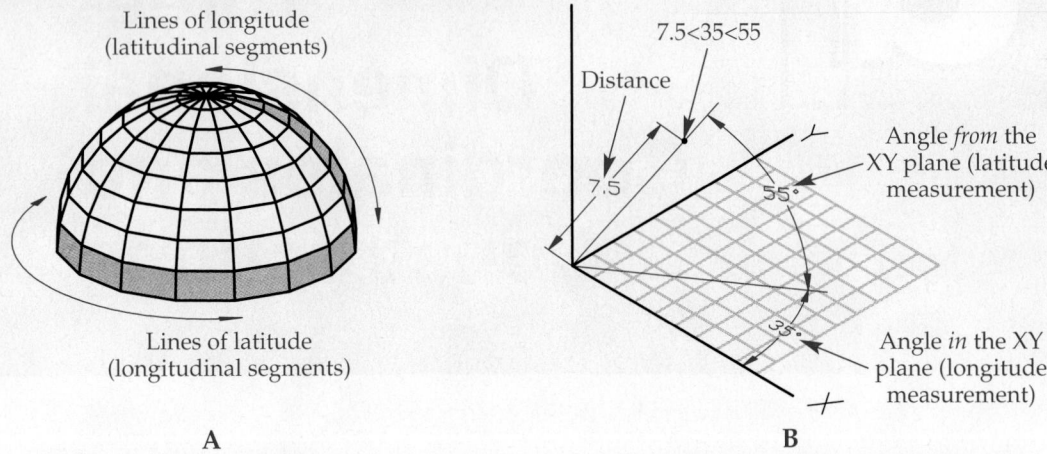

A

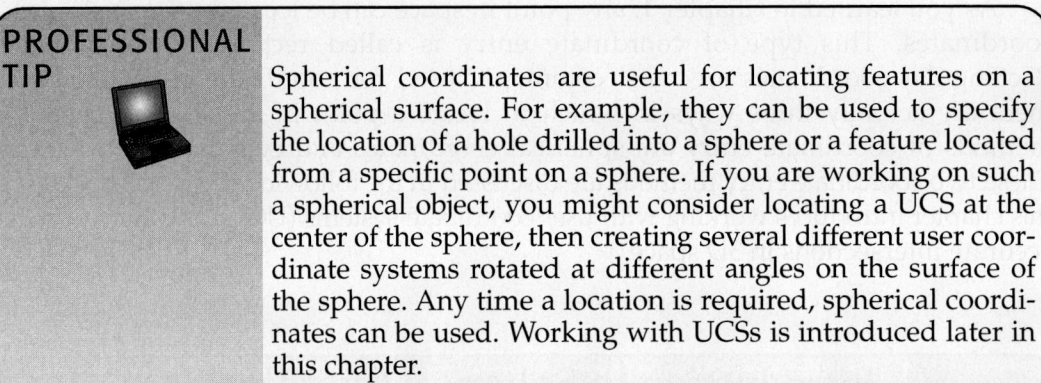

B

This coordinate represents an absolute spherical coordinate, which is measured from the origin of the current UCS. Spherical coordinates can also be entered as relative coordinates. For example, a point drawn with the relative spherical coordinate @2<35<45 is located 2 units from the last point, at an angle of 35° *in* the XY plane, and at a 45° angle *from* the XY plane.

> **PROFESSIONAL TIP**
>
> Spherical coordinates are useful for locating features on a spherical surface. For example, they can be used to specify the location of a hole drilled into a sphere or a feature located from a specific point on a sphere. If you are working on such a spherical object, you might consider locating a UCS at the center of the sphere, then creating several different user coordinate systems rotated at different angles on the surface of the sphere. Any time a location is required, spherical coordinates can be used. Working with UCSs is introduced later in this chapter.

## Using Spherical Coordinates

Spherical coordinates are well-suited for locating points on the surface of a sphere. In this section, you will draw a solid sphere and then locate a second solid sphere with its center on the surface of the first sphere.

To draw the first sphere, pick **Sphere** from the **Solids** cascading menu in the **Draw** pull-down menu, pick the **Sphere** button on the **Solids** toolbar, or type SPHERE at the Command: prompt:

    Command: **SPHERE**↵
    Current wire frame density: ISOLINES=4
    Specify center of sphere <0,0,0>: **7,5**↵
    Specify radius of sphere or [Diameter]: **1.5**↵
    Command:

**Figure 2-2.**
Note: **ISOLINES** is set to 8. A—A 3-unit diameter sphere shown from the southeast isometric viewpoint. B—A .8-unit diameter sphere with its center located on the surface of the original object. C—The objects after using the **HIDE** command.

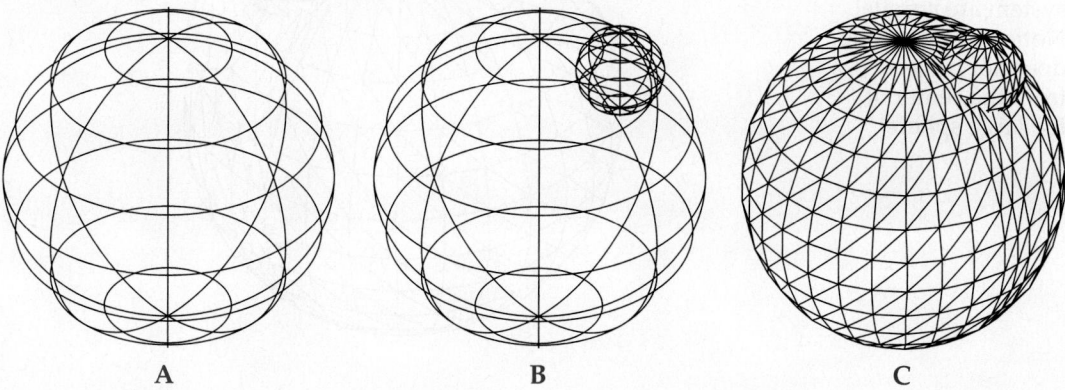

A                         B                         C

Now, display a pictorial view of the sphere by picking **SE Isometric** from the **3D Views** cascading menu in the **View** pull-down menu or the **SE Isometric View** button on the **View** toolbar. Alternately, you can use the **3DORBIT** command to create a pictorial view. Your drawing should look similar to **Figure 2-2A.**

Since you know the radius of the sphere, but the center of the sphere is not at the origin of the current UCS (the WCS), a relative spherical coordinate will be used to draw the second sphere. The sphere is a solid and, as such, you can snap to its center using the **Center** object snap. Set this as a running object snap and then enter the **SPHERE** command again to draw the second sphere:

> Command: **SPHERE**↵
> Current wire frame density: ISOLINES=4
> Specify center of sphere <0,0,0>: **FROM**↵
> Base point: *(use the **Center** object snap to select the center of the existing sphere)*
> <Offset>: **@1.5<30<60**↵ *(1.5 is the radius of the first sphere)*
> Specify radius of sphere or [Diameter]: **.4**↵
> Command:

The objects should now appear as shown in **Figure 2-2B.** The center of the new sphere is located on the surface of the original sphere. This is clear after using the **HIDE** command, **Figure 2-2C.** If you want the surfaces of the spheres to be tangent, add the radius values of each sphere (1.5 + .4) and enter this value when prompted for the offset from the center of the first sphere:

> <Offset>: **@1.9<30<60**↵

Notice in **Figure 2-2C** that the polar axes of the two spheres are parallel. This is because both objects were drawn using the same UCS, which can be misleading unless you understand how objects are constructed based on the current UCS. Test this by locating a cone on the surface of the large sphere, just below the small sphere. First, display a wireframe view of the objects by typing REGEN at the Command: prompt. Then, continue as follows.

> Command: **CONE**↵
> Current wire frame density: ISOLINES=4
> Specify center point for base of cone or [Elliptical] <0,0,0>: **FROM**↵
> Base point: **CEN**↵
> of *(pick the large sphere)*
> <Offset>: **@1.5<30<30**↵
> Specify radius for base of cone or [Diameter]: **.25**↵
> Specify height of cone or [Apex] <0>: **1**↵
> Command:

**Figure 2-3.**
The axis lines of objects drawn in the same coordinate system are parallel. Notice that the cone does not project from the center of the large sphere.

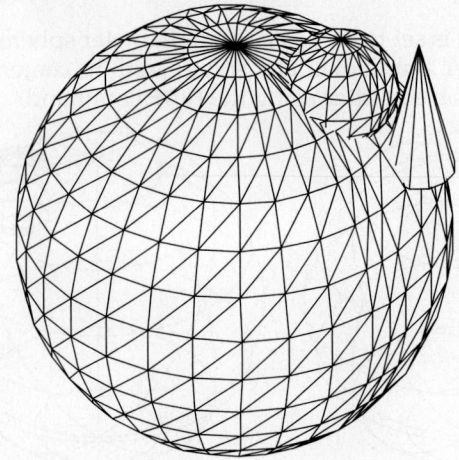

The result of this construction, after using the **HIDE** command, is shown in **Figure 2-3.** Notice how the axis of the cone is parallel to the polar axis of the sphere. To draw the cone so that its axis projects from the center of the sphere, you will need to change the UCS. This is discussed later in this chapter.

> NOTE
>
> The **REGEN** command used in the previous example will not restore hidden lines if the **SHADEMODE** command is set to an option other than **2D wireframe**. If necessary, enter this option and then use the **REGEN** command to display a wireframe view.

## Introduction to Cylindrical Coordinates

Locating a point in space with *cylindrical coordinates* is similar to locating a point on an imaginary cylinder. Cylindrical coordinates have three values. The first value represents the horizontal distance from the origin, which can be thought of as the radius of a cylinder. The second value represents the angle in the XY plane, or the rotation of the cylinder. The third value represents a vertical dimension measured up from the polar coordinate in the XY plane, or the height of the cylinder. See **Figure 2-4.** The absolute cylindrical coordinate shown in the figure is:

**7.5<35,6**

Like spherical coordinates, cylindrical coordinates can also be entered as relative coordinates. For example, a point drawn with the relative cylindrical coordinate @1.5<30,4 is located 1.5 units from the last point, at an angle of 30° in the XY plane, and at a distance of 4 units up from the XY plane.

Cylindrical coordinates work well for attaching new objects to a cylindrical shape. An example of this is specifying coordinates for a pipe that must be attached to another pipe, tank, or vessel. In **Figure 2-5,** a pipe must be attached to a 12′ diameter tank at a 30° angle from horizontal and 2′-6″ above the floor. In order to properly draw the pipe as a cylinder, you will have to change the UCS, which you will learn how to do later in this chapter. An attachment point for the pipe can be drawn using the **POINT** command and cylindrical coordinates.

**Figure 2-4.**
Cylindrical coordinates require a horizontal distance from the origin, an angle in the XY plane, and a Z dimension.

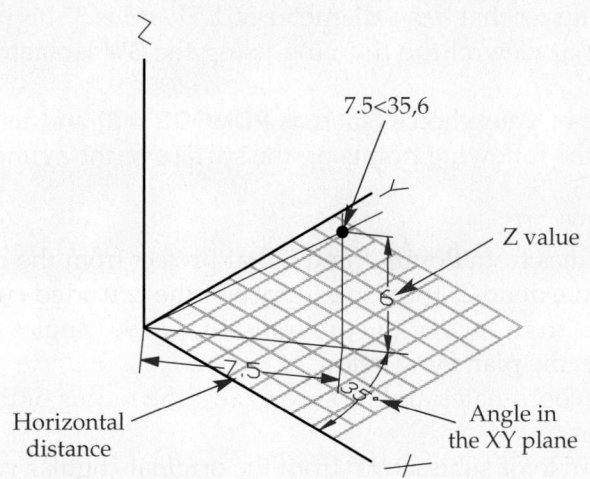

**Figure 2-5.**
A—A plan view of a tank shows the angle of the pipe attachment. B—A 3D view from the southeast quadrant shows the pipe attachment point located with cylindrical coordinates. Notice that the box representing the pipe needs to be rotated 30° for proper orientation. C—By creating a new UCS, the pipe can be drawn as a cylinder and correctly located without editing.

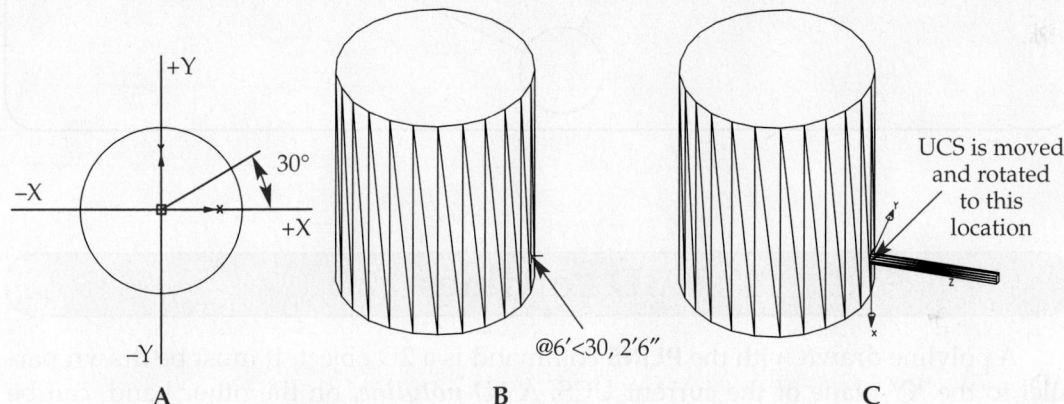

```
Command: PDMODE↵
Enter new value for PDMODE <current>: 3↵
Command: POINT↵
Current point modes: PDMODE=3 PDSIZE=0.0000
Specify a point: FROM↵
Base point: CEN↵
of (pick the base of the cylinder)
<Offset>: @6'<30,2'6"↵ (The radius of the tank is 6'.)
Command:
```

The point can now be used as the center of the pipe (cylinder), **Figure 2-5B.** However, if you draw the pipe now, it will be parallel to the tank (large cylinder). By changing the UCS, as shown in **Figure 2-5C**, the pipe can be drawn correctly. Working with the UCS is introduced later in this chapter.

○ Start a new drawing.

○ Draw a solid cylinder that has a diameter of 1.5″ and is 3″ high.

○ Display a pictorial view of the drawing using the **SW Isometric View** button on the **View** toolbar.

○ Set a point style of your choice (such as **PDMODE** = 3) and use the **POINT** command to locate the following points on the surface of the cylinder.
  ○ Point 1 = <25,.75
  ○ Point 2 = <295,.75

○ Draw separate lines from Points 1 and 2 that project from the center of the circle cross section and extend 2″ from the surface of the extruded circle.

○ Project new lines from each of the previous lines at 90° angles so that they intersect, as shown in the plan view below.
  ○ Use relative coordinates and be sure to add the radius of the cylinder to the 2″ dimension.
  ○ Either add 90° to or subtract 90° from the original angular value to determine the angle at which to draw the new lines.

○ Save the drawing as EX2-1.

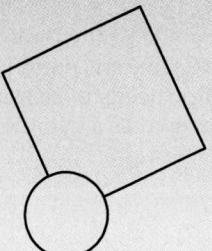

# 3D Polylines

A polyline drawn with the **PLINE** command is a 2D object. It must be drawn parallel to the XY plane of the current UCS. A *3D polyline,* on the other hand, can be drawn in 3D space. The Z coordinate value can vary from point to point in the polyline. A 3D polyline is the same type of object as a regular polyline.

The **3DPOLY** command is used to draw 3D polylines. To access this command, pick **3D Polyline** from the **Draw** pull-down menu or enter 3P or 3DPOLY at the Command: prompt. Any form of coordinate entry is valid for drawing 3D polylines.

**3DPOLY**
**3P**

Draw
↳ 3D Polyline

> Command: **3P** *or* **3DPOLY**↵
> Specify start point of polyline: **4,3,6**↵
> Specify endpoint of line or [Undo]: **@2,0,1**↵
> Specify endpoint of line or [Undo]: **@0,2,1**↵
> Specify endpoint of line or [Close/Undo]: ↵
> Command:

The **Close** option can be used to draw the final segment and create a closed shape. There must be at least two segments in the polyline to use the **Close** option. The **Undo** option removes the last segment without canceling the command.

The **PEDIT** command can be used to edit 3D polylines. The **PEDIT Spline** option is used to turn the 3D polyline into a B-spline curve based on the vertices of the polyline. A regular 3D polyline and the same polyline turned into a B-spline curve are shown in **Figure 2-6.** The **SPLFRAME** system variable controls the display of the original polyline frame and is either turned on (1) or off (0).

Figure 2-6.
A regular 3D
polyline and the
B-spline curve
version after using
the **PEDIT**
command.

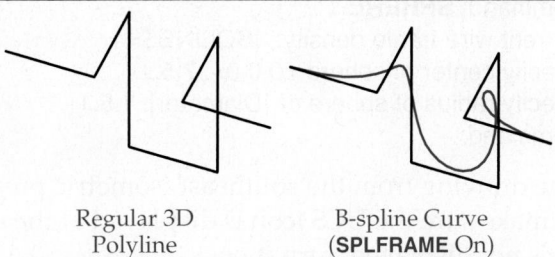

Regular 3D
Polyline

B-spline Curve
(**SPLFRAME** On)

A

B

PROFESSIONAL
TIP

A **3D Polyline** toolbar button can be placed in a custom tool-bar or added to an existing toolbar. Refer to Chapter 19 for information on customizing toolbars.

### Exercise 2-2

○ Start a new drawing.
○ Enter the **3DPOLY** command and draw a polyline using these coordinates:
  ○ 0,5,0
  ○ 5,5,0
  ○ 5,2.5,3
  ○ 5,0,0
  ○ 10,0,0
  ○ 10,2.5,3
  ○ 10,5,0
  ○ 15,5,0
○ Use the southwest isometric preset to display a pictorial view of the drawing. Your drawing should look similar to **Figure 2-6A**.
○ Set the **SPLFRAME** system variable to 1.
○ Use the **PEDIT** command to turn the 3D polyline into a B-spline curve.
○ Your drawing should look similar to **Figure 2-6B**.
○ Save your drawing as **EX2-2**.

## Introduction to Working with the UCS

Earlier in this chapter you used spherical coordinates to locate a small sphere on the surface of a larger sphere. You also drew a cone with the center of its base on the surface of the large sphere. However, the axis of the cone, which is a line from the center of the base to the tip of the cone, is not pointing to the center of the sphere, **Figure 2-3**. This is because the Z axes of the large sphere and cone coincide with the world coordinate system (WCS) Z axis. The WCS is the default coordinate system of AutoCAD.

In order for the axis of the cone to project from the sphere's center point, the UCS must be changed using the **UCS** command. Working with different UCSs is discussed in detail in Chapter 3. However, the following is a quick overview and describes how to draw a cone with its axis projecting from the center of the sphere. First, draw the large sphere:

```
Command: SPHERE↵
Current wire frame density:  ISOLINES=4
Specify center of sphere <0,0,0>: 7,5↵
Specify radius of sphere or [Diameter]: 1.5↵
Command:
```

Display the drawing from the southeast isometric preset. To help see how the UCS is changing, make sure the UCS icon is displayed at the origin of the current UCS. Also, if the icon is not displayed, turn it on.

```
Command: UCSICON↵
Enter an option [ON/OFF/All/Noorigin/ORigin/Properties] <ON>: OR↵
Command: USCICON↵
Enter an option [ON/OFF/All/Noorigin/ORigin/Properties] <ON>: ON↵
Command:
```

Now, the sphere is drawn and the UCS icon is displayed at the origin of the current UCS. However, the WCS is still the current user coordinate system. You are ready to start changing the UCS to meet your needs. Begin by moving the UCS origin to the center of the sphere.

```
Command: UCS↵
Current ucs name: *WORLD*
Enter an option [New/Move/orthoGraphic/Prev/Restore/Save/Del/Apply/?/World]
    <World>: M↵
Specify new origin point or [Zdepth]: <0,0,0>: CEN↵
of (pick the sphere)
Command:
```

Notice that the UCS icon is now displayed at the center of the sphere, **Figure 2-7**. Study **Figure 2-8** and continue as follows. Keep in mind that the point you are locating—the center of the cone on the sphere's surface—is 30° from the X axis and 30° from the XY plane.

```
Command: UCS↵
Current ucs name: *NO NAME*
Enter an option [New/Move/orthoGraphic/Prev/Restore/Save/Del/Apply/?/World]
    <World>: N↵
Specify origin of new UCS or [ZAxis/3point/OBject/Face/View/X/Y/Z] <0,0,0>: Z↵
Specify rotation angle about Z axis <90>: 30↵ (See Figure 2-8B.)
Command: (press [Enter] or the spacebar to reissue the UCS command)
Current ucs name: *NO NAME*
Enter an option [New/Move/orthoGraphic/Prev/Restore/Save/Del/Apply/?/World]
    <World>: N↵
Specify origin of new UCS or [ZAxis/3point/OBject/Face/View/X/Y/Z] <0,0,0>: Y↵
```

**Figure 2-7.**
The UCS origin is
moved to the center
of the sphere.

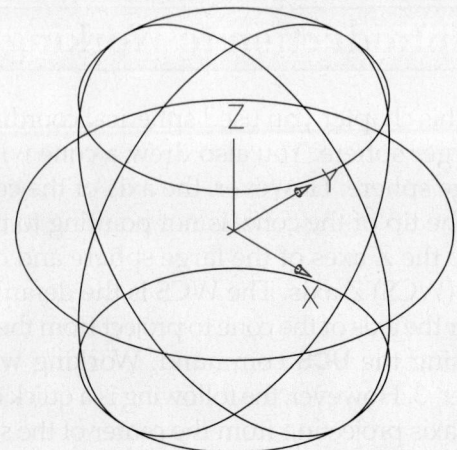

**Figure 2-8.**
A—The world coordinate system. B—The new UCS is rotated 30° in the XY plane about the Z axis. C—A line rotated up 30° from the XY plane represents the axis of the cone. D—The UCS is rotated 60° about the Y axis. The centerline of the cone coincides with the Z axis of this UCS.

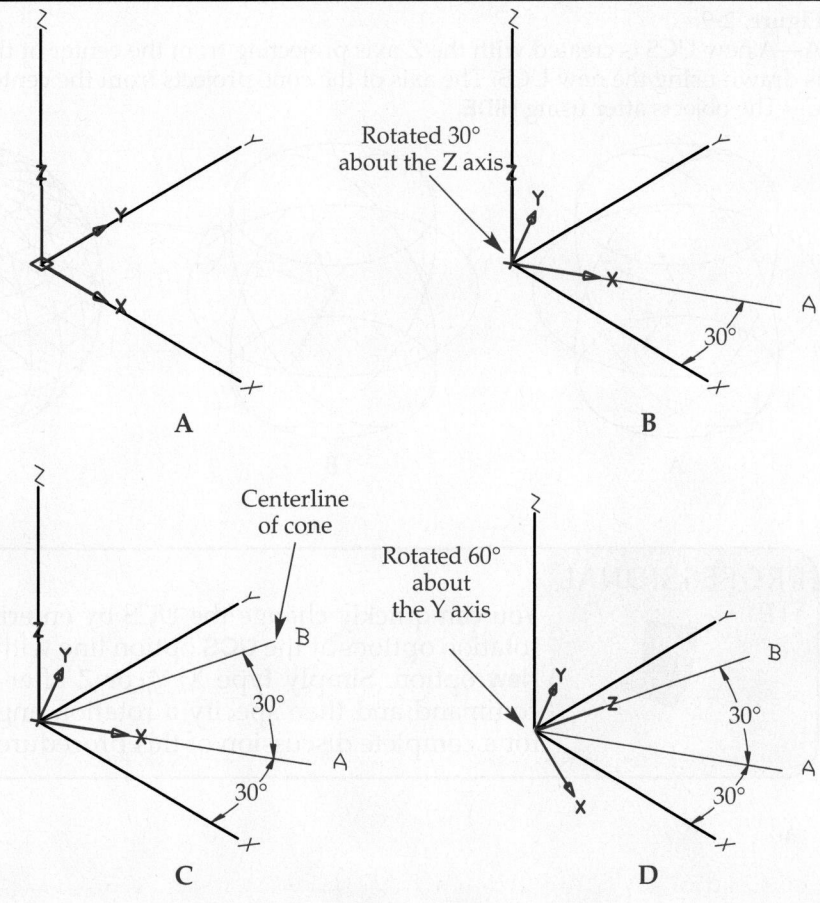

Specify rotation angle about Y axis <90>: **60**↵ *(See Figure 2-8D.)*
Command:

This new UCS can be used to construct a cone with its axis projecting from the center of the sphere. **Figure 2-9A** shows the new UCS located at the center of the sphere. With the UCS rotated, rectangular coordinates can be used to draw the cone:

Command: **CONE**↵
Specify center point for base of cone or [Elliptical] <0,0,0>: **0,0,1.5**↵ *(The radius of the sphere is 1.5 units.)*
Specify radius for base of cone or [Diameter]: **.25**↵
Specify height of cone or [Apex]: **1**↵
Command:

The completed cone is shown in **Figure 2-9B.** You can see that the axis projects from the center of the sphere. **Figure 2-9C** shows the objects after using the **HIDE** command.

This same basic procedure can be used in the tank and pipe example presented earlier in this chapter. To correctly locate the pipe (cylinder), first rotate the UCS 30° about the Z axis. Then, rotate the UCS 90° about the Y axis. The Z axis of this new UCS aligns with the long axis of the pipe. Finally, use rectangular coordinates to draw the cylinder with its center at the point drawn in **Figure 2-5B.**

Once you have changed to a new UCS, you can quickly return to the WCS. The WCS provides a common "starting place" to create new UCSs.

Command: **UCS**↵
Current ucs name: *NO NAME*
Enter an option [New/Move/orthoGraphic/Prev/Restore/Save/Del/Apply/?/World]
    <World>: **W**↵
Command:

**Figure 2-9.**
A—A new UCS is created with the Z axis projecting from the center of the sphere. B—A cone is drawn using the new UCS. The axis of the cone projects from the center of the sphere. C—The objects after using **HIDE**.

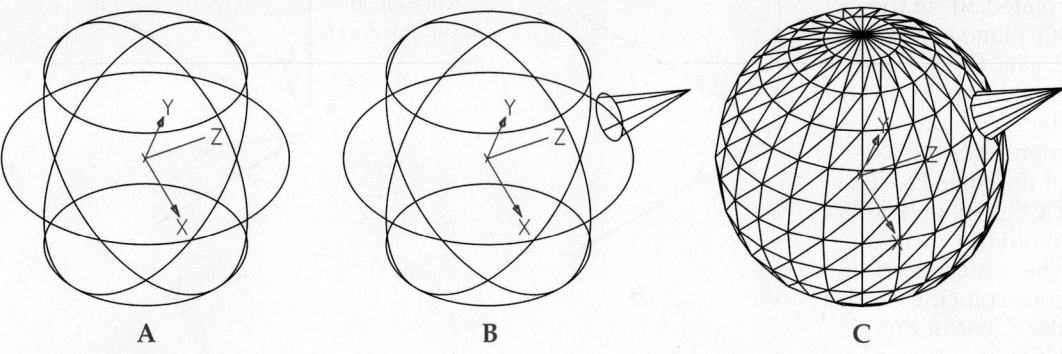

A                                    B                                    C

**PROFESSIONAL TIP**

You can quickly change the UCS by entering one of the axis rotation options at the **UCS** option line without first using the **New** option. Simply type X, Y, or Z after entering the **UCS** command and then specify a rotation angle. See Chapter 3 for a complete discussion of this procedure.

## Exercise 2-3

○ Start a new drawing for this exercise.
○ Change the **PDMODE** system variable setting to 3. Set the color to blue and draw a point at the coordinates 6,4.
○ Set the color to white and draw a Ø4″ sphere centered on the point. Use the **Node** object snap.
○ Display the drawing from the southeast isometric preset.
○ Set the color to red and draw two Ø.75″ spheres. Center both on the surface of the Ø4″ sphere.
   ○ For the first sphere, use angular coordinates of 15° *in* the XY plane and 50° *from* the XY plane.
   ○ For the second sphere, use angular coordinates of –15° *in* the XY plane and 50° *from* the XY plane.
○ Set the color to green and draw a cone with a .5″ diameter base. Center the cone on the surface of the Ø4″ sphere using angular coordinates of 0° *in* the XY plane and 30° *from* the XY plane. Specify a height of one unit for the cone.
○ Create a new UCS and construct another cone of the same dimensions with its centerline projecting from the center of the sphere. The center of the base should be at the same location as the previous cone.
○ Use the **HIDE** command.
○ Save the drawing as EX2-3.

# Constructing Accurate Intersections

When an object is located on a curved surface, there may be a small gap between the curved surface and the object. See **Figure 2-10A**. For example, there is a gap between the cone and sphere drawn in the previous section, as indicated by the visible line on the cone's base in **Figure 2-9C**. When rendered, this gap may produce an unwanted shadow. In order for the model to display properly when rendered or animated, you need to adjust for this gap.

First, lay out an orthographic view of the radius of the sphere. You may want to do this on a construction layer or in a new drawing. Then, draw a radial centerline for the intersecting cone. Draw a line tangent to the curve with a length equal to the diameter of the cone's base. This line should be centered on the point of tangency. Refer to **Figure 2-10B**. Project a new line perpendicular from one end of the tangent line through the curve. Then, move the baseline of the cone to the intersection of the projection line and the curve. This is the new base location. See **Figure 2-10B**. Next, measure the distance from the center of the sphere perpendicular to the new base location. See **Figure 2-10C**. Use this distance when relocating the cone. See **Figure 2-10D**.

The original and relocated cones are shown in **Figure 2-11** after using the **HIDE** and **SHADEMODE** commands. Notice in **Figure 2-11A** and **Figure 2-11B** that the base edge of the original cone can be seen as a line. This is because the cone is sitting above the surface of the sphere. In **Figure 2-11C** and **Figure 2-11D**, the base edge of the relocated cone cannot be seen because it is *inside* the sphere. Therefore, after rendering, the objects appear correct.

You may have expected a line to define the intersection of the cone and the sphere in **Figure 2-11C** and **Figure 2-11D**. However, AutoCAD retains the definitions of two separate objects and does not automatically create a line at intersections. If you want a line to be placed at the intersection of two objects, it may be necessary to draw them as solids and then join them in a Boolean operation. Solid model construction and editing is covered in Chapter 6 through Chapter 10.

---

**Figure 2-10.**
A—A small gap is created when the base of the cone is located tangent to the sphere's curved surface. B—The base of the cone is moved so that its edge meets the intersection of the projection line and the surface of the sphere. C—The distance from the center of the sphere to the base of the cone is determined. D—The new cone intersects the surface of the sphere with no gap.

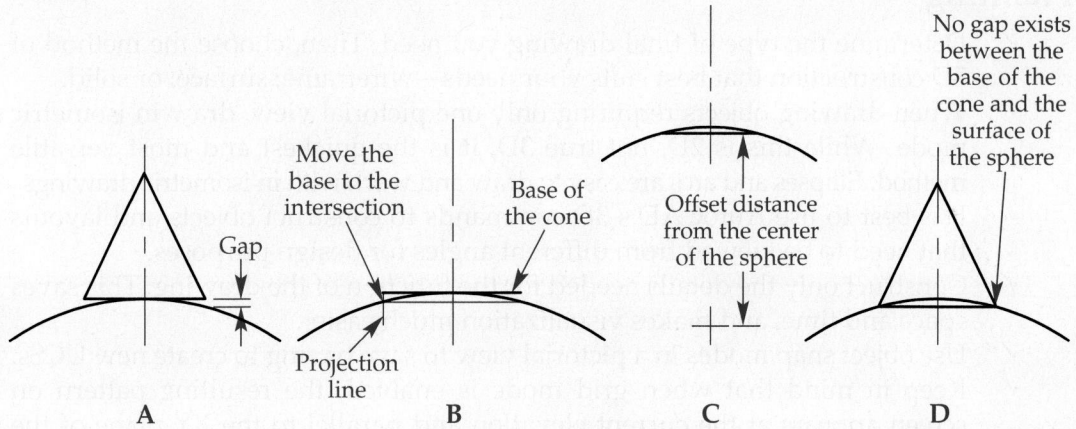

**Figure 2-11.**
A—A cone with the center of its base located on the surface of the sphere. B—When rendered, the edge of the base is visible. C—A cone with the edge of its base intersecting the surface of the sphere. D—When rendered, the edge of the base is not visible.

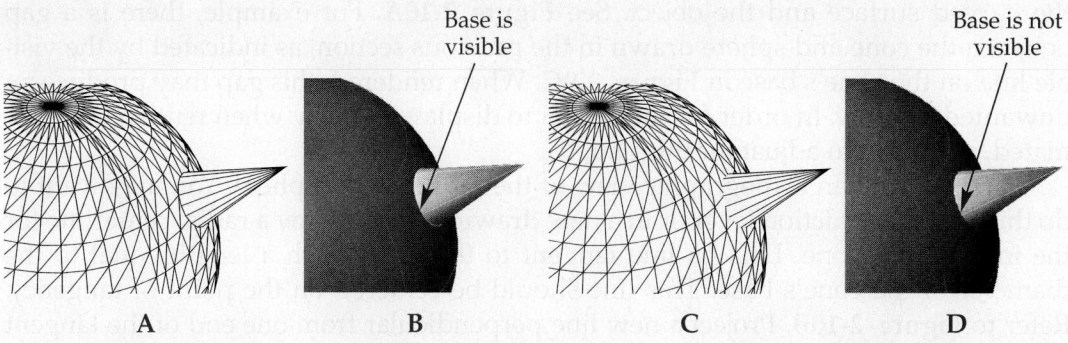

Base is visible

Base is not visible

A            B            C            D

**PROFESSIONAL TIP**

This procedure actually decreases the distance that the cone extends above the surface of the sphere. For rendering, this is OK. However, for engineering analysis and prototyping, this small discrepancy may not be acceptable. The gap may need to be filled with a cylinder, similar to creating a boss. Or, a cone with a larger base and greater height may need to be drawn to correct for the portion of the cone that is inside the sphere.

## Guidelines for Working with 3D Drawings

Working in 3D, like working with 2D drawings, requires careful planning to efficiently produce the desired results. The following guidelines can be used when working in 3D.

### Planning

✓ Determine the type of final drawing you need. Then, choose the method of 3D construction that best suits your needs—wireframe, surface, or solid.

✓ When drawing objects requiring only one pictorial view, draw in isometric mode. While this is 2D, not true 3D, it is the quickest and most versatile method. Ellipses and arcs are easy to draw and work with in isometric drawings.

✓ It is best to use AutoCAD's 3D commands to construct objects and layouts that need to be viewed from different angles for design purposes.

✓ Construct only the details needed for the function of the drawing. This saves space and time, and makes visualization much easier.

✓ Use object snap modes in a pictorial view to save having to create new UCSs.

✓ Keep in mind that when grid mode is enabled, the resulting pattern on screen appears at the current elevation and parallel to the XY plane of the current UCS.

✓ Create layers having different colors for different drawing objects. Turn them on and off as needed or freeze those not being used.

## Editing

✓ Use the **Properties** window to change the color, layer, or linetype of 3D objects.

✓ Use grips or the **STRETCH** or **LENGTHEN** commands in a 3D view to change only one dimension of a surface-modeled or wireframe object (see Chapter 13). Use the **SCALE** command in the 3D view to change the size of the entire object proportionally.

✓ **STRETCH, LENGTHEN**, and grips cannot be used to edit a solid-modeled object (see Chapter 9).

✓ Do as much editing as possible from a 3D viewpoint. It is quicker and the results are seen immediately.

## Displaying

✓ Use the **HIDE** and **SHADEMODE** commands to help in visualizing complex drawings.

✓ To change views quickly, use the preset isometric views, **3DORBIT**, and **PLAN**.

✓ Use the **VIEW** command to create and save 3D views for quicker pictorial displays. This avoids having to repeatedly use the **3DORBIT** command.

✓ Freeze unwanted layers before displaying objects in 3D, and especially before using **HIDE**. AutoCAD regenerates layers that are turned off, which may cause an inaccurate hidden display to be created. Frozen layers are not regenerated.

✓ Before using **HIDE**, zoom in on the part of a drawing to display. This saves time in regenerating the view because only the objects that are visible are regenerated.

✓ You may have to slightly move objects that touch or intersect if the display removes a line you need to see or plot.

## Chapter Test

*Answer the following questions on a separate sheet of paper.*

1. Explain *spherical coordinate entry.*
2. Explain *cylindrical coordinate entry.*
3. A new point is to be drawn 4.5″ from the last point. It is to be located at a 63° angle *in* the XY plane, and at a 35° angle *from* the XY plane. Write the proper spherical coordinate notation.
4. Write the proper cylindrical coordinate notation for locating a point 4.5″ in the horizontal direction from the origin, 3.6″ along the Z axis, and at a 63° angle in the XY plane.
5. Name the command that is used to draw 3D polylines.
6. Why is the command in Question 5 needed?
7. Which command is used to change a 3D polyline into a B-spline curve?
8. How does the **SPLFRAME** system variable affect the B-spline curve created with the command in Question 7?
9. What effect does the **ORigin** option of the **UCSICON** command have on the UCS icon display?
10. Which command is used to create a new UCS?
11. Which option of the command in Question 10 is used to place the origin of the UCS in a new location?
12. Describe how to rotate the UCS so that the Z axis is tilted 30° toward the WCS X axis.
13. How do you return to the WCS from any UCS?

# Drawing Problems

For Problems 1–4, draw each object as a wireframe. Measure the objects directly to obtain the necessary dimensions. Plot the drawings at a 3:1 scale with hidden lines removed. Save the drawings as **P2-**(problem number).

1.

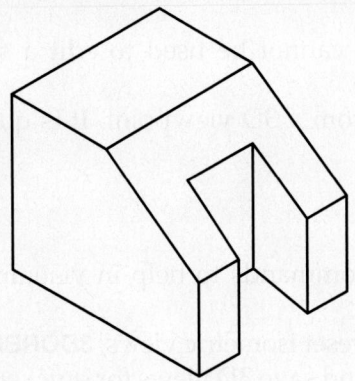

2.

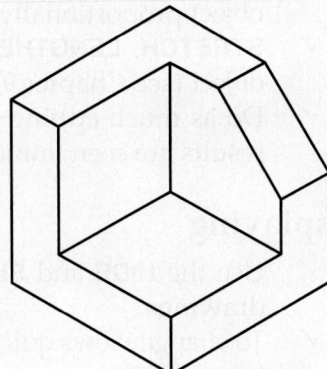

3.

4.

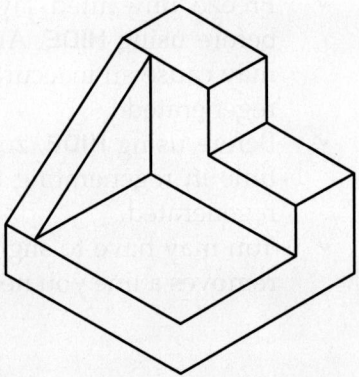

For Problems 5–7, draw each object using the dimensions given. Use solid primitives to create the models. Change UCSs and use editing commands as needed. Do not dimension the objects. Display the objects with hidden lines removed. Save the drawings as **P2-**(problem number).

5.

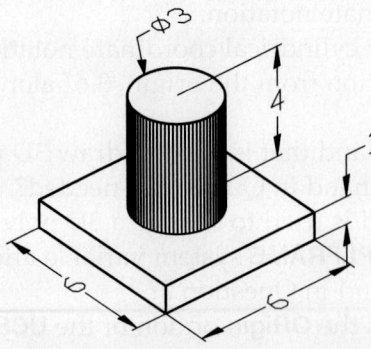

**Pedestal #1**

6.

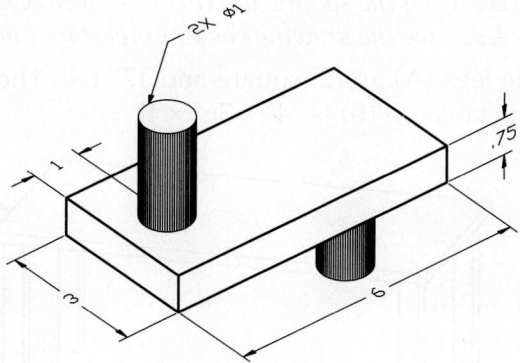

**Pivot Bracket**

7.

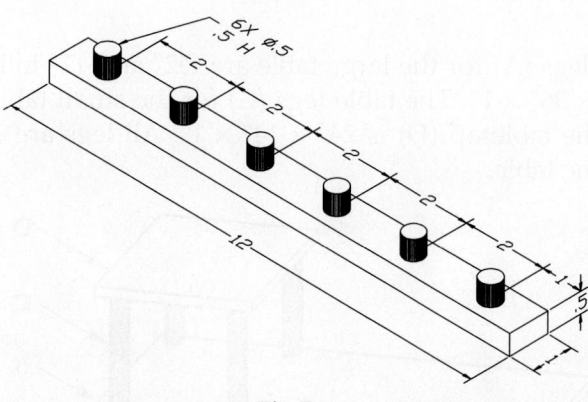

**Pin Bar**

8. Draw the Ø8" pedestal shown .5" thick. Four Ø.75" feet are centered on a 7" diameter circle and are .5" high. Save the drawing as P2-10.

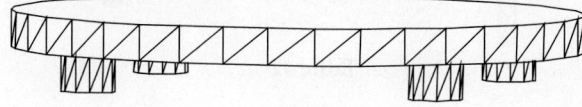

**Pedestal #2**

9. Four legs (cones), each 3" high with a Ø1" base, support this Ø10" globe. Each leg tilts at an angle of 15° from vertical. The base is Ø12" and .5" thick. The bottom surface of the base is 8" below the center of the globe. Save the drawing as P2-11.

**Globe**

*For Problems 10–15, construct 3D models of each of the objects shown. Use only solid primitives. Construct each object using the specific instructions given. Change UCSs and use editing commands as needed. Save the drawings as* P2-*(problem number).*

10. The table legs (A) are 2″ square and 17″ tall. They are 2″ in from each edge. The tabletop (B) is 24″ × 36″ × 1″.

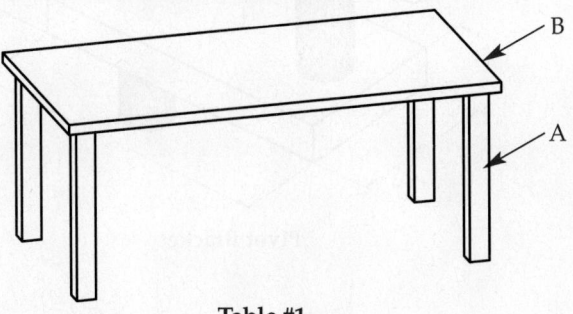

**Table #1**

11. The table legs (A) for the large table are ∅2″ and 17″ tall. The tabletop (B) is 24″ × 36″ × 1″. The table legs (C) for the small table are ∅2″ and 11″ tall. The tabletop (D) is 24″ × 14″ × 1″. All legs are 1″ in from the edges of the table.

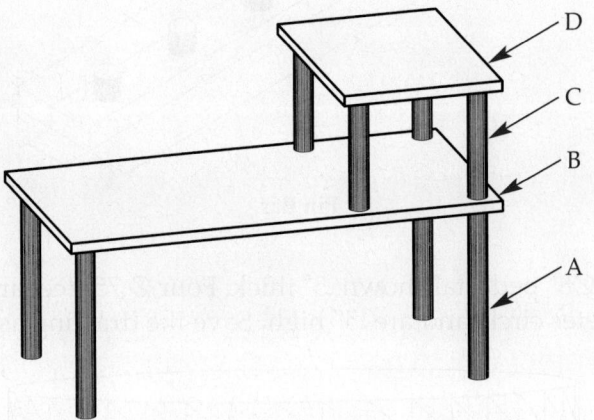

**Table #2**

12. The spherical objects (A) are ∅4″. Object B is 6″ long and ∅1.5″.

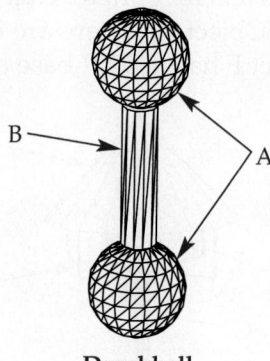

**Dumbbell**

13. Object A is a ∅8″ cylinder that is 1″ tall. Object B is a ∅5″ cylinder that is 7″ tall. Object C is a ∅2″ cylinder that is 6″ tall. Object D is a .5″ × 8″ × .125″ box, and there are four pieces. The top surface of each piece is flush with the top surface of Object C. Object E is a ∅18″ cone that is 12″ tall.

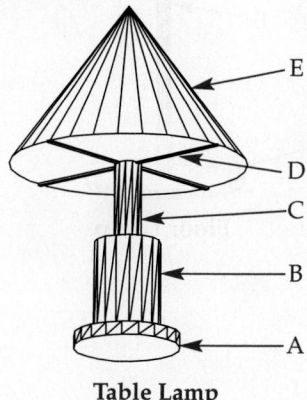

**Table Lamp**

14. Objects A and B are brick walls that are 5′ high. The walls are two courses of brick thick. Research the dimensions of standard brick and draw accordingly. Wall B is 7′ long and Wall A is 5′ long. Lamps are placed at each end of the walls. Object C is ∅2″ and 8″ tall. The center is offset from the end of the wall by a distance equal to the width of one brick. Object D is ∅10″.

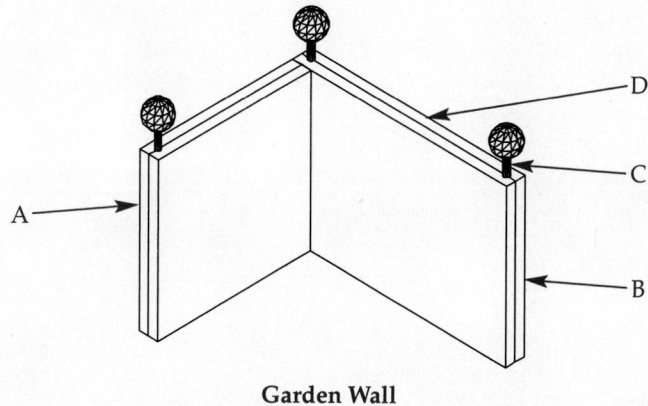

**Garden Wall**

15. Object A is ∅18″ and 1″ tall. Object B is ∅1.5″ and 6′ tall. Object C is ∅6″ and .5″ tall. Object D is a ∅10″ sphere. Object E is an L-shaped bracket to support the shade (Object F). There are eight items. Draw these an appropriate size. Object F has a ∅22″ base and is 12″ tall.

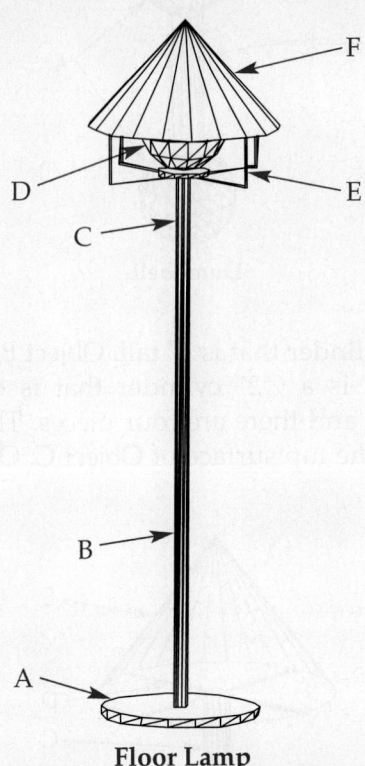

**Floor Lamp**

AutoCAD and its Applications—Advanced

# Understanding User Coordinate Systems

## Learning Objectives

After completing this chapter, you will be able to:

- Describe the function of the world and user coordinate systems.
- Move the user coordinate system to any surface.
- Rotate the user coordinate system to any angle.
- Change the user coordinate system to match the plane of a geometric object.
- Save and manage named user coordinate systems.
- Restore and use named user coordinate systems.
- Control user coordinate system icon visibility in viewports.
- Create text with a thickness.
- Draw text that is plan to the current view.
- Dimension a 3D drawing.

Part of the flexibility of 3D construction with AutoCAD is the ability to create and use different 3D coordinate systems. All drawing and editing commands can be used in any coordinate system you create. Objects that are drawn will always be parallel to the plane, or coordinate system, you are working in. This chapter provides you with detailed instructions for constructing and working with user coordinate systems. This will allow you to draw any type of 3D shape that you need.

## Introduction to User Coordinate Systems

All points in a drawing or on an object are defined with XYZ coordinate values (rectangular coordinates) measured from the 0,0,0 origin. Since this system of coordinates is fixed and universal, AutoCAD refers to it as the *world coordinate system (WCS).* A *user coordinate system (UCS),* on the other hand, can be defined with its origin at any location and with its three axes in any orientation desired, while remaining at 90° to each other. The **UCS** command is used to change the origin, position, and rotation of the coordinate system to match the surfaces and features of an object under construction. When set up to do so, the UCS icon reflects the changes in the orientation of the UCS and placement of the origin.

The available options for creating and managing a UCS, as well as controlling the display of the UCS icon, are found in the **Tools** pull-down menu and related cascading menus, **Figure 3-1A.** In addition, UCS options can be selected in the **UCS** and **UCS II** toolbars or by entering the **UCS** command at the Command: prompt. See **Figure 3-1B.** Notice in the **UCS** toolbar that the button for the WCS is labeled **World UCS.**

Four UCS selections in the **Tools** pull-down menu provide access to all UCS options. Each of these selections is introduced here and discussed in detail later in this chapter.

- **Named UCS.** This item displays the **UCS** dialog box. The three tabs in the dialog box contain a variety of UCS and UCS icon options and settings. These options and settings are described as you progress through this chapter.
- **Orthographic UCS.** This menu item displays a cascading menu with a list of the six preset UCSs. The **Preset...** option in the cascading menu displays the **Orthographic UCSs** tab in the **UCS** dialog box.

**Figure 3-1.**
UCS options can be accessed in several ways. A—The UCS selections in the **Tools** pull-down menu. B—The **UCS** and **UCS II** toolbars.

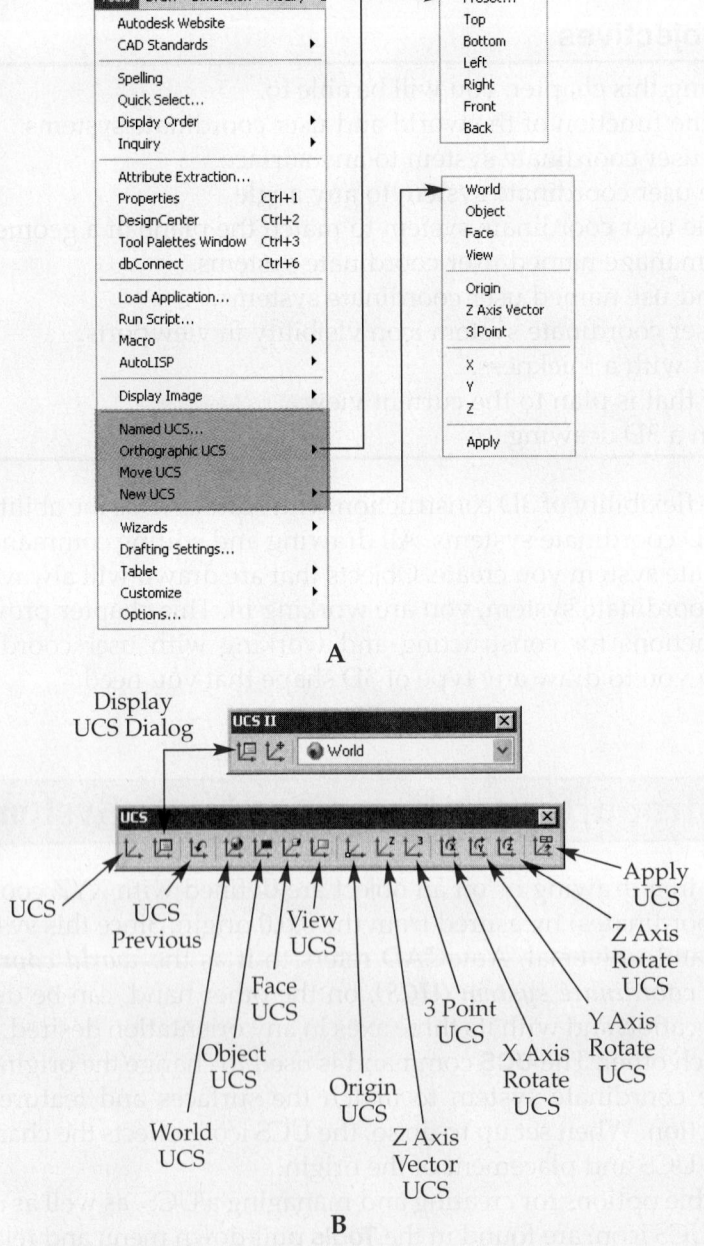

A

B

- **Move UCS.** Selecting this menu item allows you to specify a new UCS origin point or adjust the Z depth of the UCS.
- **New UCS.** This menu item displays a cascading menu containing many UCS command options.

## Working with User Coordinate Systems

Once you understand a few of the basic options of user coordinate systems, creating 3D models becomes an easy and quick process. The following sections show how to display the UCS icon, change the UCS in order to work on different surfaces of a model, and name and save a UCS.

### Displaying the UCS Icon

The symbol that identifies the orientation of the coordinate system is called the *UCS icon.* It is located in the lower-left corner of the viewport when AutoCAD is first launched. The display of this symbol is controlled by the **UCSICON** command. If your drawing does not require viewports and altered coordinate systems, you may want to turn the icon off:

    Command: **UCSICON**⏎
    Enter an option [ON/OFF/All/Noorigin/ORigin/Properties] <*current*>: **OFF**⏎
    Command:

The icon disappears until you turn it on again using the **ON** option of the **UCSICON** command. You can also turn the icon on or off and set the icon to display at the origin using the options under **UCS Icon** in the **Display** cascading menu in the **View** pull-down menu or in the **Settings** tab of the **UCS** dialog box. Refer to **Figure 3-2.**

### Modifying the UCS Icon

The appearance of the UCS icon can be changed using the settings in the **UCS Icon** dialog box. See **Figure 3-3.** This dialog box is accessed by selecting **UCS Icon** and then **Properties...** from the **Display** cascading menu in the **View** pull-down menu or by using the **Properties** option of the **UCSICON** command. You can modify three characteristics of the UCS icon.
- **Style.** Select either a 2D or 3D icon in the **UCS icon style** area. You can also specify the line width as 1, 2, or 3 pixels. If the **3D** style is selected, the **Cone** option is available. The **2D** style is the same style of UCS icon used by earlier releases of AutoCAD.
- **Size.** The **UCS icon size** area contains a text box and a slider. The value in the text box is the size of the UCS icon expressed as a percentage of the viewport size. Enter a new value in the text box or adjust the slider.
- **Color.** Use the drop-down lists in the **UCS icon color** area to set the color of the UCS icon. Notice that different colors can be set for the **Model** tab and **Layout** tab.

### Changing the Coordinate System

To construct a three-dimensional object, you must draw shapes at many different angles. Different planes are needed to draw features on angled surfaces. To construct these features, it is easiest to rotate the UCS to match any surface on an object. The following example illustrates this process.

**Figure 3-2.**
A—The **Settings** tab allows you to adjust UCS and UCS icon settings. B—The UCS icon can be turned on and off and set to the origin in the **UCS Icon** cascading menu.

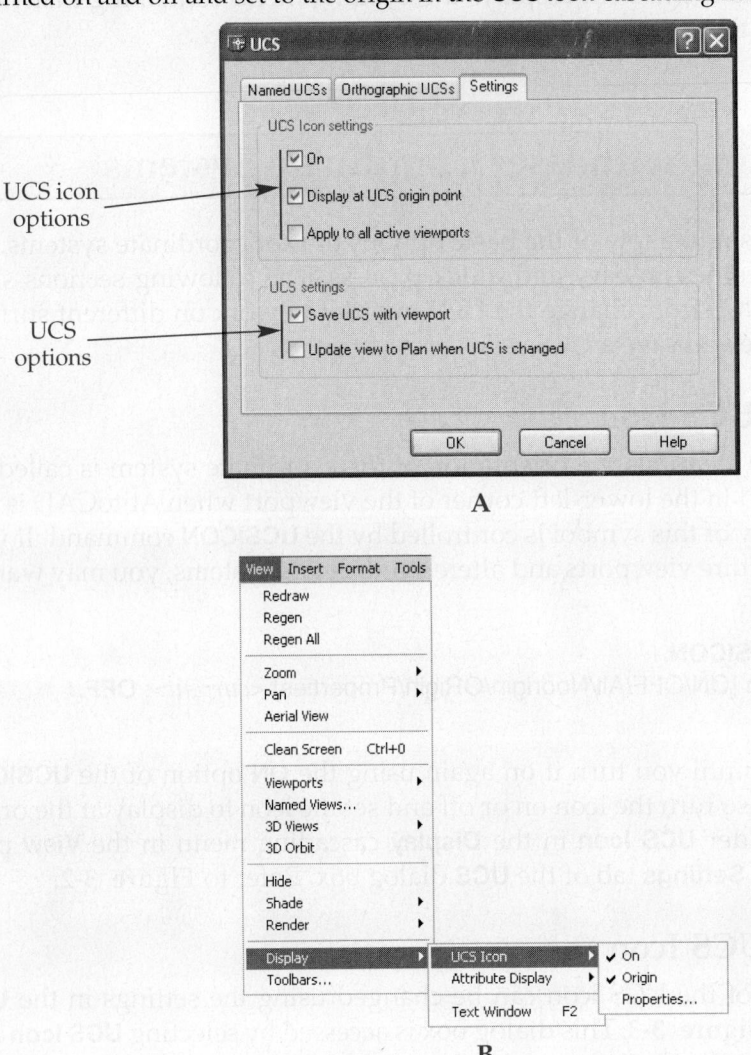

UCS icon
options

UCS
options

A

B

**Figure 3-3.**
The **UCS Icon** dialog box allows you to change the appearance of the UCS icon.

Set line
thickness

Preview
of settings

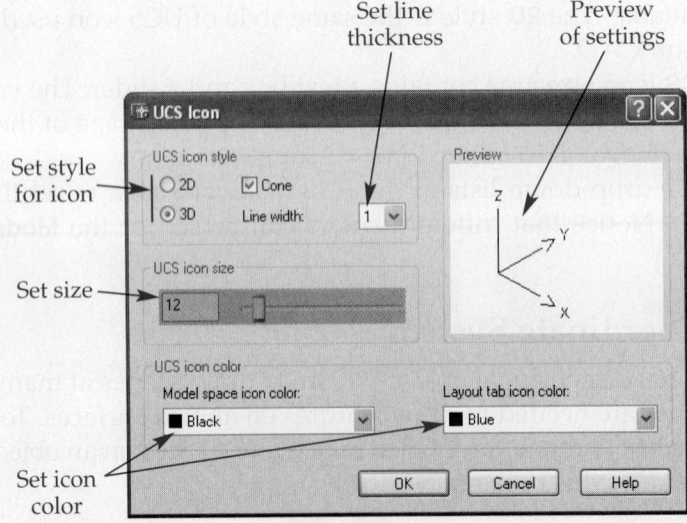

Set style
for icon

Set size

Set icon
color

**Figure 3-4.**
This object can be constructed by changing the orientation of the coordinate system. You will learn how to construct and dimension this object in this chapter.

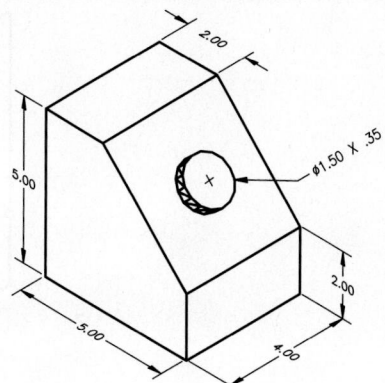

The object in **Figure 3-4** has a cylinder on the angled surface. A solid modeling command called **EXTRUDE**, which is discussed in Chapter 7, is used to create the base of the object. The cylinder is then drawn on the angled feature. Later in this chapter, you will learn how to dimension the object as shown in **Figure 3-4.**

The first step in creating this model is to draw the side view of the base as a wireframe. You could determine the X, Y, and Z coordinates of each point on the side view and enter the coordinates. However, a lot of typing can be saved if all points share a Z value of 0. By rotating the UCS, you can draw the side view entering only X and Y coordinates. Start a new drawing and display the southeast isometric view. Now, rotate the UCS so it is parallel to the side of the object. Also, turn the UCS icon on and display it at the origin.

```
Command: UCS↵
Current ucs name:  *WORLD*
Enter an option [New/Move/orthoGraphic/Prev/Restore/Save/Del/Apply/?/World]
    <World>: N↵
Specify origin of new UCS or [ZAxis/3point/OBject/Face/View/X/Y/Z] <0,0,0>: X↵
Specify rotation angle about X axis <0>: 90↵
Command: UCSICON↵
Enter an option [ON/OFF/All/Noorigin/ORigin/Properties] <ON>: ON↵
Command: UCSICON↵
Enter an option [ON/OFF/All/Noorigin/ORigin/Properties] <ON>: OR↵
Command:
```

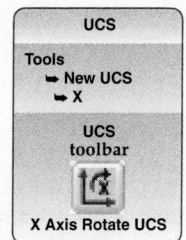

The current UCS is now parallel to the side of the object and the UCS icon is displayed at the origin of the UCS. You may want to pan the screen so the UCS icon is near the center. Then, use the **PLINE** command to draw the outline of the side view:

```
Command: PLINE↵
Specify start point: 5,2↵
Current line-width is 0.0000
Specify next point or [arc/Halfwidth/Length/Undo/Width]: 5,0↵
Specify next point or [arc/Halfwidth/Length/Undo/Width]: 0,0↵
Specify next point or [arc/Halfwidth/Length/Undo/Width]: 0,5↵
Specify next point or [arc/Halfwidth/Length/Undo/Width]: 2,5↵
Specify next point or [arc/Halfwidth/Length/Undo/Width]: C↵
Command:
```

A wireframe of one side of the object is created. See **Figure 3-5.** Notice the orientation of the UCS icon. The **PLINE** command was used instead of the **LINE** command because a closed polyline can be extruded into a solid.

**Figure 3-5.**
A wireframe of one side of the base is created. Notice the orientation of the UCS.

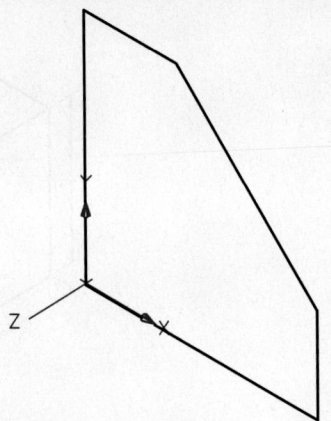

Now, the **EXTRUDE** command is used to create the base as a solid. This command is covered in detail in Chapter 7. On the same UCS used to create the wireframe side, enter the command:

```
Command: EXTRUDE↵
Current wire frame density: ISOLINES = 4
Select objects: (pick the polyline)
Select objects: ↵
Specify height of extrusion or [Path]: -4↵
Specify angle of taper for extrusion <0>: ↵
Command:
```

By entering a negative value for the height of the extrusion, the resulting object extends behind (negative Z) the XY plane of the current UCS. The base is created as a solid. See **Figure 3-6.**

**Figure 3-6.**
The wireframe is extruded to create the base as a solid.

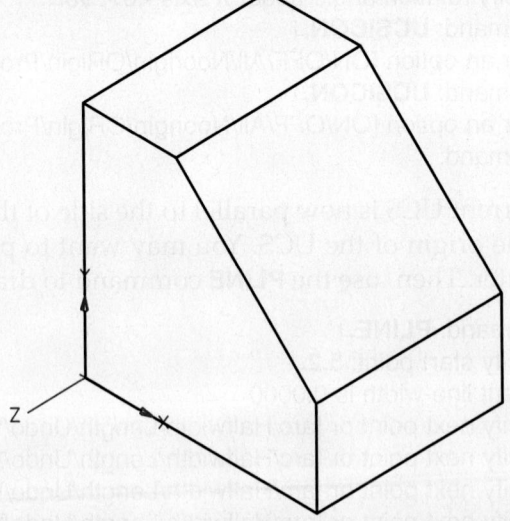

## Saving a Named UCS

Once you have created a new UCS that may be used again, it is best to save the UCS for future use. For example, you have created a UCS that you used to create the wireframe of one side of the object. You can save this UCS in the **UCS** dialog box.

First, pick **Named UCS...** from the **Tools** pull-down menu to display the **Named UCSs** tab of the **UCS** dialog box. Then, right-click on the entry **Unnamed** and pick **Rename** in the shortcut menu. See **Figure 3-7.** You can also pick once or double-click on the highlighted name. Then, type the new name in place of **Unnamed** and press [Enter]. A name can have up to 255 characters. Numbers, letters, spaces, dollar signs ($), hyphens (–), and underscores (_) are valid. Use this method to save a new UCS or to rename an existing one. A UCS can also be saved using the **Save** option of the **UCS** command:

Tools
➡ Named UCS...

Command: **UCS.**↵
Current ucs name: *current*
Enter an option [New/Move/orthoGraphic/Prev/Restore/Save/Del/Apply/?/World]
 <World>: **S.**↵
Enter name to save current UCS or [?]: *(enter a name for the UCS, such as* Side) ↵
Command:

Now, the coordinate system is saved and can be easily recalled for future use.

---

**Figure 3-7.**
Saving a new UCS. Select **Rename** to enter a name and save the **Unnamed** UCS.

Right-click on a UCS name to display the shortcut menu

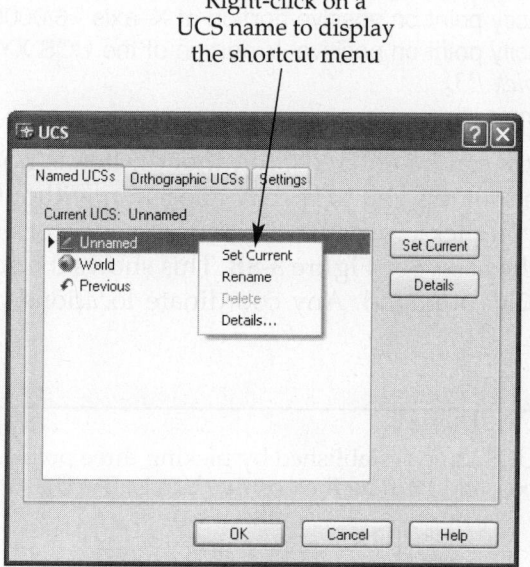

---

**PROFESSIONAL TIP**

Most drawings can be created by rotating the UCS as needed without saving it. If the drawing is complex with several planes, each containing a large amount of detail, you may wish to save a UCS for each detailed face. Then, restore the proper UCS as needed. For example, when working with architectural drawings, you may wish to establish a different UCS for each floor plan and elevation view, and for roofs and walls that require detail work.

---

# Aligning the UCS with an Angled Surface

With the base of the object drawn, the cylinder needs to be drawn on the angled surface. Notice in **Figure 3-4** that the axis of the cylinder is perpendicular to the angled surface. In 2D drafting, an angled surface is seen in its true shape and size only when projected to an auxiliary view. An auxiliary view places your line of sight perpendicular to the angled surface. This means that you see the angled surface as a plan view. A plan view is always perpendicular to your line of sight.

AutoCAD draws objects aligned with the plan view of the current UCS. Therefore, a new UCS needs to be created in which the XY plane is parallel to the angled surface. Once this is done, the cylinder can be correctly drawn.

The **3point** option of the **UCS** command can be used to change the UCS to any flat surface. This option requires that you locate a new origin, a point on the positive X axis, and a point on the positive Y axis. To use this option, pick the **3 Point UCS** button in the **UCS** toolbar; select **New UCS**, then **3 Point** from the **Tools** pull-down menu; or use the **3point** option of the **UCS** command. Refer to **Figure 3-8A** for pick points as you use the following command sequence. Use the **Endpoint** or **Intersection** object snap to select points that are not on the current XY plane.

```
Command: UCS↵
Current ucs name: current
Enter an option [New/Move/orthoGraphic/Prev/Restore/Save/Del/Apply/?/World]
   <World>: 3↵
Specify new origin point: <0,0,0>: (pick P1)
Specify point on positive portion of X–axis <6.0000,2.0000,0.0000>: (pick P2)
Specify point on positive–Y portion of the UCS XY plane <5.0000,3.0000,0.0000>:
   (pick P3)
Command:
```

Notice that 3 can be entered even though this is not listed as an option at the first prompt. This allows you to specify a location without having to first specify **New**.

After you pick P3, the UCS icon changes its orientation to align with the angled surface of the base. See **Figure 3-8B**. This shows the advantage of the **ORigin** option of the **UCSICON** command. Any coordinate locations you enter will be relative to the new origin.

**Figure 3-8.**
A—A new UCS can be established by picking three points. P1 is the origin, P2 is on the positive X axis, and P3 is on the positive Y axis. B—The new UCS is created.

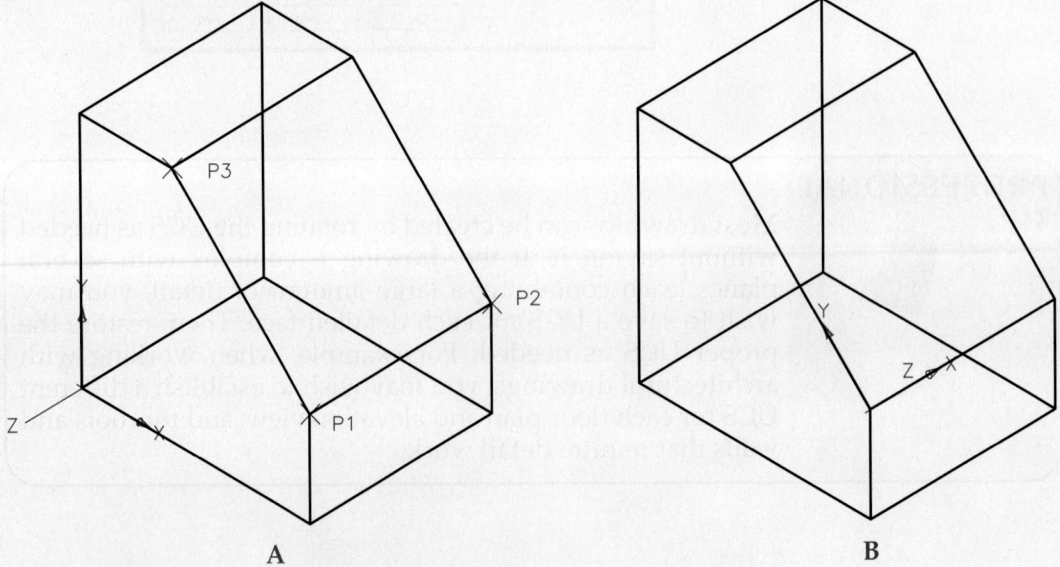

A                                                    B

The cylinder can be drawn in the isometric (3D) view or plan to the current UCS. For this example, the current 3D view is used. In this example, AutoCAD's AutoTracking feature is used to locate the center of the face. First, set **Midpoint** as a running object snap and turn object snap and object snap tracking on.

> Command: **CYLINDER**↵
> Specify center point for circle or [3P/2P/Ttr (tan tan radius)]: *(acquire the midpoint of one side of the angled face)*
> *(acquire the midpoint of a side of the angled face perpendicular to the first side and pick to place the center)*
> Specify radius for base of cylinder or [Diameter] <*current*>: **.75**↵
> Specify height of cylinder or [Center of other end]: **.35**↵
> Command: ↵

The cylinder appears in the correct orientation on the angled surface, **Figure 3-9.**

**Figure 3-9.**
The cylinder is properly drawn on the angled surface.

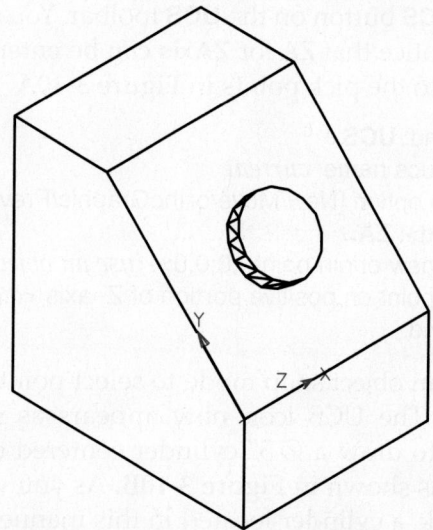

### Exercise 3-1

O Construct the 3D object shown below as a wireframe using the techniques discussed in this section. Do not include dimensions. Rotate and save the UCS as needed.
O Save the drawing as EX3-1.

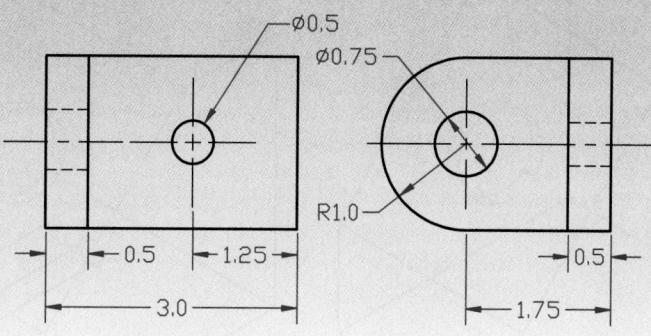

## Additional Ways to Change the UCS

There are other ways to change the UCS. These options include selecting a new Z axis, picking a new origin for the UCS, rotating the Y and Z axes, and setting the UCS to an existing object. The next sections cover these options.

### Selecting a New Z Axis

The **ZAxis** option of the **UCS** command allows you to select the origin point and a point on the positive Z axis. Once the new Z axis is defined, AutoCAD sets the new X and Y axes. You will now add a cylinder to the lower face of the base created earlier. The cylinder extends into the base. Refer to the location of the Z axis in **Figure 3-9.** This Z axis does not project perpendicular to the lower face. Therefore, a new UCS with a positive Z axis pointing into the object must be created.

Pick **New UCS** and then **Z Axis Vector** from the **Tools** pull-down menu or pick the **Z Axis Vector UCS** button on the **UCS** toolbar. You can also enter the **UCS** command as shown next. Notice that ZA for **ZAxis** can be entered directly without first entering N for **New**. Refer to the pick points in **Figure 3-10A.**

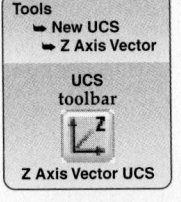

Tools
↳ New UCS
  ↳ Z Axis Vector
UCS
toolbar
Z Axis Vector UCS

> Command: **UCS**↵
> Current ucs name: *current*
> Enter an option [New/Move/orthoGraphic/Prev/Restore/Save/Del/Apply/?/World]
>    <World>: **ZA**↵
> Specify new origin point <0,0,0>: *(use an object snap to pick P1)*
> Specify point on positive portion of Z–axis <current>: *(use an object snap to pick P2)*
> Command:

You must use an object snap mode to select points P1 and P2 because they are not in the XY plane. The UCS icon now appears as shown in **Figure 3-10B.** Now, use AutoTracking to draw a ∅.5″ cylinder centered on the lower face and extending 3″ into the base, as shown in **Figure 3-10B.** As you will learn in the solid modeling section of the book, a cylinder located in this manner can be used to create a hole in the solid object.

**Figure 3-10.**
A—These pick points are used to establish a new UCS with the **ZAxis** option of the **UCS** command. B—Once the new UCS is created, a cylinder can be drawn that extends into the base.

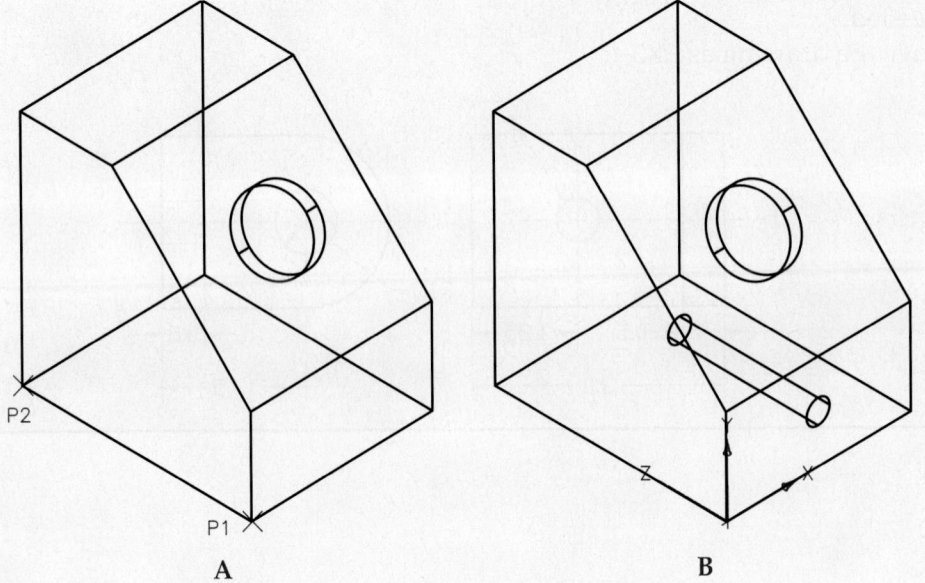

A                      B

         AutoCAD and its Applications—Advanced

## Selecting a New Origin

The **Origin** and **Move** options of the **UCS** command are basically the same; they set a new origin point. The **Origin** option can be accessed by picking the **Origin UCS** button on the **UCS** toolbar, selecting **New UCS** and then **Origin** from the **Tools** pull-down menu, or using the **UCS** command. The **Move** option can be accessed by picking **Move UCS** from the **Tools** pull-down menu, picking the **Move UCS Origin** button on the **UCS II** toolbar, or using the **UCS** command.

```
Command: UCS↵
Current ucs name: current
Enter an option [New/Move/orthoGraphic/Prev/Restore/Save/Del/Apply/?/World]
    <World>: O↵
Specify new origin point <0,0,0>: (pick the new origin)
Command:
```

The origin of the UCS moves to the specified point. The XY plane remains parallel to that of the previous UCS. **Figure 3-11** shows the UCS moved to three different origin points using the **Origin** option. Notice how the XY planes of the new locations are all parallel.

**Figure 3-11.**
The XY plane of the new UCS remains parallel to the XY plane of the previous UCS when using the **Origin** option.

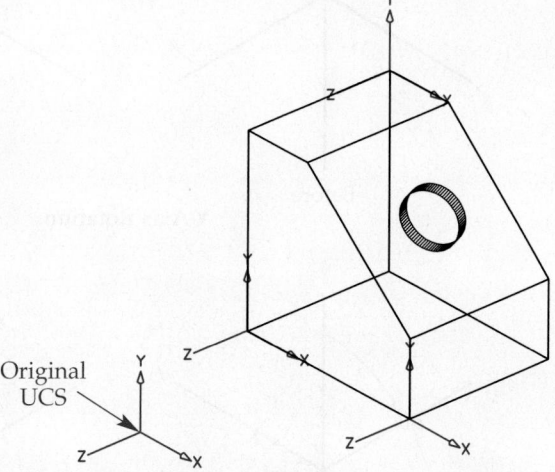

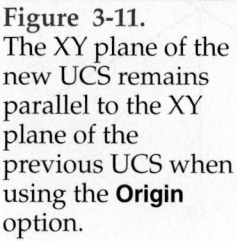

## Rotating the X, Y, and Z Axes

Earlier, you rotated the UCS about the X axis so you could draw the side view of the object before using the **EXTRUDE** command. This same technique is used to rotate the UCS about the Y or Z axis. Rotating about a single axis is useful when you need to rotate the UCS to match the angle of a surface on a part. **Figure 3-12** shows the direction of rotation around each axis when a 90° angle is specified. You can enter negative or positive angles. The following sequence rotates the UCS 90° about the Z axis. If you are having trouble visualizing the X, Y, and Z axis rotations, try using the right-hand rule. The right-hand rule is covered in Chapter 1.

```
Command: UCS↵
Current ucs name: current
Enter an option [New/Move/orthoGraphic/Prev/Restore/Save/Del/Apply/?/World]
    <World>: N↵
Specify origin of new UCS or [ZAxis/3point/OBject/Face/View/X/Y/Z] <0,0,0>: Z↵
Specify rotation angle about Z axis <90>: 90↵
Command:
```

**Figure 3-12.**
The UCS icon can
be rotated around
the X, Y, and Z axes
by entering an
angle. The angle can
be positive or
negative, as
appropriate.

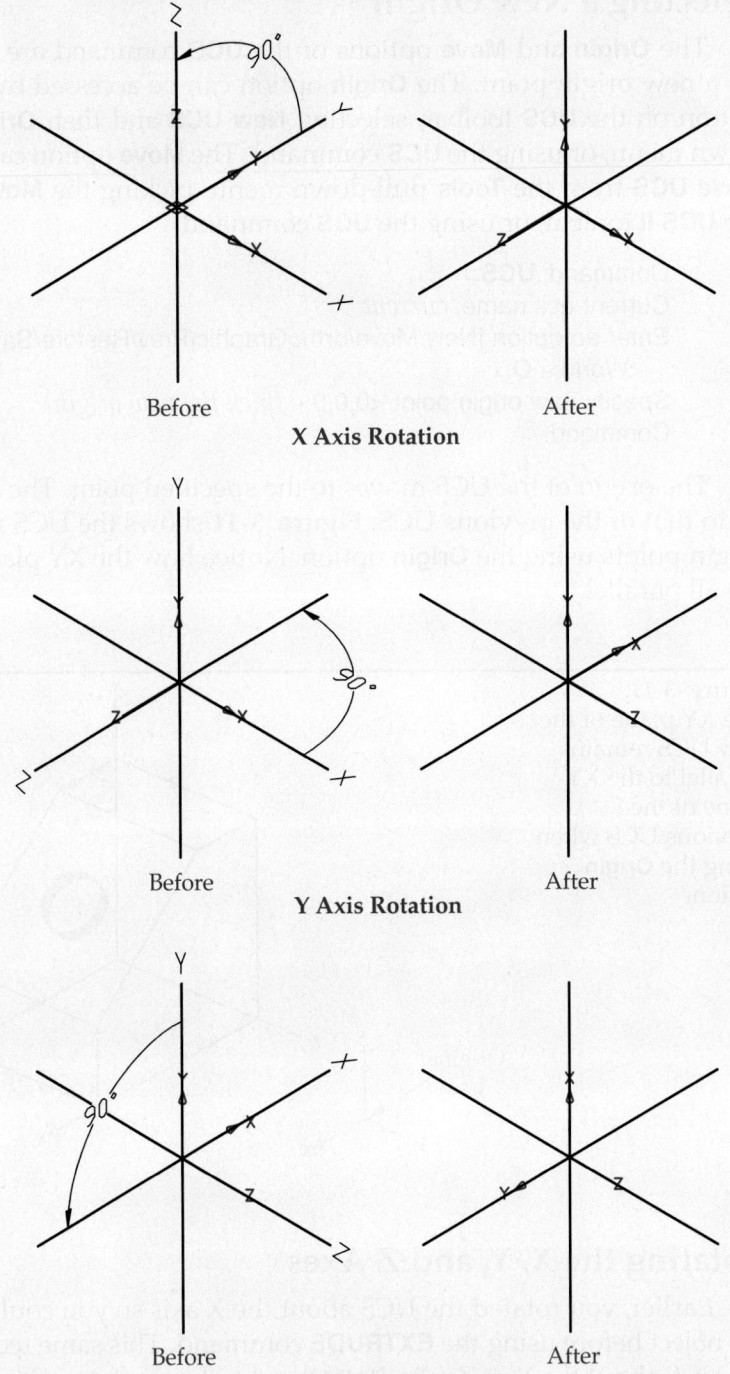

Before       After

**X Axis Rotation**

Before       After

**Y Axis Rotation**

Before       After

**Z Axis Rotation**

**PROFESSIONAL TIP**

You do not need to enter N for **New** when using the **UCS** command. All options shown at the second prompt can be entered at the first prompt. However, to enter the **Front** option at the first prompt you must type FRONT, not F. Entering F at the first prompt changes the UCS to the front orthographic UCS. Orthographic UCSs are discussed later in this chapter.

## Setting the UCS to an Existing Object

Tools
  ↳ New UCS
    ↳ Object

UCS
toolbar

Object UCS

The **OBject** option of the **UCS** command can be used to define a new UCS on an object, except a 3D solid, 3D polyline, 3D mesh, spline, multiline, region, or ellipse. This option can be accessed by picking the **Object UCS** button on the **UCS** toolbar, or selecting **New UCS** and then **Object** in the **Tools** pull-down menu, or entering the command at the Command: prompt.

There are certain rules that control the orientation of the UCS. For example, if you select a circle, the center point becomes the origin of the new UCS. The pick point on the circle determines the direction of the X axis. The Y axis is relative to X, and the UCS Z axis is the same as the Z axis of the object selected. Look at **Figure 3-13A.** The circle is rotated an unknown number of degrees from the XY plane of the WCS. However, you need to create a UCS in which the circle is lying on the XY plane. In the following example, the circle is selected for the new UCS.

Command: **UCS**↵
Current ucs name: *WORLD*
Enter an option [New/Move/orthoGraphic/Prev/Restore/Save/Del/Apply/?/World]
   <World>: **OB**↵
Select object to align UCS: *(pick the circle)*
Command:

The UCS icon may look like the one shown in **Figure 3-13B.** Notice how the X and Y axes are not aligned with the quadrants of the circle, as indicated by the grip locations. This may not be what you expected. The X axis orientation is determined by the pick point on the circle. Notice how the X axis is pointing at the pick point. To rotate the UCS in the current plane so the X and Y axes of the UCS are aligned with the quadrants of the circle, use the **ZAxis** option of the **UCS** command. Refer to **Figure 3-13C.**

Command: **UCS**↵
Current ucs name: *current*
Enter an option [New/Move/orthoGraphic/Prev/Restore/Save/Del/Apply/?/World]
   <World>: **ZA**↵
Specify new origin point <0,0,0>: **CEN**↵
of *(pick the circle)*
Specify point on positive portion of Z–axis <0.0000,0.0000,1.0000>: ↵ *(pressing [Enter] uses the current Z axis location, which also forces the X and Y axes to align with the object)*
Command:

---

**Figure 3-13.**
A—This circle is rotated off the WCS XY plane an unknown number of degrees. It will be used to establish a new UCS. B—The circle is on the XY plane of the new UCS. However, the X and Y axes do not align with the circle's quadrants. C—The **ZAxis** option of the UCS command is used to align the UCS with the quadrants of the circle.

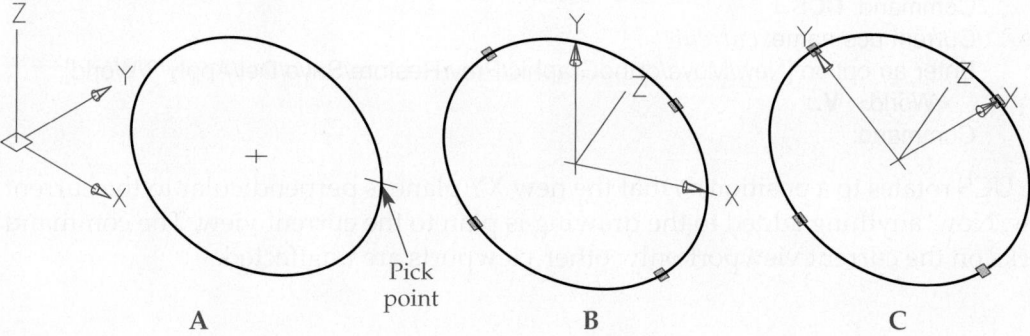

# Setting the UCS to the Face of a 3D Solid

Tools
↳ New UCS
↳ Face

UCS
toolbar

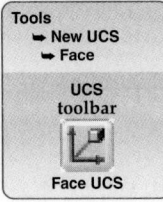

Face UCS

The **Face** option of the **UCS** command allows you to orient the UCS to any face on a 3D solid object. This option works on solids only, not wireframes or surface objects. Access this option by picking the **Face UCS** button on the **UCS** toolbar, selecting **New UCS** and then **Face** in the **Tools** pull-down menu, or entering the **UCS** command at the Command: prompt.

```
Command: UCS↵
Current ucs name: current
Enter an option [New/Move/orthoGraphic/Prev/Restore/Save/Del/Apply/?/World]
    <World>: FACE↵ (do not enter F)
Select face of solid object: (pick a face on the object)
Enter an option [Next/Xflip/Yflip] <accept>: ↵
Command:
```

After you have selected a face on a 3D solid, you have the options of moving the UCS to the adjacent face or flipping the UCS 180° on the X, Y, or both axes. Once you achieve the UCS orientation you want, press [Enter] to accept. Notice in **Figure 3-14** how many different UCS orientations can be selected for a single face.

**Figure 3-14.**
Several different UCSs can be selected from a single pick point using the **Face** option of the **UCS** command. This option can only be used on solids.

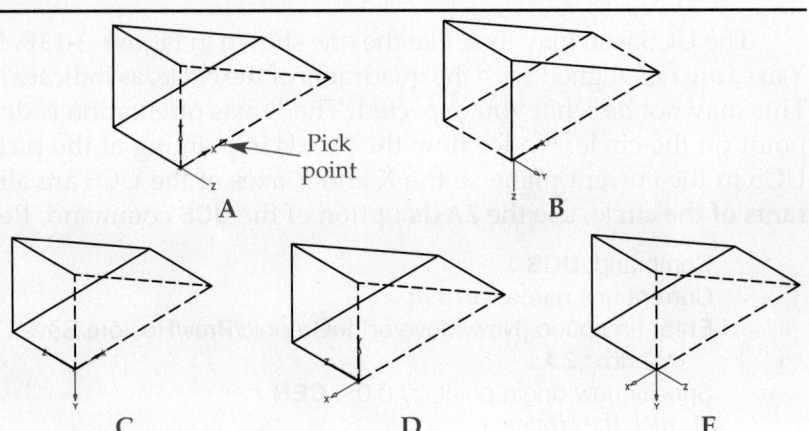

Pick point

A  B

C  D  E

# Setting the UCS Perpendicular to the Current View

Tools
↳ New UCS
↳ View

UCS
toolbar

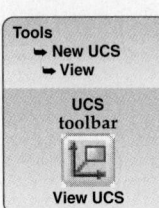

View UCS

You may need to add notes or labels to a 3D drawing that are plan to the current view, such as that shown in **Figure 3-15**. An application of this appears later in this chapter. The **View** option of the **UCS** command makes this easy to do. Access the **View** option by picking the **View UCS** button on the **UCS** toolbar, selecting **New UCS** and then **View** in the **Tools** pull-down menu, or entering the **UCS** command at the Command: prompt.

```
Command: UCS↵
Current ucs name: current
Enter an option [New/Move/orthoGraphic/Prev/Restore/Save/Del/Apply/?/World]
    <World>: V↵
Command:
```

The UCS rotates to a position so that the new XY plane is perpendicular to the current view. Now, anything added to the drawing is plan to the current view. The command works on the current viewport only; other viewports are unaffected.

**Figure 3-15.**
The **View** option allows you to place text plan to the current view.

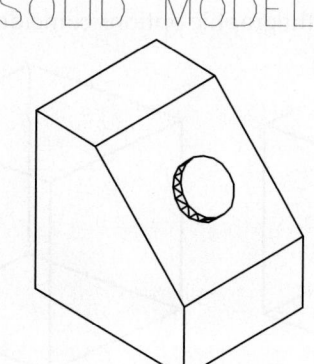

SOLID MODEL

## Applying the Current UCS to a Viewport

The **Apply** option of the **UCS** command allows you to apply the UCS in the current viewport to any or all model space or paper space viewports. This is different from the **View** option in that the **View** option applies the UCS to the current viewport only. Using the **Apply** option, you can have a different UCS displayed in every viewport, or you can apply one UCS to all viewports.

Access the **Apply** option by picking the **Apply UCS** button on the **UCS** toolbar, selecting **New UCS** and then **Apply** in the **Tools** pull-down menu, or entering the **UCS** command.

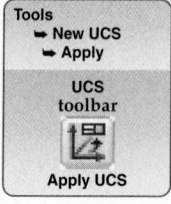

Tools
➥ New UCS
  ➥ Apply

UCS
toolbar

Apply UCS

Command: **UCS**↵
Current ucs name: *current*
Enter an option [New/Move/orthoGraphic/Prev/Restore/Save/Del/Apply/?/World]
    <World>: **A**↵
Pick viewport to apply current UCS or [All] <current>: *(pick a viewport or type A for **All**)*
Command:

## Preset UCS Orientations

AutoCAD has six preset orthographic options that match the six standard orthographic views. With the current UCS as the top view (plan), all other views are arranged as shown in **Figure 3-16.** These orientations can be selected in the **Orthographic UCS** cascading menu in the **Tools** pull-down menu or in the drop-down list that appears on the **UCS II** toolbar. They can also be selected in the **Orthographic UCSs** tab of the **UCS** dialog box. To open the UCS dialog box, select **Preset...** from the **Orthographic UCS** cascading menu in the **Tools** pull-down menu or enter UC, UCS-MAN (UCS manager), or DDUCSP (dynamic dialog UCS presets) at the Command: prompt. Six preset UCS orientations are listed in the **Orthographic UCSs** tab. These are **Top** (or plan), **Bottom**, **Front**, **Back**, **Left**, and **Right**.

DDUCSP
UC
UCSMAN

Tools
➥ Orthographic
  UCS
  ➥ Preset...

UCS II
toolbar

The **Relative to:** drop-down list at the bottom of the tab specifies whether the orthographic UCS is relative to a named UCS or absolute to the WCS. For example, suppose you have a saved UCS named Front Corner that is rotated 30° about the Y axis of the WCS. If you set the **Top** UCS current relative to the WCS, the new UCS is perpendicular to the WCS, **Figure 3-17A.** However, if **Top** is set current relative to the named UCS Front Corner, the new UCS is also rotated from the WCS, **Figure 3-17B.**

The Z value, or depth, of a preset UCS can be changed in the **Orthographic UCSs** tab of the **UCS** dialog box. First, right-click on the name of the UCS you wish to change. Then, pick **Depth** from the shortcut menu, **Figure 3-18A.** This displays the **Orthographic UCS depth** dialog box. See **Figure 3-18B.** You can either enter a new depth value or specify the new location on screen by picking the **Select new origin** button. Once the new depth has been selected, it is reflected in the preset UCS list.

---

*Chapter 3   Understanding User Coordinate Systems*

Figure 3-16.
The standard UCS orthographic options coincide with the six basic orthographic views.

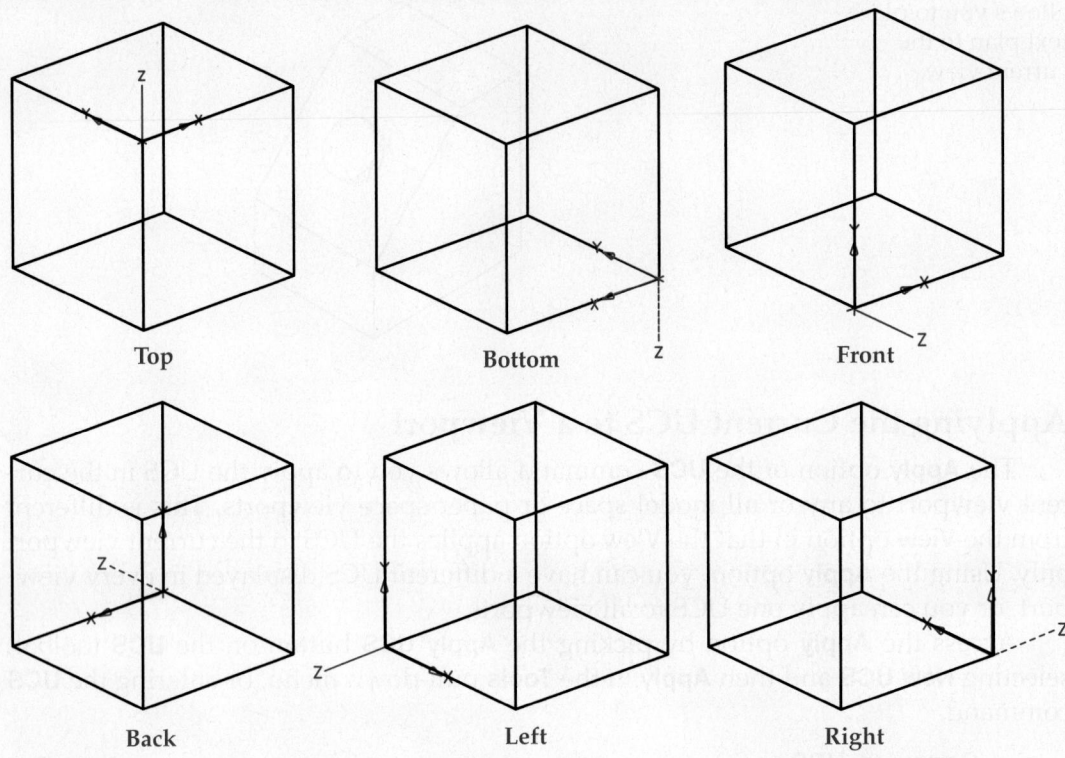

Top             Bottom             Front

Back             Left             Right

Figure 3-17.
The **Relative to:** drop-down list entry in the **Orthographic UCSs** tab determines whether the orthographic UCS is based on a named UCS or the WCS. The UCS icon here represents the named UCS. A—Relative to the WCS. B—Relative to a selected named UCS.

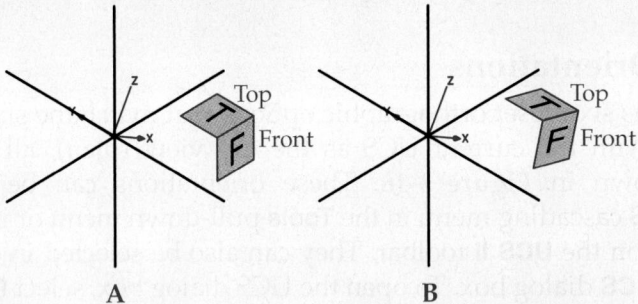

A             B

**PROFESSIONAL TIP**

Changing the **Relative to:** setting affects *all* preset UCSs *and all* preset viewpoints! Therefore, leave this set to **World** unless absolutely necessary to change it.

**Figure 3-18.**
A—The Z value, or depth, of a preset UCS can be changed by right-clicking on its name and selecting **Depth**. B—Enter a new depth value or pick the **Select new origin** button to pick the new location on the screen.

Right-click to display the shortcut menu

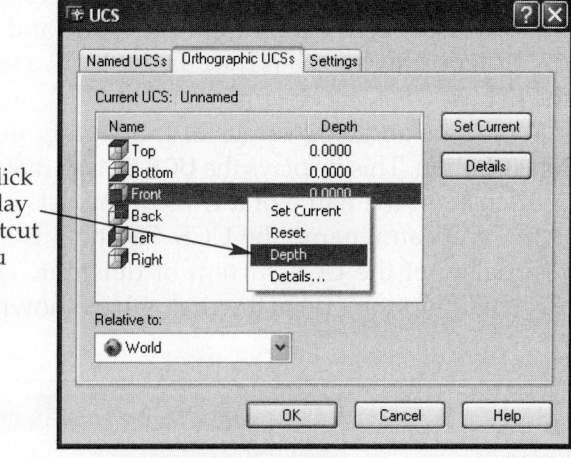

A

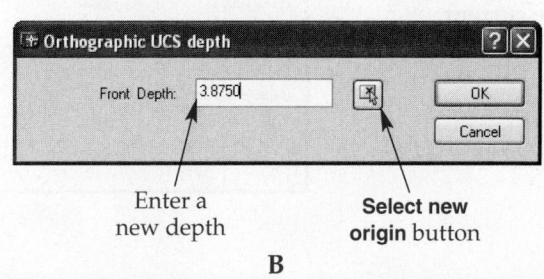

Enter a new depth

**Select new origin** button

B

## Managing User Coordinate Systems and Displays

You can create, name, and use as many user coordinate systems as needed to construct your model or drawing. AutoCAD allows you to name coordinate systems for future use. User coordinate systems can be created, renamed, set current, and deleted using the **Named UCSs** tab of the **UCS** dialog box, **Figure 3-19**. This tab is accessed by picking **Named UCS...** from the **Tools** pull-down menu; picking the **Display UCS Dialog** button in the **UCS** toolbar; or entering UC, UCSMAN (UCS manager), or DDUCS (dynamic dialog UCS) at the Command: prompt.

The **Named UCSs** tab contains the **Current UCS:** list box. This list box contains the names of all saved coordinate systems plus **World**. If other coordinate systems have been used in the current drawing session, **Previous** appears in the list. **Unnamed**

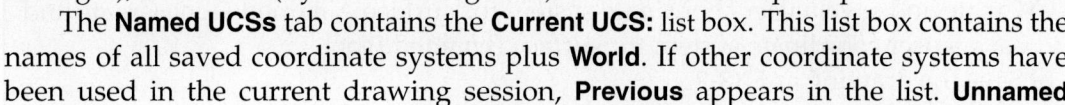

DDUCS
UC
UCSMAN

Tools
➥ Named UCS...

UCS
toolbar

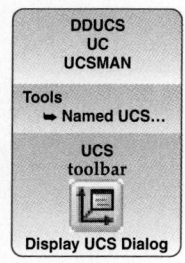

**Display UCS Dialog**

**Figure 3-19.**
The **UCS** dialog box allows you to rename, list, delete, and set current an existing UCS.

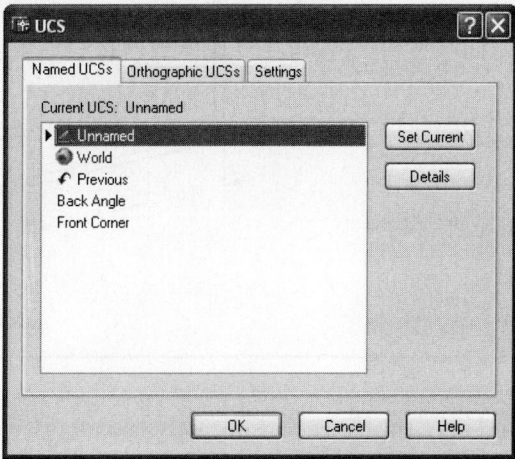

appears if the current coordinate system has not been named. To make any of the listed coordinate systems active, highlight the name and pick the **Set Current** button. If one of the UCSs listed in this tab is the current UCS, a small triangle appears next to its name in the list.

A list of coordinate and axis values of the highlighted UCS can be displayed by picking the **Details** button. This displays the **UCS Details** dialog box shown in **Figure 3-20.**

If you right-click on the name of a UCS in the list, a shortcut menu is displayed. Using this menu, you can rename the UCS. Saving a UCS is discussed earlier in this chapter. You can also set the UCS current or delete it. The **Unnamed** UCS cannot be deleted. The **Details...** option opens the dialog box shown in **Figure 3-20.**

**Figure 3-20.**
The **UCS Details** dialog box displays the coordinate values of the current UCS.

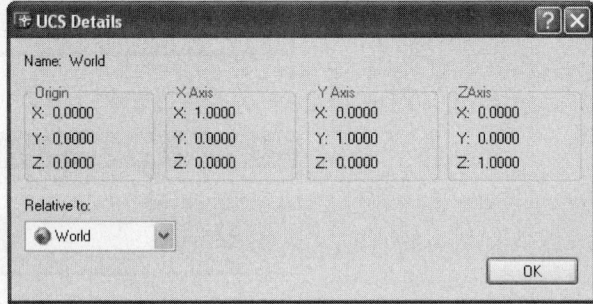

PROFESSIONAL TIP

You can manage UCSs on the command line using the **UCS** command.

---

**Exercise 3-2**

○ Construct the wireframe object shown below. Do not include dimensions or labels.
○ Rotate and relocate the UCS as needed.
○ Create and save a user coordinate system for surface A named Front. Create and save a user coordinate system for surface B named Right.
○ Save the drawing as EX3-2.

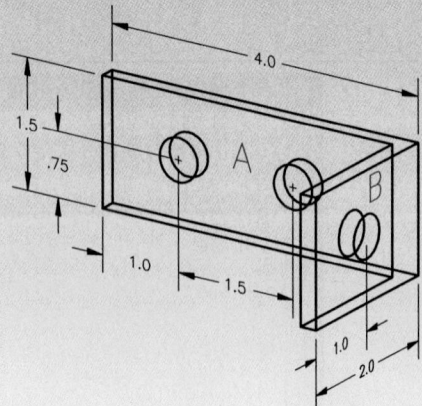

## Setting an Automatic Plan Display

After changing the UCS, a plan view is often needed to give you a better feel for the XYZ directions. While you should try to draw in a pictorial view when possible as you construct a 3D object, some constructions may be much easier in a plan view. AutoCAD can be set to automatically make your view of the drawing plan to the current UCS. This is especially useful if you will be changing the UCS often, but want to work in a plan view.

The **UCSFOLLOW** system variable is used to automatically display a plan view of the current UCS. When it is set to 1, a plan view is automatically created in the current viewport when the UCS is changed. Viewports are discussed in Chapter 4. The default setting of **UCSFOLLOW** is 0 (off). The **UCSFOLLOW** variable can be set for each viewport individually.

> Command: **UCSFOLLOW**↵
> Enter new value for UCSFOLLOW <0>: **1**↵
> Command:

A plan view will be automatically generated the next time the UCS is changed. The **UCSFOLLOW** variable generates the plan view only after the UCS is changed, not immediately after the variable is changed.

---

**PROFESSIONAL TIP**  To get the plan view displayed without changing the UCS, use the **PLAN** command, which is discussed in Chapter 5.

---

## UCS Settings and Variables

As discussed in the previous section, the **UCSFOLLOW** system variable allows you to change how an object is displayed in relation to the UCS. There are also system variables that display a variety of information about the current UCS. These variables include:

- **UCSNAME.** (Read only) Displays the name of the current UCS.
- **UCSORG.** (Read only) Displays the XYZ origin value of the current UCS.
- **UCSXDIR.** (Read only) Displays the XYZ value of the X axis direction of the current UCS.
- **UCSYDIR.** (Read only) Displays the XYZ value of the Y axis direction of the current UCS.

UCS options and variables can also be managed in the **Settings** tab of the **UCS** dialog box. See **Figure 3-2A.** The settings in this tab are:

- **Save UCS with viewport.** If checked, the current UCS settings are saved with the viewport and the **UCSVP** system variable is set to 1. This variable can be set for each viewport in the drawing. Viewports in which this setting is turned off, or unchecked, will always display the UCS settings of the current active viewport.
- **Update view to Plan when UCS is changed.** This setting controls the **UCSFOLLOW** variable. When checked, the variable is set to 1. When unchecked, the variable is set to 0.

---

# Creating Text with Thickness

PROPERTIES
[Ctrl]+[1]

Tools
➥ Properties
Modify
➥ Properties

Standard
toolbar

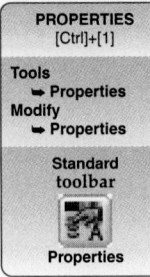

Properties

A thickness can be applied to text after it is created. This is done using the **Properties** window, which can be accessed by picking the **Properties** button on the **Standard** toolbar, selecting **Properties** from the **Tools** or **Modify** pull-down menus, or typing PROPERTIES at the Command: prompt. The thickness setting is located in the **General** section. Once a thickness is applied, the hidden lines can be removed using the **HIDE** command. **Figure 3-21** shows six different fonts as they appear after being given a thickness with hidden lines removed.

Only text created using the **TEXT** and **DTEXT** commands (text object) can be assigned thickness. Text created with the **MTEXT** command (mtext object) cannot have thickness assigned to it. In addition, only AutoCAD SHX and PostScript PFM fonts can be given thickness. AutoCAD SHP shape fonts and PostScript PFB fonts can be compiled into SHX and PFM fonts with the **COMPILE** command. The compiled fonts can then be used to create text with thickness. Windows TrueType fonts *cannot* be used to create text with thickness.

**Figure 3-21.**
Six different fonts
with thickness after
hidden lines are
removed.

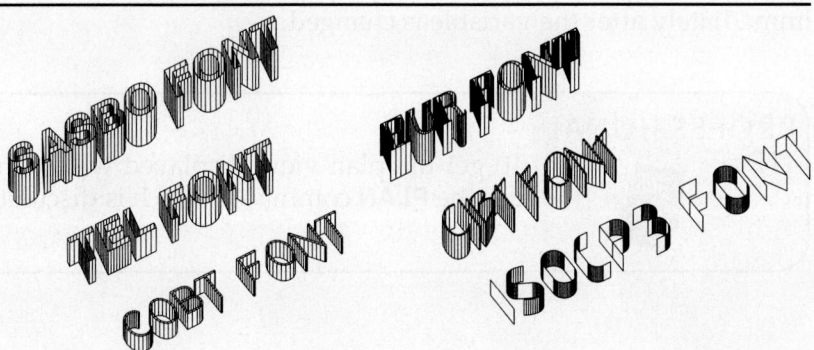

# Text and the UCS

Text is created parallel to the XY plane of the UCS in which it is drawn. Therefore, if you wish to show text appearing on a specific plane, establish a new UCS on that plane before placing the text. **Figure 3-22** shows several examples of text on different UCS planes.

**Figure 3-22.**
Text located using
three different
UCSs.

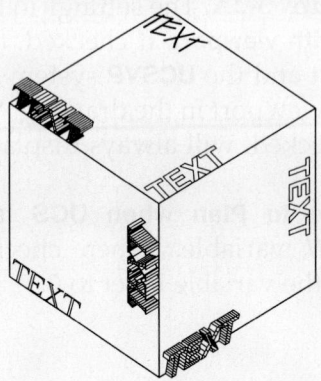

## Changing the Orientation of a Text Object

If text is placed improperly or created using the wrong UCS, it can be edited using grips or editing commands. Editing commands and grips are relative to the current UCS. For example, if text is drawn with the WCS current, you can use the **ROTATE** command to change the orientation of the text in the XY plane of the WCS. However, to rotate the text so it tilts up from the XY plane of the WCS, you will need to change the UCS. Rotate the UCS as needed so the Z axis of the new UCS aligns with the axis about which you want to rotate. Then, the **ROTATE** command can be used to rotate the text.

## Using the UCS View Option to Create a Title

It is often necessary to create a pictorial view of an object, but with a note or title that is plan to your point of view. For example, you may need to insert the title of a 3D view. See **Figure** 3-23. This is done with the **View** option of the **UCS** command, which was introduced earlier.

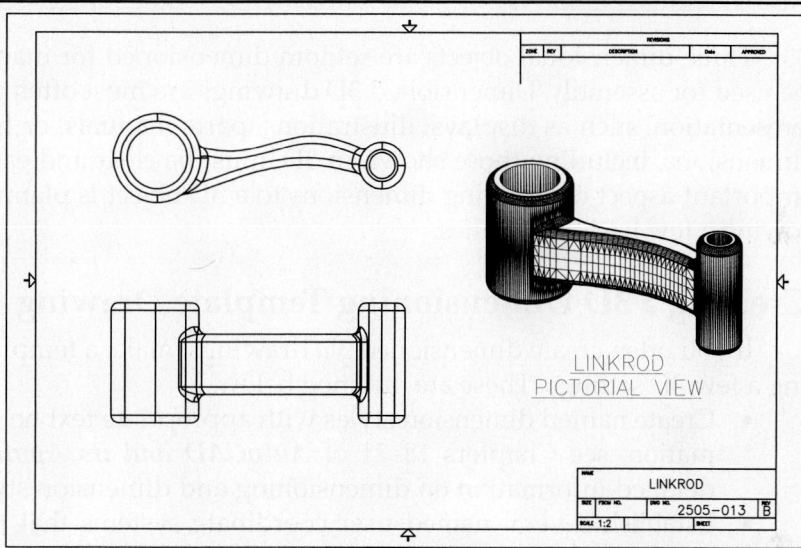

**Figure** 3-23.
This title (shown in color) has been placed correctly using the **View** option of the **UCS** command.

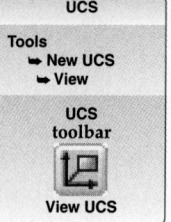

To set the UCS plan to the current viewpoint, pick the **View UCS** button in the **UCS** toolbar, select **View** from the **New UCS** cascading menu in the **Tools** pull-down menu, or enter the following at the Command: prompt.

```
Command: UCS↵
Current ucs name: current
Enter an option [New/Move/orthoGraphic/Prev/Restore/Save/Del/Apply/?/World]
    <World>: V↵
Command:
```

A new UCS is created perpendicular to your viewpoint. However, the view remains a 3D view. Inserted text will be horizontal (or vertical) in the current view. Name and save the UCS if you will use it again.

# Dimensioning in 3D

Three-dimensional objects are seldom dimensioned for manufacturing, but may be used for assembly. Dimensioned 3D drawings are most often used for some sort of presentation, such as displays, illustrations, parts manuals, or training manuals. All dimensions, including those shown in 3D, must be clear and easy to read. The most important aspect of applying dimensions to a 3D object is planning. That means following a few basic guidelines.

## Creating a 3D Dimensioning Template Drawing

If you often create dimensioned 3D drawings, make a template drawing containing a few 3D settings. These are outlined below.

- Create named dimension styles with appropriate text heights. For more information, see Chapters 18–21 of *AutoCAD and its Applications—Basics* for detailed information on dimensioning and dimension styles.
- Establish several named user coordinate systems that match the planes on which dimensions will be placed.
- If the preset isometric viewpoints will not serve your needs, establish and save several 3D viewpoints that can be used for different objects. These viewpoints will allow you to select the display best for reading dimensions.

## Placing Dimensions in the Proper Plane

The location of dimensions and the plane on which they are placed are often a matter of choice. For example, **Figure 3-24** shows several options for placing a thickness dimension on an object. All of these are correct. However, several of the options can be eliminated when other dimensions are added. This illustrates the importance of planning.

The key to good dimensioning in 3D is to avoid overlapping dimension and extension lines in different planes. A freehand sketch can help you plan this. As you lay out the 3D sketch, try to group information items together. Dimensions, notes, and item tags should be grouped so that they are easy to read and understand. This technique is called *information grouping.*

**Figure 3-25A** shows the object from **Figure 3-24** fully dimensioned using the aligned technique. Notice that the location dimension for the hole is placed on the top surface. This avoids dimensioning to hidden points. **Figure 3-25B** shows the same object dimensioned using the unilateral technique.

**Figure 3-24.**
A thickness dimension can be located in many different places. All locations shown here are acceptable.

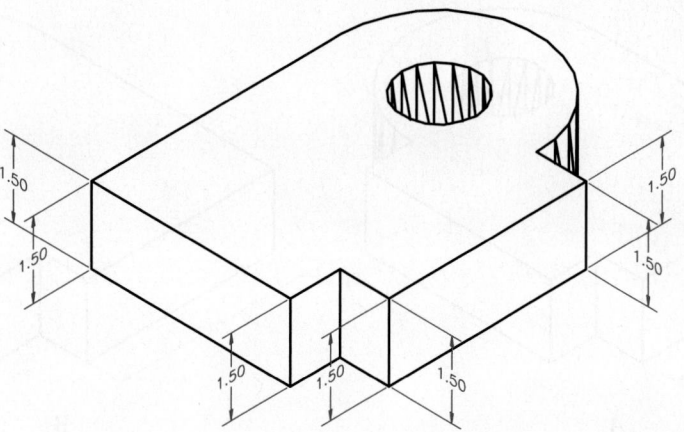

**Figure 3-25.**
A—An example of a 3D object dimensioned using the aligned technique. B—The object dimensioned with unilateral dimensions.

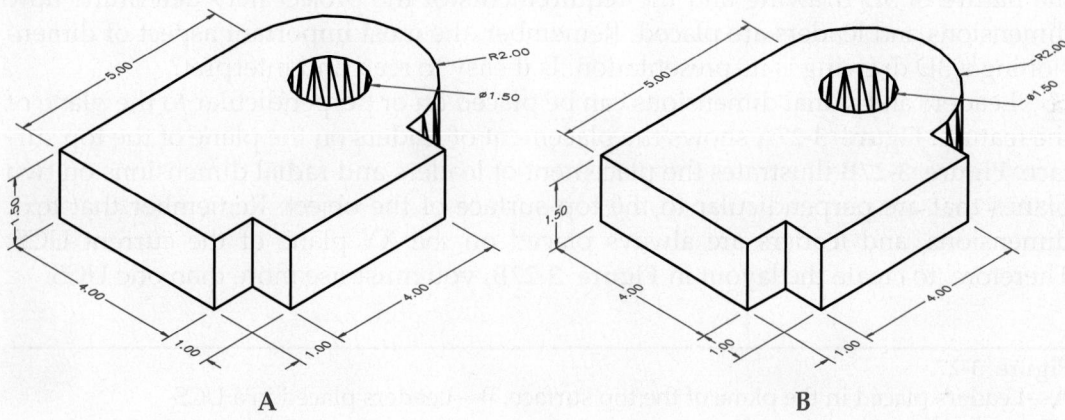

To create dimensions that display properly, it may be necessary to modify the dimension text rotation. The dimension shown in **Figure 3-26A** is inverted because the positive X and Y axes are oriented incorrectly. Using the **Properties** window, change the text rotation value to 180. The dimension text is then displayed properly, **Figure 3-26B.** Alternately, you can rotate the UCS before drawing the dimension, but this may be more time-consuming.

**PROFESSIONAL TIP**

Prior to placing dimensions on a 3D drawing, you should determine the purpose of the drawing. For what will it be used? Just as dimensioning a drawing for manufacturing purposes is based on the function of the part, 3D dimensioning is based on the function of the drawing. This determines whether you use chain, datum, arrowless, architectural, or some other style of dimensioning. It also determines how completely the object is dimensioned.

Figure 3-26.
A—This dimension text is inverted. B—The rotation property of the text is changed and the text reads correctly.

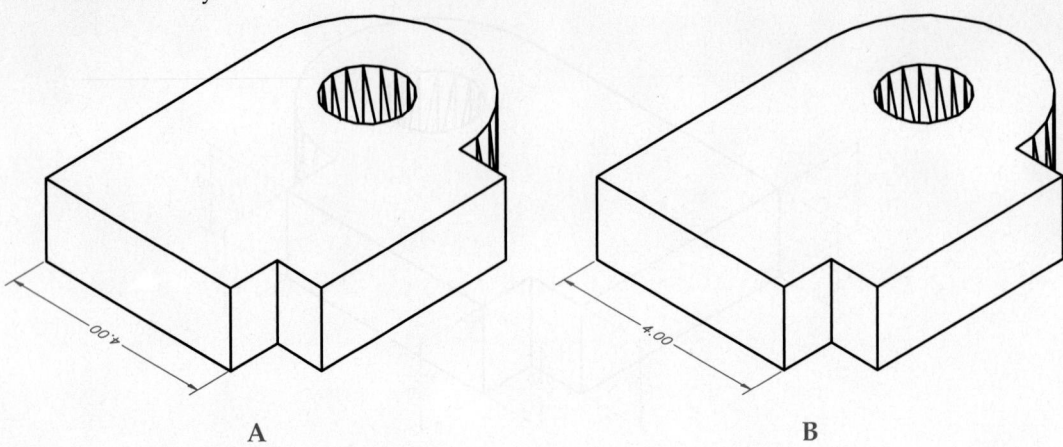

Figure 3-26.
A—This dimension text is inverted. B—The rotation property of the text is changed and the text reads correctly.

A                                    B

## Placing Leaders and Radial Dimensions in 3D

Although standards such as ASME Y14.5M should be followed when possible, the nature of 3D drawing and the requirements of the project may determine how dimensions and leaders are placed. Remember, the most important aspect of dimensioning a 3D drawing is its presentation. Is it easy to read and interpret?

Leaders and radial dimensions can be placed on or perpendicular to the plane of the feature. **Figure 3-27A** shows the placement of leaders on the plane of the top surface. **Figure 3-27B** illustrates the placement of leaders and radial dimensions on two planes that are perpendicular to the top surface of the object. Remember that text, dimensions, and leaders are always placed on the XY plane of the current UCS. Therefore, to create the layout in **Figure 3-27B**, you must use more than one UCS.

Figure 3-27.
A—Leaders placed in the plane of the top surface. B—Leaders placed in a UCS perpendicular to the top surface.

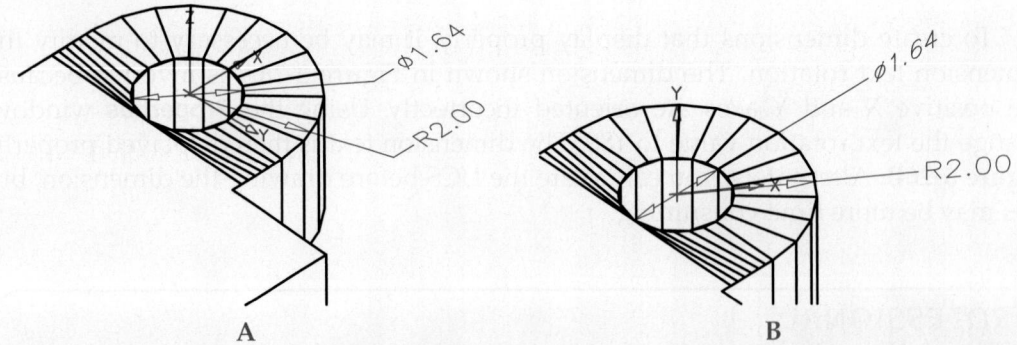

A                                    B

### Exercise 3-4

○ Begin a new drawing.
○ Draw the object shown in **Figure 3-25** as a wireframe using the dimensions given. Create and save as many user coordinate systems needed to draw and dimension the object.
○ Place dimensions and leaders to achieve the best presentation.
○ Save the drawing as EX3-4.

## Chapter Test

*Answer the following questions on a separate sheet of paper.*

1. What is the WCS?
2. What is a *user coordinate system (UCS)*?
3. Which command controls the display of the user coordinate system icon?
4. What is the function of the **3point** option of the **UCS** command?
5. How do you automatically create a display that is plan to a new UCS?
6. How is the UCS icon displayed at the origin of the current coordinate system?
7. When you use the **OBject** option of the **UCS** command, how does AutoCAD determine the X axis if you pick a circle for the new UCS?
8. How do you move the UCS along the current Z axis?
9. What is the function of the **OBject** option of the **UCS** command?
10. The **Face** option of the **UCS** command can be used on which types of objects?
11. What is the function of the **Apply** option of the **UCS** command?
12. How can you make sure that a view will always be plan to the current UCS?
13. In which dialog box is the **Orthographic UCSs** tab?
14. Which command displays the **UCS** dialog box?
15. What appears in the **Named UCSs** tab of the **UCS** dialog box if the current UCS has not been saved?
16. How can you create 3D text with thickness?
17. If text is placed using the wrong UCS, how can it be edited to appear on the correct one?
18. How can text be placed horizontally in your viewpoint if the object is displayed in 3D?
19. Name three items that should be a part of a 3D dimensioning template drawing.
20. What is *information grouping?*

## Drawing Problems

*Problems 1–3. These problems are engineering design sketches. They are the types of sketches a drafter is expected to work from in a real-world situation. Therefore, they may contain dimensioning errors and some information may be incomplete. It is up to you to supply appropriate information as needed.*

1. This is a concept sketch of a desk organizer. Create a 3D wireframe drawing using the dimensions given. Create new UCSs as needed. Length dimensions of the compartments are up to you. Plot your drawing to scale on a B-size sheet of paper. Save the drawing as P3-1.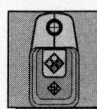

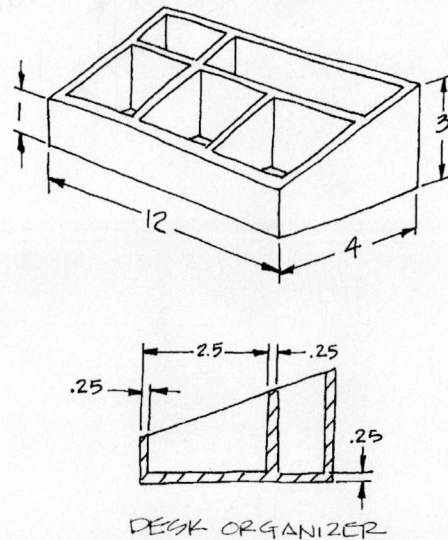

DESK ORGANIZER

2. This is a concept sketch of a desk pencil holder. Create a 3D wireframe drawing using the dimensions given. Create new UCSs as needed. Plot your drawing to scale on a B-size sheet of paper. Save the drawing as P3-2.

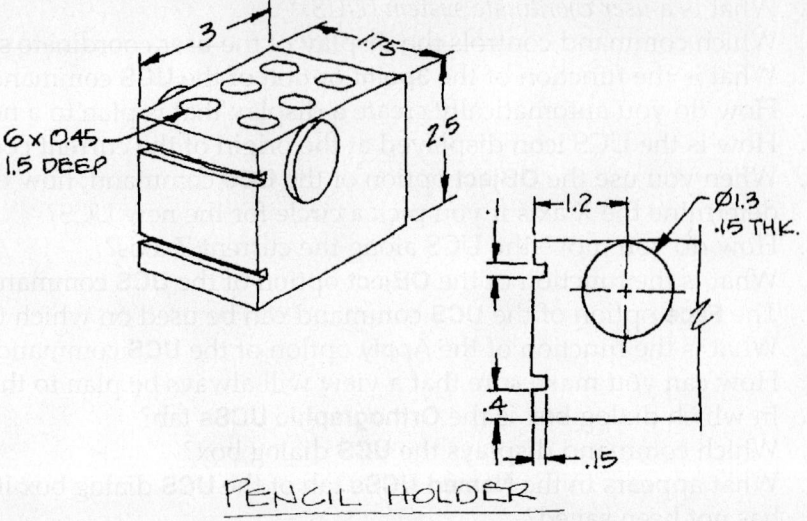

PENCIL HOLDER

3. This is an engineering sketch of a window blind mounting bracket. Create a 3D wireframe drawing using the dimensions given. Create new UCSs as needed. Plot two views of your drawing to scale on a C-size sheet of paper. Save the drawing as P3-3.

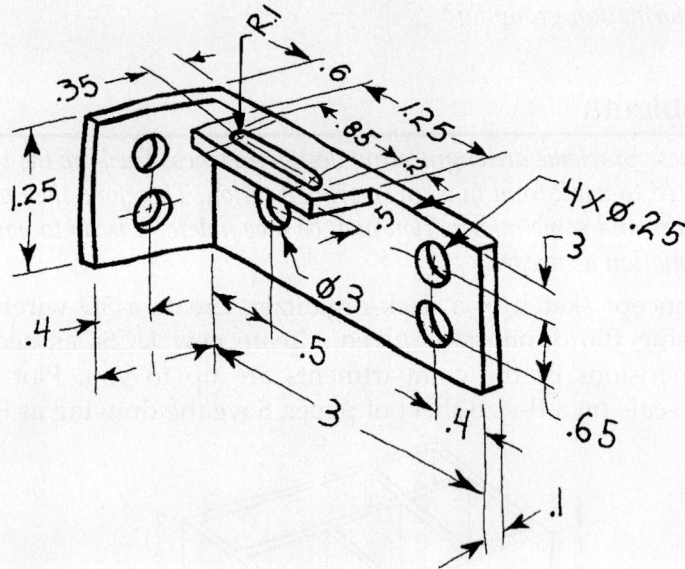

4. This is a two-view orthographic drawing of a window valance mounting bracket. Convert it to a 3D wireframe drawing. Use the dimensions given. Similar holes have the same offset dimensions. Create new UCSs as needed. Display an appropriate pictorial view of the drawing. Then, add dimensions. Finally, add the material note so it is plan to the view. Plot the drawing to scale on a C-size sheet of paper. Save the drawing as P3-4.

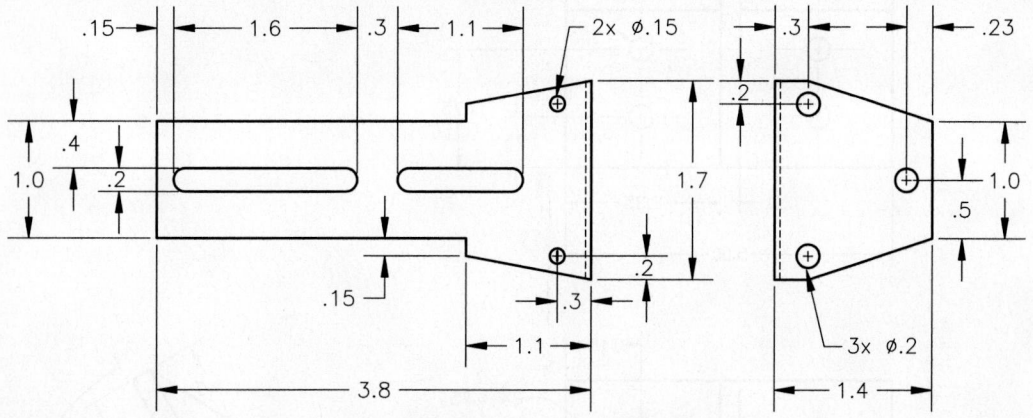

MATERIAL THICKNESS = .125"

5. This is an orthographic drawing of a light fixture bracket. Convert it to a 3D wireframe drawing. Use the dimensions given. Similar holes have the same offset dimensions. Create new UCSs as needed. Display an appropriate pictorial view of the drawing. Then, add dimensions. Plot the drawing to scale on a C-size sheet of paper. Save the drawing as P3-5.

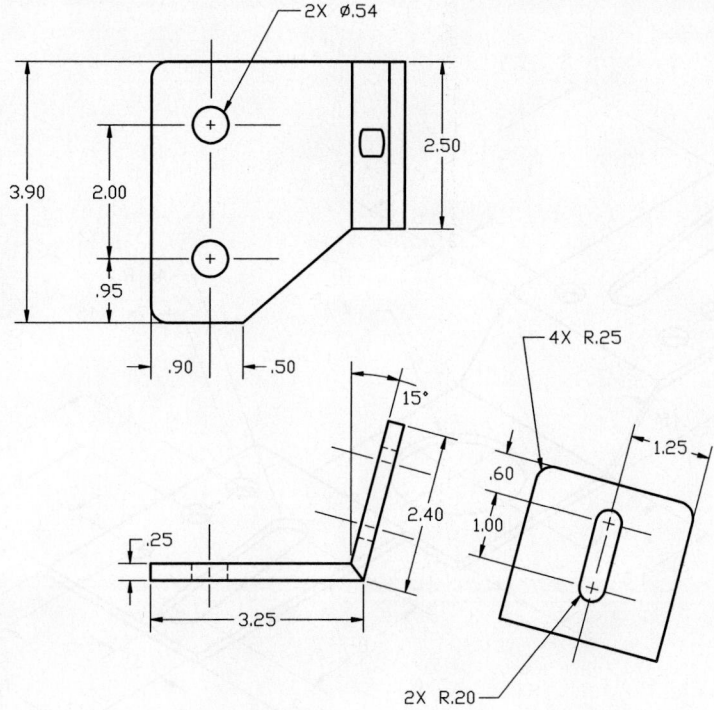

*Problems 6–8. These problems are mechanical parts. Create a 3D wireframe drawing of each part. Dimension each model. Place the title of each model so it is plan to the pictorial view. Plot the finished drawings on B-size paper.*

6.

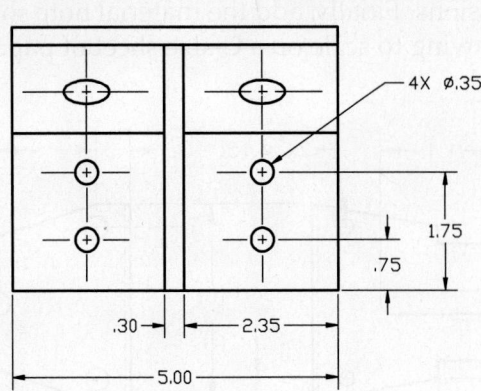

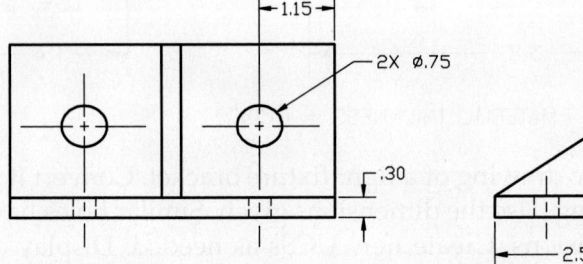

**Angle Bracket**

7.

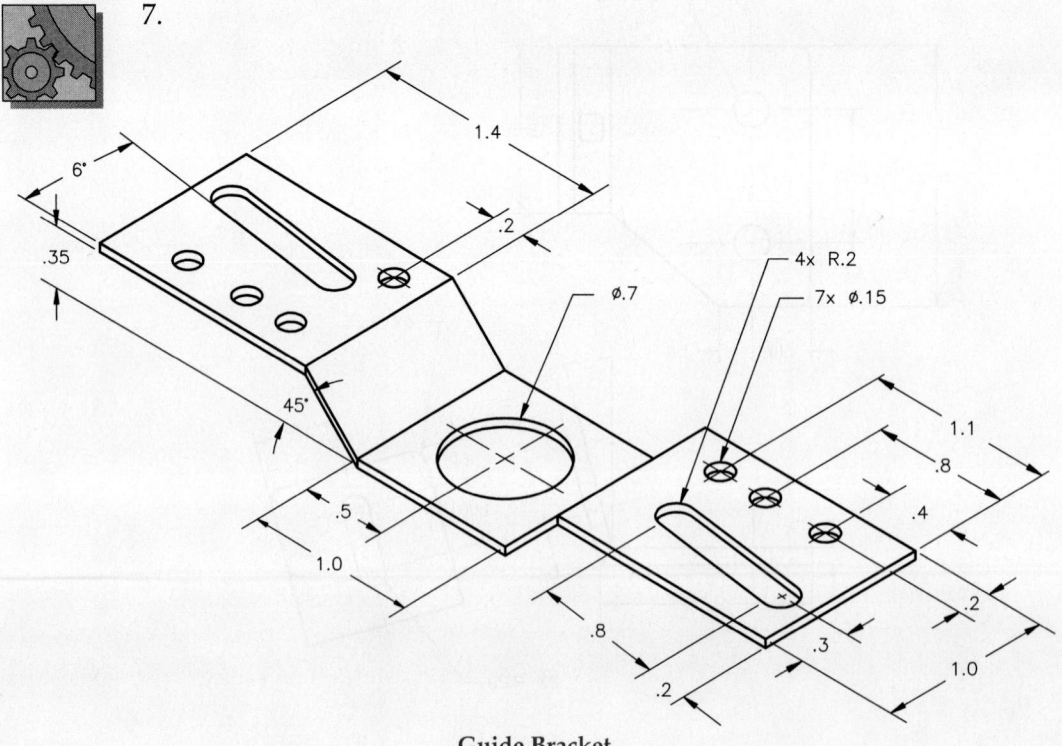

**Guide Bracket**

8.

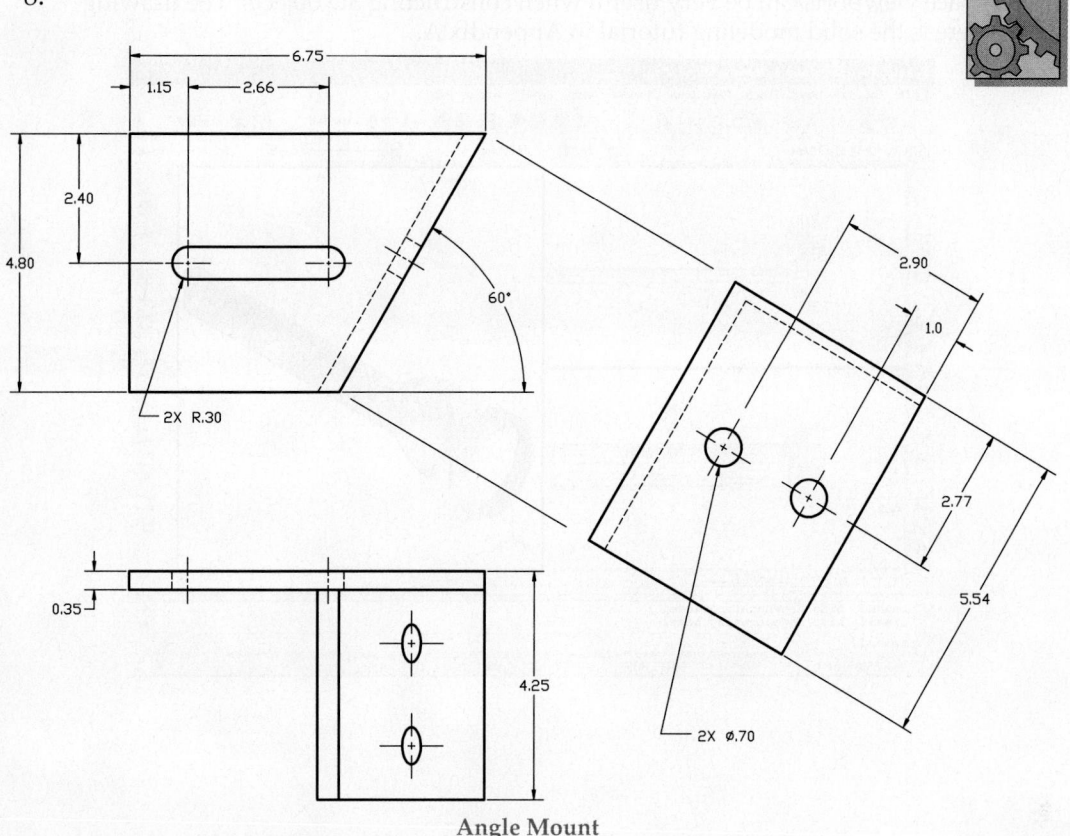

Angle Mount

Model space viewports can be very useful when constructing 3D objects. The drawing shown here is the solid modeling tutorial in Appendix A.

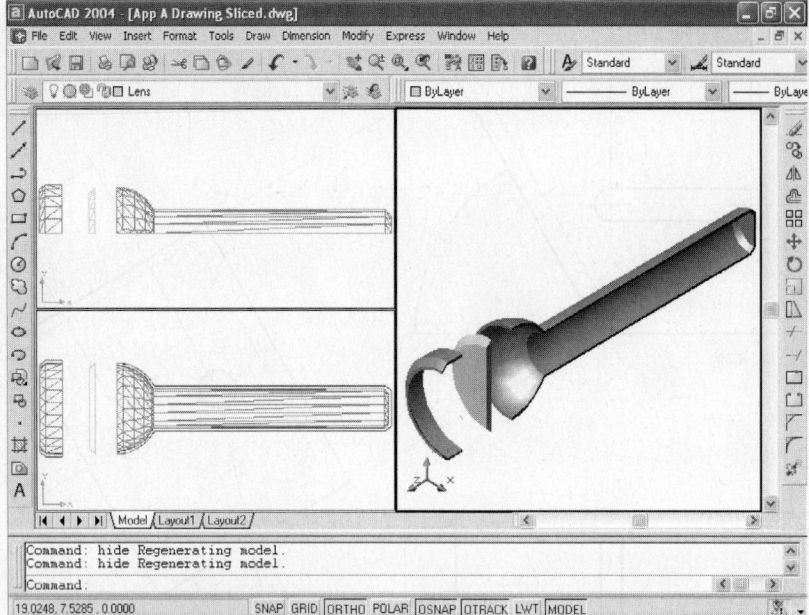

## CHAPTER 4

# Using Model Space Viewports

## Learning Objectives

After completing this chapter, you will be able to:
- Describe the function of model space viewports.
- Create and save viewport configurations.
- Alter the current viewport configuration.
- Use multiple viewports to construct a drawing.
- Create a standard engineering layout.

A variety of views can be displayed in a drawing at one time using model space viewports. This is especially useful when constructing 3D models. Using the **VPORTS** command, you can divide the drawing area into two or more smaller areas. These areas are called *viewports.* Each viewport can be configured to display a different 2D or 3D view of the model.

The *active viewport* is the viewport in which a command will be applied. Any viewport can be made active, but only one can be active at a time. As objects are added or edited, the results are shown in all viewports. A variety of viewport configurations can be saved and recalled as needed. This chapter discusses the use of viewports and shows how they can be used for 3D constructions.

## Understanding Viewports

The AutoCAD drawing area can be divided into a maximum of 64 viewports. However, this is impractical due to the small size of each viewport. Four viewports is usually the maximum number practical to display at one time. The number of viewports you need depends on the model you are drawing. Each viewport can show a different view of an object. This makes it easier to construct 3D objects.

NOTE  The **MAXACTVP** (maximum active viewports) system variable sets the number of viewports that can be used at one time. The initial value is 64.

There are two types of viewports used in AutoCAD. The type of viewport created depends on whether it is defined in model space or paper space. *Model space* is the space, or mode, where the drawing is constructed. *Paper space* is the space where a drawing is laid out to be plotted. Viewports created in model space are called *tiled viewports.* Viewports created in paper space are called *floating viewports.*

Model space is active by default when you start AutoCAD. Model space viewports are created with the **VPORTS** command. These viewport configurations cannot be plotted because they are for display purposes only. If you plot from model space, the contents of the active viewport are plotted. Tiled viewports are not AutoCAD objects. They are referred to as *tiled* because the edges of each viewport are placed side to side, as with floor tile, and they cannot overlap.

Floating (paper space) viewports are used to lay out the views of a drawing before plotting. They are described as *floating* because they can be moved around and overlapped. Paper space viewports are objects, and they can be edited. These viewports can be thought of as "windows" cut into a sheet of paper to "see into" model space. You can then insert, or *reference*, different scaled drawings (views) into these windows. For example, architectural details or sections and details of complex mechanical parts may be referenced. Detailed discussions of paper space viewports are provided in Chapters 9, 10, and 24 of *AutoCAD and its Applications—Basics.*

The **VPORTS** command is used to create viewports in a paper space layout. The process is very similar to that used to create model space viewports, which is discussed next. You can also use the **MVIEW** command to create paper space viewports.

## Creating Viewports

Creating model space viewports is similar to working with a multiview layout in manual drafting. In a manual multiview layout, several views are drawn on the same sheet. You can switch from one view to another simply by moving your pencil. With model space viewports, you simply pick with your pointing device in the viewport in which you wish to work. The picked viewport becomes active. Using viewports is a good way to construct 3D models because all views are updated as you draw. However, viewports are also useful when creating 2D drawings.

The project you are working on determines the number of viewports needed. Keep in mind that the more viewports you display on your screen, the smaller the viewports. Small viewports may not be useful to you. Four different viewport configurations are shown in **Figure 4-1.** As you can see, when 16 viewports are displayed, the viewports are very small. Normally, two to four viewports are used.

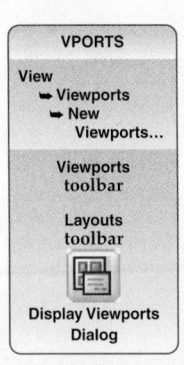

VPORTS

View
➥ Viewports
 ➥ New
  Viewports...

Viewports
toolbar

Layouts
toolbar

Display Viewports
Dialog

A layout of one to four viewports can be quickly created by using the **Viewports** dialog box or by selecting from the options in the **Viewports** cascading menu of the **View** pull-down menu. See **Figure 4-2.** The **Viewports** dialog box is accessed by entering VPORTS at the Command: prompt. A list of preset viewport configurations is provided in the **New Viewports** tab, **Figure 4-3.** You can access this tab automatically by picking the **Display Viewports Dialog** button from the **Viewports** or **Layouts** toolbar. You can also select **New Viewports...** from the **Viewports** cascading menu.

There are twelve preset viewport configurations from which to choose, including six different options for three-viewport configurations. See **Figure 4-4.** When you pick the name of a configuration in the **Standard viewports:** list, the viewport arrangement is displayed in the **Preview** area. After you have made a selection, you can save the configuration by entering a name in the **New name:** text box and then picking **OK** to close the dialog box. When the **Viewports** dialog box closes, the configuration is displayed on screen.

**Figure 4-1.**
A—Two vertical viewports. B—Two horizontal viewports. C—Three viewports, with the largest viewport positioned at the right. D—Sixteen viewports.

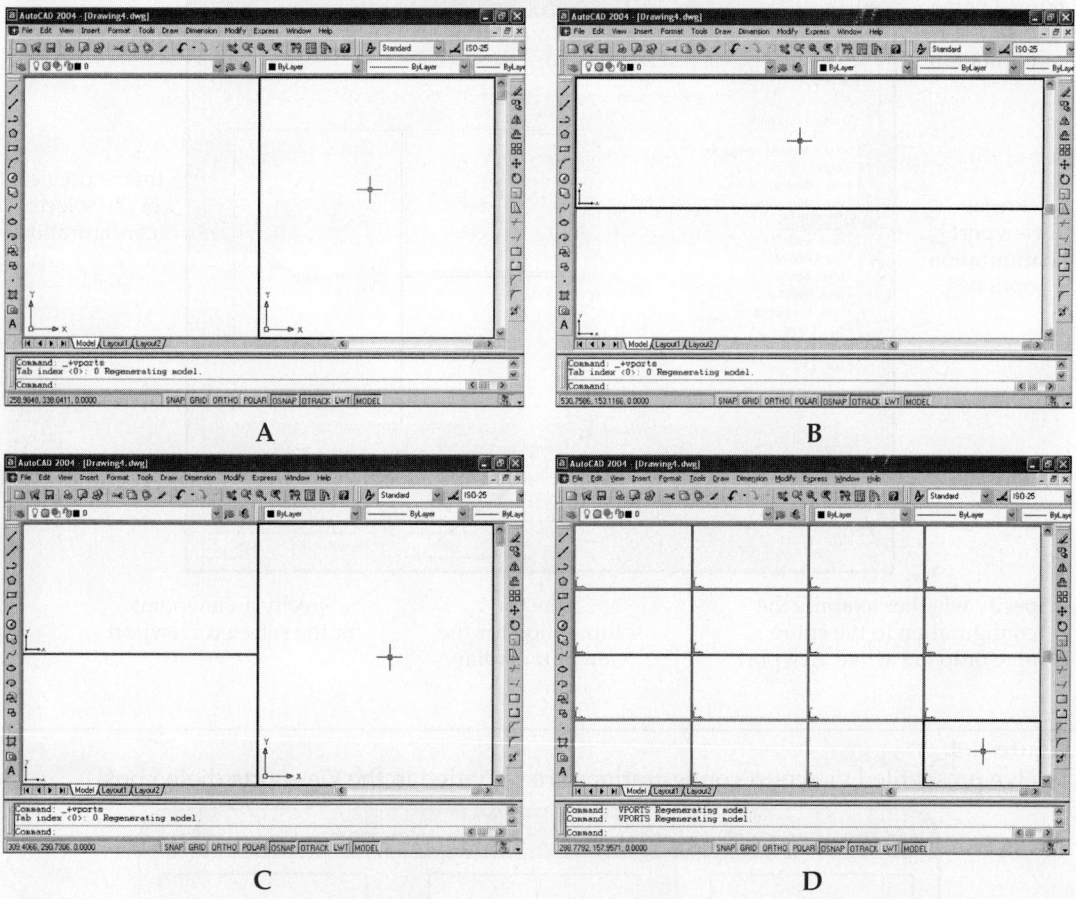

A

B

C

D

**Figure 4-2.**
Viewport configuration options can be selected from the **Viewports** cascading menu in the **View** pull-down menu.

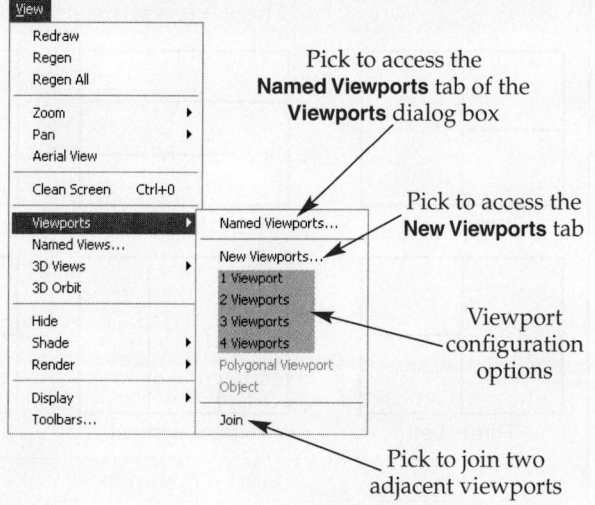

**Figure 4-3.**
Viewports are created using the **New Viewports** tab of the **Viewports** dialog box.

Enter a name to save a configuration

Preset viewport configuration options

Image preview of the selected configuration

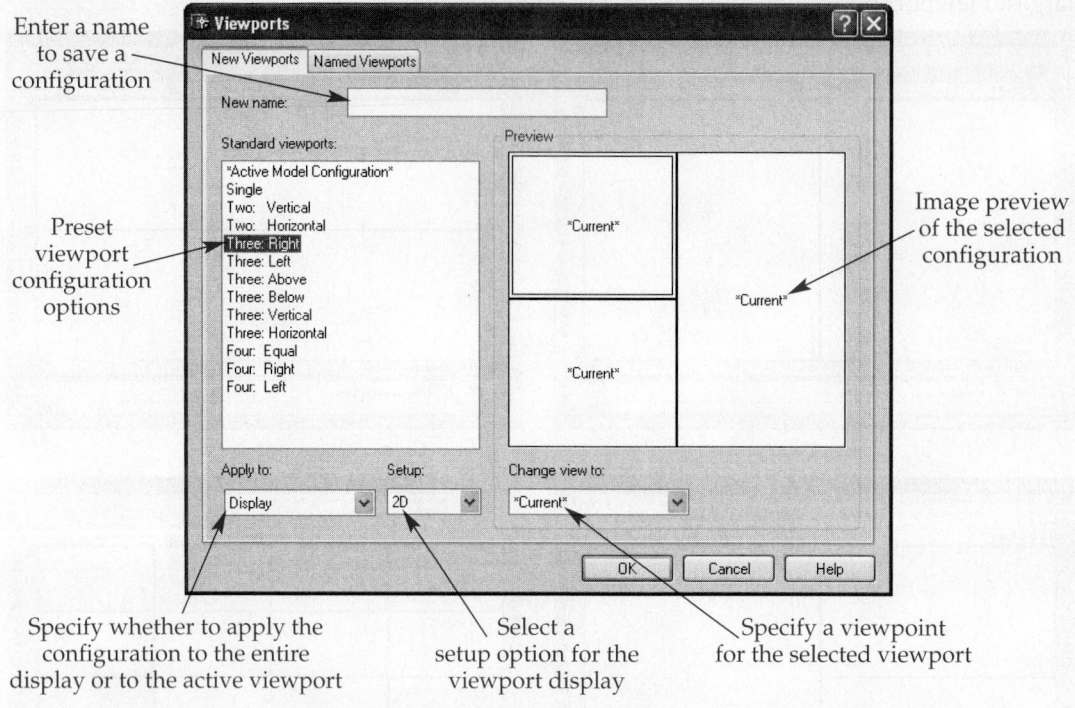

Specify whether to apply the configuration to the entire display or to the active viewport

Select a setup option for the viewport display

Specify a viewpoint for the selected viewport

**Figure 4-4.**
Twelve preset tiled viewport configurations are provided in the **Viewports** dialog box.

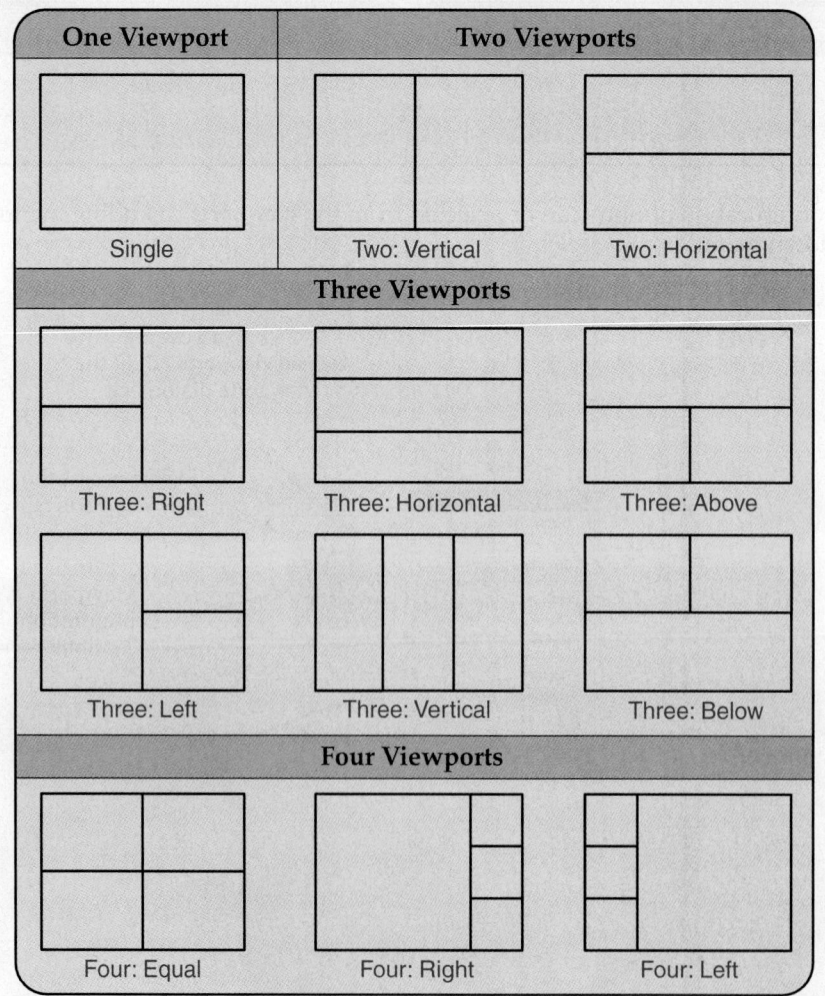

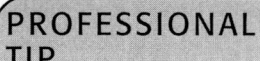

## Making a Viewport Active

After a viewport configuration has been created, a thick line surrounds the active viewport. When the screen cursor is moved inside the active viewport, it appears as crosshairs. When moved into an inactive viewport, the screen cursor becomes an arrow.

Any viewport can be made active by moving the cursor into the desired viewport and pressing the pick button. You can also press the [Ctrl]+[R] key combination to switch viewports, or use the **CVPORT** (current viewport) system variable. Only one viewport can be active at a time.

Command: **CVPORT**↵
Enter new value for CVPORT <*current*>: **3.**↵
Command:

The current value given is the ID number of the active viewport. The ID number is automatically assigned by AutoCAD. To change viewports with the **CVPORT** system variable, simply enter a different ID number. Using the **CVPORT** system variable is also a good way to determine the ID number of a viewport. The number 1 is not a valid viewport ID number.

## Managing Defined Viewports

If you are working with several different viewport configurations, it is easy to restore, rename, or delete existing viewports. You can do so using the **Viewports** dialog box. To access a list of named viewports, open the dialog box and select the **Named Viewports** tab. See **Figure 4-5**. This tab can be displayed automatically by picking **Named Viewports...** from the **Viewports** cascading menu in the **View** pull-down menu. To display a viewport configuration, highlight any of the names in the **Named viewports:** list and then pick **OK**.

Assume you have saved the current viewport configuration. Now, you want to work in a specific viewport, but do not need other viewports displayed on screen. First, pick the viewport you wish to work in to make it active. Open the **Viewports** dialog box, pick the **New Viewports** tab, and then pick **Single**. The **Preview** area displays the single viewport. Pick **OK** to exit. The active viewport you selected is displayed on screen. To restore the original viewport configuration, redisplay the **Viewports** dialog box, pick the **Named Viewports** tab, and then select the name of the saved viewport configuration. The **Preview** area displays the selected viewport. Pick **OK** to exit.

**Figure 4-5.**
The **Named Viewports** tab of the **Viewports** dialog box lists all named viewports and displays the selected configuration in the **Preview** area.

Select a named viewport to display

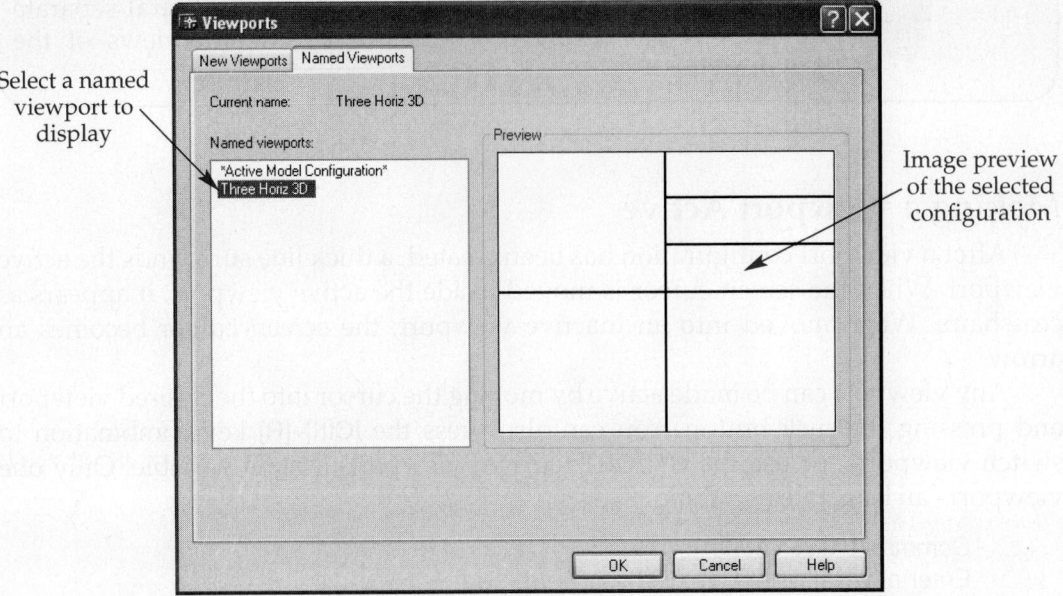

Image preview of the selected configuration

Viewports can also be renamed and deleted using the **Named Viewports** tab of the **Viewports** dialog box. To rename a viewport, right-click on the viewport name and pick **Rename** from the shortcut menu. You can also single-click on a highlighted name. When the name becomes highlighted text, type the new name and press [Enter]. To delete a viewport configuration, right-click on the viewport name and pick **Delete** from the shortcut menu. You can also press the [Delete] key to delete the highlighted viewport. Press **OK** to exit the dialog box.

---

**PROFESSIONAL TIP**

The **-VPORT** command can be used to manage viewports on the command line. This may be required for some LISP programs where the dialog box cannot be used. AutoLISP is covered later in this text.

---

## Using the Viewports Toolbar

The **Viewports** toolbar, shown in **Figure 4-6,** is used with both model space and paper space viewports. As discussed earlier, the **Display Viewports Dialog** button on the toolbar displays the **Viewports** dialog box. The **Single Viewport** button allows you to create a single-viewport configuration of the active viewport. The remaining three buttons and the drop-down list apply to paper space viewports in a layout. Complete discussions of paper space viewports are given in Chapters 9, 10, and 24 of *AutoCAD and its Applications—Basics.*

**Figure 4-6.**
The **Viewports** toolbar.

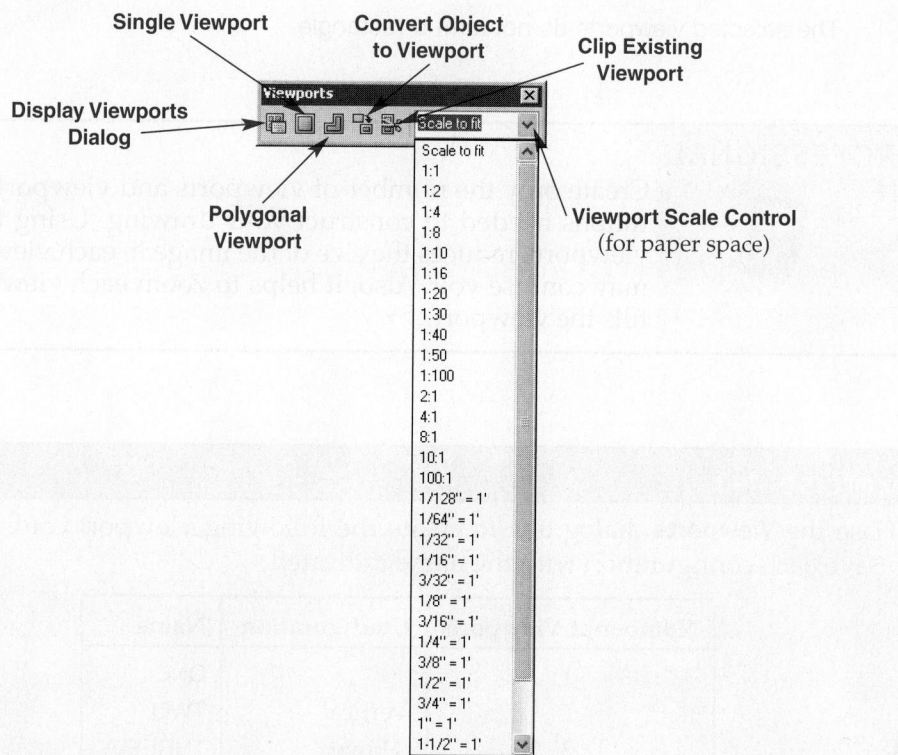

## Joining Two Viewports

You can join two adjacent viewports in an existing configuration to form a single viewport. This process is quicker than creating an entirely new configuration. However, the two viewports must form a rectangle when joined, **Figure 4-7.** You can join viewports by selecting **Join** from the **Viewports** cascading menu in the **View** pull-down menu.

When you enter the **Join** option, AutoCAD first prompts you for the *dominant viewport.* All aspects of the dominant viewport are used in the new (joined) viewport. These aspects include the limits, grid, UCS, and snap settings.

> Select dominant viewport <current viewport>: *(select the viewport or press* [Enter] *to set the current viewport at the dominant viewport)*
> Select viewport to join: *(select the other viewport)*
> Regenerating model.
> Command:

**Figure 4-7.**
Two viewports can be joined if they will form a rectangle. If the two viewports will not form a rectangle, they cannot be joined.

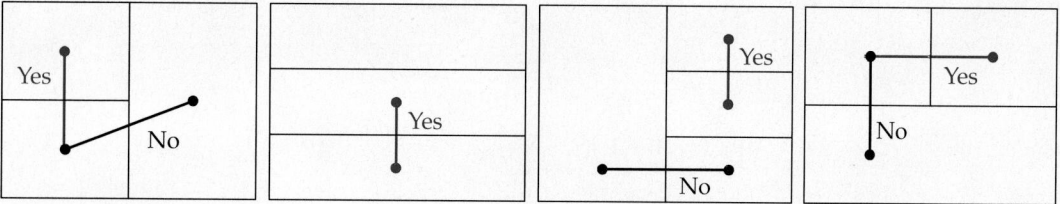

The two viewports selected are joined into a single viewport. If you select two viewports that do not form a rectangle, AutoCAD returns the message:

The selected viewports do not form a rectangle.

PROFESSIONAL TIP

Create only the number of viewports and viewport configurations needed to construct your drawing. Using too many viewports reduces the size of the image in each viewport and may confuse you. Also, it helps to zoom each view so that it fills the viewport.

### Exercise 4-1

○ Use the **Viewports** dialog box to create the following viewport configurations. Save each configuration with the name indicated.

| Number of Viewports | Configuration | Name |
|---|---|---|
| 1 | | ONE |
| 2 | Vertical | TWO |
| 3 | Above | THREE-A |
| 3 | Left | THREE-L |
| 3 | Right | THREE-R |
| 4 | Equal | FOUR |

○ Verify in the **Named Viewports** tab of the **Viewports** dialog box that each configuration was saved.
○ Restore each named configuration, one at a time.
○ Restore configuration THREE-A and join the two small viewports. Save the new configuration under the name TWO. Confirm you want to save when asked if you wish to replace the existing configuration named TWO.
○ Delete configuration THREE-A.
○ Restore configuration THREE-L. Set the grid and snap spacing in each viewport to different values. Save the configuration as THREE-L.
○ Change the display to a single viewport.
○ Restore configuration THREE-L. Check the drawing aids in each viewport to be sure they have the same values previously set.
○ Save the drawing as EX4-1.

AutoCAD and its Applications—Advanced

# Applying Viewports to Existing Configurations and Displaying Different Views

You have total control over what is displayed in model space viewports. In addition to displaying various viewport configurations, you can divide an existing viewport into additional viewports or assign a different viewpoint to each viewport. The options for these functions are provided in the **New Viewports** tab of the **Viewports** dialog box. Refer to the options located along the bottom of the dialog box in **Figure 4-3.**

- **Apply to.** When a preset viewport configuration is selected from the **Standard viewports:** list, it can be applied to either the entire display or the current viewport. The previous examples have shown how to create viewports that replace the entire display. Applying a configuration to the active viewport rather than the entire display can be useful when you need to display additional viewports. For example, first create a configuration of three viewports using the **Right** configuration option. With the right viewport active, open the **Viewports** dialog box again. Notice that the drop-down list under **Apply to:** is grayed-out. Now, pick one of the standard configurations. This enables the **Apply to:** drop-down list. The default option is **Display**, which means the selected viewport configuration will replace the current display. Pick the drop-down list arrow to reveal the second option, **Current Viewport**. Pick this option and then pick **OK**. Notice that the selected viewport configuration has been applied to only the active (right) viewport. See **Figure 4-8.**

- **Setup.** Viewports can be set up to display views in 2D or 3D. The **2D** and **3D** options are provided in the **Setup:** drop-down list. Displaying different views while working on a drawing allows you to see the results of your work on each view, since changes are reflected in each viewport as you draw. The viewport setup option controls the types of views available in the **Change view to:** drop-down list.

- **Change view to.** The views that can be displayed in a selected viewport are listed in the **Change view to:** drop-down list. If the **Setup:** drop-down list is set to **2D**, the views available to be displayed are limited to the current view and any named views. If **3D** is active, the options include all of the standard orthographic and isometric views along with named views. When an orthographic or isometric view is selected for a viewport, the resulting orientation is shown

**Figure 4-8.**
The selected viewport configuration has been applied to the active viewport within the original configuration.

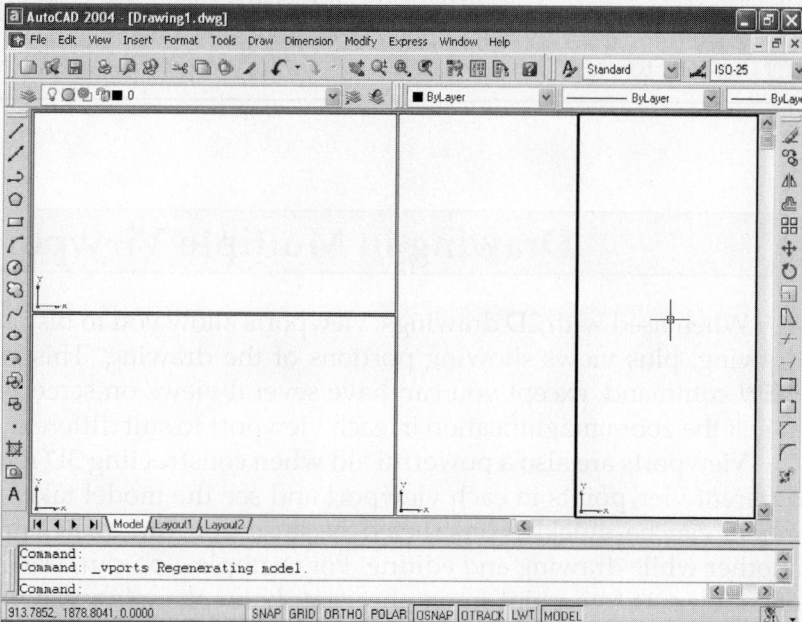

in the **Preview** area. To assign a different viewpoint to a viewport, simply pick within a viewport in the **Preview** area to make it active, and then pick a viewpoint from the **Change view to:** drop-down list. Important: If you set the viewport to one of the orthographic preset views, the UCS is also changed to the corresponding preset in that viewport.

**PROFESSIONAL TIP**

Displaying saved viewport configurations can be automated by using custom menus. Custom menus are easy to create. If a standard naming convention is used, these named configurations can be saved with template drawings. This creates a consistent platform that all students or employees can use.

---

### Exercise 4-2

○ Open the drawing named Oil Module in the AutoCAD **Sample** folder. Note: This is a large model and commands may take a few seconds to initiate.

○ Zoom in on the ladder in the middle of the model. Use the **VIEW** command to create a new view named Ladder. Zoom in on the green valve assembly just to the left of the ladder. Create a new view named Valve Ass'y.

○ Use the **Viewports** dialog box to create an arrangement of three viewports, with the largest on the right. Pick inside the large viewport to make it current.

○ Open the **Viewports** dialog box again and select an arrangement of two horizontal viewports. In the **Apply to:** drop-down list, pick **Current Viewport**. Pick **OK** to exit the dialog box and view the results.

○ In the **Viewports** dialog box, pick **3D** from the **Setup:** drop-down list. Then use the **Change view to:** drop-down list to set the following views in the four viewports:

| Viewport | View |
|---|---|
| Upper-left | Top |
| Lower-left | Southwest isometric |
| Upper-right | Named view Ladder |
| Lower-right | Named view Valve Ass'y |

○ Pick **OK** to view the results. Close the drawing without saving.

---

## Drawing in Multiple Viewports

When used with 2D drawings, viewports allow you to display a view of the entire drawing, plus views showing portions of the drawing. This is similar to using the **VIEW** command, except you can have several views on screen at once. You can also adjust the zoom magnification in each viewport to suit different areas of the drawing.

Viewports are also a powerful aid when constructing 3D models. You can specify different viewpoints in each viewport and see the model take shape as you draw. A model can be quickly constructed because you can switch from one viewport to another while drawing and editing. For example, you can draw a line from a point in one viewport to a point in another simply by changing viewports while inside the **LINE** command. The result is shown in each viewport.

**Figure 4-9.**
You will construct the object from Chapter 3 using multiple viewports.

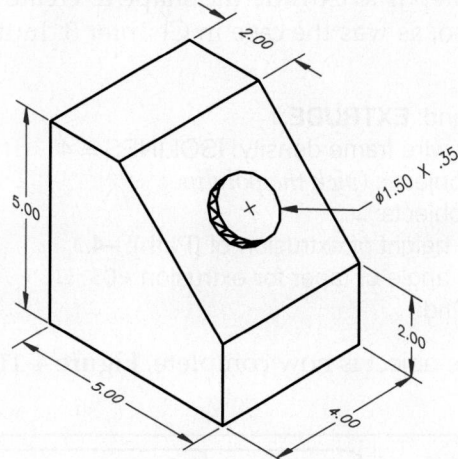

In Chapter 3, you constructed a solid object. It was a base that had an angled surface from which a cylinder projected. See **Figure 4-9.** Now, you will construct the object using two viewports. First, create a vertical configuration of two viewports. In the **Viewports** dialog box, set the right-hand viewport to display the southeast isometric. Set the left-hand viewport to display the front view. Close the dialog box and make the left-hand viewport active. Then, use the following command sequence.

```
Command: PL↵
Specify start point: 5,2↵
Current line-width is 0.0000
Specify next point or [arc/Halfwidth/Length/Undo/Width]: 5,0.↵
Specify next point or [arc/Halfwidth/Length/Undo/Width]: 0,0.↵
Specify next point or [arc/Halfwidth/Length/Undo/Width]: 0,5.↵
Specify next point or [arc/Halfwidth/Length/Undo/Width]: 2,5.↵
Specify next point or [arc/Halfwidth/Length/Undo/Width]: C.↵
Command:
```

As you construct the side view, you can clearly see the true size and shape of the side view in the left-hand viewport. At the same time, you can see the construction in 3D in the right-hand viewport, **Figure 4-10.**

**Figure 4-10.**
The screen is divided into two viewports. A side view of the object appears in the left-hand viewport and a 3D view appears in the right-hand viewport. Notice the UCS icons.

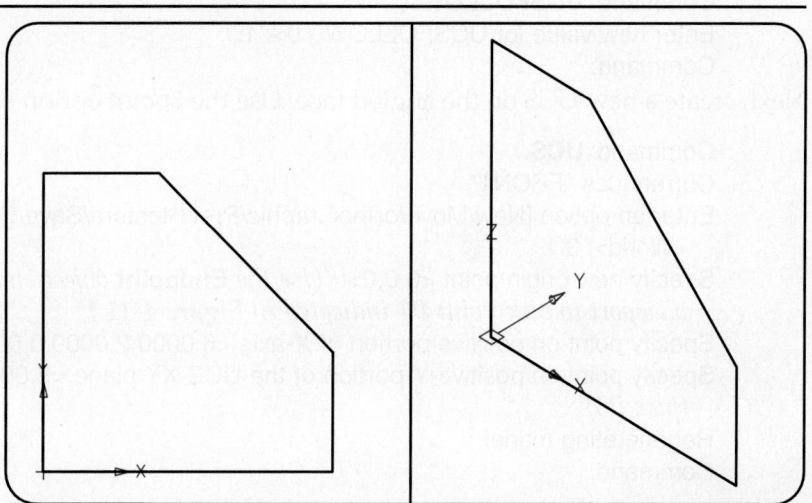

The next step is to extrude the shape to create the base. The **EXTRUDE** command is used to do so, as was the case in Chapter 3. In the left-hand viewport, continue as follows.

Command: **EXTRUDE**↵
Current wire frame density: ISOLINES = 4
Select objects: *(pick the polyline)*
Select objects: ↵
Specify height of extrusion of [Path]: **–4**↵
Specify angle of taper for extrusion <0>: ↵
Command:

The base of the object is now complete, **Figure 4-11.**

**Figure 4-11.**
The base of the object is now complete. A new UCS needs to be created based on the pick points shown here.

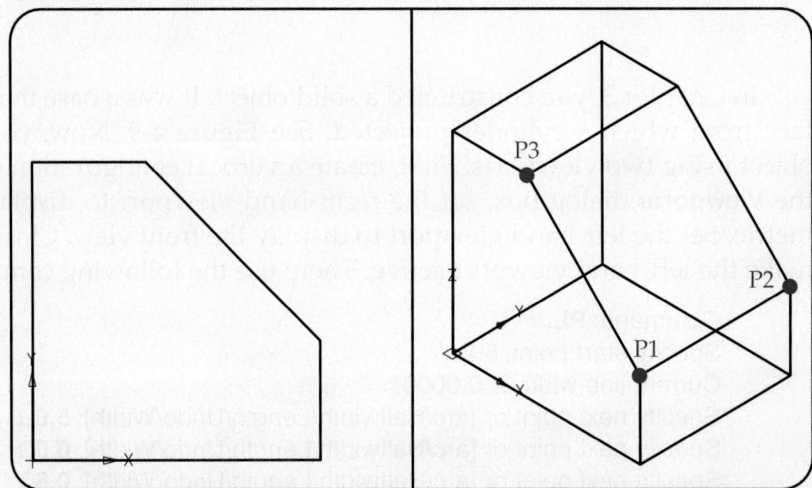

Now, the cylinder needs to be created on the angled face. First, split the left-hand viewport into two horizontal viewports using the **New Viewports** tab of the **Viewports** dialog box. Set both of the new viewports to display the current view. Pick **OK** to close the dialog box. Then, make the upper-left viewport current and set it up to always display a plan view of the current UCS:

Command: **UCSFOLLOW**↵
Enter new value for UCSFOLLOW <0>: **1**↵
Command:

Next, create a new UCS on the angled face. Use the **3point** option of the **UCS** command:

Command: **UCS**↵
Current ucs *FRONT*
Enter an option [New/Move/orthoGraphic/Prev/Restore/Save/Del/Apply/?/World]
   <World>: **3**↵
Specify new origin point <0,0,0>: *(Use the **Endpoint** object snap in the right-hand viewport to pick Point P1 indicated in Figure 4-11.)*
Specify point on positive portion of X-axis <6.0000,2.0000,0.0000>: *(pick P2)*
Specify point on positive-Y portion of the UCS XY plane <5.0000,3.0000,0.0000>:
   *(pick P3)*
Regenerating model.
Command:

Notice how the view in the upper-left viewport automatically changed to a plan view of the new current UCS. Now, set the **Midpoint** object snap and turn on AutoTracking to draw the cylinder. Work in the right-hand viewport.

Command: **CYLINDER.**↵
Specify center point for base of cylinder or [Elliptical] <0,0,0>: *(acquire the midpoint of one side of the angled surface)*
*(acquire the midpoint of the perpendicular side of the angled surface)*
Specify radius for base of cylinder or [Diameter]: **.75.**↵
Specify height of cylinder or [Center of other end]: **.35.**↵
Command:

The object is now complete, **Figure 4-12.** Notice how the lower-left and right-hand viewports have different UCSs. Each viewport can have its own UCS. The view in the upper-left viewport is the plan view of the current UCS. If the lower-left viewport is made active, the plan view will be of the UCS in that viewport. The UCS orientation in one viewport is not affected by a change to the UCS in another viewport. If a viewport arrangement is saved with several different UCS configurations, every named UCS remains intact and is displayed when the viewport configuration is restored.

**Figure 4-12.**
The cylinder is drawn to complete the object. Notice the plan view in the upper-left viewport.

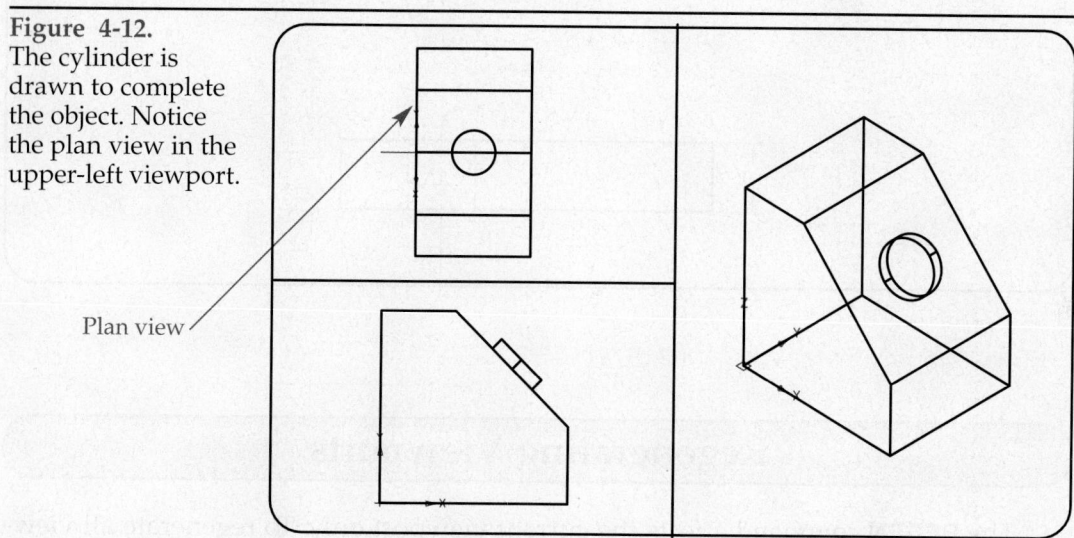

Plan view

---

 **NOTE**

The UCS configuration in each viewport is controlled by the **UCSVP** system variable. When **UCSVP** is set to 1 in a viewport, the UCS is independent from all other UCSs, which is the default. If **UCSVP** is set to 0 in a viewport, its UCS will change to reflect any changes to the UCS in the current viewport.

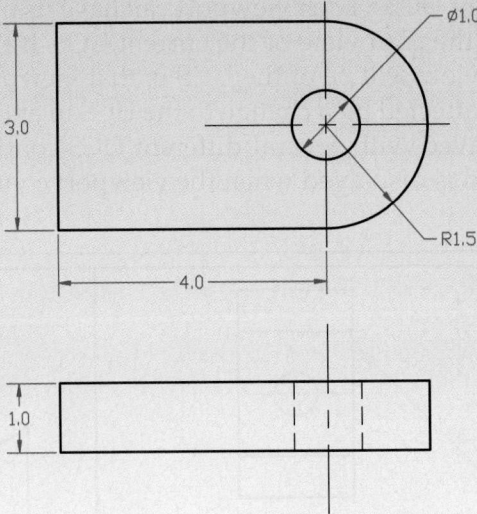
## Regenerating Viewports

The **REGEN** command affects the current viewport only. To regenerate all viewports at the same time, use the **REGENALL** command. This command can be entered by selecting **Regen All** from the **View** pull-down menu or entering REGENALL at the Command: prompt.

The Quick Text mode is controlled by the **REGEN** command. Therefore, if you are working with text displayed with the Quick Text mode in viewports, be sure to use the **REGENALL** command in order for the text to be regenerated in all viewports.

## Creating a Standard Engineering Layout

Often, objects created with 3D modeling techniques need to be transferred to 2D paper plots. A *standard engineering layout* is a layout of a 3D object that includes three orthographic views and an isometric view. An experienced print reader can use the views in the standard engineering layout to visualize the 3D object.

A simple 3D model is shown in **Figure 4-13.** To create the orthographic and isometric views needed to fully describe this object in a two-dimensional plot, you can access a layout tab (paper space) and create several floating viewports. Then, set the correct viewpoint in each viewport and scale the model. However, this process can be done much more easily using the **Create Layout** wizard. The following basic procedure is described more thoroughly in the text below.

1. Create the 3D model.
2. Start the **Create Layout** wizard.

Figure 4-13.
A simple 3D model
displayed in model
space (**Model** tab).

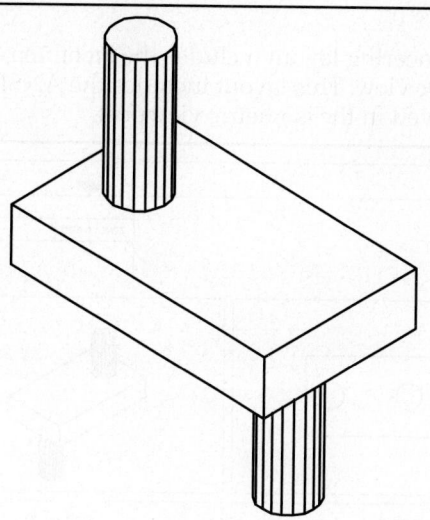

3. Select a title block.
4. Select the standard engineering viewport configuration.

The first step is to create the 3D model. This is done in model space (**Model** tab). When the model is complete, access the **Create Layout** wizard by selecting **Create Layout...** from the **Wizards** cascading menu in the **Tools** pull-down menu. The wizard steps through requests for a name of the layout, the plotter associated with the layout, the paper size, the paper orientation, and title block to include in the layout.

After you select a title block, the wizard asks you to define viewports. In the **Viewport Setup** area of the wizard panel, pick the **Std. 3D Engineering Views** radio button. See **Figure 4-14.** Once you select a viewport setup, you can adjust the spacing between viewports using the text boxes at the lower-right of the panel. You can also specify the scale factor for the viewports using the drop-down list at the upper-right of the panel. When all settings are made, pick the **Next>** button to continue.

The next panel requests the location for the layout in the drawing. After you specify the location, pick the **Next>** button to continue. The final panel gives you a message indicating that you have created a layout and the name of the layout. Pick the **Finish** button to complete the process. A standard engineering layout for the object shown in **Figure 4-13** appears in **Figure 4-15.**

Tools
➥ Wizards
　➥ Create
　　 Layout...

Figure 4-14.
Creating a standard
engineering layout
using the **Create
Layout** wizard.

Select a setup　　Specify a scale　　Adjust the spacing between viewports

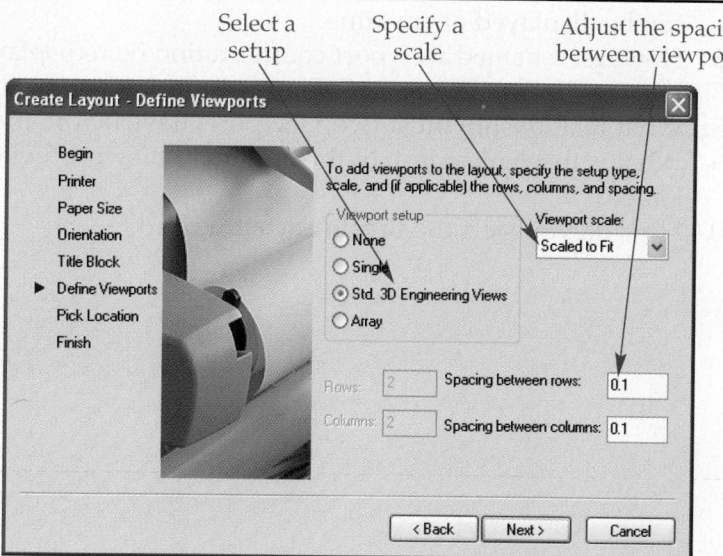

**Figure 4-15.**
A standard engineering layout includes the Front, Top, and Right orthographic views along with an isometric view. This layout includes the ANSI A-size title block and hidden lines have been removed in the isometric viewport.

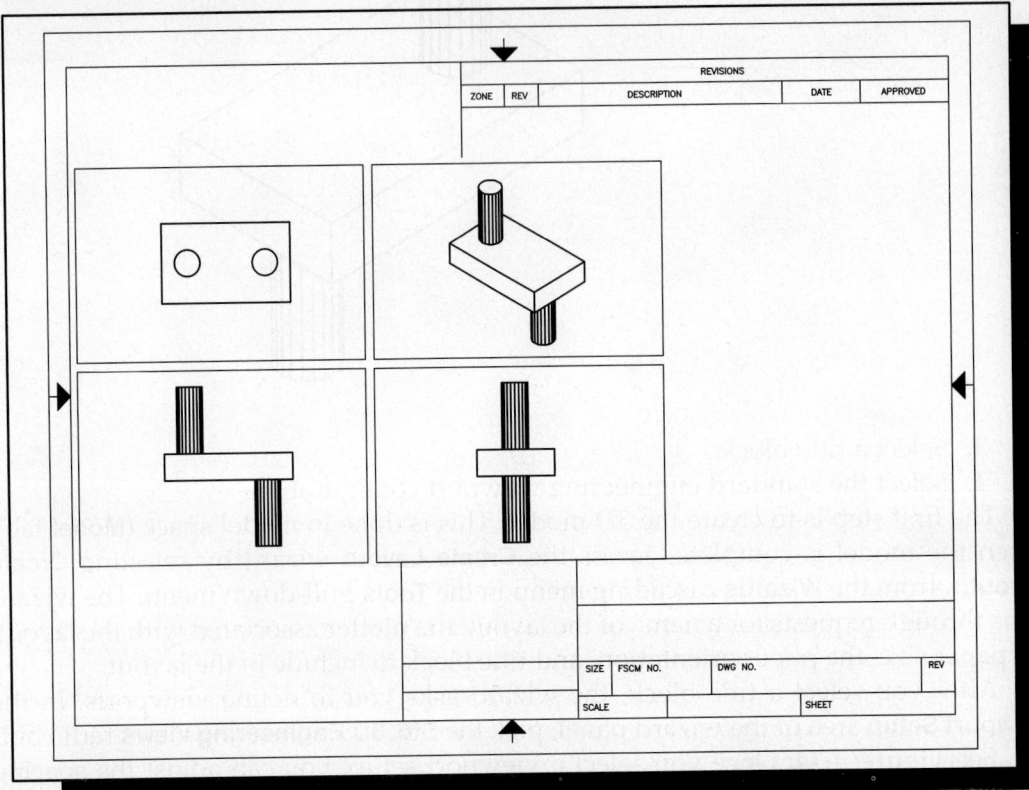

## Chapter Test

*Answer the following questions on a separate sheet of paper.*

1. What is the purpose of *viewports*?
2. How do you name a configuration of viewports?
3. What is the purpose of saving a configuration of viewports?
4. Explain the difference between *tiled* and *floating* viewports.
5. Name the system variable controlling the maximum number of viewports that can be displayed at one time.
6. How can a named viewport configuration be redisplayed on screen?
7. How can a list of named viewport configurations be displayed?
8. What relationship must two viewports have before they can be joined?
9. What is the significance of the dominant viewport when two viewports are joined?
10. How do you start the **Create Layout** wizard?

## Drawing Problems

1. Construct seven template drawings, each with a preset viewport configuration. Use the following configurations and names. Save the templates under the same name as the viewport configuration.

| Number of Viewports | Configuration | Name |
|:---:|:---:|:---:|
| 2 | Horizontal | TWO-H |
| 2 | Vertical | TWO-V |
| 3 | Right | THREE-R |
| 3 | Left | THREE-L |
| 3 | Above | THREE-A |
| 3 | Below | THREE-B |
| 3 | Vertical | THREE-V |

2. Construct one of the problems from Chapter 3 using viewports. Use one of your template drawings from Problem 4-1. Save the drawing as P4-2.

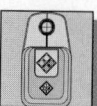

The seven **SHADEMODE** options are shown here on the drawing from the solid modeling tutorial in Appendix A. A—**2D wireframe**. B—**3D wireframe**. C—**Hidden**. D—**Flat**. E—**Gouraud**. F—**fLat+edges**. G—**gOuraud+edges**.

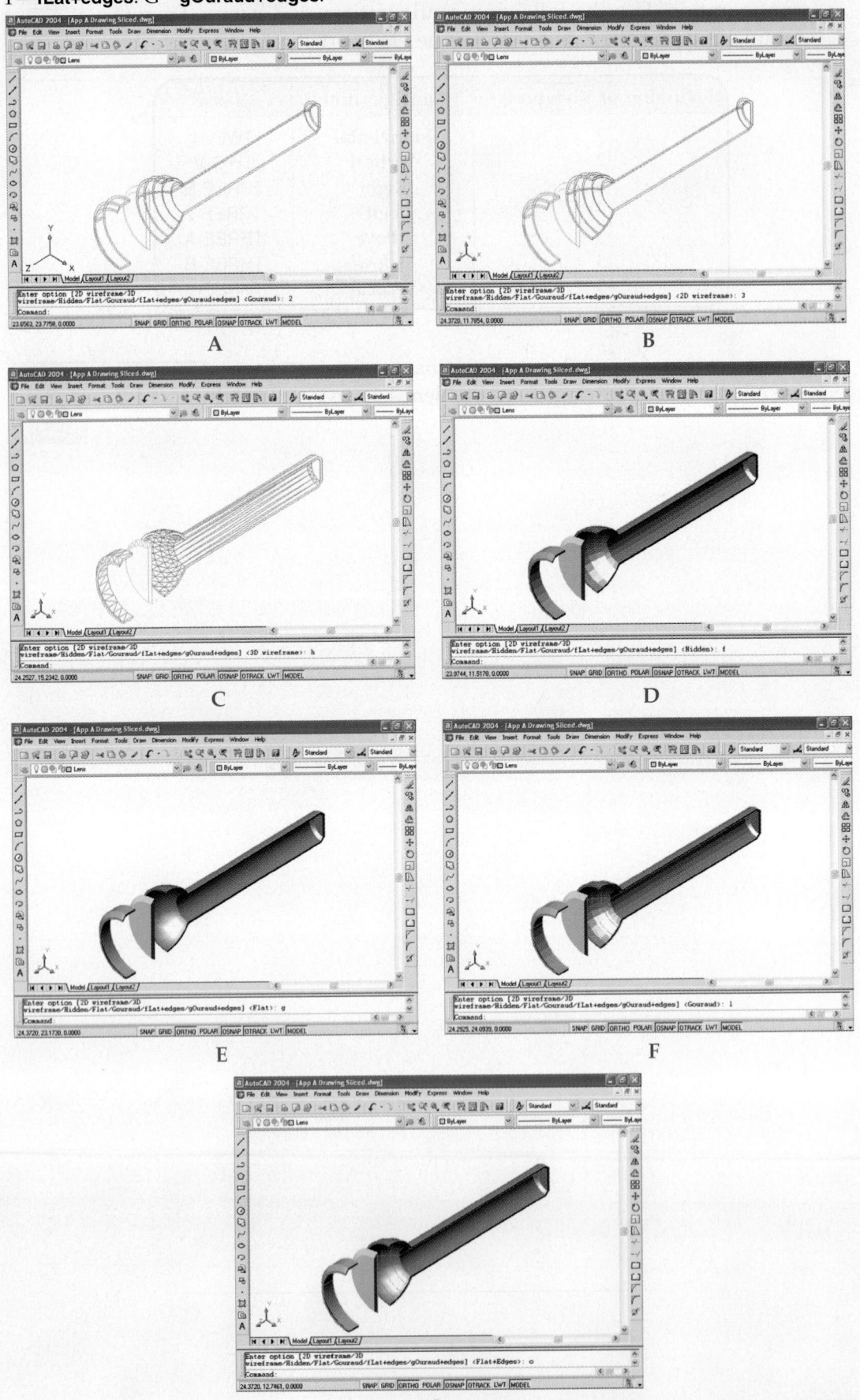

AutoCAD and its Applications—Advanced

## CHAPTER 5

# Viewing and Displaying Three-Dimensional Models

## Learning Objectives

After completing this chapter, you will be able to:
- Use the **3DORBIT** command to dynamically rotate the display of a 3D model.
- Use the **SHADEMODE** command options to create shading variations.
- Render a 3D model.
- Render selected parts of a 3D model.

There are two basic ways to select a pictorial (3D) viewpoint for 3D models. These are the preset isometric viewpoints and the **3DORBIT** command. The preset isometric viewpoints are discussed in detail in Chapter 1. The **3DORBIT** command is introduced in Chapter 1 and discussed in detail in this chapter. It enables you to rotate, pan, and zoom a 3D model while it is fully shaded. This provides a powerful design tool when working in 3D. In addition, you can display a continuously rotating model set in motion by just the movement of the mouse. This is ideal for design, demonstrations, and training.

Once a viewpoint has been selected, you can enhance the display in several ways, such as panning and zooming. You can use the **HIDE** command to temporarily remove hidden lines. This command is discussed in Chapter 1 and used in previous chapters. You can also use the **SHADEMODE** command to create a shaded display, or simple rendering, of the model. A more advanced rendering can be created with the **RENDER** command. It produces the most realistic image with highlights, shading, and materials, if applied. **Figure 5-1** shows a 3D model of a cast iron plumbing cleanout after using **HIDE**, **SHADEMODE**, and **RENDER**. Notice how different the three displays are.

> **PROFESSIONAL TIP**
>
> In addition to **3DORBIT**, AutoCAD has two other commands for displaying pictorial views—**DVIEW** and **VPOINT**. The functionalities of these commands have been replaced by the more useful **3DORBIT** command.

**Figure 5-1.**
A—Hidden display (hidden lines removed). B—Shaded. C—Rendered with materials and lights.

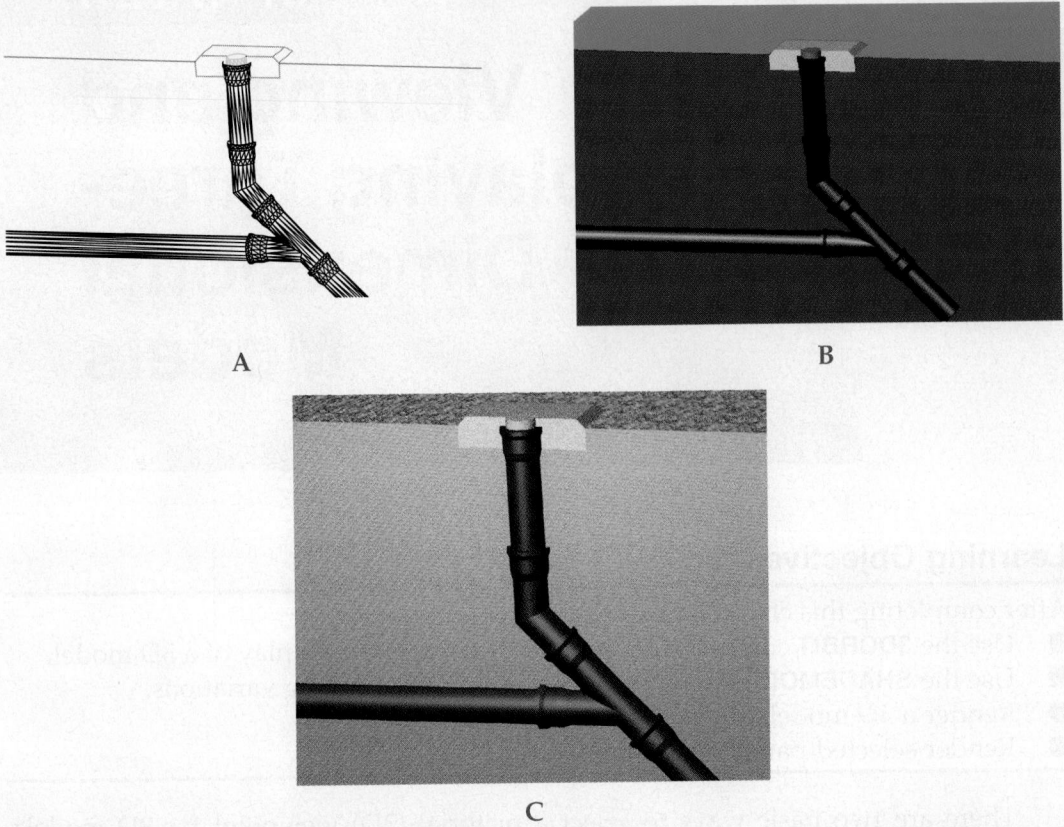

A

B

C

# PLAN Command Options

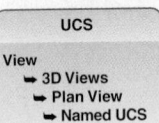

PLAN

View
→ 3D Views
   → Plan View
      → Current UCS

UCS

View
→ 3D Views
   → Plan View
      → Named UCS

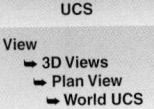

UCS

View
→ 3D Views
   → Plan View
      → World UCS

You can quickly create a plan view of any UCS or the WCS using the **PLAN** command, which was introduced in Chapter 1. This command can be accessed by picking **Plan View** from the **3D Views** cascading menu in the **View** pull-down menu. Then, select the appropriate option in the cascading menu. You can also type PLAN at the Command: prompt. The command options are:

- **Current UCS.** This creates a view of the object that is plan to the current UCS.
- **World UCS.** This creates a view of the object that is plan to the WCS. If the WCS is the current UCS, this option and the **Current UCS** option produce the same results.
- **Named UCS.** This displays a view plan to a named UCS. The preset UCSs are not considered named UCSs. This option is **UCS** on the command line.

The **PLAN** command automatically performs a **ZOOM Extents**. This fills the graphics window with the plan view.

# Dynamically Changing a 3D View

The **3DORBIT** command is a powerful and easy-to-use command for creating pictorial views of a 3D object. It allows you to dynamically rotate the view of a 3D object in real time. In addition, the model can be displayed in wireframe, hidden, or shaded display as the view is rotated.

The **3DORBIT** command was introduced in Chapter 1. To initiate the command, pick **3D Orbit** on the **3D Orbit** toolbar, select **3D Orbit** from the **View** pull-down menu, or type 3DO or 3DORBIT at the Command: prompt. A green circle is then displayed in the middle of the current viewport. This is called the trackball, or arcball. By dragging inside or outside of the trackball, the view of the object is dynamically changed. When the trackball is displayed, a variety of options are available from the shortcut menu. In addition, you can select many display options using the **3D Orbit** toolbar. See **Figure 5-2.** These options are discussed in the following sections.

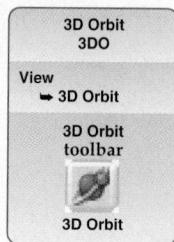

**3D Orbit**
**3DO**

**View**
→ **3D Orbit**

**3D Orbit toolbar**

**3D Orbit**

**Figure 5-2.**
A—**3DORBIT** command options are easily selected using the shortcut menu available when the command is active. B—You can select many of the **3DORBIT** display options using the **3D Orbit** toolbar.

The active display control option is identified with a check

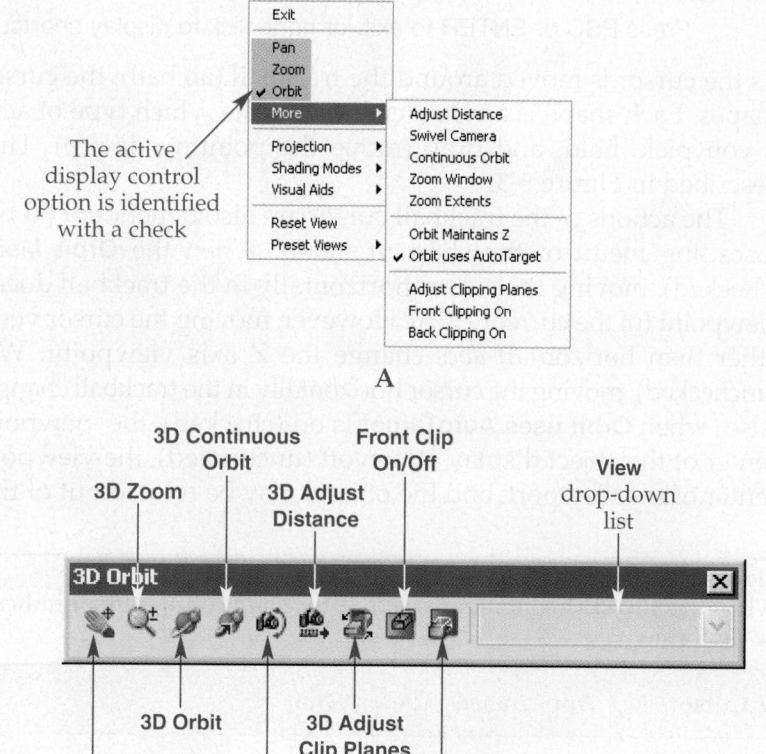

A

3D Continuous Orbit

3D Zoom

Front Clip On/Off

3D Adjust Distance

View drop-down list

3D Orbit

3D Pan

3D Swivel

3D Adjust Clip Planes

Back Clip On/Off

B

---

**PROFESSIONAL TIP**

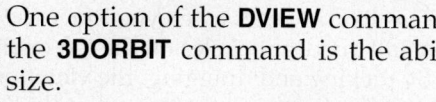

One option of the **DVIEW** command that is *not* available with the **3DORBIT** command is the ability to set the camera lens size.

---

## Basic 3D Orbit Display Controls

Within the **3DORBIT** command, you have the ability to toggle between orbit, realtime pan, and realtime zoom. The shortcut menu displays these options. See **Figure 5-2A**. A check mark appears next to the current setting, with **Orbit** being the default. The realtime pan and zoom cursors are displayed when the respective options are selected. The **Zoom Window** and **Zoom Extents** options can also be selected in the shortcut menu by first picking **More**, then picking the option in the cascading menu.

The **Pan** and **Zoom** functions within the 3D orbit view are actually the **3DPAN** and **3DZOOM** commands. These commands can also be entered outside of the **3DORBIT** command. Type 3DPAN or 3DZOOM at the Command: Prompt or select the **3D Pan** or **3D Zoom** button on the **3D Orbit** toolbar.

## Using the 3D Orbit Cursors

When you enter the **3DORBIT** command, the UCS icon is changed to a shaded 3D UCS icon. If the UCS icon display is turned off, no icon appears. The following prompt is also displayed on the command line when the **3DORBIT** command is active.

Press ESC or ENTER to exit, or right-click to display shortcut-menu.

As the cursor is moved around the trackball (arcball), the cursor takes on one of four shapes. Each shape is a visual cue to indicate which type of action will be performed if you pick, hold, and drag (move the pointing device). These cursor shapes are described in **Figure 5-3**.

The actions of the trackball cursor are also dependent on two settings in the **More** cascading menu of the shortcut menu. When the **Orbit Maintains Z** option is on (checked), moving the cursor horizontally in the trackball does not change the Z axis viewpoint (of the current UCS). However, moving the cursor vertically (or any direction other than horizontal) *does* change the Z axis viewpoint. When this option is off (unchecked), moving the cursor horizontally in the trackball changes the Z axis viewpoint. Also, when **Orbit uses AutoTarget** is on (checked), the viewpoint is rotated about the center of the object display. When off (unchecked), the viewpoint is rotated about the center of the viewport, and the objects may be rotated out of the viewport display.

Figure 5-3.
When the **3DORBIT** command is active, the shape of the cursor indicates which function will be performed.

| Cursor | Appearance | Description |
|--------|-----------|-------------|
| Two ellipses |  | This icon appears when you move the cursor inside the trackball. When you pick and drag, the viewpoint can be moved in any direction—horizontally, vertically, and diagonally. |
| Circular arrow |  | The circular arrow icon appears when the cursor is moved outside the trackball. When you pick and drag, the viewport is "rolled" around an axis that projects perpendicular to the screen. |
| Horizontal ellipse |  | This icon appears when you move the cursor into one of the small quadrant circles on the left or right of the trackball. By picking and dragging, the viewpoint can be rotated on an axis of rotation that is vertical in the viewport. |
| Vertical ellipse | 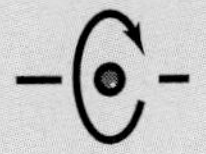 | This icon appears when you move the cursor into one of the small quadrant circles on the top or the bottom of the trackball. By picking and dragging, the viewpoint can be rotated on an axis of rotation that is horizontal in the viewport. |

AutoCAD and its Applications—Advanced

## Projection, Shading, and Visual Aids

Using the **3DORBIT** command, a 3D model can be displayed using a wide variety of options. These include projection methods, such as parallel and perspective; smoothness and edge display of the model; and visual aids such as a spherical compass, grid, and shaded UCS icon. These options are selected in the shortcut menu available after the **3DORBIT** command has been entered. The **Projection**, **Shading Modes**, and **Visual Aids** cascading menus are illustrated in **Figure** 5-4 and described in the following sections.

### Projection

The projection of a pictorial view refers to how lines that recede into the background are treated. Projection of a 3D model can be either parallel or perspective. **Figure** 5-5 shows the difference between a parallel and perspective projection.

In parallel projection, sides of objects project parallel to each other. Axonometric views (isometric, dimetric, and trimetric) are all parallel projections.

In perspective projection, sides of objects project toward one or more vanishing points. In 2D drafting, it is common to represent an object in pictorial as a one- or two-point perspective, especially in architectural drafting. While the **3DORBIT** command is active, you can pan and zoom a perspective view. However, once you exit the command, you cannot pan, zoom, or edit objects. If you wish to edit the object, you must first switch back to parallel projection.

---

Figure 5-4.
The **Projection**,
**Shading Modes**, and
**Visual Aids**
cascading menus in
the **3DORBIT**
shortcut menu.

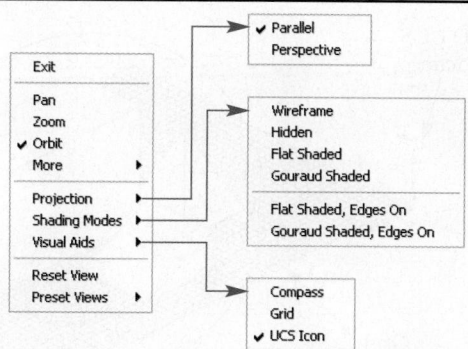

---

**Figure 5-5.**
In a parallel projection, parallel lines remain parallel. In a perspective projection, parallel lines converge to a vanishing point. Notice the three receding lines on the box.

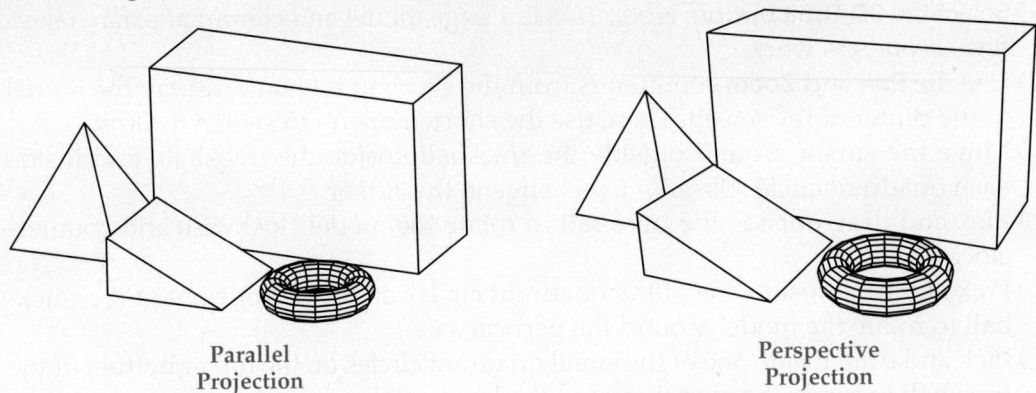

Parallel
Projection

Perspective
Projection

## Shading modes

Six shading options are available. These options are identical to the **SHADEMODE** command options, and are also available in the **Shade** cascading menu of the **View** pull-down menu. These options are described in detail later in this chapter.

## Visual aids

Visual aids help relate the view to the UCS. There are three visual aid options in the **3DORBIT** command. **Figure 5-6** illustrates the following visual aids.

- **Compass.** When on, a spherical 3D compass with the same diameter as the trackball appears. The compass has tick marks and labels indicating the X, Y, and Z axes. The compass can provide a reference for the current UCS. The **COMPASS** system variable controls this display, and is set to 0 if this item is not checked.

- **Grid.** The grid is displayed within the drawing limits when this item is checked. As you zoom in on a drawing, AutoCAD can display up to ten grid lines between major grid lines. As you zoom out, grid lines are deleted in order to maintain a clear view of the object. Every tenth line is a *major grid line*. The grid setting corresponds to the setting in the **Drafting Settings** dialog box.

- **UCS icon.** The shaded 3D UCS icon shows the orientation of the UCS. The X axis is red, Y axis is green, and Z axis is blue. When the UCS icon is on (checked), the UCS icon is displayed. When off (unchecked), the UCS icon is not displayed. The **UCSICON** command also controls the visibility of this icon. The 3D UCS icon is very useful and should be displayed.

**Figure 5-6.**
Visual aids are available in the **3DORBIT** command that can be used to help you visualize the coordinate system.

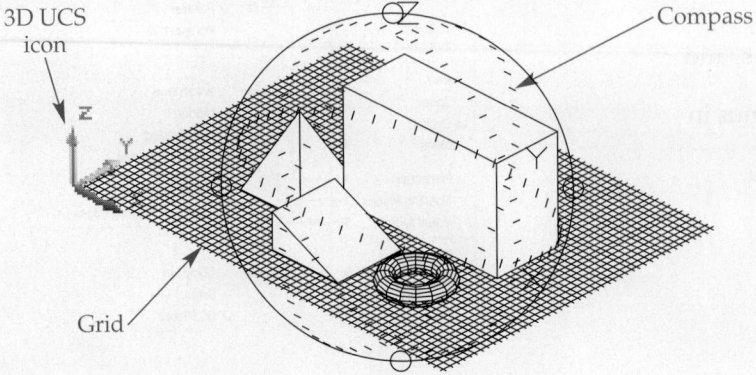

3D UCS
icon

Compass

Grid

## 3DORBIT View Options

The **3DORBIT** command is extremely versatile because you can use a variety of established views to create a display. In addition, you can use the **3DORBIT** command to rotate the viewpoint and then reset the viewpoint to the view that was displayed prior to using the command. The last three items in the 3D orbit view shortcut menu allow you to set views. See **Figure 5-7.**

- **Reset View.** Resets the view that was displayed before **3DORBIT** was invoked. The command remains active.
- **Preset Views.** Displays a list of the six orthographic and four isometric preset viewpoints. The same viewpoints are found in the **3D Views** cascading menu in the **View** pull-down menu. Note: Selecting a preset orthographic view here does *not* change the UCS.
- **Saved Views.** The named views in the drawing are displayed in this cascading menu. This menu item is not displayed if the drawing does not contain named views.

When the **3DORBIT** command is active, the drop-down list in the **3D Orbit** toolbar displays all preset and named views. See **Figure 5-8.** Simply select a view from this list to display it.

Figure 5-7.
Saved and preset views can be accessed from the **3DORBIT** shortcut menu.

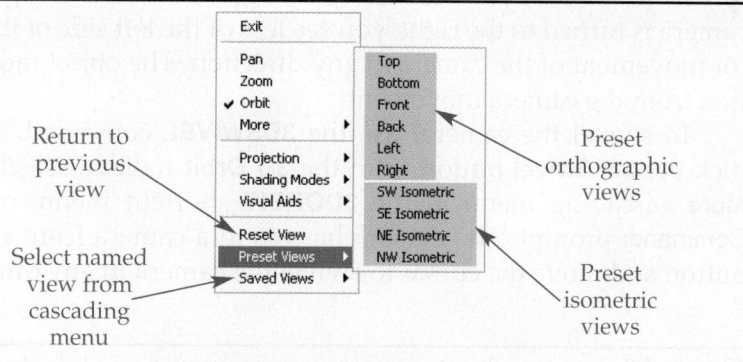

Figure 5-8.
When the **3DORBIT** command is active, the drop-down list in the **3D Orbit** toolbar displays all preset and named views.

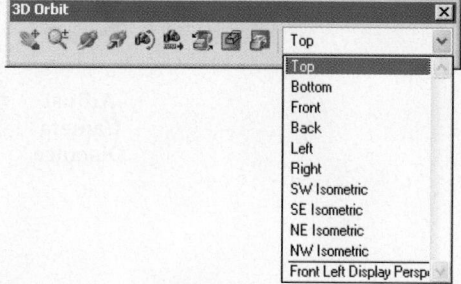

## 3DORBIT Camera Settings

Two **3DORBIT** command options enable you to change the 3D display based on functions of a camera. The distance between camera and object can be adjusted, as well as the amount the camera is "swiveled" on a tripod. These options can be selected from the **3DORBIT** shortcut menu, the **3D Orbit** toolbar, or typed at the keyboard.

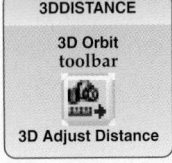

3DDISTANCE
3D Orbit toolbar
3D Adjust Distance

The distance between the viewer and the object can be set by adjusting the camera distance using the **3DDISTANCE** command. To access this command, pick the **3D Adjust Distance** button on the **3D Orbit** toolbar, select **Adjust Distance** from the **More** cascading menu in the **3DORBIT** shortcut menu, or type 3DDISTANCE at the Command: prompt. The cursor changes to arrows pointing up and down, **Figure 5-9.** Hold the pick button and move the cursor up to get closer to the object, or move it down to increase the camera distance from the object. Be warned, however, that this can distort the objects in the display.

In addition to adjusting the camera distance, you can also change the view by swiveling the camera. Imagine that the camera is on a tripod. When the camera is turned to the left, you see less of the right side of the object. Conversely, when the camera is turned to the right, you see less of the left side of the object. The same is true for movement of the camera in any direction. The object moves in the opposite direction from the camera movement.

3DSWIVEL
3D Orbit toolbar
3D Swivel

To swivel the camera, use the **3DSWIVEL** command. To access this command, pick the **3D Swivel** button from the **3D Orbit** toolbar, select **Swivel Camera** from the **More** cascading menu in the **3DORBIT** shortcut menu, or type 3DSWIVEL at the Command: prompt. The cursor changes to a camera icon, **Figure 5-9.** Hold the pick button and move the cursor to swivel the camera in any direction.

Figure 5-9.
These cursors appear when you adjust the camera distance or swivel the camera.

Adjust
Camera
Distance

Swivel
Camera

**PROFESSIONAL TIP**

When in the **3DDISTANCE** or **3DSWIVEL** command, you have access to the **3DORBIT** shortcut menu, even if the command was not entered from within the **3DORBIT** command.

**Exercise 5-4**

○ Open the Oil Module drawing from the AutoCAD Sample folder.
○ Execute the **3DORBIT** command. Change to a perspective projection and use the pan option to center the objects on the screen.
○ Adjust the camera distance to zoom in on the ladder. Pan as needed so the ladder is in the center of the screen. Notice how the model appears distorted. Adjust the camera distance to fill the screen with the model.
○ Swivel the camera to view only the left side of the model. Swivel the camera to view only the right side of the model.
○ Close the drawing without saving.

## Using Clipping Planes

An excellent design and visualization feature is the ability to apply front and rear *clipping planes* to the model. These imaginary planes slice through the model and can be compared to the cutting-plane lines used in drafting to create sections. AutoCAD allows you to adjust these clipping planes, and turn them on or off, with the **3DCLIP** command. Clipping planes are always parallel to the screen regardless of the current UCS.

Clipping planes are set and adjusted in the **Adjust Clipping Planes** window. To open this window, pick the **3D Adjust Clip Planes** button in the **3D Orbit** toolbar, select **Adjust Clipping Planes** from the **More** cascading menu in the **3DORBIT** shortcut menu, or type 3DCLIP at the Command: prompt. See **Figure 5-10**.

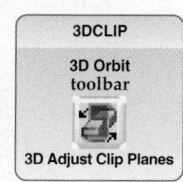

3DCLIP

3D Orbit toolbar

3D Adjust Clip Planes

The view shown in the **Adjust Clipping Planes** window looks down on the top edges of the clipping planes. The clipping planes are always parallel to the screen (current view). Therefore, if you consider the current view of the model as the front view, the **Adjust Clipping Planes** window shows the top view, hence an edge view of the clipping planes. See **Figure 5-11**.

**Figure 5-10.**
Clipping plane options are found in the **More** cascading menu in the **3DORBIT** shortcut menu.

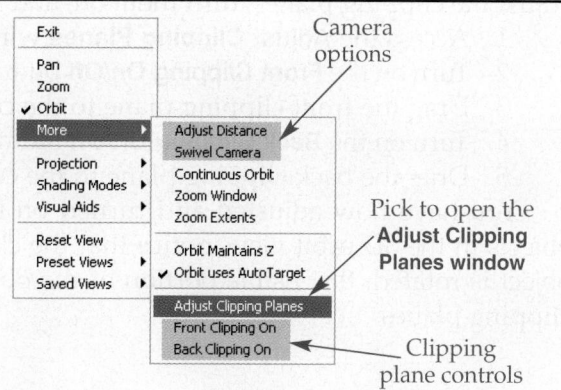

Camera options

Pick to open the **Adjust Clipping Planes window**

Clipping plane controls

**Figure 5-11.**
The view shown in the **Adjust Clipping Planes** window looks down on the top edges of the clipping planes.

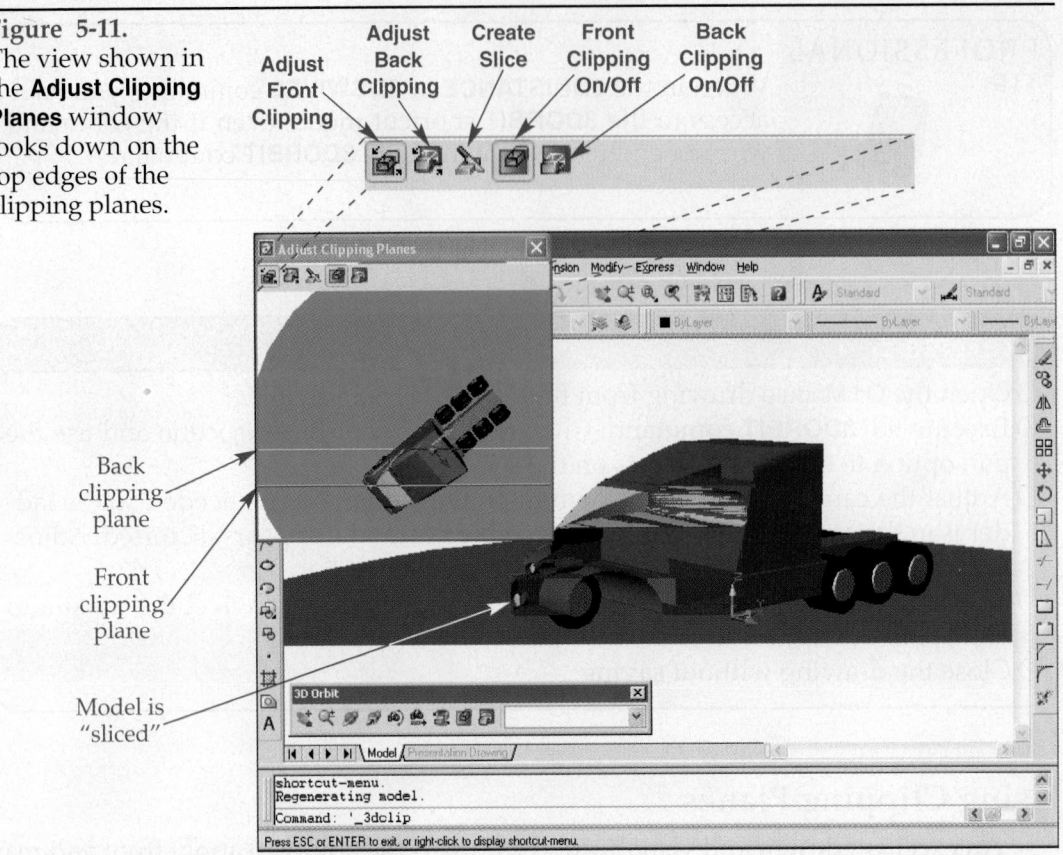

Notice the buttons at the top of the **Adjust Clipping Planes** window. They control the clipping plane options. These options can also be selected from a shortcut menu by right-clicking inside the **Adjust Clipping Planes** window.

- **Adjust Front Clipping.** Activates the front clipping plane for adjustment. The front clipping plane is the line closest to the bottom of the window. Pick and drag up or down to move the clipping plane.
- **Adjust Back Clipping.** Activates the back clipping plane for adjustment. The back clipping plane is the line closest to the top of the window.
- **Create Slice.** Creates a slice through the model, like cutting a slice of bread. When this option is selected, both the front and back clipping planes move as a single unit.
- **Front Clipping On/Off.** Toggles the front clipping plane on or off.
- **Back Clipping On/Off.** Toggles the back clipping plane on or off.

A clipping plane must be on to slice the objects. Use the following procedure to adjust the clipping planes, turn them on, and view the results.

1. Access the **Adjust Clipping Planes** window.
2. Turn on the **Front Clipping On/Off** button. Pick the **Adjust Front Clipping** button.
3. Drag the front clipping plane to the correct location.
4. Turn on the **Back Clipping On/Off** button. Pick the **Adjust Back Clipping** button.
5. Drag the back clipping plane to the correct location.

You have now adjusted and turned on both clipping planes. If you rotate the objects in the 3D orbit view, notice that the clipping planes remain stationary. As an object is rotated, the visible portion of the object varies based on the location of the clipping planes.

**Exercise 5-5**

○ Open the Oil Module drawing from the AutoCAD Sample folder.
○ Activate the **3DORBIT** command. Using the shortcut menu, display the objects from the southeast isometric preset viewpoint.
○ Open the **Adjust Clipping Planes** window.
○ Move the front clipping plane to cut through the right-front corner.
○ Move the back clipping plane to cut through the left-rear corner.
○ Be sure that both front and back clipping planes are turned on.
○ Pick the **Create Slice** button. Move the slice along the length of the model in short increments.
○ Close the drawing without saving.

## Creating a Continuous 3D Orbit

The most dynamic aspect of the **3DORBIT** command is the ability to create a continuous orbit of a model. By moving your pointing device, you can set the model in motion in any direction and at any speed, depending on the power of your computer. An impressive display can be achieved by first adjusting the clipping planes or creating a slice through the model. Then, activate a continuous orbit and watch as the model rotates in and out of the clipping planes.

To access continuous orbit mode, select **Continuous Orbit** from the **More** cascading menu of the **3DORBIT** shortcut menu, pick the **3D Continuous Orbit** button from the **3D Orbit** toolbar, or type 3DCORBIT at the Command: prompt. The continuous orbit cursor is displayed. See **Figure 5-12**.

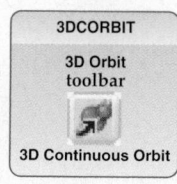

3DCORBIT

3D Orbit toolbar

3D Continuous Orbit

Pick and hold the left button and move the pointer in the direction that you want the model to rotate and at the desired speed of rotation. Release the button when the pointer is moving at the appropriate speed. The model will continue to rotate until you pick the left mouse button, press [Enter] or [Esc], or right-click and pick **Exit** or another option. At any time while the model is orbiting, you can left-click and adjust the rotation angle and speed by repeating the process for starting a continuous orbit.

**Figure 5-12.**
This is the continuous orbit cursor in the **3DORBIT** command. Pick and hold the left button and move the cursor in the direction you want the model to rotate.

## Shading a 3D Model

The *display* of a 3D model is how the model is presented. This does not refer to the viewing angle. An object can be shaded from any viewpoint. A shaded model can be edited while still keeping the object shaded. This can make it easier to see how the model is developing without having to reshade the drawing. However, when editing a shaded object, it may also be more difficult to select features.

There are four basic ways in which a model can be displayed. The first is called a wireframe, which is a display in which all lines are shown. The simplest "shaded" display technique is to remove hidden lines using the **HIDE** command. You have done this in previous chapters. However, this is not really a shaded display. A shaded model can be created with the **SHADEMODE** command. A more detailed shaded model, a rendered model, can be created with the **RENDER** command. A rendering is the most realistic presentation. This section discusses the **SHADEMODE** command and introduces rendering in AutoCAD. Detailed discussions on rendering, materials, lights, and scenes appear in Chapter 14 through Chapter 16.

## Exercise 5-6

○ The 3D model created in this exercise is used in the remainder of the chapter. You can use this model or substitute one of your own. As you create the model, create and save UCSs and views as needed. Create and save viewport configurations as needed, too.
○ Begin a new drawing.
○ Create the following layers and colors.

| Layer Name | Color |
|------------|---------|
| Box | red |
| Cone | yellow |
| Cylinder | magenta |
| Torus | blue |
| Floor-Wall | white |

○ Make the Floor-Wall layer current. Draw a solid box for the floor that is $8 \times 8 \times -.1$ units with its first corner located at the WCS origin.
○ Display the drawing from the southwest isometric viewpoint.
○ Draw another box for the wall with the same dimensions at 90° to the floor, as shown below.
○ Switch to the WCS. Then, draw the following solid objects by typing their name at the Command: prompt.
  ○ Make the Cube layer current. Draw a **BOX** with its first corner at (5.5,5.5,2). Select the **Cube** option with a length of 2.
  ○ Make the Cone layer current. Draw a **CONE** with its center at (4,4), a base diameter of 3, and a height of 6.
  ○ Make the Torus layer current. Draw a **TORUS** with the center at (7,1,2), a diameter of 3, and a tube radius of 1.
  ○ Make the Cylinder layer current. Draw a **CYLINDER** with the center at (1,6.5), base diameter of 1.5, and a height of 6.
○ Use the **3DORBIT** command to rotate the display so your drawing looks like the one shown below. Save the view.
○ Save the drawing as EX5-6. Leave AutoCAD open.

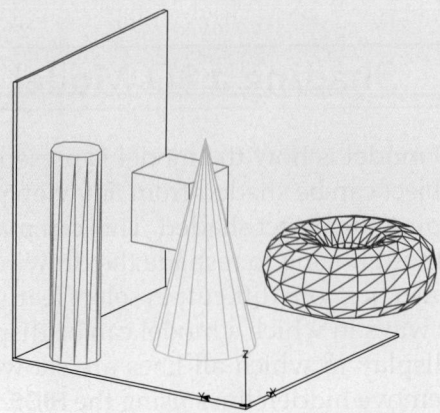

# Using the SHADEMODE Command

The **SHADEMODE** command displays a shaded view of your model. There are several options that allow varying degrees of displayed quality. The color of the shaded image is controlled by the color of the model. A single light source located behind and to the left of the viewer points at the model. Though not as realistic as a rendering, **SHADEMODE** can provide a good quality preview of a rendered object.

The **SHADEMODE** command options can be accessed by selecting the **Shade** cascading menu in the **View** pull-down menu, using the **Shade** toolbar, or typing SHADEMODE at the Command: prompt. See **Figure 5-13**. There are seven options to **SHADEMODE**, which are illustrated in **Figure 5-14**.

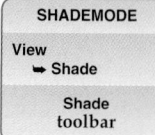

- **2D Wireframe.** This option displays normal wireframe view. It is used to restore a normal wireframe after the other options are used. Lines and curves are used to represent the edges of 3D objects. Raster images, OLE objects, linetypes, and line weights are visible when this option is used.
- **3D Wireframe.** This option displays the same type of wireframe view as the **2D Wireframe** option. However, raster images, OLE objects, linetypes, and line weights are *not* visible. The UCS icon changes to the 3D UCS icon when this option is used.
- **Hidden.** This option is the same as using the **HIDE** command on a 3D wireframe display. The lines representing backfaces are hidden. This option is slightly different from using **HIDE** on a 2D wireframe.
- **Flat Shaded.** This option applies shading to the faces of objects. The edges of the faces are not highlighted. Smoothing is not applied to the objects. Therefore, curved surfaces appear flat and faceted. Highlights are applied to objects. Raster images, OLE objects, linetypes, and line weights are not visible when this option is used.
- **Gouraud Shaded.** This option applies smoothing to the edges between the faces on an object and shades the faces. This produces a smooth, realistic appearance. Highlights are applied to objects. Raster images, OLE objects, linetypes, and line weights are not visible. This is considered the highest level of shading without producing a rendering.

**Figure 5-13.**
Shading options can be selected from the **Shade** cascading menu in the **View** pull-down menu or from the **Shade** toolbar.

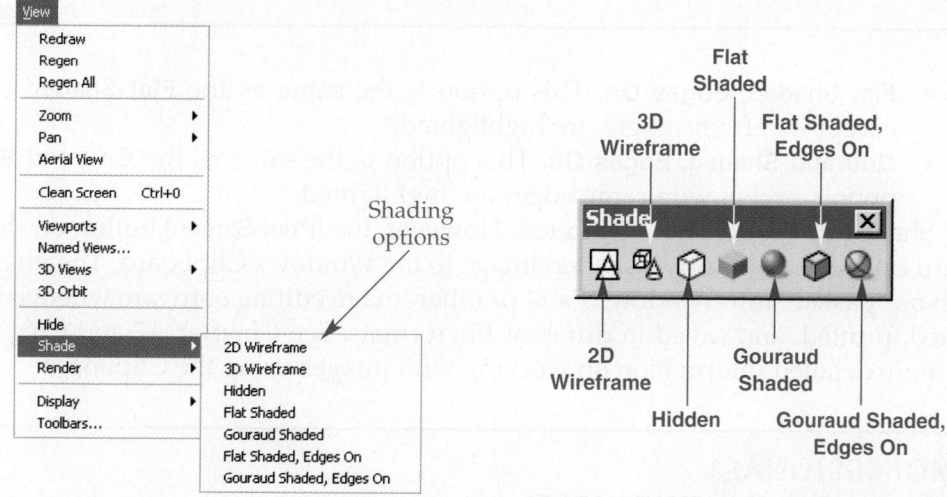

**Figure 5-14.**
The **SHADEMODE** command options produce a variety of displays.

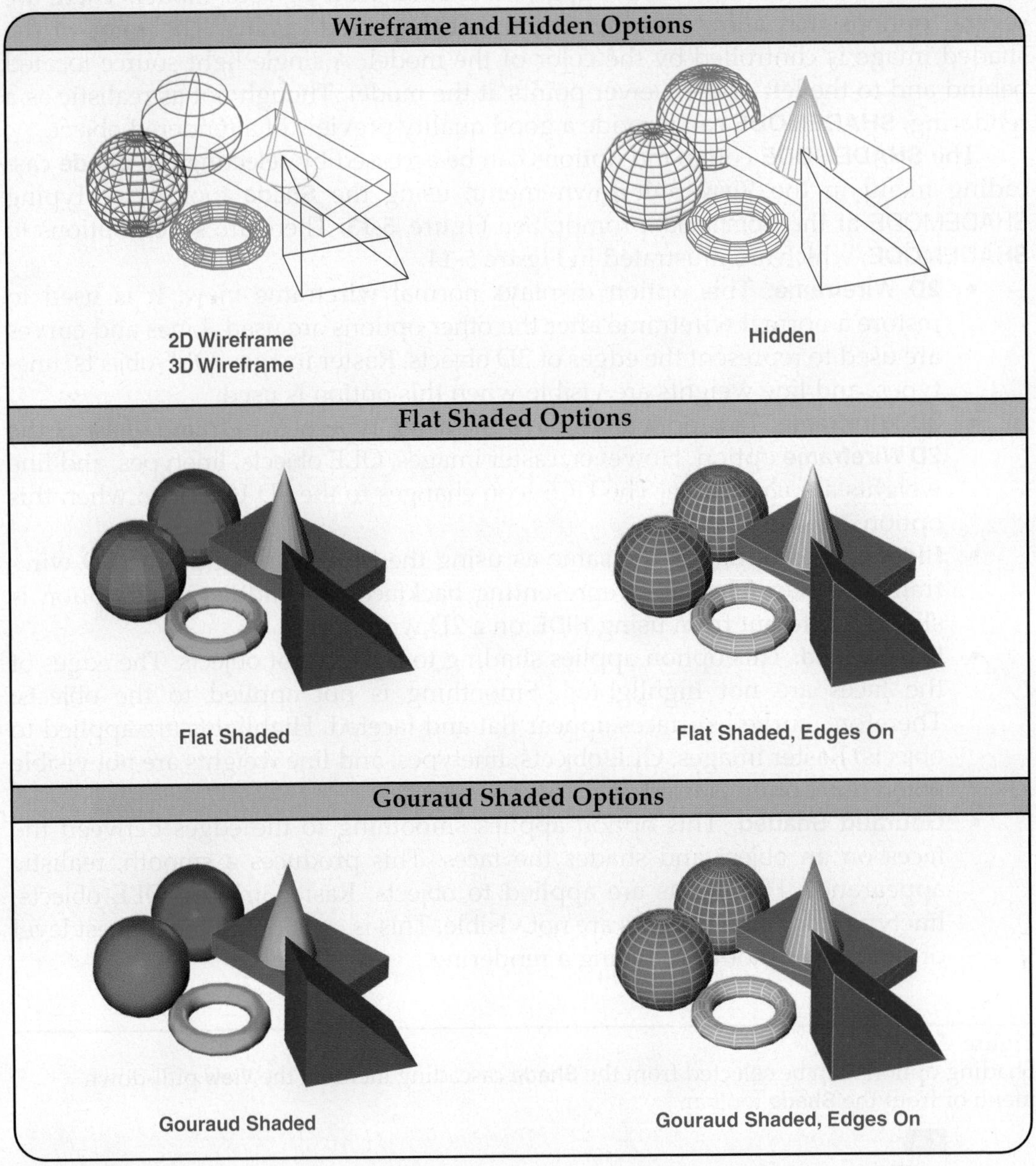

| Wireframe and Hidden Options |
|---|

2D Wireframe
3D Wireframe

Hidden

| Flat Shaded Options |
|---|

Flat Shaded

Flat Shaded, Edges On

| Gouraud Shaded Options |
|---|

Gouraud Shaded

Gouraud Shaded, Edges On

- **Flat Shaded, Edges On.** This option is the same as the **Flat Shaded** option, except wireframe edges are highlighted.
- **Gouraud Shaded, Edges On.** This option is the same as the **Gouraud Shaded** option, except wireframe edges are highlighted.

Shaded images cannot be plotted. However, the [Print Screen] button on the keyboard can be used to copy a shaded image to the Windows Clipboard. The image can then be "pasted" into Windows Paint or other image editing software where it can be edited, printed, and saved in different file formats. See Chapter 17 and Chapter 27 for more detailed information on working with images using the Clipboard.

**PROFESSIONAL TIP**

**SHADEMODE** is a good command to set up an alias for, such as **SM**. See Chapter 27 in *AutoCAD and its Applications—Basics* for instruction on customizing aliases.

○ Open the drawing named EX5-6 if it is not displayed on your screen.
○ Use the **SHADEMODE** command to shade the model. Two samples are shown below.
○ Display the model using each **SHADEMODE** option. How did each display differ?
○ Do not save the drawing.

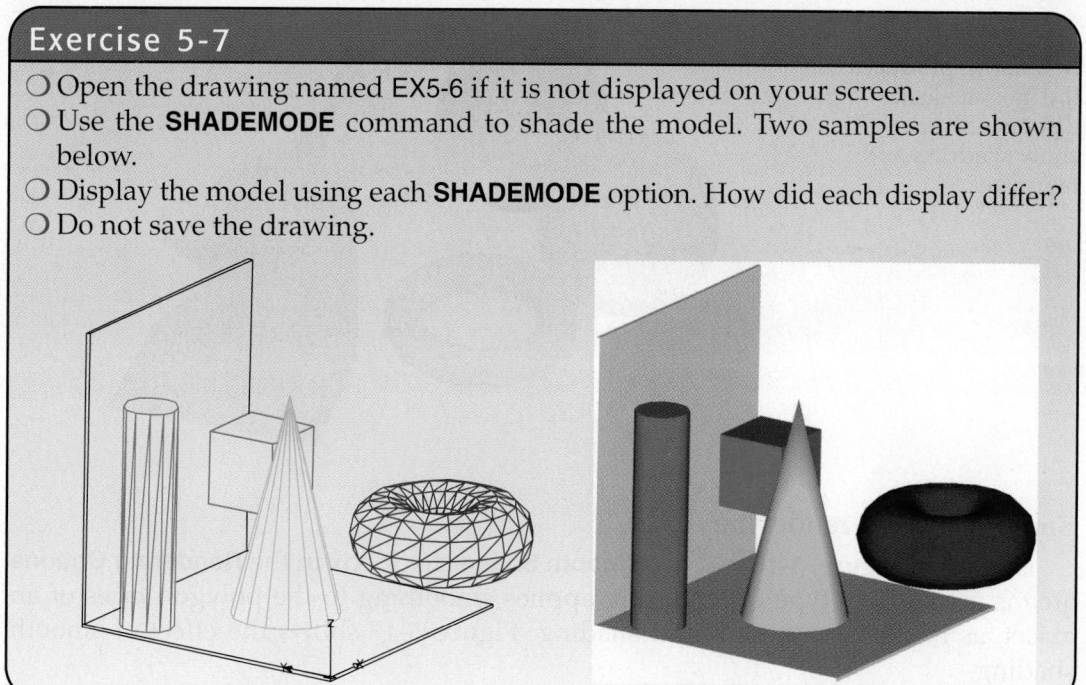

## 3DORBIT Shading Options

When the **3DORBIT** command is active, you can right-click in the viewport to display a shortcut menu. Most of the options in this shortcut menu are described earlier in the chapter. The **Shading Modes** entry displays a cascading menu. This cascading menu contains six options—**Wireframe**; **Hidden**; **Flat Shaded**; **Gouraud Shaded**; **Flat Shaded, Edges On**; and **Gouraud Shaded, Edges On**. Using each option is exactly the same as using the same **SHADEMODE** command option. **Wireframe** is equivalent to the **SHADEMODE 3D Wireframe** option. If you use the **SHADEMODE** command after setting a shading mode within the **3DORBIT** command, you will see that the default has changed to the shading mode set within **3DORBIT**.

## Rendering a Model

The **RENDER** command creates a realistic image of a model, **Figure 5-15**. However, rendering an image takes longer than shading an image. There are a variety of settings that you can change with the **RENDER** command that allow you to fine-tune renderings. These include scenes, lights, materials, backgrounds, fog, and preferences. Render settings are discussed in detail in Chapter 14 through Chapter 16.

The default render settings display an image that is rendered in the current viewport using a single light source located behind the viewer. The light intensity is set to 1 and the objects are rendered with a matte material that is the same color as the object display color.

To produce a simple rendering of your model, select **Render...** from the **Render** cascading menu in the **View** pull-down menu. You can also pick the **Render** button in the **Render** toolbar or type RR or RENDER at the Command: prompt. The **Render** dialog box appears, **Figure 5-16**. Make sure that **Viewport** is selected in the **Destination** drop-down list. Then, accept the default options by picking the **Render** button. The rendered model is displayed in the drawing area of the current viewport.

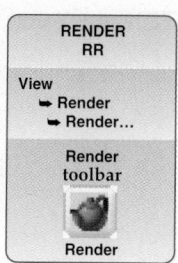

RENDER
RR

View
➡ Render
➡ Render...

Render
toolbar

Render

Figure 5-15.
Rendering produces
the most realistic
display and can
show shadows and
materials.

## Smooth shaded rendering

Notice in **Figure 5-16** that the **Smooth Shade** check box in the **Rendering Options** area is active. This type of rendering applies smoothing to the polygon faces of an object, as happens with Gouraud shading. **Figure 5-17** shows the effect of smooth shading.

To redisplay a wireframe view of the model, use the **REGEN** command. If you used any of the **SHADEMODE** options before rendering, the **REGEN** command will not restore the wireframe display. The previous **SHADEMODE** display is returned. In this case, use the **2D Wireframe** option of the **SHADEMODE** command to restore the wireframe.

Figure 5-16.
Basic rendering
options are set in
the **Render** dialog
box.

Check
to create
a smooth
shading

Check
to render
applied
materials

Destination

**Figure 5-17.**
A—A rendering without smooth shading. B—A rendering with smooth shading applied.

A                                                    B

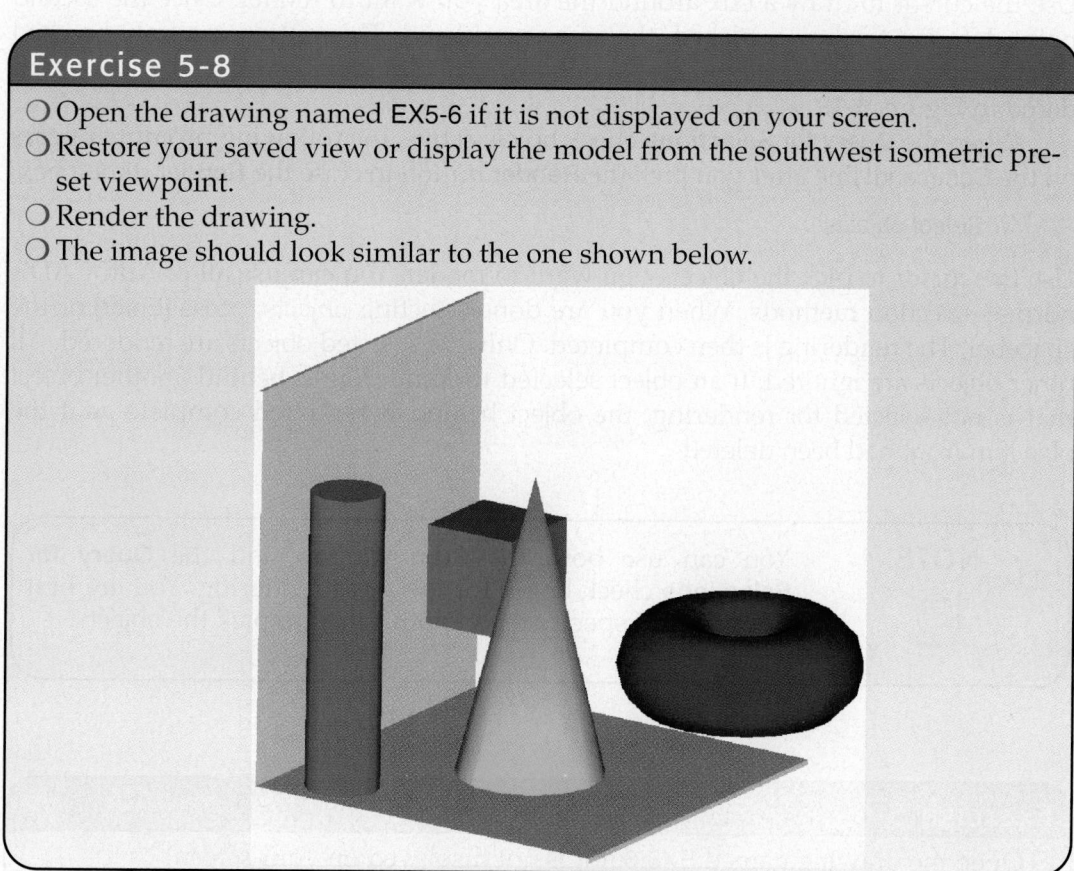

## Exercise 5-8

○ Open the drawing named **EX5-6** if it is not displayed on your screen.
○ Restore your saved view or display the model from the southwest isometric preset viewpoint.
○ Render the drawing.
○ The image should look similar to the one shown below.

## Rendering specific areas

There are two time-saving options found in the **Render** dialog box. These are **Crop Window** and **Query for Selections**. Check boxes for these options are in the **Rendering Procedure** area of the **Render** dialog box.

Checking the **Crop Window** check box allows you to draw a window around a portion of the drawing area. Only the area inside the window is rendered. When this check box is active, the following prompt appears on the Command: line after you pick the **Render** button in the **Render** dialog box.

Pick crop window to render:

**Figure 5-18.**
The model from
Exercise 9-1
rendered using the
**Crop Window** check
box.

Use the cursor to draw a box around the area you want to render. Once the second point defining the box is picked, the area is rendered. This option can only be used when rendering to the viewport. A small area of the model from Exercise 5-6 is rendered in **Figure 5-18.**

When the **Query for Selections** check box is active, the following prompt appears on the Command: line after you pick the **Render** button to close the **Render** dialog box.

Select objects:

Use the cursor to pick the objects you want to render. You can use all of AutoCAD's normal selection methods. When you are done selecting objects, press [Enter] or the spacebar. The rendering is then completed. Only the selected objects are rendered. All other objects are ignored. If an object selected for rendering is behind another object that is not selected for rendering, the object behind is rendered complete as if the object in front had been deleted.

---

NOTE   You can use both the **Crop Window** and the **Query for Selections** check boxes for the same rendering. You are first prompted to specify the window, then to pick the objects.

---

**Exercise 5-9**

○ Open the drawing named **EX5-6** if it is not displayed on your screen.
○ Restore the saved view or display the drawing from the southwest isometric preset viewpoint.
○ Create a rendered display of only the cylinder.
○ Change the color of the torus. Render only the torus.
○ Do not save the drawing.

AutoCAD and its Applications—Advanced

## Chapter Test

*Answer the following questions on a separate sheet of paper.*

1. Which command can be used to produce a view that is perpendicular to the current UCS?
2. When the **3DORBIT** command is active, what is the function of a circular arrow cursor?
3. When using the **3DORBIT** command, where must the cursor be located in order to rotate the model dynamically in any direction?
4. Which shade mode is considered the highest level of shading?
5. How can you select named views while the **3DORBIT** command is active?
6. What is the function of clipping planes?
7. Which command generates a continuous 3D orbit? Give the command line entry.
8. Which command produces the most realistic shaded image?
9. What is the difference between the **HIDE** and **SHADEMODE** commands?
10. What determines the color of shaded objects?
11. After using the **Gouraud Shaded** option of the **SHADEMODE** command, how do you return the display to a wireframe display?
12. Where is the light source located when shading objects?
13. What is the function of the **RENDER** command?
14. When rendering, what are the benefits of checking the **Crop Window** check box?
15. When active, what does the **Query for Selections** check box in the **Render** dialog box allow?

## Drawing Problems

1. Open one of your 3D drawings from a previous chapter that was created with solid primitives. Do the following.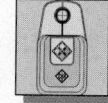
   A. Use the **3DORBIT** command to create a pictorial view of the drawing.
   B. While in the **3DORBIT** command, shade the object so that faces are shown in object colors and edges are highlighted.

2. Open one of your drawings from a previous chapter that was created with solid primitives or open the Oil Module drawing from the AutoCAD Sample folder.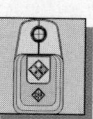
   A. Display the drawing using Gouraud shading.
   B. Change the projection to perspective and turn on the grid and compass.
   C. Create four named views of different parts on the model. Redisplay these views using the **Saved Views** cascading menu in the **3DORBIT** shortcut menu.
   D. Create a slice through the model, then put the model into a continuous orbit.
   E. Save the drawing as P5-2.

3. Open one of your 3D drawings from a previous chapter that was created with solid primitives and do the following.
   A. Create an arrangement of three floating model space viewports in a paper space layout.
   B. Display the drawing from a different viewpoint in each viewport.
   C. Use a different shading option in each viewport.

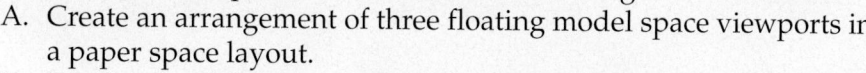
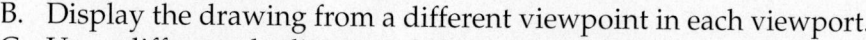

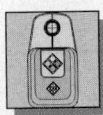

4. Open one of your 3D drawings from a previous chapter that was created with solid primitives and do the following.
   A. Create an arrangement of three floating model space viewports in a paper space layout.
   B. Display the drawing from a different viewpoint in each viewport.
   C. Make the necessary settings to display hidden lines as a dashed linetype in one of the viewports. Use the **HIDE** command to create a hidden display in that viewport.
   D. Create a rendering of the objects in one of the viewports.

5. Open one of your 3D drawings from a previous chapter that was created with solid primitives and do the following.
   A. Create a standard engineering layout.
   B. Create dimensioning layers for each of the three orthogonal viewports and apply some basic dimensions to each view.
   C. Use the **Shadeplot** option of the **MVIEW** command to hide the hidden lines in the 3D viewport.
   D. Plot the drawing from the layout tab using a scale of 1:1.

# Introduction to Solid Modeling

## Learning Objectives

After completing this chapter, you will be able to:
- Construct 3D solid primitives.
- Create complex solids using the **UNION** command.
- Remove portions of a solid using the **SUBTRACT** command.
- Create a new solid from the interference volume between two solids.
- Create regions.

## Overview of Solid Modeling

In Chapter 1, you were introduced to the three basic forms of 3D modeling—wireframe objects, solid models, and surface models. Solid models are probably the most useful, and hence most common, type of 3D modeling. A solid model accurately and realistically represents the shape and form of a final object. In addition, a solid model contains data related to the object's volume, mass, and centroid.

Solid modeling is very flexible. You can start with solid primitives, which were introduced in Chapter 1, and perform a variety of editing functions. You can think of creating a solid model as working with modeling clay. Starting with a basic block of clay, you can add more clay, remove clay, drill holes, round edges, etc., until you have arrived at the final shape and form of the object. To achieve the same results with surface modeling, complicated procedures may be required, if the result can even be achieved.

## Constructing Solid Primitives

As you learned in Chapter 1, a primitive is a basic building block. The six *solid primitives* in AutoCAD are a box, sphere, cylinder, cone, wedge, and torus. These primitives can also be used as building blocks for complex solid models. To this point, you have drawn most of the primitives to create simple objects. However, this section provides detailed information on drawing all of the solid primitives.

## Figure 6-1.
A—The **Solids** cascading menu. B—The **Solids** toolbar.

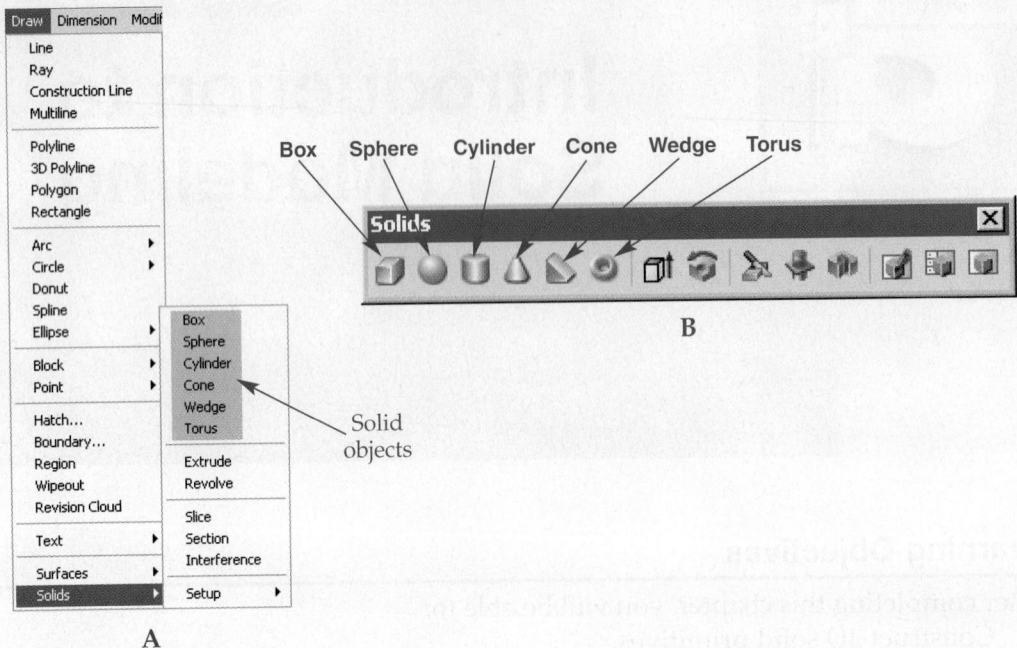

A

B

Box   Sphere   Cylinder   Cone   Wedge   Torus

Solid objects

To create a solid primitive, pick the appropriate button in the **Solids** toolbar, select the object from the **Solids** cascading menu in the **Draw** pull-down menu, or type the primitive name at the Command: prompt. See **Figure 6-1.**

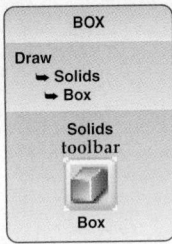

BOX

Draw
  ➡ Solids
    ➡ Box

Solids toolbar

Box

## Box

A solid box can be constructed from an initial corner or the center. These options are available by picking the **Box** button from the **Solids** toolbar, selecting **Box** from the **Solids** cascading menu in the **Draw** pull-down menu, or entering BOX at the Command: prompt. Refer to **Figure 6-2** as you read the following command sequence.

Command: **BOX**↵
Specify corner of box or [CEnter] <0,0,0>: *(pick a corner or type C for the* **Center** *option)*
Specify corner or [Cube/Length]: **L**↵ *(pick the diagonal corner of the base, or type L and press [Enter] to provide a length and width)*
Specify length: **1**↵
Specify width: **3**↵
Specify height: **2**↵

## Figure 6-2.
A—A box created using the **Cube** option. B—A box created by selecting the center point.

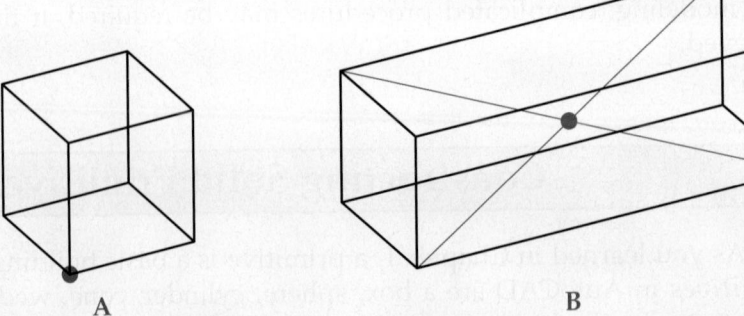

A

B

If the **Cube** option is selected, the length value is applied to all dimensions. In order to pick the opposite corner, you must have a pictorial (3D) view displayed or enter coordinates.

## Sphere

SPHERE

Draw
➡ Solids
➡ Sphere

Solids toolbar

Sphere

A solid sphere is drawn by first picking its center point, then entering a radius or diameter. To draw a sphere, pick the **Sphere** button in the **Solids** toolbar, select **Sphere** from the **Solids** cascading menu in the **Draw** pull-down menu, or enter SPHERE at the Command: prompt.

Command: **SPHERE**↵
Current wire frame density: ISOLINES=*current*
Specify center of sphere <0,0,0>: *(pick a point or enter coordinates)*
Specify radius of sphere or [Diameter]: *(pick a point or enter a value)*
Command:

Notice in **Figure 6-3A** that iso lines define the shape. Also, there is no outline or silhouette. The **DISPSILH** system variable controls the display of wireframe silhouettes. This variable is set to 0 by default. When **DISPSILH** is set to 1, the silhouette shown in **Figure 6-3B** is displayed. When hidden lines are removed, only the silhouette appears, **Figure 6-3C**. *Tessellation lines* are lines that define the curved shape of the object in a hidden display. These lines are not shown when **DISPSILH** is set to 1. The sphere is shown with hidden lines removed and **DISPSILH** set to a value of 0 in **Figure 6-3D**. Tessellation lines are shown. System variables that affect display are discussed in detail in Chapter 10.

**Figure 6-3.**
A—The basic wireframe display of spheres. B—The **DISPSILH** system variable is set to 1. C—The **DISPSILH** system variable is set to 1 and the **HIDE** command used. D—Spheres displayed after using **HIDE** with the **DISPSILH** system variable set to 0.

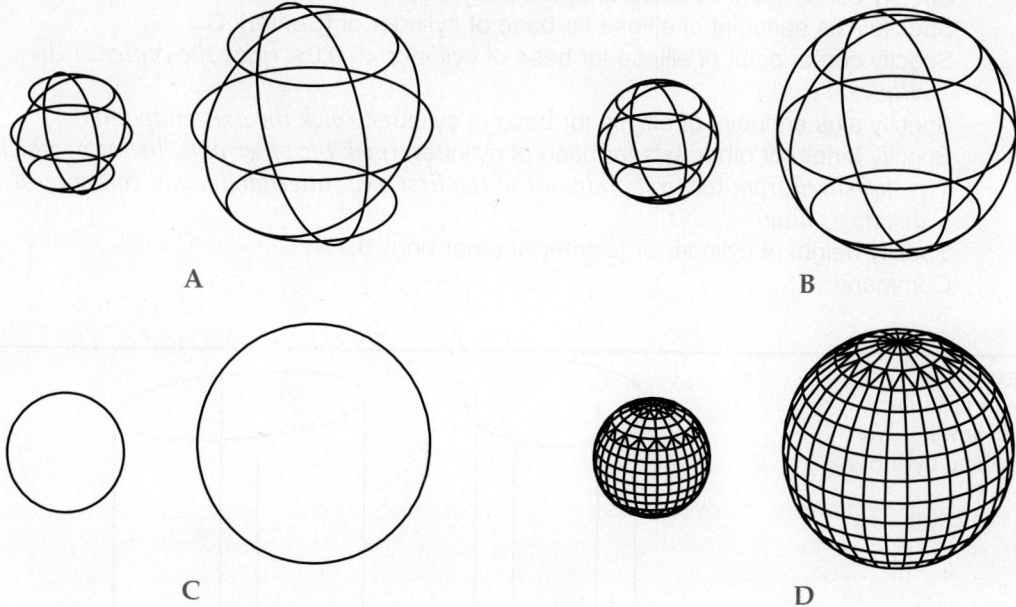

A

B

C

D

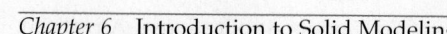

CYLINDER

Draw
  ↪ Solids
    ↪ Cylinder

Solids
toolbar

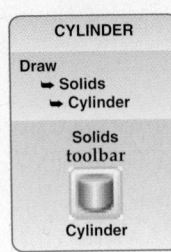

Cylinder

# Cylinder

A solid cylinder can be drawn either circular or elliptical. To draw a solid cylinder, pick the **Cylinder** button in the **Solids** toolbar, select **Cylinder** from the **Solids** cascading menu in the **Draw** pull-down menu, or enter CYLINDER at the Command: prompt.

```
Command: CYLINDER↵
Current wire frame density: ISOLINES=current
Specify center point for base of cylinder or [Elliptical] <0,0,0>: (pick a center point)
Specify radius for base of cylinder or [Diameter]: 1↵
Specify height of cylinder or [Center of other end]: 3↵
Command:
```

The cylinder shown in **Figure 6-4A** is displayed.

You can draw an elliptical cylinder in one of two ways. The default method prompts you to specify the two endpoints of the first axis and the second axis distance of the elliptical base. This prompt sequence is:

```
Specify center point for base of cylinder or [Elliptical] <0,0,0>: E↵
Specify axis endpoint of ellipse for base of cylinder or [Center]: (pick the first axis
    endpoint)
Specify second axis endpoint of ellipse for base of cylinder: (pick the second axis
    endpoint)
Specify length of other axis for base of cylinder: (pick the other axis distance, which
    is measured from the first endpoint of the first axis; alternately, you can enter a
    distance value)
Specify height of cylinder or [Center of other end]: 3↵
Command:
```

The cylinder in **Figure 6-4B** is created. The second option allows you to select the center point.

```
Specify center point for base of cylinder or [Elliptical] <0,0,0>: E↵
Specify axis endpoint of ellipse for base of cylinder or [Center]: C↵
Specify center point of ellipse for base of cylinder <0,0,0>: (pick the center of the
    ellipse)
Specify axis endpoint of ellipse for base of cylinder: (pick the axis endpoint)
Specify length of other axis for base of cylinder: (pick the other axis distance, which
    is measured from the first endpoint of the first axis; alternately, you can enter a
    distance value)
Specify height of cylinder or [Center of other end]: 3↵
Command:
```

**Figure 6-4.**
A—A circular
cylinder. B—An
elliptical cylinder.

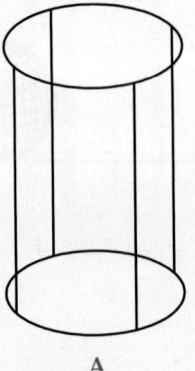

A

B

To set the height, pick two points with the cursor. The distance between the two pick points is set as the height of the cylinder. You can also enter a value at the keyboard instead of picking the distance. When setting the height, you also have the option of picking the center point of the opposite end of the cylinder. This is useful if you are placing a cylinder inside another object to create a hole. The cylinder can then be subtracted from the other object to create a hole. Refer to **Figure 6-5** as you go through the following sequence.

> Specify height of cylinder or [Center of other end]: **C**↵
> Specify center of other end of cylinder: **CEN**↵
> of (*pick the top end of the first cylinder*)
> Command:

---

**Figure 6-5.**
A—A cylinder is drawn inside another cylinder using the **Center of other end** option.
B—The large cylinder has a hole after **SUBTRACT** is used to remove the small cylinder.

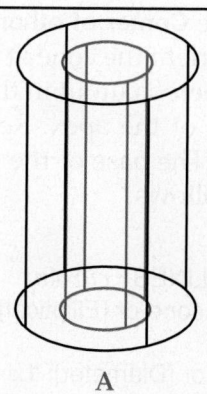 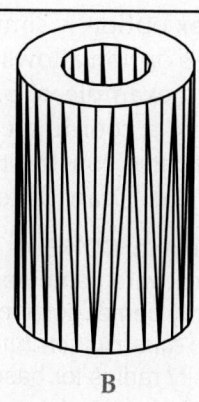

A          B

## Cone

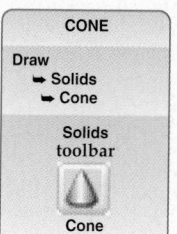

A solid cone can be drawn either circular or elliptical. To draw a cone, pick the **Cone** button in the **Solids** toolbar, select **Cone** from the **Solids** cascading menu in the **Draw** pull-down menu, or enter CONE at the Command: prompt.

> Command: **CONE**↵
> Current wire frame density: ISOLINES=*current*
> Specify center point for base of cone or [Elliptical] <0,0,0>: (*pick the center point*)
> Specify radius for base of cone or [Diameter]: **1**↵
> Specify height of cone or [Apex]: **3**↵
> Command:

The cone in **Figure 6-6A** is displayed. An elliptical cone can be created as follows.

> Specify center point for base of cone or [Elliptical] <0,0,0>: **E**↵
> Specify axis endpoint of ellipse for base of cone or [Center]: (*pick the axis endpoint*)
> Specify second axis endpoint of ellipse for base of cone: (*pick the other axis endpoint*)
> Specify length of other axis for base of cone: (*pick the other axis distance, which is measured from the center of the first axis; alternately, you can enter a distance value*)
> Specify height of cone or [Apex]: **3**↵
> Command:

The cone shown in **Figure 6-6B** is displayed. Just as with a cylinder, you can select the center of the cone at the following prompt.

> Specify axis endpoint of ellipse for base of cone or [Center]:

---

The toolbar panel reads:

> CONE
>
> Draw
> → Solids
> → Cone
>
> Solids toolbar
>
> Cone

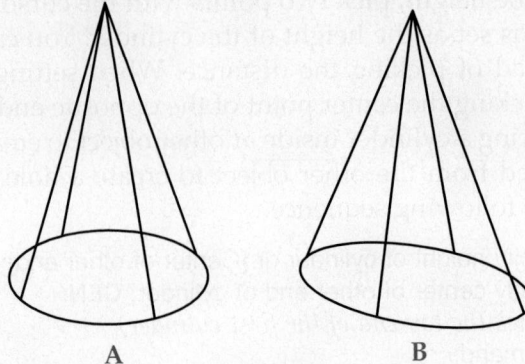

**Figure 6-6.**
A—A circular cone.
B—An elliptical cone.

A          B

The **Apex** option is similar to the **Center of other end** option for drawing a solid cylinder. This option allows you to orient the cone at any angle, regardless of the current UCS. For example, to place a tapered cutout in the end of a block, locate the cone base and give a coordinate location of the apex. Refer to **Figure 6-7.** First, draw a diagonal line as a construction line. The base of the cone will be located at the midpoint of the line. Draw the cone as follows.

Command: **CONE.**↵
Current wire frame density: ISOLINES= *current*
Specify center point for base of cone or [Elliptical] <0,0,0>: *(select the midpoint of the construction line)*
Specify radius for base of cone or [Diameter]: **1**↵
Specify height of cone or [Apex]: **A**↵
Specify apex point: **@2,0,0**↵
Command:

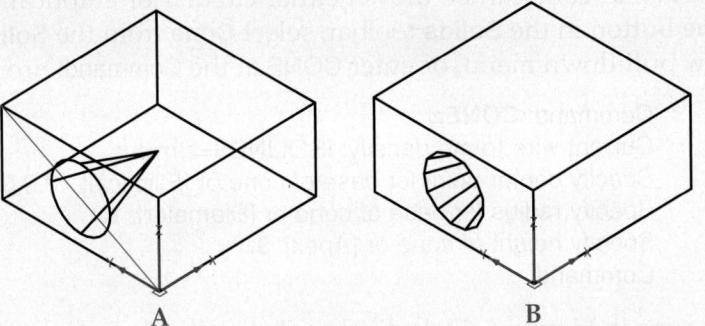

**Figure 6-7.**
A—Cones can be positioned relative to other objects using the **Apex** option. B—The cone is subtracted from the box.

A          B

WEDGE
WE

Draw
➥ Solids
➥ Wedge

Solids
toolbar

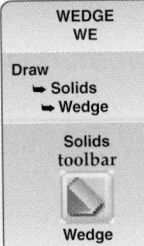

Wedge

## Wedge

A solid wedge can be constructed by picking corners or by picking the center point. The center point of a wedge is the middle of the angled surface. To draw a solid wedge, pick the **Wedge** button from the **Solids** toolbar, select **Wedge** from the **Solids** cascading menu in the **Draw** pull-down menu, or enter WE or WEDGE at the Command: prompt.

Command: **WE** *or* **WEDGE.**↵
Specify first corner of wedge or [CEnter] <0,0,0>: *(pick a corner location)*
Specify corner or [Cube/Length]: *(pick the diagonal corner location)*
Specify height: **2**↵
Command:

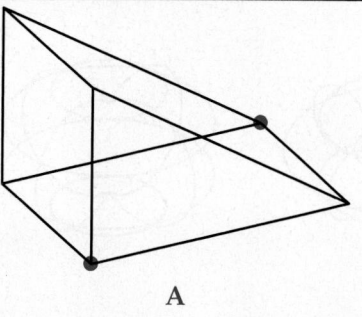
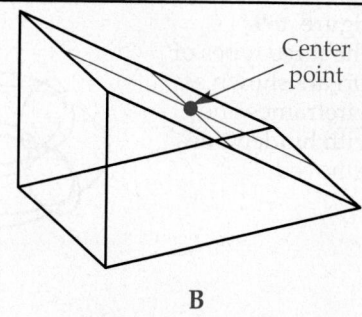

Figure 6-8.
A—A wedge drawn by picking corners.
B—A wedge drawn using the **Center** option. Notice the location of the center.

Center point

A                    B

See **Figure 6-8A.** If you pick the second corner in 3D space (different X, Y, and Z values), you are not prompted for the height. You can also specify the length, width, and height instead of picking the diagonal corner.

> Specify corner or [Cube/Length]: **L**↵
> Specify length: **3**↵
> Specify width: **2**↵
> Specify height: **2**↵
> Command:

The **Center** option is used as follows. Refer to **Figure 6-8B.**

> Specify first corner of wedge or [CEnter] <0,0,0>: **C**↵
> Specify center of wedge <0,0,0>: *(pick the center point)*
> Specify opposite corner or [Cube/Length]:

At this point, you can pick a corner of the wedge or use the **Length** option to specify length, width, and height. The **Cube** option uses the length value for all three sides.

## Torus

A solid torus can be drawn in one of three different ways. Refer to **Figure 6-9.** To draw a torus, pick the **Torus** button in the **Solids** toolbar, select **Torus** from the **Solids** cascading menu in the **Draw** pull-down menu, or enter TOR or TORUS at the Command: prompt.

> Command: **TOR** *or* **TORUS**↵
> Current wire frame density: ISOLINES=*current*
> Specify center of torus <0,0,0>: *(pick the center point)*
> Specify radius of torus or [Diameter]: **1**↵
> Specify radius of tube or [Diameter]: **.4**↵
> Command:

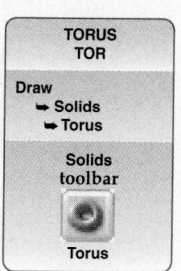
Notice that you can enter either a diameter or a radius. The basic torus shown in **Figure 6-9A** is drawn.

A torus with a tube diameter that touches itself has no center hole. This is the second type of torus and is called *self-intersecting.* See **Figure 6-9B.** To create a self-intersecting torus, the tube radius must be greater than the torus radius.

The third type of torus looks like a football. It is drawn by entering a negative torus radius and a positive tube diameter of greater value, i.e. –1 and 1.1. See **Figure 6-9C.**

---

**PROFESSIONAL TIP**

You can use snaps on solid objects. For example, you can snap to the center of a solid sphere using the **Center** object snap. The **Endpoint** object snap can be used to select the corners of a box, apex of a cone, corners of a wedge, etc.

---

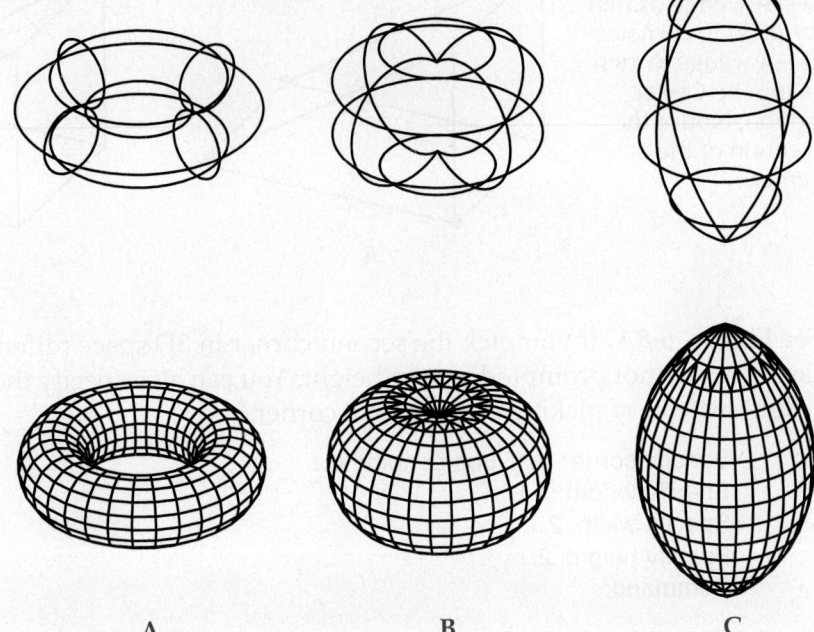

**Figure 6-9.**
The three types of tori are shown as wireframes and with hidden lines removed.

A      B      C

## Exercise 6-1

○ Begin a new drawing.
○ Display the drawing from the southwest isometric viewpoint.
○ Construct the following solid primitives.
 ○ A sphere 1.5″ in diameter.
 ○ A box that is 3″ × 2″ × 1″.
 ○ A cone 2.5″ high with a base diameter of 1.5″.
 ○ An elliptical cone 3″ high with a major base diameter of 2″ and a minor base
  diameter of 1″.
 ○ A wedge 4″ long, 3″ wide, and 2″ high.
 ○ A cylinder 1.5″ in diameter and 2.5″ high.
 ○ An elliptical cylinder with a major axis of 2″, a minor axis of 1″, and 3″ high.
 ○ A basic torus with a radius of 2″ and a tube diameter of .75″.
 ○ A self-intersecting torus.
 ○ A football-shaped torus.
○ Save your drawing as EX6-1.

## Creating Composite Solids

 A *composite solid* is a solid model constructed of two or more solids, often primitives. Solids can be subtracted from each other, joined to form a new solid, or overlapped to create an intersection or interference. The commands used to create composite solids are found in the **Solids Editing** cascading menu in the **Modify** pulldown menu and on the **Solids Editing** toolbar. See **Figure 6-10**.

**Figure 6-10.**
Boolean commands can be selected from the **Modify** pull-down menu or the **Solids Editing** toolbar.

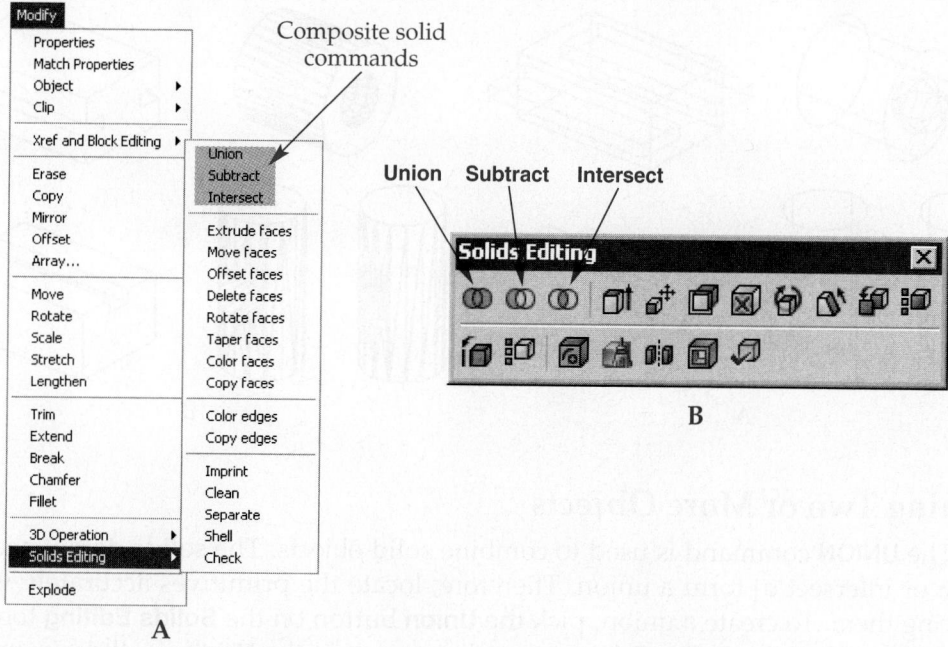

Composite solid commands

A

Union   Subtract   Intersect

B

## Introduction to Booleans

There are three operations that form the basis of constructing many complex solid models. Joining two or more solids is called a *union* operation. Subtracting one solid from another is called a *subtraction* operation. Forming a solid based on the volume of overlapping solids is called an *intersection* operation. Unions, subtractions, and intersections as a group are called *Boolean operations.* George Boole (1815–1864) was an English mathematician who developed a system of mathematical logic where all variables have the value of either one or zero. Boole's two-value logic, or *binary algebra,* is the basis for the mathematical calculations used by computers, and specifically for those required in the construction of composite solids.

## Subtracting Solids

The **SUBTRACT** command allows you to remove the volume of one or more solids from another solid. Several examples are shown in **Figure 6-11.** The first object selected in the subtraction operation is the object *from* which volume is to be subtracted. The next object is the object to be subtracted from the first. You can subtract solids by picking the **Subtract** button on the **Solids Editing** toolbar, selecting **Subtract** from the **Solids Editing** cascading menu in the **Modify** pull-down menu, or entering SU or SUBTRACT at the Command: prompt.

```
Command: SU or SUBTRACT↵
Select solids and regions to subtract from...
Select objects: (pick the object)
Select objects: ↵
Select solids and regions to subtract...
Select objects: (pick the objects to subtract)
Select objects: ↵
Command:
```

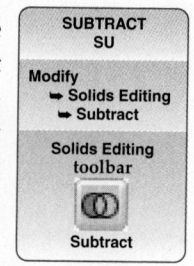

SUBTRACT
SU

Modify
➥ Solids Editing
➥ Subtract

Solids Editing
toolbar

Subtract

**Figure 6-11.**
A—The solid primitives shown here have areas of intersection and overlap. B—Composite solids after using the **SUBTRACT** command.

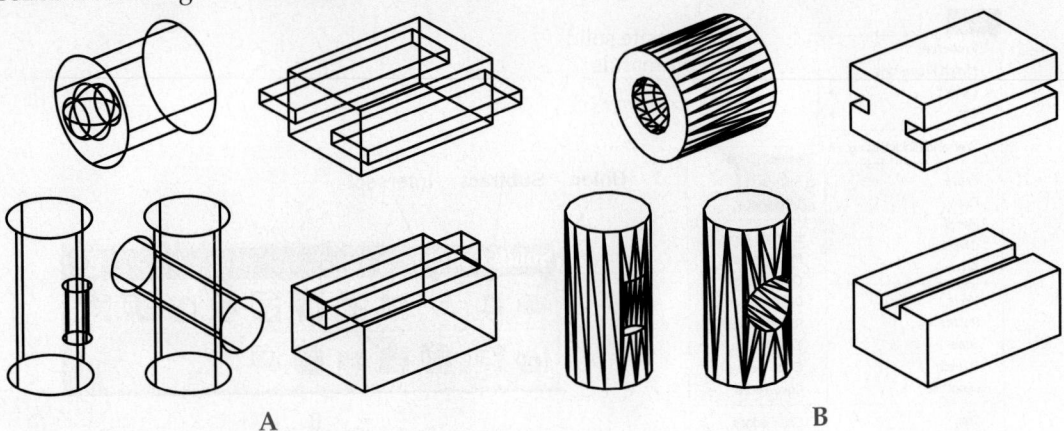

A                                                                    B

## Joining Two or More Objects

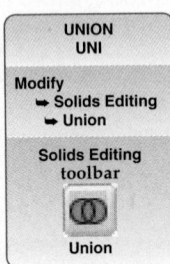

UNION
UNI

Modify
➡ Solids Editing
➡ Union

Solids Editing
toolbar

Union

The **UNION** command is used to combine solid objects. The solids do not need to touch or intersect to form a union. Therefore, locate the primitives accurately when drawing them. To create a union, pick the **Union** button on the **Solids Editing** toolbar, select **Union** from the **Solids Editing** cascading menu in the **Modify** pull-down menu, or enter UNI or UNION at the Command: prompt.

    Command: **UNI** or **UNION**↵
    Select objects: *(select all primitives to be joined)*
    Select objects: ↵
    Command:

In the examples shown in **Figure 6-12B,** notice that lines, or edges, are shown at the new intersection points of the joined objects.

**Figure 6-12.**
A—The solid primitives shown here have areas of intersection and overlap. B—Composite solids after using the **UNION** command.

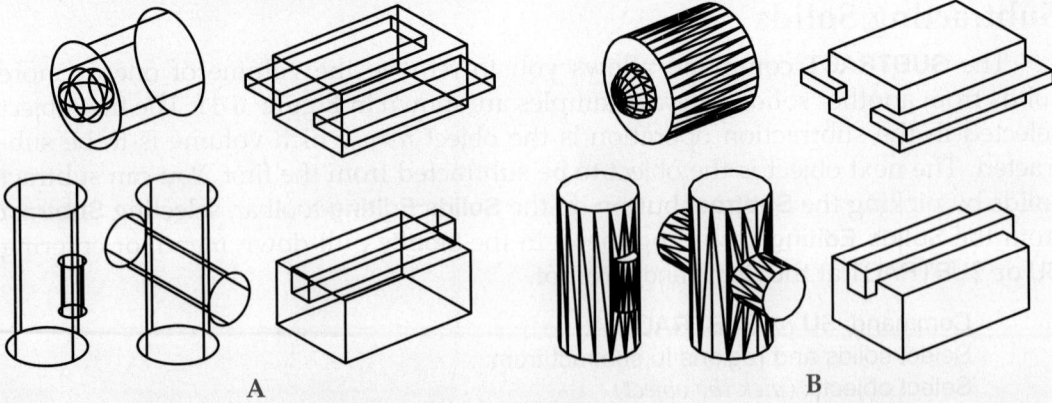

A                                                                    B

# Creating New Solids from the Intersection of Solids

When solid objects intersect, the overlap forms a common volume. This is an area in space that both primitives share. This shared space is called an *intersection.* An intersection (common volume) can be made into a composite solid using the **INTERSECT** command. **Figure 6-13** shows several examples. To use the command, pick the **Intersect** button on the **Solids Editing** toolbar, select **Intersect** from the **Solids Editing** cascading menu in the **Modify** pull-down menu, or enter IN or INTERSECT at the Command: prompt.

Command: **IN** *or* **INTERSECT**↵
Select objects: *(select the objects that form the intersection)*
Select objects: ↵
Command:

**Figure 6-13.**
A—The solid primitives shown here have areas of intersection and overlap.
B—Composite solids after using the **INTERSECT** command.

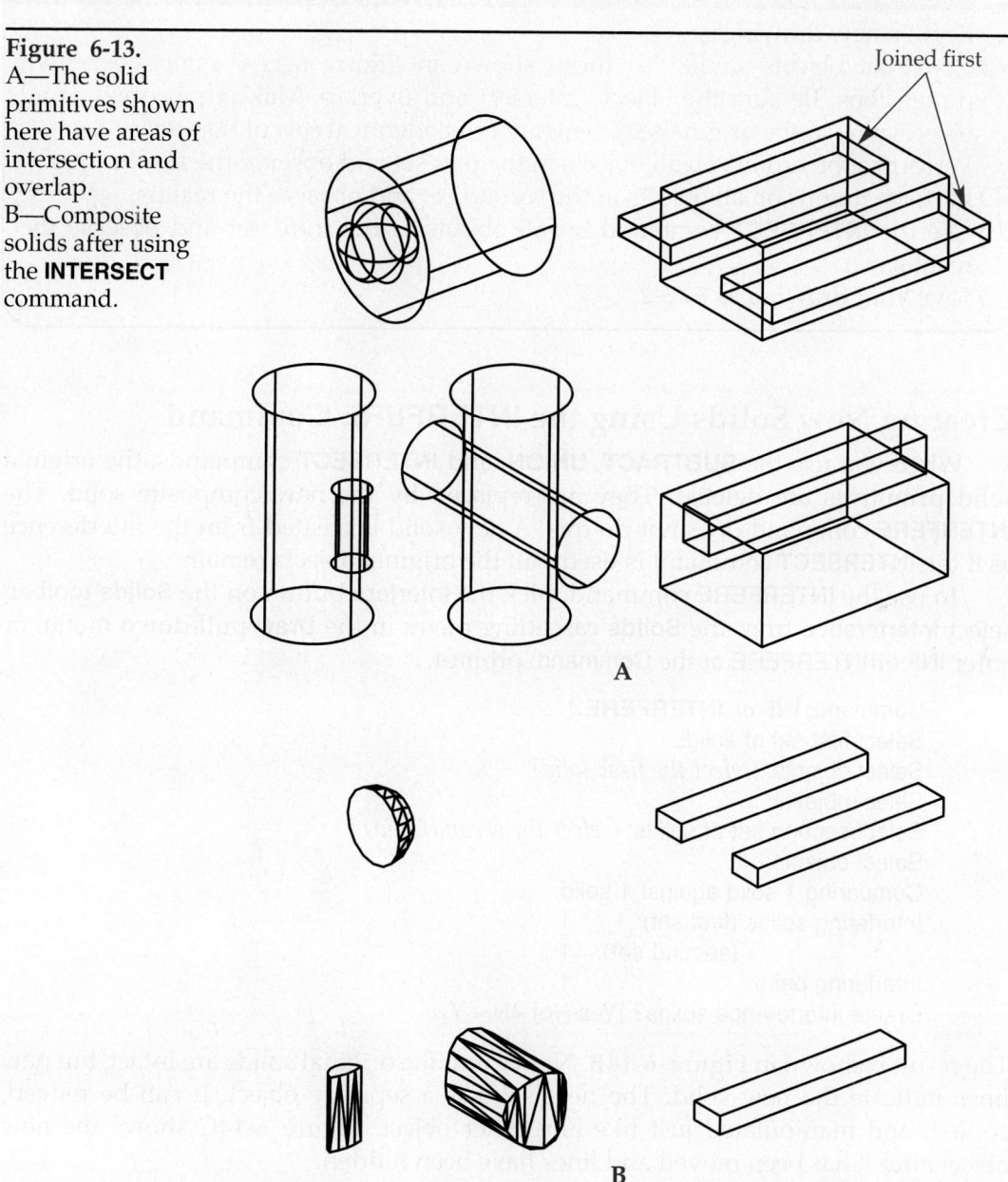

Joined first

A

B

## Exercise 6-2

○ Begin a new drawing.
○ Construct objects similar to those shown in **Figure 6-11A** using your own dimensions. Be sure the objects intersect and overlap. Make two copies of all objects next to the originals so there are three identical sets of objects.
○ Perform subtractions on all objects in the first set and observe the results.
○ Perform unions on all objects in the second set and observe the results.
○ Use the **INTERSECT** command on all objects in the third set and observe the results.
○ Save your drawing as EX6-2.

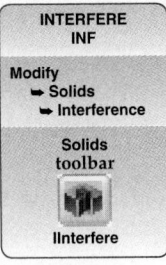

INTERFERE
INF

Modify
➡ Solids
　➡ Interference

Solids
toolbar

IInterfere

## Creating New Solids Using the INTERFERE Command

When you use the **SUBTRACT**, **UNION**, and **INTERSECT** commands, the original solid primitives are deleted. They are replaced by the new composite solid. The **INTERFERE** command does not do this. A new solid is created from the interference as if the **INTERSECT** command is used, but the original objects remain.

To use the **INTERFERE** command, pick the **Interfere** button on the **Solids** toolbar, select **Interference** from the **Solids** cascading menu in the **Draw** pull-down menu, or enter INF or INTERFERE at the Command: prompt.

```
Command: INF or INTERFERE↵
Select first set of solids:
Select objects: (select the first solid)
Select objects: ↵
Select second set of solids: (select the second solid)
Select objects: ↵
Comparing 1 solid against 1 solid.
Interfering solids (first set):        1
                 (second set):   1
Interfering pairs:                     1
Create interference solids? [Yes/No] <N>: Y↵
```

The result is shown in **Figure 6-14B**. Notice that the original solids are intact, but new lines indicate the new solid. The new solid is a separate object. It can be moved, copied, and manipulated just like any other object. **Figure 6-14C** shows the new object after it has been moved and lines have been hidden.

AutoCAD compares the first set of solids with the second set. Any solids that are selected for both the first and second sets are automatically included as part of the first selection set and eliminated from the second. If you do not select a second set of objects, AutoCAD calculates the interference between the objects in the first selection set. You can do this by pressing [Enter] instead of picking the second set.

**Figure 6-14.**
A—Two solids form an area of intersection.
B—After using **INTERFERE**, a new solid is defined (shown in color) and the original solids remain.
C—The new solid can be moved or copied.

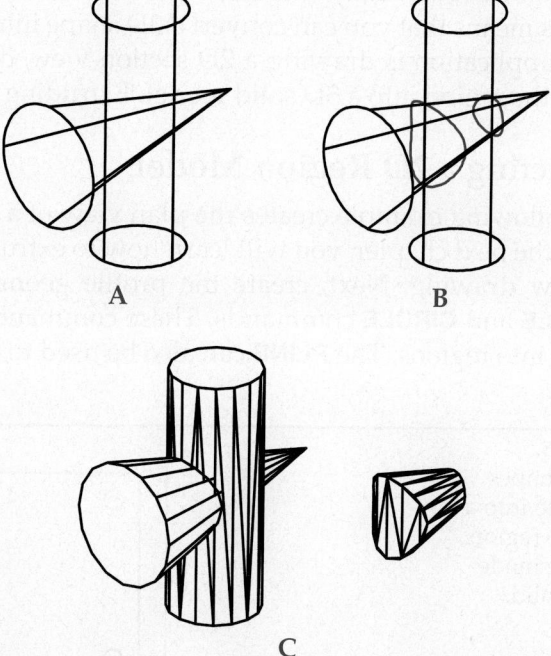

If you select multiple objects, you are given the opportunity to highlight intersecting pairs after creating the interference solid:

```
Highlight pairs of interfering solids? [Yes/No] <N>: Y↵
Enter an option [Next pair/eXit] <Next>:
```

The pairs are shown in dashed lines. You can cycle through pairs of intersecting objects. When done, use the **eXit** option and the command is completed.

---

### Exercise 6-3

○ Begin a new drawing.
○ Construct objects similar to those shown in **Figure 6-14A** using your own dimensions. Be sure the objects intersect and overlap.
○ Use the **INTERFERE** command on the objects and observe the results. Be sure to make a solid of the interference. Use the **HIDE** command.
○ Move the new solid to a new location.
○ Save your drawing as EX6-3.

---

## Working with Regions

A *region* is a closed, two-dimensional solid. It is a solid model without thickness (Z value). A region can be analyzed for its mass properties. Therefore, regions are useful for 2D applications where area and boundary calculations must be quickly obtained from a drawing.

Boolean operations can be performed on regions. When regions are unioned, subtracted, or intersected, a *composite region* is created. A composite region is also called a *region model*.

A region can be quickly and easily given a thickness, or *extruded* into a 3D solid object. This means that you can convert a 2D shape into a 3D solid model in just a few steps. An application is drawing a 2D section view, converting it into a region, and extruding the region into a 3D solid model. Extruding is covered in Chapter 7.

## Constructing a 2D Region Model

The following example creates the plan view of a base for a support bracket as a region. In the next chapter, you will learn how to extrude the region into a solid. First, start a new drawing. Next, create the profile geometry in **Figure 6-15** using the **RECTANGLE** and **CIRCLE** commands. These commands create 2D objects that can be converted into regions. The **PLINE** can also be used to create closed 2D objects.

**Figure 6-15.**
These 2D shapes can be made into a region. The region can then be made into a 3D solid.

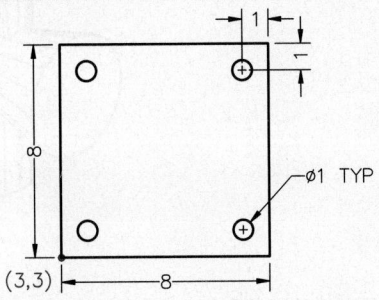

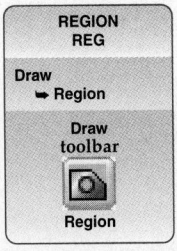

The **REGION** command allows you to convert closed, two-dimensional objects into regions. Select the **REGION** command by picking the **Region** button on the **Draw** toolbar, selecting **Region** in the **Draw** pull-down menu, or typing REG or REGION at the Command: prompt.

> Command: **REG** *or* **REGION.**↵
> Select objects: *(pick the rectangle and circles)*
> Select objects: ↵
> 5 loops extracted.
> 5 Regions created.
> Command:

The rectangle and each circle are now separate regions. You can pick them individually. If you pick a circle, notice that a grip is displayed in the center, but not at the four quadrants. This is because the object is not a circle anymore.

In order to create the proper solid, the circle regions must be subtracted from the rectangle region. Use the **SUBTRACT** command:

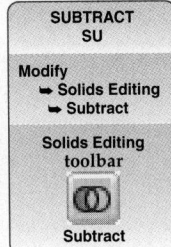

> Command: **SU** *or* **SUBTRACT.**↵
> Select solids and regions to subtract from...
> Select objects: *(pick the rectangle)*
> Select objects: ↵
> Select solids and regions to subtract...
> Select objects: *(pick the four circles)*
> Select objects: ↵
> Command:

Now, if you select the rectangle or any of the circles, you can see that a single region has been created from the five separate regions.

# Using the BOUNDARY Command to Create a Region

BOUNDARY
BO

Draw
➥ Boundary...

The **BOUNDARY** command is often used to create a polyline for hatching or an inquiry. In addition, this command can be used to create a region. To do so, pick **Boundary...** from the **Draw** pull-down menu or type BO or BOUNDARY at the Command: prompt. The **Boundary Creation** dialog box is displayed. See **Figure 6-16.**

Next, select **Region** from the **Object Type** drop-down list. You can refine the boundary selection method by picking the type of island detection method. Two options are found at the bottom of the **Boundary Creation** dialog box.

- **Flood.** When you select an internal point on an object, AutoCAD includes any islands that reside inside the object as part of the new region.
- **Ray casting.** When you select an internal point on an object, AutoCAD projects a ray to the nearest object and follows it counterclockwise to create the region. Therefore, islands are not included in the new boundary object.

Finally, select the **Pick Points** button. You are returned to the graphics display and prompted to select an internal point. Pick a point inside the object you wish to convert to a region. Press [Enter] when you are finished and the region is created. You can always check to see if an object is a polyline or region by using the **LIST** command and selecting the object.

**Figure 6-16.**
Regions can be created using the **Boundary Creation** dialog box.

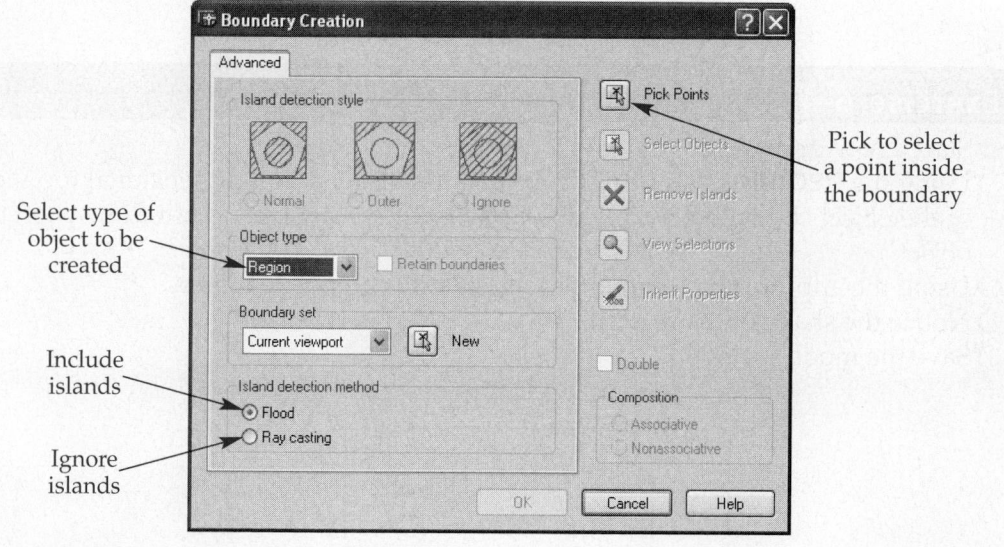

PROFESSIONAL TIP

A **Boundary** button can be added to a custom or existing toolbar. Refer to Chapter 19 for information on customizing toolbars.

## Calculating the Area of a Region

A region is not a polyline. It is an enclosed area called a *loop.* Certain values of the region, such as area, are stored as a value of the region primitive. The **AREA** command can be used to determine the length of all sides and the area of the loop. This can be a useful advantage of using a region.

For example, suppose a parking lot is being repaved. You need to calculate the surface area of the parking lot to determine the amount of material needed. This total surface area excludes the space taken up by planting dividers, sidewalks, and light posts because you will not be paving under these items. If the parking lot and all objects inside it are drawn as a region, the **AREA** command can give you this figure in one step. If a polyline is used to draw the parking lot, all internal features must be subtracted each time the **AREA** command is used.

PROFESSIONAL TIP

Regions can prove valuable when working with many items:
- Roof areas excluding chimneys, vents, and fans.
- Bodies of water, such as lakes, excluding islands.
- Lawns and areas of grass, excluding flower beds, trees, and shrubs.
- Landscaping areas excluding lawns, sidewalks, and parking lots.
- Concrete surfaces, such as sidewalks, excluding openings for landscaping, drains, and utility covers.

You can find many other applications for regions that can help in your daily tasks.

## Exercise 6-4

○ Start a new drawing.
○ Using the **RECTANG** and **CIRCLE** commands, draw a two-dimensional top view of the object shown below. Use the dimensions given, but do not dimension the object.
○ Using the appropriate commands, create a 2D composite region.
○ Notice the shape of the region.
○ Save the model as **EX6-4**.

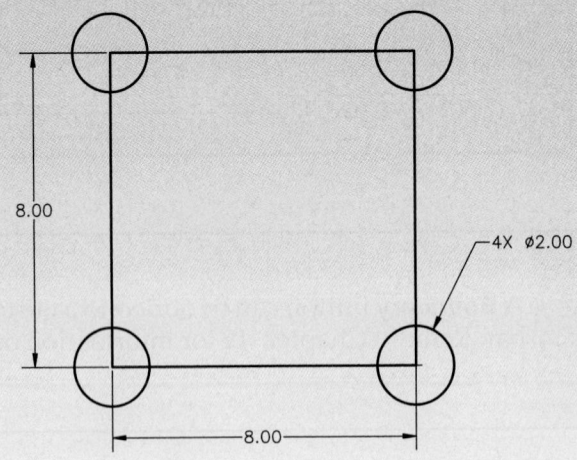

## Chapter Test

*Answer the following questions on a separate sheet of paper.*

1. What is a *solid primitive?*
2. How is a solid cube created?
3. How is an elliptical cylinder created?
4. Where is the center of a wedge located?
5. What is a *composite solid?*
6. Which type of mathematical calculations are used in the construction of solid models?
7. How are two or more solids combined to make a composite solid?
8. What is the function of the **INTERSECT** command?
9. How does the **INTERFERE** command differ from **INTERSECT** and **UNION**?
10. What is a *region?*
11. How can a 2D section view be converted to a 3D solid model?
12. What is created when regions are added to or subtracted from one another?
13. Which command allows you to remove the area of one region from another region?
14. What are the two island detection methods available with the **BOUNDARY** command?

## Drawing Problems

1. Construct the object in Problem 1 of Chapter 1 as a solid model. Save the drawing as P6-1.

2. Construct the object in Problem 2 of Chapter 1 as a solid model. Save the drawing as P6-2.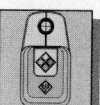

3. Construct the object in Problem 3 of Chapter 1 as a solid model. Save the drawing as P6-3.

4. Construct the object in Problem 4 of Chapter 1 as a solid model. Save the drawing as P6-4.

5. Construct the object in Problem 5 of Chapter 1 as a solid model. The final result should be a single object. Save the drawing as P6-5.

6. Construct the object in Problem 6 of Chapter 1 as a solid model. The final result should be a single object. Save the drawing as P6-6.

7. Construct the object in Problem 7 of Chapter 1 as a solid model. The end result should be a single object. Save the drawing as P6-7.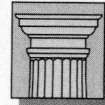

8. Construct a solid model of the object in Problem 10 of Chapter 1. The end result should be a single object. Save the drawing as P6-8.

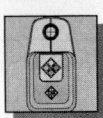

9. Construct the object in Problem 1 of Chapter 3 as a solid model. Save the drawing as P6-9.

10. Construct the object in Problem 2 of Chapter 3 as a solid model. Save the drawing as P6-10.

11. Construct the object in Problem 3 of Chapter 3 as a solid model. Save the drawing as P6-11.

12. Construct the object in Problem 4 of Chapter 3 as a solid model. Save the drawing as P6-12.

13. Construct the object in Problem 6 of Chapter 3 as a solid model. The end result should be a single object. Save the drawing as P6-13.

14. Construct the object in Problem 8 of Chapter 3 as a solid model. Save the drawing as P6-14.

## CHAPTER 7

# Solid Model Extrusions and Revolutions

## Learning Objectives

After completing this chapter, you will be able to:
- Create solid objects by extruding closed 2D profiles.
- Revolve closed 2D profiles to create symmetrical 3D solids.
- Use solid extrusions and revolutions as construction tools.

Complex shapes can be created by applying a thickness to a two-dimensional profile. This is called extruding the shape. Two or more profiles can be extruded to intersect. The resulting union can form a new shape. Symmetrical objects can be created by revolving a 2D profile about an axis to create a new solid.

## Creating Solid Model Extrusions

An *extrusion* is a closed two-dimensional shape that has been given thickness. The **EXTRUDE** command allows you to create extruded solids from closed objects such as polylines, polygons, splines, regions, circles, ellipses, and donuts. Objects in a block cannot be extruded. Extrusions can be created along a straight line or along a path curve. A taper angle can also be applied as you extrude an object. **Figure 7-1** illustrates a polygon extruded into a solid.

Create an extruded solid by picking the **Extrude** button on the **Solids** toolbar, selecting **Extrude** from the **Solids** cascading menu in the **Draw** pull-down menu, or typing EXT or EXTRUDE at the Command: prompt.

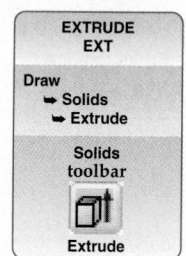

EXTRUDE
EXT

Draw
➡ Solids
 ➥ Extrude

Solids
toolbar

Extrude

> Command: **EXT** or **EXTRUDE**↵
> Current wire frame density: ISOLINES=*current*
> Select objects: *(pick the closed 2D object to extrude)*
> Select objects: ↵
> Specify height of extrusion or [Path]: **.35**↵
> Specify angle of taper for extrusion <0>: ↵
> Command:

The height of extrusion is always applied along the Z axis of the object. A positive value extrudes above the XY plane. A negative height value extrudes below the XY plane.

**Figure 7-1.**
The **EXTRUDE**
command creates a
solid by adding
thickness to a closed
2D profile. A—The
initial 2D profile.
B—The extruded
solid object shown
with hidden lines
removed.

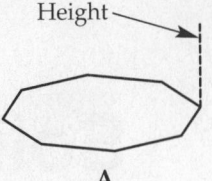
Height

A

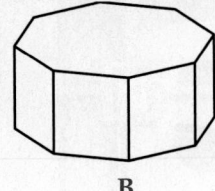

B

**Figure 7-2.**
A—A positive angle
tapers to the inside
of the object from
the base. B—A
negative angle
tapers to the outside
of the object.

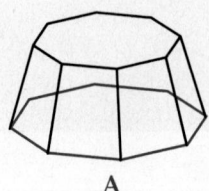

A

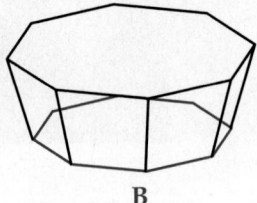

B

The taper angle can be any value between +90° and –90°. A positive angle tapers to the inside of the object from the base. A negative angle tapers to the outside of the object from the base. See **Figure 7-2**. However, the taper angle cannot result in edges that "fold into" the extruded object.

## Extrusions along a Path

A closed 2D shape can be extruded along a path to create a 3D solid. The path can be a line, circle, arc, ellipse, polyline, or spline. Line segments and other objects can be joined to form a polyline path. The corners of angled segments on the extruded object are mitered, while curved segments are smooth. See **Figure 7-3**.

```
Command: EXT or EXTRUDE↵
Current wire frame density: ISOLINES=current
Select objects: (pick object to extrude)
Select objects: ↵
Specify height of extrusion or [Path]: P↵
Select extrusion path or [Taper angle]: (pick the path)
Command:
```

Notice that you can specify a taper angle before selecting the path, if needed.

Objects can also be extruded along a line at an angle to the base object, **Figure 7-4**. Notice that the plane at the end of the extruded object is parallel to the original object. Also notice that the length of the extrusion is the same as that of the path.

**Figure 7-3.**
A—Angled
segments are
mitered when
extruded. B—
Curves are
smoothed when
extruded.

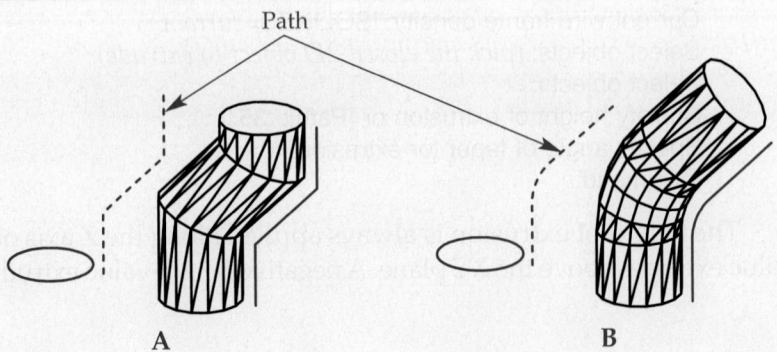
Path

A

B

**Figure 7-4.**
A—An object
extruded along a
path. B—The end of
an object extruded
along an angled
path is parallel to
the original object.

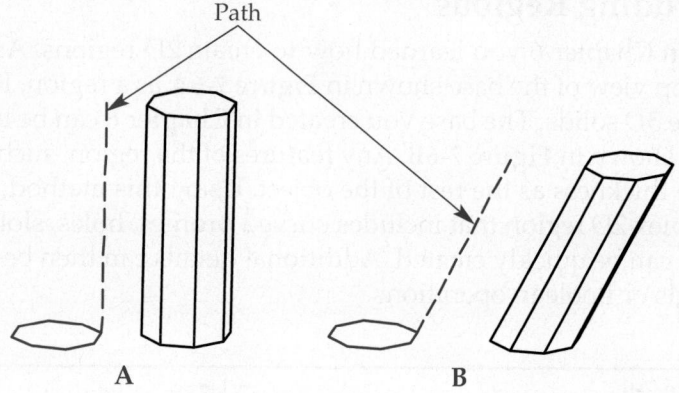

The path does not need to be perpendicular to the object. However, if the path is a spline, the new solid is created so its base is perpendicular to the path. See **Figure 7-5.** Also, one of the endpoints of the path should be on the plane of the object to be extruded. If it is not, the path is temporarily moved to the center of the profile. The following prompts may appear after the path is selected.

> Select path: *(pick the path)*
> Path was moved to the center of the profile.
> Profile was oriented to be perpendicular to the path.
> Command:

**Figure 7-5.**
When the spline
path is not
perpendicular to the
2D profile (both are
shown here in
color), the base
profile is rotated to
be perpendicular to
the path.

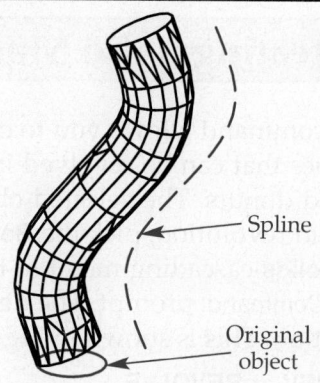

Spline

Original
object

---

## Exercise 7-1

○ Begin a new drawing.
○ Construct a hex head bolt, excluding threads, as a solid model. Make the bolt body 5/16″ diameter and 2″ long. Make the hex head 1/2″ across the flats and 3/16″ thick. Make the head and body a single solid.
○ Orient the bolt vertically with the head at the top.
○ Construct a second bolt oriented vertically with the head at the bottom.
○ Construct a flat-head wood screw, excluding threads, as a solid model. Make the body 3/16″ diameter at the base of the head, 7/8″ long, and taper to a point. Make the head 3/8″ in diameter, taper to the 3/16″ diameter body, and 1/8″ thick. Make the head and body a single solid.
○ Orient the wood screw so the head faces to the left of the screen at a 90° angle to the bolts.
○ Save the drawing as EX7-1.

---

## Extruding Regions

In Chapter 6 you learned how to create 2D regions. As an example, you created the top view of the base shown in **Figure 7-6A** as a region. Regions can be extruded to create 3D solids. The base you created in Chapter 6 can be extruded to create the final solid shown in **Figure 7-6B.** Any features of the region, such as holes, are extruded the same thickness as the rest of the object. Using this method, you can construct a fairly complex 2D region that includes curved profiles, holes, slots, etc. Then, a complex 3D solid can be quickly created. Additional details can then be added using editing commands or Boolean operations.

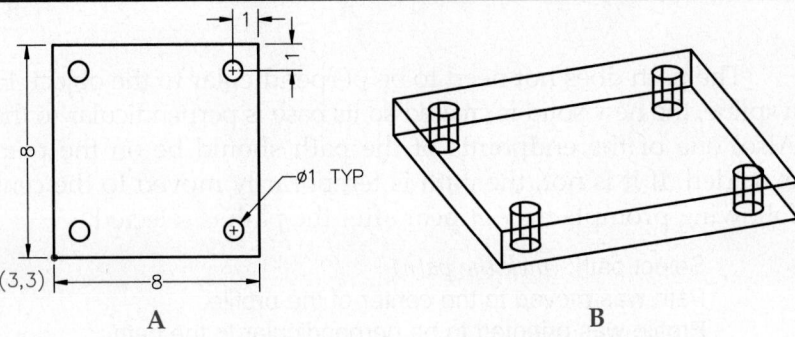

Figure 7-6.
A—The 2D region that will be extruded. B—The solid object created by extruding the region.

## Creating Solid Model Revolutions

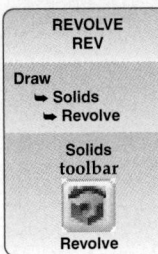
The **REVOLVE** command allows you to create solids by revolving a closed shape about an axis. Shapes that can be revolved include circles, ellipses, polylines, closed splines, regions, and donuts. The selected object can be revolved at any angle up to 360°. To create a solid revolution, pick the **Revolve** button on the **Solids** toolbar, select **Revolve** from the **Solids** cascading menu in the **Draw** pull-down menu, or enter REV or REVOLVE at the Command: prompt. The default option is to pick the two endpoints of an axis of revolution. This is shown in **Figure 7-7.**

Command: **REV** *or* **REVOLVE.**↵
Current wire frame density: ISOLINES=*current*
Select objects: *(pick the object to revolve)*
Select objects: ↵
Specify start point for axis of revolution or define axis by [Object/X (axis)/Y (axis)]:
    *(pick P1)*
Specify endpoint of axis: *(pick P2)*
Specify angle of revolution <360>:↵
Command:

Figure 7-7.
Points P1 and P2 are selected as the axis of revolution.

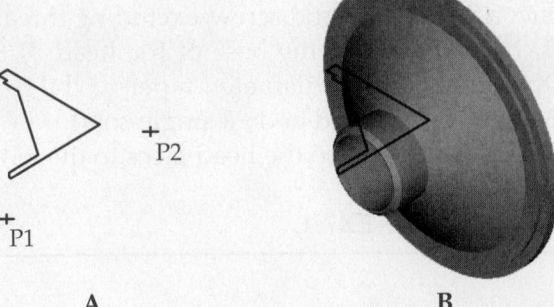

A                                    B

# Revolving about an Axis Line Object

You can select an object, such as a line, as the axis of revolution. **Figure 7-8** shows a solid created using the **Object** option of the **REVOLVE** command. Both a full circle (360°) revolution and a 270° revolution are shown.

Specify start point for axis of revolution or define axis by [Object/X (axis)/Y (axis)]: **O**↵
Select an object: *(pick the axis line)*
Specify angle of revolution <360>: ↵
Command:

**Figure 7-8.**
An axis of revolution can be selected using the **Object** option of the **REVOLVE** command. Here, the line is selected as the axis.

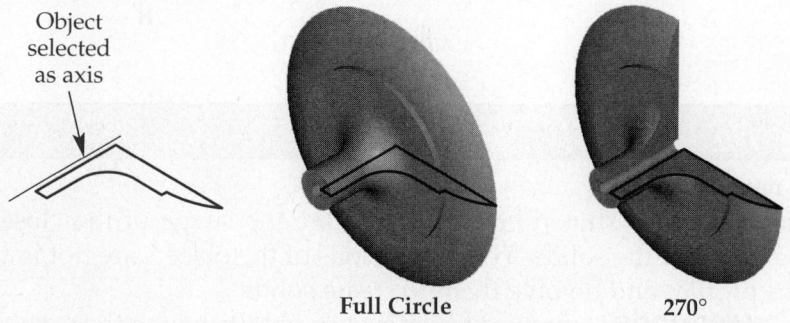

Object
selected
as axis

Full Circle                    270°

# Revolving about the X Axis or Y Axis

The X axis of the current UCS can be used as the axis of revolution by selecting the **X** option of the **REVOLVE** command. The origin of the current UCS is used as one end of the X axis line. Notice in **Figure 7-9** that two different shapes can be created from the same 2D profile by changing the UCS origin. No hole appears in the object in **Figure 7-9B** because the profile was revolved about an edge that coincides with the X axis. The Y axis can also be used as the axis of revolution. See **Figure 7-10**.

Specify start point for axis of revolution or define axis by [Object/X (axis)/Y (axis)]: **X**↵
Specify angle of revolution <360>: ↵
Command:

**Figure 7-9.**
A—A solid is created using the X axis as the axis of revolution. B—A different object is created with the same profile by changing the UCS origin.

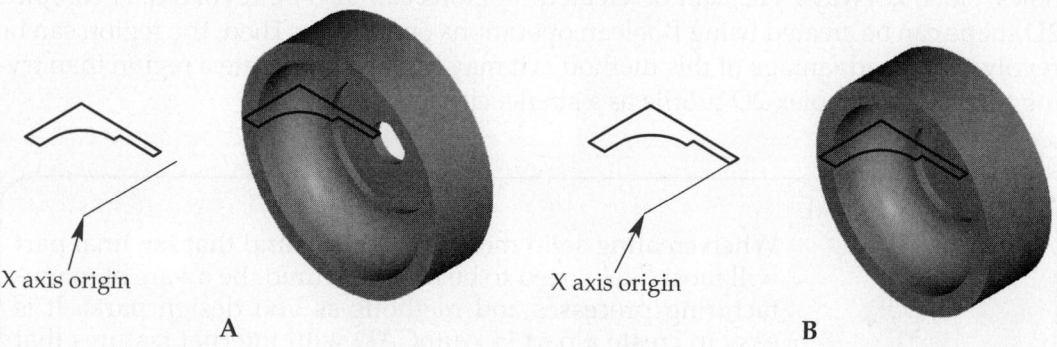

X axis origin                              X axis origin

A                                         B

**Figure 7-10.**
A—A solid is created using the Y axis as the axis of revolution. B—A different object is created by changing the UCS origin.

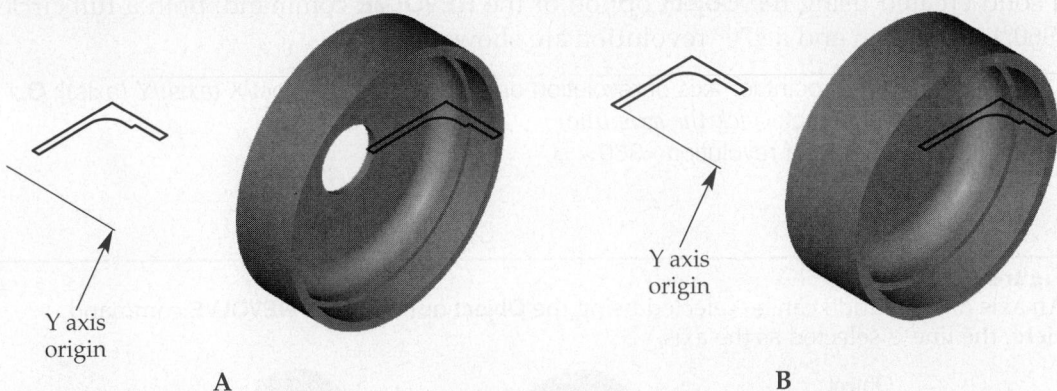

Y axis
origin

Y axis
origin

A

B

## Revolving Regions

Earlier in this chapter you learned that regions can be extruded. In this manner, holes, slots, keyways, etc., can be created. Regions can also be revolved. A complex 2D shape can be created using Boolean operations on regions. Then, the region can be revolved. One advantage of this method is it may be easier to create a region than trying to create a complex 2D profile as a single, closed polyline.

**PROFESSIONAL TIP**

When creating solid models, keep in mind that the final part will most likely need to be manufactured. Be aware of manufacturing processes and methods as you design parts. It is easy to create a part in AutoCAD with internal features that may be impossible to manufacture, especially when revolving a profile.

# Using **EXTRUDE** and **REVOLVE** as Construction Tools

It is unlikely that an extrusion or revolution will result in a finished object. Rather, these operations will be used with other solid model construction methods, such as Boolean operations, to create the final object. The next sections discuss how to use **EXTRUDE** and **REVOLVE** with other construction methods to create a finished object.

## Creating Features with **EXTRUDE**

You can create a wide variety of features with the **EXTRUDE** command. Study the shapes shown in **Figure 7-11.** These detailed solid objects were created by drawing a profile and then using the **EXTRUDE** command. The objects in **Figure 7-11C** and **Figure 7-11D** must first be constructed as regions before they are extruded. For example, the five holes (circles) in **Figure 7-11D** must be removed from the base region using the **SUBTRACT** command.

Look at **Figure 7-12.** This is part of a clamping device used to hold parts on a mill table. There is a T-slot milled through the block to receive a T-bolt and one side is stair-stepped, under which parts are clamped. If you look closely at the end of the object, most of the detail can be drawn as a 2D region and then extruded. However, there are also two holes in the top of the block to allow for bolting the clamp to the mill table. These must be added to the extruded solid.

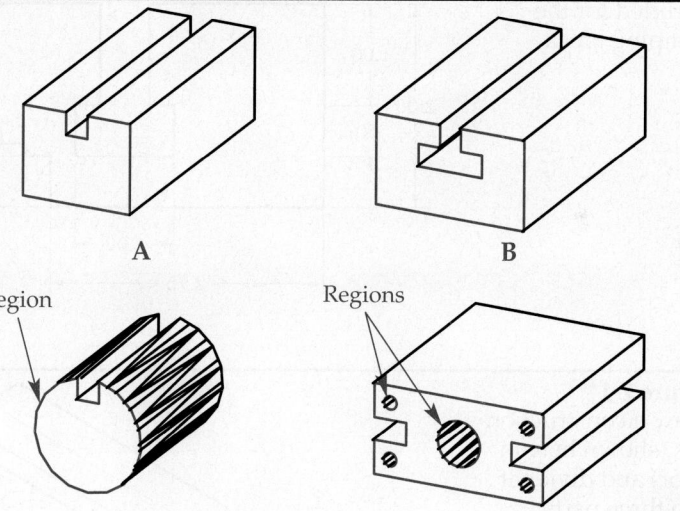

**Figure 7-11.**
Detailed solids can be created by extruding the profile of an object. The profiles are shown here in color.

A      B

Region      Regions

C      D

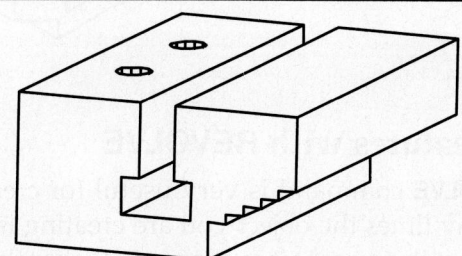

**Figure 7-12.**
Most of this object can be created by extruding a profile. However, the holes must be added after the extruded solid is created.

First, change the UCS to the front preset orthographic UCS. Display a plan view of the UCS. Then, draw the profile shown in **Figure 7-13** using the **PLINE** command. You can draw it in stages, if you like, and then use the **PEDIT** command to join all segments into a single polyline.

Next, use the **EXTRUDE** command to create the 3D solid. Extrude the profile a distance of –6 units with a 0° taper. This will extrude the object away from you. Display the object from the southeast isometric preset viewpoint or use the **3DORBIT** command. The object should look similar to **Figure 7-12** without the holes in the top.

The two holes are ∅.5 and evenly spaced on the surface through which they pass. Change to the WCS and draw a construction line from midpoint to midpoint, as shown in **Figure 7-14**. Then, set **PDMODE** to an appropriate value, such as 3, and use the **DIVIDE** command to divide the construction line into three parts. The two points created by the **DIVIDE** command are equally spaced on the surface and can be used to locate the two holes.

There are two ways to create the holes. You can draw a circle and extrude it or you can draw a solid cylinder. Either way, you need to subtract the cylinder to create the hole. Drawing a solid cylinder is probably easiest. When prompted for a center, use the **Node** object snap to select the point. Then, enter the diameter. Finally, enter a negative height so that the cylinder extends into the solid.

You can either copy the first cylinder to the second point or draw another cylinder. When both cylinders are located, use the **SUBTRACT** command to remove them from the solid. The object is now complete and should look like **Figure 7-12**.

**Figure 7-13.**
This is the profile that will be extruded for the clamping block.

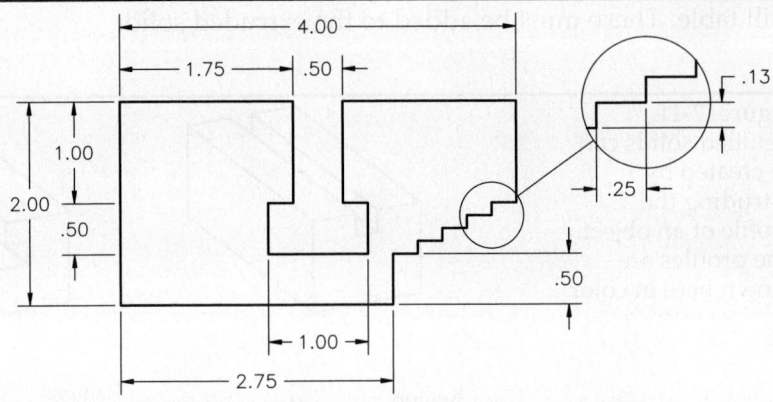

**Figure 7-14.**
Draw a construction line (shown here in color) and divide it into three parts.

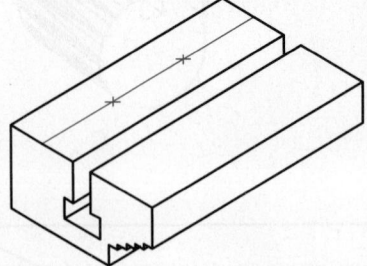

## Creating Features with REVOLVE

The **REVOLVE** command is very useful for creating symmetrical, round objects. However, many times the object you are creating is not completely symmetrical. For example, look at the camshaft in **Figure 7-15**. For the most part, this is a symmetrical, round object. However, the cam lobes are not symmetrical in relation to the shaft and bearings. The **REVOLVE** command can be used to create the shaft and bearings. Then, the cam lobes can be created and added.

**Figure 7-15.**
For the most part, this object is symmetrical about its center axis. However, the cam lobes are not symmetrical about the axis.

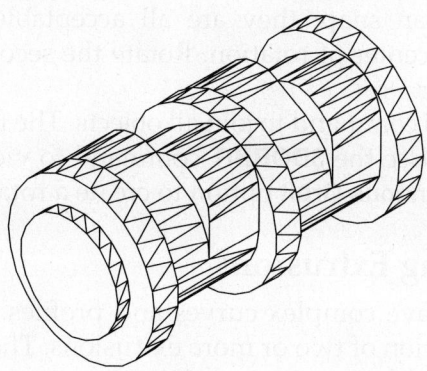

Start a new drawing and make sure the WCS is the current UCS. Using the **PLINE** command, draw the profile shown in **Figure 7-16A.** This profile will be revolved through 360°, so you only need to draw half of the true plan view of the cam profile. The profile represents the shaft and three bearings.

Next, display the drawing from the southwest isometric preset viewpoint. Then, use the **REVOLVE** command to create the base camshaft. Pick the endpoints shown in **Figure 7-16A** as the axis of revolution. Revolve the profile through 360°. Zoom extents and use the **HIDE** command to clearly see the object.

Now, you need to create one cam lobe. Change the UCS to the left orthographic preset. Then, draw a construction point in the center of the left end of the camshaft. Use the **Center** object snap and an appropriate **PDMODE** setting. Next, draw the profile shown in **Figure 7-16B.** Use the construction point you drew as the center of the large radius. You may want to create a new layer and turn off the display of the base camshaft.

Once the cam lobe profile is created, use the **REGION** command to create a region. Then, use the **EXTRUDE** command to extrude the region a height of –.5 units. The extrusion should have a 0° taper. If you turned off the display of the base camshaft, turn it back on now.

One cam lobe is created, but it is not in the proper position. Make sure the left UCS is current. Then, move the cam lobe –.375 units on the Z axis. This places the front surface of the cam lobe on the back surface of the first bearing. Now, make a copy of the lobe that is located –.5 units on the Z axis. Finally, copy the first two cam lobes –1.25 units on the Z axis.

**Figure 7-16.**
A—This profile will be revolved to create the shaft and bearings. The pick points for the axis of revolution are shown. B—This is the profile of one cam lobe, which will be extruded.

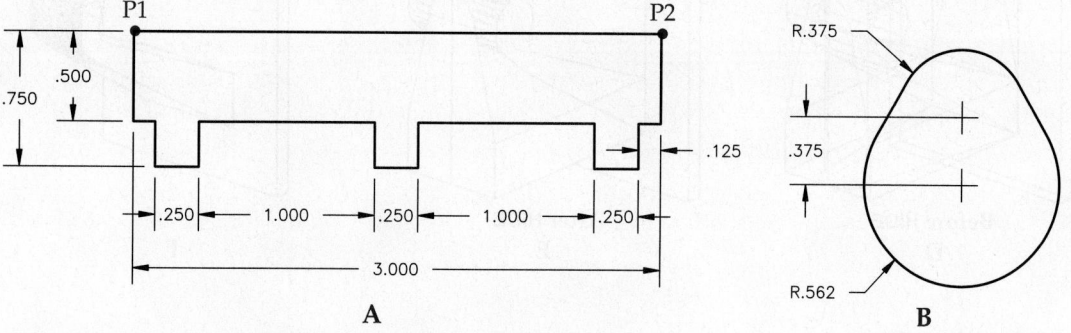

You now need to rotate the four cam lobes to their correct orientations. Make sure the left UCS is still current. Then, rotate the first and third cam lobes 30°. The center of rotation should be the center of the shaft. There are many points on the shaft to which the **Center** object snap can snap; they are all acceptable. You can also use the construction point as the center of rotation. Rotate the second and fourth cam lobes −30° about the same center.

Finally, use the **UNION** command to join all objects. The final object should appear as shown in **Figure 7-15**. Use the **3DORBIT** command to view all sides of the object. You can also use the **Continuous Orbit** option to create a rotating display.

## Multiple Intersecting Extrusions

Many solid objects have complex curves and profiles. These can often be constructed from the intersection of two or more extrusions. The resulting solid is a combination of only the intersecting volumes of the extrusions. The following example shows the construction of a coat hook.

1. Construct the first profile, **Figure 7-17A.**
2. Construct the second profile located on a common point with the first, **Figure 7-17B.**
3. Construct the third profile located on the common point, **Figure 7-17C.**
4. Extrude each profile the required dimension into the same area. Be careful to specify positive or negative heights for each extrusion, **Figure 7-17D** and **Figure 7-17E.**
5. Use the **INTERSECT** command to create a composite solid from the volume shared by the three extrusions, **Figure 7-17F.**

**Figure 7-17.**
Constructing a coat hook. A—Draw the first profile. B—Draw the second profile. C—Draw the third profile. All three profiles should have a common origin. D—Extrude each profile so that the extruded objects intersect. E—The extruded objects with hidden lines removed. F—Use **INTERSECT** to create the composite solid. The final solid is shown here with hidden lines removed.

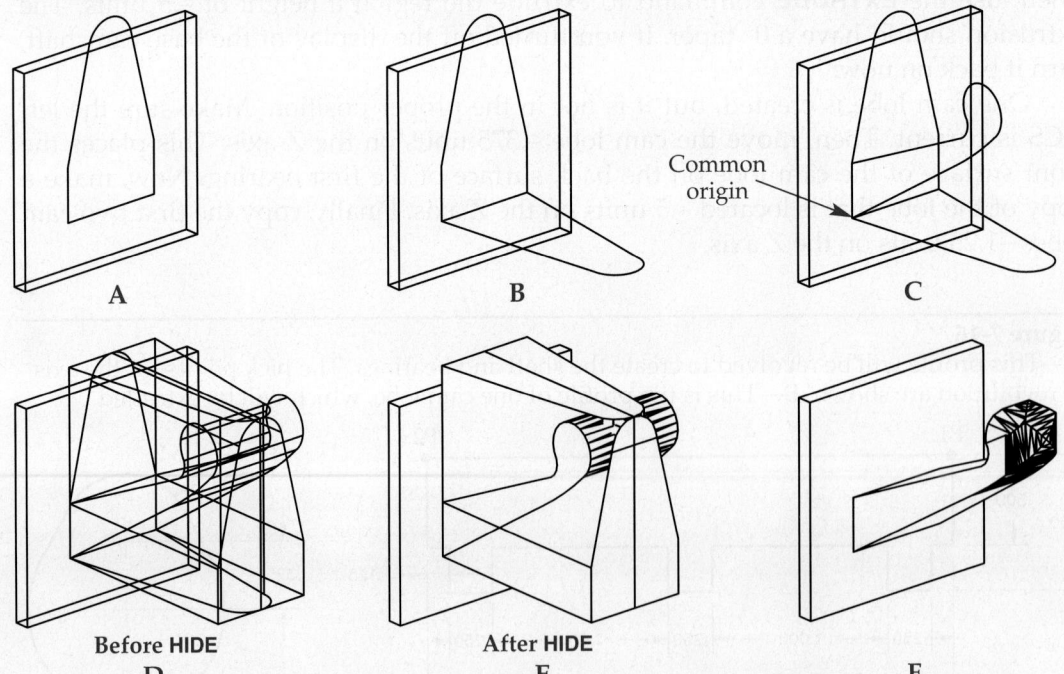

## Chapter Test

*Answer the following questions on a separate sheet of paper.*

1. What is an *extrusion*?
2. How can an extrusion be constructed to extend below the current UCS?
3. What is the range in which a taper angle can vary?
4. How can a curved extrusion be constructed?
5. If an extrusion is created as indicated in Question 4, what must be true if the base is reoriented perpendicular to the path by the command?
6. How is the height of an extrusion applied in relation to the original object?
7. What must be true of a 2D shape that is to be revolved?
8. What are the four different options for selecting the axis of revolution for a revolved solid?
9. How can a profile be revolved twice (or more) about the same axis and create different shaped solids?
10. What is one advantage of revolving a region over revolving a polyline?

## Drawing Problems

1. Construct a 12' long section of wide flange structural steel with the cross section shown below. Use the dimensions given. Save the drawing as P7-1.

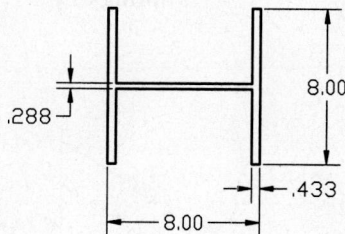

*Problems 2–7. These problems require you to use a variety of solid modeling methods to construct the objects. Use* **EXTRUDE**, **REVOLVE**, *solid primitives, and new UCSs to assist in construction. Save each as* **P7-xx.**

2.

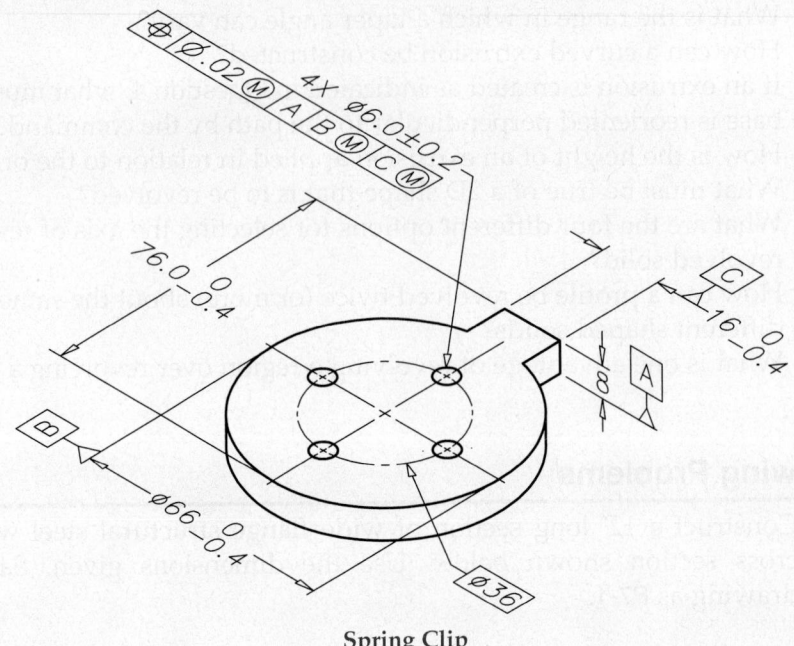

**Spring Clip**

3.

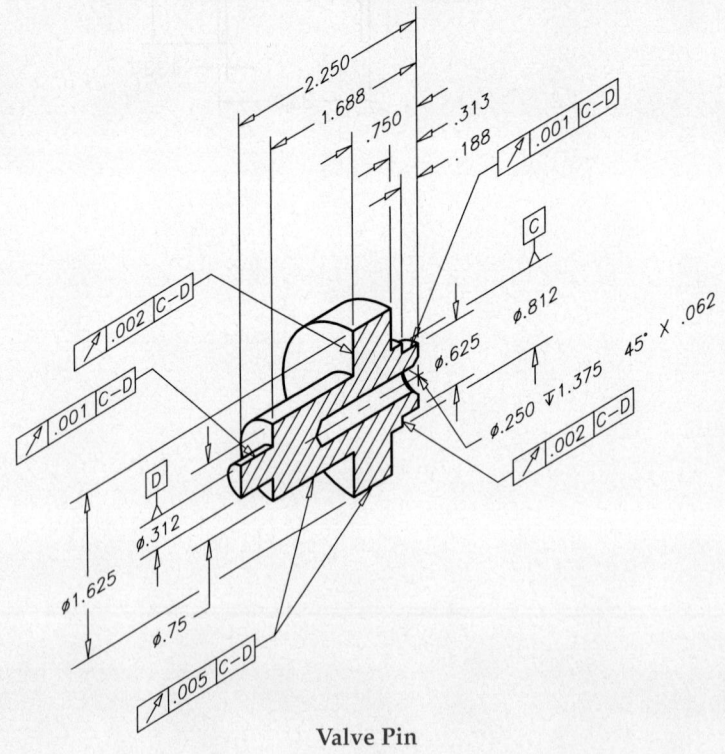

**Valve Pin**

4.

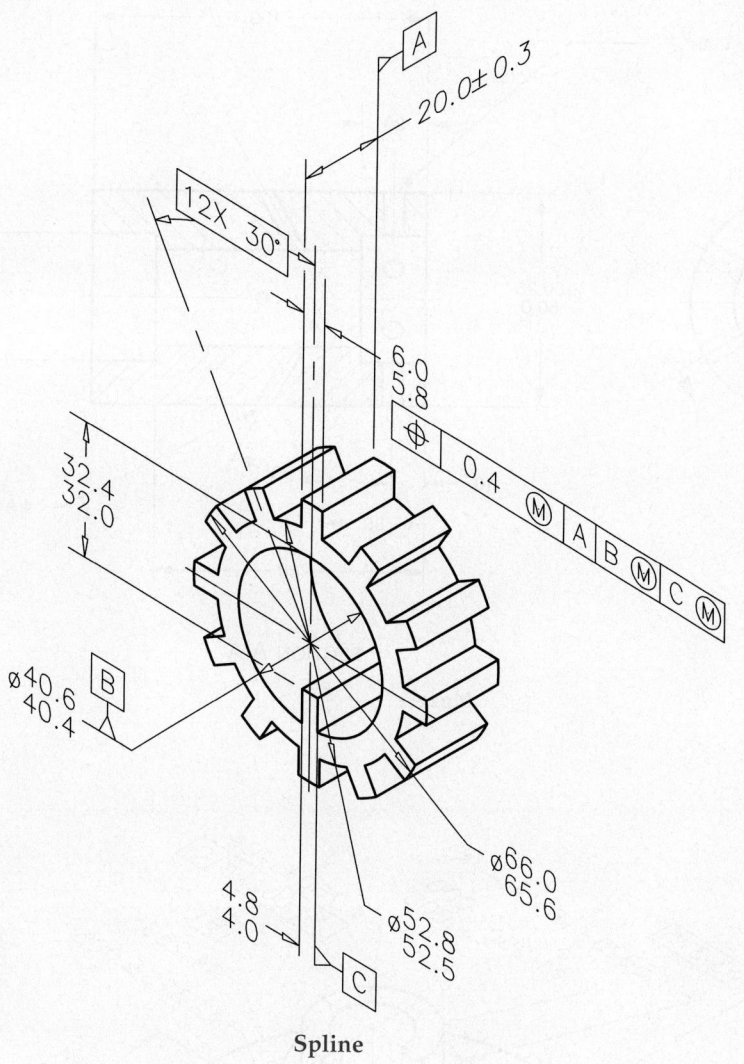

A

20.0± 0.3

12X  30°

6.0
5.8

⌖ 0.4 Ⓜ A B Ⓜ C Ⓜ

32.4
32.0

ø40.6
40.4  B

ø66.0
65.6

4.8
4.0

ø52.8
52.5  C

**Spline**

5.

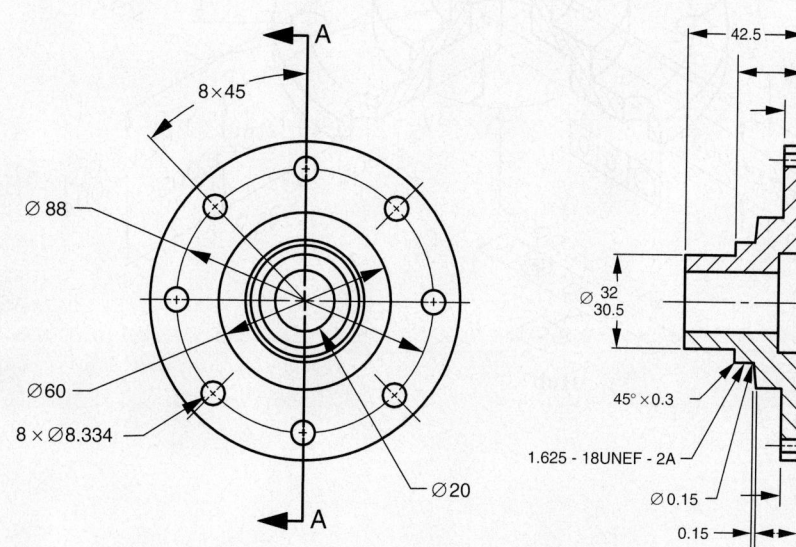

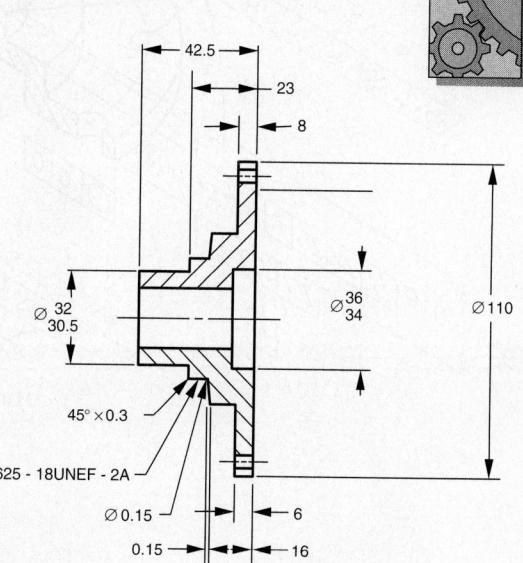

A

8×45

Ø 88

Ø 60

8 × Ø8.334

Ø 20

A

42.5

23

8

Ø 32
30.5

Ø 36
34

Ø 110

45° × 0.3

1.625 - 18UNEF - 2A

Ø 0.15

6

0.15

16

**Flange**

6.

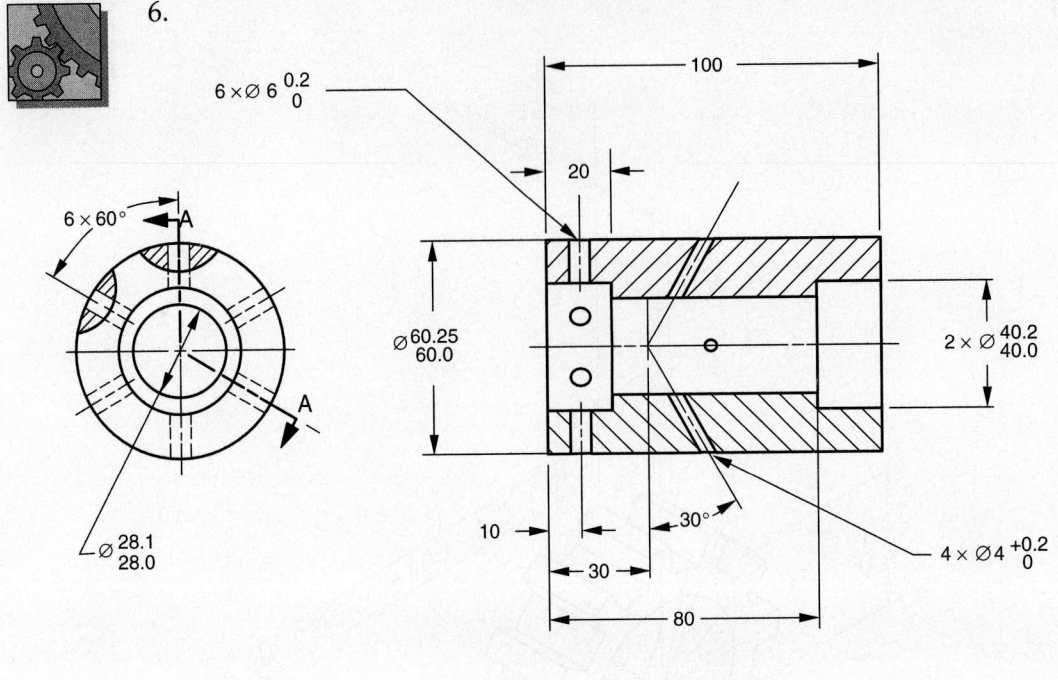

$6 \times \varnothing 6 \begin{smallmatrix} 0.2 \\ 0 \end{smallmatrix}$

$6 \times 60°$

100

20

$\varnothing \begin{smallmatrix} 60.25 \\ 60.0 \end{smallmatrix}$

$2 \times \varnothing \begin{smallmatrix} 40.2 \\ 40.0 \end{smallmatrix}$

$\varnothing \begin{smallmatrix} 28.1 \\ 28.0 \end{smallmatrix}$

10

$30°$

30

$4 \times \varnothing 4 \begin{smallmatrix} +0.2 \\ 0 \end{smallmatrix}$

80

SECTION A-A

**Nozzle**

7.

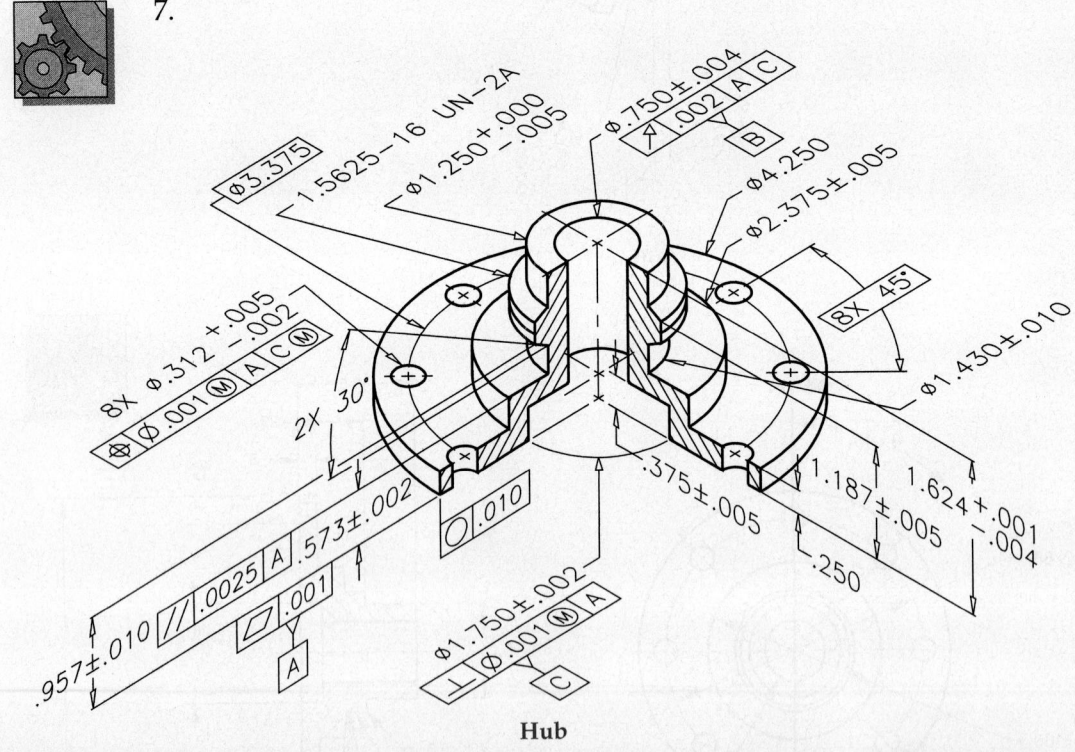

$\varnothing 3.375$

1.5625–16 UN–2A

$\varnothing 1.250 \begin{smallmatrix} +.000 \\ -.005 \end{smallmatrix}$

$\varnothing .750 \pm .004$

| ∡ | .002 | A | C |

| B |

$\varnothing 4.250$

$\varnothing 2.375 \pm .005$

| 8X | 45° |

$\varnothing 1.430 \pm .010$

8X $\varnothing .312 \begin{smallmatrix} +.005 \\ -.002 \end{smallmatrix}$

| ⌖ | $\varnothing .001$ Ⓜ | A | C | Ⓜ |

$2X \ 30°$

| ⬭ | .010 |

$.375 \pm .005$

$1.187 \pm .005$

$1.624 \begin{smallmatrix} +.001 \\ -.004 \end{smallmatrix}$

.250

$.573 \pm .002$

| ⫽ | .0025 | A |

| ⟋ | .001 |

| A |

$.957 \pm .010$

$\varnothing 1.750 \pm .002$

| ⊥ | $\varnothing .001$ Ⓜ | A |

| C |

**Hub**

AutoCAD and its Applications—Advanced

8. Construct picture frame moldings using the profiles shown below.
   A. Draw each of the closed profiles shown. Use your own dimensions for the details of the moldings.
   B. The length and width of A and B should be no larger than 1.5″ × 1″.
   C. The length and width of C and D should be no larger than 3″ × 1.5″.
   D. Construct 8″ × 12″ picture frames using moldings A and B.
   E. Construct 12″ × 24″ picture frames using moldings C and D.
   F. Save the drawing as P7-8.

A

B

C

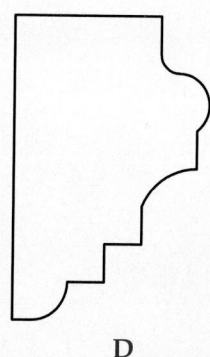

D

9. Construct a solid model of the faucet handle shown below.
   A. Create three user coordinate systems. Use a common origin for each UCS.
   B. Draw each profile using the dimensions given.
   C. Extrude each profile into a common space. Be sure to use the proper Z value when extruding.
   D. Create an intersection of the three profiles to produce the final solid.
   E. Save the drawing as P7-9.

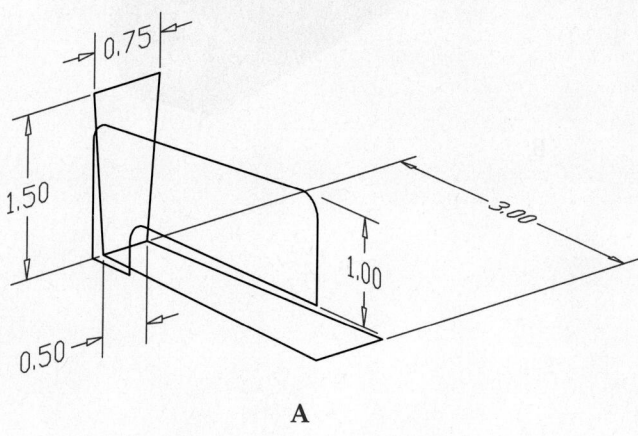

A

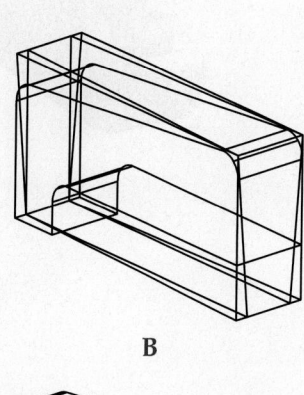

B

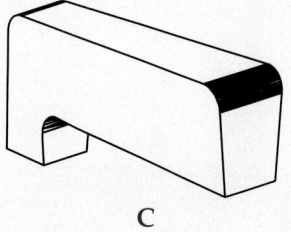

C

A—These three primitives will be used to create a completed solid model. B—By using editing commands such as **COPY**, **MOVE**, **ARRAY**, **UNION**, **SUBTRACT**, and **SOLIDEDIT**, the primitives are quickly turned into a side cover for a chainsaw.

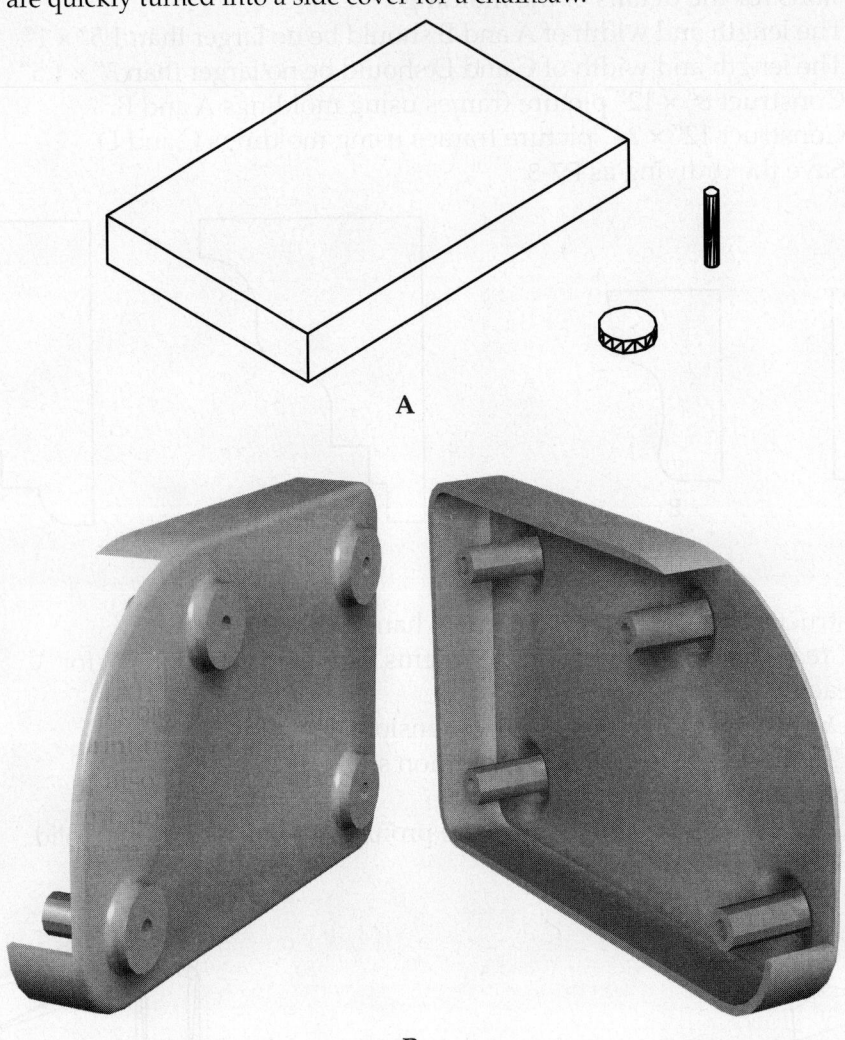

A

B

# Solid Modeling Details

## Learning Objectives

After completing this chapter, you will be able to:
- Change properties on solids.
- Align objects.
- Rotate objects in three dimensions.
- Mirror objects in three dimensions.
- Create 3D arrays.
- Fillet solid objects.
- Chamfer solid objects.
- Construct details on solid models.
- Remove features from solid models.

## Changing Properties

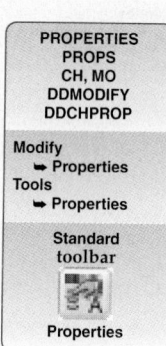

PROPERTIES
PROPS
CH, MO
DDMODIFY
DDCHPROP

**Modify**
➥ Properties
**Tools**
➥ Properties

**Standard**
**toolbar**

Properties

Properties of 3D objects can be modified using the **Properties** window, which is discussed thoroughly in *AutoCAD and its Applications—Basics.* This window is accessed by picking the **Properties** button on the **Standard** toolbar; picking **Properties** from the **Modify** or **Tools** pull-down menus; or typing CH, MO, PROPS, PROPERTIES, DDMODIFY, or DDCHPROP at the Command: prompt. You can also double-click on a solid object or press [Ctrl] + [1] on the keyboard.

The **Properties** window lists the properties of the currently selected object. For example, **Figure 8-1** lists the properties of a selected solid sphere. For a solid, only the **General** category is displayed. AutoCAD is not a parametric solid modeling program. A parametric program would allow you to change the parameters, such as a sphere's diameter, in the **Properties** window. You can, however, change a solid's linetype, linetype scale, color, layer, and lineweight. Remember, the shaded color of an object is determined by its display color.

To modify an object property, select the property. Then, enter a new value in the right-hand column. The drawing is updated to reflect the changes. You can leave the **Properties** window open as you continue with your work.

Surface models, which are discussed later in this book, may have other properties that can be changed. Other object types, such as 3D polylines, also have additional properties that can be changed.

**Figure 8-1.**
The **Properties** window can be used to change certain properties of a solid object.

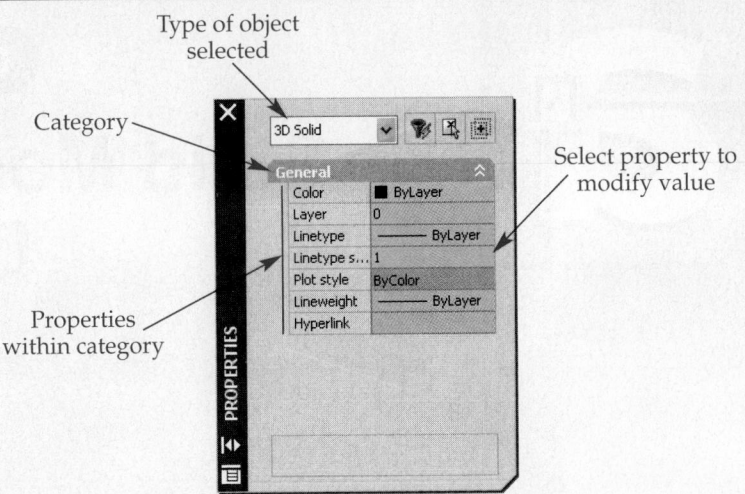

Type of object selected

Category

Select property to modify value

Properties within category

---

NOTE

The **CHANGE** command can also be used to change the base point and some properties of 3D objects from the Command: prompt. However, it has some limitations when an object is not perpendicular to the Z axis of the current UCS. The **CHPROP** command is similar to the **CHANGE** command, but can only be used to modify a few object properties.

---

## Aligning Objects in 3D

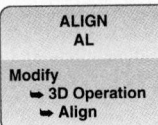

ALIGN
AL

Modify
➥ 3D Operation
➥ Align

The **ALIGN** command allows you to reorient an object in 3D space. Using it, you can correct errors of 3D construction and quickly manipulate 3D objects. **ALIGN** requires existing points (source) and the new location of those existing points (destination). The **ALIGN** command can be selected by picking **Align** from the **3D Operation** cascading menu of the **Modify** pull-down menu or entering AL or ALIGN at the Command: prompt.

For example, refer to **Figure 8-2**. The wedge in **Figure 8-2A** is aligned in its new position in **Figure 8-2B** as follows. Set the **Intersection** or **Endpoint** running object snap to make point selection easier. Refer to the figure for the pick points.

Command: **AL** or **ALIGN**.↵
Select objects: (*pick the wedge*)
Select objects: ↵
Specify first source point: (*pick P1*)
Specify first destination point: (*pick P2*)
Specify second source point: (*pick P3*)
Specify second destination point: (*pick P4*)
Specify third source point or <continue>: (*pick P5*)
Specify third destination point: (*pick P1 again*)
Command:

**Figure 8-2.**
The **Align** command can be used to properly orient 3D objects.

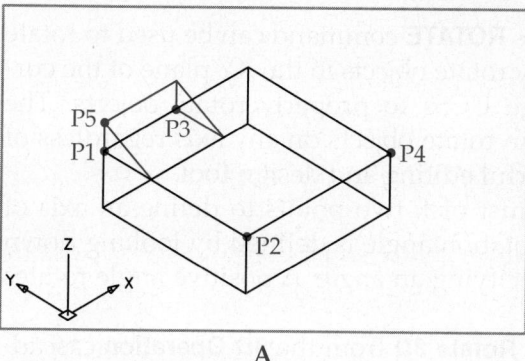

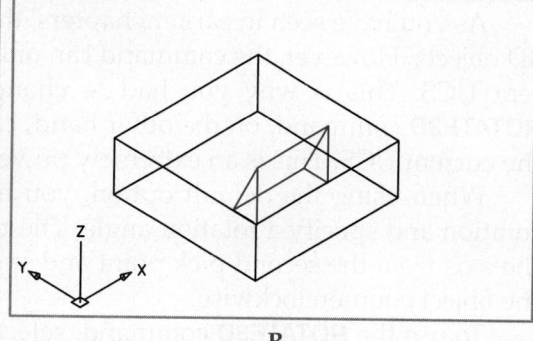

A

B

---

**PROFESSIONAL TIP**

The **Align** button can be placed on a custom or existing toolbar. Refer to Chapter 19 for information on customizing toolbars.

---

**PROFESSIONAL TIP**

Before using 3D editing commands, set running object snaps to enhance your accuracy and speed.

---

## Exercise 8-1

○ Begin a new drawing.
○ Draw a box and a wedge arranged like those shown in **Figure 8-2A**.
○ Use the **ALIGN** command to create the arrangement shown below.
○ Save the drawing as EX8-1.

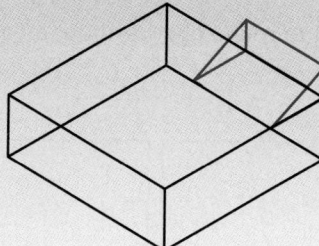

---

# 3D Rotating

As you have seen in earlier chapters, the **ROTATE** command can be used to rotate 3D objects. However, the command can only rotate objects in the XY plane of the current UCS. This is why you had to change UCSs to properly rotate objects. The **ROTATE3D** command, on the other hand, can rotate objects on any axis regardless of the current UCS. This is an extremely powerful editing and design tool.

When using the default option, you must pick two points to define an axis of rotation and specify a rotation angle. The rotation angle is defined by looking down the axis from the second pick point and specifying an angle. A positive angle rotates the object counterclockwise.

To use the **ROTATE3D** command, select **Rotate 3D** from the **3D Operation** cascading menu in the **Modify** pull-down menu or enter ROTATE3D at the Command: prompt. The following example rotates the wedge in **Figure 8-2B** –90° on a selected axis. See **Figure 8-3A** for the pick points. The rotated object is shown in **Figure 8-3B**.

ROTATE3D

Modify
➡ 3D Operation
➡ Rotate 3D

```
Command: ROTATE3D↵
Current positive angle: ANGDIR=(current) ANGBASE=(current)
Select objects: (pick the wedge)
1 found
Select objects: ↵
Specify first point on axis or define axis by
    [Object/Last/View/Xaxis/Yaxis/Zaxis/2points]: (pick P1)
Specify second point on axis: (pick P2)
Specify rotation angle or [Reference]: –90↵
Command:
```

There are several different ways to define an axis of rotation with the **ROTATE3D** command. These are explained as follows.

- **Object.** Objects such as lines, arcs, circles, and polylines can define the axis. A line becomes the axis. The axis of a circle or arc passes through its center, perpendicular to the plane of the circle. For a polyline, the selected segment (line or arc) is used to determine the axis.
- **Last.** Uses the last axis of rotation defined.
- **View.** The viewing direction of the current viewport is aligned with a selected point to define the axis.

Figure 8-3.
The **ROTATE3D** command is used to rotate objects about an axis in 3D space regardless of the current UCS.

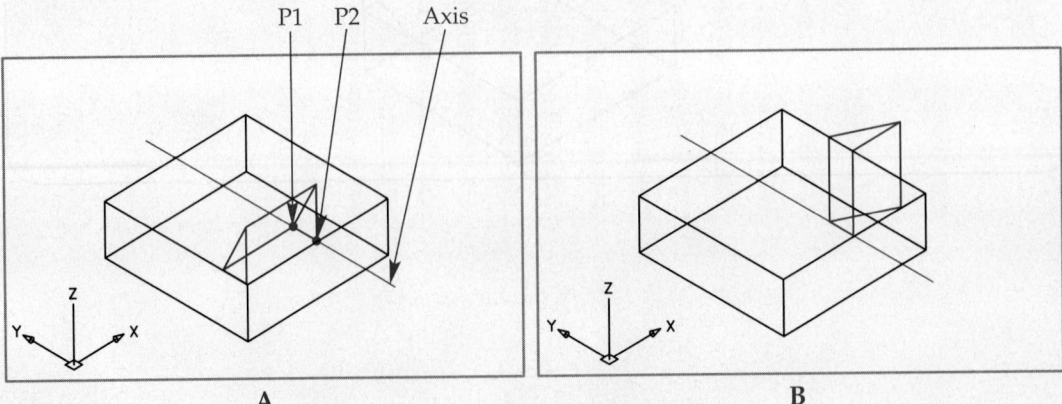

- **Xaxis/Yaxis/Zaxis.** Aligns the axis of rotation with the X, Y, or Z axis of the current UCS and a selected point.
- **2points.** Allows you to pick two points to define the axis.

### Exercise 8-2

○ Open the drawing created in the last exercise (EX8-1).
○ Use the **ROTATE3D** command to rotate the wedge to the position shown below.
○ Save the drawing as EX8-2.

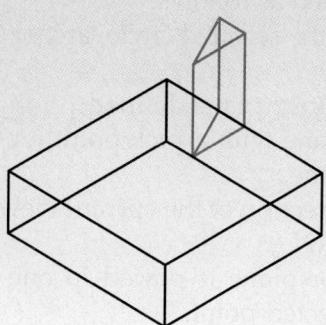

## 3D Mirroring

The **MIRROR** command can be used to rotate 3D objects. However, like the **ROTATE** command, the **MIRROR** command can only mirror objects in the XY plane of the current UCS. Often, to properly mirror objects with the command, you have to change UCSs. The **MIRROR3D** command, on the other hand, allows you to mirror objects about any plane regardless of the current UCS.

To use the **MIRROR3D** command, select **Mirror 3D** from the **3D Operation** cascading menu in the **Modify** pull-down menu, or type MIRROR3D at the Command: prompt. The default option is to define a mirror plane by picking three points on that plane, **Figure 8-4A.** Object snap modes should be used to accurately define the mirror plane.

To mirror the wedge in **Figure 8-3B,** set the **Midpoint** running object snap and use the following command sequence. The resulting drawing is shown in **Figure 8-4B.**

MIRROR3D<br>
Modify<br>
➥ 3D Operation<br>
➥ Mirror 3D

```
Command: MIRROR3D↵
Select objects: (pick the wedge)
1 found
Select objects: ↵
Specify first point of mirror plane (3 points) or
[Object/Last/Zaxis/View/XY/YZ/ZX/3points] <3points>: (pick P1)
Specify second point on mirror plane: (pick P2)
Specify third point on mirror plane: (pick P3)
Delete source objects? [Yes/No] <N>: ↵
Command:
```

**Figure 8-4.**
The **MIRROR3D** command allows you to mirror objects about any plane regardless of the current UCS. A—The mirror plane defined by the three pick points is shown here in color. B—A copy of the original object is mirrored.

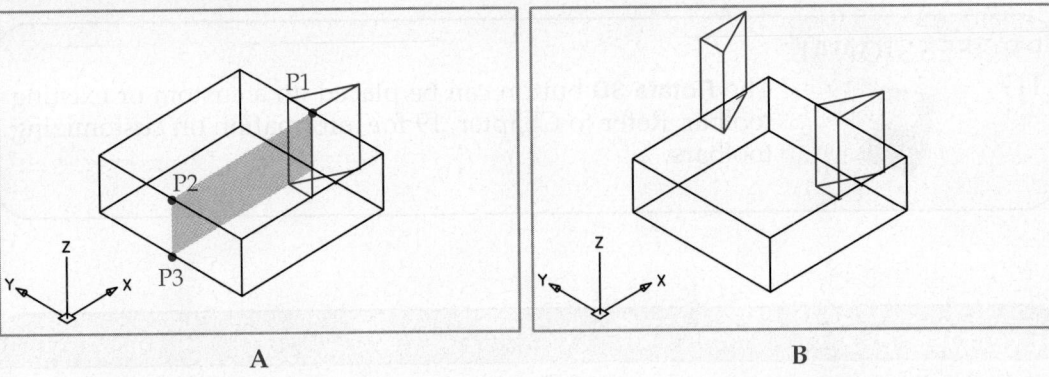

A                                            B

There are several different ways to define a mirror plane with the **MIRROR3D** command. These are explained as follows.

- **Object.** The plane of the selected circle, arc, or 2D polyline segment is used as the mirror plane.
- **Last.** Uses the last mirror plane defined.
- **Zaxis.** Defines the plane with a pick point on the plane and a point on the Z axis of the mirror plane.
- **View.** The viewing direction of the current viewpoint is aligned with a selected point to define the axis.
- **XY/YZ/XZ.** The mirror plane is placed in one of the three basic planes, and passes through a selected point.
- **3points.** Allows you to pick three points to define the mirror plane.

**PROFESSIONAL TIP**

The **Mirror 3D** button can be placed on a custom or existing toolbar. Refer to Chapter 19 for information on customizing toolbars.

## Exercise 8-3

○ Open the drawing created in the last exercise (EX8-2).
○ Use the **MIRROR3D** command to mirror the wedge to the position drawn below.
○ Save the drawing as EX8-3.

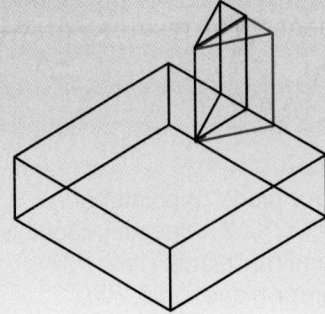

AutoCAD and its Applications—Advanced

# Creating 3D Arrays

The **ARRAY** command can be used to create either a rectangular or polar array of a 3D object on the XY plane of the current UCS. You probably used this command to complete some of the problems at the end of Chapter 7. The **3DARRAY** command allows you to array an object in 3D space. In a rectangular 3D array, as with a 2D rectangular array, you must enter the number of rows and columns. However, you must also specify the number of *levels,* which represents the third (Z) dimension. The command sequence is similar to that used with the 2D array command, with two added prompts. There are two types of 3D arrays—rectangular and polar.

## Rectangular 3D Arrays

An example of where a rectangular 3D array may be created is the layout of structural steel columns on multiple floors of a commercial building. In **Figure 8-5A,** you can see two concrete floor slabs of a building and a single steel column. It is now a simple matter of arraying the steel column in rows, columns, and levels.

To use the **3DARRAY** command, select **3D Array** from the **3D Operation** cascading menu in the **Modify** pull-down menu or enter 3A or 3DARRAY at the Command: prompt. Then, specify the **Rectangular** option when prompted.

    Command: **3A** *or* **3DARRAY**↵
    Select objects: *(pick the object)*
    1 found
    Select objects: ↵
    Enter the type of array [Rectangular/Polar] <R>: **R**↵
    Enter the number of rows (---) <1>: **3**↵
    Enter the number of columns (¦¦¦) <1>: **5**↵
    Enter the number of levels (…) <1>: **2**↵
    Specify the distance between rows (---): **10'**↵
    Specify the distance between columns (¦¦¦): **10'**↵
    Specify the distance between levels (…): **12'8**↵
    Command:

The result is shown in **Figure 8-5B.** Constructions like this can be quickly assembled for multiple levels using the **3DARRAY** command only once.

---

**Figure 8-5.**
A—Two floors and one steel column are drawn. B—A rectangular 3D array is used to place all the required steel columns on both floors at the same time.

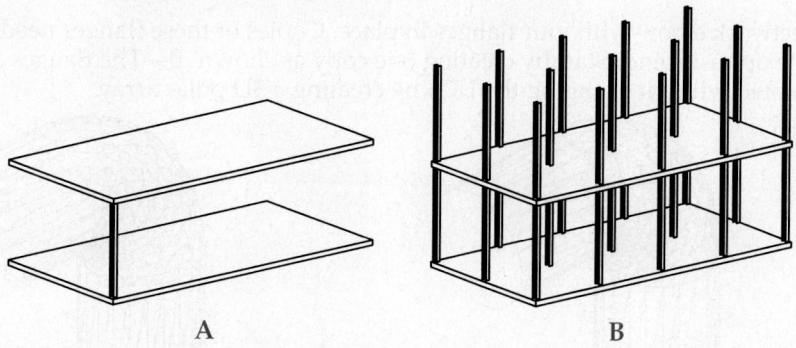

## Polar 3D Arrays

A polar 3D array is similar to a polar 2D array. However, the axis of rotation in a 2D polar array is parallel to the Z axis of the current UCS. In a 3D polar array, you can define a centerline axis of rotation that is not parallel to the Z axis of the current UCS. You can array an object in a UCS different from the current one. Unlike a rectangular 3D array, a polar 3D array does not allow you to create levels of the object. The object is arrayed in a plane defined by the object and the selected centerline (Z) axis.

To use the **3DARRAY** command, select **3D Array** from the **3D Operation** cascading menu in the **Modify** pull-down menu or enter 3A or 3DARRAY at the Command: prompt. Then, specify the **Polar** option when prompted.

For example, the four mounting flanges on the lower part of the duct in **Figure 8-6A** must be placed on the opposite end. However, notice the orientation of the UCS. First, copy one flange and rotate it to the proper orientation. Then, use the **3DARRAY** as follows. Make sure ortho is on.

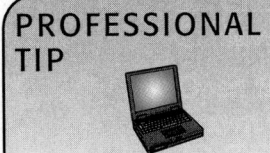

3DARRAY
3A

Modify
➡ 3D Operation
➡ 3D Array

> Command: **3A** *or* **3DARRAY**↵
> Select objects: *(select the copied flange)*
> 1 found
> Select objects: ↵
> Enter the type of array [Rectangular/Polar] <R>: **P**↵
> Enter the number of items in the array: **4**↵
> Specify the angle to fill (+=ccw, −=cw) <360>: ↵
> Rotate arrayed objects? [Yes/No] <Y>: ↵
> Specify center point of array: **CEN**↵
> of: *(pick the center of the upper duct opening)*
> Specify second point on axis of rotation: *(move the cursor so the ortho line projects out of the center of the duct opening and pick)*
> Command:

The completed 3D polar array is shown in **Figure 8-6B**. If additional levels of a polar array are needed, they can be created by copying the array just created.

---

**PROFESSIONAL TIP**

**3D Rectangular Array** and **3D Polar Array** buttons can be placed on a custom or existing toolbar. Refer to Chapter 19 for information on customizing toolbars.

---

Figure 8-6.
A—A 90° ductwork elbow with four flanges in place. Copies of these flanges need to be located on the opposite end. Start by creating one copy as shown. B—The flanges are properly oriented without changing the UCS by creating a 3D polar array.

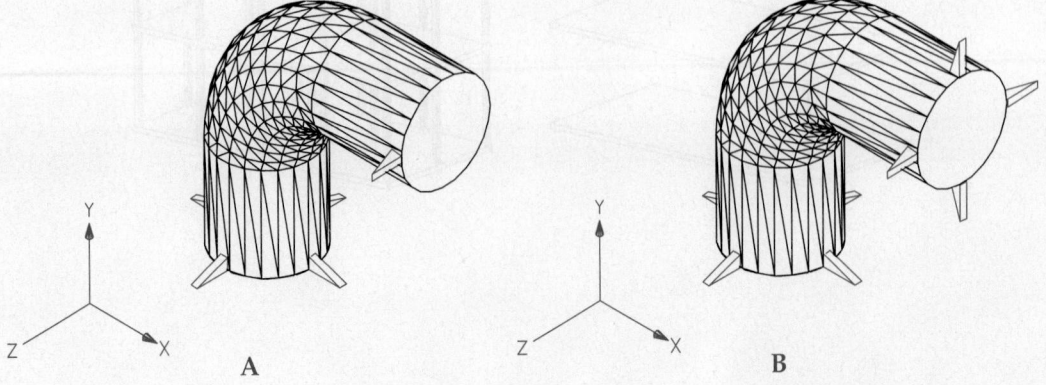

A      B

# Filleting Solid Objects

A fillet rounds the edges of an object, such as a box. Before a fillet is created at an intersection, the solid objects that intersect need to be joined using the **UNION** command. Then, use the **FILLET** command. See **Figure 8-7**. Since the object being filleted is actually a single solid and not two objects, only one edge is selected. In the following sequence, the fillet radius is set at .25, then the fillet is created.

Command: **F** *or* **FILLET**.↵
Current settings: Mode = TRIM, Radius = *current*
Select first object or [Polyline/Radius/Trim]: **R**↵
Specify fillet radius <*current*>: **.25**↵
Select first object or [Polyline/Radius/Trim]: *(pick edge to be filleted)*
Enter fillet radius <.25>: ↵
Select an edge or [Chain/Radius]: ↵ *(this fillets the selected edge, but you can also select other edges at this point)*
1 edge(s) selected for fillet.
Command:

Fillets are on internal edges. Rounds are on external edges. Examples of fillets and rounds are shown in **Figure 8-8**.

**Figure 8-7.**
A—Pick the edge where two unioned solids intersect to create a fillet.
B—The fillet after rendering.

Pick the edge

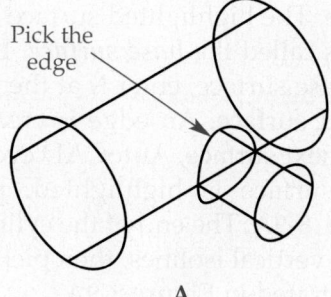
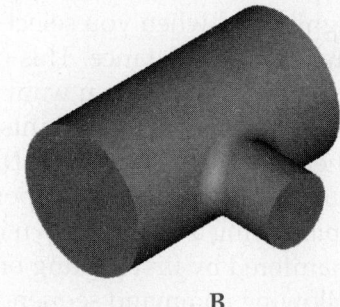

A                                          B

**Figure 8-8.**
Examples of fillets and rounds.

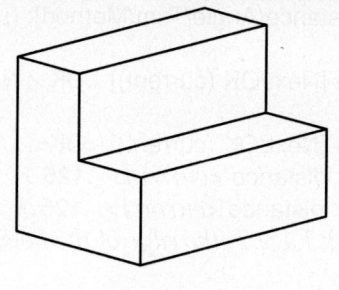

A

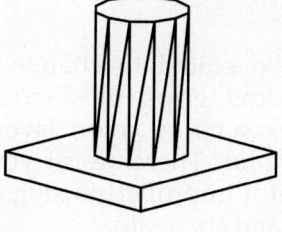

B

## Chamfering Solid Objects

To create a chamfer on a 3D solid, use the **CHAMFER** command. Just as when chamfering a 2D line, there are two chamfer distances. Therefore, you must specify which surfaces correspond to the first and second distances. The detail to which the chamfer is applied must be constructed before chamfering. For example, if you are chamfering a hole, the object (cylinder) must first be subtracted to create the hole. If you are chamfering an intersection, the two objects must first be unioned.

After you enter the command, you must pick the edge you want to chamfer. The edge is actually the intersection of two surfaces of the solid. One of the two surfaces is highlighted when you select the edge. The highlighted surface is associated with the first chamfer distance. This surface is called the *base surface.* If the highlighted surface is not the one you want as the base surface, enter N at the [Next/OK] prompt and press [Enter]. This highlights the next surface. An edge is created by two surfaces. Therefore, when you enter N for the next surface, AutoCAD cycles through only two surfaces. When the proper base surface is highlighted, press [Enter] for **OK**. Chamfering a hole is shown in **Figure 8-9A.** The end of the cylinder in **Figure 8-9B** is chamfered by first picking one of the vertical isolines, then picking the top edge. The following command sequence is illustrated in **Figure 8-9A.**

Command: **CHA** *or* **CHAMFER**↵
(TRIM mode) Current chamfer Dist1 = *current*, Dist2 = *current*
Select first line or [Polyline/Distance/Angle/Trim/Method]: *(pick Edge 1)*
Base surface selection...
Enter surface selection option [Next/OK (current)] <OK>: **N**↵ *(the top surface should be highlighted)*
Enter surface selection option [Next/OK (current)] <OK>: ↵
Specify base surface chamfer distance <*current*>: **.125**↵
Specify other surface chamfer distance <*current*>: **.125**↵
Select an edge or [Loop]: *(pick Edge 2, the edge of the hole)*
Select an edge or [Loop]: ↵
Command:

**Figure 8-9.**
A—A hole is chamfered by picking the top surface, then the edge of the hole. B—The end of a cylinder is chamfered by first picking the side, then the end. Both ends can be chamfered at the same time, as shown here.

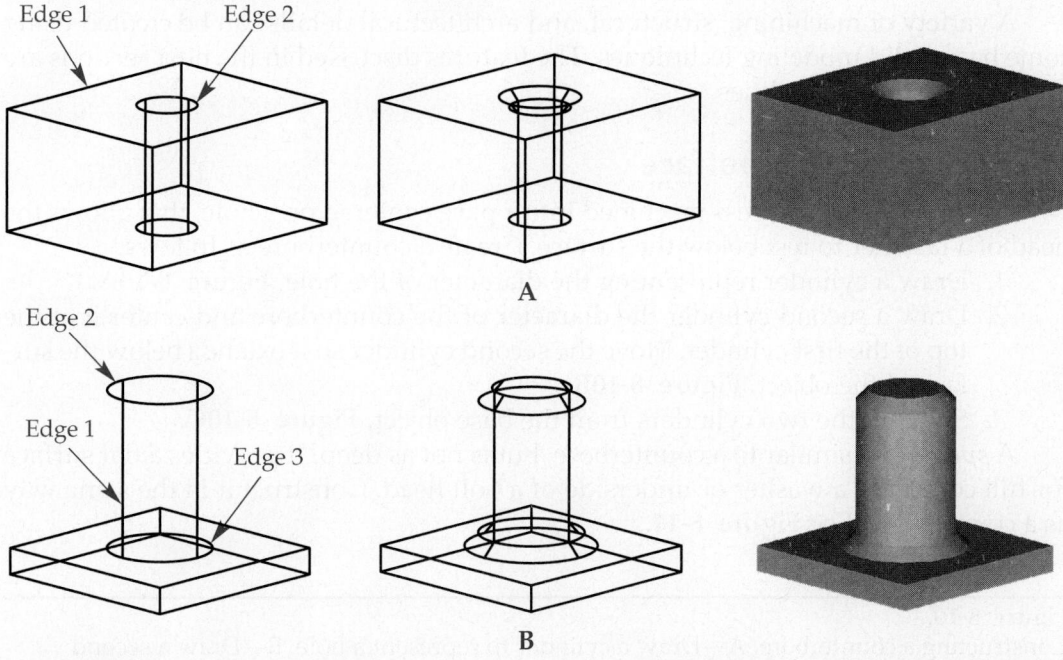

A

B

## Exercise 8-4

○ Begin a new drawing.
○ Draw the locking pin shown below using the appropriate solid modeling and editing commands.
○ The pin is 3″ long and .5″ diameter.
○ The two cotter pin holes are .2″ diameter and .35″ from each end.
○ The chamfer on each end is .1″ × .1″ and the fillet on each hole has a .02″ radius.
○ When you complete the object, display the object in pictorial and use **SHADEMODE**.
○ Save the drawing as EX8-4.

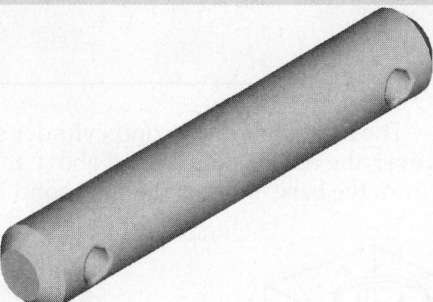

# Constructing Details and Features on Solid Models

A variety of machining, structural, and architectural details can be created using some basic solid modeling techniques. The features discussed in the next sections are just a few of the possibilities.

## Counterbore and Spotface

A *counterbore* is a recess machined into a part, centered on a hole, that allows the head of a fastener to rest below the surface. Create a counterbore as follows.

1. Draw a cylinder representing the diameter of the hole, **Figure 8-10A.**
2. Draw a second cylinder the diameter of the counterbore and center it at the top of the first cylinder. Move the second cylinder so it extends below the surface of the object, **Figure 8-10B.**
3. Subtract the two cylinders from the base object, **Figure 8-10C.**

A *spotface* is similar to a counterbore, but is not as deep. It provides a flat surface for full contact of a washer or underside of a bolt head. Construct it in the same way as a counterbore. See **Figure 8-11.**

---

**Figure 8-10.**
Constructing a counterbore. A—Draw a cylinder to represent a hole. B—Draw a second cylinder to represent the counterbore. C—Subtract the two cylinders from the base object. The object is shown here rendered.

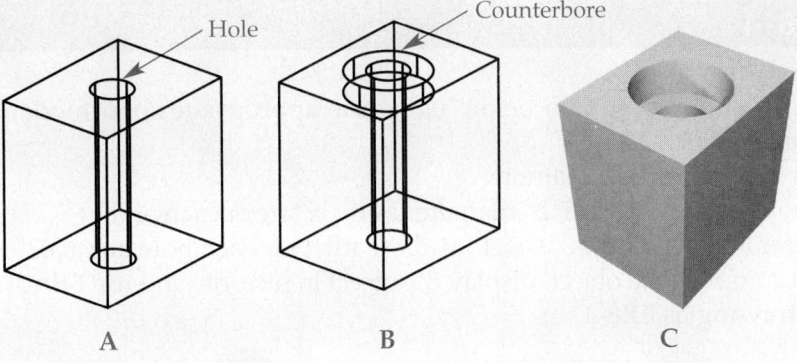

---

**Figure 8-11.**
Constructing a spotface. A—The bottom of the second cylinder should be located at the exact depth of the spotface. However, the height may extend above the surface of the cube. Then, subtract the two cylinders from the base. B—The finished solid after rendering.

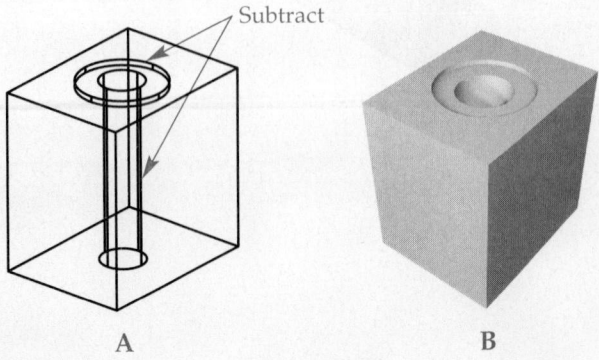

# Countersink

A *countersink* is like a counterbore with angled sides. The sides allow a flat head machine screw or wood screw to sit flush with the surface of an object. A countersink can be drawn in one of two ways. You can draw an inverted cone centered on a hole and subtract it, or you can chamfer the top edge of a hole. Chamfering is the quickest method.

1. Draw a cylinder representing the diameter of the hole, **Figure 8-12A**.
2. Subtract the cylinder from the base object.
3. Select the **CHAMFER** command and enter the chamfer distance(s).
4. Select the top edge of the base object, then pick the top edge of the hole.

# Boss

A *boss* serves the same function as a spotface. However, it is an area raised above the surface of an object. Draw a boss as follows.

1. Draw a cylinder representing the diameter of the hole. Extend it above the base object higher than the boss is to be, **Figure 8-13A**.
2. Draw a second cylinder the diameter of the boss. Place the base of the cylinder above the top surface a distance equal to the height of the boss. Give the cylinder a negative height value so that it extends inside the base object, **Figure 8-13B**.
3. Union the base object and the second cylinder. Subtract the hole from the unioned object, **Figure 8-13C**.
4. Fillet the intersection of the boss with the base object, **Figure 8-13**.

---

**Figure 8-12.**
Constructing a countersink. A—Subtract the cylinder from the base. B—Chamfer the top of the hole to create a countersink. The object is shown here rendered.

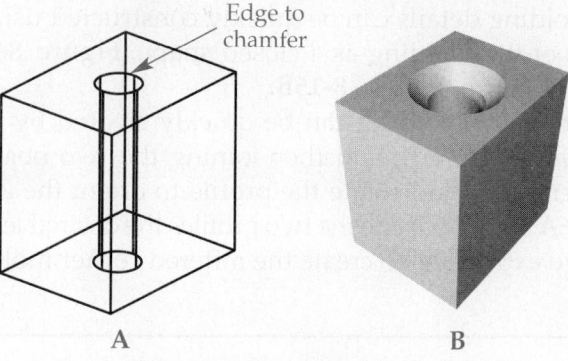

---

**Figure 8-13.**
Constructing a boss. A—Draw a cylinder for the hole extending above the surface of the object. B—Draw a cylinder the height of the boss on the top surface of the object. C—Union the large cylinder to the base. Then, subtract the small cylinder (hole) from the unioned objects. D—Fillet the edge to form the boss. The final object is shown here rendered.

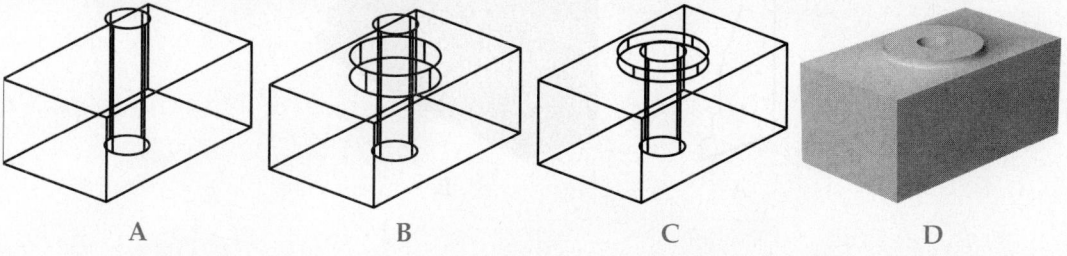

---

## O-Ring Groove

An *O-ring* is a circular seal that resembles a torus. It sits inside a groove constructed so that at least half the O-ring is above the surface. The groove can be constructed by placing the center of a circle on the outside surface of a cylinder. Then, revolve the circle around the cylinder. Finally, subtract the revolved solid from the cylinder.

1. Construct the cylinder to the required dimensions, **Figure 8-14A.**
2. Rotate the UCS on the X axis (or appropriate axis).
3. Draw a circle with a center point on the surface of the cylinder, **Figure 8-14B.**
4. Revolve the circle 360°, **Figure 8-14C.**
5. Subtract the revolved object from the cylinder, **Figure 8-14D.**

**Figure 8-14.**
Constructing an O-ring groove. A—Construct a cylinder. B—Draw a circle centered on the surface of the cylinder. C—Revolve the circle 360°. D—Subtract the revolved object from the cylinder. E—The completed O-ring groove on a rendered object.

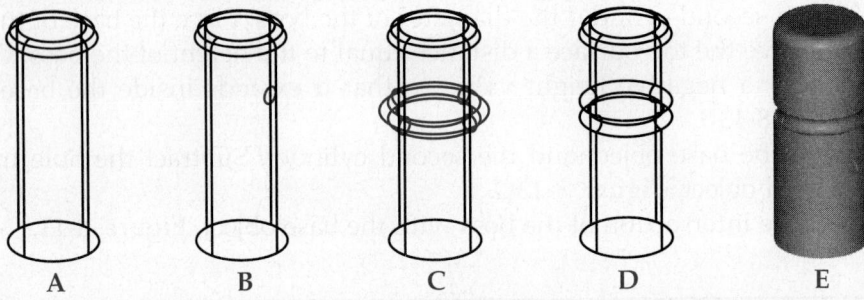

## Architectural Molding

Architectural molding details can be quickly constructed using extrusions. First, construct the profile of the molding as a closed shape, **Figure 8-15A.** Then, extrude the profile the desired length, **Figure 8-15B.**

Corner intersections of molding can be quickly created by extruding the same shape in two different directions, and then joining the two objects. First, draw the molding profile. Then, copy and rotate the profile to orient the Z axis in the desired direction, **Figure 8-16A.** Next, extrude the two profiles the desired lengths, **Figure 8-16B.** Finally, union the two extrusions to create the mitered corner molding, **Figure 8-16C.**

**Figure 8-15.**
A—The molding profile. B—The profile extruded to the desired length and rendered.

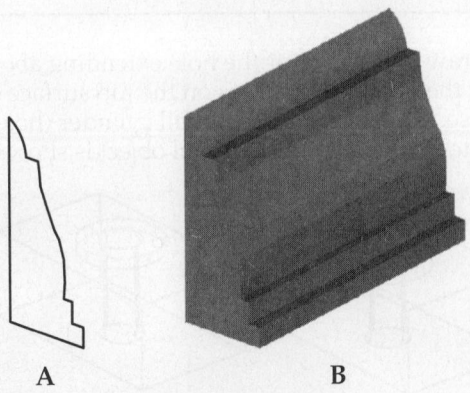

**Figure 8-16.**
Constructing corner molding. A—Copy and rotate the molding profile. B—Extrude the profiles to the desired lengths. C—Union the two extrusions to create the mitered corner. D—A rendered view of the molding.

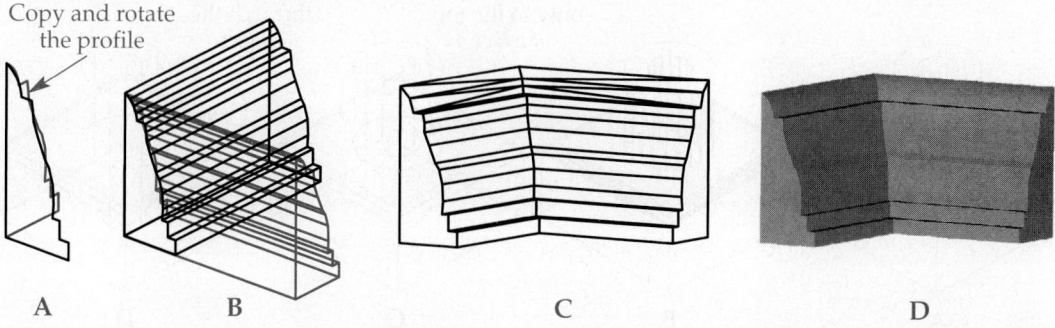

Copy and rotate
the profile

A          B                    C                    D

---

## Exercise 8-5

○ Begin a new drawing using architectural units.
○ Construct a closed profile of a piece of corner molding that is 2″ wide by 1.5″ deep. Create your own design with arcs and corners.
○ Copy the profile and rotate it 90°.
○ Extrude the first molding profile to a length of 12″.
○ Extrude the rotated molding profile to a length of 8″.
○ Union the two pieces of molding.
○ Alter your viewpoint to get different views of the molding.
○ Use the **SHADEMODE** command to shade the model.
○ Save your drawing as EX8-5.

---

## Removing Details and Features

Sometimes, it may be necessary to remove a detail that has been constructed. For example, suppose you placed a .5R fillet on an object based on an engineering sketch. Then, the design is changed to a .25R fillet. The **UNDO** command can only be used in the current drawing session. Also, even if the command can be used, you may have to step back through several other commands to undo the fillet. In another example, suppose an object has a bolt hole that is no longer needed. You will need to remove this feature.

In Chapter 6, solid modeling was described as working with modeling clay. If you think in these terms, you can remove features by adding "clay" to the object. Then, the new "clay" can be molded as needed.

For example, look at the object in **Figure 8-17A**. There are .5R fillets (rounds) on the top surface of the base. However, these should be .25R fillets. You cannot simply place the new fillets on the object. You must first add material to create a square edge. Then, the new fillets can be added.

1. Draw a solid box with the same dimensions as the base. Center the new box on the base.
2. Use the **UNION** command to add the new box to the object. This, in effect, removes the fillets.
3. Use the **FILLET** command to place the .25R fillets on the top edge of the base, **Figure 8-17B**.

---

**Figure 8-17.**
Removing fillets. A—The original object. B—The new fillets are created. C—The hole no longer passes through the object. D—The corrected object.

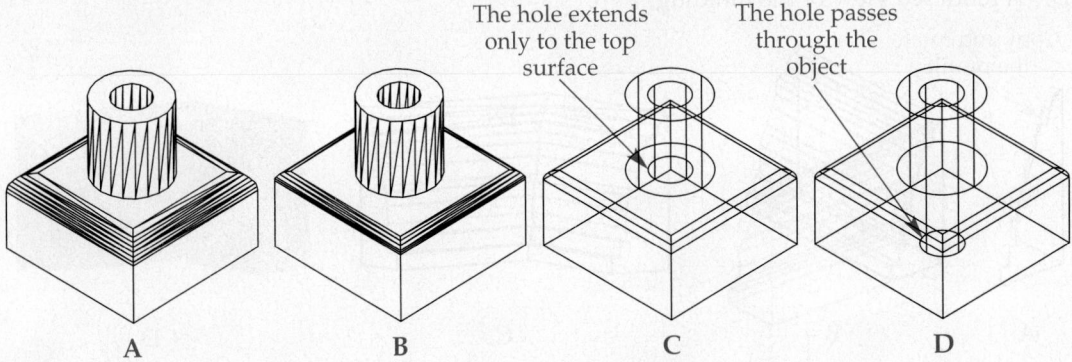

The fillets have now, in effect, been changed from .5R to .25R. However, there is an unseen problem. Display the object in wireframe. Notice how the hole no longer passes through the object, **Figure 8-17C**. To correct this problem, draw a solid cylinder of the same dimensions as the hole and centered in the hole. Then, subtract the cylinder from the object. The hole now passes through the object, **Figure 8-17D**.

This technique of adding material can be used to remove any internal feature and some external features, such as fillets (rounds). Other external features, such as a boss, can be removed by drawing a solid over the top of the feature. The feature to be removed must be completely enclosed by the new solid. Then, subtract the new solid from the original object. Be sure to "redrill" holes and other internal features as needed.

---

**PROFESSIONAL TIP**  There are several editing tools specifically for solids. These are covered in detail in Chapter 9.

---

## Chapter Test

*Answer the following questions on a separate sheet of paper.*

1. Which properties of a solid can be changed in the **Properties** window?
2. What is the purpose of the **ALIGN** command?
3. How does the **ROTATE3D** command differ from the **ROTATE** command?
4. What does the **Last** option of the **ROTATE3D** command do?
5. How does the **MIRROR3D** command differ from the **MIRROR** command?
6. Which command allows you to create a rectangular array by defining rows, columns, and levels?
7. How does a 3D polar array differ from a 2D polar array?
8. How many levels can a 3D polar array have?
9. Which command is used to fillet a solid object?
10. Which command is used to chamfer a solid object?

## Drawing Problems

1. Construct an 8″ diameter tee pipe fitting using the dimensions shown below. Hint: Extrude and union two solid cylinders before subtracting the cylinders for the inside diameters.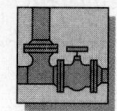
   - A. Use **EXTRUDE** to create two sections of pipe at 90° to each other, then **UNION** the two pieces together.
   - B. Use **FILLET** and **CHAMFER** to finish the object. The chamfer distance is .25″ × .25″.
   - C. The outside diameter of all three openings is 8.63″ and the pipe wall thickness is .322″.
   - D. Save the drawing as P8-1.

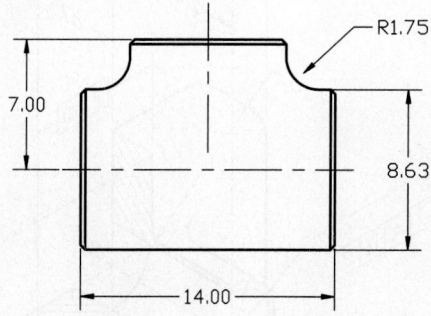

2. Construct an 8″ diameter 90° elbow pipe fitting using the dimensions shown below.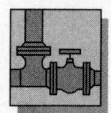
   - A. Use **EXTRUDE** to create the elbow.
   - B. Chamfer the object. The chamfer distance is .25″ × .25″. Note: You cannot use the **CHAMFER** command.
   - C. The outside diameter is 8.63″ and the pipe wall thickness is .322″.
   - D. Save the drawing as P8-2.

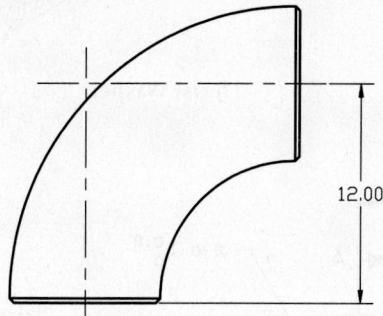

*Problems 3–6. These problems require you to use a variety of solid modeling functions to construct the objects. Use* **EXTRUDE**, **REVOLVE**, **FILLET**, *and* **CHAMFER** *to assist in construction. Create new UCSs as needed. Save each as* P8-*xx.*

3.

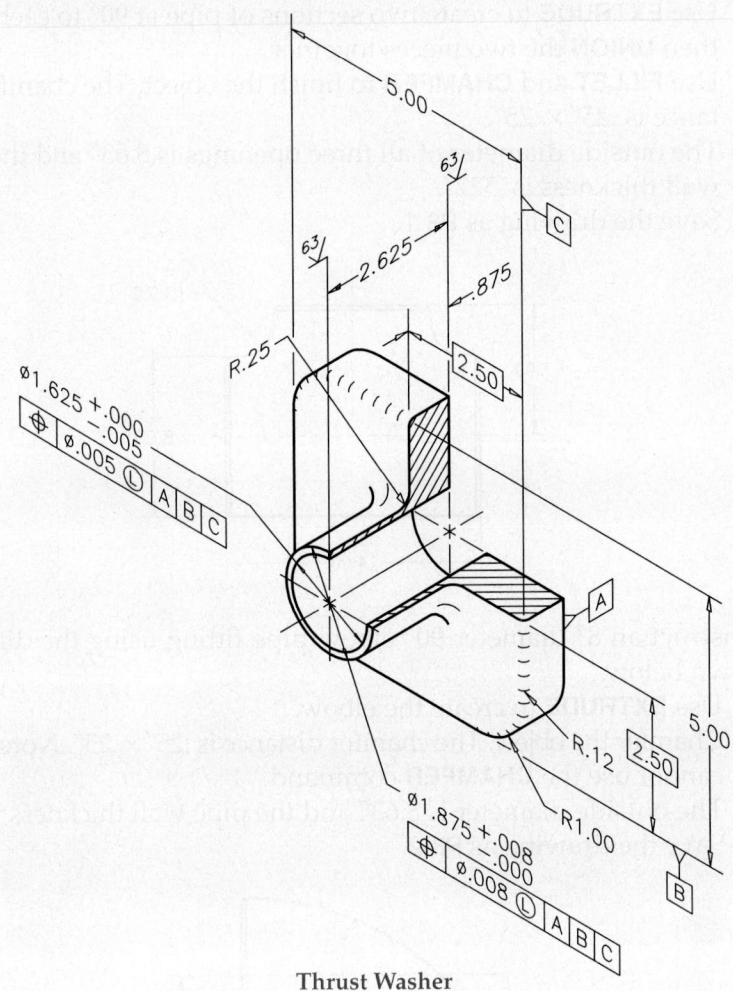

**Thrust Washer**

4.

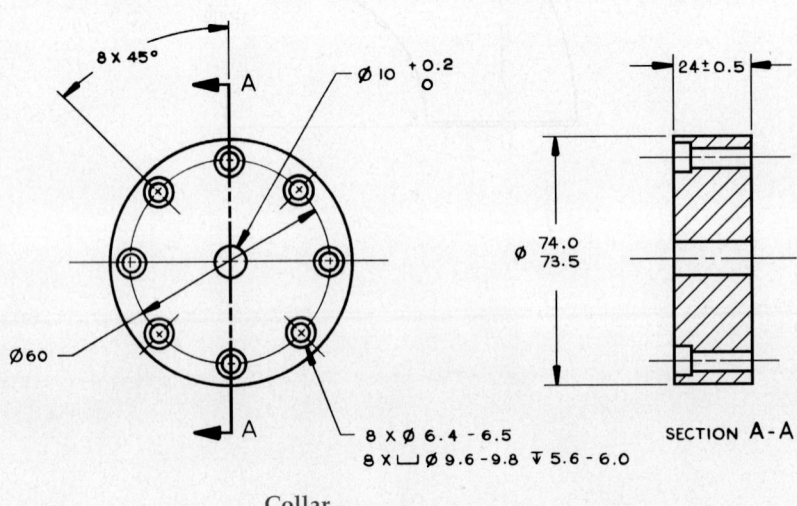

**Collar**

AutoCAD and its Applications—Advanced

5.

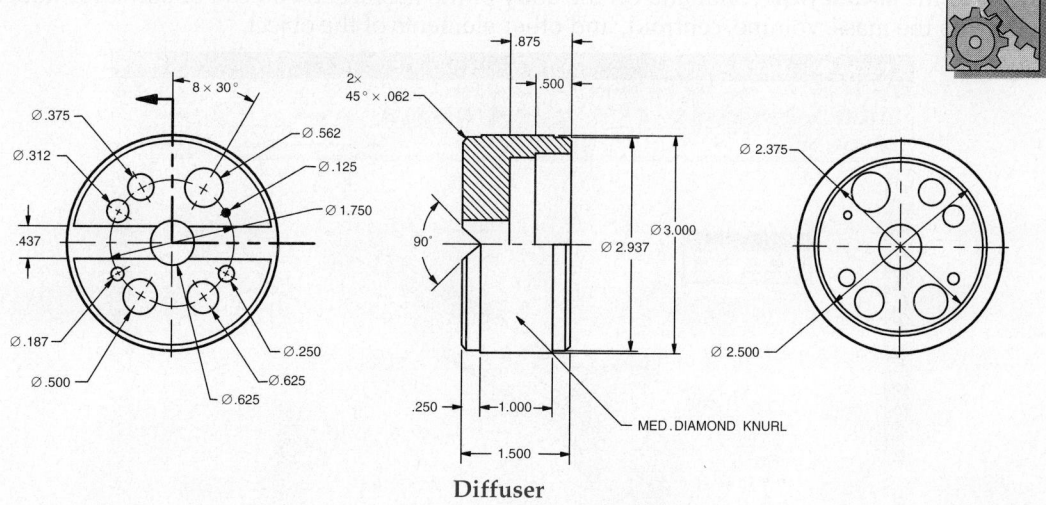

**Diffuser**

6.

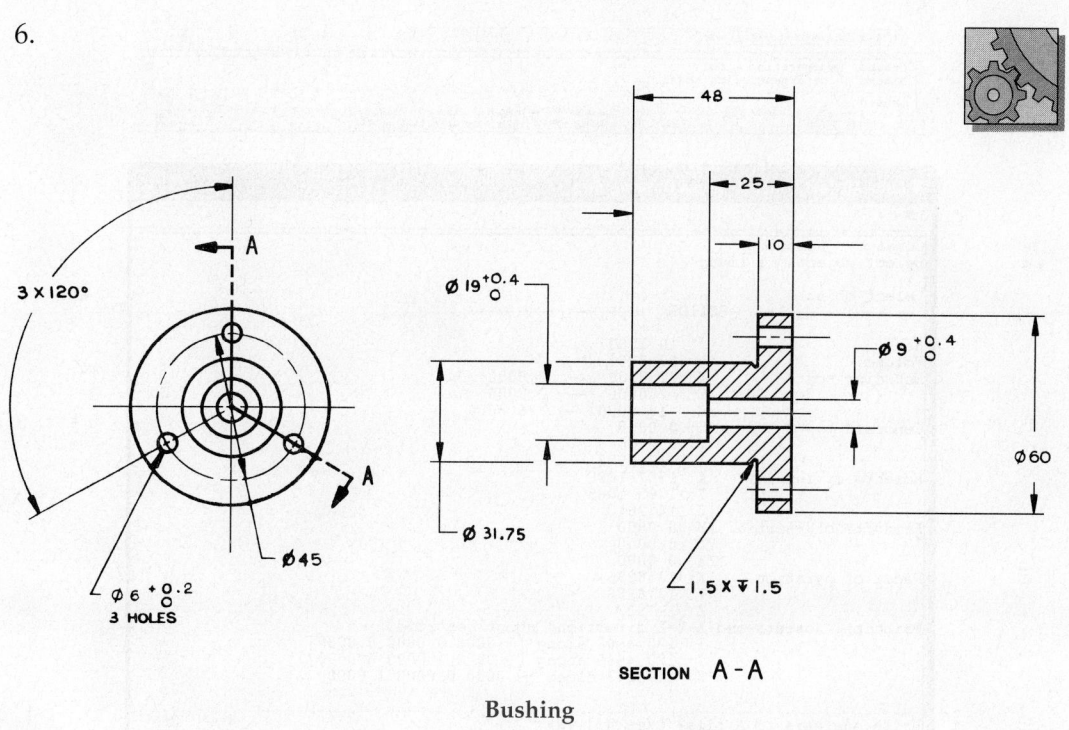

SECTION A-A

**Bushing**

By using the **MASSPROP** command on the body of the flashlight, you can obtain information related to the mass, volume, centroid, and other elements of the object.

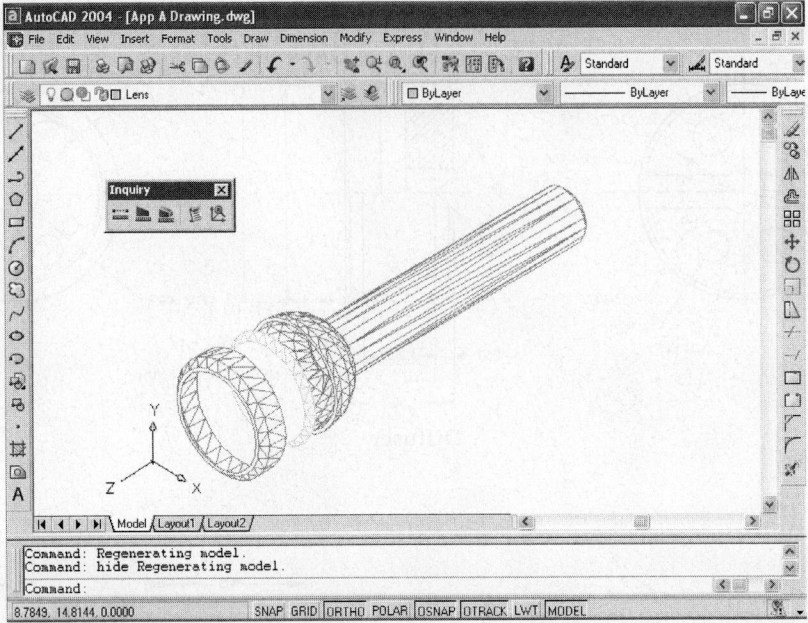

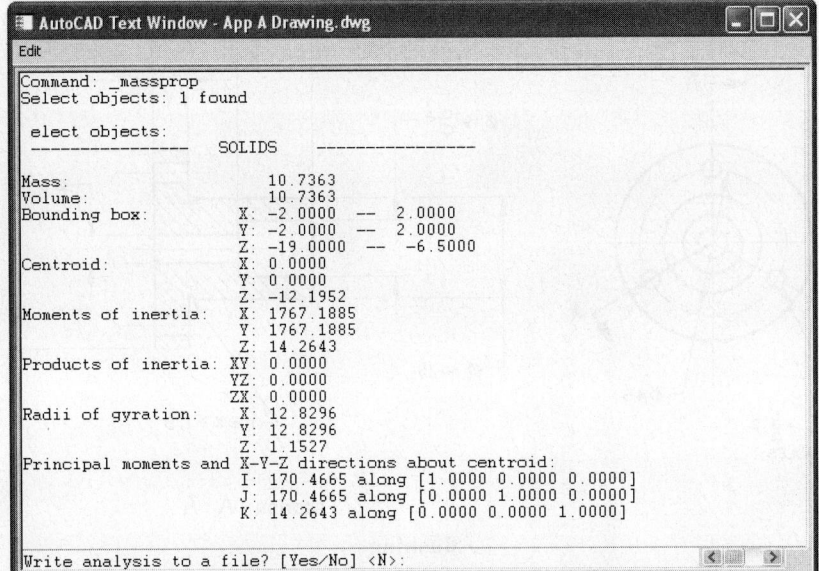

## CHAPTER 9

# Solid Model Editing

## Learning Objectives

After completing this chapter, you will be able to:
- Change the shape and configuration of solid object faces.
- Copy and change the color of solid object edges and faces.
- Break apart a composite solid composed of physically separate entities.
- Use the **SOLIDEDIT** command to construct and edit a solid model.

AutoCAD provides expanded capabilities for editing solid models. A single command, **SOLIDEDIT**, enables you to edit faces, edges, or the entire body of the solid. These features are accessed by typing SOLIDEDIT at the Command: prompt, picking an option from the **Solids Editing** cascading menu in the **Modify** pull-down menu, or using the **Solids Editing** toolbar. See **Figure 9-1**.

**Figure 9-1.**
The **SOLIDEDIT** command options are found in the **Solids Editing** cascading menu in the **Modify** pull-down menu (A) and the **Solids Editing** toolbar (B).

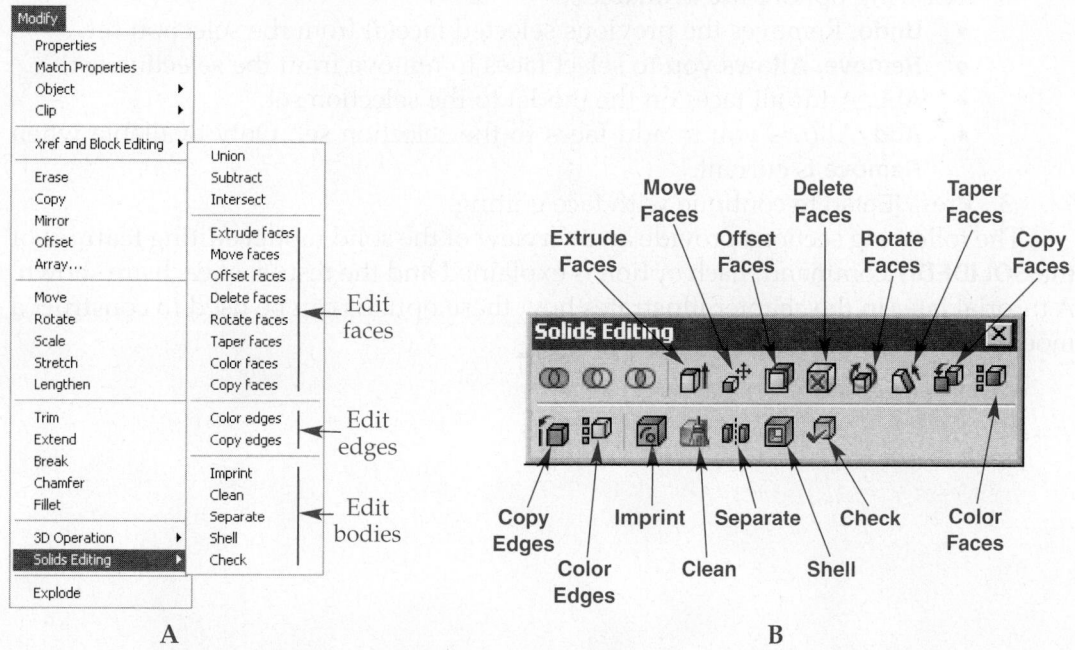

For editing purposes, a solid model has three types of components: the entire solid body, individual faces, and edges. You should first decide which component of the solid you wish to alter. Most editing will be done to faces and the body, because edge editing involves only copying or coloring.

If the **SOLIDEDIT** command is entered at the Command: prompt, you are first asked to select the portion of the solid with which you wish to work. After selecting either **Face**, **Edge**, or **Body**, the editing options are then displayed. In the following example, the **Face** option is selected.

> Command: **SOLIDEDIT**↵
> Solids editing automatic checking: SOLIDCHECK=1
> Enter a solids editing option [Face/Edge/Body/Undo/eXit] <eXit>: **F**↵
> Enter a face editing option
> [Extrude/Move/Rotate/Offset/Taper/Delete/Copy/coLor/Undo/eXit] <eXit>: **E**↵
> Select faces or [Undo/Remove]: *(select an edge)* 2 faces found.
> Select faces or [Undo/Remove/ALL]: **R**↵
> Remove faces or [Undo/Add/ALL]:

---

**NOTE**   Selecting either **Face**, **Edge**, or **Body** is not required if you pick **SOLIDEDIT** command options on the **Solids Editing** toolbar or the **Solids Editing** cascading menu.

---

It is important to make sure you select the correct part of the model for editing. Remember the following three steps when using any of the face editing options.

1. First, select a face to edit. If you pick an edge, AutoCAD selects the two faces that share the edge. If this happens, use the **Remove** option to deselect the unwanted face. A more intuitive approach is to select the open space of the face as if you were touching the side of a part. AutoCAD highlights only that face.
2. Adjust the selection set at the Select faces or [Undo/Remove/ALL]: prompt. The following options are available.
   - **Undo.** Removes the previous selected face(s) from the selection set.
   - **Remove.** Allows you to select faces to remove from the selection set.
   - **ALL.** Adds all faces on the model to the selection set.
   - **Add.** Allows you to add faces to the selection set. Only available when **Remove** is current.
3. Press [Enter] to continue with face editing.

The following sections provide an overview of the solid model editing features of the **SOLIDEDIT** command. Each option is explained and the results of each are shown. A tutorial later in the chapter illustrates how these options can be used to construct a model.

AutoCAD displays a variety of error messages when illegal solid editing operations are attempted. Rather than trying to interpret the wording of these messages, just realize that what you tried to do will not work. Actions that may cause errors include trying to rotate a face into other faces or extruding and tapering an object at too great an angle. When an error occurs, just try it again with different parameters.

# Editing Faces

The basic components of a solid are its faces, and the greatest number of **SOLIDEDIT** options are for editing these faces. All eight face editing options ask you to select faces. Remember, to select specific faces it is quicker to pick inside the boundary of the face.

## Extruding Faces

An *extruded face* is one that is moved, or stretched, in a selected direction. The extrusion can be straight or have a taper. To extrude a face, select **Extrude faces** from the **Solids Editing** cascading menu in the **Modify** pull-down menu or pick the **Extrude Faces** button on the **Solids Editing** toolbar. You can also select the **Face** option of the **SOLIDEDIT** command and then enter E for the **Extrude** option.

Modify
→ Solids Editing
↳ Extrude faces

Solids Editing
toolbar

Extrude Faces

> Command: **SOLIDEDIT**↵
> Solids editing automatic checking: SOLIDCHECK=1
> Enter a solids editing option [Face/Edge/Body/Undo/eXit] <eXit>: **F**↵
> Enter a face editing option
> [Extrude/Move/Rotate/Offset/Taper/Delete/Copy/coLor/Undo/eXit] <eXit>: **E**↵
> Select faces or [Undo/Remove]: *(select the face to edit)*

The prompt verifies the number of faces selected. For example, when an edge is selected, the prompt reads 2 faces found. If you wish to extrude a single face, use the **Remove** option to deselect one of the faces. If you pick the same edge that you selected the face with, both faces will be removed, so pick an edge that is not common to both faces.

> Select faces or [Undo/Remove/ALL]: **R**↵
> Remove faces or [Undo/Add/ALL]: *(pick the face to be removed)*
> 2 faces found, 1 removed.
> Remove faces or [Undo/Add/ALL]: ↵

Next, you need to specify the height of the extrusion. A positive value adds material to the solid, while a negative value subtracts material from the solid. A taper, or draft angle, can also be given.

> Specify height of extrusion or [Path]: *(enter height)*
> Specify angle of taper for extrusion <0>: *(enter an angle or accept the default)*
> Solid validation started.
> Solid validation completed.
> Enter a face editing option
> [Extrude/Move/Rotate/Offset/Taper/Delete/Copy/coLor/Undo/eXit] <eXit>: ↵
> Solids editing automatic checking: SOLIDCHECK =1
> Enter a solids editing option [Face/Edge/Body/Undo/eXit] <eXit>: ↵
> Command:

**Figure 9-2** shows the original solid object and the result of extruding the top face with a 0° taper angle and a 30° taper angle.

Figure 9-2.
The original object,
the result of
extruding the top
face with a 0° taper
angle, and the same
extrusion with a 30°
taper angle.

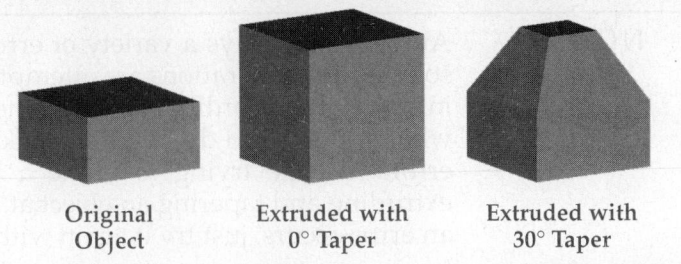

Original
Object

Extruded with
0° Taper

Extruded with
30° Taper

The extruded face can follow a path. Select the **Path** option at the Specify height of extrusion or [Path]: prompt. The path of extrusion can be a line, circle, arc, ellipse, elliptical arc, polyline, or spline. The extrusion height is the exact length of the path. See **Figure 9-3.**

Figure 9-3.
The path of
extrusion can be a
line, circle, arc,
ellipse, elliptical arc,
polyline, or spline.
Here, the paths are
shown in color.

## Exercise 9-1

○ Begin a new drawing.
○ Draw the solid shapes shown below using a color other than black. The dimensions of the shapes are not important.
○ Copy the shapes and leave the original ones intact. Perform edits on the copies.
○ Extrude the shapes to resemble the extruded shapes shown below.
○ Use the **3DORBIT** command and shading to view your work.
○ Save the drawing as EX9-1. This drawing is used for other exercises in this chapter.

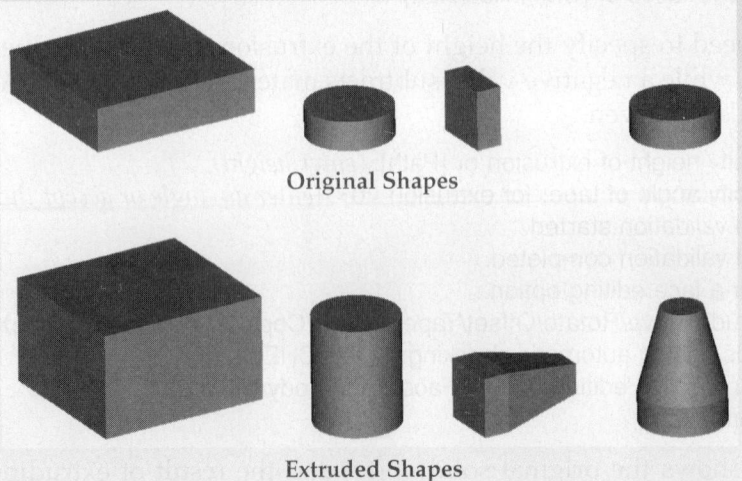

Original Shapes

Extruded Shapes

# Moving Faces

The **Move Faces** option moves a face in the specified direction and lengthens the solid object. A solid model feature (such as a hole) that has been subtracted from an object to create a composite solid can be moved with this option. Object snaps may interfere with the operation of this option.

To move a solid face, pick the **Move Faces** button on the **Solids Editing** toolbar or select **Move faces** from the **Solids Editing** cascading menu of the **Modify** pull-down menu. At the Command: prompt, you can select the **Face** option of the **SOLIDEDIT** command.

```
Enter a face editing option
[Extrude/Move/Rotate/Offset/Taper/Delete/Copy/coLor/Undo/eXit] <eXit>: M↵
Select faces or [Undo/Remove]: (pick a face to move)
1 face found.
Select faces or [Undo/Remove/ALL]: ↵
Specify a base point of displacement: (pick a base point)
Specify a second point of displacement: (pick a second point or enter coordinates)
Solid validation started.
Solid validation completed.
Enter a face editing option
[Extrude/Move/Rotate/Offset/Taper/Delete/Copy/coLor/Undo/eXit] <eXit>: ↵
Solids editing automatic checking: SOLIDCHECK =1
Enter a solids editing option [Face/Edge/Body/Undo/eXit] <eXit>: ↵
Command:
```

Faces are moved in a direction perpendicular to the face, so the new position keeps the face parallel to the original. If you are moving a face that is not "square" to the current UCS, you must enter coordinates for the second point of displacement. Faces that are "square" to the current UCS can be moved by picking a new location or entering a direct distance. See **Figure 9-4.**

**Figure 9-4.**
Faces are moved in a direction perpendicular to the face, so the new position keeps the face parallel to the original.

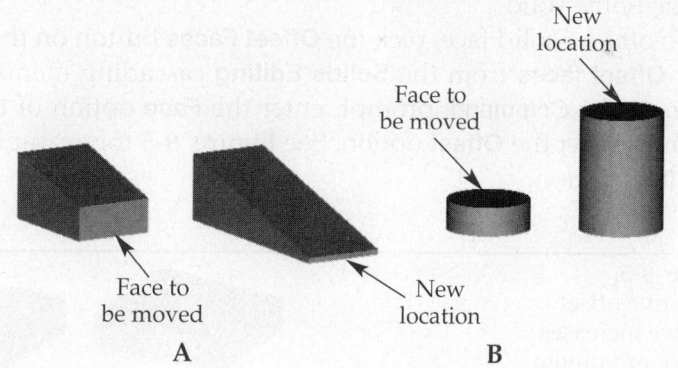

New location

Face to be moved

Face to be moved

New location

A

B

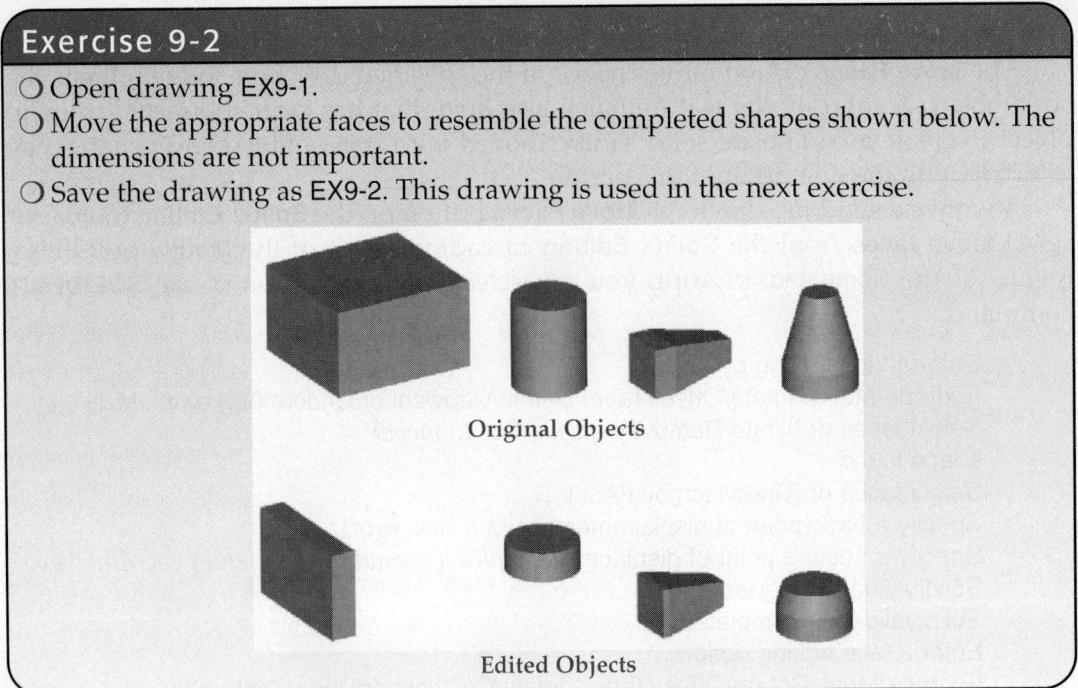
## Offsetting Faces

The **Offset** option may seem the same as the **Extrude** option because it moves faces by a specified distance or through a specified point. Unlike the **OFFSET** command in AutoCAD, this option moves all selected faces a specified distance. It is most useful when you wish to change the size of features such as slots, holes, grooves, and notches in solid parts. A positive offset distance increases the size or volume of the solid, a negative distance decreases the size or volume of the solid. Therefore, if you wish to make the width of a slot wider, provide a negative offset distance to decrease the size of the solid.

To offset a solid face, pick the **Offset Faces** button on the **Solids Editing** toolbar or select **Offset faces** from the **Solids Editing** cascading menu of the **Modify** pull-down menu. At the Command: prompt, enter the **Face** option of the **SOLIDEDIT** command, and then select the **Offset** option. See **Figure 9-5** for examples of features edited with the **Offset** option.

Modify
➡ Solids Editing
↦ Offset faces

Solids Editing
toolbar

Offset Faces

Figure 9-5.
A positive offset distance increases the size or volume of the solid. A negative offset distance decreases the size or volume of the solid.

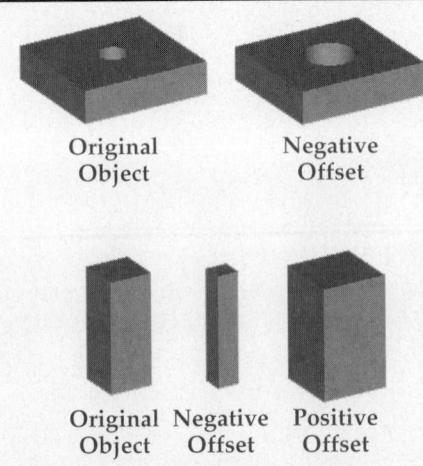

Original Object

Negative Offset

Original Object    Negative Offset    Positive Offset

○ Open drawing EX9-2.
○ Use the **Offset Faces** option to edit the original solid shapes shown below. The dimensions are not important.
○ The edited objects should resemble the completed shapes shown below.
○ Shade the drawing to better view your work.
○ Save the drawing as EX9-3.

Original Objects

Edited Objects

## Deleting Faces

The **Delete** option deletes selected faces. This is a quick way to remove features such as chamfers, fillets, holes, and slots. To delete a solid face, pick the **Delete Faces** button on the **Solids Editing** toolbar or select **Delete faces** from the **Solids Editing** cascading menu of the **Modify** pull-down menu. At the Command: prompt, enter the **Face** option of the **SOLIDEDIT** command and then select the **Delete** option.

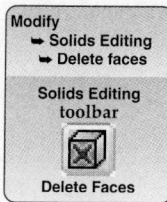

Modify
➥ Solids Editing
➥ Delete faces

Solids Editing
toolbar

Delete Faces

## Rotating Faces

The **Rotate** option rotates a face about a selected axis. To rotate a solid face, pick the **Rotate Faces** button on the **Solids Editing** toolbar or select **Rotate faces** from the **Solids Editing** cascading menu of the **Modify** pull-down menu. At the Command: prompt, enter the **Face** option of the **SOLIDEDIT** command and then select the **Rotate** option.

After a face has been selected, the Command: prompt provides several methods by which a face can be rotated.

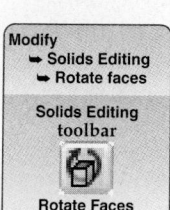

Modify
➥ Solids Editing
➥ Rotate faces

Solids Editing
toolbar

Rotate Faces

Specify an axis point or [Axis by object/View/Xaxis/Yaxis/Zaxis] <2points>:

- **2 points.** This is the default option. Pick two points to define the "hinge" about which the face will rotate, then provide the rotation angle.
- **Axis by object.** This option allows you to use an existing object to align the axis of rotation. You can select the following objects.
    - **Line.** The selected line becomes the axis of rotation.
    - **Circle, Arc, Ellipse.** The Z axis of the object becomes the axis of rotation. This Z axis is a line that passes through the center of the circle, arc, or ellipse and is perpendicular to it.
    - **Polyline, Spline.** A line connecting the polyline or spline's start point and endpoint becomes the axis of rotation.
- **View.** When you select this option, the axis of rotation is perpendicular to the current view, with the positive direction coming out of the screen. This axis is identical to the Z axis when the **UCS** command **View** option is used.
- **Xaxis/Yaxis/Zaxis.** The X, Y, or Z axis that passes through the selected point becomes the axis of rotation.

**Figure** 9-6 provides several examples of rotated faces. Notice how the first and second pick points determine the direction of positive and negative rotation angles.

Figure 9-6.
When rotating faces, the first and second pick points determine the direction of positive and negative rotation angles.

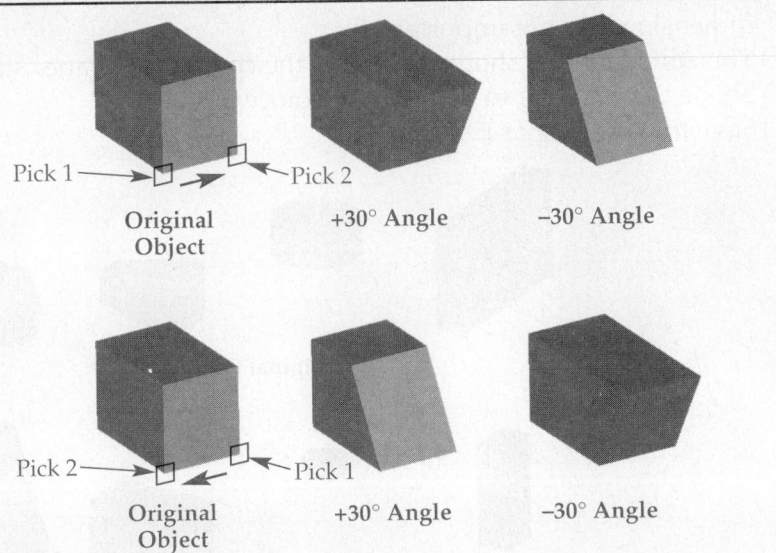

NOTE

A positive rotation angle moves the face in a clockwise direction looking from the first pick point to the second. Conversely, a negative angle rotates the face counterclockwise. If the rotated face will intersect or otherwise interfere with other faces, an error message indicates that the operation failed. In this case, you may wish to try a negative angle if you previously entered a positive one. In addition, you can try selecting the opposite edge of the face at the axis of rotation.

### Exercise 9-4

○ Begin a new drawing.
○ Draw the solid wedge (A) shown below. Dimensions are not important.
○ Rotate the two side faces at equal angles toward the center of the wedge so the object looks like (B) below.
○ Shade the drawing.
○ Save the drawing as EX9-4.

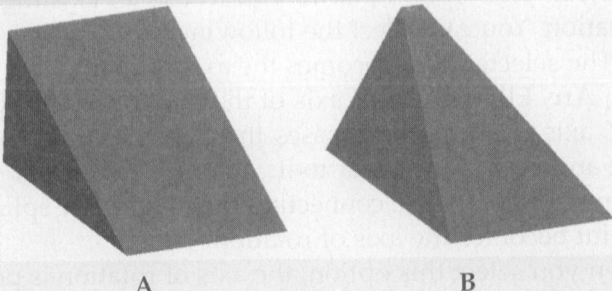

AutoCAD and its Applications—Advanced

# Tapering Faces

The **Taper** option tapers a face at the specified angle, from the first pick point to the second, if it is allowable. To taper a solid face, pick the **Taper Faces** button on the **Solids Editing** toolbar or select **Taper faces** from the **Solids Editing** cascading menu of the **Modify** pull-down menu. At the Command: prompt, select the **Face** option of the **SOLIDEDIT** command, and then select the **Taper** option.

> [Extrude/Move/Rotate/Offset/Taper/Delete/Copy/coLor/Undo/eXit] <eXit>: **T**↵
> Select faces or [Undo/Remove]: *(pick the object to taper)*
> 1 face found.
> Select faces or [Undo/Remove/ALL]: ↵
> Specify the base point: *(pick the base point)*
> Specify another point along the axis of tapering: *(pick a point along the taper axis)*
> Specify the taper angle: *(enter a taper value)*

Tapers work differently on separate objects and on features inside another object. For example, if a positive taper angle is entered for a solid cylinder, the selected object is tapered in on itself from the base point along the axis of tapering. A negative angle tapers the object out, to increase its size along the axis of tapering. See **Figure 9-7.**

**Figure 9-7.**
The effect of pick points and taper angle on an object.

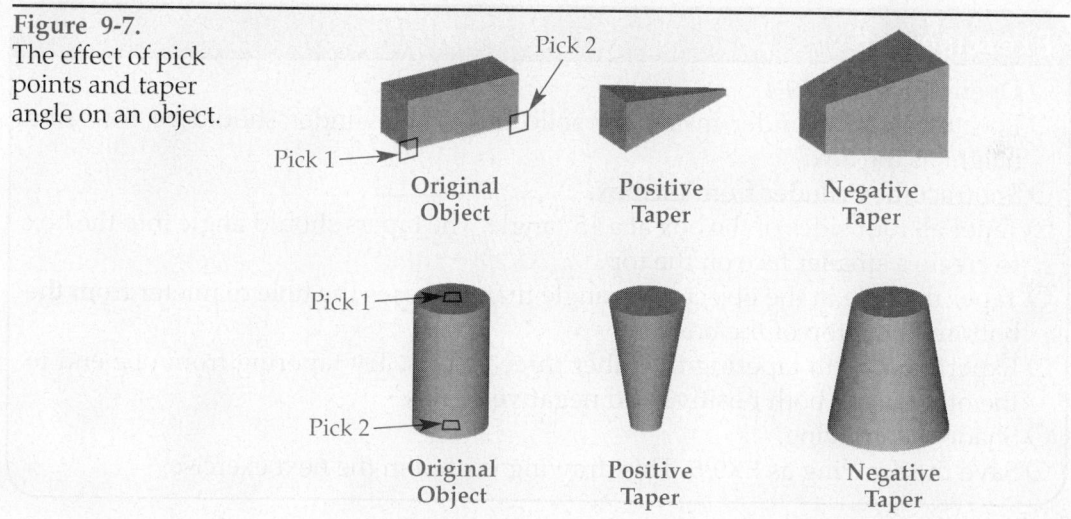

On the other hand, if a feature such as a slot or hole inside a solid object is tapered, a positive taper angle increases the size of the feature along the axis of tapering. For example, if a round hole is tapered using a positive taper angle, its diameter increases from the base point along the axis of tapering, thus removing material from the solid. **Figure 9-8** shows some examples of this function.

**Figure 9-8.**
If a hole or slot is tapered using a positive taper angle, its diameter increases from the base point along the axis of tapering, thus removing material from the solid. A negative taper angle increases the volume of the solid.

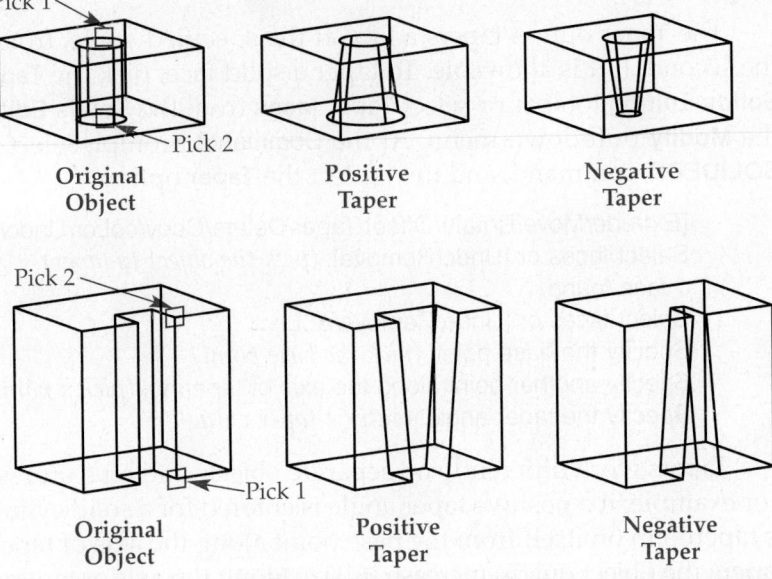

Pick 1
Pick 2

Original Object

Positive Taper

Negative Taper

Pick 2

Pick 1

Original Object

Positive Taper

Negative Taper

---

### Exercise 9-5

○ Open drawing EX9-1.
○ Locate a solid cylinder inside the solid box. The cylinder should be the same height as the box.
○ Subtract the cylinder from the box.
○ Taper all four sides of the box at a 15° angle. The tapers should angle into the box to create a smaller face on the top.
○ Taper the hole in the object at an angle that increases the hole diameter from the bottom to the top of the box.
○ Experiment with tapering the other three objects. Try tapering from one end to the other using both positive and negative angles.
○ Shade the drawing.
○ Save the drawing as EX9-5. This drawing is used in the next exercise.

---

## Copying Faces

The **Copy** option copies a face to the location or coordinates given. The copied face is not part of the original solid model. This may be useful when you wish to construct mating parts in an assembly that has the same features on the mating faces, or the same shape outline. This option is quick to use because you can pick a base point on the face, then enter a single direct distance value for the displacement. Be sure an appropriate UCS is set if you wish to use direct distance entry.

To copy a solid face, pick the **Copy Faces** button on the **Solids Editing** toolbar or select **Copy faces** from the **Solids Editing** cascading menu of the **Modify** pull-down menu. At the Command: prompt, enter the **Face** option of the **SOLIDEDIT** command, and then select the **Copy** option. See **Figure 9-9** for examples of copied faces.

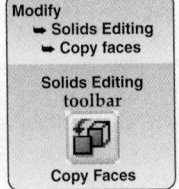

Modify
↳ Solids Editing
↳ Copy faces

Solids Editing toolbar

Copy Faces

```
Enter a face editing option
[Extrude/Move/Rotate/Offset/Taper/Delete/Copy/coLor/Undo/eXit] <eXit>: C↵
Select faces or [Undo/Remove]: (Select a face)
1 face found.
Select faces or [Undo/Remove/ALL]: ↵
Specify a base point or displacement: (pick a point on the face)
Specify a second point of displacement: (enter or pick a displacement value)
```

AutoCAD and its Applications—Advanced

Figure 9-9.
A face can be copied
quickly by picking a
base point on the
face and then
entering a direct
distance value for
the displacement.

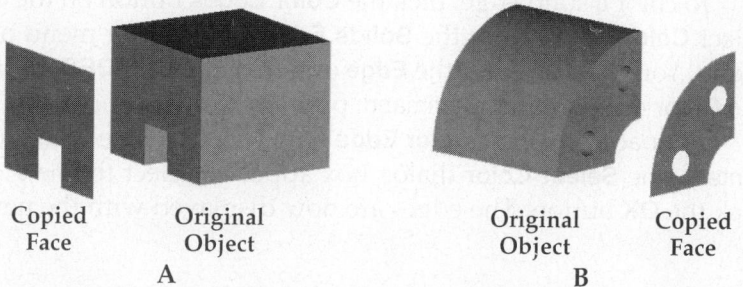

Copied
Face

Original
Object

A

Original
Object

B

Copied
Face

**PROFESSIONAL TIP**

Copied faces can also be useful for creating additional views. For example, you can copy a face to create a separate plan view with dimensions and notes. A copied face can also be enlarged to show details and to provide additional notation for design or assembly.

## Coloring Faces

You can quickly change a selected face to a different color by picking the **Color Faces** button on the **Solids Editing** toolbar or selecting **Color faces** from the **Solids Editing** cascading menu of the **Modify** pull-down menu. You can also enter the **Face** option of the **SOLIDEDIT** command at the Command: prompt, and then select the **Color** option. After accessing the option, simply pick the face, press [Enter], then choose the desired color from the **Select Color** dialog box. Remember, the color of the object (or face) determines the shaded color when the **SHADEMODE** command is used.

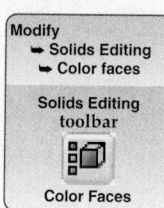

Modify
➥ Solids Editing
➥ Color faces

Solids Editing
toolbar

Color Faces

### Exercise 9-6

○ Open drawing EX9-5.
○ Use the **Color Faces** option to change the color of the tapered box and the interior of the hole.
○ Copy the bottom face of the box down and away from the object.
○ Extrude the copied face to a thickness of your choice.
○ Save the drawing as EX9-6.

## Edge Editing

Edges can be edited in only two ways. They can be copied or their color can be changed.

To copy a solid edge, pick the **Copy Edges** button on the **Solids Editing** toolbar or select **Copy edges** from the **Solids Editing** cascading menu of the **Modify** pull-down menu. You can also enter the **Edge** option of the **SOLIDEDIT** command at the Command: prompt, and then select the **Copy** option.

Copying an edge is similar to copying a face. First, select the edge(s) to copy, then select a base point and a second point. The edge is copied as a line, arc, circle, ellipse, or spline.

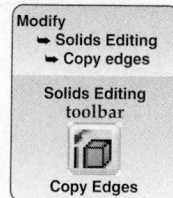

Modify
➥ Solids Editing
➥ Copy edges

Solids Editing
toolbar

Copy Edges

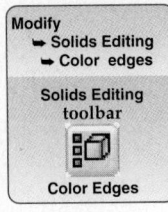

Modify
➥ Solids Editing
➥ Color edges

Solids Editing
toolbar

Color Edges

To color a solid edge, pick the **Color Edges** button on the **Solids Editing** toolbar or select **Color edges** from the **Solids Editing** cascading menu of the **Modify** pull-down menu. You can also enter the **Edge** option of the **SOLIDEDIT** command, and then select the **Color** option at the Command: prompt.

After accessing the **Color Edge** option, select the edge(s) to be modified and press [Enter]. The **Select Color** dialog box appears. Select the new color for the edges and pick the **OK** button. The edges are now displayed with the new color.

## Body Editing

The body editing options of the **SOLIDEDIT** command perform editing operations on the entire body of the solid model. The more commonly used options are **Imprint**, **Shell**, and **Clean**.

### Imprint

Arcs, circles, lines, 2D and 3D polylines, ellipses, splines, regions, bodies, and 3D solids can be imprinted onto a solid, if the object intersects the solid. The imprint becomes a face on the surface regardless of how much overlap exists between the two intersecting objects. Once the imprint has been made, the new face can then be extruded into or out of the solid.

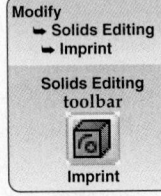

Modify
➥ Solids Editing
➥ Imprint

Solids Editing
toolbar

Imprint

To imprint an object on a solid, pick the **Imprint** button on the **Solids Editing** toolbar or select **Imprint** from the **Solids Editing** cascading menu of the **Modify** pull-down menu. You can also enter the **Body** option of the **SOLIDEDIT** command at the Command: prompt, and then select the **Imprint** option.

Once the command is activated, you are prompted to select the solid. This is the object on which the other objects will be imprinted. Then, select the objects to be imprinted. You have the option of deleting the source objects. The imprinted face can then be modified using face editing options. **Figure 9-10** illustrates objects imprinted onto, and then extruded into, the solid model.

Figure 9-10.
Imprinted objects form new faces that can be extruded into the solid. A—Solid box with three objects in the plane of the top face. B—The objects are imprinted, then the faces are extruded through the solid. The solid model is shown with hidden lines removed.

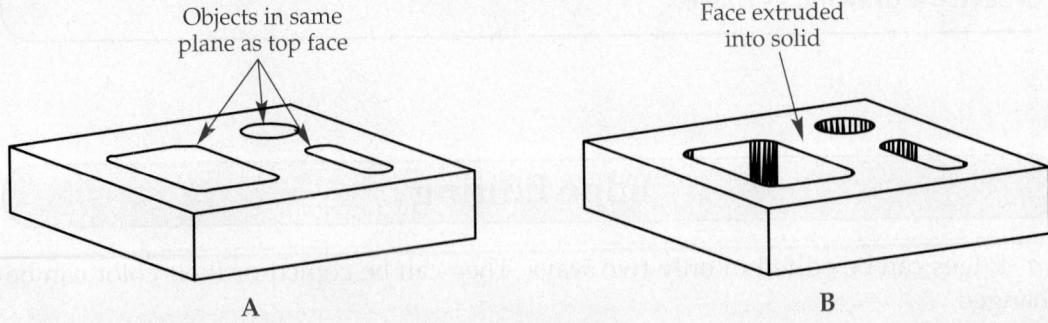

Objects in same plane as top face

Face extruded into solid

A

B

## Separate

This option separates two objects that are both a part of a single solid composite, but appear as separate physical entities. This may be a seldom-used option, but it has a specific purpose. If you select a solid model and an object physically separate from the model is highlighted, the two objects are parts of the same composite solid. If you wish to work with them as individual solids, they must first be separated.

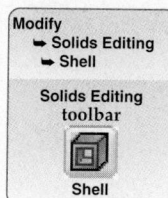

Modify
→ Solids Editing
→ Separate

Solids Editing
toolbar

Separate

To separate a solid body, pick the **Separate** button on the **Solids Editing** toolbar or select **Separate** from the **Solids Editing** cascading menu of the **Modify** pull-down menu. You can also enter the **Body** option of the **SOLIDEDIT** command at the Command: prompt, and then select the **Separate** option.

After picking the **Separate** option, you are prompted to select a 3D solid. After you pick the solid, it is automatically separated. No other actions are required and you can exit the command. However, if you select a solid in which the parts are physically joined, AutoCAD indicates this by prompting The selected solid does not have multiple lumps. A "lump" is a physically separate solid entity. In order to separate a solid, it must be composed of multiple lumps.

## Shell

A *shell* is a solid that has been "hollowed out." The **Shell** option creates a shell of the selected object using a specified offset distance, or thickness.

Modify
→ Solids Editing
→ Shell

Solids Editing
toolbar

Shell

To create a shell of a solid body, pick the **Shell** button on the **Solids Editing** toolbar or select **Shell** from the **Solids Editing** cascading menu of the **Modify** pull-down menu. You can also enter the **Body** option of the **SOLIDEDIT** command at the Command: prompt, and then select the **Shell** option.

```
Enter a solids editing option [Face/Edge/Body/Undo/eXit] <eXit>: B↵
Enter a body editing option
[Imprint/seParate solids/Shell/cLean/Check/Undo/eXit] <eXit>: S↵
Select a 3D solid: (select a solid)
Remove faces or [Undo/Add/ALL]: ↵
```

After selecting the solid body, you have the opportunity to remove faces. If you do not remove any faces, the new solid object will appear identical to the old solid object when shaded or rendered. The thickness of the shell will not be visible. If you wish to create a hollow object with an opening, select the face to be removed (the opening). After selecting the object and specifying any faces to be removed, the following prompt appears.

```
Enter the shell offset distance: (enter an offset value)
```

A positive shell offset distance creates a shell on the inside of the solid body. A negative shell offset distance creates a shell on the outside of the solid body. See **Figure 9-11.**

If you shell a solid that contains internal features, such as holes, grooves, and slots, a shell of the specified thickness is placed around those features. This is shown in **Figure 9-12.**

Figure 9-11.
A—The front, back, and bottom faces (marked here by gray lines) are removed from the selection. B—The resulting object after using the **Shell** option.

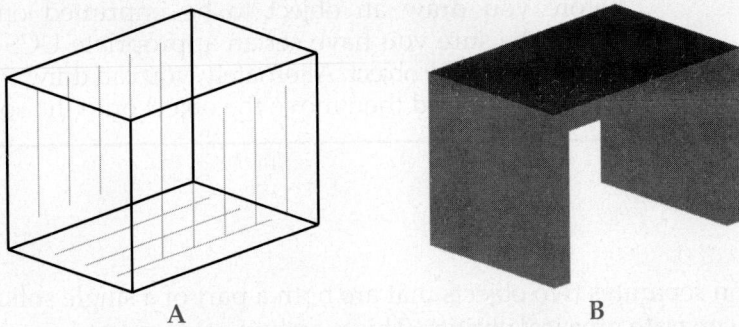

A                                                              B

Figure 9-12.
If you shell a solid that contains internal features, such as holes, grooves, and slots, a shell of the specified thickness is also placed around those features. A—Solid object with holes subtracted. B—Wireframe display after shelling. C—Rendering of the object.

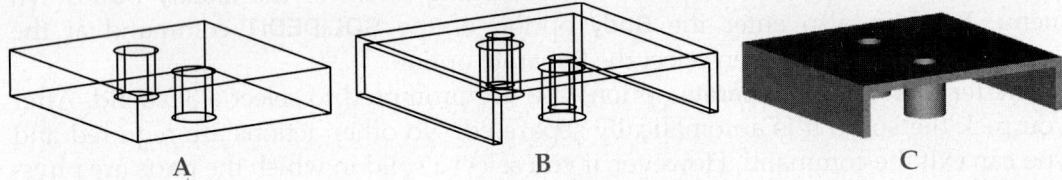

A                                    B                                    C

PROFESSIONAL TIP

The **Shell** option of the **SOLIDEDIT** command is very useful in applications such as solid modeling of metal castings or injection-molded plastic parts.

## Exercise 9-7

○ Create a solid box with the dimensions of 4 × 3 × 2.
○ Draw a ∅.75 circle in the center of the top face of the box.
○ Create an imprint of the circle on the top face of the box.
○ Extrude the circle 1.5 units below the top face. Picking the circle edge selects two faces—the face within the circle and the top face of the box. Remove the top face of the box before extruding.
○ Select the **Shell** option and pick the object. Remove the front, back, and bottom faces.
○ Shell the box using a shell offset distance of .25. Your drawing should look like the one shown below.
○ Save the drawing as EX9-7.

# Clean

The **Clean** option removes all unused objects and shared surfaces. This is useful for removing imprints that are not further modified. It is accessed by picking the **Clean** button on the **Solids Editing** toolbar or selecting **Clean** from the **Solids Editing** cascading menu of the **Modify** pull-down menu. You can also enter the **Body** option of the **SOLIDEDIT** command at the Command: prompt, and then select the **Clean** option. Select the solid to be cleaned and no further input is required. You can exit the command.

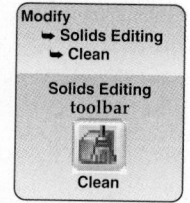

# Check

The **Check** option simply determines if the object selected is a valid 3D solid. If a true 3D solid is selected, AutoCAD displays the prompt This object is a valid ShapeManager solid. and you can exit the command. If the object selected is not a 3D solid, the prompt reads A 3D solid must be selected. and you are prompted to select a 3D solid. To access this option, pick the **Check** button on the **Solids Editing** toolbar or select **Check** from the **Solids Editing** cascading menu of the **Modify** pull-down menu. You can also enter the **Body** option of the **SOLIDEDIT** command at the Command: prompt, and then select the **Check** option.

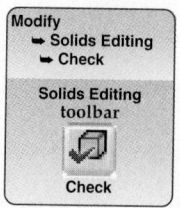

## Using SOLIDEDIT as a Construction Tool

This section provides an example of how the **SOLIDEDIT** command can be used not only to edit, but also construct, a solid model. As you have noticed, all the solid model editing functions are actually options of the **SOLIDEDIT** command. This makes it easy to design and construct a model without selecting a variety of commands, and also gives you the option of undoing a single editing operation, or an entire editing session, without ever exiting the command.

You can select the **SOLIDEDIT** command options on the **Solids Editing** toolbar, from the **Solids Editing** cascading menu, or by simply typing a single letter of the options while the command is active.

In the following example, **SOLIDEDIT** command options are used to imprint shapes onto the model body, then extrude those shapes into countersunk holes. Then the model size is adjusted, and an angle and taper are applied to one end. Finally, one end of the model is copied to construct a mating part.

### Creating Shape Imprints on a Model

The basic shape of the solid model in this tutorial is drawn as a solid box, then shape imprints are added to it. Throughout this exercise, you may wish to change the UCS to assist in the construction of the part.

1. Draw a solid box using the dimensions shown in **Figure 9-13.**
2. On the top surface of the box, locate a single ∅0.4 diameter circle using the dimensions given, then copy or array the circle to the other three corners as shown.
3. Use the **Imprint** option of the **SOLIDEDIT** command to imprint the circles onto the solid box. Delete the source objects.

Figure 9-13.
The initial set up for
the model.

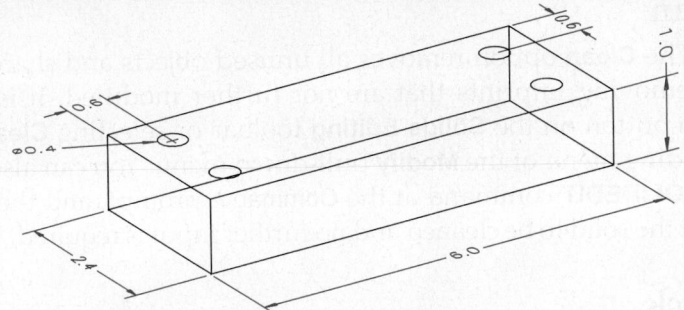

## Extruding Imprints to Create Features

The imprinted 2D shapes can now be extruded to create new 3D solid features on the model. Use the **Extrude Faces** option to extrude all four imprinted circles.

1. When you select the first circle, all features on that face are highlighted, but only the circle you picked has actually been selected. Therefore, be sure to pick the remaining three circles.
2. Remove the top face of the box from the selection set.
3. The depth of the extrusion is 0.16 units. Remember to enter −.16 for the extrusion height since the extrusion goes into the solid. The angle of taper for extrusion should be 35°. Your model should look like **Figure 9-14A.**
4. Extrude the small diameter of the four tapered holes so they intersect the bottom of the solid body. Select the holes by picking the small diameter circles. Your model should now look like **Figure 9-14B.**

Figure 9-14.
A—The imprinted circles are extruded.
B—Holes are created by further extrusion.

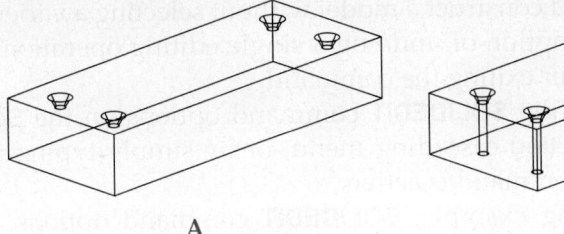
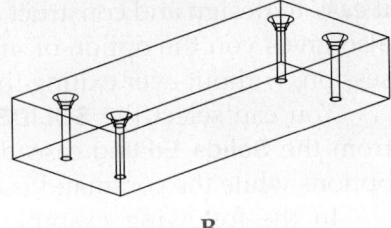

A                                                           B

## Moving Faces to Change Model Size

The next step is to use the **Move Faces** option to decrease the length and thickness of the solid body.

1. Select either end face and the two holes nearest it. Be sure to select the entire hole. Move the two holes and end face two units toward the other end, thus changing the object length to 4 units.
2. Select the bottom face and move it 0.5 units up toward the top face, thus changing the thickness to 0.5 units. See **Figure 9-15.**

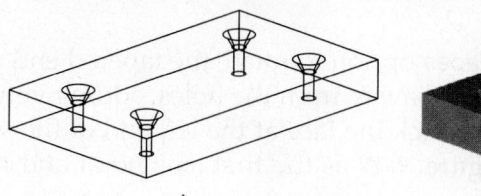
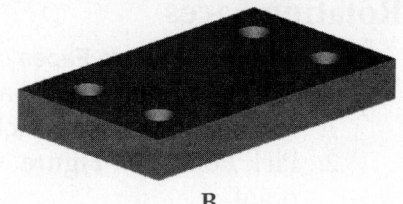

Figure 9-15.
A—The object is shortened and the height is reduced.
B—The object is rendered.

A

B

## Offsetting a Feature to Change Its Size

Now, the **Offset Faces** option is used to increase the diameter of the four holes, and to adjust a rectangular slot that will be added to the solid.

1. Using **Offset Faces**, select the four small hole diameters. Be sure to remove the bottom face from the selection set.
2. Enter an offset distance of –0.05. This increases the hole diameter and decreases the solid volume. Exit the **SOLIDEDIT** command.
3. Select the **RECTANGLE** command. Set the fillet radius to 0.4 and draw a $2 \times 1.6$ rectangle centered on the top face of the solid. See **Figure 9-16A**.
4. Imprint the rectangle on the solid. Delete the source object.
5. Extrude the rectangle completely through the solid (0.5 units). Remember to remove the top face from the selection set when you pick the rectangle.
6. Offset the rectangle using an offset distance of 0.2 units. You will need to select all edges on the rectangle. This decreases the size of the rectangular opening and increases the solid volume. Your drawing should appear as shown in **Figure 9-16B**.

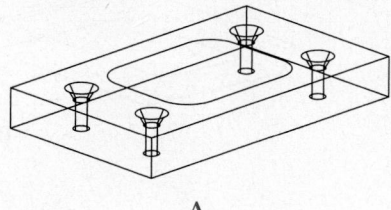
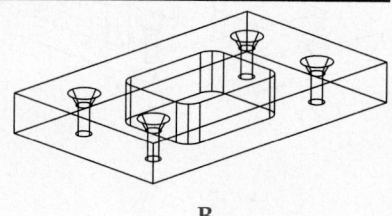

Figure 9-16.
A—The diameter of the holes is increased and a rectangle is imprinted on the top surface. B—The rectangle is extruded to create a slot.

A

B

## Tapering Faces

One side of the part is to be angled. The **Taper Faces** option is used to taper the left end of the solid.

1. Using **Taper Faces**, pick the face at the left end of the solid.
2. Pick Point 1 in **Figure 9-17** as the base point, and Point 2 as the second point along the axis of tapering.
3. Enter a value of –10 for the taper angle. This moves the upper-left end away from the solid, creating a tapered end. See **Figure 9-17**.

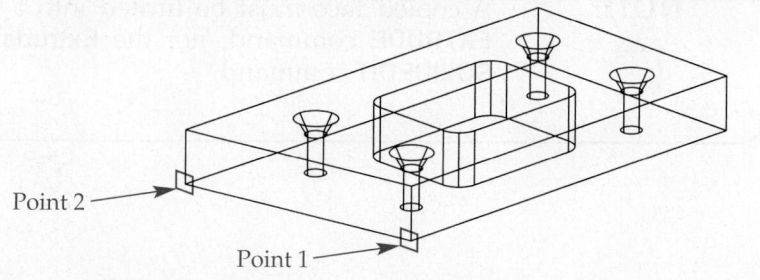

Figure 9-17.
The left end of the object is tapered. Notice the pick points.

Point 2

Point 1

## Rotating Faces

Next, use the **Rotate Faces** option to rotate the tapered end of the object. The top edge of the face will be rotated away from the holes, adding volume to the solid.

1. Using **Rotate Faces**, pick the face at the left end of the solid.
2. Pick Point 1 in **Figure 9-17** as the first axis point and Point 2 as the second point.
3. Enter a value of –30 for the rotation angle. This rotates the top edge of the tapered end away from the solid. See **Figure 9-18.**

**Figure 9-18.**
The tapered end of the object is modified.

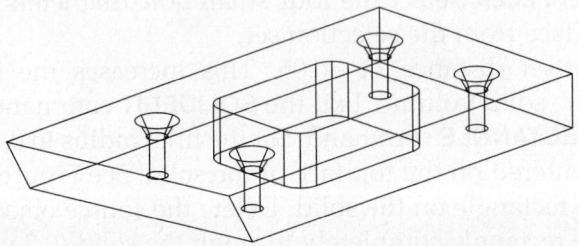

**Figure 9-19.**
A mating part is created by copying a face, and then extruding it to create a solid.

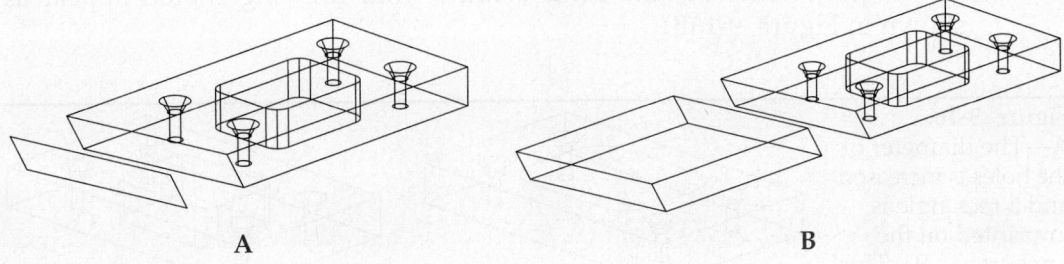

A                                                                                          B

## Copying Faces

A mating part will now be created. This is done by first copying the face on the tapered end of the part.

1. Using the **Copy Faces** option, pick the angled face on the left end of the solid.
2. Pick one of the corners as a base point and copy the face 1 unit to the left. This face can now be used to create a new solid. See **Figure 9-19A.**
3. Draw a line 4 units in length on the negative X axis from the lower-right corner of the copied face. Extrude the copied face 4 units to the left by using the line as the extrusion path. See **Figure 9-19B.** If you do not use the **Path** option, the extrusion will be projected perpendicular to the face.

> NOTE
>
> A copied face must be turned into a solid body using the **EXTRUDE** command, not the **Extrude Faces** option of the **SOLIDEDIT** command.

AutoCAD and its Applications—Advanced

## Creating a Shell

The bottom surface of the original solid will now be shelled out. Keep in mind that features such as the four holes and the rectangular slot will not be cut off by the shell. Instead, a shell will be placed around these features. This becomes clear when the operation is performed.

1. Select the **Shell** option and pick the original solid.
2. At the Remove faces prompt, pick the lower-left and lower-right edges of the solid. This removes the two side faces and the bottom face.
3. Enter a shell offset distance of 0.15 units. The shell is created and should appear similar to **Figure 9-20A.**
4. Use the **3DORBIT** command to view the solid from the bottom. Shade the model with Gouraud shading. Your model should look like the one shown in **Figure 9-20B.**

---

**Figure 9-20.**
A—The shelled object. B—The viewpoint is changed and the object is rendered.

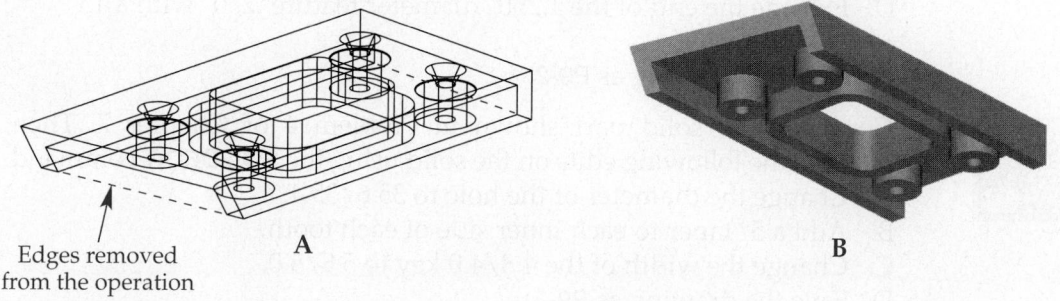

Edges removed
from the operation

## Chapter Test

*Answer the following questions on a separate sheet of paper.*

1. What are the three components of a solid model?
2. When using the **SOLIDEDIT** command, how many faces are highlighted if you pick an edge?
3. How do you deselect a face that is part of the selection set?
4. How can you select a single face?
5. Which two operations can the **Extrude Faces** option perform?
6. How does the shape and length of an object selected as the path of an extrusion affect the final extrusion?
7. What is one of the most useful aspects of the **Offset Faces** option?
8. How do positive and negative offset distance values affect the volume of the solid?
9. How is a single object, such as a cylinder, affected by entering a positive taper angle when using the **Taper Faces** option?
10. When a shape is imprinted on a solid body, which component of the solid does the imprinted object become, and how can it be used?
11. In which situation would you use the **Separate** option?
12. How does the **Shell** option affect a solid that contains internal features such as holes, grooves, and slots?
13. How can you determine if an object is a valid 3D solid?

---

## Drawing Problems

1. Complete the tutorial presented in this chapter. Then, perform the following additional edits to the solid.
   A. Lengthen the right end of the solid by 0.5 units.
   B. Taper the right end of the solid with the same taper angle used on the left end, but taper it in the opposite direction.
   C. Fillet the two long top edges of the solid using a fillet radius of 0.2 units.
   D. Rotate the face at the right end of the solid with the same rotation angle used on the left end, but rotate it in the opposite direction.
   E. Save the drawing as P9-1.

2. Construct the solid part shown in Problem 7 of Chapter 7. Use as many **SOLIDEDIT** options as possible to construct the part. After completing the object, make the following modifications.
   A. Lengthen the 1.250″ diameter feature by .250″.
   B. Change the .750″ diameter hole to .625″ diameter.
   C. Change the thickness of the .250″ thick flange to .375″.
   D. Extrude the end of the 1.250″ diameter feature .250″ with a 15° taper inward.
   E. Save the drawing as P9-2.

3. Construct the solid part shown in Problem 4 of Chapter 7. Then, perform the following edits on the solid using the **SOLIDEDIT** command.
   A. Change the diameter of the hole to 35.6/35.4.
   B. Add a 5° taper to each inner side of each tooth.
   C. Change the width of the 4.8/4.0 key to 5.8/5.0.
   D. Save the drawing as P9-3.

4. Construct a solid model of the object in Problem 6 of Chapter 8. Use as many **SOLIDEDIT** options as possible to construct the part. Perform the following edits on the solid.
   A. Change the depth of the counterbore to 10mm.
   B. Change the color of all internal surfaces to red.
   C. Save the drawing as P9-4.

5. Open the drawing for Problem 3 from Chapter 8. If you have not yet drawn this object, do so now. Perform the following edits to the solid.
   A. Change the 2.625″ height to 2.325″.
   B. Change the 1.625″ internal diameter to 1.425″.
   C. Taper the outside faces of the .875″ high base at a 5° angle away from the part. Hint: The base cannot be tapered directly.
   D. Save the drawing as P9-5.

6. Open drawing Problem 6 from Chapter 7. If you have not yet drawn this object, do so now. Perform the following edits to the solid.
   A. Change the dimensions on the model as follows.
   B. Save the drawing as P9-6.

| Existing | New |
|---|---|
| 100 | 106 |
| 80 | 82 |
| Ø60 | Ø94 |
| Ø40 | Ø42 |
| 30° | 35° |

## CHAPTER 10

# Solid Model Display and Analysis

## Learning Objectives

After completing this chapter, you will be able to:
- Control the appearance of solid model displays.
- Construct a 2D section through a solid model.
- Construct a 3D section of a solid model.
- Create a multiview layout of a solid model using **SOLVIEW** and **SOLDRAW**.
- Construct a profile of a solid using **SOLPROF**.
- Perform an analysis of a solid model.
- Export and import solid model data.

Certain aspects of a solid model's appearance is controlled by the **ISOLINES**, **DISPSILH**, and **FACETRES** system variables. The **ISOLINES** system variable controls the number of lines used to define solids in wireframe displays. The **FACETRES** system variable controls the number of lines used to define solids in hidden displays. The **DISPSILH** system variable was introduced in an earlier chapter and is used to display a silhouette.

Internal features of the model can be shown using the **SLICE** and **SECTION** commands. This chapter looks at how these sections can be combined with 2D projections created with the **SOLVIEW** and **SOLDRAW** commands to create a drawing layout for plotting. This chapter also covers how a profile of a solid can be created using the **SOLPROF** command.

## Controlling Solid Model Display

AutoCAD solid models can be displayed as wireframes, with hidden lines removed, shaded, or rendered. A wireframe is the default display and is the quickest to display. The hidden, shaded, and rendered displays require a longer regeneration time.

### Isolines

The appearance of a solid model in a wireframe display is controlled by the **ISOLINES** system variable. *Isolines* represent the curved surfaces of a solid model. This setting does *not* affect the final shaded or rendered object. The default **ISOLINES** value is 4. It can have a value from 0 to 2047. All solid objects in the drawing are affected by changes to the **ISOLINES** value. Figure 10-1 illustrates the difference between **ISOLINES** settings of 4 and 12.

Figure 10-1.
Isolines define curved surfaces. A—**ISOLINES** = 4. B—**ISOLINES** = 12.

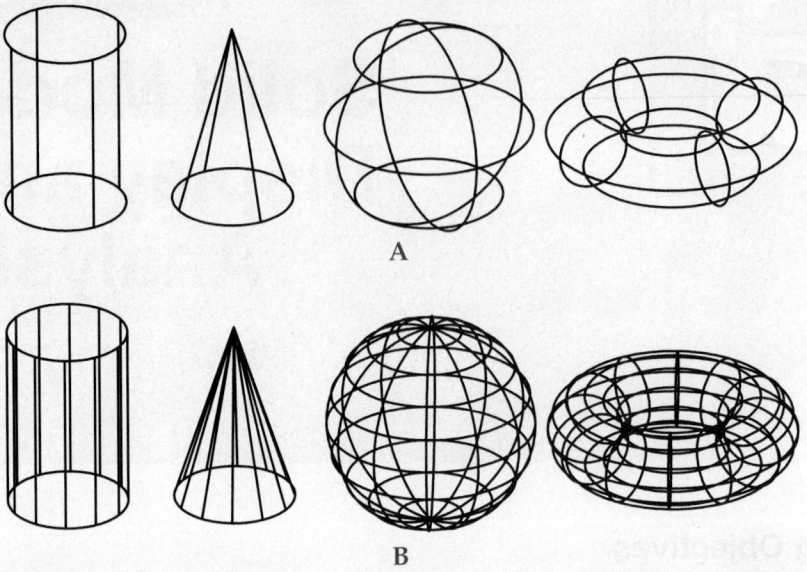

The setting of the **ISOLINES** system variables can be changed by typing ISOLINES at the Command: prompt and then entering a new value. The **ISOLINES** setting can also be changed in the **Contour lines per surface** text box found in the **Display resolution** area of the **Display** tab in the **Options** dialog box. See **Figure 10-2.**

## Creating a Display Silhouette

Solids can appear in two forms when the **HIDE** command is used. The default form shows the model as if it is composed of many individual faces. These faces are defined by tessellation lines. The number of tessellation lines is controlled by the

**Figure 10-2.**
The **ISOLINES**, **FACETRES**, and **DISPSILH** system variables can be set in the **Options** dialog box.

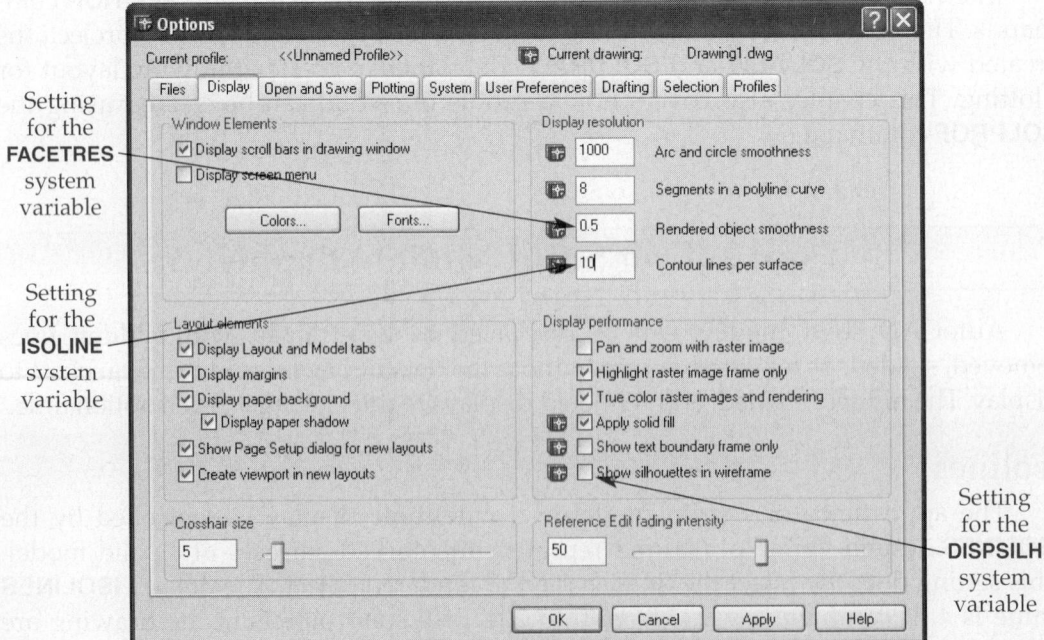

**FACETRES** system variable, which is discussed in the next section. The model can also appear smooth with no tessellation lines on the surface. This is controlled by the **DISPSILH** (display silhouette) system variable, which was introduced in Chapter 6.

The **DISPSILH** system variable has two values, 0 (off) and 1 (on). The setting can be changed by typing DISPSILH at the Command: prompt and entering a new value. You can also set the variable using the **Show silhouettes in wireframe** check box in the **Display performance** area of the **Display** tab in the **Options** dialog box. Refer to **Figure 10-1**. **Figure 10-3** shows solids with **DISPSILH** set to 1 after using **HIDE**.

The **DISPSILH** system variable only affects the display when the **HIDE** command is accessed with the shading mode set to **2D Wireframe**. The **Hidden** option of the **SHADEMODE** command is not affected by **DISPSILH** system variable. If you type HIDE while a **SHADEMODE** option other than **2D Wireframe** is active, you are actually selecting the **Hidden** option of the **SHADEMODE** command. However, the silhouette is displayed when **DISPSILH** is set to 1 and the shading mode is set to **3D Wireframe**.

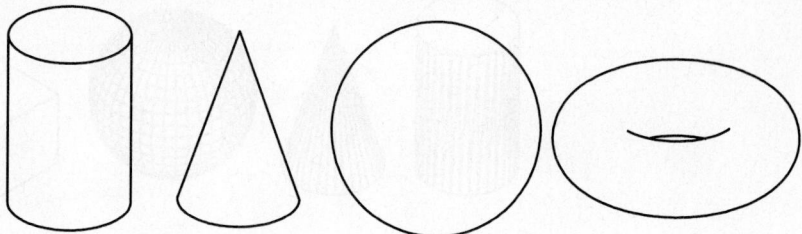

**Figure 10-3.**
Hidden solids appear as smooth objects with no facets when **DISPSILH** is set to 1 and **SHADEMODE** is set to **2D Wireframe**.

## Controlling Surface Smoothness

The smoothness of curved surfaces in hidden, shaded, and rendered displays is controlled by the **FACETRES** system variable. This variable determines the number of polygon faces applied to the solid model. The default value is .5 and can range from .01 to 10.0. This system variable can be changed at the Command: prompt or in the **Options** dialog box. Refer to **Figure 10-1**. **Figure 10-4** shows the effect of two different **FACETRES** settings.

CAUTION

Avoid setting **FACETRES** any higher than necessary. Trying to plot even one solid object with a high **FACETRES** setting can overload system resources and take considerable time. Always use the lowest setting that will produce the results required by the project.

**Figure 10-4.**
The images in the
top row have
hidden lines
removed, while the
bottom row is
rendered. A—The
**FACETRES** setting
of .5 produces these
images. B—The
**FACETRES** setting
of 5.0 produces
smoother surfaces.
Notice how the box
is not affected.

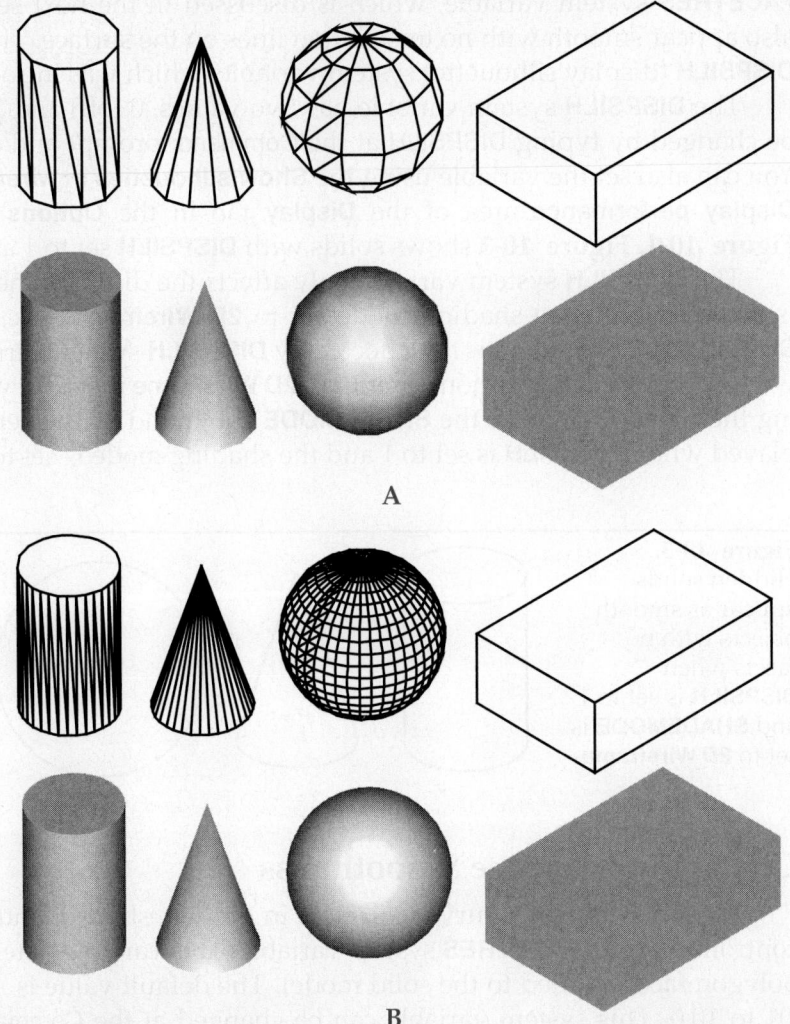

A

B

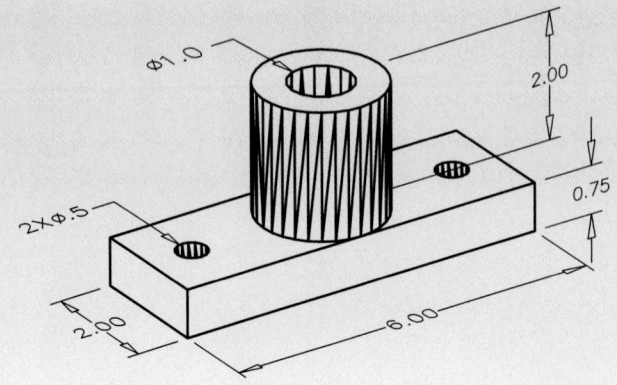

# Viewing Internal Features of a Solid Model

You can "cut" through a 3D solid model to view its internal features and profiles. The **SECTION** command allows you to create a 2D region of the model that is cut. The **SLICE** command allows you to create a 3D cutaway view of the model. These commands can be selected from the **Solids** cascading menu in the **Draw** pull-down menu or on the **Solids** toolbar. See **Figure 10-5**.

**Figure 10-5.**
The **SECTION** and **SLICE** commands can be accessed from the **Solids** cascading menu in the **Draw** pull-down menu.

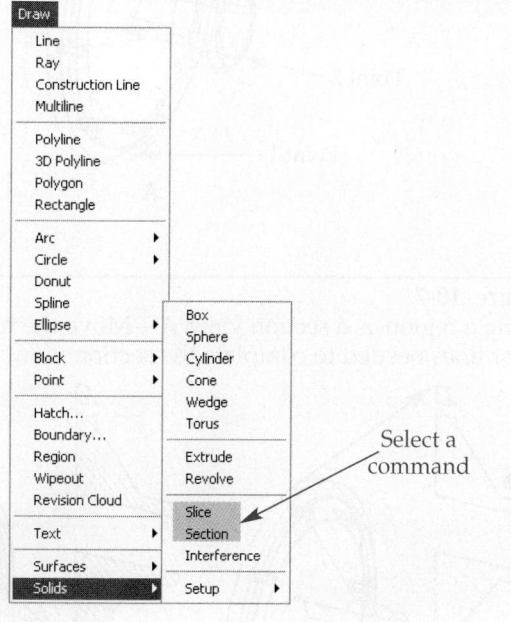

## Creating a 3D Solid Model Section

The **SECTION** command places a cutting-plane line through your model in the selected location. The default option of **SECTION** is to select three points to define the cutting plane. To access the command, select **Section** from the **Solids** cascading menu of the **Draw** pull-down menu, pick the **Section** button on the **Solids** toolbar, or type SEC or SECTION at the Command: prompt. The following example selects three points on the object in **Figure 10-6** to define the cutting plane.

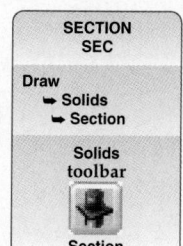

SECTION
SEC

Draw
↪ Solids
 ↪ Section

Solids
toolbar

Section

>   Command: **SEC** *or* **SECTION**↵
>   Select objects: *(pick the solid to be sectioned)*
>   Select objects: ↵
>   Specify first point on Section plane by [Object/Zaxis/View/XY/YZ/ZX/3points]
>       <3points>: *(pick Point 1)*
>   Specify second point on plane: *(pick Point 2)*
>   Specify third point on plane: *(pick Point 3)*
>   Command:

The section created is a 2D region. It has no section lines and is created on the current layer. See **Figure 10-6B**. If you wish to use the new region as the basis for a 2D hatched section view of the model, do the following.

1.  Move or copy the region to a new location. See **Figure 10-7A**.
2.  Explode the region to create individual regions if needed.
3.  Use boundary hatching commands to draw section lines inside the regions. See **Figure 10-7B**. Be sure that the XY plane of the UCS is parallel to the plane of the area to be hatched. If it is not, a boundary definition error will appear when an object is selected.

**Figure 10-6.**
A—Three points are picked to define a cutting plane. B—The section is drawn as a region, without section lines.

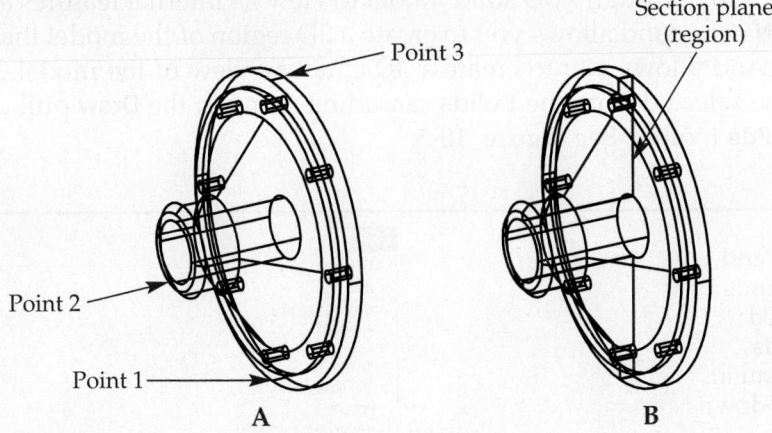

Section plane (region)

Point 3

Point 2

Point 1

A

B

**Figure 10-7.**
Using a region as a section view. A—Move the region. B—Add section lines. C—Add any other lines needed to complete the section view.

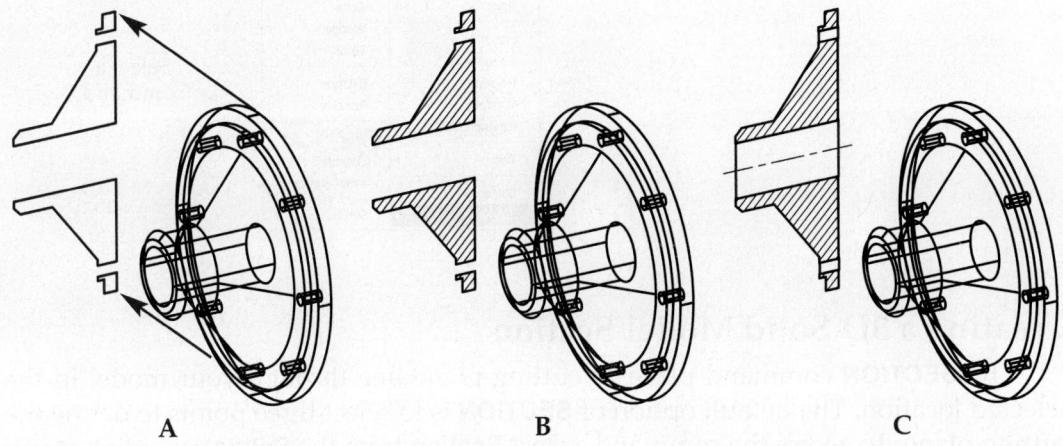

A

B

C

4. Draw any connecting lines required to complete the section view. See **Figure 10-7C.**

Additional options of the **SECTION** command enable you to specify sectioning planes in a variety of ways. These are explained below.

- **Object.** The section plane is aligned with a selected object, such as a circle, arc, ellipse, 2D spline, or 2D polyline.
- **Zaxis.** Select a point on the new section plane, then pick a point on the positive Z axis of that plane.
- **View.** Select a point on the new section plane and AutoCAD aligns the section perpendicular to the viewpoint in the current viewport.
- **XY.** The new section plane is aligned with the XY plane of the current UCS. The point selected specifies the location of the plane.
- **YZ.** The new section plane is aligned with the YZ plane of the current UCS. The point selected specifies the location of the plane.
- **ZX.** The new section plane is aligned with the ZX plane of the current UCS. The point selected specifies the location of the plane.

# Slicing a Solid Model

A true 3D sectioned model is created with the **SLICE** command. You can create a new solid by discarding one side of the cut, or both parts of the sliced object can be retained. **SLICE** does not draw section lines or create regions.

To slice an object, select **Slice** from the **Solids** cascading menu in the **Draw** pull-down menu, pick the **Slice** button on the **Solids** toolbar, or type SL or SLICE at the Command: prompt. The options of the **SLICE** command are the same as those of the **SECTION** command. In the following example, the **YZ** option is used to define the cutting plane. Refer to **Figure 10-8.**

> Command: **SL** *or* **SLICE**↵
> Select objects: *(pick the solid)*
> Select objects: ↵
> Specify first point on slicing plane by [Object/Zaxis/View/XY/YZ/ZX/3points]
>     <3points>: **YZ**↵
> Specify a point on YZ-plane <0,0,0>: ↵
> Specify a point on desired side of the plane or [keep Both sides]: *(pick Point 1 to keep the far side of the object)*

Both sides of the slice can be kept if desired. To do so, select the **keep Both sides** option. The slice plane appears the same as the section plane shown in **Figure 10-8B,** but the solid is now two separate objects. Test this by picking one side to display grips. Either side can be moved, copied, or rotated. See **Figure 10-9.**

---

**Figure 10-8.**
A—Specify the cutting plane and pick the side of the object to keep.
B—The completed slice. C—The sliced object after **HIDE.**

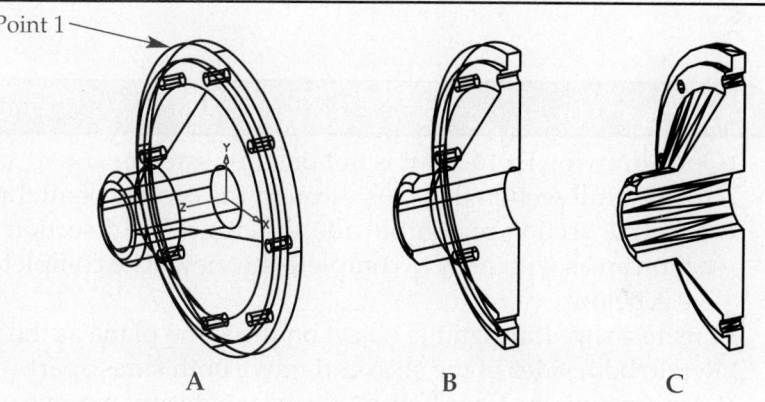

**Figure 10-9.**
Keeping both halves of a slice. A—The slice plane appears as a section.
B—Each part of the sliced object can be moved, copied, or rotated.

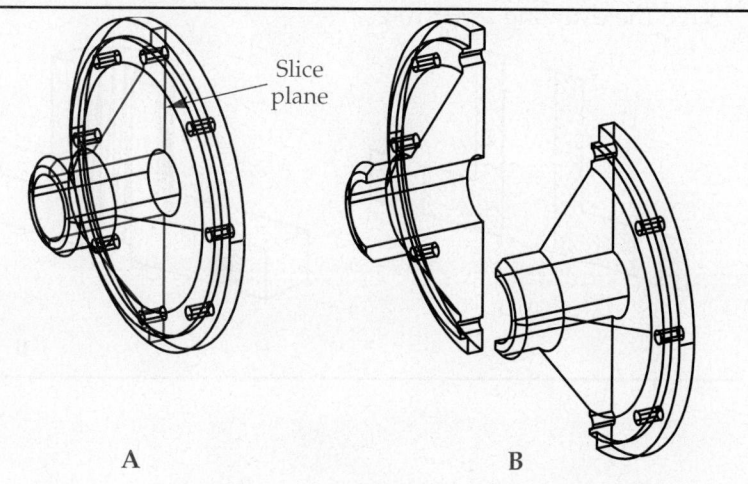

---

# Creating Special Sections with SLICE

You are not limited to a single slice through an object. For example, you can create a half section of the object in Figure 10-10 by using the **SLICE** command a second time to cut away the top half of the object nearest to you. The example shown in Figure 10-10A shows the use of the **3points** option of **SLICE** to remove one quarter of the original object. The results are shown in Figure 10-10B and Figure 10-10C.

Figure 10-10.
A—A cutting plane is selected to remove one quarter of the original object. B—The cutaway view in wireframe. C—A rendered view of the cutaway.

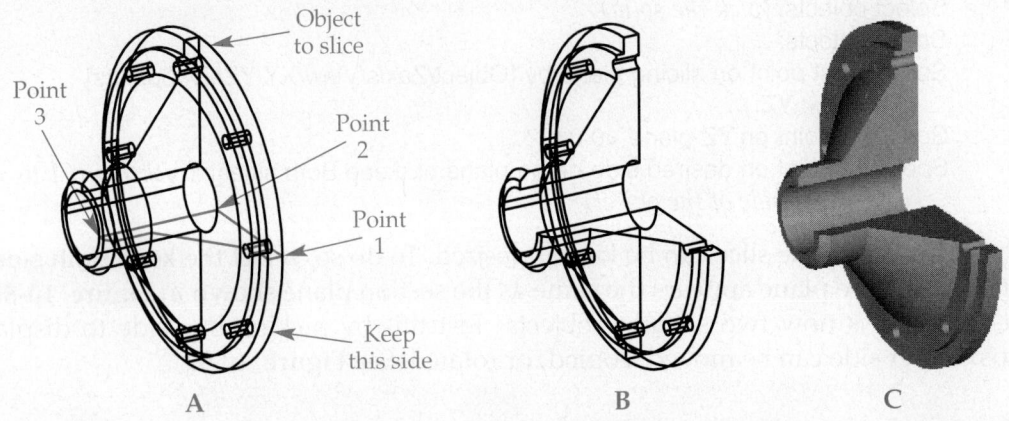

## Exercise 10-2

○ Open drawing EX10-1 if it is not on your screen.
○ Create a full section that cuts through the centers of all three holes.
○ Move the section region outside the object. Add section lines and connect the section areas with lines to complete the view. The completed section should look like A below.
○ Create a slice through the object on the same plane as the previous section.
○ Retain both sides of the slice and move both sides apart.
○ Slice through the large hole on the near side and remove one half of the side. The completed objects should look like B below.
○ Save the drawing as EX10-2.

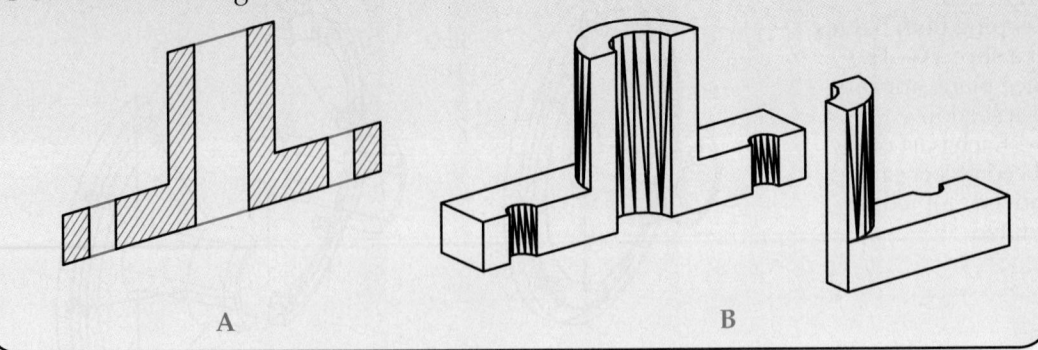

# Creating and Using Multiview Layouts

Once a solid model has been constructed, it is easy to create a multiview layout using the **SOLVIEW** command. This command allows you to create a layout containing orthographic, section, and auxiliary views. The **SOLDRAW** command can then be used to complete profile and section views. **SOLDRAW** must be used after **SOLVIEW**. The **SOLPROF** command can be used to create a profile of the solid in the current view.

## Creating Views with **SOLVIEW**

To use the **SOLVIEW** command, first restore the WCS. This will help avoid any confusion. Then, display a plan view. See **Figure 10-11**. It helps to have additional user coordinate systems created prior to using **SOLVIEW**. This allows you to construct orthographic views based on a specific named UCS.

When you enter the **SOLVIEW** command while the **Model** tab is active, AutoCAD automatically switches to the **Layout1** tab. The **SOLVIEW** command is used to create new floating viewports and to establish the display within those viewports. Therefore, you may want to delete the default viewport in the **Layout1** tab before using the **SOLVIEW** command.

Next, create an initial view from which other views can project. This is normally the top or front. In the following example, the top view is constructed first by using the plan view of a UCS named Leftside.

To initiate the **SOLVIEW** command, select **View** from the **Setup** cascading menu after selecting **Solids** from the **Draw** pull-down menu, pick the **Setup View** button on the **Solids** toolbar, or type SOLVIEW at the Command: prompt.

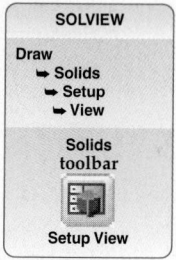

Command: **SOLVIEW**↵
Regenerating layout.
Regenerating model-caching viewports.
Enter an option [Ucs/Ortho/Auxiliary/Section]: **U**↵
Enter an option [Named/World/?/Current] <Current>: **N**↵
Enter name of UCS to restore: **LEFTSIDE**↵
Specify view scale <1.0000>: **.5**↵
Specify view center: *(pick the center of the view)*
Specify view center <specify viewport>: ↵
Specify first corner of viewport: *(pick the first corner of a paper space viewport outside the object)*
Specify opposite corner of viewport: *(pick the opposite corner of the viewport)*
Enter view name: **TOPVIEW**↵ *(left of object in AutoCAD is the top of the part)*
UCSVIEW = 1 UCS will be saved with view
Enter an option [Ucs/Ortho/Auxiliary/Section]: *(leave the command active at this time)*

Figure 10-11.
Before using
**SOLVIEW**, display
the plan view of the
WCS.

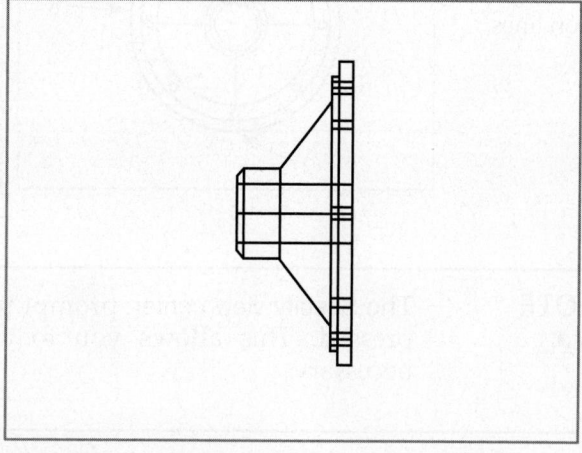

**Figure 10-12.**
The initial view
created with the **Ucs**
option of **SOLVIEW**.

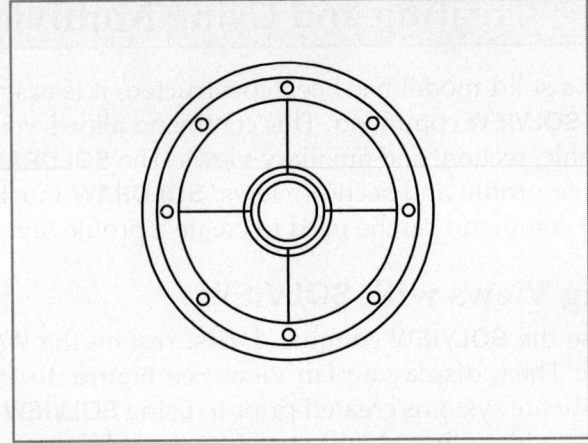

You must provide a name for the view. The result is shown in **Figure 10-12.**

The **SOLVIEW** command remains active until you press the [Enter] or [Esc] key. If you exit **SOLVIEW**, you can still return to the drawing and create additional orthographic viewports. With the command active, continue and create a section view to the right of the top view as follows:

> Enter an option [Ucs/Ortho/Auxiliary/Section]: **S**↵
> Specify first point of cutting plane: *(pick the quadrant at Point 1 in* **Figure 10-13**)
> Specify second point of cutting plane: *(pick the quadrant at Point 2)*
> Specify side to view from: *(pick Point 3)*
> Enter view scale <0.5000>: ↵
> Specify view center: *(pick the center of the new section view)*
> Specify view center <specify viewport>: ↵
> Specify first corner of viewport: *(pick one corner of the viewport)*
> Specify opposite corner of viewport: *(pick the opposite corner of the viewport)*
> Enter view name: **SECTION**↵
> Enter an option [Ucs/Ortho/Auxiliary/Section]: ↵
> Command:

Notice in **Figure 10-13** that the new view is shown as a wireframe and not as a section. This is normal. **SOLVIEW** is used to create the views. The **SOLDRAW** command draws the section lines. **SOLDRAW** is discussed later in this chapter.

**Figure 10-13.**
The section view
created with
**SOLVIEW** (shown on
the right) does not
show section lines.

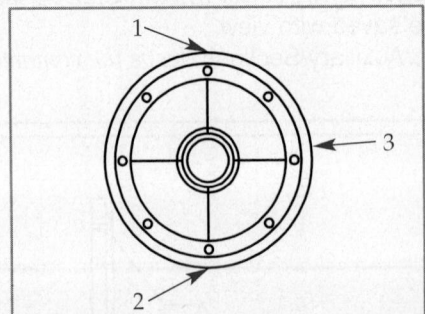
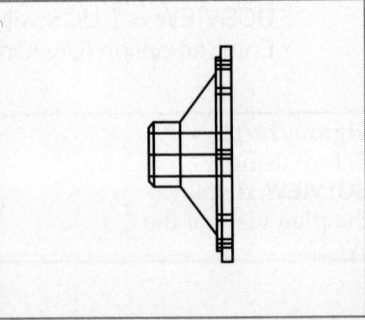

**NOTE**

The Specify view center: prompt remains active until [Enter] is pressed. This allows you to adjust the view location if necessary.

AutoCAD and its Applications—Advanced

**Figure 10-14.**
An orthographic front view is created with the **Ortho** option of **SOLVIEW**. This is the view shown at the lower left.

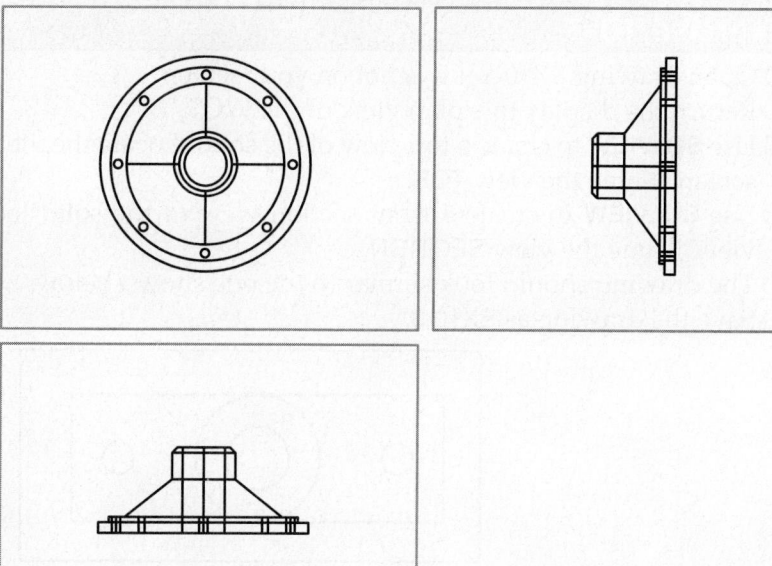

A standard orthographic view can be created using the **Ortho** option of **SOLVIEW**. This is illustrated in the following example. The new orthographic view is shown in **Figure 10-14.**

> Enter an option [Ucs/Ortho/Auxiliary/Section]: **O**↵
> Specify side of viewport to project: *(pick the bottom edge of the left viewport)*
> Specify view center: *(pick the center of the new view)*
> Specify view center <specify viewport>: ↵
> Specify first corner of viewport: *(pick one corner of the viewport)*
> Specify opposite corner of viewport: *(pick the opposite corner of the viewport)*
> Enter view name: **FRONTVIEW**↵

The **SOLVIEW** command creates new layers that are used by **SOLDRAW** when profiles and sections are created. The layers are used for the placement of visible, hidden, dimension, and section lines. Each layer is named as the name of the view with a three letter tag, as shown in the following table. The use of these layers is discussed in the next section.

| Layer Name | Object |
|---|---|
| *view name*-VIS | Visible lines |
| *view name*-HID | Hidden lines |
| *view name*-DIM | Dimension lines |
| *view name*-HAT | Hatch patterns (sections) |

○ Open drawing EX10-1 if it is not on your screen.
○ Return the display to a plan view of the WCS.
○ Use **SOLVIEW** to create a top view of the solid. Locate the view near the top of the screen. Name the view TOP.
○ Use **SOLVIEW** to create a front section view of the solid located below the top view. Name the view SECTION.
○ The drawing should look similar to the one shown below.
○ Save the drawing as EX10-3.

## Creating Finished Views with SOLDRAW

The **SOLVIEW** command saves information specific to each viewport when a new view is created. This information is used by the **SOLDRAW** command to construct a finished profile or section view. **SOLDRAW** first deletes any information currently on the *view name*-VIS, *view name*-HID, and *view name*-HAT layers for the selected view. Visible, hidden, and section lines are automatically placed on the appropriate layer. Therefore, you should avoid placing objects on any layer other than the *view name*-DIM layer.

The **SOLDRAW** command automatically creates a profile or section in the selected viewport. If you select a viewport that was created using the **Section** option of **SOLVIEW**, the **SOLDRAW** command uses the current values of the **HPNAME**, **HPSCALE**, and **HPANG** system variables to construct the section. These three variables control the angle, boundary, and name of the hatch pattern.

If a view is selected that was not created as a section in **SOLVIEW**, the **SOLDRAW** command constructs a profile view. All new visible and hidden lines are placed on the *view name*-VIS or *view name*-HID layer. All existing objects on those layers are deleted.

To initiate the **SOLDRAW** command, select **Drawing** from the **Setup** cascading menu after selecting **Solids** from the **Draw** pull-down menu, pick the **Setup Drawing** button on the **Solids** toolbar, or type SOLDRAW at the Command: prompt.

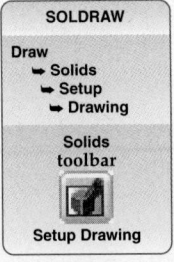

SOLDRAW

Draw
↦ Solids
  ↦ Setup
    ↦ Drawing

Solids
toolbar

Setup Drawing

Command: **SOLDRAW**↵
Select viewports to draw…
Select objects: *(pick the viewport outlines)*
Select objects: ↵
One solid selected.

After the profile construction is completed, lines that should be a hidden linetype are still visible (solid). This is because the linetype set for the *view name*-HID layer is Continuous. Change the linetype to Hidden and the drawing should appear as shown in **Figure 10-15**.

**Figure 10-15.**
The new front profile view shows hidden lines after the linetype is set to Hidden for the FRONTVIEW-HID layer.

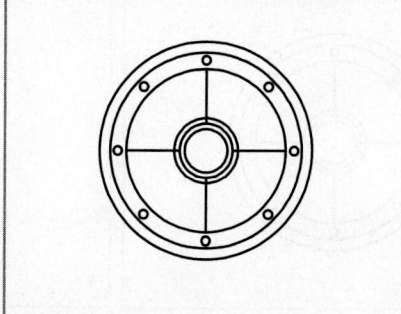
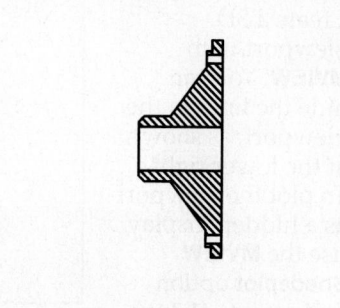
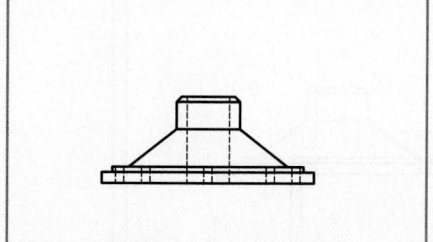

**NOTE**

AutoCAD Release 12 created solid models with a feature called the Advanced Modeling Extension® (AME®). AutoCAD now uses a different method of calculating solid models. In order to use **SOLDRAW** on AutoCAD Release 12 drawings that contain views created with **SOLVIEW**, you must first use **AMECONVERT** to update the solids in the views. Simply enter **AMECONVERT** at the Command: prompt and select the solids to be converted.

**PROFESSIONAL TIP**

If you wish to dimension views created with **SOLVIEW** and **SOLDRAW**, use the view-specific DIM layers. These layers are created for that purpose and are only visible in one view. **SOLDRAW** does not delete information on the DIM layers when it constructs a view.

## Adding a 3D View in Paper Space to the Drawing Layout

If you want to add a paper space viewport that contains a 3D (pictorial) view of the solid, use the **MVIEW** or **VPORTS** command. Create a single viewport by picking the corners. The object will appear in the viewport. Next, use the **3DORBIT** command or a preset isometric viewpoint to achieve the desired 3D view. Pan and zoom as necessary. You can also use the **HIDE** command to create a hidden display in the viewport. See **Figure 10-16.** Remember, you can use the **Hidden Line Settings** dialog box to set the linetype and display color of hidden lines.

In order to have the hidden display plotted correctly, use the **MVIEW Shadeplot** option on the 3D viewport. Select the viewport, enter the command, and select the option. Then, set the option to **Hidden**. If you have a hidden display shown in the viewport, you can also select **As displayed**. Alternately, you can select the viewport and use the **Properties** window to set the **Shade plot** property to **As Displayed** or **Hidden**. A rendered view of the viewport can also be plotted in this manner by setting **MVIEW Shadeplot** to **Rendered**.

**Figure 10-16.**
Create a 3D viewport with **MVIEW**. You can hide the lines in the viewport, as shown at the lower right. To plot the viewport as a hidden display, use the **MVIEW Shadeplot** option and set it to **Hidden**.

## Tips

Remember the following points when working with **SOLVIEW** and **SOLDRAW**.

- Use **SOLVIEW** first and then **SOLDRAW**.
- Do not draw on the *view name*-HID and *view name*-VIS layers.
- Place dimensions for each view on the *view name*-DIM layer for that specific view.
- After using **SOLVIEW**, use **SOLDRAW** on all viewports in order to create hidden lines or section views.
- Change the linetype on the *view name*-HID layer to Hidden.
- Create 3D viewports with the **MVIEW** or **VPORTS** command. Remove hidden lines when plotting with the **MVIEW Shadeplot** option set to **Hidden**.
- Plot the drawing in paper space at the scale of 1:1.

### Exercise 10-4

○ Open drawing EX10-3 if it is not on your screen.
○ Use **SOLDRAW** to create profile and section views of the two views on your screen. Adjust layer linetypes so hidden lines show properly.
○ Add a 3D view to the right of the first two. The drawing should look similar to the one shown below.
○ Save the drawing as EX10-4.

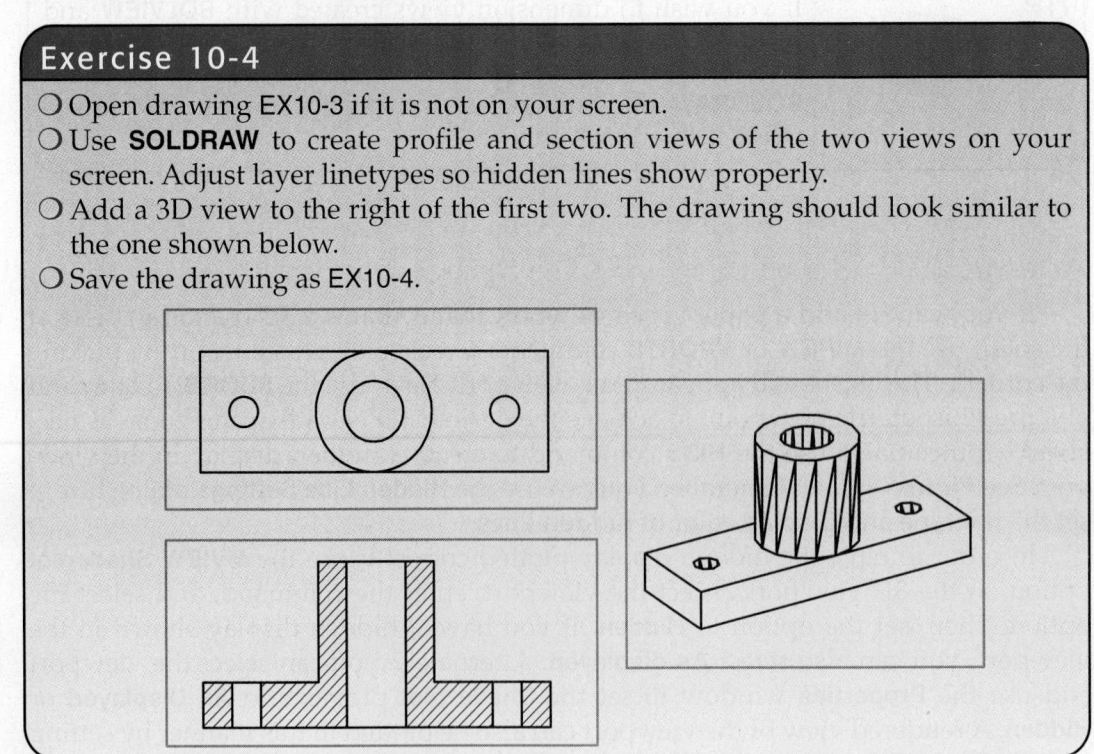

# Creating a Profile with SOLPROF

The **SOLPROF** command creates a profile view from a 3D solid model. This is similar to the **Profile** option of the **SOLVIEW** command. **SOLPROF** is limited to creating a profile view of the solid for the current view only.

**SOLPROF** creates a block of all lines forming the profile of the object. It also creates a block of the hidden lines of the object. The original 3D object is retained. Each of these blocks is placed on a new layer with the name of PH-*view handle* and PV-*view handle*. A *view handle* is a name composed of numbers and letters that is automatically given to a viewport by AutoCAD. For example, if the view handle for the current viewport is 2C9, the **SOLPROF** command creates the layers PH-2C9 and PV-2C9. You must be in a layout tab with a floating viewport active to use **SOLPROF**.

To initiate the **SOLPROF** command, select **Profile** from the **Setup** cascading menu after selecting **Solids** from the **Draw** pull-down menu, pick the **Setup Profile** button on the **Solids** toolbar, or type SOLPROF at the Command: prompt. You must be in paper space and have a model space viewport active.

> Command: **SOLPROF**↵
> Select objects: 1 found
> Select objects: ↵
> Display hidden profile lines on separate layer? [Yes/No] <Y>: ↵
> Project profile lines onto a plane? [Yes/No] <Y>: ↵

If you answer yes to this prompt, the 3D profile lines are projected to a 2D plane and converted to 2D objects. This produces a cleaner profile.

> Delete tangential edges? [Yes/No] <Y>: ↵

Answering yes to this prompt produces a proper 2D view by eliminating lines that would normally appear at tangent points of arcs and lines. The original object and the profile created with **SOLPROF** are shown in **Figure 10-17**.

**SOLPROF**

Draw
➥ Solids
 ➥ Setup
  ➥ Profile

Solids toolbar

Setup Profile

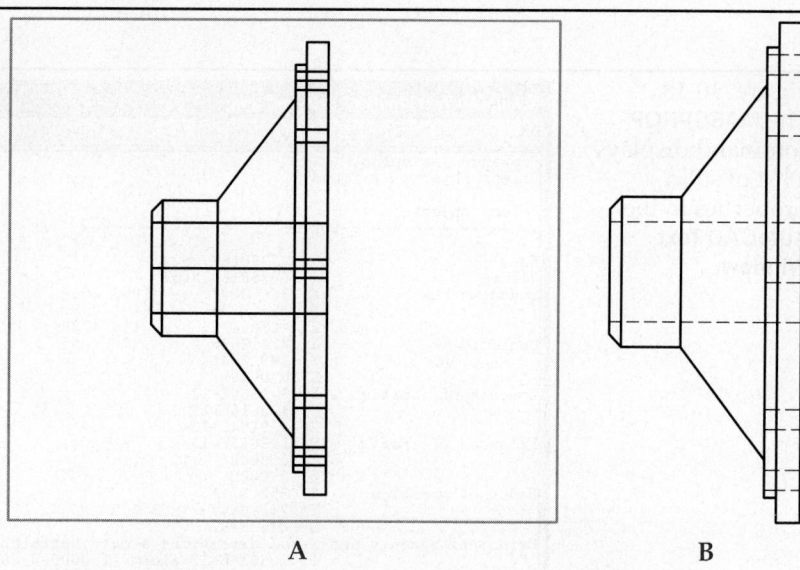

**Figure 10-17.**
A—The original solid. B—A profile created with **SOLPROF**.

A

B

> **NOTE**
>
> When plotting views created with **SOLPROF**, hidden lines may not be displayed unless you freeze the layer that contains the original 3D object.

# Solid Model Analysis

The **MASSPROP** command allows you to analyze a solid model for its physical properties. The data obtained from **MASSPROP** can be retained for reference by saving it to a file. The default file name is the drawing name. The file is an ASCII text file with a .mpr extension (mass properties). The analysis can be used for third party applications to produce finite element analysis, material lists, or other testing studies.

Select the **MASSPROP** command by selecting **Inquiry** in the **Tools** pull-down menu and then picking **Region/Mass Properties** in the cascading menu, picking the **Region/Mass Properties** button on the **Inquiry** toolbar, or typing MASSPROP at the Command: prompt.

MASSPROP

Tools
→ Inquiry
→ Region/Mass
   Properties

Inquiry
toolbar

Region/Mass
Properties

> Command: **MASSPROP**↵
> Select objects: *(pick the solid model)*
> Select objects: ↵

AutoCAD analyzes the model and displays the results in the **AutoCAD Text Window**. See **Figure 10-18**. The following properties are listed.

- **Mass.** A measure of the inertia of a solid. In other words, the more mass an object has, the more inertia it has. Note: Mass is *not* a unit of measurement of inertia.
- **Volume.** The amount of 3D space the solid occupies.
- **Bounding box.** The dimensions of a 3D box that fully encloses the solid.
- **Centroid.** A point in 3D space that represents the geometric center of the mass.
- **Moments of inertia.** A solid's resistance when rotating about a given axis.
- **Products of inertia.** A solid's resistance when rotating about two axes at a time.
- **Radii of gyration.** Similar to moments of inertia. Specified as a radius about an axis.
- **Principal moments and X-Y-Z directions about a centroid.** The axes about which the moments of inertia are the highest and lowest.

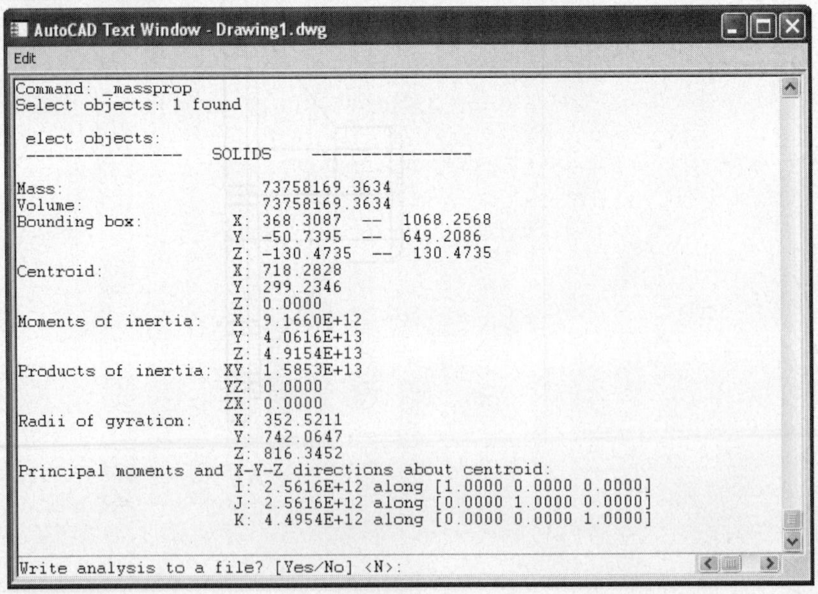

**Figure 10-18.**
The **MASSPROP** command displays a list of solid properties in the **AutoCAD Text Window.**

```
AutoCAD Text Window - Drawing1.dwg
Edit
Command: _massprop
Select objects: 1 found

 elect objects:
---------------- SOLIDS ----------------

Mass:                      73758169.3634
Volume:                    73758169.3634
Bounding box:        X:  368.3087   --   1068.2568
                     Y:  -50.7395   --   649.2086
                     Z: -130.4735   --   130.4735
Centroid:            X:  718.2828
                     Y:  299.2346
                     Z:  0.0000
Moments of inertia:  X:  9.1660E+12
                     Y:  4.0616E+13
                     Z:  4.9154E+13
Products of inertia: XY: 1.5853E+13
                     YZ: 0.0000
                     ZX: 0.0000
Radii of gyration:   X:  352.5211
                     Y:  742.0647
                     Z:  816.3452
Principal moments and X-Y-Z directions about centroid:
                     I: 2.5616E+12 along [1.0000 0.0000 0.0000]
                     J: 2.5616E+12 along [0.0000 1.0000 0.0000]
                     K: 4.4954E+12 along [0.0000 0.0000 1.0000]

Write analysis to a file? [Yes/No] <N>:
```

**PROFESSIONAL TIP**

Advanced applications of solid model design and analysis are possible with Autodesk's Mechanical Desktop® and Inventor® software. These products allow you to create parametric designs and assign a wide variety of materials to the solid model.

## Solid Model File Exchange

AutoCAD drawing files can be converted to files that can be used for testing and analysis. Use the **ACISOUT** command or **Export Data** dialog box to create a file with a .sat extension. These files can be imported into AutoCAD with the **ACISIN** command or by using the **Select ACIS File** dialog box.

Solids can also be exported for use with stereolithography software. These files have a .stl extension. Use the **STLOUT** command or the **Export Data** dialog box to create STL files.

### Importing and Exporting Solid Model Files

A solid model is frequently used with analysis and testing software or in the manufacture of a part. The **ACISOUT** command allows you to create a type of file that can be used for these purposes. You can type ACISOUT at the Command: prompt and select solid objects. After selecting the objects, the **Create ACIS File** dialog box is displayed.

You can also use the **Export Data** dialog box by picking **Export...** from the **File** pull-down menu or typing EXPORT at the Command: prompt. Pick the **ACIS (*.sat)** selection in the **Save as type:** drop-down list. See **Figure 10-19**. After entering a file name and file type, pick the **Save** button. The dialog box is closed and you can select which solid objects to include.

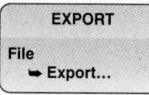

EXPORT

File
↳ Export...

**Figure 10-19.**
Pick **ACIS (*.sat)** in the **Export Data** dialog box to export a solid model to a file for exchange with other software.

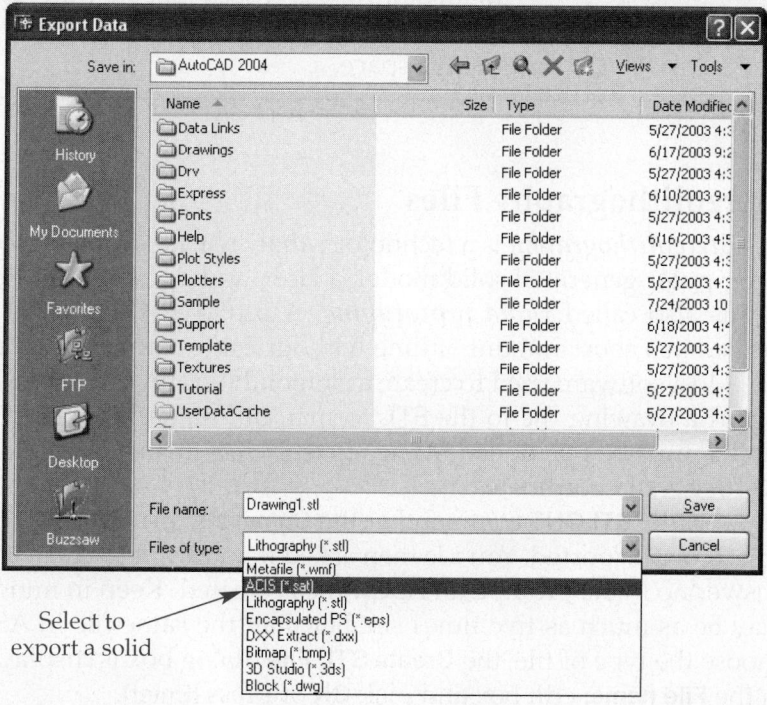

Select to
export a solid

ACISIN

Insert
→ ACIS File...

An SAT file can be imported into AutoCAD and automatically converted into a drawing file by selecting **ACIS File...** from the **Insert** pull-down menu or entering ACISIN at the Command: prompt. This displays the **Select ACIS File** dialog box. Select the SAT file and pick the **Open** button.

You can also import a file using the **IMPORT** command. Type IMP or IMPORT at the Command: prompt to display the **Import File** dialog box. Pick the **ACIS (*.sat)** selection in the **Files of type:** drop-down list, **Figure 10-20.** Then, select the SAT file and pick the **Open** button.

**Figure 10-20.**
Pick **ACIS (*.sat)** in the **Import File** dialog box to import a solid model file.

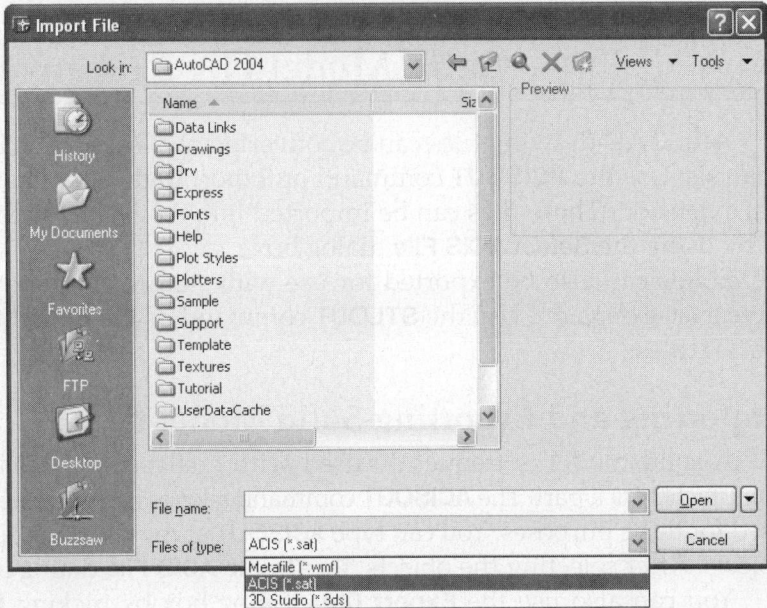

**PROFESSIONAL TIP** Solid model drawing files can be saved as SAT files for archive purposes. These files require far less disk space than DWG files and may be a good option when you have limited storage space.

## Stereolithography Files

*Stereolithography* is a technology that creates plastic prototype 3D models using a computer-generated solid model, a laser, and a vat of liquid polymer. This technology is also called *rapid prototyping.* A prototype 3D model can be designed and formed in a short amount of time without using standard manufacturing processes.

Most software used to create a stereolithograph can read STL files. AutoCAD can export a drawing file to the STL format, but *cannot* import STL files. Also, the solid model must be positioned in the current UCS in such a way so the entire object has positive XYZ coordinates.

Use the **STLOUT** command at the Command: prompt. You can only select a single object to be exported. You are then asked if you want to create a binary STL file. If you answer no to the prompt, an ASCII file is created. Keep in mind that a binary STL file may be as much as five times smaller than the same file in ASCII format. After you choose the type of file, the **Create STL File** dialog box is displayed. Type the file name in the **File name:** edit box and pick **OK** or press [Enter].

You can also use the **Export Data** dialog box to export an STL file. In this method, you name the file in the dialog box and then select the solid object. After you select the object and press [Enter], the file is created. You are not given the option of selecting a binary or ASCII format for the file.

**PROFESSIONAL TIP**

The **FACETRES** setting affects the "resolution" of the solid in an exported STL file and, thus, the final stereolithograph.

---

**Exercise 10-5**

○ Open drawing EX10-4 if it is not on your screen.
○ Perform a mass properties analysis of the solid.
  ○ What is the mass?
  ○ What is the volume?
  ○ What are the bounding box dimensions?
  ○ What are the centroid coordinates?
○ Export an SAT file and name it EX10-5.
○ Begin a new drawing. Import the SAT file named EX10-5.
○ Export an STL file and name it EX10-5.
○ Do not save the drawing.

---

## Chapter Test

*Answer the following questions on a separate sheet of paper.*

1. What is the function of the **ISOLINES** system variable?
2. Which variable controls the display of a solid primitive silhouette?
3. What is the function of the **FACETRES** system variable?
4. Which command creates a 2D region that represents a cutting plane through the solid?
5. Which command can display the true 3D shape of internal features and object profiles?
6. Which command should be used first, **SOLDRAW** or **SOLVIEW**?
7. Which command allows you to create a multiview layout from a 3D solid model?
8. Which option of the command in Question 7 is used to create an orthographic view?
9. Name the layer(s) that the command in Question 7 automatically creates.
10. Which layer(s) in Question 9 should you avoid drawing on?
11. Which command can automatically complete a section view using the current settings of **HPNAME**, **HPSCALE**, and **HPANG**?
12. When plotting, how are hidden lines removed in a viewport that contains a 3D view?
13. Which command creates a profile view from a 3D model?
14. What is the function of the **MASSPROP** command?
15. What is the extension of the ASCII file that can be created by **MASSPROP**?
16. What is a *centroid*?
17. Which commands export and import solid models?
18. Which type of file has a .stl extension?

---

## Drawing Problems

1. Open one of your solid model problems from a previous chapter and do the following.
   A. Set the **DISPSILH** variable to 1 and use **HIDE**.
   B. Set the **FACETRES** variable to .5 and shade the model. Set **FACETRES** to 1 and shade the model again. Set **FACETRES** to 2 and shade the model.
   C. Create a rendering of the model.
   D. Save the drawing as P10-1.

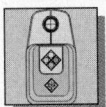

2. Open one of your solid model problems from a previous chapter and do the following.
   A. Construct a section through the model. Cut through as many features as possible.
   B. Move the new section region to a location outside the 3D solid.
   C. Place section lines in the appropriate areas. Add lines to complete the section.
   D. Cut a slice through the original solid in the same location as the previous section.
   E. Retain the piece of the solid that is the same side as the section.
   F. Remove the other side of the slice.
   G. Save the drawing as P10-2.

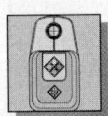

3. Open one of your solid model problems from a previous chapter and do the following.
   A. Create a multiview layout of the model. One of the views should be a section view. Use a total of three 2D views.
   B. Use **SOLVIEW** and **SOLDRAW** to create the views. Be sure that section lines and hidden lines are displayed properly.
   C. Create a fourth viewport that contains a 3D view of the solid. Place the label PICTORIAL VIEW within the viewport.
   D. Plot the drawing so the 3D view is displayed with hidden lines removed.
   E. Save the drawing as P10-3.

4. Open one of your solid model problems from a previous chapter and do the following.
   A. Display the model in a plan view.
   B. Use **SOLPROF** to create a profile view. Wblock the profile view to a file named P10-4PLN.
   C. Display the original model in a 3D view.
   D. Use **SECTION** to construct a front-view section of the model. Delete the original 3D solid.
   E. Display the section as a plan view.
   F. Insert the wblock P10-4PLN above the section view. Adjust the views so that they align properly.
   G. Save the drawing as P10-4.

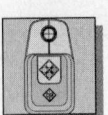

5. Choose five solid model problems from previous chapters and copy them to a new folder. Then, do the following.
   A. Open the first drawing. Export it as an SAT file.
   B. Do the same for the remaining four files.
   C. Compare the sizes of the SAT files with the DWG files. Compare the combined sizes of both types of files.
   D. Begin a new drawing and import one of the SAT files.

CHAPTER 11

# Introduction to Surface Modeling

## Learning Objectives

After completing this chapter, you will be able to:
- Explain surface modeling.
- Draw 3D faces.
- Set the visibility for edges of 3D faces.
- Draw surface model primitives

## Overview of Surface Modeling

In Chapter 1, you were introduced to the three basic forms of 3D modeling—wireframe objects, solid models, and surface models. Solid modeling is covered in detail in Chapter 6 through Chapter 10. You learned that a solid model accurately and realistically represents the shape and form of a final object and contains data related to the object's volume, mass, and centroid.

Surface modeling, on the other hand, also accurately and realistically represents the shape and form of a final object. However, a surface model does not contain data about the object's volume, mass, etc. A surface model is simply a skin used to represent the form of an object.

Surface modeling is not nearly as flexible as solid modeling. There are surface primitives, just as there are solid primitives. However, surface models are not quite as easy to edit. For example, you cannot perform Boolean operations on surface models.

This chapter introduces surface modeling. You will learn how to create surface primitives and a special type of surface called a 3D face.

## Creating 3D Faces

Surfaces that appear solid and not as wireframes are called *3D faces.* These are created using the **3DFACE** command. All of the surface modeling techniques in AutoCAD create 3D faces, whether individually or as a group that represents a shape. For example, a surface primitive is really a collection of 3D faces. A single 3D face is a flat surface that has either three or four sides.

217

**Figure 11-1.**
This T-shaped object is constructed as a surface model using 3D faces.

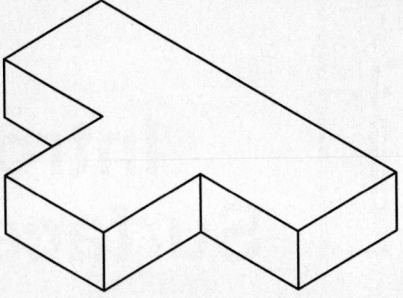

To provide an example of creating 3D faces, you will create the T-shaped object shown in **Figure 11-1.** The object is first partially modeled as a wireframe to help in creating the 3D faces. First, draw the 2D shape shown in **Figure 11-2A** using the **LINE** command. Then, copy the shape one unit up on the Z axis. Display a pictorial view of the model, **Figure 11-2B.** Now, as much of the wireframe object as needed has been created. You can now create a surface model consisting of 3D faces.

**Figure 11-2.**
A—Start constructing the surface model by drawing this 2D profile. B—The 2D profile is copied up the Z axis. The pick points for creating the first 3D face are shown.

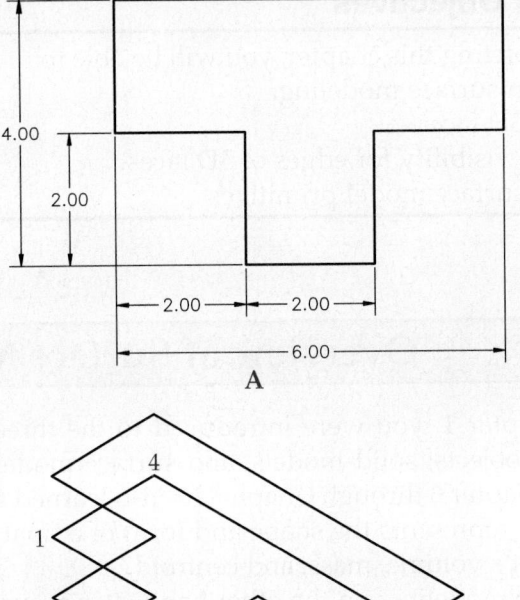

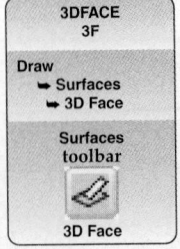

First, add the bottom surface and then the top surface. Access the **3DFACE** command by selecting **3D Face** from the **Surfaces** cascading menu in the **Draw** pull-down menu, picking the **3D Face** button on the **Surfaces** toolbar, or typing 3DFACE or 3F at the Command: prompt. For the drawing you are creating, set the **Endpoint** object snap and turn it on. Then, continue as follows.

Command: **3DFACE** or **3F**↵
Specify first point or [Invisible]: (*pick Point 1 in Figure 11-2B*)
Specify second point or [Invisible]: (*pick Point 2 in Figure 11-2B*)
Specify third point or [Invisible]: <exit> (*pick Point 3 in Figure 11-2B*)
Specify fourth point or [Invisible]: <create three-sided face>: (*pick Point 4 in Figure 11-2B*)
Specify third point or [Invisible]: <exit> ↵
Command:

AutoCAD and its Applications—Advanced

The first part of the bottom surface is created. Since a 3D face has either three or four sides, the shape of a 3D face must be either triangular or rectangular. Therefore, the bottom and top surfaces have to be constructed from two 3D faces. Draw another 3D face on the smaller part of the bottom surface. Then, copy the two 3D faces to the top surface of the object.

You may have noticed in the command sequence that after picking a fourth point, you are prompted for a third point. This allows you to create an adjoining 3D face using the last side of the previously created 3D face. This can be very beneficial, as you will see as you complete the object. Refer to **Figure 11-3** for the pick points.

Command: **3F**↵
Specify first point or [Invisible]: *(pick Point 1 in **Figure 11-3**)*
Specify second point or [Invisible]: *(pick Point 2 in **Figure 11-3**)*
Specify third point or [Invisible]: <exit> *(pick Point 3 on the right side in **Figure 11-3**)*
Specify fourth point or [Invisible]: <create three-sided face>: *(pick Point 4 on the right side in **Figure 11-3**)*
Specify third point or [Invisible]: <exit>

Continue picking Points 3 and 4 around the object until each face has been completed. Press [Enter] after completing the back face to exit the command. The finished object should appear similar to that shown in **Figure 11-4** after the **HIDE** command is used. Notice that a line appears between the two sections of the top face. This problem can be solved by making the edges invisible.

**Figure 11-3.**
Starting with Point 1, use these pick points to create the 3D faces for all sides without exiting the **3DFACE** command.

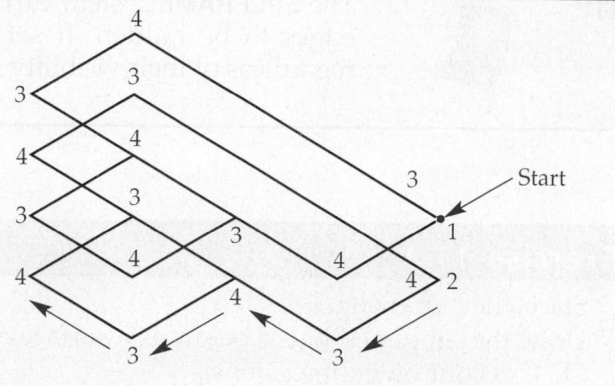

**Figure 11-4.**
The surface model after the **HIDE** command is used. Notice the visible edge between the two 3D faces on the top surface.

# Creating Invisible 3D Face Edges

The **Invisible** option of the **3DFACE** command allows you to remove, or hide, edges that should not appear as lines on a surface. The **Invisible** option must be entered before picking the first point of the invisible edge. The option remains active for one edge only.

Instead of trying to keep track of which edges are supposed to be invisible as you draw them, you can use the **Properties** window after the 3D faces are created. Simply select the 3D face containing an edge that should be invisible. Then, open the **Properties** window. In the **Geometry** area, the edges of the 3D face are listed, Edge 1 through Edge 4, with its current visibility state. The edges are numbered in the order in which they were created. Edge 4 is listed even if the face has three sides. Simply change the visibility of the appropriate edge to **Hidden**.

For the T-shaped object, select one of the 3D faces on the top surface. Then, change the appropriate edge visibility to **Hidden**. Now, use the **HIDE** command. The line is still visible because there are actually two edges there, only one of which is hidden. Select the other 3D face and change the visibility of the corresponding edge to **Hidden**. Now, the surface model should appear as shown in **Figure 11-1.** You also need to change the visibility on the two 3D faces on the bottom surface.

---

**PROFESSIONAL TIP**

The **SPLFRAME** system variable must be set to 0 for invisible edges to be hidden. If set to 1, hidden edges are shown regardless of their visibility setting.

---

## Exercise 11-1

◯ Start a new drawing.
◯ Draw the simplified house below as a surface model.
  ◯ Use your own dimensions.
  ◯ Use the **3DFACE** command to construct the surfaces.
  ◯ You may want to draw a wireframe of the house first.
◯ Save the drawing as EX11-1.

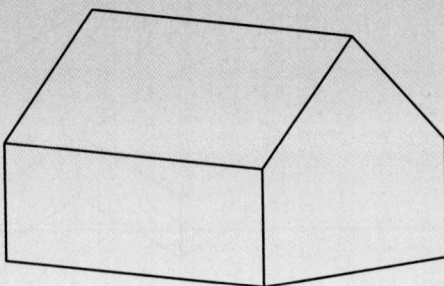

---

# Drawing Surface Primitives

AutoCAD's surface primitives can be used to create a design that can then be imported into presentation and animation programs, such as Autodesk VIZ or 3ds max®. These primitives can be drawn using the **Surfaces** toolbar or the **3D Objects** dialog box. The **Surfaces** toolbar displays buttons for all of the surface primitives, **Figure 11-5**. Picking **3D Surfaces...** from the **Surfaces** cascading menu in the **Draw** pull-down menu displays the **3D Objects** dialog box.

The surface primitives you can draw include a box, pyramid, wedge, dome, sphere, cone, torus, dish, and mesh. There is not a cylinder surface primitive. After making a selection, you only need to specify basic dimensions and an insertion location. The result is a surfaced 3D object. The **HIDE** command makes hidden lines in the object invisible, causing the object to appear solid. The next sections discuss AutoCAD's surface primitives.

Each of these objects is created as a 3D mesh and treated as a single object. If you wish to edit any part of the object, first use the **EXPLODE** command. After exploding, each object is composed of individual 3D faces.

AutoCAD has solid primitives and surfaced primitives, **Figure 11-6**. If you enter the name of one of the solid primitives at the Command: prompt, the solid model version of that shape is created. If you want to draw the surface primitive version, access the **Surfaces** toolbar or the **3D Objects** dialog box, or enter 3D at the Command: prompt. You can also enter AI before the object name. For example, the following entry can be used to draw a cone surface primitive.

Command: **AI_CONE**↵

In this instance, "AI" refers to an "Autodesk Incorporated" AutoLISP command definition that is found in the 3d.lsp file. When you select a button on the **Surfaces** toolbar, you will notice this entry on the command line. The underscore character (_) is used in the acad.mnu file to enable commands to be automatically translated in foreign language versions of AutoCAD. If you do not type AI_ before the command, a solid primitive is created instead of a surface primitive.

Figure 11-5.
AutoCAD's surface primitives can be selected on the **Surfaces** toolbar.

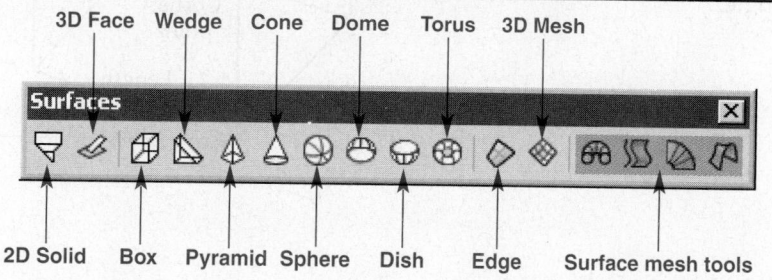

Figure 11-6.
Available surface and solid primitives.

| Solid Primitives | Surface Primitives |
|---|---|
| Box | Box |
| Cone | Cone |
| Cylinder | Dish |
| Sphere | Dome |
| Torus | Mesh |
| Wedge | Pyramid |
| | Sphere |
| | Torus |
| | Wedge |

## Box

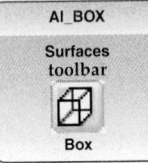

AI_BOX

Surfaces
toolbar

Box

You can construct a box surface primitive by picking the **Box** button on the **Surfaces** toolbar or the **Box** image in the **3D Objects** dialog box. You can also enter AI_BOX at the Command: prompt. You must provide the location of one corner, the box dimensions, and the rotation angle about the Z axis (with the first corner as the base). Enter the values using the keyboard or pick them with your pointing device.

> Command: **AI_BOX**↵
> Specify corner point of box: **3,3**↵
> Specify length of box: **1**↵
> Specify width of box or [Cube]: **C**↵
> Specify rotation angle of box about the Z axis or [Reference]: **0**↵
> Command:

If you enter the **Cube** option, AutoCAD applies the value entered for the length to the width and height. If you enter a value for the width, you are prompted for the height. See **Figure 11-7.**

**Figure 11-7.**
A box surface primitive requires a location for the first corner point, and values for the length, width, height, and rotation angle.

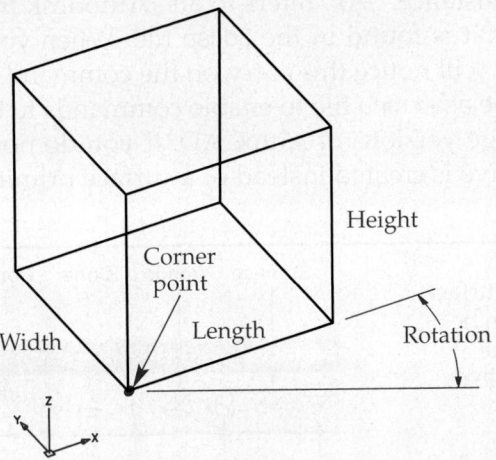

## Wedge

AI_WEDGE

Surfaces
toolbar

Wedge

You can quickly create a right-angle wedge surface primitive by picking the **Wedge** button on the **Surfaces** toolbar, selecting the **Wedge** image in the **3D Objects** dialog box, or entering AI_WEDGE at the Command: prompt. You are then prompted for a corner of the wedge, followed by the length, width, height, and rotation angle. A wedge and its basic dimensions are shown in **Figure 11-8.**

> Command: **AI_WEDGE**↵
> Specify corner point of wedge: **6,3**↵
> Specify length of wedge: **3**↵
> Specify width of wedge: **2**↵
> Specify height of wedge: **2**↵
> Specify rotation angle of wedge about the Z axis: **15**↵
> Command:

**Figure 11-8.**
A wedge surface primitive requires a corner point location, length, width, height, and rotation angle.

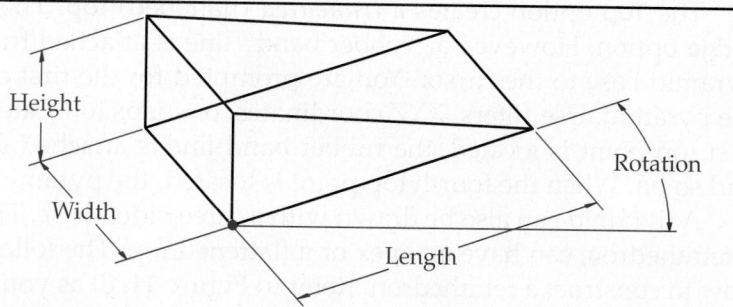

## Pyramid

Five varieties of pyramid surface primitives are available in AutoCAD. You can draw three types of four-sided pyramids, **Figure 11-9.** You can also draw two types of three-sided pyramids, called *tetrahedrons.*

To draw a pyramid surface primitive, pick the **Pyramid** button on the **Surfaces** toolbar, select the **Pyramid** image in the **3D Objects** dialog box, or enter AI_PYRAMID at the Command: prompt. First, you must draw the base of the pyramid. When you have located the third point, you can draw a tetrahedron or enter the fourth point of the base. If you draw the fourth point on the base, you can then specify an apex point, or select from the two other four-sided options (**Ridge** and **Top**). When drawing the apex, use XYZ filters, enter an XYZ coordinate, or snap to an existing object. The following example shows how to draw a four-sided pyramid with an apex.

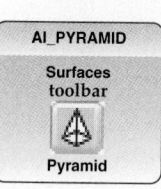

AI_PYRAMID

Surfaces toolbar

Pyramid

```
Command: AI_PYRAMID↵
Specify first corner point for base of pyramid: 2,6↵
Specify second corner point for base of pyramid: @2,0↵
Specify third corner point for base of pyramid: @0,2↵
Specify fourth corner point for base of pyramid or [Tetrahedron]: @–2,0↵
Specify apex point of pyramid or [Ridge/Top]: 3,3,7↵
Command:
```

The **Ridge** option requires two points to define the ridge at the top of the pyramid. When you enter this option after drawing the fourth point on the base, the last line drawn on the base is highlighted. This indicates that the first point of the ridge will begin perpendicular to the highlighted line. However, the first point does not need to touch the highlighted line. Use filters, enter coordinates, or snap to existing objects.

```
Specify apex point of pyramid or [Ridge/Top]: R↵
Specify first ridge end point of pyramid: .XY↵
of (pick a point inside the base)
(need Z): 3↵
Specify second ridge end point of pyramid: .XY↵
of (pick a point inside the base)
(need Z): 3↵
Command:
```

**Figure 11-9.**
Three options are available for pyramid surface primitives with four-sided bases.

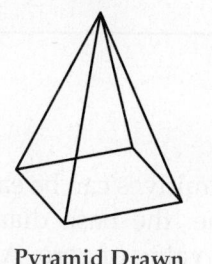

Pyramid Drawn with an Apex

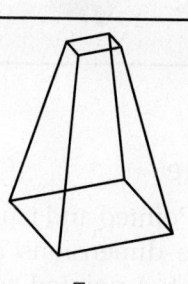

Ridge Option

Top Option

The **Top** option creates a *truncated* (flattened) top. This option is similar to the **Ridge** option. However, a "rubber band" line is attached from the first corner of the pyramid base to the cursor. You are prompted for the first corner point of the top of the pyramid. Use filters, XYZ coordinates, or snaps to locate the top points. After the first top point is located, the rubber band line is attached to the second base point, and so on. When the fourth top point is located, the pyramid is complete.

A pyramid can also be drawn with a three-sided base. The resulting shape, called a tetrahedron, can have an apex or a flattened top. The following example illustrates how to construct a tetrahedron. Refer to **Figure 11-10** as you proceed.

Command: **AI_PYRAMID**↵
Specify first corner point for base of pyramid: **2,2**↵
Specify second corner point for base of pyramid: **@3,0**↵
Specify third corner point for base of pyramid: **@0,3**↵
Specify fourth corner point for base of pyramid or [Tetrahedron]: **T**↵
Specify apex point of tetrahedron or [Top]: **4,3,3**↵
Command:

A truncated (flattened) top can be given to a tetrahedron by entering the **Top** option. Refer to **Figure 11-10B**.

Specify fourth corner point for base of pyramid or [Tetrahedron]: **T**↵
Specify apex point of tetrahedron or [Top]: **T**↵
Specify first corner point for top of tetrahedron: *(enter coordinates or use filters to pick the first top point)*
Specify second corner point for top of tetrahedron: *(enter coordinates or use filters to pick the second top point)*
Specify third corner point for top of tetrahedron: *(enter coordinates or use filters to pick the third top point)*
Command:

Figure 11-10.
A—A tetrahedron is a pyramid with a three-sided base.
B—A truncated tetrahedron requires three pick points for the top surface.

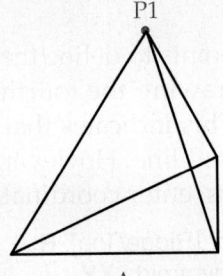
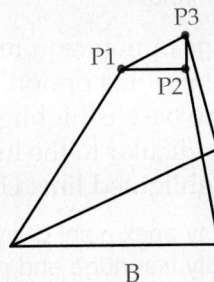

**PROFESSIONAL TIP**

Try constructing pyramids in the plan view using XYZ coordinates or filters. Your constructions will be more accurate, and you can easily see the symmetry or asymmetry required.

## Cone

Pointed and truncated cone surface primitives can be easily created in AutoCAD. Three dimensions are required for a cone: the base diameter, top diameter, and height. A pointed cone has a top diameter value of zero. A truncated cone has a top diameter value other than zero.

AutoCAD and its Applications—Advanced

To draw a cone surface primitive, pick the **Cone** button on the **Surfaces** toolbar, select the **Cone** image in the **3D Objects** dialog box, or enter AI_CONE at the Command: prompt:

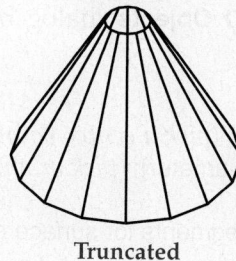
> Command: **AI_CONE**↵
> Specify center point for base of cone: **3,3**↵
> Specify radius for base of cone or [Diameter]: **1**↵
> Specify radius for top of cone or [Diameter] <0>: **.15**↵
> Specify height of cone: **2**↵
> Enter number of segments for surface of cone <16>: ↵
> Command:

If you want a pointed cone, simply press [Enter] when prompted for the top radius value. The two types of cones are shown in **Figure 11-11.**

**Figure 11-11.**
Cone surface
primitives can be
truncated or
pointed.

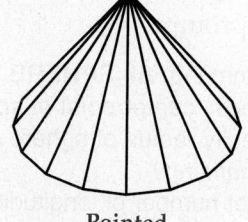

Truncated
Cone

Pointed
Cone

## Dome and Dish

A dome or a dish can be thought of as a hemisphere, or half of a sphere. If a dome is placed on top of a dish, a sphere is formed. When constructed, the top of the dome represents the north pole. The bottom of the dish represents the south pole. A spherical object has longitudinal segments around its equator; each segment runs from the north pole to the south pole. Latitudinal segments run east and west. Refer to **Figure 11-12.**

To draw a dome or dish surface primitive, pick the **Dome** or **Dish** button on the **Surfaces** toolbar or select the **Dome** or **Dish** image in the **3D Objects** dialog box. You can also enter the following at the Command: prompt.

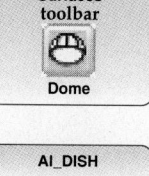
> Command: **AI_DOME**↵ *(or* **AI_DISH** *to draw a dish)*
> Specify center point of dome: *(pick a point)*
> Specify radius of dome or [Diameter]: **2**↵
> Enter number of longitudinal segments for surface of dome <16>: *(enter a value or*
> *press* [Enter]*)*
> Enter number of latitudinal segments for surface of dome <8>: *(enter a value or*
> *press* [Enter]*)*
> Command:

**Figure 11-12.**
A—This dome is
divided into 16
longitudinal
segments. B—This
dome is divided
into 8 latitudinal
segments.

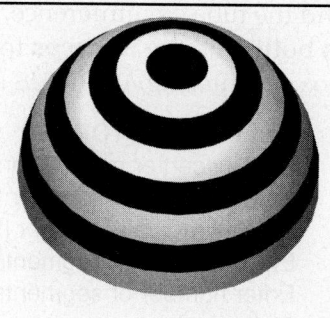

A

B

| NOTE | The more segments you use for an object, the smoother the curved surface, but the longer the drawing regeneration time. Use as few segments as possible. |
|---|---|

## Sphere

**AI_SPHERE**

**Surfaces toolbar**

**Sphere**

A sphere requires the same basic dimensions specified for a dome or dish. Since the sphere is a complete globe, the default values for the number of latitudinal and longitudinal segments are the same.

To draw a sphere surface primitive, pick the **Sphere** button on the **Surfaces** toolbar or the **Sphere** image in the **3D Objects** dialog box, or enter AI_SPHERE at the Command: prompt.

> Command: **AI_SPHERE**↵
> Specify center point of sphere: *(pick a center point)*
> Specify radius of sphere or [Diameter]: *(pick or enter a radius, or type D to provide a diameter)*
> Enter number of longitudinal segments for surface of sphere <16>: *(enter the number of segments and press [Enter])*
> Enter number of latitudinal segments for surface of sphere <16>: *(enter the number of segments and press [Enter])*
> Command:

**Figure 11-13** shows an 8-segment sphere, a 16-segment sphere, and a 32-segment sphere.

**Figure 11-13.**
Examples of sphere surface primitives. The more segments in a sphere, the smoother it appears, but the longer it takes to regenerate.

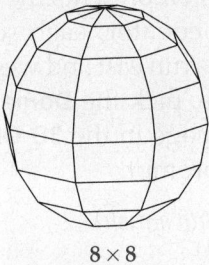 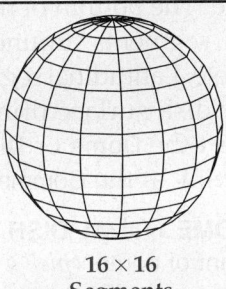 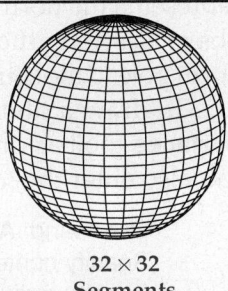

8 × 8
Segments

16 × 16
Segments

32 × 32
Segments

## Torus

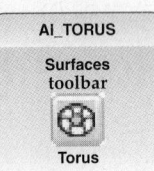
**AI_TORUS**

**Surfaces toolbar**

**Torus**

A *torus* resembles an inflated inner tube. See **Figure 11-14.** To draw a torus, you must enter values for the diameter (or radius) of the torus and the tube. The other dimensions required are the number of segments around the torus circumference and around the tube circumference. A torus surface primitive can be drawn by picking the **Torus** button on the **Surfaces** toolbar, selecting the **Torus** image in the **3D Objects** dialog box, or entering AI_TORUS at the Command: prompt.

> Command: **AI_TORUS**↵
> Specify center point of torus: *(pick the center point)*
> Specify radius of torus or [Diameter]: **2**↵
> Specify radius of tube or [Diameter]: **.5**↵
> Enter number of segments around tube circumference <16>: ↵
> Enter number of segments around torus circumference <16>: ↵
> Command:

**Figure 11-14.**
To draw a torus
surface primitive,
you must specify the
radius (or diameter)
values of the torus
and the tube. You
must also specify the
number of segments
around each.

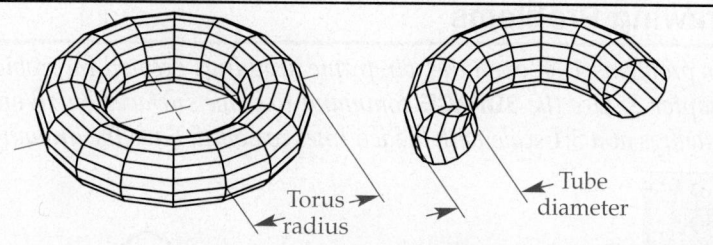

Torus → radius

Tube diameter

---

### Exercise 11-2

○ Start a new drawing.
○ Draw one of each type of surface primitive.
○ Space the primitives evenly in the drawing.
○ Make note of the information required to draw each primitive.
○ Use the **SHADEMODE** command to shade the drawing.
○ Save the drawing as EX11-2.

---

## Chapter Test

*Answer the following questions on a separate sheet of paper.*

1. What is the minimum number of edges for a 3D face?
2. What is the maximum number of edges for a 3D face?
3. Which option of the **3DFACE** command allows you to set the visibility of an edge as you are drawing the face?
4. How can you set the visibility of 3D face edges after the 3D face is drawn?
5. From which dialog box can you select one of AutoCAD's surface primitives? List the primitives that are available.
6. How many different types of pyramids can you draw with the **AI_PYRAMID** command, *not* including tetrahedrons?
7. Define *longitudinal segments* in relation to drawing a dome or dish.
8. Which command can you enter at the keyboard to draw a cone surface primitive?
9. Which command is used to draw a surface-modeled tetrahedron?
10. Which two measurements are required to draw a torus?

---

# Drawing Problems

*For problems 1–4, open the wireframe drawings created in problems P2-1 through P2-4 from Chapter 2. Use the **3DFACE** command to place surfaces on all sides of the objects. Plot the drawings at a 3:1 scale with hidden lines removed. Save the drawings as P11-(problem number).*

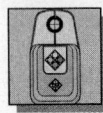 1.

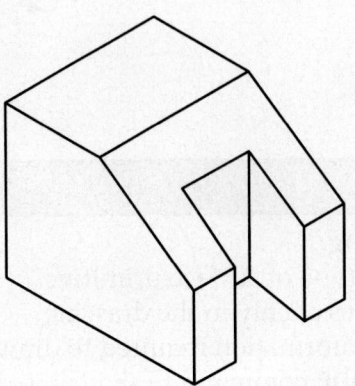

 2.

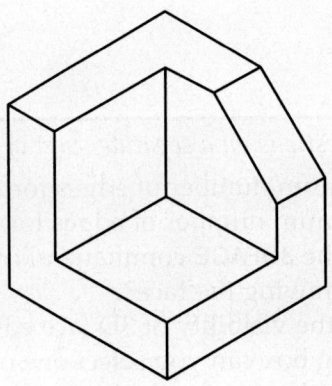

 3.

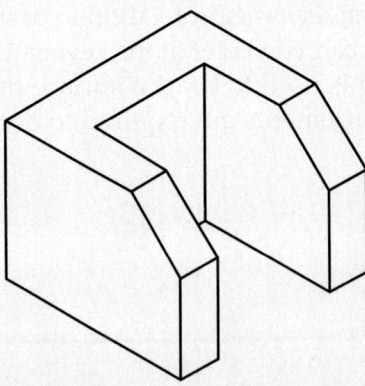

4.

*For problems 5 through 7, construct 3D models of the objects shown. Use only the surface primitives available on the **Surfaces** toolbar. Construct each object using the specific instructions given. Save the drawings as* P11-*(problem number).*

5.  The desktop (A) is 36″ × 66″ × 1.5″. The drawer section (B) is 30″ × 18″× 30″. The right leg (C) is 30″× 1.5″ × 30″. The feet (D) are ∅1.5″, and are tangent to all adjacent box sides.

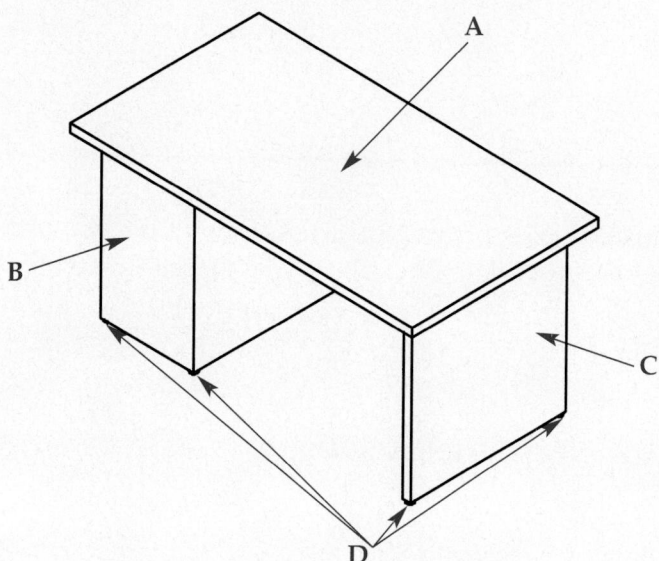

6.

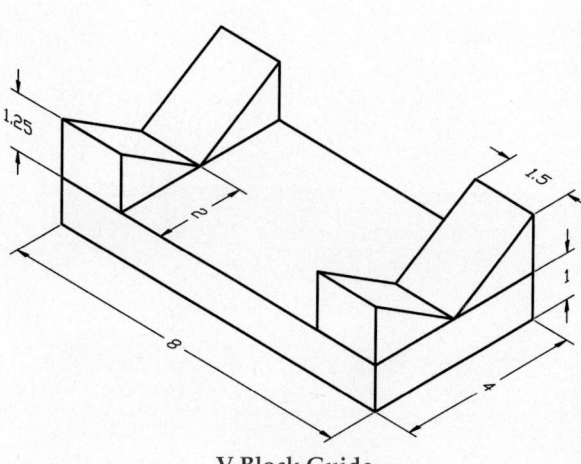

V-Block Guide

7.

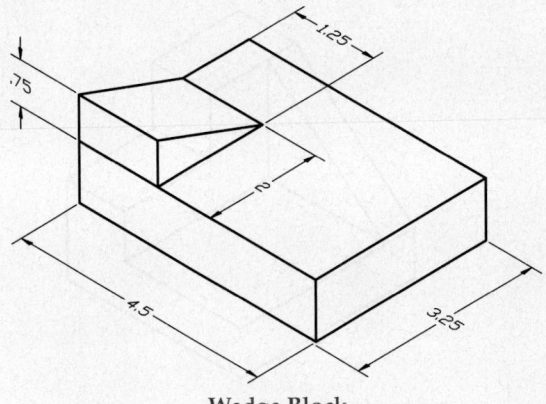

**Wedge Block**

## CHAPTER 12

# Three-Dimensional Surface Modeling Techniques

## Learning Objectives

After completing this chapter, you will be able to:

- Construct a 3D surface mesh.
- Create a variety of surface-modeled objects using the **EDGESURF**, **TABSURF**, **RULESURF**, and **REVSURF** commands.
- Draw wireframe holes.
- Surface around holes.

There are several ways to construct surface models using AutoCAD. The method you use will depend on the object you are creating. A surface mesh, or "patch," can be created using either the **3DMESH** or **PFACE** command. The **EDGESURF** command creates a surface mesh using four edges joined at the endpoints. The **RULESURF** command creates a mesh of ruled surfaces between two curves or lines. The **TABSURF** command creates a tabulated surface mesh using a curve and a specified direction to extend the surface. The **REVSURF** command creates a surface by rotating a profile around an axis.

## 3D Mesh Techniques

Three-dimensional face meshes are used to create surface models that cannot be constructed using surfacing commands. There are four types of 3D face meshes: planar mesh, 3D mesh, pface mesh, and surface patch.

A *planar mesh* is made up of four sides. The corners can have different Z values. However, the mesh lies in a single plane. In other words, the mesh is "flat." However, the mesh can be edited to create an irregular surface. A planar mesh is created with the **Mesh** option of the **3D** command.

A *3D mesh* is a polygon mesh composed of 3D faces. This type of mesh is not restricted to a single plane. The **3DMESH** command is used to create a 3D mesh.

A *pface mesh,* or *polyface mesh,* is a general polygon mesh of 3D faces. Each face can have an infinite number of vertices and can occupy a different plane. The **PFACE** command is used to create a polyface mesh.

The fourth type of mesh is a *surface patch.* This is created with the **EDGESURF** command.

# Constructing a 3D Mesh

The **3DMESH** command creates a 3D mesh. The mesh is defined in rows and columns. The *N value* defines the number of rows. An N value of three produces two rows. The *M value* defines the number of columns. An M value of four produces three columns. See **Figure 12-1**.

When using the **3DMESH** command, each vertex in the mesh must be given an XYZ coordinate location. The vertices of the mesh are its definition points. A mesh must have between 2 and 256 vertices in each direction.

---

Figure 12-1.
A 3D polygon mesh is similar to a grid of XY coordinates. M values define columns and N values define rows. This example has an M value of 4 and an N value of 3.

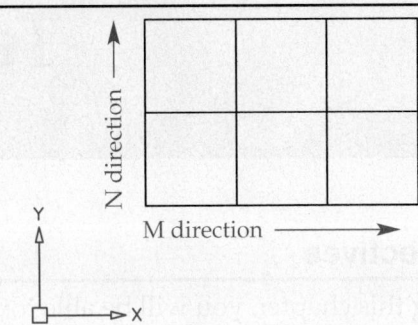

---

When prompting for coordinates, the M and N location of the current vertex is indicated. See the command sequence below. The values for each vertex of the first M column must be entered. Then, values for the second, third, and remaining M columns must be entered.

To draw a 3D mesh, select **3D Mesh** from the **Surfaces** cascading menu in the **Draw** pull-down menu, pick the **3D Mesh** button on the **Surfaces** toolbar, or type 3DMESH at the Command: prompt. Use the following command sequence to get the feel for the **3DMESH** command. When complete, use **3DORBIT** to view the mesh from different angles. The mesh should look like the one shown in **Figure 12-2** after using **3DORBIT**.

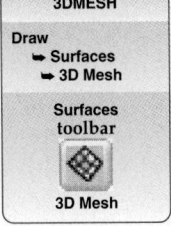

3DMESH

Draw
➡ Surfaces
➡ 3D Mesh

Surfaces
toolbar

3D Mesh

```
Command: 3DMESH↵
Enter size of mesh in M direction: 4↵
Enter size of mesh in N direction: 3↵
Specify location for vertex (0,0): 3,2,1↵
Specify location for vertex (0,1): 3,3,1.5↵
Specify location for vertex (0,2): 3,4,1↵
Specify location for vertex (1,0): 4,2,.5↵
Specify location for vertex (1,1): 4,3,1↵
Specify location for vertex (1,2): 4,4,.5↵
Specify location for vertex (2,0): 5,2,1.5↵
Specify location for vertex (2,1): 5,3,1↵
Specify location for vertex (2,2): 5,4,1.5↵
Specify location for vertex (3,0): 6,2,2.5
Specify location for vertex (3,1): 6,3,2↵
Specify location for vertex (3,2): 6,4,2.5↵
Command:
```

> **PROFESSIONAL TIP**
>
> The **3DMESH** command is not often used because it is tedious. However, AutoLISP programmers can create specialized meshes using this command.

---

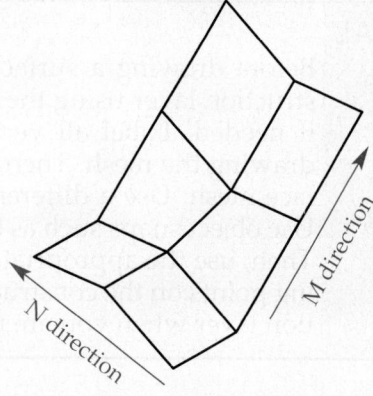

**Figure 12-2.**
A 3D polygon mesh.
The M value is 4
and the N value is 3.

N direction

M direction

## Constructing a Single-Plane Mesh

A *planar mesh* is a 3D mesh that lies in a single plane. It has between 2 and 256 vertices in both M and N directions. To draw a planar mesh, pick **3D Surfaces...** from the **Surfaces** cascading menu in the **Draw** pull-down menu. This displays the **3D Objects** dialog box. Pick **Mesh** from the list or pick the **Mesh** icon. You can also create a single-plane mesh by selecting the **Mesh** option of the **3D** command or entering AI_MESH at the Command: prompt:

> Command: **3D.↵**
> Enter an option
> [Box/Cone/DIsh/DOme/Mesh/Pyramid/Sphere/Torus/Wedge]: **M.↵**

or

> Command: **AI_MESH.↵**

You are then asked for the four corners of the mesh and the number of vertices.

> Specify first corner point of mesh: **4,3.↵**
> Specify second corner point of mesh: **9,3.↵**
> Specify third corner point of mesh: **9,8.↵**
> Specify fourth corner point of mesh: **4,8.↵**
> Enter mesh size in the M direction: **10.↵**
> Enter mesh size in the N direction: **8.↵**
> Command:

A plan view of the resulting mesh is shown in **Figure 12-3**.

**Figure 12-3.**
A planar mesh has
between 2 and 256
vertices in each
direction.

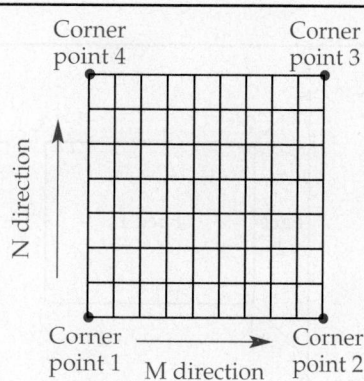

Corner point 4

Corner point 3

N direction

Corner point 1    M direction    Corner point 2

## Constructing a 3D Polyface Mesh

A general polygon mesh can be constructed using the **PFACE** command. This creates a mesh similar to the **3DFACE** command. However, you do not need to pick vertices that join another face twice. You can also create faces that have an infinite number of vertices, rather than the maximum of four specified by the **3DFACE** command. You can use the **PFACE** command to construct surfaces that cannot be "faced" using any of the standard surfacing commands. However, using this command is time-consuming and best suited for AutoLISP, ObjectARX, or other programming applications.

To create a pface mesh, first define all the vertices for the mesh. Then, assign those vertices to a face. Each face in the mesh is constructed from the vertices that you assign and is given a number. While creating a pface, you can change the layer or color by entering the **LAYER** or **COLOR** commands when [Color/Layer] appears in the prompt. The following example creates a pface mesh consisting of two faces. See Figure 12-4A. The first portion of the command defines all the vertices of the two faces.

```
Command: PFACE↵
Specify location for vertex 1: 3,3↵
Specify location for vertex 2 or <define faces>: 7,3↵
Specify location for vertex 3 or <define faces>: 7,6↵
Specify location for vertex 4 or <define faces>: 3,6↵
Specify location for vertex 5 or <define faces>: 2,7,3↵
Specify location for vertex 6 or <define faces>: 2,2,3↵
Specify location for vertex 7 or <define faces>: 3,3↵
Specify location for vertex 8 or <define faces>: ↵
```

Figure 12-4.
A—Creating a pface mesh with two faces. B—When you change the viewpoint and use **HIDE**, you can see that each face is a surface. Notice that Face 2 partially blocks the view of Face 1.

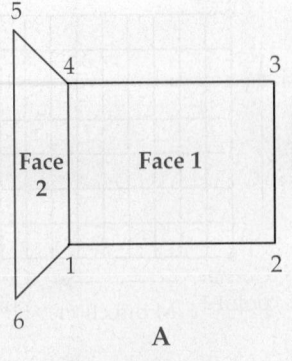

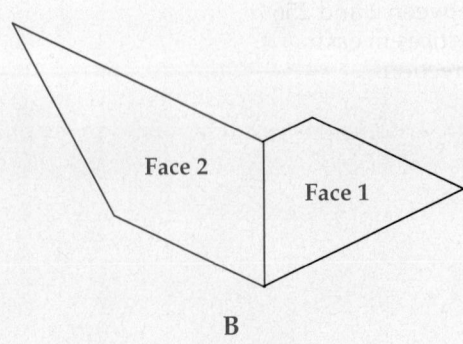

A

B

The next sequence assigns vertices to face number 1.

> Face 1, vertex 1:
> Enter a vertex number or [Color/Layer]: **1**↵
> Face 1, vertex 2:
> Enter a vertex number or [Color/Layer] <next face>: **2**↵
> Face 1, vertex 3:
> Enter a vertex number or [Color/Layer] <next face>: **3**↵
> Face 1, vertex 4:
> Enter a vertex number or [Color/Layer] <next face>: **4**↵
> Face 1, vertex 5: ↵

Now you can change the color of the second face without exiting the command.

> Enter a vertex number or [Color/Layer] <next face>: **COLOR**↵
> New color [Truecolor/COlorbook] <BYLAYER>: **BLUE**↵

The last sequence assigns vertices to face number 2.

> Face 2, vertex 1:
> Enter a vertex number or [Color/Layer]: **4**↵
> Face 2, vertex 2:
> Enter a vertex number or [Color/Layer] <next face>: **5**↵
> Face 2, vertex 3:
> Enter a vertex number or [Color/Layer] <next face>: **6**↵
> Face 2, vertex 4:
> Enter a vertex number or [Color/Layer] <next face>: **1**↵
> Face 2, vertex 5:
> Enter a vertex number or [Color/Layer] <next face>: ↵
> Face 3, vertex 1:
> Enter a vertex number or [Color/Layer]: ↵
> Command:

Now use the **3DORBIT** and **HIDE** commands to view the faces, **Figure 12-4B.**

## Polygon Mesh Variations

A polygon mesh created with **3DMESH** can be smoothed using the **PEDIT** command. The smoothness of the surface depends on the value set in the **SURFTYPE** system variable.

| SURFTYPE setting | Surface type |
|---|---|
| 5 | Quadratic B-spline |
| 6 | Cubic B-spline (default) |
| 8 | Bézier surface |

Before smoothing a polygon mesh, set the **SURFU** (M direction) and **SURFV** (N direction) system variables larger than the M and N values. If you do not change these values, the resulting surface may have less 3D faces than the original. **Figure 12-5** illustrates the different types of surfaces that can be created by adjusting the **SURFTYPE** system variable and using **PEDIT** smoothing.

> **NOTE**  A 3D mesh must have at least three vertices in each direction in order to smooth the surface.

Figure 12-5.
A—The **SPLFRAME** variable set to 1 to show the control polygon. (Note: For B–D, the **SPLFRAME** variable is set to 0 to show the smoothed mesh.) B—A quadratic B-spline (**SURFTYPE** = 5). C—A cubic B-spline (**SURFTYPE** = 6). D—A Bézier surface (**SURFTYPE** = 8).

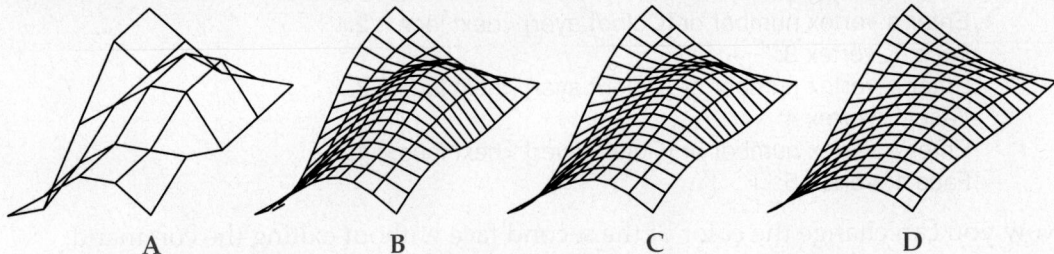

A          B          C          D

## Constructing Enclosed Surfaces with EDGESURF

The **EDGESURF** command allows you to construct a 3D mesh between four edges. The edges can be lines, polylines, splines, or arcs. The endpoints of the objects must meet precisely. However, a closed polyline *cannot* be used. The four objects can be selected in any order. The resulting surface is a smooth mesh, similar to a planar mesh. The AutoCAD help file calls this type of surface mesh a *Coons surface patch*.

The number of faces are determined by the variables **SURFTAB1** (M direction) and **SURFTAB2** (N direction). The default value for each of these variables is 6. Higher **SURFTAB** values increase the smoothness of the mesh. Change these values as follows.

    Command: **SURFTAB1**↵
    Enter new value for SURFTAB1 <*current*>: **12**↵
    Command: **SURFTAB2**↵
    Enter new value for SURFTAB2 <*current*>: **12**↵

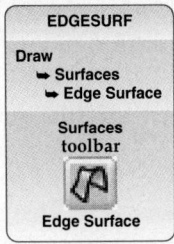

EDGESURF

Draw
➥ Surfaces
➥ Edge Surface

Surfaces
toolbar

Edge Surface

The current **SURFTAB** values will always be displayed on the Command: line when one of the surfacing commands is executed, as shown in the example below.

To draw an edge surface, pick **Edge Surface** from the **Surfaces** cascading menu in the **Draw** pull-down menu, pick the **Edge Surface** button on the **Surfaces** toolbar, or enter EDGESURF at the Command: prompt.

    Command: **EDGESURF**↵
    Current wire frame density: SURFTAB1=*current* SURFTAB2=*current*
    Select object 1 for surface edge: (*pick edge 1*)
    Select object 2 for surface edge: (*pick edge 2*)
    Select object 3 for surface edge: (*pick edge 3*)
    Select object 4 for surface edge: (*pick edge 4*)

A completed surface patch with the **SURFTAB** variables set to 12 is shown in Figure 12-6.

Figure 12-6.
A completed surface patch with both **SURFTAB** variables set to 12.

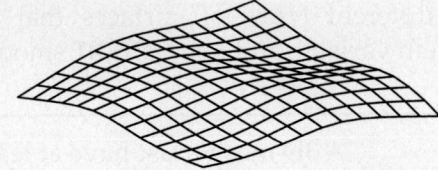

# Creating a Surface Mesh with RULESURF

A surface mesh can be constructed between two objects using the **RULESURF** command. This mesh is called a *ruled surface.* The two objects can be points, lines, arcs, circles, polylines, splines, or enclosed objects. A ruled surface can be created between a point and any of the objects listed. However, AutoCAD *cannot* generate a ruled surface between an open and a closed object, such as an arc and a circle. A variety of possible constructions are shown in **Figure 12-7.** A ruled surface is useful for surfacing holes in parts, exterior fillets (rounds), interior fillets, or flat surfaces of various shapes.

The number of elements that compose the ruled surface is determined by the **SURFTAB1** system variable. The greater the number of elements, the smoother the surface appears.

Figure 12-7.
Many different
objects can be used
to create a ruled
surface.

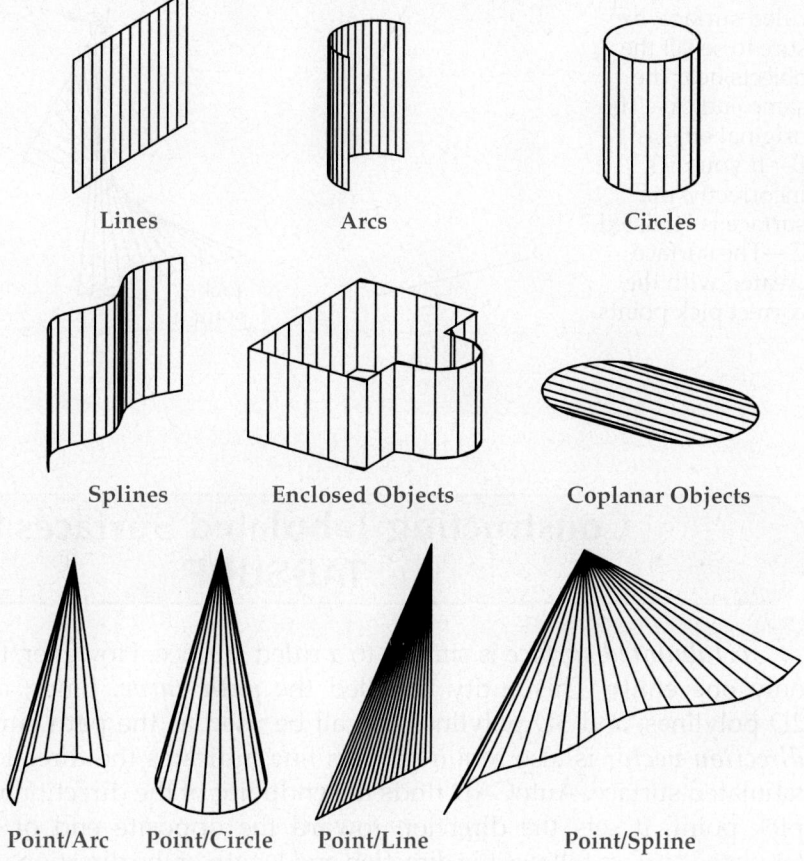

Lines          Arcs          Circles

Splines     Enclosed Objects     Coplanar Objects

Point/Arc   Point/Circle   Point/Line   Point/Spline

**PROFESSIONAL TIP**

When constructing holes in surface-modeled objects, always draw the original circles on a separate construction layer. After the hole has been surfaced with the **RULESURF** command, turn off or freeze the construction layer. If you do not turn off the construction layer, the inside of the hole will not be displayed when **HIDE** is used or the object is rendered.

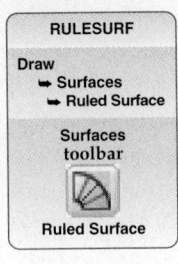

RULESURF

Draw
➡ Surfaces
➡ Ruled Surface

Surfaces
toolbar

Ruled Surface

Select the **RULESURF** command by picking **Ruled Surface** from the **Surfaces** cascading menu in the **Draw** pull-down menu, picking the **Ruled Surface** button on the **Surfaces** toolbar, or entering RULESURF at the Command: prompt.

Command: **RULESURF**↵
Current wire frame density: SURFTAB1=*current*
Select first defining curve: (*pick first object*)
Select second defining curve: (*pick second object*)
Command:

When using **RULESURF** to create a surface between two objects, such as those shown in **Figure 12-8A**, it is important to select both objects near the same end. If you pick near opposite ends of each object, the resulting figure may not be what you want, **Figure 12-8B**. The correctly surfaced object is shown in **Figure 12-8C**.

Figure 12-8.
When creating a
ruled surface, be
sure to select the
objects near the
same end. A—The
original objects.
B—If you pick
incorrectly, the
surface is "twisted."
C—The surface
created with the
correct pick points.

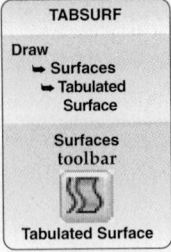

## Constructing Tabulated Surfaces with TABSURF

A *tabulated surface* is similar to a ruled surface. However, the shape is based on only one entity. This entity is called the *path curve*. Lines, arcs, circles, ellipses, 2D polylines, and 3D polylines can all be used as the path curve. A line called the *direction vector* is also required. This line indicates the direction and length of the tabulated surface. AutoCAD finds the endpoint of the direction vector closest to your pick point. It sets the direction toward the opposite end of the vector line. The tabulated surface follows the direction and length of the direction vector. The **SURFTAB1** system variable controls the number of "steps" that are constructed. **Figure 12-9** shows the difference the location of the pick point makes when selecting the vector.

TABSURF

Draw
➡ Surfaces
➡ Tabulated
  Surface

Surfaces
toolbar

Tabulated Surface

To create a tabulated surface, select **Tabulated Surface** from the **Surfaces** cascading menu of the **Draw** pull-down menu, pick the **Tabulated Surface** button on the **Surfaces** toolbar, or enter TABSURF at the Command: prompt.

Command: **TABSURF**↵
Current wire frame density: SURFTAB1=*current*
Select object for path curve: (*pick the curve*)
Select object for direction vector: (*pick the correct end of the vector*)
Command:

**Figure 12-9.**
The point you pick on the direction vector determines the direction of extrusion for the tabulated surface.

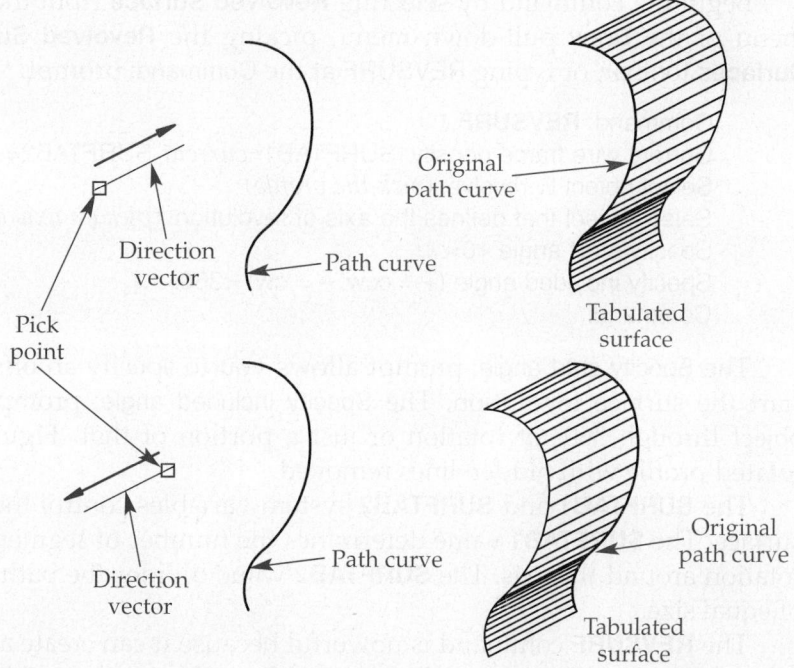

## Constructing Revolved Surfaces with REVSURF

With the **REVSURF** command, you can draw a profile and then rotate that profile around an axis to create a symmetrical object. This is a powerful tool and will greatly assist anyone who needs to draw a symmetrical three-dimensional surface. The profile, or *path curve,* can be drawn using lines, arcs, circles, ellipses, elliptical arcs, polylines, or donuts. The rotation axis can be a line or an open polyline. Notice the initial layout for a revolved surface shown in **Figure 12-10A.**

**Figure 12-10.**
A—A path curve (profile) and an axis are needed to create a revolved surface.
B—The revolved surface. The viewpoint is changed to see "inside" the object.

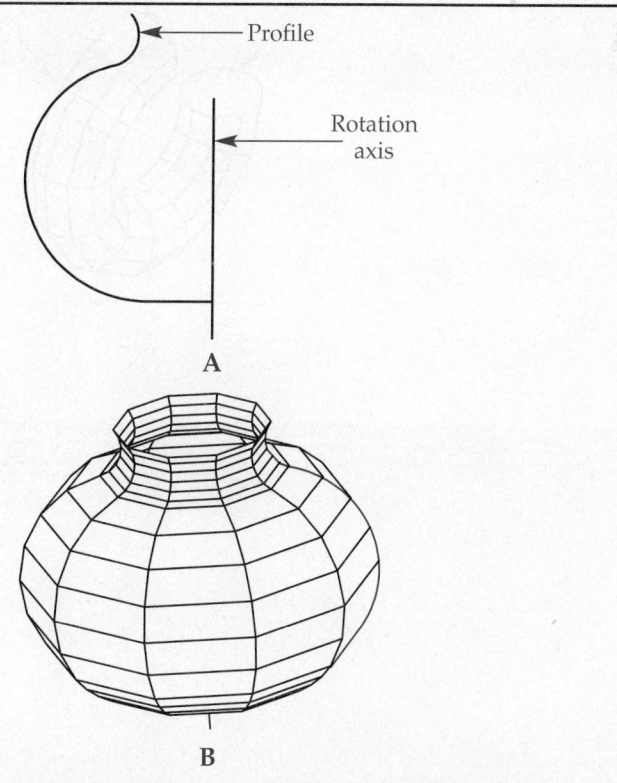

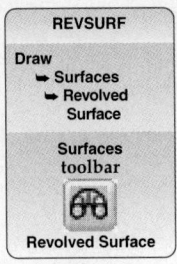

REVSURF

Draw
➥ Surfaces
 ➥ Revolved
   Surface

Surfaces
toolbar

Revolved Surface

Begin the command by selecting **Revolved Surface** from the **Surfaces** cascading menu of the **Draw** pull-down menu, picking the **Revolved Surface** button on the **Surfaces** toolbar, or typing REVSURF at the Command: prompt.

Command: **REVSURF**↵
Current wire frame density: SURFTAB1=*current* SURFTAB2=*current*
Select object to revolve: *(pick the profile)*
Select object that defines the axis of revolution: *(pick an axis line)*
Specify start angle <0>: ↵
Specify included angle (+ = ccw, − = cw) <360>: ↵
Command:

The Specify start angle: prompt allows you to specify an offset angle at which to start the surface revolution. The Specify included angle: prompt lets you draw the object through 360° of rotation or just a portion of that. **Figure 12-10B** shows the rotated profile with hidden lines removed.

The **SURFTAB1** and **SURFTAB2** system variables control the mesh of a revolved surface. The **SURFTAB1** value determines the number of segments in the direction of rotation around the axis. The **SURFTAB2** value divides the path curve into segments of equal size.

The **REVSURF** command is powerful because it can create a symmetrical surface from any profile. **Figure 12-11** illustrates additional examples of **REVSURF** constructions.

**Figure 12-11.**
Revolved surfaces
created with a
variety of profiles.

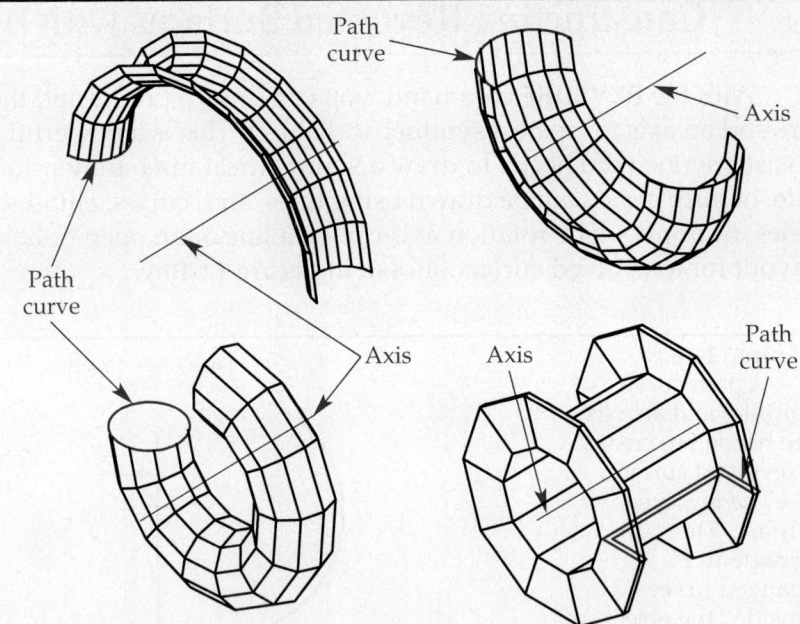

AutoCAD and its Applications—Advanced

○ Draw the objects shown below and display them in a pictorial view.
○ Set the **SURFTAB1** and **SURFTAB2** variables to values of your choice.
○ Create the surface model constructions using the command indicated.
○ Save your drawing as EX12-1.

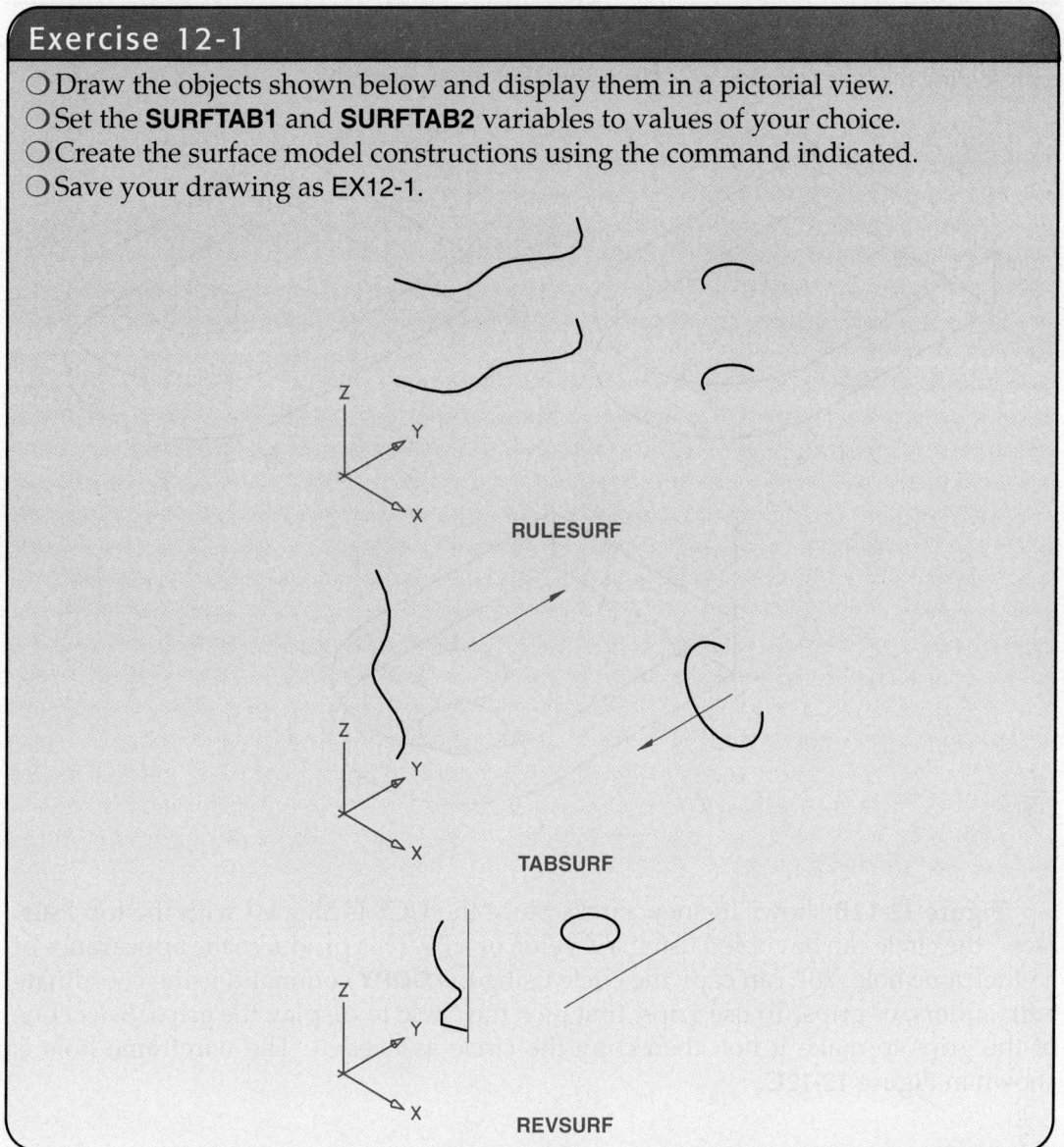

RULESURF

TABSURF

REVSURF

## Drawing Wireframe Holes

Wireframe holes can be created by drawing a circle and copying it to a new location. To add a hole to the object in **Figure 12-12**, first move the UCS. Use the **3point** option of the **UCS** command with the pick points shown in **Figure 12-12A** to place the new UCS on the top "surface." Then, draw the first circle using AutoTracking as follows.

Command: **CIRCLE**↵
Specify center point for circle or [3P/2P/Ttr (tan tan radius)]: *(acquire the midpoint of the line lying on the Y axis)*
*(acquire the endpoint of the line lying on the X axis)*
Specify radius of circle or [Diameter] <*current*>: **.5**↵
Command:

**Figure 12-12.**
A—Use the **3 Point** option of the **UCS** command to change the UCS. B—The first circle representing the hole is drawn. C—The completed wireframe hole.

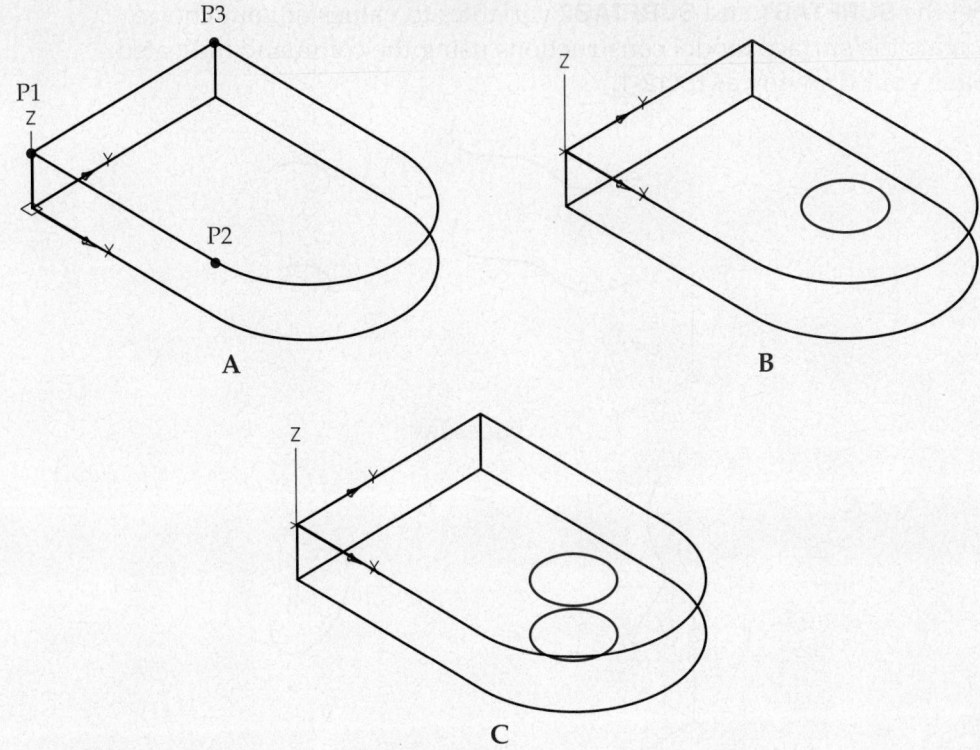

**Figure 12-12B** shows the new circle. Since the UCS is aligned with the top "surface," the circle can be copied using a Z value of –.75. This produces the appearance of a wireframe hole. You can copy the circle using the **COPY** command using coordinate entry, filters, or grips. To use grips, first pick the circle to display the grips. Select one of the grips to make it hot, then copy the circle as needed. The wireframe hole is shown in **Figure 12-12C**.

## Surfacing around Wireframe Holes

AutoCAD cannot automatically create surfacing around a hole. A series of steps is required to do this. A common method is to use the **RULESURF** and **3DFACE** commands to create the required surfaces.

For example, the object in **Figure 12-13A** must be surfaced. This object has a hole through it. To surface the hole, first construct two 180° arcs where the hole is. Use a construction layer. Next, use **RULESURF** to create the surface connecting the large arc and the hole. Use **RULESURF** again to create the surface connecting the arc and the left end of the object. The two remaining surfaces can be created using **3DFACE**. The result is shown in **Figure 12-13B**.

Another example is surfacing the space between two holes, as shown in **Figure 12-14A**. Again, create arcs where the circles are. Then, use **RULESURF** to create the surface connecting the two inside arcs. Also use **RULESURF** to create the surface between the outer arcs and the outside edges. Use **3DFACE** to surface the remaining faces. The surfaced object is shown in **Figure12-14B**.

**Figure 12-13.**
AutoCAD cannot automatically surface a hole. To do so, you must use a combination of ruled surfaces and 3D faces.

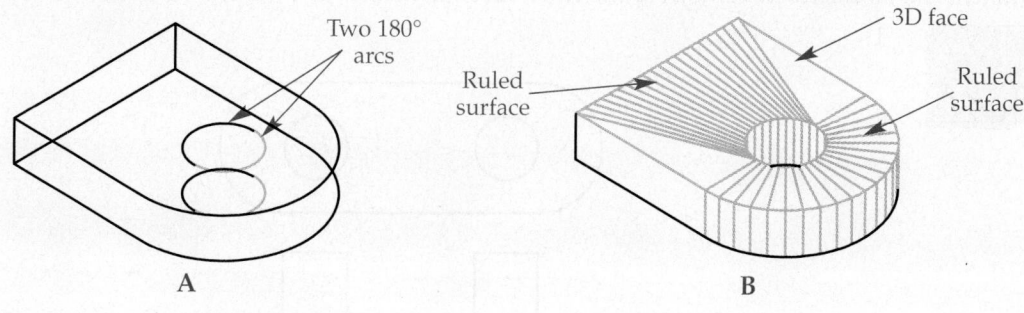

**Figure 12-14.**
Surfacing an object with two holes.

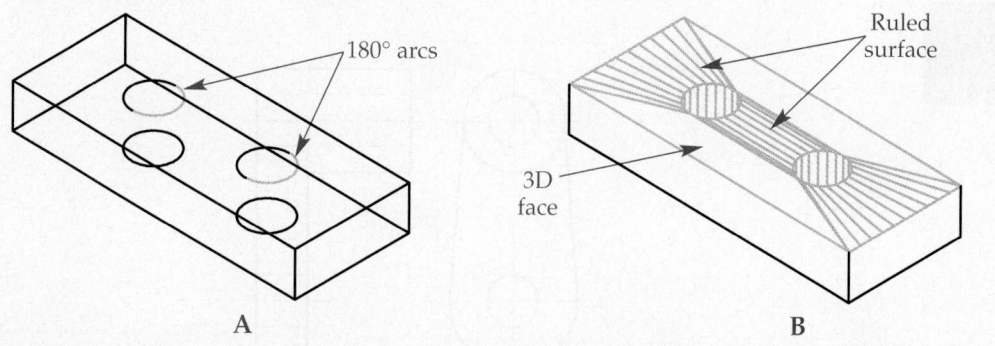

## Chapter Test

*Answer the following questions on a separate sheet of paper.*

1. Name three commands that allow you to create different types of meshes.
2. Which command creates a surface mesh between four edges?
3. How must the four edges be related when using the command in Question 2?
4. What values does AutoCAD need to know for a 3D mesh?
5. AutoCAD's surface meshing commands create which type of entities?
6. Which surface mesh command allows you to rotate a profile about an axis to create a symmetrical object?
7. Which object does **TABSURF** create?
8. What do the **SURFTAB1** and **SURFTAB2** variables control?
9. Name three entities that can be connected with the **RULESURF** command.
10. When using **RULESURF**, what happens if the two objects are selected near opposite ends?

# Drawing Problems

*Problems 1–6. Construct 3D surface models of the following objects. For objects without dimensions, measure directly from the text. Save the models as* **P12-1**, **P12-2**, *etc.*

 1.

 2.

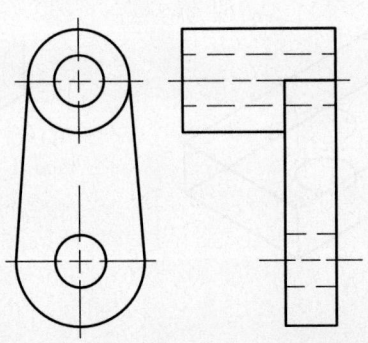

 3.

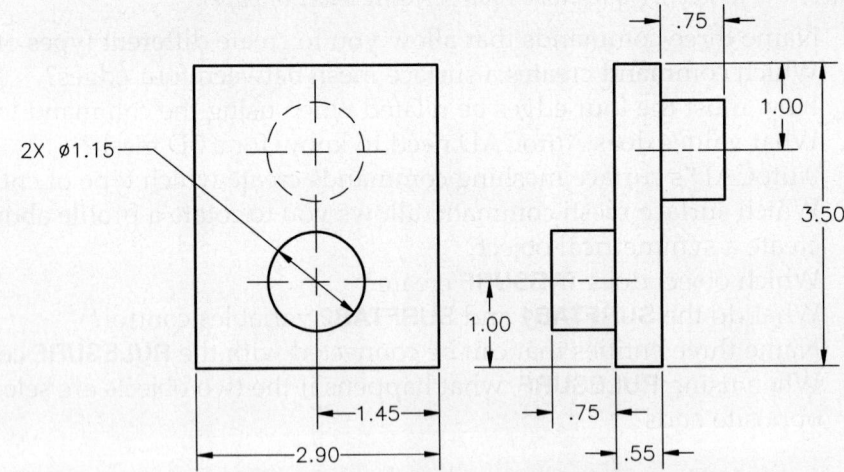

4.

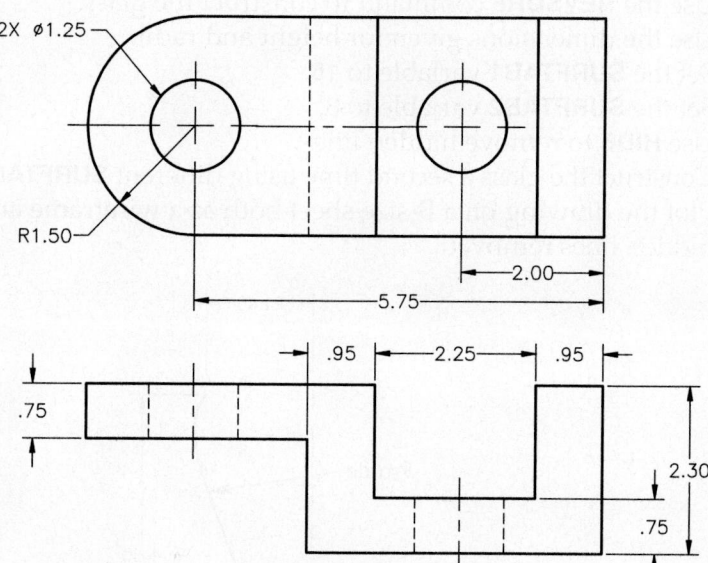

5.

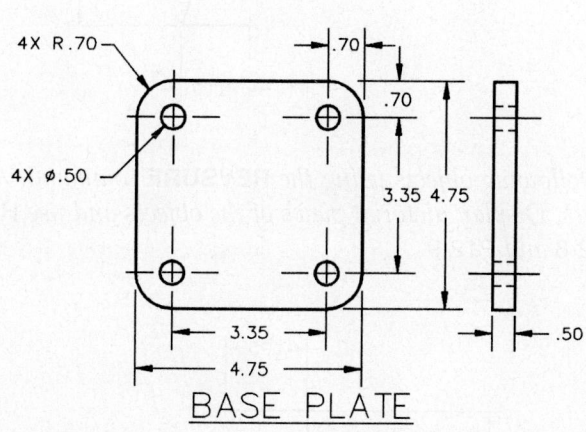

BASE PLATE

6.

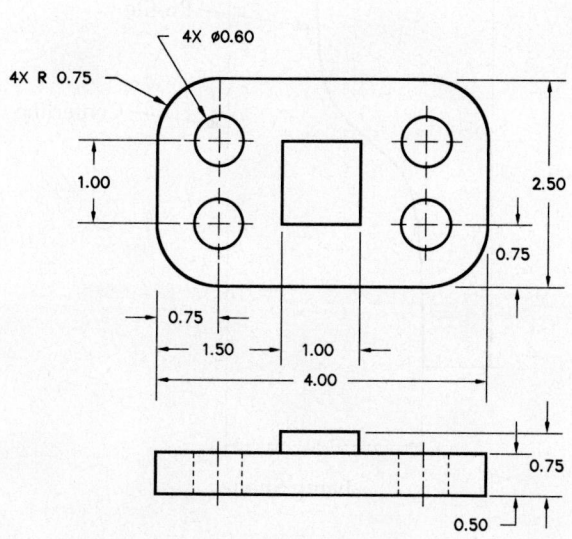

7. Create a surface model of a glass using the profile shown.
   A. Use the **REVSURF** command to construct the glass.
   B. Use the dimensions given for height and radii.
   C. Set the **SURFTAB1** variable to 16.
   D. Set the **SURFTAB2** variable to 8.
   E. Use **HIDE** to remove hidden lines.
   F. Construct the glass a second time using different **SURFTAB** settings.
   G. Plot the drawing on a B-size sheet both as a wireframe and with hidden lines removed.

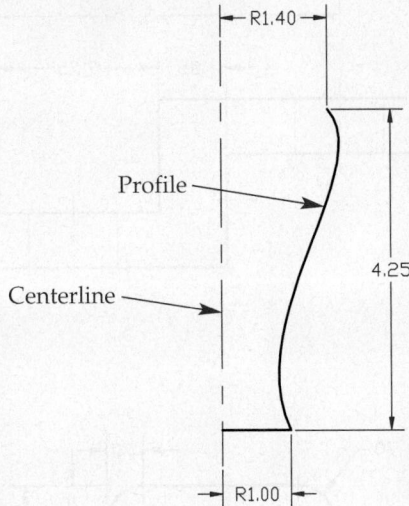

*Problems 8–9. Draw the following objects using the **REVSURF** command. Accept the default values for segments. Display pictorial views of the objects and use **HIDE** on each. Save the drawings as P12-8 and P12-9.*

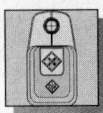

8.

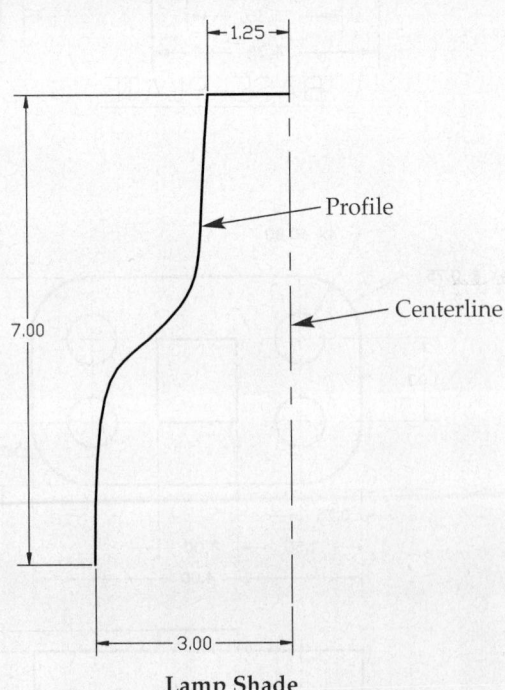

**Lamp Shade**

AutoCAD and its Applications—Advanced

9.

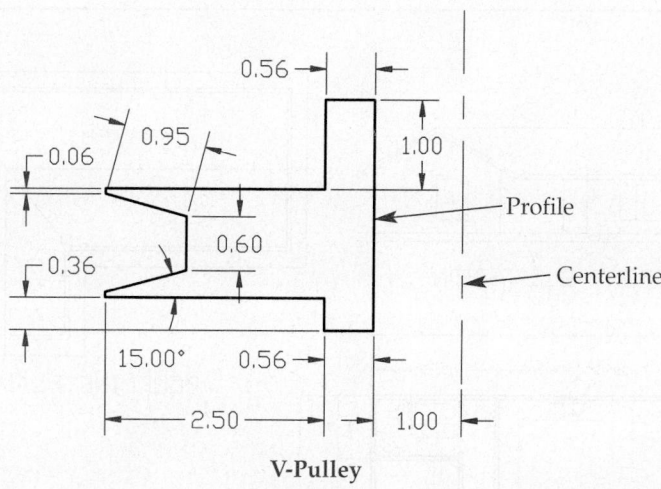

**V-Pulley**

*Problems 10–12. Problems 10 through 12 are plans of two houses and a cabin. Create a 3D model of the house(s) assigned by your instructor. Use all modeling techniques covered in this chapter.*

A.  Establish multiple viewports.
B.  Create named user coordinate systems for the floor plan and the various wall elevations.
C.  Create named viewport configurations (using one viewport) of single floors or walls so you can display the working areas as large as possible on the screen.
D.  Use the dimensions given or alter the room sizes and arrangements to suit your own design. Use your own dimensions for anything not specified.
E.  Plot the model on a B-size or C-size sheet with hidden lines removed.

10.

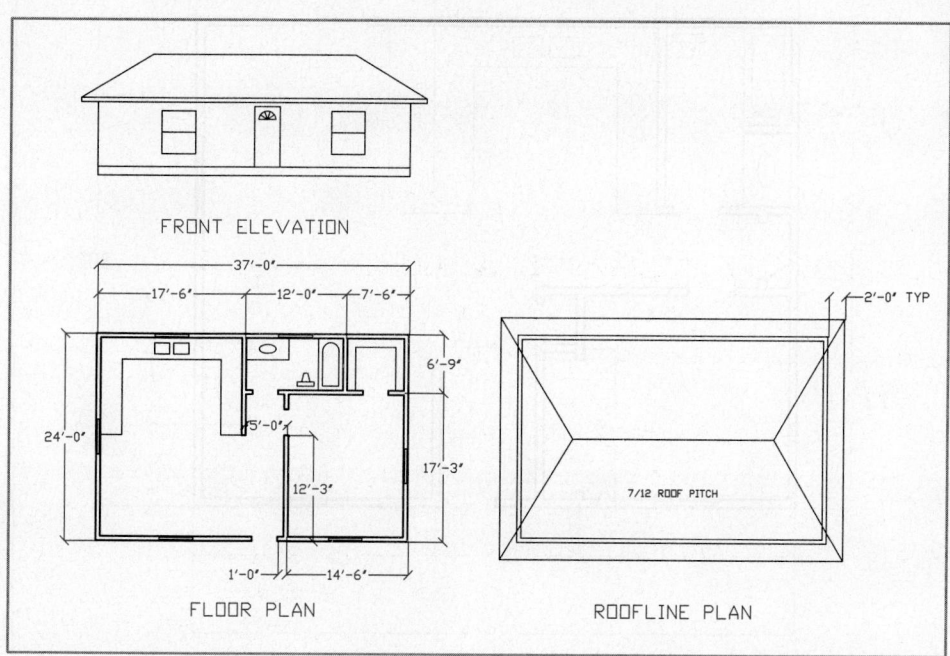

11.

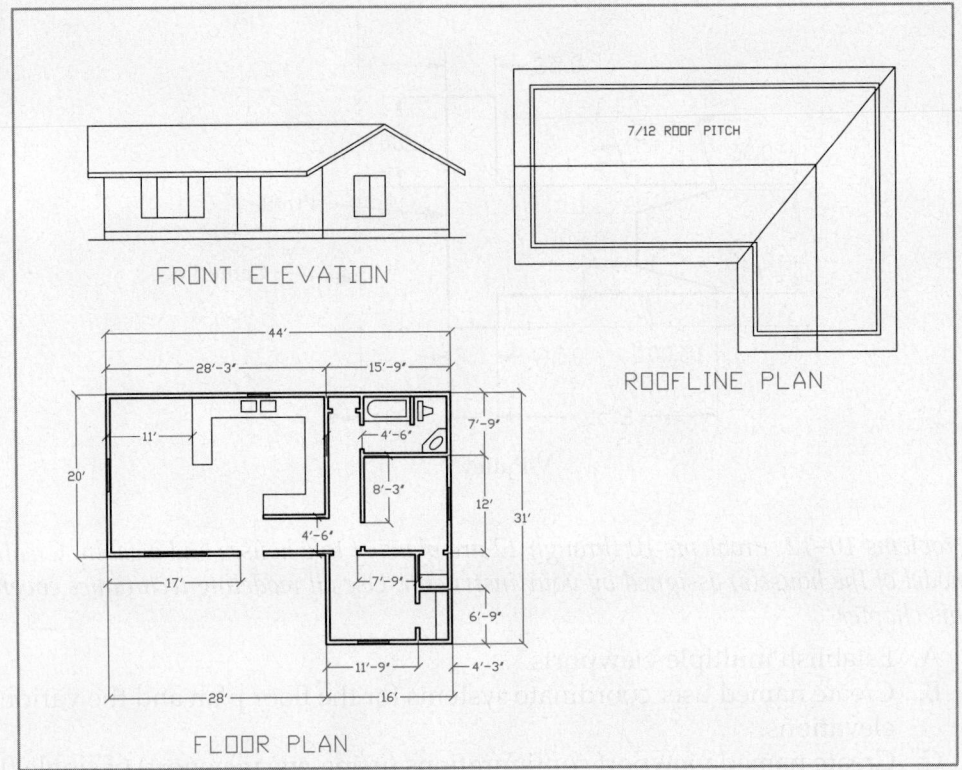

7/12 ROOF PITCH

FRONT ELEVATION

ROOFLINE PLAN

FLOOR PLAN

12.

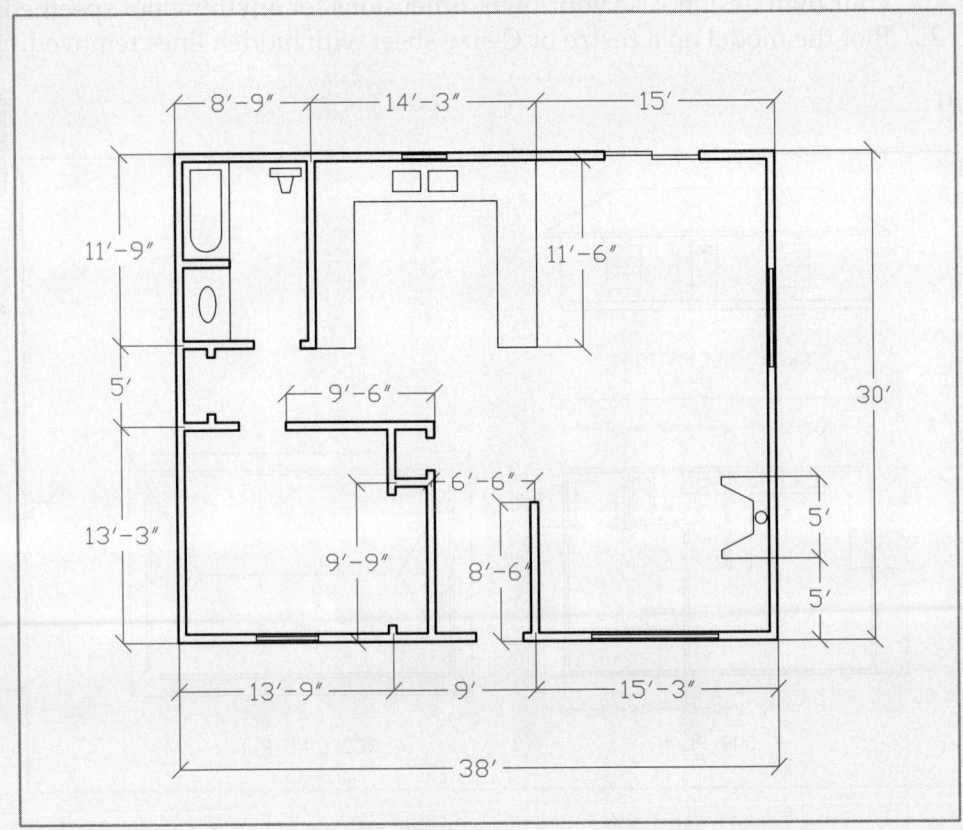

## CHAPTER 13

# Editing Surface Models

## Learning Objectives

After completing this chapter, you will be able to:
- Use grips to edit surface objects.
- Trim and extend objects in 3D.
- Create fillets and rounds on surface models.
- Edit polygon meshes.

It is always important to use proper editing techniques and commands. This is especially true when using a variety of user coordinate systems and 3D objects. Editing solid models is covered in Chapter 9. This chapter covers the correct procedures for editing surface models.

Many of the editing commands discussed for solid modeling can also be used for surface models. For example, **MIRROR3D**, **ROTATE3D**, and **3DARRAY** can be used on any object, not just solid models. Also, the **ALIGN** command can be used to align surface models in 3D space just as easily as solid models.

## Using Grips to Edit Surface Models

Using grips is an efficient way to edit surface objects. For an in-depth discussion on using grips, refer to Chapter 12 of *AutoCAD and its Applications—Basics*. Editing should be done in a pictorial (3D) view where you can see the change in "space." For example, to change the height of a cone using grips, first change to the southwest isometric preset view or another pictorial view. Next, pick anywhere on the cone and the grips appear, **Figure 13-1A**. Then, pick the grip at the apex of the cone so it becomes hot, **Figure 13-1B**. A hot grip is a red square that is filled solid. The **STRETCH** operation can be completed as follows.

```
**STRETCH**
Specify stretch point or [Base point/Copy/Undo/eXit]: @0,0,5↵
Command:
```

As you move a hot grip around the screen with your pointing device, it appears that the grip is moving in all three (XYZ) directions when in a pictorial view. However, this is misleading. You are actually moving the grip in the XY plane of the current UCS. Therefore, use XYZ filters or enter relative coordinates to edit objects in a pictorial view.

**Figure 13-1.**
Using grips to edit a 3D object. A—First, pick on the object to display the grips. Then, pick the grip to edit so that it becomes hot. B—Next, enter coordinates at the keyboard for the new location of the grip. C—The edited object.

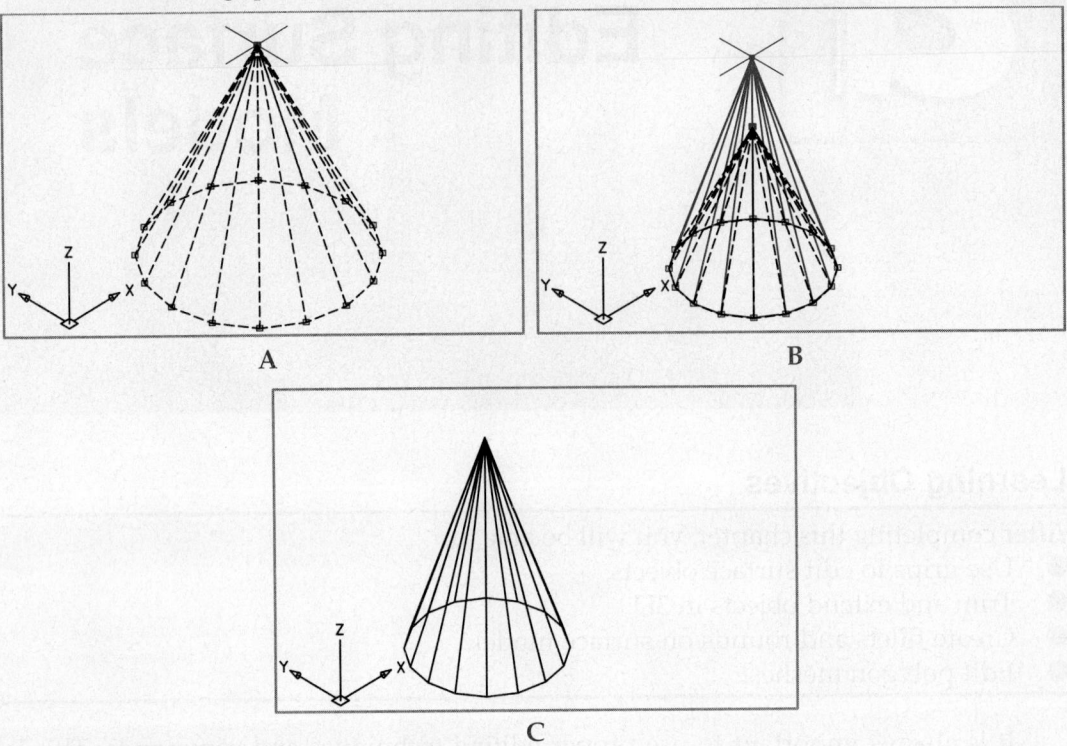

A

B

C

# Trimming and Extending Objects in 3D

As you saw in Chapter 12, surface models often start as wireframe objects on which the surface is placed. Drawing wireframes often requires using editing commands such as **TRIM** and **EXTEND**. Using the **TRIM** and **EXTEND** commands on 3D objects may be confusing at first. However, both of these commands can be powerful tools when working in 3D. This section covers using these commands on 3D objects. The discussion centers on the **TRIM** command, but also applies to the **EXTEND** command.

You can access the **EXTEND** command while using the **TRIM** command. After selecting the cutting edge, hold the [Shift] key while selecting an object to extend the object to the cutting edge. You can also access the **TRIM** command while using the **EXTEND** command. After selecting the boundary edge, hold the [Shift] key while selecting an object to trim the object at the boundary edge.

AutoCAD and its Applications—Advanced

**Figure 13-2.**
Three wireframe objects in 3D space that will be trimmed. The left view is a plan view. The right view is a 3D view.

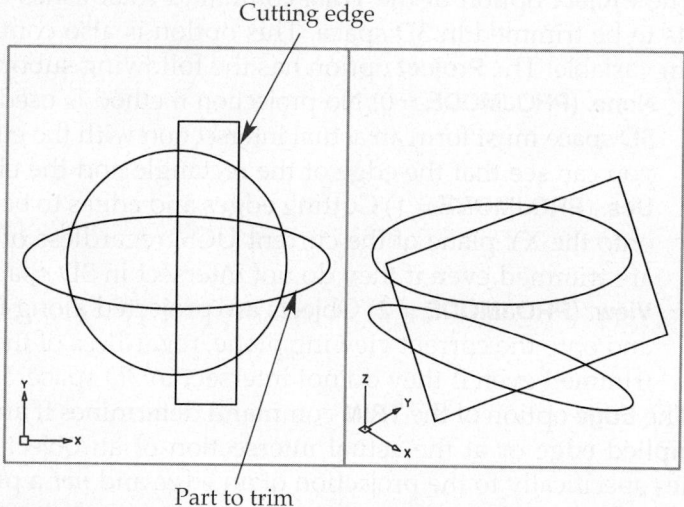

Cutting edge

Part to trim

**Figure 13-2** shows three wireframe objects. The left viewport is a plan view of the objects. The right viewport is a 3D view. The circle is three inches directly above the ellipse on the Z axis. The bottom edge of the rectangle sits on the same plane as the ellipse. The rectangle passes through the circle at an angle. The right edge of the rectangle in the left viewport is used as the cutting edge for the **TRIM** command in the following example. **Figure 13-3** shows the results.

```
Command: TRIM↵
Current settings: Projection=(current) Edge=(current)
Select cutting edges…
Select objects: (pick the bottom-right edge of the rectangle)
1 found
Select objects: ↵
Select object to trim or shift-select to extend or [Project/Edge/Undo]: P↵
Enter a projection option [None/Ucs/View] <Ucs>: N↵
Select object to trim or shift-select to extend or [Project/Edge/Undo]: (pick the right
    side of the ellipse)
Select object to trim or shift-select to extend or [Project/Edge/Undo]: ↵
Command:
```

**Figure 13-3.**
With the **None** suboption of the **TRIM** command **Project** option, the ellipse is trimmed where it actually intersects the rectangle.

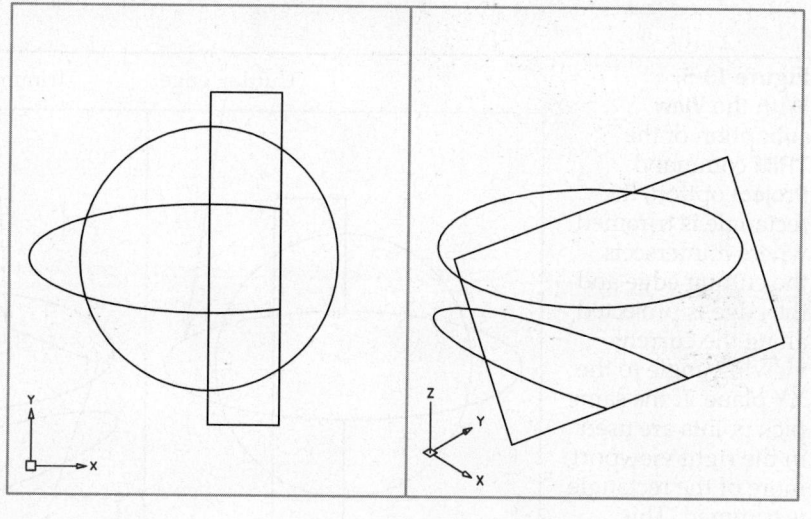

The **Project** option of the **TRIM** command establishes the projection method for objects to be trimmed in 3D space. This option is also controlled by the **PROJMODE** system variable. The **Project** option has the following suboptions.

- **None. (PROJMODE = 0)** No projection method is used. Objects to be trimmed in 3D space must form an actual intersection with the cutting edge. In **Figure 13-3,** you can see that the edge of the rectangle and the ellipse actually intersect.
- **Ucs. (PROJMODE = 1)** Cutting edges and edges to be trimmed are all projected onto the XY plane of the current UCS, regardless of the current view. Objects are trimmed even if they do not intersect in 3D space. See **Figure 13-4.**
- **View. (PROJMODE = 2)** Objects are projected along the current view direction and onto the current viewing plane, regardless of the current UCS. Objects are trimmed even if they do not intersect in 3D space. See **Figure 13-5.**

The **Edge** option of the **TRIM** command determines if an object is to be trimmed at an implied edge or at the actual intersection of an object in 3D space. This option applies specifically to the projection of an edge and *not* a plane. The **Edge** option has the following suboptions.

- **Extend.** The cutting edge is extended into 3D space to intersect objects to be trimmed.
- **No extend.** The cutting edge is not extended, and the object to be trimmed must intersect the cutting edge in 3D space.

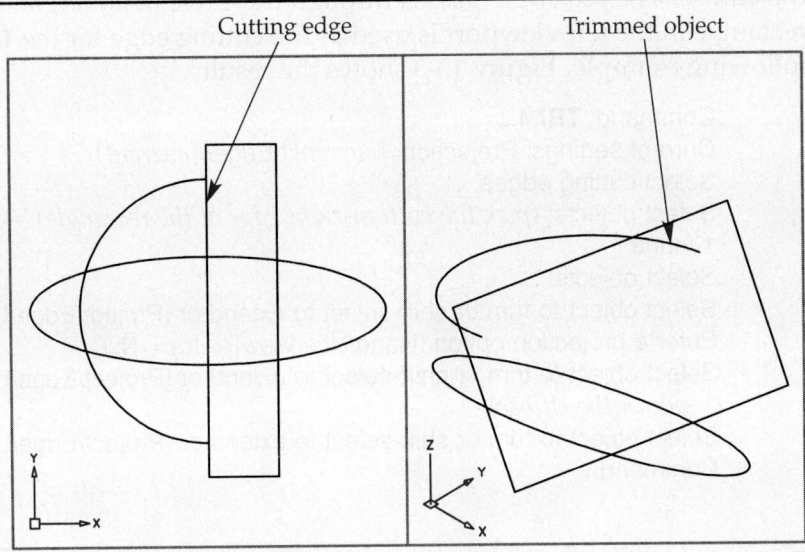

**Figure 13-4.**
With the **Ucs** suboption of the **TRIM** command **Project** option, the circle is trimmed where it intersects the cutting edge as the edge is projected to the current UCS.

Cutting edge          Trimmed object

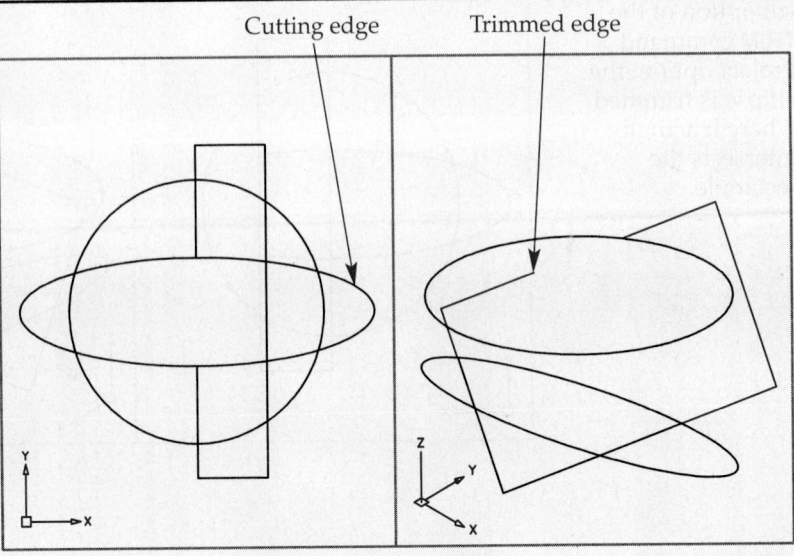

**Figure 13-5.**
With the **View** suboption of the **TRIM** command **Project** option, the rectangle is trimmed where it intersects the cutting edge and the edge is projected along the current viewing angle to the XY plane. If the same pick points are used in the right viewport, more of the rectangle is trimmed. This portion is shown in color.

Cutting edge          Trimmed edge

# Creating Surfaced Fillets and Rounds

*Fillets* are rounded inside corners. *Rounds* are rounded outside corners. Both of these are easily created with the surfacing commands **RULESURF** and **TABSURF**. Choose the one you prefer. Notice in **Figure 13-6A** that arcs have been drawn on the inside and outside corners of a wireframe object in order to create a fillet and round. The arcs are copied to the opposite side and lines are drawn connecting the tangent points of the arcs.

If you use **TABSURF**, you then only need to give direction vectors. If **RULESURF** is used, the lines connecting the arcs are not needed. Select one arc as the first defining curve and the opposite arc as the second defining curve. The result of either process is shown in **Figure 13-6B**.

The face of the arcs on both sides of the object must be surfaced with **RULESURF**. First, put points at the center of the arc on the round and at the intersection of the two inside edges of the part. See **Figure 13-6C**. Then, pick the point and the arc as the two defining curves. Now, the **3DFACE** command can be used to construct faces on the object. Three 3D faces must be drawn on the left side of the object. The completed object is shown in **Figure 13-6D**.

**Figure 13-6.**
A—To construct fillets and rounds, arcs are drawn first to serve as path curves. The direction vectors are needed if **TABSURF** is used. B—The "edges" of the fillet and round. C—Use construction points and **RULESURF** to surface the "faces" of the fillet and round. D—Use the **3DFACE** command to complete the surfacing of the entire object.

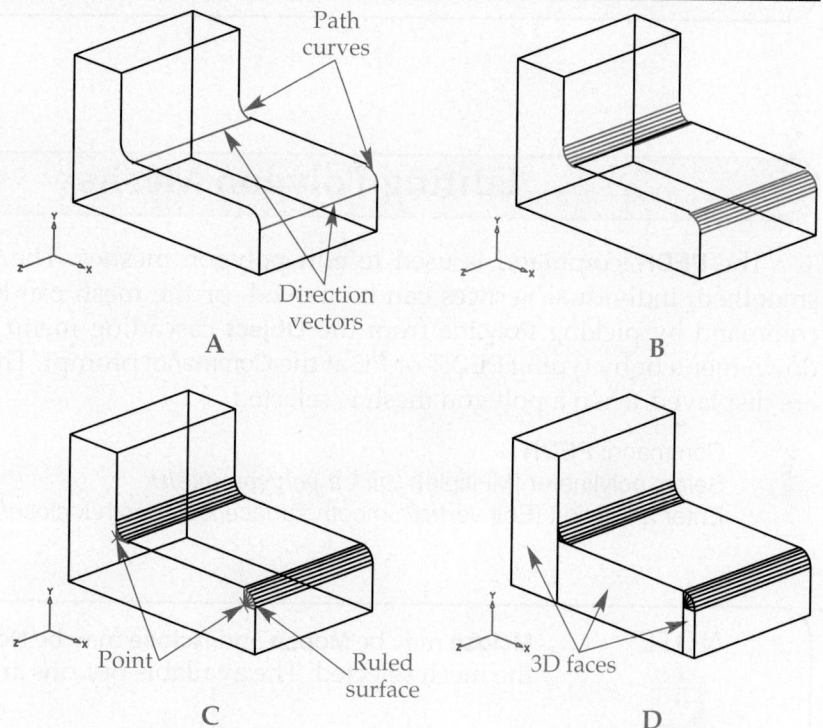

Notice in **Figure 13-6D** that the 3D face edges are visible on the left side of the object. These edges can be created as hidden edges by using the **Invisible** option of the **3DFACE** command while drawing them. You can also change the visibility of edges on an existing 3D face using the **Properties** window. However, you can quickly hide an edge with the **EDGE** command. To use this command, pick **Edge** from the **Surfaces** cascading menu in the **Draw** pull-down menu, pick the **Edge** button on the **Surfaces** toolbar, or enter EDGE at the Command: prompt.

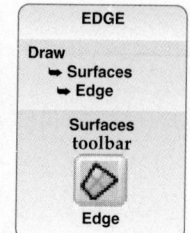

EDGE

Draw
➡ Surfaces
➡ Edge

Surfaces toolbar

Edge

```
Command: EDGE↵
Specify edge of 3dface to toggle visibility or [Display]: (pick the edge to hide)
Specify edge of 3dface to toggle visibility or [Display]: ↵
Command:
```

**Figure 13-7.**
The **EDGE** command can be used to make the edges shown in **Figure 13-6D** invisible.

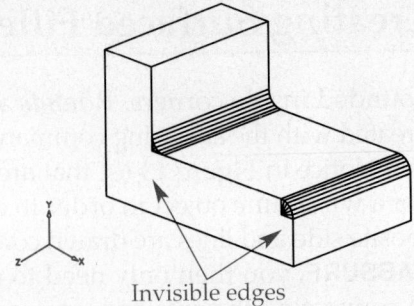

Invisible edges

The edge is hidden and the object appears as shown in **Figure 13-7**. Invisible edges can be made visible using the **Display** option of the **EDGE** command.

PROFESSIONAL TIP

Remember, the **SPLFRAME** system variable can also be used to control the visibility of 3D face edges.

# Editing Polygon Meshes

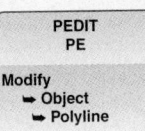

PEDIT
PE

Modify
➥ Object
  ➥ Polyline

The **PEDIT** command is used to edit polygon meshes. The entire mesh can be smoothed, individual vertices can be moved, or the mesh can be closed. Enter the command by picking **Polyline** from the **Object** cascading menu in the **Modify** pull-down menu or by typing PEDIT or PE at the Command: prompt. The following options are displayed when a polygon mesh is selected.

Command: **PEDIT**↵
Select polyline or [Multiple]: *(pick a polygon mesh)*
Enter an option [Edit vertex/Smooth surface/Desmooth/Mclose/Nclose/Undo]:

NOTE

**Mclose** may be **Mopen** and **Nclose** may be **Nopen**, depending on the mesh selected. The available options are explained below.

- **Smooth surface.** Applies a smooth surface to the mesh based on the value of the **SURFTYPE** variable.

| SURFTYPE Setting | Surface Type |
|---|---|
| 5 | Quadratic B-spline |
| 6 | Cubic B-spline |
| 8 | Bézier surface |

- **Desmooth.** Removes smoothing and returns the mesh to its original vertices.
- **Mclose.** The polylines in the M direction are closed if the M direction mesh is open.

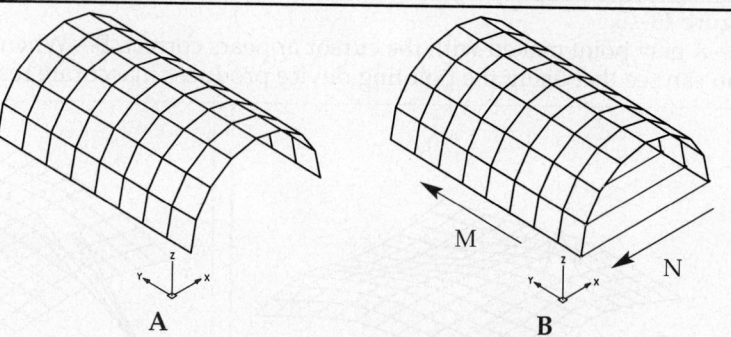

Figure 13-8.
A—A polygon mesh
with a smoothed
surface. B—The
mesh after using the
**Nclose** option of
**PEDIT**.

A        B

M N

- **Mopen.** Opens the polylines in the M direction if they are closed.
- **Nclose.** The polylines in the N direction are closed if the N direction mesh is open. See **Figure 13-8.**
- **Nopen.** Opens the polylines in the N direction if they are closed.

The **Edit vertex** option of the **PEDIT** command allows you to move individual vertices of the polygon mesh. When you select the **Edit vertex** option, you get several suboptions:

Enter an option [Edit vertex/Smooth surface/Desmooth/Mopen/Nclose/Undo]: **E⏎**
Current vertex *(current).*
Enter an option [Next/Previous/Left/Right/Up/Down/Move/REgen/eXit] <N>:

Notice in **Figure 13-9A** that an X marker appears at the first vertex. This X can be moved to the vertex you want to edit. The **Edit vertex** suboptions are explained as follows. Refer to **Figure 13-9B.**

- **Next.** The X moves to the next vertex in the order drawn. When the end of a line is reached, the X jumps to the start of the next line.
- **Previous.** The X moves to the previous vertex in the order drawn.
- **Left.** The X moves to the previous vertex in the N direction.
- **Right.** The X moves to the next vertex in the N direction.
- **Up.** The X moves to the next vertex in the M direction.
- **Down.** The X moves to the previous vertex in the M direction.
- **Move.** The vertex where the X is can be moved to a new location.

You may notice in **Figure 13-9B** that the **Right** option is actually moving the vertex to the left of the screen. This is because the right/left and up/down directions are determined by the order in which the vertices were drawn.

When the **Move** option is selected, a rubber band line appears between the vertex and the crosshairs. The following prompt appears.

Specify new location for marked vertex:

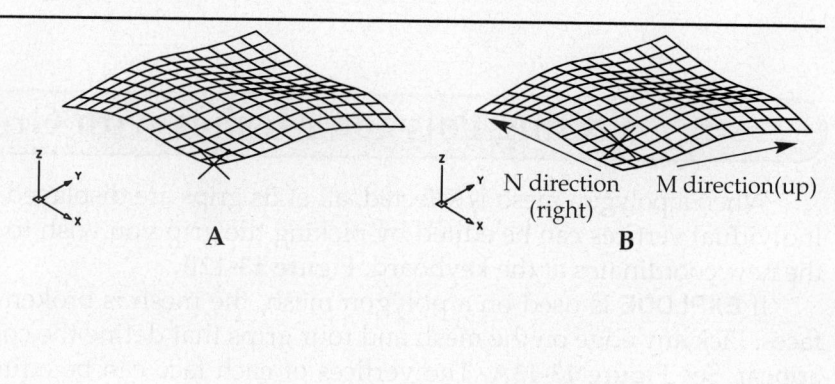

Figure 13-9.
A—An X marker,
shown here in color,
appears at the first
vertex of a polygon
mesh selected using
**PEDIT**. B—Move the
X marker in the N
direction with the
**Left** and **Right**
options. Move the X
in the M direction
with the **Up** and
**Down** options.

A      B

N direction
(right)  M direction(up)

Figure 13-10.
A—A new point picked with the cursor appears correct. B—When the viewpoint is changed, you can see that using the pointing device produces inaccurate results.

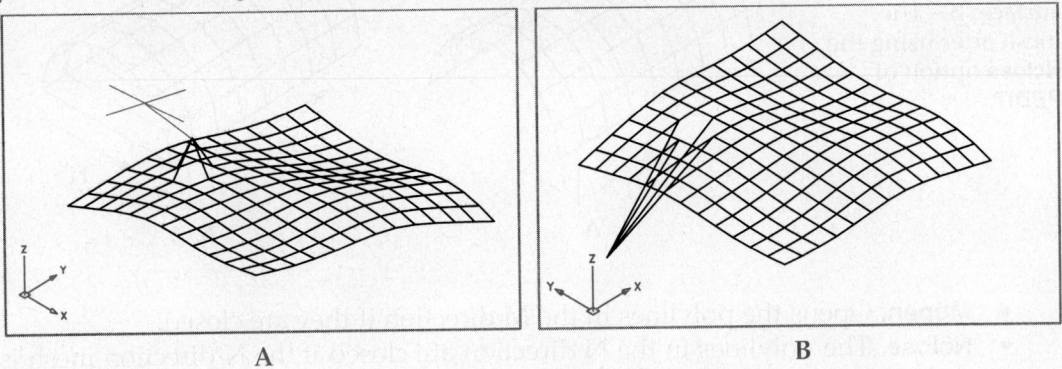

A                                         B

If a new point is picked with the cursor, the mesh may appear to be altered properly, **Figure 13-10A.** However, when the viewpoint is changed, it is clear that the new point does not have the intended Z value, **Figure 13-10B.** This is because the Z value will always be zero on the current XY plane. Therefore, do not pick a new polygon mesh location with the pointing device. Instead, enter the coordinates or use XYZ filters.

Specify new location for marked vertex: **@0,0,.6.**↵

The new location in **Figure 13-11A** appears similar to **Figure 13-10A.** However, when viewed from another direction, it is clear that entering coordinates produced the correct results, **Figure 13-11B.**

Figure 13-11.
A—When coordinates are entered at the keyboard, the results at first appear the same as when using the pointing device. B—When the viewpoint is changed, you can see that entering coordinates produces correct results.

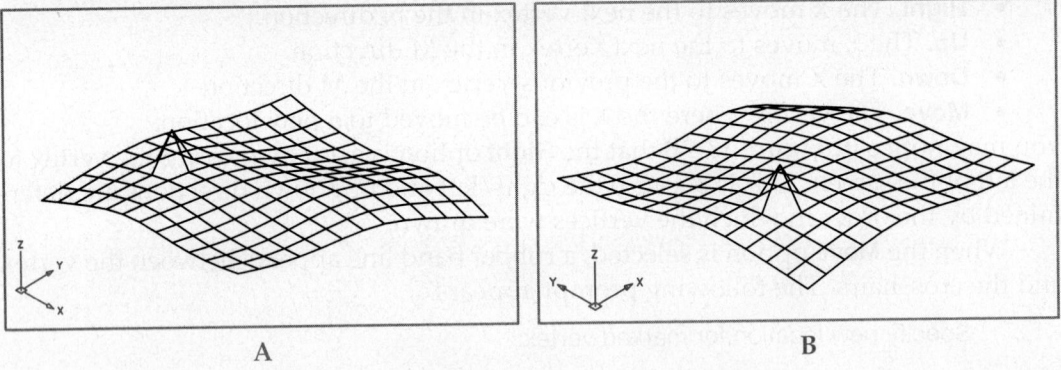

A                                         B

## Editing Polygon Meshes with Grips

When a polygon mesh is selected, all of its grips are displayed. See **Figure 13-12A.** Individual vertices can be edited by picking the grip you wish to move and entering the new coordinates at the keyboard, **Figure 13-12B.**

If **EXPLODE** is used on a polygon mesh, the mesh is broken into individual 3D faces. Pick any edge on the mesh and four grips that define the corners of the 3D face appear. See **Figure 13-13A.** The vertices of each face can be edited using grips. See **Figure 13-13B.** If you edit a vertex of a 3D face created by exploding a polygon mesh, the vertex will no longer be attached to the original mesh. See **Figure 13-13C.**

**Figure 13-12.**
A—When a polygon mesh is selected, the grips are displayed. B—Select a single grip to make it hot. This grip can then be moved.

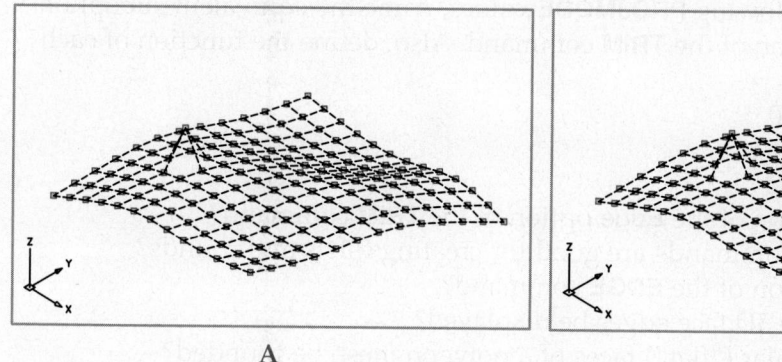
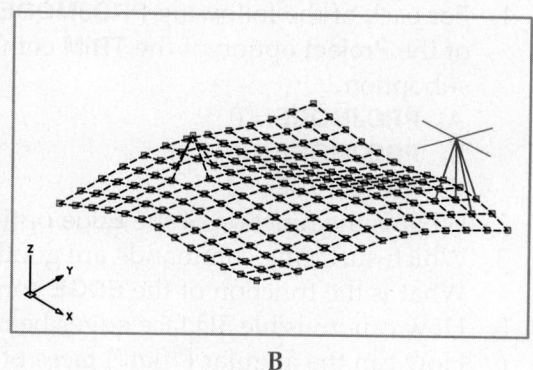

A

B

**Figure 13-13.**
A—When you select an edge of an exploded polygon mesh, you can see that it is made up of 3D faces. B—A single vertex on a 3D face can be edited using grips. C—The edited 3D face vertex is detached from the original mesh.

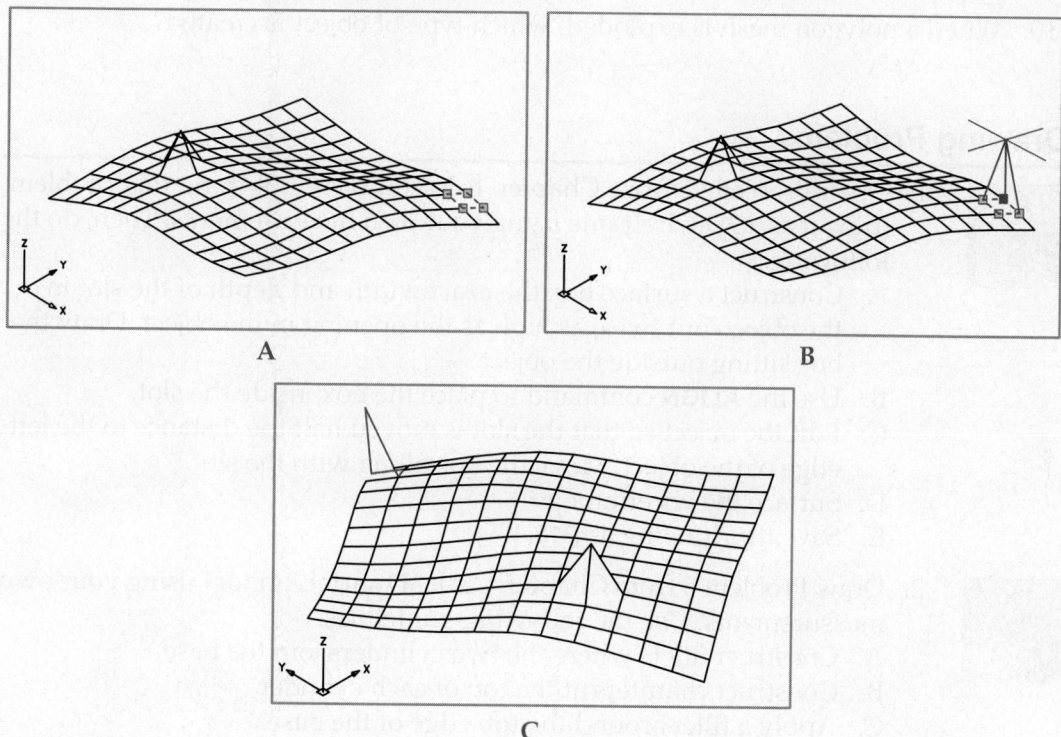

A

B

C

---

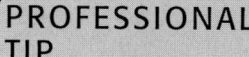

**PROFESSIONAL TIP**

With careful planning, you can minimize the number of faces you construct. Draw only the number needed and use editing commands to create the rest. As shown in **Figure 13-12**, a 3D face is easily edited using grips. Use all of the grip editing functions—move, rotate, scale, and mirror—to quickly manipulate 3D faces.

---

## Chapter Test

*Answer the following questions on a separate sheet of paper.*

1. For each of the following **PROJMODE** values, name the equivalent suboption of the **Project** option of the **TRIM** command. Also, define the function of each suboption.
   A. **PROJMODE** = 0
   B. **PROJMODE** = 1
   C. **PROJMODE** = 2
2. What is the function of the **Edge** option of the **TRIM** command?
3. Which surfacing commands are good for creating fillets and rounds?
4. What is the function of the **EDGE** command?
5. How can invisible 3D face edges be displayed?
6. How can the angular ("flat") faces of a polygon mesh be rounded?
7. Name the three types of smooth surfaces that can be applied to a polygon mesh, and give their **SURFTYPE** values.
8. Which command, option, and suboption are used to relocate a single vertex of a polygon mesh?
9. What is the most accurate way to move a polygon mesh vertex when using grips?
10. When a polygon mesh is exploded, which type of object is created?

## Drawing Problems

1. Open Problem 2 from Chapter 1. If you have not done this problem, draw it as a 3D wireframe using your own measurements. Then, do the following.
   A. Construct a surface box the exact width and depth of the slot in the object, but twice as high as the opening in the object. Draw the box sitting outside the object.
   B. Use the **ALIGN** command to place the box inside the slot.
   C. Edit the object so that the slot is moved half the distance to the left edge of the object. Move the box along with the slot.
   D. Surface the wireframe.
   E. Save the drawing as P13-1.

2. Draw Problem 5 from Chapter 1 as a 3D surface model using your own measurements. Use the following guidelines.
   A. Construct fillets where the two cylinders join the base.
   B. Construct chamfers at the top of each cylinder.
   C. Apply a fillet around the top edge of the base.
   D. Save the drawing as P13-2.

3. Draw Problem 4 from Chapter 1 as a 3D surface model using the dimensions given. Use the following guidelines.
   A. Create a 2mm × 45° chamfer on the top edge along the long dimension.
   B. Add a ⌀5mm × 15mm pin (cylinder) centered on the top surface.
   C. Place a chamfer on the top of the pin. Use your own dimensions.
   D. Save the drawing as P13-3.

4. Draw Problem 7 from Chapter 2 as a 3D surface model using the dimensions given. Use the following guidelines.
   A. Draw a bar of the same dimensions to fit over the pin bar. Construct it alongside the pin bar.
   B. Use **RULESURF** to construct the holes in the new bar, and be sure to erase the original circles used to construct the holes.
   C. Use **ALIGN** to place the new bar over the pin bar.
   D. Rotate the entire assembly 90°.
   E. Save the drawing as P13-4.

5. Draw Problem 9 from Chapter 2 as a 3D surface model using the dimensions given. Then, do the following.
   A. Explode the sphere mesh. Remove 20 of the 3D faces—12 above the equator and 8 below.
   B. Draw a new sphere in the exact center of the existing one, and 1/2 its diameter.
   C. Draw a small diameter tube protruding at a 45° angle from the center of the new sphere into the northern hemisphere. It should extend out through the large sphere.
   D. Create a 3D polar array of six tubes.
   E. Save the drawing as P13-5.

6. Draw Problem 1 from Chapter 3 as a 3D surface model. Use the following guidelines.
   A. Place a .25" radius fillet on all inside vertical corners.
   B. Place a .125" radius round on all outside vertical corners.
   C. Save the drawing as P13-6.

7. Draw Problem 3 from Chapter 3 as a 3D surface model using the dimensions given. Use the following guidelines.
   A. Give the object a .25" radius bend at the "L."
   B. Save the drawing as P13-7.

8. Draw Problem 8 from Chapter 3 as a 3D surface model using the dimensions given. Use the following guidelines.
   A. Draw the 4.80 side at a 15° angle from vertical, as shown in the top view below.
   B. Give the object a .25" inside radius at the bend.
   C. Save the drawing as P13-8.

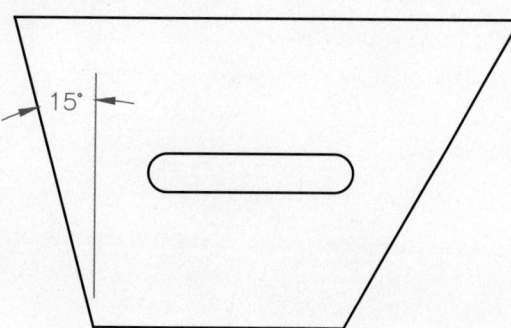

---

The sliced solid model from the tutorial in Appendix A is rendered after lights were added to the drawing. Notice the shadows and highlights. Also, the coloring of the faces on the objects is in accordance with the instructions in Appendix A.

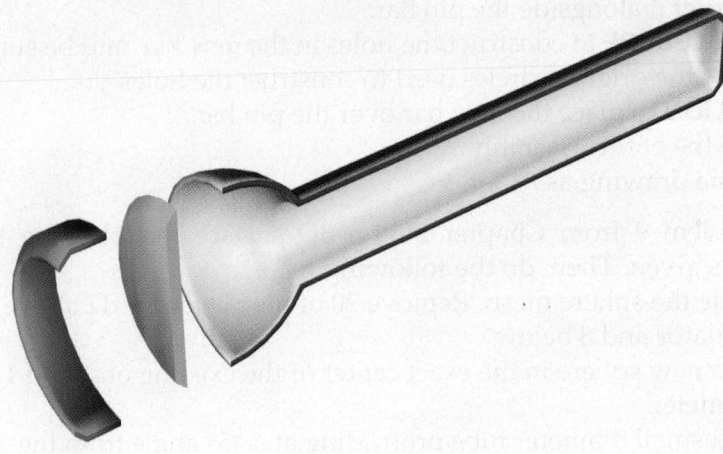

# Lights, Scenes, and Rendering

## Learning Objectives

After completing this chapter, you will be able to:
- Explain the different types of lighting in AutoCAD.
- Place light sources.
- Create scenes.
- Render and save images.
- Display rendering statistics.

Three-dimensional computer models can provide more information than a set of two-dimensional blueprints. The computer allows you to visualize the model from all sides, including the inside. The model can also be placed in a scene with lights. Views and scenes can then be created and saved, rendered, and placed in documents or on a website.

The **SHADEMODE** command, which is covered in Chapter 5, produces a shaded drawing. However, there is no control over lighting. In addition, materials can be added to a model, but are not rendered with the **SHADEMODE** command. The **RENDER** command gives you complete control over the lighting and surfaces of your model.

You have almost unlimited options and variations when rendering 3D models. Adjusting components such as color, light, shadow, sunshine, time of year, location on earth, material, texture, reflections, roughness, viewpoint, and scene can lead to a wide variety of renderings. The purpose of this chapter is to introduce you to the rendering features available in AutoCAD. The more advanced aspects of creating realistic models, such as materials and shadows, are covered in Chapter 15 and Chapter 16.

## Lights

AutoCAD uses four types of lighting. These are ambient, distant, point, and spot. See **Figure 14-1**. It is important to understand how each type applies light to a model.

### Types of Lights

*Ambient light* is like natural light just before sunrise. It is the same intensity everywhere. All faces of the object receive the same amount of ambient light. Ambient light cannot create highlights. The intensity of ambient light can be changed or turned off, but ambient light cannot be concentrated in one area.

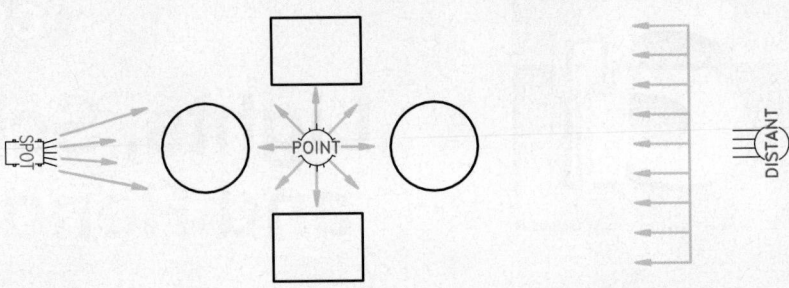

**Figure 14-1.**
AutoCAD uses ambient, spot, point, and distant light. Ambient light is an overall light and does not have an icon representation. You can see here how the other three lights strike objects.

A *distant light* is a directed light source with parallel light rays. This acts much like the sun, striking all objects in your model on the same side and with the same intensity. The direction and intensity of a distant light can be changed.

A *point light* is like a lightbulb, shining out in all directions. A point light can create highlights. The intensity of a point light falls off, or weakens, over distance. Other programs, such as Autodesk VIZ or 3ds max, may call these lights *omni lights.*

A *spotlight* is like a distant light, but it projects in a cone shape. Its light rays are not parallel. A spotlight is placed closer to the object than a distant light. Spotlights have a hotspot and a falloff.

**PROFESSIONAL TIP** Advanced lighting features, such as hotspot, falloff, and shadows, are covered in Chapter 15.

## Adding Lights

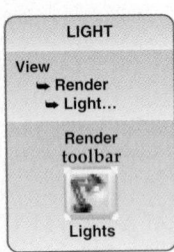

LIGHT

View
➥ Render
  ➥ Light...

Render toolbar

Lights

Lights are usually added to a drawing after the objects in the model are finalized. Consider the properties for each type of light when choosing the lights for the model. Place as many lights as you want.

Lights are placed using the **LIGHT** command. Access this command by picking the **Lights** button on the **Render** toolbar, selecting **Light...** from the **Render** cascading menu in the **View** pull-down menu, or typing LIGHT at the Command: prompt. The **Lights** dialog box is displayed, **Figure 14-2.**

Each light you add to the model must be named. The name can be up to eight characters long. Uppercase and lowercase letters can be typed, but AutoCAD changes the name to all uppercase. Spaces cannot be used in a light name. All light names must be different.

Ambient light is also set in the **Lights** dialog box. Use the slider bar or type a value in the text box in the **Ambient Light** area to adjust the intensity. You can also change the ambient light color by adjusting the appropriate slider bars. Adjusting light color is discussed in Chapter 15. Ambient light is not named.

When placing lights in a drawing, use XYZ coordinates or filters to specify a 3D location. Once a light is placed, an icon representing the light appears in the drawing. The icons representing point, distant, and spotlights are shown in **Figure 14-3.**

After lights are created, you can fine-tune them by changing their intensity, location, and color. Lights can also be turned off or deleted if needed. Once a light is selected from the list in the **Lights** dialog box, pick the **Modify...** button to adjust its intensity, position, color, and falloff.

**Figure 14-2.**
The **Lights** dialog box.

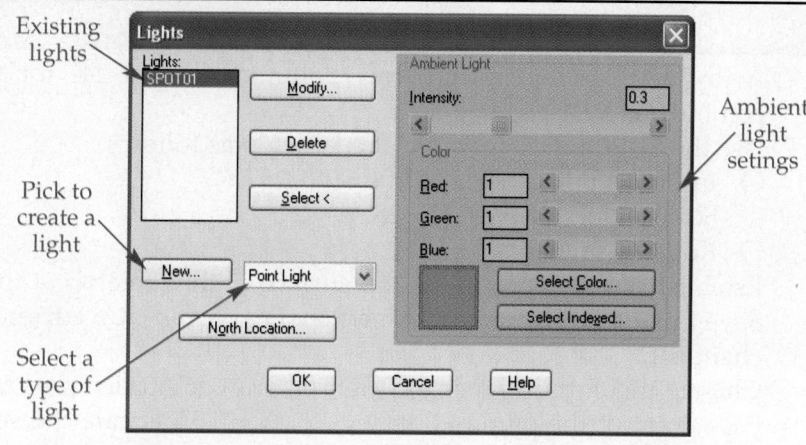

Existing lights

Ambient light settings

Pick to create a light

Select a type of light

**Figure 14-3.**
Point lights, spotlights, and distant lights appear as icons in the drawing.

## Exercise 14-1

○ Begin a new drawing. The drawing you create in this exercise is used throughout this chapter.

○ Set units to architectural.

○ Set the limits to 24', 18'. Set the grid to 6" and snap to 2". Zoom all.

○ Create the following layers and assign the colors indicated.

| Layer | Color |
|-------|-------|
| Floor-Wall | Cyan |
| Table | Red |
| Pyramid | Yellow |
| Cone | Green |
| Torus | Blue |

○ Make the Floor-Wall layer current.

○ Using the **3DFACE** command, draw the floor 8' square starting at (0,0). Draw the wall 8' long and 6' high. You may have to change your viewpoint and the UCS to draw the wall. This forms the background.

○ Use the **3DORBIT** to display a view similar to the one shown below. You may want to use the southwest preset isometric viewpoint as a starting point. Save the view.

○ Create a UCS at the lower-front corner of the floor. Save this UCS orientation as **FLOOR**. Note: Depending on how you drew the floor and wall, this UCS may coincide with the WCS. If it does, you do not need to save the UCS.

○ Create a 1" solid cube on layer 0. Save the cube as a block named CUBE with an insertion point at one corner. Delete the cube.

○ Set the Table layer current. Use the CUBE block to construct the table. Insert one cube for the first leg and enter the following values.

　　○ Insertion point: X = 2'10", Y = 2'
　　○ Scale factors: X = 4, Y = 4, Z = 16
　　○ Rotation angle = 0°

*(Continued)*

○ Array the first leg using a row/column offset of 24″ for two rows and two columns.

○ Use the **CUBE** block again for the tabletop as follows.
  ○ Insertion point: X = 2′10″, Y = 2′, Z = 16″
  ○ Scale factors: X = 28, Y = 28, Z = 2
  ○ Rotation angle = 0°

○ Establish a new UCS on the top surface of the tabletop at the lower-left corner. Save this UCS orientation as Tabletop. Leave this UCS current until instructed to change it.

○ Change the current layer to Pyramid. Draw a surface pyramid. Locate the first base point of the pyramid at X = 12″, Y = 10″. Locate the second base point as @0,–8″. Locate the third point as @8″,0. Locate the fourth point as @0,8″. Locate the apex point at 16″,6″,12″. Rotate the pyramid 45° about the point closest to the Tabletop UCS origin.

○ Set the Cone layer current and draw a solid cone centered at X = 8″, Y = 20″ with an 8″ diameter base and a 12″ height.

○ Set the current layer to Torus. Draw a solid torus centered at X = 14″, Y = 14″, Z = 22″. The torus diameter is 18″ and the tube diameter is 5″.

○ The drawing should look like the one shown below.

○ Restore the UCS orientation named FLOOR (or the WCS).

○ Save the drawing as 3DSHAPES and leave it open. These objects are used throughout this chapter.

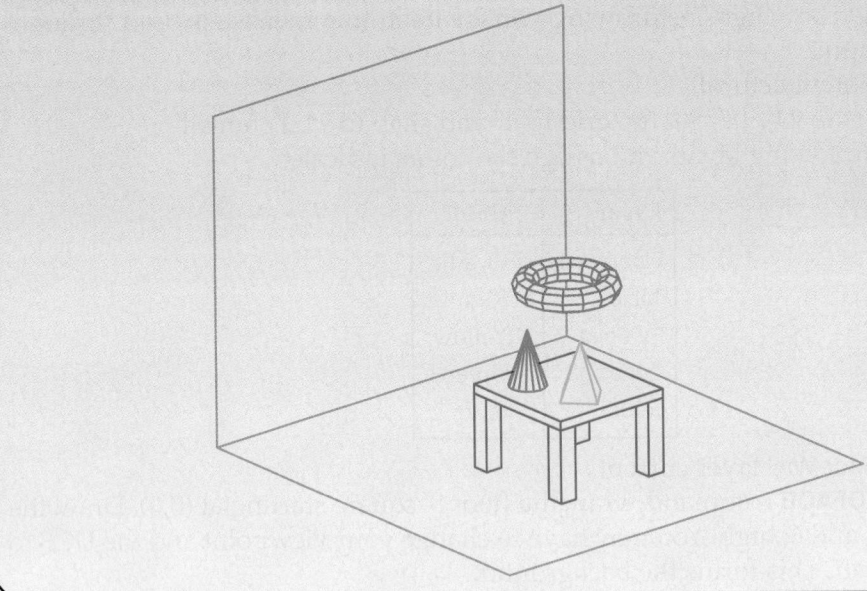

## Placing Point Lights in the Model

A point light can be placed in the drawing using the **Lights** dialog box. A location and a name are required. Remember, a name can have up to eight characters.

To place a point light in the 3DSHAPES drawing created in Exercise 14-1, first open the **Lights** dialog box. Then, select **Point Light** in the drop-down list at the left of the **Lights** dialog box. Next, pick the **New...** button. This displays the **New Point Light** dialog box shown in **Figure 14-4A.** Enter the name, such as P-1, in the **Light Name:** text box and pick **OK**. The **Lights** dialog box returns and P-1 is displayed and highlighted in the **Lights:** list box.

**Figure 14-4.**
Specifying a point light. These two dialog boxes are identical except for the title bar. A—The **New Point Light** dialog box. B—The **Modify Point Light** dialog box.

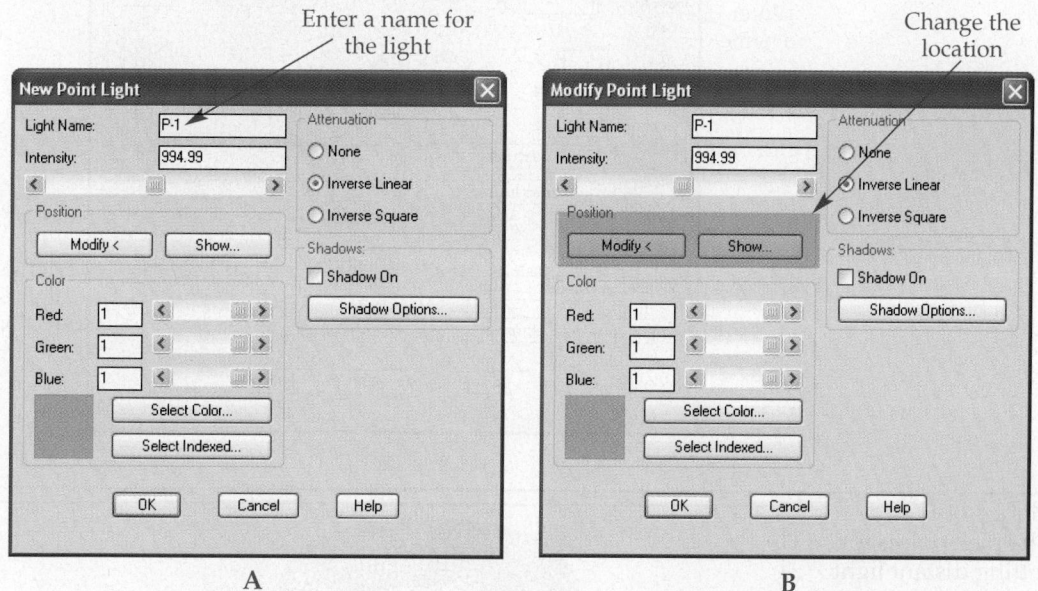

A                                      B

Now, pick **Modify...** with P-1 highlighted and the **Modify Point Light** dialog box shown in **Figure 14-4B** is displayed. Pick the **Modify<** button in the **Position** area and you are returned to the drawing. The prompt on the command line requests a light location. You can pick the location, use filters, or enter coordinates at the keyboard as follows.

Enter light location <*current*>:**4',3'2",8'**↵

The dialog box reappears once you press [Enter]. Pick **OK** in the **Modify Point Light** and **Lights** dialog boxes to complete the command.

Now, zoom all. Also, turn off grid and snap if they are on. Notice the light icon above the 3D objects. The icon is currently very small. In Chapter 16, you will learn how to change the display size of the light icons to suit your application.

## Placing Distant Lights in the Model

The Sun's rays are approximately parallel when they reach Earth and strike all objects with the same intensity. A distant light is used to simulate the Sun's rays in your model. If needed, an accurate representation of the Sun's angle can be achieved using the sun angle calculator. This feature is discussed in Chapter 16.

Distant lights are placed in the same way as point lights. However, a target location is needed as well as a light location. To place a distant light, first open the **Lights** dialog box. Then, pick **Distant Light** from the lights drop-down list. Pick the **New...** button to display the **New Distant Light** dialog box, **Figure 14-5.** Notice that this dialog box is different than the **New Point Light** dialog.

Enter a name, such as D-1, in the **Light Name:** text box. The location of the distant light can be entered as XYZ values in the **Light Source Vector** text boxes. Remember, these coordinates are relative to the origin of the current UCS. In addition, you can graphically select the location of the light using the **Azimuth:** and **Altitude:** image tiles. The *azimuth* is the angle *in* the XY plane. This can also be thought of as the angular direction of the Sun, looking south from the North Pole. The *altitude* is the angle *from* the XY plane. This measurement represents the angle of the Sun above the horizon. The location can also be set by picking the **Modify** button and entering coordinates at the Command: prompt as follows.

Enter light direction TO <*current*>: (*pick point P1 in Figure 14-6*)
Enter light direction FROM <*current*>: **6',–4',30"**↵

Figure 14-5.
The **New Distant Light** dialog box.

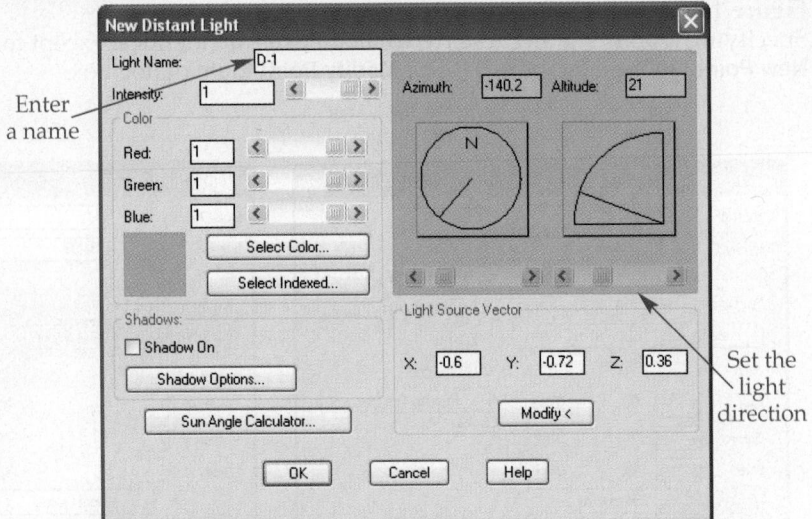

Enter a name

Set the light direction

Figure 14-6.
The pick points for setting distant light directions in the tutorial.

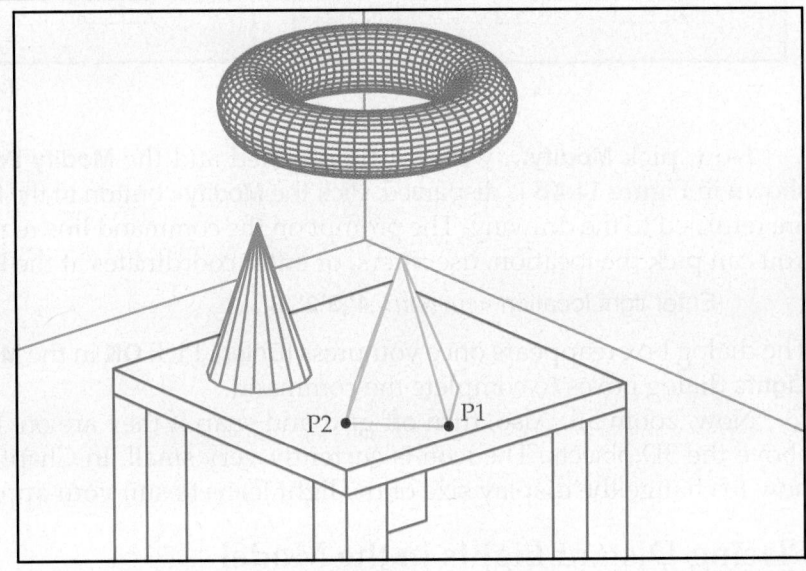

The "new" dialog box reappears. Pick **OK** to return to the **Lights** dialog box. Pick **OK** in that dialog box to return to the graphics window. The distant light is placed in the drawing. You may need to zoom out in one or more viewports to see the new light icon.

Place one more distant light in the model using the following information. The model should look like **Figure 14-7** after the second distant light is placed. However, the light icons in your drawing may be much smaller than shown in the figure.

| Name | Light direction to | Light direction from |
|------|-------------------|----------------------|
| D-2  | Point P2 in **Figure 14-6** | –2',0,30" |

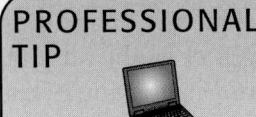

**PROFESSIONAL TIP**

Distant lights are especially important in architectural models and any model in which sunlight is a factor. It is good practice to locate as many distant lights in the model as you will need to create scenes at different times of day. Locate distant lights at the extents of the drawing, and always choose only one distant light per defined scene. Defined scenes are discussed later in this chapter.

AutoCAD and its Applications—Advanced

**Figure 14-7.**
The tutorial model with distant lights placed. The light icons in your drawing may look much smaller than shown here.

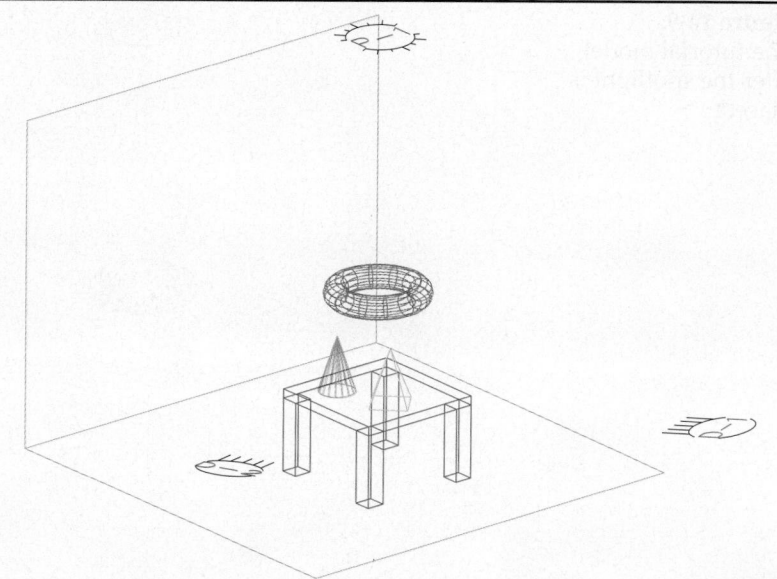

## Placing Spotlights in the Model

Spotlights are located in the same way as distant lights. First, pick **Spotlight** in the **Lights** drop-down list of the **Lights** dialog box. Then, pick the **New…** button. This displays the **New Spotlight** dialog box, **Figure 14-8.** There are several features of this dialog box that are discussed in Chapter 16.

For the 3DSHAPES drawing, name the spotlight S-1. Pick the **Modify** button to locate the light in the drawing area. Enter the location at the Command: prompt as follows.

> Enter light target <*current*>: *(pick the apex of the pyramid)*
> Enter light location <*current*>: **@24",–36",48"**↵

The dialog box returns. Pick **OK** in both dialog boxes to complete the command and return to the graphics window. Your drawing should look like **Figure 14-9.**

**Figure 14-8.**
The **New Spotlight** dialog box.

Enter a name →

Select the position and direction of the spotlight →

| New Spotlight | |
|---|---|
| Light Name: S-1 | Hotspot: 44 |
| Intensity: 994.75 | Falloff: 45 |
| **Position** | **Attenuation** |
| Modify <    Show... | ○ None |
| **Color** | ● Inverse Linear |
| | ○ Inverse Square |
| Red: 1 | **Shadows:** |
| Green: 1 | ☐ Shadow On |
| Blue: 1 | Shadow Options... |
| Select Color... | |
| Select Indexed... | |
| OK   Cancel   Help | |

**Figure 14-9.**
The tutorial model
after the spotlight is
placed.

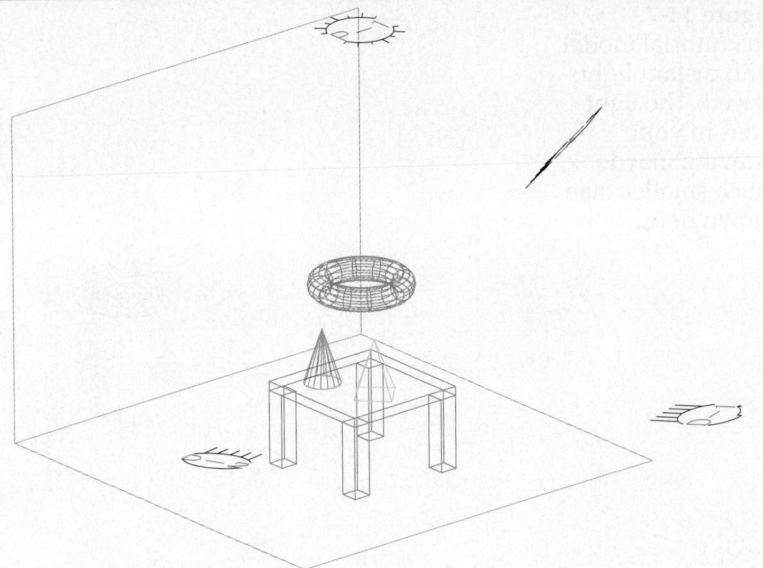

## Creating Scenes

A *scene* is like a photo studio for your model. It is made up of a view and one or more lights. You can have as many scenes in a model as you want. A scene does not have to include all lights in the drawing. When you create a scene, pick only the lights needed to illuminate the view in the scene. You can select a different combination of lights for each scene.

### Preparing to Create a Scene

The current view in the active viewport is used as the "camera" for the scene. Therefore, use the **3DORBIT** command or a preset viewpoint to set the viewpoints you want. Then, use the **VIEW** command to create named (saved) views to recall that particular view in any viewport at any time.

For the 3DSHAPES drawing, first restore the FLOOR UCS (or WCS). Then, use **3DORBIT** to adjust the view so it appears similar to **Figure 14-10.** This view is similar

**Figure 14-10.**
The model with
VIEW1 displayed.

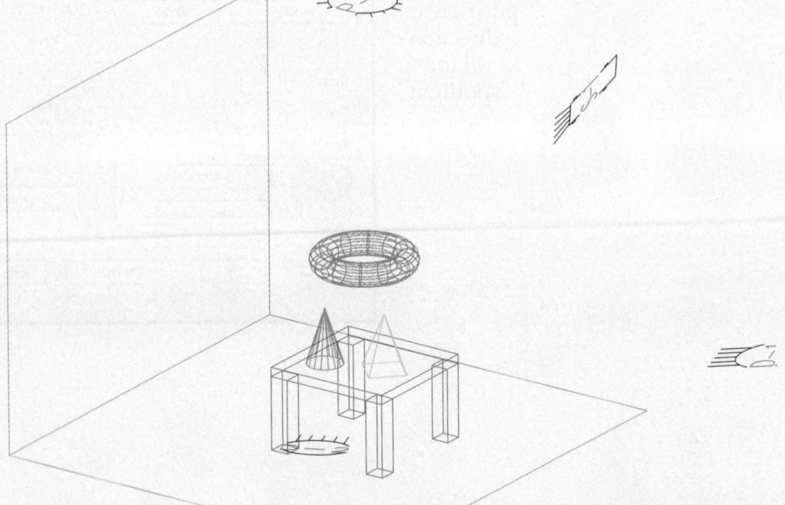

AutoCAD and its Applications—Advanced

**Figure 14-11.**
The model with
VIEW2 displayed.

to the original view setup. Save this view as VIEW1. Next, adjust the view using **3DORBIT** so the view looks similar to **Figure 14-11.** Make the projection a perspective. Save this view as VIEW2.

In addition to saving views, you must have at least one light in the drawing. Add lights as needed, as described in previous sections.

## Defining a Scene

Now that views have been saved and lights have been created, you can define scenes. Pick the **Scenes** button on the **Render** toolbar, select **Scene...** from the **Render** cascading menu in the **View** pull-down menu, or type SCENE at the Command: prompt. This displays the **Scenes** dialog box. See **Figure 14-12A.** Pick **New...** to display the **New Scene** dialog box, **Figure 14-13.** This dialog box lists all views and lights in the drawing.

For the 3DSHAPES drawing, open the **New Scene** dialog box. Then, enter FRONT in the **Scene Name:** text box; this is the name of the scene. Now you need to assign a view and lights to the new scene. Pick VIEW2, then hold the [Ctrl] key and pick lights D-1 and P-1. Pick the **OK** button to save the scene. Pick **New...** again and make another scene named SIDE. Use VIEW1 and lights D-2 and S-1. The **Scenes** dialog box now lists the two scenes, as shown in **Figure 14-12B.** Pick **OK.**

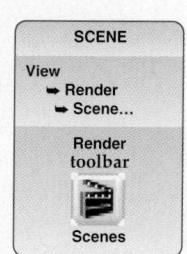

SCENE

View
➡ Render
➡ Scene...

Render
toolbar

Scenes

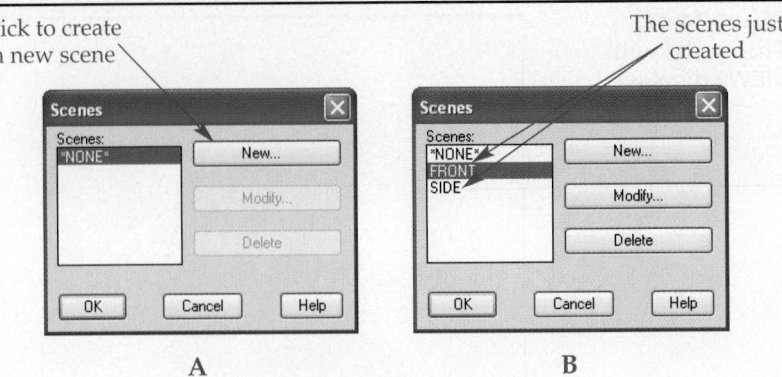

**Figure 14-12.**
A—The **Scenes** dialog box. B—The **Scenes** dialog box with new scenes created.

Pick to create a new scene

The scenes just created

A

B

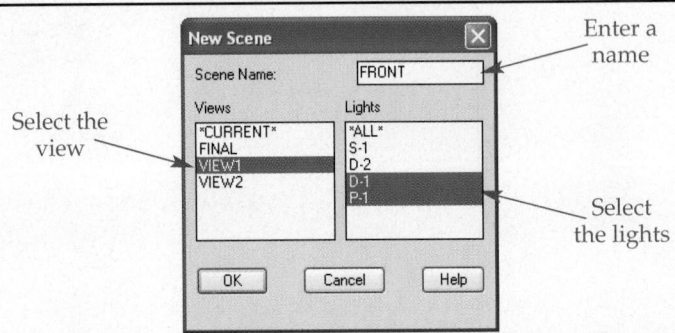

**Figure 14-13.**
The **New Scene** dialog box.

Enter a name

Select the view

Select the lights

## Rendering the Model

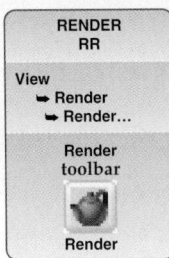

RENDER
RR

View
→ Render
→ Render...

Render
toolbar

Render

You can render your model at any time. To render your model, pick the **Render** button on the **Render** toolbar, select **Render...** from the **Render** cascading menu in the **View** pull-down menu, or type RR or RENDER at the Command: prompt. The **Render** dialog box is opened. Make sure **Viewport** is selected in the **Destination** drop-down list. Pick the **Render** button in this dialog box. AutoCAD displays a rendering of your model in the active viewport. See **Figure 14-14.**

**Figure 14-14.**
The tutorial model rendered after the lights are placed. Note: The lighting in your rendering may appear slightly different. The lights have been adjusted here for illustration purposes.

AutoCAD and its Applications—Advanced

If there are no lights in your model, AutoCAD places one behind your viewpoint (behind you). If you have placed lights in your model but have not yet constructed a "scene," AutoCAD uses all the lights and renders the current view in the active viewport. However, you can select a scene to render from the list in the **Scene to Render** list box of the **Render** dialog box. In this case, only the lights in the scene are used to illuminate the view in the scene.

AutoCAD can produce three different types of renderings. These are the default render, photo real, and photo raytrace. These options appear in the **Rendering Type:** drop-down list at the top of the **Render** dialog box, **Figure 14-15.**

**Figure 14-15.**
The **Render** dialog box.

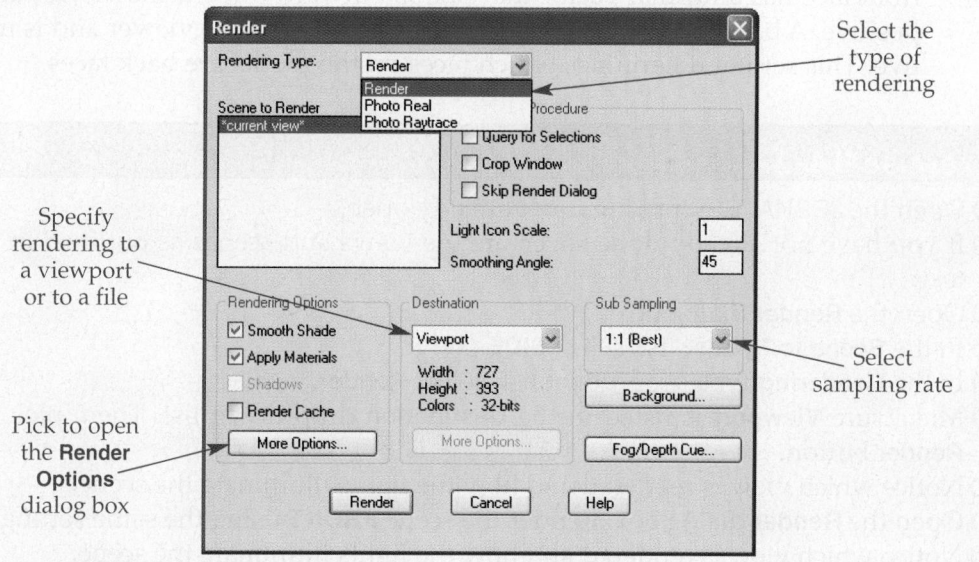

Specify rendering to a viewport or to a file

Pick to open the **Render Options** dialog box

Select the type of rendering

Select sampling rate

## Standard Rendering

The **Render** option is considered a low-level rendering. Notice that the **Shadows** check box in the **Rendering Options** area is disabled. Shadows, which are discussed in Chapter 16, are not cast when rendering a model using the **Render** option. Picking the **More Options...** button displays the **Render Options** dialog box, **Figure 14-16.** In this dialog box, you can choose the render quality and the 3D face controls.

**Figure 14-16.**
The render quality and face control options for the **Render** selection are set in the **Render Options** dialog box.

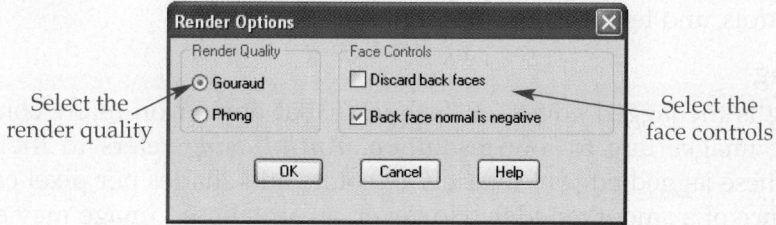

Select the render quality

Select the face controls

The type of render quality determines the points where light intensity is calculated. The two options are:

- **Gouraud.** Light intensity is calculated at each vertex with this type of rendering. The intensity of the space between vertices is estimated. This is the least realistic of the two options.
- **Phong.** With this type of rendering, light intensity is calculated at each pixel. This creates realistic lighting.

The **Face Controls** area contains two items that determine whether or not hidden faces are calculated. These two items are:

- **Discard back faces.** When checked, AutoCAD does not calculate hidden faces when rendering. This setting can speed the rendering process.
- **Back face normal is negative.** A *normal vector* is perpendicular to a face. A front face has a normal vector that points outward toward the viewer and is positive. A back face normal vector points away from the viewer and is negative. This setting determines which faces on the model are back faces.

---

## Exercise 14-2

○ Open the 3DSHAPES drawing if not already open.
○ If you have not already done so, create the views and scenes as outlined in the text.
○ Open the **Render** dialog box.
○ In the **Scene to Render** list, select **SIDE**.
○ In the **Rendering Type** drop-down list, select **Render**.
○ Make sure **Viewport** is listed in the **Destination** drop-down list. Then, pick the **Render** button.
○ Notice which view is rendered and how the lights illuminate the scene.
○ Open the **Render** dialog box. Render the scene **FRONT** using the same settings.
○ Notice which view is rendered and how the lights illuminate the scene.
○ Leave the drawing open.

---

## Photo Real Rendering

The **Photo Real** rendering type produces a more realistic image than the **Render** option. It is the default rendering type. This type of rendering can cast shadows. To display shadows in the rendering, the **Shadows** check box must be checked. In addition, for shadows to be cast, the lights in the 3D model must be set up to display shadows. Shadows are discussed in Chapter 16.

You can refine the rendered image by selecting the **More Options...** button to display the **Photo Real Render Options** dialog box. See **Figure 14-17.** In addition to the face controls discussed previously, you can adjust the antialiasing, depth map shadow controls, and texture map sampling.

### Antialiasing

*Aliasing* is the jagged edges, or "jaggies," that appear on many computer text and graphic images due to low resolution. *Antialiasing* refers to the process of smoothing these jagged edges. A variety of colors and shades per pixel can produce the appearance of a smoother edge. However, an antialiased image may also appear fuzzy or "out of focus." AutoCAD provides four different levels of antialiasing. Each successive option requires a longer time to render the image.

- **Minimal.** This level is the default and uses only horizontal antialiasing. This level of antialiasing requires the least amount of time to render.
- **Low.** This level uses horizontal antialiasing and four shading samples per pixel.

**Figure 14-17.**
This dialog box is used to select settings for a photo real rendering.

Select the level of antialiasing

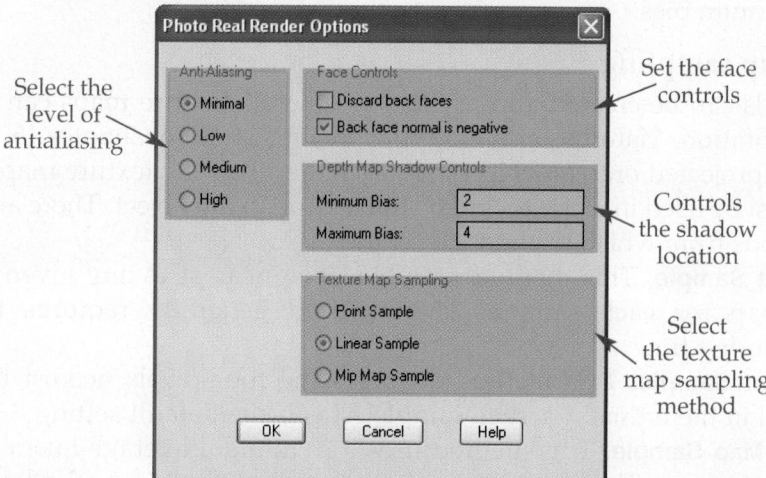

Set the face controls

Controls the shadow location

Select the texture map sampling method

- **Medium.** This level uses horizontal antialiasing and nine shading samples per pixel.
- **High.** This level uses horizontal antialiasing and sixteen shading samples per pixel. This level of antialiasing requires the most rendering time.

### Depth map shadow controls

Lights can be set up to cast shadows. This is discussed in Chapter 16. The settings in the **Depth Map Shadow Controls** area control the location of the shadow in relation to the object casting the shadow. This helps prevent detached and misplaced shadows. The higher the settings, the greater distance from the object to the shadow. See **Figure 14-18.** The following settings are available. You may need to try several different settings to get the best display. For most models, the default settings work fine.

- **Minimum Bias.** The default setting is 2. In general, a value no higher than 20 should be used.

**Figure 14-18.**
A—Photo real rendered objects with the default minimum bias 2 and maximum bias 4.
B—The same rendering with a minimum bias of 20 and maximum bias of 30.

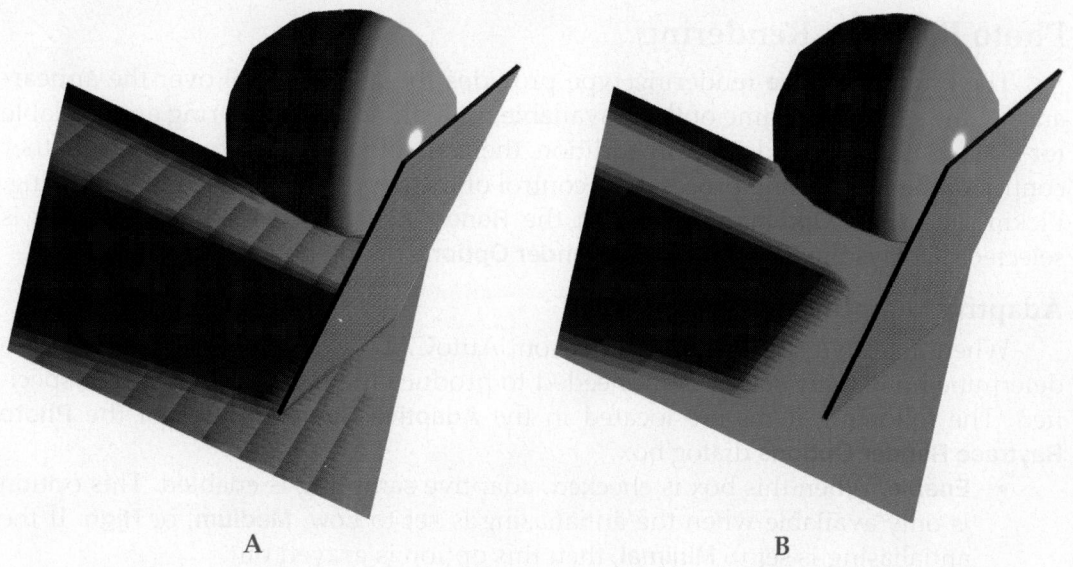

A                                                    B

- **Maximum Bias.** The default setting is 4. In general, a value no higher than 20 should be used. This value should also be no more than 10 greater than the minimum bias.

## Texture map sampling

Materials can be created and applied to objects. Texture maps can be part of a material definition. Materials and mapping are discussed in Chapter 15. When a texture map is projected onto an object that is smaller than the texture map, a sampling method must be used in order to "map" the texture to the object. There are three sampling methods from which to choose.

- **Point Sample.** This method uses the pixel nearest to any given pixel in the bitmap for each sample. This method generally requires the shortest rendering time.
- **Linear Sample.** This method averages the four pixels nearest to any given pixel in the bitmap for each sample. This is the default setting.
- **Mip Map Sample.** This method uses a pyramidal average taken from square sample areas. This averaging process is called the *mip* method and generally requires the longest rendering time.

---

### Exercise 14-3

○ Open the 3DSHAPES drawing if not already open.
○ Create the views and scenes as described in the text if you have not already done so.
○ Open the **Render** dialog box.
○ In the **Scene to Render** list, pick **SIDE**.
○ In the **Rendering Type** drop-down list, pick **Render**.
○ Make sure **Viewport** is selected in the **Destination** drop-down list and then pick the **Render** button.
○ Notice how the scene appears.
○ Open the **Render** dialog box. Select **Photo Real** in the **Rendering Type** drop-down list. Then, render the **SIDE** scene again.
○ Notice how the scene appears. Especially notice the change in how the lights illuminate the scene.
○ Leave the drawing open.

---

## Photo Raytrace Rendering

The **Photo Raytrace** rendering type provides the most control over the appearance of the scene. The same options available for a photo real rendering are available for a photo raytrace rendering. In addition, there are other options to provide further control of the antialiasing process and control of the depth of rays used in raytracing. Picking the **More Options...** button in the **Render** dialog when **Photo Raytrace** is selected displays the **Photo Raytrace Render Options** dialog box. See **Figure 14-19.**

### Adaptive sampling

When adaptive sampling is turned on, AutoCAD uses a contrast threshold to determine how many samples are needed to produce the level of antialiasing specified. The following items are located in the **Adaptive Sampling** area of the **Photo Raytrace Render Options** dialog box.

- **Enable.** When this box is checked, adaptive sampling is enabled. This option is only available when the antialiasing is set to **Low**, **Medium**, or **High**. If the antialiasing is set to **Minimal**, then this option is grayed out.

Figure 14-19.
The **Photo Raytrace Render Options** dialog box is used to control photo raytrace renderings.

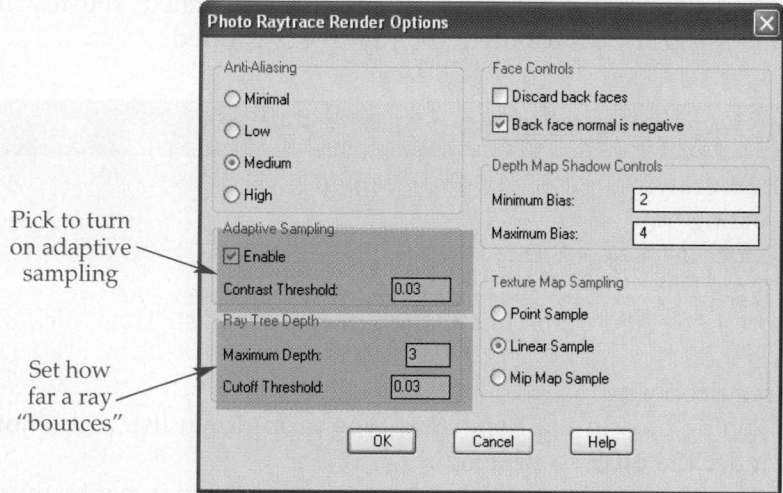

Pick to turn on adaptive sampling

Set how far a ray "bounces"

- **Contrast Threshold.** The value in this text box determines the number of samples AutoCAD will use to achieve the selected level of antialiasing. A low value means that a greater number of samples will be taken. The greater the number of samples, the longer the rendering time. This value can be between 0.0 and 1.0.

## Ray tree depth

The *ray tree* is the path that a light ray takes from the light source. Each path segment is a *branch* of the tree. See **Figure 14-20.** The **Ray Tree Depth** area contains two ray tree settings. These settings control the depth of the ray tree used to track rays. In other words, these settings determine how far a ray bounces (reflects).

- **Maximum Depth.** This value represents the maximum length a branch can extend. If a ray does not strike another object before the maximum depth is reached, the tree is "pruned." A value as high as 9999 can be entered. However, a value between 3 (default) and 10 is suggested.

Figure 14-20.
The ray tree is the path a light ray takes from the light source.

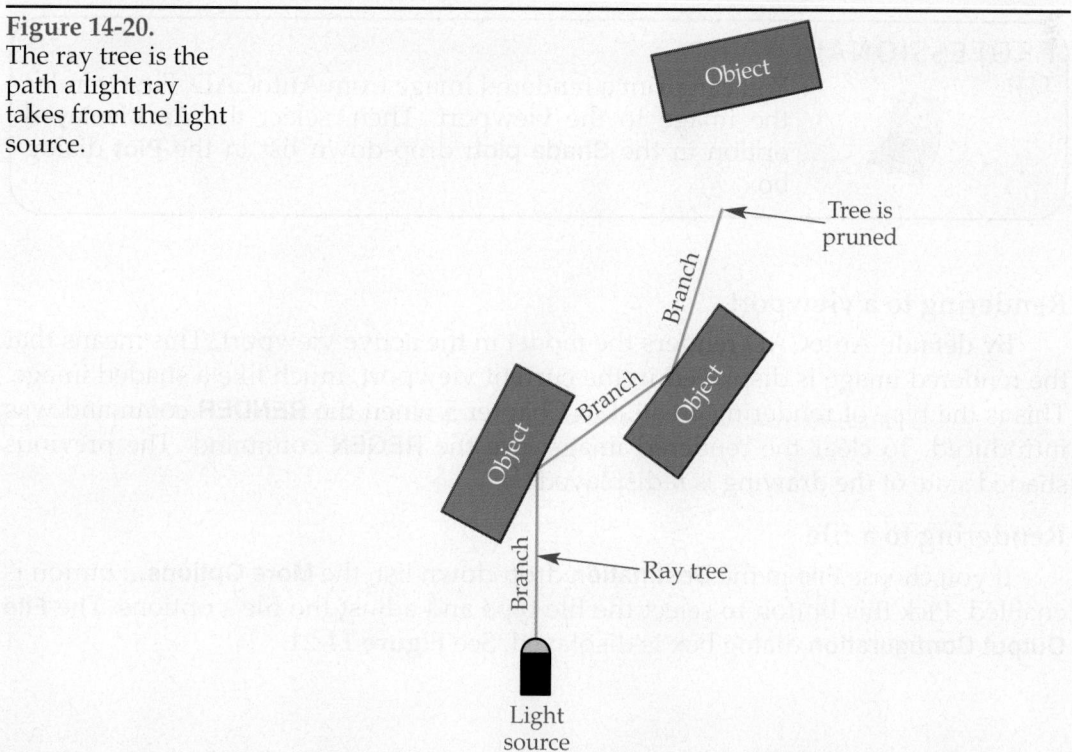

- **Cutoff Threshold.** This value defines a percentage that the next branch must add to the last pixel in the branch. A value of .05 means that at least 5% must be contributed to the final pixel value. If the 5% is reached, the ray tree continues. If the 5% is not contributed, the ray tree is pruned.

---

### Exercise 14-4

○ Open the 3DSHAPES drawing if it is not already open.
○ Open the **Render** dialog box.
○ In the **Scene to Render** list, select **SIDE**.
○ In the **Rendering Type** drop-down list, pick **Photo Real**.
○ Make sure **Viewport** is selected in the **Destination** drop-down list. Then, pick the **Render** button.
○ Notice how the scene appears.
○ Open the **Render** dialog box. In the **Rendering Type** drop-down list, pick **Photo Raytrace**. Then, render the **SIDE** scene again.
○ Notice how the scene appears. This is a simple scene, so there may not be much difference between a photo real rendering and a photo raytrace rendering.
○ Leave the drawing open.

---

## Rendering Destination

The drop-down list in the **Destination** area of the **Render** dialog box allows you to specify where a rendered image will be "placed." You can also render to an image file or to the **Render** window. The **Render** window is a carryover from early rendering capabilities of AutoCAD. Generally, it is better to render to a viewport to see the image. If you need to use the image in documents or on websites, print the image, or perform "touch ups" on the image, render to a file. This allows you to control the resolution of the image. Then, use other software, such as photo editing software, to enhance, touch up, or print the image.

---

**PROFESSIONAL TIP**  You can print a rendered image from AutoCAD. First, render the image to the viewport. Then, select the **As Displayed** option in the **Shade plot:** drop-down list in the **Plot** dialog box.

---

### Rendering to a viewport

By default, AutoCAD renders the model in the active viewport. This means that the rendered image is displayed in the current viewport, much like a shaded image. This is the type of rendering created in Chapter 5 when the **RENDER** command was introduced. To clear the rendered image, use the **REGEN** command. The previous shaded state of the drawing is redisplayed.

### Rendering to a file

If you choose **File** in the **Destination** drop-down list, the **More Options...** button is enabled. Pick this button to select the file type and adjust the file's options. The **File Output Configuration** dialog box is displayed. See **Figure 14-21.**

**Figure 14-21.**
When rendering to a file, parameters can be set in the **File Output Configuration** dialog box.

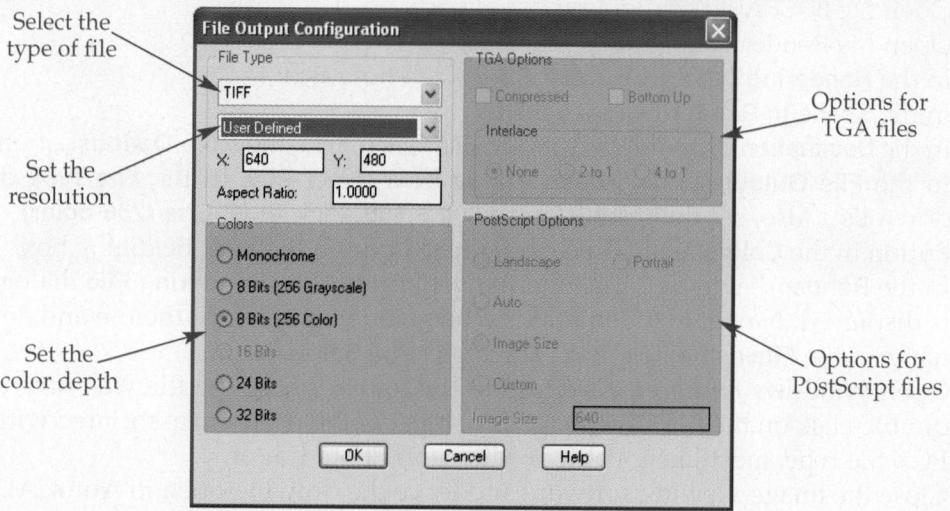

The type of image file to create and the resolution are specified in the **File Type** drop-down lists. The type of file selected determines which options are available in the dialog box. The file types to select from are BMP, PCX, PostScript, TGA, and TIFF. Pick each one of these file types and notice the different options that are available. The following four areas are found in the **File Output Configuration** dialog box.

- **File Type.** In this area, select the type of output file and the file resolution in the drop-down lists. The X and Y values of resolution and the aspect ratio are displayed grayed out at the bottom of this area. These values can be manually set if **User Defined** is picked in the resolution drop-down list.
- **Colors.** This area is where the color depth per pixel is set. The options available in this area depend on the file type.
- **TGA Options.** The options in this area are available for the TGA file type only. You can select a compressed file, specify an image that is scanned from the bottom left, or choose between an interlaced or noninterlaced image. The default **None** produces a noninterlaced image. Pick **2 to 1** or **4 to 1** to create an interlaced file.
- **PostScript Options.** These are available only when the PostScript file type is selected. You can choose between landscape and portrait format, and you can select the method of image sizing. **Auto** instructs AutoCAD to automatically scale the image. **Image Size** uses the exact image size. When **Custom** is selected, you can enter the image size in pixels in the **Image Size** text box.

## Preview Renderings

Large models may require some time to render. In general, the **SHADEMODE** command is intended to produce a preview of how the objects will look when rendered. However, there are certain aspects of a rendering that do not show in a shaded view. You can create a low-resolution preview rendering by adjusting the sub sampling. In this way, you can see the shadows and highlights without spending the time to create a high-resolution rendering.

The **Sub Sampling** drop-down list in the **Render** dialog box allows you to specify the sampling rate for the rendering. The amount of rendering time and the image quality are related to the sampling rate. The **1:1** setting produces the best-quality image and takes the longest to render. The **8:1** setting provides the lowest-quality image, but takes the shortest time to render. Other effects you have selected, such as shadows and materials, are still applied in the rendering. **Figure 14-22** shows a model rendered with three different sub sampling settings.

## Rendering Procedures

By default, everything visible in the active viewport is rendered. However, there may be times when you want to render only some of the objects or a portion of the viewport. Also, you may want to "skip" the **Render** dialog box and perform the rendering with the current settings. The options listed in the **Rendering Procedure** area of the **Render** dialog box can be used in these situations. See **Figure 14-23**. These options are described as follows.

- **Query for Selections.** When checked, this option allows you to select specific objects to be rendered. This option is covered in detail in Chapter 5.
- **Crop Window.** Check this option to draw a window around a specific area of the model for rendering. This option is only available when the destination is the viewport. It is covered in detail in Chapter 5.
- **Skip Render Dialog.** If this is checked, the **Render** dialog box is not displayed for future uses of the **RENDER** command. This is a good option if the same render settings are used for a series of renderings. You can use the **Rendering Preferences** dialog box to change this setting so that the dialog box appears. Rendering preferences are discussed later in this chapter.

**Figure 14-22.**
A drawing rendered at various sub sampling settings. Notice the change in image quality.
A—1:1 (Best). B—4:1. C—8:1 (Fastest).

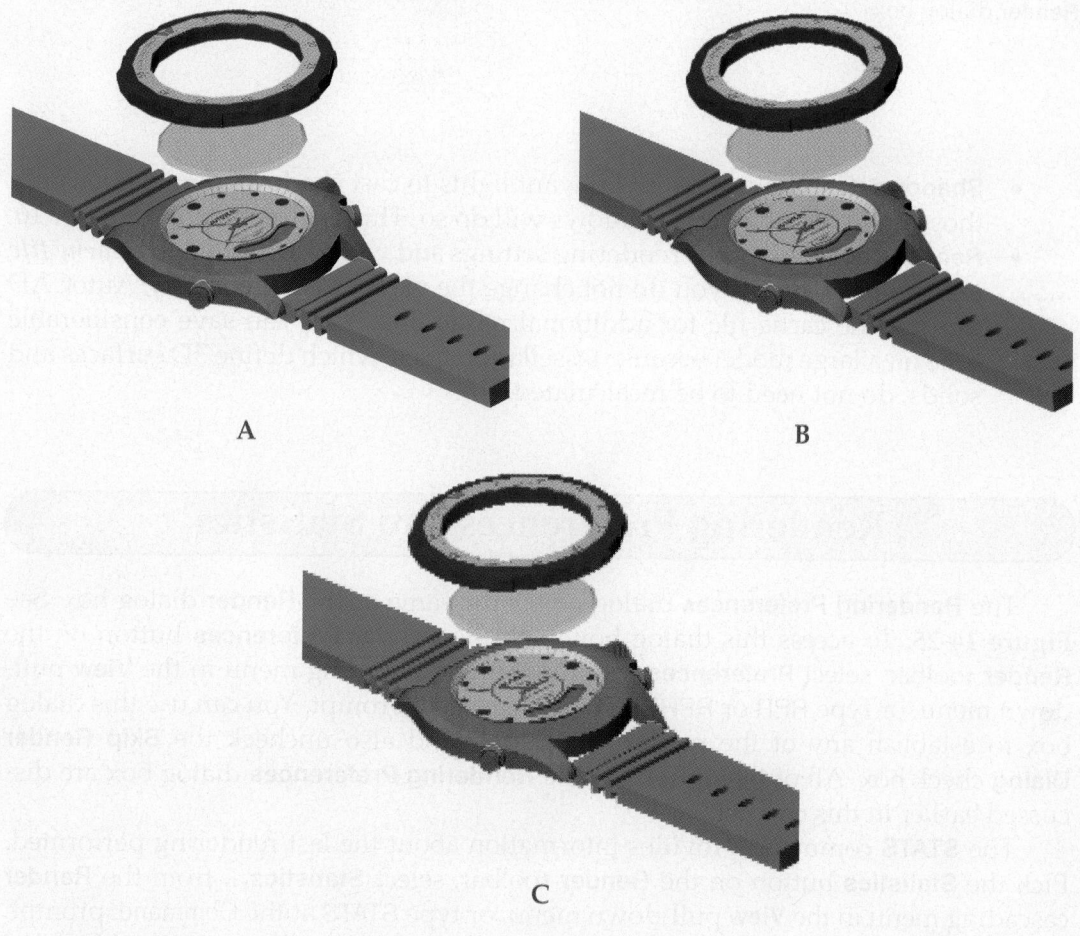

A

B

C

**Figure 14-23.**
The **Rendering Procedure** area of the **Render** dialog box.

```
Rendering Procedure
☐ Query for Selections
☐ Crop Window
☐ Skip Render Dialog
```

## Additional Rendering Options

The **Rendering Options** area of the **Render** dialog box has four options that give you a wide range of control over how the model is rendered. See **Figure 14-24.** These options not only control the appearance of the rendering, but also affect the rendering speed.

- **Smooth Shade.** When this option is checked, AutoCAD blends colors between faces to produce a smooth surface. When on, the rendering time is increased. The **Smoothing Angle** setting (located above the **Sub Sampling** area) determines the angle at which an edge is defined. Angles less than the setting are smoothed. Angles greater than the setting are not smoothed.
- **Apply Materials.** If materials have been assigned to objects in the model, AutoCAD renders them if this box is checked. When unchecked, the objects are rendered in their display color. Rendering materials increases the rendering time. The amount of increase depends on the number and complexity of the textures and materials.

Figure 14-24.
The **Rendering Options** area of the **Render** dialog box.

- **Shadows.** Check this box if you want lights to cast shadows. Remember, only those lights set up to cast shadows will do so. This is discussed in Chapter 16.
- **Render Cache.** All of the rendering settings and values are saved to a *cache file* on the hard drive. If you do not change the view or any geometry, AutoCAD can use the cache file for additional renderings. This can save considerable time on a large model because tessellation lines, which define 3D surfaces and solids, do not need to be recalculated.

## Rendering Preferences and Statistics

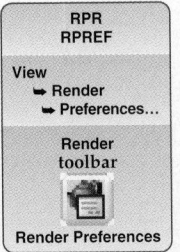

The **Rendering Preferences** dialog box is the same as the **Render** dialog box. See **Figure 14-25.** To access this dialog box, pick the **Render Preferences** button on the **Render** toolbar, select **Preferences...** in the **Render** cascading menu in the **View** pull-down menu, or type RPR or RPREF at the Command: prompt. You can use this dialog box to establish any of the rendering options, and also uncheck the **Skip Render Dialog** check box. All of the options in the **Rendering Preferences** dialog box are discussed earlier in this chapter.

The **STATS** command provides information about the last rendering performed. Pick the **Statistics** button on the **Render** toolbar, select **Statistics...** from the **Render** cascading menu in the **View** pull-down menu, or type STATS at the Command: prompt. The **Statistics** dialog box is displayed, See **Figure 14-26.** The information in the dialog box cannot be altered, but it can be saved to a text file. Place a check in the **Save Statistics to File:** check box, type in a name, and use the **Find File** button to specify the location of the saved file. You must add a .txt extension to the name. Then, pick the **OK** button.

Figure 14-25.
The **Rendering Preferences** dialog box is used to establish all the rendering options.

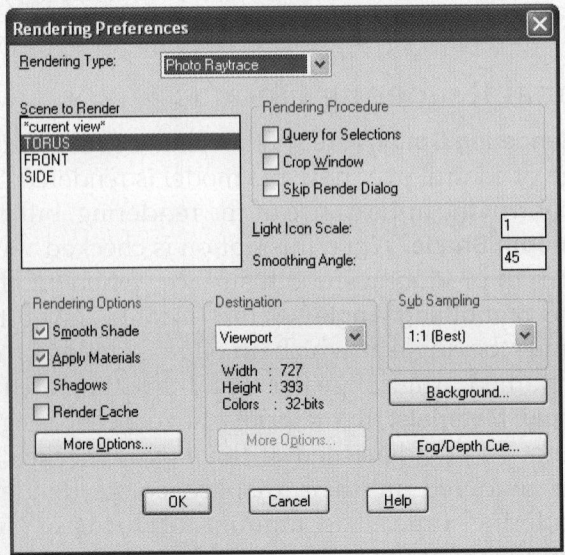

AutoCAD and its Applications—Advanced

**Figure 14-26.**
Displaying the
rendering statistics.

Check to
save to
a file

Enter a
file name

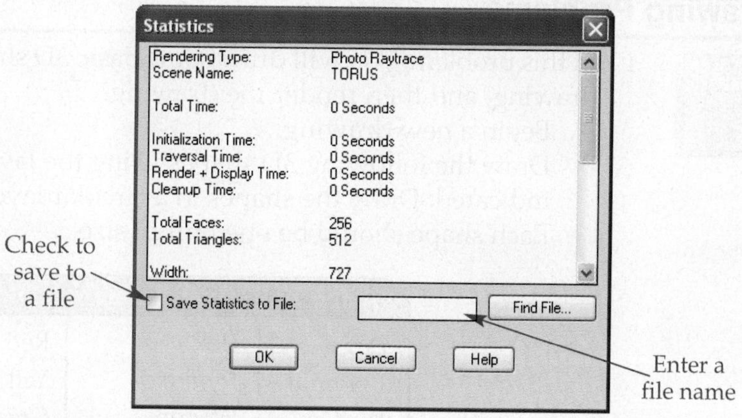

## Exercise 14-6

○ If you have not completed Exercise 14-5, do so now.
○ Type STATS on the command line to open the **Statistics** dialog box.
○ Check the **Save Statistics to File** check box.
○ Enter a name and the .txt file extension in the text box. Pick the **Find File...** button and navigate to the folder where you want to save the file. Pick the **Save** button and then the **OK** button.
○ Open Microsoft Notepad or WordPad. Then, open the TXT file that contains the rendering statistics. Print the file.
○ Close the word processor.

## Chapter Test

*Answer the following questions on a separate sheet of paper.*

1. Define the following terms:
   A. Ambient light.
   B. Distant light.
   C. Point light.
   D. Spotlight.
2. What does a defined scene in AutoCAD consist of?
3. What is the meaning of *altitude* and *azimuth?*
4. Which types of renderings can produce shadows?
5. What is *antialiasing?*
6. How do you render to a file?
7. What effect does selecting **Smooth Shade** have on the model when rendering?
8. What are the advantages of rendering to a file?
9. What is the difference between point lights and distant lights?
10. How do you prevent the display of the **Render** dialog box when the **RENDER** command is used?

## Drawing Problems

1. In this problem, you will draw some basic 3D shapes, place lights in the drawing, and then render the drawing.
   A. Begin a new drawing.
   B. Draw the following 3D shapes using the layer names and colors as indicated. Draw the shapes in a circular layout, as shown below. Each shape should be one unit in size.

| Shape | Layer Name | Color |
|-------|------------|-------|
| Box | Box | Red |
| Pyramid | Pyramid | Yellow |
| Wedge | Wedge | Green |
| Cone | Cone | Cyan |
| Dome | Dome | Blue |
| Dish | Dish | Magenta |
| Sphere | Sphere | White/Black |

   C. Place a point light in the center of the objects, three units above them.
   D. Place two distant lights as shown in the drawing, having target points in the center of the objects. Light D-1 should be located at Z = 3 and light D-2 should be located at Z = 2.
   E. Place two spotlights as shown in the figure. Light S-1 has a target of the cone apex and light S-2 has a target of the pyramid apex. Light S-1 should be located at Z = 2.5 and light S-2 should be located at Z = 2.
   F. Display a pictorial view of the drawing.
   G. Render the drawing.
   H. Save the image as a bitmap file named P14-1.
   I. Save the drawing as P14-1.

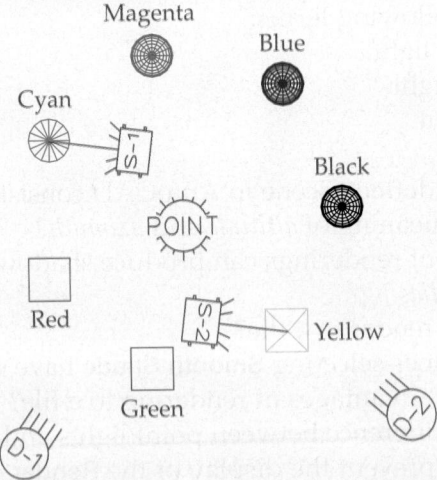

2. This problem adds additional light to a drawing. You will then render the scene and place the image into a document.
   A. Open the drawing P14-1.
   B. Place a new point light directly over the cone and a new distant light to one side and slightly below the "ground." Render the drawing to a BMP file.
   E. Open a word processor, such as Microsoft WordPad.
   F. Type the following sentence.
      This is an example of what AutoCAD can do for documents.
   G. Insert the rendered drawing into the document. Save the document as P14-2.

3. Open a 3D drawing from a previous chapter. Do the following.
   A. Place two point lights around the model.
   B. Place two distant lights around the model.
   C. Place two spotlights around the model.
   D. Create and save three different views of the model.
   E. Create three scenes of the model. Choose two different lights and a different view for each scene.
   F. Render each scene to the viewport.
   G. Render one scene as a TGA file, one as a TIF file, and one as a BMP file.
   H. Save the drawing as P14-3.

4. Open problem P14-3. Do the following.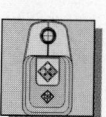
   A. Modify each of the three scenes to include only one light.
   B. Render each scene to a file. Use the file type of your choice.
   C. Save the rendering statistics of the last rendering to a file.
   D. Open a word processor, such as Microsoft WordPad. Open the rendering statistics text file.
   E. Insert one of the rendered images at the beginning of the document.
   F. Under the image, add the text:
      The rendering statistics for this image are as follows.
   G. Print the document.
   H. Save the document as P14-4.

Materials allow you to change the appearance of an object. All of these renderings have the same basic color. However, using materials, you can represent cast metal (A), transparent plastic (B), shiny opaque plastic (C), and shiny plastic with a company logo (D).

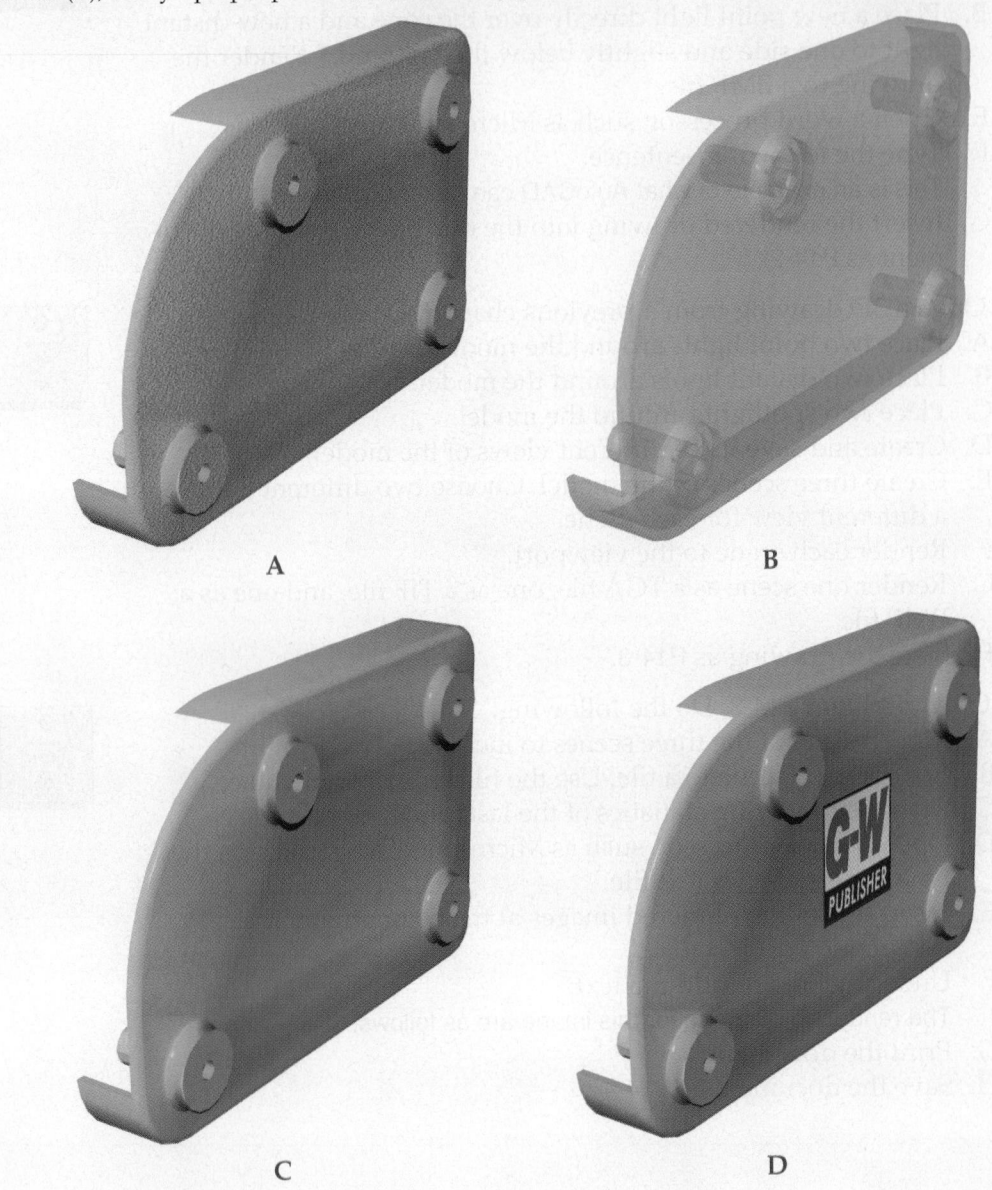

A

B

C

D

## CHAPTER 15

# Materials in AutoCAD

## Learning Objectives

After completing this chapter, you will be able to:
- Create new materials.
- Apply surface textures and materials to models.
- Map materials onto AutoCAD objects.
- Load materials from a material library.
- Save materials to a material library.

In Chapter 14, you learned how to add lights to a drawing and create scenes. You also learned how to create different types of renderings. In this chapter, you will learn how to create surface finishes, called materials, and apply them to objects in the drawing. You will also learn how to work with material libraries.

## Creating Surface Finishes with Materials

A surface finish, or *material,* defines various visual properties, such as color, roughness, and shininess. These properties are used by the **RENDER** command to create realistic representations of the objects in your drawing. You can create a variety of materials by specifying how a surface reflects light. You can also add images to represent textures and bumps. For example, you may add an image to represent wood grain or the grout lines for a tile floor.

To create a material from scratch, first pick the **Materials** button on the **Render** toolbar, select **Materials...** from the **Render** cascading menu in the **View** pull-down menu, or type RMAT at the Command: prompt. This displays the **Materials** dialog box, **Figure 15-1A.** The drop-down list below the **New...** button on the right of the dialog box provides four material types: **Standard**, **Marble**, **Granite**, and **Wood**. Select **Standard**, then pick the **New...** button to display the **New Standard Material** dialog box, **Figure 15-1B. Standard** refers to the type of material being created. The other three material types are discussed later in this chapter.

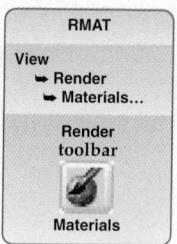

RMAT

View
➥ Render
  ➥ Materials...

Render
toolbar

Materials

**Figure 15-1.**
A—The **Materials** dialog box. Pick the **New...** button to display the **New Standard Material** dialog box. B—The **New Standard Material** dialog box.

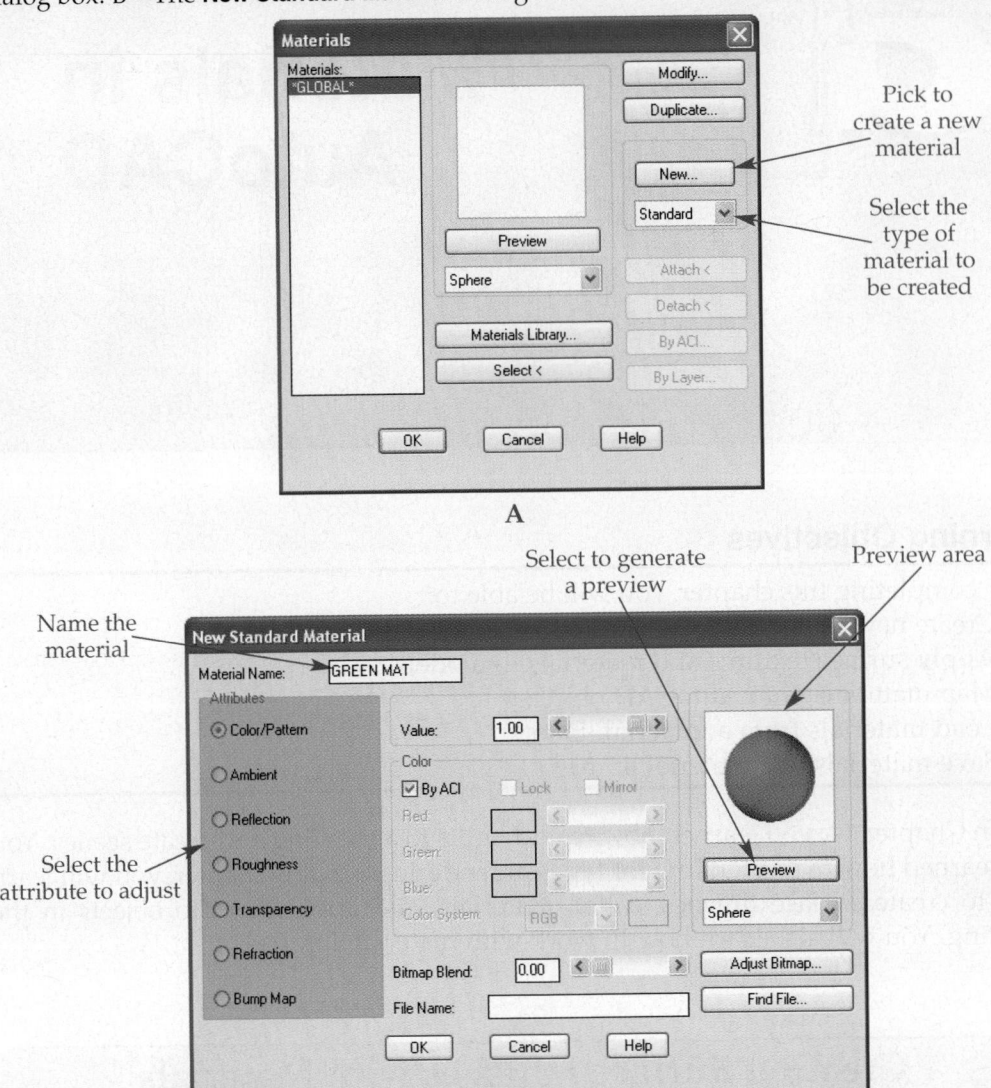

You must name the material in the **Material Name:** text box. Then, define the material attributes. Material attributes are selected for editing in the **Attributes** area of the **New Standard Material** dialog box. The following seven attributes are available. These are discussed in detail in the next sections. Also, refer to **Figure 15-2.**

- **Color/Pattern.** This color is the main color of the object.
- **Ambient.** This is the color of the ambient light reflected from the object.
- **Reflection.** This is the color of the highlight. The highlight is the shiniest spot on the object.
- **Roughness.** This controls the size of the reflection.
- **Transparency.** This controls how transparent the object is.
- **Refraction.** The refraction value specifies how much a light ray is "bent" as it enters a material.
- **Bump Map.** This is used to assign a bitmap image to represent a "bumpy" or embossed surface.

**Figure 15-2.**
Color, ambient, and reflection all combine to create the "color" of a material.

Color

Reflection

Ambient

## Exercise 15-1

○ Draw the simplified felt-tip pen and cap shown below. There are three objects.
   ○ The cap is a solid ∅.375" sphere and ∅.375" × 1" solid cylinder. Union the objects.
   ○ The body is a ∅.25" solid sphere and ∅.25" × 2" solid cylinder that are unioned.
   ○ The point is a ∅.25" × .5" solid cone. Do not union it to the body.
○ Use the **3DORBIT** command to create a pictorial display similar to the one shown. Save the view.
○ Add two point lights, one about 5" above the cap and one about 5" above the body. Both lights should be slightly in front of the pen based on your viewpoint.
○ Place another point light about 5" directly below the objects.
○ Create two scenes, each including the lower light and one of the upper lights.
○ Save the drawing as EX15-1. This drawing is used throughout this chapter.

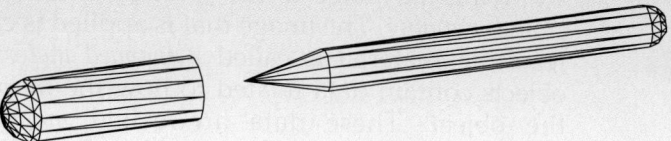

## Color/Pattern

When the **Color/Pattern** radio button is active, use the **Color** controls to change the color. By default, the **By ACI** check box is active for color. This means that the main material color is determined by the display color of the object to which you assign the material. To make the color independent, uncheck the **By ACI** check box. Then, adjust the color values using the **Red:**, **Green:**, and **Blue:** sliders.

The value set by a slider represents a percentage of 255; at 1.00 (255) there is 100% of the color. For example, setting the **Red:** slider to 1.00 adds a red value of 255, or the maximum, to the color definition. All three sliders set to 1.00 (255) creates white; all three at 0.00 (0) creates black. Using the three sliders, you can create any color you want. If you want to use the hue, saturation, luminance (HLS) color system instead of RGB, select **HLS** from the **Color System:** drop-down list.

A bitmap image can be used as a pattern. It can be used as all of the "color" or it can be blended with the color defined by the sliders (or ACI). For example, in **Figure 15-3** the checker.tga bitmap file supplied with AutoCAD has been used for a material attached to the floor of the 3DSHAPES drawing you created in Chapter 14. Any bitmap file can be used as the pattern. Either type in the path and file name in the **File Name:** text box or pick the **Find File...** button and locate the file.

Adjust the **Bitmap Blend:** setting to show more or less of the material color through the bitmap. A value of 1.00 means that none of the material color will show through the bitmap image. A value of 0.00 means that none of the bitmap image will be shown.

**Figure 15-3.**
A bitmap, such as the checker pattern, can be attached to an object. Notice the floor in this scene.

**PROFESSIONAL TIP**

Applying an image to any part of a material definition is called *mapping*. The image that is applied is called a *map*. The resulting material is called a *mapped material*. In addition, objects contain data related to how the map is rendered on the object. These data are called *mapping coordinates*. Mapping coordinates can be adjusted, as discussed later in this chapter.

## Ambient

The ambient color is the color of the object in areas that are not directly illuminated by a light. The shadows created by the object will have some of the ambient color. To adjust the ambient color, pick the **Ambient** radio button in the "new material" dialog box. By default, ambient color is locked to the main color (the **Color/Pattern** color). However, to change the ambient color, uncheck the **Lock** check box. Make sure the **By ACI** check box is not checked. Then, use the sliders in the **Color** area to adjust the ambient color.

## Reflection

The reflection is also called the *specular* reflection or highlight. This is the "shiny" part of the material. A very reflective material, such as plastic, often has a reflection that is pure white. By default, the reflection color is locked to the main color. To change the reflection color, pick the **Reflection** radio button in the "new material" dialog box. Then, uncheck the **Lock** check box. Make sure the **By ACI** check box is not checked. Then, use the sliders in the **Color** area to change the color.

A bitmap can be selected as a *reflection map.* A material like chrome, for example, often has an image attached to simulate a reflection. This makes the material appear shiny enough to reflect other objects, as chrome does. The strength of the reflection bitmap that appears on the object is based on the value set in the **Bitmap Blend:** text box. The higher this value, the clearer the mapped "reflection" is seen.

When assigning a reflection map, be sure that the reflection value is high. Also, set the roughness value low. Roughness is discussed in the next section.

## Roughness

*Roughness* is a measure of how shiny a material is. The rougher a material is, the less shiny it is. Think of cast iron. That material is very rough. Therefore, there is not much of a "shiny spot" anywhere on a cast iron object. A high roughness value creates a larger highlight area, but the reflected light is not as bright. See **Figure 15-4.**

To set the roughness, first pick the **Roughness** radio button in the "new material" dialog box. Then, use the **Value:** slider to set the value. The smaller the value, the smaller the area of highlight. A small specular highlight makes the surface appear shiny. Set a high value for **Roughness** and a low value for **Reflection** if you want the surface to appear rough or dull.

**Figure 15-4.**
Adjusting material attributes affects the rendering. A—The material on this torus has high roughness and color values and a low reflection value. B—The material on this torus has low values for roughness and color and a high reflection value.

A                              B

## Transparency

*Transparency* is a measure of how "see-through" a material is. A glass window is very transparent. However, a white plastic kitchen garbage bag is almost completely opaque. A transparency value of 1.0 makes the material appear completely transparent. Transparency falls off toward the edges of closed objects when photo real and photo raytrace renderings are used.

To change the transparency of the material, pick the **Transparency** radio button in the "new material" dialog box. Then, use the **Value:** slider to set the value.

**Figure 15-5.**
Bitmaps can be used for transparency and "bump" effects. A—The window material is completely transparent and the brick material appears "flat." B—A bitmap has been assigned to the window material as an opacity map. A different bitmap has been assigned to the brick material as a bump map. C—The opacity map used on the window material.

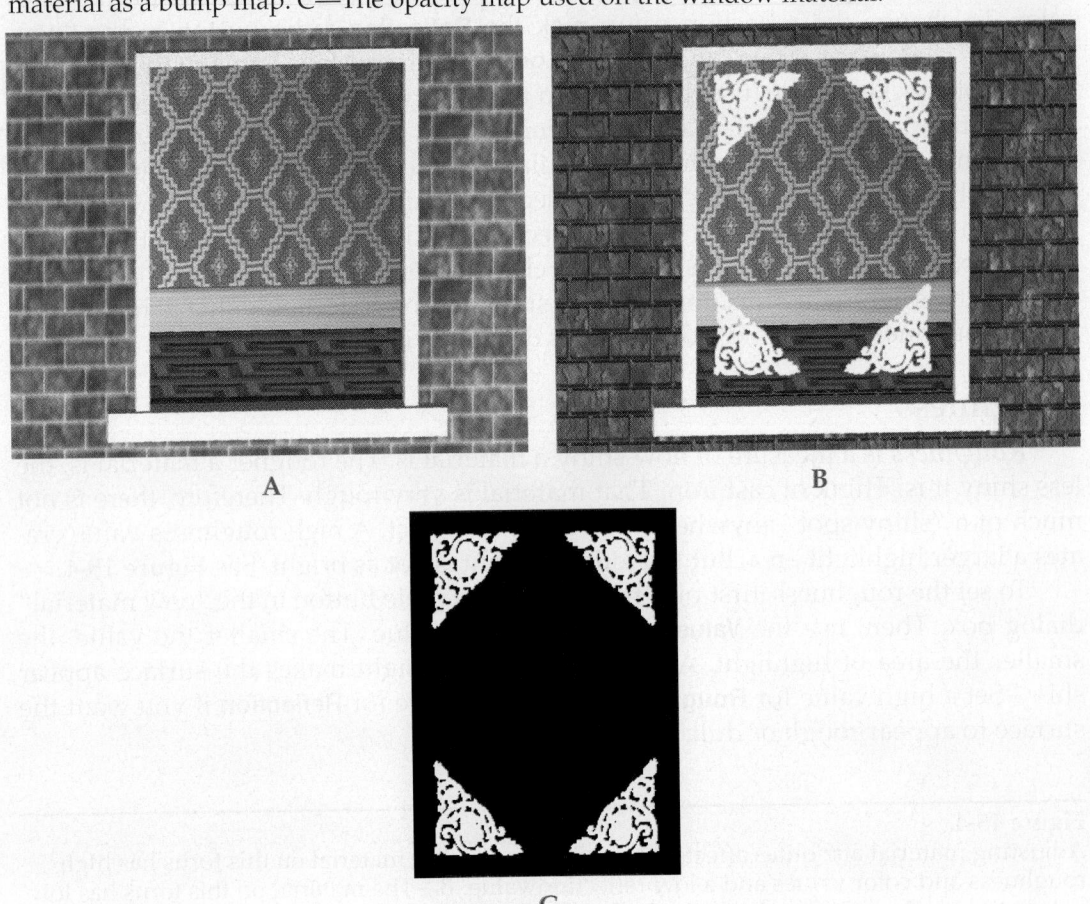

A bitmap can be assigned as a map to control transparency. This map is called an *opacity map.* See **Figure 15-5.** An opacity map is usually a black and white or grayscale image. The white areas of the bitmap are opaque and the black areas are completely transparent. Colors between black and white have varying degrees of transparency, depending on their equivalent grayscale value.

## Refraction

The *refraction* value for a material determines how much a light ray is bent when it enters a transparent material. Refraction is what makes images distort when seen through a glass of water. The higher the refraction value, the more the ray is bent. The refraction value also affects the effective transparency of a material. If a material has a very high refraction value, you may not be able to see through the material even if the transparency is set high.

To set the refraction for a material, pick the **Refraction** radio button in the "new material" dialog box. Then, use the **Value:** slider to set the value. The refraction setting only applies when creating a photo raytrace rendering.

# Bump Map

*Bump maps* are used to give the illusion of raised or lowered areas to a flat surface. For example, you can specify a brick image as the **Color/Pattern** bitmap. Then, use the same image as the **Bump Map** bitmap using the same mapping scale. Using a bump map gives a 3D appearance to the original pattern. See **Figure 15-5.** You can increase or decrease this effect by adjusting the bitmap blend value. The higher the blend value, the "deeper" the holes. Bump maps increase the rendering time.

To assign a bump map, pick the **Bump** radio button in the "new material" dialog box. Then, type the path and file name in the **File name:** text box. Or, you can pick the **Find File...** to locate and select a file. Finally, adjust the "depth" of the effect using the **Bitmap Blend:** slider.

## Changing Values

There is also a **Value:** area in the "new material" dialog box. This represents the level, or intensity, of the attribute. As you have seen, the **Value:** slider is used to adjust the transparency, roughness, and refraction of a material. However, it is also used to adjust the color/pattern, ambient, and reflection attributes.

Notice that the default **Value:** setting for **Color/Pattern** is 1.00. When combined with a 0.20 value for **Reflection**, a matte finish is produced. A polished finish is created with a 0.20 setting for **Color/Pattern** and a 1.00 setting for **Reflection**. To have the brightest reflection, keep the **Color** value low and the **Reflection** value at least 0.70.

The greater the **Ambient** value, the more pale the object appears. The default setting of 0.70 is best here, combined with a setting of 0.30 in the **Lights** dialog box. Advanced lighting is discussed in Chapter 16.

## Previewing the Material

Preview the results of your settings by picking the **Preview** button in the "new material" dialog box. AutoCAD renders a sample sphere with the material created by the settings. See **Figure 15-6.** Picking the drop-down list allows you to choose between a cube and a sphere preview. After you preview, you can make any changes necessary and preview again. If the **By ACI** box is checked, AutoCAD creates a preview of the material in a green color. The settings for reflection, roughness, etc., are reflected in the preview, but the actual color is based on an object's display color. If the color sliders have been used to set the material color, that color is reflected in the preview.

**Figure 15-6.**
A preview can be generated of the material.

Preview of the material

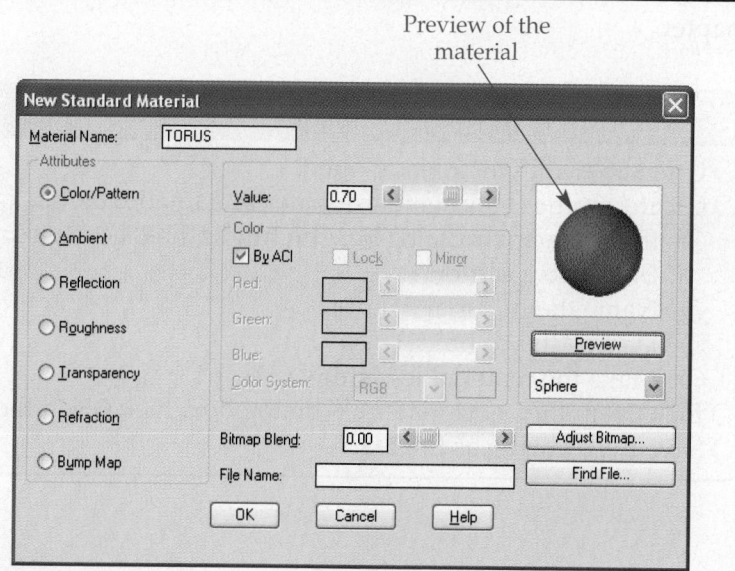

## Other Features of the Materials Dialog Box

There are several other features of the **Materials** dialog box that help you work with materials. These features are:

- **Preview.** Picking this button displays a sphere or cube with the material that has been selected in the **Materials:** list. To choose between a cube and a sphere preview, select the **Preview** drop-down list and pick the type.
- **Materials Library... button.** Picking this displays the **Materials Library** dialog box. This dialog box is discussed later in this chapter.
- **Select.** Picking this button returns to the graphics screen and allows you to pick an object. The dialog box returns and the material assigned to the object is listed at the bottom of the dialog box.
- **Modify... button.** Picking this button opens the "modify material" dialog box. This is the same as the "new material" dialog box and allows you to adjust material attributes for the highlighted material.
- **Duplicate... button.** Picking this button opens the "new material" dialog box. The settings for the material highlighted in the **Materials:** list are automatically placed in the "new material" dialog box. This allows you to create a new, but similar, material by editing the attributes.

The **Attach**, **Detach**, **By ACI...**, and **By Layer...** buttons are used for applying materials to or removing materials from objects. These features are discussed later in this chapter.

# Granite, Marble, and Wood

When creating a material from scratch, you can select from **Standard**, **Granite**, **Marble**, and **Wood** types. These are found in the **New...** drop-down list in the **Materials** dialog box. Think of these options as "templates" for creating a new material. Creating a new **Standard** material has been discussed to this point. Creating the other materials is basically the same, with some different attributes to set. **Figure 15-7** shows the different attributes for granite, marble, and wood, and samples of each. Select the type of material and pick the **New...** button to open the **New** *(type)* **Material** dialog box.

**Figure 15-7.**
The various material "templates" have different attributes available.

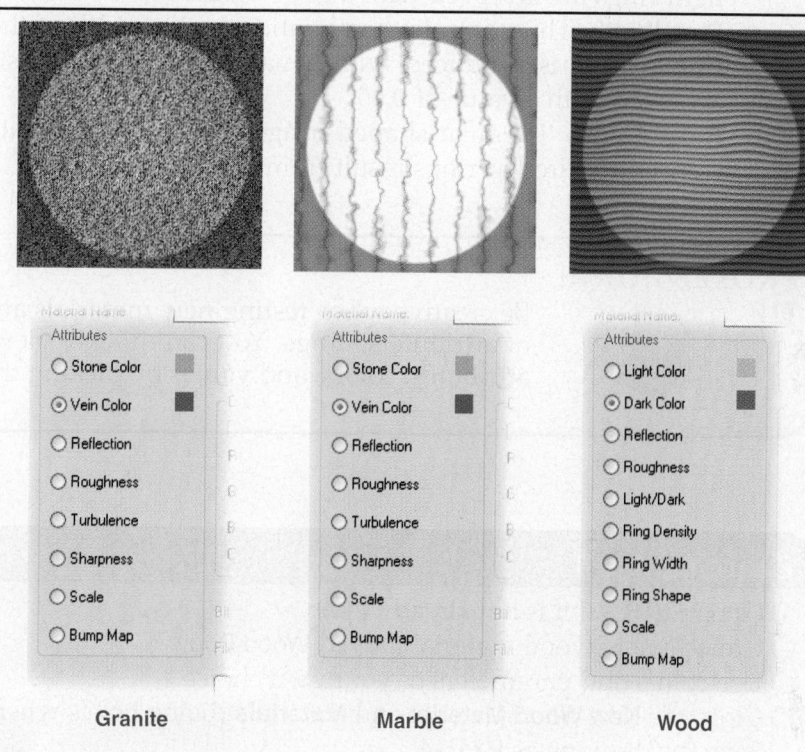

Granite       Marble       Wood

## Granite

To create a granite material, pick **Granite**, then pick the **New...** button in the **Materials** dialog box. The **New Granite Material** dialog box is displayed. Granite can be composed of up to four colors. If you want only one or two colors, set the colors you do not need to a **Value:** of zero. **Sharpness** determines how blurred or distinct the different granite colors are. A value of 1.0 produces distinct colors and a value of 0 creates blurred colors.

## Marble

To create a marble material, pick **Marble**, then pick the **New...** button in the **Materials** dialog box. The **New Marble Material** dialog box is displayed. Marble allows you to choose the stone color and the color of the veins that run through the stone. **Turbulence** refers to how much vein color is present and the amount of swirling the veins display. A higher turbulence value increases swirling and vein color.

# Wood

To create a wood material, pick **Wood**, then pick the **New...** button in the **Material** dialog box. The **New Wood Material** dialog box is displayed and provides several attributes that help refine the appearance of the wood color and grain.

- **Light Color.** Controls the color of light wood. This is usually the "base" color of the wood.
- **Dark Color.** Controls the color of dark wood. This is usually the "ring" color.
- **Light/Dark.** This controls the ratio of light to dark rings in the wood. A value of 1.0 creates a material with mostly light color. A value of 0.0 creates a material with mostly dark color.
- **Ring Density.** This is a scale that sets the number of rings in the wood. Fine, tight rings are achieved with a large value.
- **Ring Width.** This controls the variation in the width of the rings. A variety of ring widths is produced with a value of 1.00. A consistent ring width is achieved with a value of 0.00.
- **Ring Shape.** Irregular-shaped rings are produced with a value of 1.00. Concentric circular rings result from a value of 0.00.

---

**PROFESSIONAL TIP**

Be creative when testing new materials and try out a variety of attribute settings. You can quickly view the result of new attributes, colors, and values by picking the **Preview** button.

---

## Exercise 15-4

○ Open EX15-3 if it is not already open.
○ Create a new wood material named Wood Body.
○ Use colors and parameters of your own choice.
○ Close the **New Wood Material** and **Materials** dialog boxes when done.
○ Save the drawing as EX15-4.

---

## Assigning Materials to Objects

Once materials are created, they must be assigned to the objects in the drawing. AutoCAD refers to this process as attaching materials. Removing a material from an object is called detaching a material. There are several ways to attach materials to the objects in your drawing. These are initiated from the **Materials** dialog box.

The easiest method of attaching a material is by using the **Attach<** button. First, highlight the material name in the **Materials** dialog box. Then, pick the button. The graphics screen is displayed. Pick the objects to which you want the material attached. Press [Enter] to return to the dialog box. The material highlighted in the dialog box is now attached to the selected objects.

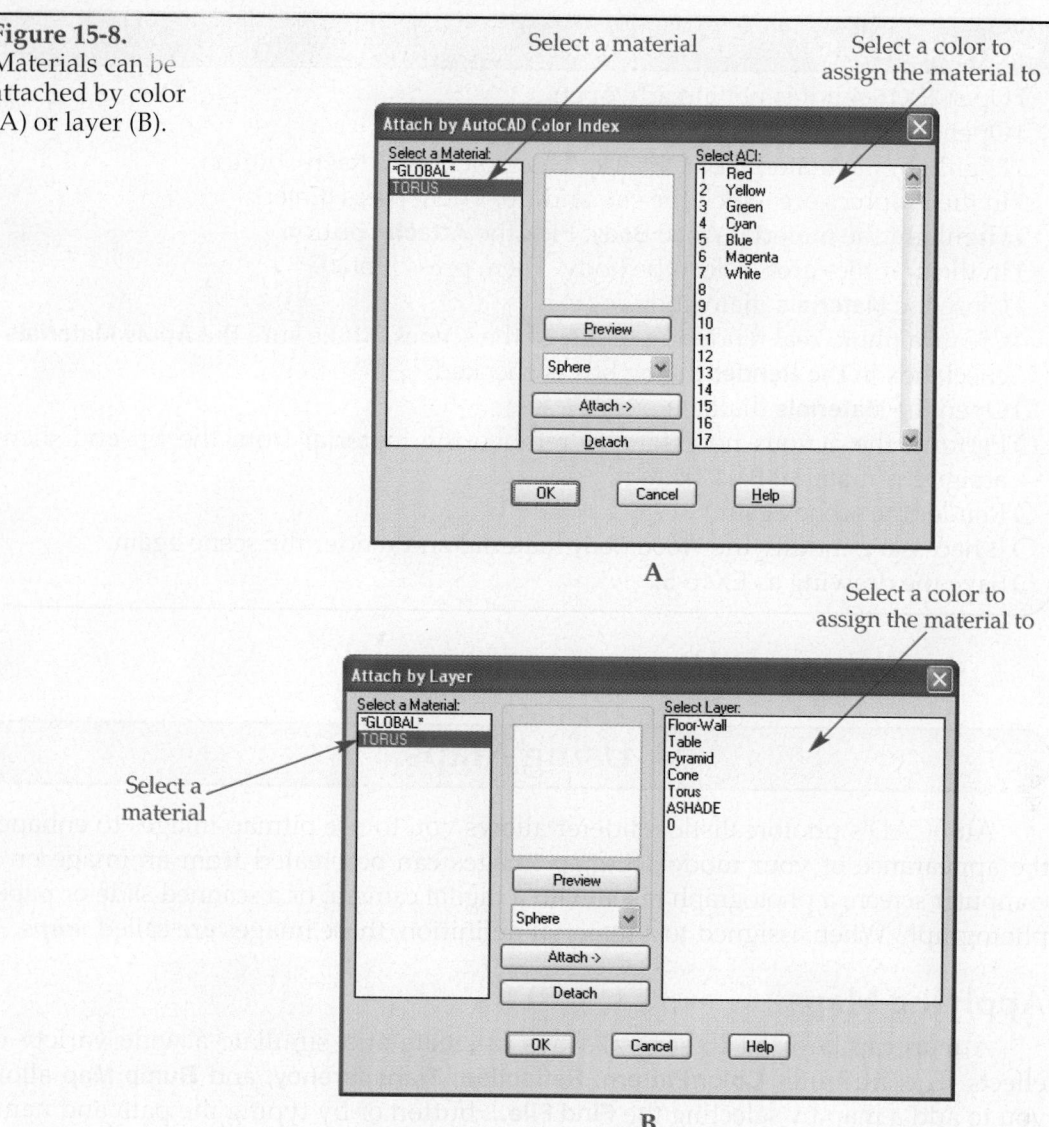

**Figure 15-8.**
Materials can be attached by color (A) or layer (B).

Select a material

Select a color to assign the material to

A

Select a color to assign the material to

Select a material

B

You can also attach a material to all objects in the drawing that share the same display color. First, highlight the material in the **Materials** dialog box. Then, pick the **By ACI...** button. The **Attach by AutoCAD Color Index** dialog box is opened, **Figure 15-8A.** The material highlighted is attached to all objects in the drawing with the color that you pick from the **Select ACI:** list. All existing and any new objects created with that color will have the material attached to them. You can attach the same material to several colors.

A material can be attached to all objects on a given layer. First, highlight the material in the **Materials** dialog box. Then, pick the **By Layer...** button. The **Attach by Layer** dialog box is opened, **Figure 15-8B.** The material highlighted is attached to all objects on the layer you select. All existing and any new objects created on that layer will have the material attached to them. You can assign the same material to several layers.

Once an object has a material attached to it, you can attach a different material using any of the methods described above. However, if you want to remove the material from an object, use the **Detach<** button in the **Materials** dialog box. Picking this button returns to the graphics screen. Pick the objects from which you want a material removed. It does not matter which material was highlighted in the **Materials** dialog box. Press [Enter] when done selecting objects to return to the dialog box. The selected objects no longer have materials attached to them.

## Using Maps

AutoCAD's photorealistic renderer allows you to use bitmap images to enhance the appearance of your model. Bitmap images can be created from an image on a computer screen, a photograph taken with a digital camera, or a scanned slide or paper photograph. When assigned to a material definition, these images are called *maps.*

### Applying Maps

A map can be used in several ways to create and simulate a wide variety of effects. The attributes **Color/Pattern**, **Reflection**, **Transparency**, and **Bump Map** allow you to add a map by selecting the **Find File...** button or by typing the path and name of the bitmap in the **File Name:** text box. Maps can be used for the following purposes.

- **Texture maps.** These maps are used to define object and surface colors and patterns. Use the **Color/Pattern** attribute setting to specify these maps.
- **Reflection maps.** Also called *environment maps,* these maps simulate a reflection on the surface of a shiny object. **Figure 15-9** shows one object rendered before and after applying the reflection map file named sunset.tga. Use the **Reflection** attribute to specify a reflection map.
- **Opacity maps.** These maps specify areas of opacity and transparency. Any black area in the map is transparent when applied to the object. Any area that is white is opaque. For example, if the bitmap image is a black circle in the middle of a white rectangle, the surface appears to have a hole in it where the circle maps onto the object. Use the **Transparency** attribute to specify an opacity map.
- **Bump maps.** These maps create the appearance of raised areas similar to an embossed effect. Use the **Bump Map** attribute to specify a bitmap to use as a bump map.

If you plan to work with 3D models and apply photorealistic textures and patterns, you should begin collecting a variety of bitmap images to use with those models. For example, architects and interior designers use a variety of carpeting textures, wallpaper designs, flooring tiles, vinyls, and window covering samples. These images can all be easily created using one of the wide variety of digital cameras on the market. Images can also be purchased or downloaded from the Internet. AutoCAD comes with a number of TGA bitmap files that can be used as maps.

A                                                    B

> **NOTE**    Mapped materials will only display correctly when the photo real or photo raytrace rendering option is used.

## Adjusting Bitmaps

All of the "new material" dialog boxes provide similar options for adjusting maps. Each dialog box allows you to select bitmap textures and provides a means to adjust and scale the bitmap texture on the object. First, assign a bitmap to an attribute. Then, pick the **Adjust Bitmap...** button in the "new material" dialog box to display the **Adjust Material Bitmap Placement** dialog box. See **Figure 15-10.**

The **Offset:** option controls the location of the bitmap on the object(s) and the **Scale:** option controls the size of the bitmap. You may see the results of your adjustments easier by selecting the **Cube** option for the **Preview** image. Offset and scale values are shown as **U** and **V**. The **U** value represents a horizontal offset/scale and the **V** value represents the vertical offset/scale.

**Figure 15-10.**
The **Adjust Material Bitmap Placement** dialog box.

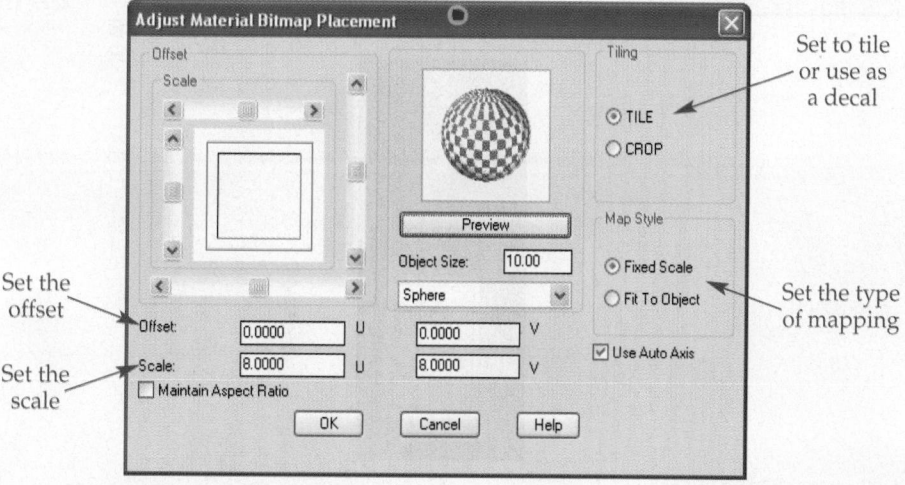

For example, enter .2 in the **Offset: U** text box and press [Enter]. Notice that the red box remains in place and the box with the magenta bottom and right side moves to the right in the **Scale** image tile. You have just moved the bitmap texture's origin on the object.

Now, pick the **CROP** radio button in the **Tiling** area. To see how this will appear when the object is rendered, pick the **Preview** button. When **CROP** is selected, all areas outside the bitmap are rendered in the material colors. This is also called a *decal map*. See **Figure 15-11.** If you want the entire object covered with the bitmap after the origin has been adjusted, pick the **TILE** radio button. The pattern (image) will be repeated all over the object.

The bitmap image can be scaled using the **Scale: U** and **V** text boxes or by adjusting slider bars. If you want the **U** and **V** values of the bitmap scale to remain proportional to each other, check the **Maintain Aspect Ratio** check box. Then, when you change one scale value, the other automatically changes. Set the scale values to .5 and do a preview. Then, set the scale values to 2.0 and do another preview. How is the bitmap affected?

The **Map Style** area of the **Adjust Material Bitmap Placement** dialog box contains two options. The **Fixed Scale** option is only used for "tiled" bitmaps, such as a quarry tile image applied to a countertop. The U and V scale values control at what scale the bitmap will be tiled onto the object being rendered. The **Fit to Object** option is used

**Figure 15-11.**
A decal map is created by cropping the bitmap. In this example, the bitmap is offset. A—The dialog box settings. B—The rendered image. C—A label on a bottle is an example of when a decal map might be used.

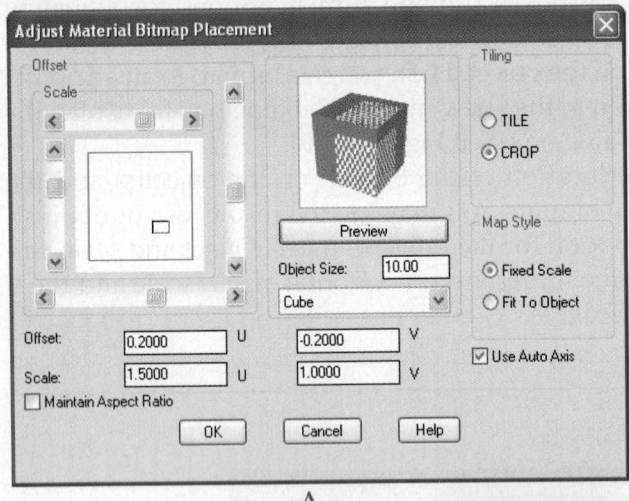

A

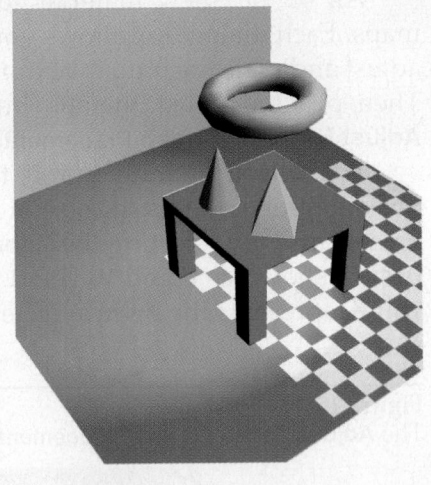

B

C

AutoCAD and its Applications—Advanced

when placing a single image bitmap onto an object. For example, you would use the **Fit to Object** option on a bitmap image of a mountain used in a living room model as a painting. The biggest difference between the two options is that increasing the U/V scale with **Fit to Object** decreases the relative size of the image, while increasing the relative size with the **Fixed Scale** option. Set the scale values to .5 with **Fit to Object** selected and do a preview. Use the same scale with **Fixed Scale** selected and do another preview. How are the two previews different?

When checked, the **Use Auto Axis** check box places the bitmap image on the XY, YZ, and XZ surfaces of the object. If this box is not checked, the bitmap image is only applied to the XY oriented surface of the object. This placement is reflected in the preview when **Cube** is selected.

> **NOTE**
>
> The values of **U** and **V** are used for horizontal and vertical adjustments to bitmaps, relative to the object. They are called *mapping axes* and are independent from the WCS and UCS coordinate axes.

### Exercise 15-6

○ Open EX15-5 if it is not on your screen.

○ Open the **Materials** dialog box. Highlight the Blue Plastic material and pick the **Modify...** button.

○ In the **Modify Standard Material** dialog box, pick the **Color/Pattern** radio button. Then, pick the **Find File...** button.

○ If the AutoCAD Textures folder is not displayed, navigate to it. It is located in the \Documents and Settings\\*username*\Local Settings\Application Data\Autodesk\AutoCAD 2004\R16.0\enu folder. Then, select the file usflag.tga and pick the **Open** button.

○ In the **Modify Standard Material** dialog box, pick the **Adjust Bitmap...** button.

○ In the **Adjust Material Bitmap Placement** dialog box, pick the **CROP** radio button. Then, set the preview shape to **Cube** and pick the **Preview** button.

○ Pick the **Fixed Scale** radio button. Also, enter 2 in the **Scale: U** and **V** text boxes. Make another preview.

○ Close the **Adjust Material Bitmap Placement**, **Modify Standard Material**, and **Materials** dialog boxes.

○ Create a photo real rendering of one of the scenes.

○ Save the drawing as EX15-6.

## Mapping Textures to Objects

If a mapped material is created, it is not enough to simply attach the material to an object. In addition, the material must be properly mapped to the object. *Mapping* is the process of specifying the orientation of a material on the surface of an object. This process is also known as applying or adjusting *mapping coordinates*. Mapping is important for materials with bitmap images, wood materials, granite materials, and marble materials. When one of these types of materials is selected and attached to an object, it is mapped in a default direction. Mapping allows you to adjust the material's scale, rotation, and to which surface the material is being applied. Once mapping coordinates are set for an object, they are retained until changed, even if the material is removed.

It is always best to preview the material or do a quick rendering to see if it is mapped to your liking. If not, change the offset, scale, and tiling in the material definition first. If sides of the object are not rendered properly, as in a stretched or "streaked" material, you can use mapping to adjust the texture. Use mapping to rotate the currently assigned texture or to move it to a different plane.

The **Mapping** dialog box is accessed by picking the **Mapping** button on the **Render** toolbar, selecting **Mapping...** from the **Render** cascading menu in the **View** pull-down menu, or typing SETUV at the Command: prompt. Mapping applies to individual objects, so when the command is invoked, a Select objects: prompt appears on the Command: line. Pick the object(s) to map and press [Enter]. The **Mapping** dialog box is displayed. See **Figure 15-12**.

SETUV

View
  → Render
    → Mapping...

Render
toolbar

Mapping

Figure 15-12.
The **Mapping** dialog box allows you to pick mapping planes and surfaces on which textures are applied.

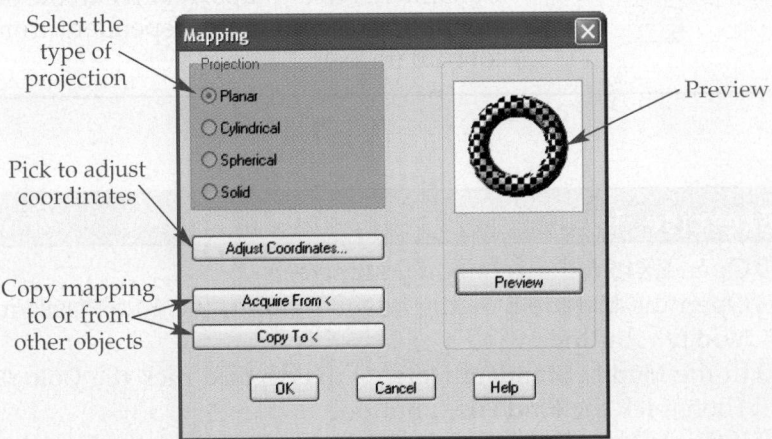

Select the type of projection

Pick to adjust coordinates

Copy mapping to or from other objects

Preview

> **NOTE**
>
> The adjustments made when mapping a material, such as scale, are cumulative with adjustments made to a bitmap in the **Adjust Bitmap Placement** dialog box.

## Setting the Type of Mapping

There are four types of projection that can be used for mapping. In the **Mapping** dialog box, select the **Planar**, **Cylindrical**, **Spherical**, or **Solid** radio button. A planar projection places the material flat onto a plane. A cylindrical projection "wraps" the material around an axis. A spherical projection "pushes" the image out from a center point. Pick the type of projection and then pick the **Preview** button to see the results. These options specify how the material is projected onto the selected object. If the mapping appears correct, pick **OK** to exit the **Mapping** dialog box.

If another object in your model has the mapping variables you wish to use, pick the **Acquire From<** button, then pick the other object. If you want to give the mapping properties of the current object to another, pick the **Copy To<** button and pick the other object(s).

# Adjusting Mapping Coordinates

If the preview of the mapping in the **Mapping** dialog box does not appear correct, you can refine the mapping coordinates. After selecting a projection, pick the **Adjust Coordinates...** button to open the **Adjust (projection) Coordinates** dialog box. This dialog box varies slightly for each type of projection. The **Adjust Planar Coordinates** dialog box is shown in **Figure 15-13**.

The **Parallel Plane** area in the **Adjust Planar Coordinates** dialog allows you to choose to which plane the map is projected. The three preset planes include the world coordinate system (WCS) XY plane, the WCS XZ plane, or the WCS YZ plane. In addition, you can pick any plane by selecting the **Picked Plane** option or the **Pick Points<** button. Picking either of these returns you to the drawing screen and you are prompted to pick three corners of the plane. Use object snaps for accuracy.

Place the lower left corner of the mapping plane: *(pick lower-left corner)*
Place the lower right corner of the mapping plane: *(pick lower-right corner)*
Place the upper left corner of the mapping plane: *(pick upper-left corner)*

The **Adjust Planar Coordinates** dialog box is redisplayed and the **Picked Plane** radio button is on.

---

**Figure 15-13.**
The **Adjust Planar Coordinates** dialog box is used to position a bitmap being used on an object. This dialog box is similar to the dialog boxes used with **Cylindrical** and **Spherical** projections.

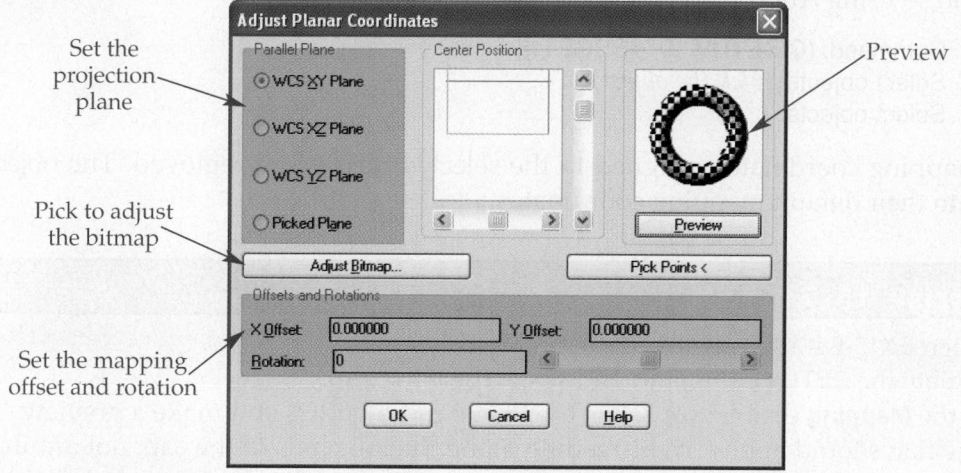

NOTE

If the points you pick are the same as one of the WCS orthographic planes, AutoCAD saves this as the WCS axis. When the **Adjust Planar Coordinates** dialog box is returned, the button indicates the selected WCS plane, rather than the **Picked Plane**.

The **Center Position** area of the **Adjust (projection) Coordinates** dialog box indicates the orientation of the object on the current projection plane. The object is displayed as red lines. The current projection for the mapped image shows as a blue outline with a small tick mark on the top. The blue outline represents the extent of the object's parallel projection. The right edge of the projection is displayed in green. Use the scroll bars to change the position of the projection axis.

The **Adjust Bitmap...** button in the **Adjust (projection) Coordinates** dialog box displays the **Adjust Object Bitmap Placement** dialog box. This is the same dialog discussed for the **RMAT** command, with the addition of the **DEFAULT** radio button in the **Tiling** area. This radio button uses the default tiling set in the material definition. The **TILE** and **CROP** buttons override the tiling set in the material definition.

The **Offsets and Rotations** area in the **Adjust (projection) Coordinates** dialog box allows you to offset or rotate the mapping coordinates. The **X Offset:** and **Y Offset:** adjustments shift the mapping similar to how the U/V offset adjustments shifted the bitmap image earlier in this chapter. However, these are X/Y offsets because they adjust the map plane, not the bitmap image.

If **Cylindrical** projection is selected, the **Adjust Coordinates...** button displays the **Adjust Cylindrical Coordinates** dialog box. This provides the same options as the "planar" dialog, except the cylindrical shape is displayed in the **Central Axis Position** area and the **Pick Points** button is used to set the **Picked Axis** projection.

If **Spherical** projection is selected, the **Adjust Coordinates...** button displays the **Adjust Spherical Coordinates** dialog box. The spherical shape is displayed in the **Polar Axis Position** area, and the red mesh of the object is shown perpendicular to the current axis. A green radius line indicates the wrap line, and the blue circle is the projection axis.

## Removing Mapping Coordinates

If for any reason you need to detach mapping coordinates from an object, you must do so using AutoLISP at the Command: prompt as follows.

Command: **(C:SETUV "D" (SSGET))**↵
Select objects: *(pick the object)*
Select objects: ↵

The mapping coordinates assigned to the selected objects are removed. The objects revert to their default mapping coordinates.

---

### Exercise 15-7

○ Open EX15-6 if it is not already open.
○ Initiate the **SETUV** command and select the pen cap.
○ In the **Mapping** dialog box, select the **Planar** radio button and make a preview.
○ The flag should appear right-reading along the long axis of the cap, not around the cap. If not, make adjustments to the mapping coordinates as needed. Adjust the map as needed by accessing the **Adjust Object Bitmap Placement** dialog box through the **Adjust Planar Coordinates** dialog box.
○ Adjust mapping coordinates for the Wood Body material as needed.
○ Create a photo real rendering of one scene. See the sample shown below.
○ Save the drawing as EX15-7.

---

AutoCAD and its Applications—Advanced

A *material library* is a saved file with definitions for one or more materials. Any material in this library can be recalled and assigned to an object without having to recreate the material. The standard AutoCAD material library is a file named render.mli located in the user's AutoCAD support folder. There is also a small library file called mini.mli in the folder. The materials listed in the **Current Library** area of the **Materials Library** dialog box are contained in these two files. This dialog box is used to import/export materials and to perform "housekeeping" functions.

The **Materials Library** dialog box is accessed by picking the **Materials Library** button on the **Render** toolbar, selecting **Materials Library...** from the **Render** cascading menu in the **View** pull-down menu, or typing MATLIB at the Command: prompt. In addition, you can pick the **Materials Library...** button in the **Materials** dialog box.

```
MATLIB

View
 ➡ Render
  ➡ Materials
     Library...

Render
toolbar

[icon]

Materials Library
```

## Using Existing Materials

The **Current Drawing** area is on the left side of the **Materials Library** dialog box. This list displays all the materials defined in or "loaded into" the current drawing. See **Figure 15-14.** The **Current Library** area on the right side of the dialog box displays all of the materials in the current library file. The name of the current library file appears in the **Current Library** drop-down list. Notice that the file name appears, but not the .mli extension.

You can use a material from the current library by highlighting the material name in the **Current Library** list and picking the **<-Import** button. This copies the material from the library list to the **Current Drawing** list, making it available in the current drawing. That material can then be attached to objects using the options in the **Materials** dialog box, as discussed earlier.

You can delete a material from the current drawing. Highlight the name in the **Current Drawing** list. Then, pick the **Delete** button. The material is removed from the drawing. If the selected material is attached to an object, a warning is displayed, however the material is still deleted. You are allowed to delete materials that are attached to objects. However, if the definition is not saved to a library, it is lost. Be careful when deleting materials. The **Purge** button removes *all* materials not attached to objects from the current drawing.

**Figure 15-14.**
The **Materials Library** dialog box.

Materials in the current drawing

Preview of the selected material

Current library file

Materials available in the current library

Use to open or save a library

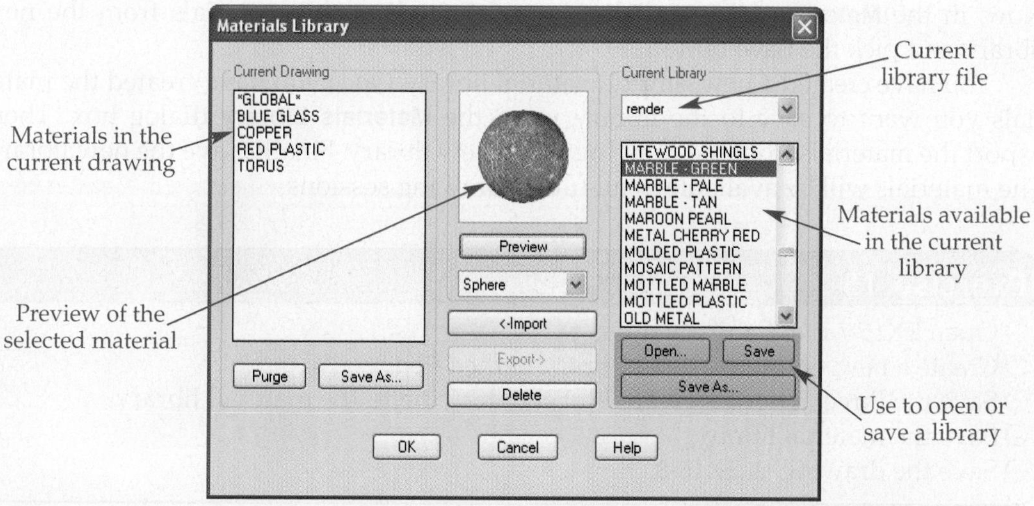

You may want to use a different library file than the default render.mli or mini.mli. For example, you may have created unique libraries for different projects or customers. A different library file (.mli) can be used by picking the **Open...** button, which displays the **Library File** dialog box. Change to the folder where the library file is located. Then, highlight the file name and pick **OK**. The materials in that library file are now displayed in the **Current Library** list.

Any material libraries that have been opened appear in the **Current Library** drop-down list. You can quickly change the current library by selecting a different library in the drop-down list.

## Saving Materials to a Library

If you want to use a material that you have created in the current drawing for other applications, you need to export it to the library file. To do so, first highlight the material in the **Current Drawing** list and then pick the **Export->** button. The material name appears in the **Current Library** list. Next, pick the **Save** button and AutoCAD saves the current library file with the new material in it. You can also select the **Save As...** button, which displays the **Library File** dialog box. This allows you to save a copy of the current library file with a new name. The new library file is also set as the current library file when you do this.

If you make changes to the library list in the **Materials Library** dialog box and pick **OK** without saving, the **Library Modification** dialog box appears. This gives you the chance to save the changes, discard the changes, or cancel and return to the **Materials Library** dialog box. Pick the appropriate button and continue.

You can delete a material from the current library file. Highlight the name in the **Current Library** list. Then, pick the **Delete** button on the left side of the dialog box below the **Current Drawing** list. The material is removed from the library. Be sure to save the library file or the material will be in the library the next time it is opened. The current material library file is unaffected by the **Purge** button.

## Creating a New Material Library

You may find it very useful to have several material libraries, each containing similar materials. For example, an architect may want to create a library for fabric, one for wood, and another for tile and brick. A mechanical drafter may want to create a library for painted finishes and another for anodized finishes.

To create a new material library, open the **Materials Library** dialog box. Then, pick the **Save As...** button. It does not matter which library is current. In the **Library File** dialog box, enter the name of the library you are creating and pick the **Save** button. Now, in the **Materials Library** dialog box, delete all of the materials from the new library and pick the **Save** button.

You have created a new, empty material library. Once you have created the materials you want to save to the library, open the **Materials Library** dialog box. Then, export the materials from the drawing to the new library. Finally, save the new library. The materials will be available in all future drawing sessions.

### Exercise 15-8

○ Open EX15-7 if not already open.
○ Create a new, empty material library named Pen.
○ Save the three materials created for the drawing to the material library.
○ Save the material library.
○ Save the drawing as EX15-8.

AutoCAD and its Applications—Advanced

## Chapter Test

*Answer the following questions on a separate sheet of paper.*

1. Define *roughness*.
2. Define *refraction*.
3. Which dialog box allows you to specify the shininess and roughness of a surface?
4. What is the relationship between the numerical value of roughness and the size of the highlight on a shiny surface?
5. When working with materials, which attributes allow the use of a bitmap?
6. What is the function of a bump map?
7. List the steps involved in loading a material, customizing the material, and applying it to a surface.
8. What is *mapping*?
9. How do you remove mapping coordinates from an object?
10. What is a *mapped material*?
11. List the four types of materials that can be created in AutoCAD.
12. What are the two color systems that can be used to define a material's color?
13. By default, the **Lock** check box is checked for both the ambient and reflection attributes. What does this mean?
14. What is the purpose of the **Bitmap Blend:** setting?
15. Briefly describe how to create a new, empty material library.

## Drawing Problems

1. In this problem, you will draw a basic 3D object, place lights and create scenes, create a material, and render the drawing.
   A. Begin a new drawing.
   B. Draw a solid cube. Use the **3DORBIT** command to display a pictorial view with perspective projection. Save the view.
   C. Add two point lights above the cube, one to the right and one to the left.
   D. Create two scenes, each containing one light.
   E. Create a new wood material. The light and dark colors should both be light beige, but slightly different. Make other attribute settings of your choice.
   F. Attach the material to the cube.
   G. Create a photo real rendering of one scene.
   H. Adjust the scale of the wood definition as needed.
   I. Create a photo real rendering of the second scene.
   J. Save the drawing as P15-1.

2. Open drawing P14-1. If you have not completed the problem, do so now. Then, create and attach the following materials. When done, save a photo real rendering to a file and save the drawing as P15-2.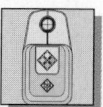

| Object | Material type | Overall color |
|--------|---------------|---------------|
| Box | Standard | Green with a decal map of your choice |
| Pyramid | Marble | Light blue stone; light purple vein |
| Wedge | Standard | Orange, very shiny |
| Cone | Wood | Light brown and dark red |
| Dome | Granite | Green; use only three colors |
| Dish | Wood | Two colors of your choice; assign a bump map |
| Sphere | Granite | Four colors of your choice; assign a bump map |

3. Open any solid or surface model from a previous chapter.
   A. Create a wood material and attach it to the object(s).
   B. Save a photo real rendering to a file.
   C. Create a granite or marble material and attach it to the object(s).
   D. Save a photo real rendering to a file.
   E. Create a standard material to represent plastic and attach it to the object(s).
   F. Save a photo real rendering to a file.
   G. Create a new, empty material library. Copy the materials you created to the library and save it.
   H. Save the drawing as P15-3.

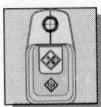

4. Open any solid or surface model from a previous chapter, other than the one used in Problem 3.
   A. Create four materials to represent metals of different colors.
   B. Create four materials to represent plastics. Use the same colors as for the metals.
   C. Make seven copies of the object(s) in your drawing.
   D. Apply a material to each of the eight objects (or group of objects).
   E. Save a photo real rendering to a file.
   F. Create a new, empty material library. Copy the materials you created to the library and save it.
   G. Save the drawing as P15-4.

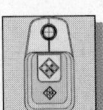

5. Open Problem 9 of Chapter 6. This is a solid model of a desk organizer.
   A. Place two distant lights around the model.
   B. Place two spotlights around the model.
   C. Create three different standard materials representing plastic. Each material should be of a different color and transparency.
   D. Save the materials in a new, blank material library named Plastics.
   E. Attach one of the materials to the desk organizer and save a photo raytrace rendering to file.
   F. Similarly, attach the other two materials and save photo raytrace renderings to files.
   G. Save the drawing as P15-5.

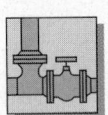

6. Open Problem 1 from Chapter 8. Do the following.
   A. Create materials representing PVC, cast iron, and copper. You may be able to use materials in the default material library as starting points for your materials.
   B. Create a new, empty material library named Pipe.
   C. Save the three material definitions in the material library. Save the library.
   D. Make two copies of the tee pipe fitting.
   E. Attach one of the three materials to each fitting.
   F. Add lights as needed.
   G. Save a photo real rendering to a file.
   H. Save the drawing as P15-6.

# Reflectivity

The angle at which light rays are reflected off a surface is called the *angle of reflection.* The angle of reflection is always equal to the angle of incidence. Refer to **Figure 16-2.**

The "brightness" of light reflected from an object is actually the number of light rays that reach your eyes. A surface that reflects a bright light, such as a mirror, is reflecting most of the light rays that strike it. The amount of reflection you see is called the *highlight.* The highlight is determined by the angle of the viewpoint relative to the angle of incidence. Refer to **Figure 16-2.**

The surface of the object affects how light is reflected. A smooth surface has a high specular factor. The *specular factor* indicates the number of light rays that have the same angle of reflection. Surfaces that are not smooth have a low specular factor. These surfaces are called *matte.* Matte surfaces *diffuse,* or "spread out," the light as it strikes the surface. This means that few of the light rays have the same angle of reflection. **Figure 16-3** illustrates the difference between matte and high specular finishes. Surfaces can also vary in *roughness.* Roughness is a measure of the polish on a surface. This also affects how diffused the reflected light is.

**Figure 16-3.**
Matte surfaces produce diffuse light. This is also referred to as a low specular factor. Shiny surfaces reflect light evenly and have a high specular factor.

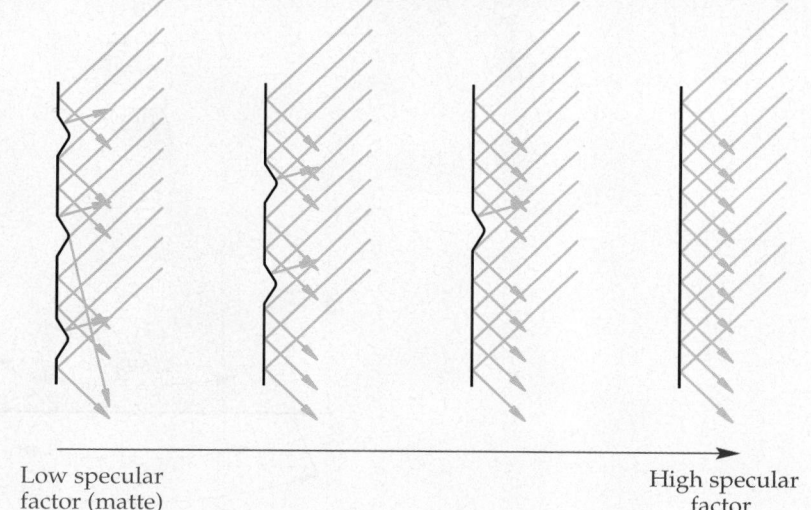

Low specular factor (matte)

High specular factor

# Hotspot and Falloff

A spotlight produces a cone of light. The *hotspot* is the central portion of the cone, where the light is brightest. See **Figure 16-4.** The *falloff* is the outer portion of the cone, where the light begins to blend to shadow. The hotspot and falloff of a spotlight are not affected by the distance the light is from an object. Spotlights are the only lights with hotspot and falloff properties.

# Attenuation

The farther an object is from a point light or spotlight, the less light will reach the object. See **Figure 16-5.** The intensity of light decreases over distance. This decrease is called *attenuation.* In AutoCAD, attenuation only applies to point lights and spotlights. Often, attenuation is called falloff. However, do not confuse this with the falloff of a spotlight, which is the outer edge of the cone of illumination. The following attenuation settings are available.

- **None.** Applies the same light intensity regardless of distance. In other words, no attenuation is calculated.

**Figure 16-4.**
The hotspot of a spotlight is the area that receives the most light. The falloff receives light, but less than the hotspot. A—The smaller cone is the hotspot. The larger cone is the falloff. B—Hotspot and falloff are set as an angular measurement.

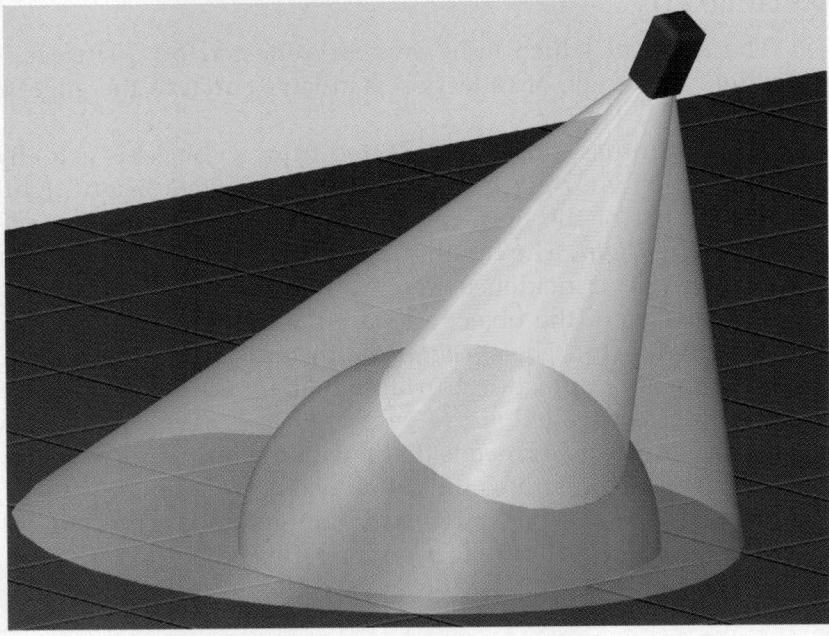

A

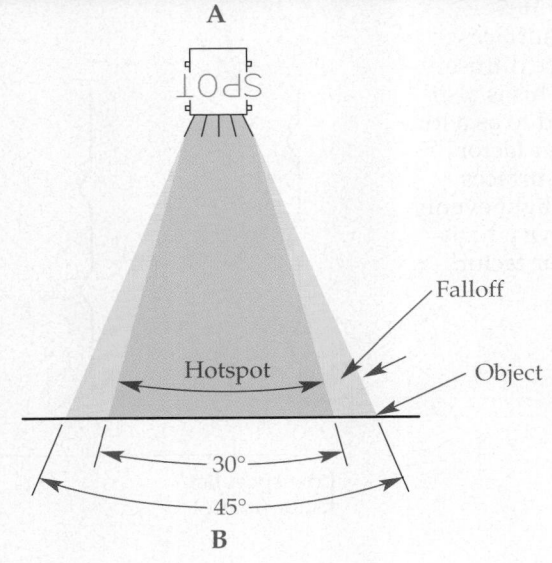

B

**Figure 16-5.**
This is an anodized, brushed-aluminum bracket. Notice how the portion of the bracket nearest to you receives full illumination while the back of the bracket receives less illumination. This decrease in illumination over distance is the attenuation of the light.

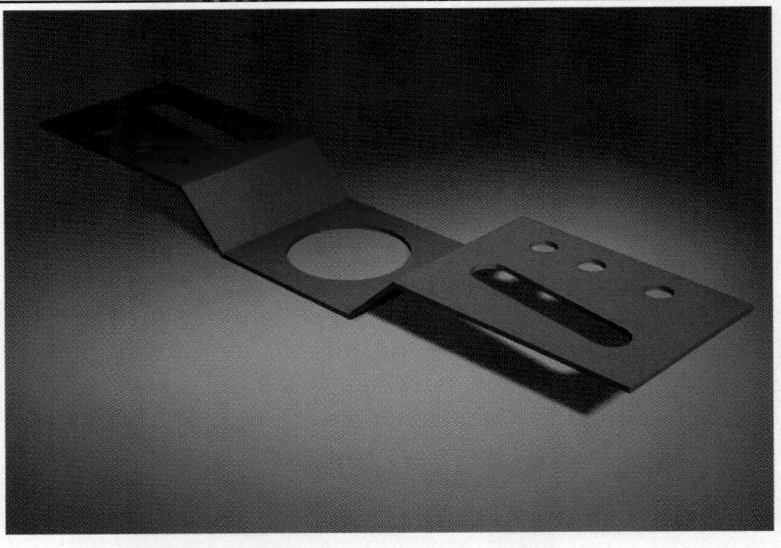

- **Inverse Linear.** The illumination of an object decreases in inverse proportion to the distance. For example, if an object is two units from the light, it receives 1/2 of the full light. If the object is four units away, it receives 1/4 of the full light.

- **Inverse Square.** The illumination of an object decreases in inverse proportion to the square of the distance. For example, if an object is two units from the light, it receives $(1/2)^2$, or 1/4, of the full light. If the object is four units away, it receives $(1/4)^2$, or 1/16, of the full light. As you can see, attenuation is greater for each unit of distance with the **Inverse Square** option than with the **Inverse Linear** option.

**PROFESSIONAL TIP**

The intensity of the Sun's rays do not diminish from one point on Earth to another. They are weakened by the angle at which they strike Earth. Therefore, since distant lights are similar to the Sun, attenuation is not a factor with distant lights.

## AutoCAD Lights

As you learned in Chapter 14, AutoCAD uses four types of lighting. Ambient light is like natural light. It is the same intensity everywhere. A distant light is a directed light source with parallel light rays. A point light is like a lightbulb, shining out in all directions. A spotlight is like a distant light, but it projects in a cone shape. In this section, you will learn how to adjust the various properties of AutoCAD lights.

### Ambient Light Properties and Settings

Ambient light has two properties that can be set—color and intensity. Both settings are made in the **Lights** dialog box, **Figure 16-6.** To change the intensity of ambient light, type a value in the **Intensity:** text box. You can also use the slider to change the value. The maximum value is 1.00. However, ambient light is usually set low. In most instances, the default of 0.30 should not be changed. *Do not attempt to illuminate your drawing with ambient light!*

**Figure 16-6.**
The ambient light settings are made in the **Lights** dialog box.

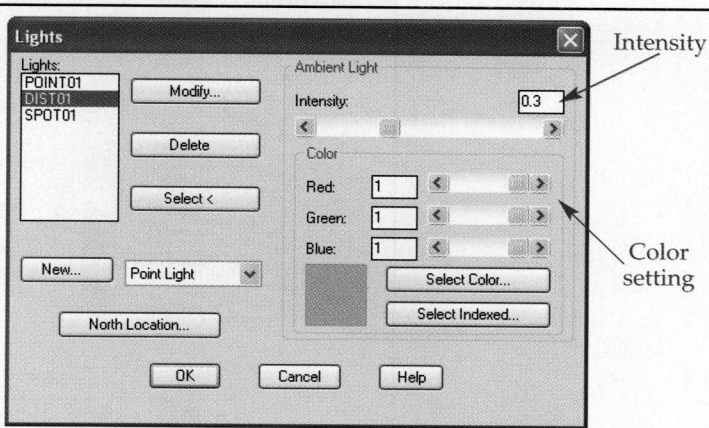

In most instances, ambient light should be white. There are instances, however, where you may want to change the color of ambient light. For example, if you are modeling a foundry, you may want to set ambient light to a very light red. This will give the impression of heat to all objects in the scene. Conversely, if you are modeling the underwater viewing area of an oceanarium, you may want to change ambient light to a light blue to give the impression of light passing through water. Always set ambient light to a light color; do not use dark colors for ambient light.

Setting the color for a light is very similar to setting the color for a material. There are sliders and text boxes for the red, green, and blue values of the light. As with a material, the sliders represent a percentage of 255, where 1.00 equals 255 and represents 100% of the color. The current color of the light is shown in the color swatch.

You can also set the color by picking either the **Select Color...** or **Select Indexed Color...** button. Both buttons open the **Select Color** dialog box, **Figure 16-7.** Using this dialog box, you can select an AutoCAD Color Index (ACI) color, true color (RGB or HSL), or color book color (such as Pantone®). Once a color is selected for ambient light, pick the **OK** button to return to the **Lights** dialog box.

**Figure 16-7.**
You can set the color of a light using the **Select Color** dialog box. A—Selecting an ACI color. B—Setting an RGB color. C—Selecting a Pantone® color.

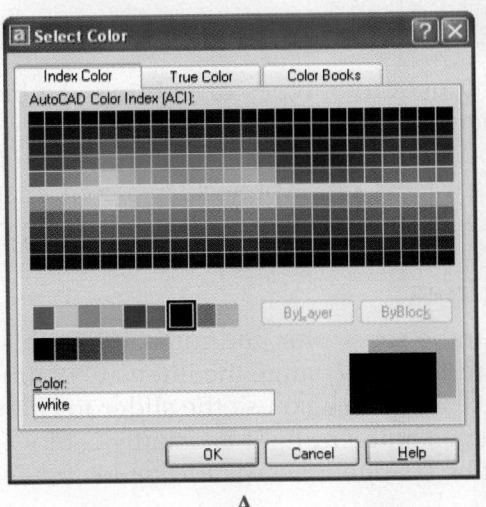

A

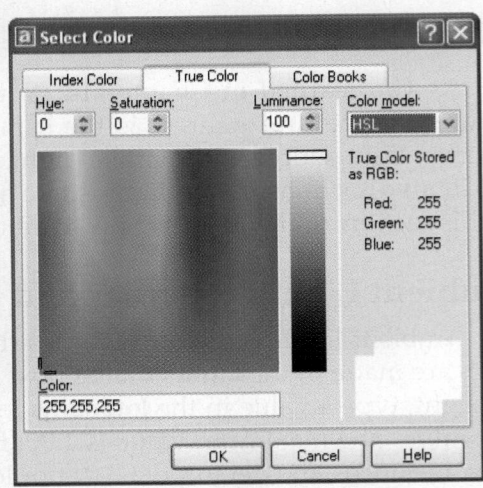

B

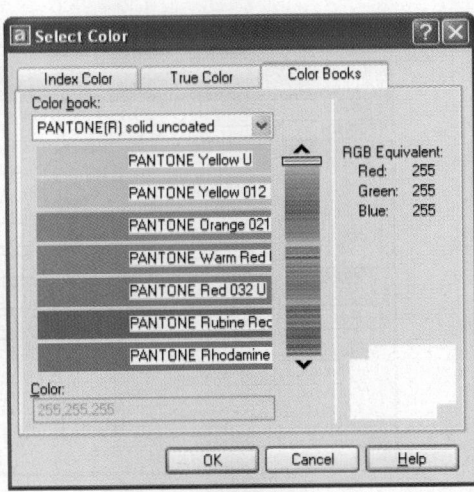

C

## Distant Light Properties and Settings

A distant light has several properties that can be set, **Figure 16-8.** You have already learned how to create a distant light and change its azimuth and altitude settings. You can also change a distant light's intensity and color and set the light to cast shadows.

To set the light to cast shadows, check the **Shadow On** check box in the **Shadows** area of the **Modify Distant Light** (or **New Distant Light**) dialog box. You can make specific shadow settings by picking the **Shadow Options...** button. Shadows are covered in detail later in this chapter.

The intensity of a distant light is set in the **Intensity:** text box. You can enter a value or use the slider to change the value. The maximum value is 1.0. To turn the light off, set the intensity to 0.00.

A distant light is often used to simulate sunlight. Therefore, you may want to change the color of the light to a light blue. A light yellow will simulate very hot sunlight.

The color of a distant light is set in the same manner as for ambient light. Use the sliders in the **Color** area to change the red, green, and blue values for the light. The current color is shown in the color swatch. You can also set the color in the **Select Color** dialog box by picking the **Select Color...** or **Select Indexed Color...** button.

**Figure 16-8.**
Modifying the parameters of a distant light.

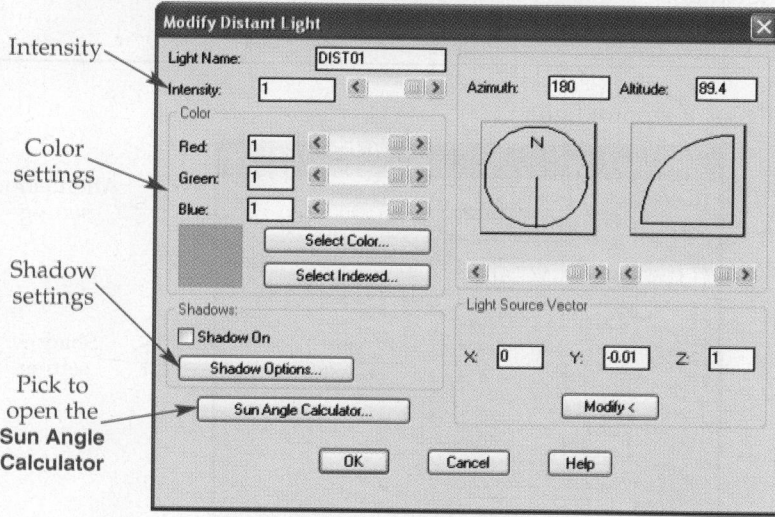

# Point Light Properties and Settings

You can change the color and intensity of a point light. You can also set the light to cast shadows and set attenuation for the light, **Figure 16-9.**

To set the light to cast shadows, check the **Shadow On** check box in the **Shadows** area of the **Modify Point Light** (or **New Point Light**) dialog box. You can make specific shadow settings by picking the **Shadow Options...** button. Shadows are covered in detail later in this chapter.

To set the attenuation, pick the appropriate radio button in the **Attenuation** area. You can select between **None**, **Inverse Linear**, and **Inverse Square**. These options are discussed earlier in this chapter.

The intensity of a distant light is set in the **Intensity:** text box. You can enter a value or use the slider to change the value. As you pick the different radio buttons in the **Attenuation** area, you will notice that the intensity setting changes. Therefore, set the appropriate attenuation first and then set the intensity of the point light. Also, the maximum value varies based on which type of attenuation is selected. To turn the light off, set the intensity to 0.00.

A point light may be used as an incandescent lightbulb, such as in a table lamp. Most of these lightbulbs cast a yellow light. In these cases, you may want to change the color of the light to a light yellow. Other colors can be used to give the impression of heat or colored lights.

The color of a point light is set in the same manner as for ambient and distant lights. Use the sliders in the **Color** area to change the red, green, and blue values for the light. The current color is shown in the color swatch. You can also set the color in the **Select Color** dialog box by picking the **Select Color...** or **Select Indexed Color...** button.

## Spotlight Properties and Settings

Spotlights and point lights have similar settings, **Figure 16-10.** You can change the color, intensity, and attenuation as described in the previous section. As with a point light, select the attenuation before setting the intensity. You can also set the light to cast shadows, as described in the previous section. However, a spotlight also has hotspot and falloff settings.

**Figure 16-9.**
Modifying the parameters of a point light.

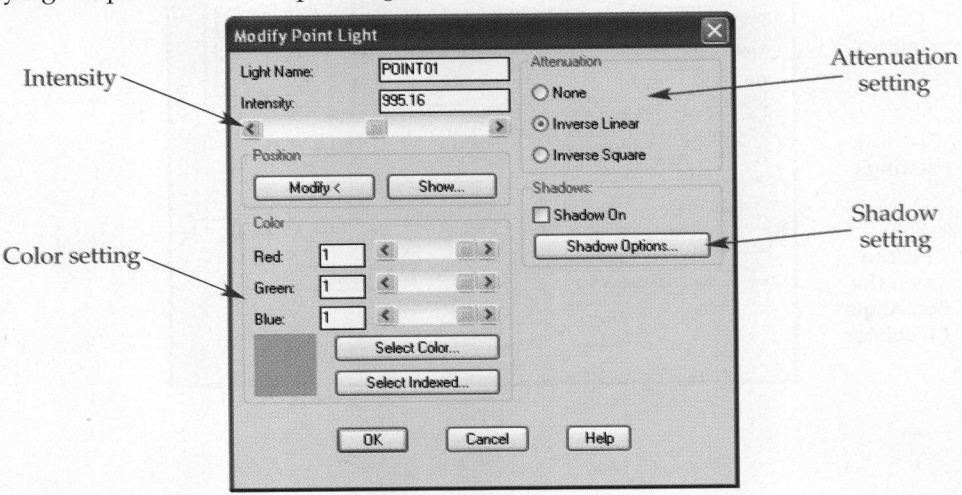

AutoCAD and its Applications—Advanced

**Figure 16-10.**
Modifying the parameters of a spotlight.

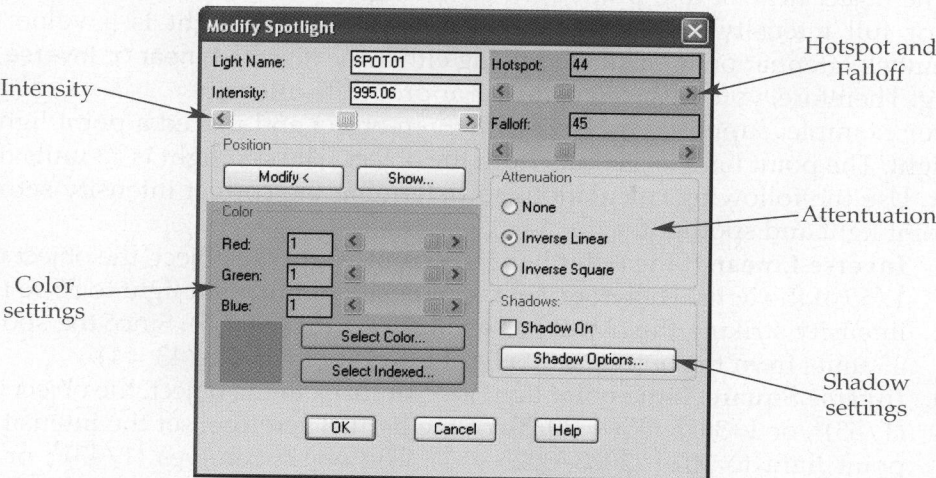

Intensity

Color settings

Hotspot and Falloff

Attentuation

Shadow settings

As described previously, the hotspot is the inner cone of illumination. The setting in the **Hotspot:** text box is the angle of this cone, as projected from the light. See **Figure 16-4B.** You can change the hotspot by entering a value in the text box or using the slider to change the value.

The falloff, not to be confused with attenuation, is the outer cone of illumination. The value in the **Falloff:** text box is the angle of this cone, as projected from the light. See **Figure 16-4B.** Change the falloff by entering a value in the text box or using the slider to change the value.

The falloff value must be greater than or equal to the hotspot value. It cannot be less than the hotspot value. In practice, the falloff value is often much greater than the hotspot value.

**PROFESSIONAL TIP**

The best way to see how colored lights affect your model is to experiment. Remember, you can render individual objects in the model. This allows you to see how light intensity and color change each object.

**Exercise 16-2**

○ Start a new drawing.
○ Draw a solid cone of your own dimensions. Change the display color to white.
○ Create and save a pictorial view of the object.
○ Place a point light, distant light, and spotlight in the drawing. Evenly space the lights around the circumference of the cone.
○ Change the color of the spotlight to blue, the distant light to yellow, and the point light to red.
○ Create a photo real rendering of the drawing in the viewport.
○ Save the drawing as EX16-2.

# Determining Proper Light Intensity

The object nearest to a point light or spotlight should receive the full illumination, or full intensity, of the light. Full intensity of any light is a value of one. Remember, attenuation is calculated using either the **Inverse Linear** or **Inverse Square** setting. Therefore, you must calculate the appropriate intensity.

For example, suppose you have drawn an object and placed a point light and a spotlight. The point light is 55 units from the object. The spotlight is 43 units from the object. Use the following calculations to determine the correct intensity settings for the point light and spotlight.

- **Inverse Linear.** If the point light is 55 units from the object, the object receives 1/55 of the light. Therefore, set the intensity of the point light to 55 so the light intensity striking the object has a value of 1 (55/55 = 1). Since the spotlight is 43 units from the object, set its light intensity to 43 (43/43 = 1).
- **Inverse Square.** If the point light is 55 units from the object, the object receives $(1/55)^2$, or 1/3025 ($55^2 = 3025$), of the light. Therefore, set the intensity of the point light to 3025 (3025/3025 = 1). The object receives $(1/43)^2$, or 1/1849 ($43^2 = 1849$), of the spotlight's illumination. Therefore, set the intensity of the spotlight to 1849 (1849/1849 = 1).

**PROFESSIONAL TIP**

If you render a scene and the image appears black, you may have selected a scene in which all the lights have been turned off (intensity 0).

---

## Exercise 16-3

○ Open EX16-2.
○ Determine the proper intensity setting for the spotlight.
○ Determine the proper intensity setting for the point light.
○ Change the intensity of the spotlight and point light as needed based on your calculations.
○ Render the drawing to the viewport.
○ Make adjustments to the lights as needed. Then, render the drawing to a file.
○ Save the drawing as EX16-3.

---

# Shadows

Shadows are critical to realism in a rendered 3D model. A model without shadows appears obviously fake. On the other hand, a model with realistic materials and shadows may be hard to recognize as computer generated. In AutoCAD, distant, point, and spotlights can all cast shadows. Ambient light does not cast shadows. There are three types of shadows that AutoCAD can create. These are shadow map, volumetric, and raytrace. Remember, shadows can only be cast when the rendering type in the **Render** dialog box is set to **Photo Real** or **Photo Raytrace**. When set to **Render**, the **Shadows** check box is grayed out.

**Figure 16-11.**
Each type of light,
other than ambient,
has a **Shadows** area in
the "light" dialog box.

## Casting Shadows

The options for creating shadows are the same for all lights, and are selected in the **Shadows:** area of all the individual light dialog boxes. See **Figure 16-11.** The **Shadow On** check box must be checked in order for the individual light to create shadows.

Picking the **Shadow Options...** button opens the **Shadow Options** dialog box. See **Figure 16-12.** In this dialog box, you select between shadow-mapped and raytraced shadows. Also, you make settings related to shadow-mapped shadows. These options are discussed in the next sections.

**Figure 16-12.**
The type of shadow
cast by a light is set
in the **Shadow
Options** dialog box.

Check for
raytraced
shadows

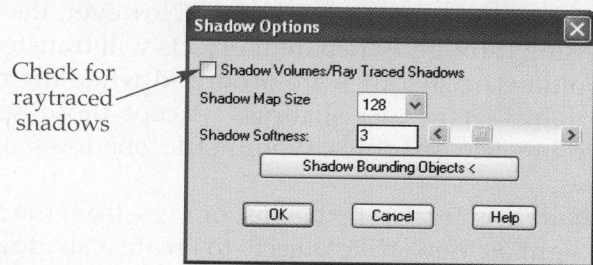

## Shadow-Mapped Shadow Settings

A *shadow-mapped shadow* is a bitmap generated by AutoCAD. A shadow map has soft edges that can be adjusted. A shadow map is the only way to produce a soft-edge shadow. Shadow maps do not transmit object color from transparent objects onto the surfaces behind the object. Shadow-mapped shadows take the least amount of time to render. **Figure 16-13** shows the difference between shadow-mapped shadows and raytraced shadows.

**Figure 16-13.**
The shadow from
the object in the
foreground is a
shadow-mapped
shadow. The
shadow from the
object in the
background is a
raytraced shadow.

The setting in the **Shadow Map Size** drop-down list in the **Shadow Options** dialog box determines the quality, or resolution, of the shadow. In effect, the value is the number of subdivisions or samples used to create the shadow. The higher the setting, the better quality of the shadow generated. However, the higher the setting, the longer it will take to render.

The value in the **Shadow Softness:** text box determines how soft the edge of the shadow is. The higher the value, the softer or blurrier the edge of the shadow. A low value can produce a very hard edge.

By picking the **Shadow Bounding Objects** button in the **Shadow Options** dialog box, you can select objects for which the light will cast shadows. After picking the button, you are returned to the graphics screen. Select the objects to create a selection set. You can also type R to remove objects from the selection set. When done, press [Enter] to return to the **Shadow Options** dialog box.

## Volumetric and Raytraced Shadow Settings

A *volumetric shadow* is generated based on the volume of the object that casts the shadow. These shadows have a hard edge. However, the shadow is an approximation. Light passing through transparent objects will transfer the color of the object to the shadow. Volumetric shadows are produced when the rendering type is set to **Photo Real**. All lights set to cast shadows, except those set for shadow-mapped shadows, cast volumetric shadows. Volumetric shadows appear very similar to raytraced shadows.

A *raytrace shadow* is created by beams, or rays, from the light source. These rays trace the path of light as they strike objects to create a shadow. In addition, rays can pass through transparent objects, such as green glass, and project color onto surfaces behind the object. Raytrace shadows have a well-defined edge. They cannot be adjusted to produce a soft edge. Raytraced shadows are produced when the rendering type is set to **Photo Raytrace**. All lights set to cast shadows, except those set for shadow-mapped shadows, cast raytraced shadows. Raytraced shadows take the greatest amount of time to render.

To turn on volumetric or raytrace shadows, check the **Shadows Volumes/Raytrace Shadows** check box in the **Shadow Options** check box. The type of shadow created (volume or raytrace) is determined by the rendering type in the **Render** dialog box. The remainder of the options in the **Shadow Options** dialog box are grayed out.

**PROFESSIONAL TIP**

If casting shadows is an important aspect of the model, be sure that shadows are turned on for each of the lights in the model. Create a variety of defined scenes and carefully place a distant light in each representing the time of year and day. Simulating sunlight is discussed in the next section.

If you wish to experiment with different lighting effects in your scenes, it may also be helpful to create a full set of lights for each scene. This is especially true if you will be using several scenes for rendering purposes. Remember, you can place an unlimited number of lights in the model and then create as many scenes as you need using any of the lights.

AutoCAD and its Applications—Advanced

## Simulating Sunlight

AutoCAD has a feature that allows you to quickly set a distant light to replicate the lighting effects of the Sun. This feature is called the **Sun Angle Calculator**. To access the **Sun Angle Calculator**, first open either the **Modify Distant Light** or **New Distant Light** dialog box. Both dialog boxes are exactly the same except for the name. Next, pick the **Sun Angle Calculator...** button. This displays the **Sun Angle Calculator** dialog box, **Figure 16-14.**

### Using the Sun Angle Calculator

The angle of the light representing the Sun is adjusted using the values on the left side of this dialog box. The **Azimuth:** and **Altitude:** image tiles on the right side graphically represent all the values on the left.

- **Date.** Enter the month and day in the text box or move the slider bar to set the date desired. One pick on the slider bar arrow changes the date by one day, and one pick in the space to the left or right of the slider bar changes the date by one month. Pick and hold the slider bar and move it left and right. As you do, watch the azimuth and altitude image tiles automatically adjust.
- **Clock Time.** This is a 24-hour clock. One pick on the slider bar arrow changes the time by ten minutes, and one pick in the space to the left or right of the slider bar changes the time by one hour. As you move the slider bar, the azimuth and altitude image tiles automatically adjust. Select your time zone from the drop-down list, and pick the **Daylight Savings** check box if it applies.

**Figure 16-14.**
The **Sun Angle Calculator** can be used to create a distant light that simulates the sun.

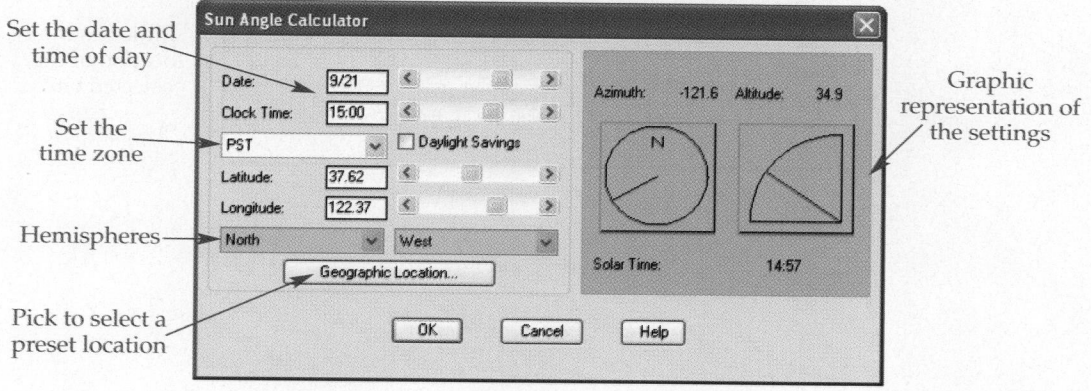

Set the date and time of day

Set the time zone

Hemispheres

Pick to select a preset location

Graphic representation of the settings

- **Latitude.** This is the angular location of the Sun from the equator to the North or South Poles. This is an angular measurement from the center of the earth, with the equator being 0° and the North and South Poles 90°. This measurement represents the seasonal and daily movements of the Sun, and most directly affects the altitude.
- **Longitude.** This represents the east/west location of the Sun as Earth rotates. It most directly affects the angle of the sun above the horizon (altitude). This angle determines shadow length.
- **Hemispheres.** Below the **Longitude** text box are two drop-down lists where you can select either the north or south hemisphere, and either the east or west hemisphere. North America is located in the northern and western hemispheres.

If you are unsure of the exact latitude and longitude of your model, you can select a location by picking the **Geographic Location...** button. This displays the **Geographic Location** dialog box, **Figure 16-15.** Use the following steps to select your location.

1. Pick the continent (or country) in the drop-down list above the map.
2. Pick the city in the **City:** list on the left of the dialog box. Its latitude and longitude are displayed in the lower left of the dialog box.

If you do not know the city nearest to your location, do the following.

1. Pick the continent (or country) in the drop-down list.
2. Check the **Nearest Big City** check box.
3. Pick your location on the map using your cursor. The nearest big city is located by the blue crosshairs, and its name is highlighted in the **City:** list.

The lower-left area of this dialog box displays the latitude and longitude of the selected city. You can change the latitude and longitude values, but the changes are not graphically updated on the map. When you pick the **OK** button, your changes are displayed in the **Sun Angle Calculator** dialog box.

Once all settings have been made in the **Sun Angel Calculator**, pick the **OK** button. You are returned to the **Modify Distant Light** or **New Distant Light** dialog box. Then, pick **OK** to create the light or save the changes to the light.

**Figure 16-15.**
Selecting the geographic location of your model automatically sets the latitude and longitude.

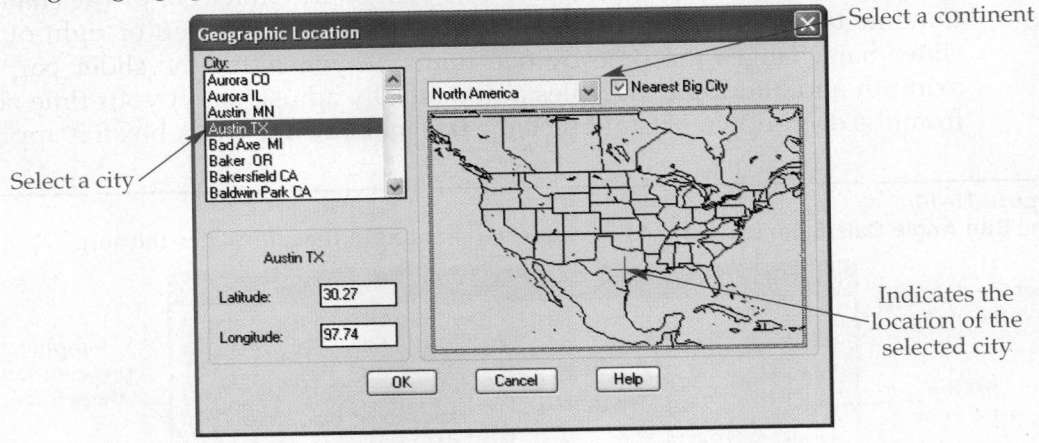

## Setting North

In order for shadows to be displayed accurately in the model, the north direction must be set properly. By default, AutoCAD locates north in the positive Y direction of the world coordinate system. To change the north direction in your model, pick the **North Location...** button in the **Lights** dialog box. This displays the **North Location** dialog box shown in **Figure 16-16.**

A new north direction can be assigned by entering an angle in the **Angle:** text box or moving the slider bar. The north line changes in the image tile as the slider bar moves. You can also pick on the image tile or enter a value in the text box. For example, if you want north to be the X direction in the WCS, enter 90 in the **Angle:** text box.

You can also orient north along the Y axis of any named UCS. All named UCSs appear in the list in the **Use UCS:** area at the right of the dialog box. Pick the UCS name from the list and pick **OK**. Before selecting a UCS, be sure that the **X/Y Plane** angle is 0.

Figure 16-16.
The **North Location** dialog box.

Set the north direction

Pick the **UCS** to use the Y axis as north

**PROFESSIONAL TIP**

If it appears shadows are being cast incorrectly for the location and time of day specified, it is possible that the north direction is improperly set. Check the north location to be sure it coincides with the north direction established for the model.

## Adding a Background

A *background* is the backdrop for your 3D model. The background for your scene can be a solid color, a gradient of colors, a bitmap file, or the current AutoCAD drawing background color. By default, the background is the drawing background color.

Establish a background by picking the **Background** button on the **Render** toolbar, picking **Background...** in the **Render** cascading menu in the **View** pull-down menu, or typing BACKGROUND at the Command: prompt. The **Background** dialog box is displayed, **Figure 16-17A.** Four radio buttons at the top of the dialog represent the four types of backgrounds. These are **Solid**, **Gradient**, **Image**, and **Merge**. The **Merge** option uses the current AutoCAD drawing background image as the background. The other three options are discussed in the next sections.

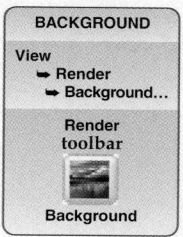

BACKGROUND

View
➡ Render
➡ Background...

**Render toolbar**

Background

---

**Figure 16-17.**
A—The **Background** dialog box. B—By creatively using materials and backgrounds, you can produce a variety of scenes, from the average to the fantastic.

Pick the background type

Set the color(s)

Select an image

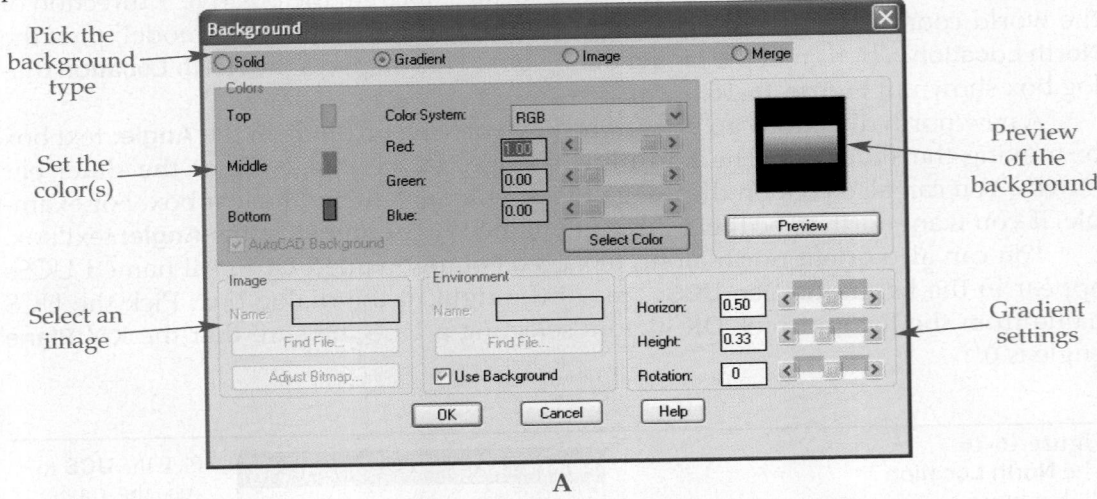

Preview of the background

Gradient settings

A

B

## Solid Backgrounds

The default background option is **Solid**, with the AutoCAD background color as the solid color. When the **AutoCAD Background** check box in the **Colors** area is unchecked, you can select a background color using either the RGB or HLS color system. Enter numeric values or use the slider bars to set the **Top** color swatch, which indicates the background color. Pick the **Preview** button to see a sample of the background. A color can also be selected from the **Color** dialog box by picking the **Select Color** button.

## Gradient Backgrounds

A **Gradient** background can be composed of two or three colors. These are shown in the **Colors** area of the dialog box as **Top**, **Middle**, and **Bottom**. By selecting one of the color swatches, you are selecting the color to be modified. The current color swatch has a black border. Use the color slider bars or the **Select Custom Color** button to adjust the color for each swatch. When **Gradient** is picked, the three values in the lower-right corner are activated.

- **Horizon.** This is a percentage value that determines where the center of the gradient is to be placed.
- **Height.** The starting location of the second color in a three-color gradient is determined by this percentage. A two-color gradient is created, composed of the top and bottom colors, if this value is 0.
- **Rotation.** The angle at which the gradient background is rotated.

Pick the **Preview** button to preview how the gradient will appear. Convincing, clear blue skies can be simulated using the **Gradient** option. Initially, set the **Top**, **Middle**, and **Bottom** color values the same. Then, change the lightness in the **Colors** dialog box.

### Using an Image as a Background

Any bitmap image can be used as a background. This technique can be used to produce realistic or imaginative settings for your models. First, pick the **Image** radio button. This activates the **Image** and **Environment** areas of the **Background** dialog box. Use the **Find File...** button in the **Image** area to select the bitmap. Use the **Adjust Bitmap...** button to alter the offset and scale.

An *environment* is a bitmap image mapped onto a sphere that surrounds the scene. This "environment-in-a-sphere" is used by the photo raytrace renderer to project additional images onto objects that have reflective surfaces. This option can provide a realistic "surrounding" environment in your scene. The **Use Background** check box must be inactive in order to use an environment.

---

### Exercise 16-5

- ○ Open EX16-4.
- ○ Add a solid background to the drawing. Select a color that complements the material color of the cone.
- ○ Render the scene containing the point light to the viewport.
- ○ Add a gradient background to the drawing. Use colors that complement the cone.
- ○ Render the scene containing the spotlight to the viewport.
- ○ Save the drawing as EX16-5.

---

## Adding Atmospheric Fog

Fog is actually a way of using colors to visually represent the distance between the camera and objects in the model. This is similar to looking at an object from a distance and seeing that the object is a little obscured from the haze in the sky. To use fog, pick the **Fog** button on the **Render** toolbar, select **Fog...** from **Render** cascading menu in the **View** pull-down menu, or type FOG at the Command: prompt. This displays the **Fog/Depth Cue** dialog box. See **Figure 16-18.**

Turn on fog by checking the **Enable Fog** check box. Checking the **Fog Background** check box also applies fog to the background in the model. Fog is composed of three components: color, distance, and percentage.

FOG

View
➡ Render
➡ Fog...

Render toolbar

Fog

---

**Figure 16-18.**
The **Fog/Depth Cue**
dialog box is used
to visually portray
the distance
between the camera
and objects in the
model.

Check to
enable fog

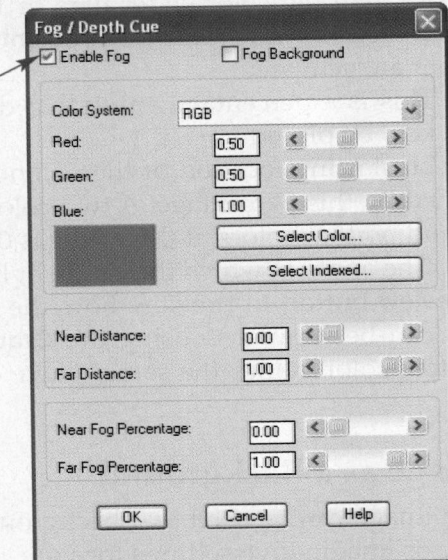

- **Color.** The color controls are the standard AutoCAD color controls previously discussed. First, select a color system. Then, enter values for each color or use the slider bars. You can also select a color by picking the **Select Color...** button or the **Select Indexed...** button.
- **Distance.** The distance values are percentages of the distance from the viewer to the rear of the model, or its back "clipping plane." The viewer has a value of 0 and the back of the model is 1.0, or 100%. Enter values in the text boxes or use the slider bars. These values determine where the fog starts and ends.
- **Fog percentage.** These values are the percentages of fog at the near distance and far distance. A value of 0 is no fog, and a value of 1.0 is 100% fog. The **Near Fog Percentage** value takes effect at the **Near Distance** value (front of the camera) and increases to the **Far Fog Percentage** value at the back of the model.

---

**PROFESSIONAL TIP**

If the **Fog Background** button has been selected, try adjusting the **Far Fog Percentage**. By default, this value is set to 1.0 (100%) which will completely render any background placed using the **BACKGROUND** command with the fog color.

---

**Exercise 16-6**

○ Open EX16-5.
○ Add fog to the drawing. Fog the background, but you should still be able to see the background in the final rendering.
○ Adjust the near and far distances so that about half of the cone is in fog.
○ Render the scene containing the spotlight to the viewport.
○ Save the drawing as EX16-6.

---

AutoCAD and its Applications—Advanced

# Landscaping (Entourage)

You can easily landscape your model by adding bushes, trees, road signs, and people. These items are called entourage; AutoCAD calls them landscaping. Pick the **Landscape New** button on the **Render** toolbar, select **Landscape New...** from the **Render** cascading menu in the **View** pull-down menu, or type LSNEW at the Command: prompt. This displays the **Landscape New** dialog box, **Figure 16-19A**. The list on the left side shows the objects in the current library file. A landscape library file can be modified and saved in a manner similar to managing material libraries. Managing a landscape library is discussed later in this chapter.

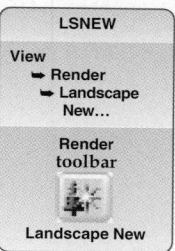

**Figure 16-19.**
A—Landscape objects can be placed and sized using the **Landscape New** dialog box.
B—Single-face and crossing-face object symbols are shown after placement in the model.
C—The same two objects after rendering.

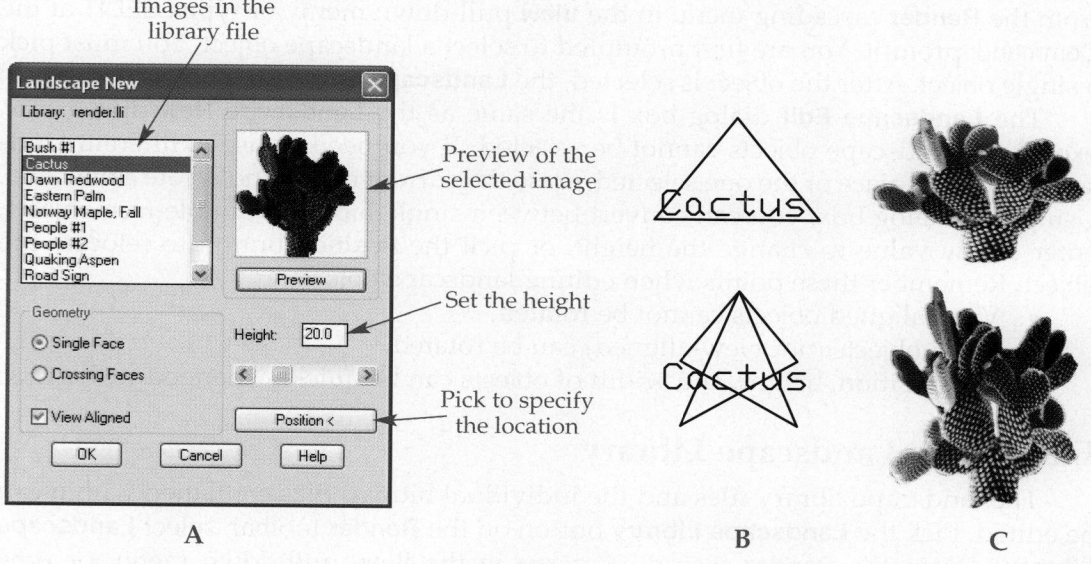

## Placing Landscaping

Select an object from the list in the **Landscape New** dialog box and pick the **Preview** button to view it. Adjust the height by entering a value in the **Height:** text box or use the slider bar. Changes in the height value are not reflected in the preview. The height is specified in the current drawing units. For example, if architectural units are the current units, then the height of the landscape object is in inches.

Pick the **Position<** button and locate the object in your model. The dialog box is hidden and the drawing screen displayed. Use standard AutoCAD methods, such as zooming and object snaps, to locate the object. Once you pick a position, the **Landscape New** dialog box is redisplayed.

The **Geometry** area allows you to specify the number of faces on the landscape object and how the view is aligned. Pick **Single Face** to display the object as a single plane. If the **View Aligned** box is checked, the object's face is placed perpendicular to the line of sight. A single-face object renders faster than a crossing-face object. The **Crossing Faces** option creates objects with two faces that intersect at a 90° angle. This object creates more realistic images and raytraced shadows. The faces are oriented at a 45° angle to the line of sight if they are view aligned.

A single-face, view-aligned object is identified by a single triangle with the name of the object at the bottom. This object cannot be rotated. A single-face, fixed object (not view-aligned) is displayed as a rectangle, and its name may be right- or wrong-reading. This type of object can be rotated. The objects are drawn to the specified height. A crossing-face object is drawn as two intersecting triangles. If they are view-aligned, they cannot be rotated. **Figure 16-19B** and **Figure 16-19C** show the difference between the object symbols and the rendered versions.

## Editing Landscape Objects

The triangular shapes of landscape objects can be edited using standard AutoCAD methods. The objects have grips at the apex, base, and corners of the triangle. The objects can be moved using the grip at the middle of the base. The size and height of the object is changed using the top and lower corner grips. The size always remains proportional.

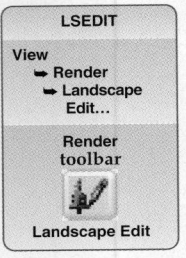

LSEDIT

View
↦ Render
  ↦ Landscape
     Edit...

Render
toolbar

Landscape Edit

The geometry, position, and height of individual landscape objects can also be edited. Pick the **Landscape Edit** button on the **Render** toolbar, select **Landscape Edit...** from the **Render** cascading menu in the **View** pull-down menu, or type LSEDIT at the Command: prompt. You are first prompted to select a landscape object. You must pick a single object. After the object is selected, the **Landscape Edit** dialog box is displayed.

The **Landscape Edit** dialog box is the same as the **Landscape New** dialog box, except the landscape objects cannot be selected. If you need to use a different landscape object in place of the one selected, erase the current object and create a new one. Using this dialog box, you can convert between single-face and double-face objects, enter a new value to change the height, or pick the **Position** button to relocate the object. Remember these points when editing landscape objects:

- View-aligned objects cannot be rotated.
- Fixed objects (not view-aligned) can be rotated.
- The position, height, and width of objects can be quickly changed with grips.

## Editing the Landscape Library

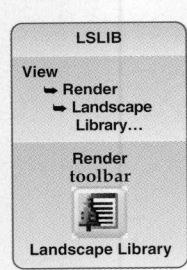

LSLIB

View
↦ Render
  ↦ Landscape
     Library...

Render
toolbar

Landscape Library

The landscape library files and the individual bitmap files contained within can be edited. Pick the **Landscape Library** button on the **Render** toolbar, select **Landscape Library...** from the **Render** cascading menu in the **View** pull-down menu, or type LSLIB at the Command: prompt. The **Landscape Library** dialog box is displayed, **Figure 16-20.** This dialog box contains the following buttons.

- **Modify.** Highlight the landscape object you want to edit, then pick the **Modify...** button. The **Landscape Library Edit** dialog box appears, **Figure 16-21.** The current name of the object is listed in the **Name:** text box. Each object has an image file and an opacity map file. The image file is the image displayed when the object is rendered. The opacity map file is used to outline the object and make it see-through. An opacity map is a file that displays the silhouette of your image in a white color and the area surrounding the image in a black color. You can change the name of this item and replace the current image and opacity files with different ones. You can also change the default geometry settings displayed when inserting a landscape object through the **Landscape New** dialog box.
- **New.** Displays the **Landscape Library New** dialog box, which is exactly the same as the **Landscape Library Edit** dialog box. In this dialog box, name the new landscape object, select the image and opacity map files to define it, and specify the default geometry settings.
- **Delete.** Removes the highlighted object from the library list.
- **Open.** Displays the **Open Landscape Library** dialog box where you can open a different landscape library file (.lli).

**Figure 16-20.**
The landscape library files, and the individual objects contained within, can be edited using the **Landscape Library** dialog box.

**Figure 16-21.**
Individual landscape objects can be edited using the **Landscape Library Edit** dialog box.

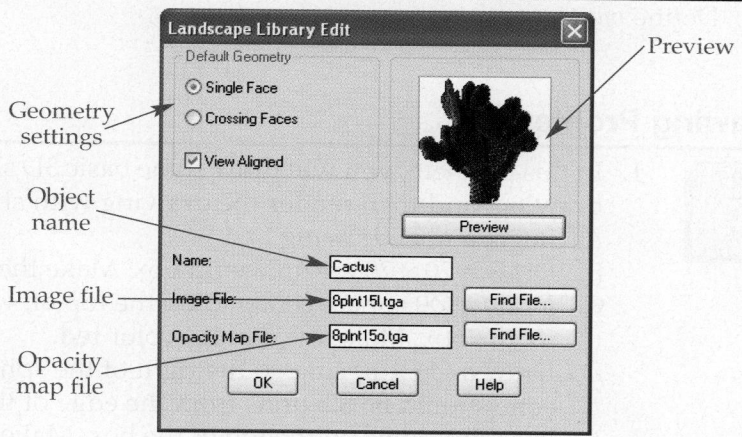

- **Save.** Displays the **Save Landscape Library** dialog box used to save the revised landscape library file.

---

### Exercise 16-7

○ Open EX16-6.
○ Add two landscape objects to the drawing, one to the left of the cone and one to the right.
○ Size the right-hand landscape object so it is about as tall as the cone.
○ Size the left-hand landscape object so it is about 1/2 as tall as the cone.
○ Render the scene containing the spotlight to the viewport.
○ Make any adjustments needed to lighting, shadows, fog, the background, or the landscape objects.
○ Render the scene containing the spotlight to a file.
○ Save the drawing as EX16-7.

---

## Chapter Test

*Answer the following questions on a separate sheet of paper.*

1. What is the meaning of *altitude* and *azimuth* in the **Sun Angle Calculator**?
2. When using the **Sun Angle Calculator**, how can you set the light up for a specific location?
3. How must the values of **Hotspot** and **Falloff** relate to each other?
4. Which lights have **Hotspot** and **Falloff** values?

---

5. Which types of renderings can produce shadows?
6. In which dialog box can you change the size of the icons that represent lights in viewports?
7. What is the difference between *point lights* and *distant lights?*
8. What is *attenuation?* Which lights have this attribute?
9. How many different types of shadows can be produced in AutoCAD? List them.
10. Name the different types of backgrounds that can be applied to a model.
11. Name two ways in which landscape objects can be displayed.
12. Which aspects of a landscape object can be edited?
13. What is the function of fog?
14. What is the function of the **View Aligned** check box for a landscape object?
15. Define *matte.*

## Drawing Problems

1. In this problem, you will draw some basic 3D shapes, place lights in the drawing, and then render the drawing with shadows.
   A. Begin a new drawing.
   B. Draw a 70 × 70 × 1 unit solid box. Make the display color white.
   C. Draw a Ø9 sphere centered on the top of, with its bottom tangent to, the box. Make the display color red.
   D. Draw a Ø6 × 10 cone to the right of the sphere. The edge of the cone should be 8.5 units from the edge of the sphere. The cone's base should be on the top of the box. Make the display color green.
   E. Draw a 20 × 10 × 3 unit box located 6 units behind the center of the sphere. The bottom of the box should be on the top of the first box. Also, the second box should be approximately centered left-to-right behind the sphere and cone. Make the display color blue.
   F. Add a single spotlight to the drawing. The light should point from the front of the first box toward the second box with the sphere and cone in between. Move the light so it is approximately 50 units above the large box. Calculate and set the proper intensity.
   G. Create and save a pictorial view.
   H. Render the drawing using the **Photo Real** rendering type.
   I. Set up the light to cast shadow-mapped shadows. Render the drawing again.
   J. Adjust the light's parameters to produce a good result.
   K. Save the drawing as P16-1.

2. Open Problem 1 from Chapter 14. Generate the following scenes using the light values given. Adjust the values of the spotlights based on their distance from the objects and include both in all three scenes. Set up the distant lights to cast shadows. See the illustration below for proper view orientations.

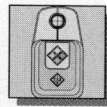

| View Name | Scene Name | Ambient | Point | D-1 | D-2 |
|-----------|-----------|---------|-------|-----|-----|
| VIEW1 | ONE | .7 | 2 | 1 | 0 |
| VIEW2 | TWO | .3 | 2 | 0 | 1 |
| VIEW3 | THREE | 0 | 5 | 1 | 0 |

A. Create a material for the sphere with a color of 0.3, reflection of 0.7, and roughness of 0.1. Name it SPHERE1.

B. Create a second material for the sphere named SPHERE2 with a color of 0.7, reflection of 0.3, and roughness of 1.0.

C. Create a third material for the sphere named SPHERE3 with a roughness of 0.7, color of 0.5, and a reflection of 0.5.

D. Attach the material SPHERE1 to the sphere and render scene ONE with shadows.

E. Attach the material SPHERE2 to the sphere and render scene TWO with shadows.

F. Attach the material SPHERE3 to the sphere and render scene THREE with shadows.

G. Save the drawing as P16-2.

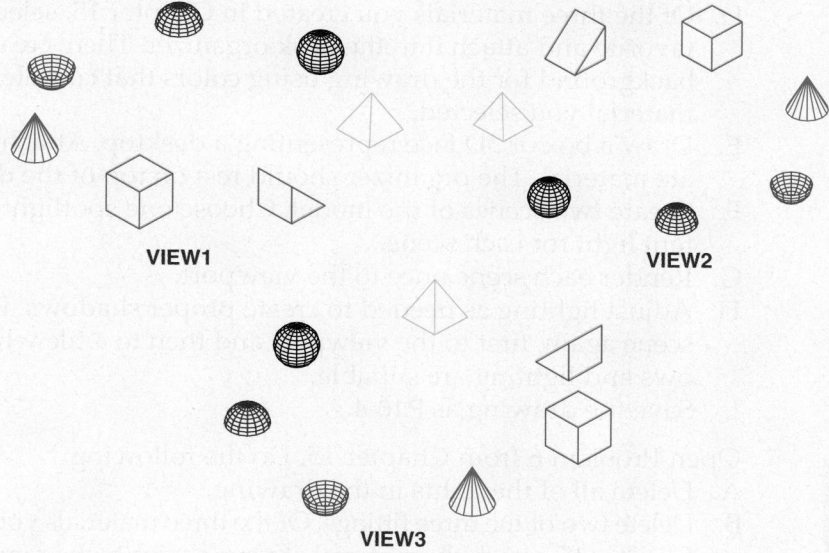

3. In this problem, materials and textures are attached to some of the objects in your drawing.
   A. Open the drawing P16-2.
   B. Define and attach materials to the following objects as indicated. Give the wood a dark color with narrow rings of a concentric shape. The marble should have a lot of vein color and swirling. The granite should have a highly polished look. Choose your own colors for the marble and granite.

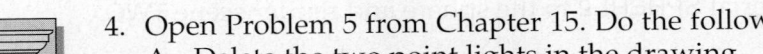

| Object | Material |
|---------|----------|
| Box | Wood |
| Pyramid | Marble |
| Dome | Granite |

   C. Create a rendering of these three objects only using each of the three rendering types.
   D. Create a rendering of all objects using raytraced shadows. Make the necessary adjustments to cast this type of shadow. Save the drawing as P16-3.

4. Open Problem 5 from Chapter 15. Do the following.

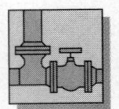

   A. Delete the two point lights in the drawing.
   B. Set up the two distant lights to cast raytraced shadows.
   C. Calculate and set the proper intensity for the two spotlights in the drawing.
   D. Of the three materials you created in Chapter 15, select your favorite and attach it to the desk organizer. Then, create a gradient background for the drawing using colors that complement the material you selected.
   E. Draw a box or 3D face representing a desktop. Attach an appropriate material. The organizer should rest on top of the desktop.
   F. Create two scenes of the model. Choose one spotlight and one distant light for each scene.
   G. Render each scene once to the viewport.
   H. Adjust lighting as needed to create proper shadows. Render each scene again, first to the viewport and then to a file when the shadows and lighting are suitable.
   I. Save the drawing as P16-4.

5. Open Problem 6 from Chapter 15. Do the following.
   A. Delete all of the lights in the drawing.
   B. Delete two of the three fittings. Of the three materials you created in Chapter 15, attach the material of your choice to the remaining fitting.
   C. Draw a box or 3D face representing a tabletop. Change the display color to white or create a material of your own and attach it to the tabletop. Arrange the fitting so that the plane of the three openings is parallel to the tabletop.
   D. Add a spotlight to the drawing. Place the light so it points at one corner of the fitting. Set up the light to cast shadows.
   E. Create a photo raytrace rendering in the viewport.
   F. Place a point light on the opposite front corner of the fitting. Set the intensity low; just high enough to illuminate the dark area of the fitting. Do not wash out the shadows from the spotlight.
   G. Create another photo raytrace rendering. When the lighting is appropriate, render the drawing to a file.
   H. Save the document as P16-5.

AutoCAD and its Applications—Advanced

## CHAPTER 17

# Using Raster and Vector Graphics

## Learning Objectives

After completing this chapter, you will be able to:
- Compare raster and vector files.
- Import and export raster files using AutoCAD.
- Import and export vector files using AutoCAD.
- Set image commands to manipulate inserted raster files.
- Replay an image file.

One of the important aspects of drawing in AutoCAD is the ability to share information. Generally, this means sharing drawing data and geometry between CAD software, either other AutoCAD workstations or workstations using a different software. AutoCAD creates drawing data files in a format known as a vector file. However, you can also share your work, as images, with photo editing and desktop publishing software. In Chapter 14 through Chapter 16, you learned how to create realistic scenes and render them to files. A scene rendered to a file is a raster image. However, images do not always need to be high quality. This chapter introduces using AutoCAD to work with raster and vector graphics files. This includes importing, exporting, and setting various parameters.

## Introduction to Raster and Vector Graphics

In the world of electronic imaging, there are two basic types of files—raster and vector. AutoCAD drawings are called vector graphics. A *vector* is an object defined by XYZ coordinates. In other words, AutoCAD stores the mathematical definition of an object. *Pixels* (picture elements) are the "dots" or "bits" in the monitor that make up your display screen. When drawing vector objects in AutoCAD, your monitor uses pixels to create a representation of the object on the monitor. However, there is no relationship between the physical pixels in your monitor and a vector object. Pixels simply show the object at the current zoom percentage. Some common vector files are DWG, DXF, AI, and EPS.

Many illustrations created with drawing, painting, and presentation software are saved as raster files. A *raster file* creates a picture or image file using the location and color of the screen pixels. In other words, a raster file is made up of "dots." Raster files are usually called *bitmaps.* There are several types of raster files used for presentation graphics and desktop publishing. Some common raster file types include TIFF, JPEG, and GIF.

## Replaying Image Files

Images saved as TGA, TIFF, and BMP files can be displayed in AutoCAD with the **REPLAY** command. These files are raster files, which are discussed in the next section. Access the command by selecting **Display Image** and then **View...** from the **Tools** pull-down menu or by typing REPLAY at the Command: prompt. This displays the **Replay** dialog box. Select the folder and file you want to display and pick the **Open** button. The **Image Specifications** dialog box then appears. See **Figure 17-1.** This dialog box allows you to specify the exact portion of the image you want to display, along with the on-screen location.

The image tile on the left side of the dialog box is titled **IMAGE**. The size of the image is given in pixels just above the image tile. You can pick two points inside this tile to crop the image for display. When you do this, notice that the offset location of the image in the **SCREEN** image tile changes. You can also change the image size by entering the cropped size of the image in the **Image Offset** and **Image Size** text boxes. The image offset defines the lower-left corner of the image. The image size defines the upper-right corner of the image.

In addition to cropping the size of the image, you can determine where it will be displayed on the screen. Do this visually by picking a point in the **SCREEN** image tile. This point becomes the center of the image on your screen. You can also specify the location by entering **Screen Offset** values in the boxes below the tile. Notice that the **Screen Size** values cannot be changed. The **Reset** button returns the image and screen values to their defaults. Pick **OK** when you are ready to display the image in the viewport.

You cannot use **PAN**, **ZOOM**, the scroll bars, or any other command to adjust the display of the image. Doing so regenerates the screen, which removes the displayed image. As you can see, the **REPLAY** command is useful for small files only.

REPLAY

Tools
➥ Display Image
➥ View...

**Figure 17-1.**
The **Image Specifications** dialog box used with the **REPLAY** command.

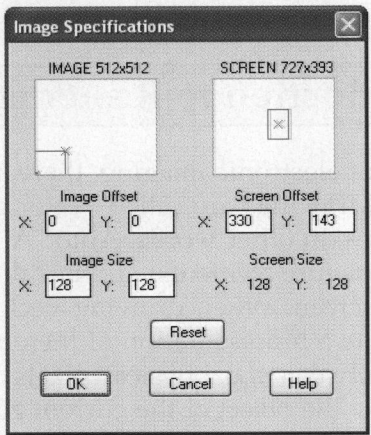

## Working with Raster Files

Raster images are inserted into AutoCAD drawings using the **IMAGE** command. These images are treated much like externally referenced drawings (xrefs). They are not added to the drawing database, but are attached and referenced by a path name to the raster file's location. Any changes to the image content must be made to the original file. Settings and commands in AutoCAD can, however, control the portion of the image shown and its appearance. Images can be inserted, removed, and modified using commands found on the **Reference** toolbar, **Figure 17-2**. These functions are discussed in detail in this section.

Some of the most common raster files used in industry today are:

- **TIFF (Tagged Image File Format).** A file format developed by Aldus Corporation and Microsoft Corporation. This is one of the most commonly used image file types.
- **JPEG (Joint Photographic Experts Group).** Creates a highly compressed graphics image file. This type of file is very common on websites. Also known as a JPG file.
- **GIF (Graphics Interchange Format).** A file format developed by CompuServe to exchange graphic images over an online computer service. This type of file is sometimes found on websites.
- **PCX (Personal Computer Exchange).** A file format developed by Z-Soft Corporation. This type of file has certain applications, but is not used much anymore.

**Figure 17-2.**
The **Reference** toolbar contains buttons for the **Image** family of commands.

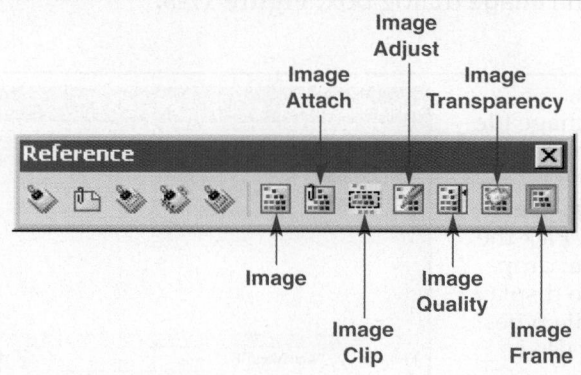

- **BMP (Bitmap).** A file format developed by Microsoft Corporation. Like PCX, there are certain applications for this type of file. However, overall, this file type is not used much anymore.

Other raster file types can also be imported into AutoCAD. If you have a raster image that cannot be imported directly, you will need to first import the file into a paint or draw program. Then, export the image in a format that AutoCAD can read.

To activate the **IMAGE** command, select **Raster Image...** in the **Insert** pull-down menu, pick the **Image** button on the **Reference** toolbar, or type IM or IMAGE at the Command: prompt. This displays the **Image Manager** dialog box, **Figure 17-3.** This dialog box lists the images currently attached to a drawing. From this dialog box, you can insert a new image, delete an image from the drawing, and view information about an attached image.

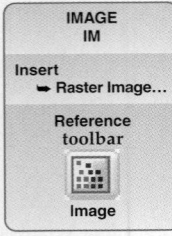

IMAGE
IM

Insert
➡ Raster Image...

Reference
toolbar

Image

Figure 17-3.
Raster images can be inserted or deleted using the **Image Manager** dialog box.

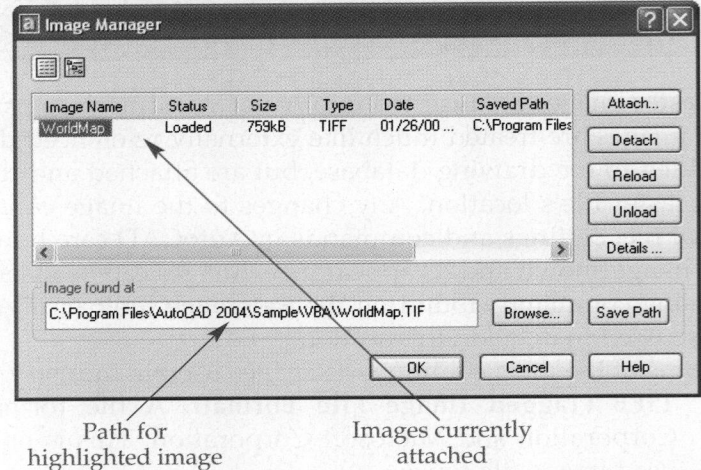

Path for highlighted image

Images currently attached

## Inserting Raster Images

The **IMAGEATTACH** command is used to attach an image file to a drawing. To access this command, pick the **Attach...** button in the **Image Manager** dialog box, pick the **Image Attach** button on the **Reference** toolbar, or type IAT or IMAGEATTACH at the Command: prompt. The **Select Image File** dialog box is displayed, **Figure 17-4.** Pick the **Files of type:** drop-down list to display all the raster file types that can be used. If a folder contains a wide variety of raster files, you can quickly narrow your search by picking one of the file types in this list. Then, select the raster file and pick **Open.** This displays the **Image** dialog box, **Figure 17-5.**

IMAGEATTACH
IAT

Reference
toolbar

Image Attach

Figure 17-4.
Select the image file to be attached to the drawing in the **Select Image File** dialog box. Pick the **Files of type:** drop-down list to display the raster file types that can be used.

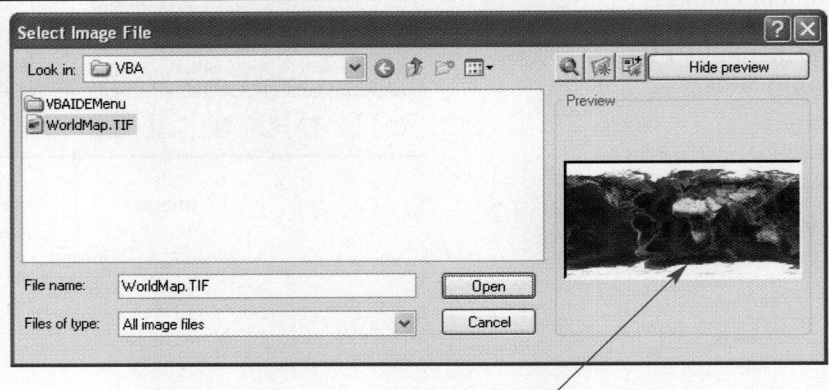

Preview of selected image

AutoCAD and its Applications—Advanced

**Figure 17-5.**
The image name
and current path are
displayed in the
**Image** dialog box.
The dialog box
expands to include
the **Image
Information** area
when the **Details<<**
button is picked.

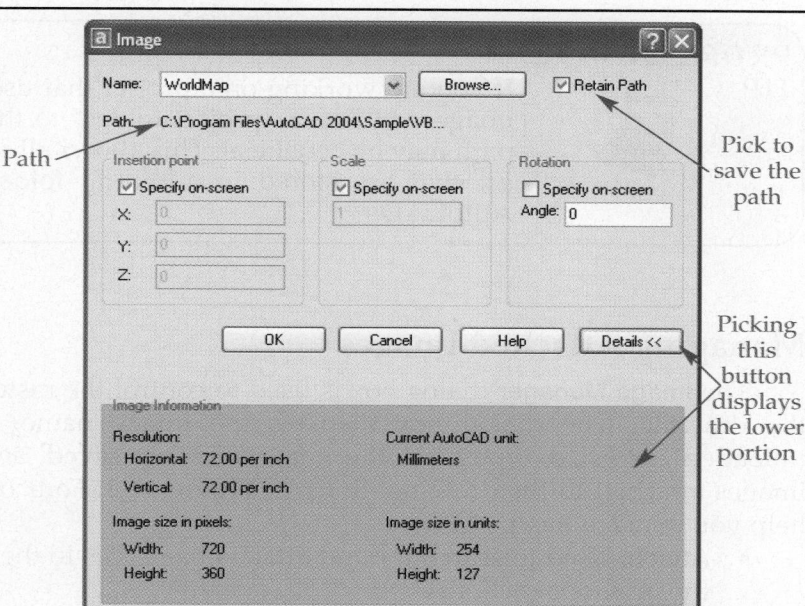

The image name and current path are displayed in the **Image** dialog box. You can preset image parameters or choose to specify them on-screen. The **Retain Path** box is checked by default. When checked, the path to the image is saved with the drawing file. If this box is not checked, AutoCAD searches through the Support Files Search Path defined in the **Files** tab of the **Options** dialog box. If the image is not located in this path, AutoCAD will not be able to find it.

You can view image resolution information in the **Image** dialog box by picking the **Details** button. See **Figure 17-5.** When the **OK** button is picked and the image placed, it is displayed in the drawing area. See **Figure 17-6.**

**Figure 17-6.**
The raster image
attached to an
AutoCAD drawing.

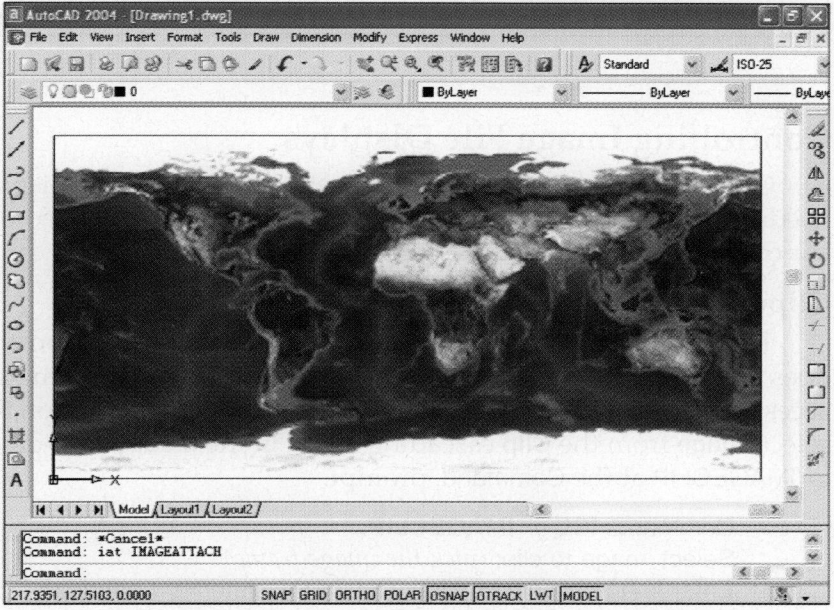

## Managing Attached Images

The **Image Manager** dialog box is used to control the raster images inserted into the drawing. The dialog box displays the image name, its status (loaded or unloaded), file size, type, date the image was last saved, and the file path for all images attached to the drawing. Refer to **Figure 17-3.** Four options are available to help you manage the images.

- **Attach.** Used to search for and attach image files to the drawing; discussed in the previous section.
- **Detach.** Removes or detaches the selected image file from the drawing.
- **Reload.** Reloads the selected image file. The **Status** column will show Reload if this option is selected. The image is loaded after the dialog box is closed.
- **Unload.** Unloads the selected image, but retains its path information. The **Status** column will show Unload if this option is selected. The image is unloaded after the dialog box is closed. An unloaded image is displayed only as a frame until reloaded.

## Controlling Image File Displays

Once an image is attached to the current drawing, its display can be adjusted if needed. The commands used to adjust images can be accessed on the **Reference** toolbar or in the **Modify** pull-down menu, **Figure 17-7.**

### Clipping an image

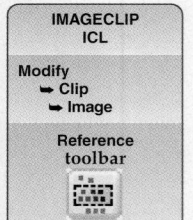

IMAGECLIP
ICL

Modify
➥ Clip
➥ Image

Reference
toolbar

Image Clip

The **IMAGECLIP** command allows you to trim away a portion of the image that does not need to be seen. The clipping frame can be rectangular or polygonal. To access the **IMAGECLIP** command, pick the **Image Clip** button on the **Reference** toolbar, select **Image** from the **Clip** cascading menu in the **Modify** pull-down menu, or type ICL or IMAGECLIP at the Command: prompt.

Command: **ICL** *or* **IMAGECLIP**↵
Select image to clip: *(pick the image frame)*
Enter image clipping option [ON/OFF/Delete/New boundary] <New>: **N**↵
Enter clipping type [Polygonal/Rectangular] <Rectangular>: **R**↵
Specify first corner point: *(pick the first corner of the clipping boundary)*
Specify opposite corner point: *(pick the second corner)*
Command:

**Figure 17-7.**
Commands used to control image files are found in the **Modify** pull-down menu.

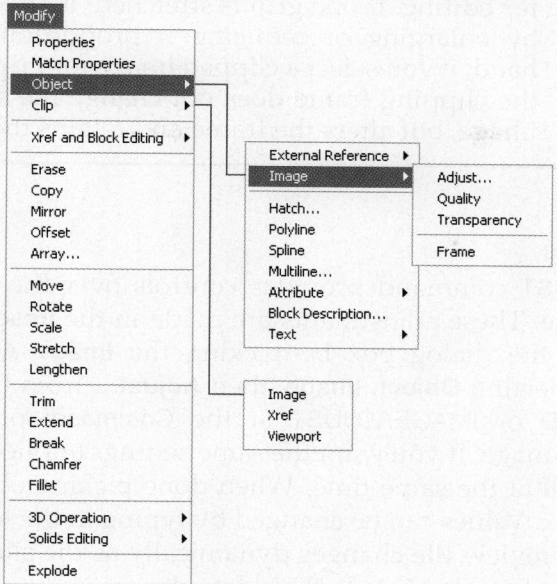

The **Polygonal** option allows you to construct a clipping frame composed of three or more points as follows.

Enter clipping type [Polygonal/Rectangular] <Rectangular>: **P**↵
Specify first point: *(pick first point to be used for the clipping boundary)*
Specify next point or [Undo]: *(pick second point)*
Specify next point or [Undo]: *(pick third point)*
Specify next point or [Close/Undo]: *(pick additional points as needed)*
Specify next point or [Close/Undo]: ↵
Command:

**Figure 17-8** shows the results of using the **Rectangular** and **Polygonal** options of the **IMAGECLIP** command on a raster image. Three additional options of **IMAGECLIP** allow you to work with the display of the clipped image.
- **ON.** Turns the clipping frame on to display only the clipped area.
- **OFF.** Turns off the clipping frame to display the entire original image and frame.
- **Delete.** Deletes the clipping frame and displays the entire original image.

**Figure 17-8.**
A—A rectangular image clip. B—A polygonal image clip (shown here in color for illustration).

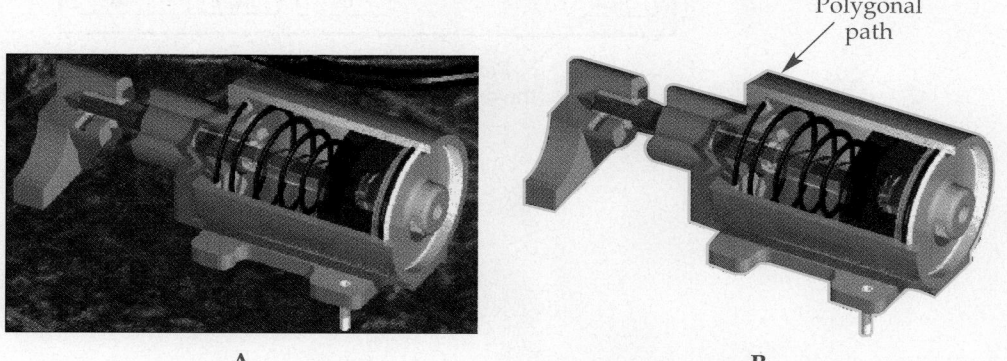

A                                              B

## Adjusting an image

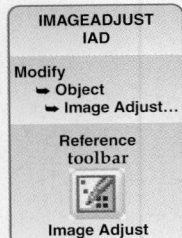

IMAGEADJUST
IAD

Modify
➡ Object
  ➡ Image Adjust...

Reference
toolbar

Image Adjust

The **IMAGEADJUST** command provides controls over the brightness, contrast, and fade of the image. These adjustments are made in the **Image Adjust** dialog box, **Figure 17-9.** Access the dialog box by picking the **Image Adjust** button on the **Reference** toolbar; selecting **Object**, **Image**, then **Adjust...** from the **Modify** pull-down menu; or typing IAD or IMAGEADJUST at the Command: prompt. You are first prompted to pick an image. If you want the same settings applied to multiple images, you can pick them all at the same time. When done picking objects, press [Enter] to display the dialog box. Values can be changed by typing in the text boxes or by using the slider bars. The preview tile changes dynamically as the sliders are moved. Pick the **Reset** button to return all values to their defaults.

- **Brightness.** Controls pixel whiteness and indirectly affects the contrast. Values can range from 0 to 100, with 50 as the default value. Higher values increase the brightness.
- **Contrast.** Controls the contrast of the image, or how close each pixel is moved toward its primary or secondary color. Values can range from 0 to 100, with 50 as the default value. Higher values increase the contrast.
- **Fade.** Controls the fading of the image, or how close the image is to the background color. Values can range from 0 to 100, with 0 as the default value. Higher values increase the fading.

**Figure 17-9.**
Brightness, contrast, and fade values can be entered numerically or set using the slider bars in the **Image Adjust** dialog box.

Preview of settings

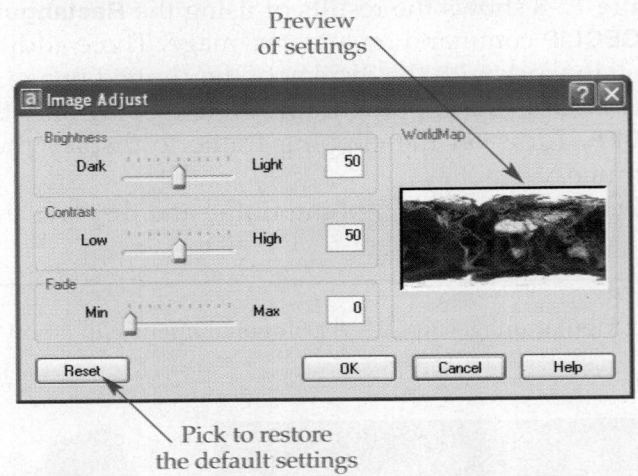

Pick to restore the default settings

## Image quality

The **IMAGEQUALITY** command provides two options: **High** and **Draft**. The high quality setting produces the best image display, but requires longer to generate. If you are working with several images in a drawing, it is best to set the **Draft** option. The image displayed is lower quality, but requires less time to display.

Change the **IMAGEQUALITY** setting by picking the **Image Quality** button on the **Reference** toolbar; selecting **Object**, **Image**, then **Quality** from the **Modify** pull-down menu; or typing IMAGEQUALITY at the Command: prompt. The setting applies to all images in the drawing.

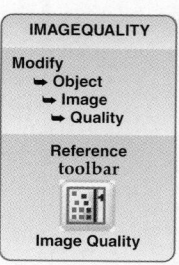

## Transparency

Some raster images have transparent background pixels. The **TRANSPARENCY** command controls the display of these pixels. If **TRANSPARENCY** is on, the drawing will show through the image background. Images are inserted with this feature turned off.

The **TRANSPARENCY** setting can be changed by picking the **Image Transparency** button on the **Reference** toolbar; selecting **Object**, **Image**, then **Transparency** from the **Modify** pull-down menu; or typing TRANSPARENCY at the Command: prompt. The setting applies to individual images. Multiple images can be selected at the same time. Remember, only images containing transparent pixels are affected.

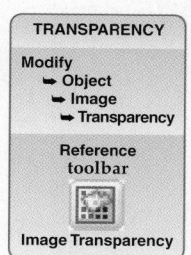

## Image frame

The **IMAGEFRAME** command controls the appearance of frames around all images in the current drawing. When attaching (inserting) images, AutoCAD places a frame around the image in the current layer color and linetype. There are two settings for the **IMAGEFRAME** command: on and off. When **IMAGEFRAME** is on, a frame appears around the image.

The **IMAGEFRAME** setting can be changed by picking the **Image Frame** button on the **Reference** toolbar; selecting **Object**, **Image**, then **Frame** from the **Modify** pull-down menu; or typing IMAGEFRAME at the Command: prompt. The setting applies to all images in the drawing.

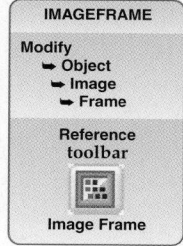

# Uses of Raster Files in AutoCAD

One use of raster images is as a background for sketching or tracing. For example, you may need a line drawing of an image only available as a photo. The photo can be scanned, which produces a raster image. After importing the raster image using the **IMAGE** command, use the appropriate drawing commands to sketch or trace the image. After the object is sketched, the original raster image can be deleted, frozen, or unloaded, leaving the tracing. You can then add other elements to the tracing to create a full drawing. See **Figure 17-10.**

Raster files can be combined with AutoCAD drawing and modeling features in many ways to complete or complement the design. For example, company marks or logos can be easily added to title blocks, style sheets, and company drawing standards. Drawings that require designs, labels, and a variety of text fonts can be created using raster files in conjunction with the wide variety of TrueType fonts available with AutoCAD. Archived manual drawings can also be scanned, brought into AutoCAD, and then traced to create a CAD drawing.

You can add features to complement raster files. For example, you can import a raster file, dimension or annotate it, and even add special shapes to it. Then, export it as the same type of file. Now you can use the revised file in the original software in which it was created. As with any creative process, let your imagination and the job requirements determine how you use this capability of AutoCAD.

**Figure 17-10.**
Using a raster image as a model for a drawing. A—The imported raster image. B—Use
AutoCAD commands to trace the image. Then, either delete the image or freeze its layer.
C—The completed drawing plotted on a title block.

A

B

C

## Exporting a Drawing to a Raster File

You can save a rendering to a raster file. This is discussed in Chapter 14.
However, 2D objects are not rendered and, therefore, do not appear in the file. If you
want what is displayed in the current viewport, including 2D objects, saved as a
raster file, you must use the **SAVEIMG** command.

The **SAVEIMG** command saves wireframe and hidden displays. Shaded displays
cannot be saved with **SAVEIMG**. Also, there are only three file types available in this
command. This command can save the drawing as BMP, TGA, and TIFF raster files.

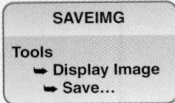

To access the command, pick **Save...** from the **Display Image** cascading menu in
the **Tools** pull-down menu or type SAVEIMG at the Command: prompt. This displays
the **Save Image** dialog box, **Figure 17-11.**

On the left side of the **Save Image** dialog box, pick the radio button for the type of
file you want to create. The TGA and TIF formats can be saved as compressed files.
Pick the **Options...** button to open the **TGA Options** or **TIFF Options** dialog box. The
compressed form for TGA files is **RLE** (run length encoded). A TIF file can be compressed as **PACK** for Macintosh computers.

The image can be cropped by specifying the XY pixel values. The pixel values
shown at the top-right of the **Save Image** dialog box next to **Size:** represent the size in
pixels of the current viewport. The **Offset X:** and **Y:** text boxes define the lower-left
corner of the image. The **Size X:** and **Y:** text boxes define the upper-right corner of the
image. You can also use the pointing device and pick the two corners in the **Active**

Figure 17-11.
The **Save Image**
dialog box.

File type

Image portion

Viewport size in pixels

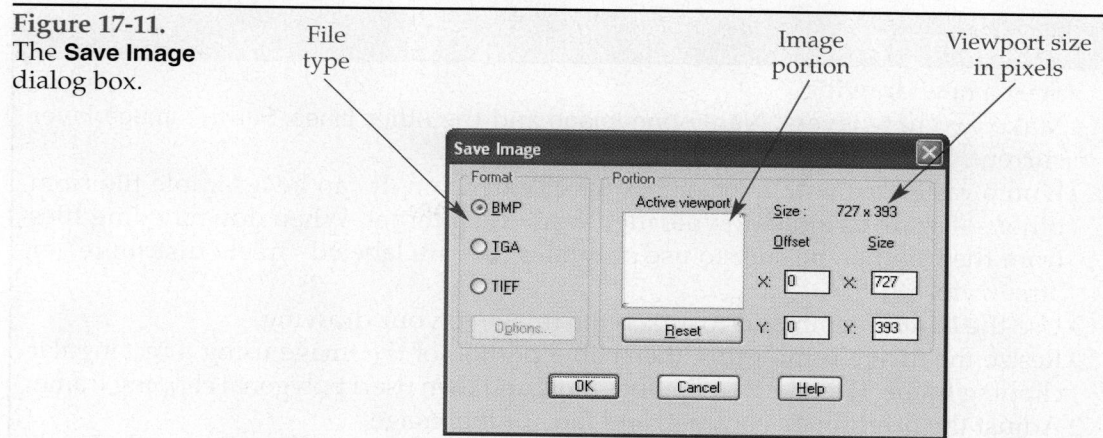

viewport image tile of the dialog box to define the image area. Pick the **Reset** button to return the portion to its default size.

Pick **OK** to close the **Save Image** dialog box. The **Image File** dialog box appears. See **Figure 17-12.** Enter a file name and location. Then, pick **Save** to save the image.

As mentioned, the **SAVEIMG** command can be used to save the current viewport as a BMP file. You can also export a BMP using the **EXPORT** or **BMPOUT** command. In this manner, you can select individual objects that will be included in the image. You can also save shaded images with this method.

Figure 17-12.
Once you pick **OK** in the **Save Image** dialog box, the **Image File** dialog box appears.

Specify a location

Enter a name

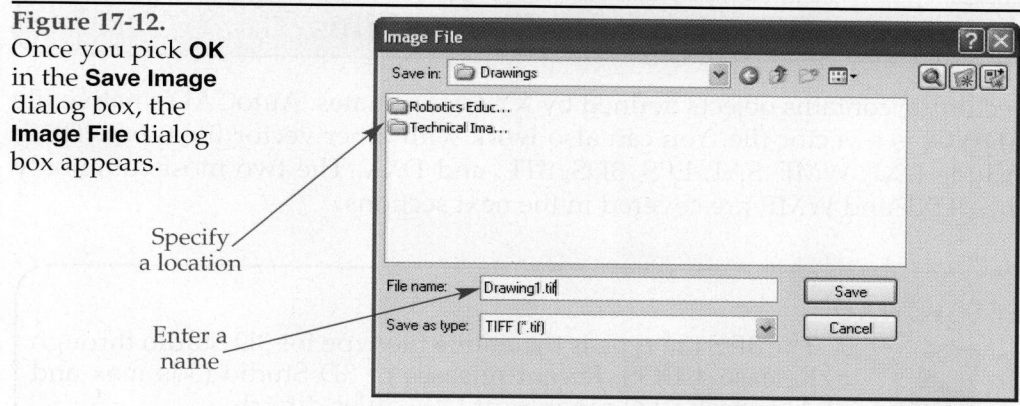

NOTE

The **SAVEIMG** command does not work with certain viewport configurations. If you encounter this problem, either temporarily switch to a single viewport or render the image to a file.

PROFESSIONAL TIP

You can use the **SAVEIMG** command to save a rendering that was rendered to the viewport. However, the result is a low-resolution image. Most images that will be in print, such as in a magazine or book, need to be high resolution. Check with the magazine or book publisher for image resolution requirements.

## Working with Vector Files

A vector file contains objects defined by XYZ coordinates. AutoCAD's native file format (DWG) is a vector file. You can also work with other vector file types. These types include DXF, WMF, SAT, EPS, 3DS, STL, and DXX. The two most commonly used types, DXF and WMF, are covered in the next sections.

**PROFESSIONAL TIP**
The 3DS file type is the native file type for 3D Studio through Release 4 DOS. Recent releases of 3D Studio (3ds max and Autodesk VIZ) can import DWG files directly.

### Exporting and Importing DXF Files

The DXF file is a generic file type that defines AutoCAD geometry in an ASCII text file. Other programs that recognize the DXF format can then "read" this file. The DXF file format retains the mathematical definitions of AutoCAD objects in vector form. The DXF objects imported into other vector programs, or opened in AutoCAD, can be edited as needed.

#### Exporting DXF files

To export DXF files, select **Save As...** from the **File** pull-down menu or type SAVEAS or DXFOUT at the Command: prompt. This opens the **Save Drawing As** dialog box. See **Figure 17-13.** Select the DXF file type from the **Files of type:** drop-down list. If you type DXFOUT, the DXF file type is automatically selected. Name the file and specify a location where you want to save it. Notice that you can select different

SAVEAS
DXFOUT

File
➥ Save As...

**Figure 17-13.**
The **Save Drawing As** dialog box is used to save a DXF file.

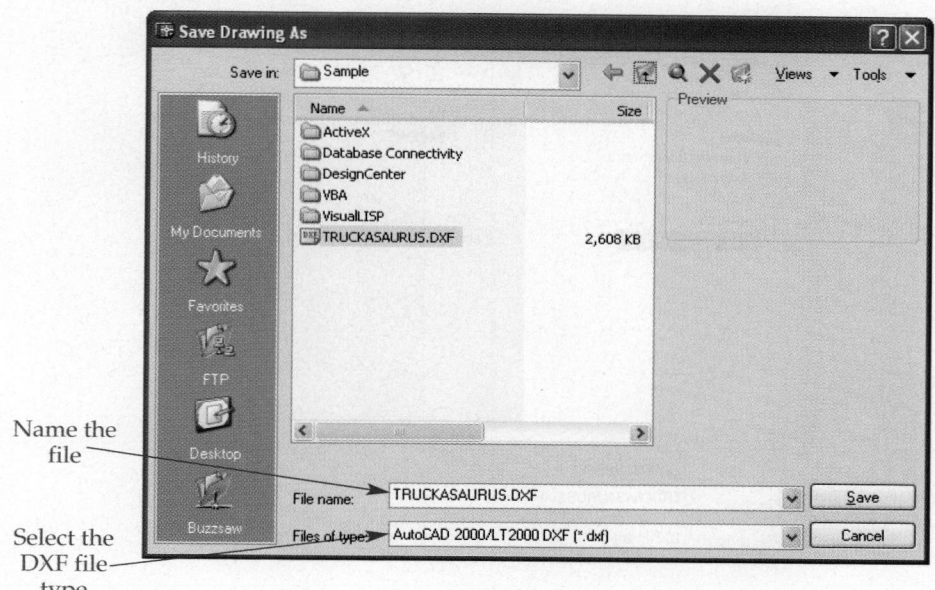

Name the file

Select the DXF file type

"versions" of DXF. This is to ensure that the file you save is "backward compatible." For example, if you are sharing the file with somebody using AutoCAD 2000, save the DXF as that "version" to ensure AutoCAD 2000 can read the file.

Since this is a "save as" operation, the current drawing is saved as a DXF file. If you continue to work on the drawing, you are working on the DXF version, *not* the DWG version. In order to work on the original drawing, you must open the DWG file. However, if you continue to work on the drawing in DXF form, save, and then attempt to close the drawing, you are warned that the drawing is not DWG. You are given the opportunity to save the drawing as a DWG file.

When a DXF file is saved, all geometry in the drawing is saved, regardless of the current zoom percentage or selected objects. However, the current zoom percentage is saved in the DXF file. As explained later, this differs from the WMF format.

The DXF file format saves any surfaced or solid 3D objects as 3D geometry. When a DXF file containing 3D geometry is opened, the surfaced or solid 3D geometry remains intact. In addition, the current **SHADEMODE** setting is saved in the DXF file.

> **NOTE**
> Not all programs that can import DXF files are capable of correctly "reading" 3D objects or the **SHADEMODE** setting.

### Importing DXF files

To open a DXF file, select **Open** from the **File** pull-down menu, pick the **Open** button on the **Standard** toolbar, press [Ctrl]+[O], or type OPEN or DXFIN at the Command: prompt. The **Select File** dialog box appears, **Figure 17-14.** Select **DXF (*.dxf)** from the **Files of type:** drop-down list. If you type DXFIN, this is automatically selected. Then, select the DXF file you want to open. Notice that there is no preview when the file is selected. AutoCAD does not support previews for the DXF file type. Finally, pick the **Open** button.

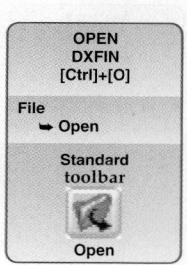

OPEN
DXFIN
[Ctrl]+[O]

File
➡ Open

Standard
toolbar

Open

**Figure 17-14.**
The **Select File** dialog box is used to import a DXF file.

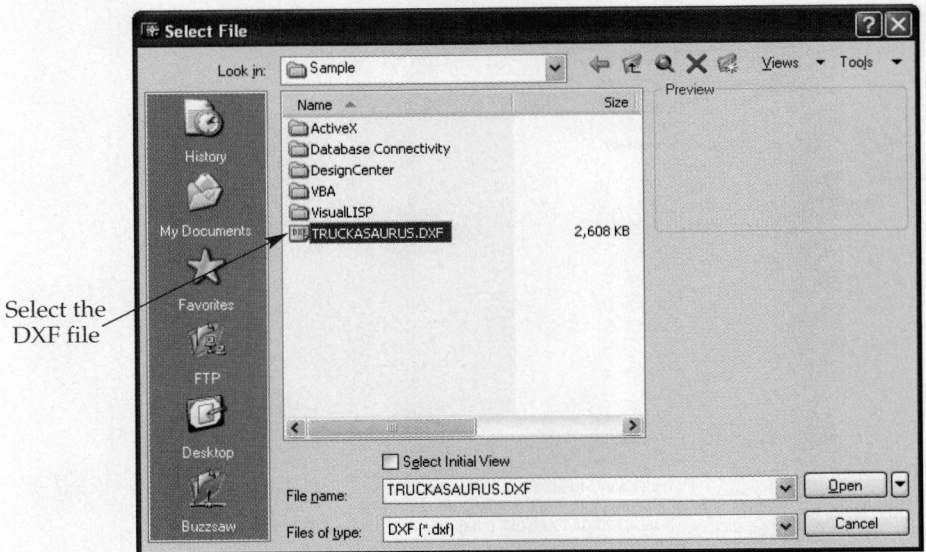

Select the DXF file

The DXF file is opened in a new document window. To place a DXF file into the *current* drawing, insert it as a block. If you do not want it inserted as a block, open the file (**DXFIN**), copy it to the clipboard ([Ctrl]+[C]), and paste ([Ctrl]+[V]) it into the current drawing.

> **NOTE**
>
> If you open a DXF file and try to save it, the **Save Drawing As** dialog box appears. You can save it as DXF, overwriting the existing file, or under a new name or as another file type.

## Exporting and Importing Windows Metafiles

The Windows metafile (WMF) file format is often used to exchange data with desktop publishing programs. It is a vector format that can save wireframe and hidden displays. Shaded and rendered images cannot be saved.

A WMF file cannot retain the definition of all AutoCAD object types. For example, circles are translated to line segments. Also, a WMF file does *not* save three-dimensional data. The view in the current viewport is projected onto the viewing plane and saved as a two-dimensional projection.

### Exporting WMF Files

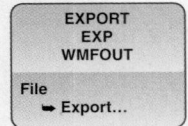

To create a WMF file, select **Export...** from the **File** pull-down menu or type EXPORT, EXP, or WMFOUT at the Command: prompt. This displays the **Export Data** dialog box. Select Metafile (*.wmf) in the **Files of type:** drop-down list. Typing WMFOUT at the Command: prompt displays the **Create WMF File** dialog box. This is the same dialog box with Metafile (*.wmf) file type automatically selected (and the only option in the drop-down list). After specifying the file name and folder location in either dialog box and picking the **Save** button, you must select the objects to place in the file. Press [Enter] when all of the objects are selected and the WMF file is saved.

Only the portions of selected objects visible on-screen are written into the file. If part of a selected object goes off the screen, that part is "clipped." Also, the current view resolution affects the appearance of a Windows metafile. For example, when **VIEWRES** is set low, circles in your AutoCAD drawing may look like polygons in the WMF file. When saved to a Windows metafile, the objects are polygons (line segments) rather than circles.

### Importing WMF Files

To import a Windows metafile, select **Windows Metafile...** from the **Insert** pull-down menu or type IMP or IMPORT at the Command: prompt. This opens the **Import File** dialog box. Select Metafile (*.wmf) in the **Files of type:** drop-down list, then select a file. You can also type WMFIN at the Command: prompt. This displays the **Import WMF** dialog box. Both dialog boxes have a preview window where you can see the image before you import it.

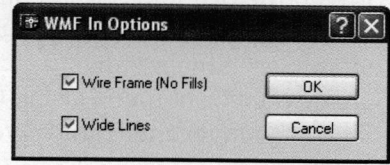

A Windows metafile is imported as a block made up of all the objects in the file. You can explode the block if you need to edit the objects within it. If an object is not filled, it is created as a polyline when brought into AutoCAD. This includes arcs and circles. Objects composed of several closed polylines to represent fills are created from solid fill objects, as if created using the **SOLID** command with the **FILL** system variable off.

There are two settings used to control the appearance of Windows metafiles imported into AutoCAD. Type WMFOPTS at the Command: prompt or pick the **Options...** button in the **Tools** drop-down menu in the "import" dialog box. The **WMF In Options** dialog box is displayed, **Figure 17-15.** The dialog box contains the following two check boxes.

- **Wire Frame (No Fills).** When checked, filled areas are imported only as outlines. Otherwise, filled areas are imported as filled objects (when **FILL** is on).
- **Wide Lines.** When this option is checked, the relative line widths of lines and borders from the WMF file are maintained. Otherwise, they are imported using a zero width.

**Figure 17-15.**
Setting options for imported WMF files.

## Chapter Test

*Answer the following questions on a separate sheet of paper.*

1. Name four common formats of raster images that can be imported into AutoCAD.
2. Which command allows you to attach a raster file to the current AutoCAD drawing?
3. What is the display status of an inserted image that has been unloaded?
4. Which two shapes can be used to clip a raster image?
5. What is the function of the **IMAGEADJUST** command?
6. Name two commands that allow you to export bitmap files.
7. Give the name and file type of the vector file that can be exchanged between object-based programs (object definitions are retained).
8. Name the commands that allow you to import and export the file type in Question 7.
9. How are three-dimensional objects treated when exported to a WMF file?
10. How can a DXF be inserted into the *current* drawing?

## Drawing Problems

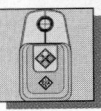

1. Locate some sample raster files with the .jpg, .pcx, or .tif file extensions. These files are often included as samples with software. They can also be downloaded from the Internet. With the permission of your instructor or supervisor, create a folder on your hard drive and copy the raster files there. Create a new drawing and attach each of the raster files. Save the drawing as P17-1.

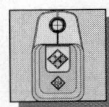

2. Choose a small raster file and attach it to a new AutoCAD drawing.
   A. Insert the image so it fills the entire screen.
   B. Undo and insert the image again using a scale factor that fills half the screen with the image.
   C. Stretch the original object using grips, then experiment with different clipping boundaries. Stretch the image after it has been clipped and observe the result.
   D. Create a layer named Raster. Create a second layer named Object. Give each layer the color of your choice. Set the current layer to Raster.
   E. Import the same image next to the previous one at the same scale factor.
   F. Set the current layer to Object and use any AutoCAD drawing commands to trace the outline of the second raster image.
   G. Unload the raster image or freeze the Raster layer.
   H. Save the drawing as P17-2.

3. For this problem, you will import several raster files into AutoCAD. Then, you will trace the object in each file and save it as a block or wblock to be used on other drawings.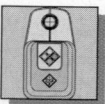
   A. Find several raster files that contain simple objects, shapes, or figures that you might use in other drawings.
   B. Create a template drawing containing Object and Raster layers.
   C. Import each raster file into AutoCAD on the Raster layer using the appropriate command. Set the Object layer current and trace the shape or objects using AutoCAD drawing commands.
   D. Detach the raster information, keeping only the traced lines of the object.
   E. Save the object as a block or wblock using an appropriate file-naming system.
   F. After all blocks have been created, insert each one into a single drawing and label each with its name. Include a path if necessary.
   G. Save the drawing as P17-3.
   H. Print or plot the final drawing.

4. In this problem, you will create a memo outlining your progress on a hypothetical project.
   A. Open Problem 4 or Problem 5 from Chapter 16.
   B. Create a hidden display.
   C. Export a WMF file of the hidden display. Take the steps necessary so that only the object is exported.
   D. Create a photo raytrace rendering of the drawing. Render the drawing to a BMP file.
   E. Open a word processor capable of importing WMF and BMP files, such as Microsoft Word or WordPad.
   F. Write a memo related to the project. A sample appears below. The memo should discuss how you created the drawing, the WMF file, and the rendered file. Insert the rendered and WMF files as appropriate.
   G. Save the document as P17-4. Print the document.

---

**MEMO**

| | |
|---|---|
| **To:** | Otto Desque |
| **From:** | Ima Drafter |
| **Date:** | Thursday, March 14 |
| **Subject:** | Project Progress |

Dear Otto,

I have completed the initial drawing. As you can see from the drawing shown here, the project is complying with design parameters. The drawing is ready for transfer to the engineering department for approval.

I have also included a rendered image of the project. The material spec'ed by the engineering department is represented in the rendering. This may help in evaluation of the design.

Respectfully,

Ima

---

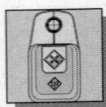

5. Begin a new drawing.
   A. Insert the blocks you created in Problem 3. Arrange them in any order you wish.
   B. Add any notes you need to identify this drawing as a sheet of library shapes. Be sure each shape is identified with its file name and location (path).
   C. Print the file on an appropriate sheet size.
   D. Save the drawing as P17-5.

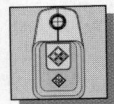

6. Add a raster image to one of your title block template drawings as a design element or a company logo. Import an existing raster image or create your own using a program such as Windows Paint. Save the template drawing.

## CHAPTER 18

# Customizing the AutoCAD Environment

## Learning Objectives

After completing this chapter, you will be able to:
- Set environment variables.
- Assign colors and fonts to the text and graphics windows.
- Control general AutoCAD system variables.
- Set options that control display quality and AutoCAD performance.
- Control shortcut menus.
- Modify program icon properties.
- Set up AutoCAD for multiple configurations.

AutoCAD provides a variety of options to customize the user interface and working environment. These options permit users to configure the software to suit personal preferences. These options include defining colors for the individual window elements, assigning preferred fonts to the command line window, controlling shortcut menus, and assigning properties to program icons.

The options for customizing the AutoCAD user interface and working environment are found in the **Options** dialog box, **Figure 18-1.** This dialog box is accessed by selecting **Options...** from the **Tools** pull-down menu, entering OP or OPTIONS at the Command: prompt, or right-clicking in the drawing area and selecting **Options...** from the shortcut menu.

Changes made in the **Options** dialog box do not take effect until either the **Apply** or **OK** button is picked. If you pick the **Cancel** button, all changes are discarded. Each time you change the options settings, the system registry is updated and the changes are used in subsequent drawing sessions. Settings that are stored within the drawing file have the AutoCAD icon next to them. Settings without the icon indicate that the option affects all AutoCAD drawing sessions.

> OPTIONS
> OP
>
> Tools
> ➥ Options...

**Figure 18-1.**
The **Options** dialog box is used to customize the AutoCAD working environment. Each tab contains a variety of options and settings.

Select the appropriate tab

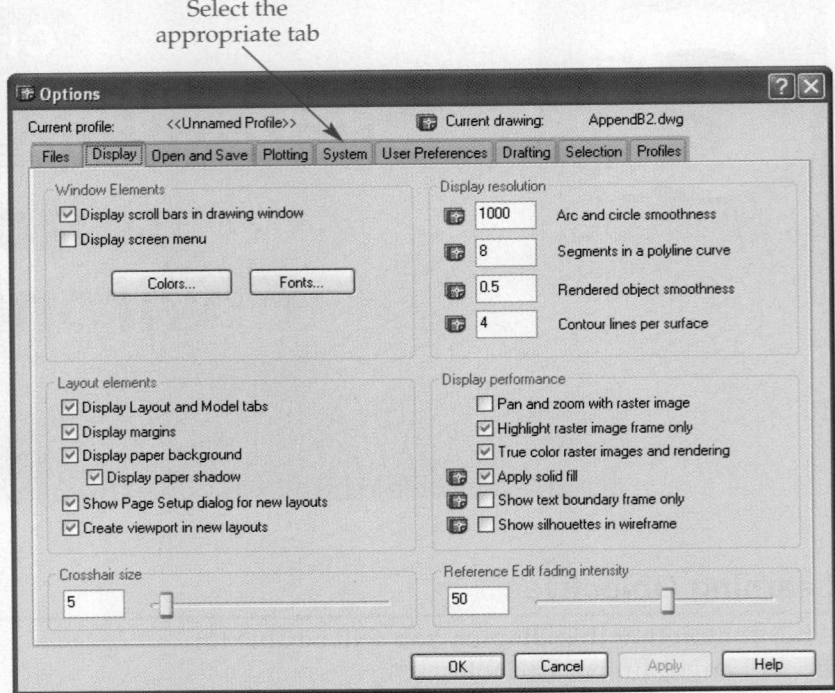

# Setting AutoCAD Environment Variables

There are numerous settings that control the manner in which AutoCAD behaves in the Windows environment. These settings are made through the use of environment variables. These variables are used to specify such items as which folders to search for driver and menu files and the location of your temporary and support files. The default settings created during installation are usually adequate, but changing the settings may result in better performance.

## File Locations

When AutoCAD is used in a network environment, some files pertaining to AutoCAD may reside on a network drive, so all users can access them, and some files may reside in folders specifically created for a particular AutoCAD user. These files may include drawings containing blocks, external reference files, and custom menu files.

While several different options exist for setting many of the environment variables, the simplest method is to use the **Options** dialog box. The **Files** tab of the **Options** dialog box is used to specify the path AutoCAD searches to find support files and driver files. It also contains the paths where certain types of files are saved, and where AutoCAD looks for specific types of files. Support files include text fonts, menus, AutoLISP files, ObjectARX files, blocks, linetypes, and hatch patterns.

The folder names shown under the Support File Search Path heading in the **Search paths, files names, and file locations:** list are automatically created by the AutoCAD during installation. As previously mentioned, some of these paths are created for a specific user. For example, **Figure 18-2** shows that the support files are saved in Documents and Setting folder path set by the AutoCAD 2004 Support File Search Path. The *username* listing will indicate the specific user.

**Figure 18-2.**
Folder paths can be customized in the **Files** tab of the **Options** dialog box.

Folder for specific user

Folders in support search path

Add a new folder or file to the selected path

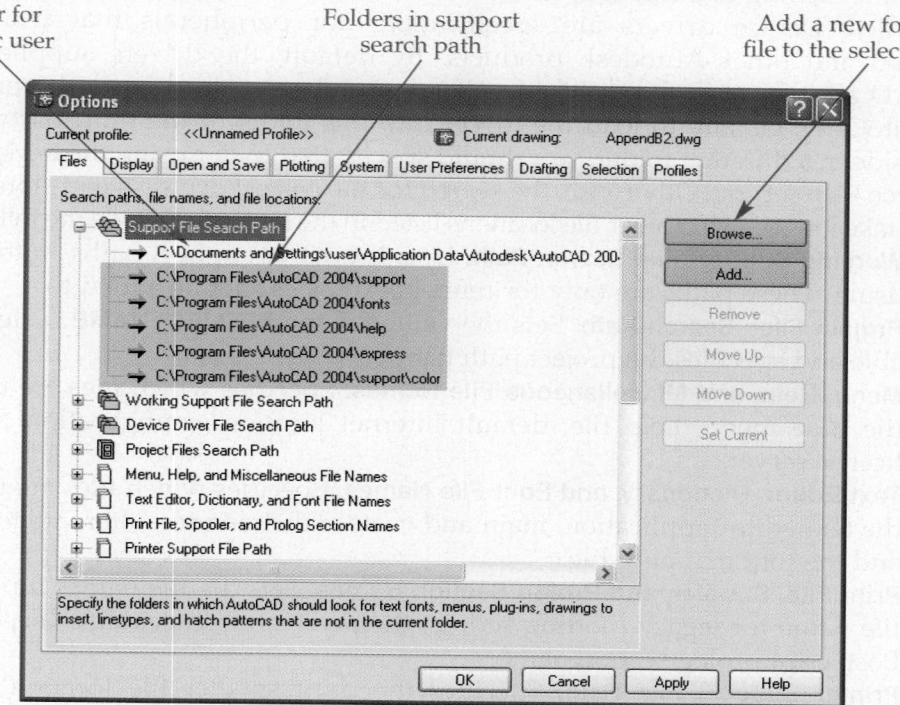

You can add the path of any new folders you create that contain support files. As an example, suppose you store all the blocks you typically use in a separate folder named Blocks. Unless this folder name is placed in the support files search path, AutoCAD will not be able to find your blocks when you attempt to insert them, unless you specify the entire folder path location.

You can add this folder to the existing search path in two ways. The first method is to highlight the Support File Search Path heading and pick the **Add...** button. This places a new, empty listing under the heading. You can now type C:\BLOCKS to complete the entry. Alternatively, instead of typing the path name, you can pick the **Browse...** button after picking **Add...** to display the **Browse for Folder** dialog box. You can then use this dialog box to select to the desired folder. The new setting takes effect as soon as you pick **Apply** or the **OK** button and close the **Options** dialog box.

## Specifying the Help File

The AutoCAD help file is named acad.chm. During installation, this file is placed in the \Help folder. You can use the Help File heading under the Menu, Help, and Miscellaneous File Names entry to specify a different path and file name for the help file. This is particularly handy if you want to locate the help file on a network drive or if you are using a custom help file.

AutoCAD is able to use any CHM, HLP, or BIN help file, so custom help files can be generated as needed. This can be a formidable undertaking and is usually done by third-party developers to supplement their software add-ons. If you are using a third-party application with AutoCAD, you may have an alternate help file.

# Other File Settings

Another setting that can be specified from the **Files** panel is the location of device driver files. Device drivers are specifications for peripherals that work with AutoCAD and other Autodesk products. By default, the drivers supplied with AutoCAD are placed in the \drv folder. If you purchase a third-party driver to use with AutoCAD, be sure to load the driver into this folder. If the third-party driver must reside in a different folder, you should specify that folder using the Device Driver File Search Path setting. Otherwise, the search for the correct driver is widespread and likely to take longer. Some other file locations listed in the **Files** tab include the following.

- **Working Support File Search Path.** Lists the active support paths AutoCAD is using. These paths are only for reference; they cannot be added to.
- **Project Files Search Path.** Sets the value for the **PROJECTNAME** system variable and specifies the project path names.
- **Menu, Help, and Miscellaneous File Names.** Specifies which files are used for the base menu, help file, default Internet location, configuration file, and license server.
- **Text Editor, Dictionary, and Font File Names.** Specifies which files are used for the text editor application, main and custom dictionaries, alternate font files, and the font mapping file.
- **Print File, Spooler, and Prolog Section Names.** Sets the file names for the plot file name for legacy plotting scripts, the print spool executable file, and the PostScript prolog section name.
- **Printer Support File Path.** Specifies the print spooler file location, printer configuration search path, printer description file search path, and plot style table search path.
- **Automatic Save File Location.** Sets the path where the autosave (.sv$) file is stored. An autosave file is only created if the **Automatic save** option is checked in the **Open and Save** tab of the **Options** dialog box.
- **Color Book Locations.** Specifies the path for color book files that can be used when specifying colors in the **Select Color** dialog box.
- **Data Sources Location.** Specifies the path for database source files (.udl).
- **Drawing Template Settings.** Specifies the default location for drawing template files and the default drawing template file name.
- **Tool Palettes File Locations.** Specifies the path for tool palette support files.
- **Log File Location.** Specifies the path for the acad.log file. A log file is only created if the **Maintain a log file** option is checked in the **Open and Save** tab of the **Options** dialog box.
- **Temporary Drawing File Location.** Sets the folder where AutoCAD stores temporary drawing files.
- **Temporary External Reference File Location.** Indicates where temporary external reference files are placed.
- **Texture Maps Search Path.** Location of texture map files for rendering.
- **i-drop Associated File Location.** Specifies the folder used by default to store downloaded i-drop content.

**Figure 18-3.**
Use the **Display** tab to set many visual elements of the AutoCAD environment.

Display options

Set appearance of graphics window

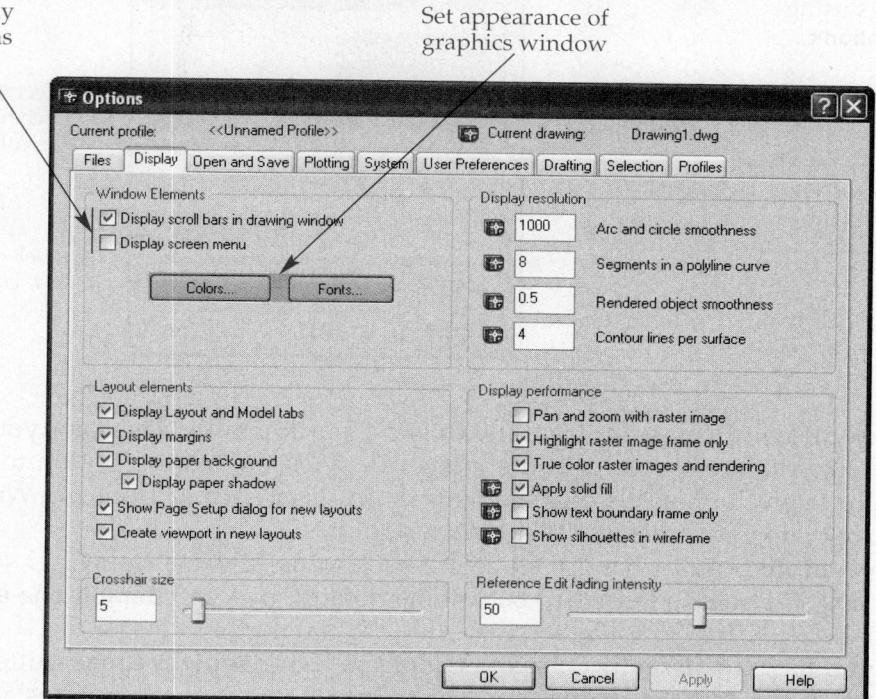

---

## Customizing the Graphics Window

Numerous options are available to customize the graphics window to your personal liking. Select the **Display** tab in the **Options** dialog box to view the display control options, **Figure 18-3.**

The **Window Elements** area has settings used to turn the scroll bars and screen menu on or off, set the number of visible command lines, and select the color and font settings. At the bottom of the tab, the **Crosshair size** setting is a percentage of the drawing screen area. The higher the value, the further the crosshairs extend. The **Reference edit fading intensity** value determines the display intensity of the unselected objects in reference edit mode. A higher value means the unselected objects are less visible.

### Changing Colors

By customizing colors, you can add your personal touch and make AutoCAD stand out among other active Windows applications. AutoCAD provides this capability with the **Color Options** dialog box, **Figure 18-4.** This dialog box is accessed by picking the **Colors...** button in the **Window Elements** area of the **Display** tab in the **Options** dialog box.

The **Window Element:** drop-down list allows you to select elements of the graphics and text windows. You can also pick on the image tiles to select an element. These elements include the model space background and pointer, the layout space background and pointer, the command line background, and the command line text. To customize colors, do the following.

1. Pick the **Color...** button in the **Display** tab of the **Options** dialog box. The **Color Options** dialog box appears.
2. Select the feature to have its color changed.

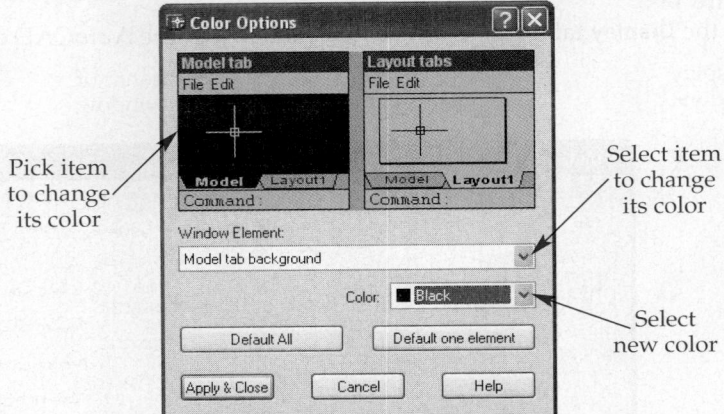

**Figure 18-4.**
Change AutoCAD color settings using the **Color Options** dialog box.

Pick item to change its color

Select item to change its color

Select new color

3. Pick the color you want from the **Color:** drop-down list. The color you select is immediately reflected in the image tile. Pick the **More...** option to pick a color from the **Select Color** dialog box. To select a color from the Windows Color dialog box, pick the **Windows...** option.

The **Default All** button changes all colors back to the default AutoCAD settings. To change only the selected element back to its default, pick the **Default one element** button.

Once you have made your color selections, pick the **Apply & Close** button, and then pick **OK** in the **Options** dialog box. The graphics window regenerates and displays the color changes you made.

## Changing Fonts

You can also change the fonts used in the command line window. The font you select has no effect on the text in your drawings, nor is the font used in the AutoCAD dialog boxes, pull-down menus, or screen menus.

To change the font used in the command line window, pick the **Fonts...** button in the **Display** tab of the **Options** dialog box. The **Command Line Window Font** dialog box appears, **Figure 18-5.**

The default font used by AutoCAD for the graphics window is Courier. The font style for Courier is Regular (not bold or italic), and it defaults to a size of 10 points. Select a new font from the **Font:** list. This displays the system fonts available for use. Also, set a style and size. The **Sample Command Line Font** area displays a sample of the selected font. Once you have selected the desired font, font style, and size for the command line window, pick the **Apply & Close** button to assign the new font.

**Figure 18-5.**
The command line window font can be changed to suit your preference.

Select a font

Select a size

Select a style

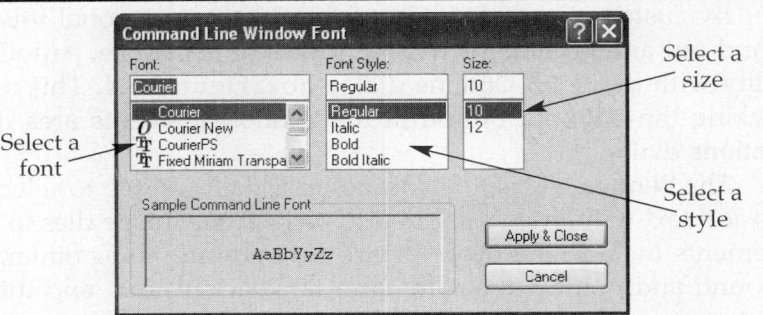

**Exercise 18-1**

○ Start AutoCAD.
○ Use the **Options** dialog box to change the color elements and fonts for the command line window to your personal liking.
○ Once you are satisfied with your modifications, exit the **Options** dialog box.

## Command Line Window Size

In addition to changing the colors and fonts used in the command line window, the number of visible lines can be changed. The number of visible lines increases if the size of the command line window is increased. The window size is changed dynamically by using the resizing cursor shown in **Figure 18-6**. Remember, changing the size of the command line window affects the size of your drawing area.

---

Figure 18-6.
This cursor appears when resizing the command line window.

## Layout Display Settings

The appearance of a layout tab is different than the appearance of the **Model** tab. The theory behind the default layout tab settings is to provide a picture of what the drawing will look like when plotted. You can see if the objects will fit on the paper or if some of the objects are outside the margins. The following options, which are found in the **Layout elements** area of the **Display** tab in the **Options** dialog box, are illustrated in **Figure 18-7**.

- **Display Layout and Model tabs.** Displays the **Model** and **Layout** tabs at the bottom of the drawing screen area.
- **Display margins.** The margins are shown as dashed lines on the paper. Any object outside the margins is not plotted.
- **Display paper background.** Displays the paper size specified in the page setup.

---

**Figure 18-7.**
Customizing the display of layouts.

Display margins

Display paper background

Create viewport in new layouts

Display paper shadow

Display **Layout** and **Model** tabs

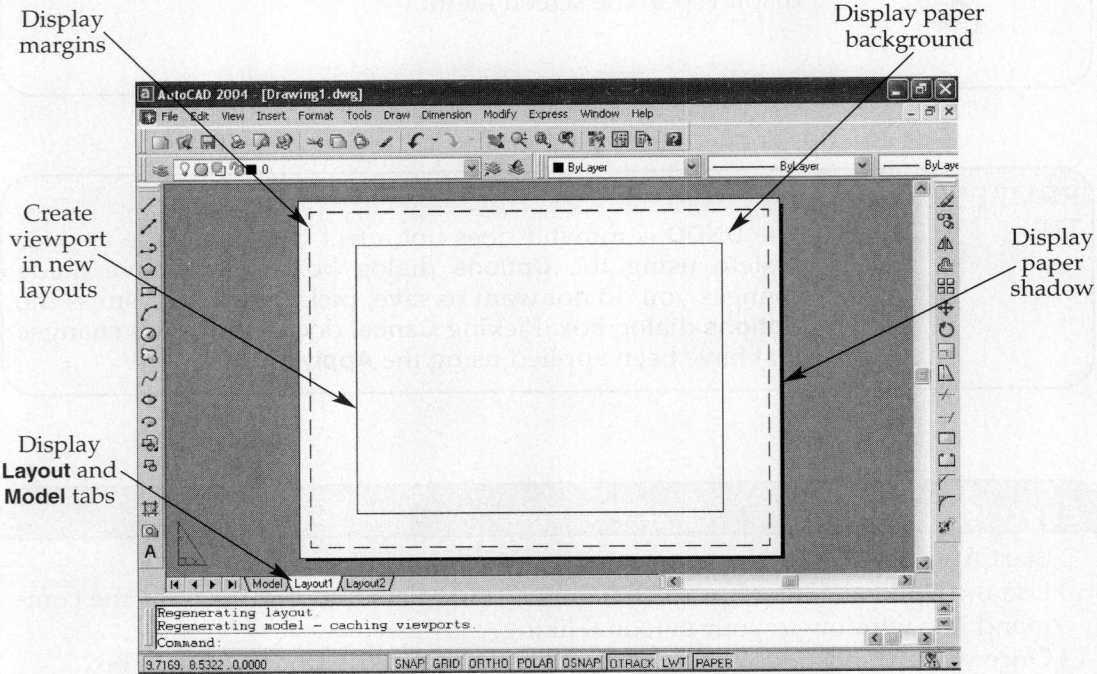

- **Display paper shadow.** Displays a shadow to the right and bottom of the paper. This option is only available if **Display paper background** is checked.
- **Show Page Setup dialog box for new layouts.** Determines if the **Page Setup** dialog box is displayed when a new layout is selected or created.
- **Create viewport in new layout.** Determines whether a viewport is created automatically when a new layout is selected or created.

## Performance Display Settings

The settings in the **Display resolution** and **Display performance** areas of the **Display** tab in the **Options** dialog box affect the performance of AutoCAD. The settings can affect regeneration time and realtime panning and zooming. The following options are available in the **Display resolution** area.

- **Arc and circle smoothness.** This setting controls the smoothness of circles, arcs, and ellipses. The default value is 1000; the range is from 1 to 20,000. The system variable equivalent is **VIEWRES**.
- **Segments in a polyline curve.** This value determines how many line segments will be generated for each polyline curve. The default value is 8, the range is a nonzero value from –32768 to 32767. The system variable equivalent is **SPLINESEGS**.
- **Rendered object smoothness.** This setting controls how smooth curved solids are when hidden, shaded, or rendered. This value is multiplied by the **Arc and circle smoothness** value. The default value is 0.5; the range is from 0.01 to 10. The system variable equivalent is **FACETRES**.
- **Contour lines per surface.** Controls the number of contour lines per surface on solid objects. The default value is 4; the range is from 0 to 2047. The system variable equivalent is **ISOLINES**.

The following options are available in the **Display performance** area.

- **Pan and zoom with raster image.** If this is checked, raster images are displayed when panning and zooming. If it is unchecked, only the frame is displayed. The system variable equivalent is **RTDISPLAY**.
- **Highlight raster image frame only.** If this is checked, only the frame around a raster image is highlighted when the image is selected. If this option is unchecked, the image displays a diagonal checkered pattern to indicate selection. The system variable equivalent is **IMAGEHLT**.
- **True color raster images and rendering.** When checked, this setting allows AutoCAD to display raster images and renderings at the highest display quality set for the Windows system.
- **Apply solid fill.** Controls the display of solid fills in objects. Affected objects include hatches, wide polylines, solids, multilines, and traces. The system variable equivalent is **FILLMODE**.
- **Show text boundary frame only.** This setting controls the Quick Text mode. When checked, text is replaced by a rectangular frame.
- **Show silhouettes in wireframe.** Controls whether or not the silhouette curves are displayed for solid objects. The system variable equivalent is **DISPSILH**.

---

**NOTE**    After changing display settings, use the **REGEN** or **REGENALL** command to make the settings take effect on the objects in the drawing.

---

**PROFESSIONAL TIP**    If you notice performance slowing down, you may want to adjust display settings. For example, if there is a lot of text in the drawing, you can activate Quick Text mode to improve performance. When the drawing is ready for plotting, deactivate Quick Text mode.

---

## File Saving Options

The settings specified in the **Open and Save** tab of the **Options** dialog box deal with how drawing files are saved, safety precautions, xrefs, the loading of ObjectARX applications, and proxy objects. This tab is shown in **Figure 18-8.**

### Default Settings for Saving Files

The settings in the **File Save** area determine the defaults for saving files. The setting in the **Save as:** drop-down list determines the default file type. You may want to change this setting if you are saving drawing files as a previous release of AutoCAD or saving drawings as DXF files. If the **Save a thumbnail preview image** box is checked, a preview image for the drawing is displayed in the **Select File** dialog box when opening a drawing. The **Incremental save percentage** value determines how much of the drawing is saved when a **SAVE** or **QSAVE** is performed. If the quantity of new data in a drawing file reaches the specified percentage, a full save is performed. To ensure that a full save is performed, set the value to 0.

---

**Figure 18-8.**
The **Open and Save** tab settings control default save options, file safety features, xref options, and ObjectARX application options.

Set default values for saving files

Autosave options

Safety options

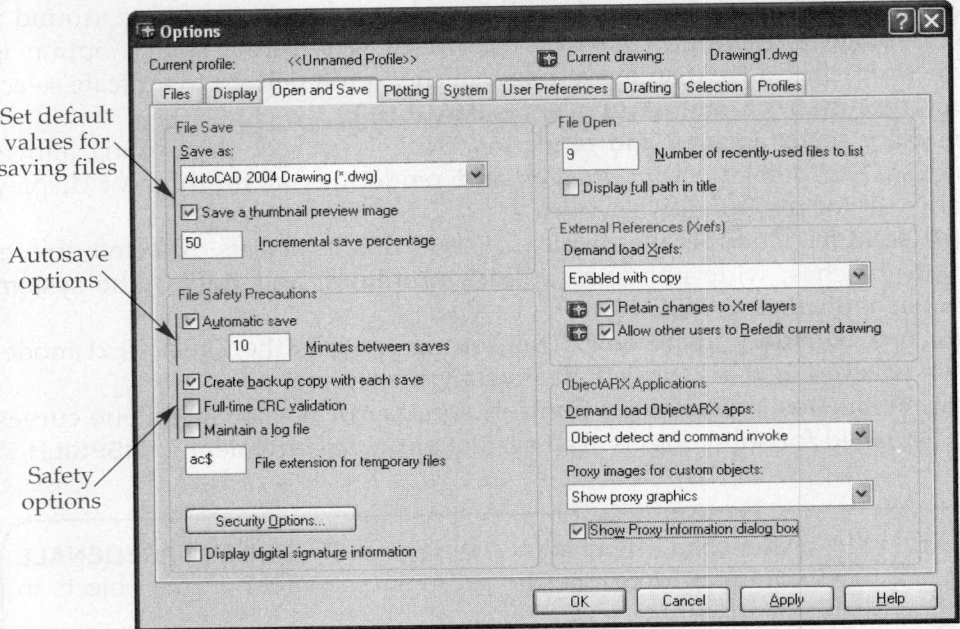

## Autosave Settings

When working in AutoCAD, data loss can occur due to a sudden power outage or an unforeseen system error. AutoCAD provides several safety precautions to help minimize data loss when these types of events occur. These settings are found in the **File Safety Precautions** area in the **Open and Save** tab of the **Options** dialog box.

When the **Automatic save** check box is enabled, AutoCAD automatically creates a backup file at a specified time interval. The **Minutes between saves:** edit box sets this interval. This is the value of the **SAVETIME** system variable. Removing the check sets **SAVETIME** to 0.

The automatic save feature does not overwrite the source drawing file with its incremental saves. Rather, AutoCAD saves temporary files. The path for autosave files is specified in the **Files** tab in the **Options** dialog box, as discussed earlier. The autosave file is stored in the location specified until the drawing is closed. When the drawing is closed, the autosave file is deleted. Autosave files have a .sv$ extension with the drawing name and some random numbers generated by AutoCAD. If AutoCAD quits unexpectedly, the autosave file is not deleted and can be renamed with a .dwg extension so it can be opened in AutoCAD.

The interval setting should be based on working conditions and file size. It is possible to adversely affect your productivity by setting your **SAVETIME** value too small. For example, in larger drawings, a **SAVE** command can take a significant amount of time. If a save takes two minutes and your autosave is set to save every five minutes, you would spend more than twenty minutes of every hour waiting on AutoCAD to finish saving the file. Ideally, it is best to set your **SAVETIME** variable to the greatest amount of time you can afford to repeat. While it may be acceptable to redo the last fifteen minutes or less of work, it is unlikely that you would feel the same about having to redo the last hour.

Setting and resetting the **SAVETIME** variable according to any given situation is often the best approach. The factors that should influence the current setting include not only file size, but also the working conditions. If your computer system is experiencing frequent lock-ups or crashes, your automatic saves should occur often. Weather can also be a factor. Wind or electrical storms should be an immediate cue to reduce the value of the **SAVETIME** variable.

## Backup Files

AutoCAD can also create a backup of the current drawing file. The backup file uses the same name as the drawing, but has a .bak file extension. The backup is not overwritten when a different drawing is opened or saved. When the **Create backup copy with each save** option in the **Open and Save** tab is checked, the backup file feature is enabled. If not checked, the file is not backed up when you save. Unless you prefer to take unnecessary risks, it is usually best to leave this feature enabled.

## CRC Validation

A *cyclic redundancy check,* or CRC, verifies that the number of data bits sent is the same as the number received. **Full-time CRC validation** is a feature you can use when drawing files are being corrupted and you suspect a hardware or software problem. When using full-time CRC validation, the CRC check is done every time data is read into the drawing. This ensures that all data is received correctly.

## Log Files

The log file can serve a variety of purposes. The source of drawing errors can be determined by reviewing the commands that produced the incorrect results. Additionally, log files can be reviewed by a CAD manager to determine the need for training and customization of the system.

When the **Maintain a log file** check box is activated in the **Open and Save** tab, AutoCAD creates a file named acad.log. The name and location of the log file can be specified using the Log File Location listing under the **Files** tab of the **Options** dialog box. When activated, all prompts, messages, and responses that appear in the command line window are saved to this file. Exiting AutoCAD or turning off this check box disables the log file feature.

The log file status can also be set using the **LOGFILEON** and **LOGFILEOFF** commands. Each individual session of AutoCAD contained in a single log file is separated by a line of dashes with a date and time stamp.

## External Reference and ObjectARX Options

The external reference options in the **Open and Save** tab are important if you are working with xrefs. These options are found in the **External Reference (Xrefs)** area of the tab. The **Demand load Xrefs:** setting can affect performance and the ability for another user to edit a drawing currently referenced into another drawing. This setting is also controlled by the **XLOADCTL** system variable. If the **Retain changes to Xref layers** option is checked, xref layer settings are saved with the drawing file. The **VISRETAIN** system variable also controls this setting. The **Allow other users to Refedit current drawing** setting controls whether or not the drawing can be edited in-place when it is referenced by another drawing. This setting is also controlled by the **XEDIT** system variable.

The **ObjectARX Applications** area controls the loading of ObjectARX applications and the displaying of proxy objects. The **Demand load ObjectARX apps:** setting specifies if and when AutoCAD loads third-party applications associated with objects in the drawing. The **Proxy images for custom objects:** setting controls how objects created by a third-party application are displayed. When a drawing with proxy objects is opened, the **Proxy Information** dialog box is displayed. To disable the dialog box, uncheck the **Show Proxy Information dialog box** option.

## File Opening Settings

The **File Open** area of the **Open and Save** tab in the **Options** dialog box contains two settings. The value in the **Number of recently-used files to list** text box controls the number of drawing files listed at the bottom of the **File** pull-down menu. The **Display full path in title** check box controls whether the entire drawing file path or just the file name is displayed in the title bar of the AutoCAD window.

## System Settings

Options for the pointing device, graphic settings, general system options, and dbConnect can be found in the **System** tab of the **Options** dialog box, **Figure 18-9.** These settings affect the interaction between AutoCAD and your operating system.

In the **Current 3D Graphics Display** area, you can set the 3D graphics display system using the drop-down list and modify its properties. AutoCAD is configured with the Heidi 3D graphics display system (GSHEIDI10).

**Figure 18-9.**
General AutoCAD system options and hardware settings can be controlled in the **System** tab.

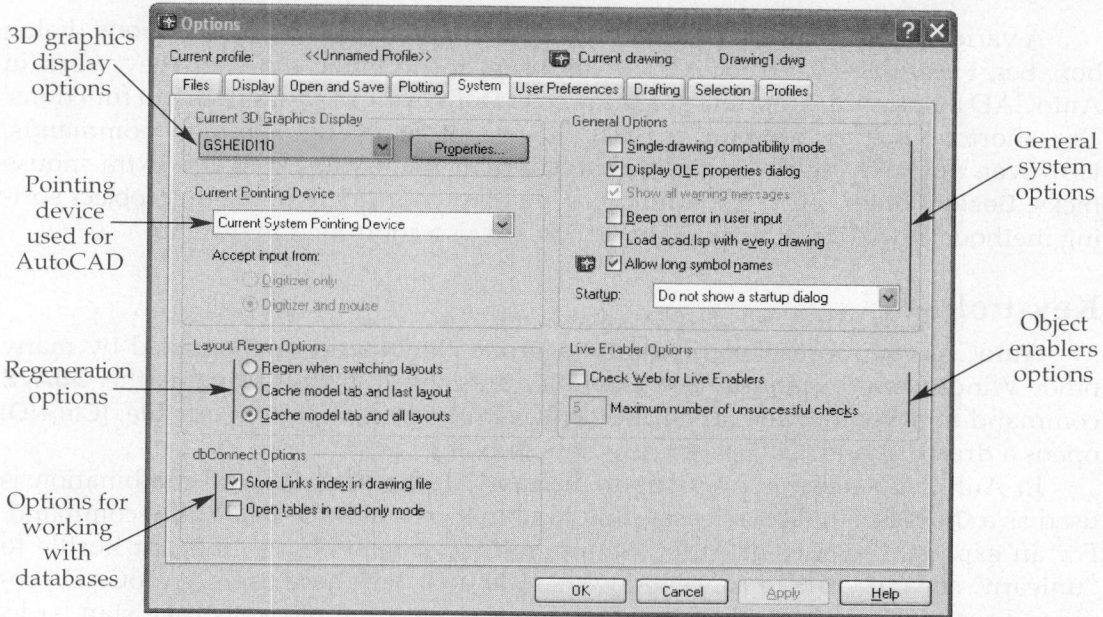

The **Current Pointing Device** area determines the pointing device used with AutoCAD. The default is the current system pointing device (usually your mouse). If you have a digitizer tablet, you will want to select the Wintab Compatible Digitizer option. You must configure your tablet before it can be used. For detailed instructions on using your tablet as a digitizing device, see Chapter 22 of this text.

The **Layout Regen Options** setting determines what is regenerated and when it is regenerated when working with layout tabs. The **Live Enabler Options** specifies when the Autodesk web site is checked for object enablers.

The settings in the **General Options** area control general system functions. The following options are available.

- **Single drawing compatibility mode.** By default, you can open multiple drawings in a single session of AutoCAD. To allow only one drawing to be open in a session, check this option. This is also controlled by the **SDI** system variable.
- **Display OLE properties dialog.** When inserting an OLE object, the **OLE Properties** dialog box is displayed if this option is checked.
- **Show all warning messages.** Controls the display of dialog boxes that include a **Don't Display This Warning Again** option.
- **Beep on error in user input.** Specifies whether AutoCAD alerts you of incorrect user input with an audible beep.
- **Load acad.lsp with every drawing.** This setting turns the persistent AutoLISP feature on or off.
- **Allow long symbol names.** Determines if long symbol names can be used in AutoCAD. If this option is checked, up to 255 characters can be used for layers, dimension styles, blocks, linetypes, text styles, layouts, UCS names, views, and viewport configurations. The system variable is **EXTNAMES**.
- **Startup.** This option controls whether the **Startup**, **AutoCAD Today**, or no dialog box is displayed when you begin an AutoCAD session.

The following options are available from the **dbConnect Options** area.

- **Store Links index in drawing file.** When this option is checked, the database index is saved within the drawing file. This makes the link selection operation quicker, but increases the drawing file size.
- **Open tables in read-only mode.** Determines whether tables are opened in read-only mode.

# User Preferences

A variety of settings are found in the **User Preferences** tab of the **Options** dialog box. See **Figure 18-10**. AutoCAD allows users to optimize the way they work in AutoCAD by providing options for the accelerator keys and shortcut menu functions. The shortcut menus provide an easy means of accessing common commands. However, you may want to disable the shortcut menus to avoid the extra mouse picks. **DesignCenter** units, hyperlink icon display, coordinate data entry, object sorting methods, and default lineweight setting are also controlled in this tab.

## Keystrokes

AutoCAD supports the common keystroke combinations recognized by many other Windows applications. For example, pressing [Ctrl]+[S] activates the **QSAVE** command to save your file. The [Ctrl]+[P] keystroke prints (plots) your file, [Ctrl]+[O] opens a drawing, and [Ctrl]+[N] starts a new drawing.

In AutoCAD releases previous to Release 13, the [Ctrl]+[C] key combination is used as a **CANCEL**. In later releases, this combination starts the **COPYCLIP** command. For an experienced user of AutoCAD upgrading, it may be a significant hurdle to "unlearn" several years of canceling with a [Ctrl]+[C]. For these users, AutoCAD provides a way to switch the new keystroke model with the old keystroke standards. Unchecking **Windows standard accelerator keys** in the **Windows Standard Behavior** area enables the old-style keystroke model.

## Shortcut Menus

AutoCAD has shortcut menus that make common commands easy to access. These shortcut menus are context sensitive, meaning the options available in the shortcut menu are determined by the active command, cursor location, or selected object.

**Figure 18-10.**
The **User Preferences** tab allows you to set up AutoCAD in a manner that works best for you.

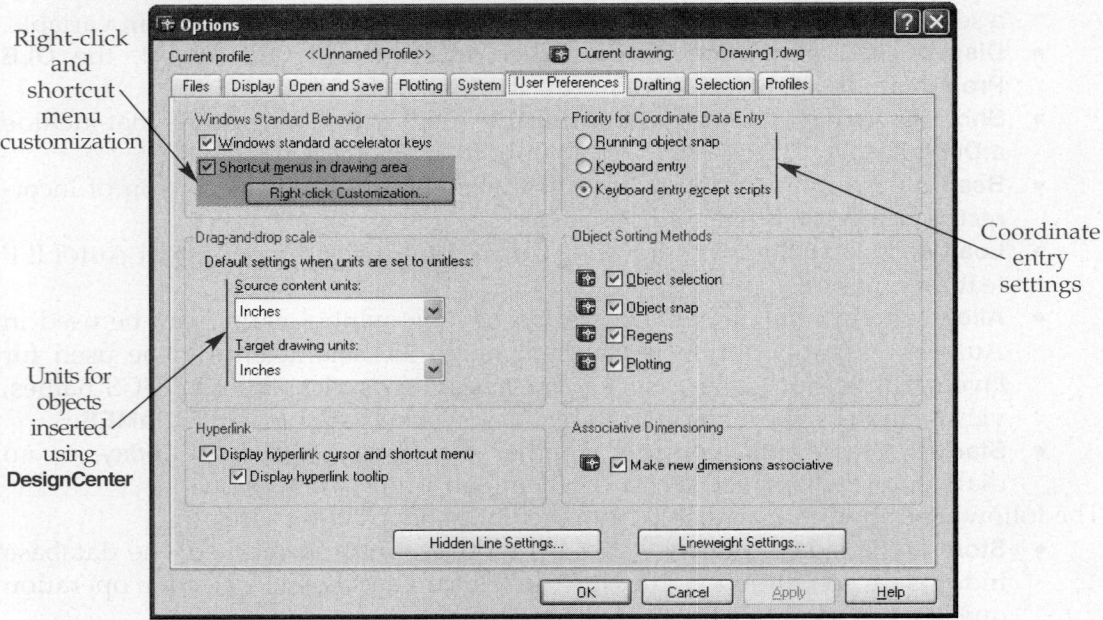

Right-click and shortcut menu customization

Coordinate entry settings

Units for objects inserted using **DesignCenter**

The shortcut menu settings are located in the **Windows Standard Behavior** area in the **User Preferences** tab of the **Options** dialog box. To disable the shortcut menus, uncheck the **Shortcut menus in drawing area** option.

You can also customize the setting for the right mouse button. Pick the **Right-click Customization...** button to access the **Right-Click Customization** dialog box. See **Figure 18-11.** The **Turn on time-sensitive right-click** check box controls the right-click behavior. A quick click is the same as pressing [Enter]. A longer click will display a shortcut menu. You can set the duration of the longer click in milliseconds. Different settings can be used for the three different shortcut menu modes.

- **Default Mode.** In this mode, no objects are selected and no commands are active. The **Repeat Last Command** option activates the last command issued. This is the right mouse button behavior in previous releases of AutoCAD.
- **Edit Mode.** In this mode, an object is selected, but no command is active.
- **Command Mode.** In this mode, a command is active. The **ENTER** option corresponds to the behavior in previous releases of AutoCAD.

**Figure 18-11.**
Use this dialog box to customize the right mouse button.

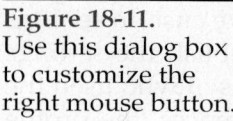
Controls right-click behavior

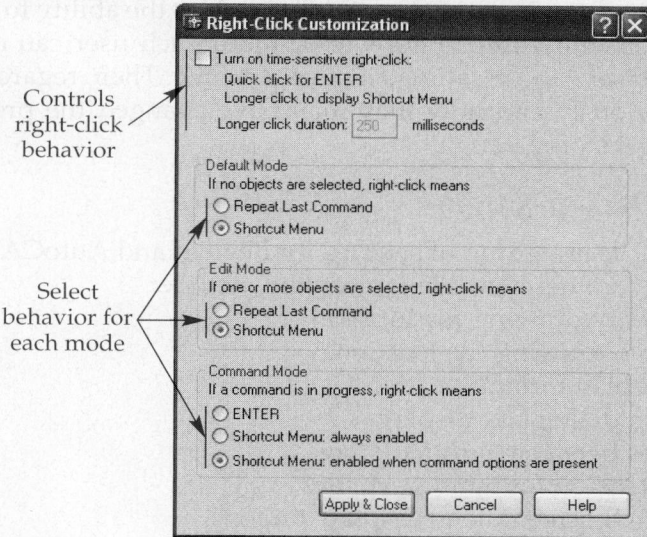

Select behavior for each mode

## Associative Dimensions

By default, all new dimensions are associative. This means that the dimension value changes automatically when a dimension's defpoints are moved. However, you can turn this option off in the **User Preferences** tab of the **Options** dialog box. When the **Make new dimensions associative** check box is unchecked, any dimensions drawn do not have associativity.

## Other User Preferences Options

In the **Drag-and-drop scale** area of the **User Preferences** tab, unit values can be set for objects when they are inserted into a drawing. The **Source content units:** setting specifies the units for objects being inserted into the current drawing. The **Target drawing units:** setting determines the units in the current drawing. These settings are used when there are no units set with the **INSUNITS** system variable.

Options for the hyperlink display can be set in the **Hyperlink** area of the **User Preferences** tab. If **Display hyperlink cursor and shortcut menu** is checked, the hyperlink icon appears next to the crosshairs when they are over an object containing a hyperlink. Additional hyperlink options are available from the shortcut menu when an object with a hyperlink is selected. The **Display hyperlink tooltip** option controls whether the text from the **Link to file or URL** text box for the hyperlink target is displayed when the cursor is held over an object with a hyperlink.

The **Priority for Coordinate Data Entry** area controls how AutoCAD responds to input of coordinate data. The system variable equivalent for this is **OSNAPCOORD**.

The sort order of objects is controlled in the **Object Sorting Methods** area of the **User Preferences** tab, or by the **SORTENTS** system variable. When an option is checked, AutoCAD sorts selectable objects from those created first to those created last. If the option is unchecked, AutoCAD sorts selectable objects randomly.

## User Profiles

In a school or company, there is often more than one person who will use the same AutoCAD workstation. Each drafter has a unique style for creating a drawing. While there are often general rules to follow, many times the method used to arrive at the end result is not important. AutoCAD provides the ability to save custom settings for each drafter who will use the workstation. Each user can establish the settings they prefer and save those settings in a user profile. Then, regardless of who used the computer previously and how they may have changed the preferences, the profile settings can be restored.

### What Is a User Profile?

A *user profile* is a group of settings for devices and AutoCAD functions. Some of the settings and values a profile can contain include:
- Temporary drawing file location.
- Template drawing file location.
- Text display format.
- Start-up dialog box display.
- Minutes between automatic saves.
- File extension for temporary files.
- AutoCAD screen menu display (on/off).
- Colors and fonts for AutoCAD's text and graphics screens.
- Type of pointer and length of crosshairs.
- Default printer or plotter.

Multiple profiles can be saved by a single user for different applications, or several users can create individual profiles for their own use. A user profile should not be confused with settings found in a drawing. Template files are used to save settings relating to a drawing session, such as units, limits, object snap settings, drafting settings, grip settings, arc and circle smoothness, dimension styles, and text styles. A user profile, on the other hand, saves settings related to the performance and appearance of the software and hardware.

### Creating a User Profile

A user profile is basically a collection of all things you have customized in AutoCAD. These customizations are usually done to make AutoCAD easier for you to use. For example, as you gain experience in AutoCAD, you realize that you:
- Like the crosshairs extending to the edges of the graphics window.
- Often use the **Inquiry** toolbar.
- Prefer the graphics window background color to be gray.

Through the course of several drawing sessions, you have customized AutoCAD to reflect these preferences. Now, so you do not lose your preference settings, you should create a user profile.

**Figure 18-12.**
Settings can be saved in a profile.

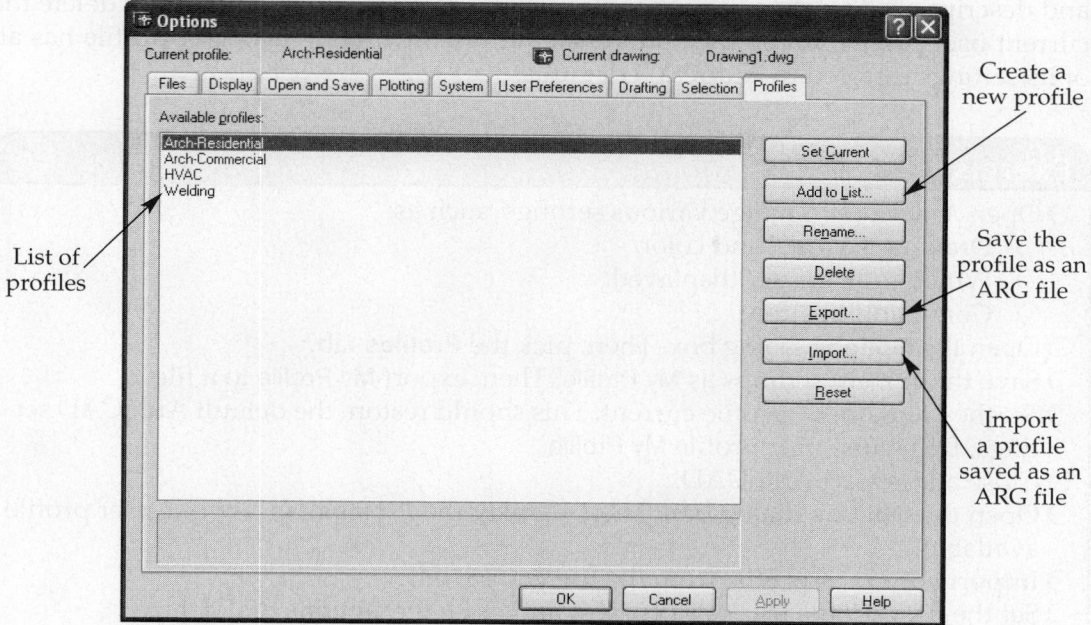

First, access the **Options** dialog box and pick the **Profiles** tab in the **Options** dialog box, **Figure 18-12.** Pick the **Add to List...** button on the right side of the tab. The **Add Profile** dialog box is opened, **Figure 18-13.** Enter a name and description. Then, pick the **Apply & Close** button to close the **Add Profile** dialog box.

The new user profile is now listed in the **Profiles** tab of the **Options** dialog box. The user profile is saved and will be available in future AutoCAD drawing sessions. To set any user profile as the current user profile, first highlight the user profile name in the **Profiles** tab. Then, pick the **Set Current** button. All of the settings in the user profile are applied while the **Options** dialog box is still open.

You can also export a user profile. You may want to do this to take your user profile to a different AutoCAD workstation. Pick the **Export...** button in the **Profiles** tab to open the **Export Profiles** dialog box. Then, select a folder and name the file. When you pick the **Save** button, the user profile is saved with the .arg file extension. To import a user profile, pick the **Import...** button in the **Profiles** tab. Then, select the proper ARG file and pick the **Open** button. The **Import Profile** dialog box is displayed. You can rename the user profile, change the description, and choose to include the file path. Then, pick the **Apply & Close** button. The user profile is then available in the **Profiles** tab.

**Figure 18-13.**
The **Add Profile** dialog box is used to create a new profile.

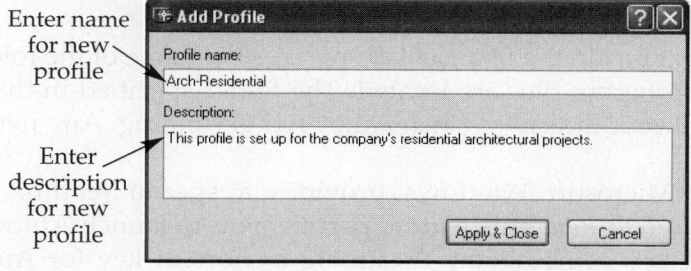

Additional buttons are available in the **Profiles** tab. To change the name of a user profile, pick the **Rename** button. In the **Change Profile** dialog box, enter a new name and description. To delete a user profile, pick the **Delete** button. You cannot delete the current user profile. If you pick the **Reset** button, the highlighted user profile has all of its settings restored to AutoCAD defaults.

---

### Exercise 18-2

○ Open AutoCAD. Change various settings, such as:
  ○ Drawing background color.
  ○ Which toolbars are displayed.
  ○ Command line font.
○ Open the **Options** dialog box. Then, pick the **Profiles** tab.
○ Save the current settings as My Profile. Then, export My Profile to a file.
○ Set the "unnamed" profile current. This should restore the default AutoCAD settings. Delete the user profile My Profile.
○ Close and restart AutoCAD.
○ Open the **Options** dialog box. Then, display the **Profiles** tab. Is your user profile available?
○ Import your user profile from the file you saved.
○ Set the user profile My Profile current and close the **Options** dialog box.
○ Exit AutoCAD.

---

## Changing Program Properties

When AutoCAD is first installed on your computer, the installation program automatically creates the AutoCAD group and several program items, and then places a program icon on the Windows desktop. If desired, you can modify the program icon properties. These properties include such things as the file attributes, the folder where AutoCAD is started, and the icon for the shortcut.

To modify the AutoCAD program icon properties, right-click on the AutoCAD 2004 icon on the desktop and then select Properties from the shortcut menu. See **Figure 18-14.** You can also pick the icon and then use the [Alt]+[Enter] key combination. Either action displays the AutoCAD 2004 Properties dialog box, **Figure 18-15.** There are three main tabs, General, Shortcut, and Compatability. Additional tabs, such as Security, may be listed, depending on your Windows setup.

- **Target.** This text box in the Shortcut tab contains the name of the executable program and its path. If the folder that contains the AutoCAD executable has changed, this line can be edited so it still links to the correct file. If you are not sure of the exact path name, you can pick the Find Target... button to locate the executable.
- **Start in.** This text box in the Shortcut tab specifies the name of the folder where the AutoCAD program files are located. The folder specified in this text box becomes the current directory when AutoCAD is running. Any new files are placed here.
- **Shortcut key.** Microsoft Windows provides a special feature called an *application shortcut key*. This feature permits you to launch AutoCAD with a user-defined key combination. Assigning a shortcut key for AutoCAD is described later in this section.

AutoCAD and its Applications—Advanced

**Figure 18-14.**
This shortcut menu
appears when you
right-click on an
icon in the
Windows desktop.

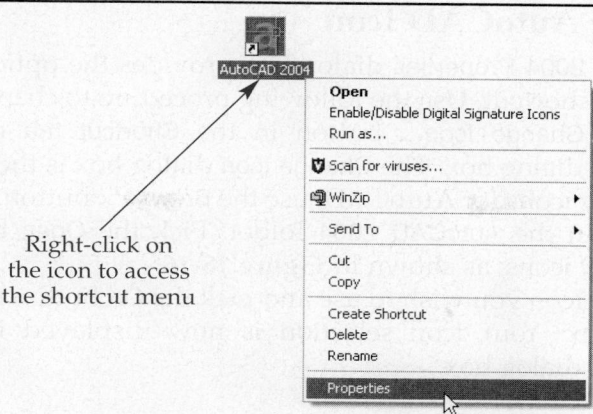

Right-click on
the icon to access
the shortcut menu

**Figure 18-15.**
The AutoCAD 2004
Properties dialog
box.

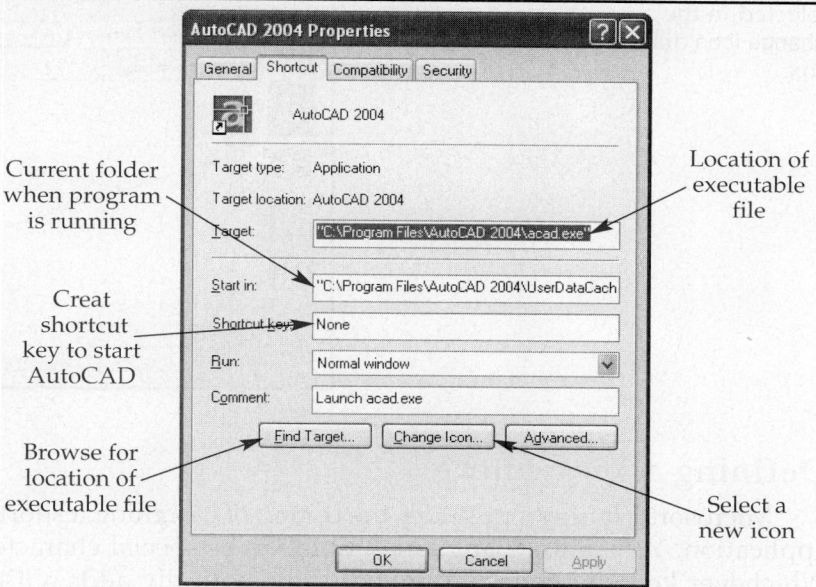

Current folder
when program
is running

Location of
executable
file

Creat
shortcut
key to start
AutoCAD

Browse for
location of
executable file

Select a
new icon

- **Run.** This listing offers options to run the program in a normal, maximized, or minimized window. Do not run the program minimized, otherwise AutoCAD appears only as a button on the taskbar when you start it. You can easily restore or maximize it, but when it does not automatically appear on screen, it may be confusing to newer users.

When you are finished making your changes, pick the OK button to exit the AutoCAD 2004 Properties dialog box. Any changes you make take effect immediately, so there is no need to restart Windows.

---

**NOTE**

Be sure to check with your instructor or system administrator before modifying the AutoCAD program properties.

---

## Changing the AutoCAD Icon

The AutoCAD 2004 Properties dialog box provides the option to change the program icon for the shortcut. Use the following procedure to change the icon.

1. Pick the Change Icon... button in the Shortcut tab of the AutoCAD 2004 Properties dialog box. The Change Icon dialog box is then displayed.
2. To display icons for AutoCAD, use the Browse... button to find the file named acad.exe in the AutoCAD 2004 folder. Pick the Open button to display the AutoCAD icons, as shown in **Figure 18-16**.
3. Select the icon you wish to use and pick the OK button to exit the Change Icon dialog box. Your icon selection is now displayed in the AutoCAD 2004 Properties dialog box.

**Figure 18-16.**
A new icon can be selected in the Change Icon dialog box.

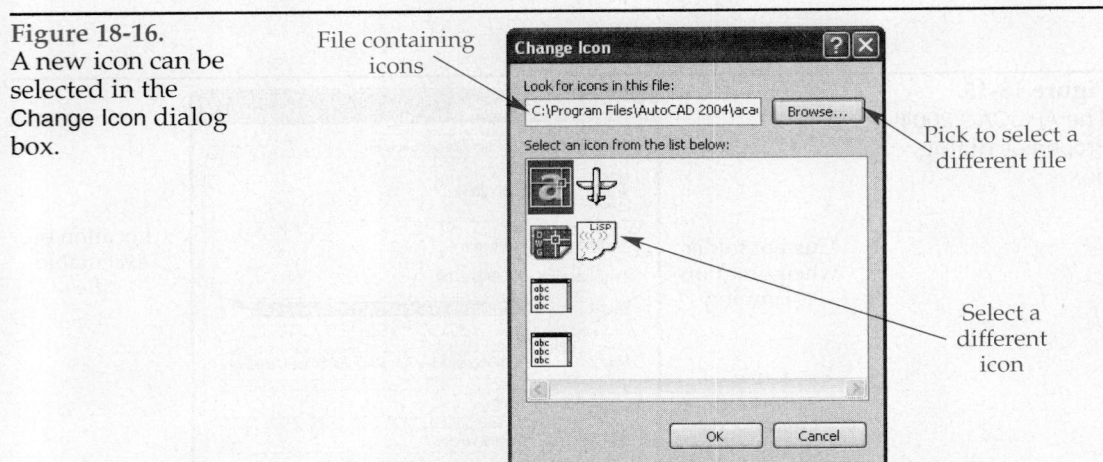

File containing icons

Pick to select a different file

Select a different icon

## Defining a Shortcut Key

Microsoft Windows provides the option of assigning a shortcut key that starts an application. You can use any letter, number, or special character for a shortcut key. Whichever key you choose, Windows automatically adds a [Ctrl]+[Alt] in front of it. You can also use function keys. To assign a shortcut key for launching AutoCAD, do the following.

1. Open the AutoCAD 2004 Properties dialog box.
2. Pick in the Shortcut key: text box. The flashing vertical cursor appears at the end of the word None.
3. Now, press A (or whichever key you prefer).
4. The character string Ctrl + Alt + A appears in the text box, **Figure 18-17.** If you press a function key, the Ctrl and Alt are not added.
5. Pick OK to exit the AutoCAD 2004 Properties dialog box.

Your new shortcut key is immediately active. Now, no matter which Windows-based application is running, you can start AutoCAD with the keyboard combination [Ctrl]+[Alt]+[A]. Refer to the Microsoft Windows *User's Guide* or online help for more information regarding shortcut keys.

## Creating Alternate AutoCAD Configurations

The information you specify for AutoCAD regarding the pointing and printing devices is recorded in a configuration file. Your pointing and printing devices are specified in the **Options** dialog box, but the information is stored in the current configuration file.

Figure 18-17.
Setting the
[Ctrl]+[Alt]+[A] key
combination to
automatically start
AutoCAD.

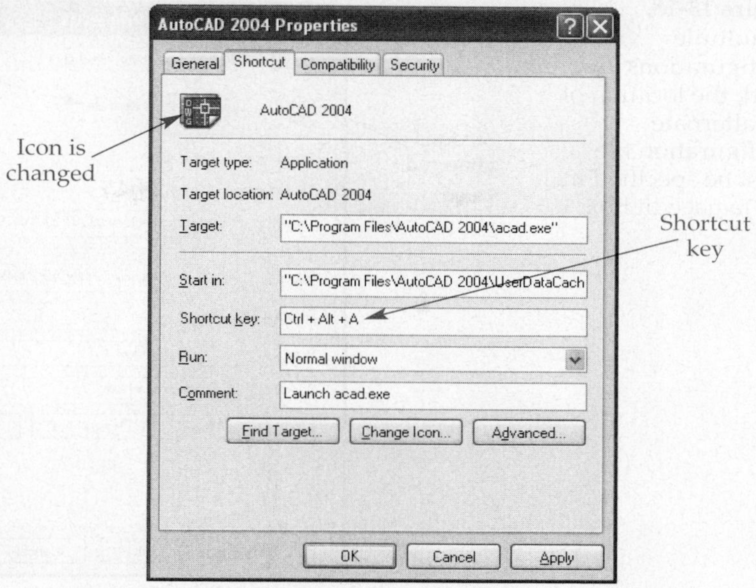

Icon is
changed

Shortcut
key

The default configuration file is acad2004.cfg. You can determine the current location for this configuration file by going to the **Menu, Help and Miscellaneous File Names** selection of the **Files** tab in the **Options** dialog box. Each time you specify a new pointing or printing device, the existing acad2004.cfg file is overwritten with the new information.

Under most circumstances, a single configuration file is all that is necessary. Some users, however, may require multiple configurations. As an example, if you use a mouse most of the time but sometimes need a digitizer tablet, you may find it convenient to set up AutoCAD to use multiple configurations. This can save you the time required to reconfigure AutoCAD each time you need to switch your pointing devices.

To save multiple configurations, you must specify a new location for AutoCAD to store the acad2004.cfg so that it does not overwrite the previous version. This way, you actually have more than one configuration file, with each file located in a specific folder. It is recommended that these folders be placed under the AutoCAD "user" folder so they are easy to locate. For this example, create a folder named \Altcfg. Now, find the acad2004.cfg file in its current folder and copy it to the new folder.

On the Windows desktop, press the [Ctrl] key and move the AutoCAD 2004 icon to create a copy. This new icon is for the new configuration. Open the AutoCAD 2004 Properties dialog box for the new icon and go to the Shortcut tab. In the Target: edit box, place /c after the existing target, followed by the directory path location for the alternate configuration. For example, in **Figure 18-18**, the configuration directory is entered as:

"C:\Program Files\AutoCAD 2004\acad.exe" /c "C:\Documents and Settings\*username*\Local Settings\Application Data\Autodesk\AutoCAD 2004\R16.0\enu\altcfg"

The *username* listing indicates the specific AutoCAD user. The new path must be placed in quotation marks due to the space in the path name. The /c is not in quotation marks. Command line switches (the /c) are separated by spaces, and the space is interpreted as the end of the path name.

It is also recommended that you change the title of the shortcut icon on the desktop to match the configuration. For example, one shortcut icon could be called AutoCAD 2004 Original and the other could be called AutoCAD 2004 Alternate. Do this by right-clicking on the icon and selecting Rename. Now you can enter the new text.

**Figure 18-18.**
If multiple configurations are used, the location of the alternate configuration file must be specified in the Target edit box.

Icon is changed

Shortcut has been renamed

Path is changed

When you start AutoCAD using the new icon, the alternate configuration file directory is used. This means that any configuration changes you make are stored in the new configuration file and do not affect other configurations.

**NOTE**

You can set up unique shortcut keys for each AutoCAD shortcut on your desktop.

**PROFESSIONAL TIP**

A profile can be accessed directly from an AutoCAD shortcut on the desktop using a /p switch and the exact profile name. For example, if you created a profile called Project 0256, the **Target:** text box in the AutoCAD 2004 Properties dialog box may read:

"C:\Program Files\AutoCAD 2004\acad.exe" /p "Project 0256"

## Chapter Test

*Answer the following questions on a separate sheet of paper.*

1. List three methods used to open the **Options** dialog box.
2. How do you open the **Color Options** dialog box?
3. What are the advantages of toggling the log file open? The disadvantages?
4. Name the two commands that toggle the log file on and off.
5. AutoCAD resides in the C:\Program Files\AutoCAD 2004 folder on your workstation. You have created two folders under \AutoCAD 2004 named Projects and Symbols. You want to store your drawings in the Projects folder and your blocks in the Symbols folder. What should you enter in the Support File Search Path area so these folders are added to the search path?

6. How do you select the folder in which the autosave file is saved?
7. How would you set the right mouse button to perform an [Enter], rather than displaying shortcut menus?
8. What is a *profile?*
9. How and why are profiles used?
10. What is the file extension used for a profile when it is exported?
11. Which file must be copied to a separate folder before creating an alternate AutoCAD configuration?

## Problems

1. Create an alternate configuration for AutoCAD dedicated to 3D modeling and rendering using the methods described in this chapter. Use the following instructions.
   A. Assign a different program icon for the 3D configuration.
   B. Name the program icon AutoCAD 3D.
   C. Define a shortcut key for the configuration.
   D. Add a directory to the support path that contains 3D shapes.

2. Create an alternate configuration for AutoCAD dedicated to dimensioning. Use the following instructions to complete this problem.
   A. Assign a different program icon for the dimensioning configuration.
   B. Name the program icon AutoCAD Dimensioning.
   C. Define a shortcut key for the configuration.

Custom toolbars increase your efficiency when performing repetitive tasks. Toolbars can be created with groups of related commands, as is the case with the default toolbars. They can also be created with dissimilar commands to make it easier to perform routine tasks. Of the four custom toolbars shown here, the **Landscapes** toolbar and the **Quick Snaps** toolbar group similar commands. The **Solid Modeling** toolbar and **Materials and Rendering** toolbar contain a mixture of commands that make modeling and rendering easier.

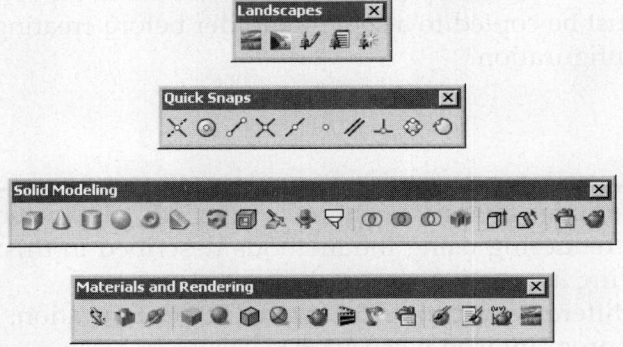

## CHAPTER 19

# Creating Custom Toolbars

## Learning Objectives

After completing this chapter, you will be able to:
- Display and hide toolbars.
- Modify existing toolbars.
- Create new toolbars.
- Create new toolbar buttons.
- Construct new button images.
- Create and modify flyouts.
- Describe the purpose and function of the AutoCAD menu files.

One of the easiest ways to alter the AutoCAD environment is by customizing toolbars. This requires no programming and little use of text editors. Existing toolbars can be quickly modified by removing and adding buttons, or by changing the toolbar shape. New buttons can also be created and assigned to an existing toolbar. The most powerful aspect of customizing toolbars is the ability to quickly create entirely new functions and buttons to help you in your work.

## Working with Toolbars

Toolbars provide access to most AutoCAD commands with one or two quick "picks." This graphical interface provides much flexibility. Toolbars can be quickly and easily resized, repositioned, hidden from view, or made visible. Toolbars are moved, resized, docked, and floated in the same way as in all Windows-compatible software.

In addition to positioning and sizing toolbars, you can customize the toolbar interface. You can add new buttons or place existing buttons in new locations for quicker access. Infrequently used buttons can be deleted or moved. Entirely new toolbars can be created and filled with redefined buttons or custom buttons. Toolbars are customized using the **Customize** dialog box.

## Toolbar Visibility

You can adjust the AutoCAD screen so that only the toolbars you need are visible. This helps conserve drawing window space. If too many toolbars are displayed, the drawing window can become small and crowded. When your drawing area is small, too much of your time is spent making display changes so you can clearly see parts of the drawing.

**Figure 19-1** shows an example of a small and crowded drawing window. Also, look closely at the toolbars docked on the left side and top of the window. They are partially hidden from view. The length of some of the toolbars is longer than the available space. Remember this when arranging your toolbars. You should have access to all of the buttons.

AutoCAD provides a shortcut menu for fast and convenient control of toolbar visibility. To access the toolbars shortcut menu, point at any toolbar and right-click. As shown in **Figure 19-2,** a check mark is displayed next to the currently visible toolbars. Pick any menu name to toggle its visibility.

Toolbars can also be turned on and off using the **Customize** dialog box. Open this

| TOOLBAR TO |
| --- |
| View |
| ➥ Toolbars... |

dialog box by picking **Customize...** from the toolbars shortcut menu, selecting **Toolbars...** from the **View** pull-down menu, or entering TO or TOOLBAR at the Command: prompt. The **Customize** dialog box is shown in **Figure 19-3.** There are several options available in this dialog box for controlling the visibility and appearance of toolbars.

If there are toolbars defined in more than one menu, select the appropriate menu from the **Menu Group** list. If you loaded partial menus in addition to your primary menu, you must make the menu group name current to access the toolbars defined in that menu.

**Figure 19-1.**
Too many toolbars visible at once can cut down on the useful drawing area.

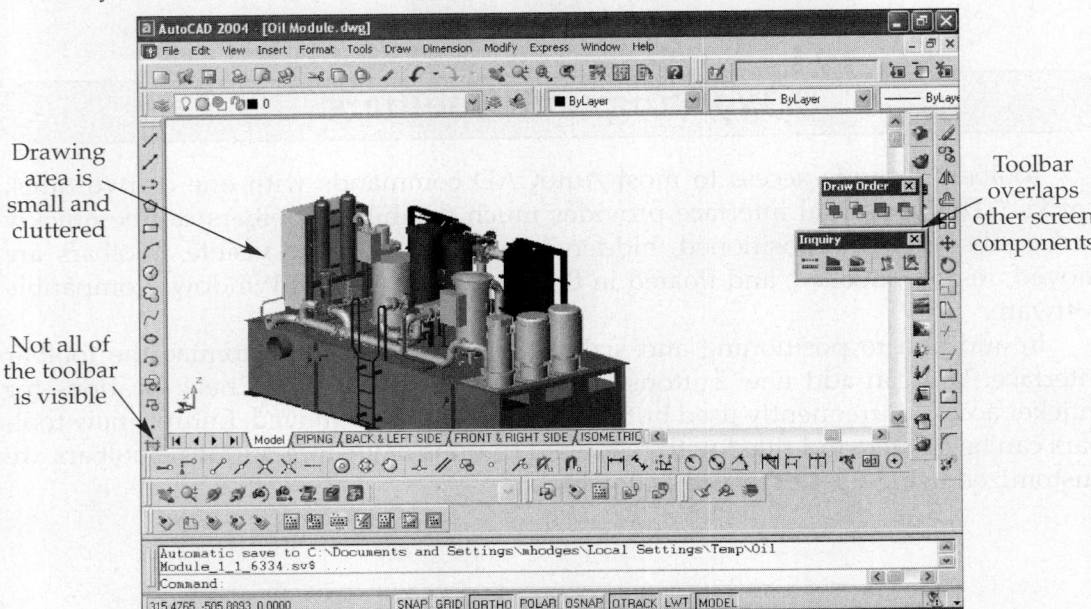

Drawing area is small and cluttered

Not all of the toolbar is visible

Toolbar overlaps other screen components

**Figure 19-2.**
The toolbars shortcut menu is accessed by right-clicking on any toolbar.

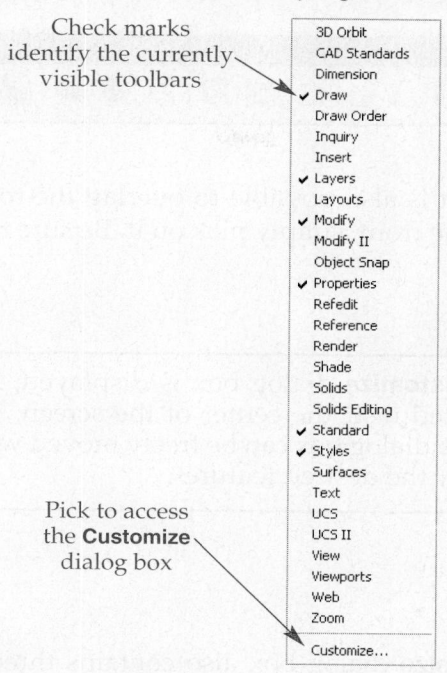

Check marks identify the currently visible toolbars

Pick to access the **Customize** dialog box

**Figure 19-3.**
The **Customize** dialog box is used to turn toolbars on and off, create new toolbars, and rename existing toolbars.

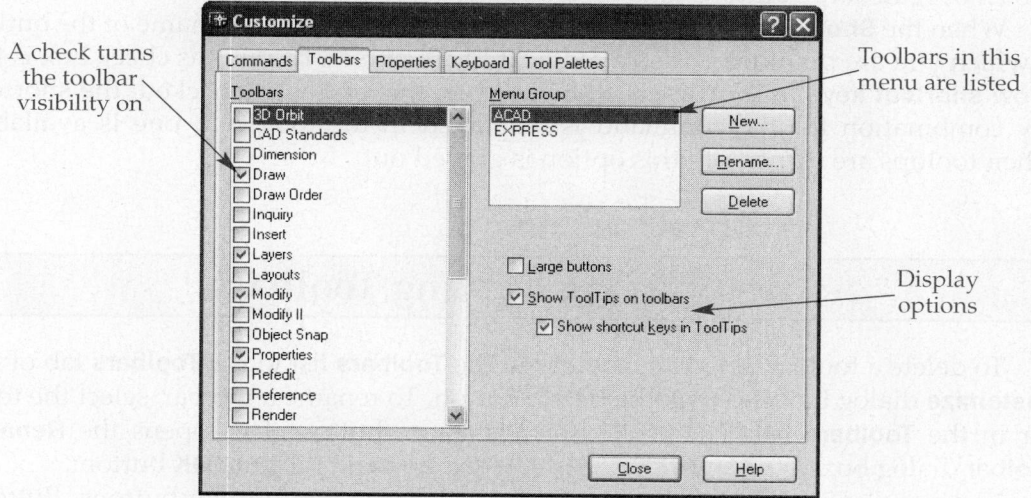

A check turns the toolbar visibility on

Toolbars in this menu are listed

Display options

The **Toolbars** list shows all the toolbars defined in the selected menu group. To make a toolbar visible, place a check in the check box next to the toolbar name by picking the box. To hide a toolbar, remove the check. The results are immediate. When you are finished, pick the **Close** button.

Another way to hide a floating toolbar is to pick its menu control button, **Figure 19-4.** If you wish to hide a docked toolbar, you can first move it away from the edge to make it a floating toolbar. Then, pick the menu control button. However, if you hide a docked toolbar in this manner, it will appear in the floating position when you make it visible again. When the **Customize** dialog box is used to hide a docked toolbar, it will appear in its docked position when reactivated.

**Figure 19-4.**
Pick the menu
control button and
the toolbar is
hidden.

Menu control
button

When using floating toolbars, it is also possible to overlap the toolbars to save screen space. To bring a toolbar to the front, simply pick on it. Be sure to leave part of each toolbar showing.

>  **NOTE** When the **Customize** dialog box is displayed, it may cover toolbars located near the center of the screen. Toolbars and the **Customize** dialog box can be freely moved whenever necessary to view the desired features.

## Toolbar Display Options

The **Toolbars** tab of the **Customize** dialog box also contains three check boxes. These check boxes provide display options for toolbar buttons.

When the **Large buttons** check box is checked, the size of toolbar buttons is increased from 16×15 pixels to 24×22 pixels. At higher screen resolutions, such as 1280×1024, the small buttons may be difficult to see. At lower screen resolutions, such as 800×600, the large buttons take up too much of the display area.

When the **Show ToolTips on toolbars** check box is checked, the name of the button to which you are pointing is displayed next to the cursor. Below this check box is the **Show shortcut keys in ToolTip** check box. When this option is checked, the shortcut key combination for the command is displayed in the tooltip, if one is available. When tooltips are turned off, this option is grayed out.

## Customizing Existing Toolbars

To delete a toolbar, select the toolbar in the **Toolbars** list in the **Toolbars** tab of the **Customize** dialog box and pick the **Delete** button. To rename a toolbar, select the toolbar in the **Toolbars** list. Then, pick the **Rename...** button. This opens the **Rename Toolbar** dialog box. Type a new name in the text box and pick the **OK** button.

You can also modify existing toolbars by deleting and adding buttons. Buttons can be copied or moved between toolbars, and buttons for commands that are not available in the default toolbars can be added. In order to customize existing toolbars, both the **Customize** dialog box and the toolbar to be modified must be displayed.

To delete a button from a toolbar, simply pick the toolbar button, hold down the left mouse button, and drag the button into the drawing area away from any toolbar. Release the pick button and a warning box asks if you want to delete the button. Pick the **OK** button to delete the button.

When adding buttons to a toolbar, you can select the button to be added from an existing toolbar or from the **Commands** tab of the **Customize** dialog box. See **Figure 19-5**. Many commands are available in this tab that are not included in the default toolbars.

Figure 19-5.
The **Commands** tab
of the **Customize**
dialog box is used
to add buttons for
existing commands
to toolbars.

Selected category

Commands within the selected category

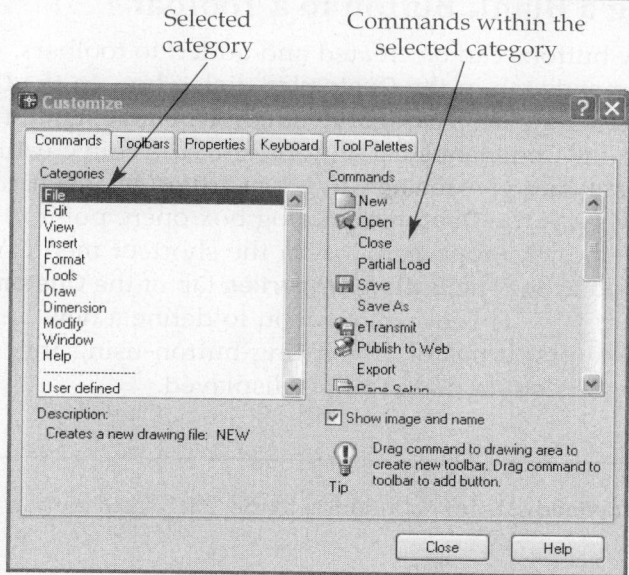

To select a button from the **Commands** tab, first select the category in which the command is grouped. Then, locate the command and button in the **Commands** list. Pick on the button image or command name, hold the left mouse button, and drag the button onto the toolbar to which the button is being added. An "I bar" cursor appears in the toolbar. Position the cursor in the location where you want the new button inserted. Release the left mouse button and the button is added to the toolbar.

You can move and copy toolbar buttons between existing toolbars using a similar process. To move a button, pick and hold on the button, and drag the cursor to the other toolbar. Position the cursor and release the left mouse button. The button is moved from the first toolbar to the second. Use this same process to copy a button between toolbars, but hold the [Ctrl] key before you release the left mouse button. The button remains on the first toolbar, and a copy is placed on the second toolbar. Keep in mind that the **Customize** dialog box must be displayed in order to transfer buttons between existing toolbars.

## Creating New Toolbars and Buttons

AutoCAD has many predefined toolbars. However, entirely new toolbars can be created and filled with redefined buttons or custom buttons. For ease of access, toolbars can be created containing buttons related to specific projects or tasks.

### Creating a New Toolbar

To create a new toolbar, pick the **New...** button in the **Toolbars** tab of the **Customize** dialog box. This opens the **New Toolbar** dialog box. Enter a name for the toolbar and select the menu group in which the toolbar is to be saved. Unless multiple menu groups are loaded, only one will be displayed in the drop-down list. Pick the **OK** button to create the new toolbar. It initially appears as a floating toolbar with no buttons. You can now add buttons to the new toolbar using the methods discussed in the previous section.

# Adding a Blank Button to a Toolbar

New buttons can be created and added to toolbars. To create a new button, pick the **Commands** tab in the **Customize** dialog box. In the **Categories** list, pick the **User defined** category. This category contains a blank standard button and a blank flyout button in the **Commands** list, **Figure 19-6.** To begin creating your own custom button, drag a blank button to the new toolbar. Custom flyouts are discussed later in this chapter.

Now, with the **Customize** dialog box open, point to the blank button and right-click. Then, pick **Properties...** from the shortcut menu. You can also simply pick on the blank button. The **Button Properties** tab of the **Customize** dialog box is displayed. See **Figure 19-7.** This tab allows you to define a new button. You can also view and modify the properties of an existing button using this tab. Simply pick the button while the **Customize** dialog box is displayed.

**Figure 19-6.**
The **User defined** category contains a blank "standard" button and a blank flyout.

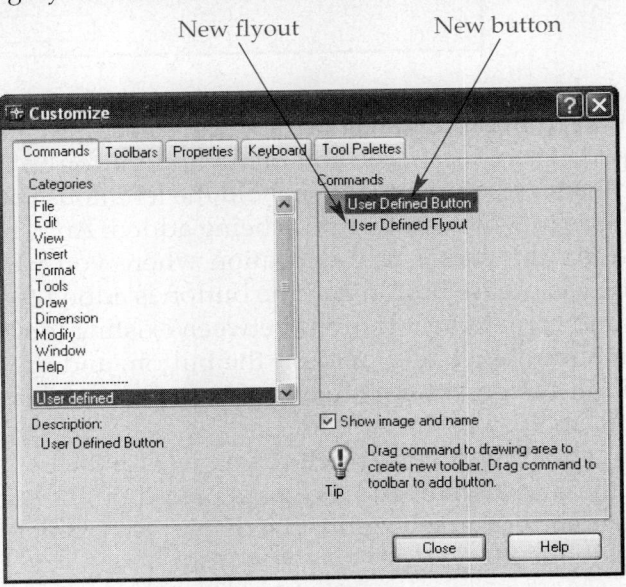

**Figure 19-7.**
Setting the properties for a button.

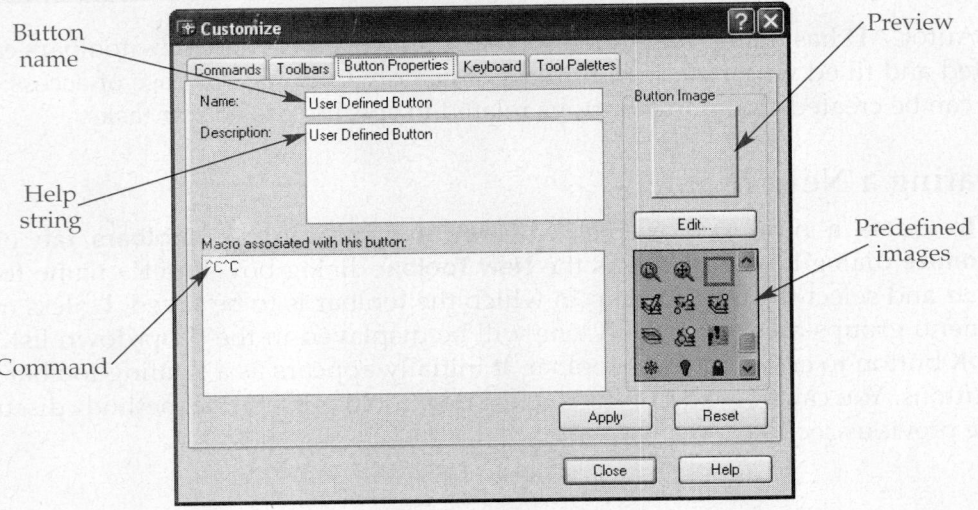

AutoCAD and its Applications—Advanced

By default, the button name is User Defined Button. The button name is what appears in the tooltip. The name should be logical, such as Draw Box. The text that appears in the **Description:** text box appears on the status line below the Command: prompt. This text, called the help string, should also be logical, but can be longer than the button name.

As an example, you will create a button that draws a rectangular border for an E-size sheet (44″ × 34″) using a wide polyline, sets the drawing limits, and finishes with **Zoom Extents**. Therefore, enter E Border as the button name. Also, enter Draws E-size Border, Sets Limits, and Zooms Extents in the **Description:** text box.

## Creating a Button Image

Next, you should create an image for the button. A predefined image can be selected from the list in the **Button Image** area of the **Button Properties** tab. However, having duplicate images can be a source of confusion. It is best to use the **Button Editor** to either modify an existing image or create a new image.

Consider the needs of the persons who will be using your custom toolbar when you design buttons. Simple abstract designs may be recognizable to you because you created them. However, when someone else uses the toolbar, they may not recognize the purpose of the button. For example, the standard buttons in AutoCAD show a graphic that implies something about the command that the button executes. Buttons you create will be most effective if they graphically represent the actions they will perform.

Rather than edit an existing button for the **E Border** button, an entirely new button will be created. With the blank button highlighted in the list of images, pick the **Edit...** button. The **Button Editor** dialog box is displayed, **Figure 19-8.**

The **Button Editor** dialog box has basic "pixel painting" tools and several features to simplify the editing process. The four tools are shown as buttons at the top of the dialog box. The pencil paints individual pixels in the current color. The line tool allows you to draw a line between two points. The circle tool allows you to draw center/radius style ellipses and circles. The erase tool clears the color from individual pixels. The current color is selected from the color palette on the right side of the dialog box. Anything you draw appears in the current color.

Drawing a graphic is usually much easier with the grid turned on. The grid provides outlines for each pixel in the graphic. Each square represents one pixel. Picking the **Grid** check box toggles the state of the grid. The area just above the **Grid** check box

Figure 19-8.
Using the **Button Editor** to create a button image from scratch.

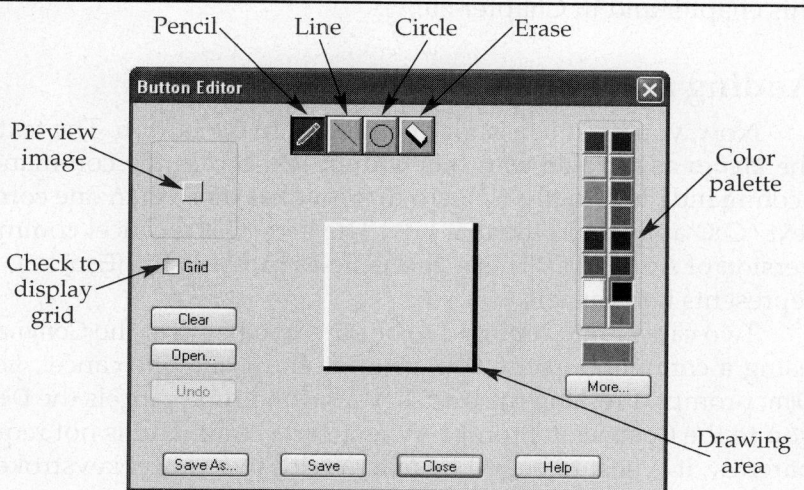

Pencil   Line   Circle   Erase

Preview image

Color palette

Check to display grid

Drawing area

provides a preview of the button in its actual size while you draw the image.

When the toolbar buttons are set in their default size, the button editor provides a drawing area of 15 pixels high by 16 pixels wide. If **Large Buttons** is turned on in the **Toolbars** tab, then this image will be 24×22 pixels. Buttons require two separate images, one at 16×15 and one at 24×22. If you only create a 16×15 pixel image, your custom button will be blank when you switch to large buttons because there is no image defined at that size. You must create a second 24×22 pixel image for the large button.

There are several other tools available in the **Button Editor**. These include the following.

- **Clear.** If you want to erase everything and start over, pick the **Clear** button to clear the drawing area.
- **Open.** Use this button to open an existing bitmap (BMP) file, up to 380×380 pixels in size. The image is automatically resized to fit the current button size.
- **Undo.** You can undo the last operation by picking this button. Only the last operation can be undone. An operation that has been undone cannot be redone.
- **Save As.** Saves a file using the **Save As** dialog box. Use this when you have opened a file and want to save it as well as keep the original file.
- **Save.** Saves the current bitmap file. If the current image has not yet been saved, then the **Create File** dialog is displayed.
- **Close.** Ends the **Button Editor** session. A message is displayed if you have unsaved changes.
- **Help.** Provides context-sensitive help.

All images saved as the button images must be where AutoCAD will find them. You could simply drop all your bitmap images into one of AutoCAD's support directories, but this may not be the best choice. A better option might be to create a folder just for your bitmap images and add this directory to the support directories specified in the **Files** tab of the **Options** dialog box.

**Figure 19-9A** shows a 16×15 pixel image created for the **E Border** button with the **Grid** option activated. After saving your button image, pick the **Close** button to return to the **Button Properties** tab of the **Customize** dialog box. Your newly created image appears above the **Edit...** button, as shown in **Figure 19-9B**. Pick the **Apply** button in the **Button Properties** tab to apply the changes to the custom button. Your button displays the new image, **Figure 19-9C**. You can now close the **Customize** dialog box.

After you apply the changes in the **Customize** dialog box, the menu file is recompiled, adding your new changes. More discussion of menu files is found at the end of this chapter and in Chapter 20.

## Adding a Command to a Button

Now, you need to assign a command to the button. The text string that appears in the **Macro associated with this button:** text box is the command. In many cases, this "command" is actually a macro that invokes more than one command. By default, the text ^C^C appears in the text box. The text ^C is a cancel command, regardless of the version of AutoCAD. This is the same as pressing the [Esc] key. The default text, then, represents two cancels.

Two cancels are required to be sure you begin at the Command: prompt. If you are using a command at the Dim: prompt and issue one cancel, you are returned to the Dim: prompt. Pressing the [Esc] key a second time cancels the Dim: prompt and returns you to the Command: prompt. Whenever a command is not required to operate transparently, it is best to begin the macro with two cancel keystrokes (^C^C) to cancel any current command and return to the Command: prompt.

**Figure 19-9.**
A—A custom button image is created. B—The button image completes the button definition.
C—The new button on the custom toolbar. Notice the tooltip.

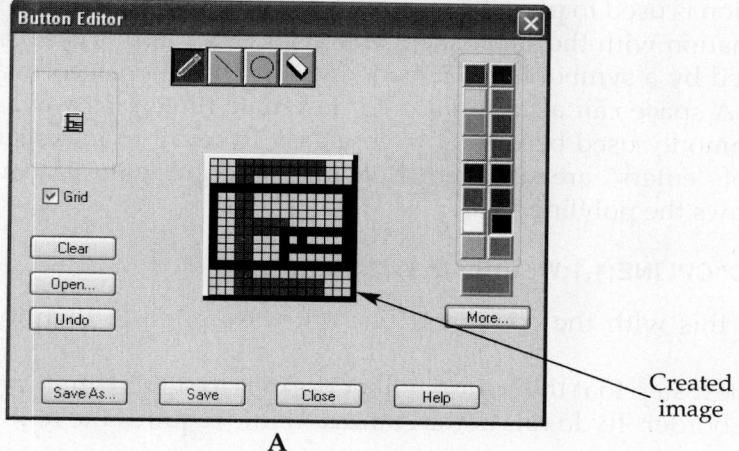

Created image

A

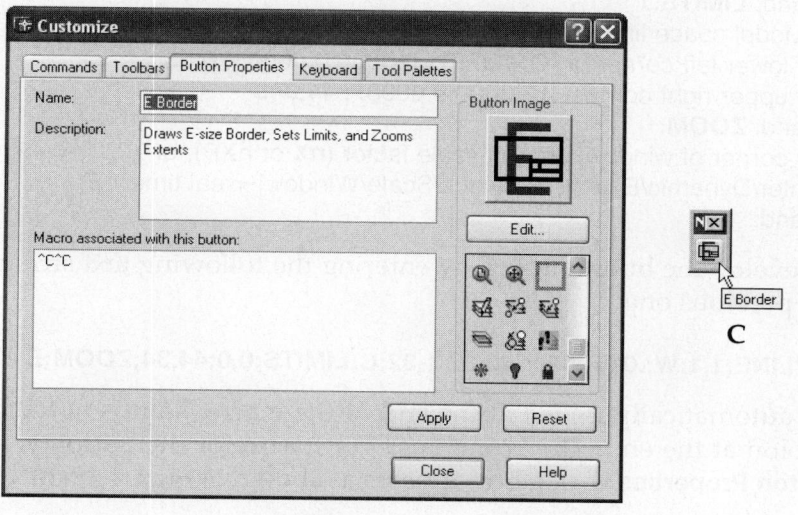

B

C

The macro must match the requirements of the activated commands perfectly. For example, if the **LINE** command is issued, the subsequent prompt expects a coordinate point to be entered. Any other data is inappropriate and will cause an error in your macro. It is best to "walk through" the desired macro manually, writing down each step and the data required by each prompt. The following command sequence creates the rectangular polyline border with a .015 line width.

```
Command: PLINE↵
Specify start point: 1,1↵
Current line–width is 0.0000
Specify next point or [Arc/Halfwidth/Length/Undo/Width]: W↵
Specify starting width <0.0000>: .015↵
Specify ending width <0.0150>: ↵
Specify next point or [Arc/Halfwidth/Length/Undo/Width]: 42,1↵
Specify next point or [Arc/Close/Halfwidth/Length/Undo/Width]: 42,32↵
Specify next point or [Arc/Close/Halfwidth/Length/Undo/Width]: 1,32↵
Specify next point or [Arc/Close/Halfwidth/Length/Undo/Width]: C↵
Command:
```

Creating the button macro involves duplicating the above keystrokes, with a couple of differences. Some symbols are used in menu macros to represent keystrokes. For example, a cancel (^C) is not entered by pressing [Esc]. Instead, the [Shift]+[6] key combination is used to place the *caret* symbol, which is used to represent the [Ctrl] key in combination with the subsequent character (a 'C' in this case). Another keystroke represented by a symbol is the [Enter] key. An [Enter] is placed in a macro as a semicolon (;). A space can also be used to designate [Enter]. However, the semicolon is more commonly used because it is very easy to count to make sure that the correct number of "enters" are supplied. Keeping these guidelines in mind, the following macro draws the polyline border.

**^C^CPLINE;1,1;W;.015;;42,1;42,32;1,32;C;**

Compare this with the command line entry example to identify each part of the macro.

The next step that the button will perform is to set the limits and zoom to display the entire border. To do this at the command line requires the following entries.

```
Command: LIMITS↵
Reset Model space limits:
Specify lower left corner or [ON/OFF] <0.0000,0.0000>: 0,0↵
Specify upper right corner <12.0000,9.0000>: 44,34↵
Command: ZOOM↵
Specify corner of window, enter a scale factor (nX or nXP), or
[All/Center/Dynamic/Extents/Previous/Scale/Window] <real time>: E↵
Command:
```

Continue to develop the button macro by entering the following text string immediately after the previous one.

**^C^CPLINE;1,1;W;.015;;42,1;42,32;1,32;C;LIMITS;0,0;44,34;ZOOM;E**

An "enter" is automatically issued at the end of the macro, so it is not necessary to enter a semicolon at the end. The "command" or macro for the button is now complete. The **Button Properties** dialog box appears as shown in **Figure 19-10**.

Figure 19-10.
The "command" or macro for the **E Border** button is entered in the **Button Properties** dialog box.

Completed macro

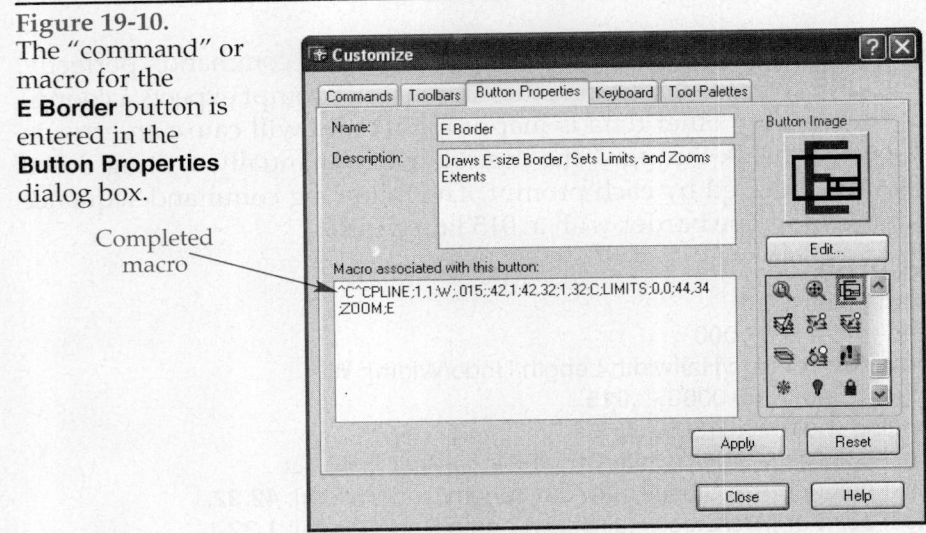

## Exercise 19-1

○ Begin AutoCAD. Open the **Customize** dialog box and display the **Toolbars** tab.

○ Create a toolbar named **Borders and Layouts**.

○ Add a button to the toolbar named **E Border**. Use the macro given in the text; however, add an "erase all" statement to the beginning. Also, enter a short description for the button and create a button image.

○ Add another new button named **Switch to Layout**. The button should execute the **LAYOUT** command, select the **Set** option, and wait for you to enter a layout name. Write the macro, enter a short description for the button, and create a button image.

○ Add another new button named **Pspace Viewports**. The button should execute the **MVIEW** command, select the **4** option to construct four viewports, and wait for you to pick corners of the rectangle border. Write the macro, enter a short description, and create a button image.

○ Arrange the buttons on the **Borders and Layouts** toolbar from left to right as **Switch to Layout**, **E Border**, and **Pspace Viewports**. Close the **Customize** dialog box to save the new toolbar configuration.

○ Test the new buttons. The three buttons allow you to enter paper space, erase the default viewport ("erase all"), create an E-size border, and divide it into four paper space viewports. When you first switch to a layout after picking the **Switch to Layout** button, the **Page Setup** dialog box appears. Be sure to select ANSI E (44 × 34) as the paper size.

## Working with Flyouts

A *flyout* is a single button that can display a number of other buttons, usually for related commands. A single pick on a flyout button activates the command assigned to the currently visible toolbar button. When you pick and hold on a flyout button, the other buttons in the flyout are displayed in a "flyout," which can be thought of as a pop-up toolbar. A flyout is really a button associated with a toolbar. While holding the mouse button, move the cursor to the desired button, and then release the mouse button. This activates the associated command or macro, and displays the selected button as the current button in the flyout.

Creating custom toolbars can help save time and increase productivity. However, each displayed toolbar takes up some of the available screen area. If many toolbars are displayed at once, the drawing area can be drastically reduced, especially with low-resolution displays. You can conserve on-screen space by using flyouts in your custom toolbars. The following discussion shows how to create a customized toolbar flyout for 3D projects.

First, open the **Customize** dialog box. Then, select the **Toolbars** tab and create a new toolbar named **3D Tools**. The "blank" toolbar appears on the screen, ready to be customized. Pick the **Commands** tab. Using the **Categories** list, add predefined buttons found in the **Draw** and **View** categories to set up your new toolbar as shown in **Figure 19-11**.

**Figure 19-11.**
A custom toolbar for working in 3D.

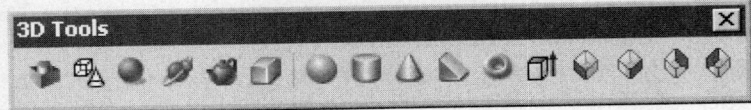

**Figure 19-12.**
This warning appears to indicate that a toolbar has not been associated with the blank flyout.

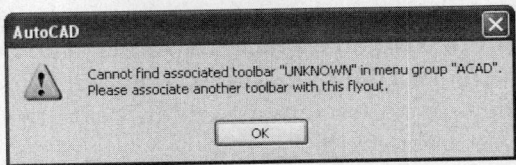

After you have set up your **3D Tools** toolbar, select the **User defined** category. Drag-and-drop a blank flyout button onto the **Modify** toolbar above the **Erase** button. Next, with the **Customize** dialog box open, pick on the blank flyout. The warning shown in **Figure 19-12** appears. Pick the **OK** button and the **Flyout Properties** tab in the **Customize** dialog box is displayed. See **Figure 19-13**. Highlight the name of your toolbar, **3D Tools**, in the list. A preview appears on the right of the tab. Then, pick the **Apply** button. The toolbar is now associated with the flyout.

Close the **Customize** dialog box. Now, when you pick the flyout, your custom **3D Tools** toolbar is displayed, as shown in **Figure 19-14**. When you point at the flyout button, the name and help string of the most recently used button (the "top" button) is displayed.

**Figure 19-13.**
Associating a toolbar with a flyout.

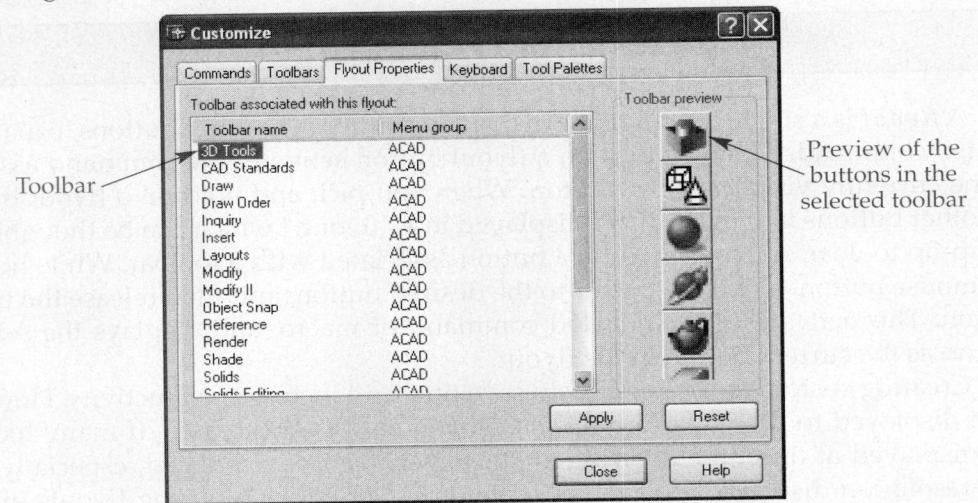

## Exercise 19-2

○ Begin AutoCAD. If you have not yet completed Exercise 19-1, do so now.
○ Open the **Customize** dialog box and display the **Commands** tab.
○ Add a blank flyout button to the **Borders and Layouts** toolbar to the right of the **Pspace Viewports** button. Associate the **Layouts** toolbar with the flyout.
○ Close the **Customize** dialog box.
○ Test the new flyout in the **Borders and Layouts** toolbar.

**Figure 19-14.**
The **3D Tools** flyout
button placed in the
**Modify** toolbar.

New flyout with
its associated
toolbar

# Toolbars and Menu Files

As toolbars are adjusted and customized, the changes are stored in files. AutoCAD maintains a record of these changes in one of several files associated with its menu system. Each of these files has the same file name, but different file extensions. The standard menu provided with the AutoCAD software is named acad, and the files associated with this menu are located in the AutoCAD Support folder.

It is important to understand how AutoCAD handles menu files. Otherwise, it is very easy for your toolbar customization work to simply disappear. The menu files associated with the acad menu are as follows.

- **ACAD.MNU.** This is the fully documented *template* file. The template file provides the initial menu setup. If this menu is edited and then loaded using the **MENU** command, it creates a new menu source file.
- **ACAD.MNS.** This is the menu *source* file. Most documentation is stripped from the file to reduce its size. All code changes to the toolbar menu are recorded into this file. This is the file that is used in the creation of a compiled menu file.
- **ACAD.MNC.** This is a *compiled* menu file. AutoCAD creates this optimized file to handle the menus in your drawing sessions.
- **ACAD.MNR.** This is the menu *resource* file. It stores all bitmap images associated with the menu for quick access.

The MNS file is the location for code changes to the toolbars. However, when an MNU file is loaded, it overwrites the current MNS file and all of your changes to the toolbars are lost. A warning to this effect is displayed whenever you attempt to load an MNU file. In order to make your changes permanent, you should open both files in a text editor, cut and paste the new or changed data from the MNS file to the MNU file, and save the MNU file. That way, when the MNU file is loaded, it keeps these changes and writes them again to the new MNS file.

The toolbar information is placed in the text files under the heading ***TOOLBARS. You can find the listings in each file for changed toolbars and update the MNU file using the code in the MNS file. New toolbars can be copied and pasted into the MNU file. More information on editing menu files is found in Chapter 20 of this text.

If you wish to keep the original MNU file available, you should make a copy of the MNS file before you modify the toolbar menus. Keep this file in an alternate directory as a backup in case you accidentally overwrite the original MNS file.

**PROFESSIONAL TIP** When editing a menu file in a text editor, be sure to save the file as "plain" ASCII text. If you do not, codes may be saved in the file that AutoCAD will not recognize.

## Working with Toolbars at the Command Line

Use the **–TOOLBAR** command to work with toolbars at the command line. This command is most useful when creating menu macros, script files, or AutoLISP functions to perform automated toolbar setups. When using this method, you are prompted for the toolbar name. The complete toolbar name consists of the menu group and toolbar name, separated by a period. For example, the toolbar name for the **Draw** toolbar defined in the acad.mnu menu is ACAD.DRAW. The menu group name can be omitted when only one menu is currently loaded, or if the toolbar name is not duplicated in another menu group. After specifying the toolbar name (or selecting **ALL** for all toolbars), you can select an option.

    Command: –TOOLBAR⏎
    Enter toolbar name or [ALL]: ACAD.DRAW⏎
    Enter an option [Show/Hide/Left/Right/Top/Bottom/Float] <Show>:

These options are used to hide, show, or specify a location for the toolbar.

* **Show.** This option makes the toolbar visible. Selecting this option is identical to activating the check box next to the toolbar name in the **Toolbars** dialog box.
* **Hide.** This option causes the toolbar to disappear. Selecting this option is identical to disabling the check box next to the toolbar name in the **Toolbars** dialog box.
* **Left.** Places the toolbar in a docked position at the left side of the window.
* **Right.** Places the toolbar in a docked position at the right side of the window.
* **Top.** Places the toolbar in a docked position at the top of the window.
* **Bottom.** Places the toolbar in a docked position at the bottom of the window.
* **Float.** Places the toolbar as a floating toolbar.

For example, to dock the **Zoom** toolbar on the left side of the AutoCAD window, use the following command sequence.

    Command: –TOOLBAR⏎
    Enter toolbar name or [ALL]: ACAD.ZOOM⏎
    Enter an option [Show/Hide/Left/Right/Top/Bottom/Float] <Show>: LEFT⏎
    Enter new position (horizontal,vertical) <0,0>: ⏎
    Command:

The **Float** option places the toolbar in a floating position anchored at the pixels in the Position <0,0>: prompt. The anchor point of a floating toolbar is the upper-left corner. If you place the toolbar at 400,300, the upper-left corner of the toolbar is at this location. You are then asked to establish the shape of the new toolbar by specifying the number of rows of buttons for the toolbar. For example, the following sequence places the **Solids** toolbar as shown in **Figure 19-15.**

**Figure 19-15.**
Locating a floating toolbar at a 400,300 position using the **–TOOLBAR** command.

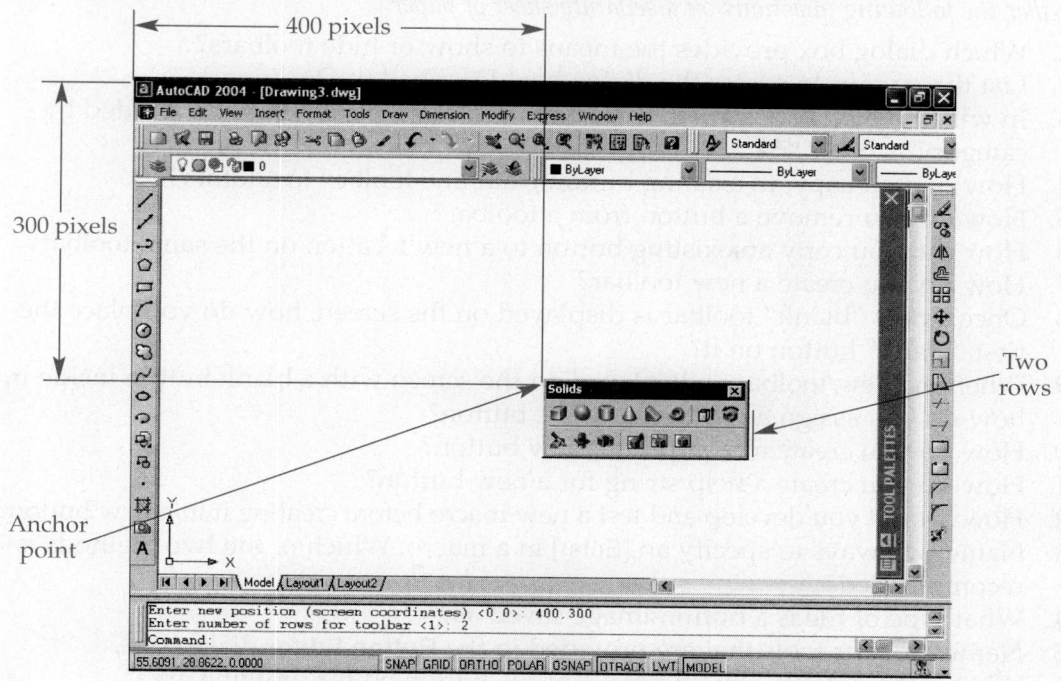

Command: **–TOOLBAR.**↵
Enter toolbar name or [ALL]: **ACAD.SOLIDS.**↵
Enter an option [Show/Hide/Left/Right/Top/Bottom/Float] <Show>: **F**↵
Enter new position (screen coordinates) <0,0>: **400,300.**↵
Enter number of rows for toolbar <1>: **2.**↵
Command:

Another capability of the **–TOOLBAR** command is to show or hide all toolbars at once. When prompted for the toolbar name, enter ALL. The only two options that appear are **Show** and **Hide**. If you use the **Hide** option, all toolbars are hidden. Then, you can use the **Customize** dialog box to select the toolbars you need.

**Exercise 19-3**

○ Open AutoCAD and maximize it so that it occupies the entire screen.
○ Use the appropriate method to display and float the **Draw**, **Modify**, and **Dimension** toolbars.
○ Move the toolbars to several different floating positions around the screen.
○ Move the **Draw** and **Modify** toolbars to a docked position at the top of the screen.
○ Move the **Dimension** toolbar to a docked position at the right side of the screen.
○ Position all three toolbars in a docked position at the right side of the screen.
○ Position each of the toolbars in two additional docked positions on the screen.
○ Return the screen to the original configuration.

## Chapter Test

*Answer the following questions on a separate sheet of paper.*

1. Which dialog box provides the means to show or hide toolbars?
2. List three ways to access the dialog box described in Question 1.
3. In which dialog box and tab can you find all predefined buttons divided by category?
4. How do you copy an existing button from one toolbar to another?
5. How do you remove a button from a toolbar?
6. How can you copy an existing button to a new location on the same toolbar?
7. How do you create a new toolbar?
8. Once a new "blank" toolbar is displayed on the screen, how do you place the first "blank" button on it?
9. When the new toolbar is displayed on the screen with a blank button inside it, how do you assign a command to the button?
10. How do you create a tooltip for a new button?
11. How do you create a help string for a new button?
12. How should you develop and test a new macro before creating it in a new button?
13. Name two ways to specify an [Enter] in a macro. Which of the two methods is recommended?
14. What type of file is a button image saved as?
15. Name the four tools that are provided in the **Button Editor** dialog box.
16. What is the default size (in pixels) of the button editor drawing area?
17. Where is the **Large Buttons** check box located? What function does this check box perform?
18. How do you insert a flyout button into a toolbar?
19. How do you assign a command to a "blank" flyout?
20. What is the name and extension of the AutoCAD menu file in which all code changes to the toolbar are recorded?
21. Which AutoCAD menu file is fully documented and is used to create a new menu source file?
22. Explain how to display a toolbar without using a dialog box.

## Drawing Problems

*Before customizing or creating any menus, check with your instructor or supervisor for specific instructions or guidelines.*

1. Create a new toolbar using the following information.
   A. Name the toolbar **Draw/Modify**.
   B. Copy at least three, but no more than six, commonly used drawing buttons onto the new toolbar. Use only existing buttons, do not create new ones.
   C. Copy at least three, but no more than six, commonly used editing buttons onto the new toolbar. Use only existing buttons, do not create new ones.
   D. Remove the default **Draw** and **Modify** toolbars from the display.
   E. Dock the new **Draw/Modify** toolbar at the upper-left side of the screen.

2. Create a new toolbar using the following information.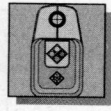
    A. Name the toolbar **My 3D Tools**.
    B. Display the **Solids** toolbar. Then, copy the following buttons from the **Solids** toolbar onto the new toolbar.

| | |
|---|---|
| **Box** | **Sphere** |
| **Cone** | **Torus** |
| **Cylinder** | **Wedge** |

    C. Display the **View** toolbar. Then, copy the following buttons from the **View** toolbar onto the new toolbar.

| | | |
|---|---|---|
| **Top View** | **Bottom View** | **Left View** |
| **Right View** | **Front View** | **Back View** |

    D. Display the **UCS** toolbar. Then, copy the following buttons from the **UCS** toolbar onto the new toolbar.

| | | |
|---|---|---|
| **Display UCS Dialog** | **Object UCS** | **World UCS** |
| **Origin UCS** | **3 Point UCS** | **UCS Previous** |

    E. Dock the toolbar in a location of your choice.

3. Create a new toolbar using the following information.
    A. Name the toolbar **Paper Space Viewports**.
    B. The toolbar should contain eight buttons that use the **MVIEW** command to create paper space viewports as follows.
    • 1 viewport—allow user to pick location
    • 2 viewports—(horizontal)—allow user to pick location
    • 3 viewports—allow user to pick orientation and location
    • 4 viewports—allow user to pick location
    • 1 viewport—fit
    • 2 viewports—vertical
    • 3 viewports—right
    • 4 viewports—fit
    C. Construct button graphics for the new buttons. Save the images in a new folder, and add the folder to the AutoCAD support environment.
    D. Dock the toolbar on the right side of the screen.

4. Create a new toolbar for inserting title block drawings. Name the toolbar **Title Blocks**.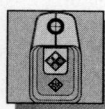
    A. The toolbar should contain six buttons that do the following.
    • Insert the ANSI A title block drawing
    • Insert the ANSI B title block drawing
    • Insert the ANSI C title block drawing
    • Insert the ANSI D title block drawing
    • Insert the ANSI E title block drawing
    • Insert the Architectural Title Block drawing
    B. Create button images for each of the new buttons. Save the images in a new folder, and add the folder to the AutoCAD support environment.
    C. Dock the toolbar on the left side of the screen.

5. Add a flyout to the **Standard** toolbar that will display the toolbar created in Problem 4. Place the flyout next to the **Open** button.

# Creating Custom Tool Palettes

Tool palettes can be quickly created from the blocks in existing drawings using the **DesignCenter**. First, open **DesignCenter**, if it is not already open. Then, navigate to the existing drawing. Expand the drawing tree, highlight the **Blocks** branch, and right-click to display the shortcut menu. See Figure A below. Finally, select **Create Tool Palette** from the shortcut menu. The new tool palette is created and added to the **Tool Palettes** window. See Figure B below. You can now use the tool palette to quickly insert the blocks contained in the drawing. For more information on working with tool palettes, including changing the appearance, arranging tool palettes, modifying tool properties, and adding hatch patterns to a tool palette, refer to *AutoCAD and its Applications—Basics*, Chapter 22 *Creating Symbols for Multiple Use.*

Figure A.

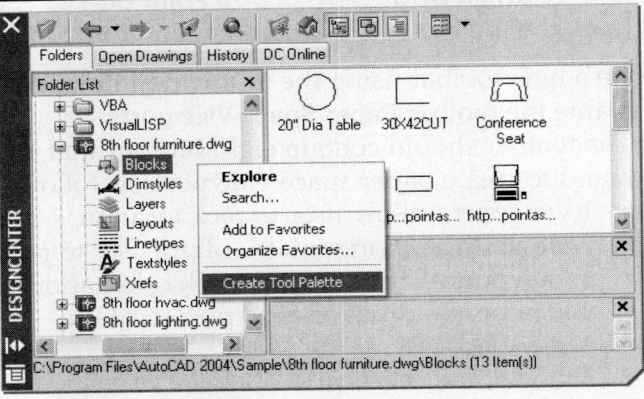

Figure B.

## CHAPTER 20

# Customizing Screen and Button Menus

## Learning Objectives

After completing this chapter, you will be able to:
- Describe the structure of button and screen menus.
- Create new button menus.
- Customize existing screen menus and create new ones.

In Chapter 19, you learned how to customize AutoCAD toolbars to suit your needs. AutoCAD menus can also be customized to suit specific needs. Users can add special commands to the standard menus, or create their own menu system from scratch. As with customized toolbars and toolbar buttons, existing commands can be used in a macro. All aspects of the menu system can be changed. This includes the cursor button functions, standard screen menus, pull-down menus, and image file menus.

## AutoCAD's Menu Structure

Before constructing your own menus, look at AutoCAD's standard menu structure to get a feel for the layout. This will give you a better understanding of the tools and techniques you can use to build custom menus. The basic components of a menu are the main sections, submenus, item titles, and command codes.

For Chapters 20–25, it is assumed you are familiar with a programmer's text editor or word processor program. You must be familiar with the commands or keys in your text editor that allow you to scroll or page through a file.

**PROFESSIONAL TIP**

It is best to do your customization using a programmer's text editor. These types of editors typically offer powerful editing features. If you do not have this type of editor, it is possible to do your menu customization using Microsoft WordPad program. If you use WordPad, save the file as a Text Document or the file may become unreadable by AutoCAD.

Whichever text editor you decide to use should have a text search function to find specified text within a file. This is the best way to navigate through the large menu file.

# AutoCAD's Menu Files

Several files are used to produce AutoCAD's menu system. The file extensions may vary, but the file names are the same. AutoCAD comes with one primary menu file named acad. **Figure 20-1** shows the AutoCAD screen with this menu loaded.

The acad menu files are discussed in this chapter. The primary files are acad.mnu, acad.mns, acad.mnl, acad.mnc, and acad.mnr. The acad.mnl is a menu LISP file that holds the AutoLISP program code. This defines any AutoLISP functions used in the menu. The acad.mnc and acad.mnr files are automatically created and updated by AutoCAD whenever an edited acad.mnu or acad.mns is loaded and compiled. More information on menu files is provided later in this chapter.

You can directly edit both the MNU and MNS files. As mentioned in Chapter 19, the MNU file is more completely documented and is, therefore, a bit easier to navigate through and understand. All work in this chapter requires the MNU file to be edited.

Loading an edited MNU file overwrites the existing MNS file of the same name. Since your interactive toolbar modifications are written to the MNS file, they are lost when an MNU file is loaded.

Rather than edit the current menu structure, a copy of the MNU file should be created. This way, any changes you make to the menu will not affect your standard menu. Additionally, since the menu you will be editing will have a different name, previous toolbar changes will not be lost as you work in this chapter.

To give you a clear idea of how the MNU and MNS files differ, look at the excerpts of menu code in **Figure 20-2**. Note that the acad.mnu file has documentation that explains the purpose of the code.

**Figure 20-1.**
The AutoCAD screen with the acad menu loaded and screen menus turned on.

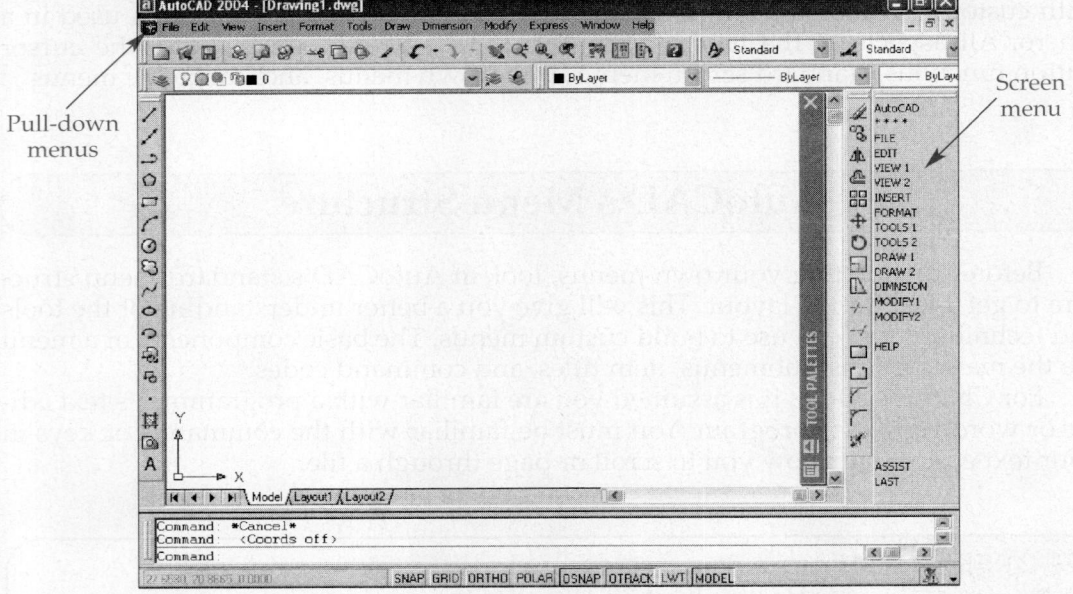

Pull-down menus

Screen menu

AutoCAD and its Applications—Advanced

Figure 20-2.
The acad.mnu file contains helpful documentation not found in the acad.mns file.

| ACAD.MNU | ACAD.MNS |
|---|---|
| //<br>//     Default AutoCAD NAMESPACE declaration:<br>//<br>\*\*\*MENUGROUP=ACAD<br><br>//<br>//  Begin AutoCAD Digitizer Button Menus<br>//<br>\*\*\*BUTTONS1<br>//   Simple + button<br>//   if a grip is hot bring up the Grips Cursor<br>     Menu (POP 500), else send a carriage return<br>//   If the SHORTCUTMENU sysvar is not 0 the<br>     first item (for button 1) is NOT USED.<br>$M=$(if,$(eq,$(substr,$(getvar,cmdnames),1,5),G<br>   RIP\_),$P0=ACAD.GRIPS $P0=\*);<br>$P0=SNAP $p0=\*<br>^C^C<br>^B<br>^O<br>^G<br>^D<br>^E<br>^T | //<br>//     AutoCAD menu file - C:\Documents and<br>Settings\\_username_\Application<br>Data\Autodesk\AutoCAD<br>2004\R16.0\enu\Support\acad.mns<br>//<br><br>\*\*\*MENUGROUP=ACAD<br><br>\*\*\*BUTTONS1<br>$M=$(if,$(eq,$(substr,$(getvar,cmdnames),1,5),<br>   GRIP\_),$P0=ACAD.GRIPS $P0=\*);<br>$P0=SNAP $p0=\*<br>^C^C<br>^B<br>^O<br>^G<br>^D<br>^E<br>^T |

**PROFESSIONAL TIP**

Regardless of your level of experience in working with menu files, it is best to maintain appropriate backup copies of prior revisions. This way, you always have something to refer back to if you encounter problems or data loss.

One approach is to create backup copies of the menu in a separate folder. Another approach is to make a copy of the current menu with a different name for your customization work. For example, make a copy of the acad.mns file named acad_work.mns and do your customization in the new file to protect the original menu. Also, this would give you something to refer back to if you have difficulties getting the new menu to function.

## Menu Section Labels

Open the acad.mnu file found in the AutoCAD Support folder using your text editing program. Use your keyboard cursor keys and the [Page Up]/[Page Down] keys to page through the file.

As you look through the menu file, notice the menu section headings. Major menu headings are identified by three asterisks (\*\*\*) in front of the name. Submenus are listed with two asterisks (\*\*) in front of the name. The following are the major menu headings.

    \*\*\*MENUGROUP
    \*\*\*BUTTONS1
    \*\*\*BUTTONS2
    \*\*\*BUTTONS3

```
***BUTTONS4
***AUX1
***AUX2
***AUX3
***AUX4
***POP0 through POP11
***POP500 through POP512
***TOOLBARS
***IMAGE
***SCREEN
***TABLET1
***TABLET2
***TABLET3
***TABLET4
***HELPSTRINGS
***ACCELERATORS
```

In this chapter, you will be working with button and screen menus. Pull-down menus and image tiles are discussed in Chapter 21. Tablet menus are discussed in Chapter 22. The AUX menu headings are used for system pointing devices.

## Menu Layout

Before beginning any editing of the acad.mnu file, take a few minutes and look through it. Load the acad.mnu file into your text editor and locate the line containing ***BUTTONS1. That portion of the menu should look like:

```
***BUTTONS1
// Simple + button
// if a grip is hot bring up the Grips Cursor Menu (POP 500), else send a carriage return
// If the SHORTCUTMENU sysvar is not 0 the first item (for button 1) is NOT USED.
$M=$(if,$(eq,$(substr,$(getvar,cmdnames),1,5),GRIP_),$P0=ACAD.GRIPS $P0=*);
$P0=SNAP $p0=*
^C^C
^B
^O
^G
^D
^E
^T

***BUTTONS2
// Shift + button
$P0=SNAP $p0=*

***BUTTONS3
// Control + button

***BUTTONS4
// Control + shift + button
```

This is the first part of the acad.mnu file. The entire file has over 4600 lines. The line ***BUTTONS1 is the beginning of the button menu. The items under that heading are specific assignments to the buttons on your pointing device.

Scroll down until you see the ***POP1 heading. This is the first pull-down menu, which appears at the left end of the menu bar near the top of the AutoCAD window. Notice that the first word on each line under the **FILE heading is preceded with the characters "ID_". This is known as a *name tag.* AutoCAD associates other lines in the menu with these name tags. Name tags are covered later in this chapter. The next item is the label, enclosed in square brackets ([ ]). Any word or character string appearing inside these brackets is displayed in the pull-down menu or on the menu bar. Also note that one of the characters within the brackets is preceded by an ampersand (&).

AutoCAD and its Applications—Advanced

The character preceded by an ampersand in a pull-down menu label defines the keyboard access key used to enable that item. This key is also called a mnemonic key. Thus, since the title of the **File** pull-down menu is defined as [&File], it can be accessed by pressing the [Alt] key to toggle the access keys on and pressing [F] for **File**.

Once a pull-down menu is displayed, a menu item within it can be selected using a single menu shortcut key. The menu shortcut keys defined for the **New...** and **Open...** items in the **File** pull-down menu appear in the acad.mnu file as &New and &Open. Therefore, these menu items are selected with the [N] and [O] keys, respectively.

## Menu Item Titles

Use the search function of your text editor or the [Page Down] key to find the **09_DRAW1 menu. Remember, the two asterisks represent a subheading under a major section. The **09_DRAW1 menu is the first page of the **DRAW1** screen menu. In Figure 20-3, the **DRAW1** screen menu as seen in AutoCAD is shown on the left, and the same page is shown on the right as it appears in the acad.mnu file.

Notice that the menu entry is the same as its label inside the brackets ([ ]). The text to the right of the closing bracket is the menu macro. Figure 20-4 shows the difference between label information and a menu macro. As a general rule, a screen menu name can be up to eight characters long. You can have longer names and descriptions inside the brackets. However, the width of the screen menu area is fixed and longer names may be truncated. The number of usable characters varies based on the properties of the current Windows system font.

**Figure 20-3.**
On the left is the **DRAW1** screen menu as it appears on screen. On the right is the related command lines from the acad.mnu file.

| AutoCAD Screen Menu (DRAW1) | ACAD.MNU Menu Code |
|---|---|
| Line | **09_DRAW1 3 |
| Ray | [Line     ]^C^C_line |
| Xline | [Ray      ]^C^C_ray |
| Mline | [Xline    ]^C^C_xline |
|  | [Mline    ]^C^C_mline |
| Pline |  |
| 3Dpoly | [Pline    ]^C^C_pline |
| Polygon | [3Dpoly ]^C^C_3dpoly |
| Rectang | [Polygon          ]^C^C_polygon |
|  | [Rectang          ]^C^C_rectang |
| Arc |  |
| Circle | [Arc      ]^C^C_arc |
| Donut | [Circle   ]^C^C_circle |
|  | [Donut    ]^C^C_donut |
| Spline |  |
| Ellipse | [Spline  ]^C^C_spline |
|  | [Ellipse  ]^C^C_ellipse |

**Figure 20-4.**
A—The first eight characters in the label appear as the screen menu selection. Additional comments can be included in the label. B—The menu macro, which follows the closing bracket, is processed by AutoCAD.

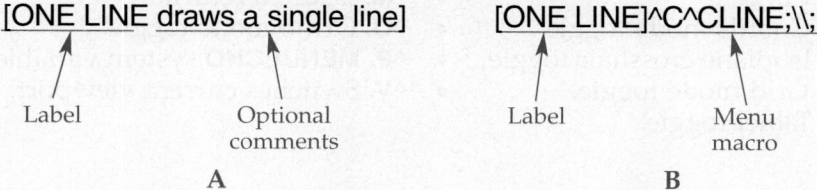

[ONE LINE draws a single line]          [ONE LINE]^C^CLINE;\\;

Label          Optional          Label          Menu
               comments                          macro

A                    B

## Menu Syntax

When paging through the menu file, you probably noticed several characters and symbols that did not make much sense, such as $S=ACAD.01_FILE and \. These are menu codes, and have explicit functions in the menu. You will be using these codes to create menus.

Figure 20-5 is a list of characters and their functions. The characters listed here can be used for button and screen menus. Special characters for pull-down menus are described later.

Figure 20-5.
Special characters are used for buttons and screen menus. Listed are the characters and their functions.

| Character | Function |
|-----------|----------|
| *** | Major menu sections—Must be placed directly in front of the name of the section, for example: ***SCREEN. |
| ** | Submenu section—Appears in front of the submenu name. The **Draw1** screen menu shown in the previous section has the name **09_DRAW1. |
| [ ] | The label, which contains the menu selection, is enclosed in brackets. Only the first eight characters inside the brackets are displayed in the screen menu. |
| $S= | This indicates that another screen menu is to be displayed and enables AutoCAD to move between submenus. Other similar codes are $B (BUTTONS), $T (TABLET), $I (IMAGE), $P (POP), and $A (AUX). |
| ^C^C | This represents two "cancels" to completely exit any command. |
| ; | The semicolon represents pressing [Enter]. |
| \ | The backslash represents a pause for user input, where information must be typed at the keyboard or entered with the pointing device. |
| + | The plus symbol is placed at the end of a long menu line and tells AutoCAD that there is more of this sequence on the next line. |
| =* | The current shortcut, pull-down, or image tile menu is displayed. |
| (space) | A blank space between items is the same as pressing [Enter] or the space bar. |
| *^C^C | Creates a repeating command. |
| si | Specifies immediate action on a single selected item. Placed at the occurrence of a Select objects: prompt during a macro. For example: Erase;si |

## Using Variables and Control Characters

AutoCAD system variables and control characters can be used in screen menus. They can be included to increase the speed and usefulness of your menu commands. Become familiar with these variables so you can make use of them in your menus.

- **^B.** Snap mode toggle.
- **^C.** Cancel.
- **^D.** Coords mode toggle.
- **^E.** Isoplane crosshair toggle.
- **^G.** Grid mode toggle.
- **^T.** Tablet toggle.
- **^H.** Issues a backspace.
- **^M.** Issues a return.
- **^O.** Ortho mode toggle.
- **^P. MENUECHO** system variable toggle.
- **^V.** Switches current viewport.

# Creating Button Menus

Button menus control the functions of the pointing device buttons. If you use a stylus or a mouse with only one or two buttons, you will not be using button menus. If you have a pointing device with more than two buttons, you can alter the functions of the buttons to suit your needs. This can add to your drawing productivity and speed the access of commonly used commands.

The BUTTONS*n* menu sections (where *n* represents a number from one to four) are used for pointing devices such as digitizer pucks. The AUX*n* menus are used for a system mouse, such as the mouse you use in Windows. A standard mouse does not provide as much room for customization as a digitizer puck. The pick button on a mouse cannot be changed by editing the menu file. Therefore, a two-button mouse has a single button that can be customized, and a three-button mouse has two customizable buttons. Still, by using the [Shift]+, [Ctrl]+, and [Ctrl]+[Shift]+ combinations described in this section, added functionality is possible even for a standard mouse.

The main button menu is BUTTONS1. It is arranged for a device with nine programmable buttons. A list of this button menu and its functions is shown in **Figure 20-6**.

**Figure 20-6.**
On the left is the ***BUTTONS1 menu and on the right is the meaning of the command lines and the associated buttons. Button #1 is the pick button and cannot be customized in the menu file.

| Menu File Listing | Button Number | Function |
|---|---|---|
| ***BUTTONS1 | | Menu section name |
| //  Simple + button | | Comment |
| //  if a grip is hot bring up the Grips Cursor Menu (POP 500), else send a carriage return | | Comment |
| //  If the SHORTCUTMENU sysvar is not 0 the first item (for button 1) is NOT USED. | | Comment |
| $M=$(if,$(eq,$(substr,$(getvar,cmdnames),1,5), GRIP_),$P0=ACAD.GRIPS $P0=*); | 2 | Return, or display grips shortcut menu |
| $P0=SNAP $p0=* | 3 | Displays Object Snap shortcut menu |
| ^C^C | 4 | Cancel |
| ^B | 5 | Snap mode toggle |
| ^O | 6 | Ortho mode toggle |
| ^G | 7 | Grid mode toggle |
| ^D | 8 | Coords mode toggle |
| ^E | 9 | Isoplane crosshair toggle |
| ^T | 10 | Tablet toggle |

## Additional Button Menus

If you are using a digitizer puck, you can have instant access to the four button menus, BUTTONS1 through BUTTONS4. Each of these menus can be accessed with a keyboard and puck button combination and can contain any commands you need. For example, you can place a variety of display commands in the BUTTONS2 menu. To access these commands, simply hold down the [Shift] key on the keyboard and press the appropriate puck button, as shown in **Figure 20-7**.

Figure 20-7.
Keyboard and puck
button combination
can be used to
access the four
button menus.

| Action | Button Number |
|---|---|
| puck button only | BUTTONS1 |
| [Shift]+ puck button | BUTTONS2 |
| [Ctrl]+ puck button | BUTTONS3 |
| [Ctrl]+[Shift]+ puck button | BUTTONS4 |

**PROFESSIONAL TIP**

You must understand how commands work to create AutoCAD menus. Know the command options, when they can be used, and how they are used. Always plan your commands and macros using the following steps.

1. Write out what you want the command or macro to do.
2. Write the macro as it will appear in the menu file using command codes.
3. Check the written macro to be sure it has the proper commands, options, and syntax.
4. Add the macro to the menu file.
5. Test the macro.

## Replacing Button Menu Items

The process of replacing button menu items is the same as editing a line in a text file. Before you edit the acad.mnu file, make a backup copy. An example is replacing the existing button commands shown in Figure 20-8 with the new commands given. Place a double cancel before each command. This cancels the current command when the button is picked. When you have finished editing, the new button menu should look like this:

```
***BUTTONS1
$M=$(if,$(eq,$(substr,$(getvar,cmdnames),1,5),GRIP_),$P0=ACAD.GRIPS $P0=*);
$P0=SNAP $p0=*
^C^C
^B
^C^CLINE
^C^CERASE
^C^CCIRCLE
^C^CARC
^T
```

Figure 20-8.
Existing button
functions can be
easily replaced with
new commands.

| Button Number | Existing Function | New Command |
|---|---|---|
| 6 | Ortho mode toggle | LINE |
| 7 | Grid mode toggle | ERASE |
| 8 | Coords mode toggle | CIRCLE |
| 9 | Isoplane crosshair toggle | ARC |

Before testing the new menu, you must load it into memory with the **MENU** command, otherwise AutoCAD will work with the old copy. The **MENU** command displays the **Select Menu File** dialog box, **Figure 20-9**. In the **Files of type:** drop-down list you can specify either Menu Files (*.mnc,*.mns) or Menu Template (*.mnu) files. Select the Menu Template (.mnu) option and find your menu file using the directory windows. Then, pick your menu from the file list and select the **OK** button. A warning appears indicating that the MNS file will be redefined and asking if you want to continue. In this case, you want to load the MNU file, so pick the **Yes** button. There may be a slight delay as AutoCAD compiles the MNU file into an MNC file. The status bar shows the progress as the menu is compiled. The MNC file is written in a format that makes it usable by AutoCAD. You cannot directly edit the MNC file.

**Figure 20-9.**
The **Select Menu File** dialog box is used to load the new menu file.

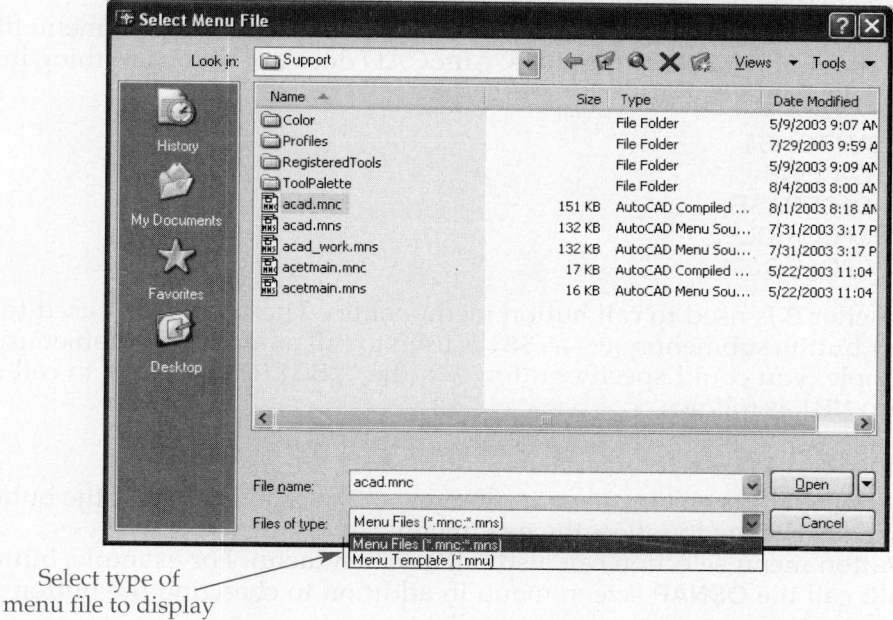

Select type of menu file to display

## Providing for User Input

Most AutoCAD commands require some form of user input—picking a location on the screen or entering values at the keyboard. The symbol used to indicate a pause for user input is the backslash (\). Inserting returns, or specifying when the [Enter] key is pressed, is handled with the semicolon (;).

When a command is listed in a menu file, AutoCAD automatically inserts a space after it, which is interpreted as a return. The following command in a menu file executes the **LINE** command and prompts Specify first point:.

    LINE

If the command is followed by a semicolon, backslash, or plus sign, AutoCAD does not insert a space. Therefore, there is no automatic return. If you want to allow for user input, and then provide a return, you should end the line with a semicolon.

    LINE;\\;

This executes the **LINE** command, waits for the user to pick the start and end points of a line, and then terminates the command.

The button menus perform additional functions with the user input symbols. If a backslash is provided after the command, the coordinates of the crosshairs on the screen are recorded when the pick button is pressed. Therefore, the following button menu entry accepts the current location of the crosshairs as the Specify first point: for the **LINE** command when the button is pressed, and the Specify next point or [Undo]: prompt is displayed.

LINE;\

This "instant input" can be used for other applications. For example, object snap modes can be executed transparently using a button menu.

## Adding New Button Menus

You are not limited to the four button menus. You can create as many as needed. However, one button should be used to switch menus. Here are a few things to keep in mind when creating new button menus.

✓ There is no screen display of button names. Use brackets in your menu file to contain button labels or numbers. AutoCAD does not act on anything inside brackets. For example:

```
***BUTTONS4
[6]^C^CLINE
[7]^C^CERASE
[8]^C^CCIRCLE
[9]^C^CARC
```

✓ The letter B is used to call button menu names. The code $B= is used to call other button submenus, just as $S= is used to call other screen submenus. For example, you could specify button 9 in the ***BUTTONS1 menu to call submenu **B1 as follows.

```
[9]$B=B1
```

Now, when button 9 is pressed, submenu **B1 is activated, and the button functions change to reflect the new menu.

✓ A button menu selection can also call a screen menu. For example, button 9 could call the **OSNAP** screen menu in addition to changing the button submenu to B1. The entry in the menu file is:

```
[9]$B=B1 $S=OSNAP
```

You will alter the **OSNAP** screen menu for using buttons in one of the chapter problems.

✓ A button menu selection can display a pull-down menu. The entry is:

```
$P11=*
```

The P11 calls for pull-down menu 11, which is the **Help** pull-down menu, and the =* displays it on screen.

✓ In the file, a space is not required after a button submenu to separate it from its submenus.

The following example shows revisions to the ***BUTTONS1 menu. The revised menu includes a function for button 10 that switches to the B1 button menu and also displays the **OSNAP** screen menu. The B1 menu provides eight object snap options, and button 10 returns to the BUTTONS1 menu and displays the **S** screen menu.

```
***BUTTONS1
[2]$M=$(if,$(eq,$(substr,$(getvar,cmdnames),1,5),GRIP_),$P0=ACAD.GRIPS $P0=*);
[3]$P0=SNAP $p0=*
[4]^C^C
[5]^B
[6]^C^CLINE
```

```
[7]^C^CERASE
[8]^C^CCIRCLE
[9]^C^CARC
[10]$B=B1 $S=OSNAP
**B1
[2]ENDpoint
[3]INTersect
[4]MIDpoint
[5]PERpendicular
[6]CENter
[7]TANgent
[8]QUAdrant
[9]NEArest
[10]$B=BUTTONS1 $S=S
```

## PROFESSIONAL TIP

When using button submenus, it is a common technique to combine menu calls with the macro in order to automatically reset the previous button menu. For example:

```
**B1
[2]$B=BUTTONS1 ENDpoint
```

## Exercise 20-1

○ Copy the acad.mnu file to a file named mymenu.mnu.
○ Create a button submenu named **B2.
○ Include three drawing commands and three editing commands in the submenu.

## Creating Standard Screen Menus

Once enabled, standard screen menus are located along the right side of the screen. They are created with the same techniques used for button menus. Screen menus are more versatile than button menus because you can see the command titles.

The positions of commands within the screen menu are referred to as *screenboxes*. The number of boxes available depends on the current size of the AutoCAD window. You can find out how many boxes are available using the **SCREENBOXES** system variable. If screen menus are turned off, the value is 0.

Command: **SCREENBOXES**↵
SCREENBOXES = 27 (read only)

Most people rarely use all the commands found in AutoCAD's screen menus. In time, you will find which commands you use most often, and those you seldom use. Begin to develop an idea of what the menu structure should look like. Then, start constructing custom menus, even though you may not completely know what to include. Menus are easy to change, and can be revised as many times as needed.

Develop a plan for your menus, but build them over time. Create one command or macro and then test it. It is much easier to create one macro and test it than to create an entire untested menu. Building menus a small portion at a time is also more efficient. It can be done as you work or study, or when you have a spare minute.

## Screen Menu Items

A screen menu item is composed of the item label and menu macro. The label is enclosed in brackets. The menu macro is a combination of commands, options, and characters that instruct AutoCAD to perform a function or series of functions. Take a look at the example in **Figure 20-10.** The following parts are included in the macro.

- Brackets ([ ]) enclose the item label. The first eight characters within the brackets are displayed on the screen.
- The command name **ONE LINE** is displayed on the screen. Try to give descriptive names to your commands so they indicate what the command does.
- The double cancel (^C^C) cancels out any command that is active when you pick the menu item.
- AutoCAD commands determine what function the macro performs (**LINE**).
- A return (;) represents pressing the [Enter] key after typing LINE at the keyboard.
- The two backslashes (\\) pause for user input at the Specify first point: and Specify next point or [Undo]: prompts. Remember, each backslash indicates a value entered at the keyboard or a selection made with the pointing device.
- A final return (;) represents pressing the [Enter] key to end the **LINE** command.

As you can see, you need to know the commands, prompts, options, and entries required to perform AutoCAD functions before you can modify screen menus. Look at the following menu item and try to determine what it is doing.

[Erase 1]^C^CERASE;si;\

The title should give you a clue. It erases a single object. The **ERASE** command is followed by a return, "si" to allow a single selection, and then a single backslash to pause for the user selection. This allows a single selection and then automatically executes the **ERASE** command. Here is another one.

[Extend 1]^C^CEXTEND;\;\;

This macro issues the **EXTEND** command, then allows for one user input to pick a boundary edge. A return ends boundary selection. One additional user input is for selecting the object to extend. After one object is picked, the last return completes the command automatically.

**Figure 20-10.**
The components of a screen menu item.

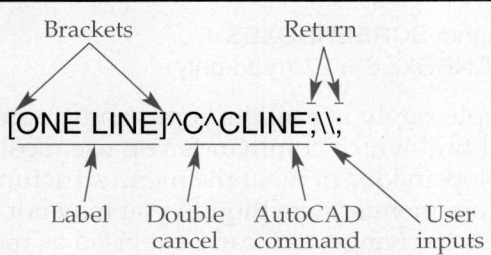

AutoCAD and its Applications—Advanced

Look at one more menu item that combines two commands. What function do you think this macro performs?

[Line T]^C^CLINE;\\;;MID;\\;

Notice that the first half of the item is exactly the same as the macro shown in **Figure 20-10.** That portion draws a single line. The return before MID issues the **LINE** command again. MID specifies an object snap mode at the Specify first point: prompt. At the first backslash, pick the line on which the midpoint is needed. The second back-slash is for selection at the Specify next point or [Undo]: prompt. The final return ends the command.

**PROFESSIONAL TIP**

When writing menu commands and macros, write them as if you are entering the commands and options at the keyboard. Use the semicolon (;) for the [Enter] key. Use first letters where appropriate for command options.

## Constructing Menu Commands

When you think of a useful command or function to include in a menu, the first step is to write it out in longhand. This gives you a clear picture of the scope of the command. The second step is to list the keyboard steps required to execute the new function. Third, write out the menu item as it will appear in the menu file. The following examples each use this three-step process. Example 6 is more involved than the first five.

### Example 1

1. Make a menu pick called ERASE L to erase the last object drawn.
2. **ERASE.**↵
   **LAST.**↵
   ↵
3. [ERASE L]^C^CERASE;L;;

### Example 2

1. Make a menu pick called ERASE 1 that erases a single selection and returns to the Command: prompt.
2. **ERASE.**↵
   *(select entity)*↵
3. [ERASE 1]^C^CERASE;si;

### Example 3

1. Make a menu pick called ZOOM D that enters the **ZOOM Dynamic** display without the user having to pick the **Dynamic** option.
2. **ZOOM.**↵
   **DYNAMIC.**↵
3. [ZOOM D]^C^CZOOM;D

### Example 4

1. Make a menu pick called ZOOM P that zooms to the previous display.
2. **ZOOM.**↵
   **PREVIOUS.**↵
3. [ZOOM P]^C^CZOOM;P

### Example 5

1. Make a menu pick that draws as many circles as needed.
2. **MULTIPLE.**↵
   **CIRCLE.**↵
3. [M CIRCLE]^C^CMULTIPLE;CIRCLE or *^C^CCIRCLE

**Example 6**

1. Create a new menu pick called DWG AIDS that sets the grid to .5, sets the snap grid to .25, and turns ortho mode on.
2. GRID↵
   .5↵
   SNAP↵
   .25↵
   ORTHO↵
   ON↵
3. [DWG AIDS]^C^CGRID;.5;SNAP;.25;ORTHO;ON

## Adding Macros to the Menu File

After the macros are written, you need to add them to the menu file. Then, test the menus. Create a new submenu after the **S menu. Load your copy of the acad.mnu file into your text editor and search for the following.

    ***SCREEN
    **S

Listed below **S is AutoCAD's familiar root menu. Find the last sequential command in that menu, which is [LAST]. Move your cursor to the end of that line and press the [Enter] key twice. Your cursor is on a blank line separated from the previous menu by a blank line.

The first screen menu listed in the ***SCREEN section is displayed when you enter the drawing editor. If you insert your submenu above the **S menu, yours will be the first displayed when you enter the drawing editor.

Name your submenu TEST. Type the entries in your text editor exactly as they are shown below. Be sure to press [Enter] at the end of each line. Then, save your menu file.

    **TEST 3 (the "3" begins the menu on the third line from the top of the screen)
    [ TEST]
    [ MENU]
    [Erase L]^C^CERASE;L;;
    [Erase 1]^C^CERASE;\;
    [Zoom W]^C^CZOOM;W
    [Zoom P]^C^CZOOM;P
    [M Circle]^C^CMULTIPLE;CIRCLE
    [Dwg Aids]^C^CGRID;.5;SNAP;.25;ORTHO;ON

## Long Menu Items

If a menu item occupies more than one line, you need to instruct AutoCAD that there is more to the item. Type a plus symbol (+) at the end of the line. Do not put spaces before or after the mark. Use the long-line technique to create a command that does the following.

- Perform a **ZOOM All**.
- Set the limits to 0,0 and 20,12.
- Set the snap grid to 0.25.
- Set the grid to 0.50.
- Draw a polyline border from 0.5,0.5. The border should be 17″ × 11″.
- Set the **MIRRTEXT** system variable to zero.
- Set the **APERTURE** system variable to 3.
- Set ortho mode on.
- Set grid mode on.
- Perform a **ZOOM Extents**.

The item name and code for this macro is written as follows. Add it below [Dwg Aids].

    [B-11x17]^C^CZOOM;A;LIMITS;;20,12;SNAP;.25;GRID;.5;PLINE;0.5,0.5;+
    17.5,.5;17.5,11.5;0.5,11.5;C;MIRRTEXT;0;APERTURE;3;ORTHO;+
    ON;GRID;ON;ZOOM;E

## Place Your Menu in the Root Menu

You have created your first screen menu, but how do you access it from the root menu of AutoCAD? There is nothing in the root menu that calls the **TEST** menu. You need to add that item to the root menu now.

Look again at the **S menu and notice that only 18 lines are occupied with commands inside brackets. You can insert your menu name on the line after [HELP], or any other blank line in this area. Insert the following item.

        [TEST] $S=ACAD.TEST

Do not press [Enter] at the end of the line or you will insert an additional line in the menu. This could push the last menu item off the screen if the AutoCAD window displays only 26 lines in the menu area. Save the menu file.

## The Menu Stack

The item you entered above calls your submenu TEST. A screen menu call is different from other menu calls because the previous menu is not removed prior to displaying the subsequent menu. Instead, the new menu is overlaid on the existing menu, with the first item being placed on the specified line. This creates a *menu stack.*

For example, the **TEST menu has a 3 following the menu name. This indicates that the first two lines are to remain unchanged and the menu data placement begins on line 3 of the screen menu display area. The new items are then used to replace existing screen menu selections.

In the **TEST menu, nine items are defined with the menu beginning on the third line. The previous menu, **S, has many additional lines. Since the **TEST menu only redefines lines 3 through 11, lines 12 and on remain unchanged. To clear these lines out when the submenu is displayed, place an appropriate number of blank lines after the code for the submenu. **Figure 20-11A** shows the **S menu with the addition of the TEST menu item, and **Figure 20-11B** shows the screen menu after calling the **TEST menu.

The standard approach is to begin submenus on the third line of the menu display area. This results in the first two lines of the **S menu being preserved regardless of which submenu is currently displayed. This is important due to the functions performed by these two items. The first two items of the **S menu are:

        AutoCAD
        * * * *

Picking the word **AutoCAD** displays the **S menu (the root menu), and picking the four asterisks displays an object snap menu. This way, no matter where you are in the menu system, it takes only one pick to get to these frequently needed items.

Figure 20-11.
A—The screen
menu with the TEST
menu item added
below HELP.
B—Calling the
**TEST submenu
results in this
display.

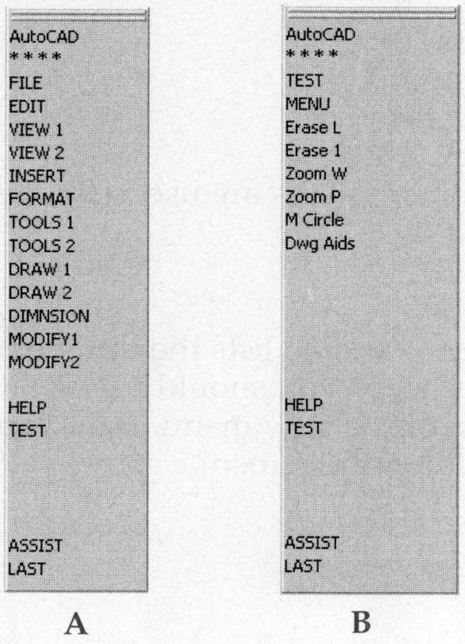

| A | B |
|---|---|
| AutoCAD | AutoCAD |
| * * * * | * * * * |
| FILE | TEST |
| EDIT | MENU |
| VIEW 1 | Erase L |
| VIEW 2 | Erase 1 |
| INSERT | Zoom W |
| FORMAT | Zoom P |
| TOOLS 1 | M Circle |
| TOOLS 2 | Dwg Aids |
| DRAW 1 | |
| DRAW 2 | |
| DIMNSION | |
| MODIFY1 | |
| MODIFY2 | |
| HELP | HELP |
| TEST | TEST |
| ASSIST | ASSIST |
| LAST | LAST |

**PROFESSIONAL TIP**

When creating screen menus, always use the standard convention for menu label appearances. On the AutoCAD screen menu, the label for an item that calls another menu is shown with all UPPERCASE characters. Items that start a command are shown in Title Case, with the first character of each word in uppercase.

---

## Exercise 20-2

○ Using a text editor and the three-step process, write the menu items given below. Save the text file as ex20-2.mnu.
  ○ [SNAPGRID]. Toggle the snap mode and grid mode on or off.
  ○ [MTEXT-S.1]. Set the snap at .1 and select the **MTEXT** command.
  ○ [MIRROR]. Turn the **MIRRTEXT** system variable off and select the **Window** option of the **MIRROR** command for a single selection. Do not delete the old objects. This command should return the user to Command: prompt.
  ○ [BREAK @]. Break a line into two parts with a single pick.
  ○ [CHMFER.5]. Set a chamfer distance of .5 and allow two lines to be picked.

## Chapter Test

*Answer the following questions on a separate sheet of paper.*

1. The name and extension of the file that contains the fully documented standard menus for AutoCAD is _____.
2. List the names of the major sections in AutoCAD's default menu.
3. All interactive toolbar modifications are written to which file?
4. Why should you edit a copy of the acad.mnu file when customizing menus?
5. Can you have more than four button menus?
6. What kind of symbol is used to indicate a screen submenu?
7. Describe the function of each of the following screen menu commands.
    A. ^C^CTRIM;\;\;
    B. ^C^CCOPY;W;\\
    C. ^C^CCHANGE;\;
8. Give the function of the following menu command codes.
    A. Brackets ([ ])
    B. Semicolon (;)
    C. Backslash (\)
    D. Plus sign (+)
    E. Single (si)
9. What key combinations are used to access the following button menus?
    A. BUTTONS2
    B. BUTTONS3
    C. BUTTONS4
10. Which system variable lists the number of screen menu items?
11. List the three steps you should use when creating a new menu command.
12. Suppose you add a new menu to the acad.mnu file. How does the new menu get displayed on the screen?
13. Define *menu stack*.

14. Define the use of the following control characters.
    A. ^B
    B. ^G
    C. ^O
    D. ^V

## Drawing Problems

1. Begin an entirely new AutoCAD menu composed of a general button section and an object snap button menu. Name the menu P20-1.MNU. Plan your menu items before you begin. Write the menus in small segments and be sure to test all items. Generate a printed copy of the menu file. The main button menu (***BUTTONS1) should have the following items.

| Button Number | Function |
|---|---|
| 2 | **DDEDIT** command. |
| 3 | **LINE** command. |
| 4 | **CIRCLE** command. |
| 5 | **ZOOM** Dynamic. |
| 6 | Leave blank. |
| 7 | Erase one object and end the **ERASE** command. |
| 8 | **ZOOM Window**. |
| 9 | [Enter]. |
| 10 | **ZOOM Previous**. |

The ***BUTTONS2 menu is an object snap interrupt menu. All object snap items should activate the object snap mode specified and select a point when the button is pressed. The ***BUTTONS2 menu should contain the following items.

| Button Number | Function |
|---|---|
| 2 | **Endpoint** object snap mode. |
| 3 | **Intersection** object snap mode. |
| 4 | **Perpendicular** object snap mode. |
| 5 | **Midpoint** object snap mode. |
| 6 | **Center** object snap mode. |
| 7 | **Tangent** object snap mode. |
| 8 | **Quadrant** object snap mode. |
| 9 | Return to main button and screen menus. |
| 10 | **Node** object snap mode. |

2. Add the screen menu given below to the P20-1.MNU file you created in Problem 1. The section name should be ***SCREEN. The main menu name should be **S. Plan your menu items before entering them in the text editor. The following items should be included. Test all menu items to ensure that they are working properly before going to the next problem. Generate a printed copy of the menu file.

| Position | Menu Items |
|---|---|
| 1 | Menu title [HOME] |
| 2 | Cancel and **ARC**. |
| 3 | Cancel and **POLYGON**. |
| 4 | Cancel and **PLINE**. |
| 5 | Cancel and **LIST**. |
| 6 | Cancel and **DIST**. |
| 7 | Cancel and **SCALE**. |
| 8 | Cancel and **OFFSET**. |
| 9 | Cancel and **ROTATE**. |
| 10 | Cancel and **STRETCH**. |
| 11 | Blank. |
| 12 | Cancel and **ZOOM**. |
| 13 | Blank. |
| 14 | Rotate crosshairs axis to user-specific angle. Allow user to set base point and leave Snap mode on. |
| 15 | Reset crosshairs axis to zero and turn Snap mode off. |
| 16 | Allow user to pick a single object and change it to a new layer. |

3. Add the following screen menu to your P20-1.MNU file. This is an editing menu and should be named **EDIT. At position 18 in your main screen menu (see Problem 2), add an item that calls the **EDIT** menu. Place the following items in the **EDIT** menu. Generate a printed copy of the menu file.

| Position | Menu Items | Function |
|---|---|---|
| 1 | [Erase-F] | Erase with **FENCE** option. |
| 2 | [Copy-WP] | Copy with **Window Polygon** option. |
| 3 | [Move-W] | Move with **Window** option. |
| 4 | [Break-F] | Activate **BREAK**, allow user to select object, then pick first and second points without entering F. |
| 5 | [Change-1] | Activate **CHANGE**, select object, and stop for user input. |
| 6 | [Reword-M] | Allow user to edit a line of text. |
| 7 | [0-Fillet] | Select two lines and clean up corners with zero radius fillet. Allow selection of five clean-ups. |
| 8 | [0-Break] | Select line or arc and split into two parts. |
| 9 | [0-Corner] | Select two intersecting lines at the inter-section. Clean up corner using two picks. |

AutoCAD and its Applications—Advanced

4. Add an item to the main button menu at button 6 that calls the **BUTTONS2 menu and a new screen menu called **OSNAP. The line should read:

[6]$B=BUTTONS2 $S=OSNAP

The new **OSNAP screen menu should contain the following items. Generate a printed copy of the menu file.

| Position | Menu Items | Function |
|---|---|---|
| 1 | [BUTTONS] | Label |
| 2 | [2=Endpt] | Show button assignment and activate **Endpoint** object snap mode if picked from the screen. |
| 3 | [3=Inter] | Show button assignment and activate **Intersection** object snap mode if picked from the screen. |
| 4 | [4=Perp] | Show button assignment and activate **Perpendicular** object snap mode if picked from the screen. |
| 5 | [5=Midpt] | Show button assignment and activate **Midpoint** object snap mode if picked from the screen. |
| 6 | [6=Center] | Show button assignment and activate **Center** object snap mode if picked from the screen. |
| 7 | [7=Tangent] | Show button assignment and activate **Tangent** object snap mode if picked from the screen. |
| 8 | [8=Quad] | Show button assignment and activate **Quadrant** object snap mode if picked from the screen. |
| 9 | [9=HOME] | Page back to main button and screen. |
| 10 | [10=Node] | Show button assignment and activate **Node** object snap mode if picked from the screen. |
| 11 | [Nearest] | Activate **Nearest** object snap mode from screen. |
| 12 | [Insert] | Activate **Insert** object snap mode from screen. |

5. Alter the **OSNAPB menu in a copy of acad.mnu to function with a button menu in the same manner as given in Problem 4. If you have not added a **BUTTONS2 menu to your acad.mnu file (explained earlier in this chapter), do so for this problem.

You can create custom pull-down menus in AutoCAD. A—The code needed to define a custom pull-down menu for drawing and working with solids. B—The resulting pull-down menu structure.

```
***POP10
**Solids_Commands
ID_3D01      [&Solids Commands]
ID_3D02      [->Solid &Primitives]
ID_3D03          [&Box]^C^C_box
ID_3D04          [&Sphere]^C^C_sphere
ID_3D05          [C&ylinder]^C^C_cylinder
ID_3D06          [C&one]^C^C_cone
ID_3D07          [&Wedge]^C^C_wedge
ID_3D08          [<-&Torus]^C^C_torus
ID_3D09      [->Solid &Commands]
ID_3D10          [&Union]^C^C_union
ID_3D11          [&Subtract]^C^C_subtract
ID_3D12          [Inter&sect]_intersect
ID_3D13          [Inter&fere]^C^C_interfere
ID_3D14          [&Revolve]^C^C_revolve
ID_3D15          [&Extrude]^C^C_extrude
ID_3D16          [<-Re&gion]^C^C_region
ID_3D17      [->&Layout Setup]
ID_3D18          [Setup &View]^C^C_solview
ID_3D19          [Setup &Drawing]^C^C_soldraw
ID_3D20          [<-Setup &Profile]^C^C_solprof
ID_3D21      [->SOLID&EDIT]
ID_3D22          [->&Face]
ID_3D23              [&Extrude]^C^C_solidedit;f;e
ID_3D24              [&Move]^C^C_solidedit;f;m
ID_3D25              [&Rotate]^C^C_solidedit;f;r
ID_3D26              [&Offset]^C^C_solidedit;f;o
ID_3D27              [&Taper]^C^C_solidedit;f;t
ID_3D28              [&Delete]^C^C_solidedit;f;d
ID_3D29              [Cop&y]^C^C_solidedit;f;c
ID_3D30              [<-&Color]^C^C_solidedit;f;l
ID_3D31          [->&Edge]
ID_3D32              [Cop&y]^C^C_solidedit;e;c
ID_3D33              [<-&Color]^C^C_solidedit;e;l
ID_3D34          [->&Body]
ID_3D35              [&Imprint]^C^C_solidedit;b;i
ID_3D36              [&Separate Solids]^C^C_solidedit;b;p
ID_3D37              [S&hell]^C^C_solidedit;b;s
ID_3D38              [C&lean]^C^C_solidedit;b;l
ID_3D39              [<-<-Chec&k]^C^C_solidedit;b;c
ID_3D40      [Mass Properties]^C^C_massprop
```

A

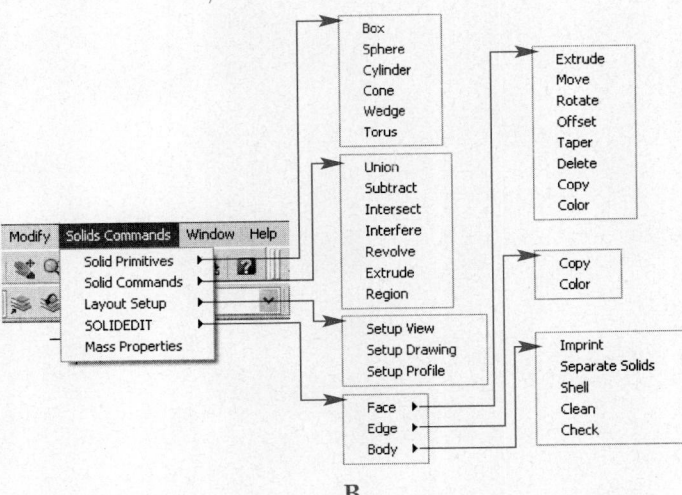

B

# Customizing Pull-Down Menus and Image Tiles

## Learning Objectives

After completing this chapter, you will be able to:

● Understand the structure of pull-down menus.
● Create single- or multiple-page pull-down menus.
● Load pull-down menus from multiple menu groups.
● Create user-defined shortcut keys.
● Describe the purpose and function of image tile menus.
● Describe the purpose and the function of a slide library.
● Create slides for image tile menus.
● Create a slide library for an image tile menu.
● Create an image tile menu file listing.

## Shortcut and Access Keys

*Shortcut keys,* also called *accelerator keys,* are key combinations used to initiate a command. For example, when the **Windows standard accelerator keys** check box in the **Windows Standard Behavior** area of the **User Preferences** tab in the **Options** dialog box is checked, [Ctrl]+[C] initiates the **COPYCLIP** command. Custom shortcut keys can be created to initiate specific AutoCAD commands or to perform macros. Creating custom shortcut keys is covered later in this chapter.

*Access keys,* also called *mnemonic keys,* are keys used to access a menu or a menu item using the keyboard. Pressing the [Alt] key will toggle the access keys for the pull-down menus on and off. The access keys are shown as underlined letters. While the access keys are on, notice that the letter M is underlined in the word **Modify**. Pressing the [M] key will access the **Modify** pull-down menu. Any letter in the menu or menu item name can be the access key, but an access key must be unique for its menu or submenu. Notice on the **Modify** pull-down menu that the M is used for **Match Properties**, so **Mirror** and **Move** use the i and v, respectively. The letter T can be used for both **Trim** and **Text** because **Text** is on the **Object** submenu.

The **MENU** command initially loads a base menu in its default condition, and provides no menu display options. However, it is possible to load multiple menus at one time and use only the desired elements of each, or modify the way a base menu is displayed, by using the **MENULOAD** command. Thus, you can customize your menu so you have access to desired features from two or more different menu files.

AutoCAD menu files are assigned menu group names. For example, near the beginning of the acad.mnu file, you will find the line:

　　　***MENUGROUP=ACAD

This assigns the group name ACAD to this menu. However, if you open the sample menu file dbcon.mnu, which is found in the Support folder, you will find the specification:

　　　***MENUGROUP=dbConnect

This identifies items in this menu as being in the dbConnect menu group. This allows you to identify items from different menus easily. For example, when working with screen menus, your calls to submenus were preceded by ACAD. This identified the group containing the desired menu. In Chapter 20, your call to the TEST screen submenu appeared as:

　　　$S=ACAD.TEST

If the dbConnect menu was loaded and also had a screen submenu named TEST, your menu call would specify from which group to obtain the definition for the TEST menu.

If you try to use **MENULOAD** to load a menu that uses the same group name as a current menu, you will get an error message. You can force AutoCAD to replace existing group definitions with newly loaded menu data.

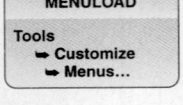

The **MENULOAD** command can be accessed by picking **Customize** and then **Menus...** from the **Tools** pull-down menu, or it can be typed directly at the Command: prompt. Entering the **MENULOAD** command displays the **Menu Customization** dialog box, **Figure 21-1**. There are several options available.

- **Menu Groups.** This list shows the currently loaded menu groups. Items on this list can be highlighted in preparation for other actions.
- **File Name.** This edit box shows the name of the currently selected menu file.

Figure 21-1.
The **Menu Groups** tab of the **Menu Customization** dialog box.

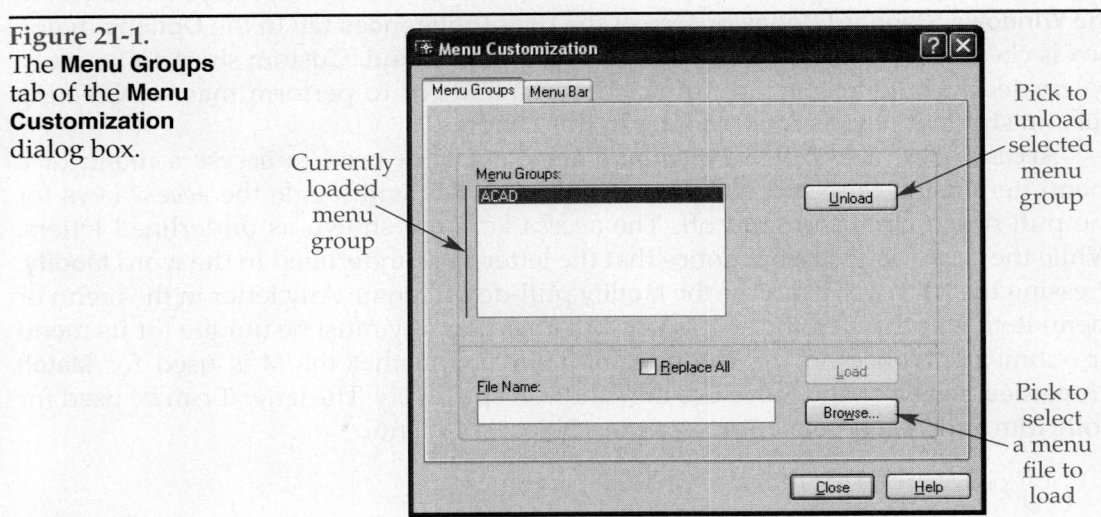

- **Replace All.** A check in this check box forces newly loaded group names to replace existing duplicate names.
- **Unload.** This button unloads the definition for the menu group highlighted in the **Menu Groups:** list box.
- **Load.** This button loads the menu file specified in the **File Name:** edit box and places its associated group name in the **Menu Groups:** list box.
- **Browse.** Select this button to specify a new menu file name for loading. It displays the **Select Menu File** dialog box and allows you to select a menu file.

To practice loading an additional menu, use the **Select Menu File** dialog box to find the dbcon.mnu file. Remember, when loading a menu template file, you must first specify *.mnu in the **Files of type:** drop-down list.

After selecting the dbcon.mnu file, you are returned to the **Menu Customization** dialog box. The dbcon.mnu file and path name appear in the **File Name:** edit box. Pick the **Load** button to load the menu definition and the new group name is displayed in the **Menu Groups:** list box.

Now that you have loaded an additional menu definition, you can specify which menus to display. First, pick the **Menu Bar** tab, **Figure 21-2.** The features of this tab are as follows.

- **Menu Group.** This drop-down list provides access to the currently loaded menu group names.
- **Menus.** All pull-down menu names defined in the selected group are displayed here.
- **Menu Bar.** This list shows the pull-down menus that are currently available on the menu bar. The top item of the list takes a position at the far left of the menu bar, and each subsequent menu title is displayed to the right of the previous one.
- **Insert.** Picking this button inserts the menu currently highlighted in the **Menus:** list above the highlighted position in the **Menu Bar:** list.
- **Remove.** Removes the currently highlighted menu title from the **Menu Bar:** list.
- **Remove All.** Removes all menu titles from the **Menu Bar:** list.

By selecting the desired group name and adjusting the various individual menu titles, you can completely customize the menu bar to have only the pull-down menus that are necessary for your current project.

---

**Figure 21-2.**
The **Menu Bar** tab of the **Menu Customization** dialog box.

Select a menu group

Select a menu

Inserted menu

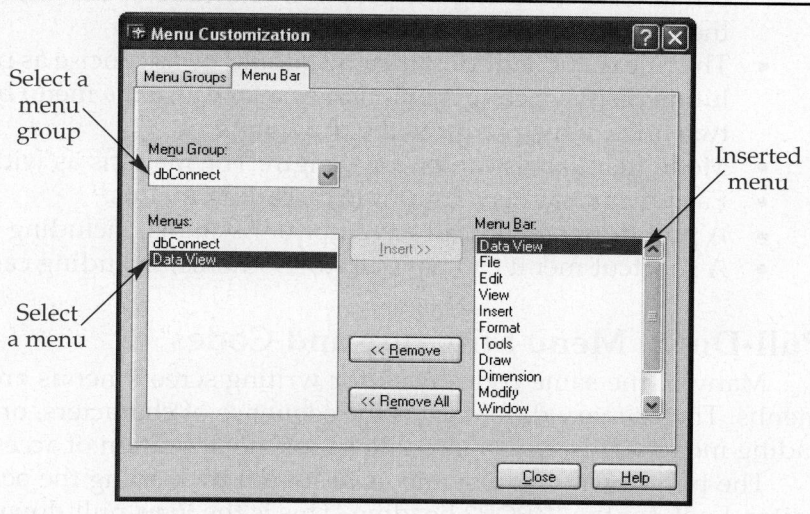

## Pull-Down Menus

The names of the standard pull-down menus appear in the menu bar at the top of the AutoCAD graphics window. The menus are selected by placing the cursor over the menu name and picking to select it. You can also use the access keys to select menus.

Pull-down menus are referred to as "POP" menus in the menu file, and are given numerical designations such as POP0 and POP1. Pull-down menus are defined in the POP1 through POP499 sections. POP0 is the object snap shortcut menu, which is enabled by simultaneously pressing the [Shift] key and the [Enter] button on your mouse or digitizer tablet puck. For example, [Shift]+right-click when using a mouse displays the POP0 object snap menu. By default, this shortcut menu displays each of the object snap modes. Context shortcut menus are defined in the POP500 through POP999 sections. The grips shortcut menu is defined in the POP500 section of the menu file. Right-clicking while a grip is hot displays this menu. Some shortcut menus, such as the zoom and toolbars shortcut menus, are handled by AutoCAD and are not defined in the menu file.

Once you understand how pull-down menus are designed, you can customize existing menus and create your own. Some basic information about pull-down menus follows.

- The titles of POP menus 1 through 16 are shown along the menu bar.
- If no POP1 through POP16 menus are defined, AutoCAD inserts default **File** and **Edit** menus. This is similar to when AutoCAD is displayed without a drawing open.
- POP menus 17 through 499 are not shown on the menu bar by default. They can be inserted using the proper menu code or the **MENULOAD** command, or they can be used for menu swapping.
- The title of the pull-down menu should be as concise as possible. On low-resolution displays, long menu names may cause the menu bar to be displayed on two lines, which reduces the drawing area.
- Menu item labels can be any length. The menu is as wide as its longest label.
- Each menu can have multiple cascading menus.
- A pull-down menu can have up to 999 items, including cascading menus.
- A shortcut menu can have up to 499 items, including cascading menus.

### Pull-Down Menu Structure and Codes

Many of the same codes used for writing screen menus are used for pull-down menus. The primary difference is the sequence of characters, or *syntax*, used for cascading menus. This syntax also allows for the definition of access and shortcut keys.

The pull-down menu syntax is best seen by loading the acad.mnu file into a text editor. Look for the ***POP3 heading. This is the **View** pull-down menu. The first part of this menu is shown in **Figure 21-3**. Compare the appearance of the menu file syntax and the pull-down menu. A few new menu syntax characters are found in this menu. These characters are explained in **Figure 21-4**. They provide a separator line, indicate where cascading menus begin and end, and define access keys.

AutoCAD and its Applications—Advanced

**Figure 21-3.**
The first part of the POP3 (**View**) pull-down menu. Note the placement of the ampersand character (&) to define access keys.

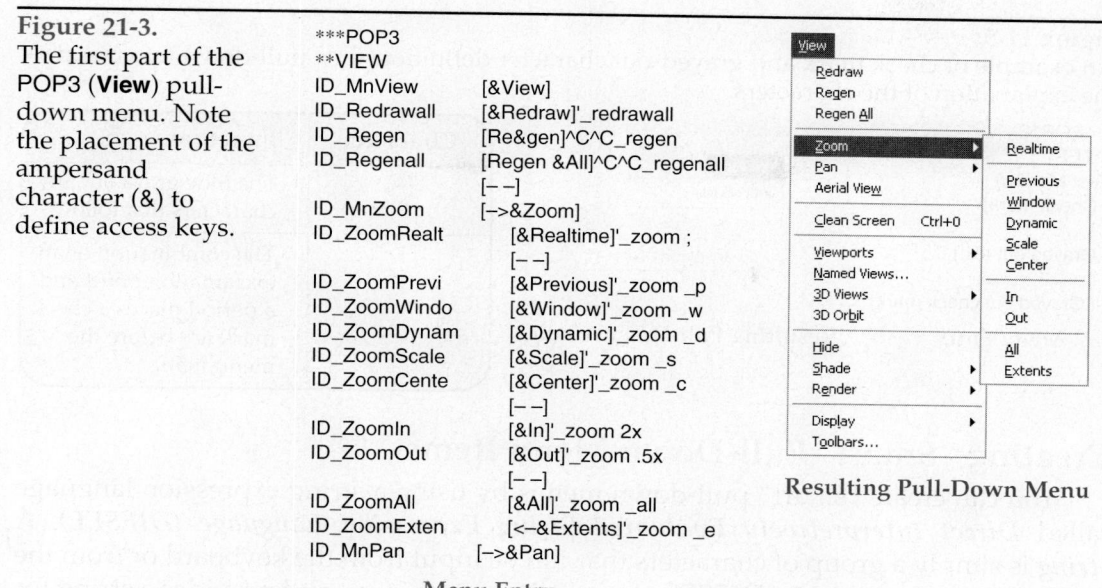

```
***POP3
**VIEW
ID_MnView        [&View]
ID_Redrawall     [&Redraw]'_redrawall
ID_Regen         [Re&gen]^C^C_regen
ID_Regenall      [Regen &All]^C^C_regenall
                 [– –]
ID_MnZoom        [–>&Zoom]
ID_ZoomRealt         [&Realtime]'_zoom ;
                     [– –]
ID_ZoomPrevi         [&Previous]'_zoom _p
ID_ZoomWindo         [&Window]'_zoom _w
ID_ZoomDynam         [&Dynamic]'_zoom _d
ID_ZoomScale         [&Scale]'_zoom _s
ID_ZoomCente         [&Center]'_zoom _c
                     [– –]
ID_ZoomIn            [&In]'_zoom 2x
ID_ZoomOut           [&Out]'_zoom .5x
                     [– –]
ID_ZoomAll           [&All]'_zoom _all
ID_ZoomExten         [<–&Extents]'_zoom _e
ID_MnPan         [–>&Pan]
```
**Menu Entry**

**Resulting Pull-Down Menu**

**Figure 21-4.**
Menu syntax characters and their function.

| Character | Function |
|---|---|
| [– –] | Two hyphens are used to insert a separator line across the pull-down menu. The line is automatically drawn the width of the menu. |
| –> | Indicates that the item has a cascading menu. |
| <– | Indicates the last item in the cascading menu. |
| <–<– | Indicates the last item in the cascading menu and the last item of the previous menu (parent menu). |
| &c | The ampersand specifies the access key in a pull-down or shortcut menu label. The "c" shown here represents any character. |

**PROFESSIONAL TIP**

Notice in the POP3 pull-down menu listing in **Figure 21-3** that indentation has been used to indicate cascading menus. Indenting is not necessary to write a valid menu file, but it gives the file an appearance similar to the actual menus. It makes the file easier to read and understand.

## Marking Menu Items

Menu items can be marked with a check mark (✓) or other character of your choosing. You can also have items "grayed out." When these marking characters are used in a menu, they mark an item permanently. This may be desirable for the separator line and for graying out specific items, but a check mark is often related to an item that is toggled on or off. Look at the sample menu file, its pull-down menu, and the explanation of the characters in **Figure 21-5**.

Figure 21-5.
An example of check mark and grayed-out character definitions in a pull-down menu and
the explanation of the characters.

```
***POP12
**TEST
[Test Men&u]
[!.Check mark]
[--]
[~Grayed out text]
[--]
[~!.Grayed out check mark]
```

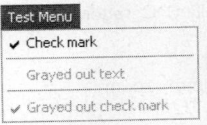

Menu Entry                Resulting Pull-Down Menu

| Character | Function |
|-----------|----------|
| [~] | The tilde grays out any characters that follow. |
| !. | The combination of an exclamation point and a period places a check mark (✓) before the menu item. |

## Creating "Smart" Pull-Down Menu Items

You can create "smart" pull-down menus by using a string expression language called *Direct Interpretively Evaluated String Expression Language (DIESEL)*. A *string* is simply a group of characters that can be input from the keyboard or from the value of a system variable. DIESEL uses a string for its input and provides a string for output. In other words, you give DIESEL a value, and it gives something back to you.

Adding a menu check mark is an excellent example of how DIESEL can be used for menu items. For example, you may want to toggle the ortho mode from a pull-down menu and indicate when it is on with a check mark. Use the following syntax.

[$(if,$(getvar,orthomode),!.)&Ortho]^O

The first $ signals the pull-down menu to evaluate a DIESEL macro. This macro gets the value (getvar) of the **ORTHOMODE** system variable, and places the check mark by the item if the value is 1 (on). Notice that the ortho mode toggle is executed (^O) when the item is picked.

**Figure 21-6** shows how two DIESEL additions to a menu named **Test** look in the menu file and the pull-down menu. The pull-down menu shows that ortho mode is on and snap mode is off.

Adding DIESEL expressions to your menus can make them more powerful and "intelligent." Refer to the online documentation for a complete discussion of the DIESEL language.

## Referencing Other Pull-Down Menus

A menu pick can activate, or "reference," another pull-down menu. A menu pick can also gray out or place a marking character by another pull-down menu item. The character codes shown in **Figure 21-7** are used for these purposes.

When referencing other pull-down menus, you can combine the marking symbols to "gray out" items or place check marks. Study the following menu item examples. The first example activates and displays POP12.

$p12=*

Figure 21-6.
An example of
DIESEL macros
added to a pull-
down menu. Note
that ortho mode is
on and snap mode
is off.

```
***POP12
**TEST
[Test Men&u]
[$(if,$(getvar,orthomode),!.)&Ortho]^O
[$(if,$(getvar,snapmode),!.)&Snap]^B
[!.Check mark]
[--]
[~Grayed out text]
[--]
[~!.Grayed out check mark]
```

Menu Entry                    Resulting Pull-Down Menu

**Figure 21-7.**
Character codes
used for graying out
or placing a check
mark by another
pull-down menu
item.

| Character | Function |
|-----------|----------|
| $pn= | Makes another pull-down menu current, where $n$ is the number of the menu. Alternately, any specified alias for the menu can be referenced. The alias is defined by the **alias label after the menu section name. |
| $pn=* | Displays the currently active pull-down menu. |
| $pn.1= | References a specific item number on another pull-down menu. |

The next menu item places a check mark on item 4 of POP12.

> $p12.4=!.

This entry grays out item 3 of POP6.

> $p6.3=~

The following menu item places a check mark by item 2 of POP8 and grays it out.

> $p8.2=!.~

The next menu item removes all marks and any "gray out" from item 2 of POP8.

> $p8.2=

The following examples show how these techniques can be combined in a macro.

> [Insert desk]^C^C-insert;desk;\\\\$p12=*
> [Setup .5]^C^Cgrid;.5;snap;.25;$p12.1=!. $p12.2=!.~
> [Defaults]^C^Cgrid;off;snap;off;$p12.1= $p12.2=

**Figure 21-8** shows a menu example containing similar macros, and the resulting pull-down menu.

---

**Figure 21-8.**
A sample of linking
pull-down menu
items.

```
***POP12
**TEST
[Test Men&u]
[$(if,$(getvar,orthomode),!.)&Ortho]^O
[$(if,$(getvar,snapmode),!.)&Snap]^B
[!.Check mark]
[Item 4]
[--]
[~Grayed out text]
[--]
[~!.Grayed out check mark]
[--]
[Check Mark Item 4]$p12.4=!. $p12=*
[Gray Out Item 4]$p12.4=~ $p12=*
[Gray/Check Item 4]$p12.4=~!. $p12=*
[Clear Item 4]$p12.4= $p12=*
```

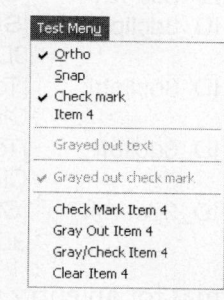

**Menu Entry**          **Resulting Pull-Down Menu**

---

**NOTE**
Menu item numbering begins with the first line of the pull-down menu below the title and continues to the bottom of the file. Separator lines are also counted when determining line numbers. AutoCAD numbers items consecutively through all menus without considering menu levels.

---

○ Create a copy of the acad.mnu file named EX21-1.MNU. Use the renamed copy for this exercise.
○ Use your text editor and put the following three commands in a new ***POP12 menu titled **Custom**.
  ○ [Copy Two M]—Make multiple copies after two selections.
  ○ [Rotate45]—Rotate an object 45° counterclockwise.
  ○ [Fillet .5]—A repeating command that applies a .5 fillet.
○ All commands should display appropriate access keys.
○ Write out the commands before you enter them in the computer.
○ Save EX21-1.MNU for the next exercise.

## Creating Help Strings for Pull-Down Menus

*Help strings* are the brief descriptions that appear on the status line describing the menu item currently highlighted. These can provide helpful information to those who are using your menu. It becomes very important to create appropriate help strings when you are adding new items to the menu, since these items may be unfamiliar to even experienced AutoCAD users.

To get an idea of the ideal content of a help string for your menu item, carefully review some of AutoCAD's existing help strings. Help string definitions are placed in the ***HELPSTRINGS section in your menu file, but references to a help string can be placed throughout your menu file. For example, if a 0.5" wide polyline option is added to a pull-down menu, the menu code might look like this:

    [0.5 Polyline]^C^Cpline;\w;0.5;0.5;

To create a help string for this entry, open the menu file and find the ***HELPSTRINGS section. The beginning of the ***HELPSTRINGS section looks like this:

```
***HELPSTRINGS
ID_2doptim      [Set viewport to 2D wireframe: SHADEMODE 2]
ID_3darray      [Creates a three-dimensional array: 3DARRAY]
ID_3dclip       [Starts 3DORBIT and opens the Adjust Clipping Planes window:
                3DCLIP]
ID_3dclipbk     [Toggles the back clipping plane on or off in the 3D Orbit Adjust
                Clipping Planes window: DVIEW ALL CL B]
ID_3dclipfr     [Toggles the front clipping plane on or off in the 3D Orbit Adjust
                Clipping Planes window: DVIEW ALL CL F]
ID_3dcorbit     [Starts the 3DORBIT command with continuous orbit active in the
                3D view: 3DCORBIT]
```

The format for an entry in the ***HELPSTRINGS section is:

    ID_*name tag* [*Help message*]

The ID_ *name tag* should be unique. Duplicate name tags can cause unexpected results. Using your text editor's "find" function, see if the name tag you want to use is already in use. The help message should be short enough to fit along the bottom of the screen, and as clearly worded as possible. A search of the acad.mnu file reveals that the name tag ID_Wpline for a wide polyline is not already in use. To prepare the help string for use, find the ***HELPSTRINGS section of the menu file and enter the following line.

    ID_Wpline [Draws a 0.5" wide polyline.]

Now that the help string definition has been created, any menu item referencing the ID_Wpline tag will display this help string. To place a reference to this help string, you need to precede the menu item label with the name tag as follows.

ID_Wpline [0.5 Polyline]^C^Cpline;\w;0.5;0.5;

When the **0.5 Polyline** menu item is highlighted, the help string "Draws a 0.5" wide polyline" is displayed on the status line.

**PROFESSIONAL TIP**

A new help string can be placed anywhere within the help string section. Since this section is rather extensive, it can be helpful to place all of your custom help string definitions together at the bottom. This makes them easy to locate when you need to edit them.

**Exercise 21-2**

○ Use your text editor and open the menu file EX21-1.MNU from Exercise 21-1.
○ Create a help string for each of the three new commands you developed in Exercise 21-1.
○ Test each command to be sure each help string is displayed properly.
○ Save the menu file for the next exercise.

## Creating Shortcut Keys

You can define your own custom shortcut keys for menu items. The shortcut key definitions are located in the ***ACCELERATORS section of the menu file. The TOOLBAR entry found in some of the definitions is used to restrict the search for ID name tag to the toolbars section of the menu file.

```
***ACCELERATORS
// Bring up hyperlink dialog
ID_Hyperlink    [TOOLBAR+CONTROL+"K"]
// Toggle Orthomode
[CONTROL+"L"]^O
// Next Viewport
[CONTROL+"R"]^V
ID_SelAll       [CONTROL+"A"]
ID_Copyclip     [TOOLBAR+CONTROL+"C"]
ID_New          [TOOLBAR+CONTROL+"N"]
ID_Open         [TOOLBAR+CONTROL+"O"]
ID_Print        [TOOLBAR+CONTROL+"P"]
ID_Save         [TOOLBAR+CONTROL+"S"]
ID_Pasteclip    [TOOLBAR+CONTROL+"V"]
ID_Cutclip      [TOOLBAR+CONTROL+"X"]
ID_Redo         [CONTROL+"Y"]
ID_U            [CONTROL+"Z"]
ID_Ai_propch    [TOOLBAR+CONTROL+"1"]
ID_Content      [TOOLBAR+CONTROL+"2"]
ID_dbConnect    [CONTROL+"6"]
ID_VBARun       [ALT+"F8"]
```

ID_VBAIDE       [ALT+"F11"]
[CONTROL+"H"]+
'_setvar;pickstyle;$M=$(if,$(eq,$(getvar,pickstyle),0),1,$(if,$(eq,$(getvar,+ pick-
      style),1),0,$(if,$(eq,$(getvar,pickstyle),2),3,2)))

There are two different ways to specify a shortcut key. The [CONTROL+"L"]^0 entry defines the [Ctrl]+[L] keystroke as an ortho mode toggle. This method allows you to specify the keystroke as a label, followed by any menu code required. For example, to define a [Ctrl]+[I] keystroke to start the **DDINSERT** command, enter the following line in the ***ACCELERATORS section.

[CONTROL+"I"]^C^CDDINSERT

It is also possible to create macros associated with shortcut keys. Simply enter the menu code just as you would for any other menu area. For example, to create a [Ctrl]+[SHIFT]+[A] shortcut key that automatically sets up A-size drawing limits and draws a 0.15 wide polyline border, enter the following in the ***ACCELERATORS section:

[CONTROL+SHIFT+"A"]^C^CLIMITS;;11,8.5;PLINEWID;0.15;REC-
      TANG;0.5,0.5;10.5,8;ZOOM;A

The second shortcut key definition method references an ID_*name tag* for a menu pick as the source code, followed by the keystroke definition. Any item in the menu file that displays a name tag can be used in this manner. For example, under the **Viewports** cascading menu in the **View** pull-down menu, the **4 Viewports** selection includes the label ID_Vports4. The following code is associated with this menu pick.

ID_Vports4 [&4 Viewports]^C^C_–vports _4

The ID_Vports4 tag can be referenced in the ***ACCELERATORS section to execute the menu code listed for this item as follows.

ID_Vports4 [CONTROL+"4"]

Pressing [Ctrl]+[4] now activates the **4 Viewports** menu selection. Entering the following in the ***ACCELERATORS section produces a similar result.

[CONTROL+"4"]^C^C_–vports _4

Either way works equally well, but it is unnecessary to duplicate existing menu code if you reference the name tag.

---

**PROFESSIONAL TIP**  Shortcuts have some specific limitations. For example, a shortcut cannot pause for user input or use repeating commands.

---

**Exercise 21-3**

○ Open the menu file you used in Exercise 21-2 in your text editor.
○ Create a shortcut key for each of the three new commands you developed in Exercise 21-1.
○ Test each command to be sure that each shortcut functions properly.

---

AutoCAD and its Applications—Advanced

## Some Notes about Pull-Down Menus

Here are a few more things to keep in mind when developing pull-down menus.
- Pull-down menus are disabled during the following commands.
  - ✓ **DTEXT**, after the rotation angle is entered.
  - ✓ **SKETCH**, after the record increment is set.
- Pull-down menus that are longer than the screen display are truncated to fit on the screen.
- The object snap shortcut menu is named POP0. It can contain items that reference other pull-down and screen menus.

## Creating a New Pull-Down Menu

When adding a new pull-down menu, first scroll through the acad.mnu file until you find the ***POP500 pull-down menu. If you want to add any additional pull-down menus, they should be inserted before the ***POP500 section. Your new pull-down menus will be located in the menu bar after the **Help** menu. Be sure to leave an empty line between pull-down menu definitions. A pull-down menu item can be as long as needed, but should be as brief as possible for easy reading. The pull-down menu width is automatically created to fit the width of the longest item.

Test each item of a new menu to make sure it works properly. Remember, when you return to the drawing editor, you must use the **MENU** command to reload the revised MNU file. If you neglect to do this, you will be working with the old version of the menu.

The following examples show how AutoCAD commands and options can be used to create pull-down or screen menu items. Remember, an ampersand (&) preceding a character in a pull-down menu label defines the keyboard access key used to enable that item. The following examples are listed using the three-step process:
- Step 1. A description of the macro.
- Step 2. The keyboard strokes required for the macro.
- Step 3. The actual macro as it appears in the menu file.

## Example 1

1. This **HEXAGON** command will start the **POLYGON** command and request a six-sided polygon inscribed in a circle.
2. **POLYGON**↵

   **6**↵

   *(select center)*

   **I**↵
3. [&Hexagon]*^C^Cpolygon;6;\I

The asterisk in front of the ^C^C repeats the command continuously until it is canceled. As mentioned in Chapter 20, you can indicate a return in a command or macro by using either a space or a semicolon. Notice the following two commands. Both commands perform the same function.

    [Hexagon]*^C^Cpolygon 6 \I
    [Hexagon]*^C^Cpolygon;6;\I

The first example uses spaces and the second example uses semicolons to represent pressing the [Enter] key. The technique you use is a matter of personal preference, but it is recommended that you use semicolons.

## Example 2

1. This **DOT** command draws a solid dot .1 unit in diameter. Use the **DONUT** command. The inside diameter is 0 (zero) and the outside diameter is .1.
2. **DONUT.**
   **0.**
   **.1.**
3. [&Dot]^C^Cdonut;0;.1

## Example 3

1. This **X-POINT** command sets the **PDMODE** system variable to 3 and draws an X at the pick point. The command should be repeated.
2. **PDMODE.**
   **3.**
   **POINT.**
   *(Pick the point)*
3. [&X-Point]*^C^Cpdmode;3;point

## Example 4

1. This command, named **Notation**, could be used by a drawing checker or instructor. It allows them to circle features on a drawing and then add a leader and text. It first sets the color to red, then draws a circle, snaps a leader to the nearest point that is picked on the circle, and prompts for the text. User input for text is provided, then a cancel returns the Command: prompt and the color is set to Bylayer.
2. **–COLOR.**
   **RED.**
   **CIRCLE.**
   *(Pick center point)*
   *(Pick radius)*
   **DIM.**
   **LEADER.**
   **NEA.**
   *(Pick a point on the circle)*
   *(Pick end of leader)*
   *(Press* [Enter] *for automatic shoulder)*
   *(Enter text)*.
   *(Press* [Esc] *to cancel)*
   **–COLOR.**
   **BYLAYER.**
3. [&Notation]^C^C-color;red;circle;\\dim;leader;nea;\\;\^C-color;bylayer

> **PROFESSIONAL TIP**
>
> Some commands, such as the **COLOR** command, display a dialog box. Menu macros can provide input to the command line, but cannot control dialog boxes. To access the command line version of a command, prefix the command name with a hyphen (–).

## Example 5

1. This is a repeating command, named **Multisquare**, that draws one-inch squares oriented at a 0° horizontal angle.
2. **RECTANG**⏎
   *(Pick lower-left corner)*
   **@1,1**⏎
3. [&Multisquare]*^C^Crectang;\@1,1

## Image Tile Menus

*Image tile menus* contain graphic symbols displayed in dialog boxes. They appear in certain dialog boxes, such as the **3D Objects** dialog box, **Figure 21-9**. This dialog box is accessed by selecting **3D Surfaces...** from the **Surfaces** cascading menu in the **Draw** pull-down menu. The dialog box shown contains several small boxes. Each box contains a small image. These displays are AutoCAD slides.

Slides are saved in a file created with the **SLIDELIB** program. This DOS-based program creates a file with an SLB extension. The slides can be used in an image tile menu by entering the required data in the menu file. Chapter 27 of *AutoCAD and its Applications—Basics* explains the use of the **SLIDELIB** program.

### Image Tile Menu Guidelines

Custom image tile menus can enhance the operation of AutoCAD. However, you must create images and menus using certain guidelines.

✓ Keep images simple. This saves display time and storage space. The image can be a simplified version of the actual symbol.

✓ When making slides, fill the screen with the image to be sure the image tile is filled. Center long items on the screen using **PAN**. This centers them in the image tile.

✓ Use image tile menus for symbols only. Do not clutter your program with image tile menus of text information. This slows the system down.

✓ AutoCAD does not display solid filled areas in image tiles. If you use fills, such as arrowheads, shade the display prior to making the slide image file.

✓ A maximum of 20 slides can be displayed in one image tile menu. The names of the images (up to 19 characters) are automatically displayed in a list box to the left of the image tiles.

**Figure 21-9.**
The **3D Objects** dialog box has an image tile menu.

List box can display the slide name or text label

Image tile menu

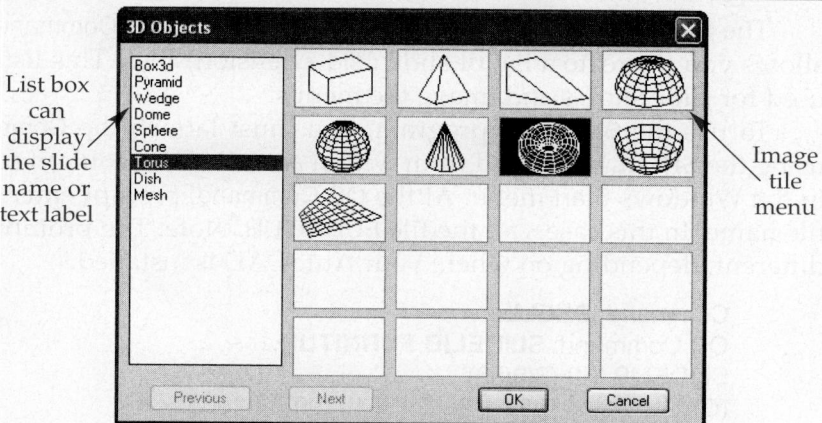

✓ If an item label in an image tile menu has a space before the first character, no image is displayed for that label, but the label name is shown. This can be used to execute other commands or call other image tile menus.

✓ If you have more than 20 slides in an image tile menu, AutoCAD creates additional "pages," each containing a **Next** and a **Previous** button for changing pages. The **OK** and **Cancel** buttons are automatically provided in the image tile menu.

## Making Symbols and Slides for the Image Tile Menu

Image tile menus can be used for a variety of purposes, but they are most commonly used to display images of blocks. Regardless of the types of symbols used, follow these steps when making image tile menus.

1. Draw the symbol or block.
2. Center the drawing on the display screen. When the drawing appears in the image tile menu, it is displayed in a box with a 1.5:1 ratio of width to height. With your drawing on the screen, switch to a layout tab (paper space), and create a 3 × 2 viewport. Now, **ZOOM Extents** and then switch back to model space. The drawing is now at the correct ratio.
3. Make a slide of the symbol using the **MSLIDE** command.
4. Write the **SLIDELIB** file.
5. Write the image tile menu file and test it.

Draw the three shapes shown in **Figure 21-10**. They represent a table, desk, and chair. Draw them any size you wish. Save each as a wblock in the Program Files\AutoCAD 2004 folder, and name them TABLE, DESK, and CHAIR. Do not include text or attributes.

Use the **MSLIDE** command to make a slide of each block, centering the slide as previously discussed. Give the slides the same name as the block. Save the slides to the Program Files\AutoCAD 2004 folder. This completes Step 3. Now you will use the **SLIDELIB** program to make the slide file.

Figure 21-10.
These objects are saved as blocks and used in a new image tile menu.

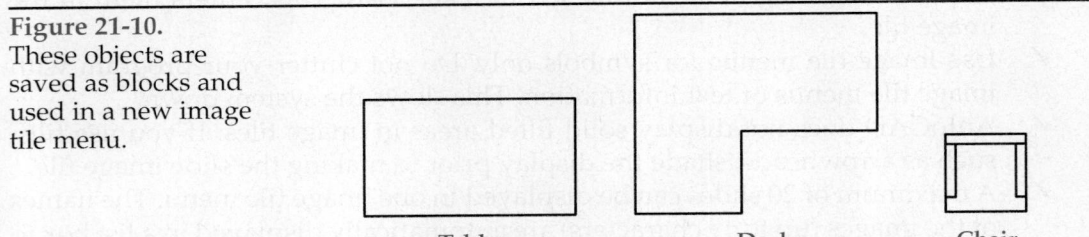

Table          Desk          Chair

## Using the SLIDELIB Program for an Image Tile Menu

The **SLIDELIB** program operates in DOS using the Command Prompt window and allows you to create a list of slide (.sld extension) files. This list of slides can then be used for slide shows and image tile menus.

To use the **SLIDELIB** program, you must launch the Command Prompt window using the **SHELL** command from within AutoCAD or you can select Command Prompt in the Windows Start menu. At the OS Command: prompt enter the name of the slide file name. In this case, call the file FURNITUR. Note: The prompt may appear slightly different, depending on where your AutoCAD is installed.

Command: **SHELL**↵
OS Command: **SLIDELIB FURNITUR**↵
SLIDELIB 1.2 (3/8/89)
(C) Copyright 1987–1989, 1994, 1995 Autodesk Inc.
  All Rights Reserved
**\Program Files\AutoCAD 2004\TABLE**↵

```
\Program Files\AutoCAD 2004\CHAIR.↵
\Program Files\AutoCAD 2004\DESK.↵
↵
↵
Command:
```

The second [Enter] after the last slide name exits the **SLIDELIB** program. Check to see that the slide library file was created by listing all files with a .slb extension.

```
C:\Program Files\AutoCAD 2004> DIR *.SLB↵
```

The file should be listed as furnitur.slb. Type EXIT to close the Command Prompt window.

A second method of creating a slide library involves using an existing list of slides in a text file. This method is useful if you add slide names to a text file (.txt) as the slides are made. The method is discussed in Chapter 27 of *AutoCAD and its Applications—Basics.*

## Creating an Image Tile Menu File Listing

Load your menu file or a copy of the acad.mnu file into a text editor. Page through the file until you find the ***image section. You can insert your new image tile menu between any of the existing ones. Be sure to leave a space between the previous and following menus.

The first item in the menu is used as the title. If you neglect to put a title here, the first line of the menu will be used as the title. Your new menu should look like the following.

```
**image_furniture
[Select Furniture]
[furnitur(Table)]^C^C–insert;table
[furnitur(Desk)]^C^C–insert;desk
[furnitur(Chair)]^C^C–insert;chair
[ Plants]$I=plants $I=*
```

Notice the space after the left bracket in the last entry, [ Plants]. This produces a label without an image tile. This label is used to execute other commands or, as in this case, display other image tile menus. These are called *branching* image tile menus. In this example, the Plants menu may show images of several types of plants. You can have as many branching image tile menus as needed.

The new image tile menu is still not usable because there is no selection that calls this menu to the screen. The **Draw** pull-down menu is a good place to put the call for this menu. Insert the following line in the pull-down menu definition (POP7).

```
[Furniture]$I=image_furniture $I=*
```

The first part of this entry, $I=image_furniture, calls the new furniture menu. The second part, $I=*, displays the menu and makes the items selectable.

Save the file and use the **MENU** command to load the menu. Test all the items in the menu and correct any problems. The new image tile menu should look like the one in **Figure 21-11.**

### Exercise 21-4

○ Using your text editor, create an image tile menu named EX21-4 using three wblocks that you have saved.
○ Plan this menu so you can add to it in the future.
○ Remember to include an entry in the **Draw** pull-down menu that calls the new image tile menu.

**Figure 21-11.**
This customized image tile menu uses previously created objects.

A block can be selected with the label or the image

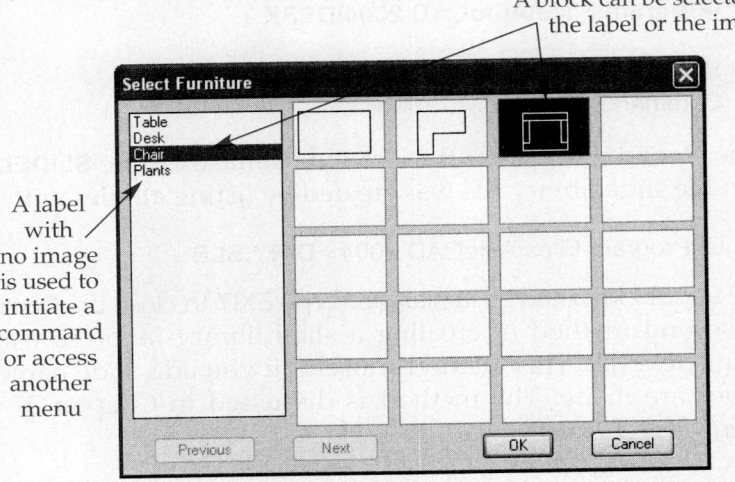

A label with no image is used to initiate a command or access another menu

## Chapter Test

*Answer the following questions on a separate sheet of paper.*

1. How many items can a pull-down menu contain?
2. Define the function of the following pull-down menu characters.
   A. ->
   B. <-
   C. <-<-
   D. &
3. Provide the character(s) required to perform the following functions.
   A. Insert a separator line across the pull-down menu.
   B. "Gray out" characters.
   C. Place a check mark before the menu item.
   D. Specify a menu access key.
4. What code is used to make pull-down menus display and be selectable?
5. Name two ways to represent a return in a menu item.
6. How many pull-down menus can be displayed on one screen?
7. How wide is a pull-down menu?
8. What is the function of the following DIESEL expression?

   [$(if,$(getvar,snapmode),!.)Snap]^B

9. What is the function of the following menu item characters?
   A. $p3=*
   B. $p4.1=~
   C. $p6.7=!.
10. Interpret the following menu item.

   ^C^Crectang;\@1,1

11. Why is it a good idea to make a copy of the acad.mnu file before you begin experimenting or customizing?
12. Write the general syntax for an entry in the ***HELPSTRINGS section of the acad.mnu file.
13. You wish to create a new macro that executes the **PURGE** command, and uses the **Blocks** option. Write the macro as it would appear in the menu file, and the correct notation in the ***HELPSTRINGS section of the acad.mnu file.
    A. Menu file
    B. Help string
14. What is the key combination called that allows you to press the [Ctrl] key and one additional key to execute a command?
15. Write the proper notation to define the type of key mentioned in Question 14 using the [M] key to execute the **MVIEW** command.
16. What is the purpose of the **MENULOAD** command?
17. Which command is used to create a slide file?
18. What is the first line of an image tile menu called?
19. List the steps required to create an image tile menu.
20. Describe the function of the following entry in an image tile menu file.

    [Fittings]$I=fittings $I=*

## Drawing Problems

1. Create a dimensioning pull-down menu. Place as many dimensioning commands as you need in the menu. Use cascading menus if necessary. One or more of the cascading menus should be dimensioning variables. Include menu access keys.

2. Create a pull-down menu for 3D objects. Add it to your copy of acad.mnu. Include menu access keys. The contents of the menu should include the following items.
   - 3D solid objects
   - 3D surface objects
   - **HIDE** command
   - **SHADEMODE** command
   - **VPORTS** command
   - **3DORBIT** command

3. Create a new pull-down menu named **Special**. The menu should include the following drawing and editing commands.
   - **LINE**
   - **ARC**
   - **CIRCLE**
   - **POLYLINE**
   - **POLYGON**
   - **RECTANGLE**
   - **DTEXT**
   - **ERASE**
   - **MOVE**
   - **COPY**
   - **STRETCH**
   - **TRIM**
   - **EXTEND**
   - **CHAMFER**
   - **FILLET**

   Use cascading menus if necessary. Include a separator line between the drawing and editing commands, and specify appropriate menu access keys.

4. Create a single pull-down menu to insert a variety of blocks or symbols. These symbols can be for any drawing discipline that you use. Use cascading menus and menu access keys if necessary. This menu should have a special group name that will enable it to be loaded with the **MENULOAD** command. This menu can be added to the existing pull-downs in the ACAD menu, or it can replace one of them.

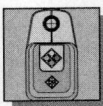

5. Choose one of the previous problems and create help strings for each of the new menu items. Use existing defined help strings whenever possible. When you define new help strings, always do a search of the menu file first to see if the string is being used elsewhere.

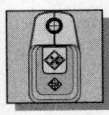

6. Refer to Problem 3. Create a shortcut key for each of the drawing and editing commands in that problem. Search the menu file to see if any of the commands are currently tagged with a shortcut key to avoid duplication.

7. Construct an image tile menu of a symbol library that you use in a specific discipline of drafting or design. Create this menu so it can be selected from the **Draw** pull-down menu, or from a new pull-down menu of your own creation. Use as many image tiles as needed. You can call additional image tile menus from the initial one. The following are examples of disciplines that could be used.
   - Mechanical
   - Architectural
   - Civil
   - Structural
   - Piping
   - HVAC
   - Electrical
   - Electronics
   - PC board layout
   - Geometric tolerancing
   - 3D construction

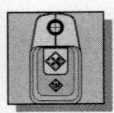

8. Modify the existing **3D Objects** dialog box and image tile menu to include additional 3D objects of your own creation. Create additional menus, or "pages," if needed.

9. Create a new image tile menu and dialog box that illustrates a variety of hatch patterns. When an image is selected, it should set a specific hatch pattern, then execute the **HATCH** command so that the user can set the scale and angle for the hatch pattern. Be sure to include the proper name of the hatch pattern in your menu file so that the user does not have to enter it when the **HATCH** command is executed.

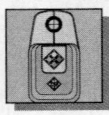

10. Create a new image tile menu that provides images of a variety of dimensioning styles. When a specific image is picked, it should automatically set the appropriate dimension variables in order to achieve the appearance of the dimension in the selected image. Test each of these selections carefully before incorporating them into the file. This may be an excellent menu for using branching image tile dialog boxes in order to display variations in different dimension styles.

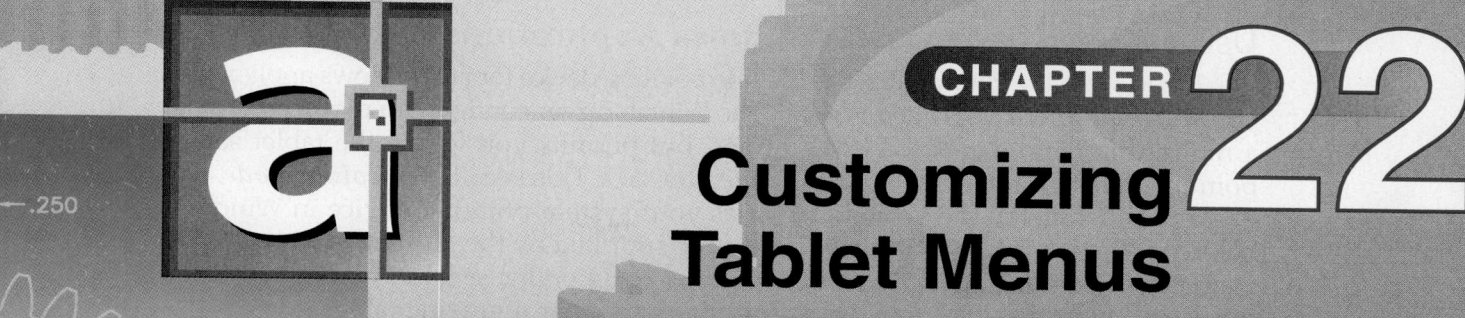

## Learning Objectives

After completing this chapter, you will be able to:
- Configure and use the AutoCAD tablet menu template.
- Customize the AutoCAD tablet menu.
- Create a new tablet menu.

If you have a digitizer, the AutoCAD standard tablet menu is an alternative to keyboard entry or picking commands on screen. The tablet menu template supplied by Autodesk is a thick piece of plastic that measures approximately 11″ × 12″. Printed on it are many of the commands available in AutoCAD. See **Figure 22-1.** Some commands are accompanied by icons that indicate the function of the command. The menu template is helpful because it provides a clear display of AutoCAD's various commands.

Most people discover that many of the commands in the AutoCAD tablet menu are not used for specific types of drawings. Like screen menus, the tablet menu can be customized. Notice the empty space at the top of the template. This space is available for adding commands and symbols. You can have several overlays for this area. Creating a custom tablet menu is similar to creating custom screen menus and is the focus of this chapter.

## Using the AutoCAD Tablet Menu

To use a tablet menu, the digitizer and digitizing tablet must first be configured for your specific hardware and the type of menu you will be using. When you initially configure AutoCAD to recognize a digitizer, the entire surface of the digitizing tablet represents the screen pointing area. The **TABLET** command allows you to configure the digitizer to recognize the tablet menu template, or overlay. When using this command, you inform AutoCAD of the exact layout of the menu areas and the size and position of the screen pointing area. Depending on the type of pointing device you are using with Microsoft Windows, there are additional aspects of tablet configuration to be considered.

## Using a Digitizer for All Windows Applications

If you are using your digitizer as the sole pointing device for all Windows applications, you will require a driver called Wintab. The Wintab driver configures a digitizer to act as a mouse for Windows-based applications, but permits you to use the tablet screen pointing area and menus when running AutoCAD. This is called *absolute mode.*

You must install the Wintab driver as your system pointing device in Windows before starting AutoCAD. Wintab drivers are supplied by the digitizing tablet manufacturers, not by Autodesk. If you have access to an online service, you can typically download the current Wintab driver for your particular digitizing tablet.

## Tablet Menu Layout

The AutoCAD tablet menu presents commands in related groups. Referring to **Figure 22-1**, notice the labels below each menu area. The labels identify the types of commands available. Find the **TABLET** command in the **TOOLS** section of the menu. This command is used to configure, calibrate, and toggle your tablet.

**Figure 22-1.**
The AutoCAD standard tablet menu template. The large area across the top of the template is used for customization. (Autodesk, Inc.)

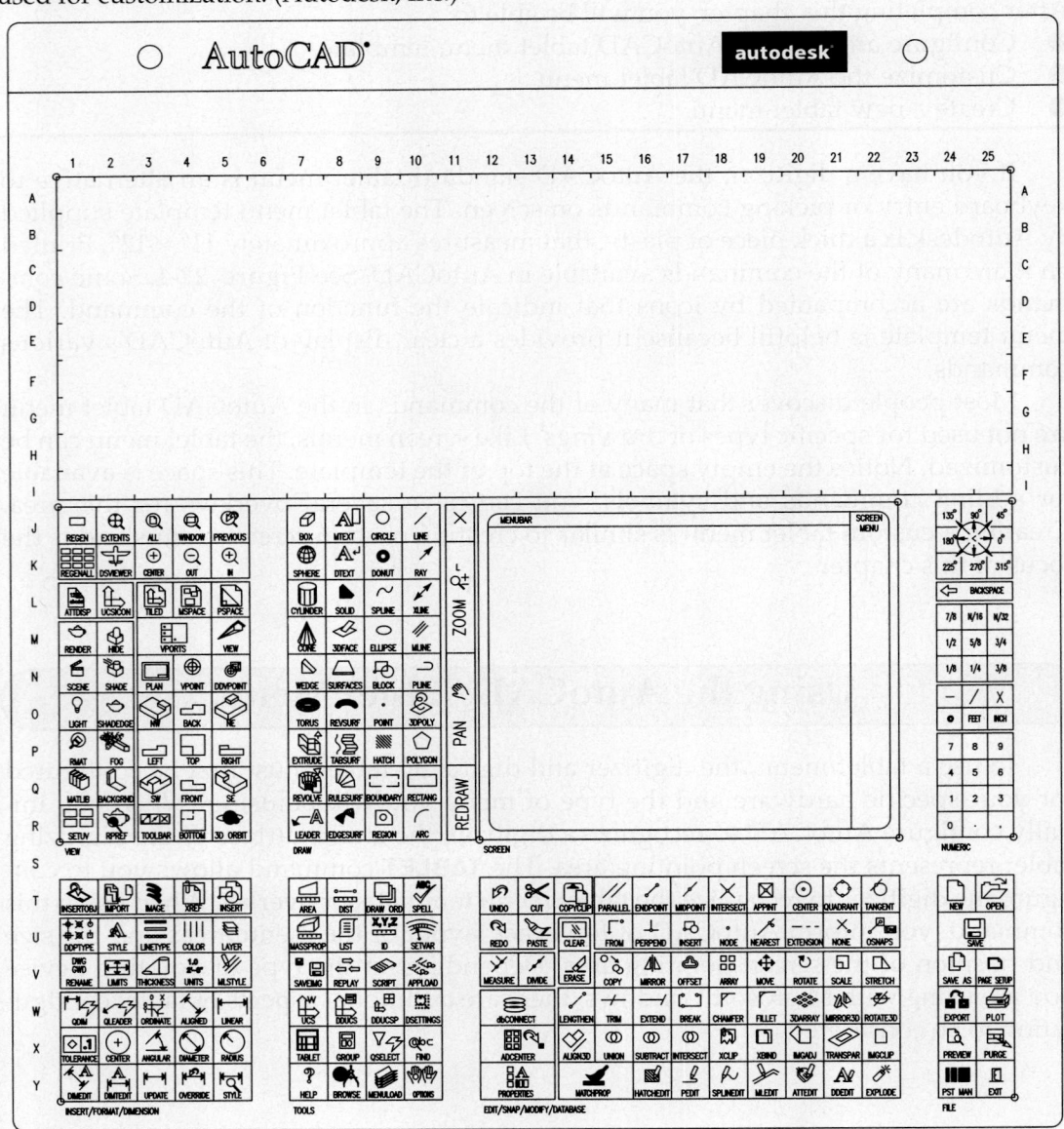

The available menu space near the top of the template is called Menu Area 1. As you develop your own customized tablet menu, make a point of taking advantage of this unused space. Suggestions and instructions for customizing Menu Area 1 appear later in this chapter.

## Configuring the Tablet Menu

As previously mentioned, the **TABLET** command is used to tell AutoCAD the layout of the tablet menu. It prompts for three corners of each menu area and the number of columns and rows in each area. The screen pointing area is defined by picking two opposite corners. Three corners of each menu area are marked with small donuts. As you read the following example, look at **Figure 22-2**, which illustrates the configuration of the AutoCAD standard tablet menu and shows the donuts marking the menu area corners.

Command: **TABLET**↵
Enter an option [ON/OFF/CAL/CFG]: **CFG**↵
Enter number of tablet menus desired (0-4): **4**↵

**Figure 22-2.**
Small donuts mark the corners of the menu areas on the AutoCAD tablet menu template.

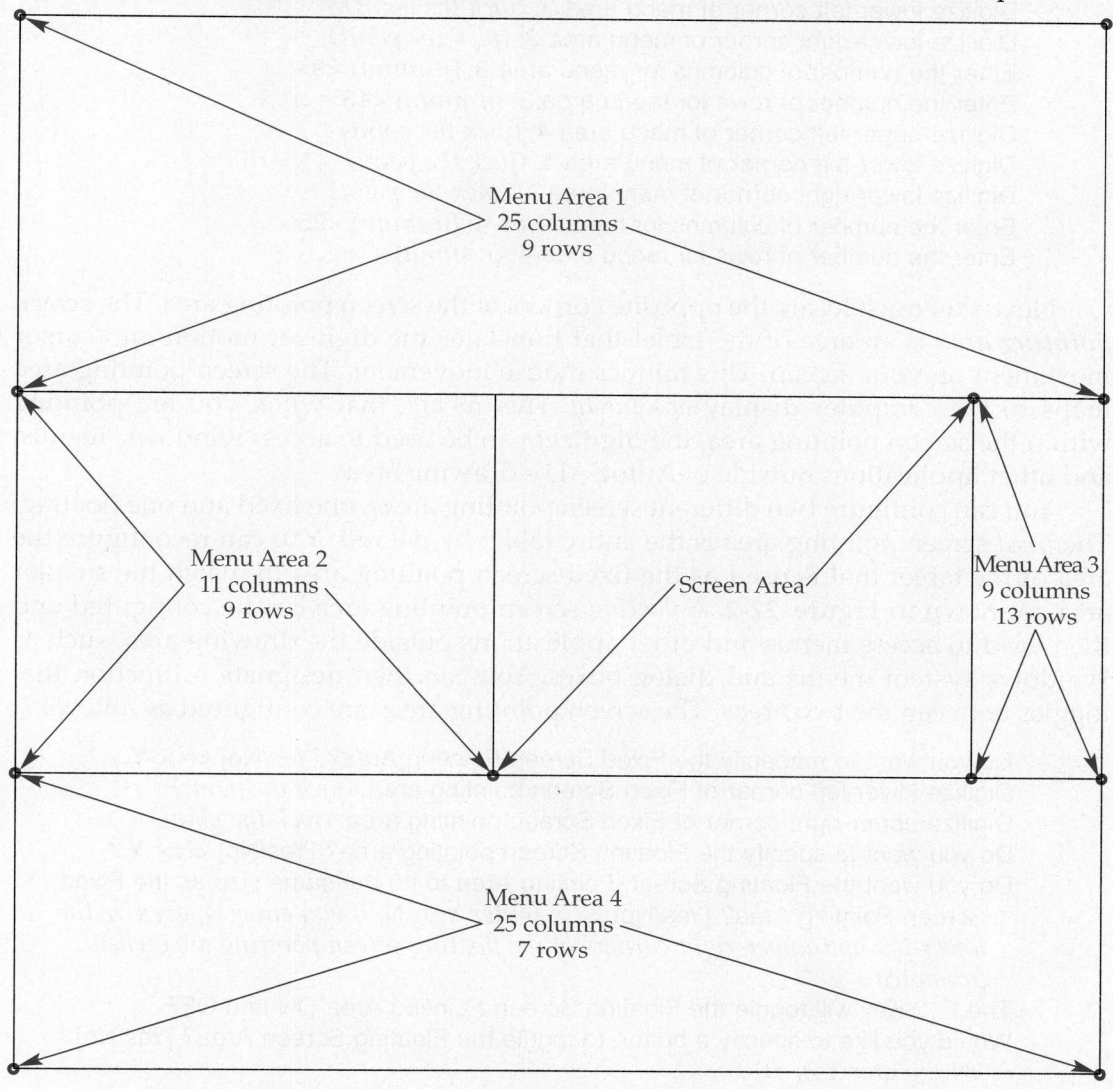

Menu Area 1
25 columns
9 rows

Menu Area 2
11 columns
9 rows

Screen Area

Menu Area 3
9 columns
13 rows

Menu Area 4
25 columns
7 rows

If tablet menus are currently in use and the same number is specified for menu areas, AutoCAD issues the following prompt.

Do you want to realign tablet menus? [Yes/No] <N>: **Y**↵

Next, you are prompted to select the points that define each menu area with the digitizer pointing device.

Digitize upper-left corner of menu area 1: *(pick the donut at the upper-left corner)*
Digitize lower-left corner of menu area 1: *(pick the point)*
Digitize lower-right corner of menu area 1: *(pick the point)*
Enter the number of columns for menu area 1: *(n-nnnn)* <25>: ↵
Enter the number of rows for menu area 1: *(n-nnnn)* <9>: ↵

You have now given AutoCAD the location of Menu Area 1 and specified the number of selection boxes that are available. The command continues with Menu Area 2.

Digitize upper-left corner of menu area 2: *(pick the point)*
Digitize lower-left corner of menu area 2: *(pick the point)*
Digitize lower-right corner of menu area 2: *(pick the point)*
Enter the number of columns for menu area 2: *(n-nnnn)* <11>: ↵
Enter the number of rows for menu area 2: *(n-nnnn)* <9>: ↵
Digitize upper-left corner of menu area 3: *(pick the point)*
Digitize lower-left corner of menu area 3: *(pick the point)*
Digitize lower-right corner of menu area 3: *(pick the point)*
Enter the number of columns for menu area 3: *(n-nnnn)* <9>: ↵
Enter the number of rows for menu area 3: *(n-nnnn)* <13>: ↵
Digitize upper-left corner of menu area 4: *(pick the point)*
Digitize lower-left corner of menu area 4: *(pick the point)*
Digitize lower-right corner of menu area 4: *(pick the point)*
Enter the number of columns for menu area 4: *(n-nnnn)* <25>: ↵
Enter the number of rows for menu area 4: *(n-nnnn)* <7>: ↵

Next, you must locate the opposite corners of the screen pointing area. The *screen pointing area* is an area of the tablet that translates the digitizer motion into cursor movement on your screen. This mimics mouse movement. The screen pointing area maps to the computer display *absolutely.* This means that when you are pointing within the screen pointing area, the digitizer can be used to access windows, menus, and other applications outside of AutoCAD's drawing area.

You can configure two different screen pointing areas, one fixed and one floating. The *fixed* screen pointing area is the entire tablet by default. You can reconfigure the area of the tablet that is used as the fixed screen pointing area to match the smaller area as shown in **Figure 22-2.** A *floating* screen pointing area can be configured and then used to access menus and other applications outside the drawing area, such as Windows system menus and dialog boxes. You can then designate a function that toggles between the two areas. The screen pointing areas are configured as follows.

Do you want to respecify the Fixed Screen Pointing Area? [Yes/No] <N>: **Y**↵
Digitize lower-left corner of Fixed Screen pointing area: *(pick the point)*
Digitize upper-right corner of Fixed Screen pointing area: *(pick the point)*
Do you want to specify the Floating Screen pointing area? [Yes/No] <N>: **Y**↵
Do you want the Floating Screen Pointing Area to be the same size as the Fixed Screen Pointing Area? [Yes/No] <Y>: *(enter Y or N; if you enter N, digitize the lower-left and upper-right corners of the floating screen pointing area when prompted.)*
The F12 Key will toggle the Floating Screen Pointing Area ON and OFF.
Would you like to specify a button to toggle the Floating Screen Area? [Yes/No] <N>: *(enter Y or N)*

AutoCAD and its Applications—Advanced

If you choose to use a digitizer puck button as the toggle, the following prompt is issued.

Press any non-pick button that you wish to designate as the toggle for the Floating Screen Area.

Press the button of your choice. Do not press the pick button.

Use the same configuration process outlined above when configuring the tablet for your custom menus. The tablet configuration is saved in the acad2004.cfg file, which is in user's Documents and Settings Autodesk folder. The system reads this file when loading AutoCAD to determine which kind of equipment you are using. It also determines which menu is current.

It is easier to configure the AutoCAD standard tablet menu by selecting the **Reconfig** option from the **Tablet:** screen menu. First, enable the screen menu display by activating the **Display screen menu** check box in the **Display** tab of the **Options** dialog box. Then, pick **TOOLS2** from the AutoCAD root menu. Next, pick **Tablet** and then select **Reconfig**. The **Tablet:** screen menu options are shown in **Figure 22-3**.

When the **Reconfig** option is selected, the configuration prompts appear as shown in the previous example. However, you do not need to enter the number of columns and rows. The **Reconfig** option assumes you are realigning the AutoCAD tablet menu template. Therefore, it only requires the locations of the menu areas and the screen pointing area. Use this screen menu option when you wish to return to the AutoCAD standard tablet menu after using a custom menu.

Figure 22-3.
Selecting **Reconfig** from the **Tablet:** screen menu allows you to quickly configure the AutoCAD standard tablet menu.

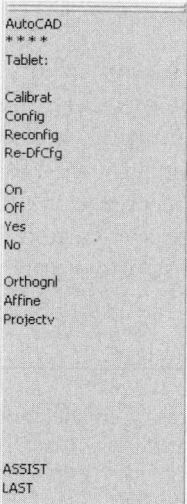

| AutoCAD |
| * * * * |
| Tablet: |
| |
| Calibrat |
| Config |
| Reconfig |
| Re-DfCfg |
| |
| On |
| Off |
| Yes |
| No |
| |
| Orthognl |
| Affine |
| Projectv |
| |
| ASSIST |
| LAST |

**NOTE**

Shortcut menus are not available during the digitizer configuration process. When you finish configuring the digitizer, shortcut menus are available to both the mouse and the digitizer.

# Customizing the Tablet Menu

The empty upper portion of the AutoCAD tablet menu can be used to add custom commands. As mentioned earlier, this portion of the tablet is Menu Area 1. It contains 225 selection boxes that can be programmed for commands, macros, scripts, and blocks. It is a good place to locate frequently used symbols and shapes.

An overlay containing block names and drawings can be plotted and slipped under the plastic menu template. Several overlays can be used for different disciplines, and structured to operate in different ways.

## Plan the Overlay

Before adding items to the AutoCAD tablet menu, take time to think about what the overlay should include. Ask yourself the following questions.

- ✓ For which kind of drawings will the overlay be used?
- ✓ Which commands or macros should be a part of the overlay?
- ✓ Which kind of symbols should be placed in the overlay?
- ✓ Should the symbols be stored as blocks or drawing files?
- ✓ Which symbols and blocks are used most often?
- ✓ If the symbols are blocks, should they be stored in a prototype drawing or a template file?

After answering these questions, you will be able to lay out a quality overlay. The next step is to draw the overlay.

## Draw the Overlay

Part of your customization plan should be to draw or sketch the menu area before creating the actual drawing file for the custom menu. The quickest way to make an accurate representation of the menu is to plot Menu Area 1 from the Tablet drawing file. This drawing is located in the AutoCAD 2004 Sample folder. The following steps should be used to create the drawing of Menu Area 1.

1. Open the drawing file named Tablet.dwg.
2. Perform a **ZOOM Window** and zoom into the drawing around Menu Area 1. See **Figure 22-4**.

---

**Figure 22-4.**
A representation of Menu Area 1 in the Tablet drawing. The area contains a grid of 225 selection boxes within its borders.

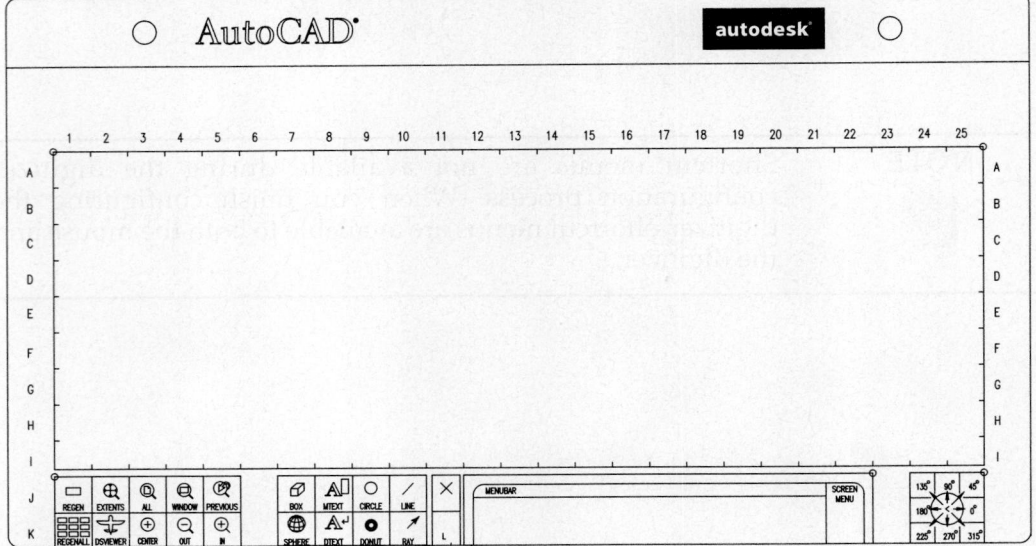

3. Freeze all layers except the Borders layer. The drawing should now appear as shown in **Figure 22-5A**.
4. Make a new layer named Area1, and give it the color cyan.
5. Use the **PLINE** command to trace over the outline of Menu Area 1.
6. Draw a vertical line between two tick marks on the right or left side and array it in 24 columns. Use object snap modes to set the correct spacing. See **Figure 22-5B**.
7. Draw a horizontal line between two tick marks at the top or bottom and array it in 8 rows. Use object snap modes to set the correct spacing.
8. Erase the remaining lines in the drawing outside Menu Area 1. See **Figure 22-5C**.
9. Plot the drawing on B-size or larger paper. A plot using a 1.5 = 1 or 2 = 1 scale provides a larger drawing, which is easier to work with for initial menu design purposes.
10. Erase all unnecessary layers.
11. Save the drawing with a new name (such as menu area 1.dwg) for future use.

Make several copies of your drawing. Pencil in the command and symbol names. Try more than one arrangement based on some of the considerations previously discussed. Keep in mind the purpose of the overlay you are making. Symbols that are used frequently should be placed along the outer edges for quick selection.

**Figure 22-5.**
A—The Tablet drawing in its unedited form, after freezing each layer except the Borders layer. B—Menu Area 1 after drawing vertical lines. C—The completed drawing of Menu Area 1.

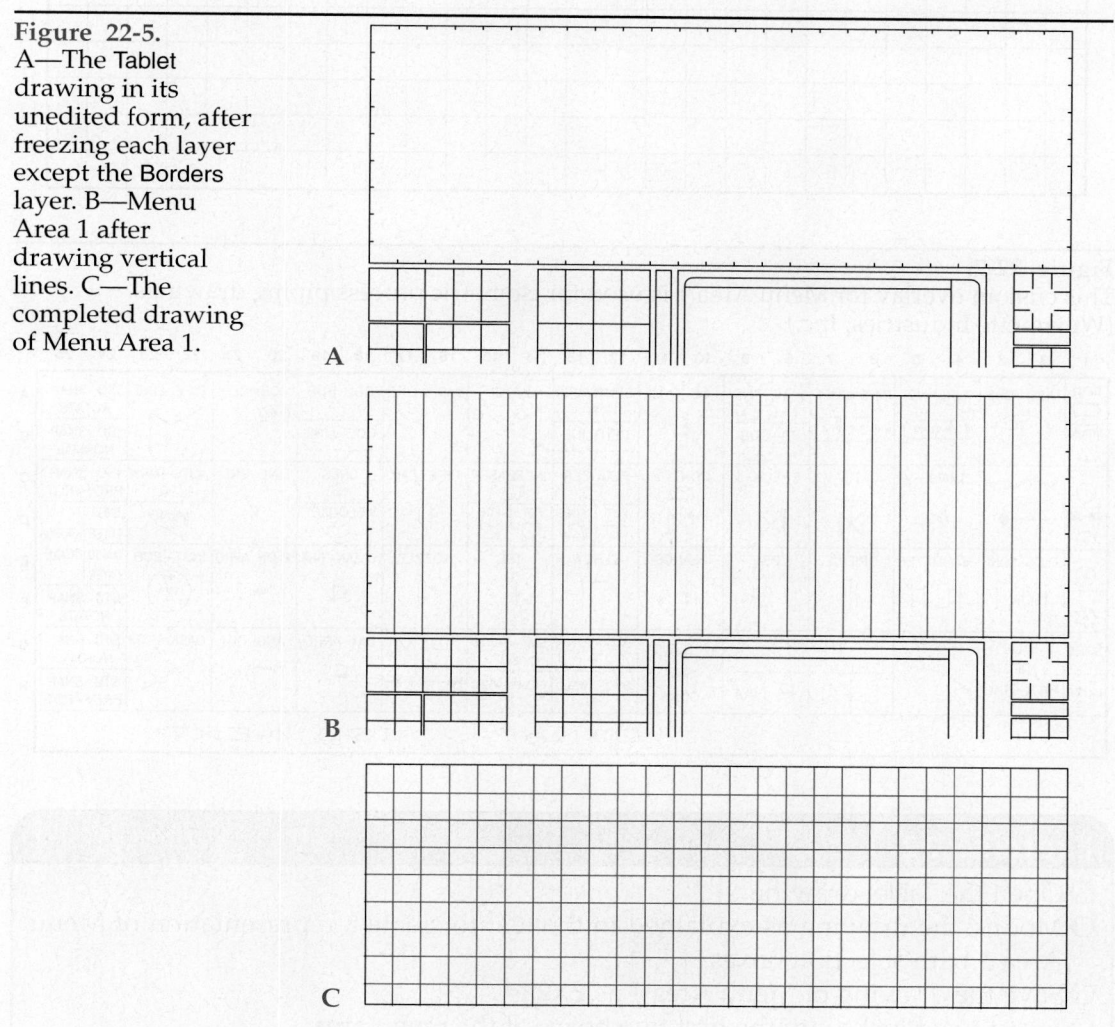

# Complete the Menu Drawing

The next step in creating your customized AutoCAD tablet menu is to draw the symbols in the menu. This should be relatively easy if the symbols are already in the form of blocks. If so, they can be inserted into the selection boxes of the menu in your Menu Area 1 drawing. You will need to scale the symbols down to make them fit. A sample menu with symbols is shown in **Figure 22-6.**

After you are finished drawing the menu, plot it at full scale (1 = 1). Use vellum or polyester film and wet ink. Use black ink rather than colored ink. This produces a high-quality plot that can be clearly seen when slipped under the AutoCAD tablet menu template.

The custom menu area can be modified to suit your needs. The symbols shown in **Figure 22-7** are used for isometric process piping drawings.

**Figure 22-6.**
Symbols saved as blocks are inserted into the boxes of the menu in the Menu Area 1 drawing.

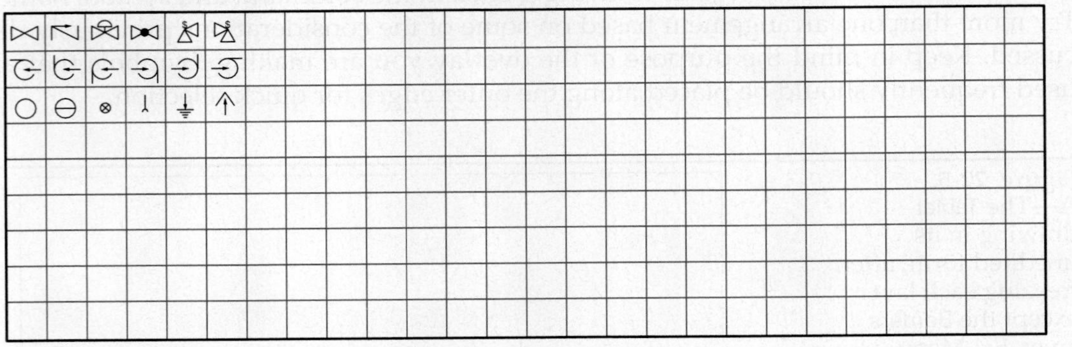

**Figure 22-7.**
This custom overlay for Menu Area 1 is used for isometric process piping drawings.
(Willamette Industries, Inc.)

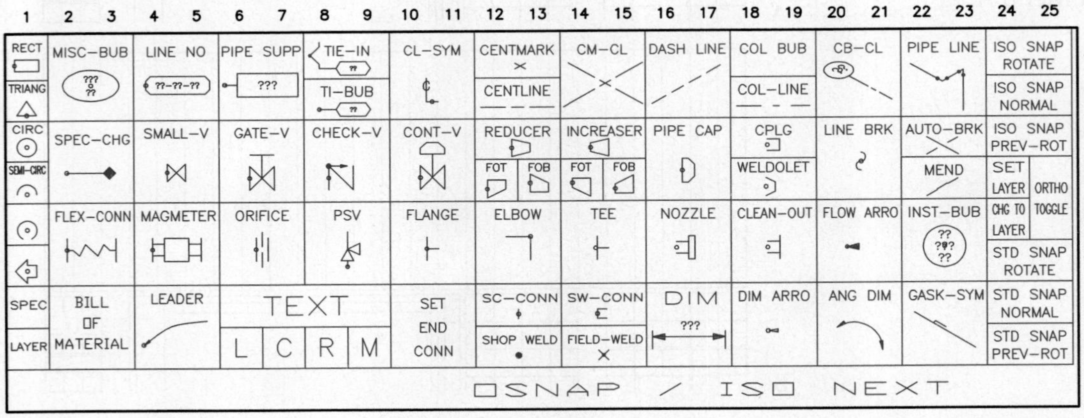

## Exercise 22-1

- Open the Tablet drawing.
- Modify the drawing as explained in the text to create a representation of Menu Area 1 with selection boxes.
- Save the drawing of Menu Area 1 as EX22-1.
- Insert two blocks into the first two boxes of the menu area.
- Scale the blocks so they fit inside the boxes.
- Save the drawing as EX22-1.

# Write the Menu File

The final step in customizing the AutoCAD tablet menu is to write the menu file in the ***TABLET1 section of the acad.mnu file. Load the file into your text editor and find the menu section ***TABLET1. It should look like:

```
***TABLET1
**TABLET1STD
[A-1]\
[A-2]\
[A-3]\
[A-4]\
[A-5]\
```

Referring to the tablet menu template in **Figure 22-4**, notice the column and row numbers and letters along the top and sides of the tablet. These correspond to the numbers in brackets in the acad.mnu file under the ***TABLET heading. Each row contains 25 selection boxes numbered from left to right. There are 225 boxes in all. Therefore, box number 70 is identified as C-20.

Referring to **Figure 22-6**, notice that the symbols placed in the menu occupy the first six boxes of the top three rows. The first box of each row is labeled [A-1], [B-1], and [C-1], respectively.

The macros for the tablet menu file can be entered in two ways. They can replace the selection box numbers listed in the menu file, or they can be entered after the box numbers. The latter method is recommended because it leaves you with reference numbers for the selection boxes. There are no screen labels for tablet menus. Thus, anything inside brackets is not displayed, nor is it read by AutoCAD. The notations inside the brackets can be left as helpful reminders.

Before making changes to the acad.mnu file, make a copy of the file. Then load the copy into the text editor. The following example gives the menu entries for the customized tablet menu shown in **Figure 22-6**.

```
**TABLET1STD
[A-1]^C^C–insert;gatevalve
[A-2]^C^C–insert;checkvalve
[A-3]^C^C–insert;controlvalve
[A-4]^C^C–insert;globevalve
[A-5]^C^C–insert;safetyvalv-r
[A-6]^C^C–insert;safetyvalv-l

[B-1]^C^C–insert;pumpr-top
[B-2]^C^C–insert;pumpr-up
[B-3)^C^C–insert;pumpr-dn
[B-4]^C^C–insert;pumpl-dn
[B-5]^C^C–insert;pumpl-up
[B-6]^C^C–insert;pumpl-top

[C-1]^C^C–insert;instr-loc
[C-2]^C^C–insert;instr-pan
[C-3]^C^C–insert;trans
[C-4]^C^C–insert;instr-con
[C-5]^C^C–insert;drain
[C-6]^C^C–insert;vent
```

After you edit or create a new menu in this manner, save the menu file and exit the text editor. Use the **MENU** command to load your copy of the acad.mnu file. Be sure to enter the proper path to the file.

PROFESSIONAL TIP

If you will be editing your menu often, consider defining a menu pick on the screen that automatically loads the menu file:

[LOADMENU]^C^Cfiledia;0;menu;*file path/menu name*;filedia;1

In this example, the **FILEDIA** system variable is set to 0 and then changed back to its default value of 1 after loading the menu file. The **FILEDIA** system variable controls the display of file selection dialog boxes. Setting the variable to 0 enables entry at the command line after the **MENU** command is issued and suppresses display of the **Select Menu File** dialog box. If you have previously set the **FILEDIA** system variable to 0, simply change the setting after using the menu pick above.

## Alternate Ways to Customize the Tablet Overlay

The customization method previously discussed uses blocks that have been saved in a prototype drawing file. In order to use the blocks, the file must first be inserted into the current drawing. As an alternative, a new drawing can be started based on a template file containing the blocks. For example, suppose the piping flow diagram symbols are saved in a template drawing named pipeflow.dwt. You can use the symbols if you specify this template when starting a new drawing.

The method used in the previous discussion inserts blocks located in another drawing. You can insert one drawing into another using the **–INSERT** command. You may consider putting an insertion command in your tablet menu.

Command: **–INSERT**↵
Enter block name or [?]: **PIPESYM**↵
Specify insertion point or [Scale/X/Y/Z/Rotate/PScale/PX/PY/PZ/PRotate]: *(press [Esc] to cancel)*

As long as the drawing is located within a folder in the AutoCAD support file search path, you do not need to enter the full path for the drawing. If the drawing is in a folder that is not part of the search path, you must enter the complete folder path. Press the [Esc] key to cancel the command when prompted for the insertion point. This allows you to insert all named items, such as blocks, views, and layers, into the drawing without inserting the actual drawing on screen. You can insert prototype drawings containing blocks (DWG files), but you cannot insert template drawings (DWT files). The **Insert Prototype Drawing** pick in your tablet menu file could be written as:

^C^C–INSERT;PIPESYM;^C

A third way to customize the overlay is to use separate drawing files for the symbols instead of blocks in a prototype drawing. The drawing files can be located on the hard disk or on diskettes. Remember that symbols stored as individual drawing files require more disk storage space. In addition, disk access time is often slower.

Evaluate your present use of blocks and drawing files when making or modifying tablet menus. Take into account your current method of symbol creation, storage, and usage when developing tablet menus that incorporate symbols. If symbol drawings (prototypes) are working best for your application, develop your tablet menu around these. If individual drawing files are used, the menus should access these. While **DesignCenter** also provides access to external symbols and drawing data, a menu macro can automatically load all required information with a single pick.

## Designing a New Tablet Menu

Planning is important when developing new tablet menus. There are several preliminary steps that should be taken before designing a menu.

✓ List the commands that you use most often.
✓ Develop macros that automate your CAD work as much as possible.
✓ List the different types of symbol overlays you may need.
✓ List each group of symbols in order of most frequently used to least frequently used.

When designing macros, think of the commands and functions you use most often. Automate these first. Keep in mind that your goal is to create a drawing or design. This requires knowledge of the specific discipline. You want to spend more time using your knowledge and skills rather than picking the proper succession of AutoCAD commands and options. Therefore, for each function that you automate, reduce the number of picks required to complete the function. In doing so, your time spent at the computer will be more productive.

After identifying the commands, macros, and symbols you will add to the menu, you can begin creating the commands, macros, and menus.

1. Develop and test individual macros in a screen menu or tablet menu.
2. Determine major groups of commands and macros based on their frequency of use.
3. Design the tablet menu layout. Draw it larger than actual size using a pencil. This gives you room for lettering and sketches. You can have up to four menu areas and a screen pointing area. Several sample layouts are shown in **Figure 22-8.**
4. Draw the basic menu layout with AutoCAD. This should be a preliminary test menu. Do not add text or graphics yet. Pencil in commands on a plotted copy of the menu.
5. Write the macros for the menu and test each function for convenience.
6. Add text and graphics to the menu in AutoCAD, then plot it. Revise the menu as needed to make it more efficient.

---

Tablet menus can get dirty and smudged with use. Plot the final copy on single-matte polyester film, which has emulsion on one side only. Use the following process to plot the menu.

- Display the menu drawing on screen.
- Mirror the menu and delete the original. Be sure that the **MIRRTEXT** system variable is set to 1 (on). The menu should appear reversed.
- Plot the menu full size using wet ink.
- Punch registration holes in the top of the menu to match those in the AutoCAD tablet menu template.
- Trim excess material from the menu and attach it to your digitizer tablet. The inked side should be facing the tablet surface.

This process creates a tablet menu template with a protected, inked menu. If single-matte film is used, a smooth surface is provided for the digitizer puck to slide on.

## Creating Your New Tablet Menu

The overlay area at the top of the AutoCAD standard tablet menu template provides limited room and flexibility for customization. For some applications, you may wish to develop an entirely new tablet menu. The process of developing your own menu is similar to customizing the AutoCAD tablet menu. Of course, it takes additional planning because you are creating the entire tablet menu.

It is not required to configure four separate menu areas for your tablet menu. You can refer to the sample menus in **Figure 22-8** when creating a layout, or you can design something completely new. When planning your tablet menu, it is a good idea to first sketch out the entire menu area. You can use the Tablet drawing as a source drawing, or you can create an entirely new drawing based on the size of your digitizer tablet and your custom menu needs. Start with a simple grid and sketch in the details, just as if you were customizing the overlay area of the AutoCAD tablet menu.

**Figure 22-8.**
Some common tablet menu layouts.

Although you are laying out selection boxes on a grid, it is not necessary to make the selection areas square or even completely rectangular. The same menu macro can be entered for any number of selection boxes, and the boxes may be interconnected or placed in separate locations. This means that there may be several boxes on the tablet menu that represent the same function. Look at the **FILE** area of the AutoCAD standard tablet menu and notice the **SAVE** selection box shown in **Figure 22-9.** AutoCAD does not designate the **SAVE** selection box as one large box because Menu Area 4 of the tablet is divided into 175 equally sized boxes. The **SAVE** command on the tablet menu is located across two boxes. Therefore, two macro lines in the menu file are required to define the **SAVE** command.

Load the acad.mnu file into your text editor and page to the ***TABLET4 section. You should notice several lines with just a backslash (\). These lines specify the blank space above Menu Area 4 of the tablet menu. Now, scroll down until you find two lines that read ^C^C_qsave. These lines correspond to the U-24 and U-25 selection boxes. The default acad.mnu file does not show the labels for these boxes, but you can place labels in the tablet menu area where needed for your own reference.

**Figure 22-9.**
A—The **SAVE** selection box on the AutoCAD tablet menu is actually composed of two smaller boxes. B—Two commands are required in the menu file.

| ^C^C_new | ^C^C_open |
|---|---|
| ^C^C_qsave | ^C^C_qsave |
| ^C^C_saveas | ^C^C_pagesetup |
| ^C^C_export | ^C^C_plot |
| ^C^C_preview | ^C^C_purge |
| ^C^C_stylesmanager | ^C^C_exit |

A                                      B

**PROFESSIONAL TIP**

Always place a backslash on the menu file lines for selection boxes that have no function. In the menu file, AutoCAD automatically places a space at the end of every line that does not end with a semicolon, plus sign (+), space, or backslash. Since a space issues an [Enter] keystroke, if there is no entry on a line for a selection box in the menu file, the previously used command is repeated when the corresponding tablet menu selection box is picked. By placing a backslash on such lines, you specify for AutoCAD to continue to await input and nothing actually happens if the related box is picked.

## A Sample Tablet Menu

An example of a custom tablet menu is shown in **Figure 22-10.** It is similar to the AutoCAD standard tablet menu, but it contains fewer boxes. The template is made up of a grid with numbers along the top and letters down the left side. The selection box locations are identified at the beginning of each macro in the menu file for reference, similar to:

```
***TABLET1STD
[A-1]
[A-2]
[A-3]
```

**Figure 22-10.**
A sample layout of a custom tablet menu.

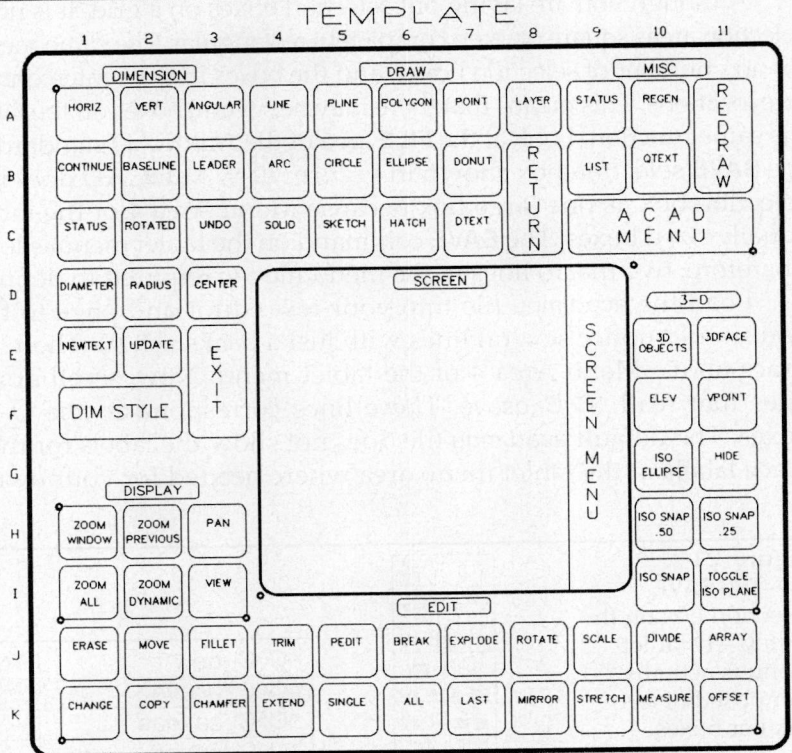

Anything inside brackets in the tablet menu section is not displayed, and does not affect the macro. This notation can be used in the acad.mnu file to indicate each tablet menu section, and the selection box number within the section. Numbers used in tablet menus are not displayed on screen. Numbers in screen menu macros must follow the eighth space in the command name. Otherwise, they are displayed on screen.

In **Figure 22-10,** notice that the most frequently used commands are placed inside large boxes. These commands include **RETURN**, **ACADMENU** (a command that loads the AutoCAD menu file), **DIM STYLE**, and **EXIT** (a command that exits from the Dim: mode). This allows you to pick them quickly.

Look at the menu file in **Figure 22-11** and compare the entries to the corresponding selection boxes in **Figure 22-10.** The grid locations of each menu item are indicated in brackets for quick identification. The button menu is for a 12-button pointing device.

If you plan to try this menu, enter the macros with your text editor. Assign the name MENU1.MNU. The new menu cannot be used until it is loaded into AutoCAD using the **MENU** command. In the following example, the **FILEDIA** system variable is currently set to 0.

> Command: **MENU**↵
> Enter menu file name or [. (for none)] <*current*>: **SUPPORT\MENU1**↵

The compiled version of the menu file has an .mnc extension. AutoCAD looks for the latest version of the compiled menu file when you begin a new drawing. If there is no such file, AutoCAD compiles the menu file again.

After loading your new menu, enter the **TABLET** command and configure the new tablet menu. If you are using the **Tablet:** screen menu, do not pick the **Reconfig** option. This starts the configuration routine for the AutoCAD tablet menu. Instead, use the **Config** option.

**Figure 22-11.**
The menu file macros for the custom tablet menu shown in **Figure 22-10.**

### MENU1.MNU

| | | |
|---|---|---|
| ***BUTTONS | [B-9]^C^Clist | ***TABLET3 |
| ; | [B-10]^C^Cqtext | [D-10]\ |
| 'REDRAW | [B-11]'redraw | [D-11]\ |
| ^C | [C-1]^C^Cdim;status | [E-10] $i=3dobjects $l=* |
| ^B | [C-2]^C^Cdim;rotated | [E-11]^C^C3dface |
| ^O | [C-3]^C^Cdim;undo | [F-10]^C^Celev |
| ^G | [C-4]^C^Csolid | [F-11]^C^Cvpoint;; |
| ^D | [C-5]^C^Csketch | [G-10]^C^Cellipse;i |
| ^E | [C-6]^C^Chatch | [G-11]^C^Chide |
| ^T | [C-7]^C^Cdtext | [H-10]^C^Csnap;s;i;.5 |
| | [C-8]^C^C; | [H-11]^C^Csnap;s;i;.25 |
| | [C-9]^C^Cmenu;acad | [I-10]^C^Csnap;s;i;; |
| | [C-10]^C^Cmenu;acad | [I-11]^E |
| | [C-11]^C^Cmenu;acad | |
| | | ***TABLET2 |
| ***TABLET1 | ***TABLET2 | [J-1]^C^Cerase |
| | [D-1]^C^Cdim;diameter | [J-2]^C^Cmove |
| | [D-2]^C^Cdim;radius | [J-3]^C^Cfillet |
| [A–1]^C^Cdim;horiz | | [J-4]^C^Ctrim |
| [A-2]^C^Cdim;vert | | [J-5]^C^Cpedit |
| [A-3]^C^Cdim;angular | [D-3]^C^Cdim;center | [J-6]^C^Cbreak |
| [A-4]^C^Cline | [E-1]^C^Cdim;newtext | [J-7]^C^Cexplode |
| [A-5]^C^Cpline | [E-2]^C^Cdim;update | [J-8]^C^Crotate |
| [A-6]^C^Cpolygon | [E-3]exit | [J-9]^C^Cscale |
| [A-7]^C^Cpoint | [F-1]^C^Cdim;style | [J-10]^C^Cdivide |
| [A-8]^C^Clayer | [F-2]^C^Cdim;style | [J-11]^C^Carray |
| [A-9]^C^Cstatus | [F-3]exit | [K-1]^C^Cchange |
| [A-10]^C^Cregen | [G-1]\ | [K-2]^C^Ccopy |
| [A-11]'redraw | [G-2]\ | [K-3]^C^Cchamfer |
| [B-1]^C^Cdim;continue | [G-3]\ | [K-4]^C^Cextend |
| [B-2]^C^Cdim;baseline | [H-1]'zoom;w | [K-5]single |
| [B-3]^C^Cdim;leader | [H-2]'oom;p | [K-6]all |
| [B-4]^C^Carc | [H-3]'pan | [K-7]last |
| [B-5]^C^Ccircle | [I-1]'zoom;a | [K-8]^C^Cmirror |
| [B-6]^C^Cellipse | [I-2]'zoom;d | [K-9]^C^Cstretch |
| [B-7]^C^Cdonut | [I-3]^C^Cview | [K-10]^C^Cmeasure |
| [B-8]^C^C; | | [K-11]^C^Coffset |

### PROFESSIONAL TIP

The name of the particular menu you use to construct a drawing is saved in the drawing file. If you use different menus, be sure that they are in the same directory as the drawings, or use the proper path when loading the menu. This path is saved with the drawing file. If AutoCAD cannot find a menu, the following message appears (if the **FILEDIA** system variable is set to 0).

Menu load failed. File not found: menu1.mnu

At this time, you can reissue the **MENU** command and enter the proper path to the menu, or enter the name of another menu.

The configuration routine prompts for the number of tablet menus. The MENU1 template requires four. You are then asked if you want to realign the tablet menu areas. Enter Y (Yes). Now, digitize the upper-left, lower-left, and lower-right corners of each of the four tablet menu areas. When prompted, provide the number of columns and rows in each area. The corners of the MENU1 tablet menu are shown in **Figure 22-12.** The number of columns and rows in each area also appears in the

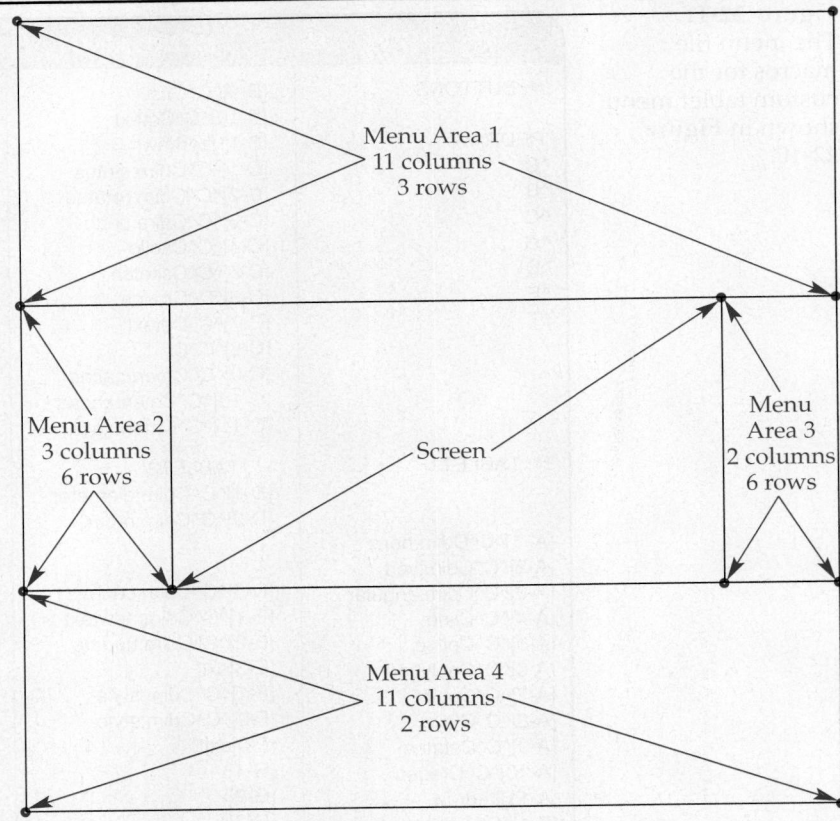

**Figure 22-12.**
Digitize the corners of the MENU1 tablet menu areas as indicated here. Complete the configuration process by picking the lower-left and upper-right corners of the screen pointing area.

Menu Area 1
11 columns
3 rows

Menu Area 2
3 columns
6 rows

Screen

Menu
Area 3
2 columns
6 rows

Menu Area 4
11 columns
2 rows

figure. The final prompt in the configuration process asks you to specify the lower-left and upper-right corners of the screen pointing area. Refer to **Figure 22-12.**

Test all of the menu items to be sure they function properly. Correct any mistakes you find. You may encounter one shortcoming if you select the **ACAD MENU** item in Menu Area 1. The AutoCAD menu will be loaded, but how do you return to the MENU1 tablet menu? There must be a call, or item in the AutoCAD menu, that loads the MENU1 tablet menu. Load the acad.mnu file into your text editor and add the following line to the **S menu, or to a pull-down menu. If you insert this entry between two existing items, do not press [Enter]. Otherwise, you will insert a blank line into the menu.

[MENU1]^C^Cmenu;menu1

## Automating the Menu Editing Process

Modifying screen or tablet menus requires opening the text editor on a regular basis. This can become tedious. The process can be automated if you create a menu macro that opens the text editor and loads the MNU file. If you are using the Notepad text editor, add the following item to your menu.

[EDITMENU]^C^CNOTEPAD;menu1.mnu;

When picked, this item cancels the current command and executes the **NOTEPAD** command to access the text editor. The file name of the menu is entered automatically.

If you use a text editor other than Notepad, just substitute its name in place of Notepad. For example, suppose an application named TextPad is used. The following entry could be placed in the screen menu section of the menu file.

[EDITMENU]^C^CTEXTPAD;menu1.mnu;

The **TEXTPAD** command will not work unless you have altered the acad.pgp file, which is discussed in Chapter 27 of *AutoCAD and its Applications—Basics.* To continue, add the following line to the acad.pgp file.

Textpad, Start txtpad32, 0,*File to edit:,

Be sure the information in the second entry, shown above as txtpad32, is the proper name of your text editor's executable file. In this case, txtpad32.exe is the file name used for the TextPad program.

> **PROFESSIONAL TIP**
>
> When creating screen or tablet menus, create small sections at a time and test them. When satisfied with their performance, add the menu items to your main menu file. In this way, you can build a large menu over time.

## Tablet Menu Tips

Tablet menus can be as simple or as complex as you want, and can contain just about any function you need. As you experiment with helpful commands and options, think of the problems you face when drawing. Design AutoCAD macros to solve problems and eliminate tedious tasks. Add them to your menu. Keep in mind the following guidelines.

✓ Use tablet menu picks to call button, screen, and image tile menus.
✓ Use tablet menu picks to call other tablet menus.
✓ Use a tablet menu pick that inserts a group of blocks from a prototype drawing into the current drawing. If the prototype drawing name is elec001, the menu macro should look like:

   ^C^C–insert;elec001;^C

This inserts only the blocks and other named objects in the file, not the actual drawing on screen.

✓ Use tablet menu picks to display help screens and frequently used slides.
✓ Plot menu overlays on heavy polyester film for durability.
✓ Be sure your template does not extend beyond the active area of your tablet.
✓ When customizing Menu Area 1 of the AutoCAD tablet menu, change the number of selection boxes to any number you need. Draw a new overlay containing the revised boxes. When configuring the customized tablet menu, be sure to use the **Config** option (not **Reconfig**) from the **Tablet:** screen menu. Enter the revised number of columns and rows.
✓ Any portion of the AutoCAD tablet menu can be changed to suit your needs. Just alter the part of the acad.mnu file that you wish to change.
✓ When customizing the acad.mnu file, always work with a copy, not the original file.
✓ If you work at a computer that other people use, restore the original tablet and menu configuration for the next user.
✓ Build your tablet menu in small pieces as you work.

## Chapter Test

*Answer the following questions on a separate sheet of paper.*

1. How many menu areas are on the standard AutoCAD tablet menu template?
2. Provide the command and option entries that allow you to initially set up the AutoCAD tablet menu template.
   A. Command: _____
   B. Enter an option [ON/OFF/CAL/CFG]: _____
3. List the number of columns and rows found in each of the four menu areas in the AutoCAD tablet menu.
4. If you are using the **Tablet:** screen menu, which option allows you to quickly set up the AutoCAD tablet menu without entering the number of rows and columns?
5. How many selection boxes are provided in Menu Area 1 of the AutoCAD tablet menu?
6. Identify the first step used to customize the AutoCAD tablet menu.
7. Describe how the Menu Area 1 selection boxes are numbered in the acad.mnu file.
8. Which command is used to load a menu file?
9. Which commands should you automate first when designing a screen or tablet menu?
10. What file extension does AutoCAD use for the compiled version of the menu file?
11. How can you automate the process of loading a text editor and a menu file for editing purposes?
12. Provide the tablet menu macro that will insert the blocks in a prototype drawing named pipe1 without inserting the actual drawing on screen. A single pick should execute the menu function.

## Drawing Problems

1. Add ten new commands to Menu Area 1 of the AutoCAD tablet menu template. Follow these guidelines:
   A. Place the commands along the bottom row (I) of the menu area. They should occupy selection boxes I-1 through I-10.
   B. Plot a drawing of the Menu Area 1 grid and sketch the commands in the selection boxes. Sketch graphic symbols to represent the commands.
   C. Draw the command symbols and save them as blocks in AutoCAD. Place the command text and symbols in the Menu Area 1 drawing.
   D. Plot a final copy of the overlay on vellum or polyester film.
   E. Make a copy of the acad.mnu file and write the macros for the new commands.

2. Create an overlay for Menu Area 1 of the AutoCAD tablet menu using graphic symbols for one of the following drafting disciplines.
   - Architectural
   - Structural
   - HVAC
   - Mechanical
   - Industrial piping
   - Electrical
   - Electronics
   A. Use existing blocks or symbols that you have on file, or create new ones.
   B. Provide a tablet menu pick that allows you to insert all symbols of a prototype drawing file into a drawing without inserting the actual drawing on screen.
   C. Provide a tablet menu pick that calls the AutoCAD menu file.

3. Redesign Menu Area 1 of the AutoCAD tablet menu so that it contains a complete selection of dimensioning commands, options, and settings. Follow these guidelines: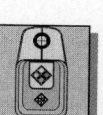
   A. Use the standard configuration of 225 selection boxes or change the configuration to suit your personal requirements.
   B. Draw graphic symbols representing the various dimensioning commands in the related selection boxes.
   C. Plot a menu overlay on vellum or polyester film that can be slipped under the AutoCAD tablet menu template.

4. Design a custom tablet menu that occupies only the lower half of your digitizer tablet. Follow these guidelines:
   A. Design the menu so that it contains a screen pointing area and two menu areas.
   B. Sketch graphic symbols that represent frequently used commands and design an area for special commands that you have created.
   C. Make a drawing of the new tablet menu and plot it on vellum or polyester film. Plot the overlay as a mirror image of the original, as discussed in this chapter.

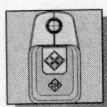

5. Design a new tablet menu that occupies the entire active area of your digitizer tablet. Follow these guidelines:
   A. Provide four menu areas and a screen pointing area.
   B. Provide access to the AutoCAD tablet menu.
   C. Include an area for custom commands you have created, plus an area for drawing symbols saved as blocks or separate files. Allow the user to change the symbols area of the menu to use a different set of drawing symbols.
   D. Draw an overlay for the new tablet menu. Draw two separate, smaller overlays for the two sets of drawing symbols.
   E. Draw graphic symbols to represent the commands and place them in the menu overlay.
   F. Insert scaled-down copies of the blocks into the symbol overlays of the menu.
   G. Plot test copies of the tablet menu and the two symbol overlays and use them for several days.
   H. Plot final copies of the template and symbol overlays on vellum or polyester film. Plot them as mirror images of the originals, as discussed in this chapter.

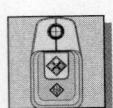

6. Design a custom tablet menu for a specific drafting discipline, such as electronics, piping, or mapping. Follow these guidelines:
   A. Create as many menu areas as you need, up to four.
   B. Provide space for a complete selection of drawing symbols. The symbols should reflect the field of drafting for which you are designing the menu.
   C. Include only the commands that you will use often for the selected discipline.
   D. Provide the ability to load a variety of prototype drawings from the tablet menu.
   E. Create menu selections that allow you to do the following.
      • Edit a file using your text editor or word processor.
      • Edit the menu file that you design for this problem.
   F. Plot the tablet menu template on vellum or film using the mirroring technique discussed in this chapter.

AutoCAD and its Applications—Advanced

## CHAPTER 23

# Introduction to AutoLISP

## Learning Objectives

After completing this chapter, you will be able to:
● Locate, load, and run existing AutoLISP programs.
● Use basic AutoLISP functions at the command line.
● Define new AutoCAD commands.
● Write AutoLISP programs using the **Visual LISP** editor.

## What Is AutoLISP?

*AutoLISP* is a derivative, or dialect, of the LISP programming language. *LISP,* which is an acronym for *list processing,* is a high-level computer programming language used in artificial intelligence (AI) systems. In this reference, the term *high-level* does not mean *complex,* rather it means *powerful.* As a matter of fact, many AutoCAD users refer to AutoLISP as the "nonprogrammer's language" because it is easy to understand.

AutoLISP is specially designed by Autodesk to work with AutoCAD. It is a flexible language that allows the programmer to create custom commands and functions that can greatly increase productivity and drawing efficiency.

Knowing the basics of AutoLISP gives you a better understanding of how AutoCAD works. By learning just a few simple functions, you can create new commands that make a significant difference in your daily productivity. Read through this chapter slowly while you are at a computer. Type all of the examples and exercises as you read them. This is the best way to get a feel for AutoLISP. An excellent resource for learning AutoLISP is *AutoLISP Programming* published by The Goodheart-Willcox Company, Inc.

### AutoLISP and AutoCAD

AutoLISP can be used in several ways. It is a built-in feature of AutoCAD and is therefore available at the Command: prompt. When AutoLISP commands and functions are issued inside parentheses on the command line, the AutoLISP interpreter automatically evaluates the entry and carries out the specified tasks. AutoLISP functions can be incorporated into the AutoCAD menu as toolbar buttons, screen menu items, and tablet menu picks. AutoLISP command and function definitions can be saved in a file and then loaded into AutoCAD when needed. Items that are used frequently can be placed in the acad2004.lsp file, which is automatically loaded for the first drawing when AutoCAD starts. The acad2004doc.lsp file should contain functions that are to be available in all concurrent drawings during a session.

AutoCAD also provides a special editing method called *Visual LISP.* Visual LISP and the **Visual LISP** editor offer powerful features designed specifically for writing and editing AutoLISP programs.

The benefits of using AutoLISP are endless. A person with a basic understanding of AutoLISP can create new commands and functions to automate many routine tasks. After working through this chapter, you will be able to add greater capabilities to your screen, tablet, and toolbar menu macros. You can also enter simple AutoLISP expressions at the Command: prompt. More experienced programmers can create powerful programs that quickly complete very complex design requirements. Examples of possible new functions that might be designed using AutoLISP include:

- Automatic line breaks when inserting schematic symbols.
- Automatic creation of shapes with associated text objects.
- Parametric design applications that create geometry based on numeric entry.

---

 **NOTE** For additional information on using AutoLISP, refer to the Visual LISP, AutoLISP, and DXF book located in the Contents tab of the online help documentation.

---

## AutoLISP Basics

As stated earlier, LISP stands for *list processing,* which indicates that AutoLISP processes lists. In the LISP language, a list can be defined as any number of data enclosed in parentheses. Each item in a list must be separated from other items by a space.

When any entry is made at the Command: prompt, it is checked to see if the first character is a parenthesis. The opening parenthesis tells AutoCAD that an AutoLISP expression is being entered. AutoCAD then sends the expression to the AutoLISP interpreter for evaluation. The initial input can be supplied as direct keyboard entry or even a menu macro. The format for an AutoLISP expression, called *syntax,* is:

    (FunctionName AnyRequiredData...)

The first item in the AutoLISP expression is a function name. Some functions require additional information. For example, the addition function requires numeric data:

    Command: (+ 2 4)↵
    6
    Command:

Any required data for a function is called an *argument.* Some functions use no arguments; others may require one or more. When entering an AutoLISP expression, it is important to *close* it using a closing parenthesis prior to pressing [Enter]. When you press [Enter], the AutoLISP interpreter checks to see that the number of opening and closing parentheses match. If they do not, you are prompted:

    Command: (+ 2 4↵
    (_>

The (_> indicates that you are missing one closing parenthesis. In this example, all that is necessary is to enter the single missing parenthesis and the function is complete.

```
(_> )↵
6
Command:
```

When the AutoLISP interpreter evaluates an AutoLISP expression, it *returns* a value. An expression entered at the Command: prompt instructs the system to return its value to the command line, such as 6 in the previous example. If a different prompt is active, the returned value is used as input for that prompt. For example, this next sequence uses the result of adding two numbers as the input at the Specify radius of circle or [Diameter]: prompt. Checking the **CIRCLERAD** system variable verifies that the value returned by AutoLISP was in fact applied to the circle radius.

```
Command: C or CIRCLE↵
Specify center point for circle or [3P/2P/Ttr (tan tan radius)]: (pick a point)
Specify radius of circle or [Diameter]: (+ 14.25 3.0)↵
Command: CIRCLERAD↵
Enter new value for CIRCLERAD <17.2500>: ↵
```

## Basic AutoLISP Functions

The best way to get started learning AutoLISP is to enter a few functions at the command line and see what they do. The following discussion includes basic AutoLISP functions that are part of the foundation for all AutoLISP programs. Practice using the functions as you read. Then, begin using them in menus and macros. At first, these functions and expressions will be entered at the command line. Later in this chapter, and in Chapter 24, you will learn about creating and using AutoLISP program files.

### AutoLISP Math Functions

AutoLISP provides many different mathematical operators for performing calculations. All real number calculations in AutoLISP are accurate to 15 decimal places. AutoLISP distinguishes between real numbers and integers, handling each data type differently. *Real numbers* are numbers with a decimal point, such as 1.25, 7.0, and –0.438. *Integers* are whole numbers without a decimal point, such as 3, 91, and –115. If a mathematical expression has only integer arguments, the result is returned as an integer. If at least one real number is used, the result is returned as a real number. The following symbols are used for the four basic math functions.

| Symbol | Function |
|--------|----------|
| + | Addition; returns the sum of all the supplied number arguments. |
| – | Subtraction; subtracts the sum of the second through the last number from the first number and returns the result. |
| * | Multiplication; returns the product of all the supplied number arguments. |
| / | Division; divides the first number by the product of the second through the last numbers. |

*Real numbers* are technically defined as those that have no imaginary part. They include integers and fractions, as well as decimal numbers. In applications involving AutoLISP, and throughout this discussion, real numbers are classified as those that always have a decimal part.

The following examples illustrate AutoLISP math expressions entered at the Command: prompt. As you practice entering these expressions, use the following procedure.

1. Start with an open parenthesis.
2. Separate each item in the expression with a space.
3. Close the expression with a closing parenthesis.

Using these steps, enter the following expressions at the Command: prompt. If you get lost at any time or do not return to the Command: prompt when expected, press the [Esc] key to cancel the AutoLISP entry.

```
Command: (+ 6 2)↵
8
Command: (+ 6.0 2)↵
8.0
Command: (– 15 9)↵
6
Command: (* 4 6)↵
24
Command: (/ 12 3)↵
4
Command: (/ 12 3.2)↵
3.75
Command: (/ 19 10)↵
1
```

An "incorrect" answer is returned in the last example. The result of dividing 19 by 10 is 1.9. When only integers are supplied as arguments, the result is returned as an integer. If the result is rounded, it rounds to 2. However, the result returned is simply the integer portion of the actual answer. The result is not rounded, it is truncated. To get the correct result in division expressions such as the one above, specify at least one of the arguments as a real number.

```
Command: (/ 19.0 10)↵
1.9
```

When entering real numbers between 1 and –1, you must include the leading zero. If the zero is not entered, you will get an error message:

```
Command: (+ .5 16)↵
; error: misplaced dot on input
Command:
```

The correct entry is:

```
Command: (+ 0.5 16)↵
16.5
```

○ Solve the following equations by using AutoLISP functions at the Command: prompt. Write down the expression you use for each equation and your answers on a separate sheet of paper.
- ○ 57 + 12
- ○ 86.4 + 16
- ○ 24 + 12 + 8 + 35
- ○ 8 – 3
- ○ 29 – 17
- ○ 89.16 – 14.6
- ○ 8 × 4
- ○ 16 × 5 × 35
- ○ 7.3 × 22
- ○ 45 ÷ 9
- ○ 60 ÷ 2
- ○ 76 ÷ 27.3

## Nested Expressions

The term *nested* refers to an expression that is used as part of another expression. For example, to add 15 to the product of 3.75 and 2.125, you can nest the multiplication expression in the AutoLISP addition expression. Notice the two closing parentheses:

```
Command: (+ 15 (* 3.75 2.125)).↵
22.9688
```

Nested expressions are evaluated from the deepest nested level outward. In the previous expression, the multiplication operation is evaluated first, and the result is applied to the addition operation. Here are some examples of nested expressions:

```
Command: (+ 24 (* 5 4)).↵
44
Command: (* 12 (/ 60 20)).↵
36
Command: (/ 39 (* 1.6 11)).↵
2.21591
```

## Significant Digits

AutoLISP performs all mathematical calculations to 15 decimal places, but only displays six significant digits. For example, take a close look at this expression:

```
Command: (+ 15 (* 3.75 2.125)).↵
22.9688
```

The actual result is 22.96875, but AutoLISP displays only six significant digits at the command line and rounds the number for display only. This is true for large and small numbers alike. The next example shows how AutoLISP uses exponential notation to display larger numbers using only six digits:

```
Command: (* 1000 1575.25).↵
1.57525e+006
```

This final example uses a numeric printing function set to show eight decimal places in order to indicate that the number is not actually rounded and that no precision is lost:

```
Command: (RTOS (+ 15 (* 3.75 2.125)) 2 8).↵
"22.96875000"
```

## Variables

All programming languages make use of *variables* to temporarily store information. The variable name can be used in another expression anywhere in the program. When AutoLISP encounters a variable in an expression, it uses the value of the variable to evaluate the expression. An AutoLISP variable name cannot be made up of numeric characters only, nor can it contain any of the following characters.

- ✓ Open parenthesis (()
- ✓ Close parenthesis ())
- ✓ Period (.)
- ✓ Apostrophe (')
- ✓ Quotation marks ("")
- ✓ Semicolon (;)

The **SETQ** AutoLISP function is used to set variable values. A **SETQ** expression requires a variable name and value as arguments. The following example shows an expression that creates a variable named A and assigns it a value of 5.

Command: **(SETQ A 5)**↵
5

If you try to use an illegal variable name, an error message is returned. The following example tries to create a variable named 2 with an assigned value of 7. Since 2 is not a valid variable name, an error message is returned.

Command: **(SETQ 2 7)**↵
; error: syntax error

Once a variable name has been assigned, it can be used in subsequent AutoLISP expressions, or even accessed directly at the command line. To access a variable value at the command line, precede the variable name with an exclamation mark (!). For example:

Command: **C** *or* **CIRCLE**↵
Specify center point for circle or [3P/2P/Ttr (tan tan radius)]: *(pick a point)*
Specify radius of circle or [Diameter] <17.2500>: **!A**↵
5
Command:

To use the value of a variable in any expression, simply include the variable in the appropriate location. The following sequence sets and uses a series of variables.

```
Command: (SETQ A 5)↵
5
Command: (SETQ B (– A 1))↵
4
Command: (SETQ C (– A B))↵
1
Command: (SETQ D (* (+ A B) 2))↵
18
```

Look closely at the example illustrated in **Figure 23-1**. Find the three separate expressions inside parentheses. AutoLISP evaluates Expression 3 first. The result is applied to Expression 2, which is then evaluated. The result of Expression 2 is applied to 1. The final evaluation determines the value of Variable D.

**Figure 23-1.**
Each AutoLISP expression must be enclosed with parentheses. In this evaluation of Variable D, Expression 3 is evaluated first, then Expression 2, and finally Expression 1.

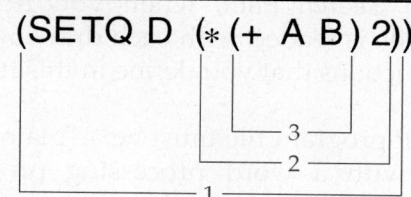

**PROFESSIONAL TIP**

When working at the command line with AutoLISP, use AutoCAD's command line editing features to your best advantage. Remember that you can use the up and down arrow keys to display previously entered lines of code. Additionally, you can use the left and right arrow keys to position the cursor to delete or insert text within a line.

**Exercise 23-3**

○ Using a separate sheet of paper, write AutoLISP expressions for the following variables in the proper format. After writing each expression, enter it into the computer to test your solution.
  A.  Assign the value of 4 to the variable ONE.
  B.  Assign the value of 3 + 2 to the variable TWO.
  C.  Assign the value of ONE + TWO to the variable THREE.
  D.  Assign the value of THREE + (TWO – ONE) to the variable FOUR.

# AutoLISP Program Files

Entering AutoLISP expressions at the command line is suitable for applications that are simple or unique. However, when more complex expressions are required or when the expressions you are using may be needed again, it is best to save them in an AutoLISP program file. This can be easily accomplished using the **Visual LISP** editor provided with AutoCAD. AutoLISP programs can be more effectively developed using the **Visual LISP** editor. Creating AutoLISP program files is discussed in the following sections.

A very common feature found in most AutoLISP programs is a function definition. A *function definition* is a collection of AutoLISP code that performs any number of tasks. The function is assigned a name that is used to activate it. Some function definitions create new AutoCAD command names that can be entered at the command line.

Once written and saved, an AutoLISP program can be loaded and used whenever it is needed. AutoCAD automatically loads the acad2004.lsp file, if it is located in the Support File Search Path, when you first begin a drawing session. The acad2004doc.lsp file is loaded with each drawing that is opened. Any new AutoLISP commands or functions that you define in this file will be available in every drawing during a session.

An AutoLISP program file must be a "plain" text file. If you choose to edit your AutoLISP files with a word processing program such as Microsoft Word or WordPerfect, be sure to save the files as text only. Word processing files use special codes that AutoLISP cannot understand. It is recommended that you use the **Visual LISP** editor, because it has tools specifically designed for use in writing and editing AutoLISP programs.

# Introduction to the Visual LISP Editor

The **Visual LISP** editor provides powerful editing features. The editor is an *interactive development environment* (IDE) that features AutoLISP development tools not available in standard text editing programs. The **Visual LISP** editor is an application containing many powerful tools and features. The interactive nature of the **Visual LISP** editor simplifies the task of creating AutoLISP program files. This section provides only a brief introduction to Visual LISP. For a more detailed discussion of the features and applications of Visual LISP, refer to AutoCAD's online documentation.

VLISP
VLIDE

Tools
➥ AutoLISP
  ➥ Visual LISP
    Editor

Open the **Visual LISP** editor by picking **Visual LISP Editor** from the **AutoLISP** cascading menu in the **Tools** pull-down menu or by entering VLISP or VLIDE at the Command: prompt. When the **Visual LISP** editor is first displayed, it appears as shown in **Figure 23-2**. The windows within the editor can be minimized or maximized, and the editor itself can be temporarily closed to return to AutoCAD as necessary.

To create a new AutoLISP program using the **Visual LISP** editor, pick the **New file** button or select **New File** from the **File** pull-down menu. This opens a window for an untitled document on the **Visual LISP** editor desktop. See **Figure 23-3**. The windows and features in the **Visual LISP** editor are:

- **Desktop.** This is the main area of the editor window. It is similar to the main program window in AutoCAD and can be used to relocate toolbars or windowed components, such as the **Visual LISP Console** or a text editor window.
- **Text editor window.** Text editor windows are used to write and edit AutoLISP programs. Different windows can be used to create new files or view existing programs. The **Visual LISP** editor provides interactive feedback as you enter material to help you avoid errors.

**Figure 23-2.**

The primary features of the **Visual LISP** editor.

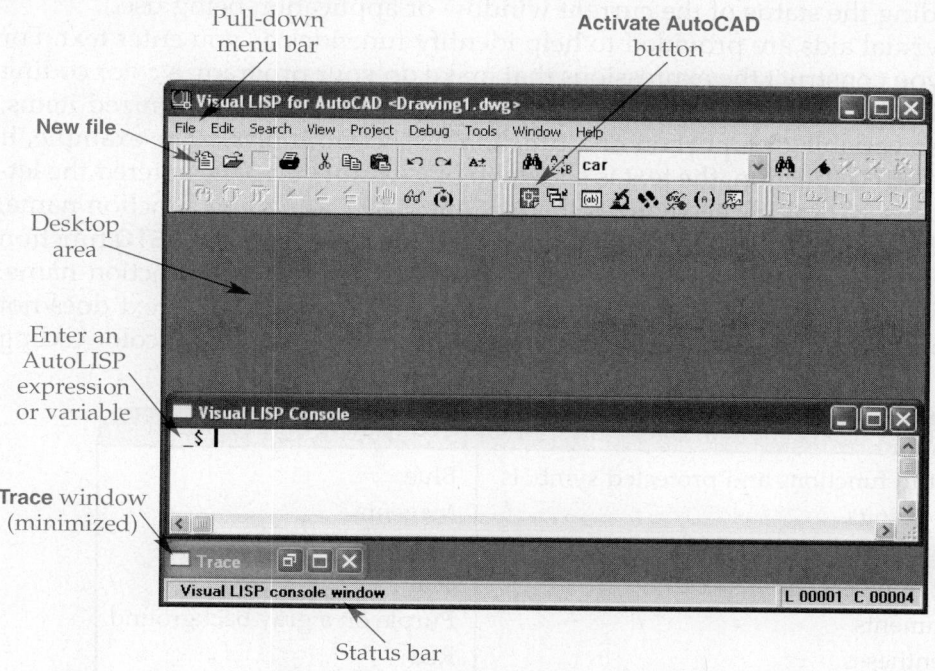

**Figure 23-3.**

Picking the **New file** button or selecting **New File** from the **File** pull-down menu displays a text editor window in the **Visual LISP** editor.

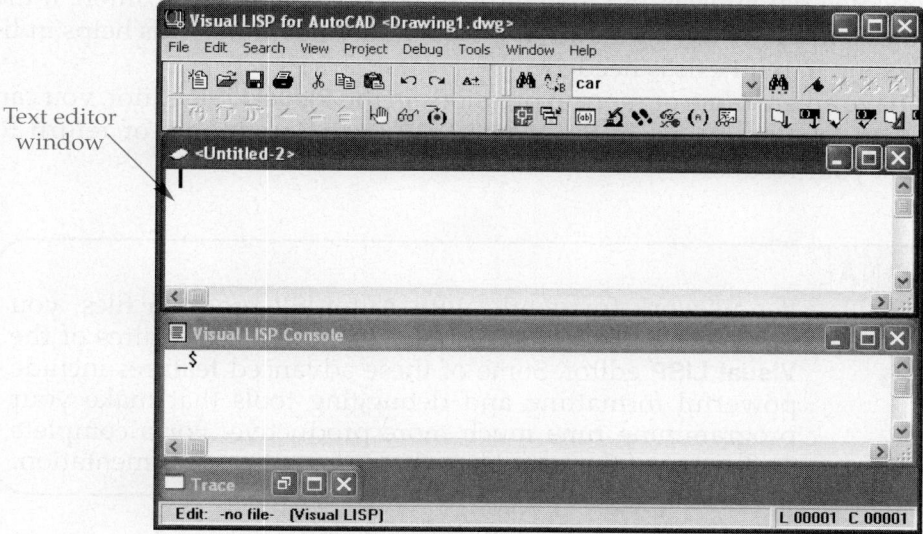

- **Visual LISP Console window.** This window provides several functions. You can use it to enter any AutoLISP expression to immediately see the results, or you can enter any AutoLISP variable to determine its value. You can also enter Visual LISP commands from this window, and copy the text from the window to a text editor window.
- **Trace window.** This window is minimized when you first display the **Visual LISP** editor. It records a history of the functions within your program and can be used to trace values when developing or debugging a program.

- **Status bar.** This area at the bottom of the **Visual LISP** editor is similar to the status bar in AutoCAD's main program window. It provides feedback regarding the status of the current window or application being used.

Several visual aids are provided to help identify functions as you enter text. For example, as you construct the expressions that make up your program, a color coding system provides immediate feedback as you type. Text for any unrecognized items, such as a user variable or a portion of a function, is shown in black. For example, if you enter the **SETQ** function, the text is shown in black until you have entered the letters SET. Because AutoLISP recognizes the text entry SET as a valid function name, the color of the text is changed to blue. When you have entered the full **SETQ** function name, the text remains blue because AutoLISP also recognizes this function name. This can be very useful, because if you enter a function name and the text does not turn blue, you know that you have made an incorrect entry. The default color coding system used in the **Visual LISP** editor appears in the following chart.

| AutoLISP Text Elements | Associated Color |
|---|---|
| Built-in functions and protected symbols | Blue |
| Text strings | Magenta |
| Integers | Green |
| Real numbers | Teal |
| Comments | Purple on a gray background |
| Parentheses | Red |
| Unrecognized items | Black |

Another valuable visual aid provided by the **Visual LISP** editor is instant parenthesis matching. When you enter a closing parenthesis in an expression, the cursor jumps to the opening parenthesis and then returns back to the current position. If the closing parenthesis does not have a match, the cursor does not jump. This helps indicate that a matching parenthesis is needed.

Once you have entered one or more expressions in the **Visual LISP** editor, you can save the file, then test the results in the **Visual LISP Console** window or return to AutoCAD to test your results.

---

**PROFESSIONAL TIP**

If you work frequently with AutoLISP program files, you may wish to learn more about the advanced features of the **Visual LISP** editor. Some of these advanced features include powerful formatting and debugging tools that make your programming time much more productive. For a complete discussion of these topics, refer to the online documentation.

---

# Defining New AutoCAD Commands

In this section, you will use several of the built-in AutoLISP functions to create a new AutoCAD command. The **DEFUN** (define function) function is used for this. The syntax for this function is:

```
(DEFUN FunctionName (ArgumentList)
  (Expression)...
)
```

The function name can be any alphanumeric name and is subject to the same conditions used for any variable name assigned with the **SETQ** function. If you prefix the function name with C:, the name can be entered at the Command: prompt.

You must include an argument list in every function definition, even if it is empty. The argument list is used to declare local variables and, in more advanced applications, to indicate which arguments are required by a function. For many applications, the argument list is simply left empty.

Any number of expressions can be included in a function definition. All of the expressions contained in the definition are evaluated when the function name is called.

A very powerful, yet simple, application for a function definition is to create a shortcut command similar to one of the command aliases in the acad.pgp file. However, a shortcut command defined using AutoLISP can specify command options and even multiple commands to use. Remember that the command aliases defined in the acad.pgp file can only start a single command; they cannot specify any command options.

This first example shows the definition for a new function named **ZX**. The function issues the **ZOOM** command and performs the **Previous** option.

```
(DEFUN C:ZX ()
  (COMMAND "ZOOM" "PREVIOUS")
)
```

To see this function work, enter the definition at the command line as:

Command: **(DEFUN C:ZX () (COMMAND "ZOOM" "PREVIOUS"))**↵
C:ZX

Notice that the new function name is returned by the **DEFUN** expression. The C: prefix indicates that it can be entered at the Command: prompt.

Command: **ZX**↵
Command: nil
Command:

When activated, defined functions return the value of the last expression evaluated in the definition. Since the **COMMAND** function always returns a value of "nil," this is also returned when using the **ZX** function. The "nil" value has no effect. You can suppress it if you do not want it to appear each time you use a defined function. To suppress the value, add the **PRINC** function using no arguments to the end of the definition:

```
(DEFUN C:ZX ()
  (COMMAND "ZOOM" "PREVIOUS")
  (PRINC)
)
```

Entering a function definition at the Command: prompt is an inconvenient way to define custom functions. By storing such definitions in a text file, they can be loaded whenever needed.

## Creating Your First AutoLISP Program

As discussed earlier, a typical use for an AutoLISP program file is to hold function definitions. An AutoLISP program file can contain a single function, or it can contain several.

Many AutoLISP programs are created to perform a single specific task. Other AutoLISP programs hold a large number of function definitions, all of which become available when the program file is loaded. One common application for the acad2004doc.lsp file is to create a series of function definitions for shortcut commands used to speed up routine drafting tasks.

### Writing the Program

To create your first AutoLISP program, open the **Visual LISP** editor or another text editing application. Begin by entering two function definitions into the program. The first is the **ZX** function from the previous example. The second defines a command named **FC** (fillet corner) that sets the fillet radius to 0 and allows the **FILLET** command to continue.

```
(DEFUN C:ZX ()
    (COMMAND "ZOOM" "PREVIOUS")
    (PRINC)
)

(DEFUN C:FC ()
    (COMMAND "FILLET" "R" 0 "FILLET")
    (PRINC)
)
```

When using the **Visual LISP** editor, the final closing parenthesis is not automatically "flush left." You will need to delete the spaces added. It is a good habit to place the final closing parenthesis "flush left" to help keep your program organized.

Adding the appropriate documentation to your program files is recommended. When a semicolon (;) is encountered in a program (except when it is part of a text string), any information to the right of the semicolon is ignored. This enables you to place *comments* and documentation in your AutoLISP programs. The example below shows the appropriate documentation for this program file, called myfirst.lsp.

```
; MyFirst.lsp
; by A. Novice
;C:ZX – To key ZOOM Previous command
(DEFUN C:ZX ()
    (COMMAND "ZOOM" "PREVIOUS")
```

*(Continued on the next page)*

```
        (PRINC)
    )

    ;C:FC – Fillet Corner, Sets fillet radius to 0 and allows FILLET command to continue.
    (DEFUN C:FC ()
        (COMMAND "FILLET" "R" 0 "FILLET")
        (PRINC)
    )
```

After entering these functions and comments into the new LISP program, save the file as myfirst.lsp in the AutoCAD Support folder.

## Loading the Program

The **APPLOAD** command is used to load applications, such as AutoLISP program files, into AutoCAD. To use this command, pick **Load...** from the **AutoLISP** cascading menu in the **Tools** pull-down menu or enter AP or APPLOAD at the Command: prompt. The **Load/Unload Applications** dialog box appears, **Figure 23-4**.

A list of currently loaded applications appears in the **Loaded Applications** tab. To load an application file, select it in the file selection window near the top of the dialog box. You can highlight any number of files in the file list. Picking the **Load** button loads the currently selected application files. If the **Add to History** check box is activated, the loaded file will be added to the list in the **History list** tab. This tab provides convenient access to saved files during subsequent **APPLOAD** sessions, and keeps you from having to search for frequently used files every time they are needed. Picking the **Unload** button removes any highlighted files from the **History list** tab or **Loaded Applications** tab.

You can also load an AutoLISP file by highlighting the file in Windows Explorer and dragging and dropping it into the AutoCAD drawing area. This method is extremely convenient if Windows Explorer is open.

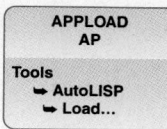

APPLOAD
AP
Tools
  ↳ AutoLISP
    ↳ Load...

**Figure 23-4.**
The **Load/Unload Applications** dialog box is used to load AutoLISP program files into AutoCAD.

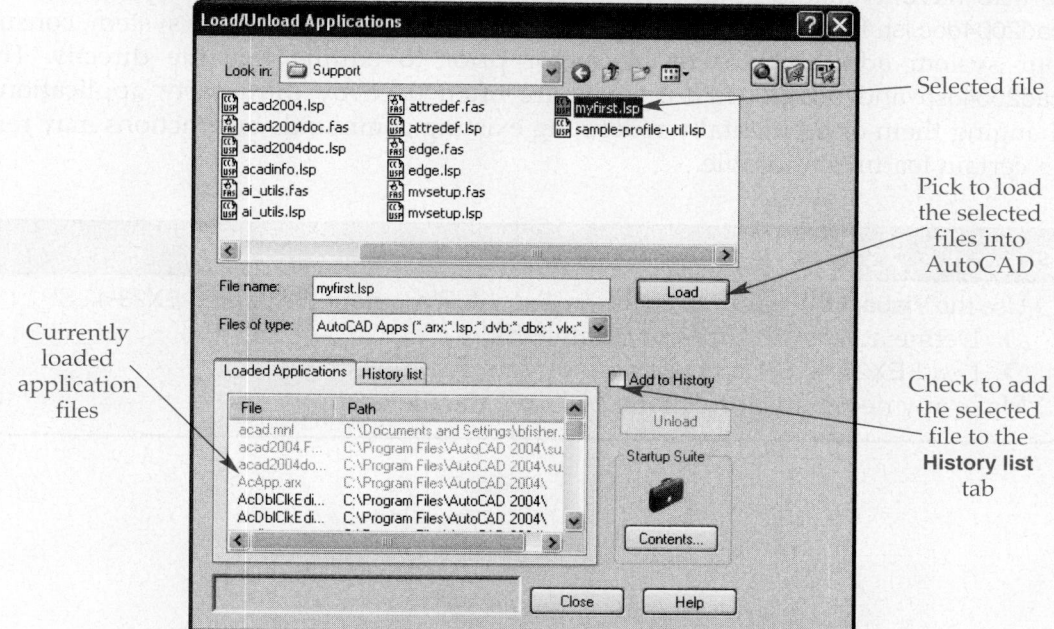

Selected file

Pick to load the selected files into AutoCAD

Check to add the selected file to the **History list** tab

Currently loaded application files

The **LOAD** function allows you to load an AutoLISP program file at the command line. This function requires an AutoLISP file name as its argument and requires that the name be enclosed in quotation marks. To load the myfirst.lsp file using the **LOAD** function, the following sequence is used.

```
Command: (LOAD "MYFIRST").⌐
C:FC
Command:
```

When the file has an LSP file extension, it is not necessary to include the extension in the **LOAD** expression. Therefore, you should use the standard LSP file extension for all AutoLISP files you create. If you are loading an AutoLISP file that does not use an LSP file extension, the actual extension must be included in the file name argument.

When an AutoLISP program file is loaded and no errors are encountered, the result of evaluating the last expression in the file is returned to the screen. In the example above, the last expression in the file is the definition for the **FC** function, so that function name is returned.

The **LOAD** function locates AutoLISP files residing in the Support File Search Path. To load a file that exists elsewhere, the path name must also be specified. In the following example, the myfirst.lsp file is stored in the C:\My Documents\AutoLISP folder.

```
Command: (LOAD "C:/MY DOCUMENTS/AUTOLISP/MYFIRST").⌐
C:FC
```

Notice that backslashes are not used in the path specification. In an AutoLISP text string, the backslash is used to specify special characters. For example, the string \n indicates a new line, or carriage return. When specifying file paths, you can use either forward slashes or double-backslashes (\\). Therefore, in the example above, the file to load could also have been specified as C:\\My Documents\\AutoLISP\\myfirst.

If you frequently load files that are in a folder not found in the Support File Search Path, it may be helpful to include the folder in the path. This is done using the **Options** dialog box. After displaying this dialog box, pick the **Files** tab and select Support File Search Path. Then, pick the **Add...** button and enter the desired folder.

As indicated previously, when you have defined one or more functions that you want to have available in all editing sessions, the definitions can be placed in the acad2004doc.lsp file. If the acad2004doc.lsp file already exists on your system, consult your system administrator or instructor prior to editing this file directly. The acad2004.lsp and acad2004doc.lsp files are often used by third-party applications. Changing them or accidentally redefining existing commands or functions may render certain features unusable.

## Exercise 23-4

○ Use the **Visual LISP** editor to create an AutoLISP program file named EX23-4.LSP.
　○ Define at least 10 shortcut commands.
　○ Load EX23-4.LSP and test each of your functions.
○ Make any necessary corrections and save the file again.

# Creating Specialized Functions

Although shortcut commands are a powerful use for AutoLISP, AutoLISP can also be used to create highly specialized functions. Input can specify how the program should function in any given situation. This aspect of AutoLISP allows you to customize AutoCAD to meet the specific needs of your industry or department.

AutoLISP is a versatile tool, offering many different functions for working effectively with numeric data, text data, data files, and AutoCAD drawing objects. This section introduces several basic AutoLISP functions, including some that are used for acquiring input from the user.

## Providing for User Input

AutoLISP can prompt the user for various types of data. Depending on its function, a program may need numeric input, text input, or specification of a coordinate location. The **GETPOINT** function prompts for a point entry and pauses the program until the point is entered. For example:

Command: **(SETQ PT1 (GETPOINT)).**⏎

After you press [Enter], AutoLISP waits for a value to be input for the PT1 variable. A prompt can be added to the original expression to clarify it as follows.

Command: **(SETQ PT1 (GETPOINT "Enter a point: ")).**⏎
Enter a point:

Now, pick a point on screen. The coordinates for the selected point are assigned to PT1 and displayed at the command line. If you know the coordinates, you can enter them at the keyboard.

The following example shows how closely AutoCAD and AutoLISP work together. First, define the two variables PT1 and PT2 as shown below. Then, enter the **LINE** command and use AutoLISP notation to return the values of PT1 and PT2 as the endpoints of the line.

Command: **(SETQ PT1 (GETPOINT "From point: ")).**⏎
From point: **2,2**⏎
(2.0 2.0 0.0)
Command: **(SETQ PT2 (GETPOINT "To point: ")).**⏎
To point: **6.25,2**⏎
(6.25 2 0)
Command: **LINE**⏎
Specify first point: **!PT1**⏎
(2.0 2.0 0.0)
Specify next point or [Undo]: **!PT2**⏎
(6.25 2.0 0.0)
Specify next point or [Undo]: ⏎

The following is a sample function definition named **1LINE** that uses expressions similar to those given in the previous example. This function will draw a line object based on user input.

```
(DEFUN C:1LINE ()
   (SETQ PNT1 (GETPOINT "From point: "))
   (SETQ PNT2 (GETPOINT "To point: "))
   (COMMAND "LINE" PNT1 PNT2 "")
   (PRINC)
)
```

The pair of quotation marks near the end of the fourth line is equivalent to pressing [Enter] after the second point entry, thus ending the **LINE** command.

When developing AutoLISP routines, you may need to assign the length of a line or the distance between two points to a variable. The **GETDIST** function allows you to assign a distance to a variable. A command line prompt is not added to the following example; the "second point" prompt is automatic.

>Command: **(SETQ LGTH (GETDIST))**↵
>*(pick the first point)*
>Specify second point: *(pick the second point)*
>*distance*

Use object snaps as needed or enter absolute coordinates. After the second point is specified, the distance value is shown and assigned to the variable. In this example, the distance is assigned to the variable LGTH. You can confirm the setting by retrieving the value of the variable.

>Command: **!LGTH**↵
>*distance*

The **DISTANCE** function is similar to the **GETDIST** function. However, the **DISTANCE** function does not require picking two points. Instead, it measures the distance between two *existing* points. This function can be used to display a distance or to assign a distance to a variable.

>Command: **(DISTANCE PT1 PT2)**↵
>*distance between PT1 and PT2*

>Command: **(SETQ D1 (DISTANCE PT1 PT2))**↵
>*distance between PT1 and PT2*

The first example returns the distance between the previously defined points PT1 and PT2. The second example displays the distance and applies it to the variable D1.

---

**PROFESSIONAL TIP**
The sample AutoLISP expressions in this section are entered at the command line. However, AutoLISP expressions are more effective as part of a saved program file.

---

## Exercise 23-5

○ Use the proper AutoLISP code to write expressions for the functions given below. Write the expressions on a separate sheet of paper. Then, test the functions by entering them into the computer.
  A. Assign a point picked on screen to the variable PNT1.
  B. Assign a point picked on screen to the variable PNT2.
  C. Assign the distance between PNT1 and PNT2 to the variable DIS.
  D. Create a function named LINE1 that draws a line between PNT1 and PNT2.
  E. Use the **DISTANCE** function to return the distance between PNT1 and PNT2.

## Assigning Text Values to AutoLISP Applications

Values assigned to AutoLISP variables do not have to be numeric. In some applications, you may need to assign a word or line of text to a variable. To do so, use the **SETQ** function and enclose the word(s) in quotation marks.

> Command: **(SETQ W "What next?")**↵
> "What next?"

You can also assign a word or line of text to a variable with the **GETSTRING** function. This function is similar to the **GETPOINT** function in that the user must enter a value.

> Command: **(SETQ E (GETSTRING))**↵

Nothing is displayed on the command line because the optional prompt was not specified. AutoLISP is waiting for a "string" of characters. You can enter as many characters (numbers and letters) as needed. Once you press [Enter] or the space bar, the string is entered and displayed. To allow spaces in the response, place the letter T, without quotation marks, after the **GETSTRING** function:

> Command: **(SETQ E (GETSTRING T))**↵
> **HI THERE**↵
> "HI THERE"
> Command:

The **PROMPT** function can be used to simply display a message. The resulting message has no variable value. AutoLISP indicates this by printing nil after the prompt.

> Command: **(PROMPT "Select an object:")**↵
> Select an object: nil

You can use prompts in AutoLISP programs to provide information or to prompt the user.

---

**CAUTION**

The symbol T is a built-in AutoLISP constant defined as a *protected symbol*. However, it is possible to change its value using the **SETQ** function. Do *not* change its value. Be certain not to use the variable name T for any of your own variables, or other functions referencing this symbol may not function properly. If it is accidentally changed, you can reset the value of T using the following expression.

Command: **(SETQ T 'T)**

---

### Exercise 23-6

○ Use the proper AutoLISP syntax to write expressions for the functions given below. Write out the expressions on a separate sheet of paper and then test them by entering them into the computer.

A. Assign the word Void to the variable VO.
B. Assign the text Enter text height to the variable TE.
C. Create the variable JP as a point that is picked on the screen. Issue the prompt Pick a point:.
D. Create the variable KP as a point that is picked on the screen, and issue the prompt Pick a point:.
E. Set the distance between points JP and KP to the variable LP.
F. Issue a prompt that says This is only an exercise.

---

Before applying the functions you have learned to an AutoLISP program, take a few minutes to review the following list. These functions are used in the next chapter, which discusses more advanced AutoLISP applications.

- **(+, −, *, /).** These are the basic math functions used in AutoLISP. They must be entered as the first part of an expression. For example: (+ 6 8).
- **(SETQ).** The **SETQ** (set quote) function allows a value to be assigned to a variable. For example, the expression (SETQ CITY "San Francisco") sets the value San Francisco to the variable CITY.
- **(!).** An exclamation point entered before a variable returns the value of the variable. For example, !CITY returns the value San Francisco for the above expression.
- **(GETPOINT).** This function allows you to define a point location by entering coordinates at the keyboard or using the pointing device. The resulting value can be applied to a variable. For example, the expression (SETQ A (GETPOINT)) assigns a point to the variable A.
- **(GETDIST).** This function provides a distance between two points entered at the keyboard or picked on screen. The value can be applied to a variable, and a prompt can be used. For example, the expression (SETQ D2 (GETDIST "Pick two points:")) allows you to determine a distance and assign it to the variable D2.
- **(DISTANCE).** This function returns a distance between two existing points. For example, the expression (DISTANCE P1 P2) returns the distance between the defined points P1 and P2. The distance can also be assigned to a variable. For example: (SETQ D (DISTANCE P1 P2)).
- **(GETSTRING).** This function returns a word or string of characters entered by the user. The resulting text can be assigned to a variable. For example, the expression (GETSTRING) waits for a string of characters and displays the string when [Enter] or the space bar is pressed. Spaces are allowed in the text string if T follows the **GETSTRING** function. For example, the expression (SETQ TXT (GETSTRING T "Enter text:")) assigns the text entered, which can contain spaces, to the variable TXT.
- **(PROMPT).** Messages or prompts can be issued in a program using the **PROMPT** function. For example, the expression (PROMPT "Select an entity:") prints the Select an entity: prompt.

**PROFESSIONAL TIP**

Design your AutoLISP programs to closely resemble the AutoCAD interface. For example, it is easier for the user to read "back-to-back" prompts when the prompts appear on separate lines. Use the \n string to specify a new line for a prompt. For example: (SETQ PT2 (GETPOINT "\nTo point:"))

## Exercise 23-7

○ Write an AutoLISP program that places the text NOTES: at a location that you pick on screen. Name the file EX23-7.LSP.
○ On a separate sheet of paper, write a description of the program in longhand. Then, write out each line of code.
○ Create the program using the **Visual LISP** editor and then test it in AutoCAD.
○ Use the following guidelines when writing the program.
  ○ Provide a comment line giving the author, date, and name of the file.
  ○ Define a function named NOTES with two variables, P1 and TXT.
  ○ Specify the value for the variable P1 as the insertion location of the text. Include a prompt for the user to enter the text location.
  ○ Give the variable TXT the text value NOTES:.
  ○ Write an expression for the **TEXT** command that uses P1 as the text location, enters a text height of 0.25", enters a rotation angle of 0, and uses the value for the variable TXT as the text.

## Chapter Test

*Answer the following questions on a separate sheet of paper.*

1. What is the standard extension used for AutoLISP program files?
2. A comment is indicated in an AutoLISP file with a _____.
3. When in the drawing area, what are three ways to load the contents of the AutoLISP file named chgtext.lsp?
4. Define the terms *integer* and *real number* as related to AutoLISP.
5. Write expressions in the proper AutoLISP format for the following arithmetic functions.
   A. 23 + 54
   B. 12.45 + 6.28
   C. 56 – 34
   D. 23.004 – 7.008
   E. 16 × 4.6
   F. 7.25 × 10.30
   G. 45 ÷ 23
   H. 147 ÷ 29.6
   I. 53 + (12 × 3.8)
   J. 567 ÷ (34 – 14)
6. Explain the purpose of the **SETQ** function.
7. Write the proper AutoLISP notation to assign the value of (67 – 34.5) to the variable NUM1.
8. What does the **GETPOINT** function allow you to do?
9. Write the proper AutoLISP notation that creates a list of the coordinate values X = 3.5 and Y = 5.25 and assigns it to the variable PT1.
10. Which AutoLISP function allows you to find the distance between two points?
11. Explain the purpose of the **GETSTRING** function.
12. Write the proper AutoLISP notation for assigning the string This is a test: to the variable TXT.
13. How do you allow spaces in a string of text when using the **GETSTRING** function?
14. Write the proper notation for using the **PLINE** command in an AutoLISP expression.
15. Which prefix must you enter before a function name in an expression to indicate it is accessible at the Command: prompt?
16. What is a *function definition*?
17. Define an *argument*.
18. Which AutoLISP function is used to create new AutoCAD commands?
19. What is the purpose of the **Visual LISP** editor?
20. How is the **Visual LISP** editor accessed?

21. When entering text in the **Visual LISP** editor, which color indicates that you have entered a built-in function or a protected symbol?

22. Explain the purpose of the \n text string in AutoLISP.

## Drawing Problems

*Write AutoLISP programs for the following problems. Use the **Visual LISP** editor. Save the files as **P23**-(problem number) with the .lsp extension.*

1. Write an AutoLISP program to draw a rectangle. Use the **GETPOINT** function to set the opposite corners of the rectangle. Follow these guidelines:
   A. Set P1 as the first corner.
   B. Set P3 as the opposite corner.
   C. Set points P2 and P4 using the list functions of AutoLISP.
   D. Use the **LINE** command to draw the rectangle.

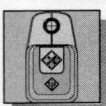

2. Create an AutoLISP program to draw a square. Follow these guidelines:
   A. Set a variable for the length of one side.
   B. Set the variable P1 as the lower-left corner of the square.
   C. Use the **LINE** command to draw the square.

3. Revise the program in Problem 2 to draw a square using the **PLINE** command.

4. Use the program in Problem 3 to create a new command that draws a square and allows you to change the line thickness.
   A. Use the **PLINE** or **POLYGON** command to draw the square.
   B. Set a variable that enables the user to input the line thickness.

5. Write an AutoLISP program that allows the user to draw parallel rectangles.
   A. Use the rectangle program from Problem 1, but replace the **LINE** command with the **PLINE** command.
   B. Provide a prompt that asks the user to enter an offset distance for a second rectangle to be placed inside the first rectangle.
   C. Use the **OFFSET** command to allow the user to draw the parallel rectangle inside the original.

## CHAPTER 24

# Beyond AutoLISP Basics

## Learning Objectives

After completing this chapter, you will be able to:
● Identify ways to provide for user input.
● Retrieve and use system variable values in AutoLISP programs.
● Work with lists using AutoLISP.
● Use angular input in AutoLISP programs.

As you practice using AutoLISP, you will develop ideas for programs that require additional commands and functions. Some of these programs may require that the user pick two corners of a windowed selection set. Another program may use existing points to draw a shape. You may also need to locate a point using polar coordinate notation or determine the angle of a line. All of these drawing tasks can be done with AutoLISP programs.

## Providing for Additional User Input

The **GETREAL** function allows you to define a variable value by entering a real number at the keyboard. Remember, as defined by AutoLISP, real numbers are classified separately from integers. A real number is considered to be more precise than an integer because it has a decimal value.

The **GETREAL** function works with numbers as units. You cannot respond with a value of feet and inches. Once issued, the function waits for user input. A prompt can be included. The real number is returned after a response is entered. The **GETREAL** function can be used to set the value of a variable as follows.

```
Command: (SETQ X (GETREAL "Enter number: "))↵
Enter number: 34.↵
34.0
```

The **GETCORNER** function allows the user to pick the opposite corner of a rectangle and define it as a point value. This is similar to placing a window around objects to define a selection set in a drawing. An existing point serves as the first corner of the rectangle. When locating the opposite corner, the screen cursor appears as a "rubber band" box similar to the window used when defining a selection set.

The **GETCORNER** function can also be used to set the value of a variable. The second corner can be picked with the pointing device or entered at the keyboard. The following is an example of using the **GETCORNER** function.

> Command: **(SETQ PT1 (GETPOINT "\nPick a point:")).**↵
> Pick a point: *(pick the point)*
> Command: **(SETQ PT2 (GETCORNER PT1 "\nPick the second corner:")).**↵
> Pick the second corner: *(pick the corner)*

Notice that the value of PT1 is set first. The point represented by PT1 becomes the base point for locating PT2. The two points (corners) located in this example can be used to construct an angled line, rectangle, or other shape. The points can also be applied to other functions.

## Using the Values of System Variables

AutoCAD's system variables can be read and changed from within AutoLISP applications with the **GETVAR** and **SETVAR** functions. These functions can be useful if an application requires you to store the value of a system variable in an AutoLISP variable, change the system variable setting for your program, and then reset it to its original value.

The **GETVAR** function is used to return the value of a system variable. In the following example, two system variable settings are saved as variable values.

> Command: **(SETQ V1 (GETVAR "TEXTSIZE")).**↵
> *current value of the* **TEXTSIZE** *system variable*
> Command: **(SETQ V2 (GETVAR "FILLETRAD")).**↵
> *current value of the* **FILLETRAD** *system variable*

The **SETVAR** function is used to change an AutoCAD system variable setting. You can assign a new value to a variable as follows.

> Command: **(SETVAR "TEXTSIZE" 0.25).**↵
> 0.25
> Command: **(SETVAR "FILLETRAD" 0.25).**↵
> 0.25

Suppose you need to save a current system variable setting, change the variable, and then reset the variable to its original value after the command is executed. The **GETVAR** function can be used to assign the original value to a variable, such as V1 shown in the first example on the **TEXTSIZE** system variable above. When the program is complete, the **SETVAR** function can be used to reset **TEXTSIZE** to its original value.

> Command: **(SETVAR "TEXTSIZE" V1).**↵
> 0.125

This returns the value of **TEXTSIZE** to the value of the variable V1, which is the original system variable setting.

○ For this exercise, enable the AutoSnap aperture box for use with the object snap modes. Use the proper AutoLISP syntax to write expressions for the functions given below. Write out the expressions on a separate sheet of paper and then test them by entering them into the computer.

A. Display the current **APERTURE** system variable setting and save it to the new variable APER.

B. Create the new variable APER4 and set it to the aperture size of four pixels.

C. Use the **LINE** command to draw two lines on screen. Next, use the **Endpoint** object snap mode to connect the endpoints of the two lines.

D. Reset the **APERTURE** system variable to the original setting.

○ Add the following capabilities to the EX23-7.LSP file that you created in Exercise 7 of Chapter 23. If you have not completed that exercise, do so now.

A. Create a variable named V1 to store the current text size. Insert a line for this function after the **DEFUN** function line.

B. At the end of the program, insert a function that resets the text size to its original value.

## Working with Lists

In AutoLISP, a *list* is defined as a stored set of values that are enclosed in parentheses. Lists are commonly used to provide point locations and other data for use in functions. A list is created, for example, when you pick a point on screen in response to the **GETPOINT** function. The list is composed of three numbers—the X, Y, and Z coordinate values. You can tell it is a list because AutoLISP returns the numbers enclosed in parentheses. A number entered in response to the **GETREAL** function is returned as a real number (it is not enclosed in parentheses). A single number is not a list. The following expression returns a list.

```
Command: (SETQ P1 (GETPOINT "Enter point:"))↵
Enter point: (pick a point)
(2.0 2.75 0.0)
```

The individual values in a list are called *atoms* and can be used in an AutoLISP program to create new points. The **CAR** function retrieves the first atom in a list. The variable P1 in the example above is composed of the list (2.0 2.75 0.0). Thus, using the **CAR** function with this variable returns a value of 2.0.

```
Command: (CAR P1)↵
2.0
```

The second atom in a list is retrieved with the **CADR** function. Find the second atom of the list related to the variable P1 by entering the following.

```
Command: (CADR P1)↵
2.75
```

You can create a new list of two coordinates by selecting values from existing points using the **CAR** and **CADR** functions. This is done with the **LIST** function. Values returned by this function are placed inside parentheses. The coordinates of the first variable, P1, can be combined with the coordinates of a second point variable named P2 to form a third point variable named P3. Study the following example and **Figure 24-1**. The coordinates of variable P1 are (2.0,2.75).

---

**Figure 24-1.**
A third point identified as P3 has been created using the **CAR** list value of P2 and the **CADR** list value of P1.

+ P2
X = 6.0 **(CAR)**
Y = 4.5 **(CADR)**

+ P1
X = 2.0 **(CAR)**
Y = 2.75 **(CADR)**

+ P3
X = 6.0 **(CAR P2)**
Y = 2.75 **(CADR P1)**

Command: **(SETQ P2 (GETCORNER P1 "Enter second point: "))**↵
Enter second point: **6,4.5**↵
(6.0 4.5 0.0)
Command: **(SETQ P3 (LIST (CAR P2) (CADR P1)))**↵
(6.0 2.75)

In AutoLISP, a function is followed by an argument. An argument consists of data that a function operates on or with. An expression must be composed of only one function and any required arguments. Therefore, the functions **CAR** and **CADR** must be separated because they are two different expressions combined to make a list. The **CAR** list value of P2 is to be the X value of P3, so it is given first. The **CADR** list value of P1 is placed second because it is to be the Y value of P3. Notice the number of closing parentheses at the end of the expression.

Now, with three points defined, there are many things you can do. For example, you can draw lines through the points to form a triangle, **Figure 24-2**. To do so, use the **COMMAND** function as follows.

Command: **(COMMAND "LINE" P1 P2 P3 "C")**↵

The **CAR** and **CADR** functions allow you to work with 2D coordinates. The **CADDR** function allows you to use the third atom of a list. This can be the Z coordinate of a point. Enter the following at your keyboard.

Command: **(SETQ B (LIST 3 4 6))**↵
(3 4 6)

You have created a list of three atoms, or values, and assigned it to the variable B. The third value is retrieved with the **CADDR** function.

Command: **(CADDR B)**↵
6

Since 6 is a single value, not a list, it is not enclosed in parentheses. Now use the **CAR** and **CADR** functions to find the other two atoms of the list.

Command: **(CAR B)**↵
3
Command: **(CADR B)**↵
4

**Figure 24-2.**
Once the third point (P3) is created, a triangle can be drawn.

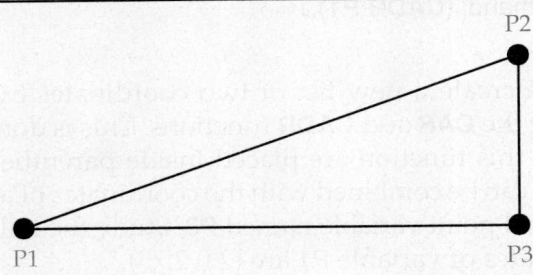

The following is a short AutoLISP program that uses the **CAR** and **CADR** retrieval functions to place an X at the midpoint of two selected points.

```
(DEFUN C:MDPNT ()
  (SETQ PT1 (GETPOINT "\nEnter the first point: "))
  (SETQ PT2 (GETPOINT "\nEnter the second point: "))
  (SETQ PT3 (LIST (/ (+ (CAR PT1) (CAR PT2)) 2) (/ (+ (CADR PT1) (CADR PT2)) 2)))
  (SETVAR "PDMODE" 3)
  (COMMAND "POINT" PT3)
)
```

The **CDR** function is also used to work with lists. It allows you to retrieve the second and remaining values of a list. Earlier in this discussion, the list (3 4 6) was assigned to variable B. In the following example, the **CDR** function is used to return the list (4 6).

Command: **(CDR B).**⏎
(4 6)

This returns a list of two values, or coordinates, that can be further manipulated with the **CAR** and **CADR** functions. Study **Figure 24-3** and the following examples.

Command: **(CAR (CDR B)).**⏎
4
Command: **(CADR (CDR B)).**⏎
6

The first example is asking for the first atom (**CAR**) of the list generated from the last two atoms (**CDR**) of variable B. In the second example, the second atom (**CADR**) of the list generated from the last two atoms of variable B is returned.

The four functions used to manipulate lists—**CAR**, **CADR**, **CADDR**, and **CDR**—may seem confusing at first. Practice using them to see how they work. Practice with a list of numbers, coordinate values, or text strings. Remember, text strings must be enclosed in quotation marks. Try the following examples to see what happens. Enter the expressions at the Command: prompt exactly as shown and press [Enter] at the end of each line.

```
(SETQ NOTES (LIST "DO" "RE" "MI"))
(CAR NOTES)
(CADR NOTES)
(CADDR NOTES)
(CDR NOTES)
(SETQ LASTNOTES (CDR NOTES))
(CAR (CDR NOTES))
(CADR (CDR NOTES))
(CAR LASTNOTES)
(CADR LASTNOTES)
```

Figure 24-3.
The **CDR** function creates a list containing the second and remaining atoms of a list. The new list can be manipulated as necessary with the **CAR** and **CADR** functions.

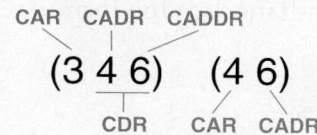

As you continue to work in AutoLISP, you will find many uses for the functions that allow you to work with lists. Remember the following review.

- **(CAR).** Returns the first atom in a list.
- **(CADR).** Returns the second atom in a list.
- **(CADDR).** Returns the third atom in a list.
- **(CDR).** Returns the second and remaining atoms of a list. The returned values are placed in a list. If the original list contains two atoms, only the second atom is returned, and it is placed in a list.
- **(LIST).** Creates a list of all values entered after the function name.

---

### Exercise 24-2

○ Write an AutoLISP program that draws a right triangle using points provided by the user. The 90° angle can be on the left or right side.
○ Use the following guidelines to write the program.
  ○ Define a function named TRIANGLE.
  ○ Set the variable P1 as the first point of the triangle. Provide a user prompt.
  ○ Set the variable P2 as the endpoint of the hypotenuse using the **GETCORNER** function. Place a user prompt on the next line.
  ○ Set the variable P3 to the X coordinate of P2 and the Y coordinate of P1.
  ○ Write an expression that draws a triangle through all three points.
○ Write the program in proper AutoLISP syntax. Use the **Visual LISP** editor and save the file as EX24-2.LSP.
○ Before saving the file, check for matching parentheses and quotation marks. Save the program and then test it.

---

## Using Polar Coordinates and Angles

The ability to work with angles is vital if you plan to do much AutoLISP programming. Four functions—**ANGLE**, **POLAR**, **GETANGLE**, and **GETORIENT**—allow you to use angles when writing program files. AutoLISP works with these functions using the radian system of angle measurement. This system of measurement is explained in the next section.

### Measuring Angles in Radians

The **ANGLE** function is used to calculate the angle in the XY plane of a line between two given points. The value of the angle is given in radians. *Radian angle measurement* is a system in which 180° equals "pi" ($\pi$). Pi is approximately equal to 3.14159.

AutoLISP functions use radians for angular measurement, but AutoCAD commands use degrees. Therefore, to use a radian angle in an AutoCAD command, it must first be converted to degrees. Conversely, a degree angle to be used by AutoLISP must be converted to radians. The following formulas are used for those conversions.

- To convert degrees to radians, use the formula:

    (* pi (/ *ad* 180.0))

  where *ad* = angle in degrees.
- To convert radians to degrees, use the formula:

    (/ (* *ar* 180.0) pi)

  where *ar* = angle in radians.

AutoCAD and its Applications—Advanced

The following table gives common angles measured in degrees, the AutoLISP expressions used to convert the angular values to radian values, and the resulting values in radians.

| Angle (degrees) | AutoLISP expression | Angle (radians) |
|---|---|---|
| 0 | | 0 |
| 30 | (/ pi 6) | 0.5236 |
| 45 | (/ pi 4) | 0.7854 |
| 60 | (/ pi 3) | 1.0472 |
| 90 | (/ pi 2) | 1.5708 |
| 135 | (/ (* pi 3) 4) | 2.3562 |
| 180 | (+ pi) | 3.1416 |
| 270 | (/ (* pi 3) 2) | 4.7124 |
| 360 | (* pi 2) | 6.2832 |

The following example illustrates how the angle between two points can be set to a variable, then converted to degrees.

Command: **(SETQ P1 (GETPOINT "Enter first point: "))**↵
Enter first point: **1.75,5.25**↵
(1.75 5.25 0.0)
Command: **(SETQ P2 (GETPOINT "Enter second point: "))**↵
Enter second point: **6.75,7.25**↵
(6.75 7.25 0.0)
Command: **(SETQ A1 (ANGLE P1 P2))**↵
0.380506

The angle represented by the variable A1 is measured in radians (0.380506). To convert this value to degrees, use the following expression.

Command: **(/ (* A1 180.0) PI)**↵
21.8014
Command: **!A1**↵
0.380506

The value 21.8014 is the angle in degrees between P1 and P2. However, notice that this conversion does not set the variable A1 to the value in degrees. Make the degree value permanent by assigning it to the variable using the following expression.

Command: **(SETQ A1 (/ (* A1 180.0) PI))**↵
21.8014
Command: **!A1**↵
21.8014

The variable A1 now has a value of 21.8014°.

## Exercise 24-3

○ Using AutoLISP expressions, locate the endpoints of a line and store each endpoint as a variable.
○ Use the **ANGLE** function to find the angle of the line. Set the value to the variable A.
○ Use the proper formula to convert the radian value to degrees.
○ Use the proper expression to assign the degree value to the variable A.

---

# Providing for Angular Input by the User

The **GETANGLE** function allows the user to input an angular value for use in an application. This function is often used to set a variable that can be used by another function. The **GETANGLE** function automatically issues a Specify second point: prompt. The following example illustrates how you can set a variable to an angular value that is input by the user.

> Command: **(SETQ A (GETANGLE "Pick first point: "))**↵
> Pick first point: *(pick the first point)*
> Specify second point: *(pick the second point)*
> *angle (in radians)*

The angular value is given in radians. To convert it to degrees, use the formula presented in the previous section.

The **GETANGLE** function uses the current **ANGBASE** (angle 0 direction) and **ANGDIR** (clockwise or counterclockwise) system variables. Therefore, if you have angles set to be measured from north (where **ANGBASE** = 90°), angles picked with the **GETANGLE** function will be measured from north. If the **ANGDIR** system variable is set to measure angles clockwise, the **GETANGLE** function will accept input of clockwise values, but returns counterclockwise values.

A companion function to **GETANGLE** is **GETORIENT**. It is used in exactly the same manner as the **GETANGLE** function. However, **GETORIENT** always measures angles counterclockwise from east (0°), regardless of the current **ANGBASE** and **ANGDIR** system variable settings.

---

## Exercise 24-4

○ Use the **GETANGLE** function to assign an angular value to the variable ANG1.
  ○ Convert the radian value to degrees using the proper AutoLISP expression. Assign the degree value to ANG1.
  ○ Convert the degree value back to radians using the proper AutoLISP expression. Redefine the variable ANG1 with the radian value.
○ Use the **GETORIENT** function to find the angle (in radians) from the X axis to a line between any two points.
○ Using the proper AutoLISP expression, save the current setting of the **ANGBASE** system variable to the variable AB. Then, change the system variable setting to 90 using the **SETVAR** function and the proper AutoLISP expression for converting the degree value to radians (/ pi 2).
  ○ Use the **GETORIENT** function again to find the angle from the X axis to a line between the same two points.
  ○ Use the **GETANGLE** function to find the angle from the X axis to a line between the same two points.
  ○ Reset the **ANGBASE** system variable to its default value.
  ○ Compare the values obtained with the **GETORIENT** and **GETANGLE** functions. Explain the results.

---

## Using Polar Coordinates

The **POLAR** function allows you to specify a new point based on the angle and distance from an existing point. Two variables must be set for the **POLAR** function to work properly. One variable must contain the coordinate location of the point from which you are locating the new point. The other variable must contain the distance value from the existing point to the new point. The syntax for the **POLAR** function is:

> (POLAR *base_point angle distance*)

For example, suppose you want to specify a point as P1 and locate another point, P2, at a specific distance and angle from P1. Enter the following expressions.

```
Command: (SETQ P1 (GETPOINT "Enter point: "))↵
Enter point: 4.0,4.5↵
Command: (SETQ D (GETDIST P1 "Enter distance: "))↵
Enter distance: 3.0↵
Command: (SETQ A (/ PI 3))↵
1.0472
```

In this example, the desired angle is 60°. However, AutoLISP uses radians for angular values. Therefore, the degree value is converted to radians. The resulting value, 1.0472, is saved as the variable A. Next, use the **POLAR** function to locate the second point relative to P1 at the specified angle and distance. A line can then be drawn from P1 at 60° to the X axis using the **COMMAND** function. The sequence is:

```
Command: (SETQ P2 (POLAR P1 A D))↵
(5.5 7.09808 0.0)
Command: (COMMAND "LINE" P1 P2 "")↵
```

### Exercise 24-5

○ Write an AutoLISP program that draws a right triangle. Refer to EX24-2. However, use the **POLAR** function instead of the **LIST** functions. Write the program in proper AutoLISP format using the **Visual LISP** editor.
○ Use the following guidelines for writing the program.
  ○ Define a function named POLARTRI.
  ○ Set the variable P1 as the first corner of the triangle. Provide a user prompt.
  ○ Set the variable D as the length of one side.
  ○ Set the variable P2 as the second corner located 0° from P1 at a distance of D.
  ○ Set the variable P3 as the third corner located 90° from P2 at a distance of D.
  ○ Write an expression that draws a line through all three points and closes the triangle.
○ Save the file as EX24-5.LSP and load the program into AutoCAD. Test the program.

## Locating AutoCAD's AutoLISP Files

One of the best ways to become familiar with AutoLISP is to enter expressions and programs into your computer. Look for programs in books or magazines that you read. Get a feel for how the functions and arguments go together and how they work in AutoCAD. Make a habit of reading through one of the AutoCAD journals and experiment with the AutoLISP routines printed in them. Also, refer to the online documentation for other samples.

AutoLISP files are typically saved with the .lsp extension. A variety of AutoLISP programs are supplied with AutoCAD. These are saved in the AutoCAD folder structure. You can use Windows Explorer to search the AutoCAD folder structure and list the .lsp files.

The AutoLISP files found in the Support folder are standard files that support many of AutoCAD's built-in features. When the command that starts the function is entered, the associated program file is automatically loaded. The following is a short list of some AutoLISP files in the Support folder, along with descriptions of the functions associated with each.

- **ddptype.lsp.** This file supports the function of the **DDPTYPE** command, providing the dialog-based interface for controlling point display options.
- **3d.lsp.** This routine is activated when you select **3D Surfaces…** from the **Surfaces** cascading menu in the **Draw** pull-down menu. It activates the **3D Objects** dialog box.
- **3darray.lsp.** This routine makes it possible to create an arrangement of rows, columns, and levels of an object with the **3DARRAY** command.

The files in the Sample\VisualLISP folder provide some sample AutoLISP programs, as well as some examples of AutoLISP working with external database applications. The Tutorial folder provides a group of lesson files that are part of a tutorial program used to complete a drawing project with Visual LISP.

> **PROFESSIONAL TIP**
>
> For easier access to any AutoLISP program file, add its folder in the Support File Search Path listing located in the **Files** tab of the **Options** dialog box.

## Sample AutoLISP Programs

The following programs are provided for you to copy and add to your acad2004doc.lsp file or to your custom menus. Practice using the routines for a few minutes a couple of times a week. This will help you begin to better understand and use AutoLISP. Train yourself to learn a new function every week. Before long, you will be writing your own useful programs.

### Erasing the Entire Screen

This program sets two variables to the minimum and maximum screen limits. It then erases everything within those limits and redraws the screen. Name this program ZAP.LSP.

```
; ERASES ENTIRE LIMITS
(DEFUN C:ZAP ()
  (SETQ LMIN (GETVAR "LIMMIN"))
  (SETQ LMAX (GETVAR "LIMMAX"))
  (COMMAND "ERASE" "C" LMIN LMAX "")
  (COMMAND "REDRAW")
)
```

### Setting the Current Layer

Similar to the built-in **Make Object's Layer Current** tool, this program asks for the user to pick an object on the layer to be set current. The program finds the layer of the object picked and sets it current. Name this program LP.LSP.

```
; AUTHOR : ROD RAWLS
(DEFUN C:LP (/ E)
  (WHILE (NOT (SETQ E (ENTSEL "\nSelect object on target layer…")))
    (ALERT "No object selected!")
  )
  (SETQ LN (CDR (ASSOC 8 (ENTGET (CAR E)))))
```

```
        (COMMAND "-LAYER" "S" LN "")
        (PRINC)
    )
```

## Cleaning Overlapping Corners

This program allows you to trim the overlapping ends of intersecting lines. You are requested to pick the two lines that intersect and overlap. The points you pick are on the portion to keep. The program does the rest. Name the program CLEANC.LSP. Note: The value returned at the end of the program is the original **OSMODE** setting.

```
; AUTHOR: GEORGE HEAD
; PRINTED IN THE JANUARY 1988 ISSUE OF "CADENCE" MAGAZINE
(DEFUN C:CLEANC (/ O1 P1 P2)
    (SETQ O1 (GETVAR "OSMODE"))
    (SETVAR "OSMODE" 512)
    (COMMAND "FILLET" "R" 0)
    (SETQ P1 (GETPOINT "\nPick a line "))
    (SETQ P2 (GETPOINT "\nPick other line "))
    (COMMAND "FILLET" P1 P2)
    (SETVAR "OSMODE" O1)
)
```

## Calculating the Length of Lines

This program calculates the length of all lines on a specified layer. It can be used for estimating and material takeoffs. This program works only with lines, not with polylines. Name the program LINEAR.LSP. After loading it into AutoCAD, respond to the first prompt by entering the name of the layer that contains the lines you wish to total. The calculation is given in current drawing units. Also, the layer name is case sensitive.

```
; AUTHOR : JOE PUCILOWSKI
; COMPANY : JOSEPH & ASSOCIATES
; ADDRESS : 7809A RIVER RESORT LANE, TAMPA, FL
; NOTE :          THIS PROGRAM FIGURES THE TOTAL NUMBER OF LINEAR
;          UNITS (FEET, INCHES, ETC.) OF LINES ON A SPECIFIC LAYER.
; REVISED : BY ROD RAWLS
;
(DEFUN C:LINEAR      ( )
    (SETQ       TOTAL 0
            E              (ENTNEXT)
            NUMLIN         0
            LAYPIK         (GETSTRING T "\nAdd up lines on layer: ")
    )
    (IF (TBLSEARCH "LAYER" LAYPIK)
    (PROGN
    (WHILE      E
        (SETQ  ENTTYP (CDR (ASSOC 0 (SETQ EG (ENTGET E)))))
            LAYNAM      (CDR (ASSOC 8 EG))
        )
        (IF
    (AND
            (EQUAL ENTTYP "LINE")
            (EQUAL LAYNAM LAYPIK)
        )
        (PROGN
            (SETQ  LINLEN (DISTANCE (CDR (ASSOC 10 EG)) (CDR
```

```
                                (ASSOC 11 EG)))
                                               TOTAL (+ TOTAL LINLEN)
                                               NUMLIN (+ 1 NUMLIN)
                          )
                        )
                      )
                      (SETQ E (ENTNEXT E))
                )
                (PRINC
                      (STRCAT           "\nFound "
                        (ITOA NUMLIN)
                      " lines on layer < "
                      LAYPIK
                      "> with a total of "
                        (RTOS TOTAL)
                      " linear units."
                        )
                  )
            )
            (PRINC "\nLayer does not exist.")
      )
      (PRINC)
    )
```

## Changing the Grid Rotation

This first routine, titled S, rotates the grid to the angle between the X axis and any picked line. The second routine, SS, returns the grid to zero rotation. These functions are achieved by rotating the snap. Save the file as ROTGRID.LSP.

```
    ; AUTHOR : EBEN KUNZ
    ; COMPANY : KUNZ ASSOCIATES ARCHITECTS
    ; ADDRESS : 38 GREENWICH PARK, BOSTON, MA
    ;
    (DEFUN C:S (/ PT1 PT2)
        (SETVAR "ORTHOMODE" 0)
        (SETQ PT1 (OSNAP (GETPOINT "\nPick line to match new Grid angle: \n")
        "NEA"))
        (SETQ PT2 (OSNAP PT1 "END"))
        (COMMAND "SNAP" "R" PT1 PT2)
        (SETVAR "SNAPMODE" 0)
    )
    (DEFUN C:SS ()
        (PROMPT "\nReturn Grid to zero.")
        (COMMAND "SNAP" "R" "" 0.0)
        (SETVAR "SNAPMODE" 0)
    )
```

## Moving Objects to the Current Layer

This simple program, titled CL.LSP, quickly changes selected objects to the current layer. You can select multiple objects using any AutoCAD selection method.

```
; AUTHOR : BILL FANE
; COMPANY : WEISER, INC.
; ADDRESS : 6700 BERESFORD ST., BURNABY, B.C.
;
(DEFUN C:CL (/ THINGS)
   (SETQ THINGS (SSGET))
   (COMMAND "CHANGE" THINGS "" "P" "LA"
         (GETVAR "CLAYER") "" )
)
```

## Moving Objects to a Selected Layer

This routine, named LA.LSP, allows you to move objects to a layer by picking an object on the destination layer. After you select an object on the destination layer, you can select multiple objects using any AutoCAD selection method.

```
; AUTHOR : SHELDON MCCARTHY
; COMPANY : EPCM SERVICES LTD.
; ADDRESS : 2404 HAINES ROAD, MISSISSAUGA, ONTARIO
;
(DEFUN C:LA ()
   (SETQ 1A (CDR (ASSOC 8 (ENTGET (CAR (ENTSEL "Entity on destination+
   layer: "))))))
   (PROMPT "Objects to change...")
   (SSGET)
   (COMMAND "CHANGE" "P" "" "P" "LA" 1A "")
)
```

## Chapter Test

*Answer the following questions on a separate sheet of paper.*

1. Name the function that allows you to return a real number and use it as a variable value.
2. Which two functions allow you to work with system variables?
3. Define the following AutoLISP functions.
   A. **CAR**
   B. **CADR**
   C. **CDR**
   D. **CADDR**
   E. **LIST**
4. Write the proper AutoLISP notation to return the last two values of the list (4 7 3).
5. Write an expression to set a variable named A to the result of Question 4.
6. Write an expression to return the second value of the list created in Question 5.
7. Compare and contrast the **GETANGLE** and **GETORIENT** functions.
8. Write an expression to set the angle between points P3 and P4 to the variable A.
9. Which system of angle measurement does AutoLISP use?
10. How do you express a 270° angle in the angular system that AutoLISP uses?
11. Explain the purpose of the **POLAR** function.

## Drawing Problems

*Write AutoLISP programs for the following problems. Use the* **Visual LISP** *editor. Save the files as* **P24-***(problem number) with the* .lsp *extension.*

1. Add the following capabilities to the right triangle function developed in Exercise 24-2.
   A. Use the **GETDIST** function instead of **GETCORNER**.
   B. Allow the angle of the hypotenuse to be picked.
   C. Allow the length of a side or the hypotenuse length to be picked.

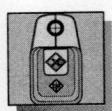

2. Create an AutoLISP program similar to that in Problem 1, but write it so that it draws an equilateral triangle (with equal angles and equal sides). Use the **POLAR** function.

3. Revise the program in Problem 1 in Chapter 23 to draw a rectangle using the **GETCORNER** function to find the second corner.

4. Add a **Fillet 0** command to your **Modify** pull-down menu. Use menu macros and AutoLISP expressions to create the command. Follow these guidelines:
   A. Retrieve the current fillet radius setting and assign it to an AutoLISP variable.
   B. Set the fillet radius to 0.
   C. Allow the user to select two lines and enter a 0 fillet.
   D. Reset the fillet radius to the original value.
   E. Assign an appropriate mnemonic key to the new menu command.

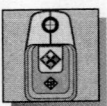

5. Write an AutoLISP program that allows the user to measure the distance between two points using the **DIST** command. Use AutoLISP expressions to do the following.
   A. Assign the current unit precision for read-only linear units to an AutoLISP variable.
   B. Prompt for the desired unit precision from the user and store the value as a variable.
   C. Set the unit precision with the user-defined variable value.
   D. Allow the user to measure the distance between two selected points with the **DIST** command.
   E. Reset the unit precision to the original value.

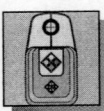

6. Write an AutoLISP program to draw a rectangle and place a circle having a user-specified diameter in the center of the rectangle.
   A. Incorporate the rectangle program from Problem 3.
   B. Use the **ANGLE**, **POLAR**, and **DISTANCE** functions to find the center point of the rectangle.
   C. Prompt the user to enter the diameter of the circle.
   D. Use the **CIRCLE** command to draw the circle at the center point of the rectangle.

7. Write a program to draw a leader with a diameter dimension having plus and minus tolerances.
   A. Issue prompts that allow the user to set the **DIMTP** and **DIMTM** system variables and save the specified values to AutoLISP variables.
   B. Set the new values to the **DIMTP** and **DIMTM** system variables.
   C. Activate the **DIM** command and turn the **DIMTOL** system variable on.
   D. Activate the **DIAMETER** command. Using the **ENTSEL** function, issue a prompt that allows the user to select the circle being dimensioned. Set the selection specification to a variable as follows.

   (SETQ SC (ENTSEL "\nSelect arc or circle: "))

   E. Using the **GETPOINT** function, issue a prompt that allows the user to pick a location for the leader line and the default dimension text.
   F. Turn tolerancing off and exit the **DIM** command.

8. Write an AutoLISP program to draw a leader with a bubble attached to the end.
   A. Prompt the user for the start point of the leader and set it to the variable P1.
   B. Prompt the user for the endpoint of the leader and set it to the variable P2.
   C. Prompt the user for the text height and set it to a variable.
   D. Issue a prompt that asks for the text string (specify a maximum of two characters) and set the resulting text to a variable.
   E. Calculate the circle diameter at 2.5 or 3 times the text height and set it to a variable.
   F. Set the center point of the circle to a point relative to P2 using the **POLAR** function. Set the relative distance as the radius of the circle. Assign the center point to the variable P3.
   G. Use the **LEADER** command to draw a leader from P1 to P2.
   H. Draw the leader line with no shoulder and no annotation text.
   I. Draw a circle with the center point at P3.
   J. Draw text in the center of the circle using the appropriate justification option of the **TEXT** command.

9. Develop a program that draws a line of text and places a box around it.
   A. Prompt the user for the text height and set it to the variable TXHT.
   B. Prompt the user for a point representing the lower-left corner of the box and set it to a variable.
   C. Prompt for the text string from the user.
   D. Set the text string length to the variable LG1. Use the **STRLEN** function. The following is an example of using this function.

   (SETQ TEXT (GETSTRING T "Enter Text: "))
   (SETQ LG1 (STRLEN TEXT))

   E. Set the X length of the box to a variable using the expression: (* LG1 TXHT).
   F. Set the Y length of the box to a variable using the expression: (* 3 TXHT).
   G. Draw the box using the variables set in E and F.
   H. Calculate the center point of the box, and set it to the variable CEN1.
   I. Draw the text string inside the box. Use the **MC** text justification option for point CEN1.

AutoCAD allows almost unlimited customization to help you draw. A—You can add a custom image menu to the acad.mnu file that offers the solid primitives. B—Using DCL and AutoLISP, you can define your own dialog box that offers the solid primitives.

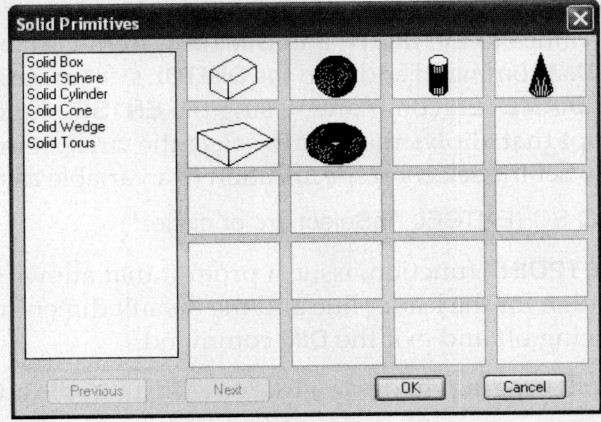

A

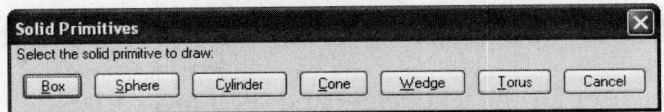

B

## CHAPTER 25

# Introduction to Dialog Control Language (DCL)

## Learning Objectives

After completing this chapter, you will be able to:
- Describe the types of files that control dialog boxes.
- Define the components of a dialog box.
- Write a DCL file for a basic dialog box.
- Write an AutoLISP file to control a dialog box.
- Associate an action with a dialog box tile.

Programmable dialog boxes can be used to completely customize the interface of AutoLISP programs. These dialog boxes allow LISP programs to work like many of AutoCAD's built-in functions. Using dialog boxes improves efficiency and reduces data entry errors.

Dialog boxes minimize the amount of typing required by the user. Rather than answering a series of text prompts on the command line, the user selects options from the dialog box. Dialog box fields can be filled in by the user in any order. While the dialog is still active, the user can revise values as necessary.

AutoLISP provides basic tools for controlling dialog boxes, but the dialog box itself must be defined using *Dialog Control Language (DCL).* The definition is written to an ASCII file with a .dcl file extension. When creating and editing DCL files, the **Visual LISP** editor provides many helpful tools, including color coding.

This chapter is only an introduction to DCL. It covers basic DCL file construction and a few common tile types. For a full discussion of DCL and dialog creation and management techniques, refer to *AutoLISP Programming* published by The Goodheart-Willcox Company, Inc.

## DCL File Formats

A DCL file is formatted as an ASCII text file with a .dcl file extension. These files can have any valid file name, but a file name with 1 to 8 characters is recommended. Writing DCL is easy. Many of the components of a DCL file are normal English words.

The components of a dialog box—such as edit boxes, images, and drop-down lists—are referred to as *tiles.* Tiles are defined by specifying various *attribute* values. Each attribute controls a specific property of the tile, such as size, location, and default values.

When writing a DCL file, you do not use parentheses as you do with AutoLISP. When defining a dialog box or tile, all the required attributes are placed within {braces}. As with AutoLISP programs, indentation helps to separate individual elements, making the file more readable. Comments are preceded by two forward slashes (//). Semicolons are used at the end of an attribute definition line.

To view an example of DCL code, open the acad.dcl and base.dcl files in a text editor. These two files are found in the user's Support folder, not the AutoCAD Support folder. A portion of the acad.dcl file is shown in **Figure 25-1**.

**Figure 25-1.**
A portion of the
acad.dcl file.

```
acad_snap : dialog {                          ← Dialog definition
    label = "Drawing Aids";  ←
    : row {                                     Label attribute
        : column {                              adds a text string
            : boxed_column {
                label = "Modes";
                : toggle {
                    label = "&Ortho";          Key attribute
                    key = "ortho";  ←          identifies a text string
                {                              that associates the dialog
                : toggle {                     tile with an AutoLISP
                    label = "Solid &Fill";     function
                    key = "fill";
                }
```

CAUTION

The base.dcl file contains standard prototype definitions. The acad.dcl file contains definitions for all the dialog boxes used by AutoCAD. *Do not edit either one of these files!* Altering them can cause AutoCAD's built-in dialog boxes to crash.

# AutoLISP and DCL

A DCL file simply defines a dialog box. The dialog box cannot actually do anything without a controlling application. AutoLISP is frequently used to control dialog sessions. This section shows examples using the AutoLISP dialog handling functions.

In order to display a dialog box, the controlling AutoLISP application must first load the dialog definition. The **LOAD_DIALOG** function loads the specified dialog definition file:

(load_dialog *"filename*.dcl")

The file name is enclosed in quotation marks. The **LOAD_DIALOG** function returns a positive integer that identifies the loaded DCL file. If the attempted load was unsuccessful, a negative integer is returned.

The next step is to activate a specific dialog box definition contained within the DCL file. The **NEW_DIALOG** function activates the dialog box specified, where *dlgname* is the name of the dialog box:

(new_dialog *dlgname dcl_id*)

This function is case sensitive. Suppose the dialog definition is named main. Specifying Main or MAIN will not activate this dialog box, since the text string does not match exactly. The *dcl_id* argument represents the integer value returned by **LOAD_DIALOG**.

This value is often assigned to a variable, as you will see later. **NEW_DIALOG** also supports additional, optional arguments, which are not discussed here.

To actually begin accepting input from the user, the **START_DIALOG** function must be used.

```
(start_dialog)
```

This function has no arguments. It allows for input to be received from the dialog box initialized by the previous **NEW_DIALOG** expression.

With these basic AutoLISP functions, it is possible to display the dialog box shown in Figure 25-2. You will create this dialog box in the next section. After the AutoLISP program is written and saved, it can be loaded into AutoCAD using the **LOAD** function or the **APPLOAD** command. Enter the controlling AutoLISP application named EXAMPLE1.LSP as follows.

```
(setq EX1_DCL_ID (load_dialog "EXAMPLE1.DCL"))
(if (not (new_dialog "main" EX1_DCL_ID))
    (exit)
)
(start_dialog)
```

**Figure 25-2.**
A sample custom dialog box.

Text item — Title bar — Predefined button

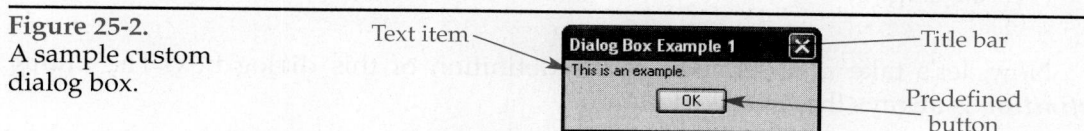

Now, let's take a closer look at the controlling code for this dialog box:

```
(setq EX1_DCL_ID (load_dialog "EXAMPLE1.DCL"))
(if (not (new_dialog "main" EX1_DCL_ID))
    (exit)
)
(start_dialog)
```

This expression loads the dialog definition found in example1.dcl and assigns the value returned by **LOAD_DIALOG** to the variable EX1_DCL_ID.

```
(setq EX1_DCL_ID (load_dialog "EXAMPLE1.DCL"))
(if (not (new_dialog "main" EX1_DCL_ID))
    (exit)
)
(start_dialog)
```

If **NEW_DIALOG** is unable to activate the specified dialog box for any reason, the expression in the next three lines exits (terminates) the application. This is an important safety feature. In many cases, loading an incorrect or incomplete definition can cause your system to lock up, often requiring that the system be rebooted.

```
(setq EX1_DCL_ID (load_dialog "EXAMPLE1.DCL"))
(if (not (new_dialog "main" EX1_DCL_ID))
    (exit)
)
(start_dialog)
```

The last expression opens the dialog box indicated by the previous **NEW_DIALOG** expression.

Once the descriptions within a specific DCL file are no longer needed, they can be removed from memory using the AutoLISP **UNLOAD_DIALOG** function.

```
(unload_dialog dcl_id)
```

Do not unload a dialog definition until your application is finished using the DCL file. Otherwise, your application may fail to function properly.

Your work in AutoCAD has provided you with a good background in how dialog boxes work. By now, you should be familiar with the use of buttons, edit boxes, radio buttons, and list boxes. This will be helpful as you design dialog interfaces for your AutoLISP programs.

DCL tiles are used individually or combined into structures called *clusters.* For example, a series of button tiles can be placed in a column tile to control the arrangement of the buttons in the dialog box. The primary tile is the dialog box itself.

The best way to begin understanding the format of a DCL file is to study a simple dialog box definition. The following DCL code defines the dialog box shown in Figure 25-2.

```
main : dialog {
    label = "Dialog Box Example 1";
    : text_part {
        value    = "This is an example.";
    }
    ok_only;
}
```

Now, let's take a closer look at the definition of this dialog box. The *dialog definition* is always the first tile definition.

```
main : dialog {
    label = "Dialog Box Example 1";
    : text_part {
        value    = "This is an example.";
    }
    ok_only;
}
```

Everything within the braces defines the features of the dialog box. The word "main" indicates the name of the dialog box. This name is referenced by the controlling AutoLISP application. A colon (:) precedes all tile callouts. In the case of a dialog tile, the colon separates the name from the tile callout.

```
main : dialog {
    label = "Dialog Box Example 1";
    : text_part {
        value    = "This is an example.";
    }
    ok_only;
}
```

The *label* attribute of the dialog tile controls the text that appears in the title bar of the dialog box. The line is terminated with a semicolon. All attribute lines must be terminated with a semicolon.

```
main : dialog {
    label = "Dialog Box Example 1";
    : text_part {
        value    = "This is an example.";
    }
    ok_only;
}
```

The *text_part* tile allows placement of text items in a dialog box. The *value* attribute is used to specify the text that is displayed. Just as with the dialog tile, all of the attributes are defined between braces.

```
main : dialog {
    label = "Dialog Box Example 1";
    : text_part {
        value   = "This is an example.";
    }
    ok_only;
}
```

There are many predefined tiles and subassemblies in the base.dcl file. A *subassembly* is a cluster of predefined tiles, such as OK_CANCEL and OK_HELP. The OK_ONLY tile places an **OK** button at the bottom of the dialog box, as shown in **Figure 25-2.** The statement is not preceded by a colon because it is not a specific definition. This line is terminated with a semicolon, just like an attribute. Braces are not required because the statement is a reference to a predefined tile, rather than a tile definition.

Once you have defined a dialog box, the definition must then be saved in a DCL file. For this example, the dialog definition above is saved in the file EXAMPLE1.DCL. This is treated as any other support file and should be saved in the AutoCAD support path.

For examples of other DCL functions, look at the **Viewpoint Presets** dialog box shown in **Figure 25-3.** Various tiles of this dialog box are identified with the corresponding DCL code needed to define the tile. In previous releases of AutoCAD, this dialog box was defined by a stand-alone DCL file named ddvpoint.dcl. However, this file no longer exists.

**Figure 25-3.**
Some of the tile definitions and attributes associated with the **Viewpoint Presets** dialog box.

```
ddvpoint : dialog {                                         : row {
  aspect_ratio = 0;                                           : radio_row {
  label = "Viewpoint Presets";                                  : radio_button {
  fixed_height = true;                                            label = "Absolute to WCS";
  fixed_width  = true;                                            key = "ddvp_abs_wcs";
  : column {                                                      mnemonic = "W";
    : row {                                                       value = "1";
      : text {                                                  }
        label = "Set Viewing Angles";                         : radio_button {
        key = "ddvp_header";                                    label = "Relative to UCS";
      }                                                         key = "ddvp_rel_ucs";
    }                                                           mnemonic = "U";
                                                              }
                                                            }
                                                          }

: row {                                                    : row {
    fixed_width = true;                                      : edit_box {
    fixed_height = true;                                       label = "From:  X Axis:";
    : image_button {                                           mnemonic = "A";
      alignment = top;                                         key = "ddvp_val_x";
      fixed_width = true;                                      fixed_width = true;
      fixed_height = true;                                     edit_width  = 6;
      key = "ddvp_image";                                    }
      width  = 39;                                          : edit_box {
      height = 12;                                            label = "XY Plane:";
      color  = 0;                                             mnemonic = "P";
      is_tab_stop = false;                                    key = "ddvp_val_xyp";
    }                                                         fixed_width = true;
  }                                                           edit_width  = 6;
                                                            }
: row {                                                    }
    : button {                                            }
      label = "Set to Plan View";
      key = "ddvp_set_plan";
      mnemonic = "V";
    }
  }
}
}
```

spacer_1;
ok_cancel_help_errtile;
}

○ Use the examples in the text to create EXAMPLE1.DCL and EXAMPLE1.LSP. Create each file in the **Visual LISP** editor.
○ Load the AutoLISP program file to test the files. The dialog box should automatically open and remain displayed until you pick the **OK** button.

## Associating Functions with Tiles

Most tiles can be associated with actions. These actions vary from run-time error checking to performing tasks outside the dialog session. The **ACTION_TILE** AutoLISP function provides the basic means of associating tiles with actions.

(action_tile "*key*" "*action-expression*")

The *key* references the attribute assigned in the DCL file. The *action-expression* is the AutoLISP expression performed when the action is called. When the desired action requires a large amount of AutoLISP code, it is best to define a function to perform the required tasks. This function is then called within the action-expression. Both the key and action-expression arguments are supplied as text strings.

In order to access a specific tile from AutoLISP, the key of the tile must be referenced. The key is specified as an attribute in the DCL file. Tiles that are static (unchanging) do not require keys. Any tile that must be referenced in any way—such as setting or retrieving a value, associating an action, or enabling/disabling the tile—requires a key.

The next example changes the previous dialog box by adding a button that displays the current time when picked. The new or changed DCL code is shown in color. Save this file as EXAMPLE2.DCL.

```
main : dialog {
    label  = "Dialog Box Example 2";
    : text_part {
        value  = "";
        key    = "time";
    }
    : button {
        key     = "update";
        label   = "Display Current Time";
        mnemonic    = "C";
    }
    ok_only;
}
```

Notice the addition of a key attribute to the text_part tile. This allows access by the AutoLISP application while the dialog box is open. Another addition is the button tile. A key is provided in the button tile so an association can be created in the AutoLISP program with an action-expression. The label attribute provides the text displayed on the button. The mnemonic attribute underlines the specified letter within the label to allow keyboard access. The AutoLISP application used to manage this dialog session is as follows. Save the program as EXAMPLE2.LSP.

```
        (setq EX2_DCL_ID (load_dialog "EXAMPLE2.DCL"))
(if        (not (new_dialog "main" EX2_DCL_ID))
           (exit)
)
 (defun  UPDTILE ()
    (setq CDVAR (rtos (getvar "CDATE") 2 16)
          CDTXT (strcat "Current Time: "
                 (substr CDVAR 10 2)
                 ":"
                 (substr CDVAR 12 2)
                 ":"
                 (substr CDVAR 14 2)
                 )
    )
    (set_tile "time" CDTXT)
)
 (UPDTILE)
 (action_tile "update" "(UPDTILE)")
 (start_dialog)
```

The "update" button displays the current time when the button is picked. The dialog box displayed by this code is shown in **Figure 25-4.** Note: Some AutoLISP functions that are not covered in this text are used in the above programming to retrieve and display the current date.

Commands that change the display or require user input (outside of the dialog interface) cannot be used while a dialog box is active. These AutoLISP functions cannot be used with DCL:

| | | | | |
|---|---|---|---|---|
| **command** | **getangle** | **getpoint** | **grread** | **prompt** |
| **entdel** | **getcorner** | **getreal** | **grtext** | **redraw** |
| **entmake** | **getdist** | **getstring** | **grvecs** | **ssget (interactive)** |
| **entmod** | **getint** | **graphscr** | **menucmd** | **textpage** |
| **entsel** | **getkword** | **grclear** | **nentsel** | **textscr** |
| **entupd** | **getorient** | **grdraw** | **osnap** | |

**Figure 25-4.**
The dialog box defined by EXAMPLE2.DCL and controlled by EXAMPLE2.LSP.

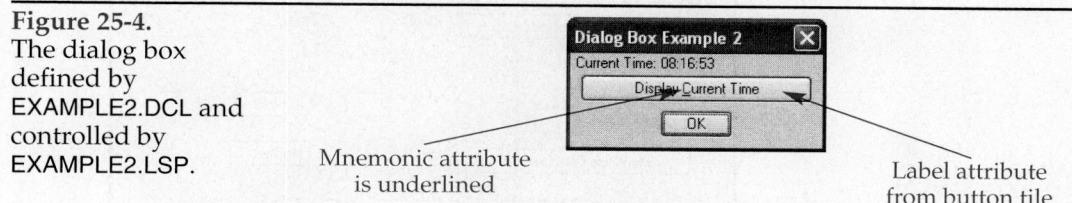

Mnemonic attribute is underlined

Label attribute from button tile

## Exercise 25-2

○ Use the examples in the text to create EXAMPLE2.DCL and EXAMPLE2.LSP. Load and run the AutoLISP program. What happens when the "time" button is picked?

There are many types of DCL tiles available. You can provide edit boxes for users to enter information directly, such as numeric or text information. You can create lists and drop-down lists to allow users to choose from preset selections. You can also add buttons to provide a simple means of initiating an action.

Images can be used to enhance dialog boxes. For example, you can place company or personal logos in your dialog boxes. An interactive image, such as those that appear in the **New Distant Light** dialog box in **Figure 25-5**, can also be used. Tools such as text tiles, sliders, and clusters are used to control the layout of tiles in a dialog box.

A wide variety of attributes are available for controlling the appearance and function of a dialog session. In addition, several AutoLISP functions are provided to control your dialog session. You can disable or enable tiles and change the active tile. It is even possible to change the value or state of a tile based on an entry in another tile.

You have already seen two examples of dialog boxes created using DCL and AutoLISP. The following sections provide two additional applications that use various dialog boxes. Study these examples for additional insight into the creation of dialog boxes. Be sure to have an appropriate reference handy, such as the online documentation, to look up DCL and AutoLISP terms. You can adapt or modify these programs to produce dialog sessions of your own.

**Figure 25-5.**
The **New Distant Light** dialog box contains two interactive images.

Interactive images

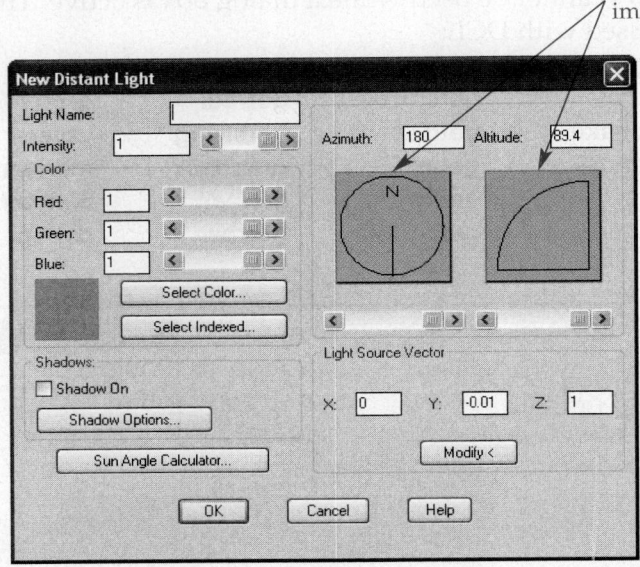

**Figure 25-6.**
The dialog box displayed using the EXAMPLE3 DCL and LSP files.

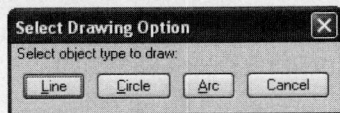

## Dialog Example 3

Create the following DCL and AutoLISP programs. Save the programs as EXAMPLE3.DCL and EXAMPLE3.LSP. Then, load the AutoLISP program file. To open the dialog box, type DRAW at the Command: prompt. See **Figure 25-6.**

```
//EXAMPLE3.DCL
//Defines a dialog box that presents three drawing options to the user.
//
draw : dialog {
  label = "Select Drawing Option";
  :      text_part {
         label = "Select object type to draw: ";
  }
  : row {
       : button {
                key       = "line";
                label     = "Line";
                mnemonic        = "L";
                fixed_width     = true;
       }
       : button {
                key       = "circle";
                label     = "Circle";
                mnemonic        = "C";
                fixed_width     = true;
       }
       : button {
                key       = "arc";
                label     = "Arc";
                mnemonic        = "A";
                fixed_width     = true;
       }
       : button {
                key       = "cancel";
                label     = "Cancel";
                is_cancel       = true;
                fixed_width     = true;
       }
  }
}
```

```
;EXAMPLE3.LSP
;This file displays the dialog box defined in EXAMPLE3.DCL and begins the
; selected drawing command as specified by the user.
;
(defun C:DRAW (/ EX3_DCL_ID)
  (setq EX3_DCL_ID (load_dialog "EXAMPLE3.DCL"))
  (if     (not (new_dialog "draw" EX3_DCL_ID))
          (exit)
  )
  (action_tile "line" "(setq CMD $key) (done_dialog)")
  (action_tile "circle" "(setq CMD $key) (done_dialog)")
  (action_tile "arc" "(setq CMD $key) (done_dialog)")
  (action_tile "cancel" "(setq CMD nil) (done_dialog)")
  (start_dialog)
  (unload_dialog EX3_DCL_ID)
  (command CMD)
)
```

# Dialog Example 4

This example allows you to select a new current layer from a drop-down list in a dialog box. Save the files as EXAMPLE4.DCL and EXAMPLE4.LSP. Then, load the AutoLISP file. To access the dialog box, type GOFOR at the Command: prompt. See **Figure 25-7**.

```
//EXAMPLE4.DCL
// Presents a list of layers to the user.
fourth : dialog {
  label = "Select Layer";
  : popup_list {
        label     = "New Current Layer:";
        mnemonic        = "N";
        key     = "lyr_pop";
        allow_accept    = true;
        width   = 32;
  }
  ok_cancel;
}
```

```
;;EXAMPLE4.LSP
;;
(defun   CHECKOUT ()
  (setq LD (tblsearch "LAYER" (nth (atoi (get_tile "lyr_pop")) LL))
        LN (cdr (assoc 2 LD))
        LS (cdr (assoc 70 LD))
  )
  (if     (and
                (/= 1 LS)
                (/= 65 LS)
          )
          (progn
                (setvar "CLAYER" (nth (atoi (get_tile "lyr_pop")) LL))
                (done_dialog)
          )
          (alert "Selected layer is frozen!")
) )
(defun C:GOFOR ()
  (setq EX4_DCL_ID (load_dialog "EXAMPLE4.DCL"))
  (if (not (new_dialog "fourth" EX4_DCL_ID)) (exit))
  (start_list "lyr_pop")
  (setq LL '()
        NL (tblnext "LAYER" T)
        IDX 0
  )
  (while        NL
        (if     (= (getvar "CLAYER") (cdr (assoc 2 NL)))
                (setq CL IDX)
                (setq IDX (1+ IDX))
          )
          (setq   LL (append LL (list (cdr (assoc 2 NL))))
                NL (tblnext "LAYER")
  )             )
  (mapcar 'add_list LL)
  (end_list)
  (set_tile "lyr_pop" (itoa CL))
  (action_tile "lyr_pop" "(if (= $reason 4) (mode_tile \"accept\" 2))")
  (action_tile "accept" "(CHECKOUT)")
  (start_dialog)
  (unload_dialog EX4_DCL_ID)
  (princ)
)
```

Figure 25-7.
The dialog box
displayed using the
EXAMPLE4 DCL and
LSP files.

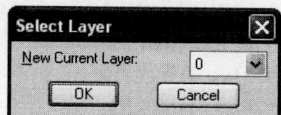

## Chapter Test

*Answer the following questions on a separate sheet of paper.*

1. What are the two types of files that must be created to construct a *functioning* dialog box?
2. When referring to a dialog box, what is a tile?
3. When defining a dialog or tile, inside of which character are all of the required attributes for a tile definition placed?
4. Which symbol indicates a comment inside a DCL file?
5. Write the appropriate notation for the first line of a DCL file that defines a dialog box named **Test**.
6. Write the appropriate notation in a DCL file that defines the text in the title bar of a dialog box named **Select Application**.
7. Write the notation in a DCL file for defining a cluster of four buttons labeled **OK**, **NEXT**, **CANCEL**, and **HELP**.
8. Which type of file is commonly used to control a DCL file?
9. Write the notation that would appear in the file in Question 8 that loads a dialog file named PICKFILE.
10. What is a *key* in a DCL file?
11. What is the function of a *mnemonic* attribute?
12. Write the proper DCL file notation for the first line that identifies a button.

## Problems

1. Create a dialog box that contains the following items. Write the required DCL and AutoLISP files.
   A. Title bar—**Dialog Box Test**
   B. Label—**This is a test.**
   C. **OK** button

2. Create a dialog box that contains the following items. Write the required DCL and AutoLISP files.
   A. Title bar—**Date**
   B. Label—**Current date:**
   C. Action button—**Display Current Date**
   D. **OK** button

3. Create a dialog box that performs the following tasks. Then, write the required DCL and AutoLISP files.
   A. Displays the current date.
   B. Displays the current time.
   C. Displays the current drawing name.
   D. Contains buttons to update current date and time.
   E. Contains an **OK** button.

# AutoCAD and the Internet

## Learning Objectives

After completing this chapter, you will be able to:

● Explain the Internet and its basic operation.
● Launch a web browser from within AutoCAD and access websites.
● Create Drawing Web Format (DWF) files.
● View a DWF file using a web browser.
● Attach hyperlinks to an AutoCAD drawing.
● Open and insert drawings from the World Wide Web.
● Create a webpage containing AutoCAD drawings.

The Internet started in 1969 as a network consisting of four computers. It now includes millions of computers worldwide, connected to one another through the use of telecommunication lines. The Internet is a powerful and versatile communication medium. One of the most widespread uses of the Internet is for sending and receiving electronic mail. Electronic mail, or *e-mail*, is used to create, send, and receive text messages and other files by telecommunication.

Another widely known application of the Internet is the World Wide Web (WWW). The *World Wide Web*, often called "the web," uses Hypertext Markup Language (HTML) files to provide a graphic interface to access Internet information. However, it is important to remember that the web is not the Internet, it *uses* the Internet.

The term *hypertext* refers to an object, such as text or a picture, that is linked to other information. This additional information is displayed when the hypertext is picked. These links are also called *hyperlinks*. A *website* is a collection of HTML documents, which may include text, graphics, and sound files, that can be accessed using a *web browser*. The *Uniform Resource Locator* (*URL*) refers to the location, or address, of a web file on the Internet.

AutoCAD incorporates tools that allow you to communicate AutoCAD drawing information over the Internet using the web or e-mail. For example, a drawing can be saved in a format that can be viewed using a web browser and then placed on a website. In this way, drawings can be shared with others who do not have AutoCAD.

Coupling AutoCAD with the Internet opens up whole new worlds of possibilities. With geographic restrictions and the need for special software removed, designs can be communicated to anyone, anywhere in the world. This ease of communication lends itself to creating effective virtual workgroups. A *virtual workgroup* is a group of individuals separated by geographic distances who collaborate on a project through the use of telecommunication technologies, such as e-mail and the World Wide Web.

## Getting Connected to the Internet

The Internet uses telecommunications lines, such as phone lines or cable television lines, to send information between computers. Home Internet users generally use modems and standard phone lines or cable connections to get "online." A *modem* is a device that converts computer data into signals that can be sent through phone or cable services to another computer modem. The other modem receives the signals and converts them back to computer data. In many areas, integrated services digital network (ISDN) or "T-carrier" connections are available. These connections offer much higher speeds than traditional phone lines, but special modems are required. There is usually a higher cost involved with these high-speed connections than with traditional phone lines or cable connections.

### Internet Service

An *Internet Service Provider* (*ISP*) is required to use the Internet. An ISP is the company or organization that you "dial up" to get access to the Internet. There are typically several different ISPs in any given region. Online service providers such as Earthlink® and America Online® (AOL) also provide Internet access. In order to take advantage of the Internet tools in AutoCAD, you need to have access to an ISP.

### Launching a Web Browser

A web browser is required to access the World Wide Web. There are several different browsers available. Most have features common to all browsers. It is a matter of personal preference which browser software you use. In order to take advantage of the newest Internet features, your browser should be the most current version.

Selecting the **Browse the Web** button from the **Web** toolbar, **Figure 26-1,** automatically launches your default web browser. The **BROWSER** command can also be entered at the Command: prompt by entering BROWSER.

BROWSER

Web toolbar

Browse the Web

PROFESSIONAL TIP

When using both AutoCAD and your web browser, you can easily move between the two applications by using the taskbar or by using the [Alt]+[Tab] keystroke. To see both windows at once, right-click on the Windows taskbar and select Cascade Windows or one of the Tile Windows options.

Figure 26-1.
The **Web** toolbar.

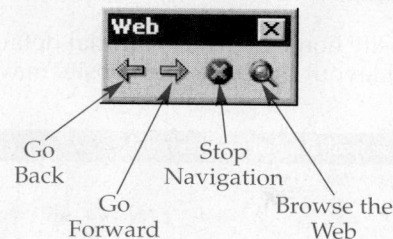

Go
Back

Go
Forward

Stop
Navigation

Browse the
Web

When you pick the toolbar button, the **BROWSER** command uses the default URL, which is initially http://www.autodesk.com. The default URL is stored in the **INETLOCATION** system variable. You can change this value at the Command: prompt as follows.

> Command: **INETLOCATION**↲
> Enter new value for INETLOCATION <"http://www.autodesk.com">: *(Enter new location, such as* http://www.g-w.com*)*
> Command:

The default URL should be the location you most frequently access when you start your browser. This may be your own website, a client's website, or any other site that you frequently access. The variable value is saved in the registry, not the drawing file.

When entered at the keyboard, the **BROWSER** command allows you to enter a specific URL or accept the default URL.

> Command: **BROWSER**
> Enter Web location (URL) < http://www.autodesk.com >: *(this is the default installation URL)*

**Figure 26-2** shows the Autodesk website home page as it appears in Microsoft Internet Explorer. From this page you can select a particular country or region. Select **United States** and you will get the Autodesk United States page. This page offers a great deal of information and many valuable resources—product support information, reviews, tips and tricks, white papers, discussion group access—for AutoCAD users of every experience level.

---

## EXERCISE 26-1

○ Ask your system administrator or instructor for guidance on accessing the Internet and the web.

○ Start AutoCAD.

○ Pick the **Browse the Web** button.

○ Once you have reached the Autodesk United States website page, select the search tool.

○ From the search window, initiate two or three searches to get a feel for how to find things. After each search is complete, select the browser's Back button to return to the search page.

---

**Figure 26-2.**
The Autodesk website home page is the initial default URL for the **BROWSER** command. Due to content and layout updates, the website may or may not appear as shown here. (Autodesk, Inc.)

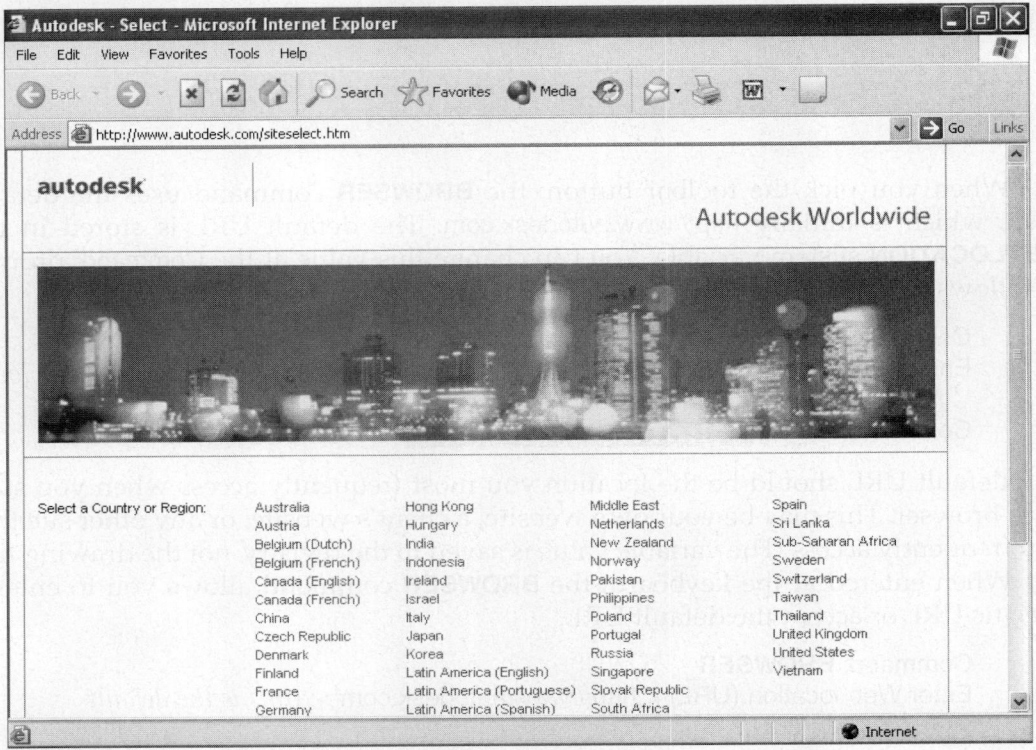

## AutoCAD Internet Utilities

AutoCAD provides powerful tools and options for data communication with clients, vendors, and colleagues through the web. For example, you can open drawings from a website using the **Search the Web** button in the **Select File** (open) dialog box. With Autodesk Express Viewer or Volo View program, drawing files in DWF format can be viewed, printed, and saved from the web using a browser.

### The Browse the Web Button

Many "open" and "save" dialog boxes in AutoCAD have the **Search the Web** button. Picking this button displays a web browser titled **Browse the Web**–*command name*, **Figure 26-3**. The current AutoCAD command is displayed in the title bar. The default page is set with the **INETLOCATION** variable. Typing the URL of a website in the **Look in:** text box and pressing [Enter] will display that site.

If you are accessing a website frequently, you can save the URL so you do not need to type it in every time. First, navigate to the website. Then, pick the **Favorites** button and select **Add To Favorites...** from the menu. The **Add to Favorites** dialog box is displayed, which allows you to save the URL in the Windows Favorites folder. The contents of this folder are displayed when the **Favorites** button is picked in a dialog box, or when Favorites is selected in the Windows Start menu.

Figure 26-3.
The **Browse the Web**
dialog box gives
you access to files
on the Internet.

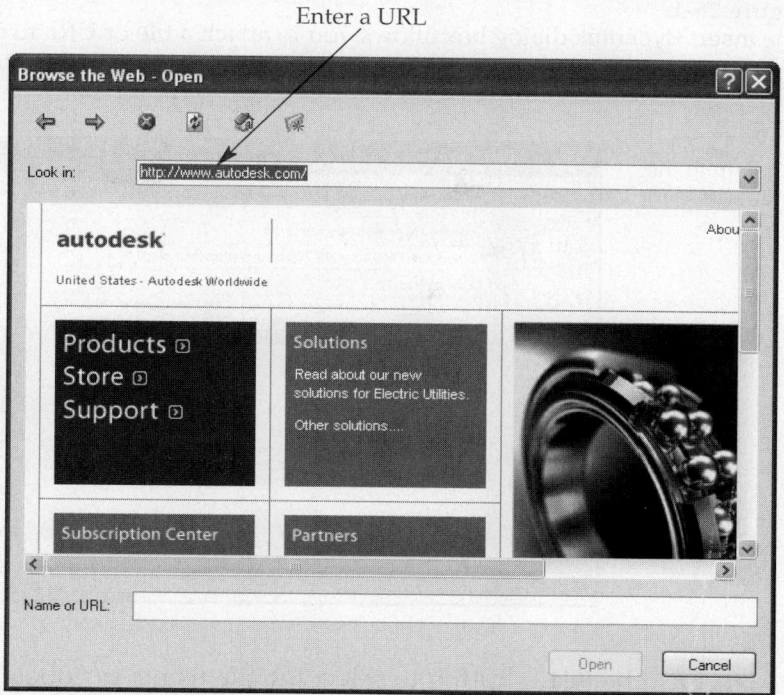

Enter a URL

## Inserting a Hyperlink into a Drawing

You can hyperlink drawing objects to a URL, e-mail address, or other files, such as drawings or text files. Once set, these links can be picked to display the other files. For example, an assembly drawing can be created with each part linked to its detail drawing. Or, the individual parts can be linked to a webpage that contains part numbers, supplier name, and prices. The assembly drawing could also have a link to a spreadsheet that is the bill of materials for all the parts in the assembly.

To attach a hyperlink to an object, pick **Hyperlink...** from the **Insert** pull-down menu, or enter HYPERLINK at the Command: prompt. The key combination [Ctrl]+[K] can also be used. A prompt appears on the Command: line asking you to select objects. Pick the objects that you want to attach a file or URL to and press [Enter]. The **Insert Hyperlink** dialog box is displayed, **Figure 26-4.** The next section describes this dialog box in detail.

## Insert Hyperlink Dialog Box

On the left side of the **Insert Hyperlink** dialog box is the **Link to:** area. The three options in this area are buttons that determine the type of hyperlink that is added. You can choose to create a hyperlink to an existing file or webpage, a view of the current drawing, or an e-mail address.

By default, the file path and name are displayed in a tooltip when the cursor is held over the hyperlink for a moment. However, you can specify the text that appears in the tooltip in the **Text to display:** text box at the top of the dialog box.

### Linking to an existing file or webpage

To create a link to an existing file or webpage, select the **Existing File or Web Page** button in the **Link to:** area of the **Insert Hyperlink** dialog box. Then, use one of the following methods to select the file or webpage to which you are linking.

- Use the **Recent Files**, **Browsed Pages**, and **Inserted Links** buttons to display the desired content in the list in the middle of the **Insert Hyperlink** dialog box. Then, pick the file or website from the list.
- Enter the path to the file or URL in the **Type the file or Web page name:** text box. Include the file name.

**Figure 26-4.**
The **Insert Hyperlink** dialog box allows you to attach a file or URL to objects.

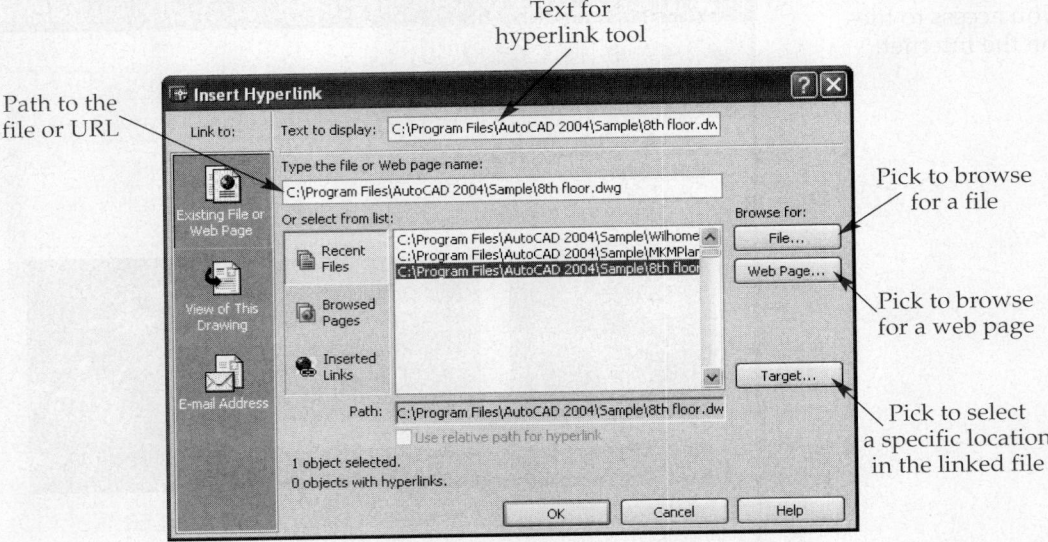

Text for
hyperlink tool

Path to the
file or URL

Pick to browse
for a file

Pick to browse
for a web page

Pick to select
a specific location
in the linked file

- Pick the **File...** button to select the file using an "open" dialog box.
- Pick the **Web Page...** button to select a webpage using the **Browse the Web** dialog box.

If you create a link to an AutoCAD drawing, you can specify a named view or tab to be displayed when the link is picked. Pick the **Target...** button to access the **Select Place in Document** dialog box, **Figure 26-5**. This dialog box lists the named views, model tab, and layout tabs contained within the linked drawing. Pick the view or tab you want initially displayed and then pick the **OK** button.

### Linking to a view in the current drawing

In addition to linking to other drawing files or webpages, you can also create a hyperlink to another view or layout within the same drawing. Pick the **View of This Drawing** button in the **Link to:** area of the **Insert Hyperlink** dialog box. The **Select a view of this** list is displayed in the middle of the dialog box. See **Figure 26-6.** The list includes any named views and layout tabs. Select the item to be accessed by the link and then pick the **OK** button.

**Figure 26-5.**
If an inserted hyperlink is to an AutoCAD drawing, you can specify the view or tab to which the link points.

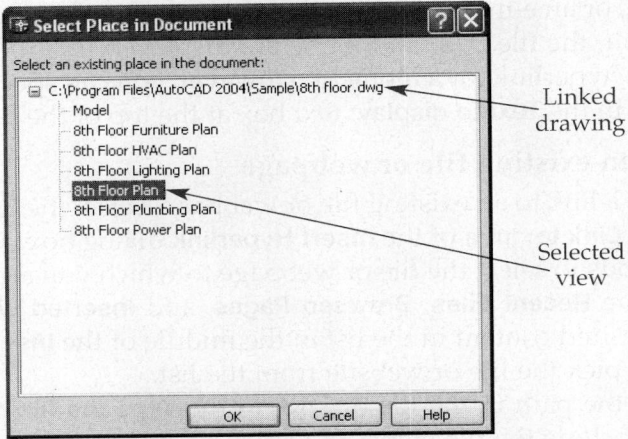

Linked
drawing

Selected
view

AutoCAD and its Applications—Advanced

**Figure 26-6.**
You can insert a
hyperlink to a view
or tab within the
current drawing.

Selected view

Current drawing

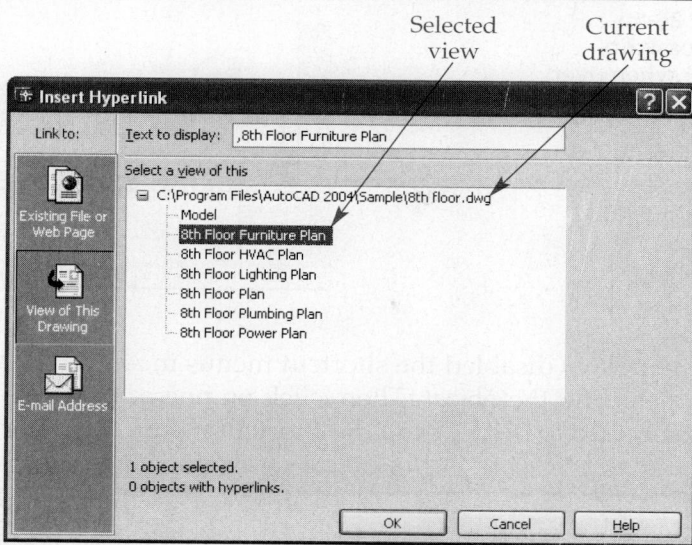

## Linking to an e-mail address

You can also create hyperlinks that access e-mail addresses. When the hyperlink is activated, the default e-mail program opens with a message addressed to the linked e-mail address. To do so, pick the **E-mail Address** button in the **Link to:** list of the **Insert Hyperlink** dialog box. The options shown in **Figure 26-7** are displayed. Type the e-mail address in the **E-mail address:** text box or select an e-mail address from the **Recently used e-mail addresses:** list. Pick the **OK** button to set the hyperlink.

## Using hyperlinks

When the cursor is held over the object in AutoCAD that has a hyperlink, an icon appears next to the crosshairs. See **Figure 26-8.** To open the hyperlink, first select the object. Next, right-click anywhere in the viewport. Select **Hyperlink** and then **Open** from the shortcut menu. The path and file name are displayed next to **Open**.

The linked file or URL is opened in the program with which it is associated. For example, the file type BMP, by Windows default, is associated with Microsoft Paint. Therefore, if you open a hyperlinked BMP file, it is opened in Microsoft Paint. If you do not have a program associated with that file type, you will get an alert box message from AutoCAD.

**Figure 26-7.**
An inserted
hyperlink can
automatically
initiate an e-mail to
a specific address.

Enter an e-mail address

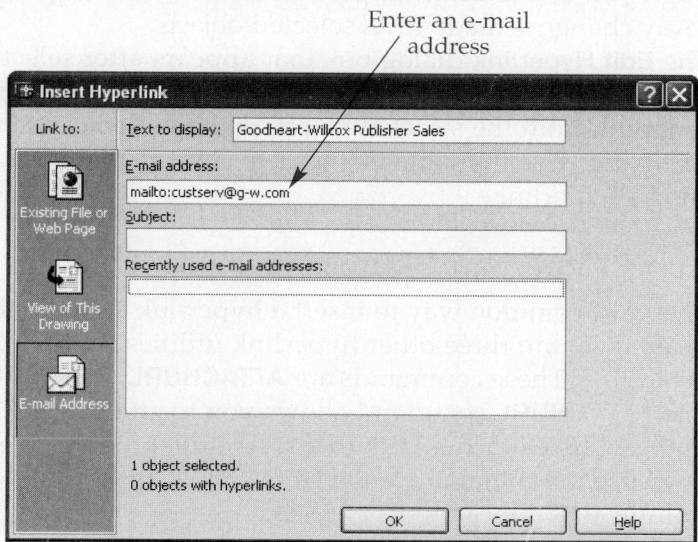

Figure 26-8.
The crosshairs
change when over
an object that
contains a
hyperlink.

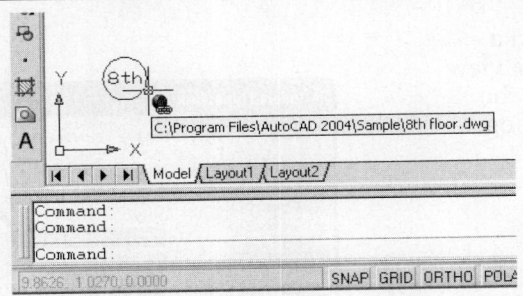

If you have disabled the shortcut menus in AutoCAD, you can open a hyperlink file by selecting the object. Then, click on one of the grips to make it hot and right-click. Select **Go to URL...** from the shortcut menu. This shortcut menu is not disabled.

---

**EXERCISE 26-2**

○ Start a new drawing. Set the limits to 0,0 and 12,9 and then **ZOOM All**.
○ Draw a rectangle from 3,3 to 10,6.
○ Pick the **Insert Hyperlink** button and select the rectangle.
○ In the **Insert Hyperlink** dialog box, pick the **Existing File or Web Page** button in the **Link to:** area. Then, pick the **Browse...** button on the right side of the dialog box. Select any type of word processing document or image file, such as a Word, Excel, or JPEG file, that has an association for your version of Windows.
○ Apply the link.
○ Select the rectangle, right-click, and select **Open** from the **Hyperlink** cascading menu. Observe the results. Then, return to AutoCAD.
○ Save the file as EX26-2.

---

## Editing a Hyperlink

If the path to a linked URL or file is changed, you will need to open the AutoCAD drawing and edit the hyperlink. Otherwise, AutoCAD will never "find" the link. To edit a hyperlink, select the **Insert Hyperlink** button, pick **Hyperlink...** from the **Insert** pull-down menu, or enter HYPERLINK at the Command: prompt. The [Ctrl]+[K] key combination also works. Then, select the hyperlinked object you want to edit. Although you can select multiple objects when editing a hyperlink, this may not be wise. Any change is made to *all* selected objects.

The **Edit Hyperlink** dialog box that appears after selecting objects is the same as the **Insert Hyperlink** dialog box, with the addition of the **Remove Link** button. To delete the hyperlink from the selected object, pick the **Remove Link** button at the bottom of the dialog box. Use the same methods to edit the hyperlink path as you would when attaching a hyperlink.

## Optional Command Line Hyperlink Utilities

The most common way to insert a hyperlink is to use the **HYPERLINK** command. However, there are three other hyperlink utilities that can be accessed only from the command line. These commands are **ATTACHURL**, **DETACHURL**, and **SELECTURL**.

The **ATTACHURL** command allows you to attach a URL to an object in the drawing. You can also attach a URL to a rectangular area of the drawing using this command. To use the command, enter ATTACHURL at the Command: prompt. Then, follow the prompts that appear.

When the **ATTACHURL** command is used to attach a URL to a rectangular area of the drawing, a red rectangle appears in the drawing to show the defined area. The rectangle is on a new layer named URLLAYER. The URLLAYER layer must be visible when you plot the DWF file, but the rectangle will not show in the DWF file. The DWF file type is covered later in this chapter.

The **DETACHURL** command is used to remove a hyperlink from selected objects or an area in the drawing. Objects that do not have a URL are filtered out of the selection set. When an area is removed, the message Remove, deleting the Area appears indicating the area was deleted. Erasing an area also removes the associated URL link. To use the command, enter DETACHURL at the Command: prompt. Then, follow the prompts that appear.

Using the **SELECTURL** command is an easy way to see which objects in the drawing have a hyperlink attached. The command selects all objects and areas in the drawing to which a hyperlink is attached. However, only the objects at least partially visible in the current viewport are selected by the command. Also, using the command to select all objects with hyperlinks and then using the **DETACHURL** command is a convenient way to remove all URLs from a drawing.

## Opening a Drawing from the Web

The **OPEN** command displays the **Select File** dialog box, which can be used to open a drawing from the web. Type the URL and the drawing file name in the **File name:** text box and pick the **Open** button. If you do not know the specific URL, you can pick the **Search the Web** button and manually locate the file on the web. When the drawing is opened, AutoCAD copies the drawing to a temporary file on your hard drive and loads it into the drawing editor. The drawing can then be edited and saved to a local hard drive or network drive.

**PROFESSIONAL TIP**

AutoCAD does not confirm that an Internet connection exists before attempting to open a drawing from the web. If you are not connected to the Internet when attempting to open a drawing from the web, a dialog box will appear with a message indicating that the drawing file is not a valid format. If this occurs, you will need to establish an Internet connection, restart AutoCAD, and then open the file. If you do not restart AutoCAD after establishing the Internet connection, you may continue to get the error message.

### Inserting a Drawing from the Web

You can insert a drawing from the web into the current drawing using the **INSERT** command. The **INSERT** command is accessed by picking the **Insert Block** button from the **Draw** toolbar, picking **Block...** from the **Insert** pull-down menu, or by entering I or INSERT at the Command: prompt. The **Insert** dialog box is displayed.

In the **Insert** dialog box, pick the **Browse...** button. This displays the **Select Drawing File** dialog box. Type the URL path and the file name in the **File name:** text box and pick the **Open** button. Or, pick the **Search the Web** button to locate the file in the **Browse the Web–Open** dialog box.

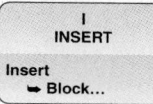

Once the file is selected, the **Insert** dialog box is redisplayed. You can now insert the drawing as a locally defined block. As with other applications of the **INSERT** command, an insertion point, scale factor, and rotation angle must be specified.

## Saving a Drawing to the Web

The **SAVE** command allows you to save a drawing directly to the web. It is accessed by picking **Save As...** from the **File** pull-down menu or by typing SAVE at the Command: prompt. This displays the **Save Drawing As** dialog box. Enter the URL and file name using the syntax:

ftp://*server name*/*path name*/*file name*.dwg

Pick the **Save** button to save the drawing. You must have the appropriate permissions in order to save the file in this manner.

AutoCAD has another way of placing your drawings on the web. This involves a file type called DWF, which is discussed in the next section. Also, refer to the section later in this chapter called *Publishing a DWF File on the Web*.

---

### EXERCISE 26-3

○ Open the drawing EX26-3.
○ With the permission of your system administrator, use the **SAVE** command to save the file to an appropriate location on your Internet server. Close AutoCAD.
○ Start a new drawing session. Now, use **OPEN** to open the drawing that you just saved from the Internet.
○ Start a new drawing session again. This time, use **INSERT** to insert the drawing into the current drawing. Save this drawing as EX26-3.

---

## Drawing Web Format (DWF) Files

You can save an AutoCAD drawing as a *Drawing Web Format (DWF)* file. A DWF file is a highly compressed vector file that can be viewed in 2D using the Autodesk Express Viewer or Volo View program. In addition, when either of these programs is installed in conjunction with Microsoft Internet Explorer 5.01 or later, you can view DWF files on the web. The Autodesk Express Viewer program is installed when AutoCAD is installed.

A DWF file is created using the **PLOT** command. The AutoCAD documentation refers to this as the "ePlot" feature. First, open the **Plot** dialog box. In the **Plotter configuration** area of the **Plot Device** tab, the **Name:** drop-down list gives you a few choices for creating files. The option for DWF files is **DWF ePlot.pc3**, Figure 26-9. The **DWF ePlot.pc3** is designed to create files that will be viewed, downloaded, and plotted. There are three other PC3 options, which are used with the **PUBLISHTOWEB** command discussed later in this chapter.

Once you select the DWF option, specify the name for the file in the **File name:** text box in the **Plot to file** area. Also, specify a location for the file in the **Location:** text box. Use all the other settings in the **Plot Device** and **Plot Settings** tabs just as you would when plotting a hard copy. Refer to Chapter 10 in *AutoCAD and its Applications—Basics* for detailed information on plotting.

**Figure 26-9.**
When plotting to a DWF file, the ePlot PC3 configuration is optimized for plotting and viewing.

Select the
DWF option

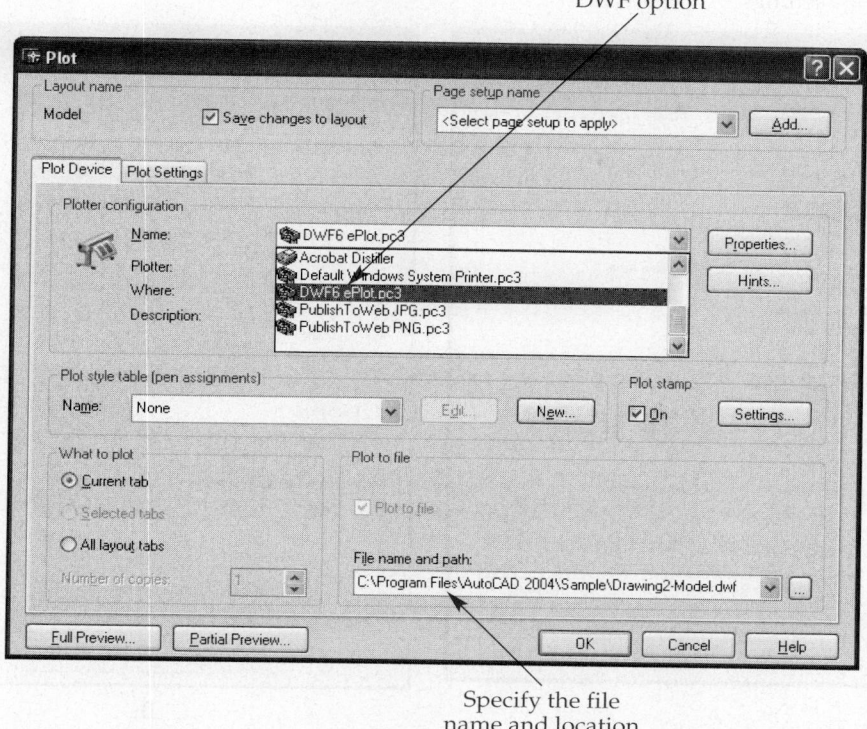

Specify the file
name and location

There are several settings for a DWF file that affect the final output. After the ePlot configuration is selected, pick the **Properties...** button in the **Plotter configuration** area of the **Plot Device** tab. In the **Plotter Configuration Editor** dialog box, select **Custom Properties** from the **Device and Document Settings** tab, **Figure 26-10A.** Then, pick the **Custom Properties...** button to display the **DWF Properties** dialog box, **Figure 26-10B.**

The **Resolution** and **Format** areas in the **DWF Properties** dialog box are primarily used to control the size of the DWF file. The **Resolution** setting controls the accuracy of the resulting DWF file. A medium resolution is best in most cases. A DWF created with high resolution may be too large for practical electronic transmission. A lower resolution will create a smaller DWF file. Small files make for easy electronic transmission. However, the resulting DWF file may not display as accurately as one created at a higher resolution.

The **Format** area has three options. The **Compressed Binary (recommended)** option is the default selection. It produces a small, binary file. The **ASCII** option creates an ASCII file.

Once you have made all settings as needed, pick the **OK** button. Then, pick **OK** in the **Plotter Configuration Editor.** If changes were made to the settings, a dialog box appears asking if you want to apply the changes on a one-time basis or save the configuration to a PC3 plotter configuration file.

> **NOTE**  Commands that control the display of geometry on screen, such as **VIEWRES**, **FACETRES**, and **DISPSILH** also affect the resulting DWF file.

**Figure 26-10.**
A—Setting up custom properties for a DWF. B—The **DWF Properties** dialog box.

Pick to adjust
settings

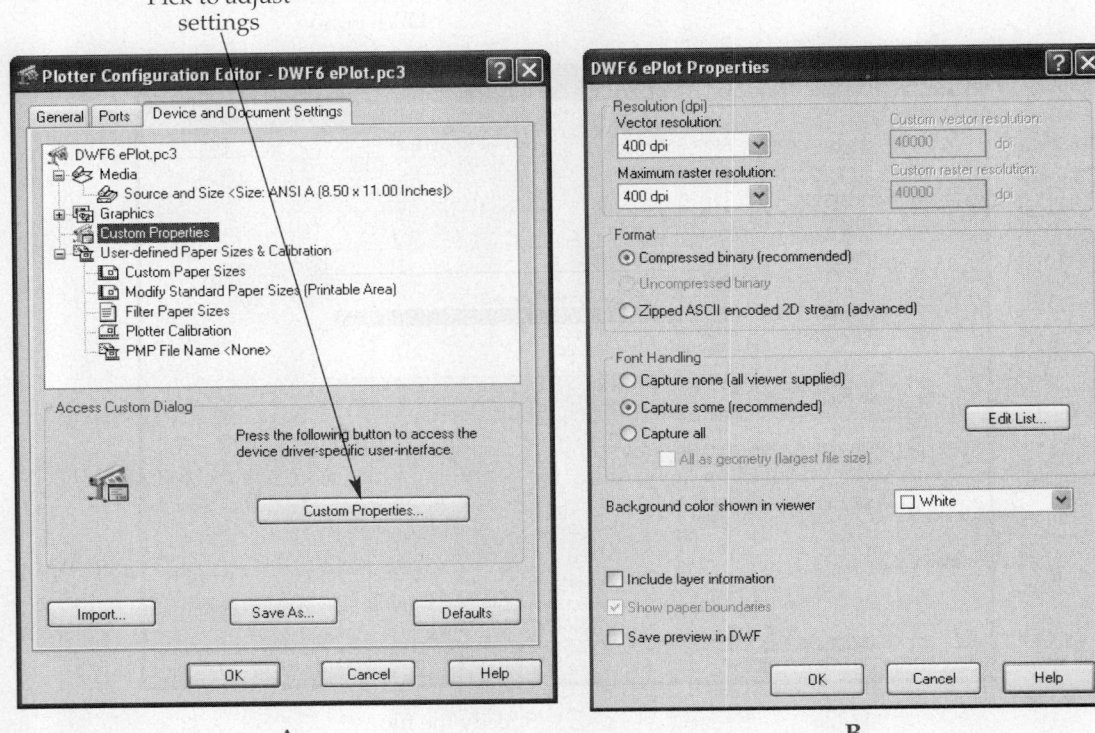

A

B

## Using Autodesk Express Viewer

This section briefly introduces the features of Autodesk Express Viewer. Many of these features are shared with Volo View. Once Autodesk Express Viewer is started, pick the **Open** in the **File** pull-down menu. Then, navigate to the folder where the DWF file is located and select it. You can open the file using Autodesk Express Viewer or from the Internet Explorer. See **Figure 26-11.**

Autodesk Express Viewer has a toolbar and several pull-down menus from which commands can be selected. It also has a shortcut menu that can be accessed by right-clicking in the display area with a file open. Depending on the drawing setup of the open file, some options may not be available. For detailed information on using the commands, refer to the online documentation in Autodesk Express Viewer.

- **Pan.** Allows you to shift the drawing around in the display area. Works like the realtime pan feature in AutoCAD.
- **Zoom.** Allows you to zoom the display in or out. Works like the realtime zoom feature in AutoCAD.
- **Zoom Rectangle.** Allows you to zoom in on a rectangular area of the drawing. Works like the **ZOOM Window** command in AutoCAD.
- **Fit in Window.** Allows you to zoom so that the area of the drawing fits into the Autodesk Express Viewer window.
- **Layers.** Allows you to turn layers within the file off and on. A dialog box appears, which has similar functions to the **Layer Properties Manager** dialog box in AutoCAD. The command is available from the **View** pull-down menu or the shortcut menu.

**Figure 26-11.**
A—A DWF file as
seen in Autodesk
Express Viewer. B—
The DWF file
shown opened with
Microsoft Internet
Explorer.

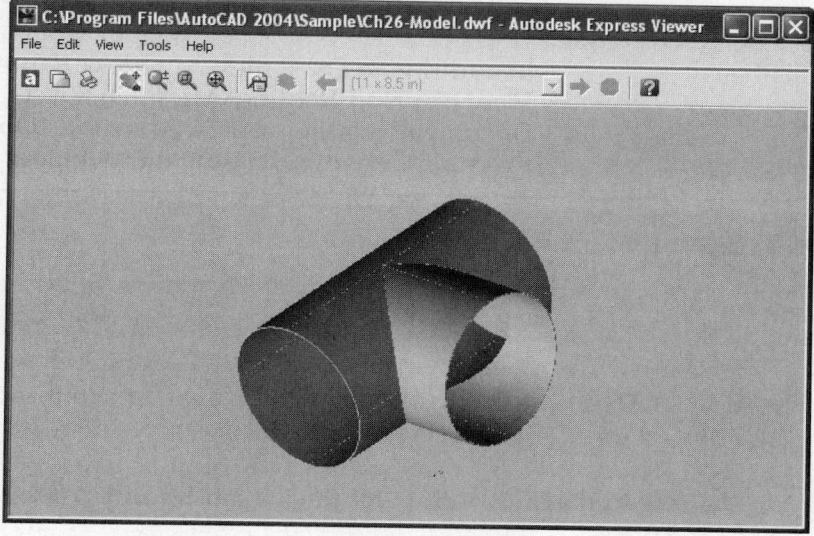

A

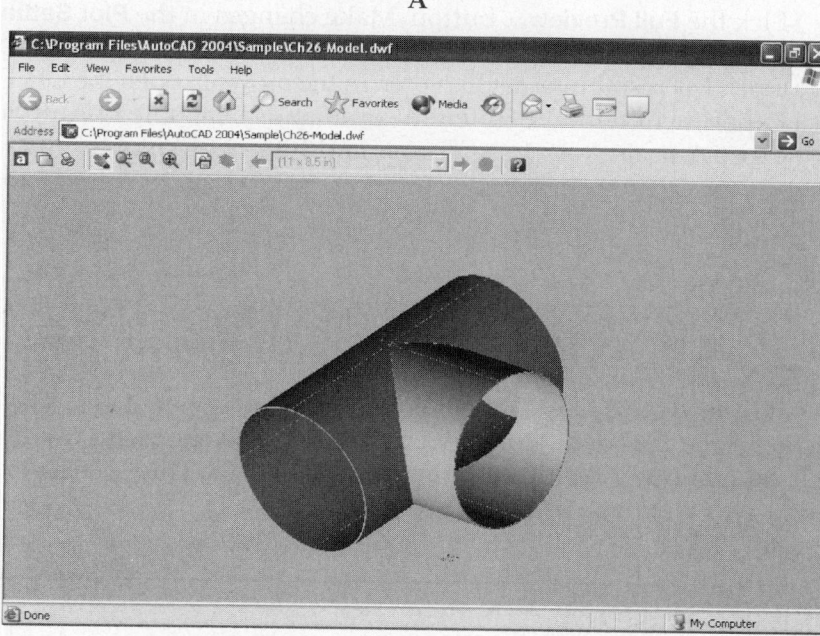

B

- **Views.** Enables you to change to a named view or reset the view to the initial view.
- **Sheets.** Displays a dialog box containing the names of the sheets contained in the current drawing file. The active sheet is highlighted and you can select a sheet from the list to make it active in the viewer.
- **Show.** Accesses a secondary menu containing the additional display options.
- **Print.** Prints the file.
- **Copy.** Copies the current view to your computer's Clipboard. You can then paste it into a different file.
- **Help.** Accesses Autodesk Express Viewer help file.

### EXERCISE 26-4

○ Open a drawing of your own or one from the AutoCAD "sample" folder.
○ Use the **PLOT** command to open the **Plot** dialog box. In the **Plot Device** tab, select the **DWF ePlot** configuration from the **Name:** drop-down list in the **Plotter configuration** area.
○ In the **Plot to file** area of the **Plot Device** tab, specify a file name and location to save the file.
○ Pick the **Full Preview...** button. Make changes in the **Plot Settings** tab as necessary.
○ Pick the **OK** button to create the DWF file.
○ Open Microsoft Internet Explorer. In the browser, open the DWF file you just created.
○ Experiment with the different commands available in Autodesk Express Viewer.
○ Close Autodesk Express Viewer and Internet Explorer.

## Publishing a Drawing on the Web

Using AutoCAD, you can create your own webpages. These pages can be published, or "uploaded," to the web. You can also choose to use the pages internally on a local computer or intranet (internal network). This section explains how to create your own webpage using AutoCAD.

### I-Drop

When publishing a drawing on the web, you can choose to enable the drawing as an i-drop drawing. An *i-drop enabled* drawing can be quickly inserted by somebody viewing your webpage. This is done by simply "dragging and dropping" the image from the web into an open AutoCAD drawing. This can be used very effectively by manufacturers who have created a web-based "block inventory" of their products. However, if you are simply sharing information on the web and do not want users to have direct access to the drawing, this feature should not be used.

# Publishing to the Web

The **PUBLISHTOWEB** command is used to create a formatted hypertext markup language (HTML) file using standard templates and DWF or JPEG versions of a drawing. The **Publish to Web** wizard is used to step you through the creation process. To open the wizard, select **Publish to Web...** from the **File** pull-down menu, select **Publish to Web...** from the **Wizards** cascading menu in the **Tools** pull-down menu, or enter PUBLISHTOWEB at the Command: prompt.

## Creating a webpage

The first panel of the **Publish to Web** wizard is the **Begin** panel. You must first select to create a new webpage or edit an existing webpage. This section explains how to create a new webpage. Editing an existing webpage is discussed in the next section. Pick the **Create New Web Page** radio button. Then, pick the **Next>** button to display the **Create Web Page** panel of the wizard. See **Figure 26-12**. Three components of the webpage are defined on this panel.

- **Webpage name.** The name of the webpage appears at the top of the webpage that will be created.
- **Webpage folder location.** Select the folder in which the webpage is to be located. This is typically on the local hard drive, and then is uploaded to the web server later.
- **Webpage description.** The text entered in this box appears on the webpage below the title.

After specifying this information, pick the **Next>** button to continue.

The next panel is the **Select Image Type** panel. On this panel, select the type of image that will be generated from your drawing. You can select DWF, JPEG, and PNG image file types. A description of the type appears in the panel when you select it from the drop-down list. If you select JPEG or PNG, you must also select an image size from the right-hand drop-down list. Once you have selected an image type and size, if required, pick the **Next>** button to continue.

The next panel is the **Select Template** panel, **Figure 26-13**. You can choose one of four different templates for your webpage. When you pick one of the templates, a preview image and template description are displayed. The following templates are available.

PUBLISHTOWEB

File
  ⮡ Publish to Web...
Tools
  ⮡ Wizards
    ⮡ Publish to
      Web...

**Figure 26-12.**
Using the **PUBLISHTOWEB** command to create a webpage.

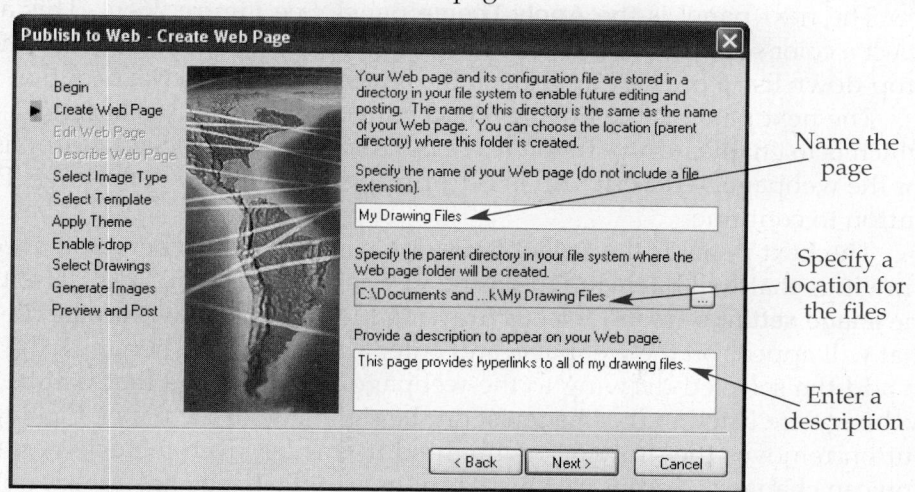

**Figure 26-13.**
When creating a webpage, you can choose from four different templates.

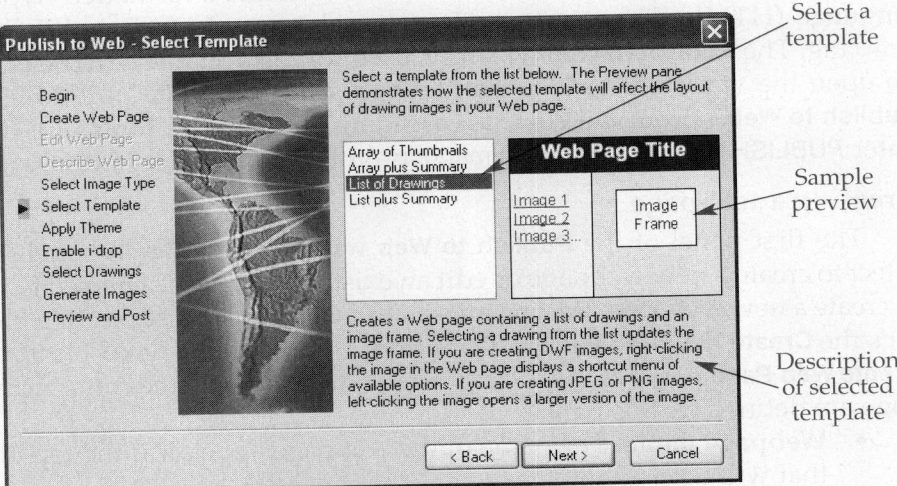

Select a template

Sample preview

Description of selected template

- **Array of Thumbnails.** This template creates a webpage with an array of thumbnail images of each drawing you specify, which you will do later. A user will pick one of the thumbnails on your webpage to display a larger version of the image.
- **Array plus Summary.** This template creates a webpage similar to the one produced by the above template, but also provides a summary area at the bottom. When a user pauses their mouse over a thumbnail, information is displayed in the summary area.
- **List of Drawings.** This template creates a webpage with a list of drawings. When a user picks a drawing from the list, the preview on the right side of the webpage displays a thumbnail of the drawing. Picking the thumbnail displays a larger view of the drawing.
- **List plus Summary.** This template creates a webpage similar to the one produced by the above template, but also provides a summary area at the bottom. When a user selects a drawing from the list, in addition to displaying a thumbnail, information about the drawing is displayed in the summary area.

Any summary information displayed is contained within the **Summary** tab of the **Drawing Properties** dialog box *for that drawing*. After picking the webpage template, pick the **Next>** button to continue.

The next panel is the **Apply Theme** panel. See **Figure 26-14.** This allows you to select a color scheme, or "theme," for your webpage. When you select a theme from the drop-down list, a preview appears in the image tile. Pick the **Next>** button to continue.

The next panel is the **Enable i-drop** panel. There is only one setting in this panel, which is to enable i-drop. If you leave the check box unchecked, i-drop is not enabled for the webpage. A description of i-drop appears at the top of the page. Pick the **Next>** button to continue.

The next panel is the **Select Drawings** panel. This is where you specify all of the drawings that will be included on the webpage. See **Figure 26-15.** Use the options in the **Image settings** area to select a drawing file and a view within the file, enter a label that will appear on the webpage, and enter a description. Then, pick the **Add->** button to add the selected drawing to the webpage. All drawings that will be added to the webpage are listed in the **Image list** on the right side of the panel. Picking the **Remove** button removes the drawing highlighted in this list from inclusion on the webpage. You can change the order in which drawings in the **Image list** appear on the webpage by highlighting the name and using the **Move Up** or **Move Down** buttons. When complete, pick the **Next>** button to continue.

**Figure 26-14.**
You can select from several preset color schemes when creating a webpage.

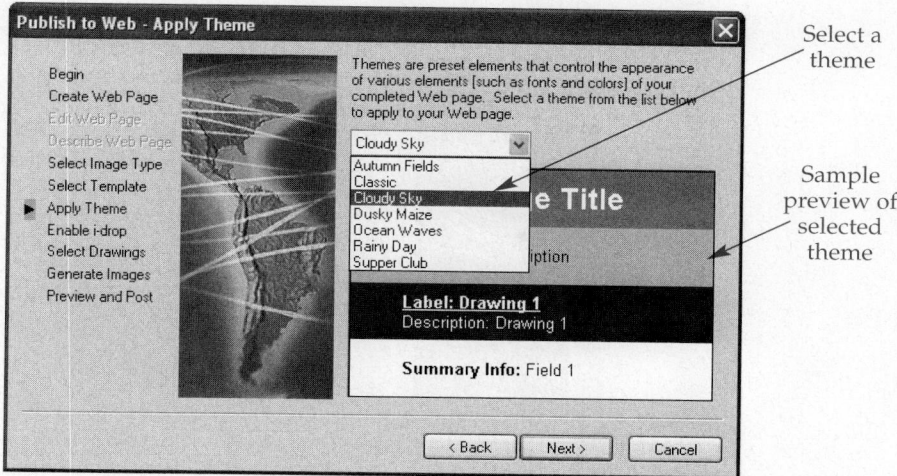

Select a theme

Sample preview of selected theme

**Figure 26-15.**
Specifying which drawings and views will be included on the webpage.

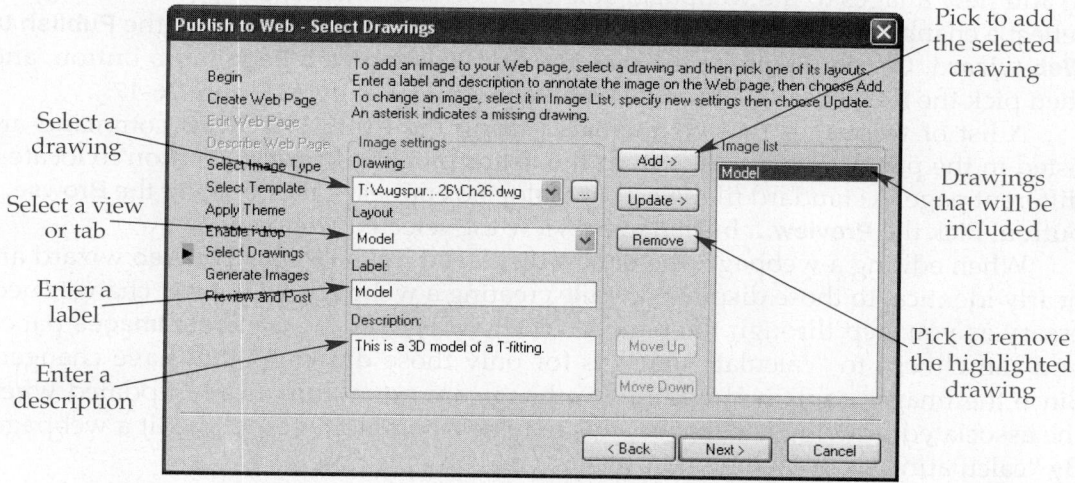

Pick to add the selected drawing

Select a drawing

Select a view or tab

Enter a label

Enter a description

Drawings that will be included

Pick to remove the highlighted drawing

The next panel is the **Generate Images** panel. The two options on this panel allow you to select which images are "calculated." If you are creating a new webpage, pick the **Regenerate all images** radio button. The **Regenerate images for drawings that have changed** radio button should be selected to "calculate" images for only those drawings that have changed since the last time the webpage was updated. After selecting the appropriate radio button, pick the **Next>** button to continue.

After AutoCAD has generated the webpage, which may take some time, the **Preview and Post** panel appears. See **Figure 26-16.** Pick the **Preview** button to view the webpage in your browser. When done previewing the page, close the browser and return to AutoCAD. Pick the **Finish** button to complete the webpage and save it to the folder you specified earlier in the wizard. If you pick the **Post Now** button, the **Posting Web** dialog box appears. This is a "save" dialog box that allows you to save the webpage to your web server.

**Figure 26-16.**
You have the option of previewing your webpage before completing the operation.

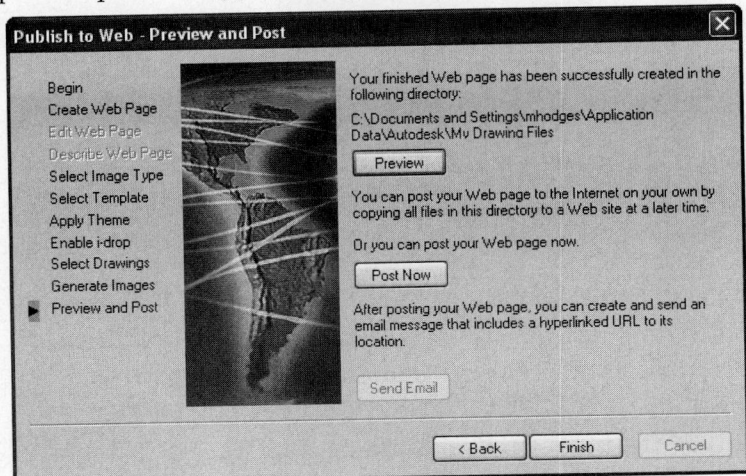

## Editing a webpage

There are many instances in which a webpage requires updating. You may want to add new images to the webpage, delete out-of-date images, or update an image to reflect a change in the drawing. To edit an existing webpage, first open the **Publish to Web** wizard. On the **Begin** panel, pick the **Edit Existing Web Page** radio button, and then pick the **Next>** button. The **Edit Web Page** panel is shown, **Figure 26-17.**

A list of webpages that were created using the **PUBLISHTOWEB** command are listed in the panel. Select a page from the list or pick the **Browse...** button to locate a different page. A standard file selection dialog box appears after picking the **Browse...** button. Pick the **Preview...** button to preview the selected webpage.

When editing a webpage, the panels displayed by the **Publish to Web** wizard are nearly identical to those displayed while creating a webpage. Make any changes necessary as you step through the panels. When you get to the **Generate Images** panel, you can choose to "calculate" images for only those drawings that have changed. Since the images contained within a webpage are not automatically updated when the associated drawing is changed, this may be a common reason to edit a webpage. By "calculating" only changed drawings, you can save time.

**Figure 26-17.**
Editing a webpage.

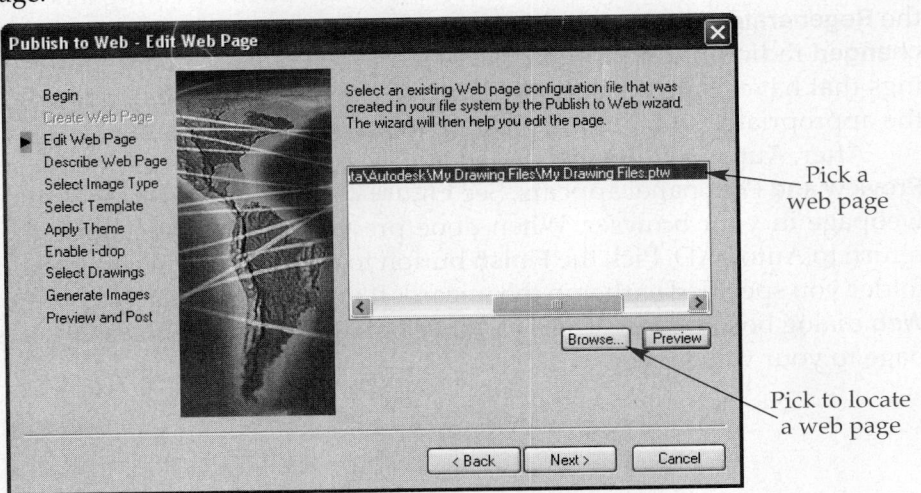

Pick a web page

Pick to locate a web page

## EXERCISE 26-5

○ Select six drawings to be included on a webpage. You can use completed drawing problems or sample drawings provided with AutoCAD.
○ Create a webpage containing the six drawings. Name the webpage My Drawings. Specify a folder approved by your instructor as the parent directory. Set the image type to DWF and select the **Array of Thumbnails** template.
○ Create a second webpage named My Drawings as JPEG. Use the same six drawings and settings, but set the image type to JPEG and medium size.
○ Open Internet Explorer and open each webpage. Notice the differences between the two types of images.

## Preparing E-Mail Transmittals

There are many instances when drawing files are transmitted using e-mail. To do this, select **Send...** from the **File** pull-down menu in AutoCAD. This automatically starts your default e-mail service and supplies the current drawing as an attachment file. If e-mail service has not been set up, this option is unavailable.

However, the recipient of your drawing may not have the font files, plot style table files, and xref files associated with the transmitted drawing. When this occurs, at best the drawing features will be displayed differently on the recipient's computer. At worst, critical components can be absent from the drawing.

The **eTransmit** feature of AutoCAD simplifies the process of sending a drawing file by e-mail by creating a transmittal file. The transmittal file contains the DWG file and all font files, plot style table files, and xrefs associated with the drawing.

To use the **eTransmit** feature, select **eTransmit...** from the **File** pull-down menu or enter ETRANSMIT at the Command: prompt. This opens the **Create Transmittal** dialog box, Figure 26-18. Use the **General** tab to specify the settings for the transmittal file. The following options are available.

- **Notes: text box.** Text entered in this text box is included in the transmittal report, which is a text file included in the transmittal.
- **Type: drop-down list.** The transmittal can be created in one of three formats. The files can be compressed into a self-extracting zip (EXE) file. The recipient can then simply double-click on the file and the individual files are automatically extracted. Another option is compressing the files into a single zip (ZIP) file. With this option, the user must have a utility program designed to work with ZIP files. The third option is to create a folder containing all files to be transmitted. The EXE and ZIP transmittals are smaller in size than the transmittal created with the "folder" option.

File
⮕ Send...

ETRANSMIT

File
⮕ eTransmit...

**Figure 26-18.**
Creating an e-mail transmittal.

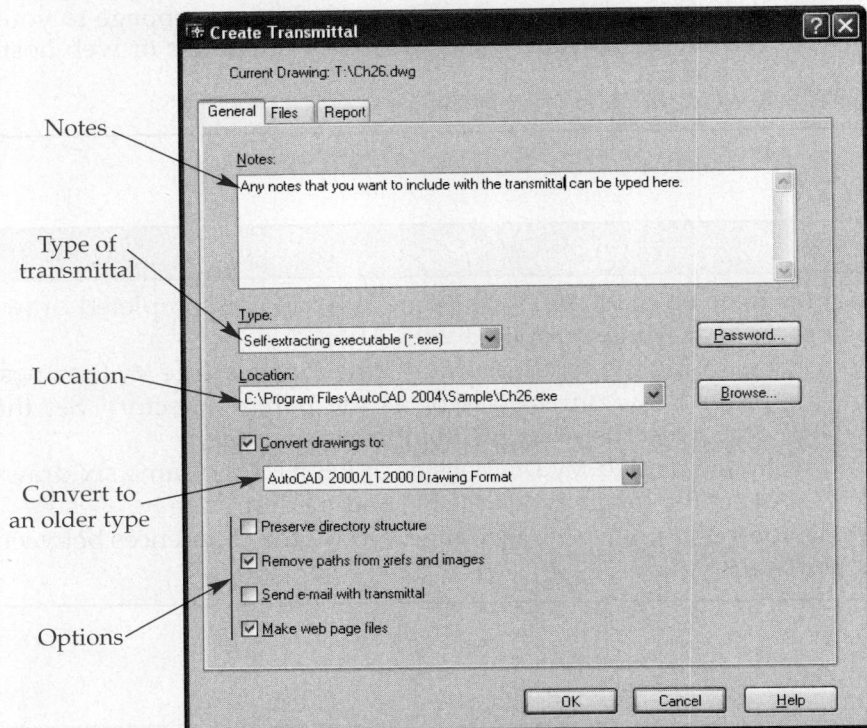

Notes

Type of
transmittal

Location

Convert to
an older type

Options

- **Location: drop-down list.** This drop-down list specifies the location of the final transmittal file or folder. Select from a previous location in the drop-down list or pick the **Browse...** button to select a different location.
- **Convert drawings to.** Pick this check box if you want to convert the drawing files to an older version of AutoCAD. This option is useful when the recipient is using an older version of AutoCAD. Select the version from the drop-down list.
- **Preserve directory structure.** This option maintains the folder locations of the transmitted files. When the transmittal is extracted, the folder structure from which the transmitted files originated will be duplicated on the recipient's computer.
- **Remove paths from xrefs and images.** Pick this option to remove the paths of these associated files. This allows the recipient to relocate the xrefs and image files.
- **Send e-mail with transmittal.** When this option is checked, the default e-mail program is automatically started when a transmittal is created.
- **Make web page files.** Select this option to produce a webpage with a link to the transmittal.

The **Files** tab of the **Create Transmittal** dialog box displays the files to be included in the transmittal. See **Figure 26-19.** There are four categories of associated files that can be included in the transmittal. These are:

- Font maps
- Shape files
- Plot style table files
- Xrefs

The **Include fonts** check box determines if font map files and shape files are included in the transmittal. If the drawings being transmitted use standard AutoCAD fonts, it is likely that the recipient already has these files. Therefore, there is no need to send them.

**Figure 26-19.**
These are the files
that will be
included in the
e-mail transmittal.

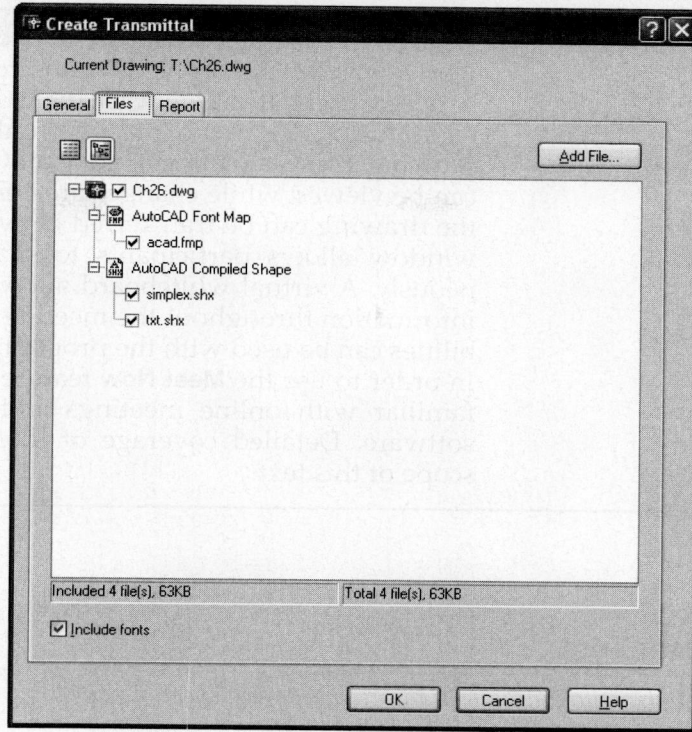

Pick the **Add File...** button to access the **Add file to transmittal** dialog box. Select any other files to be included in the transmittal. These do not need to be drawing files.

A transmittal report is included in the transmittal. The report records the time and date when the transmittal is created, lists the files included in the transmittal, and includes some general notes regarding the file types included in the transmittal. The report is saved as a TXT file with the same name as the transmittal. The **Report** tab in the **Create Transmittal** dialog box displays the text to be included in the transmittal report. You can save this as a separate text file by picking the **Save As...** button.

---

**EXERCISE 26-6**

○ Open the 8th floor.dwg drawing provided in the Sample folder.
○ Use **eTransmit** to create a self-extracting transmittal file. Save the file in the folder of your choice.
○ Prepare a second transmittal as a set of folders. Preserve the original folder structure. Save the set of folders in the same folder where the self-extracting file is located.
○ Using Windows Explorer, determine the size of the self-extracting file. Also, expand the folder structure created as the second transmittal. Determine the size of the second transmittal. How does this compare to the size of the self-extracting file?
○ Delete the self-extracting file and the folder structure from your computer

---

**Note** AutoCAD includes a feature called **Meet Now. Meet Now** works with Microsoft NetMeeting to allow online meetings between users at different locations. With this feature, up to eight AutoCAD users can meet online and collaborate on drawing files using a shared AutoCAD session. Drawings can be viewed while changes are being made and control of the drawing can be transferred between participants. A chat window allows participants to share comments instantaneously. A virtual whiteboard allows participants to record information throughout the meeting. Audio and video capabilities can be used with the proper hardware.

In order to use the **Meet Now** feature efficiently, you must be familiar with online meetings and Microsoft NetMeeting software. Detailed coverage of these topics is beyond the scope of this text.

## Chapter Test

*Answer the following questions on a separate sheet of paper.*

1. Define *hypertext/hyperlink.*
2. What does URL stand for, and what is a URL?
3. What value is stored in the **INETLOCATION** system variable?
4. What does the **BROWSER** command do?
5. What is the function of the **Browse the Web** button?
6. What is the function of the **Favorites** button?
7. Which command is used to attach hypertext to an object?
8. Which dialog box is used by the command in Question 7?
9. How do you activate a hyperlink in an open AutoCAD drawing?
10. What does *DWF* stand for?
11. How do you create a DWF file?
12. What are Autodesk Express Viewer and Volo View used for?
13. Which command is used to create a formatted webpage containing your drawings?
14. What is *i-drop?*
15. Other than simply attaching a drawing to an e-mail message, how can you send drawing data via e-mail?
16. What are some advantages of the method in Question 15?
17. What are the three basic "type" options for the method in Question 15?
18. What is the purpose of the **Meet Now** command?

## Problems

1. Create two HTML documents. Use Windows Notepad or another text editor to enter the code below. Save the text files as P26-1A.HTM and P26-1B.HTM in the folder of your choice.

   ```
   <html>
   <head>
      <title>Chapter 26 Links Problem</title>
   </head>
   <body>
   <h2>
   (Write one or two lines of information. Assume the text is describing an object or part in a drawing.)
   </h2>
   </body>
   </html>
   ```

2. Open an existing drawing. Save the drawing as P26.dwg in the folder where you saved the HTML files. Use the **HYPERLINK** command and attach URLs to two objects in the drawing. Specify the new URLs to be P26-1A.HTM and P26-1B.HTM. Then, open the hyperlink for each object within AutoCAD.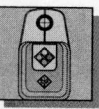

3. Use the **PUBLISHTOWEB** command to create a webpage for the P26.dwg drawing. Name the page Chapter 26 Problem. Set the image type to JPEG. Preview the webpage and pick on the thumbnail to make sure the link works. Then, finish the operation. Open the webpage in your browser to verify operation.

Using OLE, you can link drawings, spreadsheets, and other files to documents or other applications.

## CHAPTER 27

# OLE and AutoCAD

## Learning Objectives

After completing this chapter, you will be able to:

● Identify and use advanced Clipboard text and graphics options.
● Copy and reference AutoCAD drawing data to other Windows applications using Object Linking and Embedding (OLE).
● Describe the differences between linking and embedding.

## Using the Clipboard with AutoCAD

Copying, cutting, and pasting are the primary methods for relocating and duplicating data in Windows-based applications. With the help of the Windows Clipboard, AutoCAD allows you to copy objects within a drawing, from one drawing to another, or from one application (software program) to another.

The Windows Clipboard provides a simple means of taking information from one application into another application, or from one drawing into another. Think of the Clipboard as a temporary storage area, or buffer, for text and graphic information. Any time you cut or copy data in a Windows application, it is automatically placed on the Clipboard. The contents of the Clipboard can then be pasted as desired into any Windows program file, such as a word processor document, a spreadsheet, or even an AutoCAD drawing. Information copied to the Clipboard remains there until it is replaced by copying new information, or Windows is restarted.

### Copying, Cutting, and Pasting

The copy, cut, and paste features are typically found in the Edit pull-down menu of the Windows application you are using. Like most other Windows applications, AutoCAD has an **Edit** menu with these options. See **Figure 27-1A.** You can also right-click in the drawing area and access these options from the shortcut menu. See **Figure 27-1B.** Depending on what is on the Clipboard, some options may be grayed out.

- **Cut.** Removes the selected text or graphic objects and places them on the Clipboard. Can also be accessed using the [Ctrl]+[X] key combination. In AutoCAD, this activates the **CUTCLIP** command.

Figure 27-1.
Selecting Clipboard-based options in AutoCAD.
A—Options in the **Edit** pull-down menu. B—Options in the shortcut menu.

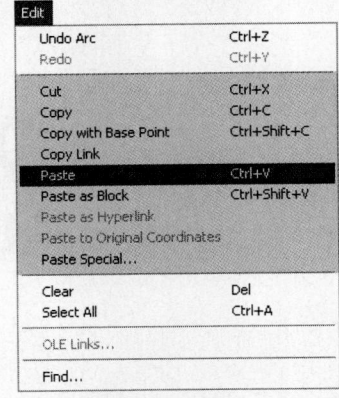

A                                                    B

- **Copy.** Copies the selected text or graphic objects and places them on the Clipboard. Can also be accessed using the [Ctrl]+[C] key combination. In AutoCAD, this starts the **COPYCLIP** command.
- **Copy with Base Point.** Copies selected objects and allows you to specify a base point. In AutoCAD, this starts the **COPYBASE** command.
- **Copy Link.** Copies objects to the Clipboard in preparation to link the information to another application. In AutoCAD, this starts the **COPYLINK** command. This option is used when copying AutoCAD objects to be inserted into another application.
- **Paste.** Pastes the contents of the Clipboard into the current drawing. Can also be accessed using the [Ctrl]+[V] key combination. Pasted objects are not removed from the Clipboard. They can be pasted into multiple locations in your drawing. In AutoCAD, this starts the **PASTECLIP** command.
- **Paste as Block.** Pastes the contents of the Clipboard as a block. In AutoCAD, this accesses the **PASTEBLOCK** command.
- **Paste as Hyperlink.** If the Clipboard contains a hyperlink, pastes the hyperlink to another object or objects. A hyperlink can be copied to the Clipboard by selecting and right-clicking on an object that has a hyperlink attached to it, selecting **Hyperlink**, and then selecting **Copy Hyperlink** from the cascading menu.
- **Paste to Original Coordinates.** Pastes objects from the Clipboard to the coordinates from which they were cut or copied. Same as the **PASTEORIG** command.
- **Paste Special.** Opens the **Paste Special** dialog box, where additional parameters can be set for the incoming data. In AutoCAD, this starts the **PASTESPEC** command.
- **Clear.** Starts the **ERASE** command. This option is included for Microsoft Office compliance only and is in no way different than the standard **ERASE** command in AutoCAD.

## COPYCLIP and CUTCLIP

The **COPYCLIP** (copy) and **COPYCUT** (cut) commands place drawing information on the Clipboard in the same manner. The difference between the commands is similar to the relationship between the **MOVE** and **COPY** commands in AutoCAD. The **COPYCUT** command works like the **MOVE** command—it removes the drawing information from its original location and places it on the Clipboard. The **COPYCLIP** command places the same information on the Clipboard, but leaves the original objects in place. Deciding which one to use depends on whether or not you require the original objects to remain in place.

To use the **COPYCLIP** command, select **Copy** from the **Edit** pull-down menu, pick the **Copy to Clipboard** button on the **Standard** toolbar, press the [Ctrl]+[C] key combination, or type COPYCLIP at the Command: prompt. To use the **COPYCUT** command, select **Cut** from the **Edit** pull-down menu, pick the **Cut to Clipboard** button on the **Standard** toolbar, press the [Ctrl]+[X] key combination, or type COPYCUT at the Command: prompt. With either command, you are prompted to select the objects to copy (or cut). If objects are selected when the command is initiated, those objects are copied (or cut) to the Clipboard and the command ends.

## PASTECLIP

The **PASTECLIP** command takes the information from the Clipboard and inserts it into the current drawing session. The inserted information is identical to the original information. AutoCAD drawing objects are inserted as drawing objects. If the Clipboard contains a block, the information is inserted as a block. Other information, such as text or graphics, is inserted as an OLE object. OLE is discussed later in this chapter.

To use the **PASTECLIP** command, select **Paste** from the **Edit** pull-down menu, pick the **Paste from Clipboard** button on the **Standard** toolbar, press the [Ctrl]+[V] key combination, or type PASTECLIP at the Command: prompt. You are then prompted for an insertion point. Either pick a point with your cursor or enter coordinates. Use object snaps as needed. Once the insertion point is selected, the command ends. Pasting an OLE object is a little different and discussed later in this chapter.

If you use the **Paste as Block** option in the **Edit** pull-down menu, the AutoCAD objects on the Clipboard are inserted as an unnamed block, even if the original objects were not a block. This option can also be accessed using the [Ctrl]+[Shift]+[V] key combination. An *unnamed block* is a block that AutoCAD has named through an automated process. Unnamed blocks typically have names similar to A$C48534010. You need to explode the pasted objects if you wish to edit them.

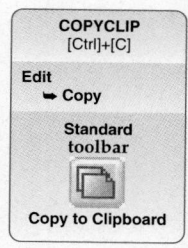

**COPYCLIP**
[Ctrl]+[C]

Edit
➥ Copy

**Standard
toolbar**

Copy to Clipboard

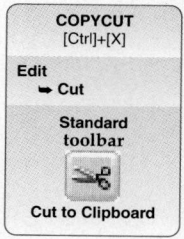

**COPYCUT**
[Ctrl]+[X]

Edit
➥ Cut

**Standard
toolbar**

Cut to Clipboard

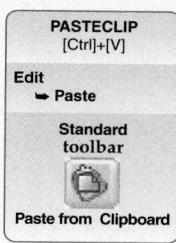

**PASTECLIP**
[Ctrl]+[V]

Edit
➥ Paste

**Standard
toolbar**

Paste from Clipboard

---

### PROFESSIONAL TIP

Copying, cutting, and pasting are not limited to the drawing. You can use copying and pasting to transfer information between dialog boxes. For example, suppose two dimensions on a drawing need the same note to appear after the dimension text. Modify the first dimension, then use [Ctrl]+[C] to copy the note. Then, modify the second dimension by using [Ctrl]+[V] to place the copied note behind the dimension text. To take it one step farther, you could have typed the original note in a word processor, copied it, and then pasted it into the first dimension.

---

### Exercise 27-1

○ Open two drawings from previous chapters.
○ Go to the drawing window that contains the geometry you wish to copy.
○ Press [Ctrl]+[C] to initiate the **COPYCLIP** command.
○ Select the objects you wish to copy and press [Enter].
○ Go to the drawing window that contains the drawing you are copying *to*.
○ Press [Ctrl]+[V] to initiate the **PASTECLIP** command.
○ Specify an insertion point and the objects are inserted.
○ Repeat the process to paste a different object from the first drawing into the second drawing.
○ Close both drawings without saving.

---

## Dragging and Dropping between Open Drawings

AutoCAD allows multiple drawings to be opened in a single session at the same time. This provides a powerful means for bringing partial drawing information from one drawing to another. You can use the copy and past functions described earlier. You can also use the drag-and-drop method.

To copy objects between drawings using the drag-and-drop method, first open both drawings and tile the windows. Then, select the object to copy so the object's grips are displayed. To copy the object to the other drawing, place the cursor on any part of the selected object except a grip. Use the pick button to pick and hold. The drag-and-drop cursor appears. Drag the object into the other drawing and release the pick button. The object is copied to the new drawing with the same properties as the source object. To cancel the operation, press the [Esc] key before releasing the pick button.

If you right-click and hold on the object and then drag it into another drawing, a shortcut menu appears. See **Figure 27-2**. This menu provides a choice of how the object is to be inserted into the drawing.

- **Copy Here.** Copies the object at the location where the pick button is released.
- **Paste as Block.** Copies the object as a block at the selected location.
- **Paste to Orig Coords.** Copies the object to the same XYZ coordinates as in the original drawing.
- **Cancel.** Aborts the copy activity.

Figure 27-2.
If you right-click on an object and then drag it into another drawing, this shortcut menu appears.

```
Copy Here
Paste as Block
Paste to Orig Coords
Cancel
```

## Pasting Objects from Other Applications

When the content of the Clipboard is text from a standard "plain text" editor, such as the Windows Notepad, pasting into an AutoCAD drawing brings it in as a multiline text object. AutoCAD places the new object at the upper-left corner of the current drawing display area. Other object types pasted from the Clipboard, such as Microsoft Word text, are brought in as OLE objects. OLE objects are covered later in this chapter. Text from any word processor can be pasted into dialog boxes as text field entries.

## Introduction to Object Linking and Embedding (OLE)

*Object Linking and Embedding (OLE)* is a feature of the Windows operating system that allows data from many different source applications to be combined into a single document. A technical document will often present data in several forms to ensure effective communications. For example, the technical documentation for a product might include formatted text from a word processor, technical drawings from AutoCAD, charts and graphs from a spreadsheet program, and even graphic images from a paint program. Understanding the use of OLE will help you to produce high-quality documentation to communicate your ideas effectively.

As implied by the name, there are two distinct aspects to OLE: *linking* and *embedding*. Both linking and embedding allow you to insert data from one application into another, but they differ in the way information is stored. The following terms are important to understand.

- **Object.** A piece of data created by a Windows application that supports OLE server functions. Such data can be text from a word processor, an AutoCAD drawing, or a graphic image.
- **OLE server.** A source application. For example, when using OLE to bring an AutoCAD drawing into your word processor, AutoCAD becomes the OLE server.
- **OLE client.** A destination application. AutoCAD is an OLE client when you use OLE to bring an object into AutoCAD from another application.

## Object Embedding

The term *embedding* refers to storing a copy of an OLE object in a client document. Embedding differs from importing because an imported object maintains no association with its source application. An embedded object is edited using the source application, or server. For example, if a Corel Photo-Paint picture is embedded in an AutoCAD drawing, double-clicking on the picture starts the Corel Photo-Paint application and loads the selected picture. On the other hand, using the **Image** command to bring an image file into AutoCAD brings in the graphic image, but the image has no association with the original application.

### Embedding Objects in AutoCAD

A simple way to embed an OLE object in an AutoCAD drawing is to first copy it to the Clipboard from the source application. Then, return to AutoCAD and paste the Clipboard contents using **PASTECLIP**. When the content of the Clipboard is not AutoCAD data and contains OLE information, it is embedded in the AutoCAD drawing.

One application for using embedded graphics is placing a picture in a title block for a logo design. In **Figure 27-3**, the Paint program has been used to design a logo graphic. Selecting the graphic image and pressing [Ctrl]+[C] copies the selected image to the Clipboard.

**Figure 27-3.**
A graphic image can be designed in the Paint program.

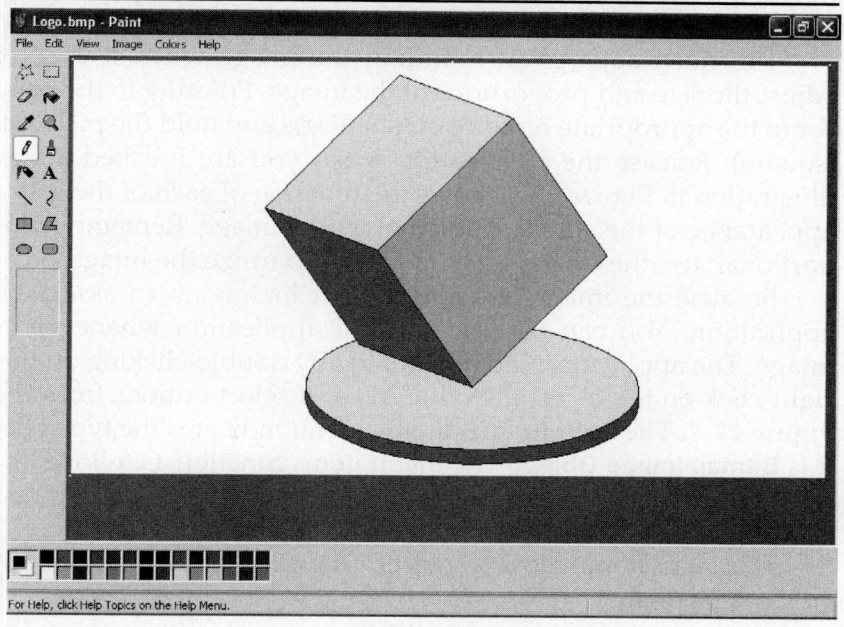

**Figure 27-4.**
Pasting an object into AutoCAD. The pasted image appears in the upper-left corner.

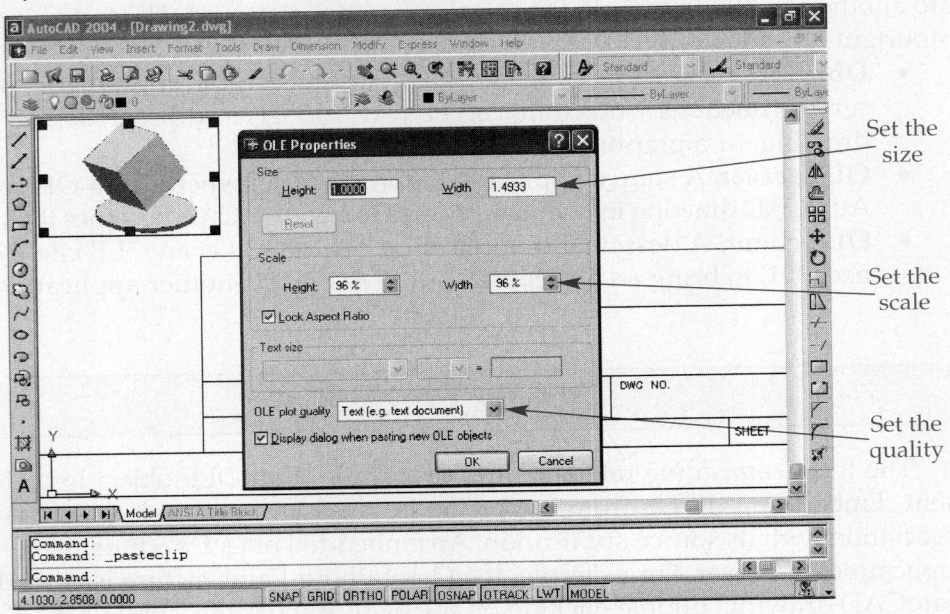

Once you have copied the image to the Clipboard, return to AutoCAD. Now press [Ctrl]+[V] to paste the Clipboard contents into the AutoCAD drawing. A pasted image appears in the upper-left corner of the graphics screen, along with the **OLE Properties** dialog box. See **Figure 27-4.**

The **OLE Properties** dialog box has settings that allow you to change the size and scale of the embedded image. If the embedded object is text, you can specify the text size. Pick **OK** to accept the settings and close the dialog box. This dialog box can be accessed after the object is embedded by right-clicking on the object and selecting **Properties...** from the shortcut menu.

Moving your cursor to point at the pasted image changes your cursor into a four-way arrow. Press and hold the pick button to move the image. Release the pick button when the image is in the desired location.

Once the image is positioned correctly, pick anywhere on the screen that is not on the image and the grips will disappear. You can also press the [Esc] key. **Figure 27-5** shows the image in its final position within the title block.

The filled squares surrounding the image when it is selected can be used to adjust the size and proportions of the image. Pointing to the squares changes the cursor to the appropriate resizing cursor. Press and hold the pick button to move the grip (square). Release the pick button when you are finished adjusting the image. The illustration in **Figure 27-6** shows the function of each of the grip points, as well as the appearance of the cursor when moving an image. Remember, to keep the image proportional, use the corner grips (squares) to resize the image.

Because the image is embedded, it maintains an association with the original application. You can use the original application whenever you need to edit the image. The application can be initiated by double-clicking on the image. You can also right-click on the object in AutoCAD and select options from the shortcut menu. See **Figure 27-7.** The bottom line on this menu indicates the type of object. In **Figure 27-7,** it is **Bitmap Image Object.** The menu items function as follows.

- **Cut.** Removes the OLE object and copies it to the Clipboard.
- **Copy.** Copies the object to the Clipboard.
- **Clear.** Removes the object from the drawing without copying it to the Clipboard.

AutoCAD and its Applications—Advanced

**Figure 27-5.**
The image moved to
the proper location.

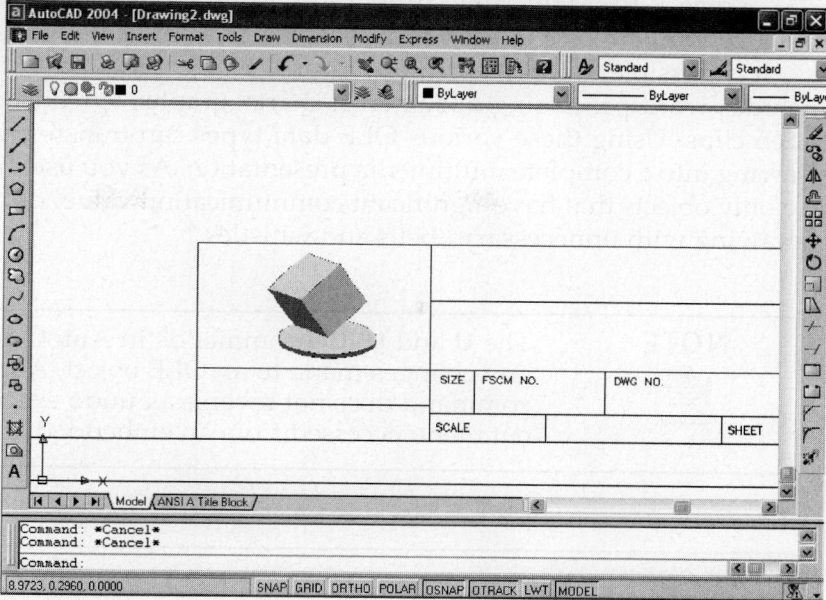

**Figure 27-6.**
The resize and
move cursor shapes
for pasted images.

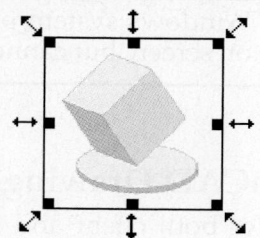

**Figure 27-7.**
Right-clicking on an
embedded object
displays a shortcut
menu with options
for modifying the
object.

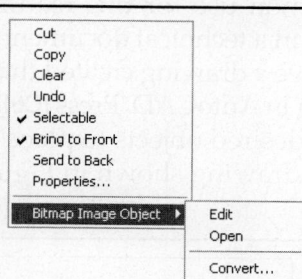

- **Undo.** Reverses the last action performed with this menu. Similar to AutoCAD's **UNDO** command, this can be used repeatedly. This will *not* undo object updates done by the server application. This will also not undo other AutoCAD commands.
- **Selectable.** Controls whether the OLE object can be selected when using AutoCAD's editing commands. When a check mark appears by this option, the object can be selected by pointing at it and picking. Whether an item is selectable or not, right-clicking on it displays the shortcut menu.
- **Bring to Front.** Brings the item to the front, similar to the function of the **DRAWORDER** command.
- **Send to Back.** Sends the item to the back, similar to the function of the **DRAWORDER** command.
- **Properties.** Displays the **OLE Properties** dialog box.
- **Object Type Cascading Menu.** Displays options for editing, opening, and converting the object to other object types. For example, a bitmap image object can be converted into a picture object. When converted to a picture object, the

object has the same properties as an image attached using the **IMAGE** command and it loses its association with the paint program.

It is possible to embed virtually any OLE object into an AutoCAD drawing. This includes word processing documents, charts, graphs, spreadsheets, audio clips, and video clips. Using these various OLE data types can transform a standard technical drawing into a complete multimedia presentation. As you use these techniques, try to use only objects that have significant communication value, rather than cluttering up a drawing with unnecessary "bells and whistles."

 **NOTE** The **U** and **UNDO** commands in AutoCAD have no effect on any changes made to an OLE object. Additionally, the **REDO** command does not reverse an undo executed from the short-cut menu accessed from an embedded object.

 **PROFESSIONAL TIP** OLE objects that are linked or embedded in an AutoCAD drawing only print on printers or plotters that use the Windows system printer driver. They will still be displayed on screen, but cannot be printed using non-Windows drivers.

## Embedding AutoCAD Drawings in Other Applications

AutoCAD provides both client and server OLE functions. This means that in addition to using embedded OLE objects, AutoCAD can provide objects for other applications. A common use for this feature is to combine technical drawings and illustrations with text in a technical document created with a word processing program.

If you already have a drawing created that you need to embed in another document, first open the drawing in AutoCAD. Press [Ctrl]+[C] or select **Copy** from the **Edit** pull-down menu and select the desired objects to place them on the Clipboard. For this example, the entire AutoCAD drawing shown in **Figure 27-8** is copied to the Clipboard.

**Figure 27-8.**
To embed a drawing, first copy it to the Clipboard.

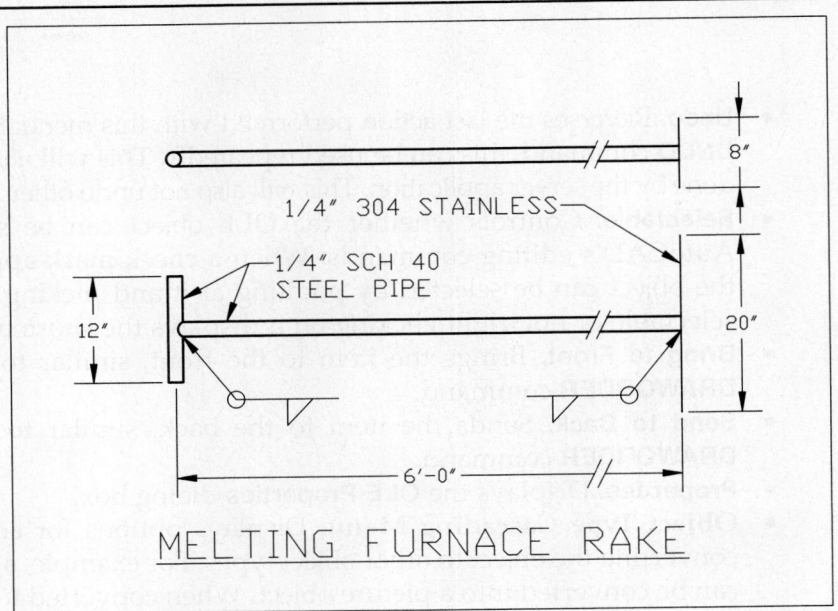

MELTING FURNACE RAKE

In this example, the Windows WordPad program is used as the client application. Open the destination document in WordPad, **Figure 27-9A.** Then, select the **Edit** menu and pick the **Paste** option to embed the AutoCAD drawing. The embedded drawing is placed at the current cursor location. You are not prompted for a location or a size. If you need to change either the location or the size, you can do so by picking on the drawing or on the grips at the edges or corners and dragging the image. **Figure 27-9B** shows the document with the drawing embedded, resized, and moved to the center of the document.

**Figure 27-9.**
Inserting an
AutoCAD drawing
object into a
WordPad
document. A—The
original document.
B—The document
after the drawing is
embedded.

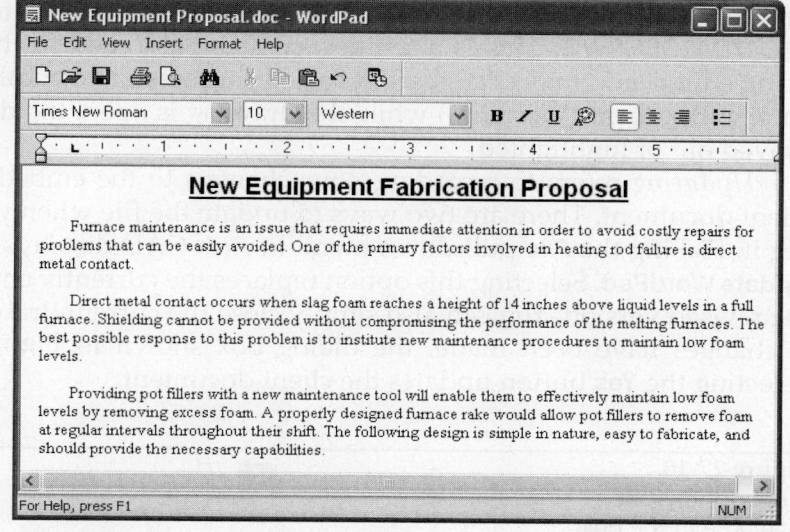

A

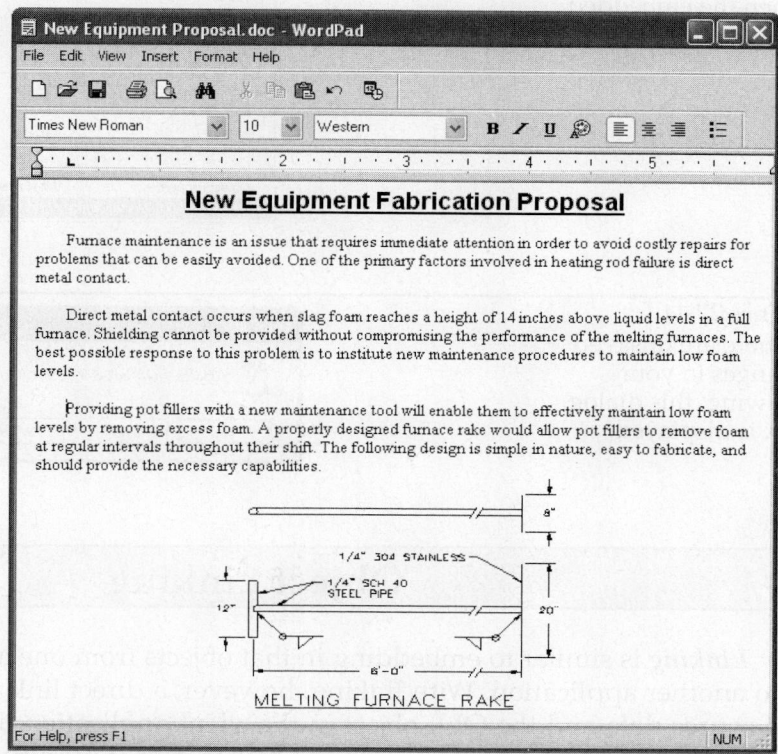

B

Embedding an OLE object in an application also modifies the "edit" menu to display new options when the object is highlighted. The Edit pull-down menu in the WordPad program appears as shown in **Figure 27-10** after highlighting the embedded drawing.

Once the drawing is embedded, it loses all connection with the original drawing file. This means that subsequent editing of this drawing will not affect the original source file. In order to edit the embedded drawing, highlight the image in WordPad and select Edit Drawing Object from the Edit pull-down menu or simply double-click on the drawing. When the AutoCAD window opens, examine the title bar and note the specified file name. The title bar shows the drawing name as Drawing in Document. If you access the **SAVEAS** command, the current file name is set to something similar to A\$C37DA7DFF.DWG. This is a temporary name assigned to the drawing while it is being edited, and may change from one editing session to another. Also, if you switch back to the client (WordPad) while the drawing is open, the drawing in the client is grayed out or highlighted.

*Updating* refers to recording your changes to the embedded object within the client document. There are two ways to update the file when you have finished editing it. Picking the **File** pull-down menu in AutoCAD displays a new option, such as **Update WordPad**. Selecting this option replaces the currently embedded drawing with the revised version. You can also simply close the current drawing or exit AutoCAD. If changes have been made, the dialog box shown in **Figure 27-11** is displayed. Selecting the **Yes** button updates the client document.

**Figure 27-10.**
New options are available in the Edit pull-down menu when the embedded drawing is selected.

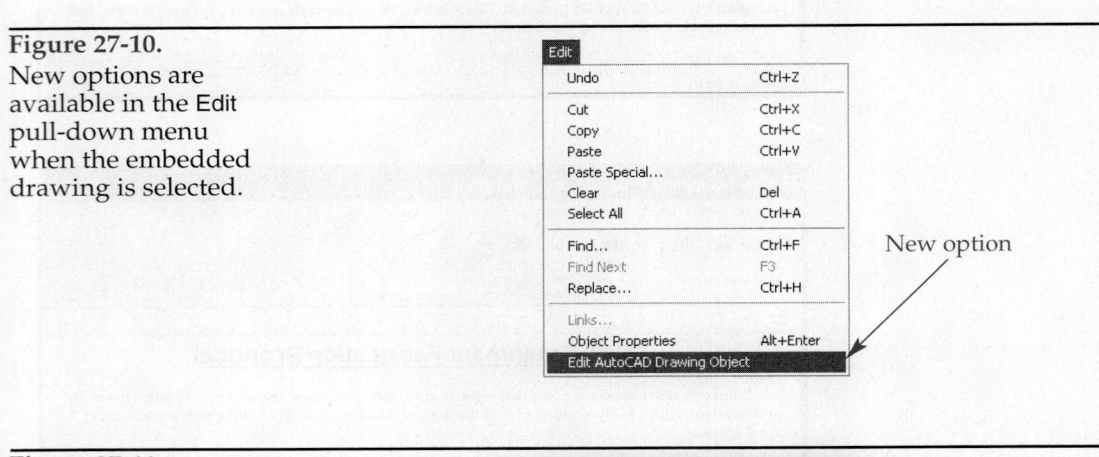

New option

**Figure 27-11.**
If there are unsaved changes in your drawing, this dialog box is displayed.

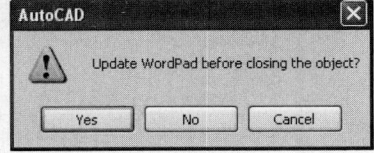

# Object Linking

*Linking* is similar to embedding in that objects from one application are brought into another application. With linking, however, a direct link is maintained between the source data and the OLE object in the client application. Linked objects support *Dynamic Data Exchange* (*DDE*). As the source data is modified, the link in the client application is updated.

## Linking Objects in AutoCAD

To link an object within AutoCAD, it must first be copied to the Clipboard. When bringing the object into AutoCAD, select **Paste Special...** from the **Edit** pull-down menu. Using this option activates the **Paste Special** dialog box, see **Figure 27-12.**

Edit
➥ Paste
Special...

The source of the information currently on the Clipboard is displayed in the upper-left area of the dialog box. Two radio buttons allow you to specify whether or not to copy the information as a link. If **Paste** is active, the object will be embedded. If the **Paste Link** option is active, the object will be brought in as a link. If you are embedding the object, you may have several format options, depending on the type of data being pasted. These formats are shown in the **As:** list box. An object that is being linked, on the other hand, is pasted as the file type associated with the server application.

**Figure 27-12.**
The **Paste Special** dialog box. The Clipboard in this example contains text from a Word document. A—The **Paste** option embeds the object, and several formats are available. B—The **Paste Link** option creates a link to the object, and only a single format can be used.

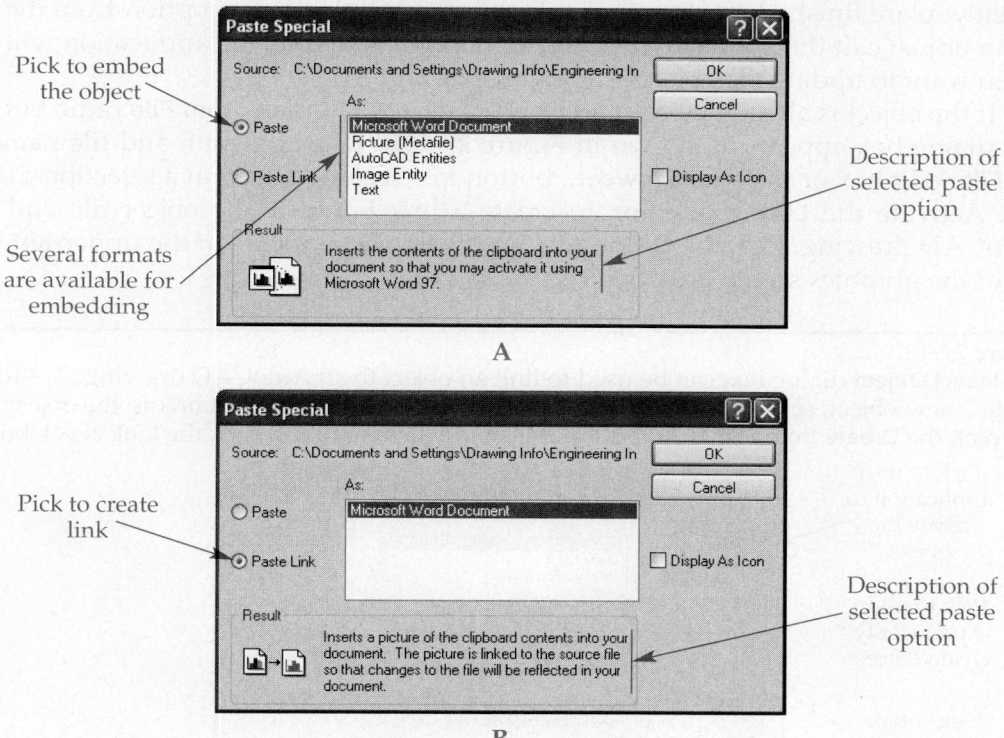

**PROFESSIONAL TIP**

Objects can only be linked through OLE if they exist as a file on disk. If you copy data from an application without first saving it to disk, the **Paste Link** radio button is disabled (grayed out). In addition, you may not be able to link to files across a network. A link maintains a direct association with the original source file, meaning that editing a linked OLE object changes its source file as well. Pasting an object when the **Paste Link** option is not available creates an embedded OLE object.

INSERTOBJ
IO

Insert
➡ OLE Object...

Insert
toolbar

OLE Object

# Inserting Linked Objects into AutoCAD

A linked object can also be inserted using the **INSERTOBJ** command. Select this command by picking the **OLE Object** button on the **Insert** toolbar, selecting **OLE Object...** from the **Insert** pull-down menu, or typing IO or INSERTOBJ at the Command: prompt. The following example shows how to use this command.

First, create a simple image in Windows Paint and save the image as a bitmap (BMP) file. Then, in AutoCAD, initiate the **INSERTOBJ** command. The **Insert Object** dialog box appears, **Figure 27-13A.**

The **Create New** radio button is selected by default. The **Object Type:** list box shows the registered applications that support OLE functions. This list varies based on the software installed on your system. Read each selection carefully, because some programs can produce varied types of data. For example, if you have Microsoft Word installed, you may see options for producing a picture or a document. The option you select affects how the specified program is started, and the data type it will be sending back to AutoCAD.

To create a new object from scratch, highlight the desired program and pick the **OK** button. The appropriate application is opened and you can create the object. When you are finished creating the OLE object, select the Update option from the File menu or just exit the application. If you exit before you save, the application will ask if you want to update the object before you exit.

If the object is already created and saved, select the **Create from File** radio button. The dialog box appears as shown in **Figure 27-13B.** Enter the path and file name in the **File:** edit box or pick the **Browse...** button to select the file from a selection dialog box. Activate the **Link** check box to create a link between the object file and the AutoCAD drawing. Pick the **OK** button, and the object appears in the upper-left corner of the graphics screen area. See **Figure 27-14.**

**Figure 27-13.**
The **Insert Object** dialog box can be used to link an object to an AutoCAD drawing. A—To create a new object, select the type of object and pick **OK**. B—To create a link to the object's file, pick the **Create from File** radio button, select the file name, and pick the **Link** check box.

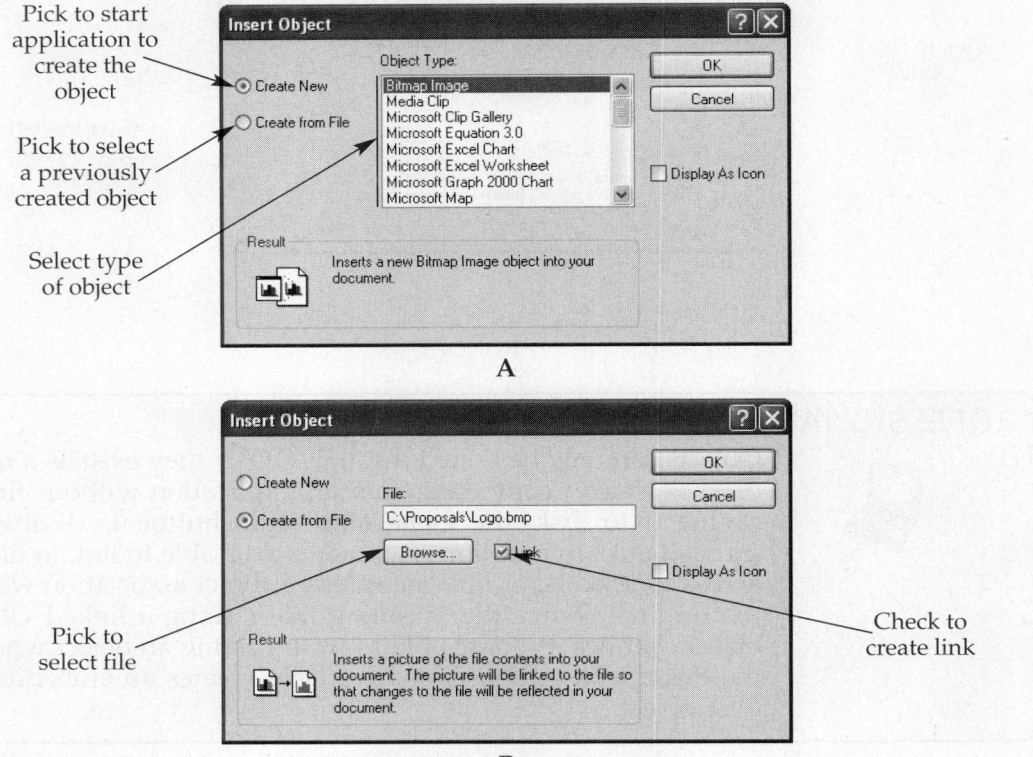

A

B

Figure 27-14.
The linked object is inserted in the upper-left corner of the drawing area.

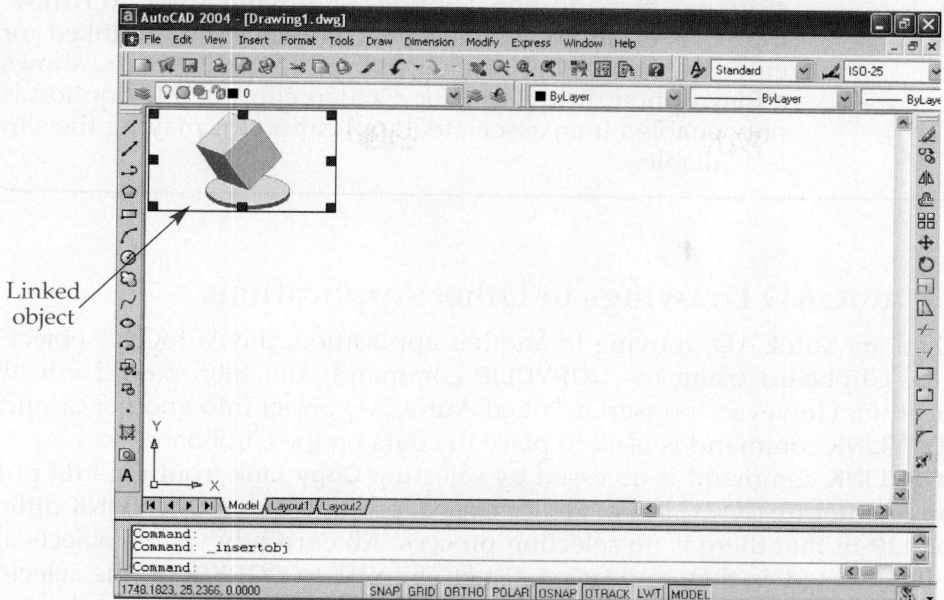

To edit the linked OLE object, double-click on it. This opens the server application, which is Paint in this example. Any changes you make to the image are updated in both the OLE object in the drawing and in the source file.

All linked OLE objects behave in much the same manner as the previous example. In certain applications, the updates may be slower, but they are still automatic. To change the way a link is updated or to adjust current links in a drawing, select **OLE Links...** from the **Edit** pull-down menu. This opens the **Links** dialog box, as shown in Figure 27-15. If no links are present in the current drawing, this item is grayed-out in the pull-down menu.

> Edit
> ➥ OLE Links...

The **Links:** list box in the **Links** dialog box displays all active links in the current drawing. The file name of the link and the update method are also shown. By default, a link is automatically updated. If you do not want the updates to be automatic, pick the **Manual** radio button. To force an update, select the **Update Now** button. The **Break Link** button removes link information from the OLE object and removes any association with the source file, effectively converting a linked object into an embedded object. Select the **Change Source...** button to change the source application with which the link is associated. Selecting **Open Source** opens the linked file using the originating application.

Figure 27-15.
The **Links** dialog box displays all active links.

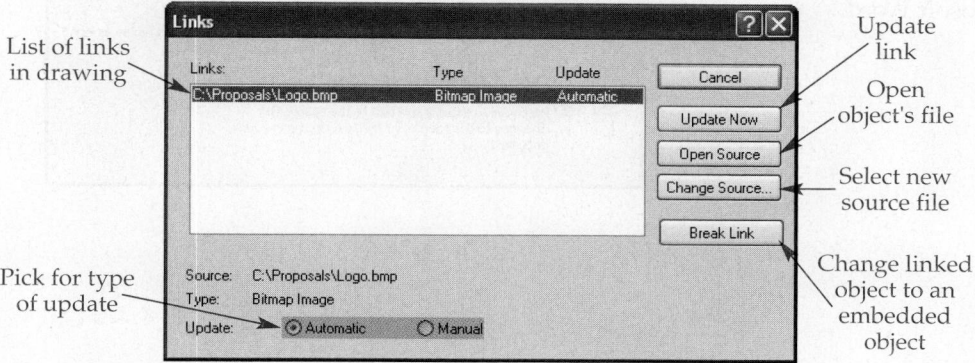

## Linking AutoCAD Drawings in Other Applications

To embed an AutoCAD drawing in another application, the AutoCAD object is copied to the Clipboard using the **COPYCLIP** command, and then pasted into the other application. However, to insert a linked AutoCAD object into another application, the **COPYLINK** command is used to place the data on the Clipboard.

The **COPYLINK** command is accessed by selecting **Copy Link** from the **Edit** pull-down menu or entering COPYLINK at the Command: prompt. Using **COPYLINK** differs from **COPYCLIP** in that there is no selection process. All currently visible objects are automatically selected as they appear on screen. Similar to **COPYCLIP**, the selected objects are displayed in a client application in the view that was active when the copy was made.

The Paste Special... selection found in the Edit pull-down menu of most Windows applications is used to paste a linked OLE object. The Paste Special dialog box displayed by picking this option may vary slightly from one application to the next, but several basic features are standard. See **Figure 27-16.** You can also select Object from the Insert pull-down menu in most applications. This is similar to using the **INSERTOBJ** command in AutoCAD.

Remember that the Paste Link option is only available if the source drawing has been saved to a file. Selecting AutoCAD Drawing Object as the data type maintains the pasted material as AutoCAD drawing data. Selecting Picture brings the information in as a WMF file and Bitmap converts the incoming data to a BMP file. Using bitmaps ensures that what you see on the screen is exactly what will print, but tends to make the client files very large and uses more memory. Your choice for the incoming data type has no effect on the original file, and the link is still maintained if the data type supports linking.

**COPYLINK**

Edit
➥ Copy Link

**Figure 27-16.**
The Paste Special dialog box is similar in most Windows applications. This is the dialog box in Microsoft Word.

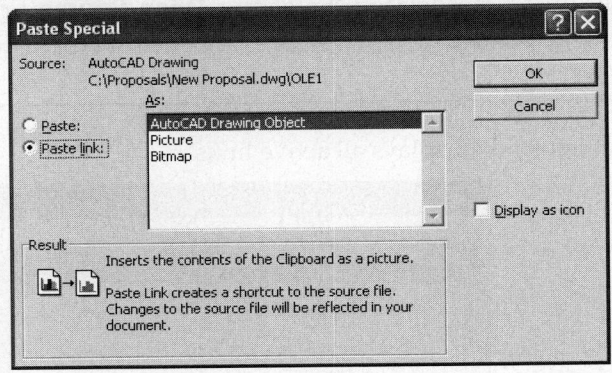

## Chapter Test

*Answer the following questions on a separate sheet of paper.*

1. Which Windows application assists in copying objects from one software program to another?
2. How long does information copied to the application in Question 1 remain there?
3. What are the functions of the [Ctrl]+[C] and [Ctrl]+[V] keystrokes?
4. Which two commands are used to copy drawing information from one AutoCAD drawing to another?
5. What does *OLE* stand for?
6. Define the following terms.
   A. Object
   B. OLE server
   C. OLE client
7. What does *embedding* mean?
8. How can you resize an object that has been pasted into another application?
9. How can you edit an object that has been embedded into an application?
10. What does *linking* mean?
11. How do you insert a new object that has not yet been created into an AutoCAD drawing?

## Drawing Problems

1. Begin a new drawing and save it as P27-1. Then, do the following.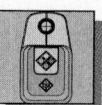
   A. Insert a title block.
   B. Open the Windows Paint program.
   C. Draw a company logo. Copy the design to the Clipboard.
   D. Paste the design into the AutoCAD drawing.
   E. Position the design in the title block.
   F. Save the drawing.

2. Open one of your 3D drawings from a previous chapter. Then, do the following.
   A. Display the object in a hidden display.
   B. Copy the object to the Clipboard.
   C. Open a word processing program and paste the Clipboard contents to create an embedded object.
   D. Create a memo to a coworker or instructor in which you describe the process used to create the document.
   E. Save the document as P27-2 but do not close the application. Return to AutoCAD and close the drawing without saving.
   F. Return to the word processor and double-click on the pasted object.
   G. Edit the object in some way and save the drawing.
   H. Return to the document and save it.

3. Open one of your 3D drawings from a previous chapter. Perform the same functions outlined in Problem 2, but this time create a link between the AutoCAD drawing and the word processing document. Edit the drawing in AutoCAD and observe the results in the document file. Save the document as P27-3 and close the word processor.

The Autodesk website provides a wealth of information, such as how-to articles and tutorials. (Autodesk, Inc.)

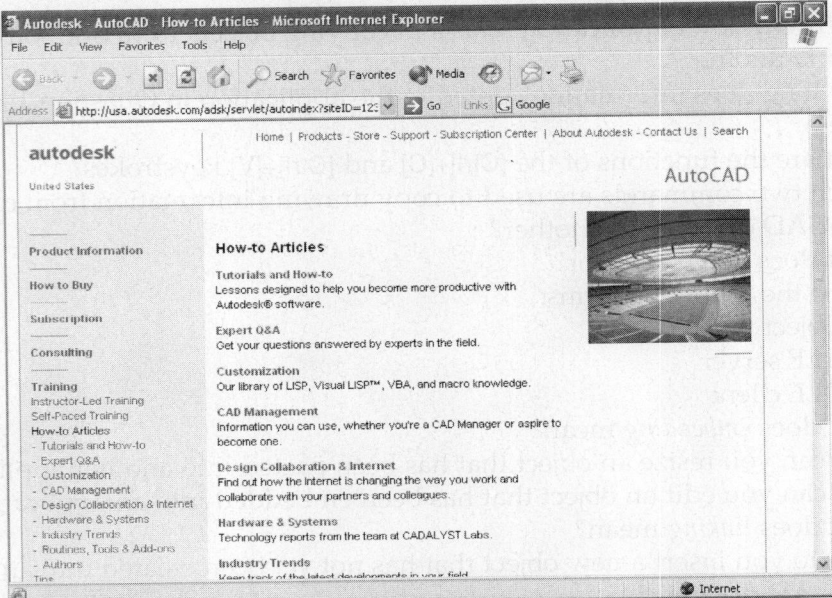

## CHAPTER 28

# Introduction to dbConnect

## Learning Objectives

After completing this chapter, you will be able to:

● Define the term *database*.
● List the components of a database table.
● Explain SQL.
● Explain dbConnect.
● Describe database and SQL applications.
● Load a database into an AutoCAD drawing.
● Initialize a database to work within an AutoCAD drawing.
● Add and edit database table records using the **dbConnect Manager**.
● Create links between a database and an AutoCAD drawing object.
● Add displayable attributes to the drawing.
● Use SQL queries to ask questions of a database.

When creating an AutoCAD drawing, you are actually creating a very powerful graphic database. This database can be linked to other database software applications, allowing you to use drawing data in a variety of ways. *Structured Query Language (SQL)* is the industry-standard language used to manage and exchange data between database applications. AutoCAD's *dbConnect* feature is a way to exchange data between AutoCAD drawings and other database applications using SQL. This chapter introduces the dbConnect feature and explains how to use it to maximize the functionality of your AutoCAD drawings.

> **NOTE**
>
>
>
> This chapter is intended to be only an *introduction* to the capabilities of dbConnect. It is suggested that you go through the documentation in the online help files. Begin to create your own small database and create a drawing that relates to it. This project should be a subject that is useful for you, and one that you can update and maintain easily. You will begin to see the value of working with a text and graphic relational database.

# What Is a Database?

A ***database*** is a collection of information with contents that can be easily accessed, managed, and updated. The information stored in many databases represents large collections of data records or files, such as inventories, employee records, and customer files. Modern databases are most often stored in computer files. There are many different software programs used to create, edit, and manage these databases. Such programs are called ***database management systems (DBMS)***. Most DBMS applications provide capabilities such as quick retrieval of files, report generation, and the ability to exchange information with other software programs.

Microsoft Access, Oracle, and dBASE are a few popular DBMS applications. The following external applications can be used with AutoCAD 2004. AutoCAD itself is a very powerful database management system. The examples in this chapter use AutoCAD and a Microsoft Access database.

- Microsoft Access
- dBASE
- Microsoft Excel®
- Oracle
- Paradox
- Microsoft Visual FoxPro®
- SQL Server

With many DBMS programs, data are created and managed by entering text information in specific locations. These locations are called fields, records, and cells. A ***field*** is a column within a database. A ***record*** is a row in a database. The location where a field and a row intersect is called a ***cell***. For example, the table in **Figure 28-1** represents a portion of an employee record database. Each row represents a single record, and each column represents a field within the record.

An AutoCAD drawing file is a database. It stores a collection of graphic information that makes up the drawing. In the AutoCAD database, each record contains the information needed to define a single object, such as a line, arc, circle, or block. For example, a line object is defined by starting and ending points, color, layer, and linetype.

The data in an AutoCAD drawing are represented graphically rather than in a table with rows and columns. The interface for creating and editing an AutoCAD database is the drawing editor. An AutoCAD database can be linked to an outside database with dbConnect. This establishes an information pool that can be edited and updated by either AutoCAD or the external database application.

**Figure 28-1.**
Databases are usually shown as tables. Each row is called a record. Each column is called a field.

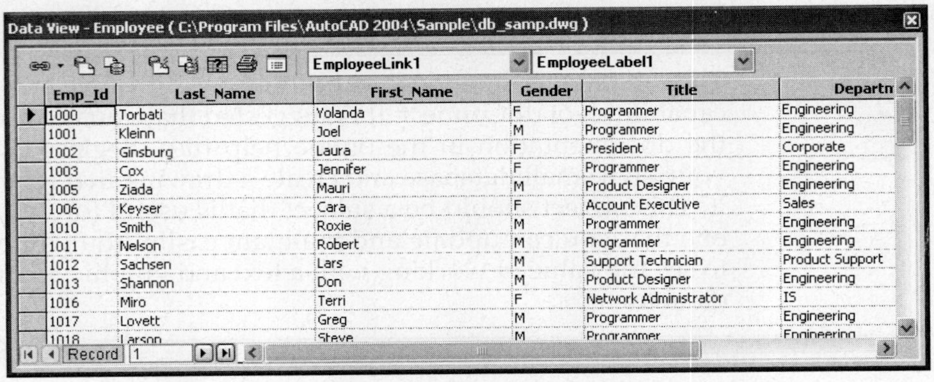


| Emp_Id | Last_Name | First_Name | Gender | Title | Departn |
|---|---|---|---|---|---|
| 1000 | Torbati | Yolanda | F | Programmer | Engineering |
| 1001 | Kleinn | Joel | M | Programmer | Engineering |
| 1002 | Ginsburg | Laura | F | President | Corporate |
| 1003 | Cox | Jennifer | F | Programmer | Engineering |
| 1005 | Ziada | Mauri | M | Product Designer | Engineering |
| 1006 | Keyser | Cara | F | Account Executive | Sales |
| 1010 | Smith | Roxie | M | Programmer | Engineering |
| 1011 | Nelson | Robert | M | Programmer | Engineering |
| 1012 | Sachsen | Lars | M | Support Technician | Product Support |
| 1013 | Shannon | Don | M | Product Designer | Engineering |
| 1016 | Miro | Terri | F | Network Administrator | IS |
| 1017 | Lovett | Greg | M | Programmer | Engineering |
| 1018 | Larson | Steve | M | Programmer | Engineering |

## Linked Database Applications

There are many applications for linking drawings to outside databases. One common application in industry is for facilities management. *Facilities management* involves the management of buildings, furnishings, equipment, and resources. An effective facilities management system maintains a record of all physical assets of a company. This record helps the company use existing resources effectively by reducing the number of unnecessary purchases. The records of personnel, physical assets, budgets, and company growth plans can be combined and used to control spending and ensure that the needs of the company are met.

Most companies maintain floor plans in CAD and maintain conventional database records of equipment and furnishings. When the conventional data is linked directly to the graphic data using dbConnect, changes in one database are automatically applied to the other. Therefore, changes to the database are reflected in the drawing, and the database records are updated if the drawing is edited.

The real power of dbConnect is the capability it gives a designer or planner to organize spatial information sources by linking AutoCAD data directly to related text data. This streamlines the process of generating reports and plans regarding space inventory, furniture and equipment inventories, and asset deployment. Equipment and furniture can be tracked when they are moved from one location to another. Any physical asset can be instantly located whenever it is needed.

## Database File Structure

The terminology used to describe the components in a database file can be confusing at first. Therefore, read this section carefully. When you understand the nature of a database table, working with dbConnect becomes much easier.

### Sample Database Layouts

In the simplest form, a database is a list of items. This list usually appears in a table. A *table* is data arranged in rows and columns. A *row* (record) is a horizontal group of entries. A *column* (field) is a vertical group of entries. A sample Microsoft Access database file named db_samples.mdb is installed with AutoCAD. A portion of the Employee table from this file is shown in **Figure 28-1.** In a table, the top row of the table contains the name of each column, such as Emp_Id, Last_Name, and First_Name.

### Database File Components

A record (row) is shown highlighted in **Figure 28-2.** The first entry in the row is in the Emp_Id column. Six additional items complete the row. All the fields in a record (row) go together. In this example, all fields in a record are related to the employee identified by the employee number. Each column represents a specific cell, also called a field, within the record. For example, the Last_Name, First_Name, and Department columns define fields within each record. The First_Name column is highlighted in **Figure 28-3.**

A database table usually has a key. A *key* is assigned to a column in the table and is used as a search option to identify different rows in the table. For example, the key for a sales projection table may be the Month column. The key can then be used to identify all the sales projections for a certain month, such as February (the February row).

**Figure 28-2.**
A record is a row in a table. Every cell in the record (row) is related to the "key field." In this example, all cells in a record are related to the employee's ID number.

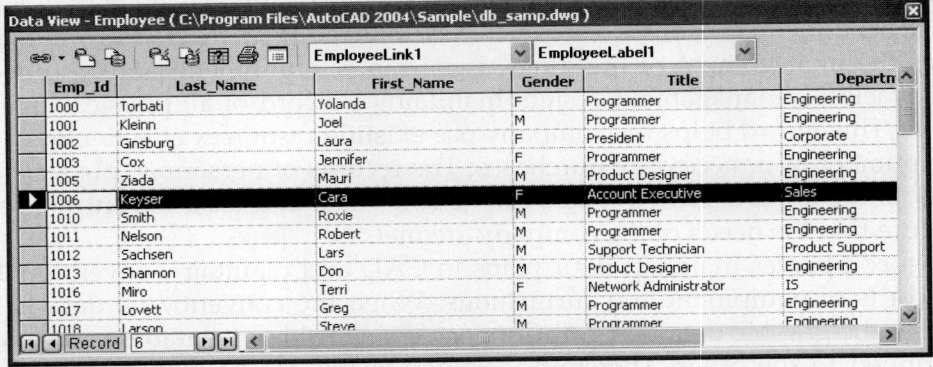

**Figure 28-3.**
The fields (columns) define specific elements of the record (row). In this example, the employee's first name appears in the highlighted column.

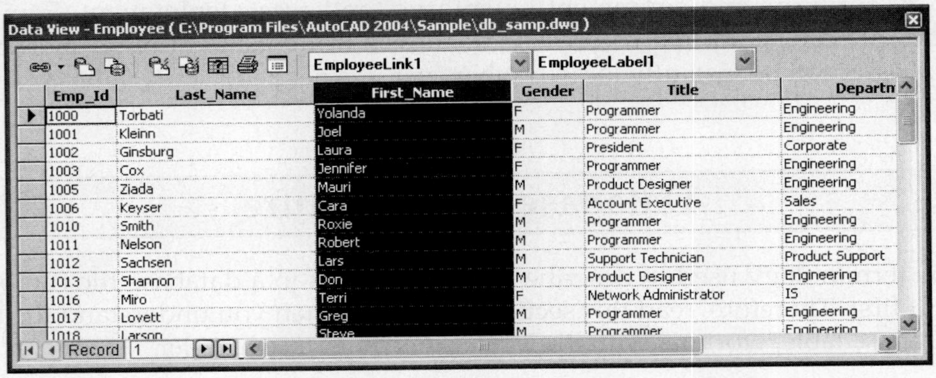

In some cases, a single key may not provide a sufficiently specific search. In such cases, additional columns must be specified for the key. For example, a company may want to identify the number of hours a particular employee worked during a particular week. In this example, the *Employee Id* column alone cannot serve as the key because a new record for that employee is created each week the employee works. Additionally, the *Date* column cannot be used alone because a separate record is created for each employee every week. The key must specify both the *Employee Id* and the *Date* columns in order to identify a unique record. A key created from multiple columns is called a ***compound key.***

## Getting Started with dbConnect

Now that you are familiar with the meaning and structure of databases and their files, you can develop an understanding of how the various components of databases and AutoCAD fit together. **Figure 28-4** illustrates the relationship of the DBMS tools used in this chapter.

**Figure 28-4.**
The relationship of database application software, database files, tables, and queries.

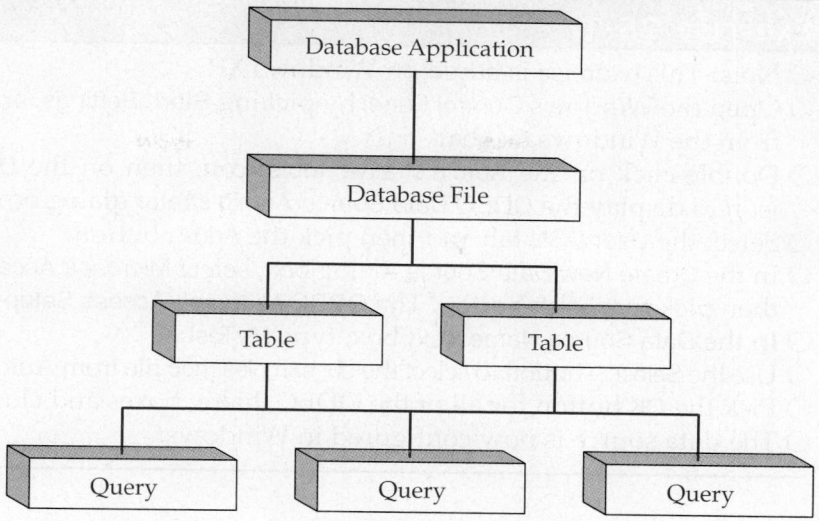

**NOTE** Before working through this chapter, make backup copies of the db_samp.dwg and db_sample.mdb files located in AutoCAD's Sample folder. When you want to restore the original files, simply copy them back to the original location.

Before you can get started using a database application with AutoCAD, an ODBC data source needs to be configured within your Windows operating system. ODBC stands for "open database connectivity" and is an interface provided by the Windows operating system that allows application software to access the data in an SQL database. This configuration is necessary to ensure the correct drivers are used by all applications that access the database, including AutoCAD.

AutoCAD has a preconfigured setup that allows you to connect to the db_sample Microsoft Access database from AutoCAD. Exercise 28-1 is a step-by-step tutorial for configuring a new data source within Windows XP.

**PROFESSIONAL TIP**  When configuring an ODBC data source in Windows, you need to decide if you want the data source to be accessible by other computers. If you create the data source under the User DSN tab, it will only be available to that computer. Use the System DSN tab to configure a data source that can be used by computers that are networked together.

## The dbConnect Manager

**DBCONNECT**
**DBC**
**[Ctrl]+[6]**

**Tools**
➡ dbConnect

The **dbConnect Manager** provides the interface that allows you to connect to an external database and then work with the data. To display the **dbConnect Manager**, type DBC or DBCONNECT at the Command: prompt, select **dbConnect** from the **Tools** pull-down menu, or use the [Ctrl]+[6] key combination. The **dbConnect Manager** is opened (by default) as a floating palette on the left-hand side of the screen, **Figure 28-5**.

The **dbConnect Manager** palette can be docked or floating, and it can be resized. To dock the palette, pick and drag it by the vertical title bar on the left or right side of the palette to a location near the left or right side of the graphics window. To float the **dbConnect Manager**, double-click on the two horizontal bars at the top of the window or grab the double horizontal bars and drag it to a different location on the screen. You can close the palette by picking the "X" button in the upper-right or upper-left corner. By right-clicking in the **dbConnect Manager** palette title bar and selecting **Auto-hide** from the shortcut menu, you can reduce the palette to just the title bar. The palette can be redisplayed by moving your cursor over the title bar.

Figure 28-5.
By default, the **dbConnect Manager** is located in the upper left corner of the AutoCAD drawing area.

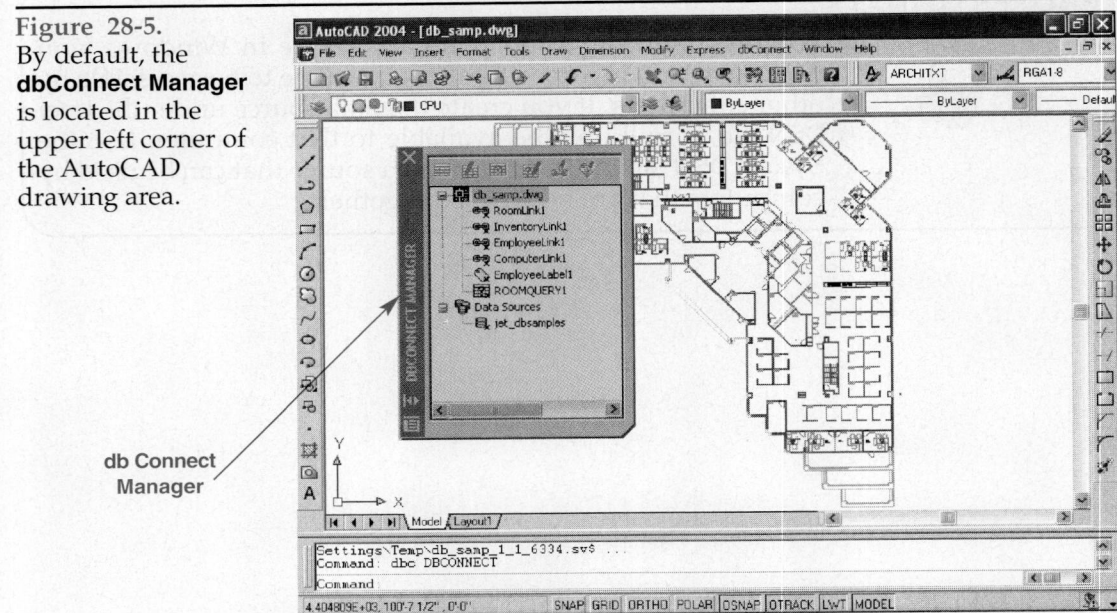

db Connect Manager

The **dbConnect Manager** palette shows two main things. First, all open drawing files are shown along with any database objects associated with each file. These are called *drawing nodes.* The palette also shows all configured data sources and their components. These are shown under the *data sources node.*

When the **dbConnect Manager** is activated, a **dbConnect** pull-down menu is added to the menu bar. The commands used with the **dbConnect Manager** are located in this pull-down menu. The commands can also be accessed in shortcut menus by right-clicking on the components in the **dbConnect Manager** or from the toolbar in the **dbConnect Manager**.

## Configuring a Data Source in AutoCAD

Once a data source has been configured in Windows, as in Exercise 28-1, you can use it to configure a data source connection in AutoCAD. Simply creating the data source in Windows does not automatically "connect" it to AutoCAD. AutoCAD comes with a preconfigured data source for the db_samp drawing. The jet_dbsamples data source should appear in the **dbConnect Manager** along with any other configured data sources. A small red "X" to the left of the jet_dbsamples name indicates that the data source is not connected.

To configure a data source in AutoCAD, right-click on **Data Sources** in the **dbConnect Manager**. Then, select **Configure Data Source...** from the shortcut menu. You can also select **Configure...** from the **Data Sources** cascading menu in the **dbConnect** pull-down menu. The **Configure a Data Source** dialog box appears. You can reconfigure an existing data source by selecting its name in the **Data Sources:** list and picking the **OK** button. To configure a new data source, enter a name in the **Data Source Name:** text box. This name does not have to be the same name as the data source you will be using. Then, pick the **OK** button to display the **Data Link Properties** dialog box. If reconfiguring an existing data source, the **Connection** tab is displayed. If configuring a new data source, the **Provider** tab is displayed, **Figure 28-6A.**

| dbConnect |
| ➥ Data Sources |
|     ➥ Configure... |

**Figure 28-6.**
The **Data Link Properties** dialog box is used to configure a data source for AutoCAD. A—The **Provider** tab is used to specify which type of database will be used when configuring a new data source. B— The **Connection** tab is used to connect a specific ODBC Sourse.

Pick to display configured
ODBC sources

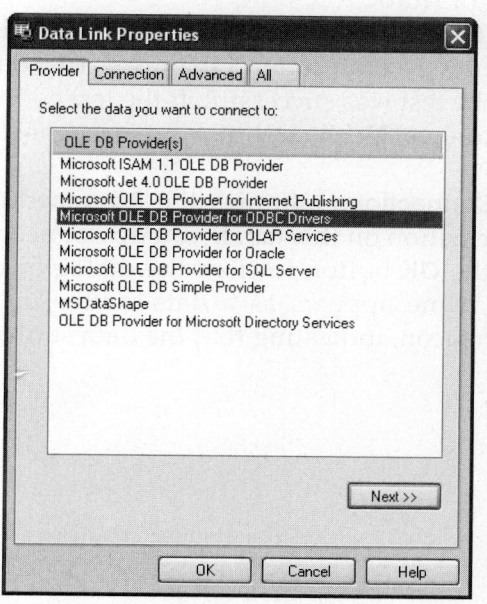

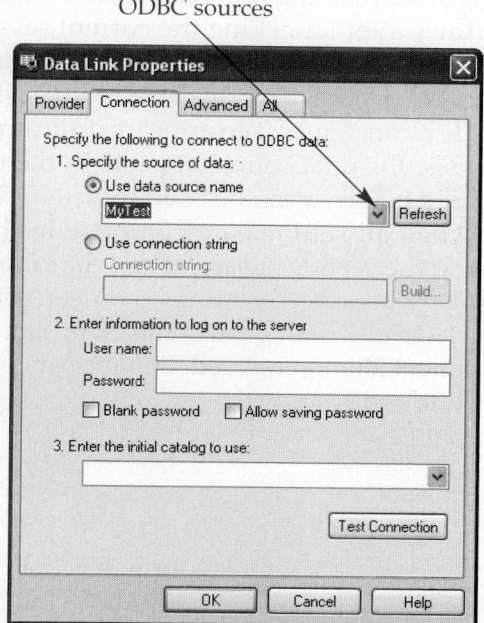

A                           B

## Reconfiguring an existing data source

When reconfiguring an existing data source, the information in the **Provider** tab is automatically set to match the data source. If you need to alter this information, pick the **Provider** tab. Then, select a new provider as needed.

In the **Connection** tab, the name of the database file is displayed in the **Use data source name** drop-down list. The drop-down list contains the names of all the data sources that are configured in Windows. You can select a new database file from this list.

At the bottom of the **Connections** tab is the **Test Connection** button. Pick this button to see if AutoCAD can connect to the external database. If it can, a message appears indicating that the test was successful. If the test connection fails, the data source appears in the **dbConnect Manager**, but an external database file must be specified later before the source can be used in AutoCAD. If a failure occurs, make sure the database file has not been moved since it has been configured. Also, make sure the settings are typed correctly. Spelling errors can cause a failure.

When all settings are complete in the **Connections** tab, pick the **Advanced** tab. Refer to the section *Advanced and All* for information on this tab. If you do not need to make any advanced settings, you can pick the **OK** button to close the dialog box. If you close the dialog box, the data source name appears as a data source in the **dbConnect Manager**. A red "X" appears on the icon, indicating that the data source is disconnected.

## Configuring a new data source

When configuring a new data source, you must first select a provider. This is similar to selecting an ODBC data source in the Windows Control Panel. Under the **Provider** tab in the **Data Link Properties** dialog box is a list of the OLE database providers installed on your system. An OLE database provider allows your drawing data to work with a specific database. Select the correct OLE database provider for the type of database that will be connected. Once the provider is selected, pick the **Next** button to open the **Connection** tab.

The **Connection** tab settings are used to specify which Windows ODBC data source is going to be used, **Figure 28-6B.** This is the data source configured using the Windows Control Panel, and the name you entered during its setup appears in the **Use data source name** drop-down list. Select the Windows-configured data source you want to use from that drop-down list. If the source does not appear in the list, but is configured, pick the **Refresh** button. This is necessary if you configured the source in Windows after launching the current session of AutoCAD.

At the bottom of the **Connections** tab is the **Test Connection** button. Once a data source is selected, pick this button to see if AutoCAD can connect to the external database. If it can, a message appears indicating the test was successful. If the test connection fails, the data source appears in the **dbConnect Manager**, but a database must be specified before it can be used in AutoCAD.

When all settings are complete in the **Connections** tab, pick the **Advanced** tab. Refer to the section *Advanced and All* for information on this tab. If you do not need to make any advanced settings, you can pick the **OK** button to close the dialog box. If you close the dialog box, the data source name appears as a data source in the **dbConnect Manager**. A red "X" appears on the icon, indicating that the data source is disconnected.

## Advanced and All

The **Advanced** tab can be used to set a timeout limit and permission rights for the data source. When a value is entered in the **Connect timeout:** text box, an error message is displayed if connecting to the data source takes longer than the specified time. This is very similar to "time out" errors you may have encountered while using the World Wide Web. In the **Access permissions:** area, different read and write permissions can be set. For example, the **Read** option allows a user to "look at" the external database, but not edit it. By default, all access options are unchecked, giving users full access.

The first three tabs are similar to a Windows "wizard." They guide you through the configuration process. The **All** tab lists all the current configuration settings. You can change an individual setting by highlighting it in the list and picking the **Edit Value...** button. Once you have become skilled at configuring a data source, use the **All** tab to streamline the process.

Once you close the dialog box, the data source name appears as a data source in the **dbConnect Manager**. A red "X" appears on the icon, indicating that the data source is disconnected.

### Exercise 28-2

○ Make sure you have completed Exercise 28-1 before starting this exercise.
○ In AutoCAD, open the **dbConnect Manager**.
○ Right-click on **Data Sources** and select **Configure Data Source...** from the shortcut menu.
○ In the **Data Source Name:** text box of the **Configure a Data Source** dialog box, type ACAD Test and then pick **OK**.
○ In the **Provider** tab of the **Data Links Properties** dialog box, select the Microsoft OLE DB Provider for ODBC Drivers. Then, pick the **Next>>** button to display the **Connection** tab.
○ In the **Connection** tab, make sure the **Use data source name** radio button is selected and select **MyTest** from the drop-down list. If you do not see **MyTest** and you have completed Exercise 28-1, pick the **Refresh** button.
○ Pick the **Test Connection** button to ensure a proper connection can be established. Once you pass the test, pick the **OK** button to close the dialog box.
○ The **ACAD Test** data source should now be listed in the **dbConnect Manager** under the **Data Sources** node.
○ Save the drawing as EX28.

## Connecting a Data Source in AutoCAD

Once a data source is configured in AutoCAD and appears in the **dbConnect Manager**, it must be connected. Once connected, you will be able to view, edit, and link the data from within AutoCAD.

dbConnect
➥ Data Sources
➥ Connect...

The easiest way to connect a data source is to double-click on its name in the **dbConnect Manager**. If the connection can be established, the source is automatically connected. You can also right-click on the data source name in the **dbConnect Manager**, and select **Connect** from the shortcut menu, or select **Connect...** from the **Data Sources** cascading menu in the **dbConnect** pull-down menu. The tables and queries stored in the external database appear below the data source name, **Figure 28-7**. Notice how this appears similar to the folder structure of Windows Explorer.

To hide the tables and queries under a data source, pick the minus sign to the left of the data source or double-click on the data source name. To disconnect a data source, right-click on its name and select **Disconnect** from the shortcut menu. Disconnecting a data source automatically hides the tables and queries.

dbConnect
➥ Synchronize...

Links can become broken or invalid if the source table structure is changed, or if the source table is moved to a different location. The **Synchronize** tool detects errors in links. To synchronize a link, right-click on the data source name and select **Synchronize...** from the shortcut menu or select **Synchronize...** from the **dbConnect** pull-down menu. Then, in the **Select a Database Object** dialog box, pick the link template to synchronize. A link template must be attached to the drawing. If errors are detected, the **Synchronize** dialog box lists the errors and a description. The **Fix** and **Delete** tools can be used on the error that is currently selected.

**Figure 28-7.**
Once a data source is connected, the tables stored in the data source appear below its name in the **dbConnect Manager**.

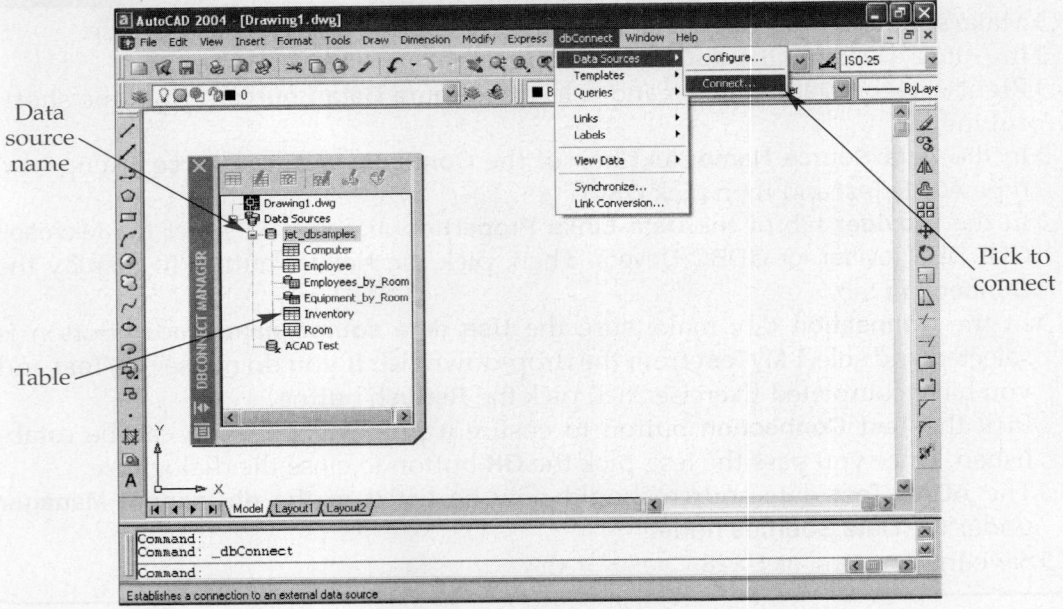

## Deleting Data Sources

When a data source is configured in AutoCAD, a UDL file with the same name as the data source is placed in the user's Data Links folder. Any configured data source appears in all sessions of the **dbConnect Manager** in all drawings. To remove a data source from the **dbConnect Manager**, delete the UDL file from the user's Data Links folder. AutoCAD can only use the database source files that are in the Data Links folder.

## Data Source Path

You can change where AutoCAD saves and looks for database source files by changing the default path. To do this, select **Options...** from the **Tools** pull-down menu or type OP or OPTIONS at the Command: prompt. In the **Files** tab of the **Options** dialog box, select the plus sign next to **Data Sources Location** to expand the tree. The current path for database source files is shown, **Figure 28-8**. To change the path, highlight it and use the **Browse...** button to specify a different location.

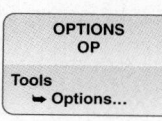

OPTIONS
OP

Tools
➡ Options...

Figure 28-8.
The location of the database source files can be specified using the **Options** dialog box.

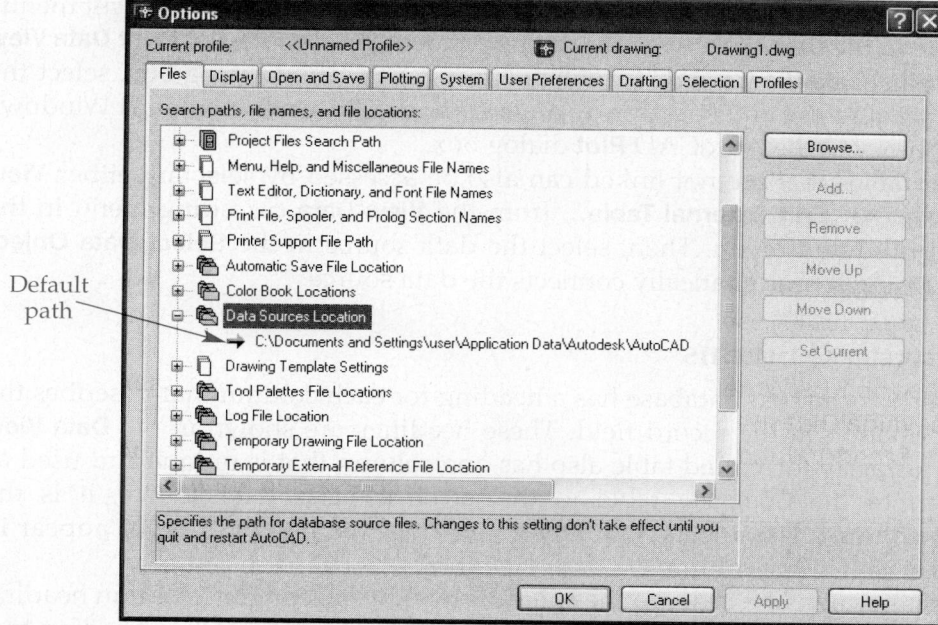

Default path

```
NOTE    After you change the data source path, the changes will not
        take effect until AutoCAD is restarted.
```

## Working with a Data Source

With a connection established to an external database, AutoCAD can serve as a database viewer and editor. You can link records to objects, add records to the database, and query information from tables. There are many other possibilities as well. This section covers how to work with a connected database.

The **Data View** window is used to view external database information within AutoCAD. It displays the data in columns and rows. The **Data View** window has its own toolbar and shortcut menus. To view a table in the **Data View** window, right-click on the table name in the **dbConnect Manager** and select either **View Table** or **Edit Table** from the shortcut menu. Selecting **View Table** allows you to view the data, but not edit it. The data background is shaded to indicate the "view mode." If **Edit Table** is selected, data can be edited, deleted, or added to the database. The data background is the Windows background color to indicate the "edit mode." The **Edit Table** option is only available if you have "write" permissions.

When the **Data View** window is activated, the **Data View** pull-down menu is added to the AutoCAD menu bar next to the **dbConnect** pull-down menu. When the **Data View** window is closed, the **Data View** pull-down menu is removed.

The **Data View** window can be open while working in an AutoCAD drawing and can be docked or floating. To dock the **Data View** window, right-click on the toolbar in the **Data View** window and select **Allow Docking** from the shortcut menu. To make it floating once it has been docked, select **Allow Docking** again from the shortcut menu.

The table in the **Data View** window can be printed by selecting the **Print Data View** button from the **Data View** window toolbar. Then, in the **Print** dialog box, select the printer you want to use and specify any other settings. This is the standard Windows print dialog box, not the AutoCAD **Plot** dialog box.

External tables that are not linked can also be accessed by selecting either **View External Table...** or **Edit External Table...** from the **View Data** cascading menu in the **dbConnect** pull-down menu. Then, select the data source in the **Select Data Object** dialog box. Doing so automatically connects the data source.

dbConnect
➡ View Data
  ➡ View
      External
      Table...

dbConnect
➡ View Data
  ➡ Edit
      External
      Table...

### Working with Columns

A properly formatted database has a heading for each column that describes the type of information in the record field. These headings are shown in the **Data View** window. A properly formatted table also has one column that is unique and used as an identifier. In the Computer table in the jet_db samples data source, it is the Tag_Number column. This means that any given "tag number" will never appear in more than one cell in the column.

You can rearrange the order of the columns by first selecting the column heading to be moved. The entire column is highlighted. Then, drag the column heading to a different location. When rearranging the order of columns, the changes are only effective for that session of **Data View**. To permanently change the order of columns, the changes need to be made to the external database file.

One of the most powerful features of any database is the ability to sort. *Sorting* is arranging the data in a column in a certain order that you specify. A sort can be done by ascending (lowest to highest) or descending (highest to lowest) values. Right-clicking a column heading displays a shortcut menu with **Sort** and other column tools. Selecting **Sort** displays the **Sort** dialog box, **Figure 28-9**. In this dialog box, you can specify the sort settings. You can specify the primary sort column, which is usually the identifier column, such as Tag_Number. You can further refine the sort by specifying other columns to use in the sorting process. You can also specify whether each sorted column appears in ascending or descending order.

**Figure 28-9.**
Use the **Sort** dialog box to specify sort settings.

Specify primary sort column

Specify order

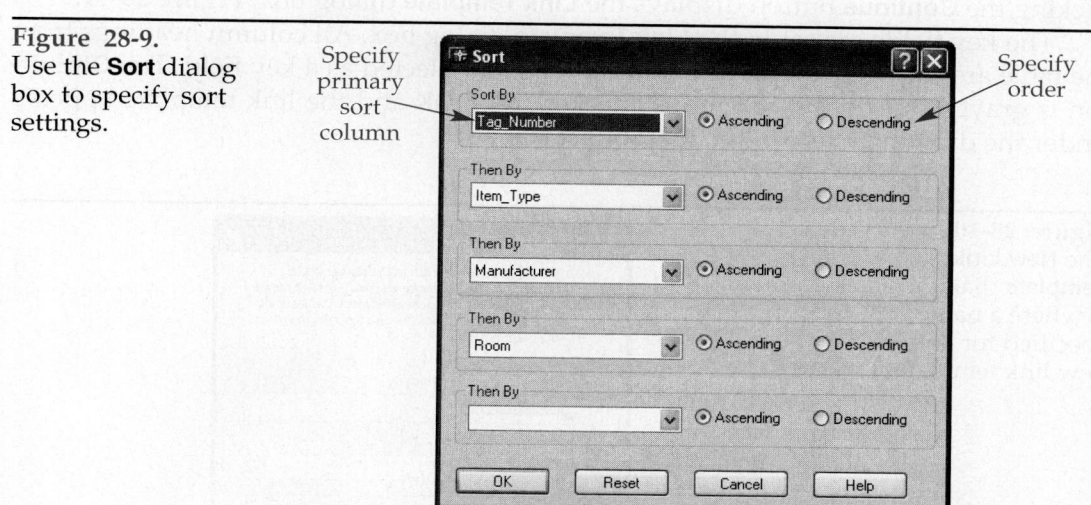

PROFESSIONAL TIP

Double-clicking a column heading sorts in ascending order by that column's data. Double-clicking the same column heading a second time sorts in the reverse order.

## Copying Database Information

The cells from the **Data View** window can be copied and pasted into another program, such as Microsoft Excel. To copy an individual cell's data, right-click in the cell and select **Copy** from the shortcut menu. To copy a record (row), right-click on the row's header and select **Copy** from the shortcut menu. An entire column can be copied by selecting the column header and using the [Ctrl]+[C] keyboard shortcut. To paste the column into another application, use that application's paste function.

## Link Templates and Linking Data

Before data can be linked to AutoCAD objects, a link template must be created. A *link template* is used to identify which fields from a database are used for the link. Each table that has data linked to AutoCAD has a link template. More than one link template can be made for a table. The difference between the templates is key value, or identifier, settings. Link templates are saved with the drawing.

## Creating a Link Template

To create a link template, highlight the table name in the **dbConnect Manager**. Then, select **New Link Template...** from the shortcut menu or pick the **New Link Template** button from the **dbConnect Manager** toolbar. The **New Link Template** dialog box is displayed, **Figure 28-10.**

Enter a name in the **New link template name:** text box. A name based on the table name appears in the text box as a suggestion. You do not have to use the suggested name. If a template is already created for the table, it is listed in the **Start with template:** drop-down list. An existing link template can be used as a base for a new one. Picking the **Continue** button displays the **Link Template** dialog box, **Figure 28-11.**

The key fields are set in the **Link Template** dialog box. All column headings from the table are shown. At least one column must be selected as a key field. The **OK** button is grayed out until a column is checked. Pick **OK** and the link template appears under the drawing name in the **dbConnect Manager**.

Figure 28-10.
The **New Link Template** dialog box is where a name is specified for the new link template.

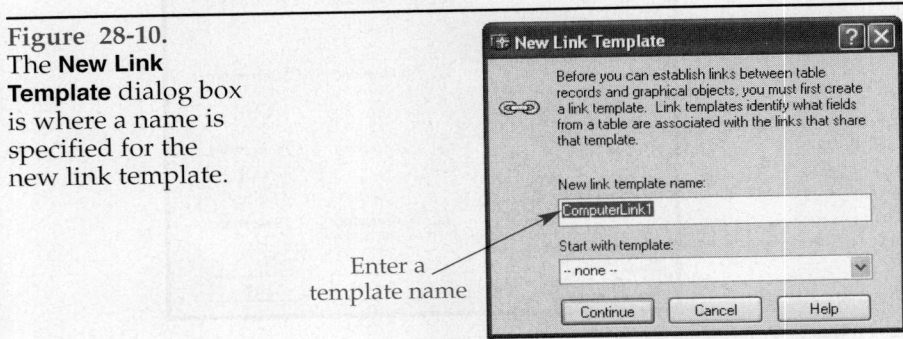

Enter a template name

Figure 28-11.
The **Link Template** dialog box.

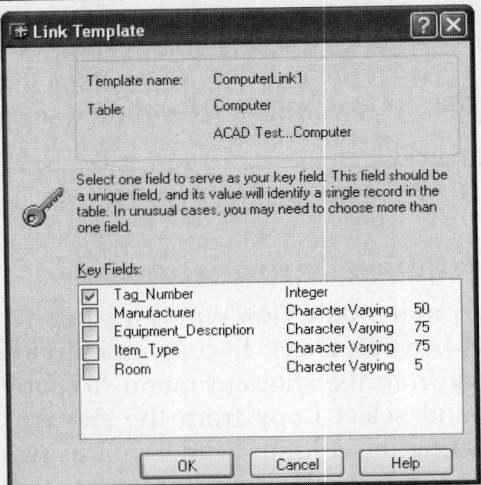

## Deleting a Link Template

To delete a link template, right-click on its name in the **dbConnect Manager** and select **Delete** from the shortcut menu. If **Delete** is shaded out, there is at least one active link using that link template. All links using a template can be deleted by right-clicking on the template and selecting **Delete links** from the shortcut menu. Then, the link template itself can be deleted.

You can also delete a link template by selecting **Delete Link Template...** from the **Templates** cascading menu in the **dbConnect** pull-down menu. Doing this opens the **Select a Database Object** dialog box. All link templates in the current drawing are listed in this dialog box. You can pick one or multiple link templates to delete. Pick **OK** to close the dialog box and delete the templates.

dbConnect
➡ Templates
   ➡ Delete Link
      Template...

---

### Exercise 28-4

○ Open EX28 if not already open. Complete Exercises 28-1 through 28-3 if you have not already done so.
○ Create a new link template using the Computer table and ACAD Test. Name it My ACAD Link and use Tag_Number as a key field.
○ Save the drawing.

---

## Linking Data to AutoCAD Objects

After creating a link template, records (rows) from a table can be linked to AutoCAD objects. To link a record, first select a link template under the current drawing node in the **dbConnect Manager**. Then, right-click and select **View Table** or pick the **View Table** button in the **dbConnect Manager** toolbar. You can also pick **View Linked Table...** from the **View Data** cascading menu in the **dbConnect** pull-down menu and select the table to view from the **Select a Database Object** dialog box. The table is displayed in the **Data View** window, **Figure 28-12.**

Next, in the **Data View** window, pick the record (row) header to highlight all the fields in the record. If you have more than one link template tied to a particular table, use the **Select a Link Template** drop-down list to choose the link template you want to use.

The setting in the **Link and Label Settings** drop-down list, located on the far left of the **Data View** window toolbar, determines if a link or a label is created. Labels are discussed later in this chapter. The icon for the drop-down list reflects the current setting, **Figure 28-13.** These same options are available in the **Link and Label Settings** cascading menu of the **Data View** pull-down menu. To create a link, make the setting **Create Links**.

dbConnect
➡ View Data
   ➡ View Linked
      Table...

dbConnect Manager
toolbar

View Table

---

**Figure 28-12.**
A table displayed in the **Data View** window.

Link and Label Settings
drop-down list

Select a Link Template
drop-down list

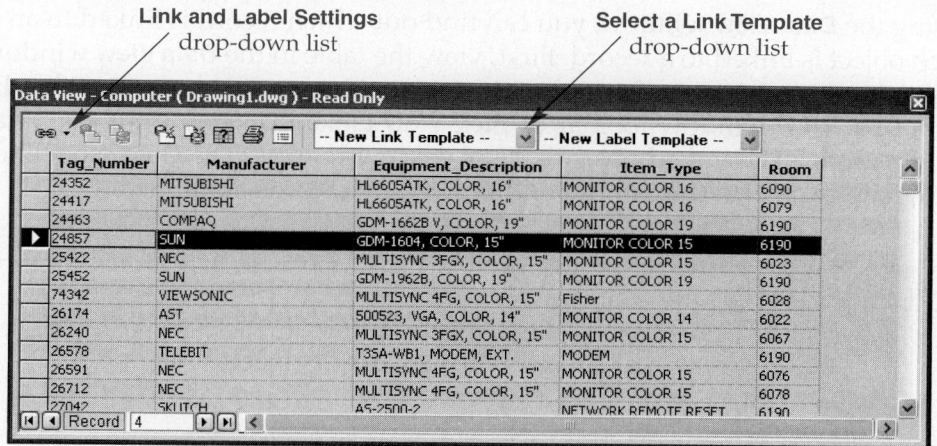

**Figure 28-13.**
The setting in the **Link and Label Settings** drop-down list specifies the current method of linking records. A—The icon when the **Create Links** setting is selected. B—The icon when the **Create Attached Label** setting is selected. C—The icon when the **Create Freestanding Label** setting is selected.

Link!

A

Create Attached Label

B

Create Freestanding Label

C

> **NOTE**
> Remember, the **Data View** pull-down menu is located on the main AutoCAD menu bar, not in the **Data View** window.

With the record (row) highlighted, pick the **Link!** button from the **Data View** window toolbar or select **Link!** from the **Data View** pull-down menu. If the **Data View** window is floating, it disappears so objects can be selected. Select the object to which the record needs to be linked. Multiple objects can be selected. When done selecting objects, press [Enter] and the **Data View** window reappears.

The external data is now linked to the AutoCAD object. The linked record (row) is highlighted yellow until another record is linked or the **Data View** window is closed. One record can be linked to more than one object. Also, an object can have more than one record linked to it.

> **NOTE**
> Links can only be viewed and modified in the file where they are created. Link information cannot be accessed in externally referenced files.

## Viewing Linked Data and Objects

Data View
→ View Linked Objects

Data View toolbar

View Linked Objects in Drawing

Using the **Data View** window, you can find out which record is linked to an object or which object is linked to a record. First, view the table in the **Data View** window and highlight the record (row). Then, select the **View Linked Objects in Drawing** button from the **Data View** window toolbar or pick **View Linked Objects** from the **Data View** pull-down menu. The linked object is displayed with grips. The Command: line indicates how many objects were found and how many records are linked.

> **PROFESSIONAL TIP**
>
> Docking the **Data View** window at the bottom of the screen may make it easier to see linked objects.

To see which record is attached to an object, pick the **View Linked Records in Data View** button or select **View Linked Records** from the **Data View** pull-down menu. The Command: line prompts you to select objects. Pick the object and press [Enter]. The **Data View** window now displays the record(s) linked to the object that was selected. If more than one object is selected, all the records linked to the objects are displayed.

Picking the **AutoView Linked Objects in Drawing** button automatically shows any linked objects when a record is selected. This allows you to quickly select different records and see the linked objects. You can also select **AutoView Linked Objects** from the **Data View** pull-down menu to use this option. Picking the **AutoView Linked Records in Drawing** button or selecting **AutoView Linked Records** from the **Data View** pull-down menu automatically shows the records attached to an object when it is selected. To turn off AutoView, pick the button or menu selection again.

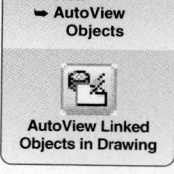

Data View
➡ View Linked Records

View Linked Records in Data View

Data View
➡ AutoView Objects

AutoView Linked Objects in Drawing

## Saving a Link

Links can be saved as an external text file. This allows you to create a file of the data for other uses when you do not want to have a link to the database, such as a chart for a website. First, select **Export links...** from the **Links** cascading menu in the **dbConnect** pull-down menu. Then, select the linked objects. In the **Export Links** dialog box, the field (column) headings are shown in the **Include Fields:** area. See **Figure 28-14**. Select the headings of the fields you want to save. More than one can be selected. In the **Save as type:** drop-down list, select to save the file in a comma-delimited, space-delimited, or native database format. "Delimited" indicates how the information is separated, by commas or spaces. Finally, name the file in the **File name:** text box and specify where to save the file.

Data View
➡ AutoView Linked Records

AutoView Linked Records in Drawing

**Figure 28-14.**
When exporting a link, you must select which fields to include.

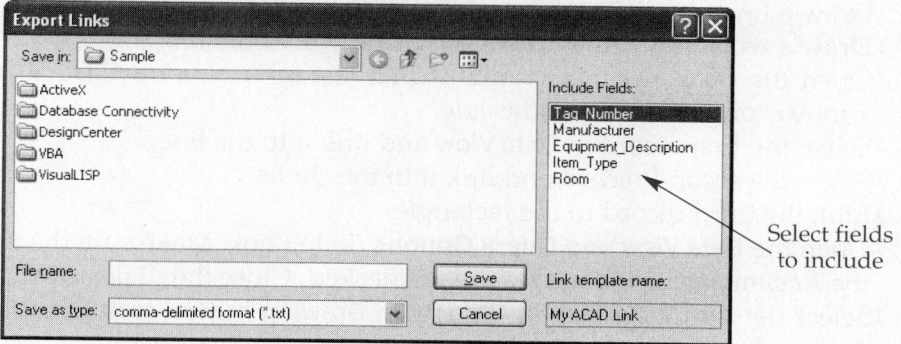

Select fields to include

## Options for Viewing Data and Object Links

To change the settings for viewing linked data and objects, select **Options...** from the **Data View** pull-down menu or pick the **Data View and Query Options** button in the **Data View** window toolbar. This displays the **Data View and Query Options** dialog box, **Figure 28-15.**

The **Record Indication Settings** area contains controls for changing the way records are presented when viewing linked data from objects. Selecting **Show all records, select indicated records** shows all records in the table and highlights the records linked to the selected objects. The highlight color is set from the **Marking Color** drop-down list. Selecting **Show only indicated records** displays only the records linked to the selected objects and hides all others.

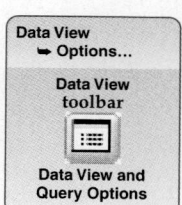

Data View
➡ Options...

Data View toolbar

Data View and Query Options

Figure 28-15.
There are various
options for viewing
data and objects.

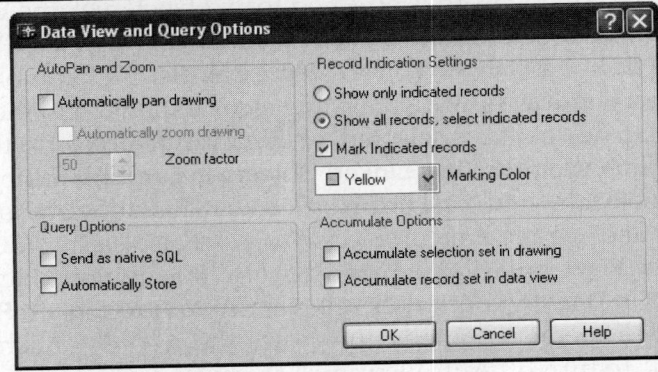

In the **Accumulate Options** area, if **Accumulate selection set in drawing** is checked, objects are added to the selection set when viewing additional linked objects. **Accumulate record set in data view** can only be selected if **Show all records, select indicated records** is chosen. If this is checked, records are added to the highlighted "record set" as additional objects are selected.

The **Automatically pan drawing** setting in the **AutoPan and Zoom** area controls whether or not the drawing is panned when viewing linked objects. If **Automatically zoom drawing** is checked, a **Zoom factor** can be set. AutoCAD then uses that zoom percentage instead of the current zoom factor when viewing linked objects.

---

### Exercise 28-5

○ Open EX28 if not already open.
○ Set the limits to 0,0 and 12,9.
○ Draw a circle centered at 1,3 with a radius of 1.5.
○ Draw a line from 0,7 to 4,7.
○ Draw a rectangle with corners at 5,3 and 9,5. Zoom all.
○ Open the Computer table under ACAD Test in "edit view." Dock the **Data View** window or move it off to the side.
○ Select the first record in **Data View** and link it to the line.
○ Select the second record and link it to the circle.
○ Link the third record to the rectangle.
○ Open the **Data View and Query Options** dialog box. Make sure the two options in the **Accumulate Options** area are unchecked. Close the dialog box.
○ Select the **AutoView Linked Objects in Drawing** button from the **Data View** window toolbar.
○ Select the header for each of the records, starting with the first one. Then, turn off "auto view."
○ Select the line and circle. Pick the **View Linked Records in Data View** button from the **Data View** window toolbar.
○ Save the drawing.

# Working with Labels

A *label* is a multiline text object that shows data from a table field. For example, a label might be placed in a floor plan drawing to display the contents of an employee name field. Then, as employees move to different offices or leave the company, the database is updated. The drawing always displays the name of the person who currently has the office.

A label can be linked to an object (attached) or "freestanding." Attached labels have a leader line connecting the label to an object. A freestanding label is simply inserted text from the record.

## Creating a Label Template

A label template must be created before any labels. A *label template* specifies which fields from the database table are displayed in the label and determines the formatting of the label text. The **Label Template** editor is used for creating label templates. This editor is the same as the multiline text editor with two additional tabs. These tabs are used for specifying which fields to use and for determining label formatting.

To create a label template, first highlight a table in the **dbConnect Manager**. Then, right-click and select **New Label Template...** from the shortcut menu or pick the **New Label Template** button in the **dbConnect Manager** toolbar. This activates the **New Label Template** dialog box.

dbConnect Manager toolbar

New Label Template

In the **New label template name:** text box, name the label. A name based on the highlighted table appears as a suggestion, but you do not have to use it. If a label already exists for the table, that name appears in the **Start with template:** drop-down list. Pick the **Continue** button and the **Label Template** editor opens, **Figure 28-16.**

The **Label Fields** tab is where fields (columns) from the table are specified to be included in the label. Notice the table name appears to the right of the **Add** button. Select a column heading from the **Field:** drop-down list. Then, pick the **Add** button. The field is added to the label and appears in the editor. A label can contain text as well as column fields. For example, if there are two fields on the same line in the editor, a comma can be added between them. A label must contain at least one field (column).

The **Start:** setting on the **Label Offset** tab determines the direction the leader line arrowhead points in relation to an imaginary bounding box around the selected object. See **Figure 28-17.** Use the **Leader offset** settings to make the leader line longer. The **Leader offset** and **Start:** settings only affect attached labels. The **Tip offset** settings represent how far, in drawing units, the arrowhead is offset from the **Start:** position. For example, if an object is a 1 × 1 box and **Middle Center** is used for the **Start:** setting, the arrowhead points to the middle of the box. If the **Tip offset** settings for **X:** and **Y:** are changed to .5, the arrowhead points to the upper-right corner of the box.

---

**Figure 28-16.**
A label is created using the **Label Template** dialog box.

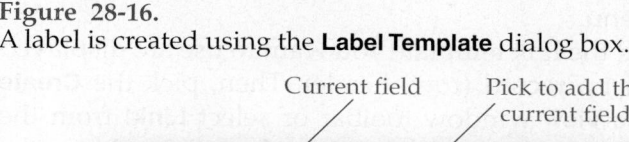

Current field

Pick to add the current field

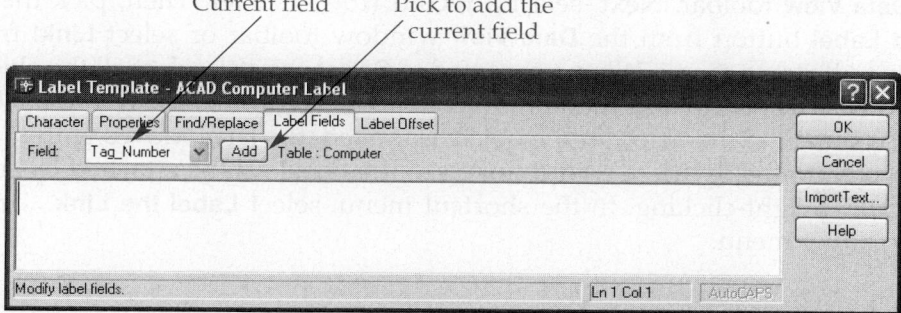

**Figure 28-17.**
There are nine different justification options in the **Start:** drop-down list. Each has a
distinctive icon shown next to the option in the list.

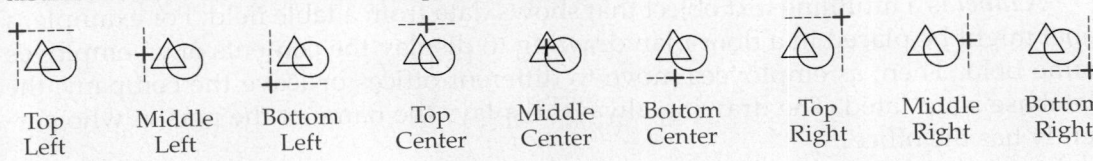

| Top<br>Left | Middle<br>Left | Bottom<br>Left | Top<br>Center | Middle<br>Center | Bottom<br>Center | Top<br>Right | Middle<br>Right | Bottom<br>Right |

Pick the **OK** button in the **Label Template** dialog box to create the label. The label name appears under the drawing name node in the **dbConnect Manager**, **Figure 28-18**.

**Figure 28-18.**
The new label template appears in the **dbConnect Manager**.

New label
template

NOTE

The **Character**, **Properties**, and **Find/Replace** tabs in the **Label Template** editor are the same as in the multiline text editor.

## Inserting an Attached Label

Data View
➡ Link and Label
   Settings
   ➥ Create
      Attached
      Labels

Data View
➡ Link!

Data View
toolbar

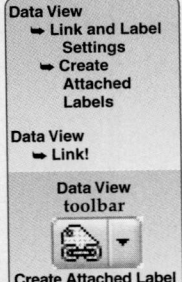

Create Attached Label

To insert an attached label, first open the table used to create the template using the **Data View** window. For example, if the Computer table is used to create a label template, open the Computer table in the **Data View** window. Next, select **Create Attached Labels** from the **Link and Label Settings** drop-down list in the **Data View** window. You may also select **Create Attached Labels** from the **Link and Label Settings** cascading menu in the **Data View** pull-down menu.

Make sure the label template and the link template you want to use are displayed on the **Data View** toolbar. Next, select a record (row) header. Then, pick the **Create Attached Label** button from the **Data View** window toolbar or select **Link!** from the **Data View** pull-down menu. When prompted to Select objects:, select all the objects the label is to be attached to and then press [Enter]. The record is linked to the label and the label is linked to the object. If the object is moved, the label moves with it.

If an object already has a record linked to it, a label can be attached by selecting the object and right-clicking. In the shortcut menu, select **Label the Link...** from the **Label** cascading menu.

## Inserting a Freestanding Label

A *freestanding label* can be inserted anywhere in the drawing. To insert this type of label, first open the table used to create the label template in the **Data View** window. Then, select **Create Freestanding Labels** from the **Link and Label Settings** drop-down list in the **Data View** window or select **Create Freestanding Labels** from the **Link and Label Settings** cascading menu in the **Data View** pull-down menu. Next, select the record (row) header in the **Data View** window. Then, pick the **Create Freestanding Label** button from the **Data View** window toolbar or select **Link!** from the **Data View** pull-down menu. Finally, pick a point in the drawing where you want the label.

Data View
➡ Link and Label Settings
➡ Create Freestanding Labels

Data View
➡ Link!

Data View toolbar

Create Freestanding Label

## Editing Label Templates and Labels

A label template can be edited by double-clicking on the template name in the **dbConnect Manager** or right-clicking on it and selecting **Edit...** from the shortcut menu. The **Label Template** dialog box used to create the label template is displayed. Different column fields can be added, formatting can be changed, or a different text style can be specified. Changes made in this dialog box are applied to *all* labels in the drawing that are based on this template once the **OK** button is selected.

## Label Visibility

The visibility of labels can be controlled globally or individually in a drawing. To control them globally, right-click on the drawing name node in the **dbConnect Manager** to display the shortcut menu. **Show Labels** displays all the labels in the drawing, including hidden ones. **Hide Labels** hides all labels. The **Reload** option updates the labels if the database record label template has changed.

**Show Labels** and **Hide Labels** can be set on individual templates by right-clicking on the template name to display the shortcut menu. In this menu, there is also a **Delete Labels** option. This option deletes all the labels in the drawing inserted using that template.

Individual label properties can also be changed. First, select the label in the drawing area and right-click. Then, choose **Label** from the shortcut menu to display the cascading menu. The label editing menus for attached and freestanding labels are shown in **Figure 28-19**. Both have the following options.

- **Reload.** Resets or updates the label data.
- **Restore Properties.** Restores the formatting settings from the label template.
- **Change Label Template.** Allows you to select a different label template.
- **Show Label.** Displays the label if it is hidden. The object must be selected when using this option.
- **Hide Label.** Hides the label.

The following options are available for attached labels.

- **Detach Label.** Changes the label to a freestanding label. The link to the object is retained.
- **Delete Label (keep link).** Deletes the label, but the link to the object is retained.

Freestanding labels have two different options.

- **Attach to an Object.** Allows you to attach the label to an object.
- **Delete Label and Link.** Deletes the label and the link.

**Figure 28-19.**
A— The shortcut menu for editing an attached label. B— The shortcut menu for editing a freestanding label.

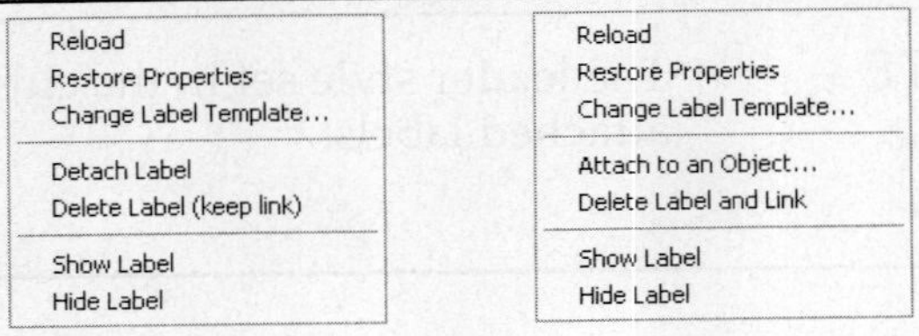

| A |
|---|
| Reload |
| Restore Properties |
| Change Label Template... |
| Detach Label |
| Delete Label (keep link) |
| Show Label |
| Hide Label |

A

| B |
|---|
| Reload |
| Restore Properties |
| Change Label Template... |
| Attach to an Object... |
| Delete Label and Link |
| Show Label |
| Hide Label |

B

> **NOTE**
>
> Do not edit labels using the multiline text editor. If the labels are reloaded, their values change back to match the label template settings.

## Exercise 28-6

○ Open EX28.
○ Create a new label template based on the Computer table under ACAD Test. Name it ACAD Computer. Add the Tag_Number, Item_Type, and Room fields.
○ Open the Computer table in the **Data View** window.
○ Create an attached label for the circle using the first record (row) and the ACAD Computer label template.
○ Create a freestanding label placed inside the rectangle using the second record (row) and the ACAD Computer label.
○ Close **Data View**. Zoom all.
○ Right-click on the ACAD Computer label template in the **dbConnect Manager** and select **Hide Labels** from the shortcut menu. Observe what happens. Then, select **Show Labels** from the shortcut menu.
○ Save the drawing.

## Editing Data in the Data View Window

An important reason for linking to a database is to ensure there is only one data source. This means that a change in data needs to be entered only once. An external database can be edited in AutoCAD's **Data View** window. Records can be added, deleted, or modified, and information in individual fields (cells) can be changed.

To edit an existing record, begin by selecting the appropriate table in the **dbConnect Manager**. Next, pick the **Edit Table** button on the **dbConnect Manager** toolbar or select **Edit Linked Table...** (or **Edit External Table...** if the table is not currently linked) from the **View Data** cascading menu in the **dbConnect Manager**. This opens the table for editing in **Data View**. Next, double-click inside the field (cell) to be modified. When you make a change in any cell in a row, the record header changes to a pencil icon to indicate that a cell in the record is being edited, **Figure 28-20.** After you select another record, a "delta" icon is displayed in the header for the record that was changed. A delta icon also appears at the top of the record header column. These icons indicate that the table has been modified, but the database has not been updated.

**Figure 28-20.**
The pencil icon in a record header indicates that the record is in "edit mode." A delta icon appears in the header of any record that has been changed.

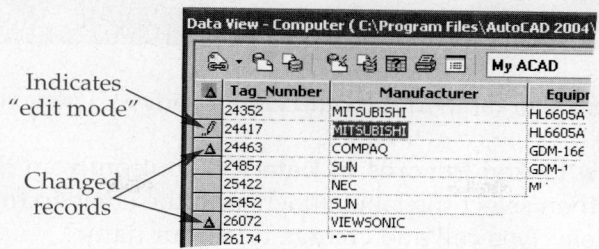

Indicates "edit mode"

Changed records

To update the external database, right-click on the top of the header column and select **Commit** from the shortcut menu. This updates the changes that were made in the **Data View** window to the external database. Closing the **Data View** window also commits the changes to the database. If the changes have not yet been committed, they can be undone by right-clicking on the top of the header column and selecting **Restore** from the shortcut menu.

**PROFESSIONAL TIP**
You can move from cell to cell in the **Data View** window using the arrow keys on the keyboard.

To add a new record (row) to a table, right-click on any record header and select **Add new record** from the shortcut menu. The new record is inserted at the bottom of the table. Edit each cell by clicking in it and typing new text. A record can be deleted by right-clicking on the record's header and selecting **Delete record** from the shortcut menu. You are asked to confirm the deletion.

If records that have labels in the drawing are modified, the labels need to be updated. To update all labels using a label template, right-click on the label template name in the **dbConnect Manager** and select **Reload** from the shortcut menu. Individual labels can be updated by selecting either the object with the attached label or the label itself and right-clicking. In the shortcut menu, select **Reload** from the **Label** cascading menu.

If a change is made to the key column assigned in a link template, the **Reload** option *cannot* be used to update the label. Instead, select **Link Manager...** from the **Links** cascading menu in the **dbConnect** pull-down menu. When prompted to Select objects:, select the object with the attached label or the label itself. In the **Link Manager** dialog box, the **Key** columns are listed with the **Value** of its cell. Pick inside the "value" cell that needs to be changed and then select the ellipsis (...) button that appears at the far right of the same cell. Select the correct value from the **Column Values** dialog box. Now, the **Reload** option can be used to update the label in the drawing.

dbConnect
➥ Links
  ➥ Links
    Manager...

**NOTE**

If you get an error message stating Unable to reload some of labels, the **Link Manager** needs to be used to update the label before **Reload** can be used.

# Working with Queries

The ability to use queries is one of the biggest advantages of a database. A *query* is a request for data that meets specified criteria from a table. If you have ever used an Internet search engine, you have used queries. For example, suppose you need to find out how many computers are in room 102. A query could be created with the criteria being "102" in a Room column and "computer" in an Equipment_Type column of the table. The resulting data are displayed just like the table with only the records that meet the specified criteria shown. Queries are very powerful and easy to create once you get the hang of them. AutoCAD provides four ways to create queries. These are quick query, range query, query builder, and SQL query.

dbConnect
➥ Queries
➥ New Query
  on an
  External
  Table...

dbConnect Manager
toolbar

New Query

To create a query, first open the **dbConnect Manager** and highlight the table to be used for the query. Then, right-click and select **New Query...** from the shortcut menu or pick the **New Query** button in the **dbConnect Manager** toolbar. You can also select **New Query on an External Table...** from the **Queries** cascading menu of the **dbConnect** pull-down menu. Then, in the **Select Data Object** dialog box, pick the table for the query. This opens the **New Query** dialog box. Enter a name for the query in the **New query name:** text field. If saved queries already exist for the table, one can be selected from the **Existing query names:** drop-down list. The existing query is then used as a base for the new query. Next, pick the **Continue** button to display the **Query Editor**. This is where you specify the type of query, parameters, and options.

> **PROFESSIONAL TIP**
>
> New queries can be created and saved in an external database file for use in AutoCAD.

## Creating a Quick Query

A *quick query* is a "template" designed to introduce queries to the beginner. In the **Quick Query** tab, a query can be created based on the data in a single field (column). In the **Field:** area, highlight the name of the field you want to use, **Figure 28-21.** The **Operator:** drop-down list sets the conditional operator. A *conditional operator*, like **Equal to** or **Greater than or equal to**, specifies parameters for the values being

**Figure 28-21.**
A quick query is a simple, fast way to create a query.

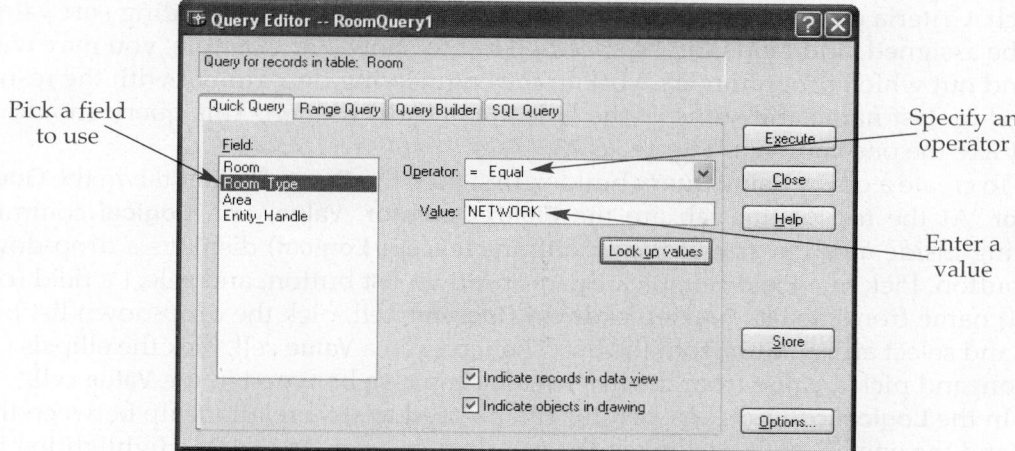

Pick a field to use

Specify an operator

Enter a value

looked for in the table. The value being looked for in the table is entered in the **Value:** text box. Picking the **Look up values** button shows a list of all the values in the highlighted field. A value can be picked from this list or typed in the **Value:** text box. Checking the **Indicate records in data view** check box returns query matches in the **Data View** window. Checking the **Indicate objects in drawing** check box returns query matches by selecting all objects in the drawing linked to matches. Pick the **Execute** button to complete the query.

## Creating a Range Query

A *range query* is basically the same as a quick query. However, two values are specified to create a range for the query. To create a range query, pick the **Range Query** tab in the **Query Editor**, **Figure 28-22.** As with a quick query, you must specify a single field (column) for the query. The **From:** text box is where one range value is specified. The **Through:** text box is where the other range value is specified.

Once executed, the query results show everything matching the **From:** and **Through:** values, and everything that falls in between. For example, if the range values are 4 and 9, and the query is for whole numbers, the numbers 4, 5, 6, 7, 8, and 9 are returned as matches to the query.

**Figure 28-22.**
A range query is used to find all values between the specified range.

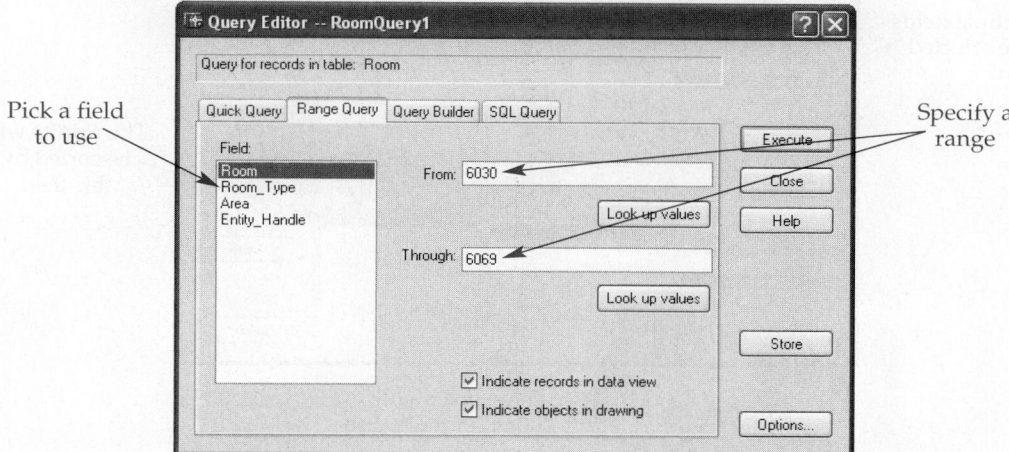

Pick a field to use

Specify a range

# Creating a Query Using the Query Builder

In a query created with *query builder,* multiple columns can be used for the search. Criteria can be parenthetically grouped, ascending or descending sort values can be assigned, and fields can be specified not to show. For example, you may want to find out which programmers work in the engineering department with the results sorted by last name and some of the fields (columns) hidden. This query should be built like the one shown in **Figure 28-23**.

To create a query using query builder, first pick the **Query Builder** tab in the **Query Editor**. At the top of this tab are the **Field**, **Operator**, **Value**, and **Logical** columns. Picking inside a cell in any of these columns (except **Logical**) displays a drop-down list button. Pick in a **Field** cell, pick the drop-down list button, and select a field (column) name from the list. Next, pick in an **Operator** cell, pick the drop-down list button, and select an operator from the list. Then, pick in a **Value** cell, pick the ellipsis (**...**) button, and pick a value from the list. A value can also be typed in the **Value** cell.

In the **Logical** column, an operator can be used to set a relationship between that row and the one below it. Picking in the cell changes from **And** to **Or**. Highlighting the cell and pressing the delete key clears the cell. If **And** is used, the resulting records meet the criteria specified in that row *and* the one below it. If **Or** is used, the resulting records meet the criteria specified in that row *or* the one below it.

The **Fields in table:** area shows a list of all the field (column) headings in the table. To show a field in the query results, highlight the name in the **Fields in table:** area and pick the **Add** button above the **Show fields:** area. The name appears in the **Show fields:** area. Only the columns listed in the **Show fields:** area are displayed in the query results. If you do not add selected field names, all fields are automatically added when the query is executed. To remove a field name from the **Show fields:** area, right-click on the name and select **Clear field name** from the shortcut menu.

To specify a sort on a field listed in the **Show fields:** area, highlight the name and pick the **Add** button above the **Sort by:** area. The name appears in the **Sort by:** area with an "up arrow" next to it. This arrow indicates that the field will be sorted in ascending order. To sort in descending order, select the button with the up and down arrows. More than one field can be sorted, but the first field in the list takes precedence over the others. To remove a field name from the **Sort by:** area, right-click on the name and select **Clear field name** from the shortcut menu.

**Figure 28-23.**
The query builder allows you to create an advanced query.

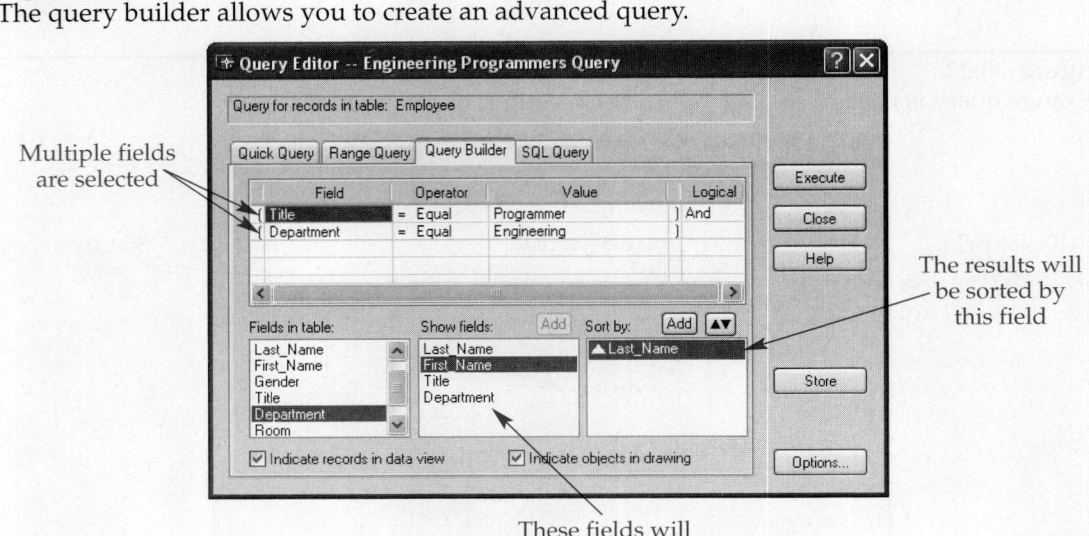

To complete the query, pick the **Execute** button. The results are displayed in the **Data View** window if the **Indicate records in data view** check box is checked. The matching objects are selected in the drawing if the **Indicate objects in drawing** check box is checked.

## Creating an SQL Query

When creating a query using any of the first three tabs in the **Query Editor**, AutoCAD translates your settings into an *SQL statement.* The SQL statement created for a query can be seen by switching to the **SQL Query** tab after making the settings, but before executing the query. Advanced users can create an SQL statement directly in this tab by typing the statement or using the tools in the **SQL Query** tab.

Notice the **Table:** area lists all the tables from the external database, Figure 28-24. When constructing a query from the **SQL Query** tab, multiple tables can be used. Suppose a report needs to be created that shows what type of computer each employee is using. The Computer table contains a column that shows the employee ID number, but not their name. The ID number is also in the Employee table, which has columns for employee names. Therefore, both tables need to be used to create the report.

To add criteria to an SQL statement, highlight a table from the **Table:** area and pick the **Add** button. Then, add a field, an operator, and a value by selecting each and picking the **Add** button above each area. Picking the **Check** button tests the SQL statement for valid syntax. When an SQL statement is complete and the syntax valid, pick the **Execute** button to perform the query.

---

**Figure 28-24.**
The SQL statement for a query can be written or viewed in the **SQL Query** tab.

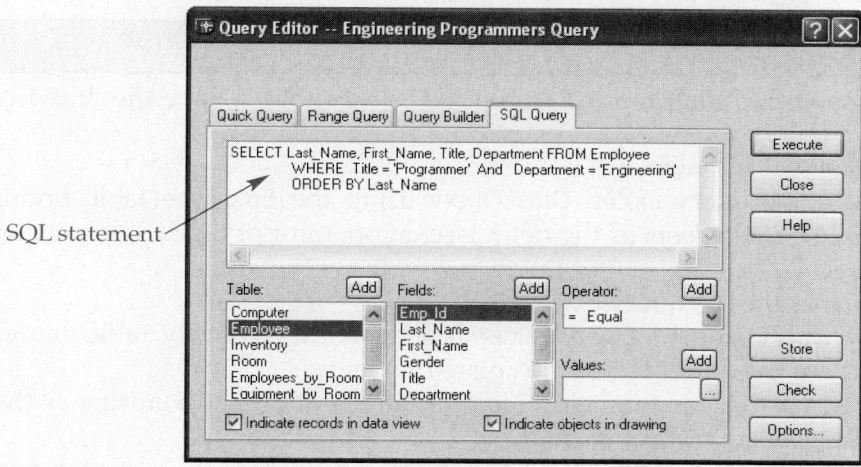

SQL statement

## Saving, Executing, and Editing a Query

Before executing a query, it can be saved in the current drawing by picking the **Store** button. Once the **Execute** button is picked, the query settings are lost. When a query is stored, the query name appears in the **dbConnect Manager** under the drawing name node, Figure 28-25.

After a query is stored, it can be executed by double-clicking on the name in the **dbConnect Manager** or right-clicking on the name and selecting **Execute** from the shortcut menu. Also, selecting **Execute Query...** from the **Queries** cascading menu of the **dbConnect** pull-down menu opens the **Select a Database Object** dialog box. Saved queries appear in this dialog box. Pick the name of the query to execute from the list and pick the **OK** button. This executes the query.

---

Figure 28-25.
The saved query
appears in the
**dbConnect Manager**.

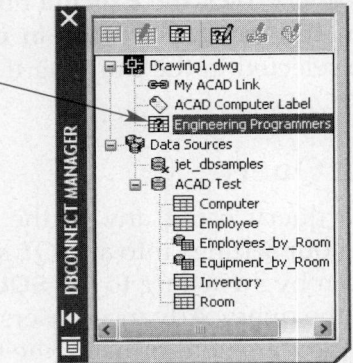

Saved query

A saved query can be edited by right-clicking on the name and selecting **Edit...** from the shortcut menu. You can also pick **Edit Query...** from the **Queries** cascading menu in the **dbConnect** pull-down menu. Then, in the **Select a Database Object** dialog box, pick the query you want to edit. To save the changes to an edited query, you must pick the **Store** button after the changes have been made.

NOTE

The **Data View** options can be set to automatically save a query when it is executed.

## Exercise 28-8

○ Open the db_samp.dwg file from the AutoCAD Sample folder. Save the drawing as EX28-8.
○ Open the **dbConnect Manager**.
○ Create a new quick query called QuickQuery using the Employee table under jet_dbsamples. Use Department as the field. Use an operator of Equal. Use a value of Engineering.
○ Save and then execute the query.
○ Create a new query named QueryBuilder based on the Inventory table under jet_dbsamples. Use the query builder to create the query.
○ In the first row, use Type as the field, Equal as the operator, and Furniture as the value. In the **Logical** column, enter And.
○ In the second row, use Price as the field, Greater than or equal as the operator, and 500 as the value.
○ Save, then execute the query.
○ Save the drawing.

## Creating Selection Sets from Queries

AutoCAD's **Link Select** can be used to construct a selection set of AutoCAD objects. The selection set can then be refined. A selection set can be created by either selecting linked AutoCAD objects or by making a database query. This initial selection set is referred to as set A. To refine set A, another selection set is created. This set is called set B. Relationship operators can then be used on the two selection sets to create one selection set.

To open the **Link Select** dialog box, right-click on a link template in the **dbConnect Manager** and select **Link Select...** from the shortcut menu or select **Link Select...** from the **Links** cascading menu in the **dbConnect** pull-down menu. The **Link Select** dialog box is displayed, **Figure 28-26.** Notice the **Quick Query**, **Range Query**, and **Query Builder** tabs in the middle of the box. These are the same as the ones found in the **Query Edit** dialog box.

To create a selection set using a query, pick the **Use Query** radio button. Use any of the query methods to create the query. Then, pick the **Execute** button to create the selection set.

To create a selection set by selecting objects in the drawing, pick the **Select in Drawing<** radio button. Notice that the "query settings" disappear from the dialog box. Then, pick the **Select** button and pick the objects in the drawing.

The **Do:** drop-down list in the **Link Select** dialog box contains the relationship operators. The following options are available.

- **Select.** Creates an initial selection set.
- **Union.** The results of the new selection set (set B) are added to the first selection set (set A).
- **Intersect.** Displays the records and objects that set A and set B have in common.
- **Subtract A – B.** Subtracts the records and objects from the new selection set (set B) from the first selection set (set A).
- **Subtract B – A.** Subtracts the records and objects from the first selection set (set A) from the new selection set (set B).

The link template that you want to use can be selected in the **Using:** drop-down list. This drop-down list contains all the link templates in the current drawing. Picking the **Reset** button discards the current settings so a new link selection operation can be defined. Picking the **Finish** button closes the **Link Select** dialog box and displays the selection set of AutoCAD objects and/or the **Data View** window records. The **Indicate records in data view** and **Indicate objects in drawing** check boxes in the **Link Select** dialog box determine how the selection set is displayed.

**Figure 28-26.**
The **Link Select** dialog box is used to build a selection set based on linked objects.

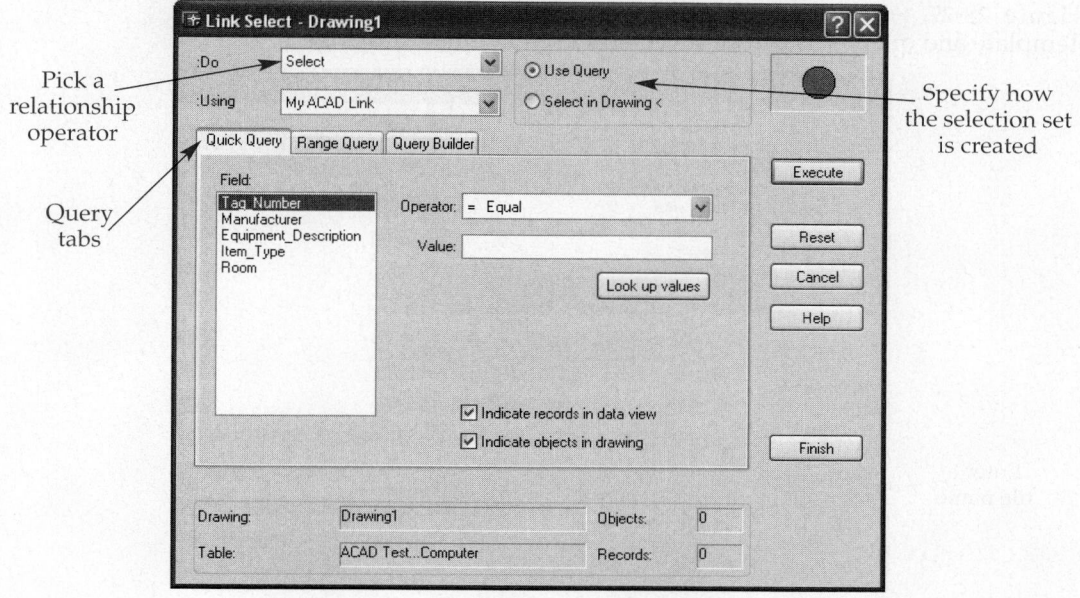

# Exporting and Importing Templates

Link, label, and query templates are saved in the drawing in which they are created. However, they can also be saved as an external file and used in other drawings. Link and label templates are saved as a "set" in a DBT file. All of the queries in a drawing are also called a "set" and can be saved as a DBQ file.

To save a link and label template set, highlight the name of the drawing node in the **dbConnect Manager**. Then, right-click and select **Export Template Set...** from the shortcut menu or select **Export Template Set...** from the **Templates** cascading menu in the **dbConnect** pull-down menu. In the **Export Template Set** dialog box, specify the file name and the location where you want to save it, **Figure 28-27.** Then, pick the **Save** button.

To import a template set, highlight the drawing name node in the **dbConnect Manager**. Then, right-click and select **Import Template Set...** from the shortcut menu or select **Import Template Set...** from the **Templates** cascading menu in the **dbConnect** pull-down menu. Browse to the DBT file and select it. Pick the **Open** button to import the file.

To save a query set, first highlight the drawing name node in the **dbConnect Manager**. Then, right-click and select **Export Query Set...** from the shortcut menu or select **Export Query Set...** from the **Queries** cascading menu in the **dbConnect** pull-down menu. In the **Export Query Set** dialog box, specify the file name and the location where you want to save it. Then, pick the **Save** button.

To import a query set, highlight the drawing name node in the **dbConnect Manager**. Then, right-click and select **Import Query Set...** from the shortcut menu or select **Import Query Set...** from the **Queries** cascading menu in the **dbConnect** pull-down menu. Browse to the DBQ file and select it. Pick the **Open** button to import the file.

dbConnect
➡ Templates
➡ Export
Template
Set...

dbConnect
➡ Templates
➡ Import
Template
Set...

dbConnect
➡ Queries
➡ Export Query
Set...

dbConnect
➡ Queries
➡ Import Query
Set...

> **NOTE**  An imported template set can only be used if the data source it was created with is configured and connected.

**Figure 28-27.**
Template and query sets can be saved and used in other drawings.

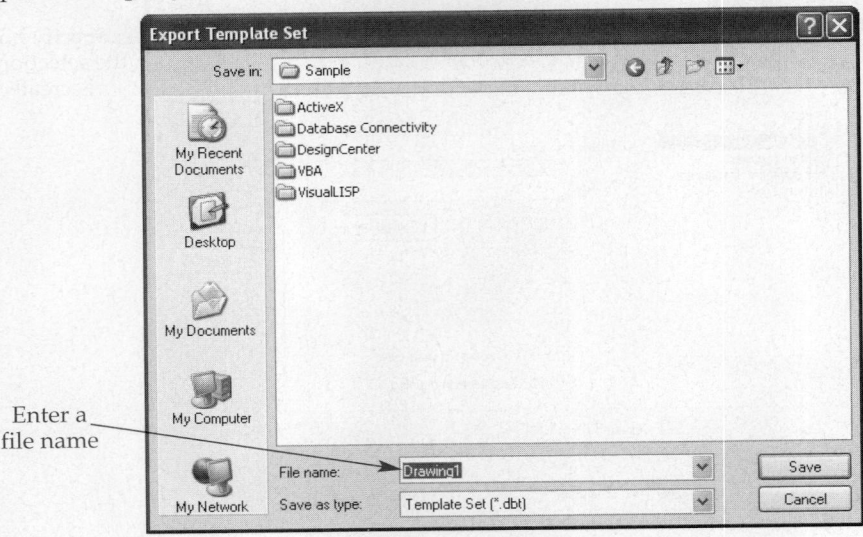

Enter a file name

# Converting Links from Previous Versions of AutoCAD

ASE links in versions of AutoCAD drawings previous to AutoCAD 2000 need to be converted to work. If a file is opened from a previous version of AutoCAD that has links, AutoCAD attempts to convert the information automatically. This may not always be successful. To manually convert a link, select **Link Conversion...** from the **dbConnect** pull-down menu. The **Link Conversion** dialog box appears, **Figure 28-28.** Select the AutoCAD drawing version that needs to be converted using the **Link Format:** radio buttons. In the **Old Link Format** area, enter the settings from the old link. In the **New Link Format** area, enter the new settings. After selecting the **OK** button, you can open the old drawing in AutoCAD and save it to convert the links.

dbConnect
➡ Link
    Conversion...

Figure 28-28.
Older AutoCAD links can be converted using the **Link Conversion** dialog box.

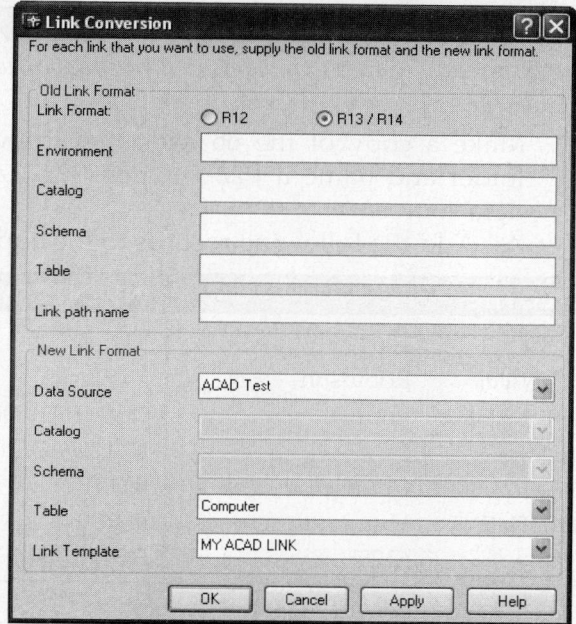

## Chapter Test

*Answer the following questions on a separate sheet of paper.*

1. What is a *database*?
2. What is a *DBMS*?
3. What is a *field*?
4. What does *SQL* stand for?
5. What is a *database table*?
6. A row in a table is called a(n) _____.
7. A column in a table is called a(n) _____.
8. A data source needs to be ____ in Windows and then ____ and ____ in AutoCAD.
9. In which AutoCAD folder are data source files stored by default?
10. How is the **Data View** window docked?
11. How can a column in **Data View** be sorted quickly?
12. Why does a link template need to be created?

13. Which of the following table components can be linked to AutoCAD objects?
    A) cell
    B) record
    C) field
14. What are the two types of labels that can be created?
15. Which type of label can be inserted without linking to an object?
16. Which shortcut menu option updates a label in the drawing?
17. Which **Data View** shortcut menu option updates the external database when changes have been made?
18. What is a *query*?
19. Which type of a query retrieves records that fall between two values?
20. Which types of queries allow more than one column to be used?

## Drawing Problems

*Make a copy of the* db_samples.mdb *file found in AutoCAD's* Sample *folder before completing any of these problems. When finished with the problems, restore the original file.*

1. Make a copy of the db_samp.dwg drawing in the AutoCAD Sample folder and name it P28-1. Open P28-1 and connect the jet_dbsamples data source.
    A. Add the following records to the appropriate tables.

| EMPLOYEE | | INVENTORY | |
|---|---|---|---|
| EMP_ID | 1064 | INV_ID | 1268 |
| LAST_NAME | Robinson | TYPE | Hardware |
| FIRST_NAME | Lonnie | DESCRIPTION | Laser Printer |
| GENDER | F | MANUFACTURER | Quasar Lasers |
| TITLE | Counselor | MODEL | QLP-600 |
| DEPARTMENT | Human Resources | PRICE | 1250 |
| ROOM | 6125 | ROOM | 6125 |

    B. View the new records to check for errors and then commit the changes.
    C. Use the **View Linked Objects in Drawing** button to find room 6125 in the drawing.
    D. Zoom in on the drawing so you can see about four cubicles that contain furniture.
    E. Link the new employee and the new laser printer (added above) to room 6125. Save the drawing as P28-1.

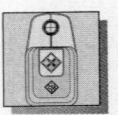

2. Open drawing P28-1 and make the following changes to the indicated tables. Check each table for errors when done.
    A. EMPLOYEE table: Change EMP_ID 1006's last name to Wilson-Jenkins, and change her title to International Sales Mgr.
    B. INVENTORY table: Change the price of INV_ID 1141 to 5300 and change the manufacturer to Tradewinds Computers.
    C. COMPUTER table: For Tab_Number 29733, change the manufacturer to SUN, and the room to 6180.

3. If you have database software, create a new database called Facilities and add a new table called Computers. Columns in the table should be: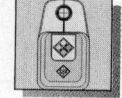
   - COMP_ID
   - CPU
   - HDRIVE
   - INPUT
   - MFR
   - RAM
   - FDRIVE
   - GRAPHICS
   A. Make a list of each computer in your drawing lab. Make note of the above information for each. Enter all of the data into the database.
   B. Make a printout when you have completed the database.

4. Construct a drawing of your computer lab. Create blocks for each workstation.
   A. Set the proper database and table in order to work with the computers in your drawing.
   B. Link each one of the computers in the drawing with the appropriate record in your database table created in Problem 3.
   C. View the links you created to check for accuracy. Edit any links that are not correct.
   D. Create labels for each workstation. The labels should use the COMP_ID and MFR columns.
   E. Place a label in the title block, or as a general note, referring to the database name that is linked to this drawing.
   F. Save the drawing as P28-4 and print or plot a copy of the drawing.

Maintaining symbols libraries is an important aspect of managing electronic data for a CAD department. This is an example of sheet that can be distributed to every drafter that indicates the symbols in the symbols library.

## Single Line Piping Symbols

| Name | Screwed | | | Buttwelded | | |
|------|---------|---|---|------------|---|---|
| | Left Side | Front | Right Side | Left Side | Front | Right Side |
| 90° Elbow | | | | | | |
| 45° Elbow | | | | | | |
| Tee | | | | | | |
| 45° Lateral | | | | | | |
| Cross | | | | | | |
| Cap | | | | | | |
| Concentric Reducer | | | | | | |
| Eccentric Reducer | | | | | | |
| Union | | | | | | |
| Coupling | | | | | | |

## CHAPTER 29

# Managing Electronic Data and Drawing Standards

## Learning Objectives

After completing this chapter, you will be able to:

- Explain the need for drawing standards.
- Create a drawing standards file (*.dws).
- Identify which aspects of a drawing can be maintained via a drawing standards file.
- Associate a drawing standards file with other drawings.
- Check a drawing for adherence to the associated drawing standards file.
- Use the **Layer Translator** to map a layering scheme from one drawing to another.
- Explain basic file, server, and hard drive management.

AutoCAD is a powerful tool used in a computer-aided drafting (CAD) environment to fulfill a wide range of drafting needs. However, it is important to maintain consistency in drawing files between users and projects. In large companies, this task falls on a system administrator or CAD manager. In smaller companies, each individual drafter may share in the responsibility. This chapter introduces some of the aspects of CAD drawings that lead to consistency between drawings.

## Introduction to Drawing Standards

There are four areas of AutoCAD drawings that lend themselves to rather easy customization: layer schemes, dimension styles, text styles, and linetypes. As a result, company standards and drawing consistency can, unfortunately, sometimes take a backseat to a drafter's personal preference. In order to present a professional drawing to a customer, contractor, or another department, the way in which these areas are presented needs to be standardized. These standards should be developed, maintained, and practiced within any organization that uses AutoCAD.

A place to start in maintaining consistency within an organization or department is the AutoCAD drawing template file. A custom template file can hold all of the standard settings for layer schemes, dimension styles, text styles, and linetypes. When a drafter starts a new drawing based on the custom template, the standards of the department are loaded. Template files are covered in detail in Chapter 3 of *AutoCAD and its Applications—Basics* published by The Goodheart-Willcox Company, Inc.

A template file, however, is merely a starting point. A drafter can still easily stray from the standards by creating nonstandard layers, linetypes, text styles, and dimension styles. Fortunately, AutoCAD has two commands that allow a drafter, manager, or administrator to make sure a drawing follows company standards. These commands are the **STANDARDS** and **CHECKSTANDARDS** commands.

## Creating a Drawing Standards File

Before you can maintain drawing standards, the standards themselves must be created. AutoCAD allows you to create and maintain standards for layers, dimension styles, text styles, and linetypes. These properties can be used as a benchmark against which all other drawings are compared.

- **Layers.** The names, color assignments, linetype assignments, and lineweight assignments are all stored in the drawing standards file. The layer states, such as on/off and frozen/thawed, are *not* stored.
- **Dimension styles.** The dimension style names and all of their variable settings are stored in the drawing standards file. Although dimension variable overrides are stored in the drawing standards file, they are *not* used in the checking process.
- **Text styles.** The text style names and all attributes of the styles are stored in the drawing standards file. This includes fonts, font styles, height, and effects such as upside down, backward, vertical, width, and oblique angle.
- **Linetypes.** The linetype names, their segment length, and spacing definitions are stored in the drawing standards file.

To create the standards, first create a new drawing. Starting with an appropriate template drawing can reduce the setup time. Next, establish all of the desired settings for layers, dimension styles, text styles, and linetypes that will comprise the standard. Finally, save the drawing as a drawing standards (.dws) file using the **SAVEAS** command. In the **Save Drawing As** dialog box, select **AutoCAD Drawing Standard (*.dws)** in the **Files of type:** drop-down list. Then, name and save the file. See **Figure 29-1**.

**Figure 29-1.**
Drawing standards files are saved with a .dws file extension.

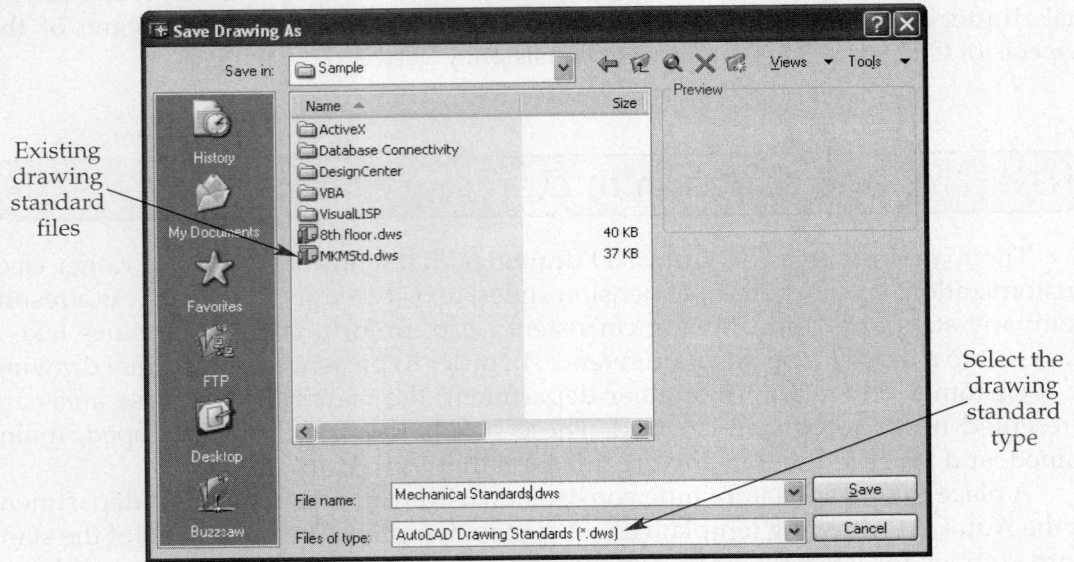

Existing drawing standard files

Select the drawing standard type

       AutoCAD and its Applications—Advanced

To avoid potential compliance "problems," be sure to include the Defpoints layer in the drawing standards file if your requirements include dimensions.

## Exercise 29-1

○ Develop a mechanical drawing standards file based on the following information.

  ○ Load the linetypes needed for the layers shown below. Do not load any additional linetypes. If any additional linetypes are loaded, purge them from the drawing.

  ○ Create the layers shown below.

| Layer Name | Color | Linetype |
|---|---|---|
| Object | Green | Continuous |
| Hidden | White | Hidden2 |
| Center | Yellow | Center |
| Phantom | Cyan | Phantom |
| Dimension | Red | Continuous |
| Annotation | Red | Continuous |
| Hatch | Magenta | Continuous |

○ Create two dimension styles based on the default "standard" style. Use the following settings.

| Description | Dimension Style Name | |
|---|---|---|
| | Dec-2 | Dec-3 |
| Arrow size | 0.21 | 0.21 |
| Dim line spacing | 0.5 | 0.5 |
| Ext line extension | 0.09 | 0.09 |
| Ext line offset | 0.09 | 0.09 |
| Precision | 0.00 | 0.000 |
| Text height | 0.125 | 0.125 |
| Tolerance method | Symmetrical | Limits |
| Tol precision | 0.00 | 0.000 |

○ Create these two text styles. Use the default settings with the following exceptions.

| Name | Font | Height | Width |
|---|---|---|---|
| Normal | ROMANS.SHX | 0.125 | 0.9 |
| Section | ROMAND.SHX | 0.25 | 0.9 |

○ Save the drawing as EX29-1.dws in the folder of your choice. Close the drawing.

# Configuring Drawing Standards

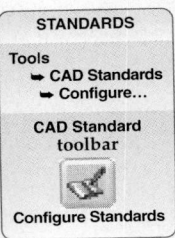
Before you can check for standards compliance, you must associate a drawing standards file with the current drawing. This is done with the **Configure Standards** dialog box. To open this dialog box, type STANDARDS at the Command: prompt, select **Configure...** from the **CAD Standards** cascading menu in the **Tools** pull-down menu, or pick the **Configure Standards** button on the **CAD Standards** toolbar. The **Configure Standards** dialog box contains two tabs. These are the **Standards** and **Plug-ins** tabs. When you pick the **OK** button to close the dialog box, the changes made are applied.

## Plug-ins tab

The **Plug-ins** tab shows the currently supported objects included in the checking process. See **Figure 29-2.** A checkbox is included to the left of each of the object name that can be included in the checking process. You do not have to check all of the plug-ins for standards compliance. When you highlight a "plug-in" in the left-hand list, a brief description appears on the right-hand side of the tab. The description includes a brief statement regarding what the plug-in checks for, a version number for the plug-in, and the name of the company that published the plug-in. Third-party software developers may have plug-ins that appear in this tab. If this is the case, you may be able to create drawing standards for properties other than layers, dimension styles, text styles, and linetypes.

**Figure 29-2.**
The **Plug-ins** tab of the **Configure Standards** dialog box.

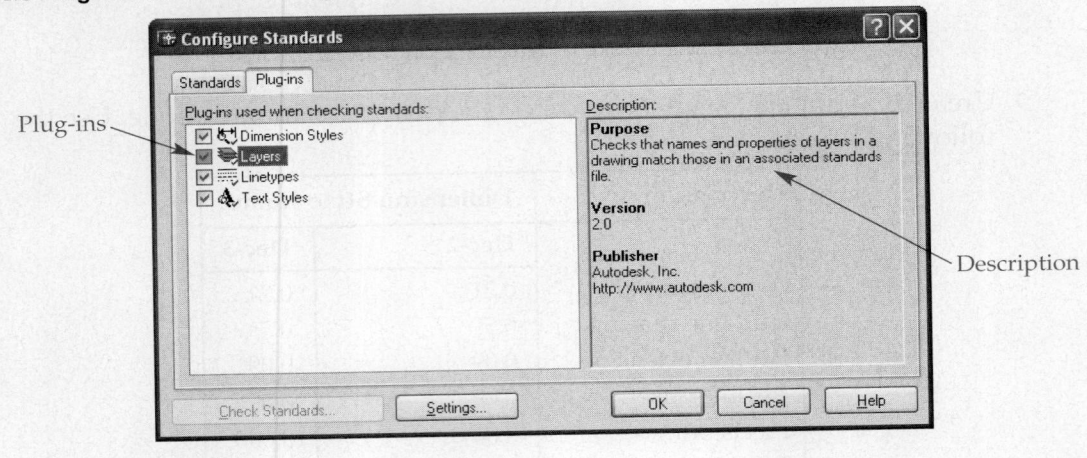

## Standards tab

The **Standards** tab has two main areas. The left side shows all drawing standards files (.dws) associated with the current drawing. The right side provides a brief description of the highlighted drawing standards file. See **Figure 29-3.** The description consists of the file name and path, the date the drawing standards file was last modified, and the AutoCAD version of the drawing standards file. A drawing standards file saved from AutoCAD 2000, 2000i, or 2002 is listed as an AutoCAD 2000 drawing format.

To associate a drawing standards file with the current drawing, pick the **Add Standards File** button that appears at the top-middle of the **Configure Standards** dialog box. You can also press the [F3] key. The **Select standards file** dialog box is opened. This dialog box is a standard "file select" dialog box. Navigate to the folder where the drawing standards file is located. Then, select the file and pick the **Open** button. The drawing standards file is added to the **Standards** tab in the **Configure Standards** dialog box.

**Figure 29-3.**
The **Standards** tab of the **Configure Standards** dialog box.

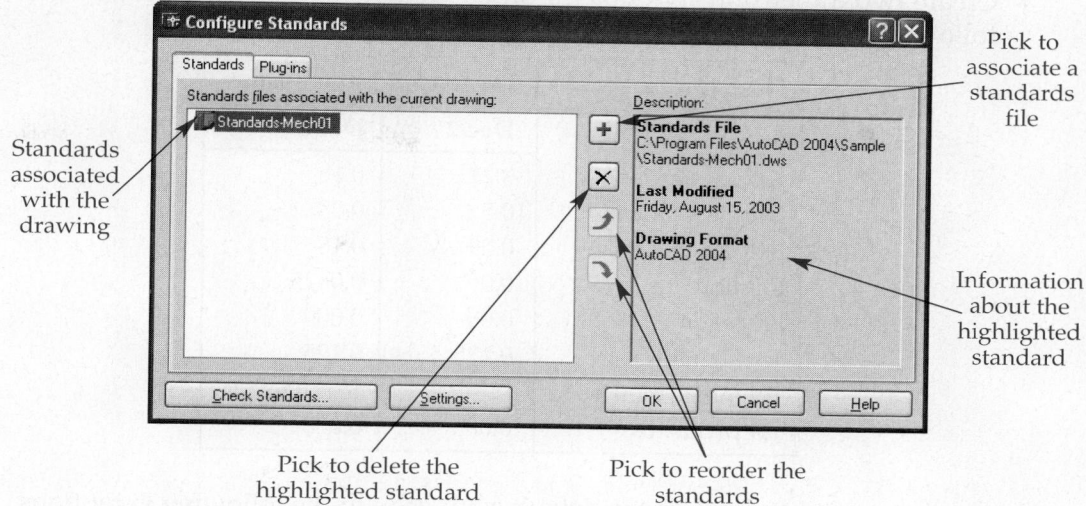

Standards associated with the drawing

Pick to associate a standards file

Information about the highlighted standard

Pick to delete the highlighted standard

Pick to reorder the standards

Multiple drawing standards can be associated with a single drawing. However, the order in which drawing standards are listed in the **Standards** tab of the **Configure Standards** dialog box is important. When conflicts arise between multiple drawing standards, such as identical layer names with differing properties, the drawing standards file listed first takes precedence. To reorder the list of drawing standards files, highlight the file to be reordered. Then, pick the **Move Up** or **Move Down** button to move the file up or down in the list. You can also pick the [F4] key to move the file up or the [F5] key to move the file down.

Drawing standards files can be deleted from the list by highlighting the name and picking the **Remove Standards File** button. You can also press the [Delete] key on the keyboard. If you accidentally remove a drawing standards file from the list, you can always add it again and reorder it as needed.

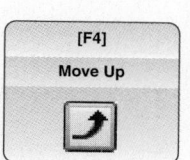

[F4]
Move Up

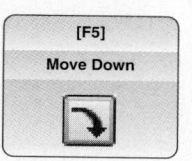

[F5]
Move Down

[Delete]
Remove Standards File

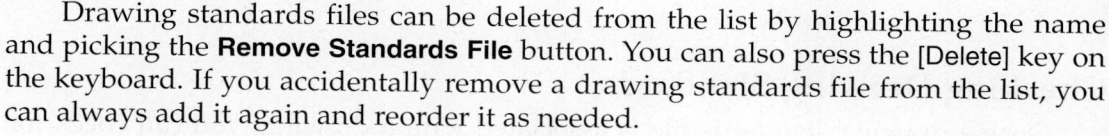

## Exercise 29-2

○ Begin a new drawing.
  ○ Load the linetypes needed for the layers shown below. Do not load any additional linetypes. If any additional linetypes are loaded, purge them from the drawing.
  ○ Create the layers shown below. Use the exact settings.

| Layer Name | Color | Linetype |
|------------|-------|----------|
| Obj | Blue | Continuous |
| Hidden | White | Hidden2 |
| Center | Yellow | Center2 |
| Pha | Cyan | Phantom |
| Dim | Red | Continuous |
| Annotate | Red | Continuous |
| Hatching | Magenta | Continuous |

*(Continued)*

○ Create two dimension styles based on the default "standard" style. Use the following settings. Match the information exactly.

| Description | Dimension Style Name | |
|---|---|---|
| | Dec-2 | Dec-3 |
| Arrow size | 0.21 | 0.18 |
| Dim line spacing | 0.5 | 0.38 |
| Ext line extension | 0.09 | 0.18 |
| Ext line offset | 0.09 | 0.0625 |
| Precision | 0.00 | 0.000 |
| Text height | 0.125 | 0.125 |
| Tolerance method | Limits | Symmetrical |
| Tol precision | 0.00 | 0.000 |

○ Create two text styles. Use the default settings with the following exceptions.

| Name | Font | Height | Width |
|---|---|---|---|
| Norm | ROMANS.SHX | 0.125 | 0.9 |
| Section | ROMANT.SHX | 0.1875 | 1.0 |

○ Use the **Configure Standards** dialog box to associate the drawing standards file EX29-1 created in Exercise 29-1 with the drawing.
○ Save the drawing as EX29-2.dwg in the folder of your choice.

## Checking Drawing Standards

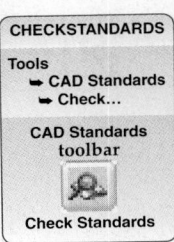

CHECKSTANDARDS

Tools
↳ CAD Standards
  ↳ Check...

CAD Standards
toolbar

Check Standards

Once a drawing standards file is associated with a drawing, you can check for standards compliance. This is done in the **Check Standards** dialog box. To open this dialog box, type CHECKSTANDARDS at the Command: prompt, pick **Check...** in the **CAD Standards** cascading menu of the **Tools** pull-down menu, or pick the **Check Standards** button on the **CAD Standards** toolbar. You can also open the dialog box by picking the **Check Standards...** button in the **Configure Standards** dialog box. The **Check Standards** dialog box is divided into three main areas. See **Figure 29-4**. A drawing standards file must be associated with the drawing in order to open the **Check Standards** dialog box.

The **Problem:** area of the **Check Standards** dialog box displays any properties that do not match the associated drawing standards file. Problems are displayed one at a time. You must address the first problem before moving on to the next.

In the **Replace with:** area of the **Check Standards** dialog box, possible solutions to the problem are shown. The possible solutions are properties from the drawing standards file that can be used to replace the property listed in the **Problem:** area. When you select a possible solution, the **Preview of changes:** area displays the values that will change if you choose to use the highlighted "solution." Sometimes, a recommended solution appears with a check mark next to it.

Once you have selected a "solution" in the **Replace with:** area, pick the **Fix** button. The property listed in the **Problem:** area is brought into compliance with the drawing standards file by replacing it with the "solution." The next property that does not comply with the drawing standards is now displayed in the **Problem:** area. When a property is fixed, the nonstandard named items are purged from the drawing. Once

**Figure 29-4.**
The **Check Standards** dialog box.

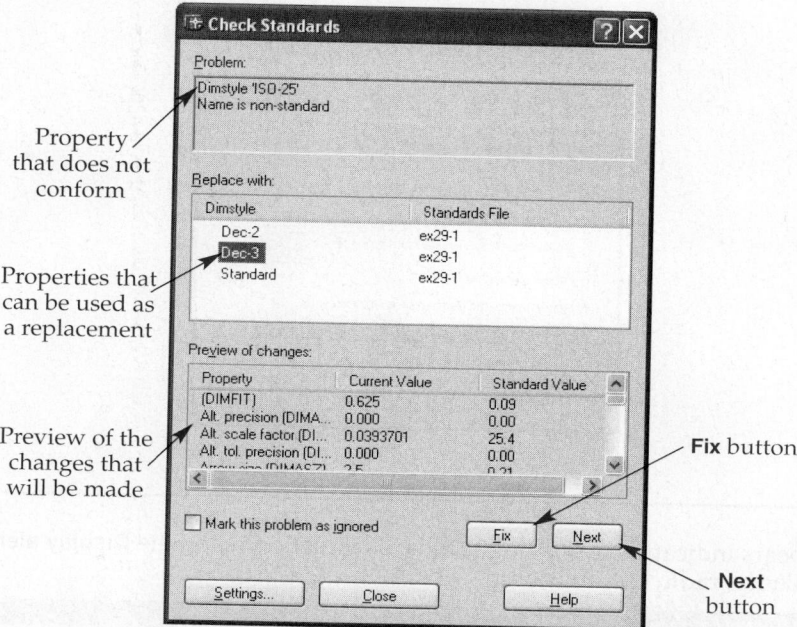

Property that does not conform

Properties that can be used as a replacement

Preview of the changes that will be made

Fix button

Next button

all problems are fixed, the **Problem:** area displays a summary and you can close the **Check Standards** dialog box.

You can choose to skip the currently displayed problem by picking the **Next** button. The next problem is then displayed and can be addressed. The skipped problem is not fixed, however, and will be shown in subsequent standards checks.

You can choose to ignore a problem during standards checks by checking the **Mark this problem as ignored** check box. When this box is checked, the user name of the checker who ignored the problem is recorded and displayed below the check box. Then, pick the **Next** button to continue to the next problem. The error will not appear in future standards checks, unless the standards checking settings are changed.

To change standards checking settings, open the **CAD Standards Settings** dialog box by picking the **Settings...** button in the **Check Standards** dialog box. See **Figure 29-5.** When the **Show ignored problems** check box is checked, any problem that is marked as "ignored" is displayed in standards checks. When the **Automatically fix non-standard properties** check box is checked, all properties of identically named objects are changed to match the properties settings in the preferred drawing standards file. The **Preferred standards file to use for replacements:** drop-down list is used to select which drawing standards file is preferred. Automatic fixes can only take place if the drawing being checked has a standard object with an identical name to a standard object found in the standards file listed in the drop-down list.

The upper area of the **CAD Standards Settings** dialog box allows you to adjust the notifications settings. When the **Display alert upon standards violation** radio button is selected, an alert box is displayed when a standards violation occurs in a drawing (as you draw), **Figure 29-6.** The alert box will let you know that a standards violation has occurred and give you the choice of fixing or not fixing the problem. Picking the **Fix** button opens the **Check Standards** dialog and allows you to fix the problem. Picking the **Don't Fix** button will close the alert box and bypass the violation until the **CHECKSTANDARDS** command is executed.

**Figure 29-5.**
Specifying settings for standards checking.

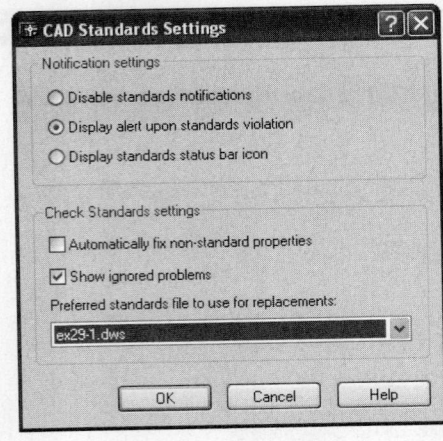

**Figure 29-6.**
This alert appears indicating a drawing standards violation when the **Display alert upon standards** violation radio button is on.

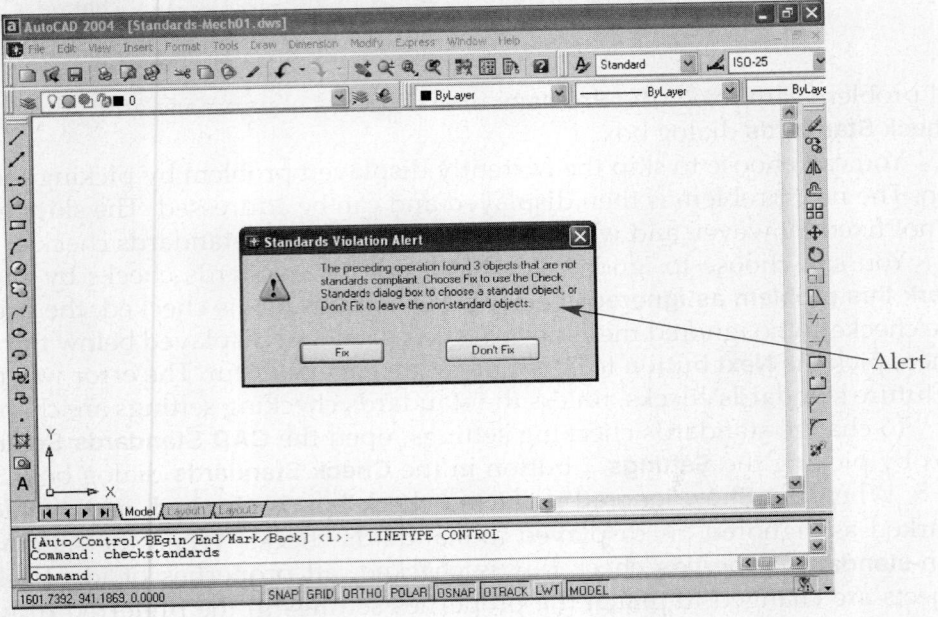

Alert

When the **Display standards status bar icon** radio button is selected, you are notified of a standards violation via a balloon from a status bar icon. See **Figure 29-7**. If you wish to fix the problem immediately, you can select **Run Check Standards**. You can also bypass the problem for the meantime by selecting the **X** in the upper-right corner to close the balloon.

You can turn off notification of standards violations. Select the **Disable standards notification** radio button in the **CAD Standards Settings** dialog box. No alert is displayed when a standards violation occurs. However, this setting does not affect standards checking.

**Figure 29-7.**
This alert appears indicating a drawing standards violation when the **Display standards status bar icon** radio button is on.

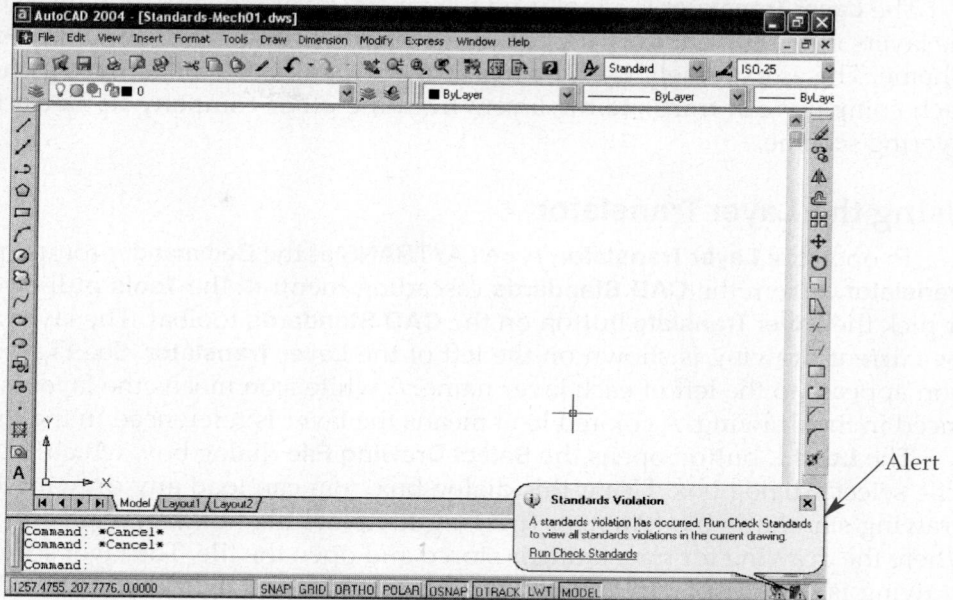

Alert

---

PROFESSIONAL
TIP

There is no undo within the **Check Standards** dialog box. When you exit the dialog box and perform an undo, all fixes are undone.

---

### Exercise 29-3

○ Open drawing EX29-2 if it is not already open.
○ Using the **Check Standards** dialog box, bring the drawing into compliance with the drawing standards file EX29-1.dws following these directions:
   ○ Ignore one of the problems. Then, open the **Check Standards** dialog box again and recheck the drawing. What happens?
   ○ Use the **CAD Standards Settings** dialog box to show ignored problems. Then, recheck the drawing for standards compliance. What happens?
   ○ Use the **CAD Standards Settings** dialog box to select **Display alert upon standards violation**. Make a new, nonstandard layer. What happens?
   ○ Use the **CAD Standards Settings** dialog box to select **Display standards status bar icon**. Make a new, nonstandard layer. What happens?
○ Save the drawing as EX29-3.

---

# Layer Translator

The **Layer Translator** is a tool used to manage layer schemes. It allows you to map the layers in the current drawing to those in another drawing, or to a whole new layer scheme. This is extremely useful when two companies are collaborating on a project. Each company can translate the layers from the other company to match their own layering scheme.

## Using the **Layer Translator**

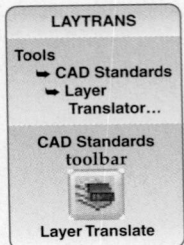

LAYTRANS

Tools
➥ CAD Standards
  ➥ Layer
     Translator...

CAD Standards
toolbar

Layer Translate

To open the **Layer Translator**, type LAYTRANS at the Command: prompt, pick **Layer Translator...** from the **CAD Standards** cascading menu in the **Tools** pull-down menu, or pick the **Layer Translate** button on the **CAD Standards** toolbar. The layer scheme of the current drawing is shown on the left of the **Layer Translator**. See **Figure 29-8**. An icon appears to the left of each layer name. A white icon means the layer is not referenced in the drawing. A colored icon means the layer is referenced in the drawing.

The **Load...** button opens the **Select Drawing File** dialog box, which is a standard "file select" dialog box. Using this dialog box, you can load any drawing file (.dwg), drawing standards file (.dws), or drawing template file (.dwt). Navigate to the folder where the drawing for translating is stored and open the file. The layer scheme in that drawing is then displayed in the **Translate To** list at the right of the **Layer Translator**. You can load more than one drawing.

**Figure 29-8.**
The **Layer Translator** dialog box.

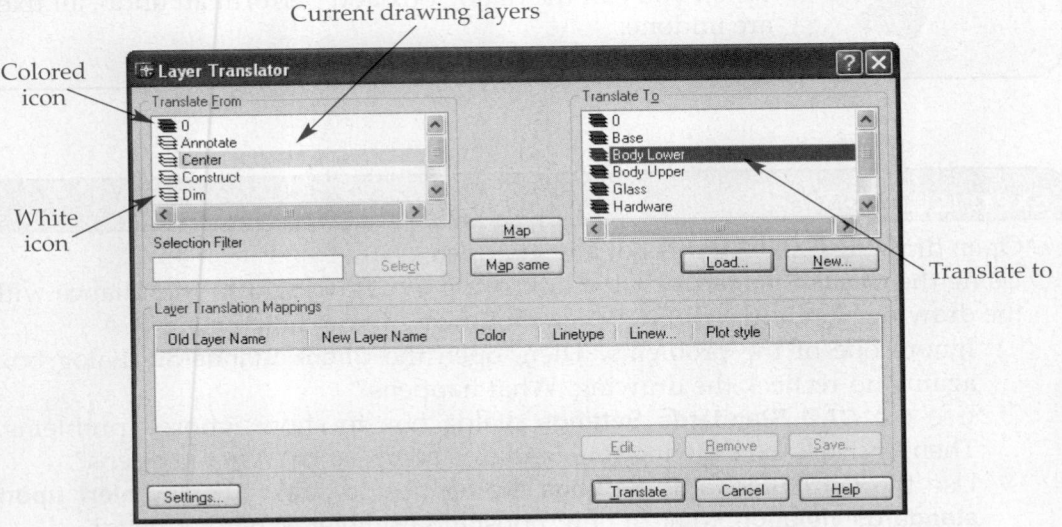

The **New...** button in the **Layer Translator** opens the **New Layer** dialog box. See **Figure 29-9**. This dialog box allows you to create a new layer that does not exist in the **Translate To** list. Enter a layer name, assign a color, select a linetype, and specify a lineweight. If named plot styles are being used, you can also select a plot style. Then, pick the **OK** button and the layer is added to the **Translate To** list.

To map layers, first select a layer in the **Translate From** list. Then, select a layer in the **Translate To** list and pick the **Map** button. All of the properties of the "from" layer will be changed to the properties of the "to" layer. This includes the layer name. Multiple layers can be selected in the **Translate From** list using the standard Windows

Figure 29-9.
The **New Layer**
dialog box allows
you to create a layer
that is not in the
"to" drawing.

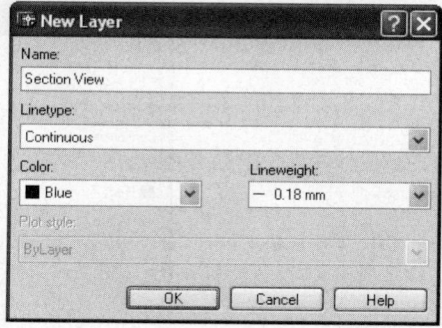

selection keys [Ctrl] and [Shift] in conjunction with mouse picks. You can also type a wildcard combination in the **Selection Filter** edit box. Then, pick the **Select** button to select all layers with names that match the wildcard. For example, if you enter la*, all layers with names that begin with la, such as Layer 1, will be selected. If you pick the **Map Same** button, layers in the **Translate From** list are automatically mapped to identically named layers in the **Translate To** list.

Once a layer is mapped, it appears in the **Layer Translation Mappings** area. This area is discussed in the next section. To apply the mapping shown in the **Layer Translator Mappings** area, pick the **Translate** button. The old layer properties are replaced by the mapped layer properties. Unmapped layers are not affected.

If you have not saved the mapping scheme when you pick the **Translate** button, the **Layer Translator Alert** dialog box appears. See **Figure 29-10**. This dialog box indicates that the mapping scheme is not saved and asks if you want to do so. Pick the **Yes** button to save the scheme. Saving a mapping scheme is discussed in the next section.

Figure 29-10.
If you translate
mapped layers
without saving the
scheme, you are
given the
opportunity to save
the scheme.

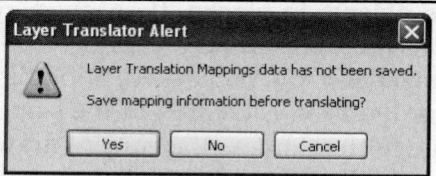

## Layer Translation Mappings Area

The list in the **Layer Translation Mapping** area shows all of the layer translations that are mapped. Each entry in the list shows the existing layer name; the name to which the layer name will be changed; and the color, linetype, lineweight, and plot style settings that the translated layer will assume. Using the buttons at the bottom of the **Layer Translation Mapping** area, you can edit the mapping, remove a layer from mapping, and save the mapping scheme.

To edit a mapping setting, select the entry in the list. Then, pick the **Edit...** button. The **Edit Layer** dialog box appears, **Figure 29-11**. Notice that the **Name:** area is grayed out. You cannot change the layer name. However, you can change the linetype, color, lineweight, and plot style. Make any changes and pick the **OK** button. Once you change any of the properties, the change is applied to all mappings that use the same new layer name.

If you have added a layer to the mapping scheme that you do not want to map, it can be removed from the scheme. Highlight the entry in the list in the **Layer Translation Mapping** area. Then, pick the **Remove** button. The entry is removed from the mapping scheme. The layer name reappears in the **Translate From** list at the top of the **Layer Translator**.

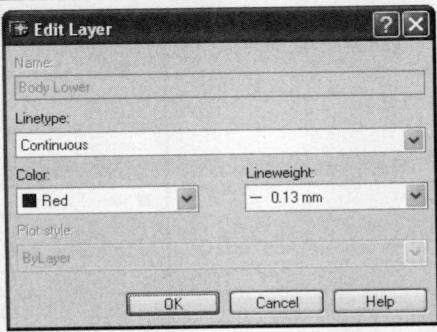

**Figure 29-11.**
The **Edit Layer** dialog box is used to change the properties of a "to" mapped layer.

If you will be using the same mapping scheme again, you can save the scheme. Picking the **Save...** button opens the **Save Layer Mappings** dialog box. This is a standard "save" dialog box that allows you to create a drawing file or drawing standards file containing all of the "translate to" layers shown in the **Layer Translation Mappings** area and their properties. However, the file contains only layers. No objects are included. The new drawing file can then be "loaded" in future translations as needed.

## Layer Translator Settings

There are a five settings that can be changed to control how layer translations are handled. To change these settings, pick the **Settings...** button in the **Layer Translator**. The **Settings** dialog box is displayed, which contains five check boxes. See **Figure 29-12**.

- **Force object color to ByLayer**. If checked, the layer name and its properties are translated *and* all objects on that layer are changed to the **ByLayer** color.
- **Force object linetype to ByLayer.** If checked, the layer name and its properties are translated *and* all objects on that layer are changed to the **ByLayer** linetype.
- **Translate objects in blocks.** If checked, objects that are nested within block definitions are translated.
- **Write transaction log.** If checked, a log file, which has all the layer translation data recorded in it, is created in the same folder of the current drawing. The file is named the same as the current drawing with the .log file extension. This is very useful if you need to review the layer scheme used prior to translation.
- **Show layer contents when selected.** If checked, only objects on the layer highlighted in the **Translate From** list in the **Layer Translator** are displayed in the AutoCAD drawing area. If unchecked, objects on all layers that are not turned off or frozen in the current drawing are displayed in the drawing area. Objects on layers that are frozen are never displayed, regardless of this check box state.

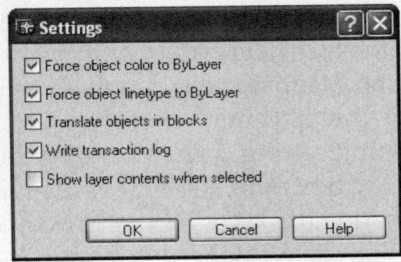

**Figure 29-12.**
The **Settings** dialog box provides options for layer translation.

○ Begin a new drawing. Load the linetypes needed to create the following layers. Then, create the layers.

| Name | Color | Linetype |
|------|-------|----------|
| Obj | Blue | Continuous |
| Hidden | White | Hidden2 |
| Center | Yellow | Center2 |
| Pha | Cyan | Phantom |
| Dim | Red | Continuous |
| Annotate | Red | Continuous |
| Hatching | Magenta | Continuous |

○ Draw a couple of objects on each layer to the left side of the drawing area.
○ Freeze the Center layer.
○ Turn the Pha layer off.
○ Open the **Layer Translator**.
  ○ Load the drawing standards file you created in Exercise 29-1.
  ○ Pick the **Settings...** button to open the **Settings** dialog box. Check the **Show layer contents when selected** check box and close the **Settings** dialog box.
  ○ Map Annotate to Annotations, Center to Center, Dim to Dimensions, Hatching to Hatch, Hidden to Hidden, Obj to Object, and Pha to Phantom. As you select each "from" layer, notice the objects in the drawing area. You may need to move the **Layer Translator** around on the screen to see objects.
  ○ When all layers are mapped, translate the layers.
  ○ Close the **Layer Translator**.
○ Open the **Layer Properties Manager** dialog box and review the new layer settings. Then, close the dialog box.
○ Save the drawing as EX29-4.

## Managing Electronic Data

All organizations require structure, organization, and standard procedures to operate efficiently. Electronic data and computer systems can be used within the company structure for organization and procedure. The computers may also contain the structural and organizational procedures themselves. In either case, the method in which electronic data are managed greatly affects the operation of the entire organization. Effective management of an AutoCAD system requires careful attention to:

- The structure and makeup of hard drives and mass storage devices.
- The location of all files and drawings.
- Storage procedures for drawing files.
- Drawing file backup procedures.
- Template drawings for specific projects.
- Use and location of symbols libraries and reference drawings.
- Creation and maintenance of drawing standards files.
- Use and location of special screen and digitizer tablet menus.
- Drawing file creation procedures and naming conventions.
- Creation and distribution methods for new symbols and menus.

- Updating methods for software and hardware.
- Hardware maintenance.

## Management Procedures

One of your goals as an AutoCAD user should be to keep the computer system as efficient as possible. This means being organized and having knowledge of school or company standards. You should also be aware of who has the authority to manage the system and follow the system manager's guidelines.

### The system manager

There should always be a *system manager* who is responsible for all functions of the computer system. In a large company, this may be one or two people. In a small company, the system manager's duties may often be part of a drafter's job. The system manager has control over the computer system and is in charge of preventing inconsistencies in procedure, drawing format, and file storage. The system manager is responsible for:

- Scheduled use of computers.
- Structure of hard drive folders.
- Administration of the network server and user access to its files.
- Appearance and function of start-up menus.
- Network log-in procedures.
- Implementation of file naming techniques.
- File storage and backup procedures.
- Password maintenance.
- Drawing file access.
- Creation of symbols libraries.
- Development and maintenance of drawing standards files.
- Development and distribution of written standards.
- Software and hardware upgrading.
- Hardware "hygiene" and maintenance.

The system manager should always check and approve all revisions to drawings, menus, templates, and drawing standards files before distributing them to users.

### Developing operating standards and procedures

A foundation of good system management is ensuring that everyone performs jobs using the same procedures, symbols, and drawing standards. A department that operates smoothly is probably using standards related to:

- File naming conventions.
- Methods of file storage that identify the location and name.
- File backup methods.
- Standard drawing sheet sizes and title blocks.
- Template drawings.
- Creation of blocks and symbols.
- Standard dimensioning techniques.
- Standard usage of layers, colors, linetypes, and text styles.
- Plot styles and color schemes for plotting.
- Creation of screen and tablet menus.
- Organized storage of printed or plotted drawings.

Study the needs of the school or company. Meet with other department managers and users to determine the nature of their drawings. Always gain input from people who use the system. Avoid making "system-wide" decisions without input.

Once needs have been established, develop the required standards and procedures. When developing procedures, begin with start-up procedures and work through the drawing process. First, develop template drawings for specific types of projects. Next, create a set of drawing standards files that can be used for standards checking. These files should be developed for each type of drawing in all disciplines in which the school or company is engaged. Finally, create screen and tablet menus and custom programs.

Now, assemble the materials and create the necessary documentation. Then, distribute the materials, documentation, and procedures to all users who require them.

## File, Hard Drive, and Server Management

The central storage device, such as a network server or local hard drive, is the heart of the AutoCAD computer system. It is the storage center for AutoCAD and other software applications. In addition, the central storage device may hold thousands of "support" files, including drawings, templates, CAD standards, custom programs, slides, menu files, script files, databases, spreadsheets, and text files. The manner in which you work with the central storage device and arrange its contents can affect your productivity and drawing efficiency. Take time to assess the needs of your school or company and then organize your central storage device accordingly.

### File maintenance

Ensuring the security of saved files must be part of everyone's responsibility who works with the system. Files of every type, including DWG, DWT, DWS, SLD, BAT, LSP, MNU, and BAK files, must have a secure storage area. Procedures for file maintenance must be documented. Any hard drive folders, floppy disks, CD-RWs, optical discs, and magnetic tapes must be kept clean of nonessential files. In addition, drawings should not be saved in the AutoCAD "root" folder. File maintenance procedures should include the following documentation.
- Location of essential AutoCAD files.
- Location of backup AutoCAD files.
- Printed contents of all hard drive folders for each workstation.
- Location and contents of all template drawings.
- Location and contents of all custom programs and associated menus.
- Location of all user files, including templates, standards, drawings, slides, and data files.

Regardless of *what* data you store, have a plan for *how* to store data. Decide on the nature of the folder structure and then stick to it. Make sure that all users are informed by documenting and distributing the standards and procedures accordingly. Place printed copies of the procedures at each workstation or provide quick access to electronic files.

When planning the folder structure, allow for future software. New programs should be installed in their own folders and the files should be managed in the same fashion as the AutoCAD files. An example of a well-planned and closely managed folder structure is shown in **Figure 29-13.**

Files used to support AutoCAD can be located in subfolders of the AutoCAD "root" folder. Other support files may be located in subfolders in the user's Documents and Settings folder. Possible subfolders include folders for drawings, AutoLISP files, drivers, templates, standards, slides, and user data. The individual files should reside within the subfolders. When specific types of files are kept in their own subfolders, file maintenance is easier.

### Maintaining symbols libraries and menus

Developing symbols libraries and customized menus is a primary function of a system manager who is managing a system on which AutoCAD is installed. Symbols must be consistent and up-to-date. Custom menus must be consistent throughout the department or company. The following guidelines should be used for developing and maintaining symbols libraries and custom menus.

**Figure 29-13.**
The folder structure of a well-managed hard drive appears clean and organized.

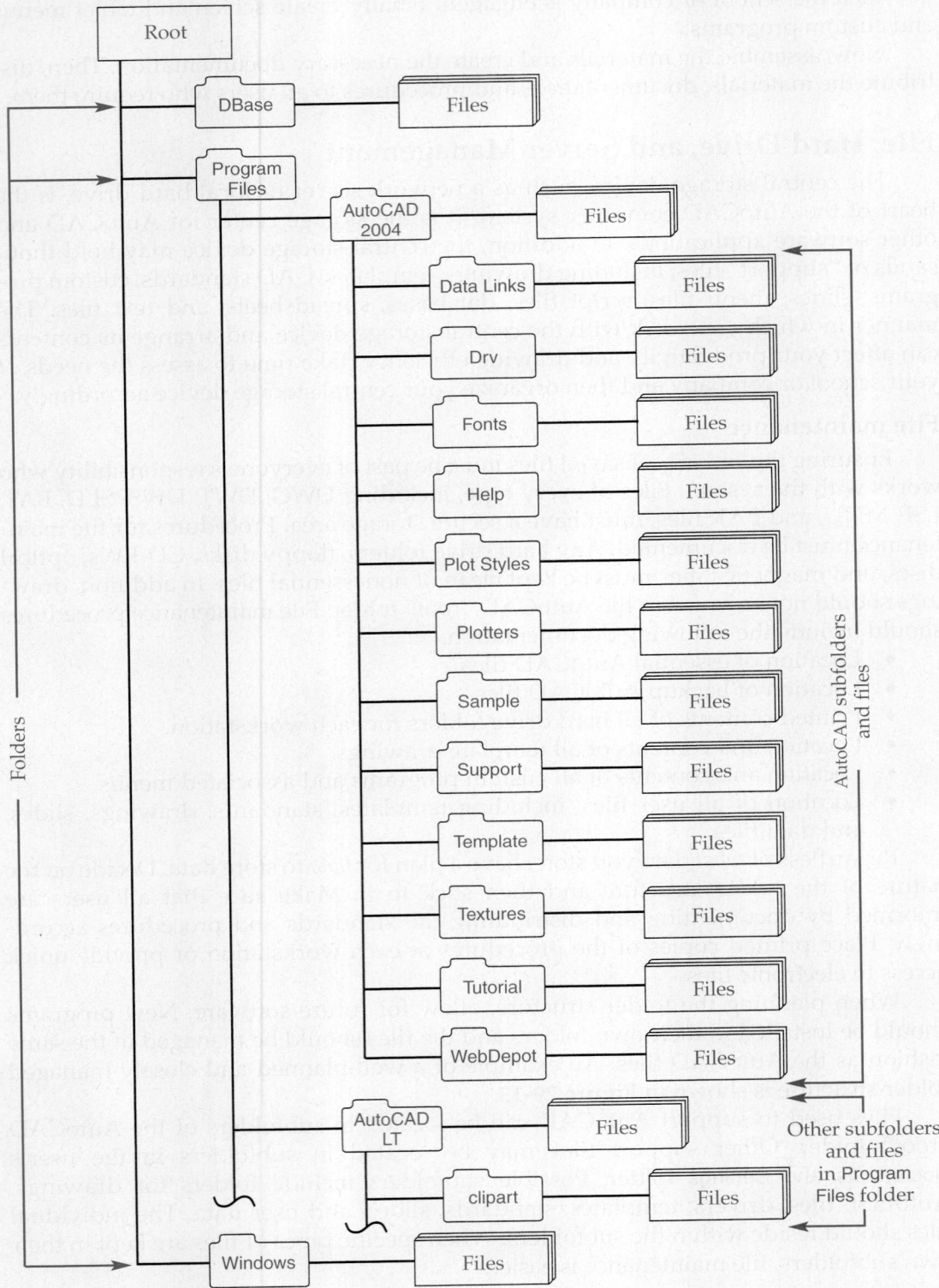

- Establish and distribute drawing standards for the creation of symbols.
- Develop a symbol-naming convention and storage system.
- Post a printed copy of all symbols libraries listing their names and locations.
- Use standards when creating and maintaining custom menus and toolbars.
- Create and assign specific custom menus to specific departments.
- Make revisions to custom menus when necessary.

### Maintaining the software

Software upgrades and maintenance releases, or "patches," are issued regularly. The transition is usually smooth with little, if any, production downtime. Establish a procedure for upgrading all computers in the classroom or office. Inform all users of changes by providing a printed listing of new features. If you work for a large company, schedule professional upgrade training for managers and employees at an authorized Autodesk Training Center (ATC), local community college or university, or authorized Autodesk dealer. You can also get valuable training information on the World Wide Web at http://www.autodesk.com, which is the Autodesk home page. You can use the **BROWSER** command in AutoCAD to log on to this site.

## Chapter Test

*Answer the following questions on a separate sheet of paper.*

1. List the four drawing properties that can be managed using drawing standards.
2. What is the file extension for an AutoCAD drawing standards file?
3. Which drawing file types can be associated with the current drawing for checking drawing standards?
4. Which of the following will *not* be evaluated when checking drawing standards?
   A. Layer color.
   B. Layer visibility.
   C. Layer name.
   D. Layer lineweight.
5. In which pull-down menu are the drawing standards commands located?
6. What information is listed in the **Plug-ins** tab in the **Configure Standards** dialog box?
7. When the **Configure Standards** dialog box is open, what function do the following keys perform?
   [F3]
   [F4]
   [F5]
   [Delete]
8. How can you open the **Check Standards** dialog box from within the **Configure Standards** dialog box?
9. When checking standards and a problem is marked as ignored, what information is displayed below the **Mark this problem as ignored** check box?
10. When checking standards, what relationship must exist between properties in the current drawing and in the standard for a problem to be automatically fixed?
11. List the types of drawing files that can be used by the **Layer Translator** for the **Translate To** list.
12. What is the purpose of the **New...** button in the **Layer Translator**?
13. Which layer properties can be mapped using the **Layer Translator**?
14. Effective management of an AutoCAD system requires careful attention to several areas. List five of these areas.

## Drawing Problems

1. Choose a field that is of interest to you, such as mechanical, architectural, electrical, civil, or facilities management. For the field you select, identify drawing properties that are considered typical or standard. Include a layer scheme, dimension styles, text styles, and linetypes. Then, create and save a drawing standards file.

2. Using the drawing standards file created in Problem 1, perform a standards check on five drawings from earlier chapters in this text.

*Using the procedures in Problem 3 and Problem 4, two companies can collaborate on a project while using their own layering scheme.*

3. Create two drawing templates, each with a simple layer scheme of at least three layers. The two schemes should not be identical, but should be similar. Save one of the drawing templates as P29-3A and the other as P29-3B. Create a new drawing based on the P29-3A template. Draw three objects of your choice on each layer. Then, use the **Layer Translator** to map the layers to the P29-3B template. Save the drawing as P29-3.

4. Open the drawing P29-3 from Problem 3. Save the drawing as P29-4. Using the **Layer Translator**, map the layers to their "original settings" located in the template file P29-3A. Then, save the drawing.

# Solid Modeling Tutorial

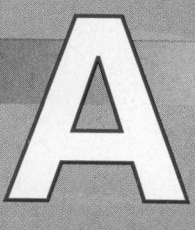

## Introduction

This tutorial is provided as a supplement to the solid modeling techniques presented in Chapter 6 through Chapter 10. It is a step-by-step process intended as a guide. Directions are given for each step of the process, but exact details regarding which commands to use, where to find commands, and exact coordinate locations are not always given. This allows you to use your knowledge of AutoCAD, consult the online help files, and refer to the text for answers. The model for this tutorial is the injected plastic handle, cap, and lens for a flashlight shown in **Figure A-1**.

**Figure A-1.**

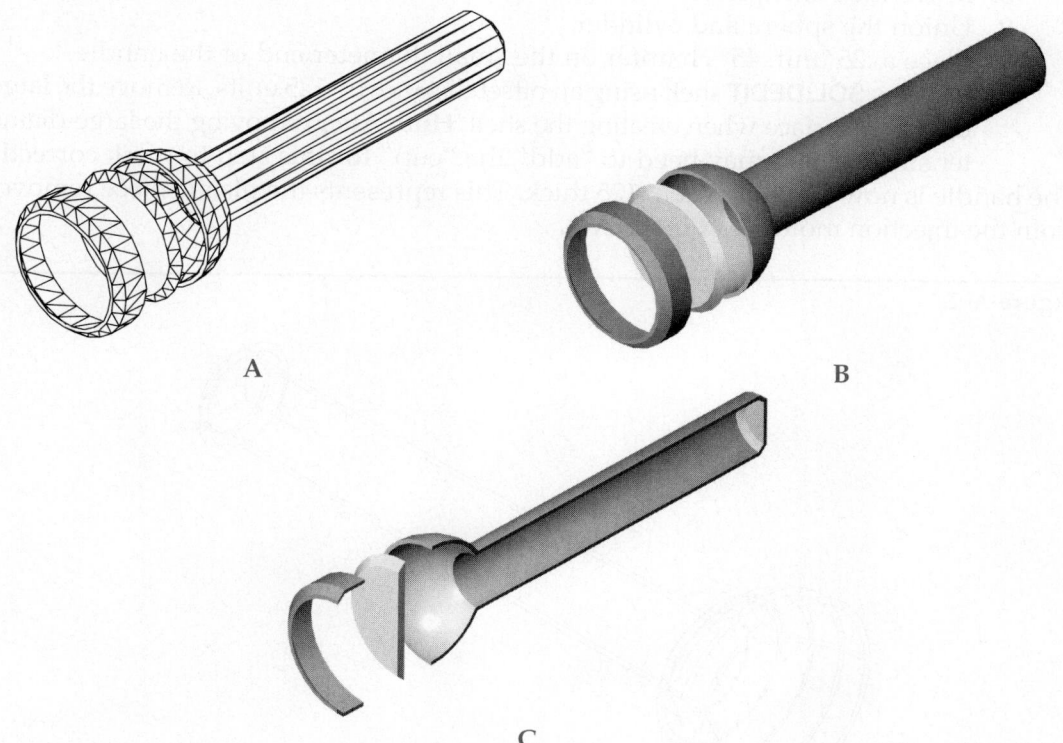

A

B

C

## Drawing Setup

Start a new drawing using the acad.dwt template. Set **FACETRES** to 2.000. Set your preferred object snaps. The **Center** object snap may be especially useful for this tutorial. Finally, create the following four layers with the indicated colors.

| Layer | Color |
|---|---|
| Handle | color 253 |
| Cap | color 30 |
| Lens | color 50 |
| Construct | green (or your preference) |

## Constructing the Handle

The handle is the portion of the flashlight where the batteries are inserted. This is constructed from two solid primitives—a cylinder and a sphere.

1.  Make the Handle layer current.
2.  Change to the southwest isometric preset viewpoint.
3.  Rotate UCS to the LEFT UCS.
4.  Draw a solid cylinder at 0,0,0 with a diameter of 2 units and height of 12 units.
5.  Draw a solid sphere centered on the near end of the cylinder with a diameter of 4 units.
6.  Make the Construct layer current.
7.  Draw a 5 unit cube. Use the cube to remove the front half of the sphere. **Hint:** Use object snaps to align a corner of the cube in the center of the sphere. Then, change to different plan views to line up the cube.
8.  Move the hemisphere .5 units along +Z axis of the LEFT UCS.
9.  Union the sphere and cylinder.
10. Place a .25 unit, 45° chamfer on the small diameter end of the handle.
11. Create a **SOLIDEDIT** shell using an offset distance of .125 units. Remove the large-diameter surface when creating the shell. **Hint:** After removing the large-diameter surface, you may need to "add" the "cup" for this step to work correctly.

The handle is now a hollow shell .125 thick. This represents the plastic piece removed from the injection mold. See **Figure A-2.**

Figure A-2.

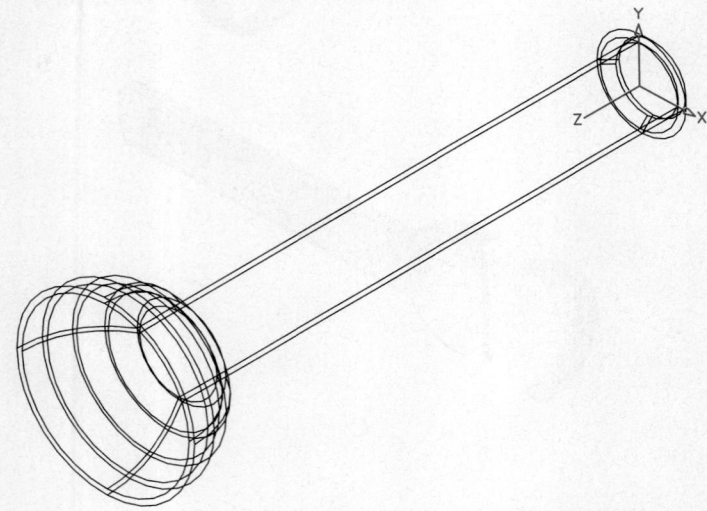

AutoCAD and its Applications—Advanced

## Constructing the Cap

Now, the cap for the flashlight is created. The cap is the portion that snaps onto the handle and contains the lens. The cap is created from a cylinder.

1. With the LEFT UCS current, move the UCS origin 15 units along the +Z axis. Save the new UCS as CAP.
2. Make the Cap layer current.
3. Draw a cylinder with a diameter of 4.25 units and a height of 1 unit centered at the CAP UCS origin.
4. Chamfer the near end of the cylinder with a .25 unit, 45° chamfer.
5. Make the Construct layer current.
6. Draw a circle with a diameter of 4 units centered at the CAP UCS origin.
7. Imprint the circle onto the cylinder body. Delete the source object.
8. Extrude the new face (imprint) into the cylinder .75 units with a 0° taper. **Hint:** Change to the southeast isometric preset viewpoint.
9. Extrude the face an additional .25 units into the cylinder with a 45° inward taper. **Hint:** Switch back to the southwest isometric preset viewpoint.

The cap is now a hollow shell with a thickness of .125 units. See **Figure A-3**. Like the handle, this represents the plastic piece removed from the injection mold.

**Figure A-3.**

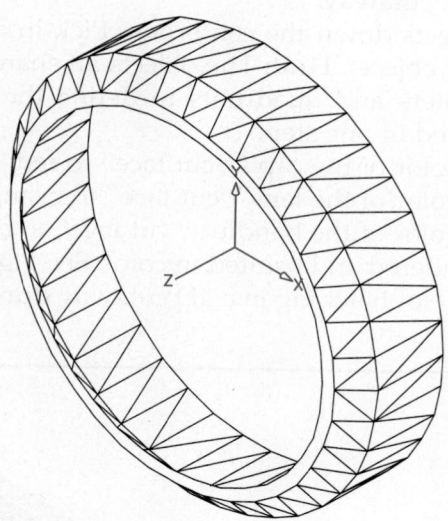

## Constructing the Lens

The lens is the clear plastic piece inserted into the cap that light from the bulb passes through. This is simply a circle extruded with a taper.

1. With the CAP UCS current, move the UCS origin 4 units along the +Z axis. Save the new UCS as LENS.
2. Make the Lens layer current.
3. Draw a circle with a diameter of 4 units centered at the origin of the LENS UCS.
4. Extrude the circle +.25 units with a 45° taper.
5. To place the lens between the cap and the handle, move it −5.5 on the Z axis of the LENS UCS.

The model now looks like an exploded assembly view. You can also render or shade the scene. See **Figure A-4**.

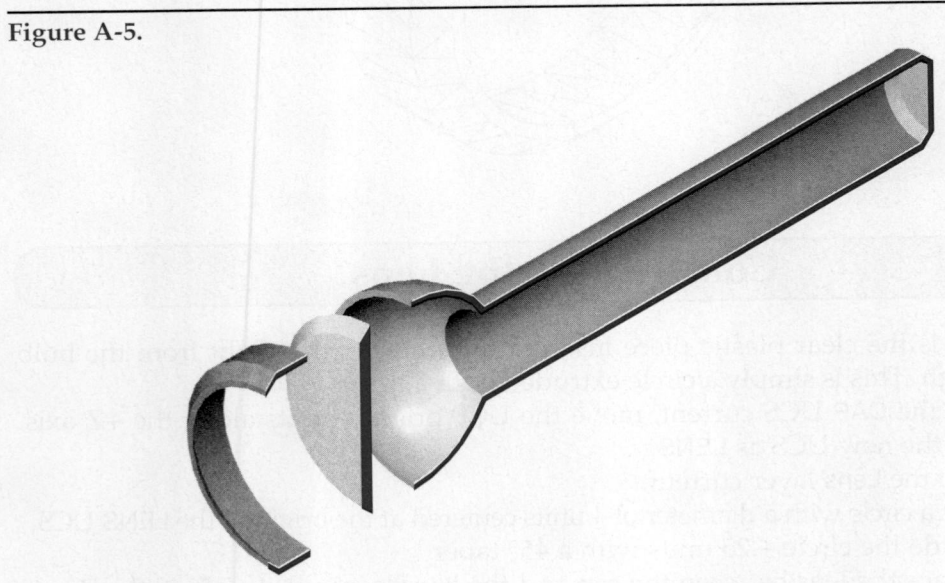

A

B

## Creating the Cutaway View

The three objects represent the plastic pieces removed from the injection molds. Now, suppose you want to create a cutaway drawing to use in a presentation. First, save the current drawing as app-a.dwg. Then, save a copy as app-a-slice.dwg. This is the drawing used to create the cutaway.

1. Slice all three objects down the centerline. Pick in a manner that keeps the "back half" of the objects. **Hint:** The objects all share the same centerline, so you can pick centers and quadrants to define the slicing plane. All three objects can be sliced in one step.
2. Change the face color of the cap's "cut face" to red.
3. Change the face color of the lens' "cut face" to cyan.
4. Change the face color of the handle's "cut face" to blue.

Now, the object can be rendered and printed in color. See **Figure A-5.** The color of the cut surfaces takes the place of hatching in a 2D cutaway drawing.

Figure A-5.

## Displaying the Model

With the cutaway model complete, you may want to create a "dynamic display" of the model. This may be useful to have on screen in AutoCAD as you discuss the design with others.

1. Shade the model using Gouraud shading.
2. Using the **3DORBIT** command, set the display to a slow, continuous spin around the object.

## Optional Additions

Once you have completed the model, you may want to add more detail. See **Figure A-6.** For example, you may want to create two batteries and insert them in the handle. You may also want to model a small lightbulb and design a metal reflector to hold it inside the cap. Add knurling around the circumference of the cap and handle to help grip the flashlight. Once you have modeled details, assign materials and place lights. Then, render the model. Make adjustments as necessary to achieve a realistic display.

**Figure A-6.**

# Surface Modeling Tutorial

## Introduction

This tutorial is provided as a supplement to the surface modeling techniques presented in Chapter 11 through Chapter 13. It is a step-by-step process intended as a guide. Directions are given for each step of the process, but exact details regarding which commands to use, where to find commands, and exact coordinate locations are not always given. This allows you to use your knowledge of AutoCAD, to consult the online help files, and to refer to the text for answers. The model for this tutorial is twelve-button digitizer puck shown in **Figure B-1.** It is not necessary to complete this tutorial in one drawing session. Complete what you can, save your work, and return when you have available time.

**Figure B-1.**

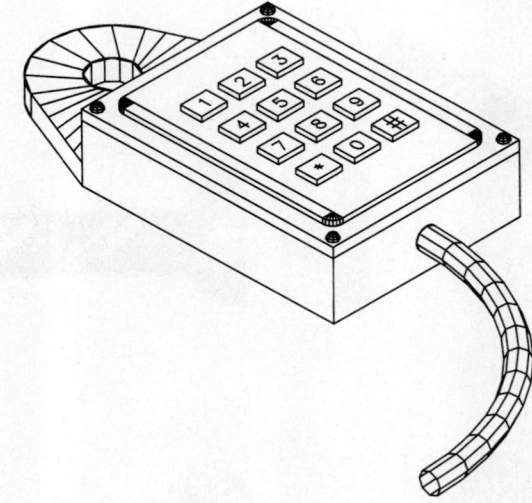

## Drawing Setup

Begin your drawing by setting units as decimal and setting limits to 18, 12. Set the grid and snap spacing to your preference. Then, create the following layers with the color indicated.

| Layer | Color |
|-------|-------|
| Body | red |
| Body Cap | white |
| Buttons | magenta |
| Button1 | magenta |
| Button2 | blue |
| Cable | green |
| Construct | blue |
| Edgesurf | green |
| Eyepiece | yellow |
| Eyesurf | yellow |
| Face1 | green |
| Face2 | cyan |
| Numbers | cyan |
| Screws | red |

## Creating the Body

The individual parts of the digitizer puck are shown in **Figure B-2**. The following steps walk you through the creation of the puck body.

1. Create a one-unit surface primitive cube on Layer 0 at 0, 0, 0.
2. Make a block of the cube. Name it BOX.
3. In an isometric view, pick one of the corners as an insertion point, **Figure B-3**.

Figure B-2.

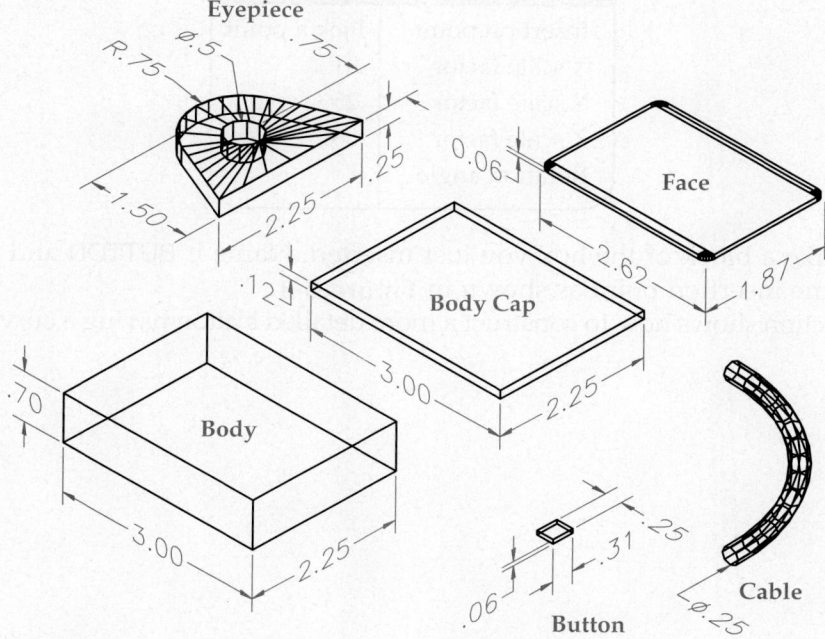

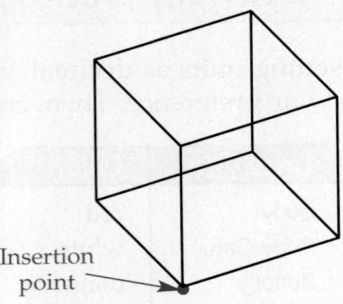

Insertion
point

4. Remove the cube from the drawing.
5. Change the current layer to Body and display a plan view of the WCS.
6. Insert the block to create the body of the puck. Use the following values:

| Setting | Value |
|---|---|
| Insertion point | 0,0,0 |
| X scale factor | 2.25 |
| Y scale factor | 3 |
| Z scale factor | .7 |
| Rotation angle | 0 |

## Creating a Button

The following instructions tell you how to create a block for the puck's buttons. This block is used later to create an array of buttons on the finished puck.
1. Change to the southwest isometric preset viewpoint.
2. Insert the BOX block on Layer 0 using the following values.

| Setting | Value |
|---|---|
| Insertion point | Pick a point |
| X scale factor | .31 |
| Y scale factor | .25 |
| Z scale factor | .06 |
| Rotation angle | 0 |

3. Make a block of the box you just inserted. Name it BUTTON and give it the same insertion point as shown in Figure B-3.

The next section shows how to construct a more detailed button having a curved surface.

# Constructing a Curved Button

The following example shows one way to create a curved button by drawing a wireframe model and surfacing it.

1. Make Layer 0 current and pick a starting point for a line.
2. Place the second point at @.31,0, the third point at @0,.25, the fourth point at @−.31,0, and then close the line. This creates the base of the button.
3. Zoom in on the object so that it nearly fills the screen.
4. Draw the vertical lines of the corners as shown in **Figure B-4A**. The line at P1 has a length of .03. The line at P2 has a length of .06.
5. Change the UCS so it matches the one in **Figure B-4B**.
6. Draw an arc, with an included angle of 20°, between the pick points specified in **Figure B-4C**.
7. Copy the two vertical lines and the arc to the opposite end of the button
8. Connect the top edges of the button with straight lines. The completed drawing should look like **Figure B-4D**.

**Figure B-4.**

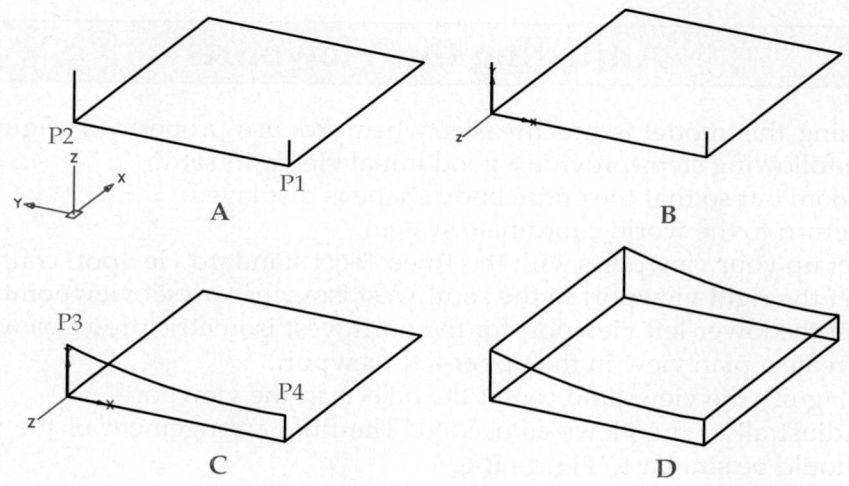

Now that the wireframe of the button has been drawn, the next step is to add the surfaces.

1. Set the current layer to Button1.
2. Set the **SURFTAB1** variable to 6 and the **SURFTAB2** variable to 2.
3. Use **EDGESURF** to create a surface patch for the side of the button, as shown in **Figure B-5A** and **Figure B-5B**.
4. Copy the surface patch to the opposite end of the button. Your object should look like **Figure B-5C**.
5. Make layer Button2 current and turn off layer Button1.
6. Create a surface patch for the curved top surface of the button. Pick one of the ends that is already surfaced as the first edge.
7. Turn on layer Button1.
8. Create 3D faces on the two remaining sides. The button should look like **Figure B-5D**.

This surfaced shape can now be saved as a block or wblocked as a file. Before doing so, place all the surfaces on Layer0. You will use the blocks you have created to complete the digitizer puck. It is a good idea to save your drawing at this point.

Figure B-5.

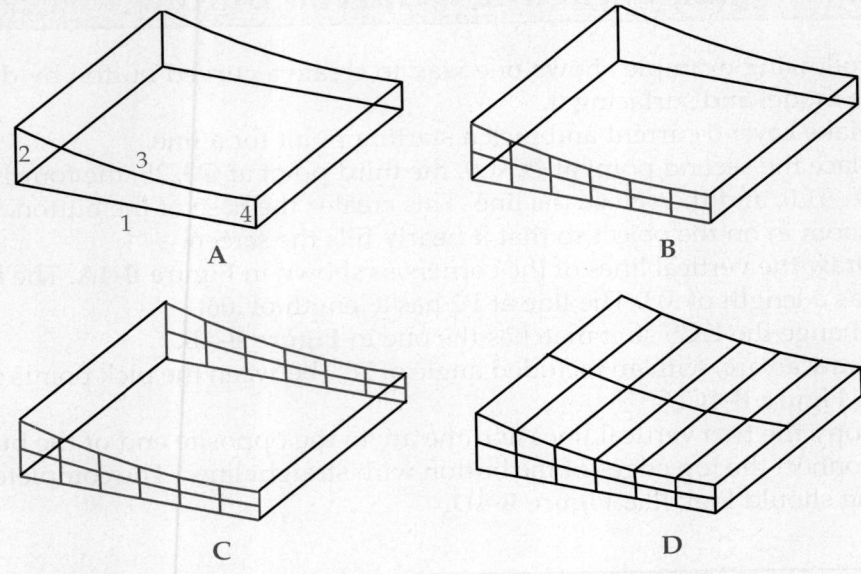

## Adjusting the Viewports

Finishing this model is much easier when you use properly configured viewports. The following steps provide a good initial viewport setup.

1. Zoom out so that the entire body shape is displayed.
2. Return to the world coordinate system.
3. Set up your viewports with the Three: Right standard viewport configuration.
4. Set the right viewport to the southwest isometric preset viewpoint.
5. Set the lower-left viewport for the northwest isometric preset viewpoint.
6. Create a plan view in the upper-left viewport.
7. Magnify the views and center the objects in the viewports.
8. Adjust all of the views as needed. The final arrangement of the viewports should be similar to **Figure B-6**.
9. Save the viewport configuration as THREE.

Figure B-6.

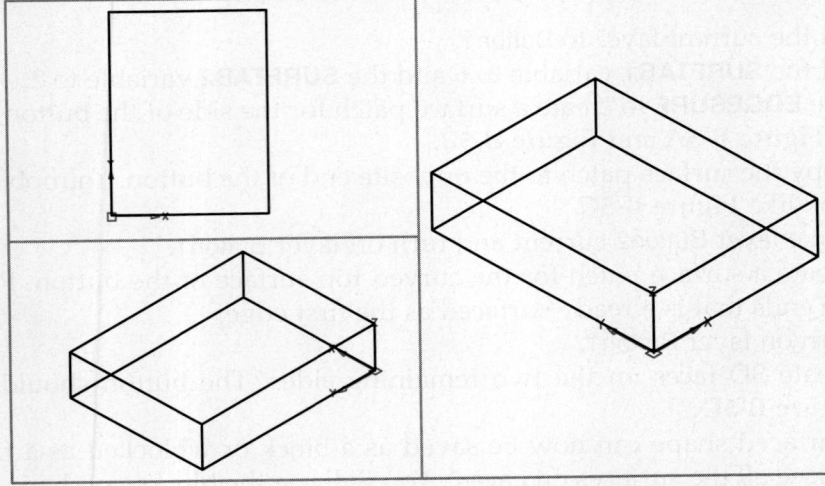

AutoCAD and its Applications—Advanced

# Adding a Cap to the Puck

Next, you need to add a "cap" to the puck body.
1. Set the current layer to Body Cap.
2. Make the large viewport active.
3. Insert the BOX block and attach it to the body at the insertion point shown in **Figure B-7A**.
4. Use the following values for the block insert. The inserted body cap is shown in **Figure B-7B**.

| Setting | Value |
|---|---|
| X scale factor | 2.25 |
| Y scale factor | 3 |
| Z scale factor | .12 |
| Rotation angle | 0 |

**Figure B-7.**

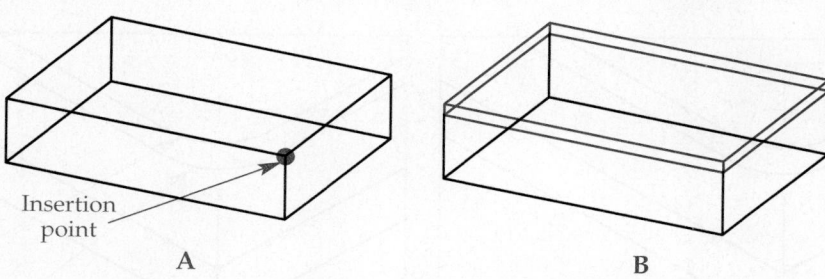

Insertion point

A

B

## Constructing the Face of the Puck

The following are instructions to construct the polyline wireframe of the face of the puck. Notice in **Figure B-2** that the face has filleted corners.
1. Create a new UCS with its origin at 0, 0, .82. Save the UCS and make it the current UCS in all viewports.
2. Change to the layer Face1.
3. Draw the polyline "face" in the upper-left viewport from the starting point .19, .19. Use the dimensions provided in **Figure B-2**. After completing the polyline, your drawing should look like **Figure B-8**.
4. Place a .125 radius fillet on the corners of the polyline.
5. Copy the filleted polyline and place the copy .06 units up the positive Z axis.

## Surfacing the Face of the Puck

In the following steps, ruled surfaces are created for the rounded areas of the face. To do this efficiently, the viewports must be adjusted.
1. Make a single viewport display of the large viewport. Save this viewport configuration as ONE.
2. Zoom in so that the object fills the screen. Save the current display as ALL.
3. Zoom in on the front corner (insertion point) of the face and body cap. Save this display as CORNER.
4. Change to the Construct layer.
5. Set **PDMODE** to 3 and set **PDSIZE** to .04.
6. Place a point at the center of the arc, **Figure B-9A**.
7. Explode the two polylines that represent the face, **Figure B-9B**.

Figure B-8.

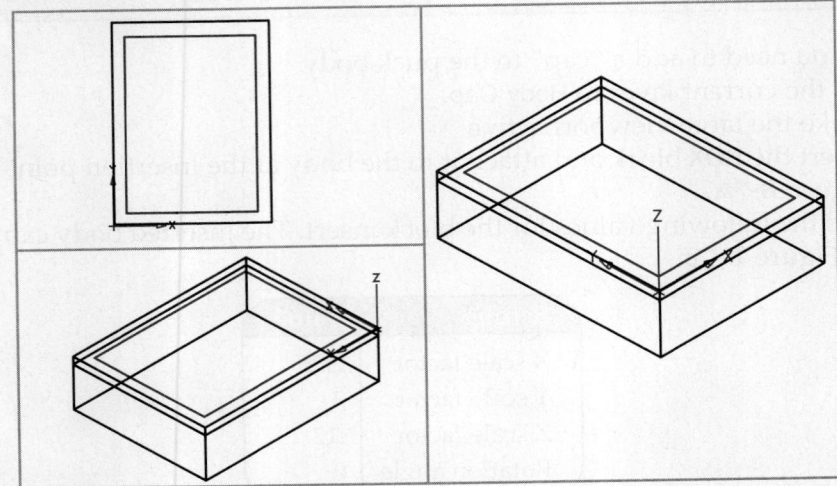

Z
Y
X
Z


Figure B-9.

Z
Y
X
A
Z
Y
X
Curve 2
Curve 1
B
Z
Y
X
C
Pick the
point symbol
Pick the
corner curve
Z
Y
X
D
Z
Y
X
E

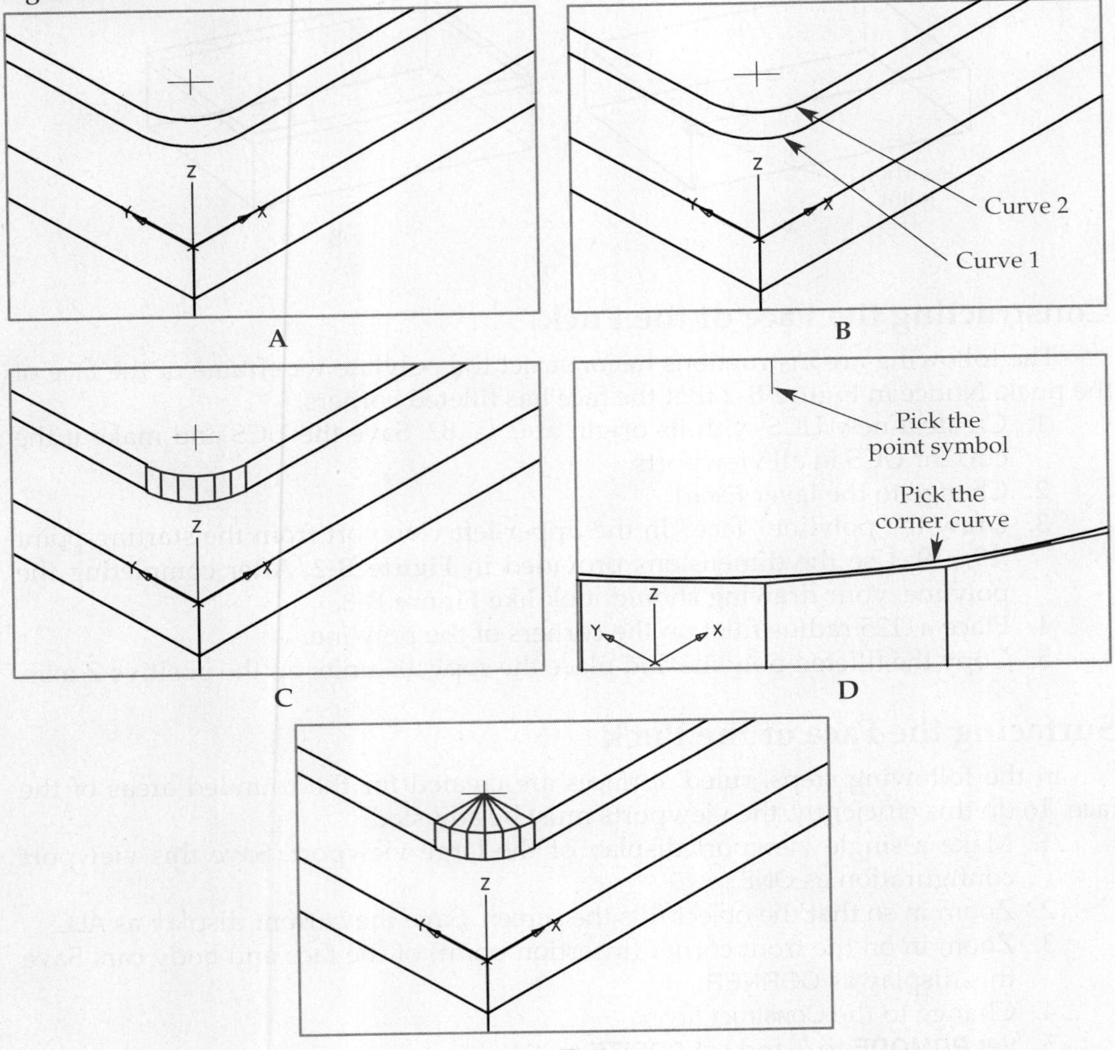

8. Change to the Face2 layer.
9. Set **SURFTAB1** to 6.
10. Create a ruled surface between the two arcs. The corner is now surfaced with six segments. See **Figure B-9C**.
11. Create a ruled surface between the top arc and the point at the center of the arc. Be sure to pick the arc as the first defining curve, not the ruled surface, **Figure B-9D**.
12. Erase the point. The corner should look like **Figure B-9E**. Save your work before continuing.

## Surfacing the Other Three Corners

The surfaces created in the previous steps are mirrored to surface the remaining three corners of the puck face.
1. Be sure you have a single viewport and restore the **ALL** view.
2. Turn **Ortho** mode on and mirror the corner surfaces along the X axis.
3. Mirror *both* corners along the Y axis. Do not delete the old objects.

## Adding 3D Faces

Next, 3D faces must be added to finish surfacing the puck face.
1. Create a view of the upper-left corner. Name this view CORNER2.
2. Adjust the viewports to a two-viewport vertical configuration. Save it as TWO.
3. Restore the CORNER2 view in the left viewport and the CORNER view in the right viewport.
4. Adjust the CORNER view so that it more closely matches CORNER2. Your screen should look like **Figure B-10**.
5. Apply 3D faces to the vertical side of the puck face and the top surface between the rule-surfaced corners. Make sure the Face2 layer is current.
6. Draw the vertical 3D face using the pick points shown in **Figure B-11A**.
7. Draw the top face between the centers of the arcs and the edge of the previous face, **Figure B-11B**.
8. Restore the ONE viewport configuration and the ALL view.
9. Use the **MIRROR** command to copy the 3D faces and ruled surfaces to the opposite side of the face. See **Figure B-12**.

Figure B-10.

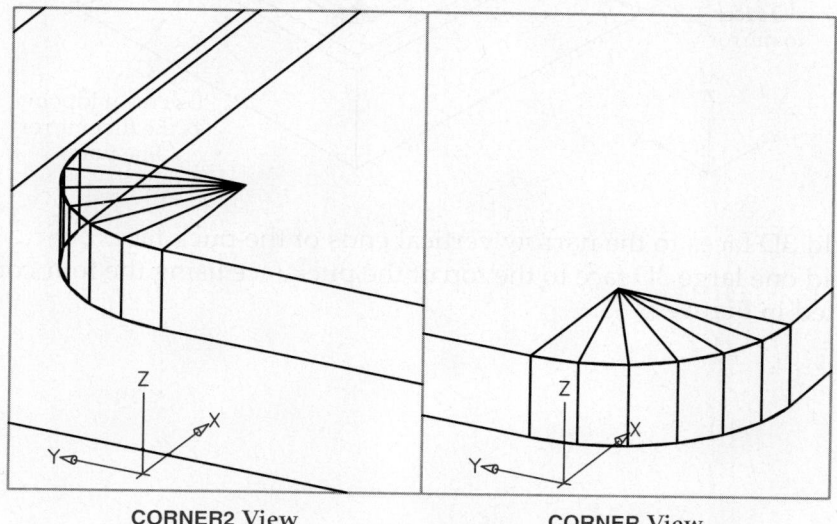

CORNER2 View          CORNER View

**Figure B-11.**

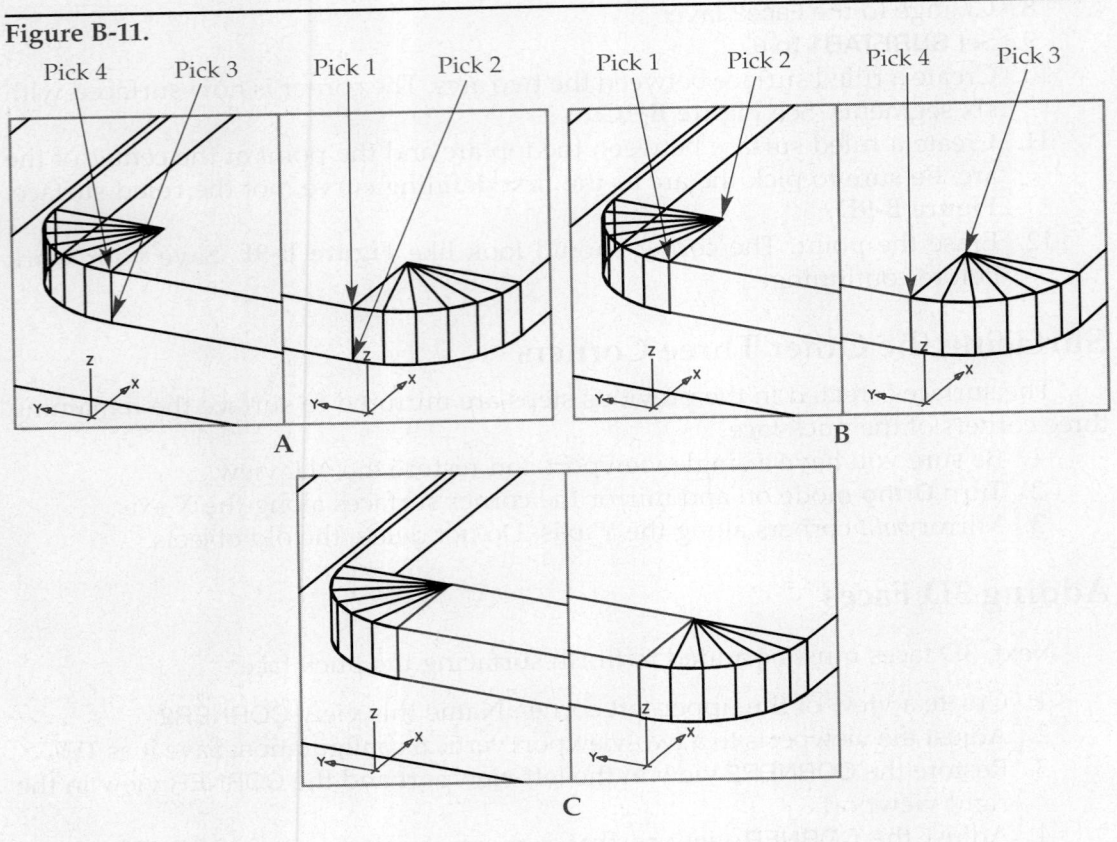

A

B

C

**Figure B-12.**

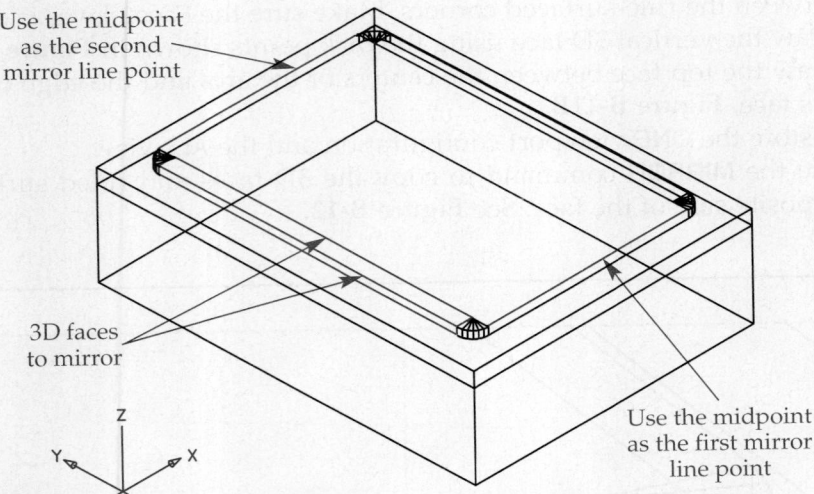

Use the midpoint as the second mirror line point

3D faces to mirror

Use the midpoint as the first mirror line point

10. Add 3D faces to the narrow vertical ends of the puck face.
11. Add one large 3D face to the top of the puck face using the four corners indicated in **Figure B-13.**

AutoCAD and its Applications—Advanced

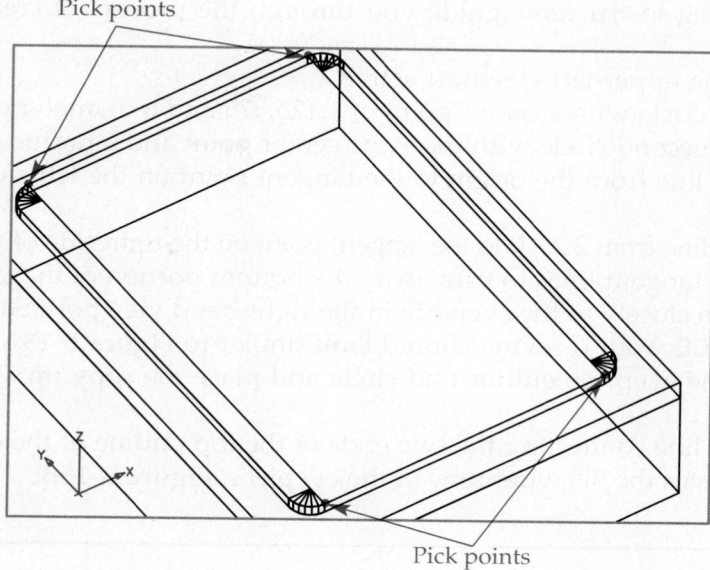

Pick points

Pick points

## Constructing the Eyepiece

Like the curved button and the puck face, the eyepiece is first created as a wire-frame and is then surfaced.

### Setup

Adjusting the display and UCS make creating the eyepiece much simpler. The following instructions provide you with the necessary setup.

1. Set the Eyepiece layer current and restore the viewport configuration THREE.
2. Make the upper-left viewport active and display a plan view showing the upper half of the object.
3. Make the large viewport active. Create a display that looks similar to **Figure B-14A**. Also change the view in the lower-left viewport to match the figure.
4. Create a new UCS by moving the origin to where the eyepiece attaches to the body. See **Figure B-14B**.
5. Save the new UCS as EYEPIECE, and restore it in all viewports.
6. Save this viewport configuration as THREE EYE.

Figure B-14.

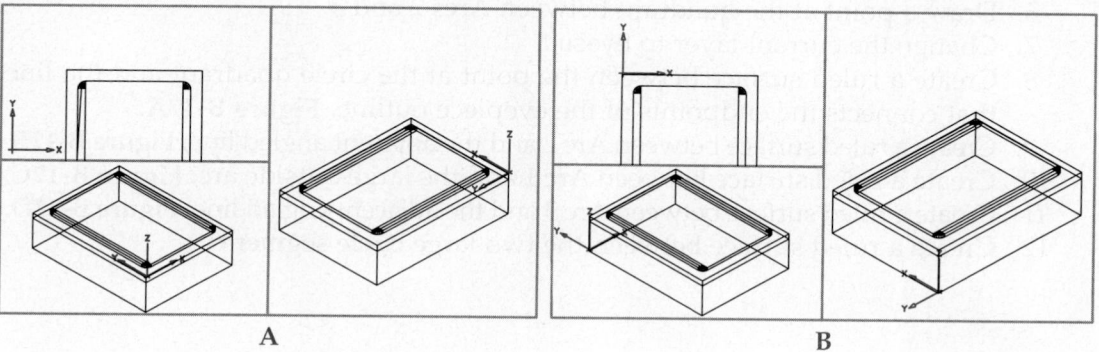

A                                                            B

## Creating the Wireframe

The following instructions guide you through the process of creating the eyepiece wireframe.

1. Make the upper-left viewport active.
2. Draw a circle with a center point of 1.125, .75 and a diameter of .5.
3. Draw a second circle with the same center point and a radius of .75.
4. Draw a line from the origin to the tangent point on the left side of the large circle.
5. Draw a line from 2.25, 0 to the tangent point on the right side of the large circle.
6. Use the tangent lines to trim away the bottom portion of the large circle.
7. Zoom in closely to the eyepiece in the right-hand viewport. Save the view as EYEPIECE. Your drawing should look similar to **Figure B-15A**.
8. Copy the eyepiece outline and circle and place the copy up .25 units on the +Z axis.
9. Draw a line connecting the two ends of the top outline of the eyepiece.

This completes the 3D wireframe of the eyepiece, **Figure B-15B**.

**Figure B-15.**

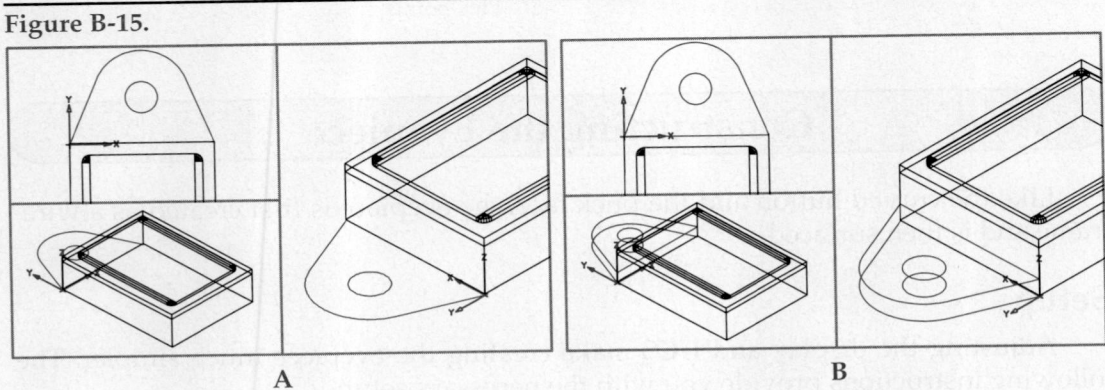

A

B

## Surfacing the Eyepiece

As with the face of the puck, the eyepiece is surfaced with a combination of ruled surfaces and 3D faces.

1. Set the Construct layer current.
2. Move the UCS origin to the top surface of the eyepiece directly above the current origin.
3. Zoom in on the top circle of the eyepiece.
4. Draw three arcs on top of the previously drawn circle. Create the arcs in the positions indicated in **Figure B-16A**.
5. Set **PDMODE** to 3 and **PDSIZE** to .08.
6. Draw a point at the quadrant between Arcs 2 and 3.
7. Change the current layer to Eyesurf.
8. Create a ruled surface between the point at the circle quadrant and the line that connects the endpoints of the eyepiece outline, **Figure B-17A**.
9. Create a ruled surface between Arc 2 and the adjacent angled line, **Figure B-17B**.
10. Create a ruled surface between Arc 1 and the large outside arc, **Figure B-17C**.
11. Create a ruled surface between Arc 3 and the adjacent angled line, **Figure B-17D**.
12. Create a ruled surface between the two large circle segments.

**Figure B-16.**

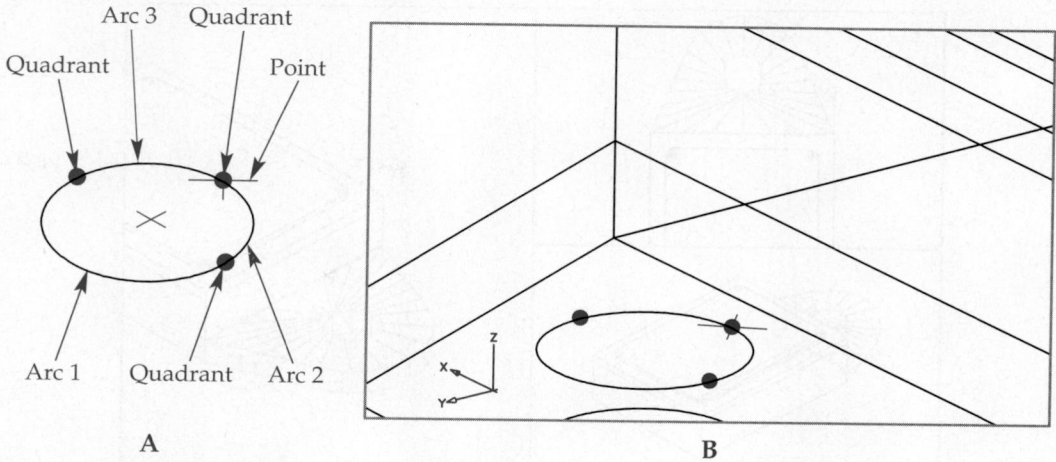

A

B

**Figure B-17.**

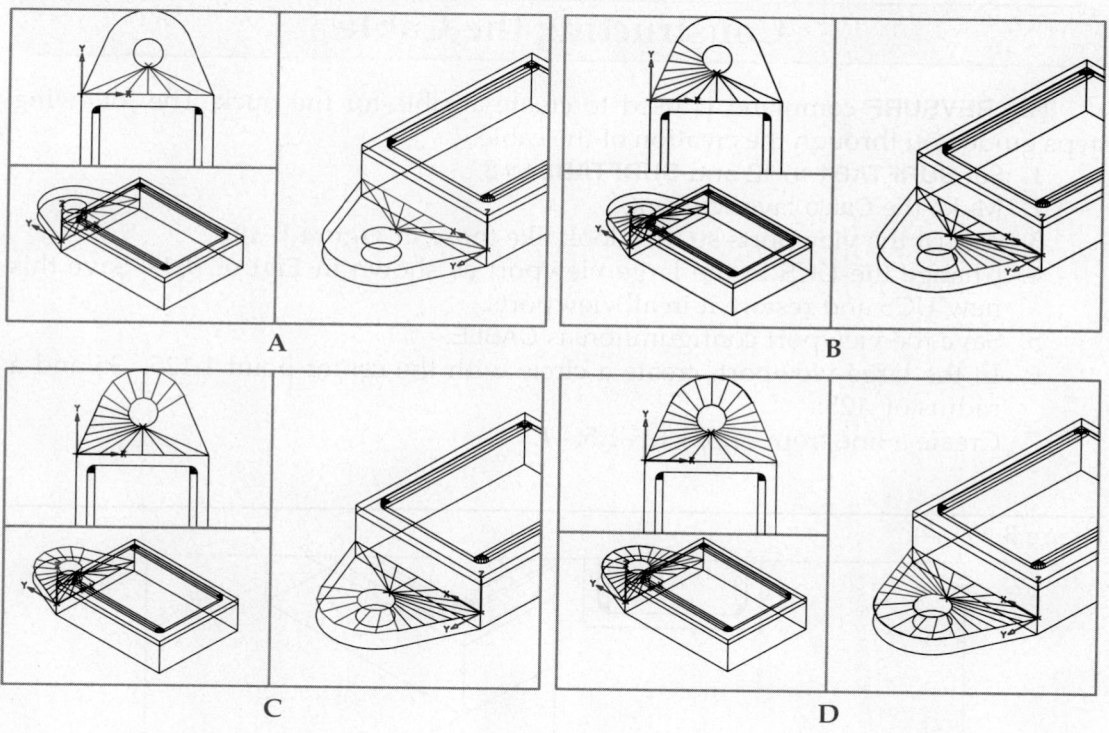

A

B

C

D

13. Set **SURFTAB1** to 8. Create a ruled surface between the top circle and lower circle, **Figure B-18.**
14. Create a 3D face on each vertical side of the eyepiece.
15. Use the **HIDE** command to be sure that you have created all of the needed surfaces.

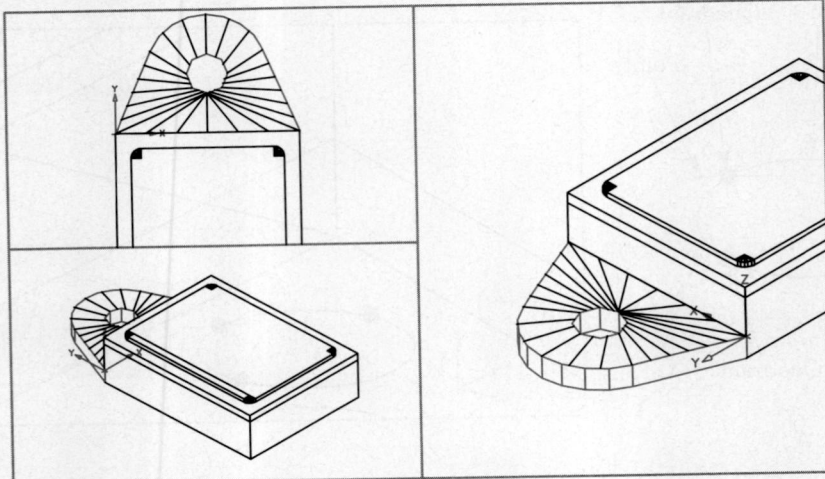

## Constructing the Cable

The **REVSURF** command is used to create a cable for the puck. The following steps guide you through the creation of the cable.

1. Set **SURFTAB1** to 12 and **SURFTAB2** to 8.
2. Make the Cable layer current.
3. Adjust the viewports so they look like those in **Figure B-19**.
4. Change the UCS in the large viewport as shown in **Figure B-19**. Save this new UCS and restore it in all viewports.
5. Save the viewport configuration as CABLE.
6. In the large viewport, create a circle with the center point 1.125, .35 and a radius of .125.
7. Create a line from –1.5, 1 to –1.5, –1.

Figure B-19.

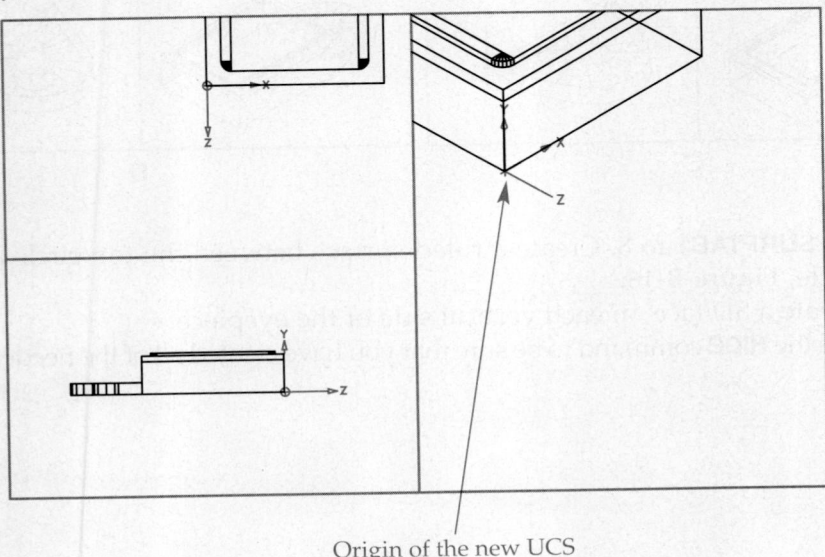

Origin of the new UCS

8. Create a revolved surface by revolving the circle around the line from 0° to −90°, **Figure B-20A.**
9. Erase the axis line.

The completed cable is shown in **Figure B-20B.** Save your work before continuing.

**Figure B-20.**

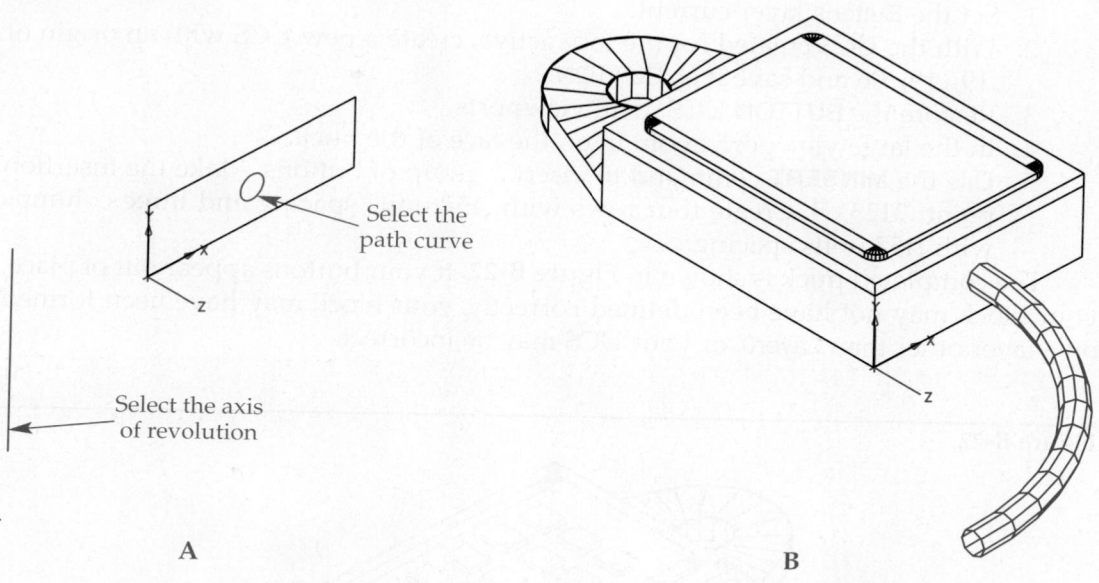

Select the path curve

Select the axis of revolution

A

B

## Adding the Screw Heads

For this tutorial, domes are used to represent screw heads on the face of the puck. The following instructions step you through the process of adding the screw heads.

1. Set the Screws layer current.
2. Restore the UCS created on the face in all viewports.
3. Create a dome with a center point of .095, .095 and a diameter of .125. Give the dome eight longitudinal segments and four latitudinal segments, **Figure B-21A.**
4. Create an array of the screw heads consisting of two rows and two columns. Set the row offset to 2.81 and the column offset to 2.06.

**Figure B-21B** shows the array of four domes on the digitizer puck from the southwest isometric preset viewpoint.

**Figure B-21.**

A

B

# Inserting the Button 3D Block

The last thing to do is add the buttons. This digitizer has twelve buttons. Earlier, you created a block called BUTTON. If you completed the optional, curved button, you may also have saved that as a block. In such a case, you may want to complete the following steps with the block you created from the optional curved button.

1. Set the Buttons layer current.
2. With the UCS created for the face active, create a new UCS with an origin of .19, .19, .06 and save it as BUTTON.
3. Restore the BUTTON UCS in all viewports.
4. In the large viewport, zoom in on the face of the puck.
5. Use the **MINSERT** command to insert a group of buttons. Make the insertion point .3125, .5. Create four rows with .457 units spacing and three columns with .457 units spacing.

The completed puck is shown in **Figure B-22.** If your buttons appear out of place, your block may not have been defined correctly, your block may have been formed on a layer other than Layer0, or your UCS may be incorrect.

**Figure B-22.**

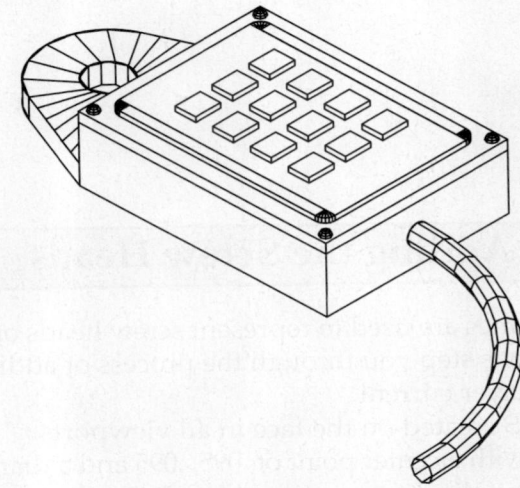

| File Extension | Description |
| --- | --- |
| 3DS | This is a native 3D Studio file, through DOS R4. |
| AC$ | A temporary work file. |
| ADS | An AutoCAD Development System application. Type (XLOAD *"filename"*) at the Command: prompt to load. |
| ADT | Audit report files created with the **AUDIT** command. |
| ARG | When you export a profile, you create a registry (.arg) file. |
| ARX | An AutoCAD Runtime Extension application file. |
| BAK | Backup drawing files created by AutoCAD the second time a drawing is saved and all times thereafter. |
| BAT | An MS-DOS batch file that executes a series of commands. |
| BK$n$ | Emergency backup files numbered sequentially. (BK1, BK2, BK3, etc.) when AutoCAD unexpectedly terminates. |
| BMP | A Windows bitmap file. |
| C | An ADS source code file. |
| CC | An ADS source code file. |
| CDF | An attribute extract file in the comma delimited format. |
| CFG | A configuration file. |
| CUS | A custom dictionary file. |
| DB2 | dBase II Database file. |
| DB3 | dBase III Database file. |
| DBC | Visual FoxPro Database file. |
| DCC | An ASCII text file that contains color settings for all dialog box elements. |
| DCE | A dialog box error report file created if errors are found when trying to load a DCL file. |
| DCL | AutoCAD dialog control language description file. |
| DEF | ADS source code file |
| DLL | A platform-specific, dynamic-linked library file. |
| DWF | Drawing Web format file for posting drawings on the Internet. |
| DWG | The native AutoCAD drawing file extension. |
| DWK | An AutoCAD drawing lock file. |
| DWL | A temporary lock file for an externally referenced drawing. |
| DXB | A drawing interchange file in binary format. |
| DXF | A drawing interchange file in ASCII format. |
| DXX | An attribute extract file in DXF format. |
| EPS | An encapsulated PostScript file. |
| ERR | An error file, created when AutoCAD "crashes," containing diagnostic information. |
| EXE | An executable program file. |
| FAS | Binary, compiled version of a single LSP program file. |

| File Extension | Description |
|---|---|
| FMP | AutoCAD Font Map. |
| GIF | A graphics interchange format raster file. |
| H | An ADS include file. |
| HLP | A Windows help file. |
| HTM/HTML | Hypertext Markup Language file for use with Internet applications. |
| INI | A program initialization file where basic settings for an application are stored. |
| LIN | A linetype library file. |
| LOG | This file is a history of all commands and variables used in a drawing session. |
| LSP | An AutoLISP file. |
| MAX | The native format for 3ds max and 3D Studio VIZ. |
| MID | An identification information file. |
| MLI | A materials library file. |
| MLN | A multiline library file. |
| MNC | A compiled menu file. |
| MND | A menu description file created for use with the mc.exe program. |
| MNL | A menu AutoLISP file. |
| MNR | A menu resource file. |
| MNS | A menu source file. |
| MNU | A menu template file in ASCII format. |
| OLD | The original version of a converted drawing file. |
| PAT | A hatch pattern library file. |
| PC2 | Complete plot configuration file for AutoCAD releases prior to AutoCAD 2000. |
| PC3 | Complete information about a given plot device. Replaces PC2 and PCP files. |
| PCP | A plot configuration parameters file for AutoCAD releases prior to AutoCAD 2000. |
| PCX | A bitmap raster image file that can be imported into AutoCAD. |
| PFA | A PostScript font file ASCII format. |
| PFB | A PostScript font file binary format. |
| PFM | A PostScript font metric file. |
| PGP | AutoCAD program parameter file |
| PLT | A plot output file. Also called a "plot file." |
| PS | A PostScript interpreter initialization file. |
| PSF | A PostScript font file. |
| RX | The acad.rx file contains a list of the ARX program files, which are loaded automatically when you start AutoCAD. |
| SAB | A binary file that stores solid model geometry. |
| SAT | An ASCII file that stores solid model geometry. |
| SCR | A command script file. |
| SDF | An attribute extract file in the space delimited format. |
| SHP | This file extension is used for both AutoCAD shape and font source files. |
| SHX | A compiled AutoCAD shape and font file. |
| SLB | A slide library file. |
| SLD | A slide file. |
| STL | A stereolithography file. |
| SV$ | An automatically saved drawing file. |
| TGA | A Truevision rendered replay file. |
| TIF | A Tagged Image File format file. |
| TTF | A TrueType font file. |
| TXT | An ASCII text file. |
| UNT | A units conversion file. |
| VLX | A compiled set of one or more LSP and/or dialog control language (DCL) files. |
| WMF | A Windows Metafile format vector file. |
| XLG | An external references log file. |
| XLS | Excel Spreadsheet file. |
| XMX | An external message file. |

# AutoCAD Command Aliases

The following aliases for AutoCAD commands are found in the acad.pgp file. This file is located in the AutoCAD \Support folder. The examples given in this file are aliases for the most frequently used commands.

You can easily create your own aliases. The first part of the alias in the PGP file is the character(s) you type at the keyboard. The second part must begin with an asterisk followed by the name of the command the alias will execute. Do not put a space between the asterisk and the command. Always consult your instructor or supervisor before altering any file crucial to the operation of AutoCAD.

| Command | Alias | | Command | Alias |
|---------|-------|---|---------|-------|
| 3DARRAY | 3A | | DDUCS | UC |
| 3DFACE | 3F | | DDUCSP | UCP |
| 3DORBIT | 3DO, ORBIT | | DDVPOINT | VP |
| 3DPOLY | 3P | | DIMALIGNED | DAL |
| ADCENTER | ADC | | DIMANGULAR | DAN |
| ALIGN | AL | | DIMBASELINE | DBA |
| APPLOAD | AP | | DIMCENTER | DCE |
| ARC | A | | DIMCONTINUE | DCO |
| AREA | AA | | DIMDIAMETER | DDI |
| ARRAY | AR | | DIMDISASSOCIATE | DDA |
| -ARRAY | -AR | | DIMEDIT | DED |
| ATTDEF | ATT | | DIMLINEAR | DLI |
| -ATTDEF | -ATT | | DIMORDINATE | DOR |
| ATTEDIT | ATE | | DIMOVERRIDE | DOV |
| -ATTEDIT | -ATE, ATTE | | DIMRADIUS | DRA |
| BHATCH | BH, H | | DIMREASSOCIATE | DRE |
| BLOCK | B | | DIMSTYLE | D, DST |
| -BLOCK | -B | | DIST | DI |
| BOUNDARY | BO | | DIVIDE | DIV |
| -BOUNDARY | -BO | | DONUT | DO |
| BREAK | BR | | DRAWORDER | DR |
| CHAMFER | CHA | | DSETTINGS | DS, SE |
| CHANGE | -CH | | DTEXT | DT |
| CIRCLE | C | | DVIEW | DV |
| COLOR | COL, COLOUR | | ELLIPSE | EL |
| COPY | CO, CP | | ERASE | E |
| DBCONNECT | DBC | | EXPLODE | X |
| DDEDIT | ED | | EXPORT | EXP |
| DDGRIPS | GR | | EXTEND | EX |
| DDRMODES | RM | | | |

*(Continued on next page)*

| Command | Alias |
|---|---|
| EXTRUDE | EXT |
| FILLET | F |
| FILTER | FI |
| GROUP | G |
| -GROUP | -G |
| HATCH | -H |
| HATCHEDIT | HE |
| HIDE | HI |
| IMAGE | IM |
| -IMAGE | -IM |
| IMAGEADJUST | IAD |
| IMAGEATTACH | IAT |
| IMAGECLIP | ICL |
| IMPORT | IMP |
| INSERT | I |
| -INSERT | -I |
| INSERTOBJ | IO |
| INTERFERE | INF |
| INTERSECT | IN |
| LAYER | LA |
| -LAYER | -LA |
| -LAYOUT | LO |
| LENGTHEN | LEN |
| LINE | L |
| LINETYPE | LT, LTYPE |
| -LINETYPE | -LT, -LTYPE |
| LIST | LI, LS |
| LTSCALE | LTS |
| LWEIGHT | LINEWEIGHT, LW |
| MATCHPROP | MA |
| MEASURE | ME |
| MIRROR | MI |
| MLINE | ML |
| MOVE | M |
| MSPACE | MS |
| MTEXT | MT, T |
| -MTEXT | -T |
| MVIEW | MV |
| OFFSET | O |
| OPTIONS | OP, PR |
| OSNAP | OS |
| -OSNAP | -OS |
| PAN | P |
| -PAN | -P |
| -PARTIALOPEN | PARTIALOPEN |
| PASTESPEC | PA |
| PEDIT | PE |
| PLINE | PL |
| PLOT | PRINT |
| POINT | PO |
| POLYGON | POL |
| PREVIEW | PRE |
| PROPERTIES | CH, MO, PROPS |
| PROPERTIESCLOSE | PRCLOSE |
| PSPACE | PS |

| Command | Alias |
|---|---|
| PUBLISHTOWEB | PTW |
| PURGE | PU |
| -PURGE | -PU |
| QLEADER | LE |
| QUIT | EXIT |
| RECTANGLE | REC |
| REDRAW | R |
| REDRAWALL | RA |
| REGEN | RE |
| REGENALL | REA |
| REGION | REG |
| RENAME | REN |
| -RENAME | -REN |
| RENDER | RR |
| REVOLVE | REV |
| ROTATE | RO |
| RPREF | RPR |
| SCALE | SC |
| SCRIPT | SCR |
| SECTION | SEC |
| SETVAR | SET |
| SHADE | SHA |
| SLICE | SL |
| SNAP | SN |
| SOLID | SO |
| SPELL | SP |
| SPLINE | SPL |
| SPLINEDIT | SPE |
| STRETCH | S |
| STYLE | ST |
| SUBTRACT | SU |
| TABLET | TA |
| THICKNESS | TH |
| TILEMODE | TI |
| TOLERANCE | TOL |
| TOOLBAR | TO |
| TORUS | TOR |
| TRIM | TR |
| UNION | UNI |
| UNITS | UN |
| -UNITS | -UN |
| VIEW | V |
| -VIEW | -V |
| VPOINT | -VP |
| WBLOCK | W |
| -WBLOCK | -W |
| WEDGE | WE |
| XATTACH | XA |
| XBIND | XB |
| -XBIND | -XB |
| XCLIP | XC |
| XLINE | XL |
| XREF | XR |
| -XREF | -XR |
| ZOOM | Z |

# Advanced Application Commands

| Command | Description |
|---------|-------------|
| **3D** | This command allows you to create box, cone, dish, dome, mesh, pyramid, sphere, torus, and wedge 3D mesh objects using the command line. |
| **3DARRAY** | This command allows you to create a three-dimensional polar or rectangular array of objects. |
| **3DCLIP** | This command enables the 3D orbit view and allows you to manipulate the view interactively using the **Adjust Clipping Planes** window. |
| **3DCORBIT** | This command enables the 3D orbit view functions and allows you to set the objects in continuous motion. |
| **3DDISTANCE** | This command establishes a closer or more distant view of the objects in the 3D orbit view. |
| **3DFACE** | This command creates a three-dimensional face. The face must have at least three and no more than four vertices. |
| **3DMESH** | This command creates a polygon mesh. You must give the coordinate location for each of the vertices in the mesh. |
| **3DORBIT** | This command enables the 3D orbit view and its interactive viewing functions. |
| **3DPAN** | This command permits the panning of objects in the 3D orbit view. |
| **3DPOLY** | This command creates a polyline in 3D space. |
| **3DSIN** | This command is used to import a 3D Studio file in 3DS format into AutoCAD. |
| **3DSOUT** | This command is used to save an AutoCAD drawing in the older native 3D Studio file format. Only 3D objects are saved. Any 2D objects are lost. |
| **3DSWIVEL** | When using the 3D orbit view, this command allows you to adjust the target view of objects by creating the effect of turning a camera with the screen cursor. |
| **3DZOOM** | This command enables you to zoom in or out in the 3D orbit view. |
| **ACISIN** | This command allows you to import an ACIS solid model (SAT) file into AutoCAD. |
| **ACISOUT** | This command allows you to save solid objects created in AutoCAD to an ACIS solid model (SAT) file. |
| **ALIGN** | This command is used to move and rotate a selected object to align with other objects in 2D or 3D. |
| **AMECONVERT** | This command converts solid models created in an AME application to AutoCAD solids. |
| **APPLOAD** | This command is used to load and unload application files and define which applications are automatically loaded at startup. |
| **AREA** | This command calculates the area and perimeter of selected objects or of defined areas. |
| **ARX** | This command loads and unloads ObjectARX applications and lists information about currently loaded applications. |

| Command | Description |
|---|---|
| **BACKGROUND** | This command sets up the rendering background for your drawing. |
| **BMPOUT** | This command saves selected objects to a bitmap (BMP) format file. |
| **BOX** | This command creates a three-dimensional solid box. |
| **BROWSER** | This command launches your system's default Web browser. |
| **CAMERA** | This command is used to set the camera location and target point. |
| **CHAMFER** | This command is used to bevel the edges of objects. A chamfer can be applied to a 2D or 3D object. |
| **COMPILE** | This command compiles shape and PostScript font files. |
| **CONE** | This command creates a three-dimensional solid cone. |
| **COPYCLIP** | This command is used to copy selected objects to the Windows Clipboard. |
| **COPYLINK** | This command copies the current view to the Windows Clipboard for linking to Object Linking and Embedding (OLE) applications. |
| **CUTCLIP** | This command removes selected objects from the drawing and places them on the Windows Clipboard. |
| **CYLINDER** | This command creates a three-dimensional solid cylinder. |
| **DBCCLOSE** | This command closes the **dbConnect Manager**. |
| **DBCONNECT** | This command opens the **dbConnect Manager** for access to database tables. |
| **DBLIST** | This command lists all data for every object in the current drawing in the **AutoCAD Text Window**. |
| **DDUCS** | See **UCSMAN**. |
| **DDUCSP** | This command allows you to select from several preset orthographic user coordinate systems (UCS) using the **UCS** dialog box. |
| **DDVPOINT** | This command is used to set the 3D viewing direction. |
| **DELAY** | This command is used to specify a timed pause within a script file. |
| **DSVIEWER** | This command allows you to change your view of the drawing using the **Aerial View** window. |
| **DVIEW** | This command allows you to define a parallel projection or perspective view of selected objects. |
| **DXBIN** | This command is used to import binary format files. |
| **EDGE** | This command is used to make an edge of a 3D face visible or invisible. |
| **EDGESURF** | This command creates a three-dimensional polygon mesh using four objects to define the edges. |
| **ELEV** | This command is used to set the current elevation and thickness. |
| **ETRANSMIT** | This command creates a transmittal for sharing drawings using e-mail. |
| **EXPORT** | This command outputs objects using a specified file format. |
| **EXTRUDE** | This command is used to create 3D solid primitives by extruding existing 2D objects. |
| **FILLET** | This command is used to place fillets and rounds on the edges of 2D or 3D objects. |
| **FOG** | This command is used to set up fog for rendering. |
| **HIDE** | This command is used to display 3D objects with hidden lines removed. |
| **HYPERLINK** | This command is used to attach a hyperlink to a graphical object or edit an existing hyperlink. |
| **HYPERLINKOPTIONS** | This command is used to control the display of the hyperlink cursor and related tooltips. |
| **IMAGE** | This command allows you to insert images and manage the display of existing images. |
| **IMAGEADJUST** | This command controls the brightness, contrast, and fade values of the selected image. |
| **IMAGEATTACH** | This command is used to attach a new image object and definition. |
| **IMAGECLIP** | This command creates new clipping boundaries for individual image objects. |
| **IMAGEFRAME** | This command controls the visibility of the frame used for images. |

| Command | Description |
|---------|-------------|
| **IMAGEQUALITY** | This command enables a setting that controls the display quality of images. |
| **IMPORT** | Various types of files can be imported into AutoCAD using this command. |
| **INSERTOBJ** | This command enables you to insert an object from an Object Linking and Embedding (OLE) application. |
| **INTERFERE** | This command creates a composite solid from the volume created by the interference of two or more solids. |
| **INTERSECT** | This command creates a composite solid or region from the intersection of two or more solids or regions and removes the nonintersecting areas. |
| **LIGHT** | This command is used to manage lights and lighting effects. |
| **LOGFILEOFF** | This command closes the file created by the **LOGFILEON** command. |
| **LOGFILEON** | When this command is enabled, the contents of the **AutoCAD Text Window** are recorded to a log file. |
| **LSEDIT** | This command is used to edit a landscape object. |
| **LSLIB** | This command is used to maintain landscape object libraries. |
| **LSNEW** | This command lets you add realistic landscape items, such as trees and bushes, to drawings. |
| **MASSPROP** | This command calculates and displays the mass properties of regions or solids. |
| **MATLIB** | This command opens the **Materials Library** dialog box, which is used to import and export materials to and from a library of materials. |
| **MEETNOW** | This command provides tools for using AutoCAD with Microsoft NetMeeting for online meetings. |
| **MENU** | This command is used to load a menu file. |
| **MENULOAD** | This command is used to load partial menu files. |
| **MENUUNLOAD** | This command is used to unload partial menu files. |
| **MIRROR3D** | This command is used to construct a mirror image of selected objects in 3D space using a mirror plane. |
| **MODEL** | When in a layout tab, this command allows you to switch to the **Model** tab and make it current. |
| **MVIEW** | This command is used to create floating viewports in paper space. It is also used to turn on existing floating viewports. |
| **MVSETUP** | This command allows you to set up the specifications of a drawing. It can be used in the **Model** tab or in a layout tab. |
| **OLELINKS** | This command is used to update, change, and cancel existing Object Linking and Embedding (OLE) links. |
| **OLESCALE** | The **OLE Properties** dialog box is opened with this command after an OLE object is selected. It is used to resize OLE objects, scale text, and control OLE plot quality. |
| **OPTIONS** | This command accesses the **Options** dialog box, which is used to customize the AutoCAD environment. |
| **PASTECLIP** | This command inserts the contents of the Windows Clipboard into the current drawing. |
| **PASTEORIG** | This command pastes an object containing AutoCAD data from the Windows Clipboard and uses the same coordinates from the original drawing for insertion. |
| **PASTESPEC** | This command inserts the contents of the Windows Clipboard and allows you to control the format of what is being inserted. |
| **PEDIT** | This command allows you to edit 2D or 3D polylines, and three-dimensional polygon meshes. |
| **PFACE** | This command allows you to create a three-dimensional polyface mesh. Each vertex must be individually specified. |
| **PLAN** | Entering this command displays a plan view of the current User Coordinate System (UCS), a saved UCS, or the World Coordinate System (WCS). |
| **PSFILL** | This command is used to fill a two-dimensional polyline outline with a PostScript pattern. |

| Command | Description |
|---|---|
| **PSOUT** | This command saves the drawing as an encapsulated PostScript file. You can save the entire drawing or a portion of the drawing. |
| **PSPACE** | This command switches the drawing from model space to paper space when in a layout tab. |
| **PUBLISHTOWEB** | This command accesses a wizard that automatically creates Web pages for displaying drawings. |
| **REGION** | This command is used to create a region from selected objects. |
| **REINIT** | This command is used to reinitialize the digitizer, I/O port, and program parameters (acad.pgp) file. |
| **RENDER** | This command opens the **Render** dialog box and initializes the AutoCAD **Render** window. The **Render** dialog box is used to create a realistically shaded image of a three-dimensional object. |
| **RENDSCR** | This command displays the last rendering created using the **RENDER** command. |
| **REPLAY** | This command is used to display a BMP, TGA, or TIF raster image file. |
| **REVOLVE** | This command is used to create a 3D solid by revolving a closed two-dimensional object about an axis. |
| **REVSURF** | This command creates a revolved surface by rotating a 2D object about a selected axis. |
| **RMAT** | The **Materials** dialog box is opened with this command. This dialog box allows you to manage materials used for rendering. |
| **ROTATE3D** | This command rotates selected objects about an axis in 3D space. |
| **RPREF** | This command allows you to set rendering preferences. |
| **RULESURF** | This command creates a 3D ruled surface between two path curves. The curves can be points, arcs, lines, splines, circles, or polylines. |
| **SAVEAS** | This command allows you to save or rename a drawing using the desired file extension. |
| **SAVEIMG** | This command saves a rendered image to a BMP, TIF, or TGA file. |
| **SCENE** | This command is used to manage scenes in a drawing. |
| **SECTION** | This command creates a region from the intersection of a plane and a solid. The region can then be used to create a section view. |
| **SETUV** | This command is used to apply mapping coordinates to an object. |
| **SHADEMODE** | This command displays a shaded image of the drawing in the current viewport. There are seven levels of quality from which to choose. |
| **SHOWMAT** | This command lists information about the material attached to a selected object and the attachment method used. |
| **SLICE** | This command is used to slice or "cut" a set of solids with a plane. |
| **SOLDRAW** | This command is used to generate profiles and sections in floating viewports created with the **SOLVIEW** command. |
| **SOLID** | This command is used to draw polygons that are filled solid. |
| **SOLIDEDIT** | This command is used to edit 3D solid objects by modifying faces and edges. |
| **SOLPROF** | This command is used to create profile images of 3D solid objects in floating viewports. |
| **SOLVIEW** | Using orthographic projection, this command creates floating viewports for multiview and section view drawings of 3D solid and body objects. |
| **SPHERE** | This command creates a three-dimensional solid sphere. |
| **STATS** | This command displays information about rendering functions. |
| **STLOUT** | This command is used to save a solid object to a ASCII or binary format file. |
| **SUBTRACT** | This command creates a composite by subtracting the area or volume of one selection set from another selection set. It can be used on 2D regions and 3D solids. |
| **TABLET** | This command is used to calibrate and configure a digitizer tablet, and to toggle its activation. |

| Command | Description |
|---|---|
| **TABSURF** | This command creates a 3D tabulated surface from a path curve and direction vector. |
| **TORUS** | This command creates a three-dimensional solid that resembles a donut. |
| **TRANSPARENCY** | The setting activated by this command controls whether the background pixels in a selected image are transparent or opaque. |
| **TREESTAT** | This command allows you to display information about the tree-structured spatial index of the current drawing. |
| **UCS** | This command is used to create and manage user coordinate systems (UCS) at the command line. |
| **UCSICON** | The setting activated by this command controls the visibility and placement of the UCS icon. |
| **UCSMAN** | This command opens the **UCS** dialog box, which is used to manage defined user coordinate systems (UCS). |
| **UNION** | This command creates a composite by adding the area or volume of two selection sets. It can be used with 2D regions or 3D solids. |
| **VBAIDE** | This command opens the **Visual Basic** editor. |
| **VBALOAD** | The **Open VBA Project** dialog box is opened with this command. It allows you to load a global VBA project into the current drawing. |
| **VBAMAN** | This command opens the **VBA Manager** dialog box, which is used to load, unload, save, create, embed, and extract VBA projects. |
| **VBARUN** | This command is used to run a VBA macro. |
| **VBASTMT** | This command is used to enter a VBA statement, or expression, on the command line. |
| **VBAUNLOAD** | This command is used to unload a global VBA project on the command line. |
| **VIEW** | This command is used to create and restore saved views. |
| **VIEWRES** | The setting made with this command controls object resolution in the current viewport. |
| **VLISP** | This command opens the **Visual LISP** editor. |
| **VPOINT** | This command is used to set the viewing direction for a 3D display of the current drawing. |
| **WEDGE** | This command creates a three-dimensional solid wedge. |
| **WMFIN** | This command is used to import a Windows metafile (WMF file) into AutoCAD. |
| **WMFOPTS** | This command is used to set importing options for use with the **WMFIN** command. |
| **WMFOUT** | This command is used to save selected objects to a Windows metafile (WMF file). |

# Advanced Application System Variables

| Variable | Saved In | Default Value | Description |
|---|---|---|---|
| ACADLSPASDOC | Registry | 0 | Determines if acad.lsp is loaded in every drawing or just the first in a drawing session.<br><br>0   Loads in just the first drawing.<br>1   Loads in every drawing. |
| ACISOUTVER | Not saved | 70 | Determines the ACIS version of SAT files. |
| BACKZ | Drawing | 0.000 | Saves the back clipping plane offset from the target plane for the current viewport. |
| BINDTYPE | Not saved | 0 | Controls how xref names are handled when binding or editing in place.<br><br>0   Traditional binding behavior.<br>1   Insert-like behavior. |
| CELWEIGHT | Drawing | –1 | Determines the line weight of new objects.<br><br>–1   ByLayer.<br>–2   ByBlock.<br>–3   Default (controlled by **LWDEFAULT**).<br>Other widths in millimeters can be entered. |
| CHAMFERA | Drawing | 0.000 | First chamfer distance. |
| CHAMFERB | Drawing | 0.000 | Second chamfer distance. |
| CHAMFERC | Drawing | 0.000 | Chamfer length. |
| CHAMFERD | Drawing | 0 | Chamfer angle. |
| CHAMMODE | Not saved | 0 | Sets the method for creating chamfers.<br><br>0   Two chamfer distances are used.<br>1   One chamfer length and an angle are used. |
| CMDACTIVE | Not saved | 1 | Stores the bitcode that indicates whether an ordinary command, transparent command, script, or dialog box is active. The value is the sum of:<br><br>1   Ordinary command active.<br>2   Ordinary command and a transparent command active.<br>4   Script active.<br>8   Dialog box active<br>16   AutoLISP active. |

| Variable | Saved In | Default Value | Description |
|---|---|---|---|
| **CMDECHO** | Not saved | 1 | Determines if AutoCAD echoes prompts and input during AutoLISP.<br><br>0   Echo off.<br><br>1   Echo on. |
| **COMPASS** | Not saved | 0 | Determines if 3D compass is on or off in the current viewport.<br><br>0   Off.<br><br>1   On. |
| **CPLOTSTYLE** | Drawing | ByLayer | Plot style for new objects. |
| **CPROFILE** | Registry | Unnamed | Name of current profile (read only). |
| **CTAB** | Drawing | Model | Displays the current drawing tab name. |
| **CVPORT** | Drawing | 2 | Identification number of the current viewport. The identification number you specify must correspond to an active viewport. Also, the cursor must not be locked in that viewpoint. Tablet mode must be off. |
| **DEFLPLSTYLE** | Registry | Normal | The default plot style for new layers. |
| **DEFPLSTYLE** | Registry | Normal | The default plot style for new objects. |
| **DELOBJ** | Registry | 1 | Determines if objects used to create other objects are kept in the drawing database.<br><br>0   Keep objects.<br><br>1   Delete objects. |
| **DIASTAT** | Not saved | 1 | Stores how the most recently used dialog box was exited.<br><br>0   Cancel.<br><br>1   OK. |
| **DIMALTRND** | Drawing | 0.0000 | Determines the rounding of alternate dimensions. |
| **DIMATFIT** | Drawing | 3 | Determines arrangement of dimension text and arrows when both do not fit inside the extension lines.<br><br>0   Places both outside extension lines.<br><br>1   Relocates arrows before text.<br><br>2   Relocates text before arrows.<br><br>3   Relocates either for best fit. |
| **DIMAZIN** | Drawing | 0 | Suppresses leading and trailing zeros for angular dimensions.<br><br>0   Displays leading and trailing zeros.<br><br>1   Suppresses leading zeros.<br><br>2   Suppresses trailing zeros.<br><br>3   Suppresses leading and trailing zeros. |
| **DIMDSEP** | Drawing | . *(period)* | Sets a character to use as the decimal point for decimal dimensions. |
| **DIMFRAC** | Drawing | 0 | Sets the format for fractional dimensions.<br><br>0   Horizontal.<br><br>1   Diagonal.<br><br>2   Not stacked. |
| **DIMLDRBLK** | Drawing | *current* | Sets the type of arrowhead for leaders. |

| Variable | Saved In | Default Value | Description |
|----------|----------|---------------|-------------|
| **DIMLUNIT** | Drawing | 2 | Sets dimension units, except angular. |
| | | | 1    Scientific. |
| | | | 2    Decimal. |
| | | | 3    Engineering. |
| | | | 4    Architectural. |
| | | | 5    Fractional. |
| | | | 6    Windows desktop. |
| **DIMLWD** | Drawing | -2 | Sets the lineweight for dimension lines. |
| | | | -3   ByLayer. |
| | | | -2   ByBlock. |
| | | | Number (100th of mm). |
| **DIMLWE** | Drawing | -2 | Sets the lineweight for extension lines. |
| | | | -3   ByLayer. |
| | | | -2   ByBlock. |
| | | | Number (100th of mm). |
| **DIMTMOVE** | Drawing | 0 | Specifies rules for moving dimension text. |
| | | | 0    Moves dimension line with text. |
| | | | 1    Adds a leader when dimension text is moved. |
| | | | 2    Allows text to be moved freely (no leader). |
| **DISPSILH** | Drawing | 0 | Sets the displays of silhouette curves for solids when in hidden line mode. |
| | | | 0    Off. |
| | | | 1    On. |
| **DWGCHECK** | Registry | 0 | Sets the dialog box display when determining if the current drawing was last edited by a product other than AutoCAD. |
| | | | 0    Suppresses the dialog box. |
| | | | 1    Displays the dialog box. |
| **EDGEMODE** | Registry | 0 | Determines how cutting and boundary edges for the **TRIM** and **EXTEND** commands are calculated. |
| | | | 0    Uses only the selected edge. |
| | | | 1    Creates an imaginary extension from the selected object. |
| **ELEVATION** | Drawing | 0.0000 | Stores the current 3D elevation relative to the current UCS for the current space. |
| **EXTNAMES** | Drawing | 1 | Determines which parameter set is used for object names stored in symbol tables. |
| | | | 0    Release 14 parameters. |
| | | | 1    AutoCAD 2000 and later parameters. |
| **FACETRATIO** | Not saved | 0 | Sets the faceting aspect ratio (mesh density) for cylindrical and conic solids. |
| | | | 0    Mesh is $N$ by 1. |
| | | | 1    Mesh is $N$ by $M$. |
| **FACETRES** | Drawing | 0.5000 | A relative measure of the number of tessellation lines used to display solids with **HIDE**. Value can range from 0.01 to 10.0. |
| **FILLETRAD** | Drawing | 0.5000 | The default radius used for fillets. |
| **FRONTZ** | Drawing | 0.0000 | The front clipping plane offset from the target plane for the current viewport. |

| Variable | Saved In | Default Value | Description |
|---|---|---|---|
| **FULLOPEN** | Not saved | 1 | Indicates if the current drawing is fully or partially open (read only). |
| | | | 0   Partially open. |
| | | | 1   Fully open. |
| **HIDEPRECISION** | Not saved | 0 | Sets the accuracy of hides and shades to either double or single precision. |
| | | | 0   Single precision. |
| | | | 1   Double precision. |
| **HYPERLINKBASE** | Drawing | *current* | Sets the path for all relative hyperlinks in the current drawing. |
| **IMAGEHLT** | Registry | 0 | Determines if a raster image frame or the entire image is highlighted when selected. |
| | | | 0   Frame only. |
| | | | 1   Entire image. |
| **INETLOCATION** | Registry | www.autodesk.com | The default URL used by the **BROWSER** command. |
| **INSUNITS** | Drawing | 1 | Determines the drawing unit value when a block or image is "dragged" from the AutoCAD DesignCenter. |

INSUNITS values:

| | | | |
|---|---|---|---|
| 0 | No units. | 11 | Angstroms. |
| 1 | Inches. | 12 | Nanometers. |
| 2 | Feet. | 13 | Microns. |
| 3 | Miles. | 14 | Decimeters. |
| 4 | Millimeters. | 15 | Decameters. |
| 5 | Centimeters. | 16 | Hectometers. |
| 6 | Meters. | 17 | Gigameters. |
| 7 | Kilometers. | 18 | Astronomical Units. |
| 8 | Microinches. | 19 | Light Years. |
| 9 | Mils. | 20 | Parsecs. |
| 10 | Yards. | | |

| Variable | Saved In | Default Value | Description |
|---|---|---|---|
| **INSUNITSDEFSOURCE** | Registry | 1 | Specifies the source content units value. Can be from 0 to 20. |
| **INSUNITSDEFTARGET** | Registry | 1 | Specifies the target drawing units value. Can be from 0 to 20. |
| **ISOLINES** | Drawing | 4 | Specifies the number of isolines per surface. Values can range from 0 to 2047. |
| **LENSLENGTH** | Drawing | 50.0000 | Indicates the lens length (in millimeters) for perspective viewing (read only). |
| **LISPINIT** | Registry | 1 | Determines if AutoLISP-defined functions and variables are preserved when a new drawing is opened or valid in the current drawing session only. |
| | | | 0   Preserved. |
| | | | 1   Valid in current drawing only. |
| **LWDEFAULT** | Registry | 25 | Sets the default lineweight value (in mm). |
| **LWDISPLAY** | Drawing | 0 | Determines if lineweights are displayed. |
| | | | 0   Not displayed. (OFF) |
| | | | 1   Displayed. (ON) |
| **LWUNITS** | Registry | 1 | Determines if lineweight units are shown as inches or millimeters. |
| | | | 0   Inches. |
| | | | 1   Millimeters. |

| Variable | Saved In | Default Value | Description |
|---|---|---|---|
| **MAXACTVP** | Drawing | 64 | Determines the maximum number of viewports that can be displayed at one time. |
| **MBUTTONPAN** | Registry | 1 | Determines the action of the third mouse button or mouse wheel. |
| | | | 0    Action is defined in the AutoCAD menu file. |
| | | | 1    Allows panning by holding and dragging the button or wheel. |
| **NOMUTT** | Not saved | 0 | Suppresses the displaying of messages. |
| | | | 0    Displays messages. |
| | | | 1    Suppresses messages. |
| **OFFSETGAPTYPE** | Registry | 0 | Determines how polylines are offset when a gap is created by offsetting individual polyline segments. |
| | | | 0    Segments are extended to fill the gap. |
| | | | 1    Gaps are filleted. |
| | | | 2    Gaps are chamfered. |
| **OLEHIDE** | Registry | 0 | Sets display of OLE objects. |
| | | | 0    All OLE objects visible. |
| | | | 1    OLE objects visible in paper space only. |
| | | | 2    OLE objects visible in model space only. |
| | | | 3    No OLE objects visible. |
| **OLEQUALITY** | Registry | 1 | Sets the default quality of embedded OLE graphics. |
| | | | 0    Line art quality. |
| | | | 1    Text quality. |
| | | | 2    Graphics quality. |
| | | | 3    Photograph quality. |
| | | | 4    High-resolution photograph. |
| **OLESTARTUP** | Drawing | 0 | Determines if the source application of an embedded OLE object loads when plotting. |
| | | | 0    No load. |
| | | | 1    Load. |
| **PAPERUPDATE** | Registry | 0 | Determines if a warning dialog is displayed when trying to print a layout with a paper size different from the paper size specified by the plotter configuration file. |
| | | | 0    Displays a warning dialog box. |
| | | | 1    Sets paper size to the configured paper size of the plotter configuration file. |
| **PFACEVMAX** | Not saved | 4 | Determines the maximum number of vertices per face (read only). |
| **PLQUIET** | Registry | 0 | Determines if optional dialog boxes and nonfatal errors for batch plotting and scripts are displayed. |
| | | | 0    Displays plot dialog boxes and nonfatal errors. |
| | | | 1    Logs nonfatal errors; suppresses the display of plot-related dialog boxes. |
| **POLARADDANG** | Registry | *current* | Stores up to 10 user-defined polar angles. |
| **POLARANG** | Registry | 90 | Determines the increment for polar angles. |
| **POLARDIST** | Registry | 0.0000 | Determines the snap increment for polar snap. |

| Variable | Saved In | Default Value | Description |
|---|---|---|---|
| POLARMODE | Registry | 0 | Determines the setting for polar and object snap tracking. The value can be from 0 to 15 and is the sum of: |
| | | | **Polar angle measurements** |
| | | | 0   Measure polar angles based on the current UCS. |
| | | | 1   Measure polar angles from selected objects. |
| | | | **Object snap tracking** |
| | | | 0   Track orthogonally only. |
| | | | 2   Use polar tracking settings in object snap tracking. |
| | | | **Use additional polar tracking angles** |
| | | | 0   No. |
| | | | 4   Yes. |
| | | | **Acquire object snap tracking points** |
| | | | 0   Acquire automatically. |
| | | | 8   Press [Shift] to acquire. |
| PROJECTNAME | Drawing | *current* | Assigns a project name for the drawing. |
| PROJMODE | Registry | 1 | Projection mode for **Trim** and **Extend**. |
| | | | 0   No projection. |
| | | | 1   Project to the XY plane of the current UCS. |
| | | | 2   Project to the current view plane. |
| PSTYLEMODE | Drawing | 0 | Shows if the current drawing is in color-dependent or named plot style mode (read only). |
| | | | 0   Named plot style. |
| | | | 1   Color-dependent plot style. |
| PSTYLEPOLICY | Registry | 0 | Determines if an object's color property is associated with its plot style. |
| | | | 0   No association. |
| | | | 1   Associated. |
| PSVPSCALE | Drawing | 0 | Determines the view scale factor for all new viewports. A value of 0 means scaled to fit. |
| PSQUALITY | Registry | 75 | Controls the rendering quality of PostScript images. |
| | | | 0   Disables PostScript image generation. |
| | | | < 0   Sets the number of pixels per drawing unit for the PostScript image. |
| | | | > 0   Sets the number of pixels per drawing unit and shows PostScript paths as unfilled outlines. |
| PUCSBASE | Drawing | *current* | Sets the UCS that defines the origin and orientation of orthographic UCS settings in paper space. |
| RASTERPREVIEW | Registry | 1 | Determines if a BMP preview image is saved with the drawing. |
| | | | 0   No preview. |
| | | | 1   Preview. |
| REFEDITNAME | Not saved | *current* | Shows if the drawing is in reference-editing state (read only). |
| SAVEFILEPATH | Registry | User's temp folder | Sets the location for automatic save files. The default value is based on which OS you are using. |

| Variable | Saved In | Default Value | Description |
|---|---|---|---|
| **SDI** | Registry | 0 | Determines if AutoCAD runs in single or multiple document interface. |
| | | | 0   MDI on. |
| | | | 1   MDI off. |
| | | | 2   (Read only, not saved) MDI disabled because AutoCAD has loaded an application that does not support multiple drawings. |
| | | | 3   (Read only, not saved) MDI is disabled because the user has set SDI to 1 and AutoCAD has loaded an application that does not support multiple drawings. |
| **SHORTCUTMENU** | Registry | 11 | Determines if default, edit, and command mode shortcut menus are available in the drawing area. Value is a sum of: |
| | | | 0   Disables shortcut menus (R14 behavior). |
| | | | 1   Enables default mode shortcut menus. |
| | | | 2   Enables edit mode shortcut menus. |
| | | | 4   Enables command mode shortcut menus. |
| | | | 8   Enables command mode shortcut menus only when command options are currently available on the command line. |
| **SHADEDIF** | Drawing | 70 | Ratio of diffuse reflective light relative to ambient light for SHADEDGE 0 or 1. |
| **SHADEDGE** | Drawing | 3 | Controls shading of edges in shadings. Corresponds to **SHADEMODE** settings. |
| | | | 0   Faces shaded, edges not highlighted. |
| | | | 1   Faces shaded, edges drawn in background color. |
| | | | 2   Faces not filled, edges in object color. |
| | | | 3   Faces in object color, edges in background color. |
| **SNAPTYPE** | Registry | 0 | Sets the snap style for the current viewport. |
| | | | 0   Standard (grid) snap. |
| | | | 1   Polar snap. |
| **SOLIDCHECK** | Not saved | 1 | Determines if solid validation is on or off for the current drawing session. |
| | | | 0   Off. |
| | | | 1   On. |
| **SPLFRAME** | Drawing | 0 | Controls display of spline and spline-fit polylines. |
| | | | 0   Does not display the control polygon. |
| | | | 1   Displays the control polygon. |
| **SPLINESEGS** | Drawing | 8 | Number of line segments for each spline-fit polyline generated by **PEDIT Spline**. |
| **SPLINETYPE** | Drawing | 6 | Type of spline curve to be generated by **PEDIT Spline**. |
| | | | 5   Quadratic B-spline. |
| | | | 6   Cubic B-spline. |
| **SURFTAB1** | Drawing | 6 | Number of tabulations generated for **RULESURF** and **TABSURF**. Also, mesh density in the $M$ direction for **REVSURF** and **EDGESURF**. |
| **SURFTAB2** | Drawing | 6 | Mesh density in the $N$ direction for **REVSURF** and **EDGESURF**. |

| Variable | Saved In | Default Value | Description |
|---|---|---|---|
| **SURFTYPE** | Drawing | 6 | Controls the surface-fitting of **PEDIT Smooth**. |
| | | | 5    Quadratic B-spline surface. |
| | | | 6    Cubic B-spline surface. |
| | | | 8    Bézier surface. |
| **SURFU** | Drawing | 6 | Surface density in the *M* direction for **PEDIT Smooth**. |
| **SURFV** | Drawing | 6 | Surface density in the *N* direction for **PEDIT Smooth**. |
| **TARGET** | Drawing | 0.00,0.00,0.00 | Location of the target point for the current viewpoint in UCS coordinates (read only). |
| **TDUCREATE** | Drawing | 2452867.425 42034 | Stores the universal time and date a drawing is created (read only). |
| **TDUPDATE** | Drawing | 2452867. 42542034 | Stores the local time and date of the last update (read only). |
| **THICKNESS** | Drawing | 0.0000 | Sets the current 3D thickness. |
| **TILEMODE** | Drawing | 1 | Sets the model tab or last layout tab current. |
| | | | 0    Makes the last active layout tab current. |
| | | | 1    Makes the model tab current. |
| **TRACKPATH** | Registry | 0 | Controls the display of polar and object snap tracking alignment paths. |
| | | | 0    Displays the object snap tracking path as full screen. |
| | | | 1    Displays the object snap tracking path between the alignment point and "from" point to the cursor location. |
| | | | 2    Polar tracking path is not displayed. |
| | | | 3    Polar and object snap tracking paths are not displayed. |
| **TRIMMODE** | Registry | 1 | Controls edge trimming for chamfers and fillets. |
| | | | 0    Leaves edges intact. |
| | | | 1    Trims edges. |
| **TSPACEFAC** | Not saved | 1.0000 | Sets multiline text line spacing as a factor of text height. Can be from 0.25 to 4.0. |
| **TSPACETYPE** | Not saved | 1 | Controls the type of line spacing used in multi-line text. |
| | | | 1    At least. (tallest character) |
| | | | 2    Exactly. (character independent) |
| **TSTACKALIGN** | Drawing | 1 | Determines vertical alignment of stacked text. |
| | | | 0    Bottom aligned. |
| | | | 1    Center aligned. |
| | | | 2    Top aligned. |
| **TSTACKSIZE** | Drawing | 70 | Percentage of stacked text fraction height relative to the height of the text. Can be from 25 to 125. |
| **UCSAXISANG** | Registry | 90 | Default angle value for rotating the UCS around one of its axes. |
| **UCSBASE** | Drawing | *current* | The UCS that defines the origin and orientation of orthographic UCS settings. |
| **UCSFOLLOW** | Drawing | 0 | Generates a plan view in a viewport whenever the UCS is changed in that viewport. Each viewport has its own setting. |
| | | | 0    UCS does not affect the view. |
| | | | 1    Any UCS change generates a new plan view. |

| Variable | Saved In | Default Value | Description |
|---|---|---|---|
| **UCSICON** | Drawing | 3 | Controls the displays of the user coordinate system icon in the current viewport. |
| | | | 0    No display. |
| | | | 1    Icon is displayed. |
| | | | 2    If icon is displayed, it is shown at the UCS origin, if possible. |
| | | | 3    Icon is displayed at the UCS origin. |
| **UCSNAME** | Drawing | *current* | Indicates the name of the active coordinate system in the active viewport (read only). |
| **UCSORG** | Drawing | 0.0000,0.0000, 0.0000 | Indicates the origin point in World coordinates of the current UCS in the active viewport (read only). |
| **UCSORTHO** | Registry | 1 | Sets if an orthographic UCS is automatically set current when the related orthographic view is restored. |
| | | | 0    Current UCS is retained. |
| | | | 1    Orthographic UCS is set current. |
| **UCSVIEW** | Registry | 1 | Controls if the current UCS is saved when a view is named. |
| | | | 0    UCS is not saved. |
| | | | 1    UCS is saved. |
| **UCSVP** | Drawing | 1 | Controls if the UCS in all viewports change to reflect the UCS of the active viewport. Each viewport has its own setting. |
| | | | 0    Changes. |
| | | | 1    Does not change. |
| **UCSXDIR** | Drawing | | The X direction of the active UCS for the active viewport (read only). |
| **UCSYDIR** | Drawing | | The Y direction of the active UCS for the active viewport (read only). |
| **VIEWCTR** | Drawing | | The center of view in the current viewport, in UCS coordinates (read only). |
| **VIEWDIR** | Drawing | | The viewing direction in the current viewport, in UCS coordinates (read only). |
| **VIEWMODE** | Drawing | | Determines the viewing mode for the current viewport (read only). The value is the sum of: |
| | | | 0    Disabled. |
| | | | 1    Perspective view active. |
| | | | 2    Front clipping on. |
| | | | 4    Back clipping on. |
| | | | 8    UCS follow mode on. |
| | | | 16   Front clip not at eye. |
| **VIEWSIZE** | Drawing | | Height of the view in the active viewport (read only). |
| **VIEWTWIST** | Drawing | | View twist angle for the active viewport (read only). |
| **VSMAX** | Drawing | | Upper-right corner of the virtual screen in the active viewport, in UCS coordinates (read only). |
| **VSMIN** | Drawing | | Lower-left corner of the virtual screen in the active viewport, in UCS coordinates (read only). |
| **WHIPARC** | Registry | 0 | Sets the display smoothness of circles and arcs. |
| | | | 0    Circles and arcs are shown as a series of vectors. |
| | | | 1    Circles and arcs are shown as true circles and arcs. |

| Variable | Saved In | Default Value | Description |
|---|---|---|---|
| **WMFBKGND** | Not saved | 1 | Determines if the background of AutoCAD objects is transparent in other applications. |
| | | | 0    Transparent background. |
| | | | 1    Background is the AutoCAD drawing area color. |
| **WORLDUCS** | Not saved | 1 | Shows if the UCS coincides with the WCS (read only). |
| | | | 0    UCS and WCS are different. |
| | | | 1    UCS and WCS coincide. |
| **WORLDVIEW** | Drawing | 1 | Controls whether UCS changes to WCS during **DVIEW, 3DORBIT,** or **VPOINT**. |
| | | | 0    UCS does not change. |
| | | | 1    UCS changes to the WCS until the command is terminated. |
| **WRITESTAT** | Not saved | 1 | Shows if a drawing can be edited and saved (read only). |
| | | | 0    Read only. |
| | | | 1    Can be saved. |
| **XEDIT** | Drawing | 1 | Determines if the current drawing can be edited in place when referenced by another drawing. |
| | | | 0    Cannot be edited in place. |
| | | | 1    Can be edited in place. |
| **XFADECTL** | Registry | 50 | Sets the percentage of fading for references being edited in place. Can be from 0% to 90%. |
| **ZOOMFACTOR** | Registry | 60 | Sets zoom increments for the mouse wheel. Can be between 3 and 100. |

# Basic AutoLISP Commands

The following is a list of basic AutoLISP commands with a brief definition of each command. These commands are covered in Chapter 23 and Chapter 24 of this text. Detailed definitions of these and all other AutoLISP commands are found in the online documentation.

| Command | Description |
|---|---|
| **+** *(addition)* | Adds all numbers. |
| **–** *(subtraction)* | Subtracts the second and following numbers from the first and returns the difference. |
| **\*** *(multiplication)* | Multiplies all numbers. |
| **/** *(division)* | Divides the first number by the product of the remaining numbers and returns the quotient. |
| **=** *(equal to)* | Returns a total if all arguments are equal. Returns *nil* otherwise. |
| **ANGLE** | Returns the angle from the X axis of the current UCS to a line defined by two endpoints, as measured counterclockwise. The value is given in radians. |
| **ARXLOAD** | Loads an AutoCAD Runtime Extension application. |
| **ARXUNLOAD** | Unloads an AutoCAD Runtime Extension application. |
| **CADDR** | Returns the third element of a list. |
| **CADR** | Returns the second element of a list. |
| **CAR** | Returns the first element of a list. |
| **CDR** | Returns the second and remaining elements of a list. If the list contains more than two elements, the returned values are placed in a list. |
| **DEFUN** | Defines a function. |
| **DISTANCE** | Returns the distance between two points. The distance is measured in 3D space. |
| **GETANGLE** | Waits for a user-input angle and returns the angle in radians. The user can input the angle at the keyboard or use the pointing device to pick points on screen. |
| **GETCORNER** | Waits for the user to input the second corner of a rectangle. |
| **GETDIST** | Waits for a user to input distance. The distance can be entered at the keyboard or using the pointing device to pick points on screen. |
| **GETORIENT** | Waits for a user-input angle and returns the angle in radians. This is similar to the **GETANGLE** function, but the **ANGBASE** and **ANGDIR** system variables do not affect it. |
| **GETPOINT** | Waits for a user-input point and returns the coordinates of the point. |
| **GETREAL** | Waits for a user-input real number and returns the real number. |
| **GETSTRING** | Waits for a user-input string and returns the string. |
| **GETVAR** | Returns the value assigned to a specified AutoCAD system variable. |

| Command | Description |
|---|---|
| **GRAPHSCR** | If the text screen is currently displayed, switches to the AutoCAD graphics screen. This is the same as pressing [F2] to close the text window. |
| **LOAD_DIALOG** | Loads a Dialog Control Language (DCL) file. |
| **NEW_DIALOG** | Opens a specified dialog box. This function can also specify a default action of the dialog box. |
| **POLAR** | Returns the coordinates of a 3D point that is a specified angle and distance from a specified point. |
| **PRINC** | Prints a specified expression on the command line. This function can also be used to write a specified expression to a file. |
| **PROMPT** | Displays a specified string on the command line. |
| **START_DIALOG** | Opens a specified dialog box and readies AutoCAD for user input. |
| **STRLEN** | Reports the number of characters in a string. |
| **TERPRI** | Prints a new line on the command line. |
| **TEXTSCR** | If the graphics screen is currently displayed, switches to the AutoCAD text screen. This is the same as pressing [F2] to display the text window. |
| **UNLOAD_DIALOG** | Unloads a Dialog Control Language (DCL) file. |

# Index